Family Law in
the World Community

Family Law in the World Community

Cases, Materials, and Problems in Comparative and International Family Law

D. Marianne Blair
PROFESSOR OF LAW
UNIVERSITY OF TULSA

Merle H. Weiner
ASSOCIATE PROFESSOR OF LAW
UNIVERSITY OF OREGON

CAROLINA ACADEMIC PRESS
Durham, North Carolina

ISBN 0-89089-284-9
LCCN 2003106096

CAROLINA ACADEMIC PRESS
700 Kent Street
Durham, North Carolina 27701
Telephone (919) 489-7486
Fax (919) 493-5668
www.cap-press.com

Printed in the United States of America

This book is dedicated to Henry, Eli, and Tom.

Merle

———————————

This book is also dedicated

to Sean, whose creativity, courage, and humor
inspire me,

to Sarah, whose affectionate nature, perception, and determination
bring me joy,

to Meagan, whose smile I will always treasure, and

to Chris, who has stood by me through the laughter
and tears, and without whom I would never have
fully known the fulfillment family can bring.
With all my love,

Marianne

Contents

Part Two
Rights and Responsibilities of Parents, Children, and the State

Table of Cases

Principal cases are set in italics, while cases cited in the text and in the authors' notes are set in roman type. Where a principal case is also referenced elsewhere in the text, the principal pages are also italicized.

Preface for Instructors

Before we began writing this book in 1999, we surveyed the courses in comparative and/or international family law offered by American law schools, both on campus and in their overseas programs. Our examination confirmed our suspicion that the courses were extremely diverse, both in structure and content. Some of these courses were two credit hours, others were three; some of these courses were seminars, others were not. The instructors' pedagogical goals and coverage fell along a continuum: some focused almost exclusively on training students for the practice of transnational family law; others concentrated mostly on examining discrete family law issues from a comparative perspective; some emphasized international human rights conventions affecting the family. Notwithstanding this variety, several generalizations were evident. The majority of the instructors utilized a combination of public international law, private international law, and comparative law sources. In addition, all taught with materials that they or others had gathered, as no casebook yet existed in this field.

Ours is the first casebook created for American law students in the field of comparative and international family law. As such, we tried to create a book that can be used flexibly in many types of courses. We included more material than can be taught in a course of two- or three-credit hours in order to ensure sufficient content to meet each instructor's interests and goals. We used recurring themes throughout the book to try to provide coherence regardless of the material chosen.

The first chapter presents an overview of the comparative and international law disciplines. We have presumed that students have not had either an international or comparative law course. Therefore, we use family law topics not covered elsewhere in the book to introduce the skills and information necessary to explore effectively the topical chapters that follow. The first chapter also contains a section on researching international and comparative family law, which may prove particularly useful for seminar students.

The remaining chapters are divided into two parts. Chapters Two through Six focus primarily on relationships between adult partners. Chapters Seven through Fourteen concentrate largely upon the relationships between children and their parents and other caregivers.

For those instructors who want to teach a mixture of comparative, international, and transnational law, and consequently will seek material by topic rather than by discipline, Chapters Two through Fourteen offer a range of options. The book is organized topically because we believe that the study of family law is particularly rich and exciting when one explores a particular topic through a combination of comparative law, public international law, and private international law. However, for those instructors who want to organize materials around a specific discipline, we offer the following suggestions. Instructors who want to emphasize transnational family law will find most useful

Chapters One (section B), Two (section E), Five, Eight, Ten, and Twelve. Chapter Six (sections B.3.c. and C.1), addressing the ability of family violence victims to successfully obtain asylum in the United States, might also be a beneficial addition to a transnational course. Instructors who wish to concentrate mostly on comparative family law might want to select Chapters One (section A), Two, Three, Four, Six (sections A and B), Seven, Nine, Eleven, Thirteen, and Fourteen. Chapter Eight might also be usefully included in such a course, as certain portions take a comparative approach to examining the topics of child abduction and custody jurisdiction, and many of the cases provide significant insight into the substantive custody law of the nations involved. Instructors who seek to focus on the intersection of international human rights law and family law will find most relevant Chapters One (section B), Two (sections B.4 and E), Four (section B), Six, Seven, Eleven, Thirteen, and Fourteen.

The book incorporates a broad range of materials, including judgments from international tribunals and domestic courts of many nations, statutes from around the world, and excerpts from professional journals in law and related fields. Each chapter includes problems and exercises that permit instruction through problem-solving and role-playing. Each chapter also contains both specific and open-ended questions to facilitate policy discussions and socratic dialogue.

A separate paperback, entitled *International Family Law: Conventions, Statutes, and Regulatory Materials*, complements this casebook and is also available through Carolina Academic Press. It contains the edited text of global and regional international conventions relevant to the field of family law, selected U.S. federal statutes and regulations, and the text of the Uniform Interstate Family Support Act (1996) and the Uniform Child Custody Jurisdiction and Enforcement Act (1997). We placed these materials in a separate supplement because these materials are referred to throughout the book and because they are lengthy. An instructor certainly could make available these treaties and statutory materials through other means; we have only sought to eliminate that inconvenience for those who would prefer not to have it.

This book was not created for the basic domestic Family Law course taught in most U.S. law schools, and this book is not well suited for that purpose. Although the book contains some U.S. cases, legislative materials, and summaries of legal doctrine, this material is provided solely for comparative purposes or to contextualize a discussion of transnational or public international law. Rather, our goals were to create a book that would allow students to explore family law issues from a global or comparative perspective, to understand the influence and limitations of international law in resolving familial conflicts, and to prepare for the practice of transnational family law. To those of you who share these goals, we hope that this book provides you a useful tool for exploring this fascinating and rapidly expanding field of law with students. We welcome your comments and suggestions. Please direct comments about Chapters 1.B, 3–5, 7, 8.B, 8.C, and 10–12 to Marianne Blair and comments about Chapters 1.A, 1.C, 2, 6, 8.A, 9, 13, and 14 to Merle Weiner.

Acknowledgments

We gratefully acknowledge Mary Clayton and Dennis Hyatt, law librarians at the University of Oregon, who made a significant contribution to this book by writing for us *Researching International and Comparative Family Law*, which appears in section C of Chapter One. We would also like to thank Anne Goldstein and her students at George Washington University Law School, and Theresa Glennon at Temple University, for their helpful comments to earlier drafts of this book. Barbara Stark at University of Tennessee College of Law receives our appreciation for her encouragement.

We appreciate the many individuals who agreed to share their expertise with us about various substantive issues, including Barbara Atwood, Nicholas Bala, Phil Bates, Tom Bennett, Raquel Hecht, Marie-Therese Meulders, Patrick Parkinson, June Sinclair, Robert Spector, and Paul Ward.

We both have been fortunate to have had some excellent research assistance during the course of this project. Merle would like to thank the following students (and now former students) for their help: James Alfieri, Tom Boes, Brittany Carroll, Michael Drobac, Shannon Eddy, Daniel Foster, Ivan Gardzelewski, Russell Gray, Sharon Griffin, Andrew Heinz, Heather Hepburn, Jennifer Hisley, Catherine Hoskins, Stacey Lowe, Annie Mortland, Matt Mues, Chris O'Connor, Kristin Olson, Spencer Parsons, David Pebworth, Jared Phillips, Aoife Cox Rinaldi, Leilani Robinson, Devorah Signer, Ted Tollefson, Christi Shaffner, Amber Sun, Jane Trost, Ryan Valentin, Ross Williamson, and Melissa Wright. As they all know, she could not have completed her chapters without their help. Merle would also like to thank Julianna Coons and Katie Birnie for their comments. Marianne wishes to express her appreciation to each of the following students, who worked long hours to assist her with researching and proofreading both this book and the accompanying supplement: Kristen Reser Baker, Vicki Brandt, Kristin Cherry, Patricia K. Curtis, Eric Hallett, Michelle Harris, Jennifer Kern, Merrit M. Klapperich, Emily Maples, Deborah Martin, Judy Monroe, Christopher Ray, Matthew Sandgren, and Lorentia Suwana. Special recognition must be given to the contribution of Eric Hallett, whose research for Chapters Four and Seven was invaluable.

At both of our institutions we enjoyed supportive colleagues and talented support staff. Professor Larry Backer deserves Marianne's thanks for inspiring her to begin this journey, and Professors Paul Finkelman and Garrett Epps deserve our gratitude for their assistance when we were circulating our book proposal. Professors David Clark and Linda Lacey also provided helpful advice to Marianne along the way. Professors Leslie Harris, Garrett Epps, Mary Wood, and Rennard Strickland offered very helpful suggestions to Merle in the final stages of this project. Merle is also especially indebted to Karyn Smith for her consistently excellent secretarial support. Marianne wishes to thank Cyndee Jones and Sharon Miller, who provided secretarial support on the supplement for this book. Kathy Kane, Carol Arnold, and David Gay, librarians in the law library of the University of Tulsa, deserve her sincere thanks for the many hours they devoted to assisting her with obtaining foreign sources. Angus Nesbit and Stephanie Midkiff, librarians at the University of Oregon, were also very helpful in tracking down often obscure pieces of information.

Both of our schools provided financial support for this project. Merle appreciates the summer research support she received, and particularly acknowledges the Stoel Rives Faculty Fellowship and the Board of Visitors' Faculty Endowment Fund. Marianne appreciates the assistance of Dean Martin Belsky and the University of Tulsa for providing sabbatical and summer research support.

We also acknowledge the following people and entities for their generous permission to include their materials in our book:

Abrams, Paula, *Population Politics: Reproductive Rights and U.S. Asylum Policy*, 14 Geo. Immigr. L. J. 881 (2000). Reprinted with permission of the publisher, Georgetown Immigration Law Review © 2000, and the author.

Abrahamson, Shirley S. & Michael J. Fischer, *All the World's a Courtroom: Judging in the New Millennium*, 26 Hofstra L. Rev. 273 (1997). Reprinted with permission of Hofstra Law Review and the authors.

Al-Hibri, Azizah Y., *Marriage Laws in Muslim Countries: A Comparative Study of Certain Egyptian, Syrian, Moroccan, and Tunisian Marriage Laws*, 4 Int'l Rev. of Comp. Pub. Pol'y 227 (1992). Reprinted with permission of the International Review of Comparative Public Policy, Michigan State University, and the author.

American Academy of Pediatrics, *Guidance for Effective Discipline*, 101 Pediatrics 723 (1998). Used with permission of the American Academy of Pediatrics.

Andrews, Lori B., *Reproductive Technology Comes of Age*, 21 Whittier L. Rev. 375 (1999). Reprinted with permission of Whittier Law Review and the author.

Appleton, Susan Frelich, *Surrogacy Arrangements and the Conflict of Laws*, 1990 Wis. L. Rev. 399 (1990). Copyright 1990 by The Board of Regents of the University of Wisconsin System; Reprinted by permission of the Wisconsin Law Review and the author.

Apy, Patricia E., *Managing Child Custody Cases Involving Non-Hague Contracting States*, 14 J. Am. Acad. Matrim. Law. 77 (1997). Reprinted with permission of the copyright holder, Journal of the American Academy of Matrimonial Lawyers.

Armatta, Judith, *Getting Beyond the Law's Complicity in Intimate Violence Against Women*, 33 Willamette L. Rev. 773 (1997). Reprinted with permission of Willamette Law Review, owner of the copyright.

Barksdale, Yvette Marie, *And the Poor Have Children: A Harm Based Analysis of Family Caps and the Hollow Procreative Rights of Welfare Beneficiaries*, 14 Law & Ineq. 1 (1995). Reprinted with permission of Law & Inequality: A Journal of Theory and Practice, University of Minnesota Law School.

Barsh, Russel Lawrence, *Putting the Tribe in Tribal Courts: Possible? Desirable?*, 8 Kan. J. L. and Pub. Pol'y 74 (1999). Reprinted with permission of the Kansas Journal of Law and Public Policy and the author.

Bartholet, Elizabeth, *International Adoption: Propriety, Prospects, and Pragmatics*, 13 J. Amer. Acad. Matrim. Law. 181 (1996). Reprinted with permission of the copyright holder, Journal of the American Academy of Matrimonial Lawyers.

Bennett, T.W., Human Rights and African Customary Law 48 (1995). Reprinted with permission of Juta & Co., Ltd. and the author.

Billings, Peter W., *A Comparative Analysis of Administrative and Adjudicative Systems For Determining Asylum Claims*, 52 Admin. L. Rev. 253 (2000). Reprinted by permission of the American Bar Association.

Blumberg, Grace Ganz, Reporter's Memorandum to the Members of the Institute, Principles of the Law of Family Dissolution, Tentative Draft No. 3, Part II, March 7, 1998. Copyright 1998 by the American Law Institute. Reprinted with permission. All rights reserved. The final text of the Principles of the Law of Family Dissolution: Analysis and Recommendations is now available on the ALI website at www.ali.org.

Boland, Reed, *Civil and Political Rights and the Right to Nondiscrimination: Population Policies, Human Rights and Legal Change*, 44 Am. U. L. Rev. 1257 (1995). Reprinted with the permission of the American University Law Review and the author.

Boland, Reed, *Symposium on Population Law: The Environment, Population, and Women's Human Rights*, 27 Envtl. L. 1137 (1997). Reprinted by permission of Environmental Law, Northwestern School of Law at Lewis & Clark College and the author.

Bowman, Cynthia Grant, *A Feminist Proposal to Bring Back Common Law Marriage*, 75 Or. L. Rev. 709 (1996). Reprinted with permission of the Oregon Law Review and the author.

Bradley, Curtis, A., *Customary International Law and Private Rights of Action*, 1 Chi. J. Int'l L. 421 (2000). Reprinted with permission of the copyright holder, The Chicago Journal of International Law.

Bryant, Taimie L., *For the Sake of the Country, for the Sake of the Family: The Oppressive Impact of Family Registration on Women and Minorities in Japan*, 39 UCLA L. Rev. 109 (1991). Originally published in 39 UCLA L. Rev. 109. Copyright 1991, The Regents of the University of California. All Rights Reserved. Reprinted with permission.

Burman, Sandra, *Illegitimacy and the African Family in Changing South Africa*, 1991 Acta Juridica 38 (1991). Reprinted with permission of Juta & Co., Ltd. and the author.

Butler, William E., International Law in Comparative Perspective 5. Copyright © 1980. Reprinted with the kind permission of Kluwer Law International, and with the permission of the author, William E. Butler.

BVerfG [Constitutional Court], BverfGE 39 (1975), 1 (1-68) (F.R.G.), translated in Robert E. Jonas & John D. Gorby, *West German Abortion Decision: A Contrast to Roe v. Wade*, 9 J. Marshall J. Prac. & Proc. 605 (1976). Reprinted with permission from the John Marshall Journal of Practice & Procedure.

Chambers, David L., *Civilizing the Natives: Customary Marriage in Post-Apartheid South Africa*. In Engaging Cultural Differences: The Multicultural Challenge in Liberal Democracies, edited by Richard Shweder, Martha Minow, and Hazel Rose Markus. © 2002 Russell Sage Foundation, 112 East 64th Street, New York, NY, 10021. Reprinted with permission of the Russell Sage Foundation and the author.

Charlesworth, Hilary, Christine Chinkin & Shelley Wright, *Feminist Approaches to International Law*, 85 Am. J. Int'l L. 613 (1991). Reproduced with permission from 85 AJIL 613 (1991), © The American Society of International Law.

Chen, Janie, *The Right to Her Embryos: An Analysis of Nachmani v. Nachmani and Its Impact on Israeli In Vitro Fertilization Law*, 7 Cardozo J. Int'l & Comp. L. 325 (1999). Reprinted with the permission of the Cardozo Journal of International and Comparative Law.

Chief Adjudication Officer v. Kirpal Kaur Bath, 1999 WL 819134 (Eng. C.A. Oct. 21, 1999). Reprinted with permission from Westlaw.

Clarke, Donald C., *What's Law Got to Do With It? Legal Institutions and Economic Reform in China*, 10 UCLA Pac. Basin L. J. 1 (1991). Reprinted by permission of the UCLA Pacific Basin Law Journal and the author.

Close v. Close [1999] 50 R.F.L.4th 342 (N.B.Q.B.). Reproduced with permission of *Access Copyright*, The Canadian Copyright Licensing Agency.

Coello, Isabel, *Female Genital Mutilation: Marked by Tradition*, 7 Cardozo J. Int'l. & Comp. L. 213 (1999). Reprinted with permission of the Cardozo Journal of International and Comparative Law and the author.

Coester-Waltjen, Dagmar, & Michael Coester, *Formation of Marriage*, IV International Encyclopedia of Comparative Law 7 (1997). Reprinted with permission of the authors.

Cohen, Cynthia Price, *The Developing Jurisprudence of the Rights of the Child*, 6 St. Thomas L. Rev. 1 (1993). Reprinted with permission of the St. Thomas Law Review and the author.

Cohen, Cynthia Price, The *Jurisprudence of the Committee on the Rights of the Child*, 5 Geo. J. on Fighting Poverty 201 (1998). Reprinted with permission of Georgetown Journal on Fighting Poverty and the author.

Committee on School Health, *Corporal Punishment in Schools*, 88 Pediatrics 173 (1991). Used with permission of the American Academy of Pediatrics.

Cooper, Cynthia L., *Poll on Welfare, Birth Control Misleading*, Women's Enews, July 12, 2001, *available at* http://www.womensnews.org/article.cfm/dynaid/612/context/archive. Reprinted with permission of the editor-in-chief of Women's Enews.

Copelon, Rhonda, *Recognizing the Egregious in the Everyday: Domestic Violence as Torture*, 25 Colum. Hum. Rts. L. Rev. 291 (1994). Reprinted by permission of the Columbia Human Rights Law Review and the author.

Cox, Susan Soon-Keum, *Ritual*, 9 Yale J. L. & Feminism 17 (1997). Reprinted by permission of The Yale Journal of Law & Feminism, Inc., from The Yale Journal of Law & Feminism Vol. 9, No.1.

Dailey, Anne C., *Federalism and Families*, 143 U. Pa. L. Rev. 1787 (1995). Reprinted with permission of the University of Pennsylvania Law Review and the author.

DeKoker, Jeanne Y., *African Customary Family Law in South Africa: A Legacy of Many Pasts, in* The Changing Family: International Perspectives on the Family and Family Law 321 (John Eekelaar & Thandabantu Nhlapo eds., 1998). Reprinted with permission of Hart Publishing, Ltd.

Demleitner, Nora V., *Combating Legal Ethnocentrism*, 31 Ariz. St. L.J. 737 (1999). Reprinted with permission of the Arizona State Law Journal and the author.

Dewar, John, *Family Law and its Discontents*, 14 Int'l J. L., Pol'y & Fam. 59 (2000). Reprinted with permission of Oxford University Press and the author.

Dillon, Susan A., Comment, *Yoni in the Land of Isis: Female Genital Mutilation is Banned (Again) in Egypt*, 22 Hous. J. Int'l L. 289 (2000). Reprinted with permission from Houston Journal of International Law and the author.

Donoho, Douglas Lee, *Relativism Versus Universalism in Human Rights: The Search For Meaningful Standards*, 27 Stan. J. Int'l L. 345 (1991). Reprinted with permission of the Stanford Journal of International Law and the author.

Dorff, Elliott, *A Jewish Approach to Assisted Reproductive Technologies*, 21 Whittier L. Rev. 391 (1999). Reprinted with permission of Whittier Law Review.

Eekelaar, John, *Are Parents Morally Obliged to Care for Their Children?*, 11 Oxford J. Leg. Stud. 340 (1991). Reprinted with permission of Oxford University Press and the author.

Eekelaar, John, *Child Support as Distributive and Commutative Justice: The United Kingdom Experience, in* Child Support: The Next Frontier 151 (J. Thomas Oldham & Marygold S. Melli eds. 2000). Reprinted with permission of the University of Michigan Press.

Fagan, Jeffrey & Angela Brown, *Violence Between Spouses and Intimates: Physical Aggression Between Women and Men in Intimate Relationships*, 3 Understanding and Preventing Violence 115 (Albert J. Reiss, Jr. & Jeffrey A. Roght eds., 1994). Reprinted with permission from Understanding and Preventing Violence, copyright 1994 by the National Academy of Sciences. Courtesy of the National Academies Press, Washington, D.C.

Field, Martha A., *The Differing Federalism of Canada and the United States*, 55 Law & Contemp. Probs. 107 (1992). Reprinted with permission of Law and Contemporary Problems, Duke University School of Law, and the author.

Fineman, Martha Albertson, *Child Support Is Not the Answer: The Nature of Dependencies and Welfare Reform, in* Child Support: The Next Frontier 209 (J. Thomas Oldham & Marygold S. Melli, eds. 2000). Reprinted with permission of the University of Michigan Press.

Fleishman, Rishona, Comment, *The Battle Against Reproductive Rights: The Impact of the Catholic Church on Abortion Law in Both International and Domestic Arenas*, 14 Emory Int'l

L. Rev. 277 (2000). Reprinted with permission of Emory International Law Review and the author.

Fox, Sanford J., *Beyond the American Legal System for the Protection of Children's Rights*, 31 Fam. L. Q. 237 (1997). Reprinted by permission of the American Bar Association.

Friedman, Lawrence M., *A Dead Language: Divorce Law and Practice Before No-fault*, 86 Va. L. Rev. 1497 (2000). VIRGINIA LAW REVIEW by LAWRENCE FRIEDMAN. Copyright 2000 by VIRGINIA LAW REVIEW. Reproduced with permission of VIRGINIA LAW REVIEW in the format Textbook via Copyright Clearance Center.

French Civil Code (1804), *available at* http://www.napoleon-series.org/research/government/c_code.html. Reprinted with permission.

Frenkel, David A., *Legal Regulation of Surrogate Motherhood in Israel*, 20 Med. & the L. 605 (2001). Reprinted with permission of Yozmot Initiative Center and the author.

Garfinkel, Irwin, *The Limits of Private Child Support and the Role of an Assured Benefit*, in Child Support: The Next Frontier 183 (J. Thomas Oldham & Marygold S. Melli eds., 2000). Reprinted with permission from the University of Michigan Press.

Garrison, Marsha, *The Goals and Limits of Child Support Policy in* Child Support: The Next Frontier 16 (J. Thomas Oldham & Marygold S. Melli eds., 2000). Reprinted with permission of the University of Michigan Press.

George, Erika et al., Scared At School: Sexual Violence Against Girls in South African Schools (Joe Saunders et al. eds., 2001), *at* http://www.hrw.org/reports/2001/safrica. Reprinted with permission from Human Rights Watch.

Glendon, Mary Ann, The Transformation of Family Law (1989). Reprinted with permission of the author, and the publisher and copyright holder, The University of Chicago Press. © 1989 by The University of Chicago.

Goldberg, Deborah, *Developments in German Abortion Law: A U.S. Perspective*, 5 UCLA Women's L. J. 531 (1995). Reprinted with permission from the UCLA Women's Law Journal.

Goldsmith, Jack, *Should International Human Rights Law Trump U.S. Domestic Law*, 1 Chi. J. Int'l L. 327 (2000). Reprinted with permission of the copyright holder, The Chicago Journal of International Law.

Gunning, Isabelle R., *Arrogant Perception, World-Travelling and Multicultural Feminism*, 23 Colum. Hum. Rts. L. Rev. 189 (1992). Reprinted by permission of the Columbia Human Rights Law Review and the author.

Gunning, Isabelle R., *Global Feminism at the Local Level: Criminal and Asylum Laws Regarding Female Genital Surgeries*, 3 J. Gender Race & Just. 45 (1999). Reprinted with permission from the Journal of Gender, Race and Justice, University of Iowa College of Law, and the author.

Halpern v. Toronto (A.G.), [2002] 28 R.F.L.5th 41 (Ont. Div. Ct.). Reprinted with permission of the publisher and copyright holder, Canada Law Book.

Harris, Susan R., *Race, Search, and My Baby-Self: Reflections of a Transracial Adoptee*, 9 Yale J. L. & Feminism 5 (1997). Reprinted by permission of The Yale Journal of Law & Feminism, Inc. from The Yale Journal of Law & Feminism Vol. 9, No. 1.

Hartog, Hendrick A., Man and Wife in America: A History. Reprinted by permission of the publisher, Cambridge, Mass.: Harvard University Press, Copyright © 2000 by the President and Fellows of Harvard College.

Hathaway, Oona A., *Do Human Rights Treaties Make A Difference?*, 111 Yale L.J. 1935 (2002). Reprinted by permission of The Yale Law Journal Company, William S. Hein Company and the author.

Hernandez-Truyol, Berta Esperanza, *Law, Culture, and Equality — Human Rights' Influence on Domestic Norms: The Case of Women in the Americas*, 13 Fla. J. Int'l L. 33 (2000). Reprinted with permission by the Florida Journal of International Law © 2000 and the author.

Hernandez-Truyol, Berta Esperanza, *Latinas, Culture and Human Rights: A Model for Making Change, Saving Soul*, 23 Women's Rts. L. Rep. 21 (2001). Reprinted with permission from the Women's Rights Law Reporter and the author.

Hernandez-Truyol, Berta Esperanza, *Sex, Culture, and Rights: A Re/Conceptualization of Violence for the Twenty-First Century*, 60 Alb. L. Rev. 607 (1997). Reprinted by permission of the Albany Law Review and the author.

Hitchcock, David, Asian Values and the United States (1994). Reprinted by permission on a one-time basis from Center for Strategic and International Studies and the author.

Hobson v. Gray, [1958] 25 W.W.R. 82 (Alta. Sup. Ct.). Reprinted with permission of Carswell Publishing, through *Access Copyright*, The Canadian Copyright Licensing Agency.

Hong, Lawrence K., *Potential Effects of the One-Child Policy on Gender Equality in the People's Republic of China*, 1 Gender & Soc'y 317 (1987). Reprinted by permission of Gender & Society, Sage Publications, Inc., and the author.

I. O'T. v. B., [1998] 2 I.R. 321 (Ir. S.C.). Reprinted with permission of the publisher and copyright holder, Incorporated Council of Law Reporting for Ireland.

Islam v. Secretary of State for the Home Dep't; Regina v. Immigration Appeal Tribunal and Another *ex parte* Shah (conjoined appeals), 38 I.L.M. 827 (Eng. H.L. 1999). Reprinted with the permission of the American Society of International Law.

Jordan, Ann D., *Human Rights, Violence Against Women, and Economic Development (The People's Republic of China Experience)*, 5 Colum. J. Gender & L. 216 (1996). Reprinted with permission of the Columbia Journal of Gender & Law.

Kabeberi-Macharia, Janet & Celestine Nyamu, *Marriage by Affidavit: Developing Alternative Laws on Cohabitation in Kenya, in* The Changing Family: International Perspectives on the Family and Family Law 197 (John Eekelaar & Thandabantu Nhlapo eds., 1998). Reprinted with permission of Hart Publishing, Ltd.

Kerr v. Kerr, [1934] S.C.R. 72 (Can.). Reproduced with permission of Canada Law Book through *Access Copyright*, The Canadian Copyright Licensing Agency.

Kilbourne, Susan, *U.S. Failure to Ratify the U.N. Convention on the Rights of the Child: Playing Politics with Children's Rights*, 6 Transnat'l L. & Contemp. Probs. 437 (1996). Reprinted with permission of Transnational Law and Contemporary Problems, University of Iowa College of Law, and the author.

Kindregan, Charles P., *State Power over Human Fertility and Individual Liberty*, 23 Hastings Law J. 1401 (1972). Reprinted with permission of the Hastings Law Journal and the author.

King, Michael, *Against Children's Rights*, 1996 Acta Juridica 28. Reprinted by permission of Juta & Co., Ltd. and the author.

Kirgis, Frederic L., *International Agreements and U.S. Law*, ASIL Insight, *at* http://www.asil.org/insigh10.htm, May 1997. Reproduced with permission from ASIL Insight, http://www.asil.org/insigh10.htm, May 1997, © The American Society of International Law.

Kligman, Gail, The Politics of Duplicity: Controlling Reproduction in Ceausescu's Romania (1998). Reprinted with permission of the University of California Press and the author.

Law No. 194 of 22 May 1978 on the social protection of motherhood and the voluntary termination of pregnancy (Gazzetta Uficialee della Repubblica Italiana, Part I, 2 May 1978, No. 140, pp. 3642–3646) (Italy), *available at* http://cyber.law.harvard.edu/population/abortion/Italy.abo.htm. Reprinted by permission of Terry Martin, Librarian and Professor of Law, Harvard Law School and produced by the International Digest of Health Legislation at the World Health Organization.

Law No. 350 of 13 June 1973 on the interruption of pregnancy (Lovitidende for Kongeriget Danmark, Part A, 6 July 1973, No. 32, pp. 993–995) (Denmark), *available at* http://cyber.law.harvard.edu/population/abortion/denmark.abo.htm. Reprinted by permission of Terry Martin, Librarian and Professor of Law, Harvard Law School and produced by the International Digest of Health Legislation at the World Health Organization.

Legler, Paul K., *The Impact of Welfare Reform on the Child Support Enforcement System, in* Child Support: The Next Frontier 57 (J. Thomas Oldham & Marygold S. Melli eds., 2000). Reprinted with permission of the University of Michigan Press.

Levesque, Roger J.R., *Educating American Youth: Lessons from Children's Human Rights Law*, 27 J. L. & Educ. 173 (1998). Reprinted with permission from Journal of Law and Education, Jefferson Law Book Company, and the author.

Levesque, Roger J.R., *International Children's Rights Grow Up: Implications for American Jurisprudence and Domestic Policy*, 24 Cal. W. Int'l L.J. 193 (1994). Reprinted with the permission of the California Western International Law Journal and the author.

Levi-Strauss, Claude, "The Family," from MAN, CULTURE, AND SOCIETY, edited by Harry L. Shapiro, copyright 1956 by Oxford University Press, Inc. Used by permission of Oxford University Press, Inc.

Levy, Richard E. and Alexander Somek, *Paradoxical Parallels in the America and German Abortion Decisions,* originally published in 9 Tul. J. Int'l & Comp. L. 109 (2001). Reprinted with permission of the Tulane Journal of International and Comparative Law, which holds the copyright.

Li, Xiaorong, *License to Coerce: Violence Against Women, State Responsibility, and Legal Failures in China's Family Planning Program,* 8 Yale J. L. & Feminism 145 (1996). Reprinted with permission of the Yale Journal of Law and Feminism and the author.

Liebowitz-Dori, Iris, *Womb for Rent: The Future of International Trade in Surrogacy,* 6 Minn. J. Global Trade 329 (1997). Reprinted with permission from Minnesota Journal of Global Trade.

Lilith, Ryiah, *Buying a Wife But Saving a Child: A Deconstruction of Popular Rhetoric and Legal Analysis of Mail-Order Brides and Intercountry Adoption,* 9 Buff. Women's L. J. 225 (2000–2001). Reprinted with permission of the copyright holder, Buffalo Women's Law Journal.

Lininger, Tom, *Overcoming Immunity Defenses to Human Rights Suits in U.S. Courts,* 7 Harv. Hum. Rts. J. 177 (1994). Reprinted with permission of the President and Fellows of Harvard College, the Harvard Human Rights Journal, and the author.

Lloyd, Kathryn A., *Comment, Wives for Sale: The Modern International Mail-Order Bride Industry,* 20 Nw. J. Int'l L. & Bus. 341 (2000). Reprinted with permission of the author.

Lopez, Antoinette Sedillo, *Evolving Indigenous Law: Navajo Marriage—Cultural Traditions and Modern Challenges,* 17 Ariz. J. Int'l & Comp. L. 283 (2000). Reprinted with permission of the Arizona Journal of International and Comparative Law and the author.

M. v. H., [1999] 2 S.C.R. 3. Reprinted for educational purposes with the knowledge and authorization of Crown Copyright and Licensing, Canadian Government Publishing.

Margulies, Peter, *Democratic Transitions and the Future of Asylum Law,* 71 U. Colo. L. Rev. 3 (2000). Reprinted with permission of the University of Colorado Law Review and the author.

Martinez-Torron, Javier, Anglo-American Law and Canon Law (1998). Reprinted with permission of Duncker & Humblot and the author.

Mattern, Michael G., *Notes and Comments, German Abortion Law: The Unwanted Child of Reunification,* 13 Loy. L.A. Int'l & Comp. L. Rev. 643 (1991). Reprinted with permission of the Loyola of Los Angeles International and Comparative Law Review and the author.

McA v. McA, [2000] 1 I.R. 457 (Ir. H. Ct.). Reprinted with permission of the publisher and copyright holder, Incorporated Council of Law Reporting for Ireland.

McBain v State of Victoria (2000) 99 F.C.R. 116 (Austl.). Reprinted with the expressed permission of the © Lawbook Co., part of Thomson Legal & Regulatory Limited, www.thomson.com. au.

Meeusen, Johan, *Judicial Disapproval of Determination Against Illegitimate Children,* 43 Am. J. Comp. L. 119 (1995). Reprinted with permission of the American Journal of Comparative Law, University of California at Berkeley School of Law (Boalt Hall) and the author.

Melli, Marygold S., *Guideline Review: The Search for an Equitable Child Support Formula, in* Child Support: The Next Frontier 118 (J. Thomas Oldham & Marygold S. Melli eds., 2000). Reprinted with permission of the University of Michigan Press.

Merryman, John G., David S. Clark, & John O. Haley, The Civil Law Tradition: Europe, Latin America, and East Asia © 1994 Matthew Bender, Michie Publishing. Reprinted with permission of Matthew Bender.

Mezey, Susan Gluck, *Constitutional Adjudication of Children's Rights Claims in the United States Supreme Court, 1953–92*, 27 Fam. L. Q. 307 (1993). Reprinted by permission of the American Bar Association.

Minow, Martha, *Whatever Happened to Children's Rights?*, 80 Minn. L. Rev. 267 (1995). Reprinted with permission of the Minnesota Law Review and the author.

Miron v. Trudel, [1995] 2 S.C.R. 418. Reprinted for educational purposes with the knowledge and authorization of Crown Copyright and Licensing, Canadian Government Publishing.

Mlyniec, Wallace J., *A Judge's Ethical Dilemma: Assessing a Child's Capacity to Choose*, 64 Fordham L. Rev. 1873 (1996). Reprinted with permission of the Fordham Law Review and the author.

Moodie, Michael, et al., *Symposium on Religious Law: Roman Catholic, Islamic, and Jewish Treatment of Familial Issues, Including Education, Abortion, In Vitro Fertilization, Prenuptial Agreements, Contraception, and Marital Fraud*, 19 Loy. L. A. Int'l & Comp. L. J. 9 (1993). Reprinted with permission of the Loyola of Los Angeles International and Comparative Law Journal.

Morse, Adrian M., Jr. & Sayeh, Leila P., *Tunisia: Marriage, Divorce, and Foreign Recognition*, 29 Fam. L.Q. 701 (1995). © American Bar Association. Reprinted by permission.

Mosikatsana, Tshepo, *Children's Rights and Family Autonomy in the South African Constitution: A Comment on Children's Rights under the Final Constitution*, 3 Mich. J. Race & L. 341 (1998). Reprinted with permission of the Michigan Journal of Race and Law and the author.

Murphy, Sean D., *Non-State Entities in International Law*, 94 Am. J. Int'l L. 111 (2000). Reprinted with permission of the author.

Mutua, Makau, *Savages, Victims, and Saviors: The Metaphor of Human Rights*, 42 Harv. Int'l L.J. 201 (2000). Reprinted by permission © 2000 by the President and Fellows of Harvard College, the Harvard International Law Journal, and the author.

Mutua, Makau, *What is Twail?*, 94 Am. Soc'y Int'l L. Proc. 31 (2000). Reproduced with permission from 94 ASIL Proc. 33 (2000), © The American Society of International Law.

National Conference of Commissioners on Uniform State Laws, Selected portions of the text and comments to the Uniform Child Custody Jurisdiction Act, © 1968, the Uniform Child Custody Jurisdiction and Enforcement Act, © 1997, the Uniform Interstate Family Support Act (1996) © 1996, and the Uniform Interstate Family Support Act (2001) © 2001. Reprinted with permission of the copyright holder, the National Conference of Commissioners on Uniform State Laws.

Neuman, Gerald L., *Casey in the Mirror: Abortion, Abuse and the Right to Protection in the United States and Germany*, 43 Am. J. Comp. L. 273 (1995). Reprinted with permission of the American Journal of Comparative Law, University of California at Berkeley School of Law (Boalt Hall), and the author.

Oldham, J. Thomas, *New Methods to Update Child Support*, in Child Support: The Next Frontier 128 (J. Thomas Oldham & Marygold S. Melli eds., 2000). Reprinted with permission of the University of Michigan Press.

Orsy, Ladislas, Marriage in Canon Law (1985). Reprinted by permission of The Liturgical Press and the author.

Paust, Jordan J., *Human Rights Purposes of the Violence Against Women Act and International Law's Enhancement of Congressional Power*, 22 Hous. J. Int'l. L. 209 (2000). Reprinted with permission of Houston Journal of International Law and the author.

Penal Code, Proclamation No. 158 of 1957, §2 (Ethiopia), available at http://cyber.law.harvard.edu/population/abortion/ethiopia.abo.html. Reprinted by permission of Terry Martin, Librarian and Professor of Law, Harvard Law School and produced by the International Digest of Health Legislation at the World Health Organization.

Perry, Twila, *Transracial and International Adoption: Mothers, Hierarchy, Race, and Feminist Legal Theory*, 10 Yale J. L. & Feminism 101 (1998). Reprinted by permission of The Yale Journal of Law & Feminism, Inc. from The Yale Journal of Law & Feminism Vol. 10, No. 1.

Pitrolo, Elizabeth Ann, *The Birds, The Bees, and the Deep Freeze: Is There International Consensus in the Debate Over Assisted Reproductive Technologies?*, 19 Hous. J. Int'l L. 147 (1996). Reprinted with permission from Houston Journal of International Law.

Re J, 1999 WL 1142460 (Eng. C.A. Nov. 25, 1999). Reprinted with permission of Westlaw.

Reitz, John C., *How to Do Comparative Law*, 46 Am. J. Comp. L. 617 (1998). Reprinted with permission of the American Journal of Comparative Law, University of California at Berkeley School of Law (Boalt Hall), and the author.

Resnik, Judith, *"Naturally" Without Gender: Women, Jurisdiction, and the Federal Courts*, 66 N.Y.U. L. Rev. 1682 (1991). Reprinted with permission of the New York University Law Review and the author.

Rosettenstein, David S., *Trans-Racial Adoption in the United States and the Impact of Considera- tion Relating to Minority Population Groups on International Adoptions in the United States*, 9 Int'l J. Law & Fam. 131 (1995). Reprinted with permission of the author and of the pub- lisher and copyright holder, Oxford University Press.

Roth, Kenneth, *Domestic Violence as an International Human Rights Issue*, from Human Rights of Women, edited by Rebecca J. Cook. Copyright © 1994 University of Pennsylvania Press. Reprinted with permission of the University of Pennsylvania Press and the editor.

Roth, Kenneth, *The Charade of U.S. Ratification of International Human Rights Treaties*, 1 Chi. J. Int'l L. 347 (2000). Reprinted with permission of the copyright holder, The Chicago Journal of International Law.

Russell v Russell, [1976] 134 C.L.R. 495. Reprinted with the expressed permission of the © Law- book Co., part of Thomson Legal & Regulatory Limited, www.thomson.com.au.

Sachs, Justice Albie, *Introduction* to The Changing Family: International Perspectives on the Family and Family Law xii (John Eekelaar & Thandabantu Nhlapo eds., 1998). Reprinted with permission of Hart Publishing, Ltd.

Sarkin, Jeremy, *The Drafting of South Africa's Final Constitution from a Human Rights Perspective*, 47 Am. J. Comp. L. 67 (1999). Reprinted with permission of the American Journal of Com- parative Law, University of California at Berkeley School of Law (Boalt Hall), and the author.

Scholes, Robert J. & Anchalee Phataralaoha, The "Mail-Order Bride" Industry and its Impact on U.S. Immigration (1999), *at* http://www.ins.usdoj.gov/graphics/aboutins/repsstudies/ Mobappa.htm *or* http://www.clas.ufl.edu/users/rscholes/homepage.htm. Reprinted with permission of the authors.

Schwartz, Laura J., *Models for Parenthood in Adoption Law: The French Conception*, 28 Vand. J. Transnat'l L. 1069 (1995). Reprinted with permission of the copyright holder, Vanderbilt Journal of Transnational Law.

Sloth-Nielsen, Julia, *Chicken Soup or Chainsaws: Some Implications of the Constitutionalisation of Children's Rights in South Africa*, 1996 Acta Juridica 6. Reprinted by permission of Juta & Co., Ltd.

Stark, Barbara, *Women and Globalization: The Failure and Postmodern Possibilities of International Law*, 33 Vand. J. Transnat'l L. 503 (2000). Reprinted with permission of Vanderbilt Journal of Transnational Law, who is the copyright holder, and the author.

Teitelbaum, Lee E., *Children's Rights and the Problem of Equal Respect*, 27 Hofstra L. Rev. 799 (1999). Reprinted with permission of the Hofstra Law Review Association.

Thomas, Dorothy Q. and Michele E. Beasley, *Domestic Violence as a Human Rights Issue*, 58 Alb. L. Rev. 1119 (1995). Reprinted with permission of Albany Law Review.

Torfs, Rik, *Church and State in France, Belgium, and the Netherlands: Unexpected Similarities and Hidden Differences*, 1996 B.Y.U. L. Rev. 945 (1996). Reprinted with permission of the Brigham Young University Law Review and the author.

Treitel, Andrew, *Conflicting Traditions: Muslim Shari'a Courts and Marriage Age Regulation in Is- rael*, 26 Colum. Hum. Rts. L. Rev. 403 (1995). Reprinted with permission of the Columbia Human Rights Law Review.

Van de Perre v. Edwards, [2001] 2 S.C.R. 1014. Reprinted for educational purposes with the knowl- edge and authorization of Crown Copyright and Licensing, Canadian Government Publishing.

Vergara, Vanessa B.M., Comment, *Abusive Mail-Order Bride Marriage and the Thirteenth Amend- ment*, 94 Nw. U. L. Rev. 1547 (2000). Reprinted by special permission of Northwestern Uni- versity School of Law Law Review and the author.

Wardle, Lynn, *International Marriage and Divorce Regulation and Recognition: A Survey*, 29 Fam. L. Q. 497 (1995). © American Bar Association. Reprinted by permission.

Weiner, Merle, *International Child Abduction and the Escape from Domestic Violence*, 69 Fordham L. Rev. 593 (2001). Reprinted with permission of the Fordham Law Review and the author.

Weisbrod, Carol, *Universals and Particulars: A Comment on Women's Human Rights and Religious Marriage Contracts*, 9 S. Cal. Rev. L. & Women's Stud. 77 (1999). Reprinted with permission of the Southern California Review of Law and Women's Studies and the author.

Willekens, Harry, *Long Term Developments in Family Law in Eastern Europe: An Explanation, in* The Changing Family: International Perspectives on the Family and Family Law 55 (John Eekelaar & Thandabantu Nhlapo eds., 1998). Reprinted with permission of Hart Publishing, Ltd.

Woodhouse, Barbara Bennett, *The Constitutionalization of Children's Rights: Incorporating Emerging Human Rights into Constitutional Doctrine*, 2 U. Pa. J. Const. L. 1 (1999). Reprinted with permission of the University of Pennsylvania Journal of Constitutional Law and the author.

Wright v. Zaver, [2002] 211 D.L.R.4th 260 (Ont. C.A.). Reproduced with permission of Carswell Publishing, through *Access Copyright*, The Canadian Copyright Licensing Agency.

Editorial Note: In many of the cases and materials that we have excerpted, citations and footnotes have been omitted. Footnotes, in particular, were frequently omitted without notes or symbols indicating their omission. When we have retained footnotes from cases or excerpted materials, we have retained the original footnote numbers.

Part One

Family Formation, Regulation, and Dissolution

Chapter 1

Introduction to the Study of Family Law in the World Community

A competent practitioner of family law cannot ignore the legal world outside the country in which he or she practices. "Globalization"—or, if you prefer, "globalism"—has occurred. Not only are enormous transfers of wealth and information occurring across borders, often through cyberspace, but also vast numbers of people move daily from country to country. Regardless of whether globalization is to be applauded or condemned, it has had the undeniable effect of bringing more people and cultures together. The result for the family law practitioner is a world of new and challenging legal issues as well as new possibilities prompted by the cross-fertilization of legal ideas. For policy makers, globalization has required the adoption of international instruments that address transnational family law matters. This book is a first attempt to capture some of the legal challenges, doctrines, and possibilities that students of family law will one day encounter when they practice in our interconnected world.

This casebook is an amalgam of a vast array of information. All of the world's legal resources were possible sources of information for this book. Not surprisingly, we had to be very selective. The materials chosen are deliberately diverse to reflect the breadth of information available. The material should allow you to come away from the course with a sense that the world, indeed, has much to offer us here in the United States, and that your continued inquiry into comparative and international family law materials will be fruitful, if not challenging.

The materials that follow can be categorized into three groups: comparative, international, and U.S. legal materials. Since many students have not yet studied comparative and international materials, we provide some basic information and concepts in the first two parts of this first chapter. The last part of the chapter provides some tips on researching international and comparative family law—tips that should prove useful both when writing law school papers and when conducting legal research for a client.

A. An Introduction to Comparative Law

Throughout this casebook, you will encounter a variety of legal materials from countries as diverse as China and Canada, the Philippines and South Africa, and Romania and

France, to name just a few. At the outset, you may be wondering, why is such a course of study beneficial to me since I intend to practice family law in the United States?

1. Why Study Comparative Law?

There are many potential benefits to engaging in comparative legal analysis. As described below, comparative legal analysis can benefit domestic and international law reform efforts, can aid lawyers representing a particular client, and can further harmonization efforts. Most importantly, it can foster an open-mindedness that is particularly useful in the practice of law.

First, other nations' approaches to legal problems may provide ideas for the improvement of law in the United States. Using comparative law for the improvement of one's own law is common in Europe. As one commentator recently observed, "[A] comparative study involving American law is generally perceived to be very important for the development in the European Union and the individual European countries...." Gerda A. Kleijkamp, Family Life and Family Interests: A Comparative Study on the Influence of the European Convention of Human Rights on Dutch Family Law and the Influence of the United States Constitution on American Family Law 4 (1999). This justification is "the most traditional and widely accepted view" of the usefulness of comparative studies, *see* Xavier Blanc-Jouvan, *Centennial World Congress on Comparative Law: Closing Remarks*, 75 Tul. L. Rev. 1235, 1237 (2001), and has very ancient roots. "The comparison of laws, at least in their geographical diversity, is as old as the science of law itself. Aristotle (384–322 B.C.), in considering what form of political community would be best, studied 153 constitutions of Greek and other cities...." René David & John E.C. Brierley, Majority Legal Systems in the World Today: An Introduction to the Comparative Study of Law 1 (3d ed. 1985). It would be parochial and wrong to think that legislators and policy makers in the United States could not gain from examining the laws of other nations.

Second, the study of comparative law may also help us craft international legal solutions to problems, and may help the United States aid other nations in designing their own solutions to problems. Individuals from the United States are involved in a variety of multilateral and international law-making projects. To work effectively on these projects, or to know when to undertake new ones, it is important to have some understanding of the legal systems of other participants. Similarly, Americans are involved in the domestic legal reform of other countries. For example, the American Bar Association's Central and East Europe Law Initiative ("CEELI") sends Americans abroad, principally into former Soviet republics and Eastern Europe, to help formulate laws. It is important that we do not blindly recommend our own laws for others when better models may exist.

Third, apart from the benefits to the future legislator or policy maker, a study of comparative family law may assist the future lawyer. It is no longer unusual to have clients who come from abroad, or who marry, divorce, or have children while living abroad. American nationals may want to know, for example, what protection one can expect abroad from an abusive spouse, or whether a court in another country would award a woman custody if she were to divorce. Or a client may have fled to the United States from abroad with her children, and the children's father may be seeking the children's return. The lawyer would need to know something about the law of the child's habitual residence as well as the law of the country to which the child was taken. Comparative study also provides law students with insight into laws and legal systems that can impact, or have impacted, "foreign"-born clients. *See* Nora v. Demleitner, *Challenge, Opportunity and Risk: An Era of Change in Comparative Law*, 46 Am. J. Comp. L. 647, 649 (1998). For example, whether a person can be admitted to this country as a spouse of an American citizen may depend on whether the marriage was valid where entered. *See* Cosulich Societa Triestina Di Navigazione v. Elting, 66 F.2d 534 (2d Cir. 1933). Similarly, whether a child is legitimated, for purposes of immigration, may also depend, in part, upon the law of another country. *See* 8 U.S.C. § 1409(a)(4)(A); Ng Suey Hi v. Weedin, 21 F.2d 801 (9th Cir. 1927). Or a client, or client's adversary, may try to use cultural practices to excuse intra-family criminal conduct such as domestic violence or child abuse. *See, e.g.,* People v. Wu, 286 Cal. Rptr. 868 (Cal. Ct. App. 1991); Valerie L. Sacks, *Note, An Indefensible Defense: On the Misuse of Culture in Criminal Law*, 13 Ariz. J. Int'l & Comp. L. 523, 528–29 (1996) (citing People v. Chen, No. 87-7774 (N.Y. Sup. Ct. 1989)). Sometimes these sorts of questions will be resolved by the application of rules on the conflict of laws, but the issues still require an understanding of the other nations' rules. While often it will be important to contract with counsel from the other country in order to provide the expertise required in these cases, the study of comparative family law can nurture a cultural sensitivity essential to the understanding of the issues involved.

In addition, lawyers can use comparative law to advocate on behalf of their clients, even when their clients' cases do not involve issues of foreign law. It is perhaps illustrative that the authors of a widely read text on comparative law for American law students include in their book the case *Greenspan v. Slate*, decided by the Supreme Court of New Jersey in 1953. *See* Rudolf B. Schlesinger et al., Comparative Law: Cases, Text, Materials 2 (5th ed. 1988). The issue posed was whether the parents of an infant child were liable for necessaries furnished to their child in an emergency, in the absence of an express or implied contract. Greenspan v. Slate, 97 A.2d 390 (N.J. 1953). In the face of conflicting rules, the New Jersey Supreme Court was influenced by a civil-law system's approach to the problem. The court ultimately adopted the equitable rule that such a legal obligation existed. The case illustrates that practitioners can successfully cite foreign solutions in domestic cases. The casebook authors state in a note: "The principal case is not unique. There are many other English and American decisions, especially in cases involving novel problems, in which the court's opinion reflects successful resort by counsel to civil-law authorities." Schlesinger, *supra*, at 6.

Just as competent practitioners of private international law require an ability to engage in comparative analysis, so do specialists in public international law. Article 38 of the Statute of the International Court of Justice indicates that a source of international law is "the general principles of law recognized by civilized nations," and that "judicial decisions and the teachings of the most highly qualified publicists of the various nations" are a "subsidiary means for" determining the law. William E. Butler's *International Law in Comparative Perspective* 5 (1980) elaborated upon some of the various uses of comparative law in the practice of public international law:

> [T]he comparative method has been found useful in identifying trends in the emergence of general principles of international law (and the same would hold true for regional or subsystems of international law), as a means of filling gaps in or interpreting international treaties and even customary international law, of evaluating state practice as a constituent element in the formation of customary rules of international law, of exploring parallels between rules of municipal law and international law and the possibility that the former may comprise part of the latter, as a means of probing and clarifying the underlying ideologies, values, legal institutions, and cultures of states in order to better comprehend the inter-

national legal system, avert misunderstandings and misconceptions, and lay the groundwork for a more viable world order, of elaborating, exploring, and developing the law of international institutions, of assisting international tribunals, of codifying international law and developing individual branches of international law, of clarifying goals and values held by policymakers whose actions and decisions affect international law, [and] of assessing compliance by states with international law....

Fourth, comparative law is useful for those seeking the harmonization of laws. Professors Merryman, Clark, and Haley explain:

> Since the late 19th century, scholars and politicians have advocated the international unification of private law, an enterprise that necessarily calls for the description and evaluation of different private law systems. The idea of international unification inspired the first International Congress of Comparative Law held in Paris in 1900 and remains on the agenda of subsequent congresses of comparative law that are now held every fourth year. That ideal also led to establishment of the International Institute for the Unification of Private Law in Rome, which is supported by a large number of nations, including the United States.

John Henry Merryman et al., The Civil Law Tradition: Europe, Latin America, and East Asia 2 (1994).

Despite the potential benefits to be derived from studying (and later using) comparative law, one has to be somewhat cautious about expecting to experience these benefits. One commentator, for example, has said, "[Comparative law] has not been used much by state or federal legislators and law commissions." Vernon Valentine Palmer, Insularity and Leadership in American Comparative Law: The Past One Hundred Years, 75 Tul. L. Rev. 1093, 1097 (2001). David Clark has revealed that with the exception of two recently emerging fields (international civil procedure and international criminal law), "there is scant legal literature on the use of foreign and comparative law in United States courts because courts rarely cite foreign law." David S. Clark, The Use of Comparative Law by American Courts, 42 Am. J. Comp. L. 23, 23 (1994). In fact, Professor Reimann has stated, "Law students stand virtually no chance ever to pursue [domestic law reform through the adoption of foreign models] because, in contrast to many other countries, American judges and legislators pay next to no attention to foreign ideas." Mathias Reimann, The End of Comparative Law as an Autonomous Subject, 11 Tul. Eur. & Civ. L.F. 49, 56 (1996). This is in contrast to "most states of the world" that "have persisted in the use of persuasive [non-national] authority throughout the nineteenth and twentieth centuries." H. Patrick Glenn, Comparative Law and Legal Practice: On Removing the Borders, 75 Tul. L. Rev. 977, 986 (2001) (citing recent examples from English, Dutch, and French courts).

Nor do we expect students to become proficient in harmonizing the law, assuming such harmonization is a beneficial process in the family law area. Comparative law has not been used much to harmonize family law. "As with legal unification (both today and in 1900), there is more effort to harmonize commercial and contract law, and perhaps to establish a broader obligations law, than to put much time into harmonized family or successions law." David S. Clark, Nothing New in 2000? Comparative Law in 1900 and Today, 75 Tul. L. Rev. 871, 905 (2001). In fact, it is a hotly debated political question whether more harmonization, unification or integration is desirable, especially in the sphere of family law where unification has been described as "clearly pointless—and even dangerous" because "national traditions and moral values have an important role to play." Blanc-

Jouvan, *supra*, at 1240. Moreover, this book does not strive to have students harmonize the law of various legal systems because harmonization cannot be learned in the classroom. *See* Reimann, *supra*, at 57. "Even if one could [teach harmonization in the classroom], it would not make for good teaching material because it requires highly-detailed studies of individual rules on a very technical level and often in the most tedious manner." *Id.* We spare students this sort of exercise, for better or worse.

In addition, this book is not structured to prepare students for some of the other possible benefits, and hence they are unlikely to materialize either. For example, a true preparation for an international legal practice would require the study of various international and foreign procedures, and this book hardly addresses such issues.

Given the list of potential benefits, and then caveats, you may still be wondering whether the study of comparative law is worth the effort. We now come to our fifth, and perhaps most important, reason for the study of comparative law. It is the reason that motivated the authorship of this casebook. The study of other systems' laws fosters a certain open-mindedness. As one scholar stated, "Comparative legal analysis introduces legal concepts, styles, organizations and categorizations previously unknown, opening unsuspected possibilities in the very notion/of law. The differences discovered in foreign legal cultures should propel law students and scholars to greater acuity in distinguishing the actual from the inevitable; and historically contingent happenstances from causally connected phenomena." Vivian Grosswald Curran, *Dealing in Difference: Comparative Law's Potential for Broadening Legal Perspectives*, 46 Am. J. Comp. L. 657, 665 (1998). "Law" comes to be better understood as dependent upon its social, economic, historic and political surroundings. Another scholar put it this way: "[Studying foreign law] delivers the student from dogmatism. A student confronted with only one solution to a legal problem has a tendency to assume it is the right one. When he is confronted with two, he is encouraged to think." James Gordley, *Comparative Law and Legal Education*, 75 Tul. L. Rev. 1003, 1008 (2001). As a result, comparative analysis gives us profound insight into our own system and a better understanding of our own laws. "Comparative law in the proper sense means an observation of one's own law from outside, in order to evaluate it critically." *See* Max Rheinstein, *Comparative Law and Conflict of Laws in Germany*, 2 U. Chi. L. Rev. 232, 237 (1934).

There exists some danger in using comparative law to evaluate our own laws. As Professor Nora Demleitner describes, this type of self-evaluation can reinforce ethnocentrism, parochialism, and intolerance. To prevent that result, Professor Demleitner offers some important insights and advice. In the following excerpt, Professor Demleitner explains how "Comparative law can reveal and equalize the relationships between different legal cultures." She suggests that this equalization then has its own benefits: for example, it may help us view international law from a new and healthier perspective.

Nora V. Demleitner, *Combating Legal Ethnocentrism*
31 Ariz. St. L.J. 737, 741–61 (1999)

Comparative law promotes "thinking with another set of legal concepts and categories, [so that] we can then look back at our own legal world with a sense of it as newly strange." Not unlike feminist legal scholarship, at its best, comparative law can be sensitive to the consequences of laws, skeptical of the legal system's claim to encompass all of social reality and practice, and critical of the law's discourse of dominance. "It confronts us with our own hidden conceptual, ideological framework." Consequently, it offers different perspectives on the traditional view of the legal system in which we matured as people and as lawyers.

But there must be more to comparative law. If its sole goal were to learn about our own law and culture, then modern jurisprudential theories which explain the operation of the domestic legal system would be equally useful. Yet even more disturbingly, comparative law—when its exclusive aim is to provide a reflection of ourselves—may lead to a merely superficial analysis of the foreign system. Therefore, it can become a tool of ethnocentrism and prejudice. Only awareness of its destructive potential will allow comparativists to avoid those pitfalls and develop a comparative law adequate to combat the ethnocentrism already embedded in law.

At its worst, comparative law will merely confirm personally, communally, and systemically preconceived notions about the comparativist's own system, and most distressingly, other legal systems and cultures....

The challenge in comparative law is not merely an intellectual one. Legal comparativists share with religious comparativists an emotional attachment to their own religion/law: "For doctrinal law is a parochial science in the sense that it is of little concern to the traditional lawyer how other legal systems are treated, as long as his own system is approached with the proper respect." The affinity for one's own system implies that any negative findings about that system will be reinterpreted so as to be reconcilable with a world view that elevates one's domestic system. For example, abuses that would lead to the conclusion that a violation of human rights has occurred are considered mere aberrations at home. If the same abuses take place abroad, however, they are deemed systemic, sometimes even culturally ingrained. For example, in the Western world, sati, or "widow burning," as previously practiced in India, is viewed as a serious human rights violation indicative of the low value Indian culture assigns women. Because of the Western definition of free will, however, we do not deem face lifts and cosmetic breast enlargements to be human rights violations. Even though frequently bemoaned, most of society views them as singular events rather than gauges of female oppression. On the other hand, Westerners often see sati as characteristic of a larger societal problem. While sati is defined as a crime in India, no pressure group has arisen in Western countries to advocate the criminalization of so-called "cosmetic surgery."...

While legal ethnocentrism affects the view of all other legal systems, its effect is most noticeable on the legal systems in non-Western, non-Christian, non-white, and economically less developed countries. Colonialism and Social Darwinism were the primary contributors to the ethnocentric illusion of the superiority of Western cultures, and with it Western law. The economic and political success of Western regimes has continued to reinforce that attitude....

Comparative law can reveal and equalize the relationships between different legal cultures. The recalibration of comparative law and its potential are exemplified in two situations. First, the interplay between the legal culture of the host country and the migrants can illuminate legal changes in both systems, as well as create new, mixed systems. Second, comparative law can provide a crucial role in the human rights debate by deconstructing the static notions of universality and relativism....

While the original purpose of comparative law was to facilitate European cross-border trade through a comparison of legal rules, today it can assist in mediating conflicts that may arise from the cross-border movement of persons who are imbued with the values of the legal culture into which they were born. Such a practical component can lead to greater insights. Comparative law can reveal how another person perceives the world, and how law contributes to and reflects the culture of a country. The ultimate goal of such an inquiry is to establish our own identity. But rather than seeing the others as not so much like us, we should see ourselves as very similar to others while acknowledging, accepting, embracing, and even admiring our differences. Instead of taking ourselves as the yard-stick, or as the norm, we must situate ourselves equidistant from the "others" in the world, whoever they might be. This will require us to "defin[e] ourselves neither by dis-tancing others as counterpoles nor by drawing them close as facsimiles but by locating ourselves among them."

After recognizing commonalities and similarities, it is then necessary to manage the difference, not to abolish it. Even an internationalized world and a global world society should not connote uniformity but rather equality in diversity and difference, since differ-ence often drives creativity. The difference between men and women, for example, which leads to different perceptions and experiences, is frequently portrayed as complementary and necessary to create a whole. The differences between individuals from different legal cultures should be viewed similarly. Only if difference is conceived in this positive, affirm-ing light can it also make interdependency—whether between men and women, between states, or between individuals in a multi-cultural society—appear non-threatening and even enriching. Should this perceptual reevaluation fail, difference will continue to stand for a threatening, alien quality....

Comparative law and human rights so far have largely failed to intersect even though they could enrich each other's discourse. Comparative law has remained trapped in the belief that laws and legal institutions in a country are shaped solely by national character-istics, without any regard to the global society or even regional developments. Therefore, human rights law with its global perspective has found comparative law inhospitable and unsuitable for analysis. On the other hand, to a large extent, the failing ability on part of the discussants to enter the legal and cultural understanding of the "other" has driven the false dichotomy in the human rights debate between universalism and relativism. One's own often limited and biased perspective has dominated any analysis of other systems. Comparative law can provide a mechanism to control for such biases and allow for a more nuanced comprehension and appreciation of other systems.

While we have come to recognize and permit some plurality and diversity at home, the human rights debate itself continues to center around the universality of law and legal norms.

> [T]he fact that so many fundamental features of culture are universal, or at least occur in many isolated places, interpreted by the assumption that the same fea-tures must always have developed from the same causes, leads to the conclusion that there is one grand system according to which mankind has developed every-where; that all the occurring variations are no more than minor details in this grand, uniform evolution.

However, with respect to legal universality such a conclusion may be fatally flawed since existing variations might conceal very substantial differences, and/or the same phenom-ena might result from distinct causality.

While universality may exist for some values at least at some level of abstraction, it might not be the general norm. Any general assumption of universality, however, will foreclose a searching, independent analysis of the norms underlying different legal cul-tures. Such norms can only be discovered through a study of the acceptance of the exist-ing legal structure in a society. That requires recognition of the fact that those within another legal system will fundamentally disagree with each other about particular values and practices in their own legal culture. While we recognize such multiplicity within our own society and legal system, there is often still reluctance to accept the absence of a uniform legal system and experience in other countries....

An analysis of the impact of human rights norms will also reveal the contingency and often domestically driven choice of issues that dominate the international human rights debate. For example, much of the U.S. and Western European discussion surrounding the position of women in Central Europe centers on domestic violence even though these might not be the most prominent or pressing issues for the women in these countries. The agenda, however, is set by human rights advocates and feminists abroad for whom those are the most salient issues because they are of preeminent importance at home....

The absence of a "common core" of values and legal norms, however should not be interpreted as lack of a common humanity but rather as recognition of different normative values and possibly institutional processes. Moreover, a group's identification of difference may serve to "'create[]' the community and 'create[]' the difference with the outside world." Such a process may be psychologically necessary to counteract the perceived pressure to achieve cultural and legal uniformity, as expressed through universal human rights standards....

Problem 1-1

Imagine that you are a jurist on the European Court of Human Rights ("the Court"). As you will see in the next subsection, the Court is the adjudicatory body for disputes arising under the European Convention on Human Rights, a regional treaty. The applicants are a mother and her infant daughter. The mother is unmarried and was so when she gave birth to her daughter.

The law of the country where the mother and child live states that no legal bond between an unmarried mother and her child results from the mere fact of birth. The birth certificate recorded at the registrar's office suffices to prove the maternal affiliation of a married woman's children, but maternal affiliation of an "illegitimate" child must be established either by a voluntary recognition by the mother on the birth certificate or by court declaration in an action instituted by the child or the child's legal representative.

The establishment of maternal affiliation of an "illegitimate" child has limited legal effects with respect to the child's family relationships for matters of inheritance. Once such affiliation has been established, it creates a legal bond with the mother alone. The child does not become a member of his or her mother's family. Consequently, the recognized "illegitimate" child has no rights through intestacy in the estates of the mother's relatives. In addition, a recognized "illegitimate" child receives only three-quarters of the share that the child would have taken if the child had been "legitimate" when the mother dies intestate.

If the mother of a recognized "illegitimate" child remains unmarried, she has but one means of improving her child's status, namely, "simple" adoption. The adopted child acquires over the adopter's estate the rights of a "legitimate" child. However, unlike the "legitimate" child, the adopted child has no rights on intestacy to the estates of the mother's relatives. Only legitimation and legitimation by adoption place an "illegitimate" child on exactly the same footing as a "legitimate" child; both of these measures presuppose the mother's marriage.

The mother recognized and adopted her daughter pursuant to the country's law. However, the mother and daughter claim that the illegitimacy laws in the country infringe various provisions of the European Convention on Human Rights, including the right to respect for family life and the non-discrimination provision (both for these children and their mothers). Assume that the only international instrument that would apply in this case is the European Convention on Human Rights.

Would a comparative legal analysis presented by the advocates be helpful? Why or why not? If you think it would be helpful, what would you want to know and why? What functions can comparative law serve here?

2. What Is Comparative Family Law?

The study of comparative law potentially offers so much to a future family law practitioner. But let us be a little more specific with our terminology. What exactly is "comparative law"? For newcomers to the discipline, it may surprise you that this question is hotly debated. The President of the International Association of Legal Science, Xavier Blanc-Jouvan, recently stated, "One knows less and less what comparative law really is, how it should be approached, and what use can be made of it. There are epistemological debates that obscure, rather than clarify, that matter." Xavier Blanc-Jouvan, *Centennial World Congress on Comparative Law: Opening Remarks*, 75 Tul. L. Rev. 859, 863 (2001). In our opinion, one of the best answers to that question was offered by Professor John Reitz. We like Professor Reitz's answer because it does not require an analysis of the origins of comparative law, but rather offers a practical and modern explanation of the discipline. Professor Reitz's description of comparative law occurs in the context of scholarship. While we will draw some important distinctions between scholarship and classroom learning after the excerpt, the methodology Professor Reitz describes is still a useful starting point.

John C. Reitz, *How to Do Comparative Law*
46 Am. J. Comp. L. 617 (1998)

I offer the following nine principles about comparative law scholarship and the closely allied field of foreign law. The first principle considers the relationship between the study of comparative law and the study of foreign law. The next four principles (Nos. 2–5) concern the basic technique of comparing law in different legal systems and the special value of that type of study. There follow three principles (Nos. 6–8) concerning specific guidelines for carrying out a comparison involving legal subjects. The final principle concerns the attitude which I believe to be indispensable for good comparative work. While I am interested in providing guidance in order to strengthen the quality of comparative law studies and increase interest in the field, I think it important to concede that there is no simple recipe for good scholarship. I am simply trying to list the most important characteristics of good comparative scholarship, with the caveat that deviations may always be made for good cause....

1. Comparative law involves drawing explicit comparisons, and most non-comparative foreign law writing could be strengthened by being made explicitly comparative....

I wish to insist that the comparative method involves explicit comparison of aspects of two or more legal systems. Some may object that any description of foreign law is implicitly comparative because all descriptions of foreign law are at a minimum trying to make the law of one system comprehensible for those trained in a different system. But I reject that argument on the grounds that the step of actually drawing the comparison is crucial to realizing the intellectual benefits of comparison. Actually framing the comparison makes one think hard about each legal system being compared and about the precise ways in which they are similar or different....

2. The comparative method consists in focusing careful attention on the similarities and differences among the legal systems being compared, but in assessing the significance of differences the comparatist needs to take account of the possibility of functional equivalence.

Comparison starts by identifying the similarities and differences between legal systems or parts of legal systems under comparison. However, in performing the basic comparative job of identifying similarities and differences, one has to consider the scope of comparison: What is going to be compared with what? Here the comparatist comes face to face with the enigma of translation. In one sense every term can be translated because there are things in each legal system that are roughly the functional equivalent of things in the other legal system. In another sense nothing can be translated because the equivalents are different in ways that matter at least for some purposes. At a minimum, generally equivalent terms in each language often have different fields of associated meaning, like, for example, "fairness" and "loyaute."

One is thus always in some sense comparing apples and oranges....

Comparatists dispute vigorously among themselves how big a problem the lack of congruity is in general and with respect to specific areas of comparison. But I think there is a high degree of consensus that good comparative analysis should pay careful attention to the problem of equivalency by probing how similar and how different the aspects of each legal system under study are. A comparative study of the consideration doctrine in British, French, and German law that simply reported that neither French nor German law recognizes the doctrine without considering whether French and German law achieve some of the same purposes with other rules would simply be a very weak effort....

Before leaving the discussion of the basic procedure of comparing, we need to discuss one technical term, the tertium comparationis, which a number of well-known writers insist upon as an essential element of the comparative method. This imposing bit of jargon refers to nothing more than the common point of departure for the comparison, typically either a real-life problem or an ideal. For example,...a comparative study of the consideration doctrine might take a functional approach by asking how each legal system under study determines which promises to enforce....In large measure, the notion of a common point of departure seems inherent in the process of comparison. Either one legal system has the same legal rule or legal institution as another, or it has different rules or institutions which perform the same function, or it provides different results for a particular problem, or it does not seem to address that problem at all. A diligent search for similarities and differences ought to encompass all of those possibilities, so one may simultaneously agree that the term is essential to the comparative method and question whether one needs the special term at all....

In using ideals as a common point of departure for comparison, one must be on guard against the natural human tendency to use without reflection the ideals of one's own system as the normative measure for systems that may not accept the ideal. For example, the rule of law is an ideal that developed first in Western Europe and the United States. Some would argue today that it enjoys nearly universal acceptance; others would dispute that it does, pointing out how its development is tied to the development of society, law, and forms of government in the West. Thus, if one wishes to argue that one legal system is better or more highly developed than another because it better or more fully institutes the rule of law, one should not only consider carefully the question of functional equivalence, but also confront directly the question why it is appropriate to apply the rule of law as a normative measure....

3. The process of comparison is particularly suited to lead to conclusions about (a) distinctive characteristics of each individual legal system and/or (b) commonalities concerning how law deals with the particular subject under study.

What should the point of the comparison be? Comparative study of law can be undertaken simply to inform the reader about foreign law, perhaps for the practical purpose of facilitating an international transaction or resolving a conflict of laws problem. It may be part of a campaign of law reform. It may be part of a comparative study of human culture or part of a critical project aimed at exposing the way law masks the exercise of power. It can even be used to spoof legal scholarship. There is no reason why comparative studies should be limited to any particular set of purposes. The comparative method is just a tool.

From the nature of comparative studies, as outlined in the foregoing section, however, it can be seen that comparative law naturally and primarily leads in two directions at once. Because comparison focuses on both differences and similarities, comparative law studies cast light on (1) the special or unique natures of the legal systems being compared and (2) their commonalities with respect to the issue in question. The first direction leads toward defining the distinctive features of each legal system. The second direction leads toward appreciation of commonalities, maybe even universal aspects, of legal systems and insight into fundamental aspects of the particular legal issue in question....

It is important to bear in mind that comparison by itself is at best a "weakly normative" exercise. As every adolescent in U.S. society learns, there is some normative force in the statement, "Everyone else is doing it," or "Nobody else's family does that," but, as we parents immediately counter, "So what?" Comparison is a relatively weak basis for normative argument. Rather, it is a sign that hard thinking about the normative basis for the apparently deviant behavior or rule is in order. Thus comparative studies may uncover interesting ideas for domestic law reform, but in the end the case for adoption of a foreign model cannot rest on the fact that many other countries have the rule or legal institution. The argument for domestic law reform has to be made in terms of normative claims acceptable within the domestic legal system, and probably the foreign transplant will have to be modified in significant ways precisely because each legal system reflects an at least partially unique legal system....

4. One of the benefits of comparative analysis is its tendency to push the analysis to broader levels of abstraction through its investigation into functional equivalence.

The fact that after careful analysis the aspects to be compared in each legal system remain in some important senses apples and oranges is not bad. The real power of comparative analysis arises precisely from the fact that the process of comparing "apples" and "oranges" forces the comparatist to develop constructs like "fruit." It forces the comparatist to articulate broader categories to accommodate terms that are at least in some significant way functional equivalents and to search on broader levels for functional similarities and differences.... [T]he search for functional equivalence with U.S. civil discovery procedures leads to the broader question of how different legal systems handle the inequality between the parties with respect to access to information.

5. The comparative method has the potential to lead to even more interesting analysis by inviting the comparatist to give reasons for the similarities and differences among legal systems or to analyze their significance for the cultures under study.

Comparative study could end with a delineation of relevant similarities and differences. This would satisfy the minimum goal of comparative study.... However, once one has carefully determined similarities and differences between the legal systems under study, a broader field of inquiry presents itself, one that poses fascinating questions of great general interest. One may ask what the reasons are for the similarities and differences among the legal systems under study. Alternatively, to avoid simplistic notions of causality in human society, one may ask what the significance of the identified similarities and differences is for an understanding of the respective legal systems and the broader cultures of which they are a part. In either case, the point of the inquiry is to pay attention to the connections (or lack of connections) between the specific differences and similarities under study and broader, more systemic contrasts among legal systems, and most particularly, broader contrasts among societies and cultures.

Seeking answers to these questions will cause the comparatist to consider not only global comparison of legal systems, but also similarities and differences in the respective political, economic, and social systems and historical traditions of which they are a part. This is the aspect of comparative law that leads the student beyond law to the rest of the humanities and social sciences, maybe even to the natural sciences....

6. In establishing what the law is in each jurisdiction under study, comparative law (and, for that matter, studies of foreign law, as well) should (a) be concerned to describe the normal conceptual world of the lawyers, (b) take into consideration all the sources upon which a lawyer in that legal system might base her opinion as to what the law is, and (c) take into consideration the gap between the law on the books and law in action, as well as (d) important gaps in available knowledge about either the law on the books or the law in action.

I have now described the basic method and value of comparing law, but I need to say more about the specific rules for carrying out the comparison. This section lays down guidelines for determining what the law is in each country under comparison....

(a) Focus on the Normal Conceptual World of the Lawyers

[T]he primary task for which comparative lawyers are prepared by their training and experience is to compare law from the interior point of view—that is, to help lawyers from one legal system see how lawyers in another legal system think about certain legal problems. I do not want to lay down narrow definitions of what is and what is not comparative law for fear of choking off interesting work that might not fit my definition. Moreover, comparative law by definition takes one outside of one's own legal tradition and therefore facilitates the taking of an exterior viewpoint of the law. I also have no problem with the kind of political science that treats law as the output of a black box and seeks to explain that output by correlation with other factors exterior to the law, and I have no objection to lawyers contributing to that kind of study as long as they do a good job. Indeed, I think that lawyers should be interested in such studies especially insofar as they shed light on the workings of the legal system and suggest factors at work other than those called out explicitly by legal doctrine. But I do wish to insist that comparative law studies should normally compare the interior views of legal systems, whatever else they may also do. Comparative work therefore usually ought to address the question, "How does the foreign lawyer appear to think about this question and how does that compare to the way we think about it in our legal system?"

This focus on the conceptual world of the lawyer suggests first and foremost a focus on formal legal reasoning. What counts as a source of law in each system under study? Using the law stated in the formal sources of law, what arguments can be made in each system with respect to the legal question under study and how would they be evaluated by well-trained lawyers in each system respectively? In some systems, like that of the United States with its common law heritage and explicitly political ways of selecting judges, lawyers tend to include a consideration of broader questions of policy in their formal legal reasoning and may also take into consideration the political dimensions of a legal problem in ana-lyzing how a court will likely decide a given issue. These kinds of policy considerations and political calculations should also be included as part of the mental world of the well-trained lawyer in such a system. [A]ppreciating what does and does not count as a good argument in a foreign legal system requires an understanding of the general philosophical traditions of that culture, at least to the extent that they may have influenced the jurists.

(b) Taking Account of All Sources of Information About the Law

The focus on lawyers' argumentation will counteract the tendency to focus on statu-tory materials only and will force the comparatist to consult cases and the commentary of scholars, as well. In Sacco's terms, the comparatist will have to deal with the variety of "legal formants"—that is, all the authorities a lawyer working in a given system might consult to find the law, from formal sources of law like constitutions and statutes to au-thorities that are not recognized as formal sources of law but which are nevertheless influ-ential, such as the writings of jurists.... [T]here are likely to be in any legal system that has any substantial degree of autonomy from other political institutions a number of conflict-ing opinions about what the legal rule is. By paying attention to all the relevant legal for-mants, the comparatist will be saved from taking a more simplistic view of the law than does the foreign legal culture the comparatist is studying.

(c) The Gap Between Law on the Books and Law in Action

The discussion of legal formants shows that one cannot confine one's search for foreign law to the statute books. Other legal formants, such as court opinions or the writings of scholars, may show that what is regarded as the law in that society is quite different from what one might have thought it to be if one looked only at the statutes. There thus may be, and probably are in most legal systems, important gaps between the law in the statute books and the law actually applied by the courts. Comparative law should be interested in both, and especially in the explanations and rationales given by participants in the legal system to explain the gap because these explanations may reveal a great deal about legal reasoning in that system....

(d) Gaps in Information About Foreign Law

Those who study U.S. law in the large research libraries in the United States become ac-customed to having a great deal of information available about their subject, from com-plete collections of statutes and regulations to extensive case reports, a burgeoning "how-to" literature for the actual practice, and an extensive academic literature. There is even a growing literature about empirical studies of the real-world effects of many aspects of law in the United States. But comparative law studies are dogged by enormous gaps in the in-formation available. First, libraries' collections of foreign law are hardly ever as complete as the best libraries in the foreign country itself. Second, countries of the civil law tradition do not publish the decisions of appellate courts with the thoroughness and persistence of common law countries. Third, despite the growth of fields like legal sociology,... it is even more difficult to find relevant empirical studies for many other countries, especially third-world countries.

Good comparative writing should show concern for this issue and should deal honestly and forthrightly with it. The reader should bear this concern in mind in evaluating comparative and foreign law studies. Has the author cited the most recent sources for what is represented to be current law? Are there reasons to believe that the sources available to the author are not current? Has the author cited such a reasonable assortment of commentators or such distinguished commentators that the views represented to be the dominant views in a given legal system are not likely to be the idiosyncratic views of one person or group? Has the author presented any information about law in action so that the reader can see whether or not there is a gap between it and the law on the books? If so, does the author cite reliable sources for that information? (Anecdotal evidence is not necessarily objectionable. Much comparative law is based on anecdotal evidence of law in action. It is not, however, systematic and hence may not accurately represent the norm, and careful comparative analysis should recognize this limitation.)

In short, good comparatists should be sensitive to the ever present limitations on information available about foreign legal systems and should qualify their conclusions if they are unable to have access to sufficient information or if they have reason to suspect that they are missing important information. If the gaps are too large, the study should not be undertaken at all because its conclusions about foreign law will be too uncertain to be useful.

7. Comparative and foreign law scholarship both require strong linguistic skills and maybe even the skills of anthropological field study in order to collect information about foreign legal systems at first hand, but it is also reasonable for the comparative scholar without the necessary linguistic skill or in-country experience to rely on secondary literature in languages the comparatist can read, subject to the usual caution about using secondary literature....

There are two points I wish to make about the knowledge and experience needed to gain a proper understanding of foreign law. First, the burden involved in obtaining it is a good reason why some scholars choose to specialize in foreign law and minimize explicit comparison.... Specialization and team efforts comprise a better solution than asking every scholar to spread himself too thin....

Second, it is quite legitimate for comparatists to base their comparisons on literature produced by foreign law specialists, at least to a substantial degree. The comparatist need not have first-hand knowledge of all the foreign law upon which he bases his comparisons, but she needs to be a discriminating consumer of the available scholarly writing, whether it is explicitly comparative or not. The comparatist should evaluate secondary literature on foreign law in accordance with the foregoing observations about what is required. Does the author possess the necessary linguistic knowledge? Do his citations show that he has canvassed adequately the various legal formants? Has she made good use of translations of important, relevant legal literature from the foreign country if there are any? Has he reported on actual practices in the country based on his own experiences or on reliable reports by others? Do the author's comments appear to be informed by a deep understanding of the nation's cultural and religious traditions and history? It may be difficult for the non-foreign-law-specialist to make these judgments with any confidence. As in all types of research beyond personal knowledge, healthy skepticism, a search for corroboration from multiple sources, and attention to academic reputation should help.

8. Comparative law scholarship should be organized in a way that emphasizes explicit comparison.

Finally, I come to the nitty-gritty detail of organization. I do not wish to dictate matters of form narrowly. Good writers find the organization that best fits their subject. However, I want to encourage the use of organization for comparative writing that emphasizes the comparative task being accomplished.... I advocate trying as much as possible to make every section comparative. For example, if the subject is antitrust law, one section might compare and contrast the development of antitrust law in each country, another the two countries' treatment of horizontal restraints of trade, another the vertical restraints, another the enforcement mechanisms and remedies, etc. Try to break the subject down into the natural units that are important to the analysis and then describe each country's law with respect to that unit and compare and contrast them immediately. Let the contrasts documented in each section build toward your overall conclusion. Of course, for certain subjects it may be necessary to describe the law of one country in a block before comparing it. This seems especially likely, for example, when what is being compared is the historical development of a field or legal system. But the shorter these blocks, the more effective will be the comparison.

9. Comparative studies should be undertaken in a spirit of respect for the other.

The last point concerns the attitude a comparatist should have. So much in foreign legal systems seems so bizarre that it shocks us. Why do the Germans and French disdain the U.S. practice of intrusive party-led discovery in civil cases? To the U.S. lawyer, it almost seems as if the Germans and French must not be that interested in finding the truth. To the German and French lawyers, it seems as if the U.S. system fails to protect individual privacy. Neither system is contemptible simply because it is different from the other. In analyzing a foreign legal system, the comparative scholar has to make extraordinary efforts to discern the sense of foreign rules and arrangements.

I want to emphasize that I mean by this to suggest a working method only, not a limit on what comparative scholars may say. I have already said...above that comparative law may be undertaken for any purpose, including a critical one. Indeed, constructive criticism is a sincere form of respect. Moreover, at the end of the day, criticism should be judged, not by the critic's attitude, but by the reasonableness of her premises and the force of her logic. However, before the comparatist criticizes, she must make all possible efforts to avoid a narrowly chauvinistic view. She must try to see the sense of the foreign arrangements even if they are strangely different from her own and seem to represent values directly contrary to her own.

The comparatist must also bear in mind that criticism coming from an outsider is always suspect on the grounds of chauvinism. This is all the more reason to be cautious in criticizing foreign law, but it is much less of a problem when the same piece of scholarship levels the same or a similar criticism against the author's own legal system. Criticism of a foreign legal system is also less likely to be dismissed as chauvinistic if it is supported by citation to domestic critics of the system. Nevertheless, sometimes a foreign legal system's disregard for certain values compels one to criticize even in the absence of support from the target legal system, especially in situations involving authoritarian governments, in which only the foreigners may have the possibility of publishing their criticism. God grant us the wisdom to know when to speak out forcefully!

The foregoing nine principles comprise, I believe, the basic elements of the comparative method for studying law. The method is not complicated.... It is difficult to do well. Nevertheless, it is ever more indispensable in our interconnected and shrinking world.

———————

Ideally students of comparative family law would have the time to compare different countries' substantive laws, legal cultures, legal histories, and legal machinery on a particular topic. There is no doubt that in a limited amount of time and space a better "comparative" analysis would be had by studying, for example, only two countries, as opposed to a variety of countries. Yet for our purposes, such a limited comparison would not work. Our goal is to challenge students to think differently about our own family law system, not to become foreign law experts. Law school papers are the place for students to engage in a more in-depth comparative analysis, and Professor Reitz's article undoubtedly will help students in that task. If this book were to focus on only one or two other countries, we would be required to forego many interesting points of comparison on a sufficiently broad range of topics. Hence, while Professor Reitz's article is unassailable in the context of comparative legal scholarship, the rigor it demands must be balanced with other goals in the context of the classroom.

Our challenge is to provide you with materials on a wide range of family law topics that allow more than superficial comparisons with other jurisdictions. In addition, we must do so in a manner that is coherent. To help with coherency, several themes will recur throughout these materials: the role of the state and religion in regulating the family; the legal position of women and children in the family; the difference between "law on the books" and "law in action;" and the tension between the respect for cultural diversity and the advancement of human rights.

Since our approach to comparative law is to inspire new thoughts and reflection about United States' family law, we recognize that at times we favor this goal at the expense of exploring other systems in appropriate depth. As Professor Reitz suggests, one needs to be honest about the limits of one's work, and we concede there are many in ours for the true comparatist. Yet if we help some students recognize the possibility that the world presents for creative advocacy at home, or if we help some readers think about American family law in a slightly different way, we will have accomplished our goal.

Shirley S. Abrahamson & Michael J. Fischer, *All the World's a Courtroom: Judging in the New Millennium*
26 Hofstra L. Rev. 273, 285–88 (1997)

I can already hear the objections. You cannot glean the substance of a legal system from an examination of its particular rules of substantive law, let alone from a smattering of opinions interpreting a narrow issue. The law of a particular country is deeply rooted in that country's history and traditions. It gives voice to aspirations, fears, and priorities specific to that country's culture. Although the rhetoric and terminology used by different jurisdictions may sound and even feel similar, the same words and phrases can and often do convey different meanings. As one commentator has stated, "[A] good comparatist is one who, while studying the law of any country, looks not merely at the particular rules of its substantive law, but rather at the many processes and institutions by which substantive law is transformed into reality...."

But the risks inherent in exploring different legal systems are risks that American lawyers and state court judges take every day. We are already comparatists. We just don't think of ourselves that way.

The American federal system has made seasoned comparatists of all of us. Every American law school class and casebook uses the comparative law method, drawing upon examples and opinions from numerous states and state courts. Every American lawyer and judge must pay attention to the law developing in other state jurisdictions.

So when I, as a state court judge, figuratively leave my jurisdiction searching for insights from court opinions issued in places like Alabama or Alaska, I venture into unfamiliar terrain. I may feel insecure, but I go nevertheless. And thanks to my training as an American federalist, I know what to do when I get there.

Of course, when I cite to or draw upon the reasoning of an insurance case arising in Alabama or a products liability case arising in Alaska, I never for a moment imagine that I have magically become an expert in the law of either jurisdiction. Opinions from other American state courts may respond to wrinkles and nuances in their own particular legal and political histories about which I know little or nothing. Nevertheless, those courts will frequently see such problems in a light which, from my vantage point, is fresh and provocative. Those courts inform and illuminate. They may help me formulate or clarify issues. They may suggest a solution or possible alternatives. They may challenge my perspective. In short, I wouldn't dream of doing without the insights provided by these trips into unfamiliar terrain, even though they can leave me feeling apprehensive.

Why shouldn't our experiences as American comparatists embolden more American lawyers and judges to explore the law of non-American jurisdictions in the same spirit? Why shouldn't we take advantage of the comparatist instincts learned in our law schools and practiced in our courts by venturing farther afield?

Indeed, we can cross the divide separating us from other jurisdictions around the world. And if we do so with the modest intent to borrow ideas on classifying, discussing, and solving a particular problem, we should not be deterred by unfamiliarity with foreign legal systems. We may fail to understand a particular system of law or even misinterpret some foreign decisions. Nevertheless, we may also find unexpected answers or new challenges to domestic legal issues.

Problem 1-2

Problem 1-1 was modeled on an actual case, *Marckx v. Belgium*. The European Court of Human Rights issued a judgement in the case, a small portion of which is included immediately below. As you read the excerpt, imagine that you represent the Government of Belgium. Consider what mistakes, if any, the Court demonstrates in its use of comparative law. Do not worry about the actual legal analysis that occurs under Articles 8 or 14 of the European Convention on Human Rights; the Convention's provisions and the Court's jurisprudence are covered in more detail elsewhere. For now, focus solely on the Court's response to the Government's argument that, even assuming that "the law at issue may appear open to criticism," "the problem of reforming it arose only several years after the entry into force of the European Convention on Human Rights in respect of Belgium (14 June 1955), that is, with the adoption of the Brussels Convention of 12 September 1962 on the Establishment of Maternal Affiliation of Natural Children...." In short, the Government was arguing that discrimination against illegitimate children was typical and permissible when the European Convention on Human Rights was adopted; therefore, such discrimination could not be a violation of that Convention.

Marckx v. Belgium
2 Eur. H.R. Rep. 330, 346–47 (1979)

It is true that, at the time when the [European Convention on Human Rights] of 4 November 1950 was drafted, it was regarded as permissible and normal in many European countries to draw a distinction in this area between the 'illegitimate' and the 'legitimate' family. However, the Court recalls that this Convention must be interpreted in the light of present-day conditions. Tyrer v. U.K. (1978), 2 E.H.R.R. 1, 10, para. 31. In the instant case, the Court cannot but be struck by the fact that the domestic law of the great majority of the member States of the Council of Europe has evolved and is continuing to evolve, in company with the relevant international instruments, towards full juridical recognition of the maxim *mater semper certa est.*

Admittedly, of the ten States that drew up the Brussels Convention, only eight have signed and only four have ratified it to date. The European Convention of 15 October 1975 on the Legal Status of Children Born out of Wedlock has at present been signed by only ten and ratified by only four members of the Council of Europe. Furthermore, Article 14(1) of the latter Convention permits any State to make, at the most, three reservations, one of which could theoretically concern precisely the manner of establishing the maternal affiliation of a child born out of wedlock (Art. 2).

However, this state of affairs cannot be relied on in opposition to the evolution noted above. Both the relevant Conventions are in force and there is no reason to attribute the currently small number of Contracting States to a refusal to admit equality between 'illegitimate' and 'legitimate' children on the point under consideration. In fact, the existence of these two treaties denotes that there is a clear measure of common ground in this area amongst modern societies.

What mistakes, if any, might the Court have committed in reaching its conclusion based upon its comparative analysis? The Court cites only European trends. Would a reference to U.S. practices and laws have been helpful? Why or why not?

Notes and Questions

1. *Spiraling Comparisons.* Does one need to engage in a separate comparative analysis of how Europeans perceive comparative law in order to understand and judge the use of comparative law by the European Court of Human Rights?

2. *Danger.* Comparatists often say that bad comparative law is dangerous. For example, "The legal rules must be put back in their original context—social, economic, political, and cultural; they must be appraised not only from the point of view of their formal expression (notably in codes), but also of their actual implementation (hence the importance of case law), their real effectiveness, and their practical consequences. If such conditions are not met, the comparison is not only useless, but it may become dangerous and the source of serious mistakes." Xavier Blanc-Jouvan, *Centennial World Congress on Comparative Law: Closing Remarks*, 75 Tul. L. Rev. 1235, 1237 (2001). What is the danger?

3. *Sources of Information.* Judge Sir Gerald Fitzmaurice, in his dissenting opinion in *Marckx*, stated the following:

> I do not think any breach of the Convention is involved by this, because I do not think these matters are matters of family life, but of affiliation and civil status with which the Convention does not deal. However, even if this was not my opinion, and even if I subscribed to the view taken on this matter in the Judgment, I should still feel strongly that the Belgian Government ought not to be condemned for the operation of a law which, while some may consider it defective or inequitable, has in fact (as clearly emerged in the course of the proceedings) much that can be urged in favour of it, and in any event lies well within the margin of appreciation or discretion that any Government, acting bona fide, ought to be accorded. I fail to see how States can possibly be required to have uniform laws in matters of this kind. It is, I think, an exaggeration to say, as was maintained on behalf of the applicants, that the old forms of family relationships, and in particular the old distinction between legitimate and illegitimate children, are in the process of obliteration. But, in any event, States must be allowed to change their attitudes in their own good time, in their own way and by reasonable means—States must be allowed a certain latitude.

There is obviously a disagreement between the majority and Judge Sir Gerald Fitzmaurice on the factual question of whether the "old distinction between legitimate and illegitimate children are in the process of obliteration." As comparatists, who are we to believe? Can we use either opinion as a source of information for drawing comparisons?

4. *Functional Equivalents.* The Belgium government justified its law in part with the following statement: "[W]hilst the married mother and her husband 'mutually undertake...the obligation to feed, keep and educate their children,' there is no certainty that the unmarried mother will be willing to bear on her own the responsibilities of motherhood; by leaving the unmarried mother the choice between recognizing her child or dissociating herself from it, the law is prompted by a concern for protection of the child, for it would be dangerous to entrust it to the custody and authority of someone who has shown no inclination to care for it; many unmarried mothers do not recognize their child." Given this statement, can one conclude that the system in Belgium in the 1970s has a functional equivalent in the laws of most U.S. states today?

5. *Timeframe Sensitivity.* For law students studying today in the United States, the law in Belgium in the 1970s might appear very peculiar. After all, today "[a]ll states...permit nonmarital children to inherit from and through their mothers." Katheleen Guzman, *Essay: What Price Paternity?*, 53 Okla. L. Rev. 77, 98 n.2 (2000). The maxim *mater semper certa est* is enshrined in the Uniform Parentage Act, section 3. Yet one always needs to be cognizant of whether one's comparative information comes from similar time periods. Historically, at common law, a nonmarital child could not inherit from his or her mother or father. *See* William M. McGovern et al., Wills, Trusts, and Estates, Including Taxation and Future Interests 32 (1988). Although the Uniform Parentage Act was adopted by the National Conference of Commissioners on Uniform State Laws in 1973, when did the change in the United States occur? Did the Uniform Parentage Act reflect state law or cause state law to change? It appears that by 1934, it was the "virtually universal" rule that nonmarital children could inherit from their mothers, although not their fathers. Guzman, *supra*, at 98 n.2 (citing McGovern, *supra*, at 37).

6. *Larger Context.* It is often dangerous to extrapolate about a given society merely from its statutory laws. For example, as you will learn in Chapter Four, various Scandina-

vian countries have adopted registered partnership systems. Vermont also has a registered partnership system called "civil unions." Can one draw any conclusions from the mere fact that both of these places have registered partnerships, assuming they afford similar legal status, without knowing why they were adopted? Think for a moment about Vermont and the adoption of its law permitting civil unions. The Vermont legislature created this status after its supreme court held that Vermont's system of limiting marriage benefits to opposite-sex couples was a violation of the Vermont Constitution's Common Benefits Clause. *See* Baker v. State, 744 A.2d 864 (Vt. 1999). The court gave the legislature the choice of extending marriage to same-sex couples or enacting a new status that would give the benefits and protections of marriage to same-sex couples. *Id.* at 887. The legislature chose the latter. *See* Vt. Stat. Ann. tit. 15 § 1202. This new status, therefore, was the more conservative option and was enacted pursuant to court order. On the other hand, "The registered partnership systems introduced in Denmark, Norway and Sweden reflect priorities of Scandinavian social democracy." David Bradley, *Convergence in Family Law; Mirrors, Transplants and Political Economy,* Maastricht J. Eur. & Comp. L. 127 (1999). This topic is discussed further in Chapter Four on the Emerging Rights and Duties of Nontraditional Partners. Here the point is simply that one cannot conclude based upon the black-letter law that the population in Vermont is equally tolerant of this family form as are the people in Denmark. Similarly, without knowing the larger context of treatment for nonmarital children in Belgium and the United States, can one conclude that the United States was more tolerant of nonmarital births than was Belgium?

7. *State Practices toward Nonmarital Children and Fathers.* In the United States, the Supreme Court has held that states can impose certain procedural requirements on nonmarital children before these nonmarital children can inherit intestate from their fathers. *See* Lalli v. Lalli, 439 U.S. 259 (1978). Consequently, there have sometimes been time limits for establishing paternity during the father's lifetime, or heightened pleading or evidentiary burdens. Recently, the U.S. Supreme Court upheld a distinction between nonmarital children living abroad who seek to acquire American nationality depending upon whether the child's mother or father is an American citizen. The acquisition of American citizenship for a nonmarital child born abroad to an American mother is almost automatic, but the acquisition of American citizenship for a nonmarital child born abroad to an American father requires that a number of steps be taken. These steps include that a blood relationship between the child and father be established by clear and convincing evidence, that the father agree in writing to provide financial support for the child until the child reaches the age of eighteen years, and that before the child reaches eighteen either a court establishes paternity, the father legitimates the child, or the father acknowledges paternity in writing under oath. *See* Nguyen v. I.N.S., 121 S. Ct. 2053 (2001) (upholding 8 U.S.C. § 1409(a)). Using an intermediate level of scrutiny to evaluate the law's gender-based classification, the Court stated that the law served the important governmental objectives of ensuring a biological parent-child relationship exists, and providing an opportunity for a parent-child relationship to develop. "To fail to acknowledge even our most basic biological differences—such as the fact that a mother must be present at birth but the father need not be—risks making the guarantee of equal protection superficial, and so disserving it." *Id.* at 2066. The Court also noted that Congress was afforded wide deference in the exercise of its immigration and naturalization power. *Id.* at 2065. Four justices vigorously dissented. Although the litigation focused on the alleged gender discrimination, the result probably would have been the same if the case had focused on discrimination between nonmarital and marital children. The standard applied to evaluate a gender discrimination claim is at least as strong

as the standard applied to evaluate a discrimination claim by nonmarital children, *see* Trimble v. Gordon, 430 U.S. 762 (1977), especially in the immigration context, *see* Miller v. Albright, 523 U.S. 420, 451 (1998) (O'Connor and Kennedy, JJ. concurring) (suggesting only rational basis scrutiny would apply).

8. *Terminology Sensitivity.* "Common law marriage" is a well known term in this country. It is also a well-known term in Canada. In *Taylor v. Rossu*, [1998] 161 D.L.R.4th 266, 280 (Alta. C.A.), the Alberta Court of Appeal stated, "Most Canadian jurisdictions have extended their family legislation to provide for support for common law partners. However, the definition of common law spouse is not consistent among jurisdictions. Some require a two year relationship and application within one year of separation, and others impose five, three or one year qualifying periods. One jurisdiction simply specifies a relationship of 'some permanence.' Most jurisdictions agree that partners who have had a natural child together constitute common law partners, and some provide that partners who have adopted a child together constitute common law partners." Can you now describe the law in Canada on "common law marriage" as we understand the term, or make a comparison with the situation in the United States? Before answering, it is important to know that "In Canada the term 'common law marriage' is often used to describe an opposite-sex couple who reside together without being legally married." *See* Nicholas Bala, *Court Decisions on Same-Sex and Unmarried Partners, Spousal Rights and Children, in* The International Survey of Family Law 43, 49 n.28 (2001). Understanding differences in terminology not only avoids comparing very different situations to each other, but it also facilitates appropriate comparisons. For example, fairly recently, cohabitating couples in Canada have made tremendous gains in their ability to claim benefits typically reserved to married couples. *See, e.g.,* Taylor v. Rossu, [1998] 216 A.R. 348 (awarding interim support to a woman who had lived with a man for thirty years despite the fact that the Domestic Relations Act (DRA) limited spousal support to married parties; the DRA violated the equality provisions found in section 15 of the Canadian Charter of Rights and Freedoms). More information on the topic of cohabitants' rights and the important developments in Canada are found in Chapter Four. Here we simply note that comparative legal analysis requires an understanding of terminology.

9. *The Holding in Marckx.* In *Marckx,* the European Court of Human Rights determined for the first time that the respect for family life protected by article 8 encompassed both the "legitimate" and "illegitimate" family. It also held that article 8 required the state both to abstain from such interference and to ensure effective "respect" for family life. In short, article 8 imposed negative and positive obligations on the state. For example, a state must provide legal safeguards that render possible, from the moment of birth, the child's integration in his or her family. The court found Belgium breached article 8, as well as article 14 (which is a non-discrimination provision) taken in conjunction with article 8, with respect to both the mother and the daughter. Belgium law impeded the daughter's maternal affiliation and the daughter's other familial relationships. There was no "objective and reasonable justification" for the distinctions between nonmarital and marital children. Among other things, the European Court thought the law did not encourage marriage and that the adoption procedure left children exposed to the whims of their parents. For similar reasons, the law violated the mother's right to be free from discrimination, since she was treated differently with respect to her child than a mother who was married.

10. *The Events in Belgium Post-Marckx.* "In order to comply with the *Marckx* decision, Belgium adopted the Act amending the legal provisions concerning affiliation and inheritance (03/31/1987, B.S., 05/27/1987). The new art. 334 of the Belgian Civil Code for-

mally guarantees the equality of all children, regardless of their status at birth." Johan Meeusen, *Judicial Disapproval of Discrimination Against Illegitimate Children*, 43 Am. J. Comp. L. 119, 142 (1995). However, the old law continued to apply until the new law entered into force in 1987. Consequently, in *Vermeire v. Belgium*, 15 Eur. H.R. Rep. 488 (1993), an illegitimate child who could not inherit from her grandfather when he died intestate in 1980, although *Marckx* had been decided in 1978, successfully challenged the application of the old law to her under articles 8 and 14 of the European Convention on Human Rights.

11. *The Establishment of Maternal Affiliation.* "Recognition of maternity is particular to the Roman legal systems, *i.e.*, those legal systems which have been influenced by the French civil code." Rainer Frank, *The Establishment and the Consequences of Maternal and Paternal Affiliation, in* Council of Europe, *Legal Problems Relating to Parentage*, Proceedings of the XXVIIth Colloquy on European Law Foundation for International Legal Studies 84 (1997). In fact, Belgium adopted the French Civil Code of 1804 after achieving independence from the Dutch domination in 1830. That Code embodied the rule that maternity should not be automatically established for nonmarital children without voluntary recognition. "The reason was to protect the unmarried mother and to put her on par with the father since the judicial establishment of paternity was nearly completely impossible according to the Civil Code, absent a voluntary recognition by the father. Moreover in order to protect the mother, the French Court of Cassation admitted in 1854 that the name of the unmarried mother should not be compulsorily mentioned in the birth certificate." Letter from Professor Marie-Therese Meulders to Merle H. Weiner (Oct. 27, 2002) (on file with author).

Today the majority of countries in Europe, including Belguim, require that the birth certificate bear the mother's name and that establishes maternal affiliation. *See* Frédérique Granet, *Parentage and Civil Status Matters in the States of the International Commission on Civil Status, in* Council of Europe, *Legal Problems Relating to Parentage, supra*, at 61. However, in several countries, for example France, Italy, Luxembourg and Spain, the mother's name need not appear on the birth certificate because "the woman is entitled to give birth anonymously." *Id.* at 62. In France and Italy, even if the mother's name is on the birth certificate, the mother must still recognize her child. *Id.* at 62. In France, legal recognition can be achieved by status, most typically by the mother bringing up her child. While a child can institute maternal affiliation proceedings in Spain, Italy and Luxembourg, the situation differs in France where the Family and Social Welfare Code specifies that giving birth anonymously is an absolute bar to a subsequent maternal affiliation action brought by the child. *See id.* at 62 (citing article 341-1). What are the values underlying the French Code? Do you see the same clash of values in our law? Is it resolved similarly or differently?

One commentator believes that the reasoning in *Marckx* requires that States Parties to the European Convention recognize the maxim *mater semper certa est* in order to fulfill the fundamental right of mother and child to be affiliated from birth. *See* Patrick Senaeve, *Parentage and Human Rights, in* Council of Europe, Legal Problems Relating to Parentage, *supra*, ¶ 20. Permitting affiliation from the fact of birth certainly seems to be the trend in Europe. The Committee of Experts on Family Law of the Council of Europe recently issued a draft report on principles concerning the establishment and legal consequences of parentage. The first principle is "The woman who gives birth to the child shall be considered as the mother." *Draft Report on Principles Concerning the Establishment and Legal Consequences of Parentage*, Council of

Europe, Draft No. 1 (2001), *at* http://www.legal.coe.int/family/Default.asp?fd=general&fn=IntroReportParentageE.htm.

12. *Europe and Nonmarital Children.* "In Europe, the legal status of children born out of wedlock was profoundly influenced by the decisions of the European Court of Human Rights.... Especially the famous *Marckx* decision was fundamental for the cause of illegitimate children in Europe. The Court's decision in the *Johnston* case confirmed and refined the *Marckx* holding." Meeusen, *supra*, at 136. In *Johnston v. Ireland*, 9 Eur. H.R. Rep. 203 (1986), Mr. Johnston and Ms. Williams-Johnston formed a marital-like relationship. At all times, Mr. Johnston was married to another woman. He was unable to divorce his wife because the Constitution of Ireland made divorce impossible. Mr. Johnston and Ms. Williams-Johnston had a child after seven years of cohabitation. Irish law considered the child illegitimate, and she suffered many legal disabilities vis-à-vis her father, including under the law of succession. Also, there was no system by which the child could be affiliated to her father for all purposes. Each member of the family claimed a violation of article 8, among other articles, and the Court agreed: "[As observed in *Marckx*], 'respect' for family life, understood as including the ties between near relatives, implies an obligation for the State to act in a manner calculated to allow these ties to develop normally. And in the present case the normal development of the natural family ties between the first and second applicants and their daughter requires, in the Court's opinion, that she should be placed, legally and socially, in a position akin to that of a legitimate child." *Id.* ¶ 74. Other decisions from the Court have similarly disapproved of discrimination against children on the basis of their parents' marital status. *See, e.g.*, Inze v. Austria, 10 Eur. H.R. Rep. 394 (1988) (finding a violation of article 14 taken together with article 1 of Protocol No. 1 when legitimate child was given preference over illegitimate child under Austrian intestacy law); *see also* Mazurek v. France, App. No. 34406/97 (Eur. Ct. H.R. Feb. 1, 2000), *available at* http://hudoc.echr.coe.int/hudoc/ViewRoot.asp?Item=0&Action=Html&X=1003190648&Notice=0&Noticemode=&RelatedMode=0 (finding France's law violated the Convention because whenever the nonmarital child's claim competed with any legitimate child's claim the nonmarital child of an adulterous relationship could inherit only half the portion of his deceased parent's estate that a legitimate child could claim). *See also* Veronique Chauveau, *Children and Wedlock in France*, [2000] IFL 87 (citing Civil Code art. 759).

Fifteen countries have ratified the European Convention on the Legal Status of Children Born out of Wedlock, but numerous countries still have not, including Belgium, Finland, France, Germany, Italy, and Spain, not to mention most of the newer members of the Council of Europe. Of course, failure to ratify the Convention does not mean that a country necessarily discriminates against nonmarital children. The European Convention on the Legal Status of Children Born out of wedlock is set forth in the Statutory Supplement.

13. *Nonmarital Children and International Law.* On its face, international human rights law does not prohibit discrimination against nonmarital children. The U.N. Convention on the Rights of the Child does not have any explicit provision against such discrimination because consensus could not be reached on whether such a provision was appropriate. Some countries believe that article 2(1) bans such discrimination, and certain countries entered reservations or declarations saying that their adoption of the Convention was without prejudice to national law provisions that discriminated between marital and nonmarital children. *See, e.g., Reservations, Declarations and Objections Relating to the Convention on the Rights of the Child*, U.N. CRC, at 22–23, U.N. Doc. CRC/C/2/Rev.8 (1999) ("The Federal Republic of Germany... declares that the provisions of the Convention are

also without prejudice to the provisions of national law concerning: (c) Circumstances under family and inheritance law of children born out of wedlock."). The International Covenant on Civil and Political Rights (ICCPR) has also been cited as supporting the principle that discrimination between marital and nonmarital children is prohibited. *See* art. 24(1). The U.N. Human Rights Committee has given a General Comment which suggests that this is its view. *See* General Comment 17, ¶ 5 UNHRC, 35th Sess., *reproduced in* Compilation of General Comments and General Recommendations Adopted by Human Rights Treaty Bodies, Human Rights Committee, at 133, U.N. Doc. HRI/Gen/1/Rev.5 (2001). However, like the Convention on the Rights of the Child, an attempt to specifically address nonmarital status in the ICCPR was rejected. As one author stated, "Opinions differed considerably.... [E]mphasis was placed on the highly different ways in which legal systems dealt with the whole question of children born out of wedlock, and it was observed that the problem was a difficult one to deal with in an international human rights convention." Sharon Detrick, A Commentary on the United Nations Convention on the Rights of the Child 77 (1999).

It is useful to end this section with some comments by an individual who looked at *Marckx* in detail. Johan Meeusen has compared the European Court of Human Rights' decisions on nonmaterial children's rights with those of the U.S. Supreme Court. The conclusions drawn reflect what Professor Reitz means by "good comparative scholarship."

Johan Meeusen, *Judicial Disapproval of Discrimination Against Illegitimate Children*
43 Am. J. Comp. L. 119, 143–45 (1995)

Both in Europe and the U.S., the patrimonial rights of illegitimate children has much improved during the past 25 years. In Europe, that legal revolution was accomplished by two decisions of the European Court of Human Rights. In the U.S., the Supreme Court needed numerous, and sometimes contradictory, decisions throughout the seventies to reach a similar result.

Both Courts struggled with vigorous dissenting opinions, rejecting interventionism and pleading for a return to the more traditional "hands off" attitude. It has been suggested that the U.S. Supreme Court de facto federalized the law of illegitimacy, while the *Marckx* majority has been accused of reading a Code of Family Law into art. 8 ECHR.

While both Courts admitted that the encouragement and support of the traditional family is a legitimate legislative goal, they firmly rejected the punishment of the innocent child as a way to deter the parents. The status of illegitimacy as such was not condemned. In its *Johnston* decision, the European Court required that an illegitimate child "should be placed, legally and socially, in a position akin to that of a legitimate child." Art. 8 ECHR obliges the states to establish an appropriate legal regime for illegitimate children. This refusal to require that all children have a completely identical patrimonial situation explains the American *Mathews* and *Lalli* decisions and was made explicit in *Trimble*, where the Court admitted that "[T]he more serious problem of proving paternity might justify a more demanding standard for illegitimate children claiming under their father's estates than that required either for illegitimate children claiming under their mothers' estates or for legitimate children generally."

Both Courts made abundantly clear that illegitimates must not be given a "lesser status" because of their birth out of wedlock. They must have the same substantive rights as all other children. Nevertheless, the fact that they are born outside of marriage can justify certain qualifications of their rights in order to satisfy legitimate state interests.

In Europe, those distinctions on the basis of birth must have an "objective and reasonable justification," i.e., a reasonable relationship of proportionality must exist between the means employed and the legitimate aim sought to be realized. This test requires an adequate balancing of the public and private interests involved.

The formulation and application of that European standard resembles the traditional "rational basis" test, used in Equal Protection matters by the Supreme Court. But the European Court has given proof of a strong sensitivity to potential discrimination of illegitimates. Its attitude therefore is similar to the U.S. Supreme Court's heightened scrutiny, demonstrated by the requirement of a "substantial relationship" between the classification and the state purpose.[173] The Supreme Court has not been extremely consistent in the application of that standard, and appears to adapt its flexible test to the specific facts of each case. Furthermore, the Court's standard in this sensitive matter varied very much according to the political orientation of the Court members.

Both Courts' case law can be summarized as follows. The illegitimate child must have the same substantive patrimonial rights as the legitimate child; procedural qualifications of these rights are permitted in those categories of patrimonial cases where difficulties of proving paternity are involved. The continuous scientific progress concerning medical evidence is therefore an important factor in the evolution towards a completely identical legal status for all children.

In spite of the many similarities, it appears that the legal developments on both sides of the Atlantic were quite autonomous. Although the last major American case was decided seven months prior to the first European decision, there is no apparent evidence that the European Court took account, or was even aware, of the series of Supreme Court rulings. Nor did the European law journals pay much attention to Levy [v. Louisiana, 391 U.S. 68 (1968)] and its progeny. The fundamental change in attitude towards illegitimates can probably be explained by a concurrent shift in societal organization (important rise in the number of births out of wedlock), values (rights-consciousness and value-neutrality of the western societies) and perceptions (refusal to victimize the innocent child, reflecting the strong anti-discrimination sensitivity present in the western societies since a few decades). It would require the collaboration of a sociologist and a historian to fully explain those recent evolutions. But a mere reading of the Supreme Court and European Court decisions clarifies both Courts' choice to give priority to fairness to the child, instead of strictly adhering to public values as agreed upon by the different (state and national) legislative bodies. Both Courts refused to deny the importance of encouraging stable and "legitimate" family relationships. But in the light of the contemporary emphasis on individual rights, and also the growing hesitation to infringe upon private lifestyle decisions, that goal could not be invoked to justify unequal protection. It is telling that the value-neutral considerations of preventing fraudulent claims retained their strength and can allow procedural classifications of the childrens' substantive rights.

---

173. It is remarkable, though not surprising, that both Courts developed precisely in illegitimacy cases a non-traditional interpretation of traditional provisions (art. 8 ECHR; Equal Protection clause) and new standards of scrutiny. This way, they adapted the law to new social situations and insights. The traditional disapproval of illegitimacy has given way to the contemporary realities of limited public welfare budgets and vastly expanded numbers of non-traditional families: Cf. Dale, "The Evolving Constitutional Rights of Nonmarital Children: Mixed Blessings," 5 Ga. St. U. L. Rev. 523, 523 (1989); Poll, "The Fourteenth Amendment Rights of Children Born Out Of Wedlock," 1 Am. J. Fam. L. 123, 123 (1987)....

If these considerations really inspired the Supreme Court and the European Court, then they underscore again the importance of comparative legal research and of an interdisciplinary approach. The extremely close ties between the evolution of family law and the changes in society's organization and the few values that are deemed sufficiently fundamental to be shared on a large scale, become clear through the observation of similar but autonomous developments in different legal systems and cannot be fully explained through a perspective that is merely legal.

B. An Introduction to International Law

Because this book examines the doctrine and practice of family law from the perspectives of comparative law and public and private international law, it might be helpful at this juncture to clarify the distinctions between these disciplines. As you learned from Section A, the focus of study in the field of *comparative law* is the internal (often referred to as "domestic") law of foreign nations, using a comparative methodology. International law encompasses the law governing the relations between nations, typically referred to as *public international law*, and the law controlling transborder transactions and legal disputes of individuals, corporations, and private entities, which is often termed *private international law*.

These last two designations can be somewhat misleading, as private individuals and transactions can frequently be affected by conventions or international organizations falling within the domain of public international law; and private international law often involves public entities. With the tremendous growth both branches of international law have experienced in recent decades, the boundaries between public and private international law are becoming increasingly blurred. Nevertheless, generally speaking, public international law addresses the political interaction of the governments of sovereign nations. Private international law concerns conflict of law rules, cooperation among the courts and legal systems of different nations in resolving disputes among individuals and private entities, and regulation of various aspects of the international economy. *See* Mark W. Janis, An Introduction to International Law 2 (3d ed. 1999); Malcolm N. Shaw, International Law 1–2 (4th ed. 1997); Edith Brown Weiss, *The Rise or the Fall of International Law*, 69 Fordham L. Rev. 345 (2000).

All three fields are important to the development and practice of family law, and are increasingly intertwined. For example, imagine that you are counseling a client considering divorce whose spouse lives abroad. Your preparation for such a meeting might include a comparative analysis of the custody, property distribution, and support laws of the foreign nation and the local jurisdiction in order to provide competent advice regarding the most beneficial forum. Also critical to advising your client would be an analysis of relevant private international law, including applicable international conventions that would control the ability to move children, jurisdiction, choice of law, and recognition of foreign judgments in each potential forum. Public international law, though less often directly applicable, also plays an increasing role in the resolution of private family disputes. In the above example, a question regarding the proper interpretation of an applicable private international law convention (such as the Hague Convention on the Civil Aspects of International Child Abduction) might be resolved with reference to the Vienna Convention on the Law of Treaties, which provides general principles for treaty interpretation and is considered to be within the domain of public international law. Human rights treaties, also considered to be within the realm of public international law, are increasingly relevant to family law litigants in some regions of the world as well.

Although the significance of international law to transnational practice—divorces between spouses who are citizens or residents of different nations, international custody disputes, child support enforcement across national borders, international adoption—should be readily apparent, you may be less aware of the potential impact of international law on the development of the purely domestic family law of individual nations. Human rights conventions, in particular, increasingly shape the domestic law of countries that have ratified them. For example, the recognition of the explicit rights of children to parental care, protection from abuse, and numerous other social and political rights in the Constitution of the Republic of South Africa was heavily influenced by the United Nations Convention on the Rights of the Child and the African Charter on the Rights and Welfare of the Child. Barbara Bennett Woodhouse, *The Constitutionalization of Children's Rights: Incorporating Emerging Human Rights into Constitutional Doctrine*, 2 U. Pa. J. Const. L. 1, 37 (1999). A provision in Argentina's adoption code providing adopted individuals a right of access to their records was similarly influenced by the U.N. Convention on the Rights of the Child. Cecilia P. Grosman, *The Recent Reform of Argentine Adoption Law, in* The International Survey of Family Law 13, 15–16 (Andrew Bainham ed., 1996). The European Convention for the Protection of Human Rights and Fundamental Freedoms (hereinafter European Convention on Human Rights), enforceable against ratifying countries through the European Court of Human Rights, has prompted law reform on such issues as the Republic of Ireland's treatment of putative fathers of infants voluntarily placed for adoption, Norway's process for adjudicating termination and access within its child welfare system, and paternity proceedings in the Netherlands, to name just a few. *See* Keegan v. Ireland, 290 Eur. Ct. H. R. (ser. A) (1994); Geoffrey Shannon, *Human Rights and Family Law,* 3 Irish J. Fam. L. 1 (2000); Helen O'Driscoll, *Rights of Unmarried Fathers,* 2 Irish J. Fam. L. 18 (1999); European Court of Human Rights, *Effect of Judgments or Cases 1959–1998,* http://www.echr.coe. int/Eng/EDocs/EffectsOfJudgments.html. The United Kingdom has gone one step further by requiring in its Human Rights Act of 1998 that British courts interpret all legislation of the United Kingdom in a manner compatible with rights guaranteed by the European Convention on Human Rights, thereby permitting British citizens to directly enforce convention rights in British courts without the necessity of seeking recourse in the European Court of Human Rights. *See, e.g.,* Helen L. Conway, *The Human Rights Act 1998 and Family Law—Part One,* 1999 Fam. L. 811–14. While the efficacy of human rights conventions in achieving widespread guarantee of all of their enumerated rights is a topic that will be repeatedly examined throughout this book, there is no question that these conventions have had some impact on the evolution of familial rights and responsibilities promulgated through domestic constitutions, legislation, or common law in many regions of the world.

In the United States, the potential influence of international law on the development of family law involving purely domestic controversies has not yet been realized to a significant degree. For a variety of reasons that will be explored below in this and in subsequent chapters, the United States has been reluctant to ratify human rights conventions, and currently is party to only a few such conventions. Moreover, the ability of litigants to enforce treaty rights that provide broader protection than domestic law has been intentionally curtailed by the manner in which our government has ratified these treaties.

See Subsection 1.e, f, *infra.* Nevertheless, American family law scholars are increasingly incorporating international human rights law into their analyses of domestic issues. *See, e.g.,* Barbara Cochraine Alexander, *Convention Against Torture: A Viable Alternative Legal Remedy for Domestic Violence Victims,* 15 Am. U. Int'l L. Rev. 895 (2000); Connie de la Vega & Jennifer Brown, *Can a United States Treaty Reservation Provide a Sanctuary for the Juvenile Death Penalty?,* 32 U.S.F. L. Rev. 735 (1998); Barbara Stark, *Women and Globalization: The Failure and Postmodern Possibilities of International Law,* 33 Vand. J Transnat'l L. 503 (2000). In addition to recognizing their potential to shape substantive family law, some scholars have argued that both treaties and customary international law may in some instances supply a constitutional basis for congressional authority to enact federal legislation that protects fundamental human rights. *See* Jordan J. Paust, *Human Rights Purposes of the Violence Against Women Act and International Law's Enhancement of Congressional Power,* 22 Hous. J. Int'l L. 209 (2000).

In the area of transnational family practice, on the other hand, U.S. law is rapidly expanding. The federal government has shown increasing interest in recent decades in ratifying and implementing private international law conventions controlling transnational custody disputes and adoptions. Both federal and state governments have negotiated agreements to facilitate transborder child support enforcement. Globalization of the economy and increased international mobility have multiplied exponentially the litigation in American courts involving family members with citizenship or residence in foreign countries, resulting in an expanding body of case law addressing transnational disputes as well. As Americans increasingly cross borders to create and dissolve families and foreign immigration rises, this rapidly expanding sphere of private international law is becoming a critical component of expertise for American family law practitioners.

1. Overview of International Law[1]

For many students, this course will be your first exposure to the study of international law. It is therefore important to examine at the outset some basic terminology and doctrine common to the field, before submerging ourselves in the intricacies of various family law conventions. For those who have previously taken courses in international law, this subsection might provide a helpful review.

a. Sources of International Law

There are three primary sources of international law—explicit agreements; customary international law; and general principles of law. *See* Statute of the International Court of Justice, June 26, 1945, art. 38, 59 Stat. 1055, T.S. No. 993. The first two sources derive their authority from the consent of states. (International lawyers and documents frequently use the term *state* to denote an independent, sovereign nation, such as Denmark, rather than a component governmental unit of a nation, such as Texas.) Treaties and other types of international agreements are, of course, entered with explicit con-

---

1. For a more extensive discussion of the basic sources and rules of international law, *see* Mark W. Janis, An Introduction to International Law (3d ed. 1999); Malcolm N. Shaw, International Law (4th ed. 1997); and U.N. Office of Legal Affairs, *Treaty Reference Guide,* http://untreaty.un.org/ola-internet/Assistance/Guide.htm, from which much of the material in this subsection was condensed and adapted.

sent. Through *customary international law*, states are regarded as capable of creating binding rules of law by implied consent through their international customary practice. *See* Janis, *supra* note 1, at 42–43. The third source, *general principles of law*, is derived from the concept that rules or practices observed by the vast majority of nations as part of their municipal law are so fundamental that they should be regarded as part of international law, at least in those instances where neither explicit agreements nor customary law provide an applicable rule. *Id.* at 55. (The term *municipal law* is often used by international lawyers to refer to the domestic, or internal—as opposed to international—law of a nation, rather than to the law of a local governmental unit, such as a city or town, as the term is commonly used in other contexts within the United States.)

b. Explicit Agreements
i. Designations and Purposes

International agreements that establish rights and obligations among nations are assigned many different titles, which in some instances may reflect the particular character or importance of the instrument.

> *Treaty*, the term with which you are probably the most familiar, is often used generically to refer to any explicit international agreement between nations or international organizations, regardless of the specific title, i.e., "Convention," "Charter," etc., given to the agreement. In a more specific sense, the term "treaty" is often used in the title of a particular instrument to denote its gravity (such as the Treaty on European Union signed in Maastricht in 1992, which created the European Union), although there are no specific rules governing when this specific title is employed.

> *Convention*, like the word "treaty," has both a generic and a more specific usage. "Convention" is most commonly used as a generic term to include any type of international agreement, and is synonymous with the generic term "treaty." Although in previous centuries the more specific meaning of "convention" included *bilateral agreements* (between two parties), it is now most often used in the specific title of formal *multilateral agreements* (between more than two parties) open for participation by the entire international community, or by a large number of nations. Agreements drafted under the auspices of an international organization, such as the United Nations, or adopted by an organ of an international organization, are usually entitled "Conventions."

> *Charter* is often used in the title of instruments creating international organizations, such as the Charter of the United Nations of 1945, and other particularly formal and solemn agreements.

> *Agreement* is used generically to describe all forms of international agreements, but is used more narrowly in the titles of instruments in several situations. In the context of regional integration systems, instruments created within the framework of the constitutional treaty or by organs of the regional organizations are sometimes labeled "agreements" to distinguish them from the constitutional treaty. Less formal instruments that deal with a narrower subject matter than treaties are also typically titled "agreements." Although there is a trend to apply the term to bilateral or restricted multilateral treaties, in some areas, such as international economic law, the title "agreement" is also used for broad

multilateral agreements. The U.N. Office of Legal Affairs estimates that in recent decades the majority of international instruments are entitled agreements.

Protocols are often the title for agreements related to a convention or treaty. They serve a variety of purposes. A *Protocol of Signature* is an instrument entered by the parties to a treaty addressing the interpretation of certain clauses of the treaty, the insertion of formal clauses in the treaty, or the regulation of technical matters related to the treaty. An *Optional Protocol* creates additional rights and obligations that go beyond those of the principal treaty, and to which not all parties to the principal treaty must consent. Optional Protocols must therefore be separately ratified. Protocols may also serve to amend or supplement previous treaties, or to establish substantive obligations implementing the general objectives of an umbrella or framework treaty that has previously entered into force. Another type of protocol, a *Procès-Verbal*, records certain understandings of the contracting parties to a treaty.

Declaration is frequently the term chosen for an instrument intended to be aspirational, and not regarded by the parties as legally binding. However, the title alone is not necessarily controlling in determining the instrument's character, as declarations can also be legally binding for several reasons. The parties from the time of its creation might intend a particular declaration to establish binding obligations; the provisions of a declaration might record customary international law which is binding; or the declaration itself might, as in the case of the 1948 Universal Declaration of Human Rights, gain the status of binding customary international law as time passes. Sometimes even a series of unilateral declarations on a topic, though not directly addressed to each other, are considered to establish binding agreements that create legal bonds between the declarant nations based on their intent.

Modus Vivendi are informal records of temporary or provisional agreements, intended to be replaced by a more permanent form of agreement, and never require ratification.

Memoranda of Understanding are also less formal agreements that do not require ratification, and often address technical or detailed matters, or the operational arrangements for a framework international agreement.

An *Exchange of Notes* typically involves the exchange of two documents of identical text by government ministers, diplomats, or departmental heads to record a routine agreement, often utilized to avoid a more time-consuming treaty process.[2]

In addition to the above, *pact, statute, covenant, concordat, accord, agreed minute, memorandum of agreement, arrangement, final act,* and *general act* are among the other names frequently given to international agreements. The different titles used for explicit agreements generally have no overriding legal affect on the rules for interpretation or enforcement of the agreements. Therefore, the terms "treaties," "conventions," and "agreements," unless otherwise indicated, will be used throughout this text interchangeably in their generic sense.

---

2. U.N. Office of Legal Affairs, *Treaty Reference Guide,* http://untreaty.un.org/ola-internet/Assistance/Guide.htm. Specific examples of each type of instrument and more detailed explanations can be found at this website.

International agreements serve many different purposes. Some, such as the Charter of the United Nations, fulfill a constitutional role, creating international institutions and establishing their powers and legal foundation. Others are legislative in nature, formulating rules to guide international conduct on a particular topic, such as the Hague Convention on Protection of Children and Cooperation in Respect of Intercountry Adoption. Some serve as international contracts, or *traité-contrat,* between two or a small group of nations, often arranging a particular concession or exchange. Many of the instruments you will be examining in this course are aspirational, pronouncing goals for the international community in non-binding agreements, such as the Declaration on the Elimination of Discrimination against Women.

A large body of international law has developed governing the making, effect, amendment, invalidity, and termination of treaties. Originally formed through customary international law, it has now largely been codified in the 1969 Vienna Convention on the Law of Treaties, May 23, 1969, 1155 U.N.T.S. 331 (hereinafter Vienna Convention). Drafted under the auspices of the United Nations by an International Law Commission composed of international jurists, the Vienna Convention came into force in 1980 and has now been ratified by over 90 nations. Even in countries such as the United States,[3] which have not yet ratified it, the Vienna Convention carries significant weight. The U.S. Department of State and U. S. courts have recognized various provisions of the Convention as authoritative sources of current treaty law. Similarly, the *Restatement (Third) of the Foreign Relations Law of the United States* (hereinafter *Restatement Third*) generally regards the Convention as reflecting the law of the United States. The *Restatement Third* departs from the Convention only in those few instances where the Convention deviated or moved beyond accepted customary international law. Restatement (Third) of the Foreign Relations Law of the United States 145, Part III. International Agreements Introductory Note (1987). For example, one significant deviation is that the Vienna Convention applies only to written international agreements, whereas customary international law, and therefore the *Restatement Third*, recognize oral agreements as binding as well. *Id.* § 301 cmt. b.

ii. Treaty-Making

The Vienna Convention recognizes the capacity of every sovereign nation to enter into international agreements. The Convention neither addresses nor prohibits treaty-making by component states of a federal union. The extent to which such governmental entities have treaty-making powers is determined by the federation's domestic constitutional law. Some federations afford component states virtually no power to enter international agreements, whereas others, such as the United States, permit component states limited powers to do so. Janis, *supra* note 1, at 18–19. Although the U.S. Constitution prohibits our state governments from entering "any Treaty, Alliance, or Confederation," it also permits states to enter an "Agreement or Compact" with a foreign power, with the consent of Congress. U. S. Const. art. I, § 10. The difference between "treaty" and "agreement or compact," however, for purposes of interpreting this constitutional provision, has not been determined by the courts. Nevertheless, state governments in the United States have been considered capable of directly entering some

---

3. The United States has signed the treaty, but has not ratified it, due to a dispute between Congress and the Executive Branch regarding the allocation of authority to enter and terminate international agreements. Frederic Kirgis, *Treaties as Binding International Obligation,* ASIL Insight (1997), *at* http://www.asil.org/insight9.htm.

agreements with foreign governments without Congressional approval, by analogy to their power to enter inter-state compacts, as long as they do not encroach upon or interfere with the supremacy of the United States. *Cf.* Virginia v. Tennessee, 148 U.S. 503, 518 (1893). Therefore, our state governments have entered agreements concerning such transborder issues as local sources of pollution or police cooperation, which have not been regarded as requiring Congressional approval. Restatement (Third) of the Foreign Relations Law of the United States § 302 cmt. f (1987).

Treaties may be drafted through a variety of processes. Bilateral agreements, or those involving a small number of nations, can be negotiated directly by heads of state, diplomats, ambassadors, or, as is often the case, lower level governmental representatives with appropriate authorization. Multilateral treaties today are often negotiated through international organizations or conferences. Article 9 of the Vienna Convention provides that *adoption*, the formal act through which states agree to the form and content of the treaty, occurs when all of the states participating in the drafting agree that the text is satisfactory. Treaties negotiated at an international conference, however, may be adopted by a vote of two-thirds of the states present and voting at the conference, or by a different rule approved by the same majority.

Following adoption, a multilateral treaty is often opened for signature. In modern practice *signature* is typically made *subject to ratification, acceptance, or approval,* and does not itself signify a state's agreement to be bound by the treaty. More commonly, a nation's signature indicates that state's agreement that the text of the treaty is authentic and definitive. *See* Janis, *supra* note 1, at 20. Signature also expresses the willingness of the signatory nation to continue the process, and creates under Article 18 of the Vienna Convention an obligation "to refrain from acts that would defeat the object and purpose of the treaty," until such time as it makes clear its intention not to become a party to the treaty. Under some circumstances a representative makes a *signature ad referendum*, which simply means that the signature is conditional upon obtaining confirmation by the appropriate authority of the representative's state. *U.N. Treaty Reference Guide, supra* note 1.

International agreements become binding upon a sovereign nation only when that state has voluntarily consented to be bound. The most common methods of expressing consent to be bound today are ratification and accession. Janis, *supra* note 1, at 21.

A state that has participated in the negotiation of a treaty and signed the text consents to be bound by the terms of the treaty through *ratification*. Ratification involves (1) fulfillment of the steps necessary under the state's municipal law to enter into an international agreement (for example, the submission of certain types of agreements to Parliament in Britain or to the Senate for consent in the United States), and (2) completion of the steps required by the treaty itself or established by the negotiating states for ratification. For bilateral treaties this is often accomplished by an exchange of instruments. Multilateral treaties typically require deposit of instruments of ratification with a specified *depository*, which is charged with the duties of examining all instruments deposited to ensure compliance with formal requirements and keeping all parties informed. Often international organizations or the Secretary-General of the United Nations serve as depository for such treaties. The ratification process provides nations the time to determine public reaction, obtain the required approval for the agreement under domestic law, and enact any necessary implementing legislation. *See id.; U.N. Treaty Reference Guide, supra* note 1.

Through *accession* a state can become a party to an agreement that was negotiated and signed by other states. Accession indicates consent to be bound by the treaty, and has the same legal effect as ratification. According to Article 15 of the Vienna Convention, nations may only consent to an agreement through accession if the treaty so provides, the negotiating states so agree, or the parties to the treaty subsequently agree. Some conventions, such as the Hague Convention on the Civil Aspects of International Child Abduction, art. 38, provide that acceding states are only bound vis-a-vis those states that accept its accession. Some treaties permit accession by all other nations; others permit only certain non-signatory nations to accede.

In some instances states agree to be bound by an international agreement by depositing or exchanging instruments of *acceptance* or *approval*. This has the same legal effect as ratification, and is used when the domestic law of the state permits a simpler process for approval of certain types of agreements than formal ratification would otherwise require. In other instances states will agree to express their consent through an *exchange of letters or notes*. When this procedure is utilized, the signatures do not appear on one instrument, but rather, after the exchange, each party possesses a document signed by a representative of the other party to the agreement, typically each with identical texts. *U.N. Treaty Reference Guide, supra* note 1.

When a treaty so provides or the state otherwise clearly agrees, a state can also indicate its consent to be bound to an agreement by a *definitive signature,* a term often used for a signature which is not subject to ratification, acceptance, or approval. Bilateral treaties addressing routine matters that are not highly political often utilize this method of consent, bypassing the necessity of ratification procedures. *Id.*

It is increasingly common for nations that object to, or wish to qualify, one or more provisions of a treaty to make *reservations* at the time that they sign, ratify, or otherwise consent to be bound by the treaty. A reservation, as defined by Article 2 the Vienna Convention, is a unilateral statement through which the maker "purports to exclude or modify the legal effects of certain provisions of the treaty in their application to that state."[4] Reservations can be useful devices in the case of multilateral agreements, by encouraging wider adherence to a treaty by nations that might otherwise reject it. Professor Malcolm Shaw observes that reservations encourage "harmony amongst states of widely differing social, economic and political systems, by concentrating upon agreed, basic issues and accepting disagreement on certain matters." Shaw, *supra* note 1, at 642.

Reservations are not permitted under all circumstances, however. The treaty itself might prohibit reservations, or permit only specified reservations. Article 19 of the Vienna Convention further prohibits reservations that are "incompatible with the object and purpose of the treaty."

When a treaty has been negotiated by a limited number of nations and the treaty's purpose and object suggest that application of the entire treaty between all of the parties is an essential condition of consent to be bound by it, Article 20 of the Vienna Convention requires that a reservation must be accepted by all parties to the treaty. Article 20 further provides that a reservation is considered accepted when another consenting state raises no objection to it within twelve months of notification of the reservation, or the other state consented to the treaty after the reservation. Otherwise, express accep-

---

4. An attempt to make a reservation to a bilateral treaty would essentially constitute a counter-offer, and instigate renegotiations. If the other party agreed to the reservation, a new agreement is effectively reached. If the reservation is rejected, the underlying agreement fails. Janis, *supra* note 1, at 23.

tances must be made in writing. Reservations expressly authorized by a treaty do not require the acceptance of other parties to the treaty, unless the treaty so provides.

Even when a reservation is otherwise permissible, another state that has signed or consented to the treaty may file an *objection to the reservation*. The objecting nation may expressly provide that the objection precludes the treaty entering into force between the objecting and reserving state. Alternatively, the objecting state may choose to permit the agreement to enter into force between itself and the reserving state, in which case the treaty provisions that are the subject of the reservation will not apply between the two states to the extent of the reservation, pursuant to Articles 20 and 21 of the Vienna Convention.

Reservations modify a treaty reciprocally between the nation making the reservation and those nations that have accepted the reservation, or from whom no acceptance is required. Article 21 of the Vienna Convention further provides that such reservations do not modify the treaty as it applies to the obligations of other parties among themselves.

Many questions remain unresolved about the effect of reservations that are implicitly or explicitly prohibited by the treaty, or contrary to the object and purpose of the treaty. On some occasions, particularly when interpreting human rights treaties, there is some authority to suggest that a treaty provision addressed by the impermissible reservation applies in full to the reserving state. *Cf.* Loizidou v. Turkey, 310 Eur. Ct. H. R. (ser. A) (1995); Belilos v. Switzerland, 132 Eur. Ct. H. R. (ser. A) (1988). Alternatively, some international scholars have argued that when a reservation is found impermissible, the consent of the reserving state is invalidated and the treaty as a whole no longer applies to the reserving party. There is also disagreement regarding whether an impermissible reservation may be legitimated by the acceptance of other parties to the treaty, or whether a determination of its impermissibility is conclusive. For a more extensive discussion of the debate regarding the effect of impermissible reservations, see Professor Shaw's treatise, *supra* note 1, at 647–49.

In addition to reservations, states may make *understandings* or *interpretive declarations* at the time that they sign or deposit an international agreement to which they have consented. Understandings and interpretive declarations are statements that set forth that state's interpretation of a particular provision of the treaty, but are not intended to exclude or modify the treaty's legal effect. "Understandings" is the term most commonly used by the United States. The *Restatement (Third)* § 314(d) provides that "A treaty that is ratified or acceded to by the United States with a statement of understanding becomes effective in domestic law…subject to that understanding." "Interpretive declaration" appears to be the term synonymously used by international organizations and various other countries. Catherine Piper, Note, *Reservations to Multilateral Treaties, The Goal of Universality*, 71 Iowa L. Rev. 295, 298 n. 39 (1985); *see* U.N. Office of Legal Affairs, *Treaty Reference Guide*, http://untreaty.un.org/ola-internet/Assistance/Guide.htm.

In the United States, our government will occasionally attach reservations, understandings, and declarations (commonly referred to as "RUDs") all to the same international agreement. When differentiated from understandings in this way, declarations are statements of policy or opinion that are used to clarify a nation's position, purpose, or expectation regarding the treaty to which it is attached. Compared to reservations, understandings, or interpretive declarations, these types of declarations are regarded as having the least impact. Piper, *supra*, at 299. Like understandings, they are not to be used for the purpose of rejecting or altering treaty provisions.

The label given to a statement attached to an international agreement by the consenting party, however, is not controlling. Interpretive declarations, understandings, or declarations that evidence an intent to modify a treaty's provisions have in fact been regarded as reservations by international tribunals. In such instances they are held to the same standards set forth in the treaty for reservations, in order to determine their validity. *See* Loizidou v. Turkey, 310 Eur. Ct. H. R. (ser. A) (1995); Belilos v. Switzerland, 132 Eur. Ct. H. R. (ser. A) (1988). Otherwise, states could avoid the restrictions applicable to reservations simply by the labels they choose for their attachments.

An international agreement becomes effective on the date of its *entry into force*. The requirements necessary to trigger entry into force can be set forth in the treaty or agreed to by the negotiating states. In the absence of such a provision or agreement, a treaty enters into force when all negotiating states have consented to be bound by it. Vienna Convention, art. 24. Multilateral treaties typically require ratification or accession by certain nations, and/or a certain minimum number of nations, before they can enter into force. In some instances a treaty will provide for its entry into force on a specified date, or after a certain period of time following the last ratification, or upon the occurrence of some other event. Janis, *supra* note 1, at 26; *U.N. Treaty Reference Guide, supra* note 1.

Article 102 of the Charter of the United Nations requires that every international agreement entered into by any member of the United Nations must be registered with the Secretariat of the U.N., who thereafter is charged with the duty of publishing the agreement. Unregistered treaties may not be invoked before any organ of the United Nations, including the International Court of Justice. This registration requirement, which applies to all treaties regardless of whether they were negotiated under the auspices of the United Nations, is intended to deter secret diplomacy and ensure that the texts of all treaties are available to the public. Janis, *supra* note 1, at 26.

As changing times call for new solutions and arrangements, the parties to a treaty may wish to modify or amend it. The Vienna Convention distinguishes between the two. *Modification* occurs when fewer than all of the parties to a treaty negotiate an agreement to change some of its provisions as between themselves alone. Although they are required by Article 41 of the Convention to notify all parties to the treaty, the modification affects only those parties who enter the modification agreement. Modification is permissible whenever the international agreement provides for this possibility, or whenever it is not prohibited by the treaty and does not affect the rights and duties of other parties to the treaty or conflict with the treaty's object and purpose.

Amendments are formal changes to the terms of a treaty which could affect all parties to the treaty. According to Article 39 of the Vienna Convention, they are negotiated and entered under the same rules set forth in the Convention for the making of new treaties, unless the original treaty itself provides otherwise. All nations that are party to the original agreement must be notified of the proposed amendment; and all have the right under Article 40 to participate in the decision regarding what action should be taken concerning the proposal, and the negotiation and conclusion of any amendment agreement. Any other nations that are entitled to become a party to the original treaty have a right to become a party to the amended treaty.

Agreements to amend a treaty are treaties in their own right. Janis, *supra* note 1, at 33. States that are parties to the original treaty prior to entry into force of the amending agreement may choose not to become a party to the amending agreement, and as such, according to Article 40 of the Vienna Convention, are bound only by the original treaty.

Even in their relations with nations who have become party to the amending agreement, Article 30 of the Convention states that only the original agreement to which both states are party governs their mutual rights and obligations. As between nations that are both parties to the amending agreement, Article 30 provides that the terms of the original treaty apply only to the extent that they are compatible with the amending agreement.

Nations that become parties to a treaty after an agreement amending that treaty has entered into force are considered by Article 40 of the Vienna Convention to be parties to the amending agreement as well, unless they indicate a different intent. Their relations with another nation that is not bound by the amending agreement, however, will still be governed only by the original treaty.

iii. Effect and Interpretation of Treaties

International agreements that have entered into force are binding upon each *state party*, i.e., each nation that has consented to be bound by the treaty. States parties are required by Article 26 of the Vienna Convention, as well as by the principle of *pacta sunt servanda,* recognized long before the Convention under customary international law, to perform their treaty obligations in good faith. In accordance with fundamental international law principles respecting sovereignty and the independence of nations, only nations that are parties to a treaty or have otherwise consented can acquire either rights or obligations under a treaty.

Articles 34 through 37 of the Vienna Convention address the effect of treaties upon *third states,* i.e., states that are not party to a treaty, and provide that such nations can incur *obligations* only if the third state expressly consents to the obligation in writing and the parties to the treaty intend to establish the obligation. A *right* can be conferred if the states parties to the treaty so intend, and if the consent of the third state can be implied, i.e., there has been no indication that it would object. Although a treaty itself cannot otherwise bind a third party, some treaties establish norms that become so widely adopted that they come to be regarded as customary international law, which, as will be discussed below, then becomes binding upon all nations.

International agreements are enforced in a variety of ways. Some treaties, such as the European Convention on Human Rights, create international tribunals specifically charged with jurisdiction to apply and interpret those treaties. Some international agreements, such as the International Covenant on Civil and Political Rights (ICCPR), create committees and commissions to monitor compliance and attempt to mediate disputes between nations over reported violations. Sometimes the terms of a convention, or an optional protocol, permit these committees to also consider communications from individuals who have been victimized by a treaty violation, if the contracting parties specifically agree to submit to this authority. Other treaties may provide that disputes related to their provisions are to be resolved by an international tribunal that the treaty did not itself create. For example, Professor Mark Janis notes that as of 1995, there were at least 267 treaties that referred disputes over their terms to the International Court of Justice. Janis, *supra* note 1, at 133. Interpretation and enforcement may also occur in domestic courts of the states parties, particularly when the treaty involved is a human rights treaty affording certain protections to the citizens of a contracting nation. Given the nature of the international arena, international agreements are also often applied by nations through their diplomatic relations, by persuasion or force. *Id.* at 10.

Articles 31–33 of the Vienna Convention articulate essential norms for the construction of international agreements. A treaty must be "interpreted in good faith in accordance with the ordinary meaning to be given to the terms of the treaty in their context and in the light of its object and purpose." The "context" includes a treaty's preamble and annexes, any agreements regarding the treaty made by all of the states parties, and any instruments made in connection with the treaty that are accepted by all of the parties. In addition, any subsequent agreement of the parties or subsequent practice which establishes the parties' agreement regarding interpretation will be considered, along with any relevant rules of international law. If the parties' intent to give a term a special meaning can be established, that special meaning will control.

Professor Janis has observed that the focus of treaty interpretation under the Vienna Convention is primarily the terms of the treaty's text, "giving rather less emphasis than might some municipal laws of contract to the circumstances surrounding the explicit agreement of the parties." Janis, *supra* note 1, at 30. Students familiar with statutory interpretation in other contexts might also be surprised at the somewhat narrow role that the Convention gives to a treaty's legislative history, its *travaux preparatoires*. Article 32 provides that the "preparatory work of the treaty" and the "circumstances of its conclusion" may be used only to confirm the meaning construed from the text, context, and other sources discussed in the previous paragraph, or to interpret the agreement when those sources (1) produce an ambiguous or obscure meaning, or (2) yield a manifestly absurd or unreasonable result.

This standard leaves some discretion to the body interpreting the rule to determine the circumstances under which legislative history may be consulted, and domestic courts, in particular, may be influenced by their own traditions. Professor Janis notes that U.S. courts attempt to give treaties the same interpretation that would be rendered by an international court, but are sometimes more willing to interpret a treaty by ascertaining the parties' intended meaning, rather than confining themselves strictly to the text. U.S. courts may also tend to consider domestic legislative history regarding the treaty, such as congressional reports, more frequently than would an international tribunal, and to give deference to the meaning attributed to treaty provisions by those in the Executive Branch whose duty it is to negotiate and enforce the treaty. Janis, *supra* note 1, at 31–32.

International agreements are frequently authenticated in more than one language. Article 33 of the Vienna Convention provides that in such circumstances, each text is equally authoritative unless the parties agree or the treaty provides that a certain version will prevail. If the treaty is published in languages other than the ones in which it is authenticated, those versions are authentic only if the treaty provides or the parties agree. The rules for interpretation presume that the treaty terms have the same meaning in each authentic text. When the terms of authentic texts in different languages cannot be reconciled, none has been designated by the treaty or the parties' agreement as prevailing, and the normal rules of treaty interpretation cannot otherwise reconcile the discrepancy, Article 33 provides that the meaning which best reconciles the text in light of the object and purpose of the treaty shall be adopted.

iv. Invalidating, Terminating, and Suspending Treaties

Just as domestic contract law recognizes certain grounds for invalidating contracts, Articles 46 through 52 of the Vienna Convention set forth very limited grounds for invalidating a nation's consent to be bound by a treaty. These include, *inter alia*, consent obtained by error, fraud, corruption or coercion of the state's representative, coercion of the state itself through threat or use of force, or exercise of a state representative's authority outside of a specific restriction made known to the other negotiating states. According to Article 53, a treaty can also be found void if it "conflicts with a peremptory norm of international law," sometimes referred to as *jus cogens*. These norms are considered so fundamental by the international community as a whole that no departure from them is permitted, even by consent via the treaty process. If a new peremptory norm emerges, Article 64 recognizes its power to invalidate and terminate even existing treaties. The use of fraud, corruption, coercion, and peremptory norm as bases for invalidating treaties represents an extension by the Vienna Convention beyond grounds generally recognized in customary practice, and is therefore somewhat controversial. Janis, *supra* note 1, at 36. Moreover, while the concept of the existence of *jus cogens* is well recognized, its content and method of creation are often debated. Shaw, *supra* note 1, at 665.

States that are parties to a treaty cannot justify a violation of the treaty on the ground that the treaty conflicts with, or would otherwise not be enforceable under its domestic law. Even if an international agreement is not recognized as legally binding under the municipal law of a nation that is party to it, Article 27 of the Vienna Convention still recognizes the duty of the state to perform its treaty obligations. Although Article 46 of the Convention recognizes a rare exception when a state shows that its consent to the treaty was given in violation of its domestic law regulating authorization to enter treaties, this justification cannot invalidate that state's consent unless the domestic law violated was of "fundamental importance" and would be "objectively evident to any State conducting itself in the matter in accordance with normal practice and in good faith."

Treaties that are recognized as invalid are void, and under Article 69 of the Vienna Convention, have no legal effect. In some instances states can require other parties to restore their mutual relations to the situation that would have existed had not certain actions been taken in reliance on the treaty.

International agreements can be terminated or suspended (1) pursuant to the terms of the treaty, or (2) by consent, after consultation, of all parties to the agreement. Vienna Convention, art. 54, 57. Fewer than all of the parties to a multilateral treaty may agree to suspend a treaty among themselves, if the treaty so provides, or if (1) the suspension is not prohibited by the treaty, (2) is not incompatible with its object and purpose, and (3) would not affect the obligations and rights of other parties to the treaty. Vienna Convention, art. 58. If all of the parties to a treaty enter a subsequent treaty concerning the same subject matter, and it appears that they intend the later treaty to govern the matter, or if application of both treaties cannot be reconciled, Article 59 of the Vienna Convention provides that the earlier treaty is terminated. The earlier treaty could also be suspended in such circumstances, but only if it appears that suspension was the intention of the parties.

Material breach of an international agreement is also recognized in Article 60 as a ground for termination or suspension of both bilateral and multilateral treaties, in whole or part. In the case of a multilateral treaty, breach can be invoked as the basis for suspension or termination by unanimous agreement of all of the other contracting parties, as between themselves and the party in breach, or as between all parties. In addition, any party specifically affected by the breach may thereafter suspend the treaty as between itself and the defaulting nation. Finally, any party other than the nation in breach may invoke a breach to suspend the treaty as to itself if the nature of the breach is such that it changes the position of every party with respect to its performance under the treaty. Provisions providing humanitarian protection, however, and in particular provisions prohibiting reprisals against those protected by the treaty, cannot be suspended or terminated as the result of a breach. A material breach is regarded in Article 60 as a repudiation of the treaty not otherwise permitted by the Vienna Convention, or a violation of a term essential to accomplishing the treaty's object or purpose.

Theoretically, a nation cannot unilaterally withdraw from an international agreement unless the treaty so provides, explicitly or implicitly, or the parties' intent to permit withdrawal or denunciation is established. In such instances, Article 56 of the Vienna Convention requires that the withdrawing or denouncing party give at least a one year notice of its intention. In practice, disputes over attempted withdrawal and breach arise frequently. Treaties are frequently denounced unilaterally, typically by asserting grounds of changed circumstances. Janis, *supra* note 1, at 37–38. The Vienna Convention recognizes a very narrow ground for termination or withdrawal on this basis in Article 62, requiring, among other things, that the circumstances constituted an essential basis for the party's consent and the change "radically transforms the extent of the [treaty] obligations still to be performed." The Convention recognizes impossibility of performance as an additional ground for termination or withdrawal, but this ground has rarely been invoked. Janis, *supra* note 1, at 39.

Termination of an agreement, according to Article 70 of the Convention, releases states parties from further obligation, but does not affect any right or obligation created by the treaty prior to its termination. The effect of suspension on the obligations of parties is identical to that of termination, during the period of suspension, but the parties are obligated by Article 72 to refrain from actions that would obstruct resumption of operation of the treaty. Withdrawal of one nation from a treaty releases that nation and the other states parties from reciprocal obligations under the treaty from the date the withdrawal or denunciation takes effect. Vienna Convention, art. 70.

v. *International Agreements under Domestic Law*

Within each nation, the domestic law determines which governmental officers and bodies have the power to negotiate and enter international agreements, the steps necessary to implement them, and their effect in proceedings before domestic courts. In the following article, Professor Kirgis examines these issues under the municipal law of the United States.

Frederic L. Kirgis, *International Agreements and U.S. Law*

ASIL Insight (1997), *at* http:/www.asil.org/insigh10.htm

…"Treaty" has a much more restricted meaning under [Article II of the United States Constitution than it does under customary international law or The Vienna Convention on the Law of Treaties]. It is an international agreement that has received the "advice and consent" (in practice, just the consent) of two-thirds of the Senate and that has been ratified by the President. [Ed. Note: Because "treaty" is often used throughout this book in its broader context under international law, when it is used in this narrower context, it will be referred to as an *"Article II treaty"* or otherwise clearly differentiated.]

The Senate does not ratify treaties. When the Senate gives its consent, the President—acting as the chief diplomat of the United States—has discretion whether or not to ratify the instrument. Through the course of U. S. history, several instruments that have received the Senate's consent have nonetheless remained unratified. Those instruments are not in force for the United States, despite the Senate's consent to them.

Not all international agreements negotiated by the United States are submitted to the Senate for its consent. Sometimes the Executive Branch negotiates an agreement that is intended to be binding only if sent to the Senate, but the President for political reasons decides not to seek its consent. Often, however, the Executive Branch negotiates agreements that are intended to be binding without the consent of two-thirds of the Senate. Sometimes these agreements are entered into with the concurrence of a simple majority of both houses of Congress ("*Congressional-Executive agreements*"); in these cases the concurrence may be given either before or after the Executive Branch negotiates the agreement. On other occasions the President simply enters into an agreement without the intended or actual participation of either house of Congress (a "*Presidential,*" or "*Sole Executive*" agreement)....

Although some Senators have at times taken the position that certain important international agreements must be submitted as [Article II] treaties for the Senate's advice and consent, the prevailing view is that a Congressional-Executive agreement may be used whenever [an Article II] treaty could be. This is the position taken in the American Law Institute's Restatement Third of Foreign Relations Law of the United States, § 303, Comment e. Under the prevailing view, the converse is true as well: [an Article II] treaty may be used whenever a Congressional-Executive agreement could be.

The President's authority to enter into Sole Executive agreements, however, is thought not to be so broad. Clearly, the President has some authority to do so in his capacities as commander in chief of the armed forces and as "chief diplomat." Thus, armistice agreements and certain agreements incidental to the operation of foreign embassies in the United States could be done as Sole Executive Agreements. The agreement-making scope of these two sources of Presidential authority is nevertheless somewhat vague.... Presidents have sometimes asserted agreement-making authority stemming directly from the basic constitutional grant to the President of executive power. If this grant includes some authority to enter into Sole Executive agreements independently from more specific grants of presidential power, it would be difficult to ascertain what limits, short of those imposed on the government itself by the Bill of Rights, there might be to it. For this reason, many members of Congress and others have disputed any claim by a President to base agreement-making authority solely on the grant of executive power.

At one time there was some doubt whether a treaty (adopted with the consent of two-thirds of the Senate) must comply with the Bill of Rights, and the Supreme Court has yet to hold a treaty unconstitutional. Nevertheless, there is very little doubt that the Court would do so today if [an Article II] treaty clearly violated the Bill of Rights. Even more certainly, it would hold unconstitutional a Congressional-Executive agreement or a Sole Executive agreement that is inconsistent with the Bill of Rights.

As a matter of domestic law within the United States, Congress may override a preexisting [Article II] treaty or Congressional-Executive agreement of the United States. To do so, however, would place the United States in breach of the obligation owed under international law to its treaty partner(s) to honor the treaty or agreement in good faith. Consequently, courts in the United States are disinclined to find that Congress has actually intended to override [an Article II] treaty or other internationally binding obligation. Instead, they struggle to interpret the Congressional act and/or the international instrument in such a way as to reconcile the two.

Provisions in [Article II] treaties and other international agreements are given effect as law in domestic courts of the United States only if they are "self-executing" or if they have been implemented by an act (such as an act of Congress) having the effect of federal law. Courts in this country have been reluctant to find such provisions self-executing, but on several occasions they have found them so — sometimes simply by giving direct effect to the provisions without expressly saying that they are self-executing. There are varying formulations as to what tends to make a treaty provision self-executing or non-self-executing, but within constitutional constraints (such as the requirement that appropriations of money originate in the House of Representatives) the primary consideration is the intent — or lack thereof — that the provision become effective as judicially-enforceable domestic law without implementing legislation. For the most part, the more specific the provision is and the more it reads like an act of Congress, the more likely it is to be treated as self-executing. A provision in an international agreement may be self-executing in U.S. law even though it would not be so in the law of the other party or parties to the agreement. Moreover, some provisions in an agreement might be self-executing while others in the same agreement are not.

All treaties are the law of the land, but only a self-executing treaty would prevail in a domestic court over a prior, inconsistent act of Congress. A non-self-executing treaty could not supersede a prior inconsistent act of Congress in a U. S. court. A non-self-executing treaty nevertheless would be the supreme law of the land in the sense that — as long as the treaty is consistent with the Bill of Rights — the President could not constitutionally ignore or contravene it.

Even if [an Article II] treaty or other international agreement is non-self-executing, it may have an indirect effect in U. S. courts. The courts' practice, mentioned above, of interpreting acts of Congress as consistent with earlier international agreements applies to earlier non-self-executing agreements as well as to self-executing ones, since in either case the agreement is binding internationally and courts are slow to place the United States in breach of its international obligations. In addition, if state or local law is inconsistent with an international agreement of the United States, the courts will not allow the law to stand. The reason, if the international agreement is a self-executing treaty, is that such a treaty has the same effect in domestic courts as an act of Congress and therefore directly supersedes any inconsistent state or local law. If the international agreement is a non-self-executing treaty, it would not supersede inconsistent state or local law in the same way a federal statute would, but the courts nevertheless would not permit a state of the union to force the United States to breach its international obligation to other countries under the agreement. The state or local law would be struck down as an interference with the federal government's power over foreign affairs.

To summarize: the Senate does not ratify [Article II] treaties; the President does. Treaties, in the U. S. sense, are not the only type of binding international agreement. Congressional-Executive agreements and Sole Executive agreements may also be binding. It is generally understood that [Article II] treaties and Congressional-Executive agreements are interchangeable; Sole Executive agreements occupy a more limited space constitutionally and are linked primarily if not exclusively to the President's powers as commander in chief and head diplomat. [Article II] treaties and other international agreements are subject to the Bill of Rights. Congress may supersede a prior inconsistent [Article II] treaty or Congressional-Executive agreement as a matter of U. S. law, but not as a matter of international law. Courts in the United States use their powers of interpretation to try not to let Congress place the United States in violation of its international law obligations. A self-executing treaty provision is the supreme law of the land in the same sense as a federal statute that is judicially enforceable by private parties. Even a non-self-executing provision of an international agreement represents an international obligation that courts are very much inclined to protect against encroachment by local, state or federal law.

Notes

1. *Congressional-Executive Agreements and Sole Executive Agreements.* Professor Kirgis observes in the above article that, despite the provision in Article II of the U.S. Constitution requiring the President to obtain the consent of two-thirds of the Senate to a treaty, many treaties are made as Congressional-Executive agreements or Sole Executive agreements. These latter types of treaties are still considered under Article VI of the U.S. Constitution as the "supreme law of the land." Studies have shown that these types of treaties are in fact far more common; Article II treaties have comprised at most 10% of the international agreements entered by the United States. *See* Janis, *supra* note 1, at 94–95.

2. *Effects of Non-self-executing Treaties* Although Professor Kirgis repeats the common generalization that "treaties and other international agreements are given effect as law in domestic courts of the United States only if they are 'self-executing' or if they have been implemented" by federal legislation, he then goes on to clarify the many ways that non-self-executing treaties do have "an indirect effect" in domestic courts in the United States, such as their use to interpret relevant statutory, common law, and other legal provisions, *see, e.g.,* Ma v. Reno, 208 F.3d 815 (9th Cir. 2000) (interpreting immigration law consistently with ICCPR), and their ability to supercede inconsistent state or local law. *See* Jordan Paust, International Law as Law of the United States 62–63 (1996) for further discussion of the legal effects of non-self-executing treaties.

In addition to those effects mentioned by Professor Kirgis, some courts and scholars have recognized that non-self-executing treaties may be used defensively in proceedings in U.S. courts. Maria v. McElroy, 68 F. Supp. 2d 206 (E.D.N.Y. 1999) (defending against deportation); *contra* In re Extradition of Cheung, 968 F. Supp. 791 (D. Conn. 1997). *Cf.* United States v. Duarte-Acero, 208 F.3d 1282 (11th Cir. 2000) (considered, but found inapplicable, defense to criminal proceedings based on ICCPR, despite observing treaty was non-self-executing). In most cases in which such a treaty was used defensively, however, the doctrine of non-self executing treaties was not explicitly discussed. *See, e.g.,* Kolvart v. Oregon, 366 U.S. 187, 188–89 (1961) (defense to escheatment proceeding); Ford v. United States, 273 U.S. 593 (1927) (defense to personal jurisdiction in admiralty proceeding); Patsone v. Pennsylvania, 232 U.S. 138, 139 (1914) (criminal proceedings); United States v. Rauscher, 119 U.S. 407 (1886) (criminal proceedings). *See, e.g.,* Kristen D.A. Carpenter, *The International Covenant on Civil and Political Rights: A Toothless Tiger*, 26 N.C. J. Int'l L. & Com. Reg. 1 (2000); Connie de la Vega & Jennifer Brown, *Can a United States Treaty Reservation Provide a Sanctuary for the Juvenile Death Penalty?*, 32 U.S.F. L. Rev. 735, 762–64 (1998).

3. *Approach of Other Nations.* Although U.S. law permits some treaties to be self-executing, other nations take differing approaches to the incorporation of international agreements into their municipal law. Great Britain, Canada, and most other common law countries do not permit self-executing treaties. Treaties that affect private rights or require a modification of existing laws to implement their obligations will not be en-

forced by domestic courts in those nations until they have been incorporated into the municipal law by legislation. Some civil law countries, such as France, Japan, and Mexico, do permit self-executing treaties to a varying extent. Janis, *supra* note 1, at 97–102.

c. *Customary International Law*

The idea that custom could serve as a source of domestic law was accepted by many ancient cultures, including the Romans, and as will be discussed in more detail in Chapter Two, it is still an important source of domestic law in many parts of the world today. Throughout the centuries, custom has also been an important source of international law, and until the twentieth century was considered to be its principal source. In some ways norms created by customary international law can have a broader impact than those created by explicit agreements, because many customary rules are found to apply generally to all nations. Although some are determined to be of regional application only, and occasionally a nation is held not to be bound by a norm it has expressly rejected or repudiated through its practices, more commonly customary international law is seen to have universal application. The U.S. Supreme Court as early as 1820 recognized customary international law as "the universal law of society." United States v. Smith, 18 U.S. (5 Wheaton) 153, 161 (1820).

On the other hand, the content and formulation of customary international law is more difficult to discern than is that of law created by explicit international agreements. Determining when a particular practice ripens into a rule of law, and when inconsistent practice by a particular nation constitutes a violation, rather than a dissent or a replacement of old customary international law with new, has been described as an art rather than a science. Janis, *supra* note 1, at 44–46.

Establishing the existence of a norm of customary international law requires examination of two elements. First, it must be determined that a particular practice, while perhaps not unanimously observed, is consistently and uniformly adhered to by the international community. Second is the psychological element, *opinio juris vel necessitatis*, which requires that not only must the practice be habitual, but that it be followed out of a sense of legal obligation rather than mere convenience or courtesy. Occasionally statements by government officials made in the process of treaty-making or their other diplomatic relations provide evidence of *opinio juris*, but more often this element is derived from the writings of judges and international scholars. *See* Janis, *supra* note 1, at 45–48. Detecting *opinio juris* is often particularly problematic in the area of human rights, where norms often concern a state's treatment of its own citizens rather than its relations with other nations or their citizens. Several scholars have suggested that *opinio juris* in the human rights arena can be found in the "shared sense of moral reprehensiveness" that leads nations to collectively abandon certain practices and embrace others. Joan F. Hartman, *"Unusual" Punishment: The Domestic Effects of International Norms Restricting the Application of the Death Penalty*, 52 U. Cin. L. Rev. 655, 671 (1983). *See also* Ved P. Nanda, *The United States Reservations to the Ban on the Death Penalty for Juvenile Offenders: An Appraisal Under the International Covenant on Civil and Political Rights*, 42 DePaul L. Rev. 1311, 1334 (1993).

A variety of sources may be utilized to discern when a rule of customary international law has evolved: treaties; domestic legislation and legislative history implementing or concerning international agreements or foreign relations; decisions, reports, or other publications of domestic and international tribunals and other international bodies; scholarly publications; and digests of the international law practice of individual nations or a group of nations. These have all been recognized as important resources to detect and elucidate states' practices and motivations. Other influential evidence of the development of customary law is found in the resolutions and recommendations of the General Assembly of the United Nations, which has been charged with the duty to conduct studies and issue recommendations to promote international cooperation and the development and codification of international law. Although such studies, recommendations, and resolutions are not themselves international legislation, in some instances they may reflect international consensus, particularly for matters that have been approved through the vote of a large majority of nations, or by contrast they may reflect international disharmony. Also influential are the reports and drafts of the International Law Commission, a group of thirty-four jurists appointed by the United Nations General Assembly to codify and develop international law, although documents viewed as codification rather than those which reflect suggested development are better evidence of customary international law. Janis, *supra* note 1, at 48–53.

Even though customary international law is generally binding upon all nations, the *Restatement Third* observes that, in rare instances, when a state has indicated its dissent from a particular practice "while the law is still in the process of development," that nation "is not bound by the rule even after it matures." Restatement (Third) of the Foreign Relations Law of the United States §102, cmt. d & reporters' note 2 (1987). *See also* Malcolm N. Shaw, International Law 72 (4th ed. 1997). This exception, derived from the understanding that customary international law is based upon the implied consent of nations, is sometimes referred to as the "persistent objector" doctrine. To be entitled to the exemption, scholars contend, a state must object when the customary international norm is in its nascent stage, and continue its objection consistently thereafter. Lynn Loschin, Comment, *The Persistent Objector and Customary Human Rights Law: A Proposed Analytical Framework*, 2 U.C. Davis J. Int'l Law & Pol'y 147, 150 (1996). Because invocation of the status before international courts has been so infrequent, issues regarding the exact circumstances under which the exemption can be claimed remain unresolved. *Id.* at 154.

d. *General Principles of International Law*

General principals of international law are used primarily by courts to fill gaps when issues arise that are not resolved by international agreements or customary international law. These general principles are derived by examining and comparing the municipal law of many nations, based on the premise that some legal norms are so fundamental that they will be found in the major legal systems of the world. Restatement (Third) of the Foreign Relations Law of the United States §102 and cmt. l (1987). General principles are frequently used interstitially to resolve procedural issues before international tribunals. Other areas in which general principles have been recognized include contractual relations and administrative law. Janis, *supra* note 1, at 55–58.

Justification for the use of general principles of international law is based in part on the Statute of the International Court of Justice, to which all members of the United Nations and Switzerland are party, which recognizes these general principles as applicable in disputes before that court in Article 38(1)(c). It has also been argued that since these principles are common to the domestic laws of the world's major legal systems, there must be, in the absence of protest, some type of quasi-consent. Beyond these arguments, it is likely that use of these principles has been accepted because they are so rarely used to alter existing rules of international law, but only to fill gaps, or, on occasion, to support a finding regarding customary international law. *Id.* at 57.

Some scholars advocate that general principles of law have at times also been derived from natural law, *jus cogens*, and equity; others sometimes categorize these as separate sources for international law. Both positions have generated considerable controversy. Natural law is based on the notion that "there is a law so natural," whether derived from religious principles or the rule of reason, "that it is to be found in any community," including the international community. *Id.* at 62. Natural law was viewed as a primary source of international law in the sixteenth through eighteenth centuries, and the font of such principles as the equality of nations, non-aggression, and the national rights of nations to independence and self-preservation. In modern times natural law has come to be viewed primarily as a historical source rather than a modern source of international law. *Id.* at 59–62. *See* Shaw, *supra* note 1, at 43–44, 88.

The doctrine of *jus cogens*, discussed above as a ground for invalidating treaties, accepts the existence of certain norms as so fundamental that they can invalidate customary international law as well as the provisions of international agreements. Such norms are considered so essential that they cannot be derogated by the consent of nations. Characterized by some as a modern version of natural law, the doctrine developed in part as a reaction to Nazism in the mid-20th century. Janis, *supra* note 1, at 62–64. Professor Janis suggests that the doctrine of *pacta sunt servanda*, requiring contracts between nations to be legally binding, might itself be an example of such a fundamental norm. *Id.* at 66. The rights not to be subject to genocide, enslavement, murder, prolonged arbitrary detention, and systematic racial discrimination, along with other basic human rights, have similarly been identified as norms achieving the status of *jus cogens*. Restatement (Third) of the Foreign Relations Law of the United States § 702 and reporter's note 11 (1987). Although treaties have rarely, if ever, been voided on the basis of *jus cogens*, the existence of these peremptory norms has in fact been recognized in judicial opinions in both international and domestic tribunals, Janis, *supra* note 1, at 64–66, including a case in the U.S. Ninth Circuit that found the "right to be free from official torture" to be a norm of *jus cogens*. Siderman de Blake v. Argentina, 965 F.2d 699, 715, 717 (9th Cir. 1992).

The use of equitable principles by judges and arbitrators in international disputes has been particularly controversial. Absent specific authorization by the parties, the use of equitable principles as a basis for judicial discretion to achieve the intent of rules of international law or to fill gaps is premised in part on the notion that equitable principles are found in the traditions of both common law and civil law countries, and thus is a derivation of the use of general principles of law. Despite some scholarly debate, equitable principles have in fact frequently been used by courts, particularly in disputes over maritime and other boundaries, to apply other rules of international law or to fill gaps. The substitution of equitable principles for strict rules of international law that should otherwise be applicable, however, has been viewed as particularly suspect and subject to intense criticism. *See* Janis, *supra* note 1, at 66–75; Shaw, *supra* note 1, at 82–86.

In the United States, customary international law, general principles of law, and related court opinions are often considered together as *international common law*, rather than being treated as discrete sources of international law. Janis, *supra* note 1, at 103. Federal courts recognize international common law as part of federal common law. *E.g.,* The Paquete Habana, 175 U.S. 677 (1900); Filartiga v. Peña-Irala, 630 F.2d 876, 884 (2d Cir. 1980) (determining official torture is prohibited by the law of nations). International common law is therefore binding on both federal and state courts, and equally entitled to supremacy over state law as would be treaties. Restatement (Third) of the

Foreign Relations Law of the United States § 111 (1987). Federal statutory law enacted later in time, however, would prevail in U.S. courts over pre-existing international common law. *Id.* § 115. Whether new international common law could supercede preexisting federal statutes is uncertain, but in practice is rarely problematic, as courts try to reconcile conflicts. Janis, *supra* note 1, at 105–06.

The approach taken by other common law countries to the incorporation of international common law into their municipal common law is similar to that of the United States. Many civil law countries recognize non-treaty international law through various constitutional provisions, sometimes affording it supremacy over domestic law. *Id.* at 106–09.

Notes and Questions

1. *Interrelationship of Sources.* Explicit international agreements, customary international law, and general principles of law are typically categorized by international scholars as separate sources of international law, yet there are many ways in which they interrelate. Based on the above reading, identify several ways in which the law of treaties, customary international law, and general principles of law affect each other's development and application.

2. *An Exercise in the Application of Treaty Law.* In your Supplement you will find the International Covenant on Civil and Political Rights (ICCPR), along with information regarding its status. For a current list of nations that have signed and ratified the agreement and those that have become states parties through accession, see http://untreaty. un.org.

Skim the Preamble and Articles of the ICCPR. In light of your reading in the foregoing subsections, consider the following questions:

a. Will the ICCPR's Preamble have any effect when courts or other tribunals have occasion to interpret the covenant?

b. The Covenant's Preamble mentions the 1948 Universal Declaration of Human Rights, which is also set forth in your Supplement. If you skim this Declaration, you will see that its articles recognize many of the same rights set forth in the ICCPR. Given the existence of the Declaration, what would be the necessity for creating the ICCPR?

c. What does it mean to say that the ICCPR was "opened for signature" on December 19, 1966? Costa Rica signed the ICCPR on the date that it was opened for signature and ratified the Convention on November 29, 1968. Was the agreement binding on the date that Costa Rica signed the Convention? If not, what was the purpose of its signature? When did the ICCPR become binding upon Costa Rica?

d. Austria signed the agreement on December 10, 1973, and ratified it on September 10, 1978. When did the ICCPR become binding upon Austria? See Article 49 of the ICCPR.

e. Some nations have become states parties through ratification, others through accession. What is the difference? Does it affect their obligations under the Covenant? Can any nation accede to the ICCPR? See Article 48 of the ICCPR.

Some nations, such as Croatia, joined the agreement through *succession.* Under the Vienna Convention on Succession of States in Respect of Treaties,

August 22, 1978, 17 I.L.M. 1488 (1978), as well as customary international law, a new nation can choose to succeed to the treaty obligations of a predecessor nation that has ceased to exist, and whom it has replaced for the purposes of assuming responsibility for the international relations of a specific geographic area.

f. Who is the depository for the ICCPR? What duties does that entail? See Articles 40, 48, 51, 52, and 53 of the ICCPR.

g. Review the Reservations, Understandings, and Declarations made by the United States at the time of its ratification of the ICCPR, found in your Supplement following the text of the Convention.

What does the United States regard as the difference in the effect of these three types of statements attached to a treaty?

Read in your Supplement the objections filed by Finland to the reservations, understandings, and declarations of the United States. How can Finland object to an "understanding"?

Note Finland's objection to the United States' third reservation? What authority might Finland have used to support its argument? Is Finland's argument well taken as a basis for an objection to a reservation?

In light of Finland's objections, is the ICCPR in force between the United States and Finland?

h. According to Article 51 of the ICCPR, the Convention can be amended. Are the procedures proposed in Article 51 consistent with those generally recognized under the Vienna Convention for the Law of Treaties?

Assume an amendment was properly approved and entered into force under Article 51. Assume that Finland and Norway became parties to the amendment and Denmark did not. Would the amendment bind Finland and Norway in their relations with each other? Would it bind either Finland or Denmark in their relations with each other?

i. Following the ICCPR in your Supplement are two Optional Protocols to the International Covenant on Civil and Political Rights. The first Optional Protocol entered into force on the same date at the ICCPR itself. What is an Optional Protocol? Why do you think these provisions were not simply included in the original Covenant?

j. On August 25, 1997, the Democratic People's Republic of Korea (DPRK) gave notification to the Secretary-General of its withdrawal from the ICCPR. In October 1997, the Human Rights Committee, created by Article 28 of the ICCPR, responded with a General Comment on the question of withdrawal from the ICCPR. In November 1997, the Secretary-General of the U.N. also responded with a communication to the DPRK, explaining the Secretary-General's view of the legal status of the withdrawal. The notification of withdrawal and the responding communication, called an *aide-mémoire*, were circulated to all of the states parties. C.N.1997. Treaties-10 of 12 November, 1997. Based upon your reading above, what do you think these communications might have said about the possibility of withdrawal?

For those who are curious to learn more information about this withdrawal, *see* Elizabeth Evatt, *Democratic People's Republic of Korea and the ICCPR: Denunciation as an Exercise of the Right of Self-defence*, Australian

Journal of Human Rights, http://www.austlii.edu.au/au/other/ahric/V5N1/ajhr518.html [General Comment of the HRC annexed].

k. The U.S. Senate gave its advice and consent to ratification of the ICCPR on April 2, 1992. Does that mean the treaty is ratified by the United States as of that date?

l. What mechanisms do the ICCPR and its first Optional Protocol create for enforcement of the rights recognized in the Covenant? How effective do you anticipate these mechanisms will be?

m. Note the declaration of the United States, following its reservations and understandings, which states that the Covenant is not self-executing. What does that mean?

e. A Closer Look at U.S. Policy Regarding Ratification of Human Rights Agreements

Problem 1-3

Two years ago, Philby Turner, who was then sixteen years of age, brutally murdered a young mother and her five-year-old daughter in their home during a botched burglary. When he was seventeen years of age, Turner was convicted of one count of first degree murder, one count of first degree murder with a deadly weapon, and one count of robbery with the use of a deadly weapon. He was sentenced to death for the two murder convictions. The state supreme court upheld the murder convictions and sentence. Turner's lawyer then filed a motion for correction of an illegal sentence, arguing that execution of a juvenile offender violates the International Covenant on Civil and Political Rights (ICCPR), customary international law, and *jus cogens*. Case law in this state has clearly recognized the power of a court in this state to correct a facially illegal sentence.

Some background information on the juvenile death penalty might be helpful. From August 1993 through January 2001, only four countries other than the United States executed persons for crimes committed before the age of eighteen. These were the Democratic Republic of Congo, Iran, Nigeria, and Pakistan (which changed its law to prohibit such executions in late 2000). Patricia Puritz, Editorial, *Ban the Juvenile Death Penalty*, The Wash. Post, Jan. 22, 2001. In December 1999, Amnesty International observed that of the 19 juvenile offenders executed throughout the world between 1990 and 1999, the United States executed ten of them. Jennifer Gonnerman, *Kids on the Row, The U.S. Gets Ready to Execute Three Juvenile Offenders*, The Village Voice, Jan. 11, 2000.

In addition to the ICCPR, the American Convention on Human Rights (ACRH) and the Convention on the Rights of the Child (CRC) prohibit the death penalty for crimes committed before the age of eighteen. The Convention on the Rights of the Child has been ratified by every nation in the world, except the United States and Somalia. In addition, the United Nations Economic and Social Council adopted a resolution prohibiting the juvenile death penalty in 1984, which has subsequently been endorsed by other U.N. bodies.

As of June 2002, twenty-two U.S. states permitted imposition of the death penalty for crimes committed before the age of eighteen, and 80 people were on death row in the U.S. for crimes committed before their 18th birthdays. Victor L. Streib, *The Juvenile Death Penalty Today: Death Sentences and Executions for Juvenile Crimes, January 1, 1973 to June 30, 2002, at* http://www.law.onu/faculty/streib/juvdeath.htm. Opponents of capital punishment observed in January 2000 that 43% of those on death row for juvenile crimes at that time were African American (as compared to 13% of the nation's population which is African-American) and 20% were Hispanic-American (as compared to 12% of the nation's population which is Hispanic-American). Gonnerman, *supra.* As of June 2002, similar disparities existed, as 49% of those receiving death sentences for juvenile crimes were African-American, and 14% were Latino. Streib, *supra.*

Although in the 19th century the United States is reported to have executed an African-American boy and a Cherokee Indian boy as young as age ten, and as recently as 1944 a fourteen-year-old child was executed in South Carolina, Stan Grossfeld, *U.S. Leads World in Sentencing Teens to Death; Other Nations Say We Violate Three Treaties,* Seattle Post-Intelligencer, Dec. 6, 1999, the U.S. Supreme Court in 1988 determined that imposition of the death penalty for a crime committed at age fifteen constituted cruel and unusual punishment, thus violating the Eighth Amendment of the U.S. Constitution. Thompson v. Oklahoma, 487 U.S. 815 (1988). However, in 1989 a plurality of the Supreme Court affirmed the death sentences of a sixteen-year-old and a seventeen-year-old, holding that such sentences did not constitute cruel and unusual punishment. Stanford v. Kentucky, 492 U.S. 361 (1989). Since that time, state and federal courts in the United States have regarded the imposition of the death penalty for crimes committed by persons over the age of fifteen as permissible under the U.S. Constitution. Though the Court has recently revisited the issue of imposition of the death penalty upon the mentally retarded, and determined such executions constitutionally impermissible as cruel and unusual punishment, Atkins v. Virginia, 536 U.S. 304 (2002), the Court has not yet reversed *Stanford.*

The United States participated in the drafting and negotiation of the ICCPR, the American Convention on Human Rights, and the Convention on the Rights of the Child. The United States has signed, but thus far failed to ratify the latter two conventions, in part based on objections to the juvenile death penalty provisions. At the time that the U.S. participated in the drafting of the ICCPR and ACRH, however, the United States had discontinued executions for crimes committed by juveniles (none took place between 1964 and 1985) and thus raised no objection to the juvenile death penalty provisions of those conventions. The United States did not resume executions for crimes committed by juveniles until after it had signed the ICCPR, but before it had ratified it. The United States has also ratified the Fourth Geneva Convention Relative to the Protection of Civilian Persons in Time of War, which prohibits the death penalty for offenses committed as a juvenile by persons held by a party to armed conflict or by an occupying force.

The United States signed the ICCPR in 1977, and it was transmitted to the Senate by the Carter Administration in 1978. Domestic and international events prevented the Senate Foreign Relations Committee from moving to a vote on the ICCPR during the Carter Administration, and the Reagan Administration did not indicate interest in ratifying the Covenant. The Committee therefore took no action until President Bush asked the Committee in 1991 to renew its consideration of the Covenant, and submitted a package of conditions similar in many respects to those submitted by the Carter Administration. The Report of the Committee on Foreign Relations, accompanying its recommendation to the Senate favoring ratification, included the explanation of the Bush Administration for their proposals for reservations, understandings, and declarations. Regarding the non-self-executing declaration, the Bush administration stated that "[t]he intent is to clarify that the Covenant will not create a private cause of action in U.S. courts." S. Exec. Rep., No. 102-23, 102d Congress, 2d Session, 19; 31 I.L.M. 645, 657 (1992).

As the lawyer for defendant Turner, what arguments would you make to the state supreme court in support of your motion?

What counter-arguments would you expect the prosecution to make, and how would you respond to them?

In preparing your answer to this problem, consider Articles 2, 4, and 6 of the ICCPR, the U.S. reservations, understandings, and declarations to the ICCPR, Articles 19 through 23 of the Vienna Convention on Treaties, and the information in the forgoing subsection of this text regarding international agreements, customary law, and general principals of law. You may also find it interesting to review the objections of other nations to the U.S. reservations to the ICCPR, which can be found at http://untreaty.un.org.

Consider the following materials, which debate the broader issue regarding the appropriate approach the United States should take to ratification of human rights treaties.

Kenneth Roth, *The Charade of U.S. Ratification of International Human Rights Treaties*
1 Chi. J. Int'l L. 347 (2000)

...[O]n the few occasions when the U.S. government has ratified a human rights treaty, it has done so in a way designed to preclude the treaty from having any domestic effect. Washington pretends to join the international human rights system, but it refuses to permit this system to improve the rights of U.S. citizens.

This approach reflects an attitude toward international human rights law of fear and arrogance—fear that international standards might constrain the unfettered latitude of the global superpower, and arrogance in the conviction that the United States, with its long and proud history of domestic rights protections, has nothing to learn on this subject from the rest of the world. As other governments increasingly see through this short-sighted view of international human rights law, it weakens America's voice as a principled defender of human rights around the world and diminishes America's moral influence and stature.

The U.S. government's approach to the ratification of international human rights treaties is unique. Once the government signs a treaty, the pact is sent to Justice Department lawyers who comb through it looking for any requirement that in their view might be more protective of U.S. citizens' rights than pre-existing U.S. law. In each case, a reservation, declaration, or understanding is drafted to negate the additional rights protection. These qualifications are then submitted to the Senate as part of the ratification package....

After this exercise of stripping human rights treaties of any protections that might add to U.S. law, the government takes out a sort of insurance policy against the possibility that the Justice Department lawyers might have made a mistake. To ensure that some new hidden right is not lurking in parts of the treaty for which no reservation, declaration or understanding was entered, the U.S. government first declares that the treaty is "not self-executing," meaning that it has no force of law without so-called implementing legislation. This step is not necessarily objectionable in itself, since it ensures that new rights are endorsed by both houses of Congress through the traditional legislative process, rather than through the unicameral ratification process, which requires the consent of only the Senate. But then, the government announces that implementing legislation is unnecessary because, according to the Justice Department lawyers, all the rights for which reservations, declarations or understandings were not registered are already protected by U.S. law. The result is that U.S. citizens are left with no capacity to invoke the treaty in the U.S. courts. The non-self-executing declaration precludes stating a cause of action under the treaty, and the lack of implementing legislation means that there is no alternative route to assert a claim.

One other way that U.S. citizens might have invoked their treaty rights would have been by appealing to one of the United Nations...review committees established by many human rights treaties. For example, the ICCPR creates the Human Rights Committee—a group of independent experts elected by the states party to the Covenant with the responsibility, among others, of hearing complaints brought by people who believe their treaty rights have been violated. However, complaints can be heard only against governments that have ratified the (first) Optional Protocol to the ICCPR, which the US government has not done. Nor has it consented to have individual complaints of rights violations heard by any of the other treaty bodies.

Another possible way to give meaning to the ratification of human rights treaties is to take seriously the periodic self-assessment—a report to the relevant treaty body of experts—that is required of all participating states. But the U.S. government has treated these reports as little more than an opportunity for self-congratulation. Its first report under the ICCPR, in July 1994, was a lengthy review of relevant U.S. laws with minimal reference to actual practices. Its first report under the Torture Convention, in October 1999, was only slightly better. As of May 2000, the U.S. government is five years overdue in submitting what may be its most sensitive report—its first report under the International Convention on the Elimination of All Forms of Racial Discrimination.

This refusal to apply international human rights law to itself renders U.S. ratification of human rights treaties a purely cosmetic gesture. It allows the U.S. government to pretend to be part of the international human rights system, but in fact it does nothing to enhance the rights of U.S. citizens. This approach suggests a view that human rights treaties should be embraced only insofar as they codify existing U.S. practice, not if they would compel any change in U.S. behavior. Indeed, one is hard-pressed to identify any U.S. conduct that has changed because of the government's supposed embrace of international human rights standards. The only two ratification-induced changes that come to mind are the government's establishment and enhancement of criminal and civil liability in the United States for those responsible for torture and other severe mistreatment in other countries, as required by the Torture Convention, and the outlawing of genocide, as required by the Convention on the Prevention and Punishment of the Crime of Genocide....

In February 2000, for the first time of which I am aware, the U.S. government vowed to change not only its laws but also its conduct because of a human rights treaty—in this case a proposed treaty. At issue was the use of children under eighteen years of age as soldiers—a severe problem that plagues an estimated 300,000 children in conflicts around the world. A broad coalition sought to enact a prohibition against such abuse of children by adding an optional protocol to the Convention on the Rights of the Child. To the dismay of many, the U.S. government at first opposed the protocol because it wanted to continue recruiting youths immediately upon their graduation from high school, whether or not they had turned eighteen. Indeed, quite apart from rejecting the protocol, the U.S. government blocked other governments from adopting it for fear that its existence would make the United States look bad....

In January 2000, the U.S. government agreed to a compromise. It would accept a rule barring the deployment of children under eighteen in combat and the involuntary drafting of them. But the proponents of a child-soldiers ban were forced to allow continued voluntary recruitment of children under eighteen. This was a problematic compromise because in civil wars the line between voluntary and coerced recruitment is often blurred. But if the U.S. government ratifies the protocol as it has suggested it will and then changes its military recruitment and deployment practices, it would at least mark the first time that government behavior, rather than law, has changed because of a human rights treaty. Whether this marks a new attitude toward international human rights law remains to be seen, but its very rarity suggests how entrenched the view is in Washington that the U.S. government ordinarily should not embrace international human rights law except insofar as it parallels existing U.S. practice.

Informing this view is the assumption that the United States has nothing to learn from the rest of the world when it comes to human rights—that U.S. human rights protections are already state-of-the-art—and that improvement upon them is either inconceivable or undesirable. The ratification process is treated not as an opportunity to bring U.S. conduct up to the level of international standards, but as a legal exercise in "dumbing down" international standards to equate them with U.S. practice.

Such arrogance might be understandable if U.S. human rights practice were beyond reproach, but it is not. The United States certainly has much to boast about when it comes to human rights. The fact that I can criticize the government in this article without fear of an official "knock on the door" is one illustration of the many rights and liberties that U.S. citizens in fact enjoy. But many U.S. citizens, particularly those who are politically weak and disfavored, continue to suffer violation of their rights. The arbitrary application of the death penalty, the lack of accountability for police abuse or misconduct by prison officials, the racially discriminatory impact of the war on drugs, and the lack of legal protection against discrimination for gays and lesbians are among the serious human rights violations in the United States that existing law does not adequately address.

The ratification process might have been considered an opportunity to examine critically these deficiencies in U.S. human rights practice and to commit the government to improvements. It might have been seen as an opportunity to build a backstop of international legal protection should constitutional or statutory guarantees fail. Instead, this opportunity was squandered; ratification was treated as a mere charade for external consumption, with no impact on these or any other human rights problems in the United States.

The U.S. government's attitude toward human rights treaties differs from its view of other international accords. Washington routinely accepts changes in its conduct when negotiating trade or security agreements—by, for example, lowering trade barriers or reducing missile or bomb deployments. But when it comes to human rights treaties, ratification will evidently be considered only if it is cost-free.

...One possible explanation [for the U.S. attitude] is isolationism—the determination not to sacrifice U.S. sovereignty to rule by "furiners." But...even if the U.S. government were to declare human rights treaties to be self-executing or enact implementing legislation, the effect would simply be that alleged victims of human rights abuse in the United States would have an opportunity to state a claim *before a U.S. judge*....

Washington's cynical attitude toward international human rights law has begun to weaken the U.S. government's voice as an advocate for human rights around the world. Increasingly at U.N. human rights gatherings, other governments privately criticize Washington's "a la carte" approach to human rights.... For example, at the March–April 2000 session of the U.N. Commission on Human Rights, many governments privately cited Washington's inconsistent interest in international human rights standards to explain their lukewarm response to a U.S.-sponsored resolution criticizing China's deteriorating human rights record.

The U.S. government should be concerned with its diminishing stature as a standard-bearer for human rights.... Much of why people worldwide admire the United States is because of the moral example it sets. That allure risks being tarnished if the U.S. government is understood to believe that international human rights standards are only for other people, not for U.S. citizens.

Note

1. *Reservations Protecting Constitutional Rights.* Mr. Roth made clear in a footnote that was omitted from the above excerpt that he distinguishes the U.S. practice of drafting reservations that would negate additional protection for U.S. citizens, which he opposes, from the "legitimate effort to ensure that the ratification process enhances U.S. citizens rights by identifying and entering reservations to any treaty provision that might detract from pre-existing rights." An example of his conception of the appropriate use of reservations is the U.S. reservation to the ICCPR's Article 20. Article 20 provides that "any propaganda for war" and "any advocacy of national, racial or religious hatred that constitutes incitement to discrimination, hostility or violence" must be prohibited by law. The first U.S. reservation to the ICCPR provides that "article 20 does not authorize or require legislation or other action by the United States that would restrict the right of free speech and association protected by the Constitution and laws of the United States."

Jack Goldsmith, *Should International Human Rights Law Trump U.S. Domestic Law*
1 Chi. J. Int'l L. 327 (2000)

The human rights community has fiercely criticized the United States' failure to make international human rights treaties a source of law in the domestic realm. In this essay, I defend U.S. practice against these criticisms. To focus the analysis, I simplify in two ways. First, I consider only the ICCPR, the most ambitious of the international human rights treaties. Second, I assume that the U.S. practice of not incorporating the ICCPR into the domestic realm is legally valid under both international law and domestic constitutional law. I thus concentrate only on the policy question whether the U.S. should apply the ICCPR in the domestic realm.

Critics maintain that the United States should consent to all of the terms in the ICCPR, and should make the ICCPR directly enforceable by courts on the domestic plane. In short, the critics would like the ICCPR to be the functional equivalent of a domestic federal statute. The appropriate normative questions are thus (a) should the United States enact a domestic federal law with the content of the ICCPR and (b) should this domestic federal law be made by the President and two-thirds of the Senate rather than through the bicameral legislative process?

The ICCPR touches on every conceivable political and civil right. If proposed as a federal statute, it would be the most ambitious domestic human rights law ever introduced, touching on topics regulated by the Bill of Rights, the Reconstruction Amendments, dozens of civil and political rights statutes, and numerous state tort laws. The domesticated ICCPR would supersede prior inconsistent state and federal law. When ICCPR rights were more protective than domestic constitutional rights, the ICCPR would apply. The ICCPR could not violate domestic constitutional protections; if it purported to do so, domestic constitutional rights would trump.

Neither the treatymakers (President and Senate) nor the lawmakers (President, House, and Senate) could responsibly enact the ICCPR as domestic federal law. To see why, consider first the ICCPR analogues to U.S domestic law. The ICCPR protections are couched in different terms than domestic legal protections. Thus its differently worded terms would lead to litigation in every circumstance in which the terms differed. Consider Article 26, the ICCPR's equal protection provision. Would its guarantee of equal protection without "any" discrimination eliminate all forms of affirmative action in the United States? How would its guarantee of "effective" in addition to "equal" protection change domestic anti-discrimination law? Would its "protection against discrimination on any ground," including "status," extend to discrimination on the basis of homosexuality? Age? Weight? Beauty? Intelligence?...These are just a few of the broader questions raised by Article 26. There are hundreds of other smaller details of domestic anti-discrimination law—statutes of limitation, burdens of proof, disparate impact analysis, immunity rules, and scores of other case-law intricacies—that would be open to litigation and potential change.... In short, a domesticated ICCPR would generate enormous litigation and uncertainty, potentially changing domestic civil rights law in manifold ways.

Human rights protections in the United States are not remotely so deficient as to warrant these costs. Although there is much debate around the edges of domestic civil and political rights law, there is a broad consensus about the appropriate content and scope of this law. This consensus has built up slowly over the past century. It is the product of years of judicial interpretation of domestic statutory and constitutional law, various democratic processes, lengthy and varied experimentation, and a great deal of practical local experience. Domestic incorporation of the ICCPR would threaten to upset this balance. It would constitute a massive, largely standardless delegation of power to federal courts to rethink the content and scope of nearly every aspect of domestic human rights law. To see its implications this way is to see why a domesticated ICCPR is unacceptable.

Two further considerations should be mentioned. First, the traditional bicameral process, and not the treatymaking process, is the appropriate venue to make domestic civil rights law. There is a powerful case to be made that human rights treaties, which do not involve reciprocal obligations, and which only regulate domestic relations between a nation and its citizens, are beyond the scope of the treaty power. Conventional academic wisdom suggests that the treaty power has no subject matter limitation. But... the Supreme Court has long recognized that the treaty power contains subject matter limits. It has never backed away from this view. Just as important, the treatymakers have recognized these limits. In the non-self-execution clauses attached to human rights treaties, for example, they acknowledge that domestic civil and political rights law should be made by Congress and the President, not the Senate and the President.

Second, a domesticated ICCPR would raise a concern about excessive delegation. When federal courts interpret international human rights norms, they look to "writings of jurists" as a genuine source to give the norms content. They do so in part out of fealty to a common law tradition that has no relevance in the modern world. And they do so in part because of their relative ignorance about international law. Who are these jurists? For the most part, they are legal academics, human rights activists, and international institutions like the ICCPR's Human Rights Committee. These are not groups whose democratic pedigrees inspire confidence. Academic commentary and the work of the HRC are far more progressive than American political (and judicial) institutions.

For these reasons, the double-delegation entailed by a domesticated ICCPR—first to unelected federal courts, and then to unelected "jurists"—is unwarranted. This is so whether one views the problem in constitutional terms (excessive delegation, or an appointments clause violation) or from the perspective of democratic legitimacy.

* * *

I can imagine at least two objections to the analysis thus far. The first is that Congress could diminish the uncertainties of a domesticated ICCPR by enacting implementing legislation to clarify the details of its domestic scope. I doubt that it is possible to capture by code the variety of issues that will arise under a document as broadly worded as the ICCPR....

A second objection is that I have overlooked the many deficiencies of domestic human rights protection that might be rectified by a domesticated ICCPR. Nothing in my analysis suggests that U.S. domestic human rights protections are perfect, either as written or as enforced. Many contend, and I do not here argue otherwise, that domestic U.S. law and enforcement are inadequate in many respects, especially concerning immigration, discrimination, police abuse, and the death penalty. Even assuming this is so, these deficiencies should not be viewed as costs of failing to incorporate the ICCPR, and certainly not costs that warrant incorporating the ICCPR. In the United States, enactment of a vaguely worded international human rights treaty is not an appropriate or effective remedy for particular gaps in domestic human rights protection. Any such deficiencies will be most effectively and legitimately rectified through targeted democratic lawmaking, not through wholesale incorporation of what would in effect be a new constitution for civil and political rights.

* * *

...U.S. practice with respect to human rights treaties shows no disrespect for international law. To the contrary, when the United States refuses to consent to a small number of treaty norms (such as the ICCPR's prohibition on hate speech protection or the juvenile death penalty), it takes international law very seriously because it declines to make a legal commitment it cannot uphold. This is not an aberrational practice—many western European nations also decline to consent to ICCPR terms that are inconsistent with fundamental domestic law commitments. (These practices can profitably be compared to ICCPR ratifications by Iraq and Libya, which contain no such conditions.)...

The (inaccurate) charge of disrespect toward international law is often tied to a broader claim that the U.S. failure to bring human rights law home weakens U.S. human rights influence abroad. This purported connection is belied by the fact that the extraordinary achievements in international human rights have come during a period when the United States resisted ratification, much less domestication, of international human rights treaties. The United States exercises an enormous influence on human rights practices abroad through three mechanisms: (a) the example of its domestic human rights practices; (b) selective economic and military sanctions; and (c) victory in the cold war. The failure to domesticate human rights treaties has had no effect on these mechanisms. Nor will it going forward. As the United States' assumption of financial and military responsibilities for punishing Serbia last summer suggests, U.S. leadership and resources will remain crucial to the enforcement of human rights norms....

Nations that increase protection for their citizens' human rights rarely do so because of the pull of international law. Europe appears to be, but is not, a counterexample.... [T]he successful European human rights system was made possible by a "prior convergence of domestic practices and institutions" in support of democracy and human rights. The European system provided the monitoring, information, and focal points that assisted domestic governments and groups already committed to human rights protections but unable to provide these rights through domestic institutions. The European system contrasts with the international human rights regime in Latin America, which, though legally similar, has been relatively unsuccessful because it has little support from domestic groups there....

Similarly, neither the act of nor the success of human rights shaming strategies depend on the legal status of moral norms. China was criticized for its human rights abuses long before it signed the ICCPR. The United States was shamed before the world by its race discrimination practices in the 1950s and 1960s long before there was an international law prohibition against such discrimination. When nations criticize the United States for its juvenile death penalty, it matters not a bit that there is no international rule binding on the United States that prohibits this practice.... [I]t is the moral quality of the act, and not its legal validity, that provokes such criticisms. When shaming works, it is the perceived moral quality of the shamed practice, and not its illegality, that matters.

The United States has a long, deeply felt tradition of resisting international entanglements. Since World War II, human rights treaties have been a special cause for concern, for they strike at the heart of domestic self-governance. Opposition to ratifying these treaties was overcome only recently, and only because of the conditions to ratification that precluded these treaties from having domestic force.... If the U.S. treatymakers' only option were to consent to all ICCPR provisions and incorporate them fully into the domestic realm, there is no doubt that they would reject this option.... It is hard to see how the failure to ratify the human rights treaties—the only viable option to the present approach—would help the international human rights movement.

Problem 1-4

You are a professor of law with considerable expertise in the areas of international law, family law, and human rights. Assume that it is late 1991, and the Senate Foreign Relations Committee is holding a public hearing on the ratification of the International Covenant on Civil and Political Rights. The Bush Administration [George Bush, Sr.] has just submitted a package of proposed U.S. reservations, understandings, and declarations. [Assume they are identical to the text of the United States' RUDs following the ICCPR in your Supplement.] These RUD's are in fact very similar to the package of proposed conditions previously proposed by the Carter Administration, which, due to the hostage crisis in Iran and the press of other international events, never came to a vote before the Committee.

You have been asked to testify before the Committee at the public hearing, and to offer your opinion regarding whether the ICCPR should be ratified, and whether reservations, understandings, and declarations should be recommended to the Senate in the Foreign Relations Committee's report to the Senate. What position will you take?

Notes

1. *Scholarly Debate.* The articles excerpted above provide only a glimpse of the intensity and breadth of the scholarly debate regarding the stance adopted by the United States towards the use of reservations, its ratification of the ICCPR, and its involvement with human rights treaties in general. Well-respected academics and scholars weigh in on both sides of the controversy. For additional insights from those critical of the U.S. approach, see, *e.g.,* M. Cherif Bassiouni, *Reflections on the Ratification of the Interntational Covenant*

on Civil and Political Rights by the United States, 42 Depaul L. Rev. 1169 (1993); Lori Fisler Damrosch, *The Role of the United States Senate Concerning "Self-executing" and "Non-self-executing" Treaties,* 67 Chi.-Kent L. Rev. 515 (1991); Louis Henkin, *U.S. Ratification of Human Rights Conventions: The Ghost of Senator Bricker,* 89 Am J. Int'l L. 341 (1995); Jordan J. Paust, *Avoiding "Fraudulent" Executive Policy: Analysis of Non-self-execution of the Covenant on Civil and Political Rights,* 42 Depaul L. Rev. 1257 (1993); William A. Schabas, *Invalid Reservations to the International Covenant on Civil and Political Rights: Is the United States Still a Party,* 21 Brook. J. Int'l L. 277 (1995). For more detailed analysis from scholars supporting U.S. practice, *see, e.g.,* Curtis Bradley & Jack Goldsmith, *Treaties, Human Rights, and Conditional Consent,* 149 U. Pa. L. Rev. 399 (2000); Madeline Morris, *Few Reservations About Reservations,* 1 Chi. J. Int'l L. 341 (2000).

2. *Legislative History.* A brief legislative history reflecting the views of the Senate Foreign Relations Committee on the ICCPR and U.S. reservations can be found at the following: United States: Senate Committee on Foreign Relations Report on The International Covenant on Civil and Political Rights, S. Exec. Rep., No. 102-23, 102d Congress, 2d Session, 31 I.L.M. 645 (1992).

3. *Juvenile Death Penalty Scholarship.* Those of you particularly interested in the topic of international law and the juvenile death penalty may find interesting the following articles: Connie de la Vega & Jennifer Brown, *Can a United States Treaty Reservation Provide a Sanctuary for the Juvenile Death Penalty?,* 32 U.S.F. L. Rev. 735 (1998); Ved P. Nanda, *The United States Reservations to the Ban on the Death Penalty for Juvenile Offenders: An Appraisal Under the International Covenant on Civil and Political Rights,* 42 DePaul L. Rev. 1311 (1993). *See also* Joan F. Hartman, *"Unusual" Punishment: The Domestic Effects of International Norms Restricting the Application of the Death Penalty,* 52 U. Cin. L. Rev. 655 (1983); Lynn Loschin, Comment, *The Persistent Objector and Customary Human Rights Law: A Proposed Analytical Framework,* 2 U.C. Davis J. Int'l Law & Pol'y 147 (1996); Michael J. Spillane, Comment, *The Execution of Juvenile Offenders: Constitutional and International Law Objections,* 60 U.M.K.C. L. Rev. 113 (1991); Erica Templeton, Note, *Killing Kids: The Impact of Domingues v. Nevada on the Juvenile Death Penalty as a Violation of International Law,* 41 B.C. L. Rev. 1175 (2000).

f. Enforcing Claims under International Common Law as Private Rights of Action in U.S. Courts

Claims by individuals based upon customary international law have on occasion been successfully litigated in state and federal courts in the U.S. *See, e.g.,* Republica v. De Longchamps, 1 U.S. (1 Dallas) 111 (1794); The Paquete Havana, 175 U.S. 677 (1900). In the area of human rights standards, however, Professor Bradley observes that U.S. federal courts have taken a limited approach to recognizing private rights of action for monetary damages.

Curtis A. Bradley, Customary International Law and Private Rights of Action

1 Chi. J. Int'l L. 421 (2000)

[In 1980,] the U.S. Court of Appeals for the Second Circuit issued its landmark decision in Filartiga v. Pena-Irala [630 F.2d 876]. In upholding federal court jurisdiction over a suit between aliens concerning violations of international human rights standards in a foreign country, the court in *Filartiga* paved the way for modern international human rights litigation....

Since *Filartiga*, U.S. courts have been confronted with two waves of international human rights litigation. The first wave has primarily involved suits, like *Filartiga* itself, between aliens concerning alleged human rights abuses occurring outside the United States. This wave has been moderately successful. While enforcement of judgments is often a problem in these cases, many courts have at least been receptive to hearing the plaintiff's claims. In recent years, litigants have increasingly attempted to apply the principles developed in this first wave litigation to suits against domestic defendants. This "second wave" litigation has been much less successful than the first wave....

Even if customary international law is federal law, this does not mean that it necessarily confers a private right of action. Not all federal law, even federal constitutional law, carries with it a private right to sue. Former Judge Bork, [i]n a concurrence in ... Tel-Oren v Libyan Arab Republic, [726 F.2d 774 (D.C. Cir.1984),] argued that it was in fact inappropriate for courts to imply...a private cause of action under customary international law. Among other things, he noted that the political branches rather than the courts have principal responsibility for foreign relations issues, that the domestic implementation of international law is generally governed by domestic rather than international law, and that even the international law governing human rights does not generally purport to require private civil remedies.

Judge Bork's argument generated...sufficient concern...that in 1991 Congress was persuaded to enact the Torture Victim Protection Act ("TVPA"). By its terms, this statute creates a private right to sue in U.S. courts for claims of torture and extrajudicial killing, subject to a statute of limitations, an exhaustion requirement, and other provisions. The TVPA covers only torture and extrajudicial killing committed under "actual or apparent authority, or color of law, of any *foreign nation*," and thus does not apply to actions by U.S. officials. Importantly, however, its cause of action is available to both domestic and foreign plaintiffs.

The TVPA does not apply to claims based on conduct other than torture or extrajudicial killing.... Some courts have addressed this problem by holding that another statute, the Alien Tort Statute ("ATS"), creates a private right of action. This statute, which was enacted in 1789 as part of the first Judiciary Act, states that "[t]he district courts shall have original jurisdiction of any civil action by an alien for a tort only, committed in violation of the law of nations or a treaty of the United States."...[T]he ATS has a major limitation built into its scope: it applies only to suits by alien plaintiffs and thus cannot be relied upon to create a right to sue in cases brought by U.S. plaintiffs.

There have been a number of cases in recent years in which alien plaintiffs have sued domestic defendants for violations of international human rights law, including several cases brought against U.S. corporations. In this category of second wave cases, the plaintiffs can invoke the Alien Tort Statute, which, as noted above, has been held by some courts not only to confer statutory jurisdiction but also to create a cause of action. One might assume, therefore, that these suits would be as successful as the alien-versus-alien cases described above. In fact, with rare exceptions, these suits have failed.

These suits have encountered a variety of doctrinal and procedural barriers. As in first wave litigation, the plaintiffs are generally disallowed in these cases from bringing claims directly under human rights treaties because the United States either has not ratified them or has declared them to be non-self-executing. In addition, courts have held that customary international law cannot be applied by U.S. courts when there is a controlling executive or legislative act to the contrary. Courts also have been strict about the requirements for pleading and proving the international law violations. Furthermore, they have applied domestic law restrictions, such as statutes of limitation and the act of state doctrine, to bar the international law claims.... In sum, although there are a variety of specific reasons why courts have rejected claims in this context, it appears that, in general, courts are more resistant to allowing international human rights claims when they are brought against domestic defendants.

There have been several recent international human rights cases brought by U.S. citizens against domestic defendants. These cases have involved claims concerning unauthorized medical experiments conducted on state prisoners and patients, and the improper use of force to restrain a state criminal defendant. Because the plaintiffs in these cases were not aliens, they could not invoke the ATS as a basis for their cause of action. And, in each of these cases, courts have held that there is no private right of action under customary international law.... These courts have offered several reasons for their conclusion.

First, the Supreme Court has held that private rights of action should not be implied under domestic law when there are "special factors counseling hesitation"—for example, if the right of action issue raises difficult policy questions best left for Congress in the first instance. Courts have reasoned that, if anything, this separation of powers concern is higher with respect to cases involving international law issues, since foreign affairs matters are particularly the province of the legislative and executive branches of government....

Second, courts have noted that there are extensive domestic remedies available for abusive actions by federal and state officials—such as the remedies available under the civil rights statute, 42 U.S.C. § 1983; under the Federal Tort Claims Act; and under state tort law.... Such domestic remedies...reduce the need, courts have reasoned, for implying private rights of action under customary international law.

Third, courts have reasoned that Congress already looked at the issue of a right to sue under customary international law when it enacted the TVPA, and it codified only torture and extrajudicial killing, not other customary international law claims. By implication, the courts have said, Congress has not approved private rights of action under other customary international law claims....

Fourth, courts have sought to avoid allowing litigants to circumvent limitations imposed by the U.S. treatymakers. Many of the customary international law rights asserted in U.S. courts are also reflected in human rights treaties, either because the treaties codified customary international law or because the customary international law has been derived in part from the treaties. To the extent that the United States has ratified these treaties, it has consistently declared their substantive provisions to be non-self-executing—that is, not enforceable in court unless and until Congress passes implementing legislation. As a result, courts consistently have disallowed private claims under these treaties. If courts concluded that customary international law conferred a private right of action, litigants would be able to do an end run around this case law and, more importantly, the actions of the U.S. treatymakers....

Notes

1. *Asymmetrical Rules.* Professor Bradley comments in another part of the article on the anomaly of permitting alien plaintiffs greater opportunities than domestic plaintiffs to invoke customary international law as a basis for private rights of action in U.S.

courts. Nevertheless, he finds the arguments against recognition of a private right of action based on customary international human rights law persuasive. Do you? You may wish to reflect upon this further, as you read in the next subsection about the European Court of Human Rights, in which private litigants are permitted by the European Convention for the Protection of Human Rights and Fundamental Freedoms to seek damages for violations of their human rights.

2. *Broader Debate.* It is perhaps prudent to be aware that Professor Bradley, along with Professor Goldsmith, are central voices among a group of academics who argue for a decreased role for customary international law in American courts. Prominent among their articulated concerns is that customary international law, to the extent that it alters a result that might otherwise be reached under domestic law, undermines choices that have been made through more democratic institutions. Curtis A. Bradley & Jack L. Goldsmith, *Customary International Law as Federal Common Law: A Critique of the Modern Position,* 110 Harv. L. Rev. 815 (1997). *See also* Paul Stephens, *International Governance and American Democracy,* 1 Chi. J. Int'l L. 237, 238, 241 (2000). An opposing group of academics contend that the attempt of Professors Bradley and Goldsmith to undermine customary international law disregards two hundred years of judicial precedent supporting the treatment of customary international law as federal common law. Moreover, they assert, "judicial application of customary international law" has long been viewed as consistent with "the American understanding of democracy," and is consonant with our system of common law judging, whereby courts frequently apply legal norms not created by the legislative bodies of their sovereigns. Harold Hongju Koh, *Is International Law Really State Law?,* 11 Harv. L. Rev. 1824, 1831–41, 1851–60 (1998). *See* Joel Richard Paul, *Is Global Governance Safe for Democracy,* 1 Chi. J. Int'l L. 263 (2000). Furthermore, to suggest that customary international law is the creature of "other" nations is to ignore the predominant role that U.S. state practice and U.S. academics have played in shaping customary international law. Michael Byers, *International Law and the American National Interest,* 1 Chi. J. Int'l L. 257, 260 (2000).

In assessing the potential of customary international law to offer remedies to U.S. citizens litigating family law matters, it is important to consider the obstacles encountered by litigants asserting private rights of action in federal court, described by Professor Bradley in the above excerpt. It is also important to understand, however, that his observations about the underlying rationale for constricting private rights of action and the approach courts should take may be influenced by his views on customary international law in general, which is the subject of some controversy among international scholars.

3. *Act of State Doctrine.* The excerpt above refers to a common law rule, the "act of state" doctrine, which prohibits U.S. courts from questioning the validity of the actions of a foreign government within its own territory. Recognized in a long line of U.S. Supreme Court cases, the doctrine has been justified based on the notions of international comity and respect for the sovereignty of other nations, as well as principles of separation of powers, that prevent courts from interfering with the conduct of foreign relations. W.S. Kirkpatrick & Co. v. Environmental Tectonics Corp., 493 U.S. 400 (1990); First National City Bank v. Banco Nacional de Cuba, 406 U.S. 59 (1972); Octjen v. Central Leather Co., 246 U.S. 297 (1918); Underhill v. Hernandez, 168 U.S. 250 (1897). Foreign courts in general do not apply an equivalent doctrine. Joel Richard Paul, *Is Global Governance Safe for Democracy,* 1 Chi. J. Int'l L. 263, 265–66 (2000).

4. *Related Statutory Claims.* Professor Bradley observes that alien plaintiffs can successfully bring claims against alien defendants in U.S. courts under the Alien Tort Claims Act and the Torture Victim Protection Act for abuses committed abroad. Personal jurisdiction in these cases is often obtained over an alien defendant by "tag" service, i.e., personal service upon the defendant within the territory of the court. *See, e.g.,* Kadic v. Karadzic, 70 F.3d 232 (2d Cir. 1995). Enforcement of these judgments, however, is sometimes problematic. For an interesting discussion of how the proposed Hague Convention on International Jurisdiction and Foreign Judgments in Civil and Commercial Matters might facilitate or inhibit enforcement of these judgements, *see* Thomas Vanderbloemen, Note, *Assessing the Potential Impact of the Propose Hague Jurisdiction and Judgments Convention on Human Rights Litigation in the United States,* 50 Duke L.J. 917 (2000). The Alien Tort Claims Act and the Torture Victims Protection Act are discussed further in Chapter Six on Domestic Violence.

2. International Institutions

In order to put the materials in the following chapters in context, it will be useful to have a brief introduction to the history, structure, and operation of the international bodies that play a dominant role in the development and enforcement of international law affecting the field of family law. All of the organizations discussed in this section are *public international organizations.* Because they are created by treaties, they are considered to have an independent legal personality, theoretically justified by the fact that states have delegated to them through their constituent treaties some small portion of the states' sovereign powers. Public international organizations are not viewed under international law as states, nor do they have the same rights and duties as states. They do, however, have their own status under international law and possess those limited rights, duties, and powers conferred upon them by the treaty that created them. Janis, *supra* note 1, at 196–97. International *nongovernmental organizations (NGOs)*, by contrast, are nonprofit private associations that are incorporated under the laws of a particular state. Although they often make important contributions to international relations and the development of international law, they are not created by treaties, and thus have no similar international legal personality derived from an express delegation by states. *Id.* at 198–99.

Although a vast number of international organizations, both governmental and nongovernmental, influence the development of international law, there are a few key institutions that have been particularly influential in the field of family law. The United Nations and the Hague Conference on Private International Law have been the primary sources of global multilateral conventions addressing family law issues. In addition, numerous regional family law conventions have been drafted and negotiated under the auspices of the Council of Europe. One of those conventions, the Convention for the Protection of Human Rights and Fundamental Freedoms (European Convention on Human Rights), preserves familial rights in several of its articles, and is enforced through the Council's judicial arm, the European Court of Human Rights. The European Union has become actively involved in regulating the exercise of jurisdiction by its member nations in a variety of family law proceedings. In the future, the Charter of Fundamental Rights, drafted for the European Union, could also potentially have significant influence over the resolution of many family matters in Europe as well. Other important regional human rights and family law conventions have been prepared through the Organization of American States and the Organization of African Unity.

a. United Nations

The U.N. Charter was signed in San Francisco on June 26, 1945 by representatives of the 50 nations that participated in the Charter's drafting. In addition to maintaining international peace and security and developing friendly relations among nations, the United Nations seeks to address social, economic, cultural, and humanitarian problems; advance human rights; and foster the codification and development of international law. Today, nearly every nation in the world is a member of the United Nations. *The U.N. in Brief,* http://un.org/overview/brief.html.

The Charter establishes six principal organs of the United Nations: the General Assembly, the Security Council, the Economic and Social Council, the Trusteeship Council, the Secretariat, and the International Court of Justice. The first five are located at the United Nations headquarters in New York City. The International Court of Justice, the judicial organ of the United Nations, is located at The Hague, in the Netherlands.

Each member state of the United Nations is represented in the General Assembly, and each nation has one vote. The General Assembly may discuss and study any matter related to the United Nation's mission, and make recommendations to U.N. members, the Security Council, or both, with the exception that it may not make recommendations regarding disputes or other situations that are currently being handled by the Security Council. Decisions on those issues deemed important under Article 18 of the Charter must be by two-thirds vote; all other issues are decided by simple majority vote, or in some cases, by consensus rather than by formal vote.

The Security Council bears primary responsibility under the Charter for the maintenance of international peace and security. It is composed of fifteen members. Five nations are permanently represented—China, France, the Russian Federation, the United Kingdom, and the United States—and the other ten countries with representatives on the Security Council are elected by the General Assembly for two-year terms.

The Economic and Social Council (ECOSOC) consists of representatives of 54 member nations, each of whom is elected for a three-year term by the General Assembly. It meets throughout the year, and holds a major session each summer to discuss key economic and social issues. The Economic and Social Council is the central forum for initiating studies, discussions, recommendations, and draft conventions regarding international economic, social, cultural, educational, and health matters, and human rights issues. Of the six principal U.N. organs, ECOSOC has been the one most involved in matters related to international family law. ECOSOC has established and oversees the work of subsidiary U.N. commissions and bodies in the fields of economic and social development and human rights. ECOSOC also coordinates efforts with, and obtains reports from, a variety of specialized agencies, such as the World Health Organization and the U.N. Educational, Scientific, and Cultural Organization (UNESCO). These specialized agencies are autonomous bodies created by their own constituent treaties and are linked to the United Nations by cooperative agreements.

The Secretariat, consisting of various departments and offices and a staff of almost 9,000, performs much of the substantive and administrative work of the United Nations. At its head is the chief administrative officer of the United Nations, the Secretary General, who is appointed by the General Assembly upon the recommendation of the Security Council.

The International Court of Justice (ICJ), also known as the World Court, is governed by the Statute of the International Court of Justice, which is annexed to the U.N. Charter and to which every member of the U.N. is a party. Composed of 15 judges elected by the General Assembly and the Security Council, the Court hears disputes between states and will issue advisory opinions on questions submitted by international organizations. Unlike several other international courts, however, private parties are prohibited from appearing before the court. States that have specifically agreed to accept the Court's compulsory jurisdiction can bring a dispute against another such state on matters regarding the interpretation of a treaty, any question of international law, and the breach of an international obligation or reparations for such a breach. Any disputes between states not covered by this compulsory jurisdiction, either because they do not fall within the specified subject matter or because one or both disputants did not agree to be subject to the compulsory jurisdiction of the ICJ, may be submitted to the court by special agreement, called a *compromis,* of both disputing nations. As a result of the limitations on the jurisdiction of the Court, it issues an average of only three decisions per year. Janis, *supra* note 1, at 126–32.

Many of the important human rights declarations and conventions about which you will read in subsequent chapters were created through the United Nations. The Universal Declaration of Human Rights, prepared by the Commission of Human Rights and adopted by resolution of the General Assembly on December 10, 1948, recognized many of the social, political, and cultural rights that became the cornerstone of subsequent conventions. Although declarations issued by resolution of the General Assembly are not legally binding treaties, the Universal Declaration of Human Rights is viewed by many scholars as evidence of customary international law, and was the first step in developing an international bill of rights. The second step comprised the International Covenant on Civil and Political Rights (ICCPR) and the International Covenant on Economic, Social, and Cultural Rights (ICESCR), Dec. 16, 1966, 993 U.N.T.S. 3, both of which were adopted by resolution of the General Assembly in 1966, and entered into force in 1976.

Due to the jurisdictional restrictions on the International Court of Justice, the Court does not serve as the primary enforcement mechanism for these covenants. The ICESCR merely requires periodic reports on implementation, which are submitted to ECOSOC and reviewed by the Committee on Economic, Social and Cultural Rights and, when appropriate, various specialized agencies. The ICCPR enforcement system is more complex. As you learned from your study of the ICCPR in the previous subsection, the Covenant creates a Human Rights Committee (HRC) to monitor implementation reports from member states. In addition, however, if both states have specifically agreed to submit to this authority, the HRC may consider a complaint, referred to as a "communication," from a member state regarding another state's alleged violation of an ICCPR obligation. The HRC then solicits information from both parties, attempts to resolve the dispute, and if unresolved, submits a report. The HRC may also appoint a Conciliation Commission to gather information, attempt to facilitate a resolution, and submit its own report and recommendations.

If a country ratifies the first Optional Protocol to the ICCPR, individuals claiming to be victims of a violation of the ICCPR by that nation may also submit communications to the HRC. These communications undergo a similar information gathering process, and a report is ultimately issued to the state party and individual concerned. Decisions of the HRC are also published. Approximately two-thirds of the parties to the ICCPR have ratified this Protocol, but the United States has not chosen to ratify.

In addition to enforcement mechanisms available through treaty-based organs such as the Human Rights Committee, which are specifically created through a convention, the United Nations also fosters the enforcement of human rights standards through charter-based organs, i.e., bodies such as ECOSOC that are mandated by the Charter and bodies created by Charter-mandated organs. For example, the U.N. Commission on Human Rights, created by ECOSOC, addresses consistent patterns of gross violations of human rights, both within particular countries and across borders, through various methods of investigating, reporting, and attempting conciliation efforts through both confidential and public channels.

The United Nations has been active in drafting international documents and sponsoring other programs and activities addressing the situation of families throughout the world. In addition to the two broad human rights conventions, many important specialized conventions addressing women's and children's concerns were drafted and adopted through various bodies of the United Nations, including the Convention on the Political Rights of Women, the Convention on the Nationality of Married Women, the Convention on the Recovery Abroad of Maintenance, the Convention on the Consent to Marriage, the Minimum Age of Marriage and Registration of Marriages, the Convention on the Elimination of All Forms of Discrimination Against Women, and the Convention on the Rights of the Child. The General Assembly has also issued important declarations, including the Declaration on the Elimination of Violence Against Women in 1993. That same year, a Special Rapporteur on Violence Against Women was appointed to investigate and report to the U.N. Commission on Human Rights on an ongoing basis regarding violence against women throughout the world. Four world conferences on women have been sponsored by the United Nations in Mexico City (1975), Copenhagen (1980), Nairobi (1985), and in Beijing (1995).

In addition to the Special Rapporteur, several other important bodies within the United Nations have been established to promote the rights of women. In 1946 the Commission on the Status on Women(CSW) was established by ECOSOC to prepare recommendations and reports on women's issues and serve as a global advocate for equality between men and women. The Commission is an intergovernmental body of representatives from 45 countries who are elected every four years pursuant to a specific geographic formula ensuring representation for all regions of the world. In addition to drafting many of the Conventions set forth above and initiating the world conferences, the Commission brings women's concerns to the attention of many other U.N. bodies and specialized agencies.

Another important organization, the Committee on the Elimination of Discrimination Against Women (CEDAW Committee), was established in 1982 to monitor the implementation of the Convention on the Elimination of Discrimination Against Women. The Committee's membership is composed of twenty-three experts nominated by their governments and elected by those countries that have ratified the Convention. They serve four-year terms in their individual capacities and not as the representatives or delegates of their countries of origin. The Committee meets annually to review the implementation reports submitted by nations that have ratified the Convention, make recommendations to those nations, solicit reports from UN specialized agencies, and submit its own report to ECOSOC, the Commission on the Status of Women, and the General Assembly.

In December 2000, a Protocol to the Convention on the Elimination of Discrimination against Women entered into force that permits the CEDAW Committee to also consider communications submitted by individuals who claim to be victims of a violation of the Convention by a state that has ratified the Protocol. Upon receipt of the communication, the Committee may gather information, request the state party to take interim measures to avoid irreparable damage to the alleged victim, make recommendations to the parties and monitor subsequent compliance. In addition, the Committee may engage in a special inquiry, including a site visit, in response to information indicating grave or systematic violations, unless a ratifying nation specifically declines to accept such competence on the part of the Committee.

Two additional autonomous bodies within the U.N. system focus on integrating women in the development process. Working through ten regional offices, the United Nations Development Fund for Women (UNIFEM) provides direct technical and financial support for development projects for women and promotes the inclusion of women in the decision-making of mainstream development programs. The United Nations International Research and Training Institute for the Advancement of Women (INSTRAW) conducts research projects to identify barriers that prevent women from achieving equality in social, political, and economic development programs and develops training and information activities to overcome those obstacles. *The United Nations and the Status of Women,* http://www.un.org/Conferences/Women/PubInfo/Status/Text Only.htm.

Implementation of the Convention on the Rights of the Child is monitored by the Committee on the Rights of the Child, consisting of eighteen experts elected by the states that are party to the Convention. The Committee meets three times per year to review periodic reports on implementation from the governments of the states parties, as well as from international organizations, such as UNICEF and WHO, and national and international NGOs, such as Human Rights Watch. The Committee then issues its own reports, Concluding Observations and Recommendations, for each country reviewed. The Committee is discussed in more detail in Chapter Fourteen.

b. The Hague Conference on Private International Law

The Hague Conference on Private International Law is an intergovernmental organization whose principal purpose is to negotiate and draft multilateral conventions in a variety of fields, with the goal of furthering the progressive unification of private international law. Although sessions of the Hague Conference were convened sporadically by the government of the Netherlands beginning in 1893, it was not until 1955 that the Statute of the Hague Conference on Private International Law entered into force, creating for the first time a permanent organization. States that had participated in at least one of the earlier sessions could become members by accepting the Statute, and other nations willing to accept the Statute are admitted by a majority vote of the member states. Although originally all of the founding members except Japan were European states, by March 2003 over sixty nations, representing every continent, were members of the Hague Conference. The United States became a member in 1964.

Beginning in 1956, the Hague Conference has met every four years in diplomatic sessions, called Plenary Sessions, to discuss and adopt conventions that have been prepared by Special Commissions composed of governmental experts, and to set the agenda for subjects to be included in the future work of the Conference. On occasion, Extraordinary Sessions are held when needed. At Plenary and Extraordinary sessions, each member state has one vote, and decisions are reached by majority vote of the delegations of the member states present. Non-member states are sometimes invited to participate on the same footing as member states, and in such circumstances they also have the right to vote. Since 1960, conventions have been drawn up in both French and English. Following adoption of a convention, all texts are brought together into a final act to be signed by the delegation of each nation.

The activities of the Hague Conference are coordinated by a secretariat, the Permanent Bureau, which is located in the Hague, Netherlands. The Permanent Bureau prepares and organizes the Plenary Sessions, conducts preparatory research, and supports the Special Commissions that draft the conventions and subsequently monitor their implementation. The Permanent Bureau also maintains communication with the governments of the member states through a National Organ designated by each government (the National Organ for the United States is the Department of State), as well as through the Central Authorities designated by member states to perform various functions under particular conventions. Coordination is also facilitated with other international organizations, including the United Nations, the Council of Europe, the Organization of American States, and the Asian-African Legal Consultative Committee, and with NGOs such as the International Bar Association and the International Society of Family Law, which often send observers to the meetings.

Since 1955, the Hague Conference has produced 35 conventions in a variety of fields. Thirteen of these conventions concern international family law. In recent years, two in particular, the Convention on the Civil Aspects of International Child Abduction and the Convention on the Protection of Children and Cooperation in Respect of Intercountry Adoption, have been widely ratified and significantly impact the practice of transnational family law. In addition to producing conventions, the Conference participates in numerous international symposia on topics related to international family law, and has provided expertise to various nations drafting domestic legislation. Further information regarding the Hague Conference, current copies of all of the Hague Conventions, and news about work in progress on conventions currently under consideration can be found at the Conference's official website, http://www/hcch.net. *See also* K. Lipstein, *One Hundred Years of Hague Conferences on Private International Law,* 42 Int'l & Comp. L.Q. 533 (1993).

c. *Council of Europe*

In addition to organizations seeking global membership, the post-World War II era also witnessed the formation of several regional intergovernmental organizations that have played a major role in shaping human rights and family law issues. In Europe, the first such organization was the Council of Europe, created when ten European countries signed its constituent treaty, the Statute of the Council of Europe, on May 5, 1949. Inspired by the need to escape the economic and social devastation in Europe following the war and avoid repetition of this tragedy, the Council of Europe pledged itself to (1) the protection of human rights, pluralist democracy, and the rule of law, (2) the development of European cultural identity and diversity, (3) collectively seeking solutions to discrimination against minorities, xenophobia and intolerance, environmental problems, and other issues facing Europe, and (4) facilitating democratic stability in Europe by promoting political, democratic, legislative, and constitutional reform. With permanent headquarters in Strasbourg, France, the organization now has a membership of over 40 European nations.

The Council operates through several organs. The principal decision-making body is the Committee of Ministers, composed of the Minister for foreign affairs of each member state. The Committee meets twice annually. Day-to-day work is conducted by the Ministers' Deputies, who are appointed by the Ministers to act as the Permanent Representatives of each member state. The decisions of Ministers' Deputies, who meet two or three times per month, carry the same authority as the Committee of Ministers. The responsibilities of the Committee of Ministers include concluding conventions and agreements, adopting recommendations to member states, admitting new members, monitoring the Council's program of activities, following up on commitments by member states, and supervising the execution of judgments of the European Court of Human Rights.

The Parliamentary Assembly, the deliberative body of the Council, is composed of over 300 members who are elected or appointed by the national parliaments of the member states from among their own members. Each nation has between two and eighteen representatives, depending on the size of its population.

In addition to providing a forum for debate on European and world events, the Assembly initiates the many European conventions and agreements that have been drafted and negotiated under the auspices of the Council of Europe. After the Council of Ministers has adopted the text of a proposed convention or agreement, it is opened for signature by member states. These conventions and agreements are not statutory acts of the Parliamentary Assembly of the Council of Europe. Instead they have the same legal effect as any other treaties, and bind their member states only when they have been properly ratified or otherwise accepted by the governments of the member states.

Among the many conventions created through the Council of Europe, four deal exclusively with family law matters: (1) the European Convention on the Adoption of Children (1967), (2) the European Convention on the Legal Status of Children Born out of Wedlock (1975), (3) the European Convention on Recognition and Enforcement of Decisions Concerning Custody of Children and on Restoration of Custody of Children (1980), and (4) the European Convention on the Exercise of Children's Rights (1996). The Council has also issued several recommendations in the field of family law and children's rights, and sponsored the European Social Charter, a synthesis of social objectives that includes many provisions calling for the social protection of mothers, children, and families. Giacomo Oberto, *International Conventions in the Field of Family Law: A Report*, 48 Chitty's L. J. & Fam. L. Rev. 1 (1999). Perhaps its most important contributions in the family law field, however, are the European Convention on Human Rights, and its enforcement mechanism, the European Court of Human Rights, which serves as the judicial arm of the Council.

d. European Convention on Human Rights and the European Court of Human Rights

The Convention for the Protection of Human Rights and Fundamental Freedoms, Nov. 4, 1950, 213 U.N.T.S. 221, as amended by Protocol 11, May 11, 1994, Eur. T.S. No. 155, better known as the European Convention on Human Rights, has been hailed by the Council of Europe as its most significant achievement. Adopted in 1950 and entered into force in 1953, the goal of the Convention was to secure and provide effective enforcement for certain rights set forth in the United Nation's 1948 Universal Declaration of Human Rights. As of March 2003, 44 of the 45 members of the Council of Europe were parties to the Convention, and the newest member had signed but not yet ratified it.

The Convention is remarkable in two respects. The first is its unprecedented scope. The Convention and its subsequent Protocols address the rights to life, liberty, property, and security; abolition of the death penalty; the prohibition of torture, slavery, forced labor, ex post facto criminal punishment, double jeopardy, imprisonment for debt, expulsion of nationals or collective expulsion of aliens, and discrimination; freedom of thought, conscience, religion, expression, movement, assembly and association; and the rights to education, free elections, a fair trial, criminal appeals, compensation for wrongful convictions, and an effective judicial remedy. Particularly important in the field of family law are its recognition of the right to marry, the right to respect for private and family life, and the right to equality between spouses. The Convention guarantees these rights to each individual within the jurisdiction of the nations that are party to it.

The other notable aspect of the Convention is the rigor with which these rights have been enforced through the specific international judicial institutions created by the Convention for that purpose. Under the Convention, when contracting states have so agreed, individuals and non-governmental organizations, as well as states, may lodge complaints against contracting nations for denial of the rights guaranteed in the Convention and seek monetary awards as just compensation.

Initially three institutions were allocated responsibility for resolving claims under the Convention. The European Commission of Human Rights reviewed the complaints preliminarily to determine their admissibility, explored the possibility of friendly settlement, and prepared a report on unsettled disputes that established the facts and included a recommendation on the merits, which was then transmitted to the Committee of Ministers. Subsequently, the Commission, contracting states, and eventually the individual involved could then choose to bring a case before the European Court of Human Rights (ECHR), a court created by the Convention for this express purpose. Cases not selected by the Court's Screening Panel or otherwise referred were decided by the Committee of Ministers.

Skyrocketing caseloads and the accession of many new contracting states in the 1990s prompted the amendment of the Convention through Protocol 11, which entered into force in 1997. Following a transitional period, the Commission was abolished[5] and a new European Court of Human Rights came into operation in 1998. Contracting states or individuals or nongovernmental organizations claiming to be victims of a violation of the Convention may now file applications alleging breach of the Convention directly with the Court.

Under the Convention as amended, the number of judges on the Court equals the number of nations that have ratified the Convention. Judges are elected for a term of six years by the Parliamentary Assembly. Since judges sit in their individual capacity and

---

5. The Commission actually remained in operation until October 31, 1999 to handle cases that had been declared admissible prior to November 1, 1998 under the old system. Just as the European Commission of Human Rights was going out of existence, the Council of Europe created a new office, the Commissioner for Human Rights, in May 1999. The Commissioner for Human Rights, who is elected by the Parliamentary Assembly, is delegated the responsibilities of fostering awareness of human rights, identifying possible human rights shortcomings in member states, and promoting compliance with Council of Europe instruments. The Commissioner may contact the governments of Council of Europe members directly, provide advice and information on the prevention of human rights violations, and cooperate with national human rights organizations or ombudsmen and other international human rights institutions. The Commissioner and staff of the Commissioner's office do not consider individual complaints, however, nor can they advocate on behalf of an individual before any national or international court or national government. Unlike the former European Commission of Human Rights, the office of the Commissioner is a non-judicial institution. See http://www.commissioner.coe.int/.

not as representatives of any nation, there is no restriction on the number of judges that may be of the same nationality. The Court is divided into four Sections for three-year cycles, each Section being balanced for the judges' gender and geographic origin, as well as taking into account the differing legal systems of the states parties. The entire Court elects a President, two Vice-Presidents who also serve as Section Presidents, and the Section Presidents of the two additional sections.

Within each Section, Committees of three judges are established for twelve-month periods, which carry out much of the screening formerly accomplished by the Commission. In addition, Chambers of seven members are selected by rotation within each Section. For each case, the Section President and the judge elected in respect of the state concerned participate. If the latter is not a Section member, that judge serves as an ex officio member of the Chamber.

Every application alleging a breach of the Convention is first assigned to one of the four Sections. A rapporteur, appointed by the Section President, decides after a preliminary review of cases filed by individuals if the case should be first screened by a Committee or go directly to a Chamber of the Section. If sent to a Committee, the Committee may strike an application or declare it inadmissible by unanimous vote. Those cases surviving Committee review, those sent directly to the Chamber, and those applications filed by a state are examined by a Chamber, which proceeds to determine both admissibility and merits, usually in separate decisions. A Chamber may at any time, however, refer a case regarding an important question of interpretation or risking departure from existing case law to a Grand Chamber. The Grand Chamber is composed of seventeen judges, formed by rotation within two groups, and includes the President, Vice-Presidents, and Section Presidents, who serve ex officio.

Proceedings before the European Court of Human Rights are adversarial and generally public. Legal representation is required after a decision declaring an application admissible, and for all hearings. Legal aid has been established by the Council of Europe for applicants who cannot afford counsel. Although a Chamber may hold a hearing on admissibility, the first stage of the proceeding is generally on the papers. Chamber decisions on admissibility are made by majority vote, and must contain the reasons for the decision. To be admissible a complaint must be made by an eligible complainant, i.e., a person or group who is a victim of a violation of the Convention or one of its Protocols by a nation that is a party to the Convention or to the Protocol at issue, occurring within the jurisdiction or control of that nation. Complaints are only admissible after domestic remedies through the national court system have been exhausted, and must be made within six months of the exhaustion of the last domestic remedy. Anonymous complaints are inadmissible, as are petitions that are substantially the same as previous applications or manifestly ill-founded. Luke Clements, Nuala Mole, & Alan Simmons, European Human Rights: Taking a Case under the Convention 13–40 (2d ed. 1999).

In those cases in which admissibility is approved by the Chamber, parties may be invited to submit further evidence or written observations, and a public hearing is held. States that are parties to the Convention, but not parties to the proceeding, and other concerned non-party individuals may be permitted by the Chamber President to submit written comments, or on rare occasions, to participate in the hearing. A state whose national is the applicant is entitled to intervene as of right. While a case is pending, negotiations towards a friendly settlement may be conducted confidentially, with the assistance of the Registrar.

Chamber decisions on the merits are also by majority vote. Any judge who has participated in consideration of the case is entitled to attach to the judgment a separate opinion, concurring or dissenting, or simply a statement of dissent. After the Chamber has delivered its opinion on the merits, any party may request, within three months, a referral to the Grand Chamber to review a serious question of interpretation or of general importance. Serious issues of general importance might include issues that are politically sensitive, such as cases where the decision is critical of a domestic legal system, and substantial policy issues, such as state practices that might routinely violate the Convention. *Id.* at 71. A judgment of the Chamber becomes final if the parties do not request the referral within three months or a five judge panel of the Grand Chamber rejects the referral. If the referral is accepted, the Grand Chamber then renders its decision by majority vote and its judgment is final.

Final judgments of the Court are binding on the respondent states. When the Court determines that the Convention has been violated, and if the domestic law of the respondent state permits only partial reparation to be made, Article 41 of the Convention permits the Court to award "just satisfaction" to the victim, which typically involves reimbursement of costs and expenses, and compensation for pecuniary and non-pecuniary damages, when appropriate. The Council of Europe reports that states that have been ordered to make payments by the Court have consistently complied thus far. *See Effects of Judgments or Cases 1959–1998,* http://www.echr.coe.int/Eng/EDocs/EffectsOfJudgments.html.

Aside from compensation and costs, however, the European Court of Human Rights has no power under the Convention to order injunctive or any other kind of relief. Thus, it cannot order a state to take any particular action, or prohibit it from taking any particular action. *Id.* at 79. Nevertheless, judgments may result in the respondent state adopting other concrete measures of their own volition affecting the individual complainant. Moreover, a finding that a state is in violation of a convention often results in general measures to comply with the decision as well, such as expedited amendments to legislation or regulations, and adaptations in case law by domestic courts of the respondent nation. The Committee of Ministers supervises execution of the judgments and verifies whether states have taken adequate remedial measures to comply with all obligations under the Court's judgment.[6]

The Committee of Ministers of the Council of Europe may also request advisory opinions from the Court on questions regarding interpretation of the Convention and Protocols. Advisory opinions are made by the Grand Chamber by majority vote.

The following judgment by the European Court of Human Rights illustrates the role undertaken by the Court in a review of the internal actions of a member of the Council of Europe under the Convention.

L. v. Finland
31 E.H.H.R. 737 (2000)

[Ed. Note: The father and grandfather of two children placed in public care by the government of Finland filed applications in 1994 alleging violations of their rights under the European Convention on Human Rights. In 1996, the Commission invited the Government to submit observations on admissibility and merits. The Commission had ap-

---

6. *See Effects of Judgments or Cases 1959–1998,* http://www.echr.coe.int/Eng/EDocs/EffectsOfJudgments.html, for a summary of the effects of particular judgments entered by the Court between 1959 and 1998, based on resolutions adopted by the Committee of Ministers made in the context of supervising execution of these judgments.

parently not yet made recommendations when Protocol 11 took effect, and the case was forwarded to the reorganized Court and assigned to the Fourth Section. Further information was submitted to the Court by the applicants and the government in 1999. An in camera hearing then took place on the admissibility and merits of the claims. At that hearing, the Court declared certain claims admissible, and received throughout the remainder of 1999 various documents submitted by the applicants and the government.

Following the procedural history of the case, the opinion sets forth a statement of the facts. In January 1992, governmental authorities placed the father's two daughters in public care, based on their suspicion that P, who was then six years old, had been sexually abused and fear that her eight-month-old sister was at risk of similar abuse. Both the father and mother opposed the public care order. Although psychiatric investigation did not result in any finding that P had been subject to sexual abuse, the Social Welfare Board continued to keep the children in public care on the ground that the mother was suffering from mental illness, the parents had been planning a divorce, and the Board considered the parents incapable of providing the children with basic security and the necessary stimulation for their growth and development. The children were placed in a foster home and the parents' visitation was severely restricted. The parents' appeal of the public care order to a Finnish tribunal was subsequently rejected and their request for an oral hearing on the matter was denied.

The parents separated in 1994, at which time the father moved in with his parents, and subsequently divorced in 1996. By 1999, when the Court heard the action, the mother had developed a cooperative relationship with the foster family and a satisfactory visitation arrangement. The father's visitation, however, was restricted to seeing the children four times per year in the home of the foster family, and the paternal grandparents were prohibited from visiting.

Following a review of the relevant domestic law of Finland, the Court proceeded to analyze the claims under the Convention.]

I. Alleged Violation of Articles 8 and 13 of the Convention

* * *

98. The applicants complained that the taking of the children into public care was too drastic a measure and that especially after that measure, the authorities had not aimed at effectively reuniting the family.... The applicants claimed that the taking into care of the applicant father's children P. and S., the refusal to terminate the care and the deprivation of the applicants' right of access as well as access prohibitions constituted a violation of their right to respect for their family life protected by Article 8 of the Convention. That Article, insofar as is relevant, reads as follows:

1. Everyone has the right to respect for his...family life....

2. There shall be no interference by a public authority with the exercise of this right except such as is in accordance with the law and is necessary in a democratic society...for the protection of health or morals, or for the protection of the rights and freedoms of others.

99. The Court has examined this complaint together with the complaints concerning Article 13 of the Convention which reads as follows:

Everyone whose rights and freedoms as set forth in this Convention are violated shall have an effective remedy before a national authority notwithstanding that the violation has been committed by persons acting in an official capacity.

A. Whether there was an interference with the applicants' right to respect for their family life under Article 8 of the Convention

100. The Government accepted, in their written observations, that there had been an interference with the applicants' right to respect for their family lives as guaranteed by Article 8 § 1 of the Convention....

101. The Court recalls that the mutual enjoyment by parent and child, as well as by grandparent and child, of each other's company constitutes a fundamental element of family life, and domestic measures hindering such enjoyment amount to an interference with the right protected by Article 8 of the Convention.... Such interference constitutes a violation of this Article unless it is "in accordance with the law," pursues an aim or aims that are legitimate under paragraph 2 of Article 8 and can be regarded as "necessary in a democratic society."

B. Were the interferences justified?

1. "In accordance with the law"

102. It was undisputed before the Court, with two exceptions, that the impugned measures had a basis in national law and, to that extent, the Court is satisfied that such was the case.

103. The exceptions were allegations by the applicants that no care plan was drawn up which would comply with domestic law, and that the care orders could not be based on suspicions of sexual abuse which were never corroborated by expert findings.... The applicants maintained that the care plan made on 21 February 1996 did not fulfil the requirements set forth for such a plan in Section 4 of the Child Welfare Decree, as it did not involve the parents, as required by the law [of Finland]. Moreover, the plan did not contain any consideration on how and under what conditions the family reunification could take place. On the contrary, it was stated in the plan that the taking into care would be continued at least for two years....

105. The Court recalls that the expression "in accordance with the law," within the meaning of Article 8 § 2, requires firstly that the impugned measures should have a basis in domestic law. It also refers to the quality of the law in question, requiring accessibility and foreseeability so as to give the individual adequate protection against arbitrary interference.... Whilst it is true that no interference or decision can be considered to be "in accordance with the law," unless it complied with the relevant domestic legislation, the logic of the system for safeguarding rights established by the Convention sets limits upon the scope of the power of review exercisable by the Court in this respect. It is in the first place for the national authorities, notably the courts, to interpret and apply the domestic law....

106. ... The Court notes that, according to the document setting out the care plan of 21 February 1996, the first applicant had been present when the plan was drawn up but he declined to sign the document. The plan mentions the first applicant's wishes, indicates several measures to be resorted to for the benefit of the children and states that the care will continue until further notice since the conditions for its termination are, for the time being, not fulfilled.

107. The Court finds nothing to suggest that the care plan did not comply with domestic law and thus was not "in accordance with the law" within the meaning of Article 8 § 2 of the Convention. The Court, accordingly, finds this requirement to be satisfied.

2. Legitimate aim

108. In the Court's view the relevant Finnish law was clearly aimed at protecting "health or morals" and "the rights and freedoms" of children. There is nothing to suggest that it was applied for any other purpose in the present case.

3. "Necessary in a democratic society"

109. The applicants alleged that the measures at issue could not be regarded as "necessary in a democratic society." They argued that the taking the children into public care was too drastic a measure to begin with. The allegation of sexual abuse of P. was first made on 4 December 1991 by her mother in connection with the announced intention of the father to seek a divorce and to demand the care and custody of both children. Medical and psychological investigation of P. resulted, on 12 March 1992, in a finding that there was no indication of sexual abuse. The measures recommended in the same statement did not include the taking into care of P.

110. The applicant's further argued that the taking into care on the basis of the alleged sexual abuse by the grandfather was not a genuine reason, especially since the parents had agreed to move to a living environment separate from that of the grandparents. The authorities were aware of this agreement when they decided to take the children into care on 19 March 1992....

* * *

113. The Government regarded the interferences with the applicants' right to respect for their family life as "necessary in a democratic society." Taking a child into care often represents a measure of long duration — insofar as his or her childhood is concerned — and thus can be considered a completely normal measure. The Government questioned whether the ultimate aim of reuniting the natural parent and the child really could be the purpose of Article 8 of the Convention under the notion of the right to respect for family life that normally should be aimed at and sought by the implementing measures. Attention should rather be paid to the particular circumstances of each case, and especially the reasons for taking the child into care and maintaining the care decision in force. In this respect it should be remembered that childhood is a short but very important period in a person's life, considering his or her future development. Mistakes made by the parents towards their children are thus serious and cannot always be repaired. Therefore it may be necessary for the stability of the child that the family situation, modified already once, will not be changed back again. In this respect it should be remembered that a child is entitled to respect for his or her family life, in accordance with Article 8 of the Convention, also in his or her foster family and children's home.

114. The Government did not foresee the physical reunification of the children and the applicants, and accordingly, no measures aimed at such a reunification had been carried out. A child often becomes strongly attached to his foster parents and it is therefore harmful for the child to detach him or her from the foster family and the relationships built within that family. The younger the child is, the faster the psychological relationship between the child and the foster parents develops. It may be necessary for the stability of the child that the family situation not be changed back again. Ultimately, the termination of the public care as well as the taking into public care have to be decided in the best interests of the child.

115. The Government stressed that the taking of both children into care, as is evident from the County Administrative Court's decision of 17 August 1992, was based on defi-

ciencies in their care, and that the conditions in their home seriously risked to jeopardise their development.

116. The Government also observed that the mother and the applicant father have joint custody of the children after their divorce. The mother has accepted the children's stay in the foster home and is not willing to allow that the children be handed over to their father or his parents. She and her mother, the other grandmother of the children, have a positive co-operative relationship with the authorities and the foster family. They are satisfied with the care the children receive in the foster family; and in their opinion the family placement is in the best interests of the children. Their wish is that the stabilised conditions of the children should no longer be changed. Also, the children have a close relationship with the mother and her mother, and have several times visited their home. Further, it is not clear what the "reunification of the family" would mean in this case as the reunification of the family is not possible in its usual form in the present case, because the biological parents have lived separately since 1993 and have been officially divorced in 1996. The applicant father has lived with his... parents since the beginning of 1994, and the applicants' request for reuniting the family has referred to returning the children to the common home of the applicant father and his parents.

117. The Government further argued that the most important obstacle is, however, the fear, tension and anguish of P. caused by the contacts with her father and his parents. P., who was 6 years old when she was taken into care and is now 14 years old, has expressed this several times. It was recalled that, with a view to finding out P.'s own wishes and thoughts concerning the meeting arranged with her father, she was submitted to a child psychiatric investigation at the Central Hospital of S. In his conclusions Dr L. noted that P. spontaneously described her sexual abuse by the applicant father as well as by the applicant grandfather.

The Government underlined that the children... have lived [with the foster family] since the beginning of 1992 and have become attached to and feel at home in the foster family. Indeed, S. was only eight months old when she was taken into care and does not remember having lived anywhere else. The Government finally noted that in the present situation the right to respect for family life from the children's point of view means above all the right to live in the foster family which is their *de facto* family, and to live together. In this kind of a case the mutual family ties between a child who has been taken into care and her biological parents shall, as far as possible, be ensured in some other way than by reuniting the family into a physical entity, for example by visits and letters to the extent required and allowed by the interest of the child.

118. In determining whether the impugned measures were "necessary in a democratic society", the Court will consider whether, in the light of the case as a whole, the reasons adduced to justify them were relevant and sufficient for the purposes of paragraph 2 of Article 8 of the Convention.... In so doing, the Court will have regard to the fact that perceptions as to the appropriateness of intervention by public authorities in the care of children vary from one Contracting State to another, depending on such factors as traditions relating to the role of the family and to State intervention in family affairs and the availability of resources for public measures in this particular area. However, consideration of what is in the best interest of the child is in every case of crucial importance. Moreover, it must be borne in mind that the national authorities have the benefit of direct contact with all the persons concerned, often at the very stage when care measures are being envisaged or immediately after their implementation. It follows from these considerations that the Court's

task is not to substitute itself for the domestic authorities in the exercise of their responsibilities for the regulation of the public care of children and the rights of parents whose children have been taken into care, but rather to review under the Convention the decisions that those authorities have taken in the exercise of their power of appreciation....

The margin of appreciation to be accorded to the competent national authorities will vary in the light of the nature of the issues and the seriousness of the interests at stake. Thus, the Court recognises that the authorities enjoy a wide margin of appreciation in assessing the necessity of taking a child into care. However, a stricter scrutiny is called for both of any further limitations, such as restrictions placed by those authorities on parental rights and access, and of any legal safeguards designed to secure an effective protection of the right of parents and children to respect for their family life. Such further limitations entail the danger that the family relations between the parents and a young child are effectively curtailed....

119. The Court observes that the children were taken into care in a situation in which an allegation of sexual abuse had arisen. However, the Social Welfare Board's decision to take the children into care on 19 March 1992 was based on other grounds, such as the parents' incapacity of providing the children with the stimulation necessary for their growth and development and the mother's mental illness. For several years before the decision to take the children into care, there had been contacts between the family and the social welfare authorities, who had afforded various open-care measures in view of the family's economical and social difficulties. P.'s development at the time did not correspond to the average for her age, and it seemed that the child was at a stage on her development where it was crucial that she should be attached to stable and secure persons without putting her further development at risk. The younger daughter, S., was found to be in a similar situation, even though her development was at an earlier stage....

120. In these circumstances the Court sees no reason to doubt that the authorities could consider that the care in the foster home had better prospects of success than the continuation of the open-care measures. The Court also considers that there is nothing to suggest that the decision-making process leading to the taking into public care failed to involve the applicants to a degree sufficient to provide them with the requisite protection of their interests....

121. In the light of the foregoing, the Court is satisfied that the taking of the applicant father's children P. and S. into care [was] based on reasons which were not only relevant but also sufficient for the purposes of paragraph 2 of Article 8 of the Convention and that the decision-making procedure satisfied the requirements of that provision. It considers that in taking the above care measures the national authorities acted within the margin of appreciation afforded to them in such matters. The Court accepts also that the appeals which were open to the applicants before the County Administrative Court and the Supreme Administrative Court satisfy the conditions of Article 13 of the Convention. Accordingly, the taking into public care did not constitute a violation of Articles 8 and 13.

122. The Court recalls that taking a child into care should normally be regarded as a temporary measure to be discontinued as soon as circumstances permit, and that any measures of implementation of temporary care should be consistent with the ultimate aim of reuniting the natural parent and the child.... In this regard a fair balance has to be struck between the interests of the child in remaining in public care and those of the parent in being reunited with the child.... In carrying out this balancing exercise, the Court will attach particular importance to the best interests of the child, which, de-

pending on their nature and seriousness, may override those of the parent. In particular, the parent cannot be entitled under Article 8 of the Convention to have such measures taken as would harm the child's health and development.

* * *

123. The question of whether the continuation of the implementation of the care measures was justified must be assessed in the light of the circumstances and their development since 1992. In this regard it is observed that the applicant father and the mother of the children had separated before the request was made and did not constitute a family any more. The rights and interests of the mother have also to be taken into account. In these circumstances the national authorities could, in the exercise of their discretion, consider the maintenance of the care order to be in the best interest of the children. The Court therefore concludes that...the failure of the authorities to terminate the care at a later date [does not] in the Court's view violate that Article.

* * *

127. ...The Court notes that while the applicant father's access has been considerably restricted, he has been able to meet the children regularly. Moreover, his right to see the children was increased by the County Administrative Court in 1995, only to be decreased again in the light of the child psychiatric examination suggesting sexual abuse of P. While such abuse has never been confirmed by a judicial finding, the Court concludes that the children's interest made it justifiable for the Finnish authorities to reduce the right of access of the applicant father.

In these circumstances the decisions concerning the applicant father's access can be regarded as fulfilling the principle of proportionality and therefore as necessary in a democratic society. The applicant grandfather has been suspected of the sexual abuse of P. since the children were taken into care. Both children, P. and S., have later indicated that they do not wish to meet him at all. The applicant grandfather indeed has been denied any access to the children. While this restriction is very drastic even in case of a child/ grandparent relationship, the Court accepts that in the circumstances of the present case the national authorities could reasonably consider that restriction to be necessary in a democratic society.

128. ... [T]he Court thus considers that the national authorities acted within the margin of appreciation afforded to them in such matters. The Court is also satisfied that the appeals which were open to the applicants before the County Administrative Court met the conditions of Article 13 of the Convention. Accordingly, these measures did not constitute a violation of Articles 8 and 13 of the Convention.

II. Alleged Violation of Article 6.1 of the Convention

129. The applicants further complain that the County Administrative Court refused to hold an oral hearing in the proceedings ending on 17 March 1997, even though it was requested by the applicants. The Court has examined this complaint under Article 6 § 1 of the Convention which reads, in so far as relevant, as follows:

"In the determination of his civil rights and obligations..., everyone is entitled to a... public hearing...."

* * *

132. The Court recalls that the instrument of ratification of the convention deposited by the Finnish Government on 10 May 1990 contained a reservation according to which Finland could not guarantee a right to an oral hearing before the courts mentioned in the reservation. Their reservation was, however, withdrawn, insofar as administrative courts

are concerned as from 1 December 1996, i.e., before the proceedings leading to the decision of the County Administrative Court of 17 March 1997 had been instituted.... While, for reasons relating to the Finnish reservation, the Court is only competent to deal with the lack of an oral hearing as regards the decision of 17 March 1997, it must take into account the previous court proceedings as a background to the issue before it....

In this respect the Court notes that at no stage of the previous proceedings had there been an oral hearing. In view of this, the nature of the issues and of what was at stake for the applicants, the Court is not satisfied that there were exceptional circumstances which...would have justified dispensing with a hearing.

133. Accordingly, the Court finds that there has been a violation of Article 6 § 1 of the Convention on account of the lack of an oral hearing before the County Administrative Court....

III. Application of Article 41 of the Convention

* * *

A. Damages

137. The Court notes that in the present case an award of just satisfaction could only be based on the fact that the applicants did not have the benefit of the right to an oral hearing as guaranteed in Article 6 § 1 of the Convention. The applicants had not sought any compensation under Article 6 § 1 of the Convention, as pointed out by the Government. In any case, whilst the Court cannot speculate as to the outcome of the trial had the position been otherwise, it considers that a finding of a violation of Article 6 § 1 constitutes in itself sufficient just satisfaction for the applicants' alleged non-pecuniary damage.

B. Costs and Expenses

* * *

140. Taking into account that the applicants' complaints have only been partially approved, the Court, making its assessment on an equitable basis, awards the applicants a total of FIM 35,000, in respect of the proceedings before the Commission and the Court and for domestics costs together with any relevant value-added tax, from which must be deducted the FRF 24,560.60 already received for legal fees from the Council of Europe by way of legal aid.

* * *

Notes and Questions

1. *Format.* The opinion above is heavily edited. Typically judgments of the European Court of Human Rights begin with a list of the judges in the Chamber that heard the case, followed by a summary of the procedural history of the case, a list of the attorneys and representatives for the parties, a lengthy recitation of the facts, and then a summary of the relevant domestic law and practice. In cases decided under the previous procedural system, in which the Commission issued an opinion, that opinion is also presented. The full opinion then sets forth as to each alleged violation of the Convention a summary of the facts and arguments presented by the applicant and by the government, followed by the reasoning of the Court on that issue. In the unedited judgement, citations to previous decisions of the Court follow many of the statements of legal principles upon which the Court relies.

2. *Margin of Appreciation.* In its ruling on whether the removal of the children into state custody was justified, the Court discusses the *margin of appreciation* that it must afford the national governments. The "margin of appreciation" has been described as a certain latitude, or degree of discretion, that is afforded by the Court to national governments regarding the manner in which they implement Convention rights. Douglas Lee Donoho, *Autonomy, Self-Governance, and the Margin of Appreciation: Developing a Jurisprudence of Diversity within Universal Human Rights,* 15 Emory Int'l L. Rev. 391, 451–52 (2001). One commentator observed that the principle "essentially allows the ECHR to take account of the fact that the social situation in one country may make necessary a particular limitation which would not be justifiable in another country with a different social situation." Helen Conway, *The Human Rights Act 1998 and Family Law — Part One,* 1999 Fam. L. 811, 814. Though initially invoked in contexts relating to the regulation of potentially harmful activities and matters of national security, Enyal Benvenisti, *Margin of Appreciation, Consensus, and Universal Standards,* 31 N.Y.U. J. Int'l L. & Pol. 843, 845 (1999), the doctrine is now frequently applied by the Court when evaluating the scope of personal liberties, enabling the Court to "strike a balance between a European (international) human rights standard and the cultural, social, or religious preferences of the state and its democratic majority." Donoho, *supra,* at 455–56. Proponents observe that the doctrine enables the Court to accommodate national prerogatives, self-governance, and diversity of culture and tradition, but to temper national discretion when the importance of the right at issue so requires or the Court perceives a contrary European consensus on the issue. *Id.* at 456–58. Critics of the doctrine suggest that its acceptance of moral relativism is inconsistent with the notion of the universality of human rights, and contend that inconsistent adjudication of similar cases undermines confidence in the Court and its ability to develop universal standards. Benvenisti, *supra,* at 844.

3. *Comparing Systems.* What document within our American political system serves the function of the European Convention on Human Rights? If the state officials of Oklahoma had removed children from their parents' custody and subsequently restricted a parent's visitation under similar circumstances, and the parent's attempt to appeal these actions through the Oklahoma court system had been unsuccessful, what would be the parent's recourse for further appeal?

Consider the similarities and differences between that system and the opportunity of a European parent to file an application for relief with the European Court of Human Rights.

Is the relationship between the State of Oklahoma and the U.S. Supreme Court the same as the relationship between the government of Finland and the European Court of Human Rights?

What is the analytical framework used by the Court in *L. v. Finland* for assessing under the Convention the validity of the decisions to place and retain children in permanent foster care and to restrict parental access? Is it similar to an analysis that might be used within the U.S. system for assessing the validity of a governmental action affecting fundamental rights?

4. *Comparing Rights.* Under the European Convention on Human Rights, as interpreted by the Court in *L. v. Finland,* who has rights that matter? If more than one individual has rights, how are these conflicting rights claims resolved?

Consider the weight the Court in *L v. Finland* places on the bonding of the children with the foster family. Is this similar or different from your perception of American child protection cases? Are foster families entitled to protection under the European Convention of Human Rights?

Compare the approach of the European Court of Human Rights with the approach of the U.S. Supreme Court in *Smith v. Organization of Foster Families for Equal. & Reform*, 431 U.S. 816 (1977). In that case, foster parents brought a civil rights class action pursuant to 42 U.S.C. § 1983, on their own behalf and on behalf of children for whom they had provided homes for a year or more. They alleged that the state procedures governing the removal of foster children from foster homes violated the Due Process Clause of the Fourteenth Amendment. The parties' arguments were the following:

> [The foster parents argued] that when a child has lived in a foster home for a year or more, a psychological tie is created between the child and the foster parents which constitutes the foster family the true 'psychological family' of the child. See J. Goldstein, A. Freud, & A. Solnit, Beyond the Best Interests of the Child (1973). That family, they argue, has a "liberty interest" in its survival as a family protected by the Fourteenth Amendment.... Upon this premise they conclude that the foster child cannot be removed without a prior hearing satisfying due process. Appointed counsel for the children,... however, disagrees, and has consistently argued that the foster parents have no such liberty interest independent of the interests of the foster children, and that the best interests of the children would not be served by procedural protections beyond those already provided by New York law. The intervening natural parents of children in foster care...also oppose the foster parents, arguing that recognition of the procedural right claimed would undercut both the substantive family law of New York, which favors the return of children to their natural parents as expeditiously as possible,...and their constitutionally protected right of family privacy, by forcing them to submit to a hearing and defend their rights to their children before the children could be returned to them. *Id.* at 839–40.

Despite the foster families' assertions, the Court in *Smith* did not decide whether the relation of foster parent to foster child was sufficiently akin to the concept of "family" recognized in other cases to merit similar 14th Amendment protection. *Id.* at 842. Rather, it held that even on the assumption that appellees have a protected liberty interest, the District Court erred in holding that the pre-removal procedures presently employed by the State are constitutionally defective. *Id.* at 855–56. Yet, in *obiter dictum*, it discussed the relationship between the foster family and child in great detail. While acknowledging that foster families will hold the same place in a child's emotional life as a natural family when an infant is placed in foster care, does not know his natural parents, and has remained continuously in the care of the same foster parents for several years, *id.* at 844, the Court still concluded "there are also important distinctions between the foster family and the natural family." First, "unlike the earlier cases recognizing a right to family privacy, the State here seeks to interfere, not with a relationship having its origins entirely apart from the power of the State, but rather with a foster family which has its source in state law and contractual arrangements." *Id.* at 845. It was necessary "to ascertain from state law the expectations and entitlement of the parties." *Id.* at 846. Here the contracts made any "liberty" interest in the foster family limited, as the foster parents knew the arrangements were to be temporary. Second, "ordinarily procedural protection may be afforded to a liberty interest of one person without derogating from the substantive liberty of another. Here, however, such a tension is virtually unavoidable," especially where the proposed removal from the foster family is to return the child to his natural parents. *Id.* at 847. The Court also dropped a footnote, where it acknowledged that "recognition of a liberty interest in foster families for purposes of the procedural protections of the Due Process Clause would not necessarily require that foster families be treated as fully equivalent to biological families for purposes of substantive due process review." *Id.* at 842 n.48.

How is the children's interest defined in *Smith* as compared to *L v. Finland*? How much weight is given to the children's interest in *Smith* in distinguishing foster families from biological families? Should foster families be considered families for purposes of constitutional and ECHR protection?

Would the father's argument have been more forceful if the children had entered care with the consent of their parents? In *Smith*, it was noted that approximately "80% of the children in foster care in New York City are voluntarily placed." *Id.* at 825 n.9.

5. *Care v. Access Determinations.* The Court suggests that there is a wider margin of appreciation in assessing the necessity of taking a child into care than, for example, limiting parental access once the child is in care. *See* para. 118. Can this distinction be defended?

Would it be within a country's margin of appreciation to decide that certain types of child abusers, say parents who commit sexual abuse, should never be able to see their children again, assuming procedural protections at the outset for making the determination of child abuse?

6. *Companion Case: K. and T.* On the same day that the judgment in *L.v. Finland* was issued, the same Section of the European Court of Human Rights issued a judgment in another case, *K. and T. v. Finland*, 31 E.H.H.R. 484 (2000). Despite the wide margin of appreciation that the Court in *L.* recognized in assessing the necessity of placing a child in public care, the Court in *K. and T.* found Finland in violation of Article 8 for removing a child at birth from the care of her parents, as well as a three-year-old half-brother, due to the mother's history of mental illness. The Court also found the authorities' lack of efforts to reunify the family, including the unreasonable restriction of parental visitation to only one visit per month at the outset, to be a further violation of Article 8.

Despite the fact that the removal and lack of reunification efforts violated the Convention, the Court nevertheless accepted the access restrictions of one visit per month at the current time. The fact that the children had now been in the care of the foster parents for almost seven years led the Court to accept that the imposition of this restriction was within the margin of appreciation of the authorities and did not constitute an additional violation of Article 8. The Court therefore awarded each parent FIM 40,000 (approximately $6,000) for non-pecuniary damages, plus an amount for costs and legal fees. Although the applicants in *K. and T.* were more successful than the applicants in *L. v. Finland*, do you think they were satisfied with the relief they received?

Following the decision of the Chamber, the government of Finland requested review of the judgment by the Grand Chamber. On March 16, 2001, *K. and T.* became the first case to be presented in an oral hearing before the seventeen judges of the Grand Chamber. On July 12, 2001, the Grand Chamber held, by a vote of 14 to 3, that taking the newborn infant into emergency care and, by unanimous vote, that the failure to take proper steps to unify the family, both constituted violations of the right to respect for family life guaranteed by Article 8. By a vote of 11 to 6, the court held that the emergency care order concerning the three-year-old did not violate Article 8. The Grand Chamber also ruled unanimously that the normal care orders regarding both children, and the current access restrictions did not violate Article 8. The Court affirmed the amount of the monetary award, and awarded further costs for expenses on appeal. K. and T. v. Finland, HUDOC Ref. No. 2663 (July 12, 2001), *available at* http://hudoc. echr.coe.int. Further information on the *K. and T.* case can be found in a lecture by the applicant's advisor, Anu Suomela, given on June 17, 2000, available at http://nkmr.org/ k_and _t_v_finland.htm.

For an excellent summary of the law developed by the European Court of Human Rights on the placement of children in public care, *see* Ursula Kilkelly, *Child Protection and the European Convention on Human Rights*, 2 Irish J. Fam. L. 12 (2000).

7. *Reunification.* The European Court of Human Rights scrutinized the reunification efforts of the governmental authorities to a greater extent in *K. and T. v. Finland* than in *L. v. Finland.* What circumstances, do you think, accounted for the different emphasis? Do you think it was justified?

It is interesting to compare the approach of the Finnish state authorities, and the European Court in *K. and T.*, with the recent change in policy regarding the emphasis given to reunification in the United States.

In an effort to achieve permanence and avoid "foster care drift," Congress enacted the Adoption Assistance and Child Welfare Act of 1980. Under this Act, states were encouraged to make reasonable efforts to keep families together and encourage reunification. The Act discouraged termination of parental rights except in situations in which the child was so imperiled that reunification was untenable.

However, burgeoning foster care caseloads, increasing numbers of children "growing up" in foster care, and serious incidents of child abuse occurring during reunification efforts caused a shift in child welfare policy. In 1997 Congress passed the Adoption and Safe Families Act ("ASFA"), which promotes adoption of foster children and shortens the time agencies had to wait to terminate parental rights. ASFA establishes timelines for state welfare agencies. For example, if a child has been in foster care for fifteen out of the most recent twenty-two months, a petition for termination of parental rights must be filed, unless the child is in kinship care, or there are "compelling reasons" why such a petition would not be in the child's best interest, or inadequate services have been provided to the family. *See* The Adoption and Safe Families Act of 1997, Pub. L. No. 105-89, 111 Stat. 2115 (codified in 42 U.S.C. §675(5)(E) (2000)). AFSA now requires a permanency hearing within twelve months of a child's entry into foster care, with follow up hearings annually thereafter. 42 U.S.C. § 675(5)(C) (2000)). In addition, there are now specific circumstances when reasonable efforts to preserve or reunify can be dispensed with, such as sexual abuse. *See* 42 U.S.C. §671(a)(15)(D)(i) (2000). *See, e.g.,* Libby S. Adler, *The Meanings of Permanence: A Critical Analysis of the Adoption and Safe Families Act of 1997,* 38 Harv. J. on Legis. 1 (2001).

Assume the facts of *L v. Finland* and *K. and T. v. Finland* occurred in the United States. What would be the outcome under ASFA for the children?

8. *Human Rights Act of 1988.* The United Kingdom has gone one step further. The Human Rights Act 1998 requires British courts to apply all legislation in a manner that gives effect to those rights under the European Convention on Human Rights that are specified in the Act, taking into account all decisions by the European Court of Human Rights, the Commission of Human Rights, and the Committee of Ministers. The intent is to make Convention rights more directly accessible to the British populace, circumventing the need to seek relief from the ECHR. Individuals who believe they have been a vic-

tim of a violation of those Convention rights specified in the Act at the hands of a public authority may bring an action based upon the breach alone, or rely upon the breach in an action based upon another pre-existing right under domestic law. The British court can afford such relief within its powers as would be appropriate, and may award damages if the court normally has the power to award them, and if they are necessary to afford "just satisfaction." The Act creates no right to damages against private individuals for infringement of a right recognized by the Convention (such as denial of visitation), but where there is a pre-existing cause of action against an individual, courts, as public authorities, will be obligated to interpret the domestic law in accordance with the rights guaranteed by the Convention. Conway, *supra,* at 811–12. The Republic of Ireland is also considering legislation incorporating the Convention into domestic law. E.g., Carol Coulter, *Human Rights Bill Is Flawed—Senator,* The Irish Times, June 14, 2002; Miriam Donohoe, *European Human Rights to Become Irish Law,* The Irish Times, September 22, 2000.

e. The European Union, the European Community, and the Charter of Fundamental Rights

Another regional intergovernmental institution in Europe that is increasingly influencing the practice of family law is the European Union (E.U.). Formed by the Maastricht Treaty on European Union, which entered into force in 1993, the European Union is a superstructure founded upon three pre-existing European Communities and their institutions, which were established in the aftermath of World War II to promote European economic integration. The European Coal and Steel Community, formed in the early 1950s to integrate regulation of the coal and steel industry, was followed in 1957 by the Treaty of Rome, which created the European Economic Community and established a European common market, and by creation that same year of the European Atomic Energy Community, which coordinates research and the development of atomic energy among the member nations. Although each Community initially established its own institutions, in 1967 the Communities merged their parallel institutions into a common parliament, council, commission, and court, which are today the European Parliament, the Council of the European Union, the European Commission, and the Court of Justice. Nevertheless, the Communities and their constituent treaties remain distinct. Each institution acts under the authority of the relevant treaty when addressing matters within that treaty's scope.

The Maastricht Treaty did not replace the Communities. Instead, it was joined with a renamed version of the Treaty of Rome, dropping the word "economic" from the former title to reflect the expanded political and social roles that the Communities assumed. The full name of the resulting document is now the "Treaty on European Union together with the Treaty Establishing the European Community."[7] The Community,

---

7. This document, signed at Maastricht and entered into force in 1993, was later revised in the Amsterdam Treaty, signed in 1997 and entered into force in 1999, which made certain amendments to and renumbered the Maastricht document. Treaty of Amsterdam Amending the Treaty on European Union, the Treaties Establishing the European Communities, and Certain Related Acts, Oct. 2, 1997, O.J. C340/1 (1997). *See* Ralph Folsom, *European Union Law in a Nutshell* 29–30 (3d ed.1999). Although, as of March 2003, the European Union had fifteen member nations, it was preparing for the accession of thirteen additional eastern and southern European countries. Amendments to the constituent treaties facilitating the enlargement of the European Union were incorporated in the Treaty of Nice, which was signed by the member nations on February 26, 2001 and entered into force on February 1, 2003. A Treaty on the Accession of 10 new Member States was expected to be signed on April 16, 2003 and to enter into force on May 1, 2004.

which consists of the three original Communities, is considered the first "pillar" of the European Union. Its institutions, under the three constituent treaties that created the Communities, have been delegated with certain powers by the member states, and they exercise sovereignty on behalf of the member states within the areas and limitations established by the treaties. Because the sovereign powers delegated to the Community far exceed the powers normally delegated to an international organization, its institutions have been described as supranational, rather than international or intergovernmental. The other two pillars of the European Union, designated as a "Common Foreign and Security Policy" and "Co-operation in the Fields of Justice and Home Affairs," are essentially distinct policy-making systems that operate on an intergovernmental model through which decisions are reached by consensus of the member states without any transfer of sovereignty to the institutions. The complexity of this hybrid framework reflects the members' divergent preferences, some favoring the model of a federal union and others preferring an intergovernmental model with minimum surrender of sovereignty. Jörg Monar, *European Union,* in Butterworths Expert Guide to the European Union 157–60 (Jörg Monar, et al. eds., 1996); Folsom, *supra* note 7, at 1–10, 26–30.

The institutional system of the European Union boasts a unique composition. The membership of its principal decision-making body, the Council of the European Union, consists of ministers of the governments of the member nations. As of March 2003, when there were fifteen members of the E.U., there were fifteen Council members at each meeting, but the ministers who fill those roles vary depending upon the topics on the agenda. The national ministers of finance, foreign affairs, education, economy, agriculture, etc. each attend meetings of the Council to discuss and vote on issues within their competence, and several different Council meetings can in fact take place simultaneously. A Committee of high-ranking national civil servants based in Brussels, known as the Committee of Permanent Representatives (COREPER), and working groups of other civil servant experts, assist the Council in reviewing legislative proposals. All legislative acts of the European Union must be approved by the Council of the European Union, by majority, qualified majority, or unanimous vote, depending upon the issue. Each nation within the Union has a prescribed number of votes within the Council, roughly based upon its population. For a detailed description of the complex voting procedures of the Council, *see* Folsom, *supra* note 7, at 49–60.

Not to be confused with the Council of the European Union (or the Council of Europe) is the European Council, which is a political body composed of the heads of state or government of each member of the European Union and the President of the European Commission. Summit meetings of the European Council are held twice annually to formulate broad policy declarations and launch initiatives for the E.U. Simon Bulmar, *European Council,* in Monar, *supra,* at 142.

Members of the European Parliament are directly elected every five years by the citizens of each member nation of the European Union. Initially the Parliament's role in the legislative process of the E.U. was limited to reviewing legislative proposals and sharing its opinion on legislation with the Commission and the Council. Many types of legislation, however, are now subject to a "co-decision" procedure that effectively gives the Parliament a veto power. Most of the legislation subject to co-decision is therefore the result of a legislative compromise reached between the Council of the European Union and the Parliament through conciliation committees formed under this procedure. Some types of legislation are the product of a "cooperation procedure," which gives Parliament less of a voice than the co-decision procedure, but still provides Parliament the opportunity to reject or amend legislative proposals from the Commission. Folsom, *supra* note 7, at 37–42.

Although the Secretariat of the Parliament is located in Luxembourg, meetings of the Parliament and its committees take place in Strasbourg, France and Brussels, Belgium.

The European Commission, the executive body of the Union, is composed of civil servants appointed by the member states and approved by the European Parliament. Commission members are required to act in the interests of the Community, and not as representatives of their respective governments. In fact, they are forbidden by the Treaties from taking instructions from their governments. Beneath the Commissioners is an administrative staff of over 15,000 officials, headed by a Secretary General, and subdivided into various services, including twenty-five Directorates General (DGs) that operate like small ministries with competence in specific areas of expertise. Martin Westlake, *European Commission*, in Monar, *supra*, at 131–34. The Commission and the majority of the staff are located in Brussels, Belgium.

Although the Council and the Parliament may request the Commission to submit certain legislative proposals, only the Commission has the right to initiate and draft legislation. The Commission is also responsible for implementing E.U. legislation, as well as the programs and budget adopted by the Council and Parliament, and for negotiating international agreements on behalf of the E.U. *Id.* at 136; *Institutions of the European Union*, http://europa.eu.int/inst-en.htm.

The above institutions have generated a rapidly expanding body of E.U. law over the past several decades. The two primary types of legislative acts are directives and regulations. Directives establish European Union policy, which then must be implemented in member states through whatever mechanism—statute, administrative act, constitutional amendment, etc.—is appropriate in the context of the member's domestic legal system. Directives are considered binding as to the result to be achieved, leaving to the member states the choice of methods to realize the objective. Regulations of the European Union, by contrast, are binding and directly applicable in all member states. They are similar in nature to administrative regulations in the U.S. legal system. Recommendations and opinions that may be issued through the Commission, Parliament, and Council have no binding force, but may be used to interpret related E.U. law or domestic law of the member nations. Folsom, *supra* note 7, at 35.

Another significant source of regional law has been the judgments issued by the Court of Justice. Located in Luxembourg, the Court is charged with the responsibility to ensure that Community law is interpreted uniformly and applied effectively. The Court's jurisdiction includes many types of proceedings, including (1) actions brought by the Commission or a member state against another member state for failure to fulfill an obligation under Community law, or failure to comply with a Court judgment; (2) proceedings by the Council, Commission, Parliament, or a member state to annul Community legislation; (3) proceedings against a Community institution for breach of the Treaty by failure to act; (4) actions for noncontractual damages caused by Community institutions or employees; and (5) references from domestic courts of member states seeking preliminary rulings concerning the interpretation or validity of Community law. In addition, the Court of Justice hears appeals from the Court of First Instance, which include, inter alia, actions against the Community for annulment, failure to act, or damages brought by individuals directly affected; and disputes between the Community and its employees. *See A Court for Europe*, http://curia.eu.int/en/pres/jeu.htm; K.P.E. Lasok, *Court of Justice*, in Monar, *supra*, at 77–83. Although the Court is recognized as part of the institutional framework of the European Union, the actions of the second and third pillars of the E.U. generally fall outside of the Court's cognizance. Folsom, *supra* note 7, at 27, 81.

The Court of Justice is composed of one justice from each member nation (plus a rotating justice when there is an even number of member states) and a specified number of Advocates General (generally eight), appointed by agreement of the governments of the Member States. An Advocate General plays a role unfamiliar to most American lawyers. One Advocate General is assigned to each case, sitting with the judges for any hearing that may occur, and then submitting to the judges, prior to their deliberation, an opinion setting forth the background of the case, relevant legislation and case law, a statement of the issues, a summary of the parties' arguments, a personal assessment of how the issues should be resolved, and a proposed course of action for the Court. The opinion is not binding on the Court, although one scholar estimates that it is followed in approximately 70% of the cases. David T. Keeling, *Advocates General*, in Monar, *supra*, at 9–11.

Through its powers of judicial review, the Court of Justice plays a critical role in maintaining the balance of power among the institutions of the European Union, and between the Community and the member states. In this last regard, decisions of the Court have established two essential principles: (1) the primacy of Community law over national law, and (2) the direct effect of community law in member states. As early as 1964, the Court ruled that in instances of conflict with national law, Community law is supreme. Since that time, the Court has invalidated numerous domestic laws of member states under its supremacy doctrine. The direct effects doctrine requires domestic courts of member nations to permit litigants to raise rights and defenses under Community treaties, regulations, and directives in proceedings before their domestic courts, as long as domestic law has provided a plaintiff with an initial right to litigate, i.e., a cause of action. As a result, the courts and tribunals of member nations now hear the bulk of litigation concerning Community law issues, and their decisions constitute another significant source of E.U. law. *See A Court for Europe, supra;* Folsom, *supra* note 7, at 31–32, 71–75, 82.

Though the primary focus of the European Union institutions has been economic, in recent years the European Union has issued several regulations addressing the exercise of jurisdiction and recognition of judgments in divorce, custody, and maintenance proceedings by national courts in its member nations, which are discussed in Chapters Eight and Ten. Council Regulation 1347/2000, 2000 O.J. (L 160) 19; Council Regulation 44/2001, 2001 O.J. (L 012) 1; Proposal for a Council Regulation Concerning Jurisdiction and the Recognition and Enforcement of Judgments in Matrimonial Matters and in Matters of Parental Responsibility, COM (2002) 222 final/2. In addition, E.U. institutions have in many instances supported the recognition and enforcement of human rights and undertaken initiatives that significantly influence the well-being of European families. Article 6 of the Maastricht Treaty on European Union itself requires the Union to respect fundamental rights, as guaranteed by the European Convention on Human Rights, as well as the constitutional traditions common to member nations. Folsom, *supra* note 7, at 67–71. The Court of Justice has recognized a duty to respect fundamental rights as part of general principles of law, a type of common law that the Court recognizes as capable of overriding even legal acts of the Community. Issues regarding gender pay equality and family employment policies, family immigration issues, health care issues, and employment benefits are just some of the issues addressed by E.U. institutions that affect European families. *See, e.g.,* Merle H. Weiner, *Fundamental Misconceptions about Fundamental Rights: The Changing Nature of Women's Rights in the EEC and Their Application in the United Kingdom,* 31 Harv. Int'l L.J. 565 (1990).

The Charter of Fundamental Rights of the European Union, 2000 O.J. (C 364) 1, was proclaimed at the European Council meeting in Nice on December 7, 2000, and signed thereafter by the Presidents of the European Parliament, the Council of the European Union, and the European Commission. The Charter has the potential to significantly increase the involvement of the Court of Justice and possibly other E.U. institutions in family law issues. The Charter was drafted at the bequest of the European Council by a special body, referred to as the "Convention," composed of members of the European Parliament, national parliaments, a Commissioner, and representatives of the fifteen heads of government. The Charter incorporates the rights recognized in the European Convention on Human Rights, as well as the constitutional traditions of the E.U. member states, the Council of Europe's Social Charter, the Community Charter of Fundamental Social Rights of Workers, and other international agreements to which the European Union or its member states are parties. Gioia Scappucci, *Road Taken Towards a Charter of Fundamental Rights for the EU Unveiled*, 64 E.U. Focus 2, 4 (2000). Specific recognition of the right to respect for family life, the rights to marry and found a family, the right of equality between men and women, and children's rights are contained within its provisions.

The legal status of the Charter has been controversial. The Convention drafted the Charter as if it would be a legally binding text, *id.* at 3, and both the European Parliament and the European Commission support conferring this status upon the Charter. Resolution A5-0064/2000 of the European Parliament, Minutes of Plenary Session of March 16, 2000, 2000 O.J. (C 377) 167; Communication from the Commission on the Legal Nature of the Charter of Fundamental Rights of the European Union, E.U. Com (2000) 644. Nevertheless, the United Kingdom strongly opposed this approach, preferring that the Charter remain merely declaratory. As a result, the European Council decided not to incorporate the Charter into the Treaty of Nice, but instead issued it in Nice by proclamation, deferring further discussion of its legal status. Nevertheless, the European Commission and European Parliament have affirmed their intention to be guided by the Charter in their formulation and implementation of policy. Europarl, *The Charter of Fundamental Rights of the European Union*, http://www.europarl.eu.int/charter/default_en.htm; Andrew Duff, *Frequently Asked Questions: European Union Charter of Fundamental Rights*, http:/eld.europarl.eu.int/charter.htm (2001). Though the Charter has been referenced by Advocates General and the Court of First Instance in its first year of existence, scholars continue to speculate concerning the treatment it will be afforded by the European Court of Justice. Clare McGlynn, *Families and the European Union Charter of Fundamental Rights: Progressive Change or Entrenching the Status Quo?*, 26 E.L. Rev. Dec. 582 (2001); John Morlin, *Judicial Reference to the EU Fundamental Rights Charter, available at* http://europa.eu.int/futurum/documents/other/oth000602_en.pdf.

The purpose of the Charter is primarily to codify the rights of citizens of the member nations as they are affected by the supranational authority of the European Union. Duff, *supra*. Thus the Charter protections were intended to apply to any rule or action by E.U. institutions, or those of member nations when applying E.U. law. Nevertheless, the drafters chose to include in the Charter a complete list of human rights, even when they did not relate to matters within the legal sphere of the E.U., such as the abolition of capital punishment. One commentator suggests that the drafters intended that those rights that concern only the areas of competence of the member nations should be protected by national law. Scappucci, *supra*, at 3.

In the area of family law, Professor McGlynn suggests that the Charter's specific recognition of the familial rights of E.U. citizens and of the entitlement of the family to "legal, economic, and social protection," Article 33(1), "cements the developing process of family regulation" by the European Union. Though she concedes that it is unlikely that the family provisions of the Charter will provide a legal basis for the adoption of new measures, since the Union treaties themselves contain no specific provisions relating to family law, she predicts that the Charter's family provisions will enable the existing E.U. family law regulations "to be interpreted more broadly and in a more extensive fashion," and "create a climate in which the future inclusion of new legal bases in the Union treaties will not be seen as so radical, novel or dangerous." McGlynn, *supra*, at 586–87.

Because, when the Charter was drafted, all of the members of the European Union had also ratified the European Convention on Human Rights, the relationship between the Charter and the European Convention was an important consideration for the Charter's drafters. Ultimately, for those rights that are guaranteed by the European Convention, they chose to follow the text of the Convention closely, but not word for word, and in some areas the scope of protection offered by the Charter is wider. For example, the accompanying explanation to Article 7 of the Charter, which protects the rights of family and private life, establishes that the rights guaranteed in Article 7 correspond to those guaranteed by Article 8 of the European Convention. By comparison, the accompanying explanation to Article 9 of the Charter, which guarantees the rights to marry and found a family in accordance with national law, clarifies that Article 9 may have a wider scope than the corresponding Article 12 of the European Convention, because the Charter language would afford protection to same-gender unions if such unions were recognized by the domestic legislation of a member state. The Charter ensures in Article 53 that it must not be construed to restrict or in any way adversely affect the rights afforded by the European Convention or other international agreements that its member states have ratified. Charter of Fundamental Rights of the European Union, Articles 7, 9, 53, and explanatory notes, http://europarl.eu.int/charter/default_en.htm; Scappucci, *supra*, at 3. In some spheres, however, the Charter may provide more extensive protection. Duff, *supra*.

Another issue yet to be fully resolved is the relationship between the European Court of Human Rights in Strasbourg and the Court of Justice. One possibility is that the Court of Justice might have a relationship with the Court in Strasbourg similar to that of the domestic court system of a member state of the Council of Europe. The European Parliament has in fact suggested that the European Union itself ratify the European Convention on Human Rights, which would result in a formal protocol addressing the relations between the two courts. *Id.* Despite the many uncertainties at present, the Charter, with its explicit protections for the family, children, and gender equality, certainly creates the potential for increased attention by E.U. institutions, and the Court of Justice in particular, to family-related matters.

f. *Organization of American States*

One of the oldest regional organizations is the Organization of American States (OAS). Building upon the work of its predecessors, the International Union of American Republics, formed in 1890, and the Pan American Union, established in 1910, the OAS was conceived in 1948 when the twenty-one original members signed the Charter of the Organization of American States and the American Declaration of the Rights and Duties of Man. Since that time, the OAS has pursued a multi-faceted mission to strengthen democracy in its member nations, promote peaceful resolution of regional disputes, advance human rights, foster economic integration and regional free trade, promote sustainable development, and address the complex problems of the region, such as international drug trafficking. Today all thirty-five nations of the Caribbean and North, South, and Central America belong to the OAS.

Major policies and directives of the OAS are produced in the annual meeting of the General Assembly, composed of a representative of each member state, and the Meeting of Consultation of Ministers of Foreign Affairs, which convenes when necessary to address urgent problems. The Permanent Council, to which each member nation appoints an ambassador, manages ongoing administrative and political issues through regular meetings at the OAS headquarters in Washington, D.C. The Inter-American Council for Integral Development, the fourth principal governing body, addresses the elimination of poverty through economic, social, cultural, educational, scientific, and technological initiatives. The Secretariat, headed by the Secretary General, implements programs and policies and provides administrative support. Numerous other councils, commissions, and committees, including the Inter-American Commission of Women and the Inter-American Children's Institute, draft international instruments, reports, and proposals and assist the governing bodies. Organization of American States, *The OAS and the Inter-American System,* http://www.oas.org/en/OAS/oas.htm; Charter of the Organization of American States, http://www.oas.org/juridico/english/charter.html.

The OAS has produced several significant human rights documents. The American Declaration of the Rights and Duties of Man (American Declaration), to which each member of the OAS is subject, recognizes fundamental substantive and procedural human rights, including the right to establish a family, the right to protection of private and family life, and the right to protection for mothers and children, as well as essential duties of individuals, including the duty of parents to educate and protect their children and the duty of children to honor, aid, support, and protect their parents. The American Convention on Human Rights (American Convention), which legally binds the twenty-five member nations that have ratified the treaty, elaborates upon those rights in further detail and establishes an enforcement mechanism through two organs of the OAS, the Inter-American Commission on Human Rights and the Inter-American Court. Additional conventions affecting issues of family and gender include the Inter-American Convention on the Granting of Civil Rights to Women (1949), the Inter-American Convention on the Granting of Political Rights to Women (1949), the Inter-American Convention on Conflict of Laws Concerning the Adoption of Minors (1988), the Inter-American Convention on the International Return of Children (1994), the Inter-American Convention on the Prevention, Punishment and Eradication of Violence Against Women (1995), the Inter-American Convention on Support Obligations (1996), and the Inter-American Convention on International Traffic in Minors (1997).

Implementation of the Inter-American system for the protection of human rights is accomplished largely through its two principle organs, the Inter-American Commission on Human Rights and the Inter-American Court. The Commission, composed of seven members elected by the General Assembly, meets in sessions throughout the year at its headquarters in Washington, D.C., as well as in member countries. The Commission monitors the compliance of all OAS member countries with the American Declaration. Although the United States argues that the obligations being monitored are not legal ones, the Commission and Court have taken the view that the rights set forth in the Declaration are "indirectly legally binding" on all member nations of the OAS, because they define the human rights obligations imposed by the OAS Charter, which all member nations have ratified. David Harris, *Regional Protection of Human Rights: The Inter-American Achievement,* in The Inter-American System of Human Rights 4–6 (David

Harris & Stephen Livingstone eds., 1998). In addition, the Commission monitors compliance with the American Convention by those nations that are states parties to it.

The Commission fulfills its mission in many ways. In the past, on site-visits were frequently conducted to countries suspected of large-scale abuses, in order to foster public awareness of the importance of human rights and to produce reports documenting violations. Rapporteurs and working groups are now often appointed by the Commission to investigate specific types of human rights issues in a member nation, and offer proposals for reform. The Commission also issues advisory opinions, at the request of a member state, on domestic legislation that might violate human rights.

A primary mode of implementation by the Commission is hearing petitions filed by individuals asserting violation of their human rights against the government of an OAS member. Pursuant to the American Declaration, or the American Convention if the respondent state is a party to it, the Commission may investigate the complaint, hear evidence, attempt to facilitate a friendly settlement, and if no settlement is reached, prepare an initial report of the facts and its conclusions, including recommendations for remedial measures, such as protective orders, where appropriate. The respondent state is given a specific period of time following receipt of this report in which to resolve the situation and comply with Commission recommendations. If the matter is not resolved to the Commission's satisfaction, the Commission may, following a second report and period for resolution, publish the report, or the Commission may refer the case to the Inter-American Court, if the respondent state is a party to the American Convention that has accepted the Court's compulsory jurisdiction. *See* American Convention on Human Rights, Nov. 22, 1969, art. 58–63, 68, O.A.S. Treaty Series No. 36, http://www.oas.org/juridico/english/Treaties/b-32.htm; Claudio Grossman, *Moving Toward Improved Human Rights Enforcement in the Americas*, 27 Human Rights 16 (Summer, 2000); Leslie Kurshan, *Rethinking Property Rights as Human Rights: Acquiring Equal Property Rights for Women Using International Human Rights Treaties*, 8 J. Gender Soc. Pol'y & L. 353, 367–70 (2000); Victor Rodriguez Rescia & Marc David Seitles, *The Development of the Inter-American Human Rights System: A Perspective and a Modern-Day Critique*, 16 N.Y.L. Sch. J. Hum. Rts. 593 (2000); *Inter-American Commission on Human Rights*, http://www.cidh.oas.org/WhatstheIACHR.htm.

Conclusions of the Commission are not legally binding upon the parties, and particularly in cases confirming gross violations by military regimes, the Commission's recommendations have frequently not been followed. Unlike the European Commission, and now the European Court, whose decisions receive supervision of enforcement from the Committee of Ministers, there is no counterpart to supervise enforcement in the Inter-American system, and the OAS has at times been unsupportive of the Commission's criticism of member states. Harris, *supra*, at 20–21.

The Inter-American Court, located in San Jose, Costa Rica, is composed of seven judges elected in the General Assembly by the states parties to the American Convention. The Court has both contentious and advisory jurisdiction. Under its contentious jurisdiction, the Court may hear cases referred by either the Commission or a member state, but cannot hear cases filed directly with the Court by individuals. If the Commission decides to refer a case for resolution under the Court's contentious jurisdiction, the Commission acts as counsel for the individual victim before the Court, although the victim's own representative may present arguments to the Court in the reparations stage regarding appropriate damages. The Court hears evidence and arguments, often in a series of hearings. If it determines that there has been a violation of a right, the Court may issue a legally binding decision ordering that the respondent state ensure the injured party the enjoyment of that right, and award compensatory damages or other reparations, which can be executed using the domestic procedures of the respondent nation for execution of judgments. American Convention, art. 58–63, 68; Kurshan, *supra,* at 367–70; Rescia, *supra,* at 593.

At the request of an OAS member state, the Commission, or other OAS organs, the Court under its advisory jurisdiction may issue opinions interpreting the American Convention or any other OAS conventions concerning the protection of human rights. In addition, any OAS member state may request and receive from the Court an advisory opinion concerning the compatibility of any of its domestic laws with the American Convention or any other OAS human rights conventions. American Convention, art. 64.

Though the caseload of the Court is steadily increasing, to date it has heard far fewer cases than the European Court of Human Rights. Janis, *supra* note 1, at 272, 278. One factor affecting this is the different political climate in which the Inter-American system must operate. The presence of military dictatorships and violent political repression has forced the system to focus on gross violations of human rights involving forced disappearances, killing, torture, and arbitrary detention rather than the individual cases of ordinary human rights violations involving familial rights, freedom of expression, and civil due process that the European system has been able to address. Harris, *supra,* at 2. Another contributing factor is that, as of March 2003, only twenty-five OAS members had ratified the American Convention, and two large nations in the region, the United States and Canada were not yet states parties. Furthermore, even fewer nations have submitted themselves to the Court's contentious jurisdiction. Richard Wilson & Jan Perlin, *The Inter-American Human Rights System: Activities During 1999 Through October 2000,* 16 Am. U. Int'l L. Rev. 315, 319 (2001) (observing that of the twenty-one nations that had submitted, two of those countries, Trinidad and Tobago in 1998 and Peru in 1999, had subsequently attempted to withdraw from the court's jurisdiction). In addition, because the Commission and Court meet only three to four times per year, cases frequently take eight years to make their way through the system. Rescia, *supra,* at 622–23. Nevertheless, the decisions issued by both the Court and the Commission are increasing, Wilson, *supra,* at 316, and their impact on domestic legislation and the policies of many OAS member nations is steadily expanding. Moreover, the body of law created by the Court and Commission is increasingly considered by domestic courts in the region, particularly in the areas of due process, detention, torture, kidnaping, amnesty laws, and the direct applicability of the norms of the American Convention. Grossman, *supra,* at 18.

g. African Union

A third regional human rights system developed under the aegis of the Organization of African Unity (OAU), and operates today within the framework of the African Union (AU), which replaced the OAU in July 2002. When it was founded in 1963 with the adoption of the Charter of the Organization of African Unity, the OAU's initial focus was the eradication of colonialism on the continent. Henry Steiner & Philip Alston, International Human Rights in Context: Law, Politics, Morals 921 (2d ed. 2000). The need to broaden the scope of the organization's objectives, streamline its operation, and integrate its political activities with the economic and social development activities of the African Economic Community led to the adoption of the Constitutive Act of the African Union by the heads of state of the fifty-three OAU member nations in July 2000. The Constitutive Act entered into force on May 26, 2001, and following a one-year transition, the African Union began operation. Though it is loosely based on the European Union model, the AU is a unique organization that has chosen to move away from the "state-centric" model of the OAU and to encourage the cooperation of African NGOs, civil societies, labor unions, and business organizations in its quest for economic integration and social development. *AU2002: Transition from the OAU to the African Union, at* http://www.au2002.gov.za/docs/background/oau_to_au.htm.

Principal institutions of the African Union include the Assembly of Heads of State and Government (Assembly), the Executive Council, the Pan-African Parliament, the Court of Justice, and the Commission. The heads of state of each member nation meet annually in the Assembly to coordinate and direct the general policy of the organization. The foreign ministers, or another minister designee, meet twice per year in the Executive Council to implement Assembly decisions and oversee the work of seven Specialized Technical Committees, which coordinate the projects and programmes of the Union. The powers of the Pan African Parliament are defined in a separate Protocol, adopted in 2000, which provides that for the first five years the Parliament is in operation, it will have advisory and consultative powers only. As of mid-2002, that Protocol had not yet entered into force, and a separate protocol defining the composition and functions of the Court of Justice had not yet been adopted. *AU2002: Transition, supra.* The Commission operates as the Secretariat for the Union. Along with the Permanent Representatives Committee, the Commission provides administrative and support services to the other organs and conducts the daily work of the Union through its staff, located at AU headquarters in Addis Ababa, Ethiopia.

The principal human rights instrument adopted through the OAU, and now implemented through the AU, is the African Charter on Human and Peoples Rights, also known as the Banjul Charter. The Charter entered into force in 1986 and was ratified by all fifty-three member nations. Nsongurua H. Udombana, *Toward the African Court on Human and Peoples' Rights: Better Late than Never,* 3 Yale Hum. Rts. & Dev. L.J. 45, 46 (2000). The Charter recognizes many basic human rights common to other human rights treaties, including the right of the family to state protection and assistance, the duty of the state to ensure elimination of discrimination against women, and the protection of the rights of women and children as provided in "international declarations and conventions." African Charter on Human and Peoples' Rights, June 27, 1981, art. 18, OAU Doc. CAB/LEG/67/3 rev.5, 21 I.L.M. 58 (1982).

The Banjul Charter is distinctive, in comparison with other regional human rights conventions, in that it recognizes the rights of peoples as well as individuals; it includes economic, social and cultural rights in addition to civil and political rights; and it emphasizes duties of individuals to a greater degree than other human rights instruments. These characteristics reflect the culture and history of Africa, its traditional focus on collective and community needs, its struggle with poverty and underdevelopment, and its efforts to redress its colonial heritage. Udombana, *supra,* at 60–61. The duties recognized in the Charter go beyond those that are simply inherent in the protection of the enumerated rights, and extend from individuals to the state as well as to other individuals and groups. Some scholars have expressed concern that the recitation of duties could be interpreted in a manner that could impinge on the protection of rights. Because the articles setting forth duties have not as yet been interpreted or enforced, and their language is broad, the extent to which they might affect enforcement of rights, or the extent to which the duties themselves are binding and enforceable, is not yet determined. Steiner, *supra*, at 357–61.

At present the only enforcement mechanism under the Charter is the African Commission on Human and Peoples Rights. The Charter bestows upon the Commission three tasks: to promote, interpret, and protect the Charter provisions. Observers have noted that thus far the Commission's primary focus of activity has been promotional—organizing conferences, appointing Special Rapporteurs to investigate specific problems, and collecting documents. The Commission is empowered to interpret the Charter, at the request of a member state or AU institution, but this responsibility has been infrequently utilized. Udombana, *supra*, at 64–66; Vincent Orlu Nmehielle, *Towards an African Court of Human Rights: Structuring and the Court*, 6 Ann. Surv. Int'l & Comp. L. 27, 30–34 (2000).

The Commission's protective powers are exercised in two ways. The Commission is expected to review periodic compliance reports from the member states, though the quality and timeliness of these reports in the past has been viewed as problematic. Udombana, *supra*, at 69. The Commission is also mandated to hear complaints, referred to as "communications," from member states, and is permitted to hear communications from individuals and groups, if a majority of the Commissioners choose to consider the communication. After deliberation, the Commission transmits reports regarding the facts and its findings to the states involved and the Assembly. If the Commission finds a violation under the Charter has occurred, it has no power to award damages, restitution, or reparations, or to condemn the offending state. It can make recommendations to the parties and report to the Assembly. Proceedings before the Commission are confidential, and the Commission's reported findings can only be made public if the Assembly authorizes publication. Although the Assembly exhibited some reluctance in the past to permit publication, recently more decisions are being published. Scholars have also observed that the Commission has been hampered by a lack of resources, and at times, a lack of activist conviction of its members, who can simultaneously hold important government positions within their own countries. Some assert that the language of the Charter further hampers effective enforcement, as many of the rights are qualified by clauses such as "in accordance with the provisions of the law," that define those rights as limited by domestic legislation. Nmehielle, *supra*, at 29–34; Udombana, *supra*, at 62–73. That same language, of course, is found in other human rights instruments, and in fact many of these criticisms have been leveled at other regional and global human rights systems as well, particularly in their nascent stages.

Human rights activists in Africa have celebrated the recent Protocol to the African Charter on the Establishment of the African Court on Human and Peoples' Rights, June 9, 1998, OAU/LEG/EXP/AFCHPR/PROT III (1999), which was adopted by the OAU Assembly in June, 1998. The Protocol, if it enters into force, would create a court similar to the European and Inter-American Courts of Human Rights. The Court would have advisory jurisdiction to issue opinions, at the request of the AU, its members or organs, or African organizations recognized by the AU, on any matter related to the Charter or other relevant human rights instruments. Under its contentious jurisdiction, the Court could hear cases submitted by the Commission, states that have been party to a proceeding before the Commission or whose citizen has been the victim of a violation, and African intergovernmental organizations. In addition, NGOs and individuals would be permitted to institute cases directly with the Court, if a ratifying nation specifically accepts the competence of the Court for such matters.

Another recent African development is the entry into force in 1999 of the African Charter on the Rights and Welfare of the Child, July 1, 1990, OAU Doc. CAB/LEG/24.9/49. The scope of the Charter is extremely broad. It recognizes that the best interests of the child must be the primary consideration in all actions concerning a child; affirms a child's rights to survival and development, name and nationality, education, health and health services, freedom of expression, association, thought, and religion; and requires protection against child labor, child abuse, and harmful social and cultural practices. It requires certain procedural protections in juvenile justice proceedings and armed conflicts. The Charter also requires that parents have equal rights with regard to children, during marriage and in the event of divorce; mandates child support regardless of parental marital status; and sets standards for child protective proceedings. Standards for adoption, where permitted, are addressed, as are requirements to provide protection against sexual exploitation, apartheid and discrimination, trafficking, and drug abuse. Special protections for children of imprisoned mothers and mentally and physically challenged children are also included.

This African Charter on the Rights and Welfare of the Child is more than a compendium of rights. States parties to this Charter are specifically required to adopt domestic legislation or other measures to give effect to the Charter's provisions. In addition, the Charter provides that custom, tradition, cultural or religious practices inconsistent with the Charter's rights and obligations must be discouraged. The African Committee of Experts on the Rights and Welfare of the Child was established under this Charter, as part of the AU, to monitor implementation, interpret Charter provisions, and oversee member state's reports. In addition, the Committee may receive communications from individuals, organizations, or member states regarding any matter covered by the Charter, and investigate and report to the Assembly. The African Court on Human and Peoples Rights, when it begins operations, would also be permitted to hear matters raised by the Charter.

A working group of the African Commission on Human and Peoples' Rights has also been drafting an additional protocol to the African Charter, specifically addressing the rights of women in Africa. Anticipation of the entry into force of the Protocol on the African Court of Human Rights, the recent entry into force of the African Charter on the Rights and Welfare of the Child, and the efforts to produce this new Protocol on the Rights of Women all suggest that the regional activity of the AU may increasingly affect the future development of familial rights in Africa in the coming decades.

Problem 1-5

In the rural area in which you reside, the local governmental authorities that issue documents recognizing a marriage (the equivalent of a license or certificate in our culture) refuse to issue those documents unless the application has been signed by the prospective bride's father (regardless of her age). Though the long-standing tradition of giving a father full authority to choose a spouse for his daughter has waned in other parts of your country, it is still common in your area, and this local governmental practice fosters its entrenchment. Many adult women in your area have been unable to marry the partner whom they chose, or have been forced to marry a spouse they did not wish to marry, as a result of the power this local practice provided to their fathers.

As the head of a local women's collective, you and your members wish to change this local governmental practice, but your efforts to challenge it through your domestic legal system have been futile. Your local organization receives some resources and support from an international women's organization, and you have been advised to try to challenge the practice through your regional human rights system. Look at Articles 1, 8, 12, and 14 of the European Convention on Human Rights, Articles 1, 2, 11, 17, 24, and 32 of the American Convention on Human Rights, and Articles 2, 3, 18, and 29 of the African Charter on Human and Peoples' Rights, and the descriptions above of the enforcement mechanisms available under each instrument.

What arguments would you make under each, what counter-arguments would you anticipate, what remedies might you realistically expect under the enforcement mechanisms of each system, and how useful would they be in achieving the reform you desire?

Notes and Questions

1. *Purpose of Regional Human Rights Systems.* Given the existence of global human rights documents, such as the ICCPR (see Articles 3 and 23) and CEDAW (see Articles 2, 5, and 16) which have been ratified by most, if not all of the countries that participate in the regional conventions, what purpose is served by the regional human rights systems? What relief would be available to you, in Problem 1-5, under the ICCPR and CEDAW?

2. *Interaction.* As you continue to reflect upon the interaction between global and regional human rights systems, consider the following two excerpts:

> One can parse the African Charter, looking as it were for difficulties and inherent violations of universal human rights norms, looking for ways to criticize the prevalence of duties. One can also view it as an instrument that will be sensibly understood and interpreted, even while it seeks to preserve some small degree of the cultural distinctiveness systematically denied Africa by the West as the West invaded, colonized and manipulated Africa for its strategic values, and now penetrates Africa by trade and by imposing media conditions on national or international aid. The Charter should be seen as an affirmation of a modern degree of cultural relativism or particularism, the very occasion and reason for regional as well as universal human rights systems. That particularity speaks to the African Tradition and constitutes a fundamental value in the entire human rights movement, namely the preservation of difference.

* * *

> Whatever the African Charter says, African states are subject like all states to the universal human rights system expressed through the UDHR [Universal Declaration of Human Rights] and the two basic Covenants [ICCPR and ICESCR]. If there is a conflict, if this regional regime requires or permits state conduct that universal norms prohibit, or prohibits state conduct that universal norms require, those norms must prevail. Else the human rights movement collapses into a hopeless regional anarchy, and we encourage the development of additional regional systems that will simply flout universal imperatives by asserting their own distinctive norms.

> Henry Steiner & Philip Alston, International Human Rights in Context: Law, Politics, Morals 696 (1996).

3. *Other Human Rights Systems.* The above subsections highlight the major regional human rights systems of Europe, the Americas, and Africa. There are, of course, other significant intergovernmental human rights documents, although they are not yet associated with enforcement mechanisms of the same complexity, nor have they yet developed a substantial body of interpretive law.

For example, in 1995 the states that were formerly part of the Soviet Union adopted a Commonwealth of Independent States Convention on Human Rights in Minsk. Observers have commented that it has not as yet generated much activity. Steiner (2000), *supra,* at 780. Several members of the former Soviet bloc have recently become or are in the process of becoming members of the Council of Europe, and states parties to the European Convention on Human Rights.

The Organization for Security and Co-operation in Europe (OSCE), currently the largest intergovernmental organization in Europe with 55 members (as of 2003), is also focusing increasing attention on human rights. OSCE was transformed in 1995 from the former Conference on Security and Co-operation in Europe, to which the United States, Canada, the countries of Eastern and Western Europe, and the former Soviet Union belonged. Although its primary focus initially was the development of a cooperative security system and resolution of regional conflicts, a number of nonbinding human rights documents have been concluded by its members. Its principal institutions include a Secretariat and a Representative on Freedom in the Media in Vienna, an Office for Democratic Institutions and Human Rights in Warsaw, and a High Commissioner on National Minorities located at The Hague. A mechanism for OSCE human rights fact-finding missions is in place. OSCE agreements contain strong statements on minority rights, and the High Commissioner has intervened in more than ten states under OSCE mechanisms to provide assistance and conciliation in instances of conflict among national minorities. Steiner (2000), *supra,* at 791–793; Clements, *supra,* at 249–250. *See* the OSCE official website, http://www.osce.org.

The League of Arab States, composed of over twenty Arab countries in Africa and the Middle East, has adopted an Arab Charter on Human Rights, Sept. 15, 1994, *reprinted in* 18 Hum Rts. L.J. 151 (1997), which recognizes a right of privacy in family affairs, the inviolability of the home, and the duty of the state to protect the family, mothers, children, and the aged. The Charter creates a Committee of Experts on Human Rights that is charged with the duty to review periodic reports submitted by member states, and submit its own report to the Standing Committee on Human Rights at the Arab League. The Arab system at present has been described as "largely dormant." Steiner (2000), *supra,* at 780. A translated copy of the text of the Arab Charter on Human Rights can be found at http://ecolu-info.unige.ch/FormaConti/Droits-Homme/A27.html.

There is no intergovernmental regional human rights system, as yet, for the Asia-Pacific region. A group of nongovernmental organizations drafted the Bangkok NGO Declaration on Human Rights in 1993, setting forth their human rights aspirations for the region. *See* The Center for International Human Rights Law, Inc., *The Rights International Research Guide for the International Human Rights Lawyers,* http://www.rightsinternationalorg/ricenter/instruments.html. Another group of human rights activists, the Asian Human Rights Commission, has drafted and "declared" the Asian Human Rights Charter, described as a people's charter, which is intended to encourage the development of human rights mechanisms in the Asian region. *See* Asian Human Rights Commission, *More About AHRC,* http:www.ahrchk.net/about/mabout.html. These documents are not intergovernmental agreements, however, and have no binding effect upon the nations of the region.

C. Researching International and Comparative Family Law

The following article was written specifically for this casebook by two law librarians from the University of Oregon School of Law. The information it contains will prove useful to anyone undertaking foreign law or international law research. The authors warn of potential pitfalls as well as suggest specific sources, both print and internet, that may assist with a project. The insights provided are certain to save the researcher time and frustration.

Dennis Hyatt & Mary Clayton, Researching International and Comparative Family Law

(2003)

Introduction

In the latter part of his stellar career, Adolf Sprudzs, renowned foreign law librarian and lecturer in legal bibliography at the University of Chicago, characterized international legal research as a potential "infinite paper chase."[1] The documents flooding into the ocean of literature that is international law manifest today's increasingly complex, interrelated world. The number of members of the international community continues to grow.[2] As the number of geographic boundaries grow their significance diminishes because of the blossoming of world trade, international travel, and global communication. A multitude of treaties are attempting to bring unification and harmonization of laws. This greater interdependence results in the publication of a tremendous quantity of legal information at national, regional, and international levels. The scope of international law has expanded to include greater concern for individual human rights, and as a result subject areas once outside the ambit of international law, such as criminal law and family law, are now within its purview. The number of international and regional organizations has increased dramatically; the number of non-governmental organizations has grown exponentially. The involvement of all these organizations in advocacy and fact-finding not only helps change the methods of international law-making, but also changes the nature and sources of international law. Researching the traditional sources of international law has always been a challenge, but an ever-changing, growing global community adds to the range of legal materials that must be consulted. International legal research now includes the primary law of all nations, plus secondary sources in a wide variety of disciplines, including comparative law. The international legal researcher, especially a beginner who is perhaps "accustomed only to the well-organized

---

1. Adolf Sprudzs, *International Legal Research: An Infinite Paper Chase*, 16 Vanderbilt J. Transnat'l L. 521–36 (1983). The increase in the number of documents world-wide that constitute the sources of international law, coupled with the lack of adequate indexing and updating tools, were recurring concerns for this international legal research expert. *See also* Adolf Sprudzs, *Status of Multilateral Treaties — Researcher's Mystery, Mess or Muddle?* 66 Am. J. Int'l L. 365–76 (1972), and Adolf Sprudzs, *Problems with Sources of Information in International Law and Relations: The Case of the World-Wide Treaty Jungle,* 9 Int'l J. L. Libr. 195–202 (1981).

2. In 1945, the United Nations was established with 51 founding members; in 2002, the number of member nations is 189.

predictability and effectiveness of United States legal research sources,"[3] is faced with two dilemmas that echo Sprudzs's assessment of the research difficulties ahead: In which direction do I run? How do I know when I'm done?

Traditional legal research methods, as taught in most first-year legal research and writing courses, are indeed well-suited for sifting through the finely-structured law of the United States. Students discover that U.S. law is a well-defined literature composed of comprehensive sets of statutes, court reports, and administrative agency regulations and rulings. They learn that sophisticated subject guides, such as digests for court decisions, and updating tools, such as citators for cases and statutes, are powerful finding aids that help link a literature composed of millions of small documents into an overall structure of crystalline elegance. Students realize that although the most frequently used titles may contain a large number of documents in a large number of volumes, the total number of U.S. law titles that must be consulted for any particular research problem is fairly small. First-year legal research courses concentrate on the most commonly consulted titles.

Over time these traditional research methods have created strong presumptions that some of the most useful and often-used publications are also the most accurate and reliable. In return, the high quality of the publications has given additional legitimacy to the research process. This reiterated feedback between methodology and the publication of familiar forms of legal information has been instrumental in conferring cognitive authority on a select group of titles.

> For most of the twentieth century, the legal world had agreed to confer cognitive authority on a small set of resources. By 'cognitive authority' I mean the act by which one confers trust upon a source.... One of the major features of legal information in the twentieth century has been the deeply rooted and stable array of cognitive authorities. Legal researchers learned that certain sets of books were authoritative and reliable. If used correctly, such sources provided 'the' information. One didn't need to look behind such a publication and evaluate its worth. The process of critically judging its value had been performed long ago. The topography of legal information was so accepted, and it functioned so well, that researchers gave it little thought.[4]

New and fast-changing subjects of law, such as international family law, are not well-represented in the canon of cognitive authorities taught in first-year legal research courses. When beginning researchers first locate apparently useful titles in international legal research, they are unlikely to know how reliable and authoritative the titles are. Increases in the amount of available information, reorganization throughout the law publishing industry, and the widespread use of computer technologies have combined to break down the established research routines used for finding these materials. In wandering outside the scope of books and familiar formats that have enjoyed a long-unexamined trustworthiness in the United States, researchers are left wondering whether their research efforts have located the most authoritative information available.

---

3. Sprudzs, *supra* note 1, at 523.
4. Robert C. Berring, *Legal Information and the Search for Cognitive Authority*, 88 Calif. L. Rev. 1673, 1676–77 (2000). *See also* Patrick Wilson's observations about the need for everyone, including librarians and other information specialists, to be concerned with social epistemology and the ways people come to distinguish information from misinformation. "All I know of the world beyond the narrow range of my own personal experience is what others have told me. It is all hearsay. But I do not count all hearsay as equally reliable. Some people know what they are talking about, others do not. Those who do are my cognitive authorities." Patrick Wilson, Second-Hand Knowledge: An Inquiry into Cognitive Authority 13 (1983).

Bibliographic Awareness

At the most basic level of bibliographic awareness,[5] researchers in international law will encounter some differences in international publications. Book layout may vary and descriptive elements usually found on a title page and verso may be missing or printed in different places throughout the text block. In Canada, for example, the challenge of bilingual publication of statutes has led to an unusual book design. In each volume the French text block begins at one 'front' of the book. The book is flipped over for the English text block to begin at the other 'front.' There are two title pages with two sets of page numbers. The two languages meet in the middle of the book with the ending text of one version upside down and facing the ending text of the other version.

Bibliographic awareness also allows researchers to understand the rules of citation. Researchers accustomed to applying citation rules to U.S. legal materials may find the rules more difficult to apply to international legal materials,[6] and language is only one complication to consider.[7] In response to changes in the format of legal information, the conventional rules of legal citation have changed rapidly over the past few years. Be aware, in looking at citations, that computer databases now separate citation information from the printed artifacts that have historically served as the sole source of the authoritative record. To include databases the new rules are format-neutral, but because the rules now separate the citation from the publishers of the print record, they are also called vendor-neutral rules.[8]

By using basic bibliographic awareness skills to search the catalog of an academic law library, researchers can readily locate a variety of published legal research guides that provide excellent orientations to legal materials and the research process. Overviews to research in international law are found in *Chapter 11, International Law*, in Morris L. Cohen & Kent C. Olson, Legal Research in a Nutshell (7th ed. 2000); Jonathan Pratter, *Chapter 20, International Law*, in Roy M. Mersky & Donald J. Dunn, Fundamentals of Legal Research (8th ed. 2002); *Chapter 15, International Law*, and *Chapter 17, Foreign and Comparative Law*, in Morris L. Cohen, Robert C. Berring & Kent C. Olson, How to Find the Law (9th ed. 1989). For a slightly more general introduction to research in in-

---

5. 'Bibliographic awareness' is a term of art largely subsumed by a newer, broader term 'information literacy.' Whereas bibliographic awareness is concerned primarily with an understanding of the layout and organization of print materials, information literacy refers first to the ability to 'read' all kinds of information formats, a set of skills considered essential for using the variety of media saturating the information age. Consider Virgil L.P. Blake's discussion of the connections between listening comprehension skills, the mission of libraries, and bookcassettes in *Something New Has Been Added: Aural Literacy and Libraries, in* Virgil L. P. Blake & Renee Tjoumas, eds., Information Literacies for the Twenty-First Century 203–218 (1990). Information literacy has an expanded meaning applied to the research skills needed to understand and appreciate how information is gathered, manipulated, packaged, and retrieved. For example, law librarians and legal research instructors promote computer training as an essential component of preparation for the practice of law.

6. "Citation of foreign materials should conform as closely as possible to local citation practice, as modified by rule 20." *Rule 20, Foreign Materials*, A Uniform System of Citation 151 (17th ed. 2000).

7. "Translate all titles, names, or words cited that are not in the Roman alphabet, using a standard transliteration system." *Rule 20.1.4, Languages That Do Not Use the Roman Alphabet*, A Uniform System of Citation, *supra* note 6, at 152.

8. Separating legal information from well-known, reliable law book publishers, such as West Publishing Company, has contributed to the loss of cognitive authority that researchers have attached to their publications.

ternational, foreign and comparative law, delivered with a broader perspective in more casual narrative essays, see Accidental Tourist on the New Frontier: An Introductory Guide to Global Legal Research (Jeanne Rehberg & Radu D. Popa, eds., 1998). The George Washington University Journal of International Law and Economics, Guide to International Legal Research (3d ed. 1998), with annual supplements, strives for more exhaustive coverage of resources. Its commendable effort to include the specific contents of hundreds of internet sites and commercial database services that have foreign and international law materials is useful, but may eventually make the work too bulky and awkward to use easily. Newcomers to international legal research may benefit also from introductory textbooks that describe the nature, structure, and processes of international law. The catalog of any academic law library will indicate its holdings of several international law treatises.

The researcher who is bibliographically aware is concerned not only with finding and citing materials, but also with their dates of coverage and how up-to-date they are. Law is time-sensitive; therefore, legal research is time-sensitive. Concern for time pervades the law. Clients pay attorneys for their expertise based on increments of time. Attorneys are willing to pay commercial vendors high prices for timely delivery of quality legal information. The law imposes procedural time limits. When events occur is one determinant of the law that applies to them. To determine coverage dates, start by consulting the spines of books, title pages, and prefatory statements. Because publications can be in production for several months after the compiler or author has completed research, a copyright or issue date is only a partial indication of how current information may be. It is incorrect to assume that the currency of the information actually extends to the date of copyright or issue date. For example, the verso of the title page of the 2000 edition of the U.S. Department of State's Treaties in Force shows that this publication was released in June 2000. However, a time sensitive researcher will be more aware of the coverage of this edition by noticing its subtitle, "A List of Treaties and Other International Agreements of the United States in Force on January 1, 2000."

At every level of bibliographic awareness computer databases are altering the traditional assumptions and methods of research that grew from print publications. Foremost among the changes is the different awareness of time fostered by computers. The act of printing and the permanence of the printed page help give certainty and linearity to time, and this simplifies the concept of 'before and after' as a measure of a document's dates of coverage and currency. Time-sensitive researchers may find great difficulty in determining the scope of coverage and timeliness of electronic files because new information can be added continuously and transparently by database managers. Careful researchers will keep a record of when they conduct each computer database search as one measure of the contents and currency of the database they are searching. Recognizing the time-related problems that database files pose for their most sophisticated users, database vendors are beginning to provide improved scope notes and updating information online.

It is a natural tendency for researchers to incorporate bibliographic awareness of one literature into their expectations for researching another literature. The more closely the disciplines resemble each other, the stronger the expectations may be that the same research process will produce similar results. Researchers whose bibliographic awareness of legal research is founded on the experiences of what is learned in first-year legal research and writing courses must approach international and foreign legal research carefully because their expectations of the literature may be unrealistically high. Because the bases of authority in international law are much broader than the sources of primary authority that constitute U.S. law, the literature of international law is less well-defined. Its basic titles are less comprehensive and more numerous. The finding aids are less polished and, for the most part, do not contribute a sense that they draw documents together to bring coherent structure to the literature. Whereas a researcher of U.S. law must have bibliographic awareness of relatively few essential titles that embrace the search for authority, international law researchers must be aware of the several titles that together comprise the most comprehensive—but likely incomplete—set of documents, or that together constitute the most inclusive—but likely mismatched—set of indexing and updating aids. It is not surprising that the researcher may feel uncomfortably uncertain whether a research process that relies primarily on bibliographic awareness is sufficiently thorough to find all essential documents and titles of publications.

In using their bibliographic awareness skills in an academic law library, most researchers can locate an enormous number of documents relating to international and comparative family law. The challenge of legal research, especially in unfamiliar subjects, quickly shifts from finding documents to creating information filters for them. These filters establish a hierarchy of importance to the documents, restrict the search for information to the most relevant and authoritative materials, and limit the time devoted to the research process. Without these filters, research lacks direction, becomes unending, and risks failure. Each filter provides a context for focusing research.

Finding the Text of Treaties

Treaties have become the single most important means by which nations regulate their relations with each other. Since the creation of the United Nations in 1945, more than thirty thousand treaties have been registered with the organization. It is little wonder that many legal research textbooks suggest that any research in international law begin with the search for applicable treaties. The steps in treaty research are logical and few, although not always easy to navigate. First, locate the text of the treaty in an authoritative source. Second, determine its current status—is it in force? Who are the parties? What reservations apply? Third, interpret the treaty, which may include looking at other agreements or instruments between the parties, the subsequent practices of the parties, legislative history, and judicial decisions.

Finding the text of treaties is one of the more straight-forward tasks in international legal research. Nonetheless, because the researcher must be aware of so many titles, elaborate charts of titles, usually arranged by dates of coverage, have been created to show the different sources of text in relation to the various titles the researcher must use to find and update them. See, for example, the useful charts compiled by Jeanne Rehberg in *Chapter 6: Finding Treaties and Other International Agreements*, Accidental Tourist on the New Frontier: An Introductory Guide to Global Legal Research, *supra*, in which she uses a select list of forty sources recommended for treaty research.

Extensive collections of treaties help make locating the text of a particular treaty a relatively easy part of the research process. Taken together, three comprehensive print collections, each covering a specific time period, provide the text of treaties of many nations from 1648 to the present. Treaties in the 243 volumes of the Consolidated Treaty Series are arranged chronologically and cover the period 1648–1919.[9] A supplemental

---

9. Although many earlier treaties are known from the Italian city-states of the Middle Ages, as well as from the Roman Empire and Greek city-states, coverage of the Consolidated Treaty Series begins with the Peace of Westphalia of 1648 that concluded the Thirty Years War. This treaty—the

collection of colonial and postal treaties left out of the original compilation was published, along with a multi-volume guide to the entire set that includes an index to parties. The 205 volumes of the League of Nations Treaty Series covers 1920–1946, and contains treaties between members as well as between members and non-members of the League. The 2016 (and counting) volumes of the United Nations Treaty Series covers 1947 to date. Under the U.N. Charter, all member nations are required to register their treaties, and while some nations do not comply, this series is the single most complete collection of modern treaties available.[10]

Researchers should note that the United Nations Treaty Series is now four years behind in publication. This delay in availability is not an obstacle to finding the text to treaties to which the United States is a party, because those treaties will appear in other more timely U.S. publications. For treaties to which the United States is not a party, quite often the print resource of first resort for recent treaties is International Legal Materials, a bi-monthly journal of the American Society of International Law. The treaties and other international materials, such as judicial decisions and documents of international organizations, are chosen for inclusion based on an estimation of their current and future legal significance.[11]

Some treaty sets, such as the Organization of American States Treaty Series,[12] are collections of the treaties between members of regional international organizations. The European Treaty Series includes the treaties of the 25 nations who are members of the Council of Europe. Several countries have established separate national treaty series as well. The United Kingdom Treaty Series began coverage in 1892, and the Canada Treaty Series began in 1928. While print versions may be available in only a few libraries, official national internet sites may be excellent sources for the text of a nation's treaties. One example is the Australian Treaties Library, maintained by the Australia Department of Foreign Affairs and Trade.[13]

Prior to 1950, the text of U.S. treaties was published in various volumes of the United States Statutes at Large. Since 1950, the Department of State has published treaties as sequentially numbered pamphlets in the Treaties and Other International Agreements Series (T.I.A.S.).[14] Several years later, these pamphlets are compiled in numerical order and published in hardbound volumes—with continuous pagination through each volume—titled United States Treaties and Other International Acts (U.S.T.). As a convenience to

---

product of the first great international conference—dismantled feudalism and paved the way for the rise of modern nations. It is considered a foundation document of modern international law. The Consolidated Treaty Series was compiled and edited by bibliographer Clive Perry, who declared in the preface that his goal was to include all treaties from 1648 until "the date of commencement of the *League* series (approximately 1918–1920), to reproduce such prints of treaties in their original languages as can be found in whatsoever collection along with such translations into English or French as again, which is very often the case, can be found." 1 Consolidated Treaty Series vi (1969).

10. The United Nations Treaty Collection, http://untreaty.un.org, is the single most comprehensive internet source for treaties and is more up to date than the U.N.T.S print collection. However, a subscriber fee is charged for access.

11. International Legal Materials is also available online through Lexis-Nexis and Westlaw. On a subscription or fee basis, I.L.M. may also soon be available to researchers through the American Society of International Law internet site, http://www.asil.org.

12. The O.A.S. Treaty Series was preceded by the Pan-American Union Treaty Series (1934–1956).

13. Australian Treaties Library, *at* http://www.austlii.edu.au/au/other/dfat/.

14. Executive agreements are included in T.I.A.S., but were not included in the United States Statutes at Large because they were not considered legislative action.

researchers, the pre-1950 treaties were collected into a 13-volume set called Treaties and Other International Agreements of the United States of America, 1776–1949 (Bevans). Published by the Department of State, this set is usually cited by the last name of the compiler, Charles Bevans.

T.I.A.S. and U.S.T. are the official source of text for all U.S. treaties. Because both are slow to publish, the researcher can first find the text of recent U.S. treaties in a variety of unofficial sources. In addition to International Legal Materials (which prints treaties on a selective basis), the foremost print resource for recent U.S. treaties and international documents is Consolidated Treaties & International Agreements.[15] Online access to the text of U.S. treaties is provided through GPO Access[16] (the internet site of the U.S. Government Printing Office) and Thomas[17] (the Library of Congress site). Lexis-Nexis and Westlaw database files also provide the text of U.S. treaties.

Collections of treaties help focus research on particular subject areas. One of the first compilations of treaties published specifically to facilitate research in international and comparative family law is D. Marianne Blair & Merle H. Weiner, International Family Law: Conventions, Statutes, and Regulatory Materials (2003), which organizes treaties into specific topics, such as treaties relating to women, marriage and dissolution, domestic violence, and children. This collection also includes selected Conventions of the Hague Conference on Private International Law, European conventions, Inter-American conventions, African and Arab charters on human rights, as well as selected U.S. federal statutes, regulations, and uniform acts. Women's Human Rights Resources,[18] maintained by the University of Toronto Bora Laskin Law Library, is just one example of a useful internet site that provides the text of a range of related human rights treaties. Particularly in using internet resources, the researcher must be attentive to the accuracy, authenticity, and current status of the text of the treaties.

Several indexes to treaties are published separately from a specific collection. Unfortunately, most are too outdated to provide useful guidance in identifying the text of treaties in new areas of concern in international law. Published by the United Nations, Multilateral Treaties Deposited with the Secretary General (1982) is available not only in print, but also online by subscription. It is an especially useful index, because it also includes status information as well as reservations and other declarations of the parties.

The most comprehensive index to U.S. treaties is the United States Treaty Index, a multi-volume set that provides multiple points of access to all U.S. treaties.[19] It is up-

---

15. Consolidated Treaties & International Agreements (Erwin C. Surrency, comp. & ed., 1990–). Now issued in bound volumes, the goal of this service, as stated in the foreword of each volume, is publication "within ninety days of release or ratification, newly concluded international agreements, both executive agreements as well as formal treaties, which have been ratified." Because this publication pre-dates official publication and the assignment of T.I.A.S. numbers, an internal control number ('CTIA' number) is assigned to each document. Country and subject indexes are attached as appendices to each volume, a statement in the foreword of each volume noting that it is "a herculean task to attempt to comprehensively index all American treaties other than to the title of the treaty." *See* United States Treaty Index, *infra.*, which is just such an attempt.

16. United States Government Printing Office, *at* http://www.access.gpo.gov.

17. The Library of Congress, *at* http://thomas.loc.gov.

18. Women's Human Rights Resources, *at* http://www.law-lib.utoronto.ca/diana/mainpage.htm.

19. United States Treaty Index: 1776–1990 Consolidation (Igor I. Kavass, ed., 1991–). This extremely helpful publication, currently consisting of 13-volumes plus a one-volume supplement, is updated with revised volumes. "The set presents information about the treaties in many different ways—chronologically, by country, by the names of international organizations, by subject, numerically, and by a geographical-subject combination—so as to ease the process of

dated every six months, and because the current index is published more quickly than T.I.A.S. pamphlets, the documents are given temporary 'KAV' numbers to facilitate tracking them through the various indexes. Unfortunately, 'KAV' control numbers used for tracking the indexing of recent U.S. treaties and 'CTIA' control numbers[20] assigned to the text of recent U.S. treaties are not related to each other. By using chronology tables and subject indexes in both sets, it is possible to convert one control number to the other and use these two sets from different publishers in tandem.

Treaty Status, Analysis, and Interpretation

Once an authoritative text of the treaty is available, the next step is to determine the status of the treaty: who are the signatories, when is the treaty entered into force, what declarations and reservations have been made. As mentioned, the United Nations index of Multilateral Treaties Deposited with the Secretary General includes status information for many treaties, as well as declarations and reservations. The European Treaty Series also includes reservations and declarations, which is unusual for a treaty collection.

Under the terms of many multilateral treaties, treaty secretariats are established and charged with tracking subsequent signatures, ratifications, and other status documents relating to the treaty. Started in 1992, the Multilaterals Project of the Fletcher School of Law & Diplomacy at Tufts University is working to make available the text of multilateral conventions and other agreements.[21]

The primary source for determining the status of agreements to which the United States is a party is Treaties in Force, published annually by the Department of State. It is available in print and online,[22] but the online version is no more current than the print version. Treaties in Force consists of two lists: a list of bilateral agreements arranged alphabetically by country and sub-divided by subject categories, and a list of multilateral treaties arranged by broad subject headings. Unfortunately, there is little consistency in the terms used as subject categories for bilateral treaties and the terms used as subject headings in multilateral treaties. Treaties in Force is more difficult to use than it should be.[23] The U.S. Department of State internet site includes Treaty Actions,[24] which provides updates to the changes in status of U.S. treaties and international agreements. A researcher may also contact the Department of State Office of Treaty Affairs by telephone at (202) 647-1345 for the most current treaty information.

Travaux préparatoires are the legislative history of international agreements—the documents, such as reports and debates, produced during the process of drafting a treaty. The Vienna Convention on Treaties recognizes them as a valid means of interpreting and clarifying treaty language. Increasingly, the travaux are being published in commercial sources,[25] but for most treaties the travaux are not readily available except

---

research." ix, vol. 1 (1998 revision). The Current Treaty Index is a looseleaf supplement to the United States Treaty Index that contains information on current actions by the United States regarding treaties.

20. *See infra* note 24 and accompanying text.

21. Edwin Ginn Library, Multilaterals Project, *at* http://www.fletcher.tufts.edu/multilaterals.html.

22. U.S. Dep't of State, *at* http://www.state.gov/www/global/legal_affairs/tifindex.html.

23. The researcher should consider using A Guide to the United States Treaties in Force (Igor I. Kavass, ed., 1982–) in conjunction with Treaties in Force. The guide contains approximately the same information, but has in-depth indexing presented in a more useful format.

24. U.S. Dep't of State, Treaty Actions, *at* http://www.state.gov/s/l/c3428.htm.

25. Some examples include Marc J. Bossuyt, Guide to the 'Travaux Préparatoires' of the International Covenant on Civil and Political Rights (1987); Council of Europe, Collected Edition of the

as separate documents (which may be deposited with the United Nations or other international organizations). The researcher's quest for interpretative commentary and travaux for particular treaties must include not only the search for documents in organization archives, but also the search for books through library catalogs, for articles through periodical indexes, and for text files through internet sites.

The procedural record of a treaty's ratification in a particular nation may also serve as documentation for interpreting and clarifying the treaty's meaning, including whatever reservations and declarations have been made by that country. In the United States, most of the documents which constitute the legislative history of treaty ratification arise from the activities of the U.S. Senate,[26] especially from the Senate Committee on Foreign Relations. Beginning with the 97th Congress in 1981, proposed treaties referred to the Senate have been printed and issued in a series called Senate Treaty Documents.[27] The Foreign Relations Committee makes its recommendations to the full Senate in reports printed in a series called Senate Executive Reports. The recommendations often include a reprint of the proposed treaty with a section-by-section analysis, which will include any declarations, reservations, and conditions that are recommended to the full Senate. The Senate Treaty Documents and the Senate Executive Reports are often the only official source for these interpretive materials. Fortunately, they are available in a variety of sources.[28] For current information on recent treaty actions, the researcher should consult the Senate's Legislative Activities Treaties internet site,[29] which has links to treaties transmitted from the President, treaties on the Executive calendar, treaties approved by the Senate, and other treaty status actions.

Judicial Interpretation of Treaties

Article 59 of the Statute for the Permanent Court of International Justice provides that ICJ court decisions have "no binding force except between the parties and in respect of that particular case." This restriction diminishes the value of judicial opinions as prece-

---

'Travaux Préparatoires' of the European Convention on Human Rights, 8 vols. (1975–1985); The United Nations Convention on the Rights of the Child: A Guide to the 'Travaux Préparatoires' (Sharon Detrick, comp. and ed., 1992); B.G. Ramcharan, *The Travaux Préparatoires of the African Commission on Human Rights*, 13 Hum. Rts. L. J. 307–314 (1992); Lars Adam Rehof, Guide to the Travaux Préparatoires of the United Nations Convention on the Elimination of all Forms of Discrimination Against Women (1993); Anna-Lena Svensson-McCarthy, The International Law of Human Rights and States of Exception: with Special Reference to the Travaux Préparatoires and Case-Law of the International Monitoring Organs (1996).

26. Under the Constitution, the President has the "Power, by and with the Advice and Consent of the Senate, to make Treaties, provided two thirds of the Senators present concur...." U.S. Const. art. II, §2.

27. Prior to the 97th Congress, proposed treaties were printed in a series called Senate Executive Documents.

28. The separate Treaty Documents and Executive Reports are eventually printed in bound volumes of the U.S. Serial Set, a huge collection of government documents available in most large libraries that are designated U.S. government depositories. Since 1970, they are also reproduced in microfiche format by the Congressional Information Service, which provides comprehensive indexing and abstracting to all Congressional documents. Congressional Information Service also provides similar information through its commercial internet site called Congressional Universe. The Treaty Documents and Executive Reports are available in Lexis-Nexis and Westlaw databases relating to treaties. Beginning with the 104th Congress in 1995, they are available through the U.S. Congress Senate, House, and Executive Reports internet site, *at* http://www.access.gpo.gov/congress/cong006.html. Other sources of documents and reports include the Weekly Compilation of Presidential Documents, and the Public Papers of the Presidents.

29. U.S. Senate, Treaties, *at* http://www.senate.gov/activities/treaties.html.

dent; nonetheless, published decisions of international law courts do provide evidence for defining customary law, for recognizing international practice, and for interpreting treaties.[30] Almost all international judicial proceedings, including disputes brought before special commissions and international arbitral bodies, involve interpretation of treaties.

The decisions of the ICJ are available in print,[31] at the court's internet site,[32] and on Westlaw. Regional international court decisions are also published in print, but are most readily available at the regional courts' internet sites. Examples include decisions of the European Court of Justice,[33] the European Court of Human Rights,[34] and the Inter-American Court of Human Rights.[35] Westlaw and Lexis-Nexis also have databases of international court opinions.

The vast majority of adjudications involving family law arise in national courts and administrative tribunals, including disputes which involve international law. National court decisions are also recognized under Article 38 of the Vienna Convention on the Law of Treaties as one of the "subsidiary means for the determination of the rules of law." The sources and research techniques necessary to find cases will vary from country to country. For example, in addition to official and unofficial reports series, the decisions of national courts on international law issues are sometimes published or summarized in national yearbooks and periodicals, as well as in digests of international law.[36] There are also specialized case reports dealing with international law.[37]

International Law Reports[38] is a compilation of international law court decisions from both international and national courts. However, its coverage is limited. "The

---

30. For in-depth discussion of international case law, leading treatises include Shabtai Rosenne, The Law and Practice of the International Court (3d ed. 1997); A. S. Muller, D. Raic, J. M. Thuránszky, eds., The International Court of Justice: Its Future Role After Fifty Years (1997); Christine D. Gray, Judicial Remedies in International Law (1987); Georg Schwarzenberger, International Law as Applied by International Courts and Tribunals, 4 vols. (3d ed. 1957–1986); Edward McWhinney, The World Court and the Contemporary International Law-Making Process (1979); L.C. Green, International Law Through the Cases (4th ed. 1978).

31. International Court of Justice, Reports of Judgments, Advisory Opinions, and Orders (1947–). There are 30 bound volumes of reports through 1997, but the opinions are first published as separate pamphlets.

32. International Court of Justice, *at* http://www.icj-cij.org.

33. CURIA, *at* http://www.europa.eu.int/cj/en/index.htm.

34. European Court of Human Rights, *at* http://www.echr.coe.int, and the Court's Reports of Judgments and Decisions. Another option for decisions of the Court is the series, European Human Rights Reports, which started publication in 1979. Significant decisions of the Court have also been compiled in Leading Cases of the European Court of Human Rights (1997).

35. Corte Interamericana de Derechos Humanos, *at* http://www.corteidh.or.cr/juris_ing/index.html. The Court's advisory decisions are printed in Series A, Advisory Opinions, while contentious cases are included in Series C, Decisions and Judgments.

36. Marjorie M. Whiteman, Digest of International Law, 15 vols. (1963–1973) is the most recent compiled digest of United States practice. As a supplement to the Whiteman digest, for 1974–1980 the U.S. Department of State published the annual Digest of Practice in International Law, concluding with a cumulative index for this period. This was followed by a three-volume set covering 1981–1988. In 2001, the State Department announced that it had contracted with the International Law Institute to recommence publication of the annual digest commencing with the 2000 volume, and eventually ILI will publish volumes covering the preceding years.

37. American International Law Cases (1971–) includes reprints of U.S. federal and state court cases beginning 1793. Now in its 3d series, it is currently edited by Bernard Reams.

38. The first 16 volumes of International Law Reports (Elihu Lauterpacht, C. J. Greenwood & A.G. Oppenheimer, eds., 1919–) were published under the title Annual Digest and Reports of Public International Law Cases.

number of decisions on questions of international protection of human rights has increased considerably in recent years and it is now impossible for the Reports to cover them all.... Decisions of national courts on the application of conventions on human rights will not be published unless they deal with a major point of substantive human rights law or a matter of wider interest to public international lawyers such as the relationship of international law and national law, the extent of the right of derogation or the principles of the interpretation of treaties."[39] A useful consolidation of finding aids has been created for volumes 1–100 of the reports (a two-volume consolidation covers volumes 1–80, and a one-volume supplement covers volumes 81–100). Tables of treaties and tables of case names direct the researcher to specific cases. The subject index for volumes 1–35 of the reports has no subject entry under "family," whereas the subject index for volumes 36–80 has an entry for "family, protection of" with references to six cases, and the index for volumes 81–100 has an entry for "family life, respect for" with references to five cases.

Research in international family law is built first on a consideration of applicable treaties and their interpretation. Interpretative documents arise from the treaty-making process as well as from the cases in international and national courts that involve those treaties. While court decisions have limited authority as precedent in international law, they do reflect international practice of law and evidence of underlying customary principles.

Comparative and Foreign Law

There is growing academic interest in researching the laws of other nations (foreign law to anyone not from that country), as well as in researching the differences in legal systems and cultural contexts of law in those nations (comparative law). Treaty provisions invoked by private parties in national tribunals have also heightened consideration of foreign laws and comparative law concepts. The literature of foreign law and comparative law is massive, and generally, the researcher who needs a basic understanding of the law of a foreign country will seek information on the legal system, the cultural context in which it operates, and the primary sources of law. Examples of recent books[40] in English that provide these types of information include:

Richard A. Haigh & Lee Poh-York, Researching Australian Law (1997)

Herbert Hausmaninger, The Austrian Legal System (1998)

Paul Graulich et al., Guide to Foreign Legal Materials—Belgium, Luxembourg, Netherlands (1968)

Jacqueline R. Castel & Omeela K. Latchman, The Practical Guide to Canadian Legal Research. (2d ed. 1996)

Charles Szladits & Claire M. Germain, Guide to Foreign Legal Materials—French. (2d ed. 1985)

Nigel G. Foster, German Law & Legal System (1993)

David J. Stott, Legal Research (2d ed. 1999) (Great Britain & Wales)

Thomas O'Malley, The Round Hall Guide to the Sources of Law: An Introduction to Legal Research and Writing (1993) (Ireland)

---

39. International Law Reports, *supra* note 38, Editorial Note, vol. 118, ix–x.

40. In addition to books, there are hundreds of useful pamphlets, journal articles, and internet sites available to the researcher that summarize the legal systems and legal bibliography of individual countries.

Esther M. Snyder, Israel: A Legal Research Guide (2000)

Angelo Grisoli, Guide to Foreign Legal Materials—Italian (1965)

G. Leroy Certoma, The Italian Legal System (1985)

Meryll Dean, Japanese Legal System: Text and Materials (1997)

Francisco A. Avalos, The Mexican Legal System. (2d ed. 2000)

Margaret Greville & Scott Davison, Legal Research and Writing in New Zealand (2000)

Sung Yoon Cho, Law and Legal Literature of North Korea: A Guide (1988)

Heather Creech, A Guide to Legal Research in Papua New Guinea (1990)

Fortunato Gupit & Daniel T. Martinez, A Guide to Philippine Legal Materials: A Text on Philippine Legal Bibliography, Philippine Legal History, Philippine Legal System, Legal Philosophy, Methods of Legal Research (1993)

William E. Butler, Russian Law (1999)

Gennady M. Danilenko, Law and Legal System of the Russian Federation (2d ed. 2000)

Karen Fullerton & Megan Macgregor, Legal Research Skills for Scots Lawyers (1999)

James W. Colquhuon, Finding the Law: A Handbook for Scots Lawyers (1999)

Elena Merino-Blanco, The Spanish Legal System (1996)

Stig Strömholm, ed., An Introduction to Swedish Law (2d ed. 1988)

F. Dessemontet & T. Ansay, eds., Introduction to Swiss Law (2d rev. ed. 1995).

How a nation receives and incorporates treaty obligations into its legal system depends on the nature of the division of functions and powers between the legislative, judicial, and administrative branches of its government. Researchers must be wary in assuming too much about how the legal system operates in another nation.[41] For unfamiliar jurisdictions researchers may be hard-pressed to discover which branches of government deal with family law matters and how. Regardless of the type of legal system in a country, there are also conceptual differences in the appropriate scope of family law. In Germany, for example, matrimonial property is part of family law, while in France it is considered part of the law of property. Abortion, surrogate motherhood, rights of unmarried persons, same-sex marriages, and protection of children from violence are all subjects of interest in family law, but are not necessarily included in the statutory codifications, digests, or indexes devoted to family law.

Begun in 1980 and still in progress, the International Encyclopedia of Comparative Law is a monumental scholarly work that can provide the researcher with detailed background of family law issues from a comparative law perspective. Each chapter of each volume is a substantial, separately-published work. All of the chapters of volume 4 deal with family law.[42] Some chapters of volume 3 of the encyclope-

---

41. Civil law and common law systems are both traditions growing out of western European history. Their differences are not particularly useful in analyzing the organization of government and system of laws of different cultures of Asia and Africa, and religion-based governments, such as those of Islamic countries, that were not heavily influenced by European colonial rule.

42. Of the 11 chapters planned for volume 4, only chapter 5 dealing with divorce remains to be published. The published chapters are M. Rheinstein & R König, ch. 1, Introduction—The Family and the Law (1974); A. Heldrich et al., ch. 2, Persons (1995), dealing with the legal personality and

dia touch on conflicts of laws and other private international law concerns that affect the family.[43]

Eventually, the researcher is left with the daunting task of understanding international family law in the context of the various legal systems and laws of specific nations. Five resources, taken together, provide a beginning for finding the laws of a foreign country. Modern Legal Systems Cyclopedia[44] outlines the legal systems with individual narrative analyses for more than 175 countries. Another useful source is the International Encyclopedia of Laws, Family and Succession Law (Walter Pintens, ed., 1997), which contains extensive monographs on the national law of sixty countries and the international law of fourteen international organizations, and is supplemented regularly. Constitutions of the Countries of the World[45] provides the text of the constitutions of more than 180 countries. Text in the official language is always provided, and, when available, a translation in English is provided if the official language is not English. Foreign Law: Current Sources of Codes and Legislation[46] is a country-by-country bibliography of the major publications of statutory authority and court reports. The listings include citations to the official codifications of the civil code, code of civil procedure, commercial code, criminal code, and code of criminal procedure. For each country a subject guide cites to specific statutory acts, and 'family' is one of the subject terms used.[47] The Bibliography on Foreign and Comparative Law[48] is a comprehensive bibliography of foreign law, English language treatises, and periodical articles arranged by

---

capacity of parties, names, domicile and residence, nationality, and registration of civil status; D. Coester-Waltjen & M. Coester, ch. 3, Formation of Marriage (1997), including freedom to marry and the consequences of a defective marriage; M. Rheinstein & Mary Ann Glendon, ch. 4, Inter-spousal Relations (1980), surveying spousal ownership and control of property; H.D. Krause, ch. 6, Creation of Relationships of Kinship (1976), examining legitimacy and illegitimacy, ascertainment of paternity and maternity, adoption, and artifical insemination; S. Stoljar, ch. 7, Children, Parents, and Guardians (1974), addressing the care and protection of children, and the property, litigation and capacity of children; Salvatore Patti, ch. 9, Intra-Family Torts (1998), including torts between spouses and torts between parent and child; Marko Mladenovi, Marina Janji-Komar & Christa Jessel-Holst, ch. 10, The Family in Post-Socialist Countries (1998); P.H. Neuhaus et al., ch. 11, The Family in Religious and Customary Laws (1983), providing a survey of Christian, Jewish, Islamic, Hindu, and customary family law concepts.

43. Fewer than half of the 44 chapters planned for volume 3 are published. Lennart Pålsson, ch. 16, Marriage and Divorce (1978), and Christian von Bar, ch. 17, Personal Effects of Marriage (1986) are complete. Yet to be published are chapters 18–20, covering private international law problems of the effects of marriage, children, and succession.

44. Modern Legal Systems Cyclopedia, 10 vols. (Kenneth Robert Redden & Linda L. Schlueter, eds., 1984–), is published in compression binders and updated on a regular basis.

45. Constitutions of the Countries of the World, 20 vols. (A. P. Blaustein & G.H. Flanz, eds., Permanent ed. 1971–). The constitutions are published as pamphlets and stored alphabetically by country in compression binders.

46. Thomas H. Reynolds & Arturo A. Flores, Foreign Law: Current Sources of Codes and Legislation in Jurisdictions of the World. 6 vols. (1989–). Six times per year the compression binders are updated with new and revised material.

47. After locating citations to statutes and court decisions, the researcher can undertake the search for the text. Fortunately, a considerable amount of foreign law, including English translations, is available on the internet, and several law metasites provide electronic gateway access to the appropriate databases.

48. Szladits' Bibliography on Foreign and Comparative Law (Daniel L. Wade, S. Blair Kauffman & Tracy L. Thompson, comps. and eds., 1955–). Charles Szladits' began this bibliography in 1949, the first volume appearing in 1955 and covering 1790–1952. Subsequent bound volume 'supplements' cover additional chronological time periods, including the most recent three-volume update published in 2000 which covers 1995–1996.

subject with author and geographic indexes. The literature has grown so much that only books, and not periodical articles, were included beginning in 1991.[49] A variety of subject headings relating to family law are used: 'children law and legislation', 'marriage law and legislation', 'divorce law and legislation', and 'family policy.'

The researcher is well-prepared to begin research in international family law when bibliographic awareness is coupled with the ability to identify appropriate titles, to appreciate how differences in legal systems may affect research strategies and outcomes, and to locate the text of applicable treaties, constitutions, legislation, and court decisions of a particular jurisdiction. Expert opinions and factual setting both provide additional important information that facilitate researching particular issues.

Finding Facts and Expert Opinion

Acquiring the facts which give rise to a client's particular legal problems is essential for setting the context for the practicing attorney's legal research. Without facts, most legal issues are hypothetical debating points, and research lacks the direction needed to come to precise conclusions. Facts make legal research a manageable enterprise by grounding legal theory in reality. Any publication may be a source of facts, but the sources that stand out for finding facts of relevance to international law problems are the publications of international organizations and the publications of non-governmental organizations.

International government organizations (IGOs) are created by formal agreement among nations. They generate a tremendous number of documents and publications in fulfilling their mission. None are more productive than the United Nations and its affiliated agencies such as the United Nations Economic and Social Council (UNESCO), the International Labour Organization, the Food and Agriculture Organization, and the World Health Organization. Regional international organizations, such as the Council of Europe and the Organization of American States, also collect and disseminate large quantities of factual information. Depository libraries, commercial publishers, database services such as Westlaw and LexisNexis, and official internet sites all provide the researcher with access to IGOs' publications.[50]

Non-governmental organizations (NGOs) are typically created by private individuals, usually as non-profit corporations with particular goals and objectives. Many of the largest have established informal affiliations with their international government organization counterparts.[51] Although NGOs are not law-making bodies, they play an increasingly important role in drafting treaties, lobbying nations to sign and ratify them, and monitoring compliance.[52]

---

49. Subject access to periodical articles in English is provided by the same legal periodical indexes that had become the principal source for creating the bibliography. The bibliographic entries were unnecessarily duplicating the work of the indexes.

50. For a comprehensive overview of basic information about international organizations, how they operate, and what they publish, see Introduction to International Organizations (Lyonette Louis-Jacques & Jeanne S. Korman, eds., 1996).

51. For example, the NGO Global Network, at http://www.ngo.org, is an internet site maintained for NGOs associated with the United Nations. Links to affiliated NGOs are arranged by subject—13 links to NGOs under 'children and youth,' a link to the National Council on Family Relations under 'family,' nine links to 'human rights' NGOs, and nine links under 'status of women.'

52. For the role that non-governmental organizations play in international human rights activities, see NGOs and Human Rights: Promise and Performance (Claude E. Welch, Jr., ed., 2001). Citing other sources, the editor notes that "NGOs provide 85 percent of the information provided to the UN Centre for Human Rights...." Id. at 8. "NGOs are by far the main providers of information

There are hundreds of IGOs and NGOs relating to the protection of human rights. Some have a particular focus, such as women, children, and family. They have goals in advocacy, education, assistance, and fundraising that lead to the gathering of information and its distribution through internet sites, as well as through the publication of journals and books. For many publications there is no indexing, and bibliographic control is scant. Two directories provide assistance in locating international organizations.[53] Research starts with identifying the organizations that may provide relevant information.

The opinions of experts and scholars are valuable for their expressions of what the law is and what the law should be. In citing these writings as persuasive authority, the researcher must be careful to distinguish between an author's descriptive statements and normative pronouncements. The Restatement of Foreign Relations Law[54] is considered one of the most authoritative treatises on U.S. international law practice. It is not an official document and, as a secondary source of law, has no binding authority. Similarly, the Restatement of Conflict of Laws,[55] which also is accorded high authoritative value as a secondary source, details U.S. practice regarding issues of private international law.

Over 1300 English language journals are devoted to the publication of articles relating to law. Journal articles are the principal means of scholarly communication, and they provide the following: analysis of the law; economic, cultural, and historic background to legal issues; and citation to authorities which support the author's text. Several journals are devoted to particular subject areas, including family law and international law. These subject journals are shown on the list below. Omitted are the several additional journals relating to women's rights. This list has been compiled primarily to show which law periodical indexes cover their contents and which texts are available in Lexis-Nexis or Westlaw. The most significant point for a researcher to consider from the list is the bibliographic fact that no one index or commercial online source of text covers all of these journals. For comprehensive coverage of law journals, a sophisticated researcher must search all indexing sources.

Key

1	indicates the title is indexed in the Legal Resources Index, 1980 -
2	indicates indexing in the Index to Legal Periodicals, 1908 -
3	indicates indexing in the Index to Foreign Legal Periodicals, 1960 -
4	indicates indexing in the European Legal Journals Index, 1993 -
5	indicates indexing in the Legal Journals Index, 1986 -
W	indicates full text available in Westlaw
L	indicates full text available in LexisNexis

---

to the UN human rights system.... [I]f it had been dependent on governments, it would have ground to a halt long ago." Helena Cook, *Amnesty International at the United Nations, in* 'The Conscience of the World': The Influence of Non-Governmental Organisations in the UN System 198 (Pete Willetts, ed., 1996).

53. Yearbook of International Organizations (1948–) is an annual. The 38th edition for 2001/2002 is five volumes. Each entry for the 40,000+ organizations includes the organization's name, address, contact information, internet site addresses, history and goals, and publications by title. The Yearbook is also available as a fee-based internet site *at* http://www.uia.org/homeorg.htm.

The Encyclopedia of Associations: International Associations (1989–) is also an annual, providing similar information for nonprofit organizations that are international in scope. It is indexed by name of organization, keyword, location, and names of executive personnel.

54. Restatement (Third) of the Foreign Relations Law of the United States. 2 vols. (1987).

55. Restatement (Second) of the Conflict of Laws. 4 vols. (1971–1980).

Journals

	3 4 5			African Journal of International and Comparative Law, v. 1 - 1989 -
	3			African Journal of International Law
	3			African Yearbook of International Law, v. 1 - 1993 -
1 2 3				American Journal of Comparative Law, v. 1 - 1952 -
1 2				American Journal of Family Law, v. 1 - 1987 -
1 2 3		W L		American Journal of International Law, v. 1 - 1907 -
1 2		W L		American University International Law Review
2		W L		Annual Survey of International and Comparative Law, v. 1 - 1994 -
3				Arab Law Quarterly, v. 1 - 1985 -
				Asia-Pacific Journal on Human Rights and the Law, v. 1 - 2000 -
1 2		W L		Arizona Journal of International and Comparative Law, v. 1 - 1982 -
3				Asian Yearbook of International Law, v. 1 - 1991 -
1 2		L		Australian Journal of Family Law, v. 1 - 1986 -
1 2 3				Australian Year Book of International Law, v. 1 - 1965 -
3				Austrian Journal of Public and International Law,
3				Austrian Review of International and European Law, v. 1 -1996 -
1 2		W L		Berkeley Journal of International Law, v. 14 - 1996 - (continues International Tax and Business Lawyer, v. 1-13, 1983-1996)
1 2		W L		Boston College International and Comparative Law Review, v. 1 - 1977 -
1 2 3		W L		Boston College Third World Law Journal, v. 1 - 1980 -
1 2		W L		Boston University International Law Journal, v. 1- 1982 -
1 2				Brandeis Journal of Family Law, v. 37 - 1998 - (continues Journal of Family Law, v. 1-36, 1961-1997)
1 2 3 4 5				British Year Book of International Law, v. 1 - 1920 -
1 2		W L		Brooklyn Journal of International Law, v. 1 - 1975 -
2		W		Buffalo Human Rights Law Review, v. 4 - 1998 - (continues Buffalo Journal of International Law, v. 1-3, 1994-1997)
1 2		W L		California Western International Law Journal, v. 1 - 1970 -
1				Canadian Family Law Quarterly, v. 1 - 1986-
1 3				Canadian Human Rights Yearbook, 1983 -
1 2		W L		Canadian Journal of Family Law, v. 1 - 1978 -
1 2 3				Canadian Yearbook of International Law, v. 1- 1963 -
2		W L		Cardozo Journal of International and Comparative Law, v. 3 - 1995 - (continues New Europe Law Review, v. 1-2, 1993-1994)
1 2 3				Case Western Reserve Journal of International Law, v. 1 - , 1968 -
4 5				Child and Family Law Quarterly, v. 7 - 1995 - (continues Tolley's Child and Family Law Quarterly, v. 1-6, 1995)
1 2				Children's Legal Rights Journal, v. 1 - 1979 -
4 5				Childright
3				Chinese Yearbook of International Law and Affairs, v. 1 - 1981 -
1 2		W L		Columbia Human Rights Law Review, v. 4 - 1972 - (continues Columbia Survey of Human Rights Law, v. 1-3, 1967-1970)
1 2 3		W L		Columbia Journal of Transnational Law, v. 1 - 1961 -

	3					Comparative and International Law Journal of Southern Africa, v.1 - 1968 -
1				W	L	Connecticut Journal of International Law, v. 1 - 1985 -
1	2			W	L	Cornell International Law Journal, v. 1 - 1968 -
1	2			W	L	Denver Journal of International Law and Policy, v. 1 - 1971 -
1	2			W	L	Dickinson Journal of International Law, v. 1- 1983 -
1	2			W	L	Duke Journal of Comparative and International Law, v. 1 - 1991 -
		3				East African Journal of Peace and Human Rights, v. 1 - 1993 -
1	2			W	L	Emory International Law Review, v. 4 - 1990 - (continues Emory Journal of International Dispute Resolution, v. 1-3, 1986-1989)
			5	W		European Human Rights Law Review, 1995 -
	2 3 4 5					European Journal of International Law, v. 1 - 1990 -
1				W		Family Advocate, v. 1 - 1978 -
1	2			W		Family Court Review, v. 39 - 2001 - (continues Family and Conciliation Courts Review, v. 1-38, 1965-2000)
1		4 5				Family Law, v. 1 - 1971 -
		4 5				Family Law Bulletin
		4 5				Family Matters
		4 5				Family Mediation
1	2			W		Family Law Quarterly, v. 1 - 1967 -
1				W	L	Fletcher Forum on World Affairs, v. 1 - 1976 -
1	2			W	L	Florida Journal of International Law, v. 1 - 1984 -
1	2			W	L	Fordham International Law Journal, v. 1 - 1977 -
1						George Washington International Law Review, v. 33 - 2000 - (continues George Washington Journal of International Law and Economics, v. 1-32, 1968-1999)
1	2			W	L	Georgia Journal of International and Comparative Law, v. 1 - 1970 -
		3				German Yearbook of International Law, v. 1 - 1958 -
	3					Hague Yearbook of International Law, v. 1 - 1988 -
1	2			W	L	Harvard Human Rights Journal, v. 1 - 1988 -
1	2 3			W	L	Harvard International Law Journal, v. 1 - 1958 -
1	2			W	L	Hastings International and Comparative Law Review, v. 1 - 1977 -
1	2			W	L	Houston Journal of International Law, v. 1 - 1978 -
1						Human Rights, v. 1 - 1970 -
1						Human Rights Law Journal, v. 1 - 1980 -
		3				Human Rights Quarterly, v. 1 - 1979 -
1						Human Rights Review, v. 1 - 1999 -
1	2			W	L	ILSA Journal of International and Comparative Law, v. 1 - 1995 -
		3				Indian Journal of International Law, v. 1 - 1960 -
1	2			W	L	Indiana International and Comparative Law Review, v. 1 - 1991 -
1	2			W	L	Indiana Journal of Global Legal Studies, v. 1 - 1993 -
						Inter-American Juridical Yearbook, 1948 -
						Inter-American Yearbook on Human Rights, 1985 -

1 2 3					International and Comparative Law Quarterly, v. 1 - 1952 -
					International Children's Rights Monitor (Defence for Children International), v. 1 - 1983-
					International Court of Justice Yearbook, 1946 -
					International Family Planning Perspectives (Alan Guttmacher Institute), v.1 - 1979 -
		4 5			International Family Law, v. 1 - 1997 -
					International Journal of Child and Family Welfare, v. 1 - 1996 -
	3				International Journal of Children's Rights, v. 1 - 1993 -
					International Journal of Family and Marriage, v. 1 - 1993 -
	3				International Journal of Human Rights, v. 1 - 1997 -
1 2		4 5			International Journal of Law, Policy and the Family, v. 10 - 1996- (continues International Journal of Law and the Family, 1987-1995)
1			W L		International Legal Perspectives, v. 1 - 1987 -
					International Survey of Family Law, 1994 -
		4 5			Irish Journal of Family Law
	3				Islamic and Comparative Law Review, v. 1 - 1981 -
	3				Islamic Law and Society, v. 1 - 1994 -
	3				Israel Yearbook on Human Rights, v. 1 - 1971 -
	3				Italian Yearbook of International Law, v. 1 - 1975 -
	3				Japanese Annual of International Law, v. 1 - 1957 -
1 2 3					Journal of African Law, v. 1 - 1957 -
	3				Journal of Chinese and Comparative Law, v. 1 - 1995 -
	3				Journal of Islamic Law, v. 1 - 1996 -
1	3				Journal of Legal Pluralism and Unofficial Law, v. 19 - 1981 - (continues African Legal Studies, v. 1-18, 1969-1980)
					Journal of Malaysian and Comparative Law, v. 1 - 1974 -
		4 5			Journal of Social Welfare and Family Law, v. 1 - 1991 -
1			W L		Journal of the American Academy of Matrimonial Lawyers, v. 1 - 1985 -
	2		W		Journal of Transnational Law and Policy, v. 1 - 1992 -
1					Juvenile & Family Court Journal, v. 1 - 1978 -
	3				Korean Journal of International and Comparative Law, v. 1 - 1973 -
	3				Law and Anthropology, v. 1 - , 1986 -
1	3				Leiden Journal of International Law, v. 1 - 1988 -
1					Liberty, Life, and Family
1 2			W L		Loyola of Los Angeles International and Comparative Law Journal, v. 1 - 1978 -
	3	5			Maastricht Journal of European and Comparative Law, v. 1 - 1994 -
1 2 3			W L		Michigan Journal of International Law, v. 1 - 1978 -
	3				Netherlands International Law Review, v. 1 - 1953 -
		4 5			Netherlands Quarterly on Human Rights
	3				Netherlands Yearbook of International Law, v. 1 - 1970 -
1 2			W		New York International Law Review, v. 1 - 1987 -
1			W		New York Law School Journal of Human Rights, v. 1 - 1983 -

1			W	L	New York Law School Journal of International and Comparative Law, v. 1 - 1979 -
1	2	3	W		New York University Journal of International Law and Politics, v.1 - 1968 -
		3			Nihon University Comparative Law, v. 1 - 1983 -
		3			Nordic Journal of International Law, v. 1 - 1930 -
	2		W	L	Pace International Law Review, v. 1 - 1989 -
		3			Palestine Yearbook of International Law, v. 1 - 1984 -
	2	3			Parker School Journal of East European Law, v. 1 - 1994 -
		3			Philippine Yearbook of International Law, v. 1 - 1966 -
		3			Polish Yearbook of International Law, v. 1 - 1966 -
		3 4 5			Review of Central and East European Law, v. 18 - 1992 - (continues Review of Socialist Law, v. 1-17, 1975-1991)
		3			Scandinavian Studies in Law, v. 1 - 1957 -
	2	3			Singapore Journal of International and Comparative Law, v. 1 - 1997 -
		3			South African Human Rights Yearbook, v. 1 - 1990 -
		3			South African Journal on Human Rights, v. 1 - 1985 -
		3			South African Yearbook of International Law, v. 1 - 1975 -
		3			Spanish Yearbook of International Law, v. 1 - 1991 -
					Sri Lanka Journal of International Law, v. 1 - 1989 -
1	2	3	W	L	Stanford Journal of International Law, v. 1 - 1965 -
1	2		W	L	Suffolk Transnational Law Review, v. 1 - 1977 -
1	2		W	L	Temple International and Comparative Law Journal, v. 1 - 1985 -
1	2	3	W	L	Texas International Law Journal, v. 1 - 1965 -
1		3			Third World Legal Studies, v. 1 - 1982 -
1			W		Touro International Law Review, v. 1 - 1990 -
1	2		W	L	Transnational Law and Contemporary Problems, v. 1 - 1991 -
1	2		W	L	Tulane Journal of International and Comparative Law, v. 1 - 1993 -
	2		W	L	Tulsa Journal of Comparative and International Law, v. 1 - 1993 -
					United Nations Juridical Yearbook, 1962 -
1	2		W	L	Vanderbilt Journal of Transnational Law, v. 1 - 1967 -
1	2	3	W	L	Virginia Journal of International Law, v. 1- 1960 -
					Waseda Bulletin of Comparative Law, v. 1 - 1981 -
1	2		W	L	Wisconsin International Law Journal, v. 1 - 1982 -
1	2		W	L	Yale Journal of International Law, v. 10 - 1984 - (continues Yale Journal of World Public Order, v. 1-9, 1974-1983)
		5		L	Yearbook of European Law, v. 1 - 1981 -
					Yearbook/European Convention on Human Rights, 1958 -
					Yearbook on Human Rights, 1947 - , biennial beginning 1973/1974

Internet Resources

Because there is already so much legal material available on the web, a researcher might be led to two erroneous conclusions. The first one is that everything is already on the web, and the second is that everything there is easy to find. Although the number of sites increases every day, the primary law, legislation, court decisions and administrative law is simply not available in full text for every country. Most of the legal material available is from the United States, Canada, Australia, Latin America, and some European and developing countries.[56]

The second issue is that even if the information that a researcher is looking for is available on the web, it might be very difficult to locate.[57] Catalogs and search engines are the two tools available to researchers to locate legal materials on the web. Catalogs involve a human indexer classifying and sometimes briefly describing a web site. A couple of examples of annotated lists of legal sites are provided below. The sheer volume of material on the web means that any catalog will be selective. Search engines are programs that search the web and create indexes to the pages they locate. For a variety of reasons, described in the articles cited, general search engines search only about sixteen percent of the web, missing millions of pages of information. The question for the researcher is how to proceed. Using gateway or portal sites that have already identified relevant and significant sites for legal information is one option. Web sites which deal with a specific issue, such as human rights, also offer more focused research. Examples of both are provided below.

LLRX.com[58] is a free web journal with very up-to-date information on internet legal research. The site has several Resource Centers, including one on International/Foreign Law, which contains chapters written by librarians, attorneys, information technology specialists, and legal technology consultants. The site includes chapters on Researching U.S. Treaties and Agreements and Researching Non-U.S. Treaties. There is also a chapter on International Family Law: A Selective Resource Guide. These chapters cover print and internet resources in detail, with links to a wide variety of documents.

The American Society of International Law web site is a valuable tool for locating related web sites and also contains useful materials for the beginning researcher.[59] From the home page select "Resources"; this takes you to a list of information resources on international law, one of which is the ASIL Guide to Electronic Resources for International Law.[60] The Guide has chapters on the United Nations, Human Rights, Treaties, and Private International Law, among others. There is also an Introduction to the Guide, which covers researching international law on the internet and contains suggestions for evaluating the content you find. Each chapter includes "Quick Links," which are lists of links to additional relevant web sites for that topic. The Introduction includes in its "Quick Links" section a list of sources that evaluate legal web sites.

The Law Library of Congress site[61] has links to Guide to Law Online and the Global Legal Information Network (GLIN). The Guide is prepared by the Library of Congress for GLIN and is an annotated hypertext guide to government and legal information

---

56. Graham Greenleaf, *Solving the Problems of Finding Law on the Web: World Law and DIAL*, 29 Int'l J. Legal Info. 383–84 (2002). This author details why general search engines are inadequate.

57. This is because of the phenomenon of what has been called the deep or invisible web, which has been addressed in research and described in several articles. *See* Diana Botluk, Mining Deeper Into the Invisible Web, *at* http://www.llrx.com/features/mining.htm; Steven Whittle, *Finding Law in the 21st Century: An Introduction to the SOSIG Law Gateway*, 29 Int'l J. Legal Info. 360–82 (2002). Both authors cite the research of S. Lawrence and C.L. Giles, *Accessibility of Information on the Web*, 400 Nature 107 (July 8, 1999).

58. LLRX.com, *at* http://www.llrx.com.

59. ASIL, *at* http://www.asil.org.

60. *Id.*, *at* http://www.asil.org/resource/Home.htm.

61. Law Library of Congress, *at* http://lcweb2.loc.gov/lawweb/public/htdoc/index.html.

available free online. The Nations Guide has links to sources of information on nations from Afghanistan to Zimbabwe. The International and Multinational Guide leads to a section on Multinational Reference Sources. One of the sources is an article by Timothy Mulligan, Foreign and International Law Librarian at the University of Houston Law Center.[62] His object was to list only sites that contain foreign primary law either in the original language or a translation. Many of the foreign law sites offer digests of the law rather than full text, so the selectivity of this site makes it valuable to the researcher. GLIN[63] provides a database which contains summaries in English of laws, regulations, and other legal information of many countries. The documents are supplied by the governments of the member nations to the Library of Congress.

The University of Minnesota has developed an extensive Human Rights Library site which leads to treaties, UN documents, bibliographies, and research guides, and also has links to over 3,000 other sites that deal with various aspects of human rights.[64] The list of treaties purports to be "complete." The treaties are also organized by subject matter and are searchable by key word. The Bibliographies and Guides section includes both a bibliography and a guide on researching international human rights law. The links to other human rights sites are organized by documents, regions and specific topics, including Children and Human Rights and Women and Human Rights. There are also links to search engines that will search multiple human rights sites.

Cornell University's Legal Information Institute site has links to national law material as well as international law.[65] This site also has a selective guide to web sites, providing links to primary and secondary national legal materials, that includes brief annotations describing the organization of each site and pointing out noteworthy links. The University of Chicago Library site includes an extensive list of research resources and a list of recommended readings on Women in International Law.[66]

The Australasian Legal Information Institute has developed a portal site, AUSTLII,[67] which is attempting to develop "a world-wide catalog created by intellectual indexing effort, which at least catalogs significant national law sites in all countries world-wide and the major subject-oriented resources."[68] The World Law section of the site offers categories by country, region, subject, and type of material, such as law journals. The subject offerings include family law, which is further broken down by country, journals, indexes, Children, and Women & the Law. The World Law section has expanded with Project DIAL (Development of the Internet for Asian Law), funded by the Asian Development Bank. "Stored Searches" are a valuable feature of this site. The stored searches are created by the legal indexers who maintain the catalog, and whose search expertise will exceed that of most researchers. There are several stored searches on various topics under Family Law and Women & the Law. The stored searches can also be good starting points for research on the law of a specific

---

62. Mulligan, Timothy F., *Foreign Primary Law on the Web*, at http://www.law.uh.edu/librarians/tmulligan/foreignlaw.html.

63. GLIN, *at* http://www.loc.gov/law/glin.

64. University of Minnesota Human Rights Library, *at* http://www1.umn.edu/humanrts.

65. Legal Information Institute, *at* http:www.law.cornell.edu/world.

66. Women in International Law: Research Resources, *at* http:www.lib.uchicago.edu/~llou/women.html, written by Lyonette Louis-Jacques, Foreign and International Law Librarian and Lecturer in Law, University of Chicago Law School.

67. AUSTLII, *at* http://www.austlii.edu.au.

68. *See* Greenleaf, *supra* note 1, at 395.

country. All the pages in the World Law section have a "translate" button which leads the researcher to Alta Vista's automated translation service, Systran. The translation facility works from English to French, Spanish, Portuguese, Italian, and German, and back. It is useful for menu pages and lists and can translate search terms into another language.[69]

The Social Science Information Gateway (SOSIG), Law Gateway is a descriptive database of web legal information sources.[70] It is part of the United Kingdom's Resource Discovery Network initiative and is being developed by the University of London Institute of Advanced Legal Studies and the University of Bristol. The Project Manager indicates, "The service identifies and evaluates legal resource sites, offering descriptive records and links both to service cites publishing primary and secondary materials and to specific documents...."[71] The site offers a wide range of browsing and searching options. While it initially emphasized the United Kingdom and European Union countries, the range of countries covered is expanding. The record of each site includes the site title, keywords, url, and a description, which includes the source of the site, its authority, accuracy, and coverage.[72] Human Rights law is one of the topics under International Law, and the Subject Area section includes the topics Family Law, Human Rights, and Gender Law.

Conclusion

A research strategy requires focus on specific issues. The less research experience, the fewer facts, and the less contextual awareness the researcher has available, the more likely the researcher will flounder through the literature and end with opaque search results. The novice researcher should consider beginning research in secondary sources, such as periodical literature, where scholars and experts provide sound context, considered opinions, relevant facts, and citations to legal authority and precedent. Experienced researchers will already know reliable, accurate, and trustworthy sources on which they have conferred cognitive authority. For issues of international and comparative family law, they can more confidently start their research by locating applicable treaties and other binding authority.

No matter how good the research strategy, how insightful and knowledgeable the researcher, there remains the awareness and the fact that most legal research problems—especially in new and complicated areas such as international family law—have more resources to consult than the time or energy of the researcher will permit. If the researcher understands the law and authorities that apply to a particular problem, and if a coherent answer (with citation to relevant authorities) can be given to the specific legal questions involved, it is usually the sign that research on that problem can end.

---

69. See *Id.* at 397, 410–12, 414–15.
70. SOSIG, Law Gateway, *at* http:www.sosig.ac.uk/law.
71. See Whittle, *supra* note 2, at 360.
72. *See id.* at 369, 374–75.

Chapter 2

Regulation of Marriage

A. The Importance of Marriage

There is a perception that marriage is a nearly universal institution, regardless of time, place, or culture: "[A]ll societies, both past and present, prescribe marriage for the majority of their members. Marriage...is a universal social institution, and, although extramarital sexual contacts frequently are permitted, it is the marriage arrangement that is most strongly sanctioned for most men and women during most of their life spans." Harold T. Christensen, *Development of the Family Field of Study, in* Handbook of Marriage and the Family 3–4 (Harold T. Christensen ed., 1964). Marriage, of course, may not always take the form we know. For example, marriage may not be monogamous, but may be polygamous (having more than one spouse at a time). A polygamous marriage can be either polygynous (having multiple wives at the same time) or polyandrous (having multiple husbands at the same time). What binds the concept of "marriage" together cross-culturally, however, is that it is an institution in which individuals tend to live together in relations "of a more or less durable character." Edward Westermarck, The History of Human Marriage 14–15 (3d ed. 1903). In addition, marriage "nearly always" begins with "an elaborate ceremonial, which may include feasting, fancy dress, processionals, perhaps religious observances of some kind, and large-scale financial outlay by either the groom, the groom's parents, or the bride's parents. At the very least, bride and groom announce their marriage to society." William N. Stephens, The Family in Cross-Cultural Perspective 6 (1963). Another common feature of marriage cross-culturally is that this group-sanctioned status tends to confer obligations and benefits upon its members. Consider the following:

Claude Levi-Strauss, *The Family, in* Man, Culture, and Society
261, 268–70 (Harry L. Shapiro ed., 1956)

The important thing is that every society has some way to operate a distinction between free unions and legitimate ones. There are several levels at which that distinction is made.

In the first place, nearly all societies grant a very high rating to the married status. Wherever age-grades exist, either in an institutional way or as non-crystallized forms of grouping, some connection is established between the younger adolescent group and bachelorhood, less young and married without children, and adulthood with full rights, the latter going usually on par with the birth of the first child. This three-fold distinction was recognized not only among many primitive tribes but also in peasant western Europe, if only for the purpose of feasts and ceremonies, as late as the early twentieth century.

What is even more striking is the true feeling of repulsion which most societies have toward bachelorhood. Generally speaking it can be said that, among the so-called primitive tribes, there are no bachelors, simply for the reason that they could not survive. One of the strongest field recollections of this writer was his meeting, among the Boróro of central Brazil, of a man about thirty years old; unclean, ill-fed, sad, and lonesome. When asked if the man were seriously ill, the natives' answer came as a shock: what was wrong with him?—nothing at all, he was just a bachelor. And true enough, in a society where labor is systematically shared between man and woman and where only the married status permits the man to benefit from the fruits of woman's work, including delousing, body painting, and hair-plucking as well as vegetable food and cooked food (since the Boróro woman tills the soil and makes pots), a bachelor is really only half a human being.

This is true of the bachelor and also, to a lesser extent, of a couple without children. Indeed they can make a living, but there are many societies where a childless man (or woman) never reaches full status within the group, or else, beyond the group, in this all important society which is made up of dead relatives and where one can only expect recognition as ancestor through the cult, rendered to him or her by one's descendants. Conversely, an orphan finds himself in the same dejected condition as a bachelor. As a matter of fact, both terms provide sometimes the strongest insults existing in the native vocabulary. Bachelors and orphans can even be merged together with cripples and witches, as if their conditions were the outcome of some kind of supernatural malediction.

The interest shown by the group in the marriage of its members can be directly expressed, as it is the case among us where prospective spouses, if they are of marriageable age, have first to get a license and then to secure the services of an acknowledged representative of the group to celebrate their union. Although this direct relationship between the individuals, on the one hand, and the group as a whole, on the other, is known at least sporadically in other societies, it is by no means a frequent case. It is almost a universal feature of marriage that it is originated, not by the individuals but by the groups concerned (families, lineages, clans, et cetera), and that it binds the groups before and above the individuals. Two kinds of reasons bring about this result: on the one hand, the paramount importance of being married tends to make parents, even in very simple societies, start early to worry about obtaining a suitable mate for their offspring and this, accordingly, may lead to children being promised to each other from infancy. But above all, we are confronted here with that strange paradox...namely, that although marriage gives birth to the family, it is the family, or rather families, which produce marriage as the main legal device at their disposal to establish an alliance between themselves. As New Guinea natives put it, the real purpose of getting married is not so much to obtain a wife but to secure brothers-in-law. If marriage takes place between groups rather than individuals, a large number of strange customs become immediately clearer. For instance, we understand why in some parts of Africa, where descent follows the father's line, marriage only becomes final when the woman has given birth to a male child, thus fulfilling its function of maintaining her husband's lineage. The so-called *levirate* and *sororate* should be explained in the light of the same principle: if marriage is binding between two groups to which the spouses belong there can be without contradiction a replacement of one spouse by his brothers or by her sisters. When the husband dies, the levirate provides that his unmarried brothers have a preferential claim on his widow (or, as it is sometimes differently put, share in their deceased brother's duty to support his wife and children), while the sororate permits a man to marry preferentially in polygamous marriage his wife's sisters, or—when marriage is monogamous—to get a sister to replace the wife in case the latter remains childless, has to be divorced on account of bad conduct, or dies. But whatever the way in which the collectivity expresses its interest in the marriage of its members, whether through the authority vested in strong consanguineous groups, or more directly, through the intervention of the State, it remains true that marriage is not, is never, and cannot be a private business.

As the Levi-Strauss excerpt suggests, most societies have viewed marriage, at least until very recently, as an essential prerequisite to becoming a full member of society. In the United States, marriage has been called "the most important relation in life" and "the foundation of the family and of society, without which there would be neither civilization nor progress." Zablocki v. Redhail, 434 U.S. 374, 384 (1978) (quoting Maynard v. Hill, 125 U.S. 190 (1888)). Is marriage currently a prerequisite to becoming a full member of society in the United States? Do we view the never-married adult with a certain feeling of "repulsion?" Alternatively, are there economic or legal benefits conferred on married individuals that makes a single person "only half a human being?"

Levi-Strauss also mentions the "almost" "universal feature of marriage:" that marriage is "originated, not by the individuals but by the groups concerned," and that it "binds the groups before and above the individuals." For students of U.S. family law, it seems odd to suggest that marriage takes place between groups and not individuals. Yet the phenomenon Levi-Strauss identifies relates to the way "in which the collectivity expresses its interest in the marriage," and he admits that the collectivity's interest is also expressed "more directly, through the intervention of the State." Therefore, to the extent that there is commonality across time and culture, it is society's interest in marriage. What is society's interest in marriage today that justifies state intervention?

For Western nations, the strength of society's interest in the institution of marriage is manifested, in part, by the level of state regulation. Mary Ann Glendon, reviewing the law in the United States, England, France, and former West Germany, commented upon the "significant deregulation of the formation of marriage" that has occurred from the 1800s forward. She suggests that this deregulation "might be seen as an indication of the declining importance of marriage as a determinant of social standing and economic security in modern societies." *See* Mary Ann Glendon, The Transformation of Family Law 35 (1989).

Another indication of a society's interest in the institution of marriage is the magnitude of benefits individuals receive upon marrying. In this respect, some countries' interest in marriage also appears to be waning to some extent. "Evolution of legal policy on unmarried heterosexual cohabitation is entering a new phase in West-European jurisdictions." David Bradley, *Regulation of Unmarried Cohabitation in West-European Jurisdictions—Determinants of Legal Policy*, 15 Int'l J.L., Pol'y & Fam. 22, 22 (2001). Simply, the legal differences between marriage and cohabitation are declining. "This development takes two forms: enactment of a comprehensive status for cohabitation or, alternatively, a major extension of statutory rights involving, for example, support and property adjustment." *Id.* at 23. A good example is the registered partnership law in the Netherlands, enacted in 1997. That law makes marriage and partnership virtually equivalent, with some minor exceptions (for example, partners are not eligible for a judicial separation). *Id.* at 28–33. This particular law will be explored more in Chapter Four, which addresses the rights and obligations of non-marital partners.

Yet, to this day, legal differences between marriage and cohabitation still exist in most countries. "In practically all European jurisdictions, cohabitation does not lead to a legally recognized status." Barbara E. Graham-Siegenthaler, *Principles of Marriage Recognition Applied to Same-Sex Marriage Recognition in Switzerland and Europe*, 32 Creighton L. Rev. 121, 126 (1998). While "parties are generally free to make contractual arrangements and can stipulate that the rules that apply to married couples on marriage breakdown apply to them," those rules do not apply automatically merely as a result of the parties' status. *Id.* Differences also continue even in countries that have enacted legislation that affords cohabitants significant legal benefits. For example, the Pacte Civil de Solidarité, enacted by France in 1999, provides registration of an opposite-sex or same-sex couple, and affords certain benefits like "mutual material assistance" and "liability to creditors for household debts." Yet there is no provision in the law regulating cohabitants' obligations for maintenance at the relationship's end, for property succession upon death of one of the parties, or for automatic tax concessions. *Id.* at 33–34.

As demographics change in "many western, common-law derived jurisdictions," the coveted status of marriage will continue to be challenged. *See* John Dewar, *Family Law and its Discontents*, 14 Int'l J.L., Pol'y & Fam. 59, 60 (2000).

> Marriage is a convenient conceptual device for making families visible in law, provided that most family life is conducted within marriage.... The growth in extra-marital cohabitation, and in the numbers of children born outside marriage, has had two consequences, both of which have decentered marriage as a legal concept. The first is growing practical and political pressure to grant non-marital relationships some form of legal "recognition." The second is an increased prominence for the legal status of parenthood.

Id. at 62.

Given these observations—the deregulation of marriage formation, the extension of marital-like benefits to alternative family forms, and the pronounced demographic changes—it is, perhaps, as Professor Glendon notes, somewhat of a paradox that over the same period of time one has seen the legal recognition of marriage as a basic human right. *See* Glendon, *supra*, at 35. Also, somewhat paradoxically, one has witnessed powerful institutions both within and outside of nations competing to regulate the institution. Marriage, in most places today, is still worthy of the fight.

This chapter examines four topics related to the legal institution of marriage. First, the chapter explores which groups or institutions in society regulate marriage and how various conflicts are managed. Second, the chapter focuses on procedural requirements for entering the marital state and raises questions about how entrance into marriage can and should be regulated. Third, the chapter looks at the substantive impediments that can exist to marriage, but does so only briefly because Chapters Four and Five address the topic. Finally, the chapter considers the practice of finding a spouse through an international "mail-order" service and uses the topic to expand and apply much of the foregoing material in this chapter.

B. The Power to Regulate Marriage

Marriage is often regulated by one or more powerful institutions in society; these institutions can include the central government, cultural communities, and religious entities. Professor Wardle makes the point that conflict between these powerful forces in society can occur regardless of whether the legal system is "pluralistic" (*i.e.*, civil, customary, and religious law coexist and regulate marriage), "federal" (*i.e.*, power is divided between a central government and other autonomous, yet constituent, governmental units) or "unitary" (*i.e.*, the geographical entity has one general body of law). *See* Lynn D. Wardle, *International Marriage and Divorce Regulation and Recognition: A Survey*, 29 Fam. L.Q. 497, 499 (1995). Today the institutions regulating marriage, or attempting to regulate marriage, are not merely within a country's borders, but include international organizations associated with the human rights system. We first consider some of the potential conflicts within municipal systems; we will then return to explore international-municipal conflicts at the end of this section.

The topic has particular relevance for American students for a multitude of reasons. On a practical level, our courts are occasionally asked to recognize customary marriages or religious marriages; these marriages can occur either in other countries or within our own country. In addition, sometimes our courts are also asked to give effect to terms in prenuptial agreements that are premised on customary or religious law. Therefore, knowing something about these systems of law, and recognizing the difficulties inherent in knowing something about these systems of law, is beneficial. On a more theoretical level, however, the topic raises a host of questions that are relevant to issues that we in the United States are currently facing with respect to the regulation of marriage and the family. By reflecting more broadly on who in society should be regulating marriage and the values that undergird marriage regulation, we can think more deeply about common law marriage, Native American tribal marriages, federal marriage initiatives (including the Defense of Marriage Act), the domestic relations exception to diversity jurisdiction, and international efforts to regulate marriage.

1. Customary Law

One level of lawmaking related to marriage occurs in some countries under the rubric of "customary law." Customary law refers to the recognized legal practices within a community as opposed to the state-created legislative or judicial law. Systems vary in the amount of formal recognition they give to customary law. For those countries that recognize customary marriages, there are logistical questions about how one proves either the existence of a customary marriage or even the content of customary law. Customary marriage also evokes the general question, "Which group in society should be responsible for marriage regulation?"

David L. Chambers, *Civilizing the Natives: Marriage in Post-Apartheid South Africa,*
129 Daedalus 101–24 (2000)

South Africa is a Land of Many Cultures

For several hundred years, British and Afrikaaner whites controlled the country, systematically manipulating black people to the whites' advantage. For the most part, however, whites tolerated the continuation within black communities of traditional marriage practices that white Christians considered uncivilized. In 1994, South Africa changed governments. A black majority Parliament came to power, adopting a constitution dedicated to equality and human dignity. Four years later, Parliament adopted a new marriage law that, though permitting some of the external trappings of the traditional marriage system to continue, eliminated by law much of the core of its male-centered rules.

From the point of view of the legislators who voted for it, the new law was required in order to promote gender equality under the new constitution. From the point of view of traditional leaders and some other rural dwellers, the new law was unjustifiable because it failed to honor black people's traditions in a new black South Africa....

The Customary Rules and Practices

About 78 percent of South Africa's population is black, about 12 percent is white, and the rest is primarily Indian or of mixed race, called "coloured." Nearly half of all black Africans still live in rural areas, the great majority in traditional groups headed by hereditary kings or chiefs and by headmen and subchiefs. The largest of these groups are the Zulu, the Xhosa, the Pedi, the Sotho, the Tswana, the Tsonga, and the Swazi. All are hierarchically organized, and, in nearly all, only men can be chiefs or senior counselors.

Each of these cultural groups has its own customs and rules—rituals and practices at birth, at the coming of age, at marriage, and at death. Indeed, within each group are subgroups with their own variations. The customary rules are not unalterable. Though certain common patterns persist through time, the actual content of rules—the so-called customary law—is revealed at any given time through the practices of the people who live by them, and practices change with changing conditions. Whether these practices are appropriately regarded as "law" is debatable, for they have no definitive textual form and are modified over time by the actions of those who adhere to them. Still, Africans of all sorts speak as if these practices were "law," and, as we will see, South Africa's new constitution itself directs courts to apply "customary law" in appropriate circumstances. The chiefs, of course, also believe in customary laws and consider themselves the authoritative voice of their content. They or other senior leaders preside over local customary courts where they apply their view of the "law" to resolve disputes. Most black South Africans who live in rural areas follow customary practices in their daily lives. For them, the chiefs still play central roles as the keepers and promoters of traditions and as political leaders. In last year's parliamentary elections, for example, the presidential candidates of all the major national political parties courted the traditional chiefs because they believed that the chiefs could deliver large numbers of votes.

During the years of white rule, the only sort of coupling relationship denominated as "marriage" by law was the form of Christian or civil marriage that white people practiced. The rules for entry into civil marriage and the legal consequences of it are similar to those in the United States....

During the twentieth century, black South Africans who wished to marry had a choice. They could marry under civil law, and indeed, by the mid-twentieth century, many black Christians did so. (Most blacks who married under civil law also observed some customary marriage rituals as well.) The remaining black South Africans, probably close to a majority even today, marry solely within the customary group of which they consider themselves a part.

The customary rules determining how a marriage is formed vary widely across groups but share common characteristics, many of which reach back many centuries.

At root, customary marriage marks not the joining of two individuals but the joining of two families or two kinship groups and is a vehicle for ensuring the continuation of the male's family line. In nearly all groups, the groom or members of his family enter into highly stylized negotiations with the parents of the bride and agree on an amount of bridewealth, called lobolo, bogadi, and various other names (hereafter, lobolo), that the groom will convey to the parents of the bride. In the past, the lobolo was nearly always paid in cattle. Today the parties nearly always agree on a sum of money, though the amount is still commonly determined by the current cost of a certain number of cows. The equivalent of several hundred American dollars would be a common figure. That is a very large sum for most black South African men in their twenties.

Upon payment of all or part of the lobolo, the performance of ceremonies that vary widely, and, in some groups, a period of cohabitation or the birth of a child, the couple is considered married within their customary group. They were never, however, considered "married" under the laws of South Africa. Instead, they were treated as partners in a mere "customary union," which was a legally recognized relationship that carried consequences for pensions, taxation, and so forth, but civil "marriage" was accorded higher legal status.[4]

Just as the rules of lobolo were determined by customary law, so too were most of the consequences of a customary marriage. As a broad generalization, in nearly all these groups, a woman upon marriage became a part of the husband's family and shifted from living under the control of her father to living under the control of her husband, her mother-in-law, and the head of her husband's family. Any children of the marriage became part of the husband's family. She had no power to enter into contracts or to own property in her own name. She could appear in a tribunal only through her husband or the head of her husband's family. Her husband was free to marry additional women, but she was not free to marry additional men. If a wife left the marriage, her parents would usually be expected to repay or return all or part of the lobolo, and any children would remain with the husband or his family. If she outlived her husband, she would not inherit his property. Rather, a male member of his biological family—his oldest son, his brother, his father—was considered the only appropriate heir, though the heir was obliged to provide in some way for the widow. In some groups, the widow was expected to marry another male member of her husband's family, especially if she had not yet borne any children. This was the custom of levirate marriage.

The cornerstone of the customary marriage system is the lobolo transaction. Lobolo retains positive and complex meaning to most black Africans, including most urban black Africans. It stands variously as a symbol that the wife is valued, as a mark of the bond between families, as compensation to the bride's parents for the cost and effort to raise her, and, today, as a symbol of continuity with African traditions. For married women, it remains an important source of status in both rural and urban areas, despite the fact that some practices, such as levirate marriage, grow out of a view that the husband's family, through the payment of lobolo, has acquired the woman's reproductive capacity (yet another "meaning" of lobolo).

---

4. Thus, for example, a person in customary union could invalidate the union by entering into a civil marriage with someone else, but not vice versa. Bennett, Application of Customary Law in Southern Africa, 172–182.

Do women who live in rural customary groups today lead lives of subordination and degradation? That is a difficult question to answer, not solely because of the difficulty of deciding what should count as a degrading life. I have done no empirical work of my own in the rural areas, and though many studies have been written about the experiences of black South African women, few are available that are recent and methodologically rigorous. It is certainly easy to find accounts from the twentieth century of women who saw themselves as having been "sold" by their fathers to an older man they did not know, who experienced intercourse with him as a physical violation, and who were treated much like a servant. At the same time, most accounts of women's lives are mixed but more positive. H. J. Simons, one of the most thoughtful white South African observers of customary practices, believed that in circumstances in which rural husbands and wives lived in an extended family of the husband's, most women, while not equals, were at least "junior partners in a joint family enterprise." The system of rules, when it worked, ensured that no woman was without a man responsible for her well-being. And, during the marriage, especially after bearing children, women typically exercised considerable authority in the operation of their households. The beleaguered new wife became the powerful mother-in-law a generation later. Customary unions continued to be potentially polygamous, but fewer and fewer men could afford second wives.

By the mid-twentieth century, however, large numbers of black Africans no longer lived in rural settings or in extended family arrangements, and the practice of male control of wealth no longer matched many urban or rural women's lives or needs. Many black women lived in cities and worked in the labor force—primarily as domestic workers—were paid directly by their employers, and controlled the income they earned. Large numbers of rural men worked in the cities or mines and provided neither support nor protection for their wives who remained in the country. Polygamy was frequently a warped parody of its earlier form: many men took a wife in the country, then moved to the city, leaving wife and children behind, and married again.

By moving to the cities, many women (and young men) largely evaded the control of the male elders, but many rural women still suffered under the old practices. Some stayed in marriages they wanted to leave because of pressure from their fathers, who sided with their husbands and who did not want to return lobolo. Others were left without resources on the death of their husbands when a male relative of the husband claimed the family assets but failed to provide for the widow's care. Moreover, the tradition of male dominance, coupled with the decline of extended family living arrangements, has probably contributed to the extremely high levels of physical abuse to which African men subject their wives.

To be sure, among white South Africans married under civil law, it is equally debatable whether wives experience the equality in their relationships that the official rules now proclaim. In South Africa as elsewhere, white men earn more than white women, and neither British nor Afrikaaner South African men are known for egalitarian attitudes toward marriage. Still, by the 1990s, married women were formal equals under the common-law rules but not under the customary practices.

Dominance and Tolerance

The story of the positions South African colonial settlers took toward customary rules and practices during the nineteenth and twentieth centuries is far too complex to relate in a short essay. As a broad generalization, the British and Afrikaaner settlers regarded black African marital practices as barbaric—at worst, lobolo as a transaction in which a man sold his daughter into slavery, polygamy as uncurbed lust—but in the end, colonial and settler governments generally tolerated the practices because, in a context in which blacks greatly outnumbered whites, tolerance was consistent with efficient administration.... As part of their system of control, the British government created special "native" courts to apply customary law in disputes between black South Africans. In some parts of the country, the customary rules were codified by British lawmakers, who learned the rules from chiefs and other headmen and rendered them into English legal language that was often inaccurate in translation and often more male-centered than actual practice. Courts routinely applied these codified customary rules, but, even so, there were limits on the degree to which they were willing to give such rules legal effect. In each of the ordinances and statutes that authorized courts to apply customary laws in suits between blacks, a proviso always directed the court not to do so when it found a particular custom "repugnant to the general principles of humanity recognized throughout the whole civilized world" or "opposed to the principles of public policy or natural justice." In addition, the same courts refused to treat women within customary unions as wives for purposes of certain common law and statutory benefits....

By the late twentieth century, courts rarely invoked the repugnancy clauses and Parliament had extended some statutory benefits of civil marriage to spouses in customary unions. The unions of rural black people were accepted as "marriages" by all the people who mattered to them, and, for most, the state recognized their relationship in the few contexts in which it made any difference. Unlike the U.S. government in its campaign against the Mormon church in the late nineteenth century, the whites in South Africa, however brutal their policies, never declared polygamy a crime for people living in customary unions, never prosecuted and imprisoned thousands of polygamists or drove thousands of others into hiding, and never sought to remove the children of polygamous parents on the grounds that their practices were inherently harmful.

The New Constitutional Order

After World War II, the Afrikaaner-led National Party won control of South Africa's government and, over time, imposed its apartheid policy of rigid segregation. Blacks ceased to be citizens of South Africa. Those who were needed by whites for labor were forced to live as migrants at the mines or in all-black townships outside the cities, and those who were not needed were relegated to "homelands" ruled by black leaders who were in large part puppets of the South African government. In 1994, after years of internal struggle and international condemnation, the National Party agreed to relinquish control to the black majority. Parliament adopted a new constitution, called the Interim Constitution, hammered out between the National Party and the African National Congress (ANC) with the participation of other smaller parties, and the homelands were reabsorbed into South Africa. The promulgation of the Constitution led directly to the elections in 1994 in which black South Africans, voting for the first time, brought a black-controlled government into power. Two years later, in 1996, a Final Constitution was adopted, drafted by a committee of Parliament dominated by the ANC.

The Interim and Final Constitutions sound many themes—individual freedom, human dignity, universal suffrage, reconciliation between racial groups, a parliamentary system of government—but no theme is sounded more forcefully than that of equality. That is hardly a surprise given the nation's sordid history. Somewhat surprising to many, however, is that the new constitutions emphasize equality based on sex as strongly as they do equality based on race. The prominent place of sex equality grew out of the ANC's adoption in the 1960s of Western human-rights ideology as well as the participation of South African women and women's groups in the anti-apartheid liberation efforts and in the negotiations over the Constitution....

The Constitutions' drafters were well aware of the potential impact of the equality clauses on the gender-based family rules of the customary groups. So too were the traditional leaders. In the deliberations, the leaders advocated that customary rules, and particularly customary family rules, be treated as a separate system of laws exempt from the Constitution. The chiefs and other traditional leaders argued that traditional ways, tolerated but demeaned during apartheid, deserved to be embraced in a new black nation.

As eventually adopted, however, the Interim and Final Constitutions took a quite different approach to the customary leaders and customary rules....

Thus, in the end, the Final Constitution, adopted by a black majority Parliament, reflects a mixed view of blacks' own traditional cultures. On the affirming side, the Final Constitution declares that the country's official languages, formerly Afrikaans and English, were now to be "Sepedi, Sesotho, Setswana, Siswati, Tshivenda, Xitsonga, Afrikaans, English, isiNdebele, isiXhosa, and isiZulu." The Constitution further guarantees to all the right "to participate in the cultural life of their choice" and directs courts to "apply customary law when that law is applicable." It even provides that "the institution, status, and role of traditional leadership, according to customary law, are recognized." On the other hand, the Constitution simultaneously makes customary rules and the traditional leaders subordinate to Parliament and the Bill of Rights. Yes, all citizens have the right to participate in the cultural life of their choice, "but," continues the same provision, "no one exercising these rights may do so in a manner inconsistent with any provision of the Bill of Rights," and the traditional leadership may continue to hold their offices but "subject to the Constitution." And yes, courts are to apply customary law, but they are to do so "subject to the Constitution and any applicable legislation that specifically deals with customary law." Customary law, that is, may be changed by Parliament as freely as it can change judge-made common law or its own prior legislation.

Given these constitutional provisions, it may appear that the old gender-based customary family rules must be rejected today as unconstitutional, inconsistent with the equality clause of the Bill of Rights. And perhaps the new Constitutional Court will someday so hold. But remember that the Constitution does not prohibit all discrimination, only discrimination that is "unfair." And even "unfair discrimination" (an elusive notion under the court's early jurisprudence) will be tolerated if the state can demonstrate that a discriminatory regulation comes within the terms of a general limitations clause in the Constitution that permits restricting any of the rights in the Bill of Rights "to the extent that the limitation is reasonable and justifiable in an open and democratic society based on human dignity, equality, and freedom."

The Recognition of Customary Marriages Act of 1998

In November of 1998, four years after coming to power, Parliament adopted new legislation regarding customary marriage....

As adopted, the first substantive section of the act—called the Recognition of Customary Marriages Act of 1998—declares that all customary unions entered into in the past are relabeled "marriages" and that, for the future, all customary marriages that comply with the provisions of the act are valid. The rest of the act regulates the content of customary marriage. Three themes dominate. The first is to ensure that each partner truly chooses to marry. Marriage must be with "consent." The second is to declare women and men formal equals within the marriage relationship. In the absence of a prenuptial contract, spouses in customary marriages will be treated as holding property equally as community property. Married women are given the power to acquire and dispose of assets, to enter into contracts, and to litigate in their own names. The final theme is to inject the state bureaucracy into the regulation of customary marriages, first by requiring that all marriages be registered with a government agency and second by permitting divorce only when it is granted by a family court judge. The judge will divide the couple's property, award alimony where appropriate, and decide which parent is the more appropriate custodian for the children.

Within this structure, some important aspects of customary marriage are permitted to continue. Most significantly, the customary groups are free to retain lobolo as a condition of a valid marriage. In addition, child marriage can still occur if a group's rules permit it and if, in the particular case, the child "consents" and both parents concur. Levirate marriage—the widow's marrying of her late husband's brother—can still occur as long as the widow consents.

And even polygyny is permitted to continue as long as the interests of the first wife are protected. A man may have a valid second marriage during the course of a first marriage as long as he enters into a written contract with his first wife fairly dividing the property accrued to that point and persuades a family court, after a hearing, that the contract is equitable to everyone concerned.

How much of customary marriage remains? If lobolo is the heart of customary marriage, customary marriage still has its heart. If polygyny is of symbolic importance even if in decline, it too survives. From another perspective, however, the new act maintains the trappings of customary marriage but empties it of most of its content. Women are now the formal equals of men. Customary courts no longer have any formal authority to resolve disputes. The act replaces a patriarchal view of marriage with a partnership view. Even the polygamy provision is structured to make sure that the first wife or wives get their full share of the partnership out of the marriage up to that point. And, although customary courts may perform mediation, they cease to have any formal authority to order a resolution of a marital dispute.

Notes and Questions

1. *Then and Now.* What is your assessment of the outcome in South Africa? Does it sufficiently protect black peoples' traditions? How does the process by which change was achieved affect your view of the outcome? Consider, for example, that the constitutional drafters included members of customary groups who were elected as black members of Parliament. However, the African National Congress (ANC) "dominated" the Committee of Parliament that drafted the final Constitution, and the ANC was not a proponent of customary law. The Parliament that drafted the Recognition of Customary Marriages Act of 1998 was comprised of a majority of black members, although the Parliament is not elected by districts. Rather, candidates are chosen by their parties and voters can vote only for the party. Consequently, tribal candidates have been underrepresented in Parliament. Chambers, *supra.*

2. *Constitutional Right to Marry and to Family Life.* The South Africa Constitution does not encompass the right to freely marry and establish a family life, a right popular

in various other countries' constitutions and in various international instruments. *See, e.g.,* Namibian Constitution § 14(3) (providing for the protection of the family as the basic unit of society). The Constitutional Court of South Africa set forth the benefits of not having such a provision when it assessed whether the final Constitution of South Africa was in accordance with various Constitutional Principles set forth in Schedule 4 of the interim Constitution. The Constitutional Court had to find compliance with the Constitutional Principles before the final Constitution could become effective and replace the interim Constitution. Constitutional Principle II required that everyone must enjoy "all universally accepted fundamental rights, freedoms and civil liberties" and that such rights must be "protected by entrenched and justiciable provisions in the Constitution." The Constitutional Court of South Africa was not troubled by the omission of a right to family life. The following excerpt sets forth the Court's opinion on the matter. Its use of the term "New Text" refers to the final Constitution in its draft form:

> From a survey of international instruments it is clear that, in general, states have a duty, in terms of international human rights law, to protect the rights of persons freely to marry and to raise a family. The rights involved are expressed in a great variety of ways with different emphases in the various instruments. Thus the African Charter on Human and Peoples' Rights expressly protects the right to family life (article 18), but says nothing about the right to marriage. Similarly the Convention on the Elimination of All Forms of Discrimination against Women departs from many other international documents by emphasizing rights of free choice, equality and dignity in all matters relating to marriage and family relations (article 16), without referring at all to the family as the basic unit of society.

> A survey of national constitutions in Asia, Europe, North America and Africa shows that the duty on the states to protect marriage and family rights has been interpreted in a multitude of different ways. There has by no means been universal acceptance of the need to recognize the rights to marriage and to family life as being fundamental in the sense that they require express constitutional protection.

> The absence of marriage and family rights in many African and Asian countries reflects the multi-cultural and multi-faith character of such societies. Families are constituted, function and are dissolved in such a variety of ways, and the possible outcomes of constitutionalising family rights are so uncertain, that constitution-makers appear frequently to prefer not to regard the right to marry or to pursue family life as a fundamental right that is appropriate for definition in constitutionalised terms. They thereby avoid disagreements over whether the family to be protected is a nuclear family or an extended family, or over which ceremonies, rites or practices would constitute a marriage deserving of constitutional protection. Thus, some cultures and faiths recognize only monogamous unions while others permit polygamy. These are seen as questions that relate to the history, culture and special circumstances of each society, permitting of no universal solutions.

> International experience accordingly suggests that a wide range of options on the subject would have been compatible with [Constitutional Principle II]. On the one hand, the provisions of the [New Text] would clearly prohibit any arbitrary state interference with the right to marry or to establish and raise a family. [New Text] 7(1) enshrines the values of human dignity, equality and freedom, while [New Text] 10 states that everyone has the right to have their

dignity respected and protected. However these words may come to be interpreted in the future, it is evident that laws or executive action resulting in enforced marriages, or oppressive prohibitions on marriage or the choice of spouses, would not survive constitutional challenge. Furthermore, there can be no doubt that the [New Text] prohibits the kinds of violations of family life produced by the pass laws or the institutionalized migrant labour system, just as it would not permit the prohibitions on free choice of marriage partners imposed by laws such as the Prohibition on Mixed Marriages Act 55 of 1949.

On the other hand, various sections in the [New Text] either directly or indirectly support the institution of marriage and family life. Thus, [New Text] 35(2)(f)(i) and (ii) guarantee the right of a detained person to communicate with, and be visited by, his or her spouse or partner and next of kin.

There are two further respects in which the [New Text] deals directly with the issue, and both relate to family questions of special concern. The first deals with the rights of the child, wherein the right to family and parental care or appropriate alternative care is expressly guaranteed ([New Text] 28(1)(b)). The second responds to the multi-cultural and multi-faith nature of our country. [New Text] 15(3)(a) authorizes legislation recognizing "marriages concluded under any tradition or a system of religious, personal or family law," provided that such recognition is consistent with the general provisions of the [New Text].

In sum, the [Constitutional Assembly] was free to follow either those states that expressly enshrined protection of marriage and family rights in their constitutions, or else those that did not. It took a middle road and, in the circumstances, the objection cannot be sustained.

In re Certification of the Constitution of the Republic of South Africa, 1996 (4) SA 744, at ¶¶ 97–103. (S. Afr.) The Court's analysis was further described by Justice Albie Sachs of the Constitutional Court of South Africa:

We did a study of constitutions throughout the world and came up with interesting results. Many constitutions contain clauses expressly defending the family and a right to create a family, and there are enormous variations within that, but many constitutions do not. Germany has a clause, Austria does not; Pakistan has, India does not; China has, Taiwan and Singapore do not. There is no automatic correspondence even with national origin or history. It is an option that constitution makers have. And the reason we felt that so many countries do not constitutionalise the family and family law is that the very nature of the family, particularly in multicultural and multifaith societies, is so diverse that it is best to leave the fundamental rights and liberties in relation to family life to the basic principles of freedom, security and choice. Then, through legislation, the development of precedent in the courts, social custom and practice, the different forms of family life will manifest themselves and be appropriately protected.... The minute you constitutionalise the family, the courts are obliged to establish a prototype of what is meant by the family, and families take on such diverse forms in South Africa that this could impose a straitjacket on future development.

Justice Albie Sachs, *Introduction, in* The Changing Family: International Perspectives on the Family and Family Law xii–xiii (John Eekelaar & Thandabantu Nhlapo eds., 1998). Who does Justice Sachs think should, and should not, be regulating marriage? What does Justice Sachs mean when he suggests that the law will "appropriately protect" different forms of family life? Would a constitutional right to marry and raise a family potentially invalidate portions of the Recognition of Customary Marriage Act of 1998? Does the omission of a constitutional right to marry or to establish and raise a family free South African courts from ever having to establish a prototype of the "family"? The courts in the United States have not been spared the task despite the U.S. Constitution's silence regarding the right to marry and raise a family. *See* Village of Belle Terre v. Boraas, 416 U.S. 1 (1974) (upholding ordinance that restricted land use to one-"family" dwellings and precluded six college students from living together); Moore v. City of East Cleveland, 431 U.S. 494 (1977) (invalidating housing ordinance that defined "family" to exclude grandmother, her son, her son's son, and another grandson).

3. *Registration.* When countries permit marriage by customary means, they sometimes adopt mechanisms to minimize the logistical problems involved with proving that such marriages exist. Sometimes, as in South Africa, customary marriages must be registered. Lack of registration may mean the marriage is not recognized at all, or it is recognized only for limited purposes. For example, in Zimbabwe, unregistered customary law unions are not valid, except for the purposes of status, guardianship, and rights of succession of children. Consequently, an individual may be denied certain benefits afforded to married couples. *See* David M. Bigge & Amelie von Briesen, Note, *Conflict in the Zimbabwean Courts: Women's Rights and Indigenous Self-Determination in Magaya v. Magaya,* 13 Harv. Hum. Rts. J. 289, 310 n.97 (2000) (citing section 3 of the African Marriages Act). In South Africa, failure to register does not affect the validity of a customary marriage. Chambers, *supra.*

4. *Registration Problems.* There is some question whether the South African registration system will be effective. "There is, said [SA Law Commission representative Thandabatu] Nhlapo, abundant research that African people don't think highly of registration. He cited a similar law enacted in Swaziland to try to coerce couples to register customary marriages, which he said was an abysmal failure. There is a saying that an African marriage is a process and not an event. The processes in African marital unions were so public that Africans saw no need for registration to validate them." *See* Bonile Ngqiyaza, *SA Gets Divorce from Apartheid Marriage Law,* Business Day (South Africa), Nov. 20, 2000, *available at* 2000 WL 27222181. Should the government impose a registration requirement if many individuals will not register their marriages? Should registration be a precondition to validity? Requiring registration as a condition of validity can sometimes operate unjustly. How? For a good explanation of how the registration requirement has worked unjustly in China, *see* Michael Palmer, *The People's Republic of China: More Rules but Less Law,* 29 J. Fam. L. 325 (1991).

5. *Proving the Fact of Marriage.* If a country does not want to rely on a system of registration, how else might it allow parties to prove the fact of marriage? Consider the following excerpt.

Janet Kabeberi-Macharia & Celestine Nyamu, *Marriage by Affidavit: Developing Alternative Laws on Cohabitation in Kenya, in* The Changing Family: International Perspectives on the Family and Family Law

197–98, 206–07
(John Eekelaar & Thandabantu Nhlapo eds., 1998)

At the official level, unions will count as valid marriages if they are created under any of four systems of family laws in Kenya, namely:

- Any of the various African customary law systems in Kenya;

- Hindu religious practice, provided for under the Hindu Marriage and Divorce Act (chapter 157 of the Laws of Kenya);

- Islamic religious practice, provided for under the Mohammedan Marriage and Divorce Act (chapter 156 of the Laws of Kenya); or

- The statutory system set up under the Marriage Act (chapter 150) and the African Christian Marriage and Divorce Act (chapter 151).

Multiple systems of family law therefore operate side by side....

Although marriage under customary law is recognized as one of the valid forms of marriage under Kenya law, the marriages are not officially registered, and there are no official records of customary law marriages. This makes it necessary for a couple married under customary law to prove the existence of the marriage by means of an affidavit, every time documented proof of the official status of their union is required, for example, in any official dealing. The affidavit will usually indicate the particular customary law system under which they are married (i.e. which ethnic group's system), and the date on which the ceremony was held.

[Ed. Note: The authors explain that individuals can swear an affidavit for a specific purpose. Affidavits sworn for a particular purpose are valid only for the purposes for which they are sworn. Couples can also swear a general affidavit of marriage "that suffices as proof of marriage for all types of purposes. This type of affidavit remains valid for one year. The legal basis for the swearing of affidavits generally is the Oaths and Statutory Declaration Act, chapter 15 of the laws of Kenya.... The effect of this [system] is that couples, or, as is sometimes the case, only the women, have to constantly swear a general affidavit every year to show that they are married. In reality, many swear only one affidavit." Folks fail to renew it because they believe it remains valid even after its expiration. These individuals presume the affidavit has the same effect as a marriage certificate since it is an official document.]

An affidavit containing an assertion that parties were married under custom is usually taken as *prima facie* evidence that they do, indeed, have a valid marriage. It is not usual practice for officials to go behind the affidavit to require further or more specific evidence of marriage. It is presumed that they have complied with their community's essentials of a marriage which may include marriage payments and agreement between the two families. Thus, here lies the appeal of the affidavit to couples cohabiting informally. All they need to do is allege marriage under custom, even though they never actually went through the recognized formalities of it. Thus, an affidavit of marriage sworn by a cohabiting couple will, more often than not, allege that the parties are married by virtue of customary law. This is because the very idea of swearing an affidavit of marriage is rooted in the practice of documentary proof of customary marriage.

The use of affidavits has been taken up by other couples who cohabit as man and wife, but do not want to undergo either a customary or civil ceremony, but at the same time want to enjoy the same "benefits" as those who have undergone either of the ceremonies. That way, they get to by-pass both customary and statutory civil law marriage requirements; hence our argument that a new form of marriage has been shaped, that is "neither customary nor legal"....

[Ed. Note: The authors explain that there are several reasons why people may cohabit without getting married, "but a common reason is the costs involved. Cost refers not only to the expenses of the marriage ceremony, but also the marriage payments (bridewealth) expected by the woman's family in many African communities.... Affidavits, therefore, offer an affordable alternative to some people...."]

Although we pointed out that officials will rarely go beyond an affidavit that alleges marriage by customary law to require evidence of a ceremony, the courts do insist on precisely this kind of proof. The courts insist on detailed proof of the ceremony, and witnesses have to testify that the prerequisites of a customary law marriage were complied with. In addition to oral testimony, there has emerged a practice of referring to documented "sources" or compilations of marriage customs of the various groups in Kenya. This rigid requirement for strict proof hardens the distinction between customary law marriages, and cohabitation unions. Since many people who seek affidavits of marriage only interact with administrative officials other than courts... they rarely need to worry about this strict level of proof.

---

6. *Registration and Discrimination.* Some have suggested that registration systems can facilitate discrimination against individuals. In Japan, for example, the family registration system (Koseki) has caused problems for women and minorities, especially Burakumin (Japanese whose ancestors held certain occupations that made them "unclean" under Buddhist doctrine). *See generally* Taimie L. Bryant, *For the Sake of the Country, for the Sake of the Family: The Oppressive Impact of Family Registration on Women and Minorities in Japan*, 39 UCLA L. Rev. 109 (1991). In addition, the way in which registration occurs can support discriminatory marriage policies. For example, transsexuals were stopped from marrying by the registration system in France. In France, marriages are recorded on an individual's birth certificate. *See* The French Civil Code, art. 70, ord. no. 59-71 (John H. Crabb trans., 1995) (1959). Since the certificate must be presented to the public official administering the marriage, and since the birth certificate includes information on a person's sex at birth, transsexuals had difficulty marrying individuals whose gender matched the transsexuals' gender as recorded on the transsexuals' birth certificates. *See* French Civil Code, arts. 57 & 70. The French system was challenged as a violation of the European Convention on Human Rights. In *B. v. France*, 16 Eur. H.R. Rep. 1 (1992), the European Court of Human Rights held that France violated article 8, which guarantees "the right to respect for... private and family life," when France refused to alter the birth certificate of a post-operative transsexual to reflect the transsexual's new gender. Various official documents were based on the birth certificate, and the Court stressed the inconveniences faced by a transsexual whose physical appearance did not comport with various official documents that indicated gender, for example, European Community passports. *Id.* at 33–34. Although the applicant did not emphasize her inability to marry, a dissenting judge pointed out that the desire to marry motivated the application. *Id.* at 38 (Penero Farinha, J., dissenting). Chapter Four discusses the ability of transsexuals in Europe to marry. Do the licensing requirements in the United States buttress discriminatory marriage laws?

7. *Valuing Diversity.* A society might not recognize customary marriages, but might still give legal status to a couple's relationship so long as the relationship fell within some category that already existed within the formal legal culture: *e.g.,* common-law marriage or domestic partnerships. Alternatively, a society might permit customary marriages even though the marriages varied greatly from marriages permitted by the dominant legal culture. What is the benefit or disadvantage of each approach? One reason that a society might want to recognize customary marriages as its own entity is to value and honor the diversity that exists in that society. Yet, are there no limits to a soci-

ety's need to tolerate diversity? The Australian Law Commission considered whether Australian family law is appropriate to a multicultural society, and formulated two principles by which to evaluate its laws.

> First, unless there is good reason to do otherwise, the law should not inhibit the formation of family relationships. Secondly, the law should recognize, support and protect the family relationships people choose for themselves. Limitations on these principles arise from the need to protect the rights and freedoms of others who may be in a position of relative powerlessness, such as children and victims of violence. The law should not support relationships in which rights and freedoms of individuals are violated, but should intervene to protect them.

Justice Elizabeth Evatt, *Multiculturalism and Family Law, Summary of Discussion Paper No. 46,* 5 Aust. J. Fam. L. 86, 86 (1991). What do you think of these two principles and the allowable limitations? Assuming that the people in South Africa agreed with these principles, does the Recognition of Customary Marriage Act of 1998 adequately reflect them?

8. *Uniform or Parallel Systems.* Legal dualism refers to countries that have two coexisting legal systems. Legal pluralism refers to countries that have more than two legal systems. What is the advantage to a society of having two or more types of legal systems that govern marriage, *e.g.,* civil and customary, with different formalities and substantive rules? Are there any disadvantages? One commentator noted that individuals living in countries with parallel systems "rarely confine their actions within one system of law." *See* Bart Rwezaura, *Tanzania: Building a New Family Law Out of A Plural Legal System,* 33 Louisville J. Fam. L. 523 (1994–95) (describing enactment of Law of Marriage Act 1971, which was to integrate and reform different systems). Rather people often "draw from all the various systems whenever it suited them best," causing choice of law problems, undermining certainty of status, allowing the powerful to manipulate the systems and victimize those less experienced, and causing different (and some would say discriminatory) remedies to apply. *Id.* A solution to this problem might involve forcing individuals into one system or the other. For example, in the United States, the Indian Child Welfare Act of 1978, Pub. L. No. 95-608, 92 Stat. 3069 (codified as amended in scattered sections of 28 U.S.C., 43 U.S.C.), is a congressional effort to recognize tribal authority. Among other things, the act gives tribal courts exclusive jurisdiction over the adoption of Indian children domiciled on a reservation. *See* 28 U.S.C. § 1902. Alternatively, a country might choose to have one law of general applicability, but make it flexible enough to accommodate differences. The latter approach might be a marriage law that allows individuals below the age of eighteen to marry with court approval. The court, in such a situation, could take into account the cultural traditions of the couple. Which of the various approaches is preferable?

9. *Choice.* A legal system could allow couples to choose the marital regime they want. In Zimbabwe, for example, customary law governs a dispute only when the parties both want it to govern. *See* Zimb. Const. § 23(3)(b). Should the initial choice of law bind a couple in all aspects of their marriage? If there is a disagreement as to which set of rules should apply later, which should be the default rules? Why? A related question is where disputes between the parties should be litigated when at least one party seeks to invoke customary law. In Botswana, the High Court in Lobatse ruled that "it is erroneous for a plaintiff who wants to dissolve a customary law marriage to seek to base his grounds of divorce on the legal grounds provided under the Matrimonial Causes Act," and to invoke the jurisdiction of the High Court and not the customary court at first instance. *See* Letshiviti Tutwane Mmegi, *"Give Customary Courts a Chance" Rules High Court,*

Africa News Service, Dec. 1, 2000, *available at* 2000 WL 30131771. *Compare* Section 16 of the Zimbabwean Customary Marriage Act, 1 Statute of Zimb. 249, 5:07, § 16 (1996) (divorce must only occur in those courts dictated by the Matrimonial Causes Act, including the High Court and for customary divorces, a magistrates court; traditional courts are not included). *See also* Matrimonial Causes Act, 1 Statute Law of Zimb. 277, 5:13, § 2 (1996).

A. *Customary Law.* In South Africa, the answer to the questions "to whom does customary law apply" is guided by legal principles developed under the 1927 Native Administration Act, Act 38 of 1927, § 11(1), and the Law of Evidence Amendment Act 45 of 1988. One author has stated that two principles emerge from the case law: "The first is a deference to the personal inclinations of the parties.... If the courts can discover no common intention in the parties' actions to be bound by the common law, they fall back on the second principle: to apply customary law to those who adhere to an African culture. The courts impute a cultural affiliation to individuals by reason of their integration into a community. The test is strictly objective, normally entailing investigation of a person's participation in culturally marked activities. At its most fundamental level the choice of law process is dictated by the parties' reasonable expectations in the circumstances of the case. If they had agreed that a certain law should apply, the courts simply give effect to the agreement. Such an understanding might be express, but more frequently it has been inferred from conduct...." T. W. Bennett, Human Rights and African Customary Law 52–54 (1995). What kinds of facts would support the application of customary law? Section 31 of the Black Administration Act, 1927 (Act No. 38 of 1927), allows an individual "who is deemed to be sufficiently acculturated to western lifestyle to apply for permanent exemption from customary law. Very few people made use of this procedure, which is hardly surprising in view of the paternalistic way in which it was conceived." Bennett, *supra*, at 53.

B. *Customary Courts.* What difference might it make if customary or civil courts hear claims for divorce and nullity that involve an application of customary law? In South Africa, under the Recognition of Customary Marriages Act of 1998, the family court has exclusive jurisdiction to issue divorces and decrees of nullity. However, the proprietary consequences of customary marriages entered before the Act are still governed by customary law. *See* § 7(1). These provisions differ from the prior rule, whereby the Black Administration Act allowed a ruler, once approved by the minister, to hear "civil claims arising out of Black law and custom brought before [him] by Blacks against Blacks resident within [his] area of jurisdiction," excluding questions of nullity and divorce in civil/christian marriages. Bennett, *supra*, at 76 n.93. However, even under the prior law the Constitutional Court had the final word over any conflict between customary law and the Constitution. *Id.* at 48. The "repugnancy clause," mentioned in the next note, permitted the civil courts to invalidate customary law when they thought it appropriate.

10. *Coequal Marriages?* Although a country has two or more legal systems operating simultaneously, the marriages from each system may not have an equivalent status. For example, some have stated that customary law has never been treated as the equal of the civil law in South Africa given the repugnancy clause of section 1(1) of the Law of Evidence Amendment Act 45 of 1988. *See* Jeanne Y. DeKoker, *African Customary Family Law in South Africa: A Legacy of Many Pasts, in* The Changing Family: International Perspectives on the Family and Family Law 321 (John Eekelaar & Thandabantu Nhlapo eds., 1998). Section 1(1) provides that "Any court may take judicial notice of the law of a foreign state and of indigenous law in so far as such law can be ascertained readily and with

sufficient certainty: Provided that indigenous law shall not be opposed to the principles of public policy and natural justice: Provided further that it shall not be lawful for any court to declare that the custom of lobolo or bogadi or other similar custom is repugnant to such principles." Section 1(4) explains that "indigenous law" means the law or custom as applied by black tribes in the Republic. Interestingly, the Recognition of Customary Marriage Act 1998 did not make the repugnancy clause inapplicable to matters covered by the new act. Professor Tom Bennett reports that efforts currently exist to repeal the clause.

Yet lately, judicial practice has rendered the repugnancy clause less important. "In practice the [repugnancy] clause has, to a large degree, fallen into disuse." *Id.* at 331 n.82. In fact, the Supreme Court of Appeal of South Africa expressly refused to apply it in *Mthembu v. Letsela,* 2000 (3) SA 867 (A), ¶¶ 43–45 (S. Afr.). Under attack in that case was a rule of customary law, incorporated through legislation, that made it impossible for illegitimate children to inherit from a father who died intestate. The Court rejected the application of the repugnancy clause and upheld the customary law. The Court emphasized that the law was not repugnant because the law permitted the decedent to bypass the customary law rules by writing a will. In addition, since the decedent could have achieved the same discriminatory result with a will, it was not contrary to public policy to give effect to customary law that obtained that result. Finally, the Court refused to apply the repugnancy clause because it would strike down a statute, even though the statute incorporated the discriminatory customary rule.

Does a system that tries to accommodate diversity with legal pluralism inevitably create new distinctions that might prove discriminatory? For example, with passage of the Recognition of Customary Marriage Act of 1998, there are now differences between the favorable treatment given African customary marriages under the act and the treatment of religious marriages. While the act permits customary polygynous marriages, if certain requirements are met, the same is not extended to Muslim polygynous marriages. *See* June Sinclair, *South Africa: Giving Effect to the Spirit of the Constitution, in* The International Survey of Family Law 341, 347 (2000) (citing Ryland v. Edros, 1997 (2) SA 690 (CC) (S. Afr.). Apparently the distinction is causing resentment among Muslims, a small minority in the country. *Id.* at 348, 350. As of July 2002, there had not been any legislation passed in South Africa that addresses the problem of Muslim polygamous marriages being treated less favorably than customary polygamous marriages. Nor had there been any constitutional challenges based upon "unfair discrimination" on the basis of religion or culture. However, Professor June Sinclair reports that there is a Law Commission Paper containing a draft bill on Muslim marriages that addresses this issue. Letter from June Sinclair to Merle H. Weiner (July 17, 2002) (on file with author).

11. *Gender Equality.* Is the Recognition of Customary Marriage Act of 1998 unconstitutional because it permits polygyny? The Constitution requires that family law not embody "unfair discrimination." *See* The Constitution of the Republic of South Africa Act 108 of 1996, §§ 9(4), 15(3)(b). The Recognition of Customary Marriage Act of 1998 tries to minimize the harmful aspects of polygamy by giving the family court a role in deciding whether a man gets to marry a second woman. The court must approve an application that appends a written contract regulating the future matrimonial property system of the applicant's marriages. *See* § 6. The court may deny the application if the interests of any party would not be "sufficiently safeguarded" by the contract. *See* § 7. *But see generally Report of the Committee on the Elimination of Discrimination Against Women,* U.N. GAOR, 49th sess., Supp. No. 38, ¶ 14, U.N. Doc. A/49/38 (1994) (General Recommendation No. 21) ("Polygamous marriage contravenes a woman's right to equality with men, and can have such serious emotional and financial consequences for her and her dependents that such marriage ought to be discouraged and prohibited.").

Assuming polygyny violates principles of gender equality, should the principles of gender equality prevail over custom as a normative matter? A similar question arises with respect to the act's imposition of equality between men and women during marriage. The Recognition of Customary Marriage Act now treats property acquired during the marriage as community property, absent a contract to the contrary. Should the principles of gender equality prevail over custom?

In classic African customary law, the laws that govern the household are patriarchal. "In monogamous marriages, the husband owns and manages the entire estate except for odd items of personal property of a ritual or intimate nature, which belong to the individual concerned." Bennett, *supra*, at 122. All property earned by the wife becomes part of the husband's estate. In polygynous households, management of property during the marriage belongs to the family head, although he is to manage it for the family's benefit and he could not transfer property between houses without his wife's consent. Property acquired by anyone in the house is "house property," except that property acquired by the family head belongs to the family estate. The house property is inherited by the heir to the house; the family estate is inherited by the family head's general heir. *Id.* at 122–23. The oldest son of the first wife is heir to the house, and acquires both the rights and the obligations of that status. The rules of primogeniture require that the general heir must be a male. *Id.* at 126. "In monogamous families, the eldest son of the family head is his heir, failing him the eldest son's eldest male descendant. Where the eldest son has predeceased the family head without leaving male issue the second son becomes heir; if he be dead leaving no male issue the third son succeeds and so on through the sons of the family head. Where the family head dies leaving no male issue his father succeeds." Mthembu v. Letsela, 2000 (3) SA 867 (A), ¶8 (S. Afr.).

Although African customary law disadvantaged women in many ways, customary law also conferred certain benefits upon women. When a woman's husband dies, she had the right either to a levirate union or to maintenance out of the estate. *Id.* The heir to the head of the family becomes "liable for the debts of the deceased and assumes the deceased's position as guardian of the women and minor sons in the family. He is obliged to support and maintain them, if necessary from his own resources, and not to expel them from his home." *Id.* Because the rules of primogeniture impose on men a reciprocal duty to provide for the women, at least one court has held that the system is not one of "unfair discrimination," as is prohibited in the Constitution. *Id.* ¶11 (citing trial court opinion in *obiter dictum*).

Not all countries elevate principles of equality over custom. In fact, in Zimbabwe, the Supreme Court recently held that the Constitution exempts customary law from constitutional scrutiny. Justice Muchechetere said: "Whilst I am in total agreement with the submission that there is a need to advance gender equality in all spheres of society, I am of the view that great care must be taken when African customary law is under consideration." Magaya v. Magaya, S.C. No. 210-98 (Zimb. 1999). In that case, a man's son from his second wife was made administrator of the man's estate instead of the man's oldest child, a daughter from his first wife. As the Administration of Estates Act required, the court had based its decision on customary law. The relevant custom is that a man has preference over a woman in administering an estate. The Supreme Court of Zimbabwe affirmed. *See generally* Bigge, *supra* note 3, at 292–95. Two commentators concluded: "*Magaya* offends principles of equality for women. Yet just as clearly, it upholds important emerging principles of group self-determination. The conflict between these areas is evident; its resolution less so." *Id.* at 299. How should this conflict be resolved? Why?

12. *Ethnocentrism.* Any assessment of marriage practices as discriminatory or immoral must involve a close look at our own practices. Compare, for example, the substantive law of polygamy. In South Africa, the Recognition of Customary Marriages Act of 1998 allows couples to register polygamous marriages at home affairs offices and be issued a marriage certificate. Women can avoid a polygamous marriage by divorcing their husbands. Upon divorce they would have the same legal protection as women in civil marriages. *See generally* Sizwe samaYende, *Applause for Recognition of Polygamy,* Africa News Service, Nov. 20, 2000, *at* 2000 WL 29193357. In commenting on the family law in Norway, Sweden, Denmark, Belgium, France, Spain, Portugal, Italy, Switzerland, Austria, Germany, the United Kingdom, and the Netherlands, one author noted:

> The principle of *monogamy* has been maintained, but surreptitiously polygamy has been introduced in many family law systems. This is obvious as far as serial polygamy is concerned: where the remarriage of the widowed and divorced is allowed, serial polygamy will ensue; but this is nothing special, and, with a few exceptions, common to all known societies. But, less obviously, simultaneous polygamy has been introduced. This follows from four developments. First, insofar as western legal orders are confronted with the legal consequences of polygamous marriages entered into validly in legal systems which explicitly recognize polygamy, there is a tendency to accept (some of) these consequences, which in earlier times used to be considered to be contrary to public order. Secondly, the combination of remarriage with the (sometimes) lifelong subsistence of some of the economic rights and duties of a former marriage has the effect that one person can have simultaneous institutional relations with two or more partners. Thirdly, the institutionalization of unmarried cohabitation does just as well produce situations in which the same person has institutional rights and duties *vis-a-vis* two partners (one the spouse, the other the cohabitee). Fourthly, the fact that it has now become possible for a man simultaneously to have children with a fully legal status with two or more different women, would in any other society be considered to be the surest sign of the legality of polygamy, it being the case that in all societies hitherto marriage was co-defined by its monopoly of legitimacy.

Harry Willekens, *Long Term Developments in Family Law in Eastern Europe: An Explanation, in* The Changing Family: International Perspectives on the Family and Family Law 57 (John Eekelaar & Thandabantu Nhlapo eds., 1998). Similarly, South Africa now has a community property system for ownership of property that gives parties the equal right to manage it. Some states in the United States still allocate management of property during the marriage to the person holding title. *See, e.g.,* Uniform Marital Property Act § 5, 9A U.L.A. 97 (1987).

13. *Bridewealth.* Bridewealth is a necessary prerequisite to a valid customary marriage in many cultures. Be clear, however, that an agreement to marry plus the payment of bridewealth itself is not sufficient for a marriage to exist. There must also be appropriate formalities. *See* Mthembu v. Letsela, 2000 (3) SA 867 (A), ¶ 17 (S. Afr.). How does bridewealth affect the notion of consent to the marriage? What practical problems do you suppose may exist with a system that makes the payment of bridewealth a prerequisite to a valid marriage? Consider that "a customary-law union, in practice if not as clearly in the textbooks, is a process rather than an event.... But the payment of bridewealth may take many years or, indeed, may never be completed." Sandra Burman, *Illegitimacy and the African Family in a Changing South Africa,* 1991 Acta Juridica 38, 41. Alternatively, sometimes a portion of the bridewealth is paid, but formalities never occur; the parties may still live their lives as a married couple. *See* Mthembu, 2000 (3)

SA 867, ¶8. For a comprehensive look at lobolo, *see* Angeline Shenje-Peyton, *Balancing Gender, Equality, and Cultural Identity: Marriage Payments in Post-Colonial Zimbabwe,* 9 Harv. Hum. Rts. J. 105 (1996).

14. *Collateral Effects of Bridewealth.* If bridewealth is necessary to create the marriage, its payment may also serve as a marker for who has rights and responsibilities toward children born of the couple. Consider the following excerpt from an article by Sandra Burman, entitled *Illegitimacy and the African Family in a Changing South Africa,* 1991 Acta Juridica 38, 41, 44.

> By paying bridewealth (termed "lobolo" among the Xhosa) to a woman's natal family, a man obtains rights over her and her offspring, and undertakes certain corresponding duties. In this way the woman and children are incorporated into his patriliny and the wife's guardian forfeits his claims to them, though he retains residual rights of guardianship for the rest of her life.... While the maternal family may invoke their right to the children until such time as bridewealth is paid, they are very unlikely to do so as long as there remains the expectation— or hope—that the father will yet honour the bridewealth agreement.

> If he does not, or if there has never been such an agreement, the children belong to their mother's family. Her father—or, if he is dead, the senior male agnate indicated by customary law—assumes all the rights over, and responsibilities for, the children that their father would have had, if he had paid bridewealth. Theoretically, therefore, in most instances the children are not discriminated against for purposes of maintenance or status within the family, though they generally have an inferior jural position as regards inheritance. Their jural relationship to their mother is unclear, especially where her father or brother is legally father of her children....

> Once bridewealth is paid, any progeny of the wife remain part of the husband's family, even if conceived after the husband's death. But if no bridewealth has been paid, the child is attached to the mother's natal family and the father has no rights in, or duties to, it. If he wishes to bring the child into his family, he must—at least in the official version of Southern Nguni law, to which the Xhosa-speaking groups belong—make a special payment to the mother's natal family (or, if the mother is a widow who has conceived after her husband's death, to her late husband's family)....

> [If the parents have never married] the natural father may pay seduction damages to the mother's family (which immediately legally brings the child into his family) and, on payment of an extra beast, termed isondlo, he may claim physical custody of the child as well.

15. *Asymmetrical Treatment of Customary Law.* South Africa has adopted a system in which only some customary law will be binding. The constitutionally recognized principle of gender equality, for example, takes precedence over conflicting customary law. Asymmetrical treatment may be appropriate, especially when one considers the broad scope of customary law. For example, Kenyan customary law permits female circumcision. *See* Chege Mbitiru, *Women Lawyers Call for Law Against Female Circumcision,* Assoc. Press Newservices, Dec. 14, 2000. Should a country be consistent in its treatment of customary law? What limits should exist? Should equality be the only limit on permissible customary law? What about the standard embodied in the Law of Evidence Amendment Act, *see* note 10 *supra,* that customary law cannot violate "the principles of public policy and natural justice"?

Problem 2-1

Tembi was married under customary law to Tebalo. When Tembi was twenty-three, Tebalo died. Tebalo's brother, Sedise, wanted to enter a levirate union by marrying Tembi and thereby assuming Tebalo's obligations to Tembi. Tembi did not want to marry Sedise. She thought he was a vile and evil man. Tembi's father, her guardian, insisted that Tembi marry Sedise. Tembi's father would have had to return some portion of the bridewealth if Tembi did not marry Tebalo's brother. Under threat of harm, Tembi very reluctantly agreed to marry Sedise. A few months later, she seeks an annulment. Assume that the marriage to Sedise was valid under customary law. Would she be able to get an annulment in South Africa?

Some states in the United States also have a customary marriage law in addition to state-enacted marriage law. Most obviously, common law marriage constitutes a form of customary marriage. Today approximately ten states and the District of Columbia permit common law marriage, although at the turn of the nineteenth century a majority of states permitted the practice. Are there parallel issues between the recognition of customary marriages in South Africa and the recognition of common law marriage here? If so, what are those issues? What are the differences? Keep in mind your knowledge about common law marriage as you consider the following material.

Kalyton v. Kalyton
74 P. 491 (Or. 1903)

This is a suit by Agnes Kalyton, a minor, by her mother, as guardian ad litem, to establish her right to certain real property. The transcript shows that about April 21, 1891, Joe Kalyton, an Indian, and a member of the Cayuse Tribe, was allotted in severalty 157 acres of land in the Umatilla Indian Reservation. He thereafter lived with the plaintiff's mother, and died intestate about January, 1899, seised of the real property allotted to him, and after his death the plaintiff was born. The defendant Mary Kalyton, his sister, claiming to be his sole heir, took possession of the premises in question, and secured the rents therefrom. The complaint, after alleging the facts, in substance, as hereinbefore stated, avers that about 1893 plaintiff's mother married Kalyton according to the customs and laws of the tribe to which they belonged; that thereafter they lived and cohabited as husband and wife; and that plaintiff is the issue of such marriage, and the sole heir of the deceased. The answer denies the material allegations of the complaint, and, for a further defense, avers that the alleged marriage was not performed according to law, and therefore was void. For a further defense, it is averred that Kalyton and plaintiff's mother, being allottees of land in severalty, were citizens of this state, and that he died unmarried and without lineal descendants. A demurrer to the first separate defense having been overruled, a reply was filed putting in issue the averments of new matter in the answer, whereupon a trial was had, resulting in a decree that the defendant Mary Kalyton was the sole heir of the deceased, and entitled to the real property of which he died seised, and the plaintiff appeals.

Moore, C.J.

The Cayuse Indians were recognized as a tribe by the United States June 9, 1855, when a treaty was concluded with them and other Indians, which was ratified by the Senate March 8, 1859, and approved by the President April 11th of that year, setting apart for their exclusive use certain territory in Oregon, which has since been known as the "Umatilla Indian Reservation." 12 Stat. 945. An act of Congress approved March 3, 1885, authorized the President of the United States, with the consent of the Indians, to allot to the Cayuse and other Indians residing upon the Umatilla Reservation certain areas of land in severalty....

Section 6 of an act of Congress approved February 8, 1887, generally known as the "Dawes Act," providing for the allotment of land in severalty to the Indians on the various reservations, is as follows:

> That upon the completion of said allotments and the patenting of the lands to said allottees, each and every member of the respective bands or tribes of Indians to whom allotments have been made shall have the benefit of and be subject to the laws, both civil and criminal, of the state or territory in which they may reside; and no territory shall pass or enforce any law denying any such Indian within its jurisdiction the equal protection of the law. And every Indian born within the territorial limits of the United States to whom allotments shall have been made under the provisions of this act, or under any law or treaty, and every Indian born within the territorial limits of the United States who has voluntarily taken up, within said limits, his residence separate and apart from any tribe of Indians therein, and has adopted the habits of civilized life, is hereby declared to be a citizen of the United States, and is entitled to all the rights, privileges, and immunities of such citizens, whether said Indian has been or not, by birth or otherwise, a member of any tribe of Indians within the territorial limits of the United States without in any manner impairing or otherwise affecting the right of any such Indian to tribal or other property. 24 Stat. 390, c. 119.

Section 5 of an act of Congress approved February 28, 1891, amending and extending the benefits of the act approved February 8, 1887, is, so far as deemed applicable, as follows:

> That for the purpose of determining the descent of land to the heirs of any deceased Indian under the provisions of the fifth section of said act, whenever any male and female Indian shall have co-habited together as husband and wife according to the custom and manner of Indian life the issue of such co-habitation shall be, for the purpose aforesaid, taken and deemed to be the legitimate issue of the Indians so living together, and every Indian child, otherwise illegitimate, shall for such purpose be taken and deemed to be the legitimate issue of the father of such child. 26 Stat. 794, c. 383.

These excerpts and quotations from the acts of Congress disclose the policy pursued by the United States in dealing with Indians residing upon reservations to whom land has been allotted in severalty, and though these people have been invested with the rights of citizenship and guarantied [sic] the protection of the laws, and rendered amenable thereto, the object evidently intended to be subserved by such legislation was to encourage them to forsake their primitive ways and to adopt a higher civilization. Reforms of this character are necessarily radical, and not cheerfully submitted to or acquiesced in by uneducated Indians. The change from savagery to refinement is slow, and results from convincing the ignorant of the superior advantages which the latter state affords. The general government, realizing that the task of persuading the older Indians was difficult, has established schools to teach their children the English branches, and to instruct them in the use of tools and implements, thus rendering them self-supporting and partially qualified to compete with the Caucasian race. It is to the younger Indians, then, when removed from the influence of the examples of their parents, and from the teachings and traditions of their tribes, during the formation of their characters, and when educated in the schools provided for them, that the government must look, to elevate their race. It is quite probable that this conclusion induced the passage of section 5 of the act of Congress approved February 28, 1891 (26 Stat. 794, c. 383).... Congress thus recognized the validity of Indian marriages, and, though the union may have occurred subsequent to the acceptance of an allotment of land in severalty in an Indian reservation, we believe that if the nuptials were celebrated according to the custom of the tribe of which the parties were members, or to which one of them belonged, and, in pursuance of such union, they have cohabited as husband and wife, the marriage is valid.... To reach any other conclusion might in some instances thwart the beneficent purpose of the government, and transfer the title of land donated by it to induce the elevation of a race into another channel, never contemplated, for if a marriage entered into by members of a tribe, according to the customs thereof, is to be held invalid, and the issue illegitimate, the offspring could never inherit from the father, whose real property, if he had no collateral kinsmen, following the rule of descent in Oregon, would escheat to the state. Laws 1903, p. 127....

The principal inquiry, therefore, is whether Joe Kalyton and plaintiff's mother were married according to the customs of the Cayuse Indians. Lee Moorehouse, who had been Indian agent at the Umatilla Reservation, appearing as plaintiff's witness, testified that he had observed the customs of the Indians on that reservation, and was asked: "Can you tell the habits of these Indians in regard to marrying, by the Indian custom?" and, over objection and exception, replied: "There doesn't appear to be any regular form they go through in an Indian marriage, and, to get married, they simply go to living together, as near as I understand it." This witness further says that when these Indians concluded to marry they entered into the agreement by mutual consent, and went to living together; that sometimes the man, if he had any property, purchased his wife; and that he understood the Indians considered their form of marriage as sacred as any other. In *Henry v. Taylor* (S.D.) 93 N.W. 641, it was held that in order to show a marriage between two Indians according to the Indian custom, consisting of an agreement to live together, followed by cohabitation, it was necessary to show an express agreement and pursuant cohabitation, which contract must be evidenced by words disclosing a meeting of minds, uttered in the present tense, for the purpose of establishing the marriage relation. The plaintiff's mother, testifying by an interpreter, says that she lived with Joe Kalyton as his wife five years immediately prior to his death; that they were not married by any regular custom; that he asked her if she would live with him, and she consented; that the young and the old Indians are married in that manner; and that it is an old custom, and she could not tell when it commenced. The testimony of this witness is corroborated by that of Joe Allen, who says that Kalyton and plaintiff's mother lived together as other Indian husbands and wives belonging to that tribe. The defendant Mary Kalyton testifies that her brother and plaintiff's mother lived together as husband and wife according to the Indian customs, in speaking of which she says she was first married in that manner, and lived with her husband one summer, and that they were thereafter married according to the laws of this state. We think the testimony clearly shows a valid and subsisting custom of the Cayuse Tribe of Indians, in observing which Kalyton and plaintiff's mother entered into an express agreement, evidenced by words disclosing a meeting of their minds, followed by cohabitation, and, under the rule announced, established the existence of a valid marriage.

It is maintained by defendants' counsel, however, that plaintiff's mother was not competent to enter into a marriage contract at the time or after she commenced living with Kalyton, and, this being so, plaintiff's illegitimacy is established, and no error was committed in decreeing the real property of which he died seised to his sister, as his sole heir. The testimony shows that plaintiff's mother had lived with the following named Indians, as the wife of each, respectively, to wit, Ish-lo-wal-ko, White Wolf, and Top-la-won. The transcript does not show whether or not the first-named person is dead, but it discloses that the others were living during all the time she lived with Kalyton, Top-la-won having remarried. The plaintiff's mother testifies that she was married to these persons in the Indian manner, and that she ceased to live with and separated from each according to the custom of her tribe. The following question was propounded to the interpreter: "Ask her if she separated or was divorced from White Wolf and these other Indians according to Indian custom, the same as Indians always separated?" and she answered, through him, as follows: "Yes, sir; separated in the Indian way." No evidence was offered tending to show how an Indian divorce is secured, and it is argued by defendants' counsel that the testimony of plaintiff's mother is the mere statement of a legal conclusion, and insufficient to establish the probative facts of the dissolution of the marital relation according to the Indian custom. The legal principle insisted upon would ordinarily be sufficient to defeat the plaintiff's right of recovery, but in the present instance we do not think the rule invoked applicable, for, in settling the pleadings, the court having held that after the allotment of land in severalty a marriage according to law was a prerequisite to the legitimacy of the issue of cohabitation, the subordinate question of the capacity of plaintiff's mother to enter into a marriage contract with Kalyton was not given that degree of attention which its importance demanded. No objection was interposed to the questions propounded to her in relation to her separation from her prior husbands, nor was she cross-examined as to the customs of her tribe in the manner of securing divorces, in view of which we believe the testimony was sufficient to show that she was divorced from them, and was capable of entering into a valid marriage with Kalyton.

It is contended by defendants' counsel that the plaintiff was not born within the period of gestation after the death of Kalyton, and hence no error was committed in rendering the decree complained of. The testimony shows that Kalyton died, as plaintiff's mother testified, a "few days" after the New Year, and that her daughter was born "late in the fall—the time the leaves fall off the trees"; that the witness did not know the names of the months, but that plaintiff was born about one month before Christmas, and at the trial her age was "four snows." When it is considered that the knowledge of plaintiff's mother concerning the year seems to be limited to the holidays, and that a "few days" or "one month" are to her vague and indefinite terms, we believe her testimony that Kalyton was the father of her daughter to be true, without discussing the question of how long gestation might be protracted. No testimony having been offered tending to show that plaintiff's mother was dissolute, we conclude that her daughter, the plaintiff herein, was born in lawful wedlock, and is the sole heir of Joe Kalyton, deceased, and, as such, entitled to the possession of the real property of which he died seised.

The decree will therefore be reversed, and one entered here in accordance with this opinion.

Notes and Questions

1. *Marriage Recognition by Common Law.* In *Kalyton*, Congress made customary marriages valid for the limited purpose of the allotment policy. Would the doctrine of *lex loci celebrationis* have obtained the same result? Earlier in *McBean v. McBean*, 61 P. 418 (Or. 1900), Chief Justice Wolverton stated,

As a general proposition, it is well settled that a marriage valid according to the law or custom of the place where it is contracted is valid everywhere.... And it is the adjudged policy of the law to treat the Indian tribes who adhere to their peculiar customs, as separate communities or distinct nationalities, with full and free authority to manage their own domestic affairs, and to pursue their own peculiar habits and customs, especially as it concerns the marriage relation. And this is so although their territory is located within the state lines, and the federal government manages their affairs through agencies designated for the purpose.... [I]t would seem that where the marriage is between members of the tribe wholly, or between white persons and members of the tribe, conforming to tribal customs, the union will be recognized as constituting a valid marriage in the state and federal courts.

Marriage recognition issues are discussed more fully in Chapter Five.

2. *Marriage Recognition in Kalyton. Kalyton* appears to be a marriage recognition case, albeit one in which the federal statute required recognition. However, was the court in *Kalyton* actually recognizing a customary marriage, or was it, rather, merely equating the situation to a form that was already recognized? One author has concluded that the courts in the nineteenth century that recognized Indian customary marriages "[l]ooked for indicia of the marital relationship in ways in which it appeared that the parties satisfied the requirements of a common law marriage." Antoinette Sedillo Lopez, *Evolving Indigenous Law: Navajo Marriage-Cultural Traditions and Modern Challenges*, 17 Ariz. J. Int'l & Comp. L. 283, 304 (2000). Was the court doing the same in *Kalyton*, an early twentieth century case?

3. *Contrast Choice of Laws for Incidents. Kalyton* was not a case where the court was asked to apply Indian substantive law regarding the rights and obligations of marriage. Are marriage recognition cases different in kind from cases where a party or the parties want "foreign law" applied to resolve a dispute other than the mere existence of a valid marriage? These issues are covered in Chapter Five on marriage recognition.

4. *Capacity to Marry.* Why did the *Kalyton* court reject the defendant's argument that the mother was already married to another when she supposedly married Joe Kalyton? Would the following cases have helped the defendant? Roche v. Washington, 19 Ind. 53, 57-58 (1862) (refusing to recognize Miami Indians' marriage because, inter alia, informal divorces made "state of concubinage" "not a marriage"); State v. Ta-Cha-Na-Tah, 64 N.C. 614, 616 (1870) (refusing to recognize Cherokee marriage because "it can never be held that mere cohabitation, with an understanding that it may cease at pleasure, can constitute a marriage"); Bethell v. Hildyard, 4 T.L.R. 319 (Eng. Ch. 1888) (refusing to recognize Baralong tribal marriage because tribe permitted polygamy so parties did not intend to contract a "marriage").

5. *Outcome in Kalyton.* The *Kalyton* case was eventually appealed to the United States Supreme Court. The Supreme Court reversed and remanded for further proceedings; it held that the Oregon state court was "without jurisdiction to entertain the controversy." McKay v. Kalyton, 204 U.S. 458, 469 (1907). The defendant had argued that "the court had erred in taking jurisdiction of the case, for the reason that it involved the title and right to possession of public land held in trust by the United States for the benefit of Indians, and hence the United States was a necessary party defendant, and not subject to the jurisdiction of a state court." *Id.* at 460. The United States Supreme Court agreed. Consequently, in actions by Indians over their rights to allotments, the federal courts, and not the state courts, have jurisdiction. It is uncertain whether this federal jurisdic-

tion preempts tribal court jurisdiction. See Felix S. Cohen's Handbook of Federal Indian Law 343 (Rennard Strickland, ed. 1982). In *Kalyton,* the Supreme Court made clear, however, that it was not "intimating an opinion that we deem that the principles applied by the court in disposing of the merits of the case [to be] erroneous." McKay, 204 U.S. at 469.

6. *Establishing Custom.* How courts determine what constitutes customary law is a persistent problem around the world. This issue differs from the question of whether a marriage actually took place, once customary law is understood. That factual question was addressed in notes 3–5 following the David Chambers' article on South African customary marriages, *supra.* Sometimes countries have statutes that specifically address how litigants prove the content of customary law. For example, the Law of Evidence Amendment Act, 1988, in South Africa states, "The provisions of subsection (1) [permitting judicial notice of indigenous law] shall not preclude any party from adducing evidence of the substance of a legal rule contemplated in that subsection which is in issue at the proceedings concerned." Law of Evidence Amendment Act § 1(2) (1988) (S. Afr.). *See also* Application and Ascertainment Act § 11 (1969) (Bots.). How was custom established in *Kalyton v. Kalyton?*

a. *Who Can Testify.* One of the important questions in proving customary law is whether the court considers customary law to be a matter of fact or opinion. If the latter, the court may require that an expert testify. An expert, in this context, may be someone who has studied the laws in a formal manner, such as an anthropologist, a political scientist, or a lawyer. Alternatively, a court might consider someone an expert by virtue of that person's experience in a community.

b. *Hearsay.* Another important question is whether the court will exclude hearsay. The answer can be critical if the witness bases his or her opinion on both what the witness has observed and what the witness was told, as is common among anthropologists.

c. *Judicial Notice.* If the customs have become so notorious, courts will sometimes take judicial notice of them. *See, e.g.,* Angu v. Attah, Gold Coast Privy Council Judgments 1874–1928 (1916).

d. *Treatises.* Typically statutory provisions allow courts to consider textbooks or other documents of reference when determining the content of customary law. *See, e.g.,* Mthembu v. Letsela, 2000 (3) SA 867 (A), ¶16, 20 (S. Afr.). What are the limitations to these sources, if any?

e. *Fact or Law.* Once the trial court rules on the content of customary law, there is the question of whether that ruling is one of fact or law, the latter generally being considered de novo on appeal.

f. *Proving Custom in the United States.* There is no statute that tells courts in the United States how to ascertain the content of customary law. What do you make of the provision in the Federal Rules of Evidence 44.1 that states, "The court, in determining foreign law, may consider any relevant material or source, including testimony, whether or not submitted by a party or admissible under the Federal Rules of Evidence. The court's determination shall be treated as a ruling on a question of law." At times, this rule has allowed a litigant in the United States to prove the content of customary law in a foreign country. *See, e.g.,* Kaho v. Ilchert, 765 F.2d 877 (9th Cir. 1985).

7. *Custom Fluidity.* The problem of what constitutes customary law becomes more complicated because custom is not necessarily static, and disputes can arise about what constitutes the relevant customary practice at a particular time. For example, "The cul-

tural norms about marriage [in the Navajo nation] have undoubtedly evolved since pre-European contact. Indeed, 'iii nel kad' the Navajo phrase meaning that there is going to be a wedding, literally means 'bringing in the horses' referring to the exchange of traditional gifts between the uniting families. However, horses did not appear on the scene until after the Spaniards arrived." Sedillo Lopez, *supra*, at 301. Today, the Navajo Tribal Code provides:

> The contracting parties engage in a traditional Navajo wedding ceremony which shall have substantially the following features:
>
> 1. The parties to the proposed marriage shall have met and agreed to marry;
>
> 2. The parents of the man shall ask the parents of the woman for her hand in marriage;
>
> 3. The bride and bridegroom eat cornmeal mush out of a sacred basket;
>
> 4. Those assembled at the ceremony give advice for a happy marriage to the bride and groom;
>
> 5. Gifts may or may not be exchanged;
>
> 6. The person officiating or conducting the traditional wedding ceremony shall be authorized to sign the marriage license.

Sedillo Lopez, *supra*, at 299 n.131 (citing Navajo Code, tit. 9, §3(d)). In addition, the Tribal Council in 1993 enacted a provision that permits common law marriage. *See generally* Sedillo Lopez, *supra*, at 292–300. *See also* In re Validation of Marriage of Francisco, 16 Indian L. Rep. 6113 (Navajo 1989). Marriage recognition issues, as well as questions about the effects of marriage, can be complicated if the marriage occurs in a community without a written code, *see, e.g.,* Manychief v. Poffenroth, [1995] 3 W.W.R. 210 (Alta. Q.B.), or in a community with a code that no longer is, or never was, reflective of customary practice.

8. *Multiple Versions of Customary Law.* Consider what one author has said about the establishment of customary law in South Africa as a historical matter. This history has had an impact on what is considered customary law today in South Africa.

Jeanne Y. DeKoker, *African Customary Family Law in South Africa: A Legacy of Many Pasts, in* The Changing Family: International Perspectives on the Family and Family Law
321, 333–34
(John Eekelaar & Thandabantu Nhlapo eds., 1998)

Rules of customary law were adduced by calling expert witnesses and by attaching people whom the colonials regarded as having first hand experience of customary law as assessors to the courts to give advice when questions involving African customary law arose. African customary law proved in evidence was derived from oral or written sources. Witnesses and assessors were usually male elders from the communities concerned. The colonial administration and courts relied heavily on the male elders as the local leaders in order to ascertain the content of African customary law because they regarded them as the custodians of traditional African customary law. Written evidence was mainly derived from textbooks and manuals which were compiled by missionaries, traders, colonial officials and anthropologists. Gradually from a stock of precedents, a general body of customary law was built up and thus "official" African customary law was created.

In this process of incorporating African customary law into the formal legal system it was transformed to comply with the requirements of the dominant western legal culture. Indigenous institutions were described in terms of European legal concepts and the social contexts of rules were regarded as rather unimportant.... This process of "inventing" a "tradition" of "official" African customary law created a distorted version of African customary law which was claimed to be a body of rules which represented a genuine precolonial tradition or a continuing evolution of social norms. In reality, this body of law reflected the preconceptions and biases of its translators.

———

Earlier in the article, the author explains that today there are three forms of African customary law: "Autonomic" [also referred to as "living" or "non-official"], "official" African customary law, and "academic" African customary law. *Id.* at 322. The author continued:

The content of the different forms of African customary law, particularly that of "official" and "non-official" African customary law, differs. "Official" African customary law is embodied in legislation and acknowledged in law reports and government papers. It is a rigid set of written rules which are applied in the official courts and state bureaucracy in South Africa. This form of African customary law is generally regarded as a distortion of "living" African customary law. "Living" African customary law, on the other hand, is a fluid and dynamic legal system, practiced by the people and applied in various traditional and informal tribunals. "Academic" African customary law is mainly distinguished for teaching purposes. It is a flawed mixture of "official" and "non-official" African customary law which is presented to students in order to introduce them to the dichotomy of modern African customary law. The existence of these different forms of African customary law are regarded as one of the results of colonialism.

9. *Native American Marriage Law Today.* Native American tribes in the United States set their own rules regarding marriage to varying degrees. Some tribes have left the regulation of marriage to the states, others have set up their own requirements. *See* National American Indian Court Judges Association, Indian Family Law and Child Welfare 1 (1986).

10. *Tribal Courts' Jurisdiction.* So far, most of this section has focused on the litigation of claims in the civil law courts. As David Chambers mentioned, the customary courts in South Africa have been stripped of their power to resolve marital disputes. *Kalyton* too was litigated in an Oregon state court. Where a dispute involving a Native American party is litigated typically depends upon a combination of party desire and jurisdictional rules established by the civil and tribal governments. These rules of jurisdiction are beyond the focus of this casebook, although a few point can be made. Tribal jurisdiction over marriage extends to tribal members in tribal territory. The extent to which tribal jurisdiction extends to nonmembers in tribal territory or tribal members outside tribal territory is more complex. This brief statement by Professor Atwood regarding tribal courts in the United States is helpful:

[Tribal jurisdiction] may extend to nonmembers where the nonmember is involved in a consensual relationship with the tribe or where the nonmember's conduct poses a direct threat to the tribe's welfare. Although enormous uncertainties exist as to the controls of a tribe's civil jurisdiction, the cases indicate that in the realm of family law, where tribes traditionally have enjoyed a prominent sovereign role, a tribe's civil jurisdiction may be at its strongest. By their own tribal codes, moreover, tribes often assume the power to resolve domestic disputes between members and nonmembers.

Barbara Ann Atwood, *Tribal Jurisprudence and Cultural Meanings of the Family*, 79 Neb. L. Rev. 577, 594–95 (2000). Whether tribal jurisdiction is exclusive of state court jurisdiction is another matter. Tribal jurisdiction is exclusive when the matter is between Indians in Indian Country. It may be exclusive even when the matter involves a non-Indian. *See* Williams v. Lee, 358 U.S. 217 (1959) (state court lacked jurisdiction over a claim by a non-Indian against an Indian when the claim arose in Indian territory). However, state courts may have concurrent jurisdiction, especially when both parties are domiciled outside of Indian territory, or in certain instances state courts may even have exclusive jurisdiction. An important factor determining the extent of state and tribal jurisdiction is whether a state is subject to Public Law 280. *See* Act of Aug. 15, 1953, ch. 505, 67 Stat. 588 (codified as amended at 18 U.S.C. §1162, 25 U.S.C. §§1321–1326, 28 U.S.C. §1360). Public Law 280 affords the civil courts of some states jurisdiction over Indians and Indian Country, but it has been interpreted narrowly. *See generally* Felix S. Cohen's Handbook of Federal Indian Law 246, 249, 341–48 (Rennard Strickland ed., 1982). The extent to which tribal decisions will be respected in state court also depends upon considerations of full faith and credit and comity. For an excellent summary of the current complexity regarding tribal sovereignty over family law, see Lesley M. Wexler, Comment, *Tribal Court Jurisdiction in Dissolution-Based Custody Proceedings*, 2001 U. Chi. Legal F. 613, 616–27 (2001).

11. *Tribal Courts Generally.* Native American tribal courts are very diverse, although they often encounter similar issues (*e.g.*, about choice of law and evidence of custom) as those encountered by the civil courts.

a. *Diversity.* In the United States, of the 500-plus federally recognized tribes, bands, and villages, "today more than 200 federally recognized tribes have some form of judicial system qualifying as a 'court,' but the diversity among these many courts is enormous." Atwood, *supra*, at 592. Diversity among tribal courts is found in many areas, including who can practice before the courts (in some courts, for example, advocates without law school training are common), whether traditional dispute resolution methods are used (*e.g.*, the Pueblo communities have talking circles facilitated by elders to resolve marital conflicts), and the extent of reliance on tribal custom and tradition. Sometimes the tribal code mandates the application of customary law. *See* Navajo Code tit. 7, §204(a) (1977).

b. *Customary Law.* Determining the content of customary law can be difficult. Often the heritage of the tribal court is "rooted firmly in Western thinking: in codes drafted by Western-trained, frequently non-Indian lawyers, and in interpretations of those codes and the 'tribal common law' by Western-trained, often non-Indian judges." Russel Lawrence Barsh, *Putting the Tribe in Tribal Courts: Possible? Desirable?*, 8 Kan. J.L. & Pub. Pol'y 74, 75 (1999). One scholar described the jurisprudence as "weaving strands from native culture, tribal law, Western culture, and Anglo-American law." Barbara Ann Atwood, *Tribal Jurisprudence and Cultural Meanings of the Family*, 79 Neb. L. Rev. 577, 579 (2000). Some courts are particularly dedicated to "reclaim[ing] and continu[ing] its culture and manag[ing] its own affairs" through an articulation of authentic tribal custom. Sedillo Lopez, *supra*, at 283. Professor Sedillo Lopez has described how the Navajo Nation has used marriage regulation "to reclaim traditional values and to resist (at least in part) the dominant values imposed on the Navajo Nation." *Id.* at 283–86. One author suggests that this may be a hard task to actually accomplish. The author examined 359 cases published since January 1995 in the Indian Law Reporter; the Navajo tribal courts were heavily represented in the cases examined. The author stated, "Especially intriguing (and counterintuitive) is the reliance of tribal courts on state law when ruling on family and property matters." Barsh, *supra*, at 80. The author also found that "tribal judges tend to require proof of the contexts of indigenous jurisprudence, as if it were foreign law, while presuming that they can pronounce and elaborate principles of federal and state common law without such proof." *Id.* at 82.

c. *Evidence of Custom.* Consider how Navajo custom is proven before the tribal courts:

> Navajo custom and tradition may be shown...through recorded opinions and decisions of the Navajo courts or through learned treatises on the Navajo way; it may be judicially noticed; or it may be established by testimony of expert witnesses who have substantial knowledge of Navajo common law in an area relevant to the issue before the court.... Where no question arises regarding custom or usage, the court need not avail itself of experts in Navajo culture.... Thus, if a custom is generally known within the community, or if it is capable of accurate determination by resort to sources whose accuracy cannot reasonably be questioned, it is proven.

In re Estate of Belone v. Yazzie, 5 Navajo Rptr. 161, 165 (Navajo Sup. Ct. 1987).

d. *Differing Methodology.* Notwithstanding the similar problems encountered by tribal and state courts when needing to assess the content of customary law, the application of the rules might differ. One author's insights are interesting: "Western legal methodology begins with categorization of the case and a selection of applicable rules. Tribal methodology begins with an analysis of the litigants' relationships with each other and with others, focusing on duties and legitimate expectations attached to those relationships. Kinship structure provides the basic set of principles for determining what is just. Justice is a function of individuals' family histories, and the historical relationships between their families." Barsh, *supra*, at 76.

12. *Tribal Law and its Relationship to the U.S. Bill of Rights.* Imagine that a particular tribe had a rule of family law that clearly discriminated on the basis of gender. Could the party who was to be disadvantaged by the law claim that the U.S. Constitution prohibited its application? Put another way, does the constitutional guarantee of equality trump customary laws that are discriminatory? As a matter of constitutional law, the answer is no. According to the U.S. Supreme Court in *Talton v. Mayes*, 163 U.S. 376, 382 (1896), the Constitution limits the government that it created and not the tribes. *Talton*, 163 U.S. at 382. As commentators have noted, "Even though the Court has over the years held that most of the Bill of Rights applies to the states through the 14th Amendment, it has never applied these provisions to tribal governments." John T. Cross & Kristin M. Lomond, *The Civil Rights of the Aboriginal Peoples of the United States and Canada*, 10 Ariz. J. Int'l & Comp. L. 253, 287 n.149 (1993). The only exception is the Thirteenth Amendment to the Constitution which abolished slavery throughout the United States. *See* United States v. Choctaw Nation, 38 Ct. Cl. 558 (1903), aff'd, 193 U.S. 115 (1904). Consequently, various tribal laws that discriminate on the basis of gender have not been subject to constitutional challenge.

However, Congress has passed an act called the Indian Civil Rights Act (ICRA) that applies to tribes. *See* 25 U.S.C. § 1302 *et seq.* ICRA incorporates many provisions of the Bill of Rights and applies them to tribes, including a guarantee of equal protection of the laws. *See* 25 U.S.C. § 1302(8). ICRA, however, can only be invoked in tribal court itself. Tribal sovereignty precludes suing a tribe in a state or federal court and invoking ICRA unless the tribe has consented to suit or Congress has waived its immunity. Consequently, in *Santa Clara Pueblo*, a woman's suit on behalf of her children against the tribe in federal court was barred. *Santa Clara Pueblo v. Martinez*, 436 U.S. 49 (1978) (tribe may refuse tribal membership to children of females who marry outside the tribe, even though it affords membership to children of similarly situated males). While claims can be brought in tribal court, "tribal fora have sometimes proven inadequate to enforce ICRA. The problem often does not lie with the tribal tribunals themselves since many have expressed a desire to enforce the restrictions of ICRA. Instead, the problem lies in the nature of tribal government. Many tribal adjudicative bodies have no authority to compel the tribal council or other governing body to abide by their orders. For these tribes, Congress has essentially created a right without any real remedy." Cross & Lomond, *supra*, at 290. *See also* Rennard J. Strickland, *Indian Bill of Rights*, in The Oxford Companion to the Supreme Court of the United States 427 (Kermit L. Hall et al. eds., 1992).

13. *Comparison.* What comparisons can you make between the treatment of customary family law in South Africa and in the United States?

2. Religious Law

Various religions have laws regarding marriage, including Catholicism, Judaism, Islam, and Hinduism. Since marriage between baptized persons is a sacrament in Catholicism, the Church claims the right to legislate for all Catholics. *See* Stanislaus Woyowd, A Practical Commentary on the Code of Canon Law 643 (1957) (citing canon 1055). Hinduism law also believes that marriage is a sacrament, and therefore its rules apply to all Hindus. *See* Srikanta Mishra, Ancient Hindu Marriage Law and Practice 10 (1994). Jewish law, *halakhah*, likewise applies to all Jews. "In Islamic law, '[t]he religious law, the *Shari'a* claims competence to regulate the formation of marriage for all Muslims.'" Dagmar Coester-Waltjen & Michael Coester, *Formation of Marriage, in* IV International Encyclopedia of Comparative Law 9 (1997). The Protestant Church, in contrast, has traditionally considered marriage a civil act. *Id.* at 8.

The extent to which religious law is reflected in a civil legal system differs depending upon whether the legal system is unitary or pluralistic and depending upon whether there is a recognized doctrine of separation between church and state. In a unitary system that lacks the doctrine of separation between church and state, religious law may constitute the only law. For example, *Shari'a* is the only law in Saudi Arabia. In a unitary legal system that has a separation between church and state, religion may have a minimal role, if any, on the formal level. In pluralistic systems, religious law may have a coequal status with civil law. In some pluralistic systems, religious law is made mandatory for family law matters even though the country formally recognizes a separation between church and state. For example, India's Constitution embodies freedom of religion, but India also retains plural systems of religious personal law (Muslim, Hindu, Parsi, and Christian) to govern family law matters. *See* Martha C. Nussbaum, *India: Implementing Sex Equality Through Law*, 2 Chi. J. Int'l L. 35, 40 (2001).

In most legal systems, even those with a constitutionally mandated separation of church and state, governments allow religion to play some role. For example, states in the United States recognize marriages solemnized by religious authorities. Similarly, "more than 80% of all states [in Europe and North America] at least allow the marriage to be contracted in a religious form." *See* Rene David & John E.C. Brierley, Major Legal Systems in the World Today 10 (2d ed. 1968). Moreover, even in places where the religious form is today prohibited or is insufficient to contract marriage, religion may have left a mark on the institution of marriage. Since religious organizations have had a large historical role in the regulation of marriage, a legacy often exists from this involvement. *See* Chapter 3.A; *see also* Chapter 2.C notes 20–21. Yet the influence of religion has not been omnipresent in all societies. "[R]eligious bodies have never played a predominant role in regulating the formation of marriage in China, Japan and other Asian states not influenced by Catholic or Islamic religion. Here marriage was traditionally a family-controlled procedure without church or state involvement." Coester-Waltjen & Coester, *supra,* at 9.

As an example of how religious law regulates marriage, we consider the law of Islam, or *Shari'a.* We chose to focus on Islamic law because "secular law has become the pre-dominant regulative authority as to the formation of legal marriage [in] ... all countries of the world except to those of the Islamic sphere." Coester-Waltjen & Coester, *supra,* at 10. "In most Islamic states in Asia and Africa, the *Shari'a* is recognized as compulsory for all Muslims." *Id.* In addition, there is concern among Muslims and others about the treatment and understanding of Islamic law in U.S. courts. *See, e.g.,* Asifa Quraishi, American Muslims and American Law (Apr. 1996), *available at* http://www.zawaj.com/articles/legalities.html (last visited Mar. 1, 2003); Pascale Fournier, *The Erasure of Islamic Difference in Canadian and American Family Law Adjudication,* 10 J.L. & Pol'y 51 (2001).

The *Shari'a* is "the code of law based on religious principles that regulates the conduct of all Muslims, a code that covers social, commercial, domestic, criminal, and political affairs as well as devotional practices." Thomas W. Lippman, Understanding Islam: An Introduction to the Muslim World 71 (1990). In addition, *Shari'a* principles "form the basis of a society's moral code." *Id.* at 86. There are multiple branches of Islamic law. While all branches of Islamic law are based on the *Koran* (God's word as revealed to the Prophet Muhammad) and on the *sunna* (the Prophet Muhammad's sayings and teachings), the interpretations of the *sunna* differ and are reflected in the *ijtihad* of five schools: *Hanafi, Maliki, Shafi'i, Hanbali,* and *Ja'fari.* Judges often turn to the *ijtihad* when Islamic law is not clear. Despite the resulting complexity, some generalizations on a few topics are attempted here.

1. *Guardian.* Traditional Islamic law gives great power to a father or a grandfather to arrange a minor's marriage. Such an arranged marriage cannot even be annulled at puberty, unlike child marriages arranged by other guardians. *See* John L. Esposito & Natana J. DeLong-Bas, Women in Muslim Family Law 16 (2001).

In Islamic law, even a woman past puberty has a guardian for marriage matters. In most states with modern legal codes, however, guardians are not allowed to compel a woman into marriage. *Id.* at 100. Rather, the guardian's consent is necessary if the woman wants to marry.

> It is generally recognized that a Muslim woman who has never been previously married needs a *wali* (guardian) to enter into a marriage.... The *wali* is usually her father. Schools differ as to the duration and nature of the *wilayah* (guardianship) of marriage. The Hanafi view is, in many ways, the most liberal on this matter. Under this view the *wali* acts only as an advisor to the female who has reached puberty and shares in her decision-making process.... The Hanafi view, however, provides the *wali* with an important deterrent to ensure that his advice is taken seriously. If a female who has reached puberty discards her *wali*'s advice and marries someone "unsuit-

able," the *wali* can move to void the marriage if no pregnancy has oc-curred....

Azizah Y. al-Hibri, *Marriage Laws in Muslim Countries: A Comparative Study of Certain Egyptian, Syrian, Moroccan, and Tunisian Marriage Laws*, 4 Int'l Rev. of Comp. Pub. Pol'y 227, 231–32 (1992). Many modern codes provide that the woman can petition the court for permission to marry when the marriage is beneficial to her, and yet her guardian withholds consent. Esposito & DeLong-Bas, *supra*, at 100.

2. *Suitability*. At a minimum, suitability refers to the groom's religion. In classic Islamic law, a Muslim woman could only marry a Muslim man, although a Muslim man had slightly more ability to select a partner with a different religion. *See* Esposito & De-Long-Bas, *supra*, at 19. Beyond that, however, the meaning of suitability varies. As Professor al-Hibri explained:

> "Suitability" is a term of art. Its meaning differs from one school to another and even within a school. Generally, however, the Hanafi school's definition includes lineage, religion, financial condition, piety, and skill or profession.... This definition differs from the *sunnah*. The Prophet's established view is that the only relevant measure for preferring one Muslim over another is piety....

See al-Hibri, *supra*, at 232.

3. *Polygamy*. Traditional Islamic law recognizes a husband's right to have up to four wives. There is the requirement, however, that he be able to treat all equally. The modern trend is one "of restricted polygamy if not monogamy outright." Jamal J. Nasir, The Status of Women Under Islamic Law and Under Modern Islamic Legislation 25 (1990).

4. *Rights and Obligations of the Marital Parties*. Wives have an obligation of obedience and to engage in domestic activities, and husbands have the obligation of support. One source explained, "The major corollary of this duty of obedience is that the husband may prevent his wife from leaving the marital home without his permission." The husband has the right to restrain his wife's movements, including showing herself in public. *See* Esposito & DeLong-Bas, *supra*, at 22–26. Violation of the duty of obedience "leads to wide-ranging consequences which affect her maintenance, marriage, and divorce rights." al-Hibri, *supra*, at 238. The husband has the obligation to provide his wife with the necessities of life, i.e., "maintenance" or "nafaqah." A woman is also entitled to "mahr" (dower), as described in note 6, *infra*. Neither party acquires an interest in the property of the other because of marriage. Each may own and manage his or her own property throughout the marriage. Each may inherit from the other. Esposito & De-Long-Bas, *supra*, at 22–26.

Some of these basic tenants of Islamic law have changed over time. For example, many modern Muslim codes specifically give the wife the right to work, and some guarantee her right to visit her family. *See* al-Hibri, *supra*, at 238–39. Tunisia and Somalia, for example, require both the husband and wife to contribute to the financial support of the family. Esposito & DeLong-Bas, *supra*, at 96.

5. *Islamic Law and the Contractual Conception of Marriage*. Under Islamic law, as under Jewish law, marriage is a contract between the parties. Islamic law recognizes the right of the parties to agree upon specific terms of the marriage contract, including the right of the wife to stay in her home town, to divorce herself at will, to work, or to be her husband's only spouse. Violation of a contract term allows the marriage to be dissolved. The wife will maintain her marital rights if the husband violates a term or the husband will be released from deferred dower and *iddat* maintenance if the wife violates

a term. Nasir, *supra*, at 14–15. Terms against public policy are void. *Id.* Some countries have facilitated contracting out of the traditional rules. For example, in Iran, marriage contracts issues after 1982 contained a list of twelve conditions to which the husband and wife could agree, including the equal division of property upon divorce and the right of a woman to initiate divorce. *See* Esposito & DeLong-Bas, *supra*, at 103.

How does the Islamic conception of marriage as a contract differ from how our law conceives of marriage? Professor Carol Weisbrod has written:

> That the Islamic marriage contract is conceptually contractual (rather than having an emphasis on status or covenant) is clear in the following description from a Pakistani judge: 'The rights arising out of an Islamic marriage contract are not the gifts of any legislative body of a country; they emanate from the proposal and the acceptance of the parties made at marriage time.' The contract is understood as simultaneously temporal and religious. The religious marriage contract suggests that the current conversation on the "commercialization" of marriage through contract, a conversation common in the United States, makes most sense against a particular background, Western, which focuses on romantic love. Further, it suggests that the idea that there is little room for variations in the marriage contract is perhaps more culturally specific than we as Americans ordinarily see.

Carol Weisbrod, *Universals and Particulars: A Comment on Women's Human Rights and Religious Marriage Contracts*, 9 S. Cal. Rev. L. & Women's Stud. 77, 88 (1999).

6. *Mahr.* Mahr, otherwise known as *sadaq*, is dower: it is a reasonable payment the groom makes to the bride when the parties marry. The payment belongs to the bride and not to her family. If the mahr has not been paid, it becomes due at the time of divorce or death. Mahr is perhaps the most important part of the marriage contract for Muslims, and if it is not written into the contract, the wife is still entitled to it. *See* Jamila Hussain, Islamic Law and Society: An Introduction 66 (1999). However, entitlement to mahr and the amount of mahr turn on consummation of the marriage; if the marriage is annulled prior to consummation, the wife is entitled to none of it and if she is divorced before consummation, she is entitled to only half. *See* Ziba Mir-Hosseini, Marriage on Trial, A Study of Islamic Family Law, Iran and Morocco Compared 73 (1993). Mahr is meant to provide the woman with some resources in the event of divorce or her husband's death. In fact, some have stated that the purpose of mahr is to compensate the wife for the husband's right to divorce at will under Islamic law. *See* In re Marriage of Shaban, 105 Cal. Rptr. 2d 863, 869 n.6 (Cal. Ct. App. 2001).

7. *Mutà Marriage.* A *mutà* marriage is a marriage established by cohabitation of a fixed term, even a day, with dower. Normally dower is not required for the validity of other marriages, but it is for a *mutà* marriage. Any children born during a *mutà* marriage are legitimate. The husband can terminate the marital relationship, but termination gives the wife entitlement to full dower if they have consummated the relationship. The wife can also end a *mutà* marriage, but she will receive less dower. If they have never consummated the *mutà* marriage, and the husband terminates the relationship, the wife gets one half the dower. A *mutà* wife has no entitlement to maintenance. Also, neither party inherits from the other. At the end of the *mutà* marriage, the woman must maintain a period of sexual abstinence (*idda*), to help establish the father of any child conceived from the union. *See* Shahla Haeri, *Mutà: Regulating Sexuality and Gender Relations in Postrevolutionary Iran*, *in* Islamic Legal Interpretation: Muftis and Their Fatwas 251, 252 (Muhammad Khalid Masud et al. eds., 1996). This form of marriage is recognized only by some Muslim sects, and Muslims debate whether the Koran sup-

ports the institution. *See generally* Nasir, *supra*, at 16–18, 43; Kristen Cherry, Comment, *Marriage and Divorce Law in Pakistan and Iran: The Problem of Recognition*, 9 Tulsa J. Comp. & Int'l L. 319, 323 (2001); Ja'far, Mutà Marriage, *at* http://www.1ummah.org/understand/muta.htm.

In the prior section on customary law, we observed tribal leaders and federal legislators competing for power over marriage. Now religious bodies are added as competitors. In a pluralistic system, some individuals try to use the multiplicity of law to their own advantage and to their spouse's detriment. For example, in India, it had recently become "very common amongst the Hindu males who cannot get a divorce from their first wife…[to] convert to Muslim religion solely for the purpose of…second marriage, but again become recovert[ed] so as to retain their rights in the properties…and continue their service and all other business in their old name and religion." *See, e.g.*, Lily Thomas v. Union of India, 2 L.R.I. 623 (India 2000) (holding wife could institute criminal proceedings for bigamy against husband who converted to Islam solely to be able to marry another woman). Even in legal systems in which religious law has no formal role, some individuals find the rules complex enough that their partners can defraud them. In these situations, a defrauded person may honestly believe that he or she is married, even through he or she is not. A court resolving a subsequent dispute between the parties must then balance its desire to honor a party's good faith expectations with its own perceived need to protect the dominant institution's authority over marriage and to have administrable rules.

In re Marriage of Vryonis
248 Cal. Rptr. 807 (Cal. Ct. App. 1988)

Klein, J.

Appellant Speros Vryonis, Jr. (Speros) purports to appeal a judgment on bifurcated issues wherein the trial court held respondent Fereshteh R. Vryonis (Fereshteh) had the status of a putative spouse. Because Fereshteh reasonably could not believe she was validly married under California law, we order the issuance of a peremptory writ.

Factual & Procedural Background

Speros was the director of and a teacher at the Center for Near Eastern Studies at UCLA. Fereshteh was a visiting professor at the Center, and the parties met there in the fall of 1979. She was an Iranian citizen, a member of the Shiah Moslem Twelve Imams religious sect, and involved in the local Islamic community. Speros was a nonpracticing member of the Greek Orthodox Church. Prior to arriving in the United States in 1979, Fereshteh spent six years in England, where she earned a Ph.D. at Cambridge University. She had been married before and was the mother of two children.

The parties saw each other occasionally during 1980 and 1981 in connection with Center activities. They dated in February and March of 1982, but Fereshteh repeatedly stated she could not date Speros without marriage or a commitment because of her strict religious upbringing. Speros responded he could not marry as he did not know her and that he was a "free man." Nonetheless, on March 17, 1982, at her Los Angeles apartment, Fereshteh performed a private marriage ceremony. According to Fereshteh, the marriage conformed to the requirements of a time specified, "Muta" marriage, authorized by the Moslem sect of which she was an adherent. Fereshteh was unfamiliar with the requirements of American or California marriage law. However, she believed the ceremony created a valid and binding marriage, and Speros so assured her.

The parties kept the marriage secret and did not hold themselves out as husband and wife. All indicia of marriage were lacking. The parties did not cohabit, but rather, maintained separate residences. They did not inform relatives or friends of the marriage. Speros did not have a key to Fereshteh's apartment, and Fereshteh only had a key to Speros' house for three months. Speros continued to date other women. Fereshteh did not use Speros' surname. The parties did not commingle their finances, nor did they assume any support obligations for one another. They did not take title to any property jointly. During the period of time in question, Speros and Fereshteh filed separate tax returns, each claiming single status. They spent 22 nights together in 1982, only a few in 1983, and none in 1984. On frequent occasions, Fereshteh requested Speros to solemnize their marriage in a mosque or other religious setting, which Speros refused.

In July 1984 Speros informed Fereshteh he was going to marry another woman, after which time Fereshteh began informing people of the purported marriage. In September 1984, about two and one-half years after the date of the private marriage ceremony, Speros married the other woman.

Fereshteh thereafter petitioned for dissolution on October 15, 1984, seeking attorney's fees, spousal support and a determination of property rights. Speros moved to quash the summons based on lack of jurisdiction in that a marriage did not exist. The motion was denied. The trial court held a bifurcated hearing in March 1985 to determine first the validity of the marriage and putative spouse status.

In the statement of decision and judgment on bifurcated issues, the trial court held Fereshteh had a good faith belief a valid marriage existed between her and Speros, and specifically found:

> On March 14, 1982, in Los Angeles, California, the Petitioner performed a private religious marriage ceremony between herself and the Respondent which conformed to the requirements of a Muslim Mota [sic] marriage. No marriage license was obtained. And only the Petitioner and Respondent were present during the ceremony. No written documents were made to declare or record or otherwise authenticate the existence of a marriage between the parties, either at the time of the ceremony or thereafter. The Respondent required the Petitioner to keep the marriage secret and to live in a separate residence. The Petitioner believed in good faith that a valid marriage existed as a result of the ceremony, the consent expressed by Respondent, Respondent's subsequent actions, and statements of the Respondent. The Petitioner had no knowledge of the marriage laws of California and was ignorant as to any impediment to the validity of the marriage and justifiably relied on Respondent's assertions that the Petitioner and Respondent were husband and wife. On March 14, 1982, when the marriage ceremony was performed, the Respondent stated his consent to the marriage but did not intend such statements and participation in the ceremony to constitute a valid California marriage. The ceremony performed between the parties on March 14, 1982, did not constitute a valid California marriage due to the Respondent's lack of intention that such ceremony constituted a valid marriage and due to the subsequent lack of recordation or authentication of such marriage ceremony. The Petitioner has the status of a putative spouse...."

The finding of putative marriage would allow Fereshteh in subsequent proceedings to assert claims for spousal support and property division. The trial court ordered Speros to pay $10,000 as a partial contributory share of Fereshteh's attorney's fees. Speros filed the purported appeal.

Contentions

Speros contends: (1) the trial court erred as a matter of law in finding putative spouse status because (a) there was no evidence of a void or voidable marriage in that neither party made any attempt to comply with the statutory requirements of solemnization and recordation, and (b) there was no objective evidence to sustain the finding of Fereshteh's good faith belief in the existence of a valid marriage without the existence of the usual indicia of a marriage....

Discussion

1. *General principles of putative marriage doctrine.*

Civil Code section 4100 defines the marriage relationship as "a personal relation arising out of a civil contract between a man and a woman, to which the consent of the parties capable of making that contract is necessary. Consent alone will not constitute marriage; it must be followed by the issuance of a license and solemnization as authorized by this Code...." Section 4200 sets forth the procedural requirements for a valid California marriage as one which "must be licensed, solemnized, authenticated, and the certificate of registry of marriage filed as provided in this article; but noncompliance with its provisions by others than a party to a marriage does not invalidate it."

Where the marriage is invalid due to some legal infirmity, an innocent party nevertheless may be entitled to relief under the long recognized protection of the putative marriage doctrine....

Section 4452 sets forth the rights of a putative spouse as follows: "Whenever a determination is made that a marriage is void or voidable and the court finds that either party or both parties believed in good faith that the marriage was valid, the court shall declare the party or parties to have the status of a putative spouse, and, if the division of property is in issue, shall divide, in accordance with Section 4800, that property acquired during the union which would have been community property or quasi-community property if the union had not been void or voidable. The property shall be termed 'quasi-marital property.'" In addition to enjoying property rights in the nature of those afforded marital partners (4452, 4800), a putative spouse may also obtain spousal support. (4455).

2. *Requirement of a void/voidable marriage construed to mean invalid marriage.*

As set forth *ante*, section 4452 requires a threshold determination of a void or voidable marriage. A void marriage is an incestuous (4400), bigamous or polygamous one. (4401). A voidable marriage is defined as one where there was (a) no capacity by one party to consent due to youth or unsoundness of mind, (b) fraudulently or forcibly obtained consent, (c) physical incapacity of entering into a marriage, or (d) a living spouse of either party who has been absent five years or more and believed dead. (4425).

The circumstances here do not give rise to either a void or a voidable marriage. However, that in and of itself does not preclude relief under the putative marriage doctrine.

A fact situation may involve neither a void nor a voidable marriage, and yet relief is afforded, based upon the reasonable expectations of the parties to an alleged marriage entered into in good faith....

[S]ection 4452 merely codified the substantive case law...defining a putative spouse. ... Before time, it was well settled that the essential basis of a putative marriage was a belief in the existence of a valid marriage.... Were section 4452 limited to situations where a marriage is void or voidable as those terms are defined by statute (4400, 4401, 4425), the putative marriage doctrine would cease to apply to many invalid marriages. Because in enacting section 4452 the Legislature intended merely to declare existing law, we construe the void/voidable aspect as simply requiring a threshold determination that a legal infirmity in the formation renders a marriage invalid. In the instant case, the purported marriage was plainly defective.

3. Inquiry into good faith belief in a valid marriage.

Fereshteh seeks affirmation of the trial court's finding she had a good faith belief she was validly married to Speros, urging the only necessary finding to establish a putative marriage is that one spouse believed in good faith a valid marriage existed. Speros urges more than a "good faith belief, however wild" is required. He posits the requisite state of mind must be a good faith belief in a valid California marriage, and that there must also be some objective indicia of a valid marriage by which to measure such belief.

It is unclear from the statement of decision whether the trial court found Fereshteh believed she had celebrated a valid Muta marriage and held thereby a belief sufficient to confer putative spouse status, or whether the trial court determined Fereshteh had a good faith belief she was validly married under California law. If the trial court based its putative marriage finding on Fereshteh's belief she had celebrated a valid Muta marriage, the ruling was error because the required good faith belief is in the existence of a lawful California marriage. If the trial court found Fereshteh had a good faith belief she was validly married under California law, the ruling was error because the requisite good faith belief must have a reasonable basis.

a. Good faith belief must be objectively reasonable.

While a trial court may be tempted to base a finding of putative spousal status merely on the subjective good faith in a valid marriage held by a credible and sympathetic party, more is required. "Good faith belief" is a legal term of art, and in both the civil and criminal law a determination of good faith is tested by an objective standard.

[Ed. Note: The court then cites a contract case in which that court had said that "[t]he essence of the good faith covenant is objectively reasonable conduct. Under California law, an open term in a contract must be filled in by the party having discretion within the standard of good faith and fair dealing." It also cited a Fourth Amendment case that held that an officer's subjective good faith is not enough by itself to save an otherwise defective warrant. The court cited yet another case that suggested that a warrantless search can only be based on a probable cause determination based on objective facts, not merely the subjective good faith of the police officers.]

Without question, the hallmark of the law is reasonableness, and " '[r]easonableness,' of course, is an objective standard, requiring more than good faith." (*In re Arias* (1986) 42 Cal. 3d 667, 696, 230 Cal. Rptr. 505, 725 P.2d 664.)

A proper assertion of putative spouse status must rest on facts that would cause a reasonable person to harbor a good faith belief in the existence of a valid marriage.

Where there has been no attempted compliance with the procedural requirements of a valid marriage, and where the usual indicia of marriage and conduct consistent with a valid marriage are absent, a belief in the existence of a valid marriage, although sincerely held, would be unreasonable and therefore lacking in good faith.

While solemnization is not an absolute prerequisite to establishing a putative marriage...it is a major factor to be considered in the calculus of good faith. Lacking some diligent attempt to meet the requisites of a valid marriage...a claim of good faith belief in a valid marriage would lack any reasonable basis. Consideration of such factors provides a framework for determining whether a petitioner had reason to believe a valid marriage existed. Without a reasonable basis for an alleged good faith belief, even an honestly held belief in the existence of a valid marriage will not be in good faith and therefore insufficient to come within section 4452....

Fereshteh testified her belief in the validity of the purported marriage rested on her having performed the Muta ceremony, combined with Speros' assurances the marriage was valid. As indicated, Fereshteh performed a private marriage ceremony at her apartment, with only the two of them present. The ceremony was not solemnized by a third party. No license was obtained and there was no authentication or recordation. In short, there was no attempt to meet the statutory requirements of section 4200 with respect to the formation of a valid California marriage. Because the parties made no colorable attempt at compliance, Fereshteh could not believe reasonably a valid California marriage came into being. Fereshteh's ignorance of the law does not compel a contrary conclusion. Further, her reliance on Speros' assurances is unavailing. Unlike *Monti*, wherein Shirley relied on Clifford's statement that the divorce dissolving their undisputable valid marriage was never finalized (*In re Marriage of Monti, supra*, 135 Cal. App. 3d at p. 53, 185 Cal. Rptr. 72), there was no endeavor here to comply with legal formalities.

We are aware of *In re Marriage of Recknor*, (1982) 138 Cal. App. 3d 539, 544-547, 187 Cal. Rptr. 887, which held a woman did not qualify as a putative spouse because she *knew* at the time she entered into the second marriage her first marriage had not yet been dissolved, but she was entitled to recover support and attorney's fees because the man was estopped from denying the validity of their 15 year marriage. It appears *Recknor* failed to give due consideration to an essential element of estoppel, namely, the party asserting it must have been ignorant of the true state of facts. (*LaRue v. Swoap* (1975) 51 Cal. App. 3d 543, 551, 124 Cal. Rptr. 329.) In order to prove this element, "'it is necessary that the evidence show not only that the party claiming the estoppel did not have actual knowledge of the true facts but that he did not have notice of facts sufficient to put a reasonably prudent [person] upon inquiry, the pursuit of which would have led to actual knowledge; the convenient or ready means of acquiring knowledge being the equivalent of knowledge [citations].'" (*Ibid.*) Notwithstanding Speros' assurances, because Fereshteh was on notice the purported marriage was defective, estoppel does not lie.

Subsequent events are not germane to whether there was a proper effort to create a valid marriage in the first instance. However, later conduct sheds further light on whether Fereshteh had reason to believe she was married to Speros. We observe the parties did not reside together, but continued to maintain separate households. They did not assume any support obligations for one another. They spent no more than five or six nights together in any given month during the marriage. Speros continued to date other women, of which fact Fereshteh was aware. Fereshteh did not use Speros' name. There was no merging of finances, nor was there any joint accumulation of real or personal property. Fereshteh and Speros filed separate tax returns, each claiming single status. For the two and one-half year period following the purported marriage, the parties did not hold themselves out as husband and wife. It was only when Speros told Fereshteh he was to be married that Fereshteh published the fact of their purported marriage.

In sum, the alleged private marriage went unsolemnized, unlicensed and unrecorded. Thereafter, the parties did not cohabit, or hold themselves out as husband and wife, and in no way approximated the conduct of a married couple. Because the facts were at odds with the formation and existence of a valid marriage pursuant to California law, Fereshteh could not rely on Speros' statements reasonably to believe she was married. Notwithstanding Fereshteh's sincerity, her belief was unreasonable and therefore not in good faith.

b. *Required belief in valid marriage construed to mean lawful marriage.*

As noted, the trial court may have based its finding of putative spouse status on Fereshteh's belief she had conducted a valid Muta marriage. However, case law reflects the requisite belief is in a *lawful* marriage, that is to say, a marriage which complies with statutory requirements. *Schneider v. Schneider* (1920) 183 Cal. 335, 339, 191 P. 533, recognized the putative marriage doctrine serves to protect persons domiciled in a community property state who "believ[ed] themselves to be *lawfully* married to each other...." (Italics added.) Along similar lines, *Feig v. Bank of Italy etc. Assn.* (1933), 218 Cal. 54, 58, 21 P.2d 421, held a plaintiff who "innocently and in good faith believed himself at all times to be the *lawful* husband of the decedent" was entitled to an equitable apportionment of their gains. (Italics added.) Two years before *Feig,* in *Flanagan v. Capital Nat. Bank* (1931) 213 Cal. 664, 666, 3 P.2d 307, the essential basis of recovery under the doctrine was stated as a bona fide belief "in the existence of a *valid* marriage." (Italics added.) "Lawful" and "valid" are nearly synonymous, and subsequent cases tended to use the latter term in enunciating the doctrine, as does section 4452....

Although in many situations, there is little practical difference between lawful and valid, the use of the latter term in this context may engender confusion. The putative marriage doctrine protects the expectations of innocent parties who believe they are *lawfully* married. (*Schneider v. Schneider, supra*, 183 Cal. at 339–340, 191 P. 533). When the basis of the doctrine is stated as a good faith belief in a valid marriage, Fereshteh's belief she had celebrated a valid Muta marriage initially might seem sufficient to come within the doctrine. However, our overview discloses the doctrine requires a belief a marriage is lawful within the meaning of the Civil Code. Assuming the trial court based its finding of putative marriage on Fereshteh's belief she had conducted a valid Muta marriage, the ruling was error.[7]...

Let a peremptory writ of mandate issue, directing the trial court to vacate its judgment on bifurcated issues and to make a different order consistent with this opinion....

Notes and Questions

1. *Marriage Recognition Distinguished. In re Marriage of Vryonis* is not a marriage recognition case because the *mutà* marriage occurred in California. If the parties were domiciled and contracted the marriage in a place that permitted *mutà* marriage, the

---

7. Moreover, the putative marriage doctrine operates to protect expectations in property acquired through joint efforts. (Schneider v. Schneider, *supra*, 183 Cal. at 339–340, 191 P. 533.) Where, as here, there is neither cohabitation, pooling of earnings, acquisition of jointly owned property, nor any economic interdependence, the rationale of section 4452 would not be served.

question would have been whether California public policy permits recognition of this type of marriage. Recognition issues are discussed in Chapter Five.

2. *Significance of Holding.* What is the holding of *In re Marriage of Vryonis*? Should the California appellate court have found that a marriage existed? Should it have applied the putative spouse doctrine? Why was Speros not estopped from challenging the marriage's validity? If you like the outcome in *Vryonis*, do you also like the reasoning? After all, could the court have found that Fereshteh did not have a good faith belief that she entered a *mutà* marriage, rather than hold that she needed, and lacked, a good faith belief that she entered a legally valid marriage? One commentator has stated that Fereshteh undoubtedly knew that she did not have a valid *mutà* marriage because she claimed to be an expert in Islamic law and she would know that she could not marry anyone but a Muslim. *See* Kristen Cherry, Comment, *Marriage and Divorce Law in Pakistan and Iran: The Problem of Recognition,* 9 Tulsa J. Comp. & Int'l L. 319, 350 (2001).

3. *Religious Courts.* What if Fereshteh had petitioned for dissolution, spousal support, and property rights in a Muslim court in the United States? Such courts are operating. *See, e.g.,* Shikoh v. Murff, 257 F.2d 306 (2d Cir. 1958) (refusing to recognize divorce that occurred before the Islamic Mission of America, Inc.). These courts may have substantive and procedural rules much different than our own. *See, e.g.,* Anne Hellum, *Human Rights and Gender Relations in Post Colonial Africa: Options and Limits for the Subjects of Legal Pluralism,* 25 Law & Soc. Inquiry 635 (2000) (book review) (rules of evidence in the Islamic court made relevant the gender and number of witnesses to factual determinations). Other religions also have such courts. For example "[e]very Catholic diocese has a marriage court, and these courts, in the United States, process over 70,000 petitions regarding marital status each year. Church personnel in the hundreds and funds in the millions support this activity." James A. Coriden, An Introduction to Canon Law 132 (1991). The Beth Din of America provides similar services for members of the Jewish community.

What would be the effect of a religious court's judgment in the United States? In Kovacs v. Kovacs, 633 A.2d 425 (Md. App. Ct. 1993), two Orthodox Jews sought to dissolve their marriage through "arbitration" in a Beth Din, a Jewish court proceeding before a panel of three rabbinic judges. The Beth Din ruled on matters related to the divorce, including custody, child support, visitation, and property. After the Beth Din ruled, the wife petitioned for divorce in civil court. The husband requested that the circuit court confirm the award. The trial judge confirmed the award, finding that the proceeding was in accordance with the Maryland Uniform Arbitration Act, and both parents had participated voluntarily. The Maryland Court of Appeals reversed the part of the award relating to custody and child support since the trial judge failed to exercise independent judgment before adopting the ruling of the Beth Din. The appellate court emphasized that the trial court had a *parens patriae* role to ensure the best interests of the children. Just as a parental agreement could not bind the court with respect to child custody or child support, neither could a parental agreement to allow an arbitrator to decide custody and child support. However, the alimony and property award by the Beth Din could be binding on the trial court, provided it was not facially unjust or inequitable. The court equated the arbitration award to a valid settlement agreement. Although the wife had alleged various procedural irregularities regarding the Beth Din proceeding, the appellate court emphasized that her allegations were inadequately supported, and, more importantly, would not matter "so long as the litigants voluntarily and knowingly agree to the arbitration procedures." The court recognized a narrow exception if the proceedings failed to conform to notions of basic fairness or due process, but basic fairness and due process existed here.

4. *Choice of Law.* Could the parties bind themselves at the outset of their marriage to have another system's law apply to disputes arising during or at the conclusion of the marriage? *See* In re Marriage of Shaban, 105 Cal. Rptr. 2d. 863 (Cal. Ct. App. 2001) (refusing in a dissolution proceeding to give any weight to premarital agreement entered in Egypt whose only term was that the marriage was made in accordance with "Islamic Law" and allegedly was to be governed by the same, since parol evidence could not be used to establish the substance of the alleged agreement); Kaddoura v. Hammound, [1998] 168 D.L.R.4th 503 (Ont. Div. Ct.) (Muslim marriage certificate, which had term for mahr, was "as unsuitable for adjudication in the civil courts as is an obligation in a Christian religious marriage, such as to love, honour and cherish" because "the issue must be determined with reference to religious doctrine and principle" and the "civil court is...lacking in expertise" and "constitutionally beyond its proper territory."). Chapter 4.C.1. addresses whether parties can use religious law to restrict their ability to divorce and whether an agreement to submit a dispute to a religious court is enforceable. Note 3 of that section mentions the constitutional concerns associated with these issues.

5. *Understanding Difference.* The California court in *Vryonis* stated, "All indicia of marriage were lacking." What is the court's factual basis for reaching this conclusion? What do you make of the fact that the "changing of the wife's family name on marriage is not required by fiqh, and indeed has not been a characteristic of most Muslim communities. And second, Muslim women often keep separate bank accounts to protect their right under Islamic law to exclusive control over their personal property." Asifa Quraishi & Najeeba Syeed-Miller, No Alters: A Survey of Islamic Family Law in the United States, II.A., *at* http://els41.law.emory.edu/ifl/cases/USA.htm#note1 (citing Azizah al-Hibri). According to one author, the parties kept their marriage quiet because they were both professors in the same department and "found it a bit uncomfortable to announce the marriage." *See* Azizah al-Hibri, Challenges and Opportunities Facing American Muslim Women, Part IV, *at* http://www.zawaj.cm/articles/challenges_women_4.html.

6. *Functionalist Approach.* One commentator has suggested that judges should try to ascertain the purpose and values of a religious rule, and then act to honor the purpose and values. *See* Pascale Foournier, *The Erasure of Islamic Difference in Canadian and American Family Law Adjudication,* 10 J.L. & Pol'y 51, 71 (2001). The same could be said for a cultural rule. Is this a good idea? Did this occur in *Vryonis?* This arguably occurred in *Shayegan v. Baldwin,* 566 A.2d 1164, 1166 (N.J. Super. Ct. App. Div. 1989), where the court held that the transfer of $400,000 in securities by an Iranian woman to her husband was not a gift. Rather, the court found that the wife was engaging in the Iranian custom whereby the husband administers his wife's assets. Consequently, the court refused to apply the presumption that a resulting trust does not arise when the transfer occurs within the marital relationship.

7. *Functional Equivalents.* What is the purpose of *mutà* marriage? One commentator on *mutà* marriage notes that the institution is "given for difficult circumstances." He suggests that most women prefer a permanent marriage, and it is her right and her guardian's right to insist on a permanent marriage. However, if "one is compelled to a lower alternative we must not look at it insultingly." Ja'far, *Mutà Marriage, in* Let Us Understand Each Other, *at* http://www.1ummah.org/understand/muta.htm. Sheikh Hussein al-Khishin, a Shi'ite religious law teacher, explains: "Temporary marriage is for solving a problem that human beings suffer from, a problem that is basically sexual.... This is solving a huge crisis for young people; it saves them from [having sex outside of marriage]." Joseph Logan, God's Loophole: Lebanon's Tempo-

rary Shi'ite Marriage, *at* http://ca.news.yahoo.com/020527/5/mnra.html. Is there anything like *mutà* marriage in U.S. law?

8. *Outsiders' Perspectives.* The Immigration Appellate Authority in the United Kingdom has issued gender guidelines to be used in evaluating claims for asylum. In discussing what constitutes "serious harm" for purposes of asylum eligibility, the guidelines identify *mutà* marriage and indicate "it may be, in effect, a form of legal prostitution or even rape." The example supporting the term "legal prostitution" is from Iran, where article 1075 of the civil code recognizes temporary marriage and specifies that "a man may have an unlimited number of temporary wives." Immigration Appellate Authority, Asylum Gender Guidelines ¶ 2A.24 (2000) (citing Canadian Documentation, Information and Research Branch, Human Rights Briefs: Women in the Islamic Republic of Iran ¶ 2.6.1 (1994)). The example of rape comes from Algeria, where "armed groups have abducted women and girls for forced temporary 'marriages' in which the captive women and girls are raped, sexually abused and often mutilated and killed." *Id.* (citing Report of the U.N. Rapporteur on Contemporary Forms of Slavery, 22 June 1998). What might Fereshteh Vryonis say about the claim that "mutà marriage" may constitute legal prostitution or even rape?

9. *Insiders' Perspectives.* Debates about *mutà* marriage within societies where it is permitted reveal a variety of competing perspectives. Most obviously, the schools of Islamic thought disagree about the legitimacy of the practice. Islamic political leaders also frequently disagree. For example, the Iranian government has taken different positions, reflecting various political interests at work. The Ayatollah Khomeini issued a fatwa reaffirming the necessity of a father's permission for the temporary marriage of a virgin. This helped maintain parental control over a woman's choice of her marital partner and over her sexuality. However, the practice of *mutà* marriage had become so popular that his fatwa had little impact during his life and terminated upon his death. Subsequently, President Rafsanjani, the "highest ranking Iranian political leader with a religious title," reiterated the benefits of the *mutà* marriage and suggested loosening some of the requirements in Iran, such as having it performed by a mullah, registering it, or having the ceremony conducted in Arabic. Parents and women who feared *mutà* marriage as a "threat to the stability and security" of marriage were outraged. Since *mutà* marriage in Iran is predominantly an urban phenomenon, there is a clear geographical divide. *See generally* Shahla Haeri, *Mutà: Regulating Sexuality and Gender Relations in Postrevolutionary Iran, in* Islamic Legal Interpretation: Muftis and Their Fatwas 249 (Muhammad Khalid Masud et al. eds., 1996).

10. *Evidence of Religious Law.* Expert testimony is often used to establish the content of Islamic law in the United States. However, note the warning of Professor al-Hibri:

> Many Muslim men, whether imams of mosques or professors of religion, are not sufficiently familiar with Islamic law. Often, they confuse their cultural beliefs and practices with Islam itself. An American judge has no way of discerning the difference in the absence of more reliable sources of information. If I am a non-Muslim American judge and a Muslim expert witness, a Muslim professor of Islam (how more reliable can an expert witness be?) or the imam of a masjid [mosque] walks into my court, then I am inclined to believe that I am going to get the real story. But that is not always the case.

Azizah Y. al-Hibri, Marriage Contract in American Courts, *at* http://www.minarek. org/azizah.htm. Note what one commentator has said about the testimony in *Vryonis:* "Interestingly, Fereshteh, had held herself out to be an expert on Shi'i Islamic law."

Cherry, *supra*, at 350. Yet, she did not tell the court that she could not validly marry anyone but a Muslim, nor did she tell the court that under Islamic law a *mutà* marriage does not give rise to an obligation for maintenance. Are there fundamental issues about the courts' ability to adjudicate fairly these sorts of claims? If so, do you think courts should construct the law to exclude these sorts of claims altogether?

As note 9 suggests, religious institutions, or religious factions, can be caught in overt turf wars with the secular state over the regulation of marriage. The regulation of the marriage age in Israel serves as an interesting example of the interaction of state law and religious law. Andrew Treitel explored this topic in *Conflicting Traditions: Muslim Shari'a Courts and Marriage Age Regulation in Israel*, 26 Colum. Hum. Rts. L. Rev. 403 (1995). He explains that Israel has both secular courts and government-sanctioned tribal and religious courts. "Tribal courts are found in the sub-district of Beer-Sheva in the south where sheikhs appointed by the minister of justice may apply tribal custom, so long as the custom is not repugnant to natural justice or morality. There are four officially sanctioned religious court systems: Rabbinical (Jewish), Shari'a (Muslim), Christian, and Druze." *Id.* at 411. Appointment of judges, or quadis, to the *Shari'a* courts are made by the president of Israel. "Quadis must pledge their allegiance to the state and promise to dispense justice in accordance with its laws." *Id.* at 416. All of the religious courts have exclusive jurisdiction over marriages for their respective populations. *Id.* at 411–13. The judgments of these courts are executed by the civil courts, and execution may be refused if the religious court exceeded its jurisdiction or its judgment is contrary to natural justice. The Israeli Supreme Court, sitting as the High Court of Justice, would hear these appeals. *Id.* at 413.

In 1950, the Israeli Knesset passed the Marriage Age Law § 5(a), 4 L.S.I. 158, (1950), which enabled only the secular courts, not the religious courts, to permit marriage of girls under 17 under certain circumstances. It also allowed welfare officers to seek the dissolution of marriages of girls under 17. Marriage Age Law § 3(b). This legislation particularly impacted Muslims because marriage of minor girls was frequent in that community. Under Islamic law, girls were considered mature for purposes of marriage at the onset of menstruation. Treitel, *supra*, at 422, 434.

The law was simply not implemented by the Islamic community.

> [The] Sheikh Tahir Hammad, quadi of Yaffo and later head of the Shari'a Appeals Court, felt that underage marriages should not be terminated. He claimed that "age does not affect the validity of the marriage," thereby reflecting the prevailing Muslim sentiment that secular intrusions into traditionally religious realms should be disregarded. The quadis' response to the state's usurpation of a power formerly exercised by the religious courts was to ignore the new (Israeli) provisions and simply follow the [Ottoman Law of Family Rights of 1917] and Hanafi fiqh as it was previously observed. Indeed, in the first meeting of the quadis, in 1950, they agreed that, regardless of the secular legislation barring underage marriages, they felt no obligation to enforce the new minimum age requirement for marriage. Thus, it was due to Muslim pressure that the minimum age rules were later softened if the girl was pregnant or had already given birth. Even though this permission to allow underage marriages was granted to the civil courts, not to the Shari'a courts, the quadis began conducting themselves as if they had received these broad new

powers, allowing and performing underage marriages without the civil courts' pre-approval.

Id. at 433. Furthermore, secular welfare officers never requested dissolutions for marriages involving minors, nor did the husbands who were told that requesting dissolution would mitigate any possible penal sanction that they might face. *Id.* at 433. Consequently,

> within the first decade after passage of the Marriage Age Law, there were hundreds of marriages sanctioned by the Shari'a courts in violation of the minimum age requirement. Indeed, the 1961 census showed that 42.7% of all Israeli Muslims had been married before the age of seventeen. The actual number becomes much higher when one calculates those marriages performed by local custom and not registered with the state courts.

Id. at 434. Treitel concluded, "The ideas echoing in the halls of Parliament were barely heard by the people in the villages." *Id.* at 436.

Notes and Questions

1. *Law in Action.* What was the practical impact of Israel's imposition of marriage requirements that were out of sync with the Islamic religious community? For another story about the effectiveness of civil marriage law in combatting child marriages, see Mark Cammack et al., *Legislating Social Change in Islamic Society—Indonesia's Marriage Law*, 44 Am. J. Comp. L. 45 (1996) (suggesting Indonesia's National Marriage Act did not have a direct effect on raising the actual marriage age because individuals thought Islamic marriage would still be valid; however, it had an indirect effect because the act emphasized individual autonomy and choice, and this emphasis encouraged later marriages).

2. *Islamic Law and Age.* Under classic Islamic law, "No contract whatever can be concluded by one who has not reached the age of discernment (*tamyîz*—usually reckoned at about seven), but children below this age can be given in marriage by their marriage guardians. Between the age of discernment and that of full legal capacity, a child may himself conclude certain contracts, including marriage, subject to the consent of his guardian. If this consent is forthcoming, the contract is ratified; if it is withheld, the contract is void *ab initio*. Alternatively, and more usually, children of this age can be contracted in marriage by their guardians. Full legal capacity is reached when a boy or girl attains puberty *(bulûgh)*—which is usually presumed, in the absence of physical evidence, to be at the completion of the fifteenth year together with adequate mental development *(rushd)*. The whole subject is complicated, in the matter of marriage, by the fact that only the *Hanafîs* and *Ithnâ' Asharîs* allow even an adult woman to conclude her own contract of marriage; and also by the fact that marriage guardians sometimes have the right to give their wards in compulsory marriage *(idjbâr)* and sometimes to do this only with their consent." Sir Norman Anderson, *Islamic Family Law, in* IV International Encyclopaedia of Comparative Law 55, 58 (1983).

Today, most of the Muslim world imposes a minimum marriage age. That lowest official age for marriage is fifteen in several countries, although judges sometimes have authority to "bypass the minimum age requirements in cases where the guardian agrees and there is some perceived benefit or necessity to the marriage." In these places, the marriage age can be as low as nine for girls and fifteen for boys, so long as the child is mature. *See* Esposito & DeLong-Bas, *supra*, at 99.

3. *Age gap.* Some Islamic countries require judicial permission to marry if the parties are vastly different in age. For example, Jordanian law states, "No marriage contract shall be solemnized for a woman under 18 years of age if the husband-to-be is over 20 years older than her, unless the judge makes sure of her consent and free choice, and that the marriage is in her interests." Jamil Nasir, The Status of Women Under Islamic Law and Under Modern Islamic Legislation 8 (1990).

4. *Comparing Customary and Religious Law.* Many of the issues that we have covered already with respect to customary law also arise with respect to religious law. For example, the state's requirement that a marriage be registered might be seen as unnecessary, and therefore disregarded, by those entering a religious marriage. Followers of the *Shari'a* believe that a marriage exists if it occurs in the presence of two witnesses, regardless of its registration. *See, e.g.,* Nadya Haider, *Islamic Legal Reform: The Case of Pakistan and Family Law,* 12 Yale J.L. & Feminism 287, 310 (2000). In addition, just as some customary practices discriminate on the basis of gender, so too do some religious practices, although these practices should be distinguished from religious doctrine itself. *See* al-Hibri, *supra,* at 228 (discussing sources of Islamic law and how interpretations of the Koran developed in a patriarchal culture). What other similarities, or differences, do you see between customary law and religious law?

5. *Reform.* "One of the earliest abuses tackled by the reformers in several Muslim countries has been the question of child marriage." Anderson, *supra,* at 62. As explained by one scholar, three fundamental principles of Islamic jurisprudence make change possible within the confines of the Koran and *sunna:*

> 1. Islamic laws may change with the passage of time or with the change of place or circumstance....

> A corollary of this principle permits change in the law whenever related customs change.

> 2. Islamic laws must avoid harm....

> This principle is also referred to as the principle of choosing the lesser of two evils.

> 3. Islamic laws must serve the public interest....

See al-Hibri, *supra,* at 230. Of course, these principles can permit change that we might consider beneficial as well as change that we might consider harmful. For example, in 1975, Iran set the minimum age for marriage at eighteen for girls and twenty for boys. However, it returned the ages to nine years for girls and fifteen for boys under the Ayatollah Khomeini's rule. Subsequently, the age for girls was raised to fifteen to prevent harm from sex and pregnancy. No exceptions are permitted. *See* Esposito & DeLong-Bas, *supra,* at 99.

6. *Religion and the State in the United States.* Try to describe the relationship between religious law and secular law in the United States on the topic of marriage. There is much to consider in such an exercise. As a constitutional matter, the government is not supposed to either inhibit the free exercise of religion or establish religion. However, one sees a subtle hostility on the part of the state, as embodied through the courts, for example, when parties try to argue that their religious beliefs constrain the state's ability to award a divorce. *See, e.g.,* Trickey v. Trickey, 642 S.W. 2d 47 (Tex. Ct. App. 1982) (no fault divorce provision was constitutionally applied to Christian marriage). Sometimes even overt hostility exists; such hostility was evident, for example, toward individuals who tried to practice polygamy. Starting with the Morrill Act in 1862, Congress passed

several acts criminalizing polygamy in the territories. Then in *Reynolds v. U.S.*, 98 U.S. 145 (1878), the Supreme Court upheld the criminalization of polygamy against a First Amendment challenge. It held that "laws are made for the government of action, and while they cannot interfere with mere religious belief and opinions, they may with practices," at least when the practices are "subversive of good order." *Id.* at 164, 166. The underlying rationale was that a monogamous family was critical to democracy; society is built on marriage and polygamy leads to patriarchy and despotism. *See* Mary K. Campbell, *Mr. Peay's Horses: The Federal Response to Mormon Polygamy, 1854–1887*, 13 Yale J.L. & Feminism 29, 41 (2001). The hostility towards polygamy by state actors has waned substantially. While the Mormon Church has officially condemned the practice, polygamy is still practiced by 25,000 to 50,000 polygamists in the West who claim to be Mormon. *See* Keith E. Sealing, *Polygamists Out of the Closet: Statutory and State Constitutional Prohibitions Against Polygamy are Unconstitutional Under the Free Exercise Clause*, 17 Ga. S. Univ. L. Rev. 691, 693–94 (2001). Tom Green's prosecution in 2001 was the first prosecution in Utah for bigamy in five decades. Richard A. Vazquez, Note, *The Practice of Polygamy*, 5 N.Y.U. J. Leg. & Pub. Pol'y 225 (2001–02).

Also consider that some individual decision-makers, both judges and legislators, undeniably base their view of "marriage" on their faith. Perhaps one of the most infamous examples is the trial court's decision in *Loving v. Virginia*, where the trial court upheld Virginia's antimiscegenation statute and stated, "Almighty God created the races white, black, yellow, malay and red, and he placed them on separate continents. And but for the interference with his arrangement there would be no cause for such marriages. The fact that he separated the races shows that he did not intend for the races to mix." *See* Loving v. Virginia, 388 U.S. 1, 3 (1967).

Finally, make sure to consider that the U.S. marriage regime grows out of a history that was dominated, at times, by religious institutions, particularly the Catholic Church. In England, canon law was specifically applied by the ecclesiastical courts, from approximately the eleventh century forward. Secularization of marriages did not occur until 1857, with the establishment of the Court for Divorce and Matrimonial Causes. *See generally* Javier Martinez-Torron, Anglo-American Law and Canon Law 93-100 (1998). As a consequence of the English experience, marriage law in the United States is also strongly influenced by canon law. See Chapter 3.A. *See also* John Witte, Jr., From Sacrament to Contract: Marriage, Religion, and Law in the Western Tradition 16–41 (1997).

Is the somewhat contradictory approach to religion by state institutions a preferable way to resolve tensions than the adoption of a pluralistic legal system?

3. Constitutional Law

In many countries, governmental institutions constitute another source of intra-societal competition over marriage. In a federal system, the competition can exist between the federal government and its constituent states. Competition can also exist between branches of government, *e.g.*, the legislature, the executive, and the courts. Particularly interesting is whether the courts from one level of government have the power to adjudicate claims based upon the legislation from another level of government. These types of struggles often take place against the backdrop of a constitution that allocates power among the contestants. These struggles and the constitutional law that guides the outcomes again raise the following question: Which group in society should be responsible for marriage regulation?

a. *Constitutional Allocation of Power between the Legislative Branches*

For a country with a federal system of government, like the United States, either the federal government and/or the state governments might have the power to regulate entry into marriage. In the United States, the substantive and formal requirements for marriage have mostly been regulated by the states. The United States Supreme Court declared that "domestic issues [are] an area that has long been regarded as a virtually exclusive province of the states." Sosna v. Iowa, 419 U.S. 393, 404 (1975) (upholding durational residency requirement for filing of divorce petition). In Pennoyer v. Neff, 95 U.S. 714, 734-35 (1878), the Court commented in dicta that "the State...has absolute right to prescribe the conditions upon which the marriage relation between its own citizens shall be created, and the causes for which it may be dissolved." The states regulate marriage in the United States because any power not enumerated in the U.S. Constitution and allocated to the federal government is reserved to the states by virtue of the Tenth Amendment.

It would be wrong, however, to infer that the federal government in the United States is uninvolved in the marriage question. After all, the federal government can bind and has bound the United States, including the individual states, to treaties that address marriage, such as the International Covenant on Civil and Political Rights, Mar. 23, 1976, 999 U.N.T.S. 171. Even apart from international legal measures, there certainly has been the occasional federal foray into the area. The American Bar Association recently listed forty-three federal statutes relating to family law, and fifty-four Supreme Court rulings on family law topics "that include a federal interest or a federal issue." *See Federal Statutes Relating to Family Law*, 23 Fam. Advoc. 13 (2001); *Supreme Court Cases*, 23 Fam. Advoc. 15 (2001). Some of these forays are quite direct. *See, e.g.*, Cleveland v. U.S., 329 U.S. 14, 26 (1946) (holding that transportation of multiple wives across state lines violates the Mann Act); Reynolds v. U.S., 98 U.S. 145, 166 (1878) (holding that federal law forbidding polygamy within U.S. territories did not unconstitutionally interfere with freedom of religion). *See also, e.g.*, 25 U.S.C. § 181 (limiting rights of white men marrying Indian women to tribal property); the Anti-Polygamy Acts, July 1, 1862, ch. 126, 12 Stat. 501; Mar. 22, 1882, ch. 47, 22 Stat. 30; Mar. 3, 1887, ch. 397, 24 Stat. 635, *repealed by* Act of Mar. 4, 1909, ch. 321, 35 Stat. 1156 & Act of Mar. 3, 1911, ch. 231, 36 Stat. 1168. At other times, federal regulation occurs more indirectly, for example through federal tax laws and federal benefit laws. *See generally* Patricia A. Cain, *Heterosexual Privilege and the Internal Revenue Code*, 34 U.S.F. L. Rev. 465, 467 (2000).

The proper role of the federal government has been raised recently as part of the debate over the Defense of Marriage Act, 23 U.S.C. § 1738(C) (1996). The Defense of Marriage Act (DOMA) was passed when it appeared that some states might permit same-sex marriage. DOMA defines marriage as between a man and a woman for purposes of federal benefit laws. It also says that no state need recognize a same-sex marriage from another state. During the debate, Representative Farr, a democrat from California, said:

> Our country has just gone through 220 years without Federal law on marriages. Think about it. We do not have a Federal marriage license. People get

married under State law. Some States allow people to marry cousins. Some States allow persons committing statutory rape to have the rape dropped if they marry the person. States do not regulate how many times someone can get married, they do not regulate how many times someone can get a divorce. So why is this bill called the Defense of Marriage Act? It does not improve marriages, and it takes away States' rights.

142 Cong. Rec. 7441 (1996) (statement of Rep. Farr). *See also* Joan Biskupic, *Same-Sex Marriage Issues to Take Center Stage in Senate*, Wash. Post., Sept. 3, 1996, at A1 (quoting Representative Lynn C. Woolsey, a democrat from California); 142 Cong. Rec. 7441 (1996) (statement of Rep. Jackson-Lee).

In contrast to the United States, some countries expressly allocate legislative power over marriage to the central, or federal, government. For example, Part V of the Australian Constitution lists those matters over which the Commonwealth government has legislative power. Section 51 states, "The Parliament shall, subject to this Constitution, have the right to exercise power to make laws for the peace, order, and good government of the Commonwealth with respect to...(xxi) Marriage...(xxii) Divorce and matrimonial causes; and in relation thereto, parental rights, and the custody and guardianship of infants." In fact, in the debates leading up to the establishment of the Commonwealth of Australia in 1901, advocates of the Constitution referred to the " 'great mistake' of the framers of the Constitution of the United States, which left these matters, of 'vital and national importance,' in state hands; the result, conflict and confusion, should not be allowed to occur in Australia." Leonie Star, Counsel of Perfection: The Family Court of Australia 44 (1996) (citing Malcolm Broun, *Historical Introduction, in* Paul Toose et al., Australian Divorce Law and Practice (1968)). Opponents of the Australian Constitution, in contrast, felt "that states should retain sovereignty over the personal affairs of their citizens." J. Neville Turner, *Australia, in* International Encyclopaedia of Laws: Family and Succession Law 22 (Walter Pintens & R. Blanpain eds., 1997). Justice Jacobs of the High Court of Australia commented that the marriage and divorce provisions in section 51 "are the only subject matters of Commonwealth power which are not related to what may be broadly described as public economic or financial subjects but which are related to what are commonly thought of as private or personal rights." Russell v. Russell (1976) 134 C.L.R. 495, 546-47. He continued:

> The reason for their inclusion appears to me to be twofold. First, although marriage and the dissolution thereof are in many ways a personal matter of the parties, social history tells us that the state has always regarded them of matters of public concern. Secondly, and perhaps more importantly, the need was recognized for a uniformity in legislation on these subject matters throughout the Commonwealth. In a single community throughout which intercourse was to be absolutely free, provision was required whereby there could be uniformity in the laws governing the relationship of marriage and the consequences of that relationship as well as the dissolution thereof. Differences between the States in the laws governing the status and the relationship of married persons could be socially divisive to the harm of the new community which was being created. But because these subject matters enter so deeply into the field of personal and private rights, a field largely left within the legislative power of the States, it is difficult to resist the tendency in oneself to regard the Commonwealth power as an intrusion into an area solidly filled by State laws on a variety of subject matters which govern personal and private rights.

Id.

In Australia, this federal power over divorce was only first exercised in 1959 with passage of the Matrimonial Causes Act, and the power over marriage was only first exercised with the passage of the Marriage Act of 1961. The Marriage Act, which addresses both capacity to marry and formalities as well as legitimation of children, had the effect of standardizing marriage law throughout Australia. *See* H.A. Finlay, Family Law in Australia 60 (1983). The Australian courts, following the canon of construction that legislative powers conferred by the Constitution should be construed liberally, have broadly interpreted the power allocated by the Constitution to Parliament. The High Court of Australia, for example, in *Att'y-Gen.(Vict.) v. The Commonwealth* (1962) 107 C.L.R. 529, 558 (Austl.), held that section 51 did not refer only to the solemnization of marriage. The Court held that it was constitutional for Parliament also to specify the legal consequences of marriage, and in particular, that the marriage of a child's parents legitimatizes the child. However, since Parliament has no power to regulate the consequences of nonmarital relationships, any legal issues relating to these relationships fall to the states or territories. Consequently, for example, state or territory law governs the financial consequences of the dissolution of non-marital ("de facto") relationships.

Some countries, like Canada, have a bifurcated approach to the regulation of marriage. For example, The Constitution Act of 1867, which serves as Canada's written Constitution, states that "[T]he exclusive Legislative Authority of the Parliament of Canada extends to all Matters coming within the Classes of Subjects next hereinafter enumerated; that is to say,... Marriage and Divorce." Can. Const. (Constitution Act, 1867) pt. VI (Distribution of Legislative Powers), § 91(26). The Constitution Act goes on to say that "In each Province the Legislature may exclusively make Laws in relation to... [t]he Solemnization of Marriage in the Province." Can. Const., *supra,* §§ 92(12). Consequently, the federal government has exclusive jurisdiction over the capacity to marry, but the formalities are determined by the provinces. "While federal legislation typically supersedes contrary provincial legislation, in the area of marriage, however, the Privy Council has held that the 'solemnization of marriage' was an exception carved out of the federal power over 'marriage' and that federal legislation cannot supersede valid provincial legislation." Donald J. MacDougall, *Marriage Resolution and Recognition in Canada,* 29 Fam. L.Q. 541, 541 (1995).

Although Canadian law authorized the federal government to regulate the entrance into marriage, until very recently the "only federal legislation [was] the Marriage (Prohibited Degrees) Act, 1990 which is a short Act defining the prohibited degrees of relationships." *Id.* at 542. Professor MacDougall continues, "In the absence of federal legislation, the provinces... made imaginative use of the 'solemnization of marriage' power, and the courts have generally accommodated a broad interpretation of provincial power." *Id.* In 2000, federal legislation was finally passed that indirectly touches upon the topic of who may marry whom by setting forth a definition of marriage. The Modernization of Benefits and Obligations Act (2000) is designed to ensure that both same-sex and opposite-sex "common-law" relationships are treated equally under federal law. The "Interpretation" section of the act states: "For greater certainty, the amendments made by this Act do not affect the meaning of the word 'marriage,' that is, the lawful union of one man and one woman to the exclusion of all others." The implications of this act, and this section in particular, are only starting to be understood. *See infra* note 6 following *Kerr* (discussion of *Halpren v. Toronto*).

In Canada, the constitutional bifurcation of powers related to marriage regulation has lead to interesting questions about the validity of particular marriages. As mentioned above, despite federal power to regulate entry into the institution, the Dominion has seldom done so. In the absence of federal legislation, the provinces have passed statutes regulating the institution of marriage. Questions about the constitutionality of these statutory provisions have occasionally reached the Supreme Court of Canada, as the next case illustrates.

Kerr v. Kerr
[1934] S.C.R. 72 (Can.)

Lamont, J....

The facts of the case are not in dispute. The parties first met in April 1930, and sexual intercourse took place between them on some four occasions. In September 1930, Frances Margaret Smith found herself to be pregnant and she and some of her friends urged the appellant to marry her. He objected claiming that he was not the cause of her condition. Yielding, however, to their importunities, the appellant, on December 2, 1930, went through a form of marriage with her at Hamilton, Ontario, where they both resided. To obtain the marriage license, Frances Margaret Smith made an affidavit that she was 18 years of age, although she was then only seventeen. When the affidavit was made both the appellant and Miss Smith knew that the statement therein contained as to her age was false, and knew also that it was made for the purpose of procuring the marriage license. The ceremony was performed without the knowledge of the parents or family of either of the parties. No consent to the marriage was obtained from the mother of Frances Margaret Smith as required by s. 17 of the Marriage Act. The marriage was never consummated and the parties, since the ceremony, have not co-habited or lived together as man and wife.

On these facts the trial Judge gave judgment for the appellant, declaring the marriage ceremony between the parties to be null and void upon the ground that the consent of the girl's mother to the marriage (her father being dead) had not been obtained, and that s. 34 of the Act was ultra vires of the Provincial Legislature.

From that judgment an appeal was taken to the Court of Appeal by the respondent, Frances Margaret Kerr. The Court of Appeal ([1932] 4 D.L.R. 288) reversed the judgment of the trial Judge holding that s. 34 was within the competence of the provincial legislature. The appellant now appeals....

The appeal turns upon the construction to be placed upon §§ 17 and 34 of the Marriage Act. The relevant parts of these sections are:

17(1) Save in cases provided for by subsections 3 and 4 of this section and by section 18, where either of the parties to an intended marriage, not a widower or a widow, is under the age of eighteen years, the consent in writing of the father if living, or, if he is dead, or living apart from the mother and child, and is not maintaining or contributing to the support of such child, the consent in writing of the mother if living, or of a guardian if any has been duly appointed, shall be obtained from the father, mother or guardian before the license is issued...and such consent shall be deemed to be a condition precedent to a valid marriage, unless the marriage has been consummated or the parties have after the ceremony cohabited and lived together as man and wife.

34(1) Where a form of marriage is gone through between persons either of whom is under the age of eighteen years without the consent of the father, mother or guardian of such person, when such consent is required by the provisions of this Act... such form of marriage shall be void and the Supreme Court shall have jurisdiction and power to entertain an action by the person who was at the time of the ceremony under the age of eighteen years, to declare and adjudge that a valid marriage was not effected or entered into, and shall so declare and adjudge if it is made to appear that the marriage has not been consummated and that such persons have not, after the ceremony, cohabited and lived together as man and wife, and that the action is brought before the person bringing it has attained the age of nineteen years.

(2) The Court shall not declare a marriage void where carnal intercourse has taken place between the parties before the ceremony.

The contention of the appellant is:

1. That s. 17(1) is competent provincial legislation in so far as it requires the consent of the parents or guardians of a contracting party... before the issue of the license if the party is under the age of 18 years, and also in so far as it enacts that such consent shall be a condition precedent to a valid marriage.

2. That s. 34 is ultra vires of the Provincial Legislature, as it is legislation on the subject of marriage and divorce which, by s. 91(26) of the [British North American Act 1987 (BNA Act)], is exclusively assigned to the Dominion Parliament.

3. That, as the consent required by s. 17(1) was not obtained and, as s. 34 is ultra vires, the marriage should be held null and void by virtue of the Divorce Act (Ontario), 1930, enacted by the Dominion Parliament.

By the BNA Act, the power to make laws respecting marriage and its solemnization was distributed between the Dominion Parliament and the Provincial Legislatures. To the Dominion was assigned the exclusive legislative jurisdiction over the subject of "Marriage and Divorce" (s. 91(26)) while to the Provinces was given the exclusive legislative jurisdiction over the "Solemnization of Marriage" in the Provinces (s. 92(12)). The solemnization of marriage might readily have been included within the general description of "Marriage and Divorce," but it seemed wise to the framers of our constitutional Act to carve out of the field which marriage and divorce would otherwise have covered, a small but distinct and essential part designated "The Solemnization of Marriage in the Province" and give the Provincial Legislatures the exclusive right to make laws in respect thereof. Each legislative body is supreme within its own sphere and the question we have to determine is, does the impeached legislation (s. 34) fall within any one of the subjects exclusively assigned to the Provincial Legislatures?

[I]t has been settled law that the exclusive power of the Provincial Legislatures to make laws relating to the solemnization of marriage in the Province operates by way of exception to the powers conferred upon the Dominion Parliament as regards marriage by s. 91(26), and enables the Provincial Legislatures to enact conditions as to the solemnization which may affect the validity of the contract.

"Solemnization of Marriage" within the meaning of s. 92 includes not only the essential ceremony by which the marriage is effected, but also parental consent where such consent is required by law. In Sottomayor v. De Barros (1877), 3 P.D. 1, Cotton, L.J., at p. 7, says:

It only remains to consider the case of Simonin v. Mallac, 2 Sw. & Tr. 67 [164 E.R. 917]. The objection to the validity of the marriage in that case, which was solemnized in England, was the want of the consent of parents required by the law of France, but not under the circumstances by that of this country. In our opinion, this consent must be considered a part of the ceremony of marriage, and not a matter affecting the personal capacity of the parties to contract marriage.

The Provincial Legislature is, therefore, competent by apt legislation to make the preliminaries, leading up to the marriage ceremony, conditions precedent to the solemnization of the marriage. From this it follows, in my opinion, that the Legislature is also competent to declare that in the event of these conditions precedent not being complied with no valid marriage has taken place....

Then are s-ss. (1) and (2) of s. 34 competent provincial legislation?...

The object of these two sections is, I think, clear. By them the Legislature was endeavoring, (1) To provide that a failure to furnish the consent to an intended marriage, required by s. 17 in case of a contracting party thereto under the age of 18 years who has gone through a form of marriage, would in certain cases have the effect of preventing a valid marriage from taking place, and (2) To bestow on the Supreme Court of Ontario jurisdiction to entertain an action and to declare and adjudge that the going through of such a form of marriage, under the circumstances, would not constitute a valid marriage. This jurisdiction was bestowed on the Court only in those cases in which the conditions prescribed by the statute had been complied with....

[T]he whole enactment in these two sections concerns the bestowal of jurisdiction on the Supreme Court of Ontario to try an action and make a declaration that there has been no valid marriage in certain cases and under certain conditions, and the withholding of such jurisdiction in others, particularly s-s. (2) where the Act expressly states that the Court should not "declare a marriage void where carnal intercourse has taken place between the parties before the ceremony." Is it within the competence of the Legislature to give jurisdiction to the Court in some cases and withhold or deny it in others?

In the case of a marriage void by the law of the place where it was celebrated, on account of lack of essential formalities, a declaration that it is invalid has been described as "merely a judicial ascertainment of facts." It ascertains but does not change the status of the parties. If that is so, and I think it is, it is difficult to see why the Legislature should not be competent to invest the Courts with jurisdiction to ascertain a fact. The jurisdiction of the Supreme Court of Ontario is statutory. Without this enactment the Court would have no jurisdiction to declare null and void the going through of a form of marriage.

In this case I have no doubt that the Provincial Legislature had full power, under s. 92(14), to enact the impeached legislation.... [Ed. Note: Section 92(14) of the BNA Act gives the provinces the exclusive right to make laws respecting the "Administration of Justice in the Province, including the Constitution, Maintenance, and Organization of Provincial Courts, both of Civil and of Criminal Jurisdiction, and including Procedure in Civil Matters in those Courts."]

Crocket, J.

I regret that I cannot agree with my brethren upon the question of the constitutionality of the provisoes of s. 34 of the Ontario Marriage Act....

The report of the Judicial Committee of the Privy Council on the Canadian Marriage Reference of 1912 (7 D.L.R. 629) distinctly laid down the principle that s. 92(12) enables the Provincial Legislature "to enact conditions as to solemnization which may affect the validity of the contract" of marriage. I have no doubt that in accordance with the principle of this decision, this exclusive legislative authority in the Provincial Legislature comprises not only the power to declare void a marriage for want of the required consent of a parent or guardian in the case of a marriage solemnized between persons, one of whom is under the age of 18 years, but the power to confer upon the Supreme Court jurisdiction to pronounce a decree of nullity for want of such consent in such case, or for any other reason which in reality pertains to the subject-matter of the solemnization of marriage.

I find it impossible, however, to assent to the view that the conditions prescribed by the provisoes in s. 34 as conditions, not as to the validity or invalidity of the marriage ceremony, but as conditions to the right of the Court to pronounce a decree of nullity in the case of such a marriage, are conditions which do pertain in any way to the subject-matter of the solemnization of marriage. The manifest intent, and the real pith and substance of these provisoes is to prevent the Supreme Court from declaring void any marriage ceremony for want of the required consent of a parent or guardian of a person under the age of 18 years, except at the instance of the party to the marriage ceremony, who was under the prescribed age at the time of the performance of that ceremony; and, even where an action for annulment is brought by such party, to prohibit the Court from granting such a decree if, after the ceremony, there has been consummation and cohabitation as husband and wife between the parties; or, if the plaintiff has failed to bring his or her action for such annulment before attaining the age of 19 years; or, further, if the parties to the marriage have had carnal intercourse before the performance of the ceremony.

The provisoes prescribe conditions which, whether they do or do not themselves strictly affect the validity of the marriage contract, make a judicial declaration or judgment of annulment impossible in such a case. They are an absolute bar to such a decree, and in reality dispense with the requirement of a parent's or guardian's consent to the solemnization of the marriage ceremony.... None of these conditions pertain to any of the requisite preliminaries or formalities of the marriage ceremony. They treat of matters which are wholly extraneous thereto, i.e., the conduct of the parties before and after the ceremony. Consummation and cohabitation as husband and wife are, no doubt, the natural consequences of a marriage ceremony, but obviously, whether consummation or subsequent cohabitation take place or not, could not conceivably affect the right of any person, possessing the requisite governmental authority for the purpose, to solemnize or perform the ceremony, or even the right or capacity of the parties themselves to have it solemnized; neither could the neglect or laches of either party to bring an action for annulment before attaining the age of 19 years. In my opinion, they go entirely beyond the subject-matter of the solemnization of marriage and consequently invade the exclusive legislative authority of the Dominion Parliament in relation to all other matters pertaining to the larger subject of marriage and divorce....

It seems to me that if it is now to be held that the Provincial Legislatures can validly impose any such restrictions as are here in question upon the right of the Supreme or any other provincial Court to grant decrees of annulment for want of the requisite consent of a parent or guardian to the solemnization of a marriage ceremony, they may quite as logically impose any other imaginable restrictions, not only as conditions to the granting of such decrees, but as conditions to the validity of a marriage, and thus exhaust and effectively control the whole field of validity. If they can prescribe the fact of no previous carnal intercourse having taken place between the parties to the solemnization of a marriage ceremony, either as a condition of the validity of the marriage or as a condition of the power of the Court to grant a decree of annulment, why may they not likewise, for instance, prescribe the condition that the parties be not related by consanguinity or that there is no impotence upon the part of either as further conditions of validity or of the jurisdiction of the Court to pronounce a decree of annulment in such a case?...

[Ed. Note: The separate opinions of Duff, C.J.C., Rinfret, Cannon and Smith, JJ., have been omitted. These justices all believed the appeal should be dismissed for reasons similar to Justice Lamont's.]

Notes and Questions

1. *Clarifying Terms.* The British North America Act, 1867 ("BNA Act") was passed by the British Imperial Parliament. "The BNA Act created the Dominion of Canada as a single federal entity under a governor general appointed by the Queen, with an appointed Senate, and an elected House of Commons." L. Kinvin Wroth, *Notes for a Comparative Study of the Origins of Federalism in the U.S. and Canada,* 15 Ariz. J. Int'l & Comp. L. 93, 118 (1998). The BNA Act was renamed the Constitution Act, 1867 in 1982, and included, for the first time, a Charter of Rights. The BNA Act contains the basic constitutional framework for Canada's federal system. Canada has now attained its autonomy from Britain through the Statute of Westminster and the Canada Act, 1982.

Justice Crocket spoke of "the real pith and substance" of the Marriage Act's provisos, and Justice Lamont spoke of their object. "Canadian courts reviewing the constitutionality of a challenged legislative enactment have the duty to examine the purpose and effect of the law and to uphold it only if 'the pith and substance' of the enactment is within the jurisdiction of the enacting legislature." Martha A. Field, *The Differing Federalism of Canada and the United States,* 55 Law & Contemp. Probs. 107, 115 (1992). "Ultra vires" means that the governmental body performed acts unauthorized by its constituent instrument, therefore, the acts are void for want of legal capacity or power.

2. *Outcome.* Did the Supreme Court of Canada's decision mean that the parties were, or were not, married? Justice Crocket ultimately agreed with Justice Lamont that the appeal should be dismissed. Although Justice Crocket believed that section 34 was *ultra vires,* he also believed (unlike Justice Lamont) that the Supreme Court of Ontario lacked statutory or inherent jurisdiction to pronounce a decree of annulment. Justice Crocket did not think the province conferred jurisdiction by statute, and he read the Divorce Act (Ontario), 1930 (Can.), enacted by the Dominion Parliament, as not conferring jurisdiction in this situation either.

3. *Formalities versus Capacity.* Both Justice Crocket and Justice Lamont agree that rules requiring parental consent address marital "solemnization." What if the law had said that a person must divorce any prior living spouse as a precondition to solemnization? Is that a law related to solemnization? Try to answer that last question in light of *Kerr* and also *Neilson v. Underwood,* [1934] S.C.R. 635 (Can.), where the Supreme Court of Canada further elaborated on the meaning of laws related to solemnization. There the Supreme Court of Canada again upheld a provincial law making parental consent a condition precedent to a valid marriage for minors, citing *Kerr v. Kerr & Att'y Gen. Ont.* Rinfret, J. stated: "The whole question depends upon the distinction to be made between the formalities of the ceremony of marriage and the status or capacity required to contract marriage. Solemnization of marriage is not confined to the ceremony itself. It legitimately includes the various steps or preliminaries leading to it. The statute of Alberta, in its essence, deals with those steps or prelimi-

naries in that Province. It is only territorial. It applies only to marriages solemnized in Alberta and it prescribes the formalities by which the ceremony of marriage shall be celebrated in that Province (Brook v. Brook, [1861] 9 H.L.C. 193). It does not pretend to deprive minors domiciled in Alberta of the capacity to marry outside the Province without the consent of their parents. Moreover, it requires that consent only under certain conditions and it is not directed to the question of personal status." *Neilson*, [1934] S.C.R. at 639.

4. *Allocation of Power I. Kerr* helped define the boundaries of the provinces' enumerated powers. In Canada, the courts have interpreted the provincial solemnization power in section 92(12) broadly. To see this more clearly, answer the following questions: Which legislative body passed the Marriage Act? What was the argument that section 34 was *ultra vires* the BNA Act? Why did this argument not succeed?

5. *Allocation of Power II.* A different type of constitutional issue could also present itself in Canada: Whether the federal government has exceeded its powers when regulating marriage. Section 91 of the Canadian Constitution allocates legislative power in enumerated areas to the Canadian Parliament and also provides that Parliament may legislate for "the Peace, Order, and Good Government of Canada" in relation to all subjects not specifically allocated to the provinces. Consequently, while federal power is enumerated, the federal government also has residual powers similar to the states in the United States. This clause might be relevant, for example, to Parliament's power to regulate "same-sex marriage" if the definition of marriage were fixed at the time of the Constitution Act's adoption. *Cf.* Egale Canada Inc. v. Canada (Att'y-Gen.), [2001] 11 W.W.R. 685 (B.C. Sup. Ct.) (holding that "marriage" in section 91(26) was a union of opposite-sex parties and that the issue did not fall under section 92(13) which gives the provinces jurisdiction over "Property and Civil Rights" in the provinces).

Despite the broad constitutional language, the Canadian courts have confined federal power to those areas enumerated in the Constitution, even though that was not the intent of its framers (who witnessed the U.S. Civil War before the adoption of the Canadian Constitution of 1867 and therefore wanted to strengthen federal power). *See* Keith S. Rosenn, *Federalism in the Americas in Comparative Perspective*, 26 U. Miami Inter-Am. L. Rev. 1, 11–12 (1994). The Privy Council stated:

> [T]he exercise of legislative power by the Parliament of Canada, in regard to all matters not enumerated in section 91, ought to be strictly confined to such matters as are unquestionably of Canadian interest and importance, and ought not to trench upon provincial legislation with respect to any of the classes of subjects enumerated in section 92. To attach any other construction to the general power which, in supplement of its enumerated powers, is conferred upon the Parliament of Canada by section 91, would, in their Lordships' opinion, not only be contrary to the intendment of the Act, but would practically destroy the autonomy of the provinces.

Att'y-Gen. of Ontario v. Att'y-Gen. for the Dominion, [1896] A.C. 348, 360-61 (P.C.) (holding that both the federal and provincial governments have authority to regulate liquor, and that provincial legislation was valid since it did not conflict with federal legislation). *See also* In re Authority of the Parliament of Canada to Enact "The Marriage Act," [1912] A.C. 880 (Can. P. C.) (Privacy Council) (holding Parliament had no power to enact legislation making a marriage valid throughout Canada if valid where performed because such federal power would render provincial power virtually meaningless).

6. *Contemporary Example of Tension. Halpern v. Toronto (A.G.)*, [2002] 28 R.F.L.5th 41 (Ont. Div. Ct.) is an excellent example of how the jurisdictional tensions are presently playing out in Canada with respect to marriage. The case arose because the clerk of the city of Toronto refused to grant a marriage license to some same-sex couples, and the registrar general of Ontario refused to register the same-sex marriages of some other couples. The officials cited the Ontario Marriage Act and the Vital Statistics Act as justifying their refusals. The Divisional Court of the Ontario Superior Court of Justice held that the officials' acts were unconstitutional. The officials' decisions had rested upon the common law definition of marriage (that marriage is exclusively between a man and a woman) and that definition violated the equality provisions of section 15(1) of the Canadian Charter of Rights and Freedoms.

The constitutional federalism issues loomed large in the court's opinion. First, the divisional court held that the province had no power to address the capacity of same-sex parties to marry. To the extent that the province's statutory law could be read to define marriage as between a man and a woman, that legislation was ultra vires the province's authority. *See* LaForme, J., ¶92; Smith, A.C.J.S.C., ¶2(a); Blair, R.S.J., ¶21. Second, the court rejected the argument that Parliament had defined marriage by statute and had thereby created a statutory impediment to the issuance of marriage licenses to same-sex couples. One of the three judges stated:

> It is the federal government that has the constitutional authority to define marriage, by virtue of the division of powers in sections 91 and 92 of the Constitution Act. Section 91(26) gives Parliament authority over marriage and divorce. Parliament has not legislatively defined what is meant by "marriage," however.
>
> The closest Parliament has come to doing so is in section 1.1 of the Modernization of Benefits and Obligations Act, S.C. 2000, c. 12 (the "MBOA"). Section 1.1 is the "interpretation" clause in the legislation—which was an omnibus bill designed to amend a large number of federal statutes to comply with the law respecting gays and lesbians following the decision of the Supreme Court of Canada in *M. v. H.* It states that "the amendments made by this Act do not affect the meaning of the world 'marriage,' that is, the lawful union of one man and one woman to the exclusion of all others." While this statutory provision may provide a strong indication of Parliament's view on marriage, at the time of the enactment of MBOA, it does not constitute a statutory definition of marriage that would feed the Ontario legislation governing the issuance of marriage licenses and registration of marriages performed under the authority of banns, and preclude the relief sought by the Applicants....

Blair, R.S.J., ¶¶ 26–27; *see also* LaForme, J., ¶ 93–95; Smith, A.C.J.S.C., ¶ 2.

Third, the court held that it could interpret the word "marriage" in the Constitution to include the union of same-sex couples. One of the litigants, the Association of Marriage and the Family, had argued that the use of the word marriage in sections 91(26) and 92(12) of the Constitution Act, 1982, meant, as a constitutional matter, that marriage was a union between a man and woman. Therefore, it argued, the federal government had no authority to legislate on same-sex marriage, and the provinces were prohibited from solemnizing same-sex unions. It contended that any change to the word "marriage" found in the Constitution required a formal amendment to the Constitution Act. *See* LaForme, J., ¶¶ 99–101. In response, LaForme, J. explained that the word "marriage" was part of a living instrument, and that the understanding of marriage at the time of the Constitution's enactment did not freeze the word's meaning for all time. LaForme, J., ¶¶ 105–06.

The three judges disagreed about the correct remedy. In the end, the court invalidated the common law definition of marriage, but put a twenty-four month hold on the effective date of the declaration of invalidity in order to give Parliament (and the provincial legislature where appropriate) time to reform the law. One judge explained: "The Court should defer to the legislative branch to make policy choices from a number of possible remedial options. The legislative branch of government is especially suited to assess and take into account the competing values and interests of all societal participants, as well as to assess the legal effects of a state-recognized union between same-sex partners.... The fact that the definition of marriage under consideration is one developed under the common law does not change the need for deference to the legislative branch." Smith, A.C.J.S.C. ¶¶ 6, 9.

After the decision, Ralph Klein, the Premier of Alberta, indicated that "Alberta will never allow gay marriage, and if Ottawa drafts such a law, the province will invoke the notwithstanding clause of the Charter of Rights and Freedoms to protect the 'sanctity of marriage' between man and woman." Robert Benzie, *Klein Draws the Line at Gay Marriage,* National Post, July 19, 2002, at A8. The "notwithstanding clause," found in section 33 of the Canadian Charter of Rights and Freedoms, allows a government to enact a statute to declare a law's validity for up to five years, with the possibility of renewal, notwithstanding that the law violates the Charter. *See generally* Jeffrey L. Friesen, *The Distribution of Treaty-Implementing Powers in Constitutional Federations: Thoughts on the American and Canadian Models,* 94 Colum. L. Rev. 1415, 1445 (1994). "The clause represents a response to an established constitutional tradition of parliamentary supremacy, a more recent tradition of provincial autonomy, and the felt political necessities surrounding patriation of the Canadian Constitution." Calvin R. Massey, *The Locus of Sovereignty: Judicial Review, Legislative Supremacy, and Federalism in the Constitutional Traditions of Canada and the United States,* 1990 Duke L.J. 1229. The power under the notwithstanding clause has rarely been used. *See* Keith S. Rosenn, *Federalism in the Americas in Comparative Perspective,* 26 U. Miami Inter-Am. L. Rev. 1, 43 (1994). Since a government can only invoke the notwithstanding clause within its own sphere of power, can the Premier of Alberta successfully invoke the notwithstanding clause in this context? *See* North v. Matheson, 52 D.L.R. (3d) 280, ¶ 6 (Man. Country Ct. 1974) (provincial legislature lacked constitutional authority to authorize same-sex marriage). *Halpren* is discussed further in Chapter 4.B.1.

7. *Treaty-Making Power.* Despite what has been stated so far, the federal government in the United States may have more power than the federal government in Canada to regulate marriage. The U.S. Constitution gives the President the power to make treaties, subject to the Senate's ratification. *See* U.S. Const. art. II, s. 2, c. 1. The states are prohibited from entering into any treaty, but might enter into an "agreement or compact" with a foreign state, with the consent of Congress. *See id.,* art. II, s. 10, c. 1. Article VI, clause 2, makes treaties "the supreme Law of the Land." If the treaty's terms are self-executing, then implementing legislation need not be passed. If its terms are not self-executing, then Congress has full power to enact the necessary legislation. *See* Missouri v. Holland, 252 U.S. 416 (1920). Consequently, the federal government has the power to regulate the formalities and substance of marriage pursuant to a treaty obligation. "Although the issue has never been free from substantial controversy," "the dominant view" is an expansive understanding of federal power pursuant to a treaty obligation. *See* David M. Golove, *Treaty-Making and the Nation: The Historical Foundations of the*

Nationalist Conception of the Treaty Power, 98 Mich. L. Rev. 1075, 1078 (2000). For two outstanding discussions of the validity of this view compare Professor Golove's article, *id.,* with Curtis A. Bradley, *The Treaty Power and American Federalism,* 97 Mich. L. Rev. 391 (1998).

However, the U.S. federal government exercises self-restraint. The senate, where each state is equally represented, almost always ratifies treaties subject to a federalism reservation. For example, the U.S. reservation to the Charter of the Organization of American States says that none of the Charter's provisions "shall be considered as enlarging the powers of the Federal Government of the United States or limiting the powers of the several states of the Federal union with respect to any matters recognized under the Constitution as being within the reserved powers of the several states." See Charter of the Organization of American States, Apr. 30, 1948, 2 O.S.T. 2394, 119 U.N.T.S. 3. *See generally* Chapter 2.B. *See also* Greg Craven, *Federal Constitutions and External Relations, in* Foreign Relations and Federal States 7 (Brian Hocking ed., 1993).

Contrast the situation in the United States with that in Canada. In Canada, "treaty-making is an exercise by the federal government of Canada of what is historically the crown's prerogative. It is the old common law right of the sovereign to enter into agreements, on behalf of the state, with other states. And in Canada this prerogative power is exercised by the Governor General. In a formal sense this power is delegated by Queen Elizabeth II to the Governor General. The treaty-making power is exercised completely in Canada upon advice of Canadian (federal) ministers.... There is no requirement in the Canadian Constitution that treaties be submitted to the federal parliament for approval. Treaty-making is purely an executive act." Ton Zuijdwijk, *Presentation of the Canadian Delegation,* 22 Md. J. Int'l L. & Trade 221, 259–60 (1999). Although the Constitution Act does not expressly say that the federal power to enter treaties is exclusive of the provinces, that is how the allocation of power has worked in practice. *See* Peter Hogg, Constitutional Law of Canada 283 (3rd ed. 1992).

The federal power to implement treaty obligations appears quite broad from the text of the Constitution Act, although in reality the federal government's power is much narrower than in the United States. Section 132 of the Constitution Act, 1867 provides, "The Parliament and Government of Canada shall have all Powers necessary or proper for performing the Obligations of Canada or of any Province thereof, as Part of the British Empire, towards Foreign Countries, arising under Treaties between the Empire and such Foreign Countries." The federal power, however, is limited by the constitutional division of powers. In the *Labour Conventions Case* (Canada (Att'y-Gen.) v. Ontario (Att'y-Gen.), [1937] A.C. 326 (P.C.)), the provinces challenged the Dominion's ability to ratify three International Labour Organization conventions and then pass labor legislation intruding upon provincial jurisdiction. The Privy Council held:

> [I]n a federal State where legislative authority is limited by a constitutional document, or is divided up between different Legislatures in accordance with the classes of subject-matter submitted for legislation, the problem is complex. The obligations imposed by treaty may have to be performed, if at all, by several Legislatures; and the executive have the task of obtaining the legislative assent not of one Parliament to whom they may be responsible, but possibly of several Parliaments to whom they stand in no direct relation.

Id. at 348.

Hence, while the federal government in Canada has the necessary power to sign treaties, it often remains within the power of the individual provinces to implement the treaties. As a consequence of the *Labour Conventions Case,* the federal government must gain provincial cooperation to ensure the performance of treaties. In fact, the federal government consults with the provinces before assuming treaty obligations that would require provincial implementation. *See* William A. Schabas, *Canada and the Adoption of the Universal Declaration of Human Rights,* 43 McGill L. J. 403, 440 (1998). If Canada adheres to a treaty and a province subsequently enacts legislation in contravention of the treaty, Canada would be in breach of its treaty obligation. The provincial statute, however, would not be void or inoperative simply because it violates a treaty. *See* Thomson v. Thomson, [1993] 3 S.C.R. 551, ¶ 126 (Can.) (L'Heureux-Dube J., concurring).

The Canadian government has used its jurisdictional limitations as a "pretext" for opposing various international instruments. For example, Canada cited jurisdictional considerations when it voted against the Universal Declaration of Human Rights in the Third Committee of the United Nations General Assembly. *See* Schabas, *supra.* In reality, Canada had substantive concerns about the Declaration in light of Canada's own treatment of communists and Japanese. *See id.* Similarly, Canada has not yet ratified the American Convention on Human Rights. "The standard and somewhat unconvincing explanation for this failing is that the provinces are not yet in agreement." *See id.* at 441.

Despite the differences in the constitutional allocation of power over marriage in Canada and the United States, what similarities exist regarding the regulation of marriage in Canada and the United States?

b. Constitutional Allocation of Power between the Judiciaries

The federalism description so far has been somewhat simplistic because it has focused primarily on lawmaking by legislative bodies. However, courts also help determine the content and parameters of marriage law. Conflict can occur between courts and legislators, but such conflict takes on an additional dimension when the courts from one level of government adjudicate claims based upon legislation passed by another level of government. Some have called this type of conflict "judicial federalism." *See, e.g.,* Thomas Baker, *A Catalogue of Judicial Federalism in the United States,* 46 S.C. L. Rev. 835 (1995). In the United States, the issue might take the following form: Should federal courts adjudicate family law actions if the parties meet the statutory prerequisites for diversity jurisdiction under 28 U.S.C. § 1332(a)? In Australia, the issue is slightly different because the law regulating marriage and divorce is federal. There the question is as follows: Should provincial courts be adjudicating divorce actions since strong federal interests may be involved? In Canada, one gets both types of questions: Should the provincial courts be adjudicating issues of federal marriage law and should federal courts be adjudicating issues related to provincial marriage law?

A comparative analysis of the allocation of judicial power in Australia, Canada, and the United States raises interesting questions about people's reluctance to have federal courts in the United States hear domestic relations cases, and casts doubt on some of the reasons for this reluctance. Yet, the comparison also demonstrates a desire in all jurisdictions for courts with family law expertise to adjudicate family law matters. In fact, the use of specialized family courts in Australia and Canada suggests that the United States' approach may be somewhat consistent with the approaches in those jurisdictions. The comparison also shows the possibility of cooperation among judiciaries within a country. Although the reason for judicial cooperation in Canada and Australia differs from what would be the reason for cooperation in the United States, nonetheless the Canadian and Australian experiences present a hopeful lesson in possibilities.

In Australia, although the Constitution gave the federal government the power to make laws with respect to marriage, the Matrimonial Causes Act 1959 gave state courts jurisdiction over issues arising under federal parliamentary acts dealing with marriage. Matrimonial Causes Act 1959 § 23 (Austl.). This state of affairs continued until the Family Law Act of 1975, which established the Family Court of Australia. The Family Court of Australia is a superior court of the federal, not state, system. *See generally* Mary Crock & Ronald Mc-Callum, *Australia's Federal Courts: Their Origins, Structure and Jurisdiction*, 46 S.C. L. Rev. 719, 753 (1995). The new court was given jurisdiction in all matters under the Family Law Act of 1975, which includes dissolution of marriage, child custody and visitation, and property distribution upon dissolution, and in all matters under the Marriage Act 1961, which addresses both marriage capacity and formalities. Family Law Act 1975 § 31 (Austl.). The Family Court's jurisdiction is "largely exclusive of that of the states." Brian R. Opeskin, *Federal Jurisdiction in Australian Courts: Policies and Prospects*, 46 S.C. L. Rev. 765, 794 (1995). A significant factor in the establishment of the Family Court was the desire to have a forum with substantial expertise in family law matters. However, since Parliament could only give the Family Court jurisdiction over areas that Parliament could constitutionally regulate, and since state magistrates' courts have a limited jurisdiction to decide family law issues and to make consent orders, "split jurisdiction" problems arose, such as the ability of the Family Court to hear disputes relating to marital, but not non-marital, children. *See* Justice Linda Dessau, *A Unified Family Court*, (Oct. 24, 1998), *at* http://www.familycourt. gov.au/papers/html/dessau2.html (detailing other aspects of fragmentation). The problems have been generally addressed with judicial and legislative solutions. *See* Opeskin, *supra*, at 794–95. As a general matter, most family law matters are now decided by the federal Family Court, *see* Crock & McCallum, *supra*, at 754–55, or the Federal Magistrates' Service. The latter was created by the Commonwealth Parliament at the end of 1999 to deal with less complicated cases, thereby relieving the Family Court of some of its tremendous workload.

In Canada, any congruence between the legislative body that makes the law and the judicial entity that applies or interprets the law ends once a case is appealed, at least for cases based on provincial law. In Canada, "Each province has superior courts, the judges of which are appointed by the federal government, and inferior courts, the judges of which are appointed by the provincial government. Each province administers its own inferior and superior courts, and these courts may deal with matters of both federal and provincial legislative jurisdiction." Martha Bailey et al., *Canada, in* International Encyclopaedia of Laws: Family and Succession Law 29 (Walter Pinten & R. Blanpain eds., 1999). Ontario serves as an example. There, the Ontario Court of Justice, a provincial court with provincially appointed judges, can hear certain family law matters, including custody, access, and support (if not part of a dissolution action), enforcement of child support, and adoption. Appeals would be heard by the Superior Court of Justice, a court with federally appointed judges. In contrast, divorce matters (including custody, access, support, and property issues) are heard by the federal trial court of general jurisdiction, the Superior Court of Justice. Appeals from the Superior Court of Justice go to the Ontario Court of Appeal and then to the Supreme Court of Canada. The judges who sit on the Ontario Court of Appeal and the Supreme Court of Canada are federally appointed.

The potential problems associated with judicial federalism appear quite pronounced in Canada, at least for family law issues grounded in provincial law. In particular, the Supreme Court of Canada has far more power to interpret provincial legislation than the U.S. Supreme Court has to interpret state legislation. The Supreme Court of Canada is a true appellate court, hearing appeals from the superior courts of the provinces and from the appellate division of the federal court regardless of the subject of litigation. Consequently, it equally develops federal and provincial law. This, of course, is in stark contrast to the U.S. Supreme Court, which cannot hear appeals of state law claims unless the state law violates a federal statute or the Constitution, and upon appeal it is prohibited from interpreting state law.

Canada, like Australia, also has faced problems of "split jurisdiction." There has been a trend in the Canadian provinces towards the creation of unified family courts that are empowered to deal with all matters of family law, including the formation and validity of marriage, in order to eliminate problems of split jurisdiction. *See, e.g.,* Unified Family Court Act, Nfld. R.S., ch. U-3, §6 (1990) (Can.). These courts are created with the cooperation of the federal and provincial governments. In Ontario, for example, the Unified Family Court is administered as part of the Superior Court of Justice (with federally appointed judges). *See generally* Ontario Women's Justice Network, *A Map of the Courts, at* http://www.owjn.org/info/map.htm. They are heralded for being especially able to deal with the "special nature of family-law problems," and often involve simplified court procedures, specialized judges, and a wide range of services. *See* Unified Family Court Task Force, Part 2: Report and Recommendations 1 (2001), *available at* http://www4.gov.ab.ca/just/pub/family_court/part2.htm.

The allocation of judicial power in the United States differs from Australia and Canada. Although state courts can adjudicate most issues of federal law, domestic relations matters are typically state law matters and these state law matters must be heard by state court judges. In fact, our federal courts refuse to entertain most family law matters at first instance absent a constitutional issue. This allocation of power is not set forth in the U.S. Constitution, but is the result of a conscious decision by the U.S. Supreme Court to reaffirm a commitment to the domestic relations exception to federal diversity jurisdiction. *See* Ankenbrandt v. Richards, 504 U.S. 689 (1992). *See also* Anne C. Dailey, *Federalism and Families,* 143 U. Pa. L. Rev. 1787, 1823 (1995) ("the exception exists as a matter of statutory construction" rather than constitutional construction).

In *Ankenbrandt,* the issue was whether the federal district court had jurisdiction to hear a lawsuit brought by two girls, through their mother, against their father and his female companion for alleged sexual and physical abuse. While the Supreme Court permitted the tort suit, the Court also emphasized the continuing vitality of the domestic relations exception to federal jurisdiction. The exception covers suits "involving the issuance of a divorce, alimony, or child custody decree." *See Ankenbrandt,* 504 U.S. at 704. The Court stated that its conclusion was "rooted in respect for this long-held understanding," and also in "sound policy considerations." In particular, it mentioned,

> As a matter of judicial economy, state courts are more eminently suited to work of this type than are federal courts, which lack the close association with state and local government organizations dedicated to handling issues that arise out of conflicts over divorce, alimony, and child custody decrees. Moreover, as a matter of judicial expertise, it makes far more sense to retain the rule that federal courts lack power to issue these types of decrees because of the special proficiency developed by state tribunals over the past century and a half in handling issues that arise in the granting of such decrees.

Id. Other courts have provided additional policy rationale: "the strong state interest in domestic relations matters, the competence of state courts in settling family disputes, the possibility of incompatible federal and state court decrees in cases of continuing judicial supervision by the state, and the problem of congested dockets in federal courts." Crouch v. Crouch, 566 F.2d 486, 487 (5th Cir. 1978). Many scholars have criticized the U.S. Supreme Court's decision in *Ankenbrandt v. Richards*. *See, e.g.,* Naomi R. Cahn, *Family Law, Federalism, and the Federal Courts*, 79 Iowa L. Rev. 1073, 1075 (1994) ("Given the lack of a persuasive rationale for excepting some types of family law cases, and in light of the need for diversity jurisdiction to help litigants overcome local bias, federal courts should consider exercising jurisdiction over these cases in the same manner as they do over other diversity cases."); Thomas H. Dobbs, *The Domestic Relations Exception Is Narrowed After Ankenbrandt v. Richards*, 28 Wake Forest L. Rev. 1137, 1161–62 (1993) ("The most questionable conclusion...was that congressional silence amounted to congressional approval of [the Court's interpretation of the diversity statute].").

In evaluating the domestic relations exception to federal diversity jurisdiction, what can we take away from the experiences of Canada and Australia? For example, what features in those countries make judicial federalism a non-issue? If those same features exist in the United States, perhaps the domestic relations exception is not needed. In Canada, the potential problems presented by provincial court judges interpreting federal legislation or federal judges interpreting provincial legislation are minimized because no judges are elected. Canadian judges are appointed until the age 75, and are removable only for cause by the governor general upon a joint address to Parliament. *See* Constitution Act 1867, § 99. Since Canadian judges are insulated from politics, they are less apt to reflect local interests, unlike the state court judges in the United States who are subject to reelection and local political pressure. In addition, since the Supreme Court of Canada can hear appeals from the superior courts of the provinces regardless of the subject matter, a federal court can correct any overreaching by provincial courts.

For similar reasons, one might imagine that federal judges would be fairly faithful to state law enactments in the United States. The Erie doctrine obligates federal courts adjudicating cases pursuant to diversity jurisdiction to apply the law of the state in which it sits. *See* Erie R.R. Co. v. Tompkins, 304 U.S. 64 (1938); Rules of Decision Act, 22 U.S.C. § 1652. Federal judges have life tenure, and their interpretations of state law are always subject to correction by the state courts themselves, albeit in subsequent cases. To the extent that judicial expertise is an important reason for the continued vitality of domestic relations exception, Canada and Australia demonstrate the possibility of specialized family courts and show that these courts can exist at the federal level. To the extent that resource concerns undergird the continued vitality of the exception, including the need for social workers to assist the courts in their adjudications, Canada and Australia also demonstrate that cooperation between state and federal entities is possible. After all, if the federal and provincial governments in those countries can agree to share power, is it impossible to imagine that our federal and state governments would agree to share resources?

Somewhat ironically, the U.S. Supreme Court itself is now the principal threat to state autonomy on family law matters in the United States. The Supreme Court is currently cabining congressional power under both the Commerce Clause and under the Fourteenth Amendment. *See, e.g.,* U.S. v. Morrison, 120 S. Ct. 1740 (2000) (invalidating federal civil remedy for victims of gender-motivated violence). The Supreme Court's denial of federal trial court jurisdiction in domestic relations actions may be seen as an effort to maintain strong state control over family law matters, although as mentioned above, the fear of federal court overreaching is probably non-existent. Of course, the

U.S. Supreme Court, a federal court, impacts state family law dramatically through its constitutional decisions regarding individual rights. For instance, the Supreme Court has decided cases about marriage that have had an important effect. *See, e.g.,* Loving v. Virginia, 388 U.S. 1, 12 (1967) (holding that a Virginia miscegenation statute violates Equal Protection and Due Process Clauses of the Fourteenth Amendment); Zablocki v. Redhail, 434 U.S. 374, 383-87 (1978) (striking down a Wisconsin statute that prohibited any resident from marrying without court approval if he had minor children not in his custody that he had to support). However, the Court's recent case law suggests that some members of the Court are attempting to restrain the impact of the Court's own decisions on state practices. *See* Troxel v. Granville, 530 U.S. 57 (2000) (invalidating Washington State's third-party visitation statute as applied).

The Canadian Supreme Court's constitutional decisions may also standardize provincial practices. *See* M. v. H., [1999] 171 D.L.R. (4th) 577 (Can.) (invalidating portion of Ontario Family Law Act that denied same-gender partners the opportunity to obtain spousal support like opposite-gender couples). This possibility may not appear troublesome to Canadians from a federalism perspective, however, because many family law matters are already regulated by the federal government; instead, it may principally raise concerns about the role of the judiciary versus the role of elected representatives.

For an excellent summary of recent constitutional law as it applies to families, see Sylvia Law, *Families and Federalism,* 4 Wash. U. J. L. & Pol'y 175, App. I & II (2000). For an informative article on the comparison between the allocation of judicial power in Canada and the United States, *see* John T. Cross, *The Constitutional Federal Question in the Lower Federal Courts of the United States and Canada,* 17 Hastings Int'l & Comp. L. Rev. 143 (1993).

---

c. Reconsidering the Allocation of Power in the United States

Given this background, it is useful to consider, afresh, some of the justifications for allocating power to regulate marriage, both substantively and procedurally, to the states in the United States. The next two excerpts, by Hendrick Hartog and Anne Dailey, provide information relevant to this question. The third excerpt, by Judith Resnik, discusses the policy behind the continued validity of the domestic relations exception to federal diversity jurisdiction. Most of her comments also seem very applicable to the question of the allocation of legislative power.

Hendrick Hartog,
Man & Wife in America: A History
16–19 (2000)

For the better part of two centuries, the agencies of the federal government claimed little constitutional responsibility or interest over the law of marriage. During the framing of the Constitution in 1787 the topic never arose. The implicit denial of constitutional responsibility was reaffirmed, explicitly and consciously, during the debates over the Fourteenth Amendment after the Civil War. From the middle of the nineteenth century until the constitutional revolution of the 1960s, there were repeated moments of passionate talk about the need for a national law of marriage and for uniformity, particularly in the face of the threat posed by Mormon polygamy in the Utah territory. And there were particular institutional responsibilities of the federal government, such as immigration law, that implicated marriage. Nonetheless, throughout the first 175 years of national government, marriage law was not the business of Washington....

All of which is not to say that the federal Constitution was not of significance in the constitution of marriage in America. [T]he "full faith and credit clause" played a crucial and determinative role in the legal history of marriage.... Although full faith and credit was a clear constitutional mandate, nineteenth-century state courts interpreted the clause through the lens of state sovereignty and insisted on their right to act as if their state were a separate country. They talked in the language of conflicts of law, of "private international law," as if the laws of other states belonged to other nations, as if Nebraska were France or Argentina....

Two kinds of critics observed this system and called it corrupt. One, whom we today would identify with woman's rights and feminism, saw through the jurisdictional multiplicity and found the continuity of male power and authority, the constitution of marriage as an oppressive structure. There were lots of states, but there were only men in control.... After the Civil War, these critics looked to the federal government and the federal courts as institutional locations where new, more universal, rights could be constructed, and they claimed that the federal Constitution embodied an ungendered and critical standard that delegitimated the received laws.... The others, pious men and other conservatives (and more conservative women), looked at the federal system and saw only a field of action for manipulative and strategic men. To them, the weakness of the federal system threatened to destroy the constitution of Christian marriage. It tempted fallible men and women toward the sin of believing that they could undo what only God could undo. The only remedy, they believed, lay in a unitary national law of marriage, incorporating a national (anti-) divorce law. Both shared a general revulsion of the diversity and complexity of the system, and both participated in the construction of a widely shared perception, one that resonates with us still: that marriage was in a state of constitutional crisis requiring drastic and immediate national action.

Disorder may have been the rule in law and in many personal lives. Nonetheless, this was a country in which Americans lived their marital lives—one with many jurisdictions with imperfect forms of policing and regulation, with a national post office and a developing communication structure, yet with inadequate and locally based forms of property and marriage recordation.

Anne C. Dailey, *Federalism and Families*
143 U. Pa. L. Rev. 1787, 1790 (1995)

States enjoy exclusive authority over family law, not because families are in some sense noncommercial, as the *Lopez* majority suggested,* but instead because of the fundamental role of localism in the federal design. The theory of localism presented here rests on the view that the law of domestic relations necessarily promotes a shared moral

---

* Ed. Note: In *U.S. v. Lopez*, 514 U.S. 549, 559-561 (1995), the Supreme Court held that the Gun-Free School Zones Act, a criminal law, was an unconstitutional extension of Congress' power under the Commerce Clause because the Act did not substantially affect interstate commerce, and had nothing to do with economic enterprise.

vision of the good family life. Although in law, as elsewhere, we are accustomed to thinking of the family as a private realm free from governmental influence and control, the domestic sphere is deeply patterned by state laws regulating the formation, maintenance, dissolution, and boundaries of family life. Legal regulation of the family forms domestic roles, directs intimate relationships, and consequently shapes human identity in profoundly normative ways. Legal decision-makers confront fundamental questions concerning the meaning of parenthood, the best custodial placements for children, the rights and obligations of marriage, the financial terms of divorce, and the standards governing foster care and adoption. In answering such questions, state legislatures and courts draw upon community values and norms on the meaning of the good life for families and children.

Judith Resnik, *"Naturally" Without Gender: Women, Jurisdiction, and the Federal Courts*
66 N.Y.U. L. Rev. 1682, 1751–57 (1991)

The central question is what "business is the federal business," and it is time to answer this question by recognizing that there already is joint federal and state governance of an array of issues, from land use and torts to families. Once understood as a joint endeavor, the next issue is how to allocate authority.

A first possibility is that federal court involvement in family life is bad, per se, at a structural level.... Under this vision, the states (and indian tribes) as smaller units of government are closer to "the people" and thus a more appropriate level of government to determine matters affecting intimate life.

Possible justifications for this view exist. Contemporary invocations of the domestic relations exception discard arguments based on ecclesiastical authority, the alleged lack of jurisdictional diversity between married couples, and the claim that divorces lack monetary value—all in favor of a "modern view that state courts have historically decided these matters and have developed both a well-known expertise in these cases and a strong interest in disposing of them." Whether based in nineteenth-century or twentieth-century conceptions, the claims of affiliation and expertise require consideration. "Communitarianism" has strong adherents in contemporary debates on political theory; respecting groups' self-constitution may entail state governance of the family. Further, the existence of some form of an exception to federal court jurisdiction based on probate reveals another justification for state control—an implicit sense of marriage as a status existing within the state's borders and an ongoing link between sovereign authority and territorial borders. Holding aside the ever-present question of boundaries, doctrine might shift in a variety of ways when ideological claims about the relationship between federal courts and family are revised.

First, one could insist that, despite recognition of federal laws of the family, the claim of deference to state governance remains strong and, as a matter of doctrine, complete abstention (a form of reverse preemption) is desirable. To the extent recent federal law in bankruptcy, pensions, and benefits law points in the other direction, that erosion should be stopped—by legislation or judicial interpretation. But were one to really press this claim—that states are specially situated and should be controlling family life—one would not seek only to cabin the federal courts. This position would also require urging Congress and agencies to avoid defining families by rewriting statutes and regulations to incorporate state law, so as to permit state governance of interpersonal relations. An array of federal statutes would have to incorporate state definitions of families, and what would be lost in uniformity and national norms would be gained in recognition of the special relationship of states in defining family life....

A different conception rejects a view that the states are the embodiment of communities that legitimate state governance of intimate life. While a few states may be relatively homogeneous, the vast majority have no special claim to a communitarian vision. Therefore, federal court involvement in family life is not bad, per se, as a matter of federalism. Nonetheless, federal court jurisdiction might still be undesirable, given federal judicial history-either of noninvolvement or of disclaimers of such involvement with domestic life. Here the question of the "quality of the federal bench," as well as that of the "nature of federal law," reemerges. Arguments in support of this approach could be tied to two other strains in the case law claiming a "domestic relations" exception to federal court jurisdiction. First, in light of this "time-honored boundary," the federal courts lack the requisite knowledge and "are not, as a matter of fact, competent tribunals to handle" typical domestic relations cases. Translated, the claim is that federal judges are neither selected on the basis of knowledge of family law nor trained, once judges, to become knowledgeable and also lack support staff who might mitigate these problems. Moreover, given the composition of the docket, federal courts would be unlikely to gain expertise because their involvement would be sporadic. Second, the federal courts are too important or the issues of family law too unappealing, trivial, and "non-national" for federal court decisionmaking.

The competency claim, at least in the subset of family law dealing with interpersonal familial relations, has some appeal. In the words of one federal court, some questions are:

> too hard and too remote from the experience of federal judges.... Our experience and sense of fairness teach us that this is not a case where the application of a federal rule...is likely to provide the best answer. We must rely on a judge in a court of family law-with its more flexible standards...to balance the equities and seek compromises that best accommodate the interests of the parties.

Feminism similarly counsels attention to experience, to the knowledge gained by firsthand understanding of problems. But the imagined state competence is undermined to some extent by the many state gender bias task forces that found state judges were biased in this very area of the assumed expertise—family law cases. Further, some of those reports also detail a parallel devaluation of family law. Trivialization of family life is a problem that defies jurisdictional boundaries. While the federal courts may lack the experience, the lesson from state bias studies is that experience alone is insufficient....

The current hierarchy stipulates the federal courts as most powerful; the supremacy clause confirms that sense of authority. Further, federal courts theorists might affirmatively argue that federal courts are needed in this area—either because of their special capacity to protect the politically disfavored or because federal sovereign and administrative interests are at stake. While neither the appeal to the community envisioned by the claim of closeness of the state to the family nor the concern about attitudes and knowledge of federal judges should be discounted, the "inevitability of federal involvement" in family life remains, as does a sense that the rejection of that role by federal courts reconfirms the marginalization of women and families from national life.

Notes and Questions

1. *Practical Effects.* What is the significance, if any, of the allocation of marriage issues in the United States to the state governments instead of the federal government? Is
it a false distinction, *i.e.*, is the allocation of power truly exclusive or enduring? What is
the significance, if any, of the continuing vitality of the domestic relations exception to
federal diversity jurisdiction?

2. *Uniformity.* Uniformity is repeatedly mentioned as a benefit of the Australian system. Why might uniformity be important? Is it because uniformity provides certainty to
individuals? What do you make of the fact that the Family Law Act 1975 was amended
more than forty times in approximately the first twenty years after its passage? J. Neville
Turner, *Australia, in* International Encyclopaedia of Laws: Family and Succession Law
22 (Walter Pintens & R. Blanpain eds., 1997). Does a system like the United States' tend
toward uniformity in substantive marriage laws even without a uniform marriage law?
If so, why?

3. *Efficiency.* One obvious advantage of centralized power over marriage is efficiency.
For example, the attorney general of Australia asked the Australian Law Reform Commission to review laws that relate to marriage, among others, and to assess whether they
were "appropriate to a society made up of people from differing cultural backgrounds
and from ethnically diverse communities." *Terms of Reference, Multiculturalism* (Aug. 2,
1989), *in* Multiculturalism and the Law, Rep. No. 57, xxii (The Law Reform Comm'n
1992). The Law Reform Commission then proposed various changes to federal legislation. *Id.* at xxvii–xxx. Imagine how such a review would be done in the United States, if
at all.

4. *Expertise.* Another claimed benefit of the Australian system is the specialization
that has occurred with its creation of the federal Family Court. Brian R. Opeskin, *Federal Jurisdiction in Australia Courts: Policies and Prospects*, 46 S.C. L. Rev. 765, 778
(1995). Are there any disadvantages to specialization? If the domestic relations exception to diversity jurisdiction were eliminated, should Congress create a federal family
court in each federal judicial district?

5. *Resources.* What of the fact that in the United States the fifty state judiciaries comprise over 28,000 trial judges while the federal system has approximately 650 trial
judges? *See* Thomas Baker, *A Catalogue of Judicial Federalism in the United States*, 46
S.C. L. Rev. 835, 839, 841 (1995). If the domestic relations exception to diversity jurisdiction were eliminated, should Congress create more federal district courts to address
the new cases? Could states share their resources with the federal courts?

6. *Comparing Systems I.* Linda Elrod has recently stated, "Many still feel that states
should legislate all aspects of family law. Yet, some issues transcend state boundaries.
When the issues involve protecting children, as in sheltering children from abuse, neglect, abduction, or ensuring health insurance coverage or enforcement of child support, the proverbial village has grown to a national size." Linda Henry Elrod, *Chair's
Column*, 23 Fam. Advoc. 2 (2001). Could you make a similar argument about marriage?
Would you differentiate between marriage formalities, marriage capacity, and incidents
of marriage? Is the Australian or Canadian model preferable?

7. *Comparing Systems II.* Are the split jurisdictional problems that arose in Canada or
Australia likely to arise here if the domestic relations exception were eliminated?

8. *Sources.* Many scholars have thought about family law and federalism in the
United States. A few citations are provided here. *See, e.g.,* Libby S. Adler, *Federalism and*

Family, 8 Colum. J. Gender & L. 197 (1999); Naomi Cahn, *Family Law, Federalism, and the Federal Courts*, 79 Iowa L. Rev. 1073 (1994); Ann Laquer Estin, *Federalism and Child Support*, 5 Va. J. Soc. Pol'y & L. 541 (1998); Jill Hasday, *Federalism and the Family Reconstructed*, 45 UCLA L. Rev. 1297 (1998); Sylvia Law, *Families and Federalism*, 4 Wash. U. J. L. & Pol'y 175 (2000); Kenneth R. Redden, The Federal Regulation of Family Law (1982).

4. International Law

Many public international law instruments address the topic of marriage, both directly and indirectly. International instruments deal to varying degrees with marriage formalities, capacity, and the effects of marriage. For example, the Universal Declaration of Human Rights (UDHR), art. 16, states:

> 1. Men and women of full age, without any limitation due to race, nationality or religion, have the right to marry and to found a family. They are entitled to equal rights as to marriage during marriage and at its dissolution.
>
> 2. Marriage shall be entered into only with the free and full consent of the intending spouses.
>
> 3. The family is the natural and fundamental group unit of society and is entitled to protection by society and the state.

The International Covenant on Civil and Political Rights, art. 23(2)-(4), has similar language. The Convention on the Elimination of All Forms of Discrimination against Women (CEDAW), art. 16, embodies much of the same. *See* art. 16(1)(a)-(c), (g), (h).

Several themes reappear throughout the international instruments. The idea that marriage and procreation must be available to all, regardless of race, nationality or religion, is grounded in the historical context of the instruments. The Universal Declaration of Human Rights was adopted in the aftermath of World War II and the Nazi's regulation and restriction of Jews' ability to marry and have a family.

Another theme is that marriage requires the voluntary consent of both parties. Although the UDHR states this generally, other instruments target specific practices. For example, the 1956 Supplementary Convention on the Abolition of Slavery, the Slave Trade and Institutions and Practices Similar to Slavery requires States Parties to bring about the abolition of any practice, regardless of whether it is "slavery," whereby "[a] woman, without the right to refuse, is promised or given in marriage on payment of a consideration in money or in kind to her parents, guardian, family or any other person or group; or... [t]he husband of a woman, his family, or his clan, has the right to transfer her to another person for value received or otherwise; or a woman on the death of her husband is liable to be inherited by another person." Supplementary Convention of the Abolition of Slavery, the Slave Trade and Institutions and Practices Similar to Slavery, Sept. 7, 1956, art. a(c)(i)-(iii), 18 U.S.T. 3201, 266 U.N.T.S. 3.

International law recognizes that some individuals are too young to give meaningful consent. CEDAW contains an explicit prohibition on "child" marriages: "The betrothal and the marriage of a child shall have no legal effect, and all necessary action, including legislation, shall be taken to specify a minimum age for marriage and to make the registration of marriages in an official registry compulsory." CEDAW, *supra*, art. 16(2). This provision in CEDAW mirrors, to some extent, language in the U.N. Convention on Consent to Marriage, Minimum Age for Marriage and Registration of Marriages, Dec.

10, 1962, 521 U.N.T.S. 231 and the U.N. Recommendation on Consent to Marriage, Minimum Age for Marriage and Registration of Marriages, G.A. Res. 2018, U.N. GAOR, 20th Sess., Supp. No. 14, at 36, U.N. Doc. A/6014 (1965). These documents can be found in the Statutory Supplement. *See also* G.A. Res. 843, U.N. GAOR, 9th Sess., Supp. No. 21, at 23, U.N. Doc. A/2890 (1954).

The problem of child marriages has been addressed at the international level by setting a minimum age for marriage at 15. This number does not appear in CEDAW or in the U.N. Convention on Consent to Marriage, Minimum Age for Marriage and Registration of Marriage, but in the U.N. Recommendation of the same name, which followed a year after the U.N. Convention. When the U.N. Convention on Consent to Marriage was being negotiated, there was no agreement on the minimum age for marriage. "Proposals ranged from 14 to 18 years and in the absence of any consensus it was decided to leave the matter open to each State Party to prescribe the age." *Report of the Committee on Progress Achieved in the Implementation of the Convention: Note by the Secretariat*, CEDAW, 14th Sess., ¶51, U.N. Doc. CEDAW/C/1995/7 (1995). *See also* U.N. Convention on Consent to Marriage, *supra*, at art. 2. Yet the U.N. Recommendation states, "Member States shall take legislative action to specify a minimum age for marriage, which in any case shall not be less than fifteen years of age; no marriage shall be legally entered into by any person under this age, except where a competent authority has granted a dispensation as to age, for serious reasons, in the interest of the intending spouses." *See* U.N. Recommendation on Consent to Marriage, *supra*, principle II. The Recommendation provides guidelines for Governments who ratified the Convention as well as those who were not in a position to ratify the Convention. *See* Report of the Committee, *supra*, at ¶52. As of May 2000, there were forty-nine States Parties to the Convention on Consent to Marriage, Minimum Age for Marriage and Registration of Marriages.

Another theme relates to the importance of registration. Article 3 of the U.N. Convention on Consent to Marriage states, "All marriages shall be registered in an appropriate official register by the competent authority." The Committee on the Elimination of Discrimination Against Women discussed article 16(2) of CEDAW and indicated why such an obligation exists: "States Parties should also require the registration of all marriages, whether contracted civilly or according to custom or religious law. The State can thereby ensure compliance with the Convention and establish equality between partners, a minimum age for marriage, prohibition of bigamy and polygamy and the protection of the rights of children." *Report of the Committee, supra*.

The U.N. Convention on Consent to Marriage also speaks to the form of the ceremony. One needs the consent to be expressed "in person after due publicity and in the presence of the authority competent to solemnize the marriage and of witnesses, as prescribed by law." U.N. Convention on Consent to Marriage, *supra*, art. 1(1). The reason for these sorts of requirements will be explored in the next section, Procedural Requirements for Entry into Marriage, in the context of French law.

Another theme that emerges from several of the instruments is that men and women "are entitled to equal rights as to marriage during marriage and its dissolution." UDHR, *supra*, at art. 16(1). *See also* ICCPR, art. 23(4). Article 16 of CEDAW goes even further by requiring States Parties to take measures to eliminate discrimination in a variety of areas related to marriage and family relations, including, for example, having and caring for children.

Finally, international law also addresses the consequences of marriage. For instance, the Convention on the Nationality of Married Women, Feb. 20, 1957, 309 U.N.T.S. 65, was enacted because of "conflicts in law affecting the nationality of married women which in some instances imposed serious disabilities on a woman who married a man of a different nationality. She could lose important personal rights where nationality affected rights and duties in private law. Conflicts in laws might also place her in danger of becoming stateless." *Report of the Committee, supra,* at 48. Articles 1 and 2 of the Convention on the Nationality of Married Women state that "neither the celebration nor the dissolution of a marriage between one of its nationals and an alien, nor the change of nationality by the husband during marriage, shall automatically affect the nationality of the wife" and that "neither the voluntary acquisition of the nationality of another State nor the renunciation of its nationality by one of its nationals shall prevent the retention of its nationality by the wife of such national." The full Convention is set forth in the Statutory Supplement. As of May 9, 2000, there were sixty-nine parties to the Convention on the Nationality of Married Women. The United States is not a participant.

The conventions mentioned above vary in their approach to reservations. For example, CEDAW allows them, so long as they are not incompatible with the object and purpose of the Convention. *See* CEDAW, *supra,* art. 28. The Convention on the Nationality of Married Women does not permit reservations to articles 1 and 2. *See* Convention on the Nationality of Married Women, *supra,* art. 8. The Convention on Consent to Marriage, Minimum Age for Marriage and Registration of Marriages is silent on the issue of reservations.

The treaties discussed impose both specific obligations (*e.g.,* no child marriages permitted), and more general ones (*e.g.,* equal rights during marriage). Should international law address these issues regarding marriage? Is your answer to this question informed by the federalism debate in the United States? Does the material on customary law and religious law also help you reach an answer? Assuming international law should address these issues, how should adherence to its provisions be achieved?

As you think about the answers to these questions, consider the following three excerpts. The first excerpt suggests that some of the practices that violate international law are deeply ingrained in community practice and local norms. The second and third excerpts reflect the approach of a human rights monitoring body, the Committee on the Elimination of Discrimination Against Women, for eliminating these objectionable practices.

Fact Sheet No. 23, Harmful Traditional Practices Affecting the Health of Women and Children, Office for the High Commission for Human Rights
at http://www.unhchr.ch/html/menu6/2/fs23.htm (1987)

Early marriage is another serious problem which some girls, as opposed to boys, must face. The practice of giving away girls for marriage at the age of 11, 12 or 13, after which they must start producing children, is prevalent among certain ethnic groups in Asia and Africa. The principal reasons for this practice are the girls' virginity and the bride-price. Young girls are less likely to have had sexual contact and thus are believed to be virgins upon marriage; this condition raises the family status as well as the dowry to be paid by the husband. In some cases, virginity is verified by female relatives before the marriage....

Neglect of and discrimination against daughters, particularly in societies with strong son preference... contribute to early marriage of girls.... In some countries, girls as young as a few months old are promised to male suitors for marriage. Girls are fattened up, groomed, adorned with jewels and kept in seclusion to make them attractive so that they can be married off to the highest bidder. . . .

Some states have argued that girls attain their physical maturity earlier, but it is the view of the Committee that maturity cannot simply be identified with physical development when social and mental development are lacking and that, on the basis of such criteria, girls are considered adults before the law upon marriage, thus being deprived of the comprehensive protection ensured by the Convention on the Rights of the Child. . . .

Although many countries have raised the legal age for marriage, this has had little impact on traditional societies where marriage and child-bearing confer "status" on a woman.

Report of the Committee on the Elimination of Discrimination against Women

U.N. GAOR, 56th Sess. Supp. No. 38,
at 70, U.N. Doc. A/56/38 (2001)
(Reviewing second and combined third and
fourth periodic reports of Viet Nam).

250. The Committee expresses concern that patriarchal attitudes and behavior, reflected, inter alia, in women's inferior role in the family, the non-recognition of women's work, son-preference and men's failure to share household and family responsibilities, are deeply entrenched.

251. The Committee recommends that the Government take urgent and wide-ranging measures, including targeted educational programmes, the revision of curricula and textbooks, and mass media campaigns, to overcome traditional stereotypes regarding the role of women and men in the society.

252. The Committee expresses concern about the low representation of women in decision-making bodies in political and public life at all levels.

253. The Committee recommends increasing the number of women in decision-making at all levels and in all areas, including macroeconomic policy. It also recommends that the State party introduce temporary special measures, in accordance with article 4, paragraph 1, of the Convention, to strengthen its efforts to promote women to positions of power, supported by special training programmes and awareness-raising campaigns promoting the importance of women's participation in decision-making at all levels.

Report of the Committee on Progress Achieved in the Implementation of the Convention: Note by the Secretariat

CEDAW, 14th Sess., U.N. Doc. CEDAW/C/1995/7 (1995)

Reservations

41. The Committee has noted with alarm the number of States Parties that have entered reservations to the whole or part of article 16, especially when a reservation has also

been entered to article 2, claiming that compliance may conflict with a commonly held vision of the family based, inter alia, on cultural or religious beliefs or on the country's economic or political status.

42. Many of these countries hold a belief in the patriarchal structure of a family which places a father, husband or son in a favorable position. In some countries where fundamentalist or other extremist views or economic hardships have encouraged a return to old values and traditions, women's place in the family has deteriorated sharply. In others, where it has been recognized that a modern society depends for its economic advance and for the general good of the community on involving all adults equally, regardless of gender, these taboos and reactionary or extremist ideas have progressively been discouraged.

43. Consistent with articles 2, 3 and 24 in particular, the Committee requires that all States Parties gradually progress to a stage where, by its resolute discouragement of notions of the inequality of women in the home, each country will withdraw its reservation, in particular to articles 9, 15 and 16 of the Convention.

44. States Parties should resolutely discourage any notions of inequality of women and men which are affirmed by laws, or by religious or private law or by custom, and progress to the stage where reservations, particularly to article 16, will be withdrawn.

45. The Committee noted, on the basis of its examination of initial and subsequent periodic reports, that in some States Parties to the Convention that had ratified or acceded without reservation, certain laws, especially those dealing with family, do not actually conform to the provisions of the Convention.

46. Their laws still contain many measures which discriminate against women based on norms, customs and socio-cultural prejudices. These States, because of their specific situation regarding these articles, make it difficult for the Committee to evaluate and understand the status of women.

47. The Committee, in particular on the basis of articles 1 and 2 of the Convention, requests that those States Parties make the necessary efforts to examine the de facto situation relating to the issues and to introduce the required measures in their national legislation still containing provisions discriminatory to women.

Reports

48. Assisted by the comments in the present general recommendation, in their reports States Parties should:

(a) Indicate the stage that has been reached in the country's progress to removal of all reservations to the Convention, in particular reservations to article 16;

(b) Set out whether their laws comply with the principles of articles 9, 15 and 16 and where, by reason of religious or private law or custom, compliance with the law or with the Convention is impeded.

Legislation

49. States Parties should, where necessary to comply with the Convention, in particular in order to comply with articles 9, 15 and 16, enact and enforce legislation.

Encouraging Compliance with the Convention

50. Assisted by the comments in the present general recommendation, and as required by articles 2, 3 and 24, States Parties should introduce measures directed at encouraging

full compliance with the principles of the Convention, particularly where religious or private law or custom conflict with those principles.

Problem 2-2

Lisa married Frank when she was 13. The marriage was arranged by her father, in conformity with the family's religious and cultural practices. She had never met Frank before the marriage. As an 18-year-old, Lisa now wants to marry Tim. Assume that under the laws of the country in which she lives, she has no grounds for divorce or annulment. Assume also that the country has ratified all the international instruments mentioned in this subsection. The country, however, has entered a general reservation to CEDAW that says it will not comply with article 16 "to the extent that the laws on personal status which are binding on various religious communities do not conform with the provisions of that article." Does international law help her? Should it?

Notes and Questions

1. *Competing Rights.* Is valuing multiculturalism a legal mandate? Look at the International Covenant on Civil and Political Rights (ICCPR), in particular, articles 14, 26, and 27. What about article 30 of the Convention on the Rights of the Child? Can you use these provisions to argue for or against a particular approach to customary law? What about article 23(1) of the ICCPR regarding the protection of the family unit? Do these support deferring to customary law? How? How does one reconcile those provisions with article 18(3) of the ICCPR?

2. *International Law and Age.* Would a country be in violation of CEDAW if it permitted the marriage of boys and girls over thirteen years old?

3. *Purpose of Registration.* Is registration merely a method for the state to effectuate its substantive marriage policy? If so, how effective is it? In the United States, the Uniform Marriage and Divorce Act § 206(c) has a registration requirement. *See* Unif. Marriage and Divorce Act, § 206(c), 9A U.L.A. 182 (1998). Does marriage registration help effectuate states' substantive marriage policies in the United States? What else might be the purpose of registration? Is a registration requirement imposed by international law beneficial? What problems might develop from such a requirement?

4. *A View of Marriage?* Human rights instruments stress "equality" between spouses. *See, e.g.,* CEDAW, *supra,* art. 16. What does this mean? Consider the following excerpt from Egypt's reservation to article 16:

> Reservation to the text of Article 16 concerning the equality of men and women in all matters relating to marriage and family relations during the marriage and upon its dissolution, without prejudice to the Islamic Sharia's provisions whereby women are accorded rights equivalent to those of their spouses so as to ensure a just balance between them. This is out of respect for the sacrosanct nature of the firm religious beliefs which govern marital relations in Egypt and which may not be called in question and in view of the fact that one of the most important bases of these relations is an equivalency of rights and duties so as to ensure complementary which guarantees true equality between the spouses.

See Convention on the Elimination of All Forms of Discrimination against Women: Declarations and Reservations, Human Rights Internet, *at* http://www.hri.ca/fortherecord1998/documentation/reservations/cedaw.htm.

5. *Other International Law Provisions.* The Human Rights Committee stated, "The Committee wishes to note that such legal provisions [on marriage] must be compatible with the full exercise of the other rights guaranteed by the [ICCPR]; thus, for instance the right to freedom of thought, conscience and religion implies that the legislation of each State should provide for the possibility of both religious and civil marriages. In the Committee's view, however, for a State to require that a marriage, which is celebrated in accordance with religious rites, be conducted, affirmed or registered also under civil law is not incompatible with the Covenant." *Protection of the Family, the Right to Marriage and Equality of Spouses (Art. 23): General Comment 19*, CCPR, 39th Sess., (1990), *at* http://www.unhchr.ch/tbs/doc.nsf/(Symbol)/6f97648603f69bcdc12563ed004c3881?Opendocument.

C. Procedural Requirements for Entry into Marriage

United States family law scholars used to discuss, as a matter of course, other countries' procedures for regulating entry into marriage. *See, e.g.,* Frederick Pollock & Frederic Maitland, 2 The History of English Law 364 (2nd ed. 1911); Otto E. Koegel, Common Law Marriage and Its Development in the United States 49–50 (1922). A renewed focus on other countries' procedures is useful for several reasons. First, other countries provide examples of possible legal solutions to problems we encounter. Second, contrasting other countries' approaches to our own, and exploring why our laws differ, tells us something about the role and influence of religion in regulating marriage in our own society.

The discussion focuses now on what is often called marriage "formalities." Generally, formalities are much less important today than they were in the past. "Clearly the predominant policy among nations today is to prefer marriage, and to impose relatively few conditions on marriage.... Accommodating personal autonomy seems to be a stronger part of marriage policy today than in the past." Lynn D. Wardle, *International Marriage and Divorce Regulation and Recognition: A Survey*, 29 Fam. L.Q. 497, 514 (1995). Yet, at least in the United States, there is a renewed interest in pre-event formalities as a way to encourage certain social norms. *See, e.g.,* Elizabeth S. Scott, *Social Norms and the Legal Regulation of Marriage*, 86 Va. L. Rev. 1901, 1956–57 (2000). As you read this material, think about what social norms are being encouraged and how well they are being encouraged.

1. France: Age, Consent, Banns, and Compulsory Civil Ceremony

French law serves as our focus. France has a civil law system; its marriage law has been heavily influenced by roman law and canon law. Marriage preliminaries are still quite important in France, as they have been historically, especially when compared to the United States. The next excerpt is from the French Civil Code of 1804, otherwise known as the Napoleonic Code. One commentator has said of contemporary French marriage law, "The winds of change that have blown on family law have left marriage intact, governed with minor exceptions, by the original texts of the Code Napoleon." Jacqueline Rubellin-DeVichi, *How Matters Stand Now in Relation to Family Law Reform*, *in* The International Survey of Family Law 143, 152 (Andrew Banham ed., 2000) (quoting Dean Carbonnier).

The Napoleonic Code gives us a detailed and comprehensive approach to marriage preliminaries. "[F]rench law is very heavily based on legislation, but this is not a feature peculiar to French law. The pace of social change and the importance of government direction in society and the economy has meant that most modern societies have a large amount of law-making from legislatures and government. The distinctive feature of France and a number of continental European countries is the perception that the written legislative rules provide a coherent and self-contained framework for the solution of contemporary social problems." *See generally* John Bell, Sophie Boyron & Simon Whittaker, Principles of French Law 5 (1998).

The French Civil Code (1804)

available at

http://www.napoleon-series.org/research/government/c_code.html

Book I: Of Persons.
Title II: Of Acts Before the Civil Authorities.
Chapter III: Of Acts of Marriage.

63. Before the celebration of a marriage, the civil officer shall make two publications, with an interval of eight days between them, one being on a Sunday, before the gate of the town-hall. These publications, and the act which shall be drawn up relating to them, shall set forth the Christian names, surnames, professions, and domiciles of the parties about to be married, the circumstance of their majority or minority, and the Christian names, surnames, professions, and domiciles of their fathers and mothers. This act shall set forth, moreover, the days, places, and hours at which the publications shall have been made; it shall be inscribed on one single register, which shall be endorsed and marked as directed in article 41, and deposited at the end of every year among the rolls of the court of the circle.

64. An extract from the Act of Publication shall be affixed to the door of the town-hall, and remain so during the interval of eight days between the one and the other publication. The marriage shall not be celebrated until the third day exclusive after that of the second publication.

65. Where a marriage has not been celebrated within a year, to be computed from the expiration of the interval between the publications, it shall not be celebrated until new publications have been made according to the forms hereinbefore prescribed.

66. Acts of opposition to a marriage shall be signed, both original and copy, by the parties opposing, or by their attorneys, specially and authentically appointed; they shall be communicated, with a copy of the appointment, to the party, or delivered at the domicil of the parties, and to the civil officer, who shall put his visa on the original.

67. The civil officer shall, without delay, make mention concisely of the opposition on the register of the publications; he shall likewise make mention, on the margin of the copy of the said opposition, of the judgments or acts of renunciation which shall have been sent to him.

68. Where opposition has been made, the civil officer shall not be at liberty to celebrate a marriage, until he shall have had a renunciation transmitted to him, upon pain of a fine of 300 francs, together with all costs.

69. If there has been no opposition, a memorandum thereof shall be made in the act of marriage; and where publications have been made in several communes, the parties shall transmit a certificate from the civil officer of each commune, certifying that there is no opposition.

70. The civil officer shall cause to be transmitted to him the act of birth of each party about to be married. Where either party shall be unable to produce it to him, its place may be supplied by showing an act of notoriety delivered by the magistrate at the parties' place of birth, or at that of his domicil.

71. The act of notoriety shall contain the declaration of seven witnesses of either sex, relations or otherwise, the christian names, surnames, professions, and domicil of the future husband or wife, and those of the father and mother, if they are known; the place, and as nearly as possible, the date of birth, and the causes which prevent the producing of the act of birth. The witnesses shall sign the act of notoriety with the magistrate; and if there are any witnesses who are unable or too ignorant to sign their names, mention shall be made of that circumstance.

72. The act of notoriety shall be presented to the court of first instance in the place where the marriage is to be celebrated. The court, after having heard the commissioner of the government, shall give or refuse its approval accordingly, as it shall find the declarations of the witnesses, and the causes which prevent the production of the act of birth sufficient or insufficient.

73. The authentic act of the consent of fathers and mothers, or of grandfathers and grandmothers, or in defect of these; that of the family, shall contain the Christian names, the surnames, the professions, and domiciles of the future husband, or wife; and of all those who shall have concurred in the act, together with their degree of relationship.

74. The marriage shall be celebrated in the commune in which one or other of the parties shall be domiciled. This domicil, as regards the marriage, shall be established by six months' continued habitation within the same commune.

75. On the day appointed by the parties after the interval for the publications, the civil officer in the town hall, in the presence of four witnesses, relations, or otherwise, shall read to the parties the before-mentioned documents, relating to their condition and to the formalities of the marriage, and from Chap. 6. title "Of Marriage:" "On the respective rights and duties of married persons." He shall receive from each party, in succession, a declaration that they are willing to take each other for husband and wife; he shall pronounce, in the name of the law, that they are united in marriage, and he shall forthwith draw up an act to that effect.

76. In the act of marriage shall be set forth,

1st. The Christian names, surnames, professions, ages, places of birth, and domiciles of the married persons;

2nd. If they are of full age or minors;

3rd. The Christian names, surnames, professions, and domiciles of the fathers and mothers;

4th. The consent of the fathers and mothers, grandfathers and grandmothers, and that of the family, in the cases in which they are requisite;

5th. The respectful acts, if any have been made;

6th. The publications within the different places of domicil;

7th. The opposition, if any have been made; the relinquishment of them, or the memorandum that no opposition has been made.

8th. The consent of the contracting parties to take each other as husband and wife, and the declaration of their union by the public officer;

9th. The Christian names, surnames, ages, professions, and domiciles of the witnesses, and their declaration whether they are relations or allied to the parties, on which side and in what degree....

Title V: Of Marriage.
Chapter I: Of the Qualities and Conditions Required in Order to be Able to Contract Marriage.

144. A man before the age of 18, and a woman before 15 complete, are incapable of contracting marriage.

145. The government shall be at liberty, nevertheless, upon weighty reasons, to grant dispensations of age....

148. The son who has not attained the full age of 25 years, the daughter who has not attained the full age of 21 years, cannot contract marriage without the consent of their father and mother; in case of disagreement, the consent of the father is sufficient.

149. If one of the two be dead, or under an incapacity of manifesting his or her will, the consent of the other is sufficient.

150. If the father and mother are dead, or if they are under an incapacity of manifesting their will, the grandfathers and grandmothers shall supply their place; if there be a disagreement between the grandfather and grandmother of the same line, the consent of the grandfather shall suffice. If the disagreement be between the two lines, this division shall import consent.

151. Where the children of a family have attained the majority fixed by article 148, they are required, previously to contracting marriage, to demand, by a respectful and formal act, the advice of their father and mother, or that of their grandfathers and grandmothers when their father and mother are dead, or under an incapacity of manifesting their will.

152. From the majority fixed by article 148 to the age of 30 years completed for sons, and until the age of 25 years completed for daughters, the respectful act required by the preceding article and on which consent to marriage shall not have been obtained, shall be renewed two several times, from month to month; and one month after the third act it shall be lawful to pass on to the celebration of the marriage.

153. After the age of 30 years, it shall be lawful, in default of consent, upon a respectful act, to pass on, after the expiration of a month, to the celebration of the marriage.

154. The respectful act shall be notified to such person or persons of the ascending line as are pointed out in article 151, by two notaries, or by one notary and two wit-

nesses; and in the statement which shall be drawn up thereof, mention shall be made of the answer.

155. In case of the absence of the ancestor to whom the respectful act ought to have been made, the celebration of the marriage may be proceeded in, on producing a judgment given declaring absence, or in default of such judgment that which shall have directed an inquiry, or if such latter judgment shall not yet have been pronounced, an act of notoriety delivered by the justice of the peace of the place where the ancestor had his last known domicil. This act shall contain the deposition of four witnesses officially summoned by the justice of the peace.

156. The officers of the civil power who shall have proceeded to the celebration of marriages contracted by sons not having attained the full age of twenty-five years, or by daughters not having attained the full age of twenty-one years, without having the consent of the fathers and mothers, that of the grandfathers and grandmothers, and that of the family, in a case requiring them, declared in the act of marriage, shall, on the prosecution of the parties interested, and of the government commissioner in the tribunal of first instance of the place where the marriage shall have been celebrated, be condemned to the fine inflicted by article 192, and further to an imprisonment, whose duration shall not be less than six months.

157. Where respectful acts shall have been omitted to be made in cases in which they are prescribed, the civil officer who shall have celebrated the marriage, shall be condemned to the same fine, and to an imprisonment of not less than one month.

158. The regulations contained in articles 148 and 149, and those of articles 151, 152, 153, 154, and 155, relative to the respectful act required to be made to the father and mother in the case contemplated by those articles, are applicable to natural children legally recognized.

159. The natural child who has not been acknowledged, and the child who after having been so, has lost his father and mother, or whose father and mother are unable to manifest their will, shall not be at liberty, before the full age of twenty-one years, to marry without the consent of a guardian ad hoc, who shall be nominated for him.

160. If there is neither father nor mother, neither grandfathers nor grandmothers, or if they are all found to be under an incapacity of manifesting their will, male or female children under the age of twenty-one years cannot contract marriage without the consent of a family council....

Chapter II: Of the Formalities Relative to the Celebration of Marriage.

165. The marriage shall be celebrated publicly, before the civil officer of the domicil of one of the two parties.

166. The two publications directed by article 63, under the title "Of the acts of the civil power," shall be made to the municipality of the place where each of the contracting parties shall have his domicil....

170. A marriage contracted in a foreign country between natives of France, and between a native of France and a foreigner, shall be valid, if celebrated according to the forms used in that country, provided that it has been preceded by the publications prescribed in article 63, under the title "Of acts of the civil power," and that the Frenchman has not infringed the regulations contained in the preceding chapter.

171. Within three months after the return of a Frenchman into the territory of the republic, the act of the celebration of marriage contracted in a foreign country, shall be transcribed into the public register of marriages, at the place of his domicil.

Chapter III: Of Opposition to Marriage.

172. The right of opposing the celebration of marriage belongs to the person connected by marriage with one of the two contracting parties.

173. The father, and in default of the father, the mother, and in default of the father and mother, the grandfathers and grandmothers, may oppose the marriage of their children and descendants, although they have accomplished twenty-five years.

174. In default of ancestors, the brother or sister, the uncle or aunt, cousin or cousins german, being of age, can make no opposition except in the two following cases:

> 1st. Where the consent of the family-council, required by article 160, has not been obtained.

> 2nd. Where the opposition is founded on a state of insanity in the future spouse: This opposition, of which the court is empowered to pronounce the pure and simple abrogation, shall never be received except on condition by the opponent of urging the interdiction, and causing a decree to be made thereon, within the interval which shall be fixed by judgment.

175. In the two cases contemplated by the preceding article, the guardian or curator shall not, during the continuance of the guardianship or curatorship, make opposition, except so far as he shall have been authorized by a family-council, which he is at liberty to convoke.

176. Every act of opposition shall set forth the quality which gives to the opponent the right to make it; it shall contain the election of domicil in the place where the marriage is to be celebrated; it shall, in like manner, unless it is made at the request of an ancestor, contain the motives of opposition: the whole on pain of nullity, and of suspension of the ministerial officer, who shall have signed the act containing the opposition.

177. The tribunal of first instance shall pronounce within ten days, on the petition for revocation.

178. If an appeal be made, a decision shall be made thereon within ten days from the citation.

179. If the opposition be rejected, the opponents, other nevertheless than ancestors, may be sentenced to damages.

Chapter IV: Of Petitions for Nullity of Marriage....

182. A marriage contracted without the consent of the father and mother, of the ancestors, or of the family council, in cases where such consent was necessary, can only be impeached by those whose consent was requisite, or by such of the two married persons as stood in need of that consent.

183. A suit for nullity is no longer maintainable either by the married persons, or by the relations whose consent was required, in those cases where the marriage has been approved, either expressly or tacitly, by those whose consent was necessary; or when a year has elapsed without complaint on their part, subsequently to their knowledge of

the marriage. Such suit is no longer maintainable by a spouse, after the lapse of a year without complaint on his part, subsequently to his having attained the competent age for consenting to the marriage in his own person.

184. Every marriage contracted in contravention of the regulations contained in article[] 144…may be impeached either by the married parties themselves, or by those who have an interest therein, or by the public authorities.

185. Nevertheless a marriage contracted by parties who have not yet reached the required age, or of whom one has not attained that age, is no longer liable to be impeached, 1st, where six months have expired since the married person or persons have attained the competent age; 2d, where the woman not having reached that age has conceived before the expiration of six months.

186. The father, the mother, the ancestors, and the family having consented to a marriage contracted under the circumstances mentioned in the preceding article, are inadmissible as plaintiffs in a suit for nullity.

187. In all those cases where, conformably to article 184, a suit for nullity may be instituted by all those who have an interest therein, such suit shall not be maintained by collateral relations, or the children born of another marriage of the survivor of the parties, but only where they have an actual and existing interest therein….

190. The commissioner of government may and shall, in all cases to which article 184 can be applied, and subject to the modifications contained in article 185, demand the nullity of the marriage,…and cause them to be sentenced to separation.

191. Every marriage not publicly contracted, and not celebrated before the competent public officer, may be impeached by the married parties themselves, by the father and mother, by the ancestors, and by all those who have an actual and existing interest therein, as well as by the public authorities.

192. If the marriage has not been preceded by the two publications required, or if the dispensations permitted by the law have not been obtained, or if the intervals prescribed between the publications and celebrations have not been observed, the commissioner shall cause a fine to be awarded against the public officer, which shall not exceed 300 francs; and against the contracting parties, or those under whose control they have acted, a fine proportioned to their fortune.

193. The punishments awarded in the preceding article shall be inflicted on the persons designated therein, for every contravention of the rules prescribed by article 165, even though such contravention shall not be adjudged sufficient, whereon to pronounce a nullity of the marriage.

194. No person shall be at liberty to claim the title of spouse, and the civil consequences of marriage, unless upon the production of an act of celebration inscribed upon the register of the civil power, saving the cases provided for by article 46, under the title "Of acts before the civil authorities."…

197. Where, nevertheless, in the cases of articles 194 and 195, there are children, the issue of two individuals who have lived publicly together as husband and wife, and who are both deceased, the legitimacy of such children cannot be contested on the single ground of the non-production of the act of celebration, whenever such legitimacy is proved by an actual marriage uncontradicted by the act of birth….

201. A marriage which has been declared null draws after it, nevertheless, civil consequences, as well with regard to the married parties as to their children, where the marriage has been contracted in good faith.

202. Where good faith exists only on the part of one of the married persons, the marriage is only attended by civil consequences in favor of such persons, and the children of the marriage.

Chapter VI: Of the Respective Rights and Duties of Married Persons.

[Ed. Note: Section 75 of the code requires the civil officer to read to the parties, among other things, the sixteen articles contained in this chapter. The first three are included here to give a flavor of the provisions. The rest are omitted. Many of the other provisions reflect the fact that the code rejected a model of equality for family members and instead elevated the husband's authority above the wife's.]

212. Married persons owe to each other fidelity, succor, assistance.

213. The husband owes protection to his wife, the wife obedience to her husband.

214. The wife is obliged to live with her husband, and to follow him to every place where he may judge it convenient to reside: the husband is obliged to receive her, and to furnish her with everything necessary for the wants of life, according to his means and station.

Notes and Questions

1. *The Influence of the French Code.* Christian Dadomo and Susan Farran, authors of *The French Legal System* (1993), describe how the Napoleonic Code had a tremendous impact: "[N]apoleon's codification process was to have a wide impact on the rest of Europe, as a consequence of French political and military aggrandizement, with the result that a number of countries came to share a common legal heritage, not only of Roman law, but of the French Codes which were either imposed on them as a result of conquest, voluntarily adopted, or used as models for codes of their own." *Id.* at 9–10. It also influenced the development of legal codes in Latin America and the Arab world when countries there were rejecting the law of their conquerors. *See* The French Civil Code (John H. Crabb trans., rev. ed. xxiii 1995) (1959).

2. *Change.* While various articles of the Napoleonic Code still regulate marriage, many others have been repealed or amended. "General tendencies have been to remove the restrictions upon the capacity of married women; to modernize the matrimonial regimes; to facilitate marriage; and to augment the rights of illegitimate children." F.H. Lawson et al., Amos and Walton's Introduction to French Law 19 (3d ed. 1967).

3. *Parental Consent.* Are the French provisions on consent different in kind from the parental consent requirements in some American states? *See, e.g.,* Or. Rev. Stat. §§ 106.010, 106.060 (2001):

> *Marriage as civil contract; age of parties.* Marriage is a civil contract entered into in person by males at least 17 years of age and females at least 17 years of age, who are otherwise capable, and solemnized in accordance with ORS 106.150.

> *Consent of parent or guardian if party under 18.* A marriage license shall not be issued without the written consent of the parent or guardian, if any, of an applicant who is less than 18 years of age, nor in any case unless the parties are each of an age...capable of contracting marriage. If either party under 18 years of age has no parent or guardian resident within this state and either party has resided within the county in which application is made for the

six months immediately preceding the application, the license may issue, if otherwise proper, without the consent of the nonresident parent or guardian.

What justifies these types of provisions? One commentator has said "the Civil Code draftsmen brought forward these consent rules from the prerevolutionary law because they seemed a necessary feature of a system in which marriage created responsibilities on the part of the family of origin of each spouse and potentially involved the dispersal of family wealth." Mary Ann Glendon, The Transformation of Family Law 41 (1989). The Napoleonic Code itself imposed specific obligations on the families to their sons-in-laws and daughters-in-laws, *see, e.g.,* The French Civil Code 1804, *supra*, at Book I, tit. II, ch. V, §§ 206, 207, although the larger concern was the potential transfer of family assets. *See* Dagmar Coester-Waltjen & Michael Coester, *Formation of Marriage, in* IV International Encyclopedia of Comparative Law 7 (1997) ("The state was interested in these rules because it wanted to protect and further the interests of the (leading) families who seemed to guarantee the exercise and the continuity of the political institutions in power."). Are these provisions serving the same purpose in the United States today?

4. *Parental Disagreement.* Article 148 was amended in 1927 to state "in the case of dissent between the father and mother, such division imports consent." Law of 11 July 1927, The French Civil Code, art. 148 (John H. Crabb trans., rev. ed. xxiii 1995) (1959). A similar change was made to article 150. *Id.* The Code could have been changed to make division dispositive of a lack of consent. What use is the consent requirement if division implies consent?

5. *Consequence of No Consent.* The Code makes the remedy for violation of the consent provision explicit. Consider, for example, articles 182–190. How does the doctrine of ratification work when the necessary third party consent is missing?

6. *Unreasonable Opposition.* When a relative's opposition to marriage can constitute an impediment to marriage, some mechanism may be needed to stop the relative from abusing the privilege. What is that mechanism in the French Civil Code? Does it matter if the relative opposes the marriage for reasons that have nothing to do with the compatibility of the parties? Consider the following amendment made in 1919: "After the judicial withdrawal of an opposition to marriage made by an ascendant, no new opposition made by an ascendant is either receivable nor capable of retarding the celebration." *Id.* art. 173, Law of Aug. 1919. Instruments of opposition are valid for one year, although they can be renewed unless there has been a judicial withdrawal of the opposition to marriage. *Id.* art. 177, Law of 15 Mar. 1933. Parties to the marriage, even minors, can petition for the withdrawal of the opposition. Is there a remedy for an unreasonable withholding of consent? Mary Ann Glendon has suggested that when a parent unreasonably withholds approval, a child may have a claim for "abuse of right." Glendon, *supra*, at 42. One commentator has said the French Civil Code balanced "freedom of marriage and family solidarity." James Frederick Traer, Marriage and the Family in French Law and Social Criticism from the End of the Ancient Regime to the Civil Code 286 (Univ. of Mich. 1970) (dissertation submitted in completion of a Ph.D.). Do you agree? Today the procedure for formal opposition still exists, *see* French Civil Code, arts. 172–79, but is "very rarely used." Coester-Waltjen & Coester, *supra*, at 17.

7. *Third-Party Involvement.* The need for third-party consent to a marriage, or the ability of a third-party to object, perhaps suggests that the marital relation has implications for the third parties. Who in our society is often impacted by marriage, but has no ability to object to the marriage? What about children of the parties or former spouses?

Why not allow those who are impacted to have a say about whether the marriage occurs? What do you make of the English law that requires any descendant of George II (other than the offspring of princesses who have married foreigners) to gain the consent of the reigning sovereign to marry? If the descendent is over twenty-five, however, the person can marry if the Privy Council is given one year's notice and both houses of Parliament do not expressly disapprove during that period. If any such person goes through the form of marriage in defiance of these provisions, the marriage is held by English law to be null and void. Royal Marriage Act, 1772, 12 Geo. 3, 11 (Eng.). *See also* 10 Halsbury's Statutes of England and Wales 68 (1995). The Act was passed because "Marriages in the Royal Family are of the highest Importance to the State."

8. *Age and Consent Today.* The marriage age today in France is the same as it was in 1804. The need for parental advice was abolished in 1933, although not for those under 18. *See* French Civil Code, art. 148. There is still no judicial procedure to bypass the parental consent requirement, as is common in some other countries such as Germany. *See* Marriage Law § 3, ¶ 2. *See generally* Coester-Waltjen & Coester, *supra,* at 16–18.

9. *Post-mortem Marriage.* In one situation, the French Civil Code today does not require both parties' consent to be married. The Code allows the marriage of a dead person. To state the obvious, a dead person cannot consent to anything. These marriages can occur "provided (1) the marriage intent of the parties can be proven and has been expressed beforehand by the preparation of the preliminaries to marriage, (2) there is an important reason for marriage (mostly pregnancy), (3) the French President has given his approval, and (4) all other conditions for entering a valid marriage are fulfilled." Coester-Waltjen & Coester, *supra,* at 27 (citing art. 171). Although the rule is criticized by scholars, it has been used. The primary benefit seems to be the legitimation of a child the woman was carrying. *Id.* at 28. Do we have a comparable process in the United States?

10. *Respectful Acts.* What were respectful acts? *See* French Civil Code, arts. 151–57. Was this formality a significant barrier to marriage?

11. *Banns.* Articles 63–65 reflect the requirement that banns be published before a marriage occurs. What is the purpose of the banns? Does the United States have anything similar to the publication of the banns? Is the license requirement equivalent? Consider, for example, the law of the State of Georgia, which is the only state that still talks about "banns." In Georgia, banns serve as a substitute for a marriage license and permit recordation in the same book where licenses are recorded. *See* Ga. Code Ann. §§ 19-3-39, 19-3-46 (2000).

12. *Modern Banns.* Although the French Civil Code of 1804 has undergone many changes, often the new provisions still harken back to the older requirements. For example article 63, which required the publication of the banns twice on the gate of the townhall door, has been amended to require only one publication on the door of the communal hall. In addition, the law now specifies that the publication cannot be made until "after the remittance by each one of the future spouses of a medical certificate dating from less than two months, attesting...that the interested party has been examined in prospect of marriage." Failure to obtain the certificate subjects the public officer to prosecution and a fine. The requirement of the medical certificate may be dispensed with "in exceptional cases." *See* art. 169. Interestingly, the medical certificate is confidential, and each spouse need not reveal the results to the other.

13. *Official Investigations.* Germany has a "compulsory official investigation into all necessary conditions of marriage. The banns are only an additional, but dispensable means of discovering existing marriage impediments." Coester-Waltjen & Coester, *supra,* at 66. Similarly, Austria carries out an official investigation. *Id.*

14. *Compulsory Civil Ceremony.* Look at the French Civil Code §§ 75–76, 165, 191. These provisions have stayed virtually the same over time. What is the effect of a religious marriage in France? What is the purpose of the French system? Does it help convey social norms? Contrast the idea of a mandatory civil ceremony with the Uniform Marriage and Divorce Act, § 206(a): "A marriage may be solemnized by a judge of a court of record, by a public official whose powers include solemnization of marriages, or in accordance with any mode of solemnization recognized by any religious demonstration, Indian Nation or Tribe, or Native Group. Either the person solemnizing the marriage, or, if no individual acting alone solemnized the marriage, a party to the marriage, shall complete the marriage certificate form and forward it to the [marriage license] clerk." 9A U.L.A. 182 (1973). Few states, if any, require a particular form of the ceremony. What is the disadvantage of a compulsory civil ceremony for all? One author, speaking about a similar requirement in Germany, suggested that there might be a fiscal motivation behind the requirement or, perhaps, the compulsory civil ceremony reflects "a legal culture intent on telling people what they can do in addition to what they cannot do." Thomas Lundmark, *Introduction to German Law*, 47 Am. J. Comp. L. 677, 677–85 (1999) (reviewing Introduction to German Law (Werner F. Ebke & Matthew W. Finkin eds. 1996)).

15. *Covenant Marriage.* Some states, such as Louisiana and Arizona, have provided couples with the option of covenant marriage. *See, e.g.,* La. Rev. Stat. Ann. 9:272–275.1, 307–309 (2000); Ariz. Rev. Stat. 25–901 (1998). Parties selecting this type of marriage must generally have premarital counseling that emphasizes the seriousness and permanency of marriage. They must sign a declaration of their intent to take all reasonable efforts to preserve the marriage, including pre-divorce counselling. Parties to a covenant marriage are restricted in their access to divorce, at least within the state in which they enter the covenant marriage and arguably in other places as well. *See* Katherine Shaw Spaht & Symeon C. Symeonides, *Covenant Marriage and the Law of Conflicts of Laws*, 32 Creighton L. Rev. 1085 (1999). In Louisiana, a covenant marriage restricts no-fault divorce to couples who have lived separate and apart continuously without reconciliation for a period of two years, or who satisfy one of the four fault grounds for divorce (adultery, serious felony, abandonment for one year, or physical or sexual abuse of the spouse or a child). Does a covenant marriage offer the same advantages as the French civil marriage ceremony?

16. *The Long-Arm of the French Civil Code?* Is the notion of covenant marriage directly traceable to the Napoleonic Code? "It would come as no surprise…that Louisiana, whose private civil law is derived from continental sources consisting principally of French and Spanish sources, would be the first state to address issues of divorce and the breakdown of families through law that attempts to persuade and educate." *See* Katherine Shaw Spaht, *For the Sake of the Children: Recapturing the Meaning of Marriage*, 73 Notre Dame L. Rev. 1547 (1998).

17. *A Model?* With approximately half of the marriages in this country ending in divorce, should states adopt some more exacting marriage preliminaries? Would states be best advised to follow the early French model, or is it preferable to require couples to engage in premarital counseling and/or the drafting of premarital agreements? *See* Kaylah Campos Zelig, Comment, *Putting Responsibility Back Into Marriage: Making a Case for Mandatory Prenuptials*, 64 U. Colo. L. Rev. 1223 (1993). For your information, the divorce rate in France in 1996 was 38%, and has been increasing steadily since 1960 when the rate was 9%. *Recent Demographic Developments in Europe*, 1999

Eur. Y. B. (Council of Eur.), *at* http://www.coe.int/t/e/dg3/population/demographic_year_book/Countries/1999/France/Ftabl4.asp. If one likes some of the provisions of the French Civil Code, could one cherry pick some provisions or is the Code a cohesive framework that does not work when disassembled? Remember that the 1804 Code elevated the husband's authority above the wife's authority.

18. *Conclusions?* "The preliminaries required by modern legal systems before a marriage can take place are revealing indications of the degree to which the state is actively interested in regulating marriage formation, as opposed to contenting itself with the promulgation of rules which prescribe desirable behavior but which have no real sanctions. To the extent that the various compulsory marriage preliminaries are contrived to identify problem cases, and to prevent marriages in violation of the rules concerning who may marry whom, they indicate how seriously the various marriage restrictions in a given country are to be taken." Glendon, *supra*, at 59. What can be said about how seriously marriage restrictions were taken in France in 1804 and in the United States today?

19. *The Role of the Catholic Church.* French marriage law has been heavily influenced by canon law, starting in the early Middle Ages. In response to the French Royalists in the early 17th century who emphasized that marriage was solely a contract, the Church stressed the inseparability of sacrament from the contract and claimed that it had the right to set the conditions for legitimacy and were the only judges of its validity. Ladislas Orsy, Marriage in Canon Law 55–56 (1986). The Church was successful in establishing jurisdiction over marriage, in whole or in part in France, until the Revolution of 1789. *See* Christian Dadodmo & Susan Farran, The French Legal System 6 (1993). The French Code of 1804, conceived of as a break with France's past, had a variety of provisions that would vest control of marriage in the state. Compulsory civil ceremonies are an obvious example. Less obvious perhaps is the strict nullity provision in article 191. One scholar has stated, "The prohibition was clearly an effort to support the requirement of civil marriage and deter individuals from celebrating only a religious ceremony before a priest." Traer, *supra*, at 287. Yet the new Code itself drew on canon law. "Neither the content of the Code, nor the idea of codification itself marked a total break with the past." Dadomo & Farran, *supra*, at 9–10. As Mary Ann Glendon explained, when the monarchy assumed jurisdiction over marriage, the government "took over much of the ready-made set of rules of the canon law.... Thus, many rules which had been developed in the canon law continued to govern marriage, although they received new interpretations on certain points." Mary Ann Glendon, The Transformation of Family Law 31 (1989).

Modernly, French marriage law and canon law are quite different. In canon law, an essential property of the marriage is its indissolubility. The Code of Canon Law 189 (The Canon Law Society of Great Britain trans., 1984) (1983) (canon 1056). Since the adoption of the 1804 Code, divorce has been possible in France. *See* French Civil Code, arts. 229–45. Canon law forbids marriage between a Catholic and an unbaptized person unless the impediment is dispensed with after several conditions are met, including the Catholic party's assurance that the children will be raised as Catholics. The Code of Canon Law, *supra*, at 193, 195 (canons 1086, 1125, 1126). French law has no such religious matching. One even sees a distinction in the formalities. For example, France currently insists upon a civil marriage ceremony, and the church insists that the marriage be "contracted in the presence of the local ordinary, or of the parish priest, or of a priest or a deacon delegated by either of them, who must assist, and in the presence of two witnesses." Orsy, *supra*, at 160–61 (citing canon 1108).

The way each system responds to the others' rules says something about the power of the state and the church.

F. J. Sheed, Nullity of Marriage
88, 90–94 (1959)

Both state and church insist on certain forms being observed: in both, there are some forms whose absence is illegal, but not fatal to the marriage, and some whose absence is fatal....

In the Catholic church, the form is clearly laid down. Since the Council of Trent so decided in 1563, a Catholic must be married before the parish priest (or his delegate) and two other witnesses; otherwise the marriage is clandestine, and therefore null.... [T]his form is obligatory on Catholics: any Catholic who tries to marry not observing this rule simply is not married.

There are...certain exceptions to the strictness of the requirement that a priest be present. In danger of death, for instance, two witnesses suffice, even without a priest. The same rule applies if the parties could get to the priest (or the priest to the parties) only with serious difficulty: the priest is to be regarded as unobtainable; and if the situation is likely to last for a month, the parties may marry without his presence. But if their belief that the priest is unobtainable happens to be wrong, then their marriage is invalid.

One special form of "unobtainability" is worth mentioning. In countries where... the law forbids a church marriage under heavy penalties unless there has first been a civil marriage...then Catholics may be married in the presence of two witnesses, with no priest present.

Apart from such exceptional cases, a Catholic who goes through a civil form of marriage only is not merely committing a most grave sin, but is not married at all. If his wedding is in a non-Catholic church, the marriage is still null and the sin is greater. If, however, the civil law requires marriage before one who is in fact a protestant minister, Catholics do not sin who go through the form of marriage before him, regarding him simply as a state official, and without his performing any religious ceremony.

Apart from accommodation as to form, the Church also recognizes the competence of civil authorities over the civil effects of marriage. *See* The Code of Canon Law 189 (The Canon Law Society of Great Britain trans., 1984) (1983) (canon 1059). To further assess how the conflicts between the church and state on this topic have been formally resolved, recall the civil law's treatment of religious marriages. Review articles 165 and 191 of the French Civil Code (1804). The essence of these provisions still exists today. What conclusions can be drawn about the formal power of the State and the Church over marriage in France?

Of course, the Church's diminished formal power over marriage in France says nothing about its informal power. It is difficult, however, to draw conclusions one way or another. Despite the fact that the French are not very religious, the Church appears to be somewhat important to them in the context of marriage. While "[a]pproximately 90% of French people call themselves Catholics,...only about 15% regularly go to Sunday mass." Rik Torfs, *Church and State in France, Belgium, and the*

Netherlands: Unexpected Similarities and Hidden Differences, 1996 BYU L. Rev. 945, 950 (1996). In fact, "A European values poll in 1990 indicated that...[in France, 38%] of the population, among them many baptized Catholics, declare that they are without religion." *Id.* at 966. Notwithstanding this secularization, French people still like to solemnize their marriages in church ceremonies after the civil ceremony. "The secularization of marriage in France had little effect...on the custom of having a religious wedding ceremony. It is still very common in France for couples to proceed directly from their civil wedding (which is required by law to take place before any religious ceremony) to a wedding in church." Glendon, *supra*, at 71.

Today the Church's influence in France is achieved by its collaboration with the State, and the Church implicitly agrees "to function within the framework of the state." Torfs, *supra*, at 966. Professor Rik Torfs explains that cooperation between the State and the Catholic church has replaced the formal competition between those institutions that was evident in "the nineteenth-century battle over administrative control of marriage," which "led to stipulations requiring civil marriages to precede church marriages." *Id.* at 965–66. The collaboration paradigm is important because churches "help establish a common morality, and prevent social problems stemming from an atomic society and loneliness." *Id.* at 951. Torfs emphasizes that this cooperative relationship is not limited to the Catholic church, but rather is now pluralistic because France professes religious neutrality. *Id.* at 953 (citing Law of December 9, 1905 on Separation).

---

2. The Importance of Formalities

The importance that a society attaches to its marriage formalities can be judged in several ways. For example, if the state attaches criminal penalties to a failure to follow formalities and if it prosecutes violators, a society presumably takes its formalities very seriously. Another indicator may be whether the courts recognize marriages that fail to comply with formalities, *e.g.*, whether formalities are found to be directory or mandatory. In addition, the degree to which the society allows exceptions to the requirements indicates something about the importance of the requirements. A still further indication of the significance of formalities is whether the legislature or courts have developed legal alternatives to render marriage, and its formalities, less important overall. *See generally* Cynthia Grant Bowman, *A Feminist Proposal to Bring Back Common Law Marriage*, 75 Or. L. Rev. 709, 776–78 (1996).

These criteria do not always give a clear answer to the question about the importance of marriage formalities because sometimes the signals conflict. For example, in canon law, failure to publish the banns might subject the parties and the witnesses to ecclesiastical punishment, and the priest might be punished by a temporary removal from office. Yet the marriage would not be invalid, and parties could receive a dispensation from publication of the banns for a sufficient reason. *See generally* Thomas J. Shahan, *Banns of Marriage*, *in* 2 Catholic Encyclopedia 256–57 (Robert Appleton Co. 1907).

The next case allows us to consider why a society might impose certain requirements, and then excuse violations of those same requirements. The case also demonstrates methods courts employ to excuse violations.

Chief Adjudication Officer v. Kirpal Kaur Bath
1 Fam. 8 (Eng. C.A. 2000)

Evans, L.J.

[The Respondent] is a lady now aged 59 who in 1956 at the age of 16 went through a Sikh marriage ceremony with Zora Singh Bath, who was then aged 19 and was also a Sikh. They lived together as man and wife for 37 years until he died on 23 January 1994. They had two sons, born in 1963 and 1965. He built up a successful cash and carry business and in later years, as her sons grew up, she helped him in the business. He paid income tax and social security contributions on the basis, which was never queried, that he was a married man. When he died, she applied for the pension payable to a widow under section 38 of the Social Security Contributions and Benefits Act 1992. That was on 3 February 1994.

Her application was refused and the refusal was belatedly justified on the ground that she was not a widow, because there was no evidence of a valid [marriage] ceremony in accordance with the Marriage Act 1949. She appealed to the Social Security Appeals Tribunal (S.S.A.T.) where the Adjudication officer said that...the ceremony could not be accepted as a valid marriage.... The Appeal Tribunal found that:

> The Tribunal had enormous sympathy with the appellant's predicament. Unfortunately, at the time of her marriage ceremony the Sikh temple was not registered for performing marriages, nor had the marriage been registered in a Registry Office. As a result there had not been a valid ceremony in accordance with the Marriage Act 1949, and this meant that the appellant is not entitled to Widows Pension.

[On appeal, the Social Security Commissioner held:] "In my view that marriage is validated by the common law presumption from long cohabitation, in pursuance of the policy of the law that, in the absence of the clearest possible reason why there should not be such a presumption, a ceremony of marriage bona fide entered by parties who thereafter live monogamously and bring up children of the union should be respected and accorded the proper legal status of marriage."

Notwithstanding this decision in her favor, dated 7 May 1998, Mrs. Bath has not been paid the pension to which the Commissioner held she is entitled, because, we were told, the department, now the Benefits Agency, exercised its power to withhold payment pending the present appeal. Nearly six years after her claim was first made, she has not received a penny....

These [facts] were not in dispute. The Sikh marriage ceremony took place at the Sikh Temple, the Central Gurdwara, at 79 Sinclair Road, London W.14. There was a marriage ceremony duly administered by a Sikh priest in accordance with the Sikh custom and religion. There were up to fifty persons present and photographs were taken. In a letter dated 1st November 1995, Mrs. Bath wrote: "Like most other first wave immigrants, we had no knowledge of the law, were completely illiterate and led to believe, by our elders and peers, that we had followed the correct procedures. Both my husband and I have always been religious and we would have been very concerned if our marriage had not been carried out in accordance with the Sikh custom and religion or thought that our marriage was not valid."

Enquiries revealed that the temple moved from Sinclair Road to 62 Queensdale Road, London W1 sometime between 1956 and 1983. It was registered for marriages at the new address with effect from 26 September 1983. There was no evidence that it was not registered at either address before 1983, apart from the following correspondence. On 29 September 1994, the District Manager of the Benefits Agency wrote to the Temple asking "Could you please advise whether, in 1956, this Sikh temple was a registered building for performing marriages?" and the President replied, by letter dated 4 October: "please note that I came in this country in 1960 and at that time the Sikh temple as far as I know was not registered in performing the marriages. Some other old members of the temple had confirmed me this point."

Under section 41 of the Marriage Act 1949, the Registrar General was required to keep a book in which buildings which were places of religious worship could be registered for the purposes of the Act. There was no evidence as to the state of the book at any time. On the other hand, the respondent accepted in her letter dated 1 November 1995 that the building was not registered, and the Commissioner proceeded on the basis that it was not. He referred to a later letter from the Office for National Statistics dated 25 June 1997 which confirmed that Queensdale Road was registered on 28 September 1983, but which made no express reference to the position of Sinclair Road before that date.

[The Marriage Act 1949] was a consolidation Act which permits the solemnization of a marriage in a building, being a place of worship registered for that purpose (section 41) according to such form and ceremony as those persons [the couple being married] may see fit to adopt (section 44(1)) provided that a Registrar or an authorized person is present (section 43) and subject to certain requirements including the presence of two or more witnesses (section 44(2)) and an exchange of appropriate undertakings (section 44(3)). Section 49 reads:

> Void marriages
>
> If any persons knowingly and wilfully inter-marry under the provisions of this Part of this Act....
>
> (e) In any place other than the church, chapel, registered building office or other place specified in the notice of marriage and certificate of the superintendent registrar:
>
> (f) In the case of a marriage in a registered building (not being a marriage in the presence of an authorized person), in the absence of the registrar of the registration district in which the registered building is situated;....
>
> The marriage shall be void.

This section, therefore, renders the marriage void, notwithstanding the exchange of vows, if the parties to it have knowingly and wilfully failed to comply with the relevant statutory provisions....

There can be no suggestion in the present case that either of the couple was aware of any defect. On the contrary, they were aged 16 and 19, they had recently come to this country and the ceremony was conducted by a senior churchman at the Temple in the presence of their family and friends. A marriage contract was made between them. There is no statutory provision which renders their marriage void.... [T]he common law presumed from the fact of extended cohabitation as man and wife that the parties had each agreed to cohabit on that basis, and the presumption was extended to include an inference that the statutory requirements first introduced by Lord Hardwickes Marriage Act 1753 had been duly complied with; but in each case the presumption was capable of being rebutted by clear and convincing evidence. It is understandable why clear evidence was required to rebut the presumption after a long period of unchallenged cohabitation as man and wife, because the evidence in rebuttal would by definition refer to events many years in the past and might be concerned with matters that were not easily susceptible of proof at that distance of time....

I would agree with the Commissioners Decision R(G) 2/70 that when there is positive evidence that the statutory requirements were not complied with, then the presumption cannot be relied upon to establish that they were.

However, that is not the end of the matter. Mr. McManus' submission assumes that if the place of worship where the ceremony takes place is not registered in accordance with the Act then the marriage is invalid, or more precisely, that it does not count as a marriage for the purposes of the social security legislation regarding widows pensions. This leads to the remarkable conclusion, apart from the injustice of which the Respondent complains, that a valid marriage ceremony may be presumed where there is no evidence from the surviving widow, as where she refuses to co-operate by providing information, but it may not be presumed when, as here, she gives a truthful account which leads to the discovery that there was a failure to comply with the requirements of the Act, of which she was and remained unaware. Likewise, when as here she accepts the truth of what the department alleges against her, she is in a worse position than if she had insisted on their producing positive evidence of non-registration (which they have not done). Even more remarkable is the consequence referred to by the Commissioner.... A marriage could be presumed from long cohabitation when there was no ceremony, but not when a bona fide ceremony failed to comply with all the requirements of the Act, perhaps for some trivial reason.

In my judgment, the submission is fallacious, for this reason. There is no statutory provision that a marriage, otherwise carried out in proper form, by an authorized celebrant and at a place of worship eligible to be registered under the Act, is invalid merely on the ground that the building was not registered, for whatever reason. The marriage was not void or voidable under the law in force before 1971 (see Halsburys Laws (4th ed.) Vol. 13 paras. 538–39) nor was it rendered void by section 49 of the 1949 Act....

For this reason, I would hold that Mr. and Mrs. Bath were validly married in 1956 by reason of the ceremony at the Sikh temple at Sinclair Road, notwithstanding that the Temple was not registered at that date pursuant to the Act. This assumes, of course, that they were unaware of that fact. The contrary is not and cannot be suggested. It is noteworthy that guilty knowledge by both parties is necessary for the marriage to be void under section 49 (Halsburys Laws Vol. 22 para. 914 no. 23). Unless both participate, it is not invalid (ibid.)....

I would also be prepared to hold, notwithstanding the finding that the Temple was not registered under the Act, that the evidence relied upon by the department was not sufficiently positive to displace a presumption that the building was registered. The letters from the current senior officers of the Temple in its new location are not even the best evidence, which could and should be produced, in the form of the book, which there was a statutory obligation to keep. The applicant simply does not know, and her admission therefore is of no weight as evidence in support of the department's case....

Robert Walker, L.J.

I agree with Evans L.J. that this appeal should be dismissed. I reach that conclusion by reference to the presumption of marriage arising from long cohabitation, and the absence of compelling evidence to rebut that presumption.... Nevertheless there was (on the Chief Adjudication Officers view of the facts, and apart from any presumption) a manifest non-compliance with the provisions of Part III of the 1949 Act: no notice of marriage under s.27, no declaration under s.28, no entry in the marriage notice book under s.31, no certificate under s.32, no registered building under s.41, and no registrar or authorized person present under s.44. If in this case the husband and wife had been compelled by adverse circumstances to separate soon after the ceremony, so that no presumption arose from cohabitation, I feel real doubt whether they could have been regarded as lawfully married under English law, despite the logic of the argument based on the mental state required for a marriage to be void under s.49.

Notes and Questions

1. *Basis for Decision.* In *Kirpal Kaur Bath,* what are the reasons why Lord Justice Evans finds the widow's claim for social security valid? Imagine a widow whose husband died two days after the ceremony. Would she still be able to recover under Lord Justice Evans' reasoning? What if she knew the temple was not registered, but her husband, now deceased, did not?

2. *Comparison with U.S. Law.* How would *Kirpal Kaur Bath* be decided in most states in the United States? Are the legal doctrines that might be employed by a court in the United States the same or functional equivalents of the doctrines employed by the court in *Bath*?

3. *Saving Devices.* Countries have various mechanisms for conferring marital status upon individuals who live their lives as married, even when those marriages are technically invalid. The court in *Kirpal Kaur Bath* used presumptions to help establish the marriage's validity. We have previously seen presumptions operating. Recall that presumptions were also used in Kenya, where an affidavit asserting the parties were married under customary law serves as prima facie evidence of a marriage for administrative matters. *See supra* Chapter 2.B.1., note 5.

The putative spouse and common law marriage doctrines are two other devices used to uphold parties' expectations regarding the validity of their marriage. These devices have spread all over the world as a result of imperialism and the Catholic Church's influence. The putative marriage doctrine derives from canon law, and was popular in civil code jurisdictions. It is evident in article 201 and 202 of the French Civil Code, *supra.* The doctrine can be found in early English family law as well. The doctrine typically requires that one or both parties have a good faith belief that there is no impediment to the marriage, and that they go through a marriage ceremony. *See generally* Christopher L. Blakesley, *The Putative Marriage Doctrine,* 60 Tul. L. Rev. 1, 7–8 (1985). Islamic law has the category of *fasid* marriages, which is similar to the putative marriage doctrine. *Fasid* marriages are also typically invalid, either because the woman married during her *iddat* (the period of time a woman is supposed to wait after divorce or the death of her spouse before remarriage) or because a defect exists in the formalities. A woman who is party to a *fasid* marriage is still entitled to her mahr and the children are considered legitimate.

Common-law marriage also has its origins in canon law. Although the Catholic Church has always encouraged marriages with religious ceremonies, as early as A.D. 1145 it also tolerated informal marriages. While the Church outlawed informal marriages in the mid-1500s, informal marriages continued to be permissible in England because England formally rejected canon law with the Act of Supremacy of 1534. Informal marriages continued at least until Lord Hardwicke's Act, passed in 1752; this act was meant to end secret "fleet" marriages among young people performed by unscrupulous clergy. Scholars debate whether common-law marriage was still permissible after that act, but by 1843 the House of Lords held that England did not permit common law marriage. *See generally* Merle H. Weiner, *Common-Law Marriage, in* 1 The Family in America: An Encyclopedia 217 (2001). Other societies far removed from the Catholic Church and the British Empire also have similar categories. For example, in China, "de facto" marriages, *i.e.*, proper marriages in all respects except for a failure to register, were cured once the parties registered their marriage, and the effect can be "dated back to the beginning of the de facto marriage." *See* Xiaoqing Feng, *A Review of the Development of Marriage Law in the People's Republic of China*, 79 U. Det. Mercy L. Rev. 331, 347–48 (2002) (discussing the apparent recent elimination of this remedy).

Ratification is another common legal device, which is also seen in the French Civil Code §§ 183, 185, *supra*. If the parties continue to live together as husband and wife after a defect is rectified (*e.g.*, nonage), then the parties will be considered married. Similarly, other equitable principles might convince the court to deny an annulment, including unclean hands or laches.

Other legal devices may help establish the validity of the parties' marriage, including estoppel and jurisdictional rules. For example, it is difficult in the United States to claim that a marriage is bigamous, even if one of the parties' prior divorce is invalid. The Full Faith and Credit Clause, as interpreted by the Supreme Court, makes collateral attacks on the validity of divorce decrees very difficult, even if the court issuing the decree lacked jurisdiction because neither party was domiciled in the jurisdiction. *See* Sherrer v. Sherrer, 334 U.S. 343 (1948) (holding Full Faith and Credit Clause requires states to reject collateral attack on subject matter jurisdiction of court issuing decree if defendant had opportunity to litigate issue of subject matter jurisdiction); Johnson v. Muelberger, 340 U.S. 581 (1951) (precluding attack by daughter of one of the parties); Cook v. Cook, 342 U.S. 126 (1951) (precluding attack by husband). Estoppel similarly would preclude a party from later attacking a decree that he or she has obtained. Standing is an important device that may limit which people may challenge a marriage for a particular defect. For example, section 182 of the French Civil Code, *supra*, only permits petitions for nullity by those whose consent was requisite to a marriage and the two persons who stood in need of that consent. In Chinese law, there are time limits for seeking the repeal of a marriage that was coerced. *See* Marriage Law of the People's Republic of China (1980), as amended in accordance with Decision Regarding the Amendment of Marriage Law of the People's Republic of China, 21st sess. Standing Committee of the Ninth National People's Congress, art.11 (Apr. 28, 2001), *available at* http://www.fmprc.gov.cn/eng/28840.html.

Can one draw some conclusions about the policies that undergird these devices?

4. *Form and Canon Law.* The Catholic Church had been known to insist on the canocial form for marriage validity. The 1917 Code "displayed a certain intransigence about the observance of the form. Apart from emergency situations (danger of death, no priest available) the form was absolutely binding to the extent that an inadvertent omission of some technical requirements (*e.g.*, about delegation) could invalidate the marriage and deprive the substantially correct intention of the parties from its effect. The form took precedence over the substance. The new Code is more flexible. Dispensation from the form can be obtained whenever a Catholic marries a non-Catholic person, Christian or not. Delegation has been made easier. In the case of a technical fault the church is more willing to supply what is missing. The substance has come to the fore." Ladislas Orsy, Marriage in Canon Law 159–160 (1986). Yet Canon 1160 still states that a

defect of form must be cured by contracting marriage again according to the canonical form. *See* Orsy, *supra*, at 43. Would that requirement have worked for Ms. Bath?

5. *Other Mechanisms for Upholding Parties' Expectations.* Sometimes legal systems try to uphold the expectations of parties by developing an alternative status that, at times, rivals the marriage status, but often is inferior to it. Some alternative status categories are discussed in Chapter 4.A.2 (discussing, inter alia, registered partnership regimes). The creation of alternative status categories is not a new phenomenon. Concubinage, for example, was a known status at various times in different parts of the world including China and Hong Kong, as well as France and Louisiana. In the following case, Lord Millett gave a good concise description of concubinage in China.

Suen Toi Lee v. Yau Yee Ping
[2002] 1 HKLRD 197, 212–14 (Court of Final Appeal)

Concubinage is an institution peculiar to Oriental societies. For centuries it served a valuable social function by providing women, some of whom would otherwise be left destitute, with a home and family, a recognized place in society, and economic security for life....

The right of the man to take one or more concubines was an accepted part of a Chinese customary marriage. While it seems that in theory an unmarried man could take a concubine, this very rarely happened in practice. Only a man who was of Chinese ethnic origin was capable of entering into a Chinese customary marriage and taking a concubine in accordance with Chinese law and custom. As the White Paper on Chinese Marriages in Hong Kong published on 13 December 1961 was at pains to emphasize, women in Hong Kong who claimed to be concubines but were not attached to a Chinese customary marriage were mistresses only and had no legal status.

No particular ceremony was required to enter into a union of concubinage: *see* Cheang Thye Phin v. Tan Ah Loy [1920] AC 369. All that was needed was: (i) that the man should intend to take the woman into his family as a member of his household as his concubine (tsip) and publicly hold her out as such; (ii) the woman's consent to become his concubine and to occupy a position inferior to that of the principal wife (tsai); and (iii) acceptance of her status as his concubine by his principal wife (if any).

A Chinese customary marriage was monogamous in the sense that a man could have only one principal wife at a time: a man who purported to take a second tsai during the lifetime of the first was guilty of an offence. But the existence of the institution of concubinage meant that it was not "a voluntary union for life of one man and one woman to the exclusion of all others," and hence was regarded as potentially polygamous for the purposes of English matrimonial law: see Hyde v Hyde (1865–69) LR 1 P & D 130....

Being unknown to Western legal systems, the status of a concubine is difficult to describe with any degree of accuracy in terms of those systems. But this much can be stated. A union of concubinage was a particular matrimonial relationship recognized by law. The relationship was an open one and was not adulterous. A concubine was more than a mistress and less than a second wife. Unlike a mistress, she had a recognized legal status, though it was inferior to that of the principal wife. She was entitled to be maintained by her consort while he was alive and out of his estate after his death. Her children were legitimate and regarded as full brothers and sisters of her consort's children, whether born to the principal wife or to another concubine. It is not surprising to find that she has often been described as a secondary wife, or that the courts of Hong Kong have accorded her some of the rights and subjected her to some of the disabilities of a wife. Thus she is entitled to apply for Letters of Administration to the estate of her deceased consort, subject to the prior claim of the principal wife; and she is not a competent or compellable witness in any criminal proceedings against her consort.

Lord Millett went on to describe the abolition of concubinage in Mainland China in 1931. At that time, the Civil Code replaced the institution of concubinage with the institution of "the household." "Permanent members of a household were to be entitled to be maintained by the head of the household whether they consorted with him or not. [T]his was intended (inter alia) to give women who had been concubines, or who became concubines in a purely factual sense in future, financial rights which would compensate them for the loss of the right of maintenance which was an incident of the status of concubine under Chinese customary law and custom previously in force." *Id.* at 214. In Hong Kong, the legal institution of concubinage was abolished in 1971, although the Marriage Reform Ordinance abolished the status only prospectively. Those who had the status previously would have their status and rights preserved. *See* § 5(2).

Concubinage also was known in societies other than those identified by Lord Millett. As in China, it was typically a subordinate status to marriage. During the Roman Empire, concubinage was "widely recognized but only existed as an inferior or secondary status to marriage and was afforded only certain types of legal recognition." *See* Succession of Bacot, 502 So.2d 1118, 1127-28 (La. Ct. App. 1987). The Romans used this status to give some support and succession rights to children of these relationships. *See* Neely S. Griffith, Comment, *When Civilian Principles Clash with the Federal Law: An Examination of the Interplay between Louisiana's Family Law and Federal Statutory and Constitutional Law,* 76 Tul. L. Rev. 519, 525 (2001). *See generally* Kathryn Venturatos Lorio, *Roman Sources and Constitutional Mandates: The Alpha and Omega of Louisiana Laws on Concubinage and Natural Children,* 56 La. L. Rev. 317 (1995). Concubinage was also a recognized status in Louisiana until fairly recently. It required that non-marital couples openly live together as husband and wife, and not reasonably believe that they were married. *See* Succession of Bacot, 502 So.2d at 1127-29. For many years, Louisiana prohibited donations to concubines of any immovables or movables worth more than one-tenth of the value of an estate, whether by donation inter vivos or mortis cuasa. *See* La. Civ. Code art. 1481 (1870), repealed by 1987 La. Acts No. 468. In addition, before 1990, entering into concubinage could make one ineligible for permanent alimony from one's former spouse. *See* La. Civ. Code art. 160. Now concubinage is not explicitly relevant to the maintenance determination. *See* La. Civ. Code art. 112.

Intermediate status categories sometimes spawn the development of additional legal rules to assist parties who want to claim the status. Presumptions may develop to help parties achieve even an intermediate status. This is not surprising since it is just as difficult to establish a party's intent and consent to be a concubine as it is to establish a party's intent and consent to become a common-law spouse. Consequently, for example, some courts infer agreements and intent from circumstantial evidence. *See, e.g.,* Leung Kat v. Lee Chin Tooy Yook, [1986] HKLRD 503 (H.K.C.A.) (sufficient evidence of reputed concubinage existed to give rise to inference of concubinage when there was evidence of cohabitation, acceptance of concubine by wife, and recognition of concubine by the rest of the family).

What intermediate categories exist in the United States? *See Connell v. Francisco,* 898 P.2d 831 (Wash. 1995) (en banc) (allowing a "just and equitable" division of property that would have been community property if the parties were married when the parties had a long-term relationship that was stable and meretricious). Are the intermediate categories always "status" categories? *See, e.g.,* Marvin v. Marvin, 557 P.2d 106 (Cal. 1976) (recognizing express, implied, and quasi-contract claims to uphold parties' expectations). For more on intermediate status categories, see Chapter Four.

D. Capacity to Marry

Part C of this chapter has focused primarily on formalities. It would be wrong to leave you with the impression that form is all that matters. To the contrary, there are important substantive rules regarding entry into marriage in all societies. These often go to "capacity." In the United States, capacity requirements typically include that the parties have mental competency, be single, be unrelated by blood or affinity, and be of different genders. However, the requirements can go further. For example, in the Catholic Church, the diriment impediments which make a marriage void include marriages by or with one impotent, unbaptized, bound by a vow of chastity, or ordained a deacon, presbyter, or bishop. Also void are marriages where the groom abducts his bride (unless she has been freed and agrees to marry), where one party kills or conspires to kill his or her spouse or his or her lover's spouse, or public propriety. *See generally* The Code of Canon Law 193–94 (The Canon Law Society of Great Britain trans., 1984) (1983) (Canons 1083–1094). Some of the prohibitions can be dispensed with, like the age requirement, but others cannot, like marriage by one who is already married. *See* James A. Coriden, An Introduction to Canon Law 135 (1991). "[L]ocal ordinaries have the power to dispense from them, unless a case is explicitly reserved to the Holy See." Orsy, *supra,* at 86.

Some scholars have tried to generalize about capacity requirements across societies. *See, e.g.,* Lynn D. Wardle, *International Marriage and Divorce Regulation and Recognition: A Survey,* 29 Fam. L.Q. 497, 500 (1995); Barbara E. Graham-Siegenthaler, *Principles of Marriage Recognition Applied to Same-Sex Marriage Recognition in Switzerland and Europe,* 32 Creighton L. Rev. 121, 125 (1998). Generalizations are difficult, however. For example, in many African and Asian states polygamy is allowed. As one author stated, "The idea of polygamy seems to be still so strong in many Islamic societies that its abolition is unthinkable." Dagmar Coester-Waltjen & Michael Coester, *Formation of Marriage, in* IV International Encyclopedia of Comparative Law 32 (1997). Even in Europe one has significant differences between countries. For instance, some countries have abolished affinity restrictions and limited consanguinity restrictions (Sweden) and others strongly adhere to the restrictions (England). *See* David Bradley, *Convergence in Family Law: Mirrors, Transplants and Political Economy,* 6 Maastricht J. Eur. & Comp. L. 127 (1999). Despite the difficulties of generalizing, one generalization is perhaps unassailable: All societies have some substantive restrictions.

These types of marriage restrictions are not addressed here because this topic is often discussed in basic family law classes and because these sorts of restrictions are encountered later in the book. Chapter Four addresses same-sex marriage and Chapter Five discusses capacity issues in the context of the recognition of marriage.

Finally, it is worth remembering that while we tend to think of procedural and substantive requirements for marriage as distinct, the two often interact. The procedural requirements are often meant to give teeth to the substantive requirements. To use an example from this country, the lawsuit in *Baehr v. Lewin,* 852 P.2d 44 (Haw. 1993), which involved whether same-sex individuals could marry each other in Hawaii, stemmed from the refusal of the Hawaii Department of Health to issue marriage licenses to three same-sex couples. Hawaii law required that a marriage license be secured before a couple could be married. Haw. Rev. Stat. §572-1(6) (2000).

E. Mail-Order Marriages

An analysis of "mail-order marriages" serves as an opportunity to apply much of the information found previously in this chapter. As you read the material in this section, consider the following questions: 1) Is there a "problem" that needs addressing if the parties involved desire these marriages? 2) Assuming there is a problem, at what level (local, state, international) should this problem be addressed? 3) What institutional and other interests might oppose a solution? 4) What solutions are preferable and why? 5) Can marriage preliminaries help the parties avoid the pitfalls that may attend these types of marriage? 6) Will a legal solution work?

1. The Factual Background

Robert J. Scholes & Anchalee Phataralaoha, The "Mail-Order Bride" Industry and its Impact on U.S. Immigration, App. A (1999)

at http://www.ins.usdoj.gov/graphics/aboutins/repsstudies/Mobappa.htm

The Industry

An American man seeking a foreign bride may avail himself of over 200 different services in which foreign women advertise for husbands. There are two types of such services. In one type, the so-called "mail-order bride" industry (representatives of the industry prefer the term "international correspondence service"), women's names, photos, biographical sketches, and addresses are presented in hard copy brochures or on the Internet. In these services, the agency provides the photos and descriptions of the women, who are not charged for this listing. Men who wish to obtain the mailing address of any of the women they would like to contact are charged a fee of from $2 to $5 for each of the mailing addresses.

The other way to contact potential spouses is through e-mail "pen-pal" clubs. These services are generally free of charge. In them, men and women provide biographical data, an e-mail address, and an indication of what type of relationship they seek....

In these clubs, one can find nearly 10,000 foreign women seeking marriage or long-term relationships. Since these services require access to computers, the women tend to be older and better educated than those listed in the "mail-order bride" catalogs and to reside in more developed countries such as Japan and Russia.

The women are obtained through advertisements in local newspapers and popular women's magazines and, most commonly, through word of mouth.

Based on a scanning of the services listed and information provided by the agencies themselves, we may estimate that between 100,000 and 150,000 women from a variety of countries (including the United States, Canada, Europe, and Australia) annually advertise themselves as available for marriage. The great majority of these women are from two major areas: Southeast Asia, including the Philippines, and Russia and other countries of the former Soviet Union.

The Women...

Why do foreign women want American husbands? Many sources suggest that these women are searching for a "better life" in terms of socio-economic factors—they do, for the most part, come from places in which jobs and educational opportunities for women are scarce and wages are low. However, when the women themselves are asked this question, the answer generally indicates an attraction to American men (they look like movie stars) and an aversion to native men. Americans, they say, make good husbands while Filipino (Thai/Indonesian/Russian/etc.) men do not. Americans are thought to be faithful to their wives, while the native men are cruel and run around with other women. True or not, this is the perception.

The Men...

David Jedlicka (1988)...surveyed 607 American men seeking mail-order brides and received 206 responses. He found that the men were generally white (94 percent); highly educated (50 percent with two or more years of college, 6 percent with M.D.'s or Ph.D.'s, only five did not complete high school); politically and ideologically conservative; and generally economically and professionally successful (64 percent earned more than $20,000 a year; 42 were in professional or managerial positions). Their median age was 37. The men came from 44 states, with 22 percent from California, and 84 percent lived in metropolitan areas. Fifty-seven percent had been married at least once; most had been divorced after an average of seven years of marriage, 35 percent had at least one child, and 75 percent wished to father additional children. When asked about their religious affiliations, 48 percent of the men identified themselves as Protestant, 23 percent as Catholic, 15 percent as belonging to other religions, and 14 percent as having no religious affiliation.

Why do American men want foreign wives? Most of the personal reports from American men who have married women through these agencies talk about "traditional values." That is, American women are thought not content to be wives and mothers but seek personal satisfaction through their own careers and interests, while the foreign woman is happy to be the homemaker and asks for nothing more than husband, home, and family. Again, true or not, this is the perception....

Of the 30 mail-order bride couples Mila Glodava (Glodava and Onizuka, 1994) encountered between 1986 and 1993, only two were close in age (4–6 years difference). In the other 28 there was a 20 to 50 year difference in age. Older men, says Glodava, often want women "they can mold" and therefore do not want those who are too educated. "They would just become like any other American woman," they said. She concludes that, "It is apparent that power and control are critical for the men."

It is interesting to note that the views above on native and foreign men and women are not limited to the Occident—a similar attitude exists in Taiwan. According to "Taiwan Moves to Boost Women's Marriage Prospects" (The Associated Press, Aug. 30, 1996, by Annie Huang), many Taiwanese men prefer brides from other Asian countries because they feel Taiwanese women—who tend to be better educated and more affluent—expect too much from their husbands. Due to this attitude, Taiwan has imposed a limit on the number of brides from certain countries that can enter Taiwan each year— 360 from Indonesia, 420 from Burma, and 1,080 from China. On the women's side, many of them are seeking Western men since, they say, Taiwanese men want to marry only hard-working obedient drudges while Taiwanese women have discarded this traditional role and are seeking equality and mutual respect in marriage.

Success Rates for International Services...

According to the women themselves (in written replies to a 1996 questionnaire from the author), approximately 10 percent of these women are successful—they find and marry a man through the service. There are, then, around 10,000 marriages a year between women listed by these agencies and men who use the services. Of these 10,000, around 4,000 involve U.S. men. The remainder is distributed among Canadian, Australian, European, and, increasingly, Japanese clients.

Based on these data, we may estimate that 4 percent of the 100,000 to 150,000 women seeking U.S. husbands through international services find them; that is, "mail-order bride" and e-mail correspondence services result in 4,000 to 6,000 marriages between U.S. men and foreign brides each year....

Impact on U.S. Marriages

According to data supplied by the U.S. Census Bureau, there were 2,395,000 marriages in the United States in the 12 months ending June 1997 (and 1,154,000 divorces in the same period). The 4,000 to 6,000 marriages involving international services represent, then, a tiny portion (.021 percent) of the women who marry U.S. men.

It is interesting to note that, based largely on data provided by the agencies themselves (along with the Commission on Filipinos Overseas report cited above), marriages arranged through these services would appear to have a lower divorce rate than the nation as a whole, fully 80 percent of these marriages having lasted over the years for which reports are available.

Impact on U.S. Immigration

Statistics provided by the Immigration and Naturalization Service for the years 1994–96 show that there have been over 800,000 immigrants per year, of whom about 18 percent enter as spouses of U.S. citizens; e.g., 169,760 of 915,900 in 1996. An additional 14 percent (130,000) of the total immigrants involves parents and children of U.S. citizens.

In any case, the 4,000 to 6,000 women who immigrate through international correspondence agencies represent less than 6 percent of the new citizens. The majority of the women who gain permanent resident alien status through marriage do so through more traditional means, such as by meeting their spouse at work or in school or through marriage to U.S. servicemen stationed overseas....

Fraud

There is no question that many of the alien women who advertise for U.S. husbands are far more interested in gaining permanent residence alien status than in gaining a good marriage. What portion of the women intend to use marriage to gain permanent resident alien status cannot be ascertained, of course, since we cannot know what is in the woman's mind, but a reading of the self-descriptions they offer and their willingness to marry men of advanced age and dubious character attests to this intention. The true character of the men is well expressed in Glodava and Onizuka (1994:26), who note, "those who have used the mail-order bride route to find a mate have control in mind rather than a loving and enduring relationship."

The most common times for mail-order brides to leave the marriage, according to Martin are "immediately, 3 months after marriage (receipt of the green card), and 2 years after marriage (receipt of nonconditional permanent residence)."

There are reports of a different kind of fraud—namely, one in which women are recruited into prostitution through the international matchmaking services. This new slave trade has not, however, to the author's knowledge, occurred in the United States, although it is a well documented trade involving Russian women imported into Israel (Specter, 1998).

Abuse

According to "The Health Care Response to Domestic Violence" (anon. 1994), "Within the last year 7 percent of American women (3.9 million) who are married or are living with someone as a couple were physically abused, and 37 percent (20.7 million) were verbally or emotionally abused by their spouse or partner."

While no national figures exist on abuse of alien wives, there is every reason to believe that the incidence is higher in this population than for the nation as a whole. Authorities agree that abuse in these marriages can be expected based on the men's desire for a submissive wife and the women's desire for a better life. At some point, after the alien bride has had time to adjust to the new environment, to make new friends, and to become comfortable with the language, her new independence and his domination are bound to conflict....

Current INS Regulations....

The Immigration and Nationality Act, as amended, provides U.S. citizens with two options for facilitating the immigration of future spouses to the United States: the K-1 fiancé(e) visa and the alien-spouse immigrant visa.

U.S. citizens may file an I-129F petition with INS for the issuance of a K-1 fiancé(e) visa to an alien fiancé(e). A citizen exercising this option must remain unmarried until the arrival of the fiancé(e) in the United States, and the wedding must take place within 3 months of the fiancé(e)'s arrival if he/she is to remain in status. Also, the alien and U.S. citizen must have met personally at least once in the 2 years before the petition was filed....

If a U.S. citizen marries an alien abroad, an I-130 petition must be filed after the marriage to begin the immigration process for the alien spouse.... The U.S. [petitioner] must...prove that the marriage is bona fide, that is, entered into for love rather than simply for the foreign-born spouse to obtain a green card.... Simultaneously, the foreign-born spouse must submit an application for adjustment of status (form I-485) which is an application for a green card.... The spouse can also file an OF-230 with the consulate and be issued an immigrant visa. In both the immigrant visa and adjustment of status cases, the petitioning U.S. citizen...must also complete an affidavit of support, INS form I-864, on behalf of the alien spouse....

2. Legal Responses of Countries of Destination

8 U.S.C § 1375 (Supp. 2003)

Mail-Order Bride Business

...

(b) Information dissemination

    (1) Requirement

Each international matchmaking organization doing business in the United States shall disseminate to recruits, upon recruitment, such immigration and naturalization information as the Immigration and Naturalization Service deems appropriate, in the recruit's native language, including information regarding conditional permanent residence status and the battered spouse waiver under such status, permanent resident status, marriage fraud penalties, the unregulated nature of the business engaged in by such organizations, and the study required under subsection (c) of this section.

    (2) Civil penalty

        (A) Violation

Any international matchmaking organization that the Attorney General determines has violated this subsection shall be subject, in addition to any other penalties that may be prescribed by law, to a civil money penalty of not more than $20,000 for each such violation....

(e) Definitions

    As used in this section:

    (1) International matchmaking organization

        (A) In general

The term "international matchmaking organization" means a corporation, partnership, business, or other legal entity, whether or not organized under the laws of the United States or any State, that does business in the United States and for profit offers to United States citizens or aliens lawfully admitted for permanent residence, dating, matrimonial, or social referral services to nonresident noncitizens, by:

        (i) an exchange of names, telephone numbers, addresses, or statistics;

        (ii) selection of photographs; or

        (iii) a social environment provided by the organization in a country other than the United States.

        (B) Exception

Such term does not include a traditional matchmaking organization of a religious nature that otherwise operates in compliance with the laws of the countries of the recruits of such organization and the laws of the United States.

    (2) Recruit

The term "recruit" means a noncitizen, nonresident person, recruited by the international matchmaking organization for the purpose of providing dating, matrimonial, or social referral services to United States citizens or aliens lawfully admitted for permanent residence.

3. Legal Responses of Countries of Origin

Many mail-order brides come from the Philippines. "An analysis of the listings in recent issues of five popular catalogs featuring 1,400 Asian women found that 70 percent were Filipino." Scholes & Phataralaoha, *supra*, at 3. The Philippines has enacted laws to deal with the practice, including Republic Act No. 6955.

Republic Act No. 6955 (1990)
(Phil.)

Section 1. It is the policy of the State to ensure and guarantee the enjoyment of the people of a decent standard of living. Towards this end, the State shall take measures to protect Filipino women from being exploited in utter disregard of human dignity in their pursuit of economic upliftment.

Section 2. Pursuant thereto, it is hereby declared unlawful:

(a) For a person, natural or juridical, association, club or any other entity to commit, directly or indirectly, any of the following acts:

(1) To establish or carry on a business which has for its purpose the matching of Filipino women for marriage to foreign nationals either on a mail-order basis or through personal introduction;

(2) To advertise, publish, print or distribute or cause the advertisement, publication, printing or distribution of any brochure, flier, or any propaganda material calculated to promote the prohibited acts in the preceding subparagraph;

(3) To solicit, enlist or in any manner attract or induce any Filipino woman to become a member in any club or association whose objective is to match women for marriage to foreign nationals either on a mail-order basis or through personal introduction for a fee;

(4) To use the postal service to promote the prohibited acts in subparagraph 1 hereof.

(b) For the manager or officer-in-charge or advertising manager of any newspaper, magazine, television or radio station, or other media, or of an advertising agency, printing company or other similar entities, to knowingly allow, or consent to, the acts prohibited in the preceding paragraph.

Section 3. In case of violation of this Act by an association, club, partnership, corporation, or any other entity, the incumbent officers thereof who have knowingly participated in the violation of this Act shall be held liable.

Section 4. Any person found guilty by the court to have violated any of the acts herein prohibited shall suffer an imprisonment of not less than six (6) years and one (1) day but not more than eight (8) years, and a fine of not less than eight thousand pesos (P8,000) but not more than twenty thousand pesos (P20,000): Provided, that if the offender is a foreigner, he shall be immediately deported and barred forever from entering the country after serving his sentence and payment of fine.

Section 5. Nothing in this Act shall be interpreted as a restriction on the freedom of speech and of association for purposes not contrary to law as guaranteed by the Constitution.

Section 6. All laws, decrees, orders, instructions, rules and regulations, or parts thereof inconsistent with this Act are hereby repealed or modified accordingly.

Section 7. This Act shall take effect upon its publication for two (2) consecutive weeks in a newspaper of general circulation.

In addition to the above law, it appears that "the Philippines [has] set up a special mandatory counseling program" for women travelling abroad. *RP Mail-Order Brides in Demand*, Filipino Reporter, Jan. 23, 1997, *available at* 1997 WL 11616970.

Despite the law, many mail-order catalogues contain the listings of women from the Philippines. Why are the criminal penalties not working? In fact, "Since the law took effect seven years ago, not one person has been arrested." *Id.* Why? The answer is undoubtedly shaped by the following two facts. First, "economic [business] realities have allowed the industry to prevail. Informal recruiting practices have replaced formal advertising." Kathryn A. Lloyd, Comment, *Wives for Sale: The Modern International Mail-Order Bride Industry*, 20 Nw. J. Int'l L. & Bus. 341, 350 (2000). Second, the industry is too valuable to the Philippines' economy. "[A]s a third world country, the Philippines relies heavily on exports to the first world, and one of its most valuable exports is its women. Each year, close to half a million Filipino women go to foreign countries, many as nurses and maids; some as prostitutes, and others as brides, it says. And these women send millions of dollars a year back home." *RP Mail-Order Brides in Demand*, *supra.* Yet why else would some girls and women not heed the counselors' warnings of potential danger?

Notes and Questions

1. *Immigration Fraud.* The U.S. Congress adopted the legislation on mail-order brides in 1996 as part of the Illegal Immigration Reform and Immigrant Responsibility Act. A study was conducted by the government pursuant to that act. Among other things, the study found that only 1% of the individuals denied permanent resident status for cause involved mail-order marriages and fraud. It concluded, "at a rate of 1 percent...this study did not demonstrate a significant role played by the matchmaking industry in marriage fraud." Immigration and Naturalization Service, International Matchmaking Organizations: A Report to Congress 14 (1999).

2. *Regulations.* As of May 2001, the INS was still preparing the brochures that matchmaking organizations would have to give to women recruits. Unified Agenda, 66 Fed. Reg. 25,635, 25,637 (2001). Yet the State Department has developed literature regarding trafficking which includes how victims can get assistance in the United States. The literature was distributed in 1998 in the waiting rooms of the U.S. embassies in Poland and Ukraine. *See* Immigration and Naturalization Service, *supra*, at 18. Expanded distribution was planned. *Id.* at 19.

3. *A problem?* Is there a difference between an international introduction service and either a national dating service or personal advertisements? What exactly is wrong, if anything, with the practice? Are women forced to marry? How does the practice differ from the picture-bride phenomenon popular in the United States from 1908 until 1921? Picture-bride marriages were marriages that tended to be arranged through a mutual family friend or a relative of the groom. The man, typically an immigrant laborer in the United States, would have his photo sent to the bride and her family in Japan, Korea, or

Okinawa. The bride was typically from the same village as the groom. If the bride was interested, the bride's picture would be sent to the intermediary. The marriage would then be arranged, and would be "considered legal when the bride's name was entered into the Koseki (family register) of the groom's family even if she had been married by proxy or in a groom's absentia." This practice of using a go-between was an extension of Japanese marriage custom, begun during the feudal period. *See generally* Alice Yun Chai, *Picture Brides: Feminist Analysis of Life Histories of Hawaii's Early Immigrant Women from Japan, Okinawa and Korea, in* Seeking Common Ground: Multidisciplinary Studies of Immigrant Women in the United States 123, 125–27 (1992).

4. *Big Business.* "These businesses can be highly profitable. Bob Burrows, president of Cherry Blossoms, reports that this agency serves over 1,000 men per month who pay up to $200 each." Robert J. Scholes & Anchalee Phataralaoha, The "Mail-Order Bride" Industry and its Impact on U.S. Immigration, App. A (1999), *at* http://www.ins.usdoj. gov/graphics/aboutins/repsstudies/Mobappa.htm. "Mail-order bride businesses do not make their money exclusively from selling women's addresses and charging fees to their recruits. The primary profit comes from 'romantic bridal tours,' which agencies offer to potential grooms." Vanessa B.M. Vergara, Comment, *Abusive Mail-Order Bride Marriage and the Thirteenth Amendment*, 94 Nw. U. L. Rev. 1547, 1554 (2000).

5. *Age of Brides.* According to one study, mail-order brides tend to be young: "20 percent are 16–20 years of age, 41 percent are 21–25, 24 percent are 26–30, 11 percent 31–35, and just 4 percent are over the age of 35." The Asian women tend to be younger overall than women from the former Soviet Union. *See* Scholes & Phataralaoha, *supra,* at 3.

6. *Securities Law Model?* U.S. law requires issuers of stocks that are publicly traded to disclose certain information to prospective stockholders, including audited financial statements and, to some extent, risk factors. Should individuals seeking foreign brides be required to give the prospective spouses certain information, including information about their criminal records, before marriage? What other information might need to be disclosed? As a practical matter, how would this be done? Is there any reason to limit such disclosure to foreign fiancées? Are there any problems with imposing this requirement on everyone?

7. *French Formalities.* Perhaps a system like that found in the Napoleonic Code would be appropriate to apply to couples entering these marriages? Would such a system work in this context?

8. *Annulment.* Should it be easier for mail-order brides to obtain an annulment than others? After all, they may consent to marriage, but their consent may not be fully informed. They may not know much about American life, or more importantly, they may not know much about their prospective husbands. The men may lie to their prospective brides about both America and themselves. Yet these sorts of lies may not be legally sufficient to secure an annulment. *See generally* Homer H. Clark, The Law of Domestic Relations in the United States 119 (1988).

9. *Immigration.* When a mail-order bride finds her marriage untenable, she faces a host of issues collateral to the break up of the marital relationship. Concerns about her immigration status probably top the list. An immigrant spouse who has been married less than two years has a conditional residency status for approximately two years from the time she is interviewed by immigration authorities. To obtain permanent resident status, she and her citizen spouse must file a petition for removal of conditional status within ninety days of the expiration of her conditional status. There are three grounds on which this joint spousal filing could be waived. The Immigration Marriage Travel

Amendments of 1986, Pub. L. No. 99-639, 100 Stat. 3537 (1986) embodied the first two grounds for waiver described below. The Immigration and Marriage Fraud Act (IMFA) of 1990 established another procedure to request waiver of the requirements of joint spousal filing for the removal of the conditional permanent residency status.

The first of these three hardship waivers is based on extreme hardship. In deciding whether to waive any of the requirements for removal of conditional status, the Attorney General may only consider factors that arose after the alien obtained CPR [conditional permanent resident] status. For example, marital abuse prior to the joint petition for CPR would be irrelevant to assessing an extreme hardship waiver. In addition, the Attorney General is required to bear in mind that removal from the United States would cause anyone a degree of hardship, thus, only in exceptional cases "where the hardship is extreme" should a waiver be properly granted.

The second type of waiver is based on an alien's claim that the marriage was entered into in good faith but has been terminated for reasons other than death of spouse, and the alien was not at fault in failing to meet the requirements for removal of the conditional basis. Evidence of a marriage entered into in good faith may include evidence of commingling of financial assets, documentation of the length of time in cohabitation after the marriage and after the alien received CPR status, birth certificates of children born to the marriage, and other evidence deemed pertinent by INS.

Finally, the third type of waiver is based on battery or extreme cruelty. This waiver requires an alien to establish that the marriage was entered into in good faith, that during the marriage the alien [or her child] suffered battery or extreme cruelty.... The battery or extreme cruelty waiver may be invoked even after CPR status has been terminated, regardless of the alien's marital status, so long as the alien has not yet departed from the United States.

All three hardship waivers discussed above may only be invoked by aliens who have obtained CPR status. In other words, where an alien's citizen spouse has failed to petition for his wife's CPR status, none of these waivers are applicable because there is no conditional status to remove or, for that matter, requirements for removal to waive. Many alien spouses, who are often battered spouses of American citizens, fall into this category. By passing [the Violence Against Women Act (VAWA)], Congress has made an attempt to account for battered immigrant women who would otherwise fall through the statutory and regulatory cracks. Specifically, one provision allows battered spouses of U.S. citizens to self-petition for conditional permanent resident status or to self-petition for adjustment in status. Essentially, the hardship waiver provisions discussed above are mechanisms by which battered spouses, who have at least attained CPR status because their citizen spouses filed for their CPR status, may self-petition for the removal of the condition. Similarly, the VAWA provision allows battered spouses of U.S. citizens to file for CPR status or adjustment of status on their own.

Vergara, *supra*, at 1565–66. Information about the waiver application and the grounds for waiver can be found at 8 C.F.R. § 1216.5 (2003).

As the author suggests, federal law now allows some women to self-petition for an adjustment of status. *See, e.g.,* 8 U.S.C. §§ 1154(a)(1)(A)(iii). See also 8 C.F.R § 204.2. The ability to self-petition requires that the alien demonstrate the following: 1) the marriage was entered into in good faith by the alien; 2) during the marriage, the alien or the alien's child "has been battered or has been the subject of extreme cruelty perpetrated by the alien's spouse or intended spouse"; 3) the alien is a spouse or a putative spouse (so long as the reason for the putative status is bigamy of the spouse) of a U.S. citizen or lawful permanent resident (LPR), or must have been a spouse of a U.S. citizen/LPR within the past two years and the citizen/LPR spouse died, or the parties divorced for reasons related to domestic violence, or the citizen/LPR spouse lost citizenship or LPR status due to domestic violence; 4) the parties resided together; and, 5) the petitioner is "a person of good moral character." Divorce after the date of filing does not terminate the right to self-petition under §1154 (a)(1)(A)(iii). *See* 8 U.S.C. §1154(h). However, the self-petition will be denied if the petitioner remarries before filing, or after filing and before the petition is approved. Unmarried children under 21 who live in the United States can be included as derivative beneficiaries on the petition of the self-petitioner. *See* 8 U.S.C. §§1154(a)(1)(A)(iii); 1154(a)(1)(B)(ii). The Violence Against Women Act 2000, which incorporates the Battered Immigrant Women Protection Act of 2000, permits battered spouses living abroad to self-petition for entry into the United States if their spouses are a U.S. government employee or a member of the armed service or if their spouses subjected them to battery or extreme cruelty in the United States. *See* 8 U.S.C. §1154 (a)(1)(A)(v).

In addition, if a domestic violence victim is in removal proceedings or she does not qualify for the self-petition process, she can seek a suspension of deportation, now called cancellation of removal under a special provision. *See* 8 U.S.C. §1229(b). This would be the remedy for a battered woman who divorced the U.S. citizen or legal permanent resident more than two years before she filed her self-petition, or who is placed into removal proceedings, or who is not married to her abuser, but has a child with him. "The basic requirements of 'cancellation of removal' for battered immigrants are: 1) inadmissible or deportable under certain grounds; 2) battery or extreme cruelty by a citizen or permanent resident spouse or parent; 3) physical presence in the United States for a continuous period of three years; 4) good moral character for the past three years; 5) extreme hardship to the alien, alien's child or alien's parent (if the alien is a child). IIRIRA §304 (codified at INA §240A(b)(2), 8 U.S.C. §1229b(b)(2))." Linda Kelly, *Stories from the Front: Seeking Refuge for Battered Immigrants in the Violence Against Women Act,* 92 Nw. U. L. Rev. 665, 672 n.35 (1998). The Violence Against Women Act 2000 gives the Attorney General discretion under both the Immigration and Nationality Act, section 212 (admissibility) or section 237 (deportability) to find good moral character if the applicant's bad acts were related to the domestic abuse.

Finally, U-visas allow domestic violence victims new immigration protection. The Violence Against Women Act of 2000

> [c]reates a new nonimmigrant U-visa for victims of certain serious crimes, including domestic violence, sexual assault, stalking, and trafficking crimes if the victim has suffered substantial physical or mental abuse as a result of the crime, the victim has information about the crime, and a law enforcement official or a judge certifies that the victim is or is likely to be helpful in investigating or prosecuting the crime. The number of visas is capped at 10,000 per year. The Attorney General may adjust U-visa holders to lawful permanent resident status if they have been present in the U.S. for three years and it is justified on humanitarian grounds, to promote family unity, or is otherwise in the public interest.

See The Violence Against Women Act of 2000 Summary, *available at* http://www.ojp. usdoj.gov/vawo/laws/vawa_summary 2.htm.

Although undoubtedly some mail-order marriages involve violence, it is difficult to know the prevalence of violence. Current statistics are unsatisfying. For example, only 0.5% of the women self-petitioning for permanent resident alien status because of domestic violence were involved in mail-order introductions. *See* Immigration and Naturalization Service, *supra,* at 16. Yet this statistic tells us nothing about the number of women who experience violence and whose abusers petition for removal of conditional status, or the number of women who experience violence but obtain a waiver on another ground, or the number of women who remain in the country illegally. For more detailed information on immigration benefits and domestic violence, *see* INS, How Do I Apply for Immigration Benefits as a Battered Spouse or Child?, *available at* www.ins. usdoj.gov/graphics/howdoi/battered.htm.

10. *Thirteenth Amendment and Slavery?* The Thirteenth Amendment to the U.S. Constitution reads: "(1) Neither slavery nor involuntary servitude, except as a punishment for crime whereof the party shall have been duly convicted, shall exist within the United States, or any place subject to their jurisdiction. (2) Congress shall have power to enforce this article by appropriate legislation." Vanessa B.M. Vergara argues for the applicability of the Thirteenth Amendment to mail-order marriages that are abusive, i.e., where "women are treated like slaves." Vergara, *supra,* at 1548. She contends, "Women are bought and sold on the mail-order bride market, physically tortured, and sexually dominated in a way similar to past episodes of African slavery." *Id.* at 1568. Might some mail-order marriages be akin to slavery?

Slavery has been defined by the courts for the purposes of 18 U.S.C. § 1583, which makes it a crime, among other things, to kidnap or carry away "any other person, with the intent that such other person be sold into involuntary servitude, or held as a slave; or Whoever entices, persuades, or induces any other person to go on board any vessel or to any other place with the intent that he may be made or held as a slave...." 18 U.S.C. § 1853. The generally accepted definition of "slavery" under this section is as follows: "A slave is a person who is wholly subject to the will of another, one who has no freedom of action and whose person and services are wholly under the control of another, and who is in a state of compulsory service to another." United States v. Ingalls, 73 F. Supp. 76, 78 (S.D. Cal. 1947).

Assuming the applicability of the Thirteenth Amendment, could a mail-order bride use the amendment to sue her husband for his treatment of her? It is unclear whether a claim can be brought directly under the Thirteenth Amendment. *Compare* Terry Properties, Inc. v. Standard Oil Co., 799 F.2d 1523 (11th Cir. 1986) *with* Bascomb v. Smith Barney Inc., 1999 WL 20853 at 6 (S.D.N.Y. Jan. 15, 1999) (citing cases), *overruled on other grounds* Lauture v. International Business Machines Corp., 216 F.3d 258 (2d Cir. 2000). However, pursuant to clause 2 of the Thirteenth Amendment, Congress has the power to pass laws that give private individuals a cause of action. *See, e.g.,* Jones v. Alfred H. Mayer, Co., 392 U.S. 409 (1968) (upholding law prohibiting private racial discrimination in real estate transactions because housing discrimination was one of the "badges and incidents of slavery").

11. *Thirteenth Amendment and Involuntary Servitude.* The Thirteenth Amendment prohibits both slavery and involuntary servitude. The term "involuntary servitude" has been interpreted in the context of 18 U.S.C. § 1584, which made it a crime if one "knowingly and willfully holds to involuntary servitude or sells into any condition of involuntary servitude, any other person for any term, or brings within the United States any per-

son so held." Violation of 18 U.S.C. § 1584 can result in life imprisonment if its violation includes aggravated sexual abuse or an attempt to commit aggravated sexual abuse. Consider the following three cases and assess whether some mail-order brides may be subjected to "involuntary servitude."

In *U.S. v. Kozminski*, 487 U.S. 931 (1988), the Supreme Court reversed the convictions of the defendants and remanded. The defendants had been convicted pursuant to 18 U.S.C. § 1584. They operated a farm, employed two mentally disabled men, forced them to work long hours for virtually no pay. The Court held that psychological coercion alone was insufficient to sustain the convictions. "[C]ompulsion of services by the use or threatened use of physical or legal coercion is a necessary incident of a condition of involuntary servitude." *Id.* at 953.

In *U.S. v. Shackney*, 333 F.2d 475 (2d Cir. 1964), the appellate court reversed the conviction of a farmer who had hired two Mexican families and then made them work in squalor. The farmer threatened them with deportation if they were to quit. The court explained, "[H]olding in involuntary servitude means...action by the master causing the servant to have, or to believe he has, no way to avoid continued service or confinement, in Mr. Justice Harlan's language, 'superior and overpowering force, constantly present and threatening,' not a situation where the servant knows he has a choice between continued service and freedom, even if the master has led him to believe that the choice may entail consequences that are exceedingly bad." The court held that the statute was not meant to cover threats of deportation as a means for extracting involuntary servitude, even though the statute could cover threats of imprisonment, unless the deportation was equivalent to imprisonment or worse. *Id.* at 486.

In *U.S. v. Alzanki*, 54 F.3d 994 (1st Cir. 1995), the court upheld the conviction of a man who employed a Sri Lankan woman as his housekeeper. Among other things, the employer confiscated her passport, forbade her to leave the apartment alone, and prohibited use of the telephone or mail. He told her that the American police would shoot unaccompanied undocumented aliens. He assaulted her twice, once throwing her against a wall and another time spitting in her face. She was denied medical treatment and adequate food and was compelled to work fifteen hours a day. She was also threatened with deportation, death, or serious harm if she disobeyed. The First Circuit stated that compulsion was a necessary component of involuntary servitude, but it could exist if there were actual physical restraint or physical force, legal coercion, or plausible threats of physical harm or legal coercion. Here there was sufficient evidence to find the defendant used or threatened physical restraint, bodily harm, and legal coercion. *Id.* at 1000.

After these three cases, Congress passed the Victims of Trafficking and Violence Protection Act of 2000 (VTVPA), described in the next note. A congressional finding states, "Involuntary servitude statutes are intended to reach cases in which persons are held in a condition of servitude through nonviolent coercion." 22 U.S.C. § 7101(13). The finding then cites the narrow interpretation the Supreme Court gave 18 U.S.C. § 1584 in *Kozminksi*. The VTVPA defines "involuntary servitude" for purposes of the Act: it "includes a condition of servitude induced by means of (A) any scheme, plan, or pattern intended to cause a person to believe that, if the person did not enter into or continue in such condition, that person or another person would suffer serious harm or physical restraint; or (B) the abuse or threatened abuse of the legal process." 22 U.S.C. § 7102(5).

12. *VTVPA.* The Victims of Trafficking and Violence Protection Act of 2000, Pub. L. No. 106-386, 114 Stat. 1460 (codified as amended in scattered sections of 8 U.S.C., 18

U.S.C., 20 U.S.C., 22 U.S.C., 28 U.S.C., 42 U.S.C.,) was passed to "combat trafficking in persons, a contemporary manifestation of slavery whose victims are predominantly women and children, to ensure just and effective punishment of traffickers and to protect their victims." 22 U.S.C. § 7101(a). Although the findings do not mention marriage as a method of trafficking, might the act apply? The act addresses severe forms of trafficking in persons, *i.e.,* situations in which the person is subjected either "(1) to sex trafficking in which a commercial sex act is induced by force, fraud, or coercion, or in which the person induced to perform the commercial sex act is under 18 years of age, or (2) to the recruitment, harboring, transportation, provision, or baiting of a person for labor or services, through the use of force, fraud, or coercion for the purpose of subjection to involuntary servitude, peonage, debt bondage, or slavery." *See* Protection and Assistance for Victims of Trafficking, 66 Fed. Reg. 38,514, 38,515 (2001) (to be codified at 28 C.F.R. pt. 1100). The Act defines "commercial sex act" as "any sex act on account of which anything of value is given to or received by any person." 22 U.S.C. § 7102(3).

Among other things, the act establishes an interagency task force to monitor and combat trafficking, *see* 22 U.S.C. § 7103; calls on the president to initiate economic programs to reduce trafficking by providing opportunities to potential trafficking victims, *see* 22 U.S.C. § 7104; charges the secretary of state with establishing and carrying out programs in foreign countries that are meant to ease integration, reintegration, or resettlement of trafficking victims, *see* U.S.C. § 7105; authorizes the president to provide assistance to foreign countries to meet minimum standards for the elimination of trafficking, *see* 22 U.S.C. §§ 2152d & 7106; and authorizes the president to withhold nonhumanitarian, nontrade-related foreign assistance to those countries that do not meet minimum standards. *See* 22 U.S.C. § 7107. The act also provides certain benefits for victims of trafficking, including the crime victim rights specified in 42 U.S.C. § 10606(b) and the crime victim services specified in 42 U.S.C. § 10607(c). *See* 28 C.F.R. § 1100.29. Also, if a victim is in federal custody, the federal government is obligated to provide various services. *See* 28 C.F.R. § 1100.31. Perhaps most importantly for some victims, the act allows the INS to grant permission for the victim's continued presence in the United States if the victim is a "potential" witness to trafficking. *See* 28 C.F.R. § 1100.35(a).

13. *Consent.* Most women consent to be mail-order brides. How does this fact affect the various legal remedies that may exist? Can one say that a mail-order bride consents to being treated like a slave or to the trafficking?

14. *Existing Laws.* In the United States there are a variety of laws that potentially apply to international matchmaking organizations. Apart from 8 U.S.C. § 1375 (set forth at the beginning of Chapter 2.E.2) and the anti-trafficking provisions (8 U.S.C. §§ 1324(a), 1325(d), 1584, 2421), provisions address immigration marriage fraud, *see* 8 U.S.C. §§ 1154, 1227, 1325(c), document fraud, *see* 8 U.S.C. § 1324(c), 18 U.S.C. §§ 1001, 1028, 1546, 1583, racketeering (maintaining businesses through criminal activity), *see* 18 U.S.C. §§ 1961–63, mail or wire fraud, *see* 18 U.S.C. §§ 1341–42, and the importation of an alien for immoral purposes, *see* 8 U.S.C. § 1328. Do these laws get at the problem?

15. *Potential Reforms.* What legislative changes would you make, if any, to address mail-order marriages? Should law reform efforts target individuals who seek spouses from abroad, the industry, or the prospective mail-order brides themselves? Could the adoption of marriage formalities address these disparities, or is there a fundamental issue of capacity involved that makes these marriages invalid? Should law reform occur mostly in countries from which the brides originate or in countries to which they are

destined? Should solutions be adopted on a local or national level? What role, if any, might women's economic development have in minimizing the practice? Are there any problems with regulation?

16. *Countries of Transit.* So far, attention has focused on countries of origin and countries of destination. Countries of transit might also have a part to play in any additional reform efforts. These countries might be especially important if a particular country served as the Las Vegas of mail-order-bride marriages.

17. *The Constitutionality of Solutions.* Could the U.S. government ban mail-order marriages? Would such a ban be constitutionally permissible? *Cf.* Zablocki v. Redhail, 434 U.S. 374 (1978) (subjecting state restriction on marriage to heightened scrutiny under equal protection clause). Would a ban be beneficial for women overall?

18. *Regulation of Lawyers.* Is a potential solution the regulation of lawyers? "On the Mail Order Bride Warehouse site, potential customers can hyperlink directly to a page entitled the Law Offices of Livingston and Associates to answer their questions concerning immigration law and obtain the services of an attorney. The Sunshine International website offers an 'Immigration, Visa, Travel Info, Writing Tips, and Much More' information packet for $25, which offers 'step-by-step' directions and all necessary paperwork for applying for a Fiancée Visa with INS.... The Sunshine Girls International website refers Los Angeles residents to the Los Angeles County Bar Immigration Projects (sic), listed as a non-profit organization, that gives in-person consultations for only $10 and offers to handle a fiancee visa petition for $50 (plus, it may be assumed, the INS filing fee of $95)." *See Lawyers and the Mail Order Bride Industry,* at http://www.unc.edu/courses/law357c/cyberprojects/spring99/mailorder/lawyers.html. What role should the lawyers themselves play in regulating this industry? Are the matchmaking organizations engaging in the unauthorized practice of law when lawyers are not involved but the organization provides information on U.S. immigration law? *See* 8 C.F.R. § 292.2(a) (allowing representation of clients before the INS and BIA (including before the immigration court) by representatives of qualified and recognized organizations, such as non-profit religious, charitable, social service, or similar organizations, so long as representative is of good moral character and has "at its disposal adequate knowledge, information, and experience").

4. International Legal Responses

International law addresses many of the concerns that may exist with mail-order marriages. In particular, those concerned about power imbalances in these marriages may find some comfort in international instruments addressing discrimination against women (*e.g.,* the Convention on the Elimination of All Forms of Discrimination against Women (CEDAW)), trafficking of persons, or slavery. Yet none of the older instruments on these topics specifically mention mail-order marriages and their applicability or position on the practice is subject to interpretation.

a. Discrimination against Women

Is a country's failure to vigorously regulate mail-order marriages a violation of CEDAW? Which provisions, if any, suggest that this might be the case? Does article 16 offer assistance? Consider the following.

General Recommendation No. 21, ¶ 16, *in*
Report of the Committee on Progress Achieved
in the Implementation of the Convention
CEDAW, 14th Sess., ¶ 465, U.N. Doc. CEDAW/C/1995/7 (1995)

A woman's right to choose a spouse and enter freely into marriage is central to her life and to her dignity and equality as a human being. An examination of States parties' reports discloses that there are countries which, on the basis of custom, religious beliefs, or the ethnic origins of particular groups of people, permit forced marriages or remarriages. Other countries allow a woman's marriage to be arranged for payment or preferment, and in others, women's poverty forces them to marry foreign nationals for financial security. Subject to reasonable restrictions, based, for example, on a woman's youth or consanguinity with her partner, a woman's right to choose when, if, and whom she will marry must be protected and enforced at law.

---

b. Trafficking

One of the provisions of CEDAW that might be relevant is article 6. Article 6 says, "State parties shall take all appropriate measures, including legislation, to suppress all forms of traffic in women and exploitation of prostitution of women." Various commentators equate mail-order marriages with trafficking. For example, one commentator stated, "The mail-order bride industry is one of the most open forms of trafficking women into developed nations...." *See* Kathryn A. Lloyd, Comment, *Wives for Sale: The Modern International Mail-Order Bride Industry*, 20 Nw. J. Int'l L. & Bus. 341, 344 (2000). *See also, e.g.,* Janice G. Raymond & Donna M. Hughes, *Sex Trafficking of Women in the United States*, Coalition Against Trafficking in Women, March 2001, at 24 ("Mail order bride industries, or marriage marketing, can be viewed as a form of marriage trafficking in which women are marketed as products, and transported across borders for purposes of a commercial sexual transaction, a transaction that often involves fraud, deception and inducement."); Shelley Case Inglis, *Expanding International and National Protection Against Trafficking for Forced Labor Using a Human Rights Framework*, 7 Buff. Hum. Rts. L. Rev. 55 (2001); Becki Young, Note, *Trafficking of Humans Across United States Borders: How United States Laws Can be Used to Punish Traffickers and Protect Victims*, 13 Geo. Immigr. L.J. 73, 79 (1998); Donna R. Lee, Note & Comment, *Mail Fantasy: Global Sexual Exploitation in the Mail-Order Bride Industry and Proposed Legal Solutions*, 5 Asian L.J. 139, 170–71 (1998).

Apart from CEDAW, there are seventeen U.N. documents that address trafficking, and twelve Council of Europe or European Union initiatives. *See* Kathrina Knaus, et al., Combat of Trafficking in Women for the Purpose of Forced Prostitution: International Standards 19–31, 37–42 (Ludwig Boltzmann Institute of Human Rights ed., 2000), *at* http://www.univie.ac.at/bim/download/international.pdf (listing documents and relevant provisions). The problem with all of these instruments in this context is that none of them explicitly applies to the mail-order marriage industry and the analogies are strained. For the U.N. treaties, one has to make an argument that a mail-order marriage involves slavery (Slavery Convention, art. 1 (1926), International Covenant on Civil and Political Rights, art. 8 (1966)), debt-bondage (Supplementary Convention on the Abolition of

Slavery, the Slave Trade, and Institutions and Practices Similar to Slavery, art. 1 (1956)), forced labour (Forced Labour Convention, art. 1, 2 (1930), International Covenant on Economic, Social and Cultural Rights, art. 6, 7 (1966), Abolition of Forced Labour Convention (1957)), servitude (Universal Declaration of Human Rights, art. 4 (1948)), prostitution (Convention for the Suppression of the Traffic in Persons and of the Exploitation of the Prostitution of Others, art. 1, 2 (1949)), economic or sexual exploitation or sale of a child (Convention on the Rights of the Child, art. 32, 34, 35 (1989)), migrant work (International Convention on the Protection of the Rights of All Migrant Workers and Members of Their Families (1990)), or discrimination against women (CEDAW, art. 6).

The argument that mail-order brides are trafficked also has been hindered, until recently, because trafficking itself has been defined in terms of prostitution or has not been defined at all. For example, article 1 of the U.N. Convention for the Suppression of the Traffic in Persons and of the Exploitation of the Prostitution of Others of 1949, contained in the Statutory Supplement, states that signatories "agree to punish any person who, to gratify the passion of another...procures, entices, or leads away, for purposes of prostitution, another person, even with the consent of that person." Prostitution is not defined, and the 1949 Convention was adopted before the mail-order-bride industry exploded. *See* Janice G. Raymond, Guide to the New U.N. Trafficking Protocol 2 (European's Women's Lobby 2001). While CEDAW contains language that is obviously broader than the 1949 Convention, it is still unclear whether or not it covers mail-order marriages because traffic is not defined in CEDAW. The Special Rapporteur on Violence against Women has defined trafficking and stated that at "the core of any definition" is its "non-consensual nature." While she specifically mentioned "forced marriage," she did not mention mail-order marriage. *See Integration of the Human Rights of Women and the Gender Perspective: Violence Against Women*, U.N. ESCOR, 56th Sess., Agenda Item 12(a), U.N. Doc. E/CN.4/2000/68/Add. 4 (2000).

A new international instrument, however, contains a broad definition of trafficking. The Protocol to Prevent, Suppress and Punish Trafficking in Persons, especially Women and Children, supplements the U.N. Convention Against Transnational Organized Crime. It was adopted by the General Assembly on November 15, 2000, and appears in the Statutory Supplement. Article 3 defines "trafficking in persons." It states:

(a) "Trafficking in persons" shall mean the recruitment, transportation, transfer, harbouring or receipt of persons, by means of the threat or use of force or other forms of coercion, of abduction, of fraud, of deception, of the abuse of power or of a position of vulnerability or of the giving or receiving of payments or benefits to achieve the consent of a person having control over another person, for the purpose of exploitation. Exploitation shall include, at a minimum, the exploitation of the prostitution of others or other forms of sexual exploitation, forced labour or services, slavery or practices similar to slavery, servitude or the removal of organs;

(b) The consent of a victim of trafficking in persons to the intended exploitation set forth in subparagraph (a) of this article shall be irrelevant where any of the means set forth in subparagraph (a) have been used;

(c) The recruitment, transportation, transfer, harbouring or receipt of a child for the purpose of exploitation shall be considered "trafficking in persons" even if this does not involve any of the means set forth in subparagraph (a) of this article;

(d) "Child" shall mean any person under eighteen years of age.

The interpretative notes for the travaux préparatoires state that the "reference to the abuse of a position of vulnerability is understood to refer to any situation in which the person involved has no real and acceptable alternative but to submit to the abuse involved." *Report of the Ad Hoc Committee on the Elaboration of a Convention Against Transnational Organized Crime on the Work of Its First to Eleventh Sessions,* 55th Sess., Agenda item 105, U.N. Doc. A/55/383/Add.1 (2000). Various non-governmental organizations were "pivotal" in getting the broad definition of trafficking in the new Trafficking Protocol. Raymond & Hughes, *supra,* at 3. Does the definition in the new Protocol cover mail-order brides? What if no fraud is involved at the outset? Also, who exactly is doing the trafficking? Are members of the industry trafficking women or information? Would a mail-order bride business be guilty of trafficking if it was intentionally ignorant of the abuse that might occur in some of these marriages? What about an airline that is a critical link in the trafficking chain, but has no reason to suspect any particular individuals are trafficking?

The Protocol has provisions relating to the criminalization of trafficking (art. 5), the provision of assistance to and protection of victims of trafficking (art. 6), the status of trafficked persons in receiving States (art. 7), the repatriation of trafficked persons (art. 8), and the prevention of trafficking (art. 9). As of December 2000, eighty nations, including the United States, have signed the Protocol. *See* U.S. Dep't of State, Bureau of Int'l Narcotics & Law Enforcement Affairs, *Protocol to Prevent, Suppress, and Punish Trafficking in Persons, Especially Women and Children, and Protocol Against the Smuggling of Migrants by Land, Sea, and Air* (Jan. 21, 2001), *at* http://www.state.gov/g/inl/crm/fs/index.cfm?docid=562. It will enter into force when forty countries ratify it. *Id.* As of June 15, 2001, the treaty was not yet in force. *See* United Nations, *Protocol to Prevent, Suppress, and Punish Trafficking in Persons, Especially Women and Children, Supplementing the United Nations Convention Against Transnational Organized Crime, at* http://untreaty.un.org/English/TreatyEvent2001/17.htm (last visited Aug. 8, 2001).

Notes and Questions

1. *Scope of Legal Response.* Is an international solution better than a municipal one? Why or why not?

2. *Comparing the Old and the New.* Assume for purposes of analysis that both the 1949 Convention and the new Protocol cover mail-order marriages. What are the critical differences between the two instruments? Among other things, compare the role of consent in the 1949 Convention and the new Protocol. Can a bride consent to enter an abusive marriage? Should she be able to do so?

3. *Prostitution of Wives and Fiancées.* You should not assume that the 1949 Convention is irrelevant to mail-order marriages, even if you cannot equate the category "mail-order marriage" to "prostitution." Sometimes men use a mail-order marriage service to acquire a bride who they then force into prostitution. One study indicates that mail-order bride agencies have served as a conduit for some U.S. men who have brought international women into the United States for the sex industry (many of whom have never before been prostitutes). Janice G. Raymond & Donna M. Hughes, *Sex Trafficking of Women in the United States,* Coalition Against Trafficking in Women, March 2001, at 51. The phenomenon of husbands serving as pimps to their foreign wives is not new. The same study indicated that "Often the servicemen marry prostituted women around military bases abroad, bring them to the United States and pressure them into prostitution. A large number of foreign military wives become victims

of domestic violence, displaced or homeless, and end up in prostitution around U.S. military bases." *Id.* at 9, 23, 48 (finding 20% of international women said husbands/ boyfriends acted as pimps). Sometimes traffickers pay U.S. servicemen to marry women and bring them into the United States for use in the sex industry. *Id.* at 24. The report recommends the following: "There should be some way of tracking U.S. men who travel to the same or different countries, and return to the United States with serial foreign fiancées or wives." *Id.* at 14.

4. *Proposed Convention Against Sexual Exploitation.* Various non-governmental organizations have proposed even broader definitions of trafficking than exists in the Protocol to Prevent, Suppress and Punish Trafficking in Persons, especially Women and Children (2000). In 1995, the Coalition Against Trafficking in Women (CATW) sought adoption of a draft Convention Against Sexual Exploitation. The Convention would obligate states to take all necessary measures to eliminate all forms of sexual exploitation. *See* art. 1. Consider the following provisions:

> Article 2. Sexual exploitation is the sexual violation of a person's human dignity, equality, and physical and mental integrity. It is a practice by which some people (primarily men) achieve power and domination over others (primarily women and children) for the purposes of sexual gratification, financial gain, and/or advancement.

> Article 3. For purposes of the present Convention, sexual exploitation takes the forms of, but is not limited to sexual violence and murder; sexual abuse and torture including sadistic, mutilating practices; genital mutilation; prostitution, sex trafficking, sex tourism and mail order bride markets; rape, incest, sexual harassment and pornography; involuntary sterilization and childbearing; female seclusion, dowry and bride price; temporary marriage or marriage of convenience for the purpose of sexual exploitation.

> Article 10. States Parties shall prohibit and punish persons or enterprises who promote, profit from, or engage in any business involving the matching of women in marriage to foreign nationals by mail order or pseudomarriage.

See Coalition Against Trafficking in Women, Proposed United Nations Convention Against Sexual Exploitation (1995). The convention criminalizes sexual exploitation, and requires States to develop policies to prevent sexual exploitation and to protect the victims of sexual exploitation. The convention would require States Parties to enact quite broad preventive measures, including to "[r]eject state economic policies and practices of development that help precipitate persons into situations of sexual exploitation." *Id.* art. 5(1)(a). What are the strengths and weaknesses of this proposed convention? Would the criminalization of the mail-order bride industry force the practice underground?

5. *Enforcement.* What are the enforcement mechanisms in the 1949 Convention and the new Protocol? One author has stated that "since [the] creation [of the 1949 Convention] there has been no enforcement of state parties' obligations." Shelley Case Inglis, *Expanding International and National Protections Against Trafficking for Forced Labor Using a Human Rights Framework*, 7 Buff. Hum. Rts. L. Rev. 55, 60 (2001). The Proposed Convention Against Sexual Exploitation would establish, inter alia, a Committee on the Elimination of Sexual Exploitation (art. 18), which would review reports submitted by State Parties every four years (art. 20), require states to respond to its inquiries (art. 21), and entertain complaints from other states (art. 22). It also provides a procedure whereby states can agree that the Committee will receive individual complaints (art. 23).

6. *Involuntary Labor.* The International Labor Organization's Forced Labor Convention (No. 29) and the 1957 Abolition of Forced Labor Convention (No. 105) provide a definition of forced labor for purposes of those instruments. The ILO Convention defines forced labor as "all work or service which is extracted from any person under the menace of any penalty and for which the said person has not offered himself voluntarily." Convention Concerning Forced or Compulsory Labor, *entered into force* May 1, 1932, 39 U.N.T.S. 55 (modified 1949). It is questionable whether the ILO would consider a mail-order marriage to constitute "work or service," since the ILO has even "shied away from directly dealing with prostitution as an economic sector.'" Inglis, *supra*, at 84. "Although mail order bride marriages are in effect an exchange of sexual and domestic services for material and financial support, these relationships have not been defined as or treated as work." *Id.* at 91. Moreover, are these marriages involuntarily entered?

7. *Other Violations of International Law.* Can you identify other potential violations of international instruments by countries who are not adequately combatting the mail-order marriage phenomenon?

8. *Age.* The Convention on the Rights of the Child prohibits the trafficking of children. *See* Convention on the Rights on the Child (1989), art. 35. A child is defined as anyone under 18. *See* art. 1. The new Protocol to Prevent, Suppress and Punish Trafficking in Persons, especially Women and Children treats trafficking in children differently than trafficking in adults. *See* arts. 3(c), 6(4). *See also Report of the Ad Hoc Committee on the Elaboration of a Convention Against Transnational Organized Crime on the Work of Its First to Eleventh Sessions*, U.N. GAOR, 5th Sess., Agenda Item 105, at 53, U.N. Doc. A/55/383 (2000), *available at* http://www.undcp.org/palermo/convmain.html. What is "trafficking" in the context of children? Are mail-order brides under 18 trafficked? Are there reasons to treat the trafficking of children differently than the trafficking of adults?

9. *Other Types of Suspect Marriage Practices.* Mail-order marriages are not the only situation in which a party might be either coerced into the marital relationship and/or coerced once inside the marital relationship. Consider, for example, what the State Department reported recently about the practice of obtaining brides in the country of Georgia: "Kidnapping of women for the purpose of marriage sometimes occurred in rural areas, although the practice was declining. If an eager or spurned suitor holds his intended fiancée as a hostage for more than 24 hours, her family considers her to be no longer suitable for marriage except to her kidnaper. If she consents to marriage, the incident is considered part of a traditional courtship ritual; if not, future marriage may become problematic. In such cases, the woman occasionally is raped." *See* U.S. Dep't of State, Bureau of Democracy, Human Rights, and Labor, *1999 Country Reports on Human Rights Practices* (Feb. 25, 2000), *at* http://www.state.gov/www/global/human_rights/1999_hrp_report/georgia.html. Similarly, in China, the trafficking of women and children is "rampant in rural areas." Abducted women are, among other things, sold as brides in prosperous regions. Four men who trafficked women in this manner were recently sentenced to death. *See China: Campaign Against Trafficking*, Int'l Children's Rts. Monitor, May 2001, at 9.

c. *Slavery*

Equating mail-order marriages to slavery was briefly raised above as a possibility under U.S. law. It is also possible to conceive of mail-order bride marriages as slavery under international law. A state violates *jus cogens* if it "practices, encourages, or condones... (b) slavery or slave trade,... (d) torture or other cruel, inhuman, or degrading treatment or punishment" Restatement (Third) of Foreign Relations Law § 702 cmt. n (1987) "A *jus cogens* norm is a principle of international law that is 'accepted by the international community of States as a whole as a norm from which no derogation is permitted....'" Committee of U.S. Citizens in Nicaragua v. Reagan, 859 F.2d 929, 940 (D.C. Cir. 1988) (quoting Vienna Convention on the Law of Treaties, May 23, 1969, art. 53, U.N. Doc. A/Conf. 39/27, 8 I.L.M. 679). Slavery is also a violation of customary international law. *See* M. Cherif Bassiouni, *Enslavement as an International Crime*, 23 N.Y.U. J. Int'l L. & Pol. 445 (1991). In addition, the practice is governed by treaties. "Seventy-nine separate international instruments and documents have addressed the issue of slavery, the slave trade, slave-related practices, forced labor, and their respective institutions." *See* Bassiouni, *supra*, at 454. For example, the Slavery Convention of 1926 (League of Nations Slavery Convention, 60 L.N.T.S. 253, *reprinted in* 21 Am. J. Int'l L. 171 (Supp. 1927)), the first convention to define slavery, and the Supplementary Convention on the Abolition of Slavery, the Slave Trade and Institutions and Practices Similar to Slavery (1956) 18 U.S.T. 3201, 226 U.N.T.S. 3, define slavery as "the status or condition of a person over whom any or all of the powers attaching to the right of ownership are exercised." Article 2(2) of the Supplementary Convention obligates States Parties to prevent slave trade and end slavery. It also addresses "compulsory or forced labour" and requires states to take actions so that forced labour does not develop into conditions analogous to slavery, and to put an end to it expeditiously. *See* art. 5.

Lest you think the notion of marriage as slavery is novel in international law, consider that the Supplementary Convention specifically mentions marriage. The Supplementary Convention directs parties to bring about progressively and as soon as possible the complete abolition or abandonment of various marriage practices including the sale of a woman into marriage. *Id.* art. 1(c). The Supplementary Convention also suggests that states establish "suitable" minimum marriage ages, that states encourage the ceremony to occur in a setting where both parties can freely express their consent, and that states encourage the registration of marriage. *Id.* art. 2. Similarly, lest you think action between family members is exempt from the concept of slavery, consider the Conclusions and Recommendations of the Special Rapporteur in *Updating of the Report on Slavery Submitted to the Sub-Commission on Prevention of Discrimination and Protection of Minorities in 1966*, UNHCHR, U.N. Doc. No. E/CN.4/Sub.2/1982/20/Add.1 (July 7, 1982). He wrote: "[W]hether by economic or sexual exploitation or physical brutality,...the power exercised over children (inside or outside the family) can, in their worst manifestations, amount to a widespread equivalent of slavery." *Id.* at 72(xvi).

Notes and Questions

1. What arguments would a husband make that he has not enslaved his mail-order bride?

2. *Private Right of Action.* Do any of the international instruments discussed above provide a private right of action for a mail-order bride against her husband? Could she directly sue either the state of origination, transit, or destination, alleging violations of international law?

3. For an excellent overview of the international instruments on slavery, see Bassiouni, *supra.*

Problem 2-4

Svitlana is a twenty-three-year-old school teacher in an impoverished Eastern European country. She is paid about $100 per month for her work. At times, two or three months may pass during which Svitlana does not receive any pay. She does not have health or disability insurance.

Svitlana is single. She responded to an advertisement in a local newspaper placed by a "matchmaking service." She found out the service was essentially a brokerage service for mail-order brides. However, she agreed, at no cost to her, to place a picture of herself, along with a brief personal description, in an international catalogue featuring potential mail-order brides.

Five men from the United States inquired about Svitlana through the service. Each paid $200 to have access to the catalogue of potential brides. After two months of internet correspondence, Svitlana received a proposal from a fifty-year-old divorced man from a Midwestern state. The man earns $50,000 per year, is a university professor, and clearly indicated that he expects his new wife to devote herself to caring for the home and raising children. His new wife would not be "permitted" to attend school or seek employment. Svitlana accepted his offer of marriage, even though she had no personal contact with the man until the day she married him. The parties married three months after the correspondence began. They traveled together almost immediately to the United States.

Svitlana's new husband does not physically assault her. He provides a very comfortable middle-class lifestyle. She spends her time at home performing domestic chores. After about a month of living with her husband she became pregnant. Svitlana has no relatives in town, her husband does not permit her to leave the house much, and she speaks little English. Consequently, she feels extremely isolated. Svitlana wants out of the marriage, but she wants to stay in the United States. In light of the foregoing materials, consider whether there is anything wrong with the arrangement and whether this arrangement violated any international or domestic law. Assuming Svitlana divorces her husband, can she stay in the United States?

Chapter 3

Dissolution of Marriage: A Continuing Conundrum

Questions regarding who should control marital dissolution and the circumstances under which it should occur have generated the same intensity of debate and disparate resolution over time and geography as have the issues examined in Chapter Two regarding access to marriage. In the United States, a wave of legislative reform during the past four decades has spawned controversy over the high incidence of divorce and its economic impact, fueling public and political discourse and, in some states, providing renewed impetus for further reform. To better inform an understanding of the historical and cultural roots of our own law of dissolution and enhance the assessment of alternatives, the regulation of marital dissolution is explored in this chapter from both historical and comparative perspectives.

Because the origins of family law in the United States are found primarily in Western Europe, Section A begins with a brief overview of the evolution of marital regulation in that region over several millennia, examining both the progression from customary to religious to state dominion over marriage, and the shift from relatively unfettered marital termination to the notion of indissolubility. The impact of that heritage is then explored through a survey of the divorce system that prevailed throughout much of the first two centuries in the United States, setting the stage for an appraisal of modern reform movements in Section B.

Comparative study is often facilitated by the examination of legal systems that develop within similar cultural, religious, political, economic, and social climates. Section B therefore focuses primarily on the similarities and differences in divorce reform undertaken in the past four decades in the United States, Great Britain, and the Republic of Ireland. In less detail, the modern transformation of divorce regulation in other nations in Western Europe and around the globe will be surveyed, both to illustrate the remarkable coincidence and convergence of reform, but also to observe some striking variations. In each instance, the struggle to maintain an appropriate balance among the interests of the individual partners and societal needs is complex and ongoing.

Currently many nations with Western legal systems and predominantly Christian populations have assumed exclusive control over the termination of the *civil* marital status of their citizens, but disclaimed any authority over their *religious* marital status. Nevertheless, the extent to which governmental entities in some of these countries have mandated court action that affects religious marital status belies the impenetrability of these constructs, raising interesting constitutional and policy issues. Nations with substantial populations that are non-Christian often utilize religious norms to regulate legal marital status, and many authorize religious bodies, either exclusively or in combination with civil courts, to hear dissolution matters. The extent to which the civil termination of marriage is and should be regulated by religious norms and institutions, and conversely the extent to which civil authorities should attempt to affect religious marital status today, are the focus of Section C.

A. Historical Origins of Western Law of Dissolution: From Customary to Religious to State Control

Those of us steeped in American legal tradition might take for granted the power our legal system confers upon secular governmental authorities, not only to bestow marital status, but also to dissolve it. Yet study of the evolution of the regulation of marital dissolution in Western Europe, from which much of the U.S. legal system was transplanted, indicates that the notions of civil marriage and state control of its termination are relatively recent constructs.

Mary Ann Glendon,
The Transformation of Family Law
19–34 (1989)

Regulation through enacted legal norms is but one mode of social control. Moreover, it is one which has appeared on a large scale only rather late in history, as a characteristic component of those processes of rationalization and consociation that have gradually penetrated all aspects of social life. Thus, it might occur to an inquisitive person, contemplating the elaborate modern systems of family law that now surround us, to wonder how marriage and family matters once governed only by custom, ethics, manners, or religion came to be regulated so extensively by law.... How is it...that, in the West, the innovations of law became, to a great extent, our marriage customs?

* * *

With respect to the Germanic and Roman antecedents of modern Western marriage systems, historians are able to tell us something about how community or kinship-group interest in mating manifested itself, and about the early forms of rank and status derived from marriage and birth. Marriage was a definite social status, but the wedding, or marriage rite, seems to have been important only under special circumstances, in particular where property was exchanged.... Among the early Germans, marriage differed from other sexual unions in that the wife and children of the marriage enjoyed a more secure position in relation to the husband and his kinship group than other women with whom he may have cohabited and their offspring. The distinction between legitimate marriage and other unions which, though not disapproved, are of lower status appears not only in primitive systems but also in Roman law and in the civil law of many continental countries until early modern times.

From a sociological point of view, the significance of the legitimate marriage is that it enables the family to function as a status-conferring institution. Only the legitimate wife and children share the social rank of their husband and father. In the widespread custom of high-ranking families to give away their daughters only on assurances of preferred status for the daughter and her children, Max Weber saw the origin of the earliest *legal* characteristics of marriage: dowry, the agreement to support the wife and pay her compensation upon abandonment, and the successoral position of her children.

In cultures or social groups where marriage is simply the decision of the partners to live together and to raise common children, and where marriage involves no exchange of property, the couple relationship tends to be dissolved simply by desertion or separation. But as marriage formation becomes more complex, the procedure for dissolving it typically does too. The emphasis on procedures for both seems to vary with the roles of rank and property. Where these are important, rules appear to distinguish clearly which sexual relationships will give rise to rights. The need arises to justify the dissolution of marriage and to furnish reasons to neutralize the objections of relatives.

This was already beginning to be the case in the earliest periods of Roman and Germanic customary law. It is said that the early Germanic folk were relatively monogamous, although plurality of wives was permissible among them, and that Rome, for its first five hundred years, had a tradition of marital stability, despite the fact that marriages were dissoluble there. In the morally strict society of early republican Rome, a man would incur disapproval if he repudiated his wife without some cause, such as barrenness or infidelity. Old Germanic law recognized marriage dissolution by agreement between the husband and the wife's relatives and permitted the husband, and eventually the wife, to end the marriage unilaterally for certain serious reasons.

* * *

Over the long period of Roman history, marriage customs varied considerably.... *Free consensual marriage...*, in which the man and woman married simply by starting life in common [with] *affectio maritalis,* [i.e., regarding] each other as husband and wife,...was known at the time of the earliest Roman code of laws, the Twelve Tables (451–450 B.C.). It was common in the third and second centuries B.C., and became the usual mode of marriage in the late Republic. There was nothing but *affectio maritalis* to distinguish free marriage from any other type of sexual union. If this state of mind ceased on either side, the marriage, in principle, was at an end. Legally, the free marriage was treated as dissolved when the parties separated by agreement, or when one spouse departed and notified the other of his or her intention to terminate the relationship. At one time, it may have been the case that only the husband could unilaterally terminate the marriage. But the parties were on an equal footing in this respect at least by the end of the third century B.C..... Thus one can say that in Rome, marriage had become a formless transaction dissoluble at the will of either party, and remained so at the time of the first Christian Emperor, Constantine (c. A.D. 285–337).

The Christian emperors made little effort to regulate family behavior. From Constantine until Justinian, Roman marriage legislation had no ambitions beyond punishing unjustified repudiations. If one spouse repudiated the other without some good reason, he or she might have to give back the marriage portion or lose other property rights. Eventually, the offending spouse could even be deported, confined within a monastery, or subjected to restrictions on remarriage. But even these more restrictive laws permitted repudiation for cause, and they did not affect divorce by mutual agreement.... Justinian broke with Roman tradition and established penalties for mutual consent divorce.... [H]owever,...[h]is restrictions...were short lived, being repealed by Justinian's successor in one of his first acts after ascension to the throne.

At the close of the Roman period, then, it can be said that the law had little direct involvement with the social institution of marriage. The idea of legal regulation of marriage formation or the conduct of married life was unknown and legal control of marriage dissolution had been attempted only to a very limited degree by the legislation of the Christian emperors, which implicitly accepted the premise that marriage was dissoluble. In Rome and among the Germanic peoples, marriage was thus not a legal institution....

After the Roman empire in the West broke down in the course of the fifth century A.D., the Christian Church not only remained intact but grew stronger than ever. The new kingdoms of the West had not yet developed those political organizations on the Roman pattern that were to develop subsequently into various forms of feudalism and still later into what we now call the state. The Church was able to exercise great influence over, and was closely associated with, the secular power of the early Visigothic kings and the later Merovingian and Carolingian dynasties. Even so, the establishment of the doctrine of the indissolubility of marriage and the acquisition of ecclesiastical jurisdiction over matrimonial matters took centuries.

* * *

The greatest obstacle to the direct enforcement by the Church of the new Christian ideas about sex and marriage was that marriage was regarded everywhere in Europe in the first half of the Middle Ages as a personal and purely secular matter. Conversion to Christianity in the Roman empire and in the lands inhabited by the Germanic tribes did not automatically result in immediate acceptance of the Christian notions that marriage had to be strictly monogamous and that all sexual relations outside marriage were prohibited. Nor did the Church insist on this. Marriage continued to be regulated by social rules about marriage age, choice of partners, and legitimate descent. Sometimes these rules were grounded in custom and convention, sometimes in ancient pagan religion. Ecclesiastical jurisdiction over marriage was acquired only very gradually, and in large part, through a process of compromise with, adaptation to, and even incorporation of indigenous practices....

The idea of the indissolubility of marriage did not easily gain a foothold in the ancient world. Within the early Church, some held the opinion that the passages in the Apostolic Writings, upon which Church fathers based the principle of indissolubility, did not absolutely prohibit divorce, at least in the case of adultery. Eventually the point was more or less settled in ecclesiastical doctrine, but the Church still had to contend with deeply rooted secular customs. The Anglo-Saxons, the Franks, the other Germanic tribes, and the Romans all had permitted divorce. Marriages were dissoluble (without intervention of any judge) by mutual consent or by unilateral repudiation, sometimes with payment of a penalty. For centuries, when all that the Church had to back up its norms was its disciplinary power over Christians, it was compelled to exercise a great deal of tolerance. To some extent, it even accepted divorce and remarriage.

* * *

Ecclesiastical jurisdiction over matrimonial causes and the rudiments of a canon law system were established in what is now France and the Germanies by the end of the tenth century, and in England by the middle of the twelfth century.... The development of the doctrine of sacramental marriage, [...the Christian idea that marriage is not only a natural institution and a contract between the spouses, but also...a channel of divine grace], furnished the theoretical basis for the assertion of ecclesiastical authority over an area of life which previously had not been subject to any kind of systematic official control....

The acquisition of jurisdiction over marriage by ecclesiastical courts and the application by these courts of the various church doctrines which eventually coalesced into a body of canon law was something new in human history.... The norm system of the canon law, formulated and systematically organized after the manner of the law of the late Roman empire, did not gain immediate acceptance in social life, but over time it had far-reaching and long-lasting effects on all Western marriage law, effects which have lasted down to the present day.... The Church bided its time, winning social acceptance of its doctrines in much the same way as it had acquired jurisdiction, through a long patient process of action and interaction with everyday life. Meanwhile, the canon law of marriage assumed the form that was to be of such crucial importance for the future....

Once the rule of indissolubility was established,... [i]t had to be spelled out in minute detail exactly which unions were of the type that now could not be dissolved and outside of which all sexual intercourse was unlawful. Marriage had to be defined with more precision than ever before. Out of this need came the whole complex canon law system of marriage impediments and prohibitions. The multiplication of these causes of nullity in turn led to the need to investigate in advance of marriage whether impediments in fact existed and thus to the origin of the publication of the banns and the Church's increasing insistence on public marriage, as well as to the elaboration of procedures for declaring marriages invalid.... The result was that the apparent rigidity of the principle of indissolubility was considerably mitigated in practice by the rules on consent and by the existence of a variety of potential grounds for annulment.... The proliferation of bases for annulment has been variously viewed as logically compelled by the theory of marriage; related to money and power in the sense that annulments gave the Church a source of revenue and a certain amount of control over families; a humane response to the desires of some individuals to escape from intolerable situations and to remarry; and a "safety valve," substituting for the necessary but missing institution of divorce. No doubt all these factors played a role.

* * *

The Church alleviated the severity of its indissolubility rule by establishing a procedure for judicial separation as well as by providing many causes for annulment. Separation could be decreed in situations where one spouse had committed adultery, apostasy, or heresy, or had deserted or seriously mistreated the other. But unlike annulment, judicial separation did not permit the parties to remarry.... Foreshadowed itself by the grounds of justifiable repudiation in the imperial Roman decrees, the canon law of judicial separation prefigures [the] doctrine of divorce as a sanction for marital misconduct....

* * *

Up to the time of the Council of Trent, the Church had only gone so far as to make a public blessing in church a religious duty, sanctioned by penance or censure. To find out why a public formal ceremony was made a condition for the validity of marriage (by the Decree *Tametsi* in 1563), we must look, not to ecclesiastical doctrine, but to pressures and events in the secular world.... [S]ocial and economic changes...increasingly caused families in certain levels of society to seek control over the shifts of wealth and power that marriages could produce.... [T]he time-honored doctrine that Christian marriages could be formed by consent alone...had the effect of liberating individuals from the constraints which parents, kinship groups, or political authorities might try to impose on their choice of spouses. But it was this very liberating effect which began to be perceived as troublesome in sixteenth-century Europe, in those circles where large amounts of money could change hands upon the right sort of marriage.

...[In addition, so] long as informal marriages were permitted, the difficulty of either proving or disproving them would allow some persons to slip out of the bonds of valid marriages, and others to profit through inheritance or in other ways by falsely alleging the existence of a secret marriage. This longstanding potential for abuse became an increasingly serious issue with the rise of the new economy and the appearance of the merchant class. Such secular concerns may explain in part why the same bishops who were the chief proponents of compulsory ceremonial marriage at the Council of Trent also endeavored to have the Council make parental consent an ecclesiastical marriage requirement.... The validity of informal marriage had been defended by theological purists, who maintained that one's spiritual liberty to marry or not should be protected from interference by others, particularly parents. But...the advocates of change claimed that informal marriages threatened property rights, and endangered social peace and private morality.

[T]he Decree *Tametsi*...provided that henceforth no marriage was valid which had not been celebrated in the presence of a priest and other witnesses. The Decree also mandated the publication of banns of marriage and the keeping of official records of marriages. Thus, the Church helped families at least to keep up with the marriage plans of their children, but it did not go so far as some delegates to the Council would have liked in reinforcing family control.

Those seeking legal support for parental control over marriage found a warmer response from the secular authorities in many places. A French royal edict of 1556 empowered parents to disinherit children who married without their consent and provided punishments for anyone assisting such a marriage. After Martin Luther condemned clandestine marriages for enabling strangers to marry into wealthy families without prior parental approval and to obtain a share of estates, a minister's presence at weddings was made mandatory in the Reformation ordinances of the Protestant principality of Württemberg (1553) and the Palatinate of the Rhine (1563)...[and] in Geneva in 1561.... [A]ll these ordinances required couples to obtain the consent of their parents before they could marry. England, however, long remained a case apart. The Church of England, which had deprived the Roman Catholic Church of jurisdiction over matrimonial causes in 1534, continued to recognize informal marriages as valid until 1753.

It seems likely that the Decree *Tametsi* and all its secular counterparts had little effect on the marriage practices of persons other than the well-to-do.... The Church, as we have noted, did not even try to impose its new ceremonial marriage requirement on all the peoples in all the territories subject to its influence. [T]he Church made no effort to enforce it in places like the New World, where priests were scarce. Thus informal marriages continued to be valid under canon law in many parts of the world....

...From the sixteenth to the eighteenth century, in great parts of Western Europe, the Catholic Church lost its jurisdiction over marriage. In Protestant regions this occurred as a consequence of the Reformation, and in France it took place in connection with Gallicanism and the progress of the monarchy. When the Church lost its monopoly over matrimonial causes, the newly emerging states acquired jurisdiction more or less by default. Rather than develop an entirely new body of law to apply in such cases, secular governments simply took over much of the ready-made set of rules of the canon law, modeling their new divorce law on the ecclesiastical rules governing separation from bed and board. Thus, many rules which had been developed in the canon law continued to govern marriage, although they received new interpretations on certain points.

...Luther and others had claimed that marriage was properly subjected to the control of civil, rather than church, courts.... The reformers rejected the notion that marriage was a sacrament, but they took for granted that secular marriage regulations should conform to Christian teaching. Christian teaching was, of course, reinterpreted by them to permit divorce as a punishment for grave violation of marital duties—for adultery in particular, but gradually for other causes as well. Even the significance of this well-known instance of departure from Catholic doctrine should not be exaggerated, however, for it was accompanied by a tightening up of nullity, which the Church had at times offered rather freely. Protestantism did not return divorce to the private order by any means: no divorce by mutual consent was recognized, and divorce for cause had to be granted by the state.

...[T]he appearance of the humanistic and individualistic thought of the Enlightenment and the rise of the absolutist state...in France and the various regions of Germany...led in both places to unprecedented attempts at legal regulation of ongoing family relationships. England, once again, remained in this respect a special case, and so, in consequence, did the United States.

* * *

With Reformation and Enlightenment, the idea of marriage as a contract took a new turn.... [C]onsent was the essence of marriage in ecclesiastical law. But thinkers as diverse as Martin Luther and John Locke began to emphasize the aspect of marriage as a civil contract. This was a point of view that appealed especially to the French revolutionaries who were eager to eliminate the last vestiges of ecclesiastical jurisdiction. Several consequences followed from accentuation of the contractual aspect of marriage, the most important of which were laying the groundwork for divorce by mutual consent and for state regulation not only of the formation and dissolution of the marriage contract, but of its very content. The great continental codifications enclosed the spouses in a network of legal rights and duties that gave each spouse a full set of claims against the other that could be made on the basis of legal action before a judge....

In France, the penchant for legislative regulation during this period gave rise to the development of two important modern institutions affecting the family: the compulsory civil marriage ceremony and the system of comprehensive public registration of civil status. The civil marriage ceremony had been available as an option in the Calvinist Netherlands and in New England, but it was made mandatory by a French revolutionary decree of 20 September 1792. From France, the civil ceremony spread all over the world, as at least an optional method of marrying. France also furnished the model for the systems of secular registration of civil status which are now in worldwide use....

As mentioned, England followed a somewhat different course. The ecclesiastical jurisdiction of the Church of England over marriage continued without significant interference until the middle of the nineteenth century. Briefly under Cromwell...civil marriage was available, and divorce may have been permitted. But with that brief exception, civil marriage did not appear in England until 1836—in connection with passage of a spate of bureaucratic legislation concerning registration of vital statistics. Informal marriages remained valid in England until...1753.... Divorce became available after 1660, but could be obtained only by special parliamentary act, and then only for adultery. It was expensive, complicated. and rarely used. Judicial divorce was not introduced until 1857.

Notes and Questions

1. *Societal Functions of Marriage Underpinning Regulation.* Professor Glendon identifies two societal functions that marital relationships have historically fulfilled, which have influenced a society's need to regulate recognition of marital relationships and control their dissolution, through custom, religion, or law. What are these functions and how have they interacted over the centuries in Western Europe with evolving requirements for marital formation and dissolution?

Are these functions equally important to all levels of society? Even if they are not, do the resulting norms regulating marriage and its dissolution impact all levels of society, historically and today?

Have changes in modern Western society affected the importance of these functions? Are there other functions today that the institution of marriage fulfills?

2. *Evolution of Control.* Professor Glendon traces the transfer of the control of marital dissolution in Western Europe from predominantly customary control, to control by religious hierarchy, to control by the secular state. What historical forces shaped this evolution?

Subsequent sections of this chapter will examine various models of interaction between governmental and religious authorities concerning the regulation of marital dissolution. Given their constitutional law training regarding the separation of church and state, American law students might categorize the regulation of civil dissolution of marriage in the United States as completely secular. While authority to regulate dissolution in the United States is vested in a secular governmental legislature and judiciary disassociated from a religious organization, what light does Professor Glendon's research cast upon the source of much of our marital dissolution law?

3. *Historical Pendulum.* Americans today might well view the notion that one or both partners should be able to terminate the marital bond as a product of late twentieth century reform. Yet Professor Glendon illustrates that attitudes towards indissolubility in Western marriage regulation reveal a circular rather than a linear pattern. For additional information regarding the history of divorce in Western Europe, see Roderick Phillips, Putting Asunder: A History of Divorce in Western Society (1988).

European colonists brought with them to America their conceptions of marriage and its legal regulation. Professor Glendon relates that those colonies in which Protestants settled had divorce laws early in their history. Colonies, and later states, in which the influence of Anglicans (members of the Church of England) prevailed initially had no divorce at all. As a result of these settlement patterns, Professor Lawrence Friedman has noted that some northern states developed a system of judicial divorce by the late eighteenth century, whereas in many southern states divorce could only be obtained from the state legislature by individual petition well into the nineteenth century. By 1900, however, all states had established a system of judicial divorce, with the exception of South Carolina, which did not permit divorce of any kind until 1949. The operation of this system, which we now refer to as the "fault system," prevailed in the United States throughout the nineteenth and much of the twentieth century, and is described by Professor Friedman in the following excerpt.

Lawrence M. Friedman, *A Dead Language: Divorce Law and Practice Before No-Fault*
86 Va. L. Rev. 1497, 1501–07, 1512, 1516,
1518–20, 1523, 1530–31 (2000)

A divorce action was, in form, an adversary lawsuit. The plaintiff came before the court as an innocent victim arguing that the defendant, husband or wife, had broken the marriage contract. State statutes contained lists of bad deeds that constituted "grounds" for divorce. Each state had its own version, and its own procedures, differing in large and small details. The typical list of grounds included adultery, desertion, and some form of cruelty. In many states, habitual drunkenness was also grounds for divorce, and so was impotence; a few threw in narcotic addiction as well. Non-support and conviction of a felony were also common grounds. There were also some idiosyncratic statutes: In Hawaii, leprosy was grounds for divorce; in Virginia, if a husband discovered his wife had been a prostitute, he had the right to get out of the marriage. Tennessee quite reasonably provided that if one spouse tried to kill the other spouse "by poison or any other means showing malice," the victim was entitled to divorce. A few states were much more stringent than the norm.... In New York, under a notably severe statute, adultery was basically the only grounds for divorce.

In spite of such restrictions, the actual demand for divorce rose substantially during the last part of the nineteenth century. The divorce rate in 1870 was 1.5 per 1000 marriages; in 1900 it was 4 per 1000 marriages. This was small by modern standards—still, the rate had more than doubled in thirty years. In short, more people seemed to want to get out of their marriages.... [P]ressure on legislatures to ease up on the stringency of the law...undoubtedly existed, and there were reform movements, led at times by prominent women reformers. But in many or most states, it came to almost nothing. The laws were frozen in place.

The reasons are hardly mysterious. Many influential people disapproved of divorce, the Catholic church positively forbade it, the clergy in general were hostile, and divorce carried considerable stigma in society.... There was certainly the idea that divorce was, if not a cause, then at least an indicator of moral dry rot. In any event, it proved almost impossible, politically, to loosen the laws in most of the states. In fact, some states in the late nineteenth century went the other direction: They tightened their laws.... National opinion polls suggested that the public shared the views of their moral betters well into the twentieth century.... These attitudes were apparently shifting by the 1940s, at least somewhat, but they provide more evidence of why, despite the enormous subterranean demand, divorce laws were so inelastic.

It was a situation in which an irresistible force met an immovable object. The result was a kind of stalemate, and what we might call a dual system. The divorce laws in practice had almost nothing in common with the divorce laws on the books. After 1870, as far as we can tell, most divorces were collusive; there was no real courtroom dispute. In the vast majority of cases, all the issues were decided beforehand. That is, the parties had already agreed on a divorce, for whatever reason, whether reluctantly or not. Once this agreement was in place, one of the two, usually the wife, filed suit, accusing the other party, usually the husband, of violating the marriage in some statutory way. The defendant would let the case go by default. He or she would simply not show up, or not enter a defense. The judge would decree a divorce. The "lawsuit" was essentially a sham.

In most of the divorces granted in the hundred years between 1870 and the birth of no-fault, the collusion was direct. In the case of migratory divorce, it was a bit more indirect. To escape states with harsh laws, people with money (or, more frequently, wives of people with money) could get on a train and head for a "divorce mill." Throughout much of the twentieth century, the divorce mill was Nevada. It needed the business, and moral qualms, for whatever reason, have never played a big role in Nevada jurisprudence. In 1927, Nevada reduced its residence period to three months, and in 1931,... Nevada reduced the residence period still further, to six weeks.... In 1946, riding a wave of postwar divorces, Nevada recorded 143.9 divorces per 1000 inhabitants, and in 1950, 55 per 1000. This was more than fifty times the rate in New York, the least divorce-prone state, and almost fifteen times the rate in California. Obviously, a husband could, in theory, get on board the next train, travel to Reno, and fight his wife's divorce action in the Nevada courts, but this was a rare event indeed.

* * *

The "theory of antagonistic divorce" was just that—theory. Anyone with "time and money—and a cooperative spouse" could get a divorce, no matter what the statutes said.

* * *

Every study of divorce in the period, in every jurisdiction, found collusion to be the norm.... Collusion, in divorce law, means pretending to have grounds for divorce when in fact you have none, or when you choose (as often happened) not to tell the truth about the ones you do have. It must therefore be molded to the list of statutory grounds for divorce. New York, to take the classic example, basically allowed divorce only for adultery....

In light of this, there developed a most interesting practice, which we might call soft-core adultery. This involved a little drama performed in a hotel. The cast of characters included the husband, a woman (generally a blonde who was hired for the occasion), and a photographer, of course. An article in the New York Sunday Mirror magazine section, published in 1934, had the intriguing title: "I was the Unknown Blonde in 100 New York Divorces." The "unknown blonde" usually charged $50 for her work. She was in fact a woman named Dorothy Jarvis, who (according to the Mirror) had "retired as a professional co-respondent in view of her forthcoming marriage to a man she met while performing her role." Whatever sins the blonde may have committed in her young life, sex with the men who paid her was not among them....

* * *

To be sure, this does not mean that judges and lawyers liked the system. Most of them, in fact, hated it. The laws were "a farce," they were "insulting." They were described by attorneys as "ridiculous," "cockeyed," "stupid," "inhuman," and words to that effect. Yet the lawyers were caught in a bind; they had to act "like blind monkeys" to help their clients in New York or "help them engage in the sophistry of an out-of-state divorce." Either way was repellant. For lawyers, the only alternative—and hardly a practical one—was to get out of the divorce business and do something else.

New York was also...the nation's annulment capital. In most states, annulment was a fairly rare legal action. After all, to annul a marriage meant that a court decree wiped out its legal existence.... But New York was another story. In New York, thousands of marriages were annulled on all sorts of grounds—for example, fraud, a concept that could be quite liberally interpreted.... In 1950, in New York state, there were 6604 divorces granted and 4599 annulments—a truly amazing figure.

* * *

California law, as of 1931, gave a plaintiff six grounds for divorce, but only four were significant: desertion, adultery, extreme cruelty, and neglect. California was no exception to the general rule that divorce was a trumped-up, collusive affair. "Extreme cruelty" made the plaintiff's job that much easier; there was no need for hotel shenanigans. "Extreme cruelty" made it possible to get a divorce in California on ground of incompatibility, or in short, on the grounds that the marriage had simply gone sour, regardless of what the statute said. Cruelty was a charade, but a cheaper one than the soft-core adultery of New York.

As in New York..., the judges in California were perfectly aware of what was going on. In 1934, one judge in San Francisco, Walter Perry Johnson, more or less dropped the mask of ignorance, and talked openly about realities. The occasion was a divorce case; the plaintiff, one Jessie Trower, used cruelty as her ground for divorce, as was typical. And what did the cruelty consist of? Her husband's "absence from home without explanation, his statement that he did not love her, and his objection to her music studies." The judge remarked, quite rightly, that these allegations did not "really constitute cruelty in the proper meaning of the term." They amounted to nothing more than "incompatibility." But that was true of most of the "cruelty" charges, he said, and, in his view, "incompatibility" should be grounds for divorce. Of course, the legislature had never made such a move. No matter, Judge Johnson granted the divorce.

* * *

Every state had its peculiarities, no doubt. What was common to all of them, as far as one can tell, is some sort of system of collusion and perjury.

* * *

The divorce charade...had a paradoxical result. It paraded before the courts an endless procession of men, and mostly men, who confessed by their silence to adultery, cruelty, gross neglect of their obligations, and other deep-stained sins. But everybody knew the allegations were often or mostly lies. Hence in a way the system protected men (and mostly men) from revelations that would be much more damning. New York adultery was fake adultery—adultery with an imaginary woman. But nobody doubts that there was real adultery in New York, and that it was mostly husbands who cheated on wives, not the other way around. There was surely real cruelty—even "extreme cruelty" in California. There were violent husbands, husbands who beat their wives, drunk or sober, night and day. Yet the law paid little attention to real domestic violence. If there was a deeper rottenness and disloyalty in the marriages that ended up in court, it was hidden in the dark, in the fathomless reserves of private life, beyond the reach of legal proceedings.

...The divorce laws, in theory, were available to give a remedy to spouses whose partners broke the rules. In practice, divorce law almost forced women into a posture of submission and humility, into a mold of tender, injured femininity.

Notes

1. *Historical Roots.* As you read Professor Friedman's description of the limited grounds for divorce and the utilization of annulment, consider again Professor Glendon's observations of the historical foundations of this system. Why, for example, do you think adultery became a ground for divorce in every jurisdiction?

2. *Defenses under the Fault System.* The restricted fault grounds for divorce were accompanied by an elaborate system of defenses. For example, a divorce could be denied

on the ground of recrimination, i.e., that the "innocent" spouse was also guilty of a marital offense that would serve as a ground for divorce. Theoretically this was consistent with the concept of divorce as a reward for the blameless, though its practical effects made little sense. Its origins have been traced to Roman practices addressing the circumstances under which a divorcing husband should be permitted to retain his wife's dowry, and historians postulate that it found its way into American law via English equitable doctrine, by historical accident rather than deliberate policy. Other defenses that could prevent a divorce included condonation, i.e., forgiveness of the offense by the innocent spouse, which was frequently construed from a husband's (but not a wife's) engagement in intercourse with his spouse after knowledge of her misconduct; connivance, variously conceived as assisting or permitting the marital offense; and collusion of the spouses, by presentation of fraudulent testimony or the withholding of relevant facts, in those relatively rare instances in which the court chose to make an issue of it. Max Rheinstein, Marriage, Stability, Divorce, and the Law 53–56 (1972).

Rheinstein's text is an excellent source for further information regarding the history of divorce in the United States. *See id.* at 31–105. Another interesting source is Lawrence M. Friedman, A History of American Law 202–11 (2d ed. 1985).

B. Contemporary Divorce Reform

The tensions and discontent spawned by the fault system reached a crescendo on both sides of the Atlantic by the 1960s, motivating widespread reexamination of both the substantive and procedural process for marital termination in the United States and Western Europe throughout the next four decades. The nature of those reforms exhibit great similarities, but also some distinct differences.

This subsection will first explore the history of modern divorce reform in the United States, England, and the Republic of Ireland. Focusing on nations that share a common cultural heritage and similar social and economic conditions enhances, to some extent, our capacity to utilize the comparative process to understand our own law of dissolution and inspire our thinking about alternatives for further reform. The broad reach of contemporaneous reform throughout Europe will then be surveyed briefly, examining in particular those countries that chose a markedly different path. Though a comprehensive survey of divorce law in every nation is beyond the scope of this chapter, parallel divorce reform efforts in Asia will also be examined briefly. A small sample of the scholarly critique of modern reforms is then presented in preparation for the concluding problem at the end of the chapter, which will require you to fashion your own statutory scheme for divorce.

1. Modern Divorce Reform in the United States

By the 1960s, the pressure to overhaul the fault system in the United States prompted the formation of several bodies of experts to prepare proposals for major reform. As discussed in Chapter Two, marital dissolution, like most areas of family law, is reserved under the U. S. Constitution to the authority of state governments to regulate. The pace of reform, therefore, varied throughout the country. In fact, as early as 1950, Professor Friedman notes that perhaps as many as twenty states had added some ground that in reality did not require labeling one spouse as the offender. A long period of separation (two, three, or sometimes five or ten years) was typically the basis used. As early as 1933, New Mexico had added "incompatibility" to its list of grounds, and even before 1960, a few other states followed New Mexico's lead. Nevertheless, credit for leadership in the no-fault reform is usually conferred upon California, which totally removed fault grounds from its dissolution statute in the Family Law Act of 1969, and the National Conference of Commissioners on Uniform State Laws (NCCUSL), which promulgated a model no-fault dissolution statute as part of the Uniform Marriage and Divorce Act in 1970.

In California, the Governor's Commission on the Family was appointed in the mid-1960s, following a study by the California legislature, to make recommendations for reform. Two proposals were at the core of its recommendations: (1) replace fault with a marital breakdown standard as the basis for divorce, and (2) create a family court that would operate on an administrative and therapeutic, rather than an adversarial, model. The Commission envisioned the addition of professional counselors to the staff of the family courts who would initially attempt to facilitate reconciliation. The Commission's proposals were modified by the legislature, which deleted the proposal for a family court. Nevertheless, California's Family Law Act of 1969 became the first American divorce statute to completely eliminate fault grounds, substituting "irreconcilable differences, which have caused irremedial breakdown of the marriage" and incurable insanity as the sole grounds for divorce. *See* Herma Hill Kay, *From the Second Sex to the Joint Venture: An Overview of Women's Rights and Family Law in the United States During the Twentieth Century,* 88 Cal. L. Rev. 2017, 2050–55 (2000); Ira Ellman, *Divorce in the United States, in* Sanford Katz, John Eekelaar & Mavis Maclean, Cross Currents: Family Policy in the United States and England 343 (2000).

Another national group of experts appointed as an Advisory Committee by the National Conference of Commissioners on Uniform State Laws (NCCUSL) worked concurrently with the California Governor's Commission to produce the 1970 Uniform Marriage and Divorce Act, which utilized irretrievable breakdown as the sole basis for divorce. Under pressure from the American Bar Association, the UMDA was amended in 1973 to specify the findings necessary to find irretrievable breakdown. Although Kentucky chose to enact the 1970 UMDA, substituting a 60 day period of separation for the findings required by the 1973 amendment, seven other states subsequently have enacted the 1973 version, sometimes with minor revisions, which reads as follows:

§ 302. Dissolution of Marriage: Legal Separation

(a) The [...] court shall enter a decree of dissolution of marriage if:

* * *

(2) the court finds that the marriage is irretrievably broken, if the finding is supported by evidence that (i) the parties have lived separate and apart for a period of more than 180 days next preceding the commencement of the proceeding, or (ii) there is serious marital discord adversely affecting the attitude of one or both of the parties toward the marriage;

(3) the court finds that the conciliation provisions of Section 305 either do not apply or have been met;

(4) to the extent it has jurisdiction to do so, the court has considered, approved, or provided for child custody, the support of any child entitled to support, the maintenance of either spouse, and the disposition of property, or has provided for a separate, later hearing to complete these matters.

(b) If a party requests a decree of legal separation rather than a decree of dissolution of marriage, the court shall grant the decree in that form unless the other party objects.

§ 305 Irretrievable Breakdown

(a) If both of the parties by petition or otherwise have stated under oath or affirmation that the marriage is irretrievably broken, or one of the parties has so stated and the other has not denied it, the court, after hearing, shall make a finding whether the marriage is irretrievably broken.

(b) If one of the parties has denied under oath or affirmation that the marriage is irretrievably broken, the court shall consider all relevant factors, including the circumstances that gave rise to filing the petition and the prospect of reconciliation, and shall:

(1) make a finding whether the marriage is irretrievably broken; or

(2) continue the matter for further hearing not fewer than 30 nor more than 60 days later, or as soon thereafter as the matter may be reached on the court's calendar, and may suggest to the parties that they seek counseling. The court, at the request of either party shall, or on its own motion may, order a conciliation conference. At the adjourned hearing the court shall make a finding whether the marriage is irretrievably broken.

(c) A finding of irretrievable breakdown is a determination that there is no reasonable prospect of reconciliation.

By the mid-1980s, all states had abandoned the pure fault system of divorce. Their reformed divorce laws have taken a variety of approaches, however. Currently, approximately one-third of the states have abolished fault grounds completely. Linda Elrod & Robert Spector, *A Review of the Year in Family Law: State Courts React to Troxel,* 35 Fam. L.Q. 577, 620 (2002). These states recognize only no-fault grounds such as irreconcilable differences, incurable insanity (*e.g.,* Cal. Fam. Code § 2310 (West 1994)); irretrievable breakdown (*e.g.,* Colo. Rev. Stat. § 14-10-106 (2001)); incompatibility (*e.g.,* Nev. Rev. Stat. 125.010 (2001)); and/or judicial separation or living separate and apart for a certain period of time, typically between six months and three years (*e.g.,* N.C. Gen. Stat. § 50-6 (2001) (one year)), although states requiring separation periods longer than one year normally have additional no-fault grounds that have no time limit (*e.g.,* Haw. Rev. Stat. § 580-41 (1993)).

The remaining two-thirds of the states have retained at least some traditional fault grounds, such as adultery or extreme cruelty, and added one or more no-fault grounds as alternative bases to obtain a divorce. *See e.g.,* Okla. Stat. tit. 43, § 101 (2001). The vast majority of divorces in these states are obtained upon no-fault grounds as well.

Although vague terms such as irreconcilable differences and incompatibility might be assumed to generate substantial litigation concerning eligibility for divorce, at least in those instances in which one party opposes the break-up, in reality that has not proven to be the case. After some initial skirmishes when no-fault grounds were first introduced, U.S. courts have uniformly interpreted irreconcilable differences, irretrievable breakdown, or incompatibility to essentially require the same thing, as illustrated by the following Florida appellate court opinion.

Riley v. Riley
271 So. 2d 181 (Fla. Dist. Ct. App. 1972)

Johnson, J.

* * *

The parties herein had been married for almost 40 years when the appellant-husband, age 63, filed his Petition for Dissolution of Marriage in July of 1971, alleging that the parties had ceased to live together as husband and wife and that the marriage was irretrievably broken. The appellee-wife answered the petition by denying that this ground for dissolution existed and alleging that the husband had become temporarily enamored with another woman but that, within a reasonable period of time, he will wish to reconcile with appellee.

The appellant-husband testified that during the past ten or twelve years of the marriage, the parties had had no companionship, love, affection or home life, and that they had been drifting along for years with no reason for staying together except for the four children, who had now reached their majority. He admitted that prior to April of 1971, the parties had had no real domestic problems that could not be surmounted. They had had no arguments, because there was nothing to argue about, there being a feeling of indifference between them.

The appellee-wife testified that the parties had lived a happy life together until appellant met the Georgia widow who proposed marriage to him. When asked what specific acts of companionship between the parties existed within the last five or six years, appellee stated that they went to church and that they went out to dinner quite a bit. When asked what she had in common with her husband now that she could base a reconciliation on, appellee answered '39 years'.

Upon these facts, the trial judge found that the marriage had not been proven to be irretrievably broken and the petition was dismissed. The husband brings this appeal....

To our knowledge, this is a case of first impression under the new dissolution of marriage law of Florida.... We are called upon to determine whether the trial court abused its discretion in dismissing the petition in light of the reforms....

The basic substantive change in the law is the elimination of fault or guilt as grounds for granting or denying a dissolution of the marriage. The traditional fault-oriented grounds for divorce...have been abolished and replaced with only two grounds; to wit: a showing that the marriage is 'irretrievably broken' or mental incompetence of one of the parties....

* * *

...[W]e are hesitant to set forth specific circumstances which trial courts could utilize as permissible indices of an irretrievable breakdown of the marital status. Were we to attempt to do so, we feel that the basic purpose of the new dissolution of marriage law would be frustrated. Such proceedings would either again become primarily adversary in nature or persons would again fit themselves into tailor-made categories or circumstances to fit judicially defined breakdown situations. It is our opinion that these two problems are the very ones which the Legislature intended to eliminate.

While the Legislature did not define an 'irretrievably broken' marriage, it has stated that the purpose of the new law is to preserve the integrity of marriage and to safeguard meaningful family relationships. Whether or not the marriage is irretrievably broken is left to the trial court's determination based upon the evidence adduced at the hearing.

Such evidence need not be corroborated and there need be no showing of fault to determine that the marriage has in fact broken down.

Without attempting to set forth specific guidelines, we think the central inquiry in each situation should be a subjective, rather than an objective, one. In other words, observable acts and occurrences in the marriage relationship and the causes of the state in which the parties find themselves are not as important or controlling as the question of whether the marriage is in fact ended because of the basic unsuitability of the spouses for each other and their state of mind toward the relationship. Self-restrained spouses who do not permit outward manifestations of the failure of their marriage should not be penalized by the denial of the dissolution petition. If refusal of dissolution would amount to a legal perpetuation of a relationship which has ceased to exist in fact, the petition should be granted.

In every case, the important issue is the possibility of a reconciliation and the marriage as a whole must be considered. Before dissolution is granted, the court should be satisfied that the parties can no longer live together because their difficulties are so deep and substantial that no reasonable effort could eradicate them so as to enable the parties to live together in a normal marital relationship. If the trial judge doubts the petitioner's testimony that his or her marriage has irretrievably broken down, he should continue the proceedings to determine if reconciliation is possible.

Applying these principles to the case now before us, we feel that the trial judge erred in flatly dismissing the petition. If one marital partner has made the considered decision that the relationship should be terminated, perhaps it may properly be said that the marital relationship has broken down. However, as noted above, if the trial court doubts this spouse's testimony, we feel that the action should be continued to determine if reconciliation is possible. While the power of the State should be exerted to preserve the marriage if it can be preserved, it should not perpetuate a legal relationship which has or will cease to exist in fact. The power to continue the proceedings for a reasonable length of time not to exceed three months to enable the parties themselves to effect a reconciliation, or to order either or both parties to consult professional counselors, is authorized by F.S.A. s 61.052(2)(b). It is our considered opinion that either of these alternatives would be a better disposition of the present case and would be more in keeping with the new dissolution of marriage laws of this State. If, however, a temporary suspension of the proceedings or consultation with professional counselors fails to effectuate a reconciliation between the parties, the trial judge should then reconsider the issue of whether the marriage has in truth and in fact been irretrievably broken. If this issue is resolved in the affirmative, then a judgment dissolving the marriage should be rendered; otherwise, the prayer for dissolution should be denied and the complaint dismissed.

* * *

Reversed and remanded.

Spector, C.J. (dissenting)

* * *

Marriages are durable. They break, of course. But not all breaks are beyond repair. Especially when only one spouse wants out and the other is willing to reconcile upon passage of the temporary diversion which caused the rift.

* * *

In my view, all that appellant's evidence demonstrates is that he would like to enjoy the companionship of the widow lady and the comforts that her money will provide.

But, in no way has it been demonstrated that 'it's all over' between him and his wife. That is what 'irretrievably broken' means.

Appellant's effort to turn his back on the woman who ministered to his needs for some 40 years should not be assisted by this court. The mere absence of roman candles or champagne and strawberries for breakfast in the twilight years of a marriage is not proof that the marriage should be dissolved....

Most states therefore moved from a system in which spouses could not divorce easily even when both desired to do so, to a system in which one spouse could easily obtain a divorce over the objection of the other. A few states, however, including New York, have resisted this trend, permitting divorce on a no-fault ground only if both parties consent, and otherwise requiring proof of one of the traditional fault grounds. *See* N.Y. Dom. Rel. Law § 170 (McKinney 1999); Miss. Code Ann. § 93-5-2 (1999).

Some states, however, took a middle ground, permitting divorce upon a no-fault ground if both parties agreed to the divorce, but otherwise requiring either proof of a fault ground or a lengthy separation. Sometimes this is referred to as a hedged no-fault system. Missouri's divorce statute provides an example of this system.

Mo. Ann. Stat. § 452.320 (West 1997)

1. If both of the parties by petition or otherwise have stated under oath or affirmation that the marriage is irretrievably broken, or one of the parties has so stated and the other has not denied it, the court, after considering the aforesaid petition or statement, and after a hearing thereon shall make a finding whether or not the marriage is irretrievably broken and shall enter an order of dissolution or dismissal accordingly.

2. If one of the parties has denied under oath or affirmation that the marriage is irretrievably broken, the court shall consider all relevant factors, including the circumstances that gave rise to the filing of the petition and the prospect of reconciliation, and after hearing the evidence shall

(1) Make a finding whether or not the marriage is irretrievably broken, and in order for the court to find that the marriage is irretrievably broken, the petitioner shall satisfy the court of one or more of the following facts:

(a) That the respondent has committed adultery and the petitioner finds it intolerable to live with the respondent;

(b) That the respondent has behaved in such a way that the petitioner cannot reasonably be expected to live with the respondent;

(c) That the respondent has abandoned the petitioner for a continuous period of at least six months preceding the presentation of the petition;

(d) That the parties to the marriage have lived separate and apart by mutual consent for a continuous period of twelve months immediately preceding the filing of the petition;

(e) That the parties to the marriage have lived separate and apart for a continuous period of at least twenty-four months preceding the filing of the petition; or

(2) Continue the matter for further hearing not less than thirty days or more than six months later, or as soon thereafter as the matter may be reached on the court's calendar, and may suggest to the parties that they seek counseling. No court shall require counseling as a condition precedent to a decree, nor shall any employee of any court, or of the state or any political subdivision of the state, be utilized as a marriage counselor. At the adjourned hearing, the court shall make a finding whether the marriage is irretrievably broken as set forth in subdivision (1) above and shall enter an order of dissolution or dismissal accordingly. (L.1973, H.B. No. 315, p. 470, § 5, eff. Jan. 1, 1974. Amended by L.1977, H.B. No. 470, p. 629, § 1.)

In addition to expanding or replacing the substantive grounds for divorce, some states have enacted procedural reforms to make divorce more affordable and accessible to people of all income levels. Although most states still require at least one of the parties to appear before the judge even in uncontested divorce proceedings, *e.g.,* Okla. Stat. tit. 43, § 130 (2001), some states now permit uncontested divorces without a hearing. Colorado, for example, permits final orders of dissolution of marriage to be entered upon the affidavit of either or both parties, if there are no minor children, or if the spouses are both represented by counsel and have entered a separation agreement that provides for the allocation of parental responsibilities and child support. In order for this procedure to be utilized, there must be no marital property to divide, or the spouses must have entered an agreement regarding its disposition. The court may, of course, in its discretion, require a formal hearing. Colo. Rev. Stat. § 14-10-120.3 (2001).

The past decade has seen a counter-movement in the United States to curb the tide of divorces, although there is significant disagreement about the appropriate approach to undertake. Three states, Louisiana in 1997, Arizona in 1998, and Arkansas in 2001, enacted covenant marriage statutes, which give those applying for a marriage license the option to agree to more restrictive grounds for dissolution, should one party later wish to terminate the marriage. Couples entering a covenant marriage must receive premarital counseling. Previously-married couples may also file a declaration to convert their marriages to covenant marriages. In Louisiana, where non-covenant marriages may be dissolved if the spouses have lived apart for 180 days, La. Civ. Code Ann. art. 102 (West 1999), the following statute sets forth the grounds for divorce or legal separation for covenant marriages:

La. Rev. Stat. Ann § 9:307 (West 2000)

A. Notwithstanding any other law to the contrary and subsequent to the parties obtaining counseling, a spouse to a covenant marriage may obtain a judgment of divorce only upon proof of any of the following:

(1) The other spouse has committed adultery.

(2) The other spouse has committed a felony and has been sentenced to death or imprisonment at hard labor.

(3) The other spouse has abandoned the matrimonial domicile for a period of one year and constantly refuses to return.

(4) The other spouse has physically or sexually abused the spouse seeking the divorce or a child of one of the spouses.

(5) The spouses have been living separate and apart continuously without reconciliation for a period of two years.

(6)(a) The spouses have been living separate and apart continuously without reconciliation for a period of one year from the date the judgment of separation from bed and board was signed.

(b) If there is a minor child or children of the marriage, the spouses have been living separate and apart continuously without reconciliation for a period of one year and six months from the date the judgment of separation from bed and board was signed; however, if abuse of a child of the marriage or a child of one of the spouses is the basis for which the judgment of separation from bed and board was obtained, then a judgment of divorce may be obtained if the spouses have been living separate and apart continuously without reconciliation for a period of one year from the date the judgment of separation from bed and board was signed.

B. Notwithstanding any other law to the contrary and subsequent to the parties obtaining counseling, a spouse to a covenant marriage may obtain a judgment of separation from bed and board only upon proof of any of the following:

(1) The other spouse has committed adultery.

(2) The other spouse has committed a felony and has been sentenced to death or imprisonment at hard labor.

(3) The other spouse has abandoned the matrimonial domicile for a period of one year and constantly refuses to return.

(4) The other spouse has physically or sexually abused the spouse seeking the divorce or a child of one of the spouses.

(5) The spouses have been living separate and apart continuously without reconciliation for a period of two years.

(6) On account of habitual intemperance of the other spouse, or excesses, cruel treatment, or outrages of the other spouse, if such habitual intemperance, or such ill-treatment is of such a nature as to render their living together insupportable. Added by Acts 1997, No. 1380, § 4.

Arkansas' statute is very similar. Ark. Code Ann. § 9-11-808 (Michie 2002). Arizona's covenant marriage statute also contains similar grounds, but as an alternative ground permits dissolution of a covenant marriage by mutual consent. Ariz. Rev. Stat. Ann. § 25-903 (West 2000).

The impact of this most recent reform effort, however, may be small. At most, between 1% to 3% of newly-married couples in Louisiana were reported to have chosen the covenant marriage option in the first few years after the law was enacted. *See* Allen M. Parkman, *Reforming Divorce Reform*, 41 Santa Clara L. Rev. 379, 400–01 & n.83 (2001). Divorce reform legislation that would have modified or eliminated no-fault grounds was introduced in at least a dozen other states as well in the late 1990s, but these efforts also have been largely unsuccessful. *Id.* at 398–401. Although several public opinion polls taken in the United States in the late 1990s reported that roughly half of those surveyed suggested that as a general principle divorce should be more difficult to obtain, *see* Lynn D. Wardle, *Divorce Reform at the Turn of the Millennium: Certainties and Possibilities*, 33 Fam. L.Q. 783, 786 (1999), it does not appear that widespread retrenchment of no-fault grounds is on the near horizon.

A more modest approach has been to enact various procedural reforms associated with obtaining a divorce or entering marriage. Some states have recently increased the waiting period after filing to obtain a final decree of divorce. Oklahoma, for example, in 1997 imposed a ninety-day waiting period between filing a divorce petition and the issuance of a final order in cases involving minor children brought on no-fault grounds, although the period can be waived by the court if the parties attend marital counseling. Okla. Stat. tit.12, §107.1 (2001). Florida in 1999 reduced the fee for a marriage license for couples who attend a premarital preparation course. Fla. Stat. Ann. §741.0305 (West Supp. 2002). Such procedural reforms have not, however, made major inroads in the availability of divorce for spouses who seek to end their marriages.

While the second leg of the original reform efforts—the provision of state-sponsored counseling to preserve marriages—involved a commitment the states were unwilling to undertake, recent decades have seen an increase in the utilization of mediation and court-sponsored education programs, particularly involving parenting issues, to assist couples in resolving the parental and financial issues that accompany divorce outside of an adversarial context. Many states now give family court judges the discretion to refer couples to mediation before proceeding with adjudication, particularly when custody or visitation is contested, e.g., Alaska Stat. §25.24.060 (Michie 2000); Iowa Code Ann. §598.41 (West 2001), and some statutes mandate mediation as a first step in resolving those issues. E.g., Cal. Fam Code §3170 (West Supp. 2002); N.C. Gen. Stat. §50-13.1 (2001). Most of these statutes exclude from court-referred mediation those cases in which a party or a child of the parties have been physically or sexually abused by another party. E.g., id.; Minn. Stat. Ann. §518.619 (West Supp. 2002). Court-ordered participation in group parenting education classes is also commonly required for divorcing parents. E.g., Okla. Stat. tit. 12, §107.1 (2001). While these programs do not reduce the incidence of divorce, they are undertaken with the hope of reducing the emotional scarring that often accompanies the adversarial model of dissolution.

Problem 3-1

In each of the following marriages, one or both of the spouses wish to obtain a divorce. As to each, consider whether the party or parties desiring the divorce could obtain it, how long it would take to do so, and under what circumstances, applying the laws as described above in the states of:

(a) Colorado (which has enacted the Uniform Marriage and Divorce Act);

(b) Oklahoma (which has added incompatibility to its traditional fault grounds);

(c) New York;

(d) Missouri; and

(e) Louisiana (assuming a covenant marriage between the parties).

(1) Christy and Sean were married six months ago after a whirlwind college romance. Four months after setting up housekeeping together on campus, they realized this was a big mistake. They both would like a divorce at this time, as quickly as possible, although they wish to remain friends. They have acquired virtually no joint property, other than wedding gifts that they can amicably divide.

(2) Martha and Stuart have been married for fourteen years and are in their mid-thirties. They have two children in elementary school. Martha, a high school graduate, worked as a bookkeeper prior to her pregnancy with their first child twelve years ago, and has been a homemaker since that time. Stuart has completed junior college and works as a salesman for a company manufacturing plumbing supplies. For the past five

years, Stuart has been unhappy in the marriage. The couple occasionally quarreled over minor issues. He left home for a period of one year, during which time he had sexual relationships with a few women, but he then returned to attempt a reconciliation. Six months later he moved out again, and now, after a two-month period apart, he wishes to file for divorce, feeling he simply is not interested in spending time with Martha. He has refused to participate in counseling. Martha very much opposes the divorce and hopes for another reconciliation. She has attended counseling herself, hoping to improve the marriage, but would prefer to attend with Stuart. They own a small home with a mortgage and two small cars.

(3) Bart and Liza have been married for ten years. Bart has assaulted Liza on many occasions, and has twice sent her to the hospital with broken bones. Liza is currently living in the local battered women's shelter with their small child, and has no desire to return to their apartment. She has decided she wants to end the marriage, but Bart refuses to cooperate and wants her to move back in with him.

4) Clyde and Ethel have been married for thirty years. They are in their mid-fifties and their three children are grown. Clyde is an accountant and Ethel, a homemaker when the children were young, has worked in an office for the past ten years since the youngest child graduated from middle school. Ethel has been unhappy in the marriage for many years, but the couple rarely quarrel. Ethel loves playing bridge, and has met George, a widower, in a bridge club through their church. Clyde hates bridge. Ethel has decided she wants to divorce Clyde and begin a new life. She would like to be free to remarry if things work out with George, but that relationship is just a friendship at the moment. Clyde is very opposed to divorce and hopes that through counseling they can work their differences out. Ethel is not interested in counseling and wants the divorce as quickly as possible.

5) Peter and Anna have been married for thirty-five years and are in their late fifties. Anna has been a homemaker throughout the marriage, and their children are grown. Peter moved out one year ago and is living with Paula, whom he wishes to marry. Anna has severe rheumatoid arthritis, which requires expensive medical treatment. Without the treatment she would be severely disabled. Anna currently is able to afford the treatment through health insurance, for which she is eligible as Peter's spouse. Upon divorce, she would be entitled to coverage for a maximum of thirty-six months only if she paid the premiums, which she cannot afford. She also cannot afford, nor even obtain, coverage of her own. Moreover, government health benefits would not cover enough of the costs of her treatments to enable her to afford them. Though Peter works full-time in a warehouse, his income is so low that even if he were forced to pay a substantial portion of it as alimony, it would not be enough to pay for Anna's bare living expenses and the cost of the insurance premiums or the treatments themselves. Anna opposes the divorce.

2. Divorce Reform in England

Prior to 1857, English courts did not have the power to issue decrees of divorce. Ecclesiastical courts, governed by canon law, could grant annulments and decrees of divorce *a mensa et thoro*, a limited divorce that did not afford either spouse the right to remarry. The only route to an absolute divorce that permitted remarriage, instigated around 1700, was to obtain a divorce *a mensa et thoro* from an ecclesiastical court and then a judgment awarding damages for adultery from the common law court, and finally a divorce through private act from Parliament. This costly process was described and satirized in an infamous speech by Judge Maule in *R. v. Hall* when he was sentencing a bigamist in 1845:

Prisoner at the bar, you have been convicted before the court of what the law regards as a very grave and serious offense: That of going through the marriage ceremony a second time while your wife was still alive.... [One] of your irrational excuses is that your wife had committed adultery, and so you thought you were relieved from treating her with any further consideration — but you were mistaken. The law in its wisdom points out a means by which you might rid yourself from further association with a woman..., but you did not think proper to adopt it. I will tell you what that process is. You ought first to have brought an action against your wife's successor, if you could have discovered him; that might have cost you money, and you say you are a poor working man, but that is not the fault of the law. You would then be obliged to prove by evidence your wife's criminality in a Court of Justice, and thus obtain a verdict with damages against the defendant, who was not unlikely to turn out a pauper. But so jealous is the law (which you ought to be aware is the perfection of reason) of the sanctity of the marriage tie, that in accomplishing all this you would only have fulfilled the lighter portion of your duty. You must then have gone, with your verdict in your hand, and petitioned the House of Lords for a divorce. It would cost you perhaps five or six hundred pounds, and you do not seem to be worth that many pence. But it is the boast of the law that it is impartial, and makes no difference between the rich and the poor.... [A]t the end of a year, or possibly two, you might obtain a divorce which would enable you legally to do what you have thought proper to do without it. [The defendant was subsequently sentenced to imprisonment for one day, and released for time served.] R. v. Hall [1845], reprinted in Nicholas Mostyn, 'Justice Must Be Seen To Be Done" — Open Justice and Family Law, 1999 Int'l Fam. L. 80, 82–83.

Further pressure for reform was created by the fact that in Great Britain, Scotland regulates family law matters separately from England and Wales, and in Scotland divorces were available by the early nineteenth century from the Courts of Justice. Englishmen who obtained divorces in Scotland and remarried in England, however, found themselves subject to criminal prosecution in England and possible deportation to Australia for bigamy. Id. at 80.

In 1857, the Court for Divorce and Matrimonial Causes was created, which could grant annulments and decrees of divorce in both England and Wales. Husbands were permitted to divorce their spouses only on the ground of adultery. Wives who wished to divorce their husbands, however, were required to prove both that the husband committed adultery and also that he had committed some other offence, such as desertion or cruelty. It was not until 1923 that adultery alone became the sole ground for divorce when sought by either husbands or wives. In 1937, the grounds were expanded to include cruelty and desertion, as well as the "no-fault" ground of insanity. Gillian Douglas, An Introduction to Family Law 160 (2001).

During the 1960s, amid increasing pressure for liberalized access to divorce, the Archbishop of Canterbury appointed a commission to investigate the issue. Its report was a major catalyst for modern divorce reform in England and Wales, and was influential throughout the Anglo-American legal world. In Putting Asunder; A Divorce Law for Contemporary Society, The Report of a Group Appointed by the Archbishop of Canterbury in January 1964 37, 63–64 (London S.P.C.K. 1966), the commission recommended that the doctrine of marital breakdown replace the fault system and that courts actively evaluate the possibilities of reconciliation in each case:

The law...is moving away from superficiality towards a serious attempt to deal justly both with the complexities of the matrimonial relationship itself and with the interests of other persons upon whom the conduct of the spouses may have impinged. The social context of the family is thus recognized. We therefore recommend that the process be completed as soon as possible by openly substituting the principle of breakdown for the principle of the matrimonial offense.

* * *

...[I]t is implicit in the doctrine of breakdown that a decree of divorce cannot rightly be made while any reasonable hope remains that the parties might be reconciled.... We do not recommend...that the court should be put under obligation to attempt reconciliation itself, or that it should enforce recourse to counselling [since it is rarely effectual if not voluntarily sought], but that it should have a duty to inquire what attempts at reconciliation have been made (unless the nature of the case were such that it would be vain to do so) and the right, if not satisfied that the possibilities of reconciliation had been exhausted, to adjourn the hearing. This, we believe would encourage parties to avail themselves of marriage-guidance counselling or other help before coming to court....

The report was referred to the Law Commission, a law reform organization that had also engaged in extensive study of the matter. The Law Commission issued its own report, *The Field of Choice*, in 1966, which accepted the recommendation of the Archbishop's Commission to substitute marital breakdown for the fault system, but rejected the concept of a thorough inquest by the court into the possibility of reconciliation, finding the proposal too costly and time-consuming. Further discussions between the Archbishop's Group and the Law Commission resulted in the Divorce Reform Act of 1969, now consolidated into the Matrimonial Causes Act 1973, which is the current law in effect in England and Wales.

Under this Act, the only ground for divorce is irretrievable breakdown of the marriage. To avoid the necessity for a detailed inquiry, however, irretrievable breakdown cannot be established unless one of five "facts" are proven.

Matrimonial Causes Act, 1973, c.18 (Eng.)

§ 1. Divorces on Breakdown of Marriage

(1)...[A] petition for divorce may be presented to the court by either party to a marriage on the ground that the marriage has broken down irretrievably.

(2) The court hearing a petition for divorce shall not hold the marriage to have broken down irretrievably unless the petitioner satisfies the court of one or more of the following facts, that is to say—

(a) that the respondent has committed adultery and the petitioner finds it intolerable to live with the respondent;

(b) that the respondent has behaved in such a way that the petitioner cannot reasonably be expected to live with the respondent;

(c) that the respondent has deserted the petitioner for a continuous period of at least two years immediately preceding the presentation of the petition;

(d) that the parties to the marriage have lived apart for a continuous period of at least two years immediately preceding the presentation of the petition...and the respondent consents to a decree being granted;

(e) that the parties to the marriage have lived apart for a continuous period of at least five years immediately preceding the presentation of the petition....

The first three of these "facts" mirror former fault grounds. Petitioners alleging adultery are now required to also prove that living with their spouse is intolerable, so that adultery is cast as a symptom rather than the underlying cause of the breakdown. *See* Douglas, *supra*, at 161. In addition, the adultery need not be the reason that cohabitation is intolerable. *Id.* Nevertheless, the distinction between use of this "fact" and the former fault ground of adultery is probably lost on most spouses. *Id.* at 162. 'Behavior with which a spouse should not reasonably be expected to live' has replaced cruelty, and is measured against an individual standard, taking into account the personalities and circumstances of the individual couple. Though domestic violence and substance abuse might be more obvious examples, the courts have used this "fact" to find breakdown based on a broad range of conduct, including in one case the obsession of a spouse with ineptly undertaking do-it-yourself jobs around the house. *Id.* Desertion requires an unjustifiable separation without the partner's consent. The other two "facts," separation for two years with mutual consent or separation for five years, were intended to assure that divorce would not be undertaken easily, while still obviating the need for an elaborate inquest.

Subsequent sections of the Act impose two additional limitations. A petition for divorce cannot be filed within one year of the date of the marriage. Matrimonial Causes Act, 1973, c. 18, § 3. In addition, a divorce based on five years separation may be denied if the respondent can show that the divorce would cause him or her grave financial or other hardship and that based upon all of the circumstances it would be wrong to dissolve the marriage. Matrimonial Causes Act, 1973, c. 18, § 5. Opposition to divorce on this basis, however, is rarely successful, particularly if there are financial assets or state benefits that can meet the objecting spouse's needs. Douglas, *supra*, at 164.

Procedural changes that took place in the 1970s have had a far more pronounced effect on the accessibility of divorce than revision of the grounds. A "special procedure" was implemented to handle all uncontested divorces, which abolishes the need for a court hearing and permits a district judge in the county court to review the petition and accompanying documents and, if the contents appear satisfactory, certify that petitioner is entitled to a divorce. A decree *nisi prius* is then issued, and an absolute decree may be obtained by the petitioner six weeks thereafter. Thus, unless a spouse decides to challenge the documentation, the veracity of the allegations of the "fact" asserted is not effectively investigated, and the divorce itself becomes essentially an administrative process. *Id.* at 164–65; Andrew Bainham, *Exciting Times in England—Human Rights, Children and Divorce*, 2001 Int'l Fam. L. 71, 74.

One might speculate that in England, as in American states that combine fault and no-fault grounds, divorces requested on the basis of the three fault "facts" would be rare. Because of the lengthy separation periods required for a no-fault divorce, however, around 70% of divorces in England are requested based upon allegations of the fault "facts." These grounds, combined with the "special procedure," permit parties to divorce far more quickly. Divorces based on the two-year separation, when it is used, is usually reserved to upper-income petitioners who can afford to move into separate households for two years before reaching a property settlement in the divorce suit. Approximately 70% of petitioners are women, who frequently require resolution of financial and child care issues quickly, because they often need some form of assistance from their spouse or the state. Douglas, *supra*, at 161, 163.

Although counseling is not required as a prerequisite to obtaining a divorce, the petitioner's solicitor must certify to the court whether the possibility of reconciliation has been discussed with the client and the names of counselors provided. Matrimonial Causes Act, 1973, c. 18, § 6. Whatever effect this requirement has had, it does not appear to have stemmed the tide of divorces. The annual number of divorces has risen from approximately 45,000 per year in 1968 to approximately 140,000 per year in the 1990s. Douglas, *supra*, at 161. By 1999, it was estimated that there were approximately 180,000 divorces per year in England and Wales, of which all but approximately 250 per year were undefended and handled under the "special procedure." Mostyn, *supra*, at 86.

Just as in the United States, the 1990s brought a second wave of divorce reform to England and Wales. In 1990, the Law Commission proposed eliminating fault altogether from the process and replacing it instead with a twelve-month period between the beginning of the process (when the spouses would be given an informational packet regarding sources of support, counseling, mediation, and legal assistance) and the end of the process, the issuance of a final decree. During the twelve months the spouses would not be required to separate. It was suggested that the waiting period would give them the opportunity to contemplate whether they truly wished to end the marriage, and if so, to negotiate financial and parental issues before the final decree, although final resolution of these issues was not a prerequisite for the final decree of divorce under this proposal. *Id.* at 166–67.

The proposal culminated in passage of the Family Law Act of 1996 [hereinafter the 1996 Act], although with some major modifications to the Law Commission's proposal. Some members of Parliament, concerned that deletion of fault and the periods of separation would make divorce too easy, succeeded in amending the proposal to add additional procedural steps. The controversy generated by these amendments, however, and the failure in pilot projects to reap the intended consequence of "saving marriages," resulted in the government delaying implementation and ultimately repealing the Act before it ever took effect. *See id.* at 167, 170–71; Bainham, *supra*, at 75; Steve Doughty, *Killed off at Last; Reforms That Pushed More Couples Into Divorce*, Daily Mail, January 17, 2001, at 6.

As enacted, the 1996 Act would have required at the outset that a spouse contemplating a divorce attend an informational meeting, rather than simply receive a packet of information. The information made available was to relate to the following: the divorce process; the availability of counseling, free of charge if the parties qualified for free legal assistance; the importance of the welfare and wishes of the children; the availability of support services and parenting education to minimize the impact of divorce on the children; financial issues occurring in divorce; the availability of domestic violence protection and assistance; mediation; and access to legal representation, both private and publicly funded. 1996 Act § 8.

Three months after attending the informational meeting, the 1996 Act would have permitted the spouse or spouses who attended the informational meeting to file with the court a statement of marital breakdown. Once this statement had been filed, the court would have had the power to make financial and other orders, and could have required the parties to attend a meeting at which the facilities for mediation would be explained to them and they would be provided an opportunity to agree to mediate. 1996 Act § 13.

Fourteen days after the statement of marital breakdown was filed, a "period of reflection and consideration" was to commence, to permit the parties to "reflect on whether the marriage can be saved and to have an opportunity to effect a reconciliation," and "to consider what arrangements should be made for the future." Normally the period of reflection was to be a minimum of nine months, but it would have been extended to fifteen months if one spouse opposed the divorce and filed for the extension, or if the spouses had a child under the age of sixteen at the time the application for a divorce order would otherwise have been made. This six-month extension would not have applied if a domestic violence order had been issued against the spouse who was not seeking the divorce, or if the spouse seeking the divorce order could show that the delay would harm the welfare of any of the children. The spouses could also have applied to jointly toll the period of reflection for up to eighteen months for an attempted reconciliation, but either party could start it running again by filing notice that the attempted reconciliation was unsuccessful. Actual separation of the parties, however, was not required throughout any of this process. 1996 Act §§ 5, 7.

Once the period of reflection was over, either spouse, regardless of whether he or she was the one who had filed the statement of marital breakdown, could apply for a divorce order. If neither had applied within a year of the end of the reflection period, the statement of breakdown was to have lapsed and the process would have had to begin again. 1996 Act § 5. Before the final order was issued, the applicant normally would have had to prove that the financial issues had been resolved by court order or agreement, although there were a number of exceptions to this requirement. 1996 Act § 9. Parental responsibility issues would not have been required to be resolved prior to issuance of the divorce order. *See* 1996 Act § 11.

In addition to the opportunities to delay the divorce afforded to a spouse who opposes it, the 1996 Act also provided an opportunity to veto the divorce by expanding the rarely utilized grave hardship exception currently in effect under the Matrimonial Causes Act, 1973, c. 18, § 5. Under the 1996 Act, after one spouse made an application for a divorce order at the end of the period of reflection, the other spouse could have applied for an "order preventing divorce," which could be issued if the court was satisfied that the divorce would cause "substantial hardship or other hardship" to the spouse opposing divorce or to a child of the family, and that it would be wrong to grant the divorce under the circumstances, after taking into consideration the conduct of the parties and the interests of the parties' children.

In order to test the waters with this new legislation before implementation of the Act, the Government established several pilot projects that experimented with various formats for the informational meetings. The results surprised proponents of the concept. It was discovered that only a small portion of those who attended the meeting subsequently participated in marriage counseling or mediation. Douglas, *supra*, at 170. Mediation, the research showed, was likely to be used by fewer than 10% of those divorcing. Bainham, *supra*, at 75. In fact, 40% of those surveyed suggested that they were more likely to consult a lawyer as a result of the informational meeting. Douglas, *supra*, at 170. The results of this research played a role in the decision of the Government to repeal the legislation in January 2001.

Problem 3-2

Consider the five couples described in Problem 3-1. As to each, could the party or parties desiring a divorce obtain it, how long would it take to do so, and under what circumstances, (1) under the current divorce law in England, as set forth in the Matrimonial Causes Act, 1973; and (2) under the 1996 Family Law Act, if those provisions had taken effect.

Notes and Questions

1. *Cross-fertilization.* Professor Herma Hill Kay, a member of the California Governor's Commission on the Family in the 1960s, observed that the California Commission's report cited extensively to *Putting Asunder*, the final report of the Archbishop of Canterbury's commission, in support of their own divorce reform proposals, although she notes that the California Commission arrived at their reform proposals independently. Herma Hill Kay, *From the Second Sex to the Joint Venture: An Overview of Women's Rights and Family Law in the United States During the Twentieth Century*, 88 Ca. L. Rev. 2017, 2051 (2000). Anyone who doubts the influence of British reform efforts on the development of American divorce law might examine the Missouri Rev. Stat. §452.320 (enacted in 1973, and amended in 1977) and the Matrimonial Causes Act, 1973, both set forth above. Though not identical, the parallels are striking.

On the other hand, what characteristics of the English divorce process make it operate quite differently? Compare the outcomes for the couples in Problems 3-1 and 3-2 for an illustration of this point.

2. *Critique.* Was the 1996 Family Law Act system for divorce, in your mind, superior or inferior to the system under the Matrimonial Causes Act, 1973, which now remains in effect after the 1996 Act was repealed? What inadequacies, if any, do you think the 1996 Act was designed to eliminate? What shortcomings, if any, did the reform proposal contain? Would the original proposal of the Law Commission in 1990 be preferable? For an excellent critique of the 1996 Act by Professor Gillian Douglas of Cardiff Law School, see her treatise, An Introduction to Family Law 170–71 (2001).

3. *Preserving Social Institutions and Prevailing Societal Norms.* Any observer of the American political scene cannot help but be aware that a major change in divorce regulation, like many other social issues, is a hot-button political issue that is both exploited and feared by politicians. Lawrence Stone, a noted British social and economic historian, observed in 1990 that the relatively few changes in English marriage law from the twelfth century to the current day reflects the perception that the family is the "building block of all other social institutions," and the fear that tampering with its regulation could result in social or political chaos. Mostyn, *supra*, at 80 (quoting The Road to Divorce 15 (1990)).

The notion of preserving "family values," and the quest to define which values that concept should reflect, are no less controversial in Britain than in the United States. Another leading scholar of British family law, Professor Andrew Bainham of the University of Cambridge, attributes the failure of the 1996 reform to the divergence between the vision of family maintained by the political forces in Parliament who sponsored many of the restrictive measures in the 1996 Act and the values of the majority of the British populace. He suggests that "[a] liberal divorce law reflects the view that divorce is an individual entitlement and ought not to be restricted by the state," whereas restrictive divorce legislation is motivated by a desire to promote and preserve marriage "as the only 'legitimate' form of family living and the only one worthy of support." While those who sponsored the more restrictive aspects of the divorce reform, he believes, were opposed both to making divorce easier and to affording equal treatment to those who live in families outside of marriage, the majority of the British populace, he contends, do not share this vision. He observes:

> The British are not actively religious, are marrying in smaller numbers, are divorcing more often and are increasingly living together in stable, often serial unions outside of marriage. The view of divorce held by many in England is

that it is an individual right when a marriage becomes unhappy, that it should be freely available and that it is a private matter into which the state should not intrude. Bainham, *supra*, at 75.

4. *Role of the Courts.* If divorce is a private matter, what is the need for court involvement at all? Professor Douglas observes that public notification of the termination of the legal relationship could be accomplished by a simple registration procedure, as is utilized in countries such as Russia and Japan, and couples would have no need to resort to the courts unless they were unable to resolve a dispute regarding financial matters or parental responsibilities. Douglas, *supra*, at 157. What role, if any, does court supervision of the process play?

5. *Additional Restrictions for Parents.* The 1996 Act would have imposed a substantially longer period of reflection upon parties with children under the age of 16. Would such a scheme invariably be beneficial to children, or are there ways in which it might frequently operate to their disadvantage?

6. *"Marriage Saving" and Mediation.* Were reformers who wished to deter divorces through the informational meetings undercutting their goal by encouraging both counseling and mediation at the same meeting? Professor Bisset-Johnson of Dundee University in Scotland observed in a discussion of the 1996 Act that once the parties reach mediation, the mediator is normally concerned with assisting the spouses in accepting that the marriage is over, and refocusing them from looking backward and attributing blame for the marriage's failure to looking forward to concentrate on building a new life for themselves and their children after the divorce. Alastair Bissett-Johnson, *Parents and Children—A Scottish White Paper on Family Law,* 2001 Int'l Fam.L. 155, 157. Compare Professor Bisset-Johnson's depiction of the approach British mediators have preferred to the description of the role mediators have often traditionally undertaken in China, and until very recently, in Japan, discussed below in Section B.4.b.

3. Divorce Reform in the Republic of Ireland

For many centuries Brehon Law, the legal system created by the Celts, regulated the familial rights of the Irish. Though the rules were not static, and in fact were influenced by the conversion of Ireland to Christianity between the third and fifth centuries, Brehon law for over a millennium permitted both husbands and wives in Ireland to seek a divorce. Even after the Norman invasion of Ireland in the twelfth century, Brehon law still governed the legal affairs of the native Irish. It was not until the English Tudor monarchs gradually re-conquered Ireland throughout the sixteenth century that Brehon law was replaced in Ireland by English law, which permitted spouses to obtain only limited divorces (divorce *a mensa et thoro*) through the ecclesiastical courts.

After absolute divorce became available through a private act of Parliament in England, the Irish Parliament (composed only of members of the Protestant upper class) in the eighteenth century was given a similar power. Up until 1800, when the Irish Parliament voted itself out of existence through the Act of Union, the Irish Parliament passed nine bills of divorce and rejected one. Alan Joseph Shatter, Shatter's Family Law 369 (4th ed. 1997).

Between 1800 and 1922, Ireland was united politically with Britain. Although the Court of Matrimonial Causes was given jurisdiction to grant absolute divorces in England through the Matrimonial Causes Act of 1857, that Act did not apply to Ireland.

Therefore spouses domiciled in Ireland during this period could obtain an absolute divorce only by a private bill of divorce passed by the British Parliament, after obtaining a divorce *a mensa et thoro* from the Irish High Court. *Id.*

When the Republic of Ireland gained its independence from Britain in 1922, its first constitution, the Constitution of the Irish Free State, made no mention of divorce by either the Parliament or the courts. By 1925, three bills for divorce were pending with the Oireachtas, the new Irish Parliament. Amidst heated debate about the stance the new nation should take to divorce law, the Oireachtas quite publicly and explicitly refused to rule on these bills, effectively precluding legislative divorce as an option. *Id.*

In 1937, a new constitution, the Bunreacht na hEireann, or Constitution of Eire, was adopted by constitutional referendum. Its principal drafter, Eamon de Valera, incorporated into the new constitution a vision of the family that reflected the Roman Catholic mores he and the majority of the population embraced. As one scholar observed:

> Catholicism had become for the colonially oppressed Irish a force with mythic impact and had created in the Irish mind a "Holy Ireland"; after independence from England, the priests and laymen who ran the Catholic Church turned their energies, formerly dispensed on the fight for social and religious rights for Catholics in a Protestant world, inward to the delineation and monitoring of proper social conduct, as norms for living in the new state were being formed.

Christine P. James, *Cead Mile Failte? Ireland Welcomes Divorce: The 1995 Irish Divorce Referendum and the Family (Divorce) Act of 1996*, 8 Duke J. Comp. & Int'l L. 175, 177 (1997).

Article 41 of the 1937 Constitution afforded the family unit and the institution of marriage explicit constitutional protection and prohibited the enactment of laws providing for dissolution of marriage. Over the ensuing decades, the provision drew resentment from the non-Roman Catholic minority. Critics also observed that in some cases the constitutional prohibition of divorce was even more restrictive than Roman Catholic canon law, which itself permitted dissolution of marriage in very limited circumstances. Shatter, *supra*, at 372, n.17 and accompanying text.

In 1967, an all-party committee composed of members of the Dail (the body in the Irish legislature similar to the U.S. House of Representatives) recommended a constitutional amendment that would have prohibited dissolution of a marriage of a person married in accordance with the right of a religion on any ground "other than those acceptable to that religion." The Committee stated that the provision would be drafted so as to preclude changing from one religion to another in order to take advantage of "a more liberal divorce regime." The proposal was opposed by both Catholic and Anglican Irish Archbishops and was never put to a referendum. *Id.* at 373–74.

In 1985, however, a Joint Oireachtas Committee, composed of members of both the Dail and the Seanad (the other body in the Irish Legislature) published a report calling for a constitutional referendum on divorce. Though the Committee took no position on the issue of whether divorce legislation was desirable, it summarized the arguments of the opponents and proponents of such an amendment. Among those arguments recorded favoring retention of the divorce prohibition were the following:

(1) Divorce was contrary to the religious tenets of the Roman Catholic Church, of which the majority of the population were members.

(2) Spouses would put less effort into resolving marital difficulties, leading to an increased incidence of marital breakdown.

(3) Marriages and family would be undermined by the perception of marriage as a temporary institution, and society would be destabilized.

(4) More children would be damaged by parental divorce.

(5) The increased expenses resulting from two households instead of one would create financial hardship for women and children.

Arguments recorded in favor of reform included the following:

(1) With the exception of the Mormons, members and leaders of all other religions in the nation favored the amendment, perceiving the prohibition as imposing Catholic regulation and discriminating against members of other denominations and those with no religious affiliation.

(2) Marital breakdown occurred regardless of the constitutional ban on divorce, and was on the increase. Divorce was not the cause of that phenomena, but merely recognized it, giving the parties the freedom to remarry.

(3) Victims of domestic violence, in particular, deserved the right to remarry.

(4) It was marital breakdown, and not divorce, that caused financial hardship and adversely affected children, and these harms can sometimes be eased when a new family unit can be formed.

(5) Spouses who had separated were in fact entering new relationships, and their inability to obtain legal recognition for those relationships left the partners in the new relationships unprotected, rendered children in the new relationships illegitimate, and prevented the parties from entitlement to tax and social welfare benefits. Id.

A year after issuance of the report, following a bitter and divisive debate, an amendment to the Constitution permitting divorce was submitted for public vote. In June 1986, the amendment was defeated, with 63% of those voting rejecting the proposal, despite the fact that recent public opinion polls had indicated 61% of the public favored some type of divorce reform. Id. at 375–83; James, *supra*, at 193.

Almost a decade passed before another referendum on divorce was submitted to the Irish populace. This time, rather than remain neutral, leaders in all Irish political parties favored the reform, and the Government issued a report strongly supporting the amendment. Moreover, in the intervening decade, legislation regulating property division and other ancillary issues had been passed, which eliminated some anxiety about how these collateral issues might be resolved. In November 1995, the amendment to permit divorce passed by a slim margin of only 0.6%. James, *supra*, at 208–14.

As amended, Article 41 of the Bunreacht na hEireann, the Constitution of Ireland, now provides:

Article 41 — The Family

1.1 The State recognises the Family as the natural primary and fundamental unit group of Society, and as a moral institution possessing inalienable and imprescriptible rights, antecedent and superior to all positive law.

1.2 The State, therefore, guarantees to protect the Family in its constitution and authority, as the necessary basis of social order and as indispensable to the welfare of the Nation and the State.

2.1 In particular, the State recognises that by her life within the home, woman gives to the State a support without which the common good cannot be achieved.

2.2 The State shall, therefore, endeavour to ensure that mothers shall not be obliged by economic necessity to engage in labour to the neglect of their duties in the home.

3.1 The State pledges itself to guard with special care the institution of Marriage, on which the Family is founded, and to protect it against attack.

3.2 A Court designated by law may grant a dissolution of marriage where, but only where, it is satisfied that—

    i.   at the date of the institution of the proceedings, the spouses have lived apart from one another for a period of, or periods amounting to, at least four years during the previous five years.

    ii. there is no reasonable prospect of a reconciliation between the spouses;

    iii. such provision as the court considers proper having regard to the cirumstances exists or will be made for the spouses, any children of either or both of them and any other person prescribed by law, and

    iv. any further conditions prescribed by law are complied with.

3.3 No person whose marriage has been dissolved under the civil law of any other State but is a subsisting valid marriage under the law for the time being in force within the jurisdiction of the Government and Parliament established by this Constitution shall be capable of contracting a valid marriage within that jurisdiction during the lifetime of the other party to the marriage so dissolved.

Subsequently the Family Law (Divorce) Act of 1996 was passed, incorporating in §5 virtually verbatim the grounds for divorce set forth in Subsections i, ii, and iii of Section 3.2 of Article 41. To facilitate reconciliations where possible, the Divorce Act also requires solicitors, prior to institution of the proceeding, to discuss with clients applying for divorce: (1) the possibility of reconciliation, providing the names of counselors; (2) the possibility of mediation, providing the names of mediators; (3) the possibility of entering a separation agreement; and (4) the possibility of obtaining a judicial separation instead of a divorce. Certification of these discussions must be provided to the court, and served on the other spouse with the other pleadings. Family Law (Divorce) Act of 1996 §6. Solicitors representing respondents must certify that they engaged in the same discussions with their clients when they enter an appearance in the case. *Id.* at §7.

Because living apart for four out of the previous five years is essentially the only "ground" for a divorce, the meaning of "living apart" becomes crucial. In 1998, the Irish High Court, which has original jurisdiction over divorce proceedings, had occasion to further interpret the phrase "living apart," relying in part on English cases defining that concept.

McA v. McA

1 I.R. 457 (Ir. H. Ct. 2000), *available at*
http://www.ucc.ie/law/ir/irlii/cases/89m_98.htm

McCracken, J.

[Ed. Note: After over thirty years of marriage, the wife in 1999 filed for a Decree of Judicial Separation and ancillary orders relating to property division and maintenance (alimony). The husband counterclaimed for a Decree of Divorce, which the wife contested. Both parties agreed that the relationship had irretrievably broken down. At the time of the Application both children of the marriage were adults.]

* * *

...[T]he only issue which I have to decide [regarding issuance of the divorce decree] is whether the spouses have *"lived apart from one another"* for the relevant period or periods.

In 1988, the Applicant discovered that the Respondent was carrying on an affair with another lady and sometime about September 1988, having been confronted with his wife's knowledge of the affair, the Respondent left the family home and continued to conduct his affair with this lady.... Respondent...continued to reside in the family home with the two children.

In 1991 the Respondent ended his relationship and returned to live in the family home. The Applicant has said in evidence that she was glad to have him come back, because she had never really accepted that the marriage had ended, but the Respondent maintains that his primary motive for returning was that he wanted to develop a better relationship with his son, who was then just eighteen. I accept that at this time, that is in 1991, the Applicant certainly hoped that some form of normality could be achieved in the marriage. I think the Respondent did not have any such expectations, even at that stage.

There is some conflict in the evidence as to the relationship between the parties over the next few years. The parties slept in separate bedrooms and never resumed sexual relations. They did on several occasions go away on holidays with the children, but again slept in separate bedrooms while on holiday. When they were in the house together they appear to have had what might be called a civilised relationship, in that they were polite to each other and if both were present at meal times would take their meals together. When he was at home, the Respondent would tend to go to bed, or at least to his room, early and watch television and he had a separate telephone line installed into his room.

...It may be of some relevance that, following the return of the Respondent in 1991, he agreed to pay the Applicant a sum of £750 per month in cash, which sum was later increased to £1,000 per month, and her car and all motoring expenses were paid out of the Respondent's business. [Appellant was paid wages for running a shop, as part of Respondent's business, and it is not clear if the court's reference to the payments here is in addition to those wages, or a part of them. Ed.]

In 1995, while the parties were still living in the same house, the Applicant entered into a relationship, including a sexual relationship, with another gentleman and in 1996 the Respondent entered into a relationship with a lady with whom he is now living. On the evidence it seems that at the time neither of them was fully aware of the extent of the other's relationships, but undoubtedly such relationships did exist.

* * *

[The English cases reviewed by the court suggest] that the intention of the parties is a very relevant matter in determining issues such as whether [spouses] live apart....

...[I]n my view the whole purpose of the provision in section 5(1)(a) of the 1996 Act to the effect that the parties must have lived apart from one another for at least four years during the previous five years is to allow for the situation where the parties may come together for a short time in an attempt to become reconciled, and indeed has been inserted to encourage possible reconciliation. The fact that the section in effect allows the parties to live together for one year out of five and then separate again without affecting the rights under the section, seems to me to make it quite clear that it was the view of the Legislature that it was necessary to make such provision as otherwise parties who attempted but did not attain reconciliation would not be able to avail of the Act if they lived together for a short time during the preceding five years. . . .

It must be born in mind that the right to a divorce in this country is a constitutional right arising under Article 41.3.2 of the Constitution, and that the 1996 Act sets out the circumstances under which such constitutional right may be exercised. In construing the Act the court must have regard to the context in which words are used, namely the termination of a matrimonial relationship. Marriage is not primarily concerned with where the spouses live or whether they live under the same roof, and indeed there can be a number of circumstances in which the matrimonial relationship continues even though the parties are not living under the same roof as, for example, where one party is in hospital or an institution of some kind, or is obliged to spend a great deal of time away from home in the course of his or her employment. Such separations do not necessarily constitute the persons as living apart from one another. Clearly there must be something more than mere physical separation and the mental or intellectual attitude of the parties is also of considerable relevance. I do not think one can look solely either at where the parties physically reside, or at their mental or intellectual attitude to the marriage. Both of these elements must be considered, and in conjunction with each other.

Applying this test, I have no doubt that, just as parties who are physically separated may in fact maintain their full matrimonial relationship, equally parties who live under the same roof may be living apart from one another. Whether this is so is a matter which can only be determined in the light of the facts of any particular case.

. . . {T]here is some conflict between the parties as to the extent of the relationship between them between 1991 and 1997. The Respondent categorized his bedroom as his apartment, and said that it was his habit to go to bed early and watch television in the bedroom and that normally he went away at weekends unless the children were at home, and that he would be away for three weekends out of four. He further said that he would only see the Applicant for two or three hours in any one week and that he felt like a lodger in the house. On the other hand it is quite clear that when the children were in the house, he took a full part in the household arrangements, and on a number of occasions went on holidays with the Applicant and the children.

Having heard both parties give evidence, I am satisfied that the Respondent did not return with any intention of resuming a normal matrimonial relationship. . . . I have no doubt equally that the Applicant did not want the marriage to be at an end. . . . Marriage involves mutuality, and it is my view on the evidence that when Respondent returned in 1991 he did not intend to return to a marriage, but rather that he wanted to have a better relationship with his children. . . . [A]s the phrase "living apart from one another" is used in the context of a marriage, I think the Respondent never intended to live other than apart from the Applicant.

. . . [I]n the circumstances of this case I am in fact concerned with the four years preceding [the institution of divorce proceedings, August 16th, 1999.] It is not in dispute that in 1995 the Applicant formed a relationship, including a sexual relationship, with another gentleman without the knowledge of the Respondent. In my view the existence of this relationship is evidence of the mental attitude of the Applicant to the marriage in 1995. Whatever she may have hoped for in 1991 when the Respondent returned, quite clearly by 1995 she was aware that for all intents and purposes the marriage was at an end, there had been no sexual relations for many years and she, perhaps understandably, was prepared to form a relationship with another person. If I consider the mental and intellectual attitude of the parties, therefore, I am satisfied that the Respondent never considered himself to be living together with the Applicant in a marriage, and that certainly in the last four years of the marriage the Applicant did not consider herself to be living together with the Respondent in that same sense. Accordingly, I am of the view that the Respondent has satisfied the conditions set out in Section 5 of the 1996 Act and I would propose to grant a Decree of Divorce.

Problem 3-3

How would the spouses seeking dissolution of the five marriages described in Problem 3-1 fare in the Republic of Ireland under current law?

Notes and Questions

1. *Fault v. No-Fault Grounds.* The previous three subsections trace the evolution of divorce reform in the United States, England, and the Republic of Ireland, three predominantly English-speaking nations with a common legal heritage and, at least in recent decades, similar—though not identical—social, political, and economic systems. While there are strong similarities in their current divorce systems, there are substantial differences as well, as you have undoubtedly observed in considering the first three Problems. Based upon your reading in Chapter 2, the above sections, and your own general knowledge of the historic, socio-economic, and cultural forces that may have impacted the evolution of divorce reform in these three nations, which factors do you think played a significant role in the relative willingness or unwillingness of each nation to facilitate access to dissolution of marriage, and the grounds each chose to utilize?

2. *Living Apart.* One might think that one benefit of using a period of living apart as a ground for divorce is that it would be a relatively straightforward, black-and-white rule that would generate little litigation. What is the standard fashioned by Justice McCracken for living apart? Is it an objective test, a subjective test, or does it have elements of both? What are the benefits and deficiencies of using a test of this nature? What do you think should be the core characteristics that define a relationship as "marital"? For an interesting discussion of the factors that should be considered in construing "living apart," see Frank Martin, *"Living Apart" in Divorce Law*, 2 Irish J. Fam. L. 66 (2000); Frank Martin, *"To Live Apart or Not to Live Apart"; That is the Divorce Question*, 2 Irish J. Fam. L. 2 (2000).

"Living apart" for a year has also been a ground for judicial separation in Ireland since passage of the 1989 Judicial Separation and Family Law Reform Act. Due to the existence of other grounds for judicial separation, however, it was rarely utilized or litigated under that Act. Section 2(3)(a) of the Judicial Separation Act defines "living apart" as living in separate households. No similar definition, nor any definition at all, was provided for "living apart" in the 1996 Divorce Act, and *Mc A* is the first published case to discuss the criteria for living apart under this Act. In the three years under the new Divorce Act prior to the *McA* decision, most divorce proceedings filed were reported to be uncontested. Frank Martin, *'Living Apart ' in Irish Divorce Law*, 2 Irish J. Fam. L. 66 (2000).

3. *Constitutional Regulation of Divorce*

a. *Implications of Constitutional Regulation.* Although the U.S. Constitution impacts family law regulation in a number of ways, particularly through the Equal Protection and Due Process Clauses and the First Amendment, it does not specifically address familial rights and obligations in its text. In the U.S. federal system, the power to regulate family law matters has largely been reserved to the states, and state governments have also generally chosen to regulate such issues through legislation rather than their state constitutions. Consider the treatment afforded the family under Article 41 of the Irish Constitution. What are the benefits and potential drawbacks of specifically regulating familial rights and divorce through a constitutional provision?

b. Is Divorce a Constitutional Right? Prior to the 1995 constitutional amendment, the 1937 Constitution of Ireland (Bunreacht na hEireann) prohibited the enactment of laws providing for divorce. Did the new Section 3.2 of Article 41, set forth above, make divorce constitutionally permissible, or, as Justice McCracken suggests, did it create a constitutional right to divorce?

In the United States, state governments have been free to choose whether, and under what circumstances, marriages may be terminated through divorce, provided that they do so in a manner that does not violate due process or equal protection. In *Sosna v. Iowa*, 419 U.S. 393, 404 (1975), the U.S. Supreme Court reaffirmed in dicta that a state has an "absolute right to prescribe the conditions upon which the marriage relation between its own citizens shall be created, and the causes for which it may be dissolved." The Federal Constitution has never been interpreted by the Court to require a state to permit divorce. When a state does provide a judicial mechanism for termination of marriages, however, the Court has held that due process prohibits a state from denying access to the courts to plaintiffs who wish to file divorces but are unable to afford the filing fees, reasoning that resort to the judicial process is the "exclusive precondition to the adjustment of a fundamental human relationship." Boddie v. Connecticut, 401 U.S. 371, 383 (1971).

Compare this approach with the ruling of the High Court of the State of Kerala in India, which in 1995 declared the provisions of the Christian Divorce Act of 1825 unconstitutional. As recently as the mid-1990s, this Act was being applied to permit men to divorce only on grounds of adultery, and to permit women to divorce only if they could prove both adultery and desertion or cruelty. Martha Nessbaum, *India: Implementing Sex Equality Through Law*, 2 Chi. J. Int'l L. 35, 42 (2001). In *Ammini Ej v. UOI*, 82 AIR Ker 252 (1995), the Kerala High Court ruled:

> The life of a Christian wife who is compelled to live against her will, though in name only, as the wife of a man who hates her, has cruelly treated her and deserted her, putting an end to the matrimonial relation irreversibly, will be a sub-human life without dignity and personal liberty. It will be a humiliating and oppressed life, without the freedom to remarry and enjoy life in the normal course. It will be a life without the freedom to uphold the dignity of the individual in all respects as ensured by the Constitution of India in the Preamble and Article 21. [The law is] highly harsh and oppressive and as such arbitrary and violative of Article 14. (*as quoted in* Nessbaum, *supra,* at 42).

4. *Is Divorce a Human Right under International Conventions?* In Europe, the European Convention on Human Rights guarantees certain civil liberties, and authorizes the European Court of Human Rights to grant monetary damages to individuals whose rights under the Convention have been violated by the actions of contracting nations. (See Chapter 1, Section B.2.d. for more detailed information on the European Convention on Human Rights and the European Court of Human Rights.) The Republic of Ireland is a member of the Council of Europe, and a party to the European Convention on Human Rights. Prior to the constitutional referendum amending Article 41 of the Constitution of Ireland, a challenge to Ireland's constitutional prohibition of divorce was lodged in the

European Court of Human Rights by three applicants: Roy Johnston, an Irish citizen who was separated from his wife by mutual consent; Janice Williams-Johnston, the woman with whom Mr. Johnston cohabited and wished to marry; and their daughter, Nessa.

In Johnston v. Ireland, 112 Eur. Ct. H. R. (1987), the Court rejected the contention of the first two applicants that Ireland's prohibition of divorce violated their right under Article 12 of the Convention to marry in accordance with the national laws, finding that Article 12 creates no right to divorce. Similarly, affording Ireland a "wide margin of appreciation," the Court determined that the right to respect for family life under Article 8 did not impose upon Ireland the obligation to permit divorce and remarriage, nor did it require that cohabitants who could not legally marry must be afforded the same familial rights under the law to which married couples are entitled. The applicants also argued that they were victims of financial discrimination in violation of Article 14, because Ireland recognized divorces obtained abroad by those who could afford to establish domicile in a nation permitting divorce. The Court rejected this contention as well, finding that applicants were not in an analogous situation to those domiciled abroad. The Court also determined that the right to freedom of thought, conscience, and religion guaranteed by Article 9 did not create a right to divorce, despite Mr. Johnston's contention that his inability to live with Ms. Williams-Johnston other than in an extra-marital relationship offended his conscience and discriminated against him on the basis of conscience and religion. Citing Marckx v. Belgium, 31 Eur. Ct. H. R. (1979) (see Chapter 1, Section A.2.), the Court held that respect for the familial rights of the third applicant, Nessa, under Article 8 required that "she be placed, legally and socially, in a position akin to that of a legitimate child," but that this finding did not require that Ireland permit divorce and remarriage.

Although the European Convention on Human Rights is a regional convention, many of the rights unsuccessfully invoked by the Johnstons to challenge Ireland's former ban on divorce are also recognized in global human rights conventions, such as the International Covenant on Civil and Political Rights (ICCPR), although the availability of enforcement remedies to individuals under those treaties is far more limited. (See Chapter One, Sections B.1.d., note 2, and B.2.a. for a discussion of the ICCPR and enforcement mechanisms for U.N. human rights conventions).

5. *Alternatives to Divorce.* The absence of divorce from a legal system often creates pressure for other legal mechanisms to accommodate the needs of separating spouses. In Chapter Two you read about the use of annulment under canon law and civil law as a method to enforce norms regulating the entry into marriage. Annulments also can operate as an escape valve in systems in which divorce is not possible. Prior to passage of the constitutional amendment and Family (Divorce) Act of 1996, the only alternatives available for Irish citizens desiring to terminate their marriage were (1) for at least one spouse to establish domicile in a foreign country and obtain a divorce, which Irish courts would recognize under the Domicile and Recognition of Foreign Divorces Act 1986, §5, or (2) to obtain a decree of nullity. Irish legal scholar Kieron Wood observed that in the decade and a half prior to implementation of the 1996 Act, the number of civil annulments granted by the Irish courts was steadily rising and nullity jurisprudence was developing at a rapid pace. Eight decrees of nullity were granted in 1981, but by 1993 the courts issued 45 per year. Kieran Wood, *Nullity and Divorce—The New Alternatives?*, 2 Irish J. Fam. L. 12 (1999). During the 1980s and early 1990s, Irish courts applied an increasingly broad interpretation to the grounds for annulment. *See* Paul Ward, *Defective Knowledge: A New Ground for Nullity, in* 1996 The International Survey of Family Law 215 (Andrew Bainham ed., 1998). Although in the first few years after implementation of the divorce legislation, the number of nullity decrees issued re-

mained over fifty per year, the number of applications dropped from eighty-four in 1995/96 to just twenty during the year after the divorce legislation became effective. Kieran Wood, *supra,* at 12.

The other mechanism available to Irish spouses prior to implementation of the Divorce Act of 1996 was to obtain a Decree of Judicial Separation, which extinguishes the legal obligation of spouses to live together. Although such a decree did not enable spouses to remarry, it did provide a mechanism to resolve property, support, and custody issues following the separation. Even after implementation of the Divorce Act, the ability to obtain such a decree, or a deed of separation for those couples who can resolve financial and custody issues without court intervention, provides a method for resolution of financial and parental issues during the four year separation prior to eligibility for divorce proceedings. *See generally* Shatter, *supra,* at 337–68.

6. *Impact of Reform.* Though the press reported that in November 1996, over 60,000 people in Ireland had already been separated for the requisite four years, the anticipated flood of divorce actions never occurred. During the first three full years of operation for which statistics are available, 1998, 1999, and 2000, fewer than 3,400 applications for divorce were received by the courts each year, and this annual rate appeared to have stabilized. Irish barristers and solicitors suggest that many couples had settled their affairs through a decree of judicial separation, and if they had no wish to remarry, felt no need to divorce. Many also may be reluctant to disturb the status quo, as a divorce proceeding would instigate re-examination of their financial arrangements, and might prompt increased maintenance payments or redistribution of property acquired since the separation. Even uncontested divorces typically entail solicitors fees of well over a thousand dollars, and Legal Aid assistance for lower income people often requires lengthy delays of up to fifteen months just to obtain an appointment. Moreover, the social acceptance of second, cohabiting families that developed in the pre-divorce era, and the absence of a divorce culture, have been suggested as further explanations for the failure of many long-separated couples to take advantage of the new law. Jenny Burley & Francis Regan, *Divorce in Ireland: The Fear, The Floodgates, and the Reality,* 16 Int'l J. L. Pol. & Fam. 202, 214–19 (2002).

7. *Financial Consequences.* A society's view of marriage is reflected not only in the degree of restriction it incorporates into its divorce laws, but also in the provisions it creates to regulate the financial consequences after divorce. Although comprehensive treatment of the financial consequences of divorce in the United States, England, and the Republic of Ireland is beyond the scope of this chapter, it is interesting to observe that Ireland's courts have interpreted the new divorce statute to reject what academics often refer to as a "clean break" divorce. Not only can an obligation to pay spousal support be imposed upon one spouse until the death of either spouse and be subject to post-decree amendment, as is true in most U.S. states, but in some circumstances property division awards can be amended subsequent to the final allocation. In addition, one party may apply to the court for additional financial relief after the death of his or her former spouse, to be paid from the estate. The fact that the Family Law (Divorce) Act 1996 specifically permits application to the courts for ancillary relief during the lifetime of the other spouse has persuaded jurists that they should award maintenance and a lower property division, even when spouses have substantial property that could be divided in a way that would provide both spouses independent financial security and terminate future financial obligations. Rejection of the clean break approach has been attributed to the Irish tradition that a marriage entails a life-long obligation, as well as to the need to meet the criticism of opponents of the 1995 divorce referendum who pointed to the adverse consequences following divorce for women and children in the United States. It is

also influenced by the significant portion of wives in Ireland that still occupy the full-time role of homemaker. The courts have also observed the interest of the state in not assuming the burden of support for financially vulnerable ex-spouses. Frank Martin, *From Prohibition to Approval: the Limitations of the "No Clean Break" Divorce Regime in the Republic of Ireland*, 16 Int'l J.L. Pol. & Fam. 223, 229–43, 246–48 (2002).

It is interesting to contrast the Irish approach to post-divorce financial obligations with the Swedish approach. As described below, Swedish law makes access to divorce very easy. Swedish academics observe that "[t]he issue of the incontestable right to obtain a divorce is also related to the standing of the spouses as individuals and as an economic unit. Swedish law assumes as the principal rule that each spouse will support him- or herself after the divorce." Michael Bogdan & Eva Ryerstedt, *Marriage in Swedish Family Law and Swedish Conflicts of Law*, 29 Fam. L.Q. 675, 679 (1995). Alimony, other than a transitional award when needed, is described as very rare. Sweden also has a high percentage of wives employed outside of the home, and an extensive social services system. *Id.* at 679. (More on the social and economic system in Sweden can be found in Chapter 9, The Financial Support of Children.)

4. A Glimpse of Divorce Reform around Europe—and around the World

a. *Western Europe*

The past four decades have witnessed a liberalization of divorce law in most of the countries of Western Europe, generally moving, as did the United States and Britain, from legal regimes that primarily permitted the termination of marriage only for serious fault grounds to the recognition or expansion of nonfault grounds and the introduction or expansion of divorce by mutual consent. Mary Ann Glendon, The Transformation of Family Law 149 (1989). This phenomenon occurred not only in historically Protestant nations, but also in nations such as France, Italy, and Spain, whose populations are predominantly Roman Catholic. *Id.* Though divorce by mutual consent is now widely accepted, these nations varied in the degree to which they embraced unilateral divorce.

France, for example, in 1975 replaced its ninety-two year old divorce law permitting divorce only on grounds of adultery, criminal conviction, and grave violation of marital duties, with a new scheme permitting the following: two forms of divorce by mutual consent; divorce based upon reformulated fault grounds; divorce based upon mental illness; and divorce based upon a "prolonged disruption of the life in common," the French formulation for irreconcilable differences, combined with a separation of six years. While this last basis permits unilateral divorce, it typically carries greater economic disadvantages for a plaintiff when the divorce is opposed, and can also be thwarted by a judicial finding of hardship. *See* Glendon, *supra*, at 159–68. Moreover, French judges, particularly in rural areas, have applied the hardship exception more liberally than have the English, who construe hardship in purely economic terms. The French hardship exception affords judges discretion to deny the divorce if it would impose "material or moral consequences of exceptional hardship" for the objecting spouse or the children, which would include mental or physical hardship, and has been exercised when it appears to the court that granting the divorce would "in all the circumstances be wrong." *Id.* at 172, 168. Given the difficulties and lengthy separation required by the "prolonged disruption" ground, only a small percentage of divorces (estimated by Professor Glendon at 1%) are sought on this ground. *Id.* at 171. Regardless of which method of divorce is pursued, however, the process is fairly complex and involves multiple court appearances, so that even divorces by mutual consent are rarely terminated in less than a year. *Id.* at 165–72.

Italy has also been slow to embrace unilateral divorce. Divorce was not available at all in modern Italy until 1970, following a referendum, and the law was again modified in 1978 and 1987. Divorce cannot be obtained until three years after legal separation, which can occur through an agreement between the spouses ratified by a judge, or on the petition of one spouse when there is sufficient cause to discontinue the cohabitation (sometimes translated as intolerability of cohabitation) or reasons that would affect the children, a ground rarely, if ever, used. These grounds are subject to case-by-case interpretation, but in reality reliance upon intolerability of cohabitation is successful in over 99% of the cases in which it is asserted. Roberta Ceschini, *International Marriage and Divorce Regulations and Recognition in Italy*, 29 Fam. L.Q. 560, 568–70 (1995); Leonardo Lenti, *Recent Changes in the Judge-Made Law of Separation and Divorce and Perspectives on Law Reform, in* The International Survey of Family Law 207, 209–11 (Andrew Bainham ed., 2002). Both separation by agreement and judicial separation require a court to convene a hearing to attempt a reconciliation, however, before any order can be issued. Three years later, if a petition for divorce is then filed, another hearing to attempt reconciliation must be convened. Ceschini, *supra,* at 569–70. A period of reconciliation between the spouses that interrupts the initial separation starts the three-year waiting period running again. Andrea Russo & Robert Rains, *The Reform of the Italian System of Private International Law with Particular Regard to Domestic Relations Issues*, 25 N.C. J. Int'l L. & Com. Reg. 271, 284 (2000). Divorces can be obtained without satisfying the legal separation requirement only in special circumstances, such as a spouse being convicted of a serious crime or undergoing sex change surgery, Ceschini, *supra,* at 571, but these grounds account for fewer than 2% of all Italian divorces. Lenti, *supra,* at 207.

West Germany also liberalized its divorce law in the mid-1970s. A system of divorce exclusively upon fault grounds or insanity had actually been revised by the Nazis in 1938. The Nazis in fact desired to have only one ground for divorce—marital breakdown—in order to dispose of marriages that had lost their value to the "Volksgemeinschaft," the "community of all racially pure Germans." Glendon, *supra,* at 175. Recognizing that such a radical change would not be immediately accepted, however, they instead added breakdown combined with a period of three years separation as a ground for divorce, as well as new fault grounds, such as "unreasonable refusal to beget offspring." When the 1938 law came under review by the Allied Control Council in 1946 following the war, the Council eliminated its racial and eugenic aspects, such as the fault ground of refusal to beget offspring, but retained the breakdown ground, largely at the urging of an American member of the Committee who convinced his European colleagues that breakdown was not a concept tainted by Nazi ideals. The State of Louisiana at the time already permitted no-fault divorce following a three-year separation, he noted, and that state was certainly not influenced by Nazi agendas. The 1938 breakdown ground, with a hardship exception added by the Allied Council, was therefore in place even prior to the 1976 revision of German divorce law. By the late 1960s, however, its use had dwindled so that it accounted for fewer than 5% of all divorces, the West German populace preferring to agree to consensual divorces on fault grounds rather than waiting the three years. *Id.* at 175–77.

In 1976, the West German government eliminated all fault grounds. A single ground, *Scheitern,* the foundering or failure of the marriage, is conclusively presumed if both spouses consent to divorce and have lived apart for one year, or if they have lived apart for three years despite the absence of mutual consent. By statute, living apart was defined as the absence of household community between the spouses, combined with the rejection of the marital community of life by at least one spouse, which can occur even if both are residing in the marital dwelling. A hardship exception for children and opposing spouses in extraordinary circumstances was retained, and an attempt to revoke the hardship exception in 1980 was held unconstitutional by the West German Federal Constitutional Court, on the basis of a provision specifying that: "Marriage and the family are under the special protection of the state." Nevertheless, in Germany divorces are almost never denied based on the hardship exception. *Id.* at 178–81.

Sweden's divorce reform in the late 1960s and early 1970s was one of the most far-reaching in Europe in terms of its acceptance of simplified divorce procedure and unilateral divorce. Swedish family law scholars Michael Bogdan and Eva Ryerstedt have described Sweden's divorce system and its rationale:

> The only requirement for a divorce is that one of the spouses has a desire to withdraw from the marriage. Marriage is considered to be a voluntary union. Therefore, it is only natural that if one of the spouses is dissatisfied, he or she may demand a divorce. The existence of guilt or fault no longer has any significance in Swedish marital law. Furthermore, when courts pronounce divorces, they do not inquire about the reasons for the application.

* * *

> If only one of the spouses wishes to obtain a divorce, or if there is a child younger than sixteen years of age, a mandatory reconsideration period of six months is required before the marriage can be dissolved. That is also the case if both spouses request a reconsideration period. In case of bigamy, an incestuous marriage, or if the couple has been separated for at least two years, the requirement of a reconsideration period does not apply.

Michael Bogdan & Eva Ryrstedt, *Marriage in Swedish Family Law and Swedish Conflicts of Law,* 29 Fam. L.Q. 675, 678 (1995). Spouses are not required to live apart during the period of reflection. If there are no children or stepchildren under the age of sixteen and both spouses desire the divorce, they can obtain an immediate divorce. The former requirement of a year of living apart was abolished, as was a requirement for compulsory mediation, although voluntary mediation is still available. Ake Lögdberg, *The Reform of Family Law in the Scandinavian Countries, in* The Reform of Family Law in Europe 201, 202–03 (A.G. Chloros ed., 1978).

Another reason proffered for easing access to unilateral divorce in Sweden was the increasing competition the institution of marriage was facing from the rising rate of cohabitation among couples, many of whom were raising families. Between 1960 and 1971 the number of out-of-wedlock children born each year almost doubled to over 21%, and approximately two-thirds of the mothers of these children were cohabiting with the father. Given the relative ease with which cohabitants can separate, the desire to minimize disincentives to marry, as well as the philosophy prevalent in Sweden that "similar social situations should be treated equally," inspired the liberal reform of Swedish divorce law. *Id.* at 202, 204.

At the other end of the divorce spectrum in Europe is Malta, a small island nation in the Mediterranean. A heavily Roman Catholic country, marital law was regulated by canon law rather than civil law until 1975. Although it is now regulated by the state, divorce is not permitted in Malta, and the only method of dissolving a marriage is by annulment. Judicial separation is available through the court for fault grounds, or irretrievable breakdown if the marriage is of at least four years duration, but such a decree affords no right to remarry. Ruth Farrugia, *International Marriage and Divorce Regulation in Malta*, 29 Fam. L.Q. 627–32 (1995). *See also* Sandra Lonegrave, *The Maltese Version—A Hybrid Court*, 2001 Int'l. Fam. L. 112, 114.

Notes and Questions

1. *Annulment and Liberal Divorce Laws.* In Malta, just as in Ireland before the divorce referendum passed, annulment actions are commonly instigated and the law of nullity generates substantial judicial attention. Farrugia, *supra*, at 628 n.2, 631–32. In Sweden, by contrast, annulments were abolished at the same time that the divorce laws were being liberalized in the early 1970s. A marriage performed in the proper form by a duly authorized person is valid, and a bigamous, incestuous, or underage marriage can be dissolved only by divorce in Sweden, although in some cases of this type, the divorce petition can be filed by the public prosecutor even against the will of the spouses. Bogdan, *supra*, at 678. Beyond serving as a substitute for divorce, does annulment have purposes related to enforcing norms regarding the entry of marriage that require retention of the institution? If so, can these goals be as readily achieved through divorce actions when third parties are allowed to instigate them?

2. *Divorce Reform Inspired by Revolution.* The attempt of the National Socialist (Nazi) regime in Germany at social engineering through reform of the divorce laws is not the only example of the interest displayed by radical new governments on both sides of the political spectrum in the liberalization of divorce laws. In 1792, the French revolutionaries' rejection of ecclesiastical regulation of marriage prompted a new law that permitted divorce on a variety of grounds, including mutual consent and incompatibility of temperament. The latter ground, though accompanied by cumbersome procedures, created the possibility of unilateral divorce, a radical concept for the eighteenth century. Inspired by the philosophy of the enlightenment, the reformers believed that as a civil contract, marriage should be ended when the parties to it mutually desired termination. Moreover, notions of individual liberty required, in their view, that either spouse be able to seek emancipation from the restraints that marriage imposed on his or her freedom. The majority of the populace in this conservative, Catholic country did not yet share this vision of marriage, and the reforms were short-lived. Unilateral divorce disappeared in 1804, and in 1816 divorce was completely abolished. When it was again revived in 1884, it was available only for serious fault grounds, similar to those in effect in England and the United States in the late nineteenth century. Glendon, *supra*, at 159–60.

The Russian Revolution similarly abolished a very restrictive divorce regime and instigated in 1917, by Decree of the Central Executive Committee and Council of People's Commissars, a simple procedure for no-fault divorce. Subsequent reforms in the next decade enabled most couples to divorce without judicial intervention, consistent with the Bolshevik philosophy that individuals should be free from state intervention in their personal relations. In 1944, in response to a population crisis created by the shortage of men of marriageable age following World War II, the government by decree imposed a new law making divorce more difficult and complicated, which remained in effect until Soviet family law was again reformed in the late 1960s. Olga Dyezheva & Harriet Cohen, *Russian Family Law: Its Development and Comparisons with U.S. Family Law*, 6 J. E. Eur. L. 349, 350, 352–54 (1999).

Is it surprising that decades, and even centuries, before the United States and most British Commonwealth nations entertained such reforms, these three very different radical changes in European governments, at three very different times in history, all resulted in reforms, albeit some short-lived, that markedly increased access to divorce? Are there common links that explain this phenomenon?

b. East Asia

Patriarchal family structures characterized East Asian culture for many centuries, just as they did for much of the same time period in Europe and former European colonies, such as the United States. In China, Japan, and Korea, their development, and family law norms in general, were heavily influenced by Confucianism, a hierarchical belief system that taught that husbands were superior to wives, parents must be obeyed by their offspring, only sons could succeed their fathers, and married daughters must obey and respect their husbands and their in-laws. *See* Lee Wha-Sook *Marriage and Divorce Regulation and Recognition in Korea,* 29 Fam. L.Q. 603 (1995); Janice A. Lee, Note, *Family Law of the Two Chinas: A Comparative Look at the Rights of Married Women in the People's Republic of China and the Republic of China,* 5 Cardozo J. Int'l & Comp. L. 217, 219–23 (1997).

In China, Confucian codes and ethics controlled most aspects of Chinese culture. As early as the Han Dynasty (202 B.C.–A.D. 220), the concept that husbands had legal authority over their wives and children was incorporated into Chinese law. Marriages were arranged between families, and spouses often did not meet until after the marriage. *Id.* at 220, 223–24. A bride enabled the groom's family to obtain male heirs for ancestor worship, and was expected to perform household work and care for her parents-in-law as they aged.

Divorce in traditional Chinese society was extremely rare, and, like the marriage, was a matter between the families and not just the individuals. Husbands could divorce wives for failure to produce a son, adultery, stealing, jealousy, gossiping too much, being unfilial towards in-laws, or malignant diseases. Cailian Liao & Tim Heaton, *Divorce Trends and Differentials in China,* 23 J. Comp. Fam. L. Stud. 413, 413–14 (1992). Societal disapproval and the cost of the marriage, however, normally motivated the family to persuade an unhappy husband to take a concubine instead. Martha Bailey, *Mediation of Divorce in China,* 8 Can. J. L. & Soc'y, Spring 1993, at 45, 49. If a husband did initiate a divorce, the wife generally had no ability to contest, as the consent to the divorce came from the same parties who consented to the marriage, typically the parents of the spouses. Wives generally could not instigate a divorce, and in any event, a wife would have been unlikely to pursue one. A woman's bond with her own family was considered severed when she married, and she might not be welcomed back after a divorce. Moreover, divorce destroyed a woman's relationship with her children, because they belonged to the father and his family. Liao, *supra,* at 414; Lee, *supra,* at 224.

The 1930 Civil Code, the first codified domestic relations law in China, was enacted during the Nationalist Era, when China was under the leadership of Sun Yat-sen and the Kuomintang Party. The Code departed from Confucian philosophy by giving women the right to choose their own spouses and the right to own property. The Code also made it more difficult for a husband to obtain a divorce, and gave women the right to divorce. The father, however, was still legally entitled to custody of the children after a divorce, and was the legal owner and manager of the marital property. The Code was not widely publicized to the populace, and the courts often imposed stringent proof requirements upon women seeking divorce. Thus, the actual situation of women was not substantially altered. Lee, *supra,* at 231–33.

Following the rise to power of the Communist Party following World War II and civil war within China, the Communist Party denounced the inequities of the past, and encouraged women to play a significant role in the nation's social reconstruction and to gain economic independence by working outside of the home. A new Marriage Law of the Peoples Republic of China was enacted in 1950, formally and explicitly abolishing the "feudal marriage system," proclaiming equal rights for women and men, and confirming that the new marriage system was based on free choice of spouses and monogamy. *Id.* at 233–35. The new law recognized equal rights of husband and wife to possession and management of family property, *id.*, and permitted divorced women to retain their land allotment and an equal share of property acquired during the marriage. Liao, *supra,* at 414. Reversing patriarchal custom, the mother was now favored in awarding custody of children. *Id.*

In addition to recognizing divorce by mutual consent, the Marriage Law of 1950 also permitted unilateral divorce upon the request of one spouse, but only "when mediation by the district people's government and the judicial organ failed to bring about a reconciliation." Lee, *supra,* at 236, quoting the Marriage Law of 1950, *translated in* Wai-Kin Che, The Modern Chinese Family 94 (1979). Neighborhood committees, originally established to mediate disputes, were confronted with an increasing number of divorces in the early 1950s, many of which were filed by women. A backlash developed, as husbands and their families strongly opposed divorces initiated by wives, particularly since divorce entitled wives to their share of the family property and land and a right to financial support from their ex-husbands. Although the law was not amended, gradually the Party advised mediators that divorces must be handled in a manner that would not alienate male supporters. In addition, there were often ties between the local mediators and the husband's family in rural areas. Mediators thus gradually undermined the effectiveness of the new law, and divorce became increasingly more difficult for women to obtain. Mediation became synonymous with reconciliation, and scholars report that some women seeking a divorce were actually imprisoned for "forced reconciliation." Bailey, *supra,* at 53–56; Lee, *supra,* at 237–38 & n.137.

Following the upheaval of the Cultural Revolution in the mid-1970s, a new, highly publicized Marriage Law of 1980 was enacted that eased the restrictions on unilateral divorce. Although the 1980 law still directs neighborhood or workplace mediators to try to effect a reconciliation when only one party desires a divorce, it also provides that a party may appeal directly to a court for divorce. The court is also directed to attempt a reconciliation, Lee, *supra,* at 239, but the 1980 Marriage Law provides that: "In cases of complete alienation of mutual affection, and when mediation has failed, divorce should be granted." Liao, *supra,* at 415. Though the law now provides explicitly that mediation should not ultimately block a divorce, women still report substantial pressure in mediation to withdraw divorce petitions or accept unfavorable settlements. Lee, *supra,* at 239–40; Bailey, *supra,* at 59–63. In Beijing, for example, between 1981 and 1983, mediation was reported to have achieved reconciliation in 31% of all divorces filed. Bailey, *supra,* at 59.

Currently in the People's Republic of China, if both spouses wish to divorce and they have settled their property and custody issues, they may obtain a no-fault divorce without delay following application by both in person at the civil affairs office, which also handles marriage registration. This is a fairly quick and inexpensive process that requires no judicial involvement, and is generally preferred to court action, an option the Chinese regard as somewhat humiliating. Lee, *supra,* at 239; *Chinese Marriage Rule*

Change Features Privacy: Report, People's Daily Online, May 23, 2001, at http://english. peopledaily.com.cn. Amendments to the Marriage Law adopted in April 2001 retained the provisions of the 1980 Law permitting unilateral divorce and providing the option of seeking a divorce in court, but now codify guidelines to be used by the courts to determine when mutual affection no longer exists. *Marriage Law to Better Protect Women, Children,* People's Daily, May 1, 2001, and *Drastic Overhaul Planned for Current Marriage Law,* People's Daily, Oct. 24, 2000, *both available at* http://english.peopledaily. com.cn. Several of these circumstances appear equivalent to fault grounds, and include marriages in which one spouse commits domestic violence, deserts the other, commits bigamy, has an incorrigible gambling, drug or other evil habit, is criminally prosecuted, or contracts a disease that renders the spouse unfit for marriage, as well as situations in which a spouse is declared missing. In addition, living apart for two years is deemed to be a ground to determine that marital affection no longer exists. *See Revised Draft of the PRC Marriage Laws,* World News Connection, May 3, 2001, *available at* 2001 WL 20505662. A general category, "all other situations that lead to the couple no longer having mutual affection," was also created. *Id.*

The 2001 amendments could potentially restrict the availability of unilateral divorce, a prospect that drew attention from the Western media when they were in draft form. *See* Leslie Pappas, *China's New Family Values,* Newsweek, Aug. 24, 1998, at 36. On the other hand, they could potentially signal to mediation committees that are predisposed to dissuade wives from pursuing divorce that, at least when domestic violence is present, the government has acknowledged that divorce is an acceptable outcome. Domestic violence was one of the central issues addressed in the 2001 amendments. The new amendments specifically prohibit familial violence. They also provide that an "unoffending party" may seek damages in a divorce action as compensation from a spouse who has committed bigamy or had conjugal relations outside of marriage, or who has committed domestic violence or abused a family member. *See* Marriage Law of the People's Republic of China, as amended in 2001, Articles 3, 46, *available at* http://www.international-divorce.com.

Japan's family law system was also traditionally influenced by Confucian ideals, conferring upon men a superior legal status and recognizing a family (*Ie*) system in which the family head was given significant authority over other family members. After World War II, a new Constitution proclaimed that a family was to be based on the free agreement of a man and a woman, and required equality of the sexes, effectively undermining the *Ie* system and paving the way for an increasing number of marriages based on love rather than familial arrangements. Fujiko Isono & Satoshi Minamikata, *Family Law Reform and In-Court Mediation in the Japanese Family Court, in* The International Survey of Family Law 1994, 303, 311 (Andrew Bainham ed., 1996); Jun'ichi Akiba & Minoru Ishikawa, *Marriage and Divorce Regulation and Recognition in Japan,* 29 Fam. L. Q. 589, 589–90 (1995). Though the divorce rate was traditionally extremely low in Japan, and remains below U.S. rates, it has been rising steadily over the past 30 years, reaching 289,000 in 2001, twice the number that occurred in 1980. Miki Tarnikawa, *Lack of Enforcement Weakens Effects of Japan's Divorce Provisions,* Int'l Herald Trib., Feb. 2, 2002, at 15.

Over 90% of divorces in Japan are by mutual agreement. These divorces require no court intervention, because the parties have agreed concerning the divorce, custody, and financial arrangements, and merely require that the couple file a notification form with the family registry at a local government office, which can even be done by mail. Akiba, *supra,* at 592–93; Isono, *supra,* at 307.

In those cases in which the couple cannot agree, the parties are required to go through conciliation, sometimes translated as mediation, in the Family Court before a divorce proceeding can be filed in the district court. The Mediation Panel consists of a man, a woman, and a judge, although frequently the judge appears in the proceeding only to finalize an agreement. Those appointed to be mediators receive a small remuneration, and are typically elderly and well educated—male mediators are often retired public servants or businessmen, and female mediators are often graduates of a university or wives of prominent community members. Although there are no professional requirements, it is increasingly common for mediators in recent years to have studied family problems in their education. Mediators are regarded as representing the "good sense" of society. They are sometimes assisted by investigation officers, who provide information about the parties. Investigation officers are typically university graduates who studied law, sociology, psychology, or similar disciplines. They present a report to the Mediation Panel, and sometimes are requested by the Panel to counsel the parties. Isono, *supra*, at 315–17.

Japanese family law scholars, Fujiko Isono and Satoshi Minamikata, suggest that the Japanese mediation system finds its roots in "the objections of traditionalists to the recognition of individual rights for members of the family," and a somewhat paternalistic notion that the State, in the role of guardian, should solve the problems of marital partners. The requirement of mediation was originally intended to achieve marital reconciliation, and reports generated by one study in the 1960s suggested that half of the women interviewed felt that they had been pressured in the mediation to put up with the "present situation" in the marriage. In recent years, "successful" mediations typically result in a divorce agreement resolving financial and custodial arrangements. Approximately 30% of the cases going to mediation reach an agreement, which is incorporated in a mediation document that has binding force equivalent to a divorce decree. The mediation process involves very little expense for the parties, unless they choose to be represented by a legal advisor. Isono and Minamikata suggest that the system could potentially be more effectively used if the investigating officers were trained social workers competent to counsel with a guarantee of confidentiality. *Id.* at 316–18.

Parties who cannot reach agreement or are dissatisfied with the decision of the Mediation Panel may file divorce proceedings in a district court, although due to the expense and delay of this route, only a very small percentage of divorces (estimated in 1992 as fewer than 1%) are resolved in court. Five grounds for divorce exist: sexual misconduct, willful desertion, the absence of knowledge for at least three years about whether a missing spouse is alive or dead, insanity, and grave reason that makes it difficult for the spouse to continue the marriage, sometimes translated as breakdown. This final ground leaves open the possibility of unilateral divorce, even if it is sought by a spouse who might otherwise be viewed as the "guilty" party. The Japanese Supreme Court has approved unilateral divorce even when sought by a party deemed "guilty," but required that the "innocent party" be provided with sufficient financial security, that there be no dependent children, and that the parties have lived apart for a substantial period of time. An eight-year separation was deemed sufficient in one case before that court. Isono, *supra*, at 308–09; Akiba, *supra*, at 593. In recent years divorces are reported to have been granted after separations of shorter duration, when the court finds the divorce will not create undue mental or economic hardship. *See* Kawanishi Yuko, *Breaking Up Still Hard to Do*, 45 Japan Quarterly 84–89 (1998). An amendment to the Civil Code providing for a five-year separation as a ground has been discussed, but Professor Yuko, a Japanes sociologist, suggests that "no fault divorce in the Western sense...is still a far-off concept in Japan." *Id.*

Notes and Questions

1. *Comparison.* Consider the similarities and differences between divorce regulation in Japan and the People's Republic of China. What political, social, and historical factors do you think may account for those differences?

2. *Pregnancy Restriction.* China's Marriage Law specifically prohibits husbands from applying for a divorce during the wife's pregnancy, within six months of the birth of a child, or within six months after termination of a pregnancy, unless the wife also applies for a divorce, or "the people's court deems it necessary to accept the divorce application by the husband." Marriage Law of the People's Republic of China, Art. 34, as amended in 2001. Should similar restrictions, in your opinion, be considered in the United States? Would such a restriction survive constitutional challenge in the United States?

3. *Mediation.* While mandatory mediation is a relatively recent phenomena for divorce actions in the United States, it has played a significant role in the divorce process in China and Japan for many decades. What differences and similarities do you see in the manner in which mediation has been utilized in divorce proceedings in the United States, China, and Japan?

Some of the scholars cited above expressed concerns about the role mediation has played in China and Japan. *See* Isono, *supra,* at 316–18; Lee, *supra,* at 237–40; Bailey, *supra,* at 45. Though discussed more fully in their articles, some of these issues are apparent from the discussion above. Does mandatory mediation present similar concerns in the United States? The utilization of mediation in divorce proceedings in the United States has also drawn heated debate, with many feminists, in particular, opposing its use on a mandatory basis. *See e.g.,* Andree G. Gagnon, *Ending Mandatory Divorce Mediation for Battered Women,* 15 Harv. Womens L.J. 272 (1995) (contending mandatory mediation disempowers battered women and creates risk of further abuse); Trina Grillo, *The Mediation Alternative: Process Dangers for Women,* 100 Yale L.J. 1545 (1991) (arguing mandatory mediation disempowers and disadvantages subordinated groups, including women); Martha Fineman, *Dominant Discourse, Professional Language, and Legal Change in Child Custody Decisionmaking,* 101 Harv. L. Rev. 727 (1988) (asserting mandatory mediation alters the substantive rules in custody disputes, disadvantaging custodial mothers, and enabling social workers to appropriate the custody decisionmaking process). *Cf, e.g.,* Craig Mcewen & Nancy Rogers, *Bring in the Lawyers: Challenging the Dominant Approaches to Ensuring Fairness in Divorce Mediation,* 79 Minn. L. Rev. 1317 (1995) (asserting the participation of lawyers in mandatory mediation can assure fairness); Andrew Schepard, *An Introduction to the Model Standards of Practice for Family and Divorce Mediation,* 36 Fam. L.Q. 1 (2001) (extolling benefits of mediation in reducing economic and emotional transaction costs, when conducted according to high standards, but recognizing it may not be appropriate for family disputes involving domestic violence or high conflict custody disputes).

c. *Africa*

You have already read about family structures under customary law in South Africa and other parts of Southern and Central Africa, in Chapter Two, Section B.1. You may have noticed many similarities between Professor Chambers' description of customary marriage and termination of marriage in South Africa, and the description above of traditional marriage and divorce practices in China. Yet these nations have taken different paths in the development of current marriage and divorce law regarding the accommodation of traditional practices. What historical, political, and social factors may account for those differences? Do you regard one approach as preferable?

5. The Debate Continues

As nations around the globe continue to reevaluate and adjust the accessibility to divorce appropriate for their societies, discussion among scholars on this issue continues as well. One fundamental basis of disagreement relates to whether the adoption of no-fault divorce laws has increased divorce rates. Some scholars contend that such a correlation exists, particularly if states that consider fault as a factor in the financial award, even if not in the dissolution grounds, are included in the studies as fault jurisdictions. Margaret Brinig and F. H. Buckley contend that their study of divorce rates between 1988 and 1991, calculated in this manner, suggests that the removal of fault as a factor in both the dissolution and the financial awards is associated with higher divorce levels. Observing that social as well as legal variables may account for the difference, however, they suggest that divorce levels will generally be lower in societies that stigmatize divorce, which are also the societies that are more likely to incorporate fault in their divorce laws. Margaret Brinig & F. H. Buckley, *No-Fault Laws and At-Fault People,* 18 Int'l Rev. L. & Econ. 325, 340 (1998). *See also* Paul A. Nakonezney, Robert D. Shull, & Joseph Lee Rodgers, *The Effect of No-Fault Divorce Law on the Divorce Rate Across the 50 States and Its Relation to Income, Education, and Religiosity,* 57 J. Marriage & Fam. 477, 485 (1995) (concluding from statistical study that a change to no-fault divorce law in various states led to an increased divorce rate).

Other scholars contend that the bulk of studies have shown no lasting effects of no-fault reforms on divorce rates. Examining the divorce rate relative to the population in the United States over the past century, Ira Ellman and Sharon Lohr note that following a sharp rise during World War II and a period of relative stability in the 1950s, the American divorce rate then resumed climbing in the 1960s, experiencing a steep increase from the mid-1960s to 1979, when it peaked at 5.3 per 1000 people, after which it declined throughout the 1980s. They observe that the divorce rate therefore began its ascent more than a decade before the no-fault movement is generally regarded as beginning, and began its decline just as the reform was adopted nationwide. Moreover, they note that rising divorce rates have been a widespread phenomenon in western societies, despite significant differences in their divorce laws. Ira Mark Ellman & Sharon Lohr, *Marriage as Contract, Opportunistic Violence, and Other Bad Arguments for Fault Divorce,* 1997 U. Ill. L. Rev. 719, 723–25. These scholars also question the statistical analyses of the studies cited above. Ira Ellman & Sharon Lohr, *Dissolving the Relationship Between Divorce Laws and Divorce Rates,* 18 Int'l Rev. L. & Econ. 341, 345, 358–59 (1998) (observing that their own study shows that despite some short-term spurts of a year or two in divorce rates following changes to no-fault laws affecting divorce grounds or financial awards, in the long run their results parallel those of other demographers and sociologists who conclude that easier divorce laws have no long-term effect on divorce rates).

Scholars similarly disagree about whether increasing restrictions upon divorce would remedy the social ills attributed to divorce, and whether such restrictions should be mandated, or undertaken by individual couples through premarital agreement or through a state-created covenant marriage. Elizabeth Scott argues that precommitments that impose restrictions upon divorce, such as a mandatory waiting period of substantial length, not only discourage divorces motivated by transitory preferences, but also encourage cooperative behavior and trust during the marriage, as spouses understand that exit will be difficult. Elizabeth Scott, *Marriage as Precommitment* (1996), *reprinted in* Ira Ellman, Paul Kurtz, & Elizabeth Scott, Family Law 22 (3d ed. 1998). Katherine Shaw Spaht, proponent of Louisiana's covenant marriage statute, asserts that the more limited, largely fault-based grounds for divorce available to couples who choose covenant marriages "restores broader notions of objective morality to conduct within the context of marital relationship.... Such collective social condemnation, altogether missing in pure no-fault divorce statutes, is powerful and should occur," she contends, because "[g]uilt and shame, if our society can restore it, often control human behavior." She further argues that children are harmed emotionally, economically, and psychologically when raised in divorced households. Katherine Shaw Spaht, *For the Sake of the Children: Recapturing the Meaning of Marriage,* 73 Notre Dame L. Rev. 1547, 1554, 1569–71 (1998). Sharing this concern, Judith Younger has suggested that couples with minor children be precluded from divorcing unless they could prove to a court that the children would be better off after the divorce. Judith T. Younger, *Marital Regimes: A Story of Compromise and Demoralization, Together with Criticism and Suggestions for Reform,* 67 Cornell L. Rev. 45 (1981).

Others conclude that these restrictions are unwarranted, and may lead to unintended consequences. In the United States, over two-thirds of those who file for divorce are women, and studies also suggest that women instigate the separation in the majority of cases, despite the fact that the average woman's standard of living declines following divorce. Margaret Brinig & Douglas W. Allen, *"These Boots Are Made for Walking": Why Most Divorce Filers Are Women,* 2 Am. L. & Econ. Rev. 126, 127–29 (2000). Linda Lacey observes that precommitments to engage in counseling or accept a lengthy waiting period could further compromise women and children financially, if the wife cannot afford an attorney to assist in obtaining support and property during the lengthy separation, or if she must pay substantial counseling fees. Moreover, she contends, there is little reason to believe that mandatory counseling would be effective in averting divorce when raised in this context, noting that Germany repealed laws requiring mandatory attempts at reconciliation and rejected proposals for compulsory counseling, based on the perception of poor success rates of such requirements in other countries. She expresses particular concern regarding divorce restrictions that impede a battered woman's access to a swift and final divorce, cautioning that the longer a woman remains in an abusive relationship, the greater the likelihood that she will be seriously injured. Linda L. Lacey, *Mandatory Marriage "For the Sake of the Children": A Feminist Reply to Elizabeth Scott,* 66 Tul. L. Rev. 1435, 1444–45, 1458–60 (1992).

The principal effect of waiting periods, Ellman and Lohr suggest, is to delay or prevent remarriage, and the remarriage of the custodial parent often improves the financial situation of the children. Moreover, a lengthy waiting period may simply retard the adjustment process for a spouse, particularly one who opposed the divorce, preventing "victims of failed marriages from rebuilding new lives for themselves and their children." Ellman & Lohr, *supra,* at 728–32.

Scholars who have addressed the child-centered arguments also observe that while studies comparing children of divorce with those of intact families do indicate the children from divorced families suffer a negative impact, there is disagreement regarding the extent of those psychological effects. The more sophisticated studies, they suggest, show that the average effect is small and the proportion of children seriously impaired is limited. Robert Gordon, Note, *The Limits of Limits on Divorce*, 107 Yale L. J. 1435, 1447–48 (1998) (citing Paul Amato & Bruce Keith, *Parental Divorce and the Well-Being of Children: A Meta-Analysis*, 110 Psychol. Bull. 26 (1991) and numerous other studies by social scientists). Moreover, many studies have confirmed that children whose parents eventually divorce exhibit more psychological and behavioral problems many years before the divorce than children of intact families, leading most scholars to concur that the divorce itself was not the cause of a significant portion of the differences between children in the two groups. Gordon, *supra*, at 1448. In addition, divorce in high conflict families has been found by some studies to improve the well-being of children. These children might otherwise be detrimentally affected by the increased parental conflict that restrictive divorce laws may spawn. *Id.* at 1449.

The above discussion conveys only a sampling of the divergent opinions represented in this dialogue. As you consider the exercise at the end of the following section, you may wish to examine this rich body of work. *See also, e.g.,* Allen M. Parkman, No-Fault Divorce: What Went Wrong? (1992); Ann Laquer Estin, *Economics and the Problem of Divorce*, 2 U. Chi. L. Sch. Roundtable 517 (1995); Lynn D. Wardle, *Divorce Violence and the No-Fault Divorce Culture*, 1994 Utah L. Rev. 741 (1994); Lynn D. Wardle, *No-Fault Divorce and the Divorce Conundrum,*1991 BYU L. Rev. 79; Martha Heller, Note, *Should Breaking Up Be Harder to Do?: The Ramifications a Return to Fault-Based Divorce Would Have Upon Domestic Violence*, 4 Va. J. Soc. Pol'y & L. 263 (1996).

C. The Intersection of Religion and the State in Contemporary Regulation of Divorce

In Chapter Two you were introduced to a variety of models adopted around the world for allocating authority between religious and civil institutions over the regulation of entry into marriage. These diverse systems, and the resulting jurisdictional tensions generated in each, extend to the termination of marriage as well.

As you read in Section A, religious institutions directly controlled the regulation of divorce in predominantly Christian nations for many centuries in Western Europe. Between the sixteenth and the nineteenth centuries, however, in the wake of the Reformation and the Enlightenment, jurisdiction over divorce gradually transferred to civil authorities. Even in predominantly Roman Catholic nations such as the Republic of Ireland and Malta, where the influence of Catholicism is particularly strong, the grounds for obtaining divorce are now established by the state, and the process for obtaining a divorce is also administered by the government. Religious systems regulating termination of marriage may co-exist, but in most respects they have no control over the civil marital status of their followers.

In nations whose religious heritage is not primarily Christian, access to divorce is still in many instances controlled by religious norms or institutions, or a combination of religious and civil authorities. Countries in which substantial portions of the population subscribe to different religions accommodate their diverse practices in different ways. The approaches of various religious groups to the termination of marriage, and governments' responses to this diversity, are explored in this Section.

1. Nations Delegating Exclusive Control of Civil Marital Status to the State

Williams v. Williams
543 P.2d 1401 (Okla. 1975)

Hodges, V.C.J.

The sole issue on appeal is the authority of the district court to grant a divorce on the grounds of incompatibility. Appellant wife contends that the court is without such authority because it contravenes the religious oaths and vows taken by the parties, and, the authority of God, the Bible and Jesus Christ. Appellee husband does not refute these allegations of religious vows and belief but contends he is entitled to a divorce on the statutory grounds of incompatibility.

Surprisingly, we have no precedent, and the issue comes to us as a case of first impression.

A matrimonial ceremony may have two resulting aspects:

(1) A civil contract between the parties granted by law.

(2) An ecclesiastical obligation imposed by God as interpreted by the beliefs and conscience of the parties.

Appellant contends the civil contract of marriage cannot be dissolved by the State when it is in conflict with the ecclesiastical obligations of marriage of which both parties profess and proclaim. She argues, since both parties in this case believe that adultery in [sic] the only scriptural grounds [sic] for divorce, and neither has committed an act of adultery, the State must then recognize their ecclesiastical obligations and vows of marriage, and deny the appellee a divorce.

Appellant would have this court to invoke the conscience of the appellee and apply their ecclesiastical beliefs on marriage and divorce. Under the constitutional mandate of separation of church and state, we decline. We have no business or right, constitutional or statutory, to interpret and enforce the ecclesiastical vows of marriage. While this court is concerned with the mores and religious beliefs of the citizenry, our jurisdiction extends only to the civil matters of state.

Freedom of religion, which is embodied in the First Amendment to the Constitution of the United States and in the due process clause of the Fourteenth Amendment, reflects the philosophy the church and state should be separate, and that both religion and government can best work to achieve their lofty aims if each is left free from the other within its respective sphere....

We are a civil court having constitutional and legislative sanction to administer man-made laws justly, fairly and equally. We have no jurisdiction to regulate or enforce scriptural obligations.

Title 43 O.S.1971 s 1 states that:

'Marriage is a personal relation arising out of a Civil contract to which the consent of parties legally competent of contracting and of entering into it is necessary, and the marriage relation shall only be entered into, maintained or abrogated as provided by law."....

Divorce is wholly a creature of statute with absolute power to prescribe conditions relative thereto being vested in the State.... Neither the Constitution of the United States, nor the State of Oklahoma, prohibits the legislature from specifying upon what grounds, if any, divorces are to be granted. The State has a constitutional right to declare and maintain a policy in regard to marriage and divorce as to persons domiciled within its borders. The statutory grounds of divorce are exclusive, and the courts have authority in this field to do only that which is prescribed by the legislature. The legislature has vested the courts of this state with ultimate control over the dissolution of marriage....

The law does not, nor can the courts, compel a husband and wife to live together. The remedy of absolute divorce is an extraordinary remedy for situations which are unavoidable and unendurable and which cannot be relieved by any proper and reasonable exertion of the party seeking the aid of the courts.... Although the State is a silent third party in every divorce proceeding, it is not interested in perpetrating a marriage after all possibility of accomplishing any desirable purpose of such relationship is gone.

Appellant's complaint that her constitutional right for the free exercise of religion is being violated is unfounded. The action of the trial court only dissolved the civil contract of marriage between the parties. No attempt was made to dissolve it ecclesiastically. Therefore, there is no infringement upon her constitutional right of freedom of religion. She still has her constitutional prerogative to believe that in the eyes of God, she and her estranged husband are ecclesiastically wedded as one, and may continue to exercise that freedom of religion according to her belief and conscience. Any transgression by her husband of their ecclesiastical vows, is, in this instance, outside the jurisdiction of the court.

It is not within the power of the church or an individual to affect the status or civil relations of persons. This may only be regulated by the supreme civil power....

The State has absolute control over the dissolution of the civil marriage contract. Dissolution of the marital relationship or religious vows are a matter of conscience; extinguishment of the civil marriage contract and the marital status are matters of statutory construction.

* * *

[Ed. Note: The court concluded that the divorce should be granted on the grounds of incompatibility.]

Avitzur v. Avitzur
459 N.Y.S.2d 572 (N.Y. 1983), *cert. den.*, 464 U.S. 817 (1983)

Wachtler, J.

This appeal presents for our consideration the question of the proper role of the civil courts in deciding a matter touching upon religious concerns. At issue is the enforceability of the terms of a document, known as a Ketubah, which was entered into as part of the religious marriage ceremony in this case. The Appellate Division...held this to be a religious covenant beyond the jurisdiction of the civil courts. However, we find nothing in law or public policy to prevent judicial recognition and enforcement of the secular terms of such an agreement. There should be a reversal.

Plaintiff and defendant were married on May 22, 1966 in a ceremony conducted in accordance with Jewish tradition. Prior to the marriage ceremony, the parties signed both a Hebrew/Aramaic and an English version of the "Ketubah." According to the English translation, the Ketubah evidences both the bridegroom's intention to cherish and provide for his wife as required by religious law and tradition and the bride's willingness to carry out her obligations to her husband in faithfulness and affection according to Jewish law and tradition. By signing the Ketubah, the parties declared their "desire to... live in accordance with the Jewish law of marriage throughout [their] lifetime" and further agreed as follows: "[W]e, the bride and bridegroom...hereby agree to recognize the Beth Din of the Rabbinical Assembly and the Jewish Theological Seminary of America or its duly appointed representatives, as having authority to counsel us in the light of Jewish tradition which requires husband and wife to give each other complete love and devotion, and to summon either party at the request of the other, in order to enable the party so requesting to live in accordance with the standards of the Jewish law of marriage throughout his or her lifetime. We authorize the Beth Din to impose such terms of compensation as it may see fit for failure to respond to its summons or to carry out its decision."

Defendant husband was granted a civil divorce upon the ground of cruel and inhuman treatment on May 16, 1978. Notwithstanding this civil divorce, plaintiff wife is not considered divorced and may not remarry pursuant to Jewish law, until such time as a Jewish divorce decree, known as a "Get," is granted. In order that a Get may be obtained plaintiff and defendant must appear before a "Beth Din," a rabbinical tribunal having authority to advise and pass upon matters of traditional Jewish law. Plaintiff sought to summon defendant before the Beth Din pursuant to the provision of the Ketubah recognizing that body as having authority to counsel the couple in the matters concerning their marriage.

Defendant has refused to appear before the Beth Din, thus preventing plaintiff from obtaining a religious divorce. Plaintiff brought this action, alleging that the Ketubah constitutes a marital contract, which defendant has breached by refusing to appear before the Beth Din, and she seeks relief both in the form of a declaration to that effect and an order compelling defendant's specific performance of the Ketubah's requirement that he appear before the Beth Din. Defendant moved to dismiss the complaint upon the grounds that the court lacked subject matter jurisdiction and the complaint failed to state a cause of action, arguing that resolution of the dispute and any grant of relief to plaintiff would involve the civil court in impermissible consideration of a purely religious matter....

* * *

Accepting plaintiff's allegations as true, as we must in the context of this motion to dismiss, it appears that plaintiff and defendant, in signing the Ketubah, entered into a contract which formed the basis for their marriage. Plaintiff has alleged that, pursuant to the terms of this marital contract, defendant promised that he would, at plaintiff's request, appear before the Beth Din for the purpose of allowing that tribunal to advise and counsel the parties in matters concerning their marriage, including the granting of a Get. It should be noted that plaintiff is not attempting to compel defendant to obtain a Get or to enforce a religious practice arising solely out of principles of religious law.

She merely seeks to enforce an agreement made by defendant to appear before and accept the decision of a designated tribunal.

Viewed in this manner, the provisions of the Ketubah relied upon by plaintiff constitute nothing more than an agreement to refer the matter of a religious divorce to a nonjudicial forum. Thus, the contractual obligation plaintiff seeks to enforce is closely analogous to an antenuptial agreement to arbitrate a dispute in accordance with the law and tradition chosen by the parties. There can be little doubt that a duly executed antenuptial agreement, by which the parties agree in advance of the marriage to the resolution of disputes that may arise after its termination, is valid and enforceable.... Similarly, an agreement to refer a matter concerning marriage to arbitration suffers no inherent invalidity.... This agreement—the Ketubah—should ordinarily be entitled to no less dignity than any other civil contract to submit a dispute to a nonjudicial forum, so long as its enforcement violates neither the law nor the public policy of this State....

Defendant argues, in this connection, that enforcement of the terms of the Ketubah by a civil court would violate the constitutional prohibition against excessive entanglement between church and State, because the court must necessarily intrude upon matters of religious doctrine and practice. It is urged that the obligations imposed by the Ketubah arise solely from Jewish religious law and can be interpreted only with reference to religious dogma. Granting the religious character of the Ketubah, it does not necessarily follow that any recognition of its obligations is foreclosed to the courts.

It is clear that judicial involvement in matters touching upon religious concerns has been constitutionally limited in analogous situations, and courts should not resolve such controversies in a manner requiring consideration of religious doctrine.... In its most recent pronouncement on this issue, however, the Supreme Court, in holding that a State may adopt any approach to resolving religious disputes which does not entail consideration of doctrinal matters, specifically approved the use of the "neutral principles of law" approach as consistent with constitutional limitations.... This approach contemplates the application of objective, well-established principles of secular law to the dispute..., thus permitting judicial involvement to the extent that it can be accomplished in purely secular terms.

The present case can be decided solely upon the application of neutral principles of contract law, without reference to any religious principle. Consequently, defendant's objections to enforcement of his promise to appear before the Beth Din, based as they are upon the religious origin of the agreement, pose no constitutional barrier to the relief sought by plaintiff. The fact that the agreement was entered into as part of a religious ceremony does not render it unenforceable. Solemnization of the marital relationship often takes place in accordance with the religious beliefs of the participants, and this State has long recognized this religious aspect by permitting duly authorized pastors, rectors, priests, rabbis and other religious officials to perform the ceremony.... Similarly, that the obligations undertaken by the parties to the Ketubah are grounded in religious belief and practice does not preclude enforcement of its secular terms. Nor does the fact that all of the Ketubah's provisions may not be judicially recognized prevent the court from enforcing that portion of the agreement by which the parties promised to refer their disputes to a nonjudicial forum.... The courts may properly enforce so much of this agreement as is not in contravention of law or public policy.

In short, the relief sought by plaintiff in this action is simply to compel defendant to perform a secular obligation to which he contractually bound himself. In this regard, no doctrinal issue need be passed upon, no implementation of a religious duty is contemplated, and no interference with religious authority will result. Certainly nothing the Beth Din can do would in any way affect the civil divorce. To the extent that an enforceable promise can be found by the application of neutral principles of contract law, plaintiff will have demonstrated entitlement to the relief sought. Consideration of other substantive issues bearing upon plaintiff's entitlement to a religious divorce, however, is appropriately left to the forum the parties chose for resolving the matter.

* * *

[Ed. Note: The above opinion was joined by 4 judges. The dissenting opinion, in which 3 judges joined, is omitted.]

Notes and Questions

1. *Variants of an Occidental Pattern.* Max Rheinstein, a well-known comparativist, observed that nations that regulated family law matters through the secular laws of the state, a pattern he referred to as "Occidental," could be subdivided into two categories. In the first, the state "attempts to devise rules that correspond to patterns of belief or behavior that are widely shared among the groups and subgroups of which the society is composed." Applying his definitions, Mary Ann Glendon suggested a decade ago that England and France, as well as several other European countries, could be classified in this group. Because family law cannot correspond to all of the religious and cultural beliefs that might exist in a society, other nations have taken a different approach, adopting what Rheinstein refers to as "the ideology of tolerance." Nations in this category, in which Professor Glendon placed the United States and Sweden, "refrain from articulating a common morality," but rather merely define "the current outer limits of permissible diversity in family matters," such as bans on polygamy, "while leaving maximum room for choice and avoiding value judgments other than those favoring individual liberty." Glendon, *supra*, at 13–15. Would you agree with this characterization of the categories, and of the placement today of the United States in the second category?

2. *Secular Divorces Impacting Religious Commitments.* In *Williams* and *Avitzur* two American state supreme courts address claims by spouses requesting that state courts enforce commitments undertaken as part of religious marriage ceremonies, in or following the civil divorce proceedings in which their husbands sought civil termination of their marital status. In the United States, delineating the spheres of government and religion are determined not just by legislative policy choices, but also by the constrictions of the Establishment and Free Exercise Clauses of the First Amendment of the U.S. Constitution. Thus, both courts were required to consider the requests before them in light of not only legislative authority and public policy, but also constitutional directive.

In declining the wife's request in *Williams* to deny her husband a divorce, the Oklahoma Supreme Court addresses two constitutional arguments. The wife's argument was based on the Free Exercise Clause: the divorce violates her right to freely exercise her religion. The husband's argument was based upon the Establishment Clause: interpretation of the ecclesiastical vows of marriage would violate the constitutional mandate of separation of church and state. In response to the wife's Free Exercise challenge to the state's divorce statute, the court provides a classic articulation of the notion of separation of civil marital status and religious marital status, a theoretical framework that underlies divorce systems that relegate sole authority over civil marital status to the state. Does the majority opinion in *Avitzur* reject this theoretical framework? If not, how can the court's decision to order the husband in *Avitzur* to appear before the Beth Din be distinguished?

In addition to determining that granting a divorce does not violate a spouse's rights under the Free Exercise Clause, the *Williams* court also declares that denying a divorce in order to enforce the ecclesiastical beliefs of the parties would be a violation of the First Amendment's requirement of separation of church and state. In *Avitzur* the intermediate appellate court had granted the husband's motion to dismiss on the same basis, determining that a religious agreement was unenforceable by the State. The New York Court of Appeals rejects this argument as well. What is the majority's reasoning on this issue? Do you think this reasoning is persuasive? In order to fully respond to that question, additional information concerning the get and its significance in Jewish law might be helpful.

3. *Jewish Divorce Law and the Get.* Unlike Christianity, which developed the doctrine of the indissolubility of marriage during the Middle Ages, divorce has been continuously recognized in Judaism. Under Jewish law, a marriage cannot be dissolved until the husband gives his wife, and she receives, a *get.* The practice of giving a *get* was recognized in the book of Deuteronomy, and is believed to have been customary in Israelite society at least as far back as the later days of the Kingdom of Judah. Michael Freeman, *The Jewish Law of Divorce*, 2000 Int'l Fam.L. 58, 58. From the Middle Ages until the French Revolution, Jews in Western Europe were not regarded as citizens of the states in which they lived, because citizenship was reserved for Christians. Jewish communities were treated in some respects as foreign nations that had a social contract with the local sovereigns, and were permitted autonomy to regulate matrimonial matters among members of the community. Therefore, Jews had access to divorce in Europe, to the extent permitted by Jewish law, over many centuries during which most Christians did not. In the political aftermath of the French revolution, Jews gradually gained the right to citizenship throughout Western Europe, as well as in many other nations, such as the United States and Canada, that were originally colonized by Western Europeans. David Novak, *Jewish Marriage and Civil Law: A Two-Way Street*, 68 Geo. Wash. L. Rev. 1059, 1068–69 (2000). As these nations developed civil divorce, Jews, like citizens of other faiths, became subject to the requirements of civil law in order to terminate their civil marital status, while continuing to be subject to the dictates of Jewish law to determine their religious marital status.

Judaism regards marriage as a covenant between the two spouses, solemnized by a religious ceremony, rather than as a sacrament or a status conferred upon the parties. The *ketubah* is a document that sets forth the rights and duties of the spouses during the marriage. Orthodox ketubahs, written in Aramaic, remain virtually unchanged since the Middle Ages, when they were created to protect the wife in the event of a divorce, by guaranteeing her certain property rights. Heather Lynn Capell, Comment, *After the Glass Has Shattered: A Comparative Analysis of Orthodox Jewish Divorce in the United States and Israel*, 33 Tex. Int'l L.J. 331, 335 (1998).

Referring to the "Jewish law of divorce" is somewhat problematic, as within the broader Jewish community there is much disagreement today about the need for a *get*. In the United States, those who are affiliated with Reform or Reconstructionist communities would be less likely to observe traditional requirements related to a *get*, whereas members of Conservative communities would be more likely do so, and in Orthodox and Hasidic communities traditional law would normally be strictly observed. *See* Paul Finkelman, *A Bad Marriage: Jewish Divorce and the First Amendment*, 2 Cardozo Women's L.J. 131, 135 & n. 3 (1995). That being said, there appears to be some consensus about the provisions of certain traditionally recognized norms.

According to the traditional Jewish law of divorce, only a husband may initiate the process to give his wife a *get*. Until she receives a *get*, the marriage is not dissolved, and the wife cannot remarry under Jewish law. If she cohabits, or remarries civilly, she is viewed as an adulteress. Thereafter, even if her husband later gives her a *get*, she is prohibited from remarrying her partner under Jewish law. She also loses her rights to alimony (under Jewish, not civil, law) and any children with her new partner are regarded as *mamzerim* (out-of-wedlock). As *mamzerim*, under Jewish law they are restricted from certain privileges and permitted to marry only other *mamzerim* or converts, and all of their progeny are regarded as *mamzerim*. A woman who has not been given a *get*, but is civilly divorced, is referred to as an *agunah*, although there is disagreement within the Jewish community as to exactly who qualifies as an *agunah*. Freeman, *supra*, at 58; Finkelman, *supra*, at 141–44; Capell, *supra*, at 337.

Although the book of Deuteronomy originally appeared to give a husband complete discretion to divorce his wife, rabbinic interpretations in the Middle Ages modified this to require the wife's consent, and so to this day under normal conditions a wife must freely consent to receiving the *get* before the marriage can be dissolved and the spouses freed to remarry. Moreover, technical drafting requirements were added in the Middle Ages that as a practical matter required the assistance of a rabbinical court, the *Beth Din*, which imposed a level of supervision over the process. Even though Jewish law states that the husband cannot be compelled to give a *get*, it has been interpreted since the time of Maimonides in the twelfth century to permit the Beth Din to attempt to coerce him to give a *get* under certain conditions to his wife who desires a divorce, if, for example, he is habitually unfaithful, impotent, or refuses to support her. However, a *get* coerced by civil authorities may not be viewed as freely given, and may therefore be ineffective under Jewish law. Freeman, *supra*, at 58–59; Finkelman, *supra*, at 140–42.

Because normally a husband must give, and a wife must agree to accept, a *get* in order to dissolve a marriage, Jewish law might appear to create parity between the spouses. However, a husband also has an opportunity to dissolve a marriage when the wife refuses to accept a *get*, by undergoing the expensive and time-consuming procedure of *heter me'ah rabbanim* (the permission of 100 rabbis). No equivalent procedure is available to the wife. Moreover, the consequences of a failure to give a *get*, or of a refusal of a wife to receive a *get*, are not the same for husband and wife under Jewish law. Although as an *agun* the husband cannot remarry under traditional Jewish law, if he remarries civilly or cohabits with another woman he is not considered an adulterer, and children with his new partner are not *mamzerim*. If he subsequently offers and his wife accepts a *get*, he will be permitted to marry his new partner in the civil marriage under Jewish law. Because the status of *agunah* affects a wife and her children more harshly, the failure to obtain a *get* has been viewed as far more cataclysmic for a religious Jewish woman. Freeman, *supra*, at 58–59; Finkelman, *supra*, at 140–43. As a result, the ability of a husband to withhold a *get* has operated as a bargaining chip in the negotiation of the financial issues and custodial arrangements of many civil divorces. Finkelman, *supra*, at 143; Note, *The Schpiel' on Getting Divorced Under Jewish Law*, 16 The Matrimonial Strategist 6 (1998).

3. *Response of American Legal System.* A year after the *Avitzur* decision was issued, the New York legislature passed a law providing that a judgment of divorce or annulment could not be issued unless the plaintiff and the defendant, if he or she had entered an appearance, had each served a sworn statement that he or she had "taken all steps solely within his or her power" necessary "to remove all barriers to the other party's remar-

riage." "Barriers" are defined to include "any religious or conscientious restraint or inhibition" known to the verifying party that would be imposed "under the principles held by the clergyman or minister who solemnized the marriage by reason of the" verifying party's "commission or withholding of a voluntary act." N. Y. Dom. Rel. Law § 253 (McKinney 1999).

Several other states have addressed the dilemma of the *agunah* through court decisions, and these courts are split concerning the constitutionality of civil intervention. In addition to New York, courts in Illinois and Delaware have held that a Ketubah could be specifically enforced. In *Goldman v. Goldman*, 554 N.E.2d 1016 (Ill. App. 1990), *cert. den.* 555 N.E.2d 376 (Ill. 1990), the court took enforcement one step further than the court in *Avitzur*, by upholding the lower court's order to the husband to obtain and deliver a *get* to his wife, either by appearing before a Beth Din or Rabbinical Council or by obtaining a *get* by proxy or some other method recognized as valid by an Orthodox Beth Din. Rejecting the arguments that the Ketubah was not a valid contract and that it was too vague, the court found that "[b]e thou my wife according to the law of Moses and Israel" meant that their marital status would be governed by Orthodox Jewish law. 554 N.E.2d at 1021. The court also rejected the husband's contention that the order violated the Establishment Clause of the First Amendment, determining that the order served the secular purposes of enforcing a contract and mitigating harm to the wife in the divorce; that obtaining a *get* was a secular act and not an act of worship, according to expert witnesses on Judaism; and that the order avoided an excessive entanglement with religion by applying well-established contract law. The court also determined that Mr. Goldman's Free Exercise argument was without merit, observing that he had given a *get* to his first wife and that he was withholding the *get* as a bargaining tool in the custody dispute. 554 N.E.2d at 1022–24. *See also* Scholl v. Scholl, 621 A.2d 808 (Del. Fam. Ct. 1992) (when husband obtained a Conservative *get* instead of an Orthodox *get*, the court ordered husband to obtain an Orthodox *get* in order to enforce a Settlement Stipulation providing that husband would cooperate in allowing wife to obtain a *get*).

New Jersey courts have split on this issue. In *Minkin v. Minkin*, 434 A.2d 665 (N.J. Super. Ct. Ch. Div. 1981), a New Jersey Chancery court ordered a husband to secure a *get*, as specific performance of the ketubah. In a more recent decision, *Aflalo v. Aflalo*, 685 A.2d 523 (N.J. Super. Ct. Ch. Div. 1996), another court declined to order defendant either to obtain a *get* or to appear before the Beth Din. In *Aflalo*, the court observed that the defendant opposed the divorce and was not using the *get* as a negotiating chip, and that the wife had refused to appear before a Beth Din at his request to attempt reconciliation. Beyond distinguishing the case factually, however, the court also rejected the reasoning of earlier decisions, observing that a civil court cannot, consistently with the First Amendment, interpret religious law, and that the court in *Minkin* had been required to choose between the conflicting testimony of different rabbis in order to conclude that providing a *get* was not a religious act.

In addition to New Jersey, courts in Arizona, Florida, and Ohio have refused to compel a spouse to cooperate in a *get* procedure. *See* Victor v. Victor, 866 P.2d 899 (Ariz. Ct. App. 1993) (court refused to order husband to grant a *get*, finding language of ketubah too vague to be an enforceable agreement to provide a *get*); Turner v. Turner, 192 So. 2d 787 (Fla. Dist. Ct. App. 1967) (court had no authority to order husband to participate in religious ceremony); Steinberg v. Steinberg, No. 44125, 1982 WL 2446 (Ohio Ct. App., June 24, 1982) (order to perform a religious act, cooperating in obtaining a *get*, violates the Ohio Constitution). *See also* Paul Finkelman, *A Bad Marriage: Jewish Di-*

vorce and the First Amendment, 2 Cardozo Women's L.J. 131 (1995) (court intervention on behalf of an *agunah* violates the First Amendment).

4. *Other Nations' Efforts on Behalf of Agunot.* A statute similar to New York's is in effect in England and Wales. It provides that after a decree nisi has been granted, upon application of either party, the court may order that the decree of divorce not be made absolute until both parties have made a declaration that they have taken any steps required to dissolve the marriage in accordance with "the usages of the Jews," or "any other prescribed religious usages." Such an order can be entered, however: (1) only if the parties had been married in accordance with "the usages of the Jews" or another religion and they must cooperate in order to dissolve the marriage in accordance with those usages; and (2) only if the court is satisfied that under the circumstances the order is just and reasonable. If such a declaration is inaccurate, however, the validity of any decree of divorce made in reliance upon it is not affected. Divorce (Religious Marriages) Act, 2002, c.27, §1 (Eng.). For a critique of an earlier version of this Act, see Freeman, *supra,* at 59–60. A similar statue has been proposed for Scotland. Alister Bissett-Johnson, *Parents and Children — A Scottish White Paper on Family Law,* 2000 Int'l Fam. L. 160.

The above discussion has focused on the dilemma of addressing the recalcitrance of husbands who obtain civil divorces but refuse to grant a *get* in nations that relegate dissolution of civil marital status to secular courts. The problem of the *agunah* has been problematic in Israel as well, however, despite the fact that religious courts in Israel generally have jurisdiction over divorce. It has been estimated that thousands of *agunot* reside in Israel. Capell, *supra,* at 337. In an effort to address the problem, the Rabbinical Court Act (Implementation of Divorce Judgments) 1995 permits Rabbinical Courts to impose sanctions upon a husband who has been ordered by the court to grant a *get,* but refuses to do so. These sanctions include cancellation of a driver's or professional license, cancellation of a passport, and arrest. Edwin Freedman, *Religious Divorce in Israel,* 2000 Int'l Fam. L. 19, 21. A wife can also be sanctioned under the Act for refusing to receive a *get,* although the process for doing so is more complex. *Id.* On rare occasions, the civil courts have enforced orders of the rabbis to grant a *get* by imprisoning husbands who refuse. In one highly publicized case, a physically abusive husband was jailed for thirty-two years for refusing to grant a *get.* Capell, *supra,* at 342, citing C.A. 220/67 Att'y General v. Yehya & Ora Avraham, 22(1) P.D. 29.

2. Nations Regulating Termination of Marriage through Religious Norms or Institutions

In countries in which large segments of the population subscribe to different religions with varying norms regarding divorce, one common approach is for a government to permit termination of marriage to be governed by the norms of the religion with which a couple is affiliated. This is often referred to as a system of personal law. Nations that follow this approach often delegate authority to legally dissolve marriages to religious entities as well. While such arrangements have their advantages, they are not without problems.

Israel provides an example of such a system. As you read in Chapter 2, Israel has four officially sanctioned religious court systems for Jewish, Muslim, Christian, and Druze citizens. Israeli law confers exclusive jurisdiction on these courts over divorce between spouses belonging to the same religious community. In general, the legal system does not provide for civil divorce. Freedman, *supra,* at 19.

One obvious complexity arises when spouses do not share a common religion. Because no court has inherent jurisdiction, the parties must apply to the President of the Supreme Court, who must obtain the opinions of the Attorney General as well as of the religious courts potentially involved before deciding on the most appropriate court to exercise jurisdiction. In most of these cases, the President awards jurisdiction to the civil courts. Because there is no civil law establishing grounds for divorce, however, the civil judge is free to apply the judge's own criteria, and grant or deny the divorce according to his or her own discretion. *Id.*

As was observed in Chapter Two regarding entry into marriage, the interaction and competition between religious and civil courts create further complexity, and this is certainly as true at the time of marital dissolution as at the time of marital formation. According to the enabling statutes conferring jurisdiction on the courts, *Shari'a* courts have exclusive jurisdiction to determine child custody and maintenance between Moslems. Rabbinical courts, however, have concurrent jurisdiction with the civil courts to determine child custody and support rights between Jewish spouses. Rabbinical courts can only adjudicate ancillary issues if they are raised in connection with a divorce petition. Civil courts, which normally have no divorce jurisdiction, may hear actions seeking spousal support, property division, and/or custody. Because prima facie jurisdiction over ancillary issues typically is with the court in which the first petition is filed and served, this concurrent jurisdiction often results in a race to the court house and much strategic behavior, according to Edwin Freedman, an Israeli attorney. *Id.* For example, husbands often attempt to steer resolution of ancillary issues to the Rabbinical courts, which divide property by title, rather than the community property rule applied by the civil courts. Rabbinical courts also generally award lower maintenance, and will not award temporary maintenance. As a countermeasure, however, the Supreme Court of Israel, which sits as the High Court of Justice to review decisions of the Rabbinical Court, has taken a narrow view of matters "connected" to divorce proceedings. The High Court often voids Rabbinical judgements regarding ancillary matters if it believes the timing of the divorce action in the Rabbinical Court was engineered to create a tactical advantage over the wife. The High Court has also held that child support issues are not ancillary to divorce unless the wife consents to the jurisdiction of the Rabbinical Court over this issue. *Id.* at 19–20. Thus, multiple proceedings are often required to resolve all of the issues related to the termination of one marriage.

When nations confer upon religious norms or entities the task of regulating legal marital termination, the risk of conflict with international human rights norms also increases. Israeli scholar and academic, Ruth Halperin-Kaddari, has observed that both Muslim nations applying *Shari'a* law and Israel have had to make reservations to the Convention on the Elimination of all Forms of Discrimination Against Women (CEDAW) on religious grounds. Israel specifically entered a reservation to CEDAW's Article 16, which requires contracting nations to ensure equality between women and men in all matters relating to marriage and family relations, and specifically includes rights and responsibilities during marriage and at its dissolution. The reservation provides in part:

> The State of Israel hereby expresses its reservation with regard to Article 16 of the Convention, insofar as the laws of personal status binding on the several religious communities in Israel do not conform with the provision of that Article.

In response to Israel's reservation, the Committee on the Elimination of All Forms of Discrimination Against Women, which is charged with implementing CEDAW, suggested in its review of Israel's compliance in 1997 that: "In order to guarantee the same rights in marriage and family relations in Israel and to comply fully with the Convention, the [Israeli] Government should complete the secularization of the relevant legislation, place it under the jurisdiction of the civil courts and withdraw its reservations to the Convention." Ruth Halperin-Kaddari, *Women, Religion and Multiculturalism in Israel*, 5 UCLA J. Int'l L. & For. Aff. 330, 345–46, nn. 21–22 and accompanying text (2000) (citing Report of the Committee on the Elimination of All Forms of Discrimination Against Women, 16–17 Sessions, 1997, at 91).

As you have observed throughout this chapter, when a nation's law of marital dissolution is tied to religious norms that were developed many centuries earlier, it becomes difficult to make amendments to adjust to changing societal needs and mores, as well as to international standards. Adoption of religious norms has been problematic in this regard not only for predominantly Christian and Jewish nations, but for predominantly Muslim nations as well, which typically incorporate *Shari'a* law to regulate marital and familial issues. In Chapter 2 you examined Muslim law regarding entry into marriage. The following excerpt describes Muslim Law regarding termination of marriage, and the approach Tunisia has taken to modifying traditional applications of that law. In Tunisia, *Shari'a* courts were abolished in 1956, when Tunisia gained independence, and the courts with jurisdiction over family matters, including divorce, are now civil and not religious courts. Divorce is regulated by the Tunisia Code of Personal Status, which is based on unofficial draft codes of Maliki and Hanafi family law, and applies to all Tunisians regardless of religion. Islamic Family Law, http:/www.law.emory.edu/ifl/index2.html.

Adrian M. Morse Jr. & Leila P. Sayeh, *Tunisia: Marriage, Divorce, and Foreign Recognition*
29 Fam. L.Q. 701, 702–14 (1995)

Tunisia was conquered by the advancing forces of Islam in the seventh century when an important garrison was established at Qayrawan in the former Roman province of Africa. By the end of the tenth century, a large part of the population of Tunisia had converted to Islam....

The French occupied North Africa in the latter 1800s, establishing a protectorate in Tunisia by treaties in 1881 and 1883. Tunisia retained its indigenous system of government with the Bey remaining in power. Although the commercial and legal infrastructures of the country were appropriated by the French, with French citizens residing in Tunisia falling under the French *statut personnel*, the laws governing the personal status of Tunisian nationals continued to be the Muslim laws which had taken root over the previous 1,200 years. Islam thus remained inviolate in the family law area.

To understand the provisions governing marriage and divorce, it is essential to introduce the religious law upon which the modern civil law is based. Islam is a monotheistic religion which shares its roots and many of its core beliefs with Judaism and Christianity. The *Qur'an* was revealed at a time and place in history when patriarchal values reigned supreme and its laws in large part tempered and relieved some of the most egregious excesses which then subsisted by creating new regulations for society and modifying customary practices.

Islamic law has three basic foundations: the *Qur'an*, the *Sunnah*, and the tradition of *ijtihad*. There are five major schools of Islamic law: four Sunni and one Shi'i. The differences between the schools center on differences in the interpretation of some Quranic verses, disagreement among religious scholars on the authenticity of some of the *Hadith*, dissension with regard to the weight to be given to some legal sources, and differences in opinion as to what is required when faced with novel practical situations.

The four schools of Sunni Islam are: the Maliki in north, central, and west Africa; the Hanafi in the Arab Middle East and south Asia; the Shafii in east Africa, southern Arabia, and southern Asia; and the Hanbali in Saudi Arabia. The most important Shi'i school is the Ja'fari. All the religious schools accept the *Qur'an* as the primary authoritative source for religious law, and regard the *Sunnah* of the Prophet as a secondary source which may be used to shed light on the interpretation of the verses of the *Qur'an*.

Islam is receptive to change and its laws may be modified in at least three circumstances: necessity or public interest, change in the facts which originally gave rise to the law, and change in the custom or usage on which a particular law was based. Students and practitioners of the American legal system should have little difficulty in recognizing a system which is permitted to change within certain parameters, as this is the basic mechanism of the common law. One major difference, however, is that *Shari'ah* judges are severely limited in their authority to engage in interpretation, and consequently must limit their options to choosing from among the recognized schools the rule which best fits the facts before them. [Ed. Note: The authors explain in a footnote that this system is known as *takhayyur*. Although originally limited to "the adoption of divergent opinions within the particular school to which the judge belonged, or to the introduction of the dominant doctrine of another Sunni school," the practice later expanded to "the borrowing of any opinion of any jurist regardless of his school. Occasionally the doctrine of one school or jurist is combined with another, allowing reforms which are socially desirable and can be justified as not departing from the essence of Islam. In fact, what results is an entirely new principle."]

The *Shari'ah* is the whole body of Islamic law, encompassing the teachings of the various schools of law, the *Qur'an*, the *Sunnah*, and legal precedent established in individual cases. The Tunisian code expressly bases itself on the *Shari'ah* and derives its legitimacy from a modern interpretation of Islamic law. When it was devised, the authors used *takhayyur* to find the rules which the government felt best suited the needs of the Tunisian people among the various interpretations of the different schools. Despite this painstaking care to trace the Quranic pedigree of its reforms, among modern Muslim states Tunisia is widely viewed as having strayed the furthest from strict adherence to traditional Islamic law. No Muslim country has completely codified or comprehensively restated the family law as it exists in the *Shari'ah*. Therefore Tunisia, like other Muslim states, superimposes its statutory modifications to family law upon the framework provided by the *Shari'ah*.

* * *

Divorce is strongly condemned in Islam, and is very rare in Muslim countries. The Prophet reportedly considered it as the most reprehensible of all permitted practices in Islam, and declared that it should not be employed unless it is impossible for the husband and wife to live together under any circumstances. Many Quranic verses seek to limit both the frequency and ease with which divorce was practiced in pre-Islamic Arabia. Divorce is regarded as a safety valve, resorted to when the spouses find it impossible to live together in peace and continuing the marriage would defeat its very purpose. The permission to divorce comes from very specific passages in the *Qur'an*. The *Qur'an* also makes clear the various rights and obligations which flow from divorce.

A. Forms of Divorce

Classical *Shari'ah* law has made it extremely easy for the husband to obtain a divorce, and particularly difficult for the wife. There are five categories of divorce recognized by the jurists: *talaq, talaq altawfid', khul, lian* and *faskh*, and apostasy. Family law is at a crossroads in Muslim countries, where modern trade and increasing global interaction have resulted in civil codes to govern most facets of the law. There is an ongoing struggle between the religious communities, who wish to preserve what has come to be viewed as the last bastion of the *Shari'ah*, and the state, whose wish is to promulgate an integrated unified law for all the communities within its jurisdiction.

In the interest of justice and equality among women and men, Tunisia has elected to allow divorce only before a court. The statute in question states unequivocally that extrajudicial divorces are not effective in Tunisia: "Divorce may not take place except before the court." However, Tunisia does not keep the spouses from obtaining divorce. Either the husband or the wife may obtain a divorce:

The court shall grant a divorce:

with the mutual consent of the spouses;

upon the demand of either spouse on the grounds of material or moral prejudice;

upon the demand of the husband or wife.

Once the spouses (or one of them) request a divorce, the court must then make an attempt to reconcile the parties. Should the presiding judge's, or his delegate's, attempt at conciliation prove unfruitful, then a divorce may be pronounced. Many classical jurists have ruled that *talaq* is in no way subject to external limitation. Tunisia justifies the court's interference by reference to a passage from the *Qur'an* authorizing arbitration.

No other Arab Muslim country has taken judicial intervention into the process as far as Tunisia. The grounds of divorce available are as diverse as in any other country in the world, and the law is an example of social engineering. However, the Tunisians base their modifications to classical jurisprudence on modern interpretations of the Qur'an and the need for the law to change with time and circumstances.

B. Divorce Obligations

All the major schools of Islamic law agree that upon divorce various obligations come into play. The wife's main obligation is to observe her *'idda* to avoid any questions of paternity or inheritance with regard to any child, and to provide time for possible reconciliation. During the *'idda* the husband must provide maintenance, which is defined in the *Shari'ah* as food, clothing, and lodging. If the divorced woman has a young child, she may nurse him for two years, during which time the obligation to maintain both of them continues. The level of maintenance is determined according to the standard of living of the spouses.

If the marriage was not consummated, the jurists have agreed that the *Qur'an* clearly requires that the wife receive a suitable gift if the dower was not fixed in the contract, or up to one-half of an established dower. The dower will sometimes have been paid immediately after the marriage, known as the prompt dower. However, usually some, if not all, of the dower is deferred, to be paid upon dissolution of the marriage by divorce or death, or upon the occurrence of an event specified in the contract. The deferred dower is payable immediately upon divorce or death and represents an unsecured debt if unpaid. Spouses continue to inherit from one another during the *'idda* period in a revocable divorce, but such rights cease at the end of the period, or immediately in the case of an irrevocable divorce.

Tunisia has added some rather modern provisions to the traditional consequences of divorce. As is required by the *Qur'an*, a woman has the right to half of a specified dower if divorce occurs prior to consummation of the marriage. However, unlike the minimal requirements of the classical jurists, Tunisia has opted to make maintenance in cases involving "material prejudice" to the wife, meaning pecuniary or economic damages, extend far beyond the *'idda*. Where divorce is demanded at the request of either party under Article 31, a woman who has been materially injured will be compensated through a monthly allowance to begin at the end of the *'idda* in an amount sufficient to maintain the standard of living she enjoyed during marriage, including lodging. The allowance continues for the lifetime of the divorced wife, and may be revised upwards or downwards in response to changing circumstances. It terminates if the woman remarries or no longer has a need for it because she acquires sufficient property or salary. Upon the death of the ex-husband, the allowance becomes a debt on the estate and must be liquidated, either informally with the heirs, or via judicial decree, in a single lump sum payment taking into account the age of the former wife as of that date. The wife may also opt for a single lump sum upon divorce in lieu of an allowance.

The court must first rule on the divorce request and on the consequences which flow from it. If the court fails to succeed in reconciling the parties, the presiding judge issues an order providing for all necessary measures concerning the matrimonial domicile, aliments (means of support including clothing, lodging, and medical expenses), and custody and visitation rights of children, unless both parties expressly renounce the court's measures in whole or in part. The court's determination of the alimentary support will take into account the information at its disposal concerning likely future needs at the time the attempted reconciliation took place. The court's order shall be enforceable immediately upon issuance, and factual issues will not be appealable, although the order may be revised so long as the request for revision does not concern an issue of law. Tunisia has thus retained what is mandated by the *Qur'an* as appropriate upon divorce, and decided to legislate further in order to fulfill the spirit and intent, rather than simply the letter, of the holy law.

Notes and Questions

1. *Traditional Muslim Divorce Law.* Tunisia has been at the forefront of divorce reform in the Muslim world. Traditionally, Islamic law gives the husband the right to terminate the marriage at will, without showing cause, simply by pronouncing a formula referred to as the *talaq*. The precise methods of pronouncing *talaq* depend upon the type of divorce being used. The Islamic schools vary regarding the requirements of each, the possibility of revocation of the various types of divorce, and the economic consequences. Unlike Tunisia, which requires that the *talaq* be pronounced in court, most Islamic countries require only that the divorce be registered after the talaq is pronounced. Pakistan, however, requires that shortly after pronouncing the *talaq*, the husband must notify a designated official, who is then required to establish a reconciliation procedure. The divorce in Pakistan does not take effect until 90 days after the notice is

given, if the reconciliation fails. Doreen Hinchcliffe, *Divorce in the Muslim World*, 2000 Int'l Fam. L. 63, 63–64.

In addition to unilateral termination by the husband, traditional Islamic law also permits divorce by mutual consent through a procedure known as *khul*, in which the husband receives compensation from the wife in return for pronouncing the *talaq*. Generally the compensation is the return of the dower, or a commitment to forgive any outstanding portion of dower still owed to the wife. For a husband to seek greater compensation is considered reprehensible, but is legally possible in some countries. This creates the possibility for economic coercion, particularly in those schools in which it is difficult or impossible for a wife to seek dissolution on her own. *Id.* at 64.

There is significant diversity among the different schools regarding the extent and circumstances under which a wife can seek a divorce unilaterally. In the Hanafi school traditionally wives had no right to terminate a marriage. The other three Sunni schools and the Shi'a permit wives to seek dissolution if the husband is absent, has certain defects or diseases, or fails to support the wife. The Maliki school also permits a wife to seek a judicial divorce for harm resulting from the marriage. If the wife is unable to prove the harm, the court converts to an arbitration panel, consisting of the judge, two representatives of the husband, and two representatives of the wife. If the panel is unable to bring about a reconciliation, it then determines which spouse is primarily responsible for the discord. If it is the husband, the wife is granted divorce by a judicial *talaq*. If responsibility lays with the wife, she may obtain divorce only by a judicial *khul*, which requires that she pay compensation, again typically the return of the dower or forgiveness of remaining dower debt. *Id.* at 64.

Since the beginning of the twentieth century, significant reforms have been made in most Muslim countries, so that now even in most nations within the Hanafi school, at least some grounds exist upon which wives may seek a divorce. Many of these reforms followed the Maliki law. However, Tunisia's extension of the right of unilateral termination to women under the same circumstances upon which it is available to a man is still relatively unique within Muslim nations. *Id.* at 64–65.

In Egypt, where family law is also based upon *Shari'a*, divorce reform enacted by the Parliament in 2000 caused significant turmoil. Conservatives strongly opposed the new law, which permits women to seek divorce on the grounds of incompatibility, in addition to pre-existing fault grounds. Wives who pursue divorces based on incompatibility avoid the lengthy delays and years of appeals that often accompany divorces initiated by wives on fault grounds, but they must return dower and have no right to maintenance. The new law passed due to the efforts of moderate Muslim clerics, women's advocates, judges and divorce lawyers, who argued that the law was in keeping with Islamic principles. *See* Susan Sachs, *Egypt's Women Win Equal Rights to Divorce*, N. Y. Times, March 1, 2000, at 1; Elizabeth Bryant, *Egyptians Split by Proposed Divorce Law Changes*, Hous. Chron., Feb. 13, 2000, at 26; *Giving Wives a Way Out*, U.S. News & World Rep., March 6, 2000, at 35.

The above discussion is only a brief introduction to the complexities of Islamic divorce law. More information may be obtained in Jamal J. Nasir, The Status of Women Under Islamic Law 69–106 (1990); and, in a country-by-country breakdown, at Islamic Family Law, http:/www.law.emory.edu/ifl/index2.html.

2. *Alternative Judicial Models.* The above discussion has illustrated several models for allocation of judicial authority in nations that utilize religious norms to regulate termination of marriage: (1) awarding exclusive jurisdiction over divorce to religious courts, with or without the authority to adjudicate ancillary issues (Israel utilizes both models);

and (2) retaining jurisdiction in civil courts applying civil law based upon the norms of the predominant religion to all citizens (Tunisia). Egypt utilizes what might be considered a third model, having integrated its *Shari'a* courts into a national court system in 1956. Family law matters are now adjudicated in the civil courts, but by judges trained in *Shari'a* law, and there is a separate chamber of the civil court for family law issues affecting the Coptic Christian minority. Islamic Family Law, http://www.law.emory.edu/ifl/index2.html. In India, a similar system operates. Separate personal laws for members of the Hindu, Muslim, Parsi, and Christian religions govern family law matters, all administered by the civil court system. Islamic Family Law, http://www.law.emory.edu/ifl/index2.html.

3. *Impact of Colonization on Indigenous Religious Norms.* Ironically, on the Indian subcontinent the attempt by the British to codify indigenous law during the colonial period contributed heavily to the perception of Islamic law as textually based and immutable. During the eighteenth century, Muslim communities on the subcontinent differed in their application of local law, and the *qadis,* religious judges, took local customs into account. When the British replaced the local systems with colonial courts, they codified what they perceived to be Islamic law, converting a fluid system into one that was fixed. Moreover, their codification was inaccurate, as they perceived the *Qur'an* and the *Sunnah* as codes and applied them without considering the social context in which they were written or the circumstances in which they were applied. They also translated the *al-Hadiya*, a compilation of Hanafi doctrine, thus inflating its importance rather than treating it as one statement within a larger body of scholarly debate. The application of this new code in a judicial system following legally binding precedent further altered traditional application of Islamic principles. Nadya Haider, *Islamic Legal Reform: The Case of Pakistan and Family Law,* 12 Yale J.L. & Feminism 287, 294–96 (2000).

Though British codification stifled the fluidity of Islamic family law, scholars point out that by legislatively altering doctrines they found offensive, the British also weakened the perception on the subcontinent of the law as divine, and fostered acceptance of the notion that law could be reformed legislatively. When the British passed the Dissolution of Muslim Marriages Act in 1939, for example, they departed from Hanafi doctrine by permitting wives to obtain judicial divorces on one of eight fault grounds. *Id.* at 296–98.

The British codification of Hindu law similarly altered Hindu doctrine regarding marital dissolution. The Hindu religion has no single text equivalent to the Bible or the *Qur'an*. Though a series of books known as *dharmasastra* sets forth guidelines, prior to colonization most enforcement of social norms occurred through local custom at the family or community level. The *dharmasastra* does not recognize divorce, and among the high caste communities prior to colonization it was not practiced. Divorce appears to have been widely practiced among the non-Brahminical communities, however, which were largely autonomous in pre-colonial times. The British codification of *dharmasastra* in general entrenched the upper caste standards, restricting the customary divorce practices of the majority and thereby eliminating the routes many women had used to escape abusive marriages. Though the British retained the customary practice of divorce by mutual consent, they eliminated the lower caste custom of permitting a wife to leave the marriage unilaterally. But as with the Muslims, British colonization pulled in two directions. Michael R. Anderson, *Hindu Divorce—At the Intersection of Convention and Globalization,* 2000 Int'l Fam. L. 14, 14–15. As British scholar Michael Anderson has noted, "one of the ironies of colonial legal rule was that it rigidified Hindu law through a scripturalist approach to Brahminical texts and then re-liberalized the law through statutory reform." *Id.* at 15. Although later British colonial statutes made some minor inroads into the restrictions, the Hindu Marriage Act passed after independence and, subsequently amended, ultimately permitted divorce on a variety of fault grounds and mutual consent. *Id.* at 15–16.

In addition to the fossilization of Muslim and Hindu divorce practices, colonial codification of indigenous law is often credited as one of the factors that polarized the Muslim and Hindu communities during the colonial era. By ignoring the diverse practices among both groups, the essentialist approach of the British codification, it is suggested, contributed to the development of strong political identities and the conflict that later ensued. Haider, *supra,* at 295–96. Michael Anderson has observed regarding this dynamic: "The difference in divorce laws became emblematic of Hindu and Muslim identity in an environment of growing unease between the two religious communities." Anderson, *supra,* at 15. Does this cautionary tale of the ramifications of British actions during the colonial period suggest the need for temperance and reflection when considering the transplant of practices from one legal system to another, or are the problems identified related solely to the colonial context in which this transplant occurred?

Problem 3-4

Atlantica is a large island located south of Iceland and 1,000 miles west of Ireland, with a population of 5 million. It has been settled predominantly by immigrants from Western Europe and the United States. In addition, approximately 15% of the population is descended from African immigrants. The economy of the island is reasonably good, but it is not a wealthy country. The unemployment rate is normally approximately 5%, although in the recent past it has been slightly higher, as the economies of its trading partners in Europe and the United States have declined. The population is roughly half men and half women, with an age distribution similar to that of the United States. The religious affiliation of the island is as follows: 25% are Roman Catholic, 20% are members of other Christian religions, 15% are Muslim, 15% are Jewish, 5% are Unitarians, and 20% have no religious affiliation.

Because the early settlers to the country were predominantly European, Atlantica's divorce laws were initially based upon early 20th century British law, and currently are very similar to the British divorce laws in effect in the 1930s. Husbands or wives can obtain a divorce if they can prove adultery, desertion, cruelty, or insanity on the part of their spouses. The Atlantica legislature is now engaging in an intense debate regarding the revision of these laws.

As a member of the Atlantica Legislature, draft a proposal for "termination of marriage" legislation for Atlantica. Assume that you have the freedom to draft whatever you feel would be the ideal system. Obviously, if the majority of your colleagues do not agree with you, your bill will not pass; but for this draft, ignore the political realities, whatever they may be, and draft legislation that you feel will best serve the citizens of your nation.

In preparing your proposal, consider whether divorce (or dissolution, if you prefer that nomenclature), is going to be available in Atlantica, on what grounds, and through what process. Specify whether annulment and/or judicial separation will be retained. Clarify whether you will allow individual couples to alter the grounds or process by private agreement or invocation of a separate type of marriage. If your proposed law would continue to permit the termination of civil marital status, clarify whether termination of civil marital status will be governed by civil norms exclusively, or whether your legislation will incorporate religious norms for all or certain portions of the populace. Specify also whether the process for termination will involve judicial or administrative authorities, litigation, alternative dispute resolution, counseling, or a combination of some or all of these mechanisms. Will these functions be carried out by governmental employees, religious institutions, private nonprofit organizations, profit-making entities, or some combination of these groups?

Problem 3-5

Part A. A legislative committee of the Atlantica Parliament is holding a public hearing today to consider divorce reform legislation. As a lobbyist, prepare a 3–5 minute presentation to the legislative committee, advocating the position of your organization. Your presentation could be a personal (fictional) testimonial, a presentation of policy arguments, or any other format that you feel would effectively convey the position of your interest group. Be creative. The following are interest groups that would be eager to be heard on this issue. If your instructor does not assign you, individually or in groups, to represent a particular group for this Problem, then select the group you would like to represent.

Interest Groups

Organization of Atlantica Roman Catholic Clergy

Atlantica Jewish Alliance

Atlantica Muslim Federation

Atlantica Christian Federation (group representing a coalition of fundamental Christian churches)

Atlantica Legal Aid Board

Atlantica Organization for Women (a feminist organization similar to NOW)

Family Law Section of the Atlantica Bar Association

Atlantica Children's Rights Advocates

Atlantica Association of Family Counselors and Therapists

Atlantica Association of Judges and Court Personnel

Part B. As a legislator and member of the legislative committee considering divorce reform legislation, prepare a short presentation to your committee advocating the enactment of the proposed legislation that you drafted for Problem 3-4.

Chapter 4

Emerging Rights and Duties of Nontraditional Partners

Family law continues to evolve rapidly. Past orthodoxies become unsustainable, while new norms and values are ushered in.

> John Murphy, *The Recognition of Same-Sex Families*
> *in Britain: The Role of Private International Law,*
> 16 Int'l J. L. Pol. & Fam. 181, 185 (2002)

Perhaps nowhere in family law is this evolution more visible than in relation to the burgeoning recognition of rights of nontraditional couples. Within the past few decades courts, legislatures, and international bodies on every continent have confronted a myriad of issues regarding the extent to which rights and obligations formerly reserved to heterosexual married spouses should be conferred on other partners.

Individuals become unmarried partners under different circumstances. Gay and lesbian couples have historically been precluded from entering marriage. Other cohabiting couples who are eligible to legally marry choose, for a variety of reasons, not to complete the formal requirements to marry. Many individuals in both groups do not wish to undertake some or all of the panoply of legal obligations that accompany marital status. Among couples who have been historically denied eligibility to marry, however, there are many who fervently wish to make that commitment and to achieve the social recognition that accompanies marital status. Fashioning legal norms that respond to the divergent legal needs of these groups has presented unique challenges, which are compounded by pressures from other elements in society to preserve the institution of marriage in accordance with their own religious or traditional values.

One approach to respond to the needs of couples that have traditionally been denied marital status is to eliminate the substantive barrier precluding entry. Another option, which to date has been more widely utilized, is to create an alternative legal status conferring some or all of the marital rights and obligations upon couples who choose to enter it. Some governments have chosen to make this status available only to gay and lesbian or certain other couples who are not permitted to marry, while other governments have extended eligibility to any couples meeting the requisite age requirements. Section A will examine the steps taken in several nations to extend eligibility to marry or create an alternative institution, comparing the models chosen and the benefits and obligations that accompany each.

A combination of policy considerations and political pressures have influenced the willingness of some of these governments to recently accord gay and lesbian couples entitlement to certain rights or status. In other instances, however, governmental authorities responded to recognition by their courts of the right of gay and lesbian partners to equal treatment under their domestic constitutions. International conventions and institutions have also influenced change. Section B will examine the impact of domestic constitutions and international law on the recognition of rights for gay and lesbian individuals and couples.

Many governments have also conferred certain rights and imposed obligations on cohabitants who have not entered an alternative status, both between the partners themselves and in their relations with third parties. In some nations courts have determined that even heterosexual cohabitants, under certain circumstances, are constitutionally entitled to at least some of the legal rights enjoyed by marital spouses. Section C provides a comparative examination of the legal rights conferred upon those cohabitants who are not legal spouses or partners in a domestic partnership or civil union.

A. Marriage and Alternative Institutions

1. Opening Entry to Marriage

On April 1, 2001, the Netherlands became the first nation to permit partners of the same gender to marry. Although the Netherlands had already had domestic partnership legislation in effect since 1998 for both heterosexual and homosexual couples, the Government decided to take the further step of equalizing access to marriage for opposite-gender and same-gender couples, in furtherance of the principles of gender-neutrality and equal treatment. *See* Explanatory Memorandum accompanying the Act on Opening up of Marriage, Acts of 21 December 2000, Stb. 2001, no. 9 (Kees Waaldijk, trans.), *at* http//ruljis.leidenuniv.nl/user/cwaaldij/www/NHR/transl-marr.html. As amended by the Act, Articles 30, 77a, and 80f of Book 1 of the Civil Code now read as follows:

Article 30—A marriage can be contracted by two different persons of different sex or of the same sex. The law only considers marriage in its civil relations.

Article 77a—When two persons indicate to the registrar that they would like their marriage to be converted into a registered partnership, the registrar of the domicile of one of them can make a record of conversion to that effect. If the spouses are domiciled outside the Netherlands and want to convert their marriage into a registered partnership in the Netherlands, and at least one of them has Dutch nationality, conversion will take place with the registrar in The Hague.

* * *

A conversion terminates the marriage and starts the registered partnership on the moment the record of conversion is registered in the register of registered partnerships. The conversion does not affect the paternity over children born before the conversion.

Article 80f—When two persons indicate to the registrar that they would like their registered partnership to be converted into a marriage, the registrar of the domicile of one of them can make a record of conversion to that effect. If the registered partners are domiciled outside the Netherlands and want to convert their registered partnership into a marriage in the Netherlands, and at least one of them has Dutch nationality, conversion will take place with the registrar in the Hague.

* * *

A conversion terminates the registered partnership and starts the marriage on the moment the record of conversion is registered in the register of marriages. The conversion does not affect the paternity over children born before the conversion. (Kees Waaldijk, trans., *supra*).

The legal requirements for and consequences of a same-gender marriage are identical to those of a heterosexual marriage in virtually every way. The conditions for entry, in terms of restrictions on age, plural marriages, consanguinity restrictions, etc, are the same. Whether or not they are a same-gender couple, at least one of the partners must be either a Dutch national or habitually resident in the Netherlands for the Dutch marriage laws to apply. Marriage for both opposite-gender partners and same-gender partners permits one to use the other's surname, and unless a premarital agreement provides otherwise, triggers community property treatment of assets and debts of the marriage. Marriage also imposes spousal support obligations both during marriage and after divorce, joint liability for certain household debts, and restrictions upon management of joint property. Marriage impacts many other legal rights and obligations, such as inheritance, tax consequences, and entitlements to pensions and governmental benefits, all of which will apply equally to both same-gender and opposite-gender marriages. To terminate any marriage, whether between couples of the same or different genders, a court's divorce pronouncement is required. The Ministry of Justice, *Same-sex Marriages: Fact Sheets* (April 2001), *at* http://www.minjust.nl:8080/a_belcid/fact/same-sexmarriages.htm.; Wendy Schrama, *Reforms in Dutch Family Law During the Course of 2001: Increased Pluriformity and Complexity*, in The International Survey of Family Law 277, 278 (2002).

Only a few differences remain. Because the Netherlands is a hereditary monarchy and in this context genetic progeny are deemed important, the Government pronounced in deliberations on the bill that it would not apply to the king or queen or a potential successor to the throne. This objective is to be legally accomplished, in the Government's view, by interpreting Article 28 of the Constitution, which addresses the marriage of the king or queen, as referring exclusively to an opposite-gender marriage, while interpreting the Civil Code's provision opening marriage to same-gender couples to apply to everyone else. Schrama, *supra*, at 278–79. Though interesting, this restriction directly affects only certain members of the royal family.

Of broader interest is the different effect of same-gender marriage on the recognition of legal parenthood. A marriage of spouses of opposite gender creates a presumption that the husband and wife are parents of any child born of the marriage. A woman who bears a child is the mother, and her husband is presumed to be the father of a child she bears. The legislature was unwilling to extend this presumption to the same-gender partner of another man, as the biological link that created the presumption for heterosexual spouses would be absent. Therefore, the Act Opening Marriages did not amend the relevant language in the Dutch statute creating marital presumptions of parenthood. If one of the spouses is a biological parent, that parent's same-gender partner is regarded as a legal parent of the child only if he or she adopts the child.

Legal parenthood must be distinguished in the Dutch system, however, from shared parenting responsibilities. A new law, which took effect in January, 2002, provides that a spouse in a lesbian marriage, as a matter of law, will acquire automatic shared custody of a child born to her partner during the marriage, if the child has no other legal parent.

This would be the case if the child was conceived by anonymous artificial insemination. This rule does not apply to male couples, as the birth mother of the child would normally be recognized as a legal parent. A male partner of a biological father, however, or both, if neither is the legal parent, can still apply for shared custody if the other statutory requirements for shared custody are satisfied. Scharma, *supra*, at 295–96; Ministry of Justice, *supra*.

Notes and Questions

1. *Retention of the Domestic Partnership Alternative.* The Netherlands originally created domestic partnerships in 1998 in order to afford same-gender couples a status that would provide almost all of the benefits of marriage. Nevertheless, in order to provide equal access to the symbolic nature of marriage, the Government went further to enact the Act Opening Marriage three years later. Yet the Act retains the option of registered partnerships, and in fact permits a couple to convert their marriage to a registered partnership, or their registered partnership to a marriage, simply by making a record of conversion. If the goal of equality for same-gender couples has now been achieved by opening marriage, what purpose does retention of the registered partnership as an institution serve? The Act postpones a decision on the ultimate fate of registered partnerships until 2006. Are there any drawbacks to retaining it?

In the Netherlands the rights and obligations that the parties have towards each other are the same in both marriages and registered partnerships. There are some minor differences regarding the form of the ceremony for entering a registered partnership, as opposed to a marriage, but the major difference affects dissolution, in that a marriage can only be dissolved through a divorce in court, but a registered partnership can be terminated by the parties themselves. The Ministry of Justice, *supra*. In addition, a registered partnership does not establish legal parenthood of the male partner over a child born during the partnership, even when the partnership is heterosexual, and requires formal recognition of the child by the male partner who wishes to become the legal father. Schrama, *supra*, at 262–63. This last distinction would not affect the choice of a male same-gender couple regarding which institution to enter, however, as for them the legal status of father is not derived from either marriage or registered partnership. Similarly, the parental status of female same-gender partners is not altered by the fact that the relationship is a marriage rather than a registered partnership. *Id.* at 295–99.

2. *Utilization of the Marital Option.* Government statistics indicate that during the first six months in which the Act Opening Marriage was in effect, 1900 same-gender couples married in the Netherlands, which constituted 3.6% of the total marriages performed during this period. Of these couples, 55% were male couples and 45% were female couples. Schrama, *supra*, at 279.

A similar gender disparity was observed in the early years of registered partner legislation in Denmark, Norway, and Sweden. Male couples registering far outnumbered female couples initially, although as each year goes by this disparity diminishes markedly. William N. Eskridge, Jr., *Comparative Law and the Same-Sex Marriage Debate: A Step-by-Step Approach Toward State Recognition*, 31 McGeorge L. Rev. 641, 661 (2000).

3. *A Standard Progression of Rights?* Dutch law professor Kees Waaldijk and Professor William Eskridge of Yale have both observed a pattern in the legal progression towards equality in many European countries. They suggest that decriminalization of same-gender sexual behavior is typically the beginning step, followed by equalizing the age of

consent for sexual conduct, prohibition of discrimination based upon sexual orientation, limited recognition characterized by bestowing certain rights and obligations on cohabiting same-gender couples, recognition of same-gender partnerships, and finally legalization of joint adoption of children by gay and lesbian couples. Eskridge, *supra*, at 647–49; Kees Waaldijk, *Towards the Recognition of Same-Sex Partners in European Union Law: Expectations Based on Trends in National Law, in* Legal Recognition of Same-Sex Partnerships 635 (Robert Wintemute & Mads Andenaes, eds. 2001).

This sequential and incremental process, Professor Eskridge observes, has played an important role in the relative sea change that has occurred in many countries in the treatment afforded gay people by the legal system over the past fifty years:

> The recurrence of the same pattern in country after country suggests this paradox: law cannot move unless public opinion moves, but public attitudes can be influenced by changes in the law. For gay rights, the impasse suggested by this paradox can be ameliorated or broken if the proponents of reform move step-by-step along a continuum of little reforms.... Step-by-step change permits gradual adjustment of anti-gay mindsets, slowly empowers gay rights advocates, and can discredit anti-gay arguments. Eskridge, *supra*, at 648.

The Netherlands serves as a prototype for this progression theory and, completing the model, it in fact passed a law permitting same-gender couples to adopt at the same time that the Act Opening Marriage was passed. *See* Wijziging van Boek 1 van het Burgerlijk Wetboek (Adoptie Door Personen van Hetzelfde Geslacht (Amendment of Book 1 of the Civil Code, Adoption by Persons of the Same Sex), Stb. 2001 no.10. Prior to April 2001, gay couples could not adopt, even if they were registered partners, although one member of the couple could become an adoptive parent. Scott Seufert, Note, *Going Dutch?: A Comparison of the Vermont Civil Union Law to the Same-Sex Marriage Law of the Netherlands*, 19 Dick. J. Int'l L. 449, 456 (2001). Other European nations that have recognized domestic partnerships between same-gender couples have also often been slower to extend adoption rights to gay and lesbian couples. Sweden, for example, which enacted its Registered Partnership Act in 1994, did not permit registered partners to adopt until 2002. *See* Katherine McGill, *Sweden Passes Bill Allowing Homosexual Couples to Adopt*, The Independent (London), June 7, 2002, at 11. Denmark legalized adoption of a partner's child (though not other children) in 1999, ten years after it enacted its Registered Partnership Act, and Iceland approved joint adoption four or five years after its partnership legislation was enacted. *See* Nancy D. Polikoff, *Recognizing Partners but Not Parents / Recognizing Parents but Not Partners: Gay and Lesbian Family Law in Europe and the United States*, 17 N.Y.L. Sch. J. Hum. Rts. 711, 729 (2000).

Professor Eskridge observes that to some extent U.S. jurisdictions that recognize domestic partnerships have followed the steps of this progression as well. Eskridge, *supra*, at 652–53. Professor Polikoff suggests that in at least one respect, however, U.S. law has followed a different sequence. Though recognition of same-gender marriage and domestic partnerships has occurred at a much slower pace in the United States than in Europe, American courts have already approved joint adoptions by gay or lesbian couples in more than half of the U.S. states. Polikoff, *supra*, at 712–13. What factors do you think contributed to the differences in the relative willingness of European nations and U.S. states to accept joint adoption and to create a legally sanctioned partnership status for gay and lesbian couples?

4. *Is Marriage the Appropriate Trigger?* One argument for opening the institution of marriage to same-gender couples is that marriage is the qualifying event for nu-

merous legal benefits, as well as obligations, under the legal systems of most nations. Yet some scholars have questioned the extent to which marriage is the appropriate trigger for legal intervention, and whether it is a worthy institution for same-gender couples to pursue. *See* Kenneth Norrie, *Marriage is for Heterosexuals: May the Rest of Us Be Saved From It*, [2000] Child & Fam. L.Q. 363; Nancy D. Polikoff, *We Will Get What We Ask For: Why Legalizing Gay and Lesbian Marriage Will Not "Dismantle the Legal Structure of Gender in Every Marriage,"* 79 Va. L. Rev. 1535 (1993); Paula L. Ettelbrick, *Since When is Marriage a Path to Liberation*, Nat'l Gay & Lesbian Q., Fall 1989, at 9.

Would all couples be better served if other life events or incidents played the central role in the allocation of legal rights and obligations? For example, the length and stability of the relationship might be the factor that triggers entitlement to legal rights, or the birth of a child, rather than the entry into marriage. Under such a system marriage could remain a choice for personal or religious reasons, but would lose its legal significance. Although no nation has adopted such a system, Sweden, for example, has reduced the number of rights attached to marriage, emphasizing individual responsibility and equality in its allocation of governmental rights and duties. Rebecca Probert & Anne Barlow, *Displacing Marriage—Diversification and Harmonisation within Europe*, 12 Child & Fam. L. Q. 156, 162–63 (2000). What arguments might be made for substituting factors related to the substance of a relationship rather than entry into the marital status itself, as the criteria for legal rights and obligations? As you read the subsequent sections regarding alternative status options and rights afforded cohabitants, consider the extent to which some nations are partially moving in the direction of linking rights to the substantive characteristics of a relationship.

Another approach would be to abolish civil marriage completely and to tie legal consequences to civil registration of a relationship rather than to marriage or to the characteristics of the relationship. While some nations have created registration systems as alternatives to marriage, as discussed in the next subsection, no nation has to date chosen to totally replace the institution of marriage with registration as a method of affording equality to same-gender couples. The Law Commission of Canada, a federal law reform agency that advises the Canadian Parliament, has discussed the advantages and disadvantages of this approach—along with others—in Chapter 4 of its December 2001 report, *Beyond Conjugality: Recognizing and Supporting Close Personal Relationships Between Adults* (2001), *available at* http://www.lcc.gc.ca/en/themes/pr/cpra/chap4.asp:

> Creating a registration scheme that would permit all relationships, conjugal and other, to benefit from the characteristics of voluntariness, publicity, certainty and stability now afforded only to marriage could eliminate the need for marriage. It would not prevent people from marrying religiously or calling themselves "married" in addition to "registering" their unions. However, the religious marriage would not carry legal connotations nor would the public identification as "married" be of any legal consequence. In order to have legal consequences, people would have to register their relationship. Legal consequences would accompany only the additional and separate step of registering the relationship for civil purposes. The system of civil registration would be open to all, married couples and others, who want to obtain public recognition and support of their relationships while voluntarily subscribing to a range of legal rights and obligations.

The idea has many advantages. By removing the link between marriage and legal consequences, the spheres of religious and secular authority would be more clearly delineated. By establishing a civil registration scheme open to all persons in committed relationships, the state could focus more clearly and effectively on accomplishing the underlying objective currently accomplished incompletely by marriage, namely, recognizing and supporting committed personal adult relationships by facilitating an orderly regulation of their affairs.

However, one disadvantage of leaving the solemnization of marriage to religious authorities is that the option of marrying in a secular ceremony would be lost. This may be a serious disadvantage given that civil marriage ceremonies constitute a growing proportion of marriages solemnized in many Canadian jurisdictions. Nevertheless, this would not prevent couples from calling "marriage" the registration of their unions and celebrating this commitment.

It should also be noted that under this model, married persons would have the choice, currently unavailable to them, whether or not to have their relationship status formally recognized by the state. There are both advantages and disadvantages to this choice. On the one hand, it promotes the value of autonomy for married and unmarried persons alike since they all will be able to choose whether or not to register their relationships. On the other hand, it may create the undesirable situation of undermining individuals' reasonable expectations. If individuals do not understand that a religious marriage unaccompanied by a registration does not result in any legal consequences, they may be lulled into a false sense of security having entered only a religious marriage....

...While there are many principled advantages to this model, it is not likely an option that would appear very attractive to a majority of Canadians.... Removing marriage as a choice for conjugal couples prevents them from continuing to use a legal mechanism that many regard as fundamental to their commitment. While further debate about...removing the state from the marriage business... is worthwhile, we do not believe that this is a viable reform option at this time.

* * *

Ultimately the Law Commission recommended instead to Parliament and the provincial legislatures that they establish registration schemes to facilitate the private ordering of both conjugal and non-conjugal relationships, and that they remove restrictions on marriages between persons of the same sex.

2. Creating an Alternative Status

To date the majority of nations desiring to afford same-gender couples the opportunity to legally formalize their relationships have opted to create an alternative status that coexists with the institution of marriage. In 1989, Denmark became the first nation to follow this route when it enacted registered partnership legislation. It was soon joined by other Nordic countries—Norway (1993), Sweden (1994), Greenland (1994), and Iceland (1995)—whose legislation mirrored Denmark's.

Registered partnerships in these Nordic countries are open only to same-gender couples. The legislation explicitly guarantees that, with a few delineated exceptions, registered partners will have all of the same rights under law as married couples. Thus, the registered partnership creates mutual obligations of support, inheritance rights, insurance benefits, and the other economic and legal rights, between the partners themselves and in relation to third parties, that accompany marital status. The substantive exceptions in the original legislation all relate to parental rights. Denmark and Sweden, for example, restricted the ability of partners to have joint custody, and Iceland and Sweden restricted access to artificial insemination. Originally, all of these countries withheld the right to adopt, although Denmark, Sweden, and Iceland have lifted or partially lifted those restrictions subsequently, as described above in Note 3. *See* Martin DuPuis, *The Impact of Culture, Society, and History on the Legal Process: An Analysis of the Legal Status of Same-Sex Relationships in the United States and Denmark,* 9 Intl J. L. & Fam. 86, 104–05 (1995); translated texts of The Danish Registered Partnership Act, Iceland's Registered Partnership Act, Norway's Act on Registered Partnerships for Homosexual Couples, and Sweden's Registered Partnership Act, http://users.cybercity.dk/~dko12530/s2.htm.

Many of the restrictions to entry to marriage, such as under-age, consanguinity, and bigamy prohibitions, also apply to registered partnerships in these countries, and each of these nations requires that at least one partner be a citizen of the nation and domiciled therein. Solemnization requirements for registered partnerships, however, are not identical to marriage, and vary by country. In Denmark, for example, "[r]egistered partners do not have a right to a Danish church wedding," nor do they have a right by law to mediation performed by clergy. DuPuis, *supra*, at 104–05, citing Act No. 821, 19 Dec. 1989. Nevertheless, the following ceremony, similar in nature to a wedding, reportedly takes place in Copenhagen's City Hall, where registrants are asked to take vows when they go to register their partnership:

> As you have made an application to the Copenhagen City Hall in order to get your partnership lawfully registered, your wish will now be fulfilled. With this registration you will—with few exceptions—obtain the same social security as married people in Danish society.

> Before performing the registration, the municipality wishes to remind you of the meaning and importance of the promise you are giving each other. Registered partnership implies in general a pledge to live together in mutual affection, helpfulness and tolerance. In recognition of this, the municipality expresses the wish that throughout your partnership, with all its changes, you will preserve the good intentions, to live together in a harmonious and meaningful fellowship.

> I ask you, (Name), do you take (Name) to be your lawful register partner? (Repeat for each partner)

> After you now solemnly declared your desire to enter into registered partnership with each other, I hereby ask you to sign.

Partners Task Force for Gay & Lesbian Couples, at http://buddybuddy.com/d-p-scan.html. Registered partnerships in these countries are also dissolved under the same circumstances as marriages.

More recently, Germany and Finland have enacted registered partnership legislation, also limiting entry to same-gender couples. Germany's legislative scheme, the Registered Partnership Act of 2001, *Gesetz zur Beendigung der Diskriminierung gleichgeschlechtlicher Gemeishaften Lebenspartnerschaften,* 2001 BGBI. I S. 266, is of particular interest, as it deviates from the Nordic model in several respects.

Rather than grant all of the rights of marriage, with specified parental exceptions, the German legislature instead enumerated the rights and obligations that registered partnership would entail. While extensive, they deviate from the rules governing marriage in some significant respects. Registered partners commit to provide each other with appropriate financial support during the relationship, and to joint entitlement and obligations arising from contracts entered by one partner, just as in marriage. Unlike marital spouses, however, partners must declare which system of property will be applicable to their partnership —a regime of accrued gains (which secures a share of property acquired for the home-maker partner), a contract that modifies the accrued gains regime, separation of property, or communal property—at the time they establish the partnership. Registered partners have the same rights of inheritance as marital spouses, and a right to become tenant of a joint residence after the death of a partner, but do not have equal tax status in terms of inheritance tax or other tax benefits. Registered partners are accorded testimonial and immigration privileges similar to marital spouses, and one partner may acquire the right, with the consent of the other partner, to participate in day-to-day decisions regarding the partner's child. Joint adoption, or adoption of a partner's child, is not permitted, however, nor is artificial insemination of one of the partners. If one partner does live with the biological or adopted child of the other partner over an extended period of time, the former individual has a right of access following dissolution, but would not have a right to custody. Nina Dethloff, *The Registered Partnership Act of 2001, in* The International Survey of Family Law 171, 174–78 (Andrew Bainham ed., 2002); Steven Ross Levitt, *New Legislation in Germany Concerning Same-Sex Unions,* 7 ILSA J. Int'l & Comp. L. 469, 482–88 (2001).

As in marriage, dissolution of a German registered partnership requires a court decree. The grounds for dissolution of a registered partnership, however, differ in some respects from the grounds for dissolution of marriage. Dissolution of a registered partnership is permitted (1) by agreement, 12 months after the parties file a declaration of their desire for a dissolution; (2) at the request of one partner, 36 month's after that partner's declaration has been filed; or (3) on the basis of unacceptable hardship to the partner who files, for reasons related to the other partner. Unlike dissolution of a marriage, there is no irrefutable presumption based upon breakdown and separation for a specific period. Thus, registered partners will frequently have to wait longer for the decree, because partners must declare their intent at the beginning of the statutory period, whereas marital spouses may choose to file toward the end of a separation period, and separation of spouses can be deemed to include periods in which both were physically living in the same home. Dethloff, *supra,* at 179.

German registered partnerships may, under some circumstances, create an obligation to provide post-dissolution maintenance to a former partner who cannot support himself or herself, due to age or disability. Unlike the situation following dissolution of a marriage, however, the court is directed by the legislation to look first to relatives of the financially vulnerable partner to provide support, and only if support cannot be obtained from such relatives would the obligation for post-dissolution maintenance be imposed upon an ex-partner. Levitt, *supra,* at 483.

Notes and Questions

1. *Constitutional and Political Constraints.* Several unique constitutional and political factors contributed to the different model for registered partnership ultimately fashioned by the German legislature. One important constraint was the risk that the new legislation would be determined unconstitutional by the Federal Constitutional Court.

Article 6 of the German Constitution explicitly provides special protection for the institutions of marriage and the family, both by protecting the institutions from state intervention and by imposing a positive duty upon the state to support them. Ilona Ostner, *Cohabitation in Germany—Rules, Reality and Public Discourses*, 15 Int'l J.L. Pol. & Fam. 88, 99 (2001). Review of legislation by the Federal Constitutional Court does not necessitate the same kind of standing requirements the U.S. Supreme Court would demand. Instead, an abstract review can be initiated by complaint of any of the sixteen state governments asserting that the challenged law violates constitutional principles. Sensing the likelihood that opponents of the legislation would challenge the legislation under Article 6, drafters steered away from the use of the word "marriage," as well as from consideration of an alternative status for both opposite-sex and same-sex partners that might compete with marriage. Though the bill's drafters desired to provide as many rights as possible, legislative history reveals their concern that the partnership be perceived as a new institution, without all of the rights and indicia of marriage, so that it would not be regarded as a rival or an affront to the legitimacy of traditional marriage that might be found to violate the government's constitutional duty to protect marriage and family life. Levitt, *supra*, at 478–79, 488–89. *See also* Ostner, *supra*, at 99.

The drafters' calculations proved to be successful. In an action challenging the constitutionality of the German domestic partnership legislation, brought by Bavaria and two other states, the Federal Constitutional Court voted 5–3 to uphold the law's constitutionality. *German Court Oks Gay Marriage*, July 17, 2002, *at* http://www.nytimes.com/aponline/international/AP-Germany-Gay-Couples.html.

Another set of constraints was imposed by Germany's federal system. A bill regarded as affecting the rights or interests of the states requires a simple majority of votes in both the Bundestag, the lower house, and the Bundesrat, the upper house in which legislators are chosen by the state governments and each state's representatives must vote as a block. Legislation regarded as within the competency of the federal government can, under certain circumstances, become law without approval of the majority in the upper house. When it became apparent that the registered partnership legislation did not have sufficient votes in the Bundesrat, the legislation was split into two bills, separating out the matters within the competency of the federal government, which was the portion that ultimately was put into effect. Those matters regarded as impacting state governments, such as the tax benefits, were separated into a second bill, which was ultimately defeated. Levitt, *supra*, at 479–81, 488.

2. *Should Role Assumptions Impact Creditors' Rights?* German law professor Nina Dethloff questions whether imposing contractual liability on both partners for purchases made by one partner during the relationship for food, clothing, furniture, or a vehicle is creating a windfall for the creditor. She argues that insufficient data is available regarding the role assumption of same-gender partners, but postulates that differentiated division of tasks is rarer because few children are raised in German same-gender relationships. If so, she suggests that this creditor protection is unnecessary, as the principal function of joint liability is to enable a homemaker partner to make purchases for the couple independently. Dethloff, *supra*, at 175. Liability to creditors during opposite-gender marriages has been a doctrine in the state of flux during the past few decades in the United States, where the issue frequently arises in the context of imposing liability for one spouse's medical debts upon the other spouse, and U.S. states have fashioned four or five different approaches to the issue.

Does it make more sense, when fashioning an alternative status, to scrutinize each legal effect of opposite-gender marriage to determine if it is reasonably applied to same-gender couples, or rather to take a broader approach, establishing rights and obligations equivalent to marriage across the board?

If you believe scrutinizing individual rights and obligations is more appropriate, do you think Dethloff's assumption that differentiated division of tasks is far less frequent among same-gender couples would be accurate in the United States? Absent valid socio-economic studies, which Dethloff recognizes are not available, should legislatures justify differences in rights and obligations based on their individual perceptions regarding differences in role differentiation?

France introduced a very different model for an alternative status when its Pacte Civil de Solidarité (PACS), Loi no. 99-994, entered into effect in November 1999.

First, the status is open to opposite-sex as well as same-sex cohabitants.

Second, the law requires that the couple enter a cohabitation contract, the PACS, in which they set forth the terms and conditions that they wish to regulate their common life. It is the PACS, rather than the relationship, which is technically registered. Property issues regulated by private law, such as ownership of property and financial commitments towards each other, during and after the relationship, can be stipulated by the parties, subject to any restrictions the general law imposes. Alternatively, the partners may choose not to address some or all specific issues and declare that general law will regulate the PACS. In such cases, property acquired after the PACS is registered will be presumed to be owned by the partners in equal shares, unless a purchase deed specifies otherwise. Anne Barlow & Rebecca Probert, *Le PACS est arrivé—France Embraces Its New Style Family*, 2000 Int'l Fam. L. 182, 182.

A third important difference is the fact that some of the public benefits bestowed upon the couple after registration of a PACS are phased in based on the length of the relationship or birth of a child. For example, after two years PACS partners may leave an increased portion of their estate to the other partner without tax, and after three years PACS couples will be taxed as married couples. On the other hand, PACS partners can immediately take advantage of their partner's health insurance and social security contributions. *Id.* Entry into a PACS permits certain employment and immigration benefits as well. Adoption and custody are not addressed in the French PACS legislation. Collectif PACS et Caetera, http://perso.club-internet.fr/ccucs/frames/e_une.html.

Like the German registered partnership, not every feature of the PACS is equivalent to marriage. For example, partners owe each other "mutual and material assistance," which is considered a lower standard than the "help and assistance" duty imposed on married partners. Also like the German statute, the PACS law specifically sets forth enumerated rights and obligations, including the joint and several liability of each for debts incurred by either partner for household expenses. Upon desertion or death of one partner, the other is entitled to the tenancy of the partners' home, *id.*, but apart from tenancies, there are no succession rights. Claude Martin & Iréne Théry, *The PACS and Marriage and Cohabitation in France*, 15 Int'l J. L. Pol. & Fam. 135, 150–51 (2001).

Registration of the PACS requires the attendance of both partners at the local courthouse, where the declaration of their agreement is recorded. The court must be notified of any subsequent amendments to its terms. The parties may terminate a PACS immediately upon their mutual agreement, or upon marriage to each other or the marriage of one to another individual. It can also be terminated by one partner unilaterally three months after notice is given to the other party and the court. Unless the parties marry each other, dissolution of the relationship requires that property be divided according to the terms of the PACS, and the role of the court is to resolve any disputes that might arise concerning these terms or their implementation, or to determine the financial consequences regarding those issues the PACS does not address. *Id.* at 182–83. *See also* website of Collectif PACS et Caetera, *supra.*

Notes and Questions

1. *Constitutionality.* France' s PACS legislation was also the subject of constitutional challenge, and was upheld by the Conseil Constitutionnel, subject to certain *réserves d'interprétation.* The Court held that the legislation is constitutional only if the parties are required to "live as a couple" and not simply as persons sharing a household; and that PACS partners not be permitted to opt out of the obligation of mutual assistance, and may be held liable to a partner if one breaks the relationship. Eva Steiner, *The Spirit of the New French Registered Partnership Law—Promoting Autonomy and Pluralism or Weakening Marriage,* 12 Child & Fam. L.Q. 1, 4 (2000), citing Decision 99-419 DC of 9 November 1999.

2. *Demographic Changes.* The PACS legislation was a response not only to the need of same-gender couples for equality, but also to the changes that had occurred in French society over the last few decades. Between 1980 and 1997, the annual rate of marriages celebrated in France dropped from 334,000 in 1980 to 284,000 in 1997; the annual percentage of children born out of wedlock rose from 11.4% in 1980 to 40% in 1997, and by 1999 one in three couples between the ages of 25 and 39 were cohabiting. Steiner, *supra,* at 3, n.12 and accompanying text.

3. *Participation.* During the first four and one-half months in which the PACS legislation was in effect, almost 14,000 PACS were registered. During the first two years of the Dutch Registered Partnership Act, by comparison, only 2,822 Dutch couples registered. Barlow, *supra,* at 183. No confirmed statistics regarding the gender of PACS partners are available, as the registering tribunals are forbidden to release this information. Martin, *supra,* at 151. However, a media survey of court clerks indicates that the majority of couples registering PACS are heterosexual. Barlow, *supra,* at 183. Does your knowledge of French divorce law from Chapter 3 possibly shed some light on the popularity of PACS in France?

4. *Uncertainty.* French academics Claude Martin and Iréne Théry describe the PACS legislation as transitory law, observing that its "intermediate status, neither a union nor a contract, neither private nor public, expresses the ambiguity of the *French way* of responding to increasing cohabitation." Martin, *supra,* at 135. They suggest that no consensus exists among French academics regarding the appropriate approach to the needs of same-gender couples and other cohabitants. *Id.* at 135, 151. *See also* Steiner, *supra,* at 10 (observing that in contrast to U.S. and U.K. academics, the bulk of French academics have criticized same-gender marriages). Martin and Théry suggest that the diverse academic reactions reflect in part a broader public debate, noting that no consensus exists in France as yet about the changes in family and private life in general. Historically a dichotomy has existed in France between conservatives, influenced by Catholicism, promoting a traditional family model, and progressives and socialists who, from the time of the French revolution, emphasized individual liberty, secularism, and equality. These

historical tensions influenced the dramatic swings in divorce reform over the past two and a half centuries in France, as we saw in Chapter 3, and are also reflected in the new effort to define family, but have become increasingly complex with the pluralization of family forms that has occurred during the past two decades. They predict that the lack of a strong consensus and uncertainties in the application of PACS legislation will lead to further modification of the law within the next few years. Martin, *supra*, at 151–56.

5. *Alternative Status in Other Nations.* As in France, legislation in Belgium, the Netherlands, several provinces in Spain, and the Canadian province of Nova Scotia have created domestic partnerships that are open to both opposite-gender and same-gender couples. Levitt, *supra*, at 478, n. 47; R.S.N.S. c. 494, §54 (2002). In 2002 the Canadian province of Quebec created civil unions, which also appear to be open to both same-gender and opposite-gender partners. Civil Code of Quebec, c. 64, §521.1 (2002). Portugal is also reported to have enacted domestic partnership legislation in 1999, but limited eligibility to heterosexual couples. *See* http://www.ilgu.org. The news media reports, however, that additional legislation in 2001 would afford same-gender couples in Portugal who have cohabited for more than two years the same rights as opposite-gender couples in common law marriages. Data Lounge, *Portugal Adopts Same-Sex Partner Benefits*, at http://www.datalounge.com/datalounge/news/record.html.

On a local level, many cities and local governments around the globe currently permit same-gender couples to register domestic partnerships, with varying benefits associated with this status. *See* IGLHRC, *Registered Partnership, Domestic Partnership, and Marriage*, at http://www.iglhrc.org/news/factsheets/marriage_981103.html.

In the United States, currently no states permit same-gender couples to marry. Three states and the District of Columbia have created an alternative status, using a variety of models.

In 1999 Vermont established civil unions, a status open only to same-gender couples. Parties to a civil union are explicitly granted "all of the same benefits, protections and responsibilities" that are granted to marital spouses under Vermont state law. Therefore, parties to a civil union are responsible for each other's support to the same degree as spouses, and are subject to the same domestic relations law, including the law of divorce, annulment, separation, property division, and child custody and support. All areas of Vermont law, including *inter alia* adoption law, probate law, property law, entitlement to state benefits, health care law, employment benefits, and evidentiary law, apply equally to parties to a civil union. Vt. Stat. Ann. tit. 15, §§1201–1205 (2000). Benefits and obligations conferred upon marital spouses by U.S. federal law, however, cannot be conferred by Vermont's civil union statutes, and to date the federal government has not accorded parties to a civil union recognition as spouses under federal law. *Cf.* 1 U.S.C. §7 (2000) (defining marriage exclusively in terms of an opposite-gender union for purposes of federal law).

Parties entering a civil union must obtain a license from a town clerk. The civil union must then be certified by a judge, justice of the peace, or member of the clergy. Vt. Stat. Ann. tit. 18, §§5160, 5164 (2000). Age, competency, consanguinity, and affinity restrictions apply to entering a civil union just as they do to marriage, and parties are prohibited from entering a civil union if they are at the time married or a party to another civil union. Vt. Stat. Ann. tit. 15, §1203; tit. 18, §5163(2000). Out-of-state residents are permitted to enter into civil unions in Vermont. Vt. Stat. Ann. tit. 18, §§ 5160 (2000).

In 1997 Hawaii created reciprocal beneficiary relationships, which can be entered by parties meeting the requisite age requirements who are not married or in another such relationship. Only parties who are legally prohibited from marrying, however, can become reciprocal beneficiaries. Though these relationships would therefore primarily be entered by same-gender couples, they would also be open to couples whose relationship by blood or marriage violates consanguinity or affinity restrictions that prevent them from entering a legal marriage. Haw. Rev. Stat. § 572C-4 (2001). These relationships need not necessarily be conjugal. In fact, in its statement of purpose, the legislature illustrates its intent to make the rights and benefits of a reciprocal beneficiary relationship available to those in nonmarital relationships by using the example of a widowed mother and her unmarried son. Haw. Rev. Stat. § 572C-2 (2001). The relationship is entered when both parties sign and file a notarized declaration of reciprocal beneficiary relationship with the Hawaii Director of Health, and is terminated when either files a declaration of termination or enters into a legal marriage. Haw. Rev. Stat. §§ 572C-5, 572C-7 (2001).

Unlike parties to a civil union in Vermont, parties to a reciprocal beneficiary relationship in Hawaii do not have all of the rights conferred through marriage, but rather only those rights that are specifically enumerated by statute. Haw. Rev. Stat. § 572C-6 (2001). Among those rights are state income tax advantages, eligibility for public pension benefits and certain insurance benefits, the right to hold property in joint tenancy by the entirety, the ability to elect a statutory share of a deceased partner's estate, certain evidentiary privileges, a cause of action for wrongful death of a partner, and post-termination claims to maintenance and equitable property division. *See* Sanford N. Katz, *Emerging Models for Alternatives to Marriage,* 33 Fam. L.Q. 663, 674 (1999).

California has created domestic partnerships for same-gender couples and opposite-gender couples over the age of 62 who qualify for social security benefits. Partners meeting these criteria who cohabit and agree to be jointly responsible for each other's basic living expenses may jointly file a Declaration of Domestic Partnership with the Secretary of State, provided they are adults and not married or in another domestic partnership. Cal. Fam. Code § 297 (West 2001). The domestic partnership terminates when one partner dies or marries, or when the Secretary of State is notified that the partners no longer share a common residence, or that one partner has notified the other by certified mail that he or she is terminating the relationship. Cal. Fam. Code § 299 (West 2001).

The rights established by a California domestic partnership are very limited. Each partner agrees to provide for the basic living expenses of the other—food, shelter, utilities, household expenses—if the other is unable to provide for himself or herself. As this duty between the partners can easily be terminated by moving out or giving notice of termination by mail, the principal effect of this obligation is to provide creditors who relied on the existence of the domestic partnership with a basis for liability for goods or services rendered during the relationship. *See* Cal. Fam. Code § 297 (West 2001). Domestic partnerships do not create community property interests, but property held in joint title must be divided upon termination in proportion to the interest so assigned to each, unless the parties have otherwise expressly agreed in writing. Cal. Fam. Code § 299.5 (West 2001). Domestic partners also acquire visitation privileges in health facilities. Cal. Health & Safety Code § 1261 (West 2000).

The District of Columbia has also created registered domestic partnerships, which are open to any competent adult cohabitants in a "mutual caring relationship" who are not married or already in a domestic partnership. D.C. Code Ann. § 32-701 (2001). The status provides visitation privileges in health facilities, as well as family leave benefits and eligibility for family insurance benefits for District governmental employees. D.C. Code Ann. §§ 32-704, 32-705, 32-706 (2001).

Many other local and municipal governments in the United States, including New York, Chicago, Seattle, Ann Arbor, and San Francisco, have enacted some form of domestic partner registration, and provide partnership benefits for their public employees. David L. Chambers & Nancy Polikoff, *Family Law and Gay and Lesbian Family Issues in the Twentieth Century*, 33 Fam. L.Q. 523, 530–31 (1999). In Florida, the constitutionality of the Broward County Domestic Parnership Act was challenged under a provision of the Florida Constitution that prohibits county ordinances inconsistent with state law. Rejecting plaintiff's contention that the Domestic Partnership Act(DPA) of Broward County legislates within the domestic relations zone reserved for the state, a Florida Appellate Court, in Lowe v. Broward County, 766 So. 2d 1199 (Fla. Dist. Ct. App. 2000), held that the DPA did not curtail any rights incident to marriage. One provision of the Act, which permitted a domestic partner to make health care decisions on the same basis as would a spouse, was invalidated, however, as it directly conflicted with the prioritization of decision-making authority established by state statute.

Problem 4-1

You are a staff member for an advocacy group for gay and lesbian partners, drafting legislation on behalf of your members to present to the legislature when it begins its next session. Assume that at present, the state or nation in which you reside does not permit same-gender marriage, nor has it created an alternative status for partners of any type. You are meeting today with the legislative lobbyist for a local feminist organization, which is preparing draft legislation to create an alternative status for cohabitants. Slightly over 90% of the members of this particular organization are heterosexual. The two organizations have good relations and have worked together in the past to support various legislative proposals. The purpose of today's meeting is to attempt to negotiate a proposal for formal recognition of relationships that both organizations would enthusiastically support, if possible.

Which objectives of each organization might be likely to be the same? Which might be different?

Do you think either group would be more likely to prefer a bill creating predominantly contract-based rights and obligations, rather than status based rights and obligations? What are the advantages and drawbacks of each model?

Do you think either group would be more likely to prefer legislation that creates a status in which rights and obligations attach upon entry, or in which they accrue based upon the length or some other characteristic of the relationship?

Would either group be likely to desire any particular preconditions to entry, such as the absence of other marriages or formalized relationships or consanguinity restrictions?

What arguments do you anticipate encountering from opponents to your legislation when you present your draft to the legislature? What counter-arguments will you make?

Problem 4-2

While studying in a graduate program in Freiburg, Germany, you met your partner, a German computer programmer. You have been living together in Denmark, where your partner has been transferred, for several years. You are an American citizen currently teaching at the International School in Copenhagen. You and your partner have made a commitment for life, and would like to formalize your relationship. You are both the same gender, and your jobs give you flexibility to move back to Vermont, remain in Denmark, where you are now habitual residents, or relocate in Germany. From a legal perspective, in which country would you and your partner prefer to formalize your relationship and take up residence, and why?

B. The Impact of Domestic Constitutions and International Law on the Rights of Same-Gender Partners

The initiative of the Dutch legislature to open marriage to same-gender partners and the efforts of many other European nations to create registered partnerships were motivated by a combination of policy considerations. Prominent among these was the desire to foster equality and gender neutrality. Though inspired by these principles, these legislative bodies were not acting under duress of recent court directives setting forth constitutional mandates. In fact, the Government officials in the Netherlands who championed the most recent reform steadfastly maintained that opening marriage was *not* mandated by either the Netherlands Constitution, international treaties, or the case law of the Dutch Supreme Court. Schrama, *supra,* at 279.

Within some nations, however, including Canada, the United States, and South Africa, the creation of an alternative status or the conferral of benefits upon gay and lesbian partners have in some instances been heavily influenced by recent constitutional directives from appellate courts. International conventions influenced to some degree Germany's adoption of domestic partnership legislation, Levitt, *supra,* at 474, and may play an increasing role in the recognition of rights of same-gender couples in other nations. This section examines the degree to which domestic constitutions and international law have already influenced the recognition of rights for same-gender couples, and their potential for future impact.

1. Constitutional Rights of Same-Gender Couples

Halpern v. Canada (A.G.)
[2002] 60 O.R.3d 321
(Ont. Sup. C. J. Div. Ct.)

[Ed.: Eight same-gender couples and a church that married two additional same-gender couples brought actions against the Attorneys General of Canada (AGC) and Ontario, and the Clerk of the City of Toronto, seeking an order directing the Town Clerk to issue marriage licenses to the eight couples and to register the marriage certificate of the other two couples. The actions were consolidated and transferred to the Ontario Superior Court of Justice (Divisional Court). Three justices hearing the case each issued individual opinions, disagreeing about the appropriate remedy, but unanimously concurring that the existing common law rule that defines marriage as the union of "one man and one woman" infringes the rights of gays and lesbians to equal benefit of the law under § 15(1) of the Charter of Rights and Freedoms, which became part of the Canadian Constitution in 1982. Section 1 of the Charter establishes that the rights and freedoms set forth therein are "subject only to such reasonable limits prescribed by law as can be demonstrably justified in a free and democratic society," a standard the justices agreed was not met by Respondents in this action. Although the combined opinions are over 125 pages in length, the following excerpts from two of the opinions provide insight into the justices' rationale.]

Blair, R.S.J.

* * *

[30] ..."Marriage" as defined by the common law, is the lawful and voluntary union of one man and one woman to the exclusion of all others.

[31] The common law cannot isolate itself from the dictates and reality of modern society, however. It must evolve. Indeed, the essential characteristic of the common law over the centuries has been its ability to do just that....

[32] ... [T]he constitutional and *Charter*-inspired values which underlie Canadian society today dictate that the status and incidents inherent in the foundational institution of marriage must be open to same-sex couples who live in long-term, committed, relationships —marriage-like in everything but name—just as it is to heterosexual couples. Each is entitled to full and equal recognition, and the law must therefore be adapted accordingly.

* * *

[35] Section 15(1) of the *Canadian Charter of Rights and Freedoms* states:

> 15(1) Every individual is equal before and under the law and has the right to the equal protection and equal benefit of the law without discrimination and, in particular, without discrimination based on race, national or ethnic origin, colour, religion, sex, age or mental or physical disability.

[36] It is well established that the courts are to take a purposive and contextual approach to the analysis and interpretation of s. 15 equality rights. In *Law v. Canada (Minister of Employment and Immigration)*, [1999], 1 S.C.R. 497, Iacobucci J. summarized the basic elements of the Supreme Court of Canada's approach to the analysis....:

> ... [A] court that is called upon to determine a discrimination claim under s.15(1) should make the following three broad inquiries. First, does the impugned law (a) draw a formal distinction between the claimant and others on the basis of one or more personal characteristics, or (b) fail to take into account the claimant's already disadvantaged position within Canadian society resulting in substantively differential treatment between the claimant and others on the basis of one or more personal characteristics? If so, there is differential treatment for the purpose of s.15(1). Second, was the claimant subject to differential treatment on the basis of one or more of the enumerated and analogous grounds? And third, does the differential treatment discriminate in a substantive sense, bringing into play the *purpose* of s. 15(1) of the *Charter* in remedying such ills as prejudice, stereotyping, and historical disadvantage?...

* * *

[38] ...I agree with the s. 15(1) analysis and interpretation undertaken by Justice LaForme in this case [see below].... I wish simply to add some observations about the nature of marriage, because I believe that the view one takes of this subject may well be the beginning and the end of the s. 15(1) discussion.

Marriage

[39] What is the nature of marriage? In particular, what is the nature of marriage in its present-day civil context?...

[40] Anthropological, sociological and historical studies reveal that from time immemorial "marriage" has *almost* universally been viewed as a monogamous union between a man and a woman. This has been true across cultures, across religions, and across polities, and seems clearly to have been the norm. Certainly, modern Western European culture and its North American progeny, have accepted no other form of marriage....

[41] [In an affidavit submitted to the Court, Professor Witte, Director of the Center for the Interdisciplinary Study of Religion at Emory University in Atlanta, Georgia, on behalf of the Respondents] states that "marriage has, at its core, been understood in the West as a union of a man and woman, for purposes of procreation, rearing of children by both natural parents, companionship, and the uniting of two opposite sexes". [In her affidavit submitted on behalf of Respondents, Dr. Katherine Young, Professor in the Faculty of Religious Studies at McGill University,] concludes that "from [her] study of world religions (such as Judaism, Confucianism, Hinduism, Islam, and Christianity)" the institution of marriage "is a culturally approved opposite-sex relationship intended to encourage the birth (and rearing) of children...."

[42] ...[S]he states...:

> ...Marriage is supported by authority and incentives; it recognizes the interdependence of maleness and femaleness; it has a public dimension; it defines eligible partners; it encourages procreation under specific conditions; and it provides mutual support not only between men and women but also between men and women and their children....

> The following features of marriage are *nearly* universal: an emphasis on durability; mutual affection and companionship; family (or political) alliances; and the intergenerational cycle...Most large-scale societies have encouraged durable parental relationships (at least until children reach maturity)....

[43] ...[Professor Young concludes]:

> Same-sex relationships are indeed worthy of respect. But "same-sex marriage" is an oxymoron, because it lacks the universal, or *defining* feature of marriage...: a setting for reproduction that recognizes the reciprocity between the nature (sexual dimorphism) and culture (gender complementarity). [Italics in original; underlining added by Blair, R.S.J.]

[44] Nonetheless—in spite of these views—there have been societies in which gay and lesbian relationships have been accepted.... The affidavit filed by Professor William N. Eskridge, Jr., [historian and professor of jurisprudence at Yale Law School,] on behalf of the Applicant Couples, [suggests]...that Egyptian and Mesopotamian civilizations at least tolerated same-sex relationships and sometimes celebrated them to the point of treating them similarly to different-sex marriages.... [T]here is some evidence that classical Greek and republican Roman cultures recognized gay and lesbian relationships, al-

though they did not necessarily treat them as marriages. In Imperial Rome, however, same-sex marriages were recognized in some circles. The Emperors Nero and Elagabalus, for instance, are both reported as having married men.

[45] North American aboriginal, African and Asian cultures also exhibit examples of same-sex relationships with a stature at least similar to marriage between different-sex couples. Closest to home amongst these latter examples is the *berdache* tradition which was common amongst North American natives, as well as in the Aztec, Mayan and Incan civilizations.... The *berdache* was a person who deviated from his or her traditional gender role, taking on some of the characteristics and responsibilities of the opposite sex. They "married" individuals of the same-sex, and such marriages were recognized by the societal laws and customs. Professor Eskridge notes...:

> ... [B]erdaches have been an accepted and in fact valued part of culture and law in a large majority of Native American Tribes. Most academic attention has been focused on male *berdaches*, who frequently became revered leaders in their communities. Often, a male child was consciously raised to be a *berdache*, who assumed a special role in the community mediating between the spiritual and physical worlds. Marriages between men and male *berdaches* were widespread among Native American cultures.... The men who married male *berdaches* were usually attracted to women as well as to men and were not themselves considered *berdaches*. Many such men preferred *berdache* wives for economic advantages, as *berdaches* not only would do the housework, but would help with hunting and other traditionally male activities as well. Others believed that marrying a *berdache* guaranteed greater marital stability, while still other conventional men pursued male *berdaches* on the basis of simple sexual attraction.

> ... [F]emale *berdaches* comprised an important cultural institution in most Native American communities. Like her male counterpart, the female *berdache* assumed many of the responsibilities traditionally performed by the opposite sex, including hunting and heading a household. And she would commonly marry another woman. Female *berdaches* and woman-woman marriages were integral to women's ability to achieve a higher status in most Native American cultures. Thus, a female *berdache* would marry a *non-berdache* woman and would assume a position as head of the household, together with economic responsibilities for hunting and other traditionally "male" jobs.

[46] There are illustrations in other non-Western European cultures of similar traditions. In addition, the Record affords examples of marriage-like same-sex unions in China during the Yuan and Ming Dynasties (1279–1644), and of "boy-wives" or "warrior-lovers" in military settings where pair-bonding was treated as marriages. The samurai warriors of feudal and Tokugawa Japan, and the Azande warriors of the African Sudan illustrate these phenomena. Finally, there is a tradition of "woman marriage" in certain African cultures. In this latter tradition, "the term female husband...refers to a woman who takes on the legal and social roles of husband and father by marrying another woman according to the approved rules and ceremonies of her society...[and] she may belong to any one of over 30 African populations". Interestingly, the woman marriage is described as "the institution by which it is possible for a woman to give bridewealth for, and marry, a woman, over whom and whose offspring she has full control, *delegating to a male genitor the duties of procreation*", thus providing a legal and cultural way in which human procreation was carried out in those societies in relation to

same-sex unions.[quotations here are footnoted in original to scholars cited in Prof. Eskridge's Affidavit. Ed.]

[47] The evidence of Professor Eskridge...is contested by Professors Young and Duncan...[who] contend that same-sex marriages "involve only a few examples or mere analogies to marriage"...and that "they have a rarity historically"....

[48] It is unnecessary, in my view, to resolve this controversy for purposes of these Applications. I cite the foregoing examples of the recognition of same-sex marriages, or marriage-like unions, not to establish that same-sex unions have ever been considered the norm in society...[but] to illustrate that there have been *exceptions to the norm* across various cultures and polities..., including cultures in which modern Western society finds many of its roots. Coupled with the fact that the views towards marriage and family of various societies and cultures—including our own—have evolved over the centuries, these examples of same-sex marriage recognition provide context against which the question of whether modern-day civil "marriage" should be broadened to encompass such unions should be considered.

Changing Attitudes and Perspectives

[49] Different faiths and different cultures have emphasized different aspects of marriage at different times and for different reasons.... Experts on all sides of these proceedings confirm that societal concepts of marriage have changed, and that marriage is not a static institution within any society. It evolves as society changes.

[50] ...[O]n behalf of the Respondent[s], Professor Witte tracks the historical and religious development of the concept of marriage in Western society....:

> The Western Christian Church has...understood marriage as a monogamous, heterosexual union.... *Marriage is a contract*, formed by the mutual consent of the marital couple, and subject to their wills and preferences. *Marriage is a spiritual association*, subject to the creed, code, cult and cannons of the religious community. *Marriage is a social estate*, subject to special state laws of property, inheritance, and evidence and to the expectations of the local community. *Marriage is also a natural institution*, subject to the laws of nature communicated in Scripture, reason, and conscience, and reflected in tradition, custom, and experience.
>
> In Western tradition, all of these perspectives were complementary, but also stood in some considerable tension, as they were all linked to competing claims of ultimate authority over the form and function of marriage—claims by the couple, the church, the state, and by nature and God. *Some of the deepest fault lines in the historical formation and the current transformations of Western marriage break out from this central tension of perspective*.
>
> Catholics, Protestants, and Enlightenment exponents alike all constructed models to address the priority and inter-relation of these perspectives. Each of these groups recognizes multiple perspectives on marriage, but gives priority to one of them in order to achieve an integrated understanding. Catholics emphasize the spiritual or sacramental perspective of marriage. Protestants emphasize the social or public perspective. Liberal enlightenment exponents emphasize the contractual or private perspective. *Broadly, the Catholic model dominated Western marriage law until the sixteenth century. From the mid-sixteenth to the mid-nineteenth century, Catholic and Protestant models, in distant and hybrid forms, dominated Western marriage law. In the past century, the En-*

lightenment model has emerged triumphant, in many instances eclipsing the the-
ology and law of Christian models. Each model has contributed a variety of en-
during ideas and institutions to modern marriage law.

[51] From the Applicant's perspective, Professor Eskridge sees marriage as having developed from concepts based upon notions of functional or gendered division of labour to
concepts based upon notions of marriage as a "companionate" model.... [H]e states:

> ...The main change in the institution [of marriage] has been the elevation of
> women's roles within marriage. Rural societies with gendered divisions of labor
> and needs for lots of children did not emphasize companionate marriage
> among social equals; this was true for same-sex, as well as different-sex unions
> in Greece, Rome, Egypt, and elsewhere. *Urban societies offering women many*
> *opportunities outside the home and fewer economic and social pressures to bear*
> *children will press marriages to be companionate;* this will be true for same-sex
> as well as different-sex marriages. *Indeed, the demand for same-sex marriage by*
> *lesbians and gay men in countries like Canada and the United States is a direct*
> *consequence of the elevated role of women, compared with 200 years ago: as gen-*
> *der roles have come into question, women who emotionally or sexually prefer the*
> *company of other women are increasingly acting on those preferences (same for*
> *men), and demanding that state recognition is important to a neutral regime of*
> *equality for people of all orientations.*

* * *

> ...The major goal of state-recognized or socially-encouraged marriage is *uni-*
> *tive:* the state or society recognizes the committed couple as a decisionmaking
> unit, as an economic partnership, and as a mutual support group....

[52] Finally, Dr David Coolidge[, Director of the Marriage Law Project at Catholic University School of Law in Washington, D.C., who filed an affidavit on behalf of Inter-
venor, the Association for Marriage and the Family in Ontario,] describes what he calls
"the three concepts of marriage at work in the current debate" regarding the definition
of marriage....

[53] With regard to the Classical model, [he] explains...:

> ...[M]arriage is a unique community defined by sexual complementarity—the
> reality that men and women are 'different from, yet designed for' one another....

[54] The Choice model of marriage views marriage as essentially an agreement between
individuals.... Thus, there is no reason to limit it to the union of a male and female....

[55] ...[T]he Commitment model...views marriage as essentially a relationship. Marriage
is entered into by individuals, and their relationship can be institutionalized, but the core
of the institution is the relationship between the parties, which is seen to transcend and
even alter the individual selves and to give rise to specific obligations.... He concludes...:

> *If marriage is essentially a committed, intimate relationship, there is no reason to*
> *define it legally as a male-female institution.*

* * *

> *...This ethic, however, is not a return to the Classical view. It does not appear to*
> *involve a belief in universal truths, natural orders, or enduring moral boundaries.*
> *Instead, the Commitment model requires that the law make an "imaginative re-*
> *construction" of "our marital tradition" as "the provision of social support for*
> *those who wish to make a commitment to emotional interdependence."*

* * *

Marriage and the Law Today

[59] What, then, of marriage today?

[60] If the Courts are to examine the common law definitions of marriage through the prism of *Charter* rights and values, it seems to me they must recognize and appreciate the changes that have occurred over the centuries, and more rapidly in recent years, in the attitudes of society towards the family, marriage, and relationships, as outlined above. To do otherwise is to abandon the purpose of section 15—which is to promote equality and prevent discrimination arising from such ills as stereotyping, prejudice and historical wrongs—and to fail to consider the common law principle under review in a contextual fashion....

[61] Given this background of dramatically shifting attitudes towards marriage and the family, I have a great deal of difficulty accepting that heterosexual procreation is such a compelling and central aspect of marriage in 21st century post-Charter Canadian society that it—and it alone—gives marriage its defining characteristic and justifies the exclusion of same-sex couples from that institution....

[62] Yet that is the nub of the argument put forward by the Respondents....

[63] Stripped to its essentials,...[their] contention is based upon the notion that heterosexual procreation is the ultimate defining characteristic of marriage, which is thus inherently heterosexual in nature....

[64] If this understanding of marriage forms the starting point of the analysis, I agree the argument that s. 15(1) is violated by the common law definition of marriage is harder to make. Viewed from this standpoint, same-sex couples are not excluded from the institution because of their sexual orientation; rather they are simply ineligible because they fall outside of the "definitional boundaries of marriage."...

[65] On the other hand, if marriage is viewed through a looking glass with a broader focus—and not conceived as a social, cultural, religious and legal edifice built upon heterosexual procreation as its fundamental infrastructure—the s. 15(1) analysis is directly engaged. In this approach, same-sex couples are not precluded from participating by reason of its innate characteristic. They are precluded simply because of their sexual orientation. The evidence is clear: same-sex couples can and do live in long-term, caring, loving and conjugal relationships—including those involving the rearing of children (and, in a modern context, even the birth of children). In short, their relationships are characterized by all the indicia of marriage, as traditionally understood, save for classic heterosexual intercourse, and they live in unions that are marriage-like in everything but name.

* * *

[68] Cultures and social mores, however, as well as faiths and religions and laws and economies, all tend to be reflective of the physical, environmental, technological and scientific realities of the times. Those realities can and do shift....

[69] ...Scientific advances have made it possible for children to be born to couples— heterosexual or homosexual—through artificial insemination, in vitro fertilization in its various forms, surrogate motherhood, et cetera. While it remains true—at least for now—...that birth in a same-sex union by necessity must involve a third person, procreation through heterosexual coupling, as the source of the reality of children being born into a family, and therefor as the characteristic giving marriage its principal ratio-

nale and unique heterosexual nature, is becoming an increasingly narrow and shaky footing for the institution of marriage.

[70] Too narrow, and too shaky, in my opinion, to be tenable as the legal base for such a foundational institution in society as marriage. To be sure, the production, care and raising of children is a principle purpose of marriage. But that purpose...is presently sustainable through means other than heterosexual intercourse. There is much more to marriage as a societal institution, in my view, than the act of heterosexual intercourse leading to the birth of children. Moreover, the authorities are clear that marriage is not dependent upon the presence of children, nor are the incapacity or an unwillingness to have children a bar to marriage or a ground for divorce....

[71] ...Marriage has a physical sexual component to it, of course. Marriage is more fully characterized in my opinion, however, by its pivotal child-rearing role, and by a long-term conjugal relationship between two individuals—with its attendant obligations and offerings of mutual care and support, of companionship and shared social activities, of intellectual and moral and faith-based stimulation as a couple, and of shared shelter and economic and psychological interdependence—and by love. These are the indicia of the purpose of marriage in modern Canadian society....

* * *

[81] ...[O]nce it is accepted that same-sex unions can feature the same conjugal and other incidents of marriage, except for heterosexual intercourse, and if heterosexual procreation is no longer viewed as the central characteristic of marriage, giving it its inherently heterosexual uniqueness, the s. 15 argument must succeed. If heterosexual procreation is not essential to the nature of the institution, then the same-sex couples' sexual orientation is the only distinction differentiating heterosexual couples from homosexual couples in terms of access to the institution of marriage. For all of the reasons articulated by Justice LaForme, this differentiation is discriminatory of the same-sex couples' equality rights as set out in s. 15 of the *Charter* and cannot stand.

* * *

LaForme, J.

[Ed. Note: Justice LaForme begins his opinion with a review of the factual background, the issues, the positions of the parties, and preliminary issues such as jurisdiction of the court. He then concludes that Parliament has not created a statutory impediment to the issuance of marriage licenses to same-sex couples, and that Canadian common law prevents the issuance of marriage licenses to same-sex parties. Both of these are findings with which the other two justices concur. Turning to the constitutionality of this common law rule under s.15 of the *Charter*, Justice LaForme reviews briefly the evidence submitted by the parties, discussed above at greater length in Justice Blair's opinion, and the steps of the analysis, with which the excerpt from Justice Blair's opinion above begins.]

[163] In order to decide whether or not the common law rule of marriage is compatible, or in harmony, with the *Charter*, it will be necessary to measure the two together.... [T]he first step will be to assume an approach that will, (i) define the values that the law is alleged to offend, and (ii) measure them against the impugned law so as to decide their conformity.

[164] ...[T]he AGC submits that the proper approach to this analysis is contextual. That is, it argues that marriage exists and is universally understood to be in relation to only heterosexual unions....

* * *

[167] ... [T]he Applicant Couples submit that the position of the AGC amounts to an analysis based upon "definitional exclusion".... Applicants argue that this court should not solely analyze the law by deciding that contextually the definition of marriage means "only one man and woman" and does not rely upon personal characteristic....

[168] ... Applicant Couples... submit that... the proper approach to a s.15(1) analysis is the "purposive approach." That is to say...: does the law offend the purpose of s. 15(1) of the *Charter*? I agree.

* * *

[171] Regarding any evidentiary standard that will apply, the law does not require the claimants under this s. 15(1) *Charter* challenge to demonstrate that the impugned distinction amounts to unreasonableness, or that it is "invidious, unfair or irrational". All that is required for the Applicants is to show that the impugned law treats them more harshly than others. It is not a question of degree.

[172] And finally, it does not matter whether it was the law's intention to discriminate specifically against gays and lesbians....

* * *

[174] At the outset, I believe the purpose of the s. 15(1) equality guarantee is worth repeating.... I prefer the language... referenced by Iacobucci J. in [the Canadian Supreme Court decision] in *Law*:

> ... the purpose of s.15(1) is to promote a society in which all are secure in the knowledge that they are recognized at law as human beings equally deserving of concern, respect and consideration. The provision is a guarantee against evil oppression... designed to remedy the imposition of unfair limitations upon opportunities, particularly for those persons or groups who have been subject to historical disadvantage, prejudice, and stereotyping.

* * *

Differential Treatment

* * *

[184] ... [T]he AGC submits that the *Charter* guarantees the equal protection and benefit of the law, not the right to nomenclature.... [I]t says that by capturing the essence of marriage, the common law recognizes the inherent differences between opposite-sex and same-sex couples.

[185] The AGC goes on to submit that, since the recent enactment of the *Modernization of Benefits and Obligations Act,* same-sex couples receive substantive equal benefit and protection of the federal law....

[186] Respectfully, I find that I must disagree with the... conclusions of the AGC....

[187] The gist of the first part of AGC's submissions requires this court to accept that "marriage" is a word that merely identifies a unique institution. That argument implies that, if the Applicants are granted all the rights, privileges and benefits of the institution of marriage—but under some other nomenclature—then there can be no discrimination because there would be no differential treatment. That, in my opinion, is wrong.

[188] Marriage is more than nomenclature—more than just a word.... [T]he passion and sincerity of all those who argued before this court is testament to the deeply held views of marriage.... [M]arriage—to most of Canadian society is:

...the institution that accords to a union the profound social stamp of approval and acceptance of the relationship as being of the highest value.

* * *

...The power of marriage comes not from what it is in the abstract, or how it is defined, or even what it symbolizes, but from how it is transubstantiated by society's focus on marital status as key element in defining every person.

[190] ...[A] law that offers a "significant choice" may also offer a "valuable benefit." And where the definition of that law confers state recognition of the legitimacy of a particular status, denial of the ability to choose that status to lesbians and gays amounts to a violation of s.15(1)...

* * *

[192] I also reject the argument of the AGC that the benefits afforded through the institution of marriage can be remedied by amendment to legislation that otherwise grants benefits to co-habiting couples. In my opinion that submission amounts to the "separate but equal" argument that has long since been rejected in Canada as a justification for an otherwise discriminatory law.

[193] I find that it is non-answer to the concerns of the Applicants to simply say to them that, same-sex couples have—or will have—all the benefits that married couples have through other legislative measures such as "domestic partners".

[194] To accept that argument would mean that I agree that same-sex couples are entitled to all the benefits and privileges that opposite-sex couples are granted through marriage, but not the right to be recognized as married. In other words, I would have to embrace the concept that same-sex couples are entitled to be married; they just cannot appropriate the word marriage because that belongs exclusively to heterosexual couples. That would be a wrong concept for this court to embrace.

* * *

[197] ...I find that the answer to this first aspect of the s. 15(1) *Charter* analysis is— the common law rule of marriage subjects the Applicants to different treatment than others.

Analogous Ground:

[198] ...[T]he ACG agrees that, if there is a finding of different treatment it is grounded in sexual orientation, which is an analogous ground under s. 15(1) of the *Charter*. As I find that to be indeed the case, I correspondingly answer this part of the analysis in the affirmative.

Is it Substantive Differential Treatment?

[199] It is argued that, by deeming gay and lesbian people to be excluded from marriage, there is a denial of their equal opportunity to fully participate in our society. There is, it is contended, a fundamental right to marry recognized in Canada, United States, and international jurisprudence. I fully accept this argument....

[200] The first contextual factor I need to consider under this analysis is to decide whether there subsists within Canadian society a "pre-existing disadvantage, vulnerability, stereotyping, or prejudice" experienced by gay and lesbian people. In my opinion this issue has little to no contrary argument—it most assuredly does exist.

* * *

[202] Excluding gays and lesbians from marriage disregards the needs, capacities, and circumstances of same-sex spouses and their children. It declares an entire class of persons unworthy of the recognition and support of state sanction for their marriages....

[203] The next contextual factor that must be addressed is whether the denial has an "ameliorative purpose" or effect.... The AGC asserts that [marriage]...is of fundamental importance to all societies in that it provides a means—admittedly not the only one—of serving and recognizing the realities of one of the goals of marriage, namely—the nurturing and protection of children....

[204] Same-sex couples who form family units with children are not less parents and are no less entitled to the same concerns by our courts.

* * *

[206] The final contextual factor focuses on an examination of the nature and scope of the interest affected by the impugned law. That is, how harshly does the law of marriage affect gays and lesbians by their exclusion from it?...

[207] As previously noted, it appears to be universally accepted that the freedom to marry the person of one's choice and the right to have that relationship recognized by society is of fundamental importance in our society...

* * *

[210] ...I therefore find that the denial of equal marriage violates s. 15 of the *Charter*. Specifically, I find that it draws a distinction in a substantive sense on the basis of sex and sexual orientation that withholds the equal benefit of the law in a manner that offends the human dignity of gays, lesbians and bisexuals.

* * *

(v) Is there a s.1 Charter analysis required and, if so, can the infringement be justified?

[220] ...[S].1 provides that:

> The *Canadian Charter of Rights and Freedoms* guarantees the rights and freedoms set out in it subject only to such reasonable limits prescribed by law as can be demonstrably justified in a free and democratic society.

* * *

[229] ...[W]here a law gives rise to a *Charter* breach, it must then be *demonstrably justified* as a *reasonable limit* in a free and democratic society in order for it to pass judicial scrutiny.

[230] ...It is a two pronged test that requires (1) an initial examination of the objective or concerns of the law that is responsible for the limits on the...*Charter* rights, and then (ii) an examination...to determine:

(1) Whether the objective or concern is sufficiently important to warrant overriding the protected right. The objective or concern must be pressing or substantial;

(2) Whether it does so proportionately. Proportionality is measured through a three-part test that requires that the measures chosen:

    (a) are rationally connected to the objective;

    (b) impair the right or freedom as little as possible; and

(c) result in harmful effects, if any, that are proportional to both the laws salutary effects and the importance of the objective.

[233] ... [T]he AGC submits that the restriction against same-sex marriage... is essentially to further procreation and provide institutional support to families with children.

* * *

[238] I do not agree that the evidence—such as it is—supports the AGC's proposition that procreation is the essential objective of marriage. Indeed, the evidence actually demonstrates that it was only recently—when same-sex couples began to advance claims for equal recognition of their conjugal relationships—that some courts began to infer that procreation was an essential component to marriage....

* * *

[246] Given the failure of the evidentiary burden I find that, the current common law rule of marriage is one that is based upon sexual orientation and is intended to specifically exclude marriage between same-sex couples. This in turn is categorically a rights violation based upon a discriminatory objective.

* * *

[248] [However,] [a]ssuming that part of what constitutes the purpose of marriage is to foster and provide institutional support for adult relationships that allow for the possibility of procreation and child-rearing—the restriction against same-sex marriage, I find, is not rationally connected to this objective. There simply is no evidentiary basis to support the proposition that granting same-sex couples the freedom to marry would either diminish the number of children conceived by heterosexual couples, or reduce the quality of care with which heterosexual couples raise their children.

[249] Same-sex couples experience, and raise children as a result of a variety of reproductive and parenting arrangements, none of which is unique to same-sex partners....

[250] ... I find that, the restriction against same-sex marriage fails the rational connection test because it is both:

• overinclusive in that it allows non-procreative heterosexuals to marry; and

• underinclusive because it denies same-sex parents and intended parents the right to marry.

* * *

[261] In the case at bar,... "the deleterious effects of the exclusion... are numerous and clear." The restriction against same-sex marriage is an offense to the dignity of lesbians and gays because it limits the range of relationship options available to them. The result is they are denied the autonomy to choose whether they wish to marry. This in turn conveys the ominous message that they are unworthy of marriage. For those same-sex couples who do wish to marry, the impugned restriction represents a rejection of their personal aspirations and the denial of their dreams.

[262] There is no meaningful evidence that points to any legitimate benefit to the rights denial. In this case, an absolute common law bar on the freedom of same-sex couples to marry does not constitute the "least intrusive" means by which the state could achieve the purported goal of providing institutional support to couples who have and raise children....

* * *

[264] ...I find that the infringement of the Applicant's *Charter* rights cannot be justified under s. 1 of the *Charter*.

* * *

[Ed. Note: Justice LaForme determined that the appropriate remedy was to reformulate the common law rule by reading out the words "a man and a woman" and reading in "two persons." He argues that this is the appropriate remedy because there is no other appropriate response for Parliament to choose, and because there is no reason that the rights infringement should continue any longer. Justice Blair and Chief Justice Smith would declare the common law definition of marriage invalid, but suspend the operation of the declaration of invalidity for 24 months to enable Parliament to correct the violation. Justice Blair would declare the common law definition to be reformulated, as Justice LaForme proposed, if Parliament failed to act within the 24 month period, but Chief Justice Smith does not believe the court should reformulate the invalid rule even in this event. Both Justices Smith and Blair argued that major responsibility for law reform should be with the legislature, and that the consequences from this change are complex. Justice Blair expressed concerns about the possibility that a registered partnership scheme would be considered by Parliament as one option, but he did not totally reject it out of hand. He also noted that totally replacing marriage for all couples with civil union or civil registration was an option Parliament could choose. Chief Justice Smith did not discuss this option, and explicitly declined to comment on the adequacy of a domestic partnership regime under the *Charter*, asserting that it was not appropriate to comment on the constitutionality of such regimes in advance.]

Notes and Questions

1. *Relevance of Defining Marriage.* Justice Blair devotes a substantial portion of his concurring opinion to reviewing the incidence of same-gender marriages in other societies and to the different conceptions of marriage prevalent historically and in contemporary Canadian society. Why is reflection on the nature of marriage important to determining the issue of whether the exclusion of gay men and lesbian couples from the institution of marriage violates § 15(1) of the Canadian Charter of Rights and Freedoms?

2. *Comparison with U.S. Federal Constitutional Doctrine.* Section 15(1) of the Canadian Charter of Rights and Freedoms is similar in some respects to the Equal Protection Clause of the Fifth and Fourteenth Amendments to the U.S. Constitution. Consider the analytical framework initially set forth in the excerpt from Justice Blair's opinion and applied in the excerpt from Justice LaForme's opinion. In what ways is it similar to, and in what ways is it different from, Equal Protection analysis as formulated by the U.S. Supreme Court under the U.S. Federal Constitution? Are the nature of the differences such that they should make a difference in the outcome?

3. *Canadian Courts Split.* As this book goes to print, the decision of the Ontario Superior Court of Justice is the most recent word from Canadian appellate courts regarding same-gender marriage, but it is by no means the only word, nor is it the last word. Shortly after the opinion was issued, the Attorney General announced that the decision would be appealed. Chris Hornsey, *News*, Windsor Star, July 30, 2002, at A1. In early September, 2002, the Canadian press reported that a Quebec Superior Court had also ruled that the limitation of marriage to opposite-gender couples was discriminatory, echoing the ruling of the Ontario court in *Halpern*. The federal government announced its intention to appeal this decision as well. *Ottawa to Consult Public on Same-sex Mar-*

riages; Ruling on Definition of Marriage to be Appealed, Winnipeg Free Press, September 10, 2002, at B1.

The Canadian provincial courts are currently divided in their treatment of same-gender marriage. In Egale Canada Inc. v. Canada (Attorney General), [2001] B.C.J. N. 1995 (S.C.), the British Columbia Supreme Court rejected a claim by same-gender couples seeking marriage licenses. In that opinion, Justice Pittfield, writing for the entire court, first determined that changes to the common law should only be made by incremental steps. Sanctioning same-gender marriages, in Justice Pifffield's view, is not incremental, as it would have broad legal ramifications and require the formation of rules addressing the entry and dissolution of same-gender unions.

Second, in Justice Pittfield's view even the Canadian Parliament could not define marriage to include same-gender marriages. This is because, even though the term "marriage" is not specifically defined in the Canadian Constitution of 1867, when the term was first used in 1867 it unambiguously meant a "monogamous opposite-sex relationship," and any attempt to change the meaning of marriage would be equivalent to a unilateral amendment to the Canadian Constitution, which Parliament is not empowered to do.

Judge Pittfied also addressed the equal protection argument that is central to the court's decision in *Halpern,* i.e., that denying applicants' entry to marriage violated their rights under § 15 of the Charter. He conceded that denial of the choice to marry denies an equal benefit of the law, enhancing the stereotypical view that same-gender relationships are less valuable, and thus violates § 15. Nevertheless, in examining the second stage of the Charter analysis under §1, i.e., whether the violation is a reasonable limit that can be demonstrably justified, Justice Pittfield found that the objective of preserving the constitutional meaning of marriage was substantial. The requirement that married couples be of opposite gender is the primary means by which human reproduction occurs, and therefore the requisite proportionality exists between the equality violation and the purpose for it.

Moreover, because he found that "marriage" is a constitutionally defined term, Judge Pittfield ruled that the Charter cannot be used to invalidate another constitutional provision. Only a formal constitutional amendment, in the view of the British Columbia Supreme Court, can amend the definition of "marriage" to permit same-gender couples to marry.

In a much earlier action, Re North and Matheson, [1974] 52 D.L.R. (3d) 280 (Man. Co. Ct.), a Manitoba court also rejected a request by a same-gender couple for registration of their marriage, applying the common law rule that marriage is the union of a man and a woman. In fact, just nine years prior to *Halpern,* the Divisional Court in Ontario had ruled in Layland v. Ontario (Minister of Consumer & Commercial Relations, [1993], 14 O.R. (3d) 658 (Ont. Div. Ct.) that under the common law a marriage could take place only between a man and a woman, and in that decision the majority had declined to find this rule violated § 15 of the Charter.

Canadian legal scholars suggest that ultimately this issue will be addressed by the Canadian Supreme Court, and that the Court's 1999 ruling in *M. v. H.,* the next opinion to this section, could be a harbinger of the approach the Court might take. Nicholas Bala & Rebecca Jaremko Bromwich, *Context and Inclusivity in Canada's Evolving Definition of the Family,* 16 Int'l J.L. Pol. & Fam. 145, 162 (2002).

4. *Public Opinion.* Changing societal norms undeniably influence judicial willingness to expand constitutional doctrines, as well as legislative willingness to undertake re-

form. *See* Jay Michaelson, *On Listening to the Kulturkampf, or, How America Overruled Bowers v. Hardwick, Even though Romer v. Evans Didn't,* 49 Duke L.J. 1559 (2000). It is therefore interesting to observe that a recent (April 2001) survey conducted by Environics Research Group revealed that 55% of Canadians reported that they strongly (29%) or somewhat strongly (26%) support marriage between same-gender couples, with a 73% support rate from those in the 18–29 year-old age group. Bala & Bromwich, *supra,* at 165.

M. v. H.

[1999] 2 S.C.R. 3

[Ed. Note: Following the separation of two female partners who had lived together for over five years, one of the women, who allegedly had undertaken a greater share of the domestic tasks, brought an action against her former partner seeking support and challenging the constitutionality of Ontario's spousal support statute, § 29 of the Ontario Family Law Act. This section permitted heterosexual cohabitants who had lived together more than three years or had a child in a relationship of some permanence to seek spousal support after termination of their relationship, but denied the same opportunity to same-gender partners. The lower courts ruled in favor of the applicant, finding that the exclusion of same-gender partners from the opportunity to seek support at the end of a long-term relationship constituted discrimination based upon sexual orientation under § 15 of the Charter of Rights and Freedoms. Applying the same analysis set forth above in *Halpern,* the Canadian Supreme Court ruled 8–1 to affirm.]

Cory and Iacobucci, JJ.

* * *

45. The Attorney General for Ontario, displaying great candour, very fairly conceded that s. 29 of the *FLA* contravenes the provisions of s. 15 of the *Charter.* His entire argument was directed at demonstrating that the section was nonetheless justifiable and saved by s. 1 of the *Charter.* The Court is certainly not bound by this concession. Although, in my view, he was correct in taking this position, it would not be appropriate in this appeal to undertake only a s.1 analysis without considering whether s.15 has in fact been violated....

* * *

62. ... [T]he first broad inquiry in the s.15(1) analysis determines whether there is differential treatment imposed by the impugned legislation between the claimant and others. It is clear that there is differential treatment here. Under s.29 of the *FLA,* members of opposite-sex couples who can meet the requirements of the statute are able to gain access to the court-enforced system... that ensures the provision of support to a dependent spouse. Members of same-sex couples are denied access to this system entirely on the basis of their sexual orientation.

63. ... [I]t must be shown that an equality right was denied on the basis of an enumerated or analogous ground, and that this differential treatment discriminates "in a substantive sense, bringing into play the *purpose* of s. 15(1) of the *Charter*"....

64. In *Egan,*...this Court unanimously affirmed that sexual orientation is an analogous ground to those enumerated in s.15(1). Sexual orientation is "a deeply personal characteristic that is either unchangeable or changeable only at unacceptable personal costs".... In addition, a majority of this Court explicitly recognized that gays, lesbians and bisexu-

als, "whether as individuals or couples, form an identifiable minority who have suffered and continue to suffer serious social, political and economic disadvantage"....

65. The determination of whether differential treatment imposed by legislation on an enumerated or analogous ground is discriminatory within the meaning of s. 15(1) of the *Charter* is to be undertaken in a purposive and contextual manner. The relevant inquiry is whether the differential treatment imposes a burden upon or withholds a benefit from the claimant in a manner that reflects the stereotypical application of presumed group or personal characteristics, or which otherwise has the effect of perpetuating or promoting the view that the individual is less capable or worthy of recognition or value as a human being or as a member of Canadian society, equally deserving of concern, respect, and consideration....

* * *

69. In this case, there is significant pre-existing disadvantage and vulnerability, and these circumstances are exacerbated by the impugned legislation.... The...system clearly provides a benefit to unmarried heterosexual persons who come within the definition set out in s. 29, and thereby provides a measure of protection for their economic interests.... The denial of that potential benefit, which may impose a financial burden on persons in the position of the claimant, contributes to the general vulnerability experienced by individuals in same-sex relationships.

* * *

72. ...In the present case, the interest protected by s. 29 of the *FLA* is fundamental, namely the ability to meet basic financial needs following the breakdown of a relationship characterized by intimacy and economic dependence. Members of same-sex couples are entirely ignored by the statute, notwithstanding the undeniable importance to them of the benefits accorded by the statute.

73. The societal significance of the benefit conferred by the statute cannot be overemphasized. The exclusion of same-sex partners from the benefits of s. 29 of the *FLA* promotes the view that M., and individuals in same-sex relationships generally, are less worthy of recognition and protection. It implies that they are judged to be incapable of forming intimate relationships of economic interdependence as compared to opposite-sex couples, without regard to their actual circumstances.... [S]uch exclusion perpetuates the disadvantages suffered by individuals in same-sex relationships and contributes to the erasure of their existence.

74. Therefore I conclude that...the human dignity of individuals in same-sex relationships is violated by the impugned legislation. In light of this, I conclude that the definition of spouse in s. 29 of the *FLA* violates s. 15(1).

* * *

93. ...[T]he objectives of the impugned spousal support provisions were...to provide "for the equitable resolution of economic disputes that arise when intimate relationships between individuals who have been financially interdependent break down" and to "alleviate the burden on the public purse by shifting the obligation to provide support for needy persons to those parents and spouses who have the capacity to provide support to these individuals"....

* * *

95. ...Expressly included among the purposes of a spousal support order in s. 33(8) of the Act are the relief of financial hardship, the recognition of the spouse's contribution to the relationship, and the economic consequences of the relationship for the spouse.

* * *

102. ...[T]he appellant argued that the *FLA* is a remedial statute designed to address the power imbalance that continues to exist in many opposite-sex relationships. Thus, it was submitted that the inclusion of same-sex couples in a scheme established to deal with problems that are not typical of their relationships is inappropriate. Further, the appellant asserted that where persons fall outside the rationale for which a benefit was established, the legislature is justified in withholding it from those persons.

* * *

109. Even if I were to accept that...the Act is meant to address the systemic sexual inequality associated with opposite-sex relationships, [a proposition that is rejected in an earlier, omitted portion of the opinion,] the required nexus between this objective and the chosen measures is absent in this case. In my view, it defies logic to suggest that a gender-neutral support system is rationally connected to the goal of improving the economic circumstances of heterosexual women upon relationship breakdown. In addition, I can find no evidence to demonstrate that the exclusion of same-sex couples from the spousal support regime of the *FLA* in any way furthers the objective of assisting heterosexual women.

110. Although there is evidence to suggest that same-sex relationships are not typically characterized by the same economic and other inequalities which affect opposite-sex relationships..., this does not, in my mind, explain why the right to apply for support is limited to heterosexuals.... [T]he infrequency with which members of same-sex relationships find themselves in circumstances resembling those of many heterosexual women is no different from heterosexual men who, notwithstanding that they tend to benefit from the gender-based division of labour and inequality of earning power, have as much right to apply for support as their female partners.

111. Put another way, it is important to recall that the ability to make a claim for spousal support does not automatically translate into a support order. To the extent that *any* relationship is characterized by more or less economic dependence, this will affect the amount and duration, if any, of an award under s. 33(9) of the *FLA*. Thus, it is no answer to say that same-sex couples should not have access to the spousal support scheme because their relationships are typically more egalitarian....

* * *

113. Even if I were to accept that the object of the legislation is the protection of children, [a proposition that is rejected in an earlier, omitted portion of the opinion,] I would have to conclude that the spousal support provisions in Part III of the *FLA* are simultaneously underinclusive and overinclusive. They are over inclusive because members of opposite-sex couples are entitled to apply for spousal support irrespective of whether or not they are parents and regardless of their reproductive capabilities or desires. Thus, if the legislation was meant to protect children, it would be incongruous that childless opposite-sex couples were included among those eligible to apply for and to receive the support in question.

114. The impugned provisions are also underinclusive. An increasing percentage of children are being conceived and raised by lesbian and gay couples as a result of adoption, surrogacy and donor insemination. Although their numbers are still fairly small, it seems to me that the goal of protecting children cannot be but incompletely achieved by denying some children the benefits that flow from a spousal support award merely because their parents were in a same-sex relationship....

115. The same result follows from the objectives identified...in the court below. No evidence has been supplied to support the notion that the exclusion of same-sex couples

from the spousal support regime furthers the objective of providing for the equitable resolution of economic disputes that arise upon the breakdown of financially interdependent relationships. Similarly, it is nonsensical to suggest that the goal of reducing the burden on the public purse is advanced by limiting the right to make private claims for support to heterosexuals. The impugned legislation has the deleterious effect of driving a member of a same-sex couple who is in need of maintenance to the welfare system and it thereby imposes additional costs on the general taxpaying public.

116. If anything, the goals of the legislation are undermined by the impugned exclusion. Indeed, the *inclusion* of same-sex couples in s.29 of the *FLA* would better achieve the objectives of the legislation while respecting the *Charter* rights of individuals in same-sex relationships. In these circumstances, I conclude that the exclusion of same-sex couples from s. 29 of the Act is simply not rationally connected to the dual objectives of the spousal support provisions of the legislation.

117. Given this lack of a rational connection, s. 29 of the *FLA* is not saved by s. 1 of the *Charter....*

* * *

124. ... [N]either the common law equitable remedies nor the law of contract are adequate substitutes for the *FLA*'s spousal support regime. Indeed, if these remedies were considered satisfactory there would have been no need for the spousal support regime, or its extension to unmarried, opposite-sex couples. It must also be remembered that the exclusion of same-sex partners from this support regime does not simply deny them a certain benefit, but does so in a manner that violates their right to be given equal concern and respect by the government. The alternative regimes just outlined do not address the fact that exclusion from the statutory scheme has moral and societal implications beyond economic ones.... Therefore the existence of these remedies fails to minimize sufficiently the denial of same-sex partners' constitutionally guaranteed equality rights.

* * *

134. I therefore conclude that the exclusion of same-sex couples from s.29 of the *FLA* cannot be justified as a reasonable limit on constitutional rights under s. 1 of the *Charter....*

Notes and Questions

1. *Remedy.* Because affording same-gender cohabiting couples the same treatment as opposite-gender couples required alterations that could not be accomplished by substituting a few words, the majority chose to declare § 29 of no force or effect, but to temporarily suspend that remedy for six months to give the legislature the opportunity to amend the statute in conformity with the decision. Preferring not to change the definition of "spouse," the Ontario government instead added provisions to the Family Law Act that afford "same-sex partners" who "live together in a conjugal relationship for three years," or in "a relationship of some permanence, if they are the natural or adoptive parents of a child," all of the benefits and obligations afforded to unmarried opposite-gender cohabitants under Ontario law. Bala & Bromwich, *supra,* at 163, 178.

2. *Impact.* The repercussions of *M. v. H.* spread far beyond Ontario's support statutes. In Ontario alone, over 60 statutes that conferred rights or duties upon unmarried opposite-gender cohabitants were broadened by the amendment of the Family Law Act to apply to same-gender cohabitants whose relationship satisfied the same criteria. *Id.* at 163.

In addition, because the decision was based on national constitutional norms, the federal government and the governments of the other provinces were forced to examine their own legislative schemes. In 2000 the federal Parliament passed the Modernization of Benefits and Obligations Act, S.C. 2000, c.12, which amended 68 federal statutes to recognize both same-gender and opposite-gender partners as "common law partners" if they have cohabited in a conjugal relationship for at least one year. The effect of this bill was to extend to same-gender couples the rights and obligations that were already afforded under federal law to unmarried opposite-gender cohabitants in such areas as income tax benefits and federal pension eligibility. *Id.* at 163–64. Various provincial governments also amended their statutes to afford same-gender partners the same rights as opposite gender unmarried cohabitants, and Nova Scotia went further to created a registered partnership status as well. *Id.* at 164. More recently, Quebec created civil unions, which are open to same-gender partners as well as opposite-gender couples. Civil Code of Quebec, c. 64, §521.1 (2002).

Despite this broad impact, however, Justices Cory and Iacobucci stressed that none of the issues raised by the appeal required them to address the question of whether the Charter mandated that same-gender couples be afforded the right to marry, and that they were neither considering nor commenting on that issue.

Problem 4-3

Assume that the appeal of *Halpern* has just reached the Supreme Court of Canada. If you were representing the Applicants in an oral presentation to the Court, what arguments would you make to the Court? How, if at all, would you utilize *M. v. H.* in the presentation of your case?

If you were instead appearing on behalf of the Attorney General of Canada, what arguments would you present to the Court, and how would you seek to distinguish *M. v. H.?*

In the United States, the passage of the civil union legislation in Vermont and the reciprocal beneficiary legislation in Hawaii, described in Subsection A of this chapter, was prompted by the constitutional directives of those states' highest courts. Both courts determined that failure to afford entry to marriage or, in the case of Vermont, an alternate marital status, to same-gender couples violated the states' constitutions under provisions similar to, but not identical with, the Equal Protection Clause of the Federal Constitution. As you read the following excerpts from the opinion of the Vermont Supreme Court, consider whether differences in the applicable constitutional provisions, or other factors, account for the different remedial preferences of the Vermont court and the Ontario justices in *Halpern*.

Baker v. State

744 A.2d 864 (Vt. 1999)

[Ed. Note: Three same-gender couples who had each cohabited for many years brought suit seeking a declaratory judgment that the refusal to issue them marriage licenses violated the state's marriage statutes and the Vermont Constitution. After determining that the state marriage statutes reflect the understanding of marriage as a union between a man and a woman, and did not entitle plaintiffs to relief, the court next turned to examine plaintiffs' contention that, by excluding them from the legal benefits and protections accompanying marital status, the State was violating their rights under the Common Benefits Clause of Article 7 of the Vermont Constitution.

The Common Benefits Clause reads, in pertinent part:

> The government is, or ought to be, instituted for the common benefit, protection, and security of the people, nation, or community, and not for the particular emolument or advantage of any single person, family, or set of persons, who are a part only of that community.

The court began by observing that the Common Benefits Clause differs markedly from the federal Equal Protection Clause in its historical origins, purpose, and approach. Initially aimed at Great Britain as well as wealthy residents from other colonies claiming Vermont lands, the eighteenth century framers were concerned not with "the eradication of racial or class distinctions," but rather with "the elimination of artificial governmental preferments and advantages." *Id.* at 876. Eschewing the rigid categories or analytical formulas that are frequently undertaken in application of the federal Equal Protection Clause, the court observed that the approach of judicial review under the Common Benefits Clause "may be described as broadly deferential to the legislative prerogative to define and advance governmental ends, while vigorously ensuring that the means chosen bear a just and reasonable relation to the governmental objective." *Id.* at 871. Describing the analysis as a balancing approach that requires a "more stringent" reasonableness inquiry than generally associated with the "rational basis" review under the Federal Constitution, *id.*, the court stated that the case-specific analysis required by the Common Benefits Clause requires that "statutory exclusions from publicly-conferred benefits and protections must be premised on an appropriate and overriding public interest." *Id.* at 873.

Observing that the statutory classification at issue herein excludes those who wish to marry someone of the same sex, the court proceeded to scrutinize the proffered governmental purposes.]

* * *

...It is beyond dispute that the State has a legitimate and long-standing interest in promoting a permanent commitment between couples for the security of their children. It is equally undeniable that the State's interest has been advanced by extending formal public sanction and protection to the union, or marriage, of those couples considered capable of having children, i.e., men and women. And there is no doubt that the overwhelming majority of births today continue to result from natural conception between one man and one woman....

It is equally undisputed that many opposite-sex couples marry for reasons unrelated to procreation, that some of these couples never intend to have children, and that others are incapable of having children. Therefore, if the purpose of the statutory exclusion of same-sex couples is to "further the link between procreation and child rearing," it is significantly under-inclusive....

Furthermore, while accurate statistics are difficult to obtain, there is no dispute that a significant number of children today are actually being raised by same-sex parents, and that increasing numbers of children are being conceived by such parents through a variety of assisted-reproductive techniques....

...[T]o the extent that the State's purpose in licensing civil marriage was, and is, to legitimize children and provide for their security, the statutes plainly exclude many same-sex couples who are no different from opposite-sex couples with respect to these objectives. If anything, the exclusion of same-sex couples from the legal protections incident to marriage exposes their children to the precise risks that the State argues the marriage laws are designed to secure against. In short, the marital exclusion treats persons who are similarly situated for purposes of the law, differently.

The State also argues that because same-sex couples cannot conceive a child on their own, their exclusion promotes a "perception of the link between procreation and child rearing," and that to discard it would "advance the notion that mothers and fathers... are mere surplusage to the functions of procreation and child rearing." Apart from the bare assertion, the State offers no persuasive reasoning to support these claims. Indeed, it is undisputed that most of those who utilize non-traditional means of conception are infertile married couples,... and that many assisted-reproductive techniques involve only one of the married partner's genetic material, the other being supplied by a third party through sperm, egg, or embryo donation.... The State does not suggest that the use of these technologies undermines a married couple's sense of parental responsibility, or fosters the perception that they are "mere surplusage" to the conception and parenting of the child so conceived.... Nor does it even remotely suggest that access to such techniques ought to be restricted as a matter of public policy to "send a public message that procreation and child rearing are intertwined." Accordingly, there is no reasonable basis to conclude that a same-sex couple's use of the same technologies would undermine the bonds of parenthood, or society's perception of parenthood.

...Courts have upheld underinclusive statutes out of a recognition that, for reasons of pragmatism or administrative convenience, the legislature may choose to address problems incrementally.... The State does not contend, however, that the same-sex exclusion is necessary as a matter of pragmatism or administrative convenience.

* * *

The State asserts that a number of additional rationales could support a legislative decision to exclude same-sex partners from the statutory benefits and protections of marriage. Among these are the State's purported interests in "promoting child rearing in a setting that provides both male and female role models," minimizing the legal complications of surrogacy contracts and sperm donors, "bridging differences" between the sexes, discouraging marriages of convenience for tax, housing or other benefits, maintaining uniformity with marriage laws in other states, and generally protecting marriage from "destabilizing changes." The most substantive of the State's remaining claims relates to the issue of childrearing. It is conceivable that the Legislature could conclude that opposite-sex partners offer advantages in this area, although we note that child-development experts disagree and the answer is decidedly uncertain. The argument, however, contains a more fundamental flaw, and that is the Legislature's endorsement of a policy diametrically at odds with the State's claim. In 1996, the Vermont General Assembly enacted, and the Governor signed, a law removing all prior legal barriers to the adoption of children by same-sex couples.... At the same time, the Legislature provided additional legal protections in the form of court-ordered child support and parent-child contact in the event that same-sex parents dissolved their "domestic relationship."...In light of these express policy choices, the State's arguments that Vermont public policy favors opposite-sex over same-sex parents or disfavors the use of artificial reproductive technologies, are patently without substance.

Similarly, the State's argument that Vermont's marriage laws serve a substantial governmental interest in maintaining uniformity with other jurisdictions cannot be reconciled with Vermont's recognition of unions, such as first-cousin marriages, not uniformly sanctioned in other states.... In an analogous context, Vermont has sanctioned adoptions by same-sex partners,...notwithstanding the fact that many states have not.... Thus, the State's claim that Vermont's marriage laws were adopted because the Legislature sought to conform to those of the other forty-nine states is not only speculative, but refuted by two relevant legislative choices which demonstrate that uniformity with other jurisdictions has not been a governmental purpose.

The State's remaining claims (e.g., recognition of same-sex unions might foster marriages of convenience or otherwise affect the institution in "unpredictable" ways) may be plausible forecasts as to what the future may hold, but cannot reasonably be construed to provide a reasonable and just basis for the statutory exclusion. The State's conjectures are not, in any event, susceptible to empirical proof before they occur.

Finally, it is suggested that the long history of official intolerance of intimate same-sex relationships cannot be reconciled with an interpretation of Article 7 that would give state-sanctioned benefits and protection to individuals of the same sex who commit to a permanent domestic relationship. We find the argument to be unpersuasive for several reasons. First, to the extent that state action historically has been motivated by an animus against a class, that history cannot provide a legitimate basis for continued unequal application of the law.... As we observed recently... "equal protection of the laws cannot be limited by eighteenth-century standards." Second, whatever claim may be made in light of the undeniable fact that federal and state statutes—including those in Vermont—have historically disfavored same-sex relationships, more recent legislation plainly undermines the contention....

Thus, viewed in the light of history, logic, and experience, we conclude that none of the interests asserted by the State provides a reasonable and just basis for the continued exclusion of same-sex couples from the benefits incident to a civil marriage license under Vermont law....

It is important to state clearly the parameters of today's ruling. Although plaintiffs sought injunctive and declaratory relief designed to secure a marriage license, their claims and arguments here have focused primarily upon the consequences of official exclusion from the statutory benefits, protections, and security incident to marriage under Vermont law. While some future case may attempt to establish that—notwithstanding equal benefits and protections under Vermont law—the denial of a marriage license operates per se to deny constitutionally protected rights, that is not the claim we address today.

We hold only that plaintiffs are entitled under Chapter I, Article 7, of the Vermont Constitution to obtain the same benefits and protections afforded by Vermont law to married opposite-sex couples. We do not purport to infringe upon the prerogatives of the Legislature to craft an appropriate means of addressing this constitutional mandate, other than to note that the record here refers to a number of potentially constitutional statutory schemes from other jurisdictions. These include what are typically referred to as "domestic partnership" or "registered partnership" acts, which generally establish an alternative legal status to marriage for same-sex couples, impose similar formal requirements and limitations, create a parallel licensing or registration scheme, and extend all or most of the same rights and obligations provided by the law to married partners. [References were included here to the domestic partnership legislation of Hawaii, Denmark, and Norway. Ed.] We do not intend specifically to endorse any one or all of the referenced acts, particularly in view of the significant benefits omitted from several of the laws.

Further, while the State's prediction of "destabilization" cannot be a ground for denying relief, it is not altogether irrelevant. A sudden change in the marriage laws or the statutory benefits traditionally incidental to marriage may have disruptive and unforeseen consequences. Absent legislative guidelines defining the status and rights of same-sex couples, consistent with constitutional requirements, uncertainty and confusion could result. Therefore, we hold that the current statutory scheme shall remain in effect for a reasonable period of time to enable the Legislature to consider and enact implementing legislation in an orderly and expeditious fashion....

* * *

While many have noted the symbolic or spiritual significance of the marital relation, it is plaintiffs' claim to the secular benefits and protections of a singularly human relationship that, in our view, characterizes this case. The State's interest in extending official recognition and legal protection to the professed commitment of two individuals to a lasting relationship of mutual affection is predicated on the belief that legal support of a couple's commitment provides stability for the individuals, their family, and the broader community. Although plaintiffs' interest in seeking state recognition and protection of their mutual commitment may—in view of divorce statistics—represent "the triumph of hope over experience," the essential aspect of their claim is simply and fundamentally for inclusion in the family of State-sanctioned human relations.

The past provides many instances where the law refused to see a human being when it should have. See, e.g., Dred Scott.... The extension of the Common Benefits Clause to acknowledge plaintiffs as Vermonters who seek nothing more, nor less, than legal protection and security for their avowed commitment to an intimate and lasting human relationship is simply, when all is said and done, a recognition of our common humanity.

[Although all five justices concurred in finding a constitutional violation, Justice Johnson dissented to the portion of the opinion setting forth the remedy, arguing that the Common Benefits Clause required granting the relief requested—issuance of marriage licences—rather than merely affording plaintiffs the economic and other statutory benefits that accompany marital status.]

Notes and Questions

1. *Political Context.* Baker was actually the third U.S. state court decision in favor of same-gender couples seeking a constitutional right to marital status. In 1993 the Hawaii Supreme Court in a 3–2 opinion, Baehr v. Lewin, 852 P.2d 44 (Haw. 1993), ruled that the Hawaii statute restricting marriage to opposite-gender couples was a sex-based classification subject to strict scrutiny under the Equal Protection Clause of the Hawaii Constitution. In so holding, the Court rejected the State's definitional argument, similar to the one made in *Halpern*, that no discrimination on the basis of gender occurred because by definition marriage is a relationship between a man and a woman. The plurality also rejected the argument, strongly asserted by the dissenting justices, that the restriction was not based on sex, because persons of both genders were affected equally. The Court remanded the case to the trial court, to provide the State with an opportunity to overcome the presumption the statute was unconstitutional by demonstrating a compelling state interest.

On remand the trial court found that the State had failed to prove that the public interest in the well-being of children or their optimal development would be adversely affected by same-gender marriage, nor had the State demonstrated any other adverse consequences that would demonstrate a compelling state interest. Therefore the court enjoined the State officials from denying Plaintiffs a marriage license. Baehr v. Milke, No. 91-1394, 1996 WL 694235 (Haw. Cir. Ct. 1996). While that order was stayed pending appeal, the Hawaii Legislature in 1997 approved a constitutional amendment limiting marriage to opposite-gender couples, while at the same time enacting reciprocal beneficiary registration legislation that provides registered couples with significant property, probate, employment, and other benefits. The constitutional amendment was approved in 1998 by a majority of 70% of the voters, *see* David L. Chambers & Nancy D. Polikoff, *Family Law and Gay and Lesbian Family Issues in the Twentieth Century*, 33 Fam. L.Q. 523, 529 (1999), causing the Hawaii Supreme Court to reverse and remand the case by summary disposition. Baehr v. Milke, 994 P.2d 566 (Haw. 1999).

An Alaska trial court determined in 1998 that limiting marriage to opposite-gender couples denied same-gender partners their fundamental right to marry under the Alaskan Constitution. Brause v. Bureau of Vital Statistics, No. 3AN-95-6562Cl., 1998 WL 88743 (Alaska Super. Ct. Feb. 27, 1998). This decision was also mooted by a subsequent amendment of the Alaskan Constitution, passed by popular vote, which limited marriage to unions between one man and one woman. Brause v. Bureau of Vital Statistics, 21 P.3d 357 (Alaska 2001).

In *Baker*, in a portion of the opinion not included above, the majority defended their decision to refrain from issuing an immediate injunction to issue the licenses, against the dissenting justice's suggestion that such a mandate would avoid the "political cauldron" of public debate, by noting that both *Baehr* and *Bruase* had been effectively overturned by state constitutional amendments.

2. *Jurisdictional Split.* Like the Canadian courts, American courts have been split regarding the viability of constitutional claims by same-gender couples asserting a right to marry. To date, *Baker, Baehr,* and *Brause* are the only decisions in which the courts have found constitutional claims to be viable, and although two of these decisions prompted the creation of a state-wide alternative status, none of these has resulted in gay couples being permitted to marry within the United States. Many courts have rejected the viability of constitutional claims based on the Federal Constitution, state constitutional provisions, or both. *See* Jones v. Halloran, 501 S.W.2d 588 (Ky. 1973) (no constitutional violation because same-gender partners are incapable of entering a marriage); Dean v. District of Columbia, 653 A.2d 307 (D.C. 1995) (Federal Constitutional claims rejected); Goodridge v. Dept. of Public Health, 14 Mass. L. Rptr. 591, 2002 WL 1299135 (Mass. Super. 2002) (recognizing procreation as the central purpose of marriage, and therefore finding limitation of marriage to opposite-gender couples rational and permissible under state constitution); Baker v. Nelson, 191 N.W.3d 185 (Minn. 1971) (observing procreation is fundamental to marriage and finding no violation of Federal Constitution); Storrs v. Holcomb, 645 N.Y.S.2d 286 (N.Y. Sup. 1996) (New York constitution not violated); Singer v. Hara, 522 P.2d 1187 (Wash. App. 1974) (denial of license was not based on sex, but on nature of marriage itself, and thus Federal Constitution and state's Equal Rights Amendment not violated).

3. *Substantive Due Process.* Plaintiffs asserting a constitutional right to issuance of a marriage license typically assert constitutional bases in addition to equal protection in support of their claim. Frequently these include a claim based upon substantive due process. Most of these efforts, however, have been unsuccessful. In *Baehr* the Hawaii Supreme Court rejected a substantive due process claim brought under the Federal and Hawaii Constitutions. Examining construction of the right to marry under the Federal Constitution, the court found that the fundamental right had been inextricably linked with procreation in Supreme Court cases developing that right, and thus contemplated only unions between a man and a woman. The court declined to extend that fundamental right under the Hawaii

Constitution, observing that the right to same-sex marriage was not rooted in the traditions and collective conscience of the Hawaiian people. *See also* Dean v. District of Columbia, 653 A.2d 307 (D.C. 1995) (no deeply rooted tradition of same-gender marriage creates fundamental liberty interest under Federal Constitution); Storrs v. Holcomb, 645 N.Y.S. 2d 286 (N.Y. Sup. 1996) (same under New York Constitution).

It is interesting to note that in *Halpern*, in a portion of the opinion omitted from the above excerpt, the Justices rejected without discussion the additional contention of Applicants that denial of their right to marry violated their right to liberty under Section 7 of the Charter, because it undermined their dignity, privacy, and autonomy.

Only the Alaska trial court, in Brause v. Bureau of Vital Statistics, 1998 WL 88743 (Alaska Super. Ct.), found a substantive due process claim viable. Explicitly rejecting the analysis of the Hawaii Supreme Court in *Baehr* on this issue, the court observed that the issue is not whether same-sex marriage is a deeply rooted tradition. Rather, it is the freedom to make a choice of a life partner that is deeply rooted in tradition, and therefore a fundamental right protected by the right to privacy under the Alaskan Constitution. This determination became moot, however, with the substantive amendment to the Alaska Constitution specifically limiting marriage to opposite-gender unions.

———————

Unlike the Canadian Charter of Human Rights and U.S. federal and state constitutions, the Bill of Rights of the 1996 Constitution of South Africa explicitly prohibits public and private discrimination based on sexual orientation. As this book goes to press, the Constitutional Court of South Africa has not yet had the opportunity to address the issue of whether that or other provisions of the Constitution require that same-gender couples be permitted to marry in South Africa, although a case presenting that issue is working its way through the court system. *Gays Welcome Concourt Decision*, S. Afr. Press Ass'n, Sept. 10, 2002, at 2002 WL 26632075. The Constitutional Court has, however, issued a number of important decisions providing that same-gender partners who are in permanent life partnerships are entitled to various benefits to which spouses are entitled.

National Coalition for Gay and Lesbian Equality v. Minister of Home Affairs
2000 (2) SA 1 (CC)

Ackermann, J.

[1] This matter raises two important questions. The first is whether it is unconstitutional for immigration law to facilitate the immigration into South Africa of the spouses of permanent South African residents but not to afford the same benefits to gays and lesbians in permanent same-sex life partnerships with permanent South African residents. The second is whether, when it concludes that provisions in a statute are unconstitutional, the Court may read words into the statute to remedy the unconstitutionality....

* * *

[30] Section 9 of the Constitution provides:

Equality

(1) Everyone is equal before the law and has the right to equal protection and benefit of the law.

(2) Equality includes the full and equal enjoyment of all rights and freedoms. To promote achievement of equality, legislative and other measures designed to protect or advance persons, or categories of persons, disadvantaged by unfair discrimination may be taken.

(3) The state may not unfairly discriminate directly or indirectly against anyone on one or more grounds, including race, gender, sex, pregnancy, marital status, ethnic or social origin, colour, sexual orientation, age, disability, religion, conscience, belief, culture, language and birth.

(4) No person may unfairly discriminate directly or indirectly against anyone on one or more grounds in terms of subsection (3). National legislation must be enacted to prevent or prohibit unfair discrimination.

(5) Discrimination on one or more grounds listed in subsection (3) is unfair unless it is established that the discrimination is fair.

Section 10 provides:

Human Dignity

Everyone has inherent dignity and the right to have their dignity respected and protected.

[31] ... In the present case the rights of equality and dignity are also closely related and it would be convenient to deal with them in a related manner.

[32] The differentiation brought about by section 25(5) is of a negative kind. It does not proscribe conduct of same-sex life partners or enact provisions that in themselves prescribe negative consequences for them. The differentiation lies in its failure to extend to them advantages or benefits that it extends to spouses....

[33] Before this Court respondents challenged the conclusion reached by the High Court that the omission in section 25(5) of spousal benefits to same-sex life partners was a differentiation based on the ground of sexual orientation. It was submitted...that the differentiation was based on the ground that they were non-spouses, which had nothing to do with their sexual orientation, and that accordingly, because the differentiation was based on the ground that they were non-spouses, rather than marital status, it did not constitute unfair discrimination. There is no merit in this submission, as... spouse...is but the name given to the partners to a marriage.

[34] ... [I]t was argued that, even if the differentiation was on grounds of marital status, there was nothing that prevented gays and lesbians from contracting marriages with persons of the opposite sex, thus becoming and acquiring spouses and accordingly being entitled to the spousal benefits under section 25(5).... What that submission implies is that same-sex life partners should ignore their sexual orientation and, contrary thereto, enter into marriage with someone of the opposite sex.

[35] I am unable to accede to this line of argument. It confuses form with substance and does not have proper regard for the operation, experience or impact of discrimination in society. Discrimination does not take place in discrete areas of the law, hermetically sealed from one another, where each aspect of discrimination is to be examined and its impact evaluated in isolation. Discrimination must be understood in the context of the experience of those on whom it impacts....

[36] Moreover, the submission fails to recognise that marriage represents but one form of life partnership. The law currently only recognises marriages that are conjugal rela-

tionships between people of the opposite sex.... The law currently does not recognise permanent same-sex life partnerships as marriages. It follows that section 25(5) affords protection only to conjugal relationships between heterosexuals and excludes any protection to a life partnership which entails a conjugal same-sex relationship, which is the only form of conjugal relationship open to gays and lesbians in harmony with their sexual orientation.

* * *

[38] ...The respondents' submission that gays and lesbians are free to marry in the sense that nothing prohibits them from marrying persons of the opposite sex, is true only as a meaningless abstraction. This submission ignores the constitutional injunction that gays and lesbians cannot be discriminated against on the grounds of their own sexual orientation and the constitutional right to express that orientation in a relationship of their own choosing.

* * *

[40] The better view...in my judgment, is that the discrimination in section 25(5) constitutes overlapping or intersecting discrimination on the grounds of sexual orientation and marital status, both being specified in section 9(3) and presumed to constitute unfair discrimination by reason of section 9(5) of the Constitution....

[41] ...[T]he determining factor regarding the unfairness of discrimination is, in the final analysis, the impact of the discrimination on the complainant or the members of the affected group....

[42] ...The sting of past and continuing discrimination against both gays and lesbians is the clear message that it conveys, namely, that they, whether viewed as individuals or in their same-sex relationships, do not have the inherent dignity and are not worthy of the human respect possessed by and accorded to heterosexuals and their relationships. This discrimination occurs at a deeply intimate level of human existence and relationality. It denies to gays and lesbians that which is foundational to our Constitution and the concepts of equality and dignity, which at this point are closely intertwined, namely that all persons have the same inherent worth and dignity as human beings, whatever their other differences may be. The denial of equal dignity and worth all too quickly and insidiously degenerates into a denial of humanity and leads to inhuman treatment by the rest of society in many other ways....

* * *

[54] ...The message is that gays and lesbians lack the inherent humanity to have their families and family lives in such same-sex relationships respected or protected. It serves in addition to perpetuate and reinforce existing prejudices and stereotypes. The impact constitutes a crass, blunt, cruel and serious invasion of their dignity. The discrimination, based on sexual orientation, is severe because no concern, let alone anything approaching equal concern, is shown for the particular sexual orientation of gays and lesbians.

[55] We were pressed with an argument, on behalf of the Minister, that it was of considerable public importance to protect the traditional and conventional institution of marriage and that the government accordingly has a strong and legitimate interest to protect the family life of such marriages and was entitled to do so by means of section 25(5).... In the first place, protecting the traditional institution of marriage as recognised by law may not be done in a way that unjustifiably limits the constitutional rights of partners in a permanent same-sex life partnership.

[56] In the second place there is no rational connection between the exclusion of same-sex life partners from the benefits under section 25(5) and the government interest sought to be achieved thereby, namely the protection of families and the family life of heterosexual spouses.... I accordingly hold that section 25(5) constitutes unfair discrimination and a serious limitation of the section 9(3) equality right of gays and lesbians who are permanent residents in the Republic and who are in permanent same-sex life partnerships with foreign nationals. I also hold...[that] section 25(5) simultaneously constitutes a severe limitation of the section 10 right to dignity enjoyed by gays and lesbians....

* * *

[Ed. Note: Applying the balancing of different interests necessary to carry out the justification analysis once a violation of rights is identified, the court went on to conclude that there were no countervailing interests, because the protection of family in conventional spousal relationships would be in no way affected by including same-sex life partners under the protection of section 25(5). The Court then determined that the appropriate remedy was to read into the statute, after the word spouse, the words "or partner, in a permanent same-sex life partnership." The Court defined "permanent" as "an established intention of the parties to cohabit with one another permanently." ¶ 86.]

[88] Whoever in the administration of the Act is called upon to decide whether a same-sex life partnership is permanent, in the sense indicated above, will have to do so on the totality of the facts presented. Without purporting to provide an exhaustive list, such facts would include the following: the respective ages of the partners; the duration of the relationship; whether the partners took part in a ceremony manifesting their intention to enter into a permanent partnership, what the nature of that ceremony was and who attended it; how the partnership is viewed by the relations and friends of the partners; whether the partners share a common abode; whether the partners own or lease the common abode jointly; whether and to what extent the partners share responsibility for living expenses and the upkeep of the joint home; whether and to what extent one partner provides financial support for the other; whether and to what extent the partners have made provision for one another in relation to medical, pension and related benefits; whether there is a partnership agreement and what its contents are; and whether and to what extent the partners have made provision in their wills for one another. None of these considerations is indispensable for establishing a permanent partnership. In order to apply the above criteria, those administering the Act are entitled, within the ambit of the Constitution...to take all reasonable steps,...to ensure that full information concerning the permanent nature of any same-sex life partnership is disclosed.

* * *

Notes and Questions

1. *Additional Rulings.* Recently the South African Constitutional Court has determined that other statutory provisions that fail to afford same-sex life partners the same benefits as spouses violate Section 9 of the Constitution. In Satchwell v. President of Republic of South Africa, CCT 45/10, (S. Afr. July 25, 2002), *available at* http://www/con-court.gov.za/cases/2002, the Court unanimously held that the provisions of a South African statute that provided survivorship benefits to the spouses of judges must be read to provide the same benefits to permanent same-sex life partners, but only if the partners have undertaken reciprocal duties of support.

In fashioning a remedy in both *National Coalition* and *Satchwell*, the Constitutional Court confronts the necessity of defining when a same-sex relationship is equivalent to marriage. In the context of immigration law even marriages are often subject to intense factual scrutiny, at least in the United States, to ensure that the marriage is not a sham concocted for immigration purposes. That concern was also raised by the respondents in *National Coalition*. Nevertheless, the existence of a marriage, because of the formal registration requirements that normally exist, is still more susceptible to objective proof than an unregistered relationship. The Constitutional Court in *National Coalition* devised a definition for what it termed permanent same-sex life partnerships, and then created a flexible list of criteria that could be applied by immigration officials to determine when such a relationship was sufficiently "permanent" that it should be treated as equivalent to a marriage. Do you think the list of factors was appropriate? It is interesting to note that in *Satchwell*, when a different type of statutory benefit was at issue, the Court instead took a functional approach, focusing on a particular factor, the reciprocal duty of support, that was related to the benefit at issue, rather than the more flexible laundry list proposed in *National Coalition*. Should the characteristics of the same-sex relationship required in order to receive equivalent benefits to a marital spouse vary with the nature of the benefit, or would it be more appropriate to fashion an overarching definition? Is the flexibility of either approach preferable to requiring a relationship to be registered, or is the certainty of limiting benefits to those in a legislatively created permanent status preferable?

In another recent decision, Du Toit v. Minister of Welfare, CCT 40/01 (SA Sept. 10, 2002), *available at* http://www/concourt.gov.za/cases/2002, the Constitutional Court ruled in favor of two women seeking to jointly adopt two children, who challenged the constitutionality of a statute that permitted joint adoption only by married couples. Although the couple had been approved by the placing agency to adopt the siblings placed with them, as a result of the statutory restriction only one partner was permitted by the court in the original adoption proceeding to become an adoptive parent. As in *National Coalition*, the Constitutional Court unanimously determined that this restriction discriminated on the grounds of sexual orientation and marital status, and also violated section 28(2) of the Constitution, which requires that a child's best interests must be paramount in every proceeding concerning the child. The Court therefore ruled that the legislation must permit same-sex life partners to jointly adopt children if they are otherwise found to be suitable parents.

2. *Traditional Woman to Woman Marriages.* In *Satchwell*, the Court observes that same-sex unions are not new to South Africa:

> In certain African traditional societies woman-to-woman marriages are not unknown, this being prevalent in families that are childless because the woman is barren or where the woman is in a powerful position in her community, like being a queen or a chieftainness, or where she is very wealthy. *Id.* at ¶ 12.

3. *History.* For an interesting account of the historical, ideological, and political forces that led to the inclusion of explicit protection for the gay and lesbian community in South Africa, *see* Eric C. Christiansen, *Ending the Apartheid of the Closet: Sexual Orientation in the South African Constitutional Process*, 32 Int'l L. & Pol. 997 (2000).

4. *Constitutional Prohibitions of Sexual Orientation Discrimination.* In addition to South Africa, the International Lesbian and Gay Association (ILGA) reports that sexual orientation (or a similar ground that is intended to cover sexual orientation) is explic-

itly included in the nondiscrimination provisions of the national constitutions of Ecuador (1998), Fiji Islands (1997), and Switzerland (1999), in two state constitutions in Brazil (Mato Grosso and Sergipe), and in three state (länder) constitutions in Germany (Berlin, Brandenburg, and Thuringia). Robert Wintemute, *European Treaties and Legislation and National Constitutions and Legislation Expressly Prohibiting Discrimination Based on Sexual Orientation,* at http://www.ilga.org/Information/Legal_Survey/list_ of_international_treaties.htm (Last Updated Sept. 30, 2002).

2. International Law

Apart from domestic constitutions, international human rights instruments are increasingly becoming a focus of attention as members of the gay and lesbian community turn to international organizations and tribunals to challenge discriminatory practices. Though international tribunals have been slow to recognize the relationships of same-gender partners, support from international instruments for equality of treatment is developing.

a. Council of Europe and European Convention on Human Rights

The Council of Europe has addressed some of the issues facing gay and lesbian families through a series of non-binding resolutions and recommendations. Most recently, in September 2000 the Parliamentary Assembly issued Recommendation 1474 regarding the *Situation of Lesbians and Gays in Council of Europe Member States, available at* http://assembly.coe.int., in which the Assembly recommended to the Committee of Ministers that sexual orientation be added to the grounds for discrimination prohibited by the European Convention on Human Rights, and that the terms of reference of the European Commission against Racism and Intolerance be extended to cover homophobia. The resolution also urged member states, *inter alia,* to adopt legislation providing for registered partnerships, to prohibit sexual orientation discrimination in their national legislation, to decriminalize homosexual acts between consenting adults, and to take positive measures to combat homophobic attitudes. Also in 2000, the Assembly issued Recommendation 1470 (2000) on the *Situation of Gays and Lesbians and their Partners in respect of Asylum and Immigration in the Member States of the Council of Europe, available at* http://assembly.coe. int., in which the Assembly recommended to the Council of Ministers that member states be urged to reexamine their immigration policies in order to provide residence rights to a foreign partner in a bi-national partnership, analogous to those provided to spouses, and to grant refugee status to homosexuals with a well-founded fear of persecution.

The European Court of Human Rights, and the former European Commission of Human Rights, when it was in operation (*see* Chapter One, Section B.2.d.), have given a mixed reception to claims brought by gay men and lesbians under the Convention. Three articles of the Convention are particularly relevant. First, Article 14 provides that the rights set forth in the Convention are to be secured without discrimination on any ground such as sex, race, colour, and a number of other enumerated grounds. Sexual orientation is not included in the enumerated list, however. Second is Article 8, which guarantees each individual "the right to respect for his private and family life." Third is

Article 12, which guarantees men and women of marriageable age a right to marry in accordance with national laws.

Thus far the European Convention on Human Rights has not been interpreted to require contracting nations to recognize spousal or partnership rights originating from families formed by two persons of the same gender. In Simpson v. United Kingdom, DR 274, HUDOC REF 407 (1986), the European Commission on Human Rights determined that a homosexual relationship does not entitle either partner to familial rights under Article 8. The Commission ruled that neither Article 8 nor Article 14 entitled a lesbian applicant to claim a statutory spousal right to succeed to her partner's tenancy in the home they had occupied upon her partner's death. Moreover, the European Court of Human Rights, in earlier decisions addressing a related issue, the right of transsexuals to marry, stated its opinion that "the right to marry guaranteed by Article 12 refers to the traditional marriage between persons of opposite biological sex." Rees v. United Kingdom, 106 Eur. Ct. H.R. (ser. A) at 19 (1986); Cossey v. United Kingdom, 184 Eur. Ct. H. R.(ser. A) at 17–18 (1990). See also X.Y. & Z. v. United Kingdom, 35 Eur. Ct. H.R. 619 (1997).

Nevertheless, a recent decision of the European Court of Human Rights, though also addressing the right to marry of transsexuals rather than same-gender couples, may be a harbinger of changing attitudes. Sitting as a Grand Chamber, the Court in I. v. United Kingdom, HUDOC Ref. 3735 (2002), reversed its own previous decisions in Rees, Cossey, and X.Y. & Z., and determined that the United Kingdom's failure to grant legal recognition to the gender re-assignment of a post-surgical transsexual violated her right to privacy under Article 8 and her right to marry under Article 12 of the Convention. Observing that the ability of a couple to conceive a child is not a condition to enjoyment of the fundamental right to marry, the Court held that, "While it is for the Contracting State to determine inter alia the conditions under which a person claiming legal recognition as a transsexual establishes that gender re-assignment has been properly effected ... and the formalities applicable to future marriages (including, for example, the information to be furnished to intended spouses), the Court finds no justification for barring the transsexual from enjoying the right to marry under any circumstances." ¶ 83. Specifically rejected was the argument that the applicant remained free to marry a person of her former opposite sex. Observing that the applicant lived as a woman in a relationship with a man and only wished to marry a man, the Court found that denying her that possibility infringed "the very essence of her right to marry." ¶ 81.

Articles 8 and 14 of the European Convention on Human Right have thus far been the basis for several decisions by the European Court of Human Rights finding various practices discriminating against homosexuals to be in violation of the Convention. Over two decades ago, in Dudgeon v. United Kingdom, 45 Eur. Ct. H.R. (ser. A) 5 (1981), the Court held that criminalization of private sexual acts between consenting adult males contravened the right to privacy guaranteed by Article 8 of the Convention. The Court has reached similar rulings in several subsequent cases, including A.D.T. v. United Kingdom, 2000-IX Eur. Ct. H.R. 295, in which the court found prosecution for "gross indecency" for private sexual acts involving a small group of men violated Article 8. In 1999, in two separate decisions handed down the same day, Lustig-Prean and Beckett v. United Kingdom, 29 Eur. H.R. Rep. 548 (1999) and Smith and Grady v. United Kingdom, 1999-IV Eur. Ct. H.R. 45, the Court held that the applicants' discharge from the armed forces on the basis of their sexual orientation, as well as the nature of the interviews and searches that accompanied the investigation into their sexual orientation, violated the applicants' right to privacy under Article 8 of the Convention. That same year the Court determined in Salgueiro da Silva Mouta v. Portugal, 1999-IX

Eur. Ct. H. R. 309, that consideration of a father's sexual orientation and cohabitation with a male partner by a Portuguese Court of Appeals in its decision to transfer custody of his child to her mother constituted a differentiation in treatment under Article 14 that could not be justified, and in conjunction with the father's right to family life under Article 8, violated his rights under the Convention.

b. European Union

Thus far the judgments of the Court of Justice of the European Union have lent little support to gay and lesbian partners seeking recognition and entitlement to spousal rights. In Grant v. South-West Trains Ltd., 1998 E.C.R. I-621 the Court held that the refusal of an employer to provide travel concessions to an employee's same-sex partner equivalent to those that would be provided to an employee's spouse or opposite-sex partner did not constitute discrimination under the EC Treaty, nor the did it violate a Council Directive requiring equal pay for men and women. The Court determined that the restriction of benefits to opposite-sex partners was not a discrimination based on sex, since the restriction applied equally to male and female employees. In support of its decision, the Court of Justice noted that Articles 8, 12, and 14 of the European Convention of Human Rights had not been interpreted to require same-gender relationships to receive equivalent treatment to opposite-gender relationships.

Three years later the Court held in D. v. Council of Ministers, 2001 E.C.R. I-4319, that even as to its own employees, the European Union was not required under Community law then in effect to treat registered same-sex partners as equivalent to spouses. Despite the fact that D, a Swedish official of the European Communities, had entered a registered partnership recognized under Swedish law, the Court found that Staff Regulations regulating the provision of a household allowance did not require that he receive the payment to which he would be entitled if he were married. Again, the Court found that this was not discrimination based on sex because the restriction would apply to both male and female employees. Nor, in the Court's eyes, was this a restriction discriminating on the basis of sexual orientation, as in this case it was not the gender of the partner that determined whether the allowance was granted, but the legal nature of the relationship. Any decision to treat registered partnerships of employees as equivalent to marriage, the Court noted, must be made by the legislature, a change that the legislature had explicitly declined thus far to make, but which was under study.

In the opinion of the Advocate General submitted to the justices in D., the Advocate General considered Article 9 of the new Charter of Fundamental Rights of the European Union (see Chapter One, Section B.2.e. for a discussion of both the role of the Advocates General and the Charter). Rather than incorporate the wording of Article 12 of the European Convention on Human Rights, which recognizes the right to marry of "men and women of marriageable age," the Charter's drafters chose to delete the reference to "men and women" and instead provide in Article 9 that: "The right to marry ... shall be guaranteed in accordance with the national laws governing the exercise of those rights." The explanatory notes to the Charter, however, indicate that the drafters intended neither to prohibit nor require recognition of same-gender marriages, and the Advocate General therefore argued in D. that Article 9 could not be used to expand the definition of spouse under Community law. Clare McGlynn, *Families and the European Union Charter of Fundamental Rights: progressive change or entrenching the status quo?*, (2001) 26 E.L. Rev. Dec. 582, 592. Professor McGlynn observes that the Charter's preamble, which espouses the goal of protecting "fundamental rights in the light of changes in society," might support a less restrictive interpretation in the future. *Id.* at 593.

The European Parliament of the European Union has passed resolutions urging member nations to pass their own legislation providing same-gender partners access to marriage or an alternative status (1994), and to take action to end legal and social discrimination based on sexual orientation (1984). These resolutions were non-binding, however, and the European Commission questioned E.U. competence to take action prohibiting such discrimination. Heather Hunt, *Diversity and the European Union: Grant v. SWT, The Treaty of Amsterdam, and the Free Movement of Persons,* 27 Denv.J. Int'l L. & Pol'y 633, 648 (1999).

Recent changes to E.U. law, however, suggest that it may become a more useful basis to challenge discrimination on the basis of sexual orientation in the future. When the Treaty on European Union and the Treaty Establishing the European Community were amended in the Treaty of Amsterdam in 1997 (*see* Chapter One, Section B.2.e for a detailed discussion of the treaties of the European Union and its structure), Article 13 of the Treaty Establishing the European Community was amended to provide:

> Without prejudice to the other provisions of this Treaty and within the limits of the powers conferred by it upon the Community, the Council, acting unanimously on a proposal from the Commission and after consulting the European Parliament, may take appropriate action to combat discrimination based on sex, racial or ethnic origin, religion or belief, disability, age or sexual orientation.

Article 13 is not itself a "current prohibition on discrimination based on sexual orientation," but instead provides a framework for passing future laws. Hunt, *supra,* at 651. The inclusion of "sexual orientation" in the list of grounds is an important acknowledgment, creating the potential for a Community-wide prohibition of discrimination on the basis of sexual orientation, as opposed to resolutions encouraging member states to pass their own legislation. Nevertheless, the unanimity requirement places significant restrictions on the Council's ability to bring about significant change. *Id.* at 648–51.

In 2000 the Council utilized its new power to pass Council Directive 2000/78/EC, which establishes a general framework for equal treatment in employment and occupation. Directives establish European Union policy, and require member nations to implement that policy through whatever means — statute, administrative regulation, constitutional amendment — would be appropriate in the context of their own legal systems. Directive 2000/78 provides in part:

> (12)...[A]ny direct or indirect discrimination based on religion or belief, disability, age or sexual orientation as regards the areas covered by this Directive should be prohibited throughout the Community. This prohibition of discrimination should also apply to nationals of third countries but does not cover differences of treatment based on nationality and is without prejudice to provisions governing the entry and residence of third-country nationals and their access to employment and occupation.

This mandate is unlikely to affect the provision of spousal benefits to same-gender partners, however, as paragraph 22 provides: "This Directive is without prejudice to national laws on marital status and the benefits dependent thereon." On the other hand, it might well address differences in benefits afforded to same-gender and opposite-gender cohabitants. A further limitation is included in paragraph 23, which provides that, "[i]n very limited circumstances, a difference of treatment may be justified where a characteristic related to...sexual orientation constitutes a genuine and determining occupational requirement, when the objective is legitimate and the requirement is proportionate." The member nations are required to provide information regarding any such circumstances to the Commission. The Directive permits ameliorative measures intended to compensate disadvantaged groups, as well as organizations of persons of a particular sexual orientation whose purpose is to promote the special needs of that group. In addition to prohibiting employment discrimination on the basis of sexual orientation, member nations are required by the Directive to create judicial or administrative procedures for the enforcement of obligations by victims of the prohibited discrimination.

In addition, the new Charter of Fundamental Rights, proclaimed at the European Council meeting in December 2000, may provide broad protection against discrimination on the basis of sexual orientation in the future. Article 21 of the Charter of Fundamental Rights provides:

> Any discrimination based on any ground such as sex, race, colour, ethnic or social origin, genetic features, language, religion or belief, political or any other opinion, membership of a national minority, property, birth, disability, age or sexual orientation shall be prohibited.

As explained in more detail in Chapter One, Section B.2.e., the Charter is not as yet regarded as binding upon member nations in the conduct of their domestic affairs, but it may well embody the rights of citizens of member nations in their interaction with the supranational authority of the European Union itself.

c. Organization of American States

Partners in same-gender relationships have also recently begun to seek assistance from the Inter-American Commission on Human Rights in their efforts to secure equivalent benefits. In the Case of Marta Lucia Alvarez Giraldo, Case 11.656, Report No. 71/99 (1999), the Commission reviewed a complaint brought by the applicant against Columbia, alleging that the director of the prison in which the applicant was incarcerated had refused her request for intimate visits from her female life partner on the basis of her sexual orientation. Finding that Columbia law afforded prisoners a right to intimate visits, the Commission determined that the applicant had stated a colorable claim of arbitrary and abusive interference with her private life, in violation of Article 11(2) of the American Convention on Human Rights. Following unsuccessful attempts to resolve the matter by friendly settlement, the Commission declared the case admissible, and agreed to publish the decision, to continue analyzing the merits of the case, and to renew its efforts to conclude a friendly settlement. (*See* Chapter One, Section B.2.f for a detailed discussion of the Convention and the procedures and remedies available to the Commission.). A subsequent action brought by José Alberto Pérez Meza, Report No. 96/01 (2001), seeking inheritance rights on the basis of a de facto same-gender partnership equivalent to those Paraguayan law would permit opposite-gender de facto partners, was dismissed because the petitioner had not exhausted domestic remedies.

d. United Nations Human Rights System

Within the United Nations human rights system, the convention most frequently invoked in support of same-gender partners is the International Covenant on Civil and Political Rights (ICCPR). The Human Rights Committee monitors implementation of the ICCPR through its review of periodic reports from the member states. Victims of violations of the ICCPR may submit communications to the Human Rights Committee against a contracting nation only if that nation has also ratified the first Optional Protocol to the ICCPR. Complaints from a member state about another member state's violation of the ICCPR may also be heard through a communication to the Human Rights Committee, but only if both states have specifically agreed to this authority. (*See* Chapter One, Section B.2.a. for further information regarding the operation of the enforcement system under U.N. human rights conventions.) Although the limited nature of this enforcement scheme has not facilitated extensive consideration of matters involving sexual orientation issues, two cases arising out of this system have received significant attention.

The first case involved a challenge to New Zealand's refusal to permit same-gender couples to marry. Three lesbian couples who unsuccessfully sought a declaratory judgment appealed the High Court's decision to the New Zealand Court of Appeal, arguing both that the gender neutral marriage law did not preclude them from obtaining a license and that barring their entry to marriage constituted discrimination under the New Zealand Human Rights Act. In Quilter v. Attorney General [1998], 1 N.Z.L.R. 523, the Court unanimously determined that the statute permitted marriage between a man and woman only, and the majority further held that this restriction did not constitute discrimination under the Act. The couples subsequently filed a communication with the United Nations Human Rights Committee under the first Optional Protocol to the ICCPR, asserting that New Zealand's failure to permit same-gender marriage violated their rights under Articles 16, 17, 23, and 26 of the ICCPR. In Joslin v. New Zealand, Communication No. 902/1999, CCPR/C/75/D/902/1999 (July 30, 2002), the Human Rights Committee issued its determination:

* * *

... The Committee notes that article 23, paragraph 2 of the Covenant expressly addresses the issue of the right to marry.

Given the existence of a specific provision in the Covenant on the right to marriage, any claim that this right has been violated must be considered in the light of this provision. Article 23, paragraph 2, of the Covenant is the only substantive provision in the Covenant which defines a right by using the term "men and women", rather than "every human being", "everyone" and "all persons". Use of the term "men and women", rather than the general terms used elsewhere in Part III of the Covenant, has been consistently and uniformly understood as indicating that the treaty obligation of States parties stemming from article 23, paragraph 2, of the Covenant is to recognize as marriage only the union between a man and a woman wishing to marry each other.

In light of the scope of the right to marry under article 23, paragraph 2, of the Covenant, the Committee cannot find that by mere refusal to provide for marriage between homosexual couples, the State party has violated the rights of the authors under articles 16, 17, 23, paragraphs 1 and 2, or 26 of the Covenant.

The Human Rights Committee, acting under article 5, paragraph 4 of the Optional Protocol, is of the view that the facts before it do not disclose a violation of any provision of the International Covenant on Civil and Political Rights.

Just as in the European Court of Human Rights, a communication submitted to the Human Rights Committee challenging the criminalization of private same-gender sexual conduct between consenting adults was more successful. In Toonen v. Australia, Communication No. 488/1992, CCPR/C/50/D/488/1992 (April 4, 1994) the Committee determined that the provisions of the Tasmanian Criminal Code constituted an arbitrary interference with the author's privacy, in violation of Article 17 of the ICCPR, that could not be justified by the intent to prevent the spread of AIDS. The Committee suggested that as a remedy, the State of Tasmania should repeal the relevant sections of the Criminal Code within 90 days. The Committee also observed that the prohibition against sex discrimination in Article 26 of the ICCPR "is to be taken as including sexual orientation," but found it unnecessary, in light of its decision under Article 17, to determine whether there was also a violation of Article 26.

Issues regarding discrimination on the basis of sexual orientation also surface in the periodic reports submitted by member nations and the reviews of those reports conducted by the Human Rights Committee. For example, the Summary Record of the 1961st meeting of the Human Rights Committee, CCPR/C/SR.1961 (October 23, 2002), reviewing the Fifth Periodic Report of the United Kingdom, noted favorably the United Kingdom's recent legislation establishing a common age of consent for same-gender and opposite-gender sexual relations, as well as immigration rules that permit long-term same-gender cohabitants to immigrate under the same terms as opposite-gender cohabitants and married couples. In its Concluding Observations considering the report submitted by the Hong Kong Special Administrative Region of China, CCPR/C/79/Add.117 (December 11, 1999), the Committee expressed concern that no legislative remedies were available to victims of discrimination on grounds of race or sexual orientation. Such reviews, though far too numerous to review ad seriatim herein, are an important component of the response of the United Nations' human rights system to discrimination on the basis of sexual orientation. Considering that approximately 150 nations are now parties to the ICCPR, these reviews may well, over time, have some impact on discriminatory practices against sexual minorities that occur in many nations with which regional organizations have little involvement.

Problem 4-4

Elena and Sofia have resided together in a conjugal relationship in Luxembourg, their native country, for the past twelve years. They have committed to a life-long relationship, and are raising a daughter conceived by artificial insemination. Having unsuccessfully sought a marriage license in proceedings in the Luxembourg courts and exhausted all domestic remedies, they file an application with the European Court of Human Rights alleging violations of Articles 8, 12, and 14.

The European Court of Human Rights is not bound by past precedent. The Convention is viewed as a "living instrument" and its interpretation can evolve over time. As an advocate for the applicants appearing before the Court, what arguments would you make to persuade the Court to rule that denial of the ability to marry violates the applicants' rights under the Convention? As you frame your arguments, consider drawing upon analogous constitutional decisions as well as precedent under international law.

As counsel for the Grand Duchy of Luxembourg appearing before the Court, what arguments, drawing from both international and constitutional precedents from around the world, would you submit to the Court?

C. Rights of Cohabitants

The rising incidence of nonmarital cohabitation is gaining increasing attention world-wide. In the United States, the 2000 census figures indicated that approximately

5.4 million households classified themselves as "unmarried-partner households," an increase of over 70% since 1990. D'Vera Cohn, *Married-With-Children Still Fading*, Washington Post, May 15, 2001, at A01. By the mid-1990s, unmarried cohabitants constituted at least 7% of all couples in the Unites States, more than 20% of all couples in Denmark, 14% of all Canadian couples, and over 10% of Australian couples. J. Thomas Oldham, *Lessons from Jerry Hall v. Mick Jagger Regarding U.S. Regulation of Heterosexual Cohabitants or, Can't Get No Satisfaction*, 76 Notre Dame L.Rev. 1409, 1410–11 (2001). While the United States affords comparatively few legal rights to cohabitants, vis-a-vis each other or as to third parties, many countries have developed a fairly extensive network of rights and obligations for cohabitants whose relationships meet specified criteria, even if those couples have not registered for an alternative status as described in Section A.

Miron v. Trudel
[1995] 2 S.C.R. 418

McLachlin, J.

* * *

122. This appeal requires us to decide whether exclusion of unmarried partners from accident benefits available to married partners violates the equality guarantees of the *Canadian Charter of Rights and Freedoms*. I conclude that it does.

123. The record before us posits the following facts. John Miron and Jocelyne Valliere lived together with their children. They were not married, yet their family functioned as an economic unit. In 1987, John Miron was injured while a passenger in a motor vehicle owned by the respondent William James McIsaac and driven by the respondent Richard Trudel. Neither McIsaac nor Trudel was insured. After the accident, Mr. Miron could no longer work and contribute to his family's support. He made a claim for accident benefits for loss of income and damages against Ms. Valliere's insurance policy which extended accident benefits to the "spouse" of the policyholder. The insurance company, Economical Mutual, denied his claim on the ground that Mr. Miron was not legally married to Ms. Valliere and hence not her "spouse".

124. Mr. Miron and Ms. Valliere sued the insurer. The insurer brought a preliminary motion to determine whether the word "spouse", as used in the applicable portions of the policy, includes unmarried common law spouses. The motions court judge found that "spouse" meant a person who is legally married.... Mr. Miron and Ms. Valliere appealed the decision to the Ontario Court of Appeal, arguing first that Mr. Miron is a spouse under the terms of the policy, and alternatively, that the policy terms which are prescribed by the *Insurance Act*, R.S.O. 1980, c. 218, discriminate against him in violation of s.15(1) of the *Charter*. The Court of Appeal dismissed their claim.... They now appeal to this court.

* * *

133. ...The benefits in question were governed by 1980 legislation. That legislation extended the accident and loss of income benefits in question to the "spouse" of the insured, left undefined. By contrast, the same legislation included in "spouse" for the purposes of the death benefit provisions a man and woman who were not married to each other but who had cohabited continuously for five years or lived in a relationship of some permanence and had a child. In 1990, the Legislature amended the Act and expanded the definition of "spouse" in relation to the benefits Miron

and Valliere claim. The new definition of "spouse" includes a heterosexual couple who have cohabited for three years or who have lived in a permanent relationship with a child.

134. The extended definition of "spouse" in the 1980 legislation for death benefits and in the 1990 legislation for the benefits here at issue belies the suggestion that the Legislature in 1980 intended the term "spouse" to apply to unmarried partners. In fact, where the Legislature wanted to extend benefits to such persons, it expressly did so....

135. I conclude that "spouse" in the 1980 provisions relating to loss of income benefits and uninsured motorist claims did not include unmarried couples living in a common law relationship.

* * *

[The Court next addresses the issue of whether the limitation of benefits to married persons violates the equality provisions of the Charter. The Court first sets out the language of Sections 1 and 15 of the Charter, which are set forth in Section B of this chapter in the opinions of Justices Blair and LaFerme in *Halpern*.]

138. The analysis under s.15(1) involves two steps. First, the claimant must show a denial of "equal protection or equal benefit of the law", as compared with some other person. Second, the claimant must show that the denial constitutes discrimination. At this second stage, in order for discrimination to be made out, the claimant must show that the denial rests on one of the grounds enumerated in s.15(1) or an analogous ground and that the unequal treatment is based on the stereotypical application of presumed group or personal characteristics. If the claimant meets the onus under this analysis, violation of s. 15(1) is established. The onus then shifts to the party seeking to uphold the law, usually the state, to justify the discrimination as "demonstrably justified in a free and democratic society" under s.1 of the *Charter*.

* * *

153. In this case,... [t]he policy denies a person in an unmarried relationship benefits granted a similar person in a married relationship. Thus denial of equal benefit on the basis of marital status is established.

154. Section 15(1) of the *Charter* forbids discrimination, and "in particular,... discrimination based on race, national or ethnic origin, colour, religion, sex, age or mental or physical disability". The ground upon which the distinction in this case is based—marital status—is not included in the list of particularized grounds. We must therefore determine whether marital status is an analogous ground.

* * *

157. The grounds of discrimination enumerated in s.15(1) of the *Charter* identify group characteristics which often serve as irrelevant grounds of distinction between people. The history of the human rights movement is a history of reaction against persecution and denial of opportunity on the basis of irrelevant stereotypical group classifications like race, sex, and religion. It is not surprising therefore to see these as well as other common markers of irrelevant exclusion enumerated in s.15(1). But the categories are not closed, as s.15(1) recognizes. Analogous grounds of discrimination may be recognized. Logic suggests that in determining whether a particular group characteristic is an analogous ground, the fundamental consideration is whether the characteristic may serve as an irrelevant basis of exclusion and a denial of essential human dignity in the human rights tradition. In other words, may it serve as a basis for unequal treatment based on stereotypical attributes ascribed to the group, rather than on the true worth

and ability or circumstances of the individual? An affirmative answer to this question indicates that the characteristic may be used in a manner which is violative of human dignity and freedom.

158. ...One indicator of an analogous ground may be that the targeted group has suffered historical disadvantage, independent of the challenged distinction.... Another may be the fact that the group constitutes a "discrete and insular minority"...."[D]istinctions based on personal characteristics attributed to an individual solely on the basis of association with a group will rarely escape the charge of discrimination, while those based on an individual's merits and capacities will rarely be so classed."... By extension, it has been suggested that distinctions based on personal and *immutable* characteristics must be discriminatory within s.15(1).... Additional assistance may be obtained by comparing the ground at issue with the grounds enumerated, or from recognition by legislators and jurists that the ground is discriminatory....

159. All of these may be valid indicators in the inclusionary sense that their presence may signal an analogous ground. But the converse proposition — that any or all of them *must* be present to find an analogous ground — is invalid....

160. What then of the analogous ground proposed in this case — marital status? The question is whether the characteristic of being unmarried — of not having contracted a marriage in a manner recognized by the state — constitutes a ground of discrimination within the ambit of s. 15(1). In my view, it does.

161. First, discrimination on the basis of marital status touches the essential dignity and worth of the individual in the same way as other recognized grounds of discrimination violative of fundamental human rights norms. Specifically, it touches the individual's freedom to live life with the mate of one's choice in the fashion of one's choice. This is a matter of defining importance to individuals. It is not a matter which should be excluded from *Charter* consideration on the ground that its recognition would trivialize the equality guarantee.

162. Second, marital status possesses characteristics often associated with recognized grounds of discrimination under s.15(1) of the *Charter*. Persons involved in an unmarried relationship constitute an historically disadvantaged group. There is ample evidence that unmarried partners have often suffered social disadvantage and prejudice. Historically in our society, the unmarried partner has been regarded as less worthy than the married partner. The disadvantages inflicted on the unmarried partner have ranged from social ostracism through denial of status and benefits. In recent years, the disadvantage experienced by persons living in illegitimate relationships has greatly diminished. Those living together out of wedlock no longer are made to carry the scarlet letter. Nevertheless, the historical disadvantage associated with this group cannot be denied.

163. A third characteristic sometimes associated with analogous grounds — distinctions founded on personal, immutable characteristics — is present, albeit in attenuated form. In theory, the individual is free to choose whether to marry or not to marry. In practice, however, the reality may be otherwise. The sanction of the union by the state through civil marriage cannot always be obtained. The law; the reluctance of one's partner to marry; financial, religious or social constraints — these factors and others commonly function to prevent partners who otherwise operate as a family unit from formally marrying. In short, marital status often lies beyond the individual's effective control. In this respect, marital status is not unlike citizenship, recognized as an analogous ground in *Andrews*: the individual exercises limited but not exclusive control over the designation.

164. Comparing discrimination on the basis of marital status with the grounds enumerated in s.15(1), discrimination on the ground of marital status may be seen as akin to discrimination on the ground of religion, to the extent that it finds its roots and expression in moral disapproval of all sexual unions except those sanctioned by the church and state.

165. Of late, legislators and jurists throughout our country have recognized that distinguishing between cohabiting couples on the basis of whether they are legally married or not fails to accord with current social values or realities. As the amicus curiae has pointed out, 63 Ontario statutes currently make no distinction between married partners and unmarried partners who have cohabited in a conjugal relationship. For example, the right to spousal maintenance is not conditioned on marriage: see Part III, *Family Law Act*, R.S.O. 1990, c. F.3, which establishes a right to spousal support for those who have cohabited continuously for a period of not less than three years or who have cohabited in a relationship of some permanence and who have a child. Other provinces have adopted similar benefit thresholds. In the judicial domain, judges have recognized the right of unmarried spouses to share in family property through the doctrine of unjust enrichment.... All this suggests recognition of the fact that it is often wrong to deny equal benefit of the law because a person is not married.

166. ...The essential elements necessary to engage the overarching purpose of s.15(1)—violation of dignity and freedom, an historical group disadvantage, and the danger of stereotypical group-based decision-making—are present and discrimination is made out.

167. ...It remains to consider, however, the theme underlying the whole of the insurer's submissions—that marriage is a good and honourable state and hence cannot serve as a ground for discrimination.

168. These sentiments, valid as they are, do not advance the insurer's case. The argument, simply put, is that marriage is good; the grounds of discrimination evil; therefore marriage cannot be a ground of discrimination. The fallacy in the argument is the assumption that the grounds of discrimination are evil. Discrimination is evil. But the grounds upon which it rests are not. Consider the enumerated grounds—race, national or ethnic origin, colour, religion, sex, age and mental or physical disability. None of these are evil in themselves.... What is evil is not the ground of discrimination, but its *inappropriate use* to deny equal protection and benefit to people who are members of the marked groups—not on the basis of their true abilities or circumstance, but on the basis of the group to which they belong. The argument that marital status cannot be an analogous ground because it is good cannot succeed.... [I]t is not anti-marriage to accord equal benefit of the law to non-traditional couples.

* * *

171. The legislation reflected in the insurance policy at issue denies equal benefits to partners in an unmarried relationship solely on the ground of their marital status. This ground is an analogous ground under s. 15(1).... It follows that discrimination under s. 15(1) is established.

* * *

173. Determining whether it has been demonstrated that the impugned distinction is "demonstrably justified in a free and democratic society" involves two inquiries. First, the goal of the legislation is ascertained and examined to see if it is of pressing and substantial importance. Then the court must carry out a proportionality analysis to balance

the interests of society with those of individuals and groups. The proportionality analysis comprises three branches. First, the connection between the goal and the discriminatory distinction is examined to ascertain if it is rational. Second, the law must impair the right no more than is reasonably necessary to accomplish the objective. Finally, if these two conditions are met, the court must weigh whether the effect of the discrimination is proportionate to the benefit thereby achieved....

* * *

175. The goal or functional value of the legislation here at issue is to sustain families when one of their members is injured in an automobile accident. When an adult partner in a family unit is injured, economic dislocation may not be far behind. If the injured partner is a wage-earner, the family income may be reduced or eliminated. If the injured party works in the home, it may be necessary to hire replacement services. In either case, the result is economic dislocation. This, in turn, can work great hardship on the family and its members. The goal of the legislation is to reduce this economic dislocation and hardship. This is a laudable goal. And given the frequency of injuries from motor vehicle accidents, it assumes an importance which can without exaggeration be described as pressing and substantial.

* * *

178. ... [T]he [next] question is whether marital status is a reasonably relevant marker of individuals who should receive benefits in the event of injury of a family member in an automobile accident, given the goal of the legislation. The insurer defends the marker of marital status as an indicator of stability which goes to the economic interdependence of the family unit. To maintain this claim, the state (or the insurer that here stands in its stead) must show that stable, and thus economically interdependent, family units typically involve married partners, and conversely, that unmarried partners in stable relationships are but a minor anomaly. Further, given the injustice of any anomalies, one would expect a demonstration that better criteria, producing fewer anomalous cases, are not readily available. In short, it must be demonstrated that the chosen group marker is reasonably relevant to the legislative goal in all the circumstances of the case, having regard to available alternative criteria and the need to minimize prejudice to anomalous cases within the group.

179. This the insurer and the state have not done.... The [legislative] debate [concerning the Act] centred on marital equivalence. To quote the amicus curiae, "[the legislators'] search was directed towards defining a 'marriage-like' conjugal relationship, usually in terms of mutual commitment and permanence—a 'near' marriage—instead of trying to define the underlying functional values, e.g., financial interdependence, relevant to the legislative subject-matter of the *Insurance Act*." ...Having misconstrued the issue as one of marriage equivalence, the Legislature found itself unable to agree. But this provides no justification for failing, from 1980 to 1987, to deal directly with the problem of which family units were so financially interdependent and stable as to warrant provision of the benefits in question.

180. If the issue had been viewed as a matter of defining who should receive benefits on a basis that is relevant to the goal or functional values underlying the legislation, rather than marriage equivalence, alternatives substantially less invasive of *Charter* rights might have been found. For example, the Legislature was able to agree in 1980 on a formula to extend death benefits to a certain class of unmarried persons. And in 1981, in the Ontario *Human Rights Code, 1981*...the Legislature agreed on a definition of "spouse" as the person to whom a person of the opposite sex is married or with whom the person is living in a conjugal relationship outside marriage. A modified version of

the *Human Rights Code* definition requires marriage or cohabitation for at least one year or having a child together, or entering into a cohabitation agreement under s. 53 of the *Family Law Act*. This modified definition is used in 21 Ontario statutes.

181. It thus emerges that in fixing on marital status as the criterion of eligibility for family accident benefits, the Legislature chose a criterion that was at best only collaterally related to its legislative goal; a criterion, moreover, that had the effect of depriving a substantial number of deserving candidates of receipt of benefits. Better tests were available. In short, the Legislature did not choose a reasonably relevant marker.

* * *

184. ... Having determined that marital status is not a reasonable indicator of those who should obtain accident benefits — ... it is unnecessary to move to the final step to consider whether the effect of the infringement is "proportionate" to the benefit to be derived from using the discriminatory marker.

185. I conclude that the state has failed to demonstrate that the exclusion of unmarried members of family units from motor vehicle accident benefits is demonstrably justified in a free and democratic society. It follows that the *Charter* violation is established.

* * *

190. ... The 1990 amendments provide the best possible evidence of what the Legislature would have done had it been forced to face the problem the appellants raise. The only claims are monetary and readily calculable and satisfied. Most importantly, the result will be to cure an injustice which might otherwise go unremedied.

191. In this case, the benefit payments are actually made available pursuant to the insurance contract between Ms. Valliere and Economical Mutual. Because the provisions in the insurance policy were mandated by the *Insurance Act*, the effect of reading up the Act is to import the 1990 definition of spouse into the standard automobile insurance policy.

* * *

Notes and Questions

1. *Analogous Ground.* Justice McLachlin determines in *Miron* that marital status is analogous to the grounds on which discrimination is explicitly forbidden in Section 15(1) of the Charter. Under the Equal Protection Clause of the Fifth and Fourteenth Amendment of the U.S. Constitution there are no enumerated grounds. Consider your comparison after *Halpern* of the Canadian analysis under Section 15 with the equal protection doctrine developed by the U.S. Supreme Court to analyze different types of discrimination. What level of scrutiny would marital status be afforded under a U.S. federal equal protection analysis? What are the advantages and disadvantages of the Canadian approach to equal protection, as compared to the U.S. doctrine, when analyzing differential treatment on the basis of a characteristic such as marital status?

Consider the many reasons why individuals choose to cohabit rather than marry. In finding marital status an analogous ground, Justice McLachlin in ¶163 describes it as immutable, but in attenuated form. What arguments could be made in support of his proposition? In opposition? In the end, do you think immutability was central to his determination of marital status as an analogous ground? Should it make a difference, in your opinion?

2. *Cohabitant Rights Under Canadian Law—A Marriage Mirror?* Two decades before *Miron*, Canadian provincial legislatures and courts, inspired by policy considerations

rather than constitutional mandate, began to afford cohabitants certain benefits formerly available only to spouses. In 1975 British Columbia granted heterosexual cohabitants a right to seek spousal support if they "lived together as husband and wife" for at least two years. As you read in *M. v. H.*, the Ontario Family Law Act afforded cohabitants the same right if they lived together three years, or had a child together and lived in a conjugal relationship of "some permanence." By the time of *Miron,* most provinces had followed suit. In Alberta, however, where the legislature had not yet created a statutory right for cohabitants to seek support, the Alberta Court of Appeal, following *Miron,* ruled that failure to provide cohabitants a claim against a former partner for support violated the partners' constitutional rights under § 15. Taylor v. Rossu, [1998] 216 A.R. 348. In response, Alberta's legislature amended its statutes accordingly. Nicholas Bala & Rebecca Jaremko Bromwich, *Context and Inclusivity in Canada's Evolving Definition of the Family,* 16 Int'l J. L. Pol. & Fam. 145, 156–58 (2002).

Many other spousal benefits have been conferred upon cohabitants in Canada as well. In most provinces cohabitants in a conjugal relationship for a specified period of time (typically between one and three years) or who have a child together are entitled to make a claim against the estate of a deceased partner. Justice McLachlin notes in *Miron* that, at that time, 63 Ontario statutes made no distinction between married and unmarried partners. Many federal statutes have also been amended to confer upon conjugal partners the rights and obligations of spouses, including the federal income tax statute. *Id.* at 158. Canadian courts have also used the constructive trust doctrine to award one partner a share in property acquired during the partnership, based on the contribution of the partner receiving the award. That contribution can include domestic services, such as child-care.

The allocation of property rights appears to remain one of the last bastions of legal distinction between married and unmarried cohabitants in Canada. *Id.* at 159. As of 2002, no province had granted cohabitants a statutory claim to property equivalent to the statutory marital property rights of spouses, nor had cohabitants been statutorily afforded the possessory rights in the family home that a married spouse could claim. *Id.* Although a Nova Scotia appellate court ruled that failure to afford cohabitants the same property rights conferred on spouses violated § 15 of the Canadian Charter of Rights and Freedoms, the Canadian Supreme Court disagreed. Walsh v. Bono, [2002] S.C.C. 83, *rev'g* [2000] 183 N.S.R.2d 74 (N.S.C.A.). In a 7–1 decision, the Supreme Court determined that failure to extend application of the Matrimonial Property Act, R.S.N.S. 1989, c. 275, to unmarried cohabitants was not discriminatory, but rather reflected the differences between marital and non-marital relationships. Unmarried couples are free to marry, to enter domestic partnerships, to enter domestic contracts regarding property ownership, or to own property jointly, the majority observed, and remedies such as constructive trust are available to address inequities at the time of dissolution. Application of the Matrimonial Property Act to such couples, however, would deprive individuals of their freedom to choose whether to enter or avoid the institution of marriage and the legal consequences that follow, and thus, in the majority's view, be inconsistent with the very notions of liberty protected by the Charter. Therefore, although the Canadian courts and legislative bodies have afforded similar rights to married and unmarried cohabitants in numerous legal contexts, the Canadian Supreme Court appears now to be signaling in *Walsh* its belief that some legal distinction between the two groups must continue to be maintained.

3. *Defining the Relationship—Is Conjugality Essential?* Australia's experience with cohabitant rights provides an interesting contrast to that of Canada in defining the relationships that generate rights and obligations. Although many family law issues in Aus-

tralia are regulated by federal law, the rights of cohabitants upon separation are within the authority of the Australian state and territorial governments to regulate. Rather than opt for a registered partnership or civil union model, they, like Canada, have chosen to confer certain rights on unmarried cohabitants by operation of law, through state statutes most frequently referred to as De Facto Relationship Acts.

Originally in most of the statutory schemes, de facto relationships were defined as heterosexual. Beginning in the mid-90s, however, several of the provinces, including the Australian Capital Territory, Queensland, and New South Wales, have extended their definition of cohabitants entitled to benefits to include same-gender partners. Rebecca Bailey-Harris, *Dividing the Assets of the Unmarried Family—Recent Lessons from Australia,* [2000] Int'l Fam. L. 90, 91.

Aside from extending their benefits to same-gender partners, however, some of the states have defined eligible relationships more broadly than the conjugal, or "marriage" model of relationship that is prevalent elsewhere. New South Wales, for example, in 1999 renamed its De Facto Relationship Act (which conferred benefits upon de facto partners who lived as husband and wife) to become the Property (Relationships) Act, and now confers benefits upon those in a "domestic relationship." A "domestic relationship" is defined as either a de facto relationship (two adults who live together "as a couple" and are not related by marriage or family) or a close personal relationship (two adults who live together, one or both of whom provide the other with personal care and domestic support). Those in a close personal relationship may be related by family and need not have a sexual component to their relationship. *Id.* The benefits conferred include property and inheritance rights. The Australian Capital has also adopted a broader definition for entitlement to benefits, defining "domestic relationship" to include two adults who "provide personal or financial commitment and support for the material benefit of the other, and includes a de facto marriage." *Id.* at 90.

Do you think the extension of rights beyond conjugal relationships is appropriate? One factor in your consideration of this issue might be the nature of the rights awarded. In New South Wales, which utilizes a broad definition, property distribution by the court after termination of the cohabitation relationship is based on contribution to the relationship and not future needs, even though future needs would be relevant in that state in a property distribution following dissolution of a marriage. Queensland, by contrast, which utilizes a gender neutral conjugal definition of eligible cohabitants, considers factors that closely parallel those utilized in marital dissolution, which include factors relevant to need such as age, earning capacity, and standard of living. In both of these states, as well as in the majority of Australian states, cohabitants may seek a time-limited support order after termination of the relationship, if the relationship has created financial dependency. *Id.* at 91. *See also* Rebecca Bailey-Harris, *Financial Rights in Relationships Outside Marriage: A Decade of Reforms in Australia,* 9 Int'l J. L. & Fam. 233 (1995).

4. *Cohabitant Rights Widespread.* Although comprehensive review of cohabitants' rights worldwide is beyond the scope of this text, it is important to understand that Canada and Australia are not alone in their willingness to confer upon cohabitants some benefits typically awarded to spouses. Many nations afford legal rights to couples in de facto conjugal relationships.

New Zealand, for example just passed a new Property (Relationships) Amendment Act 2001, which gives the courts wide discretion to award property upon the death of one partner or dissolution of the relationship, and creates a general rule that property be divided equally if the parties have lived together for three or more years. Prior to implementation of this Act, application of constructive trust doctrine made it possible for a partner to claim a share in property at issue, but only by proof that he or she contributed to the property in question and that it was reasonable to expect to receive an interest in it. N. Richardson, *Why Marry? Controversial Legislation in New Zealand,* [2001] Int'l Fam. L. 68. *See also* Nicola Peart, *Property Rights for Married, De Facto and Same-Sex Couples — Proposals for Reform in New Zealand,* [2000] Int'l Fam. L. 93.

In Japan the courts have given special protection to partners in de facto marriages, called *nai'en,* since 1914. Damages may be awarded to one partner when the other party to the *nai'en* leaves the relationship without good cause. Judith Akiba & Minoru Ishikawa, *Marriage and Divorce Regulation and Recognition in Japan,* 29 Fam. L.Q. 587, 591 (1995).

Many European countries afford some marital rights to cohabiting couples. In Sweden, under the Cohabitees (Joint Homes) Act of 1987, the non-owning partner may request that the court, upon the couple's separation, divide equally the value of the home and household goods acquired by one for the joint use of both, when the parties live in a "marriage like condition." A surviving partner is also given certain rights against the partner's estate. Anders Agell, *Family Forms and Legal Policies: A Comparative View from a Swedish Observer,* 38 Scandinavian Studies in Law 197, 200 (1999); Ake Saldeen, *Joint Custody, Special Representative for Children and Cohabitees' Property, in* The International Survey of Family Law 2001, 405 (Andrew Bainham ed., 2001). In Portugal de facto partners are entitled to numerous statutory benefits, including wrongful death benefits upon the death of a partner; rights upon a partner's death to property, pension, and support; and certain familial employment benefits. Sofia Oliveira Pais, *De Facto Relationships and Same-Sex Relationships in Portugal, in* The International Survey of Family Law, 337 (Andrew Bainham ed., 2002). The Spanish provinces of Catalonia and Aragon also have enacted legislation that permits the courts to divide some property upon termination of a relationship, although not necessarily equally, if one partner has been unjustly enriched. Rebecca Probert & Anne Barlow, *Displacing Marriage — Diversification and Harmonisation within Europe,* 12 Child & Fam. L. Q. 153 (2000). France also recognizes a separate legal status, concubinage, which can entitle a concubine to wrongful death damages for her partner, and social security and insurance benefits in some circumstances. *See In re* Estate of Huyot, 645 N.Y.S.2d 979 (N.Y. Sur. Ct. 1996).

Many other parts of the world statutorily recognize cohabitant rights as well. In Barbados the Family Law Act provides heterosexual partners in unions of five or more years a right to seek legal distribution of accumulated assets. Norma Monica Forde, *The Emerging Legal Status of the De Facto Family in Barbados, in* The International Survey of Family Law 1995, 51 (Andrew Bainham ed., 1997). Brazil affords both same and opposite-sex de facto partners inheritance rights to each other's social security and pension benefits, as well as other tax benefits. *Brazil: Same-sex Couples Are Granted Rights, Recognition,* Minneapolis Star Tribune, June 10, 2000, at 8A. Other Latin American countries have created substantial rights for cohabitants as well, J. Thomas Oldham, *Lessons from Jerry Hall v. Mick Jagger Regarding U.S. Regulation of Heterosexual Cohabitants or, Can't Get No Satisfaction,* 76 Notre Dame L.Rev. 1409, 1421, n. 64 (2001), including Paraguay, *see* José Alberto Pérez Meza, Report No. 96/01 (2001) (referenced above) and Colombia, *see* American Airlines v. Mejia, 766 So. 2d 305 (Fla. Dist. Ct. App. 2000) (set forth in Chapter 5, Section A, *infra.*).

4. *U.S. Treatment of Cohabitants.* In the United States, cohabitants can create enforceable rights between themselves regarding property or support matters by written contract. Though at one point in history contracts between cohabitants were considered unenforceable under the illegal consideration doctrine, the modern approach is to enforce contracts that are not explicitly based on meretricious sexual consideration, *e.g.,* Marvin v. Marvin, 557 P.2d 106 (Cal. 1976), or that contemplate all of the burdens and amenities of marital life. Latham v. Latham, 547 P.2d 144 (Or. 1976). Although the statute of frauds may become problematic, in most situations oral contracts between cohabitants are enforceable as well. Some states, however, have statutes that require such contracts to be in writing. *See* Minn. Stat. §§ 513.075, 513.076 (2002); Tex. Bus. & Com. Code § 26.01(b)(3) (2002).

Absent an express contract, many states will recognize a right to division of some property acquired during the relationship on the basis of an implied contract; doctrines such as resulting trust, constructive trust, or unjust enrichment; or simply an application of their general equitable powers. *E.g.,* Marvin, *supra;* Sullivan v. Rooney, 533 N.E.2d 1372 (Mass. 1989) (constructive trust); Pickens v. Pickens, 490 So. 2d 872 (Miss. 1986) (equitable powers). The Washington Supreme Court has taken a status-based approach to the issue, permitting courts to make an equitable distribution of property acquired during a stable, marital-like relationship, which the court has termed the meretricious relationship doctrine. Connell v. Francisco, 898 P.2d 831 (Wash. 1995). Under any of these theories, same-gender partners would not be precluded from seeking property division. *Cf.* Vasquez v. Hawthorne, 33 P.3d 735 (2001). Absent a written contract, however, a claim for post-relationship support in any non-marital relationship in the United States, whether the partners are opposite-gender or same-gender, is far less likely to be successful than a claim for court distribution of property acquired by the partners during the relationship. *See* Friedman v. Friedman, 20 Cal. App. 4th 876 (1993).

Unlike the nations whose statutory schemes are examined above, no U.S. jurisdiction has legislatively created a separate status for unmarried couples. J. Thomas Oldham, *Lessons from Jerry Hall v. Mick Jagger Regarding U.S. Regulation of Heterosexual Cohabitants or, Can't Get No Satisfaction,* 76 Notre Dame L.Rev. 1409, 1413 (2001). The American Law Institute (ALI) has proposed model legislation that would enable both opposite-gender and same-gender couples to make financial claims at the termination of their relationship, similar to those spouses make, if they satisfy the durational criteria chosen by the states for cohabitation as a couple, or for cohabitation with their common child. American Law Institute, Principles of the Law of Family Dissolution: Analysis and Recommendations §§ 601–606 (2002).

Problem 4-4

You are a judge in a state appellate court of a northern U.S. state. Before you is pending an appeal filed by Nora, a woman who has been denied a claim for property division and support, following her separation from her partner, Kevin, after a twenty-five year relationship. She and her partner were intrigued by alternative life styles when they first met and moved in together. After two children were born and several moves, the idea of going through a marriage ceremony just seemed superfluous to them. Nora was formerly an artist and a potter, but primarily has been a homemaker for the past twenty years. Although their children are now grown, Nora has become disabled due to chronic fatigue syndrome, and is unable to work. At the present time she requires a wheelchair to move more than a few feet. The condition may improve in five or ten years, although her prognosis is uncertain. Most of the assets that they had accumulated during their cohabitation, including the bank accounts, were in Kevin's name.

Given your close proximity to Canada, you are very intrigued by Canadian jurisprudence in the field of cohabitant's rights. Assume the constitution of your state is virtually identical to the U.S. federal constitution. Nora asserts a constitutional right to seek property division and alimony, under the principles applicable to marriage in your state. Would you recognize such constitutional rights or not? Be prepared to describe the analysis and policy arguments that you would include in your opinion to support your position. If you would recognize a constitutional right, how would you define the group eligible to invoke it? If not, and if you feel common law remedies are inadequate, is there any particular action or approach you would recommend, in dicta, to the legislature of your state?

Chapter 5

Recognition of Foreign Marriages and Divorces

The previous three chapters illustrate the diversity of legal norms governing the formation and dissolution of marriages and alternative forms of partnership around the globe. Not surprisingly, these differences can foster conflicts when one nation is asked to recognize a marriage or an alternative status, or to give effect to a divorce, entered in another nation. This chapter focuses primarily on the treatment afforded to foreign marriages and divorces by U.S. courts. The approach other countries take to recognition issues and the regulation of recognition by international conventions will also be examined briefly. The recognition of marriages and alternative partnerships is addressed in Section A. Jurisdiction, choice of law, and recognition of decrees terminating marital status, dividing property, and awarding spousal support are discussed in Section B. Though often raised in conjunction with divorce proceedings, issues regarding jurisdiction, recognition, and enforcement of child custody and child support orders are addressed later in this book, in Chapters Eight and Ten, respectively.

A. Recognition of Marriages and Alternative Partnerships

1. U.S. Tribunals

The principles governing the recognition by U.S. courts of marriages entered in foreign nations have for the most part been created by state courts through common law, although some states have now codified their foreign marriage recognition rules. Because the substantive and procedural requirements for entry to marriage are regulated by state law in the United States, and vary somewhat from state to state, U.S. state courts have a well developed body of law governing interstate marriage recognition. The same basic principles are generally applied in the context of recognizing marriages entered in foreign countries as well. As the following cases illustrate, however, international marriage recognition can present some unique challenges.

Leszinske v. Poole
798 P.2d 1049 (N.M. Ct. App. 1990)

Minzner, J.

[Ed. Note: Following initiation of a divorce action in New Mexico, the mother, age 35, was awarded temporary custody of the parties' three children. Seven months prior to trial, while the parties were separated, she began a relationship with her uncle, a 55 year-old California resident. At the time of trial, she indicated she wished to marry her uncle following the divorce. Based on the mother's role as primary caretaker during the marriage and the father's history of depression, the court at trial expressed an intent to award primary physical custody to the mother if she and the uncle entered a valid marriage. Uncle-niece marriages were incestuous and void under the statutory law of both New Mexico, where the parties had lived, and California, where the mother and her uncle would live with the children following the divorce. Incest was also a crime in both New Mexico and California. The mother and her uncle therefore married in Costa Rica within a month after entry of the decree of divorce. The district court subsequently entered its findings of fact and conclusions of law, awarding joint legal custody and primary physical custody to the mother.

The father appealed, contending that the trial court erred in conditioning its award upon the mother's entry into a Costa Rican marriage, celebrated with the intent to avoid New Mexico law and "repugnant to the public policy" of New Mexico. *Id.* at 1051. Despite a written finding of the trial court that conditioned custody upon the mother's marriage in a jurisdiction that would recognize the marriage as valid, the appellate court viewed the trial court's oral and written comments on the marriage as acknowledgment of the mother's intent and the reality of what would occur, rather than encouragement. The appellate court also observed that for the morality of a parent's sexual conduct to be considered, there must be compelling evidence that the conduct has a significant effect upon a child's best interest. The appellate court found the issue of whether California would recognize the marriage relevant to the children's best interests, however, because if so, it would eliminate the threat of criminal prosecution for incestuous marriage or fornication. It also found the issue of whether New Mexico would recognize the mother's marriage as relevant to whether the trial court erred in taking it into account in awarding custody.]

* * *

Ordinarily...a marriage valid when and where celebrated is valid anywhere. In New Mexico, a statute, NMSA 1978, Section 40-1-4...codifies this rule and states:

> All marriages celebrated beyond the limits of this state, which are valid according to the laws of the country wherein they were celebrated or contracted, shall be likewise valid in this state, and shall have the same force as if they had been celebrated in accordance with the laws in force in this state.

An interest in comity underlies Section 40-1-4 and the rule it codifies.... "Comity refers to the spirit of cooperation in which a domestic tribunal approaches the resolution of cases touching the laws and interests of other sovereign states."... [In Societe Nationale Industrielle Aerospatiale v. United States District Court, 482 U.S. 522 (1987) the U. S. Supreme Court has observed]: "Comity, in the legal sense, is neither a matter of absolute obligation, on the one hand, nor of mere courtesy and good will, upon the other."... The desirability of uniformity in the recognition of marital status is an additional rationale for the rule....

The rule has exceptions. One such exception is derived from specific statutory restrictions voiding marriages for citizens who marry in foreign states for the purpose of evading the law in their home state.... Another exception pertains to marriages contracted in one state which are contrary to the strong public policy of another state. *See Restatement (Second) of Conflict of Laws* § 283 at 233 (1971).... The exceptions have been described respectively as (a) cases within the prohibition of positive law, and (b) cases within the prohibition of natural law....

Under the *Restatement* formulation, the two exceptions are actually one. The *Restatement* states the rule and its exception as follows: "A marriage which satisfies the requirements of the state where the marriage was contracted will everywhere be recognized as valid unless it violates the strong public policy of another state which had the most significant relationship to the spouses and the marriage at the time of the marriage." *Id.* at § 283(2). For purposes of this opinion, we assume that both New Mexico and California have a significant relationship to the spouses and the marriage.... Under the *Restatement* formulation, the first question is whether there is a statute invalidating the out-of-state marriage of local domiciliaries. *Id.,* comment k at 238–39. The *Restatement* suggests that, in the absence of a statute, the next question is whether the choice-of-law provisions in the forum state provide guidance on the question of whether that state would recognize the validity of the marriage under the laws of the foreign jurisdiction. *See id.,* comment j at 237–38. Finally, the *Restatement* indicates that, if no clear answers can be obtained from statutory or decisional law, the question is whether the marriage offends a sufficiently strong policy of the state with the most significant relationship. *Id.,* comment k at 237–38.

We note that the Uniform Marriage Evasion Act has been withdrawn, ... as inconsistent with the current comity rule contained in the Uniform Marriage and Divorce Act.... The comity rule under the Act also does not incorporate the "strong public policy" exception, suggesting a developing trend away from that exception.

Arizona, for example, currently has a statute with an evasion provision: "Parties residing in this state may not evade the laws of this state relating to marriage by going to another state or country for solemnization of the marriage." A.R.S. § 25-112(C) (1976)....

Section 40-1-4 contains no similar language, and the supreme court has indicated, in an analogous situation, that none was intended. In *Gallegos v. Wilkerson,* ... appellants argued that on public policy grounds the court ought not recognize a common law marriage between two New Mexico residents that was contracted in Texas. Our supreme court, noting that the statute contained no language denying validity to New Mexico residents evading the statute, refused to extend its meaning to include that exception.

California law provides that all marriages contracted outside California, which would be valid by the laws of the jurisdiction in which they were contracted, are valid in California. West's Ann.Cal.Civ.Code § 4104 (1983). Section 4104 also contains no language similar to the evasion language contained in the Arizona statute, and the California Supreme Court has expressly refused to void a marriage celebrated in Nevada with the intent to avoid California law....

For the reasons stated above, we believe that neither a New Mexico nor a California court would invalidate an out-of-state marriage between domiciliaries solely on the ground that the parties were attempting to avoid domestic law. Further, each state's choice-of-law rule suggests that the Costa Rican marriage would be recognized as valid....

The New Mexico penal statutes indicate that incestuous marriages are contrary to the public policy of both states.... Nevertheless, the dispositive question is whether the marriage offends a sufficiently strong public policy to outweigh the purposes served by the rule of comity.

This case involves an additional consideration, which is the district court's finding that it is in the children's present best interests to be with their mother. We cannot answer the question of how New Mexico and California would treat an incestuous marriage without taking into account the purpose of the inquiry. Here, the ultimate purpose of the inquiry of the district court was to determine who would have the physical custody of the children. We need not decide whether New Mexico and California would, in all circumstances and for all purposes, recognize the marriage as valid. We need only decide whether the district court erred in concluding that, for purposes of avoiding criminal liability, a valid marriage ceremony outside California would be recognized in California, and for purposes of awarding mother primary physical custody, a valid marriage ceremony outside New Mexico could be taken into account.

The test for public policy employed by the California Supreme Court is whether the marriage is considered odious by the common consent of nations or whether such marriages are against the laws of nature.... Although it has been suggested that uncle-niece marriages are against the laws of nature,... [citing Pennsylvania and Ohio cases], the Maryland Court of Appeals held that uncle-niece marriages were not considered incestuous according to generally accepted opinion because incest related only to persons in the direct line of consanguinity and brothers and sisters.... Despite the existence of statutes prohibiting uncle-niece marriages, the New York Court of Appeals refused to invalidate an uncle-niece marriage between citizens whose marriage was lawfully celebrated in accordance with Rhode Island law.... We note that "[t]he weight of domiciliary law on uncle-niece [marriages] looks to the law of the place of celebration, and treats a marriage valid there as valid at the domicile also."...It is difficult to conclude that uncle-niece marriages are odious by the common consent of nations. The record proper contains evidence that twenty-three South and Central American and northern European nations recognize such marriages.

* * *

For these reasons, we think the record supports the district court's decision. Under the circumstances of this case, we believe California would recognize the Costa Rican marriage as valid, and New Mexico's public policy against incest did not preclude the district court from awarding mother primary physical custody after taking into account her plans to marry her uncle.

In sum, both states recognize the general rule, which is that a marriage valid when and where performed is valid everywhere. Neither state has a judicial decision invalidating an uncle-niece marriage validly contracted outside the state. The California penal statute appears to apply to marriages within the state and to an extra-marital uncle-niece relationship and not to a relationship between persons who have been married in a jurisdiction that recognizes the ceremony as valid. Although the New Mexico criminal statute is unclear on this point, mother plans to reside in California. Under these circumstances, we believe the district court did not err in concluding that if mother married in Costa Rica, California would recognize the marriage for purposes of avoiding criminal liability, and that New Mexico's public policy did not preclude awarding mother primary physical custody where that choice was in the best interests of the children and mother and uncle intended to reside in California.

* * *

People v. Ezeonu

588 N.Y.S.2d 116 (N.Y. Sup. Ct. 1992)

Fisch, J.

Defendant stands indicted for the crimes of Rape in the First Degree and Rape in the Second Degree. The People contend the complainant was thirteen years old at the time of the alleged crimes. Defendant, a Nigerian national, seeks to raise as a defense to the charge of rape in the Second Degree that at the time of the alleged crimes the complainant was his "second" or "junior" wife, given to him by her parents in Nigeria pursuant to the laws and tribal customs of that country. Defendant acknowledges that he already was legally married under both New York and Nigerian law at the time he entered into the purported second marriage, but asserts that the laws and tribal customs of Nigeria allow one man to have multiple wives....

* * *

Penal Law § 130.30 provides that:

> A person is guilty of Rape in the Second Degree when, being eighteen years old or more, he or she engages in sexual intercourse with another person *to whom the actor is not married* less than fourteen years old. (*Emphasis added*)

* * *

Generally, a marriage is recognized in New York if it is valid where consummated.... However, it is well established that this general rule does not apply where recognition of a marriage is repugnant to public policy. Clearly, recognition of a polygamous marriage is repugnant to public policy as evidenced by Section 6 of the Domestic Relations Law which provides that:

> A marriage is absolutely void if contracted by a person whose husband or wife by a former marriage is living, unless either... [the former marriage has been annulled or dissolved.]

It is significant to note that under said statute a bigamous marriage is not "voidable" but "absolutely void". Moreover, bigamy is a crime in the State of New York. (Penal Law § 255.15)

Hence, "[i]t has been held that when this state is called upon to recognize either an incestuous or bigamous marriage, it will assert its strong public policy of condemnation thereof and refuse recognition even if that marriage was valid where consummated."... Consequently, a polygamous marriage legally consummated in a foreign country will be held invalid in New York.

Recently, the Supreme Court, New York County, reached the same conclusion in a civil matter.... There, the plaintiff alleged that she was married to the defendant in Nigeria and was one of defendant's twenty-five wives. The court refused to recognize the alleged marriage, holding that "bigamous or polygamous marriages even if legal where contracted are not considered valid as a matter of law and public policy."...

* * *

...While Nigerian law and custom may permit a "junior wife", New York does not recognize such status. Since at the time of his "marriage" to complainant, Dr. Ezeonu was married to his living wife, his "marriage" to her is absolutely void even were it legally consummated in Nigeria. Consequently, this Court holds, as a matter of law, Dr. Ezeonu is not married to Chiweta for purposes of criminal liability for Rape in the Second Degree.... Accordingly, he cannot raise the purported marriage as a defense to that crime.

* * *

Farah v. Farah
429 S.E.2d 626 (Va. Ct. App. 1993)

Coleman, J.

* * *

Ahmed Farah is a citizen of Algeria. Naima Mansur is a citizen of Pakistan. They have resided in Virginia for several years. They belong to different Muslim sects. They signed a proxy marriage form (the "Nikah") that is used to solemnize marriages by members of the Ahmadiyya Muslim community. The "Nikah" or marriage contract also provided that Ahmed Farah would receive a deferred payment of $20,000 as the wife's dower. On July 31, 1988, Ahmed Farah and Naima Mansur purported to enter into a Muslim marriage through their proxies in London, England. Neither Ahmed Farah nor Naima Mansur was present in England during the ceremony. No marriage certificate was issued by any court or governmental authority in England. According to testimony at trial, under Islamic law and Pakistani law, which generally recognizes Islamic religious law, the parties to the "Nikah" are legally married once the proxy ceremony is complete. During the ceremony, a member of the Muslim community solemnizes the marriage in the presence of the parties' proxy representatives and their witnesses.

Approximately one month after the "Nikah" was solemnized in London, the parties went to Pakistan for three days, where Naima Mansur's father held a reception (the "Rukhsati") in their honor. Under the tradition of the wife's Islamic sect, the "Rukhsati" symbolizes the sending away of the bride with her husband. The parties returned to Virginia in September of 1988 and purchased a house that was jointly titled in both names. They had intended to have a civil marriage ceremony when they returned to the United States, but they never did so. They lived together in Virginia as husband and wife for about one year when, on June 29, 1989, they separated, and Ahmed Farah filed a bill to have the marriage declared void and Naima Mansur filed for divorce and equitable distribution.

At trial, Ahmed Farah introduced testimony from a solicitor of the Supreme Court of England and Wales that a marriage performed in England is void *ab initio* unless all statutory formalities of the Marriage Act are satisfied. The Marriage Act of England requires issuance of a marriage license, fifteen-day residence in England by one of the parties before the marriage, and the issuance of a certificate of marriage by a duly authorized registrar of marriages. Ahmed Farah and Naima Mansur, in their proxy marriage, did not obtain a special license nor did they comply with any of the formalities required by the Marriage Act of England.

Naima Mansur contends that, even though they did not comply with the requirements of the Marriage Act of England, her marriage to Ahmed Farah is valid and must be recognized in Virginia. She asserts that the English law governing her marriage is not applicable because the marriage ceremony was completed in Pakistan by conducting the

"Rukhsati," and, furthermore, that the proxy marriage conducted in London was valid under Pakistani law, which recognizes a valid Islamic marriage.

A marriage that is valid under the law of the state or country where it is celebrated is valid in Virginia, unless it is repugnant to public policy.... A marriage that is void where it was celebrated is void everywhere.... Although the trial judge found that the marriage was celebrated in England, he ruled, however, that the marriage of the parties took place in London under Moslem law which was applicable to the parties, that the marriage by proxy is sanctioned under Moslem law and that the law of the state of Pakistan sanctions marriages performed under the personal law of the parties which in this case was Moslem law....

The trial court granted the parties a divorce based upon a separation of more than one year and ordered equitable distribution of their jointly owned marital residence by evenly dividing the equity of approximately $62,000.

The fact that Pakistan may recognize the parties' marriage as valid because it was valid according to Islamic religious law does not control the issue of the validity of the marriage under Virginia law. In Virginia, whether a marriage is valid is controlled by the law of the place where the marriage was celebrated.... Thus, the question is whether aspects of the marriage were performed in Pakistan, as the wife contends, so that it was a marriage celebrated in Pakistan, or whether it was a valid marriage celebrated in England.

The only aspect of the Muslim ceremony that occurred in Pakistan was the "Rukhsati," or reception, which the evidence showed is merely a custom that has no legal significance and is not a formality required for a legal marriage in Pakistan. Furthermore, at trial, evidence was presented that even Pakistan would not recognize the proxy marriage in England as valid because, contrary to Islamic law, the parties had not signed the "Nikah" at the same time and also because the wife was a member of a controversial Muslim sect that the Pakistani government did not recognize. No evidence established that a marriage ceremony, or any part of it, occurred in Pakistan or that it was celebrated in any jurisdiction other than England.

Because the marriage was contracted and celebrated in England, the validity of the marriage is determined according to English law.... The Marriage Act of England requires that a marriage be contracted in strict compliance with its statutory formalities. None of those formalities were complied with in the proxy marriage. Therefore, the marriage was void *ab initio* in England and is void in Virginia.

Furthermore,... [t]here is no evidence...that Ahmed Farah and Naima Mansur created a common-law marriage by entering into a relationship as husband and wife in any jurisdiction that recognizes common-law marriages.

...Accordingly, no marriage existed from which the trial judge could grant a divorce according to Virginia law. Therefore, we reverse the trial judge's declaratory judgment finding that the parties entered into a valid marriage, and we remand the matter for the circuit court to vacate the divorce decree and order of equitable distribution. We leave the parties to seek such other remedies as are appropriate to determine and resolve their property rights.

Notes and Questions

1. *Place of Celebration Rule.* Two significant policies have been identified as underpinning the creation of rules governing the recognition of marriage: (1) to assure each

spouse has freely consented to the union, and (2) to sustain the validity of relationships freely entered. Eugene F. Scoles et. al., Conflict of Laws 543, 549 (3d ed. 2000). As the above cases acknowledge, the basic rule of marriage recognition adopted in U.S. courts is to apply the law of the place in which a marriage was celebrated in order to determine its validity. Are these policies well served by this general rule, and if so, how?

2. *Public Policy Exception and the Importance of Context.* A widely recognized exception to this, or for that matter, any general marriage recognition rule, is the public policy exception. Though the underlying concept is easily understood, determining the circumstances under which it should be invoked can be problematic. In the United States, at least as to heterosexual marriages, the two substantive restrictions most likely to trigger this exception are the prohibitions against polygamous and incestuous marriages, as illustrated by *Leszinske* and *Ezeonu*. Nevertheless, even violations of these norms do not in all circumstances doom recognition, as *Leszinske* demonstrates.

If no statute specifically precludes recognition of a certain type of marriage, U.S. courts will look at various factors to determine when there is such a strong public policy against the marriage that it should not be recognized, despite its validity where celebrated. One factor often examined is whether a marriage of the type at issue is deemed void, or merely voidable, under the law of the forum state being asked to recognize the marriage. Although the characteristics of void and voidable marriages can vary by state, generally void marriages are considered void *ab initio*, whereas voidable marriages are in effect until annulled. The validity of a void marriage can be attacked after the death of one of the spouses, and the issue can be raised by any party in any legal proceeding in which the issue of the validity of the marriage is relevant. A voidable marriage typically cannot be attacked after the death of a spouse. Moreover, the defect in a voidable marriage can normally be raised only by specific parties, depending on the defect. Marriages deemed void are often more likely to be found to violate a strong public policy, but not in all circumstances, as *Leszinski* and cases cited therein demonstrate.

Another factor courts examine to determine the strength of public policy is whether entry into the type of marriage at issue violates the forum state's penal statutes. As *Leszinski* illustrates, however, this factor is also not dispositive. A third factor, the approach taken by California courts according to *Leszinski*, is to determine whether the marriage is "considered odious by the common consent of nations or whether such marriages are against the laws of nature." In applying this standard, the court undertakes a comparative examination of the treatment afforded this type of marriage in other states and nations.

Another significant factor is the purpose for which the determination regarding the validity of the marriage is being made. What factors affecting the context of the two decisions persuaded the courts to find that the marriage in *Leszinski* should be recognized and the marriage in *Ezeonu* should not be? Do you agree with the courts' resolution of these two cases?

Even as to polygamous marriages, context can persuade a court to grant recognition. For example, a California court in *In re* Dalip Singh Bir's Estate, 188 P.2d 499 (Cal. App. 1948), determined that it would not violate public policy to recognize both marriages and divide a decedent's estate between his two surviving wives, whom he had legally married in India and who still both resided there, particularly where both wives agreed to equal division and there were no other interested parties. In the course of the decision, the court cites other Canadian and American decisions recognizing polygamous marriages in the context of probate proceedings.

3. *Ethnocentrism Considerations.* The public policy concerns that cause courts to invalidate marriages celebrated abroad typically reflect social, religious, or cultural values held by the majority of the populace in the recognizing forum. Even if those norms are appropriate for regulating marriages entered within the forum (a debatable issue in itself), should the same restrictions be imposed upon those who created marriages within the context of another culture, particularly when facts suggesting evasion are absent?

Consider in this regard the tension reflected by the Australian Law Reform Commission's statements regarding recognition of polygamous marriages, albeit the topic under study was marriages created within Australia itself. The Commission explained: "Multiculturalism as a social policy requires a systematic examination of Australian law to consider first, whether it creates barriers to the expression of cultural identity and secondly, whether it could play a more positive role in achieving the goals of multiculturalism by promoting effective equality before the law (not just formal equality). A further question is whether the law could be administered so that it does not have an unintended discriminatory impact on the members of particular ethnic minority groups." The Law Reform Commission, Multiculturalism and the Law, Report No. 57 (1992), at 9. Yet the Commission also voiced the concern that multicultural policies must nonetheless require all Australians to accept the basic structures and principles of Australian society—the Constitution and the rule of law, tolerance and equality, parliamentary democracy, freedom of speech and religion, English as the national language and equality of the sexes. Voicing the concern that recognition would "offend the principles of gender equality that underlie Australian laws," the Commission recommended against recognizing polygamous marriages contracted in Australia. *Id.* at 94. The Commission acknowledged that its position was not consistent with the principles that the law should not inhibit the formation of family relationships and should recognize and protect the relationships people choose for themselves. *Id.* at 93. Moreover, the Commission recognized that the willingness of the government to accord some of the benefits of marriage upon de facto spouses created further inconsistency of treatment and discriminatory impact. For example, in some communities, including the Muslim community, polygamous marriages may be acceptable to all parties and recognized within the community, but a de facto relationship would be totally unacceptable within the community. *Id.* at 94.

3. *Marriage Evasion Exception.* Several states refuse to recognize the marriages of their citizens who marry elsewhere in order to avoid their home state's substantive restrictions regarding capacity to marry. In some states this exception to the general recognition rule is codified, and in others it is imposed by common law. Not all states enforce this exception, however, and many that do take the Restatement approach, as set forth in *Leszinski*, which combines both the evasion and policy exceptions into one. Although the *Leszinski* court does not elaborate upon the method for determining a state with the most significant relationship to the spouses and their marriage, some courts have suggested it would be a state where at least one of the two was domiciled prior to the marriage and both returned to establish their marital domicile after the marriage.

4. *Additional Basis for Recognition.* Some states will also recognize a marriage as valid if it was valid under the law of the place of the parties' domicile, even if not valid in the place of celebration. This is essentially the flip side of the evasion doctrine, looking to the place with the most significant relationship to the parties at the time of the marriage

as a basis to validate a marriage that does not satisfy the law of the place of celebration. If the marriage would be valid under the law of the nation in which both parties were domiciled or in which the spouses were first domiciled after the marriage, for example, the courts of those domiciliary states or other states often will recognize the marriage. Scoles et al., *supra*, at 547, 549. What policy considerations would support this alternative basis?

5. *Defects Affecting Form*. Unlike many other nations, which apply different rules to scrutinize the formal and substantive validity of foreign marriages, U.S. courts apply the law of the place of celebration to determine both the formal as well as the substantive validity of a marriage. In *Farah* there was no indication that the parties lacked the substantive capacity to marry either in England, where the proxy marriage was entered, or under the laws of Virginia, the state in which the parties were domiciled following their marriage, and which was asked to recognize the marriage. Yet the Virginia court refused to recognize the marriage because the procedural requirements for entering marriage in England were not satisfied. Does the court's decision make sense from a policy perspective?

Consider the possible functions procedural requirements serve. These might include to avoid sham marriages, to insure the partners have freely consented, to support compliance with substantive requirements, and to ensure that a proper record of the marriage is preserved. Were any of these concerns a risk in this case, under the procedures that were in fact utilized?

U.S. courts are willing to recognize marriages contracted in nations with fewer procedural requirements for entering marriage than the recognizing U.S. state, as long as the marriage is valid where celebrated. *See* Ma v. Ma (*In re* Marriage of Yi Ning Ma), 483 N.W.2d 732 (Minn. Ct. App. 1992) (recognizing Chinese marriage entered by registration with registry officer).

6. *Presumptions*. In several recent cases challenging the validity of marriages on the ground that procedural requirements of the celebrating nation were not satisfied, courts have recognized a strong presumption in favor of the marriage. In Amsellem v. Amsellem, 730 N.Y.S.2d 212 (N.Y. Sup. Ct. 2001), for example, the husband raised such a challenge in the context of a subsequent divorce proceeding, asserting that by conducting a religious ceremony in France without ever conducting a civil ceremony, they failed to satisfy French statutory requirements. Given that following their religious ceremony, the parties had cohabited for almost 10 years in New York, filed joint tax returns, and had five children, the court held that, "a presumption arises that the parties are legally married, and this presumption, especially in a case involving legitimacy, can only be rebutted by the most cogent and satisfactory evidence." *Id.* at 214. The court held that the affidavit submitted by the husband setting forth the requirements of French law did not establish that the marriage was void under French law, but only that the rabbi who performed the ceremony could have been subject to penalty for conducting a religious ceremony prior to a civil ceremony.

Similarly, in James v. James, 45 S.W.3d 458 (Mo. Ct. App. 2001), when the husband in divorce proceedings challenged the validity of the parties' marriage entered in a ceremony in Mexico, after which the parties lived together for over fifteen years and held themselves out as husband and wife, the court observed that "the performance of a ceremony with the appearance of validity creates a presumption as to the lawfulness of the form...." *Id.* at 462. Moreover, the court observed that if the parties have lived together as husband and wife, a marriage should be presumed, and the burden is on the party attacking its validity. *Id.* at 463.

By contrast, in a criminal prosecution for bigamy, a Washington appellate court has held that the burden is on the state to prove the validity of a marriage contracted in a foreign nation, as this was an essential element of the crime. State v. Rivera, 977 P.2d 1247 (Wash. Ct. App. 1999).

7. *Proof of Foreign Law.* In order to establish that a particular marriage did or did not satisfy the requirements of the nation in which the marriage was contracted, it is normally necessary to prove what the foreign law requires. One method of proving foreign law is to submit into evidence a properly authenticated copy of the relevant laws. The proper method of authentication will vary, depending upon whether the nation involved is one of over 75 parties to the Hague Convention Abolishing the Requirement of Legalization of Foreign Public Documents, Oct. 5, 1961, T.I.A.S. No. 172, 537 U.N.T.S. 189. The United States and other parties to this Convention will recognize public documents of member nations on the basis of a certification (an apostille) executed by authorities designated by the nation in which the document originates. Documents originating in nations that are not a party to this Convention are typically authenticated by a process referred to as "chain authentication," or "triple authentication."

The Federal Rules of Evidence and the evidentiary rules of many state courts also permit courts to treat foreign official documents as presumptively authentic even in the absence of all of the legalization requirements, if reasonable opportunity has been given to all parties to investigate their authenticity and accuracy. Fed. R. Evid. 902(3). *See, e.g.,* Okla. Stat. tit. 12, §902(3) (2001). Translations of foreign law must also, of course, be certified as accurate by a qualified translator. *See* Gary Caswell, *International Child Support—1999*, 32 Fam. L. Q. 525, 552 (1998).

Moreover, in two recent marriage recognition cases courts have held that where the court is presented with conflicting or insufficient proof of the foreign law, the court will presume that it is the same as their own law. Rivera, 977 P.2d at 1249 ("Washington follows the general rule that absent sufficient proof of the foreign law, it is presumed to be the same as that of the forum."); *see* James, 45 S.W. 3d at 5 (presented with conflicting affidavits from Mexican attorneys regarding the requirement for a valid marriage in Mexico over sixteen years prior to the time of trial, the court would apply Missouri law).

Same-gender marriages and same- or opposite-gender couples in an alternative status present unique challenges for courts being asked to recognize such unions. In the United States, the recognition of domestic same-gender marriages has been addressed in both federal statutes and the statutes of many states. In 1996, Congress passed the Defense of Marriage Act (DOMA), in the wake of conjecture that Hawaii was about to sanction same-gender marriage (see Chapter 4, Section B.1. for a discussion of Baehr v. Lewin, 852 P.2d 44 (Haw. 1993)). The Act provides in part, at 1 U.S.C. §7 (2000):

> In determining the meaning of any Act of Congress, or of any ruling, regulation, or interpretation of the various administrative bureaus and agencies of the United States, the word "marriage" means only a legal union between one man and one woman as husband and wife, and the word "spouse" refers only to a person of the opposite sex who is a husband or wife.

Also included in DOMA was 28 U.S.C. §1738c (2000), which provides:

> No State, territory, or possession of the United States, or Indian tribe, shall be required to give effect to any public act, record, or judicial proceeding of any other State, territory, possession, or tribe respecting a relationship between persons of

the same sex that is treated as a marriage under the laws of such other State, territory, possession, or tribe, or a right or claim arising from such relationship.

Thus, when a state or federal court is called upon to determine the validity of a marriage for purposes of applying federal law, such as in immigration or federal tax matters, Section 7 would appear to preclude recognition of a same-gender marriage even if performed in a nation in which such marriages are valid. When applying state law, on the other hand, Section 1738c does not prohibit a court from recognizing a same-gender marriage. Section 1738c was, at a minimum, an effort to clarify Congressional intent regarding the reach of the Federal Full Faith and Credit Statute, declaring that the federal statute would not *require* a state to recognize a same-gender marriage performed in another state. Much has been written about whether Section 1738c also limits the recognition that one state is required by the Full Faith and Credit Clause of the Federal Constitution to afford a marriage celebrated in another state, or whether such a limitation would itself be precluded by the Federal Full Faith and Credit Clause and Due Process Clause. *See, e.g.,* Mark Strasser, *Baker and Some Recipes for Disaster: On DOMA, Covenant Marriages, and Full Faith and Credit Jurisprudence,* 64 Brook L. Rev. 307 (1998). In any event, that debate will be left to your domestic family law class, because neither the Federal Full Faith and Credit Clause of the Constitution nor the Federal Full Faith and Credit statute require state courts to recognize the public acts of other nations. As discussed in *Leszinski,* state courts choose to recognize foreign marriages under the doctrine of comity, and their decision to recognize or deny recognition to same-gender marriages performed in the Netherlands or another nation, regarding matters governed by state law, is not affected by DOMA.

Over half of the U.S. states have enacted statutes of their own, however, that either define marriage as a union between a man and a woman, or declare same-gender marriages void, or explicitly deny recognition to out-of-state same-gender marriages. Oklahoma's statute, for example, provides: "A marriage between persons of the same gender performed in another state shall not be recognized as valid and binding in this state as of the date of the marriage." Okla. Stat. tit. 43, §3.1 (2001). Though technically this statute would not apply to marriages in other nations, it would at the least be a strong indication of public policy. *See* Paul Axellute, *Same-Sex Marriage, available at* http://www/rci.rutgers.edu/~axellute/ssm.htm., for a listing of states with similar statutes.

A same-gender alternative status, such as a civil union or a domestic partnership, might similarly be denied recognition on public policy grounds. At least one state court has already refused to hear an action to dissolve a Vermont civil union, refusing to find the action within the subject matter jurisdiction granted to its courts over matters concerning "family relations," on the basis that to do so would be inconsistent with legislative intent and that state's public policy. Rosengarten v. Downes, 802 A.2d 170 (Conn. App. Ct. 2002). Partners in an alternative status, whether they are of the same or opposite gender, face another obstacle as well. Many of the benefits for which recognition is typically sought under state law are explicitly tied to marital status, and thus courts must decide whether that language can also be read to include an alternative status.

American Airlines, Inc. v. Mejia
766 So. 2d 305 (Fla. Dist. Ct. App. 2000)

Farmer, J.

Carmen Cabrejo was a flight attendant for American Airlines (American). In December 1995, American Flight 965 crashed en route from Miami to Cali, Colombia. Carmen, a native of Colombia, died in the crash. At the time of her death she had five living siblings. She also had a "permanent companion," appellee Libardo Mejia. Claiming that he was Cabrejo's "common-law" husband, Libardo filed the wrongful death action in the United States District Court for the Southern District of Florida against American. He alleged that, as Carmen's common-law husband, he was her "surviving spouse" under the Florida Wrongful Death Act (WDA). American filed a motion for partial summary judgment on all of Libardo's claims, arguing that he was not Carmen's spouse under Colombian law and also within the meaning of WDA. The federal court stayed the action. Meanwhile Libardo filed the present probate proceeding, seeking a determination that he is Carmen's surviving spouse.

Libardo acknowledged that he and Carmen never participated in a formal, civil or religious ceremony of marriage. He argued, however, that they were entitled under Colombian law to claim the status of "*Union Marital de Hecho*" (*union*)[translated in English, "Marital Union in Fact" Ed.]. This status, he contends, equates with a common law marriage in the United States and thus makes him Carmen's surviving spouse under Florida law. Libardo adduced evidence that he and Carmen lived together, owned seven properties together, and had reciprocal wills—all in Colombia.

American argued that an *union* should be distinguished from formal and common law marriages. It pointed out that Colombia itself treats a formal marriage under its law differently from the informal *union* enjoyed by Carmen and Libardo, and that under its law an *union* is not considered a marriage at all, and its partners are not considered spouses.... The trial judge found as a matter of law that an *union* "is a marriage which a Florida Court must recognize as a valid marriage." We disagree.

We begin with the proposition that the meaning and effect of the law of a foreign nation is a question of law as to which our review is de novo.... We also follow the definitions in the controlling Florida statute as to what constitutes a marriage and who will be considered a spouse. Section 741.212 provides as follows:

> For purposes of interpreting any state statute or rule, the term 'marriage' means only a legal union between one man and one woman as husband and wife, and the term 'spouse' applies only to a member of such a union.

§741.212(3), Fla. Stat. (1999). By its clear text this definition controls determinations of marriage and the related question of who is a spouse when the question arises under the Florida Probate Code and WDA. It applies to "*any* state statute."...Under the plain meaning of this text, the *union* of Carmen and Libardo will be considered a marriage in Florida if it constitutes "a legal union between one man and one woman *as husband and wife*"...under Colombian law; and conversely Libardo will be deemed a spouse of Carmen only if their *union* is a marriage.

* * *

The law of Columbia distinguishes between marriage and *union marital de hecho*. Under its positive law, marriage is "a solemn contract by which a man and a woman join for the purpose of living together...." Colombian Civil Code (CCC), Art. 113....

* * *

Under Colombian law, an *union* is "the union between a man and a woman, *who although unmarried*...create a permanent and singular life in common...." Art. 1, Law 54 of 1990. The partners who create an *union* become "permanent companions to each other." *Id*. No formalities are necessary to establish an *union*, the fact of which may be demonstrated by the ordinary rules of evidence. Art. 4, Law 54 of 1990. An *union* is dissolved by, among other things, *the simple fact of one of the permanent companions marrying another person.* Art. 5(b), Law 54 of 1990. The effect of establishing an *union* is to create a presumptive "patrimonial society"[6] between the companions upon the condition that the *union* has existed for not less than 2 years. Art. 2, Law 54 of 1990. Unlike a surviving spouse of a marriage, a surviving permanent companion has no right of inheritance in the personal estate of the deceased companion. Arts. 5–6, Law 54 of 1990.

As we have seen, the *union marital de hecho* was codified by Law 54 of 1990. The Colombian Constitutional Court has explained the historical background of Law 54 of 1990 as follows:

> The Civil Code provides for the establishment of conjugal society solely by the mere fact of matrimony.... This is a society of community property....
>
> Contrary to above, the [Civil] Code and the laws prior to Law 54 of 1990 did not have any similar provisions with respect to concubinage.[7] This is logical if one takes into account the prevailing moral climate at the time that the [Civil] Code of Colombia was adopted, and those circumstances explain the unjust legal regulations that were especially damaging to women and to biological or extra-matrimonial children.
>
> By the middle of this century, the jurisprudence of the Supreme Court of Justice was entrusted with beginning the process of establishing justice in the case of free unions and on behalf of women, who are generally the weaker half of the relationship, due to financial, cultural or social factors in general. *... In a country where approximately half of the unions are de facto unions, it was natural that the laws that elevated the status of married women and biological children would motivate the courts to come to the defense of the concubine.*
>
> ... [C]oncubinage does not generate, as does matrimony, a society of assets that the law hastens to recognize and regulate. However, based on equity, it is [submitted] that a conjunction of interests by the lovers, whether deliberate or not, and a lengthy common work endeavor could constitute a de facto society, which is almost always a product of circumstance more than of reasoned and voluntary activity....
>
> Judgment C-239 of May 1994.

Our explication of these differences between a marriage and an *union* under Colombian law and this historical background surely demonstrate of their own force why the Colombian *union* under Law 54 of 1990 cannot be considered a marriage for purposes of Florida law, especially under section 741.212(3). The principal difference for our purposes is that marriage is a solemn contract dissoluble only by death or divorce, while an *union* is an informal circumstance that may be ended simply by one of the permanent companions marrying someone else. The children born of marriage need no recognition to be deemed legitimate, while the children born during an *union* are deemed extramarital and must be formally recognized by their father.

---

6. In civil law, *patrimony* refers to "all of a person's assets and liabilities that are capable of monetary valuation and subject to execution for a creditor's benefit." Black's Law Dictionary 1148 (7th ed.1999).

7. The Colombian court defined *concubinage* as "the result of ostensible and permanent sexual relations between a man and a woman who are not married to each other and, as such, it is a de facto situation." Judgment C-239 of May 1994.

As the Colombian Constitutional Court itself explained about the *union* under Law 54 of 1990:

* * *

Matrimony is different from free union and, therefore, the legal status of spouses and permanent companions is also different. Judgment No. C-174/95.

Accordingly, we hold that the *union* between Carmen and Libardo was not "a legal union between one man and one woman *as husband and wife*" within the meaning of Florida law, and therefore they were not the spouses of one another.

Notes and Questions

1. *Common Law Marriage.* As you read in Chapters One and Two, approximately one-fourth of the U.S. states still permit a couple to contract a valid, legal marriage by fulfilling certain requirements, originally created by common law, rather than performing the statutorily prescribed process for ceremonial marriage. Though there is some variation among the states, typically the elements of a common law marriage are that the couple (1) each have the intent to be married at the present time (an agreement), as opposed to the intent to be married at some future time; (2) cohabit; (3) hold themselves out to others as husband and wife; and (4) have the capacity to enter marriage. Where recognized, a common law marriage is a valid marriage that has the same effect under law as a cere-monially-entered marriage. Although the majority of U.S. states have now abolished common law marriage, the doctrine is of relevance in those states as well, as they will generally recognized a common law marriage created in a common law marriage juris-diction if the couple had a substantial attachment to the common law marriage jurisdic-tion. Although Florida has not recognized the validity of common law marriages con-tracted in Florida since 1968, the court in *Mejia* observed in a footnote that Florida will respect the validity of common law marriages created in jurisdictions where such mar-riages can be legally entered. The trial court ruled that the plaintiff's *union marital de hecho* should be recognized as a common law marriage, but the appellate court dis-agreed. Considering the elements of a common law marriage, which court do you think was correct?

A New York court faced a similar claim from a French "concubine" attempting to elect a spousal share against the will of her former partner, with whom she had lived for a period of eight years, although the relationship terminated four years before his death. French law recognizes a status of "concubinage," which is separate from the PACS dis-cussed in Chapter 4, and confers upon concubines certain rights, including the right to remain in the home as if she were a spouse and certain social security and insurance benefits. A concubinage is terminable at the will of either partner. Because a concubi-nage is not recognized as equivalent to marriage under French law, but rather is treated as a separate status, the court rejected petitioner's claim that she should be treated as a common law spouse. In the Matter of Estate of Robert Huyot, 645 N.Y.S.2d 979 (N.Y. Surr. Ct. 1996), *aff'd* 666 N.Y.S.2d 697 (N.Y. App. Div. 1997).

2. *Putative Spouse Doctrine.* In Chapter Two, Section B.3., you read in *In re Vryonis* about the putative spouse doctrine, which permits a partner in an invalid marriage who has a good faith belief that his or her marriage is valid to acquire some of the rights of a marital spouse, up until the point when the alleged putative spouse discovers the infir-mity. Several U.S. states recognize this doctrine. If the petitioner in *Mejia* had instead been litigating his claim in one of those states, would he have fared any better under the

putative spouse doctrine? Could it have been useful to Naima Mansur in *Farah,* if that proceeding had instead been initiated in a state recognizing the putative spouse doctrine?

2. Marriage Recognition under Foreign and International Law

Lynn Wardle, International Marriage and Divorce Regulation and Recognition: A Survey
29 Fam. L. Q. 497, 502–06 (1995)

* * *

A. Formalities

Most countries distinguish between marriage formalities and marriage essentials (usually called capacity in choice of law) in resolving international marriage recognition issues. The nearly ubiquitous rule regarding marriage formalities is to apply the law of the place where the marriage was celebrated. "[T]here is no rule more firmly established in private international law than that which applies the maxim *locus regit actum* to the formalities of a marriage." Application of the law of the place of celebration to matters of form is nearly "absolute." There are, however, exceptions. To validate marriages that are invalid under the law of the place of celebration, reference often is made either to personal law, or *renvoi* is used (the forum applies the law looked to by the choice of law rules of the place of celebration). Exceptions to the *lex loci celebrationis* rule also exist for consular marriages and marriages by members of the military serving abroad in some circumstances. Also, violation of a strong forum public policy still may result in nonrecognition of marriages valid where performed.

Requirements of religious celebration have historically provided a major source of marriage recognition problems relating to form. "The law of many religious communities ignore the distinction...between form and substance and regard the institution of marriage as an indivisible whole, for which they claim application of their own rules to the exclusion of any secular law." When such religious doctrines are incorporated rigidly into the marriage regulation and recognition laws of a state, foreign laws and marriages may be at risk. While this seems to be less a problem today in christian and socialist nations than it once was, elsewhere the problem has not entirely disappeared.

B. Essential Capacity

Regarding marriage essentials, there are two grand choice of law systems widely used for international marriage recognition. One is the rule of *lex loci celebrationis* (the law of the place of celebration). The other is the rule of personal law (the law that defines the personal status of the parties). The personal law system involves two competing rules for determining personal law: *lex patriae* (the law of one's nationality) and *lex domicilii* (the law of one's domicile).

1. Personal Law: Nationality vs. Domicile

"In most countries the substantive validity of marriages is tested by the personal law rather than by the *lex loci celebrationis.*" The parties to the prospective marriage are deemed to carry the law of a nation with them, and that law is applied to determine substantive questions regarding whether they are eligible to marry. In most civil law countries, nationality has been the primary source of personal law (*lex patriae*). This is the traditional choice of law rule for marriage recognition "nearly everywhere in Continental Europe," as well as in most of the Arab world countries with western legal systems.

The other personal law regime looks to the law of the domicile (*lex domicilii*). This is the choice of law rule for marriage recognition in the United Kingdom, many commonwealth countries, and some Latin American countries. The trend is toward using domicile ("habitual residence" is the preferred term today) rather than nationality for determining the law governing marriage capacity or essentials. In a very insightful passage, Professor Michael Bogden and Eva Ryrstedt explain the reason for this rule-change: When a country is sending its citizens to other parts of the world, where they will reside for long periods of time, it prefers the choice of law rule of nationality so that it may apply its own law to its citizens abroad and so that they may rely on the law of their own nationality wherever they have gone. When, however, a country is the recipient of many foreign immigrants (for example, foreign workers employed in nations with falling birthrates), it prefers the choice of law rule of domicile, so that it may apply its own law to the foreign nationals who have come to live and work in that nation.

When the parties are of different nationalities or domiciles, the courts traditionally gave preference to the husband's personal law on the notion that the husband is the head of the family. In light of gender equality notions now prevailing, this is no longer widely followed. The prevailing rule is to apply the personal law of each party to determine the validity of the marriage as to that party, though sometimes both sets of personal law are applied to both parties. The "dual," "interrelated," or "bilateral" concept of personal law is that some marriage requirements apply to both parties (such as polygamy or consanguinity rules); generally each of the parties must satisfy the bilateral requirements of both states, but in some states the stricter requirement is applied. There are no uniform criteria for deciding which marriage requirements are bilateral, but generally bilateral requirements are those for which the marriage policy would not be achieved if applied to only one party. Many states require the parties to satisfy the capacity requirements of the forum, also, if citizens of foreign states wish to marry there.

Typically, the law of the state of domicile or nationality at the time of (immediately before) celebrating marriage controls. To validate a marriage, some courts have looked to the domicile or nationality of the parties at the time of the suit, or even to the law of the place of celebration. *Renvoi* is sometimes applied for the same purpose. If either party is domiciled in or a citizen of the forum, another solution is to adopt the *lex fori*. Forum public policy may be invoked in exceptional cases either to validate or invalidate foreign marriages or marriage laws.

2. Lex Loci Celebrationis

The other choice of law regime, *lex loci celebrationis*, is the oldest of the prevailing choice of law systems. Some states follow the *lex loci celebrationis* principle as to substantive marriage requirements, including the United States, several Latin American countries, and Scandinavian countries *inter se*. In those states, a marriage that is valid under the law of the place of celebration is valid in the forum, unless it violates the strong public policy of the forum.

Evasion of marriage laws can be a significant problem in *lex loci celebrationis* states because the restrictive policies of the state with greatest interest in regulating marriage may be evaded by the simple expedient of crossing a border to celebrate the marriage, and then returning to the restrictive state to live. Thus, *lex loci celebrationis* countries generally refuse to recognize evasive marriage of their own citizens. This is a matter of the *ordre public* exception in choice of law; if a strong public policy is violated, a marriage valid where performed will not be recognized even in a state that generally follows the *lex loci celebrationis* rule.

International marriage recognition is actually much more complicated than this brief description suggests. Common-law courts that wrestle with these cases and civil law legislators often draw many more, and more subtle, distinctions. It may make a significant difference whether both or one or neither party is a national or domicile, where they resided at the time of marriage (and how long), the relation of the place of the marriage to the marriage, etc.

C. Treaties and International Agreements

There have been numerous bilateral treaties, conventions, and regional agreements addressing various aspects of international marriage recognition....

* * *

The Hague Conference on International Private Law has twice promulgated Conventions specifically addressing the topic of marriage recognition. In 1902 the Hague Conventions Relations to Differences in Marriage Laws, Divorce Laws, and Guardianship of Minors opened for signature. It generally adopted a *lex patriae* (law of nationality) choice of law approach for marriage recognition. Thirteen European states eventually ratified this Convention, though two of them, France and Belgium, withdrew ratification. In 1976 the Hague Conference promulgated the Convention on Celebration and Recognition of the Validity of Marriages ("Hague Convention on Marriages"). It provides, generally, that the law of the state of celebration governs the formal requirements for marriage (Art. 2) and the substantive validity of the marriage (Art. 16). However, as of June 16, 1994, only three states had ratified the Convention, and three others had signed it in the seventeen years since it opened for signature.[This statement was still true as of July 2002. Ed.]

Several notable multilateral conventions provide regional marriage recognition rules, such as the 1889 and 1940 Montevideo Treaties on International Civil Law, which are very influential in Latin America. These treaties reportedly adopt the general principle of *lex loci celebrationis* to determine marriage validity. Reportedly these treaties have not been adopted by those (Brazil and Chile) that favor the *lex patriae* choice of law rule. The 1928 Code of Private International Law (Bustamante Code), approved by at least fifteen Latin American nations, also provided that all substantive marriage issues are governed by the personal law of the parties, and each state is free to determine whether domicil or nationality (or other criteria) provides the personal law. However, the modern American Convention on Human Rights appears to reinforce the choice of law rule generally prevailing in Latin America today that the law of the place of celebration governs all questions concerning marriage celebration and validity.

The Scandinavian Convention Containing Provisions in the Field of Private International Law Relating to Marriage, Adoption and Guardianship (Denmark, Finland, Iceland, Norway and Sweden) provides generally that *lex loci celebrationis* governs capacity to marry when at least one of the parties to a marriage is a habitual resident of that place, unless the party requests application of the *lex patriae*. The European Convention for the Protection of Human Rights and Fundamental Freedoms, obligates member states to guarantee the right to marry without religious obstacle. The Paris Convention to Facilitate the Celebration of Marriages Abroad authorizes the state of celebration to grant a dispensation from marriage impediments based on the personal law of a habitual resident of the state of celebration. The Luxembourg (C.I.E.C.) Convention on the Recognition of Decisions Concerning Marital Relations, provides that when a divorce or annulment has been recognized in a contracting state, it may not refuse to allow a party to remarry on the ground that some other state (presumably the state of nationality or domicil of the applicant) would not recognize the divorce or annulment.

Most treaties however regarding marriage recognition are bilateral treaties regulating relations between only two nations and their citizens. In several countries (for example, Russia, Italy, and Argentina), conventions and treaties regulating private international law are of paramount importance. In those countries, priority is given to recognition of foreign marriage and divorce laws, judgments, and status when the terms of an international agreement are met. If recognition of marriage or divorce is sought outside the terms of some international agreement, it appears that the presumption in favor of the validity of the foreign marriage or divorce may not be as strong as it is in other countries.

Note

1. *International Recognition of Same-Gender Marriages and Alternative Relationships.* At present there is little case law supporting the proposition that tribunals in nations that do not themselves permit same-gender marriages or domestic partnerships are likely to recognize those relationships entered by same-gender couples elsewhere. Regardless of whether a nation utilizes the *lex loci celebrationis, lex patriae,* or *lex domicilii* choice of law system, most nations recognize a public policy exception, often referred to as *ordre public,* which could be used by a court to deny recognition. *See* Federal Court of March 3, 1993, BGE 119 II 266 (Swiss Federal Court ruling that recognition or registration of same-gender union entered in Denmark would violate Swiss public policy against same-sex marriage, reported in Barbara E. Graham-Siegenthaler, *Priniples of Marriage Recognition Applied to Same-Sex Marriage Recognition in Switzerland and Europe,* 32 Creighton L.Rev. 121, 139–40 (1998)). These nations could also avoid recognition by taking a definitional approach, asserting that a domestic partnership or similar status, or even a same-gender marriage itself, was not a marriage and thus they were not bound by domestic or international law to recognize it. *See* Martha Bailey, *Hawaii's Same-sex Marriage Initiatives: Implications for Canada,* 15 Can. J. Fam.L. 153, 169 (1998). Taking a similar approach, an Israeli family court denied an application by a lesbian couple to have the registered partnership they entered in Germany recognized as a civil marriage under Israeli law, on the ground that the women were not recognized as a family under Israeli law, and thus the court was not authorized to rule on their case. *See* Amotz Asa-El, *News, Week in Review,* Jerusalem Post, March 29, 2002, at 3; News, Tel Aviv, March 19, 2002., *at* http://www.planetout.xom/pno/news/article.html.

Some commentators have argued that on the basis of favorable rulings towards gay or lesbian couples on related issues in their countries, recognition of relationships entered abroad should not legitimately be denied on public policy grounds. *See* Bailey, *supra,* at 173–76 (Canada); John Murphy, *The Recognition of Same-Sex Families in Britain: The Role of Private International Law,* 16 Int'l J. L. Pol. & Fam. 181, 188–89

(2002). *Cf.* Nicholas J. Patterson, *The Repercussions in the European Union of the Netherlands' Same-Sex Marriage Law,* 2 Chic. J. Int'l L. 301 (2001).

In the absence of recognition as a status, however, it has been suggested that as a fallback, registered partnerships could be recognized as contracts under the contractual choice of law rules. This approach is deemed less appropriate, however, particularly for the Scandinavian and Dutch legislation, which focus more on the parties' status than their reciprocal obligations. Murphy, *supra,* at 189–90. *See also,* Michael Freeman, *How Should an English Court Respond to a Same-sex Union,* [1998] Int'l Fam. L. 5, 7.

B. Recognition of Foreign Marriage Dissolutions and Related Orders

1. U.S. Tribunals

a. *Status Termination*

The United States is not currently a party to any convention that regulates recognition of foreign divorce decrees. Unlike the recognition of divorce judgments of other states, which is subject to the requirements of the Full Faith and Credit Clause of the Federal Constitution, the recognition by U.S. tribunals of divorce judgments of other nations is determined largely by application of the common law doctrine of comity, subject to several limitations. Some of these limitations emanate from the jurisdictional and procedural requirements of the Due Process Clause, as the following cases illustrate.

Maklad v. Maklad
28 Conn. L. Rptr. 593, No. FA000443796S, 2001 WL 51662
(Conn. Super. Ct. Jan. 3, 2001)

Alander, J.

The plaintiff has filed for a dissolution of her marriage with the defendant. The defendant has moved to dismiss the action on the grounds that this court lacks jurisdiction due to the issuance of a prior divorce decree in Egypt.

The plaintiff and the defendant were married on November 11, 1984 in Egypt. Soon after their marriage, they moved to the United States. From 1984 until September 15, 2000, both parties continuously resided in Connecticut. The plaintiff and the defendant have four children, all of whom were born in Connecticut. The parties and their children are citizens both of the United States and Egypt.

On September 15, 2000, the defendant removed the three youngest children, ages three, nine and eleven, from school and took them to Egypt without the knowledge or permission of the plaintiff. Since that date, the defendant has resided in Egypt with the three children. On September 27, 2000, the defendant obtained a certificate of divorce in Egypt. The plaintiff had no prior notice that the defendant was seeking a divorce decree in Egypt and was given no opportunity to be heard in Egypt with respect to the certificate of divorce.

On October 4, 2000, the plaintiff initiated the current action for a dissolution of her marriage to the defendant. That same day, the court granted ex parte the plaintiff's motion for temporary custody of the four minor children....

The law governing the recognition of divorce decrees from foreign courts is well established.... [T]he Connecticut Supreme Court held that, while the full faith and credit clause of the United States constitution does not apply to judgments of foreign nations, such judgments are entitled to recognition in this state under the principle of comity.... The court also noted that the principle of comity is frequently applied in divorce cases.... Notwithstanding the respect due the decisions of foreign courts, the principle of comity is not unbounded.... A decree of divorce will not be recognized by comity where it was obtained by a procedure which denies due process of law in the real sense of the term, or was obtained by fraud, or where the divorce offends the public policy of the state in which recognition is sought, or where the foreign court lacked jurisdiction.

The defendant in this case asks the court to recognize the divorce decree he obtained on September 27, 2000 in Egypt. In order for this court to defer to the certificate of divorce issued by the court in Egypt, the court in Egypt must have had jurisdiction to issue such a decree. Essential to a court's divorce jurisdiction is that at least one of the parties had a domicile in that country.... If neither spouse was domiciled in the foreign nation granting the divorce, the court of that nation lacked jurisdiction to do so and its judgment will not be afforded comity....

A key ingredient to domicile is an intention to permanently remain in the country....

The evidence establishes that the defendant did not intend to permanently reside in Egypt. The defendant has lived continuously in Connecticut for the past sixteen years. For the last twelve years, the defendant has worked at Sikorsky Aircraft. His youngest son, Abdellah, suffered significant brain damage in an accident and is in need of substantial medical and rehabilitative services. His oldest son, Mohamed, remains in Connecticut with the plaintiff. After leaving abruptly for Egypt without the knowledge or permission of the plaintiff, the defendant, through his brother, delivered a written statement to the school of his son, Abdelrahman. The statement indicated that "due to unusual circumstances" the defendant had to leave the United States, but the child will be away for only "three to six months." The defendant has provided no evidence to contradict this written statement nor has he provided any other evidence indicating an intent on his part to permanently relocate to Egypt. Given the defendant's strong ties to Connecticut and his written statement that his absence would be temporary, I find that the defendant did not intend to permanently reside in Egypt in September 2000. The Egyptian certificate of divorce is also not entitled to comity because the decree was obtained by the defendant without affording due process to the plaintiff. The plaintiff was not present personally or through counsel in the Egyptian court at the time the decree was issued. The plaintiff received no prior notice that the defendant was seeking a certificate of divorce in Egypt and she was given no opportunity to be heard prior to the issuance of the decree. It is a fundamental tenet of the due process of law that all parties be given notice of the pendency of the proceedings and a meaningful opportunity to be heard.... Comity does not countenance a court judgment that the plaintiff had no prior notice of and no opportunity to contest....

The defendant further asserts that the doctrine of practical recognition prevents the plaintiff from contesting the certificate of divorce that he procured in Egypt. The defendant contends that the parties were married in Egypt in accordance with their Islamic religion and that they both participated in a religious ceremony on August 5, 2000 in

Connecticut during which the defendant divorced the plaintiff pursuant to the tenets of Islam. The defendant claims that the plaintiff agreed to this religious divorce and that he merely legalized the divorce on September 27, 2000 in Egypt. He asserts that it would now be inequitable to allow the plaintiff to invalidate a divorce that she previously agreed to.

The doctrine of practical recognition accords recognition to a divorce decree rendered in a foreign nation in those situations where it would be inequitable to allow the party attacking the decree to do so. Bruneau v. Bruneau,...489 A.2d 1049 (Conn. App. 1985). "The rule precluding a person from attacking the validity of a foreign divorce if, under the circumstances, it would be inequitable to do so is not limited to situations of what might be termed 'true estoppel' where one party induces another to rely to his damage upon certain representations as to the facts of the case. If the person attacking the divorce is, in doing so, taking a position inconsistent with his past conduct, or if the parties to the action have relied upon the divorce, and if, in addition, holding the divorce invalid will unset relationships or expectations formed in reliance upon the divorce, then estoppel will preclude calling the divorce in question. Thus, if one party has accepted benefits under the original decree or waited an unreasonably long time before attacking it, an invalid decree will be held immune from attack, particularly if the other party has remarried in the meantime."...Even if a divorce decree rendered in a foreign country is otherwise invalid under the exceptions to comity..., the judgment may be permitted practical recognition.

In *Bruneau,* the court prevented one spouse from invalidating a divorce obtained by the other spouse in Mexico despite the lack of domicile by either spouse in Mexico because she willingly participated in procuring the dissolution by appearing through counsel, her husband had relied on the divorce decree by remarrying, and she waited nineteen years before questioning the Mexican divorce.

Unlike the situation in *Bruneau,* it would not be inequitable under the circumstances of this case to allow the plaintiff to attack the divorce judgment that the defendant obtained in Egypt. The plaintiff did not participate in or consent to the divorce proceedings initiated by the defendant in Egypt. The plaintiff immediately questioned the validity of the Egyptian divorce decree upon learning of its existence and the defendant has not justifiably entertained expectations or formed relationships in reliance on the Egyptian judgment. The fact that the plaintiff may have participated in a religious ceremony in Connecticut does not equitably estop her from questioning the judgment procured ex parte in Egypt. It is the Egyptian judgment not the religious divorce that the defendant seeks to have this court recognize.

For the foregoing reasons, the defendant's motion to dismiss is hereby denied.

In the Matter of the Estate of Ian A. Pringle
2000 WL 1349231 (Terr.V.I.)

Steele, J.

[Ed. Note: Three years after his disappearance while piloting a small plane between islands in 1996, Decedent, Ian Pringle, was declared dead, and Petitioner sought a share of his estate as surviving spouse. Although Decedent and Petitioner were married in January, 1978, the other heirs asserted that she was no longer Decedent's spouse, based on a divorce obtained in the Dominican Republic in 1980. Following the divorce,

Petitioner continued to reside in their shared residence for an additional sixteen years until Decedent's death, gave birth to two of his children, and shared in his various business ventures. However, Decedent also openly had relationships with numerous other women, with whom he often lived on weekends, and fathered other children during this period.

Petitioner contends that the divorce was obtained at Decedent's request, so that he could persuade another women, with whom he was romantically involved, to manage one of his businesses on another island, and that Decedent had assured her the divorce would not be valid unless it was filed in the Virgin Islands, where they resided.]

* * *

The Constitution of the United States requires that our Territory grant full faith and credit to a judgment of a U.S. State.... However, judgments from a foreign nation do not garner this same type of treatment. Instead, the principles of comity are utilized, with our courts extending a prima facie validity to such foreign judgments.... It is unquestionable that a valid divorce decree will serve to sever whatever inheritance right an individual had by law to receive a distributive share of their former spouse's estate. Therefore, it must be determined whether recognition of the Dominican Republic divorce decree would offend public policy of the Virgin Islands.

1. Validity of Divorce Decree

Whether recognition is to be granted a divorce decree entered into by a foreign nation is not a novel issue before the Territory.... The court in Perrin [v. Perrin, 408 F.2d 107 (3rd Cir. 1969)] found that recognition of a bilateral Mexican divorce would not offend public policy. The spouse procuring the divorce appeared personally in the Mexican proceeding, while her husband appeared by a duly empowered attorney at law.... Significant emphasis was apparently placed upon the aspect of physical presence in the foreign forum. Although merely dictum, the court stated that "mail order" divorce decrees in which neither spouse appeared personally in the foreign jurisdiction would certainly not be recognized in the Virgin Islands....

In the case at hand, neither the Decedent nor the Petitioner were domiciles or even residents of the Dominican Republic when the divorce decree was issued. While the decree itself purports that the Decedent was momentarily in the Dominican Republic, the uncontroverted evidence presented before the Court does not support this assertion. In order to obtain their divorce, the Petitioner testified that she and the Decedent traveled to Puerto Rico where they met with the Office of Consulate General of the Dominican Republic. At no time did either party visit the Dominican Republic in reference to their divorce until the Petitioner personally went there to retrieve the decree.

* * *

A "mail-order divorce" has been defined as a situation where two persons attempt to confer jurisdiction upon a court of a foreign nation by executing a power of attorney to counsel who resides in that foreign nation and then forwarding such instruments by mail without ever visiting the nation or establishing their domicile there.... Such divorces are null and void as the foreign court has no scintilla of jurisdiction when neither party was ever in that country.... [Caldwell v. Caldwell,] 81 N.E.2d [60,] 62 [N.Y. 1948]; Rosenbaum v. Rosenbaum, 210 A.2d 5, 7 (D.C.1965); See also In Re Cohen,...93 A.2d 4, 5 (N.J.1952) (citing the well settled principle that Mexican mail-order divorce decrees obtained merely on signed waivers of jurisdiction without the personal appearance in the foreign nation of either the husband or wife are complete nullities in New Jersey).

The courts in New York have held that mail-order divorces are so patently invalid that they do not estop a person who has procured one from commencing an action to have his or her marital status judicially determined. *E.g.* Dorn v. Dorn, 112 N.Y.S.2d 90, 92 (N.Y. Sup.Ct.1952). However, these types of divorces may be divided into two separate categories.... The first category consist of cases where the plaintiff seeks to reestablish the former marital status. Included in this reestablishment are any financial benefits which are merely incidental to the status, such as support and alimony. The New York court's [sic] reasoned that such benefits derive from statute and not from the common law.... The second category involves those cases where the plaintiff attacks the divorce primarily for the purpose of obtaining financial gain.... Application of the doctrine of estoppel to this category will only deny the person guilty of misconduct from benefitting financially, and will not serve to validate the mail-order decree of the foreign nation....

Although the New York cases previously cited specifically dealt with Mexican mail-order divorce decrees, the rationale utilized in these decisions is equally applicable to similar decrees which are received from any foreign nation. Upon concluding our review of case law from other jurisdictions as well as our own, it is clear to the Court that the Dominican Republic divorce decree voluntarily entered into by the Decedent and the Petitioner may not be recognized in the Virgin Islands as terminating the marital vows. This determination must be made even though the Court does not perceive the Petitioner to be the innocent and naive party that she now claims to have been during the divorce process. For quite some time, the Petitioner has been actively involved in managing business entities. By all accounts, it appears that she is an astute entrepreneur, as was the Decedent during his lifetime.

It is the belief of the Court, and indeed the apparent testimony of the Petitioner, that the divorce was concocted for unsavory business purposes. In short, it was meant to deceive Edwina Josephine Lewis. The Petitioner and the Decedent shared what can best be described by the Court as a marriage of convenience. This relationship was more along the lines of a business partnership rather than that of a marriage. While it is true that the Petitioner gave birth to two of the Decedent's children after the divorce occurred, several other children were fathered by the Decedent during this same period. It is the opinion of the Court that the Decedent not only sought trustworthy individuals to manage his business interests, but also ones he could control emotionally. The fact that he chose to secure many of his possessions in his name alone is not merely coincidence. The Court finds that such decisions were consciously devised by the Decedent. He filed his income tax returns as a single person. Even the title to the home he shared with the Petitioner is only in his name.

The Court fully believes that the Petitioner knew of the consequences of the divorce action. Whether she agreed to this termination for questionable business tactics or simply to continue her relationship with the Decedent does not concern the Court. The public policy of the Virgin Islands would surely be offended were the Territory to allow its citizens to obtain unenforceable sham divorces. Nevertheless, the lack of physical presence by either the Decedent or the Petitioner in the Dominican Republic during the divorce restricts the Court from recognizing what should otherwise be a valid divorce decree.

2. Procurement of an Invalid Divorce Decree

Merely finding that the Dominican Republic divorce decree is invalid in the Virgin Islands does not assure that the Petitioner may assume her rights as the Decedent's surviving spouse for inheritance purposes.... [T]he Virgin Islands Code has specified certain actions which if performed by a spouse will deprive that individual of his or her distributive share. *See* V.I.Code Ann. tit. 15, §87 (1996). In particular, one such situation deals with the procurement of a foreign divorce decree not recognized as being valid in the Territory. Specifically, subsection (2) of this section provides that:

> No distributive share of the estate of a decedent shall be allowed under the provisions of this chapter, either—

> (2) to a spouse who has procured without this territory a final decree or judgment dissolving the marriage with the decedent, where such decree or judgment is not recognized as valid by the law of this territory;...

* * *

Even though a foreign judgment is not recognized in the jurisdiction as dissolving the marriage of the parties, it is still effective to bar the spouse who had obtained it from sharing in the estate of the deceased spouse. The Judiciary of New York have had several occasions in which to enforce [a similar statute upon which the Virgin Island statute is based.] *See* [In Re Rathscheck's Estate],...90 N.E.2d 887 (N.Y. 1950) (barring petitioner from sharing in the intestate's property where neither party had traveled to Mexico, but both had joined by mail in arranging and obtaining a Mexican divorce decree);...In Re Mane's Estate,...244 N.Y.S.2d 183 (N.Y.Sur.Ct.1963) (entering a voluntary appearance in a foreign divorce, the cross-petitioner was found to have assisted in the procurement of the divorce and was therefore barred from receiving a distributive share of the estate).

It is apparent from the New York case law that the lack of physical presence in the foreign jurisdiction of the divorce decree by either party will not impede the termination of inheritance rights. Thus, termination will depend on the procurement requirement of the code section. An accused spouse will be found to have not procured the divorce decree where he or she did not affirmatively participate in the divorce.... However, where a divorce is obtained by amicable arrangement, with each spouse desiring to terminate the marriage and each taking affirmative action to accomplish that result, it cannot be said that only one spouse is the procurer of the divorce. Where a decree was procured by the voluntary appearance of a spouse and the decree recited an agreement of the parties, that spouse cannot be regarded as an innocent party who has been imposed on. As each party sought the termination of their marriage, each should accept the consequences of their actions....

In the matter at hand, the Petitioner testified that she and the Decedent went to Puerto Rico and visited the Office of Consulate General of the Dominican Republic for the purpose of obtaining a divorce decree. According to the Petitioner however, it was the Decedent's idea to get the divorce. She maintains that she was initially hesitant to agree to such a termination, but did so on the Decedent's assurance that the divorce was for business purposes and would have no effect on their marital status unless filed in the Virgin Islands. The Petitioner even claimed to have lied to the Consul General in order to receive the decree. She supported the notion of a sham divorce with the fact that the couple continued to live together for an additional sixteen (16) years after the entry of the decree. Indeed, the Decedent went on to provide for the Petitioner's well-being, and they eventually had two children together.

Even if the Petitioner's allegations of deception were accepted as true, the Court would still find that she was barred from receiving a distributive share of the Decedent's Estate pursuant to 15 V.I.C. §87(2).... [T]he Petitioner voluntarily chose to appear in the divorce action. In fact, the Dominican Republic divorce was obtained by utilizing a procedure where both parties mutually consented to the action. The mere presence of the Petitioner at the Consul General's office is a sufficient act in furtherance of the divorce. More damaging is the testimony elicited from the Petitioner herself. She admitted to lying to the Office of the Consulate General in order to obtain the divorce. It is abundantly clear to the Court that such an affirmative act was conducted to assist in the procurement of the divorce. No matter which party initiated the proceedings, each played an active role in the procurement. An absence of participation from either party would have frustrated the Dominican Republic action. As such, the Court holds that both the Petitioner and the Decedent procured the divorce decree. The fact that neither individual was physically present in the Dominican Republic is of no consequence.

* * *

III. Conclusion

...As neither the Petitioner nor the Decedent were ever physically present in the Dominican Republic during the divorce proceedings, the decree may not be recognized through the principle of comity.

... [B]oth spouses may be found to have procured the decree if each performed affirmative actions in the furtherance of the divorce. As the Petitioner admitted that she voluntarily appeared and mutually consented to the divorce, the Court finds that she in fact procured the decree along with the Decedent. Thus, she is barred from receiving a spouse's distributive share of the Estate.

Notes and Questions

1. *Choice of Law.* U.S. state courts apply the law of the forum in which a dissolution action is brought to determine whether a particular marriage can be terminated. As a result, when considering whether to recognize a foreign order terminating marital status, the substantive law applied by the foreign court is rarely a concern. Because a U.S. court would have applied forum law in a domestic proceeding, U.S. tribunals accept a foreign court's application of its own law. Conversely, the fact that the foreign court applied substantive law identical to the law of the recognizing state is unlikely to be a factor favoring recognition in the U.S. court, if a jurisdictional ground for nonrecognition exists. Eugene F. Scoles et al., Conflict of Laws 628 (3d ed. 2000).

2. *Grounds for Nonrecognition—Jurisdiction.*

   a. *Requirement of Domicile.* One of the most common reasons that a U.S. tribunal refuses to recognize a foreign divorce order is that the tribunal issuing the order did not satisfy the jurisdictional standards required by the Due Process Clause of the U.S. Constitution for the exercise of personal jurisdiction. In Williams v. North Carolina, 325 U.S. 226 (1945), the U.S. Supreme Court held that due process will be satisfied in a proceeding in a U.S. court to adjudicate marital status if at least one of the spouses is domiciled in the forum state. *Macklad* and *Pringle* join a long line of cases in which U.S. courts have refused recognition to foreign divorce orders because neither party was domiciled in the nation that issued the divorce, even if domicile was not required by that nation's own jurisdictional standards. *E.g.* In re Marriage of Pascavage, No. 923-86, 1994 WL 838136 (Del. Fam. Ct. Aug. 15, 1994); Carr v. Carr, 724 So. 2d 937 (Miss. Ct. App. 1998); Atassi v. Atassi, 451 S.E.2d 371 (N.C. Ct. App. 1995); Jewell v. Jewel, 751 A.2d 735 (R.I. 2000). Courts will often justify such nonrecognition on public policy grounds. Conversely, when one or both parties are domiciled in the foreign nation at the time the foreign divorce proceeding is initiated, and no other basis for nonrecognition is present, a U.S. court will recognize the divorce under the doctrine of comity. *E.g.,* Robinson v. Shalala, Unempl. Ins. Rep. (CCH) P 15069B, 1995 WL 681044 (S.D.N.Y.) (recognizing Danish divorce based on husband's domicile); Azim v. Saidazimova, 720 N.Y.S.2d 561 (N.Y. App. Div. 2001) (recognizing Kirgistani divorce based on domicile of both spouses).

When foreign nationals obtain a divorce in a foreign nation, however, and at a later point in time, when one or both of the parties are now located in the United States, a U.S. court is asked to recognize that divorce for some purpose, the U.S. court will often do so, even if neither was domiciled in the nation issuing the divorce order, if the divorce was valid where rendered. U.S. courts have no interest in creating a "limping marriage," nor do other policy grounds justify nonrecognition of a decree entered at a time when the parties had no connection to the United States. Scoles & Hay, *supra,* at 517. For example, in Goode v. Goode, 997 P.2d 244 (Or. App. 2000), an Oregon court recognized the validity of a Dominican Republic divorce between two Columbian citizens, even though neither spouse was domiciled in the Dominican Republic at the time of the divorce, because it occurred before the wife subsequently came to the United States. Her former husband also had no connection to the United States. Justifying its recognition, the court observed, "Any public policy of the State of Oregon to prevent forum shopping could not have been violated under those circumstances, as it might have been had the wife been an Oregon resident at the time she obtained the divorce."

As you will read in the next section, many other nations recognize nationality as a basis to exercise divorce jurisdiction. In *Maklad*, the husband, wife, and children were citizens of both the United States and Egypt at the time that the husband obtained the divorce in Egypt. When both spouses have a significant connection such as this with the nation rendering a divorce, is the insistence of U.S. courts upon domicile of one of the parties in that nation as a ground for recognition justified on public policy grounds?

b. Bilateral Divorces. Despite the absence of domicile by either spouse in the divorcing nation, several U.S. states and territories will recognize a consensual divorce rendered in a foreign nation if the petitioning spouse is physically present in the divorcing nation and the other spouse voluntarily appears in person or through an attorney in the action, a practice sometimes referred to as a "bilateral" foreign divorce. *E.g.,* Perrin v. Perrin, 408 F.2d 107 (3rd Cir. 1969); Rabbani v. Rabbani, 578 N.Y.S.2d 213 (N.Y. App. Div. 1991); Terrell v. Terrell, 578 S.W.2d 637 (Tenn. 1979) (validity of divorce uncontested by parties). Other states, however, have refused recognition to such divorces. *See* 24A Am. Jur. 2d *Divorce and Separation* § 1160 (1998). Given that the Virgin Islands is one of the U.S. jurisdictions that will recognize foreign bilateral divorces, why did the court in *Pringle* find the consensual divorce entered between Bernadette and Ian Pringle invalid?

Those of you who remember your Civil Procedure might be perplexed as to why recognition would ever be denied to a decree entered in a court that assumed jurisdiction with the consent of both parties, because consent has traditionally been recognized as a separate ground for personal jurisdiction. Divorce proceedings, however, were traditionally treated as *in rem* proceedings, and the jurisdiction of a court was thought to be based on the connection of the status to the forum rather than on the connection of the defendant to the forum.

The U.S. Supreme Court's decision in *Williams v. North Carolina* established that a state court could adjudicate the status of one of its domiciliaries, even if the defendant in the divorce suit was not otherwise subject to the jurisdiction of the state on the basis of service in the state, consent, defendant's own domicile in the state, or minimum contacts with the forum. Despite the subsequent decision of the U.S. Supreme Court in *Shaffer v. Heitner*, 433 U.S. 186 (1977), requiring that all *in rem* proceedings must now meet the requirements for assertion of *in personam* jurisdiction, a footnote in *Shaffer* appears to have excluded status proceedings from this requirement, *id.* at 209, n. 30, and the vast majority of state courts thus continue to treat satisfaction of the *Williams* criteria of domicile of one of the parties as sufficient to establish personal jurisdiction to render a divorce.

The question left unresolved by *Williams*, however, is whether the existence of one of the other bases, such as service on defendant in the forum or defendant's consent, is sufficient to establish personal jurisdiction over a status adjudication in the absence of the domicile of either party in the forum. Because state courts are not required by comity to recognize foreign judgments, reticence on the part of some states to recognize bilateral foreign divorces may reflect the view expressed by some courts in other contexts that domicile is the *only* acceptable basis for the exercise of jurisdiction over status determinations, *see* Alton v. Alton, 207 F.2d 667 (3d Cir. 1953), *vacated as moot*, 347 U.S. 610 (1954): *contra* Wheat v. Wheat, 318 S.W.2d 793 (Ark. 1958) (domicile need not be the sole basis for divorce jurisdiction); or it may reflect other policy concerns, such as enforcement of the state's own restrictions on access to divorce, particularly when one or both parties were citizens of the state at the time of the divorce. Interestingly, however, New York, which has traditionally maintained one of the more restrictive legal regimes regarding access to divorce, was one of the first states to recognize bilateral foreign divorces, effectively sanctioning their use as a safety valve.

Support for recognition of bilateral foreign decrees can be found by analogy in a line of decisions of the U.S. Supreme Court interpreting the Full Faith and Credit Clause. In the context of domestic interstate recognition, the Court has held that if a defendant has appeared in the divorce proceeding, the judgment cannot later be collaterally attacked on the ground that neither party was a domiciliary of the forum state. Sherrer v. Sherrer, 334 U.S. 343 (1948); Coe v. Coe, 334 U.S. 378 (1948); Cook v. Cook 342 U.S. 126 (1951). The first judgment must be given full faith and credit. Because full faith and credit is inapplicable to the recognition of foreign decrees, these cases are not controlling. Moreover, the rationale behind them, that a defendant had the opportunity to litigate jurisdictional defects in the first suit, may be inapplicable to foreign proceedings, in which different jurisdictional standards are utilized by the foreign courts. *See* Scoles & Hay, *supra*, at 516–17. Nevertheless, when a defendant consents to the jurisdiction of a foreign court and appears therein, as in the type of bilateral foreign divorces described herein, support for recognition can be found by analogy to the *Sherrer* line of cases, and the policy they exemplify of "discouraging relitigation of marital issues when the parties made a mature choice and knowingly waived the protection available under U.S. law by participating in the foreign divorce." *Id.* at 521.

All U.S. states, however, including those which recognize bilateral foreign divorces, refuse to recognize unilateral *ex parte* divorces in which the defending party enters no appearance, when neither party is domiciled in the foreign forum issuing the divorce. *E.g.*, Blair v. Blair, 643 N.E.2d 933 (Ind. Ct. App. 1995); Carr v. Carr, 724 So. 2d 937 (Miss. Ct. App. 1998); Husein v. Husein, 2001 WL 842023 (Ohio App.); Jewell v. Jewel, 751 A.2d 735 (R.I. 2000).

    c. Mail Order Divorces. Even if both parties consent and cooperate by signing powers of attorney or similar documents in an attempt to obtain a divorce from a foreign jurisdiction in which neither is domiciled, a U.S. court will not recognize the divorce judgment if neither party physically appeared before the court, as the cases cited above in *Pringle* illustrate. *See* Scoles & Hayes, *supra,* at 522. Given that neither due process nor full faith and credit require the personal appearance of a party in a domestic consensual divorce in order for it to be recognized in another state, and given that bilateral foreign divorces are recognized in some states, what public policy grounds do you think underpin this wholesale rejection of "mail order divorces"? Is it justified?

3. *Other Grounds for Nonrecognition.* Courts have refused to recognize a foreign decree of divorce because the defendant in the foreign proceeding was not given timely notice. *E.g.,* Seewald v. Seewald, 22 P.3d 580 (Colo. Ct. App. 2001); Blair v. Blair, 643 N.E.2d 933 (Ind. Ct. App. 1995); Tal v. Tal, 601 N.Y.S.2d 530 (N.Y. Sup. Ct. 1993). Comity will also be denied, as recited in *Maklad,* if the foreign court lacks jurisdiction under its own standards.

Recognition has also been denied when one spouse was fraudulently coerced into signing documents, or otherwise defrauded by the circumstances in which the divorce was obtained. *E.g.,* Williams v. Williams, 1993 WL 331874 (Del. Fam. Ct.). Recently, a Connecticut court denied recognition to a divorce obtained in the Ukraine seventeen years previously on the ground that it was obtained to defraud, not the wife, but the state. Given the housing shortage in the Ukraine, the husband, with the wife's knowledge, obtained a divorce in order to be eligible for a separate apartment, as the family was living with the wife's relatives. After the divorce, the couple lived together another seventeen years as man and wife, eventually emigrating to the United States and becoming citizens, and continuously represented themselves in immigration and tax papers as married. Finding the divorce was procured by fraud, the court refused the husband's motion to dismiss the Connecticut divorce proceedings on the ground that the couple was already divorced. Gitelman v. Gitelman, No. FA0007 25844, 2001 WL 128927 (Conn. Super. Ct. Jan. 22, 2001).

A New York appellate court rejected a public policy defense to recognition of a Soviet decree based on similar circumstances, however, finding insufficient evidence to support the wife's contention that a divorce obtained eighteen years prior was a sham to ease the parties' efforts to emigrate. Gotlib v. Ratsutsky, 613 N.Y.S.2d 120 (N.Y. App. 1994). Unlike the *Gitelman* case, the spouses in *Gotlib* had not lived together continuously since the divorce and emigrated separately, and the plaintiff had never disclaimed the validity of the divorce until she instigated the New York divorce proceeding. Although the wife contended that the Soviet divorce should be disregarded on public policy grounds because it was the product of offensive Soviet policies that restricted the emigration of married Jews, the court noted that the emigration of the wife's married parents and siblings at the time the wife emigrated undermined her contention that her divorce was a product of such policies. Failure to recognize a divorce on the basis of vaguely asserted allegations, the court declared, "would substitute an amorphous and inadvisably open-ended escape valve" and undermine the "rare" public policy exception to the doctrine of comity. *Id.* at 122.

4. *Estoppel and Similar Doctrines.* Even a foreign divorce that is not entitled to legal recognition may under some circumstances have legal effect in U.S. courts under the doctrine of estoppel. According to a traditional definition of estoppel, an individual should be bound by his or her representations if others have relied thereon to their detriment. In the context of divorce recognition, the concept has been applied more broadly, to preclude a person from attacking the validity of a divorce in other circumstances in which it would be inequitable to permit the attack. The court in *Maklad* refers to this as the doctrine of practical recognition, although in other states this broader application is also referred to as quasi-estoppel or simply estoppel. What cir-

cumstances does the *Makald* court suggest might make it inequitable to give legal effect to an invalid divorce judgment? Do you think the court in *Maklad* was correct in finding that the Plaintiff's participation in the religious divorce was not a basis to invoke practical recognition? In reflecting on this, consider why Ms. Maklad was opposed to the recognition of the Egyptian divorce, when she also was seeking a divorce.

In *Pringle* a statute, V.I. Code Ann. tit. 15, §87(2) (1996), codified the doctrine of estoppel in a specific context. Do you think the court was correct in finding that Petitioner "procured" the divorce within the meaning of the statute? If so, was treating her as a non-spouse the equitable resolution of this estate proceeding in your opinion?

Estoppel has been recognized by many courts as a basis to prevent a spouse who obtained a foreign divorce from later attacking its validity. *E.g.,* Diehl v. U.S., 438 F.2d 705 (5th Cir. 1971) (wife who obtained Mexican divorce was estopped to assert its invalidity and thereby seek appointment as executrix of ex-husband's estate); Diamond v. Diamond, 461 A.2d 1227 (Pa. 1983) (husband was not entitled to an annulment of his second marriage on the basis that his mail-order divorce in his first marriage was invalid).

Estoppel can also be applied against a person who has accepted benefits under the decree, such as alimony, or otherwise taken advantage of the decree, such as by remarrying. In addition, the application of estoppel has been used to prevent a second spouse of an individual who terminated his or her first marriage through an invalid foreign divorce from asserting the invalidity of the prior divorce as a basis to annul the second marriage. When the second spouse instigated and financed his or her partner's first divorce, Mayer v. Mayer, 311 S.E.2d 659 (N.C. Ct. App. 1984), or even when he or she simply knows of the circumstances of the first divorce, and both partners marry and undertake marital obligations on the belief that the first divorce was valid, the second spouse cannot later rely upon the invalidity of the foreign divorce to avoid alimony obligations. Poor v. Poor, 409 N.E.2d 758 (Mass. 1980).

5. Jurisdiction of U.S. Courts to Divorce Foreign Nationals. A separate but related issue to recognition by U.S. courts is the question of when a U.S. court can exercise jurisdiction over the divorce of foreign nationals. Essentially, U.S. courts apply the same rules that are applicable to proceedings terminating the marriage of U.S. citizens, i.e., a U.S. court has jurisdiction to terminate marital status as long as one of the parties (1) is domiciled in the forum state, thus satisfying the *Williams v. North Carolina* due process standard, and (2) meets any other residency requirements imposed by the forum state's laws (typically residence for a period between 30 days to one year, the most common residency requirement being six months). Thus, the Supreme Court of Iowa in In re Marriage of Kimura, 471 N.W.2d 869 (1991), determined that an Iowa court could exercise jurisdiction over an action to dissolve the marriage of a Japanese citizen domiciled in Iowa with permanent resident status, even though his wife, also a Japanese citizen, had no contacts with Iowa. Because there was no basis for personal jurisdiction over the wife, however, the court recognized it had no jurisdiction to determine any of the financial issues.

Because Mr. Kimura had permanent resident status, he was entitled to live in the United States for as long as he desired, obtain employment on a permanent basis, and eventually apply for U.S. citizenship. Therefore, establishing his own domicile was not problematic. For foreign nationals who are not permanent residents, however, establishing domicile for purposes of divorce jurisdiction can be more difficult. Foreign nationals who enter the United States as nonimmigrants are required by U.S. immigration law to attest that they have no intention of abandoning their residence in their home country, and that they will return when the purpose for their visit is completed.

When the wife of a Korean student sought a divorce in Tennessee, her husband, a foreign student in Tennessee, objected on the ground that she could not establish domicile, and in particular, an intent to remain, since she had entered the United States on a nonimmigrant visa as the wife of a student. Observing that the clear weight of authority on this issue was that "the nonimmigrant status of 8 U.S.C. § 1101(a)(15)(F) is not a per se absolute bar to the acquisition of a new domicile in this country, but only one factor to be considered along with a myriad of other factors," the court found that aliens can have a dual intent, "an intent to remain if that may be accomplished and at the same time an intent to leave if the law so commands." Cho v. Jeong, 1997 WL 306017, at 5 (Tenn. Ct. App. 1997). Noting that the wife had lived in Tennessee for three years and desired to remain because of her fear that if she returned to Korea her husband's parents would immediately obtain custody of her son, the court found she was domiciled in Tennessee and jurisdiction over the divorce existed. *See also, e.g.,* Dick v. Dick, 18 Cal. Rptr.2d 743 (Cal. Ct. App. 1993) (husband's nonimmigrant status and entry on a tourist visa, even though he had not applied for permanent resident status, did not preclude his domicile in California, where he had lived as a continuous resident for six months, had a drivers license, and rented an apartment).

The Virginia Court of Appeals has taken a stricter view of domicile in one recent case, however. In Adoteye v. Adoteye, 527 S.E.2d 452 (Va. Ct. App. 2000), a Virginia appellate court affirmed a decision holding that a wife who had immigrated on a G-4 visa as an employee of the World Bank and who had resided in Virginia for over twelve years was not domiciled in Virginia, because she remained on a non-immigrant visa, with her right to remain dependent upon her continued employment. The court appeared to find it significant that she had taken no steps to secure an immigrant visa or citizenship, thus remaining exempt from the payment of state and federal income taxes. Nevertheless, in a subsequent decision, Hanano v. Alassar, No. 169004, 2001 WL 8763000 (Va. Cir. Ct. Jan. 23, 2001), a Virginia trial court determined that *Adoteye* indicates that an immigration status standing alone does not bar a claim of domicile, but is only one factor. Because Ms. Hanano, also living in the United States on a nonimmigrant visa, had taken preliminary steps to apply for a permanent visa and green card, the court denied her husband's plea for dismissal of the divorce action.

b. *Property Division and Alimony*

Dart v. Dart
579 N.W.2d 82 (Mich.1999)

Kelly, J.

We granted leave to determine whether the parties' English divorce judgment is entitled to full faith and credit under the principle of comity, and whether res judicata bars the action.[1]

We hold that principles of comity and res judicata mandate that the Darts' foreign divorce judgment be enforced. The English court decided the property distribution

---

1. We note that the lower courts considered whether the Uniform Foreign-Money Judgments Recognition Act (UFMJRA)…applied to the facts of this case. However, even if the UFMJRA did not apply, we can decide this issue under the general principle of comity…. We note, also, that the circuit court's jurisdiction was not raised as an issue in the Court of Appeals.

issue on the merits, and no evidence was presented showing that plaintiff Katina Dart was denied due process. We affirm the decision of the Court of Appeals.

I. Facts

Plaintiff and defendant were married in 1980 and were residents of Okemos, Michigan until 1993, when they moved to England. The couple owned a large house in Okemos, situated on thirty-nine acres of land, valued at $1,500,000. The parties had two children. The defendant is the son of the founder of Dart Container Corporation, one of the largest family-controlled businesses in the United States. The defendant's earned income for the years 1992, 1993, and 1994, was $313,009, $563,917, and $281,548, respectively. Between 1990 and 1993, the family's annual expenditures ranged from $300,000 to $600,000. The move to England made possible a September 1993 transfer of several hundred million dollars to the defendant from family trusts.

In 1974, before the marriage, the defendant's father established a trust for the benefit of defendant and his brother. For the transfer to occur, defendant had to renounce his United States citizenship and relocate outside the United States. The plaintiff refused to renounce her United States citizenship, and she also refused to renounce the citizenship of the children. She claims that, despite the relocation to London, England, she has always considered herself a resident and domiciliary of Okemos, Michigan.

In 1993, the parties jointly purchased a house near London for £2.75 million, and began renovations that took over a year to complete and cost another £3.5 million. They enrolled the children in the American School of London. Between 1993 and 1995, plaintiff asserts that she and the children made regular trips to Michigan for holidays, medical care, vacations, haircuts and other activities. Also, she maintained her Michigan driver's license and voted regularly in Michigan elections.

In September 1993, defendant received his distribution from the family trust which had a present, net value of £274 million (approximately $500,000,000). In the fall of 1994, plaintiff announced that she wanted a divorce. She revealed that what she had previously described to the defendant as a "one night stand" in 1989 had actually been a regular, adulterous affair with a man in Greece. The plaintiff asserted that she and defendant agreed to postpone the divorce action until she and the children returned to Michigan after the 1994–95 school year.

Despite the putative agreement, defendant filed for divorce in England on February 3, 1995. Plaintiff was served with process at the parties' home the following day. She contacted her American attorneys, and they filed a similar suit on her behalf in Michigan in the Ingham Circuit Court four days later. The parties remained in England until a consent order was entered in the English court on June 9, 1995, allowing plaintiff to return with the children to Michigan.

On March 21, 1995, in the Ingham Circuit Court, defendant moved for summary disposition...on the bases of lack of jurisdiction and pendency of a prior proceeding. Following a hearing, the circuit court determined that jurisdiction was proper in Michigan and assumed jurisdiction over the children and the divorce proceeding. The court reserved for future decision the issue of jurisdiction over the parties' property.

Plaintiff also brought a jurisdictional challenge. The English court ruled on June 13, 1995, that jurisdiction was proper in England. Defendant then asked the Ingham Circuit Court to defer jurisdiction to the English court on the basis of *forum non conveniens*. After a hearing on August 7, 1995, the circuit court denied the motion and assumed jurisdiction over the parties' property.

Both suits proceeded. On October 27, 1995, a "decree absolute" of divorce was entered in the English court. This was followed by a seven-day trial in March 1996 in which plaintiff filed an answer claiming the "full range of financial ancillary relief available to a wife under the Matrimonial Causes Act [of] 1973."

Both sides presented expert witnesses who testified regarding the parties' assets and plaintiff's reasonable needs. On March 21, 1996, the English court issued a lengthy opinion in which it determined defendant's total net worth to be "about £400 million.

The court ruled that the reasonable needs or requirements of plaintiff, in light of her predivorce lifestyle and habits and the available assets, entitled her to £300,000 ($450,000) a year for life. However, the court held that, "In seeking to achieve justice [the court is] not limited to the reasonable annual expenditure of the wife...or to such other matters...described as constituting her 'reasonable requirements.' "

The court awarded the plaintiff a lump sum of £9 million ($13,500,000), the amount it felt necessary to achieve an equitable distribution. The plaintiff was also awarded the house in Okemos, Michigan, and its contents, that the parties agreed were worth approximately $1.5 million. She was awarded four paintings and her jewelry. The court also set child support in the amount of $95,400 a year for both children.

Defendant was awarded four automobiles and the balance of the marital estate. The English court expressly found that plaintiff was not entitled to a substantial share of defendant's family wealth. It was not a product of the marriage and had not been generated by the efforts of either party.

On March 29, 1996, defendant moved to stay or dismiss the Ingham Circuit Court proceedings, arguing that the English judgment was entitled to enforcement under the principle of comity and under the Uniform Foreign Money-Judgments Recognition Act.... At the hearing on April 8, 1996, he urged, also, that the present action was barred by res judicata.

The circuit court judge denied the motion, finding that the English judgment was not entitled to recognition under the UFMJRA or the principle of comity. He reasoned that the English system of law was repugnant to the public policy of Michigan, and the English decision violated plaintiff's "right to have a fair and equitable distribution of property...."

On appeal, in a per curium opinion, the Court of Appeals reversed, concluding that the "entire judgment, including the property division as well as the child support and lump-sum awards," should be enforced under the UFMJRA....

With regard to whether the English law was repugnant to our public policy, the Court of Appeals explained:

> [I]t cannot reasonably be argued that plaintiff was denied due process because she was represented by counsel, given an opportunity to be heard, and presented evidence on her own behalf. Although the circuit court opined that the English judge was not impartial, a review of the lengthy opinion of the English judge fails to support a finding of bias. Further, had the issue of fault been raised, it would not have benefited plaintiff, who admitted that her continuing infidelity was the cause of the marital breakdown. Consequently, no evidence that plaintiff was prejudiced by an unfair tribunal or proceeding is present....
>
> While the Ingham circuit judge might have awarded plaintiff more of the marital estate than did the English judge, that fact alone does not render the

English judgment repugnant to the public policy of the state where the children are adequately provided for and the plaintiff has the means to maintain a lifestyle similar to the one she enjoyed throughout the greater part of the marriage....

The Court of Appeals also concluded that comity mandated that the English judgment be respected. Plaintiff had a fair hearing on the merits at which she was present, represented by counsel, and actively participated. Thus, she was accorded due process.

Finally, the Court of Appeals reasoned that res judicata barred the case from being relitigated because the English court had considered the property, alimony, and child support claims and issued a final order. The English court did not consider child custody or visitation. These issues were within the purview of the Ingham Circuit Court under the Uniform Child Custody Jurisdiction Act....

* * *

II. Analysis

The Court of Appeals correctly held that comity dictated that the judgment should be enforced because the plaintiff was accorded due process. Since the English judgment adjudicated the property issue, the plaintiff is barred from relitigating that issue under res judicata.

Comity is defined as the recognition which one nation allows within its territory to the legislative, executive, or judicial acts of another nation, having due regard both to international duty and convenience and to the rights of its own citizens or of other persons who are under the protection of its laws....

Comity mandates that this foreign judgment be given force and effect. The seminal United States Supreme Court case of Hilton v. Guyot, [159 U.S. 113 (1895)] set forth the factors that the federal courts use in recognizing and giving full effect to the judgment of foreign countries under comity:

> Where there has been opportunity for a full and fair trial abroad before a court of competent jurisdiction, conducting the trial upon regular proceedings, after due citation or voluntary appearance of the defendant, and under a system of jurisprudence likely to secure an impartial administration of justice between the citizens of its own country and those of other countries, and there is nothing to show either prejudice in the court or in the system of laws under which it was sitting, or fraud in procuring the judgment, or any other special reason why the comity of this nation should not allow it full effect, the merits of the case should not, in an action brought in this country upon the judgment, be tried afresh, as on a new trial or an appeal, upon the mere assertion of the party that the judgment was erroneous in law or in fact.

* * *

Here, both parties participated and were represented by counsel in the English court proceedings. Plaintiff initially challenged jurisdiction in the English court. She asserted that defendant had not been "habitually" a resident of England for twelve months. Justice Johnson of the Family Division of the High Court of Justice ruled in defendant's favor, concluding that England was his main home and that he intended to stay there.

Plaintiff argues that the English judgment should not be enforced because defendant was not domiciled in England. We find this argument unpersuasive.... [I]n the present case, the record does not reflect that defendant moved to England for the purpose of obtaining a divorce. Rather, he moved to England to receive a disbursement from his family's trust.

The English court heard evidence pertaining to the value of the Dart Container Corporation, as well as defendant's salary and other real and personal property. It heard evidence regarding plaintiff's nonmonetary contributions to the marriage as well. It considered the home in Michigan, paintings, jewelry, and cars.

The parties agree that the factors that the English courts examine when dividing property are substantially the same as those used in Michigan. In Sparks v. Sparks, [485 N.W.2d 893 (Mich. 1992)], this Court set forth the appropriate factors to consider in the division of marital property:

> (1) duration of the marriage, (2) contributions of the parties to the marital estate, (3) age of the parties, (4) health of the parties, (5) life status of the parties, (6) necessities and circumstances of the parties, (7) earning abilities of the parties, (8) past relations and conduct of the parties, and (9) general principles of equity....

Section 25 of the Matrimonial Causes Act requires that an English court consider nearly identical factors in dividing marital property.

Plaintiff argues that English courts apply a different rationale in cases involving large assets. In her brief, she asserts that the English court principally examined her financial needs to determine the appropriate award, not the marital assets.

In Preston v. Preston, [1981 2 FLR 331], the English court announced a formula to be applied in cases in which the available resources are large. *Preston* established that there is a maximum sum to be awarded. This so-called "*Preston* ceiling" limits the award to an amount that satisfies the court's estimation of a wife's needs for support....

Had the English court actually used this formulation to divide the parties' marital assets, we might agree with plaintiff that she was denied due process. However, the English court did not use the *Preston* ceiling. Instead, it determined that the defendant's holdings and trust income were not marital property. Justice Johnson explained:

> [I]f you had a case where the husband and wife together built up a vast property empire, I see no reason why the wife's contribution should not entitle her to 50%. There is said to be a distinction between the wife whose contribution was child care and the wife who actually worked in the business, doing the books or whatever, it was. If Mr. and Mrs. Dart had started with nothing and in a back street somewhere in Detroit they had started making plastic objects and over the period of 20 or 30 years they had [ended] up with an empire worth £1,000 million, I would see every reason for Mrs. Dart having half of it. Personally, I do not have any difficulty with that. Whether the English law permits it or not is another matter, but that is not this case.

Normally, property received by a married party as an inheritance, but kept separate from marital property, is deemed to be separate property not subject to distribution. Lee v. Lee,...477 N.W.2d 429 (Mich.1991). The trust income from the Dart Container Corporation was never marital property. Although the defendant worked for Dart Container Corporation during the marriage, his compensation was the salary and bonuses that he earned. His cumulative salary and bonuses over the course of the marriage were far less than the $14.5 million property award that plaintiff received.

The Dart fortune and defendant's interest in it exist independently of defendant's workplace activities or the marriage partnership. Thus, the English court's treatment of defendant's interests in the Dart family trusts and assets as separate property, rather than marital assets, did not violate plaintiff's right to due process.

Moreover, plaintiff's assertion that the English court failed to consider marital property is flawed. The English judgment awarded her the $1.5 million house in Okemos, some paintings, and a car. It also awarded child support in the amount of more than $90,000 a year. Certainly, the English court could not have divided these marital assets had there been no discovery. We find that the plaintiff was accorded due process in the English proceeding.

Consequently, res judicata bars the plaintiff from relitigating the property distribution issue. The English court decided this issue on the merits. Res judicata bars a subsequent action between the same parties when the evidence or essential facts are identical.... A second action is barred when (1) the first action was decided on the merits, (2) the matter contested in the second action was or could have been resolved in the first, and (3) both actions involve the same parties or their privies....

* * *

Here, the Michigan divorce action involves the same parties with the same assets and the same children as the English action. We have already determined under our comity analysis that the English judgment is valid. The fact that it does not address custody or visitation is not fatal to its preclusive effect with respect to property distribution. The Ingham Circuit Court has jurisdiction over the questions of custody and visitation, pursuant to the Uniform Child Custody Jurisdiction Act.... Accordingly, res judicata bars relitigation of the present action.

III. Conclusion

We affirm the Court of Appeals decision to give deference to the English divorce judgment under the principle of comity. It was evident from the judgment rendered in England that plaintiff had a fair hearing on the merits, that she was present, represented by counsel, and actively participated. Thus, the present action is barred by res judicata.

Cavanagh, J. (*dissenting*).

I must part company with the majority on the deference shown to the English Court's judgment. While I agree with Justice Kelly that the English Court did not apply the *Preston* "ceiling" rule in this case, but rather steered away from such a ruling to find the bulk of defendant's assets to be nonmarital property, I am unpersuaded that such a finding removes the English decision from the looming shadow of *Preston*.

As even the majority tacitly admits, the application of the *Preston* rule in a case such as this (or in any case for that matter) would likely raise serious due process concerns. The mere existence of such a rule, and the apparent statutory basis for the rule cited by Lord Justice Ormrod in adopting it, suggests that, at least in cases in which substantial assets are involved, the goals of the English judicial system in marital dissolution cases differ substantially from the framework of our state.... Where plaintiff was in the exact position necessary for her to suffer the ill effects not only of the *Preston* rule, but also the underlying statutory and judicial rationales for it, I cannot say, particularly in view of the asset division undertaken by the English Court, that she escaped unscathed by the effects of the adverse predispositions demonstrated.

In reaching this conclusion, it is necessary to consider, given the majority's reliance on the determination of the trust assets as nonmarital in nature, what sort of effect would have occurred had Justice Johnson of the English Court found the entire amount of disputed property (including the trust assets) to consist of marital assets. While the justice postulated he personally would not have had difficulty awarding plaintiff half the assets in such a case, he also noted that whether that would be permitted under law was another matter. Indeed, the *Preston* rule would appear to dictate that, regardless of his decision, plaintiff, from the beginning of the English case, was predestined to receive only a fraction of the disputed assets, regardless of the determinations of the Court on whatever substantive issues there might have been (including the marital property issue). It is difficult to give due process credence to a system in which the result would remain adverse to the plaintiff whether or not she prevailed on the point the majority determines the case should be decided upon.

Accordingly, while not, in large part, disputing the authorities cited by the majority as a general matter, I am nonetheless convinced that the operation of the English system of marital asset division in cases involving substantial assets reflects considerations very different from our own, and that such considerations cast a shadow on the decision sufficient to preclude Michigan courts, with our well-established criteria for property distribution in divorce cases, from recognizing a decision that is not only from another land, but truly foreign to the concepts underlying Michigan law. Accordingly, I respectfully dissent from the Court's decision.

Brickley, J concurs with Cavenaugh, J.

Notes and Questions

1. *Grounds for Nonrecognition—Jurisdiction.* Although the U.S. Supreme Court in *Williams v. North Carolina* determined that due process requires only that one of the spouses be domiciled in the forum state in order for a court to adjudicate marital status, adjudication of the financial issues related to a divorce proceeding—property division, alimony, child support, and attorney fee awards—requires more. One of the traditional bases for the exercise of personal jurisdiction over a defendant—service on the defendant within the forum, consent of the defendant to the court's jurisdiction, defendant's domicile in the forum, or minimum contacts of the defendant with the forum—is necessary in order for the court to resolve the financial issues within the requirements of due process. Kulko v. Superior Court of Cal., 436 U.S. 84 (1976). Thus, U.S. courts will not extend comity to recognize or enforce the financial awards of foreign courts in matrimonial actions if the defendant in the foreign action did not have a nexus with the foreign court sufficient for that court to exercise personal jurisdiction over the defendant on a ground that would satisfy U.S. standards of due process. To do otherwise, the courts suggest, would violate public policy. This principle is illustrated in the context of a child support enforcement proceeding in the case of *Country of Luxembourg v. Canderas,* which is set forth in Chapter Ten.

In Dart, did the English court have a basis to exercise personal jurisdiction over Ms. Dart according to one of these traditional bases for in personam jurisdiction? If so, what jurisdictional argument was she trying to assert?

2. *Differing Substantive Standards.* At what point should differences in substantive law standards constitute a basis to deny comity? That is the central question raised by *Dart.* The Michigan trial judge and the dissenting justices on the Michigan Supreme Court felt comity should be denied because the English substantive law for property division in cases involving substantial resources differed from the Michigan property division standards to such an extent that the English law was repugnant to the public pol-

icy of Michigan and due process. The Michigan intermediate appellate court and the majority of the justices on the Michigan Supreme Court determined that the English decision was entitled to recognition because the English court did not actually apply the *Preston* rule, although the majority observed that had the English court applied the *Preston* rule, they might have agreed that the decision should not be recognized. Do you agree?

In reflecting upon this issue, some understanding of the principles underlying financial distribution by English courts is useful. Unlike most U.S. state divorce regimes, which provide for equitable division of marital property and then award support alimony to a financially dependent spouse, if necessary, the English system does not make a distinction between alimony and property division. English judges are directed to "order one spouse to make 'financial provision' for the other by way of periodical payments, a lump sum, a transfer or settlement of property, or various combinations of these devices," and are given very broad discretion about how this is to be accomplished. Mary Ann Glendon, The Transformation of Family Law 199 (1989). The list of statutory factors to be considered, as the Michigan court noted, is very similar to those considered by most American courts, and expressly provides that in considering contributions of the spouses, homemaking as well as financial contributions are to be considered. *Id.* at 200. In making financial arrangements, courts are also directed to first consider the welfare of the children. English courts are also directed by statute to promote a clean break and self-sufficiency, if possible, by making periodic orders, if made at all, of a limited duration only, when that would not adversely impact the children. *Id.* at 202–04. The clean break concept is also codified in some U.S. states that have adopted the Uniform Marriage and Divorce Act, although in recent decades courts have been applying it less stringently to marriages of long duration.

The genesis of the significant difference between the English financial provision principles at the time of *Dart* and those of Michigan and other American jurisdictions is found not so much in English statutory provisions, however, as in the common law principles that guided English courts. Although only a handful of American states are required to equally divide marital property between the spouses (currently three community property states), most American courts use equal division as either a presumption or a starting point and then make adjustments on the basis of other factors such as contribution of the spouses and need. The majority of American jurisdictions equitably divide only marital property, i.e., property acquired during the marriage through the effort of either spouse rather than through gift or inheritance, although some states (not Michigan) are "hotchpot" states whose courts are empowered to equitably divide all property. At the time of the *Dart* case, English courts were directed by common law precedent to distribute assets in such a way as to meet the reasonable needs of each spouse, taking into account the standard of living enjoyed during the marriage. *Preston* created a formula for estimating the wife's needs for support in cases where there were significant resources. In application, this resulted in courts determining the reasonable needs of the wife, and leaving the bulk of a large marital estate with the husband. For more detail regarding this system, *see* Kary Burkholder, *Darting to England, A Comparison of the United States' and England's Divorce Laws,* 13 Temple Int'l & Comp. L J. 163 (1999).

In July 2000, the British House of Lords issued a decision in White v. White, (2000) 2 FLR 981, which significantly transformed the guidelines for financial provision in an English divorce. Rejecting the focus on reasonable requirements that the Court had utilized in *Dart*, the House of Lords directed instead that equality should become the starting point. Although the Court specified that equality was not a presumption, English courts were nevertheless directed to depart from equality only if there was good reason to do so. Financial needs were no longer to be determinative, but merely one of a number of factors, including the contribution of the parties, that were to be taken into account.

3. *Recognition and Enforcement of Spousal Support Orders.* Although the doctrine of comity is applicable to the enforcement of foreign alimony orders, many such orders will also be enforceable under the 1996 Uniform Interstate Family Support Act (1996 UIFSA), which has been enacted in all fifty U.S. states. In general, UIFSA applies to support orders issued by nations that would afford American orders reciprocity. UIFSA §§ 101. UIFSA provides various procedural and evidentiary advantages, UIFSA §§ 313–316, and requires states to recognize and enforce support orders that are covered by the Act. UIFSA §§ 501–610. Amendments to UIFSA promulgated by the National Conference of Commissioners on Uniform State Laws (NCCUSL) in 2001 are likely to gradually be incorporated into the law by most states in future years, and will further facilitate enforcement of foreign orders.

Although under U.S. law alimony orders are modifiable, UIFSA permits modification of alimony orders only by the jurisdiction in which the order was issued. Therefore, foreign spousal support orders to which UIFSA applies could not be modified by U.S. courts, nor would U.S. courts recognizes modification of their own alimony orders by other courts. UIFSA § 205 (f). In UIFSA enforcement proceedings, U.S. tribunals are required to apply the law of the nation that issued the order regarding the nature, extent, amount and duration of current payments and arrearages. In addition, when enforcing arrearages, UIFSA requires the enforcing court to use the statute of limitations of either the enforcing forum or the issuing nation, whichever is longer. UIFSA § 604. UIFSA is covered in detail in Chapter Ten, Section B, which addresses the issuance and enforcement of child support orders. Much of the material included in that section, however, is relevant to the enforcement of spousal support orders as well.

Each U.S. state has a governmental entity designated as the state IV-D agency, which is required by federal law to provide child support assistance at little or no cost. Although these agencies are not mandated to provide assistance with the collection of alimony, some will in fact provide such services to citizens of foreign nations, as well as to U.S. citizens. See Chapter Ten, Section A for additional information about these agencies.

2. Divorce Recognition under Foreign and International Law

Lynn Wardle, International Marriage and Divorce Regulation and Recognition: A Survey
29 Fam. L. Q. 497, 512–15 (1995)

* * *

The law of the forum (*lex fori*) appears to be the predominant choice of law rule in divorce cases. It appears to be strongly favored in Anglo-American legal systems. The potential for sharp conflict in a sensitive area of sovereign policy is avoided by this rule, and certainty and predictability enhanced, at the cost of some flexibility and fairness. The next most common choice of law rule is to apply the law of the domicile of the parties; reference to the law of nationality was once popular in continental Europe, but that appears to be waning in the advance of domicile in choice of law regarding personal status.

The court rendering the divorce must have had jurisdiction to adjudicate the divorce proceeding. "The domicile or the habitual residence of the parties is almost universally accepted as a basis for assuming jurisdiction in divorce and legal separation." [Lennart Poalsson, *Marriage and Divorce*, in 3(16) Private International Law, International Encyclopedia of Comparative Law 106 (1978).] However, beyond the broad statement of a general rule, there are vast differences in detail and application of the domicile rule. For instance, there are differences concerning whether the domicile of both parties is required, or the conjugal domicile, or the domicile of either of them, or of only one of them (historically the husband). And both nationality and law of the place of marriage celebration are logical, if rare, alternative bases for divorce jurisdiction.

Overall, the articles in the symposium suggest a trend toward recognition of the foreign divorce if it was valid under the laws of the place it was rendered, or the law of the parties' domicile or nationality. This is qualified in some states, however, by the requirement that the divorce was rendered by a judicial tribunal (some countries are hesitant to recognize nonjudicial divorces) that had a reasonable basis for jurisdiction (typically domicile or nationality), that accorded the parties basic procedural fairness (notice to all parties of the proceedings, and opportunity to participate), and that the ground for the divorce did not violate very strong public policy of the forum.

The Hague Conference on Private International Law has twice promulgated conventions dealing with divorce recognition, which affects marriage recognition (at least remarriageability). The first, adopted in 1902, was ratified by only eleven European states, three of whom subsequently withdrew. In 1969, a replacement Convention on the Recognition of Divorces and Legal Separations ("Hague Convention on Divorce") was promulgated. It applies *lex divortium*—the law of the place of divorce or separation (called "the State of origin")—to determine the effect of divorce or separation decrees (Art. 1), if that state had jurisdiction by reason of nationality, habitual residence, or domicile (Arts. 2, 3). Recognition may be denied if it is manifestly incompatible with the public policy of the state in which recognition is sought (Art. 10), or if both parties were nationals of a state which did not provide for divorce. [As of March 2003, eighteen] nations have ratified or acceded to this Convention.

* * *

The current status of marriage and divorce regulation and recognition law provides a powerful perspective on relations between church and state. Traditionally, the regulation of marriage and divorce often came within the jurisdiction of the religion(s) dominant in an area. The state largely deferred to religious marriage and divorce initiatives and rules. That, however, created problems of efficiency for the state as it had to address issues of foreign marriage recognition, which fell within its jurisdiction. The deregulation of marriage and divorce means fewer problems for the state, and clearly manifests a trend toward declining religious influence in marriage regulation, and greater dominance of state over church in relative influence in society—worldwide.

This review presents only a broad overview. Perhaps it is appropriate to conclude with an observation that the generalities of this survey conceal as much as they reveal in terms of qualifications, exceptions, and variations from the general rules....

Since Professor Wardle published his article, the European Union has issued Council Regulation No. 1347/2000, which legislates standards for jurisdiction and enforcement of judgments in divorce, legal separation, and annulment proceedings that are now binding law on all members states of the European Union except Denmark, which exercised its right to decline to participate under a Protocol annexed to the Treaty on European Union. Pursuant to the regulation, jurisdiction over matters related to divorce, legal separation, or annulment must be based on (1) the habitual residence of both spouses, or of one spouse if specified conditions are met, or (2) on the nationality of both spouses, or in the United Kingdom and Ireland, the domicile of both spouses. (Article 1). Member states are required to recognize each other's judgments relating to divorce, separation, or annulment, unless the recognition would be manifestly contrary to the public policy of the recognizing nation, the defendant in the first action was not properly served, or an earlier judgment entitled to recognition was entered. (Articles 14, 15). Member nations are not permitted to refuse recognition because the law of the recognizing nation would not allow divorce, separation, or annulment on the same facts. (Article 18). Between member nations, this regulation takes precedence over other relevant Hague Conventions. (Article 37).

A new Council Regulation is currently under consideration that would repeal Regulation No. 1347/2000 and incorporate its present terms into a broader regulation that would create a single instrument addressing jurisdiction over both divorce and parental responsibility proceedings. *See* European Commission, *Explanatory Memorandum, in* Proposal for a Council Regulation, COM (2202) 222 final/2, *available at* http://europa.eu.int/eur-lex/en/search/search_lip.html. For further discussion of this proposal, see Chapter Eight, Section B.2.c. ii(b).

In addition to the Hague Conventions described by Professor Wardle and the E.U. Council Regulation, all of which specifically address recognition of divorce judgments, there are also a number of global and regional conventions that address the transnational creation and enforcement of support orders, which include orders for spousal support as well as child support. Among these conventions are the New York Convention on Recovery Abroad of Maintenance, the 1973 Hague Convention on the Recognition and Enforcement of Decisions Related to Maintenance Obligations, the 1973 Hague Convention on the Law Applicable to Maintenance Obligations, the Inter-American Convention on Support Obligations, and European Union Council Regulation No. 44/2001, all of which are described in some detail in Chapter Ten, Section D. Currently the United States is not a party to any of these instruments.

The Hague Conference also has produced a Convention on the Law Applicable to Matrimonial Property Regimes. Although the Convention entered into force in 1992, as of March 2003, only three nations were parties: France, Luxembourg, and the Netherlands. Under the Convention's terms, the matrimonial property distribution would be governed first by the internal law designated by the spouses, subject to certain restrictions; or, if no designation was made, then by the law of the nation in which the spouses establish habitual residence or in which they are nationals, depending upon the circumstances.

Problems

5-1. Amgad and Fatima marry in Tunisia when they are each fifteen years of age. Assume that in Tunisia the minimum age for marriage is twelve for males and nine for females. At seventeen years of age, they immigrate to the United States, along with Amgad's parents, to live and work in North Carolina. After nine months, Fatima leaves Amgad and moves to a shelter. With the assistance of shelter staff, she files for divorce, seeking spousal support. The couple have no children and Fatima has never been pregnant.

In his answer to her petition, Amgad denies that the marriage is valid, because North Carolina law establishes eighteen as the minimum age for marriage. The North Carolina statute also permits men and women to marry with parental consent between the ages of sixteen and eighteen, and further provides: "Every person under the age of sixteen years is expressly forbidden and prohibited from entering into the marriage relation, and any marriage entered in violation of this provision is void." Judges in North Carolina are permitted, however, to authorize marriages of individuals under the age of sixteen if the prospective wife is pregnant. No criminal penalties are established by North Carolina law for attempting to marry at an earlier age, but a marriage license would not be issued to anyone whom the registrar knows to be under the statutory minimum age. What arguments would you make as counsel for Fatima that the marriage is valid? What arguments would you make as counsel for Amgad that the marriage is invalid? As judge, how would you rule?

5-2. Assume the marriage between Amgad and Fatima occurred in Tunisia, as recited above, except that Amgad was twenty-two years of age at the time of their marriage, and Fatima was twelve years of age at the time of marriage. They immigrated to North Carolina from Tunisia when Fatima was fifteen, and she moved out when she was sixteen. She moved in with a cousin, and had no resources to file for divorce. When she was eighteen, she married Robert and became pregnant shortly thereafter. Amgad learns of the marriage, and persuades the local prosecuting attorney to charge Fatima with bigamy. As defense counsel for Fatima arguing that the first marriage should be given no legal effect, what arguments would you make? As prosecuting attorney, what arguments would you make? As judge, how would you rule?

5-3. Eva and Sven were raised in Kansas. Although they have the same father, they have different mothers, and were raised in separate households with little contact. When they were ages nineteen and twenty-one, respectively, they fell in love. They decided to travel to Sweden for a year of study abroad, and to renew acquaintances with extended family who lived there. While in Sweden, they married. Half-siblings are permitted to marry under Swedish law with permission of the court, which they obtained. Three years after they returned to Kansas, Eva was killed in a car accident. Sven brought a wrongful death action against the driver of the other vehicle, who defended the action on the ground that Sven was not Eva's lawful husband, and therefore had no claim for loss of consortium. Assume that Kansas' consanguinity statute prohibits marriages between brothers and sisters of the half as well as the whole blood, and declares them to be incestuous, illegal, and void. What arguments would you make, respectively, as plaintiff's counsel and defendant's counsel? How would you rule as judge?

5-4. Tony and Maria, residents of New Jersey, fell in love and decided to elope to Italy, to be married in the small city where they would attend a graduate program in art for the upcoming year. At a large wedding attended by both families and many friends, they were married by a priest, and they met all of the capacity requirements for marriage under Italian law. However, in their haste, they posted notice of the marriage at City Hall for only six days prior to the marriage instead of the eight days required by Italian law. Following their year of study, they returned to New Jersey and had a child. Three years later, Tony was killed in a boating accident. As he died without a will, Maria filed an application to be named administrator of the estate, and to claim a statutory share of the estate as the surviving spouse. Her appointment and share were challenged by Tony's sister, Elva, who was aware of the posting requirement, and who asserted that Maria was not Tony's legal spouse. As judge, what law must you consider? How do you think the case will likely be resolved?

5-5. Anneke and Sonja fell in love in the Netherlands, where Anneke, a Dutch citizen, worked for a travel agent and Sonja was studying in a year-abroad program affiliated with Vermont Law School. After marrying, they returned to Vermont, so that Sonya could finish her degree. Four years later, by artificial insemination, Anneke gave birth to a child, whom Sonya formally adopted. Thereafter, Anneke worked only part-time, while Sonya contributed the major share of the family's support through her employment as a state prosecutor. Ten years after their marriage, while still living in Vermont, Sonya was killed in an explosion at the courthouse where she worked. Anneke applied for federal Social Security benefits as a surviving spouse, in addition to applying for benefits for their child. She also applied for a lump sum death benefit available to surviving spouses of state employees under state law. Both of the applications for spousal benefits were refused on the ground that she and Sonja were both women. In addition, the state argued that they had never entered a civil union in Vermont. As Sonja's lawyer representing her in litigation on both claims, what arguments would you make on her behalf? What arguments do you anticipate from opposing counsel? What are your chances for success on either claim?

5-6. Benjiro and Fumi, both Japanese citizens, met and married while living and working as professors at the University of Michigan. Both were permanent residents of the United States at the time. Two year after their marriage, they planned a summer trip home to see family between academic terms. By the time that they left Michigan, however, their relationship had deteriorated. While in Japan, they divorced by agreement. Their divorce was valid under the law of Japan. They returned to Michigan in the fall and lived separately thereafter.

Two years later, Fumi met and married Paul, another professor who had recently joined her department. Paul and Benjiro became acquainted through various faculty activities, and Paul was aware of Fumi's former marriage to Benjiro and the circumstances under which it was terminated. Benjiro married Joan a year after his divorce from Fumi, but the marriage was short-lived, and he and Joan divorced within six months.

Three years after her marriage to Paul, Fumi and Paul separated. If Fumi wished to annul her marriage to Paul, on the ground that her first divorce was invalid, would she be likely to be successful? If Paul wished to annul the marriage with Fumi on the ground that her first divorce was invalid, would he be likely to be successful? If Fumi died before any legal proceeding was filed regarding her marital status with Paul, and Paul and Benjiro both asserted a right to insurance benefits as her surviving spouse (assume no beneficiary had been named), which one would be more likely to succeed with his claim?

5-7. Kenji and Kaya, both citizens of Japan, met and married in Korea while employed there by a Japanese corporation. Six years later, they divorced in Japan by agreement while on a six-week trip home to visit their extended families. Their divorce was valid under the law of Japan. They returned to Korea separately and lived apart thereafter.

Three years later, Kaya was transferred to Chicago, where she subsequently married Nick and became a U.S. citizen. They had three children. After six years of marriage, Kaya filed for divorce in Illinois. Nick learned in discovery about Kaya's first marriage, and the circumstances of her divorce. He subsequently amended his petition to seek an annulment, in the hopes of avoiding alimony. Is he likely to be successful in convincing the Illinois court to annul his marriage with Kaya?

5-8. After an unhappy three-year marriage, Brenda and Jack met new loves and decided they would like a swift dissolution of their marriage in order to pursue their new relationships. Because neither wished to fabricate fault grounds, nor did they wish to wait for a year of separation, they decided to travel to Haiti to obtain a divorce. Jack and Brenda appeared personally before the court and obtained a divorce, and then both returned to New York. Brenda remarried quickly. Tragically, her new husband, Tom, was killed in a bus accident six years later. In an action against the bus company for wrongful death, the bus company defended against her claim for loss of consortium on the ground that she was not Tom's lawful spouse. What arguments would counsel for plaintiff and defendant be likely to make, and which side would be likely to prevail in a New York court? Would that same outcome be likely in all other U.S. courts?

5-9. Assume that instead of traveling to Haiti, Brenda and Jack had signed powers of attorney, each agreeing to permit separate attorneys in Haiti to appear on their behalf in the divorce proceeding. Assume also that this would create a valid divorce in Haiti. If the other facts in Problem 5-7 remained the same, what arguments would counsel for each side make, and what would be the likely outcome of the lawsuit in New York and in other U.S. state courts?

5-10. Rebecca and Herzel immigrated from Israel to New York, where they had four children and became permanent residents of the United States. Ten years later, when their marriage was deteriorating, Rebecca, who read or spoke little English, signed a separation agreement in which she waived all right to support and agreed to a split of property that left her with only an old car and $10,000. Shortly thereafter, she fled the marital home to live with relatives, escaping physical and mental abuse. The parties obtained a get in New York from a Rabbinical Court. Shortly thereafter, Herzel traveled to Israel to obtain a formal decree of divorce from the Tel Aviv Rabbinical Court, which incorporated the terms of the separation agreement that they had signed in New York. Rebecca was never notified of or served in the Israeli divorce proceeding. Two months after Herzel's return, Rebecca filed a divorce proceeding in New York, seeking alimony. Herzel sought dismissal of the proceeding (except for the custody claim, which the court dealt with separately and is not in issue herein), relying upon the Israeli divorce. What arguments would counsel for Rebecca and Herzel be likely to make, and what do you think would be the likely outcome in a New York court?

5-11. Four years after Cho and Jeong married in Korea, Jeong came to the United States on a non-immigrant student visa. Cho remained in Korea with family, as the relationship between the two was strained by this point. Two years later, Jeong filed for divorce in Ohio, where he had been attending school. At that point, Jeong had applied for an extension of his visa to attend a post-doctoral program, and he hoped to obtain a teaching position after that program, which would enable him to apply for permanent resident status. Cho, with the help of her family, hired a lawyer to seek dismissal of the Ohio proceeding. What arguments would counsel for Cho and Jeong be likely to make? What do you think would be the likely outcome in the Ohio court?

Chapter 6

Violence between Family Members

A. Violence and Context

Violence against women is ubiquitous around the world.

> Violence against women and girls continues to be a global epidemic that kills, tortures, and maims—physically, psychologically, sexually and economically. It is one of the most pervasive of human rights violations, denying women and girls equality, security, dignity, self-worth, and their right to enjoy fundamental freedoms.
>
> Violence against women is present in every country, cutting across boundaries of culture, class, education, income, ethnicity and age. Even though most societies proscribe violence against women, the reality is that violations against women's human rights are often sanctioned under the garb of cultural practices and norms, or through misinterpretation of religious tenets. Moreover, when the violation takes place within the home, as is very often the case, the abuse is effectively condoned by the tacit silence and the passivity displayed by the state and the law-enforcing machinery.
>
> The global dimensions of this violence are alarming, as highlighted by studies on the incidence and prevalence of violence. No society can claim to be free of such violence, the only variation is in the patterns and trends that exist in countries and regions....
>
> While reliable statistics are hard to come by, studies estimate that from country to country, between 20 and 50 per cent of women have experienced physical violence at the hands of an intimate partner or family member.

U.N. Children's Fund, *Domestic Violence Against Women and Girls*, 6 Innocenti Digest 2 (2000).

The topic of domestic violence raises two related issues at the outset. First, does the type of violence involved make a difference to the legal or policy discussion? Perhaps one can consider as a monolith all of the violence committed against women and girls by family members. Alternatively, perhaps one needs to consider each type of violence separately either because the practice is not "violence" in its cultural context or because it is not comparable to other types of violence. Or perhaps the violence should not be equated in order to facilitate achieving a particular legal objective. Simply put, it might or might not matter if one is talking about husband-on-wife hitting, marital rape, female genital mutilation, bride-burning, foot binding, honor-killing, or female infanticide. Second, can the violence be decontextualized from the status of women generally in the society? To varying degrees, women around the world encounter many oppressive practices, including restrictions on voting, citizenship, and holding political office. In some countries, marked discrimination exists between men and women in such areas as marriage, child custody, property ownership, travel, employment opportunities, educational opportunities, and medical care. Can one meaningfully look at the issue of violence without considering these other issues?

Your answer to the first question (whether the type of violence involved makes a difference to the legal or policy discussion) may emerge as you read the material in this chapter. Your analysis may be influenced in part by your position in the debate between cultural relativists and those who claim human rights are universal, or by your willingness to disaggregate the violence for instrumental purposes. However, your answer to the second question (whether violence can be decontextualized from women's status in society generally) requires study that extends beyond the boundaries of a course in family law. It is adequate for our purposes merely to consider some thoughts of scholars who have studied the issue in depth.

Berta Esperanza Hernandez-Truyol, Sex, Culture, and Rights: A Re/Conceptualization of Violence for the Twenty-First Century
60 Alb. L. Rev. 607, 632–634 (1997)

The United Nations has recognized that women's unequal status transcends the social and family spheres. Women's global disadvantages and marginalization also result from lack of access to economic development opportunities (in both the private and public sectors), denial of educational opportunities and restriction from social and political participation. Scrutiny of women's condition reveals that their less-than-full citizenship status can be traced to both physical and economic violence. Such violence is often widely accepted, and even embraced, under the pretext of cultural normativity. Consequently, before women can achieve social and economic equality and engage in full political participation, societies world-wide must re/conceptualize the notion of violence. This reconceptualization must include all forms of injustice for women, including injustice beyond the "A hit B" or "A shot B" paradigm. It must include economic marginalization and acts of violence justified on the grounds of culture or traditional practices. Indeed, such a framework will facilitate and permit the recognition and understanding of the many intersections of the physical abuse and economic deprivation components in the construction of violence.

Thus, here are my suggestions. On any matter, always ask the woman question: can or does the policy/practice/standard effect, facilitate, promote or ignore violent consequences to women? This inquiry must recognize that such violent consequences can be direct or indirect, and physical as well as economic, emotional, psychological, social, educational or political.... Such a model requires women's comprehensive participation in the consideration of the consequences of the specific rules and practices.... [T]he inquirer must ask women if the proposal has an impact on their real lives. The only effective way to eradicate violence against women is to understand its overt and subtle forms by deconstructing its causes and manifestations so that violence can be detected at the outset....

In looking at violence, we must expand our view from guns and fists to jobs and dignity. We must start from the bottom up rather than from the top down in defining violence. We need to ask those at the bottom of the economic ladder, the educational ladder, the health ladder and at the margins of the cultural borders—be those frontiers of sex or sexuality, religion, ability or language—what their needs are and how such needs can best be met. We must ask those who are not represented in our representative bodies what their needs are in representation. We must give a voice and render visible those who are underrepresented. A re/constructed paradigm must ask the necessary questions to bring those at the margins to the center of human rights talk. All this can be achieved through a re/conceptualization of violence that truly recognizes the needs of women around the world.

Barbara Stark, *Women and Globalization: The Failure and Postmodern Possibilities of International Law*
3 Vand. J. Transnat'l L. 503, 531–532 (2000)

[I]nternational law has failed women in at least two distinct but overlapping ways, both grounded in its failure to fully and effectively incorporate human rights law. First, on the state level, it has failed to prevent the widespread deprivation of human rights, caused by shredded safety nets, environmental degradation, and other byproducts of globalization, or to alleviate the resultant human suffering. Although the vast majority of states have ratified the International Covenant on Economic, Social and Cultural Rights... this has not deterred them from embracing policies that as a practical matter deny economic rights to massive segments of their own populations.... Second, international law has failed to compel even the most basic recognition of human rights on the part of the Major Players, that is, the non-state actors who are in fact the principal agents of globalization. Indeed, international law has failed even to bring [multinational corporations] and investment firms into the international system as participants.

Both Professor Hernandez-Truyol and Professor Stark remind us, at the outset, that violence may have a broader meaning than "A hit B," and that this broader reconceptualization of violence poses doctrinal challenges for human rights advocates. When one expands the definition of violence as Professor Hernandez-Truyol does, one certainly cannot decontextualize physical from economic (or other) violence because they all constitute injustice for women, although how important a particular type of violence is at a particular time may differ between groups of women.

With this important caveat in mind, one can try to discern what exactly is the relationship between economic development and domestic violence. Is there a causal relationship? There is certainly some evidence that domestic violence is more prevalent when women's economic status is low in society. For example, in two studies, one of a Taiwanese village and one among the Indo-Fijians, "where wife-beating used to be frequent and severe, as women increase their economic resources, redefine their gender roles, and no longer passively accept abuse, the level of gender violence in the family seems to be remaining constant or perhaps even to be dropping.'" *See* Johanna Maria Richters, Women, Culture and Violence: A Development, Health and Human Rights

Issue 102 (1994). "An even greater degree of predictability exists if, in addition to economic dependence, women also have no decision-making power, no 'female solidarity groups' for assistance and support, and few or no sanctions for wife abuse. Thus, 'women with limited or no economic resources who are restricted by socially-constructed sexual stereotypes and forced to be passive are more likely to suffer from physical abuse in the home.'" Ann Jordan, *Human Rights, Violence Against Women, and Economic Development (The People's Republic of China Experience)*, 5 Colum. J. Gender & L. 216, 265 & n.157 (1996) (quoting Jacquelyn C. Campbell, *Wife-Battering: Cultural Contexts Versus Western Social Sciences, in* Sanctions & Sanctuary: Cultural Perspectives on the Beating of Wives 229 (Dorothy Ayers Counts et al. eds., 1992)).

The evidence is somewhat equivocal, however, that economic development always helps decrease violence against women. Consider the following excerpt.

Ann D. Jordan, *Human Rights, Violence Against Women, and Economic Development (The People's Republic of China Experience)*
5 Colum. J. Gender & L. 216, 246–67 (1996)

Human rights instruments and scholarship addressing the issues of violence against women and economic development fail to recognize that mainstream development projects directly impact upon the increasing levels of violence against women in the developing world. An unstated assumption in these instruments, and in most scholarship, is that economic development is a neutral, even a positive, force for change....

[Ed. Note: The author identifies, as an example of how development contributes to violence against women, the "housewifization" of women in the development process.]

[H]ousewifization represents one of those Western values which...is brought in with development to "modernize" women in the developing world. Housewifization, because it reduces women's independence and status, renders women vulnerable to abuse by their wage-earning husbands and to exploitation in the work force.

The coming of housewifization to China means that housework is no longer recognized as contributing to the country's development. During the collective era when people earned points for working instead of money, women received work points for domestic labor, which enabled them to contribute to their families' standard of living. In today's commodity-based society, women who stay at home to raise children receive nothing, except perhaps for some rural women who make money from household production. Less money means less status because the value of domestic work can no longer be calculated in monetary terms, which renders women's labor at home invisible.

Housewifization in China supports development because it defines urban women's place in the new capitalist order. A key component of China's economic development is the downsizing of the bloated public sector labor force in order to turn loss-producing industries into efficient, profitable ones. Urban women feel the brunt of the efficiency drive as they are consistently the first fired. To encourage women to accept their second-class status in the labor market, much of the housewifization discourse in China is directed at urban women who are told to be good wives and mothers and good citizens by sacrificing their secure jobs for the benefit of their families and the greater society. The underlying message transmitted is that "feminine" women do not work in factories; they devote their energies to the private sphere. As a result, many urban women have, in fact, returned to the home, but many others have turned to the lower-paid and less secure private or informal sectors where their "feminine" skills are highly-prized, especially because they can be purchased so cheaply. As women's role in the public sector has become more insecure and narrowly defined and as women have been and are being shunted aside in order to assure men a place in the paid labor force, women's status in the home and at work is being diminished. Consequently, reports of sexual exploitation and violence in all types of workplaces, from the most prestigious to the smallest companies, are increasing.

The worst form of violence against Chinese women is the burgeoning trade in female flesh. The practice is widespread, with 15,000 reported cases in 1993, most of which involve the kidnap and sale of women to men who cannot find a wife.... A large percentage of trafficked women are raped by their procurers prior to sale to ensure that they become "damaged" goods. They are next raped by their "husbands" or johns to ensure total submission. The rapes are intended to dehumanize the women and to instill in them a sense of their powerlessness in order to ensure obedience. Rape is a successful tactic of subordination in Chinese society because women who lose their virginity have very little chance of ever leading a normal married life. Thus, whether they are forced to marry a stranger or to become a commercial sex worker, trafficked women are forced psychologically and physically to become virtual slaves....

The economic origin of trafficking in women is clear. China now has millions more men than women. [Ed. Note: This gender imbalance is attributed to China's One-Child policy, which is discussed in Chapter 13.A.1.b] This sex imbalance gives women's families leverage over men's families to extort exorbitant amounts of money from the future bridegroom's family for the purchase of newly-available commodities, such as washing machines and televisions. Poor men, when faced with the possibility of never having a male child (because they cannot find a wife/womb), turn to the market to buy a woman at a much lower cost from traffickers. These trafficking entrepreneurs kidnap, lure, or buy (from the women's families) poor, uneducated women from isolated regions, usually in western China. Even with the millions fewer women than men, reform has assured a never-ending supply of young women for these criminals to prey upon because rural women can be tricked into leaving home upon a promise of work or can be kidnapped without leaving a trace. The profits are high and the demand is great, not only for wives but also for commercial sex workers because economic reform has given male laborers and businessmen enough disposable income to enable them to purchase women's bodies.

Economic transformation is putting the lion's share of the newly created wealth into the hands of men and only a pittance into the hands of women. It is creating gender politics based on money; those with money (men) control those without (women). This represents a radical departure from China's recent socialist past, when equality was given more than token attention, women's sex was valued for its powers of reproduction, and women's work was valued for its contribution to socialist development.

Notes and Questions

1. *Disclaimer.* Ann Jordan qualifies her article with the following disclaimer:

Two final comments are in order. This Article is not intended to be read as a condemnation of the idea of economic reform or of change in developing countries. Rather, it critiques a particular form (or forms) of top-down economic development that, in many countries, violates women's human rights and contributes to, or indirectly causes, acts of violence against women. Further, this Article should not be read to imply that all women in all developing countries are disadvantaged by economic reform or that no women will ever be able to 'catch up' with men. Many women have indeed benefitted from economic reforms; many women in developing countries, including women in China, have more money and better living conditions than before development, and many women have and will overcome sex, class and race barriers. However, at the same time, many more women have realized no benefit from the development process or have seen their condition deteriorate as a result of development. Some women may even have improved living conditions while, at the same time, they may still be unable to avoid physical abuse.

Id. at 218–19.

2. *The Impact of Economic Policy on the Level of Violence.* Does violence against women in the United States help prove or disprove Jordan's thesis, or is the U.S. experience irrelevant? Consider that "In general, the lower the annual household income, the higher the rate of intimate partner violence. Among females age 16–19, rates of intimate partner violence for the households receiving $7,500 or less were at least twice those of females in the same age category but at other income levels. For women age 20–24 in the lowest income category, intimate victimization rates were at least 20% higher than those in households with a larger income." Bureau of Justice Statistics, Intimate Partner Violence and Age of Victim 1993–99, 6 (2001). What questions does Jordan's work raise about these statistics? Other questions are also raised by the material that follows.

3. *The Impact of Violence on Economic Well Being.* There are two potential ways to view the connection between development and violence. On the one hand, as the bulk of the reading above suggests, development may either increase or decrease the overall level of violence committed against women. On the other hand, violence may have economic repercussions for individual women, regardless of their country's stage of development. The preamble to the U.N. Declaration on the Elimination of Violence Against Women indicates that "violence against women is an obstacle to the achievement of equality," that "opportunities for women to achieve legal, social, political and economic equality in society are limited, inter alia, by continuing and endemic violence," and that "violence against women is one of the crucial social mechanisms by which women are forced into a subordinate position compared with men." G.A. Res. 48/104, U.N. GAOR, Supp. No. 49 at ¶ 4–6, U.N. Doc. A/48/49 (1993). Are these statements supported by the experience of victims of domestic violence in the United States? A variety of laws in the United States do reflect the belief that violence against women can hurt their economic well-being. For example, unemployment compensation may be available to victims of domestic violence who must leave their jobs because of the violence. *See, e.g.,* Wyo. Stat. Ann. § 27-3-311 (2000) (making one eligible for unemployment compensation if "forced to leave the most recent work as a result of being a victim of documented domestic violence"); *cf.* Me. Rev. Stat. Ann. tit. 6, § 850 (2000) (requiring employers to give "reasonable and necessary leave" to victims to "obtain necessary services to remedy a crisis caused by domestic violence, sexual assault, or stalking," including attending court or medical appointments). *But see* Hall v. Florida Unemployment Appeals Comm'n, 697 S.2d 541 (Fla. Dist. Ct. App. 1997) (holding claimant's move to another state to protect herself and her children from batterer was "voluntary" so that she did not

qualify for unemployment insurance, nor was there "good cause" attributable to her employer); Pagan v. Board of Review, 687 A.2d 328 (N.J. Super. Ct. App. Div. 1997) (same).

4. *International Recognition of the Link.* The Vienna Declaration and Programme of Action, which emerged from the 1993 World Conference on Human Rights, specifically stated that gender-based violence and sexual harassment and exploitation could be eliminated "by legal measures and through national action and international cooperation in such fields as economic and social development, education, safe maternity and health care, and social support." U.N. Doc. A/CONF. 157/23, ¶18. In 1995, an even stronger statement emerged in the Declaration and Platform for Action from the U.N. Fourth World Conference on Women. It stated, "Violence against women is an obstacle to the achievement of the objectives of equality, development and peace.... The low social and economic status of women can be both a cause and a consequence of violence against women." *U.N. Report of the Fourth World Conference on Women,* U.N. Doc. A/CONF. 177/20 (1995); & A/CONF. 177/20/Add.1 (1995).

5. *Using International Development Aid to Fund Violence Initiatives.* Various international organizations have attempted to combat violence against women within the context of development programs. For example, the U.N. Development Fund for Women (UNIFEM) funds projects that promote the empowerment of women and gender equality in developing countries, and it focuses some of its resources on combating violence directly. In 1998, UNIFEM started a $1.2 million trust fund dedicated to eliminating violence against women. *UNIFEM Launches Trust Fund to Eliminate Violence Against Women,* 24 WIN News 35(1) n.2 (1998). In 2002, UNIFEM chose to fund eighteen projects in sixteen countries (one project was regional); the projects included law reform initiatives, scholarly projects, educational programming, direct services, and training for law enforcement. *See* UNIFEM Trust Fund, Previous Grant Recipients, *available at* http://www.undp.org/unifem/trustfund/TFgrants.html. However, the funding of approximately $1 million a year is far exceeded by requests totalling over $12 million. *See* UNIFEM, Press Release, Women Ending Violence Worldwide, Aug. 15, 2000, *available at* http://www.unifem.undp.org/press/pr_violence.html.

6. *Tying Development Aid to Violence Initiatives.* The United States at times has tied its foreign economic aid to domestic violence reform. For example, a federal law requires that "the United States Executive Director of each international financial institution... use the voice and vote... to oppose any loan or other utilization of the funds of their respective institution, other than to address basic human needs, for the government of any country which the Secretary of the Treasury determines — (1) has, as a cultural custom, a known history of the practice of female genital mutilation; and (2) has not taken steps to implement educational programs designed to prevent the practice of female genital mutilation." 22 U.S.C. §262K-2(a)(2000). The international financial institutions covered by the law are the International Bank for Reconstruction and Development, the Inter-American Development Bank, the Asian Development Bank, the Asian Development Fund, the African Development Bank, the African Development Fund, the International Monetary Fund, the North American Development Bank, and the European Bank for Reconstruction and Development. *See* Omnibus Consolidated Appropriations Act, Pub. L. No. 104-208, §532(b), 110 Stat. 3009-152 (1996). Is the law too vague to be useful? One commentator reports that "[b]ecause of the law's vagueness, the current administration has said it will not use the law against any countries in which FGM occurs." *See* Antonia Kirkland, Note, *Female Genital Mutilation and the United States Vote at International Financial Institutions,* 20 Women's Rts. L. Rep. 147,

152 (1999). If the United States did implement the law, would women in countries that were sanctioned pursuant to the statute be better off? Instead of denying all aid, would a better solution be to give the money to the U.N. Development Fund for Women or to local groups working to end the practice?

7. *An Economic Argument for Reform.* One author suggests that the world-wide economic repercussions of violence against women must be brought to the attention of governments and international organizations. The author believes that economic arguments would better motivate nations to combat the violence than rights-oriented arguments. She cites the World Health Organization's conclusion that the lives of women fifteen to fifty-four are made shorter more often from domestic violence and rape than by "breast cancer, cervical cancer, obstructed labor, heart disease, AIDS, respiratory infections, motor vehicle accidents, and war." Kelsey S. Barnes, *The Economics of Violence: Why Freedom From Domestic Violence Must Be Treated As A Developmental Right in International Law*, 6 U. Miami Y.B. Int'l L. 97, 100 (1997). Do you agree that government officials consider violence against women "elusive, inappreciable, and, ultimately, of little genuine concern" because they do not "understand the cost to their society"? *Id.* at 133.

8. *Discrimination and Violence.* It is important to end this section with a reminder. As suggested briefly above, economic disadvantage *coupled with* other social disadvantages place women in the most vulnerable position. Laws that "trap women in abusive relationships... [can] include prohibitions and restrictions on divorce, a father's right of child custody, property distribution that favors males, discriminatory citizenship laws, laws proclaiming women perpetual minors, and restrictions on women's access to the legal system." Judith Armatta, *Getting Beyond the Law's Complicity in Intimate Violence Against Women*, 33 Willamette L. Rev. 773, 787 (1997). "In a study of ninety societies, four factors were predictive of societies with high rates of domestic violence: (1) male control of family wealth; (2) male domestic authority; (3) divorce restrictions for women; and (4) violent conflict resolution throughout the culture. 'When these four conditions are present in a society and in families, the likelihood is strong that wife beating will occur in a majority of households in the society.'" *Id.* at 841 (citing David Levinson, Family Violence in Cross-Cultural Perspective 88 (1989)).

B. Female Genital Mutilation

One type of physical violence that has received a lot of international attention is female genital mutilation (FGM). "According to Amnesty International, every year two million girls are at risk of suffering genital mutilation, and 135 million women worldwide have already endured it. An estimated 15% of all mutilations in Africa are infibulations." Isabel Coello, *Female Genital Mutilation: Marked by Tradition*, 7 Cardozo J. Int'l & Comp. L. 213, 215 (1999).

The United States' legal response to FGM has been pronounced. The response has included the criminalization of the practice, permissive immigration rules for people threatened by the practice, and as noted above, the ability to deny U.S. support for international aid to countries that inadequately address the practice. As you read the following material, consider whether FGM should be singled out for such a response. On the one hand, is FGM less reprehensible than other types of violence if the majority in the society where the women live do not view it as violence? On the other hand, is FGM more devastating to women than other forms of violence so that singling out FGM for special legal treatment in the United States is warranted?

1. The Practice

Fact Sheet No. 23, Harmful Traditional Practices Affecting the Health of Women and Children
Office of the High Commissioner for Human Rights (1987)
at http://www.unhchr.ch/html/menu6/2/fs23.htm

Female genital mutilation (FGM), or female circumcision as it is sometimes erroneously referred to, involves surgical removal of parts or all of the most sensitive female genital organs. It is an age-old practice which is perpetuated in many communities around the world simply because it is customary. FGM forms an important part of the rites of passage ceremony for some communities, marking the coming of age of the female child. It is believed that, by mutilating the female's genital organs, her sexuality will be controlled; but above all it is to ensure a woman's virginity before marriage and chastity thereafter. In fact, FGM imposes on women and the girl child a catalogue of health complications and untold psychological problems....

The origin of FGM has not yet been established, but records show that the practice predates Christianity and Islam in practicing communities of today. In ancient Rome, metal rings were passed through the labia minora of slaves to prevent procreation; in medieval England, metal chastity belts were worn by women to prevent promiscuity during their husbands' absence; evidence from mummified bodies reveals that, in ancient Egypt, both excision and infibulation were performed, hence Pharaonic circumcision; in tsarist Russia, as well as nineteenth-century England, France and America, records indicate the practice of clitoridectomy. In England and America, FGM was performed on women as a "cure" for numerous psychological ailments.

The age at which mutilation is carried out varies from area to area. FGM is performed on infants as young as a few days old, on children from 7 to 10 years old, and on adolescents. Adult women also undergo the operation at the time of marriage. Since FGM is performed on infants as well as adults, it can no longer be seen as marking the rites of passage into adulthood, or as ensuring virginity.

Among the types of surgical operations on the female genital organs listed below, there are many variations, performed throughout Africa, Asia, the Middle East, the Arabian Peninsula, Australia and Latin America.

Types of surgical forms

(a) Circumcision or Sunna ("traditional") circumcision: This involves the removal of the prepuce and the tip of the clitoris. This is the only operation which, medically, can be likened to male circumcision.

(b) Excision or clitoridectomy: This involves the removal of the clitoris, and often also the labia minora. It is the most common operation and is practiced throughout Africa, Asia, the Middle East and the Arabian Peninsula.

(c) Infibulation or Pharaonic circumcision: This is the most severe operation, involving excision plus the removal of the labia majora and the sealing of the two sides, through stitching or natural fusion of scar tissue. What is left is a very smooth surface, and a small opening to permit urination and the passing of menstrual blood. This artificial opening is sometimes no larger than the head of a match.

Another form of mutilation which has been reported is introcision, practiced specifically by the Pitta-Patta aborigines of Australia. When a girl reaches puberty, the whole tribe—both sexes—assembles. The operator, an elderly man, enlarges the vaginal orifice by tearing it downward with three fingers bound with opossum string. In other districts, the perineum is split with a stone knife. This is usually followed by compulsory sexual intercourse with a number of young men.

It is reported that introcision has been practiced in eastern Mexico and in Brazil. In Peru, in particular among the Conibos, a division of the Pano Indians in the north-east, an operation is performed in which, as soon as a girl reaches maturity, she is intoxicated and subjected to mutilation in front of her community. The operation is performed by an elderly woman, using a bamboo knife. She cuts around the hymen from the vaginal entrance and severs the hymen from the labia, at the same time exposing the clitoris. Medicinal herbs are applied, followed by the insertion into the vagina of a slightly moistened penis-shaped object made of clay.

Like all other harmful traditional practices, FGM is performed by women, with a few exceptions (in Egypt, men are known to perform the operation). In most rural settings throughout Africa, the operation is accompanied with celebrations and often takes place away from the community at a special hidden place. The operation is carried out by women (excisors) who have acquired their "skills" from their mothers or other female relatives; they are often also the community's traditional birth attendants.

The type of operation to be performed is decided by the girl's mother or grandmother beforehand and payment is made to the excisor before, during and after the operation, to ensure the best service. This payment, partly in kind and partly in cash, is a vital source of livelihood for the excisors.

The conditions under which these operations take place are often unhygienic and the instruments used are crude and unsterilized. A kitchen knife, a razor-blade, a piece of glass or even a sharp fingernail are the tools of the trade. These instruments are used repeatedly on numerous girls, thus increasing the risk of blood-transmitted diseases, including HIV/AIDS.

The operation takes between 10 and 20 minutes, depending on its nature; in most cases, anaesthetic is not administered. The child is held down by three or four women while the operation is done. The wound is then treated by applying mixtures of local herbs, earth, cow-dung, ash or butter, depending on the skills of the excisor. If infibulation is performed, the child's legs are bound together to impair mobility for up to 40 days. If the child dies from complications, the excisor is not held responsible; rather, the death is attributed to evil spirits or fate. Throughout South-East Asia and urban African communities, FGM is becoming increasingly medicalized.

FGM is known to be practiced in at least 25 countries in Africa. Infibulation is practiced in Djibouti, Egypt, some parts of Ethiopia, Mali, Somalia and the northern part of the Sudan. Excision and circumcision occur in parts of Benin, Burkina Faso, Cameroon, the Central African Republic, Chad, Côte d'Ivoire, the Gambia, the northern part of Ghana, Guinea, Guinea-Bissau, Kenya, Liberia, Mauritania, Nigeria, Senegal, Sierra Leone, Togo, Uganda and parts of the United Republic of Tanzania.

Outside Africa, a certain form of female genital mutilation exists in Indonesia, Malaysia and Yemen. Recent information has revealed that the practice also exists in some European countries and Australia among immigrant communities.

FGM is a custom or tradition synthesized over time from various values, especially religious and cultural values. The reasons for maintaining the practice include religion, custom, decreasing the sexual desire of women, hygiene, aesthetics, facility of sexual relations, fertility, etc. In general, it can be said that those who preserve the practice are largely women who live in traditional societies in rural areas. Most of these women follow tradition passively.

In the countries where the practice exists, most women believe that, as good Muslims, for example, they have to undergo the operation. In order to be clean and proper, fit for marriage, female circumcision is a precondition. Among the Bambara in Mali, it is believed that, if the clitoris touches the head of a baby being born, the child will die. The clitoris is seen as the male characteristic of the woman; in order to enhance her femininity, this male part of her has to be removed. Among women in Djibouti, Ethiopia, Somalia and the Sudan, circumcision is performed to reduce sexual desire and also to maintain virginity until marriage. A circumcised woman is considered to be clean.

Establishing identity and belongingness is another reason advanced for the perpetuation of the practice. For example, in Liberia and Sierra Leone, groups of girls of 12 and 13 of the indigenous population undergo an initiation rite, conducted by an older woman "Sowie." This involves education on how to be a good wife or co-wife, the use of herbal medicine and the "secrets" of female society. It also involves the ritual of circumcision.

Health and psychological implications

The effects of female genital mutilation have short-term and long-term implications. Hemorrhage, infection and acute pain are the immediate consequences. Keloid formation, infertility as a result of infection, obstructed labor and psychological complications are identified as later effects. In rural areas where untrained traditional birth attendants perform the operations, complications resulting from deep cuts and infected instruments can cause the death of the child.

Most physical complications result from infibulation, although cataclysmic hemorrhage can occur during circumcision with the removal of the clitoris; accidental cuts to other organs can also lead to heavy loss of blood. Acute infections are commonplace when operations are carried out in unhygienic surroundings and with unsterilized instruments. The application of traditional medicine can also lead to infection, resulting in tetanus and general septicaemia. Chronic infection can also lead to infertility and anaemia.

Hematocolpos, or the inability to pass menstrual blood (because the remaining opening is often too small), can lead to infection of other organs and also infertility.

Obstetric complications are the most frequent health problem, resulting from vicious scars in the clitoral zone after excision. These scars open during childbirth and cause the anterior perineum to tear, leading to hemorrhaging that is often difficult to stop. Infibulated women have to be opened, or deinfibulated, on delivery of their child and it is common for them to be reinfibulated after each delivery.

There has been little research in the area of the psychological implications of FGM, but evidence indicates that most children experience recurring nightmares.

In her recent book, Cutting the Rose-Female Genital Mutilation: The Practice and its Prevention, Efua Dorkenoo reports that some evidence of psychological effects is emerging among the large immigrant communities now living in Europe, the Americas, Australia and New Zealand. Teenagers, in particular, are having to live in two very different cultures, where different values prevail. At school they move within the very liberal setting of the Western culture; at home they have to conform to values held by their parents. Some of these values often conflict. For some teenagers this is proving to be problematic. Girls who have been genitally mutilated have to come to terms with the fact that they are not like their classmates. Mood swings and irritability, a constant state of depression, and anxiety have all been noted among infibulated girls. A small number, upon reaching the age of consent, are being deinfibulated without their parents' knowledge and engaging in premarital relationships, thus validating the reasoning behind their parents' wishes to have the operation performed.

There are also reports of psychological and health problems suffered by women seeking medical assistance in Western medical facilities due to lack of knowledge regarding genital mutilation. Excised and infibulated women have special needs which have been ignored or dealt with on a trial-and-error basis. In Western countries, severe forms of FGM present challenges to midwives and obstetricians in providing antenatal and postnatal care....

---

2. National Legal Responses

The governments in some countries where FGM is widespread have attempted to eliminate the practice. First we consider, for example, the situation in Egypt. Afterwards, we will examine the approach in France, where FGM is not widespread. Comparing these two countries' approaches allows us to think about legal reform generally and to better assess the approach taken in the United States. The U.S. approach is documented in section B.3, following this one.

Susan A. Dillon, Comment, *Yoni in the Land of Isis: Female Genital Mutilation is Banned (Again) in Egypt*
22 Hous. J. Int'l L. 289, 290, 309, 315–321 (2000)

Egypt is the second most populous African nation and the most populous Arab nation. Egypt is a leader in Islamic jurisprudence, and its citizenry is 90% Muslim. Female circumcision (female genital mutilation or FGM) has been practiced in Egypt for thousands of years and perhaps as many as 97% of Egyptian "ever-married" women have endured the practice. Although there is disagreement among theologians, fundamentalists continue to promote FGM as an Islamic mandate for the preservation of women's chastity.

In Egypt, female genital mutilation is known as "tahara" or purification. A 1995 health survey reported an average incidence of 97%, and an 81.6% expression of support for continuation of FGM among the 14,779 female participants. One particularly striking fact emerges from the results of the survey. Regardless of a woman's age, place of residence, her mother's education, or her work status, as an Egyptian she is more likely than not to have been subjected to FGM....

Today's efforts to abolish female genital mutilation in Egypt are only the most recent in a much longer tradition of such campaigns. Evidence of educational efforts supported by the Egyptian Doctors' Society, sheikhs (the leaders of Arab or Muslim tribes, villages, or families), governmental doctors, and the press, date back to the 1920s. Anecdotal accounts from families in which FGM was abandoned in the 1930s and 1940s demonstrate the effectiveness of some early efforts. During the 1950s, articles in health reviews, periodicals, and a women's magazine continued to urge eradication. But perhaps the best evidence of early success in the battle against FGM came in the June 24, 1959 ministerial decree, Number 74, which prohibited FGM by lay persons and government doctors. It stated:

1. It is forbidden that persons other than physicians perform female circumcision. Circumcision should be partial and not of the severe kind to those who request it.

2. Female circumcision is not to be performed in the Ministry health units in an effort to eradicate it (sic) because of its harmful effects.

3. "Dayas" are not allowed to perform any surgical procedures, including circumcision.

4. Female circumcision, as performed in Egypt now, has its harmful effects on females before and after marriage. Religious authorities "Foquahaa" have decided that it is against Islamic law (shria) to excise wholly these organs, but they differed regarding partial circumcision.

The decree was widely misconstrued, within the Egyptian medical community and internationally, as outlawing FGM completely. In fact, "it allowed medical doctors to perform a 'partial' variety of FGM in their private clinics at the request of the parents." The public, and traditional practitioners, largely ignored the decree.

In September 1994, the International Conference on Population and Development (ICPD) was held in Cairo, Egypt. On September 6, Dr. Ali Abd el Fattah, the Health Minister, stated, "FGM is rarely practiced in Egypt." On September 7, Cable News Network (CNN) aired footage of FGM being performed on a ten-year old girl by a barber in a Cairo slum. Her ankles were tied to her wrists and her family observed as she screamed in pain. The footage embarrassed public officials, outraged much of the citizenry, and resulted in several arrests and a private suit against CNN for "blacken(ing) the image of Egypt." However, a subsequent cover photo of the semi-official Al Musawwar, showing the pained face of a second girl undergoing circumcision, was impossible to dismiss as merely a Western media attack on the country. Subsequently, at an ICPD seminar, Dr. Ali Abd el Fattah "promised the international community—and not his own people—to issue a law that will penalize the practice of FGM." The Population Minister, Maher Mahran, announced that Parliament would consider a new law specifically targeting FGM and providing for sanctions.

Public debate ensued. The Great Imam ("(t)he caliph who is successor to Mohamed as leader of the Islamic community"), Sheikh Mohamed Sayed Tantawi stated that the Qur'an has no mention of FGM. In addition, those ahadith (sayings) attributed to the prophet Mohamed in support of the practice are "unauthenticated, badly worded and were passed on by men who have little credibility." He solicited medical advice on the practice from doctors and later gave support to the 1996 ban. Conversely, the Grand Sheikh Gad-El-Haq Ali Gad-El-Haq, leader of the Al-Azhar Islamic Institute, issued a religious decree supporting FGM as an Islamic practice.

On October 9, 1994, the Health Minister appointed twenty-one members to the Higher Committee for Eliminating Female Genital Mutilation, which met only once. The Committee defeated a motion to encourage new legislation aimed at criminalizing FGM. They denounced the practice, but predicted that a legal ban would simply drive it underground and discourage parents, fearful of penalties, from seeking medical treatment for daughters who needed it following the procedure.

On October 19, 1994, under pressure resulting from statements by the Grand Sheik Gad-El-Haq Ali Gad-El-Haq, the same Health Minister issued a statement to all health directorates with the following instructions:

> To forbid the performance of circumcision by any one other than physicians, and in no other places than hospitals, and to put into force the law regulating medical practice. Strict legal action should be immediately taken against those who break this law.

> All government hospitals, (general training, or local) should specify two days a week to perform male circumcision, and another day a week to receive the families desiring female circumcision.

> Each hospital should form a committee consisting of a gynecologist, anesthetist, social worker, nurse and religious leader to receive the families wishing to circumcise their daughter on that set day. This reception committee should clearly explain the physical and psychological harmful effects of the operation, and the religious views on the practice. The committee should try several times to persuade the family against the operation and help it to review its decision, and not accept to perform the operation except after many and repeated attempts of persuasion. This step may help to contain the practice and if necessary perform the operation under good medical condition in preparation for its final elimination....

Despite guidelines in the decree, there were reports that hospitals performed circumcisions daily and that no reception committees were formed to advise families against FGM. A coalition of seventeen activists, journalists, and lawyers filed suit against the Health Minister for encouraging illegal, unnecessary surgery. The plaintiffs claimed that the new decree led the public to believe there was a difference between bad circumcision (performed by lay persons) and good circumcision (performed by doctors in hospitals).

In April 1995, nine members of the Egyptian Organization for Human Rights initiated suit against the Grand Sheik Gad-El-Haq Ali Gad-El-Haq, leader of the Al-Azhar Islamic Institute. He had issued a fatwa (religious edict), that "whoever opposes circumcision (of girls) is opposing a religious obligation, and the leader of the country must kill him." In October 1995, state hospitals were secretly told to cease performing FGM. Pressure from human rights groups and fear of U.S. aid sanctions led to the private reversal.

In 1996, Dr. Ismai'l Sallam took office as the new Health Minister. On July 18 of that year, he issued order number 361/96, banning FGM by government and private hospitals and clinics except in cases where it is medically necessary as diagnosed by a "head of the gynecology department." This decision was immediately hailed by the Syndicate of Doctors as long overdue.

Dr. Mouneer Fawzy and Sheikh Youssif El-Badri, an Islamist lawyer and preacher, filed a suit in opposition to the Health Minister's ban. Their petition attacked the ban as a violation of Islamic law and therefore of the Egyptian constitution, "which states that the Islamic shari'a is the main source of legislation." On June 24, 1997, a lower administrative tribunal ruled in favor of the fundamentalists and revoked the ministerial ban on FGM. Judge Abdul Aziz Hamade declared the ban an illegal infringement by the government on doctors' authority to make medical decisions. The court also accused Health Minister Sallam of "abuse of power" because of the court's understanding that only parliament could outlaw the practice. Dr. Ismai'l Sallam appealed with support from the Doctors' Syndicate and the Prime Minister.

On December 28, 1997, the Supreme Administrative Court of Egypt (the Council of State) overturned the lower administrative tribunal and upheld the ministerial ban on FGM. Medical and paramedical personnel are prohibited from performing FGM, even with consent of the girl or her parents because it "is not a personal right sanctioned by Shari'a." The court held that the Qur'an did not authorize female circumcision and also said there is no clear proof that the practice was sanctioned by the prophet Mohamed or ordained in Islam. Egypt does not have any legislation specifically targeting FGM, but the court held that under the existing penal code, FGM is considered intentional infliction of bodily harm, punishable by three years imprisonment. The ruling is not subject to appeal.

Notes and Questions

1. *The Role of Religion.* "In Egypt, Islam is the state religion and Islamic jurisprudence (Shari'a: 'the highway of good life') is the 'principle source of legislation.' The civil code is an effort to 'synthesize Islamic principles of law' with the Napoleonic code. In 1955, the separate Shari'a courts were merged with the National Courts. Shari'a law has not been abolished, it has simply been absorbed and integrated into the National Courts." Dillon, *supra*, at 315–21. The Qur'an does not discuss FGM. At most, it is sunnah, or founded upon the customs of the Prophet. *See* Efua Dorkenoo, Cutting the Rose—Female Genital Mutilation: The Practice and its Prevention 36–37 (Minority Rights Group 2d ed. 1995). Yet the practice is not solely practiced by Muslims in Egypt. One source states "FGM is practiced throughout the country by Muslims and Christians." Anika Rahman & Nahid Toubia, Female Genital Mutilation: A Guide to Laws and Policies Worldwide 140 (2000). Does the integration of religion into a state's substantive law make a "religious practice" more or less vulnerable to eradication? Does the First Amendment to the U.S. Constitution prohibit criminalizing a religious practice that harms children?

2. *The Law on the Books.* Will the Health Minister's ban and the general criminal law end the practice of FGM in Egypt? Consider that there are deeply held beliefs that FGM "will moderate female sexuality, that it will assure a girl's purity, femininity, and later marriageability, and that it is sanctioned by religion." Omaima El-Gibaly et al., *The Decline of Female Circumcision in Egypt: Evidence and Interpretation*, 54 Soc. Sci. & Med. 205 (2002). *See also* Karen Paige Erickson, *Female Circumcision Among Egyptian Women*, 4 Women's Health: Research on Gender, Behavior, & Policy 309 (1995).

3. *Empirical Evidence.* Empirical research does suggest that FGM is on the decline in Egypt. There has been a ten percentage point decline in the number of adolescent girls who have had the procedure done compared to their mothers. The researchers identify "increased momentum" in the decline in the years following the 1994 International Conference on Population and Development in Cairo. The authors do not believe the decline is attributable to underreporting now that the procedure is illegal. They reach this conclusion in part because the court decisions surrounding the ban has made the situation "more likely to be confus[ing] than intimidat[ing]." El-Gibaly, *supra*, at 210.

Not surprisingly, the researchers also noted an increased "medicalization" of the procedure prior to the ruling of the Supreme Administrative Court of Egypt. In 1995, 13.1% of the ever-married woman indicated that the procedure was performed by a doctor, compared to 45.8% of the daughters. The 1997 ACSE survey found doctors performed 47.5% of procedures on adolescent girls. Yet approximately three-fourths of the procedures still occurred at home, not in a clinic.

4. *Criminalization versus Regulation.* The policies in Egypt over FGM reflect a tension between outlawing the practice altogether and medicalizing the practice. What are the relative merits of these approaches? What is the effect of laws prohibiting FGM if social attitudes lag behind the legal changes? Would parents who subject their daughter to the procedure necessarily be charged with a crime?

5. *Applicability of General Criminal Provisions.* Sometimes FGM is criminalized, but not by legislation particularly aimed at FGM. As suggested above, Egypt has no criminal provision specifically addressing FGM, although it has several provisions related to wounding, including the prohibition of surgery by nondoctors and a prohibition on doctors causing a wound absent medical necessity. *See* Rahman & Toubia, *supra*, at 141 (citing Egyptian Penal Code, articles 236–40). What are the advantages and disadvantages of relying on general criminal provisions if one hopes to end the practice?

6. *Criminalization versus Education.* Egypt is not alone in addressing the issue of FGM. "Some African governments have begun to take the first steps to eradicate excision, either by prohibiting the practice, as is the case of Burkina Faso, Guinea, Ghana, Central African Republic and Sudan, or by supporting, sometimes only morally, campaigns carried out by non-governmental organizations. At present, branches of the Inter-African Committee on Traditional Practices Affecting the Health of Women and Children [IAC] can be found in twenty-two countries, where it develops training and information programs aimed at local activists." Isabel Coello, *Female Genital Mutilation: Marked by Tradition*, 7 Cardozo J. Int'l & Comp. L. 213, 217–18 (1999). Those nations are: Benin, Burkina-Faso, Chad, Egypt, Ethiopia, Gambia, Ghana, Guinea, Guinea-Bissau, Kenya, Liberia, Mali, Mauritania, Niger, Nigeria, Senegal, Sierra Leone, Sudan, Tanzania, Togo, Uganda and Djibouti. *Id.* at 218 n.22. The IAC, a non-governmental organization, was given high praise by the Special Rapporteur, Halima Embarek Warzazi, in the *Third Report on the Situation Regarding the Elimination of Traditional Practices Affecting the Health of Women and the Girl Child*, U.N. ESCOR, Comm. Hum. Rts., 51st Sess., Item 5(a), at 80, U.N. Doc. E/CN.4/Sub.2/1999/14 ¶ 80 (1999) ("NGOs have been doing a remarkable job of consciousness-raising, [providing] information, training and providing material and financial assistance, thus making a substantial contribution to the campaign against such practices."). It appears that education is having an effect. *See, e.g.,* David Hecht, *Standing Up to Ancient Custom*, Christian Sci. Monitor, June 3, 1998, *available at* 1998 WL 2368217 (African NGO's educational program is helping change the practice in Senegal). The IAC is determined to see the practice eliminated by 2010. *See, e.g.,* The Ouagadougou Declaration, May 6, 1999, *cited in Third Report of the Special Rapporteur on Traditional Practices*, 13 Int'l Children's Rts. Monitor 21 (2000).

7. *Regional Efforts.* There have been a variety of regional efforts in Africa to eliminate the practice. For example, the West African Economic and Monetary Union in 1999 issued declarations condemning the practice. *See* The Ouagudougou Declaration, *supra*. Also, the OAU Council of Ministers adopted the Addis Ababa Declaration on Violence Against Women in 1997, which was endorsed by the Assembly of Heads of State and Government. *See* Warzazi, *supra*, ¶ 51.

8. *Change Afoot?* Recently a Kenyan court, for the first time, issued an injunction prohibiting a father from having the procedure done on his fifteen and seventeen-year-old daughters. *See* Chege Mbitiru, *Women Lawyers Call For Law Against Female Circumcision*, Assoc. Press Newservices, Dec. 14, 2000. The decision was premised on the notion that female circumcision constitutes assault. The judge stated that "customary law, which is recognized in the Kenyan constitution, supersedes statutory law only when it is not repugnant to justice and morality." The father claims to have wanted the procedure performed on his daughters because he did not want the girls' new husbands to return them when they discovered they were not circumcised. Then the father would have to return the dowry. If the father truly was concerned for his daughters' welfare, should the Magistrate have issued the injunction? Does the fact that the girls were older and sought the injunction themselves matter? Apparently the girls sought legal help because they were "Christians and as such had abandoned some of their traditional customs, among them circumcision." *Id.*

It is difficult to judge the potential impact of this ruling. The fact that a Kenyan court has issued this ruling at the behest of Kenyans may make the case particularly useful for those in Kenya who seek to eliminate the practice. Earlier efforts in Kenya to eradicate the practice had been instituted by British colonizers, and those efforts were counterproductive. *See* L. Amede Obiora, *Bridges and Barricades: Rethinking Polemics and Intransigence in the Campaign Against Female Circumcision*, 47 Case W. Res. L. Rev. 275, 330–31 (1996); Bruce Berman & John Lonsdale, Unhappy Valley: Conflict in Kenya & Africa 388–94 (1992).

9. *Child Abuse.* Child abuse laws might apply to parents who seek to have FGM performed on their children. Should a child be taken away from the parents and placed under the protection of a state agency if the parents indicate that they will have the procedure done to the child? Are there any problems with using child abuse laws to protect children in this context? What if the child herself wants the procedure done? In Egypt, "42 percent of the already circumcised girls...are unconvinced of the necessity of the procedure." El-Gibaly, *supra*, at 216 (suggesting the majority of such girls feel otherwise). However, it is interesting to note that the girls most at risk of the procedure, between ages eight and fourteen, typically have little or no input into the decision. *Id.* at 206.

The appropriateness of a particular response to the practice may differ depending upon whether the practice occurs in a country where FGM is endemic, like Egypt, or in a country where a small proportion of the population engages in it. "Although efforts to eradicate the practice are on the rise in Africa, the panorama looks bleak in Western countries, since female genital mutilation is increasing among immigrant communities. Cases of genital mutilation have been reported in Australia, Canada, Denmark, France, Italy, Netherlands, United Kingdom, United States and Sweden." Coello, *supra*, at 217–18 n.5. Consequently, we now examine France's efforts to eradicate the practice there.

France has relied upon the criminal law to address the practice of FGM. "[I]n France, no specific law exists, but article 312-3 of the Penal Code is applied to prosecute persons exercising violence against or seriously assaulting a child under 15, 'if the result has been mutilation, amputation or...loss of an eye or other permanent disabilities, or death not intentionally caused by the perpetrator.' The Criminal Division of the Cour de Cessation decided, by a judgment of 20 August 1983, that ablation of the clitoris resulting from wilful violence constituted a mutilation under article 312-3 of the Penal Code. While the term 'female genital mutilation' is not used in the Penal Code, this decision makes it quite clear that such practices fall within the purview of the enactment." *See generally Fact Sheet No. 23, Harmful Traditional Practices Affecting the Health of Women and Children*, OHCHR (1987), *at* http://www.unhchr.ch/html/menu6/fs23.htm.

Isabel Coello, *Female Genital Mutilation: Marked by Tradition*

7 Cardozo J. Int'l & Comp. L. 213, 221–22 (1999)

Although there are no official figures, the Commission Against Sexual Mutilations calculates that, given the number of immigrants and their children living in France, several thousand of these operations must occur each year. In February 1999, the Femmes Solidaires association announced that, in the Paris region alone, 4,500 immigrant girls are at risk of suffering genital mutilation. For a long time, these incidents went unpunished in France, but over the last few years the number of cases has decreased, due in part to the dissuading effect of several trials that resulted in jail sentences.

The wide coverage given these cases by the media has led to other results. French society has also had to face an issue that, until the trials, was taboo and posed a moral dilemma for many people. "Many people found [it] unfair to convict parents who had done nothing but respect their tradition for their children's welfare," French lawyer Linda Weil-Curiel remembers. Weil-Curiel, who has defended more than twenty cases, refuses to accept that argument. "The law has to be respected by any person being on national soil. Foreigner customs must submit to the law. If not, we would be committing an unacceptable discrimination based on the girls' origin. It would mean that, though we find the idea of cutting a white girl's clitoris scandalous we accept it being done to an African girl."

On the other hand, these penal prosecutions caused many French born girls, daughters of African immigrants, to wonder about their own fate and whether they had been mutilated when they were babies. "For these girls, who have grown up amidst French culture and values, finding out that they're marked for life and that they are never going to have a normal sex life is such a desolating experience," continues Weil-Curiel. "Very often they find out when they start having sexual relationships with boys and they ask them why they're not like the rest of girls, how come they don't feel any pleasure." These girls become filled with indignation towards their parents, but that indignation has never been so severe as to cause one of these girls to decide to put her case in the hands of Justice. The prospect of seeing their families on trial serves to check the indignation of these girls.

In France, cases of female genital mutilation were, at first, denounced only by doctors and social assistants. Ten years after she had been mutilated in Paris along with her sisters, eighteen year old Mariatou Keita broke this unspoken rule and revealed her ordeal. She became the first girl who went to trial demanding compensation for the behavior of her parents and the State, neither of whom protected her. A verdict in the case was reached in February, 1999. Seated in the chamber alongside the woman who had performed the ablation (Hawa Greou, a 52-year-old Malian woman accused of mutilating 48 girls in France), Mariatou saw her own parents and another twenty families prosecuted as accomplices in the mutilations after the investigation. In total, 22 mothers and five fathers have been tried. On February 16, 1999, the Paris Court handed down an eight-year jail sentence to Greou and sentenced the parents to terms ranging from three years suspended to two years in prison.

Isabelle R. Gunning, *Global Feminism at the Local Level: Criminal and Asylum Laws Regarding Female Genital Surgeries*

3 J. Gender Race & Just. 45, 49–51 (1999)

The criminalization approach has been popular and controversial in a number of western countries. France, for example, has had several trials regarding the surgeries....

Some twenty-five years ago when the American Academy of Pediatrics (AAP) determined that male circumcision had no particular health benefits, one could have asked then why not pass a law outlawing the practice of male circumcision under threat of fines and imprisonment? To be sure, many, but not all, forms of female circumcision are more physically invasive and possibly life threatening than male circumcision. Still, male circumcision does involve the removal of healthy human tissue that some circumcision opponents argue in fact carries negative physical, sexual and psychological consequences.... While arguments can be made for criminalization, I cannot help but wonder if the thought of rabbis, hospitals and medical doctors on trial or the image of white parents being imprisoned as torturers and child abusers for their misguided and damaging religious and cultural beliefs is more horrifying to westerners than the sight of misguided African parents (mothers in particular) being tried and imprisoned for their "own good."

Notes and Questions

1. *Ethnocentrism.* FGM raises important theoretical questions about the relationship of law and culture. For Professor Gunning, the topic made her ask "1) by what right did I, as a Western feminist, have to criticize as right or wrong the practices of an entirely different culture? and 2) should and can law, with its attribution of right and wrong, exoneration and punishment, be used to eradicate a cultural practice?" Isabelle R. Gunning, *Arrogant Perception, World-Travelling and Multicultural Feminism: The Case of Female Genital Surgeries*, 23 Colum. Hum. Rts. L. Rev. 189, 189 (1992). Can one respect other cultures and still be critical of this practice? How does one do that? How does one differentiate valid criticism from ethnocentrism? Does the validity of the criticism differ if one is criticizing the practices of a minority in one's own country versus the practices of a majority in another country?

2. *Contextualization.* Trying to contextualize the practice of FGM within any one country or cultural community would take much more space that can be allotted here. However, it is essential to appreciate, as mentioned in Fact Sheet No. 23 above, that this procedure is important for women in societies where it is practiced because it makes them "fit for marriage." As in the West, marriage often offers women gains in social status and economic security. *See* Gunning, *Arrogant Perception, supra,* at 215 (citing Ellen Gruenbaum, *Reproductive Ritual and Social Reproduction: Female Circumcision and the Subordination of Women in Sudan, in* Economic and Class in Sudan (Norman O'Neill & Jay O'Brien eds., 1988)). FGM is often associated with chastity, which can increase one's marriageability, or with health benefits, such as increased fertility. *Id.* at 217–18. The practice is often accompanied by an important ceremony for the girl. *Id.* at 220. In some cultures, grandmothers and midwives are the largest proponents of the practice, the latter group deriving significant income from the practice and the former group acting to protect "the status, health, and honor of their...

granddaughters." *Id.* at 222–23. One outcome of outlawing or medicalizing the practice is the "systematic imprisonment or economic collapse of the most relatively powerful and economically independent women within the cultures." *Id.* at 229–30.

   3. *Comparable Practices.* Ideally, the study of FGM should help us reassess practices in this country. Not only did FGM occur for many years in the United States, practiced by upper-middle class caucasians to cure psychological ailments, *see* Ben Barker-Benfield, *Sexual Surgery in Late Nineteenth Century America*, 5 Int'l J. Health Serv. 279, 285–86 (1975), but there are contemporary practices in the United States that might be comparable to FGM. For example, cosmetic surgery is a common practice in America. You may remember when Cher had her bottom rib removed to narrow her waist. *See* Kathy Davis, *Cultural Dopes and She-Devils: Cosmetic Surgery as Ideological Dilemma, in* Negotiating at the Margins 23 (Sue Fisher & Kathy Davis eds., 1993). More common plastic surgery procedures include breast lifts, buttock lifts, cheek implants, liposuction, eyelid surgery, facelifts, and tummy tucks. Breast augmentation, in fact, is a fairly widespread practice. In 1999, there were 167,318 women who had this procedure, a 413% increase over the number in 1992. National Clearinghouse of Plastic Surgery Statistics, *1999 Plastic Surgery Procedural Statistics*, at http://www.plasticsurgery.org/mediactr/trends92-99.htm. Most of these surgeries are done for cosmetic reasons. *See* Lucette Lagnado, *Women Find Breast Surgery Attractive Again*, Wall St. J., July 14, 1998, at B1. Yet, there are potential health consequences from the implants. Known risks of surgery include possible complications from general anesthesia, infection, hematoma, hemorrhage, thrombosis, and skin necrosis. Implant risks include leak or rupture, loss of sensation in the nipple or breast tissue, formation of calcium deposits in surrounding tissue, possibly causing pain and hardening, and interference with mammography readings. *See generally* Marian Segal, *A Status Report on Breast Implant Safety*, FDA Consumer (1995), *available at* http://www.FDA.gov/FDAC/Features/995_implants.html. There are additional risks associated with silicone gel breast implants. Approximately 1.8 million American women have silicone breast implants. Approximately 70% of them had the procedure for cosmetic reasons. *Panel Confirms No Major Illness Tied to Implants*, N. Y. Times, June 21, 1999, at A1. These implants have been linked to a variety of health problems, and they were finally banned in 1992. *See* Rebecca Weisman, *Reforms in Medical Device Regulation: An Examination of the Silicone Gel Breast Implant Debacle*, 23 Golden Gate U. L. Rev. 973, 978–79 (1993); FDA General and Plastic Surgery Devices: Effective Date of Requirement for Premarket Approval of Silicone Gel-filled Breast Prosthesis, 21 C.F.R. §878(A) (1990). Like FGM, breast augmentation in the United States has been justified as helpful in finding a husband. *See* Gunning, *supra*, at 191. How do you view the practice of breast augmentation? Should it be criminalized? Should we spend time and money discouraging women from having this surgery? Is the practice of breast augmentation in the United States less of a problem than access to affordable child care? What, if anything, does this exercise teach us?

3. The United States' Approach

   The legal and policy issues introduced above also exist in the United States. The Center for Disease Control estimates that in 1990, 168,000 people were subjected to or were at risk for FGM in the United States. Wanda K. Jones et al., *Who is at Risk in the U.S.?*, 112 Pub. Health Rep. 368, 372 (1997). Should the United States' concern about FGM differ depending upon whether the procedure is practiced here or practiced abroad? If so, does it matter if it is practiced abroad on children of immigrants who travel from the United States to have FGM performed on their daughters? We have already mentioned that the United States ties its development aid, at least in theory, to efforts by governments to prevent FGM through education. *See* 22 U.S.C. §262k-2(a) (2000). How does the United States address the practice at home? The material that follows considers the response to the practice in the United States through criminal, child protection, and immigration laws.

a. *Criminal Law*

Federal law states that "whoever knowingly circumcises, excises, or infibulates the whole or any part of the labia majora or labia minora or clitoris of another person who has not attained the age of 18 years shall be fined under this title or imprisoned not more than 5 years, or both." *See* 18 U.S.C. §166. There is a limited exception where necessary for the person's health and when performed by a doctor or other designated medical professional. In applying the health exception, "no account shall be taken of the effect on the person on whom the operation is to be performed of any belief on the part of that person, or any other person, that the operation is required as a matter of custom or ritual." Could a federal prosecutor use this law to prosecute parents who travel abroad with their daughter in order to obtain the procedure?

The law does not require international or even interstate travel for its violation. Can such a law be constitutional? Would the law survive a federalism challenge? Congress made six findings when it passed the law:

> (1) the practice of female genital mutilation is carried out by members of certain cultural and religious groups within the United States; (2) the practice of female genital mutilation often results in the occurrence of physical and psychological health effects that harm the women involved; (3) such mutilation infringes upon the guarantees of rights secured by Federal and State law, both statutory and constitutional; (4) the unique circumstances surrounding the practice of female genital mutilation place it beyond the ability of any single State or local jurisdiction to control; (5) the practice of female genital mutilation can be prohibited without abridging the exercise of any rights guaranteed under the First Amendment to the Constitution or under any other law; and (6) Congress has the affirmative power under section 8 of article 1, the Necessary and Proper clause, section 5 of the Fourteenth Amendment, as well as under the Treaty Clause, to the Constitution to enact such legislation.

See Criminalization of Female Genital Mutilation, Pub. L. No. 104-208, div. C, title IV, subtitle D, §645(a)(1)-(b) (1996). Would the law survive a First Amendment challenge by a parent or by a girl who wanted the procedure?

Fourteen states have also criminalized FGM. *See* Female Genital Mutilation: A Guide to Laws and Policies Worldwide 237 (Anika Rahmun & Nahid Toubia eds., 2000) (citing California, Colorado, Delaware, Illinois, Maryland, Minnesota, Nevada, New York, North Dakota, Oregon, Rhode Island, Tennessee, West Virginia, and Wisconsin). The authors explain that the laws sometimes differ from the federal law by 1) prohibiting the practice also for women over 18 years old or 2) holding parents liable if they consent to the procedure. *Id.* "To date, there have been no criminal prosecutions at the federal or state level." *Id.*

b. Child Protection Laws

Adoption of Peggy

767 N.E.2d 29 (Mass. 2002)

Greaney, J.

A judge in the Worcester Division of the Juvenile Court Department adjudicated the five year old daughter, whom we shall call Peggy of S.T. (father), an Indian national living in the Commonwealth on a temporary work visa, in need of care and protection and committed her to the permanent custody of the Department of Social Services (department).... The judge also ordered the entry of a decree...dispensing with the need for the father's consent to, or notice of, any petition for the adoption of the child. The father appealed....

A trial on the department's care and protection petition was...conducted over the course of fourteen days.... The judge found that the father was unfit to assume parental responsibility for his daughter, that his unfitness was likely to continue into the indefinite future, and that it was in the best interests of the child to terminate the father's parental rights....

We summarize the findings of fact made by the judge.... Peggy was born on October 27, 1995, to the father and his wife, A.T., in Proddatur, India. A.T. died on April 7, 1997, in a fall from the third-floor balcony of the family's residence in Hyderabad, India. Until her death, A.T. was the child's primary caretaker. After her mother's death, the child was placed in the care of her paternal grandmother. On September 12, 1997, the father married M.H. On April 23, 1998, the father immigrated to the United States on a temporary visa to work as a computer software specialist in Northborough. Shortly thereafter, he moved to Colorado, where he was engaged as a consultant for one of his employer's clients. On October 17, 1998, M.H. and the child joined him in Colorado, leaving the couple's newborn son with relatives in India. While living in Colorado, only the father and M.H. took care of the child.

On or about November 24, 1998, the child fractured her elbow. On November 26, the father and M.H. brought her to the emergency room of a hospital in Colorado Springs, but denied witnessing how the child had been injured. The examining physician advised the couple that the child needed immediate corrective surgery. Although their initial reaction was to inform the doctor that they preferred to defer such surgery until they could return to their home in India, after further discussion, they agreed to allow immediate surgery to repair the child's elbow. The operation required orthopedic follow-up, without which, the couple were informed, the child could have problems with her growth. Because the family planned to move back to the Boston area in December, they were referred to two orthopedic doctors whom they could consult in that area, but the child never received follow-up orthopedic care.

The family left Colorado on December 23, 1998, driving cross-country to Massachusetts, and arrived on December 27, 1998.... From the time of her arrival in Massachusetts until April 8, 1999, the child was in the exclusive care at all times of the father and M.H.

On April 6, 1999, M.H. informed the father that the child had a soft spot on the back of her head that she had discovered while brushing the child's hair. Her husband told her to make an appointment to see the pediatrician the next day. At approximately 2:30

a.m. on April 7, the child reportedly woke the father because she needed to use the bathroom. According to the father, the child's right eye, which had appeared fine when she went to bed, was swollen shut. Although the father, M.H., and the child shared one sleeping space, with the father in the middle, he had no explanation for the injury to the child's eye.

In the afternoon of April 7, 1999, the father brought the child to the doctor. The doctor discovered that, in addition to the swollen eye and swelling in the back of her head, the child had bruises on her body. An infected abrasion to her left ear and abrasions on her middle finger, which the father stated had been evident since March, were also present.... The doctor instructed the father and M.H. to take the child immediately to the University of Massachusetts Medical Center (UMMC).

On being admitted to UMMC the next day, the child was observed to have numerous injuries. Her principal injury consisted of the amputation of seventy-five per cent of her labia minora and the displacement of the clitoral hood from its superior position to lower down on the external genitalia. The injuries were consistent with the practice known as "female circumcision."[4] According to the pediatric surgeon at UMMC who examined the child, these injuries could not have been self-inflicted by a three and one-half year old child, and could only have been caused by a "cutting or cauterizing device." The judge found that the damage to the child's genitalia was consistent with a deliberate cutting of the clitoris, clitoral hood and labia.

The child was also observed to have an abnormally low hematocrit level, caused by the loss of blood attendant to the amputation of her genitalia. She also had severe anemia consistent with the loss of blood. The "boggy swelling" on the back of the child's head was determined to be a subdural hematoma, typically caused by a blow or trauma to the head. In addition, the child was also observed to have (a) a swollen right eye; (b) a swollen left eye; (c) a one centimeter long injury to her left upper lip; (d) multiple injuries to the fingers of both hands; (e) a "chronic injury" to her left ear comparable to a "cauliflower ear;" and (f) bruising on her back and shoulder.

The judge did not credit statements made by the father and M.H. that all the child's injuries were self-inflicted, nor did the judge credit the father's explanation that the damage to his daughter's genitalia resulted from her scratching herself. The UMMC staff observed no self-abusive behavior of any nature during the child's stay at the hospital. The judge found that the injuries to the child's genitalia were undoubtedly inflicted on her. In view of the fact that the child was in the exclusive custody of the father or M.H. at all times relevant to her injuries, the judge found that the father either participated in his daughter's mutilation or knowingly failed to take any steps to protect her from her abuser.

After receiving temporary custody, the department made reasonable efforts to locate an appropriate foster home for the child. Although the department attempted to develop a service plan for the child's family, neither the father nor his wife would cooperate with the department, on advice of counsel, due to a pending criminal proceeding stemming from the child's injuries. After a diligent search, the department failed to locate within the Commonwealth a foster family that spoke the child's native language, Telugu, or one which practiced the Hindu religion. At the time of the child's discharge from UMMC on April 20, 1999, there were no relatives with whom she could be placed within the Commonwealth. The child was originally placed in an approved foster home

---

4. The judge made a specific finding that "female circumcision" is not part of the rituals or beliefs of the Hindu religion, the religion practiced by the family. This finding is not challenged.

in which the foster father was a practicing physician, but shortly thereafter, due to her need for extraordinary care, she was placed in the care of a more experienced foster family, Mr. and Mrs. C., with a diverse, multi-cultural background.

In August, 1999, the child's paternal grandmother traveled to Massachusetts from her home in India. She resided with her son, the father, throughout her stay in the Commonwealth. On being informed of her interest in gaining custody of the child,[5] arrangements were made for the services of an interpreter so that the department could assess her suitability as a placement for the child. This assessment never took place, due to a no-contact order that prohibited any contact between the child and the grand-mother.[6] The grandmother subsequently returned to India without having seen the child. At the time of trial, the child had not seen her grandmother in nearly two years.

By the time of trial, the child had become an integral part of her new foster family and had formed strong attachments to her foster parents, Mr. and Mrs. C., and to their other children. Under the care of Mr. and Mrs. C., the child's symptoms of post-traumatic stress disorder, exhibited as a result of her recent trauma, almost entirely abated. The judge concluded that the severance of the child's new primary attachment to Mrs. C. posed an unacceptable risk that the child would develop an attachment disorder. The judge thus approved the department's proposal for the adoption of the child by Mr. and Mrs. C.

We turn now to issues raised by this appeal.... The father claims that the judge lacked authority to dispense with his consent to the child's adoption because both he and the child are Indian nationals.... General Laws c. 119, § 24, grants broad authority to the Juvenile Court to act on the petition of any person brought on behalf of any child under the age of eighteen years "within the jurisdiction of the court." This authority includes committing the child to the permanent custody of the department, if the court adjudges that the child "is in need of care and protection" as defined by the statute. See G.L. c. 119, § 26. See also Custody of a Minor (No. 1), 385 Mass. 697, 704, 434 N.E.2d 601 (1982). If the child so adjudged is under the age of twelve years, the Juvenile Court is required to enter a decree dispensing with the need for the consent to the child's adoption, if such decree would serve the best interests of the child, as defined by G.L. c. 210, § 3 (c). See G.L. c. 119, § 26(4). The decree effectively terminates the legal bond between parent and child. See G.L. c. 210, § 3....

The importance of the policy behind the statutory scheme — to protect children of the Commonwealth against "harmful effects resulting from the absence, inability, inadequacy or destructive behavior of parents or parent substitutes, and to assure good substitute parental care in the event of the absence, temporary or permanent inability or unfitness of parents to provide care and protection for their children" — cannot be overemphasized. G.L. c. 119, § 1. The child was living in Framingham.... The Juvenile Court's jurisdiction over the matter stems from the child's presence in the Commonwealth and her obvious need of care and protection. This protection is

---

5. In January, 2000, the grandmother filed a motion to intervene in the custody proceedings. The motion was denied and the grandmother did not appeal. She also filed a petition in the Juvenile Court to obtain guardianship of the child and, in May, 2000, requested that the department consider her as a placement for her granddaughter. It is not apparent what action, if any, was taken with regard to her guardianship petition. The department refused her request to have the child placed in her care.

6. The no-contact order was issued in the pending criminal suit against the father and M.H. based on their suspected abuse of the child....

mandated by G.L. c. 119 and does not depend on the immigration status of the child....

The father argues, nonetheless, that the decree dispensing with the need for his consent to the child's adoption and the judge's approval of the department's proposed adoption plan, violated Federal and international law. His primary complaint appears to be that, in light of the child's status as a foreign national, the judge erred in not considering Federal immigration law and international treaties. Thus framed, his argument presents essentially a question of choice of law, rather than one of jurisdiction. As such, it has been waived.... In any case, his argument lacks merit.

We are aware of no Federal or international law that would operate to divest the Juvenile Court of the power to reach the result it did in these proceedings. There is no question that immigration law is strictly within the purview of Federal courts. *See* 8 U.S.C. § 1101 (2000). The judge, however, made no determination relative to the child's immigration status. Although it undoubtedly will change as a result of the termination of the father's parental rights, her new immigration status will have to be determined by the proper Federal authorities. The details of how, and when, this may happen are matters that, as a State court, we do not discuss. We note, however, that Federal immigration law specifically recognizes the jurisdiction of State Juvenile Courts over determinations regarding the custody and best interests of children who have been abused or neglected, regardless of their immigration status. *See* 8 U.S.C. § 1101(a)(27)(J) (providing means by which child who has become ward of State due to abuse, neglect, or abandonment, may apply for permanent legal resident status)....

The father refers us to international law, contending that provisions of the Convention on the Rights of the Child (convention) preclude the actions taken by the judge.... The convention is not binding on our courts because, although it has been signed, it has never been ratified by the United States.... We have read the entire text of the convention, nonetheless, and conclude that the outcome of the proceedings in this case are completely in accord with principles expressed therein. Of particular relevance is language contained in art. 3 ("[i]n all actions concerning children, whether undertaken by public or private social welfare institutions, courts of law, administrative authorities or legislative bodies, the best interests of the child shall be a primary consideration") and in art. 19 ("[parties to the convention] shall take all appropriate legislative, administrative, social and educational measures to protect the child from all forms of physical... violence, injury or abuse...while in the care of parent(s)....").[11]

We reject the father's claim that the department's adoption plan violates art. 21 of the convention. Article 21 considers the topic of a country's adoption system in general, and does not appear to apply to the specific circumstance, such as here, where a State has taken custody of a child due to parental abuse. Nonetheless, regarding international adoptions, art. 21 states that "inter-country adoption may be considered...if the child cannot be placed in a foster or an adoptive family or cannot in any suitable manner be cared for in the child's country of origin." More to the point, art. 21 confirms that the paramount consideration of agencies placing children in adoptive homes, whether in

---

11. There can be no doubt that the child's extensive injuries are encompassed by this language. The injury to her genitalia, euphemistically referred to by the judge as "female circumcision," is more commonly known as "female genital mutilation" and has been unequivocally condemned by Federal and international law as a violation of the rights of women and female children. *See* Abankwah v. Immigration & Naturalization Serv., 185 F.3d 18, 23–26 (2d Cir. 1999), and authorities cited.

their country of origin or abroad, must be "the best interests of the child." We conclude that the principles of children's rights, as expressed in the convention, do not conflict, and are in total agreement, with the termination of the father's parental rights, the decree dispensing with the need for his consent to the child's adoption, and the department's plan for her adoption by her foster parents, Mr. and Mrs. C.[12]

We consider the father's remaining claims that go to the merits of the trial. The father advances numerous arguments to support his challenge to the decree dispensing with the need for his consent to the child's adoption. Primarily, he asserts that the judge's determination of his parental unfitness was unsupported by clear and convincing evidence because it was based on factual findings that were substantially ("[m]ore than one-half") erroneous and on improperly admitted evidence....

We reject the father's challenges to the judge's decree for the following reasons. The department presented clear and convincing evidence of the father's unfitness. The... judge's ultimate conclusion of parental unfitness is overwhelmingly supported by the record. *See* Adoption of Helen, 429 Mass. 856, 860, 712 N.E.2d 77 (1999)....

In determining whether the best interests of a child will be served by issuing a decree dispensing with the need for consent, a judge must consider "the ability, capacity, fitness and readiness of the child's parent...to assume parental responsibility," as well as "the plan proposed by the department or other agency initiating the petition." G.L. c. 210, §3 (c).... There was no evidence whatsoever on which the judge could find that the child, if returned to her father, would not continue to be subjected to physical abuse. At the time of the judge's decision, the child had been in foster care for approximately nineteen months and had formed a strong positive bond with her foster parents, Mr. and Mrs. C. The judge was fully warranted in concluding that the father was unfit to assume parental responsibility for the child. On the facts of this case, a conclusion other than the one reached by the judge might have constituted error....

Notes and Questions

1. *Sole Injury.* The court called the FGM the "principal injury." What, however, if it were her sole injury? Would the outcome have been the same? Should it have been?

2. *Explanation for the Injury.* What argument would you have made on the father's behalf before the trial court regarding the FGM?

3. *Choice of Law.* Had the choice of law argument been made before the trial court, what would it have looked like? Would it have been effective?

4. *Adoption.* International adoption is dealt with extensively in Chapter Twelve.

---

12. Notification of authorities at the Indian consulate, that the child, an Indian national, was the subject of custody proceedings, may have been in order. *See* art. 37 of the Vienna Convention on Consular Relations, 21 U.S.T. 77, 101, 102 (1963) (imposing duty on "competent authorities of the receiving State" to inform the appropriate consular post of any case involving appointment of guardian for minor who is "a national of the sending State"). Whether such notification was given is not established in the record. Counsel for the child asserted at oral argument, without challenge, that the child's paternal grandmother had contacted the Indian consulate "one year ago." The Indian government has asserted no interest in this case, and notice pursuant to art. 37, or the lack thereof, would not have changed its outcome. *See id.* at 102 (notification acts without prejudice to operation of laws of receiving State).

c. Immigration Law

FGM is relevant to attempts by aliens to gain entry or stay in the United States. While immigration law is not typically studied in a family law class, some aspects of immigration law are very relevant to us here. As a practical matter, clients may have specific immigration concerns and the existence of "family violence" may help them achieve their legal goals. More theoretically, immigration law, and particularly the law of asylum, tells us a great deal about how family violence is perceived by decision makers in a particular country. The law of asylum forces judges and legislators to articulate a view of family violence either as a private matter, solely between a victim and her perpetrator, or as a social phenomenon. Additionally, judges and legislators are forced to consider whether or not different types of violence against women are functionally the same. Finally, the depth of a society's commitment to human rights can arguably be measured, in part, by its asylum law because decision makers are asked to apply at home the human rights rhetoric that is used to criticize others. Understanding something about immigration law helps one evaluate how violence claims are treated.

The United States is a party to the 1951 United Nations Convention Relating to the Status of Refugees (1951 Convention) and the 1967 Protocol Relating to the Status of Refugees (1967 Protocol). The United States enacted the Refugee Act of 1980, Pub. L. No. 96-212, as a way to implement its treaty obligations. Asylum and refugee claims are resolved pursuant to this law.

Sean D. Murphy, *Non-State Entities in International Law*
94 Am. J. Int'l L. 111, 111–13 (2000)

Aliens may apply for entry as "refugees" only from outside the United States. To qualify as a refugee, the alien must show "persecution or a well-founded fear of persecution" in another country "on account of race, religion, nationality, membership in a particular social group, or political opinion."[4] The number of "refugees"—persons fleeing persecution in their home countries—that can be admitted to the United States each year is determined by the president in consultation with Congress. On that basis, up to 78,000 refugees could be admitted to the United States in [Fiscal Year] 1999, with each of five geographical regions having a specified allocation: Africa (12,000), East Asia (9,000), Europe (48,000), Latin America/Caribbean (3,000), and Near East/South Asia (4,000), with 2,000 unallocated....

Aliens who are already in the United States (such as on a temporary visa) or at a U.S. port of entry may apply to the INS [Immigration and Naturalization Service] for "asylum."[7] Even if the alien is deemed a "refugee," the decision on whether to grant an application for asylum rests with the attorney general.[8] The attorney general may not grant

---

4. 8 U.S.C.A. § 1101(a)(42)(A) (West Supp. 1999).

7. Immigration and Nationality Act, 8 U.S.C. § 1101-1537 (1994 & Supp. 1998), 8 U.S.C.A. § 1101-1537 (West Supp. 1999). The alien may apply affirmatively to the INS for asylum, in which case the application is heard by an INS asylum officer. If the application is denied, it may then be heard by an immigration judge. If the INS has brought proceedings against an alien, and the alien then requests asylum, the matter goes directly to an immigration judge.

8. 8 U.S.C.A. § 1158(b)(1) (West Supp. 1999). For the procedures followed upon an application for asylum, see 8 C.F.R. 208 (1999).

asylum, however, when, among other things, "the alien, having been convicted by a final judgment of a particularly serious crime, constitutes a danger to the community of the United States" or "there are serious reasons for believing that the alien has committed a serious nonpolitical crime outside the United States prior to the arrival of the alien in the United States." The statutory provisions and related relief for asylum closely track the U.N. Convention Relating to the Status of Refugees and the U.N. Protocol Relating to the Status of Refugees.

Separate from, but closely related to, the issue of asylum is that of "withholding" deportation (which, unlike a grant of asylum, does not necessarily lead to permanent residency in the United States). If the attorney general determines that an "alien's life or freedom would be threatened" in another country "because of the alien's race, religion, nationality, membership in a particular social group, or political opinion,"[12] the attorney general must withhold deportation (that is, there is no discretion). The standard of proof, however, is somewhat higher than the one used in cases of asylum. Whereas an alien requesting asylum need only prove a well-founded fear of persecution, an alien attempting to prevent "removal" must prove that such persecution is more likely than not. As in the case of asylum, however, the attorney general may not withhold deportation if the alien has been convicted of a serious crime or has committed a serious nonpolitical crime prior to arrival in the United States....

It is helpful to know how asylum claims are frequently adjudicated. Any alien who is physically present in the United States or at a U.S. port of entry can request asylum. Aliens apply for asylum either with an INS asylum officer or with an immigration judge if in removal proceedings.

The Illegal Immigration Reform and Immigrant Responsibility Act of 1996 specifies that individuals who appear at the border without adequate documentation will receive a "credible fear" interview with an asylum officer. The interview is not a formal hearing. The purpose is to see if the alien has a credible fear of persecution or torture and is thus eligible to apply for asylum or withholding of removal. In the credible fear interview, the alien must show that there is a significant possibility that he or she could successfully establish the grounds for the asylum. If the alien makes out this showing, then the alien can apply for asylum. An alien is often detained pending the application.

An immigration judge can review a negative determination by the INS asylum officer on the credible fear determination. Typically such review takes place very quickly, often within twenty-four hours but always within seven days. If the immigration judge agrees that there is no "credible fear," then the INS begins removal proceedings. *See* Jaya Ramji, *Legislating Away International Law: The Refugee Provisions of the Illegal Immigration Reform and Immigrant Responsibility Act,* 37 Stan. J. Int'l L. 117, 134 (2001). Aliens denied asylum by the INS may renew asylum claims with the immigration judge when they are in removal proceedings.

"The decision of the immigration judge...in removal proceedings is appealable to the Board of Immigration Appeals. From there, appeals go to the federal courts, either by statute or via an application for a writ of habeas corpus. The 1996 legislation restricted federal court review in asylum cases by moving from a 'substantial evidence standard' to an even more deferential 'abuse of discretion and manifestly contrary to

---

12. 8 U.S.C.A. § 1231(b)(3)(A) (West Supp. 1999).

law' test." *See* Peter Margulies, *Democratic Transitions and the Future of Asylum Law,* 71 U. Colo. L. Rev. 3, 12 n.19 (2000).

To make out a successful asylum claim, an applicant must establish that he or she is a refugee under the 1980 Refugee Act. *See* 8 U.S.C. § 1101(a)(42). The elements, to be explicit, are 1) a well-founded fear 2) of persecution 3) on account of 4) one of the specified grounds (race, religion, nationality, membership in a particular social group, or political opinion). Additionally, if the persecution is inflicted by a non-governmental entity, then an applicant must show that the persecutor was someone the government was "unable or unwilling to control." Sangha v. INS, 103 F.3d 1482, 1487 (9th Cir. 1997) (citing McMullen v. INS, 658 F.2d 1312, 1315 (9th Cir. 1981)). "Government action is not necessarily required; instead, police inaction in the face of…persecution [by non-governmental groups] can suffice to make out a claim." Navas v. INS, 217 F.3d 646, 656 n.10 (9th Cir. 2000).

The asylum remedy is important for reasons beyond avoiding immediate deportation. When a woman is granted asylum, she may be eligible for adjustment of status to lawful permanent resident after one year, she is eligible for employment authorization, she is eligible for state welfare benefits, she can apply to bring her family members over, and she can eventually apply for citizenship. Only citizenship gives her immunity from deportation.

In re Fauziya Kasinga
21 I. & N. Dec. 357 (B.I.A. 1996) (en banc)

Schmidt, Chairman:

This is a timely appeal by the applicant from a decision of an Immigration Judge dated August 25, 1995. The Immigration Judge found the applicant excludable as an intending immigrant, denied her applications for asylum and withholding of deportation, and ordered her excluded and deported from the United States. Upon reviewing the appellate record anew ("de novo review"), we will sustain the applicant's appeal, grant asylum, and order her admitted to the United States as an asylee.…

The applicant is a 19-year-old native and citizen of Togo. She attended 2 years of high school. She is a member of the Tchamba-Kunsuntu Tribe of northern Togo. She testified that young women of her tribe normally undergo FGM at age 15. However, she did not because she initially was protected from FGM by her influential, but now deceased, father.

The applicant stated that upon her father's death in 1993, under tribal custom her aunt, her father's sister, became the primary authority figure in the family. The applicant's mother was driven from the family home, left Togo, and went to live with her family in Benin. The applicant testified that she does not currently know her mother's exact whereabouts.

The applicant further testified that her aunt forced her into a polygamous marriage in October 1994, when she was 17. The husband selected by her aunt was 45 years old and had three other wives at the time of marriage. The applicant testified that, under tribal custom, her aunt and her husband planned to force her to submit to FGM before the marriage was consummated.

The applicant testified that she feared imminent mutilation. With the help of her older sister, she fled Togo for Ghana. However, she was afraid that her aunt and her husband would locate her there. Consequently, using money from her mother, the applicant embarked for Germany by airplane....

The applicant testified that the Togolese police and the Government of Togo were aware of FGM and would take no steps to protect her from the practice. She further testified that her aunt had reported her to the Togolese police. Upon return, she would be taken back to her husband by the police and forced to undergo FGM. She testified at several points that there would be nobody to protect her from FGM in Togo.

In her testimony, the applicant referred to letters in the record from her mother. Those letters confirmed that the Togolese police were looking for the applicant and that the applicant's father's family wanted her to undergo FGM.

The applicant testified that she could not find protection anywhere in Togo. She stated that Togo is a very small country and her husband and aunt, with the help of the police, could locate her anywhere she went. She also stated that her husband is well known in Togo and is a friend of the police....

[Ed. Note: In Germany, the applicant bought a passport and a ticket to the United States. She did not attempt a fraudulent entry into the United States, but instead immediately requested asylum. The INS detained her until April 1996, during which time she filed a formal written asylum application. As mentioned above, this application was denied by the immigration judge. On appeal, the BIA agreed with both parties that FGM can be a basis for asylum. The issues on appeal related to "the parameters of FGM as a ground for asylum in future cases" and whether this applicant was entitled to asylum on the basis of the facts in her case.]

FGM As Persecution...

While a number of descriptions of persecution have been formulated in our past decisions, we have recognized that persecution can consist of the infliction of harm or suffering by a government, or persons a government is unwilling or unable to control, to overcome a characteristic of the victim. *See* Matter of Acosta, 19 I&N Dec. 211, 222-23 (BIA 1985), modified on other grounds, Matter of Mogharrabi, 19 I&N Dec. 439 (BIA 1987).... As observed by the INS, many of our past cases involved actors who had a subjective intent to punish their victims. However, this subjective "punitive" or "malignant" intent is not required for harm to constitute persecution.

Social Group...

In the context of this case, we find the particular social group to be the following: Young women of the Tchamba-Kunsuntu Tribe who have not had FGM, as practiced by that tribe, and who oppose the practice. This is very similar to the formulations suggested by the parties.

The defined social group meets the test we set forth in *Matter of Acosta, supra,* at 233. *See also* Matter of H-, Interim Decision 3276 (BIA 1996) (finding that identifiable shared ties of kinship warrant characterization as social group). It also is consistent with the law of the United States Court of Appeals for the Third Circuit, where this case arose. Fatin v. INS, 12 F.3d 1233, 1241 (3d Cir. 1993) (stating that Iranian women who refuse to conform to the Iranian Government's gender-specific laws and social norms may well satisfy the Acosta definition).

In accordance with *Acosta,* the particular social group is defined by common characteristics that members of the group either cannot change, or should not be required to change because such characteristics are fundamental to their individual identities. The characteristics of being a "young woman" and a "member of the Tchamba-Kunsuntu Tribe" cannot be changed. The characteristic of having intact genitalia is one that is so fundamental to the individual identity of a young woman that she should not be required to change it.

Well-Founded Fear

The burden of proof is upon an applicant for asylum to establish that a "reasonable person" in her circumstances would fear persecution upon return to Togo.... The applicant has met this burden through a combination of her credible testimony and the introduction of documentary evidence and background information that supports her claim....

"On Account of"

To be eligible for asylum, the applicant must establish that her well-founded fear of persecution is "on account of" one of the five grounds specified in the Act, here, her membership in a "particular social group."...

Both parties have advanced, and the background materials support, the proposition that there is no legitimate reason for FGM. Group Exhibit 4 contains materials showing that the practice has been condemned by such groups as the United Nations, the International Federation of Gynecology and Obstetrics, the Council on Scientific Affairs, the World Health Organization, the International Medical Association, and the American Medical Association.

Record materials state that FGM "has been used to control woman's sexuality," FGM Alert, *supra*, at 4. It also is characterized as a form of "sexual oppression" that is "based on the manipulation of women's sexuality in order to assure male dominance and exploitation." During oral argument before us, the INS General Counsel agreed with the latter characterization. He also stated that the practice is a "severe bodily invasion" that should be regarded as meeting the asylum standard even if done with "subjectively benign intent."

We agree with the parties that, as described and documented in this record, FGM is practiced, at least in some significant part, to overcome sexual characteristics of young women of the tribe who have not been, and do not wish to be, subjected to FGM. We therefore find that the persecution the applicant fears in Togo is "on account of" her status as a member of the defined social group.

Country-Wide Persecution

The INS suggests, in its brief and at oral argument, that a remand is necessary because the applicant has not established that she would be unable to avoid FGM by moving to some other part of Togo. As we found in Part I of our opinion, the applicant presented credible testimony that her husband is a well-known individual who is a friend of the police in Togo. She testified that her aunt and her husband were looking for her and that there could be no refuge for her because Togo is a small country and the police would not protect her.

The applicant's testimony is consistent with the background information in the record. That information confirms that 1) FGM is widely practiced in Togo; 2) acts of violence and abuse against women in Togo are tolerated by the police; 3) the Government of Togo has a poor human rights record; and 4) most African women can expect little governmental protection from FGM.... We also take notice that Togo is a small country of approximately 22,000 square miles, slightly smaller than West Virginia.

Neither in its briefs nor at oral argument did the INS raise any claim of "new evidence" that might show changed country conditions. We assume that if the INS had any new documentation showing that the applicant could find safety from FGM elsewhere in Togo, it would have offered that evidence in support of its motion to remand.

For the foregoing reasons, we find that this record adequately supports the applicant's claim that she has a country-wide fear of persecution in Togo....

[Ed. Note: After finding the applicant eligible for asylum, the BIA exercised its discretion and granted asylum to her.]

Filppu, concurring, joined by Heilman:

I respectfully concur. I write separately in part to respond more completely to several arguments advanced by the Immigration and Naturalization Service....

Despite the absence of any major dispute between the parties in this case, the Service requests that we adopt its broad "framework of analysis" for claims of this type. Its suggestion candidly is aimed at addressing issues it sees arising in relation to claims that may be made by women from other "parts of the world where FGM is practiced" and by those "who have been subjected to it in the past."...

The Service points out that it is "estimated that over eighty million females have been subjected to FGM." It further notes that there is "no indication" that "Congress considered application of [the asylum laws] to broad cultural practices of the type involved here." The Service proceeds to argue that "the underlying purposes of the asylum system...are unavoidably in tension" in both providing protection for those seriously in jeopardy and in maintaining broad overall governmental control over immigration. The Service further argues that "the Board's interpretation in this case must assure protection for those most at risk of the harms covered by the statute, but it cannot simply grant asylum to all who might be subjected to a practice deemed objectionable or a violation of a person's human rights." It is from these underpinnings that the Service argues that the class of FGM victims who may be eligible for asylum "does not consist of all women who come from the parts of the world where FGM is practiced, nor of all who have been subjected to it in the past."...

The Service then offers its "framework of analysis." That framework includes a new "shocks the conscience" test for persecution. The advantages seen by the Service of this test evidently include: 1) the ability to define FGM as "persecution" notwithstanding any lack of intent to "punish" FGM victims on the part of the victims' parents or tribe members who may well "believe that they are simply performing an important cultural rite that bonds the individual to the society"; 2) the ability to exclude other cultural practices, such as "body scarring," from the definition of persecution as these do not shock the conscience; and 3) the ability to exclude past victims of FGM from asylum eligibility if "they consented" to it or "at least acquiesced," as in the case of a woman who experienced FGM as "a small child," since FGM would not shock the conscience unless inflicted on "an unconsenting or resisting individual."...

The Service can seek to have the Attorney General issue regulations that comprehensively address competing concerns, or it can work within the Administration for appropriate legislative action by Congress. The Service should not, however, expect the Board to endorse a significant new framework for assessing asylum claims in the context of a single novel case, especially when that framework seems intended primarily to address cases that are not in fact before the Board yet.

Information Regarding Female Genital Mutilation

8 U.S.C. § 1374 (2001)

(a) Provision of information regarding female genital mutilation

The Immigration and Naturalization Service (in cooperation with the Department of State) shall make available for all aliens who are issued immigrant or nonimmigrant visas, prior to or at the time of entry into the United States, the following information:

(1) Information on the severe harm to physical and psychological health caused by female genital mutilation which is compiled and presented in a manner which is limited to the practice itself and respectful to the cultural values of the societies in which such practice takes place.

(2) Information concerning potential legal consequences in the United States for (A) performing female genital mutilation, or (B) allowing a child under his or her care to be subjected to female genital mutilation, under criminal or child protection statutes or as a form of child abuse.

(b) Limitation

In consultation with the Secretary of State, the Commissioner of Immigration and Naturalization shall identify those countries in which female genital mutilation is commonly practiced and, to the extent practicable, limit the provision of information under subsection (a) of this section to aliens from such countries.

(c) Definition

For purposes of this section, the term "female genital mutilation" means the removal or infibulation (or both) of the whole or part of the clitoris, the labia minora, or labia majora.

Notes and Questions

1. Why might Kasinga have had difficulty obtaining asylum when her case was heard by the Immigration Judge?

2. *Persecution.* Persecution is not defined either in the 1951 Refugee Convention or the 1980 U.S. Refugee Act. In fact, Congress deliberately decided to exclude a definition, believing the term was commonly understood as the following: "the infliction of suffering or harm, under government sanction, upon persons who differ in a way regarded as offensive (e.g., race, religion, political opinion, etc.), in a manner condemned by civilized governments. The harm or suffering need not be physical, but may take other forms, such as the deliberate imposition of severe economic disadvantage or the deprivation of liberty, food, housing, employment or other essentials of life." H.R. Rep. 95-1452 at 5 (1978). The BIA follows this definition, and, as is obvious from *In re Kasinga,* no subjective intent on the part of the persecutor to "inflict harm" or "punish" the victim is required. This is important for asylum seekers because often the persecutor believes he or she is doing something to benefit the victim. *See, e.g.,* Pitcherskaia v. INS, 118 F.3d 641 (9th Cir. 1997) (remanding case of lesbian woman who claimed that she had been forced to undergo psychiatric treatments and threatened institutionalization by Soviet officials as a "cure" to change her sexual orientation). The United Nation's High Commissioner for Refugees agrees that FGM can constitute persecution. *See* Letter from U.N. High Commissioner for Refugees to British Refugee Legal Centre (July 8, 1994) (quoted at http://www.amnesty.org/ailib/intcam/femgen/fgm6.htm).

A. *Hypothetical No. 1.* Imagine that FGM is performed on adult women in a particular culture immediately before their marriage. It is never inflicted on a woman without her consent. However, if the woman does not undergo the procedure, she cannot marry. Is that persecution? The United Nations High Commissioner for Refugees believes that a woman "fleeing severe discrimination or other inhuman treatment... for her failure to conform to strict social codes" may qualify as a refugee, if the discrimination has "consequences that are significantly prejudicial." *Protecting Refugees: Questions and Answers* 12, U.N. HCR, U.N. Doc. HCR/PI/Q&A-UK1.PM5 (1996).

B. *Hypothetical No. 2.* Assume for a moment that the only basis for Kasinga's application was the arranged marriage to a man approximately thirty years her senior. If her family would have forced her to marry that man, would that be persecution?

3. *State Action.* Both of the hypotheticals in the foregoing note raise two issues: 1) whether the harm or suffering inflicted is sufficient to constitute persecution; and, 2) whether there is sufficient governmental involvement to constitute persecution. The hypotheticals in note 2 were meant to address primarily the first consideration. This note is intended to address the second consideration. Simply, must one prove state action in order to obtain asylum? *Kasinga* is consistent with the U.N. Refugee Handbook. It states: "Persecution is normally related to action by the authorities of a country. It may also emanate from sections of the population that do not respect the standards established by the laws of the country concerned. A case in point may be religious intolerance, amounting to persecution, in a country otherwise secular, but where sizeable fractions of the population do not respect the religious beliefs of their neighbors. Where serious discriminatory or other offensive acts are committed by the local populace, they can be considered as persecution if they are knowingly tolerated by the authorities, or if the authorities refuse, or prove unable, to offer effective protection." *Handbook Procedures and Criteria for Determining Refugee Status*, U.N. HCR, at ch. II, B(2)(g), §65, U.N. Doc. HCR/IP/Eng/REV.1 (1979).

4. *Well-Founded Fear.* An applicant's fear of persecution must be subjectively and objectively reasonable. In *INS v. Cardoza-Fonseca*, 480 U.S. 421 (1987), the Supreme Court held that a ten-percent possibility of persecution made an asylum-seeker's fear of returning home objectively "reasonable." A reasonable person would find even a ten-percent chance of grave harm material. The issue of "well-founded fear" is explored further in Chapter Thirteen in the context of claims for asylum brought by individuals fleeing countries with coercive population control policies.

5. *Floodgates?* To what extent does the *Kasinga* decision help women who are facing or have experienced FGM gain entry into the United States? Are the INS's fears, set forth in the concurring opinion, valid?

6. *More Facts.* Fauziya Kasinga's real name is Fauziya Kassindja, but her name was misspelled when she arrived in the United States. *See* Female Genital Mutilation, A Guide to Laws and Policies Worldwide 241 n.19 (Anika Rahmun & Nahid Toubia eds., 2000). As suggested by the facts of her transit from Togo to the United States, Ms. Kasinga was an economically privileged African. *See* Fauziya Kassindja, Do They Hear You When You Cry? 12–14 (1998).

7. *Parents.* The United Nations High Commissioner for Refugees encourages countries to grant refugee status to parents who fear persecution because of their refusal to inflict FGM on their children. *See Protecting Refugees: Questions & Answers, supra,* at 12.

8. *Education.* Look again at 8 U.S.C. § 1374(a)(1). The statute requires that certain entrants into the United States receive information about FGM. Is it possible to provide the information specified and be "respectful?" Do you think the provision of information on the harmful effects is inherently disrespectful? Why or why not?

9. *Risks of Asylum Law.* Compared to the criminal law or child protection law, asylum law might appear an attractive option for furthering a human rights agenda at home. Are there any disadvantages to this approach? One of the potential disadvantages of using asylum law to further human rights causes is that advocates may exaggerate a practice and a foreign country's acceptance of that practice in order to build their clients' cases.

4. International Law

By at least the 1950s, Western countries were aware of female genital mutilations occurring in Africa. However, they were not ready to become involved in studying, much less opposing, "cultural" practices. In 1959, the World Health Organization (WHO) refused an invitation by the Economic and Social Council of the United Nations to study "ritual operations" on girls because the study of social and cultural traditions was "outside the competence of the World Health Organization." It would be another twenty years before a true international dialogue on the topic would erupt....

In February 1984, the United Nations Working Group on Traditional Practices sponsored a seminar attended by representatives from twenty-one African nations. This resulted in formation of the Inter-Africa Committee (IAC) to promote the abolition of harmful traditional practices. At its inception, the IAC warned against "untimely haste, which would result in rash legal measures that would never be enforced." However, in 1987 it requested, and in 1990 reiterated the need for, laws against FGM, especially directed at health professionals....

In March 1998, the United Nations began a three year campaign to eliminate FGM worldwide...of girls.

Susan A. Dillon, *Healing the Sacred Yoni in the Land of Isis: Female Genital Mutilation is Banned (Again) in Egypt*, 22 Hous. J. Int'l L. 289, 300–01 (2000). *See also Report of the Committee on Progress Achieved in the Implementation of the Convention*, CEDAW, 14th Sess., U.N. Doc. CEDAW/C/1995/7 (1995).

The campaign to eliminate the practice presupposes that FGM is a violation of the human rights of women and girls. Apart from possibly constituting persecution in violation of the Refugee Convention and Protocol, what other provisions of international law are violated by the practice? After all, not all people subjected to the procedure object to it. Do the provisions related to "non-discrimination" apply? How? *See, e.g.,* Universal Declaration of Human Rights (UDHR), art. 2; International Covenant on Civil and Political Rights (ICCPR), art. 2(1); International Covenant on Economic, Social, and Cultural Rights (ICESCR), art. 2(2); Convention on the Elimination of Discrimination Against Women (CEDAW), art. 1; African Charter on Human and Peoples Rights (Banjul Charter), arts. 18(3), 28. Consider particularly article 1 of CEDAW. Is FGM discrimination against women? What about the fact that men cannot experience the procedure because they are physically different from women? The Committee on the Elimination of Discrimination Against Women has issued General Recommendation No. 14, A/45/38 (9th Sess. 1990), which concludes that FGM is discrimination against women. Also, article 2 of the Declaration on the Elimination of Violence Against Women mentions "female genital mutilation" as a type of violence that must be eliminated. *See* G.A. Res. 48/104, U.N. Doc. A/RES/48/49 (1993). Yet what about the fact that many *women* are vehemently supportive of the practice?

Other provisions of international law are also potentially relevant. Consider article 3 of the Universal Declaration of Human Rights: "Everyone has the right to life, liberty and security of person." *See also* ICCPR, art. 9(1); Banjul Charter, art. 4; American Convention on Human Rights, art. 5(1). Do girls subjected to FGM experience violations of their right to security of person? Need the girl protest the procedure in order to experience the violation? What if the girl consents? What if her parent consents? Do these provisions impose any obligation on States Parties to prohibit the practice if it is performed by non-state actors?

Perhaps FGM is a form of violence and article 19 of the U.N. Convention on the Rights of the Child (CRC) applies. As mentioned above, FGM is identified as "violence" in the U.N. Declaration on the Elimination of Violence Against Women. *See* art 2(a); *see also* General Recommendation No. 19, *Violence Against Women*, CEDAW, U.N. GOAR, 47th Sess., Supp. No. 38, U.N. Doc. A/47/38 (1992). Would article 19 be violated if the perpetrator does not view the procedure as violent or even harmful, but rather views it as beneficial to the recipient?

Perhaps the Convention Against Torture and Other Cruel, Inhuman or Degrading Treatment or Punishment, discussed later in the chapter, applies to FGM. The ICCPR and the UDHR also prohibit "torture" and "cruel, inhuman or degrading treatment or punishment." *See* ICCPR, art. 17; UDHR, art. 5.

What about provisions discussing the right to enjoy high standards of physical health? Consider, for example, article 12 of the ICESCR, which states, "Parties to the present Covenant recognize the right of everyone to the enjoyment of the highest attainable standard of physical and mental health." There are similar provisions in other international instruments. *See, e.g.,* CRC, arts. 9, 24; Declaration of the Rights of the Child, principle 2 (1959); Banjul Charter, art. 16; American Declaration on the Rights and Duties of Man, art. XI; CEDAW, article 11(1)(f). In particular, article 24(3) of the Convention on the Rights of the Child requires States Parties to "take all effective and appropriate measures with a view to abolishing traditional practices prejudicial to the health of children." What of the fact that those who practice the procedure claim FGM actually promotes physical health? *See* Charles W. Holmes, *The Plight of Women Around the World—Sexuality: Painful, Ritual Procedure Tied to Tradition,* Atlanta Constitution, Sept. 3, 1995, at 1995 WL 6547902 (citing a fundamentalist cleric who claims that uncircumcised women "face the possibility of diseases, 'bad smells' and the sinful temptation to masturbate").

Provisions in international legal instruments, however, may also be cited to support the practice. Perhaps provisions that recognize a right to practice one's culture support the legality of this practice under international law. *See, e.g.,* UDHR, art. 27(1); ICESCR, art. 15(1)(a). Arguments might also be based, similarly, on the rights of minorities, *see* ICCPR, art. 27, or the right to freedom of religion, *see* ICCPR, art. 18. Do the instruments themselves suggest how to resolve this tension? *See* UDHR, art. 30; ICESCR, art. 5(1). *See also* CEDAW, art. 5. *Compare* Banjul Charter, art. 29(7).

How this tension is resolved depends, in part, upon a larger theoretical debate about the universality of certain human rights and the importance of group rights. Pieces of that debate follow. The excerpts first address the question whether certain human rights are universal. Then the excerpts address the issue of group rights. Later in the chapter, both the substantive content of various international law provisions as well as state responsibility for the action of non-state actors will be explored. For now, however, it is sufficient to assume that a state could be responsible under international law for FGM that occurred in its country. Here we are concerned with the normative question: "Should it be responsible?"

a. The Universality of Human Rights

Katherine Brennan, Note, *The Influence of Cultural Relativism on International Human Rights Law: Female Circumcision as a Case Study*

7 Law & Ineq. J. 367, 371–72 (1989)

Universalism, which draws from the natural law tradition in Western jurisprudence, is the theory that there exists some set of standards which all cultures espouse. These universal principles transcend cultural differences and serve as the authority for adopting international human rights. This theory assumes that all cultures value the protection of individual human dignity and that they would establish similar minimum standards for protecting their individual members. The official doctrine underlying the current international human rights systems is that the instruments which make up developing international human rights law enumerates these universal minimum standards. If at least some of the rights enumerated by the U.N. human rights instruments are universal, that core of rights would provide a standard against which cultural practices could legitimately be judged.

Addressing the global system of international law, Professor Makau Mutua echoes the sentiments of many Third World commentators:

> The regime of international law is illegitimate. It is a predatory system that legitimizes, reproduces and sustains the plunder and subordination of the Third World by the West.... The construction and universalization of international law were essential to the imperial expansion that subordinated non-European peoples and societies to European conquest and domination.... Historically, the Third World has generally viewed international law as a regime and discourse of domination and subordination, not resistance and liberation.... Since the state is the central and most important actor in international law, sovereign statehood, as defined by European powers, was the difference between freedom and the conquest and occupation of a people or a society.... [Through the United Nations], European hegemony over global affairs was simply transferred to the big powers—the United States, Britain, France, the Soviet Union, and China—which allotted themselves permanent seats on the Security Council.... The primacy of the Security Council over the...General Assembly, which would be dominated by Third World states, made a mockery of the notion of sovereign equality among states.

Makua Mutua, *What is Twail?*, 94 Am. Soc'y Int'l L. Proc. 31, 33, 34 (2000). *See, e.g.,* Third World Attitudes Toward International Law (Frederick E. Snyder & Surakiart Sathiranthai eds., 1987); Mohamed Bedjaoui, *Poverty in the International Order, in* International Law: A Contemporary Perspective (Richard Falk et al. eds., 1985).

Regarding the human rights movement specifically, Professor Mutua writes:

As currently constituted and deployed, the human rights movement will ultimately fail because it is perceived as an alien ideology in non-Western societies.... In order ultimately to prevail, the human rights movement must be
moored in the cultures of all peoples.... [I] do not mean to suggest that human
rights are bad per se or that the human rights corpus is irredeemable. Rather,...
the globalization of human rights fits a historical pattern in which all high
morality comes from the West as a civilizing agent against lower forms of civilization in the rest of the world.... International law itself was founded on the
preeminence of four specific European biases: geographic Europe as the center,
and Christianity, mercantile economics, and political imperialism as superior
paradigms. Both the League of Nations and its successor, the United Nations,
revitalized and confirmed European-American domination of international affairs.... The West was able to impose its philosophy of human rights on the rest
of the world because it dominated the United Nations at its inception....

Without a doubt many of the leaders and foot-soldiers of the human rights
movement are driven by a burning desire to end human suffering, as they see it
from their vantage point. The white American suburban high school or college
student who joins the local chapter of AI [Amnesty International] and protests
FGM in far away lands or writes letters to political or military leaders whose
names do not easily roll off the English tongue are no doubt drawing partly
from a well of noblesse oblige. The zeal to see all humanity as related and the
impulse to help those defined as in need is noble and is not the problem addressed here. A certain degree of human universality is inevitable and desirable.
But what that universality is, what historical and cultural stew it is made of, and
how it is accomplished make all the difference. What the high school or college
student ought to realize is that her zeal to save others—even from themselves—
is steeped in Western and European history. If one culture is allowed the prerogative of imperialism, the right to define and impose on others what it deems
good for humanity, the very meaning of freedom itself will have been abrogated.

Makau Mutua, *Savages, Victims, and Saviors: The Metaphor of Human Rights*, 42 Harv.
Int'l L.J. 201, 208, 210, 214–15, 219 (2000).

"Cultural relativist" is a common term attached to those who share the views of
Makau Mutua. The following excerpt by Douglas Donoho explains in some detail the
variety between, and commonality among, relativists' claims.

Douglas Lee Donoho, *Relativism Versus Universalism in Human Rights: The Search For Meaningful Standards*
27 Stan. J. Int'l L. 345, 349–54 (1991)

[A] growing number of scholars, as well as governments of developing and socialist
states, have contended that states may refute accusations of non-compliance and object
to international scrutiny on the grounds of divergent cultural, ideological, or social traditions. To varying degrees, these arguments rely on the assertion that the existence, application, and meaning of human rights should be dependent upon national conditions.

Scholars commonly group states into the three competing views of human rights:
Western, socialist, and developing nations. Typically, they regard the Western view as

that reflected in current human rights instruments, which are historically derived predominately from European, liberal, democratic traditions. Commentators characterize developing countries, particularly African and Asian nations, as viewing current human rights standards as culturally biased, since they fail to reflect the varied cultural, political, and social heritages of the non-Western world. These developing states and scholars frequently object to an alleged overemphasis on individual, justiciable rights and political and civil liberties in contrast to social welfare, collective rights, consensual dispute resolution, economic development, and state interests. While asserting many of the same objections, socialist states also argue for an ideological conception of rights as a social institution and for a priority among rights which is fundamentally different from that espoused by Western nations.

Collectively, these objections reveal the considerable resistance among developing and socialist states to human rights standards cast in predominately liberal, Western terms. While such objections undoubtedly contain strong elements of political rhetoric (and rationalizations designed to support repressive tactics by ruling elites), their existence reflects significant differences among the various states' fundamental conceptions regarding the meaning of human rights and the relation of the individual to society and government.

In broad terms, all of these claims fall under the rubric of relativism. Scholars have given the term "relativism" a variety of interpretations, but in human rights discourse, it typically involves some combination of three related propositions. The first proposition simply points out that an observable divergence in moral judgments exists among societies due to their differing cultural, political, and social traditions. The second proposition, often described as "normative relativism," asserts that these divergent moral judgments and values have no meaning or validity outside their particular social context. In other words, "what is right or good for one individual or society is not right or good for another, even if the situations involved are similar. The third, less extreme version of relativism argues that no objectively justifiable moral standards or judgments exist outside particular cultural contexts. This "meta-ethical" view does not necessarily deny the possibility of universal truths or shared values, but rather contends that no valid means exist to objectively justify one culture's moral values over another's.

Advocates of a relativistic framework for international human rights rarely distinguish between competing meanings of relativism. Rather, relativist arguments tend to be based on the general proposition that members of one society may not legitimately judge or condemn the social practices of other traditions. The essence of this relativist argument is the insight that normative values take their meaning primarily from context. At its extreme, relativism denies the existence of legitimate cross-cultural standards for evaluating human rights practices and exempts certain variations in social practices and institutions from external criticism.

Not all forms of relativism necessarily require tolerance of diverse moral practices. However, without the notion of tolerance, the relativist position is reduced merely to an acknowledgement of enculturation and of the ethnocentricity inherent in cross-cultural moral judgments.* While such insights provide important lessons for human rights advocates, the relativist argument does not end here. Rather, most proponents of relativism endorse tolerance as a paramount value and reject, to some extent, the legiti-

---

* [Ed. Note: As the author states, "Enculturation is the process by which all people unconsciously absorb the cultural values of their society and learn to believe that they are 'true' values. Ethnocentricity is the belief that one's own value system is superior to all others and thereby constitutes the standard for all moral judgments."]

macy of external critiques of culturally based practices. Under this view, foreign scrutiny challenging the legitimacy of culturally or politically accepted domestic practices at best constitutes intolerance and disrespect, and at worst, cultural imperialism and a violation of domestic sovereignty.

Relativism in human rights suggests four related and somewhat overlapping claims. First, the relativist position argues that certain human values, as articulated in general and abstract rights such as equal protection or political participation, are simply inappropriate in certain cultural or political contexts. Islamic states, for example, assert that the equal treatment of women and the freedom to change religion conflict with the dictates of Shari'ah, the historically based Islamic religious law, and are therefore inappropriate in their societies.

Second, even if an abstract human right is appropriate to a culture, its specific content and application depend primarily upon the cultural and political circumstances of that society. Fundamental values such as justice, liberty, equality, and freedom from want mean markedly different things depending upon one's cultural and political assumptions. For example, Americans and Chinese will arguably interpret the meaning of abstract rights, such as due process, political participation, and the right to work, in conflicting and perhaps incommensurable ways....

A third major relativist claim, derived from the two preceding claims, asserts that respect and toleration of diverse cultural traditions should insulate certain specific, culturally based social practices from external critique and action. Discrete ethnic or linguistic minorities (and anthropologists) frequently make these culturally based "defense" claims, arguing that the international community should tolerate certain cultural practices prohibited by human rights law, such as child betrothal, widow inheritance, and female genital mutilation.

Finally, relativists contend that each state should espouse its own conception of what human rights entail as a social institution based upon its cultural preferences and political ideology. Western societies consider human rights to be individualistic, adversarial, justiciable, and inalienable, while human rights in the Asian, African, and Hindu traditions may not encompass any of these characteristics.

Justice Albie Sachs, *Introduction to* The Changing Family: International Perspectives on the Family and Family Law xiii–xiv
(John Eekelaar & Thandabantu Nhlapo eds., 1998)

Does one have to make a choice between universal principles on the one hand, and local, historical, cultural, philosophical, personality-based particularities on the other? Or does one dissolve the universal and opt for a multiplicity of particular systems, all rooted in history, culture and tradition? Well, I do not think that we are faced with an either/or choice. I would resolve or approach the resolution of this tension (and there is a tension, it's a real tension), with the following two thoughts in mind.

First, we have to distinguish between globalization and universalism. Globalization presupposes that you have an idea or technique or thing, a means that starts in one part of the globe and then spreads to encompass the whole of the globe. It does not change its character; it simply spreads itself to envelope everybody and everything. That is globalization. Universalism is just the opposite. Universalism starts everywhere where people are, with their practices and their ways, and finds that wherever people are, however they live, however they associate, there are certain commonalities, shared experiences and similar ways of seeing and doing things. Then you distill from the variety of human experience these commonalities, and they are universal. It is a complete opposite of globalization. I would not say there is no interaction between the two, but the essential underlying concept is the opposite....

I came across this universalism in a rather poignant and sad sense working, and doing research on family law, in Mozambique during the period of exile. I took a plane from Maputo up to Pemba in the North and then a car on a tarred road and then a four-wheel truck deep, deep, deep into the bush to a little village that had no radio, that had as its only contact this four-wheel-drive truck coming once a month, or once every two months. We discovered that the family law problems of a people living in that small village were exactly the same as problems you would get in Cape Town or in London—of persons living together who were destroying each other; they just cannot get on as society expects them to, and there is a certain inertia, trapped, but they are just not making it any more. What is the court going to do about it, what is going to happen to the children, what is going to happen to the house? And the house might have been a reed hut but it was the home, it was the place where the people lived. There was a public sentiment about who associates with whom, what you are in the community depended very much on whom you were living with. I could not help thinking afterwards when Charles and Diana had their highly publicized misfortunes, they were no different from the misfortunes of a family struggling in Capo Delgado in northern Mozambique. I coined the sad phrase: the universality of matrimonial misery.

There are these commonalities, positive ones, hopeful ones, idealistic ones, negative ones, sad ones, but always coping. That is what the law is doing, the law is coping; it is not creating, it is coping with, handling, creating frameworks for, minimizing the loss and damage of interpersonal relationships. All may be affected in different ways by different cultures, expressed in different languages, different procedural forms but in essence I would say it is the same processes that are involved. So we distinguish between globalization and universalism in the way that I have just mentioned.

Secondly, the value of pluralism is a universally accepted value in itself. Diversity, the right to choose how to associate with others, the right to conscience, belief, preference, taste, lifestyle; these are universally accepted as values. So there is a commonality in the acceptance of pluralism and if we can allow that pluralism then to seep into our concepts of the universal, the tension remains but it is not inherently antagonistic or conflictual.

Notes and Questions

1. *Terminology.* Of course, the use of the term "female genital mutilation" reflects a certain perspective in the debate. Those who are reluctant to criticize the practice, or who seek more neutral terminology, call the practice female circumcision. *See* Nahid Toubia, Female Genital Mutilation: A Call for Global Action 9 (1999) (stating that female circumcision is the term used "in the communities where FGM takes place," but questioning the appropriateness of the analogy). Others use the term "female genital cutting."

2. *Arguments?* Assume people in a particular nation widely practice FGM. The practice is encouraged by the government and the government bases its support on a religious text. Governmental representatives call the international human rights instru-

ments "products of Western ideology incompatible with their own." If you represent a group in the West opposed to FGM, what is your response?

3. *Cultural Diversity.* How does one determine a society's moral values? Does one look at the laws? The majority's views? The views of minority groups? What if there is a conflict, for example, between the views of the majority (who oppose FGM) and the views of those in the village where the woman lives (who favor FGM)?

4. *Universalism as Fact.* Why is the debate between cultural relativists and universalists not ended by the empirical fact of widespread acceptance of the Universal Declaration on Human Rights as well as various other international instruments? Since the prohibition against torture has reached the status of customary international law, *see* Restatement (Third) of Foreign Relations § 702 (1987), do the universalists win the debate if they can argue that FGM is torture?

5. *False Dichotomy.* Justice Albie Sachs tries to reconcile the tension between the universalists and the relativists. His two points are helpful if one conceives of international law as a framework for dialogue that may help eliminate the practice of FGM.

6. *Effectiveness.* Outside influences can improve human rights within a country. Certainly world opinion has been an important influence on the improvement of human rights in the United States. *See* Mary L. Dudziak, *Desegregation as a Cold War Imperative,* 41 Stan. L. Rev. 61 (1988). However, at times outside influences have been counter-productive and have increased fidelity to the challenged practice or have led to unintended consequences. For example, some have chronicled the important, although certainly not exclusive, role that Westerners played in the elimination of Chinese foot-binding. That practice was historically justified, like FGM today, as essential to a woman's marriagability. *See* Edward Alsworth Ross, The Changing Chinese 178 (1911). Modern efforts to ban the practice began in the late 1800s, when Western missionaries worked within China to change public opinion. *See* Allison R. Drucher, *The Influence of Western Women on the Anti-Footbinding Movement 1840–1911, in* Women in China: Current Directions in Historical Scholarship 189–90 (Richard W. Guisso & Stanley Johannesen eds., 1981). At that time, some Chinese actively opposed the practice, citing the importance of world opinion critical of China. *See* Howard S. Levy, Chinese Footbinding: The History of A Curious Erotic Custom 71 (1970) (citing K'ang Kuang-jen, founder of the Unbound Foot Association in Canton in 1894). The practice declined during the early 1900s and basically was eliminated not long thereafter. *See* Wang Ping, Aching for Beauty: Footbinding in China 36–39 (2000). *See generally* Erika Sussman, Note, *Contending With Culture: An Analysis of the Female Genital Mutilation Act of 1996,* 31 Cornell Int'l L. J. 193 (1998) (arguing that the shift in public opinion furthered by Western efforts was critical to the success of national laws outlawing the practice). However, it should be noted that the transformation in Chinese society was not without drawbacks for many women. The change caused many women to lose economic and social status because "[a] lot of older and middle-aged women were divorced or simply abandoned by their modernized husbands, who often studied or worked in the cities, with the excuse that they could not find love or common language with their footbound wives." Ping, *supra,* at 41. Also, "[t]iny-footed women...became 'unwanted goods' on the marriage market.'" *Id.* at 42. Moreover, numerous footbound women faced "emotional damage" because of public ridicule. *Id.* at 41.

Some scholars have argued that international norms have been important to the enactment of anti-FGM legislation, and they specifically point to Egypt as an example. They cite as evidence that "many individuals support the procedure [in the countries where the legislation is adopted], the time and character of national legal action [banning, not medicalizing, the procedure], and the uniformity of political action [similar rhetoric by activists from different countries]...." *See* Elizabeth Henger Boyle & Sharon E. Preves, *National Politics as International Process: The Case of Anti-Female-Genital-Cutting Laws*, 34 Law. & Soc'y Rev. 703 (2000).

7. *Other Competing Provisions?* Various provisions of international law designate the family as the "natural and fundamental group unit of society," which both deserves protection and which is responsible for the care of children. *See, e.g.*, ICESCR, art. 10; ICCPR, art. 23(1). Can one argue that these provisions provide legal support for FGM? If so, do these provisions invoke the same tension between universalism and cultural relativism? Are arguments based upon the rights of the family stronger or weaker than arguments based upon group rights? Group rights will be examined next in section B.4.b.

8. *Different Contexts.* Is it possible to resolve the tension between the universalists and the relativists without talking about the repercussions of victory in a certain context? For example, one author has stated, "[r]elativist conceptions of human rights...in the context of asylum easily become vehicles for discriminatory hierarchization of human rights protection and an uncritical reinforcement of exclusionary state practices...." *See* Jacqueline Bhabha, *Embodied Rights: Gender Persecution, State Sovereignty and Refugees*, 9 Pub. Cult. 3, 32 (1996). She continued, "Rights are not ends in themselves. They are instruments to facilitate interventions in the political and social arena. The context in which they are invoked crucially determines their potential effect; pragmatic considerations about context and goal should therefore influence decisions about the particular articulation of rights." *Id.*

9. *Feminist Criticism.* Relativists are not the only ones leveling criticism against the international human rights regime. Western feminists have also leveled criticism, but their sentiments tend to be aligned with the universalists' position. In particular, feminists have expressed concern that women's power to shape the international legal system has been meager, and that the framework of conventions and institutional structures focusing on women's concerns has been relatively ineffective. One of the seminal feminist critiques was by Hilary Charlesworth, Christine Chinkin, and Shelley Wright:

> The structure of the international legal order reflects a male perspective and ensures its continued dominance. The primary subjects of international law are states and increasingly, international organizations. In both states and international organizations the invisibility of women is striking. Power structures within governments are overwhelmingly masculine.... States are patriarchal structures not only because they exclude women from elite positions and decision-making roles, but also because they are based on the concentration of power in, and control by, an elite and the domestic legitimation of a monopoly over the use of force to maintain that control. This foundation is reinforced by international legal principles of sovereign equality, political independence and territorial integrity.... [The] structures [of international organizations] replicate those of states, restricting women to insignificant and subordinate roles.... Women are excluded from all major decision making by international institutions on global policies and guidelines, despite the often disparate impact of those decisions on women. Since 1985 there has been some improvement in the representation of women in the United Nations and its specialized agencies.... [H]owever, at the present rate...it will take until...2021...to reach equality.

Hilary Charlesworth et al., *Feminist Approaches to International Law*, 85 Am. J. Int'l L. 613, 621–22, 623 (1991).

Leslie Kurshan observes that the exclusion of women from the formulation of the early human rights documents forced women to choose the alternate route of international forums specifically addressing women's rights. She notes that their success was limited:

> These initial separate women's conferences were very successful in bringing women's rights issues to the attention of international legal bodies and obtaining legal instruments recognizing women's rights. However, the conferences had limited success in actually improving the human rights conditions of women. One reason for this failure is that the separate institutions developed to implement these instruments are comparatively weak. They simply lack the authority and resources to implement the agreements and ensure compliance....

Leslie Kurshan, *Rethinking Property Rights as Human Rights: Acquiring Equal Property Rights for Women Using International Human Rights Treaties*, 8 Am. U. J. Gender Soc. Pol'y & L. 354, 364–365 (2000). *See, e.g.,* Eve McCabe, *The Inadequacy of International Human Rights Law to Protect the Rights of Women as Illustrated by the Crisis in Afghanistan*, 5 UCLA J. Int'l. & Foreign Aff. 419 (2000). Do these criticisms ring true in the context of the FGM debate?

b. The Importance of Group Rights

A somewhat different, but related, argument to cultural relativism is the claim that communities have the "right" to have their own culture. Sometimes this culture is heavily influenced by religion, but sometimes it is not. Regardless, proponents of group rights seek to prevent undesirable homogenization fostered by globalization and "universal" human rights. Proponents suggest that individuals find it meaningful to belong to a culture, and that a diversity of cultures enhances freedom by allowing individuals to choose how they want to live their lives. *See* Will Kymlicka, Multicultural Citizenship: A Liberal Theory of Minority Rights 88–89 (1995).

Various international law provisions are cited in support of the legitimacy of group rights. Perhaps most notable is article 27 of the International Covenant on Civil and Political Rights (ICCPR) and article 17 of the African Charter on Human and Peoples' Rights. Article 27 of the ICCPR states: "In those States in which ethnic, religious or linguistic minorities exist, persons belonging to such minorities shall not be denied the right, in community with the other members of their group, to enjoy their own culture, to profess and practice their own religion, or to use their own language." Article 17(2),(3) of the African Charter states: "Every individual may freely take part in the cultural life of his community.... The promotion and protection of morals and traditional values recognized by the community shall be the duty of the State." Other human rights documents also mention cultural rights, but these other provisions seem to suggest that cultural rights are rights of the individual and not of the group. *See, e.g.,* Universal Declaration of Human Rights (UDHR), art. 22 ("everyone, as a member of society...is entitled to cultural rights indispensable for his dignity"); UDHR, art. 27(1) (everyone "has the right freely to participate in the cultural life of the community"). *See also* International Covenant on Economic, Social and Cultural Rights (ICESCR), art. 15(1); International Convention on the Elimination of All Forms of Racial Discrimination, art. 1; the Convention on the Elimination of All Forms of Discrimination Against Women, art. 1; Convention on the Rights of the Child, arts. 4, 29, 30 and 31. Group rights also find indirect support in the numerous provisions relating to the right of people to self-determination. *See, e.g.,* U.N. Charter, art. 1(2); ICCPR, art. 1(1); ICESCR, art. 1.

The concept of group rights raises a question: As a matter of law, can a claim of right by a "cultural" or "religious" group trump individual human rights, or at least be balanced against them? In some contexts, the answer is clear. For example, the South Africa Constitution makes explicit that group rights, like the right to culture or religion, can be restricted to protect the rights of others. Constitution of the Republic of South Africa § 30, 31 (1996).

At the international law level, the answer to this question is also sometimes clear. Occasionally text resolves the tension. For example, the Convention Concerning Indigenous and Tribal Peoples in Independent Countries, adopted by the International Labor Organization in 1989, gives groups the "right to retain their own customs and institutions" so long as they are not "incompatible with fundamental rights defined by the national legal system... [or] with internationally recognized human rights." Convention Concerning Indigenous and Tribal Peoples in Independent Countries, June 27, 1989, 28 I.L.M. 1382, 1386 (art. 8). Similarly, some international instruments require states to take affirmative action to eliminate certain practices, despite their foundation in "culture" or "religion." See CEDAW, art. 5, 10(c). These factors suggest that perhaps group rights are subordinate to individual rights. Others have suggested that the right to self-determination applies only to situations involving colonization and that group rights are merely derivative (and subordinate to) individual rights. *See* Roger J.R. Levesque, *Sexual Use, Abuse and Exploitation of Children: Challenges in Implementing Children's Human Rights*, 60 Brook. L. Rev. 959, 969–973 (1994).

Yet extra-legal considerations are an important part of the ultimate answer to the question. As one author stated, "In practice, restrictions on the freedom of religion for the purpose of protecting the human rights of others are readily conceded to be justified where the moral and political authority accorded to a particular human right, or set of rights, is generally acknowledged. International consensus thus demands the abolition of slavery and apartheid, notwithstanding the historical approbation of these practices by religious traditions." Donna J. Sullivan, *Gender Equality and Religious Freedom: Toward a Framework for Conflict Resolution*, 24 N.Y.U. J. Int'l L. & Pol. 795, 810–11 (1992). Whether there is an international consensus on the abolition of violence against women is discussed *infra*.

The notion of group rights also raises a normative question: Should group rights be accorded great weight and value within a human rights framework? One reason why they perhaps should not relates to the concept of group rights itself. Madhavi Sunder challenges the notion of a uniformity of views in a particular culture or religion. Madhavi Sunder has suggested that a strong legal conception of group rights may itself lead to tyranny. "Legal rights to police a culture's normative borders—granted in the name of protecting a culture against homogenization—could do more than offer a means for cultural communities to regain a degree of control over their community and expressions. Legally enforced cultural boundaries could, conceivably, accord powerful members of cultural groups the ability to suppress any rumblings for change in a culture, particularly by censoring or excluding those members who challenge power relationships within a culture and threaten the status quo." Madhavi Sunder, *Cultural Dissent*, 54 Stan. L. Rev. 495, 503 (2001). *See also* K. Anthony Appiah, *Identity, Authenticity, Survival: Multicultural Societies and Social Reproduction, in* Multiculturalism 149, 162–63 (Amy Gutmann ed., 1994) (suggesting that collective identity may assume a uniform perspective which ends up "replacing one kind of tyranny with another"). On the other hand, not every claim for group rights necessarily suffers from this particular concern.

To resolve these conflicts, Donna Sullivan suggests a "balancing approach" that is highly contextualized and assesses the rights involved for each participant. In particular, she advocates considering the relative importance of the practices involved, the degree of infringement each solution imposes on the other party, whether other human rights are implicated that tip the scale in one direction, and the proportionality of any solution. Sullivan, *supra*, at 821–23. Do you like this proposal?

C. Domestic Violence

Our study of FGM and the broader theoretical issues regarding human rights serve as a useful backdrop to our next topic. We now turn to the issue of "domestic violence" by which we mean assault or battery committed by an intimate partner. Domestic violence exists worldwide, as the next excerpts suggest. Our tasks are to consider whether the domestic and international responses to domestic violence are the same as the responses to FGM, and whether they should be the same. For example, how should we treat women who come to the United States and seek asylum because their partners abuse them? We will also expand our understanding of international law by exploring how states can be responsible for the acts of non-state actors, a question left unresolved in our study of FGM. Before turning to these questions, it is useful to consider some cross-cultural generalizations about domestic violence.

Jeffrey Fagan & Angela Brown, *Violence Between Spouses and Intimates: Physical Aggression Between Women and Men in Intimate Relationships*
3 Understanding and Preventing Violence 115, 120–21
(Albert J. Reiss, Jr. & Jeffrey A. Roght eds., 1994)

Marital violence is intrinsic to many cultures. Levinson (1988) using cross-cultural data on family violence from the Human Relations Area Files (HRAF) database identified eight varieties of marital violence in 330 societies. Levinson (1988, 1989) estimated the prevalence of wife beating in a representative sample of 90 societies from the 330 cultural groups in the HRAF database. Wife beating occurred in 84.5 percent of the 90 cultures. It occurred "at least occasionally" in all or nearly all households in 18.8 percent of the societies and in a majority (but not all) in 29.9 percent. Husband beating was reported in 6 percent of all societies; it was rare or unheard of in 73.1 percent and occurred in a minority of households in 20.2 percent. Other studies (cited in Levinson, 1989) report comparable data: Wife beating occurs in 71 to 92 percent of the societies studied.

Motivations for wife beating in these societies included sexual jealousy or infidelity (45.5%), insubordination or disobedience by the wife (25.5%), and the wife's failure to meet "household responsibilities" (23.3%). Societal responses to wife beating varied extensively. In 91.2 percent of the societies, intervention by outsiders occurred. These interventions included help or intercession by kin or neighbors (17.6%), shelter for the wife (14.7%), legal intervention (17.6%), marital violence as grounds for divorce (11.8%), and supernatural sanctions (e.g., casting a spell) in an unspecified proportion.

In 29.4 percent of the societies, interventions are limited to beatings that exceed societal norms for the "physical discipline" of wives. Interventions were reportedly unavailable in 8.8 percent of the societies. The study gave no indication of the legal status of wife or husband assaults in the societies studied....

INS Asylum and Withholding Definitions
65 Fed. Reg. 76588, 76595 (proposed Dec. 7, 2000)

The Violence Against Women Office of the Department of Justice has offered the following observations about domestic violence, based on its experience in the United States as well as with foreign governments and non-governmental organizations:

It is our experience that domestic violence manifests similar characteristics across all racial, ethnic and socioeconomic groups, and that many cultures have a variety of ways in which they condone and perpetuate domestic violence.... First, in relationships involving domestic violence, past behavior is a strong predictor of future behavior by the abuser.... Victims report patterns of abuse—rather than single, isolated incidents—that tend to include the repeated use of physical, sexual and emotional abuse, threats, intimidation, isolation and economic coercion.... Second, both domestically and internationally, domestic violence centers on power and control over the victim.... Consequently, when victims attempt to flee the abusive relationship, or otherwise assert their independence, abusers often pursue them and escalate the violence to regain or reassert control.... The risk of lethality to the victim is typically greatest when she attempts to escape the abuse and, in contrast to other persecution cases where the persecutor's desire to harm the victim may wane if the victim leaves, the victim's attempt to leave typically increases the abuser's motivation to locate and harm her.... Third, because of the abuser's intimate relationship with the victim, he is likely to possess important information about where the victim could go or to whom she would turn for assistance.

U.N. *Report of the Fourth World Conference on Women*
¶119, U.N. Doc. A/CONF.177/20 &
A/CONF.177/20/Add.1 (1995)

Violence against women is a manifestation of the historically unequal power relations between men and women, which have led to domination over and discrimination against women by men and to the prevention of women's full advancement. Violence against women throughout the life cycle derives essentially from cultural patterns, in particular the harmful effects of certain traditional and customary practices and all acts of extremism linked to race, sex, language or religion that perpetuate the lower status accorded to women in the family, the workplace, the community and society. Violence against women is exacerbated by social pressures, notably the shame of denouncing certain acts that have been perpetrated against women; women's lack of access to legal information, aid or protection; the lack of laws that effectively prohibit violence against women; failure to reform existing laws; inadequate efforts on the part of public authorities to promote awareness of and enforce existing laws; and the absence of educational and other means to address the causes and consequences of violence. Images in the media of violence against women, in particular those that depict rape or sexual slavery as well as the use of women and girls as sex objects, including pornography, are factors contributing to the continued prevalence of such violence, adversely influencing the community at large, in particular children and young people.

Cultural Differences in Types of Domestic Violence. Despite the cross-cultural similarities, there are differences. For example, an article by Subrata Paul discusses the problem of domestic violence in India. Domestic violence takes on some unique characteristics in India, where the husband and wife often live with the husband's family. Mother-in-laws contribute to the violence, either directly or through encouraging others. In addition, dowry death, or "bride-burning," occasionally occurs when dowry payments are insufficient. Subrata Paul, *Combating Domestic Violence Through Positive International Action in the International Community and in the United Kingdom, India, and Africa*, 7 Cardozo J. Int'l & Comp. L. 227, 236–38 (1999).

The legal responses in India are tailored to the specific nature of this type of violence. India passed the Dowry Prohibition Act of 1961. It has since been amended twice, once in 1984 and again in 1986. The 1986 amendment requires the police and a judicial magistrate to investigate every unnatural death of a woman married fewer than seven years. Parliament has also criminalized dowry-related violence against women as evidenced by the Indian Penal Code, amended in 1983, which outlaws dowry-related cruelty by a husband or his relatives. The Indian Penal Code was further amended in 1986 to explicitly provide that dowry deaths are punishable with imprisonment of seven years to life. *Id.* at 238–39.

Honor crimes are another type of violence women experience in certain countries. The Special Rapporteur on Violence Against Women has explained that honor crimes occur after a woman violates the family's honor by transgressing traditional sexual and familial roles. The family kills the woman, sometimes first giving her a chance to kill herself. In some countries honor crimes are legal or the perpetrator receives only a light sentence. *See generally Report of the Special Rapporteur on Violence Against Women, Its Causes and Consequences*, U.N. Comm'n Hum. Rts., 55th sess., provisional agenda item 12(a), ¶ 18, U.N. Doc. E/CN.4/1999/68 (1999). In Jordan, it is estimated that "25% of all murders" are honor crimes. *See* Bureau of Democracy, Human Rights and Labor, 2001 Country Reports on Human Rights Practices, Jordan § 5 (2002) [hereinafter 2001 Jordan Country Report]. In fact, the police "regularly" imprison women to protect them from honor crimes by male relatives. *Id.*

In Jordan, "honor crimes" are recognized, and excused, by the formal criminal law. Article 340 of the Penal Code provides an exemption from penalty for men who murder a female relative caught committing adultery, and a reduced penalty if the woman is caught in "an unlawful bed." *See* The Penal Code (No. 16, 1960), *available at* http://www.equalitynow.org/beijing_plus5_violence_eng.html. "Although few defendants are able to meet the stringent requirements for a crime of honor defense (the defendant personally must have witnessed the female victim engaging in sexual relations), most avoid trial for the crime of murder and are tried instead on the charge of manslaughter; even those convicted of murder rarely spend more than 2 years in prison. In contrast to honor crimes, the maximum penalty for first-degree murder is death, and the maximum penalty for second-degree murder is 15 years." *See* 2001 Jordan Country Report, *supra*, § 5. In 1999, the Justice Ministry in Jordan recommended abolishing article 340, but the Lower House of Parliament rejected a reform measure in both 1999 and 2000.

See Equality Now, *Words and Deeds: Holding Governments Accountable in the Beijing + 5 Review Process*, Women's Act 16.2 (1999), *available at* http://www.equalitynow.org/action_eng_16_2_links.html. In addition, "most activists believe that even if Article 340 were repealed, honor crimes likely would persist, with sentences continuing to be reduced under Article 98," which allows a "heat of passion" defense for men only. *See* 2001 Jordan Country Report, *supra*.

Differences in types of violence and the legal systems' responses should not mask the similarities. Take, for example, India and Jordan. According to a bill that was recently introduced in India, male-on-female battery of an intimate partner is "widely prevalent but has remained largely invisible in the public domain." *See* Statement of Objects and Reasons, § 2, The Protection from Domestic Violence Bill, 2002 (India). India has a criminal provision that can address such violence, but not a system of civil protection orders comparable to what exists in the United States. *See* Parliamentary Committee on Human Resource Development Invites Suggestions on the Protection from Domestic Violence Bill, 2002, *available at* http://www.indianngos.com/government/attention.htm (citing Indian Penal Code § 498-A (1860)). Although legislation has been introduced during the last several years to address this legal gap, the legislation has not yet passed. Similarly, non-lethal intimate partner violence is widely said to exist in Jordan and should not be forgotten when discussing the less frequent honor killings. *See* 2001 Jordan Country Report, *supra* ("Violence against women is common. Reported incidents of violence against women do not reflect the full extent of the problem. Medical experts acknowledge that spousal abuse occurs frequently."). While there are some legal remedies, like the right to file a complaint in court against a spouse for battery, the legal remedies are incomplete (for example, marital rape is legal) and society discourages women from using existing remedies. *See id.*

---

1. Immigration Law

Immigration law is important for women who seek entry into the United States or continued permission to remain here. It also provides insight into how the United States perceives and responds to violence against women. Historically, family violence was perceived as a private matter. It was inappropriate for the state to get involved because of the doctrine of family privacy. Martha Albertson Fineman, *What Place for Family Privacy*, 67 Geo. Wash. L. Rev. 1207, 1215 n.48 (1999). Family violence was rarely conceived of as a social problem, or as having roots in women's subordinated status in society. More recently there has been a recognition that a systemic problem exists, whereby women are in a subordinated status, thereby making them vulnerable to abuse, and that state involvement to address the violence is appropriate. *See* Elizabeth M. Schneider, Battered Women and Feminist Law Making 27–28 (2000). The following material provides a snapshot of how far the United States has come in its willingness to recognize and address the systemic nature of the violence.

After the BIA's holding in *Kasinga, supra*, and its refusal to adopt the framework suggested by the Immigration and Naturalization Service, questions arose about the extent to which refugee law could protect women subject to other types of violence. The next two cases, one before the U.S. Board of Immigration Appeals and one before the English House of Lords, address this topic.

Two issues are of major significance in both cases: whether victims of gender violence are part of a "particular social group" and whether they are persecuted for their membership in a particular social group. Gender is simply not mentioned as a relevant ground for persecution in either the 1980 Refugee Act or the international conventions on refugees. Rather, all of these instruments identify as relevant grounds "race, religion, nationality, membership of a particular social group or political opinion." *See* 1951 Convention Relating to the Status of Refugees, art. 1(2); 1967 U.N. Protocol Relating to the Status of Refugees, art. 1(2) (incorporating by reference definition of refugee in 1951 Convention). Some authors have explained that the omission of gender was a result of the policy-makers' biases and focus. Simply, the 1951 Refugee Convention was promulgated in the aftermath of World War II and during the Cold War when policy-makers focused on people who were persecuted on account of religious, racial, and political grounds. Gender persecution was not the "most apparent." *See* Bret Thiele, *Persecution on Account of Gender: A Need for Refugee Law Reform*, 11 Hastings Women's L.J. 221, 223 (2000). Notwithstanding the omission of gender, the definition of refugee contained in both the 1967 Protocol as well as the 1980 Refugee Act is gender-neutral.

In re R-A

22 I. & N. Dec. 906 (B.I.A. 1999) (en banc)

Filppu, Board Member:

The question before us is whether the respondent qualifies as a "refugee" as a result of the heinous abuse she suffered and still fears from her husband in Guatemala. Specifically, we address whether the repeated spouse abuse inflicted on the respondent makes her eligible for asylum as an alien who has been persecuted on account of her membership in a particular social group or her political opinion....

Factual Background

Testimony and Statements of Abuse

The respondent is a native and citizen of Guatemala. She married at age 16. Her husband was then 21 years old. He currently resides in Guatemala, as do their two children. Immediately after their marriage, the respondent and her husband moved to Guatemala City. From the beginning of the marriage, her husband engaged in acts of physical and sexual abuse against the respondent. He was domineering and violent. The respondent testified that her husband "always mistreated me from the moment we were married, he was always...aggressive."

Her husband would insist that the respondent accompany him wherever he went, except when he was working. He escorted the respondent to her workplace, and he would often wait to direct her home. To scare her, he would tell the respondent stories of having killed babies and the elderly while he served in the army. Oftentimes, he would take the respondent to cantinas where he would become inebriated. When the respondent would complain about his drinking, her husband would yell at her. On one occasion, he grasped her hand to the point of pain and continued to drink until he passed out. When she left a cantina before him, he would strike her. As their marriage proceeded, the level and frequency of his rage increased concomitantly with the seeming senselessness and irrationality of his motives. He dislocated the respondent's jaw bone when her menstrual period was 15 days late. When she refused to abort her 3- to 4-month-old fetus, he kicked her violently in her spine. He would hit or kick the respondent "whenever he felt like it, wherever he happened to be: in the house, on the street, on the bus." The respondent stated that "[a]s time went on, he hit me for no reason at all."

The respondent's husband raped her repeatedly. He would beat her before and during the unwanted sex. When the respondent resisted, he would accuse her of seeing other men and threaten her with death. The rapes occurred "almost daily," and they caused her severe pain. He passed on a sexually transmitted disease to the respondent from his sexual relations outside their marriage. Once, he kicked the respondent in her genitalia, apparently for no reason, causing the respondent to bleed severely for 8 days. The respondent suffered the most severe pain when he forcefully sodomized her. When she protested, he responded, as he often did, "You're my woman, you do what I say."

The respondent ran away to her brother's and parents' homes, but her husband always found her. Around December 1994, the respondent attempted to flee with her children outside the city, but her husband found her again. He appeared at her door, drunk, and as she turned to leave, he struck her in the back of her head causing her to lose consciousness. When she awoke, he kicked her and dragged her by her hair into another room and beat her to unconsciousness.

After two months away, her husband pleaded for the respondent's return, and she agreed because her children were asking for him. One night, he woke the respondent, struck her face, whipped her with an electrical cord, pulled out a machete and threatened to deface her, to cut off her arms and legs, and to leave her in a wheelchair if she ever tried to leave him. He warned her that he would be able to find her wherever she was. The violence continued. When the respondent could not give 5,000 quetzales to him when he asked for it, he broke windows and a mirror with her head. Whenever he could not find something, he would grab her head and strike furniture with it. Once, he pistol-whipped her. When she asked for his motivation, he broke into a familiar refrain, "I can do it if I want to."

Once, her husband entered the kitchen where the respondent was and, for no apparent reason, threw a machete toward her hands, barely missing them. He would often come home late and drunk. When the respondent noted his tardiness, he punched her. Once, he asked where the respondent had been. When she responded that she had been home waiting for him, he became enraged, struck her face, grabbed her by her hair, and dragged her down the street. One night, the respondent attempted to commit suicide. Her husband told her, "If you want to die, go ahead. But from here, you are not going to leave."

When asked on cross-examination, the respondent at first indicated that she had no opinion of why her husband acted the way he did. She supposed, however, that it was because he had been mistreated when he was in the army and, as he had told her, he treated her the way he had been treated. The respondent believed he would abuse any woman who was his wife. She testified that he "was a repugnant man without any education," and that he saw her "as something that belonged to him and he could do anything he wanted" with her.

The respondent's pleas to Guatemalan police did not gain her protection. On three occasions, the police issued summons for her husband to appear, but he ignored them, and the police did not take further action. Twice, the respondent called the police, but they never responded. When the respondent appeared before a judge, he told her that he would not interfere in domestic disputes. Her husband told the respondent that, because of his former military service, calling the police would be futile as he was familiar with law enforcement officials. The respondent knew of no shelters or other organizations in Guatemala that could protect her. The abuse began "from the moment (they) were married," and continued until the respondent fled Guatemala in May 1995. One morning in May 1995, the respondent decided to leave permanently. With help, the respondent was able to flee Guatemala, and she arrived in Brownsville, Texas, 2 days later.

A witness, testifying for the respondent, stated that she learned through the respondent's sister that the respondent's husband was "going to hunt her down and kill her if she comes back to Guatemala."

We struggle to describe how deplorable we find the husband's conduct to have been.

Country Conditions

Dr. Doris Bersing testified that spouse abuse is common in Latin American countries and that she was not aware of social or legal resources for battered women in Guatemala. Women in Guatemala, according to Dr. Bersing, have other problems related to general conditions in that country, and she suggested that such women could leave abusive partners but that they would face other problems such as poverty. Dr. Bersing further testified that the respondent was different from other battered women she had seen in that the respondent possessed an extraordinary fear of her husband and her abuse had been extremely severe....

The Department of State issued an advisory opinion as to the respondent's asylum request. The opinion states that the respondent's alleged mistreatment could have occurred given its understanding of country conditions in Guatemala. The opinion further indicates:

> [S]pousal abuse complaints by husbands have increased from 30 to 120 a month due to increased nationwide educational programs, which have encouraged women to seek assistance. Family court judges may issue injunctions against abusive spouses, which police are charged with enforcing. The (Human Rights Ombudsman) women's rights department and various non-governmental organizations provide medical and legal assistance.

The respondent has submitted numerous articles and reports regarding violence against women in Guatemala and other Latin American countries. One article, prepared by Canada's Immigration and Refugee Board, indicates that Guatemala has laws against domestic violence, that it has taken some additional steps recently to begin to address the problem, and that "functionaries" in the legal system tend to view domestic violence as a violation of women's rights. Nevertheless, the article indicates that Guatemalan society still tends to view domestic violence as a family matter, that women are often not aware of available legal avenues, and that the pursuit of legal remedies can often prove ineffective....

Analysis

[W]e agree with the Immigration Judge that the severe injuries sustained by the respondent rise to the level of harm sufficient (and more than sufficient) to constitute "persecution." We also credit the respondent's testimony in general and specifically her account of being unsuccessful in obtaining meaningful assistance from the authorities in Guatemala. Accordingly, we find that she has adequately established on this record that she was unable to avail herself of the protection of the Government of Guatemala in connection with the abuse inflicted by her husband. The determinative issue, as correctly identified by the Immigration Judge, is whether the harm experienced by the respondent was, or in the future may be, inflicted "on account of" a statutorily protected ground....

And, as explained below, we do not agree with the Immigration Judge that the respondent was harmed on account of either actual or imputed political opinion or membership in a particular social group.

Imputed Political Opinion

The record indicates that the respondent's husband harmed the respondent regardless of what she actually believed or what he thought she believed. The respondent testified that the abuse began "from the moment (they) were married." Even after the respondent "learned through experience" to acquiesce to his demands, he still abused her. The abuse took place before she left him initially, and it continued after she returned to him. In fact, he said he "didn't care" what she did to escape because he would find her. He also hurt her before her first call to the police and after her last plea for help.

The respondent's account of what her husband told her may well reflect his own view of women and, in particular, his view of the respondent as his property to do with as he pleased. It does not, however, reflect that he had any understanding of the respondent's perspective or that he even cared what the respondent's perspective may have been. According to the respondent, he told her, "You're my woman and I can do whatever I want," and "You're my woman, you do what I say." In fact, she stated that "(a)s time went on, he hit me for no reason at all," and that he "would hit or kick me whenever he felt like it."

Nowhere in the record does the respondent recount her husband saying anything relating to what he thought her political views to be, or that the violence towards her was attributable to her actual or imputed beliefs. Moreover, this is not a case where there is meaningful evidence that this respondent held or evinced a political opinion, unless one assumes that the common human desire not to be harmed or abused is in itself a "political opinion." The record before us simply does not indicate that the harm arose in response to any objections made by the respondent to her husband's domination over her. Nor does it suggest that his abusive behavior was dependent in any way on the views held by the respondent. Indeed... [t]he record reflects that, once having entered into this marriage, there was nothing the respondent could have done or thought that would have spared her (or indeed would have spared any other woman unfortunate enough to have married him) from the violence he inflicted....

The respondent argues that, given the nature of domestic violence and sexual assaults, her husband necessarily imputed to her the view that she believed women should not be controlled and dominated by men. Even accepting the premise that he might have believed that the respondent disagreed with his views of women, it does not necessarily follow that he harmed the respondent because of those beliefs, rather than because of his own personal or psychological makeup coupled with his troubled perception of her actions at times [INS v. Elias-Zacarias, 502 U.S. 478, 482 (1992)]; Sangha v. INS, 103 F.3d 1482, 1487 (9th Cir. 1997) ("[T]he petitioner must prove something more than violence plus disparity of views.")....

It is certainly logical and only human to presume that no victim of violence desires to be such a victim and will resist in some manner. But it is another matter to presume that the perpetrator of the violence inflicts it because the perpetrator believes the victim opposes either the abuse or the authority of the abuser. We do not find that the second proposition necessarily follows from the first. Moreover, it seems to us that this approach ignores the question of what motivated the abuse at the outset, and it necessarily assumes that the original motivation is no longer the basis, at least not by itself, for the subsequent harm. We are unwilling to accept a string of presumptions or assumptions as a substitute for our own assessment of the evidence in this record, particularly when the reliability of these presumptions as genuine reflections of human behavior has not been established....

Put another way, it is difficult to conclude on the actual record before us that there is any "opinion" the respondent could have held, or convinced her husband she held, that would have prevented the abuse she experienced....

Particular Social Group

Cognizableness

Initially, we find that "Guatemalan women who have been involved intimately with Guatemalan male companions, who believe that women are to live under male domination" is not a particular social group. Absent from this group's makeup is "a voluntary associational relationship" that is of "central concern" in the Ninth Circuit [citing, *inter alia*, Sanchez-Trujillo v. INS, 801 F.2d 1571, 1572 (9th Cir. 1986) (rejecting as a social group "young, working class males who have not served in the military of El Salvador")]....

Moreover, regardless of Ninth Circuit law, we find that the respondent's claimed social group fails under our own independent assessment of what constitutes a qualifying social group. We find it questionable that the social group adopted by the Immigration Judge appears to have been defined principally, if not exclusively, for purposes of this asylum case, and without regard to the question of whether anyone in Guatemala perceives this group to exist in any form whatsoever. The respondent fits within the proposed group. But the group is defined largely in the abstract. It seems to bear little or no relation to the way in which Guatemalans might identify subdivisions within their own society or otherwise might perceive individuals either to possess or to lack an important characteristic or trait. The proposed group may satisfy the basic requirement of containing an immutable or fundamental individual characteristic. But, for the group to be viable for asylum purposes, we believe there must also be some showing of how the characteristic is understood in the alien's society, such that we in turn may understand that the potential persecutors in fact see persons sharing the characteristic as warranting suppression or the infliction of harm....

The respondent's showing fails in another respect, one that is noteworthy in terms of our ruling in *Matter of Kasinga, supra*. She has not shown that spouse abuse is itself an important societal attribute, or, in other words, that the characteristic of being abused is one that is important within Guatemalan society. The respondent has shown official tolerance of her husband's cruelty toward her. But, for "social group" purposes, she has not shown that women are expected by society to be abused, or that there are any adverse societal consequences to women or their husbands if the women are not abused. While not determinative, the prominence or importance of a characteristic within a society is another factor bearing on whether we will recognize that factor as part of a "particular social group" under our refugee provisions. If a characteristic is important in a given society, it is more likely that distinctions will be drawn within that society between those who share and those who do not share the characteristic....

In our opinion,...the mere existence of shared descriptive characteristics is insufficient to qualify those possessing the common characteristics as members of a particular social group.... Our past case law points out the critical role that is played in "social group" analysis by common characteristics which potential persecutors identify as a basis for the infliction of harm. Matter of Kasinga, *supra*.... But the social group concept would virtually swallow the entire refugee definition if common characteristics, coupled with a meaningful level of harm, were all that need be shown.[2]

The starting point for "social group" analysis remains the existence of an immutable or fundamental individual characteristic in accordance with *Matter of Acosta*. We never declared, however, that the starting point for assessing social group claims articulated in *Acosta* was also the ending point. The factors we look to in this case, beyond *Acosta*'s "immutableness" test, are not prerequisites, and we do not rule out the use of additional considerations that may properly bear on whether a social group should be recognized in an individual case. But these factors are consistent with the operation of the other four grounds for asylum and are therefore appropriate, in our judgment, for consideration in the "particular social group" context.

On the record before us, we find that the respondent has not adequately established that we should recognize, under our law, the particular social group identified by the Immigration Judge.

Nexus

[I]n analyzing "particular social group" claims, our decisions, as well as those of the Ninth Circuit, in which this case arises, require that the persecution or well-founded fear of persecution be on account of, or, in other words, because of, the alien's membership in that particular social group....

In this case, even if we were to accept as a particular social group "Guatemalan women who have been involved intimately with Guatemalan male companions, who believe that women are to live under male domination," the respondent has not established that her husband has targeted and harmed the respondent because he perceived her to be a member of this particular social group. The record indicates that he has targeted only the respondent. The respondent's husband has not shown an interest in any member of this group other than the respondent herself. The respondent fails to show how other members of the group may be at risk of harm from him. If group membership were the motivation behind his abuse, one would expect to see some evidence of it manifested in actions toward other members of the same group....

The respondent was not at particular risk of abuse from her husband until she married him, at which point, given the nature of his focus, she was in a "group" by herself of women presently married to that particular man. Such a group, however, would fail to qualify as a "particular social group" under the Act.

The Immigration Judge nevertheless found, and the respondent argues on appeal, that her various possible group memberships account for her plight, in large measure because the social climate and the Government of Guatemala afford her no protection from her husband's abuse. Societal attitudes and the concomitant effectiveness (or lack thereof) of governmental intervention very well may have contributed to the ability of the respondent's husband to carry out his abusive actions over a period of many years. But this argument takes us away from looking at the motivation of the husband and focuses instead on the failure of the government to offer protection.

---

2. Other "social group" definitions potentially covering the respondent were suggested below or in the appeal briefs, such as "Guatemalan women" and "battered spouses." We need not now address whether there are any circumstances under which the various alternative proposals might qualify as a "particular social group," as each of them fails on this record under the "on account of," or nexus, requirement of the statute, for the reasons we identify below....

[G]overnmental inaction is not a reliable indicator of the motivations behind the actions of private parties. And this is not a case in which it has been shown that the Government of Guatemala encourages its male citizens to abuse its female citizens, nor in which the Government has suddenly and unreasonably withdrawn protection from a segment of the population in the expectation that a third party will inflict harm and thereby indirectly achieve a governmental objective.

The record in this case reflects that the views of society and of many governmental institutions in Guatemala can result in the tolerance of spouse abuse at levels we find appalling. But the record also shows that abusive marriages are not viewed as desirable, that spouse abuse is recognized as a problem, and that some measures have been pursued in an attempt to respond to this acknowledged problem. In this context, we are not convinced that the absence of an effective governmental reaction to the respondent's abuse translates into a finding that her husband inflicted the abuse because she was a member of a particular social group. The record does not support such a conclusion, as a matter of fact, when the husband's own behavior is examined. And Guatemala's societal and governmental attitudes and actions do not warrant our declaring this to be the case as a matter of law....

Importantly, construing private acts of violence to be qualifying governmental persecution, by virtue of the inadequacy of protection, would obviate, perhaps entirely, the "on account of" requirement in the statute. We understand the "on account of" test to direct an inquiry into the motives of the entity actually inflicting the harm. *See* INS v. Elias-Zacarias, *supra.* Further, the adoption of such an approach would represent a fundamental change in the analysis of refugee claims. We see no principled basis for restricting such an approach to cases involving violence against women. The absence of adequate governmental protection, it would seem, should equally translate into refugee status for other categories of persons unable to protect themselves....

The Kasinga Decision....

The respondent in this case has not demonstrated that domestic violence is as pervasive in Guatemala as FGM is among the Tchamba-Kunsuntu Tribe, or, more importantly, that domestic violence is a practice encouraged and viewed as societally important in Guatemala. She has not shown that women are expected to undergo abuse from their husbands, or that husbands who do not abuse their wives, or the nonabused wives themselves, face social ostracization or other threats to make them conform to a societal expectation of abuse. While the respondent here found no source of official protection in Guatemala, the young woman in *Kasinga* testified that the police in Togo were looking for her and would return her to her family to undergo FGM.

We recognize that the respondent's situation is similar to that in *Kasinga*, in part, because the person actually inflicting the harm or feared harm is a family member of the victim. While the cases bear some similarities in this regard, we do not find this to be a factor that supports the claim of group recognition. Rather, it is a factor to be overcome if the group is to be accepted. In the context of asylum law, persecutors typically harbor animosities and act on those animosities toward many persons known to have the "hated" characteristic. When action is directed toward but one individual, or toward a small number of close family members, it calls into question both the propriety of the group definition and the alleged group motivation of the persecutor....

Guendelsberger, dissenting, joined by Schmidt, Villageliu, Rosenberg, and Moscato....

The majority proposes a laundry list of hurdles to be cleared before she may demonstrate membership in a particular social group. This stringent approach to asylum law disregards decisions of tribunals, both domestic and foreign, which extend asylum protection to women who flee human rights abuses within their own homes. It also ignores international human rights developments and the guiding principle of the Charter of the United Nations, the Universal Declaration of Human Rights, and the 1951 Convention Relating to the Status of Refugees, "that human beings shall enjoy fundamental rights and freedoms without discrimination." United Nations Convention Relating to the Status of Refugees, preamble.... The respondent has a fundamental right to protection from abuse based on gender. When domestic abuse based on gender occurs, as here, with state acquiescence, the respondent should be afforded the protection of asylum law.

[Ed. Note: *Social Group*]....

The Immigration Judge decided the case before her consistent with our precedent decision in *Kasinga*. In both cases, the social group was defined by reference to gender in combination with one or more additional factors. In *Kasinga*, the social group was defined by gender, ethnic affiliation, and opposition to female genital mutilation ("FGM"). In the instant case, the social group is based on gender, relationship to an abusive partner, and opposition to domestic violence. As the Immigration Judge below correctly observed, the respondent's relationship to, and association with, her husband is something she cannot change. It is an immutable characteristic under the *Acosta* guidelines, which we affirmed in *Kasinga*....

[Ed. Note: *Nexus*]....

First, to assess motivation, it is appropriate to consider the factual circumstances surrounding the violence. The factual record reflects quite clearly that the severe beatings were directed at the respondent by her husband to dominate and subdue her, precisely because of her gender, as he inflicted his harm directly on her vagina, sought to abort her pregnancy, and raped her.

Second, the very incomprehensibleness of the husband's motives supports the respondent's claim that the harm is "on account of" a protected ground. This is not a case of simple assault. Nor is this a case where the factors motivating the harm arguably are limited only to some comprehensible criminal motive. Rather, this is a case where the respondent's husband treated her merely as his property, to do with as he pleased. Under these circumstances, to place undue emphasis on the respondent's explanations for her husband's motives misses the obvious point that no good reason could exist for such behavior....

Illegitimate motives can give rise to an inference that the harm has occurred on account of a statutorily protected characteristic which, in this case, is the respondent's membership in a particular social group and her actual or imputed political opinion.... The record reflects, as it did in *Matter of Kasinga*, *supra*, that "no legitimate reason" exists for the severe harm inflicted upon the respondent.

Third, we should attempt to identify why such horrific violence occurs at all.... The fundamental purpose of domestic violence is to punish, humiliate, and exercise power over the victim on account of her gender.... Moreover, it is well established in the record before us that Guatemalan society is especially oppressive of women generally.

The materials submitted reveal that extreme patriarchal notions are firmly entrenched in Guatemalan society....

It is reasonable to believe, on the basis of the record before us, that the husband was motivated, at least in part, "on account of" the respondent's membership in a particular social group that is defined by her gender, her relationship to him, and her opposition to domestic violence....

[Ed. Note: *Actual or Imputed Opinion*]....

Opposition to male domination and violence against women, and support for gender equity, constitutes a political opinion. *See* Fatin v. INS, *supra*, at 1242 (acknowledging that there is "little doubt that feminism qualifies as a political opinion within the meaning of the relevant statutes")....

The respondent's political opinion opposing male domination and domestic violence imposed upon her by her husband is clearly stated in the record—both in her statements and her actions. As he persisted in subjecting her to persecution that would affirm his dominance over her, she resisted him, tried to flee, sought governmental intervention, and filed legal actions against him.

The respondent may, in addition, establish a "political opinion" by demonstrating that such an opinion has been attributed to her by her persecutors. Opposition to male domination and violence against women may be imputed to a victim of domestic violence who protests, resists, or seeks to escape such domination and violence. *See*, e.g., Lazo-Majano v. INS, *supra*. Such a perception, whether actual or simply imputed, is a motivator for further violence and abuse....

The record reflects that the respondent not only holds an actual opinion opposing her husband's violence, but it is apparent that her husband believed that her resistance to his domination and abuse, particularly as reflected in her seeking assistance from governmental authorities, constituted an opinion opposing his male dominance. Imputing this opinion to her, he sought to overcome her opposition by escalating his abuse of her....

For example, according to the respondent's credible account, her husband explained his repeatedly striking her, whipping her with an electrical cord, threatening her with a machete, pistol whipping her, raping her, sodomizing her, breaking a mirror over her head, kicking her in the spine, attempting to abort their second child, slamming her head into furniture and dragging her by the hair, and knocking her unconscious, as his right as her husband....

Moreover, the record before us reflects that the abuser is motivated to continue and even escalate his abuse in order to stifle and overcome his victim's opposition to it. As the majority notes, the rage, abuse, and violence against the respondent escalated as the marriage progressed....

The majority insists that the respondent's husband persecuted her regardless of what she believed or what he thought she believed, claiming that the record does not reflect he was motivated by gender animus generally. The majority contends that the abuser was not, even in part, motivated by the respondent's resistance to his domination, even though he had told her he viewed women as property to be treated brutally in order to sustain his domination. This is contrary to fact, law, and logic. To reach such a conclusion, the majority must ignore entirely the mixed motive doctrine, which not only constitutes a well-established basis for asylum in cases arising before the Ninth Circuit, but also constitutes a basis for asylum in claims made before this Board. Furthermore, as we stated in conjunction with our consideration of the respondent as a member of a particular social group, illegitimate motives triggering persecution raise an inference that the harm has occurred on account of a statutorily enumerated ground....

Islam v. Secretary of State for the Home Dep't;
Regina v. Immigration Appeal Tribunal *ex parte* Shah (conjoined appeals)
38 I.L.M. 827 (Eng. H.L. 1999)

Steyn, L.

The two appeals before the House raise important questions about the interpretation of article 1A(2) of the Convention Relating to the Status of Refugees, 1951, and in particular the meaning of the words "membership of a particular social group."...The common features of the two appeals are as follows. Both appeals involve married Pakistani women, who were forced by their husbands to leave their homes. They are at risk of being falsely accused of adultery in Pakistan. They are presently in England. They seek asylum in this country as refugees. They contend that, if they are forced to return to Pakistan, they would be unprotected by the state and would be subject to a risk of criminal proceedings for sexual immorality. If found guilty the punishment may be flogging or stoning to death. In these circumstances both women claim refugee status on a ground specified in article 1A(2) of the Convention, namely that they have a well founded fear of being persecuted for reasons of "membership of a particular social group."...

Women in the Islamic Republic of Pakistan

Notwithstanding a constitutional guarantee against discrimination on the grounds of sex, a woman's place in society in Pakistan is low. Domestic abuse of women and violence towards women is prevalent in Pakistan. That is also true of many other countries and by itself...does not give rise to a claim to refugee status. The distinctive feature of this case is that in Pakistan women are unprotected by the state: discrimination against women in Pakistan is partly tolerated by the state and partly sanctioned by the state. Married women are subordinate to the will of their husbands. There is strong discrimination against married women who have been forced to leave the matrimonial home or have simply decided to leave. Husbands and others frequently bring charges of adultery against such wives. Faced with such a charge the woman is in a perilous position. Similarly, a woman who makes an accusation of rape is at great risk. Even Pakistan statute law discriminate[s] against such women. The position is described in a report of Amnesty International dated 6 December 1995 on Women in Pakistan. The report states, at pp. 5–7:

> [S]everal Pakistani laws explicitly discriminate against women. In some cases they allow only the evidence of men to be heard, not of women. In particular, the Evidence Act and the Zina Ordinance, one of four Hudood Ordinances promulgated in 1979, have eroded women's rights and denied them equal protection by the law.
>
> Women are also disadvantaged generally in the criminal justice system because of their position in society.... Women are particularly liable to be punished under the Zina Ordinance which deals with extramarital sexual intercourse.... Offenses under this law attract different punishments according to the evidence on which the conviction is based. In cases where the most severe (hadd) punishments may be imposed, the evidence of women is not admissible.

In a rape case the onus of proof falls on the victim. If a woman fails to prove that she did not give her consent to intercourse, the court may convict her of illicit sexual intercourse.... About half the women prisoners in Pakistan are held on charges of Zina.... Arrests under the Zina Ordinance can be made without a magistrate first investigating whether there is any basis for the charge and issuing a warrant. As a result, women in Pakistan are often held under the Zina Ordinance for years although no evidence has ever been produced that they have committed any offence. Men frequently bring charges against their former wives, their daughters or their sisters in order to prevent them marrying or remarrying against the man's wishes.... Most women remain in jail for two to three years before their cases are decided, often on the basis of no evidence of any offence.

For what may be a small minority, who are convicted of sexual immorality, there is the spectre of 100 lashes in public or stoning to death in public.

This brief description of the discrimination against women, which is tolerated and sanctioned by the state in Pakistan, is the defining factual framework of this case.

The Shah case

The appellant is 43. Her husband turned her out of the marital home in Pakistan. She arrived in the United Kingdom in 1992 and gave birth to a child shortly thereafter. In June 1993 she claimed asylum. She is afraid that her violent husband may accuse her of adultery and may assault her or denounce her under Sharia law for the offence of sexual immorality. In her case the evidence of state toleration and sanctioning of discrimination against women was sketchy....

The Islam case

The appellant is 45 and has two children. She arrived with her children in the United Kingdom in 1991. In the same year she claimed asylum. She is a teacher. She married her husband in 1971. He was often violent towards her. But the marriage endured. In 1990 a fight broke out in the school where she was teaching. The fight was between young supporters of two rival political factions. She intervened. One faction became hostile towards her. They made allegations of infidelity against her. These allegations were made, inter alia, to her husband who was a supporter of the same faction. Her husband assaulted her and she was twice admitted to hospital. She left her husband. She stayed briefly at her brother's house. Unknown men threatened her brother. She could not remain with him. After a brief stay in a temporary refuge she came to the United Kingdom....

Article 1A(2) in the Scheme of the Convention

The critical and operative provision of the [U.N. Refugee] Convention is article 1A(2)....* In the search for the correct interpretation of the words "membership of a particular social group" the travaux préparatoires of the Convention are uninforma-

---

* Ed. Note: Article 1A(2) defines "refugee" and states that it applies to any person who: "As a result of events occurring before 1 January 1951 and owing to a well-founded fear of being persecuted for reasons of race, religion, nationality, membership of a particular social group or political opinion, is outside the country of his nationality and is unable or, owing to such fear, is unwilling to avail himself of the protection of that country; or who, not having a nationality and being outside the country of his former habitual residence as a result of such events, is unable or, owing to such fear, is unwilling to return to it."

tive. The words in question were introduced at a late stage of the process leading to the finalization of the Convention. That fact tells one nothing about their contextual meaning. But the preambles to the Convention are significant. I set out the relevant preambles:

> Considering that the Charter of the United Nations and the Universal Declaration of Human Rights approved on 10 December 1948 by the General Assembly have affirmed the principle that human beings shall enjoy fundamental rights and freedoms without discrimination,

> Considering that the United Nations has, on various occasions, manifested its profound concern for refugees and endeavored to assure refugees the widest possible exercise of these fundamental rights and freedoms....

The relevance of the preambles is twofold. First, they expressly show that a premise of the Convention was that all human beings shall enjoy fundamental rights and freedoms. Secondly, and more pertinently, they show that counteracting discrimination, which is referred to in the first preamble, was a fundamental purpose of the Convention. That is reinforced by the reference in the first preamble to the Universal Declaration of Human Rights, 1948, which proclaimed the principle of the equality of all human beings and specifically provided that the entitlement to equality means equality "without distinction of any kind, such as race, colour, sex, language, religion, political or other opinion, national or social origin, property, birth or other status."...

Narrowing the issue

It is common ground that there is a general principle that there can only be a "particular social group" if the group exists independently of the persecution. In A. v. Minister for Immigration and Ethnic Affairs and Another (1997) 142 A.L.R. 331, 358 McHugh J. neatly explained the point as follows:

> If it were otherwise, Art. 1(A)(2) would be rendered illogical and nonsensical. It would mean that persons who had a well founded fear of persecution were members of a particular social group because they feared persecution. The only persecution that is relevant is persecution for reasons of membership of a group which means that the group must exist independently of, and not be defined by, the persecution....

The first issue: is cohesiveness a requirement for the existence of a particular social group?

[Ed. Note: The Court of Appeal below had held that "as a matter of law a particular social group can only exist if there is "some degree of cohesiveness, co-operation or interdependence." Lord Steyn, citing Sanchez-Trujillo v. I.N.S., 901 F.2d 1571 (9th Cir. 1986), recognized that "There is some authority for this view." However, Lord Steyn also mentioned that "on circuits other than the Ninth Circuit, a less restrictive interpretation of the words 'particular social group' has been adopted. The foundation of the contrary view is the earlier decision of the Board of Immigration Appeals in In re Acosta (1985) 19 I. & N. 211. This decision was not mentioned in Sanchez-Trujillo."]

In Acosta the Board dismissed the claim of a collection of Salvadoran taxi drivers who allegedly feared persecution from an organized group of taxi drivers in El Salvador. The reasoning is important. The Board observed:

> We find the well-established doctrine of ejusdem generis, meaning literally, "of the same kind," to be most helpful in construing the phrase "member-

ship in a particular social group." That doctrine holds that general words used in an enumeration with specific words should be construed in a manner consistent with the specific words.... The other grounds of persecution in the Act and the Protocol listed in association with "membership in a particular social group" are persecution on account of "race," "religion," "nationality" and "political opinion." Each of these grounds describes persecution aimed at an immutable characteristic: a characteristic that either is beyond the power of an individual to change or is so fundamental to individual identity or conscience that it ought not be required to be changed.... Thus, the other four grounds of persecution enumerated in the Act and the Protocol restrict refugee status to individuals who are either unable by their own actions, or as a matter of conscience should not be required, to avoid persecution.

Applying the doctrine of ejusdem generis, we interpret the phrase "persecution on account of membership in a particular social group" to mean persecution that is directed toward an individual who is a member of a group of persons all of whom share a common, immutable characteristic. The shared characteristic might be an innate one such as sex, color, or kinship ties, or in some circumstances it might be a shared past experience such as former military leadership or land ownership. The particular kind of group characteristic that will qualify under this construction remains to be determined on a case-by-case basis.... By construing "persecution on account of membership in a particular social group" in this manner, we preserve the concept that refuge is restricted to individuals who are either unable by their own actions, or as a matter of conscience should not be required, to avoid persecution....

I am satisfied that for the reasons given in *Acosta's* case the restrictive interpretation of "particular social group" by reference to an element of cohesiveness is not justified....

Apart from the judgment of Staughton L.J. in the present case, there is no English authority for the view that cohesiveness is an indispensable requirement for the existence of a "particular social group."... Cohesiveness may prove the existence of a particular social group. But the meaning of "particular social group" should not be so limited: the phrase extends to what is fairly and contextually inherent in that phrase.

The second issue: The different theories of "particular social group."...

Women in Pakistan as a Group. [The reasoning in *Acosta*] covers Pakistani women because they are discriminated against and as a group they are unprotected by the state. Indeed the state tolerates and sanctions the discrimination.... Historically, under even the most brutal and repressive regimes some individuals in targeted groups have been able to avoid persecution. Nazi Germany, Stalinist Russia and other examples spring to mind. To treat this factor as negating a Convention ground under article 1A(2) would drive a juggernaut through the Convention. My Lords, on careful reflection there is no satisfactory answer to the argument that the social group is women in Pakistan....

The Narrower Group. If I had not accepted that women in Pakistan are a "particular social group," I would have held that the appellants are members of a more narrowly circumscribed group as defined by counsel for the appellants.... It depends on the coincidence of three factors: the gender of the appellants, the suspicion of adultery, and their unprotected position in Pakistan. The Court of Appeal held (and counsel for the Secretary of State argued) that this argument falls foul of the principle that the group must exist independently of the persecution. In my view this reasoning is not valid. The unifying characteristics of gender, suspicion of adultery, and lack of protection, do not involve an assertion of persecution. The cases under consideration can be compared with a more narrowly defined group of homosexuals, namely practicing homosexuals who are unprotected by a state. Conceptually such a group does not in a relevant sense depend for its existence on persecution....

The third issue: The causation test....

[I]t is plain that the admitted well founded fear of the two women is "for reasons" of their membership of the social group. Given the central feature of state-tolerated and state-sanctioned gender discrimination, the argument that the appellants fear persecution not because of membership of a social group but because of the hostility of their husbands is unrealistic....

Hoffmann, L....

The problem for both women was to specify the "social group" of which they claimed their membership had given rise to persecution.... Mr. Blake Q.C. who appeared, as he did before your Lordships, for the women, defined it as "Pakistani women...accused of transgressing social mores (in the instant case, adultery, disobedience to husbands)...who are unprotected by their husbands or other male relatives."...

To what social group, if any, did the appellants belong? To identify a social group, one must first identify the society of which it forms a part. In this case, the society is plainly that of Pakistan. Within that society, it seems to me that women form a social group of the kind contemplated by the Convention. Discrimination against women in matters of fundamental human rights on the ground that they are women is plainly in pari materiae with discrimination on grounds of race. It offends against their rights as human beings to equal treatment and respect....

The reason why the appellants chose to put forward this restricted and artificial definition of their social group was to pre-empt the question of whether their feared persecution was "for reasons of" their membership of the wider group of women. It was argued for the Secretary of State that they could not fear persecution simply for the reason that they were women. The vast majority of women in Pakistan conformed to the customs of their society, did not chafe against discrimination or have bullying husbands, and were not persecuted. Being a woman could not therefore be a reason for persecution. The question is essentially one of causation. Being a woman does not necessarily result in persecution and therefore cannot be the reason for those cases in which women are persecuted....

I think that the argument on causation which it was designed to meet is fallacious.... What is the reason for the persecution which the appellants fear? Here it is important to notice that it is made up of two elements. First, there is the threat of violence to Mrs. Islam by her husband and his political friends and to Mrs. Shah by her husband. This is a personal affair, directed against them as individuals. Secondly, there is the inability or unwillingness of the State to do anything to protect them. There is nothing personal about this. The evidence was that the State would not assist them because they were women. It denied them a protection against violence which it would have given to men. These two elements have to be combined to constitute persecution within the meaning of the Convention. As the Gender Guidelines for the Determination of Asylum Claims in the UK (published by the Refugee Women's Legal Group in July 1988) succinctly puts it (at p. 5): "Persecution = Serious Harm + The Failure of State Protection."

Answers to questions about causation will often differ according to the context in which the question is asked. Suppose oneself in Germany in 1935. There is discrimination against Jews in general, but not all Jews are persecuted. Those who conform to the discriminatory laws, wear yellow stars out of doors and so forth can go about their ordinary business. But those who contravene the racial laws are persecuted. Are they being persecuted on grounds of race? In my opinion, they plainly are. It is therefore a fallacy to say that because not all members of a class are being persecuted, it follows that persecution of a few cannot be on grounds of membership of that class. Or to come nearer to the facts of the present case, suppose that the Nazi government in those early days did not actively organize violence against Jews, but pursued a policy of not giving any protection to Jews subjected to violence by neighbors. A Jewish shopkeeper is attacked by a gang organized by an Aryan competitor who smash his shop, beat him up and threaten to do it again if he remains in business. The competitor and his gang are motivated by business rivalry and a desire to settle old personal scores, but they would not have done what they did unless they knew that the authorities would allow them to act with impunity. And the ground upon which they enjoyed impunity was that the victim was a Jew. Is he being persecuted on grounds of race? Again, in my opinion, he is. An essential element in the persecution, the failure of the authorities to provide protection, is based upon race. It is true that one answer to the question "Why was he attacked?" would be "because a competitor wanted to drive him out of business." But another answer, and in my view the right answer in the context of the Convention, would be "he was attacked by a competitor who knew that he would receive no protection because he was a Jew."...

I am conscious...that there are much more difficult cases in which the officers of the State neither act as the agents of discriminatory persecution nor, on the basis of a discriminatory policy, allow individuals to inflict persecution with impunity. In countries in which the power of the State is weak, there may be intermediate cases in which groups of people have power in particular areas to persecute others on a discriminatory basis and the State, on account of lack of resources or political will and without its agents applying any discriminatory policy of their own, is unable or unwilling to protect them. I do not intend to lay down any rule for such cases. They have to be considered by adjudicators on a case by case basis as they arise. The distinguishing feature of the present case is the evidence of institutionalized discrimination against women by the police, the courts and the legal system, the central organs of the State....

Hope of Craighead, L.

I have had the advantage of reading in draft the speeches which have been prepared by my noble and learned friends Lord Steyn and Lord Hoffmann. I agree with them that these appeals should be allowed, and I would make the same orders as they have proposed.

Hutton, L.

I have had the advantage of reading in draft the speech of my noble and learned friend Lord Steyn, and I agree that the appeals should be allowed on the ground described by him as "the narrower ground" which was relied on by the appellants. I prefer to express no view on the wider issue whether women in Pakistan constitute "a particular social group" within the meaning of article 1A(2) of the Convention.

Millett, L....

Whether the social group is taken to be that contended for by the appellants, however, or the wider one of Pakistani women who are perceived to have transgressed social norms, the result is the same. No cognisable social group exists independently of the social conditions on which the persecution is founded. The social group which the appellants identify is defined by the persecution, or more accurately (but just as fatally) by the discrimination which founds the persecution. It is an artificial construct called into being to meet the exigencies of the case.... The evidence clearly establishes that women in Pakistan are treated as inferior to men and subordinate to their husbands and that, by international standards, they are subject to serious and quite unacceptable discrimination on account of their sex. But persecution is not merely an aggravated form of discrimination; and even if women (or married women) constitute a particular social group it is not accurate to say that those women in Pakistan who are persecuted are persecuted because they are members of it. They are persecuted because they are thought to have transgressed social norms, not because they are women. There is no evidence that men who transgress the different social norms which apply to them are treated more favorably.

In the course of argument an illuminating instance was put forward. Suppose, in the early years of the Third Reich, Jews in Nazi Germany were required to wear a yellow star on pain of being sent to a concentration camp and murdered if they did not. Would they have failed to qualify as refugees on the ground that they were not liable to persecution on racial grounds, but because they were defying the law? Of course we know now that they should not have failed to qualify, because the law was not merely discriminatory but a necessary part of the intended persecution. Jews were required to wear a distinguishing badge in order to mark them out for persecution. At the time this would have been a matter of evidence; but given the absence of any other rational explanation for the law, the virulence of the state-inspired racial propaganda which formed the background against which it was enacted, and the wholly disproportionate penalty for disobedience, there should have been no difficulty in satisfying the requirements of the Convention even in the absence of other evidence of persecution (of which there was an abundance). I find the example instructive precisely because of the differences between it and the present case rather than the similarities.

I am accordingly not willing to accept, as a general proposition, the submission that those who are persecuted because they refuse to conform to discriminatory laws to which, as members of a particular social group, they are subject, thereby qualify for refugee status. Such persons are discriminated against because they are members of the social group in question; but they are persecuted because they refuse to conform, not because they are members of the social group. Nor am I able to accept the submission that somehow this ceases to be the case where the persecution is sanctioned or tolerated by the state. As I have said, this goes to a different question, whether the applicant's fear of persecution is well founded. It is still necessary to establish that the persecution, whether or not sanctioned by the state, is for a Convention reason.

Of course, the fact that the persecution is sanctioned by the state may make it easier to categorize it as persecution on political grounds. In extreme cases, where persecution is employed as an instrument of state policy and is actively encouraged by the authorities, as in Nazi Germany, the distinction between discrimination and persecution may be a distinction without a difference. Persecution takes many different forms. Where the authorities perceive a particular social group to be hostile, they may persecute its members by openly withdrawing their protection and leaving them to the mercy of criminal elements. The fact that those who take advantage of the situation to use violence against members of the group do so for their own private purposes does not matter; the members should be regarded as the victims of official persecution by the state. To qualify for refugee status, however, they must still prove that the state authorities have withdrawn their protection for a Convention reason.

Such questions will depend on the evidence. The evidence in the present case is that the widespread discrimination against women in Pakistan is based on religious law, and the persecution of those who refuse to conform to social and religious norms, while in no sense required by religious law, is sanctioned or at least tolerated by the authorities. But these norms are not a pretext for persecution nor have they been recently imposed. They are deeply embedded in the society in which the appellants have been brought up and in which they live. Women who are perceived to have transgressed them are treated badly, particularly by their husbands, and the authorities do little to protect them. But this is not because they are women. They are persecuted as individuals for what each of them has done or is thought to have done. They are not jointly condemned as females or persecuted for what they are. The appellants need to establish that the reason that they are left unprotected by the authorities and are liable to be persecuted by their husbands is that they are women. In my opinion they have not done so.

I would dismiss the appeals.

Notes and Questions

1. *R-A.* Can you summarize the disagreement between the majority and dissenting opinions in *In re R-A*? How would R-A have fared under the Service's framework proposed in *Kasinga*? How would R-A have fared under the House of Lords' analysis in *Islam*? Under *R-A*, will a victim of domestic violence ever be able to fashion a successful claim for asylum? What would be the argument?

2. *Comparing.* Is the House of Lords' opinion in *Islam* in conflict with the BIA's decision in *R-A*? How can you harmonize them? The analysis in Lord Millett's dissenting opinion in *Islam* differs from the majority's analysis in *R-A*. Could his analysis be used to support the result in *R-A* or is it uniquely situated to the facts of *Islam*? How would you respond to his analysis?

3. *Particular Social Group.* What similarities exist between the "particular social group" found to exist in *Kasinga* and that advocated for in *In re R-A*? Did you find the Board's reasons in *R-A* for distinguishing *Kasinga* persuasive? Why or why not? Consider what the Seventh Circuit noted in *Lwin v. INS*: "[t]he legislative history behind the term [membership in a particular social group]... is uninformative, and judicial and agency interpretations are vague and sometimes divergent. As a result, courts have applied the term reluctantly and inconsistently." 144 F.3d 505, 510 (7th Cir. 1998). Do *Kasinga* and *R-A* support this statement?

4. *Possible Social Groups.* Social groups differ from society to society, and from time to time. Consider for example the notion of "landowners." While such a social group would have had significance at one time in American culture, it no longer has relevance

today. Different definitions of "particular social group" can be found in the case law, although relevant considerations almost always seem to include whether the members share an immutable characteristic that cannot be or should not be changed, including a past experience; whether the group has an identity in the community at large or in the eyes of the persecutors; whether the group experiences discrimination or preferential treatment; whether the group members are closely affiliated; whether the group members share common beliefs; whether there is a voluntary social membership among them; and whether the members see themselves as part of a group. Consider whether any of the following constitute a "particular social group" for a woman who was physically abused by her husband.

A. *The Family.* Is it possible to argue the family is a "social group" under the BIA's definition in *Acosta*, which is cited in *Islam*, or under the holding in *R-A*? If the family can be a particular social group, could friends also be a particular social group? Need all the family members suffer persecution by the same person in order to qualify as a particular social group? Must the family members be part of the immediate, and not extended, family? The Ninth Circuit in *Sanchez-Trujillo v. INS*, 801 F.2d 1571, 1576 (9th Cir. 1986), stated that a particular social group is "a collection of people closely affiliated with each other, who are actuated by some common impulse or interest. Of central concern is the existence of a voluntary associational relationship among the purported members, which imparts some common characteristic that is fundamental to their identity as a member of that discrete social group. Perhaps a prototypical example of a 'particular social group' would consist of the immediate members of a certain family, the family being a focus of fundamental affiliational concerns and common interests for most people." Other courts have issued opinions with similar language. *See* Gebremichael v. INS, 10 F.3d 28, 36 (1st Cir. 1993) (citing Ravindran v. INS, 976 F.2d 754, 761 n.5 (1st Cir. 1992)) ("[t]here can, in fact, be no plainer example of a social group based on common, identifiable and immutable characteristics than that of the nuclear family"); Iliev v. INS, 127 F.3d 638, 642 n.4 (7th Cir. 1997) ("case law has suggested, with some certainty, that a family constitutes a cognizable 'particular social group' within the meaning of the law").

B. *Marital Status.* Could an applicant's marital status qualify her as a member of a social group? *See, e.g.,* Matter of [name withheld], [number withheld], slip. op. at 14 (IJ Oct. 24, 2001) (N.Y., N.Y.) (Chew, IJ) (citing 65 Fed. Reg. 76593 (Dec. 7, 2000)).

C. *Broad Demographic Characteristics.* Is being a female enough to qualify one for membership in a particular social group in the United States? "[W]hile some courts have concluded as a legal matter that gender can define a particular social group, no court has concluded as a factual matter that an applicant has demonstrated that the government (or a persecutor the government could not or would not control) would seek to harm her solely on account of her gender." Phyllis Coven, Office of Int'l Affairs (INS), Memorandum: Considerations for Asylum Officers Adjudicating Asylum Claims from Women 13 (1995). Some courts, however, have rejected broad demographic characteristics. *See* Gomez v. INS, 947 F.2d 660, 664 (2nd Cir. 1991) ("Gomez failed to produce evidence that women who have previously been abused by guerrillas possess common characteristics—other than gender and youth—such that would-be persecutors could identify them as members of the purported group."). If race, religion, nationality, and political opinion can serve as grounds for asylum, why not gender?

D. *Religion.* If a woman's husband beats her because she refuses to follow the strict code of the husband's religion, will her more moderate religious beliefs allow her to argue that she is persecuted because of her religion? Does she have to show she is part of a social group at all? *See* In re S-A, 22 I. & N. Dec. 1328 (B.I.A. 2000).

E. *A Combination of Factors.* The litigants in *Kasinga, R-A,* and *Islam* all sought to combine factors to define the particular social group. Why? Does that strengthen or weaken an applicants claim?

5. *Political Opinion.* Jacqueline Bhabha has explained that "The field of human rights has undergone significant transformation since the mid-twentieth century, when the principle informative framework for refugee law was established. A gender-based approach to rights has transformed thinking about what counts as rights violations, problematizing not only the simplistic division between public, state-induced harms and private domestically caused problems, but also the very notion of the 'political.'" Jacqueline Bhabha, *Internationalist Gatekeepers?: The Tension Between Asylum Advocacy and Human Rights,* 15 Harv. Hum. Rts. J. 155, 157 (2002). There are some immigration judges who have held that the persecution of a victim of domestic violence may be on account of her political opinion. *See, e.g.,* Stephen M. Knight, *Seeking Asylum From Gender Persecution: Progress Amid Uncertainty,* 79 Interpreter Releases 689 (2002) (citing decision by Immigration Judge Glenn McPhaul). As the dissenting opinion in *R-A* makes clear, an applicant can establish persecution on account of political opinion even if the applicant does not hold a particular opinion, so long as her persecutor attributes or imputes the opinion to her. What political opinion is expressed, or potentially expressed, by domestic violence victims? If an applicant were merely neutral on the issue of women's rights, would that constitute a political opinion?

6. *Nexus.* Persecution because of one's gender does not always cause a gender-specific harm. To see the difference, assess whether a woman is persecuted "on account of" her gender in each of the following scenarios:

A. A woman is raped because she is a member of a political group.

B. A woman is stoned to death for having sex out of wedlock.

C. A woman is forced to submit to FGM because it is the custom in her community.

7. *Nexus II.* How can a woman be persecuted because of her gender if, in fact, her husband does not attack women randomly on the street?

8. *Nexus III.* Both Lords Hoffman and Millet in *Islam* discuss hypotheticals involving the Jews during Nazi Germany. Each claim their example supports their point about nexus. How can that be?

9. *U.N. Refugee Convention.* One is struck by the tone of John Guendelsberger's dissenting opinion in *R-A,* and the tone of Lord Steyn's opinion in *Islam,* especially where Lord Steyn cites to the preamble of the U.N. Refugee Convention. To what extent does *R-A* violate the spirit, or the object and purpose, of the 1951 Refugee Convention?

10. *U.N. Refugee Handbook and Guidelines.* In 1979, the U.N. Higher Commissioner for Refugees (U.N. HCR) issued a handbook to assist governments, academics and lawyers concerned with refugee problems. *See Handbook on Procedures and Criteria for Determining Refugee Status Under the 1951 Convention and the 1967 Protocol Relating to the Status of Refugees,* U.N. HCR, U.N. Doc. HCR/IP/4/Eng/REV.1 (reedited 1992). The U.N. Refugee Handbook says a social group "normally comprises persons of similar background, habits, or social status." *Id.* ¶ 77. While that definition is not particularly

helpful, in 1991 the U.N. HCR issued Guidelines on the Protection of Refugee Women. Those guidelines ask states to "[p]romote acceptance in the asylum adjudication process of the principle that women fearing persecution or severe discrimination on the basis of their gender should be considered a member of a social group for the purposes of determining refugee status." *See Information Note on U.N. HCR's Guidelines on the Protection of Refugee Women*, U.N. HCR, 42d Sess., ¶71, U.N. Doc. ES/SCP/67 (1991). What force should the U.N. Guidelines have in defining relevant terms in U.S. statutes? The U.S. Supreme Court has held that the 1979 U.N. Handbook is not binding on the attorney general, the BIA, or U.S. Courts. *See* INS v. Aguirre-Aguirres, 119 S.Ct. 1439, 1447 (1999). The BIA in *Acosta* admitted that the U.N. HCR's position in the Handbook is a "useful tool," although not controlling. *Id.* at 221. *See also* INS v. Cardoza-Fonseca, 480 U.S. 421, 437 (1987).

11. *Well-Founded Fear of Persecution and Past Persecution.* Unlike women who fear the future infliction of FGM, domestic violence victims typically will have experienced violence already. How does this affect their claims for asylum? Past persecution gives rise to a presumption that it is reasonable to fear future persecution. Surita v. INS, 95 F.3d 814, 821 (9th Cir. 1996). The INS can rebut the presumption if there has been a fundamental change in circumstances so that the fear is no longer well-founded, or if the applicant could, and reasonably should, relocate to another part of the country. *See* Establishing Asylum Eligibility, 8 C.F.R. §208.13(b)(1)(i)(A) & (B), 208.13(b)(1)(ii). If the presumption is rebutted, the applicant must then prove a well-founded fear of future persecution. The applicant may also be able to make out a successful claim if he or she proves "compelling reasons for being unwilling or unable to return to the country arising out of the severity of the past persecution," or the applicant proves there is "a reasonable possibility that he or she may suffer other serious harm upon removal to that country." 8 C.F.R. §208,13(b)(1)(iii).

12. *Differences in the Type of Violence?* What explanations exist for the Board's different conclusions in *Kasinga* and *R-A*? One commentator has suggested the following: "It seems plausible that the Board was in some way culturally biased, implicitly finding FGM outrageous and offensive to human dignity, while viewing domestic violence as so common and widespread that women subjected to it could not be regarded as belonging to a particular social group." *See* Andrea Binder, *Gender and the "Membership in a Particular Social Group" Category of the 1951 Refugee Convention*, 10 Colum. J. Gender & L. 167, 184–85 (2001). Another author speaking more generally about immigration law from the mid-1980s until the mid-1990s stated, "This body of case law...has...coincided with the fall of communism as the prime target of Western foreign policy, and the rise of Islamic fundamentalism as a movement of increasing concern to Western governments. The latter development may be associated with a decreasing deference to the state sovereignty of Islamic regimes and may contribute to a climate of opinion in refugee decision making where feminist arguments concerning women's rights are used (and at times abused) to defend an undifferentiated concept of 'Western values,' to attack a simplistic, homogenized notion of Islam and therefore to serve a new foreign policy-inspired agenda." *See* Jacqueline Bhabha, *Embodied Rights: Gender Persecution, State Sovereignty and Refugees*, 9 Pub. Cult. 3, 19 (1996). Do you agree with either of these authors' conclusions?

13. *Immigration Policy.* The INS's concern about controlling the number of successful asylum applicants was evident in its argument in *Kasinga*. It was also evident in *Aguirre-Cervantes v. INS*, 242 F.3d 1169 (9th Cir. 2001), where a domestic violence victim sought asylum for the extreme abuse perpetrated on her by her father. The nine-

teen-year-old applicant convinced the Ninth Circuit that her social group was her family and that she was persecuted because of her membership in it. That decision was vacated when the Ninth Circuit agreed to hear the case *en banc,* and then rendered moot when the applicant's father was killed pending argument. However, the government's argument for a rehearing is informative. It stated,

> Domestic violence and discrimination against women occur in many—perhaps all—countries. Even our own country is not free from these problems. These considerations indicate both that the number of potential asylum applicants who may bring claims based upon domestic violence is very large, and that the judgement as to which victims of domestic violence are "refugees" within the meaning of the asylum statute is one of great delicacy.

See Stephen M. Knight, *Seeking Asylum From Gender Persecution: Progress Amid Uncertainty,* 79 Interpreter Releases 689, 695 (2002) (citing INS Petition for Rehearing En Banc at 10–11, *Aguirre-Cervantes v. INS* (No. 97-70861)). Although the BIA disavowed interest in such an argument in *Kasinga,* could that concern help explain the BIA's decision in *R-A?*

Certainly the British have a long history of carefully controlling immigration also. *See* Mark F. McElreath, Note, *"Degrading Treatment"—From East Africa to Hong Kong: British Violations of Human Rights,* 22 Colum. Hum. Rts. L. Rev. 331 (1991). Did the House of Lords' decision in *Islam* make it too easy for certain people to get asylum in England? Some members of the British press believe this to be the case. *See, e.g.,* Auberon Waugh, Sunday Comment: *He Wants Us to Take in the Battered,* Sunday Telegraph, Mar. 28, 1999, at 41 (*Islam* decision will "encourage flood of new immigration"); George Pascoe-Watson, *Asylum Lunacy,* The Sun, Apr. 11, 2000 (stating *Islam* case "opened the floodgates").

In fact, there has been a "steady upward trend" in asylum applications over the last fifteen years in the United Kingdom, from approximately 4,000 asylum seekers in 1988 to 80,315 in 2000. The 2000 figure was 13% more than in 1999, but "the smallest percentage increase for three years (compared with year-on-year increases of 55 percent in 1999 and 42 percent in 1998)." *See* Secretary of State for the Home Department, *Secure Borders, Safe Haven: Integration with Diversity in Modern Britain* 50 (2002); The Secretary of State from the Home Department, *Fairer, Faster, & Firmer—A Modern Approach to Immigration and Asylum* 1 (July 1998). The 2002 White Paper on immigration does not break down the increase in applications by grounds for asylum or by gender of applicant. The 1998 White Paper, in contrast, stated that in 1997, 75% of the principal applicants were male and 87% of the applicants had no dependents at the time of application. *Fairer, Faster, & Firmer, supra,* at 11. As of 2000, the United Kingdom had increased the percentage of individuals granted asylum by 1% from the level in 1997 (when 10% of applicants were granted asylum). The percentage of individuals granted exceptional leave to remain for humanitarian factors increased from 9% to 12% of applicants over that same period. *See Fairer, Faster, & Firmer, supra,* at 11–12; *Secure Borders, Safe Haven, supra,* at 51. Again, there was no breakdown by grounds for asylum or by gender of applicants of those who were granted asylum or leave to remain.

14. *Asylum Guidelines.* The Department of Justice promulgated guidelines in 1995 that addressed asylum claims involving violence against women. Coven, *supra.* The DOJ Guidelines announced that "women's rights are human rights, and women's rights are universal." *Id.* at 2. The guidelines explicitly state that "rape...sexual abuse and domestic violence, infanticide and genital mutilation are forms of mistreatment primarily directed at girls and women and they may serve as evidence of past persecution on ac-

count of one or more of the five grounds." *Id.* at 4. The DOJ Guidelines recommend that asylum claims be analyzed against the background of the fundamental purpose of refugee law: to provide surrogate international protection where there is a fundamental breakdown in state protection. The DOJ Guidelines go on to state that domestic violence exemplifies just such a breakdown:

> This principle becomes crucial where the applicant alleges private actions— such as domestic violence—that the state will not protect against. In such situations, the officer must explore the extent to which the government can or does offer protection or redress, and the extent to which the risk of harm extends nationwide.

Id. at 18. The DOJ Guidelines also say that "the evaluation of gender-based claims must be viewed within the framework provided by existing international human rights instruments and the interpretation of those instruments by international organizations." *Id.* at 2. Why did the Guidelines not make a difference in *R-A*? After all, the BIA cited to the Guidelines in *Kasinga* for the proposition that FGM may serve as evidence of past persecution. *See* 21 I. & N. at 362.

15. *Proposed Regulations.* On December 7, 2000, the Department of Justice proposed a rule to amend the INS regulations that govern establishing asylum and withholding of deportation. *See* 65 Fed. Reg. 76588, 2000 WL 1783793. The regulations, if allowed to become final, would bind the INS. The portions of the proposed regulations related to "social group" and "nexus" are reproduced here. The Department of Justice explicitly stated that "The proposed new language in 208.15(b) is intended to address analytical issues that have arisen in the context of some claims based on domestic violence, and in particular in the Board's decision in *In re R-A*, Interim Decision 3403 (BIA 1999)." *Id.*

Asylum & Withholding Definitions
65 Fed. Reg. 76588, 76597–98 (proposed Dec. 7, 2000)

(b) *On account of the applicant's protected characteristic.* An asylum applicant must establish that the persecutor acted, or that there is a reasonable possibility that the persecutor would act, against the applicant on account of the applicant's race, religion, nationality, membership in a particular social group, or political opinion, or on account of what the persecutor perceives to be the applicant's race, religion, nationality, membership in a particular social group, or political opinion. In cases involving a persecutor with mixed motivations, the applicant must establish that the applicant's protected characteristic is central to the persecutor's motivation to act against the applicant. Both direct and circumstantial evidence may be relevant to the inquiry. Evidence that the persecutor seeks to act against other individuals who share the applicant's protected characteristic is relevant and may be considered but shall not be required.

(c) *Membership in a particular social group.*

(1) A particular social group is composed of members who share a common, immutable characteristic, such as sex, color, kinship ties, or past experience, that a member either cannot change or that is so fundamental to the identity or conscience of the member that he or she should not be required to change it. The group must exist independently of the fact of persecution. In determining whether an applicant cannot change, or should not be expected to change, the shared characteristic, all relevant evi-

dence should be considered, including the applicant's individual circumstances and...country conditions....

(2) When past experience defines a particular social group, the past experience must be an experience that, at the time it occurred, the member either could not have changed or was so fundamental to his or her identity or conscience that he or she should not have been required to change it.

(3) Factors that may be considered in addition to the required factors set forth in paragraph (b)(2)(i) of this section, but are not necessarily determinative, in deciding whether a particular social group exists include whether:

(i) The members of the group are closely affiliated with each other;

(ii) The members are driven by a common motive or interest;

(iii) A voluntary associational relationship exists among the members;

(iv) The group is recognized to be a societal faction or is otherwise a recognized segment of the population in the country in question;

(v) Members view themselves as members of the group; and

(vi) The society in which the group exists distinguishes members of the group for different treatment or status than is accorded to other members of the society....

How would R-A's claim be resolved if this rule were in force at the time she petitioned for asylum? What problems might she still have in establishing her claim? Are the factors in (c)(3) a checklist that an applicant must meet in order to establish a social group? The Department of Justice believes its proposed guidelines would permit case-by-case development of the law in highly fact-specific cases. Asylum and Withholding Definitions, 65 Fed. Reg. at 76594. What are the disadvantages, if any, to this approach? Would it be better to have a categorical rule that a victim of domestic violence is or can be a refugee on account of that experience or fear? Without a bright-line rule, will the new guidelines make a difference? The INS stated that it did not expect "a flood of asylum applications" if the proposed guidelines were adopted. See U.S. Dept. of Justice, INS, Questions and Answers: The R-A Rule 4 (2000). In fact, after *Kasinga*, the number of claims based on FGM did not appreciably increase. *Id.* Even if the applications based upon domestic violence were to increase 100% under the proposed guidelines, the number of women seeking asylum based upon domestic violence would still be relatively small. In 1999, the INS received 42,207 asylum applications and only 1,085 were filed by women seeking asylum based upon membership in a social group. *Id.*

As of January 20, 2002, nothing had happened to change the status of the proposed rule. See www.ins.usdoj.gov/graphics/lawsregs/q4_2000.htm.

16. *R-A Post-Script.* The BIA's decision in *R-A* was appealed by R-A to the Ninth Circuit. In January 2001, while the appeal was pending, the attorney general vacated the decision of the BIA in *In re R-A*. The attorney general's order said that R-A's case was to be remanded to the INS for reconsideration once the proposed regulations became final. The Ninth Circuit then denied a request for a continuance and dismissed the case without prejudice in light of Attorney General Reno's ruling. The Ninth Circuit probably assumed that new regulations would soon issue, although R-A's attorneys had asked the Ninth Circuit to continue the case because R-A had no other forum if the regulations never became final. Since the regulations have never become

final, R-A's case has never been reheard and R-A's status is in limbo. Although R-A had been granted asylum by the immigration judge in 1996, the INS appealed R-A's grant of asylum. At the time of press, the appeal was still pending before the BIA. "Altogether, Ms. Alvarado's claim for asylum has been pending for a total of six years, during which time she has been separated from her two children, ages nine and fourteen, who remain in Guatemala. Until she is granted asylum she has no legal right to bring her children." Amnesty International, Action Appeal, Rodi Alvarado, from Guatemala (Jan. 22, 2002), at http://www.amnestyusa.org/action/women_01222002.html. In March of 2003, Attorney General Ashcroft stated that he would "certify" the case himself and issue a decision. He also stated that the proposed regulations are still in the process of being revised. *See* Center for Gender and Refugee Studies, *Current Updates*, http://www.uhastings.edu/cgrs/campaigns/alvarado.htm#update.

17. *Asylum Today.* After R-A was vacated and the proposed guidelines were issued, a number of applicants have sought asylum based upon gender-related violence. Included among these cases are cases of domestic violence, sometimes in combination with other facts, such as forced marriage, incest, and FGM. After reviewing the cases, Stephen Knight said there is a "small but significant number of women" who have been granted asylum in the United States recently. *See* Stephen M. Knight, *Seeking Asylum From Gender Persecution: Progress Amid Uncertainty*, 79 Interpreter Releases 689 (2002). However, Knight also cites cases where the immigration judge has followed the analysis of *R-A*.

18. *Abusers.* If domestic violence qualifies as persecution, the perpetrator is barred from seeking asylum. *See* 8 U.S.C. § 1101(a)(42). In addition, the Illegal Immigration Reform and Immigrant Responsibility Act (IIRIRA) makes deportable any alien who has been convicted of a crime of domestic violence or has been found in violation of certain provisions of a domestic violence protection order. *See* 8 U.S.C. § 1227(a)(2)(E).

19. *Practical Problems.* Various other nations explicitly recognize gender, and particularly the experience of domestic violence, as a basis for a grant of asylum. For example, the Immigration Appellate Authority in the United Kingdom issued new Asylum Gender Guidelines in 2000, and these Guidelines identify domestic violence as a form of persecution. *See* Immigration Appellate Authority, Asylum Gender Guidelines § 2A.17 (2000). However, the Home Office, which makes the initial decisions about whether an applicant qualifies for asylum, does not have similar guidelines. The Home Office has been criticized for its lack of experience in human rights issues and its lack of cultural sensitivity.

The usefulness of recognizing domestic violence as a basis for asylum rests, to some degree, on decision makers' receptiveness to victims' stories. Historically in the United States, victims of domestic violence often have been disbelieved. Linda Kelly, *Domestic Violence Survivors: Surviving the Beatings of 1996*, 11 Geo. Immigr. L. J. 303, 310–11 (1997). Skepticism can pose particular problems in the asylum context where the initial fact finding is so critical. *See, e.g.*, Matter of A-S, 21 I. & N. Dec. 1106 (B.I.A. 1998) (stating that BIA will generally defer to an adverse credibility finding if the record has discrepancies and omissions, if they present a specific and cogent reason to conclude the alien is not credible, and if the alien has failed to give a convincing explanation for the discrepancies and omissions). Of particular concern is whether the process inhibits a domestic violence victim's ability to disclose and whether the decision-maker understands the dynamics of domestic violence. The U.N. High Commissioner for Refugees has recommended certain techniques for interviewing women refugees, including awareness "of gender differences in communication,... [e.g.,] ability to maintain eye contact," of "inhibitions, particularly regarding sexual abuse," of symptoms of "Rape

Trauma Syndrome...includ[ing] persistent fear, a loss of self-confidence and self-esteem, difficulty in concentration, an attitude of self-blame, a pervasive feeling of loss of control, and memory loss or distortion," and of the importance of questioning women outside other family members' presence. *See Guidelines on the Protection of Refugee Women*, U.N. HCR, ¶72, U.N. Doc. ES/SCP/67 (1991).

A. Asylum Officers' Training. Peter Billings claims that the United States has been much better than the United Kingdom in equipping primary decision-makers to make difficult decisions on credibility. The United States has an Asylum Officer Corps, and entry into it requires a university degree. In addition, the United States gathers "publicly available and verifiable sources of information from human rights monitors and analyses by non-governmental organizations (NGOs), the media, and from the governments of the states under scrutiny." Peter W. Billings, *A Comparative Analysis of Administrative and Adjudicative Systems for Determining Asylum Claims*, 52 Admin. L. Rev. 253, 297–300 (2000). All asylum officers in the United States are required to read the 1995 Gender Guidelines and receive training on them. *See* Phyllis Coven, Office of Int'l Affairs, Memorandum: Considerations for Asylum Officers Adjudicating Claims from Women 18 (1995). The Guidelines offer, among other things, recommended procedures for processing claims by women with gender-related claims. These procedures include use of female asylum officers and interviews away from family members. *Id.* at 5. The U.K. Home Office does not have comparable guidelines. Overall, "[t]he United States and Canada appear to have grasped the nettle in this regard, whereas the United Kingdom has been slower to recognize the wisdom of the need for specialized knowledge, training, and experience." Billings, *supra*.

B. Gender-Specific Obstacles. The Canadian Guidelines recognize that "women refugee claimants face special problems in demonstrating that their claims are credible and trustworthy." For example, "[w]omen from societies where the preservation of one's virginity or marital dignity is the cultural norm may be reluctant to disclose their experiences of sexual violence in order to keep their 'shame' to themselves and not dishonour their family or community." *See* Immigration and Refugee Board, Women Refugee Claimants: Fearing Gender-Related Persecution, Guidelines Issued by the Chairperson Pursuant to § 65(3) of the Immigration Act, Guideline 4, D(1) (1996). The U.S. Guidelines recognize that women who have been abused can suffer psychological trauma, which "may have a significant impact on the ability to present testimony." Coven, *supra*, at 7. The 2000 Gender Asylum Guidelines, issued by the Immigration Appellate Authority in the United Kingdom, suggests that women may be reluctant to claim asylum status independently of their family because men often deal with official matters, women may not want to offend the men by acting independently, or women may fear for their safety because of a perceived lack of confidentiality. Many of the specific recommendations in each countries' gender guidelines can be traced to recommendations by the U.N. High Commissioner for Refugees in the Guidelines on the Protection of Refugee Women, *supra*, ¶72.

C. Credibility. An applicant must establish that she has a well-founded fear of persecution. What happens if there is not objective evidence to support the applicant's claim? Domestic violence typically occurs in private and a victim may have many legitimate reasons for never before bringing the problem to anyone's attention. Can the decision-maker rely solely on the applicant's own testimony? In *Matter of Mogharrabi*, 19 I. & N. Dec. 439, 443–46 (BIA 1987), albeit in a different context, the BIA recognized that the alien's own testimony can suffice "where the testimony is believable, consistent, and sufficiently detailed to provide a plausible and coherent account of the basis for his fear." Corroborative background evidence is always helpful, but it is most essential when the basis for a claim rests on "broad allegations regarding general conditions in the respondent's country of origin," and not "specific events involving the respondent personally." *See* Matter of Dass, 20 I. & N. Dec. 120 (B.I.A. 1989).

D. The Process

Peter W. Billings, *A Comparative Analysis of Administrative and Adjudicative Systems For Determining Asylum Claims*
52 Admin. L. Rev. 253, 263–74 (2000)

[The United States]

Pre-screening procedures operate in two stages: first, claimants have to demonstrate a fear of return, and second, must also demonstrate a credible fear of persecution. An individual who arrives at a port of entry, and who, upon primary inspection by an Immigration and Naturalization Service (INS) inspection officer appears to lack valid documentation, is immediately referred to a secondary inspection. If the second inspection indicates that an alien is inadmissible for misrepresentation or for lack of proper documentation, the officer may order the removal of the alien from the country without any further proceedings, conditional on the alien not indicating an intention to apply for asylum or a fear of persecution. This removal order has the same weight as one issued by an Immigration Judge and is reviewed by a senior-level supervisory immigration inspector. The inspecting officer is obliged to afford the asylum seeker the opportunity to claim asylum by reading them a statement about the asylum process, and by asking three specific questions concerning whether they have a fear of being returned home. They are instructed to use verbal and non-verbal indications of fear, such as shaking, perspiration, sweating, hysteria and even silence. No individual can be expeditiously removed from the United States until this process is performed. This process of self-identification is of the utmost importance....

If the circumstances surrounding the interview are not humane, a claimant's ability to reveal the reasons for migrating may be adversely affected. Such a suspicion, though probably well-founded, is difficult to verify. Therefore, it is helpful to assess whether the manner in which aliens are treated leading up to, and during the interview, is ethical. For those claimants who arrive by plane, the secondary inspection will take place at the airport. Individuals are immediately escorted to the waiting area without opportunity to rest, eat, or to contact anybody....

The conditions in which claimants are expected to elucidate their fears and past experiences merit scrutiny because oppressive surroundings, or those which lack privacy for the individual, can compromise the claimants' abilities to reveal their experiences. The absence of confidentiality during secondary inspections does little to put the alien at ease and may fetter the claimant's participation in the interview. The general environment in which secondary inspections takes place does not appear to promote a feeling of trust and security, but demonstrates scant respect for the dignity of the individual. The ethicality of the entire process of secondary inspection is highly dubious....

Claimants who, in the opinion of a secondary inspector, indicate a fear of persecution or a desire to apply for asylum are detained and referred to an asylum officer. The officer then determines whether they have a credible fear of persecution....

20. *Domestic Violence and Immigration Law Generally.* We are about to leave the topic of immigration, at least until it reappears in Chapter Twelve on International Adoption, and then again in Chapter Thirteen on Reproductive Rights. Although we have focused so far on refugee law, there are other provisions in U.S. immigration law that specifically address domestic violence victims. Of utmost importance is the battered spouse waiver and the self-petitioning process. These were discussed in Chapter Two in the section on mail-order marriages. *See* Chapter 2.D.3.

Unlike the refugee quotas, there are no numerical restrictions on the numbers of immediate relations of citizens who can be lawfully admitted to the United States (there are restrictions, however, for relatives of lawful permanent residents). In fact, our immigration policy is primarily guided by the desire to keep family members together and there are immigration preferences for immediate family members. However, citizens and lawful permanent residents generally must petition for their eligible relatives (spouses and children) to gain permanent residency, *see* 8 U.S.C. § 1154(a), by filing a Petition for Alien Relative, and then, after that is approved, a petition for adjustment of status. If the marriage is less than two years old, only conditional residency will be granted initially, and then a joint application must be filed at the end of a two-year period. As described in Chapter Two, there are several grounds on which the joint filing can be waived as well as a mechanism to self-petition. *See* Chapter 2.D.3 (note 8).

While immigration law has become much more sympathetic over the last fifteen years to the plight of domestic violence victims seeking to stay in the United States, some critics believe the law still can be improved. *See, e.g.,* Elizabeth Shor, Note, *Domestic Abuse and Alien Women in Immigration Law: Response and Responsibility*, 9 Cornell J.L. & Pub. Pol'y 697 (2000). One commentator has compared the immigration law applied to immigrant women who are battered while living in the United States and to women who are battered while living abroad. She concluded that "a double standard" exists whereby "battered immigrant women living in the United States face a much easier standard than their counterparts fleeing abuse in their home countries." Lydia Brashear Tiede, *Battered Immigrant Women and Immigration Remedies: Are the Standards Too High?*, 28 Hum. Rts. 21 (2001).

Problem 6-1

Analyze the following fact pattern under U.S. law. Ms. Musse Ahmed seeks asylum. While legally in the United States with her son, she entered into an extra-marital relationship with a man and had a daughter out of wedlock. Her husband in Somalia became aware of the situation and swore to kill her when she returned to Somalia. She also fears being punished by the existing regime whose application of the Shari'a law has led to the stoning death of women considered to be adulteresses. If her husband accuses her of adultery, she faces a moderate chance of being punished severely for having violated a social norm. In addition, even if she manages to avoid her husband's violence or the government's punishment, she believes that her husband would divorce her and take custody of their son. Under Shari'a law, the divorced woman has to relinquish custody of her children to their father, because they are a part of his clan. Losing custody of her son would be devastating for Ms. Ahmed. She also fears that if she returns to Somalia, her daughter will be forced to undergo FGM. Although FGM has been outlawed in Somalia since 1947, approximately ninety-eight percent of the women experience FGM. *See* Mohamed v. Canada [1997] F.C. IMM-4742-96 (Fed. Ct.). *See generally* Tiajuana Jones-Bibbs, *United States Follows Canadian Lead and Takes an Unequivocal Position Against Female Genital Mutilation: In Re Fauziya Kasinga*, 4 Tulsa J. Comp. & Int'l L. 275, 296–305 (1997) (discussing case of Khadra Hassan Farah).

2. International Law

Previously in the chapter, we started to explore those substantive provisions of international law that may make FGM a violation of a woman's human rights. The same provisions of international law may make domestic violence a human rights violation. Similarly, the theoretical debate between "universalists" and "cultural relativists" explored within the context of FGM sometimes replicates itself in this context. Consequently, we now raise some other issues. We will explore in more detail the advantages or disadvantages of certain international law theories as tools to combat domestic violence. While we identified the relevant provisions in the context of our discussion of FGM, here we pause to think about them in more detail. We will also explore whether violence against women has reached the status of jus cogens, whether it is torture, or whether "new approaches" to human rights, specifically international and regional instruments which address explicitly violence against women, will be advantageous. Inherent in all of these topics is the issue of state responsibility for the actions of private parties.

a. *Traditional Human Rights Approaches*

Dorothy Q. Thomas & Michele E. Beasley, *Domestic Violence as a Human Rights Issue*
58 Alb. L. Rev. 1119, 1121–33, 1143–47 (1995)

A. *The Scope of International Human Rights Law*

The concept of human rights developed largely from Western political theory of the rights of the individual to autonomy and freedom. International human rights law evolved in order to protect those individual rights from limitations that might be imposed on them by states. States are bound by international law to respect the individual rights of each and every person and are thus accountable for abuses of those rights. The aim of the human rights movement is to enforce states' obligations in this regard by denouncing violations of their duties under international law. The exclusive focus on the behavior of states confines the operation of international human rights law entirely within the public sphere.

B. *Gender-Neutral Law, Gender-Biased Application*

International human rights law is facially gender neutral. The rights embodied in the Universal Declaration of Human Rights are defined as belonging to "all human beings," not just to men. All the major human rights instruments include sex as one of the grounds upon which states may not discriminate in enforcing the rights set forth.

Although international law is gender neutral in theory, in practice it interacts with gender-biased domestic laws and social structures that relegate women and men to separate spheres of existence: private and public. Men exist as public, legal entities in all countries, and, barring an overt abuse by the state, participate in public life and enjoy the full extent of whatever civil and political rights exist. Women, however, are in every country socially and economically disadvantaged in practice and in fact and in many places by law. Therefore, their capacity to participate in public life is routinely circumscribed. This gender bias, if unchallenged, becomes so embedded in the social structure that it often assumes the form of a social or cultural norm seemingly beyond the purview of the state's responsibility, rather than a violation of women's human rights for which the state is accountable....

When gender-neutral international human rights law is applied in these gender-biased social contexts, those making the application—both governments and nongovernmental organizations—do not necessarily challenge the gender bias embedded in the social structure or in the state's determination of its responsibilities. In past human rights practice, organizations often have not challenged the relegation of women and what happens to them in the private sphere, whether in law or in practice, and have allowed social or cultural justifications to deter them from denouncing restrictions on women's capacity to participate in public life. Even where abuses against women have occurred in realms they traditionally monitor, such as police custody, they have not consistently reported them.... In a very real sense, gender specific abuses—even those directly attributable to states—have until recently been "privatized" internationally and either go unchallenged or are left out of human rights practice altogether.

Nowhere is the effect on international human rights practice of the public/private split more evident than in the case of domestic violence which literally happens "in private." States dismiss blatant and frequent crimes, including murder, rape, and physical abuse of women in the home, as private, family matters, upon which they routinely take no action. Moreover, the state's failure to prosecute violence against women equally with other similar crimes or to guarantee women the fundamental civil and political right to equal protection of the law without regard to sex have largely escaped international condemnation.

At least four interrelated factors have caused the exclusion of domestic violence in particular from international human rights practice: (1) traditional concepts of state responsibility under international law and practice, (2) misconceptions about the nature and extent of domestic violence and states' responses to it, (3) the neglect of equality before and equal protection of the law without regard to sex as a governing human rights principle, and (4) the failure of states to recognize their affirmative obligation to provide remedies for domestic violence crimes. These factors, independently and in relationship to one another, are beginning to change and, with them, so is the treatment of domestic violence under international law. The following sections attempt to trace the course and direction of this emerging change.

C. The Concept of State Responsibility

The concept of state responsibility defines the limits of a government's accountability for human rights abuses under international law. Of course, all acts are done by real people, individually or with others, and not by the fictive "person" of the state. Therefore, responsibility is generally understood to arise only when an act by a real person or persons can be imputed to the state. Traditionally, the idea of vicarious responsibility for acts is a perfectly acceptable one: such responsibility flows from the authorized acts of agents of the state, or persons acting with the apparent authority or condonation of the state. In traditional human rights practice, states are held accountable only for what they do directly or through an agent, rendering acts of purely private individuals—such as domestic violence crimes, outside the scope of state responsibility.

More recently, however, the concept of state responsibility has expanded to include not only actions directly committed by states, but also states' systematic failure to prosecute acts committed either by low-level or para-state agents or by private actors. In these situations, although the state does not actually commit the primary abuse, its failure to prosecute the abuse amounts to complicity in it. For instance, in three significant cases, *Velasquez, Godinez and Fairen,* and *Solis,* decided by the Inter-American Court on Human Rights in 1988–1989, the tribunal found that the government of Honduras was responsible for a series of forced disappearances carried out between 1981 and 1984 by members of the Honduran military who were acting as private individuals.

The test of the state's responsibility for an act differs depending upon whether the actor is the state or a private individual. To hold a state accountable for the actions of state actors, one of two things must be shown: (1) the state explicitly authorized the act (i.e., a senior official committed or authorized it), or (2) the state systematically failed to prosecute abuses committed by its agent, whether or not these acts were ordered by senior officials. In the latter case, one must usually show a pattern of nonprosecution of acts that violate human rights, and that the state has agreed to enforce those human rights....

The test is different when the actors are private. For example, systematic nonenforcement of laws against armed robbery by private actors alone is not a human rights problem; it merely indicates a serious common crime problem. Nonprosecution of the crimes of private individuals becomes a human rights issue (assuming no state action or direct complicity) only if the reason for the state's failure to prosecute can be shown to be rooted in discrimination along prohibited lines, such as those set forth in Article 26 of the Covenant on Civil and Political Rights.

There are rights to bodily integrity in international human rights law which armed robbery appears to violate. However, these are rights against the state, not rights that states must enforce against all other persons. States cannot be held directly accountable for violent acts of all private individuals because all violent crime would then constitute a human rights abuse for which states could be held directly accountable under international law. The state's international obligation with regard to the acts of private individuals is to ensure that where it does protect people's lives, liberty, and security against private depredations, it must do so without discrimination on prohibited grounds. Therefore, there would have to be systematic, discriminatory nonenforcement of the domestic criminal law against murder or assault for domestic violence to constitute a human rights issue, not merely a showing that the victims' lives ended or their bodies were harmed.

The expansion of state responsibility to include accountability for some acts of private individuals as defined above is one of the factors necessary to permit analysis of domestic violence as a human rights violation. However, in many cases it is also necessary to show a pattern of discriminatory nonprosecution which amounts to a failure to guarantee equal protection of the law to women victims....

D. Widespread Violence and a Pattern of Nonprosecution

New information on domestic violence has surfaced as a result of a long international campaign by women's rights groups to raise consciousness about women's issues....

Certain characteristics of the problem become clear from the overall research: domestic violence is not unusual or an exception to normal private family life; the vast majority of crimes against women occur in the home and are usually committed by a spouse or relative in the form of murder, battery, or rape; and, domestic violence is endemic to all societies. The immensity of the problem has led researchers to conclude:

> If you are one of only 500 women in a population of 50 million then you have certainly been more than unlucky and there may perhaps be something very peculiar about your husband, or unusual about your circumstances, or about you; on the other hand, if you are one of 500,000 women then that suggests something very different—that there is something wrong not with a few individual men, or women, or marriages, but with the situation....

If violence against women in the home is inherent in all societies, then it can no longer be dismissed as something private and beyond the scope of state responsibility. Although information about government response to this problem is still minimal, the research suggests that investigation, prosecution, and sentencing of domestic violence crimes occurs with much less frequency than other, similar crimes....

E. The Underlying Right to Equal Protection of the Law

Until recently, sex discrimination has been visibly absent from the agendas of most governmental and nongovernmental bodies concerned with human rights, with the exception of the Committee on the Elimination of All Forms of Discrimination Against Women, the U.N. body which monitors state conduct under the Convention on the Elimination of All Forms of Discrimination Against Women....

However...the mainstream Geneva-based human rights bodies, which oversee instruments that have stronger protective mechanisms, have used the existence of this separate women's human rights regime as an excuse to marginalize sex discrimination and most other women's human rights violations, which nonetheless fall clearly within their own mandates.[53] Within the cumulative human rights practice of governments and governmental bodies, sex discrimination has been deemphasized and placed outside the rubric of central human rights concerns. International nongovernmental human rights organizations, including the two largest groups, Amnesty International and Human Rights Watch, have until recently reflected and perpetuated this trend....

Ultimately, women's rights activists internationally condemned many of the international governmental and nongovernmental human rights bodies for gender bias and, among other things, for their failure to adequately promote and protect women's rights to nondiscrimination and equal protection of the law. Largely as a result of this increasing pressure from women's rights activists internationally, and heightened awareness of the extent of violence against women and government tolerance of it, the nongovernmental human rights of nations began to highlight these issues within their overall human rights practice.

These separate but interrelated developments have allowed domestic violence to be placed within the context of international human rights law and practice. Develop-

---

53. For example, the United Nations Human Rights Commission established an Ad Hoc Working Group of Experts in 1967 to investigate various aspects of human rights and racial discrimination in South Africa and other parts of Southern Africa in 1967. *See United Nations Action in the Field of Human Rights,* U.N. Doc. ST/HP/2/Rev. 2 (1983). No such similar group has ever been established by the Human Rights Commission to study discrimination on the basis of sex internationally or even regionally.

ments in the concept of state responsibility, new information about the gender-specific nature of domestic violence, its pervasiveness and frequent non- or discriminatory prosecution by governments, and a new emphasis on equal protection of the law as a central human rights concern have made it possible to conceptualize domestic violence as a human rights issue and to hold governments accountable for the pervasive abuse of women worldwide....

Conclusions: The Limits and Value of the Equal Protection Human Rights Approach to Combatting Domestic Violence

[I]t is very difficult to use the human rights approach to prevent domestic violence. Positive state responsibilities such as education or economic support programs, which might help eliminate the causes of domestic violence, are less clearly prescribed by international law than prohibitions against certain abuses, even where the state may be domestically obligated to undertake certain functions. It is one thing for a human rights organization to address the state's discriminatory application of law; it is quite another to direct a state to adopt a particular social program to change discriminatory attitudes. The first instance is, in a sense, a "negative" injunction, one to stop violations of international human rights law; the second is a "positive" exhortation to adopt a particular policy. The latter statement has a more amorphous basis in international legal principles and requires a less straightforward remedy. It is more difficult for an international human rights organization to be persuasive positively than negatively.[108]

Increasingly, the positive responsibilities of states are being incorporated into international human rights law and practice. The Convention on the Elimination of All Forms of Discrimination Against Women (CEDAW), for example, requires governments to take positive measures to end legal, social, and economic gender inequality. The international human rights community has not yet reached a consensus about the ability of human rights organizations to advocate positive measures, or about states' responsibility under international law to take such actions. However, as the concept of state responsibility in international law evolves further, human rights organizations may more easily hold governments accountable for failing actively to counter the social, economic, and attitudinal biases which underpin and perpetuate domestic violence.

Finally, and perhaps most importantly, the current human rights approach to domestic violence and state responsibility only addresses the problem of equal protection; it usually cannot hold governments accountable for the domestic violence itself, just as it could not hold governments accountable internationally for other violent crimes committed by private individuals. Given the current state of international human rights jurisprudence, the nondiscrimination approach most closely resembles current thinking as regards state responsibility for private actions. However, it is possible to derive concepts of direct state accountability for private acts from human rights law...and it might be preferable to undertake such an analytic endeavor.

Addressing the state's responsibility for domestic violence per se would entail investigating in more detail the particular characteristics of domestic violence, as distinguished

---

108. That is in large part because positive exhortations usually imply that a state ought to spend its money in a particular way. Human rights practice loses its moral force when it attempts to direct spending policies; the practice is then attempting to insert itself into what is purely an internal state matter of distributive justice.

from other violent crime. To some extent domestic violence is not random, that is, it is directed at women because they are women and is committed to impede women from exercising their rights. As such, it is an essential factor in maintaining women's subordinate status.... In this sense, domestic violence is different from other violent crimes. Treating domestic violence as merely an issue of equal protection, and by inference therefore, setting up the treatment of men as the standard by which we ought to measure the treatment of women in our societies, may in fact disserve women and mask the ways in which domestic violence is not just another common crime. The norm of gender neutrality itself, embodied in the human rights treaties and international customary law, may unintentionally reinforce gender bias in the law's application and obscure the fact that human rights laws ought to deal directly with gender-specific abuse, and not just gender-specific failures to provide equal protection. The gender-neutral norm may appear to require only identical treatment of men and women, when in fact, equal treatment in many cases is not adequate....

The practical and methodological problems outlined above are not an inherent deterrent to integrating domestic violence into human rights practice. To identify practical obstacles and understand the methodological limits of the current human rights approach is to expand human rights practice, which is far from static, that much further. Moreover, to understand the limits of the human rights approach is also to clarify the particular contributions it can make as part of broader local and international efforts to combat domestic violence.

Rhonda Copelon, *Recognizing the Egregious in the Everyday: Domestic Violence as Torture*
25 Colum. Hum. Rts. L. Rev. 291, 365–66 (1994)

Jus cogens embrace values of supreme, overriding and fundamental importance to the international community. The norms designated as jus cogens occupy a privileged position in the hierarchy of international concerns. They are non-derogable: they take precedence over treaties to the contrary and bind states that are not parties to treaties. They are determined by considerations that are both positivist (the demand for consensus) and normative (the significance of the violation). At the time of the negotiation of the Vienna Convention, the International Law Commission identified, in another context, slavery, genocide, apartheid and destruction of the environment through massive pollution as likely jus cogens. More recently, in response to widespread abuses by dictatorial governments, the shorter list has come to include torture and cruel, inhuman and degrading treatment or punishment as well as prolonged and arbitrary detention, systematic racial discrimination, assassination and causing the disappearance of people.

Striking in this list is the absence of rights that reflect the ways in which women suffer gross violation of their human dignity and oppression. As Hilary Charlesworth and Christine Chinkin write, "the concept of the jus cogens is not a properly universal one: its development has privileged the experiences of men over those of women and it has provided a protection to men that is not accorded to women." They attribute this to the role of the public/private distinction in international law, as well as to the failure to explore empirically, from women's perspectives, the meaning of existing guarantees and the significance of the social and economic rights.

The absence of gender-based violence from either the categories or the debates on the scope of jus cogens is particularly striking given the centrality of violence in the agreed-upon norms. The category of jus cogens has expanded historically, however, as a result not of abstract logic, but of cataclysms in human experience and the resistance they set in motion. Today a global women's movement is challenging the historic dehumanization of women and elucidating the universality of gross, systemic and often privatized gender violence and its centrality to the subordination of women.

Given the symbolic importance of the peremptory norms in international law, gender-based violence should be included among them. Elucidating the atrociousness of gender-based violence is critical to deconstructing the public/private dichotomy that has shielded it from international attention. Moreover, understanding the reality and harm of gender-based intimate terror is essential to developing the consensus against it as well as the sense of outrage that propels recognition of a new jus cogens norm even, as with torture, in the presence of widespread violations.

On the other hand, the need for consensus among the states in the formation of both customary norms and jus cogens—while a pragmatic and necessary safeguard against destructive universalism—is also a substantial obstacle. Unlike other forms of violence recognized as jus cogens, there is no society that is free of gender-based violence; no states that can be targeted as wrongdoers while others are innocent. Virtually every society is built upon some form of brutality and degradation of women. Whether or not it is sanctioned by law, religion, or explicit custom or effective impunity, gender-based violence is deeply intertwined with economic, social and cultural structures and plays a role in shaping every man and every woman. Beyond that, women have been and continue to be excluded from equal participation in the domestic political process as well as from the upper echelons of international relations and policy-making.

Notes and Questions

1. *Challenges.* When violence against women is broadly defined, the inadequacies of the existing framework as well as the challenge of including gender-based violence as jus cogens become even more obvious. Hilary Charlesworth has succinctly made this point: "From conception to old age, womanhood is full of risks: of abortion and infanticide because of the social and economic pressure to have sons in some cultures; of malnutrition because of social practices of giving men and boys priority with respect to food; of less access to health care than men; of endemic violence against women in all states. Although the empirical evidence of violence against women is overwhelming and undisputable, it has not been adequately reflected in the development of international law." Hilary Charlesworth, *What are 'Women's International Human Rights?' in* Human Rights of Women 71–72 (Rebecca J. Cook ed., 1994). Take Charlesworth's example involving food. Using the Thomas and Beasley article, identify the doctrinal problems that exist if one seeks to convince others that gender preferencing is a human rights violation. Do these problems disappear if one calls gender-based violence jus cogens? Can one? Jus cogens was also discussed in Chapter 1.B., and you may want to review those materials.

2. *Traditional Theories.* Under what traditional human rights doctrine can domestic violence be conceived of as a violation of international human rights? Thomas and Beasley discuss the preeminence of the equal protection approach. All of the traditional instruments address equality. For example, article 3 of the International Covenant on Economic, Social and Cultural Rights (ICESCR) states, "The States Parties to the present Covenant undertake to ensure the equal right of men and women to the enjoyment of all economic, social and cultural rights set forth in the present Covenant." *See also* Interna-

tional Covenant on Civil and Political Rights, art. 26; Universal Declaration on Human Rights, art. 2. Why exactly does the equality model have limitations in this context?

For other possible provisions that might apply, please refer back to the discussion of international law in the context of FGM. *See* Chapter 6.B.4. There may, however, be additional provisions available for victims of domestic violence. For example, one author has suggested that domestic violence may violate, *inter alia*, article 6 of the International Covenant on Economic, Social, and Cultural Rights, which guarantees a "right of everyone to the opportunity to gain his living by work...." *See* Barbara Stark, *Domestic Violence and International Law: Good-Bye Earl (Hans, Pedro, Gen, Choy, etc.)*, 47 Loy. L. Rev. 255 (2001). The author explains that domestic violence causes women to miss work, to be fired, and to be threatened at work. Similarly, one might be able to argue that provisions such as article 3(2) in the U.N. Convention on the Rights of the Child require States Parties to halt violence between parents of children.

3. Possibility I: ICCPR. Liability of the state under international human rights law for domestic violence had typically been predicated on the notion of state responsibility by omission, rather than commission. For example, under the equal protection approach, it is the state's failure to address domestic violence when it addresses other crimes that gives rise to the liability. If a state never addresses any private violence, then there would be no problem under the non-discrimination approach. Can one argue, however, that a state has a positive obligation to combat crime generally? Consider article 6 of the ICCPR on the right not to be "arbitrarily deprived of life." Now look at article 2 of the ICCPR. It specifically says that States Parties are to "respect and to ensure...the rights recognized in the present Covenant...." What is the difference between respecting and ensuring? Does one impose a negative obligation and the other impose an affirmative obligation?

4. Reason for Slow Recognition of Domestic Violence As a Human Rights Issue. Traditional international human rights instruments were not used to combat domestic violence, in part, because of the following:

> [H]uman rights organizations, particularly in their early days, treated these provisions as if they applied only to the victims of politically motivated abuse (and even then only if the abuse was at the hands of a government agent).... Part of the reason for this narrow reading of the Covenant [on Civil and Political Rights] is historical accident: the large human rights organizations were born out of a concern with politically motivated abuse.... [T]he lack of a traditional political motivation behind domestic violence against women should no longer preclude its consideration by international human rights organizations. Like violence against presumed common criminals, violence against women can be said to have a political dimension in that it arguably serves as a form of social control by reinforcing the subjugation of women. But even that political dimension should not be necessary to address the issue. If international human rights organizations no longer ask the political views of a victim of execution, torture, or inhuman prison conditions, why should they care that domestic violence has little if anything to do with the political views of its victims? A woman killed by her husband for a supposed offense to his 'honor' is deprived of her life in as 'arbitrary' a fashion (to use the language of Covenant article 6(1)) as a common criminal suspect who is summarily executed by the police.

Kenneth Roth, *Domestic Violence as an International Human Rights Issue, in* Human Rights of Women 327–29 (Rebecca J. Cook ed., 1994).

5. *Evidence of Change*. The Human Rights Committee in 2000 issued General Comment 28, which addresses state reporting obligations on equality of rights between men and women (article 3 of ICCPR). *See* General Comment 28, U.N. HRC, U.N. Doc. No. CCPR/21/Rev.1/Add. 10 (2000). For example, the Comment says, "When reporting on the right to life protected by article 6, States Parties should...report on measures to protect women from practices that violate their right to life, such as female infanticide, the burning of widows and dowry killings." It continues: "[t]o assess compliance with article 7 of the Covenant [prohibiting torture or cruel, inhuman or degrading treatment], as well as with article 24, which mandates special protection of children, the Committee needs to be provided information on national laws and practices with regard to domestic and other types of violence against women, including rape." *Id.*

The Human Rights Committee now comments about gender-based violence as part of its monitoring of States Parties' compliance with the International Covenant on Civil and Political Rights. It is concerned about the absence of necessary legislation and the lack of effective implementation measures. For example, in its concluding observations to Zimbabwe, the Human Rights Committee stated, "The Committee is concerned about the extent and persistence of domestic violence against women. Legislation should be passed [to] make marital rape a criminal offence. Educational campaigns should be undertaken and institutional mechanisms should be established to address all forms of violence against women, and to provide assistance to victims of violence." *Consideration of Reports Submitted by States Parties Under Article 40 of the Covenant (Zimbabwe)*, U.N. HRC, 63rd Sess., ¶ 14, U.N. Doc. CCPR/C/79/Add. 89 (1998). Similarly, in commenting on Sweden's report, the Committee stated, "The Committee notes with concern the persistence of domestic violence despite legislation adopted by the State Party (articles 3 and 7 of the Covenant). The State Party should pursue its policy against domestic violence and, in this framework, should take more effective measures to prevent it and assist the victims of such violence." *Consideration of Reports Submitted by States Parties Under Article 40 of the Covenant (Sweden)*, U.N. HRC, 74th Sess., U.N. Doc. CCPR/CO/74/SWE (2002).

Since States Parties must now address the issue of domestic violence directly in their compliance reports, the U.S. executive branch cited the Violence Against Women Act (VAWA) in its report and claimed VAWA was enacted in fulfillment of the United States' treaty obligations under the ICCPR. *See* Jordan J. Paust, *Human Rights Purposes of the Violence Against Women Act and International Law's Enhancement of Congressional Power*, 22 Hous. J. Int'l L. 209, 211–12 (2000).

6. *Possibility II: CAT*. The nondiscrimination model poses challenges for human rights advocates because state omissions fall along a continuum. For example, at one end of the continuum is the state's failure to arrest a particular batterer. At the other end of the continuum is the state's failure to arrest any batterers. Most police inaction would fall somewhere between these two extremes. Consequently, it may be difficult as an empirical matter to establish a claim of discriminatory treatment or to hold states responsible for omissions that are not widespread. However, consider the Convention Against Torture and Other Cruel, Inhuman and Degrading Treatment or Punishment, 1987 ("CAT"). It applies even to individual occurrences so long as the act is "inflicted by or at the instigation of or with the consent or acquiescence of a public official or other person acting in an official capacity." *See* art. 1, ¶ 1. CAT is discussed further in the next section.

7. *Possibility III: CEDAW.* The non-discrimination model is the foundation of the Convention on the Elimination of All Forms of Discrimination Against Women. Does this instrument get one further in arguing that states have an obligation to end domestic violence than the other U.N. human rights treaties' that condemn discrimination? The article by Thomas and Beasley suggests this is the case. In fact, if domestic violence itself is "discrimination against women," then State Parties have a variety of actions that they must undertake to help eliminate the discrimination. *See* art. 2. This obligation includes taking "all appropriate measures to eliminate discrimination against women by any person, organization or enterprise," art. 2(e), and taking "all appropriate measures, including legislation, to modify or abolish existing laws, regulations, customs and practices which constitute discrimination against women." *See* art. 2(f). In addition, article 5 states that "States Parties shall take all appropriate measures: a) To modify the social and cultural patterns of conduct of men and women, with a view to achieving the elimination of prejudices and customary and all other practices which are based on the idea of the inferiority or the superiority of either of the sexes or on stereotyped roles for men and women." Is domestic violence "discrimination against women" under the Convention? Article 1 defines "discrimination against women" as "any distinction, exclusion or restriction made on the basis of sex which has the effect or purpose of impairing or nullifying the recognition, enjoyment or exercise by women, irrespective of their marital status, on a basis of equality of men and women, of human rights and fundamental freedoms in the political, economic, social, cultural, civil or any other field."

8. *Other Possibilities.* The international instruments that specifically address domestic violence, such as CEDAW's General Recommendation No. 19, the U.N. Declaration on the Elimination of Violence Against Women, and the Inter-American Convention to Prevent, Punish, and Eradicate Violence Against Women, are examined below in the section C.2.c, entitled "New International Law Approaches to Domestic Violence."

9. *Foundation for Federal Action.* The "Necessary and Proper Clause" of the U.S. Constitution affords Congress the power to implement U.S. treaty obligations. *See, e.g.,* Missouri v. Holland, 22 U.S. 416 (1920). Congress also has power under the "define and punish" clause of the U.S. Constitution to address "offenses against the law of Nations." See U.S. Const., art. 1, §8, cl.10 (granting Congress the power to "define and punish Piracies and Felonies committed on the high Seas and Offenses against the law of Nations"); *see also* U.S. v. Arjona, 120 U.S. 479, 483 (1887). Finally, federal judges can adjudicate claims under customary international law because customary international law is part of the U.S. law. *See* The Paquete Habana, 175 U.S. 677, 700–01 (1900). A statute conferring jurisdiction on the federal courts to adjudicate claims based upon customary law would arguably be permissible under the "Necessary and Proper Clause."

Given these sources of power, could Congress pass sweeping legislation to combat domestic violence? Of course, legislation to combat domestic violence would have to be seen as furthering a treaty obligation, punishing an "offense against the law of Nations," or furthering customary international law. Does federal legislation that addresses domestic violence qualify? An amicus brief filed in *U.S. v. Morrison*, 120 S. Ct. 1740 (2000), argued that the three sources of congressional power set forth above all supported congressional passage of the Violence Against Women Act's (VAWA) civil rights remedy. *See* Brief of Amici Curiae Int'l Law Scholars et al., U.S. v. Morrison, 1999 WL 1037253 (1999) (Nos. 99-5, 99-29). The Supreme Court did not address the amici's arguments. Instead the Supreme Court held that gender motivated crimes of violence are not economic activity, and therefore, Congress did not have authority under the Commerce Clause to enact the civil remedy provision of VAWA. It stated,

> We...reject the argument that Congress may regulate noneconomic, violent criminal conduct based solely on that conduct's aggregate effect on interstate commerce. The Constitution requires a distinction between what is truly national and what is truly local.... In recognizing this fact we preserve one of the few principles that has been consistent since the Clause was adopted. The regulation and punishment of intrastate violence that is not directed at the instrumentalities, channels, or goods has always been the province of the states.... Indeed we can think of no better example of police power, which the Founders denied the National Government and reposed in the States, than the suppression of violent crime and vindication of its victims.

U.S. v. Morrison, 529 U.S. 598, 617–18 (2000). While such language was clearly limited to the Court's discussion of the Commerce Clause, the Court's sweeping language about federalism and its failure to address the amici's arguments raise questions about whether the amici's arguments would ever be successful. The Court also held that Congress did not have the requisite power to enact VAWA under Section Five of the Fourteenth Amendment. The concurring and dissenting opinions did not address amici's arguments either. *See generally* Paust, *supra*.

b. *Convention Against Torture*

A prohibition against torture and cruel, inhuman and degrading treatment is found in a variety of international instruments, including the Universal Declaration of Human Rights (art. 5) and the International Covenant on Civil and Political Rights (ICCPR) (art. 7). On December 10, 1984, the United Nations General Assembly adopted the Convention against Torture and Other Cruel, Inhuman or Degrading Treatment or Punishment (CAT). *See* 39 U.N. GAOR Supp. (No. 51) at 197, U.N. Doc. A/39/51 (1984), annexed to Resolution 39/46. The U.S. Senate gave its advice and consent to the Convention on October 27, 1990, making ratification subject to the enactment of implementing legislation. 136 Cong. Rec. S17, 491–92 (daily ed. Oct. 27, 1990). The United States filed a declaration with its instrument of ratification that articles one through sixteen were not self-executing. *See* 136 Cong. Rec. 517486-01, 517492 (1990). The United States has subsequently taken legislative or administrative action in fulfillment of its obligations. *See, e.g.,* 18 U.S.C. § 2340A (criminalizing acts of torture that occur outside the United States); 22 C.F.R. § 95.2 (directing competent authorities to implement article 3 of the Convention prohibiting expulsion, return, or extradition of a person to a State where that person is likely to be tortured).

The Convention might be useful to victims of FGM and domestic violence in two ways. First, CAT may provide an immigration benefit, in particular the "withholding of removal" to the country of torture. Second, CAT may help hold governments accountable for domestic violence in their territory. These benefits are examined in turn. Start by examining the Convention Against Torture, which is set forth in the Supplement.

i. Immigration Law

Ali v. Reno

237 F.3d 591 (6th Cir. 2001)

Daughtrey, J.

Zainab Ali petitioned the Immigration and Naturalization Service for asylum and for protection under the Convention Against Torture and other Forms of Cruel, Inhuman or Degrading Treatment or Punishment. An immigration judge denied the petition, and on appeal the Board of Immigration Appeals affirmed the order. Ali now challenges the Board's finding that she had been firmly resettled in Denmark, thus making her ineligible for asylum, and its ruling that she did not warrant protection under the Convention. For the reasons stated below, we conclude that the Board's order must be affirmed.

Factual and Procedural Background

Zainab Ali is a native and citizen of Iraq. In August 1997, Immigration and Naturalization Service officials detained Ali for attempting to enter the country without proper authorization. The I.N.S. commenced proceedings to deport Ali to Iraq for attempting to enter the country without proper authorization and with the aid of a fraudulent document. Subsequently, Ali filed an application for asylum. After the immigration judge determined that Ali was subject to removal for attempting to enter the country with a false Danish passport, he proceeded to address Ali's asylum claim, which was based on the following circumstances.

Ali's family is Shiite Muslim, and her father was a member of the opposition Al-Da'Wa party in Iraq during the 1970s. During this period, Ali's father went into hiding to escape threats and harassment from Iraqi authorities, and because of his absence, Ali's mother was subject to threats and detainment. Due to the constant threats and harassment, the family fled Iraq in 1980 and settled in Syria for ten years. In Syria, the family rented a home for shelter, Ali attended school, and Ali's father continued his affiliation and activities with Al-Da'Wa. Because of his political activities, Ali's father was arrested several times by Syrian authorities who endeavored to persuade him to relinquish his political affiliation and spy on Iraq.

In 1990, the family returned to Iraq to visit Ali's ailing grandmother and stayed approximately two months, until the Iraqi government discovered that they were in the country. According to Ali, the government pursued the family in a high-speed car chase, during which there was an accident in which Ali suffered serious injury, but Ali and her family escaped across the border into Syria.

The family remained in Syria for two months, during which time Ali, at the age of 17, married an Iraqi citizen. Shortly thereafter, Danish authorities accepted the family into Denmark as refugees. The Danish authorities issued Ali and her family passports and residence permits, and her family continues to live in Denmark. Ali, however, without notification to Danish authorities, utilized her Danish passport and returned to Syria after staying six months in Denmark. Using an Iraqi passport that she obtained during her visit to her grandmother, Ali obtained a visa and entered the United States in 1990 to visit her husband, who had matriculated at an educational institution in Ohio.

Ali stayed in the United States for six years, during which time her visa expired, and she gave birth to two children who have United States citizenship. Following a visit from her mother, Ali and her children went to Denmark in April 1997, in response to information from her family that her father was seriously ill. Upon arrival, Danish authorities confiscated her passport because it had expired. They also informed her that she no longer had refugee status in Denmark and that she would be deported. Ali applied for asylum in Denmark, but her application was rejected.

Shortly after her arrival in Denmark, Ali discovered that the report of her father's illness was a ruse designed to persuade her to leave her husband. At one point during her five-month stay in Denmark, Ali was beaten and kicked by her father and three brothers because she refused to leave her husband. Apparently, the Danish police arrested the assailants, and an officer questioned Ali at a hospital. The Danish police report indicates that Ali told the police that she did not want her three brothers punished, although she wanted the authorities to admonish her brothers not to contact her any more. Ali testified that an officer said that he would instruct Ali's father and brothers not to bother her or go near her. However, when Ali herself requested that her brothers not be punished, the Danish chief of police decided not to pursue the case any further and released them from custody. According to Ali, after she was released from the hospital, she went to stay with her sister who lived in a location five hours from her parents' home. At her sister's home, one of Ali's brothers wielded a gun and threatened to kill her. Following this incident, Ali obtained the false Danish passport and returned to the United States with her children.

The immigration judge denied Ali's request for asylum and found her ineligible for withholding from removal. On appeal, the Board remanded the case and directed the immigration judge to correct some deficiencies in the record and rule on the motion to reconsider. On reconsideration, the immigration judge denied the request for asylum on the basis of his finding that Ali had firmly resettled in Denmark and thus was not eligible for asylum according to statutory dictate, but he granted her request for withholding of removal to Iraq and ordered instead that she be removed to Denmark or Syria. Ali now seeks reversal of the Board's order affirming that ruling.

Discussion

[Ed. Note: The Court held that the denial of asylum was proper, in part because under the Illegal Immigration Reform and Immigrant Responsibility Act of 1996 (IIRIRA) (Pub. L. No. 104-208, 110 Stat. 3009), an alien may not obtain asylum if she "was firmly resettled in another country prior to arriving in the United States." 8 U.S.C. § 1158(b)(A)(vi). It found that the Board did not abuse its discretion in finding that Ali was firmly resettled in Denmark.]

Article 3(1) of the Convention [Against Torture] provides that "[n]o State Party shall expel, return ('refouler') or extradite a person to another State where there are substantial grounds for believing that he would be in danger of being subjected to torture." Convention Against Torture and Other Cruel, Inhuman or Degrading Treatment or Punishment, *opened for signature* February 4, 1985, S. Treaty Doc. No. 100-20, at 20 (1988), 23 I.L.M. 1027, 1028 (1984). Judicial review of Convention claims is available only when such claims are heard as part of the review of a final order of removal pursuant to 8 U.S.C. § 1252. *See* Foreign Affairs Reform and Restructuring Act of 1998 (FARRA), Pub. L. No. 105-277, 2242(d), 112 Stat. 2681, 2681-821; 8 C.F.R. 208.18(e) (2000). Therefore, the applicable standard of review maintains that "a decision that an alien is not eligible for admission to the United States is conclusive unless manifestly contrary to law[,]" and, as mentioned above, "the administrative findings of fact are conclusive unless any reasonable adjudicator would be compelled to conclude to the contrary." 8 U.S.C. § 1252(b)(4)(B) and (C).

The United States deposited the instrument of ratification of the Convention with the United Nations on October 21, 1994, and the obligations under the Convention went into effect for the United States on November 20, 1994. Because the United States Senate consented to ratify the Convention with the declaration that Convention articles 1–16 are not self-executing, *see* 136 Cong. Rec. S17486-01, S17492 (1990), Congress sought to conform immigration practices to the Convention with the passage of FARRA. *See* Pub. L. No. 105-277, 2242, 112 Stat. 2681, 2681-821.[2] Pursuant to FARRA's directive instructing the appropriate agencies to implement the obligations of the United States under Article 3 of the Convention, *see* Pub. L. No. 105-277, 2242(b), 112 Stat. 2681, 2681-821, the I.N.S. and the Executive Office for Immigration Review have promulgated regulations for Convention claims.

Protection under the Convention exists in the form of withholding of removal to the country of torture. 8 C.F.R. 208.16(c)(4) (2000). The applicant for withholding of removal pursuant to the Convention bears the burden of proof to "establish that it is more likely than not that he or she would be tortured if removed to the proposed country of removal." *See id.* 208.16(c)(2) (2000). In assessing the risk of torture, the adjudicator must consider the possibility of future torture, including any evidence of past torture inflicted upon the applicant and evidence that the applicant is not likely to be tortured in another area of the country of removal. *See id.* 208.16(c)(3)(2000). The regulations define torture as follows:

> Torture is defined as any act by which severe pain or suffering, whether physical or mental, is intentionally inflicted on a person for such purposes as obtaining from him or her or a third person information or a confession, punishing him or her for an act he or she or a third person has committed or is suspected of having committed, or intimidating or coercing him or her or a third person, or for any reason based on discrimination of any kind, when such pain or suffering is inflicted by or at the instigation of or with the consent or *acquiescence* of a public official or other person acting in an official capacity. *See id.* 208.18(a)(1) (2000) (emphasis added).

The interpretation of 'acquiescence' represents the sole issue with respect to the application of the Convention to Ali's circumstances. Ali contends that the Danish police will acquiesce to the torture that will be inflicted by her father and brothers if she is removed to Denmark and, therefore, that she qualifies for protection under the Convention. The Board found that the Danish government's inability to control the activities of Ali's family members does not constitute acquiescence and that the Danish authorities did not wilfully ignore the actions of the family members. Based on the record now before us, we can only conclude that the Board's determination is not manifestly contrary to law.

According to the regulations, "the term 'acquiescence' requires that the public official, prior to the activity constituting torture, have awareness of such activity and thereafter breach his legal responsibility to intervene to prevent such activity." 8 C.F.R. 208.18(a)(7) (2000). This requirement mirrors the Senate's understanding of the term upon consenting to ratify the Convention, *see* 136 Cong. Rec. S17486-01, S17491-92 (1990), and the interpretation of the United States Department of State upon the

---

2. Section 2242(a) essentially mirrors the protection provided by Article 3 of the Convention: "It shall be the policy of the United States not to expel, extradite, or otherwise effect the involuntary return of any person to a country in which there are substantial grounds for believing the person would be in danger of being subjected to torture, regardless of whether the person is physically present in the United States." Foreign Affairs Reform and Restructuring Act of 1998, Pub. L. No. 105-277, 112 Stat. 2681, 2681-821.

President's transmission of the Convention to the Senate. *See* Message from the President of the United States Transmitting the Convention Against Torture and Other Cruel, Inhuman or Degrading Treatment or Punishment, S. Treaty Doc. No. 100-20, at 4 (1988). The Senate Committee on Foreign Relations stated that the purpose of this requirement "is to make it clear that both actual knowledge and 'willful blindness' fall within the definition of the term 'acquiescence.'" S. Exec. Rep. No. 101-30, at 9 (1990). The agencies implementing Article 3 concluded that 'acquiescence' "includes only acts that occur in the context of governmental authority." *Regulations Concerning the Convention Against Torture*, 64 Fed. Reg. 8478, 8482 (1999). This interpretation corresponds to the understanding of the Department of State, which remarked that "the Convention applies only to torture that occurs in the context of governmental authority, excluding torture that occurs as a wholly private act or, in terms more familiar in United States law, it applies to torture inflicted 'under color of law.'" Message from the President of the United States Transmitting the Convention Against Torture and Other Cruel, Inhuman or Degrading Treatment or Punishment, S. Treaty Doc. No. 100-20, at 4 (1988).

All considered, the Board's determination that the Danish police did not 'acquiesce' to torture against Ali is not manifestly contrary to law. The record shows that the Danish police arrested the assailants, incarcerated them during the investigation of Ali's charges, and offered to warn Ali's father and brothers not to harm her. The Board characterized the Danish police's actions as an "inability to control the activities" of Ali's family members, but it appears that this "inability" stems simply from Ali's refusal to allow punishment of her brothers. Because we conclude that the Danish police did not breach its "legal responsibility to intervene to prevent" torture, the Board's determination is manifestly not contrary to the law.

This is not to say that domestic violence of the sort alleged in this case could never be the basis for relief under the Convention Against Torture. In different circumstances, such as a situation in which the authorities ignore or consent to severe domestic violence, the Convention appears to compel protection for a victim. *See* Patricia A. Seith, Note, *Escaping Domestic Violence: Asylum as a Means of Protection for Battered Women*, 97 Colum. L. Rev. 1804 (1997); Barbara Cochrane Alexander, Note, *Convention Against Torture: a Viable Legal Alternative Remedy for Domestic Violence Victims*, 15 Am. U. Int'l L. Rev. 895 (2000); G. Kristian Miccio, *With All Due Deliberate Care: Using International Law and the Federal Violence Against Women Act to Locate the Contours of State Responsibility for Violence Against Mothers in the Age of Deshaney*, 29 Colum. Hum. Rts. L. Rev. 641 (1998).

Despite the sad circumstances of this case...there is no legally sufficient basis upon which to reverse the Board's decision to deny Ali's application for asylum and for protection under the Convention Against Torture. We therefore AFFIRM the Board's order.

Notes and Questions

1. *Definition of Torture: Severe Physical or Mental Pain and/or Suffering.* Examine the definition of torture in article 1 of the Convention Against Torture (CAT), found in the Statutory Supplement. Much domestic violence will probably satisfy the first requirement in the definition: "any act by which severe pain or suffering, whether physical or mental, is intentionally inflicted on a person." Note that a physical injury is not required by the definition, nor is a physical injury necessarily determinative of "severe pain or suffering."

Article 2 of the Inter-American Torture Convention also defines torture and does not require that the pain or suffering be "severe."

a. *Necessity of Physical Threats or Physical Violence?* Does torture under CAT require physical brutality or even threats of physical brutality? Consider also part of the definition of torture in Article 2 of the Inter-American Torture Convention: "Torture shall also be understood to be the use of methods upon a person intended to obliterate the personality of the victim or to diminish his physical or mental capacities, even if they do not cause physical pain or mental anguish."

b. *Compare Concept of Domestic Violence.* If torture can occur solely from acts of psychological brutality, more actions of a batterer may qualify as torture than would qualify under domestic legislation as domestic violence warranting injunctive protection. For example, insults, humiliation, and threats of reprisals against relatives might qualify under CAT, but might not satisfy domestic statutes enabling victims of domestic violence to obtain restraining orders. *Cf.* Leslye E. Orloff & Janice V. Kaguyutan, *Offering a Helping Hand: Legal Protection for Battered Immigrant Women: A History of Legislative Responses*, 10 Am. U. J. Gender Soc. Pol'y & L. 95, 106 (2001) (comparing broad definition of domestic violence for battered spouse waiver in immigration law with narrow definition in most state statutes). What does the definition of torture tell us about domestic remedies that are limited to physical abuse or threats of physical abuse?

c. *U.S. Reservation.* The United States has accepted the competence of the Committee Against Torture, pursuant to Article 21(1), to accept complaints from another State Party. *See* 136 Cong. Rec. S17486-01 (Oct. 27, 1990). What of the fact that the United States has entered a reservation to CAT, which states that "to constitute torture, an act must be specifically intended to inflict severe physical or mental pain or suffering and that mental pain or suffering refers to prolonged mental harm caused by or resulting from: (1) the intentional infliction or threatened infliction of severe physical pain or suffering; (2) the administration or application, or threatened administration or application, of mind altering substances or other procedures calculated to disrupt profoundly the senses of the personality; (3) the threat of imminent death; or (4) the threat that another person will imminently be subject to death, severe physical pain or suffering, or the administration or application of mind altering substances or other procedures calculated to disrupt profoundly the senses or personality. (b) That the United States understands that the definition of torture in Article 1 is intended to apply only to acts directed against persons in the offender's custody or physical control." *See Declarations and Reservations*, G.A. Res. 39/46, U.N. GAOR, 39th Sess., Annex 1, U.N. Doc. A/RES/39/46 (1984).

2. *The Definition of Torture: Purpose.* "[T]he intent required under the international torture conventions is simply the general intent to do the act which clearly or foreseeably causes terrible suffering." Rhonda Copelon, *Recognizing the Egregious in the Everyday: Domestic Violence as Torture*, 25 Colum. Hum. Rts. L. Rev. 291, 325 (1994). However, CAT also has a specific intent requirement. The definition of torture in article 1 of CAT says that torture is inflicted "for such purposes as obtaining from him or a third person information or a confession, punishing him for an act he or a third person has committed or is suspected of having committed, or intimidating or coercing him or a third person, or for any reason based on discrimination of any kind...." Is this requirement broad enough to cover victims of domestic violence or FGM? Why does the assailant's purpose matter at all? After all, is a heinous act any less heinous for the victim simply because the perpetrator acts for a reason not listed? The list contains both valid reasons for state action (e.g., obtaining information and punishment) and invalid rea-

sons for state action (e.g., coercion and discrimination), so why have any reasons at all? Judge Sir Gerald Fitzmaurice once stated, "Torture is torture whatever its object may be, or even if it has none, other than to cause pain, provided it is inflicted by force...." Ireland v. U.K., 25 Eur. Ct. H.R. (ser. A) at 129–30 n.19 (1978) (Fitzmaurice, J. dissenting). A member of the legal staff at the European Court of Human Rights suggests that the European Court's jurisprudence does not necessarily require that the torturer have any purpose at all. *See* Ela Grdinic, *Application of the Elements of Torture and Other Forms of Ill-Treatment, Domestic Violence*, 25 Hastings Int'l & Comp. L. Rev. 217 (2000).

3. *State Action: "By or at the instigation."* Part of the definition of torture in article 1 of CAT requires that the act be "inflicted by or at the instigation of...a public official or other person acting in an official capacity." Certainly domestic violence is rarely inflicted by or at the instigation of a public official or a person acting in an official capacity, unless, of course, the batterer's occupation is police officer or other public official. *See, e.g.,* Batista v. Fuentes-Agostini, 87 F. Supp. 2d 72 (D. P.R. 2000) (describing criminal conviction of Department of Justice employee for domestic abuse); Ward v. Tomsick, 30 P.3d 824 (Colo. Ct. App. 2001) (describing misdemeanor conviction of Denver police officer for domestic assault against his wife); Gillespie v. City of Indianapolis, 185 F.3d 693 (7th Cir. 1998) (describing guilty plea of police officer to a misdemeanor charge of battery involving his former wife). Even then, however, it is unclear whether the person needs to be acting in his official capacity when committing the violent acts.

4. *State Action: Acquiescence.* Article 1 of CAT also allows state action to exist when the violence occurs "with the consent or acquiescence of a public official or other person acting in an official capacity." The inclusion of acquiescence constitutes an expansion over the definition found in article 1 of the U.N. Declaration on Torture, art. 1(1). The Inter-American Convention to Prevent and Punish Torture, Dec. 9, 1985, O.A.S. T.S. No. 67, is similar to CAT. However, it specifically requires that the public official "being able to prevent it, fails to do so." *See* art. 3(a). Would the interpretation of "acquiescence," as set forth in *Ali v. Reno*, cover the following scenarios:

A. Despite repeated requests from human rights monitoring bodies, the state takes no action to minimize its police force's misconceptions about domestic violence. Simply, the state lacks the resources to train its officers. These misconceptions have led to a very limited response by the state's criminal justice system with regard to domestic violence.

B. Betty, the victim of severe battery by her husband, calls the police about threats her husband has recently made to kill her. The police tell Betty to go to the courthouse the next morning to obtain a civil protection order and to call them back if her husband returns. The police do not tell Betty anything else. That evening, Betty's husband returns home and he maims her before Betty can call the police. The police look for the husband, but can never apprehend him, primarily because the police force is so small.

C. Janie calls the police station and asks the officer to "come right over" because her ex-husband is breaking into her house. The police officer starts to go to Janie's house, but a bomb threat in a day care center diverts the officer from following through on Janie's call. When the officer goes to check on Janie later, he discovers that Janie's ex-husband broke into the house and raped her. The ex-husband is prosecuted and convicted for rape.

5. *State Action and the ECHR.* When you get to Chapter Fourteen on Children's Rights, you will read *A v. United Kingdom*, 27 Eur. H.R. Rep. 611 (1998). There the Euro-

pean Court of Human Rights unanimously held that the United Kingdom had violated article 3 of the European Convention on Human Rights when the United Kingdom allowed the defense of reasonable chastisement in a criminal action against a man for the caning of his nine-year-old stepson. Would a child who lived in a country with a similar defense, and whose parents believed in corporal punishment, qualify for withholding of removal if the child was legally in the United States at the time of his application and he was soon to depart back to his home country with his parents? The ability of children to seek asylum contrary to their parents' wishes will be briefly explored at the end of Chapter Eight with respect to Elian Gonzales. Here simply consider whether there is sufficient state action by the boy's home country to permit a successful asylum application.

6. *FGM.* Would Kasinga have been entitled to the CAT remedy? Would *R-A*?

7. *Danger Upon Return.* CAT demands that a woman not be sent to a state "where there are substantial grounds for believing that [s]he would be in danger of being subjected to torture." Art. 3(1). The Code of Federal Regulation says that she must show it is "more likely than not" that she would be tortured if she returned. 8 C.F.R. §208.16(c)(2) (discussing withholding of removal). What sort of facts might help establish the remedy of withholding of removal? While a beneficiary of CAT protection could not be extradited, returned, or expelled to a country where he or she might be tortured, the successful applicant could still be removed to another place. In addition, if a victim of past persecution cannot prove the likelihood of future torture, she would be ineligible for the CAT remedy.

8. *Asylum versus CAT Remedy?* Would asylum or the CAT article 3 remedy be preferable for a domestic violence victim seeking to stay in the United States?

9. *CAT and Domestic Violence.* An immigration judge has granted a domestic violence victim relief under the U.N. Convention Against Torture and Other Cruel, Inhuman or Degrading Treatment or Punishment. *See* Stephen M. Knight, *Seeking Asylum From Gender Persecution: Progress Amid Uncertainty,* 79 Interpreter Releases 689 (2002) (discussing Matter of K, [number withheld] (B.I.A. 2002)).

---

ii. State Responsibility

The Convention Against Torture can also help hold a government accountable for domestic violence in its territory. State obligations arise under CAT whether domestic violence is conceived of as "torture" or as "cruel, inhuman or degrading treatment or punishment" short of torture. *See, e.g.,* art. 16. However, the way in which domestic violence is characterized can affect the obligations of States Parties under CAT.

Rhonda Copelon, *Recognizing the Egregious in the Everyday: Domestic Violence as Torture*
25 Colum. Hum. Rts. L. Rev. 291, 358–59 (1994)

[I]f domestic violence were treated as torture under the United Nations Convention Against Torture, states would be obliged to take legal and other measures to prevent domestic violence through training, investigation and prosecution or extradition of offenders. The victim would be entitled to protection against retaliation and to fair and adequate compensation, including that needed for rehabilitation. Victims of domestic violence would not lose the possibility of redress when their aggressors leave the country. Finally, the United Nations Convention Against Torture would also prevent expulsion, return (refoulement) or extradition of a woman to another State "where there are substantial grounds for believing that [s]he would be in danger of being subjected to torture [or severe private gender-based violence unredressed by the state]."

The ill-defined distinction between torture and cruel, inhuman and degrading treatment or punishment significantly affects the scope of obligations and remedies under the United Nations Convention Against Torture, however. Only the provisions requiring training and regulation of law enforcers and public officials, and prompt and impartial investigation and review, apply to cruel, inhuman and degrading treatment. With regard to international accountability mechanisms, the [Committee Against Torture] can initiate investigations only as to torture. With state consent, however, it is competent to entertain state and individual complaints of ill-treatment. By contrast, the Inter-American Torture Convention does not distinguish cruel, inhuman and degrading treatment in terms of the obligations to punish, train and regulate officials, or to extradite alleged perpetrators or refuse to return potential victims. It does, however, reserve the obligation to investigate and prosecute every allegation and to provide compensation for torture alone.

Thus, the recognition of domestic and other forms of gender-based violence as torture and, to a lesser extent, as cruel, inhuman and degrading treatment, would trigger a substantial range of state responsibilities and potential individual responsibilities under the international torture conventions. It would also lay a foundation for individual accountability before all national courts based on the provision for universal jurisdiction. Still, given the tendency to minimize domestic violence, the suggested distinction of degree between torture and ill-treatment could present problems for women seeking the full scope of remedies....

Notes and Questions

1. *Torture versus Cruel, Inhuman and Degrading Treatment.* As Professor Copelon notes, whether an act qualifies as torture or as "cruel, inhuman or degrading treatment" can affect the remedy available to a victim. The U.S entered a reservation, among others, that states: "[t]he United States considers itself bound by the obligation under Article 16 to prevent 'cruel, inhuman or degrading treatment or punishment,' only insofar as the term 'cruel, inhuman or degrading treatment or punishment' means the cruel, unusual and inhumane treatment or punishment prohibited by the Fifth, Eighth, and/or Fourteenth Amendments to the Constitution of the United States." *See Declarations and Reservations,* G.A. Res. 39/46, U.N. GAOR, 39th Sess., Annex 1, U.N. Doc. A/RES/39/46 (1984). Of course, the meaning of those terms in the U.S. Constitution is not static. As the Supreme Court has stated in the context of the Eighth Amendment, the definition of "cruel and unusual punishment" draws "its meaning from the evolving standards of decency that mark the progress of a maturing society." Trop v. Dulles, 356 U.S. 86, 99–100 (1958). Yet the U.S. reservation still limits dramatically the scope of article 16 for the United States.

2. *Other International Instruments.* CAT, article 1(2), states that its definition of torture is without prejudice to other international or national instruments that have a wider application. CAT, in article 16(2), also states that CAT is without prejudice to the provisions of other international instruments that address "cruel, inhuman or degrading treatment." While we have focused primarily on CAT, other conventions also deal specifically with torture. *See, e.g.,* Inter-American Convention to Prevent and Punish Torture, Dec. 9, 1985, O.A.S. T.S. No. 67; European Convention for the Prevention of Torture and Inhuman or Degrading Treatment or Punishment, Nov. 26, 1987, E.T.S.

126. While the definition of torture is sometimes broader in these other instruments, the requirement of state action is often more strict. For example, the definition of torture under the Inter-American Convention to Prevent and Punish Torture is broader than under the U.N. Convention, including "any act intentionally performed whereby physical or mental pain or suffering is inflicted on a person...as a means of intimidation, as personal punishment, as a preventive measure...or for any other purpose." *Id.* art. 2. On the other hand, those who may be guilty of the crime of torture under the Inter-American Convention is quite narrow and includes only public servants or employees, or those acting at the instigation of a public servant or employee. *Id.* art. 3.

3. *ICCPR and Torture.* The general human rights instruments may prove more useful than CAT if one is equating domestic violence to torture. For example, the state action requirement may be less onerous if the claim is brought under article 7 of the International Convention on Civil and Political Rights (ICCPR). *See* Copelon, *supra,* at 353. Copelon argues that the prohibition in the ICCPR is "framed in exactly the same manner as the prohibition against slavery and servitude, which has always applied directly to private conduct. Article 2 requires a State Party to 'respect and ensure' the rights protected by the Covenant 'without distinction...such as...sex' and to adopt legislative remedies and other measures, including development of appropriate tribunals 'to give effect' to these rights." *Id.* at 353. Similarly, the American Convention on Human Rights may also be more liberal regarding the state action requirement. *See* Velazquez-Rodriguez, 28 I.L.M. 294 (Inter-Am. Ct. of H.R. 1989) (interpreting "respect" and "ensure" in article 1 to impose responsibility on Honduras for acts committed by private paramilitary groups when the state did not investigate and punish acts by private group).

4. *Executive Order.* President Clinton, by Executive Order 13107 (Dec. 10, 1998), ordered that various actions be taken in furtherance of the United States' obligations under ICCPR, CAT, the Convention on the Elimination of All Forms of Racial Discrimination (CERD), and other relevant treaties concerned with the protection and promotion of human rights. *United States: Executive Order 13107,* 38 I.L.M. 493 (1999), *available at* http://clinton6.nara.gov/1998/12/1998-12-10-executive-order-13107-on-human-rights-treaties.html. Among other things, the President ordered "All executive departments and agencies...[to] maintain a current awareness of United States international human rights obligations that are relevant to their functions and [to] perform such functions so as to respect and implement those obligations fully." *Id.* § 2(a). In addition, the Executive Order established an Interagency Working Group on Human Rights Treaties, which had as one of its principle functions "developing recommended proposals and mechanisms for improving the monitoring of the actions by the various States, Commonwealths, and territories of the United States and, where appropriate, of Native Americans and Federally recognized Indian tribes, including the review of State, Commonwealth, and territorial laws for their conformity with relevant treaties, the provision of relevant information for reports and other monitoring purposes, and the promotion of effective remedial mechanisms." *Id.* § 4(c)(v). The Group was also to "coordinat[e] and direct[] an annual review of United States reservations, declarations, and understandings to human rights treaties, and matters as to which there have been non-trivial complaints or allegations of inconsistency with or breach of international human rights obligations, in order to determine whether there should be consideration of any modification of relevant reservations, declarations, and understandings to human rights treaties, or United States practices or laws. The results and recommendations of this review shall be reviewed by the head of each participating agency." *Id.* § 4(c)(vii). The Executive Order made clear that it did not establish a private right of ac-

tion, nor did it supersede federal statutes or impose any justiciable obligations. *Id.* §6(a), (b). If you sat on the Interagency Working Group, what inquiries would you want the committee to undertake with respect to domestic violence?

5. *U.S. Torts Claims.* Article 14 of CAT provides that "[e]ach State Party shall ensure in its legal system that the victim of an act of torture obtains redress and has an enforceable right to fair and adequate compensation...." The United States signed CAT subject to the "understanding" that "Article 14 requires a State Party to provide a private right of action for damages only for acts of torture committed in territory under the jurisdiction of that State Party." *See* 136 Cong. Rec. S17486-01 (daily ed., Oct. 27, 1990). Notwithstanding this understanding, does the United States provide torture victims whose torture occurs outside the United States with remedies in its courts? For instance, assuming a victim suffers FGM or domestic violence abroad, could she bring a tort suit in the United States for her injuries, and if so, whom could she sue? Are there benefits to such suits beyond those that would accrue to the plaintiff?

Answers to these questions requires an analysis of the Alien Tort Claims Act, 28 U.S.C. §1350, the Torture Victim Protection Act, 28 U.S.C. §1350, federal common law, and the Foreign Sovereign Immunities Act, 28 U.S.C. §1602-1611. These topics were introduced in Chapter 1.B.1.f, and a review of that section may be beneficial. In addition, for an excellent article outlining the three acts, see Tom Lininger, *Overcoming Immunity Defenses to Human Rights Suits in U.S. Courts*, 7 Harv. Hum. Rts. J. 177 (1994). *See also* Adam Karp, Note, *Genitorts in the Global Context: Female Genital Mutilation as a Tort under the Alien Tort Claims Act, the Torture Victim Protection Act, and the Foreign Sovereign Immunities Act*, 18 Women's Rts. L. Rep. 315 (1997).

The Alien Tort Claims Act (ATCA) provides that "[t]he district courts shall have original jurisdiction in any civil action by an alien for a tort only, committed in violation of the law of nations or a treaty of the United States." 28 U.S.C. §1350. Thus, federal courts have jurisdiction to adjudicate any tort that violates the "law of nations" or a treaty. Does the "law of nations" afford a broader basis on which to invoke a tort suit than CAT? State-inflicted "official" torture constitutes a violation of the law of nations, even when the government mistreats its own foreign national. *See* Filartiga v. Pena-Irala, 630 F.2d 876, 884 (2d Cir. 1980). In addition, cruel, inhuman, and degrading treatment is also a violation of the law of nations. *See* Tel-Oren v. Libyan Arab Republic, 726 F.2d 774, 781 (D.C. Cir. 1984) (Edwards, J. concurring). Private non-state conduct can also violate the law of nations. *See* Kadic v. Karadzic, 70 F.3d 232, 239 (2d Cir. 1995) (holding the fact that Karadzic personally planned and ordered a campaign of murder, rape, forced impregnation, and other forms of torture violated the international law norm proscribing genocide "regardless of whether Karadzic acted under color of law or as a private individual"); Doe v. Islamic Salvation Front, 993 F. Supp. 3, 7-8 (D.D.C. 1998) (holding that members of an organization that beheaded women for failing to wear a veil, and that were responsible for the kidnaping and sexual slavery of countless young women, stated claim under the ATCA despite absence of state action). Consequently, ATCA permits suits against individuals and governments, and allows private individuals to be accountable for violations of international law even when not acting under color of governmental authority.

The Torture Victim Protection Act (TVPA) specifically addresses torture and states that "[a]n individual who, under actual or apparent authority, or color of law, of any foreign nation—(1) subjects an individual to torture shall, in a civil action, be liable for damages to that individual; or (2) subjects an individual to extrajudicial killing shall, in a civil action, be liable for damages to the individual's legal representative, or to any person who may be a claimant in an action for wrongful death." 28 U.S.C. § 1350(2)(a)(1)-(2). A U.S. citizen can bring a suit under this act, unlike under ATCA. However, the TVPA, in contrast to the ATCA, contains explicit language requiring state action, although the state action requirement does not require that the particular government be officially recognized. A private group can constitute a "de facto state." *See* *Doe*, 993 F. Supp. at 9. A plaintiff must exhaust domestic remedies in his or her own country prior to instituting suit in the United States, although this requirement is excusable if domestic remedies would be futile. *Id.*

Apart from ATCA and TVPA, there is yet another basis for federal question jurisdiction over a human rights tort suit between a victim and her torturer for actions occurring abroad. A federal statute, 28 U.S.C. § 1331, allows federal courts to hear actions "arising under" the Constitution or federal law. To the extent federal common law includes international law, see, for example, U.S. v. Schiffer, 836 F. Supp. 1164, 1170 (E.D. Pa. 1993), its violations may be justiciable in the federal courts.

Suits against governments face particular challenges because of the Foreign Sovereign Immunities Act (FSIA). This statute immunizes any "political subdivision of a foreign state or an agency or instrumentality of a foreign state," 28 U.S.C. § 1603(a), by stripping the federal courts of subject-matter jurisdiction over a claim against the foreign state. There are exceptions, but they are narrowly interpreted. One exception applies to "commercial activities," *i.e.*, acts done in connection with a foreign state's commercial activity. 28 U.S.C. § 1605(a)(2). The U.S. Supreme Court has held the "commercial activity" exception did not to apply in a case involving an American hospital worker who sued Saudi Arabia for torture committed by the Saudi police force after he reported safety defects in a Saudi-owned hospital's equipment. *See* Saudi Arabia v. Nelson, 113 S. Ct. 1471 (1993) (holding the arrest, imprisonment, and torture were not commercial activities, but were acts of the police, and also holding that the purpose of torture is irrelevant to the question of an activity's commercial character). The FSIA was amended in 1996 to permit lawsuits against certain foreign governments by U.S. nationals who are either the victim or the claimant for acts of torture. *See* 28 U.S.C. § 1605 (a)(7). Assuming FGM is not "torture," would *Saudi Arabia v. Nelson* preclude a suit based upon the performance of FGM at state-owned hospitals? Other limited exceptions exist, including for acts committed by the foreign state's officials or employees within the United States. 28 U.S.C. § 1605(a)(5).

Suits against individuals are more likely to succeed than suits against a government. *See* Lininger, *supra*, at 185. The FSIA's definition of "foreign state" does not refer to human beings or individual officials, although one court has held that the act does apply to shield individuals who are acting in an official capacity. *See* In re Estate of Marcos Litigation 978 F.2d 493, 497 (9th Cir. 1992) (finding, nonetheless, that defendant was not immune because defendant acted in her individual capacity in committing human rights violations). However, the act would not shield individual defendants who exceed the scope of their authority. *See* Chuidian v. Philippine Nat'l Bank, 912 F.2d 1095, 1106 (9th Cir.1990). The latter situation might exist if an official policy condemns FGM or domestic violence, but a state actor engages in it nonetheless.

The act of state doctrine also protects some individual defendants and bars U.S. courts from reviewing the official acts of a foreign government. *See generally* Restatement (Third) of the Foreign Relations Law of the United States § 443 (1987). The defense requires that the act be a public act, e.g., that individuals with sovereign authority are acting in an official capacity. Consequently, human rights abuses are treated skeptically. *See* Lininger, *supra*, at 189 n.78; *see also* Jiminez v. Aristeguieta, 311 F.2d 547, 558 (5th Cir. 1962) (embezzlement by chief executive of Venezuela was for private financial gain and is not an act of state). Generally the doctrine is not applied if the defendant is a former official at the time of suit. *See* Republic of the Philippines v. Marcos, 806 F.2d 344, 359 (2d Cir. 1986).

There are a variety of other immunity doctrines, but their applicability to a tort suit by a victim of domestic abuse would probably be limited. For example, the "head of state" enjoys immunity in U.S. courts pursuant to customary international law. The doctrine allows immunity for "official acts" taken while the "ruler is in power." *See* In re Grand Jury Proceedings, 817 F.2d 1108, 1110 (4th Cir. 1987); In re Doe, 860 F.2d 40, 45 (2d Cir. 1988) (noting in dictum that head of state defense does not apply to "private or criminal acts in violation of American law"). The immunity can be waived by the state. *See* In re Grand Jury, *supra*.

In addition, accredited diplomats have immunity under international law. The United States is a party to the Vienna Convention on Diplomatic Relations, Apr. 18, 1961, 23 U.S.T. 3227, T.I.A.S. No. 7502, 500 U.N.T.S. 95. Among other things, it gives diplomats of the sending state immunity from both criminal and civil process. The state of the diplomat can waive this immunity. Foreign representatives attending the United Nations in New York also have immunity. *Agreement Between the United Nations and the United States of America Regarding the Headquarters of the United Nations*, G.A. Res. 169, U.N. Doc. A/371 (1947), authorized by S.J. Res. 144, 80th Cong., 1st Sess., Pub. L. No. 80-357 (1947), reprinted following 22 U.S.C. § 287. However, this immunity does not apply if the attendee is a U.N. invitee. *See* Kadic v. Karadzic, 70 F.3d 232 (2d Cir. 1995) (allowing President of self-proclaimed Bosnian-Serb republic of "Srpska" to be sued in U.S. district court by victims of atrocities committed in Bosnia because President was personally served with process while in Manhattan as an invitee of the United Nations).

6. *Symbolic Importance.* Some of the potential benefits of CAT for domestic violence victims have been canvassed. Are there other, perhaps symbolic, benefits? Are there dangers in using these instruments for domestic violence victims' benefit?

7. *Obstacles.* Despite the potential benefits of categorizing domestic violence as torture, there are considerable obstacles. Rhonda Copelon explains: "There are two major obstacles to the recognition of intimate violence against women as a human rights violation. One is the role of the public/private dichotomy in international law. The second...is the persistent trivialization of violence against women. Intimate violence — with the exception of some of its more sensationalized and culture-specific examples — has not been considered violence. Seen as 'personal' or 'private' a 'domestic' or 'family' matter, its goals and consequences have been obscured and its use, justified as chastisement or discipline." Copelon, *supra*, at 295–96.

---

c. *New International Law Approaches to Domestic Violence*

Domestic violence is being recognized in countries around the world as a problem. Many national reforms have been prompted by action at the international level to address domestic violence. Subrata Paul chronicled the most recent "positive international action" on domestic violence in a 1999 article. It included efforts through the U.N. Convention on the Elimination of All Forms of Discrimination Against Women, the

U.N. Second World Conference on Human Rights in Vienna, the U.N. Fourth World Conference on Women in Beijing, the U.N. Development Fund for Women, the First World Conference on Family Violence, and a 1998 European Parliament resolution designating 1999 as the European Year Against Violence Against Women. *See generally* Subrata Paul, *Combating Domestic Violence Through Positive International Action in the International Community and in the United Kingdom, India, and Africa,* 7 Cardozo J. Int'l & Comp. L. 227 (1999). Some of these international efforts are described below by Professor Hernandez-Truyol. What is notable is the explicit discussion of gender-based violence. Women do not need to argue that domestic violence constitutes a violation of their human rights as they had to with the older human rights instruments.

A variety of questions can be asked about these new efforts. This section briefly addresses two of the questions. First, are these worldwide efforts of any potential use or benefit to women domestically, or rather, are they useful only in countries that lag significantly behind the rest of the world in terms of their responses to domestic violence? Second, are these efforts counterproductive because they segregate the issue of gender-based violence from other human rights issues and reduce the need for the Human Rights Committee to take responsibility and address the violence?

Berta Esperanza Hernandez-Truyol, *Sex, Culture, and Rights: A Re/Conceptualization of Violence for the Twenty-First Century,*
60 Alb. L. Rev. 607, 629–32 (1997)

To be sure, these changes are very recent. In 1985, at the World Conference of Women, held in Nairobi, women from around the world united for the first time to condemn domestic violence. The Conference recognized the heinous nature of domestic violence and re/defined it as a public act of violence against women. This strategy resulted in unprecedented successes during the World Conference of Human Rights in Vienna in 1993. Noting that the quintessential disempowerment of women is based on the public/private dichotomy, women in Vienna, from all parts of the world spoke in a unified voice in their strategic approach to the Conference: to make violence against women a focal point of the demands for inclusion of women in the Vienna agenda—a human rights agenda that, at the outset, did not include women. Fortunately, the strategy was successful. Success was achieved, however, because, unfortunately, violence against women is so prevalent that it was a common concern for all women, from every place and status in the world.

The conference document finally pierced the veil of the private closet in which women have suffered harms from time immemorial....

The consensus document that emerged from the Vienna conference (the Vienna Declaration) for the first time recognized violations of human rights and incorporated the rights of women as "an inalienable, integral and indivisible part of universal human rights." The Declaration condemned "[g]ender-based violence and all forms of sexual harassment and exploitation" and instructed the General Assembly to adopt a draft declaration on violence against women that urges states "to combat violence against women" according to U.N. mandates. The Vienna Conference thus smashed, at the gender level, the barriers between state and individual responsibilities and rights. Vienna crumbled the public/private barriers that had long caused the invisibility and untouchability of matters vital to women and their existence, subsistence and persistence....

The international community continued to dismantle the public/private dichotomy in Cairo during the International Conference on Population and Development. In Cairo, the discussion of population policies included reproductive technologies, processes, information and strategies to ensure not only maternal and infant health but women's overall well-being as well. The Cairo Conference document expressly confirms that "[t]he human rights of women and the girl-child are an inalienable, integral and indivisible part of universal human rights." The Cairo Declaration also recognized that this is central to the elimination of all forms of violence against women, to achieving gender equality and eradicating inequalities and subordination based simply on sex.

Similarly, the document emerging from the Social Summit held in Copenhagen in 1995 requires the taking of "full measures to eliminate all forms of exploitation, abuse, harassment and violence against women, in particular domestic violence and rape. Special attention should be given to violence resulting from harmful traditional or customary practices and all forms of extremism...." Finally, the Fourth World Conference on Women, produced the Beijing Declaration and Programme of Action. These documents confirmed that the mandate of equality for women and the prohibitions of violence against women, are the global expectations of human rights norms.

These global developments provide the foundation for re/defining "violence against women." Indeed, the documents themselves have started the re/defining process by recognizing notions of violence beyond direct physical assaults. Moreover, these instruments are particularly valuable because they are consensus documents. They provide the foundation for rejecting cultural and religious pretexts for the subordination and subjugation of women. They condemn such pretexts as inappropriate bases to deny women the exercise of their civil and political rights, or their social, economic and cultural rights. Finally, because of the clear and distinct nexus between physical, social, educational and psychological abuse on the one hand, and economic deprivation on the other hand, it becomes not only logical, but necessary, to recognize that denial of economic rights is part of the panoply of events that effect harm on, and constitute violence against, women.

Notes and Questions

1. *Declarations.* The Statutory Supplement contains the U.N. General Assembly Resolution 48/104 Containing the Declaration on the Elimination of Violence Against Women (February 23, 1994). The preamble indicates that the General Assembly believes the "effective implementation of the Convention on the Elimination of All Forms of Discrimination against Women would contribute to the elimination of violence against women and that the Declaration on the Elimination of Violence against Women...will strengthen and complement that process." Do you agree? What function does the Declaration serve?

2. *The Declaration and U.S. Domestic Violence Law.* Does the United States comply with the letter or spirit of Resolution 48/104? Consider, for instance, article 1 that defines "violence against women." What acts are covered by that definition that are not covered by the examples of "violence against women" in article 2? Is the legal response to domestic violence in the United States coextensive with this definition? What is "psychological violence occurring in the family"? Does the United States protect against "physical, sexual and psychological violence perpetrated or condoned by the State, wherever it occurs"? If you see inconsistencies between United States' law and the U.N. instrument, is the United States in violation of international law?

3. *The Declaration and U.S. Adherence Generally.* Article 4(j) of U.N. General Assembly Resolution 48/104 requires State Parties to "Adopt all appropriate measures, especially in the field of education, to modify the social and cultural patterns of conduct of men and women and to eliminate prejudices, customary practices and all other practices based on the idea of the inferiority or superiority of either of the sexes and on stereotyped roles for men and women." What could the United States do to adhere better to this provision? Does article 4(c) or, (g), or any other provision indicate that the United States should change its asylum law? Of what significance is the fact that the preamble recites the rights and principles enshrined in various international instruments, including the Convention against Torture and Other Cruel, Inhuman or Degrading Treatment or Punishment?

4. *U.N. Mandate.* The U.N. Declaration on the Elimination of Violence Against Women is, as you now know, quite broad in its content. Is a resolution that condemns violence between intimates an appropriate focus for the United Nations General Assembly, an organization developed in response to state mandated atrocities in Europe? The Charter of the United Nations does set out a rather broad mission. The preamble indicates that the United Nations was formed, in part, "to reaffirm faith in fundamental human rights, in the dignity and worth of the human person, in the equal rights of men and women and of nations large and small, and to establish conditions under which justice and respect for the obligations arising from treaties and other sources of international law can be maintained." Article 1(3) sets out the following as a specific purpose of the United Nations: "To achieve international co-operation in solving international problems of an economic, social, cultural, or humanitarian character, and in promoting and encouraging respect for human rights and for fundamental freedoms for all without distinction as to race, sex, language, or religion." Article 55 reads: "With a view to the creation of conditions of stability and well-being which are necessary for peaceful and friendly relations among nations based on respect for the principle of equal rights and self-determination of peoples, the United Nations shall promote: a) higher standards of living, full employment, and conditions of economic and social progress and development; b) solutions of international economic, social, health, and related problems and international cultural and educational co-operation; and c) universal respect for, and observance of, human rights and fundamental freedoms for all without distinction as to race, sex, language, or religion." Ending domestic violence falls into which provisions of Article 55?

5. *General Recommendation No. 19.* Examine General Recommendation No. 19, issued by the Committee on the Elimination of All Forms of Discrimination Against Women. The recommendation is found in the Supplement. Is its legal force greater than Resolution 48/104? A general recommendation is not binding on States Parties. The recommendation is "the Committee's authoritative statement on the meaning of the Convention with regard to violence against women, and thus forms part of a growing body of jurisprudence surrounding the Convention." *Report of the Committee on Progress Achieved in the Implementation of the Convention,* U.N. CEDAW, 14th Sess., Agenda Item 9, ¶ 491, U.N. Doc. CEDAW/C/1995/1 (1995). General recommendations are intended to guide States Parties as to the kind of information the Committee hopes to receive in their reports. *Id.* ¶ 492.

6. *Impact of Recommendation No. 19.* General Recommendation 19 "strongly influenced" the preparation of the U.N. Declaration on the Elimination of Violence Against Women by the General Assembly. *Id.* ¶ 493.

7. *Platform for Action.* The U.N. Fourth World Conference on Women had a very detailed Declaration and Platform for Action on Violence Against Women. It directed states to take a variety of actions to prevent, condemn, and punish violence against women. The United States submitted the following written statement:

> Interpretative statement on the Beijing Declaration. The United States understands that the phrase "hereby adopt and commit ourselves as Governments to implement the...Platform for Action" contained in the Beijing Declaration, and other similar references throughout the texts, are consistent with the fact that the Platform, Declaration and commitments made by States (unless such States indicate to the contrary) are not legally binding, and that they consist of recommendations concerning how States can and should promote the objectives of the Conference. The commitment referred to in the Declaration, therefore, constitutes a general commitment to undertake meaningful implementation of the Platform's recommendations overall, rather than a specific commitment to implement each element of the Platform. Accordingly, the United States accepts this phrase on this basis, on the understanding that it does not alter the status of the documents or the recommendations contained therein.

U.N. Report of the Fourth World Conference on Women, ¶ 30, U.N. Doc. A/CONF.177/20 & A/CONF.177/20/Add.1 (1995).

d. *Regional Approaches*
i. *Convention of Belém do Pará*

Perhaps the most hopeful of all the new approaches to domestic violence in international law emerges in regional human rights treaties. Various regional human rights instruments address domestic violence either explicitly or implicitly. Of particular note is the Inter-American Convention to Prevent, Punish and Eradicate Violence Against Women (*Belém do Pará*), which is the first regional human rights treaty to focus explicitly on violence against women, including domestic violence. The Convention entered into force in March 1995, and currently has approximately thirty parties. This makes it "the most widely ratified law in the Inter-American system." *See* Berta Esperanza Hernandez-Truyol, *Latina, Culture and Human Rights: A Model for Making Change, Saving Soul,* 23 Women's Rts. L. Rep. 21, 31 (2001). However, neither the United States nor Canada have even signed the Convention. *See* Secretariat for Legal Affairs, Dep't of Legal Cooperation & Information, A-61: Inter-American Convention on the Prevention, Punishment and Eradication of Violence Against Women "Convention of Belém do Pará," *at* http://www.oas.org/juridico/english/sigs/a-61.html.

The Convention differs from many other human rights treaties in a number of ways. First, its substantive provisions are quite remarkable. The Convention explicitly states that violence impairs or nullifies the ability of women to exercise and enjoy their human rights and fundamental freedoms. *See, e.g.,* art. 5. However, it also recognizes that violence against women is embedded in the larger societal inequities. For example, it obligates the state to "take all appropriate measures, including legislative measures, to amend or repeal existing laws and regulations or to modify legal or customary practices which sustain the persistence and tolerance of violence against women." *See* art. 7(e). Violence is defined broadly to include "any act or conduct, based on gender, which causes death or physical, sexual, or psychological harm or suffering to women, whether in the public or the private sphere." *See* art. 1. Second, the Convention's procedural provisions are progressive. The Convention allows individuals and NGOs to petition the Inter-American Commission on Human Rights for state violations of the treaty. *See* art. 12.

The Convention's impact has been multifold. As one commentator noted, "The Inter-American system has been instrumental in placing women's rights on the social agenda both regionally and locally and in instituting regional and local reforms aimed at advancing the legal, social, political, and economic status of women." *See* Hernandez-Truyol, *Latina, Culture and Human Rights, supra*, at 32. Many of the changes occurred voluntarily in order to bring countries into better compliance with their obligations under the Convention. Consequently, after adoption of the Belém do Pará, Argentina, Bolivia, Chile, Colombia, Costa Rica, Ecuador, Mexico, Panama, and Uruguay passed laws on domestic violence. *See* Rhonda Copelon, *Violence Against Women: The Potential and Challenge of a Human Rights Perspective, in* The Right to Live Without Violence, 1 Women's Health Collection 115–16, n.402 (1996).

The Convention, however, has also provided a mechanism to hold recalcitrant states accountable, and the Commission has found admissible a number of cases alleging violations of the Convention. In fact, the first case brought before an international tribunal asserting that domestic violence is a violation of human rights was brought before the Inter-American Commission on Human Rights. The petitioners alleged violations of the Convention of Belém do Pará, the American Convention on Human Rights, Recommendation No. 19 of CEDAW, and the Declaration on the Elimination of Violence Against Women. The case, *Trinidad and Tobago v. Ramjattan*, Case 11.837, Report No. 92/98, Inter-Am. C.H.R., OEA/ser.L/V/II.95, doc. 7 rev. at 259 (1998), involved a battered woman who was sentenced to death for the murder of her batterer, her common-law husband. She had alleged, inter alia, that no importance was attached by the system (legal aid lawyers, the court, etc.) to the abuse she suffered. *Id.* ¶ 5. The Commission found the petition admissible. *Id.* ¶ 15(1). Subsequently, the Privy Council in London, the highest appellate court for cases from Trinidad and Tobago, granted the defendant leave to appeal based on new evidence showing that the defendant had suffered from Battered Woman's Syndrome. The Trinidad and Tobago Court of Appeal, on remand, overturned the murder conviction and imposed a manslaughter verdict and a further five years in prison. *See Trinidad and Tobago: The Imminent Execution of a Battered Women's Defenders*. Women's Action 15.2 (Equality Now) July 2000, *at* http://www.equalitynow.org/action_eng_15_2.html (last visited July 23, 2002).

Now consider the following case brought against Brazil.

Maria da Penha Maia Fernandes
Case No. 12.051, Inter-Am C.H.R. 54-1 (2001)

Summary

1. On August 20, 1998, the Inter-American Commission on Human Rights (hereinafter "the Commission") received a petition filed by Mrs. Maria da Penha Maia Fernandes, the Center for Justice and International Law (CEJIL), and the Latin American and Caribbean Committee for the Defense of Women's Rights (CLADEM) (hereinafter "the petitioners"), as provided for in Articles 44 and 46 of the American Convention on Human Rights (hereinafter "the Convention" or "the American Convention") and Article 12 of the Inter-American Convention on the Prevention, Punishment, and Eradication of Violence against Women (Convention of Belém do Pará or CMV).

2. The petition alleges that the Federative Republic of Brazil (hereinafter "Brazil" or "the State") condoned, for years during their marital cohabitation, domestic violence perpetrated in the city of Fortaleza, Ceará State, by Marco Antônio Heredia Viveiros against his wife at the time, Maria da Penha Maia Fernandes, culminating in attempted murder and further aggression in May and June 1983. As a result of this aggression, Maria da Penha has suffered from irreversible paraplegia and other ailments since 1983. The petition maintains that the State has condoned this situation, since, for more than 15 years, it has failed to take the effective measures required to prosecute and punish the aggressor, despite repeated complaints. The petition alleges violation of Article 1(1) (Obligation to Respect Rights), 8 (a Fair Trial), 24 (Equal Protection), and 25 (Judicial Protection) of the American Convention, in relation to Articles II and XVIII of the American Declaration of the Rights and Duties of Man ("the Declaration"), as well as Articles 3, 4(a), (b), (c), (d), (e), (f), and (g), and 5 and 7 of the Convention of Belém do Pará....

Position of the Parties

A. *The petitioners*

8. The petition states that on May 29, 1983, Mrs. Maria da Penha Maia Fernandes, a pharmacist, was the victim of attempted murder by her then husband, Marco Antônio Heredia Viveiros, an economist, at her home in Fortaleza, Ceará State. He shot her while she was asleep, bringing to a climax a series of acts of aggression carried out over the course of their married life. As a result of this aggression of her spouse, Mrs. Fernandes sustained serious injuries, had to undergo numerous operations, and suffered irreversible paraplegia and other physical and psychological trauma.

9. The petitioners state that Mr. Heredia Viveiros was an aggressive and violent person, and that he would assault his wife and three daughters during his marriage. According to the victim, the situation became unbearable but she was too afraid to take steps to obtain a separation. They maintain that the husband tried to cover up the attack by reporting it as an attempted robbery and the work of thieves who had fled. Two weeks after Mrs. Fernandes returned from the hospital and was recovering from the attempt on her life on May 29, 1983, Mr. Heredia Viveiros again attempted to kill her by allegedly trying to electrocute her while she was bathing. At that point, she decided to seek a legal separation from him.

10. They maintain that Mr. Viveiros acted with premeditation, since the week before the attack he had tried to convince his wife to make him the beneficiary of a life insurance policy, and five days before attacking her, he tried to force her to sign a document for the sale of her car that provided no indication of the name of the purchaser. They state that Mrs. Fernandes learned subsequently that Mr. Viveiros had a criminal record, that he was bigamous, and that he had a child in Colombia, information that he had concealed from her....

12. The petitioners maintain that during the judicial investigation, which was launched a few days after the June 6, 1983, assault, statements were taken establishing that Mr. Heredia Viveiros was responsible for the assault.... [T]he Office of the Public Prosecutor filed charges against Mr. Heredia Viveiros on September 28, 1984, leading to public criminal proceedings in the First District Court of Fortaleza, in Ceará State.

13. The petitioners indicate that despite the clear nature of the charges and preponderance of the evidence, the case languished for eight years before the jury found Mr.

Viveiros guilty on May 4, 1991, sentencing him to 15 years in prison for assault and attempted murder, which was reduced to ten years because he had no prior convictions....

[Ed. Note: The Commission then described a series of out-of-time appeals which were nevertheless considered by the courts in Brazil, a retrial in which Mr. Viveiros was again sentenced to over ten years in prison, and another appeal which was pending at the date the petition was submitted to the Commission.]

19. The petitioners maintain that as of the date of the petition, the Brazilian justice system had dragged its feet for more than 15 years without handing down a final ruling against the ex-husband of Mrs. Fernandes, who has been free during that entire period, despite the serious nature of the charges, the mountain of evidence against him, and the serious nature of the crime committed against Mrs. Fernandes. The judicial system of Ceará and the Brazilian State have thus been ineffective, as seen in their failure to conduct proceedings in a prompt and efficient manner, thereby creating a great risk of impunity, since punishment in this case will be barred by the statute of limitations twenty years after the occurrence of these events, a date that is approaching. They maintain that the primary aim of the Brazilian State ought to have been to ensure compensation for the suffering of Maria da Penha, by guaranteeing her a fair trial within a reasonable time period.

20. They maintain that this complaint does not represent an isolated situation in Brazil; rather, it is an example of a pattern of impunity in cases of domestic violence against women in Brazil, since the majority of complaints filed do not lead to criminal prosecution and in the few cases where they do, the perpetrators are convicted in only a small number of cases. We note the comments of this Commission in its report on Brazil:

> The crimes which fall within the heading of violence against women constitute human rights violations under the American Convention, as well as under the more specific terms of the Convention of Belém do Pará. When committed by state agents, the use of violence against the physical and/or mental integrity of an individual gives rise to the direct responsibility of the State. Additionally, the State has an obligation under Article 1(1) of the American Convention and Article 7.b of the Convention of Belém do Pará to exercise due diligence to prevent human rights violations. This means that, even where conduct may not initially be directly imputable to a state (for example, because the actor is unidentified or not a state agent), a violative act may lead to state responsibility "not because of the act itself, but because of the lack of due diligence to prevent the violation or respond to it as the Convention requires."

[Report on the Situation of Human Rights in Brazil, 1997, Chapter VIII]....

B. *The State*

25. The Brazilian State has not provided the Commission with a response regarding the admissibility or the merits of the petition, despite the requests of the Commission to the State on October 19, 1998, August 4, 1999, and August 7, 2000....

Analysis of the Merits of the Case....

A. *Right to Justice (Article XVIII of the Declaration); and to a Fair Trial (Article 8) and Judicial Protection (Article 25), in relation to the Obligation to Respect and Guarantee Rights (Article 1(1)) of the Convention*

37. Articles XVIII of the Declaration and 8 and 25 of the American Convention on Human Rights stipulate that all persons are entitled to access to judicial remedies and to

be heard by a competent authority or court when they think that their rights have been violated, which is reaffirmed in Article XVIII (right to justice) of the Declaration, all in relation to the obligation set forth in Article 1(1)) of the Convention. Article 25(1) of the Convention states:

> Everyone has the right to simple and prompt recourse, or any other effective recourse, to a competent court or tribunal for protection against acts that violate his fundamental rights recognized by the constitution or laws of the state concerned or by this Convention, even though such violation may have been committed by persons acting in the course of their official duties.

38. More than 17 years have elapsed since the launching of the investigation into the attack on the victim Maria da Penha Maia Fernandes and to date, based on the information received, the case against the accused remains open, a final ruling has not been handed down, and remedies have not been provided for the consequences of the attempted murderer of Mrs. Fernandes.[10] The Inter-American Court of Human Rights has stated that the term "reasonable time" established in Article 8(1) of the Convention is not a concept that can be defined easily and has referred to the decisions of the European Court of Human Rights for guidance in this regard. These decisions state that the following elements must be evaluated in determining whether the time period within which proceedings take place is reasonable: the complexity of the case, the procedural activity of the interested party, and the conduct of the judicial authorities....

[Ed. Note: After analyzing these factors, the court then concluded there was "unwarranted delay in the administration of justice in the case."]

42. ... [The Inter-American Court of Human Rights] has stated the following:

> The State is obligated to investigate every situation involving a violation of the rights protected by the Convention. If the State apparatus acts in such a way that the violation goes unpunished and the victim's full enjoyment of such rights is not restored as soon as possible, the State has failed to comply with its duty to ensure the free and full exercise of those rights to the persons within its jurisdiction. The same is true when the State allows private persons or groups to act freely and with impunity to the detriment of the rights recognized by the Convention.

[Inter-American Court of Human Rights, Velásquez Rodríguez case, Judgment of July 29, 1988, para. 176; and Inter-American Court of Human Rights, Godínez Cruz case, Judgment of January 20, 1989, para. 187.]

43. With regard to the obligations of the State in situations where action has not been taken to guarantee the victim the ability to exercise his rights, the Inter-American Court has stated the following:

> The second obligation of the States Parties is to "ensure" the free and full exercise of the rights recognized by the Convention to every person subject to its jurisdiction. This obligation implies the duty of the States Parties to organize the governmental apparatus and, in general, all the structures through which public power is exercised, so that they are capable of juridically ensuring the free and full enjoyment of human rights. As a consequence of this obligation, the States must prevent, investigate and punish any violation of the rights recognized by the

---

10. During almost half of that period, since September 25, 1992, this situation has existed while the American Convention has been in effect for Brazil. The Convention of Belém do Pará has been in effect since November 27, 1995.

Convention and, moreover, if possible attempt to restore the right violated and provide compensation as warranted for damages resulting from the violation.

[Inter-American Court of Human Rights, Godínez Cruz case, Judgment of January 20, 1988, para. 175.]

44. ... The Commission holds the view that the domestic judicial decisions in this case reveal inefficiency, negligence, and failure to act on the part of the Brazilian judicial authorities and unjustified delay in the prosecution of the accused. These decisions are standing in the way of punishment of the accused and are raising the specter of impunity and failure to compensate the victim as a result of barring the offense by the statute of limitations. They demonstrate that the State has not been capable of organizing its entities in a manner that guarantees those rights. As a whole, this situation represents a separate violation of Articles 8 and 25 of the American Convention on Human Rights in relation to Article 1(1) thereof and the corresponding Articles of the Declaration.

B. Equality before the Law (Article 24 of the Convention) and Articles II and XVIII of the Declaration

45. The petitioners also allege violation of Article 24 of the American Convention in relation to the right to equality before the law and the right to justice enshrined in the American Declaration on the Rights and Duties of Man (Articles II and XVIII).

46. In that regard, the Inter-American Commission notes that it has followed with special interest developments related to respect for the rights of women, particularly those related to domestic violence. The Commission has received information on the high number of domestic attacks of women in Brazil. In Ceará alone (the place where the events related to this case took place), there were 1,183 death threats reported to special police stations handling women's affairs in 1993, out of a total of 4,755 complaints.

47. Compared to men, women are the victims of domestic violence in disproportionate numbers. A study done by the National Movement for Human Rights in Brazil compares the incidence of domestic violence against women and men and shows that in terms of murders, women are 30 times more likely to be killed by their husbands than husbands by their wives. In its special report on Brazil in 1997, the Commission found that there was clear discrimination against women who were attacked, resulting from the inefficiency of the Brazilian judicial system and inadequate application of national and international rules, including those arising from the case law of the Brazilian Supreme Court. In its 1997 Report on the Situation of Human Rights, the Commission stated:

> Moreover, even where these specialized stations exist, it remains frequently the case that complaints are not fully investigated or prosecuted. In some cases, resource limitations hinder efforts to respond to these crimes. In other cases, women refrain from pressing formal charges. In practice, legal and other limitations often expose women to situations where they feel constrained to act. By law, women have to register their complaint at a police station, and explain what happened so the delegate can write up an "incident report." Delegates who have not received sufficient training may be unable to provide the required services, and some reportedly continue to respond to victims in ways that make them feel shame and humiliation. For certain crimes, such as rape, victims must present themselves at an Institute of Forensic Medicine (*Instituto Médico Legal*), which has the exclusive compe-

tence to perform the examinations required by law to process a charge. Some women are not aware of this requirement, or do not have access to such a facility in the timely manner necessary to obtain the required evidence. These Institutes tend to be located in urban areas, and, where available, are often understaffed. Moreover, even when women take the steps necessary to denounce the use of criminal violence, there is no guarantee that the crime will be investigated and prosecuted.

Although the Supreme Court of Brazil struck down the archaic "honor defense" as a justification for wife-killing in 1991, many courts remain reluctant to prosecute and punish the perpetrators of domestic violence. In some areas of the country, use of the "honor defense" persists, and in some areas the conduct of the victim continues to be a focal point within the judicial process to prosecute a sexual crime. Rather than focusing on the existence of the legal elements of the crime in question, the practices of some defense lawyers—sustained in turn by some courts—have the effect of requiring the victim to demonstrate the sanctity of her reputation and her moral blamelessness in order to exercise the remedies legally required to be available to her. The initiatives taken by the public and private sector to confront violence against women have begun to combat the silence which customarily has concealed it, but have yet to surmount the social, legal and other barriers which contribute to the impunity in which these crimes too often languish.

48. That report also makes reference to various studies that demonstrate that in cases where statistics have been kept, they have shown that only one percent of the offenses reported to specialized stations are actually investigated. *Unido de Mulheres de Sao Paulo, A Violencia Contra a Mulher e a Impunidade: Una Questão Política* (1995). In 1994, of 86,815 complaints filed by women who were assaulted in the home, only 24,103 led to police investigations, according to that report.

49. Other reports indicate that 70% of the criminal complaints pertaining to domestic violence are put on hold without any conclusion being reached. Only 2% of the criminal complaints for domestic violence against women lead to conviction of the aggressor. (Report of the San Pablo Catholic University, 1998).

50. In this analysis examining the pattern shown by the State in responding to this kind of violation, the Commission also notes that positive measures have been taken in the legislative, judicial, and administrative spheres.[18] The Commission points to three ini-

---

18. As a result of joint action taken by the Government and the CNDM [National Council for Women's Rights], the 1988 Brazilian Constitution has been amended in a manner that reflects significant progress in women's rights. In the context of the National Program on Human Rights, the initiatives proposed by the Government aimed at strengthening the rights of women include: support for the National Council for Women's Rights and the National Program to Prevent Violence against Women; efforts to support and prevent sexual and domestic violence against women, to provide comprehensive assistance to women who are at risk, and to educate the public about discrimination and violence against women and safeguards that are available; repeal of certain discriminatory provisions in the Penal and Civil Code on parental authority; support for efforts to develop gender-specific approaches in the training of State agents and in the establishment of curriculum guidelines at the primary and secondary education levels; and support for statistical studies related to the status of women in the labor sphere. The program also recommends that the Government implement the decisions contained in the Inter-American Convention on the Prevention, Punishment, and Eradication of Violence against Women.

tiatives that are directly related to the situation seen in this case: (1) the establishment of special police stations to handle reports on violence against women; (2) the establishment of shelters for battered women; and (3) the 1991 decision of the Supreme Court to strike down the archaic concept of "honor defense" as a justification for crimes against wives. These positive and other similar initiatives have been implemented on a limited basis in relation to the scope and urgency of the problem, as indicated earlier. In this case, which stands as a symbol, these initiatives have not had any effect whatsoever.

C. Article 7 of the Convention of Belém do Pará

51. On November 27, 1995, Brazil deposited its ratification of the Convention of Belém do Pará [CVM], the inter-American instrument by means of which American States acknowledge the extent of this problem, establish guidelines to be followed, make commitments to address it, and establish the possibility for any individual or organization to file petitions and take action on a matter before the Inter-American Commission on Human Rights and through its proceedings. The petitioners are seeking a finding of violation by the State of Articles 3, 4, 5, and 7 of this Inter-American Convention on the Prevention, Punishment, and Eradication of Violence against Women, and are alleging that this case must be analyzed in a context of gender-based discrimination by Brazilian State organs, which serves to reinforce the systematic pattern of violence against women and impunity in Brazil....

53. The Convention of Belém do Pará is an essential instrument that reflects the great effort made to identify specific measures to protect the right of women to a life free of aggression and violence, both outside and within the family circle. The CVM provides the following definition of violence against women:

> Article 2
>
> Violence against women shall be understood to include physical, sexual, and psychological violence:
>
> a. that occurs within the family or domestic unit or within any other interpersonal relationship, whether or not the perpetrator shares or has shared the same residence with the woman, including, among others, rape, battery and sexual abuse;
>
> b. that occurs in the community and is perpetrated by any person, including, among others, rape, sexual abuse, torture, trafficking in persons, forced prostitution, kidnapping and sexual harassment in the workplace, as well as in educational institutions, health facilities or any other place; and
>
> c. that is perpetrated or condoned by the state or its agents regardless of where it occurs.

54. Within the scope of application of the CMV, reference is made to situations defined by two conditions: first, violence against women as described in sections (a) and (b); and, second, violence perpetrated or condoned by the State. The CMV protects, *inter alia*, the following rights of women when they have been violated by acts of violence: the right to a life free of violence (Article 3), the right to have her life, her physical, mental, and moral integrity, her personal safety, and personal dignity respected, to equal protection before and of the law; and to simple and prompt recourse to a competent court for protection against acts that violate her rights (Articles 4 (a), (b), (c), (d), (e), (f), and (g)), and the resulting duty of the State set forth in Article 7 of that instrument. Article 7...states:...

> The States Parties condemn all forms of violence against women and agree to pursue, by all appropriate means and without delay, policies to prevent, punish and eradicate such violence and undertake to:

a. refrain from engaging in any act or practice of violence against women and to ensure that their authorities, officials, personnel, agents, and institutions act in conformity with this obligation;

b. apply due diligence to prevent, investigate and impose penalties for violence against women;

c. include in their domestic legislation penal, civil, administrative and any other type of provisions that may be needed to prevent, punish and eradicate violence against women and to adopt appropriate administrative measures where necessary;

d. adopt legal measures to require the perpetrator to refrain from harassing, intimidating or threatening the woman or using any method that harms or endangers her life or integrity, or damages her property;

e. take all appropriate measures, including legislative measures, to amend or repeal existing laws and regulations or to modify legal or customary practices which sustain the persistence and tolerance of violence against women;

f. establish fair and effective legal procedures for women who have been subjected to violence which include, among others, protective measures, a timely hearing and effective access to such procedures;

g. establish the necessary legal and administrative mechanisms to ensure that women subjected to violence have effective access to restitution, reparations or other just and effective remedies; and

h. adopt such legislative or other measures as may be necessary to give effect to this Convention.

55. The impunity that the ex-husband of Mrs. Fernandes has enjoyed and continues to enjoy is at odds with the international commitment voluntarily assumed by the State when it ratified the Convention of Belém do Pará. The failure to prosecute and convict the perpetrator under these circumstances is an indication that the State condones the violence suffered by Maria da Penha, and this failure by the Brazilian courts to take action is exacerbating the direct consequences of the aggression by her ex-husband. Furthermore, as has been demonstrated earlier, that tolerance by the State organs is not limited to this case; rather, it is a pattern. The condoning of this situation by the entire system only serves to perpetuate the psychological, social, and historical roots and factors that sustain and encourage violence against women.

56. Given the fact that the violence suffered by Maria da Penha is part of a general pattern of negligence and lack of effective action by the State in prosecuting and convicting aggressors, it is the view of the Commission that this case involves not only failure to fulfill the obligation with respect to prosecute and convict, but also the obligation to prevent these degrading practices. That general and discriminatory judicial ineffectiveness also creates a climate that is conducive to domestic violence, since society sees no evidence of willingness by the State, as the representative of the society, to take effective action to sanction such acts.

57. The Commission must consider, in relation to Articles 7(c) and (h), the measures taken by the State to eliminate the condoning of domestic violence. The Commission notes the positive measures taken by the current administration towards that objective, in particular the establishment of special police stations, shelters for battered women, and others. However, in this case, which represents the tip of the iceberg, ineffective judicial action, impunity, and the inability of victims to obtain compen-

sation provide an example of the lack of commitment to take appropriate action to address domestic violence. Article 7 of the Convention of Belém do Pará seems to represent a list of commitments that the Brazilian State has failed to meet in such cases.

58. In light of the foregoing, the Commission holds the view that this case meets the conditions for domestic violence and tolerance on the part of the State, defined in the Convention of Belém do Pará, and that the State is liable for failing to perform its duties set forth in Articles 7(b), (d), (e), (f), and (g) of that Convention in relation to rights protected therein, among them, the right to a life free of violence (Article 3), the right of a woman to have her life, her physical, mental, and moral integrity, her personal safety, and personal dignity respected, to equal protection before and of the law, and to simple and prompt recourse to a competent court for protection against acts that violate her rights (Articles 4(a), (b), (c), (d), (e), (f), and (g)).

Proceedings Subsequent to Report No. 105/00

59. The Commission approved Report No. 105/00 pertaining to this case on October 19, 2000, at its 108th session. This report was transmitted to the State on November 1, 2000, and it was granted a period of two months to implement the recommendations made. The Commission informed the petitioners of the approval of a report in accordance with Article 50 of the Convention. Inasmuch as the period granted has expired and the Commission has not received a response from the State regarding these recommendations, the IACHR adopts the view that these recommendations have not been implemented.

Conclusions

The Inter-American Commission on Human Rights Decides That

60. The Inter-American Commission on Human Rights reiterates to the State the following conclusions:

1. It is competent to hear this case and that the petition is admissible pursuant to Articles 46(2)(c) and 47 of the American Convention and in accordance with Article 12 of the Convention of Belém do Pará, with respect to violation of the rights and duties established in Articles 1(1) (Obligation to Respect Rights); 8 (a Fair Trial); 24 (Equal Protection); and 25 (Judicial Protection) of the American Convention, in relation to Articles II and XVIII of the American Declaration (the Declaration); as well as Article 7 of the Convention of Belém do Pará.

2. Based on the facts, which have not been disputed, and the foregoing analysis, the Federative Republic of Brazil is responsible for violation of the right to a fair trial and judicial protection, guaranteed in Articles 8 and 25 of the American Convention, in accordance with the general obligation to respect and guarantee rights set forth in Article 1(1) of this instrument, because of the unwarranted delay and negligent processing of this case of domestic violence in Brazil.

3. The State has adopted a number of measures intended to reduce the scope of domestic violence and tolerance by the State thereof, although these measures have not yet had a significant impact on the pattern of State tolerance of violence against women, in particular as a result of ineffective police and judicial action in Brazil.

4. The State has violated the rights of Mrs. Fernandes and failed to carry out its duty assumed under Article 7 of the Convention of Belém do Pará and Articles 8 and 25 of the

American Convention; both in relation to Article 1(1) of the Convention, as a result of its own failure to act and tolerance of the violence inflicted.

Recommendations

61. Based on the foregoing analysis and conclusions, the Inter-American Commission on Human Rights recommends once more that the Brazilian State:

1. Complete, rapidly and effectively, criminal proceedings against the person responsible for the assault and attempted murder of Mrs. Maria da Penha Maia Fernandes.

2. In addition, conduct a serious, impartial, and exhaustive investigation to determine responsibility for the irregularities or unwarranted delays that prevented rapid and effective prosecution of the perpetrator, and implement the appropriate administrative, legislative, and judicial measures.

3. Adopt, without prejudice to possible civil proceedings against the perpetrator, the measures necessary for the State to grant the victim appropriate symbolic and actual compensation for the violence established herein, in particular for its failure to provide rapid and effective remedies, for the impunity that has surrounded the case for more than 15 years, and for making it impossible, as a result of that delay, to institute timely proceedings for redress and compensation in the civil sphere.

4. Continue and expand the reform process that will put an end to the condoning by the State of domestic violence against women in Brazil and discrimination in the handling thereof. In particular, the Commission recommends:

a. Measures to train and raise the awareness of officials of the judiciary and specialized police so that they may understand the importance of not condoning domestic violence.

b. The simplification of criminal judicial proceedings so that the time taken for proceedings can be reduced, without affecting the rights and guarantees related to due process.

c. The establishment of mechanisms that serve as alternatives to judicial mechanisms, which resolve domestic conflict in a prompt and effective manner and create awareness regarding its serious nature and associated criminal consequences.

d. An increase in the number of special police stations to address the rights of women and to provide them with the special resources needed for the effective processing and investigation of all complaints related to domestic violence, as well as resources and assistance from the Office of the Public Prosecutor in preparing their judicial reports.

e. The inclusion in teaching curriculums of units aimed at providing an understanding of the importance of respecting women and their rights recognized in the Convention of Belém do Pará, as well as the handling of domestic conflict.

f. The provision of information to the Inter-American Commission on Human Rights within sixty days of transmission of this report to the State, and of a report on steps taken to implement these recommendations, for the purposes set forth in Article 51 (1) of the American Convention.

Publication

62. The Commission transmitted the report adopted pursuant to Article 51 of the American Convention to the State and to the petitioner on March 13, 2001, and gave the State one month to submit information on the measures adopted to comply with

the Commission's recommendations. The State failed to present a response within the time limit.

63. Pursuant to the foregoing considerations, and in conformity with Article 51(3) of the American Convention and Article 48 of its Regulations, the Commission decides to reiterate the conclusions and recommendations of paragraphs 1 and 2, to make this Report public, and to include it in its Annual Report to the General Assembly of the OAS. The Commission, pursuant to its mandate, shall continue evaluating the measures taken by the Brazilian State with respect to the recommendations at issue, until they have been fully fulfilled....

Notes and Questions

1. *Law on the Books/Law in Action.* As mentioned in footnote 18 of Case No. 12.051, *supra*, Brazil's Constitution is notable for its attention to equality for women. In fact, "[i]n 1988, Brazil became the first country to address domestic violence explicitly in its constitution." Judith Armatta, *Getting Beyond the Law's Complicity in Intimate Violence Against Women*, 33 Willamette L. Rev. 773, 807 (1997) (citing articles 226, 227). Article 226 states: "The family, which is the foundation of society, shall enjoy special protection from the State.... (8) The State shall ensure assistance to the family in the person of each of its members, creating mechanisms to suppress violence within the family." Article 227 speaks to the "duty of the family, the society, and the State to ensure children and adolescents, with absolute priority,...[freedom] from all forms of negligence, discrimination, exploitation, violence, cruelty and oppression." Paragraph 4 of that article continues, "The law shall severely punish abuse, violence and sexual exploitation of children and adolescents." Federative Republic of Brazil, Constitution (1988) (Istvan Vajda et al. translators) (Brasília 1998). Obviously, legal prohibitions against violence do not necessarily translate into actual results for victims of violence. Nor are a state's obligations under the Belém do Pará (for example art. 7(d)) satisfied by the passage of aspirational statements, even if contained in foundational documents.

2. *Is International Law Law?* Consider Brazil's response to the proceedings. Given what appears to be its contempt for the proceedings, will Case No. 12.051 make any difference whatsoever? According to the Inter-American Commission on Human Rights, Brazil has at least partially complied with the Commission's recommendations. *See* http://www.cidh.oas.org/annualrep/2002eng/chap.3h.htm. The perpetrator was sent to prison. Contrast Brazil's response with Guatemala's response to similar proceedings, described in note 3.

3. *Women's Equality Generally.* The Inter-American Commission on Human Rights clearly sees a link between women's inequality in the family and domestic violence. For example, the Inter-American Commission found Guatemala in violation of the American Convention on Human Rights, articles 24, 17 and 11, for its discriminatory treatment of married women in Maria Eugenia Morales De Sierra, Case No. 11.625, Inter-Am C.H.R. 4-01 (2001). The provisions of Guatemalan Civil Code that were challenged were the following:

> Article 109 provides that representation of the marital union corresponds to the husband, although both spouses have equal authority within the home. Article 110 stipulates that the husband owes certain duties of protection and assistance to the wife, while the latter has the special right and duty to care for minor children and the home. Article 113 sets forth that the wife may exercise a profession or

pursue other responsibilities outside the home only insofar as this does not prejudice her responsibilities within it. Article 114 establishes that the husband may
oppose the pursuit of his wife's activities outside the home where he provides adequately for maintenance of the home and has "sufficiently justified reasons."
Where necessary, a judge shall resolve disputes in this regard. Article 115 states
that representation of the marital union may be exercised by the wife where the
husband fails to do so, particularly where he abandons the home, is imprisoned,
or is otherwise absent. Article 131 states that the husband shall administer the
marital property. Article 133 establishes exceptions to this rule on the same basis
set forth in Article 115. Article 255 states that, where husband and wife exercise
parental authority over minor children, the husband shall represent the latter and
administer their goods. Article 317 establishes that specific classes of persons may
be excused from exercising certain forms of custody, including, inter alia, women.

Id. ¶ 28.

These legal provisions had been challenged before the Guatemalan Court of Constitutionality, and that Court had ruled that the distinctions were constitutional. The provisions were upheld "essentially on the basis of the need for certainty and juridical security, the need to protect the marital home and children, respect for traditional
Guatemalan values, and in certain cases, the need to protect women in their capacity as
wives and mothers. However, the Court of Constitutionality made no effort to probe
the validity of these assertions or to weigh alternative positions...." *Id.* ¶ 37.

In the case before the Commission, Guatemala admitted that the provisions were
"out of date," but maintained that it was taking steps to modify the challenged articles
and bring them into conformity with international law norms. Governmental initiatives
to reform the laws were then pending.

The Commission concluded that the identified provisions denied the petitioner
equal protection of and before the law as set forth in article 24 of the American Convention. "A distinction which is based on 'reasonable and objective criteria' may serve a legitimate state interest in conformity with the terms of Article 24, including 'to protect
persons requiring the application of special measures.' If the distinction also is proportional to the end sought then it would not fall afoul of the Convention." *See id.* ¶ 31.
However, these provisions could not be justified.

The provisions also violated article 17(4) of the American Convention, which derives
from article 16(1) of the Universal Declaration of Human Rights, and specifies that
"States Parties shall take appropriate steps to ensure the equality of rights and the adequate balancing of responsibilities" in marriage and its dissolution. *Id.* ¶ 40. The Commission explained:

> The Commission finds that, far from ensuring the "equality of rights and ade-
> quate balancing of responsibilities" within marriage, the cited provisions insti-
> tutionalize imbalances in the rights and duties of the spouses. While Article
> 110 suggests a division of labor between a husband's financial responsibilities
> and the wife's domestic responsibilities, it must be noted that, pursuant to Ar-
> ticle 111, a wife with a separate source of income is required to contribute to
> the maintenance of the household, or to fully support it if her husband is un-
> able to do so. The fact that the law vests a series of legal capacities exclusively in
> the husband establishes a situation of de jure dependency for the wife and cre-
> ates an insurmountable disequilibrium in the spousal authority within the
> marriage. Moreover, the dispositions of the Civil Code apply stereotyped no-

tions of the roles of women and men which perpetuate de facto discrimination against women in the family sphere, and which have the further effect of impeding the ability of men to fully develop their roles within the marriage and family. The articles at issue create imbalances in family life, inhibiting the role of men with respect to the home and children, and in that sense depriving children of the full and equal attention of both parents. "A stable family is one which is based on principles of equity, justice and individual fulfillment for each member."

Id. ¶ 44.

The Commission also found a violation of the right to privacy contained in article 11 of the American Convention, which is intended "to protect individuals from arbitrary action by State authorities which infringes in the private sphere." *Id.* ¶ 47. The provision foreclosing a woman's employment if her husband opposed it "cannot be justified." *Id.* ¶ 50. "This discrimination has consequences from the point of view of her position in Guatemalan society, and reinforces cultural habits with respect to which the Commission has commented in its Report on the Status of Women in the Americas…. This situation has a harmful effect on public opinion in Guatemala, and on María Eugenia Morales de Sierra's position and status within her family, community and society." *Id.* ¶ 50.

For our purposes, it is important to know that the Commission's report linked the gender discrimination to violence against women. The Commission stated:

> The inter-American system has recognized, for example, that gender violence is "a manifestation of the historically unequal power relations between women and men." "Traditional attitudes by which women are regarded as subordinate to men or as having stereotyped roles perpetuate widespread practices involving violence or coercion, such as family violence and abuse…." De jure or de facto economic subordination, in turn, "forces many women to stay in violent relationships."

Id. ¶ 52.

The Commission's report, initially issued in 1998, found Guatemala responsible for failing to uphold its article 1 obligation to respect and ensure those rights under the Convention as well as its article 2 obligation to adopt the legislative and other measures necessary to give effect to those rights of the victim. The Commission called on Guatemala to amend, repeal or leave without effect articles 109, 110, 113, 114, 115, 131, 133, 255, and 317 of the Civil Code and to redress and adequately compensate the petitioner for the violations established.

Soon thereafter, Guatemala enacted reforms to the Civil Code, although the reforms addressed only seven of the nine challenged provisions. After another hearing before the Commission, Guatemala informed the Commission that further reform had occurred regarding Article 113. Guatemala reiterated its view that Article 317 constituted a privilege, a special consideration which may be invoked, rather than a form of discrimination.

In its Report No 4/01, the Commission concluded that Guatemala had not fully complied with its recommendations, despite the extensive legal reform that had occurred since the Commission's initial 1998 report.

> The original heading and first paragraph of Article 110, which remain in force, refer to the duty of the husband to protect and assist his wife within the marriage, a duty that, in and of itself, is consistent with the nature of the marital relationship. For its part, Article 111 of the Code establishes the obligation of the wife to contribute equitably to maintenance of the home to the extent that

she can, a duty that is also consistent with the relationship between spouses. While neither of these duties gives rise, in itself, to a situation of incompatibility, they continue to reflect an imbalance in that the legislation recognizes that the wife is the beneficiary of the husband's duty to protect and assist her, while the law does not impose the same duty on her with regard to her husband. Article 17(4) of the American Convention requires the State to "ensure the equality of rights and the adequate balancing of responsibilities of the spouses as to marriage."

With regard to Article 317, the decisive factor is not whether it is viewed as referring to a privilege or an obligation; what is dispositive is the nature of the distinction made in the provision and the justification offered for it. Essentially, the terms of Article 317 identify categories of persons who may be excused from custody or guardianship due to limitations, for example, economic or health reasons. It is not evident, nor has the State explained what limitation justifies including "women" in these categories. According to Article 17 of the American Convention, and as expressly stipulated in Article 16 of the Convention on the Elimination of All Forms of Discrimination against Women, States Parties must guarantee equal rights and duties with regard to exercising custody and other forms of guardianship of children.

In this sense, both Article 317 and the title and first paragraph of Article 110 suggest, expressly or implicitly, that women are characterized by inherent weaknesses that limit their capacity as compared to men. This affects María Eugenia Morales de Sierra in her right to equal protection of the law, in accordance with Article 24 of the American Convention, and to respect for her human dignity, pursuant to Article 11 of that Convention. Additionally, as stated in paragraph 44 above, these norms apply stereotyped notions about gender roles, thereby perpetuating de facto discrimination against women in the family sphere. Further, with regard to the question of compliance with the recommendations, the State has provided no measures of reparation to the victim in response to the findings and recommendations of the Commission.

Id. ¶ 79–81. The Commission published its 2001 report and planned to forward it to the General Assembly of the OAS.

4. *Limits of the Inter-American Commission.* The Inter-American Commission's "oversight and enforcement obligations span thirty-four countries with a population of more than 600 million human beings. Yet to carry out these tasks the Commission has only seven members, a staff of ten lawyers, a secretarial staff of seven, and an annual budget of less than $1.6 million. The Commission's tasks are rendered even more difficult by the social and economic heterogeneity of the Americas, the intermittent civil strife that still afflicts many countries, the terrorism and narcotics traffic that compound existing human rights problems and present special human rights problems of their own, and the sporadic coups." Berta Esperanza Hernandez-Truyol, *Law, Culture, and Equality—Human Rights' Influence on Domestic Norms: The Case of Women in the Americas,* 13 Fla. J. Int'l L. 33, 41 (2000). Currently it takes three to four years to proceed before the Inter-American Commission, that is after the applicant exhausts domestic remedies. *See* Victor Rodriguez Recia & Marc David Seitles, *The Development of the Inter-American Human Rights System: A Historical Perspective and a Modern-Day Critique,* 16 N.Y.L. Sch. J. Hum. Rts. 593, 623 (2000).

5. *National Legislation.* Compare articles 4(c) and 4(d) of the U.N. Declaration on the Elimination of Violence Against Women with articles 7(b) and 7(g) of the Conven-

tion of Belém do Pará. Does the inclusion of language about "national legislation" in the U.N. Declaration mean the U.N. Declaration requires nothing of nations?

6. *Continued Discrimination Against Women in OAS Member States.* In 2001, Berta Esperanza Hernandez-Truyol outlined some of the remaining areas of inequality for women in the OAS.

- Restrictions on the exercise of a profession or on work by women insofar as the authorization of the husband is required (Bolivia, Guatemala, Panama, Peru and the Dominican Republic);

- Differentiation between men and women with respect to the authorization to contract marriage (Bolivia, Brazil), or to remarry (Mexico, Costa Rica);

- Inequality between men and women in acquiring, administering, and disposing of assets of the conjugal union (Argentina gives husbands preferences over assets whose origin cannot be determined; Chile grants the husband, in certain cases, the right to administer the assets of the union as well as those of his wife; Brazil does not recognize a married woman's equal capacity with her husband to administer certain assets);

- Differences between men and women with respect to parental authority (in Chile, the father exercises parental authority which is conferred upon the mother only in his absence);

- Classification of women with minors in labor legislation (Bolivia, Costa Rica, Ecuador, and Guatemala);

- Restrictions on a woman's right to property (the Dominican Republic's Constitution restricts campesinas from owning plots of land);

- Differen[t] . . . treatment [of] women and men with respect to certain criminal offenses (El Salvador and Venezuela treat men and women differently regarding adultery).

Beyond the specific laws that we have explored, women in the Inter-American system, much like women worldwide, remain second-class citizens in the economic realm. For example, notwithstanding the principles of equality and non-discrimination, huge income gaps remain between men and women in most of the countries in the region. In Costa Rica, as of 1990, the average monthly salary of women was 82% that of men; in rural areas, 60% of the women earned less than the minimum wage; and 34% earned half that amount. In Brazil, income earned by women was 54% that of men; and in Uruguay, as in the United States, women earn 75% of men's income.

Hernandez-Truyol, *Latina, Culture and Human Rights: A Model for Making Change, Saving Soul*, 23 Women's Rts. L. Rep. 21, 39–40 (2001). Given the decisions coming down from the Inter-American Commission on Human Rights, many of these discriminatory laws may soon be challenged. What, however, about economic rights? The American Convention on Human Rights focuses on civil and political rights. Social and economic rights are also important to victims of domestic violence. Does the Convention of Belém do Pará help establish or protect these other rights?

8. *Violence Against Women and Reproduction.* In Maria Mamérita Mestanza Chávez, Case 12.191, Inter-Am C.H.R. 66-00 (2000), the Inter-American Commission on Human Rights determined the admissibility of a petition by a woman who was forcefully subjected to surgical sterilization, which ultimately led to her death. The petition

alleged that the victim was "one...of a significant number of cases of women affected by the implementation of a massive, compulsory, and systematic government policy that emphasized sterilization as a method for quickly modifying the reproductive behavior of the population, especially of poor, indigenous, and rural woman." *Id.* ¶ 3. The claim was admissible under the American Convention, articles 1, 4, 5, and 24, but also under the Convention of Belém do Pará, article 7.

9. *Torture.* The Inter-American Commission on Human Rights has held that the rape of the wife of a political activist by military officials constitutes torture under the American Convention and under the Inter-American Convention to Prevent and Punish Torture. Raquel Martin de Mejia v. Peru, Case No. 10.970, Inter-Am. C.H.R. 157 (1996). While the recognition that rape is torture is significant, you may recall that "torture" under the Inter-American Convention is limited to an act committed by "a public official or by a private person acting at the instigation of the former."

10. *Empirical Evidence of Effectiveness.* Oona Hathaway conducted a very interesting quantitative analysis to try to assess whether human rights treaties matter to state practices. She argued,

> From the standpoint of leading perspectives on international law, the results of my research are counter intuitive. Although the ratings of human rights practices of countries that have ratified international human rights treaties are generally better than those of countries that have not, noncompliance with treaty obligations appears to be common. More paradoxically, when I take into account the influence of a range of other factors that affect countries' practices, I find that treaty ratification is not infrequently associated with worse human rights ratings than otherwise expected. I do, however, find evidence suggesting that ratification of human rights treaties by fully democratic nations is associated with better human rights practices....

> My findings do not necessarily tell us that treaties lead to worse human rights practices. Countries with worse practices may be more inclined to ratify treaties, or we may simply know more about violations committed by countries that sign human rights treaties, making countries that ratify look worse than they are. Yet given that I find not a single treaty for which ratification seems to be reliably associated with better human rights practices and several for which it appears to be associated with worse practices, it would be premature to dismiss the possibility that human rights treaties may sometimes lead to poorer human rights practices within the countries that ratify them.

> This suggestion is not as outrageous as it might at first appear. The counter intuitive results may be explained at least in part...by a conception of international treaties that takes account of their dual nature as both instrumental and expressive instruments. Treaties are instrumental in that they create law that binds ratifying countries, with the goal of modifying nations' practices in particular ways. But treaties also declare or express to the international community the position of countries that have ratified. The position taken by countries in such instances can be sincere, but it need not be. When countries are rewarded for positions rather than effects—as they are when monitoring and enforcement of treaties are minimal and external pressure to conform to treaty norms is high—governments can take positions that they do not honor, and benefit from doing so....

Oona A. Hathaway, *Do Human Rights Treaties Make A Difference?*, 111 Yale L.J. 1935, 1940–41 (2002). The author's findings are provocative. Hathaway cautions, however, that treaties may have broader positive effects not captured by her analysis, and she mentions, among other things, that treaties may "chang[e] the discourse about and expectations regarding those rights." *Id.* at 2021. She admits that countries may in fact internalize the norms of the treaty over the long term, and that her study of only a few decades may have been too short to detect long-term change. *Id.* at 2022.

11. *Causal Significance.* Imagine a country ratifies the Convention of Belém do Pará and shortly thereafter its legislature passes legislation favorable to domestic violence victims. Can one conclude that the human rights treaty caused the state to enact the legislation? Think about this analogy. You go to the park on a hot summer day. You buy an ice cream cone from a vender. The ice cream cone immediately melts in the hot sun. You then get a sun burn. Can you conclude that the melting ice cream cone caused you to get a sunburn?

ii. European Convention on Human Rights

The European Convention on Human Rights also deserves our attention. Although it does not explicitly address domestic violence, its various provisions—and cases decided under those provisions—are relevant to human rights claims by domestic violence victims. What is most noteworthy about the jurisprudence under the ECHR is that the outcomes are, in some respects, remarkably close to the results achieved in the OAS with the Convention of Belém do Pará. The comparable results are materializing even without the same sorts of provisions that explicitly impose obligations on states to address family violence. However, since most of the cases have not involved male-on-female adult battery, a definitive statement about the usefulness of the ECHR must be postponed. Under the European Convention, articles 2, 3 and 8 are the principle provisions that have proven useful for victims of violence.

In the next case, *X and Y v. The Netherlands,* the European Court of Human Rights held that the Netherlands violated article 8 of the Convention, which ensures "[e]veryone…the right to respect for his private and family life, his home and correspondence." Part of the opinion is included here:

X and Y v. The Netherlands
8 Eur. Ct. H.R. 235 (1985)

[Ed. Note: Y, the sixteen-year-old daughter of Mr. X, had been raped. It was impossible to have criminal proceedings instituted against the rapist because of a gap in the Netherlands' law. Y was mentally disabled and was incapable of filing a criminal complaint herself. Her father attempted to file one for her, but the law did not permit his complaint to be a substitute for the girl's complaint, since she was already sixteen years old.]

Alleged Violation of Article 8, Taken Alone, as Regards Miss Y

21. According to the applicants, the impossibility of having criminal proceedings instituted against Mr. B violated Article 8 of the Convention….

The Government contested this claim; the Commission, on the other hand, agreed with it in its essentials.

22. There was no dispute as to the applicability of Article 8: the facts underlying the application to the Commission concern a matter of 'private life,' a concept which covers the physical and moral integrity of the person, including his or her sexual life.

23. The Court recalls that although the object of Article 8 is essentially that of protecting the individual against arbitrary interference by the public authorities, it does not merely compel the State to abstain from such interference: in addition to this primarily negative undertaking, there may be positive obligations inherent in an effective respect for private or family life. These obligations may involve the adoption of measures designed to secure respect for private life even in the sphere of the relations of individuals between themselves.

Necessity for Criminal-Law Provisions

24. The applicants argued that, for a young girl like Miss Y, the requisite degree of protection against the wrongdoing in question would have been provided only by means of the criminal law. In the Government's view, the Convention left it to each State to decide upon the means to be utilized and did not prevent it from opting for civil-law provisions.

The Court, which on this point agrees in substance with the opinion of the Commission, observes that the choice of the means calculated to secure compliance with Article 8 in the sphere of the relations of individuals between themselves is in principle a matter that falls within the Contracting States' margin of appreciation. In this connection, there are different ways of ensuring 'respect for private life,' and the nature of the State's obligation will depend on the particular aspect of private life that is at issue. Recourse to the criminal law is not necessarily the only answer.

25. The Government cited the difficulty encountered by the legislature in laying down criminal-law provisions calculated to afford the best possible protection of the physical integrity of the mentally handicapped: to go too far in this direction might lead to unacceptable paternalism and occasion an inadmissible interference by the State with the individual's right to respect for his or her sexual life.

The Government stated that under Article 1401 of the Civil Code, taken together with Article 1407, it would have been possible to bring before or file with the Netherlands courts, on behalf of Miss Y:

— an action for damages against Mr. B, for pecuniary or non-pecuniary damage;

— an application for an injunction against Mr. B, to prevent repetition of the offence;

— a similar action or application against the directress of the children's home.

The applicants considered that these civil-law remedies were unsuitable. They submitted that, amongst other things, the absence of any criminal investigation made it harder to furnish evidence on the four matters that had to be established under Article 1401, namely a wrongful act, fault, damage and a causal link between the act and the damage. Furthermore, such proceedings were lengthy and involved difficulties of an emotional nature for the victim, since he or she had to play an active part therein.

26. At the hearings, the Commission's Delegate adopted the applicants' submissions in their essentials....

27. The Court finds that the protection afforded by the civil law in the case of wrongdoing of the kind inflicted on Miss Y is insufficient. This is a case where fundamental values and essential aspects of private life are at stake. Effective deterrence is indispensable in this area and it can be achieved only by criminal-law provisions; indeed, it is by such provisions that the matter is normally regulated.

Moreover, as was pointed out by the Commission, this is in fact an area in which the Netherlands has generally opted for a system of protection based on the criminal law.

The only gap, so far as the Commission and the Court have been made aware, is as regards persons in the situation of Miss Y; in such cases, this system meets a procedural obstacle which the Dutch legislature had apparently not foreseen....

Notes and Questions

1. *Right to Private Life.* Having found that article 8 was violated, the Court did not examine the case under article 3, taken alone, or in conjunction with article 14. Nor did it examine an alleged violation of article 13. It was uncontested that article 8 applied to this situation. Would article 8 necessarily be violated if the state refused to prosecute husbands for the assault of their wives? Be sure to consider article 8(2) on permissible derogations.

2. *Monetary Award.* Under article 50 of the Convention, which requires the Court to "afford just satisfaction to the injured party," the Court awarded Miss Y 3,000 Dutch guilders, or approximately $820 U.S. dollars.

The next case caused quite a commotion when it was decided. A subsequent case has cast some doubt on the Court's holding with regard to article 6(1); that holding is set out in note 3 following the case. However, the analysis on articles 2 and 8 remains good law.

Osman v. United Kingdom
29 Eur. Ct. H.R. (ser. A) 245 (1998)

[Ed. Note: The published report by the European Commission on Human Rights contains a very detailed and lengthy recitation of events. Only some of the facts are referred to in the Court's opinion. To fill out that discussion and to give a sense of stalking behavior, many facts are presented here in narrative form from the Commission's report. However, it should be noted that the applicants and the respondent State disagreed on many essential facts, and the applicants attacked the Commission's findings of fact as being incomplete. In addition, there was never any independent judicial determination at the domestic level of the facts.

Ahmet Osman, born in 1972, was a former pupil of Mr. Paul Paget-Lewis at Homerton House School. Starting in 1986, Paget-Lewis developed an attachment to Ahmet. Mr. Prince, the headmaster, was "keeping an eye on the situation." By 1987, Paget-Lewis started harassing another student, Green, and spreading rumors about Green because of Green's friendship with Ahmet. Paget-Lewis told Ahmet that he would find him if he left school. In March 1987, Prince met with the police on various occasions; all concerned were satisfied that there was no sexual element to Paget-Lewis' attachment to Ahmet and the matter could be dealt with internally by the school.

In March, graffiti appeared around the school regarding Green. Also in March, files relating to Ahmet and Green had been stolen from the school office. Paget-Lewis denied involvement, although facts suggested his involvement in both. In April, Paget-Lewis changed his name by deed poll to Paul Ahmet Yildirim Osman. He had previously changed his name to that of another pupil called Paget-Lewis.

On May 1, 1987, Mr. Prince wrote to the Inner London Education Authority (ILEA) expressing concern that some psychological imbalance might pose a threat to the safety of Ahmet, and asking that Paget-Lewis be removed from the school as soon as possible. In May, there were further contacts between the police and the school. Notes in the school files suggested that the police stated that they would continue the investigation. In May, the ILEA psychiatrist thought Paget-Lewis gave "cause for concern" and should receive counselling, although he recommended Paget-Lewis remain teaching at the school. In May and June, a brick was thrown through the Osmans' house window, and twice tires on Ali Osman's car were slashed. All incidents were reported to the police.

In June 1987, the ILEA psychiatrist concluded that Paget-Lewis should remain away from Homerton House and was designated temporarily unfit to work; after another interview, the psychiatrist recommended a transfer on medical grounds. Paget-Lewis voluntarily left Homerton House and did not return again. On June 18, Paget-Lewis was suspended pending an ILEA investigation for "unprofessional behaviour." On August 7, ILEA sent a letter to Paget-Lewis officially reprimanding him, but lifting the suspension. However, he was not to return to Homerton House.

From August through November 1987, a series of vandalism occurred at the Osman's home. All these incidents were reported to the police. In November, the police spoke to Paget-Lewis, who denied any involvement in the acts of vandalism. Paget-Lewis alleged, but the police denied, that he told the police about his job loss and "he felt that he was in danger of doing something criminally insane."

On December 7, 1987, Paget-Lewis drove his car into a van in which Green was a passenger. The driver of the van told the police that after the accident that Paget-Lewis had said: "I'm not worried because in a few months I'll be doing life."

On December 8, 1987, Detective Sergeant Boardman contacted ILEA. There was a dispute over whether Detective Sergeant Boardman assured ILEA that the Osman family would be protected. On December 9, 1987, Green told Detective Sergeant Boardman that Paget-Lewis had threatened to "get him" whether it took "30 days or 30 years." Detective Sergeant Boardman inspected the graffiti and interviewed the Osman family in mid-December, and found "no evidence to implicate Paget-Lewis in either of these offenses." Again, there was a dispute about whether the Detective gave the Osman family assurances that he would cause the incidents to stop.

In mid-December, Paget-Lewis asked to speak with the ILEA. He felt "in a totally self-destructive mood, stating that it was all a symphony and the last chord had to be played." He blamed Mr. Perkins (a deputy head teacher who was involved with the investigation at Homerton) for all his troubles, but would not do a "Hungerford" in a school, but would see Mr. Perkins at his home. Hungerford was the scene of a 1987 massacre in which a gunman killed sixteen persons before committing suicide. The ILEA called Detective Sergeant Boardman about this interview, and a detailed message was left with the receptionist. The Government denied that the ILEA mentioned the "Hungerford" reference or suggested that the Osmans might be in danger.

The day after receiving the message from the ILEA, Detective Sergeant Boardman sent a telex to the local police station near Mr. Perkins' home asking them to arrest Paget-Lewis. Detective Sergeant Boardman then sought to find Paget-Lewis. Boardman asked an ILEA official to ask Paget-Lewis to contact the police. Again, there were conflicting versions about whether the police assured Mr. Prince that the police would protect both Mr. Perkins and the applicants. The next day, the police went to arrest Paget-Lewis, but could not find him.

In early January 1988, the police commenced the procedure of laying an information before the Magistrates' Court with a view to prosecuting Paget-Lewis for driving without due care and attention. In addition, Paget-Lewis' name was put on the Police National Computer as being wanted for the collision and for offenses of criminal damage.

Between January and March 1988, Paget-Lewis travelled around England hiring cars in the name of Osman; he was involved in a number of accidents. He spent time at his home address during this period and continued to receive mail there.

On January 17, 1988, Paget-Lewis stole a shotgun and sawed off both barrels. On three occasions in early March 1988, Green saw Paget-Lewis wearing a black crash helmet near the Osmans' home and informed the police on each occasion. The Government said that it received only one message, "phone Mrs. Green," but no phone number was left, and it didn't connect the name to the Paget-Lewis matter.

On March 7, 1988, Paget-Lewis shot and killed Ali Osman and seriously wounded Ahmet. He then drove to the home of Mr. Perkins where he shot and wounded him and killed his son. Early the next morning Paget-Lewis was arrested. He then stated "why didn't you stop me before I did it, I gave you all the warning signs?" Later that day, Paget-Lewis told the police that he had been planning the attacks ever since he lost his job, and for the previous two weeks he had been watching the Osmans' house. Paget-Lewis was convicted of two charges of manslaughter having pleaded guilty on grounds of diminished responsibility. He was sentenced to be detained in a secure mental hospital without limit of time, pursuant to section 41 of the Mental Health Act 1983.

In September 1989, the applicants commenced proceedings against the Commissioner of Police of the Metropolis, alleging negligence. They argued that although the police were aware of Paget-Lewis' activities since May 1987, they failed to apprehend or interview him, search his home or charge him with an offence before March 1988.

In October 1992, the Court of Appeal held that in light of previous authorities no action could lie against the police in negligence in the investigation and suppression of crime on the grounds that public policy required the police department's immunity from suit. Two Lord Justices on the Court of Appeal found "a very close degree of proximity amounting to a special relationship" between the police and the Osmans. However, the Court of Appeal felt bound by the House of Lords' decision in *Hill v. Chief Constable of West Yorkshire*, [1989] A.C. 53, in which the Lords had accepted an immunity for the police for their failure to investigate a crime and to protect members of the public who might be victims of the Yorkshire Ripper. In dictum, Lord Keith set out why a negligence action should not be permitted against the police for the performance of their duties investigating and suppressing crime.

> Potential existence of such liability may in many instances be in the general public interest, as tending towards the observance of a higher standard of care in the carrying on of various different types of activity. I do not, however, consider that this can be said of police activities. The general sense of public duty which motivates police forces is unlikely to be appreciably reinforced by the imposition of such liability so far as concerns their function in the investigation and suppression of crime. From time to time they make mistakes in the exercise of that function, but it is not to be doubted that they apply their best endeavors to the performance of it. In some instances the imposition of liability may lead to the exercise of a function being carried on in a detrimentally defensive frame of mind. The possibility of this happening in relation to the investigative operations of the police cannot be excluded. Further it would be reasonable to expect that if potential liability were to be imposed it would be not uncommon for actions to be raised against police forces on the ground that they had failed to catch some criminal as soon as they might have done, with the result that he went on to commit further crimes. While some such ac-

tions might involve allegations of a simple and straightforward type of failure—for example that a police officer negligently tripped and fell while pursuing a burglar—others would be likely to enter deeply into the general nature of a police investigation, as indeed the present action would seek to do. The manner of conduct of such an investigation must necessarily involve a variety of decisions to be made on matters of policy and discretion, for example, as to which particular line of inquiry is most advantageously to be pursued and what is the most advantageous way to deploy the available resources. Many such decisions would not be regarded by the courts as appropriate to be called in question, yet elaborate investigation of the facts might be necessary to ascertain whether or not this was so. A great deal of police time, trouble and expense might be expected to have to be put into the preparation of the defence to the action and the attendance of witnesses at the trial. The result would be significant diversion of police manpower and attention from their most important function, that of the suppression of crime. Closed investigations would require to be reopened and retraversed, not with the object of bringing any criminal to justice but to ascertain whether or not they had been competently conducted.

Lord Templeman commented:

[I]f this action lies, every citizen will be able to require the court to investigate the performance of every policeman. If the policeman concentrates on one crime, he may be accused of neglecting others. If the policeman does not arrest on suspicion a suspect with previous convictions, the police force may be held liable for subsequent crimes. The threat of litigation against a police force would not make a policeman more efficient. The necessity for defending proceedings, successfully or unsuccessfully, would distract the policeman from his duties.]

Judgment

Alleged Violation of Article 2 of the Convention

101. The applicants asserted that by failing to take adequate and appropriate steps to protect the lives of the second applicant and his father, Ali Osman, from the real and known danger which Paget-Lewis posed, the authorities had failed to comply with their positive obligation under Article 2 of the Convention, which provides as relevant:

1. Everyone's right to life shall be protected by law. No one shall be deprived of his life intentionally save in the execution of a sentence of a court following his conviction of a crime for which this penalty is provided by law....

102. The Government maintained that the facts of the case did not bear out the applicants' allegation and for that reason there had been no breach of Article 2. The Commission agreed with the Government's arguments....

The Court's assessment

As to the alleged failure of the authorities to protect the rights to life of Ali and Ahmet Osman

115. The Court notes that the first sentence of Article 2(1) enjoins the State not only to refrain from the intentional and unlawful taking of life, but also to take appropriate steps to safeguard the lives of those within its jurisdiction. It is common ground that the

State's obligation in this respect extends beyond its primary duty to secure the right to life by putting in place effective criminal law provisions to deter the commission of offenses against the person backed up by law-enforcement machinery for the prevention, suppression and sanctioning of breaches of such provisions. It is thus accepted by those appearing before the Court that Article 2 of the Convention may also imply in certain well-defined circumstances a positive obligation on the authorities to take preventive operational measures to protect an individual whose life is at risk from the criminal acts of another individual. The scope of this obligation is a matter of dispute between the parties.

116. For the Court, and bearing in mind the difficulties involved in policing modern societies, the unpredictability of human conduct and the operational choices which must be made in terms of priorities and resources, such an obligation must be interpreted in a way which does not impose an impossible or disproportionate burden on the authorities. Accordingly, not every claimed risk to life can entail for the authorities a Convention requirement to take operational measures to prevent that risk from materializing. Another relevant consideration is the need to ensure that the police exercise their powers to control and prevent crime in a manner which fully respects the due process and other guarantees which legitimately place restraints on the scope of their action to investigate crime and bring offenders to justice, including the guarantees contained in Articles 5 and 8 of the Convention.

In the opinion of the Court where there is an allegation that the authorities have violated their positive obligation to protect the right to life in the context of their above-mentioned duty to prevent and suppress offenses against the person, it must be established to its satisfaction that the authorities knew or ought to have known at the time of the existence of a real and immediate risk to the life of an identified individual or individuals from the criminal acts of a third party and that they failed to take measures within the scope of their powers which, judged reasonably, might have been expected to avoid that risk. The Court does not accept the Government's view that the failure to perceive the risk to life in the circumstances known at the time or to take preventive measures to avoid that risk must be tantamount to gross negligence or wilful disregard of the duty to protect life. Such a rigid standard must be considered to be incompatible with the requirements of Article 1 of the Convention and the obligations of Contracting States under that Article to secure the practical and effective protection of the rights and freedoms laid down therein, including Article 2. For the Court, and having regard to the nature of the right protected by Article 2, a right fundamental in the scheme of the Convention, it is sufficient for an applicant to show that the authorities did not do all that could be reasonably expected of them to avoid a real and immediate risk to life of which they have or ought to have knowledge. This is a question which can only be answered in the light of all the circumstances of any particular case.

On the above understanding the Court will examine the particular circumstances of this case.

117. The Court observes, like the Commission, that the concerns of the school about Paget-Lewis' disturbing attachment to Ahmet Osman can be reasonably considered to have been communicated to the police over the course of the five meetings which took place between 3 March and 4 May 1987, having regard to the fact that Mr. Prince's decision to call in the police in the first place was motivated by the allegations which Mrs. Green had made against Paget-Lewis and the school's follow-up to those allegations. It may for the same reason be reasonably accepted that the police were informed of all rel-

evant connected matters which had come to light by 4 May 1987 including the graffiti incident, the theft of the school files and Paget-Lewis' change of name.

It is the applicants' contention that by that stage the police should have been alert to the need to investigate further Paget-Lewis' alleged involvement in the graffiti incident and the theft of the school files or to keep a closer watch on him given their awareness of the obsessive nature of his behaviour towards Ahmet Osman and how that behaviour manifested itself. The Court for its part is not persuaded that the police's failure to do so at this stage can be impugned from the standpoint of Article 2 having regard to the state of their knowledge at that time. While Paget-Lewis' attachment to Ahmet Osman could be judged by the police officers who visited the school to be most reprehensible from a professional point of view, there was never any suggestion that Ahmet Osman was at risk sexually from him, less so that his life was in danger. Furthermore, Mr. Perkins, the deputy headmaster, alone had reached the conclusion that Paget-Lewis had been responsible for the graffiti in the neighborhood of the school and the theft of the files. However Paget-Lewis had denied all involvement when interviewed by Mr. Perkins and there was nothing to link him with either incident. Accordingly, at that juncture, the police's appreciation of the situation and their decision to treat it as a matter internal to the school cannot be considered unreasonable.

Like the Commission, the Court is not persuaded either that the ILEA official's memorandum and internal notes written between 14 April and 8 May are an accurate reflection of how the discussions between Mr. Prince and the police officers wound up....

[Ed. Note: The Court then reviewed the other evidence and concluded that either Paget-Lewis' acts could not be construed to be threats, or that any threats could not be construed to be against the Osman family.]

121. In the view of the Court, the applicants have failed to point to any decisive stage in the sequence of the events leading up to the tragic shooting when it could be said that the police knew or ought to have known that the lives of the Osman family were at real and immediate risk from Paget-Lewis. While the applicants have pointed to a series of missed opportunities which would have enabled the police to neutralize the threat posed by Paget-Lewis, for example by searching his home for evidence to link him with the graffiti incident or by having him detained under the Mental Health Act 1983 or by taking more active investigative steps following his disappearance, it cannot be said that these measures, judged reasonably, would in fact have produced that result or that a domestic court would have convicted him or ordered his detention in a psychiatric hospital on the basis of the evidence adduced before it. As noted earlier, the police must discharge their duties in a manner which is compatible with the rights and freedoms of individuals. In the circumstances of the present case, they cannot be criticized for attaching weight to the presumption of innocence or failing to use powers of arrest, search and seizure having regard to their reasonably held view that they lacked at relevant times the required standard of suspicion to use those powers or that any action taken would in fact have produced concrete results.

122. For the above reasons, the Court concludes that there has been no violation of Article 2 of the Convention in the circumstances of this case....

Alleged Violation of Article 8 of the Convention

124. The applicants contended that the failure of the police first to bring an end to the campaign of harassment, vandalism and victimization which Paget-Lewis waged

against their property and family and secondly, and in particular, to avert the wounding of the second applicant constituted a breach of Article 8 of the Convention....*

128. The Court recalls that it has not found it established that the police knew or ought to have known at the time that Paget-Lewis represented a real and immediate risk to the life of Ahmet Osman and that their response to the events as they unfolded was reasonable in the circumstances and not incompatible with the authorities' duty under Article 2 of the Convention to safeguard the right to life. In the Court's view, that conclusion equally supports a finding that there has been no breach of any positive obligation implied by Article 8 of the Convention to safeguard the second applicant's physical integrity....

Lopes Rocha, J., partly dissenting, partly concurring

I regret that I am unable to share the majority's view that there has been no violation of Articles 2 and 8 of the Convention.

My interpretation of the facts...leads me to conclude that the police underestimated the danger Mr. Paget-Lewis presented for the life and physical integrity of Mr. Ahmet Osman and, in all probability, of his close relatives.

In my opinion, it is not possible to say, as the Government did, that there was no causal link between the failure to take preventive action, of which the authorities are accused, and the events that occurred.

A quite different approach is required to determine liability for an omission from that required to determine liability for an act. The former must be determined according to generally accepted rules. It has to be decided whether the assault originated from the failure to take a particular measure or measures where the assailant's previous behaviour already pointed to a likelihood that he would act aggressively towards someone of whom he was particularly fond.

In the instant case, there was strong evidence of aggressive behaviour on the part of Mr. Paget-Lewis suggesting that at the first opportunity he would act violently. It should not be forgotten that he displayed rather strange traits of personality and was known to the police, although there was some doubt over whether he was homosexual.

Given, too, the professional experience one is entitled to expect of them, the police could legitimately be required to exercise caution and to take measures to protect the people at risk. Failure to take such measures renders the police and the State concerned liable. There has therefore been a breach of the aforementioned Articles.

[The concurring opinions of Judge Foighel, Judge Sir John Freeland, and Judge Jambrek have been omitted. The partly dissenting, partly concurring opinion of Judge De Meyer, joined by Judges Lopes Rocha and Casadevall, has also been omitted.]

Notes and Questions

1. *Articles 2 and 8.* How do these two articles differ? Would Y in *X and Y* have been able to make out a successful article 2 claim? Why was Y's claim under article 8 successful and Osman's claim under article 8 unsuccessful?

2. *Article 6.* In *Osman v. United Kingdom*, the Court held that the United Kingdom violated Article 6(1) of the European Convention, which provides to the extent relevant:

---

* Article 8(1) says, "Everyone has the right to respect for his private and family life, his home and his correspondence."

"In the determination of his civil rights and obligations...everyone is entitled to a... hearing by [a]...tribunal." The violation occurred because the police were immune from negligence liability on the grounds of public policy. The European Court recognized that "the Contracting States enjoy a certain margin of appreciation" in affording access to a court, but that here the immunity impaired the very essence of the right.

> The reasons which led the House of Lords in the *Hill* case to lay down an exclusionary rule to protect the police from negligence actions in the context at issue are based on the view that the interests of the community as a whole are best served by a police service whose efficiency and effectiveness in the battle against crime are not jeopardized by the constant risk of exposure to tortious liability for policy and operational decisions.

> Although the aim of such a rule may be accepted as legitimate in terms of the Convention, as being directed to the maintenance of the effectiveness of the police service and hence to the prevention of disorder or crime, the Court must nevertheless, in turning to the issue of proportionality, have particular regard to its scope and especially its application in the case at issue. While the Government has contended that the exclusionary rule of liability is not of an absolute nature and that its application may yield to other public policy considerations, it would appear to the Court that in the instant case the Court of Appeal proceeded on the basis that the rule provided a watertight defence to the police and that it was impossible to prise open an immunity which the police enjoy from civil suit in respect of their acts and omissions in the investigation and suppression of crime.

> The Court would observe that the application of the rule in this manner without further enquiry into the existence of competing public interest considerations only serves to confer a blanket immunity on the police for their acts and omissions during the investigation and suppression of crime and amounts to an unjustifiable restriction on an applicant's right to have a determination on the merits of his or her claim against the police in deserving cases.

Id. ¶¶ 149–51. The European Court's decision caused controversy in the United Kingdom. Some English lawyers accused the European Court of not understanding principles of English tort law, especially the concept of "duty."

3. *Osman Overruled, in Part.* In *Z and Others v. United Kingdom*, 34 Eur. H.R. Rep. (2002), the European Court of Human Rights heard a case involving four siblings who were inadequately cared for by their parents and also physically abused. Social services became aware of the family's problems in 1987, but took little action. Social services decided not to remove the children, despite its own monitoring of the family and numerous complaints to the agency from relatives, teachers, and others about the children's living conditions. The agency finally took the children into care in 1992 when the mother insisted that she could not cope. A child psychiatrist described the children's prior experiences as, "to put it bluntly, horrific." It was the worst case of neglect and emotional abuse that she had seen in her professional career. She believed social services had "leaned over backwards to avoid putting these children on the Child Protection Register and had delayed too long, leaving at least three of the children with serious psychological disturbance as a result."

In 1993, the Official Solicitor, acting as the children's next friend, brought suit against the local authority claiming damages for negligence and/or breach of statutory duty. The Official Solicitor argued that the authority had failed to have regard for the children's welfare as was required by statute and should have acted more quickly and more effectively when apprised of their condition. The local authority admitted that it could foresee damage to the plaintiffs from negligent performance of its statutory duties and that the relationship between the authority and the plaintiffs was sufficiently proximate.

The trial court rejected the plaintiffs' claims, and the Court of Appeal and House of Lords affirmed. In essence, the courts held that there was no duty that gave rise to an action for monetary damages absent exceptionally clear statutory language. The decisions were based upon considerations of public policy. The courts felt that a common law negligence action would upset the statutory system that emphasized cooperation among different government agencies; it would also subject the local authority to liability in an area where the decisions were "extraordinarily delicate," and perhaps, non-justiciable.

The case was then brought to Strasbourg. In contrast to the outcome in *Osman*, the European Court held there was no violation of article 6 of the Convention. Article 6 did not itself guarantee any particular content for civil rights and obligations in national law. The Court acknowledged that the "no duty" ruling by the House of Lords was well-litigated and that the applicants had access to the courts. Moreover, it noted that the decision was not a broad immunity for all aspects of the local authority's work, but concerned only one aspect of the exercise of local authorities' powers and duties. Then the court stated:

> The applicants, and the Commission in its report, relied on the *Osman* case as indicating that the exclusion of liability in negligence, in that case concerning the acts or omissions of the police in the investigation and prevention of crime, acted as a restriction on access to court. The Court considers that its reasoning in the *Osman* judgment was based on an understanding of the law of negligence which has to be reviewed in the light of the clarifications subsequently made by the domestic courts and notably the House of Lords. The Court is satisfied that the law of negligence as developed in the domestic courts...includes the fair, just and reasonable criterion as an intrinsic element of the duty of care and that the ruling of law concerning that element in this case does not disclose the operation of an immunity. In the present case, the Court is led to the conclusion that the inability of the applicants to sue the local authority flowed not from an immunity but from the applicable principles governing the substantive right of action in domestic law....

> The applicants may not therefore claim that they were deprived of any right to a determination on the merits of their negligence claims....

> It is nonetheless the case that the interpretation of domestic law by the House of Lords resulted in the applicants' case being struck out. The tort of negligence was held not to impose a duty of care on the local authority in the exercise of its statutory powers. Their experiences were described as "horrific" by a psychiatrist and the Court has found that they were victims of a violation of Article 3. Yet the outcome of the domestic proceedings they brought is that they, and any children with complaints such as theirs, cannot sue the local authority in negligence for compensation, however foreseeable—and severe—the harm suffered and however unreasonable the conduct of the local authority in failing to take steps to prevent that harm. The applicants are correct in their assertions that the gap they have identified in domestic law is one that gives rise to an issue under the Convention, but in the Court's view it is an issue under Article 13, not Article 6(1).

Article 13 addresses the right to an "effective" remedy. The Court held that where "fundamental" rights are involved, like the right to life (art. 2) or the prohibition against torture, inhuman and degrading treatment (art. 3), then there must be mechanisms for compensation, where appropriate, and "a thorough and effective investigation capable of leading to the identification and punishment of those responsible" when those responsible are part of the police or security forces. *Id.* ¶ 109. However, where the allegation is the failure of authorities to protect persons from the acts of others, article 13 "may not always require that the authorities undertake the responsibility for investigating the allegations." Here the U.K. government admitted that its existing remedies were inadequate. For example, the Criminal Injuries Compensation Board did not permit compensation for neglect short of criminal acts, and the local Government Ombudsman could not make legally binding recommendations. The Court, therefore, found a violation of article 13. *Id.* ¶ 113. The court held that no separate issue arose under article 8 of the Convention. The portion of the judgment related to article 3 is reproduced here.

Z and Others v. United Kingdom

34 Eur. H.R. Rep. 3 (2002)

The Court reiterates that Article 3 enshrines one of the most fundamental values of democratic society. It prohibits in absolute terms torture or inhuman or degrading treatment or punishment. The obligation on High Contracting Parties under Article 1 of the Convention to secure to everyone within their jurisdiction the rights and freedoms defined in the Convention, taken together with Article 3, requires States to take measures designed to ensure that individuals within their jurisdiction are not subjected to torture or inhuman or degrading treatment, including such ill-treatment administered by private individuals. These measures should provide effective protection, in particular, of children and other vulnerable persons and include reasonable steps to prevent ill-treatment of which the authorities had or ought to have had knowledge.

There is no dispute in the present case that the neglect and abuse suffered by the four child applicants reached the threshold of inhuman and degrading treatment. This treatment was brought to the local authority's attention, at the earliest in October 1987. It was under a statutory duty to protect the children and had a range of powers available to them, including removal from their home. The children were however only taken into emergency care, at the insistence of the mother, on 30 April 1992. Over the intervening period of four and a half years, they had been subject in their home to what the child consultant psychiatrist who examined them referred to as horrific experiences. The Criminal Injuries Compensation Board had also found that the children had been subject to appalling neglect over an extended period and suffered physical and psychological injury directly attributable to a crime of violence. The Court acknowledges the difficult and sensitive decisions facing social services and the important countervailing principle of respecting and preserving family life. The present case however leaves no doubt as to the failure of the system to protect these child applicants from serious, long-term neglect and abuse.

Accordingly, there has been a violation of Article 3 of the Convention....

Notes and Questions

1. *Comparison.* Try to describe when a State Party would be responsible for a violation of the European Convention on Human Rights for violence perpetrated by a private individual against another private individual. Do these affirmative state obligations to help end private violence go further than the obligations under the Belém do Pará? Do they go further than the obligations imposed, if any, by the law in the United States? Is there any international law which imposes affirmative obligations on the United States to address domestic violence?

2. *Comparative Insight.* What benefit is studying the OAS or ECHR jurisprudence on this issue? Can this jurisprudence make a difference to litigation in this country? How?

3. *Domestic Violence. X and Y v. The Netherlands, Osman v. United Kingdom,* and *Z and Others v. United Kingdom* did not involve adult male-on-female intimate violence. Do you think that it would have made a difference to the legal analysis if the cases had involved domestic violence?

4. *Exhaustion of Domestic Remedies.* Domestic legal remedies can be relevant in two different, but related ways, to a complaint filed under the regional human rights agreements. On the one hand, failure to have an "effective" remedy for a convention breach may itself constitute a breach of a convention. *See Z and Others v. United Kingdom, supra* (citing ECHR, art. 13). Similarly, the American Convention on Human Rights contains article 25, the Right to Judicial Protection. The Convention of Belém do Pará, article 4(g), gives women the right "to simple and prompt recourse to a competent jurisdiction for protection against acts that violate her rights," and article 7(f) requires states to "establish fair and effective legal procedures for women who have been subjected to violence which include, among others, protective measures."

On the other hand, various international instruments require that parties first exhaust domestic remedies in order to have standing to allege human rights violations before the international tribunal. This is true explicitly under the American Convention, *see* art. 46, and implicitly under the Belém do Pará. *See* art. 12. It is also true under the ECHR. *See* art. 35.

Consider the situation in *Velasquez Rodriguez,* 28 I.L.M. 294 (Inter-Am. Ct. H.R. 1989). The petition against the State of Honduras alleged violations of article 4 (right to life), 5 (right to humane treatment) and 7 (right to personal liberty) of the American Convention. The petition alleged that Manfredo Velasquez was detained and taken to police cells where he was "accused of alleged political crimes and subjected to harsh interrogation and cruel torture" by the National Office of Investigation and the armed forces. He was later moved to an army location, where the interrogation continued, and he then disappeared. The police and security forces denied that he had been detained. When suit was brought before the Inter-American Court of Human Rights, the Government argued "domestic remedies had not been exhausted, that the National Office of Investigations had no knowledge of the whereabouts of Manfredo Velasquez, that the Government was making every effort to find him...." *Id.* ¶ 5. The Government also provided information that the First Criminal Court dismissed the complaints against those persons supposedly responsible for the disappearance of Manfredo Velasquez.

The Court emphasized that the obligation in article 46 to exhaust domestic remedies referred to "adequate" domestic remedies, *i.e.*, remedies that were "suitable" and "effective." *Id.* ¶¶ 64, 66. In the *Velasquez Rodriguez* case, the court concluded that although there may have been legal remedies in Honduras that theoretically allowed a person detained by the authorities to be found, those remedies were ineffective in cases of disappearances. Among other things, formal requirements made the remedy inapplicable in practice; the authorities against whom remedies were brought simply ignored them; and attorneys and judges were threatened and intimidated by authorities. Therefore, the remedies "were ineffective or were mere formalities." *Id.* ¶¶ 80, 81.

The Inter-American Commission of Human Rights has rules of procedure which set forth the exhaustion requirement. It explicitly states that the exhaustion requirement does not apply in the following cases:

a. the domestic legislation of the State concerned does not afford due process of law for protection of the right or rights that have allegedly been violated;

b. the party alleging violation of his or her rights has been denied access to the remedies under domestic law or has been prevented from exhausting them; or,

c. there has been unwarranted delay in rendering a final judgment under the aforementioned remedies.

Rules of Procedure of the Inter-American Commission of Human Rights, in effect as of 1 May 2001, art. 31, *at* http://www.cohre.org/downloads/americas.pdf.

If a state failed to protect a woman against domestic violence and the failure was endemic, what sort of evidence would satisfy the requirement that she had exhausted domestic remedies before bringing her case before the Inter-American Commission on Human Rights? Would it be enough that the police had not protected her? Would it be relevant to the exhaustion question that the state had no civil remedies available to remedy such private violence? Would she have to establish that the legislative bodies refused to adopt laws addressing domestic violence?

Problem 6-2

Barbara Amat has been battered by her husband frequently since they married five years ago. On three occasions in the past when Barbara was particularly frightened, Barbara called the police. Each time, the police came to her house and took her husband on a walk around the block to "cool off." Each time, the officers left their cards and said that if Barbara's husband acted up again, she should call them. On two of the occasions after the police left, Barbara's husband escalated his abuse "because she called the police."

On this particular occasion, Barbara's husband came home and told her "today you are going to get it." Her husband had a large wooden baton in the back pocket of his pants. Barbara called the police and asked to speak with the officer whose name appeared on the last card given to her. She spoke with him briefly, told him of the situation, and then hung up the phone quickly when she heard her husband coming down the hall. The police never responded to her call, and Barbara's husband beat her so severely that evening that Barbara will spend the rest of her life hospitalized. Barbara's husband was arrested, but he was allowed to plead guilty to a simple assault. He paid a fine of $200.

Barbara brought a negligence suit against the police, but the court recently threw out the suit because, as a matter of public policy, the police did not owe her a duty. Have Barbara's human rights been denied if the country in which she lives is a party to all the human rights treaties in the OAS system? Would she have a claim if the country in which she lives is a party to the European Convention on Human Rights? How about under CAT or the other human rights treaties? How should she proceed at this point?

Part Two

Rights and Responsibilities of Parents, Children, and the State

Chapter 7

Custody:
A Comparative Prologue

In this second portion of the book we shift our attention from relationships between adult partners to the relationships between children and their parents and other caretakers. At one time orbiting on the periphery of a legal universe dominated by the marital relationship, the needs and rights of children now increasingly command center stage in the arenas of both domestic and international family law. In this Part we examine custody, the support of children, and adoption, from both comparative and transnational perspectives. We then turn to the state's role in regulating reproductive decision-making. Our final chapter explores children's rights from a broader perspective, focusing on the rights of children vis-à-vis their family members and the state.

We begin with "custody," a term we use because of its familiarity to most law students, but which is rapidly being supplanted in the English-speaking world with terms like "parental responsibility," "residence" or "parenting" orders, "contact," and "access," which better reflect the notions of parental obligations and opportunities, rather than possessory interests. Because the international regulation of abduction, jurisdiction, and choice of law is of utmost importance to the practice of transnational family law, a substantial portion of the materials devoted to custody in this book are found in Chapter Eight, which explores those topics in the context of custody proceedings in great depth. Many of the cases in Chapter Eight were selected because they also provide significant insight into the internal custody law of the nations involved in these disputes. Indeed, when practicing in the field of transnational custody litigation, it is critical to consider the substantive differences in custody law that often fuel the initial dispute between the litigants and at times motivate removal of the child. Moreover, substantive and procedural differences in the domestic custody law of the nations involved sometimes influence a court's decision to apply an international convention or domestic jurisdictional rule in a fashion that will achieve a particular result in an international dispute. Because comparative analysis thus extends into the next chapter, this chapter provides only a brief introduction to the topic of comparative custody regulation.

Virtually all nations are now guided by the precept that the primary consideration underlying any custody decision must be the best interests of a child. In fact, they have committed to this principle through Article 3 of the Convention on the Rights of the Child, Nov. 20, 1989, 1577 U.N.T.S. 3, which all but a few nations in the world have ratified. Nevertheless, societal beliefs about the custodial arrangements that best serve children's interests vary markedly across geography, economic systems, religions, and cultures. Section A will briefly explore the allocation of responsibility for decisionmaking. Section B will then turn to consider which factors should affect custodial decisions, and the extent to which international law regulates their use.

A. Decision-Makers and Participants

In the United States, the concept that a state court must establish by decree the rights and responsibilities of each parent for the care of a child following dissolution of a marriage is so ingrained in our legal system that few students question it. Nevertheless, the automatic allocation of that authority to a governmental entity is by no means universal.

In England, for example, a nation with a legal system quite similar to our own, courts are not required to issue custody orders automatically upon divorce. This approach is referred to as the Non-intervention Principle, and is codified in the first section of the Children's Act of 1989, c. 41 § 1(5), which provides:

> Where a court is considering whether or not to make one or more orders under this Act with respect to a child, it shall not make the order or any of the orders unless it considers that doing so would be better for the child than making no order at all.

The provision was inspired in part by a 1988 report of the Law Commission, which observed that courts and solicitors had become accustomed to making custody orders upon separation and divorce, a practice that is not required, and when a divorce is amicable and the parties have worked out an agreement, may not be necessary. The Law Commission observed that when a child has a good relationship with both parents, "the law should seek to disturb this as little as possible. There is always a risk that orders allocating custody and access... will have the effect of polarizing the parents' roles and perhaps alienating the child from one or the other...."

Even when the decisionmakers are not the parents, of course, not all legal systems confer the authority to decide a child's fate upon a secular court system, at least not in the first instance. In many Islamic countries, custody disputes are decided by a Shari'a court, a religious court. Under the customary law in many African societies, the family members of the two spouses, rather than a public court system, typically decide whether a child belongs to a particular family and with whom a child should reside after a separation of the parents. *See* Alice Armstrong, *A Child Belongs to Everyone: Law, Family and the Construction of the 'Best Interests of the Child' in Zimbabwe*, UNICEF International Child Development Center, Innocenti Occasional Papers (CRS 11) 4–5 (1995).

Traditionally, in the United States and many other nations around the world, a child had little voice in the resolution of a dispute regarding his or her residence, care, and access to each parent. In recent decades many international conventions have recognized the right of the child to participate in such proceedings. Article 12 of the Convention on the Rights of the Child provides that a child who is capable of forming his or her own views must be provided the opportunity to express those views in any judicial or administrative proceeding affecting the child, and the child's views must be afforded "due weight in accordance with the age and maturity of the child." The United States is one of only a handful of nations that have not ratified this Convention, a topic that will be explored further in Chapter Fourteen. The 1996 Hague Convention on Jurisdiction, Applicable Law, Recognition, Enforcement and Co-operation in Respect of Parental Responsibility and Measures for the Protection of Children, 35 I.L.M. 1391, and European Union regulations concerning the recognition and enforcement of custody decisions, both permit member nations to refuse recognition and enforcement to custody orders of other member nations, if those judgments were rendered without the child having been given an opportunity to be heard. (See Chapter Eight, Section B.2.b.ii, addressing the 1996 Hague Convention, and c.ii. a., regarding Council Regulation No. 1347/2000 of the European Union, for further discussion of these instruments.)

B. Determining "Best Interests" — Permissible Factors and Considerations

Reaching international consensus regarding the notion that decisions affecting children's lives should be guided by the "best interests of the child" is no small accomplishment, given that throughout much of history, children have been viewed as economic assets (or liabilities). Nevertheless, "best interests" is a malleable concept, shaped by culture, economic circumstances, and religious norms. The question of which factors may justifiably be considered in determining a child's best interests in a custody dispute is one that continues to plague decisionmakers. This Section examines just a few of the factors upon which decisionmakers have frequently relied to determine a child's welfare. Though you have undoubtedly considered each of these in your courses on domestic family law, the following materials provide the opportunity to examine their application within the context of other cultures and international instruments.

1. Gender

Until very recently, gender was the primary determinant of custodial rights in Anglo-American law. Under English common law, the father was the sole legal guardian of his legitimate child, and had an absolute right to custody until the child was 21. He could be divested of custody only if he was found guilty of grave misconduct. Even after his death, a father could deprive the mother of custody by appointing a testamentary guardian for his child. As recently as the early nineteenth century, even a voluntary relinquishment of parental rights by a father in a separation agreement was held void if it provided that the mother would possess the children to his exclusion, or deprived him of power over the children. Although by the end of the nineteenth century, a maternal preference had become the judicial norm, it was not until 1925 that the "best interests" standard was codified in England. *See, e.g.,* Danaya Wright, *De Manneville v. De Manneville: Rethinking the Birth of Custody Law Under Patriarchy,* 17 Law & Hist. 247, 249 (1999); Connor Power, *The Domicile of Children: Towards a New Basis,* 2 Irish J. Fam. L. 21 (2000).

Gender has dominated U.S. custody law throughout most of its history as well. In colonial America, the father was legally entitled to determine custody for his children at divorce, although divorce was rare, and even at his death. Historians note that children are rarely mentioned in American divorce decrees from the eighteenth century, however, and are unsure as to whether this was because there was no dispute, or because the law vesting custody rights with the father was so clear that the issue was not raised. As in England, a maternal preference gradually developed in U.S. state courts throughout the nineteenth century, although as late as the early twentieth century some judges still relied upon the common law rule that the father was entitled to custody unless unfit.

See June Carbone, *Child Custody and the Best Interests of Children—A Review of* From Father's Property to Children's Rights: A History of Child Custody in the United States, *by Mary Ann Mason,* 29 Fam. L.Q. 721, 722, 727–28 (1995). Under the "tender years" presumption, later codified in many states, young children were awarded to their mother, although older children, particularly older boys, were often placed with their father. The fact that in most states the preference could be overcome by a showing that the preferred custody placement was not in the child's best interests is credited in the United States, as well as in England, with paving the way for the modern best interests doctrine. During the 1970s, as the U.S. Supreme Court was striking down gender categorizations in other fields, state courts and legislatures eliminated the tender years presumption. In most states it was replaced by individualized case-by-case assessment under a broad "best interests" standard, although a few states adopted a primary caretaker presumption. More recently, presumptions favoring joint custody are increasingly being embraced by U.S. state legislatures.

Current Maternal and Paternal Preferences

Gender still plays an important role in the custody systems of many other regions of the world. Some nations utilize a maternal presumption. Malaysia's statutes, for example, declare the welfare of the child to be the paramount consideration, generally affording neither the father nor mother a superior right of custody, but *also* codify a tender years presumption favoring placement of a child under seven years of age with the mother. *See* L. v. S., 691 M.L.J.U. 1 (High Court, Sibu 2001), *available at* 2001 MLJU Lexis 696 (awarding custody of a two-year-old to his mother, applying the presumption); Rajoo v. Ravindran, 123 M.L.J.U. 1 (High Court, Melaka 2001), *available at* 2001 MLJU Lexis 379 (awarding custody of an infant boy to the mother). The Hindu Minority and Guardianship Act 1956, applied in India to all cases in which the personal law of the parties is Hindu, also provides that custody of a child "who has not completed the age of five years" shall ordinarily be with the mother. Savitri Goonesekere, *The Best Interests of the Child: A South Asian Perspective,* 8 Int'l J. L. & Fam. 117, 125–26 (1994). Courts applying this maternal presumption suggest that they perceive the infant's best interests to be served by remaining with the mother during this period of nurture. *Id.* at 126–27.

Ater attaining independence, India, Pakistan, and Bangladesh all retained the British Guardianship and Wards Act 1890, which requires that custody be awarded according to the welfare of the child, but also establishes a superior right of the father to be guardian unless he is unfit. Though guardianship and custody are not always equivalent, many Indian court decisions implement this provision by holding that the father is the preferred guardian and custodian, reflecting the belief that a paternal right to custody serves the child's interests. *Id.* at 126.

Islamic Law

Although the details vary within the various Islamic schools and Arab nations, in general Islamic law has established gendered rules favoring each parent, depending upon the age of the child. The responsibility for the child is categorized as three types of guardianship: (1) *hadhana* or *hidhana* in Arabic, the guardianship of upbringing, or custody, which is the care the child requires during the early years of life (sometimes referred to as the age of dependence), when the child is perceived to need a woman's care; (2) *wilayat at-tabiyya,* the guardianship of education, or spiritual guardianship, which is the duty of men, and is performed by the child's father or a full blooded male relative of the father; and (3) *al wilayatu alal maal,* which is the guardianship of the child's property, if the child has property, and is fulfilled by the father. Jamal J. Nasir, *The Status of Women Under Islamic Law and Under Modern Islamic Legislation* 121–22 (1990); U.S. State Dep't, *International Child Abduction: Islamic Family Law*, at http://www.travel.state.gov/islamic_family_law.html.

The mother, even if she is separated or divorced from her husband, has the right to custody of the child (the guardianship of upbringing), which lasts during the period of dependence. The mother can lose her right to custody, however, for various reasons, one of which is remarrying anyone other than certain close relatives. The law of many Islamic countries also prohibits the mother from moving any substantial distance without the father's permission. The Hanafi school of Islam also restricts the father's travel with the child, during the mother's period of custody. Nasir, *supra*, at 122–29.

The duration of the mother's period of custody varies significantly among the Islamic schools, and also under the legislation of various Islamic nations. Generally, the mother's period of custody of boys ends between the ages of 7 and 10, although one school ends the period for boys when they are weaned, and another extends it until the boy reaches puberty. The mother's period of custody of daughters varies more significantly, generally ending at various ages between 7 and 12, but under some schools of Islam the daughter remains with the mother until she is married. When the mother's period of custody ends, several schools of Islam and the legislation of some Arab nations permit the child to choose with which parent the child wishes to live, or to spend nights with the mother and daytime with the father, to pursue an education. *Id.* at 133–36. During the mother's period of custody, she may not prevent the father from seeing the child. Similarly, the father "to whom the child has been handed" must permit the mother to see the child on a regular basis. *Id.* at 152–53.

African Customary Law

All African nations, with the exception of Somalia, have ratified the Convention on the Rights of the Child. In addition, the African Charter on the Rights and Welfare of the Child, July 1, 1990, OAU Doc. CAB/LEG/24.9149, drafted under the auspices of the Organization of African Unity, provides in Article 4 that the best interests of the child shall be the primary consideration in all actions concerning the child. Article 1(3) of the Charter further declares that "any customs, tradition, cultural or religious practice that is inconsistent with the rights, duties, and obligations contained in the Charter" are null and void. This Charter has been ratified by over twenty African nations, and has been signed by most of those nations that have not yet ratified it. *See* African Charter on the Rights and Welfare of the Child—Ratification Information, University of Minnesota Human Rights Library, *at* http://www1.umn.edu/humanrts/instree/afchildratifications. html. Moreover, many, if not most, African nations have now incorporated a "best interests" standard for custody into their legislation, or standards created by common law. *See* B. Rwezaura, *The Concept of the Child's Best Interests in the Changing Economic and Social Context of Sub-Saharan Africa*, 8 Int'l J.L. & Fam. 82, 105 (1994).

In many African nations, however, the construction given to the "best interests of the child" varies depending upon whether custody is being decided by a court or by the families of the spouses, who still make the majority of the actual custody decisions. One study of custody awards in Zimbabwe, undertaken in the mid-1990s, revealed that the Community Courts generally determined "best interests" by applying the case law of the higher Zimbabwe courts as well as South African judicial opinions. The precedents applied were heavily influenced by Dutch law, and incorporated a tender years presumption favoring an award to the biological mother. In addition, the courts, applying

Western legal notions, considered it in the child's best interests to live with a biological parent, and would award custody to a relative only under exceptional circumstances. The extended families, by contrast, apply customary law, which recognizes the right of the father's family to the child in most circumstances. Although a very young child may remain with the mother for some period, the child can go to the father's family at any time. By tradition, even very young children are often separated from their mothers for a variety of reasons, and are often "mothered" by many women, each of whom they call "mother." Children frequently move among family members, and custody is viewed as a family rather than an individual matter. Armstrong, *supra*, at 19–22.

The concept that a child belongs to the father's family is common to many of the patrilineal societies in sub-Saharan Africa, and is further complicated by the complex rules that connect the status of children with the transfer of bridewealth (a topic that is covered in more detail in Chapter Two, Section B.1.). Originating in the kinship system of pre-colonial Africa, the exchange of "bridewealth," also variously called "lobolo," "bogadi," and a variety of other names, serves to reinforce social ties. The nature and amount of the bridewealth is generally set by agreement between the family of the husband and the family of the wife, and is often paid in installments. Because these customs arose in agrarian communities, the payment of bridewealth in some communities has traditionally been made in cattle, although today all or a portion is often paid in cash. The transfer of bridewealth from the family of the husband to the family of the wife not only validates the marriage, but is also regarded as transferring to the husband and his family the wife's procreative capacity. The husband and his family, by the payment of the bridewealth, become entitled to claim all children the wife bears. At the time of divorce or separation, therefore, the husband has the right under customary law in many African societies to claim custody of the children. In some tribes, if the bridewealth is refunded to the father after the divorce, he is then deprived of his custody rights. By the same token, if the father has not paid sufficient bridewealth, at the time crucial installments are due, the children belong to the wife's family. Rwezaura, *supra*, at 85–87. *See also*, E.K. Quansah, *Botswana, in* International Encyclopaedia of Laws: Family and Succession Law, Botswana—43, 57 (R. Blanpain & W. Pintens eds., 2002); Chuma Himonga, *Zambia, in* 4 International Encyclopaedia, *supra*, at Zambia—118.

Bridewealth entitles the husband not only to the children he has biologically fathered, but under some circumstances confers upon his family the right to all other children the wife bears. This concept is captured in the Zulu saying that "cattle beget children." *Id.* at 86. *See also* Raymond Verdier, *Customary Family Law, in* IV International Encyclopedia of Comparative Law 11–260 (Glendon ed., 1973). Thus, in some African societies children born after the death of the first husband are considered his children. Under another practice called "ghost marriages," bridewealth is paid on behalf of a dead relative so that children sired by another man, usually a relative of the decedent, become the children of the decedent under customary law. *Id.* at 87. One of the most interesting cases involving this principle, Morabu Chacha v. Marwa Wambura, Mwanza High Ct., Matr. Civ. App. No. 25 (1976), was reported by Prof. Rwezaura to have occurred in Tanzania:

> In this case a man aged about sixty years gave fifty-six head of cattle to marry a young woman aged about twenty years. Despite the woman's protests she was nonetheless compelled by her father to marry the chosen husband. Shortly after the wedding she 'escaped' to live with another man with whom she had eight children. Yet because the second 'husband' did not have the fifty-six cattle to refund to the first husband, his wife could not obtain a valid divorce under cus-

tomary law. The consequence was that all the children she had with her second husband were taken by the first husband, as they became available. *Id.* at 96.

According to the customs of the Igo of Nigeria, if a first wife was unable to bear children, she could pay bridewealth herself so that her husband could marry another wife, whose children would then belong to the first wife and her husband. Among the Kuria of Tanzania, a wife who was unable to conceive in her second marriage could ask her former husband to give her a son from the first marriage, in exchange for a payment of cattle by her new husband to the former husband for the child. *Id.* at 88–89.

It is important to understand the origins of these practices in the context of the societal systems in which they developed. Children were vitally important to the survival of these agrarian communities, as a source of labor and emotional support. Daughters became brides that would eventually generate cattle that could help their brothers pay for their own marriages. Children would sometimes be "given" to elderly grandparents who lived apart from their adult children, to provide company and assistance as they grew older. As Professor Rwezaura observes, the tribal economic systems depended on human labor, and the survival of the community thus "largely depended upon how efficient they were in reproducing themselves." *Id* at 92.

This customary system of assigning custody rights may thus be viewed by those within the system as serving the best interests of children, because of the economic system in which it operates. Fathers in these rural areas generally control the economic resources—land, animals, cash—and thus separating the children from the father may be injurious to both their short and long-termed interests. Women in many parts of rural Africa do not have independent land rights, and thus are dependent upon their husbands to provide them with land on which to grow food to feed themselves and their children. The possibility of child support is not a reality for many poor families, because the father has little cash with which to pay it. Moreover, when it has been ordered the amounts have typically been extremely low and not enforced. The reluctance that many mothers have exhibited to seek custody in court or otherwise try to challenge a father's customary claim to the custody of the children may also be motivated by the additional fear that to take a child, and particularly a son, away from the father or the father's family would diminish the son's chances of inheriting from the father's family, or obtaining a contribution from that family to pay his own bridewealth when he is ready to marry. Moreover, the mother may someday be dependent herself upon the ability of an adult son to provide her with land to grow food, and is thus hesitant to diminish his chances of acquiring land. *Id.* at 106–08. As the economic situation in Africa deteriorates, Professor Rwezaura suggests that the best interests of the child is likely to continue to be equated largely with the ability to satisfy the child's material needs.

2. Religion

In the United States, the extent to which a parent's religious practices may be considered in a custody proceeding is determined not only by the policy considerations that traditionally are incorporated in custody analysis, but also by the dual mandate imposed by the First Amendment of the Federal Constitution forbidding government from establishing a religion or prohibiting its free exercise. When applying the Establishment Clause of the First Amendment, laws that create a denominational preference withstand judicial scrutiny only if they are determined to be necessary to promote a compelling state interest, a standard that has rarely, if ever, been satisfied in this context. Laws that facially employ no denominational preference but in application favor or disfavor religion or provide incidental aid to a religious institution have recently been subjected by the U.S. Supreme Court to a "purpose and effects" test, requiring that the primary purpose of the law must be secular and that the primary effect neither advances nor inhibits religion. John E. Nowak & Ronald D. Rotunda, Constitutional Law 1311–14 (6th ed. 2000). *See* Agostini v. Felton, 521 U.S. 203 (1997). Recent U.S. Supreme Court decisions applying the Free Exercise Clause suggest that governmental action that is designed to punish or burden religious beliefs or practices undertaken for a religious purpose will also be subjected to strict scrutiny, and must be necessary to achieve a compelling state interest. Laws that are neutral on their face and of general applicability, however, will not be subjected to strict scrutiny even if they have the incidental effect of burdening a particular religious practice. Church of the Lukumi Babalu Aye, Inc. v. Hialeah, 508 U.S. 520 (1993); Employment Div., Dep't of Human Res. of Or. v. Smith, 494 U.S. 872 (1990).

Although both clauses may be relevant in a particular case and the lines of demarcation are not always distinct, the Free Exercise Clause has typically been used to analyze a court's reliance upon a parent's religious beliefs and practices as a basis for a negative decision in a custody dispute. The Establishment Clause, by contrast, might be implicated if a court confers a benefit on a parent in a custody dispute, as a result of the parent's religious beliefs or practices.

Although the U.S. Supreme Court has not addressed the limitations imposed by the First Amendment in the context of a custody action, many state courts have been confronted with the thorny issues that arise when one parent asserts that the religious beliefs and practices of the other present grounds to deny or limit custody. Some courts have held that religious practices may be considered in custody disputes only if the evidence indicates that the child was actually harmed by the religious practices. *See* Quiner v. Quiner, 59 Cal. Rptr. 503 (Ct. App. 1967). Others have found that the court may consider religious practices if there is a reasonable likelihood or substantial threat that they will cause a child harm. Pater v. Pater, 588 N.E.2d 794 (Ohio 1992); Zummo v. Zummo, 574 A.2d 1130 (Pa. Super. Ct. 1990). Surprisingly, the custody cases thus far have rarely referred to the standards adopted by the U.S. Supreme Court in other contexts, and there is little uniformity in the approach state courts take. *See, e.g.,* Jennifer Ann Drobac, Note, *For the Sake of the Children: Court Consideration of Religion in Child Custody Cases,* 50 Stanford. L. Rev. 1609 (1998); Carl Schneider, *Preservation of Minority Cultures: Religion and Child Custody,* 25 U. Mich. J.L. Reform 879 (1992).

The European Court of Human Rights has similarly considered whether the consideration of a parent's religious practices as a basis to deny her custody violates Article 8 of the European Convention on Human Rights. In the following action, does the Court develop any tests or principles that might enlighten our own analysis of these issues?

Hoffmann v. Austria
225 Eur. Ct. H.R. (ser. A) 45 (1993)

[Ed. Note: The applicant, Ms. Ingrid Hoffmann, is an Austrian housewife who was formerly married to Mr. S., a telephone technician. At the time of their marriage in

1980, both she and Mr. S. were Roman Catholic. Applicant and Mr. S had two children, Martin and Sandra, who were baptized Roman Catholic.

During the marriage, Ms. Hoffman became a Jehovah's witness. In 1983, when the children were ages three and one, she instituted divorce proceedings against Mr. S., and left the marital home approximately ten months later, while divorce proceedings were still pending, taking the children with her. Following the separation, both parents applied to the court for custody.

The father asserted that if the children were placed in the applicant's custody, the manner in which she brought them up would be harmful. He asserted that the educational principles of her denomination discouraged communication with non-members, expressions of patriotism, and religious tolerance. He alleged this would lead to the children's social isolation. In addition the religion's ban on blood transfusions might endanger their life or health. If the son were raised in the religion, the father noted that eventually he would have to refuse to perform military service or even the civilian service required in its place.

The applicant claimed that she was in a better position to care for the children because she could devote herself to them completely and as a mother was better able to provide them with a family environment. She alleged that Mr. S did not provide support for them, as he was legally required to do. She acknowledged her intention to bring up the children in her faith.

Based on the expert opinion of a child psychologist, the Innsbruck District Authority Youth Office recommended that parental rights be granted to the applicant. Stating that it was only considering the well-being of the children, the District Court so awarded parental rights to applicant in January 1986, finding that although both parents could take proper care of the children, the father would need the mother's help. The Court also found the children had stronger emotional ties to their mother, with whom they had then lived for a year and a half, and that the separation might cause them psychological harm. Regarding the father's religious arguments, the Court observed that a parent's religious convictions were not a relevant criteria, and cannot be a basis for withholding custody, although a court can examine whether a parent's religious convictions would negatively affect the well-being or upbringing of the children. The court noted that the mother would not allow blood transfusions, would not celebrate customary holidays, and that the children would experience a "certain tension in relation to an environment that does not correspond to their faith," and their integration into school would be made more difficult. However, the court found no dangers to the children's development had appeared from the evidence. If the children needed a blood transfusion, a court could order one, upon application by anyone. The mother had agreed to allow the father to take the children for holidays and celebrate them with him. The fact that they will find themselves in a religious minority was not so detrimental, in the opinion of the District Court, that it merited taking them from a parent with whom they had such a close psychological relationship.

The Regional Court rejected the father's appeal, noting that the Jehovah's Witnesses are not outlawed in Austria, and thus it must be assumed that their objectives neither infringe the law nor offend morality. The Court also suggested that if a child needed a blood transfusion and there was no time for a court order, it would be up to the treating physician to reach a decision, with a view to lifesaving first, before taking into account the views of the Jehovah's Witnesses. This court also observed that there was no evidence the children had been harmed by being in the mother's custody.

The Austrian Supreme Court, however, overturned the judgements of the Regional Count and the trial court, and granted parental rights to the father, on the basis of Austrian Statutes (the Federal Law of 1985 on the Religious Education of Children, which re-enacted the 1921 Act on the Religious Education of Children), which provide that a child's religious education shall be decided by agreement of the parents. If such an agreement is revoked, neither parent during the marriage may decide without the other's consent to bring a child up in a faith different than that shared by both parents at the time of their marriage, or from the religion in which the child has thus far been raised. Because these children were not Jehovah's Witnesses, the Supreme Court determined that the intermediate appellate court's failure to apply this law was error. The Supreme Court also found the lower courts did not give due consideration to the children's welfare, in that the delay caused by the necessity of seeking a court order for a transfusion could be dangerous, and their education as Jehovah's Witnesses would cause them to be social outcasts. The Supreme Court noted that although it was preferable for young children to be in the care of their mother, there was no maternal preference, and there was no evidence that the stress of transfer would cause serious psychological harm. Moreover, the paternal grandmother could care for the children, the Supreme Court found, while the father was at work.]

* * *

16. Numbering about four million worldwide not counting uninitiated sympathizers, the Jehovah's Witnesses form a particular religious movement. It originated in America in the 1870s....

17. A central feature of Jehovah's Witness doctrine is the belief that the Holy Scriptures in the original Hebrew and Greek are the revealed word of Jehovah God and must therefore be taken as literal truth.

The refusal to accept blood transfusions is based on several scriptural references....

* * *

I. Alleged Violation of Article 8..., Taken Alone and in Conjunction with Article 14...:

28. The applicant complained that the Austrian Supreme Court had awarded parental rights over the children Martin and Sandra to their father in preference to herself, because she was a member of the religious community of Jehovah's Witnesses....

29. According to Article 8..., "Everyone has the right to respect for his private and family life, his home and his correspondence."

The Court notes at the outset that the children had lived with the applicant for two years after she had left with them before the judgment of the Supreme Court...compelled the applicant to give them up to their father. The Supreme Court's decision therefore constitutes an interference with the applicant's right to respect for her family life and the case thus falls within the ambit of Article 8. The fact relied on by the Government in support of the opposite view, namely that the Supreme Court's decision was taken in the context of a dispute between private individuals, makes no difference in this respect.

* * *

30. ...Article 14 reads...:

The enjoyment of the rights and freedoms set forth in [the] Convention shall be secured without discrimination on any ground such as sex, race, colour, language, religion, political or other opinion, national or social origin, association with a national minority, property, birth or other status.

31. In the enjoyment of the rights and freedoms guaranteed by the Convention, Article 14 affords protection against different treatment, without an objective and reasonable justification, of persons in similar situations....

32. ...[Ed. Note: The Court reviewed the factors considered by the District and Regional Courts, as set forth above in the description of the facts, noting that these courts took account of the practical consequences of the religious convictions of the Jehovah's Witnesses.]

In assessing the interests of the children, the Supreme Court considered the possible effects on their social life of being associated with a particular religious minority and the hazards attaching to the applicant's total rejection of blood transfusions not only for herself but—in the absence of a court order—for her children as well; that is, possible negative effects of her membership of the religious community of Jehovah's Witnesses. It weighed them against the possibility that transferring the children to the care of their father might cause them psychological stress, which in its opinion had to be accepted in their own best interests.

33. This Court does not deny that, depending on the circumstances of the case, the factors relied on by the Austrian Supreme Court in support of its decision may in themselves be capable of tipping the scales in favour of one parent rather than the other. However, the Supreme Court also introduced a new element, namely the Federal Act on the Religious Education of Children.... This factor was clearly decisive for the Supreme Court.

The European Court therefore accepts that there has been a difference in treatment and that that difference was on the ground of religion; this conclusion is supported by the tone and phrasing of the Supreme Court's considerations regarding the practical consequences of the applicant's religion.

Such a difference in treatment is discriminatory in the absence of an "objective and reasonable justification," that is, if it is not justified by a "legitimate aim" and if there is no "reasonable relationship of proportionality between the means employed and the aim sought to be realised"....

34. The aim pursued by the judgment of the Supreme Court was a legitimate one, namely the protection of the health and rights of the children; it must now be examined whether the second requirement was also satisfied.

35. In the present context, reference may be made to Article 5 of Protocol. No. 7..., which entered into force for Austria on 1 November 1988; although it was not prayed in aid in the present proceedings, it provides for the fundamental equality of spouses inter alia as regards parental rights and makes it clear that in cases of this nature the interests of the children are paramount.

36. In so far as the Austrian Supreme Court did not rely solely on the Federal Act on the Religious Education of Children, it weighed the facts differently from the courts below, whose reasoning was moreover supported by psychological expert opinion. Notwithstanding any possible arguments to the contrary, a distinction based essentially on a difference in religion alone is not acceptable.

The Court therefore cannot find that a reasonable relationship of proportionality existed between the means employed and the aim pursued; there has accordingly been a violation of Article 8 taken in conjunction with Article 14.

* * *

[Ed. Note: In light of the above conclusions, the Court found it was unnecessary to rule on Applicant's alleged violation of Article 8, taken alone, and of Article 9. By five votes to four, the Court voted that there had been a violation of Article 8 in conjunction with Article 14, and by a vote of eight votes to one, awarded the applicant costs and expenses.]

Notes and Questions

1. *Implied Agreements.* Several decades before the European Court of Human Rights issued the above judgment, the Irish High Court was faced with a similar conflict, albeit not in the context of a divorce, a proceeding not available in the Republic of Ireland at the time. In the case of *In re* May, [1959] I.R. 74, Josephine May filed a proceeding requesting that the court make her five children wards of the court, so that the court could resolve a disagreement between Mrs. May and her husband regarding their children's religious upbringing and education. Mr. and Mrs. May were married in the Roman Catholic Church, and all five children were baptized Catholic. The three eldest children attended Catholic school. Two or three years prior to the proceeding, Mr. May converted to become a Jehovah's Witness. Thereafter, he attempted to teach the four eldest children about his religion and to place three of the children in a non-Catholic school, removing one of the children from the home for that purpose, prompting Ms. May to file the proceeding.

The Irish High Court found that parents have a joint power to determine the religious education of their children. If they make a joint decision, before or after marriage, and put it in practice, neither can unilaterally revoke the decision against the will of the other parent. When parties of the same religion marry, it is unlikely that they will have made an express agreement, because they would take for granted that they would raise the children in that religion. When parties marry according to the rights of their church, baptize their children, and teach them at home and at school about that faith, the parents are deemed to have impliedly agreed that their children should be brought up and educated in that religion, the court reasoned. Therefore, the court found that neither parent had the right to depart from this agreement in any way, and determined that as long as Mrs. May objected, Mr. May had no right to attempt to teach the children, or have them educated, other than according to the terms of their implied agreement.

Do you think that the Irish High Court in *May* could have reached that opinion after the European Court of Human Rights decision in *Hoffman*? Do you think a U.S. court could reach such a decision constitutionally? See Zummo v. Zummo, 574 A.2d 1130 (Pa. Super. Ct. 1990), for a case raising similar issues. From a policy perspective, do you agree with the decision?

2. *Religious Custody.* Post-divorce disagreements regarding religious upbringing arise even when physical custody is not in dispute. In *Re J*, 2 F.C.R. 342, 2 F.L.R. 678 (Eng. C.S., Fam. Div. 1999), a British trial judge first considered a Muslim father's request for an order that his son be raised Muslim and not be fed pork. The child was in the residential care of the mother by agreement and was five years of age at the time of the hearing. The parents had met in Turkey while the British mother was on holiday, and married there in both a religious and civil ceremony, before returning to England to live. The mother had agreed to convert to Islam before the marriage, but had thereafter failed to convert. The judge noted that the boy was considered Muslim under Islamic law, as the child of a Muslim parent. As a non-practicing Christian, the mother had

brought up the child during the three years since the parents' separation in an essentially secular household. The trial judge commented that the father also did not regularly attend the Mosque, actively practice the religion, or "mix in Muslim circles."

In denying the father's request for an order regarding religious upbringing, the judge observed that British law requiring a child to be raised in the father's religion had been abolished in 1925. Although issuance of an order to raise a child in a particular religion is within the court's authority if the order promotes the child's welfare, the court noted that such an order would be unusual if the religion was not one practiced by the residential parent. Invoking the non-intervention principle of Section 1(5) of the Children Act of 1989, set forth in Section A of this chapter, the judge ruled that in this case it would not be better for the child to make an order regarding religious upbringing, and that the father could instruct J regarding Islam during visitation. Though the judge suggested that the mother would be wise to respect the father's views regarding pork, he also declined to issue a specific order regarding such dietary restrictions. Is the trial court's approach in *Re J* consistent with that of the Irish High Court in *May*? Is it consistent with *Hoffman*?

A second, related issue before the court in *Re J* was the father's request for an order permitting the father to have the boy circumcised, in a hospital under general anesthetic, in order to fulfill his duty as a father within Islamic law and to confirm J's identity with his father and as a Muslim. The father asserted that his right to manifest his religion under Article 9 of the European Convention on Human Rights includes the right to arrange for his son's circumcision. Though agreeing with this assertion, the trial court determined that exercise of this right may be limited when it conflicts with the rights of the other parent or child, or is not in the child's best interests. Though neither this specific holding nor the court's refusal to issue an order regarding J's religious upbringing and dietary restrictions were the subject of appeal, the court's order regarding circumcision itself was appealed. The decision of the appellate court regarding circumcision, Re J, 1 F.L.R.571, 1 F.C.R.307 (Eng. C.A. 2000), 1999 WL 1142460, is set forth in Chapter Fourteen of this book, Section D.

3. *Scholarly Review.* For a comparative view of the treatment of religion by courts in England, Australia, New Zealand, Canada, and the United States, see Rex Ahdar, *Religion as a Factor in Custody and Access Disputes,* 10 Int'l J.L. Pol. & Fam. 177 (1996), in which the author observes that the courts of all five nations profess religious neutrality. Nevertheless, he concludes that in practice attention to the objective consequences of religious practices has often led the courts in these nations to view the restricted lifestyle dictated by certain sects as a negative factor, disadvantaging parents who belong to minority religions.

3. Race

The question of when, if ever, race may be considered in custody disputes is one that has not been completely resolved in U.S. courts. In Palmore v. Sidoti, 466 U.S. 429 (1984), the U.S. Supreme Court addressed the issue in the context of a post-decree modification proceeding in which a Florida judge had transferred custody of a four-year-old daughter to her father. The trial judge explicitly declared that the ground for his modification order was the Caucasian mother's relationship with, and subsequent marriage to, an African-American man, and the damaging impact on the child that he predicted would result from the social stigmatization associated with living in a mixed-race household. Upon review, the U.S. Supreme Court observed that racial classifications merited strict scrutiny under the Fourteenth Amendment to the U.S. Constitution, and therefore to be upheld such classifications must be necessary to achieve a compelling state interest. The Court agreed that awarding custody in the best interests of the child was indisputably a substantial state interest, and acknowledged that the child might be subject to a variety of pressures as a result of her mother's racially mixed marriage. Nevertheless, the Court concluded that the trial judge's order violated Equal Protection:

> The question...is whether the reality of private biases and the possible injury they might inflict are permissible considerations for removal of an infant child from the custody of its natural mother. We have little difficulty concluding that they are not. The Constitution cannot control such prejudices but neither can it tolerate them. Private biases may be outside the reach of the law, but the law cannot, directly or indirectly, give them effect. "Public officials sworn to uphold the Constitution may not avoid a constitutional duty by bowing to the hypothetical effects of private racial prejudice that they assume to be both widely and deeply held....

> ...[In a previous case] this Court invalidated a Kentucky law forbidding Negroes to buy homes in white neighborhoods. "It is urged that this proposed segregation will promote the public peace by preventing race conflicts. Desirable as this is, and important as is the preservation of the public peace, this aim cannot be accomplished by laws or ordinances which deny rights created or protected by the Federal Constitution."...

> Whatever problems racially mixed households may pose for children in 1984 can no more support a denial of constitutional rights than could the stresses that residential integration was thought to entail in 1917. The effects of racial prejudice, however real, cannot justify a racial classification removing an infant child from the custody of its natural mother found to be an appropriate person to have such custody. *Id.* at 433–34.

Since *Palmore*, there have been very few custody decisions in the United States which discuss race as a factor, in all likelihood because the malleable nature of custody law enables judges to avoid mention of this issue in the formal record of their findings and judgments (although the issue has surfaced in adoption proceedings).

Recently, the Canadian Supreme Court had the opportunity to consider the injection of race in a custody dispute between two parents, in the context of whether the racial identity of a parent should be a factor when awarding custody of a bi-racial child.

Van de Perre v. Edwards
[2001] 2 S.C.R. 1014

Bastarache, J.

1. The appellant is a single Caucasian Canadian citizen living in Vancouver. At the time of trial, she was 24 years of age. She did not finish high school and has a spotty work record. Her upbringing was not ideal due to her parents' divorce and her mother's history of illness and drug use. Presently, however, she has a good relationship with both her mother and her father. She was actively involved in the professional basketball scene in Vancouver; this is how she came to know the respondent, Mr. Edwards.

2. Mr. Edwards is an African American. At the time of trial, he was 34 years of age and living in Vancouver. He was a professional basketball player and, since 1989, was a member of numerous National Basketball Association (NBA) teams. At the time of trial and during his relationship with the appellant, Mr. Edwards was a member of the Vancouver Grizzlies NBA team and had been since 1995. Mr. Edwards has been married to the respondent Mrs. Edwards since 1991, one and a half years after the birth of their twin daughters in 1990. Although both had attended university, neither finished their university degrees. During his professional basketball career, Mr. Edwards has played for teams located in several North American cities. While the Edwards' home base is in North Carolina, the family is in the practice of moving with Mr. Edwards at the end of each trade. At the time of trial, the entire family was living in Richmond, British Columbia.

3. The appellant and the respondent Mr. Edwards met in the spring of 1996 and commenced a sexual relationship shortly thereafter. Their relationship lasted approximately 18 months. On June 3, 1997, Elijah Theodore Van de Perre was born. He is the son of the appellant and Mr. Edwards. Although disputed by the parties, it is clear from Mrs. Edwards' testimony that she learned of Mr. Edwards' extramarital affair with the appellant in December 1996 by accident, just as she did with at least two other affairs. Notwithstanding the circumstances, the respondents have remained married. Mrs. Edwards is a stay-at-home mother.

4. At the end of the 1996–1997 basketball season, the respondents returned to North Carolina. This was before the birth of Elijah; however, in September 1997, Mr. Edwards returned to Vancouver for the new basketball season and his relationship with the appellant continued. Mrs. Edwards and the twins had planned to stay in North Carolina, but after a telephone call with Mr. Edwards wherein she learned he had continued to have relations with the appellant, she decided to return to Vancouver.

5. When Elijah was 3 months old, the appellant commenced proceedings against Mr. Edwards for custody and child support. Mr. Edwards initially sought joint custody and liberal access, but later amended his pleadings to seek sole custody. The trial lasted 26 days, from October 1998 to January 1999. The trial judge's decision was released on February 25, 1999.... Warren J. awarded sole custody to the appellant. The order granted Mr. Edwards access to Elijah for four one-week periods quarterly during the calendar year. The order also entitled Mr. Edwards to share the Christmas holidays and Elijah's birthday and, when in Vancouver, to exercise access upon short notice and for periods of no more than 48 hours.

6. Mr. Edwards became a free agent in June 1998 and was then without a contract. After the trial, the family moved to Miami where Mr. Edwards obtained a one-year contract with the city's NBA team. Subsequently, Mr. Edwards signed to play basketball with the European league and moved to Athens, Greece. His wife and daughters returned to North Carolina.

7. Mr. Edwards appealed the trial decision. During the hearing, on the invitation of the Court of Appeal, Mrs. Edwards applied for admission as a party and requested joint custody with her husband. The application and joint request for custody were granted. The court did not state any access provisions except to say that the appellant was to receive generous access. The decision of the Court of Appeal...was stayed pending the appellant's application for leave to this Court.

8. The key issue here is the applicable standard of review to be followed by appellate courts in family law cases involving custody. In the present case, other issues include a determination of whether the Court of Appeal erred in finding that the trial judge erred

in his consideration, or lack thereof, of the child's mixed racial heritage, and whether the Court of Appeal erred in adding Mrs. Edwards as a party.

I. The Applicable Standard of Review for Appellate Courts in Custody Cases

9. The principal determination to be made in cases involving custody is the best interests of the child. In making this determination... the trial judge must consider numerous factors, in particular those stated in the pertinent legislation, which in this case is the *Family Relations Act*, R.S.B.C. 1996, c. 128 ("Act"). Section 24(1) of the Act states:

> 24 (1) When making, varying or rescinding an order under this Part, a court must give paramount consideration to the best interests of the child and, in assessing those interests, must consider the following factors and give emphasis to each factor according to the child's needs and circumstances:
>
> > (a) the health and emotional well being of the child including any special needs for care and treatment;
> >
> > (b) if appropriate, the views of the child;
> >
> > (c) the love, affection and similar ties that exist between the child and other persons;
> >
> > (d) education and training for the child;
> >
> > (e) the capacity of each person to whom guardianship, custody or access rights and duties may be granted to exercise those rights and duties adequately.

In addition to these factors, the Act authorizes the trial judge to consider the conduct of the parents, but only in so far as it impacts one of the aforementioned factors. Sections 24(3) and (4) state:

> (3) If the conduct of a person does not substantially affect a factor set out in subsection (1) or (2), the court must not consider that conduct in a proceeding respecting an order under this Part.
>
> (4) If under subsection (3) the conduct of a person may be considered by a court, the court must consider the conduct only to the extent that the conduct affects a factor set out in subsection (1) or (2).

10. In preparing reasons in custody cases, a trial judge is expected to consider each of these factors in light of the evidence adduced at trial; however, this is not to say that he or she is obligated to discuss every piece of evidence in detail, or at all, when explaining his or her reasons for awarding custody to one person over another. This would indeed be an unreasonable requirement at the end of a 26-day trial. Because of this, trial judges might sometimes appear to stress one factor over another and, in fact, it may be said that this is inevitable in custody cases which are heavily dependant on the particular factual circumstances at issue. This situation does not open the door to a redetermination of the facts by the Court of Appeal.

* * *

15. ... [T]he approach to appellate review requires an indication of a material error. If there is an indication that the trial judge did not consider relevant factors or evidence, this might indicate that he did not properly weigh all of the factors. In such a case, an appellate court may review the evidence proffered at trial to determine if the trial judge ignored or misdirected himself with respect to relevant evidence. This being said, I repeat that omissions in the reasons will not necessarily mean that the appellate court has

jurisdiction to review the evidence heard at trial.... [A]n omission is only a material error if it gives rise to the reasoned belief that the trial judge must have forgotten, ignored or misconceived the evidence in a way that affected his conclusion. Without this reasoned belief, the appellate court cannot reconsider the evidence.

16. In the present case, the Court of Appeal considered the decision of the trial judge and decided that it was within the scope of review to examine all the evidence and determine whether the trial judge weighed the evidence improperly. It is in reconsidering the evidence that the Court of Appeal determined that the trial judge had made material errors.... [T]his is not the proper method of appellate review. If the Court of Appeal had followed the appropriate method, it would not have reconsidered the evidence and found what it described as material errors in Warren J.'s decision. There was no scope for appellate intervention in this case. This can be illustrated by a review of the key difficulties that the Court of Appeal found in the trial decision. These difficulties can be divided into (i) concerns related to s. 24(1)(e) of the Act, (ii) the failure of the trial judge to consider the bonds that exist between Elijah and his paternal family (s. 24(1)(c)), (iii) an emphasis on the attitudes of the parties towards each other and Mr. Edwards' extra-marital affairs, and (iv) the concern that the trial judge based his decision on stereotypical views including the tender years doctrine.

* * *

C. An Emphasis on the Attitudes of the Parties Towards Each Other and Mr. Edwards' Extra-marital Affairs

23. ...[T]he Court of Appeal found that the trial judge made findings of credibility but was diverted by the arguments made concerning Mr. Edwards' extra-marital affairs and the parties' attitudes towards each other. The Court of Appeal remarked that the trial judge criticized Mrs. Edwards for blaming the appellant for the relationship with Mr. Edwards. It stated that the appellant was in part to blame but, in any event, this had nothing to do with the best interests of the child. I disagree with this conclusion. First, it is irrelevant who is to blame for the extra-marital affair. However, the parties' attitudes towards and views of each other are important. These attitudes might impact the emotional well-being of the child and, as such, must be considered pursuant to s. 24(1)(a) of the Act. A child should be with someone who fosters the relationship between him or her and the non-custodial parent. The trial judge's finding that the respondents both blame the appellant for the relationship and both believe that she is a "gold-digger" might be relevant in this respect. This discussion by the trial judge does not justify appellate intervention.

24. With respect to the discussion of Mr. Edwards' extra-marital affairs, the Court of Appeal found that Warren J. incorrectly considered the impact of these relationships on the marriage of the respondents. It held that a marriage breakdown was speculative and that the trial judge considered Mr. Edwards in isolation from his family. It found that this was a material error of law. Again, I disagree. Warren J. did not consider Mr. Edwards in isolation from his family. Rather, he considered both biological parents as individuals as well as in conjunction with their support network. This is consistent with ss. 24(1)(a), 24(1)(c) and 24(1)(e).

25. I agree with the Court of Appeal that a trial judge cannot consider a parent completely in isolation from his or her support network. Step-parents and siblings are important in a child's life.... These individuals play an important role in the child's emotional well-being...since they are a part of the family unit in which the child might end

up living. The negative and the positive traits and influences of step-parents must be considered. This being said, there is a distinction between taking a step-parent into consideration to determine the family unit in which the child would live if that biological parent were awarded custody and taking a step-parent into consideration to determine if his or her positive qualities are sufficient to override the negative qualities of his or her custody-seeking spouse. Section 24(1)(e) is clear and requires the trial judge to consider the ability of the person who can exercise custody to actually exercise the right and duties adequately. As will be discussed later in this case, this refers to Mr. Edwards and Ms. Van de Perre.

26. Section 24(1)(e) requires that the trial judge consider the merits of each applicant with regard to the whole context. In most families, the biological parent is not completely alone. He or she will have support networks to help him or her in times of need. In many cases, there is also an actual family unit that must be considered in determining if the parent applying for custody is capable of adequately parenting the child. In some cases, the family unit will assist the custodial parent; in others, it may hinder good parenting. Support networks and family units are, however, only two of many factors to be considered. Pursuant to the specific wording of s. 24(1)(e), the objective in every case is to determine the parenting abilities of the specific person who will ultimately receive custody.

27. In the present case, Mrs. Edwards and her daughters are important in determining the best interests of the child because of the bond that might exist between them and Elijah....

28. With respect to s. 24(1)(e), the trial judge considered the family unit when he discussed the stability of Mr. Edwards' marriage. He considered the factual circumstances brought out in evidence and possible problems that might arise. Pursuant to s. 24(3) of the Act, the conduct of a parent cannot generally be considered; however, if this conduct impacts a factor stated in s. 24(1), such as the emotional well-being of Elijah or the ability of Mr. Edwards to exercise custody with and without Mrs. Edwards, it is relevant. When considering the family unit, the trial judge found that Mr. Edwards has a weak and unstable marriage. As such, this might impact the parenting support he receives both during the marriage and following a possible marriage breakdown. The appellant, on the other hand, will likely have her parents' support and assistance until their death.

29. Warren J. was also obligated to consider whether Mr. Edward's conduct might impact his individual ability to exercise the duties and rights of custody. The trial judge and Court of Appeal both found that Mr. Edwards worked long periods of time away from home. He travelled extensively and Dr. Korpach stated that he was unlikely to terminate his work to care for his children. This said, it is important to add that many fathers and mothers work long hours; many are also required to travel extensively. Work commitments do not always have a negative effect on parenting. This is a circumstance which must be considered in light of all other relevant facts. In this particular case, Mr. Edwards not only has extremely long periods away from home, but it was also found by the trial judge that while at home, he is very active in the professional basketball social scene and has had several extra-marital affairs. This, combined with the findings that he leaves all the day-to-day childcare activities to his wife, and the evidence of Dr. Korpach, which indicates that he might not learn this role, raises doubt as to his ability to parent on his own.

30. A trial judge cannot give custody to a father merely because his wife is a good mother. Her presence is a factor but, overall, the court must consider if the applicant would make a good father in her absence. Even if the family were stable, this would not

be determinative in a s. 24(1)(e) analysis. Here, it is Mr. Edwards' personal capacity to exercise custody that must be considered, and the support provided by his wife is but a factor to be weighed in assessing these parental abilities.

31. As a final note, s. 24(1)(a) might also be affected by the extra-marital affairs. The trial judge found that the daughters of Mr. and Mrs. Edwards were very upset when Mr. Edwards' affair with the appellant was discovered. It is probable that Elijah would be affected in the same way if Mr. Edwards were to have another affair.

32. In this case, it may be said that Mr. Edwards' conduct impacts both ss. 24(1)(e) and 24(1)(a), and, as such, the trial judge was correct in considering his conduct. The Court of Appeal criticized Warren J. for not considering similar conduct of the appellant. It is clear from Warren J.'s reasons that he was aware of the appellant's social behaviour; yet, he did not discuss any impact that this might have on her ability to parent Elijah. Instead, he found that the appellant was a good mother. This finding is supported by the evidence of Dr. Korpach who stated that the appellant has acquired good parenting skills since learning of her pregnancy. It is unclear how her behaviour might affect her ability to exercise custody pursuant to s. 24(1)(e) either by negatively impacting the family unit or her individual ability. In addition, it is unclear how this behaviour might impact Elijah's emotional well-being. Without an impact on one of the factors in s. 24(1), her conduct is irrelevant and, pursuant to s. 24(3), should not be considered. Past or present conduct by a parent that does not, in the words of the Act, "substantially affect" the best interests of the child has no bearing on a custody determination and does not require comment.

33. Returning to the test for appellate intervention, there is no indication that Warren J. erred materially in considering the attitudes of the parties towards each other or in considering the extra-marital affairs of Mr. Edwards. He noted s. 24(3) which provides that conduct cannot be considered unless it impacts a factor listed in s. 24(1) and, although he did not explicitly refer to the factors in question, he did discuss this conduct with reference to Mr. Edwards' parenting abilities and Elijah's emotional well-being.

D. The Concern that the Trial Judge Based his Decision on Stereotypical Views Including the Tender Years Doctrine

34. The Court of Appeal stated that it was unclear whether the trial judge considered all the factors in s. 24(1) or whether he considered the "tender years" doctrine or had a stereotypical view of one or both parties. First, as noted above, the trial judge clearly stated and discussed all factors listed in s. 24(1). With respect to the tender years doctrine, the trial judge...specifically stated that stereotypical gender views have no place in custody determinations. Nowhere in his reasons does the trial judge mention this doctrine or state that it is important for the child to be with the mother during his early years. In other words, there is absolutely nothing to give any indication that the trial judge even considered the tender years doctrine....

II. The Importance of Race in the Custody Determination of a Child of Mixed Racial Heritage

36. The Court of Appeal found that the trial judge gave "no consideration" to issues of race and interracial problems that Elijah might face. In fact, the trial judge noted that there had been some testimony at trial related to the race of Elijah and the importance of being exposed to his heritage and culture as the son of an African-American father. Rather than discussing the child's race in detail, however, the trial judge noted

that this child is of mixed race and, as such, his Caucasian Canadian heritage must also be considered.

37. The interveners, the African Canadian Legal Clinic, the Association of Black Social Workers and the Jamaican Canadian Association, submit that race is a critical factor in custody and access cases. In my view, the importance of this factor will depend greatly on many factual considerations. The interveners state that there are key tools a Canadian biracial child will need in order to foster racial identity and pride: the need to develop a means to deal with racism and the need to develop a positive racial identity. The corollary to these needs is the parental ability to meet them. The interveners do not state that the minority parent should necessarily be granted custody; rather, the question is which parent will best be able to contribute to a healthy racial socialization and overall healthy development of the child. This question is one of fact to be determined by the courts on a case-by-case basis and weighed by the trial judge with other relevant factors.

38. The interveners submit that, although some studies show that Black parents are more likely to be aware of the need to prepare their children to cope with racism, the main issue is which parent will facilitate contact and the development of racial identity in a manner that avoids conflict, discord and disharmony. But again, this is only one factor to be considered by the trial judge. I would also add that evidence of race relations in the relevant communities may be important to define the context in which the child and his parents will function. It is not always possible to address these sensitive issues by judicial notice, even though some notice of racial facts can be taken; see *R. v. Williams*, [1998] 1 S.C.R.... The weight to be given to all relevant factors is a matter of discretion, but discretion must be exercised with regard to the evidence. In essence, the interveners argue that race is always a crucial factor and that it should never be ignored, even if not addressed by the parties. They favour forced judicial consideration of race because it is essential in deciding which parent is best able to cope with difficulties biracial children may face. This approach is based on the conclusions reached concerning the present state of race relations in Canada. As I have said, racial identity is but one factor that may be considered in determining personal identity; the relevancy of this factor depends on the context. Other factors are more directly related to primary needs and must be considered in priority.... All factors must be considered pragmatically. Different situations and different philosophies require an individual analysis on the basis of reliable evidence.

39. There is also a distinction between the role of race in adoption cases and those cases involving two biological parents desiring custody; see G. Pollack, "The Role of Race in Child Custody Decisions Between Natural Parents over Biracial Children" (1997), 23 *N.Y.U. Rev. L. & Soc. Change* 603, at p. 617. In adoption cases, the situation might arise whereby the court must make an either/or decision; in other words, the child is either granted or denied exposure to his or her own heritage. Here, however, we have two biological parents, each of whom shares a part of the race and culture of the child. Of these two biological parents, one will be granted custody and one will be granted access. The result here is that Elijah will have exposure to both sides of his racial and cultural heritage. There was no evidence introduced to suggest that greater exposure to one's racial background through custody as opposed to access is in the better interests of the child in every case. Consequently, cultural concerns are not the same as those involving prospective adoptive parents who do not share the same race and culture as the child. This said, I wish to note that the approach taken in this case is not new. In *H. (D.) v. M. (H.)*, [1997] B.C.J. No. 2144 (B.C. S.C.), (subsequently conf'd by [1999] 1 S.C.R. 328 (S.C.C.)), Bauman J. considered a case involving an adoption dis-

pute between two sets of grandparents: the mother's biological father and her adoptive parents. The mother of the child was aboriginal and the father was African American. The mother's adoptive parents were Caucasian and her biological father was aboriginal. In that case, counsel for the child's biological grandfather argued that the child's aboriginal heritage should be given great weight especially in light of the *Child, Family and Community Service Act*, R.S.B.C. 1996, c. 46, which notes the importance of cultural identity of aboriginal children in consideration of their well-being. Bauman J. stated... that the child's

> ... aboriginal heritage and the ability of his biological grandfather to preserve and enhance it are important considerations, but we must not overlook the obvious fact that Ishmael has an African-American background and American citizenship. That heritage is also of importance and it is equally deserving of preservation and nurturing. This is not a case of taking an aboriginal child and placing him with a non-aboriginal family in complete disregard for his culture and heritage....

> ... The submission that Ishmael's aboriginal heritage is virtually a determining factor here, oversimplifies a very complex case....

He next proceeded to consider all factors which impact the best interests of the child, including his aboriginal heritage and, having weighed all these factors, decided that the parenting and family environment of the mother's adoptive parents was superior and better served the child's best interests. This Court upheld this decision. It is therefore clear that, even in adoption cases where it might play a more important role, race is not a determinative factor and its importance will depend greatly on the facts.

40. Race can be a factor in determining the best interests of the child because it is connected to the culture, identity and emotional well-being of the child. New Brunswick, for example, has adopted legislation prescribing mandatory consideration of "cultural and religious heritage" for all custody determinations.... British Columbia has included similar language in its provisions regarding adoption, but not in those found in the *Family Relations Act* applicable in this case.... The adoption and custody contexts may differ because the adopted child will generally cease to have contact with the biological parent while custody will generally favour contact with both parents. Nevertheless, it is generally understood that biracial children should be encouraged to positively identify with both racial heritages. This suggests the possibility of a biracial identity (i.e. "forming an identity that incorporates multiple racial heritages"....). It is important that the custodial parent recognize the child's need of cultural identity and foster its development accordingly. I would therefore agree that evidence regarding the so-called "cultural dilemma" of biracial children (i.e. the conflict that arises from belonging to two races where one may be dominant for one reason or another) is relevant and should always be accepted. But the significance of evidence relating to race in any given custody case must be carefully considered by the trial judge. Although general public information is useful, it appears to be often contradictory (T. L. Perry, "The Transracial Adoption Controversy: An Analysis of Discourse and Subordination" (1993–94), 21 *N.Y.U. Rev. L. & Soc. Change* 33, at p. 59), and may not be sufficient to inform the judge about the current status of race relations in a particular community or the ability of either applicant to deal with these issues.

41. For the Court of Appeal to intervene, it would have to find a material error. Although Warren J. did not discuss in detail the role that race plays in determining the best interests of the child, he did state that there is an overarching need for the child to be in a stable and loving environment. The limited findings of the trial judge on this

issue reflected the minimal weight that the parties themselves placed on the issue at trial. Therefore, notwithstanding the role that race may play in custody determinations, it appears that the trial judge noted that this issue was not determinative and that, in this case, Elijah would be in a more stable and loving environment if custody was granted to the appellant. He clearly considered the mixed race of Elijah and implied that race may impact s. 24(1)(a) in some cases; however, the trial judge obviously was of the view that, even if the biological father provided some benefits as regards fostering a positive racial identity, these benefits did not outweigh the negative findings related to him. By intervening in the consideration of race by the trial judge, the Court of Appeal failed to apply the correct standard of review. It should not have intervened; this issue was given disproportionate emphasis at the initiative of the Court of Appeal.

42. In this case, there was absolutely no evidence adduced which indicates that race was an important consideration. As noted by the appellant in her factum, there was essentially no evidence of racial identity by reason of skin colour or of race relations in Vancouver or North Carolina; there was no evidence of the racial awareness of the applicants or of their attitudes concerning the needs of the child with regard to racial and cultural identity. The issues of race and ethnicity were not argued at trial, nor were written submissions provided in the appeal. The sole evidence relied upon by the respondents in this Court was a blanket statement by Mrs. Edwards that the appellant could not teach Elijah what it was to be Black and the testimony of Dr. Korpach that Elijah would likely be considered to be of Black colour. The Court of Appeal acknowledged this, at para. 48, where it stated:

> Perhaps because of the sensitivity of racial and cultural factors, counsel made very little reference to these matters, although Mrs. Edwards was asked in cross-examination whether she agreed that Elijah's "heritage" was a "complicating issue" between the two parents.

43. In fact, in this Court, counsel for the respondents stated that "neither of the parties wanted to touch it, because it's so *politically incorrect* to say that race has any bearing" (emphasis added). This is an unacceptable reason for counsel to fail to raise evidence on a factor that he or she believes may impact the best interests of the child. Without evidence, it is not possible for any court, and certainly not the Court of Appeal, to make a decision based on the importance of race. Unfortunately, this is what the Court of Appeal did when Newbury J.A. stated, . . . : "If it is correct that Elijah will be seen by the world at large as 'being black', it would obviously be in his interests to live with a parent or family who can nurture his identity. . . ." She further stated . . . :

> . . . it seems to me likely that being raised in an Afro-American family in a part of the world where the black population is proportionately greater than it is here, would to some extent be less difficult than it would be in Canada. Elijah would in this event have a greater chance of achieving a sense of cultural belonging and identity and would in his father have a strong role model who has succeeded in the world of professional sports.

III. The Addition of Mrs. Edwards as a Custodial Applicant at the Court of Appeal

44. The trial was conducted from October 1998 to January 1999. The *Family Relations Act* was amended to add ss. 24(1.1) and 35(1.1) on December 8, 1998. The respondent Mrs. Edwards did not apply to become a custodial parent at this time. The trial judge mentioned that Mrs. Edwards had no custody rights to Elijah and made his order accordingly.

45. During the Court of Appeal hearing, the Court of Appeal itself invited counsel to make a custody application on behalf of Mrs. Edwards. The Court of Appeal later found

that the trial judge had erred in stating that Mrs. Edwards had no custody rights. It found that the amended legislation allowed for her to request and be granted custody, and that procedural requirements were not an important impediment since Mrs. Edwards had been questioned at length at trial and the court had *parens patriae* jurisdiction to act in the best interests of the child.

46. When faced with a custody determination, the role of the Court of Appeal is to analyse the trial decision in its proper context. In other words, in making its decision, it must take notice of the persons who are the actual parties before the court. Mrs. Edwards did not apply for custody during the trial. As a result, it can hardly be said that Warren J. erred in not awarding joint custody to her and Mr. Edwards.

47. The Court of Appeal relied upon its *parens patriae* jurisdiction to award custody to a new party together with Mr. Edwards; in my view, adding a party on the initiative of the Court of Appeal is unfair to other parties and does not fall within the court's supervisory role. *Parens patriae* jurisdiction does not justify the avoidance of the rules of civil procedure.

48. For Mrs. Edwards to be added in accordance with Rule 15, the court must find that she "ought to have been joined" or "is necessary". I do not believe that it can be said that it was "necessary" that she become a party to the proceedings or that she "ought to have been joined" as a party. Rule 15(5)(a) is meant to cover situations where it is practically necessary for a person to be added as a party for the proper determination of the case; in a custody case, where the trial judge finds that both biological parents are suitable, even though they might not be perfect parents, it is not necessary for others to be added as parties, and the court should not try to find on its own a better party to whom custody should be granted. There is no indication that the trial judge in the case at bar erred in this regard, and there is therefore no reason for appellate intervention.

49. In this case, Mrs. Edwards, who was not a party, did not apply for custody at trial, and it was wrong for the Court of Appeal to initiate this process. The parties were Mr. Edwards and Ms. Van de Perre. In suggesting that Mrs. Edwards apply for custody, the Court of Appeal essentially added a party to a custody dispute on its own initiative. If Mrs. Edwards was to be considered, it would have to be by the trial judge, and a decision would have to be taken in light of all relevant evidence and pursuant to a satisfactory cross-examination on that basis. In the circumstances, since Mrs. Edwards was the cornerstone of her husband's case, she had little choice but to apply for custody after the intervention by the appellate court; otherwise, she would have risked irreparable damage to her husband's case. The Court of Appeal had no power to intervene in such a manner and, as a result, exceeded its jurisdiction.

50. It should also be noted that, even if the Court of Appeal had been correct in finding that the trial judge should have added Mrs. Edwards by reason of the court's *parens patriae* jurisdiction, it still exceeded its jurisdiction in finding that the trial judge would have awarded custody to Mr. and Mrs. Edwards jointly, had Warren J. not made this supposed error. Custody determinations are necessarily decisions of mixed law and fact. Even if it were possible in law to allow the pleadings to be amended and award custody to Mrs. Edwards jointly with her husband, this consideration is only the legal aspect of a custody decision; it does not deal with the findings of fact. The only statement made by the trial judge as to Mrs. Edwards' ability to parent Elijah was that if left to her alone, she would fulfill Elijah's best interests. The Court of Appeal inferred from this statement that if the trial judge believed he could grant custody to Mr. and Mrs. Edwards, he would have....

51. Although the trial judge thought very highly of Mrs. Edwards and her parenting ability, he *never* stated that he would prefer to grant custody to Mrs. Edwards *along with* Mr. Edwards. Rather, the trial judge said that Mrs. Edwards *alone* satisfies Elijah's best interests. The trial judge did not think highly of Mr. Edwards, nor did he think his unstable family unit was in the best interests of the child. The Court of Appeal erred in making this finding of fact, which is contrary to the actual findings of the trial judge. If it was open to the Court of Appeal to add Mrs. Edwards as a party, which it was not, this should have been returned to trial for a determination of the best interests of the child. Upon return to trial, evidence should have been adduced concerning the impact of such a decision.... [T]he Court of Appeal heard and allowed no argument on this issue. I also note in passing that a contest between biological parents and non-parents gives rise to special considerations which were not addressed here....

52. Given the above conclusions, the appeal is allowed. The judgment of the British Columbia Court of Appeal is set aside with costs throughout and the decision of Warren J. is restored.

Notes and Questions

1. *Comparing Standards.* Did the Canadian Supreme Court apply strict scrutiny to the consideration of race in the *Van Perre* case? If not, did the Canadian Supreme Court create a different standard or guidelines to discern when race may permissibly be considered in custody actions? Does the fact that, in *Van Perre*, the intent motivating consideration of race was ameliorative rather than discriminatory make a difference in the standard that should be applied to determine when race can permissibly be a factor?

2. *Custody Award to a Non-Parent.* The Supreme Court in *Van Perre* found the addition of Mrs. Edwards as a party, at the invitation of the appellate judge, violated the procedural rules for addition of parties. The Court also observes that "special considerations" would be involved in a contest between a parent and a nonparent.

In the United States, the joinder of a step-parent as a party in a contest between two parents would be unusual. Because a legal parent, biological or adoptive, has a fundamental right to a relationship with his or her child that merits enhanced protection under substantive due process, most U.S. states do not use the traditional "best interests" test in a custody dispute between a parent and a non-parent. Many states instead will award custody to a non-parent, over a parent's objection, only if the parent is unfit. Some states will award a non-parent custody if granting custody to the parent would be detrimental to the child, or utilize a presumption that awarding custody to the parent would be in the child's best interests.

The European Court of Human Rights has addressed this issue in many decisions as well. One such case is *Hokkanon v. Finland*, 299 Eur. Ct. H.R. (ser. A) (1994). Following the death of his wife, the father agreed that his one and a half year-old daughter's maternal grandparents could look after her while he dealt with various problems caused by his wife's death and the operation of his farm. He visited his daughter sporadically. Two years later, the grandparents refused to return the child to him. Custody proceedings were instituted, and the Finnish court eventually awarded custody to the father, which the grandparents appealed. Throughout the eight years of litigation, the court repeatedly made access orders so that the child could get to know her father before custody was transferred, and the grandparents repeatedly refused to comply. Although the court imposed small fines, governmental authorities never enforced compliance with the access orders. Despite his repeated attempts to enforce custody and access and engage the court's assistance over an eight-year period, the father was only able to see Sini on a few occasions at the grandparents' home when she was five or six. Ultimately, because the daughter did not know him, custody was transferred by the court back to the grandparents, and when Sini was twelve, the Finnish courts accepted psychological evidence that the child had the capacity to decide for herself, and determined that access would not be enforced against the child's wishes. The father then lodged a claim with the European Court of Human Rights, alleging that the government's failure to enforce its orders violated his right to family life under Article 8.

The European Court of Human Rights determined that the failure to use physical force in a delicate situation in which the interests of the child are the overriding consideration could not be regarded as required by the Convention. The Court observed that in cases in which a child has been taken into State custody in child protective proceedings, the parent has a right to have measures taken to reunite the parent with the child, and held that governments have this duty as well when the initial transfer is by private arrangement. The obligation of national authorities to facilitate a reunion is not absolute, however, since the reunion of a parent with a child who has lived for some time with a non-parent may require preparatory measures, and may not be able to take place immediately. The nature and extent of these preparations, the Court found, will vary with the circumstances of each case. Where contacts with the parent would appear to threaten the interests of the child, the government must strike a fair balance between them. National authorities must take all necessary steps, the Court held, to facilitate reunion, to the extent reasonable under the special circumstances of each case. Ultimately, the Court determined that the non-enforcement of the father's access rights violated his rights under Article 8, but the decision to take Sini's views into account and terminate access when she was twelve was upheld.

3. *Access.* The European Court of Human Rights on numerous occasions has recognized that "the mutual enjoyment by parent and child of each other's company constitutes a fundamental element of family life, even if the relationship between the parents has broken down, and domestic measures hindering such enjoyment amount to an interference with the right protected by Article 8 of the Convention." Elsholz v. Germany, 2000-VIII Eur. Ct. H.R. 345, 362. When visitation disputes arise between parents, Article 8 thus includes a right on the part of the parent to obtain assistance from governmental authorities with obtaining contact with the child. However, the Court has also recognized that this right is not absolute, and in some circumstances may require preparatory or phased measures. Glaser. v. United Kingdom, 33 E.H.R.R. 1 (2001). When a child opposes visitation, a fair balance must be struck between the child's interests and those of the parent, and in some circumstances the child's interests may override those of the parent. Thus, in *Elsholz* the Court found that when a five- or six-year-old child refused visitation, the failure of the domestic court to seek an independent psychological report, in combination with a failure to provide a further hearing before a higher court, constituted a breach of a father's rights under Article 8. By contrast, in *Hokkanon,* the Court found that the eventual decision of a court to terminate a contact order based on the expressed preference of the twelve-year-old daughter following expert assessment, did not constitute a violation of the Convention.

4. Sexual Conduct of Parents

In the United States, the prevailing attitude in a custody dispute towards the heterosexual conduct of parents is that such conduct is relevant only to the extent that it has directly affected the child. While formerly many courts denied custody, particularly to women, on the basis of a parent's adultery or non-marital sexual activities, on the theory that such a parent would be a poor influence on the child's moral development, that approach is rapidly disappearing.

Consider the treatment of the Canadian Supreme Court of the sexual conduct of each parent in the *Van Perrre* case above. What weight, if any, did the Court find it could be accorded in the custody determination?

Sexual preference and homosexual conduct, until recently, has also negatively impacted a parent's attempts to secure custody in the United States. Many state court judges have removed children from the custody of gay or lesbian parents, even when the alternative placement was with a non-parent, and have restricted visitation rights by forbidding the parent's partner to be present during visitation. Over the past decade, however, many state courts have revised their attitudes, and now find that a parent's sexual preference should not determine custody. These courts apply the same rule set forth above, considering sexual conduct, whatever its nature, only as it directly affects the child.

In 1999 the European Court of Human Rights addressed the consideration of sexual preference in custody disputes in the case of *Salguiero da Silva Mouta v. Portugal*, 1999-IX Eur. Ct. H.R. 309. Following separation from his wife, the father began living with a male partner. Although the parents initially agreed that the mother would have custody and the father would have access, the mother in fact placed the child with grandparents, and the father subsequently obtained custody three years later from the Lisbon Family Affairs Court. A year and a half after the child began living with her father, her mother abducted her and subsequently the Lisbon Court of Appeal awarded custody of the child, then eight years old, to the mother. In its decision, the appellate court stated that a child should live in a traditional Portuguese family environment, rather than in the shadow of an "abnormal situation," homosexuality. Although the father was awarded substantial access rights by the Court of Appeal, the mother failed to comply with them. In addition to pursuing enforcement remedies in the Portuguese courts, the father filed an application with the European Court of Human Rights, asserting that reliance upon his homosexuality as a ground to deny him custody violated his right to family life under Article 8, in conjunction with Article 14, which affords protection against discriminatory treatment.

In a unanimous decision the European Court of Human Rights held that making a distinction in a custody determination on the basis of a parent's homosexuality violated the father's rights under Articles 8 and 14 of the Convention. The father's homosexuality was clearly a decisive factor in the Court of Appeal's decision, the European Court determined. Although the protection of the health and rights of the child is a legitimate aim, the Court observed that there is no reasonable relationship of proportionality between consideration of a parent's sexual preference and achievement of that aim. Because discriminatory treatment under Article 14 is not permissible if there is no objective and reasonable justification, the Court found that making a distinction in a custody proceeding on the basis of sexual orientation is not acceptable under the Convention.

Problem 7-1

Rachel, a child with Downs Syndeome, was the fourteenth child of an orthodox Jewish rabbi and his wife. When she was an infant, she was repeatedly hospitalized for severe respiratory infections. At the age of seventeen months, she underwent surgery for insertion of a tracheotomy tube to facilitate her breathing. Rachel's parents felt that they could not deal with the constant supervision her tube would require, and asked the local governmental authorities to place her with foster parents when she was ready to be released from the hospital. Despite significant effort, the local authority was unable to find an orthodox Jewish family with whom to place Rachel, and they instead placed her with experienced foster parents, a non-practicing Roman Catholic family, for what was expected to be a short term placement.

After Rachel was placed in her foster parents' home, she slept in her foster parents' bedroom for the two years in which the tube was in place. The foster parents and an older daughter, B, shared the responsibility of keeping the tube clear of mucous and replacing it from time to time. When Rachel had been with the foster family for one year, her birth parents decided to place her for long-term foster care or adoption. With the help of a Jewish social services agency, concerted efforts were made over the next few years to find a Jewish family for the child. The only Jewish family found was rejected by the parents. In the meantime, Rachel remained with the foster family, who expressed the strong desire to continue to raise her, and to whom she was becoming very attached.

When Rachel was almost four, the foster parents instituted proceedings to become her guardians. The birth parents at that time sought her return. At the hearing, the judge came to the conclusion that Rachel had an exceptionally strong attachment to the foster parents. Experts testified that Rachel was likely to live to the age of 30 to 40, and to achieve the level of understanding of an eight-year-old. The judge accepted the unanimous opinion of the experts that Rachel should be moved only if it was necessary in her wider interests, and that because of her disability she would be unlikely to have any real perception of her Jewish heritage. The judge granted the residence order, which provided that Rachel live with the foster parents for the foreseeable future, which, because of her condition, was likely to continue throughout her life. Prior to the order, the foster parents had scrupulously observed the dietary and dress requirements requested by her birth parents. The residence order provided that the foster parents were at liberty thereafter to determine all questions regarding Rachel's education, religion, and upbringing. The birth parents' access rights were continued. The birth parents chose not to pursue an appeal.

When Rachel was seven, the birth parents filed a new proceeding seeking Rachel's return. At the time of the hearing, when Rachel was eight, she was observed to be a lively, happy, energetic child. She was attending a local school where she was mainstreamed. Experts noted that her progress with the foster family had been remarkable. One expert testified that the foster parents' care had been unconditional, and that Rachel would have great difficulty understanding the reason for a move, and a move would be difficult for her. The testimony also revealed a growing degree of mistrust between the foster parents and Rachel's birth parents following the initial residence order. Although one expert testified that Rachel might now be able to achieve an understanding of her Jewish heritage at the level of a ten- to twelve-year-old, another expert continued to believe that Rachel's level of understanding would remain at an eight-year-old level, and that her understanding of religion would remain very rudimentary. The trial court ordered that Rachel should not be moved, that contact with the parents would be reduced to four times per year, and that the foster parents were not to have Rachel baptized.

You are located in a European nation that has ratified the Convention on the Rights of the Child, the International Covenant on Civil and Political Rights, and the European Convention on Human Rights. As counsel for the birth parents before your nation's appellate court, what arguments would you make on their behalf to challenge this most recent order? As counsel for the foster parents, what arguments would you make in support of the trial judge's recent decision?

Chapter 8

Child Abduction, Jurisdiction, and Enforcement in International Custody Disputes

Judicial recognition of foreign custody decrees comports with the reality that nations are drawing closer together. Information, capital, and goods daily cross international boundaries. People likewise travel regularly from country to country. National boundaries no longer prevent people from meeting or marrying. Sometimes those marriages will end in divorce or custody disputes. International child-custody actions have become part of a global society.

Justice Pollack, Ivaldi v. Ivaldi,
685 A.2d 1319, 1324 (N.J. 1996)

As the world rapidly becomes more interconnected, in all of the ways Justice Pollack describes, children are increasingly caught in custody disputes spanning more than one nation. Such disputes arise between married and unmarried parents (and sometimes between parents and third parties), and between those who are citizens of different nations as well as those who are citizens of the same nation. When relationships between parents deteriorate, a host of reasons motivate parents to move children to, or seek a custody order in, a nation far removed from the other parent. These reasons include a yearning for old friends or familiar surroundings, the pursuit of employment or other economic opportunities, blatant forum shopping, and the need to escape domestic violence.

When a custody dispute arises, there is always the possibility that one person will remove a child from the country in which the other parent is living. This removal may occur when no judicial or administrative custody order has been issued, or, if it occurs subsequent to issuance of a custody order, it may or may not be in violation of the order's terms. The phrase "child abduction" is often used in connection with the conventions and domestic law affording remedies to the left-behind parent under this broad array of circumstances, and the phrase is used even when the removal does not violate a judicial or administrative order, or does not comport with the general public's notion of a "kidnapping."

Any analysis of available remedies for a left-behind parent must begin with these questions: from which country did a parent take the child, to which country has the child been taken, and which relevant conventions, if any, are in force between those two nations. Section A of this chapter examines in depth the most widely ratified of these conventions, the Hague Convention on the Civil Aspects of International Child Abduction ("Hague Convention on Child Abduction"). If the Hague Convention on Child Abduction is in effect between the two nations, a left-behind parent residing in one country may seek the return of a child who has been wrongfully moved to or retained in another country. The procedures in this Convention can help achieve a voluntary return of the child or an order of return from a judicial or administrative tribunal, often without the left-behind parent needing to travel personally to that country. Any custody proceedings pending in the country to which the child had been taken will be stayed pending resolution of the application for return. Assuming the child is returned, all questions on the merits of custody will typically be heard in the country to which the child is returned.

In many international custody disputes, however, the Hague Convention on Child Abduction is not in effect between the nations involved, or the child has not been wrongfully removed or retained, or for a variety of other reasons the Hague Convention on Child Abduction will not secure the return of the child or resolve the issue of where custody is to be determined. When custody proceedings are then initiated in more than one nation, or one nation is asked to modify, recognize, or enforce the custody order of another, tribunals typically look to their domestic law (*i.e.*, the law governing jurisdiction and the recognition and enforcement of foreign orders) as well as principles of comity, to determine how to proceed. International conventions addressing jurisdiction and enforcement are also in effect between some countries, and other conventions addressing these issues are in developmental stages. Section B of this chapter examines this topic of jurisdiction and enforcement in international custody disputes, focusing both on current U.S. domestic law and these emerging conventions.

Section C addresses additional remedies available in the United States to prevent and respond to abductions, and examines their efficacy. Criminal prosecution, contempt proceedings, orders restricting travel and visitation, tort claims, and self help are included in this appraisal.

A. The Hague Convention on the Civil Aspects of International Child Abduction

Of all of the family law conventions drafted and negotiated under the auspices of the Hague Conference on Private International Law, the Hague Convention on the Civil Aspects of International Child Abduction has been the one most broadly embraced by the international community to date. Over seventy nations have ratified or acceded to this Convention, including the United States, for whom the Convention entered into force on July 1, 1988. The United States has implemented the Hague Convention on Child Abduction through the International Child Abduction Remedies Act, 42 U.S.C. § 11601 (2002) ("ICARA").

Pursuant to Article 38 of the Convention, the treaty is in effect between all States who are members of the Hague Conference and who ratify the treaty. It is operative for other nations that accede to the Convention, but only to the extent that a particular contracting state accepts the accession. Thus the Convention applies only if it is in effect between both the country from which return is requested and the country to whom the child is to be returned. *See, e.g.,* Mezo v. Elmergawi, 855 F. Supp. 59 (E.D.N.Y. 1994) (holding that no injunction would issue ordering Secretary of State to perform his duties under the Hague Convention when plaintiff's children were abducted by father to Egypt and Libya, because neither country were contracting states to the Convention and bound by its terms); Mohsen v. Mohsen, 715 F. Supp. 1063 (D. Wyo. 1989) (holding Hague Convention petitioner had no rights under Convention when U.S. mother wrongfully retained child in the United States, because child's habitual residence was Bahrain and Bahrain is a noncontracting state).

Start by reading the Hague Convention on Child Abduction, which is found in the Supplement. Afterward, consider these cases that interpret the Convention and raise interesting issues about its application.

1. Wrongful Removal and Retention

a. Habitual Residence

Mozes v. Mozes
239 F.3d 1067 (9th Cir. 2001)

Kozinski, J.

In a case of first impression in our court, we interpret the term "habitual residence" in the Hague Convention on the Civil Aspects of International Child Abduction.

I

Arnon and Michal Mozes are Israeli citizens. Married in 1982, they have four children, ranging in age from seven to sixteen years. Until 1997, parents and children lived in Israel, as they had their entire lives. In April 1997, with Arnon's consent, Michal and the children came to Los Angeles. Michal had long wanted to live in the United States, and both parents agreed that the children would profit from a chance to attend school here, learn English and partake of American culture. Accordingly, Michal moved with the children to Beverly Hills, where she leased a home, purchased automobiles and enrolled the children in school. Arnon remained in Israel, but he paid for both the house and the automobiles used by his family, and stayed with them at the house during his visits to Los Angeles. The parties agree that Arnon consented to have Michal and the children remain in the United States for fifteen months, though they disagree as to what understanding existed beyond that. What we know for certain is that on April 17, 1998, a year after they arrived in the United States, Michal filed an action in the Los Angeles County Superior Court seeking dissolution of the marriage and custody of the children. The court granted temporary custody to Michal, and entered a temporary restraining order enjoining Arnon from removing the children from southern California. Less than a month later, Arnon filed a petition in federal district court, seeking to have the children returned to Israel under the Hague Convention. The oldest child elected to return to Israel, and did so by mutual agreement of the parents. Arnon now appeals the district court's denial of his petition with regard to the three younger children.

II

Adopted in 1980, the Hague Convention on the Civil Aspects of International Child Abduction ["Convention"] is intended to prevent "the use of force to establish artificial jurisdictional links on an international level, with a view to obtaining custody of a child." Elisa Perez-Vera, Explanatory Report ¶ 11, in 3 Hague Conference on Private International Law, Acts and Documents of the Fourteenth Session, Child Abduction 426 (1982) ["Perez-Vera Report"]. Despite the image conjured by words like "abduction" and "force," the Convention was not drafted in response to any concern about violent kidnappings by strangers. It was aimed, rather, at the "unilateral removal or retention of children by parents, guardians or close family members." Beaumont & McEleavy, The Hague Convention on International Child Abduction 1 (1999). Such an abductor "rarely seeks material gain; rather, he or she will aspire to the exercise of sole care and control over a son or daughter in a new jurisdiction." *Id.* The preamble to the Convention describes the signatory states as "[d]esiring to protect children internationally from the harmful effects of their wrongful removal or retention," effects which are thought to follow when a child "is taken out of the family and social environment in which its life has developed." Perez-Vera Report at ¶ 11. This may occur either through the "removal [of a child] from its habitual environment," or by "a refusal to restore a child to its own environment after a stay abroad." *Id.* at ¶ 12.

The Convention seeks to deter those who would undertake such abductions by eliminating their primary motivation for doing so. Since the goal of the abductor generally is "to obtain a right of custody from the authorities of the country to which the child has been taken," *id.* at ¶ 13, the signatories to the Convention have agreed to "deprive his actions of any practical or juridical consequences." *Id.* at ¶ 16. To this end, when a child who was habitually residing in one signatory state is wrongfully removed to, or retained in, another, Article 12 provides that the latter state "shall order the return of the child forthwith." *Id.*, art. 12. Further, Article 16 provides that "until it has been determined that the child is not to be returned under this Convention," the judicial or administrative authorities of a signatory state "shall not decide on the merits of rights of custody." Convention, art. 16. The United States and Israel are both signatories to the Convention.

The key operative concept of the Convention is that of "wrongful" removal or retention. In order for a removal or retention to trigger a state's obligations under the Convention, it must satisfy the requirements of Article 3:

> The removal or the retention of a child is to be considered wrongful where—
>
> a) it is in breach of rights of custody attributed to a person, an institution or any other body, either jointly or alone, under the law of the State in which the child was habitually resident immediately before the removal or retention; and
>
> b) at the time of removal or retention those rights were actually exercised, either jointly or alone, or would have been so exercised but for the removal or retention.

A court applying this provision must therefore answer a series of four questions: (1) When did the removal or retention at issue take place? (2) Immediately prior to the removal or retention, in which state was the child habitually resident? (3) Did the removal or retention breach the rights of custody attributed to the petitioner under the law of the habitual residence? (4) Was the petitioner exercising those rights at the time of the removal or retention?

In this case, the answer to the first question is clear. Arnon claims that Michal wrongfully retained the children from the moment on April 17, 1998, when she asked the Los Angeles County Superior Court to grant her custody of them. The district court denied Arnon's petition based on its answer to the second question: It found that as of that date, the children's "habitual residence" was in the United States, not Israel. Our central task is to review this finding, which we do immediately below.

III

The Perez-Vera Report describes "habitual residence" as "a well-established concept in the Hague Conference, which regards it as a question of pure fact, differing in that respect from domicile." Perez-Vera Report at § 66. In seeking to understand this "well-established concept," id., we discover that although the term "habitual residence" appears throughout the various Hague Conventions, none of them defines it. As one commentary explains, "this has been a matter of deliberate policy, the aim being to leave the notion free from technical rules which can produce rigidity and inconsistencies as between different legal systems." J.H.C. Morris, Dicey and Morris on the Conflict of Laws 144 (10th ed. 1980) ["Dicey & Morris"].

Clearly, the Hague Conference wished to avoid linking the determination of which country should exercise jurisdiction over a custody dispute to the idiosyncratic legal definitions of domicile and nationality of the forum where the child happens to have been removed. This would obviously undermine uniform application of the Convention and encourage forum-shopping by would-be abductors. To avoid this, courts have been instructed to interpret the expression "habitual residence" according to "the ordinary and natural meaning of the two words it contains[, as] a question of fact to be decided by reference to all the circumstances of any particular case." C v. S (Minor: Abduction: Illegitimate Child), [1990] 2 All E.R. 961, 965 (Eng. H.L.).

Certain commentators, however, have gone considerably farther than this, decrying as an unwelcome technical rule any attempt to develop guiding principles for courts to consult when making findings of "habitual residence." This has not, of course, prevented courts faced with disputes under the Convention from articulating what they understand the "ordinary and natural meaning" of the two words to be, or from looking to cases decided by other courts for help in refining and applying that meaning. Nor should it. . . . In order for decisions under the Convention to be intelligible, courts must be able to explain these conclusions and the reasoning used to reach them. To achieve the uniformity of application across countries, which depends upon the realization of the Convention's goals, courts must be able to reconcile their decisions with those reached by other courts in similar situations. . . . Cutting fact-finding tribunals adrift with only the Bellman's map to guide them does not lead to consistency; it leads only to the absence of any common standard by which inconsistency can be identified. . . .

"Habitual residence" is the central—often outcome-determinative—concept on which the entire system is founded. Without intelligibility and consistency in its application, parents are deprived of crucial information they need to make decisions, and children are more likely to suffer the harms the Convention seeks to prevent. . . .

This explains why, while a determination of "habitual residence" under the Convention is primarily factual, it has not been understood to mean that it is left entirely within the unreviewed discretion of the trial court. Rather, reviewing courts have taken the approach articulated by Lord Scarman:

> Though the meaning of ordinary words is . . . a question of fact, the meaning to be attributed to enacted words is a question of law, being a matter of statutory interpretation. So . . . a question of law arises as to the meaning of [habitual residence], even though it arises only at a preliminary stage in the process of de-

termining a question of fact.... It is with this preliminary stage that the [reviewing] courts are concerned.

Shah v. Barnet London Borough Council and other appeals, [1983] 1 All E.R. 226, 233 (Eng.H.L.). This is what we refer to in American legal parlance as a mixed question of law and fact....

IV

A. The Relevance of Intent

Perhaps the most straightforward way to determine someone's habitual residence would be to observe his behavior. As Lord Scarman put it, "in their natural and ordinary meaning the words mean that the person must be habitually and normally resident here, apart from temporary or occasional absences of long or short duration." Shah, [1983] 1 All E.R. at 234 (internal quotation marks omitted). Under this approach, we might say that if we observe someone centering his life around a particular location during a given period, so that every time he goes away from it he also comes back, we will call this his habitual residence.

This approach, while intuitively appealing, suffers from a fatal flaw: It may yield strikingly different results depending on the observer's time frame. A child who spends two months at Camp Chippewah, if observed only during that period, would appear to be habitually resident there. On the other hand, if we follow the same child through to adulthood, we might label a couple of years spent studying abroad a mere "temporary absence of long duration." This indeterminacy is unavoidable, as it is "not desirable, indeed it is not possible, to enter into any game of numbers on the duration required." Adderson v. Adderson, 51 Alta.L.R. (2d) 193, 198 (Alberta C.A.1987). The absence of an objective temporal baseline however, requires that we pay close attention to subjective intent when evaluating someone's habitual residence. Elaborating on the subjective element of the inquiry, Lord Scarman reasoned that for habitual residence to accrue, there must be a "settled purpose":

> The purpose may be one or there may be several. It may be specific or general. All the law requires is that there is [sic] a settled purpose. That is not to say that the propositus intends to stay where he is indefinitely; indeed his purpose, while settled, may be for a limited period. Education, business or profession, employment, health, family or merely love of the place spring to mind as common reasons for a choice of regular abode. And there may well be many others. All that is necessary is that the purpose of living where one does has a sufficient degree of continuity to be properly described as settled.

Shah, [1983] 1 All E.R. at 235....

None of it is very useful, however, when attempting to decide a borderline case. Even the child who goes off to summer camp arguably has a "settled purpose" to live there continuously "for a limited period." *Id.* No one would seriously contend that the summer camp is the child's habitual residence, but the notion of "settled purpose" alone is powerless to tell us why not.

The obvious reason why the camper is not regarded as habitually resident is that he already has an established habitual residence elsewhere and his absence from it—even for an entire summer—is no indication that he means to abandon it. Lord Brandon has discussed the distinction between abandoning a prior habitual residence and acquiring a new one:

[T]here is a significant difference between a person ceasing to be habitually resident in country A, and his subsequently becoming habitually resident in country B. A person may cease to be habitually resident in country A in a single day if he or she leaves it with a settled intention not to return to it but to take up long-term residence in country B instead. Such a person cannot, however, become habitually resident in country B in a single day. An appreciable period of time and a settled intention will be necessary to enable him or her to become so.

C v S (minor: abduction: illegitimate child), [1990] 2 All E.R. at 965. As this passage illustrates, the first step toward acquiring a new habitual residence is forming a settled intention to abandon the one left behind. Otherwise, one is not habitually residing; one is away for a temporary absence of long or short duration. Of course, one need not have this settled intention at the moment of departure; it could coalesce during the course of a stay abroad originally intended to be temporary. Nor need the intention be expressly declared, if it is manifest from one's actions; indeed, one's actions may belie any declaration that no abandonment was intended. If you've lived continuously in the same place for several years on end, for example, we would be hard-pressed to conclude that you had not abandoned any prior habitual residence. On the other hand, one may effectively abandon a prior habitual residence without intending to occupy the next one for more than a limited period. Whether there is a settled intention to abandon a prior habitual residence is a question of fact as to which we defer to the district court.

B. Whose intent is it, anyway?

Having concluded that a settled intention to abandon one's prior habitual residence is a crucial part of acquiring a new one, we confront an additional problem: Whose settled intention determines whether a child has abandoned a prior habitual residence? One obvious response would be, the child's. It is, after all, the child whose habitual residence we are out to determine. And indeed we sometimes find courts declaring the intentions of the parents to be irrelevant. There is an obvious problem with this approach, however. Children, particularly the ones whose return may be ordered under the Convention, normally lack the material and psychological wherewithal to decide where they will reside. This leads to the conclusion that, "in those cases where intention or purpose is relevant—for example, where it is necessary to decide whether an absence is intended to be temporary and short-term—the intention or purpose which has to be taken into account is that of the person or persons entitled to fix the place of the child's residence."

Difficulty arises, of course, when the persons entitled to fix the child's residence no longer agree on where it has been fixed—a situation that, for obvious reasons, is likely to arise in cases under the Convention. In these cases, the representations of the parties cannot be accepted at face value, and courts must determine from all available evidence whether the parent petitioning for return of a child has already agreed to the child's taking up habitual residence where it is. The factual circumstances in which this question arises are diverse....

C. Parental Intent and the Circumstances of the Child

While the decision to alter a child's habitual residence depends on the settled intention of the parents, they cannot accomplish this transformation by wishful thinking alone. First, it requires an actual "change in geography." Friedrich, 983 F.2d at 1402. Second, home isn't built in a day. It requires the passage of "[a]n appreciable period of time," C v S (minor: abduction: illegitimate child), [1990] 2 All E.R. 961, 965 (Eng. H.L.), one that is "sufficient for acclimatization." Feder, 63 F.3d at 224. When the child moves to a new country accompanied by both parents, who take steps to set up a regular household together, the period need not be long. On the other hand, when circumstances are such as to hinder acclimatization, even a lengthy period spent in this manner may not suffice.

A more difficult question is when evidence of acclimatization should suffice to establish a child's habitual residence, despite uncertain or contrary parental intent. Most agree that, given enough time and positive experience, a child's life may become so firmly embedded in the new country as to make it habitually resident even though there be lingering parental intentions to the contrary. The question is how readily courts should reach the conclusion that this has occurred. Since the Convention seeks to prevent harms thought to flow from wrenching or keeping a child from its familiar surroundings, it is tempting to regard any sign of a child's familiarity with the new country as lessening the need for return and making a finding of altered habitual residence desirable. Further, some courts regard the question whether a child is doing well in school, has friends, and so on, as more straightforward and objective than asking whether the parents share a "settled intent." Despite the superficial appeal of focusing primarily on the child's contacts in the new country, however, we conclude that, in the absence of settled parental intent, courts should be slow to infer from such contacts that an earlier habitual residence has been abandoned.

The Convention is designed to prevent child abduction by reducing the incentive of the would-be abductor to seek unilateral custody over a child in another country. The greater the ease with which habitual residence may be shifted without the consent of both parents, the greater the incentive to try.... Further, attempting to make the standard more rigorous might actually make matters worse, as it could open children to harmful manipulation when one parent seeks to foster residential attachments during what was intended to be a temporary visit—such as having the child profess allegiance to the new sovereign....

Even if deliberate manipulation were not a danger, divining from a child's observed contacts in a new country whether it has come to reside there habitually would be an enterprise fraught with difficulty. Children can be remarkably adaptable and form intense attachments even in short periods of time—yet this does not necessarily mean that the child expects or intends those relationships to be long-lived. It is quite possible to participate in all the activities of daily life while still retaining awareness that one has another life to go back to. In such instances one may be "acclimatized" in the sense of being well-adjusted in one's present environment, yet not regard that environment as one's habitual residence. It thus makes sense to regard the intentions of the parents as affecting the length of time necessary for a child to become habitually resident, because the child's knowledge of these intentions is likely to color its attitude toward the contacts it is making....

V

The district court held that the habitual residence of the Mozes children had shifted from Israel to the United States between April 1997 and April 1998. It did so based on the following understanding of the applicable standard:

> [T]o establish that the habitual residence of a child has shifted, the law requires that a child be in the new forum by mutual consent of the parents and that the child has become settled in that new forum....

Where, as here, children already have a well-established habitual residence, simple consent to their presence in another forum is not usually enough to shift it there.

Rather, the agreement between the parents and the circumstances surrounding it must enable the court to infer a shared intent to abandon the previous habitual residence, such as when there is effective agreement on a stay of indefinite duration.

Here, the district court's findings of fact with regard to the shared intentions of the parents, findings to which we defer, were as follows:

> The parties stipulate that they agreed that the children would remain in the United States until July 1998. However, there is a dispute as to whether the parties agreed that the date of return had been extended to July 1999, if it had become indefinite or remained unchanged. At the very least, the parties discussed the possibility of the children remaining in the United States for another year, and may have even come to such an understanding. In April 1998, it is clear that petitioner decided he wanted the children to return to Israel as originally planned by July 1998.

Mozes, 19 F. Supp. 2d at 1115–16. Absent from this discussion is a finding that the parents shared an understanding that their children's stay in the United States would last indefinitely. Having heard the conflicting testimony of both parties and reviewed all the evidence, the district court was able to say only that Arnon and Michal had "discussed the possibility" of extending the stay for one additional year, and that they "*may* have even come to such an understanding." *Id.* (emphasis added). The district court did not find that they had actually reached such an understanding.

The district court's reticence is not surprising, given the striking difference between this case and those where courts faced with similarly ambiguous facts have found a settled intent in favor of indefinite residence. In those cases, the country in which it had been agreed the child should spend time was the native country of one of the parents. It is entirely natural and foreseeable that, if a child goes to live with a parent in that parent's native land on an open-ended basis, the child will soon begin to lose its habitual ties to any prior residence. A parent who agrees to such an arrangement without any clear limitations may well be held to have accepted this eventuality.

The situation here is far different. Michal had never lived in the United States. Prior to their departure, all of her life and the lives of the children had been spent in Israel. All of the family's relatives were there. Further, Michal and the children left for the United States with a temporary visa, casting considerable doubt on whether they would be allowed to remain here indefinitely even if they wished to. Finally, while Michal took steps to obtain work in the United States, the economic base on which the family depended for sustenance remained entirely in Israel. Under these circumstances, the district court was clearly right to refrain from finding that the parents had agreed to an indefinite stay.

The district court reasoned, however, that "[t]he fact that a child is to remain indefinitely in a new forum...is not a necessary condition to establishing the habitual residence of a child." Mozes, 19 F. Supp. 2d at 1115. This is true; it is not a necessary condition. When a child has no clearly established habitual residence elsewhere, it may become habitually resident even in a place where it was intended to live only for a limited time. The same is true if the child's prior habitual residence has been effectively abandoned by the shared intent of the parents. Where there is no such intent, however, a prior habitual residence should be deemed supplanted only where "the objective facts point unequivocally" to this conclusion. Zenel, 1993 S.L.T. at 979. This, too, may occur during the course of a stay which is not intended to be indefinite.

The objective facts found here are as follows:

> [B]y April 17, 1998, the children had settled into their new home, were en-
> rolled and participating full time in schools and social, cultural, and religious
> activities. They had successfully completed a year of school in the United
> States, quickly learned English, made new friends, and were accustomed to
> and thriving in their new life in Beverly Hills.

Mozes, 19 F. Supp. 2d at 1116. These facts certainly show that the Mozes children, as the
district court remarked, spent a "very full year" in the United States. *Id.* But they do not
point unequivocally to the conclusion that, at the time Michal petitioned for their custody, the children had ceased to be habitually resident in Israel....

In conclusion, the district court's determination of habitual residence in this case appears to have relied upon an understanding of that term that gives insufficient weight to
the importance of shared parental intent under the Convention. Given that the Mozes
children had a clearly established habitual residence in Israel in April 1997, and that the
district court did not find an intent to abandon this residence in favor of the United
States, the question it needed to answer was not simply whether the children had in
some sense "become settled" in this country. Rather, the appropriate inquiry under the
Convention is whether the United States had supplanted Israel as the locus of the children's family and social development. As the district court did not answer this question,
we must remand and allow it to do so.... Reversed and Remanded.

Notes and Questions

1. *Unilateral Action and the Passage of Time.* In a footnote, the Ninth Circuit cites ap-
provingly to E.M. Clive, *The Concept of Habitual Residence*, 1997 Jurid. Rev. 137, 145,
who stated:

> Suppose, for example, that a child has lived for 15 years in a new country after
> a wrongful removal. It would be an abuse of ordinary language to say that the
> child had been habitually resident for all of that time in the country from
> which he or she had been removed and had not become habitually resident in
> the new country.

Mozes, 239 F.3d at 1081 n.42. Will abduction be encouraged if a parent's unilateral action can change a child's habitual residence, despite the left-behind parent's continued
disapproval of the move? Or is failure to recognize a changed habitual residence in this
situation an "absurd result?" *Id.* (citing Clive, *supra*). Some courts have said "where
both parents have equal rights of custody no unilateral action by one of them can
change the habitual residence of the children, save by the agreement or acquiescence
over time of the other parent...." *In re S.* (Minors) (Abduction: Wrongful Retention),
Fam. 70 (Eng. Fam. 1994). Is this statement consistent with the holding in *Mozes*?

2. *The Majority Approach. Mozes* is quite detailed in the rules that it lays down. Although many of its rules are obiter dictum, *Mozes* stands out as a clear departure from
the majority of cases in which courts deny that they are creating legal rules about habitual residence. *See, e.g.,* Kanth v. Kanth, 232 F.3d 901 (10th Cir. 2000) ("[A] child's habitual residence is defined by examining specific facts and circumstances and is a term
courts should not interpret technically or restrictively."). This relatively unstructured
approach has received widespread support throughout the world from courts and
scholars. *See, e.g.,* E.M. Clive, *The Concept of Habitual Residence*, 1997 Jurid. Rev. 137,
147 ("[H]abitual residence is a simple concept which should be applied by concentrat-

ing on the ordinary and natural meaning of the two words which it contains and on the facts of the particular case. It should not be embellished by technical rules.... The two words 'habitual' and 'residence' are quite capable of doing all the work which is required of them without the addition of spurious legal propositions."); Paul R. Beaumont & Peter E. McEleavy, The Hague Convention on International Child Abduction 101 (1999) ("the concept should not be given an abstract or technical interpretation").

Perhaps, more significant than the expressed approach is whether the *Mozes'* roadmap embodies a new legal standard that will change what courts are implicitly doing. Certainly in a number of cases courts express a test closer to that announced by the district court in *Mozes,* i.e., one that focuses on whether the child is ordinarily resident in a location and whether the parents have agreed that the child be there, and ignores the parents' intentions. *See, e.g., Feder v. Evans-Feder,* 63 F.3d 217, 224 (3d Cir. 1995) ("A child's habitual residence is the place where he or she has been physically present for an amount of time sufficient for acclimatization and which has a 'degree of settled purpose' from the child's perspective") (finding that child's habitual residence was Australia, after the child had lived there six months, when the parents, both U.S. citizens, moved there for the father's job, although mother was "reluctant" to do so because of "deep misgivings about the couple's deteriorating relationship"). The Ninth Circuit's approach in *Mozes* conceivably would change the outcome in some cases. In *Moses* itself, for example, the new test contributed to the parties entering a stipulation for a consent order to return the children to Israel. The order was entered and everyone did return to Israel.

3. *"Habitual Residence" Applied.* Where is the child's "habitual residence" in each of the following cases, and why?

Problem 8-1: Both parents had lived together in Australia continuously for fifteen months, during which time they had made renovations to the house they lived in, and considered purchasing another home elsewhere in the country. The mother obtained full-time employment in Australia five months prior to her decision to remove the child to Scotland. The mother's travel to Australia was part of a reconciliation by the parents, and the mother and father had agreed that if the reconciliation failed the mother and child could return to Scotland. The mother clandestinely returned to Scotland when the marriage failed to work, deciding to do so only a few days before leaving. The child was two months old when he had arrived in Australia.

Problem 8-2: An eight-year-old child lives with her mother for over two years in Sweden, pursuant to a custody arrangement under which the child was to spend a total of eight years there and four years in the United States. Pursuant to the agreement, the child was to live in the United States after her first two years in Sweden. The mother has refused to send the child to the United States. Prior to the child's two years in Sweden, the child lived in the United States, with each parent having custody for two weeks on an alternating basis.

Problem 8-3: American citizens met in Germany in 1987, had a child, and returned to the United States in 1990. The father began looking for work abroad in 1993, and the mother, his wife, had "considerable hesitation" about going abroad. After the father obtained a job offer in Australia, the mother and child, now four years old, traveled to Australia with the father in the beginning of 1994; the mother was intent on working to improve her marital relationship. She remained "ambivalent about the move; while she hoped her marriage would be saved, she was not committed to remaining in Australia." The couple put their U.S. house up for sale and bought another in Australia. In Australia, they applied to have their son admitted to a private school when he reached the fifth grade, some seven years in the future. The mother accepted a job which obligated her to work until 1995. The father completed the paperwork necessary to obtain permanent residency for the entire family, although the mother did not sign the necessary paperwork. The family obtained Australian Medicare cards, giving them access to Australia's health care system. The child attended preschool and was enrolled in kindergarten for the upcoming year. When the marriage deteriorated in the spring of 1994, the mother told the father she wanted to visit her parents in the United States, and the father bought two round-trip tickets for her and the child. Mother and child departed Australia at the end of June 1994. After two months in the United States, the mother refused to return the son to Australia.

4. *Multiple Habitual Residences.* Can there be "dual" habitual residences? *See* Paul R. Beaumont & Peter E. McEleavy, The Hague Convention on International Child Abduction 110 (1999) (suggesting that such a conclusion may be appropriate at times and would make return under the Convention unnecessary).

5. *Proving Habitual Residence.* What sort of evidence should an attorney gather to establish a child's habitual residence?

6. *Domestic Violence and Habitual Residence.* What effect should domestic violence, perpetrated by one parent against another, have on a finding of "habitual residence?" What if the father forces a mother to go and live in a foreign country or detains her there after their vacation? In *In re Ponath*, the couple met, married, lived, and had a child together in Utah during the course of approximately one year. The family then traveled to Germany. The couple disputed whether the Germany trip was to be temporary. At the end of the first three months in Germany, the mother desired to return to the United States with the child, but petitioner refused to permit her and the child to return. Petitioner continued to prevent her and the child's return by means of verbal, emotional and physical abuse. After approximately one year, the mother and child returned to the United States. Thereafter, the father was arrested in the United States for allegedly attacking a relative in the mother's home while attempting to see the mother and child. The mother presented the evidence of a clinical psychologist, who supported the mother's claims that she was verbally, emotionally and physically abused by the father. The court concluded that the child's habitual residence was Utah. It stated:

> Although it is the habitual residence of the child that must be determined, the desires and actions of the parents cannot be ignored by the court in making that determination when the child was at the time of removal or retention an infant. The concept of habitual residence must, in the court's opinion, entail some element of voluntariness and purposeful design. Indeed, this notion has been characterized in other cases in terms of "settled purpose"....

> In this case, what began as a voluntary visit to petitioner's family in Germany, albeit an extended visit, might be viewed by the court as a change of habitual residence of the minor child but for respondent's intent and desire to return to the United States with the minor child and petitioner's willful obstruction of that purpose. Petitioner's coercion of respondent by means of verbal, emotional and physical abuse removed any element of choice and settled purpose which earlier may have been present in the family's decision to visit Germany. The aim of the Hague Convention is to prevent one parent from obtaining an advantage over the other in any future custody dispute.... For the court to grant petitioner's motion, and thereby sanction his behavior in forcing continued residence in Germany upon respondent, and through her, the minor child, would be to thwart a principle purpose of the Hague Convention. In the

court's view, coerced residence is not habitual residence within the meaning of the Hague Convention. [T]he concept of habitual residence, for purposes of the Hague Convention, is viewed to be fluid and fact based. Given the specific facts of this case, the court can draw no conclusion other than that the habitual residence of the child was in Carbon County, Utah.

See In re Ponath, 829 F. Supp. 363, 367–68 (D. Utah 1993). Can a residence be coerced on less than physical violence or the threat of physical violence? *Accord* Director General v. M.S., No. SY8917 of 1997, slip op. ¶¶ 28, 29 (Austl. Fam. Ct. 1998) (habitual residence not acquired despite two years in Austria, where husband's family was hostile to wife, and wife and children were linguistically and socially isolated). What if there was a voluntary change of the child's habitual residence, but then the father batters the mother and the new country of habitual residence refuses to address the violence? Can one argue that the child's habitual residence shifts back when the mother returns with the child to the former habitual residence?

7. *Appellate Review.* What was the standard of review in *Mozes?* If habitual residence were a factual determination, one would expect that the appellate court would review it under a "clearly erroneous standard." *See* Fed. R. Civ. P. 52(a). If it is a mixed question of fact and law, *i.e.*, the application of a legal standard to facts, the appellate court typically would defer to the trial court's finding of facts, but would review de novo the legal conclusions derived from the facts. Which standard is most appropriate? Why?

8. *Rate of Return.* Petitioners' success using the Hague Convention varies widely by country. Approximately half of all Hague petitions result in a court order for return, with rates for individual countries ranging from 5% to 95%. *See* Nigel Lowe, National Center for Missing & Exploited Children, International Forum on Parental Child Abduction: Hague Convention Action Agenda 8 (1999) (describing research by Janet Chiancone and Linda Girdner in 1995). Commentators attribute part of the difference to the interpretation of "habitual residence," and describe it as "a difficult concept to pin down." *Id.* at 11. Consequently, "habitual residence" has been called a "legal loophole." *Id.* Is it a "loophole" or merely a factually-based determination? Is *Mozes* a solution to the criticism?

9. *Interpretation of Habitual Residence Abroad.* Some of our treaty partners have come under criticism for interpreting habitual residence inconsistently with the framers' understanding of the term. For example, Sweden implements its obligations under the Hague Convention through its 1989 Enforcement Act. This Act contains the term "hemvist," which is interpreted to mean "domicile" and not "habitual residence." The Swedish Supreme Administrative Court has issued decisions that have been criticized by the U.S. Department of State. *See* Johanna L. Schiratzki, *Friends at Odds— Construing Habitual Residence for Children in Sweden and the U.S.*, 15 Int'l J. of L., Pol'y & Fam. 297 (2001).

What exactly is the problem with using the concept of domicile? Domicile traditionally means the place where one resides with the absence of any present intention to live elsewhere. In the United States, the common law traditionally said that a child could not select or change its domicile, but rather was dependent on the parents' domicile. *See, e.g.*, Arredondo v. Brockette, 648 F.2d 425 (5th Cir. 1981), *aff'd sub nom* Martinez v. Bynum, 461 U.S. 321 (1983) (explaining that Texas common law fixes minor's domicile as that of father's because of "minor's presumed lack of capacity to form the requisite intention necessary to establish a separate domicile"). What potential problems arise if one were to substitute the term domicile for the term habitual residence in the Convention? Does *Mozes* create these same problems?

10. *Public International Law.* If courts of a certain nation are not acting in good faith in applying the Hague Convention, the country may be in breach of it. The nation may also be in breach of public international law obligations. For example, article 11 of the U.N. Convention on the Rights of the Child requires States Parties to "take measures to combat the illicit transfer and non-return of children abroad." Article 35 requires that States Parties "take all appropriate national, bilateral and multilateral measures to prevent the abduction...of...children for any purpose or in any form." Article 18 says "both parents have common responsibilities...[and] the primary responsibility for the upbringing and development of the child.... States' parties shall render appropriate assistance to parents...in the performance of their child-rearing responsibilities...."

Similarly, the European Convention on Human Rights states, "Everyone has the right to respect for his private and family life...." *See* art. 8(1). States are prohibited from interfering with the exercise of this right, except for one of the enumerated reasons. *See* art. 8(2). In *Ignaccolo-Zenide v. Romania*, 31 Eur. H.R. Rep. 7 (2001), the European Court of Human Rights found Romania in violation of article 8 when its courts failed to order the return of children to France pursuant to the mother's petition under the Hague Convention on Child Abduction. Rather, Romania allowed the father to evade enforcement of the French custody and visitation order and manipulate the Romanian system to his advantage.

Can a nation be in breach of public international law if it quickly and erroneously returns a child pursuant to a Hague application? In *"X" and "Z" v. Argentina*, Case No. 11.676, Rep. No. 71/00, Inter-Am. C.H.R., OEA/Ser.L./V/II.111 Doc. 20 rev. at 582 (2000), the petitioner alleged that Argentina violated her rights under the American Convention on Human Rights, in particular her right to due process (art. 8(1)), the right to protection of the family (art. 17), the rights of the child (art. 19), and the right to judicial protection (art. 25). Argentina had executed, within twenty-four hours, its court's ruling ordering the return of Z to Z's habitual residence in Spain, in the care and custody of the father, while the mother's appeal was pending. In her suit against Argentina, the mother alleged that the Hague petition should not have been granted, in part, because the removal of Z to Argentina had not been unlawful. The Inter-American Commission on Human Rights found her arguments without merit. The Commission emphasized that it would not decide whether the Hague Convention was properly interpreted or applied, but merely whether the judicial authorities acted in conformity with the American Convention. *Id.* ¶ 43. It then held that it was not per se incompatible with the Convention for a court ruling to be executed when an appeal was pending. *Id.* ¶ 49. Nor in the particular case was there a violation since an immediate return was consistent with the object and purpose of the Hague Convention. *Id.* ¶ 51. Since the mother's arguments under articles 17 and 19 were derivative of her arguments under articles 8 and 25, the Commission did not address them.

b. Rights of Custody

David S. v. Zamira S., 574 N.Y.S.2d 429 (N.Y. Fam. Ct. 1991). The parties were both Canadian nationals. Owing to marital difficulties, the parties separated and agreed that respondent would have custody of their son, the only child born at that time, and the petitioner would have regular visitation. The separation agreement further provided that the respondent "shall make [the son] available [to the petitioner] within the Metropolitan Toronto vicinity." A daughter was later born and no agreement governed her custody or visitation. After the daughter's birth, the Supreme Court of Ontario issued an interim order preventing the respondent from removing the children from Ontario and from obtaining passports for them. After being served with the interim order, the respondent and the children left Ontario and went to New York. Thereafter, the petitioner sought, and obtained, an interim order granting him temporary custody of both children. He also sought return of the children pursuant to the Hague Convention. *Held*: Removal was wrongful. Petitioner had "rights of custody." The separation agreement "gave the respondent custody of their son and the petitioner visitation with the child.... [T]he petitioner's statutory right to custody of their son was suspended by virtue of the separation agreement. There was no such formal agreement for their daughter. Thus, with respect to her, the petitioner and respondent had an equal right to custody.... [The respondent's] ability to relocate her residence with the children outside the Metropolitan Toronto area was restricted.... [R]espondent was duly served with the October 5, 1989 [interim] order and nonetheless left the country. Based on the foregoing, this Court finds that the respondent acted in contempt of the Supreme Court's order of October 5, 1989 by leaving the country." The Court then stated:

> Respondent's contention that the petitioner is not entitled under the Hague Convention to have their son returned, because he only had visitation ("access") rights and not custody, might have some merit but for the respondent's contemptuous conduct, and the subsequent orders of the Supreme Court of Ontario which give temporary custody of both children to the petitioner. Moreover, respondent's argument overlooks the fact that their daughter was not included in the provisions of the separation agreement. Therefore, the petitioner had an equal right to custody of their daughter when the respondent left Ontario. Under § 11603(f) of ICARA, this Court can find there was a "wrongful removal" in the absence of any formal declaration of custody.

Croll v. Croll
229 F.3d 133 (2d Cir. 2000)

Jacobs, J.

Petitioner-appellee Stephen Halladay Croll seeks an order compelling his wife, respondent-appellant Mei Yee Croll, to return their minor child, Christina Croll, to Hong Kong under the Hague Convention on the Civil Aspects of International Child Abduction,... implemented by the International Child Abduction Remedies Act (ICARA)....

Stephen and Mei Yee Croll, both United States citizens, were married in Hong Kong in 1982. Their daughter Christina was born in Hong Kong in 1990 and lived with both of her parents until they separated in 1998. While the separated couple remained in Hong Kong, Christina lived with her mother, and was regularly visited by her father.

At some point in 1998, Mr. Croll commenced divorce proceedings in the District Court of the Hong Kong Special Administrative Region, Matrimonial Causes. The custody order issued by the Hong Kong court—the only custody order applicable to this case—grants Mrs. Croll sole "custody, care and control" of Christina and grants Mr. Croll a right of "reasonable access."... To aid the parties' rights under the Custody Order (Mrs. Croll's custody and Mr. Croll's access), a separate paragraph directs that Christina "not be removed from Hong Kong until she attains the age of 18 years" without leave of court or consent of the other parent. Mr. Croll contends that this ne exeat clause,[1] which grants a veto power over any place of residence outside Hong Kong, gives him rights of custody within the meaning of the Convention.

Mrs. Croll brought Christina to New York on April 2, 1999, intending (she says) that Christina would interview at schools in New York City, attend school for a few weeks, and then return to Hong Kong for the summer. But (Mrs. Croll admits) "[i]n the back of her mind" she intended to remain in the United States permanently. On April 8, 1999, Mrs. Croll filed an action in Family Court in New York County seeking custody, child support, and an order of protection. Those proceedings have been stayed pending the outcome of this federal action.

When Mr. Croll returned to Hong Kong from a business trip on April 7, 1999, he learned that his wife had gone with Christina to the United States. On April 22, 1999, Mr. Croll filed a missing persons report with the police in Hong Kong, and on May 14, 1999, he filed this petition in the Southern District of New York seeking Christina's return to Hong Kong pursuant to the Hague Convention....

Mrs. Croll moved in the Southern District to dismiss the petition on the ground that Mr. Croll could not claim "custody" of Christina and that therefore (a) the court lacked subject matter jurisdiction and (b) the petition failed to state a claim upon which relief could be granted. The court denied the motion to dismiss, granted Mr. Croll's petition, and ordered that Christina be returned to Hong Kong. The court reasoned that "the Hong Kong order dated February 23, 1999 provides that Christina may not be removed from Hong Kong before her 18th birthday without either leave of court or both parents' consent. Accordingly,...Mr. Croll had a right, along with respondent, to determine Christina's place of residence and he had a corresponding right of custody within the meaning of the Convention. Christina's removal from Hong Kong—her habitual residence—was in violation of her father's right of custody and was, therefore, wrongful pursuant to the Convention...."

At issue on this appeal are two sets of rights recognized in the Convention to be distinct: rights of custody and rights of access. If Mr. Croll has custody rights, courts in the United States have jurisdiction to order return of Christina to Hong Kong, as the district court has done, and the duty to do so. If, however, Mr. Croll has the lesser rights of access, jurisdiction is lacking and Mr. Croll must rely on other remedies....

In order to "preserve the status quo and to deter parents from crossing international boundaries" to secure a more favorable forum for the adjudication of custody rights, the Convention provides for the return of children "wrongfully removed to or retained in any Contracting State." A removal or retention is to be considered "wrongful" where:

  a) it is in breach of rights of custody attributed to a person, an institution or any other body, either jointly or alone, under the law of the State in which the child was habitually resident immediately before the removal or retention; and

  b) at the time of removal or retention those rights were actually exercised, either jointly or alone, or would have been so exercised but for the removal or retention.

---

1. The custody order's ne exeat clause provides that Christina not be removed from Hong Kong without leave until she attains the age of 18 years, but provided that if either parent were to give a general undertaking to the Court to return the said child to Hong Kong when called upon to do so, and unless otherwise directed with the written consent of the other parent, that parent may remove the said child from Hong Kong for any period specified in such written consent.

Id. art. 3. Rights of custody "may arise in particular by operation of law or by reason of a judicial or administrative decision, or by reason of an agreement having legal effect under the law of that State." *Id.*

Thus an order of return is available as a remedy only for wrongful removals or retentions, and removals or retentions are wrongful only if they are "in breach of rights of custody." The Convention defines rights of custody as "rights relating to the care of the person of the child and, in particular, the right to determine the child's place of residence." *Id.* art. 5.

Rights of custody are distinguished from rights of access, which are defined in the Convention as "the right to take a child for a limited period of time to a place other than the child's habitual residence." *Id.* The Convention provides recourse in the event a child is removed from an habitual residence in breach of access rights, but those remedies do not include an order of return to the place of habitual residence. *See id.* art. 21. To vindicate the breach of access rights, the Convention authorizes signatory nations to use one or more remedies (short of return) to "promote the peaceful enjoyment of access rights," and to "take steps to remove, as far as possible, all obstacles to the exercise of such rights." *Id.* One such remedy is a writ ordering the custodial parent who has removed the child from the habitual residence to permit, and to pay for, periodic visitation by the non-custodial parent with access rights. *See id.* art. 26. The Convention makes plain that unless the petitioner has rights of custody, a court has no authority to order return.

We open the dictionary to find the ordinary meaning or meanings of "custody." *See Chan,* 490 U.S. at 128 (looking first to Webster's Second International Dictionary to construe "irregularity" under the Warsaw Convention). Dictionaries support the idea that custody entails care, and in any event confirm the intuition that custody is something other and more than a negative right or veto.

Black's Law Dictionary defines custody generally as "[t]he care and control of a thing or person for inspection, preservation or security"; parental custody as "[t]he care, control, and maintenance of a child awarded by a court"; sole custody as "[a]n arrangement by which one parent has full control and responsibility to the exclusion of the other"; and joint (or shared) custody as "[a]n arrangement by which both parents share the responsibility for and authority over the child at all times." Black's Law Dictionary 390 (7th ed. 1999).

Webster's Third defines custody as a "duty of guardianship and preservation...protection, care, maintenance, and tuition." Webster's Third New International Dictionary Unabridged 597 (1986). The Random House dictionary defines custody as "keeping; guarding; care: in the care of her father." Random House Dictionary of the English Language 357 (2d ed. 1987) (emphasis in original).

Taking these definitions together, custody of a child entails the primary duty and ability to choose and give sustenance, shelter, clothing, moral and spiritual guidance, medical attention, education, etc., or the (revocable) selection of other people or institutions to give these things. The dissent characterizes this as a "parochial definition" that reflects only "traditional American notions of custody rights," because it is distilled from American lexical sources. But this definition reflects none of the peculiar practices of American child-rearing; it includes an open-ended "etc."; and the dissent identifies no feature of custody that is missing except for the dubious addition of a ne exeat clause.

Nothing in the Hague Convention suggests that the drafters intended anything other than this ordinary understanding of custody. Article 5 of the Convention defines "rights of custody" generally as "rights relating to the care of the person of the child." Hague

Convention, art. 5. The plural "rights" references a bundle of rights exercised by one or more persons having custody, and is in some tension with the idea (critical to the district court's opinion in this case) that one can have custody by holding a single power such as the veto conferred by a ne exeat clause.

Mr. Croll emphasizes that the Convention's definitional phrase "rights relating to the care of the person of the child" continues immediately to offer as an example, "in particular, the right to determine a child's place of residence." Hague Convention, art. 5. Mr. Croll reasons that a ne exeat clause gives an otherwise non-custodial parent a power that amounts to a "right to determine the child's place of residence" and thereby creates a "right of custody" that is protected by the Convention's return remedy.

We disagree. The right to determine the "place of residence" is an apt example of a right of custody because it is indicative: the parent who decides where the child dwells is very likely to be the parent who exercises care and control, and therefore has custody. It is unhelpful and insufficient to think about the custodial right to designate a child's "place of residence" in terms of the power to pick her home country or territory. Such a power protects rights of custody and access alike, and is no clue as to who has custody. Every roof is in some country, territory or jurisdiction. A child may be profoundly affected by the ambient culture and regime of a particular country, but "place of residence," as a signal example of parental control over care and upbringing, necessarily entails more specific choices. A custodial parent cannot discharge the responsibility of deciding a child's "place of residence" by picking a country or territory. Depending on many considerations, the custodial parent must place the child in a city, suburb, or countryside; in a particular dwelling unit at some address; at home, or in a boarding school, finishing school, military academy, or institution. These choices are unavoidable for a parent who exercises the custodial right to fix the residence of a child.

The wording of the "place of residence" example buttresses our interpretation of Article 5. The right specified is the "right to determine" a child's place of residence, thereby implying an active power to choose (and change) the residential address, at will, as a matter of parental and personal judgment. See Webster's Third at 617 (defining "determine" as "to settle or decide by choice of alternative possibilities; to direct or control the end or course of"); Random House at 393 (defining "determine" as "to cause, affect or control; to fix or decide causally; to settle or decide by an authoritative or conclusive decision").

The ne exeat clause limits Mrs. Croll's custodial power to expatriate Christina, but it does not suggest that the power to "determine" Christina's "place of residence" (in Hong Kong, New York, or anywhere else) is also Mr. Croll's. The Custody Order gives Mr. Croll a veto power only—and only over Christina's expatriation—but gives him no say over any other custodial issue, including Christina's "place of residence" within Hong Kong. That single veto power, even if leveraged, falls short of conferring a joint right to determine the child's residence, particularly since an earlier clause in the custody order awards "custody care and control" solely to the mother.

Just as important, Article 3's definition of "wrongful removal" requires that for a child's removal to be "wrongful" (and a return remedy available) the removal must be in breach of custodial rights of the petitioning parent that "were actually exercised...or would have been so exercised but for the removal." Hague Convention, art. 3. The right conferred by the ne exeat clause is not one that Mr. Croll "actually exercised," and it is circular to say that he would have exercised it but for Christina's removal, because the right itself concerns nothing but removal itself, and would never have been exercised had Mrs. Croll been content to stay in Hong Kong during Christina's minority....

If we were to enforce rights held pursuant to a ne exeat clause by the remedy of mandatory return, the Convention would become unworkable. A foundational assumption in the Convention is that the remedy of return will deliver the child to a custodial parent who (by definition) will receive and care for the child. It does not contemplate return of a child to a parent whose sole right—to visit or veto—imposes no duty to give care.

In this case, for example, the custody order places all the burdens of care and custody on Mrs. Croll, and none of them on Mr. Croll. If return were ordered, perhaps Mrs. Croll (an American citizen) would expatriate herself to the People's Republic of China in order to care for her daughter; and if she does not, Mr. Croll probably will arrange for his daughter's care. But an order of return does not require Mrs. Croll to return with Christina; the Hong Kong custody decree does not require Mr. Croll to take care of the child day-to-day; we lack discretion to withhold return of a child who has been wrongfully removed; and the Convention does not allow us to alter the custodial arrangements ordered by the court in Hong Kong. Given those mandated strictures, we cannot plausibly read the Convention to compel the removal of a child from a parent who exercises all rights of care to a country in which no one has that affirmative power or duty.

The dissent points out that the Convention undoubtedly compels return of a child (accompanied or not by the parent who took her abroad) even (i) to a parent with joint custody who may receive the child upon repatriation at a time of year when custody would ordinarily be exercised by the parent who may remain abroad, or (ii) to a parent who exercises custody rights by decisional power without day-to-day care. In the first case, the child is returned to a parent who gives day-to-day care in season and who can be expected to have the facilities, resources, fitness, and inclination to give care out of season as well; in the latter case, the decision-making parent can decide in what school or in whose care the child can be placed. The dissent's analysis, however, would compel the return of the child to a parent who lacks the right or responsibility to give care or to decide who should give it, or even to a parent with access who has been found unfit to have custody. The custodial parent who expatriates the child in violation of a court order may elect to stay abroad, if only to avoid contempt proceedings; yet the dissent construes the Convention to compel return of the child to a country in which the only parent has no duty to give care and no power except to compel the return and enjoy occasional access. The dissent offers the reassurance, however, that such a child would not be neglected because "a parent's duty to care for a child" may be imposed by "the law of the country of habitual residence." No doubt, family courts in the United States would impose that obligation as a matter of family law—though of course a court cannot confer competence or fitness—but on this point the dissent is generalizing from local American law; and even if we assume that courts anywhere can in a pinch confer custodial rights and duties on the local parent if the custodial parent remains abroad, the effect of compelling return on that assumption would be to alter custody rights rather than to enforce them....

The Convention's ratification history is entirely consistent with our interpretation of "rights of custody" as defined in the Convention.... The official reporter of the Hague Conference recounts that "[a]lthough the problems which can arise from a breach of access rights, especially where the child is taken abroad by its custodian, were raised... the majority view was that such situations could not be put in the same category as the wrongful removals which [the Convention] is sought to prevent." Pérez-Vera Report 65, at 444–45.... The Convention's official reporter has explained why the Convention provides separate remedies to secure access rights versus custodial rights, and limits the return remedy to the breach of custody:

A questionable result would [be] attained had the application of the Convention, by granting the same degree of protection to custody and access rights, led ultimately to the substitution of the holders of one type of right by those who held the other.

Pérez-Vera Report 65, at 445 (emphasis added)....

Mr. Croll asks us to draw a distinction between: (i) a bare right of access, recognized as such; and (ii) the same bare right of access enforced by a ne exeat clause. The rationale for this distinction is that a parent who removes a child in violation of access rights and a ne exeat clause would otherwise succeed in frustrating the ne exeat clause altogether, so that a return remedy is needed to achieve the Convention's goal of preventing parents from unilaterally circumventing the home country's courts in search of a more sympathetic forum. But the frustration of judicial power is not the touchstone for a return remedy under the Convention. A court order that confers a right of access (without more) on a non-custodial parent of a middle-class means is utterly frustrated if a custodial parent then permanently moves the child so far away that neither parent can afford to finance court-ordered access. Yet it is undisputed that the remedy of return is unavailable in such a case.

A ne exeat provision protects parental rights of access or custody alike; it does not transmute one right into the other....

No consensus view emerges from the opinions issued by the courts of the signatory nations. Though the "opinions of our sister signatories [are] entitled to considerable weight," Air France v. Saks, 470 U.S. 392, 404 (1985), we are aware of no doctrine requiring our deference to a series of conflicting cases from foreign signatories.... Moreover, most of the cases rest on distinguishable facts, such as (a) orders of temporary custody awarded in the course of an ongoing custody battle,...or (b) consent decrees expressly granting custody rights to both parents.

Although the dissent claims "strong support" in caselaw for its point of view, the dissent itself confirms that no consensus is available: the cases worldwide are few, scattered, conflicting, and sometimes conclusory and unreasoned....

Sotomayor, J., dissenting....

The critical interpretive challenge in this case involves the definition of "rights of custody" as used in the Convention. The majority begins this undertaking by surveying a host of American dictionaries.... While traditional American notions of custody rights are certainly relevant to our interpretation of the Convention, the construction of an international treaty also requires that we look beyond parochial definitions to the broader meaning of the Convention, and assess the "ordinary meaning to be given to the terms of the treaty in their context and in the light of [the Convention's] object and purpose." Vienna Convention on the Law of Treaties, May 23, 1969, art. 31.1, 1155 U.N.T.S. 331, 340 (stating general rule on the interpretation of treaties); see also Restatement (Third) of Foreign Relations Law §325 (1987) (same).

Contrary to the majority's position that "[n]othing in the Hague Convention suggests that the drafters intended anything other than this ordinary understanding of custody," the Convention and its official history reflect a notably more expansive conception of custody rights. The report containing the official history and commentary on the Convention clarifies that "the intention [of the Convention] is to protect all the ways in which custody of children can be exercised." Elisa Pérez-Vera, Explanatory Report to the Hague Conference on Private International Law, in 3 Acts and Documents of the Fourteenth Session (Child Abduction) 426, para. 71 (1980) (emphasis in original) ("Pérez-Vera Report"). This broad notion of custody rights is also consistent with Article 3, which provides that "rights of custody" may arise from a variety of sources, including by "operation of law or by reason of a judicial or administrative decision, or by reason of an agreement having legal effect under the law of [the child's country of habitual residence]." Hague Convention, art. 3. In this way, the Convention plainly favors "a flexible interpretation of the terms used, which allows the greatest possible number of cases to be brought into consideration." Pérez-Vera Report, para. 67. Consequently, in determining whether the rights arising under a ne exeat clause constitute "rights of custody" under the Convention, I discern an intent of inclusion rather than exclusion, so as to effectuate the drafters' goal of making the treaty applicable to all possible cases of wrongful removal.

Although the treaty does not generally define its legal terms, the risk that "an incorrect interpretation of [custody and access rights] would...compromis[e] the Convention's objects" led the drafters to include Article 5, which offers further guidance on the meaning of the term "rights of custody." I note, however, that the provision was left deliberately vague due to the drafters' failure to agree on a more precise definition. See Pérez-Vera Report, para. 84. Article 5 provides that: "For the purposes of this Convention—(a) 'rights of custody' shall include rights relating to the care of the person of the child and, in particular, the right to determine the child's place of residence...." Hague Convention, art. 5. As I interpret the Convention, rights arising under a ne exeat clause include the "right to determine the child's place of residence" because the clause provides a parent with decisionmaking authority regarding a child's international relocation. Thus the ne exeat clause vests both Mr. Croll and the Hong Kong court with "rights of custody" for the purposes of the Convention....

At its core, therefore, the Convention's return remedy targets those individuals who cross international borders, presumably in search of a friendlier forum, flouting the custody law of the child's home country in the process.

In light of the Convention's broad purpose, the concept of "wrongful removal" clearly must encompass violations of ne exeat rights. When a parent takes a child abroad in violation of ne exeat rights granted to the other parent by an order from the country of habitual residence, she nullifies that country's custody law as effectively as does the parent who kidnaps a child in violation of the rights of the parent with physical custody of that child. Moreover, where, as here, the parent seeks a custody order in the new country, she seeks to legitimize the very action—removal of the child—that the home country, through its custody order, sought to prevent. To read the Convention so narrowly as to exclude the return remedy in such a situation would allow such parents to undermine the very purpose of the Convention....

The Hague Convention provides a remedy not when a parent moves the child from city to suburb or from home to boarding school, but when he or she transports the child across national borders. In light of this international context, the term "place of residence," as used in the Convention, logically contemplates decisions regarding international relocation. Accordingly, the right to choose the country in which a child lives, like the authority over the child's more specific living arrangements, constitutes a "right to determine the child's place of residence" under Article 5, and thus a "right of custody" under the Convention....

While not essential to my conclusion that ne exeat rights constitute "rights of custody" under the Convention, I note that my analysis is consistent with the decisions of most foreign courts to consider the issue. Given the desirability of uniformity in treaty interpretation, these cases lend support to my understanding of the Convention....

Notes and Questions

1. *Ne Exeat Clause.* A ne exeat clause gives the beneficiary a veto over the other parent's decision to leave the country, unless the court gives permission for the departure. The court in *Croll* characterizes the Croll custody order as containing such a clause. Did such a clause exist at the time the children were removed in *David S. v. Zamira S.*? What is the New York Family Court's basis for saying that the children's removal was "wrongful"?

2. *Care of the Child Upon Return.* In clarifying "rights of custody," the *Croll* majority mentions that if it ordered Christina's return, she might be uncared for since her father had no legal obligation to care for her. Does that assumption comport with the facts? Could the appellate court have remanded to discover the father's intentions? Could it have extracted undertakings to address this concern? Moreover, is this a legitimate concern or is this a matter for the courts in Hong Kong?

3. *Access v. Custody v. Ne Exeat Clause.* Does the majority's reference to the drafters' intent really address the dissent's view that "rights of custody" should be viewed expansively?

4. *Majority View.* Most courts believe a remedy of return is only available for a violation of rights of custody, not access. Most courts also believe a ne exeat clause establishes rights of custody. The case most often cited for this proposition is the 1989 English decision in *C v. C (Minors) (Abduction: Rights of Custody Abroad)*, 2 All E.R. 465 (Eng. C.A. 1989). In *C v. C*, the divorce decree awarded the mother custody, made both parents guardians, and restricted both parents from removing the child from Australia without the other's consent. The mother violated the order by taking the child to England. In granting the father's petition for the return of the child, the Court of Appeal held that the ne exeat clause gave the father more than just a veto over the mother's ability to leave England. Rather, it gave him a right to establish the child's residence as a condition of departure. Lord Justice Neill explained, "This consent could be limited both as to the period of absence [from Australia] and as to the place to which the child could be taken. Thus, to take an example, the father could consent to the child residing with the mother for a period of a year or so in England or some other agreed country or even at some particular address." *Id.* at 465.

5. *Enforcement of Rights of Access.* How does someone enforce his rights of access when the custodial parent takes the child abroad and refuses to make the child available for visitation? In contrast to invoking article 12, a parent denied access rights can petition the Central Authority pursuant to article 21. Practices vary greatly among Central Authorities since article 21 provides countries considerable discretion.

In the United States, despite 42 U.S.C. § 11603(b), federal courts have held that they do not have subject matter jurisdiction over claims for rights of access. *See* Janzik v. Schand, 2000 WL 1745203 (N.D. Ill. Nov. 27, 2000); Teijeiro Fernandez v. Yeager, 121 F. Supp. 2d 1118 (W.D. Mich. 2000); Bromley v. Bromley, 30 F. Supp. 2d 857 (E.D. Pa. 1998). However, civil law countries, and some common law countries, believe that article 21 provides them with jurisdiction to enforce existing access orders. *See, e.g.,* Amended Rules of the Court of Session (Scotland), Rule 70.5(2); Gumbrell v. Jones, [2001] N.Z.F.L.R. 593 (N.Z. Fam. Ct.).

Assume that a Central Authority does no more than provide general information to applicants seeking to obtain visitation, and assume further that the courts in the jurisdiction do not view article 21 as providing a basis for a judicial action regarding access rights. What should an applicant do next? Are there other remedies available to a parent who is denied access rights?

6. *Solutions to the Access Problem.* It is a complex and unresolved question whether visitation, or even more visitation, with a non-custodial parent benefits a child. *See* John Eekelaar, *Contact—Over the Limit,* [2000] Fam. L. 271, 272 (summarizing empirical data). Assuming, however, that denial of rights of access is a serious problem, what should be done about it? If the custodial parent is denying access, in part, because of a fear that the noncustodial parent will not return the child if the child is sent abroad for visitation, there may be solution. Although the Hague Convention provides a remedy in this type of situation, the custodial parent may fear the risk that her petition would be denied or may worry about the costs involved with the litigation. A possible solution is to have the noncustodial parent secure a mirror order before the child is sent abroad. A mirror order is an order entered by a court of the jurisdiction to which the child is to be sent. The order would confirm issues such as the child's custodian, the time-frame for visitation, and the child's habitual residence. This order would expedite the return of the child if the child were then wrongfully retained. A mirror order may be especially important when a non-custodial parent seeks to exercise visitation in a country that is not a party to the Hague Convention.

7. *Broader Solutions to the Access Problem.* Apart from the fact pattern described in note 6, access issues can take a variety of other forms. For example, a party may seek to establish access pending the resolution of a Hague petition, a party may want to establish access after the denial of a Hague petition, a parent may want a foreign access order enforced in the place where the child is now located, a parent may want to establish an access order independent of any Hague proceeding, or a parent may want to modify an access order entered by a foreign court or by the court in the jurisdiction where the child now lives. While most countries have laws to assist litigants with achieving their goals, the reality is that "they may carry certain disadvantages such as the absence of a supporting role by the Central Authority, slower procedures, or less favourable provision for legal aid, assistance or advice." *Transfrontier Access/Contact and the Hague Convention of 25 October 1980 on the Civil Aspects of International Child Abduction,* Hague Conference on Private International Law, at 15, Prel. Doc. No. 5 (2002). Moreover, there exists transnational variation, including inconsistent jurisdictional rules for the establishment or modification of contact orders, varied levels of assistance available to foreign applicants, different levels of protection for the child's and custodial parent's safety, and different timetables by which access matters are resolved.

The question has arisen whether the Permanent Bureau at the Hague should draft a protocol to the Hague Convention on Child Abduction that would provide in a more satisfactory and detailed manner than article 21 for the effective exercise of access/contact between children and their custodial and non-custodial parents. Recently, a Final Report by the Permanent Bureau on the issue recommended that the Conference should take a number of intermediate steps "as a matter of urgency" while the idea of a protocol is considered further. The report concludes that if the intermediate steps address most of the existing concerns, then a protocol may not be necessary. The intermediate steps recommended include the development of a Guide to Good Practice in relation to access/contact cases, the development of general advisory principles relevant to international access/contact cases, the fostering of judicial education and cooperation, the encouragement of states to ratify the Hague Convention of 19 October 1996 on Jurisdiction, Applicable Law, Recognition, Enforcement and Co-operation in Respect of Parental Responsibility and Measures for the Protection of Children (discussed in the next part), and the monitoring and dissemination of information about mediation efforts. *See generally Preliminary Doc. No. 5 of July 2002, supra.* If you were to participate in the effort to draft general advisory principles relevant to access cases, which ones would you want to see included? Do you think that the recommendations, all of which would be non-legally binding, would adequately address the problem?

8. *Bilateral or Regional Agreements.* In some jurisdictions, bilateral or regional agreements are in place on the topic of child custody. For example, the European Convention on Recognition and Enforcement of Decisions Concerning Custody of Children and on Restoration of Custody of Children, found in the Supplement, is in force among twenty-eight countries, and addresses, among other issues, child abduction. The European Convention on Recognition operates differently than the Hague Convention, and the circumstances under which a right of return might be available under the European Convention on Recognition are far narrower than under the Hague Convention on Child Abduction. Courts, in fact, have held that an unlawful removal for purposes of the Hague Convention is not necessarily an unlawful removal for purposes of the European Convention on Recognition. *See, e.g., In re S.,* A.C. 750 (Eng. H.L. 1998).

In contrast to the Hague Convention, a request for return of the child under the European Convention on Recognition must be made to a Central Authority within six months of the date of the improper removal or retention. *Id.* art. 8. In addition, the removal or retention must breach a custody order actually in existence at the time of the removal, or one obtained subsequently (sometimes referred to as a "chasing order"). *Id.* arts. 1, 8, 12. A contracting party can also enact several broad defenses to return, two of which would permit a court to engage in an extensive examination of the substantive merits. Return could be refused, for example, if "the effects of the decision are manifestly incompatible with the fundamental principles of the law relating to the family and children in the State addressed." *Id.* art. 10(1)(a). Enforcement also may be refused if "a change in the circumstances...not including a mere change in the residence of the child after an improper removal" makes "the effects of the original decision...manifestly no longer in accordance with the welfare of the child." *Id.* art. 10(1)(b). Finally, if the children or the parents have the wrong nationality (e.g., the child is a national of the state addressed), then the European Convention affords no assistance. *See* arts. 8, 10(1)(c)(i). *See, e.g., In re T* (Children), 2 Fam. Ct. Rep. 159 (Eng. Fam. 2000) (holding that a Spanish order was not enforceable in England when one of the two children was born in England and the other child's birth was registered at the British Embassy so that he too was a British citizen and a national of the State addressed and strong reasons existed not to order return under the Hague Convention). Section B.2.b.iv of this chapter discusses the way in which the European Convention on Recognition secures the recognition and enforcement of custody and visitation orders.

9. *The Need for Uniformity.* The Convention was adopted in an effort to promote uniformity among nations in their response to the problem of international child abduction. Contrary to the majority's disclaimer in *Croll v. Croll,* the outcome differs from how most other courts have decided this issue. *See* Merle H. Weiner, *Navigating the Road Between Uniformity and Progress: The Need for a Purposive Analysis of the Hague Convention on the Civil Aspects of International Child Abduction,* 33 Colum. Hum. Rts. L. Rev. 275 (2001). What problems are presented when countries interpret the Convention differently? Since foreign decisions have no precedential weight for

U.S. courts, what should be the approach of U.S. courts to foreign courts' interpretation of the Convention's terms? Professor Weiner gives various reasons why U.S. courts should be deferential, and at least treat foreign caselaw as presumptively correct. When should one consider that presumption rebutted? For an analysis of this problem, *see* Weiner, *supra*. Given the importance of uniformity, perhaps courts contemplating a departure from the prevailing approach should consider the likelihood that other nations will follow a novel interpretation. What do you think of the Second Circuit's reasoning in *Croll*? Can you envision another way to arrive at the same conclusion that might appeal more to courts in other nations?

Problem 8-4

A couple with two children divorced in Israel, and the divorce judgment incorporated the terms of the parties' separation agreement. The agreement gave the parents joint legal custody. The agreement also provided that the children would live with their mother in the United States, but not beyond July 22, four years hence. The children would then live in Israel, and study there during the following school year. The agreement entitles the father to visitation in Israel every summer, for sixty-five days, and during school vacations. The father earns a low income, so the mother agreed to pay for the children's travel to Israel. In addition, if the father travels to the United States, he can visit the children there. The parties agreed that all future modifications to their agreement would be handled solely by the District Court in Jerusalem. The mother moved to the United States with the children last year. Recently, just prior to a scheduled visit with the children in the United States, the mother filed a "Verified Complaint for Custody" in the state court, seeking to modify all visitation that might occur in Israel. The father responded, in part, by filing an action for the return of the children, alleging that the mother's actions amounted to a wrongful retention. How should the court rule on the father's Hague petition?

Whallon v. Lynn
230 F.3d 450 (1st Cir. 2000)

Lynch, J.

In May 2000, Richard Charles Whallon, Jr. petitioned for the return of his five-year-old daughter, Micheli Lynn Whallon King, to Mexico pursuant to the Hague Convention on the Civil Aspects of International Child Abduction. Micheli had been taken by her mother, Diana Lynn, from Mexico, where all three had lived, to Massachusetts. Lynn says that she was entitled to do so, inter alia, because Whallon never had the type of "rights of custody" as to Micheli that are protected by the Convention. The parties agree that this in turn requires an inquiry into what rights under Mexican law an unmarried parent (here Whallon) has under the doctrine "patria potestas," a doctrine with ancient roots in Roman law....

Micheli was born in Mexico on July 4, 1995. Micheli's parents, Diana Lynn and Richard Charles Whallon, Jr., both American citizens, never married, and they separated towards the end of 1995. Micheli lived with her mother and her half-sister Leah in Cabo San Lucas, Baja California Sur, Mexico. Following the separation, Whallon continued to spend time with Micheli. At no time did Whallon and Lynn enter into a formal custody agreement; neither has sought a custody determination as to his or her own status.

Lynn alleged that Whallon performed only a limited parental role and provided only sporadic child support during the last two years all three of them were in Mexico. Additionally, Lynn accused Whallon of subjecting her and Leah to significant verbal abuse and of allowing matters to escalate to physical violence against Lynn herself. Lynn made no such claim that Whallon acted that way towards Micheli.

In fact, the record reflects that Whallon was significantly involved in his daughter Micheli's life. From the time of Micheli's birth, Whallon saw her on an almost daily basis. And from the time Micheli was three years old, she spent every other weekend, overnights, with Whallon. Indeed, in August 1997, Whallon moved to within one hundred yards of where Lynn and Micheli lived to be closer to Micheli. Whallon also paid Lynn at least $500 of child support for Micheli each month, money that was used to pay for dental and medical work for Micheli. Whallon did the types of things that one generally expects an attentive and mindful parent to do: driving Micheli to and from nursery school every day for almost two years; buying Micheli clothes; helping her with homework and art projects; attending various school activities; and taking Micheli to the doctor when she was sick. Additionally, Whallon took Micheli—with Lynn's approval—to San Diego for medical and dental appointments and to Arizona in 1998 to meet Micheli's paternal grandfather.

In late September 1999, Whallon learned that Lynn was planning to take Micheli with her to Texas to visit Lynn's parents. Whallon filed a petition in the court of the State of Baja California Sur in Mexico to permanently deprive Lynn of all custody rights over Micheli and to grant him all such rights. The Mexican court eventually denied the petition in April 2000, concluding that Whallon had failed to establish the imminent danger, absolute abandonment, or sort of corruption or mistreatment required to terminate a mother's custody of a child under seven years of age. In the interim, Whallon's attorney attempted to block the departure of Lynn, Micheli, and Leah.... On October 1, 1999, Lynn took Micheli and Leah with her to the United States. Whallon then petitioned the district court in Massachusetts for Micheli's return to Mexico.

Following a two-day evidentiary hearing, the district court granted the petition and then denied respondent Diana Lynn's motion for a stay pending appeal. The district court reasoned that under the Hague Convention Lynn had physical custody over Micheli but that Whallon also exercised "rights of custody" over Micheli within the meaning of the Convention. Specifically, the court found that Whallon exercised patria potestas rights, a concept of parental custody rights distinct from physical custody rights on the one hand and mere visitation rights on the other. Accordingly, it concluded that Lynn's removal of Micheli violated Whallon's actual exercise of rights of custody under Mexican law, and was thus wrongful under the Convention....

The Hague Convention states that rights of custody "shall include rights relating to the care of the person of the child and, in particular, the right to determine the child's place of residence...." Hague Convention, art. 5(a).

While the Hague Convention itself provides no further definition of the term "rights of custody," and deliberately so, courts have commonly looked to the background report of the Convention for further guidance. That report states that "the law of the child's habitual residence is invoked in the widest possible sense," and that the sources from which custody rights derive are "all those upon which a claim can be based within the context of the legal system concerned." Explanatory Report, §67, at 446. The Report also states that the Convention favors "a flexible interpretation of the terms used, which allows the greatest possible number of cases to be brought into consideration."...

As the Explanatory Report instructs:

> [F]rom the Convention's standpoint, the removal of a child by one of the joint holders without the consent of the other, is...wrongful, and this wrongfulness derives in this particular case, not from some action in breach of a particular law, but from the fact that such action has disregarded the rights of the other parent which are also protected by law, and has interfered with their normal exercise. The Convention's true nature is revealed most clearly in these situations: it is not concerned with establishing the person to whom custody of the child will belong at some point in the future, nor with the situations in which it may prove necessary to modify a decision awarding joint custody on the basis of facts which have subsequently changed. It seeks, more simply, to prevent a later decision on the matter being influenced by a change of circumstances brought about through unilateral action by one of the parties.

Explanatory Report § 71, at 447–48.

Thus, to assess whether Whallon possesses "rights of custody" under Article 5 of the Convention, the court must not simply look to the relevant provisions of Mexican law but also must interpret those provisions in light of the Convention's basic principle that a child's country of habitual residence is best placed to decide upon questions of custody and access, unless an exception applies.

The law of the State of Baja California Sur, the place of Micheli's habitual residence, is the relevant source of law here. *See* Hague Convention, art. 3. That poses its own difficulties for a court of the United States, a court which comes from a different legal tradition. Care must be taken to avoid imposing American legal concepts onto another legal culture. Differently from many laws in this country, Mexican law appears to embody two concepts of importance here. The first is a preference in divorce cases toward placing what is called "custody" of a child under age seven with the mother. That preference is negated in "exceptional cases" such as those involving "serious and contagious illness, vice, mistreatment or desertion." Codigo Civil del Estado de Baja California Sur ("Civil Code"), art. 322. The preference is embodied in the Civil Code, and while it applies specifically to divorces (and there has been no divorce here since there was never a marriage), the Mexican court looked to this provision in informing its decision about whether to terminate Lynn's custodial rights. And so we find that maternal preference, as well as the Code's use of the term "custody," relevant to our determination of whether Whallon has rights of custody under the Convention.

The second concept is embodied in the doctrine of patria potestas, and represents a more generalized concept of parental authority. Although historically the doctrine protected the father's rights as to the child, originally absolute rights under Roman law, the Baja California Sur Civil Code refers to it as encompassing the rights of both parents. Article 474 provides generally that patria potestas, or parental authority, "is understood to mean the relationship of rights and obligations that are held reciprocally, on the one hand, by the father and the mother or in some cases the grandparents and, on the other hand, the minor children who are not emancipated." Civil Code, art. 474. The concept of patria potestas is defined broadly: "Paternal authority is exercised over the person and the property of the children subject to it. The purpose of its exercise is the comprehensive physical, mental, moral and social protection of the minor child, and it includes the obligation for [the child's] guardianship and education." *Id.* art. 479. Additionally, those exercising patria potestas "have the obligation to comport themselves in a manner that sets a good example for the children and shall teach them appropriate standards of social interaction." *Id.* art. 486.

The Civil Code explicitly discusses patria potestas rights in situations where, as here, the parents of a child born outside of wedlock separate. It provides that in such situations, "both [parents] shall continue to exercise paternal authority." *See id.* art. 478 (emphasis added). The Code then distinguishes patria potestas from "custody," which may be decided by agreement or, failing such agreement, by a judge. *Id.* Indeed, the existence of divisible custody rights under Mexican law—i.e., of physical custody and patria potestas is entirely consistent with the Hague Convention's statement that custody may be held "jointly or alone." Hague Convention, art. 3. Explanatory Report 71, at 447–48 (characterizing joint custody as "dividing the responsibilities inherent in custody rights between both parents").

Lynn says that Whallon's patria potestas rights are closer to what the Convention means by "rights of access" than to what it means by "rights of custody." We disagree. Article 329 of the Civil Code states that "[i]ndependently of who exercises patria potestas or custody, the relatives obliged by law to provide support have the right to visit their descendants or collateral relatives, and to have an adequate communication with them." Civil Code, art. 329. Thus, patria potestas, like physical custody, plainly means something "independent" from mere visitation rights. Importantly, the Code describes these visitation rights in terms of "adequate communication," *id.*, but describes patria potestas rights through the stronger language of "adequate connection," *id.* art. 323, which implies a meaningful, decisionmaking role in the life and care of the child, and not the mere access to the child associated with visitation rights.

Additionally, Whallon submitted into evidence the affidavit of Mexican attorney Omar Quijano Martinez further corroborating that both parents exercise patria potestas rights over a child under Mexican law and stating that both parents must consent to the removal of such child under Mexican law. Such affidavits are an acceptable form of proof in determining issues of foreign law, *see* Rule 44.1, Fed. R. Civ. P., and are likewise permitted under the Hague Convention, *see* Explanatory Report § 101, at 456–57 ("proof of the substantive law of the State of the child's habitual residence may be established by either certificates or affidavits").

In sum, the evidence of patria potestas rights under Mexican law leads us to conclude that Whallon's rights were "rights of custody" under the Convention. While Lynn had actual custody of Micheli, both parents exercised patria potestas rights over Micheli. Indeed, to date no Mexican court has given Lynn exclusive custody or denied Whallon patria potestas rights over Micheli. The pending Massachusetts custody proceedings commenced by Lynn after her removal of Micheli are inapplicable to this action because the Convention refers specifically to (Whallon's) rights of custody at "the time of removal." Hague Convention, art. 3(b)....

Notes and Questions

1. *Mechanisms for Establishing Rights of Custody.* How does one establish that one's client has "rights of custody"? Article 3 of the Convention provides three potential sources of custody rights: (1) operation of law, (2) judicial or administrative decision, or (3) an agreement having legal effect under the law of that state. From which of these sources were rights of custody established in *Whallon v. Lynn*?

2. *Burden of Proof.* It is the petitioner's burden to establish that he or she had rights of custody. Establishing that one was awarded or has rights of custody often requires considerable initiative. Consider the facts and holding of *Shalit v. Coppe*, 182 F.3d 1124 (9th Cir. 1999). In *Shalit v. Coppe*, Haim Shalit and Cheryl Coppe divorced in Alaska. The Alaska state court gave Coppe custody of their child, Yarden. Shalit was awarded visitation rights. Subsequently, Shalit and Coppe agreed that Yarden would move to Israel temporarily to live with Shalit. At the end of what was supposed to be a visit with Coppe in Alaska, Coppe refused to return Yarden to Israel. Shalit filed a petition under the Hague Convention requesting that Yarden be returned to Israel. The court rejected Shalit's application. In determining that Coppe's retention of Yarden was not "wrongful" under article 3 of the Convention, the court had to determine "whether Coppe's action was in breach of Shalit's rights of custody under the law of the state of Yarden's habitual residence." *Id.* at 1128.

As a precondition to establishing that Shalit had custody rights under "operation of law," Shalit had to show which law was controlling: Israeli law or United States law. Shalit ignored this issue and put forth no evidence either way. The court, therefore, could not determine whether Coppe had breached Shalit's rights of custody that might have arisen by "operation of law."

Nor was there a judicial or administrative decision in Shalit's favor determining custody rights. The only custody decision was the Alaska order granting Coppe legal and physical custody with visitation rights to Shalit. Shalit did not suggest any reason that Israel would refuse to acknowledge the Alaska court's ruling. Additionally, the orders of the Alaska court "were not entered surreptitiously or to gain a jurisdictional or procedural advantage." *Id.* at 1131.

Shalit argued that his rights of custody arose by an agreement having legal affect under the law of Israel. The court rejected this argument because Israeli law stated that agreements between separated parents are "'subject to the approval of the Court.'" *Id.* The oral agreement that Yarden would live temporarily with Shalit was not approved by either an Israeli or an American court. *Id.* at 1128 n.4.

3. *Patria Potestas.* Does the definition of patria potestas suggest that a grandparent could bring a Hague petition for a child's return when the parents leave a jurisdiction? For an analysis of the Hague Convention's operation between the United States and Mexico as well as a discussion of the law of patria potestas, *see* Antoinette Sedillo Lopez, *International Law—U.S./Mexico Cross-Border Child Abduction—The Need for Cooperation*, 29 N.M. L. Rev. 289 (1999).

4. *Unmarried Fathers and Rights of Custody.* Would Mr. Lehr have "rights of custody" if Ms. Robertson took their child abroad and he sought the child's return? You may recall that in *Lehr v. Robertson*, 463 U.S. 248 (1983), the Supreme Court upheld the scheme in New York which required an unmarried father to file with the "putative father registry" as a way to indicate his intent to claim paternity of his child, and thereby receive notice of any proceeding to adopt that child. No filing was necessary if the father fell into any other category of person to whom the law required notice be given, including the following: those who had been adjudicated to be the father; those who had been identified as the father on the child's birth certificate; those who had lived openly with the child and the child's mother and who held themselves out to be the father; those who had been identified as the father by the mother in a sworn written statement; and those who had been married to the child's mother before the child was six months old. Mr. Lehr had never registered, he fell into none of the other categories, he was never

given advance notice of the adoption proceeding, and his daughter was adopted by her mother's husband. The adoption occurred despite the fact that the court adjudicating the adoption knew of Mr. Lehr's commencement of a paternity proceeding in a neighboring county. What additional information might you need to determine whether Mr. Lehr had "rights of custody" for purposes of the Hague Convention? *See* H.I. v. M.G., [1999] 2 I.L.R.M. 1 (Ir.) (holding unmarried natural father had "rights of custody" under the Convention despite contrary expert testimony on status of unmarried fathers' rights in New York).

5. In *Whallon*, the mother had also argued, among other things, that Whallon was not "actually exercising" his rights of custody. The court found the argument totally without merit. The requirement of actual exercise is now explored further.

---

c. *Actual Exercise*

Friedrich v. Friedrich

78 F.3d 1060 (6th Cir. 1996)

Thomas was born in Bad Aibling, Germany, to Jeana Friedrich, an American servicewoman stationed there, and her husband, Emanuel Friedrich, a German citizen. When Thomas was two years old, his parents separated after an argument on July 27, 1991. Less than a week later, in the early morning of August 2, 1991, Mrs. Friedrich took Thomas from Germany to her family home in Ironton, Ohio, without informing Mr. Friedrich. Mr. Friedrich sought return of the child in German Family Court, obtaining an order awarding him custody on August 22. He then filed this action for the return of his son in the United States District Court for the Southern District of Ohio on September 23....

The removal of a child from the country of its habitual residence is "wrongful" under the Hague Convention if a person in that country is, or would otherwise be, exercising custody rights to the child under that country's law at the moment of removal. Hague Convention, Article 3....

The district court held that a preponderance of the evidence in the record established that Mr. Friedrich was exercising custody rights over Thomas at the time of Thomas's removal. Mrs. Friedrich alleges that the district court improperly applied German law. Reviewing de novo, we find no error in the court's legal analysis. Custody rights "may arise in particular by operation of law or by reason of a judicial or administrative decision, or by reason of an agreement having legal effect under the law of the State." Hague Convention, Article 3. German law gives both parents equal de jure custody of the child, German Civil Code 1626(1), and, with a few exceptions, this de jure custody continues until a competent court says otherwise. *See* Currier v. Currier, 845 F. Supp. 916, 920 (D.N.H.1994) ("under German law both parents retain joint rights of custody until a decree has been entered limiting one parent's rights")....

Mrs. Friedrich argues that Mr. Friedrich "terminated" his custody rights under German law because, during the argument on the evening of July 27, 1991, he placed Thomas's belongings and hers in the hallway outside of their apartment. The district court properly rejected the claim that these actions could end parental rights as a matter of German law. We agree. After examining the record, we are uncertain as to exactly what happened on the evening of July 27, but we do know that the events of that night were not a judicial abrogation of custody rights. Nor are we persuaded by Mrs. Friedrich's attempts to read the German Civil Code provisions stipulated to by the parties in such a way as to create the ability of one parent to terminate his or her custody rights extrajudicially.[2]

Mrs. Friedrich also argues that, even if Mr. Friedrich had custody rights under German law, he was not exercising those custody rights as contemplated by the Hague Convention. She argues that, since custody rights include the care for the person and property of the child, Mr. Friedrich was not exercising custody rights because he was not paying for or taking care of the child during the brief period of separation in Germany.

The Hague Convention does not define "exercise." As judges in a common law country, we can easily imagine doing so ourselves. One might look to the law of the foreign country to determine if custody rights existed de jure, and then develop a test under the general principles of the Hague Convention to determine what activities—financial support, visitation—constitute sufficient exercise of de jure rights. The question in our immediate case would then be: "was Mr. Friedrich's single visit with Thomas and plans for future visits with Thomas sufficient exercise of custodial rights for us to justify calling the removal of Thomas wrongful?" One might even approach a distinction between the exercise of "custody" rights and the exercise of "access" or "visitation" rights. If Mr. Friedrich, who has de jure custody, was not exercising sufficient de facto custody, Thomas's removal would not be wrongful.

We think it unwise to attempt any such project. Enforcement of the Convention should not to be made dependent on the creation of a common law definition of "exercise." The only acceptable solution, in the absence of a ruling from a court in the country of habitual residence, is to liberally find "exercise" whenever a parent with de jure custody rights keeps, or seeks to keep, any sort of regular contact with his or her child.

We see three reasons for this broad definition of "exercise." First, American courts are not well suited to determine the consequences of parental behavior under the law of a foreign country. It is fairly easy for the courts of one country to determine whether a person has custody rights under the law of another country. It is also quite possible for a court to determine if an order by a foreign court awards someone "custody" rights, as opposed to rights of "access." Far more difficult is the task of deciding, prior to a ruling by a court in the abducted-from country, if a parent's custody rights should be ignored because he or she was not acting sufficiently like a custodial parent. A foreign court, if at all possible, should refrain from making such policy-oriented decisions concerning the application of German law to a child whose habitual residence is, or was, Germany.

Second, an American decision about the adequacy of one parent's exercise of custody rights is dangerously close to forbidden territory: the merits of the custody dispute. The German court in this case is perfectly capable of taking into account Mr. Friedrich's behavior during the August 1991 separation, and the German court presumably will tailor its custody order accordingly. A decision by an American court to deny return to Germany because Mr. Friedrich did not show sufficient attention or concern for Thomas's

---

2. Mrs. Friedrich cites German Civil Code 1629, which says that a parent who exercises parental care alone can also represent the child in legal matters alone. Obviously, the ability of one parent to "represent" the child does not imply that the other parent has no custody rights....

welfare would preclude the German court from addressing these issues—and the German court may well resolve them differently.

Third, the confusing dynamics of quarrels and informal separations make it difficult to assess adequately the acts and motivations of a parent. An occasional visit may be all that is available to someone left, by the vagaries of marital discord, temporarily without the child. Often the child may be avoided, not out of a desire to relinquish custody, but out of anger, pride, embarrassment, or fear, vis a vis the other parent. Reading too much into a parent's behavior during these difficult times could be inaccurate and unfair. Although there may be situations when a long period of unexplainable neglect of the child could constitute non-exercise of otherwise valid custody rights under the Convention, as a general rule, any attempt to maintain a somewhat regular relationship with the child should constitute "exercise." This rule leaves the full resolution of custody issues, as the Convention and common sense indicate, to the courts of the country of habitual residence....

We therefore hold that, if a person has valid custody rights to a child under the law of the country of the child's habitual residence, that person cannot fail to "exercise" those custody rights under the Hague Convention short of acts that constitute clear and unequivocal abandonment of the child.[6] Once it determines that the parent exercised custody rights in any manner, the court should stop—completely avoiding the question whether the parent exercised the custody rights well or badly. These matters go to the merits of the custody dispute and are, therefore, beyond the subject matter jurisdiction of the federal courts.

In this case, German law gave Mr. Friedrich custody rights to Thomas. The facts before us clearly indicate that he attempted to exercise these rights during the separation from his wife. Mr. and Mrs. Friedrich argued during the evening of July 27, 1991, and separated on the morning of July 28. Mrs. Friedrich left with her belongings and Thomas. She stayed on the army base with the child for four days. Mr. Friedrich telephoned Mrs. Friedrich on July 29 to arrange a visit with Thomas, and spent the afternoon of that day with his son. Mr. and Mrs. Friedrich met on August 1 to talk about Thomas and their separation. The parties dispute the upshot of this conversation. Mrs. Friedrich says that Mr. Friedrich expressed a general willingness that Thomas move to America with his mother. Mr. Friedrich denies this. It is clear, however, that the parties did agree to immediate visitations of Thomas by Mr. Friedrich, scheduling the first such visit for August 3. Shortly after midnight on August 2, Mrs. Friedrich took her son and, without informing her husband, left for America by airplane.

Because Mr. Friedrich had custody rights to Thomas as a matter of German law, and did not clearly abandon those rights prior to August 1, the removal of Thomas without his consent was wrongful under the Convention, regardless of any other considerations about Mr. Friedrich's behavior during the family's separation in Germany....

Notes and Questions

1. *Breadth of the Holding.* The facts of *Friedrich* are quite simple. Isn't *Friedrich*, to some extent, a prototypical case of abduction? If so, the Sixth Circuit's statements re-

---

6. The situation would be different if the country of habitual residence had a legal rule regarding the exercise of custody rights clearly tied to the Hague concept of international removal. If, for example, Germany had a law stating that, for the purposes of the Convention, mere visitation without financial support during a period of informal separation does not constitute the "exercise" of custody rights, we would, of course, be bound to apply that law in this case.

garding "exercise" arguably went far beyond what was required to resolve the case. "Clear and unequivocal abandonment of the child" might set the bar too high in other cases. After all, the context of this determination is a Hague proceeding, *not* a termination of parental rights. A similar question arises with respect to the court's conclusion that acquiescence requires either "an act or statement with the requisite formality, such as testimony in a judicial proceeding; a convincing written renunciation of rights; or a consistent attitude of acquiescence over a significant period of time." Is this statement of the law not also *obiter dictum*?

2. *Foreign Law.* Is it clear from the Convention that "actual exercise" is to be determined according to the law of the child's habitual residence? *See* Adair Dyer, *The Internationalization of Family Law*, 30 U.C. Davis L. Rev. 625, 640 (1997) ("[T]he concept of "actual exercise" probably does not exist in the domestic laws of most states. Therefore it is, almost by necessity, a concept that is subject to an autonomous international interpretation. Thus, the express reference to German law [in *Friedrich*] was troubling.").

3. *Burden of Proof?* Look at article 13(a). Who has the burden of proof on the issue of actual exercise? Is it part of the petitioner's prima facie case or not?

2. The Defenses

a. *Grave Risk of Harm*

Blondin v. Dubois
189 F.3d 240 (2d Cir. 1999)

Cabranes, J.

Blondin and Dubois met in the summer of 1990 and soon began living together in France, though they never wed. [Ed. Note: Blondin was an American citizen and Dubois was a French citizen.] A daughter, Marie-Eline, was born in May 1991; a son, Francois, in August 1995. There is evidence in the record to suggest, however, that family life was turbulent. Dubois testified that Blondin began beating her in 1991; in some instances, he would do so while she was holding Marie-Eline, with the result that some of Blondin's blows would fall on Marie-Eline. She also testified that on one occasion in 1992, Blondin twisted a piece of electrical cord around Marie-Eline's neck, threatening to kill both the mother and the child. After this incident, Dubois left the home for two weeks, living with Marie-Eline in a shelter for battered women before returning to Blondin. The following year, Dubois again took Marie-Eline with her to a series of shelters, living in them over a period of approximately nine months.

In April 1993, Blondin commenced an action in France to obtain custody of Marie-Eline. That proceeding was resolved in December 1993, when Blondin and Dubois reconciled, agreeing to live together with Marie-Eline at Blondin's residence. Pursuant to their agreement, the French court terminated the proceedings, and issued an order declaring that "the parental rights over the child will be exercised in common by both parents" and that "the child will have its usual residence at the fathers' [sic]." The court's order also provided for regular visitation by Dubois, in the event that she should choose to live outside Blondin's home.

Dubois testified that despite their reconciliation, Blondin continued his abuse. She testified that both during and after her pregnancy with Francois, Blondin repeatedly beat her and threatened her life, as well as the lives of the children. Dubois sought medical attention for her injuries on at least two occasions, and once summoned the French law enforcement authorities.

In August 1997, when Marie-Eline was six years old and Francois was days short of his second birthday, Dubois and the children left France for the United States without notifying Blondin, let alone obtaining his consent. Earlier in 1997, Dubois had forged Blondin's signature in order to obtain passports for the children.

Within days of discovering that Dubois and the children had left the home, Blondin sought and obtained a preliminary order from a French court, directing that the children not leave "the metropolitan territory without the previous authorization of the father." It thus appears that Blondin was not immediately aware that they had departed the country, and that they were living with Dubois and her relatives in New York City. However, Blondin had discovered their whereabouts by June 1998, when he filed the instant petition, seeking the children's return to France under the Hague Convention.

[T]he District Court conducted a prompt evidentiary hearing on Blondin's petition. In that hearing, Dubois testified to the factual allegations set forth in the foregoing paragraphs; Blondin, for his part, denied that he had ever "hit" Dubois or the children, but admitted to having spanked Marie-Eline on infrequent occasions, and equivocated as to whether he may have "slapped" Dubois in the "heat of a dispute." Judge Chin also interviewed Marie-Eline, outside the presence of her parents or their attorneys. She told him that Blondin had hit her and her mother, and that this is why they had left France. She also explained that she did not want to return to France because she did not "want Daddy to hit me." In addition, she told Judge Chin that both parents beat her, but that Blondin did so more than Dubois.

By Memorandum Decision dated August 17, 1998, the District Court denied Blondin's petition....

"[O]nce a plaintiff establishes that removal was wrongful, the child must be returned unless the defendant can establish one of four defenses." Friedrich v. Friedrich, 78 F.3d 1060, 1067 (6th Cir. 1996) ("Friedrich II") (emphasis added); see 42 U.S.C. § 11601(a)(4) ("Children who are wrongfully removed or retained within the meaning of the Convention are to be promptly returned unless one of the narrow exceptions set forth in the Convention applies.").

Two of those exceptions may be established only by "clear and convincing evidence" — either that "there is a grave risk that [the child's] return would expose the child to physical or psychological harm or otherwise place the child in an intolerable situation," pursuant to Article 13(b) of the Convention, or that return of the child "would not be permitted by the fundamental principles...relating to the protection of human rights and fundamental freedoms," pursuant to Article 20. See 42 U.S.C. § 11603(e)(2)(A). In contrast, the other two exceptions to the presumption of repatriation need only be established by a preponderance of the evidence....

As the federal statute implementing the Convention makes clear, these four exceptions are meant to be "narrow." 42 U.S.C. § 11601(a)(4). They do not authorize a court to exceed its Hague Convention function by making determinations, such as who is the better parent, that remain within the purview of the court with plenary jurisdiction over the question of custody. Were a court to give an overly broad construction to its authority to grant exceptions under the Convention, it would frustrate a paramount purpose of that international agreement—namely, to "preserve the status quo and to deter parents from crossing international boundaries in search of a more sympathetic court." Friedrich I, 983 F.2d at 1400....

Dubois concedes that she "wrongfully abducted" the children from France, as that term is used in the Convention. Thus, she acknowledges, the children must be returned to France unless she can establish one of the exceptions provided by the Convention.

The District Court agreed with Dubois that returning Marie-Eline and Francois to Blondin would place them at "grave risk" of a "physical or psychological harm." The District Court relied principally upon the record evidence tending to show that Blondin had physically abused Dubois, often in the children's presence, and that he also had beaten Marie-Eline.... [T]he Court noted that Dubois has no financial resources of her own and was supported by relatives while in the United States. The Court continued,

> In France, Dubois and the children would be dependent upon Blondin. Under the circumstances, I would be extremely wary of requiring Dubois and the children to live in his home. Although one possibility would be to require Blondin to pay for their housing elsewhere, he represented to the Court, during discussions about scheduling a hearing, that he had "no more money" and could not afford the cost even of airfare.... Under these circumstances, requiring Dubois and the children to return to France for legal proceedings would present a grave risk of psychological harm or an intolerable situation.

Ample record evidence supported the District Court's factual determination regarding the risk of physical abuse that the children would face upon return to Blondin's custody. And the parties do not dispute that such a determination will normally provide the basis for an exception under Article 13(b)....

The question remaining before us, however, is whether the District Court could have protected the children from the "grave risk" of harm that it found, while still honoring the important treaty commitment to allow custodial determinations to be made—if at all possible—by the court of the child's home country....

For this reason, it is important that a court considering an exception under Article 13(b) take into account any ameliorative measures (by the parents and by the authorities of the state having jurisdiction over the question of custody) that can reduce whatever risk might otherwise be associated with a child's repatriation. In the exercise of comity that is at the heart of the Convention (an international agreement, we recall, that is an integral part of the "supreme Law of the Land," U.S. Const., art. VI), we are required to place our trust in the court of the home country to issue whatever orders may be necessary to safeguard children who come before it.

As the District Court properly recognized here, granting Blondin's petition would not—as a legal matter—invariably entail turning the children over to his custody. In fact, other arrangements might be available that would allow the children to return to France in some other person's care, pending a long-term custody adjudication—thus reducing or eliminating the risk of harm that might otherwise be associated with granting Blondin's petition. One possible remedy was suggested by Blondin—namely, the temporary placement (with the parties' consent) of Marie-Eline and Francois with their godmother, pending a final adjudication of custody by the courts of France. The District Court rejected this suggestion, stating "if I am going to send the children back, I am probably going to do it with Ms. Dubois." Having determined that the children would be returned, if at all, in their mother's care, the District Court subsequently determined in its written opinion that this arrangement would also be impracticable; the

Court based this determination on its belief that the family's strained circumstances would force Dubois and the children to live with Blondin.

As stated above, we find merit in the District Court's reasons for avoiding a remedy that would effectively transfer the children directly into Blondin's custody. However, that concern appears to justify only the Court's decision that the children not be returned in their mother's care, and thereby forced to live in their father's home. It does not explain the Court's determination that the children should not be returned in the temporary custody of some appropriate and suitable third party, with adequate guarantees of child protection. The District Court did not offer any basis in the Convention or any other legal authority for its determination that a temporary third-party placement would be unacceptable, and no such basis is readily apparent to us.

Under the circumstances presented, we think it appropriate to remand this matter to the District Court for further consideration of the range of remedies that might allow both the return of the children to their home country and their protection from harm, pending a custody award in due course by a French court with proper jurisdiction. In conducting that inquiry, the District Court should not limit itself to the single alternative placement initially suggested by Blondin. On remand, the Court will have the opportunity to exercise its broad equitable discretion to develop a thorough record to facilitate its decision. In so doing, the District Court should feel free to make any appropriate or necessary inquiries of the government of France—especially regarding the availability of ameliorative placement options in France—and to do so, inter alia, by requesting the aid of the United States Department of State, which can communicate directly with that foreign government. We trust that the District Court will conduct these proceedings on remand with the same dispatch that properly characterized its initial consideration of Blondin's Hague Convention petition.

We emphasize, however, that we do not disturb or modify the District Court's finding that returning Marie-Eline and Francois to Blondin's custody (either expressly or de facto) would expose them to a "grave risk" of harm, within the meaning of Article 13(b). Accordingly, if the District Court remains unable to find any reasonable means of repatriation that would not effectively place the children in Blondin's immediate custody, it should deny Blondin's petition under the Convention.

Blondin v. Dubois
78 F. Supp. 2d 283 (S.D.N.Y. 2000)

Chin, J.

Upon remand, I met with the parties and contacted the appropriate French and American authorities to develop a thorough record to aid my analysis of the arrangements by which the children possibly could be returned to France. After receiving responses from the French Central Authority and other French officials, as well as the United States Department of State, I conducted a hearing on December 20, 1999. I heard testimony from a French lawyer with expertise in French family law and international law, an expert in child psychiatry and child psychology, and Dubois. In addition, I interviewed Marie-Eline and Francois.

After due consideration of all the evidence and the arguments of the parties, I again find by clear and convincing evidence that there is a "grave risk" that the return of the children to France would expose them to "physical or psychological harm or otherwise place [them] in an intolerable situation." Convention, Art. 13b. Recognizing that the "grave risk" exception to the Convention is to be construed narrowly, I find that the extraordinary circumstances of this case require that I apply the Article 13b exception. I find that any repatriation arrangements, including even the return of the children in their mother's temporary custody with financial support by Blondin and French social services, would expose Marie-Eline and Francois to a "grave risk" of psychological harm.

The government's expert witness, Veronique Chauveau, testified generally about how French custody proceedings operate and about the social and legal support services available to Dubois and the children should they be returned to France. In addition, the letters submitted by the various French authorities in response to my inquiries detailed what specific social services and legal protections awaited Dubois and the children should they return to France.

There is pending in France a court order that granted parental authority over Marie-Eline jointly to Blondin and Dubois, with Marie-Eline's principal residence being with Blondin. Upon arriving in France, Dubois could file a request in French family court seeking a modification of the prior French order to grant her a temporary custody order, fixing the "habitual residence" of the children with her pending the completion of the evaluation and the new custody hearing. The French family judge would appoint a forensic expert (a child psychiatrist) and a welfare officer to evaluate the children and Dubois and prepare reports to the court. Chauveau estimated that the entire process of evaluating the children, preparing the reports, conducting a hearing, and rendering a final custody decision could take from one to three months, depending on the diligence of Dubois's attorney, the speed of the forensic expert and the welfare officer, and the willingness of both parties to participate in the inquiry.[5]

Moreover, Chauveau testified that while French judges "seem to have a difficulty" understanding the meaning of an undertaking, the French courts would likely enforce certain undertakings that Blondin might give, provided that they did not run "contrary to the public policy of France." For example, a French judge would likely enforce an undertaking given by Blondin promising not to enforce the existing custody order until a French family judge ruled on the custody modification request. Blondin has given such an undertaking, as well as others, including offering to pay for the airfare to France for Dubois and the children, as well as three weeks in a "one-star hotel" while Dubois applies for government housing, financial support, and other social services. Chauveau asserted that these undertakings would likely be enforced as well, for "when there is an agreement between parents that is coherent with the best interests of the child, the judge is always keen to enforce these kind of agreements."

In addition, free legal assistance will be provided to Dubois should she return to France. The French Ministry of Justice asked the Seine-Saint-Denis Bar Association in Bobigny, the jurisdiction in which Dubois resided before moving to the United States, to appoint an attorney to represent Dubois in the event she chose to file a custody modification petition. In response, the president of the bar association stated that "the Bar Association will appoint an attorney specializing in personal law as a legal representative" for Dubois if she so requests. The appointment of counsel "could occur immedi-

_____

5. A second court, the juvenile court, would also have jurisdiction over the case if there is an "immediate danger of health, security, education of a minor child." The juvenile justice could issue an immediate protective order granting temporary custody to Dubois if there is sufficient evidence of the danger to the children.

ately if Ms. Dubois were to obtain provisional authorization to receive legal aid... [from] the presiding judge of the court of competent jurisdiction."

Dubois is also eligible to receive social services and housing from the French government, if she returns to France and applies for such services. According to Chauveau, Dubois would be eligible for the "minimum revenue," a monthly sum of about 3,000 francs, as well as an "allocation famille locale, which is an allocation every month for the children." The children's allocation would vary, depending on Blondin's financial contribution to their support. In addition, the French government could contribute some amount of money towards Dubois's rent, or she could apply for residence in a shelter. Dubois could receive these various social services within two or three weeks of applying.

Finally, the Office of the Public Prosecutor of Bobigny has stated that it will not criminally prosecute Dubois for the abduction of the children, the forgery of Blondin's name on the passport documents, or the use of those forged documents, should Dubois return to France. If Dubois does not return to France with the children, however, the French Ministry of Justice warns that "it might be forced to take action at the level of international mutual assistance in criminal matters" to restore Blondin's parental rights "if no acceptable solution can be found very promptly on the basis of the Hague Convention." Chauveau understood this to mean that "we [France] will seek a civil solution as a cooperation based on the Hague. If we don't have any solution, whatever is the solution, based on the Hague, then we leave the criminal procedure on."...

Dr. Albert J. Solnit testified about the psychological impact of sending the children back to France for custody proceedings and Marie-Eline's maturity and ability to understand the purpose and meaning of these proceedings....

Dr. Solnit explained that while living in France, Marie-Eline[9] had suffered from an acute, severe traumatic disorder, caused by Blondin's physical and verbal abuse of her and her mother and the problems of living in an abusive situation. Dr. Solnit identified several manifestations of traumatic stress disorder in Marie-Eline, as described by Dubois and Marie-Eline herself; Marie-Eline had difficulty in eating, nightmares, interrupted sleeping, and fearfulness of being away from her mother.

Since leaving France, however, Marie-Eline and Francois have been living in the "secure environment of their home and extended family" in the United States and in that safe environment, they are recovering from the "sustained, repeated traumatic state created in France by their father's physically and emotionally abusive treatment of their mother and Marie-Eline."... He explained that Marie-Eline and Francois are "now embedded in an extended family in which you can predict what will happen, they have a good relationship with their cousins, with their aunt and their uncle, and [their aunt and uncle] are extensions of their mother in terms of safety, security, and nurturing."

In Dr. Solnit's clinical judgment, removing the children from this secure environment to return them to France would "almost certainly" trigger a recurrence of the

---

9. Dr. Solnit's testimony and report primarily focused on the trauma suffered by Marie-Eline in France. Dr. Solnit explained that clear manifestations of traumatic stress disorder did not emerge in his interview with Francois "because he would probably have been too young to remember it or be able to verbalize it." While Francois might not suffer the same degree of psychological trauma if he were to return to France, I will not separate the children.

traumatic stress disorder they suffered in France — *i.e.*, a post-traumatic stress disorder. A return to France "would set them back in a very harmful way" in their recovery from their "severe trauma," for "such a move would undo the benefit of the psychological and emotional roots they have established with their mother and her extended family." Specifically, Dr. Solnit explained that a return to France would confront the children with certain developmental risks, including "not feeling safe," "feeling exposed to the traumatizing uncertainty about where they will live and who will provide them with loving care and safety," and "having their fate determined by strangers."

The risk of post-traumatic stress disorder would be present in any proposed arrangement for returning the children to France, "however carefully organized." If the children were to return to France and be placed in the custody of a third party, without any contact with Blondin, they would be exposed to a grave risk of psychological harm because "the primary trauma would be removing them from the place where they are beginning to feel safety and trust.... [T]he primary trauma is the removal and the uncertainty and the lack of security that comes from leaving where they are now and going back to the scene of their original trauma [France]."

Even a return in their mother's temporary custody, with the social and legal support and protections detailed by Chauveau and the French Ministry, would not alleviate the risk of post-traumatic stress disorder, "because the removal from where they are now would open up the recurrence of the trauma."...

For all of these reasons, Dr. Solnit concluded that any return of the children to France would "almost certainly" trigger a post-traumatic stress disorder "that would impair their physical, emotional, intellectual, and social development," leading to "long-term or even permanent harm to their physical and psychological development." The removal of Marie-Eline and Francois from the environment in which they have begun their recovery to return to France "would expose them to physical risks, psychological harm and place them in an intolerable situation."...

Marie-Eline stated that she "never want[s] to go back to [her] daddy," to live with him or even just to visit him. Even if she did not have to live with her father, she would still only like to visit Paris for one day; she would not want to stay in Paris for a long period of time, because she would miss her cousins and aunt and uncle....

I again find, by clear and convincing evidence, that return of Marie-Eline and Francois to France, under any arrangement, would present a "grave risk" that they would be exposed to "physical or psychological harm" or that they would otherwise be placed in an "intolerable situation." I reach that conclusion for three reasons: first, removal of the children from their presently secure environment would interfere with their recovery from the trauma they suffered in France; second, returning them to France, where they would encounter the uncertainties and pressures of custody proceedings, would cause them psychological harm; and third, Marie-Eline objects to being returned to France.

1. Removal of the Children from their Present Environment

I accept and give great weight to Dr. Solnit's expert opinion that removing the children from the secure environment in which they now live to return them to the scene of their original trauma would expose them to a "grave risk" of harm, in view of the history of the serious abuse they suffered at the hands of their father.... I accept and agree with Dr. Solnit's conclusions, and I find that the removal of the children from their present environment, even temporarily, will expose them to a grave risk of physical and psychological harm....

2. Return of the Children to the Uncertainties of the Custody Proceedings

I also agree with Dr. Solnit's conclusion that the insecurity of the transition to France and the uncertainties surrounding the custody proceedings there would exacerbate the trauma suffered by Marie-Eline and Francois should they be returned. If I return the children to France, they will be uprooted from their stable, predictable family setting and thrown into a maelstrom of uncertainty and insecurity. The children would have only temporary living arrangements in a hotel upon their arrival in France; after three weeks, they would have to move out of the hotel, and it is unclear exactly where they will live after that. To some extent, they would essentially become wards of the state, dependent on public assistance. It is also unclear how long the custody proceedings would last; Chauveau testified that they could take anywhere from one to three months. As Dr. Solnit explained, to children who do not "march along to an adult sense of time," three months could seem eternal.

Moreover, the custody proceedings themselves will expose the children to extreme uncertainty about where they will live and who will take care of them, as well as the insecurity of having their fate decided by strangers. I could not assure that they would remain in their mother's temporary custody pending the proceedings as there is a French order in force, directing that Marie-Eline's principal residence is with Blondin. Admittedly, a certain degree of uncertainty attends any custody proceeding, but in this case, the uncertainty associated with the custody proceedings is not an isolated issue; it stands against the backdrop of serious physical abuse by the father, who seeks to gain custody of the children. Marie-Eline is particularly sensitive to this insecurity.... In combination, all of the uncertainties associated with a return to France will compound the children's trauma of being removed from their family and returned to the country where they were abused.

3. Marie-Eline's Views

Although her views are by no means dispositive, Marie-Eline objects to being returned to France, and pursuant to Article 13 of the Convention, I am taking her views into account. See Convention, Art. 13 ("The judicial or administrative authority may also refuse to order the return of the child if it finds that the child objects to being returned and has attained an age and degree of maturity at which it is appropriate to take account of [his or her] views."). Marie-Eline continues to impress me as a bright, poised, intelligent child who has an understanding of the purpose of these proceedings and who spoke thoughtfully and expressively about her views on being returned to France. Although she is only eight years old, the plain language of Article 13 requires me to consider her maturity as well as her age, and I find that Marie-Eline is a remarkably mature eight-year-old, probably in no small part due to the very adult proceedings and issues that she has been confronted with over the past two years....

My decision to deny Blondin's petition does not reflect any lack of trust in the French judicial and administrative systems. Chauveau wondered if I view the French as "undercivilized monkeys or responsible partners to an international convention." I assure her and the French Central Authority that I view them as the latter. I have every confidence in the ability of the French administrative and judicial systems to protect and support Marie-Eline and Francois pending the adjudication of the custody case. The United States, too, is a "responsible partner to an international convention."

The Convention sets up a framework for analyzing international child abduction cases, and we must work within that framework; I am endeavoring to do precisely that. The Convention provides that if I find that there is grave risk, I need not send the children back. If I decide, as I do, that the children should not be sent back under an exception to the Convention, it is not a matter of American chauvinism, or a lack of trust in the French court system, but a matter of working within the framework of the Convention....

Blondin v. Dubois
238 F.3d 153 (2d Cir. 2001)

Cabranes, J.

This is the second appeal in this case....

Blondin challenges the conclusion that repatriation would create a grave risk of psychological harm within the meaning of Article 13(b), and objects to the District Court's consideration, as part of its "grave risk" analysis, of whether Marie-Eline is settled in her new environment and whether she objects to returning to France. We consider these matters in turn....

On remand from Blondin II, the District Court inquired into what arrangements might be made in order to make possible the children's return without subjecting them to a grave risk of psychological harm....

Blondin did not present any evidence as to the psychological impact that a return to France would have on the children. We are thus presented with a rare situation in which, for unexplained reasons, no evidence was presented by one party that would contradict the conclusions of an expert procured by the opposing party. Dr. Solnit's conclusions thus stand uncontroverted. They are the only evidence that we and the District Court have available as to whether repatriation to France would cause the children to suffer a recurrence of traumatic stress disorder....

In light of Dr. Solnit's qualifications and expertise, *see, e.g.,* J. Goldstein, A. Freud, A. Solnit & S. Goldstein, In The Best Interests of The Child (1986); his examination of relevant documents; his interviews with Dubois and the children; and, we emphasize, the absence of any contravening evidence on point, we see no basis upon which to question the District Court's finding that the children will suffer from a recurrence of traumatic stress disorder if they return to France.

Blondin's evidence consisted entirely of testimony concerning the government services available to Dubois and the arrangements that Blondin and the French authorities would be willing to make to facilitate repatriation of the children. We do not underestimate the importance of this evidence, which we requested, and we appreciate the lengths to which both Blondin and the French authorities have gone to address the concerns raised by Dubois and by our courts. However, in light of the evidence presented by Dubois, Blondin's evidence is essentially inapposite, as it does not purport to cast doubt on the Court's finding that even with all of these arrangements in place, the children face an almost certain recurrence of traumatic stress disorder on returning to France because they associate France with their father's abuse and the trauma they suffered as a result. Therefore, we cannot say that the District Court's conclusion was clearly erroneous, and we decline to disturb it....

The District Court granted Dubois's request that it consider whether Marie-Eline was "so deeply rooted in the United States that returning her to France would expose her to a grave risk of psychological harm." The Court did not consider this matter under the rubric of Article 12 of the Hague Convention, under which the issue of whether a child is "settled" usually arises, because that provision applies only if the petition was filed over one year after the abduction, whereas Blondin instituted these proceedings within 10 months of the abduction. Instead, the Court accepted Dubois's argument that the issue of whether a child is "settled" in its new environment may be considered as one of several factors in the "grave risk" analysis under Article 13(b)....

As we read Article 12, it allows—but does not, of course, require—a judicial or administrative authority to refuse to order the repatriation of a child on the sole ground that the child is settled in its new environment, if more than one year has elapsed between the abduction and the petition for return. The article begins by setting forth the general rule that

> [w]here a child has been wrongfully removed or retained...and, at the date of the commencement of the proceedings before the judicial or administrative authority of the Contracting State where the child is, a period of less than one year has elapsed from the date of wrongful removal or retention, the authority concerned shall order the return of the child forthwith.

Hague Convention, art. 12. It then carves out a simple exception:

> The judicial or administrative authority, even where the proceedings have been commenced after the expiration of the period of one year referred to in the preceding paragraph, shall also order the return of the child, unless it is demonstrated that the child is now settled in its new environment.

Id. In other words, if more than one year has passed, a "demonstra[tion] that the child is now settled in its new environment" may be a sufficient ground for refusing to order repatriation.

To the extent that Article 12 permits the courts of a party to the Convention to deny repatriation on this basis, it effectively allows them to reach the underlying custody dispute, a matter which is generally outside the scope of the Convention. However, the Convention's framers recognized that although its aim is to ensure the return of abducted children without reaching the merits of underlying custody disputes, there could come a point at which a child would become so settled in a new environment that repatriation might not be in its best interest. Therefore, they settled on the one-year time limit, which, "although perhaps arbitrary, nevertheless proved to be the 'least bad' answer to the concerns which were voiced in this regard."

None of this implies that the question of whether a child is settled may not be considered at all under Article 13(b); it simply means that this factor cannot be the sole reason for repatriation, except as provided by Article 12. Under Article 13(b), the fact that a child is settled may form part of a broader analysis of whether repatriation will create a grave risk of harm. The ordinary disruptions necessarily accompanying a move would not by themselves constitute such a risk. Yet in the course of an Article 13(b) analysis, a district court may be presented with evidence that a child is now settled in a new environment, and such evidence may be relevant to the issue of grave risk. As we suggested in Blondin II, a district court may consider it as part of an analysis under Article 13(b) as long as that factor is not the sole basis for a finding that there is clear and convincing evidence that a grave risk of harm exists....

Its discussion makes clear that the evidence that the children are well-settled in the United States was not, by itself, the dispositive factor in this case. Accordingly, we conclude that the Court did not err in considering this evidence as one factor in its Article 13(b) analysis.

In declining to order the return of the children, the District Court also took into account Marie-Eline's objections to returning to France. *See* Blondin III, 78 F. Supp. 2d at 296. The Court was somewhat ambiguous as to the applicable provision in this regard. It initially cited the unnumbered provision of Article 13 that governs a court's consideration of a child's views, but it subsequently explained that it was considering Marie-Eline's views as only one factor under its Article 13(b) analysis....

Blondin challenges the factual finding that at eight years old Marie-Eline was old enough for the Court to consider her views. The United States, in turn, objects to this portion of the Court's analysis on the ground that the unnumbered provision of Article 13 "does not contemplate a general airing of a child's 'views' as part of an Article 13(b) analysis of 'grave risk'; rather, it permits, although does not require, a court to refuse return based on the separate ground of an older child's maturely considered objection to return." Brief of Amicus Curiae United States at 23.... At the same time, the United States concedes that a court may consider the testimony of a younger child as part of the "grave risk" analysis—although, in its view, such testimony must be limited to "evidence that abuse has occurred or that return to the immediate custody of an abusive parent would pose a grave risk of harm."

We agree with the government that the unnumbered provision of Article 13 provides a separate ground for repatriation and that, under this provision, a court may refuse repatriation solely on the basis of a considered objection to returning by a sufficiently mature child. We also agree with the government that a court may consider a younger child's testimony as part of a broader analysis under Article 13(b). In either case, of course, a court must take into account the child's age and degree of maturity in considering how much weight to give its views. As the government acknowledges, however, it stands to reason that the standard for considering a child's testimony as one part of a broader analysis under Article 13(b) would not be as strict as the standard for relying solely on a child's objections to deny repatriation under Article 13. Moreover, we do not find any basis in the Convention or in the relevant case law for limiting such testimony to "evidence that abuse has occurred or that return to the immediate custody of an abusive parent would pose a grave risk of harm." Rather, if a child's testimony is germane to the question of whether a grave risk of harm exists upon repatriation, a court may take it into account.

In the instant case, we conclude that the District Court properly considered Marie-Eline's views as part of its "grave risk" analysis under Article 13(b), and that it did not clearly err in finding that Marie-Eline was old and mature enough for her views to be considered in this context. However, because it is evident that the Court did not rely solely on her views in reaching its judgment, we do not reach the question of whether she had attained an age and degree of maturity sufficient for her views to be conclusive pursuant to the unnumbered provision of Article 13. For the same reason, we do not reach the question of whether, if Marie-Eline's views had been the sole basis for a denial of repatriation, the objections she expressed would have been sufficient to support such a denial....

Blondin does not argue that Marie-Eline is immature for her age; rather, he simply questions whether any eight-year-old is old enough for its views to be considered, and he observes that she is not as mature as a 12-or 13-year-old. This argument lacks merit. To accept it we would have to conclude that under the Convention, as a matter of law, an eight-year-old is too young for her views to be taken into account. We decline to do so, as this would read into the Convention an age limit that its own framers were unwilling to articulate as a general rule. *See* Explanatory Report, ¶ 30.

Blondin also questions whether Marie-Eline truly objects to returning to France, as opposed to returning to live with her father specifically. This argument has some merit: In both conversations, Marie-Eline several times distinguished between returning to France itself and returning to live with her father, and objected specifically to the latter. Nevertheless, although we doubt that the objections expressed by Marie-Eline would be sufficient, without more, to sustain the judgment in this case, we cannot say that the District Court clearly erred in finding that she objects to returning to France. This finding, relying as it (in part) did on the Court's personal observations of Marie-Eline, is of the sort "peculiarly within the province of the trier of fact and is entitled to considerable deference." ...

Affirmed.

Notes and Questions

1. *Burden of Proof.* Note that under ICARA, a petitioner must make out his or her case by a preponderance of evidence, 42 U.S.C. § 11603(e)(1) (2002), but a respondent must prove the defenses set out in article 13(b) or 20 by clear and convincing evidence. 42 U.S.C. § 11603(e)(2)(A). However, at least one court has held that any facts upon which an article 13(b) defense rests need only be proven by a preponderance of the evidence. *See* Danaipour v. McLarey, 286 F.3d 1, 13 (1st Cir. 2002). The other defenses, *i.e.*, under article 12 or 13, need only be established by a preponderance of the evidence. 42 U.S.C. § 11603(e)(2)(B).

2. *The Breadth of the Article 13 Defense.* Are there not adjustment problems in every abduction case? Why would an article 13(b) defense ever fail if a respondent invoked Judge Chin's analysis?

3. *Returning the Child with the Custodial Parent/Abductor.* The Second Circuit in *Blondin v. Dubois* said, "Although the Convention deals with the repatriation of abducted children, it is apparent from the District Court's opinion and the parties' submissions to this Court that no one contemplates the return of the children to France without the accompaniment of Dubois." 238 F.3d at 156 n.1. Often the custodial parent voluntarily returns with the child when a court orders the remedy of return. *See, e.g.,* Finizio v. Scoppio-Finizio, [1999] 124 O.A.C. 308 (Can.). However, a custodial parent may decide not to return with the child, especially if the parent faces criminal charges for the child's abduction in the state of the child's habitual residence.

4. *The Expert.* Dr. Albert J. Solnit is an expert in child psychiatry and pediatrics. He is the Sterling Professor Emeritus at Yale University. He has authored and co-authored numerous books, including *Beyond the Best Interest of the Child.* Most litigants will not have such a well-known expert testifying on their behalf. Was it Dr. Solnit's stature that led the courts to give such great weight to his opinion?

5. *One Expert Only.* What can explain Blondin's failure to put on any evidence to counter Dr. Solnit's conclusions, especially regarding the harm Marie-Eline might face if she were uprooted from the United States? If such evidence were irrelevant as a matter of law to an article 13(b) analysis, then no evidence presumably would have been necessary. Did *Blondin II* suggest that this was a correct interpretation?

6. *Stability and Grave Risk of Harm.* In *Blondin II, III & IV*, the District Court and the Second Circuit referred to the Sixth Circuit's opinion in *Friedrich v. Friedrich*, 78 F.3d 1060 (6th Cir. 1996). *Friedrich*, which you read in connection with your study of the phrase "actual exercise," also involved expert testimony about the harm a child would experience if uprooted:

> Mrs. Friedrich testified that Thomas has grown attached to family and friends in Ohio. She also hired an expert psychologist who testified that returning Thomas to Germany would be traumatic and difficult for the child, who was currently happy and healthy in America with his mother.
>
>> [Thomas] definitely would experience the loss of his mother... if he were to be removed to Germany. That would be a considerable loss.
>>
>> And there then would be the probabilities of anger both towards his mother, who it might appear that she has abandoned him [sic], and towards the father for creating that abandonment. [These feelings] could be plenty enough springboard for other developmental or emotional restrictions which could include nightmares, antisocial behavior, a whole host of anxious-type behavior.
>
> Blaske Deposition at 28–29. *See Friedrich*, 78 F.3d at 1067.

The Sixth Circuit held this evidence was insufficient for article 13(b) purposes. *Id.* at 1067. The court stated:

> Mrs. Friedrich advocates a wide interpretation of the grave risk of harm exception that would reward her for violating the Convention. A removing parent must not be allowed to abduct a child and then — when brought to court — complain that the child has grown used to the surroundings to which they were abducted. Under the logic of the Convention, it is the abduction that causes the pangs of subsequent return. The disruption of the usual sense of attachment that arises during most long stays in a single place with a single parent should not be a "grave" risk of harm for the purposes of the Convention.

Id. at 1068. It also held:

> Although it is not necessary to resolve the present appeal, we believe that a grave risk of harm for the purposes of the Convention can exist in only two situations. First, there is a grave risk of harm when return of the child puts the child in imminent danger prior to the resolution of the custody dispute — e.g., returning the child to a zone of war, famine, or disease. Second, there is a grave risk of harm in cases of serious abuse or neglect, or extraordinary emotional dependence, when the court in the country of habitual residence, for whatever reason, may be incapable or unwilling to give the child adequate protection. Psychological evidence of the sort Mrs. Friedrich introduced in the proceeding below is only relevant if it helps prove the existence of one of these two situations.

Id. at 1069. Are *Friedrich* and *Blondin IV* reconcilable?

7. *Domestic Violence.* Domestic violence existed in the Blondin/Dubois relationship. Seventy percent of respondents in Hague Convention cases are now believed to be mothers, many of whom claim to be fleeing from domestic violence. This fact pattern is one the drafters of the Convention never imagined. *See* Merle Weiner, *International Child Abduction and the Escape from Domestic Violence*, 69 Fordham L. Rev. 593, 601–02 (2001) ("Policy makers historically have tended to treat international child abduction by parents as a monolith, despite significant differences between the types of abduction. In

the United States, for example, reformers used the image of a 'typical' international child abduction to guide their efforts.... A similar image also exists in the materials that guided the formation of the Hague Convention on Child Abduction by members of the Hague Conference on Private International Law.... In the United States,...the stereo-typical image of an international child abduction was the following: the abductor was a male non-custodial parent, usually a foreign national, who removed the child from the child's mother and primary caretaker, typically an American national."). What implication does this fact pattern have for the application of the Convention? Is international child abduction equally harmful when the abduction is by the primary caretaker who departs to escape domestic violence?

Can article 13(b) cover the situation where the mother is the one threatened with direct physical abuse, and not the child? Consider *Finizio v. Scoppio-Finizio*, [1999] 124 O.A.C. 308 (Can.). In that case, the wife claimed that for the first time in her eight year marriage, her husband assaulted her, punched her in the face, and removed most of the money from their joint bank account. Approximately a month later, the wife left Italy with the two children for Canada, her home before her marriage and the home of her parents. The court rejected the article 13(b) defense because "there is no evidence that the husband has ever done anything to harm the children," and "the alleged single incident of assault...is...the only incident of a physical altercation between the spouses in their eight-year marriage." In addition, the court thought that undertakings could be used to protect the wife; in fact, the husband agreed that he would not annoy, harass or molest the wife. Does this outcome seem correct? Why or why not? *Compare* Pollastro v. Pollastro, [1999] 118 O.A.C. 169 (Can.) (finding violence solely committed against mother, primary caretaker, to be relevant to article 13(b) defense).

In cases with domestic abuse, Professor Weiner recommends that the court adjudicating the Hague petition stay enforcement of the remedy of return until the court of the child's habitual residence adjudicates custody (or transfers jurisdiction). In addition, she recommends that the victim of domestic violence be allowed to litigate custody or jurisdiction from the abducted-to state. Professor Weiner also suggests that a complete defense be available for women whose batterers forced them to live in the abducted-from country.

8. *Options to Ensure the Child's Safety.* Does *Blondin* ask too much of courts when respondents raise an article 13(b) defense? "In cases of serious abuse, before a court may deny repatriation on the ground that a grave risk of harm exists under Article 13(b), it must examine the full range of options that might make possible the safe return of a child to the home country." *Blondin IV*, 238 F.3d 153, 163 n.11 (2d Cir. 2001).

The Second Circuit's approach in Blondin tracks the advice of Professor Linda Silberman who, in two 1994 articles, warned: "Beware the Child Savers." Linda Silberman, *Hague International Child Abduction Convention: A Progress Report*, 57 Law & Contemp. Probs. 209, 267 (1994); Linda Silberman, *Hague Convention on International Child Abduction: A Brief Overview and Case Law Analysis*, 28 Fam. L.Q. 9, 32–33 (1994). Professor Silberman cautioned that "well-intentioned child savers could...frustrate the objectives of the Convention" by using article 13(b) to "frustrate return." These efforts could "undermine the Convention and transform its procedural framework into one of substance," and could "lengthen the proceedings and undercut the expeditious procedure envisioned by the Convention." Instead of over utilizing article 13(b), or adopting a new mechanism to address situations where "allegations of serious harm are made," Professor Silberman recommended that courts "fashion interim arrangements...to ensure the safety of the child," such as undertakings. She continued, "[O]nly if such alternatives are unavailable should the court proceed to a full-scale hearing to determine whether the defense has been substantively established by clear and convincing evidence, as is required under the federal statute." *Id.* at 33.

9. *Undertakings.* What if a petitioner agrees to undertakings regarding the children's safety? What is the effect of an undertaking? Should courts liberally rely upon undertakings in situations that entail a risk of harm to the abducting parent or the child? Consider this excerpt from Merle Weiner, *International Child Abduction and the Escape From Domestic Violence*, 69 Fordham L. Rev. 593, 676–82 (2001), who discussed undertakings in the context of women who have abducted their children in their attempt to flee from the petitioners' domestic abuse.

> Undertakings have become a fairly common way for some courts to try to secure the child's safety, and at times the abductor's safety, when ordering the child's return. In the context of a Hague proceeding, undertakings are verbal assurances given to the court by a litigant, typically through counsel, as a condition of the child's return. For instance, a petitioner might undertake to have no contact with the abductor upon the abductor's return to the child's habitual residence, or might agree to a series of conditions akin to what a court might award a victorious plaintiff in a civil protection order proceeding....

> While the text of the Hague Convention does not mention undertakings, undertakings can be justified as protection for the child. Without them, the abductor may choose not to return with the child, and the child would be forced to be without his or her primary caretaker.... In addition, without undertakings, violence may resume upon the abductor's return, and harm the children. Because protection of children is the raison d'être of the Convention, and since courts appear to have the legal authority to impose undertakings, the increased use of undertakings is a viable option for dealing with allegations of domestic abuse....

> For undertakings to be a widespread solution, however, the Convention itself would need to authorize them, and make them enforceable in all member states. Currently, some jurisdictions are skeptical of undertakings.... Moreover, there is currently no remedy for the violation of an undertaking.... When an undertaking is violated, the violator is typically outside the jurisdiction of the court that imposed the condition and the child has already been returned. While a court could require forfeiture of a bond if the undertaking is violated, or hold a petitioner in contempt if and when the petitioner ever reappears in the jurisdiction, or even dismiss any future Hague petitions that the petitioner files in that jurisdiction, these options offer the domestic violence victim and the court little comfort that an abuser will obey an undertaking....

> Notwithstanding the potential benefit of undertakings, this solution also has limitations, especially if judges are not educated about domestic violence. First, courts may not order the full range of relief necessary to protect a victim. Some courts elicit undertakings with financial relief provisions more readily than undertakings with conditions related to abductors' safety.... Unless judges who apply the Hague Convention receive domestic violence training and become accustomed to ordering broader relief, codifying the undertaking process would be an insufficient solution.

> Second, in some cases, a victim may not be adequately protected even with the imposition of a wide range of conditions related to her safety. Some batterers

are so determined to harm their victims that laws and court orders mean little, if anything. That is why advocates for domestic violence victims believe that safety planning is often more essential for victims than obtaining a protection order against abuse. Some victims may only be safe a continent away from their abusers, regardless of the conditions that courts could impose for their safety. Consequently, undertakings should be considered per se inappropriate in various situations, including where any of the following facts exist: the petitioner has a history of disobeying court orders; past violence has been so life-threatening that only vast geographic distances can protect the respondent; there are indications that future violence may be severe; or, the harm to the child will not be mitigated because the child will still fear renewed violence between the parents. Courts and reformers must acknowledge that undertakings may not sufficiently protect some battered women or children, and allow an Article 13(b) defense in those situations.

Third, undertakings are a remedy connected with the return of a child. Sometimes, however, the return of the child is the wrong remedy. For example, if the child's habitual residence was established by coercion of the mother, then it may be better for the court to make a factual determination that the abducted-from state never became the child's 'habitual residence' and thereby avoid the return of the child. Alternatively, another remedy—such as a domestic violence defense—might better address the equities of the situation.

Fourth, the power dynamic between the domestic violence victim and the batterer may undermine some courts' ability to assess the adequacy of undertakings. Unless there are proper procedural safeguards in place, a battered woman may tell the court that she feels safe with the proposed undertakings, but her response may be subtly coerced by the batterer. 'Intimidation can occur quite subtly—for example, with a certain look that a [judge] may not see or interpret as threatening.' Players in the family law field generally appreciate that the parties' power disparities can make mediation a 'dangerous process' for those subjected to domestic violence. [O]utcomes for women who are afraid of their husbands tend to be worse than for women who are not so afraid. While Hague proceedings are not 'mediation,' a similar power imbalance may arise when a court asks the parties to agree upon undertakings, especially if only the batterer is represented. Again, the need to train the courts on the issue of domestic violence will be critical.

Fifth, undertakings are a reasonable solution only when the jurisdiction to which the child is to be returned adequately protects domestic violence victims. If the police do not respond to domestic violence calls, for example, then undertakings should be considered an inadequate solution. Undertakings technically do not depend upon the habitual residence's response to domestic violence, but rather depend upon the petitioner's agreement and good faith. Yet batterers often violate agreements or court orders designed to stop the batterers' violence, as experience in the United States demonstrates. Courts must recognize this fact and determine whether the other country can adequately protect the victim upon her return to the country.

10. *Judicial Limits on Undertakings.* The United States Court of Appeals for the First Circuit has imposed some important restrictions on the use of undertakings, especially when they are used to shortcut the article 13(b) inquiry. *See* Danaipour v. McLarey, 286 F.2d 1 (1st Cir. 2002). In *Danaipour,* the district court had rejected an article 13(b) de-

fense. Although the district court had found "reason to believe the father had sexually abused his three-year old daughter," the district court felt that numerous undertakings "would adequately protect the children" until the courts in the children's habitual residence could decide whether the sexual abuse had actually occurred, and if so, the necessary steps to protect the children. *Id.* at 5.

The First Circuit, reversing and remanding, required that the district court determine the merit of the sexual abuse allegations. Only then could the district court assess whether the children could be safely returned to their habitual residence using undertakings. *Id.* at 14–15. The court also noted that the proponent of an undertaking bore the burden of showing that the undertaking negated the risk. *Id.* at 15–16. In *Danipour*, the proponent had not met his burden. There were serious questions about whether the forensic evaluation would occur at all in the habitual residence and whether that evaluation would be undermined by returning the children to the place of the abuse. *Id.* at 15. Finally, the court warned that comity precluded making the remedy of return conditional upon a foreign court's entry of an order embodying some of the undertakings. However, without such an order, a U.S. court should not merely assume undertakings are enforceable abroad. *Id.* at 16.

The First Circuit emphasized that Danaipour involved the sexual abuse of a young child and that such sexual abuse is an intolerable situation according to U.S. policy. It suggested that "undertakings should be used more sparingly when there is evidence that the abducting parent is attempting to protect the child from abuse." *Id.* at 26. Otherwise, "[t]he development of extensive undertakings in such a context could embroil the court in the merits of the underlying custody issues and would tend to dilute the force of the Article 13(b) exception." *Id.* at 25 (citing Department of State Comment on Undertakings).

When would undertakings be appropriate, if ever, given the First Circuit's reluctance to permit them in this sort of situation? Should the court's reasoning apply to other article 13(b) cases that do not involve child sexual abuse?

11. *Siblings.* What happens when there are siblings and the article 13(b) defense is made out with respect to only one child? Similarly, what happens if only one of the siblings is of an age and maturity so that the court must take account of his or her view, and that view is not to return? Compare the following cases.

B v. K (**Child Abduction**), 1 Fam. Ct. Rep. 382, 387–88 (Eng. Fam. 1993). Three children were removed from Germany. The judge held that the girl, nearly nine, and the boy, aged seven, had attained an age and a degree of maturity at which it was appropriate for him to take account of their views. He decided not to return the two older children to Germany. With regard to the youngest child, he said "The youngest child, is not, in my judgment, of an age and degree of maturity in which I should take account of his views, so that it seems to me that this basis of objection by the mother, which I have upheld in relation to the two elder children, cannot be upheld in relation to the youngest child, so I find myself, at least initially, in the position where I would not order the return of the two elder children to Germany but that I would find there to be no sustainable objection to the return of the youngest child. However, it is plain that these children have always lived together, and I accept the statement in his oral report this morning from (the court welfare officer) that the youngest child would be devastated to be separated from the two elder children. Accordingly, whilst I have rejected the mother's case on the other part of Article 13, namely that the children would suffer psychological or physical harm or be placed in an intolerable situation, I have no difficulty in holding that the youngest child would be exposed to psychological harm and would be placed in an intolerable situation if he were returned to Germany and the elder two children were not. Accordingly, it falls to me exercise the discretion conferred on me by the opening words of Article 13, and by that circuitous route I conclude that the youngest child shall not be returned to Germany."

Re HB (Abduction: Children Objections), 2 Fam. 392 (Eng. Fam. 1997). A boy aged thirteen ("A") and a girl aged eleven ("C") came to England from Denmark to visit their father. The father refused to return the children, and the mother brought an action under the Hague Convention for their return. The judge concluded that the views of both children should be taken into account, and then said this: "The policy of the Convention is, in my view, particularly important in cases where children come to another country for visits. It is obviously in the best interests of children whose parents live in separate countries that the parent with whom they live should feel able to send them on visits secure in the knowledge that the children will be returned at the end without difficulty. Otherwise parents may be tempted not to allow the children to come, and that would be detrimental to the children. In the case of C (the younger girl) I do not think that the real strength of her objections, the reasons for them and the evidence of relationships at home are enough to set against that policy. Furthermore there is no question in my mind that C's visit was always intended as a short-term holiday visit. The case of A (the older boy) is more difficult. He is older, he is more mature, he has stronger and, to my mind, quite rational objections. The evidence is that the mother herself is in doubt about what to do for the best. So what about treating the children separately? Mr McDowall, on behalf of the father argues that if C is ordered to return but A is not, C will suffer psychological harm from being separated from her brother. Their relationship was described by the court welfare officer as significant, intimate, relaxed.... In this case I do not think that that will be sufficient to amount to a grave risk of psychological harm or will otherwise place C in an intolerable position. She would be going back to a primary carer whom she loved. More to the point, therefore, is the conclusion that there is no good ground to refuse to return C a further reason for returning A as well? I have found this a very difficult decision, but I have reluctantly come to the conclusion that it is and that A should be returned." The case did not end there. When the children were taken to the airport by their father, A was willing to board the plane and return to Denmark, but C adamantly refused to do so. The case was then appealed to the Court of Appeal who remitted the case back to the trial judge. *See* Re HB (Abduction: Children Objections), 2 Fam. 422 (Eng. C.A. 1997). The trial judge eventually dismissed the Hague Convention proceedings given the passage of time and dealt with the matter in wardship. *See* Re HB (Abduction: Children Objections) (No. 2), 1 Fam. 564 (Eng. Fam. 1998). *See also In re* T (Children), 2 Fam. Ct. Rep. 159 (Eng. Fam. 2000).

Should a court order return of both children in this situation, neither, or separate the children? Is it a matter of numbers, *e.g.*, if only one out of three siblings does not have a valid defense, should all three children be allowed to remain? As a matter of treaty interpretation, is one approach preferable to the others? After all, the drafters of the Convention certainly must have been able to envision that there would be cases involving sibling groups and that not all of the siblings might qualify for a defense. Can you argue for any one approach as best reflecting the objects and purposes of the treaty?

As you formulate your arguments, consider Re C (Abduction: Grave Risk of Physical or Psychological Harm), 2 Fam. 478, 488 (Eng. C.A. 1998). There an English mother wrongfully removed her six-year-old son "B" from Cyprus and returned to

England bringing with her also a fourteen-year-old daughter, "A," from a previous relationship. When B's father sought B's return, A, with whom B was very close, adamantly refused to go back to Cyprus. In adjudicating the article 13(b) defense, Lady Justice Butler-Sloss said: "The mother is in an impossible position and cannot leave [A] behind. But if she did leave her behind and go with B to Cyprus she would be consumed with guilt; the children would be separated and either way B would be placed in a situation which comes within Art. 13(b)." On appeal, however, the defense was not allowed. Lady Justice Butler-Sloss stated: "The circumstances of this case provide a good example of how easily problems which arise in many child abduction cases caused by the actions of the abducting parent can be demonstrated by that parent to come within Art. 13(b) and thereby frustrate a return under Art. 12." *Id.* at 484. She continued, "The position of A is a relevant factor in the case to which the court has to have regard. But the mother had the opportunity to consider the implications of returning to England with both children.... I do not consider that the consequences of that return on A should deflect the court from concentrating on the right of B to have his future decided in the State of his habitual residence." *Id.* at 486. In his opinion, Lord Justice Thorpe stated: "In many cases a balanced analysis of the assertion that an order for return would expose the child to the grave risk of psychological harm leads to the conclusion that the respondent is in reality relying upon her own wrongdoing in order to build up the statutory defence. In testing the validity of an Article 13(b) defence, trial judges should usefully ask themselves what were the intolerable features of the child's family life immediately prior to the wrongful abduction? If the answer be scant or non-existent, then the circumstances in which an article 13(b) defence would be upheld are difficult to hypothesize." *Id.* at 487–88. If the Court of Appeal had agreed with the trial court and found that the article 13(b) defense applied, would not the abducting parent have been benefitting from his or her own wrong?

12. *War.* In *Freier v. Freier*, 969 F. Supp. 436, 443 (E.D. Mich. 1996), the respondent-mother argued that the place to which the children would be returned was a place of war, and therefore the article 13(b) defense was made out. The court rejected the claim:

> Respondent also argues that return of the child to Israel would expose the child to grave risk of harm as Israel is a "zone of war" as contemplated by the Sixth Circuit. Respondent claims this is true because of the "skirmishes" that erupted in Israel resulting from the opening of a tunnel under the Old City of Jerusalem in close proximity to the Al Aksa Mosque (the holiest Muslim shrine in Israel). The newspapers have dubbed this "the worst clashes since 1987–1993 uprising or intifada."...Respondent claims this fighting is not far from her home near the border. The maps and other documents presented to the Court seem to indicate the fighting is from 15 to 90 minutes away from the marital home. The Court notes these "clashes" began Tuesday or Wednesday, September 24 or 25, 1996, after the wrongful removal of the child.
>
> Respondent in her testimony expressed a great deal of anxiety and fear over the recent unrest as well as the ongoing tension in Israel. Respondent testified hearing about random violence such as car and bus bombings. Her testimony was supported by the testimony of her sister, Shoshana Silberstein, who is currently visiting from her home in Israel. Ms. Silberstein testified that she and her husband are contemplating on moving back to the United States and that at least one of her children feels the tension of the country.

On the other hand, Professor Rakover, an Assistant Deputy Attorney General in Israel, stated that things were regular and that he had walked to the Western Wall in Jerusalem since the unrest had taken place. He further indicated that although military presence was increased, schools and shops were not closed except for the holidays or for the purpose of demonstrating political views.

The Court would agree that at this time Israel is experiencing some unrest and that this unrest may be in relative proximity to the family's residence. However, the Court does not find sufficient evidence in this record for Israel to be the "zone of war" contemplated by the Sixth Circuit or the Hague Convention. No schools are closed, businesses are open and Petitioner was able to leave the country. It appears that the fighting is limited to certain areas and does not directly involve the city where the child resides.

With respect to Respondent's anxiety and fear about the ongoing tension in the country, it must be noted that she has lived there for a number of years, raised children there for some fourteen years and that her parents have spent extended periods of time there as well. Based on the above, the Court finds the Respondent has failed to establish by clear and convincing evidence that the child, Avital, is in grave risk of physical injury because of the unrest in Israel or that Israel is a zone of war as contemplated by the Hague Convention.

However, the same claim was accepted by a U.S. district court in *Silverman v. Silverman*, 2002 WL 971808 (D. Minn. May 9, 2002). The court noted that "Israel's currently in a state of turmoil" and "the infitada has escalated dramatically in recent months." *Id.* It distinguished *Freier*, mentioning the greater number of areas affected and the suicide bombings, which the court thought put children at greater risk. *Id.* at 10.

b. Children's Objection to Return

England v. England
234 F.3d 268 (5th Cir. 2000)

Duhe, J.

William and Deborah England ("William" and "Deborah") have two children: Karina, age thirteen, and Victoria, age four. All parties are American citizens. The England family lived in Texas until 1997, when they moved to Australia incident to William's job transfer there. In June 1999, the Englands left Australia for an extended overseas vacation. They arrived in the United States in July 1999 for the last leg of their vacation. Their itinerary scheduled their return to Australia for July 15, 1999. As planned, William returned to Australia that day. Ostensibly concerned for the health of her cancer-stricken father, Deborah remained in the United States. Since, Deborah told her husband, the England girls' last chance to see their grandfather was perhaps at hand, Karina and Victoria remained in the United States with her instead of returning to Australia with William as planned.

A few weeks later, Deborah filed for divorce from William in Texas. Shortly thereafter, she phoned William and advised him that neither she nor their daughters would be returning to Australia. After Deborah refused William's various requests to return the children, William filed in the District Court a Petition for Return of Children Under the Hague Convention. After an Australian court determined that Australia was the "habitual residence" of Karina and Victoria and that their removal from Australia was "wrongful," the District Court heard and denied William's Hague Convention petition....

The District Court, agreeing with the Australian court, held that, within the meaning of the Convention, Karina and Victoria were wrongfully removed from their place of habitual residence. The Court, however, determined that Karina, an adopted child who prior to her adoption by the Englands had a "turbulent" history in orphanages and foster care and endured "difficult" adoption proceedings, would face a grave risk of psychological harm if separated from her mother or forced to move so soon after re-settling in Texas. The District Court also found that—notwithstanding her Attention Deficit Disorder, learning disabilities, Ritalin use, and emotional itinerancy (she has had four mothers in her thirteen years of life)—Karina was sufficiently mature for the Court to credit her desire to remain with her mother and not return to Australia. The Court declined to separate Victoria from her older sister because "it would be psychologically damaging to both girls to be separated from each other during the pendency of the [Englands'] custody proceedings." Accordingly, the Court allowed Karina and Victoria to remain in the United States with their mother.

William argues that the District Court erroneously held that Karina and Victoria's return to Australia pending the outcome of custody proceedings would subject them to grave risks of psychological harm. He also argues that Karina is not mature enough for a court appropriately to consider her wishes under the Hague convention....

[W]e...discern nothing in the record constituting clear and convincing evidence that return to Australia pending the outcome of custody proceedings there would expose Karina to grave risks of psychological harm....

The District Court also erred in determining that Karina is mature enough for the Court appropriately to consider her views under the Convention. The Convention establishes that a court "may refuse to order the return of the child if it finds that the child objects to being returned and has attained an age and degree of maturity at which it is appropriate to take account of its views." Convention, art. 13. The party opposing the child's return must establish the child's maturity by a preponderance of the evidence. 42 U.S.C. § 11603(e)(2)(A) (1994). Like the grave risk exception, the "age and maturity" exception is to be applied narrowly. 42 U.S.C. § 11601(a)(4) (1994).

The Court's findings on this issue are even more limited than those on the grave risk exception:

> In addition, Karina has clearly objected to being returned to Australia and she is old enough and mature enough for the Court to take account of her views. She has maintained friendships with classmates here while living abroad, she likes it here and her situation has stabilized. The Court, in accordance with Karina's stated preference, declines to return her to Australia.

The Court's findings, while certainly sensitive to Karina's emotional plight, nevertheless constitute a non sequitur. That Karina has maintained her friendships with children in America, prefers America to Australia, and now enjoys a "situation [that] has stabilized" does not establish that she is mature enough for a court appropriately to consider her views on where she would prefer to live under the Hague Convention. Rather, these findings only establish that Karina prefers to remain in the United States and that some reasons support this preference. If anything, the preponderance of the evidence in this record suggests that Karina is not mature enough for the Court appropriately to take account of her views under the age and maturity exception. By no fault of her own, Karina has had four mothers in twelve years. She has been diagnosed with Attention

Deficit Disorder, has learning disabilities, takes Ritalin regularly, and is, not surprisingly, scared and confused by the circumstances producing this litigation. In view of this evidence and the extreme narrowness of the age and maturity exception to the Convention's rule of mandatory return, we hold that the District Court erroneously found Karina mature enough to trigger this exception to the Convention.

We reverse the District Court and remand with instructions that the district court order Karina and Victoria returned to Australia forthwith pending the outcome of custody proceedings there in accordance with the Convention and for such other proceedings as may be appropriate....

DeMoss, J., dissenting....

I think as a reviewing court we need to keep in mind that Judge Gilmore heard and saw the testimony of Karina in person and had the benefit of that person-to-person evaluation in addressing the question of whether Karina was sufficiently old enough and mature enough to make it "appropriate to take account of [her] views." I have read Karina's testimony, and I saw nothing therein which would lead me to conclude that she is too young or too immature "to take account of [her] views." Furthermore, I saw no testimony by any of the other witnesses in the record that would raise even a genuine issue as to whether Karina was too young or too immature to have her views considered....

There is no question that at the time of her testimony in this case Karina was 13 years old. I have looked for and could not find, and the majority has not cited, any case holding that, under the Hague Convention, a 13 year-old is just too young as a matter of law to take account of her views. In regard to age, the Hague Convention itself states that it shall cease to apply to a child who attains the age of 16 years or more. See Article 4. If the age and maturity exception of Article 3 is to have any meaning at all, it must be available for a child who is less than 16 years old. The Hague Convention does not fix a minimum age at which this exception would become inapplicable. The Convention does recognize that, in states within which different territorial units have their own rules of law respecting custody and children, the laws of those territorial units may be used for determining the applicable law within the Convention. See Articles 31 and 33. In this regard, section 153.008 of the Texas Family Code states that "If the child is 10 years of age or older, the child may, by writing filed with the Court, choose the managing conservator, subject to the approval of the Court." While the child's preference as to managing conservator (the person having custody) is not controlling, it seems to me that a federal district judge sitting in Texas should be instructed by this statute that a child who is ten years or older is old enough to have his objection considered by the Court. I would conclude, therefore, that Karina, as a 13 year-old, "has attained an age" sufficient to take account of her views. The majority does not separately address "age" as a factor in its decision.

We turn then to the "degree of maturity" element of this exception. From my reading of the record, I found no witness who testified as to any circumstances or events which would lead to a conclusion that Karina was "immature for her age." To the contrary, the record indicates that Karina was an average student academically, maintaining the school grade level commensurate with her age, and that she was engaged in a variety of sports and extracurricular activities. The words "degree of maturity" as used in Article 13 are inherently relative and subjective in their concept. But it seems self evident to me that a "degree of maturity" contemplates something less than actual, full, final, complete maturity. For that reason, I recognize that judges reading the same record (or hearing the original testimony) could come to different conclusions on the subject of Karina's degree of maturity. But the conclusions reached by Judge Gilmore on that subject are clearly supported by the record. I disagree specifically with the evidence that the majority cites as supporting its position that Karina is not mature enough to take account of her views.... There is no expert testimony whatsoever in the record which would support a correlation between these circumstances and immaturity. I am surprised that the majority is willing to draw these conclusions without the benefit of testimony in the record from a medical doctor or psychologist. The impression I got from reading the lay testimony in the record is that by taking Ritalin, Karina effectively overcomes any learning disability related to ADD. There is nothing in the record which would compel a conclusion that Karina evidences immature behavior as the result of taking Ritalin.

Finally, I have to disagree with the majority's legal assessment that the age and maturity exception is to be subjected to some "narrow" interpretation. Nothing in the Convention itself states that the exceptions set forth in Article 13 shall be "narrowly construed."

Notes and Questions

1. How did the Fifth Circuit's treatment of the child's opinion in *England* differ from the Second Circuit's treatment of the child's opinion in *Blondin IV*?

2. *Evidence of Maturity I.* The majority thought Deborah England failed to establish Karina's maturity by a preponderance of the evidence. What could a practitioner have done in *England* to make it more likely Karina's views would be heeded? Consider *In re S (Minors) (Abduction: Acquiescence)*, 1 Fam. 819, 827 (Eng. Fam. 1994):

> When Art. 13 speaks of an age and maturity level at which it is appropriate to take account of a child's views, the enquiry which it envisages is not restricted to a generalized appraisal of the child's capacity to form unexpressed views which bear the hallmark of maturity. It is permissible (and indeed will often be necessary) for the court to make specific enquiry as to whether the child has reached a stage of development at which, when asked the question, "Do you object to a return to your home country?" he or she can be relied on to give an answer which does not depend upon instinct alone, but is influenced by the discernment which a mature child brings to the questions, [for example considering the] implications for his or her own best interests in the long and short term.

See also Ostevoll v. Ostevoll, 2000 WL 1611123, at *19 (S.D. Ohio Aug. 16, 2000) (holding children age thirteen and eleven were of sufficient age and maturity after considering two psychologists' testimony which concluded the same); *Isaac v. Rice*, 1998 WL 527107, at *4 (N.D. Miss. July 30, 1998) (finding fifteen-year-old boy of sufficient age and maturity after considering child psychologist's opinion which concluded the same).

3. *Evidence of Maturity II.* How does the article 13 inquiry differ, for instance, from other determinations where courts assess a child's maturity? Consider, for example, the "mature minor" exception to parental consent in the abortion context.

> Those cases that have received appellate review suggest that trial judges intuit maturity from their perceptions of the children's demeanor while testifying. Such cases also indicate that judges evaluate the coherence of the child's response to questions concerning child rearing, abortion procedures and risks, adoption, and the child's postoperative plans.... The Supreme Court of Kansas has attempted to define the concept of mature minor. It has instructed trial courts to determine whether a child possesses "the intellectual capacity, experience, and knowledge necessary to substantially understand the situation at

hand and the consequences of the choices that can be made." In determining whether to grant or deny permission to obtain the abortion without parental notification, other courts also seem to concentrate on the knowledge possessed by the petitioner. This reliance on the concepts of maturity and knowledge reflects, in part, a use of the doctrine of informed consent. Researchers and doctors employ the informed consent doctrine to insure that human subjects used in medical research and patients subject to risky medical procedures understand the procedures in question. Knowledge, voluntariness, and capacity comprise the elements of informed consent. The knowledge prong requires that the person have a fair understanding of the nature of the activity and its procedure, and the attendant risks, discomforts, benefits, and alternatives to the procedure. Voluntariness suggests a volitional act devoid of undue influence. Capacity means the mental ability to use the information and to make a rational choice. The courts that use an informed consent analysis to permit an abortion without parental notification or consent inquire into the quantity of information the child possesses about the abortion process, the birth process, child rearing, and the risks and benefits arising from the various options. Such courts also examine the child's sources of information. Based upon the child's recitation of this information as well as the child's age, education, and behavior, the court rules on the child's maturity.

Wallace J. Mlyniec, *A Judge's Ethical Dilemma: Assessing a Child's Capacity to Choose,* 64 Fordham L. Rev. 1873, 1889–91 (1996).

4. *Is Maturity Enough?* In order for the court to consider the child's views, is it sufficient that there is a determination that the child possesses the requisite age and maturity? The court in *In re T (Children)*, 2 Fam. Ct. Rep. 159 (Eng. Fam. 2000), thought something more was required:

So a discrete finding as to age and maturity is necessary in order to judge the next question which is whether it is appropriate to take account of child's views. That requires an ascertainment of the strength and validity of those views which will call for an examination of the following matters, among others:

(a) What is the child's own perspective of what is in her interests, short, medium and long term? Self-perception is important because it is her views which have to be judged appropriate.

(b) To what extent, if at all, are the reasons for objection rooted in reality or might reasonably appear to the child to be so grounded?

(c) To what extent have those views been shaped or even coloured by undue influence and pressure, directly or indirectly exerted by the abducting parent?

(d) To what extent will the objections be mollified on return and, where it is the case, on removal from any pernicious influence from the abducting parent?

Are these sorts of questions appropriate once it is determined that the child is mature enough to have her views count? How does the assessment described in *In re T* differ from an assessment of maturity? What should a court do if a mature child says that she does not want to return because she is "well-settled"? *See In re Robinson*, 983 F. Supp. 1339 (D. Colo. 1997) (dismissing child's opinion because the child was coached).

5. *When a Mature Child's Wishes Do Not Control.* If a child is of an appropriate age and maturity to have her views considered, and the child's views are well-reasoned, must the court follow the child's will? Consider *In re R* (Child Abduction: Acquiescence), 1 Fam. 716, 734 (Eng. C.A. 1995) (Millett L.J.):

It is to be observed that, if a child is not of an age and degree of maturity which makes it appropriate to take his views into account, he must be returned despite his objections and without any further inquiry whether his return is in his best interests. If, on the other hand, he is of sufficient age and maturity for his views to be taken into account, the Convention clearly envisages that he will not be returned against his wishes, unless there are countervailing factors which require his wishes to be overridden.

6. *Rights of the Child Convention.* Article 12 of the U.N. Convention on the Rights of the Child assures to children "the right to express [their] views freely in all matters affecting [them], the views of the child being given due weight in accordance with the age and maturity of the child." This is not the right of self-determination, but the right to be heard. It applies to any child who is "capable of forming his or her own views." Does this article have any applicability in a contest over whether a child's views should be heeded?

7. *Philosophy Undergirding Hague Convention.* Does the application of the remedy of return make sense in the *England* case? Notice what the dissent said about the facts:

In this particular case, the interest of Australia in deciding the controversies is de minimis and the interest of the United States in deciding these controversies is overwhelming. The following facts, which are clearly established by the record in this case, support this conclusion:

1. William, Deborah, Karina, and Victoria are each citizens of the United States and not of Australia. Each of them carry U.S. passports.

2. William and Deborah were married in Houston, Texas, U.S.A. and not in Australia. During a majority of the time of their marriage they resided in Houston, Texas, U.S.A.

3. Karina was born in Chile, not Australia, and she was adopted by William and Deborah pursuant to a court decree entered in a state court of Texas, U.S.A. At the time of this controversy she was 13 years old.

4. Victoria was born in Houston, Texas, U.S.A and not Australia. At the time of this controversy she was four years old.

5. Both the parents of William and the parents of Deborah (the grandparents of the children) are citizens of and reside in the United States.

6. William entered Australia pursuant to an Australian temporary work visa; Deborah and the two daughters entered and remained in Australia solely pursuant to visas issued to them as dependents of William. The visas of the two daughters expired in August 1999.

7. William was employed in Australia by a U.S. entity and not an Australia employer.

8. When William and Deborah left for Australia in 1997, they owned a home in Houston which they had been living in for four years. They also owned other real property in the State of Texas. This property would be community property under the laws of Texas. They did not sell their home in Houston, and all

of the real property remains as jointly owned property to be dealt with in any divorce decree.

9. Prior to their departure from Australia on vacation in June 1999, neither William nor Deborah had filed any petition with any Australian court seeking a divorce or child custody decree. In fact, neither William nor Deborah could have filed such a petition for such relief because at that time they had not separated and lived apart for 12 months as required by Australian law.

10. When William and Deborah and their two daughters left Australia in June 1999 on a vacation trip home, they did so jointly, freely, and voluntarily. There was no wrongful abduction or denial of custody rights of any kind as of the time of their departure from Australia.

11. When he returned to Australia towards the end of July 1999, William agreed at least tacitly to the decision of Deborah to remain in Houston with the two children....

Under these circumstances, balancing the interests of Australia and the interests of the United States, it is self-evident that the interests of the United States greatly outweigh the interests of Australia. Consequently, the decision of Judge Gilmore to decline to return the two daughters to Australia is a sensible solution to a difficult problem: it avoids potential conflicts between separate court proceedings; it saves all parties the expense of duplicitous court proceedings; and it permits a quicker resolution of all the parties' controversies. Therefore, I would affirm the district court's decision to decline to return Karina and Victoria to Australia.

Is the test the Convention envisioned a balancing of the interests of the respective countries involved? Is such balancing a better test than the Convention's? The Convention has been criticized for being at odds with the principle of *forum conveniens. See, e.g.,* Rhona Schuz, *The Hague Child Abduction Convention: Family Law and Private International Law,* 44 Int'l & Comp. L.Q. 771, 800 (1995).

c. *Protection of Human Rights and Fundamental Freedoms*

Examine article 20 of the Hague Convention on Child Abduction, found in the Supplement. An article 20 defense is rarely, if ever, successful. Nigel Lowe et al., A Statistical Analysis of Applications Made in 1999 under the Hague Convention of 25 October 1980 on the Civil Aspects of International Child Abduction, Prel. Doc. No. 3, March 2001. The United States State Department has indicated: "[T]his exception, like the others, was intended to be restrictively interpreted and applied, and is not to be used, for example, as a vehicle for litigating custody on the merits or for passing judgment on the political system of the country from which the child was removed." Hague International Child Abduction Convention; Text and Legal Analysis, 51 Fed. Reg. 10494, 10510 (Mar. 26, 1986). Under the U.S. implementing legislation, the defense must be established by clear and convincing evidence. 42 U.S.C. §11603(e)(2)(A). The Explanatory Report to the Convention, prepared by Elisa Perez-Vera, states: "[T]o be able to refuse to return a child on the basis of...article [20], it will be necessary to show that the fundamental principles of the requested State concerning the subject matter of the Convention do not permit it; it will not be sufficient to show merely that its return would be incompatible, even manifestly incompatible, with these principles...." Elisa Pérez-Vera, Explanatory Report, ¶118, *reprinted in* Hague Conference on Private International Law, III Actes et documents de law Quatorzième Session October 6–25, 1980, at 426.

The question remains, what are "the fundamental principles of the requested State relating to the protection of human rights and fundamental freedoms"?

Freier v. Freier

969 F. Supp. 436 (E.D. Mich. 1996)

Hood, J.

[Ed. Note: Jonathan M. Freier sought the return of his four-year-old daughter Avital Freier to Israel, her habitual residence. The complaint was brought against Judith D. Freier, the mother. The parents are both dual United States and Israeli citizens. They both moved separately to Israel in the late 1970s. In 1987, they returned to Michigan to get married. They then returned to Israel, where they lived together continuously until the abduction. Judith has two children from a prior marriage (Yonathan, 14 and Michal, 11) who also lived with the parties. The couple's only child together, Avital, was born in Israel in 1992. Avital had resided in Israel since her birth. The mother regularly vacationed during the summers with her three children at her parents' home in Michigan. Avital had spent approximately eight weeks in Michigan, during two one-month visits. In 1996, on another vacation to Michigan, the mother called the father and informed him that she was not returning to Israel.]

Respondent asserts that the Court should refuse to return the child under Article 20 to protect the mother's rights and freedoms, particularly, her freedom of travel. Article 20 provides: "The return of the child under the provisions of Article 12 may be refused if this would not be permitted by the fundamental principles of the requested State relating to the protection of human rights and fundamental freedoms."

Respondent claims that Petitioner has sought and obtained an injunction which prohibits her from leaving Israel until the divorce and custody proceedings are settled. An injunction also limits the child's travel. The exhibits submitted at the hearing indicate the injunction expires September 1997. Respondent claims this injunction potentially affects her ability to see her two other children should she return to Israel without them. The record, including…a letter from Petitioner's counsel, Dr. Don I. Frimer in Israel, and the statements of Professor Rakover, indicate that Respondent has a due process right to challenge the injunction. Dr. Frimer claimed such challenge can include an immediate hearing on the merits of the injunction. While Professor Rakover seemed to suggest such proceedings could take up to three months, both agreed such an injunction could be dismissed if the freedom of travel could be secured by a bond. Dr. Frimer and Professor Rakover both noted that freedom to travel "was early on recognized as a right of constitutional character" and was included as a basic right in Israel's "Basic Law: The Dignity of Man and His Freedoms." This Court is satisfied based on the information received from Professor Rakover, Dr. Frimer and Rabbi Tsevi Weinman (Respondent's counsel in Israel) that Respondent's human rights and fundamental freedoms are not in jeopardy and are protected by the due process available in the civil and Rabbinical courts of Israel.

The Court has focused primarily on Respondent's rights even though it is not clear that the Hague Convention's focus under Article 20 is on the parents' rights as opposed to the child's rights. With respect to the child, Avital, the Court is satisfied that she also has due process rights available to her in Israel in order to challenge her injunction adequately. Avital's human rights and fundamental freedoms, especially the right to travel, are protected. Respondent has not shown by clear and convincing evidence that the return of Avital to Israel would violate the United States' fundamental principles relating to the protection of human rights and fundamental freedoms.

Notes and Questions

1. *Whose Law?* The terms "human rights" often denotes rights guaranteed in international law. Is international law the governing law for purposes of article 20? As Carol Bruch has said, "It is worth noting that this provision does not presume a controlling international law. Instead, in the tradition of private international law conventions, it supplies a choice of law rule — in this case, application of the law of the state hearing the return petition (the refuge state)." Carol S. Bruch, *Religious Law, Secular Practices, and Children's Human Rights in Child Abduction Cases Under the Hague Child Abduction Convention*, 33 N.Y.U. J. Int'l L. & Pol. 49, 52 (2000). Why was Israeli constitutional law being considered in *Freir*?

2. *U.S. Constitutional Law.* Presumably, the defense would be established if returning a child would violate the U.S. Constitution. Can you imagine such a scenario? What if the child were to be sent to a country where there was a paternal preference for custody for all children under twelve? The Pérez-Vera Report warned that the principles "must not be invoked any more frequently... than they would be in their application to purely internal matters." Pérez-Vera Explanatory Report, *supra,* ¶ 118. What significance is the fact that at least one state still has a maternal preference for children of tender years, at least when the case is a "close call"? *See* Woodall v. Woodall, 471 S.E.2d 154, 158 (S.C. 1996). Certainly the maternal preference was robust in the United States during the first half of the twentieth century. *See* Thomas Trenker, *Modern Status of Maternal Preference Rule or Presumption in Child Custody*, 70 A.L.R.3d 262 (1976).

3. *Rights of the Child Convention.* Consider the possible interaction of the Hague Convention and the U.N. Convention on the Rights of the Child.

> One reason that the political issues surrounding the ratification process [in the United States] are so complicated [for the U.N. Convention on the Rights of the Child] is that there are no legal consequences for the United States' failure to ratify the [U.N.] Convention. In June 1997, a world congress was held to discuss issues of import to families and children.... The question was asked, "Well, what about the United States? When are you all going to ratify the Convention?" I said, in what I considered to be a provocative way, "when you refuse to return children to the United States under Article 20 of the Hague Convention on Civil Aspects of Child Abduction because the United States cannot provide adequate human rights protection to children. That's when we'll start to think about the legal consequences of the failure to ratify." One of the judges across the table said, "Patricia, you would actually make that argument?" There was a palpable gasp in the room, and I said that I would if the circumstances and the best interest of the child provided that opportunity.

Patricia Apy, *The Use of the United Nations Convention on the Rights of the Child in Family Litigation Involving American Children*, 5 Geo. J. on Fighting Poverty 215, 216 (1998). What would the argument look like? Would this argument be successful?

d. Consent or Acquiescence to the Removal

In Re Ponath

829 F. Supp. 363 (D. Utah 1993)

Sam, J.

[Ed. Note: From the time of their marriage until November 1991, the family resided in Utah. In November 1991, the family traveled to Germany. The court made numerous findings of fact, including the following:]

5. On November 6, 1991, petitioner, respondent and the minor child traveled to Germany on round trip airline tickets for the purpose of visiting petitioner's family. The visit was at the suggestion and request of petitioner. Respondent had suggested a six month open airline ticket, but petitioner said they would be returning to Carbon County within three months. At the time the airline tickets were purchased, the return trip was scheduled for December 5, 1991....

7. Some two weeks after arriving in Germany, petitioner obtained employment. Petitioner, respondent and the minor child resided with petitioner's parents. Commencing on or about April 1992, petitioner began the construction of a house on property adjacent to that of his parents.

8. At the end of three months, approximately February 1992, respondent desired to return to the United States with the minor child, but petitioner refused to permit her and the minor child to return. Petitioner prevented and continued to prevent respondent and the minor child's return to the United States by means of verbal, emotional and physical abuse.

9. Some months later, during a discussion between petitioner and respondent regarding her desire to return with the minor child to the United States, petitioner told respondent that, if she desired to live without him as her husband and as the minor child's father, she and the child could leave Germany.

10. At that time, there was no judicial custody order and no legal proceedings had been commenced concerning the marriage or custody of the child.

11. Respondent and the minor child returned to the United States on September 7, 1992, and have resided in Carbon County, Utah since that time....

13. Petitioner returned to the United States at the end of February 1993. On March 1, 1993, petitioner was arrested by Carbon County police officials for allegedly attacking respondent's sister-in-law in her home while attempting to see respondent and the minor child....

15. Petitioner filed this action on July 9, 1993.

Conclusions of Law...

As an additional and/or alternative basis for the court's ruling, the court concludes that petitioner gave his consent for respondent to return to the United States with the minor child. Viewing the testimony of respondent as the more credible testimony, the court finds, for purposes of the Hague Convention, that respondent has established by a preponderance of the evidence that petitioner gave his consent for respondent to return to the United States with the minor child. This conclusion is further supported by petitioner's failure, for almost six months, to make any meaningful effort to obtain return of the minor child. Accordingly, the court concludes that removal of the child was not wrongful within the meaning of the Hague Convention.

Notes and Questions

1. *Temporal Element of Consent.* Mr. Ponath told Mrs. Ponath "some months" after February 1992 that if she "desired to live without him as her husband and as the minor child's father, she and the child could leave Germany." She then left Germany in September 1992. What if she had left, instead, in September 1993? Does consent ever expire?

2. *Formality of Consent.* Need consent or the revocation of consent be explicit? *Compare Ponath* with *Friedrich v. Friedrich*, 78 F.3d 1060, 1069–70 (6th Cir. 1996). Excerpts from *Friedrich* appear earlier in this chapter. Mrs. Friedrich had also argued, among other things, that Mr. Friedrich subsequently acquiesced in the removal of Thomas to the United States. Here is the Sixth Circuit's response:

> Mrs. Friedrich bases her claim of subsequent acquiescence on a statement made by Mr. Friedrich to one of her commanding officers, Captain Michael Farley, at a cocktail party on the military base after Mrs. Friedrich had left with Thomas. Captain Farley, who cannot date the conversation exactly, testified that: "During the conversation, Mr. Friedrich indicated that he was not seeking custody of the child, because he didn't have the means to take care of the child." Mr. Friedrich denies that he made this statement. The district court made no specific finding regarding this fact.
>
> We believe that the statement to Captain Farley, even if it was made, is insufficient evidence of subsequent acquiescence. Subsequent acquiescence requires more than an isolated statement to a third-party. Each of the words and actions of a parent during the separation are not to be scrutinized for a possible waiver of custody rights. *See Wanninger,* 850 F. Supp. at 81–82 (refusing to construe father's personal letters to wife and priest as sufficient evidence of acquiescence where father consistently attempted to keep in contact with child). Although we must decide the matter without guidance from previous appellate court decisions, we believe that acquiescence under the Convention requires either: an act or statement with the requisite formality, such as testimony in a judicial proceeding; a convincing written renunciation of rights; or a consistent attitude of acquiescence over a significant period of time.
>
> By August 22, 1991, twenty-one days after the abduction, Mr. Friedrich had secured a German court order awarding him custody of Thomas. He has resolutely sought custody of his son since that time. It is by these acts, not his casual statements to third parties, that we will determine whether or not he acquiesced to the retention of his son in America. Since Mrs. Friedrich has not introduced evidence of a formal renunciation or a consistent attitude of acquiescence over a significant period of time, the judgment of the district court on this matter was not erroneous.

The *Friedrich* court mentions that only a "convincing" written renunciation of rights would be sufficient for acquiescence. What could be an "unconvincing" written renunciation? *See* Currier v. Currier, 845 F. Supp. 916 (D.N.H. 1994).

In *Tabacchi v. Harrison*, 2000 WL 190576 (N.D. Ill. Feb. 10, 2000), the court refused to find acquiescence where the father mailed the child gifts, gave the mother money on request, talked about visiting and inquired about work, and filed a Hague petition approximately six months after mother and child departed. In *Krishna v. Krishna*, 1997 WL 195439 (N.D. Cal. Apr. 11, 1997), the court found consent when petitioner gave respondent the child's passport, knowing of respondent's plan to leave the country.

3. *Implicit Consent.* Can consent ever be implicit? What if a husband says to his wife, who is the primary caretaker of their children, "Come to Australia with me, and if you don't like it, you can leave." The couple moves there, lives there two years, and the wife then decides that she does not like life in Australia. Has the husband consented to her leaving with the children? *Cf.* Journe v. Journe, 911 F. Supp. 43 (D.P.R. 1995) (dismissing father's petition because father waived his rights under the Convention when he voluntary dismissed a custody proceeding in child's habitual residence after believing, erroneously, that couple had reconciled).

4. *Acquiescence.* What is the difference between consent to the removal and acquiescence to the removal? Isn't acquiescence a form of consent, just implied? The court in *In re Ponath* talks about the father's failure, for almost six months, to make any meaningful effort to obtain return of the minor child. Would that inaction, even absent his explicit consent, have been enough to establish the defense? Why or why not?

5. *A Review.* The term "habitual residence" was explored above, in Section A.1.a. Why exactly would the father's acts toward the mother affect the child's habitual residence? How would the *Mozes* court, with all of its rules, deal with this scenario? Is it clear from the *Ponath* opinion whether or not the mother had already formed a settled intent before the violence began? Does that matter?

e. One Year Elapsed from the Date of Wrongful Removal

Lops v. Lops
140 F.3d 927 (11th Cir. 1998)

Hull, J.

Petitioner-Appellee Christine Lops filed a petition under the International Child Abduction Remedies Act, seeking return of her two minor children to Germany. After conducting evidentiary hearings, the district court found that Petitioner's former husband, Respondent Michael Lops, and his mother, Respondent Anne Harrington, wrongfully removed Petitioner's minor children from Germany to the United States in violation of Petitioner's custody rights. [T]he district court ordered the children's return to Germany with Petitioner. [W]e affirm....

The issues in this appeal necessitate first a detailed review of the district court's findings of fact and the evidence supporting them.

A. On January 31, 1995, Petitioner Initiates Divorce And Custody Proceedings In Germany

Petitioner and Respondent Lops were married in Germany in June 1991. Until they separated in January 1995, they lived with their two minor daughters, Claire and Carmen Lops, in Rodgau, Germany. On January 31, 1995, Petitioner initiated divorce and custody proceedings in the German family court for the district that was the marital and habitual residence of the parties. Alleging that Respondent Lops physically abused her, Petitioner sought sole custody of the children. From January 1995 to early May 1995, Petitioner and the children visited relatives and friends in Belgium.

On May 2, 1995, Petitioner and Respondent Lops appeared with counsel for their first hearing before the family court in Germany. Respondent Lops also sought sole custody of the children. Since the parties could not reach a custody agreement, Judge Rudolf Giwitz, the German family court judge, instructed the parties to appear with the children the following week. Even though Petitioner had returned to Germany with the children in early May 1995, the animosity between Petitioner and Respondent Lops had increased due to Petitioner's taking the children to Belgium for four months without Respondent Lops's consent.

B. On May 10, 1995, Parties Agree To Share Custody At German Family Court Hearing

On May 10, 1995, the parties appeared again with counsel and the children before Judge Giwitz. At this "isolated proceeding of custody" hearing under German law, Judge Giwitz heard from each party and interviewed the children. In a letter written from Judge Giwitz to the district court, Judge Giwitz indicated that Petitioner expressed concerns that Respondent Lops would follow through on earlier threats to abduct the children and take them to the United States. Judge Giwitz's letter further states that Respondent Lops dispelled these concerns by arguing that he was firmly rooted in Germany and had no further connection with the United States.

As a result of the German family court proceeding, the parties agreed to share joint legal custody, with Petitioner retaining primary physical custody. Respondent Lops was allowed visitation rights based on his assurance to Judge Giwitz that he would return the children to Petitioner.

The parties' agreement regarding custody of the children resulted in a suspension of the German family court proceedings. Judge Giwitz approved of Respondent Lops's having a short visitation with the children immediately following the hearing, with the understanding that Respondent Lops would return the children that evening to Petitioner. The German court considered the parties' custody agreement announced in court as binding on both parties.

C. On May 10, 1995, Respondent Lops Violates Custody Agreement

Immediately following the May 10 hearing, Respondent Lops visited with the children as authorized by Judge Giwitz. Once Respondent Lops obtained the children physically, he did not return the children to Petitioner as agreed.... Petitioner objected and initiated efforts to contest this unilateral alteration of the parties' agreement announced before Judge Giwitz.

Over the next two weeks, Petitioner resided with Respondent Lops's aunt and visited the children daily in the marital residence, but she was never allowed to remain alone with the children. During this time, there was also some attempt at marital reconciliation, which soon failed.

D. On May 30, 1995, Respondents Fraudulently Obtain New Passports For The Children

Unbeknownst to Petitioner, Respondent planned to remove the children from Germany, but could not because the children's passports were in Petitioner's possession. The district court determined that Respondent misrepresented to Consulate officials that Petitioner had abandoned the children and thereby obtained new passports for the children on May 30, 1995. The district court expressly found, and the evidence showed, that Petitioner never abandoned the children and that she had parental custody rights not only by operation of German law but also by the agreement before and approved by the German family court judge.

E. On May 30, 1995, Petitioner Reopens Custody Proceedings In German Family Court, And On June 1, 1995, Respondent Lops Takes Children From Germany To Spain

On May 30, 1995, the same day Respondent obtained new passports for the children, Petitioner reopened the suspended custody proceedings before Judge Giwitz. However, on June 1, 1995, without Petitioner's knowledge or consent and in violation of the parties' custody agreement in Judge Giwitz's court, Respondent Lops took the children from Germany to Spain, where they stayed until approximately June 25, 1995. While Respondent Lops and the children were in Spain, Respondent Harrington, Respondent Lops's mother, remained at the former marital residence in Rodgau, Germany.

F. On June 27, 1995, Respondent Harrington Takes Children To The United States

Respondent Lops and the children returned to Germany on June 25, 1995. Only two days later, Respondent Harrington took the children to the United States, without Petitioner's knowledge or consent and in violation of her custody rights....

G. On July 3, 1995, German Family Court Conducts Another Hearing

Judge Giwitz held another custody hearing on July 3, 1995. Neither Respondent Lops nor his counsel revealed to the German family court, or Petitioner, that his mother, Respondent Harrington, had already taken the children to the United States, or that Respondent Lops was packing his furniture and belongings to leave for the United States only days later.

H. On July 8, 1995, Respondent Lops Joins Children In The United States But Conceals Whereabouts

On July 8, 1995, Respondent Lops left for the United States. Initially, Respondent Lops and the children stayed with Respondent Harrington in her home in Martinez near Augusta, Georgia. In early August 1995, Respondent Lops and the children moved into a home purchased by Respondent Harrington across Georgia's border in North Augusta, South Carolina. The district court described the transaction for "this curiously purchased house" as "peculiar." The purchase contract called for a down payment and a twenty-year mortgage, but Respondent Harrington was not to receive an executed deed to the home for twenty years. Instead, the seller of the home remained its owner, and the lender held the deed from the seller to Respondent Harrington. The deed was to be transferred to Respondent Harrington only after all of the mortgage payments were made. Thus, the title to the South Carolina home apparently remained in the seller, arguably concealing its true ownership.

The district court found that over the next two and one-half years Respondent Lops and his mother, Respondent Harrington, took other more significant measures to conceal his and the children's whereabouts from Petitioner. For example, Respondent Lops had no checking account and personally transacted business only in cash, including at times the children's private school tuition. Respondent Lops drove a $30,000 van registered under Respondent Harrington's name. Despite the fact that he earned an annual six-figure income as a foreign exchange broker in Germany, Respondent Lops did not obtain any employment in the United States, which would have required him to disclose his social security number. Instead, he worked as a part-time independent contractor with House Rentals owned by his stepfather, Wayne Harrington. Respondent Lops, Mr. Harrington, and Mr. Harrington's company did not have any real estate licenses.

Respondent Lops never reported any income or paid any federal or state income taxes in the United States during 1995, 1996, or 1997. In short, Respondent Lops had no "electronic identity." As the district court aptly noted in its findings of fact: "Mr. Lops has no conventional credit, no credit cards, engages only in cash transactions; pays no utilities; his mother takes care of those; has no lease with his mother. This is a curious existence...."

Notwithstanding his significant income reduction, Respondent Lops maintained a comfortable lifestyle, reportedly by borrowing from friends and family; yet, no loans had any documentation. Although living and driving in South Carolina for over two years, Respondent Lops never obtained a South Carolina driver's license, nor did any insurance policy list Respondent Lops as an authorized driver of the van. The district court's findings of fact concluded: "...I see Mr. Michael Lops in a situation or in a position or pattern of continuing deception and even if every word that he says about his income and his business affairs is to be believed he is committing either four or five misdemeanors to maintain this pattern and to conceal, at least himself, from any authority."...

M. Petitioner's Two-Year Efforts To Locate Children

The record is replete with evidence of Petitioner's two-year campaign to locate her children. For example, the district court found that from 1995 to 1997 Petitioner employed the assistance of approximately eleven state, national, and international agencies, including Interpol, the United States State Department, and the Georgia Bureau of Investigation ("GBI"). These agencies searched records (1) in Georgia, where Respondent Harrington lives; (2) in Virginia, where Respondent Lops's sister lives; and (3) in New York, where Respondent Lops's adoptive father lives.

The GBI conducted drive-by checks at Respondent Harrington's home. The GBI contacted local school officials and checked credit and employment tax records. These and many other concerted efforts, including the State Department's initiating database searches such as credit agency reports and the Federal Parent Locator Service, were to no avail....

A memo, dated December 12, 1996, from the United States National Central Bureau to the Diplomatic Security Service of the Department of State, states as follows:

> Incidentally, Lops' mother, who resides in Martinez, Georgia, refuses to admit knowing where [Respondent Lops] and the children can be found. I can locate no other trace as to their current whereabouts.

Ultimately, officials contacted the District Attorney's office in Georgia's Augusta Judicial Circuit, where Respondent Harrington lives. The District Attorney's office received authorization from the Superior Court of Columbia County, Georgia, also located in the Augusta Judicial Circuit, to place a wiretap on Respondent Harrington's telephone. Through wiretaps, officials ascertained the whereabouts of Respondent Lops and the children, as well as when the children would be at Respondent Harrington's home in Georgia.

On November 3, 1997, as a result of the GBI's requesting custody of the children, the Superior Court of Columbia County, Georgia issued an order directing law enforcement to seize the children and surrender custody to the Georgia Department of Family and Children Services ("DFACS"). On November 5 or 6, 1997, DFACS took custody of the children at Respondent Harrington's home. Petitioner took a leave of absence from work and immediately came to the United States....

[Respondents' Affirmative Defense Based on ICARA's Well-Settled Exception]

Respondents contend that the children should not be returned to Germany because they showed that the ICARA petition was filed more than one year after the wrongful removal of the children and that the children are now "well-settled" in their new environment. *See* Hague Convention, art. 12. After reviewing the evidence at trial, we conclude that the district court correctly determined that Respondents had not established an affirmative defense under the "well-settled" exception or any other affirmative defense available under ICARA and that the district court did not err in ordering that the children be returned to Germany with Petitioner....

Although the petition was not filed within one year of the wrongful removal, the district court first determined that this one-year time limit, which in some respects is similar to a statute of limitations, may be equitably tolled. In doing so, the district court found that it is difficult to "conceive of a time period arising by a federal statute that is so woodenly applied that it is not subject to some tolling, interruption, or suspension, if it is shown or demonstrated clearly enough that the action of an alleged wrongdoer concealed the existence of the very act which initiates the running of the important time period." We are not required to reach the issue of whether equitable tolling may apply under ICARA because the evidence supported the district court's factual finding that the children were not yet "well-settled" under the Hague Convention.

The district court found that "well-settled" means more than having a comfortable material existence. In determining whether the children were "well-settled," the district court properly considered many relevant factors, including but not limited to several peculiar circumstances surrounding the children's living environment, Respondent Harrington's being more involved with the children in certain areas than Respondent Lops,[27] the active measures Respondents were undertaking to keep Respondent Lops's and the children's whereabouts concealed from Petitioner and the German (and other) authorities, and the fact that Respondent Lops could be prosecuted for his violations of state and federal law because he was committing "four and five misdemeanors...to conceal, at least himself, from any authority." Other evidence adequately supported the district court's finding that the children were not "well-settled" as contemplated under ICARA and Article 12 of the Hague Convention....

We conclude that the district court correctly ordered that the two minor children, Claire Lops and Carmen Lops, be returned to the custody of Petitioner for immediate return to Germany. In accordance with the terms of ICARA and the Convention, the district court's judgment also correctly resolves only Petitioner's wrongful removal claim and remands any matter regarding the underlying custody dispute to be resolved by German courts where the litigation between the parties first began and should be resolved. Thus, we affirm the judgment of the district court.

---

27. The evidence indicated that although Respondent Lops worked only a few hours each week, Respondent Harrington picked the children up from school each day and attended more to the nurture and needs of the children. The district court found that Respondent Harrington was "in virtual control of the financial and other affairs of this family. I see that the grandmother [Respondent Harrington] is a co-partner, co-participant in the abduction and in the maintenance of these appearances whose only object could be to conceal the existence of the origins of the children."

Wojcik v. Wojcik

959 F. Supp. 413 (E.D. Mich. 1997)

Cohn, J....

This is a petition for the return of minor children pursuant to the Convention on the Civil Aspects of International Child Abduction at the Hague. Petitioner Eric Wojcik (the father) seeks the return of his two minor children, Jessica-Cecille and Jennifer, to France. The children are currently in the United States with their mother, respondent Karen Marie Wojcik (the mother). For the reasons which follow, the petition will be denied....

The Court makes the following findings of fact. The father is a French citizen. The mother is an American citizen. They were married in France on February 15, 1986, and made France their home. They had two children, both born in France: Jessica-Cecille, born on July 10, 1988, and Jennifer, born on March 24, 1991. Both children have dual citizenship in France and the United States. Between 1988 and 1994, the family visited the United States three times. During these visits, they stayed with the mother's family in Michigan.

On October 13, 1994, the mother took the children with her to the United States for a vacation that was supposed to last a couple weeks. The father knew and approved of this vacation. On November 1, 1994, the mother called the father from the United States and told him that neither she nor the children would return to France. She told the father they were staying with her brother in Roseville, Michigan, and gave the father the telephone number. The father had been to the brother's house on one of the family's visits.

On November 23, 1994, the father petitioned for divorce in France. The mother did not attend the hearing, but was represented by French counsel. The French court denied the mother's request for an international rogatory commission that would allow her to answer the petition in the United States. The court issued a provisional ruling that "parental authority...will be jointly shared by the two parents," and that the children "will have their usual residence" at the father's home in France. The mother filed a complaint for divorce in Macomb County, Michigan, on June 30, 1995. The record does not reflect the current status of the complaint.

On July 1, 1995, the father filed a request for the return of his children with the French Central Authority. On July 17, 1995, the French Ministry of Justice telefaxed a letter to the Office of Children's Issues at the United States Department of State, asking for help under the Convention in returning the children to France. On July 18, the Office of Children's Issues telefaxed a letter to the French Central Authority that confirmed receipt of the request and stated that the Office had sent a letter to "Ms. Janet Hayes," requesting that she agree to return the children to France voluntarily.

On July 25, 1995, the mother's counsel contacted the Office of Children's Issues and related the mother's refusal to return the children to France. On January 30, 1996, the State Department forwarded the father's application to the National Center for Missing and Exploited Children (NCMEC), a private, nonprofit corporation that handles child abduction cases arising under the Convention. NCMEC arranged for legal aid in the United States for the father to seek the return of his children.

On March 27, 1996, the father filed the present petition for the return of his children.... The Court held an evidentiary hearing on May 9, 1996, at which the mother was the sole witness. The mother testified that the father, from the beginning of their marriage, emotionally and occasionally physically abused her. The mother also testified that the father emotionally abused their daughters often and twice physically abused their eldest daughter. As to the children's life in America, the mother testified as follows: she and the children lived in Roseville with her brother for approximately eight months before she rented her own house, where they lived at the time of the hearing; both children have attended the same school or day-care since their arrival and have friends and relatives in the area with whom they are close; the oldest, Jessica-Cecille, is not involved in community or church activities, but the whole family attends the same church every Sunday; and both have forgotten French and adopted English as their spoken language. Finally, the mother testified that she has worked at the same bank for more than a year....

The Convention establishes guidelines for considering an application for the return of children:

> [w]here a child has been wrongfully removed or retained in terms of Article 3 and, at the date of the commencement of the proceedings before the judicial or administrative authority of the Contracting State where the child is, a period of less than one year has elapsed from the date of the wrongful removal or retention, the authority concerned shall order the return of the child forthwith.
>
> The judicial or administrative authority, even where the proceedings have been commenced after the expiration of the period of one year...shall also order the return of the child, unless it is demonstrated that the child is now settled in its new environment.

Art. 12....

The key question, therefore, is whether the father "commence[d]...proceedings before the judicial or administrative authority" when he contacted the Central Authority of the United States within a year of the wrongful retention, such that the "settled in [their] environment" exception to automatic return of the children does not apply. [Ed. Note: The court went on to hold that the term 'commencement of proceedings' in article 12 means, with respect to the return of a child located in the United States, the filing of a petition in a judicial proceeding. The court reached this result under its reading of ICARA and the Convention.]

Having thus interpreted Article 12, the Court must now apply it to the facts at hand. There is no reason in this case, as there might be in others, to refuse to apply Article 12 for equitable reasons. The mother did not hide the children; in fact, she called the father the first day of the wrongful retention and told him where they were. Still, eight months passed between the wrongful retention of the children in November of 1994 and the father's contacting the French Central Authority in July of 1995. The record does not reflect any action taken by the father during that time, aside from filing for divorce, to have his children returned to France. Less than one month after the French Central Authority was contacted, the mother had been asked to return the children and had refused. Therefore, the Court will order the return of the children unless the mother has shown by a preponderance of the evidence, 42 U.S.C. § 11603(e)(2)(B), that "the child[ren are] now settled in [their] new environment." Art. 12.

The mother has established by a preponderance of the evidence that, as of the hearing: the children had been in the United States for eighteen months; the mother and the children had initially lived with the mother's brother for eight months until they moved into a rented house of their own, where they still lived; both children had been attending school or day care consistently; both had friends and relatives in the area; the family attended church regularly; and the mother had stable employment with the same employer for more than a year. While not agreeing with all of the mother's testimony, the father provided no evidence to call it into question. And aside from the father's family—a family that the mother testified was indifferent to the children at best—the father has shown no evidence that the children have maintained any ties to France.

The mother has shown by a preponderance of the evidence that the children, eight and five years old at the time of the hearing, were settled in their new environment as of the time of the hearing. *Cf.* David S. v. Zamira S., 151 Misc.2d 630, 574 N.Y.S.2d 429, 433 (N.Y. Fam. Ct. 1991) (finding a three-year-old and a one-year-old were not settled in their new environment because they were too young to forge strong friendships, and they were "not yet involved in school, extra-curricular, community, religious or social activities which children of an older age would be"). The Court therefore will deny the petition. The Court's decision is not a decision on who should have custody of the children, or where the children should ultimately live, or even that the children are settled in the United States for the purposes of determining custody. The Court is merely holding that the custody decision should be made in the United States....

Notes and Questions

1. *Start of the Article 12 Clock.* Establishing that one year has elapsed since the wrongful removal or retention is important for one seeking to establish the "well-settled" defense. When would the one-year period have commenced in *Lops*? On May 10? June 1? June 27? Respondents raising the "well-settled" defense typically try to extend the length of time since the abduction by setting the earliest date possible for the abduction. Can a respondent count time that accrued after the abduction but before the respondent crossed an international border?

2. *Equitable Tolling.* The *Lops* court, unlike the *Wojcik* court, did not decide whether equitable tolling should be permitted to stop the article 12 clock. Does the concept have appeal on the facts of *Lops*? If the court had accepted the concept, how exactly would it have operated in *Lops*? Would this have been a better basis for refusing to return the children than the reasoning the court employed?

3. *Equitable Tolling II.* The *Wojcik* court's consideration of equitable tolling has been followed by other courts. *See, e.g., In re* Robinson, 983 F. Supp. 1339, 1345 n.10 (D. Colo. 1997) (explaining that "passage of time should not give advantage to the abductor who conceals the child or seeks to avoid process," although basis for equitable tolling did not exist on facts). The State Department's Legal Analysis of the Hague Convention on the Civil Aspects of International Child Abduction also states that if "the alleged wrongdoer concealed the child's whereabouts from the custodian necessitating a long search for the child and thereby delayed the commencement of a return proceeding by the applicant, it is highly questionable whether the respondent should be permitted to benefit from such conduct absent strong countervailing consideration." 51 Fed. Reg. at 10,509.

4. *Commencement of Proceedings.* As noted in *Wojcik*, a petitioner stops the article 12 clock by commencing appropriate proceedings. Why in the United States would only a court, and not the Central Authority, qualify as an appropriate "judicial or administrative authority"? Read all of articles 11 and 12, and try to make a plausible argument that the *Wojcik* court reached the correct conclusion on this issue. Pay close attention to the context in which "judicial or administrative authority" is used in these articles in order

to determine its meaning in the phrase "commencement of proceedings before the judicial or administrative authority."

5. *Domestic Abuse.* Both *Lops* and *Wojcik* involve women who alleged their partners abused them. Is this relevant to an article 12 inquiry? Why is it mentioned? Is it relevant to either court's analysis?

6. *The "Well-Settled" Determination.* The determination of whether a child is "well-settled" for purposes of the article 12 defense is highly fact intensive. How useful to the analysis are the facts that the *Lops* court identified as being persuasive? What else might you want to know if you were the judge? If you represented the father in *Wojcik*, what evidence would you gather to counter the mother's evidence?

7. *Central Authority.* Notice the procedures involved in the Hague Convention. The Convention mentions "Central Authorities." See arts. 6–7. The U.S.'s Central Authority is the Office of Children's Issues in the U.S. Department of State. In this country, the National Center for Missing and Exploited Children (NCMEC) has a cooperative agreement with the U.S. Department of State to handle cases where children have been abducted to the United States. The International Division of the NCMEC provides a variety of services, including a victim reunification program (funding travel for indigent left-behind parents in order to reunite with their children), a networking program to connect left-behind parents, and international photo distribution on its website.

8. *Attorney's Fees.* For children who are abducted to the United States, a prevailing petitioner may recover attorney fees, unless such an award "would be clearly inappropriate." International Child Abduction Remedies Act, 42 U.S.C. § 11607(b)(3). *See, e.g.,* Freier v. Freier, 985 F. Supp. 710 (E.D. Mich. 1997); Distler v. Distler, 26 F. Supp. 2d 723 (D.N.J. 1998). What about a prevailing respondent? The provision for attorney's fees is particularly important in the United States for petitioners, since the United States specifically entered a reservation to article 26 of the Convention. That article would have obligated the United States to make available to applicants, or at least applicants who qualify for legal aid, free legal representation. The fact that the United States does not offer free legal assistance to applicants has drawn much criticism from other States Parties, and means that applicants have to pay for their own attorneys or find pro bono counsel.

Attorney's fees may also be available under the Victim and Witness Protection Act (VWPA) of 1982 if the abductor is found guilty of a criminal offense, *e.g.,* violation of the International Parental Kidnapping Crime Act (IPKCA), 18 U.S.C. § 1204(a). See VWPA, 18 U.S.C. § 3663(a)(1)(A) (authorizing an award of restitution to victims of crimes). In *United States v. Cummings*, 281 F.3d 1046 (9th Cir. 2002), the appellate court upheld such an award in a child abduction case. The district court had ordered the father, who was convicted under IPKCA, to pay the attorney's fees that the mother had incurred in her civil contempt action and her Hague Convention proceeding. The restitution award was made even though the German court heard and denied the mother's Hague petition to return the children to the United States.

9. *Relocation.* Many of the abduction cases that involve the custodial parent as the abductor would not occur if courts freely granted custodial parents the ability to move abroad. In the United States, there is a diversity of approaches to the relocation issue, although there is a trend toward "giving the primary custodial parent free rein to relocate, provided the move is well-intentioned and some provision is made for the children to remain in contact with the non-custodial parent." Elizabeth M. Ellis & Jonathan Levin, *Conducting Psychological Evaluations in Relocation Cases*, 15 Am. J. Fam. L. 286, 287 (2001). International relocations may be seen to raise issues "different in kind" from

intra-state and inter-state relocations. *See, e.g., In re* Marriage of Condon, 62 Cal. App. 4th 533, 566 (1998). Should courts treat international relocation differently than others? Why or why not? For a liberal approach to international relocation, *see* Payne v. Payne, 1 Fam. 1052 (Eng. C.A. 2001).

Problems

Now that you have studied the analytical framework utilized by U.S. courts to assess petitions brought under the Hague Convention on Child Abduction, consider the following problems:

8-5. Paul and Eva are both American citizens. They were married in California and have two children, ages twelve and seventeen. Paul designs computer programs as a freelance consultant and Eva is a model. In January, Paul received an offer to collaborate with a French toy manufacturer to design computer games. The original offer was for a program that would take nine months to design. The French company assured Paul that if the relationship worked out, it would continue to employ him on a contract basis for future projects for the next several years. Paul and Eva sold their home that month and moved into an apartment in Paris with the children, who were then enrolled in a Parisian school. Paul and Eva obtained drivers licenses and they purchased a car. Eva attempted to obtain modeling jobs in Paris, but her California agent had few contacts that were helpful and she was unable to find work. She was increasingly unhappy and wanted to return to America. Paul loved his work and was entranced with Paris. In July of the same year, after a particularly stormy argument, Eva left Paul and brought the children to New York. She told Paul that the trip was a vacation and was to give her time to think. When she arrived in New York, however, she moved in with her parents and resumed her modeling career. In September of the same year, Paul filed a proceeding under the Hague Convention seeking the return of the children to France.

Assume hypothetically that under French law, a French court will assume jurisdiction in a child custody case if either parent or the child is present in France. Also assume that in the absence of a court order, French law makes each parent a joint guardian and joint custodian of the child. Also assume that French courts apply French law regardless of the child's nationality or place of domicile. Will a New York court, acting on Paul's Hague application, order the return of the children?

8-6. Franz, a German citizen, and Stella, an American citizen, were married in Berlin, where they resided for five years and where their son was born. Both moved with their son to Utah when he was two years old; Franz then began to work for Volkswagen in Utah. Stella was a homemaker. When the relationship deteriorated two years later, the parties separated and entered an agreement whereby each was given joint custody. Four months later, Franz was transferred back to Germany. During the month that he had physical custody under the agreement, he returned to Germany and enrolled the child in school. Stella visited Germany four months later, spent a week with Franz and the child, and then moved the son back to Utah without Franz's permission. Franz filed a proceeding under the Hague Convention for the return of the child. Will a Utah court, acting on Franz's request, order the return of the child?

8-7. Myra, an American citizen, and Sean, an Irish citizen, met in Boston and married. Shortly afterwards they move to Ireland, had a child, and resided there for five years. When their daughter was four, Myra and Sean obtained a decree of judicial separation. Myra was awarded custody, although both had joint guardianship, and Sean had access rights to visit every other weekend. During the six months after the decree was issued, Sean visited with the child only once. He did not show up for visitation on any other occasion, and would not speak with Myra when she tried to call him. Myra moved with the child back to Boston. Sean filed a Hague petition six months later for the return of the child to Ireland. How will the Massachusetts court rule on the Hague petition?

8-8. Fiona, an American citizen, and Hugh, a British citizen, were married in London and had a daughter, Ann. When Ann was five years old, the couple obtained a divorce. Fiona was given custody and Hugh was given visitation rights. Six months later, Ann and Fiona moved to Florida to live near Mickey Mouse. Hugh knew of Fiona's planned move and raised no objection. Seven months after the move, Hugh began a Hague proceeding. How is the Florida court likely to rule? Would it make a difference if, under British law, Fiona required permission from the court to remove the child from Great Britain?

8-9. Brigid, an American citizen, married Colm, an Irish citizen, and moved to Northern Ireland, where the couple raised three children. After suffering a broken arm and concussion from domestic abuse, Brigid obtained a barring order (excluding Colm from the marital home) and a custody order for the children, ages 6, 8, and 14. Colm retained access rights and continued to abuse Brigid when she retrieved the children from their visits with their father. After threats on her life during heated exchanges, Brigid fled with the three children to New York, despite a court order in Northern Ireland that required her to obtain court permission before leaving Ireland. She did not tell Colm where she went. Two years later, when Colm located her, he filed a petition for the return of the children. The children vigorously opposed return. Although Brigid had a job in New York, she had few funds and could not afford to return with the children. Assume Colm lives in a small town that has recently been bombed by the IRA. What arguments would Brigid make to oppose the return of the children and how is the court likely to rule?

B. Jurisdiction in International Custody Disputes and Enforcement of Foreign Orders

As with other types of disputes, when a judicial or administrative authority is faced with a request to resolve who should have custody of a child, that tribunal must first determine if it has jurisdiction, i.e., the authority to issue a binding decision in the controversy. Even if the tribunal determines that it does have jurisdiction, it then has discretion to choose whether to decline its jurisdiction and defer the controversy to the authority of another court system that it views as capable of providing a more convenient forum. In addition to requests to establish or change custody, tribunals are also frequently asked to enforce custody orders issued by the tribunals of other nations, and must then determine whether they are required by their domestic law or international agreement to recognize and enforce such orders.

When an application requesting return of a child is made under the Hague Convention on Child Abduction, the Convention often circumvents the need for a tribunal in the country in which the child is residing to determine issues regarding jurisdiction and enforcement under domestic law or other conventions. This is because Article 16 of the Hague Convention on Child Abduction prohibits the country in which the child is located from deciding the merits of a custody dispute unless its judicial or administrative authorities have determined that the child is not required to be returned under the Convention. When a child is returned under Convention proceedings to the child's country of habitual residence, typically custody is then litigated in that country, and the issue of jurisdiction at that point is not frequently contested.

Nevertheless, there are many international custody disputes that are not resolved in this manner. Most often this is because the Hague Convention on Child Abduction is not in effect between the two nations involved. Given that fewer than half of the nations of the world are currently parties to the Convention, and that contracting states are not required to accept the accessions of nations that are not members of the Hague Conference, there are many international custody cases, even in the courts of nations that are parties to the Convention, such as the United States, to which the Hague Convention on Child Abduction would not be applicable. In these cases, tribunals must look to their domestic law and any other applicable conventions to determine whether they have authority to issue an original or modified custody or visitation order, and when they must recognize and enforce the orders issued by the tribunals of other countries.

Even when a custody dispute involves two nations between which the Hague Convention on Child Abduction is in effect, however, issues regarding jurisdiction and enforcement of foreign orders may still come before a tribunal. There are a variety of situations in which this occurs:

(1) Following an application for return under the Convention, a tribunal might refuse to order the return of a child because it finds: (a) the country to which return is requested was not the child's habitual residence, (b) the removal or retention was not wrongful, or (c) one of the defenses to return is applicable. That tribunal may thereafter need to determine if it has jurisdiction to issue or modify a custody order, or if it must enforce another nation's order or defer to proceedings pending in that nation. *See* Appel v. Appel (*In re* C.A.M.A.), 103 Wash. App. 1032 (2000) (Washington court may exercise jurisdiction over custody under UCCJA, where retention by child's parent in Washington was not in breach of custody rights, and not wrongful under Hague Abduction Convention); *Cf.* Turner v. Frowein, 752 A.2d 955 (Conn. 2000) (after denying Dutch father's Hague Abduction Convention application under the "grave risk" exception, court addressed father's claim that Dutch order was entitled to recognition under the UCCJA).

(2) A left-behind parent may ask a tribunal of the country from which a child has been removed for a custody order, before a Convention application is resolved in the country in which the child is located, or even after that country refuses to return the child. *See* Stock v. Stock, 677 So. 2d 1341 (Fla. Dist. Ct. App.1996) (after mother removed children from Florida to Switzerland, custody proceedings were filed in both countries, and a Swiss tribunal denied father's Hague application, Florida court should have properly applied UCCJA simultaneous proceedings rule to determine if it could exercise original jurisdiction).

(3) The tribunal that issued an initial custody order may be asked to modify its order after a child's move to another country. *See* Johnson v. Johnson, 493

S.E.2d 668 (Va. Ct. App. 1997) (Virginia court had jurisdiction to modify its own order).

(4) On some occasions, even though the facts suggest a Convention application might have been filed, the left-behind parent does not pursue that remedy, and a tribunal in the country to which a child has been moved must determine if it has jurisdiction to initially determine or modify custody. Dincer v. Dincer, 701 A.2d 210 (Pa. 1998) (initial determination); Zenide v. Superior Ct., 27 Cal. Rptr. 2d 703 (Cal. Ct. App. 1994) (modification). *Cf.* Winton-Ibanez v. Ibanez, 690 So. 2d 1344 (Fla. Dist. Ct. App. 1997) (father did not request return under Hague Convention until U.S. custody proceeding, in which trial court declined jurisdiction under UCCJA, was on appeal).

(5) Sometimes courts in the country in which the child is located have adjudicated both a Convention application and issues of jurisdiction or enforcement simultaneously. *See* Jeffers v. Makropoulos, 992 P.2d 686 (Colo. Ct. App. 1999) (child was returned under Hague Abduction Convention to Greece and Colorado court declined to exercise jurisdiction under UCCJA); Henches v. Vogel, 103 Wash. App. 1019 (2000) (where both parents filed Convention applications and custody actions, Washington court ruled mother's removal not wrongful and father's removal wrongful, ordered return of children to Switzerland, and found Washington court should defer to the Swiss court under the UCCJA).

Therefore, a thorough understanding of the law regulating international jurisdiction and enforcement of judgments is critical for lawyers who practice in the field of family law, even in countries that are party to the Convention.

1. U.S. Domestic Law

Aside from Article 16 of the Hague Convention on Child Abduction, the United States is not currently a party to any treaties regulating the jurisdiction of custody matters or enforcement of custody orders in the international arena. U.S. courts therefore turn to domestic law to resolve jurisdictional and enforcement issues in international custody disputes.

Two uniform acts are the primary source of authority to resolve jurisdictional and recognition issues. In 1968, the National Conference of Commissioners on Uniform State Laws (NCCUSL) approved and recommended passage of the Uniform Child Custody Jurisdiction Act (UCCJA). The purposes of the Act, according to Section 1, included avoiding jurisdictional conflicts among the state courts, deterring abductions, and facilitating the enforcement of custody decrees of sister states. By 1983, the UCCJA was in force in all fifty states, the District of Columbia, and the Virgin Islands, although some states had enacted it with some significant deviations from the original text approved by NCCUSL.

In 1997, NCCUSL promulgated a new Act, the Uniform Child Custody Jurisdiction and Enforcement Act (UCCJEA), which was intended to supercede the UCCJA. Revision was thought necessary in order to bring state laws into conformity with a federal statute enacted in 1980, the Parental Kidnaping Prevention Act (PKPA), 28 U.S.C. § 1738A, which mandates that states recognize, enforce, and refrain from modifying custody orders rendered by sister states, if those orders were issued by courts assuming jurisdiction under the PKPA guidelines. PKPA standards for jurisdiction are similar to those in the UCCJA, but there are significant differences. The UCCJEA attempts to eliminate these differences, as well as the inconsistencies that had developed in the states' various versions of the UCCJA and their courts' judicial interpretations, by providing clearer standards for the assumption of original and modification jurisdiction, and harmonizing the law regarding simultaneous proceedings, forum non conveniens, and unclean hands. In addition, the UCCJEA expands the scope of the UCCJA by providing specific procedures for enforcement of interstate custody and visitation orders.

By March 2003, at least thirty states and the District of Columbia had enacted the UCCJEA and repealed their versions of the UCCJA, and legislation to enact the UCCJEA was pending in ten additional states. In those states that have not enacted the UCCJEA, the UCCJA remains in effect. (For current information on state adoptions of the UCCJEA, see http://www.nccusl.org/nccusl/uniformact_factsheets/uniformacts-fs-uccjea.asp.)

Over the years, state courts have struggled with the extent to which the provisions of the UCCJA should be applied to international custody disputes. In the following case, the New Jersey Supreme Court addresses this issue.

a. Jurisdictional Bases, Forum Non Conveniens, and Simultaneous Proceedings

Ivaldi v. Ivaldi
685 A.2d 1319 (N.J. 1996)

Pollock, J.

The primary issue is whether under the Uniform Child Custody Jurisdiction Act... New Jersey courts have subject-matter jurisdiction to determine this international child-custody dispute. A second issue is whether the courts of New Jersey provide a more convenient forum to resolve the issue of custody.

Plaintiff, Jean Jacques Marcel Ivaldi ("the father"), and defendant, Lamia Khribeche Ivaldi ("the mother"), are engaged in matrimonial actions in Morocco and New Jersey. Each seeks a divorce from the other and custody of the only child of their marriage, Lina Camille Ivaldi ("Lina" or "the child").

* * *

We hold that the jurisdictional provisions of the Act vest the Family Part with subject-matter jurisdiction to determine this custody dispute. We remand the matter to the Family Part for a determination whether New Jersey or Morocco provides the more appropriate forum. If the Family Part determines that Morocco is the more convenient forum, it should dismiss the custody claim without prejudice.

I. From the limited record, we gather the following facts. In 1990, the mother, a Moroccan citizen, and the father, a citizen of both the United States and France, met while studying hotel and restaurant management in Switzerland. On September 18, 1992, they were married in Rabat, Morocco. Following the wedding, the couple resided in France.... Lina was born in France on June 21, 1993.

...The mother asserts that in October 1993 the couple moved with Lina to Rabat, Morocco, where they remained until the end of January 1994. The father claims that before the family moved to New Jersey Lina visited, but did not reside, in Morocco.

In January 1994, the father moved to New Jersey, where his parents operate a restaurant. A month later, the mother and Lina joined him. Following their move to New Jersey, the couple experienced substantial marital difficulties. The father eventually moved into his parents' house in Flanders, Morris County.

On February 22, 1995, the mother and father, each represented by counsel, entered into a comprehensive separation agreement. The agreement specifically states that the parents will share joint legal custody of Lina and that the mother will have physical custody. Significantly, the agreement expressly allows the mother, provided that she abides by all relevant terms of the agreement, to leave the United States with Lina and to reside in France or Morocco.

Under the agreement, the father is allowed twelve weeks of visitation per year with Lina. The agreement further requires the mother to permit Lina to travel to the country in which the father resides. Finally, the parties agreed that New Jersey law governs the terms of the agreement, and that they will incorporate the agreement into any divorce judgment. The agreement does not specify the jurisdiction in which any matrimonial action, including one seeking custody of the child, will proceed.

Within a week of signing the agreement, the mother sent Lina to live with the mother's parents in Morocco. The mother joined Lina a few weeks later.

On April 27, 1995, the mother filed an action for divorce and child custody in the Primary Court of Rabat in Morocco. On May 2, 1995, the father filed a complaint in the Superior Court seeking, among other things, sole custody of Lina. Pursuant to a court order, he served the mother by overnight mail on August 8, 1995. She filed a motion to dismiss several days later [which the Family Part denied on September 29, 1995]....

The Family Part ordered the mother to return Lina to the United States within a week and temporarily awarded the father sole custody. It also restrained the mother from proceeding with her custody action in Morocco.

The Appellate Division granted a temporary stay and requested the Family Part to supplement its oral opinion with a written statement of reasons. In its opinion, the Family Part explained that the [UCCJA] did not apply because the Moroccan court had not yet entered a custody order. Finding that Morocco has not yet signed the Hague Convention on the Civil Aspects of International Child Abduction ("Hague Convention on Child Abduction"), the Family Part ruled that the Convention did not apply. The Family Part held that New Jersey was Lina's "home state" and that it had jurisdiction to determine the issue of custody. The court noted that when Lina left New Jersey, she had been a resident for more than one-half of her lifetime. Stating that the father believed the mother would return the child to New Jersey, the court found that the mother had removed Lina by "subterfuge."

...On March 15, 1996, the Appellate Division reversed.... It found "no basis in the record for the Family Part judge's conclusion that [the mother] wrongfully removed Lina from New Jersey to Morocco. The separation agreement clearly contemplated that [the mother] would leave the United States with Lina and take up residence in another country."...The Court continued:

> So too, the record is barren of anything supporting the judge's finding that [the mother] breached the agreement by denying [the father's] right of visitation. Although [the father]...alleged in conclusory fashion that he had not been permitted to visit Lina, it is undisputed that he never made any support payments as required by the agreement. He also neither tendered nor offered to

tender travel expenses, a precondition to his right of visitation, until April 17, 1995....

The Appellate Division also held that the Family Part did not have subject-matter jurisdiction. It deemed the [UCCJA] inapplicable, reasoning that the Act focuses on avoiding jurisdictional conflict between the courts of different states, not of different countries.... The court then turned to...the section of the Act [UCCJA §23] treating international custody disputes. It construed the section as conferring jurisdiction only when a New Jersey court is asked to enforce a custody decree entered by the authorities of a foreign country....

The Appellate Division...further...found inapplicable the Parental Kidnapping Prevention Act ("the PKPA"). It reasoned that the PKPA concerned the enforcement in one state of decrees entered by the courts of another state, not those of another country....

Finally, the Appellate Division held that even if the Family Part had subject-matter jurisdiction, principles of international comity mandated deference to the Moroccan court.... The court held that the Moroccan courts could fairly resolve the issue of custody in accordance with the best interests of the child....

At oral argument before us, the father's counsel stated that the parties are participating in mediation in the Moroccan proceeding. In that proceeding, the father is represented by counsel and is actively contesting the mother's claim to custody of Lina. By comparison, the mother is not represented by counsel before this Court.

II. To determine whether the [UCCJA] applies, we begin with its terms. The Act vests the Superior Court with jurisdiction to make a child-custody determination in a variety of circumstances. For example, the court has jurisdiction if New Jersey is the "home state" of the child, if the child and at least one parent have "significant connections" with New Jersey, or if no other state is the home state or has significant connections with the child and his or her parents.... [UCCJA§3 (a)(1)-(4)].

At first glance, the statutory language suggests that the [UCCJA] applies to custody disputes between residents of different states and not to such disputes when one party resides in a foreign country. The Act describes the jurisdiction of the Superior Court in relation to the jurisdiction of other "states." In addition, the legislative findings assert that the Act's purpose is to avoid jurisdictional competition and conflict with courts of other "states."...[UCCJA §1] The Act defines "state" as "any state, territory, or possession of the United States, the Commonwealth of Puerto Rico, and the District of Columbia."... [UCCJA §2] That definition does not expressly include other countries.

[UCCJA §23]..., entitled "International application," adds meaning to the definition of "state." This section extends the "general policies of [the Act] to the international area."... Thus, read as a whole, the Act applies to foreign countries as if they were states....

The comments by the original drafters of the Uniform Act support this interpretation. For example, the comment to UCCJA §23, which is identical to *N.J.S.A. 2A:34–51*, states that the Act's general policies, as delineated in UCCJA §1... "are to be followed when some of the persons involved are in a foreign country or a foreign custody proceeding is pending." One of the general purposes of the Act is to assure that custody litigation proceeds in the state where the child and the child's family have the closest connections and where significant evidence concerning the child's care, protection, training, and personal relationships is most readily available.... [UCCJA §1(a)(3)] Theoretically, New Jersey might be this "state," even if one parent or the parent and the child live in a different country.

* * *

[C]reating a distinction between the exercise of original jurisdiction and enforcement of a foreign decree [as did the Appellate Division] would ignore the terms of... [UCCJA § 23], which provides:

> The general policies of this act extend to the international area. The provisions of this act relating to the recognition and enforcement of custody decrees of other states apply to custody decrees and decrees involving legal institutions similar in nature...to custody [institutions] rendered by appropriate authorities of other nations, if reasonable notice and opportunity to be heard were given to all affected persons. [Ed. Typographical errors are corrected to reflect the original text of UCCJA § 23.]

The first sentence of the section extends all of the Act's general policies "to the international area." The second sentence requires New Jersey courts to recognize foreign custody decrees issued by similar "legal institutions" in the same manner as the courts would recognize decrees of other states, provided those institutions have accorded affected persons notice and the opportunity to be heard. The statutory language reflects the Legislature's uncertainty about the nature of foreign legal institutions. It counsels courts to verify that those institutions have proceeded in a manner consistent with the requirements of fundamental due process. Subject to those qualifications, the statute recognizes that the Act applies to international child-custody disputes.

* * *

Through [UCCJA §23], the Legislature has extended the Act's policies to the determination of jurisdictional questions in international custody cases. Those policies include the importance of the identification of the "home state" and the need to avoid jurisdictional conflicts.

The majority of state courts that have considered the issue have held, either explicitly or implicitly, that the term "state" may include a foreign nation.... Two courts [Missouri and Ohio] have held that "state" does not include a foreign country. In those states, however, the legislatures have adopted a version of the UCCJA that omits [UCCJA § 23]....

Our holding conforms also with a proposed revision of the UCCJA, entitled the Uniform Child Custody Jurisdiction and Enforcement Act ("the UCCJEA"), which is under consideration by the National Conference of Commissioners on Uniform State Laws. *Unif. Child Cust. Jur. Enf. Act* (1996) (draft). The proposed UCCJEA explicitly states that all of its provisions apply to child custody proceedings of other countries, including the jurisdictional determination of home-state priority....

III. Having determined that the term "state" includes foreign countries and that the jurisdictional provisions of the Act apply to international custody disputes, we now consider whether the Family Part has subject-matter jurisdiction. We begin by recognizing that New Jersey was the home state of the child at the time that the father commenced this proceeding.

[UCCJA § 2(e)]...defines a "home state" as the state where the child lived with one or both parents at least six months before the custody suit began. Lina lived in New Jersey with both of her parents from the time she was approximately eight months old until she was approximately one year and nine months old. Thus, she resided here for thirteen consecutive months, more than twice the six-month statutory requirement. New Jersey was Lina's home state.

The Act specifically vests the Family Part with jurisdiction when New Jersey is the child's home state within six months before the commencement of the proceeding, the child is absent from New Jersey because he or she has been removed by a person claiming her custody, and one parent continues to live in New Jersey.... [UCCJA § 3(a)(1)] The facts satisfy these jurisdictional prerequisites. New Jersey was Lina's home state within six months before the proceeding. She left for Morocco only two months before her father filed the present action. Her mother, who also seeks custody, removed Lina from New Jersey to Morocco. The father remains a New Jersey resident....

IV. We conclude that New Jersey is the child's "home state" and that the Family Part has jurisdiction. Those conclusions do not necessarily resolve the jurisdictional conflict that arises when another court exercises original jurisdiction in a concurrent custody proceeding. Remaining is the question whether "the child and [her] family have a closer connection with another state [or country]." [UCCJA § 7(c)]... If so, the courts of New Jersey should defer to the more convenient forum....

In the Appellate Division, the mother argued for dismissal on forum-non-conveniens grounds. Without deciding the issue, the Appellate Division held that the Family Part, even if it had jurisdiction, should defer to the Moroccan court. The court reached this result relying not on principles of forum-non-conveniens, but of international comity....

The better procedure is to decide the forum-non-conveniens issue under the provisions of the Act. Hence, we remand the matter to the Family Part to determine whether Morocco or New Jersey provides the more convenient forum. Essential to that determination is... [UCCJA § 7(c)], which states that a court should "consider if it is in the interests of the child that another state assume jurisdiction."... For this purpose, the Family Part may consider, among other things, whether Morocco has a closer connection with Lina and her mother; whether substantial evidence concerning Lina's present or future care, protection, training, and personal relationships is more readily available in Morocco; and whether the Family Part's exercise of jurisdiction would contravene any of the purposes of the Act....

Lina has lived in Morocco for approximately nineteen months since her father filed this action. She is now over three years old and presumably has established significant connections with Morocco. Furthermore, her mother and her maternal grandparents also reside in Morocco. Finally, the father is represented by counsel in Morocco and is participating in the Moroccan proceedings.

We encourage the Family Part to communicate directly with the Moroccan court to obtain any information needed to determine whether New Jersey or Morocco is the more convenient forum. [UCCJA §7(d)].... If language differences pose a problem in communication, the Family Part may obtain an interpreter through the vicinage trial-court administrator. Communication between courts furthers the goals of the Act by permitting the exchange of information so that the court best situated to consider the interest of the child will determine the question of custody....

If the Family Part dismisses this action, the dismissal will not preclude a New Jersey court from subsequently reviewing the enforceability of the Moroccan custody decree. For example, if the Moroccan court denies the father procedural due process or refuses to consider Lina's best interests, the Family Part may then refuse to enforce the Moroccan decree....

... [W]e... note the recently negotiated Hague Convention on Jurisdiction, Applicable Law, Recognition, Enforcement and Co-operation In Respect of Parental Responsibility and Measures For the Protection of Children ("Hague Convention on Jurisdiction").... [T]he Hague Convention on Jurisdiction further explains the application of comity principles to international custody disputes.

Morocco is the only country that has signed the October 19, 1996 draft of the Hague Convention on Jurisdiction. The United States has not yet signed the Convention, but in the Final Act of the Eighteenth Session on October 19, 1996, our delegates agreed to submit the Convention to this country's government. Although the Convention has not yet taken effect, it provides helpful guidance in arriving at a fair and reasonable resolution of this matter.

The Hague Convention on Jurisdiction addresses various aspects of the protection of children, including custody. It begins by "[c]onfirming that the best interests of the child are to be a primary consideration." Hague Convention on Jurisdiction, Oct. 19, 1996 (preamble). Among the objects of the Convention are "to determine the State whose authorities have jurisdiction to take measures directed to the protection of the person or property of the child" and "to establish such co-operation between the authorities of the Contracting States as may be necessary in order to achieve the purposes of this Convention." *Id.* at art. 1. Article 23 states that the courts of one country need not recognize a custody decree issued by the courts of another country if the decree contravenes the fundamental principles of procedure or the public policy of the country in which recognition of the decree is sought.

We trust, however, that the Moroccan court will consider the child's best interests in fashioning a custody order. In that regard, the Hague Convention on Jurisdiction seeks to assure that the best interests of the child is the primary consideration in all international disputes involving children. *See id.* at art. 8, 9, 23. We trust further that the Moroccan court will consider the parties' separation agreement, including its provision calling for the application of New Jersey law. Our goal is to further the purposes of the [UCCJA] and of the Hague Convention on Jurisdiction by avoiding jurisdictional competition while simultaneously discouraging parents from unilaterally removing their children to obtain a more favorable forum.

If the Family Part dismisses the father's claim for custody, it should inform the Moroccan court of its decision. [UCCJA§ 7 (h)] . . .

Notes and Questions

1. *International Application of UCCJA and UCCJEA to Jurisdictional Issues.* As Justice Pollack observed, the majority of courts examining the issue have interpreted Section 23 of the UCCJA to treat foreign countries as if they were states for purposes of jurisdictional determinations as well as for enforcement of foreign orders. Courts of a few states, however, have taken the approach of the Appellate Division in *Ivaldi*, and refused to treat foreign nations as states for purposes of determining jurisdiction. *See* Goldstein v. Goldstein, 494 S.E.2d 745 (Ga. App. 1998); McDaniel v. McDaniel, 693 N.Y.S.2d 778 (N.Y. App. 1999). *Cf.* Koons v. Koons, 615 N.Y.S.2d 852 (N.Y. Sup. Ct. 1994) (foreign country not a state for purposes of simultaneous proceedings and forum non conveniens provisions of UCCJA); Horiba v. Horiba, 950 P.2d 340 (Or. App. 1997) (same); Amin v. Bakhaty, 798 So. 2d 75 (La. 2001) (court may exercise discretion whether or not to find a foreign country a "state" when determining jurisdiction, based on best interests of child).

Ivaldi refers to the draft version of the UCCJEA, because the opinion was issued before the final draft of the UCCJEA was approved by NCCUSL in 1997. Read Section 105 of the UCCJEA in your Supplement. For states that have enacted the UCCJEA, will the application of the Act to jurisdictional determinations continue to be an issue?

2. *PKPA Inapplicable.* As the Appellate Division in *Ivaldi* correctly observed, the federal Parental Kidnaping Prevention Act (PKPA), 28 U.S.C. § 1738A, does not address jurisdictional conflicts between a state court and a foreign court. The PKPA establishes requirements for the exercise of custody jurisdiction that, if satisfied, entitle state court custody orders to recognition and enforcement as a matter of federal law, and restrict their modification by courts of other states. It is true that even in a custody dispute involving foreign nations, a state court that issues a custody order would generally want to be certain that it was exercising jurisdiction consistently with PKPA guidelines (this would occur automatically if it was a UCCJEA state), so that its order would be recognized and enforced in other states. However, the PKPA does not address questions regarding whether a foreign country should be treated as a state, when jurisdiction should be declined in favor of a foreign court, or when a foreign custody order should be recognized and enforced.

3. *Bases for Exercising Jurisdiction.* One of the significant contributions made by the UCCJA to deterring forum shopping was to create a limited number of bases upon which a court could exercise subject matter jurisdiction over custody disputes. UCCJA § 3 sets out the four bases: (1) home state; (2) significant connection with and substantial evidence in the forum state; (3) emergency jurisdiction, and (4) residual or default jurisdiction (i.e., no other state has jurisdiction on one of the other bases, or any state that does has declined jurisdiction in favor of the forum state, and it is in the best interests of the child for the forum state to assume jurisdiction). The UCCJEA follows the same general scheme, but with some important deviations.

(a) *Home State.* UCCJA § 2 defines "home state" as follows:

... [T]he state in which the child immediately preceding the time involved lived with his parents, a parent, or a person acting as parent, for at least 6 consecutive months, and in the case of a child less than 6 months old the state in which the child lived from birth with any of the persons mentioned. Periods of temporary absence of any of the named persons are counted as part of the 6-month or other period.

UCCJA § 3 provides that the home state can serve as the basis for exercise of jurisdiction in two circumstances: (1) when the forum state "is the home state at the time of commencement of the proceeding," and (2) when the forum state "had been the child's home state within 6 months before commencement of the proceeding and the child is absent from this State because of his removal or retention by a person claiming his custody or for other reasons, and a parent or person acting as parent continues to live in this State." This second scenario is sometimes referred to as the "extended" home state basis or the "left-behind parent" home state basis. Which type of home state basis was the court applying in *Ivaldi*?

The "time of commencement" under the UCCJA is determined by the law of the state in which the action is brought. See Draper v. Roberts (In re C.A.D.), 839 P.2d 165 (Okla. 1992). In most states, an action is commenced by filing, rather than by service. Under the UCCJEA, "commencement" is defined in the Act itself as the time of filing the first pleading in the proceeding. UCCJEA § 102(5). Under either Act, the critical date is the date of commencement of the most immediate application in the trial court, so in a modification proceeding, the critical date is the date that the motion to modify was filed.

Read the definition of "home state" in UCCJEA § 102(7) of your Supplement. You will see that the definition has been reworded slightly. The drafters observed in their Comment to this section that no substantive change was intended.

Read the description of home state basis in UCCJEA § 201 of your Supplement. There are some minor changes in the wording. Would they have made any difference in the outcome in *Ivaldi*?

(b) Significant Connection—Substantial Evidence. Read UCCJEA § 201(a)(2), which sets forth the requirements for jurisdiction under the significant connection basis. There is a *very* significant change from the circumstances under which this basis is used under the UCCJA. Justice Pollack in *Ivaldi* correctly describes the significant connection basis as an alternate basis under the UCCJA. The UCCJEA has instead prioritized the home state basis, and provides that the significant connection basis cannot be used unless there is no home state, or unless a court of the home state declines to exercise jurisdiction because a state with a significant connection and substantial evidence is a more appropriate forum. This change reflects the jurisdictional guidelines of the PKPA, which also prioritize home state.

Although the significant connection basis is defined somewhat flexibly under the UCCJA and the UCCJEA, the Comments of the Drafting Committee to UCCJA § 3 provide insight into its proper use:

> [J]urisdiction exists only if it is in the *child's* interest, not merely the interest or convenience of the feuding parties, to determine custody in a particular state. The interest of the child is served when the forum has optimum access to relevant evidence about the child and family. There must be maximum rather than minimum contact with the state.

Professor Robert Spector, who served as the Reporter for the Drafting Committee for the UCCJEA, observed that it was the intent of that Committee that these observations be applicable to the significant connection basis under the UCCJEA as well. He also noted that more than one state could conceivably be in a position to exercise significant connection jurisdiction at the same point in time, since "the significant connection jurisdiction provisions of the UCCJEA, like those of the UCCJA, do not require the court to weigh the connections of one state against those of another to find the state of the 'most significant connection.'" Robert Spector, *International Child Custody Jurisdiction and the Uniform Child Custody Jurisdiction and Enforcement Act*, 33 N.Y.U. J. Int'l L. & Pol. 251, 267–68 (2000).

(c) Emergency Jurisdiction. Under the UCCJA, a third basis for jurisdiction is satisfied if a child is present in the forum state and was abandoned, subjected to or threatened with abuse or mistreatment, neglected, or dependent Although this basis has been most frequently used in child protective proceedings, it can be used in any custody proceedings brought by private parties or public authorities.

Read UCCJEA § 204 in your Supplement. Under the UCCJEA, emergency jurisdiction is no longer a separate basis for permanent jurisdiction. Instead, it becomes a concurrent basis for temporary jurisdiction. It can be used by a court that cannot properly exercise home state or significant connection jurisdiction, to issue a temporary order of custody in order to protect a child who is present in the forum state from mistreatment or abuse or abandonment, until such time as a court of a state with proper jurisdiction under one of the other bases can enter an order.

The use of emergency jurisdiction under the UCCJEA is not as significant a departure from the UCCJA as it might appear, since the practice in many states even under the UCCJA was to issue only a temporary order when exercising emergency jurisdiction, and then refer the parties back to a state with home state or significant connection jurisdiction, particularly when that state had previously issued a custody order concerning the child. *See, e.g.,* Majors v. Majors, 645 P.2d 1039 (Okla. Ct. App. 1982).

The UCCJEA omits neglect or dependency of a child as a basis for temporary emergency jurisdiction, in keeping with the Comments to UCCJA § 3 and UCCJEA § 204, which both emphasize that this basis is to be "an extraordinary jurisdiction reserved for extraordinary circumstances."

The UCCJEA does recognize very limited circumstances in which an order entered by a court with temporary emergency jurisdiction could become permanent. If no previous order that would be entitled to enforcement under the Act has been entered by another court, and no custody proceeding is pending in another state exercising jurisdiction under one of the other bases, then a temporary order entered on the basis of emergency jurisdiction can become permanent, if the order so provides, when the child has lived in the state of the court exercising emergency jurisdiction long enough for it to become the child's home state.

(d) Default Jurisdiction. Read UCCJEA § 201(a)(3) and (4). This basis has been reworded from the UCCJA § 3, but remains substantially the same in practice. A court in a state without home state or significant connection jurisdiction cannot use this basis, even if another court declines to exercise their own jurisdiction and defers to it, unless there is no other state whose courts could exercise home state or significant connection jurisdiction.

4. *Forum non conveniens.* Since Justice Pollack in *Ivaldi* finds that New Jersey can exercise jurisdiction on the home state basis, why is the case remanded? The answer is that the UCCJA and the UCCJEA create a two-step analysis: (1) can the court exercise subject matter jurisdiction over the proceeding, i.e., is one of the jurisdictional bases satisfied; and if so, (2) should the court exercise jurisdiction over the proceeding, or decline in favor of a more convenient forum? Both UCCJA § 7 and UCCJEA § 207 suggest factors courts may wish to consider when determining whether they should decline jurisdiction, but neither list, according to the Comments, is intended to be exclusive.

Although a custody proceeding is frequently pending in another forum when a court chooses to decline jurisdiction on the basis of *forum non conveniens,* the existence of a pending custody proceeding elsewhere is not a prerequisite under either the UCCJA or the UCCJEA to declining jurisdiction on this basis. Although the UCCJA permits a court to dismiss an action on the grounds of *forum non conveniens* when no other action is pending, the UCCJEA requires a court in that situation to stay the proceeding upon the condition that a custody proceeding is promptly commenced in another designated forum. The original court could choose to issue a temporary custody order in the interim. Once a proceeding is commenced in another forum, the original court might dismiss the action, or stay it and resume jurisdiction if the other court refuses to take the case.

Often courts considering declining jurisdiction on *forum non conveniens* grounds will communicate directly with officials of the alternate court, as was recommended by Justice Pollack to the lower court in *Ivaldi.* Both UCCJA § 7 and UCCJEA § 110 provide for such communication. The UCCJEA requires that a record must be made of communications, other than those relating to schedules, calendars, court records, and similar procedural matters, and the parties must be informed promptly and given the opportunity to present factual information and legal arguments to the court before a decision on jurisdiction is made.

Considering the factors listed by the *Ivaldi* court for consideration under the UCCJA, and the factors recommended for consideration under UCCJEA § 207, how would you have resolved *Ivaldi* if you were the trial judge to whom the case was returned on remand?

5. *Simultaneous Proceedings.* Both UCCJA § 6 and UCCJEA § 206 establish procedures to address the problem of simultaneous proceedings. UCCJA § 6 provides in part:

(a) A court of this State shall not exercise its jurisdiction under this Act if at the time of filing the petition a proceeding concerning the custody of the child was pending in a court of another state exercising jurisdiction substantially in conformity with this Act, unless the proceeding is stayed by the court of the other state because this State is a more appropriate forum or for other reasons.

Compare this with UCCJEA § 206 in your Supplement and you will see that they are very similar in operation. UCCJA § 9 and UCCJEA § 209 require each party to a custody proceeding to provide the court in their first pleading with information concerning any custody proceeding, whether in the past or then pending, concerning the child. If the court learns from these pleadings or other sources that there is another custody proceeding pending in a court of another state, both UCCJA § 6 and UCCJEA § 206 require the court to stay its proceedings and communicate with the other court. Unless the court in the first action commenced agrees to decline jurisdiction and defer to the second court, the second court is required to dismiss its action if the first court is exercising jurisdiction in conformity with the UCCJA or UCCJEA, whichever is applicable in the second state. Both Acts therefore establish a first-in-time priority, and in fact the simultaneous proceedings provisions of each Act use very similar wording. Because of differences in the provisions of the two Acts regarding the bases for jurisdiction, however, the application of the simultaneous proceedings rule under the UCCJA and the UCCJEA can achieve very different results.

To understand this, consider *Ivaldi*. Although *Ivaldi* involved simultaneous proceedings to determine initial custody, UCCJA § 6 was never raised in the opinion, perhaps because the parties never raised it. (The mother was unrepresented by counsel, and submitted a letter pro se in lieu of a brief or oral argument.) Read UCCJEA § 206 in your supplement. The language of UCCJA § 6 is very similar. Would the *Ivaldi* case have come out differently if UCCJA § 6 had been applied? Would it have come out differently under UCCJEA § 206 if New Jersey had been a UCCJEA state at the time that *Ivaldi* proceeded through its courts?

6. *Unclean Hands.* UCCJA § 8, entitled "Jurisdiction Declined by Reason of Conduct," provides in part:

(a) If the petitioner for an initial decree has wrongfully taken the child from another state or has engaged in similar reprehensible conduct the court may decline to exercise jurisdiction if this is just and proper under the circumstances.

(b) Unless required in the interest of the child, the court shall not exercise its jurisdiction to modify a custody decree of another state if the petitioner, without consent of the person entitled to custody, has improperly removed the child from the physical custody of the person entitled to custody or has improperly retained the child after a visit or other temporary relinquishment of physical custody. If the petitioner has violated any other provision of a custody decree of another state the court may decline to exercise its jurisdiction if this is just and proper under the circumstances.

Compare this provision with UCCJEA § 208 in your Supplement. The Comments to this Section elaborate on the Drafting Committee's views of the difference between unjustifiable conduct and a "technical illegality," by observing that a parent who has fled with a child to escape domestic violence or child abuse should not automatically have his or her case dismissed, even if that parent's conduct was technically illegal (for example, in violation of a joint custody decree). The issue is "whether the flight was justified under the circumstances."

In *Ivaldi,* much discussion was generated by the father and the Appellate Division, in parts of the opinion omitted herein, about whether the mother's actions were wrongful. The Supreme Court found this issue to be irrelevant. Under either UCCJA §8 or UCCJEA §208, would that assessment be accurate?

7. *Comity.* Justice Pollack in *Ivaldi* notes that the Appellate Division had held that the New Jersey court should defer to the Moroccan court, on the basis of a common law doctrine of comity rather than the statutory doctrine under the UCCJA of *forum non conveniens.* You have previously read about the doctrine of comity in Chapter Five. The New Jersey Supreme Court, drawing on earlier decisions of the U.S. Supreme Court, has explained comity in this manner:

> Comity, in a legal sense, is neither a matter of absolute obligation on the one hand nor of mere courtesy and good will upon the other. But it is the recognition which one nation allows within its territory to the legislative, executive or judicial acts of another nation, having due regard both to international duty and convenience and to the rights of its own citizens or of other persons who are under the protection of its laws.... [*citing* The Disconto Gesellschaft v. Unbreit, 208 U.S. 570 (1908)] The recognition of a judgment of a foreign court under the principle of comity is subject generally to two conditions: (1) that the foreign court had jurisdiction of the subject matter; (2) that the foreign judgment will not offend the public policy of our own state. The rule of comity is grounded in the policy of avoiding conflicts in jurisdiction, unless upon strong grounds, and the general principle that the court which first acquires jurisdiction of an issue has precedence, in the absence of special equities. Fantony v. Fantony, 122 A.2d 593 (N.J. 1956).

Comity is used by courts in several different contexts, recently described by the Second Circuit in *Diorinou v. Mezitis,* 237 F.3d 133, 139–40 (2d Cir. 2001):

> In one context, the domestic court considers whether to proceed with litigation properly within its jurisdiction because of the pendency or availability of litigation in a foreign forum.... When domestic courts in that context say that they are deferring to foreign tribunals as a matter of "comity,"...they are invoking a doctrine akin to forum non conveniens.... In a second context, a domestic court considers whether to enforce a foreign judgment.... Here too, domestic courts say that the issue of whether to defer to the foreign tribunal's adjudication of the underlying matter is a matter of "comity."...In a third context,...a domestic court considers whether to accept the adjudication of a foreign tribunal on a cause of action or a particular issue,...often stating...that they are doing so as a matter of "comity."...("It is well-established that United States courts are not obliged to recognize judgments rendered by a foreign state, but may choose to give res judicata effect to foreign judgments on the basis of comity.") (quoting Gordon and Breach Science Publishers, S.A. v. American Institute of Physics, 905 F. Supp. 169, 178–79 (S.D.N.Y. 1995).

In this third context, the court in *Diorinou* was considering whether to defer to findings of a Greek court in an earlier Hague proceeding concerning whether a particular removal was wrongful, an issue that had relevance to resolution of a subsequent Hague proceeding regarding a different removal that was before the *Diorinou* court. In which context is the court in *Ivaldi* discussing the use of comity?

Comity is extended out of deference and mutual respect. Why do you think Justice Pollack recommended that the better procedure was to resolve the case on the basis of the UCCJA's provisions regarding *forum non conveniens* rather than comity?

8. *Child Absent from Forum.* Neither the UCCJA nor the UCCJEA require that the child be present in the forum in order to exercise jurisdiction. UCCJA § 3(c); UCCJEA § 210(c). When the Hague Convention on Child Abduction is in effect between the United States and the country to which a child has been taken, what might be the motivation for seeking a custody determination in the absence of the child? When the country in which the child is located is not a party to the Convention, such as in *Ivaldi*, what might the father be trying to accomplish?

If the lower court in *Ivaldi* decided on remand to exercise jurisdiction, how could it practically accomplish this goal? *See* Ali v. Ali, 652 A.2d 253 (N.J. Super. Ct. Ch. Div. 1994) (ordering a home evaluation in Gaza as well as psychological evaluations of the parties, while conceding that procurement of these "may not be feasible or particularly simple").

9. *Child Protective and Termination of Parental Rights Proceedings—Jurisdiction under the UCCJA/UCCJEA and Notice Requirements under the Vienna Convention on Consular Relations.* The UCCJA and UCCJEA have also been used as the basis for jurisdiction in child protective proceedings and proceedings terminating the rights of parents who are foreign nationals, when they are living in the United States with their children. *See, e.g.,* In re Stephanie M., 867 P.2d 706 (Cal. 1994) (where the child had lived with her parents in California for four months preceding the initiation of a juvenile proceeding, the court could exercise jurisdiction over dependency and subsequent termination actions based upon a significant connection and an emergency, and it was not an abuse of discretion to refuse to decline jurisdiction to Mexico on *forum non conveniens* basis); Arteaga v. Tex. Dept. of Prot. & Reg. Serv., 924 S.W.2d 756 (Tex. App. 1996) (court had jurisdiction to terminate rights of Mexican nationals on home state basis). *Cf.* E.H. v. Dep't of Health & Soc. Serv., 23 P.3d 1186 (Alaska 2001) (Under the UCCJA or UCCJEA, an Alaskan court had jurisdiction to adjudicate boys as children in need of aid, and subsequently terminate American mother's parental rights, despite the fact that the boys were found homeless and in need of medical care in Canada and transferred to the Alaska department by a Canadian protective worker, because the boys had lived in Alaska prior to a several month stay in Canada, and thus jurisdiction could be based upon the home state, emergency, or residual bases, and under continuing jurisdiction in a later proceeding.).

Another issue that has recently surfaced in dependency and termination proceedings involving children who are not U.S. citizens is the requirement under Article 37(b) of the Vienna Convention on Consular Relations that requires child welfare authorities to notify the consular post of the child's country "without delay" when "the appointment of a guardian or trustee appears to be in the interests" of the child. The Convention entered into force for the United States in 1969, and is a self-executing treaty. Although challenges to protective custody and termination proceedings have been made on the ground of late or insufficient notice, they have generally not been successful. In re

Stephanie M., 867 P.2d 706 (Cal. 1994) (failure to give notice of the pendency of a dependency action according to the Convention does not deprive the juvenile court of jurisdiction); E.R. v. Marion County Office of Fam. & Child., 729 N.E.2d 1052 (Ind. Ct. App. 2000) (a determination that five children were children in need of services (CHINS) would not be overturned in a case in which the Mexican government was notified by a relative two months after the children were taken into custody, despite the fact that the Convention required notification by a government official, since the parents suffered no prejudice from the violation); In re L.A.M. & R.K.M., 996 P.2d 839 (Kan. 2000) (notice given by aunt to Consulate sufficiently upheld the purpose and intent of the treaty); Arteaga v. Tex. Dept. of Prot. & Reg. Serv., 924 S.W.2d 756 (Tex. App. 1996) (letter to Mexican Consulate from a caseworker seeking information about paternal grandparents constituted notice, but the court urges the State in the future to provide "definite documentary record demonstrating the…Consulate received adequate notice affording it the opportunity for intervention if desired").

Consular officials can play a helpful role in explaining the proceedings to the family in their native language, and in the context of customs and laws in their native country; search for relatives; facilitate expedited home studies; contact the home country's social services; obtain official documents; and assist with travel arrangements if a child is to be returned to the home country. Pamela Kemp Parker, *When a Foreign Child Comes Into Care, Ask: Has the Consul Been Notified*, 19 A.B.A. Child Law Practice 177 (Feb. 2001) (includes sample notice). *See also* Consular Notification and Access, January 1998 Instructions for Federal, State, and Other Local Law Enforcement and Other Officials Regarding Foreign Nationals in the United States and the Rights of Consular Officials to Assist Them, U.S. Dep't of State, 1998, *available at* http.www.travel.state.gov/consul_notify.html.

10. *Personal Jurisdiction.* In the U.S. judicial system, personal jurisdiction is the power of a court to enter a judgment binding upon a particular party to the action. A plaintiff submits to the authority of a court by bringing an action, and is thus viewed as submitting to the court's jurisdiction by consent. There are two components to the exercise of personal jurisdiction over a defendant. First the defendant must receive valid service, satisfying both the federal constitutional requirements for notice and the applicable statutory requirements for service of process. Second, the defendant must be amenable to suit in the forum. When a suit is brought in state court, the issue is whether the defendant has a relationship with the forum state such that it is fair to subject the defendant to the power of the forum state. To satisfy this second issue of amenability, a court must have statutory authority to exercise personal jurisdiction, as well as exercise jurisdiction within the limits recognized under the Due Process Clause of the Fourteenth Amendment to the U.S. Constitution.

In custody cases, as in other types of litigation, a defendant must be properly served with process. *See* UCCJA §5 and Comment to UCCJEA §108. However, the requirements for amenability to suit generally differ from those required in most other types of cases. Both the UCCJA and the UCCJEA are premised upon the assumption that if their provisions for subject matter jurisdiction are satisfied, the court can subject the defendant to its personal jurisdiction even if the traditional grounds for exercise of personal jurisdiction under the Due Process Clause—service on defendant within the forum state, domicile of the defendant within the forum state, minimum contacts with the forum state, and consent to jurisdiction—are not satisfied. This is implied in UCCJA §12, which provides:

A custody decree rendered by a court of this State which had jurisdiction under section 3 binds all parties who have been served in this State or notified in accordance with section 5 or who have submitted to the jurisdiction of the court, and who have been given an opportunity to be heard....

The Comment to this Section explicitly states the view of the Drafting Committee that: "[t]here is no requirement for technical personal jurisdiction...." This is also explicitly stated in UCCJEA § 201(c), which is set forth in your Supplement. This view is supported by the traditional theory that a custody adjudication, like a divorce, is a proceeding affecting status, and therefore Due Process does not require one of the traditional bases for jurisdiction. Though U.S. Supreme Court validation of this theory is somewhat inconclusive, *see* May v. Anderson, 345 U.S. 528 (1953), it has been the prevailing view followed by the majority of states even prior to adoption of the UCCJA and UCCJEA. *E.g.,* Amin v. Bakhaty, 798 So. 2d 75 (La. 2001). Statutory authority is satisfied by compliance with the UCCJA or the UCCJEA itself, or by compliance with the state's general long arm statute.

Although the special dispensation from traditional Due Process requirements afforded to status proceedings is rooted in jurisdictional precedents that may be somewhat outdated, *see* Pennoyer v. Neff, 95 U.S. 714 (1877), the modern justification is that the UCCJA and the UCCJEA are both premised on the notion that the court deciding custody should be in the state "with which the child and his family have the closest connection and where significant evidence concerning his care, protection, training, and personal relationships is located." UCCJA §1. Under a variety of circumstances, it could be difficult to get personal jurisdiction over a defendant parent in a state or nation in which a child has lived for a significant period of time, and which has a great deal of evidence about his care. By the same token, the states within which a defendant parent either is domiciled or has minimum contacts could possibly have no connection with the child, thus making a forum with both subject matter jurisdiction under the UCCJA or UCCJEA bases and a traditional basis for personal jurisdiction impossible to locate.

A minority of state courts, however, continue to require satisfaction of one of the traditional grounds for exercise of in personam jurisdiction. See Ali v. Ali, 652 A.2d 253 (N.J. Super. Ct. Ch. Div. 1994) (finding defendant's contacts with the state sufficient). Might this approach be particularly justified in international custody cases, when one parent is a foreign national residing in another country?

b. *Modification Proceedings*

In *Ivaldi* the issue addressed by the New Jersey Supreme Court was whether the trial court had original jurisdiction to enter an initial custody order, at a time when the Morroccan court had not yet entered a custody order. Frequently courts are asked instead to modify custody orders they entered at an earlier time, or custody orders entered by other tribunals, and must determine if they have jurisdiction over a modification proceeding.

Bless v. Bless
723 A.2d 67 (N.J. Super. Ct. App. Div. 1998)

Levy, J.A.D.

This is an international child custody dispute in which the trial judge refused to stay his prior order denying plaintiff's motion for modification of the parties' custody agreement and ordering the return of the parties' child to Switzerland on the ground that New Jersey lacked subject matter jurisdiction because Switzerland had become the child's home state.... We conclude that New Jersey had subject matter jurisdiction, and therefore we reverse and remand.

The parties were married in 1987, their son Rudy was born in 1991 and they were divorced in 1994.... The judgment provided for joint legal custody of Rudy with plaintiff designated as the primary residential parent; defendant was granted "fair, reasonable, and liberal visitation with [Rudy]." The parties were New Jersey residents, but sometime thereafter, defendant remarried and moved to Switzerland. That change of circumstance resulted in a consent order, filed April 28, 1995, modifying defendant's visitation schedule, given his relocation to Switzerland. Rudy's visits with defendant were tied to the Easter and Christmas holidays and the summer season. The consent order further provided: "Despite defendant's relocation to Zurich, Switzerland, any questions or disputes that may arise between the parties as to child support, custody and visitation shall remain subject to the jurisdiction of New Jersey."

[Visitation occurred according to the schedule in 1995 and 1996. In the fall of 1996, plaintiff sold her condominium more quickly than expected and was unable to obtain substitute housing before the closing. Ed.] ... [P]laintiff asked defendant if he would like Rudy to finish out the kindergarten year in Switzerland, and defendant agreed. Although the unrepresented plaintiff believed that she and defendant had agreed that Rudy would be returned to her during the summer of 1997 so that he could attend first grade in New Jersey, on December 12, 1996, the parties entered into a consent order modifying their prior agreements, which stated...that the parties would continue to share legal custody... [and] designated defendant the primary physical custodial parent effective January 1, 1997, "for an indefinite period of time, with both parties agreeing to make all future decisions concerning custody of their child based on his best interests." Plaintiff was granted visitation with Rudy in Switzerland during his school vacations, with defendant having agreed to pay for up to four airline tickets per year for plaintiff's travel. According to plaintiff, the quoted terms were inserted for the following reasons:

> I therefore requested that a paragraph be included in the Consent Order which would allow Rudy to be returned to me prior to the summer of 1997 in the event that he expressed a desire to do so. Thus, my understanding with regard to the Consent Order was that, in the event that Rudy adjusted well, he would be returned to me during the summer of 1997 but that, in the event that he experienced anxiety or stress as a result of the move, he would be returned to me prior to that date.

...Rudy left New Jersey for Switzerland on December 30, 1996. After Rudy arrived, plaintiff spoke to him on the telephone nearly every day. In early February 1997, Rudy expressed the desire to return to New Jersey. When plaintiff discussed Rudy's statement with defendant, defendant requested that Rudy be given more time to adjust, and the parties agreed that plaintiff would visit Rudy during his winter vacation. A series of visits ensued, and each time Rudy expressed a desire to return to New Jersey. Defendant disagreed and eventually told plaintiff that he had enrolled Rudy in the first grade at a Swiss school. This litigation followed.

On June 9, 1997, plaintiff filed a motion seeking the return of residential custody, reinstatement of the original visitation schedule between Rudy and defendant, and the reinstatement of child support. Defendant cross moved for security to be posted to guaranty Rudy's return to Switzerland at the end of his summer visit with plaintiff. The motion judge denied the motion.... [He also granted the mother 6 weeks summer visitation, ordering the child be returned to Switzerland in the fall. He suggested that if she desired to seek a change of custody, she should obtain expert custody evaluation, which she did. The father refused to participate in the evaluation. When the mother filed a subsequent motion for a stay of the return order and to request a hearing to determine residential custody, the trial judge ruled that Switzerland was the home state and had exclusive subject matter jurisdiction under the Hague Convention on Child Abduction. Ed.]

The jurisdictional provisions of the UCCJA apply to international custody disputes.... The crux of the judge's jurisdiction ruling was that Switzerland "appears to have jurisdiction based upon the fact that the child has been there"... for "[s]ubstantially...at least six months."...We respectfully disagree...and find, instead, that New Jersey had the jurisdiction to decide the custody issues between the parties. The UCCJA defines "home state" as the state where the child "immediately preceding the time involved lived...for at least 6 consecutive months."...Thus, the state where Rudy lived for "at least 6 consecutive months" prior to the institution of this proceeding was his home state.

We have decided that a child's home state should be determined as of "the time of filing of the immediate application being considered by the court."...Read literally, the date would have been the filing of the motion that resulted in this appeal. That motion is the order to show cause filed on August 20, 1997. However, given what transpired below,... [the UCCJA] should not be read so restrictively.

Plaintiff first sought jurisdiction under the UCCJA in June 1997 when she filed the motion for modification of the December 1996 agreement. That motion was denied without prejudice to her right to seek custody based upon a custody evaluation. Perhaps the better response would have been for the judge to have ordered the custody evaluation and reserve decision pending a hearing, but nevertheless that was not done. However, in reliance upon the denial of the motion without prejudice and the judge's suggestion that an evaluation be obtained, plaintiff attempted to do just that but fell short as a result of defendant's refusal to cooperate. Plaintiff immediately returned to court armed with the best she could do without defendant's cooperation and sought an emergency stay given Rudy's imminent departure. Due to the proximity in time and the interrelationship between the two motions, we conclude that the date on which the proceedings commenced is June 9, 1997.

Using that date, it is apparent that Switzerland was not Rudy's home state. The December 12, 1996, consent order provided that defendant would become the primary physical custodial parent "effective January 1, 1997." It is undisputed that Rudy left the United States for Switzerland on December 30, 1996, pursuant to the consent order. Therefore, as of June 9, 1997 when the motion for return of residential custody was filed, Rudy had lived in Switzerland for only a little more than five months.... All petitions for modification must be addressed to the state which rendered the original decree if that state had and retains jurisdiction under the standards of the [UCCJA]....

Additionally,... [i]t is implicit in the UCCJA that a state does not automatically lose jurisdiction over custody when it is no longer the home state, if one parent remains resident in that state, the child has significant contact with the state, there is substantial relevant evidence available in the state, and it is in the child's best interest for that state to make the determination.... Thus, the "significant connection" test of jurisdiction... may be resorted to even if another forum prevails under the home state analysis. Even under this test,...New Jersey would have prevailed.... But for the order under review,

Rudy would have been residing in Switzerland for only slightly more than five months. Rudy's only relatives in Switzerland are his father, stepmother and half sister. He has a close relationship with his mother, maternal grandfather, paternal grandparents, Uncle Bill, cousins Kim and Ryan, and his good friend Kyle, all of whom are in New Jersey, where Rudy had resided all his life up until the last day of 1996 (except, of course, for his visits to Switzerland). Clearly, then, the best interest of Rudy would require that jurisdiction be retained in New Jersey even if there were no home state or there were concurrent proceedings.

Furthermore, no consideration was accorded the parties' agreements of April 28, 1995 and December 12, 1995, which expressly provide that New Jersey would have jurisdiction over custody and visitation issues. We conclude that their agreements are enforceable and should be given effect.... Although subject matter jurisdiction cannot be conferred by agreement where there is none,... such is not the case here.

We conclude that as a matter of law New Jersey has proper jurisdiction, and that jurisdiction has not been obliterated by Rudy's court-ordered presence in Switzerland since August 1997. The matter is remanded to the Family Part for further consideration of the merits....

Notes and Questions

1. *Modifying the Court's Own Order*—In *Bless*, the trial court was asked to modify its own order. Under the UCCJA and the UCCJEA, a court may modify its own decree as long as, at the time that the motion to modify is filed, that court would have jurisdiction under any of the jurisdictional bases established by the Act, and the court chooses not to decline jurisdiction on the basis of *forum non conveniens*. In *Bless*, the Appellate Court found that, at the time the initial motion to modify was filed, New Jersey was still the home state, even though Rudy had been in Switzerland at that point for over five months. Although the court was not as clear as it could have been about this issue, why (assuming we accept the court's analysis of the date the proceeding commenced) was the court correct?

The *Bless* court goes on to hold that even if New Jersey was not the home state on the date that it concluded this proceeding was commenced, and Switzerland had become the home state, the New Jersey court could still exercise jurisdiction over the modification provision on the significant connection basis. One of the significant issues over which state courts have disagreed over the past decades in their interpretation of the UCCJA has been the standard for significant connection at the time of a modification proceeding. Many courts take the approach that the court that issued the earlier custody order continues to have significant connection at the time a motion to modify is filed as long as a parent continues to reside in that state and maintains contact with the child. *See, e.g.,* Kumar v. Superior Court, 652 P.2d 1003 (Cal. 1982); G.S. v. Ewing, 786 P.2d 65 (Okla. 1990). Support for this approach is found in the Comment to UCCJA § 14, which addresses modification, and suggests that jurisdiction is lost if "all persons involved have moved away or the contact with the state has otherwise become slight...." The courts of some states, however, have taken the position that they lose significant connection at the time of a modification proceeding if the state no longer has "optimum access" to the evidence, often because the child's home state has changed. Which interpretation do you think the court in *Bless* is applying? Would it make a difference in this case?

Read UCCJEA § 202 in your Supplement. Would *Bless* have been resolved any differently if the UCCJEA had been in effect in New Jersey at the time that jurisdiction in the case was being resolved? Although the UCCJEA prioritizes home state as a basis, when a determination is made about whether a decree-issuing state retains jurisdiction to modify its own custody order, are there circumstances under which it could retain that jurisdiction even if it was no longer the home state?

2. *Modifying Another Tribunal's Order.* When a court is asked to exercise jurisdiction over a proceeding in which modification of a custody order issued in another state or nation is at issue, the court must do more than satisfy one of the jurisdictional bases at the time the motion to modify is filed, and determine that it should not dismiss on the grounds of *forum non conveniens.* It must also determine that the court of the state or nation that issued the order being modified no longer would have a basis for the exercise of subject matter jurisdiction at the time that the motion to modify was filed. UCCJA § 14(a) provides:

> If a court of another state has made a custody decree, a court of this State shall not modify that decree unless (1) it appears to the court of this State that the court which rendered the decree does not now have jurisdiction under jurisdictional prerequisites substantially in accordance with this Act or has declined to assume jurisdiction to modify the decree and (2) the court of this State has jurisdiction.

UCCJEA §§ 202 and 203 impose the same requirement. Read them in your Supplement. The principle difference between the UCCJA and the UCCJEA lies in who gets to make the decision about whether the state that issued the original decree retains jurisdiction.

Under the UCCJA, a court of the state before which the modification motion is pending must determine whether the decree-issuing state still satisfies a jurisdictional basis. Most courts recognize that they should apply the law of the decree-issuing state, which frequently requires application of that state's courts' interpretation of significant connection at the time of modification, to determine if the original state retains jurisdiction. However, the language of the UCCJA does not specifically compel that choice of law, and thus some modifying states have applied their own interpretation of significant connection when determining if the decree-issuing state retains jurisdiction.

The UCCJEA, on the other hand, compels a movant seeking modification in a new state or nation to obtain an order from the court of the original decree-issuing state declaring that it no longer has jurisdiction. This requirement ensures that the interpretation given to "significant connection" by the courts of the original state will be applied to determine if that state still satisfies a basis for jurisdiction. Only if the child, the parents, and any person acting as a parent have all moved away from the original state can the decision about whether the original state retains jurisdiction be made by a court of *either* the original state or the state being asked to consider a motion to modify.

3. *Applicability of the Hague Convention.* In *Bless,* the trial court held that Switzerland had exclusive jurisdiction under the Hague Convention on Child Abduction. It is probably not uncommon for state trial courts in international custody cases to think the Convention provides all of the answers. By the time of the *Bless* decision, Switzerland and the U.S. were both parties to the Convention. In a part of the opinion omitted herein, however, the Appellate Court correctly observed that "neither the Hague Convention nor the cases that interpret any of its provisions apply to the facts of this case." Why would that be true?

The trial court's confusion may have been sparked by concern over how any modified order issued by the New Jersey courts would be received by the Swiss courts, if defendant did not voluntarily comply with any modified order that might be issued, as well as the unspoken recognition that a Swiss court might recognize Rudy's habitual residence as Switzerland and issue its own order. Although it was not the case in *Bless* at the time these opinions were rendered, frequently courts in international custody cases facing requests for modification are also faced with simultaneous proceedings in another nation, or custody orders that have already been issued in another nation.

Johnson v. Johnson, 493 S.E.2d 668 (Va. Ct. App. 1997), illustrates how difficult such cases can be. In *Johnson*, Mom, a Swedish attorney, and Dad, an American attorney, met and married in Switzerland, where their only child was born in 1987. In 1990, Dad was posted to Washington, D.C., and moved to Virginia, and Mom was posted to New York. Their daughter spent her time equally between the parents' homes. The parents separated on December 31, 1990, and entered a settlement agreement and agreed decree in Virginia providing for joint custody and alternating two week periods of physical custody with each parent.

In June 1993, the father filed a motion to modify the time periods for alternating custody, because he learned the mother was planning on moving to Sweden with the child. In November of 1993 the parties entered an agreed order in Virginia providing that the mother would have physical custody from August 1993 to August 1995, with the father to get physical custody from August 1995 to August 1997, and vacation visitation to each during the other's period of custody. The order also provided that Virginia would have continuing, exclusive jurisdiction and neither would seek modification without permission of the court. Shortly thereafter, Mom and the child moved to Sweden.

In January 1995, Mom filed for custody in a Swedish court and refused to permit the child to visit for the upcoming Easter. In March 1995, Dad filed a motion in Virginia to find Mom in violation of the Virginia order. He also filed a Hague Convention application for the return of the child.

In Sweden a trial court dismissed Mom's claim, holding the child was domiciled in Virginia, but a Swedish appellate court reversed. Regarding Dad's Convention application, a different Swedish court first ordered the child returned, but a different appellate court reversed. Dad filed a second Hague Convention application, which the Swedish trial court again granted and the appellate court again reversed. In May 1996, the Swedish Administrative Court affirmed, finding the child was not illegally retained and the child's habitual residence was in Sweden.

Having failed in Sweden to obtain the child's return, in July 1996, Dad filed in Virginia a motion for sole custody and an application to hold the mother in contempt. The Virginia trial court, at a hearing at which the mother was represented, granted Dad sole custody, found Mom in contempt, and enjoined her from proceeding with any court actions in Sweden.

The Virginia appellate court rejected Mom's arguments that the child's connections with Virginia had dissipated, and found Virginia had jurisdiction to modify its earlier order. The Court also upheld the trial court's refusal to decline jurisdiction on grounds of *forum non conveniens*, stating:

> Virginia was and is the child's home state by agreement. Under the consent decree, father's residence in Virginia was the child's "place of residence for the purpose of all adjudications of custody and visitation." The parties agreed to this place of residence designation in anticipation of the child's stay in Sweden.

The child was to have equal time in both homes. But for the mother's wrongful retention, the child would have been returned to Virginia. While the most recent evidence concerning the child's care was in Sweden, pursuant to the terms of the... consent decree, the evidence concerning the child's future care would develop in Virginia. Finally,... the parties formally agreed that Virginia would be the only forum....

Can a child's home state be determined by agreement? This seems inconsistent with the widely accepted notion that home state is not the same as legal domicile. On the other hand, the court is quite correct in noting that an agreement of the parties is listed in both UCCJA § 7 and UCCJEA § 207 as a factor to be taken into account in a *forum non conveniens* determination. The court went on to explain:

Also relevant to the inquiry is the evidence in the record that the Swedish court system differs significantly from our own in matters of child custody. Father's expert testified that Swedish courts do not grant joint custody and that "since there is no statute in the Swedish law [requiring recognition of foreign custody orders,] foreign custody decisions cannot in principle have any effect in Sweden whatsoever." Additionally, in the instant case the Swedish appellate courts have refused to give comity to custody orders from the Virginia trial court....

Ironically, Mom in this case was the Swedish Ministry of Foreign Affairs' representative to the Hague Convention and Dad was an attorney for the U.S. Department of State. Isn't this kind of judicial quagmire exactly the situation the Hague Convention on Child Abduction was created to avoid? And if anyone could make it work, shouldn't it be these parents?

Does the information the court provides to us about Swedish law help explain why the Swedish court declined to return the child?

Was the decision of the Virginia court in *Johnson* regarding its jurisdiction to modify under the UCCJA correct? Would it have been correct under the UCCJEA? Given what you know from the opinion about Swedish law, is either the UCCJA or the UCCJEA likely to work as well in the international context as it does within the United States to avoid stalemates?

Of what use is Dad's victory in the Virginia courts going to be to him? Do you think the mother in this case is likely to agree to the father ever having visitation again with this child? What do you think Dad could or should have done differently?

Nothing in this opinion gives us any indication as to the child's views regarding this situation. The only information revealed about the child or the parenting skills of either parent (which may be all the Virginia court had access to) was that she was very well integrated into both parents' homes during the period in which both parents lived in the United States. Some of the mother's allegations regarding jurisdiction are recited, but no allegations of abuse or mistreatment of any kind are mentioned in the appellate opinion. Let's assume, for purposes of discussion, that the daughter had a reasonably good relationship with the father, but had expressed a desire to live with her mother in January of 1995. What could or should Mom have done differently?

For further information about the aftermath of this case, and Mr. Johnson's views regarding the inadequacy of the U.S. government's support for parents of children abducted to Hague countries, see the Testimony of Mr. Johnson before the U.S. House of

Representatives, Oct. 14, 1999, at http://www.house.gov/international_relations/106/full/106first/testimony/Johnson.htm, in which he reveals that despite an award of joint custody with unsupervised visitation to him by the Swedish courts in 1999, he still had been unable to obtain unsupervised visitation with his daughter, and had been permitted only a very few brief visits, supervised by Swedish police, other government employees, or the mother, in the five years since his daughter had been taken to Sweden.

c. Enforcement

Johnson highlights not only issues regarding modification of the custody orders of other nations, but also the difficulty of international enforcement. In the following case, it is the United States that is asked to enforce and not modify the custody order of another country.

Hosain v. Malik
671 A.2d 988 (Md. Ct. Spec. App. 1996)

Davis, J.

[Ed. Note: The mother, Joohi Hosain (formerly Malik) and the father, Anwar Malik, both citizens of Pakistan, were married in Pakistan, where their child was born in 1983. They lived together in Karachi, Pakistan until September 1990, when the mother and child moved to the mother's parents' home in the same city. During this period of separation, mother alleges that father appeared at the grandparents' home drunk and threatened the mother's life and also threatened to take the child by force, which caused the child substantial distress. Within the next several months, she immigrated to the United States on a student visa, bringing the child, Mahek, with her. Within a short period of time after her arrival in Maryland, the mother began living with another man, with whom she had a son in 1991, and later married during the course of this litigation.

Shortly after the mother and child moved to Maryland, the father sued for and was awarded custody. The mother was represented by counsel and her father in the Pakistani proceedings, who presented a written statement on her behalf, but she did not herself appear or produce witnesses. In 1992, after the father located the mother in Maryland through the use of private detectives, the mother filed a proceeding in Baltimore County seeking custody and a restraining order. Following an emergency hearing, the trial court determined that it had jurisdiction, awarded temporary custody to the mother, refused comity to the Pakistani order, and enjoined the father from going within 300 feet of the mother, the child, or their residence.

On appeal, in Malik v. Malik, 638 A.2d 1184 (Md. Ct. Spec. App. 1994), a three judge panel of the appellate court found that the trial court had jurisdiction to hold an emergency hearing, in light of the mother's allegations that the father was "constantly physically abusive to the minor child... in order to coerce her to follow his commands." Because the evidence at the hearing did not show the child was in imminent danger, the court did not thereafter have emergency jurisdiction. The appellate court determined that Maryland was the home state of the child at the time the mother's proceedings were commenced, but that Pakistan would have been regarded as the home state at the time the father's earlier custody proceeding commenced. The appellate court held that under the UCCJA, the lower court must decline jurisdiction, and under principles of comity, must enforce the Pakistani order, unless the Pakistani court (1) either did not apply the best interest of the child standard, or (2) arrived at its decision by applying a law (whether substantive, evidentiary, or procedural) so contrary to Maryland public policy as to undermine confidence in the outcome of the trial.

On remand, both parents produced expert testimony about Pakistani law. Finding that the father's expert (a retired Pakistani judge) was more qualified than the mother's expert (a non-lawyer and professor of political science) and that the burden of persuasion was on the mother, the trial court declined jurisdiction and granted comity to the Pakistani custody order.

The mother appealed on the grounds that the trial court's ruling was in error, and also that the trial court abused its discretion by proceeding with the hearing on remand in the absence of the attorney appointed for the child, who was out of town. The father argued the appeal should be dismissed because the mother included with her brief an attached recommendation by a professor of child psychology. This time the appeal was heard en banc by eight appellate judges. Finding that the attachment was irrelevant, and the absence of the child's attorney not properly preserved for review and non-prejudicial, Judge Davis, writing on behalf of the six judges in the majority, proceeded to the substantive rulings.]

* * *

Devotees of our national sports pastime agree that what is most important for a batter is to keep his or her eye on the ball.... Lest there be any confusion about our assigned task on this appeal from the limited remand hearing below, we must bear in mind what this case is not about. This case is not a review of legal determinations of the circuit court. Neither is this case about whether a Pakistani trial judge or a Maryland trial judge reached the "right" decision, for both judges are entitled to deference as to their factual findings.... And this case is not about whether Pakistani religion, culture, or legal system is personally offensive to us or whether we share all of the same values, mores, and customs, but rather whether the Pakistani courts applied a rule of law, evidence, or procedure so contradictory to Maryland public policy as to undermine the confidence in the trial.... We cannot now reverse the judgment of the circuit court unless we find the...court's [factual] determination to be "clearly erroneous."

III.

A. ...In view of the expert testimony and the language of [Pakistan's] Guardians and Ward's Act [of 1890]..., there was substantial evidence supporting the circuit court's determination that Pakistan follows the best interest of the child standard in child custody disputes.

Appellant, however,...maintains that...the circuit court "erred in finding that the Pakistani court applied the best interest of the child standard" because the decisions of the Pakistani courts were "based solely on the mother's failure to appear in the Pakistani proceedings."...A fair reading of the record reveals that the courts in Pakistan considered [father's] evidence, including...[his] denial of [mother's] allegations, and concomitantly refused to accord weight to those allegations. Appellee's expert testified that, as matter of practice, the only way the Pakistani court would have considered appellant's allegations is if she had appeared in person to substantiate them....

...That the Pakistani court may have considered only appellee's evidence and refused to give credence to appellant's allegations in making the best interest of the child determination does not render the determination defective.... In Maryland a court will proceed with a child custody determination in the absence of one of the parents.... In this regard, the Pakistani court proceeded in virtually the same manner in which a Maryland court would have proceeded had a parent failed to appear. Our view is bolstered by the uncontroverted fact that appellant had notice and an opportunity to present her side in Pakistan, but decided against doing so.

* * *

B. We now address whether substantial competent evidence existed from which the circuit court could have determined that the best interest of the child standard was in fact applied in Pakistan. Preliminarily, we believe it beyond cavil that a Pakistani court could only determine the best interest of a Pakistani child by an analysis utilizing the customs, culture, religion, and mores of the community and country of which the child and—in this case—her parents were a part, i.e., Pakistan.... [F]aced with the facts of a Pakistani child of two Pakistani parents who had been raised in the culture of her parents all of her life, not only did the Pakistani court properly utilize the only mores and customs by which the family had been inculcated, but it used the only principles and teaching available to it at the time.... Bearing in mind that in the Pakistani culture, the well being of the child and the child's proper development is thought to be facilitated by adherence to Islamic teachings, one would expect that a Pakistani court would weigh heavily the removal of the child from that influence as detrimental....

...Because appellant appealed appellee's Pakistani custody order, several Pakistani courts issued orders upon review thereof.... [Examining the original temporary custody order, the Maryland appellate court observed that] the court concluded that appellant lost her right of "Hazanit" [a religious or personal right to have custody depending on the age and sex of the child, which is also spelled Hizanat]...by removing the child from her father.... This...was injurious to the mental health and emotional well being of the child.... [Two appellate courts affirmed, the higher court also reciting appellee's testimony, including his allegation that his daughter was not properly cared for by appellant (no details given), that in Pakistan he paid for her to attend an Islamic school, and that she was not receiving an Islamic education in Maryland. In reaching its decision, this higher court relied upon several factors to which appellee also testified, e.g.,] that appellant lived with another man in adultery, that appellant had a child with her paramour, that the child was living in a non-Islamic society, that appellee is a businessman living in an Islamic society, and that appellee is of good moral character.

...We conclude that the record contains substantial competent evidence from which the circuit court could conclude that the Pakistani courts in fact applied the best interest of the child standard.

C. Next, appellant argues that, even if the Pakistani court did in fact apply the best interest of the child standard, the circuit court erred in failing to conclude under the second part of our mandate in *Malik* that the child custody law and procedure that the Pakistani courts followed was contrary to Maryland's public policy. We disagree....

i. We reject appellant's argument that the Pakistani court applied a rule of law contrary to Maryland's public policy...when it allegedly based its child custody order only on evidence that appellee presented. Initially, we observe that we are not called upon here to pass judgment on a trial by fire, trial by ordeal, or a system rooted in superstition, or witchcraft. In fact, the Pakistani child custody system is rooted in the Guardian and Wards Act of 1890—an enactment based on British common law. As we noted in part A, the great weight of evidence shows: (1) the Pakistani court proceeded in a manner quite similar to the manner in which a Maryland court would have proceeded had a parent failed to appear; (2) appellant had notice and an opportunity to present her side of the case in Pakistan; and (3) appellant was represented by counsel and by her father in Pakistan....

ii. Appellant also claims that the law as applied in Pakistan is repugnant to Maryland public policy because the Pakistani order was based on the right of Hazanit. In *Malik*, we stated the following:

> On the record before us, we cannot determine whether Pakistani law lacks conformity with Maryland law. We can, however, resolve the narrow issue of whether the Pakistani order should be denied comity because there is a paternal preference in Pakistani law. If the only difference between the custody laws of Maryland and Pakistan is that Pakistani courts apply a paternal preference the way Maryland courts once applied the maternal preference, the Pakistani order is entitled to comity. A custody decree of a sister state whose custody law contains a preference for one parent over another would be entitled to comity, provided, of course, the sister state's custody law applies the best interest of the child standard.
> ... A Maryland court should not, therefore, refuse to enforce a Pakistani custody order merely because a paternal preference is found in that country's law.

...As we previously noted, the doctrine of Hazanit embodies complex Islamic rules of maternal and paternal preference, depending on the age and sex of the child. Appellant describes the doctrine as follows:

> Under the Islamic law, the Doctrine of Hazanit governs child custody. Under the Doctrine of Hazanit, the mother is entitled to custody of her male child up to the age of seven (7) and of her female child up to the age of puberty. However, the mother's right to Hazanit is subject to the control of the father who is the child's natural guardian. Moreover, if the father is unfit for custody once the child reaches the requisite age, the child's paternal male relatives, and not the mother, are given custody. Further, the mother can lose custody before the child reaches the requisite age if she is an "apostate" (wicked or untrustworthy). The mother can also lose custody before the child reaches the requisite age if she can not [sic] promote the religious or secular interests of the child.

Appellant states that in this case, the Pakistani court ruled that she lost Hazanit because she removed the child to the U.S. where appellee was unable to exercise his right to control as the child's natural guardian. Appellant further notes that she was considered "apostate" for living in an adulterous household.

...The circuit court had before it the expert testimony of Justice Dogar that, under the Act, Hazanit is but one of the factors to be considered in the welfare of the child test. He stressed that a Pakistani court does not blindly apply the doctrine of Hazanit in making child custody determinations. According to Justice Dogar, "If the personal law [as expressed in the doctrine of Hazanit] was to be the only thing on the basis on which [the welfare of the child] was decided, there would have been no Guardians and Wards Act...." Given the circuit court's opinion of the credibility of this expert, from this testimony, we hold that the circuit court could reasonably have found that Hazanit was merely one factor. In addition, consideration of this factor does not make Pakistani law repugnant to Maryland public policy.

We recognize that Hazanit is different in many respects from the traditional maternal preference once followed in this State. We recognize, however, that Hazanit is nonetheless similar to the traditional maternal preference in that they both are based on very old notions and assumptions (which are widely considered outdated, discriminatory, and outright false in today's modern society) concerning which parent is best able to care for a young child and with which parent that child best belongs. Viewed in this regard, standing as a factor to be weighed in the best interest of the child examination, Hazanit is no more objectionable than any other type of preference....

Given that Hazanit is only more doctrinaire in degree from the maternal preference and because the circuit court could have reasonably found it to be only a factor, we hold that the circuit court did not err in concluding that the principles of Pakistani law which were applied were not repugnant to Maryland law. In fact, the Pakistani court arrived at the same rule of maternal preference now recognized in Maryland by virtue of its decision that appellant had forfeited her right of Hazanit, i.e., the preference no longer was applied in the custody determination. Thus, had the right of Hazanit been considered as a factor, we would be obliged to note that we are simply unprepared to hold that this longstanding doctrine of one of the world's oldest and largest religions practiced by hundreds of millions of people around the world and in this country, as applied as one factor in the best interest of the child test, is repugnant to Maryland public policy. Since the Pakistani court decided the right to Hazanit was forfeited, it was not factored in and thus the effect of the preference was the same as that now recognized under Maryland law.

iii. Next, appellant asserts that the Pakistani custody orders were founded on principles of law repugnant to Maryland public policy because the orders were allegedly based on the Pakistani presumption that an adulterous parent is unfit for custody. We disagree. The record, including the Pakistani orders and the testimony of the experts, contains substantial evidence that adultery was only one factor considered.

There is nothing "repugnant," or even foreign, in a court considering adultery as a factor in determining the best interest of the child.... [Maryland's highest court has held]:

> [T]here are now no presumptions whatsoever with respect to the fitness of a parent who has committed, or is committing, adultery. Rather, adultery is relevant only insofar as it actually affects a child's welfare. We will not presume a harmful effect, and the mere fact of adultery cannot "tip the balance" against a parent in the fitness determination. Thus, a chancellor should weigh, not the adultery itself, but only any actual harmful effect that is supported by the evidence.

While appellant argues in terms of "presumption of unfitness," the testimony at the remand hearing was sufficient to support a conclusion that adultery was only a factor. Accordingly, the circuit court did not err by failing to conclude that this aspect of the Pakistani welfare of the child test was repugnant to Maryland public policy.

iv. ...To the extent that appellant argues that the Pakistani courts placed too much weight on appellant's removal of the child, we simply state that we have already determined that the Pakistani courts cannot be faulted for proceeding based on only the evidence that was before it. A Maryland court could only consider events preceding the removal of the child if evidence of those events are presented during the proceedings....

v. Additionally, appellant asserts that the Pakistani custody orders were founded on principles of law repugnant to Maryland public policy because the Pakistani courts allegedly "penalized the mother for not appearing without considering the affect of her admission to adultery on her ability to return to Pakistan." In this regard, appellant points out that if convicted under Pakistani criminal law, her penalty could be public whipping or death by stoning. Although Dr. Malik [appellant's expert witness] opined that appellant would be arrested for adultery if she returned to Pakistan for the custody proceedings, he also conceded that punishment for adultery was extremely unlikely and that proving the crime was extremely difficult. [He testified no women in the past 50 years had been stoned for adultery.] Given this testimony, the circuit court was not clearly erroneous in not considering the effect of whether appellant's admission to adultery was "repugnant" to Maryland public policy in its failure to find that the Pakistani courts punished her for not appearing.

* * *

vii. Peppered throughout the minority opinion are sundry references to matters introduced at the initial proceeding before the Circuit Court for Baltimore County, unsupported allegations of wrongdoing by appellee, and the report of Dr. Rosenberg, not only objectionable because they are beyond the pale of *Malik*, but because they are not a part of the record on this appeal. The minority nevertheless makes reference to these extraneous materials and utterly ignores the procedural posture of this case. Consideration of matters that go to the merits of a cause before a determination of the question of jurisdiction—when there is such a question—runs counter to accepted rules of procedure.... Thus, it is only after the circuit court, pursuant to our mandate in *Malik*, determined that it would, in fact, exercise its jurisdiction that it would be empowered to consider the merits, including Dr. Rosenberg's report and other extraneous matters referred to by the dissent. Stated otherwise, a factual determination of whether the proceeding in Pakistan comported with Maryland law was antecedent to any consideration of the child's present position because the circuit court was without power to address the merits until it determined that it should exercise its jurisdiction....

* * *

To the extent that the best interest standard was not applied,...it is only because the mother and the child—[whom the court had ordered to be produced by appellant]—were not present in person to substantiate the mother's allegations.[12]

* * *

While we empathize with the minor child and fully appreciate the hardship attendant to her readjustment, we must be mindful of the precedent that our dissenting colleagues would have us set. Were we to adopt the minority's reasoning, our holding would promote the uprooting of children from their home surroundings away from the non-custodial parent, family, and friends and the [sic] absconding to this State, where a judge would be obliged to grant custody to the errant parent because personal bonding and a readjustment to the new surroundings will have occurred during the pendency of judicial proceedings. This is not simply a case where one parent having custody legally or pursuant to a lawful court order awaits the court's determination of which parent ultimately should have custody. Nor is this a case about an American citizen married to someone from a foreign country or a custodial parent from a foreign country who has come to this country and forthwith sought relief from an American court. Under such circumstances, arrangements may be made for visitation by the non-custodial parent in

---

12. ...Appellant, as a consequence of defying the court order [to produce the chid], thereby thwarted an opportunity to allow the Pakistani court to take into consideration what may have been the most persuasive evidence available as to the best interest of the child. Unfortunately, we will never know what the child's preference would have been when the Pakistani court ordered her production because, as a result of appellant's refusal to participate personally in the Pakistani proceedings, appellant has now created a five-year hiatus during which the child's preference and feelings have been influenced by the isolation from her father and dependency on appellant.

order to facilitate continuity in the relationship between the minor and the non-custodial parent. In other words, the court, acting as a referee, is in a position to issue pendente lite orders until such time as a judicial determination can be made concerning who is most fit to have custody. Here, the natural father was, for a period of over two years, not only deprived of the companionship of his child, but he was ostensibly subject to the emotional trauma occasioned by not knowing where his child was for that period of time. Appellee also was constrained to incur expenditures just to ascertain his daughter's whereabouts and, pending this protracted litigation, he continues to be denied the opportunity to observe his daughter undergoing the emotional, psychological, and physical changes all parents are entitled to witness as their children develop; once denied this opportunity, a parent is never able to recreate that phase of the child's development. More to the point, the child has been robbed of the guidance, love, and association with her natural father. Unquestionably, appellant's actions in secreting the child for over two years constituted extra legal efforts by appellant essentially to usurp the decision-making function of both the Pakistani and the American courts as to who should have custody of the minor child. Should appellant now be heard to interpose events that transpired over the two-year period she avoided detection and then, only after she was tracked down by appellee's investigators, seek to secure legal sanction for her extra legal acts?

While we are mindful that our decision today requires that the minor child readjust to her former culture and way of life, it would be manifestly unjust for us to reward appellant for her brazen disdain for the rule of law.... To decide otherwise would be to encourage all who are so inclined to circumvent the laws of their home state and remain outside the reach of any court for a period of time sufficiently long to permit the fugitive parent to argue that he or she should be awarded custody notwithstanding the fact that his or her actions occasioned the hardship upon which he or she bases his or her claim for relief. We decline to countenance such a result. [In a footnote the court noted that Appellant could petition the Pakistani court to modify the custody decree. However, a Maryland court, pursuant to UCCJA § 14, could not modify the Pakistani decree, unless a Pakistani court declined to exercise jurisdiction in favor of Maryland, because Pakistan retains modification jurisdiction under jurisdictional prerequisites substantially in accordance with the UCCJA, and utilizes similar substantive standards for modification.]

Judgment of the Circuit Court for Baltimore County Affirmed. Costs to be Paid by Appellant.

Hollander, J., dissents, in which Paul E. Alpert, Judge (Retired) concurs.

I respectfully dissent, and I do so for several reasons. In my view, the issue regarding counsel has been preserved. Additionally, I believe that the trial court and the majority have erred in characterizing as "not relevant" the child's views with respect to the critical issues that the judge had to resolve. Therefore, I conclude that the circuit court erred in proceeding when the child's court-appointed counsel failed to appear. Furthermore, my reading of the Pakistani court orders convinces me that the Pakistani courts did not apply the "best interests of the child" standard. As a result, the orders are not entitled to comity. Accordingly, I would reverse.

I.

* * *

The majority misconstrues the vital role of Mahak's counsel at the evidentiary hearing and overlooks the child's fundamental right to participate, as a party; that right, in

Mahak's case, could only be exercised through counsel. Moreover, the issues set forth in our mandate in *Malik* were the dispositive issues in the case. Indeed, the outcome would determine Mahak's fate—whether she would remain in the United States with her mother, with whom she has resided here since 1990, or whether she would be returned, against her wishes, to Pakistan and to a father she apparently feared. Consequently, the hearing was not merely an "early stage" of the proceedings; the trial court's ultimate resolution of the comity issue would necessarily turn on what occurred at that hearing and, if its ruling is upheld, it will be the only hearing of significance. In this light, Mahak's position was exactly what was relevant, and it is a travesty to conclude otherwise.

* * *

In my view, Mahak was tangibly prejudiced by her counsel's failure to participate. Included in appellant's appendix were reports from Dr. Leon Rosenberg, who examined Mahak during the pendency of the circuit court proceedings. His reports purport to show that Mahak was extremely fearful of her father....

The only way to show prejudice is to demonstrate what Mahak's counsel could have done had she participated at the hearing. The majority's reasoning is thus circular—it declares that there is no evidence of prejudice from counsel's failure to appear, and simultaneously it strips appellant of the ability to establish such prejudice. This circuitous approach means that a court's decision to proceed without counsel may never be reversible error, because practically the only way to establish prejudice is to go beyond the record and show what counsel could have introduced if he or she had participated in the hearing....

Whether a remand gives the mother a second bite at the apple is not the point; a remand would give Mahak her only real bite. Fundamental fairness requires no less....

II.

I disagree with the majority's conclusion that the Pakistani court orders show that the courts there applied the best interests standard. The majority admonishes that, in analyzing the issue, it is important "to keep [our] eye on the ball." I respectfully submit, however, that, in its ultimate analysis of the Pakistani court orders, the majority strikes out.

In the opinion of the Court of Vth Senior Civil Judge at Karachi East, issued October 23, 1991, the judge awarded custody to Mr. Malik because appellant removed the child from the "constructive custody" of her father and "the father cannot exercise his control" over the child. The court then cited a previous case for the proposition that "by removing the minor to U.S.A. the defendant has deprived the minor child of an opportunity to meet her father, which means that she has done something [injurious] to the mental and [e]motional well-being of the minor, and thereby has lost the right of Hizanat." Those were the only reasons that the court gave in support of its conclusion. Noticeably absent is any discussion or findings as to the fitness of either parent. Nor is there any consideration of the well-being of the child or the standard of living or surroundings in which Mahak would be reared. Further, the court did not attempt to ascertain the desires of Mahak, who was then eight years old, either through appointment of an attorney for her or through counsel for the parties. This is in spite of the fact that s 17(3) of the Pakistani Guardians and Wards Act ("the Act") allows the court to consider the preference of the minor "if the minor is old enough to form an intelligent preference."

* * *

In its recitation of facts, the Pakistani court noted appellant's allegations that her former husband "is ad[d]icted of Alcohol and tranquilizers and the said habits made him unable to deal with daily life and discharge his obligation to look after the welfare of [appellant] and the minor" and that Mr. Malik used to extend threats of dire consequences to the [appellant] and also used to threat[en] to snatch away the minor from the [appellant]. Due to said threats the minor started awakening at night time and used to utter words 'Bachao Bachao.' In order to save the minor from unpleasant atmosphere and in the welfare of the minor the [appellant] left Karachi for [the] U.S.A. along with the minor....

Yet the court failed to investigate, consider, or resolve the mother's serious allegations of appellee's substance and domestic abuse. As the majority concedes, Justice Dogar, appellee's expert witness, "opined that the Pakistani court did not consider appellant's allegations," because she failed to appear. Although appellant did not personally appear in Pakistan to present the allegations of abuse,[4] it is extremely unlikely that a Maryland judge would simply award custody of a child to a parent accused of abuse or misconduct, merely because the other parent fails to appear. Rather, the judge would attempt to ascertain the validity of the claims, in order to safeguard the well-being of the child....

[T]he Pakistani court order, which professes concern for the "welfare" of the child, nonetheless gives no indication that it considered all of the best interest factors. Rather, the court merely said that custody belonged with the father because appellant had interfered with the father's right to "control" the child. The court appeared to indulge a conclusive presumption that appellant's interference with Mr. Malik's ability to see his daughter meant that custody belonged with Mr. Malik. That is not the application of the best interests of the child test, as we have defined it....

The judgment of the Court of III Additional District Judge at Karachi East, to which Ms. Hosain appealed the previous court's ruling, is equally flawed. The mother's denial of the father's access to the child, and the near total emphasis on the father's "right" to "control" the child, were apparently the primary grounds on which the court based its decision.

* * *

The analysis of the Court of Vth Senior District Judge/ASJ & R.C. at Karachi East, dated August 10, 1993, is concededly closer to the best interests of the child standard. Nonetheless, while the court paid lip service to something that sounds like a best interests of the child standard, it still did not apply that standard. In awarding custody to appellee, the court reasoned that Ms. Hosain had "forcibly removed the custody of the minor M[a]hak Malik from the custody of" the father, that Ms. Hosain was "living a sin life accompanied by her lover," and that Mr. Malik was the "natural guardian" of the child. It added that the mother lived in "an unislamic society [which] will not be in the welfare and well being of the minor daughter," while Mr. Malik was "a business man living in an Islamic society with a moral character." Although the court mentioned that Ms. Hosain had a child with her paramour, who is now her husband, it did not con-

---

4. Appellant explained that she failed to return to Pakistan because, given her status as an adulterer, she could be severely punished. In view of Pakistani and Islamic laws and traditions, which the majority thoroughly reviewed, the mother also apparently recognized that the proceedings in Pakistan would likely result in an award of custody to the father, notwithstanding her claims of abuse....

sider or address Mahak's interest in remaining with her half-sibling. This is inconsistent with the policy in Maryland that courts should avoid the separation of siblings....

As for the first reason, Ms. Hosain's denial of Mr. Malik's access to Mahak sounds like the father's-right-to-control rule on which the other courts relied. As for the second reason, the court was certainly entitled to consider that Ms. Hosain lived with another man, and had a child with him, out of wedlock. But the court never established the correlation between that conduct and Mahak's best interests. It is settled policy in Maryland that the fact of adultery should be considered "only insofar as it affects the child's welfare."... Finally, the Pakistani court's reference to Mahak's living in an "unislamic society" is reminiscent of the facts of *Al-Fassi*, in which the Bahamian court had awarded custody to the father on the grounds of the risk of the children's becoming "little Americans," of "losing the cultural heritage of Saudi Arabia," and of losing their royal inheritance. Moreover, like the previous courts, the allegations of substance and domestic abuse were not considered, although the court stated in its opinion:

> It is further stated by [appellant, in her written statement] that [appellee] is addict of smoking joints, in the habit [of] consuming alcoh[o]l and also addict of using tranquilizers, which fact was transpired upon her after the marriage. And due to above addiction, the health of [appellee] is totally wrecked and his mind is unable to deal with his daily life, therefore, he cannot look after the welfare of the minor.

Consideration of these serious charges, regardless of whether the accuser appears, is essential to a meaningful application of the best interests test.

Certainly, I do not intend in any way to criticize Pakistani laws, mores, culture, or customs. Moreover, like the majority, I, too, recognize that Islam is "one of the world's oldest and largest religions." But we were clear in *Malik* that, unless the Pakistani courts applied the best interests standard, comity was not appropriate. The Pakistani courts' use of phrases such as the "welfare of the minor" does not constitute the application of the best interests of the child standard. These words are, after all, only labels.

III.

Ms. Hosain did not unlawfully abscond from Pakistan with Mahak. Early in the opinion, the majority acknowledged that appellant left Pakistan before, and not after, appellee was awarded custody. Thus, when Ms. Hosain came to this country, she was not under any legal compulsion to remain in Pakistan or to relinquish custody of Mahak. In essence, she came as an immigrant to our nation of immigrants. The majority's assertion that appellant attempted to use the Maryland court in "a conscious and apparently calculated plan to circumvent the laws" of Pakistan is also unfounded. She, like many others, has resorted to our courts to defend her current living arrangement with her child, and to contest custody orders from another country that, in her view, are inconsistent with this State's policy. She should not be chastised for contesting the Pakistani decrees in the courts of the land where she now lives, merely because she and her child are Pakistani by birth.

The majority also suggests that the adoption of my views would sanction wholesale "uprooting" of children and would lead to the influx to Maryland of parents seeking custody of children who have been snatched, or trying to re-litigate issues that have been determined by custody decrees of other courts. I certainly do not want to be understood as encouraging such conduct.... But we should not lose sight of the fact that this case concerns only one child. [The dissent noted in a footnote that the father's expert conceded that Pakistan does not recognize child custody awards issued by other nations.]

Notes and Questions

1. *Refusal to Enforce on Procedural and Policy Grounds—Legal Basis.* Before examining whether the majority or dissent better applied the public policy exception, it is important first to examine the legal bases for nonrecognition. What grounds may U.S. courts properly consider to deny enforcement to the custody orders of foreign nations?

(a) *Denial of Notice or Opportunity to Be Heard.* One ground upon which there is no disagreement is denial of the due process requirements of reasonable notice and opportunity to be heard. Under UCCJA §§ 5, 13, and 23, as well as UCCJEA §§ 105, 108, 303, and 305, the provision of adequate notice and opportunity to be heard in the original proceeding are prerequisites for enforcement of both domestic and foreign custody orders. It is common for U.S. courts to refuse recognition and enforcement to custody orders of foreign nations that were issued without affording proper notice or opportunity to be heard to one of the parties. *See, e.g.,* Godwin v. Bogart, 749 So. 2d 450 (Ala. App. 1998); Malek v. Malek, 227 Cal. Rptr. 841 (Cal. Ct. App. 1986); Kallman v. Kallman, 623 So. 2d 1213 (Fla. Dist. Ct. App. 1993); Al-Fassi v. Al-Fassi, 433 So. 2d 664 (Fla. Dist. Ct. App. 1983); Koestar v. Montgomery, 886 S.W.2d 432 (Tex. App. 1994).

(b) *Failure to Satisfy UCCJA/UCCJEA Jurisdictional Standards.* Another possible ground to deny enforcement is that the foreign nation did not have jurisdiction under the jurisdictional standards of the UCCJA, or UCCJEA, whichever is applicable in the state being asked to enforce the order. UCCJA § 13, the section of general applicability addressing recognition, provides:

> The courts of this State shall recognize and enforce an initial or modification decree of a court of another state which had assumed jurisdiction under statutory provisions substantially in accordance with this Act or which was made under factual circumstances meeting the jurisdictional standards of the Act, so long as this decree has not been modified in accordance with jurisdictional standards substantially similar to those of this Act.

The Comment to UCCJA § 23 raises a slight question as to whether this requirement applies to the enforcement of orders of foreign nations under the UCCJA. UCCJA § 23 provides in part:

> The provisions of this Act relating to the recognition and enforcement of custody decrees of other states apply to custody decrees and decrees involving legal institutions similar in nature to custody institutions rendered by appropriate authorities of other nations if reasonable notice and opportunity to be heard were given to all affected persons.

The Comment of the Drafting Committee to Section 23 suggests that when recognition of a decree rendered by the appropriate judicial or administrative authorities of another nation is at issue, the only prerequisite is reasonable notice and opportunity to be heard. Moreover, the Comment provides that "it is also to be understood that the foreign tribunal had jurisdiction under its own law rather than under section 3 of this Act." If this Comment was meant to suggest that exercise of jurisdiction under one of the UCCJA bases is not required for recognition and enforcement of a foreign nation's custody order, it does not appear that this position has been followed by the courts. *See* Al-Fassi v. Al-Fassi, 433 So. 2d 664, 666–67 (Fla. Dist. Ct. App. 1983) (even if foreign court had jurisdiction under its own laws, it was not enforceable when the "decree was not entered under factual circumstances meeting the jurisdictional standards of the Act"). The actual language of Section 23 supports the courts' interpretation, because "The provisions of the Act relating to the recognition and enforcement of custody decrees" would include the requirement of Section 13 regarding compliance with the jurisdictional provisions of the Act.

In UCCJEA states, this ambiguity is removed. See Section 105 of the UCCJEA in your Supplement. Subsection (b) and the accompanying Comment make clear that child custody orders of foreign countries are enforceable if the exercise of jurisdiction was in substantial compliance with the Act.

Of course, under both the UCCJA and the UCCJEA, an order properly issued under the relevant Acts is not enforceable if, prior to the enforcement proceeding, the order has been modified, stayed, or vacated by a court exercising jurisdiction in conformity with the Acts. See UCCJA §§ 12, 13; UCCJEA § 305.

(c) Order not Entitled to Recognition in Foreign Jurisdiction. American courts have also refused to enforce orders that were entered without jurisdiction under the laws of the nation that entered the order. In Noordin v. Abdulla (*In re* Custody of R), 947 P.2d 745 (Wash Ct. App. 1997), the Washington court declined to enforce an order of a Muslim Shari'a court in the Philippines granting the father custody, because a Philippine Regional Court had subsequently granted temporary custody to the mother, ruling that the Shari'a court order was entered after the regional court had acquired exclusive jurisdiction over the custody matter. Relying upon Restatement (Second) of Conflict of Law, §§ 98 cmt. c, 92, 104, 112–115 (1971), the court observed that American courts enforce the judgments of foreign countries only if the foreign court had jurisdiction to act and the order would be entitled to recognition in the foreign nation itself. A party challenging enforcement of the judgment of a foreign court is entitled to raise any defense to the validity of the order that could be raised in the courts of the foreign jurisdiction. Noordin, 947 P.2d. at 751.

(d) Public Policy Grounds. In *Hosain,* the Pakistani court's exercise of jurisdiction did satisfy UCCJA requirements for jurisdiction under the "left-behind parent" home state basis; as well as Pakistani jurisdictional requirements. It was undisputed that the mother was given notice of the Pakistani proceeding, and she was in fact represented at the hearings and on appeal by counsel. Given UCCJA §§ 13 and 23, you may wonder how the appellate court, in its prior decision in the *Hosain* case, Malik v. Malik, 638 A.2d 1184 (Md. Ct. App. 1994), reached the conclusion that the UCCJA permitted it to deny enforcement to the Pakistani order if it did not apply the best interest standard.

In *Malik,* the appellate court focused on UCCJA § 8(b), the unclean hands provision set forth in note 6 following the *Ivaldi* case. This provision prohibits a court from exercising jurisdiction to modify the order of another court after improper removal of a child from the person entitled to custody, or improper retention by the parent seeking modification, unless required "in the interest of the child." Unfortunately, this application of the qualifying phrase in Section 8(b) to *also* circumvent the requirements of Sections 13 and 14, which limit modification and require enforcement of the order of another state, on the ground that the other state's order was not in the best interest of the child, would eviscerate Sections 13 and 14 of the Act and permit courts to reevaluate the substantive merits of a sister state's custody order. This is exactly the scenario the UCCJA was created to avoid, and in domestic cases similar interpretations have been regarded as inappropriate. See Grubbs v. Ross, 630 P.2d 353 (Or. 1981), *overruling* In re Settle, 556 P.2d 962 (Or. 1976). Moreover, the Comment of the Drafting Committee to Section 8 suggests that Section 8(b) does not come into play unless the court already has the power under Section 14 to modify the custody decree of another state.

The other doctrine applied by the court in *Malik* was the common law doctrine of comity, discussed above in note 7 following *Ivaldi*. The court relied upon Restatement (Second) of Conflicts § 90, which provides: "No action will be entertained on a foreign cause of action the enforcement of which is contrary to the strong public policy of the forum."

May a court disregard the enforcement mandate of a state statute, i.e., Sections 13 and 23 of the state's UCCJA, in reliance upon a common law doctrine? Surely not, unless the legislature intended that the two be co-extensive. Since most states enacted Section 23 verbatim from the NCCUSL draft, the Comment of the Drafting Committee to Section 23 might be useful to consider. However, following the observation that the only prerequisite to enforcement is reasonable notice and opportunity to be heard, the Comment invites readers to "Compare Restatement of the Law Second, Conflict of Laws, Proposed Official Draft, sections 10, 92, 98, and 109(2) (1967)." Did the drafters of the UCCJA, recognizing that the custody laws of other nations could be vastly different from the custody laws of American states, intend that these differences should never be taken into account? If they did, do you agree with that approach?

Despite the problematic basis for statutory authority in UCCJA states for nonrecognition on the basis of "repugnant" substantive rules, the *Malik-Hosain* court is not alone in finding that a decree from another nation need not be enforced if the "best interests of the child standard" is not employed, or if the substantive law is otherwise found to violate the policy of the forum state. *See, e.g.,* Abu-Dalbouth v. Abu-Dalbouth, 547 N.W.2d 700 (Minn. Ct. App. 1996) (no problem with simultaneous jurisdiction if foreign court failed to consider the best interest of the child, thereby failing to conform to UCCJA); Ivaldi v. Ivaldi, 685 A.2d 1219, 1327 (1996) ("If the Moroccan court denies the father procedural due process or refused to consider Lina's best interest, the Family Part may then refuse to enforce the Moroccan decree."); Tataragasi v. Tataragasi, 477 S.E.2d 239 (N.C. Ct. App. 1996) (court ignores simultaneous proceedings rule because Turkey applied Islamic law and order did not discuss child's best interest); Noordin v. Abdulla (In re Custody of R), 947 P.2d 745, 752 (Wash Ct. App. 1997) ("Washington courts presented with foreign custody judgements should consider our strong public policy favoring the best interests of the child."). *Cf.* Zenide v. Superior Court, 27 Cal. Rptr. 2d 703, 707 (Cal. Ct. App. 1994) (court rejects parent's contention that French decree was punitive and not in child's best interests, but does not declare argument irrelevant to decree's enforceability); Amin v. Bakhaty, 798 So. 2d 75 (La. 2001) (court refused to regard Egypt as a state, for purposes of jurisdictional analysis, based on substantive differences in custody law). To the extent that they address the issue at all, most courts seem to assume that the "jurisdictional standards of the Act" include substantive standards as well, an interpretation that would be highly problematic and clearly erroneous if it was applied in a domestic, interstate context.

In those states that have enacted the UCCJEA, there is only slightly more statutory support for consideration of the substantive law of the foreign state when determining whether to enforce its custody order. UCCJEA § 303, which sets forth the general duty to enforce custody decrees of other States, is virtually identical to UCCJA § 13, and the Comment suggests that the duty to enforce established by both sections is the same. However, Section 105, which addresses the international application of the UCCJEA, provides that custody determinations of foreign courts made in conformity with UCCJEA jurisdictional standards must be recognized and enforced unless "the child custody law of [the] foreign country violates fundamental principles of human rights." The

Comment construes this exception narrowly, noting that "it is invoked only in the most egregious cases."

The Comment also observes that it is the same standard found in Section 20 of the Hague Convention on Child Abduction, which permits a court to refuse to return a child "if this would not be permitted by the fundamental principles of the requested state relating to the protection of human rights and fundamental freedoms." As you read in Section A of this chapter, there is very little case law on this particular provision of the Hague Convention. Because the defense has been interpreted so restrictively, it is rarely, if ever, successful. *See* Subsection A.2.c. of this Chapter, *supra*. *See also* March v. Levine, 136 F. Supp. 2d 831, 855 (M.D. Tenn. 2000), *aff'd* 249 F.3d 462 (6th Cir. 2001) (denying Art. 20 defense, finding no proof grandparents who removed children from Mexico would be denied a fair trial or due process under the Mexican judicial system).

2. *Refusal to Enforce on Policy Grounds—Application.* Even assuming, as many U.S. courts do, that the UCCJA or the UCCJEA permit our courts to deny recognition and enforcement to a custody order issued by another nation because its substantive law of custody is inconsistent with our own, the question then becomes—when should this discretion be exercised? This is, of course, an issue of critical importance. Efforts to achieve international cooperation and to avoid forum shopping and child-snatching can only succeed to the extent nations can transcend political, cultural, and religious differences and find common ground rules to apply to recognition and enforcement issues. On the other hand, are there situations in which the custody determination of another nation would be considered so antithetical to a child's best interests from our own cultural perspective that it should not be enforced? Is *Hosain* such a case?

The court in *Hosain* raises several important issues in this regard. Should a test for recognition and enforcement incorporate the best interests standard? If so, should American courts look at whether that is the legal standard under the custody laws of the foreign nation, or whether that is the standard the court in fact applied? And if we are looking at whether a foreign court applied this standard, should American courts assess that application using American customs, culture, religion, and mores, or those of the foreign nation?

Should it make a difference if the foreign custody laws would violate our own constitution, if applied in the manner in which the foreign court applied them in a U.S. court? Would the law applied by the Pakistani court in *Hosain* have survived constitutional muster if it had been state law applied by an American state court?

Should it make a difference if both parents are citizens of the nation that issued the custody order, or if one parent (or the child) is an American citizen? Do you think *Hosain* would have been decided the same way by the Maryland court if the mother had been an American citizen with a Christian religious heritage?

Once we resolve whose standards should be applied, should the American court deny enforcement if it would reach a different determination applying those standards, or only if there is insufficient evidence that the foreign court in fact applied those standards? How would the majority and dissent in *Hosain* each answer this question? Do you agree with the majority or dissent regarding whether the Pakistani court did in fact apply the best interests standard?

As discussed in the above note, the appellate court in *Hosain* applied the traditional comity doctrine in addition to the UCCJEA, and thus found that it may deny enforcement if the Pakistani determination was made on the basis of substantive or procedural or evidentiary law "so contrary to Maryland public policy as to undermine confidence in the outcome of the trial." Malik, 638 A.2d at 1191. Use of this additional ground, of course, permits the Maryland court to reassess the Pakistani decision, even if it does find the court applied the best interest standard.

The court first assesses the rules of Hazanit, finding them only more doctrinaire in degree from the maternal preference formerly used in many American states. Consider the following tender years statute, which is typical of those applied in many U.S. states thirty years ago:

> As between parents adversely claiming the custody or guardianship of a minor, neither parent is entitled to it as of right, but other things being equal, if the child be of tender years, it should be given to the mother; if it be of an age to require education and preparation for labor and business, then to the father. Mont. Rev. Code Ann. § 91-4515(2) (Smith 1963) (repealed 1975).

In many American states, statutes such as this one operated as a tie-breaker. In others, they shifted the burden of persuasion. In a few states, tender years statutes could only be rebutted by showing the mother was unfit. It is interesting that Pakistan's Guardians and Wards Act Ss. 16–17 (1890), the statute applied by the Pakistani court, in fact contains a tender years presumption for custody disputes between parents "who are European British subjects," which differs from the above Montana statute only in that it would award custody of all girls, as well as custody of boys of tender years, to the mother. Sardar Mohammad Iqbal Khan Mokal, The Guardians and Wards Act (VIII of 1890) & The Majority Act (IX of 1875) with Commentary 146 (1992). This section, of course, would not have been applicable to the parents in Hosain.

No American states currently retain a tender years presumption in their statutes. Do you agree that the rules of Hazanit, as described in Hosain, are comparable? In assessing whether the rules of Hazanit are contrary to public policy, should it matter why American jurisdictions have all rejected this rule? Should the constitutionality of a gender presumption be a factor in determining whether a foreign nation's custody law is contrary to public policy? Is the Hosain majority correct in asserting that the rules of Hazanit were not "factored in" by the Pakistani court and thus the effect of the preference was the same as that now recognized under Maryland law?

In Whallon v. Lynn, in Section A, you read that under Mexican law there is a preference to award custody of a child under seven to the mother in divorce cases, absent exceptional circumstances such as "serious and contagious illness, vice, mistreatment or desertion." In deciding whether or not to recognize and enforce a custody award to a mother made in Mexico utilizing this preference, should this custody law be found to be contrary to pubic policy? Would it matter if an American court would have reached a similar result applying its own custody criteria and notions of "best interests"?

Do you agree with the majority that the Pakistani court's treatment of the mother's adultery was similar enough to a Maryland court's treatment of this factor, so as not to be "repugnant" to Maryland public policy?

Was the Pakistani court's treatment of the mother's removal of the child from Pakistan and failure to inform the father of her whereabouts similar to or contrary to the reaction of an American court under similar circumstances?

The majority contends that if the reasoning of the dissent was adopted, the holding would promote child-snatching. The dissent counters that the mother brought the child to America before any custody order was in place. What are the similarities and differences between the mother's actions and the surrounding circumstances in the *Johnson* case, and the mother's actions and surrounding circumstances in *Hosain*? Do they justify different approaches or the same approach to the enforcement issue facing the Swedish court in *Johnson* and the American courts in *Hosain*?

3. *Comparison with Hague Convention on Child Abduction.* If Pakistan was a party to the Hague Convention, what would have been a likely outcome of an application by the father to U.S. courts for return of the child, Mahak? In all likelihood, the mother would have raised a grave risk of harm defense that the American court would have to resolve. There is no similar defense under the UCCJA or UCCJEA to enforcement of a foreign custody order. If such a defense existed, would it circumvent some of the struggles that some of the questions raised in Notes 1 and 2 might have posed for you? Would including such a defense in the interstate application of the Acts make sense, or would it undermine some of the basic goals of the Acts? If you would not favor its application in an interstate context, are there different justifications for including such a provision in the international applications of the Acts?

One scholar has gone further and proposes in very general terms the adoption of legislation in the U.S. that would regulate custody disputes between U.S. citizens or resident aliens and citizens of non-member nations of the Hague Abduction Convention. She would require courts to consider the child's best interests; whether the child had experienced emotional, psychological, or physical abuse in the marital home; and who was the preabduction primary caretaker. *See* June Starr, *The Global Battlefield: Culture and International Child Custody Disputes at Century's End*, 15 Ariz. J. Int'l & Comp. L. 791, 832 (1998).

4. *Comparison with English cases.* In *Re E*, (Abduction: Non-Convention Country)[2000] W.L.R. 1036, [1999] 2 F.L.R. 642, an English Court of Appeal ordered the return of a child to Sudan, following removal of the child by the Sudanese mother in defiance of a Sudanese court order awarding custody pursuant to Shari'a law to the paternal grandmother. Despite the longstanding adherence in English law to the notion that a child's best interests are served by awarding custody to a parent, the court found that it would be wrong to judge other systems using Judeo-Christian values. Rather, the court observed, the child's welfare had to be seen in the context of the customs and rules prevailing in the country of the child's habitual residence, as well as the notions of welfare of their religion, to which the mother herself subscribed.

By contrast, in 1997 an English Court of Appeal in *Re JA* (Abduction, Non-Convention Country [1998] 1 F.L.R. 231, refused to return a child to the United Arab Emirates, following a retention of the child in England without the father's consent or a court order, because the mother would have no possibility of obtaining an order granting her permission to remove the child. In comparing the two cases, Henry Setright observes that: "English judges have always seen a close relationship between the concept of returning abducted children for issues to be resolved in their countries of habitual residence, with the potential for the abducting parent, especially if that parent be a de facto or de jure primary carer, to seek by lawful means to accomplish that which he or she attempted wrongfully by abducting." Though Setright notes that in *Re E* the mother also was extremely unlikely to obtain a modification awarding her custody, he attributes the difference to the fact that *Re JA* involved an English primary caretaker mother, whereas in *Re E* the abducting mother was Sudanese and a non-primary carer. Henry Setright, *Removals to and From Non-Convention Countries—The Perspective of Courts in England and Wales*, 2000 Int'l Fam. L. 125, 126–27.

In discussing the application of the "welfare of the child" principal in these cases, Setright asks, "What is welfare?" He observes that in the recent past in England, when divorce was based on adultery, children were awarded to the non-adulterous spouse, "on the basis that the moral welfare of the child demanded nothing less. Once in England the scope and importance of access by a child with a non-primary carer parent was deemed to be relatively modest. Once in England it was thought normal and appropriate that rights of custody should not be shared between parents. Now the English law is developing so that, for example, not just the gender, but the sexual orientation of a parent, including a perspective adoptive parent, may be of itself less determinative than hitherto. All this shows a changing concept of 'welfare' that is not absolute or immutable, but is reflective of and responsible to social developments in the English population." *Id.* at 126.

5. *Methods of Enforcement of Custody and Visitation Orders.* The UCCJA specifically permits courts to order a party to appear before the court with a child. UCCJA § 11. It further provides that a court may order a petitioner who has wrongfully removed or retained a child or who has violated any other provision of a custody order to pay the travel and other expenses, including attorneys fees, of the other party or the other party's witnesses. UCCJA §§ 8, 15, 19. Even in the absence of wrongful conduct, the court has discretion to order one party to pay the travel and other necessary expenses of another party who is outside the state. UCCJA § 11.

The UCCJA is frequently used in combination with traditional custody enforcement remedies. In some states, parents might use a Motion to Enforce to initiate proceedings to enforce custody or visitation orders. In other states, a common remedy for a parent who asserts a legal right to custody of a child being physically retained by someone else is to apply to the court for a writ of habeas corpus. *See Prefatory Note to the Uniform Child Custody Jurisdiction and Enforcement Act,* 9 U.L.A. 649 (1999). A habeas corpus proceeding is an independent action designed to obtain a prompt determination of the legality of a detention, and, if found to be illegal, to secure the release of the person detained. *See, e.g.,* Thomas v. Dugger, 548 So. 2d 230 (Fla. 1989); Walt v. Walt, 574 So. 2d 205, 210 (Fla. Dist. Ct. App. 1991). In Noordin v. Abdulla (In re Custody of R), 947 P.2d 745, 752 (Wash Ct. App. 1997), a habeas proceeding commenced by a father seeking to enforce a Philippine custody order, the court observed that in order to succeed on the application for such a writ, the parent bringing the action must be able to show a "preexisting legal right to custody...of the child, paramount to the right of the other parent." When a habeas corpus action is used to enforce a custody order of a foreign court, it is subject to the requirements of the UCCJA or UCCJEA. See generally, Danny R. Veilleux, *What Types of Proceedings or Determinations Are Governed by the Uniform Child Custody Jurisdiction Act (UCCJA) or the Parental Kidnapping Act (PKPA),* 78 A.L.R. 4th 1028 (2001).

Another traditional enforcement mechanism is to bring a contempt proceeding against a party who is violating the custody or visitation provisions of a foreign custody order that has been properly registered with the court in which enforcement proceedings are being initiated, pursuant to § 15 of the UCCJA or § 305 of the UCCJEA. Violation of custody or visitation orders is generally regarded as "indirect contempt," the willful disobedience of any order lawfully issued by a court. *See, e.g.,* Davis v. Murphy, 188 P.2d 229 (Okla. 1947). It is typically punishable by imprisonment or a fine, *see, e.g.,* Okla. Stat. tit. 21, §§ 565–566 (2001), which can be averted upon compliance with the order. *See, e.g.* Davis v. Davis, 739 P.2d 1029 (Okla. Ct. App. 1987).

One of the major goals of the UCCJEA was to incorporate more effective and uniform enforcement procedures and remedies. *Prefatory Note to the UCJEA, supra,* at 652.

The first is a simple procedure for registering another forum's custody order. Upon receiving notification of the registration, if the parent or other person receiving notice fails to request a hearing contesting the validity of the order within 20 days, the order is confirmed and all further contest of the order's validity with respect to any matter that could have been asserted at the time of registration is precluded. If a hearing is requested, the only grounds for nonconfirmation of the order are that the issuing court did not have jurisdiction under the jurisdictional standards of the Act, that the order has since been vacated, stayed, or modified by a court having jurisdiction under the Act to do so, or that the person contesting registration was not given proper notice in the proceedings creating the order. UCCJEA § 305. In addition to its usefulness for parents seeking to enforce custody or visitation rights with children located in the United States, this provision may be particularly helpful in securing visitation for non-custodial parents located in the United States in international proceedings, because it reduces the risk that a visiting child will not be returned. *Prefatory Note to the UCJEA, supra,* at 653.

In addition, the UCCJEA creates an expedited enforcement mechanism that requires a court, upon the filing of a petition for enforcement, to issue an order directing the respondent to appear, with or without the child, at a hearing the next judicial day after service of the order to appear, or on the first judicial day possible. At the hearing, a petitioner entitled to custody or visitation under the order being enforced will be given immediate physical custody of the child, unless the custody order being enforced has not been registered and confirmed and one of the defenses to confirmation set forth above is established, or unless the respondent can prove that a registered and confirmed order has since been modified, vacated, or stayed by a court having jurisdiction to do so. UCCJEA §§ 308–310. Attorneys fees, investigative fees, travel expenses, witness fees, child care costs during the proceedings, and other costs can be awarded to the prevailing party. UCCJEA § 312. If a parent petitioning for enforcement convinces a court that the child is in imminent danger of suffering serious physical harm or being removed from the state, the court can issue a warrant to direct law enforcement officers to take physical custody of the child and provide for the child's placement pending final relief. UCCJEA § 311.

The UCCJEA specifically acknowledges in Section 315 that prosecutors, law enforcement officials, or other public officials may play a role in locating a child, obtaining a child's return, or enforcing a custody order in a UCCJEA enforcement proceeding or a proceeding brought under the Hague Convention on Child Abduction. When doing so, however, the prosecutor or other official acts on behalf of the court, and may not represent any party.

Problems

8-10. Joan, a resident of Wisconsin, married Ibrahim, a Jordanian citizen, while Ibrahim was a student at the University of Wisconsin. Following the birth of their oldest child in Wisconsin one year later, the family moved to Jordan, where the two youngest children were born. Joan later testified that during their seven years in Jordan, she and the children were subject to repeated beatings and mental abuse, and malnutrition. Her husband refused to buy needed medication for the family, and she was forced to abort their fourth child. Joan and the children, with the assistance of the United States Embassy, secretly moved to Wisconsin, and six and one-half months later, she filed an action for divorce in Wisconsin seeking custody. Assume Ibrahim was properly served. Several months later, Ibrahim initiated a custody proceeding in Jordan. May the Wisconsin court exercise jurisdiction under the UCCJA? Under the UCCJEA?

8-11. Fatima, an American citizen of Turkish descent who grew up in Ohio, met Fehmi, a Turkish exchange student, and married him a year later in Turkey. The couple settled immediately in Switzerland, where Fehmi became employed by an international organization headquartered there. All three of their children were born in Switzerland, and visited for one month each year with both their maternal grandparents in Ohio and their paternal grandparents in Turkey.

When the children were ages nine, seven, and three, Fatima traveled to Ohio with them with round-trip tickets for the annual grandparent visit, but failed to return. She filed a petition for custody in Ohio three weeks after she arrived, and was awarded temporary custody. One month later, Fehmi filed for divorce and custody in Switzerland. Each was served with papers from the other's actions. Following a hearing in Switzerland at which Fatima did not appear, Fehmi was awarded "provisional custody." He registered that order in the Ohio court. A hearing has now taken place before the Ohio trial court, at which Fatima and Fehmi both testified, to determine whether the Ohio court should exercise jurisdiction over the custody proceeding filed by Fatima. Within the past few years, Fehmi purchased a home in Turkey. He testified that it was purchased for a contingency plan if he was layed off due to staff reductions by his employer. Fatima testified that she believes he intends to move to Turkey with the children.

May the Ohio court exercise jurisdiction under the UCCJA, and if so, should it? May the Ohio court exercise jurisdiction under the UCCJEA, and if so, should it?

8-12. Magda, an Egyptian citizen, married Sayed, a U.S. citizen, in Egypt, and Ahmed was born one year later. Throughout their marriage, Magda lived in her father's home in Egypt raising Ahmed. Sayed has lived in the United States virtually all of his adult life. He carried on an active medical practice in Chicago, and visited Egypt up to six times per year, staying a week or two each visit. During one period of approximately two years, he did not visit Egypt at all.

When Ahmed was eight, Magda brought him to the United States without fore-warning her husband, for the purpose of visiting him and her sisters, all of whom re-side in Memphis, Tennessee. Upon reaching Chicago, she telephoned her husband, and then traveled on to Tennessee to look for an apartment, believing he was going to meet her in Memphis. Instead, she learned from her father within the week that her husband had traveled to Egypt to press criminal charges against her for removing Ahmed from the country, without the father's permission, and for obtaining Ahmed's passport fraudulently. Magda filed an action for divorce and custody less than a month after arriving in Memphis, and just one day before her husband obtained a divorce in Egypt and filed a proceeding for custody there. When Magda's action for custody went to trial in Tennessee ten months later, no custody order had yet been issued by an Egyptian court.

Magda and her son continue to reside in Tennessee, and she testified that if she returned to Egypt she would be imprisoned, as a result of the criminal charges filed by Sayed. The parties assert that Egyptian law prohibits a married woman as well as a minor child from traveling outside of Egypt without the written permission of the father. The father entered an appearance in the Tennessee action to challenge the subject matter and personal jurisdiction of the Tennessee court.

How should the court rule on the issues of subject matter and personal jurisdiction if Tennessee were a UCCJA state? How should it rule if Tennessee were a UCCJEA state?

8-13. Marta, a permanent resident of the United States, married Abdul in California, where their first daughter, Nada, was born five years later. After the family moved to Saudi Arabia, a second daughter, Reema, was born. After three years in Saudi Arabia, Marta returned alone to California. She stated that she did not bring the girls because she could not obtain an exit visa for them. Abdul obtained a divorce and custody of both girls from a court in Saudi Arabia. Marta did not get notice of either decree until after Abdul obtained them. Her contact with the girls for the next five years was limited to phone calls and a yearly two-week visit with them in the United Arab Emirates.

When the girls were ages seven and eleven, their father brought them to Orlando, Florida for a vacation, and invited Marta to join them. Several days later, Marta and Abdul got into an argument. When Nada sided with her mother, Nada asserts that Abdul punched Nada several times, and clawed her when she attempted to get away from him. Marta called the police, who arrested Abdul, and subsequently Marta brought the girls back to California and filed for a restraining order. The County Social Services Agency (SSA) were alerted by the nature of the petition's allegations, and took the girls into protective custody, filing a dependency action and releasing them to Marta's care.

In interviews with the SSA staff, Nada told them that she was afraid of her father and would kill herself if returned to his care. She stated that he would daily drive with the girls in the car while intoxicated. She related that on one occasion when she was five, her father had given her a loaded handgun to hold to her sleeping mother's head. She also alleged she had frequently been sexually abused by two family drivers and a cousin. She contends that she had recently told her father about this abuse, and he had not responded. Reena confirmed her father drank a lot and that she was also afraid of him. She also remembers being given a loaded handgun to hold as a toddler.

Abdul challenged the jurisdiction of the California court to conduct a dependency hearing and the court's failure to communicate with the Saudi Arabian court. He also seeks dismissal of the action on the ground that the California SSA failed to notify the Saudi Arabian embassy or consulate when the dependency proceeding was filed. In addition, he seeks enforcement of his decree.

At the hearing, Marta testified that she had never seen her husband physically harm either child before the Florida incident, but that he had hit her on many occasions and had twice been arrested in the United States during their marriage following physical altercations with her involving alcohol. She also confirmed the gun incidents when the children were young. Abdul testified that Marta had been drinking too much in Florida, and that Nada's bruises occurred on rides and swimming pool slides. He denied the allegations regarding alcohol and the gun. He asserts that he does not believe the allegations of sexual abuse and that he has never heard of them before.

If the UCCJA is the controlling law, what, if anything, does the California court have jurisdiction to do in this case? If the UCCJEA is the controlling law, what, if anything, does it have jurisdiction to do?

8-14. Renee and Paul were married in France, where they had two daughters. When their daughters were ages five and eight, the parents separated and divorced in France. The divorce judgment confirmed their agreement that Paul was to have sole custody of the girls, and Renee would have liberal visitation rights. Six months later, Paul moved with the girls to Seattle, Washington for employment-related reasons. The French judgement did not prohibit moving the children out of France.

Renee contends that it was her understanding that the move was only to be for the summer. Paul claims he advised her the move was permanent. When the girls did not return for the school year in September, Renee sought a custody modification from the French court. Although the trial court only adjusted her visitation, the French appellate court the following May reversed that decision and awarded custody to Renee and liberal visitation to Paul, following a hearing at which both parents appeared. The court found Renee was not properly informed of the permanent nature of the move, keeping the children for the second half of the summer in the U.S. (presumably during the mother's visitation period) violated French law, it was in the girls' best interest to maintain maximum contact with both parents and reside in their native country, and Renee could not maintain regular contact if the girls were in Seattle. Paul appealed to the French Supreme Court.

While that appeal was pending, Paul filed a motion to modify in a state court in Washington, but failed to tell the Washington court about the appeal pending in the French Supreme Court. At the point that this proceeding was filed, the girls had lived in Washington for fifteen months. Renee was given notice of the Washington proceeding but chose not to appear, on the ground that Washington had no jurisdiction. The Washington court awarded custody to Paul, with very limited monitored visitation to Renee. Two months later, the French Supreme Court affirmed the French intermediate appellate court's order awarding custody to Renee and requiring that the children be returned to France.

Shortly thereafter, Paul, his new wife, and the girls moved to Colorado. Renee registered her French decree with the Colorado court and sought enforcement. Paul filed a motion to enforce the Washington decree in the same action. At a hearing on the two motions, the girls, now ages eight and eleven, indicated a strong desire to remain with their father and stepmother. The girls at this point have not had any significant contact with their mother for over two years.

How should the Colorado court rule under the UCCJA? How should it rule under the UCCJEA?

8-15. Nomi is a U.S. citizen and Ibrahim is an Iranian citizen. Nomi and Ibrahim married in Iran, moved to the United States, and then had two children together. Nomi was a homemaker and Ibrahim was a successful doctor. After ten years of marriage, Nomi had an affair. When Ibrahim discovered Nomi's infidelity, Ibrahim told Nomi that she'd never see her children again and he removed them to Iran without her permission. Within one month, he secured a Muslim divorce, pursuant to which he was awarded sole custody of the children. Assume that one year later, Nomi hired a commando group which successfully removed the children from Iran and brought them back to the United States. If Ibrahim then brings an action in state court seeking enforcement of his custody decree, how is the court likely to rule?

2. Foreign Law and International Conventions

Lack of uniformity regarding state jurisdictional standards and unwillingness to enforce the orders of other states were significant inducements to child-snatching and forum shopping within the United States prior to enactment of the UCCJA. Similarly, the absence of uniform jurisdictional standards and inadequate enforcement have contributed to the same problems on an international level. A new Hague Convention has been created to address these issues on a global scale, and several regional conventions have attempted to provide some uniformity in jurisdiction and enforcement as well.

a. *Disparate Domestic Law Standards*

As you have just learned, American jurisdictions, under the UCCJA and UCCJEA, recognize home state and significant connections as the primary jurisdictional bases for custody and access proceedings, along with short term emergency jurisdiction and residual jurisdiction when no other state qualifies under the other bases. In other nations, a variety of different jurisdictional bases have been recognized in their domestic law.

Habitual residence was chosen as the cornerstone for return under the Hague Abduction Convention because it is a common basis for jurisdiction in many nations. England and Wales, for example, permit courts to hear custody cases regarding children who are habitual residents. If children are present in England but habitually resident elsewhere, even if they are English children, the courts will exercise jurisdiction only to the extent that emergency protections are required. If a child is neither present nor habitually resident in England, no jurisdiction will normally be exercised over custody matters concerning the child. Henry Setright, *Removals to and from Non-Convention Countries — The Perspective of Courts in England and Wales*, 2000 Int'l Fam. L. 125.

In other nations, however, presence, domicile, or nationality may be jurisdictional bases. In some nations, for example, jurisdiction over custody may be exercised for any child who is a citizen of the country, even if the child lives abroad. The use of nationality of a child as a basis for jurisdiction stems in part from the notion of *parens patriae*, that a citizen is entitled to the protection of her country's courts. In one case, the Irish High Court found nationality could serve as a jurisdictional basis even though the child had never lived in Ireland. C.M. v. Delegacion Provincial de Malaga Conserjeria De Trabajoe, [1999] 2 I.R. 363 (deferring to pending litigation in Spain on forum non conveniens grounds).

When there are pending proceedings outside the forum nation, or a child has recently been removed from another country, the courts of some nations will apply forum non conveniens principles, seeking to promote justice among the litigants and resolve the conflict in the forum with ready access to evidence concerning the child. Other nations have declared the "welfare of the child" as the paramount criteria, which might lead them to refuse deference to another forum if their court perceived that the other forum's decisions would be made on a criteria other than the child's "welfare" or "best interests." Some parties to the Hague Abduction Convention will apply Convention principles even if the other country is not a party to the Convention. Others require reciprocity, deferring only to nations that would defer to or recognize orders of the forum nation under similar circumstances. See Lara Cardin, *The Hague Convention on the Civil Aspects of International Child Abduction as Applied to Non-signatory Nations: Getting to Square One*, 20 Hous. J. Int'l L. 141, 157–69 (1997).

Similarly, the willingness of nations to recognize, enforce, and refrain from modifying the custody orders of other nations varies tremendously. Some nations will not recognize or enforce foreign custody orders. See, e.g., Johnson v. Johnson, 493 S.E.2d 668, 674 (Va. Ct. App. 1997) ("there is no statute in the Swedish law [requiring recognition of foreign custody orders]"); Hosain v. Malik, 671 A.2d 988, 1022 (dissenting opinion fn. 6) (Md. Ct. Spec. App. 1996) (Pakistani father's expert conceded Pakistan does not recognize child custody awards issued by other nations.). Other nations may enforce them depending upon the tradition of comity within the nation's legal system. U.S. Dep't of State, Bureau of Consular Affairs, International Child Abduction, Part VI (revised July, 2001), *available at* http://travel.state.gov/int'lchildabduction.html#6.

b. Hague Conventions

i. 1961 Convention on the Protection of Minors

In addition to the regional conventions discussed below, the Hague Conference on International Law has produced two conventions addressing jurisdiction and enforcement of custody that are open for global membership. The first, the 1961 Convention on the Protection of Minors, had fourteen contracting parties, as of March 2003. With the exception of Macau, a Special Administrative Region of China formerly under Portuguese control, all of the states parties are European countries. None of the common law nations of Europe agreed to participate. The 1961 Convention, though still attracting parties (Latvia and Lithuania acceded in 2001), has been criticized for permitting jurisdiction to be exercised in custody proceedings based upon both habitual residence and nationality, and for exceptions to recognition that produced substantial conflict. Linda Silberman, *The 1996 Hague Convention on the Protection of Children: Should the United States Join?*, 34 Fam. L.Q. 239, 243–44 (2000).

ii. 1996 Convention for the Protection of Children

Dissatisfaction with the 1961 Convention motivated efforts to create a revised jurisdiction and enforcement convention that would attract broader global acceptance. These efforts culminated in the Hague Convention on Jurisdiction, Applicable Law, Recognition, Enforcement and Co-operation in Respect of Parental Responsibility and Measures for the Protection of Children, 35 I.L.M. 1391 (hereinafter the 1996 Hague Protection Convention), which was adopted and opened for signature in October 1996 by the Hague Conference on Private International Law. The Convention entered into force in January, 2002. As of March 2003, only seven nations—the Czech Republic, Ecuador, Estonia, Latvia, Monaco, Morocco, and Slovakia—were parties to the Convention. Fifty nations, however, participated in the drafting of the Convention, whose text was adopted unanimously by the member nations of the Hague Conference. The United States was an active participant in the drafting process, and signature and ratification of the Convention is under active consideration by the U.S. Dept. of State. Given the potential for broad future participation in this treaty, and the possibility that the United States might become a party, the Convention merits examination.

The 1996 Hague Protection Convention would apply to a broad range of public and private proceedings involving the protection of children and their property, including custody and access proceedings, guardianships, protective care placements, kafala, and proceedings to delegate, restrict, or terminate parental rights.(Article 3). The primary basis to exercise jurisdiction over these proceedings would be the child's habitual residence. When a child's habitual residence changes to a new contracting state, jurisdiction over custody matters regarding the child passes to the courts of the country of the child's new habitual residence. (Article 5). To avoid a conflict with Council Regulation No 1347/2000 of the European Union (*see* Section B.2.c.iii.a. *infra*), however, the Convention also permits a court exercising jurisdiction over a dissolution, legal separation, or annulment proceeding to exercise jurisdiction, even if the country is not the child's habitual residence, as long as one of the parents habitually resides in the forum nation and the requirements for jurisdiction under Regulation 1347/2000 are satisfied. (Article 10). Since these requirements include agreement by both parents to the court's jurisdiction over the custody proceeding, this exception should not produce conflicting judgments.

The 1996 Hague Protection Convention permits a court with jurisdiction on the basis of the child's habitual residence to defer to a court in a nation (1) in which the child is a national; (2) in which property of the child is located; (3) in which the child has a substantial connection; (4) in which the court is "better placed" to assess the child's best interests; or (5) in which an application for divorce, legal separation, or annulment is pending, even if the requirements of Article 10 are not satisfied. (Articles 8, 9). Because exercise of jurisdiction in such countries can occur only with the approval of the court of the country of the child's habitual residence, however, these provisions also should not create the potential for conflicting judgements.

The 1996 Convention permits the exercise of jurisdiction for the issuance of temporary emergency orders (Article 11), which serve a function similar to the emergency jurisdiction basis in the UCCJA/UCCJEA. There are also provisions for default jurisdiction, for children who are displaced due to disturbances in their countries or whose habitual residence cannot be determined. (Article 6). Temporary orders could also be entered regarding matters which "have a territorial effect limited to" the forum nation, if not incompatible with orders entered by the court with primary jurisdiction under the Convention, but permanent resolution of these issues are still left with the latter court. (Article 12).

Drafters of the 1996 Hague Protection Convention were particularly concerned that this convention work in harmony with the Hague Convention on Child Abduction. They achieved this goal in two ways. First, Article 50 of the 1996 Convention affords primacy to the Hague Convention on Child Abduction by providing that the 1996 Convention "shall not affect the application" of the Abduction Convention between parties to both conventions, while permitting the 1996 Convention to be utilized to obtain the return following wrongful removal or access rights. Second, Article 7 of the 1996 Convention creates special jurisdictional rules for a child who has been wrongfully removed or retained. The nation in which the child was habitually resident immediately before the removal or retention retains jurisdiction until:

1) the child has acquired habitual residence in another state, and

2) (a) everyone with a right of custody has acquiesced to the removal or retention, or

   (b) (1) the child has resided in the new forum for at least a year after the left-behind parent or other person with custody rights had knowledge of the child's location; and

   (2) no request for return lodged within that period is still pending; and

   (3) the child is settled in his new environment.

Thus, the 1996 Convention affords a left-behind parent the same opportunity that would be provided under the Hague Child Abduction Convention to seek the child's return, and denies jurisdiction to the nation in which the child is located following removal or retention. However, it also incorporates the acquiescence and Article 12 defenses of the Hague Convention on Child Abduction. If the left-behind parent acquiesces or fails to take timely action to seek return, the nation in which the child is living can eventually acquire jurisdiction.

The 1996 Hague Protection Convention also contains choice of law rules for proceedings within the scope of the Convention. The basic rule is that courts are to apply their own substantive laws, although they are permitted to take into consideration the law of another nation with a significant connection to the situation. (Article 15). Some exceptions are created, regarding such issues as the attribution or extinction of parental responsibility by operation of law or agreement, and the effect of a child's change of habitual residence, which are addressed in Articles 15–21.

The orders made in contracting nations based on the jurisdictional guidelines of the 1996 Hague Protection Convention are entitled to recognition in other contracting states, and to enforcement to the same extent as if they had been entered by authorities of the nation in which enforcement is taking place. (Articles 23, 28). Recognition and enforcement may be denied if jurisdiction was not taken or, in transnational foster care placements, appropriate procedures were not followed according to the standards of the Convention. (Articles 23, 33). Recognition and enforcement may also be refused if the opportunity to be heard was denied in the proceeding in which the order was made, or if a later-issued incompatible order is entitled to recognition. (Article 23). Such provisions are similar to corresponding provisions of the UCCJA/UCCJEA.

In addition, recognition and enforcement may be denied if it would be "manifestly contrary to public policy of the requested state, taking into account the best interests of the child." (Article 23). While narrow in its application, this ground could still be interpreted more broadly than the corresponding provision of the UCCJEA refusing enforcement if the issuing nation's law "violates fundamental principles of human rights." Recognition and enforcement can also be denied if the child was "not provided the opportunity to be heard, in violation of the fundamental principles of procedure" of the nation in which enforcement is requested. (Article 23).

Notes and Problems

1. *Compatibility with the UCCJA/UCCJEA.* Though the 1996 Hague Protection Convention and the UCCJA or UCCJEA would produce similar results in many situations, they are not identical in their language or application. Ratification of the 1996 Convention by the United States would thus require either that implementing federal legislation itself impose the standards of the Convention, which would supercede state law by virtue of the Supremacy Clause, or that implementing legislation require states to amend their UCCJA or UCCJEA statutes, as they apply in international custody cases, to conform to the 1996 Convention. To assess whether this is desirable, read Articles 5, 7, 10, 13, 14, 23, 25, and 26 of the 1996 Hague Protection Convention in your Supplement, consider the differences highlighted in the above discussion of the 1996 Convention, and consider the following problems.

Problem 8-16. You are the state judge before whom Ms. Wojcik has brought her action seeking custody after the federal judge has denied her husband's petition for return under the Hague Abduction Convention in *Wojcik v. Wojcik*, in Section A. of this Chapter.

(a) Assume first that Mr. Wojcik never filed a custody proceeding in France. He now appears in your court and challenges the court's subject matter jurisdiction to adjudicate custody. How should you rule under the UCCJA, the UCCJEA, and the 1996 Hague Protection Convention, if both nations were contracting parties to it?

(b) Assume instead that Mr. Wojcik has in fact obtained the French order awarding him residential custody, and has taken the appropriate steps to register it in your court. He is both challenging the subject matter jurisdiction of your court to modify this order and seeking enforcement of the French court's order. How should you rule under the UCCJA, the UCCJEA, and the 1996 Hague Protection Convention, if both nations were contracting parties to it?

Problem 8-17. Kiki, a French citizen, and Nathan, a U.S. citizen, married in Switzerland and resided in the United States for fifteen years, where they have raised their son, Fritz. When Fritz was eleven, Kiki and Nathan separated. They initially agreed that Fritz could return with Kiki to France to live with his mother during the school terms, and that he would spend all school vacations with his father in Vermont, where he had grown up. After several months in France, however, Fritz and Nathan were both unhappy, and Fritz repeatedly asked to move back. Kiki disagreed. Four months after Fritz and Kiki's move to France, Nathan filed an action in Vermont for divorce, seeking joint legal custody and placement of physical custody with him for the school year. Kiki was properly served, but chose not to enter an appearance. Two months after Nathan filed in Vermont, Kiki filed a custody proceeding in France. Assume the French court determined that Fritz was habitually resident in France.

(a) What steps would the respective courts take to resolve the simultaneous proceedings issue, and what might be the likely outcome, under the UCCJEA? Under the 1996 Hague Protection Convention, if both nations were contracting parties to it?

(b) Assume that Vermont found that it could validly exercise jurisdiction under the UCCJEA, and entered judgement awarding joint custody, with residential custody to Nathan during the school year. Would France be required to enforce the judgment under the 1996 Hague Protection Convention, if both nations were contracting parties to it?

Problem 8-19. Marie and Franz, Czech citizens, were married in Paris and resided in Prague. During their marriage, Marie was frequently subjected to assaults by Franz, which hospitalized her twice. By the time their daughter, Claire, was four years old, she was becoming the target of abuse as well, causing severe bruising and a sprained wrist. Although Marie separated from Franz and obtained a protective order, Franz continued to come to her house and threaten her. When Claire was five years old, Marie brought Claire to the United States to live near Marie's sister. Franz knew only that they were living in Illinois. After a year, he located them and filed a petition for return under the Hague Abduction Convention. In the meantime, he had obtained a divorce and order awarding him custody in the Czech Republic, following service on Marie through her sister. The Illinois state court refused to order Claire's return under the Hague Abduction Convention, finding there is grave risk of harm.

Marie then filed an action seeking divorce and custody in Illinois. Assume both the United States and the Czech Republic are parties to the 1996 Hague Protection Convention. At a subsequent hearing on Franz' motions to dismiss Marie's custody proceeding for lack of jurisdiction and to enforce his custody order, which was entered eighteen months after Claire moved to Illinois and four months after Franz discovered her whereabouts, how should the Illinois court rule?

2. For a more detailed explanation of the 1996 Hague Protection Convention, see Prof. Silberman's excellent article, *The 1996 Hague Convention on the Protection of Children: Should the United States Join?*, *supra*. Additional helpful sources include: Paul Legarde, *Explanatory Report*, in Hague Conference on Private International Law, Pro-

ceedings of the Eighteenth Session, Tome II, 534 (1998), *available at* http://www. hcch.net/e/conventions/expl34e.html; Gloria Fogler Dehart, *The Relationship Between the 1980 Child Abduction Convention and the 1996 Protection Convention*, 33 N.Y.U. J. Int'l L. & Pol. 83 (2000); Peter Nygh, *The Hague Convention on the Protection of Children*, XLV Neth. Int'l L. Rev.1 (1998).

For a detailed analysis of the potential impact of the 1996 Hague Protection Convention on victims of domestic violence, see Merle Weiner, *International Child Abduction and Escape from Domestic Violence*, 69 Fordham L. Rev. 593, 682–92 (2000).

c. *Regional Conventions, Regulations, and Proposals*

In addition to conventions negotiated between nations directly (such as the Nordic Convention of 6 February 1931 between Denmark, Finland, Iceland, Norway and Sweden), several conventions related to jurisdiction and enforcement of custody and visitation orders have been adopted, converted to regional legislation, or are under consideration by regional intergovernmental organizations.

i. *Inter-American Convention on the International Return of Children*

The Inter-American Convention on the International Return of Children, July 15, 1989, O.A.S. T.S. No. 70, 29 I.L.M. 63, drafted under the auspices of the Organization of American States, operates similarly to the Hague Abduction Convention, in that its primary focus is the return of a child wrongfully removed or retained in breach of custody rights. As of March 2003, Mexico and nine Central and South American countries were parties to this Convention. Since the Convention's focus is to achieve the return of a child to the child's country of habitual residence, it can facilitate enforcement of an order that has awarded custody to a parent located in that country. Article 21 of the Inter-American Convention on the International Return of Children also permits a person with visitation rights to use the same procedures that would govern a request for a child's return, and thus could potentially provide more effective enforcement of foreign visitation orders than does the Hague Abduction Convention. Article 16 of the Inter-American Convention requires a stay of custody proceedings during the pendency of a petition for return, modeled after the Hague Abduction Convention's similar provision. Aside from Article 16, however, the Inter-American Convention, like the Hague Abduction Convention, is not in essence a convention addressing jurisdictional standards for custody proceedings, nor does it create broad guidelines for the enforcement of foreign custody orders.

ii. *European Union Regulations*

The European Union, on the other hand, has embraced the task of creating explicit jurisdictional standards for custody proceedings and promoting mutual recognition and enforcement of custody and access orders throughout the Union. In May 2000 the Council of the European Union took the first step towards this goal by adopting Council Regulation No. 1347/2000, 2000 O.J. (L. 160) 19, which establishes standards for the exercise of custody jurisdiction in certain proceedings and procedures for enforcement. During May 2002, two additional proposals that had previously been under consideration, a French Initiative to adopt a Council Regulation on Mutual Enforcement of Judgments regarding Rights of Access, and a September 2001 proposal by the European Commission to adopt a Council Regulation on Jurisdiction and the Recognition and Enforcement of Judgments in Matters of Parental Responsibility, were consolidated into a new European Commission Proposal for a Council Regulation Concerning Jurisdiction and the Recognition and Enforcement of Judgments in Matrimonial Matters and in Matters of Parental Responsibility. COM (2002) 222 final/2. If this 2002 Proposal is ultimately adopted, it would repeal Council Regulation No. 1347/2000 and incorporate its provisions into the new Regulation, while at the same time expanding the scope of proceedings covered and simplifying enforcement of access orders.

(a) Council Regulation No. 1347/2000 of the European Union—"Brussels II"

Regulation No. 1347/2000 legislates standards for jurisdiction and enforcement of custody orders issued as part of a judgment rendered in divorce, legal separation, and annulment proceedings. Initially, the Council of the European Union set forth these standards in the Convention on Jurisdiction and the Recognition and Enforcement of Judgments in Matrimonial Matters, 1998 O.J. (C. 221) 2, which was signed by representatives of the member states on May 28, 1998. The Convention became known as "Brussels II," because it was inspired by the Convention on Jurisdiction and the Enforcement of Judgments in Civil and Commercial Matters 1968 (Brussels Convention), which excluded matters of status from its coverage. However, before the Brussels II Convention could be ratified and enter into force, the Council decided to incorporate the terms of the Convention into Council Regulation No. 1347/2000, which entered into force on March 1, 2001. The Council Regulation, which will in all likelihood continue to be referred to as "Brussels II," thus became binding law on that date in the courts of all of the member states of the European Union except Denmark, which exercised its right to decline to participate created under a Protocol annexed to the Treaty on European Union.

Council Regulation 1347/2000 has a limited scope. It applies to proceedings relating to parental responsibility that: (a) are brought in conjunction with a divorce, legal separation, or annulment proceeding, (b) between both of the child's parents, (c) in the courts of a country, other than Denmark, that is a member of the European Union ("member states"). Thus, the court must satisfy the Regulation's jurisdictional standards for divorce, annulment, and legal separation proceedings, which focus on the habitual residence, nationality, or, in the United Kingdom and Ireland, domicile of the parents. Post-judgment custody modification proceedings are not covered by this Regulation, because jurisdiction under the Regulation over matters relating to parental responsibility end as soon as a final judgment regarding the divorce, separation, or annulment is issued or the proceedings otherwise end. If parental responsibility matters are still pending on that date, jurisdiction ends on the date of a final judgment in or termination of the parental responsibility proceedings. The Regulation has no application to custody proceedings involving stepchildren or non-marital children. "Parental responsibility" is not defined in the regulation itself, leaving its interpretation open, but would seem to include the decisions regarding custody typically made by American courts in the context of divorce, separation, or annulment proceedings.

The Regulation permits courts of member states that are exercising jurisdiction over divorce, legal separation, or annulment proceedings to additionally exercise jurisdiction over matters relating to parental responsibility for the couple's child if either of the following criteria are met:

(1) the child is habitually resident in the member state; or

(2) at least one of the spouses has parental responsibility in relation to the child, both spouses agree that the court may exercise jurisdiction, and the jurisdiction of the court is in the best interest of the child.

When proceedings are pending before courts of different member states, the Regulation creates a first-in-time rule (Article 11), prioritizing the first action seized. When proceedings are "seized" for purposes of this regulation is determined by the domestic laws of the forum courts. In civil law countries, generally courts are "seized" when a defendant is served, whereas in common law countries filing with the court typically causes a court to be deemed "seized." Geoffrey Shannon, *Jurisdictional and Recognition and Enforcement Issues in Proceedings Concerning Parental Responsibility under the Brussels II Convention*, 2000 Int'l Fam. L. 111, 113.

Judgments relating to parental responsibility issued pursuant to the terms of the Regulation must be recognized and enforced in other member states. However, the Regulation creates several exceptions to its recognition and enforcement requirements. Some of these are similar to the grounds American courts use to refuse recognition or enforcement of foreign custody orders, such as failure to provide proper notice or opportunity to be heard to one of the parents, or issuance of a later custody order entitled to recognition. Also similar to the practice of many American courts is a provision that permits a court to refuse recognition and enforcement if a judgment is "manifestly contrary to the public policy of the Member State in which recognition is sought taking into account the best interests of the child." (Article 15). In addition, recognition and enforcement can be denied if, absent an emergency, the judgement was rendered "without the child having been given an opportunity to be heard, in violation of fundamental principles of procedure of the Member State in which recognition is sought." *Id.* Although American courts often afford children over a certain age the opportunity to express their views, and in particularly complex cases will appoint an attorney or guardian ad litem for a child in a divorce action, failure to provide a child with the opportunity to be heard is not a ground for nonrecognition under either the UCCJA or the UCCJEA.

Notes

1. Do you think American legislatures should consider adding a provision to their states' versions of the UCCJA or UCCJEA permitting nonrecognition of a custody order entered in a proceeding in which the child had no opportunity to be heard?

2. For more detailed information about the application of the E.U. Council Regulation in custody proceedings, see Geoffrey Shannon's excellent article, cited in the above text. In addition, the following articles on the Regulation and the "Brusssels II" Convention are also of interest: David Truex, *Brussels II—It's Here*, 2001 Int'l Fam. L. 7; Nicholas Mostyn, *Brussels II Regulation: Impact on Forum Disputes in Relation to the Main Suit and Ancillary Relief Proceedings*, 2000 Int'l Fam. L. 162. *See also* Alegria Borras, Explanatory Report on the Convention on Jurisdiction and the Recognition and Enforcement of Judgments in Matrimonial Matters (approved by the European Council on May 28, 1998), Document No.498Y0716(03), *available at* http://www. europa.eu.int/ eur-lex/en/lif/dat/1998/en_498Y0716_03.html; European Union, *Judicial Cooperation in*

Civil Matters: Jurisdiction, Recognition and Enforcement of Judgments in Matrimonial Matters, http://europa.eu.int/scadplus/leg/en/lvb/l33082.htm.

(b) Proposal for a Council Regulation Concerning Jurisdiction and the Recognition and Enforcement of Judgments in Matrimonial Matters and in Matters of Parental Responsibility

The regulation proposed in 2002 would create a single instrument that would address jurisdiction over both divorce and parental responsibility proceedings. Parental responsibility is defined in Article 2 of the proposed regulation as the "rights and duties given to a natural or legal person by judgment, by operation of law or by an agreement having legal effect and relating to the person or the property of the child," including rights of custody and access. The regulation does not apply to child support matters, which are governed by Council Regulation No. 44/2001, 2001 O.J. (L. 012) 1 (discussed in Chapter 10, Section D.3.b.).

The Proposal, if adopted, would not apply to Denmark. It is anticipated that it would apply to all other member states, including Ireland and the United Kingdom, since they did not choose to opt out of Council Regulation No. 1347/2000, and have indicated they wished to take part in the French Initiative and the 2001 regulation proposed by the Commission. European Commission, *Explanatory Memorandum,* in Proposal for a Council Regulation, COM (2002) 222 final/2, *available at* http://europa. eu.int/eur-lex/en/search/search_lip.html.

Regarding custody and visitation proceedings, the proposed regulation would serve three objectives:

1) the establishment of jurisdictional rules and the extension of mutual recognition to all decisions on parental responsibility;

2) the facilitation of recognition and enforcement of access rights; and

3) the imposition of additional duties upon member states to return abducted children, which build upon the Hague Abduction Convention remedies, and permit Member States to take only provisional protective measures not to return a child. *Id.*

Under the proposed regulation, courts of E.U. member states could exercise jurisdiction over all matters of parental responsibility over a child who is habitually resident in the Member State at the time the court is seized. (Article 10). A court is seized when the document instituting the proceeding is lodged with the court, provided service is subsequently made; or, if the court requires service prior to filing, then when the document is received by the authority responsible for service, providing filing subsequently occurs. (Article 16). Several exceptions exist to this general jurisdictional basis, however. A court that issued a judgment in accordance with Article 10 has continuing jurisdiction over any matter seized in that court within six months after the child changes residence, if one of the holders of parental responsibility continues to reside in the country of the child's former residence. (Article 11). As under Council Regulation 1347/2000, a court exercising jurisdiction over a divorce, separation, or annulment proceeding may exercise jurisdiction over parental responsibility issues if both spouses agree, the child is habitually resident in an E.U. member state, and at least one of the spouses has parental responsibility in relation to the child. (Article 12). A court may also exercise jurisdiction by agreement of the parties if it would be in the child's best interests and the child has a substantial connection with the forum country, which might occur if, for example, the child is a national of the forum country or one of the holders of parental responsibility is habitually resident there. (Article 12). If a child's habitual residence cannot be established or the child is a refugee and no Member State has jurisdiction on the above bases, jurisdiction may be based on the child's presence. If no member state has jurisdiction under any of these bases, courts may then determine jurisdiction by their domestic law. (Article 14). As under the UCCJEA, a court may also issue a temporary emergency order even when another country has permanent jurisdiction. (Article 20).

Transfer to another court is permitted to serve the child's best interests, if the other court was the child's former habitual residence or place of nationality, the habitual residence of a holder of parental responsibility, or the location of property of the child; but even if one of those criteria are satisfied, transfer may only occur in exceptional circumstances, and only if the receiving court accepts jurisdiction within a month from the time it is seized. (Article 15). As under Regulation 1347/2000, when proceedings are pending before the courts of different states, the first action seized has priority. (Article 19).

The provisions of the proposed regulation regarding recognition and enforcement of parental responsibility judgments, authentic instruments, and court-approved settlements are taken from Council Regulation No. 1347/2000, described above, and simply renumbered and reproduced in the proposed new regulation. (Articles 26–44). Explanatory Memorandum, *supra*, at Section 3, Chapter IV.

Building on the earlier French Initiative, the proposed regulation simplifies enforcement of parental visitation (access) rights by abolishing *exequator,* i.e., procedures for registration or declaration of enforceability. Member nations are required to enforce a parental access order as long as the court that issued the order certifies it on a standard form that states that the judgement was not given by default in appearance and that the child, if of appropriate age and maturity, was given an opportunity to be heard. Enforcement procedures are governed by the domestic law of the enforcing nation, which is also given the authority to make practical arrangements for the visitation to the extent that such arrangements have not been included in and are not in conflict with the original judgment. (Articles 45–54).

To meet its third goal of further deterring child abduction, the 2002 proposed regulation creates specific jurisdiction and enforcement provisions applicable when a child has been abducted from one E.U. member nation to another member nation. Responding to the concern that both the 1980 Hague Child Abduction Convention and the 1996 Hague Convention for the Protection of Children under certain circumstances permit the transfer of jurisdiction to a nation to which a child has been abducted once that nation's courts have decided not to return the child, the 2002 proposed amendment would impose for E.U. member nations more stringent jurisdictional rules in abduction cases than either Hague Convention mandates.

Under the proposed regulation, the courts of the member nation in which the child was habitually resident immediately prior to the wrongful removal or retention (home country) will retain jurisdiction over parental responsibility matters. Jurisdiction to issue a custody order cannot shift to the nation to which the child has been abducted unless (1) each holder of custody rights acquiesces in the removal or retention, (2) the holder of custody rights files no application for return within a year of learning the child's location, or (3) a court in the home country effectively yields jurisdiction, as described below. (Article 21).

When the legal custodian applies to the Central Authority of the member nation to which a child has been abducted (requested country), that nation must return the child within one month of locating the child, unless proceedings have been instituted in that nation for provisional protective measures. Provisional protective measures may be ordered in the requested country only upon a showing of grave risk or the child's objection to return, defenses you are familiar with from your study of the Hague Abduction Convention in Section A of this Chapter. However, under the proposed regulation, the order may only be provisional, and the Central Authority must inform the Central Authority of the home country within two weeks of the issuance of the protective measures. The home country's Central Authority is then required within one month of receiving the information to apply to its own courts for a decision on custody, although the regulation does not prevent the holder of legal custody from also applying to those courts for the same purpose. If the home country's court orders the return of the child, that order must be enforced in the member nation in which the child is located, without requiring *exequator* or any special procedures for enforcement, and notwithstanding any appeal that may be filed. (Articles 22–24). Only if the home country's court enters a judgment that does not entail the return of the child, or issues no judgment within a year after that court has been seized, can the court of the nation to which the child has been abducted acquire jurisdiction to enter a permanent custody order. (Article 21).

Notes and Questions

1. *Interaction with Hague and other Regional Conventions.* If adopted, the 2002 proposed regulation would take precedence over the Hague Abduction Convention, the 1996 Hague Convention on Jurisdiction, and the Council of Europe Convention on Recognition and Enforcement of Decisions Concerning Custody of Children, (*see* Section B.2.c.iii. *infra*) for relations between member nations of the E.U., except Denmark. (Article 61).

2. *Debilitation of Grave Risk and Child's Objection Defenses.* The provisions in the 2002 proposal regarding child abduction are similar to those contained in the earlier 2001 proposal of the European Commission, which have generated some controversy. The earlier proposal had been criticized for weakening the application of the Hague Abduction Convention's Article 13(b) defenses by permitting them to be used only as grounds to delay return through provisional protective measures, and not, in most cases, as grounds upon which a requested nation may refuse return altogether. Proponents argue the rate of judicial refusal to return children from some E.U. member nations is high, and adoption of the proposal would deter abduction and encourage custodial parents to permit access. For articles setting forth these opposing views on the merits of the similar provisions in the 2001 proposed regulation, *see* Nigel Lowe, *Article 5(3) of the Draft EU Regulation on Parental Responsibility—Dealing with Child Abduction,* 2002 Int'l Fam. L. 36; Ian Karsten, *Article 5(3) of the Draft EU Regulation on Parental Responsibility—A Reply,* 2002 Int'l. Fam. L. 42. Do you think the approach of the proposed 2002 regulation to child abduction is preferable to that of the Hague Abduction Convention?

iii. *Council of Europe Convention on Recognition and Enforcement of Decisions Concerning Custody of Children and on Restoration of Custody of Children*

The European Convention on Recognition and Enforcement of Decisions Concerning Custody of Children and on Restoration of Custody of Children, May 20, 1980, Europ. T.S. No. 105, sometimes referred to as the "Luxembourg Convention," was drafted through the Council of Europe. As of March 2003, 29 members of the Council and one non-member nation, Serbia and Montenegro, were parties to the Convention. Because the Luxembourg Convention applies to European nations that are not members of the European Union, and because it apples to any custody order, and not just those issued in conjunction with divorce, separation, or annulment proceedings, the Luxembourg Convention will require enforcement of many orders not currently covered by the "Brussels II" regulation.

The Convention reflects in its full title its dual objectives. First, it operates similarly to the Hague Convention on Child Abduction, in that it provides for proceedings to obtain the automatic return of children improperly removed or retained. The circumstances under which a right of return is available under the Luxembourg Convention are, however, far narrower than under the Hague Convention on Child Abduction, a topic explored in Note 8 following *Croll* in Section A of this Chapter.

The second objective of the Luxembourg Convention is to secure the recognition and enforcement of custody and visitation orders. To that end, the Convention provides that custody and access decisions issued in a contracting state must be recognized and enforceable in every other contracting state, to the same extent that they would be enforceable in the nation that issued them. (Article 7). Unfortunately, the Convention includes a complex and extensive list of grounds on which recognition and enforcement may be denied.

Some of these grounds are comparable to those utilized in the UCCJA or UCCJEA. For example, lack of proper notice to defendant, if the custody order was taken by default judgment, constitutes a defense to recognition and enforcement. (Article 9). Incompatibility with another custody order rendered or enforceable in the recognizing country, under certain circumstances, would also preclude recognition and enforcement. (Articles 9, 10). When the judgment is rendered in the absence of the defendant, failure of the rendering court to exercise subject matter jurisdiction on specified grounds will render it unenforceable. The grounds set forth as sufficient bases for jurisdiction are: 1) the habitual residence of the defendant; 2) the last common habitual residence of the parents, if one still habitually resides there; or 3) the habitual residence of the child. (Article 9). Moreover, as long as no improper removal has occurred, any custody order can be denied recognition and enforcement, even if the rendering court satisfied one of those bases, and whether or not it was rendered by default, if at the time the proceedings that produced the order were initiated: 1) the child was a national or habitual resident of the recognizing nation and was not a national or habitual resident of the nation that issued the order; or 2) the child was a dual national of both the issuing and recognizing nations and was a habitual resident of the recognizing nation. (Article 10). By reservation, a state party can choose to make this final defense applicable even in situations in which an improper removal has occurred. (Article 17).

Several grounds would allow even broader examination of the substantive merits of custody and access than either the UCCJA or UCCJEA would generally permit. Recognition and enforcement can be denied to an order that is "manifestly incompatible" with the recognizing country's fundamental family and child law principles. (Article 10). The

Convention also permits a country being asked to enforce an order to consider whether a change of circumstances (other than a mere residence change subsequent to an improper removal) has occurred since issuance of the order such that it is "manifestly" no longer in the child's best interests. (Article 10). Although generally these provisions are inapplicable when an improper removal has occurred, by reservation a nation can choose to make them applicable even to cases involving improper removals, both in recognition and enforcement requests to its own courts, as well as in any other contracting nations asked to recognize the orders of the nation making the reservation. (Article 17). Finally, the Convention permits authorities in countries being asked to enforce visitation orders to create conditions for the implementation and exercise of visitation rights. (Article 11).

Notes and Questions

1. *Comparison of Jurisdictional Standards.* Although the Luxembourg Convention does not mandate jurisdictional standards, it indirectly influences jurisdictional choices by requiring enforcement of default judgments only when certain bases for jurisdiction existed. See Article 9 of the Convention in your Supplement. Do these bases indicate a different jurisdictional philosophy than that employed by the UCCJA and UCCJEA regarding the type of connections to the forum state that should be fostered? Read Article 10(1)(c). Does this basis for refusal of recognition and enforcement temper the choices made in Article 9? Would nationality be an appropriate criteria to incorporate into the standards for jurisdiction and/or enforcement in international custody disputes under the UCCJA or UCCJEA, and if so, should it be employed in the same manner?

2. *Advantages and Implementation.* Commentators have observed that although the Luxembourg Convention is less effective than the Hague Convention on Child Abduction at addressing wrongful removal and retention, it can be useful in situations in which the Hague Convention is not in effect or not applicable, particularly in regard to its provision in Article 5(3) affording applicants under the Convention free legal assistance. Paul Beaumont & Peter McEleavy, The Hague Convention on International Child Abduction 224 (1999). For further discussion of the scope of the European Convention on Recognition and Enforcement in general, and its implementation in Germany, *see* Karen Wolf, *A Tale of Two States: Successes and Failures of the 1980 Hague Convention on the Civil Aspects of International Child Abduction in the United States and Germany,* 33 N.Y.U. J. Int'l L. & Pol. 285, 309–23 (2000).

3. *Convention on Contact Concerning Children.* In the past, given the limitations of assistance available under the Hague Convention on Child Abduction for denial of visitation, the Luxembourg Convention has been viewed as a more attractive alternative for enforcement of access orders for parents in contracting states. Beaumont, *supra,* at 224. On May 3, 2002, however, the Committee of Ministers of the Council of Europe adopted the text of a draft Convention on Contact Concerning Children, *available at* http://conventions.coe.int/Treaty/EN/cadreprojects.htm. In addition to recognizing the substantive right of a child and his or her parents to maintain regular contact, (Article 4), and acknowledging that contact orders may be made in favor of non-parents as well, (Article 5), the Convention would require member nations to take "all appropriate measures to ensure that contact orders are carried into effect," (Article 9), and to incorporate into their internal law at least three safeguards and guarantees, which a court could incorporate into a contact order as a matter of discretion for the purpose of ensuring the order is carried into effect and that the child is properly returned at the end of the access period. Such safeguards and guarantees could include, *inter alia*, supervised visitation; the impo-

sition of a security deposit or other financial guarantees upon either the custodial parent or the parent exercising contact; undertakings; surrender of passports; requiring the person exercising contact to regularly present himself or herself and the child to a governmental authority in the location where contact is occurring, or to obtain an order recognizing the enforceability of the custody order in the jurisdiction in which contact is to occur; and the imposition of travel restrictions or other conditions. (Article 10).

Enforcement of contact orders would be facilitated by Central Authorities appointed under the Convention, which could assist with the transmission of information across borders between governmental entities, and particularly between judicial authorities; investigate the whereabouts of missing children; and assist children, parents, and other family members with institution of proceedings regarding transnational contact. (Articles 11–13). Rather than imposing specific mandates for recognition and enforcement, however, the Convention requires states parties to provide a system for recognition and enforcement of foreign custody and contact orders, as well as procedures for obtaining advance orders of recognition and declarations of enforceability prior to contact. (Article 14). It permits judicial authorities of the country in which contact is to occur to create conditions for implementation of foreign contact orders. (Article 15). If a child is not returned, it requires governmental authorities to ensure the child's immediate return by applying relevant international instruments and domestic law, and to make a decision on an application for return within six weeks of the application. (Article 16).

iv. *European Convention for the Protection of Human Rights and Fundamental Freedoms*

Although the European Convention on Human Rights does not specifically address the enforcement of custody or access orders, the duty in Article 8 to protect an individual's right to respect private and family life has successfully been invoked as the basis of a claim against a contracting state for failure to take sufficient steps to execute a foreign custody order. The European Court of Human Rights, in *Ignaccolo-Zenide v. Romania*, 2000-I Eur. Ct. H.R. 241, awarded non-pecuniary damages of 100,000 French francs (between $12,000 and $14,000) and costs of 86,000 French francs (approximately $12,000) against the government of Romania for: (1) its failure over the course of two years to execute the return order of a Romanian court in a Hague Abduction Convention proceeding, after the father thwarted initial attempts; (2) its failure to punish the father for his failure to present the children; and (3) its failure to utilize social services to prepare the children for reunion with their mother.

The father in this case was initially awarded custody in France of two young daughters, pursuant to the parents' agreement. When he moved to the United States in 1990 and denied the mother her summer visitation, she brought proceedings in France which ultimately produced an order changing residential custody to her. After U.S. courts ruled that this order must be enforced, following a series of proceedings in two states, *Zenide v. Superior Court*, 27 Cal. Rptr. 2d 703 (Cal. Ct. App. 1994), the father moved the children to Romania and refused to produce the two children to Romanian authorities for two years. Throughout this time, however, his residence, place of employment, and the children's school was known to the authorities. The children, who barely remembered their mother, adamantly refused to live with her. Although a home study reported that the girls were happily living in a loving home and were strongly attached to their father and stepmother, a Romanian Family Court judge also found that the father had taught them to hate their mother and denied them all contact with her. When the girls rejected the mother in their first meeting with her in seven years, in a room full of government officials, Romania's Central Authority then determined that it would deny return on the grounds of the children's objection.

Note

1. Reflecting the dilemma faced by courts in long-standing abduction cases, the one dissenting judge in the 6–1 vote of the European Court of Human Rights in *Ignaccolo-Zenide* observed:

> ... [Children] are and should be the first beneficiaries [of Article 8] where the interests of their parents are in conflict and they are mature enough to express clearly their own preferences.... It is clear from the case file that the children have been living for a long time with their father. From the standpoint of the best interests of the child, it is not of decisive importance under what circumstances that came about or what role in that situation was played by each of their parents or by the public authorities. It is also clear that the children in the instant case expressly preferred to live with their father; and their preference must have been taken into account. I much regret that this circumstance was disregarded both in the domestic and in the foreign judicial proceedings, and enforcing an old judicial decision against the will of those who were the subjects of that decision comes close to doing violence. 2000-I Eur. Ct. H.R. at 273.

Do you agree or disagree with her assessment? If so, does it address the question of whether Romania fulfilled its obligations, under either the Hague Convention on Child Abduction or the European Convention on Human Rights? Is it appropriate to use a broader, human rights convention to address matters that are addressed by more specific conventions in force between the particular nations involved regarding abduction, recognition, and enforcement? What are the benefits and risks of such an approach?

C. Other Remedies to Prevent or Respond to Abduction

Attorneys representing parents located in the United States who are concerned with preventing or responding to international abductions must consider a variety of legal responses. This section examines several preventative as well as punitive measures that are currently available to deter an abduction, locate an abducted child, facilitate return, and/or punish the abductors. Though these remedies can be utilized in connection with any potential or actual abduction, they are of particular importance when the destination is a nation that is not a state party to the Hague Convention on Abduction. Once a removal to a non-Hague contracting nation has been accomplished, however, the effectiveness of the post-abduction remedies examined herein, in comparison to return proceedings under the Hague Abduction Convention, is still quite limited.

Though a survey of remedies under foreign law available to left-behind parents is beyond the scope of this book, U.S. attorneys representing parents who have abducted children to the United States should be aware of the need to explore the existence of comparable remedies, and criminal sanctions in particular, that are often available under the laws of the country from which the child has been removed.

1. Preventative Measures and Immediate Deterrence

a. *Restricting Visitation*

Al-Silham v. Al-Silham

No. 93-A-1770, 1994 WL 102480 (Oh. Ct. App. Mar. 25, 1994)

Christley, P.J.

This is an appeal from a judgment of the Ashtabula County Court of Common Pleas. In this judgment, the court granted appellee, Lori J. Al-Silham, parental rights and responsibilities for the care of the minor child, Layla Al-Silham, and granted appellant, Reda Hassan Al-Silham, reasonable visitation rights to be exercised in Ashtabula County under the supervision of appellee or an adult approved by appellee. The court also ordered appellant to pay child support.

[Ed. Note: The appellate court summarized the history of the case, observing that the mother, a native of Ohio, met and married the father, a Saudi Arabian citizen, in Nashville, Tennessee, where the father was pursuing a masters degree. They lived together in Tennessee after the birth of their daughter in October 1990. The trial court found that during the marriage, the parties experienced a serious culture clash, and that the mother was subjected to physical and verbal abuse. When Layla was approximately one year old, the mother moved back to Ohio to live with her own mother and work in a day care, bringing Layla with her. The parties were divorced in April 1992. The father, who at the time of this appeal was a permanent resident of the United States, remained in Nashville. In awarding sole custody to the mother, the trial court considered that she had been the primary caregiver, and that shared parenting was not in the best interests of the child, given that the parties had not demonstrated the ability to cooperate or make decisions jointly, and that appellant, the father, had been dictatorial, controlling, and had "attempted to assert his authority in disregard of appellee's rights."]

* * *

The [trial] court also stated its concern over the potential for parental kidnapping by appellant. Evidence was presented at trial that, while appellant never directly threatened to remove the child to Saudi Arabia, he had threatened that appellee would lose her child if a divorce was granted. Further, there was evidence that appellant carried on his person a Saudi Arabian passport on which the child was designated, as well as a large amount of cash and a plane ticket to return to Saudi Arabia. Finally, the court considered evidence that no extradition treaties exist between the United States and Saudi Arabia; that the cultural differences between the Islamic religion and Christian religion are dramatic; and that there is no legal process to secure the return of a minor child once he or she is removed to Saudi Arabia.

The court determined that these facts required it to take extraordinary steps to ensure that the child would not be removed from the United States or the custody of appellee. Therefore, the court ordered that appellant be granted reasonable visitation rights, but under the supervision of appellee or an adult approved by appellee. The court noted that its visitation order was subject to modification in the future as the child grows older and circumstances unfold.

* * *

In his first assignment, appellant contends that the trial court committed prejudicial error by admitting into evidence four exhibits submitted by appellee, said exhibits being informational brochures or publications issued by the United States Department of State on the subjects of: marriage by United States citizens to Saudi Arabians; parental abduction cases in Saudi Arabia; Islamic family law; and international parental child abduction. Appellant argues that these publications were not admissible under any exception to the hearsay rule, and further, were never properly authenticated.

[Ed. Note: The appellate court determined that these exhibits were self-authenticating pamphlets from a government agency that did not require further authentication, but that they were inadmissible hearsay, failing to meet the public records and reports exception of Ohio Evid. Rule 803(8) (modeled after Fed. Rule Evid. 803(8)) because appellee failed to show the information contained therein "was the subject of a duty to report or that it was based on the first hand observation of the official making the report or of one with a duty to report to a government official.]

* * *

This court has great sympathy for the plight of the trial court, faced as it was with incredibly damning but inadmissible evidence. Nevertheless, appellant's arguments are well-taken that evidential rules can not be somehow subjected to a lesser standard simply because they are being applied to an emotionally disturbing situation.

Therefore, we find that the trial court erred in admitting these reports into evidence. Further, we conclude that this was prejudicial. Without this evidence, the trial court would have significantly less basis for its emphatically stated concern that appellant might remove Layla to Saudi Arabia, at which point there would be no legal process to secure her return to the United States. Further, this evidence was the express basis for the trial court's order that appellant's visitation rights be restricted by appellee's supervision.

It is clear, beyond the four exhibits at issue, that there was other evidence of the culture clash which justified awarding custody to the mother: she had been the primary caregiver since the birth of the child; appellant attempted to force the wife into the role of a subservient and isolated wife after the marriage with no hint of that expectation before the marriage; in disputes over child-rearing practices such as seatbelt usage, appellant ignored the best interests of the child; the inability of appellant to participate in joint decision making regarding the child.

While there was conflicting evidence as to much of the preceding, the trial court clearly found appellee's evidence to be more credible. We do not find such a determination to be against the manifest weight of the evidence.

It is the visitation issue which sustained the greatest impact from the admission of the four exhibits.

The question is whether the court would have come to the same conclusion without the four exhibits at issue. Put another way, if appellant were of another nationality and all the other admissible facts remained the same, would the visitation aspect of the decision have been less restrictive. We do not know, and, we hesitate to usurp the role of the trial court in this matter as it would clearly be a close call depending on the weight assigned to the evidence.

Accordingly, appellant's first assignment of error is well-taken in part, and this matter is remanded back to the trial court for reconsideration of the visitation issue.

* * *

In appellant's third assignment of error, he argues that the trial court's judgment deprived him of equal protection of the law, as the court impermissibly singled out fathers with Saudi Arabian citizenship in imposing its visitation restrictions.

Contrary to appellant's assertion, however, the trial court did not impose the visitation restrictions solely on the ground that appellant is a foreign national of the state of Saudi Arabia. Rather, the court had before it the previously recited evidence of cultural diversity, the threat of loss of the child, plus additional evidence that appellant seemed to be anticipating a hasty departure by carrying on his person his passport, which included the child, significant amounts of money, and a plane ticket to Saudi Arabia.

Thus, we do not find that the trial court denied appellant his constitutional rights under the equal protection clause of the United States Constitution or the Ohio Constitution.... Appellant's third assignment is without merit.

In light of our disposition of appellant's first assignment, we reverse and remand this matter back to the trial court in order for the court to reconsider its decision as to visitation absent the four exhibits.

Notes and Questions

1. *Constitutional Implications.* On the basis of the information presented above, and absent the four inadmissible exhibits, do you think the decision regarding supervised visitation would come out the same if the father were Irish?

The Ohio Court of Appeals rejected appellant's equal protection challenge in *Al-Silham* because "the trial court did not impose the visitation restrictions *solely* on the ground that appellant is a foreign national of the state of Saudi Arabia." (emphasis added). Was the father's nationality a constitutionally impermissible factor to consider? If so, isn't it significant for equal protection purposes if the court's analysis was *influenced* by a constitutionally impermissible factor? Would a court's fear of abduction and harm to the child be sufficient to impose restrictions on visitation even if the sole basis were the father's nationality and the increased probability that the father might abduct, given a greater rate of abductions by fathers of that nationality generally?

2. *Follow-up.* Following a hearing on remand at which additional testimony was introduced, the trial court reaffirmed its order of supervised visitation, which the father again appealed. In its decision reviewing this order, Al-Silham v. Al-Silham, No. 94-A-0048, 1995 WL 803808 (Ohio Ct. App. Nov. 24, 1995), the appellate court observed that supervised visitation is "inherently contrary to the stated intent of the visitation statute," because it is "a barrier between the free exchange of love and affection between parent and child." *Id.* at 5. Nevertheless, the appellate court declined to hold that the trial court's supervised visitation order was an abuse of discretion, finding that there was credible evidence to support the trial court's determination that appellant lacked the knowledge and experience to care for a small child and that he might abduct the child if he had the opportunity.

The father had visited for weekends fifteen times during the previous year and a half, and was permitted visits whenever he wished, but always in the company of several relatives or friends of the mother. The mother testified she had no doubt as to his love for his daughter, but that they had significant disagreements regarding her upbringing. He found car seats unnecessary and during the marriage had argued that the child could be left home alone if she was asleep.

At the time of the remand hearing, the father was not employed, had not taken classes for three years, and was, at the age of 36, still supported by his parents. He had no economic or personal ties to the U.S. other than the child. He had also had job interviews in Saudi Arabia, though he testified he had no desire to move back. The child was designated on his passport, which he kept with him at all times, and on one visit he had attempted to obtain a passport photo of Layla. His brother had returned to Saudi Arabia with his child after his divorce. Moreover, the father had repeatedly told the mother that "[she'd] be sorry" and that "[she'll] never see her baby again." He had also said Layla "would either be a Muslim or she would be a whore." He had also told the child that he would take her to see her grandparents in their country.

On the second appeal, the father again contended that the trial judge's decision resulted from racial and religious prejudice. The appellate court responded:

> The critical findings of the trial court were that: (1) appellant had little or no experience in caring for the needs and safety of a young child; (2) he had acted, in the past, in disregard of ordinary prudence in respect to the safety of the child; and (3) he had threatened abduction of the child, claiming she would be better off dead if she were not raised in his culture.

> Any parent, regardless of race or religion, who had exhibited the same behavior would undoubtedly be subjected to a similar restriction of supervised visitation, at least until such concerns were addressed to the satisfaction of the court. The needs and best interests of the child should always prevail over the needs and best interests of the parents.

The appellate court did emphasize, however, that the trial court's order limits supervision to one supervisor, and not the "entourage" that typically accompanied his visits.

b. Restricting or Intercepting Travel

Long v. Ardestani
624 N.W.2d 405 (Wisc. Ct. App. 2001)

Vergeront, J.

Lori Long appeals a trial court order denying her motion to prohibit her former husband, Mohammad Ardestani, from traveling to Iran with their minor children to visit his family. She contends the trial court erroneously exercised its discretion when it refused to grant a continuance to permit a key witness to testify, erred by placing the burden on her to prove that it was likely that Ardestani would not return with the children, and erred by failing to consider the best interests of the children. She and the guardian ad litem ask this court to rule, as a matter of law, that, if a parent objects to the other parent taking their children to visit a country with which the United States does not have diplomatic relations and which is not a signatory to the Hague Convention on the

Civil Aspects of International Child Abduction, the parent may not take the children to that country to visit.

We conclude the trial court did not erroneously exercise its discretion in refusing to grant a continuance; properly placed the burden on Long, as the moving party, to show that it was not in the children's best interests to travel to Iran with their father to visit his family; and properly considered the children's best interests in ruling on the motion. We decline to adopt the proposed ruling of law because we conclude that the existing standard of the best interests of the child, applied by trial courts in the exercise of their discretion, already allows for full consideration of all relevant concerns. Because the trial court properly exercised its discretion in its application of the best interests standard, we affirm.

BACKGROUND

Motion to Prohibit Travel

Ardestani was born in Iran and moved to the United States in 1978 when he was twenty-eight years old. He and Long were married in 1980 and have four children: Shiva, d/o/b 5/24/82; Maria, d/o/b 10/22/84; Farshaun, d/o/b 7/02/88; and Kamran, d/o/b 4/01/90. Pursuant to the stipulated judgment of divorce, entered on July 22, 1999, in Crawford County, the parties have joint legal custody of the four children. Long has primary physical placement, with Ardestani to have placement every other weekend, every Tuesday and Thursday from 3:00 p.m. to 7:00 p.m., three to six weeks in the summer depending on the children's wishes, and certain holidays. The judgment of divorce also provided, pursuant to the parties' stipulation, [that respondent give petitioner 60 days notice of his intention to take the children outside of the United States, in which case petitioner then has 30 days to move for an order prohibiting the trip or requiring respondent to post a bond.] ...

In November 1999 after Ardestani told Long he intended to take the minor children to Iran to visit, Long moved the court for an order prohibiting Ardestani from removing the minor children from the United States. She asserted as grounds for the motion that Ardestani had repeatedly stated his intentions to take the children to Iran with him and not allow them to return; that, as a woman who was not a Moslem and not a citizen of Iran, she would not have standing in an Iranian court to demand the return of the children; and her remedies under international law were severely limited because the United States does not have diplomatic relations with Iran.

At the May 5, 2000 hearing on the motion, Long, represented by counsel, presented two witnesses who testified on Iranian law as follows. Iran is not a signatory to the Hague Convention on the Civil Aspects of International Child Abduction (Hague Convention) and does not have diplomatic relations with the United States. Under Iranian law, which is based on the Koran, the mother's custody of children is restricted to the age of two for boys and seven for girls and, above those ages, the father has custody; the mother has no claim to custody. [There was testimony these ages varied in different parts of Iran.] If a mother has custody and physical placement of a child under an order of a court in the United States and the child is taken to Iran, the Iranian court does not give any weight to the United States court order, particularly if the mother is not a Moslem; if the father does not give permission to the child to leave Iran, the mother would not be permitted to take the child from Iran back to the United States. Boys need their father's permission to leave Iran up to a minimum age of eighteen, and girls need it regardless of age as long as they are unmarried. This would apply to Long's and Ardestani's children if they were in Iran, even though they are United States citizens and even though Ardestani is a United States citizen. Ardestani is still an Iranian citizen, the children are also Iranian citizens by virtue of their father's relation to Iran, and the children would be considered Iranian by Iranian authorities. If Ardestani were to die or become incapacitated or were not able to be contacted, his authority under Iranian law with regard to the children would transfer to the next male of authority within his family line.

Kristine Uhlman testified that a boy between the ages of twelve and fourteen can be drafted into the Iranian army, and this might interfere with a boy that age being able to leave Iran. According to Uhlman, Iranian families, in an effort to avoid having their boys drafted into the army, have sent them out of the country for education. She also testified that there is no existing legal mechanism that addresses the return of an abducted child if the child were taken to Iran. She agreed that, if Ardestani took the children to Iran, having the children returned would depend upon his good faith.

Long testified that she feared Ardestani would not return the children because, when she asked him for a divorce in May 1998 he said, "You know what will happen. And you haven't seen nothing yet." This meant to her that he would take the children to Iran and she would never see them, because in 1981 when she was pregnant with their first child and asked if she could have the child baptized, he made that threat explicitly saying, "If you don't raise them [sic] Moslem I will take the baby back to Iran and you'll never see it again." He also repeated that threat another time. Thereafter, during the course of their marriage when he wanted to control her he would say, "you know what will happen," and she understood he meant he would take the children and she would never see them. For this reason, when he said this in May 1998, she destroyed his American and Iranian passports and took other documents from his briefcase. During their marriage Ardestani also told her that men had sole custody of children in Iran and the mothers were never given custody. In 1997 he took the two girls, Shiva and Maria, for a visit to Iran, and when he came back he talked about some day moving to Iran: it was getting better, more open, he said. In the period just before the divorce, he said if they were divorced, he was going to leave. He has told her he "has to save face," and he wants revenge.

Long acknowledged that Ardestani took Farshaun to Iran in 1991, when he was three, and the two girls in 1997, and there was no problem with him bringing them back. She is aware that Kamran wants to go with his father to Iran. She would encourage Ardestani to bring his parents to the United States, she would help him do this, and she would give him more time with the children then.

Ardestani, representing himself, testified as follows. He moved to Prairie du Chien in 1981 and began employment at 3M. He is still employed there, now working as an operator, and has a pension plan. He denied that he ever told Long that if they got a divorce, he would take the children away. He described himself as a citizen of this country who lives and works here and helps the community. His brother and sister-in-law live here and own real estate as part of their business, and they have a child. He is trying to help his sister come here. He wants his children to see their grandparents, aunts, uncles, and cousins; his mother is ill and that is why he wants to take the children now, especially Kamran, who has not seen her. Ardestani stated he would like to take all the children, if they wanted to go, and he had four weeks of vacation time which he would like to spend there.

Ardestani testified that he would not separate his children from their mother or from this country. Ardestani agreed it would be devastating to the children if they were taken to Iran and not allowed to return. He will do whatever is necessary to guarantee that they will come back safely, including signing over his pension, and his brother would also come to court and guarantee. He, Ardestani, has his retirement and career here, ten years left to work, and he is not going to give them up.

...Ardestani explained that he has looked into bringing his parents to the United States. However, they would have to apply for a permanent residency and they do not want to live here because they are old. Also, he has to have a certain amount of income for each family member he wants to bring here, and he has only enough for one person. He talked about it with his family and they decided it made more sense to take the children to Iran so they could see the whole family, rather than bringing just one person here to see the children. In response to a question on the possibility of his parents meeting his children in a third country, Ardestani testified that his parents could not travel on their own to a third country; it would be too expensive; and he wants the children to see his culture, where he was born and where he lived. Farshaun was too young to remember and Kamran has never been there.

The therapist who had been meeting with Farshaun and Kamran since November 1999 also testified. (She had also met with Ardestani and with Long.) The boys' concern about their father's expressions of anger had been alleviated for a number of reasons, they were doing well, and they probably needed no more counseling except a session for closure. She had discussed a possible trip to Iran with them. Kamran was excited to go; Farshaun said he did not know if he wanted to be gone that long from his friends and activities, which the therapist described as a typical reaction for an eleven year old. The boys told her that some people believe their father would not bring them back, but Kamran said if something happened and they could not get back with their father, he believed their uncle, who lives in Prairie du Chien, would come to get them. Both boys are close to their uncle.

The therapist testified that she has no reason to believe that Ardestani would want to separate the children from their mother. Her view was that Ardestani has the ability now to concentrate on what is best for his children and to set aside the feelings he had about their mother and the divorce. The therapist's concern, she explained, is what would happen if a tragedy occurred in Iran, given that it has no diplomatic relations with the United States. However, because Ardestani has a brother here, and four younger siblings in Iran, there would probably be family who would help the children come back to their mother. She agreed that it would be emotionally devastating to the children if their relationship with their mother were severed because Ardestani decided to keep them in Iran.

After the evidence, the guardian ad litem recommended that the children and Ardestani be accompanied to Iran by a trusted adult male relative, preferably their uncle who lives in Prairie du Chien, and that the trip be limited to three weeks.

The court first decided that because Shiva was soon to be eighteen, it was up to her if she wanted to go with her father to Iran: the court would neither require nor prohibit that. The court then ruled that the burden was on Long, the moving party, to show that Ardestani should be prohibited from taking the other children to Iran.... The court found that Long really was afraid that Ardestani might keep the children in Iran, and she was not acting to harm or get even with Ardestani. However, the court decided that in order for Long to prevail on her motion, she had to do more than show she had a genuine fear that Ardestani would keep the children in Iran and that the harm if he did keep them, because of her lack of recourse, would be great. The court identified the critical question as the likelihood that Ardestani would keep the children in Iran....

The court described Ardestani's statements that were the basis for Long's fears as "not very specific in recent years," and as generally concerning his authority as the father and husband. The court found that much of Ardestani's conduct and statements upon which Long's belief was based were part of the culture from Iran that Ardestani still carried with him, and were not evidence he was going to take the children from their mother. Against that conduct and statements, the court weighed Ardestani's statements made "numerous times" that he has no intention of fleeing the country with the children and no motive to do so. The court also referred to psychological evaluations of Ardestani, which did not provide a basis for concerns about his personality or psychology in relation to the issue before the court, and to the therapist's testimony that she did not have a concern that Ardestani would try to keep the children from their mother. For these reasons, the court determined Long had not proved there was a likelihood Ardestani would not return the children. However, the court did permit Long to exercise some type of control over Ardestani's pension, if she chose.

The written order entered by the court on May 22, 2000, denied Long's motion and directed that, upon her request, Ardestani was to provide and sign all documents with respect to his pension and retirement benefits necessary to provide Long with security to insure the return of the children.

. . .

Motion for Reconsideration

[Ed. Note: Long appealed the order and requested a stay, arguing that the trial court had not considered the evidence of the likelihood of conscription into the Iranian army. The guardian ad litem informed the appellate court that based on this information, which he did not recall from the earlier hearing, he changed his recommendation and opposed the visit. The case was remanded for the trial court to hear a motion for reconsideration on this issue.]

* * *

At the June 23, 2000 hearing on remand, Ardestani, still proceeding pro se, presented testimony by telephone from K. Alipour. Alipour testified he was in charge of legal affairs of the Iranian Interests Section in the Pakistani Embassy. He was born and raised in Iran and served in the Iran military. According to the Iranian law and constitution, Iranian male citizens are eligible for the draft at age eighteen if they are not continuing their education. This has been the law since the end of the Iran-Iraq war. During that war, 1980–87, young males below eighteen voluntarily served in the military. Ardestani's sons are not eligible for the draft until they are eighteen, and until that age, they can travel freely in and out of Iran. Alipour was aware of no law that would allow the Iranian government to detain children between the ages of twelve and fourteen so that they would not leave the country prior to being eligible for military service and he was aware of no practice of doing that. If something happened to Ardestani while he was in Iran with his children, their mother could go to get them or a close relative could send them back to the United States. The Iranian Interests Section issues visas in the United States for travel to Iran that contain stamps granting permission to leave Iran without getting authorization in Iran. Many American citizens are now traveling to Iran on such visas.

* * *

The trial court did receive Uhlman's affidavit as evidence, while acknowledging it was hearsay, and did allow Long's counsel to make an offer of proof on what Uhlman's testimony would be. According to the offer of proof, Uhlman would testify as follows. She has specific information that there were teenagers who served in the Iranian army under the age of eighteen. She has information or is under the impression that boys were detained between the ages of twelve and fourteen so they would be available for military service at a later age. She had a case in which an Iranian/American wanted to travel with his son at age eleven or earlier to Iran because he would not be comfortable once his son turned twelve. It is common practice that teenagers are sent out of the country during their teenage years to avoid the possibility of draft. It is possible the constitution sets the age for draft at eighteen, but Iran changes its law by decree, so if there were a reason to have more young people in the military, the age could change by decree. She knew of no specific instance in which a teenager came to Iran for a visit in a situation such as this and was drafted into the military service.... In response to the court's questions, Long's counsel stated she had not asked Uhlman whether her knowledge of boys under eighteen serving in the military was based on the time of the Iran-Iraq war.

The court denied Long's motion for reconsideration....

* * *

DISCUSSION

* * *

Long...argues the trial court improperly placed the burden of proof on her, rather than Ardestani, to prove he should be prohibited from taking the children to Iran. She contends the issue, properly framed, is whether it is in the children's best interests to go to Iran with their father, and this issue was not litigated in the divorce proceedings; rather, the parties stipulated to preserving this issue for later determination by the court. Therefore, according to Long, the court is really making an initial determination on the best interests of the children, and both parties have an equal burden of showing what is in the best interests of the children....

* * *

The guardian ad litem, while also contending the court erred in placing the burden of proof on Long, takes a different position of the correct rule. The guardian ad litem contends that, when one parent wishes to travel with his or her children over the objection of the other parent to a country that is not a signatory to the Hague Convention, the parent who wishes to make the trip should have the burden of proving the trip should be allowed.

...We are persuaded that the trial court correctly concluded Long had the burden of proving that prohibiting Ardestani from taking the children to visit his family in Iran was in the children's best interests.

The general rule is that the party seeking judicial process to advance a position carries the burden of proof. In this case Long is seeking a court order prohibiting Ardestani from taking the minor children to Iran for a visit. She is doing so consistent with the procedure the parties stipulated to, which was incorporated in the judgment of divorce. Under that procedure Long has the obligation to move the court to prohibit Ardestani from taking the children to Iran; Ardestani's only obligation before taking the children is to notify Long sixty days in advance of his desire to take the children.... This indicates the parties contemplated that, if Long did not move the court to prohibit Ardestani, he could take the children without seeking any court approval, consistent with the terms of the provision.

This procedure is similar to that in the statute governing situations in which a parent wishes to remove a minor child from the state of Wisconsin for a period of more than ninety consecutive days and the other parent has periods of physical placement. Wis. Stat. § 767.327 (1999–2000). The parent wishing to do so must give the other parent notice at least sixty days in advance to allow the other parent to object.... A parent wishing to prohibit the removal must do so by motion to the court and has the burden of proof to show prohibition is in the children's best interests.

There is no statutory provision prohibiting a parent with joint legal custody and physical placement from taking the child on a visit outside Wisconsin, including to a foreign country, for less than ninety days. Also, in the absence of a provision in the divorce judgment to the contrary, there is no reason a parent with joint legal custody may not take a child on a visit to another country during the child's physical placement with that parent, without the other parent's permission, as long as the visit is less than ninety days.

We conclude that, when parents have agreed, as they have here, that one parent must move the court to prohibit the other from taking a particular trip with the children, the moving party has the burden of proof—both the burden of producing evidence and the burden of persuading the court that prohibiting the trip is in the children's best interests. Although the guardian ad litem urges us to adopt a different rule when the trip is to a country that is not a signatory to the Hague Convention, he provides us with no case law authority for such a rule....

...Long argues the trial court failed to consider the best interests of the children in making its ruling. If Long means the trial court did not apply the standard of the best interests of the children, we disagree.

...There was evidence that it would be beneficial for the children to travel with their father to the country of his birth and visit his family with him, assuming the children were returned, and there was no evidence to the contrary. There was no dispute it would be devastating to the children if they were not returned. We agree with the trial court and Ardestani that it was necessary for the court to consider not only the benefit to the children of going and the harm to them if they were not returned—neither of which were disputed—but also the likelihood of their not returning, which was the central factual dispute in this case. Accordingly, the evidence and the trial court's decision were focused on this dispute. However, this focus does not mean the trial court was not ultimately deciding what was in the children's best interests.

We understand Long to also argue that the trial court erred in applying the best interest standard because it did not give proper weight to the devastating effect on the children if they were not returned to their mother in the United States. Because the determination of a child's best interests depends on firsthand observations and experience with the persons involved, it is committed to the trial court's discretion.... We therefore examine the trial court's ruling to determine whether it properly exercised this discretion. In doing so,...we do not reverse the trial court's findings of fact unless they are clearly erroneous....

In this case the critical question of the likelihood of the children being returned has these component questions: (1) What is the likelihood that Ardestani will intentionally refuse to return the children or refuse to see that they are returned? (2) What is the likelihood that one or both boys would be detained by the Iranian government so that they could serve in the military? (3) What is the likelihood that, if Ardestani through accident becomes unable to return the children, they will be able to return nonetheless? What legal mechanisms exist to insure that if Ardestani does intentionally refuse to return the children or see that they are returned, and if his relatives refuse to or are unable to see that they are returned, Long can nonetheless secure their return?

...The trial court found Ardestani intended to bring the children back as he said he would. This is a factual finding highly dependent on the trial court's assessment of the credibility of witnesses. There is ample evidence in the record to support such a finding, which the trial court explained. Therefore, we will not set aside this finding.

The trial court's finding that there is no reasonable likelihood of detainment for military service in Iran or of conscription was based on its assessment of the persuasiveness of the testimony of Alipour as compared to the proffered testimony of Uhlman. Again, this is an assessment for the trial court to make, not this court, and we will not disturb it.

...There was no evidence suggesting that any family member who would have authority over the children under Iranian law if something happened to Ardestani would not help them return to Long.

Finally, the court considered the undisputed evidence that Iran was not a signatory to the Hague Convention, it did not have diplomatic relations with the United States, and the courts of Iran would not recognize an order of a court of the United States awarding Long custody of her children. The court did not ignore this evidence, but forthrightly addressed it: the court acknowledged that it could not absolutely rule out the possibility that Ardestani would act other than as he promised, and, if this occurred, Long would be without a legal remedy and the effect on the children would be devastating. Ultimately, the court had to weigh the benefit of the children going to Iran with their father against the likelihood that they would not be returned, along with the harm to them if they were not returned. That weighing, we conclude, is part of the exercise of the trial court's discretion in deciding what is in the children's best interests. We are satisfied the trial court properly exercised its discretion in deciding it should not prohibit Ardestani from taking the children to Iran.

Both Long and the guardian ad litem ask that we rule as a matter of law that a parent, even one having custody or joint custody, may not take a child to a country that is not a signatory to the Hague Convention if the other parent objects, even if a court finds the parent wishing to take the child intends to return the child and otherwise comply with court orders. They argue such a rule is good policy because the consequences of a failure to return the child in such situations are so severely adverse to the child.

However, none of the cases brought to our attention from other jurisdictions even hint at such a rule. Rather, in those cases in which courts have ordered restricted visitation in this country because of fear of abduction to another country, or have prohibited a parent from taking a child to, or having visitation with the child in, another country, the courts have examined the facts and circumstances of each case to arrive at the best interests of the child. In some cases the trial courts have found, based on the evidence, that there is sufficient likelihood a parent may flee the country with the child, as the other parent fears, to justify restrictions. In others cases trial courts have found, based on the evidence, there is not a sufficient likelihood of that occurring to justify either supervised visitation in this country or a prohibition on visitation in another country....

While in some cases the difficulty of obtaining the return of the child in the event of an abduction (because the other country is not a signatory to the Hague Convention or for other reasons) is one factor courts have considered in imposing restrictions,...in no case of which we are aware is this the only factor. Indeed, the Minnesota Court of Appeals has specifically rejected such an argument in the context of deciding whether visitation in this country should be supervised or not.... In addition, none of the articles to which the parties have directed us suggest the adoption of a rule such as Long and the guardian ad litem propose.

We are satisfied that the standard of the best interests of the child, comprehensive as it is, permits a full consideration of concerns both about a parent's intention in abducting a child and about the lack of a remedy should that occur....

The guardian ad litem suggests, as an alternative to adopting the rule of law he advances, that we provide guidance to trial courts by listing the factors they should take into account in deciding whether to permit one parent to take a child to another country for a visit, and that we remand to permit evidence on these factors. At oral argument the guardian ad litem mentioned such factors as: the intention of the parent to return with the child; methods of providing security that the parent will return with the child; the effect on the child; the desires of the child; the reason for the visit; and the current policies, laws, and practices of the country to which the parent wishes to take the child for a visit. While we can readily agree these are appropriate factors to consider in this case, and, perhaps in many others, we see no need to establish a definitive list of factors. The virtue of the best interests standard is that it permits the trial court to take into account all facts and circumstances bearing on the best interests of the particular child, and we view an attempt to define what those might be in a general category of cases as neither necessary nor fruitful.

Order affirmed.

Notes and Questions

1. *Comparison to Al-Silham.* Given that the relief requested by the custodial mother in *Al-Silham* is far more restrictive than the relief requested by the custodial mother in *Long*, what factors account for the different resolution of the two cases?

2. *Conclusive or Rebuttable Presumption.* On appeal in *Long* the guardian ad litem and the mother ask the court to find as a matter of law that a parent cannot take a child, over the objection of the other parent, to visit a country with which the United States does not have diplomatic relations and which is not a signatory to the Hague Abduction Convention. Later in the opinion the court phrased the guardian's position as requiring the parent who wishes to travel with a child to such a country to bear the burden of persuasion. Do you think either a conclusive or a rebuttable presumption of this nature would be preferable to the case by case approach adopted in *Long*? Would either an absolute rule or a rebuttable presumption of this nature violate equal protection or substantive due process? Was the court correct in placing the burden of persuasion on the mother, rather than placing the parents before the court on an equal footing on this issue? Would issuance of a ne exeat order in the decree have altered the court's approach to the burden of proof issue?

3. *Follow-up.* Because the final decision of the appellate court was not released until January 25, 2001, the father was prevented by the stay from traveling with the children in the summer of 2000, and by the terms of the decree was required to file a new request to travel with the boys in the summer of 2001. At the hearing before the trial court on that request, the older boy expressed strong concerns about the trip. Based on the older boy's reluctance, the trial judge issued an order permitting only the younger boy to travel. The father did not appeal that order. The younger son did travel to Iran with his father in the summer of 2001, and both returned to the United States following their visit. Ms. Long's attorney observed that the mother was reassured by the ruling that the older son need not travel. Because of the mother's perception of the importance of the eldest son in Iranian culture, the mother felt it unlikely that the father

would remain in Iran with the younger son, leaving the eldest son in the United States. Telephone interview by Marianne Blair with Lynn Rider, attorney for Ms. Long (July 30, 2001).

3. *Passport Restrictions.* U.S. citizens must enter and depart the United States with valid U.S. passports, unless they travel from countries within the Western Hemisphere, with the exception of Cuba. *See* 8 U.S.C. §1185(b) (2000); 22 C.F.R. §53.2 (2001). A parent, regardless of his or her citizenship, may apply for a U.S. passport on behalf of his or her minor child. Under current regulations, both parents of a child under the age of fourteen must execute a passport application, unless documentary evidence is supplied that the applicant is the sole parent or has sole custody of the child. Consolidated Appropriations Act, 2000, Pub. L. No. 106-113, §236, 113 Stat. 1536 (1999); 22 C.F.R. §51.27 (2001). However, there are several exceptions to the two-parent authorization requirement, such as exigent or special family circumstances. Issuance of a passport to one parent does not automatically preclude the other parent from obtaining a second passport for the child, with the Department of State's authorization. Information regarding issuance of a passport to a minor is available to any parent whose parental rights have not been terminated. *Id.*

The Department of State's Office of Children's Issues operates a Children's Passport Issuance Alert Program, which will notify a parent or court-ordered legal guardian, when requested, before issuing a U.S. passport for his or her child. A parent, guardian, legal representative, or the court must request in writing that the Office of Children's Issues enter a child's name into the program.

Under some circumstances a parent can apply to have a child's future passport application denied. The Office of Children's Issues must receive a copy of a temporary or permanent court order that provides for sole legal custody to the requesting parent; or joint legal custody to both parents (requires permission of both parents before passport issuance); or a restriction on the child's travel (requires superseding court order allowing travel, or permission of both parents before passport issuance). However, the inability to obtain a U.S. passport does not automatically prevent a dual-national child from obtaining and traveling on a foreign passport. Parents can contact the embassy or consulate of another nation to enquire about denial of that country's passport. For more information on the Children's Passport Issuance Alert Program, *see* http://travel.state.gov/pia_program.html.

Patricia E. Apy, *Managing Child Custody Cases Involving Non-Hague Contracting States*
14 J. Am. Acad. Matrim. Law. 77, 78–79, 85–94 (1997)

* * *

Seldom are clients more alarmed, less cogent and more marginalized than by a custodial dispute in which the battleground crosses continents. It is important for the attorney presented with either the perceived risk of an abduction, the threat of responding to an action filed in an international jurisdiction, or an actual child snatching to ascertain where in the process the parties currently find themselves....

...A large number of cases come into counsel without process being filed in any jurisdiction. The initial inquiry in an international custody case is to determine first the physical presence of the child, the current status of any custody dispute, the de facto and de jure custodian and the habitual residence of the child. Next, counsel should determine how many of the countries implicated by the client's history and current circumstances are signators to international treaties or agreements regarding families and children, law enforcement, extradition or civil process which might provide procedure or remedy for this international litigant....

...As an immediate and preventative measure, if the child remains within the jurisdiction, a temporary order defining custody and access rights should be sought to assure enforceable rights of custody. In order to obtain an effective order, the application should seek an immediate judicial assessment of the risk of removal and address the involvement of the non-Hague state in the lives of the family and the litigation....

* * *

If the fear is that the child is immediately in the process of being taken to a non-Hague contracting State, the attorney's analysis narrows to the possibility of intercepting the travel en route by employing international law enforcement and criminal justice remedies to facilitate the detection and potential apprehension of either parent or child.

The decision to engage the assistance of law enforcement almost assuredly requires the determination to brand the fleeing parent a fugitive from justice. In coloring the removing parent's behavior, this may have the undesired effect of motivating that individual to go into hiding or inspiring an adversarial posture with regard to future negotiations. This effect is sufficiently outweighed when the trail is still quite fresh and while the removing parent may still be ambivalent about plans and travel. Data suggest that the better planned, funded, and executed an abduction is,... [the more difficult] location and recovery [becomes].... Where travel to the non-Hague contracting State is anticipated to be accomplished through jurisdictions which are either Hague contracting States or participants in other bi-lateral law enforcement agreements, steps should be taken to maximize enforceability of both diplomatic and law enforcement measures.

Again, if the right to custody has not been judicially confirmed, an order establishing the client's right to and actual exercise of custody in the "left-behind jurisdiction" should be obtained along with factual findings that the removal of the child was without consent. Temporary custody should be designated as "sole custody" to avoid difficulties in interpretation in alternative jurisdictions. The order will usually be obtained ex parte either because of difficulties in providing notice or to avoid detection of impending apprehension, but the limitations otherwise attendant to the long-term enforceability of ex parte custody orders are not the primary concern in initiating law enforcement involvement. Still, time spent in setting forth jurisdictional prerequisites with excruciating detail can only enhance subsequent enforceability.... By providing judicial sanction for the characterization of the removing parent's conduct, police and prosecutors can take the first factual step they may need toward establishing probable cause sufficient to generate a warrant.

...As part of the family court's temporary custody order, it is sometimes possible to have the family court judge formally refer the case to the county or state prosecutor or law enforcement authority charged with enforcement. For example, the family court in New Jersey has jurisdiction under court rule to hear complaints under the Interference With Custody Statute. By evoking the criminal custodial interference laws in the jurisdiction and assessing your state's child protection statutes, the application can be made directly to the prosecutor or through the state's child protection agency to law enforcement. Of course, if the child has been taken abroad, the International Parental Kidnapping Crime Act of 1993 makes the enforcing authority the United States Attorney's Office which would charge the crime under the statute.

This may be the most expeditious way of gaining a warrant. Most state interference with custody statutes make removal of a child from the United States a felony. If it is indicated to the prosecutor that you will proceed with prosecution and are prepared to support extradition in applicable circumstances, state law enforcement officials are more likely to issue warrants. The United States Attorney can issue a warrant under 18 U.S.C. § 1204 in circumstances where state authorities are unwilling to take action. Additionally, if a state or federal warrant has been issued and notice of same has been given, a state prosecutor may request an Unlawful Flight to Avoid Prosecution (UFAP) warrant pursuant to 18 U.S.C. § 1073. Once a warrant is issued under either 18 U.S.C. § 1204 or § 1073, the Federal Bureau of Investigation undertakes the investigation and seeks to arrest the removing parent. If county or state authorities are unwilling to act quickly, instruct your client, armed with all family court orders and proofs of notice, to file a complaint with the local municipality for criminal interference with custody and request immediate assistance. Registration on the Department of Justice National Crime Information Center (NCIC) computer is mandatory in all 50 states and the first step to eventual protection.

A collateral advantage of initiating criminal prosecution and warrant power is the later ability to restrict future access by the wrongdoer to the federal courts on federal disentitlement grounds. In the case of In re Prevot, [59 F.3d 556 (6th Cir. 1995)], the court ordered the father petitioner's prayer for relief under the International Child Abduction Remedies Act (ICARA) dismissed since he was a fugitive felon from the United States. The court indicated that regardless of the merits of the analysis otherwise engaged in under the Hague Convention on the Civil Aspects of International Child Abduction, the petitioner could not invoke the treaty.

If your client is a habitual resident of the United States, it is prudent to contact the Department of State and request immediate assistance in several key areas. The Department of State's Office of Children's Issues provides the most expeditious route for access to information of other Central Authorities and through the Department of Justice to the International Criminal Police Organization (ICPO)-Interpol. Interpol is the coordinating organization of 169 member nations which works to ensure and promote mutual assistance between law enforcement authorities and contribute toward prevention and suppression of crime. According to its constitution, the agency's intervention in political, religious, racial, or military matters is prohibited. Authority for the Interpol function rests with the Attorney General; the United States National Central Bureau (USNCB) is an office in the Department of Justice.

To facilitate search and arrest of international offenders, a system of notices is circulated to member nations. For example, a red notice initiates a search for international offenders; a green notice indicates a warning of an international offender; a blue notice indicates a request to locate and identify. The red notice, while not insuring what action the foreign authority will take, will insure that each member nation's National Central Bureau will have the pertinent information as quickly as possible. Each notice contains a case summary description and reason for the notice.

The State Department can relay the information directly to Interpol. The State Department can also act quickly to alert Passport Control to withdraw the ability to obtain or replace a United States passport by the removing parent or for the children. Finally, the Department of State, by using its connections with Central Authorities of contracting states, may be able to transmit an application for location and return to the Central Authorities of those countries through which the children may travel. There is case law disfavorable to the applicability of the remedies of ICARA to abductions to non-contracting countries. However, at the juncture that the removing parent has not yet reached the non-contracting state, or is traveling on a common carrier owned or operated by a contracting state or maintains business connections to a contracting state, asserting Hague remedies through Central Authorities potentially provides a mechanism to apprehend the child.

* * *

...Most airlines, even the national airlines of non-Hague contracting states, if presented with an order and/or requests from law enforcement, will cooperate, at least, in ascertaining the legal authority of a minor child to be transported from the United States, particularly given current airline security regulations.

Because many non-Hague contracting states are in parts of the world where relatively few carriers travel directly from the United States daily, identifying which carrier is being used is easier. Computer reservation networks allow instant access to flight information.

Typically, based upon a broad "minimum contact" standard for jurisdiction, airlines can be made subject to reasonable injunctive relief. If presented to them in an organized and timely fashion, coupled with legal authority and good identification of the children and parties, voluntary cooperation by airlines can be accomplished.

* * *

Note

1. *FPLS.* The Federal Parent Locator Service (FPLS) can help locate an abducted child who is present in the United States. Regarding children abducted in the United States, requests must be made only by authorized persons to the State Parent Locator Service Office or a Title IV-D State Child Support Enforcement Agency designated in 45 C.F.R. § 302.35(b), who then in turn files the request with the Federal Parent Locator Service. Those authorized to initiate requests include a court that has jurisdiction to make or enforce a child custody or visitation determination, and any federal or state agent or attorney authorized by law to enforce a child custody or visitation determination or investigate or prosecute the unlawful taking or restraint of a child. 42 U.S.C. § 663 (d) (2000). Regarding children abducted to the United States, the National Center for Missing and Exploited Children, operating under the direction of the Office of Children's Issues in the U.S. State Department's Bureau of Consular Affairs, is authorized to obtain information from the FPLS for the purpose of locating any parent or child on behalf of an applicant to the U.S. Central Authority. 42 U.S.C. §11606 (2000). The FPLS is similarly available to the Office of Juvenile Justice and Delinquency Prevention.

All requests must contain: (1) the parent's name; (2) the parent's social security number (SSN) (or a reasonable effort to ascertain the individual's SSN) (3) whether the individual is or has been a member of the armed services, if known; (4) whether the individual is receiving, or has received, any Federal compensation or benefits, if known; (5) any other information prescribed by the Office; and a statement by the director of the IV-D agency or his or her designee, stating that the request is for a statutorily approved purpose, and that any information obtained through the FPLS will be treated as confidential. 45 C.F.R. § 303.70(c) (2001). Relevant regulations can be found at 45 C.F.R. §§ 303.69–303.70 (2001).

2. Sanctions and Tort Liability

a. *International Parental Kidnaping Crime Act and Other Federal Sanctions*

In 1993, in response to concern over the growing number of abductions to countries that were not parties to the Hague Abduction Convention, Congress passed the International Parental Kidnaping Crime Act (IPKCA), 18 U.S.C. § 1204 (2000). Though IPKCA has been construed in relatively few published decisions, Mr. Amer's appeal of his conviction in the following case afforded the Second Circuit the opportunity to explore the Act's constitutionality and construction in depth.

United States v. Amer
110 F.3d 873 (2d Cir. 1997),
cert. den. 522 U.S. 904 (1997)

Newman, C. J.

This appeal concerns several issues arising from a conviction for violation of the International Parental Kidnapping Crime Act.... The IPKCA bars a parent from removing a child from the United States or retaining outside the United States a child who has been in the United States, with the intent to obstruct the other parent's right to physical custody. We have not previously considered this statute. The specific questions raised are (i) whether the IPKCA is unconstitutionally vague, (ii) whether it is overbroad in intruding upon the free exercise of religion, (iii) whether it incorporates the affirmative defenses found in the Hague Convention on the Civil Aspects of International Parental Child Abduction ("Hague Convention"), (iv) whether the sentencing court properly imposed, as a condition of the convicted defendant's term of supervised release, a requirement that the defendant return the still-retained children to the United States, and (v) whether the sentencing court properly applied a three-level enhancement for substantial interference with the administration of justice.

[Ed. Note: Mona and Ahmed Amer were married in Egypt, where their first son, Amachmud, was born. In 1985, Ahmed emigrated to New York, where his wife, Mona, joined him two years later. Another son and a daughter were born in New York. Ahmed became a U.S. citizen in 1991, and Mona obtained permanent resident status the next year. Following several years of marital disputes over Ahmed's marriage to another woman and Mona's decision to work outside the home and apply for welfare, the couple separated in April 1994. Ahmed continued to see the children in Mona's apartment whenever he wished, and continued to physically and verbally abuse her. Mona supported herself with public assistance and loans from friends. Despite threats to kill her, Mona refused Ahmed's suggestion that the family move back to Egypt.

On January 27, 1995, during a visit, Ahmed took the children while Mona was shopping, flew to Egypt, and left them with his mother, where they continue to reside. In February, Mona filed for and was subsequently awarded custody in Queens Family Court in New York. At around the same time, Ahmed obtained an order from an Egyptian court ordering Mona to return to the "conjugal home" in Egypt. When she failed to return within three months, the Egyptian court awarded Ahmed custody in May 1995. In June 1995, Ahmed returned to the United States, where he was arrested and convicted by a jury for violation of IPKCA. He was sentenced to twenty-four months imprisonment and a one-year supervised release, on the condition that he return the three children to the United States. At the time of the appeal, the children remained in Egypt.]

I. Vagueness

Ahmed contends that three aspects of the Act render it void for vagueness by failing to give a "person of ordinary intelligence a reasonable opportunity to know what is prohibited" under the Act.... First, he asserts that the term "retains"...is vague because the Act does not define the duration or length of time that a child must be "retain[ed]" outside the United States in order to constitute a violation of the IPCKA. Second, he contends that the parenthetical phrase "([child] who has been in the United States)"...is vague because the IPKCA does not specify the length of time that a child must have been in the United States before the IPKCA will be triggered by the child's removal or retention. Third, he argues that the phrase "lawful exercise of parental rights," *id.*, is vague because the Act does not provide any guidance as to whether parental rights are to be defined by state law, federal law, Egyptian law, customary international law, or "positive law promulgated by the United Nations."

The "void-for-vagueness doctrine requires that a penal statute define the criminal offense with sufficient definiteness that ordinary people can understand what conduct is prohibited and in a manner that does not encourage arbitrary and discriminatory enforcement." Kolender v. Lawson, 461 U.S. 352, 357(1983). To succeed, however, the proponent of the vagueness argument "must demonstrate that the law is impermissibly vague in all of its applications." Village of Hoffman Estates v. Flipside, Hoffman Estates, Inc., 455 U.S. 489 (1982). Specifically, a challenger "who engages in some conduct that is clearly proscribed [by the challenged statute] cannot complain of the vagueness of the law as applied to the conduct of others."...

This limiting principle defeats Ahmed's vagueness challenge. Even if the term "retains" or the phrase "has been in the United States" might reflect some uncertainty as applied to extreme situations, the conduct for which Ahmed was prosecuted and convicted falls squarely within the core of the IPKCA. First, although it might be debatable whether a two- or three-day retention outside the United States would be sufficient to trigger the Act, there can be no doubt that Ahmed's retention of the three children from January 27, 1995, to August 4, 1995, the period set out in the indictment, was covered by the Act. Second, although there might be room for argument as to whether foreign children who were merely visiting the United States on a week-long vacation would be protected by the Act, no issue arises as to the duration of the stay of the three Amer children in the United States. The eldest child had resided in New York since leaving Egypt in 1987, and the other two children were born in New York in, respectively, 1989 and 1991, and have resided in the United States for their entire lives.

Finally, Ahmed's argument as to the clarity of the phrase "parental rights" fails because Congress made clear in the legislative history of the Act that " 'parental rights' are to be determined by reference to State law, in accordance with the Hague Convention...." H.R.Rep. No. 103-390, at 4 (1993).... Article 3 of the Hague Convention provides that parental rights are to be defined by "the law of the State in which the child was habitually resident immediately before the removal or retention."...Although the concept of the state of "habitual residence" might be unclear at the margins, there is no doubt that, in this case, New York is that place. At the time of their abduction, Amach-mud had resided in New York for eight years, and Maha and Omar had lived in New York since their birth. Moreover, there is no confusion under New York law that Mona, as the biological mother, enjoys the right to physical custody of her children unless and until this right is terminated by law.

Ahmed's act of removing long-term residents of the United States and retaining them for more than six months in Egypt in order to frustrate their mother's lawful exercise of her right to physical custody under New York law falls squarely within the coverage of the IPKCA. Because "[o]ne to whose conduct a statute clearly applies may not successfully challenge it for vagueness,"... Ahmed's first argument cannot succeed.

II. Overbreadth/Free Exercise

Ahmed next contends that the IPKCA must be invalidated because it punishes parents for engaging in the constitutionally protected act of returning their children to the land of the parents' birth for religious reasons. Although Ahmed styles this an "overbreadth" argument, his real point is that the IPKCA infringes on the free exercise of religion by proscribing removals of children from the United States even when those acts are dictated, or at least motivated, by "religious law." Ahmed contends that he returned his children to Egypt in order to provide them with a proper Muslim upbringing, and that punishing him for this act violates his rights under the Free Exercise Clause.

This argument was not raised until this appeal and is hence forfeited.... At no point during the pretrial, trial, or sentencing proceedings did Ahmed argue that his act of removing and retaining the children was religiously mandated or inspired. The only explanations that the defense proffered to justify Ahmed's conduct were that (i) Mona was neglecting the children, (ii) the children would be "better taken care of in Egypt," (iii) Ahmed had "finished [his business] in [the United States] and...wish[ed] to settle in [his] own Nation among [his] family and relatives," and (iv) "the schools over there were better."...

Moreover, there is no plain error, see Fed. R. Crim. P. 52(b), even under the somewhat less stringent version of plain-error analysis applicable to alleged "errors of constitutional magnitude."...A neutral law of general applicability does not violate the Free Exercise Clause simply because the law imposes an incidental burden on a religious practice. Employment Division, Department of Human Resources of Oregon v. Smith, 494 U.S. 872, 878–79 (1990). The IPKCA punishes conduct within its reach without regard to whether the conduct was religiously motivated. Because Ahmed does not even allege that the IPKCA targets religious beliefs or was designed to prohibit parental kidnappings motivated by the parents' religious concerns,...and because the Act punishes parental kidnappings solely for the harm they cause, it does not violate the Free Exercise Clause.[5]

---

5. Ahmed also raises the possibility that the IPKCA violates the Religious Freedom Restoration Act ("RFRA"), 42 U.S.C. §§ 2000bb to 2000bb-4, by proscribing religiously motivated removals and retentions of children. Because this argument was not raised in the District Court, it too is forfeited. In any event, Ahmed fails to meet the threshold requirement of an RFRA claim. He cannot show that the IPKCA "substantially burden[s]" a religious practice.... Even if we assume, for the sake of argument, that Ahmed in fact removed the children to Egypt in order to provide them with a religious education, there is nothing in the record to suggest that the children could not receive proper training in the tenets of Islam in the United States, or that they must go to Egypt to become religiously educated Muslims. Moreover, the IPKCA does not generally prohibit relocation of children or even make it significantly more difficult to do so. It simply prohibits relocation in one very narrow circumstance, where to do so would violate the custodial rights of the other parent. The IPKCA

III. Incorporation of Hague Convention Defenses

Ahmed contends that the District Court erred when it refused to permit him to argue in his defense that he was justified in removing and retaining the children in Egypt under the Hague Convention. The Convention, he asserts, affords him a defense where "there is a grave risk that [the children's] return would expose the child[ren] to physical or psychological harm or otherwise place the child[ren] in an intolerable situation." This risk, he argues, arises from Mona's allegedly neglectful care. Ahmed also contends that the Hague Convention allows him to argue in his defense that the children's return would not be "permitted by the fundamental principles of [Egyptian law] relating to the protection of human rights and fundamental freedoms," which allegedly do not permit Muslim children to be denied their right to an Islamic upbringing. Hague Convention, Arts. 13(b) & 20. The District Court denied Ahmed's request because it found that the three affirmative defenses specifically set forth in section 1204(c) of the Act are the only ones available to a defendant facing an IPKCA prosecution:

(c) It shall be an affirmative defense under this section that—

(1) the defendant acted within the provisions of a valid court order granting the defendant legal custody or visitation rights and that order was obtained pursuant to the Uniform Child Custody Jurisdiction Act and was in effect at the time of the offense;

(2) the defendant was fleeing an incidence or pattern of domestic violence;

(3) the defendant had physical custody of the child pursuant to a court order granting legal custody or visitation rights and failed to return the child as a result of circumstances beyond the defendant's control, and the defendant notified or made reasonable attempts to notify the other parent or lawful custodian of the child of such circumstances within 24 hours after the visitation period had expired and returned the child as soon as possible. 18 U.S.C. § 1204(c).

Since Ahmed did not qualify under any of these subsections, the Court ruled that he could not argue that he was justified in removing and retaining the children because, among other things, Mona was a poor parent or because Egyptian human rights laws protected the right of Islamic children to a proper religious education.

Ahmed argues that the District Court's construction conflicts with section 1204(d), which provides that the Act "does not detract from The Hague Convention." ... As he reads the emphasized language, the IPKCA must be construed to incorporate all the defenses available in the Hague Convention because, otherwise, the Act would "detract from" the Convention. ...

We note, as an initial matter of statutory construction, that the IPKCA's explicit listing of three, and only three, affirmative defenses is a strong indication that the defenses arguably inferred from the Hague Convention are not available in an IPKCA prosecution, at least in the absence of a clear indication that the Convention makes such defenses available. In any event, our examination of the relationship between the Hague Convention and the IPKCA reveals that, at least in this case, refusing to allow Ahmed to

---

does not "put substantial pressure on an adherent to modify his behavior and to violate his beliefs." Thomas v. Review Board of the Indiana Employment Sec. Div., 450 U.S. 707, 718 (1981).

present Hague Convention defenses not found in the IPKCA would not in any way "detract from" the Convention.

The Hague Convention...was adopted in order "to protect children internationally from the harmful effects of their wrongful removal or retention and to establish procedures to ensure their prompt return to the State of their habitual residence, as well as to secure protection for rights of access."...It created a previously unavailable civil remedy for the return of abducted children, whereby the left-behind parent can request the designated "Central Authority" of the state in which the abducted child is retained to locate the child, institute proceedings to effect its return, assist in administrative technicalities, and generally aid in the amicable resolution of the kidnapping situation.... The Convention includes no criminal punishment for the abducting parent, nor does it provide for the resolution of the underlying custody dispute. Its sole objective is to "restore the factual situation that existed prior to a child's removal or retention."

The Hague Convention's mechanisms are triggered, however, only when both the country to which the child is abducted and the country from which they are taken are parties to the Convention.... Because the Convention does not apply when children habitually resident in the United States (and who are often American citizens) are abducted from this country and retained in a non-contracting country, the perception arose that something was needed to deter parents from removing and retaining their children in these "safe haven" countries.... As the IPKCA's legislative history shows, it was against this backdrop that the Act was enacted.... Nonetheless, Congress continued to believe that the civil mechanism of the Hague Convention, when available, was the preferred route for resolving the complex and difficult problems surrounding international child abductions. It thus provided a "Sense of Congress" resolution to accompany the Act:

> It is the sense of the Congress that, inasmuch as use of the procedures under the Hague Convention...has resulted in the return of many children, those procedures, in circumstances in which they are applicable, should be the option of first choice for a parent who seeks the return of a child who has been removed from the parent.

Pub.L. No. 103-173, §2(b)....; see Statement by President Clinton upon Signing [the IPKCA], 29 Weekly Comp. Pres. Doc. 2493 (Dec. 6, 1993),... ("[The Act] reflects the Congress' awareness that the Hague Convention has resulted in the return of many children and the Congress' desire to ensure that the creation of a Federal child abduction felony offense does not and should not interfere with the Convention's continued successful operation.... [The Act] should be read and used in a manner consistent with the Congress' strong expressed preference for resolving these difficult cases, if at all possible, through civil remedies."). In that spirit, section 1204(d) of the IPKCA provides that the Act "does not detract from the Hague Convention."

Construing the IPKCA against this background, we conclude that rejecting Hague Convention defenses in Ahmed's prosecution does not "detract from" the Convention. In the first place, Egypt, the country to which the Amer children have been removed and in which they are currently being retained, is not a signatory to the Convention.... Second, because the civil mechanism of the Convention is therefore unavailable to Mona to effect the return of her children, the United States' criminal prosecution of Ahmed for the abduction and retention of the children under the IPKCA cannot in any way "detract from" the Hague Convention within the meaning of section 1204(d), and, indeed, perfectly fulfills the "enforcement-gap-closing" function for which the IPKCA was partially enacted. Although it might be a close question whether a defendant should be permitted to raise Hague Convention defenses when, for instance, there is a parallel or ongoing civil proceeding under the Convention and its implementing legislation, we do not need to decide that question in this case. The District Court acted properly in restricting Ahmed to the three available affirmative defenses found in section 1204(c) of the Act.

IV. Special Condition of Supervised Release

Ahmed next objects to the District Court's imposition of the following special condition of supervised release: "[T]he defendant [must] effect the return of the children to the United States to Mona Amer." ... [4]

(a) Guidelines limitations. Ahmed contends that the "return" condition exceeds the sentencing court's authority under 18 U.S.C. §3583 and U.S.S.G. §5D1.3(b). Although sentencing courts have "broad discretion to tailor conditions of supervised release to the goals and purposes outlined in §5D1.3(b)," this provision does not provide sentencing courts with "untrammelled discretion" in this regard.... Specifically, section 5D1.3(b) provides:

> The court may impose other conditions of supervised release, to the extent that such conditions are reasonably related to (1) the nature and circumstances of the offense and the history and characteristics of the defendant, and (2) the need for the sentence imposed to afford adequate deterrence to criminal conduct, to protect the public from further crimes of the defendant, and to provide the defendant with needed educational or vocational training, medical care, or other correctional treatment in the most effective manner.

... This Circuit has ruled that "despite the continuous use of the ... conjunctive 'and' in §5D1.3(b), taking into account the authorizing statutes, a condition may be imposed if it is reasonably related to any one or more of the specified factors." ...

The "return" condition is obviously closely related to "the nature and circumstances of the offense" of child abduction and "the history and characteristics" of Ahmed. Indeed, it is difficult to imagine a condition more closely tailored to the crime and the criminal in question than this one. Moreover, the requirement that Ahmed return the children serves the goal of general deterrence. As the District Court put it,

> It seems that often in cases such as this, a vindictive parent may be willing to possibly face a modest prison term in order to keep the children from the spouse. But if the parent recognizes that the Court has a legal mechanism to additionally order the return of the children, then recognizing that may well serve as an additional deterrent.

The condition also serves the function of specific deterrence. It deters Ahmed both from committing the offense of the unlawful retention of the children in Egypt after his release from prison, and from attempting to kidnap his children again after they have been returned to the United States.

(b) Punishment for extent of retention. Ahmed contends that the special condition essentially punishes him for the length or duration of his retention of the children because someone who retained abducted children for only a short period would not face this condition. He argues that this allegedly length-based "enhancement" is inconsistent with the Sentencing Commission's intent, and points to an analogous provision of the Guidelines—section 2A4.1 governing non-parental kidnapping offenses prosecuted

---

4. We note that the IPKCA itself does not expressly specify what should be done when a defendant refuses to return the abducted children to this country....

under, among other statutes, 18 U.S.C. § 1201 — as support. In that guideline, there is a specific offense characteristic that enhances a kidnapper's sentence based on the length of time that he held the victim....

Even if the absence of a specific offense enhancement for length of retention under the IPKCA guideline somehow implies that this factor cannot be used to "enhance" a defendant's sentence, which is doubtful, Ahmed's argument fails because the special condition is not based on the duration of the retention, but on the fact of his continued retention of the children. Regardless of how long Ahmed has held the children in Egypt, the special condition requires him to return the children if the retention continues during the term of supervised release. This condition is therefore not inconsistent with the Sentencing Commission's alleged intent not to penalize an IPKCA offender based on the duration of the retention.

(c) Double jeopardy. Ahmed argues that further imprisonment for failing to abide by this special condition, i.e., revoking his supervised release if he refuses to return the children after his release from prison, would violate the Double Jeopardy Clause by exposing him to multiple punishments for the same offense for which he was convicted. Even if this objection is ripe, which we do not think it is, no double jeopardy violation will occur if Ahmed is subsequently re-imprisoned for violating the special condition. Ahmed fails to realize that "the entire sentence, including the period of supervised release, is the punishment for the original crime, and 'it is the original sentence that is executed when the defendant is returned to prison after a violation of the terms' of his release."... Because revocation of supervised release for the violation of a condition of release is "not new punishment for a new crime,"... but "part of the whole matrix of punishment which arises out of a defendant's original crime,"... double jeopardy protection would be not violated if and when Ahmed's term of supervised release is revoked for his failure to return the children to the United States.

Moreover, we note that the key assumption underlying this objection — that Ahmed's continued retention of the children following his release from prison would constitute the "same" offense for which he was convicted — is highly questionable. The indictment charged Ahmed with removing and retaining the children during the period "from January 27, 1995 to August 4, 1995." Because the IPKCA punishes both "removals" and "retentions," and because Ahmed has not been punished for his act of retaining the children after August 4, 1995, even a subsequent criminal prosecution for this new offense — the wrongful retention of children, who have been in the United States, outside the United States from August 4, 1995 to the present — may be permitted under the Double Jeopardy Clause.

(d) Impossibility. Ahmed contends that the special condition is unfair and would be impossible for him to meet because (i) he cannot arrange for the return of the children while he is in prison, and (ii) he will be in violation of the condition as soon as he is released from prison in March 1998 (excluding good-time credit). This objection is premature, and need not be considered at this time. Any potential unfairness to Ahmed arising from an attempt to revoke his term of supervised release immediately upon his release from prison can be evaluated if and when such revocation occurs. In any event, the District Judge has already indicated her willingness to provide Ahmed with a reasonable period of time following his release from prison to effect the return of the children, and the Judge has authority under 18 U.S.C. § 3583(e) to modify or revoke the conditions and term of supervised release to account for any unforeseen or changed circumstances.

(e) Conflict with Egyptian order. Ahmed argues that the special condition conflicts with an Egyptian court's May 1995 order granting Ahmed custody over the Amer children.

This objection misconstrues the force and nature of the condition requiring Ahmed to return the children to the United States. Similar to the IPKCA, and indeed the Hague Convention, the District Court's command that Ahmed return the children does not seek to settle any underlying custody dispute that might exist between Mona and Ahmed, but merely attempts to restore the status quo prior to Ahmed's criminal removal and retention of the children, and thus to deny him the "legal advantage [he gained] from the abduction to or retention in the country where the child[ren] [are] located." ... Whatever arguable conflict with his claimed rights under the Egyptian custody order might arise from requiring return of the children to the United States cannot validly be asserted by Ahmed inasmuch as he brought the children to Egypt (and thereby obtained his claimed Egyptian custody rights) in violation of United States law.

* * *

[Ed. Note: The court also rejected the contention by Ahmed that the "three-level enhancement" included in his sentence under section 2J1.2(b)(2) for "substantial interference with the administration of justice," was improper, finding that Ahmed's act of removing the children from New York could serve as a basis for this enhancement because it prevented proper legal proceedings from occurring.]

We reject Ahmed's remaining arguments as either forfeited because not previously raised, or simply without merit. The judgment of the District Court is affirmed.

Notes

1. *Scope of IPKCA.* Read 18 U.S.C. § 1204 in your Supplement. Under IPKCA, the removal or retention of a child outside the United States with intent to obstruct the lawful exercise of parental rights is made a federal felony, punishable by up to three years imprisonment and/or a fine. At the time Mr. Amer took his children to Egypt, no custody order was in effect. Under the law of New York, both he and his wife had an equal right to custody. Nevertheless, he received a sentence of two years in prison, plus a year of supervised release on the condition that he return the children. What language in the statute covers the conduct in which Mr. Amer engaged? What purpose does imprisonment as a sanction for this conduct serve? Is this conduct that merits criminal sanction? Is the criminal sanction likely to be effective?

Would this same sanction likely be imposed upon a primary caregiver who returns to her homeland with a child upon separation from her husband prior to the filing of any court action, after several years in the United States as a result of her husband's business relocation?

2. *Hague Convention Defenses.* The court suggests that if Egypt was a party to the Hague Abduction Convention at the time of this proceeding and a parallel Hague proceeding was ongoing, it would be a close question whether a defendant should be permitted to raise Hague defenses not specifically set forth in the Act. Should different defenses be available to a defendant depending upon the country to which the children are abducted? Does this raise constitutional concerns?

3. *Additional Constitutional Challenges to IPKCA.*

(a) *Commerce Clause.* In United States v. Cummings, 281 F.3d 1046 (9th Cir. 2002), a father who removed two of his three children to Germany in violation of custody orders issued after his divorce, though conceding Congressional authority under the Commerce Clause to criminalize the *removal*, challenged the constitutional authority of Congress to criminalize *retention* of American children in a foreign country. The Ninth Circuit, however, found both IPKCA provisions validly enacted, determining that Congressional authority to keep the channels of commerce free from immoral and injurious uses reaches conduct that occurs once the unlawful transportation is completed, and that wrongful retention impedes free use of the channels of commerce for a child's return.

The IPKCA prosecution in *Cummings* was undertaken after a German court denied the mother's Hague Abduction Convention petition to return the boys, and after she had brought civil contempt proceedings. In addition to a sentence of six months in prison and a year of supervised release, the district court ordered restitution of over $15,000, which included the mother's attorney's fees for the IPKCA, Hague, and contempt proceedings. The Ninth Circuit upheld this award as well, observing that the mother had complied with IPKCA's directive to pursue Hague proceedings as the "option of first choice," and the Hague Convention's authorization to obtain a determination from the State of habitual residence that the removal was wrongful, which she did in the contempt proceedings. Thus, her fees for all three proceedings were "a direct and foreseeable result" of the father's improper removal and retention of her sons.

(b) *Equal Protection.* A father who was charged under IPKCA for abducting his two children to India asserted that IPKCA violates equal protection because it distinguishes between abductions to Hague countries and non-Hague countries by promoting the use of civil remedies under the Hague Convention, when applicable, rather than criminal remedies. In United States v. Fazal, No. CR 01-110274-PBS, 2002 WL 498922 (D. Mass. Feb. 13, 2002), the court rejected this argument, observing that the "Sense of Congress" resolution accompanying the Act did not prohibit IPKCA prosecutions when the Hague was applicable. Moreover, applying rational basis analysis, because no particular race or nationality was targeted by IPKCA, the court found that it was rational to prefer civil resolutions when available, and to use IPKCA as an "enforcement-gap-closing" tool when Hague remedies were unavailable.

4. *Protection of Grandparent Visitation Rights.* Do "parental rights" extend to grandparents? The Tenth Circuit has concluded that they do, reasoning that under IPKCA "parental rights" are defined to include "visiting rights." In United States v. Alahmad, 211 F.3d 538 (10th Cir. 2000), the court upheld a conviction under IPKCA for kidnaping against a father with sole custody who moved with his child to Jordan, in violation of a ne exeat order implementing an order that awarded visitation to his daughter's maternal grandmother, who had raised the child for the first seven years of her life.

5. *Deterrent Effect.* In addition to its usefulness as a trigger for issuance of a federal warrant and F.B.I. intervention, as described in the excerpt from Patricia Apy's article above, IPKCA, like any criminal sanction, could potentially have both a specific and a general deterrent effect. Indeed, specific deterrence was attempted by the court in *Amer*, by imposing a year of supervised release in lieu of a third year of imprisonment, subject to the requirement that Mr. Amer return the children to the United States. The subsequent history of the case, however, does not foster optimism regarding the efficacy of IPKCA in this regard.

Mr. Amer was released from prison in April, 1997, twenty-two months after his initial incarceration. For the next two months, the probation department attempted to arrange with him the return of his children, and even offered to pay their travel expenses and arrange for representation for him in the family court proceeding in New York to obtain visitation. Their efforts were to no avail. On June 5, 1997, the district court determined that Mr. Amer had made no good faith efforts to effect the children's return, and had no intention of doing so. The court's decision to return Mr. Amer to prison for the third year of his sentence, after finding that he had violated the special condition of his release, was upheld in United States v. Amer, 163 F.3d 1149 (2nd Cir. 1998). When Mr. Amer was released after serving the additional twelve months, the U.S. Attorney's Office decided not to refile charges based on the subsequent retention. The children were still residing in Egypt at that time, and their mother had not seen them since the abduction. Jacqueline D. Gola, *The International Parental Kidnapping Crime Act of 1993: The United States' Attempt to Get Our Children Back—How Is It Working?*, 24 Brook. J. Int'l L. 797, 820–21 (1999).

In *Cummings* as well, neither his incarceration for contempt nor the IPKCA prosecution prompted the father to return the boys. After serving his time, Mr. Cummings returned to Germany, where his second wife was caring for the boys. German officials refused the mother visitation when she traveled to Germany to litigate the Hague proceeding, and the father had even refused to permit her e-mail communication with the boys. Kevin Blocker, *Connection: Ruling in NW Dispute*, Spokesman Rev., June 17, 2001, at A10; Kevin Blocker, *Father Gets Prison in Custody Case; Boys Remain in Germany Despite Court Rulings*, Spokesman Rev., Jan. 19, 2001, at B3.

6. *Extradition.* The federal government has negotiated two types of extradition treaties with foreign nations. *List treaties* specifically enumerate extraditable offenses. *Dual criminality treaties* allow extradition for any crime that both nations regard as a felony. The dual criminality requirement is regarded by U.S. courts as satisfied on the part of the United States if the offense is punishable by a term of imprisonment exceeding one year under federal law, the law of the state in which the fugitive is found, or the law of the preponderance of the states. *Eg.,* Cucuzzella v. Keliikoa, 638 F.2d 105, 107 (9th Cir. 1981).

Prior to IPKCA, parental kidnaping was generally not regarded as an extraditable offense by U.S. courts under either type of treaty. IPKCA enhanced the possibility of extradition under dual criminality treaties by making international parental kidnaping a felony in the United States. Pursuant to a dual criminality extradition treaty between the United States and Canada, IPKCA was held in In re Scweidenback, 3 F. Supp. 2d 118 (D. Mass. 1998), to create an analogous offense to charges of parental abduction in a Canadian warrant against a mother with sole custody who moved to Rhode Island with her two sons, thereby obstructing the father's visitation rights. The federal court determined that IPKCA prohibits removal of a child with intent to obstruct parental rights, which is defined under IPKCA to include visitation rights.

The enactment of IPKCA did not affect list treaties, however. Despite the fact that these treaties typically included "kidnaping," the term was not construed by the United States to include parental abduction because these treaties were negotiated prior to the development of state or federal parental kidnaping laws. To facilitate extradition for parental kidnaping under list treaties, Congress declared in its findings in the Extradition Treaties Interpretation Act of 1998, Pub. L. 105-323, § 203, that, "[f]or purposes of any extradition treaty to which the United States is a party, Congress authorizes the interpretation of the terms "kidnaping" and "kidnapping" to include parental kidnapping." For further information regarding extradition for international parental abduction, see Karen Wolfe, *A Tale of Two States: Successes and Failures of the 1980 Hague Convention on the Civil Aspects of International Child Abduction in the United States and Germany*, 33 N.Y.U. J. Int'l L. & Pol. 285, 348–51(2000); Susan Kreston, *Prosecuting International Parental Kidnapping*, 15 Notre Dame J. L. Ethics & Pub. Pol'y 533, 559–63 (2001).

7. *Immigration Sanctions.* As a further remedy for international abduction, Congress in 1990 passed the International Child Protection and Recovery Act, codified at 8 U.S.C.

§ 1182 (a)(10)(C). The Act denies admission to an alien (1) who detains or retains or withholds custody of a child who is a U.S. citizen, (2) outside of the United States in a country that is not a party to the Hague Abduction Convention, (3) from a person who has been granted custody of the child pursuant to a U.S. court order. The abducting alien will be denied admission to the United States under this Act until such time as the child is surrendered to the legal custodian.

In addition, the Secretary of State has the sole and unreviewable discretion to refuse admission to the United States to:

(1) any alien known to have "intentionally assisted" the abducting alien;

(2) any alien know to be "intentionally providing material support or safe haven" to the abducting alien; and

(3) the spouse (other than the parent of the abducted child), a child (other than the abducted child), parent, sibling, or agent of the abducting alien,

until such time as the child is surrendered to the person granted custody by the U.S. court order and permitted to return to the United States or the lawful custodian's residence.

The scope of the Recovery Act is limited. It only denies visas and admission to aliens seeking entry into the United States. It does not create grounds for deportation of aliens already in the United States, or for revocation of their work or study visas. Moreover, the Act has several exceptions. U.S. government officials acting within the scope of their official duties and foreign government officials designated by the Secretary of State will not be denied admission. Moreover, Congress limited the application of the Act to abductions to countries that were not party to the Hague Abduction Convention, clearly preferring the Abduction Convention remedies where they were applicable. Nevertheless, the Act might impose some pressure to return children on aliens who take their children to live with relatives in foreign nations and wish to return to the United States to work, or to aliens whose relatives are trying to immigrate. For further discussion of the Act, see Wolfe, *supra*, at 351–54.

b. Additional Remedies under State Law

Anyanwu v. Anyanwu

771 A.2d 672 (N.J. Super Ct. App. Div. 2001)

Collester, J.A.D.

Pursuant to leave granted, plaintiff Edith Anyanwu appeals from an order of the Family Part, Morris County, on February 9, 2001. The order released the defendant, Longy Anyanwu, from custody in the Morris County Correctional Facility, to which he was confined on August 14, 1997. The parties are citizens of Nigeria who have resided in the United States for over twenty years. Defendant was a professor at Montclair State University prior to his incarceration.

The parties were married in Baltimore, Maryland, on August 25, 1984. Defendant claims an earlier marriage in Nigeria on May 26, 1984, but plaintiff maintains this was only a customary ceremony to announce their engagement and that defendant was not even present. Their two children were born in the United States: Uchechi, born June 1, 1985; Ogechi, born October 19, 1986, and now deceased. The children had dual citizenship with Nigeria.

By 1996 there were significant marital problems. Plaintiff filed a complaint under the Prevention of Domestic Violence Act...and obtained a Final Restraining Order which she later voluntarily dismissed. Defendant filed for a divorce in Nigeria in August 1996, although plaintiff contends that she was never served.

In June of 1997 the parties and their children traveled to Nigeria where they have over 100 family members. Plaintiff avers that while in Nigeria defendant told her that the marriage was over, confiscated her passport and denied her access to the children. Claiming that she was in fear for her physical safety, she returned alone to the United States in July 1997. Later that month defendant also returned. The children remained in Nigeria.

On August 5, 1997, plaintiff filed another complaint under the Domestic Violence Act,... and a Temporary Restraining Order directed defendant to return the children to plaintiff's custody. Defendant was served with the order after his return from Nigeria. At a hearing on August 11, 1997, the restraints against defendant were continued, and he was directed to produce the children in court three days later.

On August 14, 1997, both parties appeared, but the children were not present. Defendant advised the court that his father had decided to raise the children according to the customs of Nigeria and would not allow them to return to the United States. Nevertheless, the judge found that defendant could exert sufficient power over his family in Nigeria to have the children returned, held him in violation of the Final Restraining Order and...remanded defendant to the Morris County Correctional Facility until he complied with the order. Defendant has remained confined since that date.

... [Further hearings were held on September 4 and 18, 1997.] Defendant testified he called relatives in the United States to aid in convincing his father to permit the children to leave Nigeria but was advised that his father refused. He added that he was told the children were no longer living with his father but with an aunt and uncle in Nigeria.

At the hearing defense counsel also produced a letter dated September 10, 1997 from Chief Val Onugha, Chairman of the Amaraka Customary Court of Imo State, Nigeria, directed to the trial judge stating that the issue of custody of the two daughters was before the Customary Court in Nigeria as a result of the 1996 divorce action filed by defendant and that the Nigerian court ordered that the children were to remain in Nigeria. The letter also stated that jurisdiction was based on a celebration of a customary marriage in Nigeria and that plaintiff had knowledge of the suit brought by defendant. The letter concluded:

> Finally, Longy's lawyers have hinted [to] me of the possibility of Longy be[ing] forced to sign papers which would enable the children [to] be returned to America. I have taken note of this, and as long as Nigeria remains independent I shall not honor any document signed by Longy because as long as he is [in] prison and in Chains (as "the star-ledger" reports), any document he signs cannot be free of duress.

In response to the inquiry of the judge, defendant declined to sign or submit documents to the Nigerian court or other authorities because of the statements in the letter from Chief Onugha that no weight would be given to any requests from him while he remained in prison. The hearing judge found that defendant's testimony and the letter from the Nigerian court were insufficient to meet defendant's burden to prove an inability to comply with the court order. Defendant was remanded back to confinement.

On September 24, 1997, defendant appealed. We affirmed the hearing judge and emphasized that defendant was not in jail for failure to produce his children but because he had not abided by the order of the trial court to make good faith and best efforts to do so. We remanded with a direction to focus the...order more sharply to detail exactly what steps defendant needed to take to purge himself of contempt and secure his release. On remand and after considering arguments of counsel the hearing judge entered an order on January 4, 1998, setting forth the following actions by defendant that would satisfy the requirement that he act in good faith to achieve the return of his daughters to the United States:

1. Direct a letter to his father authorizing his father to turn over custody of the Defendant's children to a representative of the United States Department of State or such person as the Plaintiff may designated [sic].

2. File an application to the appropriate Court in Nigeria requesting that custody of the children be turned over to the Plaintiff/mother so that they may be returned to the State of New Jersey for further proceedings.

3. Request that the appropriate Court in Nigeria appoint a Guardian of his children, request the court to direct that custody of the children be turned over to the Guardian and that the Guardian deliver the children into the custody of the United States Department of State at the Embassy/Consulate in Lagos.

4. Direct his father to make immediate arrangements for the return of the children to New Jersey including making arrangements to take the children to the airport and place them on a flight whose ultimate destination is New Jersey.

5. Write a letter to the President and/or Prime Minister of Nigeria requesting their assistance in obtaining the return of his children to New Jersey.

6. Request his father, the government and the Courts in Nigeria to Order that the sister and brother-in-law of Defendant who last had custody of the children immediately to notify him of their latest whereabouts and medical condition.

7. File a Certification/Affidavit with the United States Department of State, the Nigerian Consulate and the United States Embassy in Lagos stating that he is the father of the children and he wants them returned to the United States. He must authorize whatever steps are necessary to effect the return of the children to New Jersey.

Unknown to the Family Part judge at that time was that on November 2, 1997, Ogechi, the youngest daughter, died at age eleven, reportedly from malnutrition.

...[A further appeal by Defendant was denied on April 2, 1998. Plaintiff filed for divorce in New Jersey on December 2, 1998, seeking custody of the surviving child, Uchechi. Defendant answered, and that case is pending trial.] Defendant submitted papers to the Family Part judge that purport to be a judgment of the Customary Court in Nigeria on August 13, 1998 dissolving the customary marriage between the parties and awarding custody to defendant based on his complaint filed in 1996. Plaintiff has responded that if the judgment is authentic, it was the product of corruption or bribery. She also asserts that she had an order of a Nigerian court incorporating the award of custody to her under the Final Restraining Order entered in New Jersey.

* * *

[Ed. Note: Defendant's March 1999 motion for release was denied, and further appeals of that denial were unsuccessful. On February 1, 2001, defendant filed a motion for review, submitting in support of his application two letters not previously considered. The first was a letter dated May 11, 1999 and signed by Michelle A. Bradford, Vice Consul at the U.S. Embassy in Lagos, Nigeria. It had been addressed to the Family Court Judge, apparently in response to his March 12, 1999 order directing plaintiff's attorney to write to "the proper Nigerian authority" to ascertain the decision of the village elders concerning the return of Uchechi and to determine "whether Nigerian culture is such as to prohibit" her return.]

The Embassy letter recites that the parties were married according to the Customary law and customs of Imo State in Nigeria on May 26, 1984 and explains under Nigerian law once a "bride price" is paid by the husband, the children and all property of marriage belong to the husband and his extended family. The letter also noted an August 19, 1997 order of the Customary court restraining plaintiff from removing or dealing with the children without consent of the court. Responding to the issue as to what steps can be taken to return Uchechi to the United States, the writer stated somewhat ominously,

> All other legal means to either resolve the case or to enforce the subsequent judgment obtained in the High Court of Lagos State and ensure that the surviving child is returned to the United States have failed. Furthermore, the recent detention of the legal guardian of the children Chris Ohuruogh on account of the death of Ogechi has not helped matters. So far it has been impossible to determine the whereabouts of Uchechi the surviving child. All the efforts of the Embassy and Edith's lawyers have also been to no avail. Edith may have to come home and settle the matter out of court with her husbands' family this will only be entertained if the charges against Longy are dropped and he is released. [sic] All in all it is a very difficult situation.

The second letter was unsolicited and sent to the trial judge on January 9, 2001 from Peter N. Njang, hereinafter the "Njang letter," an attorney at law and the executive director of the African Legal and Civil Rights center in Washington, D.C. The letter reads in pertinent part as follows:

> ...Rev. Anyanwu is locked up in jail because, it is alleged, he is deliberately keeping the child(ren) of their marriage who were born in the United State back in Nigeria. We are requesting to know how we can come in to help in this matter. As a guide to Mr. Anyanwu's predicament, we would like to beg the Hon. Judge to throw some light to the matter:

> In Nigerian Custom, as well as most African customs, children of a marriage do not belong to the husband and/or wife. Children belong to the two families even if the marriage comes to an end. To Africans, "It takes a village to mold a child". It is never heard of that divorcing couples even mention children. It is taboo! In fact, most Africans never divorce with animosity unless they come to America. Divorce is not strange to Africans, what is strange is fighting over children!

> Unfortunately, Rev. Anyanwu is caught between two elephants, the Nigerian Government and the American Government and so he is helpless. Even if he is left in prison for life, those children will not come here until they grow up to be mature to make their own decisions. Whether Rev. Anyanwu...remains in prison or comes out of prison, he cannot forcefully bring those children here to the U.S. If it were not so, what stops the children's mother from going to Nigeria, her country of origin, and to bring the children to the U.S. now that the husband is locked up and has no power to stop her from going to get the

children. Ms. Edith Anyanwu's own parents will not allow her to take the children because neither she nor Rev. Anyanwu own those children by themselves. That is our custom, i.e. the African custom....

With all due respect, your honor, we pray that you use your right judgment in deciding the fate of a man, who through no fault of his, is left in prison because he has no power over circumstances beyond his control....

... [At the review hearing on February 9, 2001, both parties were present, but neither testified.]... The defendant submitted a 128 page pro se brief setting forth his factual allegations in support of his argument that he was unable to comply with the prior orders and should therefore be released. The hearing judge indicated that the Embassy letter and the Njang letter were considered to the extent that they gave defendant support for his conclusion that he was unable to comply with the court orders. Summarizing the arguments of defendant, the judge stated the following:

His position really is that this is a conflict of cultures. Mr. Anyanwu really claims and is of the view that there are contradicting orders from two different courts in two different countries. He indicates that he's Nigerian and does not want to condemn the Nigerian court order or the Nigerian law. He will not violate, he tells me, not only when he was here last time but in his papers, the law he believes in. And he does provide some proof as to some of the things he says, although what he provides is not certified.

The judge then addressed defendant's continued detention and held as follows:

I think the issue can be framed in terms of whether there is substantial likelihood that continued confinement will cause Mr. Anyanwu to change his mind.... If the answer is no, then the likelihood of compliance does not exist and incarceration becomes or begins to become punitive, having lost its coercive effect. Bear in mind, he is incarcerated as an inducement or as a measure of coercing him to comply.... He's incarcerated since August 14, 1997. In my view, continued incarceration would no longer be coercive, but would be punitive...so I'm going to release him from incarceration.

The review hearing conducted fell short of the requirements set forth in prior case law.... [C]ontemnor had the burden of proving that continued confinement had no coercive effect and had become punitive. The...burden [must] be satisfied by competent proofs as opposed to ex parte affidavits and reports.... Factual issues...[must] be resolved only through live testimony and cross-examination.... [T]here was no live testimony presented at the review hearing, and the only new submissions were two unauthenticated letters containing hearsay statements and opinions of uncertain reliability and credibility. The hearing was therefore inadequate, necessitating a remand for a hearing consistent with the requirements of live testimony and competent evidence.

We further hold that the trial judge misapplied the standard for discharge from confinement pursuant to an order of commitment directing compliance with an earlier court order. The trial court's reliance only on the duration of confinement and the perceived refusal of defendant to comply was insufficient to carry the requisite burden of proof and persuasion. While it is inaccurate to bifurcate the legal concept of contempt into "civil contempt" and "criminal contempt,"...common legal parlance uses the terms to distinguish between coercive measures by a court to force compliance by a recalcitrant party and punitive sanctions to vindicate the authority of the court. Civil contempt is not punitive but remedial to a litigant's right to compel a recalcitrant party to "do what he ought to do."...For this reason civil contemnors are said to "carry the keys to the prison in their own pockets."...Since the legal justification for incarceration for civil contempt is to force compliance, commitment for that purpose cannot continue if it does not have or has lost its coercive power and thereby has become punitive....

Incarceration obviously loses its coercive power where the party committed is unable to comply with the court order he is charged with violating.... In the instant case, our prior opinions and the decisions of the Family Part judges at review hearings have consistently maintained and explained that defendant is not held in the Morris County Correctional Facility for failure to perform the feat of producing his living child in a New Jersey courthouse. Since 1997 he has been required only to make good faith efforts to comply with orders toward effectuating that result.

Defendant is an educated man and an educator who has demonstrated great ability to understand and communicate concerning legal concepts applicable to his case. He has had the benefit of counsel throughout this travail. Currently, he has one court-appointed attorney to represent him on this matter and another for the New Jersey divorce action brought by plaintiff. It would be fanciful to believe that he does not understand his obligation and the consequences of non-compliance. We concur with the implicit finding of the trial judge that defendant's protestations of inability to perform are disguised and contemptuous refusals of compliance.

The standard for review of commitment status...is whether there is a substantial likelihood that continued incarceration would accomplish the purpose of causing the person confined to comply with the order on which confinement is based.... No hard and fast rule or fixed period of time defines when coercive commitment becomes punitive, but refusal to comply is in itself insufficient for a finding that the commitment has lost its coercive power.... Otherwise the same willful defiance of a lawful order that precipitated the commitment would justify its dissolution and mock rather than vindicate the remedial power of the court....

* * *

Our review of the record of the last review hearing reveals that there was no additional testimony or competent evidence since Anyanwu II to support the trial judge's determination that there exists "no substantial likelihood" of compliance. The decision was based only on the passage of time of several months since Anyanwu II and the unsubstantiated opinion of the hearing judge that defendant would forever remain intransigent. In our view the record does not justify the holding that the standard of "no reasonable likelihood" of compliance was met by defendant's proofs.

* * *

Almost four years have passed since these parties first presented themselves in a New Jersey courtroom. Even a casual observer can see that their lives have gotten much worse and that they have each suffered deeply. One of their children is dead. The other somewhere far away. Their assets are depleted. The defendant lost his job and his liberty. The hostility between them remains unabated. To continue this stalemate solves nothing and assures only that defendant will remain confined for some unspecified time and plaintiff separated from her daughter. It would be naive to assume that defendant would remain within the reach of the court if released. Based on the history of this case, it appears certain that he will go to Nigeria and forever frustrate the plaintiff's search for her child.

Many legal and factual issues remain unresolved. The authenticity and effect of Nigerian court orders are disputed, including whether a valid Nigerian marriage predated the ceremony in the United States. The impact, if any, of Nigerian law and customs has not been explored to any significant extent. And of course the best interest of the child remains unknown.

We do not minimize the challenge this case presents to the hearing judge on remand, especially in light of the highly adversarial posture of the parties. We also recognize that the trial judge is relatively new to the case. We suggest therefore that the judge give consideration to appointment of a guardian ad litem to represent the interests of the child.

The guardian can proceed under the authority of the court and act impartially to report to the court on applicable issues including Nigerian law and customs. The guardian can seek out the assistance of relatives of both parties in the United States and Nigeria to assist in breaking this sad impasse. The guardian would be able to communicate with officials in Nigeria and the United States as a neutral party endeavoring to locate the child and assure the court of her status and well-being. If possible, the guardian could mediate some of the differences between the parties consistent with the best interest of the child. Furthermore, the particularized directive to defendant contained in the January 4, 1998 order must be examined and reformulated to specifically describe the action or actions required of defendant to effectuate compliance and obtain his release. The guardian would be able to assist the court in this respect as well.

In this case the private right to be vindicated and the harm resulting from defendant's non-compliance are obvious and poignant. One child died halfway around the world from her parents. Her mother was unaware both of her location and of her illness. Her father was confined to a jail. If we accept defendant's unsworn statements, the surviving child lives in an unknown place with unknown caretakers and has an uncertain future.

This is not a case of a mobster refusing to testify against criminal cohorts or of enforcement of a support order against a delinquent parent. It is not even about a conflict of cultures or the breadth or limit of judicial enforcement powers. It is about a child.

She has seen her sister die, but she has not seen either of her parents in four years, which in the life of a child can be likened to several lifetimes. While the caption of this case does not mention Uchechi Anyanwu by name, her well-being and best interests must be paramount. It is difficult to conceive of a private right of more significance and more deserving of enforcement than this one.

We have confidence in this trial judge and in the Family Part Bar to approach this troublesome matter with the sensitivity and creativity which it warrants. We believe that there should be periodic progress conferences and hearings in order to resolve this difficult matter as expeditiously as possible. Reversed and remanded. We do not retain jurisdiction.

Notes

1. *Follow-up.* In November 2001, the New Jersey Supreme Court denied the father's petition for certiorari in this case. Anyanwu v. Anyanwu, 788 A.2d 773 (2001). As of October 2001, the father was still in prison and remained steadfast in his position. The mother had no information regarding Uchechi. The trial court had not as yet been able to locate someone willing to serve as a guardian ad litem. Counsel for the mother, Mr. Thomas Snyder, suggested that fulfilling the role of guardian would probably involve a trip to Nigeria. There is some indication that the letter referred to in the above opinion from the Embassy in Lagos may have been a forgery. The U.S.

State Department subsequently advised the mother's attorney that the signature on the letter is not Ms. Bradford's signature, and that she denies having written it. The letter was sent straight to the trial court, and was not submitted by either attorney in the case. The mother has tried to hire someone to find the child in Nigeria, but that effort has been unsuccessful. She has received a letter from a member of the father's family in Nigeria suggesting that if she returns to Nigeria she will be arrested. Telephone interview by Marianne Blair with Thomas Snyder, attorney for Appellant (October 11, 2001).

If you were appointed as guardian ad litem in this case following remand, what would you recommend?

At what point does incarceration for contempt in a case of this nature become punitive rather than coercive? Does the passage of time alone, combined with the contemnor's continued refusal to perform the requested actions, ultimately transform the nature of the incarceration?

Will the contempt automatically become punitive when Uchechi turns 18, which is the age of majority in New Jersey? The mother suggests that under Nigerian customary law, there is no age of emancipation for a daughter. She remains under her father's control until she marries. Should that make a difference?

2. *State Criminal Remedies.* In addition to IPKCA, many states have imposed criminal remedies for interference with custody. Violation of these statutes is often a felony, punishable by several years in prison. *See, e.g.,* Colo. Rev. Stat. § 18-3-304 (1999); Ga. Code Ann. § 16-5-45(c)(3) (1999). Noncustodial parents, their agents, and relatives are included among those subject to prosecution. *See* State v. Vakilzaden, 742 A.2d 767 (Conn. 1999) (Uncle criminally liable for assisting his nephew in abducting nephew's daughter to Turkey during a supervised visitation); (Matsumoto v. Matsumoto, 762 A.2d 224 (N.J. Super. Ct. App. 2000) (father and paternal grandmother were indicted for conspiracy to interfere with custody, interference with custody, and endangering the welfare of a child, following their refusal to return child from Japan, where he remained after a family vacation). Some of these statutes impose higher penalties if the child is detained outside of the United States. *See* N.J. Stat. Ann. § 2C: 13-4 (1995).

State criminal statutes typically prohibit the taking, detaining, or concealing of a child from a person with court-ordered custody rights. Some also prohibit such conduct by a person with custody rights, before any order is issued, who intends to deprive another of his or her custody rights to the child, *see* Cal. Penal Code § 277 (West 1999); Mo. Rev. Stat. § 565.153.1 (1999); or who, with actual knowledge of a pending action, intends to evade the state court's jurisdiction. *See* N.J. Stat. Ann. 2C: 13-4 (1995). *See* State v. Vakilzaden, 742 A.2d 767 (Conn. 1999) (Assisting a joint custodian with abducting his daughter constitutes criminal custodial interference). Some of these statutes also impose felony imprisonment or fines for unlawful interference with visitation, as well. *See* Ariz. Rev. Stat. Ann. § 13-1302 (West 2001); N.J. Stat. Ann. § 2C: 13-4 (1995).

3. *Tort Remedies.* Abduction can create liability under a variety of tort theories. In Katjtazi v. Kajtazi, 288 F. Supp. 15 (E.D. N.Y. 1978), a federal court upheld a false imprisonment claim for compensatory and punitive damages brought on behalf of a child abducted to Yugoslavia, against both the child's father and relatives in the United States who participated in the abduction. The court also upheld claims for compensatory and punitive damages by the mother, who had been awarded temporary custody when the abduction occurred, for intentionally and maliciously abducting an infant and for intentional infliction of emotional distress.

In the decades since *Kajtazi* was handed down, the tort of intentional interference with custodial rights has been recognized by courts in approximately half of the states. Stone v. Wall, 734 So. 2d 1038, 1043 (Fla. 1999) (listing eighteen state supreme court decisions and intermediate court decisions in two other states recognizing or implying recognition of the tort; decisions in the supreme courts of four states rejecting or implying rejection of the tort; and splits in the intermediate appellate courts of two states). Where liability is recognized, damages have been pursued against not only abducting parents, *see generally* Minot v. Eckardt-Minot, 13 F.3d 590 (2d Cir. 1994), but also against relatives in other countries who are retaining the child. In Matsumoto v. Matsumoto, 762 A.2d 224 (N.J. Super Ct. App. Div. 2000), *modified and aff'd on other grounds*, 792 A.2d 1222 (N.J. 2002), a New Jersey appellate court determined that a child's paternal grandmother, who retained the child in her Tokyo home and prevented contact with his mother, was subject to the personal jurisdiction of the New Jersey courts for litigation of an interference with custody claim.

c. Self Help and Other Options

Patricia E. Apy, *Managing Child Custody Cases Involving Non-Hague Contracting States*
14 J. Am. Acad. Matrim. Law. 77, 94–95, 96–97 (1997)

Despite best efforts, removal to non-Hague contracting states is accomplished and the prospect of litigating for custody in a foreign jurisdiction looms heavy before the "left-behind" parent. An honest assessment of the circumstances must then be made and the alternatives for action must be identified and assessed.

Depending upon the country, the goal of immediate return may be unrealistic based upon the ability to compel action from the religious, legal and social systems.

The focus of the client should be directed initially on the goal of remaining in contact with and establishing access to his or her child. It is imperative to establish the physical location of the child and, by using family or friends, develop a meaningful non-adversarial conduit for communications. The litigating client must then determine whether to seek remedy from the civil or religious courts for "enforcement" of any outstanding custody orders or to initiate alternative and informal dispute resolution processes in the foreign jurisdiction. Additionally, depending on the non-Hague jurisdiction and the likelihood of future contact with the same, the cutting off of a safe jurisdiction to run to by filing for relief in the non-Hague jurisdiction may be the strongest strategy.

Here, assisting the client in locating counsel familiar with the jurisdiction and obtaining a written assessment of his opinion of the case, the likelihood of success on the merits, the application of internal law and perceived costs and time is crucial. When litigating in non-Hague jurisdictions, referral to counsel is often made through organizations and contacts not usually associated with domestic relations litigation.

Resolution of international disputes is not new territory to commercial and international private transactional law practitioners. While they may not be familiar with the family law, they are often quite knowledgeable of the political, law enforcement or religious personalities who can offer assistance both in status of the child and communications with the removing parent. Some local corporate counsel have long-standing relationships with local authorities to manage the needs of the international corporation and as a result, know who and what avenues may be available to open dialog. In addition to members of the International Academy of Matrimonial Lawyers, the International Bar Association has an extensive membership in many non-Hague jurisdictions. It is important in securing counsel to consider consulting attorneys who practice in jurisdictions who may have more frequent commercial and diplomatic ties than the United States with the non-Hague country.

* * *

...There has been no objective evidence presented that hired mercenaries have been more successful in extracting children from the non-Hague jurisdictions than alternate dispute resolution means. In fact, there is some indication that such attempts are fraught with serious personal danger for all involved, particularly the child, with no guarantee of success.

Left behind parents who have been separated from their children find seductive any possibility of return and pay extraordinary sums of money to do so. Even if the child is successfully "re-abducted," detection and fear become the lasting legacy for the family....

Children who are subjected to such tactics are at risk for unremitting psychological and physical damage not to mention that such tactics inspire additional motivation for international terrorism.

Notes

1. *Additional Opinions on Self-Help.* Ms. Apy is not alone in her criticism of self-help as a potential remedy to international child abduction. The National Center for Missing and Exploited Children, in its publication by Patricia Hoff, Judith Schretter, and Donna Aspell, *Family Abduction: How to Prevent an Abduction and What to Do If Your Child Is Abducted* (4th Ed. 1994), *available at* http://www.missingkids.com/html/index_parental. html, at 151, strongly discourages self-help in international cases. In addition to the risks of physical and psychological harm to the re-abducting parents and children and the potential financial burden, these materials stress the risk to the re-abducting parent of imprisonment in the foreign nation or deportation, which could effectively preclude any future possibility of visitation with the abducted children. Some countries are reported to impose the death penalty for child abduction. While there have been successful cases of reabduction by parents and private mercenaries (one reported an average fee of $80,000 per abduction in 1993), the risks are indeed grave. *See* Tom Harper, *The Limitations of the Hague Convention and Alternative Remedies for a Parent Including Re-Abduction,* 9 Emory Int'l L. Rev. 257, 268–70 (1995).

Information regarding one security company that attempted reabductions of American children, and its subsequent defamation action against NBC following a segment on Dateline NBC following an unsuccessful attempted reabduction from Iceland, can be found in Corporate Training Unlimited, Inc. v. National Broadcasting Company, Inc., 981 F. Supp. 112 (E.D. N.Y. 1997).

2. *Psychological Readjustment.* For an excellent discussion of the psychological adjustment issues facing families who have been reunified after an abduction, see The National Center for Missing and Exploited Children publication, *supra,* at 152–69. This publication also provides an excellent overview of the civil and criminal remedies that can be pursued in both domestic and international abductions, as well as steps that might prevent an abduction. It is a useful resource for both clients faced with an abduction and their attorneys.

3. *Postscript: Elian.* Anyone who set foot in the United States during late 1999 or the first half of 2000 may wonder how this massive chapter on international child custody disputes could be compiled without yet mentioning Elian Gonzalez, over whom the most publicized international custody dispute of the decade took place. For those who may have been trekking in Outer Mongolia that year and somehow missed the media coverage, Elian was a five-year-old rescued off the coast of Florida by two fishermen. His mother, who had attempted to immigrate to the United States with Elian, had perished along with others on the small boat in which they had attempted the crossing. The U.S. Coast Guard transported the child to a hospital for medical care. As an unaccompanied minor alien, Elian was placed in the custody of the INS and paroled to his paternal great-uncle, who resided in Miami. Elian's father, Juan Gonzalez-Quintana, who had been actively involved in the child's care following his separation and divorce from Elian's mother, immediately requested assistance from the Cuban government to have Elian returned to him, contending that the removal had been without his permission. If Cuba had been a party to the Hague Abduction Convention, how might this case have been resolved?

Elian's great-uncle sought political asylum on Elian's behalf. Following several interviews with Elian's father, the INS and the Attorney General concluded that Elian was not competent to demonstrate an intention to apply for asylum, that there was no evidence of abuse on the part of his father, who opposed the application for asylum, and that "universally accepted legal norms" support the principle that a parent is presumed to speak for his child. The application for asylum was therefore regarded by the INS as withdrawn.

The great-uncle then petitioned for and initially received temporary custody in an ex parte state court proceeding on an emergency basis, in order to pursue a challenge to the INS rejection of the asylum application. After the federal district court confirmed that the Attorney General acted within her discretion in determining that the INS need not consider Elian's asylum petition, Gonzalez v. Reno, 86 F. Supp. 2d 1167 (S.D. Fla. 2000), the Florida state court terminated its order awarding custody to the great-uncle. The state court held that it lacked subject matter jurisdiction to award the great-uncle custody for two reasons. First, the court applied the doctrine of "conflict preemption," which precludes issuance of a state court order intended to prevent or hinder a federal agency from functioning in the way Congress intended. Because immigration is exclusively a federal power, and Elian's presence in the United States was at the discretion of the federal government, the state court found it was preempted from deciding custody, and thereby subverting the decision of the federal government to return the child to his father. The fundamental nature of the case, observed the court, was "an immigration case, not a family law case." In re Gonzalez, 2000 WL 492102, at 5 (Fla. Cir. Ct. 2000). Second, the state court determined that a great-uncle did not have standing under Florida law to seek custody. Moreover, the court observed, Florida courts have determined that extended family members cannot be awarded custody over the objection of a natural parent unless the parent is unfit. *Id.* at 9. Had subject matter jurisdiction been examined under the UCCJA or the UCCJEA, what would have been the likely outcome of such an analysis?

Shortly after the state court terminated its custody order, the Eleventh Circuit granted an injunction prohibiting the removal of Elian from the United States, pending resolution of the appeal. Elian was removed a week later from his great-uncle's home by federal agents, and returned to the physical custody of his father, who had traveled to the United States. The Eleventh Circuit subsequently affirmed the ruling of the lower court, upholding the INS determination that, absent special circumstances, only a parent can represent a six-year-old in immigration matters, and that the parent's residence in a "communist-totalitarian state" is not, by itself, a special circumstance. Gonzalez v. Reno, 212 F.3d 1338, 1349–54 (11th Cir. 2000). On the day that the U.S Supreme Court denied certiorari, Gonzalez v. Reno, 530 U.S. 1270 (2000), Elian returned with his father to Cuba. While his case established a useful precedent for parents who seek the return of children brought to or retained in the United States without lawful immigration status, over the objections of both parents or the sole, living parent, this scenario arises relatively infrequently. *Cf.* Polovchak v. Meese, 744 F.2d 731, 736 (7th Cir. 1985) (twelve-year-old was at the lower end of age range in which a minor may be sufficiently mature to apply for political asylum against the wishes of his parents).

Chapter 9

Financial Support of Children

Can one draw conclusions about a country based upon how, and to what extent, that country financially supports its children? If so, what conclusions might you draw about the United States? Any analysis must focus not simply on the level at which children are supported, but it must also include questions about which private parties are obligated to support children, whether private individuals have autonomy to set the level of financial support children receive, and who bears the ultimate responsibility for ensuring that children are adequately supported.

In the United States, parents have the primary obligation to support their children, although many fail to fulfill their obligations. As Professor Marsha Garrison has stated, "There can be little doubt that child support policy is an urgent concern. At least half of all American children will be eligible for child support at some point during their minority, but most receive inadequate payments, and many receive nothing at all." Marsha Garrison, *The Goals and Limits of Child Support Policy, in* Child Support: The Next Frontier 16 (J. Thomas Oldham & Marygold S. Melli eds., 2000). The fact that so many American children rely on child support, and that so many receive inadequate support, gives rise to a series of questions about our own laws. The questions and the answers benefit from comparative analysis.

The first and perhaps most basic question is, "Who has a legal obligation to support children?" No one thinks that children should simply support themselves. In some societies, the support of children is seen primarily as a societal or group obligation. Examples of communities where communal child-rearing is the norm include the Efe, inhabitants of the Ituri Forest in the Democratic Republic of the Congo, where a caregiver responded to the question, "Who cares for Efe infants?" by stating, "All of us." Children who were eighteen weeks old spent approximately 60% of their time with individuals other than mothers, and each child was cared for on average by approximately fourteen persons. *See* Paula K. Ivey, *Cooperative Reproduction in Ituri Forest Hunter-Gathers: Who Cares for Efe Infants*, 41 Current Anthropology 856, 858, 865 (2000). Other examples include members of the Universal Brotherhood and Theosophical Society at Point Loma, a turn-of-the-century utopian society, where "family units did not include children" because "[p]arents deposited their offspring a few months after birth in a communal nursery, seeing them regularly thereafter only on Sundays." Robert Hine, California's Utopian Colonies 856, 858, 865 (1983). Perhaps best known is the Oneida community in New York, where children age two to twelve lived together in a building separate from their parents, the Children's House, with their nurses and teachers. *See* Constance Noyes Robertson, Oneida Community: An Autobiography, 1851–1876, 311 (1970). Although these examples do not differentiate between the financial and physical support of children, they still serve as reminders that not all societies allocate children's support, broadly understood, to the children's parents. Yet, in most societies, the financial and physical support of children does fall primarily upon their parents, with extended family members, the larger community, and the state playing a complementary role.

Finding the optimal balance between individual and community care is a pressing concern in the context of child support. As Irwin Garfinkel has written,

> At the most general level, child support policy reflects the extent to which the support of children is a private rather than a public responsibility. Some people take the position that child support enforcement is unnecessary because the costs of child rearing are a public responsibility. They argue that if public benefits were more generous, children would not need private child support. We do not share this position, and we would point out that no country has totally socialized the costs of children. Hence, not enforcing private child support obligations implicitly means shifting more of the costs of children onto resident mothers. The public responsibility argument, in practice becomes a smoke screen for excusing non-resident fathers from their responsibilities.
>
> Other people take the position that the support of children is purely a private responsibility. We do not agree with this position either. To begin with, society has an interest in making sure that children's basic needs are met. This means, at a minimum, that government has a responsibility to enforce private child support obligations. Even more important, just as the need for private child support enforcement would not evaporate if we had a better public income maintenance system, even a perfectly efficient child support enforcement system would not obviate the need for better income maintenance, public education, healthcare, and child care. In short, we see these two systems—public and private support for children—as complementing one another, and as reinforcing the social norm that raising healthy and secure children is a shared responsibility.

Irwin Garfinkel et al., *Conclusion, in* Father Under Fire: The Revolution in Child Support Enforcement 342 (Garfinkel et al. eds., 1998).

This chapter is concerned with how various countries strike the balance between the private and public support of children. Part A focuses on which private individuals are legally obligated to support children. Part B then examines particular state interventions in support of children. It starts with the most direct type of support, income transfers, and moves to more indirect types of support, focusing on child support assurance programs, automatic adjustments of private child support awards, and finally the initial establishment of adequate levels of private support. The aim is to better understand the balance struck in our own child support policy, and to recognize the benefits and limitations of the approach.

A. Who Must Support Children?

The answer to the question set forth immediately above is "parents." "In all [European countries and the United States]..., parents who are or were married to each other are legally obliged to support their children. In the case of unmarried parents, once paternity is established the father must also provide financial support." *See* Anne Corden & Daniel R. Meyer, *Child Support Policy Regimes in the United States, United Kingdom, and Other Countries: Similar Issues, Different Approaches*, 21 Focus 72, 75 (2000) (studying Austria,

Belgium, Denmark, Finland, France, Germany, the Netherlands, Norway, Sweden, U.K., and U.S). Whether biological or adoptive parentage should be a necessary precondition for the legal obligation, or whether some broader notion of social parentage should also obligate individuals to support children, is an issue under discussion in many countries.

Chartier v. Chartier
[1999] 1 S.C.R. 242 (Can.)

Bastarache, J.

In this appeal, the Court is asked to determine whether a person who stands in the place of a parent to a child within the meaning of the Divorce Act, R.S.C., 1985, c. 3 (2nd Supp.), can unilaterally give up that status and escape the obligation to provide support for that child after the breakdown of the marriage. The Court unanimously decided that a person cannot do so and allowed the appeal....

Facts

The parties began a common law relationship in November 1989 and married on June 1, 1991. Their child, Jeena, was born on August 29, 1990. The parties separated in May 1992, later reconciled for a month or two, then permanently separated in September 1992.

Jessica is the child of the wife from a previous relationship. While the parties lived together, the husband played an active role in caring for both children and was a father-figure for Jessica. The parties discussed, but did not proceed with, the husband's adoption of Jessica. The parties did amend Jessica's birth registration to indicate, falsely, that the husband was Jessica's natural father and to change her name to his.

On March 17, 1994, in a consent judgment in proceedings under The Family Maintenance Act, C.C.S.M., c. F20, the husband acknowledged both Jessica and Jeena as children of the marriage and was granted access to them. He agreed to pay maintenance for Jeena, but the judgment was silent as to maintenance for Jessica and for the wife. The wife commenced divorce proceedings in February 1995 and included in her claim the request for a declaration that the husband stands in the place of a parent to Jessica. The husband contested the claim. The interim order of April 19, 1995 ordered the husband to pay monthly support for Jessica and for the wife, suspended access of the husband until a further order of the court and ordered a report from Conciliation Services concerning access. That report of October 1995 recorded the husband's desire to sever his relationship with Jessica.

At trial, De Graves J. ordered spousal support, a reduction in the monthly support for Jeena, awarded costs to the wife and found that the husband had repudiated his parental relationship with Jessica.... The Court of Appeal allowed the wife's appeal on the issue of the reduction of monthly support for Jeena. The Court of Appeal dismissed the wife's appeal for support for Jessica....

Issue

Under what circumstances, if any, can an adult who is or has been in the place of a parent pursuant to s. 2 of the Divorce Act withdraw from that position?*

---

* Ed. Note: The parties agreed that their rights and obligations under the Family Maintenance Act and the Divorce Act were identical for the purposes of the action. The courts adjudicated the action as though the Divorce Act were the applicable statute.
Section 2 of the Divorce Act, R.S.C., c. 3 (2nd Supp. 1985) states:

Analysis

There is one body of case law, exemplified by *Carignan* [*v. Carignan* (1989), 61 Man. R. (2d) 66 (C.A.)], that states that a person standing in the place of a parent is entitled to make a unilateral withdrawal from the parental relationship. The other body of case law is typified by *Theriault v. Theriault* (1994), 149 A.R. 210 (C.A.); it states that a person cannot unilaterally withdraw from a relationship in which he or she stands in the place of a parent and that the court must look to the nature of the relationship to determine if a person in fact does stand in the place of a parent to a child.

Before considering these two lines of authority, I would note that in both cases the courts have engaged upon a historical review of the doctrine of loco parentis and taken the view that the words "in the place of a parent" used in the Divorce Act were intended to have the same meaning. The doctrine of loco parentis was developed in diverse contexts, trust law, tort law, master-apprentice relationships, schoolmaster-pupil relationships, wills and gifts,... at another time. Alison Diduck, in *"Carignan v. Carignan: When is a Father not a Father? Another Historical Perspective"* (1990), 19 Man. L.J. 580, explains how this common law doctrine was applied in family matters, over the years, in various jurisdictions. She concludes, at pp. 601–2, by saying:

> The in loco parentis doctrine is a creature of 19th century patriarchy. It evolved during a time when it was a morally offensive notion for a man to be held responsible for another man's child. As Mendes de Costa U.F.J. stated in a 1987 decision, it has "its roots deep in history" and "carries with it connotations of times past" (Re Spring and Spring (1987), 61 O.R. (2d) 743 at 748). Notwithstanding Parliament's choice of similar wording in the Divorce Act, 1985, it is arguably open to counsel (or to courts) to suggest that Parliament deliberately chose to reject the common law notion of in loco parentis, and that the current statute should be interpreted "free from the shadow of earlier authorities" (ibid., at 749).

I agree that the policies and values reflected in the Divorce Act must relate to contemporary Canadian society and that the general principles of statutory interpretation support a modern understanding of the words "stands in the place of a parent."...

Today there is only one principle or approach, namely, the words of an Act are to be read in their entire context and in their grammatical and ordinary sense harmoniously with the scheme of the Act, the object of the Act, and the intention of Parliament....

In my view, the common law meaning of in loco parentis is not helpful in determining the scope of the words "in the place of a parent" in the Divorce Act.

This being said, it is my opinion that the decision in *Theriault, supra*, provides the proper approach to this issue as it recognizes that the provisions of the Divorce Act dealing with children focus on what is in the best interests of the children of the mar-

---

(1) In this Act,... "child of the marriage" means a child of two spouses or former spouses who, at the material time,
    (a) is under the age of sixteen years, or
    (b) is sixteen years of age or over and under their charge but unable, by reason of illness, disability or other cause, to withdraw from their charge or to obtain the necessaries of life;...
(2) For the purposes of the definition "child of the marriage" in subsection (1), a child of two spouses or former spouses includes
    (a) any child for whom they both stand in the place of parents; and
    (b) any child of whom one is the parent and for whom the other stands in the place of a parent.

riage, not on biological parenthood or legal status of children. *Theriault* was an appeal from an interim maintenance award made to the mother and primary care-giver of two children made against the husband in a pending divorce suit. The children were not the husband's biological children. The husband gave advice and supervision to the two children from infancy but, at the hearing for interim support, he argued that his commitment to the children arose from the marriage and was conditional on the continuation of that relationship.

Kerans J.A. rejected the approach in *Carignan, supra,* and held...that once someone "has made at least a permanent or indefinite unconditional commitment to stand in the place of a parent," the jurisdiction of the courts to award support under the Divorce Act is triggered and that jurisdiction is not lost by a subsequent disavowal of the child by the parent. Underlying Kerans J.A.'s decision is the best interests of the child.... Kerans J.A. held:

> Our society values parenthood as a vital adjunct to the upbringing of children. Adequate performance of that office is a duty imposed by law whenever our society judges that it is fair to impose it. In the case of the natural parent, the biological contribution towards the new life warrants the imposition of the duty. In the case of a step-parent, it is the voluntary assumption of that role. It is not in the best interests of children that step-parents or natural parents be permitted to abandon their children, and it is their best interests that should govern. Financial responsibility is simply one of the many aspects of the office of parent. A parent, or step-parent, who refuses or avoids this obligation neglects or abandons the child. This abandonment or neglect is as real as would be a refusal of medical care, or affection, or comfort, or any other need of a child.

Other courts have also taken the view that a person who stands in the place of a parent cannot unilaterally withdraw from that relationship. In *Laraque v. Allooloo* (1992), 44 R.F.L. (3d) 10 (N.W.T.S.C.), de Weerdt J., in rejecting the notion that a person can unilaterally withdraw from a relationship in which he or she stands as a parent to a child, focused on the best interests of the children of the marriage,... [and] held:

> At the risk of being repetitious, it is well settled law that it takes a properly informed and deliberate intention to assume parental obligations for support of a child, on an ongoing basis, to bring the in loco parentis status in law into being. Given that premise, it is difficult to conclude that this status is meaningless or can be negated at whim whenever the person in loco parentis is visited by second thoughts on the matter or decides to abandon the project altogether....

In *Carignan, supra,* the wife and the husband lived together for four years before they were married in 1978. The wife's two-year-old son lived with them. The parties separated in 1981. The Court of Appeal found that the respondent did not stand in loco parentis to the child at the time of the trial and that therefore, he was not liable to pay support. Further, the court found that anyone who is in loco parentis to a child may unilaterally withdraw from that relationship simply by indicating an intention to do so.

Huband J.A. for the Court of Appeal considered the 19th century English case law with respect to two equitable doctrines in the areas of wills and estates, and trusts. In the context of wills and estates, the courts were concerned with the rules involving "double portions." In these cases, the general rule was, as stated by Huband J.A., that "a gift by deed made by a testator after he had executed a will, represents an advance as against what the child is to receive by will. A rebuttable presumption arises against the child receiving a double portion."...This rule applied both to natural parents and to adults who were in loco parentis to the child in question. The leading cases with respect to the "double portion" rule that consider loco parentis describe this relationship as being created only where the adult indicates an intention to do so. This description led Huband J.A. to conclude as follows,...

> It would seem appropriate that one would lose the status of being in loco parentis in the same manner as it is gained, by knowingly intending to terminate the relationship, and thus end the financial obligation. It is surely not a status that, once acquired, can never be shed. In dealing with double portions, the crucial issue is whether a relationship in loco parentis existed at the time the inter vivos benefit was conferred. It is entirely possible that an in loco parentis relationship might have existed for some years, and then ended by the conscious decision of the individual concerned.

Huband J.A. also examined the doctrine of advancement in the context of the law of trusts. This doctrine creates a presumption

> that where property is purchased in the name of another, or transferred to another without consideration, a resulting trust arises in favour of the person who paid the purchase price. This presumption does not operate where the purchaser stands in loco parentis to the person who receives the property. The presumption in this type of case is that the purchaser intended to confer a benefit on such a person. Again, the courts in the leading cases on this issue from the 19th century endorse the approach of the decisions made in the context of wills and estates with respect to the concept of loco parentis; the determination of whether or not this relationship exists depends on the intention of the adult.

Huband J.A. also considered a number of Canadian decisions. None of them provided him with convincing enough reasoning for him to question his view of the common law rule that an adult may end a loco parentis relationship unilaterally. Huband J.A. concluded that the respondent in *Carignan* was not liable to provide maintenance for the petitioner's son because he had ended any loco parentis relationship that existed unilaterally as he was entitled to do.

In the present appeal, the Court of Appeal, although noting that the decision has not been universally followed, confirmed the judgment in *Carignan* for essentially two reasons. The first reason is that the decision displays a "certain logic and reasonableness" because the modern institution of marriage has substantially departed from its traditional roots. Philp J.A. noted that modern marriages are "often fragile and time-limited relationships" and therefore, this raises the question of how many obligations persons must carry with them as they move from relationship to relationship. It would not be logical, in his view, for a step-parent who takes on obligations with respect to a spouse's children to be saddled with this obligation indefinitely while a step-parent who takes on no such obligation is entitled to walk away from the relationship scot-free. The finding in *Carignan* avoids this inconsistency. The second reason...relates to the fact that the decision in *Carignan* establishes "an understandable and easily determined basis for imposing or excusing responsibility."

The decision in *Carignan* has been highly criticized as seen in the decisions reviewed above and in academic commentary.... The most obvious criticism is that it nullifies the effect of the relevant provisions of the Divorce Act. If one can unilaterally terminate a relationship where a person stands in the place of a parent to a child, why define such a relationship as giving rise to obligations under the Divorce Act?

A further criticism of the analysis in *Carignan* is its treatment of the American authorities. Huband J.A. cited a number of U.S. cases from various jurisdictions which in his view support the conclusion that the loco parentis relationship can be unilaterally terminated. The application of these cases in a Canadian context is not appropriate. As Professor Farquhar stated...

> none of the cases cited involved jurisdictions where the general child support statutes impose an obligation on alternative parents to support a child. Rather, the decisions in question all involved attempts to argue that the statutory duty of a natural parent to support his or her child might also, in some circumstances, include an alternative parent. In Canada, where Parliament and the Legislatures have clearly stated that in some circumstances the duty to support a child does extend beyond natural parents to those standing in loco parentis, it may be argued that dicta from the United States should not be regarded as particularly persuasive.

I do not agree with the reasoning in *Carignan*. As noted above, the words "in the place of a parent" must be given a meaning that is independent of the common law concept and reflective of the purposive and contextual approach to statutory interpretation advocated by this Court. Once a person is found to stand in the place of a parent, that relationship cannot be unilaterally withdrawn by the adult. The interpretation of the provisions of the Divorce Act relating to "child[ren] of the marriage" should be "given such fair, large and liberal construction and interpretation as best ensures the attainment of its objects": *see* Interpretation Act, R.S.C., 1985, c. I-21, s. 12. The reasoning in *Carignan* ignores one of the fundamental objectives of the Divorce Act as it relates to children. The provisions of the Divorce Act that deal with children aim to ensure that a divorce will affect the children as little as possible. Spouses are entitled to divorce each other, but not the children who were part of the marriage. The interpretation that will best serve children is one that recognizes that when people act as parents toward them, the children can count on that relationship continuing and that these persons will continue to act as parents toward them.

What, therefore, is the proper time period for determining whether a person stands in the place of a parent? The term "at the material time" has been interpreted with reference to the parental status to mean "the time of the commencement of the proceedings," ... "the time of the hearing," ... and has also been held to mean "whatever date is appropriate."

It is clear that the court must address the needs of the child as of the date of the hearing or order. The existence of the parental relationship under s. 2(2)(b) of the Divorce Act must however be determined as of the time the family functioned as a unit. *See* Julien D. Payne, Payne on Divorce (4th ed. 1996), at p. 148. If the "material time" was to be interpreted as ["at the time of commencement of the proceedings"] it would be difficult to find a parental relationship in situations where the step-parent has little contact with the child between the separation and the divorce proceedings. This is inconsistent with the purpose of the Divorce Act.

The facts of the present case demonstrate why this interpretation is appropriate. Until Mr. Chartier's unilateral withdrawal from the relationship, Jessica saw the respondent as her father in every way. He was the only father she knew. To allow him to withdraw from that relationship, as long as he does it before the petition for divorce, is unacceptable. The breakdown of the parent/child relationship after separation is not a relevant factor in determining whether or not a person stands in the place of a parent for the purposes of the Divorce Act. Jessica was as much a part of the family unit as Jeena and should not be treated differently from her because the spouses separated. The "material time" factor does not affect the determination of the parental relationship. It simply applies to the age considerations that are a precondition to the determination of need.

What then is the proper test for determining whether a person stands in the place of a parent within the meaning of the Divorce Act? The appellant argued that the test for whether or not a person stands in the place of a parent should be determined exclusively from the perspective of the child. I cannot accept this test. In many cases, a child will be very young and it will be difficult to determine whether that child considers the person as a parental figure. Further, an older child may resent his or her step-parent and reject the authority of that person as a parent, even though, objectively, that person effectively provides for the child and stands in the place of a parent. The opinion of the child regarding the relationship with the step-parent is important, but it constitutes only one of many factors to be considered. In particular, attention must be given to the representations of the step-parent, independently of the child's response.

Whether a person stands in the place of a parent must take into account all factors relevant to that determination, viewed objectively. What must be determined is the nature of the relationship. The Divorce Act makes no mention of formal expressions of intent. The focus on voluntariness and intention in Carignan was dependent on the common law approach discussed earlier. It was wrong. The court must determine the nature of the relationship by looking at a number of factors, among which is intention. Intention will not only be expressed formally. The court must also infer intention from actions, and take into consideration that even expressed intentions may sometimes change. The actual fact of forming a new family is a key factor in drawing an inference that the step-parent treats the child as a member of his or her family, i.e., a child of the marriage. The relevant factors in defining the parental relationship include, but are not limited to, whether the child participates in the extended family in the same way as would a biological child; whether the person provides financially for the child (depending on ability to pay); whether the person disciplines the child as a parent; whether the person represents to the child, the family, the world, either explicitly or implicitly, that he or she is responsible as a parent to the child; the nature or existence of the child's relationship with the absent biological parent. The manifestation of the intention of the step-parent cannot be qualified as to duration, or be otherwise made conditional or qualified, even if this intention is manifested expressly. Once it is shown that the child is to be considered, in fact, a "child of the marriage," the obligations of the step-parent towards him or her are the same as those relative to a child born of the marriage with regard to the application of the Divorce Act. The step-parent, at this point, does not only incur obligations. He or she also acquires certain rights, such as the right to apply eventually for custody or access under s.16(1) of the Divorce Act.

Nevertheless, not every adult-child relationship will be determined to be one where the adult stands in the place of a parent. Every case must be determined on its own facts and it must be established from the evidence that the adult acted so as to stand in the place of a parent to the child.

Huband J.A., in Carignan, expressed the concern that individuals may be reluctant to be generous toward children for fear that their generosity will give rise to parental obligations. I do not share those concerns. The nature of a parental relationship is complex and includes more than financial support. People do not enter into parental relationships with the view that they will be terminated. I share the view expressed by Beaulieu J. in Siddall:

> It is important to examine the motive behind a person's generosity towards the children of the person they wish to be involved with or are involved with in a relationship. In many cases children are used as pawns by men and, on occa-

sion, women who desire the attention of the children's parent and once the relationship between the adults fail, the children are abandoned. This is not to be encouraged. If requiring men to continue their relationship, financially and emotionally with the children is a discouragement of generosity then, perhaps such generosity should be discouraged. This type of generosity which leaves children feeling rejected and shattered once a relationship between the adults sours is not beneficial to society in general and the children, in particular. After all, it is the court's obligation to look out for the best interests of the children. In too many of these situations the ultimate result is that the child is a mere object used to accommodate a person's selfish and personal interests as long as the relationship is satisfying and gratifying. As soon as things sour and become less comfortable, the person can leave, abandoning both the parent and child, without any legal repercussions.... It is important to encourage the type of relationship that includes commitment, not superficial generosity. If relationships are more difficult for a person to extricate him- or herself from then, perhaps, more children will be spared the trauma of rejection, bruised self image and loss of financial support to which they have become accustomed.

Huband J.A., in *Carignan*, also expressed the concern that a child might collect support from both the biological parent and the step-parent. I do not accept that this is a valid concern. The contribution to be paid by the biological parent should be assessed independently of the obligations of the step-parent. The obligation to support a child arises as soon as that child is determined to be a "child of the marriage." The obligations of parents for a child are all joint and several. The issue of contribution is one between all of the parents who have obligations towards the child, whether they are biological parents or step-parents; it should not affect the child. If a parent seeks contribution from another parent, he or she must, in the meantime, pay support for the child regardless of the obligations of the other parent.

Some concerns may also be raised with regard to the relevance of adoption proceedings.... I recall that Mr. Chartier did not finalize his plans to adopt Jessica. The simple answer to that is that legal adoption will nevertheless have a significant impact in other areas of the law, most notably trusts and wills; it retains its importance....

On the facts of this case, the respondent stood in the place of a parent toward Jessica. The respondent represented to Jessica and to the world that he assumed full parental responsibility for her. Mr. Chartier is the only father that Jessica has known owing to the fact that the parties led her to believe that the respondent was in fact Jessica's biological father. The respondent even considered adopting Jessica, and the parties had Jessica's birth registration amended to change Jessica's name to correspond to the respondent's. This was done by falsely submitting an application stating that the respondent was Jessica's natural father. After the separation, the respondent continued to have visits with Jessica. Eventually access was terminated with regard to both Jessica and his biological child, Jeena.

The respondent's unilateral withdrawal from the relationship with Jessica does not change the fact that he acted, in all ways, as a father during the time the family lived together. Therefore, Jessica was a "child of the marriage" when the parties separated and later divorced, with all of the rights and responsibilities which that status entails under the Divorce Act. With respect to support from the respondent, Jessica is to be treated in the same way as Jeena.

John Eekelaar, *Are Parents Morally Obliged to Care for Their Children?*
11 Oxford J. Legal Stud. 340, 351–53 (1991)

Parenthood and Duty

[I]f duties exist to care for children, are they independent or derivative from other duties? The duty to care for children is embedded in the *conjunction* of two sources. One is the *a priori* duty to promote human flourishing, which exists independently of the actual organization of any society. That moral duty binds everyone and is not specifically directed towards parents (although it will frequently fall primarily on them for no other reason than their physical proximity to their children). The other is derivative from the society itself, for social practice determines the application of that duty within its structure. There may be an independent moral duty to comply with social practice, but that is a separate matter. What is clear is that, while social practice does not itself create the duties towards children, it may place a particular responsibility on some people rather than others to discharge them with respect to particular children.

The Problem of Default

It is important to grasp this point. For it is easy to think that when a certain characteristic, say, parenthood, is identified as a basis for acquiring a duty to care for a child, it is an individual's possession of that characteristic which itself generates the moral duty. The elevation of this to a legal duty may be presented as doing no more than enforcing a moral obligation "naturally" associated with parenthood. But this is wrong. The rule might have been different while the moral duty towards the child remained intact. Of course, there are very good reasons for choosing parenthood as the basis upon which to create a dependency and, therefore, to direct the duties which parents already have towards all children, specifically towards their own child. It coincides with the wishes and instincts of most parents and will usually be well performed; it is linked to a bonding process which can be of great importance for the child's sense of identity; it allows the costs of childrearing to accrue incrementally, and marginally, to the costs of an adult household, and is therefore economically efficient.

Appreciation that social rules, not moral principles, attach duties to parenthood has important implications. The rules may be nuanced. They may except biological parenthood occurring through recognized channels of artificial generation or surrogate birth; they may impose qualifications if the parenthood occurred accidentally or contrary to the parent's will. Such rules must be rational, in conformity with other principles of equity, and never overshadow the duty everyone owes to the child. Similarly, there would seem to be no reason why a parent should not surrender responsibility provided the child's well-being is assured. (I ignore here the problem of a child's possible right, which could be provided for, later to know and perhaps meet the parent.) But suppose a father abandons his children. Apart from the mother, whose duties remain unchanged, it seems clear from this analysis that the duty to provide for the children falls back on all individuals, through the communal means constructed, or which ought to be constructed, to do this. How, then, should the community deal with the defaulter?

If the defaulter knew that, despite his departure, the child's well-being would be promoted, either by the state (as in most industrialized societies) or by wider kin, even if at a lower level than would have happened were it not for the default, the defaulter's transgression would lie more against the community's social rules than against a moral obligation towards children. What purposes, then, may justify coercive measures against such a defaulter? The following suggest themselves:

(1) To attempt to *maintain* the responsibility-allocation in this particular case: the father should be compelled to continue to devote resources for the benefit of his child to the extent that he would have done were it not for the default, or to the extent compatible with his duties towards other children for whom he has now been allocated or has assumed responsibility;

(2) To attempt to *reinforce* the rules of allocation of responsibility: the man should be compelled to contribute towards the expenses falling on others in supporting his children lest the rules lose their authority;

(3) To attempt to *redress* the imbalance that normally arises between the man and the mother in the discharge of that responsibility when the man leaves the family. The principle would be that the man should be compelled to transfer resources to the mother to the extent that in entering her parental role she has suffered economic detriment for which the continued support of the man was intended to compensate.

Although these purposes might combine in a single financial order, they nevertheless remain distinguishable objectives. The state may fulfill its duty towards the children without adopting any of the measures (although, if it omits (3), it will need to ensure that social organization is such that the risks of entering parenthood are not placed unequally on men and women). Once the primary moral duty is understood (that the community is obliged to ensure the well-being of all its children, not because or to the extent that this may be in the interests of the adult generation but because cardinal moral principles ordain the nurturing and promotion of every individual human life), the community can endeavor to produce the mix of social rules which best fulfills the obligation, remembering always, of course, that the goods of the adults must be respected as well.

Notes and Questions

1. *Relevant Provisions.* In Canada, the Divorce Act, subsection 2(2), allows a court in the context of a separation or a divorce to determine whether a spouse stands in place of a parent. Section 5 of the Federal Child Support Guidelines directs courts how to proceed if a spouse does stand in place of a parent. The guidelines state, "[w]here the spouse against whom a child support order is sought stands in the place of a parent for a child, the amount of a child support order is, in respect of that spouse, such amount as the court considers appropriate, having regard to these Guidelines and any other parent's legal duty to support the child." Federal Child Support Guidelines § 5 (1997) (Can.). The Supreme Court of Canada in *Chartier* did not refer to the Federal Guidelines because the case was tried before the guidelines came into force.

In Canada, the Federal Child Support Guidelines apply in cases brought under the Divorce Act. In other cases, for example cases involving the child support obligations of non-marital couples, the provincial child support guidelines apply. Most provinces and territories have a provision similar to section 5 in their own guidelines. In fact, many of the provinces and territories have adopted the Federal Child Support Guidelines into their law. However, four provinces, Quebec, Prince Edward Island, New

Brunswick, and Manitoba, have permission to apply their own guidelines even in cases arising under the Divorce Act, and those guidelines differ in several respects from the Federal Child Support Guidelines. *See generally* Dep't of Justice Canada, 2 Children Come First: A Report to Parliament Reviewing the Provisions and Operation of the Federal Child Support Guidelines 17–18 (2002), *at* http://canada.justice.gc.ca/en/ps/sup/pub/rp/volume_2_title.html.

Some provincial laws do extend child support obligations to individuals in a cohabiting relationship, even after the relationship ends. *See, e.g.,* Family Relations Act, R.S.B.C., c. 128, § 1 (1996) (obligating "parent" to support child and defining "parent" to include a "step-parent," which is further defined as someone who married or cohabited with a child's biological parent and contributed to the support of the child). *See, e.g.,* Dutrisac v. Ulm, [2000] 6 R.F.L.5th 132 (B.C.C.A.). The *in loco parentis* doctrine may also allow a court to reach the same result even without a favorable statutory definition. *See, e.g.,* M (S.T.) v. F (M.D.), [2002] 31 R.F.L.5th 82 (Alta. Q.B.).

2. *Obligors and Amount.* How many fathers does Jessica have? Are all equally obligated to pay child support for her? Consider again the Federal Child Support Guidelines, subsection 5, set forth in the previous note. Notice that once a court concludes that a "step-parent" stands in the place of a parent, the court does not merely apply the standard formula to determine the step-parent's liability. Rather, the court has discretion to set the relevant amount and duration of the child support obligation. In a recent report to Parliament, the Minister of Justice indicated that courts across Canada have adopted a variety of approaches to determine the proper amount and duration of child support payable by a step-parent. For example, some courts order the step-parent to pay the full guideline amount if the biological father's role in the child's life is negligible; others employ an "income-shares" model for the three adults; some courts apportion the support according to the role each adult plays in the child's life; other courts apply the full guideline amount to each adult independently and do not care about excessive support; others consider the parents' means, needs, and circumstances, the child's relationship with each adult, and the child's reliance on the support. *See generally* Dep't of Justice Canada, *supra,* at 49–50. The variety of approaches has made it "increasingly difficult for parties to agree on a child support amount." *Id.* at 48. Despite this disadvantage, the Minister of Justice recently recommended no change in the current approach to determining step-parent liability.

3. *Contribution.* Justice Bastarache stated that Mr. Chartier's liability was "joint and several," and also suggested that Mr. Chartier might be able to obtain contribution from Jessica's biological father. Other courts have decided similarly. *See generally* McBride v. McBride, [2001] N.W.T.S.C. 59 (N.W.T. Sup. Ct.) (citing cases). Some courts permit a step-father to join the biological father in the divorce action, although that option depends upon the province and whether the mother and natural father were married. For example, in *McBride*, the court allowed the step-father to join the natural father in the divorce action because the relevant legislation in the Northwest Territories permitted joinder. Even when joinder is statutorily permissible, however, courts have discretion whether to permit it in the particular case. For example, courts have declined to add a biological parent as a party when the biological parent was on welfare so that any financial contribution would be minimal. *See, e.g.,* Apthorp v. Shearing, [1998] 42 R.F.L.4th 287 (Ont. Div. Ct. 1998). As an alternative to permitting joinder, some courts limit the duration of the step-parent's liability in order to encourage the custodial parent to seek support from the biological parent. *See, e.g.,* Irwin v. Irwin, [1997] O.J. 3892 (Ont. Div. Ct.).

Step-parents are not the only ones who might seek contribution. A biological father who is paying child support, for example, may also have a claim for contribution against the step-father. In *Theriault v. Theriault*, [1994] 113 D.L.R.4th 57, 61 (Alta. C.A.), the court rejected the "universal proposition" that the biological father has primary liability. It stated that his liability would depend upon the circumstances and should be resolved in an action for contribution among those responsible for support. However, provincial guidelines may preclude a biological father from applying for apportionment of child support. *See, e.g.*, Wright v. Zaver, [2002] 211 D.L.R.4th 260, 273 (Ont. C.A.) (emphasizing that natural or adoptive parent of child could not invoke provision allowing court to impose an "appropriate" award against step-parent). For an excellent article that addresses assessment and apportionment, *see* Carol Rogerson, *The Child Support Obligations of Step-Parents*, 18 Can. J. Fam. L. 9, 106–150 (2001).

4. *Impact.* How many families in Canada were potentially impacted by the holding in *Chartier* and the "stands in the place of a parent" language found in the federal and provincial child support guidelines? In 1995, approximately 10% of married and cohabitating couples in Canada had step-children. That statistic amounts to approximately 430,000 children. *See* Statistics Canada, 2001 Census Consultation Guide: Family Characteristics, *at* http://statcan.ca/english/freepub/92-125-GIE/html/fam.htm. In the United States, approximately thirty million children under the age of thirteen live with one biological parent and the parent's current partner. *See* Larry Bumpass et al., The Changing Character of Stepfamilies: Implications of Cohabitation and Nonmarital Childbearing (1994).

5. *Step-family Formation.* How might the decision in *Chartier* impact the formation of marital relationships between an adult with minor children and the adult's romantic partner? An answer to this question requires consideration of other aspects of Canada's child-support law, at a minimum, and can become quite complicated. For example, if an obligor marries a person with children, this second family may provide a sufficient reason to reduce a preexisting support order. The Federal Child Support Guidelines indicate that on either spouse's application, a court can award an amount different from the guideline amount if the requesting spouse or the child would otherwise suffer "undue hardship." *See* Federal Child Support Guidelines § 10(1) (2001) (Can.). "Undue hardship" might exist if the obligor "has a legal duty to support a child, other than a child of the marriage." *See id.* § 10(2)(d). Yet a court must deny the downward departure if the obligor would have "a higher standard of living than the household of the other spouse" after determining the amount of child support. *See id.* § 10(3). In determining the standard of living of each household, the court includes all the income of individuals living in each household, including the new spouse's income. *See id.* at sched. II, step 1. In addition, the downward departure is always discretionary with the court, even if the factual prerequisites are satisfied. Apparently most applications for a downward departure based upon the "undue hardship" standard in section 10(2)(d) have been unsuccessful. *See* Dep't of Justice, 2 Children Come First, *supra*, at 79. Provincial guidelines often contain similar rules. *See, e.g.*, Ministry of Attorney General Ontario, Child Support Guidelines, *at* http://www.attorneygeneral.jus.gov.on.ca/html/cs/main_eng.htm.

6. *United States' and Sweden's Position.* In the United States, a step-parent's support obligation is understood to terminate upon the dissolution of the marriage, unless the doctrine of estoppel or a contract dictates otherwise. Simply, the doctrine of *in loco parentis* requires a voluntary commitment that seldom exists between the step-parent and the child at the time the court is adjudicating child support. *See, e.g.*, Jackson v. Jackson, 278 A.2d 114 (D.C. 1971). In Sweden, which is discussed extensively later in the chapter, a

step-parent has an obligation to provide for a step-child with whom he or she resides so long as the step-parent is married to the child's parent or has a child together with the parent. The obligation can continue after the child leaves home if there are "special reasons." However, the "maintenance obligation applies only to the extent that the child cannot obtain maintenance from both its biological parents." Ministry of Justice, Family Law: Information on the Rules 38 (2000).

7. *Best Interest of the Child.* The child's best interest was central to the court's analysis in *Chartier.* Why is it in a child's best interest to have a step-parent obligated for support when the non-custodial parent could also fulfill the financial obligation? Courts in the United States are also concerned with the best interest of the child. Are courts in the United States acting contrary to children's best interests when the courts refuse to impose an obligation on step-parents after marital dissolution?

8. *Establishing the Obligation.* Would the result in *Chartier* have been obtainable through the doctrine of equitable estoppel? How does the test set forth by Justice Bastarache differ from the requirements of equitable estoppel? At least one court in Canada has held that the factors in *Chartier* are only suggestive, and that they need not all exist in order for the obligation to arise. *See* R.M. v. P.M., [2000] 8 R.F.L.5th 320 (Nfld. Sup. Ct.).

9. *Same-Sex Partners.* In *A. v. R.,* [1999] N.Z.F.L.R. 249, the New Zealand High Court held that a woman ("A") had to pay child support to her lesbian lover ("R"), the mother of three children that R had by artificial insemination during their fourteen years together. A had been the guardian of the children. After R's and A's relationship deteriorated, R terminated A's guardianship without opposition from A (when the children were six, eight, and ten). R sought child support from A at the same time. The Child Support Act of 1991 allowed the imposition of a child support obligation on a "step-parent." Despite ambiguous statutory language, the court held that a step-parent was one who "entered into a relationship in the nature of marriage with the other person," and the step-parent need not have been capable of actual marriage to the parent. *See* Child Support Act 1991, §§2(1), 99 (4)(d) (N.Z.). The court reasoned, "a statute should always be read as being gender neutral, unless there is clear Parliamentary language to which a Court must defer." The court emphasized that its construction supported the policy underlying the act, which was to support children. Would the result in *A. v. R.* necessarily be the same in Canada? Should it be?

10. *Length of Obligation.* In Canada, a parent's duty to pay child support continues until the child is eighteen or nineteen, depending on the age of majority in the province or territory. The provinces are about evenly divided on the relevant age. *See* Dep't of Justice Canada, Age of Majority by Province or Territory, *at* http://canada.justice.gc.ca/en/ps/sup/steps/s2c.html. Support can be ordered for children over the age of majority if the child depends upon the parent due to illness, disability, or "other cause." "Other cause" has been interpreted by courts to include pursuit of post-secondary education. *See generally* Dep't of Justice Canada, Step 2: Determine the Number of Children, *at* http://canada.justice.gc.ca/en/ps/sup/steps/s2.html. Should a step-parent's obligation continue for as long as a biological parent's obligation might extend?

Assuming your answer is yes, would you feel the same if the parental support obligation in Canada extended for a very long period of time? In Austria, the child-support duty continues until the child is twenty-eight so long as the recipient is in school or obtaining professional training. *See* The Clearinghouse on International Developments in Child,

Youth and Family Policies at Columbia University, Child Support: Austria, at 1.52 [hereinafter *Clearinghouse*], *at* http://www.childpolicyintl.org/childsupporttables/52.htm. This is similar to the laws in Finland, Germany, and the Netherlands, which focus on the need for support. *See* Anne Corden & Daniel R. Meyer, *Child Support Policy Regimes in the United States, United Kingdom, and Other Countries: Similar Issues, Different Approaches*, 21 Focus 72, 75 (2000). In contrast, in the U.K, a child-support obligation ceases at age sixteen. This is relatively "early," as the payor is obligated in "most European countries" and in the United States, until the child is eighteen. *See* Corden & Meyer, *supra*, at 75. In most states in the United States, a court can, but is not obligated to, enter an order for the child while he or she attends post-secondary school. *See, e.g.,* Mo. Ann. Stat. § 452.340.5 (Supp. 2002) (allowing order for post-secondary education, but not past child's twenty-second birthday); Ex parte Jones, 592 So. 2d 608 (Ala. 1991) (trial courts have jurisdiction to order post-minority support for college education to non-marital children as well as marital children). Some states provide explicitly that the costs of the education itself can be covered by an order. *See, e.g.,* Colo. Rev. Stat. § 14-10-115 (1.5)(b)(I) (2002) (allowing order for postsecondary educational support, but not past child's twenty-first birthday).

11. *Who Else is Obligated?* Should extended family members be liable for the financial support of children in that family? In Austria, grandparents may have to pay child support for a grandchild if the parents cannot fulfill their obligations and the child has no property of his or her own upon which to draw. *See* Gerhard Hopf, *Austria, in* Child Support: From Debt Collection to Social Policy 98–99 (Alfred J. Kahn & Shelia B. Kamerman eds., 1988); *see also Initial Reports of States Parties Due in 1994: Austria*, CRC, ¶ 209, U.N. Doc. CRC/C/11/Add.14 (1997). The grandparents are not required to do so, however, if the payments will threaten their own livelihood. *See* Clearinghouse, *supra*, at Child Support: Austria 1.52. Similarly, in Germany, all persons in the descending line are liable for each other's support; *see* § 1601 BGB, although the grandparents' liability exists only when the parents are indigent. *See generally* Eugene Dietrich Grave, *Family Law in Germany, in* Family Law in Europe 188 (Carolyn Hamilton & Kate Standley eds., 1995).

In Canada, a court adjudicating an action under the federal Divorce Act could not as a constitutional matter impose liability on grandparents. Liability might be imposed, however, under provincial or territorial statutes. In the United States, "As a general rule, persons, other than parents, with a biological tie to a child are treated as legal strangers and have no duty to support that child." Laurence C. Nolan, *Legal Strangers and the Duty of Support Beyond the Biological Tie—But How Far Beyond the Marital Tie?*, 41 Santa Clara L. Rev. 1, 5 (2000). Grandparents would typically be obligated to support grandchildren only if they have stood *in loco parentis* to the children, *see, e.g.,* Savoie v. Savoie, 538 A.2d 762, 763–64 (N.J. Super. Ct. 1990), or if the support statutes specifically address them, *see, e.g.,* Alaska R. Civ. P. 90.3(c)(3) (permitting order against child's grandparents only if the child's parents are both minors); N.C. Gen. Stat. § 50-13.4(b) (1997).

How should a country prioritize, if at all, the legal liability of step-parents and extended family members for child support? Consider the excerpt above by John Eekelaar. Do grandparents have a moral duty to support their grandchildren? Are there good reasons for imposing a legal obligation on them? What are the disadvantages? The same questions can be asked, and answered, with respect to step-parents. If society could impose an obligation on only grandparents *or* step-parents, which would be the preferable choice and why?

12. *Public Fisc.* A major force motivating governmental involvement in the establishment of adequate child support orders against parents is preservation of the public fisc. This motivation can be seen literally around the world, from the United States, *see, e.g.,* Grace Ganz Blumberg, *Reporter's Memorandum to the Members of the Institute, in* Principles of the Law of Family Dissolution: Analysis and Recommendations (Tentative Draft No. 3, pt. II, 1998), to England, *see* Jo Roll, Child Support Provisions in the Child Support, Pensions and Social Security Bill, Research Paper 99/110 for the House of Commons 8 (1999). If saving taxpayers money were a nation's sole concern, how would a country structure liability for child support? Is there a good moral or policy reason to impose liability for child support on individuals who are more directly connected to a particular child than on the general public?

13. *Relationship between Rights and Obligation. Chartier* involved the question whether social parentage is sufficient to obligate one to support a particular child. The flip side of this issue is whether social parentage is necessary to obligate one for support. In Europe there is transnational effort to separate child support obligations from parental rights, both access and otherwise. For example, the Council of Europe recently proposed disconnecting the parental support obligation from other parental responsibilities. The Draft Report on Principles Concerning the Establishment and Legal Consequences of Parentage says that "[M]aintenance should always be an obligation of parents, even if they are no longer holders of parental responsibilities." *Working Party No. 2 of the Committee of Experts on Family Law, Draft Report on Principles Concerning the Establishment and Legal Consequences of Parentage,* ¶ 65 (Council of Europe 2001). Simply, the duty to support a child is a direct legal consequence of parentage, regardless of whether the biological parent holds other parental responsibilities. *See id.* at principle 26a. The Draft Report leaves the conditions and the duration of the duty up to national laws. *Id.* ¶ 75.

The position in the United States and Canada is similar. For example, courts in both countries generally require noncustodial parents to support their children, even if the child or custodial parent terminates or interferes with the noncustodial parent's visitation. *See, e.g.,* Myers v. Young, 427 A.2d 209, 212 (Pa. Super. Ct. 1981) (duty of support "does not depend upon satisfactory visitation arrangements"); Carter v. Carter, 479 S.E.2d 681 (W. Va. 1996); Perlow v. Berg-Perlow, 816 So. 2d 210 (Fla. Dist. Ct. App. 2002); Sharpe v. Sharpe, 902 P.2d 210 (Wyo. 1995); Twaddle v. Twaddle, [1985] 46 R.F.L.2d 337 (N. S.Sup. Ct.); Robinson v. Domin, [1998] 39 R.F.L.4th 92 (B.C. Sup. Ct.); Welstead v. Bainbridge, [1995] 2 R.F.L.4th 419 (Ont. Ct. Just. Gen. Div.). However, there are occasional exceptions in Canada, *see, e.g.,* Welstead v. Bainbridge, 2 R.F.L. 4th at 419 (recognizing in *obiter dictum* appropriateness of reducing child support, when custodial parent deprives non-custodial parent of access if custodial parent has sufficient assets and income so children will not suffer), and in the United States. *See* Or. Rev. Stat. §107.434(2)(f) (2001) (permitting reduction in child support as a remedy for reduced access).

In many states in the United States and in some provinces and territories in Canada, one large exception exists to the principle that biology is sufficient to obligate a parent to support his or her child. When parental rights are terminated, the legal obligation to support one's offspring also typically ceases. *See, e.g.,* Virginia *ex rel.* Spotsylvania County Dep't of Soc. Servs. v. Fletcher, 562 S.E.2d 327 (Va. Ct. App. 2002) (refusing to order parent whose rights had been terminated to pay support to the Department of Social Services for time when children were in the custody of DSS and in foster care and receiving public assistance); *see also* The Child and Family Services Act, C.C.S.M., C.C. 80, §45 (Man.); R(K.M.) v. R(D.E.), [2001] 14 R.F.L.5th 168 (Sask. Q.B.) (natural parent has no obligation to pay support following the child's adoption). *Cf.* Kansas, Sec'y of Soc. &

Rehab. Servs. v. Clear, 804 P.2d 961 (Kan. 1991) (holding that a parent who voluntarily surrenders a child and gives up all parental rights is not obligated to pay support for the child); Coffey v. Vasquez, 350 S.E.2d 396, 398 (S.C. App. 1986) ("a parent's obligation to feed, clothe and otherwise support a child, being correlative to the parent's rights in and to the child, does not exist where the parent's reciprocal rights in and to the child have been terminated"). *But see* Carroll County Dep't Soc. Serv. v. Edelmann, 577 A.2d 14 (Md. 1990) (holding that contractual obligation to repay social services for public assistance did not end on termination of parental rights). In Canada, the exception creates a potential asymmetry between biological parents and step-parents since step-parents have no parental rights to terminate. What should be the solution? Similarly, should step-parents and biological parents be treated differently in Canada if visitation is denied to an obligor step-parent?

15. *Identity of the Payee.* Who is the payee of the child support? In Belgium, Germany, Denmark, Finland, Norway, and Sweden, the child is the legal beneficiary. However, in some societies, notably the United States, the U.K., and Canada, the child is not the payee, but a third party is—typically either the custodial parent or the state. *See generally* Corden & Meyer, *supra*, at 75. Some courts in Canada, however, make the child support payments payable directly to children who are at or over the age of majority. *See* Dep't of Justice Canada, *Children Come First, supra*, at 39. Does it matter if the custodial parent or the child is the payee? Some commentators claim that designation of a particular payee may have "significant consequences" in terms of payor compliance or payee incentives to work. Corden & Meyer, *supra*. Should the payee differ if the obligor is the step-parent as opposed to the biological parent?

16. *Moral and Legal Obligations.* John Eekelaar's article suggests a theoretical construct by which to think about the issues related to step-parent liability for child support. Over time, our perceptions of who should be legally obligated to support children have changed. In fact, "[a]t common law, parents had no privately enforceable obligation to support their children." *See* Blumberg, *supra*. In fact, "[t]he first child support obligations [in England and the United States] were imposed by the Elizabethan poor laws, and they ran not to children but to the local parish. They were designed to save the parish the expense of supporting indigent children." *Id.* Given the materials presented, what is your opinion about the desirability of a broad step-parent obligation for child support?

17. *Other Private Support Obligations.* For an interesting article on children's obligations to support their parents, see Seymour Moskowitz, *Adult Children and Indigent Parents: Intergenerational Responsibilities in International Perspective*, 86 Marq. L. Rev. 401 (2002).

Problem 9-1

Margie and Greg married ten years ago. They separated last year. A divorce petition was recently filed by Margie. Margie has one fourteen-year-old son, Christopher, from a previous marriage. When Margie and Greg married, they agreed that Margie would limit her employment until Christopher entered middle school, so that she could be home when Christopher's school day ended. Consequently, Margie only worked outside the home part-time until Christopher was eleven years old. Christopher was thirteen years old when Margie and Greg separated.

Christopher's biological father, Wayne, has never had any relationship with Christopher. Wayne and Margie separated before Christopher was born and Wayne never has exercised any access or other form of contact. Approximately fifteen years ago, at the time Wayne and Margie separated, Wayne was earning approximately $17,000 per year.

When Margie and Greg separated, they entered into a separation agreement that obligates Greg to pay $150 per month in child support for Christopher. That support has never been paid. Margie now earns approximately $39,000 per year, and Greg earns approximately $65,000 per year.

At a hearing on various issues related to the divorce, Greg contends that he never stood *in loco parentis* to Christopher; alternatively, if he ever did assume that role, he terminated his relationship with Christopher entirely when he and Margie separated last year, thereby terminating any support obligation that he might have had. Greg also contends that Margie must first exhaust her remedies against Wayne before seeking support from him. Finally, Greg argues that in no event should his child support obligation be the full amount under the applicable guidelines because he has no current relationship with Christopher and Christopher's biological father is known and capable of paying support. There is no evidence, however, about Wayne's current financial circumstances. What would a Canadian trial court do? What would an American trial court do?

B. Parent-State Relationship for the Support of Children

When the law determines which private individuals are legally obligated to support children, the government is involved, albeit indirectly, in the support of children. The government can also be involved in other ways too. Governmental involvement in the United States primarily takes the form of establishing formulas that determine the level of support private individuals pay upon family breakup and providing mechanisms to enforce payors' obligations.

In the United States, the existing legal landscape is the result of joint federal and state efforts over the last thirty years or so. Prior to that time, states had statutes obligating parents to pay a "just and reasonable" amount of child support. State trial courts applied this vague standard inconsistently in similar cases, although they typically failed to order adequate support. The federal government became involved because it was concerned about the rising numbers of individuals claiming Aid to Families with Dependent Children (AFDC), a public assistance program enacted in 1935 to help children in single-parent households when the absent parent failed to support the child and the custodial parent was low-income. *See* Aid to Families with Dependent Children, Title IV-A of the Social Security Act of 1935, Pub. L. No. 74-271, 49 Stat. 620 (codified at 42 U.S.C. §§ 601–617).

In 1974, the federal government enacted the Child Support and Establishment of Paternity Act, which amended Title IV of the Social Security Act. *See* Social Security Amendments of 1974, Pub. L. No. 93-647, 88 Stat. 2337 (codified as amended at 42 U.S.C. §§ 651–665). The new Title IV-D law targeted recipients of public assistance and required them to cooperate in locating potential obligors, in establishing and enforcing support orders, and by assigning to the government their rights to child support. Since 1974, the federal government has enacted various laws extending the role of the federal government, often in cooperation with the states, in the establishment and enforcement of child support. The following description, while limited, gives the flavor of the federal efforts.

The Child Support Enforcement Amendments of 1984, Pub. L. No. 98-378, 98 Stat. 1305, amending 42 U.S.C. §§ 657–662 (codified as amended in scattered sections of 26 U.S.C. and 42 U.S.C.), mandated that states promulgate child support guidelines for the judiciary, although there was no requirement that the guidelines be mandatory. This act made child support services available to all who needed the services, regardless of whether they were AFDC recipients. The 1984 legislation also required that states enact expedited processes for obtaining and enforcing support orders. The 1984 act contained several important enforcement tools, including the state tax intercept program. The act also required states to enact procedures that would permit obligees to establish liens against property for past-due support.

Congress then enacted the Family Support Act of 1988. See Pub. L. No. 100-485, 102 Stat. 2343 (codified as amended in scattered sections of 42 U.S.C.). The act required that child support guidelines be applicable in all cases, and that the guideline amount be a rebuttable presumption. It also provided that any deviation from the guidelines be explained in writing, that guidelines apply in modification proceedings, and that states enact procedures for the periodic adjustments of awards. See 42 U.S.C. § 667. It also provided immediate wage withholding for all new child support orders, with limited exceptions.

Four years later, the federal government passed the Child Support Recovery Act of 1992, which criminalizes the willful failure to pay child support to a child in another state. See Pub. L. No. 102-521, 106 Stat. 3403 (codified at 18 U.S.C. § 228). A year later, the Omnibus Budget Reconciliation Act of 1993, Pub. L. No 103-66, 107 Stat. 312 (codified at 42 U.S.C. § 666(a)(5)), mandated that states adopt in-hospital programs to facilitate the voluntary acknowledgement of paternity.

In 1996, the Personal Responsibility and Work Opportunity Reconciliation Act (PRWORA) was passed. It required that additional child support collection practices be put in place by states who wanted to receive block grants under PRWORA. These practices include creating a State Case Registry database to facilitate collection and disbursement of payments, creating a New Hire Directory that reports to the Federal Parent Locator Service, adopting laws so that past due support automatically becomes liens on the obligors' property, establishing procedures so that arrearages are reported to credit bureaus, requiring states to adopt the Uniform Interstate Family Support Act, establishing procedures for license suspension for nonpayment, and expediting the process for establishment of paternity. See Personal Responsibility and Work Opportunity Reconciliation Act (Welfare Reform Act), Pub. L. No. 104-193, 110 Stat. 2105 (codified at 42 U.S.C. § 601 et seq.). See generally Samuel V. Schoonmaker, Consequences and Validity of Family Law Provisions in the 'Welfare Reform Act,' 14 J. Am. Acad. Matrimonial Law 1 (1997).

Despite the numerous federal laws on the topic of child support, federal legislation has never required that states impose a specific amount of child support on parents, that states calculate child support in a particular manner, or that calculations include child expenditures such as child care. States typically have adopted one of four models for calculating the amount of child support owed by an obligor: the Income-Shares model, the Percentage-of-Obligor-Income standard, the Delaware Melson model, or a hybrid of the Income-Shares and Percentage-of-Obligor models. "States...differ in their treatment of child expenditures not included within the basic formula." Grace

Ganz Blumberg, *Reporter's Memorandum to Members of the Institute, in* Principles of the Law of Family Dissolution: Analysis and Recommendations (Tentative Draft No. 3, pt. 2 1998). These models have been described elsewhere. *See, e.g.,* Marsha Garrison, *The Goals and Limits of Child Support Policy, in* Child Support: The Next Frontier 16–45 (J. Thomas Oldham & Marygold S. Melli eds., 2000) (footnote omitted); Jane C. Venohr & Robert G. Williams, *The Implementation and Periodic Review of State Child Support Guidelines*, 33 Fam. L.Q. 7 (1999).

The United States' approach contrasts dramatically with the approach some other countries take with respect to the support of children. We have chosen four issues by which to evaluate the United States' involvement in the adequate support of children. We start with the most direct type of state involvement and end with least direct type. In particular, we first consider state assistance given to families merely because they have children (*e.g.,* "family allowances"). We next examine state assistance given to dissolved or non-marital families when a non-custodial parent is not meeting his or her child support obligation ("child support assurance/guaranteed payment/maintenance advances"). We then consider state efforts to ensure that private child support orders hold their value over time ("automatic modification"). Finally, we explore the discretion parents have to support their children at a level below the amount dictated by the child support guidelines. While many other topics could supplement these four topics, including the manner in which child support obligations are calculated, these four topics provide a good starting point for assessing the balance struck by various nations between the public and private support of children.

1. Income Transfers/Family Allowances

Expenditures by the government on children, or on families with children, is the most overt example of public financial support for children. State support can take the form of direct cash transfers to families, either through payments or tax breaks, or in-kind benefits such as child care, food, housing, or medical care. The support can be given to all children regardless of need, or it can target the most needy. The following material contrasts Sweden and the United States in terms of public expenditures for children. While it is difficult to say conclusively why Sweden and the United States have different approaches, the following material demonstrates that they certainly do, and the notes try to suggest some possibilities for why the differences exist.

Sweden is often cited as an example of a country that has exhibited extensive concern for the support of its children. In fact, Sweden's policies in support of its children are numerous and varied.[1]

---

1. The information that follows came from a variety of sources. *See generally* International Social Security Association, Swedish Monograph to the 27th General Assembly of the International Social Security Association, Social Security in Sweden 15 (2001), *at* http://www.rfv.se/english/pdf/ssisissa.pdf; Bent Greve, Economic Support to Families With Children. A Comparison of Five Welfare States: France, Germany, the UK, Sweden and Denmark 9 (1999); Lars Gunnarsson et al., Background Report prepared for the OECD Thematic Review of Early Childhood Education and Care Policy, Early Childhood Education and Care Policy in Sweden (1999), *at* http://www.skolverket.se/pdf/ecec.pdf; Shelia Kamerman & Alfred J. Kahn, *Child and Family Policies in an Era of Social Policy Retrenchment and Restructuring, in* Child Well-Being in Rich and Transition Countries: Are Children in Growing Danger of Social Exclusion? (1999); Ministry of Health and Social Affairs, Swedish Family Policy, Fact Sheet No. 5 (2002), *at* http://social.regeringen.se/pressinfo/pdf/familj/familjepolitik_en.pdf; European Communities, Adjustment, *at* http://europa.eu.int/comm/employment_social/missoc 2001/index_en.htm; OECD Country Note: Early

Many of Sweden's policies are based on the belief that parents should be able to combine work and parenthood. Consequently, Sweden has *Parent Insurance*, which provides up to fifty days of paid leave before childbirth for pregnant mothers whose jobs are unsuitable because of their pregnancies. Sweden also has an extensive system of paid leave following the arrival of a child, whether by birth or adoption. All parents, regardless of income, are entitled to paid family leave with an assurance that their jobs are safe. Mothers receive fourteen weeks of maternity leave, and fathers receive ten days after the child arrives. Thereafter, parents receive eighteen months of parental leave. The leave is mostly paid:

> The first 13 months of leave is paid at 80 percent of wages up to a ceiling (and 100 percent for civil servants), another three months at a low flat rate, and the final three months are unpaid, but still job-protected (a non-working mother is entitled to the minimum flat rate benefit). (Employers often "top off" the first four months, thus covering 100% of salary for these months). The parental leave can be prorated (to cover 25 percent, 50 percent, or 100 percent of time off from work)....

The Clearinghouse on International Developments on Child, Youth, and Family Policies at Columbia University, *Sweden*, *at* http://www.childpolicyintl.org/countries/sweden.html [hereinafter Clearinghouse, *Sweden*]. The benefit can be invoked at anytime until the child is eight or until the end of the first school year. Both parents are entitled to an equal number of days. Apart from one month of leave which the father must take or else it is forfeited, a parent can transfer his or her benefit to the other parent. In addition, extensive paid family leave exists for use when children or the children's caregiver is sick (up to 120 days for a sick child and up to sixty days a year for a sick caregiver at 80% of qualifying income). Grandparents may also take advantage of this benefit in order to help care for a grandchild.

Sweden also has a *public childcare program*, with an emphasis on both care and education. Childcare is made available to all children over seven and under eleven whose mothers work or are full-time students, and to all children under seven regardless of their mothers' work or educational status. The government heavily subsidizes the childcare. Fees typically cost 10% of average wages; the fees meet approximately 20% of operating costs. Childcare providers receive salaries comparable to wages in other occupations. The childcare program is highly regulated, although today much power has devolved to the municipalities, which in turn has led to increased privatization in the form of non-profit parent co-operatives.

Sweden also has other programs that benefit children. For example, there is free *universal school meals, universal text books and educational materials, universal health and dental care, universal survivor's benefits*, and additional social welfare programs for the poor, refugees, and the severely handicapped. There is also a means-tested *housing allowance*. Approximately 30% of Swedish households get the housing benefit, which is at

---

Childhood Education and Care Policy in Sweden (1999), *at* http://utbildning.regeringen.se/publikationerinfo/pdfinfomat/country_note.pdf.; The Clearinghouse on International Developments on Child, Youth, and Family Policies at Columbia University, *Sweden, at* http://www.childpolicyintl. org/countries/sweden.html [hereafter Clearinghouse, *Sweden*]; *Implementation of the International Covenant on Economic, Social and Cultural Rights, Fourth Periodic Reports Submitted by States Parties under Articles 16 and 17 of the Covenant*, ECOSOC, ¶87, U.N. Doc. E/C.12/4/Add.4 (2000); David Bradley, *Family Law & Political Culture: Scandinavian Laws in Comparative Perspective* (1996); Nancy E. Dowd, *Envisioning Work and Family: A Critical Perspective on International Models*, 26 Harv. J. on Legis. 311 (1989); Ministry of Justice, Family Law: Information on the Rules (2000).

least SEK 600 per month for one child, or approximately \$60/month. Single parents are given priority for many of the benefits, including childcare and housing.

In addition, Sweden has a *family allowance system*. The "child benefit" was created by the General Child Benefit Act of 1947 as amended. It is a non-taxable cash benefit that is dispersed to all families regardless of the families' income level. The recipient must be a Swedish resident with at least one child under age sixteen, although the upper age limit is extended to twenty if the child is a student, and to twenty-three if the child has a mental disability and is attending a special school. The payee is the mother, or the father if he has custody. The benefit was approximately SEK 950/month in 2002, or approximately \$102/month, for one child. The amount is the same regardless of the child's age. There is an additional benefit for families with three or more children and for children of deceased parents and single parents. The benefit is not subject to repayment for social security received. One commentator estimated that the child allowance was equal to approximately 46% of the total expenditures a parent would make for a child, thereby making the Swedish family allowance very generous in comparison to similar allowances in France, Germany, the United Kingdom, and Denmark. *See* Bent Greve, Economic Support to Families With Children. A Comparison of Five Welfare States: France, Germany, the United Kingdom, Sweden and Denmark 15 (1999).

Sweden has no tax laws that apply exclusively to families with children. Like other countries in the Organization for Economic Co-operation and Development (OECD), direct cash benefits predominate over the use of tax benefits in the family policy arena. Nor does Sweden have "child-raising allowances," *i.e.*, money paid to parents who keep their children home instead of placing them in public daycare, except for parents of disabled children.

Sweden's extensive social programs are financed by taxes on the population, including employer taxes. The income tax is approximately 30–40% and there is a 23% sales tax on goods and services.

The United States, of course, also has benefit programs that affect or target children. Yet when the United States' initiatives are measured against Sweden's comprehensive child policy, one sees remarkable differences in the programs' breadth, eligibility requirements, administrative centralization, and justifications.

For example, the United States does not provide universal parental leave at childbirth, although limited benefits do exist. The Family and Medical Leave Act provides twelve weeks of unpaid parental leave for individuals whose employers are covered by the act, *e.g.*, employers with over fifty employees. 29 U.S.C. §§ 2601–54. A few states provide more generous benefits, allowing workers to use short-term disability insurance for parental leave. For example, workers in California can get 55% of their normal paycheck for up to six weeks after the birth of a new child or to care for a sick family member. *See* S.B. 1661, 2001–02 Leg. (Cal. 2002).

The United States, like Sweden, has a public education system. In addition, Head Start, a half-day program for children three to five years old and Early Head Start, for infants and toddlers, targets poor and vulnerable children and provides education, health and support services to their families. The Child Care and Development Fund (CCDF) makes money available to states to expand the childcare options for working parents earning less than 85% of the state median. Some states supplement the federal funding for childcare programs, although the supplementation is very uneven across the states. Also, certain tax concessions may benefit parents who utilize childcare, as described below.

Many other benefit programs assist low-income individuals, such as Medicaid, Section 8 housing benefits, and low-income energy assistance. Low-income disabled children are eligible for Supplemental Security Income (SSI). 42 U.S.C. §§ 1381–83. Children who have a parent who is entitled to old-age or disability benefits or who has died are entitled to child benefits under Social Security Disability Insurance (SSDI). *See* 42 U.S.C. § 402; 20 C.F.R. § 404.350. The Child and Adult Food Program subsidizes meals in childcare centers and schools for low-income children.

Two federal programs deserve particular mention: Temporary Assistance for Needy Families (TANF) and food stamps. The former provides cash to low income individuals who are pregnant or who have a child under eighteen, if the individual meets the program's work requirements or other requirements imposed by the states. *See* 42 U.S.C. §§ 602, 607. To qualify, the family must be subject to deprivation due to a parent's death, continued absence from the home, parental incapacity, or unemployment. *See* 45 C.F.R. § 233.10(b)(2). Single parents (separated, single, widowed, or divorced) account for around 88% of TANF claimants. U.S. Dep't of Health & Human Servs., Characteristics and Financial Circumstances of TANF Recipients: Oct. 1999–Sept. 2000, *available at* http://www.acf.dhhs.gov/programs/opre/characteristics/fy2000/analysis.htm. States can exempt unmarried recipients with children under one year old from TANF's work requirement, but otherwise recipients with children under six must work twenty hours a week and those with children over six must work thirty hours per week. *See* 42 U.S.C. §§ 607(b)(5), (c). There is an exemption for single custodial parents with children under six who cannot find suitable childcare. *Id.* § 607(e)(2). A recipient of TANF is limited to the receipt of benefits for five years during her lifetime. *Id.* § 608(a)(7). The TANF recipient must also cooperate in establishing paternity or obtaining child support, unless an exception exists, *Id.* § 608(a)(2), and fulfill certain other requirements. *See generally Id.* § 608(a).

Food stamps are vouchers to obtain food. Low-income families can qualify for them so long as the household's monthly income is below 130% of the poverty level and one family member is employed or seeking work. *See* 7 U.S.C. §§ 2011–15. States have the option of disqualifying an individual from eligibility if the individual is delinquent in any child-support payment due under a court order. *Id.* § 2015(n).

Many of the programs in the United States are administered on a decentralized basis by the states, even though the impetus for the program comes from the federal government. Although there are often national parameters for the use of federal funds, states have considerable autonomy in setting program requirements, including eligibility. For instance, there are no federal TANF rules regarding how states are to calculate benefits.

Tax benefits are the closest thing that the United States has to Sweden's "family allowances." In fact, the U.S. structures its income tax system so that children are an important determinant of the amount of tax that a person will pay. In particular, there is a *personal exemption* for dependents equal to approximately $2,000 per child, that is phased out for taxpayers with adjusted gross incomes above a certain level, *i.e.*, $150,000 for a couple filing a joint return. *See* 26 U.S.C. §§ 151, 152. This amount is adjusted for inflation under section 151(d)(4) of the Internal Revenue Code, so that the amount was actually approximately $2,900 for 2002. There is also an *earned income tax credit* that benefits those of low and middle income with a "qualifying child." 26 U.S.C. § 32. The credit works out to be worth approximately $2,400 for one child and $4,000 for more than one child for those in the lowest income brackets. Internal Revenue Service, 2001 1040A: Instructions 45 (2001). Also a *child tax credit* of approximately $600 exists for families who pay tax. 26 U.S.C. § 24. This amount is phased out for higher wage earners, *i.e.*, those with an adjusted gross income above $110,000 on a joint return. The federal government also provides a $10,000 *tax credit for adoption expenses*, which is reduced on a sliding scale for those who earn a modified adjusted gross income of more than $150,000. *See* 26 U.S.C. § 23. There is also an adoption credit of $10,000 for special needs children, which is allowed regardless of the amount of qualified adoption expense. The *dependent care tax credit* exists for childcare expenses incurred by one with a "qualifying individual," which includes a child under age thirteen for whom the taxpayer can take the personal exemption pursuant to 26 U.S.C. § 151. *See* 26 U.S.C. § 21. The dependent care tax credit is worth up to 35% of employment related expenses, which includes childcare, but the employment related expenses are capped at $3,000 for one child and $6,000 for more than one child if adjusted gross income is $15,000 or less. The credit reduces gradually to 20% of those expenses for taxpayers with adjusted gross income over $43,000. *See* 26 U.S.C. § 21(c). Finally, some taxpayers are eligible for participation in an employer's Section 129 Plan (the *Dependent Care Assistance Plan*) which allows parents to spend up to $5,000 on childcare expenses (regardless of the number of their children) and to have that amount excluded from both their income and social security taxes. *See* 26 U.S.C. § 129(a). Individual states may also have similar tax benefits. *See, e.g.,* Minnesota Dependent Care Credit, Minn. St. Ann. § 290.067 (2003).

Importantly, the description above masks the fact that many needy children in the United States are not covered by the government programs, nor benefit from the federal tax structure. For example, it is estimated that eleven million children have no health insurance and only six million of them are eligible for Medicaid or the Children's Health Insurance Program. *See* Children's Defense Fund, *Summary of the Act to Leave No Child Behind,* July 1, 2001, *at* http://www.cdfactioncouncil.org/thematic_summary_of_the_act_ to_leave_no_child_behind.htm. More than twelve million children do not get enough to eat, and over three million are regularly hungry. *Id.* Most income-eligible children do not benefit from either CCDF subsidies or Head Start. *See* OECD Country Note, Early Childhood Education and Care Policy in The United States of America 44–45 (2000). In addition, many of the federal tax benefits only assist high-income individuals.

Tax expenditures are more beneficial to wealthier taxpayers for a variety of reasons. First, except for the refundable EITC [Earned Income Tax Credit], a taxpayer cannot take advantage of a tax expenditure unless she has a tax liability. Second, even if she does have a tax liability, many tax expenditures are in the form of deductions that are available to the taxpayer only if she itemizes. In fact, most taxpayers do not itemize and those who do are, as a group, wealthier. In 1999, 67% of all individual returns filed used the standard deduction instead of itemizing, but the figures vary greatly based on income. Only 7.5% of taxpayers with adjusted gross income of $200,000 or more took the standard deduction instead of itemizing in 1999, while 96.3% of those with AGI of less than $15,000 did. See Individual Income Tax Returns, Preliminary Data 1999, in Internal Revenue Service Statistics of Income Bulletin (Spring 2001); Individual Income Tax Returns, Tax Year 1999 Preliminary Data: Selected Income and Tax Items by Size of Adjusted Gross Income 199 (1999). Preliminary statistics for the other brackets are: 85% for returns with AGI from $15,000–$29,999; 63% for returns from $30,000–$49,999; 30% for returns from $50,000–$99,999; and 9.5% for those between $100,000 and $199,999. Individual Income, *supra,* at 1.

Even when a lower bracket taxpayer does itemize and take advantage of a deduction, she saves less tax than a wealthier taxpayer. For example, if a 20% bracket takes a $100 deduction, she saves only $20, but a 30% bracket taxpayer taking the same $100 deduction would save $30. Only tax expenditures in the form of credits against actual tax liability are more beneficial to lower income taxpayers because they are dollar for dollar.

Marjorie E. Kornhauser, *A Legislator Named Sue: Re-Imagining the Income Tax*, 5 J. Gender Race & Just. 289, 325 n.55 (2002).

Notes and Questions

1. *Universalism.* Compare the United States and Sweden in terms of who is the target population of its direct government expenditures. Also, do all individuals in the United States receive the benefit of tax concessions? The explanation for the different approaches is complicated.

> Numerous hypotheses have been put forward to explain why countries have chosen universal child allowances while other countries have focused on tax concessions which are largely income-tested. Explanations usually focus on a combination of factors including the ideology of governing parties; the influence of religious parties; and the effect of political alliances among governments, trade unions and employer groups. The structure of government decision making has also been used as an explanation, especially the influence of federalism, corporatism, and the input of advocacy groups. Demographic changes such as declining birth rates or an aging population have also been used to explain pressures on governments to provide family benefits. Nations seem to value children more when it is apparent that they will be needed to pay for future social policies. Also, changing economic and labour market trends, a large deficit, and high unemployment have led to pressure by labour to create or maintain social programs and by employers and bankers to reduce social programs.

Maureen Baker, Canadian Family Policies: Cross-National Comparisons 153 (1995). The notes that follow suggest specific factors that may, or may not, be important in the comparison between the United States and Sweden.

2. *Gender Equality and Workplace Participation.* In Sweden, the "[f]amily policies are all founded on the goal of providing full employment for those able to work." Baker, *supra*, at 330. Sweden believes that both men and women need to be able to combine work and family in a way that allows each to attain economic self-sufficiency. *See* OECD, Country Note: Early Childhood Education and Care Policy in Sweden ¶ 25 (1999), *at* http://utbildning.regeringen.se/publikationerinfo/pdfinfomat/country_note.pdf.

Martha Fineman makes an argument that universal caretaking benefits are essential to allow women to be both "economic actors and mothers." *See* Martha Albertson Fineman, *Child Support Is Not the Answer: The Nature of Dependencies and Welfare Reform, in* Child Support: The Next Frontier 209 (J. Thomas Oldham & Marygold S. Melli eds., 2000). In fact, the number of children in care in Sweden has increased dramatically over time: the "proportion of children aged 1–6 in municipal child care was 12% in 1972 and 74% in 1999." Statistics Sweden, Women and Men in Sweden: Facts and Figures 2000, *at* www.scb.se/publkat/levnadsforh/1-10engtext.pdf. Consequently, today women's labor force participation is very high. Among women with children under age 7 (when compulsory school begins in Sweden), the labor force participation [was]...78 percent (and 87 percent for those with children aged 7–10)." Clearinghouse, *Sweden, supra,* at Demographic and Other Social Trends. Does the goal of "full employment for all" benefit children? How? Is it too restrictive of personal choice?

Women's workforce participation in Sweden is also encouraged in other ways. For example, Swedish tax laws are structured so that second wage earners in a family are not penalized. Individuals are the taxed unit in Sweden. This system encourages two earner couples, as opposed to the former system in which all family income was aggregated and then second-earner income was taxed at the highest marginal rate. *See* Nancy E. Dowd, *Envisioning Work and Family: A Critical Perspective on International Models*, 26 Harv. J. on Legis. 311, 322–23 (1989). In addition, the high tax rate encourages women's labor force participation because "a second income [is] a practical necessity for many two-parent families." *Id.* Finally, work force participation is encouraged because compensation is only marginally impacted by the birth of children. In fact, Sweden has the lowest pay penalty for having a child (compared to women without children) out of seven countries (Australia, Canada, Germany, Finland, Sweden, the United Kingdom, and the United States). In Sweden, the effect of children on a woman's wages was negative 0.8% for one child; negative 1.4% for two children; and, negative 2.5% for three or more children. In the United States, the respective rates were negative 3.9%, negative 7.4%, and negative 11.4%. *See* Center for Analysis of Social Exclusion, Casebrief 13, The Family Gap in Pay, tbl. 2 (1999). The variation between countries was not attributable to "differential selection into employment or to differences in wage structure." *Id.* at 2. The authors opined, but did not assess, that the difference was attributable to the variation in family policy. *Id.* at 4.

3. *Continued Gender Inequality.* Despite the official policy of gender equality, and women's high level of involvement in the paid work force, evidence suggests that most of the domestic work in Sweden is still done by women. "Swedish women spend on average 4.75 hours a week on domestic work and men 2.83 hours, a ratio of 1.7." OECD Country Note: Early Childhood Education and Care Policy in Sweden, *supra*, ¶ 28. In addition, fathers only take 10% of the total number of days used in the parental leave system. *Id.* There are ongoing efforts to alter men's participation in childcare through "personal counseling, information material, and information meetings at maternity clinics." International Social Security Association, Gen. Ass. 27th Sess., Social Security in Sweden 15 (2001). As a result, men's participation in childcare has risen during the 1990s. For example, while parents use only an average of seven days per child to care for a sick child, fathers now account for approximately 41% of those days. *Id.* Yet, despite some gains, women still take the majority of parental leave and "both parental leave and parenthood still are the responsibilities of women." Lisbeth Bekkengen, *Equal Rights, Different Practices—The Gendered Parental Leave in Sweden*, in Women Work and Health Book of Abstracts 22–23 (2002).

In addition, women currently earn on average 20% less per hour than men. Most of the difference is explainable by the high incidence of part-time work among women, education level, or choice of profession (there is obvious job segregation by sex). Yet, there is an unexplainable gap even after these other factors are taken into account. *See generally Implementation of the International Covenant on Economic, Social and Cultural Rights: Fourth Periodic Reports Submitted by States Parties Under Articles 16 and 17 of the Covenant*, ESCOR, ¶ 87, U.N. Doc. E/C.12/4/Add.4 (2000).

4. *Other Motivations for Swedish Policy.* Sweden's pronatalist policy in the 1930s was the original impetus for providing financial support for children. Greve, *supra*, at 9. Sweden's need to fulfill labor market demands motivated its initial concern with women's workforce participation. *See* Dowd, *supra*, at 346. Now Sweden's overall emphasis on social welfare drives many of these policies. Sweden's modern commitment

to social welfare began primarily after World War II, during a time of economic prosperity, when the Social Democrats took power. Family allowances were introduced in 1948, maintenance advances for single parent families in 1964, and parental insurance in 1974. Four overall goals of Swedish family policy have been identified: "— to equalize the living conditions between families with children and families without; — to give the people the economic possibility of having children when they so want; — to as far as possible within the limit [of] economic possibilities...support all in an equal way; — to give special support to vulnerable families." Greve, *supra* (*citing* the Socialdepartementet, 1996).

5. *Demographics of Sweden.* Sweden has a population of 8.8 million. It has approximately one million families with children, representing about 21% of households. Clearinghouse, *Sweden, supra,* at Demographic and Other Social Trends. Sweden ranks 15th in gross domestic product. Compare these figures with comparable figures for the United States. The United States has a population of 281.4 million. It has approximately thirty-seven million families with children, representing about 35% of households. The United States ranks first in gross domestic product.

6. *Effectiveness of Approaches.* A comparison of the level of the child benefit package in the United States and Sweden (as well as twenty other countries) has been undertaken by researchers in the United Kingdom. *See generally* Jonathan Bradshaw & Naomi Finch, *A Comparison of Child Benefit Packages in 22 Countries,* Dep't Work & Pensions Research Report No. 174, (2002), *at* http://dwp.gov.uk/asd/asd5/rrep174.html. The researchers compared not only the tax and cash benefits, but also considered the impact of housing costs and charges for childcare, health, and education. The researchers ranked the child benefit packages for a "representative" sample of families by using "purchasing power parities." The research revealed that the child benefit package in the United States is very low compared to Sweden: the United States' package is worth approximately $40 per month, and Sweden's package is worth approximately $150 per month. *Id.* at 188. Since the researchers' matrix did not attribute any value to maternity leave, paternity leave, parental leave, or leave to care for sick children, the disparity between the United States and Sweden is arguably even greater. *Id.* at 187.

The researchers also noted that the package of benefits in the United States is concentrated on low-income families. Consequently, there were notable differences between the countries regarding the level of benefits for families at different income levels. For instance, the child benefit package was considerably greater in the United States than in Sweden when the couple had three children with one earner on half the average male earnings. *Id.* at 134. The opposite was true when the family was a couple with one child and two average earners. *Id.* at 136. Despite the emphasis in the United States on providing benefits for low-income families, the United States' package was much worse for a single parent earning average female wages and needing childcare. In fact, a person in the United States in this situation who received benefits had approximately $90 less per month in net disposable income than a couple at the same income level without children. A comparable single mom in Sweden had approximately $50 more per month in disposable income than a childless couple at the same earnings level. *Id.* at 139. This difference is explainable in part because of the relatively high childcare costs in the United States and the availability of child support assurance in Sweden. *Id.* at 138.

The study noted that the level of a nation's child benefit package is not explained by a nation's wealth, its demography, or its labor market, but rather by "the overall level of social expenditure and the proportion of it going to families with children rather than the elderly." *Id.* at 189. Not only does the United States spend less of a percentage of its GNP on social expenditures than does Sweden, but the United States also spends a higher percentage of its social expenditures on the elderly than does Sweden.

A. *Income Inequality.* Income inequality refers to the distribution of income in a society. "Sweden is one of the two countries (along with Denmark) with the lowest degree of income inequality." Clearinghouse, *Sweden, supra,* at Social Protection. In contrast, the United States has a very high rate of income inequality. In Sweden, the average rich person has 2.6 times the income of the average poor person. In the United States, the average rich person has almost 6 times the income of the average low-income person. *See* David Jesuit & Timothy Smeeding, Poverty and Income Distribution, Luxembourg Income Study Working Paper No. 293, fig. 1 (1992).

B. *Child Poverty Rates.* Consider the following conclusion reached by Maureen Baker:

> Nations using social insurance programs and universal measures rather than income-tested benefits have been more effective in keeping families with children above the poverty line. These conclusions are suggested by comparison of poverty rates before and after taxes and transfers.... France, the Netherlands, and Sweden have been very effective in pulling families out of poverty by their tax and transfer systems. Despite Sweden's high tax rates, many studies have indicated that its government taxes and transfers are far more effective in pulling families out of poverty than those in Canada or the United States....

Baker, *supra,* at 153.

The specific numbers are instructive. UNICEF reports that 5.3% of Sweden's children live in households with incomes below the official poverty line, compared to 13.9% of children in the United States. *See* UNICEF, A League Table of Child Poverty in Rich Nations 7 (2000), *at* www.unicef.org.uk/news/pdf%20files/repcard1e.pdf. The numbers are more stark if one compares the percentage of children living in "relative poverty," defined as households with income below 50% of the national median. Sweden has 2.6% of its children living in relative poverty, while the United States has 22.4% of its children living in relative poverty. *Id.* at 4.

Taxes and transfers in the two countries clearly have an uneven impact on reducing child poverty. If there were no taxes and transfers at all, there would be a poverty rate in Sweden of 23.4% and in the United States of 26.7%. *Id.* at 15.

Despite the importance of state transfers to reducing child poverty, the UNICEF report concludes that the rate of child poverty is attributable to a combination of macro-economic conditions and governmental policies. In particular, relevant factors also include the percentage of single parents, the unemployment rate, and the wage disparity. In Sweden, there is a high percentage of children in single-parent households (25%), but there is also low unemployment and low wage disparity. *Id.* at 16. In the United States, there is also a high percentage of children in single-parent households (27%), but our low unemployment rate is offset by a high wage disparity. *See* Clearinghouse on International Developments in Child, Youth and Family Policies, *United States, available at* http://www.childpolicyintl.org/countries/US-html. *See also* Sheila Kamerman & Alfred J. Kahn, Child and Family Policies in an Era of Social Retrenchment and Restructuring (1999), *at* www.lisproject.org/links/cpconf/kamerman.pdf (confirming that family benefits, jobs, and adequate wages for parents are also essential to reducing poverty, although benefits certainly help); Baker, *supra*, at tbls. 3.3–.5.

C. *Other Measures of Effectiveness*. A recent report suggested that child poverty is not affected by public expenditures and that this is "not surprising given that poverty rates do not depend directly on education, nutrition, or health care expenditures." Kristen Harknett et al., *Do Public Expenditures Improve Child Outcomes in the U.S.: A Comparison Across Fifty States*, Center for Research on Child Wellbeing Working Paper #03-02 at 22 (March 2003). However, the same study, which examined the wide disparity in spending across states in the United States, indicated that "public expenditures on children are related to better child outcomes across a wide range of indicators including measures of child mortality, elementary-school test scores, and adolescent behavioral outcomes." *Id.* at 1. For example, "An extra $100 spent on Medicaid is associated with a 7 percent reduction in the child death rate.... An extra $1000 spent on education is associated with a 10 percent reduction in low math and reading scores, a 15 percent reduction in the high school dropout rate, and a 10 percent reduction in the teen birth rate." *Id.* at 21.

7. *Social Trends*. The "main demographic and social trends" in the United States and Sweden are "similar." *See* Kamerman, *supra*, at 6. The trends include "aging populations, declining or low and stable fertility rates, declining rates of marriage, high but stable divorce rates, increased cohabitation, increased lone parenting and out-of-wedlock childrearing, and medium to high rates of female labor force participation." *Id.*

8. *Political Participation by Women*. One major difference between the United States and Sweden is the rate of participation by women in political decision-making. In the United States, only 12.5% of the seats in the U.S. Congress are held by women, compared to 42.7% in Sweden. *See* OECD Country Note, *Early Childhood Education and Care Policy in The United States of America* 14 (2000).

9. *Family Allowance in the United States*. One researcher has suggested that the United States adopt a family allowance, but only for individuals who receive child support. Each year the assured benefit would be $3,000 for the first child, $1,000 for the second and third child, and $500 for each child thereafter. This benefit, with a moderate improvement in enforcement of private child support, would reduce the poverty gap in the United States among children eligible for child support by 24%. *See* Irwin Garfinkel, *The Limits of Private Child Support and the Role of an Assured Benefit, in* Child Support: The Next Frontier 183, 186 (J. Thomas Oldham & Marygold S. Melli eds., 2000). The cost of this program would be approximately $4.7 billion, although it would fall to $2.1 billion if child support enforcement improved significantly, and if that amount were remitted to the state. *Id.* at 186. Such a targeted benefit program, with reimbursement to the state by the private obligor, is considered to be "child support assurance," a program that Sweden also has and that is discussed in Section B.2. *infra.*

10. *Swedish Progressiveness*. While Sweden has been in the forefront of providing state assistance to children, Sweden has also been in the vanguard on a number of other family law issues. For example, divorce was liberalized early on in Sweden, husbands and wives were treated equally earlier than in other countries, unmarried cohabitation (including same-sex relationships) was treated favorably by Swedish family law sooner than in other countries (including by tax, welfare, and marital property law), and the conception of parental "rights" was narrowed before some other nations did the same (*e.g.*, Sweden has restricted parents' "right" to corporally punish their children, *see* Chapter 14). Harry Willekens identified these examples of "Scandinavian peculiarism" and then explained why they occurred. As you consider his explanation for

Sweden's reforms, be particularly attentive to the relationship between child support policy and other family law reforms.

Harry Willekens, *Long Term Developments in Family Law in Eastern Europe: an Explanation, in* The Changing Family: International Perspectives on the Family and Family Law

68–69 (John Eekelaar & Thandabantu Nhlapo eds., 1998)

How to explain the early timing and radicality with which reforms in Scandinavia have been pursued? I will concentrate on Sweden, in many instances the forerunner in these developments....

What is special about Sweden is not the nature of the reforms its family law has undergone—for all have evolved in the same direction—but the fact that these reforms have not been slowed down as they have been in more southern countries. An attempt at explanation should therefore in the first place look to the *absence* in Sweden of the causal elements at work in other cases.

First, the family has retained much less of a function in production relations in Sweden than in some other countries. Industrialization and capitalism came comparatively late to Sweden, were from the beginning strongly supported and influenced by the state, and led swiftly to a high degree of capital concentration; the family had only a marginal role to play in this economic development and was therefore deprived of its function in production relations in a much more brusque way than in other countries (Battail, Moyer and Fournier (1992)).

Secondly, although Sweden has a very effective system of the enforcement of the economic duties of parents (Glendon (1987)), family law is a much less needed form of protection of women and children against the risks of the breakdown of the partner relationship in Sweden than in most other countries. There are two grounds for this. Swedish women are nearly all in employment and, even if their position in the labour market is worse than men and many only work part time, they enjoy some measure of financial independence. Furthermore, abandoned partners' and children's risks are partly covered by welfare provisions (Scheiwe (1998)). This last point can also explain the extent of state intervention in the exercise of parental rights in Sweden.... [T]he more the state directly takes care of children, the more it will feel itself legitimized (and will be felt by people to be legitimized) to interfere in their upbringing.

Thirdly, political conditions in Sweden were more conducive to a rapid adaptation of the law to changes in social needs than in most other countries. If generalized democracy was a condition for the reform of family law,...then at the same time reform in most Western European democracies was hampered by the necessity to work out contorted compromises with coalition partners or social forces. In Sweden, Social Democracy dominated political life for several decades, most of the time governing alone. Moreover, Swedish society has been characterized to an uncommon degree by consensus on issues such as gender equality and the collective provision of a decent level of welfare to all; no marked difference in family policies is noticeable even in periods during which Social Democracy did not have a parliamentary majority. To a certain extent, the absence of deep ideological conflicts probably results from the incorporation of the Protestant Church in the state. Whereas the Catholic Church, being an international organization with independent infrastructures and means of existence, is a (potentially) countervailing power in both dominantly Catholic and mixed countries, therefore a power with which the state has to compromise or struggle, the Protestant Church has no such function, and is therefore much less of an impediment to family law reform than the Catholic Church can be.

---

11. *Criticism of Sweden's Approach.* Professor Nancy Dowd has been critical of Sweden's policies on a number of levels. *See* Nancy E. Dowd, *Envisioning Work and Family: A Critical Perspective on International Models*, 26 Harv. J. on Legis. 311 (1989). Among other things, she claims that the "equality model, " whereby "men and women share the same opportunities and responsibilities for family and work," discourages choice because it favors particular work-family patterns and encourages two-parent families by "not making single parent life too economically desirable." *Id.* at 317, 324–25. In addition, the equality model may have had some negative repercussions for gender equality, both practically and theoretically. Dowd claims that the model *encourages* sex discrimination because employers prefer to hire men over women given women's likelihood of taking extended parental leave and requesting part-time work. *See id.* at 317. "Most ironic[ally]," the equality model "effectively limits improvements in the status of women while simultaneously silencing women's voices" because it seems as if women have "gotten everything that they want." *Id.* at 327–28. She claims the equality model has "had the effect of resolidifying unequal roles, responsibilities, and opportunities by super-imposing an ideology and legal structure of equality upon a gendered, stratified, hierarchial work-family relationship." *Id.* at 342. She also mentions that the focus on the gender equality has excluded considerations of race and class, and that Sweden's policies are an "unconscious reflection of middle and upper-class needs." *Id.* at 340. Finally, by focusing on the equal opportunity to work, the Swedish model is premised on work-family relationships and structures as they existed and accepts a male standard as the norm. The model does not challenge the work ethic or the notion that families must adjust to work. The model does *not* require that work be restructured to accommodate families. *Id.* at 345–46.

12. *Similar Forces.* The introduction to this chapter suggested that a society's commitment to the communal physical care of children might differ from its commitment to the communal financial support of children. Yet there is often congruence. The forces that lead some societies to favor more public responsibility for the financial support of children also may lead those societies to favor more public responsibility for the physical care of children. The contrast between Sweden and the United States on the issue of early childhood education and care (ECEC) is instructive in this regard. The Organization for Economic Co-operation and Development (OECD) undertook a twelve nation review of ECEC and recently published its findings. Some of the conclusions it draws about the United States' and Sweden's approaches to childcare are also highly relevant to a discussion of the countries' approaches to children's financial support.

Two conclusions are particularly worth considering. First, the United States exhibits heavy reliance upon the market and individual choice for its ECEC. There is a feeling that "the education and upbringing of young is a private affair and not a public responsibility, that parents inherently know and are in a position to offer what is 'best' for young children."

> It seems that the policy vacuum is linked to the fairly widespread sense of mistrust against too much government intervention in the USA. Government inter-

vention is viewed as interfering with the rights and responsibilities of parents, and is only considered justifiable when the family is deemed 'in need.' This helps explain why, historically, ECEC policies [in the United States] have targeted 'at-risk,' poor, or abused children.... Policy continues to treat the family as a self-reliant entity, economically self-contained, supportive and nurturing.... In this respect, the U.S. stance differs from that in most other OECD countries, where the youngest children are viewed as society's collective responsibility.

See OECD Country Note, *Early Childhood Education and Care Policy in The United States of America* 39 (2000). Do these views about the autonomy of families in society and the distrust of government help explain the United States' child support policies too? What other values might be influencing the policy choices made in the United States regarding children's economic condition?

Second, the OECD study also noted that there is little attention in the United States to the notion of the child as having "a right to high quality education from an early age, regardless of socio-economic status or ethnic origin." The reviewers reported,

A notion of the "here and now" of childhood, of children as an independent population group to be considered in relation to other groups in the population, was one of the "missing links" in the lines of argumentation we heard—even from the most committed of advocates of high quality early education and care.. .. [C]hildren's rights...is an issue which seems to be of marginal importance. On the whole, ECEC policy initiatives have been driven by external forces, such as getting young mothers into the labour market. We are concerned that the child's perspective and acknowledged right to have a fair start in life should be taken more explicitly into consideration when considering future policy developments.

Id. at 48.

In fact, ECEC programs in the United States tend to target low-income and "at-risk" families and often have as their goal increasing workforce productivity and decreasing welfare dependency. In contrast, the following perspective undergirds Sweden's comprehensive ECEC policy:

Children are also citizens of the nation, obligated not only to carry out the social traditions, but to improve them. Children—the adults of the future—are regarded as repositories of tomorrow and as agents of social betterment. Their role is to learn and grow for themselves as individuals and as members of the society that they will create. Investing in children is analogous to investing in society.... Without manifesting a significant social investment in children, the commitment to fostering an improved, just society where all are equal would contradict the very ideas upon which the nation's social values and policies—its raison d'être—are predicated.

OECD Country Note: *Early Childhood Education and Care Policy in Sweden* ¶¶ 68, 71 (1999). Can these divergent approaches toward children, reflected in the different ECEC policies, help to explain the countries' different approaches to the economic support of children?

Problem 9-2

Assume that you are a U.S. senator. An investigator from the OECD has come to talk to you about the types and levels of benefits that the United States provides for its children.

During the conversation, the investigator asks whether you support emulating Sweden's approach to child benefits. What might the conversation between the two of you sound like?

2. Child Support Assurance

In most countries, private child support and/or governmental assistance is critical for children who live with only one parent. In the United States and in most developed countries, single mothers are unable to adequately provide for their children by themselves. *See* Leslie J. Harris, *The Proposed ALI Child Support Principles*, 35 Willamette L. Rev. 717 (1999). Professor Harris points out that "women generally earn less than men" and "rearing children simply decreases the amount of time and energy a single parent can devote to building a career." *Id.* at 726. In addition, in some countries, including the United States, the purchasing power of a low wage-earner has "declined significantly in the last thirty years." *Id.* In short, "[t]he risk of poverty is comparatively high for children in one-parent households in all first-world countries. When private resources alone are considered, cross-national studies of first-world countries show notable similarity in the economic circumstances of one-parent families." Principles of the Law of Family Dissolution: Analysis and Recommendations, § 3.03 cmt. g (Tentative Draft No. 3, pt. II, 1998).

Some countries guarantee cash support for children when the non-custodial parent fails or is unable to pay child support, even in part. The government typically pays the custodial parent a set amount, and then recoups it, when possible, from the non-custodial parent. These payments are often called "maintenance advances" or "child support assurance." Austria, Belgium, Denmark, Finland, France, Germany, Norway, and Sweden all have schemes to advance maintenance. *See* The Clearinghouse on International Developments in Child, Youth and Family Policies at Columbia University, Table 1.59: Availability of Advanced Maintenance Programs in Select Countries (2000) (*citing* Anne Corden, Making Child Maintenance Regimes Work 16, tbl. 2.3 (1999)), *at* http://www.childpolicy.intl.org/childsupporttables/table159.pdf.

Sweden's system has existed in some form since 1937 and currently pays a flat-rate maintenance advance of approximately SEK 1,173 per month for one child (approximately $126/month). "Maintenance support can be paid until children reach the age of 20 if they are still in full-time education." The Clearinghouse on International Developments in Child, Youth, and Family Policies at Columbia University, Child Support: Sweden, *at* http://www.childpolicyintl.org/childsupporttables/57.htm [hereinafter Clearinghouse, *Sweden*].

A maintenance advance in Sweden is available regardless of the custodial parent's income or employment status and regardless of whether the custodial parent remarries or cohabits. The benefit is also paid regardless of the child's income or assets. Simply, the custodial parent qualifies for an advance if the noncustodial parent defaults or pays an insufficient amount of child support. There is no requirement that the custodial parent have a child support order established or that paternity be established. *See generally* Försäkringskassan (Social Insurance Office), Child Support (2002), *at* www.a.fk.se/utland/eng/brochure%20April%202002.pdf; Anne Corden & Daniel R. Meyer, *Child Support Policy Regimes in the United States, United Kingdom, and other Countries: Similar Issues, Different Approaches*, 21 Focus 72, 77 (2000).

The primary eligibility requirement relates to residency. In cases where the custodial parent cannot satisfy the residency requirement, or in cases where the civil law permits a maintenance award larger than the advance, a civil judgment for child support is still very important. The other noteworthy eligibility requirement is that mothers must participate in establishing paternity in order to qualify for a maintenance advance. The municipal social welfare departments are responsible for ensuring that paternity is established. "The service is efficient—paternity is established in 96% of cases...." Clearinghouse, *Sweden, supra.*

The custodial parent applies for the maintenance advance from the Department of Social Welfare. The Department pays and then recoups the money from the non-resident parent. "Where the non-resident parent does not pay voluntarily the matter is referred to the crown bailiffs who collect monies by wage attachments, and also use income tax refunds." Clearinghouse, *Sweden, supra.* If the obligor is already paying maintenance to the child, the amount of maintenance support is reduced by the amount the obligor would otherwise have to repay the state. *See* Regeringskansliet (Ministry of Justice, Sweden), Family Law: Information on the Rules 42 (2000), *at* http://justitie. regeringen.se/pressinfo/pdf/famlaw.pdf.

The repayment amount is based upon the noncustodial parent's taxed income, after a standard deduction of SEK 24,000 is allowed. There are "relatively generous rules of respite...where the maintenance debtor's current economic situation is severely strained." *See Second Periodic Reports of States Parties Due in 1997: Sweden,* CRC, ¶ 530, U.N. Doc. CRC/C/65/Add.3 (1998). Under the former Maintenance Advances Act of 1964, the state was bound by the civil law maintenance award established by agreement or court judgment when seeking reimbursement. Sometimes parties deliberately set the amount of the award low, to thwart state efforts to enforce the obligor's obligation to repay the state, even when the obligor was capable of paying. *Id.* Under the current Maintenance Support Act (1996), the social insurance office does not seek recovery of maintenance that exceeds the maintenance advance, *see id.* at ¶ 392, but it does collect a flat percentage of the obligor's income until the maintenance advance is repaid. "Recovery is sought from the non-resident parent according to the number of children, as a percentage of income: 10% for 1 child, 6.25% each for 2 children, and 5% each for 3 children." Clearinghouse, *Sweden, supra.* Since the amount recovered never exceeds the maintenance advance, the custodial parent does not receive additional child support from the state's recovery efforts.

The only distorting effect of the current system occurs with support awards at the low-end. "Because maintenance support supplements child support payments which are below this level, the current system has created a disincentive for the courts to set support awards appropriately unless the non-resident parent can provide more support than is provided through the advance maintenance benefit." Clearinghouse, *Sweden, supra,* at current issues. If a court orders the noncustodial parent to pay an amount above the maintenance advance, the excess support goes to the child.

Notes and Questions

1. *Calculation of Private Child Support.* The Code Relating to Parenthood and Guardianship § 7 (1995), states that all parents must provide for their children according to their means regardless of whether they have physical contact with the children. *See generally* Försäkringskassan, *supra.* The award of private "maintenance allowance" depends upon the parents' ability to pay and the child's needs. In Sweden,

The child's needs are expressed as a proportion of a standard monthly amount, which is the basis for adult benefit rates, depending on age:

Aged 0–6   65% of standard monthly amount

Aged 7–12   80%

Aged 13+   95%

If the parents are in a position to provide more than the standard amount, then this is taken into account when assessing the child's needs. A parent is not liable to pay child support if he is not self-supporting so a deduction can be ordered for ordinary living expenses and reasonable housing costs. If there is a second family, the basic principle is to equate the needs of all the children, so that support to the first family is reduced.... There is no minimum payment which is required of all non-resident parents.

Clearinghouse, *Sweden, supra*. The base amount is provided in the National Insurance Act, and the amount is approximately SEK 1,982 for a child 0–6, and up to SEK 2,897 for a child 13 years old and above. *See* Maja Kirilov Eriksson & Johanna Schiratzki, *Sweden Family & Succession Law*, 3 Int'l Encyclop. of Laws 112 (Supp. Oct. 2001). Childcare expenses are added to this amount and government benefits, like the child benefit, are deducted. In addition to the self-support deduction, obligors can reserve an amount for the maintenance of a new spouse, registered partner, or cohabitant with whom they have a child, if there are special reasons why the new spouse or partner is at home. Special reasons include caring for young children or encountering difficulty finding work. *See* Regeringskansliet, *supra*. Additional maintenance is ordered for high income obligors pursuant to guidelines. *See* David Bradley, Family Law & Political Culture: Scandinavian Laws in Comparative Perspective 122–23 (1996). In Sweden, children are eligible for child support until they are eighteen, or until age twenty-one if they are in school (although not if the school is higher education). *See generally* Försäkringskassan, *supra*.

2. *Level of Private Support.* The amount of private child support awarded to a child in Sweden is often much less than in the U.S. Anne Corden and Daniel R. Meyer used two vignettes to get at the differences in the amount of the awards cross-nationally, using purchasing power parity in their analysis to try to standardize the awards for purposes of comparison. In the situation of unmarried parents with a two-year-old child, where the mother does not work outside the home, a noncustodial father with average earnings would be required to pay approximately $125 per month in Sweden. In Indiana and Wisconsin, the same father would be required to pay over $400 per month, and in Kansas the father would be required to pay approximately $300 per month. The gap was similarly large, and in some cases even larger, if the situation involved a divorced couple with two children, ages five and nine, a noncustodial father with a high income, and a mother with a part-time job and a need for twelve hours of childcare a week. In that situation, Sweden would award approximately $230 of child support per month, whereas Indiana and Wisconsin would award over $900, and Kansas would award over $500. *See* Anne Corden & Daniel R. Meyer, *Child Support Policy Regimes in the United States, United Kingdom, and Other Countries: Similar Issues, Different Approaches*, 21 Focus 72, 73 (2000). Is this surprising?

The value of child support can be impacted by the tax treatment of the payments. In neither Sweden nor the United States does the recipient pay taxes on the amount received. Maureen Baker, Canadian Family Policies: Cross-National Comparisons 330 (1995). In the United States and Sweden, child support is typically counted for purposes of calculating welfare benefits. *See* Corden & Meyer, *supra*, at 73.

3. *Similarities and Differences in the United States and Sweden in Setting Private Awards.* In Sweden, the private maintenance payment is calculated by multiplying the

amount that represents the child's needs by a fraction. The numerator is the noncustodial parent's financial capacity minus allowable deductions, and the denominator is the combined financial capacity of both parents minus the allowable deductions. *See* Korilova & Schiratzki, *supra*, at 112. In short, the noncustodial parent is only obligated to support the child in proportion to his income.

A couple of differences between the United States and Sweden are notable. First, the figure for the "child's needs," upon which private support is calculated, is lower in Sweden than in United States, in part because of the generous social benefits Swedish children receive, including health care and day care, and also because the "child benefit" is deducted from any calculation of their needs. Second, the allocation of child support between the custodial and noncustodial parent might differ in the two countries. More deductions are permitted to parents in Sweden in calculating their ability to pay, including for second families, than in most places in the United States.

Yet the similarities are notable too. First, most states in the United States, like in Sweden, try to allocate child support between the custodial and noncustodial parents in proportion to their ability to pay. Second, and most importantly, neither child support system is trying to achieve economic parity between the noncustodial and custodial parent households. Do these differences or similarities surprise you?

4. *Child Support Assurance Programs in the United States.* Should the federal government or states in the United States adopt a child support assurance scheme? Why or why not? Currently, "[l]ess than a third of all single mothers receive child support, a proportion that has increased only slightly in the past twenty years. In 1997, $8 billion in child support obligations were unpaid. These circumstances become more troublesome with the implementation of time-limited welfare benefits." Andrew Burwick, Child Support Assurance 2 (IDEA Brief No. 4, 2000), *at* www.ideas2000.org/issues/social_economic/child_support.pdf.

A child support assurance system was proposed during the 1970s when Congress was adopting new legislation to govern child support. *See* Irwin Garfinkel, *The Limits of Private Child Support and the Role of an Assured Benefit, in* Child Support: The Next Frontier 183 (J. Thomas Oldham & Marygold S. Melli eds., 2000). It never became law. However, starting in the 1980s, Congress allowed states to obtain waivers from the existing federal requirements in order to experiment with assured child support benefits. *Id.* at 184. Pilot programs were implemented by New York, Virginia, Connecticut, and California. Other states (Wisconsin, Iowa, Colorado, Minnesota, Missouri) have shown interest in the concept. Occasionally national efforts also emerge. During the 107th Congress, for example, Senator Dodd introduced a bill that would have provided grants to states for child support assurance demonstration projects. *See* Act to Leave No Child Behind, S. 940, 107th Cong. §§ 5141–5144 (2001). The bill was reintroduced in the 108th Congress as Senate Bill 448 and was still in committee when this book went to press.

Various barriers have inhibited the adoption of a wide-spread child support assurance program in the United States. One of the obstacles is the technological barrier of managing a system of collection and disbursement. Garfinkel, *supra*, at 185. Another obstacle is that "people in the United States consider child support as basically a private obligation," and the adoption of the Personal Responsibility and Work Opportunity Reconciliation Act of 1996 moved the United States even further away from Europe with the "norm that virtually all parents...will work, and the expectation that single parents, through work and receipt of child support, will be able to support their children without public assistance." Harris, *supra*, at 757–58.

5. *New York's CAP.* Perhaps the most developed child support assurance program in the United States existed in New York, where the Child Assistance Program (CAP) provided such benefits at one time for families on public assistance. The program included both child support assurance and broader work requirements. Eligibility for child support assurance required a child support order for each child; the amount of benefit phased out as income rose. *See generally* Tina Marie Perry & Leslie Anne Argenta, Child Support Assurance: Overcoming Political Barriers II.D (1997), *at* www.clasp.org/pubs/childassurance/manual2.html. *See also* Abt Associates, The New York State Child Assistance Program: Five-Year Impacts, Costs, and Benefits (1996). No benefit was possible if a family's income exceeded 150% of the poverty line. *See, e.g.,* Susan Price-Livingston, Child Support Assurance Programs (2001), *at* http://www.cga.state.ct.us./2001/rpt/olr/htm/2001-r-0767.htm. The program was designed to motivate participants toward greater financial self-sufficiency. *See* Abt Associates, *supra,* at i.

Under the New York program, the amount of child support assurance in 1997 was $250 per month for the first child, $125 per month for the second, and $65 per month for subsequent children. The child received the greater of this amount or the child support paid by the noncustodial parent. *See* Paula Roberts, California Child Support Assurance Legislation 2 (1997), *at* www.clasp.org/pubs/childassurance/970917.html. The program generally allowed a custodial parent to keep more of the child support as her income rose than would be the case under a cash assistance program for low-income families.

The New York program was reviewed in 1996. It was found that the total program saved the government $2,603 per household over five years. The program cost the government $237 per family over that same period in administrative costs. These results were attributable, in part, to higher rate of work participation by custodial parents. *See* Abt Associates, *supra,* at ix. The program also resulted in 21% more new support orders than occurred in a control group. *Id.* at x.

Since the New York CAP program was more than mere child support assurance (it included extensive social services to families qualifying for the benefit), the impact of the child support assurance component is difficult to assess. *See* Garfinkel, *supra,* at 187. Both the National Commission on Children and the U.S. Commission on Interstate Child Support called for more studies and suggested the possibility of expanding such programs throughout the United States. *See* The National Commission on Children, Beyond Rhetoric: A New American Agenda for Children and Families (1991); U.S. Commission on Interstate Child Support, Supporting Our Children: A Blueprint for Reform (1992).

Today the New York CAP program is no longer being administered as a demonstration program. While counties have the option of operating a CAP program under New York law, the number of counties participating has fallen from over twenty to under ten. The decline is attributed to the decreased funding for CAP and the generous amount of earned income disregard under the existing temporary welfare assistance program.

6. *Cost.* How much would it cost to adopt a child support assurance program nationwide? Consider the following statement by Andrew Burwick, Child Support Assurance, IDEA Brief No. 4 (2000), *at* http://www.ideas2000.org/Issues/Social_Economic/Child_Support.pdf:

> The costs of child support assurance would accrue from subsidies provided to single parents and, to a lesser extent, additional administrative expenses. A

number of factors would determine the precise amount of funding necessary: benefit levels, eligibility standards, and government enforcement of child support obligations.... An accurate accounting of costs must also reflect the positive impacts of child support assurance—families who leave or avoid welfare and increase their incomes. These effects would result in government savings in the form of reduced outlays for public assistance and increased tax receipts.... The wide range of possible costs for child support assurance is illustrated by estimates for a hypothetical program in Minnesota and analysis of actual costs in New York's demonstration project. Researchers modeling the cost of a universal benefit in Minnesota projected that an assured support payment of $200 a month for single-parent families with one child would cost the state $64.2 million per year, or $938 per family (taking into account the savings [from reduced outlays for public assistance and increased tax receipts]). New York's program, which enrolled only single parents eligible for welfare, actually resulted in net savings for government [of $2,366 in state and federal savings per household over five years.].... Total savings in the three counties participating in the study were estimated to be $50 million.

7. *Child Support Assurance in Europe Generally.* The benefits of a child support assurance program have persuaded many nations to adopt it. "About half the more industrialized of the OECD countries now provide some form of assured minimum financial support when the non-custodial parent fails to provide such support or provides it at an inadequate level." Sheila Kamerman & Alfred J. Kahn, *Child and Family Policies in an Era of Social Policy Retrenchment and Restructuring, in* Child Well-Being in Rich and Transition Countries: Are Children in Growing Danger of Social Exclusion? 4 (1999).

8. *Anti-family?* Can one characterize a child support assurance program as threatening the family?

9. *Maintenance Advances and Movement.* In Europe, questions have arisen under European Union law regarding whether a state can impose eligibility requirements for the receipt of maintenance advances. Two cases have come before the European Court of Justice involving Austria. The federal Austrian law on the Grant of Advances on Maintenance for Children applied to "minor children who are ordinarily resident in Austria and are either Austrian nationals or stateless." The first case, the *Offermanns* case, addressed whether the requirement of Austrian nationality violated Community law. The second case, the *Humer* case, asked whether the residence requirement violated Community law. The answer in both cases was that the Austrian legislation could not be so limited.

In Case No. C-85/99, Offermanns, 2001 E.C.R. I-2261, a German family had been living in Austria for approximately ten years when the marriage was dissolved. The children sought maintenance advances when their father failed to make child support payments in accordance with a court settlement. The children were not eligible under the Austrian program because they were not Austrian nationals or stateless. Nor were the children eligible for the German maintenance advances.

The European Court of Justice ruled that the Austrian advances on maintenance payments constituted a "family benefit" within the meaning of Article 4(1)(h) of Council Regulation (EEC) No 1408/71 of 14 June 1971 on the application of social security schemes to employed persons, to self-employed persons and to members of their families moving within the Community, as amended and updated by Council Regulation (EC) No

118/97 of 2 December 1996. "Consequently, persons residing in the territory of a Member State to which the provisions of that regulation apply are entitled, in accordance with Article 3 of that regulation, to receive such a benefit under the legislation of that member State on the same conditions as that State's nationals." *See* 2001 O.J. (C-186) 3 (provisional translation). The Council Regulation (EEC) No. 1408/71, as amended, was meant to coordinate national social security legislation within the framework of the free movement of persons. Specifically, it was designed to prohibit Member States from deterring Community workers from exercising their right to freedom of movement by making receipt of family benefits dependent on the residence or nationality of the worker's family in the Member State providing the benefits.[2]

Not long after *Offermanns* was decided, the European Court of Justice faced the question of whether an Austrian national, who moved to another Member State, would still be entitled to access maintenance advances under the Austrian legislation. *See* Case No. C-255/99, Anna Humer, 2002 E.C.R., *available at* www.curia.eu. int/en/jurisp/index.htm. In the case, Anna Humer, a minor child of divorced parents, sought three years of advance payments from the Family Costs Contribution Fund for outstanding maintenance payments due from her father. Despite repeated attempts at enforcement, her father's maintenance payments were several months in arrears and the current monthly payment had not been made at all. Humer's request was refused because the Austrian legislation applied to "minor children who are ordinarily resident in Austria." While Anna and her parents were Austrian nationals, and while the Austrian courts had adjudicated the marriage dissolution and custody, Anna and her mother had subsequently moved to France in pursuit of university study and employment. The *Humer* court found that Austria's law violated Regulation No. 1408/71, as amended, for reasons similar to those given in *Offermanns*.

10. *Advantages of Assured Child Support.* In both *Offermanns* and *Humer*, the European Court of Justice (ECJ) decided that the maintenance advance was a "family benefit" so that it fell within the scope of Regulation No. 1408/71. The *Humer* Court, referring to the judgment in *Offermanns*, explained that a family benefit was "a public contribution to a family's budget to alleviate the financial burdens involved in the maintenance...of children." In fact, the Austrian legislature specifically spoke of the financial benefits when it adopted the system of maintenance advances; the advances were adopted "to ensure the maintenance of minor children in cases where their mothers are left to cope alone with their children and, in addition to the heavy burden of raising their children, find themselves faced with the additional difficulty of obtaining maintenance for them from the father." *Humer, supra,* ¶9. Apart from the financial benefit, what other advantages flow from advanced maintenance? Advocate General Alber's opinion in the *Offermanns* case suggested some:

---

2. Article 48(1), (2) and (3)(b) of the EC Treaty (now, after amendment, article 39(1), (2) and (3)(b) EC), states:

1. Freedom of movement for workers shall be secured within the Community by the end of the transitional period at the latest.

2. Such freedom of movement shall entail the abolition of any discrimination based on nationality between workers of the Member States as regards employment, remuneration and other conditions of work and employment.

3. It shall entail the right, subject to limitations justified on grounds of public policy, public security or public health:...(b) to move freely within the territory of Member States for this purpose.

On the one hand, there is the procedural aspect, which consists in the execution of claim to maintenance or even, as the case may be, the recovery of a debt. This procedural aspect should not be underestimated since recovering outstanding payments from a parent liable for maintenance who is unwilling or incapable of making payment can be an arduous and time-consuming exercise. It is clear from the documents submitted by the national court that the legislature specifically intended to assist mothers, who generally have custody, in enforcing collection of maintenance for their children.

On the other hand, there is also a not insignificant economic aspect inherent in the advances payments on maintenance. The payment of advances has the effect of making financial resources available at the time at which they are needed. Moreover, the State bears the risk of insolvency. The Court is aware that over half the advance payments cannot be recovered from those in default of payment of maintenance. It would therefore be a simplification to dismiss the legislation on advances on maintenance as merely procedural assistance or to focus mainly on the provisional aspect of the advance financing of outstanding maintenance payments....

It cannot be ruled out that advances on maintenance payments are also intended to provide the parent having custody with a certain amount of freedom to raise a child. From this angle too it would appear appropriate to classify the advances on maintenance payments as family benefits.

Opinion of Advocate General Alber, Case No. C-85/99, *supra*, ¶¶ 33–34, 47. What is the substance of Advocate General Alber's last point? Earlier in the opinion, Advocate General Alber explained: "[T]he alleviation of subsistence concerns by the advances is also clearly intended to ensure that the parent caring for the child is able to devote him or herself more to the raising of his or her minor child by reducing the pressure to obtain the requisite financial means to fund maintenance." *Id.* ¶ 9.

Other ECJ cases have classified similar provisions in national laws as "family benefits" subject to Regulation No 1408/71. *See, e.g.,* Joined Cases Nos. C-245/94 & 312/94, Hoever and Zachow v. Land Nordrhein-Westfalen 1996 E.C.R. I-4895, ¶ 17 (German child-raising allowance is a family benefit); Case No. C-275/96, Kuusijärvi v. Riksforsakringsverket, 1998 E.C.R. I-3419 (Swedish family allowance is a family benefit); Case C-333/00, Maaheimo, 2002 E.C.R., *available at* www.curia.eu.int/en/jurisp/index.htm (Finnish home childcare allowance, which gives parents a stipend if they choose not to take up a guaranteed place in a public daycare institution, is a family benefit).

11. *Constitutional Implications.* If a resident from Minnesota went to New York and applied for its CAP program, could New York deny her application solely on the basis that she had not been a New York resident for the requisite amount of time? If a New York resident traveled to Minnesota, could New York deny her the benefit because she was not "present" in the state? *Shapiro v. Thompson*, 394 U.S. 618 (1969), which appears in Chapter 13.A.2.a. will help you answer these questions. Would a federal solution be better than a state-by-state solution if child support assurance were generally desired?

12. *Enforcement.* In contrast to a system of child support assurance, the United States and "the English-speaking countries" have "focused on the enforcement of court-awarded child support as the main policy initiative to reduce the poverty of mother-led families." Baker, *supra*, at 306. The states in the United States afford enforcement assistance to those receiving Title IV-D funds as well as to those who request help.

The United States and Canada, for example, have become quite creative in enacting mechanisms to track down obligors, to garnish state money owing to delinquent obligors, and even to deny certain licenses for those in default. For a description of some of these mechanisms in the Canadian context, *see* Dep't of Justice Canada, 2 Children Come First: A Report to Parliament Reviewing the Provisions and Operation of the Federal Child Support Guidelines 178 (2002). England has recently adopted legislation permitting the Child Support Authority to levy a fine of up to 25% on arrears, although the penalty goes to the government and not the custodial parent. Child Support, Pensions & Social Security Act of 2000 (c.19) § 18 (2) (Eng.).

The United States has focused considerable energy on the use of criminal sanctions to enforce child support obligations. It is a federal felony to fail to pay willfully $10,000 or more in child support to one living in another state, or to cross state lines to evade child-support obligations. Child Support Recovery Act of 1992, 18 U.S.C. § 228. Many states also criminalize failure to pay child support, even apart from the availability of criminal contempt. *See, e.g.,* Alaska Stat. § 11.51.120 (2002); Cal. Penal Code § 270 (2003); Or. Rev. Stat. § 163.555 (2001). The United Kingdom has recently adopted similar criminal provisions. Australia and New Zealand, in contrast, do not focus on criminal penalties. While Canada has provisions in its criminal code that might apply, its Minister of Justice prefers to use other means to secure compliance and has indicated doubt about the effectiveness of criminal sanctions. *See generally* Dep't of Justice Canada, *supra,* at 188.

Problem 9-3

Refer back to Problem 9-2. The same OECD investigator turns the discussion to the topic of child support assurance. Without repeating any of the conversation that has already occurred between the two of you, what will be the substance of your remarks about whether the United States should follow Sweden's approach to child support assurance. What might the investigator say in response and how will you answer those concerns?

3. Adjustments over Time

Child support guidelines have been adopted by many countries. In most European countries, there are rules or guidelines that help decision-makers set the correct amount of child support. *See* Anne Corden & Daniel R. Meyer, *Child Support Policy Regimes in the United States, United Kingdom, and Other Countries: Similar Issues, Different Approaches,* 21 Focus 72, 76 (2000). The justification for the adoption of guidelines is varied, but one of the cross-national themes is the minimization of discretion and inconsistency in awards. *See, e.g.,* Federal Child Support Guidelines, Objectives (1)(d) (1995) (Can.); Dep't of Social Security, 1 Children Come First: The Government's Proposals on the Maintenance of Children, Cm 1264 (1990) (Eng.).

When children rely upon child support awards for their financial support, it is important to know how the passage of time affects their awards. In particular, will an award automatically keep pace with inflation and therefore maintain its value? Will an award automatically increase as the child becomes older and the costs of raising the child increase? Will award automatically increase as the obligor's income rises?

a. The United States

Child support orders in the United States can be modified, although any change in the amount ordered may be entered only prospectively. Modification typically requires that there be a change of circumstance, and that the change could not have been anticipated at the time of the original order. It also requires that a person petition the court for the modification, and that the court agree to modify.

Starting in 1988, the federal government mandated that states provide an additional process for modification of awards. Originally, the 1988 Family Support Act required that states review and adjust public assistance cases at least every three years. Parents who were not public assistance recipients could request reviews if they were receiving Title IV-D services. Family Support Act of 1988, Pub. L. No. 100-485, §404, 102 Stat. 2343 (codified as amended in scattered sections of 42 U.S.C.). Adjustments could be made without establishing a substantial change in circumstances. The idea was that an order should be adjusted if it ceased to fall within the state's child support guidelines. States complained, however, that the review process was difficult and time consuming. Reviews required additional information from the parents and an individualized determination. States also found the individualized determinations hard to reconcile with the states' need to computerize the child support system for purposes of mass processing. *See generally* Jessica Sager & Paula Roberts, Keeping Up: State Approaches to Automatic Adjustments in Child Support Orders (1997).

The adoption of the Personal Responsibility and Work Opportunity Reconciliation Act of 1996 (PRWORA) resolved some of these issues by relaxing the requirements for mandatory review and adjustment. Federal law now requires states to implement procedures so that every three years, or sooner if the state elects, either parent, or a state agency if parents have assigned their child support to the state as part of their receipt of welfare services, can have the order adjusted. 42 U.S.C. §666(a)(10). Periodic review is mandated only when a parent or the state agency requests a review, and not even then if the review would not be in the best interest of the child. 42 U.S.C. §666 (a)(10)(A)(i). The review can be done in one of three ways: 1) a review and adjustment in accordance with the child support guidelines, or 2) application of a cost-of-living adjustment, or 3) automated methods to identify and adjust orders by "any threshold that may be established by the State." *Id.* This last method typically entails an automated comparison of orders with wage and tax data. Parties have the ability to contest the adjustment if the state implements method two or three above. Any review done outside the three-year cycle requires that there be a substantial change in circumstances. 42 U.S.C. §666(a)(10)(B). Parents must be notified every three years of the right to obtain a review. 42 U.S.C. §666(a)(10)(C).

In response to PRWORA, most states have discontinued or planned to discontinue the triennial review of public assistance cases. *See* Office of Child Support Enforcement, Automated Cost-of-Living Adjustments of Child Support Orders in Three States (2001), at Exec. Summary §1, *at* http://www.acf.dhhs.gov/programs/cse/pubs/reports/cola/pr01.html. However, "many states have yet to fully respond to the changes regarding review and modification outlined in PRWORA." *Id.* at ch. 5.

The new PRWORA system, to the extent it is operating in a state, requires parent initiative if the parent does not receive welfare. At a minimum, the parent must request Title IV-D services, and may also specifically have to request a review. Some states require parent initiative even if the family is receiving public assistance. An Assistant Commissioner at the Office of Child Support Enforcement has said, "Modification of awards is one area where the new legislation falls short. It does nothing to insure that all awards are periodically updated. PRWORA places the burden of requesting review on the parent, usually a custodial mother, but many mothers will not make such requests because they do not understand the process or do not want to rock the boat.... Closing the gap caused by failure to update awards is perhaps the principal remaining task left in reforming child support." Paul K. Legler, *The Impact of Welfare Reform on the Child Support Enforcement System, in* Child Support: The Next Frontier 57 (J. Thomas Oldham & Marygold S. Melli eds., 2000) (citations and footnotes omitted).

Oregon serves as an example. Despite the extensive administrative involvement in establishing and enforcing support orders, individual initiative by a custodial parent, whether on or off public assistance, is typically required to keep a child support order current, even after the parent is receiving Title IV-D services. While the state used to do automatic two-year reviews, work load and resource limitations forced the state to move to a service that mostly responds to requests. Consequently, individuals who receive Title IV-D services may request from the appropriate administrative agency a review of an order every two years or seek a modification at any time if there is a significant and unexpected change of circumstances. Or. Rev. Stat. § 25.287 (2001). The standard for modifying the order at the two-year review is whether the order is in "substantial compliance" with the guidelines, *i.e.,* the order must be within at least 15% or $50, whichever is less, of the amount calculated using the guidelines. If the award increases, the obligor has thirty days to object to the new amount and then receives an administrative hearing with an appeal to the circuit court. Interestingly, most of the requests in public assistance cases in Oregon come from an *obligor* seeking a downward modification.

Apart from a court-ordered modification or the adjustment processes mentioned in PRWORA, private parties are always free to try to include automatic adjustments in their orders, although these have received a mixed response from courts. Professor Oldham reports that "Courts have been generally unreceptive to the automatic adjustment of the amount of child support based upon post decree changes in the obligor's income." J. Thomas Oldham, *New Methods to Update Child Support, in* Child Support: The Next Frontier 131 (J. Thomas Oldham & Marygold S. Melli eds., 2000). In particular, orders which set the child support as a percentage of the obligor's income, and not a fixed amount, are not very widely permitted by courts. *Id.* at 131–32. While courts are more receptive to cost of living adjustments (COLA) than other mechanisms, some courts refuse to permit a COLA because they are very concerned about obligors whose incomes may not keep up with the COLA. Professor Oldham concludes:

> The current rejection of automatic adjustment mechanisms places the custodial parent at a substantial disadvantage. The custodial parent's inadequate information, the cost of legal action, and the vague standard for modification all discourage modification actions. If the award is not modified, inflation and the higher cost of children as they age force the custodial parent to bear an increasing portion of child-related expenses.

Id. at 134. The rules in the United States for child support modification and courts' reluctance to include automatic adjustment mechanisms in orders have generally contributed to the "poverty of families headed by women." *Id.* at 128.

The American Law Institute has proposed that courts include automatic escalator clauses in child support orders, for example by awarding support as a percentage of the obligor's income. It also suggests that a government attorney automatically review all orders at least every three years. *See Principles of the Law of Family Dissolution: Analysis and Recommendations* §§ 3.18–.19 (2002). However, it also allows parents to agree that no adjustment should be made to a preexisting award. *See id.* § 3.19 cmt. b.

b. England

It is interesting to compare what has happened in the United States with what has happened in England on the same topic. As the following materials suggest, England has experienced a similar disconnect between the legislative mandate and the implementation of the mandate. Some of the factors that have caused the gap are the same in both countries. England's response to the problem provides an important lesson for attorneys in the United States.

England began experimenting with national child support legislation with the Child Support Act 1991. Among other things, the act had a formula for calculating child support that looked at income, housing costs, and family responsibilities. Many criticized the act, complaining that it was rigid and complex. The act, in fact, spawned thirteen statutory instruments in 1992, eight in 1993, and two in 1994. Susan Grace Jenkinson, Child Support: A Comparison of the Old and New Approaches (2001), *at* http:/// www.childsupportanalysis.co.uk/guest_contributions/sue_paper/part_4_child%20_sup port%20_act_1991.htm. England later passed the Child Support Act 1995 which, among other things, instituted a system of departures to soften some of the harsh outcomes that were resulting under the 1991 act. Then, at the millennium, England passed the Child Support Pensions and Social Security Act 2000, which amends, but does not repeal, the prior two acts.

The Child Support Act 1991 created a new Child Support Agency (CSA), an administrative body in the Department of Social Security. The CSA was responsible for administering the act. The hope was that awards through the CSA would eliminate the discretionary approach of the courts. The CSA, however, was characterized as lacking "resources, competence, and teeth." Jenkinson, *supra.* Consequently, the CSA was subject to extensive criticism.

One of the CSA's duties was to ensure that child support awards were automatically updated so that they would keep their value.

Child Support Act 1991, c. 48, § 16 (Eng.)

Periodical reviews.

16. (1) The Secretary of State shall make such arrangements as he considers necessary to secure that, where any maintenance assessment has been in force for a prescribed period, the amount of child support maintenance fixed by that assessment ("the original assessment") is reviewed by a child support officer under this section as soon as is reasonably practicable after the end of that prescribed period.

(2) Before conducting any review under this section, the child support officer concerned shall give, to such persons as may be prescribed, such notice of the proposed review as may be prescribed.

(3) A review shall be conducted under this section as if a fresh application for a maintenance assessment had been made by the person in whose favour the original assessment was made.

(4) On completing any review under this section, the child support officer concerned shall make a fresh maintenance assessment, unless he is satisfied that the original assessment has ceased to have effect or should be brought to an end.

(5) Where a fresh maintenance assessment is made under subsection (4), it shall take effect—

(a) on the day immediately after the end of the prescribed period mentioned in subsection (1); or

(b) in such circumstances as may be prescribed, on such later date as may be determined in accordance with regulations made by the Secretary of State.

(6) The Secretary of State may by regulations prescribe circumstances (for example, where the maintenance assessment is about to terminate) in which a child support officer may decide not to conduct a review under this section.

Initially the Secretary of State issued regulations requiring annual periodic reviews. *See* The Child Support (Maintenance Assessment Procedure) Regulations (1992) SI 1813 § 17. However, the system of periodic reviews established by the 1991 act ultimately suffered an almost total demise in England. To understand why, it is essential to know more about the CSA and its workload. Before the Child Support Pensions and Social Security Act 2000, the CSA was under tremendous pressure and faced enormous criticism. It spent "90% of its resources doing assessments, and only 10% on enforcement." Jenkinson, *supra*. The complexity of the guidelines led to delays in determining liability (and getting payment to children), and inconsistency among claimants. The Stationery Office, Explanatory Notes to Child Support, Pensions and Social Security Act (2000), *at* http://www.hmso.gov.uk/acts/en/2000en19.htm. Also, while over 1.5 million children were receiving CSA services, only 300,000 received any child support payments, and only 100,000 received the full amount due. *Id.* To put this into perspective, in 1979, 50% of single parents on Income Support received child maintenance. The number receiving child maintenance fell to 23% by 1989, and stayed the same even five years after the CSA began its work. *See* Jo Roll, Child Support Provisions in the Child Support, Pensions and Social Security Bill, Research Paper 99/110 for the House of Commons 15 (1999). Moreover, the average child support assessment across all income groups was only £20 per week. *Id.* at 16.

Although the CSA was supposed to undertake yearly periodic reviews of existing assessments, the CSA's workload made yearly periodic reviews impossible. A 1995 White Paper, Improving Child Support, Cm 2745 (1995), called for, among other things, the adoption of reviews only every two years, instead of every year. This reform was adopted in 1995. The Social Security Act 1998 then abolished all periodic reviews as of December 1998, except for cases in the pipeline. At that time, "there were 371,000 periodical reviews waiting to be carried out. By July 1999, there were still 350,000 outstanding periodical reviews." Roll, *supra*, at 16.

In an effort to improve the workings of the CSA, the Child Support Pensions and Social Security Act 2000 adopted a number of changes. Part of the act simplified the determination of child support. Calculations are now essentially based upon a percentage of the obligor's net income with very few allowable departures (now termed "variations"). The act also relieved the CSA of any obligation to conduct any periodic reviews, even of those cases in the pipeline. The explanatory notes to the bill said "that this process was difficult to operate." The notes explained, "Parents, many of whom had been unwilling to co-operate in making the first assessment, failed to reply to requests for further information. Others were unable to provide all the information that the Secretary of State required. As it was impossible to clear the periodical review without this information, substantial backlogs built up. The problem became even worse as cases where a review was stalled became due for another review." Roll, *supra*, at 36.

Upon adoption of the 2000 act, the Government indicated that the CSA would publicize the new law so that parents could request to have an outstanding review finished. *Id.* The agency would then start a new program within the next two years to update assessments from a current date. *Id.* The new program will involve "periodic case checks" approximately every two years if there is a likelihood that changes have occurred. Select Committee on Social Security, *Tenth Report: The 1999 Child Support White Paper* (1999). The new system now appears to be in place. *See* Child Support Agency, Child Support: A Technical Guide 3 (2002). While the update occurs routinely if the custodial parent receives Income Support or a Jobseeker's Allowance, it will only be completed for others if a party responds to the CSA's request that it be told of changes that may affect the assessment. *Id.* at 92.

Notes and Questions

1. *Mandatory Reviews and Adjustments.* What are the benefits and drawbacks to mandatory reviews by an agency and mandatory adjustments in an order? Assuming a jurisdiction permits an automatic adjustment mechanism in an order, what type of mechanism seems the best? Why? If you favor a COLA, what should be done during periods of high inflation? Which one of these two approaches is preferable (*i.e.*, the reviews and adjustments or the automatic adjustment mechanisms in the orders themselves)? Are these two approaches mutually exclusive?

2. *Periodic Review.* Initially the periodic review in England was to occur every year. Then it was to occur every two years. Even after England eliminated its entire program of periodic reviews, it adopted a new one with periodic checks approximately every two years. In the United States, federal law requires the possibility of a review and adjustment at least every three years. How often should a periodic review be done? Why?

3. *Rationale.* How would a jurisdiction that calculated child support as a percentage of obligor income justify allowing a COLA? How would a state with an income-shares model do so?

4. *Adjustment of Benefits.* Approximately half of the member states in the European Union automatically adjust their family benefits according to the consumer price index, or some comparable index. The United Kingdom's adjustments to family benefits occur through annual legislation, and the adjustments are "usually" in line with the consumer price index. European Communities, Adjustment, at United Kingdom, *at* http://europa.eu.int/comm/employment_social/missoc2001/missoc_222_en.htm. If a country uses one of these mechanisms to keep benefits current, does it make any sense to have a different procedure for private child support orders?

5. *Change of Circumstances.* England also provides that a payor or payee can apply to the CSA for a modification of the original assessment if there has been a change of circumstance since the original assessment was made, and the amount of child support would be "significantly different." Child Support Act 1991, c. 48, §17(2). Some aspects

of the 1991 law related to modification have been changed by the Child Support Act 1995 and the Child Support, Pensions and Social Security Act 2000. However, the standard for modification remains intact. *See* Child Support Act, 1995, c. 34, §12, Child Support, Pensions and Social Security Act 2000, c. 19, §§7–9.

6. *Other Models.* The difficulties encountered in both the United States and England with periodic reviews suggests that perhaps a different, and better, approach is warranted. Alternative models exist around the world. Consider the approach in Sweden and Canada, for example.

A. *Sweden.* In Sweden, the "maintenance allowance is index-linked in order that it should retain its original value. It is adapted according to alterations in the price base amount. However, this does not apply if another index clause was included in the judgment or the agreement when the allowance was decided. The maintenance allowance has been altered every year since 1983, usually on 1 February. The alteration applies to maintenance allowance that has been decided before 1 November of the immediately preceding year. The National Social Insurance Board determines each year whether the maintenance allowance shall be altered and in that event by what percentage." Ministry of Justice, Sweden, Family Law: Information on the Rules 40–41 (2000). In addition to the increase attributable to indexing, the parties can either agree to an increase or ask the court for a modification. A party seeking court modification must establish that the change is "manifest and in excess of what one should expect as a normal variation." *Id.* at 41. However, "If a maintenance allowance has been paid at an unaltered amount for six years, ignoring alterations according to the index legislation, the court can reconsider the maintenance allowance for the future without any special reasons for reconsideration needing to be quoted.... If reconsideration is not requested, the allowance is payable as previously." *Id.*

B. *Canada.* In Canada, only Quebec's civil code provides that child support orders must be indexed. These orders are altered annually, unless the court orders otherwise. Courts in other places may order that payments be periodically adjusted to reflect changes in the cost-of-living index. According to Professor Nick Bala, indexing was common prior to enactment of the Federal Child Support Guidelines in 1997, but now indexing is infrequently done because courts expect the recipient to return to court to vary an order based upon the payor's income. For divorced couples, this would typically occur pursuant to section 17(4) of the Divorce Act, which requires a change of circumstance as provided for in the guidelines.

To facilitate modifications, the federal guidelines require that information be exchanged periodically between parents. *See* Dep't of Justice Canada, 2 Children Come First: A Report to Parliament Reviewing the Provisions and Operation of the Federal Child Support Guidelines 28 (2002). The guidelines require every obligor against whom a child support order has been made to provide income information to the custodial parent, on the custodial parent's written request, but not more than once a year. *See* Federal Child Support Guidelines §25(1) (2000) (Can.). The documents that must be exchanged include the following: a copy of every personal income tax return filed by the obligor for each of the three most recent taxation years; a copy of every notice of assessment and reassessment issued to the obligor for each of the three most recent taxation years; and where the obligor is an employee, the most recent statement of earnings indicating the total earnings paid in the year to date, including overtime, or a letter from the spouse's employer indicating the same. In addition, the obligor must provide information, in writing, about the status of any expenses included in the order and any current information about the circumstances underlying a determination of "undue hardship." The same information must be provided by an obligee to an obligor if her income was used to set the child support obligation, or if she was not ordered to pay child support because her income level was below the minimum amount required for application of the tables. Do you like the requirement that parties exchange information?

Momentum exists in Canada at the federal level to move toward automatic adjustments. Section 25.1 of the Divorce Act permits pilot projects to "recalculate, at regular intervals, in accordance with the applicable guidelines, the amount of child support order on the basis of updated income information." The new amount becomes effective in one month, unless a parent seeks court review. Various pilot projects are underway. *See* Dep't of Justice Canada, *supra*, at 209, 221–24.

7. *Administrative versus Judicial Process.* Courts have an important role in determining support obligations in many countries in Europe. However, about half the countries in Europe rely more on administrative agencies to set the level of support, and the court's role is "residual." Anne Corden & Daniel R. Meyer, *Child Support Policy Regimes in the United States, United Kingdom, and Other Countries: Similar Issues, Different Approaches*, 21 Focus 72, 74 tbl. 1 (2000). What may be more important than the decision-making body, however, is whether a country has a formula for calculating child support, what the goal of the formula is (*e.g.*, equalize household income or provide a basic level of support for a child), whether awards are indexed, and whether the state has a program of child support assurance. Information on these topics is scattered throughout the foregoing materials.

8. *Administrative Models in the United States.* States in the United States also employ administrative models in both the setting and modification of awards. For example, Oregon relies quite heavily on administrative agencies. The Department of Human Services oversees child support policy in Oregon. The Department of Justice (Division of Child Support) and the local district attorney's offices provide services to families receiving TANF or Medicaid benefits and to others who apply for Title IV-D services. Both the Department of Justice and the local district attorney's offices establish paternity and support orders, enforce support orders, and, upon request, periodically review and modify existing orders. In addition, the Department of Justice keeps records and distributes child-support for all recipients of child support.

In some respects, Oregon offers many more administrative services than other states for individuals who receive Title IV-D services, including establishing paternity by administrative order, establishing writs of garnishment by administrative order, and entering controlling order determinations under Uniform Interstate Family Support Act by an administrative process. The administrative agency can also conduct a hearing for a modification; the circuit court would hear an appeal *de novo*. Yet, as suggested above, Oregon relies heavily on parent initiative to trigger periodic reviews and modification proceedings.

The administrative process in Oregon issued 3,897 modifications in fiscal year 1999. The process also facilitated the entry of 8,678 initial administrative or court orders. *See* Div. of Child Support, Or. Dep't of Hum. Serv., 1999 Child Support Program Annual Report in Oregon (1999). The statistics do not indicate the number of modifications that produced reduced awards, or the number of modifications that were undertaken for individuals who were not recipients of public assistance.

The administrative process in Oregon is very important for keeping child support orders current. Courts in Oregon do not permit automatic increases in the child-support order, not even automatic cost of living adjustments. *See, e.g.,* In re Marriage of Maurer,

619 P.2d 964 (Or. App. Ct. 1980). While nothing precludes the obligee or obligor from utilizing the services of private legal counsel at any time to pursue modification of the support order when there has been a substantial change of circumstances, the administrative process is lauded as being quicker, cheaper, and more informal than court.

9. *Bifurcated Process in England; Escalation Provisions in Assessments.* The CSA does not have exclusive authority in England over child support, although it deals with most child support matters. The courts still have jurisdiction 1) to order child maintenance when both parties consent to the terms of an order so long as the custodial parent is not on public assistance; 2) to make a child maintenance order if a parent lives abroad; 3) to revoke existing child maintenance orders; 4) to vary existing child support orders if the CSA has not yet taken on a case; and 5) to enter "top-up" orders even if the CSA has taken action. *See* Child Support Act 1991, c. 48, § 8. Top-up orders are available in limited circumstances, *e.g.,* to address a obligor's high income, a disabled child's needs, or school fees. Since most child maintenance in England will be assessed by the CSA, it is sufficient to know that the CSA's assessment is expressed as a fixed amount and not as a percentage of the obligor's income.

10. *Individual Lawyering.* This chapter hopefully is triggering a critical assessment of child support policy in the United States. However, the comparative material may also lead you to better represent your future clients. What lessons have you learned? Imagine you represent a woman who will be awarded custody of her children and child support. What provisions in an order might you seek to help her child support order keep its value? How much faith do you now have in periodic review and adjustment of orders by the government? Given the experience in other countries, how important are automatic adjustment mechanisms within child support orders and provisions to exchange information periodically? The American Law Institute recommends that child support awards "should be, by their own terms, automatically and continuously updated as to all relevant income changes" (the ALI recommends expressing the award as a percentage of the obligor's earnings), *and* that an automatic periodic review occur at least every three years by a government agency, although exceptions exist. *See* Principles of the Law of Family Dissolution: Analysis and Recommendations §§ 3.18–.19 (2000).

4. Parents' Ability to Opt-Out of the Child Support Guidelines

Finally, we conclude this chapter by exploring the extent to which parents can decide to support their children at a level lower than is permitted by the child support guidelines. In an intact family, parents have the ability to impoverish children. Personal choices may inhibit earning capacity or dictate personal consumption to the children's detriment. When the family lives in the United States and is intact, there is no opportunity for government intervention, unless a child is "neglected" under the relevant state statutes protecting children's welfare.

The government has a convenient opportunity to intervene to protect children's interests when parents invoke the judicial system to resolve their disputes, such as a divorce. Yet children still may be impoverished despite court involvement, and despite the existence of child support guidelines, if a custodial parent can avoid requesting a child support order, can agree to a lower amount than the guidelines would dictate, or can avoid enforcement of the award when the obligor defaults. This section focuses on these issues.

a. Absence of a Child Support Order

Countless children have parents who do not live together and who have not sought court assistance to resolve the issue of child support. In fact, parental failure to seek a support order is a very large issue in some countries. In Canada, for example, "there are no child support agreements for almost one-third of Canadian children whose parents have separated." Dep't of Justice Canada, 2 Children Come First: A Report to Parliament Reviewing the Provisions and Operation of the Federal Child Support Guidelines 12 (2002) (citing National Longitudinal Survey of Children and Youth). In fact, the number was 42.2% for children whose parents had never married.

In the United States, the numbers appear similar. In 1998, there were approximately 14 million custodial parents who did not live with the other parent, and only 56% had some type of child support agreement or order for their children. See U.S. Census Bureau, Child Support for Custodial Mothers and Fathers, Current Population Reports 1, 3 (2000) (based upon self-reports). The largest reason why custodial parents did not have a legal award was because they did not feel it was necessary (32.4%). See id., fig. 4. The numbers are slightly better, although not much, for those participating in government child support enforcement services. Among that group, custodial parents in only 61.5% of cases have child support orders established. See Office of Child Support Enforcement, Statistical Overview, FY 1999 & 2000, tbl. 2, available at http://www.acf. dhhs.gov/programs/cse/pubs/2002/reports/datareport/table_2.html.

These numbers might not be alarming if custodial parents without awards were receiving at least as much support as parents with awards, or if a country had a generous program of public support. However, in the United States, the first premise is false and the second premise is debatable. Simply, child support orders are very important to children. "Children with a child support order are nearly twice as likely to receive financial support from their nonresident parent as children without an order." Elaine Sorensen & Chava Zibman, Child Support Offers Some Protection Against Poverty, in New Federalism: National Survey of America's Families 2 (Urban Instit. March 2000). The amounts received are significant.

> In 1996, children who had nonresident parents and whose families received child support received, on average, 16 percent of their family income from child support. The average amount of child support received by these families was $3,795.... Child support is an even more important source of income if the children who receive it are poor. [T]he average poor child with a nonresident parent, and whose family received child support, received $1,979 in 1996. This represents over one-quarter (26%) of their family income.

Sorensen & Zibman, supra, at 2. See also Paula Roberts, The Importance of Child Support Enforcement: What Recent Social Science Research Tells Us (2002) (statistics show that child support is an important source of income for families who have left welfare either voluntarily or because of time limits, but who are still poor).

What should be done, if anything, about parents who do not seek child support orders? The policy in the United States currently focuses on public assistance recipients. In the United States, parents who receive public assistance are obligated to help establish paternity and obtain child support orders. While there is a limited "good cause exception," *See* 42 U.S.C. § 608(a)(2), failure to cooperate in most situations can result in the loss of some or all of a public assistance grant. Most of the child support collected by the state on behalf of public welfare recipients remits to the state. While the federal government used to require states to pass through the first $50 per month of child support to the family, that requirement was eliminated in 1996. States have since taken several approaches: some states still pass through the first $50 per month, others states pass through nothing, and some states pass through greater amounts. Whether the amount remitted to the family decreases the level of public assistance, and if so by how much, also varies by state.

The current approach in public welfare cases receives mixed reviews. According to one study, the system in California (which at the time passed through $50 per month) was viewed by many low-income mothers with hostility. Mothers felt they received little economic benefit from the system and that it created conflict with fathers. Mothers also felt that their cooperation could prove harmful to their families if the establishment of child support resulted in increased contact with the fathers. *See* Maureen Waller & Robert Plotnick, Child Support and Low-Income Families: Perceptions, Practices and Policy vi (1999). Low-income fathers also had criticisms. Many found the system unappreciative of their difficult social and economic realities. "They object to high support payments, unmanageable arrears, retroactive support orders, and the system's refusal to consider current or past informal support provided directly to their children." *Id.* at viii. Men also criticized the criminalization of nonsupport. *Id.* at ix. The study indicated that "Many parents prefer informal support arrangements, including in-kind contributions from the father, because they believe that these arrangements benefit their children and their families." In addition, parents "often" fail to comply with the law because they find the law "unfair, counterproductive, or punitive." *Id.* at vi. What alternatives or improvements to this approach can you imagine?

What, if anything, should be done for those custodial parents who do not receive public assistance? Like the United States government, the Canadian government requires its welfare recipients to make reasonable efforts to seek child support. In addition, however, Canada, through its Divorce Act § 11, imposes an obligation on the court to stay any divorce application if there are no reasonable arrangements in place for the support of the children. Only very occasionally does one see a court in the United States tying the ability to divorce to the adequate provision for support. *See, e.g.,* Davis v. Davis, 143 S.E.2d 835 (Va. 1965) (suggesting chancellor could stay the divorce action until the complainant satisfactorily complied with interlocutory child support order, but disapproving of outright dismissal of action). What do you think of the statutory provision in Canada?

Close v. Close

[1999] 50 R.F.L.4th 342 (N.B.Q.B.)

Guerette, J.

The Petitioner seeks a divorce, no access to the Respondent father and no support. The child of the relationship is Dakota Hope Close, born November 4th, 1993. She has been with the mother since the separation on October 20, 1996. The parties were married on April 25, 1994.

At issue is whether the Court can ignore the Child Support Guidelines when the recipient spouse is adamant that she does not want support paid. Access has been denied through a previous court order. This arose out of incidents of violence against the Petitioner.

The last Order of the Court (Consent Order) is dated August 31, 1995 and clause 2 of the order reads as follows: "No provisions shall be made for the Respondent to have access to the aforesaid child.... Since then, the Respondent has not seen the child and has not paid any support. Nor has he made any effort to follow-up the issue of access."

In her testimony, the Petitioner declared that she is afraid of the Respondent and that he has been violent toward her in the past. No access and no contact has taken place since 1995 and she is afraid that if support is granted, he will only use it as an excuse to interfere with her and put her and her children at risk. She further testified that she is engaged to be married and will be moving to the United States after the wedding. All the needs of the child have been met and she is confident that no further arrangements need be made for the support of the child. She is, however, on social assistance at the present time....

The evidence satisfied this Court that the Petitioner is genuinely frightened of the Respondent and that there has been no contact between them since the summer of 1995. If access is granted, there is a good possibility that the Respondent will use the occasion to molest, interfere or otherwise endanger the Petitioner and the child.

In Section 11(1)(b) of the Divorce Act, R.S.C., 1985—Chp. 3 (2nd Supp.), the Court must satisfy itself that reasonable arrangements are made for the support of the child. Those arrangements can be made in accordance with Section 15.1:

> 15.1(1) A court of competent jurisdiction may, on application by either or both spouses, make an order requiring a spouse to pay for the support of any or all children of the marriage.

> 15.1(3) A court making an order under subsection (1) or an interim order under subsection (2) shall do so in accordance with the applicable guidelines.

> 15.1(4) The court may make an order under subsection (1) or an interim order under subsection (2) for a definite or indefinite period or until a specified event occurs, and may impose terms, conditions or restrictions in connection with the order or interim order as it thinks fit and just.

> 15.1(5) Notwithstanding subsection (3), a court may award an amount that is different from the amount that would be determined in accordance with the applicable guidelines if the court is satisfied

> (a) that special provisions in an order, a judgment or a written agreement respecting the financial obligations of the spouses, or the division or transfer of their property, directly or indirectly benefit a child, or that special provisions have otherwise been made for the benefit of a child; and

> (b) that the application of the applicable guidelines would result in an amount of child support that is inequitable given those special provisions.

> 15.1(6) Where the court awards, pursuant to subsection (5), an amount that is different from the amount that would be determined in accordance with the applicable guidelines, the court shall record its reasons for having done so.

It would appear that the use of the word "may" in subsection (1) and (4) leaves a discretion with the Court. If the granting of a support order is bound to result in the harassment and interference of the recipient spouse, surely the Court is entitled to take that into account. Faced with the adamant submission of the Petitioner that she does not want to face that possibility, the Court agrees that it is in the child's and the mother's best interests not to grant child support at this time.

A decree of Divorce will issue, with no access to the father and no child support.

Notes and Questions

1. *Discretion.* Other Canadian courts also have interpreted the term "may" in section 15.1(1) as giving the court discretion not to order support, especially if a prior separation agreement exists. *See, e.g.,* Fung-Sunter v. Fabian, [1999] 69 B.C.L.R.3d 18 (B.C.C.A.). Overall, seventeen percent of children of divorced parents in Canada have no child support agreement at all. *See* Dep't of Justice Canada, 2 Children Come First *supra,* at 12 (citing National Longitudinal Survey of Children and Youth).

2. *Good Cause Exception.* As *Close v. Close* suggests, victims of domestic violence sometimes do not want to seek child support from their batterers. Victims of abuse may fear that the abuser will learn of their whereabouts and/or will use an application for child support as an excuse to batter. In recognition of this fact, federal law in the United States recognizes a good cause exemption from the child support cooperation requirements in its public welfare law. The parameters of the exemption are set by the states. *See generally* Susan Notar & Vicki Turetsky, *Models for Safe Child Support Enforcement,* 8 Am. U. J. Gender Soc. Pol'y & L. 657 (2000). *See also* 42 U.S.C. § 602(a)(7) (discussing "optional" state certification that state will screen for and identify domestic violence).

3. *The Divorce Incentive.* In many places in the United States, failing to seek child support during a divorce will not stop the custodial parent from later obtaining child support. 24A Am. Jur. 2d *Divorce and Separation* §§ 1101, 1103, 1107 (2002). Consequently, in these jurisdictions, there is not even an informal mechanism, *e.g.,* the doctrine of res judicata, by which the divorce proceeding provides parents with an incentive to obtain a timely child support order.

4. *Alternative Incentives.* What other incentives might exist to encourage parents, including parents who have never been married, to obtain child support orders? As suggested above, the United States ties the receipt of welfare benefits to a custodial parent's cooperation in establishing an award, but not all custodial parents receive public assistance. Should this sort of system be expanded? What if the custodial parent's receipt of a driver's license were contingent upon the establishment of a child support award? What if a custodial parent would receive a one-time cash bonus from the state once a child support order were in place?

5. *Priority to Child Support.* The Canadian Divorce Act requires that the court "give priority to child support" when considering applications for both a child support order and for a spousal support order. *See* Divorce Act § 15.3(1). The act provides that if child support later decreases or terminates, a sufficient change of circumstance exists for varying the spousal support order. *See id.* § 15.3(3). The provision has had a large impact on what courts do: "Section 15.3 has significantly affected the way courts have determined and allocated spousal support. The most obvious effect has been to reduce or eliminate spousal support when a paying parent must first pay child support from limited funds." *See* Dep't of Justice Canada, 2 Children Come First, *supra,* at 169. The Canadian Department of Justice does not see this as a problem. The Minister of Justice notes that generally child and spousal support go to the same household and "[i]n the end, it is the total amount of support that matters." *Id.* Do you agree? The same report

suggests that some courts have found creative ways to bypass the statutory provision, including an award of spousal support under the guise of child support since the child's and parent's needs are so intertwined that they cannot be separated for support purposes. *See id.* at 170 (citing Simon v. Simon, [1999] 46 O.R.3d 349 (Ont. C.A.)).

6. *Appropriate Reasons for Deviation. Close v. Close* involved the question whether the court had to order child support at all. However, sometimes a custodial parent may accept an amount of child support that is lower than the guidelines in exchange for some other benefit, such as assured custody. These cases would be resolved under section 15.1(5) of the Divorce Act. What constitutes a "special provision" for purposes of section 15.1(5) and for parallel provincial guidelines is explored further in *Wright v. Zaver, infra,* Chapter 9.B.4.b.iii.

---

b. Private Agreements and Child Support Guidelines

Whether or not a country should be concerned about increasing the number of child support orders, and if so, what can be done to establish more orders, are complicated policy questions. A related and perhaps simpler issue is whether the legal system should require its child support orders always to conform to the child support guidelines. The question is most pressing when the guideline amount is higher than what the parents have agreed upon. This section examines, in a comparative fashion, the legal standards for reviewing private agreements, the orientation a legal system might have about this issue, and the permissibility of modifying these agreements.

i. Standards for Reviewing Private Agreements

In the United States, parties often settle the issue of child support without an adjudication. The trial court can accept or reject the agreed-upon amount. Some courts will not allow a negotiated settlement to deviate from the guidelines. *See, e.g.,* Cox v. Cox, 776 P.2d 1045, 1048 (Alaska 1989) (holding that parents may not make child support agreements that are not subject to the child support guidelines). More typically, however, courts in the United States compare the agreed-upon amount to the guideline amount. Generally, the mere fact of an agreement is not a sufficient reason to deviate from the child support guidelines. Ching v. Ching, 751 P.2d 93, 96 (Haw. Ct. App. 1988) (party agreement is not exceptional circumstance justifying deviation from guidelines where agreement is less than guideline amount). However, many courts do permit parties to deviate from the guideline amount so long as the agreement is in the best interests of the child. In some places in the United States, in fact, "a trial judge may determine that the contractual amount of child support is fair and equitable without requiring evidence and without determining the precise presumptive amount of support." *See* Moreno v. Moreno, 481 S.E.2d 482 (Va. Ct. App. 1997). As the court in *Moreno* stated, "the resources of both the court and the parties would be wasted by requiring a trial judge to sua sponte require parties to litigate a settled matter." *Id.* at 486 (so holding when amount agreed to was higher than the guideline amount).

What are the considerations that guide courts in making decisions in a particular case? Although courts often claim that the "best interest of the child" is foremost, courts may consider more than the dollar amounts involved for a particular child.

Courts may also consider the system efficiencies achieved by private agreements. Presumably, if courts readily accepted negotiated agreements, those agreements could help conserve public resources like court time. Courts may also believe that negotiated agreements further the parties' relationship and enhance the prospects for compliance with any orders entered. These considerations as well as others arguably guide judges' decisions, both at the trial and appellate levels. As you read the next case, try to identify those factors that influenced the particular outcome.

In re Marriage of Handeland
564 N.W.2d 445 (Iowa Ct. App. 1997)

Huitink, J.

This is an appeal by a wife claiming the district court should not have incorporated the parties' stipulation into their decree of dissolution. The wife claims the court should not have accepted the stipulation because it included a deviation from the child support guidelines. We affirm on appeal.

Wayne and Gail Handeland were married in 1977. They have one child, Holly, who was born in 1980. Wayne is a police officer for the City of Cedar Rapids. He has an annual income of $34,800 and a net monthly income of $2235. Gail has an annual income of $14,560 from Hunter Specialties and $4576 from Best Buy. Her net monthly income from these two jobs is $1247.

On September 18, 1995, the parties entered into a stipulation. This stipulation was incorporated by the district court into the parties' dissolution decree. Under the terms of the decree, the parties were granted joint legal custody of Holly, with Wayne having primary physical care.

Gail was ordered to pay child support of $135 per month. This amount is a deviation from the child support guidelines. Under the guidelines Gail would be required to pay child support of $268 per month. The decree provided:

> Both parties acknowledge, and the Court finds, that the amount of child support payable in this case substantially deviates from the guidelines. The reasons for said deviation are as follows:
>
> (a) The Respondent [Gail] is waiving any possible claims she may have for alimony based upon an eighteen-year marriage;
>
> (b) There is a substantial disparity in the present earnings of the parties.
>
> The foregoing constitutes just cause for deviating from the guidelines in this manner.

The decree also provided each party waived his or her right to alimony payments from the other party. Gail now appeals.

Our review of this equitable action is de novo. We are not bound by the district court's findings of fact, but we do give them deference because the district court had an opportunity to view, firsthand, the demeanor of the witnesses when testifying.

Gail contends the district court should have rejected the parties' stipulation because it improperly deviates from the child support guidelines. She believes the stipulation is unjust because she has permanently waived the ability to receive alimony, but her child support obligation could later be increased in a modification. Gail claims she is entitled to alimony. She asks to have the matter remanded to the district court on the issues of child support and alimony.

A stipulation and settlement in a dissolution proceeding is a contract between the parties; however, it becomes final only when accepted and approved by the court. When a stipulation merges into a decree, it is then to be interpreted and enforced as a final judgment of the court, not as a separate contract between the parties.

A stipulated settlement should be approved and enforced only if the district court determines the settlement will not adversely affect the best interests of the parties' children. Our child support guidelines provide:

> A stipulation of the parties establishing child support and medical support shall be reviewed by the court to determine if the amount stipulated and the medical support provisions are in substantial compliance with the guidelines. A proposed order to incorporate the stipulation shall be reviewed by the court to determine its compliance with these guidelines. If a variance from the guidelines is proposed, the court must determine whether it is justified and appropriate, and, if so, include the stated reasons for the variance in its order.

We find the district court gave sufficient reasons to deviate from the child support guidelines in this case. The deviation is based on Gail's waiver of alimony. Parties may contract away an alimony obligation and a court will give effect to the agreement absent a showing the agreement is clearly inequitable. The agreement to waive alimony was not clearly inequitable. We find the deviation from the child support guidelines was justified and appropriate. We also find the stipulation does not adversely affect the best interests of the parties' child.

We affirm the decision of the district court incorporating the parties' stipulation into the dissolution decree....

Notes and Questions

1. *Outcome.* Why did the court permit the deviation here? Is it correct that the stipulation in *Handeland* does not affect the best interests of the child? Why or why not? *Handeland* is not a typical case in many respects. Perhaps most obviously, the obligor is attacking the order because it is lower than what the guidelines would ordinarily permit. Typically the payee would be attacking the order for its inadequacy.

2. *Canada.* Canada takes a similar approach to the United States in the establishment of initial awards where the parties have negotiated an agreement. Section 15.1 of the Divorce Act (1997) (Can.) indicates when an agreement can justify deviation from the guidelines in an original application for child support. The relevant portion of that section follows:

> *Court may take agreement, etc., into account*
>
> (5) Notwithstanding subsection (3), a court may award an amount that is different from the amount that would be determined in accordance with the applicable guidelines if the court is satisfied
>
> (a) that special provisions in an order, a judgment or a written agreement respecting the financial obligations of the spouses, or the division or transfer of their property, directly or indirectly benefit a child, or that special provisions have otherwise been made for the benefit of a child; and

(*b*) that the application of the applicable guidelines would result in an amount of child support that is inequitable given those special provisions.

Reasons

(6) Where the court awards, pursuant to subsection (5), an amount that is different from the amount that would be determined in accordance with the applicable guidelines, the court shall record its reasons for having done so.

Consent orders

(7) Notwithstanding subsection (3), a court may award an amount that is different from the amount that would be determined in accordance with the applicable guidelines on the consent of both spouses if it is satisfied that reasonable arrangements have been made for the support of the child to whom the order relates.

Reasonable arrangements

(8) For the purposes of subsection (7), in determining whether reasonable arrangements have been made for the support of a child, the court shall have regard to the applicable guidelines. However, the court shall not consider the arrangements to be unreasonable solely because the amount of support agreed to is not the same as the amount that would otherwise have been determined in accordance with the applicable guidelines.

It may be difficult at first glance to understand the difference between sections 15.1(5)-(6) and sections 15.1(7)-(8). Sections 15.1(7)-(8) address the situation in which an agreement exists and both parties consent to an order for less than the guideline amount (for example, because one party received the house). In this situation, the judge would still be permitted under section 11 to grant the divorce because reasonable arrangements would have been made for the child (*see supra* Section B.4.a).

In contrast, sections 15.1(5)-(6) deal with the situation in which the custodial parent seeks a child support award, but there is an agreement or order (typically regarding maintenance or the parties' property) that would make the application of the guidelines inappropriate. In this latter situation, the obligor would need to establish that an application of the guidelines would be inequitable. In the United States, states have different approaches to this sort of situation. Sometimes state guidelines specify that an unequal division of property will not justify a deviation if the adjustment would result in a lesser economic benefit to the child. *See, e.g.,* Conn. Gen. Stat. § 466-215b(a)(2002). Other times, however, the division of personal property can justify a downward departure. *See, e.g.,* Me. Rev. Stat. Ann. tit. 19-A, § 2007 (Supp. 2002). The language of sections 15.1(5)-(6) also appears in sections 17(6.4)-(6.6) and will be discussed more in connection with *Wright v. Zaver*, which appears below.

Here we are concerned with the situation in which both parents agree to a lower amount of child support than the guidelines would otherwise permit, and the relevant provisions in Canada are sections 15.1(7)-(8). In short, parents can agree on an amount of child support, and the judge will "look at the appropriate guidelines; find the appropriate amount; and determine whether the amount the parents agreed on is reasonable." Dep't of Justice Canada, Child Support, Ten Things You Need to Know, *available at* http://canada.justice.gc.ca/en/ps/sup/10ntk/10ntk.html. Would the *Handeland* agreement have been permissible under the Canadian Divorce Act?

3. *Lump Sum Payments.* Both the Divorce Act and the Federal Child Support Guidelines allow courts in Canada to order lump sum child support. *See* Federal Child Support Guidelines § 11 (Can.). *See, e.g.,* M.R. v. S.R.R., [1998] Carswell B.C. 1192 (B.C. Sup. Ct.) (ordering lump sum child support equivalent to two and a half years of periodic support because of father's doubtful future earning potential; award was to be paid from father's only cash asset, proceeds from sale of marital home). Some state courts in the United States exercise their discretion and order support in lump sum, *see, e.g.,* In re Gonzalez, 993 S.W.2d 147 (Tex. Ct. App. 1999), although other courts expressly disapprove of lump sum orders saying the awards disregard the specific needs of children at present and they make future modification difficult, if not impossible. *See* Hobbs v. Hobbs, 275 S.W.3d 900 (Tenn. 2000). A lump-sum order also hampers the state's ability to recover reimbursement for public assistance furnished to the obligor's children, *i.e.,* if that state support is furnished after the obligor satisfies the obligations under the support order. *See* State v. Brecht, 255 N.W.2d 342 (Iowa 1977). On the other hand, lump sum payments might be particularly appropriate if the obligor may go abroad, making collection difficult. *See, e.g.,* Berge v. Berge, 536 P.2d 1135 (Colo. 1975).

---

ii. Contrasting Orientations

Two countries with very different approaches to parental agreements are Sweden and England. Sweden allows parents undergoing a divorce or separation to determine the level of child support, and the amount does not need to be ratified by the courts. Rather the courts have a residual role. Parents can freely make agreements regarding the amount of the maintenance. "If the parents agree the courts will simply ratify the parents' statement." Clearinghouse, *Sweden, supra,* at Calculation for Child Support. *See also* Anne Corden & Daniel R. Meyer, *Child Support Policy Regimes in the United States, United Kingdom, and Other Countries: Similar Issues, Different Approaches,* 21 Focus 72, 74 tbl. 1 (2000); Försäkringskassan (Social Insurance Office), Child Support (2002), *at* www.a.fk.se/utland/eng/brochure%20April%202002.pdf; Mavis Maclean & Andrea Warman, *A Comparative Approach to Child Support Systems: Legal Rules and Social Policies, in* Child Support: The Next Frontier 168 (J. Thomas Oldham & Marygold S. Melli eds., 2000) ("[p]arents may make their own arrangements, [and] the courts only become involved in disputed cases"). This is similar to the situation in Norway, but different from the situation in Austria, Belgium, Denmark, Finland, France, Germany, Netherlands, and the U.K., where the court or an administrative agency has some responsibility for ratifying the level of support. Corden & Meyer, *supra,* at 74. In Sweden, parents are also allowed to amend the maintenance allowance by writing a new agreement, even if the prior allowance had been set by the court. *See* Ministry of Justice, Sweden, Family Law: Information on the Rules 41 (2000).

That is not to say that courts exercise no supervision at all over parental agreements in Sweden. If there is a dispute, a court will set the correct amount. "The court can… adjust an agreement that is unreasonable having regard to the circumstances when the agreement was concluded and the circumstances generally." *Id.* However, such court review is discouraged, albeit indirectly. For example, "the party who loses a maintenance case before a court should in general pay both his or her own and the opposing party's litigation expenses. If it is the child that loses, the parent who represents the child should normally pay the ligation costs of the other party." *Id.*

In contrast to Sweden, England gives less deference to most written agreements. If the written agreement has not been entered into a court order, the agreement will not stop "any party to the agreement, or any other person, from applying for a maintenance assessment with respect to any child to or for whose benefit periodical payments are to be made or secured under the agreement." Child Support Act 1991, c. 48, § 9(3), (4) (Eng.). While the modification of a written agreement that has been incorporated into a court order must typically be approved by the court, this is not true if the custodial parent is receiving Income Support or a Jobseeker's Allowance. Then a written agreement, even if entered into a court order, will not stop the imposition of a new maintenance assessment by the administrative agency. The new assessment need not be based on a finding of changed circumstance or that a "significantly different" amount of support is payable because a maintenance assessment would not yet have been entered. *See id.* § 17(2). *See generally* Dep't Health & Social Serv., A Guide to Child Support Maintenance 7–8 (1999), *available at* http://www.dsdni.gov.uk/publications/documents/csa2008.pdf. In addition, once the Child Support, Pensions and Social Security Act amendments are implemented, a new assessment can be made for any court order entered after the effective date that has been in force for one year. *See* Child Support, Pensions and Social Security Act, 2000, c. 19, § 2 (Eng.).

Two commentators have reached the following conclusions: "The trend in continental European countries has been toward enabling structures and procedures which encourage parental cooperation in working out realistic support arrangements." Corden & Meyer, *supra*, at 78. "In most European countries, third-party determinations often build upon or ratify preliminary voluntary agreements between parents. This trend has been encouraged because it is believed to result in more realistic arrangements which parents are more likely to honor and reduces administration expense. The United Kingdom is unusual in Europe in providing little scope or motivation to lower-income parents to try to work together to agree upon financial liability." *Id.* at 74 tbl. 1.

Notes and Questions

1. *Amount of Awards.* The size of negotiated awards is an important consideration in assessing the desirability of private agreements. Commentators have noted that negotiated agreements in the United States are generally lower than court-imposed awards.

> Variation in award levels results largely from the negotiation process that determines the vast majority of child support orders. Many parents who negotiate support awards are poorly informed about the relevant legal standards.... In a large and apparently growing proportion of cases, lawyer representation is available to only one—or neither—parent.... Under these circumstances, each parent's resources and attitudes toward the divorce may play important roles in determining child support outcomes and produce results that bear little relationship to those lawmakers intended.

Marsha Garrison, *The Goals and Limits of Child Support Policy, in* Child Support: The Next Frontier 16 (J. Thomas Oldham & Marygold S. Melli eds., 2000) (footnote omitted).

2. *Frequency of Payment.* Evidence from Canada suggests that negotiated agreements enhance compliance with a child support obligation. In Canada, "children cov-

ered by a private agreement between the parents are more likely to receive regular support payments than are children whose parents have arrangements under a court order. Two-thirds of children under private agreements benefitted from regular support payments compared to 43% of children whose parents had a court-ordered agreement. Moreover, cases in which there have been no payments in the last six months are much more common among parents who have a court order than among those with a private agreement (30% versus 14%)." Dep't of Justice Canada, 2 Children Come First *supra*, at 13. In their study of eleven countries, Anne Corden and Daniel Meyer concluded "The Scandinavian countries appear to achieve the highest levels of compliance with payments of child support." Corden & Meyer, *supra*, at 77. "Paradoxically, high compliance rates with child maintenance orders [in Sweden] are a factor in growing criticism of the maintenance advance system." *See* David Bradley, Family Law & Political Culture, Scandinavian Laws in Comparative Perspective 124 (1996).

3. *Extent and Impact of the Practice.* It is very difficult to assess how many parents in the United States circumvent the child support guidelines through agreements. Marygold S. Melli has written about this issue and explains that some data suggests that party agreement is the most common reason courts deviate from child support guidelines, and that in the vast majority of these cases the deviation was downward. In this excerpt, Professor Melli reflects on the existing data, and in particular on the *Evaluation of Child Support Guidelines: Findings and Conclusion*, a 1996 study conducted by the American Bar Association Center on Children and the Law.

The best answer to the question of how often the states do not apply their guidelines is that it is unknown. Fewer than half of the states completed case reviews as directed by the federal regulation, deviations were not always noted, and the reasons for deviations were not always available in the record reviewed. Furthermore, the bulk of the information about the use of guidelines in the evaluation study was based on the ABA's independent analysis of a sample of 4,200 case records using a problematic methodology. The case records examined included court orders, work sheets, and supplemental data on deviations, but the records did not contain reasons for deviation that had only been placed orally on the record in the proceeding without any written documentation. The evaluation study considered all support awards to be in compliance with the guidelines unless there was some written documentation of a deviation.... This methodology resulted in the report's somewhat misleading statement that "83 percent of the cases were considered to follow the guidelines, while 17 percent of the cases were categorized as formal deviations." In fact, the 83 percent of the cases considered to be guideline cases contained a significant number that did not follow the guidelines amount.

Further data analysis examined the group of guideline cases without written documentation of a deviation to determine the extent to which the amount awarded in those cases was the same as a computed guideline amount would be for the case. If the support award agreed with the computed amount or if it was within 2 percent above or below that amount, the case was regarded as in compliance with the guideline. If the support order was not within that range, it was classified as a discrepancy case. In a significant number of cases — ranging from less than 10 percent to more than 45 percent across the twenty-one countries in the data analysis — there was a discrepancy.

The evaluation study provided an instructive analysis of the 17 percent of the cases considered formal deviations. In the vast majority of deviation cases, 83 percent, the deviation was downward, and the average amount of the decrease was 36 percent. For the 17 percent of cases with an increase, the amount of increase averaged 30 percent.

The most frequent reason for deviation, listed in 21 percent of the cases, was an agreement of the parties. Second households, extended or extraordinary visitation expenses, and low income of the noncustodial parent each accounted for deviations in 10 percent of the cases. In 8 percent of the cases the reason given was that the guideline amount would be unjust or inappropriate. In 4 percent of the cases, the reason was extraordinary needs of the parent (but the study did not specify which parent). Fifteen percent of the cases cited other reasons, and 13 percent gave no reason. Cases in which the mother was the obligor were more likely to have deviations, although fathers were the obligors in 93 percent of the cases.... More than 90 percent of the deviations because of low income of the noncustodial parent or because of a second household were downward deviations. In contrast, more than 20 percent of the deviations because of agreement of the parties were upward, as was the case with deviations because the amount of the award was inappropriate or unjust.

Marygold S. Melli, *Guideline Review: The Search for an Equitable Child Support Formula*, *in* Child Support: The Next Frontier 118–119 (J. Thomas Oldham & Marygold S. Melli eds., 2000) (citations omitted).

4. *Negotiations.* How might parental negotiations be impacted in England, Sweden and the United States in light of the countries' perspectives on the desirability and permeability of parental agreements?

5. *De Facto Priority of Child Support.* In England, the court no longer has jurisdiction over most cases of child maintenance, and the matters are resolved and appealed through administrative channels. Even where courts retain power to make an order, the administrative agency can "levy[] an assessment which will substitute the child maintenance order where the court order has been in force for one year." James Pirrie, *The Child Support, Pension and Social Security Bill*, 30 Fam. L. 199, 200 (2000). Consequently, "[t]he solicitor must tell the client to attend at the Child Support Agency as an initial step before any other family issues can be addressed. In other words, it is not possible to advise a client about the potential outcome of a family case unless support is first settled." Mary MacDonald, Expedited Child Support: An Overview of the Commonwealth Countries' and United States' Procedures for Establishing and Modifying Child Support (1997). Consequently, "the property settlement is totally separate from the child support award." *See* J. Thomas Oldham, *Lessons from the New English and Australian Child Support Systems*, 29 Vand. J. Transnat'l L. 691, 718 (1996); MacDonald, *supra*. The Child Support Act 1995, c. 34, sched. 2 §3 (Eng.), contains a limited exception that permits departure from the child support guidelines for capital or property transfers embodied in a pre-1993 decree. Generally, however, parties cannot use property as a method to provide for children. What are the advantages and disadvantages of this approach? Should child support, property issues, and spousal maintenance all be decided together? Is there an interrelationship between these awards that they should all be negotiated as a package?

6. *Presumptive Validity?* Divorce can be one of the most stressful occasions in a person's life. As one judge has noted, during a divorce many people do "very unwise things, things that are anything but mature and sensible, even when they consult legal counsel." Caron

v. Caron, [1987] 1 S.C.R. 892 (La Forest, J., dissenting.). In addition, both pro se and represented parties may not recognize the true costs of raising children, especially after divorce or separation. Should there be structures in place to review these agreements, and if so, should the decision-maker be deferential to agreements entered between the parties?

7. *ALI Principles.* At present, the approach in the United States appears to fall in between the approaches of Sweden and England. Is the United States headed in one direction or the other? The proposed new system for child support developed by the American Law Institute allows parents to agree to a lesser amount of support than the child support guidelines would ordinarily permit. *See Principles of the Law of Family Dissolution: Analysis & Recommendations,* § 3.7(2)(d) (2002). The *Principles* state that the presumptive effect of the child support guidelines is considered rebutted when "taking into account the interests of the child, the amount determined by the child-support formula would be unjust or inappropriate [because]...the parents have agreed to a greater amount, or the parents have agreed to a lesser amount and their agreement has been reviewed and approved by court pursuant to § 3.13." Section 3.13 reads as follows:

§ 3.13 Effect of Parental Agreement on the Child Support Award

(1) The child-support terms of a parental agreement should be approved and adopted by the court unless the agreement provides for substantially less child support than would otherwise be awarded under this Chapter. In that case, the court should not approve and adopt the child-support terms unless the court determines that, when read with the agreement as a whole, they are consistent with the interests of the child. In approving such child-support terms, the court should comply with the writing requirements of § 3.7(3).

(2) The child-support terms of a parental agreement, or a court order incorporating those terms, are subject to modification under §§ 3.17–3.22. However, any modification of child support should take into account all the terms of any agreement approved by the court under this section.

Id. § 3.13. The commentary indicates that a "substantial" difference might require a deviation greater than twenty percent. *See id.* cmt. a. Moreover, "the total resources of the residential household, taking into account income from all sources" is relevant to whether a "substantial" difference exists. "If the income of the residential household is large, the law has relatively little interest in insisting on the letter of the statute when the parties have agreed otherwise." *Id.* § 3.13, cmt. b. The commentary also acknowledges the importance of examining all economic aspects of the dissolution when evaluating the child support agreement, and the permissibility of trading child support for custodial responsibility and diminished access. *See id.* § 3.13, cmt. c, d. Does this recommendation make sense if children in the United States rely to such a large extent on child support ordered by the courts?

8. *Children's Rights.* Are children's rights implicated by these issues related to child support? How, and to what extent, are they implicated?

---

iii. Modification of Private Agreements Incorporated into Court Orders

The problem of low awards resulting from negotiated agreements is minimized, although not eliminated, if a party can modify the child support award and have the court or an administrative agency apply the guidelines at a later date. In the United

States, a child support award can be set aside if it is the result of fraud, coercion, or overreaching. In addition, child support awards in the United States are generally modifiable, even if they are a result of a negotiated agreement and even if the parties try to foreclose this option. *See, e.g.,* Ayo v. Ayo, 190 Cal. App. 3d 442 (1987); *see also* Marriage and Divorce Act § 306(f), 9A U.L.A. 248 (1998). The rule is often stated that a parent is unable to contract away his or her child's right to support. As noted above, the new ALI *Principles* continue to make the child support terms of a parental agreement modifiable. Generally, however, courts do not make the modification of an award retroactive because of estoppel defenses.

A party seeking modification in the United States may need to establish a "substantial change of circumstances" beyond mere non-compliance with the guidelines. *See, e.g.,* In re Marriage of O'Moore, 42 P.3d 767 (Mont. 2002.); Markofski v. Holzhauer, 799 So. 2d 162 (Miss. Ct. App. 2001). Many courts, however, will relax this standard when adjudicating the modification of an agreed-upon amount of child support. *See* Murray v. Murray, 425 N.W.2d 315, 317 (Minn. Ct. App. 1988) (adopting a relaxed standard for reviewing whether a substantial change in circumstances supporting modification had occurred where the original stipulated child-support agreement was well below statutory guidelines); Thomas v. Thomas, 120 Cal. App. 3d 33 (1981) (agreements may be modifiable without finding even a substantial change of circumstances). Today, in the United States, even a lump sum award ordered in a divorce decree will probably not fix the limit of the obligor's support obligations, although this used to be the case, *see* State v. Brecht, 255 N.W.2d 342, 345 (Iowa 1977), particularly if the lump sum is a product of an agreement. *See, e.g.,* Kelley v. Kelley, 449 S.E.2d 55 (Va. 1994).

In Canada, a parental agreement does not prohibit a court from modifying the level of child support, even if the agreement has been incorporated into a decree. Rather, the court presumes that the amount in the agreement met the child's reasonable needs at the time and then determines if the requirements for modification are met. *See generally* Willick v. Willick, [1994] 3 S.C.R. 670 (Can.). In Canada, parents do not have the ability to restrict or waive the child's right to his or her support being determined pursuant to the child support guidelines. *See* Julien D. Payne and Marilyn A. Paine, Introduction to Canadian Family Law 61 (1994) (citing cases).

The standard for modification of child support awards in Canada is set forth in federal and provincial statutes. The Divorce Act states that a change of circumstances is required. *See* Divorce Act § 17(4). Then the guidelines generally must be applied. However, the court can award a different amount for the same reasons it could vary from the guidelines in an initial order. *See* Divorce Act § 17(6.2)-(6.5). In short, if "special provisions" have been made and the guidelines would be inequitable in that situation, *see* Divorce Act § 17(6.4)-(6.6), or a consent order embodies a reasonable arrangement for the child's support, *see* Divorce Act § 17(6.2)-(6.3), then a variation is permissible.

The next case involves a prior agreement between the parties and a change of circumstances since that agreement was made. In the case, the father argued that the prior order embodied "special provisions," and that applying the guidelines would be inequitable in his situation. The case does not arise under the Divorce Act, but under the Ontario Family Law Act, R.S.O., ch. F. 3. (1990). The Ontario Family Law Act's provisions on variation are similarly worded to the provisions in the Divorce Act. Section 17 of the Divorce Act finds its counterpart in section 37 of the Family Law Act. The provisions of the Family Law Act are set forth here.

Application for variation

37. (1) [Setting forth parties with standing to make an application to the court for variation.]

Powers of court: child support

(2.1) In the case of an order for support of a child, if the court is satisfied that there has been a change in circumstances within the meaning of the child support guidelines or that evidence not available on the previous hearing has become available, the court may,

(a) discharge, vary or suspend a term of the order, prospectively or retroactively;...

(c) make any other order for the support of a child that the court could make on an application under section 33.

Application of child support guidelines

(2.2) A court making an order under subsection (2.1) shall do so in accordance with the child support guidelines.

Exception: special provisions

(2.3) Despite subsection (2.2), a court may award an amount that is different from the amount that would be determined in accordance with the child support guidelines if the court is satisfied,

(a) that special provisions in an order or a written agreement respecting the financial obligations of the parents, or the division or transfer of their property, directly or indirectly benefit a child, or that special provisions have otherwise been made for the benefit of a child; and

(b) that the application of the child support guidelines would result in an amount of child support that is inequitable given those special provisions.

Wright v. Zaver
[2000] 211 D.L.R.4th 260 (Ont. C.A.)

Simmons J.A....

Ms. Wright and Mr. Zaver were involved in an intimate relationship for slightly less than three years. Their son, Michael, was born on January 23, 1985.

Because of increasing acrimony in their relations, Ms. Wright denied Mr. Zaver and his family any contact with Michael soon after Michael's birth. In March 1985, Ms. Wright applied to the Provincial Court (Family Division) for custody, child support, and spousal support. Mr. Zaver cross-applied for custody.

The parties resolved the application by Minutes of Settlement dated May 29, 1985. The Minutes of Settlement included acknowledgments confirming that the terms would be incorporated into a court order, that the order would be subject to variation, and that Mr. Zaver did not admit paternity.

An order was made the same day incorporating the terms of the Minutes of Settlement. It awarded custody of Michael to Ms. Wright, required Mr. Zaver to pay lump sum child support of $4,000.00, and provided that Mr. Zaver would have no access to Michael.

By January 1986, Mr. Zaver began having second thoughts about the agreement. He commenced an application for access, admitted paternity, and offered to revisit the issue of child support. Ms. Wright opposed the application vigorously, contending that there had been no material change in circumstances. She also asserted that she hoped to marry and that it would not be in Michael's best interests to have Mr. Zaver involved in his life.

Faced with the prospect of acrimonious litigation, Mr. Zaver withdrew the 1986 application.

In October 1990, Ms. Wright married Mr. Wright. They separated in July 1999. During their marriage they had one child, Amanda Wright, born October 31, 1992. Throughout the marriage, Mr. Wright treated Michael as his own son.

Ms. Wright commenced this application against Mr. Zaver on October 19, 1999, claiming child support for Michael in accordance with the Ontario Guidelines and, "if necessary, a declaration that there has been a material change of circumstances." In support of her application, Ms. Wright claimed monthly living expenses of $3,819 and a gross monthly income of $2,820, leaving her with a deficit of $999 per month.

Mr. Zaver requested that Mr. Wright be added as a party to this proceeding. However, his request was made essentially meaningless by a consent order dated November 8, 1999 in divorce proceedings between Ms. Wright and Mr. Wright requiring Mr. Wright to pay child support of $879 per month for two children based on the Federal Child Support Guidelines, S.O.R./97-175, as amended (the "Federal Guidelines").

Taking account of the child support paid by Mr. Wright, Ms. Wright has a deficit of $120 per month.

Mr. Zaver is a Public Health Inspector for the City of Toronto. His gross income from all sources as disclosed on his 1998 tax return was $60,260.90. According to his financial statement, his net worth is $428,248.65.

On June 20, 2000, the applications judge found two material changes in circumstances warranting a variation of the 1985 order, first, that the lump sum payment of $4,000 was inadequate to meet Michael's continuing needs, and, second, the coming into force of the Ontario Guidelines. He accordingly ordered Mr. Zaver to pay the Ontario Guidelines table amount of $509.00 per month as child support for Michael.

The applications judge made…other findings that are in issue on this appeal. First, he found that it is immaterial whether this application is treated as an application to vary or as a fresh application for support. Second, he found that "a court is not bound by the child support provisions of an agreement, even where incorporated into a court order, where such provisions are inadequate."…

[Ed. Note: The court decided that the enactment of the Ontario Guidelines created a right to a variation of pre-existing orders for child support in accordance with the Guidelines. The enactment of the Ontario Guidelines constituted a material change of circumstances. The court also concluded that a trial court does not retain a residual discretion not to vary once the pre-condition to variation has been satisfied. Rather, the court's discretion not to apply the Ontario Guidelines is limited to the circumstances set out in §§ 37(2.3) and (2.5) of the Family Law Act. Courts in Canada are divided on whether the enactment of guidelines creates a right to variation. The Courts of Appeal of British Columbia, New Brunswick, and Alberta have held that courts retain a residual discretion not to vary. By contrast, the Courts of Appeal of Saskatchewan and Nova Scotia determined that the enactment of guidelines created a right to a variation. The court here also held the following:

> On an application to vary a pre-Guidelines order the court is required to determine child support based on the identical criteria that exist for determining

child support on an original application for support. However, because ss. 37(2.3) and 37(2.5) respectively contemplate the existence of "special provisions" and "reasonable arrangements" for the benefit or support of a child that permit the court to award an amount different than the amount that would be determined under the Ontario Guidelines, the resulting variation order need not actually change the amount of the original order.]

I accept Mr. Zaver's submission that arrangements capable of constituting special provisions were made for Michael's benefit. I am not however satisfied that application of the Ontario Guidelines would result in an amount of support that is inequitable given those provisions. I would not, accordingly, give effect to this ground of appeal.

Section 37(2.3) of the Family Law Act is one of two sections that permit the court to depart from the requirement of applying the Ontario Guidelines in making an order for child support....

Section 37(2.3) sets out a three-part test for departing from the application of the Ontario Guidelines. First, the court must find "special provisions." Second, the court must determine that the special provisions benefit the child in the specified way. Third, the court must find that applying the Ontario Guidelines would result in an amount of support that is "inequitable" given the special provisions. Only if each part of this test is satisfied can a court depart from the application of the Ontario Guidelines under s. 37(2.3).

a) Special Provisions

Section 37(2.3)(a) contemplates three types of "special provisions":

- special provisions in an order or agreement respecting the financial obligations of the parents that directly or indirectly benefit a child;
- special provisions in an order or agreement respecting the division or transfer of the parents' property that directly or indirectly benefit a child; and
- special provisions otherwise made for the benefit of a child.

Mr. Zaver asserts that the 1985 agreement and order, coupled with Mr. Wright's assumption of responsibility for Michael, fall within the third type of "special provisions."

Bateman J.A. dealt with a closely analogous situation involving a prior lump sum payment in MacKay v. Bucher.... In considering the nature of special provisions, she noted that many courts have adopted a definition of special provisions that require that they be "out of the ordinary or unusual." However, she agreed, generally, with the comments in Hall v. Hall (1997), 30 R.F.L. (4th) (B.C.S.C. Master) concerning the nature of "special provisions": "In the first place, I am of the opinion that a 'special provision' must be one which, in whole or in part, replaces the need for the ongoing support for the children...."

Like Bateman J.A., I too agree generally with this approach. In my view, however, a more precise focus would be whether the provisions replace, in whole or in part, the need for support in accordance with the Ontario Guidelines. This approach is consistent with the exercise of determining whether the Ontario Guidelines should be applied.

Moreover, I see no requirement to read s. 37(2.3) restrictively and limit its application to provisions that are "out of the ordinary or unusual," so long as the provisions replace, in whole or in part, the need for support in accordance with the Ontario Guidelines and satisfy the other requirements of s. 37(2.3).

In this respect, it is helpful to juxtapose s. 37(2.5) of the Family Law Act with s. 37(2.3). Section 37(2.5) provides the court with relatively broad discretion to recognize, where appropriate, reasonable arrangements for child support that differ from the Ontario Guidelines amount where an application is made on consent of the parents. It is clear that there is no restriction on the categories of consensual arrangements that can qualify for exemption under s. 37(2.5).

I see no reason to read such a restriction into s. 37(2.3). The enactment of the Ontario Guidelines exposed all pre-existing consent orders to variation. Although the Ontario Guidelines clearly change the ground rules for awarding child support, the simplest of domestic contracts may have involved extended negotiations and concessions that militate against their application in a particular case. Moreover, surrounding circumstances, or the terms of the agreement themselves, may make it obvious that the existence of the Guidelines would have made no difference to the agreement that was ultimately reached.

In my view, no principled reason emerges from the language or purpose of s. 37(2.3) to limit special provisions to provisions that are "out of the ordinary or unusual." Rather, they refer simply to provisions that replace, in whole or in part, the need for support in accordance with the Ontario Guidelines.

In this case, the applications judge noted that Ms. Wright "alleged [in her 1986 affidavit] that access would be upsetting for her and her son as it was her intention to move on with her life, marry, and have her future spouse take on the responsibility of fathering Michael and providing for his support.... It was her view that the father had 'sold away' his rights to parent her son and that he should not be permitted to resile from that agreement."

It is significant, in my view, that at least part of Ms. Wright's goal in entering the 1985 agreement with Mr. Zaver was to put herself in a position where she could remarry and effect for Michael what was essentially a "defacto adoption." Ms. Wright entered into the 1985 agreement expecting to be able to provide for Michael's needs either through her own resources, or with the assistance of a new partner. That expectation on her part formed part of the arrangement she and Mr. Zaver made, as did Mr. Zaver's release of any claim to access. For a significant period these arrangements completely replaced the need for any support from Mr. Zaver.

I find that the agreement entered into by the parties, the resulting court order, and the fact that Mr. Wright accepted responsibility for supporting Michael, are capable of constituting "special provisions" within the meaning of s. 37(2.3) of the Family Law Act. In my view, the support now being paid by Mr. Wright also qualifies as part of the arrangements capable of constituting "special provisions." I see nothing in the requirements relating to the third type of "special provisions" that requires that they flow entirely from the parties to the litigation or that they be entirely financial in character.

Given that it is the totality of these arrangements that are advanced as special provisions, I think it appropriate that they be assessed cumulatively, to see whether they satisfy the other two prongs of the three-part test set out in s. 37(2.3).

b) Benefit to the Child

On the issue of benefit to Michael, Mr. Wright's child support payments are a direct benefit to Michael now. Such a benefit was clearly anticipated by Ms. Wright, and, in fact, motivated the 1985 agreement between the parties, at least in part. The court endorsed the 1985 agreement at the time it was made, including the term denying Mr. Zaver access to Michael. I conclude that the 1985 agreement was clearly made for Michael's benefit.

c) Inequitability

I turn then to the question of whether the "application of the child support guidelines would result in an amount of child support that is inequitable given [these] ... provisions." ...

I ... adopt the comments of Vogelsang J. in Burns v. Burns (1998), 40 R.F.L. (4th) 32 (Ont. Ct. Gen. Div.) ...: "the term 'inequitable' ... relates to the parties and requires a consideration of both the circumstances of the parties giving rise to the order or written agreement and their circumstances at the time of the application. Such an interpretation recognizes the give and take of settlement discussions and the interrelationship of terms that will be reflected in a settlement agreement and order."

Finally, in my view, in addition to its dictionary definition of "unfair," "inequitable" as it is used in s. 37(2.3) of the Family Law Act includes a connotation that the equities between the interested parties are "out of balance." I reach this conclusion because there is no statement in the subsection of to whom "inequitable" applies. Had the legislature intended to be specific concerning to whom the concept was to apply, it could easily have said so. The interested parties include the child as well as the parties to the application.

I note the following matters relevant to Michael's needs, Ms. Wright's present ability to satisfy them, and Mr. Zaver's ability to pay:

- Ms. Wright's stated monthly shortfall, taking account of the child support she is receiving, is $120;

- on its face, Ms. Wright's budget appears not only reasonable, but "bare bones"; as an example she has no expenses for children's activities;

- given that Michael is part of a family unit which includes two children, notionally Mr. Wright pays less child support for Michael than he would if Michael was an only child, i.e. Mr. Wright is paying $879 per month, if Michael were an only child he would pay $543 per month;

- need is a relative concept, determined in part by disposable income, and in the case of a child, in part by the lifestyle of the family unit of which he is a part;

- in the case of a family unit including separated parents, the family unit includes all parents;

- assuming Michael was the only child of a payor with an income equal to the total income of Mr. Zaver and Mr. Wright, the Ontario Guidelines table amount of monthly child support would be approximately $942, a figure that is approximately equal to half of the amount paid by Mr. Wright plus the Ontario Guidelines figure for Mr. Zaver; and

- Mr. Zaver's budget includes a number of discretionary expenditures; *e.g.* his annual expenses for entertainment, recreation, vacation, gifts, alcohol/tobacco, charities/lotteries and R.R.S.P.'s (he has an OMERS pension) approximate $8000.

In my view, the most important factor affecting the determination of whether application of the Ontario Guidelines would be inequitable is the fact that Ms. Wright is no longer able to meet all of Michael's financial needs independently of Mr. Zaver, even with the benefit of the additional resources provided by Mr. Wright. Having determined that Ms. Wright is no longer able to meet all of Michael's financial needs, I do not think it appropriate to assess them on a minimalist basis. Mr. Zaver is Michael's biological father. The 1985 agreement did not relieve him of the continuing obligation to ensure that Michael's needs are properly met. The Ontario Guidelines table amounts are designed to achieve that result based on the income of the payor(s).

While it is true that neither Michael nor Mr. Zaver has had the opportunity of a personal relationship with the other, Mr. Zaver has had a holiday from support for many years. There is no indication that it will be an undue financial burden for him to pay support in accordance with the Ontario Guidelines. As the amount in issue is relatively modest, it is unlikely there will be a surplus available to somehow unfairly increase Ms. Wright's standard of living.

Taking account of all of these circumstances, I cannot conclude that the equities between the parties would be out of balance, or that it would be inequitable otherwise, if Mr. Zaver is required to pay full Ontario Guidelines support for Michael.

Sharpe J.A.

I have had the benefit of reading the reasons of Simmons J.A. and I too would dismiss this appeal. I agree, for the reasons given by my colleague, that the enactment of the Child Support Guidelines creates a right to a variation of pre-existing orders for child support. While I agree with the result she reaches, I respectfully disagree with Simmons J.A.'s analysis and interpretation of the "special provisions" exception contained in s. 37(2.3) of the Family Law Act.

I agree with the structure of the three-part test with respect to the "special provisions" exception set out at paragraph 86 of Simmons J.A.'s reasons. However, I disagree with the proposition that "special provisions" need not be out of the ordinary or unusual. Nor do I accept the contention that the subjective goals and expectations of the parties are relevant in determining whether a pre-Guidelines arrangement qualifies as a special provision within the meaning of s. 37(2.3).

For the reasons that follow, I conclude that the "special provisions" exception does not apply to the circumstances of this case. While Mr. Wright's ongoing child support arguably does qualify as a special provision, that arrangement fails to meet the test in s. 37(2.3), since applying the child support guidelines would not be inequitable.

Courts have held that "special provisions" must be out of the ordinary or unusual.... [C]ourts generally have not found that routine orders for periodic child support constitute "special provisions."...I agree with the approach in these cases.... If provisions that were not out of the ordinary or unusual could qualify as "special provisions," the word "special" in s. 37(2.3) would have no meaning.

In my view, interpreting "special provisions" to include provisions that are not out of the ordinary or unusual would undermine the general rule that the child support guidelines provide the amount of a child support order. Under s. 3(1) of the Ontario Guidelines, the presumptive rule is the guideline amount of child support. Under s. 37(2.2) of the Family Law Act, a court that varies a child support order shall do so in accordance with the child support guidelines. The "special provisions" qualification in s. 37(2.3) is an exception to the presumptive rule. Its status as an exception suggests to me that its scope must be carefully delineated. If "special provisions" were not restricted to provisions that are out of the ordinary or unusual, the exception would, in my view, effectively displace the rule.

The juxtaposition of sections 37(2.3) and 37(2.5) does not, in my view, undermine the conclusion that "special provisions" must be out of the ordinary or unusual. Whether or not s. 37(2.5) is limited to certain kinds of arrangements has no bearing on the question whether or not s. 37(2.3) is so limited. Section 37(2.3) is differently worded and contains different requirements than s. 37(2.5). While the parties must consent under s. 37(2.5), the parties need not consent under s. 37(2.3). While the arrangements under s. 37(2.5) need only be "reasonable," the provisions under s. 37(2.3) must be "special." Hence, even if it is unnecessary for arrangements to be out of the ordinary or unusual under s. 37(2.5), it does not follow that it is similarly unnecessary for provisions to be out of the ordinary or unusual under s. 37(2.3).

I do not accept the submission that the parties' goals and expectations when entering into the prior arrangement are relevant in determining whether that arrangement qualifies under the "special provisions" exception. Examining the goals and expectations of the parties would import into s. 37(2.3) an uncertainty that is, in my view, both unnecessary and inappropriate. The uncertainty is unnecessary because the question under s. 37(2.3) is not whether the parties subjectively intended to make special provisions in favour of the child. Rather, the question is whether the parties actually objectively made those provisions, which objectively replace the child's ongoing need for support. The uncertainty is inappropriate, because the objectives of the Ontario Guidelines are to enhance fairness, objectivity, efficiency, and consistency. Far from enhancing these objectives, the examination of subjective goals and expectations would undermine them by re-importing the uncertainty that characterized the former child support regime.

For the same reasons, I would hold that the goals and expectations of the parties in entering into an agreement are equally irrelevant in determining whether special provisions benefit the child. The question is not whether the parties subjectively intended to benefit the child, but whether the special provisions actually objectively benefit the child....

[Ed. Note: The other judges agreed with Simmons, J. A. on the three-part test that courts should apply under §37(2.3). However, the majority of the court agreed with Sharpe, J.A. that "special provisions" had to be out of the ordinary, and that the parties' subjective intent was irrelevant. Accordingly, all the judges thought the appeal should be dismissed.]

Notes and Questions

1. *Lump Sum Awards.* Lump sum awards are not free from modification in Canada as *Wright v. Zaver* suggests. However, is the fact that the original award was a lump sum totally irrelevant to the modification action?

2. *Rationale For "Special Provisions" Rule.* Section 15.1(5) of the Divorce Act and its Ontario counterpart are premised on the notion that child support is often negotiated as one aspect of the parties' overall financial arrangements upon divorce. In some cases, it would be unfair to upset the parties' arrangements by changing only this one component.

3. *Exceptional Special Provision.* Simmons, J. A. and Sharpe, J. A. disagree about whether there must be "exceptional" special provisions in order to disregard the presumptive effect of the guidelines. Which interpretation is better?

4. *Deference Given to Agreed-Upon Support Terms.* The trial judge in *Wright v. Zaver* found that it was immaterial whether the child support application was treated as an application to vary an existing child support award or as a fresh application for support. That was because the order had been entered before enactment of the guidelines and the new guidelines constituted a significant change of circumstances in Ontario. Consequently, under either approach, the court would be able to make a new award pursuant to the guidelines. In addition, the standard permitting variation from the guidelines was

the same in both a proceeding to modify support and a proceeding to establish an original order.

Whether a court is adjudicating an initial award or a modification action may be relevant in the United States to the deference given by the court to the agreed-upon support terms. In some places in the United States, enactment of the guidelines has been found to be an insufficient change of circumstances in and of itself. *See, e.g.,* Willingham v. Willingham, 410 S.E.2d 98 (Ga. 1991); In re Marriage of Kukes, 852 P.2d 655 (Mont. 1993). On the other hand, some courts in the United States are far more willing to modify an order that was predicated on an agreement rather than an adjudication, especially if the record is silent about the parties' financial circumstances at the time of the agreement. *See* Thomas v. Thomas, 120 Cal App. 3d 33 (1981).

5. *Comparison of Modification Approaches.* What is the standard for modification employed by most courts in the United States? How would *Wright v. Zaver* have come out differently, if at all, under this standard? What considerations of the Canadian court would likely appear, or not, in an opinion by an American court?

Like Canada, the United States generally requires a substantial change of circumstances before a modification can occur. Assuming such a change existed, a court in the United States would need to apply the child support guidelines to obtain the presumptively correct amount of support, and then see if a deviation was warranted. Deviation is normally permitted when the guideline amount would be inequitable. Federal law provides that a "written finding or specific finding on the record that the application of the guidelines would be unjust or inappropriate in a particular case, as determined under criteria established by the state" shall be sufficient to rebut the presumption in that case. 42 U.S.C. §667(b). If parents have traded-off custodial responsibility for support, as the ALI *Principles* suggest should be permissible, then it might be inequitable to later increase support. However, the *Wright v. Zaver* court rejected this sort of argument, and it is likely that a U.S. court would also reject it when faced with the insufficient financial support of a child.

6. *Larger Comparison.* The foregoing materials suggest that the United States and Canada take similar approaches to parental agreements and child support. Many of the differences are relatively minor, yet there are some notable differences between the countries when one looks at the topic of child support more generally. As discussed above in Section A of this chapter, Canada makes a much wider net of individuals potentially liable for private support. It also has some unique statutory provisions that encourage the establishment and prioritization of child support awards in a divorce. What other similarities and differences do you see?

Canada's treatment of private child support obligations must also be viewed in the context of its public support for children. A recent study suggests that Canada and the United States are virtually identical in child benefit packages when one considers also tax concessions and purchasing parities. *See* Jonathan Bradshaw & Naomi Finch, *A Comparison of Child Benefits Packages in 22 Countries,* Dep't for Work & Pensions Rpt No. 174, at 188 (2002). Yet others suggest that Canada's policies are more effective than those in the United States. *See* Shelley Phipps, An International Comparison of Policies and Outcomes for Young Children (1999) (social transfers decrease child poverty in the United States by approximately 10.5%, but social transfers decrease child poverty in Canada by 27.2%). As of 2000, the percentages of children living in relative child poverty for the United States, Canada, and Sweden respectively were 22.4%, 15.5%, and 2.6%. UNICEF, A League Table of Child Poverty in Rich Nations 4 (2000), *available at* http://www.unicef-icdc.org/publications/pdf/repcard1e.pdf. While firm conclusions are difficult to make, Canada's approach to child support, broadly understood, appears to fall somewhere in between the approach of the United States and the approach of Sweden.

7. *Approaches.* Do you agree with the following observation by Mavis Maclean and Andrea Warman? How would you identify the system in the United States?

> A clear difference exists between countries where child support is identified as primarily a legal issue for the judicial system and those in which child support is seen as primarily a matter for social policy. Under the predominantly legal approach, the aim of the system is to identify and enforce the rights of children and perhaps their resident parent to a share in the income and wealth of the other parent. In a predominantly social-policy setting, the system may seek to reduce child poverty, to reduce social security expenditure, or to enforce parental responsibility. Under a social-policy approach there will be more discussion of the distribution of resources within social groups rather than of individual rights. Whereas the legal approach can only allocate the existing resources of the parents, under a social-policy approach additional resources can be allocated from general revenue or by fiscal adjustment.

Mavis Maclean & Andrea Warman, *A Comparative Approach to Child Support Systems: Legal Rules and Social Policies, in* Child Support: The Next Frontier 166 (J. Thomas Oldham & Marygold S. Melli eds., 2000). What conclusions can you make about the relative responsibility of parents and the government in the United States in assuring an optimal level of support for children?

Problem 9-4

The parties' marital relationship ended after twenty years. The father was awarded custody of their four children. During the relationship, the mother stayed at home. At the time of separation, the mother started working as a receptionist. Also, at the time of separation, the parties agreed that, "The father shall be responsible for the maintenance and support of the children." The mother, in exchange, relinquished any claim to an inheritance from the estate of the husband's father, which was worth approximately $200,000. The father placed the inheritance funds in a trust to provide for the future support of the children. Several years later, the father enters a new relationship and seeks a variation to have the mother pay child support according to the child support guidelines. The mother now earns approximately $45,000 per year. The father concedes that he alone can support the children adequately. The mother argues that the "special provision" in the agreement negates the need to apply the guidelines. Assume that the mother had a colorable claim that she was entitled to some of the inheritance at the time the parties entered their agreement. What result in Ontario? What result in most states in the United States?

c. Failure to Seek Enforcement upon Default

In both the United States and Canada, child support orders can include their own enforcement mechanisms. For example, the Federal Child Support Guidelines in Canada allow a court to require that a child support order be secured. In *Lonergan v. Lonergan,* [1998] B.C.J. No. 150 (B.C. Sup. Ct.), the child support order was secured against the marital home. The court postponed the home's sale and allowed the children to continue to reside in it during their minority. If Mr. Lonergan defaulted on child support, the mother's family could loan her money until the house was ultimately sold. "When the home is sold, Mr. Lonergan's interest in the equity in the home will be applied first to satisfy any arrears of child support then outstanding." In the United States, "statutes commonly authorize the court to require security, such as a bond, to attach wages, or to create a lien on the obligor's property to prevent default." Harry D. Krause, Child Support in America: The Legal Perspective 74 (1981). *See, e.g.,* In re Gonzalez, 993 S.W.2d 147 (Tex. Ct. App. 1999) (approving $100,000 bond because father was Mexican citizen working for Mexican employer so income withholding was impossible).

Despite these and other private enforcement mechanisms, the government can also assist with enforcement in various ways. In the United States, the Family Support Act required immediate wage withholding as of 1990 for all new or modified orders, with limited exceptions. *See* 42 U.S.C. §666(a)(8)(B). This act led to a tremendous increase in the amount of child support collected; wage withholding is currently responsible for approximately 62% of successful collections. *See* U.S. GAO, Child Support Enforcement: Clear Guidance Would Help Ensure Proper Access to Information and Use of Wage Withholding by Private Firms 21 (2002). Notwithstanding this enforcement mechanism, in 2000 there was still at least $89 billion unpaid, but legally owed, child support in cases handled by state agencies. *Id.* at 7.

It is difficult to quantify the number of custodial parents who do not seek enforcement of their child support orders when the obligor defaults, in whole or in part. The new ALI *Principles* allow a parent to forgive any arrearage as part of a settlement, even though courts can not forgive the amount that is already due. *See Principles of the Law of Family Dissolution: Analysis & Recommendations,* §3.23 (2000). In the United States, the government only gets involved if the state agency is providing Title IV-D services to a family. These services are a mandatory condition of the receipt of public assistance, but must be requested by others. Even the criminal provisions that punish willful failure to pay child support are unlikely to be utilized without the request or cooperation of the custodial parent. Should anything be done about this type of situation? Perhaps a parent's failure to seek enforcement is not particularly problematic. If and when the family becomes sufficiently poor, it will receive public assistance and then the government's enforcement mechanisms will automatically kick in.

Perhaps more attention should focus, instead, on the government's enforcement efforts for those who receive Title IV-D services. Because of the workload, state governments over the last ten or so years have increasingly turned to private collection firms to assist in enforcement. *See* U.S. GAO, Child Support Enforcement: States Experience with Private Agencies' Collection of Support Payments (1996). In addition, because of frustration with governmental efforts, private individuals have increasingly utilized private firms to help them collect support. These firms typically charge 29% of the amount collected. *See* U.S. GAO, Clear Guidance Would Help Ensure Proper Access to Information, *supra,* at 14. The amount charged is much higher than the fees charged for the government's enforcement service. There is no fee for families receiving TANF, Medicaid, or foster care, and low fees (not to exceed $25) for others employing state collection efforts. The increased trend toward privatization of collection moves the United States even further away from other countries in its approach to child support.

This Chapter began by citing Professor Garrison's observation that "At least half of all American children will be eligible for child support at some point during their minority, but most receive inadequate payments, and many receive nothing at all." Marsha

Garrison, *The Goals and Limits of Child Support Policy, in* Child Support: The Next Frontier 16 (J. Thomas Oldham & Marygold S. Melli eds., 2000) (footnote omitted). She continues,

> After almost two decades of governmental effort, fewer than six out of ten eligible women — and less than one-third of those never married — are awarded child support. The mean child support payment, in inflation-adjusted dollars, still falls short of its 1978 value. Neither the poverty rate of children in single-parent households nor the disparity in postdivorce living standards of children and their noncustodial parents has declined.

Id. at 17 (footnotes omitted). That is not to say the reforms in the United States have had no positive effect. In particular, Professor Garrison mentions better outcomes for never-married mothers which is due, in part, to legal reform related to the establishment of paternity and the child support enforcement program. *Id.* at 18.

The limits of the approach in the United States for impoverished children rests, to some extent, on those larger societal factors mentioned by UNICEF as being important. UNICEF, A League Table of Child Poverty in Rich Nations 7 (2000), *available at* www.unicef.org.uk/news/pdf%20files/repcard1e.pdf. Those factors included the unemployment rate and the wage disparity. Professor Garrison notes that while child support policy has some potential to mitigate the number of children in poverty, its potential is limited "[b]ecause most poor children do not have 'deadbeat dads' who can contribute significantly more to their support...." *Id.* at 24. In fact, the reasons cited most often by private firms and state agencies for their failure to collect child support, apart from their inability to locate the noncustodial parent, was that the noncustodial parent had no income or assets or the noncustodial parent was in jail. *See* U.S. GAO, Clear Guidance Would Help Ensure Proper Access to Information, *supra*, at 16. Considering these facts as well as the approaches in other countries that you have seen in this chapter, what, if anything, would you propose that the United States or state governments do differently in this area? What conclusions would you draw about the United States considering how children in the United States are supported?

Chapter 10

Establishing and Enforcing Child Support Orders Transnationally

Enforcing legal duties of support against errant parents and spouses, whether divorced or not, is difficult enough when no jurisdictional lines separate the parties. Troublesome as state or provincial borders can be within a federal union, the legal barriers of intervening boundaries become much more formidable when they are national, separating, as is often the case, nations that differ in languages, legal systems, family relations, and economic conditions.

> David F. Cavers, *International Enforcement of*
> *Family Support*, 81 Colum. L. Rev. 994 (1981)

Though international agreements might help surmount some of the obstacles described by Professor Cavers, as has been the case in the areas of child abduction and international adoption, the United States has not yet become a party to any of the many multilateral treaties addressing international child support. Instead, the U.S. federal government and individual states have entered a hodgepodge of bilateral agreements and arrangements with foreign nations for reciprocal establishment and enforcement of support orders, which are examined in Section A of this Chapter. Where applicable, these agreements typically permit parents or guardians residing abroad to seek the assistance of state and federal governmental child support enforcement agencies and services, and entitle foreign orders to be treated in U.S. state courts as if they had been issued by a sister state.

Such agreements are presently in effect with only a small number of countries, however, and even in those cases to which they apply, the agreements are supplemented by other state and federal law. Section B therefore explores domestic law in the United States regulating the establishment of child support orders on behalf of parties residing abroad, and the recognition, enforcement, and modification of foreign child support orders in U.S. courts. A primary source of this law is the Uniform Interstate Family Support Act (UIFSA), a model act promulgated by the National Conference of Commissioners on Uniform State Laws (NCCUSL). Because all fifty states have been required by federal law (*see* 42 U.S.C. §666(f)(2000)) to enact UIFSA as a condition for the receipt of federal welfare funding, many issues affecting the treatment afforded foreign orders and parties in child support matters will be handled in a somewhat consistent manner throughout the country.

Section C addresses the options available for enforcing U.S. child support orders against obligors located abroad. In some circumstances, remedies may be available through American courts, governmental agencies, and employers to enforce such orders. By agreement or through voluntary cooperation, foreign courts, governmental agencies, and employers will also often provide enforcement assistance.

A brief overview of some of the multilateral child support conventions that have attracted a significant number of states parties is provided in Section D, along with an examination of some possible explanations for the failure of the United States to thus far ratify any of these agreements.

A. U.S. Participation in Bilateral Agreements

1. Foreign Reciprocating Countries

Though the U.S. federal government has been increasingly active over the past several decades in the area of domestic child support enforcement, its first foray into the realm of international child support was not until 1996, when Congress included in its welfare reform legislation, Personal Responsibility and Work Opportunity Reconciliation Act of 1996 (PRWORA), Pub. L. No. 104-193, 110 Stat. 2105, §371, provisions authorizing the declaration of individual foreign nations as *foreign reciprocating countries*. Pursuant to 42 U.S.C. §659a (2000), the U.S. Secretary of State, with the concurrence of the Secretary of Health and Human Services, may declare another nation a foreign reciprocating country if that nation has instituted procedures for the establishment and enforcement of child support obligations owed to residents of the United States, and those procedures satisfy certain specified criteria.

In order to be declared a foreign reciprocating country, a nation must have procedures available to U.S. residents to:

(1) establish paternity;

(2) establish support orders for children and custodial parents; and

(3) enforce support orders for children and custodial parents, including the collection and distribution of payments.

In addition, these procedures, including legal and administrative assistance, must be provided at no cost to U.S. residents, and the country must have a Central Authority to facilitate enforcement and ensure compliance with the statutory standards.

Although the legislation would permit declarations to be made through a variety of methods (such as the exchange of diplomatic notes in connection with corresponding foreign declarations, or a unilateral notice published in the Federal Register, if a nation already has in place the mechanisms satisfying the statutory requirements), thus far the Department of State has chosen to implement the statute by negotiating reciprocity agreements bilaterally with each individual country. The Department of State's Office of the Legal Adviser for Private International Law and the Department of Health and Human Services' Office of Child Support Enforcement (OCSE) have been conducting these negotiations with over 30 countries. Even though the advice and consent of the U.S. Senate is not required for these agreements, the progress has been somewhat slow. By March 2003, reciprocity arrangements were in force with Australia, the Canadian provinces of Alberta, British Columbia, Manitoba, New Brunswick, Newfoundland/Labrador, Nova Scotia, and

Ontario, the Czech Republic, Ireland, Netherlands, Norway, Poland, Portugal, and the Slovak Republic. A current listing of the foreign reciprocating countries can be found on the home page of the Bureau of Consular Affairs of the U.S. Department of State, at http://travel.state.gov/child_support.html. This site also contains the text of a model international reciprocity agreement, and will eventually provide links to the text of each agreement in force.

Gary Caswell, an OCSE Resource Person and advisor to U.S. delegations conducting the negotiation of these reciprocity agreements, has observed that in addition to bureaucratic obstacles and understaffing of U.S. delegations, the negotiation process has also been hindered by differences in substantive expectations. He asserts that reciprocal arrangements for enforcement only, or for establishment of support orders when paternity is not disputed, could in many cases be easily concluded. Provision of free services to U.S. residents in paternity actions is a common sticking point, however, for many nations. Because 42 U.S.C. § 659a requires provision of these services, federal negotiators have felt constrained to conclude no enforcement agreement whatsoever unless it satisfies all of Section 659a's criteria. In addition, he suggests that other nations expect governmental enforcement agencies in the United States to provide their residents assistance with the enforcement of alimony orders, even for spouses who are not custodial parents. Under UIFSA, state law empowers state courts to enforce alimony orders issued in nations that have entered reciprocity arrangements with the United States. The problem lies in the fact that the state agencies that have been created to provide child support enforcement assistance at little or no cost under the mandate of federal law (Title IV, Part D of the Social Security Act of 1975), often referred to as "IV-D agencies," are not required by federal law to provide assistance for the enforcement of spousal support to any noncustodial parents, domestic or foreign. Instead, such assistance can be provided at the discretion of the state agencies. The text of the model reciprocity agreement offered by U.S. negotiators therefore provides in Article 2(1) that "a maintenance obligation towards a spouse or former spouse, where there are no minor children, will be enforced in the United States under this Agreement only in those states and other jurisdictions of the United States that elect to do so." Moreover, even when state agencies are willing to assist foreign parties with collection of spousal support, there are many more remedies available under federal and state law for enforcement of child support than for alimony orders. Gary Caswell, *International Child Support—1999*, 32 Fam. L.Q. 525, 542, 544–45 (1998).

Although the effects of a declaration of foreign reciprocating country status within the U.S. legal system are not entirely spelled out in the federal legislation, several consequences are evident. The first is that federal agencies, such as the OCSE and the Federal Parent Locator Service (FPLS), and the state IV-D agencies that provide assistance to parents residing in the United States with the establishment and enforcement of child support or alimony obligations, are required to provide at no cost the same services to residents of foreign reciprocating countries whose petitions have been forwarded by the Cental Authority for that nation. This obligation is imposed upon the state IV-D agencies in 42 U.S. C. § 654 (2000), which mandates that requests for assistance from foreign reciprocating countries be treated in an identical manner as requests from a IV-D agency in another state. The second, implemented through UIFSA, is that state courts must recognize and enforce child support and alimony orders of foreign reciprocating countries as they would the orders of sister states. This does not mean, however, that all support orders issued in foreign reciprocating countries are always enforceable. Obligors may still utilize the same defenses that would be available to obligors defending against the enforcement of U.S. orders, including any deficiencies in the jurisdiction, notice, or other procedures utilized by the issuing tribunal that would render the order invalid under due process. Articles 7 and 8 of the model agreement suggested by the U.S. State Department specify that each nation will recognize and enforce the maintenance decisions issued by the other utilizing the applicable law and procedures, including the choice of law provisions, of the recognizing nation.

Each foreign reciprocating country must designate a body within that nation as its Central Authority to facilitate compliance with its obligations under the agreement, including the transmission of applications for assistance and other documents between nations. Additional public entities may also be designated to assist the Central Authority in carrying out its functions. The OCSE has been designated as the United States Central Authority, and is charged with the responsibility of developing uniform forms and procedures, coordinating with the Federal Parent Locator Service to locate obligors residing within the United States, and otherwise overseeing activities related to the foreign reciprocating country agreements. 42 U.S.C. §659a(c)(2000).

2. Reciprocity Arrangements Negotiated by Individual States

Even before 42 U.S.C. §659a was enacted, many state governments within the United States began negotiating reciprocal arrangements for the enforcement of child support obligations on a bilateral basis with foreign nations or their political subdivisions, i.e., individual provinces or states within those nations. Pioneered by Gloria Dehart in 1980, who was then a Deputy Attorney General in California, these arrangements required a state to enforce foreign support obligations originating in a nation or province that by its own declaration had agreed to reciprocally enforce a support order issued in that state. Peter Pfund, *The Hague Intercountry Adoption Convention and Federal International Child Support Enforcement*, 30 U.C. Davis L. Rev. 647, 658–59 (1997).

Although these reciprocal arrangements were made with the assistance and approval of the U.S. Department of State, which refers to them as *parallel unilateral policy declarations*, or PUPDs, their constitutional validity has sometimes been questioned. Article I, §10 of the U.S. Constitution prohibits a state from entering "any treaty, alliance, or confederation," but does permit states to enter an "agreement" or "compact" with a foreign nation with the consent of Congress. Though proponents of the reciprocity arrangements argued that they were neither treaties nor compacts, and therefore did not require the consent of Congress, *see* Gloria Dehart, *Comity, Conventions, and the Constitution: State and Federal Initiatives in International Support Enforcement*, 28 Fam. L.Q. 89, 102–04 (1994), the drafters of the 1996 federal legislation sought to eliminate further doubt. In 42 U.S.C. §659a (d), individual states are now explicitly authorized to enter into reciprocal support arrangements with foreign countries. These arrangements can remain in effect until such time as the nation is declared a foreign reciprocating country by the federal government. In addition, 42 U.S.C. §654 requires state IV-D agencies to treat a request for services from a foreign country with which the state has a reciprocity arrangement as if it was a request from a IV-D agency of a sister state, and to provide services at no cost to the foreign nation or foreign obligee. Though one commentator continues to raise constitutional questions, *see* Chelsea Ferrette, Note, *A Critical Analysis of the International Child Support Enforcement Provisions of the Social Security Act: The (In)ability of States to Enter Into Agreements with Foreign Nations*, 6 ILSA J.

Int'l & Comp. L. 575, 608–12 (2000) (asserting Congress cannot constitutionally delegate to states the power to enter or implement family law agreements with foreign nations), the use of PUPDs is now widely accepted by most experts in the field of international enforcement.

State reciprocal arrangements are not necessarily as comprehensive as foreign reciprocating country agreements. PUPDs are not mandated by Section 659a to include all of the requirements necessary for conferral of foreign reciprocating country status. These arrangements may thus be easier to negotiate, but will not always assure U.S. residents the level of assistance available from a foreign reciprocating country. The level of commitment on the part of the individual state or its IV-D agency also varies widely. Some PUPDs take the form of simple declarations that reciprocity exists between the state and foreign nation or province regarding child support enforcement, or letters expressing what the state or its IV-D agency intends to do for the foreign nation. For example, Texas' arrangements with several countries and provinces took the form of policy letters from its IV-D agency "declaring its will to argue for the recognition of orders and provision of judicial assistance...." Gary Caswell, *International Child Support—1999*, 32 Fam. L. Q. 525, 531–32 & n.32 (1998). On the other hand, a far more comprehensive pilot program involving coordinated training, referral, development of forms, and case tracking has been implemented between Texas and several of the Mexican states along the border. *Id.* at 553–54.

By 2002, at least 44 states had entered into reciprocal child support arrangements with over thirty nations and provinces. Information regarding the countries with which each state currently has reciprocal arrangements is available from the OCSE Online Interstate Roster, http://ocse3.acf.dhhs.gov/ext/irg/sps/selectastate.cfm; from the website of the U.S. State Department, http://travel.state.gov/child_support.html; and from the state's IV-D agency.

B. Establishing, Enforcing, and Modifying Child Support Orders in U.S. Tribunals on Behalf of Residents of Foreign Nations

During the past several decades, a large body of law has been developed in the United States to facilitate the establishment and enforcement of child support obligations. This reform was initiated in large part by the federal government, in response to serious inadequacies in the creation and collection of support awards that subjected a high percentage of U.S. children and custodial parents to a life of poverty. In addition to creation of the Federal Parent Locator Service and support services by other federal agencies to assist state collection efforts, Congress in 1975 required each state to establish child support enforcement programs—namely, the IV-D agencies referenced in Section A—to provide assistance directly to all custodial parents, regardless of their income. Successive amendments to federal law have imposed many additional requirements upon the states, as a further condition for receipt of federal funding. State legislation establishing guidelines for the amount of child support, expanded enforcement remedies and procedures, and the enactment of the Uniform Interstate Family Support

Act (UIFSA) to facilitate interstate enforcement have all been mandated by federal law. Some states have also developed creative initiatives of their own to increase the level of child support their children receive. Although this body of law merits detailed consideration, it is extensively covered in most domestic family law courses, and therefore will not be reviewed in depth in this book. However, because this law is also relevant to the creation and enforcement of support awards in U.S. tribunals on behalf of residents of foreign nations, it is in that context that we provide the following overview, examining most closely those issues of particular relevance to international application.

Many, if not most, proceedings in U.S. courts to establish, enforce, or modify child support orders on behalf of residents of foreign nations are brought under or regulated to some degree by UIFSA. Federal law required each state to enact the 1996 version of UIFSA, which incorporates the 1996 amendments promulgated by the National Conference of Commissioners on Uniform State Laws (NCCUSL). In 2001, NCCUSL again revised UIFSA, although most of the amendments were intended to provide clarification, rather than effect dramatic substantive changes. In several places the amendments address transnational proceedings more specifically than did the former version. As this book goes to press, the vast majority of states have not yet enacted the 2001 amendments, nor is there yet any federal legislation requiring their enactment. Such legislation could materialize, however, and even in its absence, states will in all likelihood gradually enact the 2001 amendments, which have been endorsed by the American Bar Association. References in this chapter to UIFSA, unless otherwise noted, are to the 1996 version. Where the 2001 amendments would effect a significant change or enhance our understanding of a particular issue, however, they are also discussed.

1. Establishing an Initial Support Order

A parent or other custodian residing outside of the United States who wishes to obtain an order of support for a minor child for whom no pre-existing order has been entered can always directly file an action seeking support in a state court with appropriate jurisdiction over such proceedings. The action must, of course, be filed in a state in which the defendant is served, domiciled, or subject to minimum contacts, unless the defendant otherwise consents to personal jurisdiction, in order to satisfy the requirements of due process under the Fourteenth Amendment of the U. S. Constitution. Kulko v. Superior Court, 436 U.S. 84 (1978). When the location of the prospective obligor is known, typically such actions are filed in the state in which the defendant resides. If the plaintiff is represented by private counsel, the case can proceed under the same law that would be applicable if both parties resided in the forum state. Moreover, there is no requirement that UIFSA even be invoked. See UIFSA §§ 103 cmt., 201 cmt., 9, Part IB U.L.A. 272, 275 (1999).

In several contexts, however, additional issues might come into play when the petitioner is a resident of a foreign nation. First, the party seeking support for a child might wish to receive the services of the state's IV-D agency at no cost or for a nominal fee, rather than incurring the expense of retaining a private attorney. If the petitioner is a resident of a foreign reciprocating country or a nation with which the forum state has a reciprocal arrangement for the establishment of child support obligations, the forum state's IV-D agency is obligated to provide representation at no cost. 42 U.S.C. §§ 654(32)(C), 659a(d)(2000). If not, then it is up to the discretion of the IV-D agency as to whether it will provide assistance. Some IV-D agencies will provide services even to residents of countries with no reciprocating arrangement with the federal or state government. In fact, the federal Office of Child Support Enforcement (OCSE) encourages them to do so, affording IV-D agencies reimbursement of federal matching funds for services to foreign support agencies and individuals residing in foreign countries even when no reciprocating arrangements are in force. Gary Caswell, *Making Long-distance Parents Pay Up*, 23-Fall Fam. Advoc. 52, 52–53 (2000).

A second issue concerns the utilization of UIFSA's special procedural provisions by foreign residents. Even though an initial order can be sought in a tribunal of the obligor's state of residence without implicating UIFSA, utilizing the Act offers some advantages. The petitioner is not required to initially pay filing fees or other costs. UIFSA § 313. Special hearsay exceptions are created for verified petitions, affidavits, and documents substantially complying with federally mandated forms. Copies of bills submitted to the adverse party at least ten days prior to trial are admissible to prove the amount charged and that they were reasonable and customary. Documents may be faxed without regard to the best evidence rule. *See* UIFSA § 316. Parties or witnesses may be allowed to testify by telephone, or audiovisual or other electronic means. *Id. But see* Dep't of Hum. Serv. v. Shelnut, 777 So.2d. 1041 (Miss. 2000) (Telephonic testimony by Canadian mother could be denied at the discretion of the court). A 2001 amendment to UIFSA § 316 would clarify that such testimony *shall* be allowed, thus eliminating court discretion to deny such permission. Courts are specifically authorized to communicate directly with a tribunal in a foreign nation to obtain information concerning provisions of foreign law, the status of proceedings, or the legal effect of an order. UIFSA § 317. These and other special procedural and evidentiary provisions facilitate litigation without the physical appearance in the forum state of the petitioner or his or her witnesses, and have proven to be very helpful in international cases. Caswell, *supra*, at 53.

UIFSA provides a mechanism for a "two-state action," whereby individuals or support enforcement agencies may file a petition seeking a support order in a tribunal in their home state (the "initiating tribunal"), which can then forward the papers to a tribunal or support enforcement agency in a state with jurisdiction over the defendant, for proceedings before a tribunal in that "responding state." UIFSA §§ 304, 305. Individuals or support enforcement agencies are permitted to bypass the tribunals of their home state, however, and still take advantage of the Act's provisions, by filing an action seeking a support order directly in a tribunal of the state in which the prospective obligor resides. UIFSA § 301(c)[1996 version], 301(b) [2001 version]. Many of the special evidentiary and procedural provisions are also applicable in a direct action filed in any state in which the obligor is subject to personal jurisdiction, even if he or she does not reside in the forum state. UIFSA §§ 202, 301(c)[1996 version], 210, 301(b) [2001 version].

Questions may arise regarding the extent to which UIFSA procedures are available in an action brought by a resident of a foreign nation, rather than a resident of another American state. The 1996 version of UIFSA § 101(19) defines "State" to include: "a foreign jurisdiction that has enacted a law or established procedures for issuance and enforcement of support orders which are substantially similar to the procedures under this [Act], the Uniform Reciprocal Enforcement of Support Act [URESA], or the Revised Uniform Reciprocal Enforcement of Support Act [RURESA]." The Comment to Section 101(19) addresses the meaning of this provision only in the context of proceedings brought to enforce foreign support orders, a topic which has generated some controversy and is examined below. For enforcement proceedings, the Comment suggests, reciprocity is critical. In the context of proceedings brought by residents of foreign nations seeking initial support orders, however, the application of UIFSA is not discussed. If reciprocity is a key component in the enforcement context, then at the very least it would seem appropriate for American courts to afford residents of foreign nations the benefits of UIFSA when those nations would permit residents of the United States to seek support orders in their tribunals against their own residents. The 2001 amendments to Section 101 make explicit a provision that is surely implicit in the 1996 version, by clarifying that under UIFSA a "state" would always include a foreign country or political subdivision given foreign reciprocating country status under 42 U.S.C. §659a, or with which the forum state has established a reciprocal arrangement for child support.

2. Simultaneous Proceedings

Questions regarding the transnational application of UIFSA may also arise when proceedings to establish a child support order are pending in both a foreign tribunal and a U.S. tribunal. When initial support proceedings are pending in two tribunals, or when modification requests are pending in two tribunals and no tribunal would have continuing exclusive jurisdiction under the Act, UIFSA provides a simultaneous proceedings rule in Section 204 that a U.S. tribunal might apply to determine priority, if the foreign nation was regarded as a "state" under the Act.

Read UIFSA §204 in your Supplement. This Section operates as a limitation upon the subject matter jurisdiction of a tribunal to establish a support order when there is a proceeding pending in another state. Although the wording of Section 204 is somewhat convoluted and there is little case law as yet interpreting it in any context, domestic or transnational, the Comment following the Section suggests that the intent of Section 204 is to give priority in competing child support proceedings to the child's "home state." If the child has no home state, the first-filed action controls. *See* UIFSA §204 cmt., 9, Part IB U.L.A. 423 (1999). "Home state" is defined by UIFSA §101 (4) as the state in which the child lived with a parent or a person acting as a parent for the six consecutive months prior to the filing of the support proceeding.

Therefore, if the first action filed is located in the child's home state, the action in that tribunal will clearly have priority. However, under Section 204, even if the action pending in the child's home state is not the first action filed, it will still have priority as long as a challenge to the jurisdiction of the first tribunal is timely made by the party contesting jurisdiction in that tribunal, and the second "home state" action is filed before expiration of the period in the first tribunal for making such a jurisdictional challenge. Otherwise, when these requirements are not satisfied or there is no home state at the time of filing, the state in which the first action was filed has priority.

3. Enforcing a Foreign Order in a U.S. Court

An obligee who wishes to enforce a child support order issued by a foreign tribunal may choose to hire a private attorney to bring an enforcement proceeding in a U.S. court, or may seek the services of the forum state's IV-D agency, either directly or by way of referral from a support enforcement agency in the obligee's home country. As mentioned above, services requested through proper channels from a foreign reciprocating country or a country with which the forum state has a reciprocity arrangement must be provided by IV-D agencies at no cost, and services to residents of other foreign countries may be provided at the discretion of the IV-D agency. In some situations, a IV-D agency might offer some advantages over private representation, because the IV-D agency has access to governmental records and services useful for locating an obligor and the obligor's assets, such as the Registries for New Hires, the IRS refund intercept program, and the Federal Parent Locator Service, as well as to other enforcement mechanisms, such as passport denial, that are not directly available to private counsel. With or without IV-D representation, however, there are obstacles an obligee may encounter when enforcing a foreign child support order utilizing either UIFSA or the common law doctrine of comity, as the following cases illustrate.

Country of Luxembourg, on behalf of Ana Ribeiro, v. Canderas
768 A.2d 283 (N.J. Super 2000)

Brock, J.S.C.

The issue presented to this court for determination is whether the plaintiff's request to enforce a judgment for child support entered against the defendant on October 5, 1998, by the Court of Conciliation of Esch-sur-Alzette in the Grand Duchy of Luxembourg should be dismissed for lack of personal jurisdiction. For the reasons which follow, this court concludes that the issuing tribunal did not have personal jurisdiction over the defendant. Therefore the registration of the judgment for enforcement under the Uniform Interstate Family Support Act (UIFSA) will be vacated and the request to otherwise enforce the judgment will be dismissed.

The relevant facts are not in dispute. The defendant admits that he lived with the mother of the child in Portugal from 1980 to 1987. During that time their daughter was conceived and born in Portugal on June 29, 1981. In September of 1987, the defendant came to the United States. He now lives in Union County, New Jersey. The plaintiff and the child moved to Luxembourg. The defendant has never been in Luxembourg and owns no property there.

In July 1998, the defendant received a summons in the mail to appear before the Court of Conciliation in Esch-sur-Alzette on September 21, 1998. The summons alleged that the defendant had left the plaintiff to go to the United States in September, 1987, and failed to support the child since then. It further stated [the amount of support] that the child's mother was seeking..., subject to a salary index plus legal fees and costs. The summons stated that the defendant is domiciled in the United States.

[In]...August of 1999, the defendant received by mail the judgment entered against him by default on October 5, 1998. It provided [the amounts] that the defendant [must] pay to the plaintiff [for past due and future support].... In addition, the support allowances were made automatically subject to adjustment to the salary index as of July 1, 1998, and the defendant was ordered to pay all the costs and expenses of the proceedings.

On...January 19, 2000, the attorney for the plaintiff in Luxembourg sent the judgment to the Central Registry of Child Support Enforcement Services of New Jersey and requested that the judgment be registered for enforcement. The judgment was assigned a docket number, forwarded to this vicinage for enforcement, and the matter was listed for a hearing before a child support hearing officer. After the defendant received notice of the hearing, his attorney filed the motion to dismiss the case for lack of jurisdiction....

The plaintiff seeks to enforce the judgment under the Uniform Interstate Family Support Act (UIFSA).... Pursuant to [UIFSA § 304]..., a party seeking to enforce a support order issued by a tribunal of another state may send the documents required for registering the order to a support enforcement agency of this State. The non-registering party may request a hearing to contest the validity or enforcement of a registered order in this state or seek to vacate the registration of the order by proving one or more enumerated defenses, including the defense that the issuing tribunal in another state lacked personal jurisdiction over the contesting party....

For purposes of this case, the statute defines a "state" as a foreign jurisdiction that has enacted a law or established procedures for issuance and enforcement of support orders which are substantially similar to the procedures under UIFSA... [UIFSA § 101(19)]....

The 1996 Welfare Reform Act authorizes the Secretary of State, with the concurrence of the Secretary of Health and Human Services, to make federal level declarations of reciprocity for child support establishment and enforcement. It further authorizes states to enter into their own arrangements with foreign jurisdictions that have not been declared to be foreign reciprocating countries under the Act to the extent consistent with federal law.... Neither the United States nor the state of New Jersey have established reciprocity with Luxembourg. Nevertheless, the UIFSA statute provides that its remedies are cumulative, and do not affect the availability of remedies under other law....

... [T]his court must consider whether or not Luxembourg has enacted a law or established procedures which are substantially similar to UIFSA....

In this case the issue is whether or not the issuing tribunal had personal jurisdiction over the defendant. UIFSA changed the former law... by adding Section 201, a broad provision for asserting long-arm jurisdiction over non-residents in the home state of the supported family.... It provides that a tribunal of this state may exercise personal jurisdiction over a nonresident individual in a proceeding to establish, enforce or modify a support order if:

a. the individual is personally served with a summons or notice within this State;

b. the individual submits to the jurisdiction of this State by consent, by entering a general appearance, or by filing a responsive document having the effect of waiving any contest to personal jurisdiction;

c. the individual resided with the child in this State;

d. the individual resided in this State and provided prenatal expense or support for the child;

e. the child resides in this State as a result of the acts or directives of the individual;

f. the individual engaged in sexual intercourse in this State and the child may have been conceived by that act of intercourse; or

g. there is any other basis consistent with the constitutions of this State and the United States for the exercise of personal jurisdiction.

Plaintiff's counsel in Luxembourg has forwarded certain sections of that country's Code of Civil Procedure on the Jurisdiction of District Court Judges. With respect to subject matter jurisdiction, Article 4(1) provides:

> He (the district judge) always hears and determines, subject to appeal, no matter what the sum of the claim...all requests for child support excepting those relating to divorce or physical separation process.

With request to territorial jurisdiction, Article 38 provides:

> Claims for payment or revision of child support described in article 4 above, may be brought, at the choice of the creditor of the child support, either before the jurisdiction of the debtor, or else before the jurisdiction of his or her own domicile.

In this case, the plaintiff/creditor chose to bring the case before the jurisdiction of her own domicile....

No statute or procedure of Luxembourg which is substantially similar to [UIFSA § 201]...has been presented to this court for review. It may be that Luxembourg has a statute or procedure for obtaining personal jurisdiction over a non-resident which has not been provided by the plaintiff. However, even if it had a similar statute or procedure, this court would still be required to determine whether or not, in this case, the issuing tribunal had a basis for exercising personal jurisdiction over this defendant.

Relying on the provisions of [UIFSA § 201]..., this court finds, based on the undisputed facts, that the first six of the seven possible bases for obtaining personal jurisdiction over the defendant under the statute do not apply in this case. The last provision of the statute permits this court to consider whether there is any basis consistent with the constitutions of New Jersey or the United States for the exercise of personal jurisdiction.

New Jersey has expressed as its policy its intent to exercise personal jurisdiction over nonresidential defendants to the extent "consistent with due process of law." R. 4:4-(b)(1)....

In International Shoe Co. v. State of Washington, 326 U.S. 310 (1945) the United States Supreme Court held that: Due process requires only that in order to subject a defendant to a judgment in personam, if he be not present within the territory of the forum, he have certain minimum contacts with it such that the maintenance of the suit does not offend traditional notions of fair play and substantial justice. In Hanson v. Denckla, 357 U.S. 235, 253(1958), the United States Supreme Court further pointed out that: [I]t is essential in each case that there be some act by which the defendant purposely avails itself of the privilege of conducting activities within the forum State, thus invoking the benefits and protections of its laws.

A state court's exercise of in personam jurisdiction over a nonresident implicates the Due Process Clause of the Fourteenth Amendment to the United States Constitution, Kulko v. Superior Court of California, 436 U.S. 48, 91, 98 (1978), and federal constitutional principles are binding on our courts in New Jersey....

* * *

Although these parties never married, they have an undisputed obligation to support the child born of their relationship. The judgment of the issuing tribunal in Luxembourg stated this, and New Jersey has long had a strong policy of requiring parents to support their children.... However, in this case,...the fact that the plaintiff lives in the forum state is insufficient to create a relationship between Luxembourg and the defendant under Hanson v. Denckla....

... [I]n this case, the defendant has no contacts at all with Luxembourg. He has never physically visited the country and he owns no property there.... There is no basis consistent with the constitution of New Jersey and the United States for the exercise of personal jurisdiction over him. As a result, this court cannot find that the issuing tribunal acted in accordance with a law or procedure which was substantially similar to that of UIFSA for obtaining personal jurisdiction over a non-resident.

Finally, to determine whether or not the judgment of the issuing tribunal should be enforced in New Jersey, principles of comity must be examined. In Fantony v. Fantony, 122 A.2d 593 (1956) the New Jersey Supreme Court delineated the standard for the application of comity:

> The recognition of a judgment of a foreign court under the principle of comity is subject generally to two conditions: (1) that the foreign court had jurisdiction of the subject matter; (2) that the foreign judgment will not offend the public policy of our own State....

The rule of comity is grounded in the policy of avoiding conflicts in jurisdiction, unless upon strong grounds, and the general principle that the court which first acquires jurisdiction of an issue has precedence, in the absence of special equities. A litigant cannot be compelled to act elsewhere, but may remain in the court which first acquires jurisdiction and abide by the terms of its decree.... The[se]...principles of comity are in accord with the decisions of the United States Supreme Court.

Applying principles of comity to this case, this court holds that the foreign court had jurisdiction of the subject matter under its own Code of Civil Procedure to determine a claim for child support in the jurisdiction of the plaintiff's domicile. However,...[because] the issuing tribunal lacked personal jurisdiction over the defendant,...this court finds that it would offend our public policy to enforce a judgment which is inconsistent with due process under our state and federal constitutions.

The court will therefore vacate the registration of the judgment with the Office of Child Support Enforcement Services of New Jersey under UIFSA, and dismiss the plaintiff's request to otherwise enforce the judgment for lack of personal jurisdiction over the defendant.

Haker-Volkening v. Haker
547 S.E.2d 127 (N.C. App. 2001)

Hudson, J.

The background facts here are not in dispute. Brigitte Haker-Volkening (petitioner) and Werner Andreas Haker (respondent) were married in 1967 and lived in Switzerland at that time. In 1984, respondent commenced a civil action in the Zuerich District Court seeking divorce. On 29 April 1985, petitioner and respondent entered into a voluntary agreement regarding alimony payments, distribution of property, and custody, visitation and support in relation to their two minor children. On 7 May 1985, the Zuerich District Court entered an order (the Swiss order) granting the divorce, determining custody of the two minor children, ordering visitation, requiring respondent to pay child support, and expressly approving the 29 April 1985 document embodying the agreement between the parties. Respondent complied with the alimony provisions of the 29 April 1985 agreement through 1994, at which time he relocated to North Carolina.

On 10 June 1998, petitioner filed a petition in the district court of Transylvania County, North Carolina, seeking to have the Swiss order registered and enforced in North Carolina pursuant to...UIFSA.... On 10 June 1998, the [court clerk]...filed a "Notice of Registration of Order," notifying respondent that the Swiss order had been registered in Transylvania County pursuant to [UIFSA § 602].... This registration order provides that respondent was, as of 22 May 1998, in arrears of 57,074 in Swiss Francs. On 22 June 1998, respondent filed a motion challenging the validity and enforcement of the registration. Following a hearing, the trial court entered an order on 27 March 2000, holding the Swiss order registered and enforced under UIFSA. Respondent appeals from this order.

* * *

...First, respondent argues that this matter does not fall within the purview of UIFSA because Switzerland does not constitute a "state" pursuant to the definition provided in UIFSA. Because we agree, and conclude that the trial court did not have the authority to register the Swiss order, we need not reach respondent's other arguments.

We first note that respondent contends that the issue of whether Switzerland constitutes a "state" under UIFSA is an issue of subject matter jurisdiction. However, a court's authority to act pursuant to a statute, although related, is different from its subject matter jurisdiction. Subject matter jurisdiction involves the authority of a court to adjudicate the type of controversy presented by the action before it. *See* 1 Restatement (Second) of Judgments s 11, at 108 (1982). This power of a court to hear and determine (subject matter jurisdiction) is not to be confused with the way in which that power may be exercised in order to comply with the terms of a statute (authority to act).... Here, UIFSA provides that the district courts of North Carolina are authorized to hear matters falling under UIFSA. Thus, there is no question that the Transylvania County District Court had subject matter jurisdiction to hear petitioner's petition for registration pursuant to UIFSA, and to hear respondent's contest of that registration.

However, only judgments or orders of "another state" may be registered under UIFSA. [UIFSA § 301(b)(3)].... UIFSA defines a "state" as including any "foreign jurisdiction that has enacted a law or established procedures for issuance and enforcement of support orders which are substantially similar to the procedures under this Act." [UIFSA § 101(19)].... In other words, UIFSA requires that "a foreign nation must have substantially similar law or procedures to...UIFSA...(that is, reciprocity) in order for its support orders to be treated as if they had been issued by a sister State." Official Comment...to [UIFSA §101(19)]. Thus, if Switzerland is not a "state" under UIFSA, then the district courts of North Carolina do not have statutory authority to register an alimony or child support order from Switzerland under UIFSA.

* * *

The record here includes the order entered by the Zuerich District Court. It also includes a document entitled "Federal Act on Private International Law," which is apparently a copy of certain Swiss laws regarding the general enforcement of foreign judgments. The record contains no evidence that Switzerland has enacted a law for the issuance and enforcement of support orders that is "substantially similar to the procedures under [UIFSA]." Furthermore, although the Swiss order itself is arguably some evidence that legal procedures have been established in Switzerland for the issuance and enforcement of support orders, there is no evidence in the record documenting that such procedures are "substantially similar to the procedures under [UIFSA]." Thus, we must conclude that the record fails to establish that Switzerland is a "state" as that term is defined by UIFSA, and that the trial court was therefore without statutory authority to register the Swiss order pursuant to UIFSA.

We note that petitioner argues in her brief that even if Switzerland is not a "state" under UIFSA, the Swiss order should still be enforced as a matter of comity. Comity has been defined as "the recognition which one nation allows within its territory to the legislative, executive or judicial acts of another nation, having due regard both to international duty and convenience, and to the rights of its own citizens." ... Under the doctrine of comity, North Carolina courts may choose to enforce foreign support orders issued by courts in foreign jurisdictions provided the foreign court had jurisdiction over the cause and the parties.... We do not disagree with petitioner that the Swiss order may be enforceable in North Carolina as a matter of comity, and our holding does not preclude petitioner from seeking enforcement of the Swiss order via a civil complaint seeking enforcement. However, petitioner did not file a civil complaint seeking enforcement, she filed a petition for registration of the Swiss order pursuant to UIFSA. Accordingly, the issue of comity is not properly before us. For the reasons stated herein, we reverse the order of the trial court denying respondent's contest of the registration of the Swiss order, and we further vacate the trial court's registration of the Swiss order.

Reversed and vacated. Judges Wynn and Timmons-Goodson concur.

Notes and Questions

1. *Personal Jurisdiction.* As the *Luxembourg* case illustrates, U.S. courts have consistently refused to enforce a foreign judgment when the foreign judgment would have been subject to collateral attack for lack of personal jurisdiction if it had been issued by a sister state.

(a) *Limitation on Collateral Attack.* In domestic actions, in which state courts are required by the Federal Constitution and federal statute to give full faith and credit to the judgments of sister states, the absence of personal jurisdiction by the issuing court may be raised in subsequent enforcement proceedings in another state only when the defendant in the first action entered no appearance and the judgement was entered by default. *See, e.g.,* Williams v. North Carolina, 325 U.S. 226 (1945); Baldwin v. Iowa State Traveling Men's Ass'n, 283 U.S. 522 (1931). This appears to have been the situation in *Luxembourg,* as the facts imply that Mr. Canderas entered no appearance in the Luxembourg proceeding that established the child support order. U.S. courts have not permitted collateral attack on a judgement of a sister state for a personal jurisdiction defect if the defendant entered an appearance in the first action, regardless of whether the appearance was special or general, or whether the defendant raised and contested the defect in the first action or did not. *See, e.g.,* Sherrer v. Sherrer, 334 U.S. 343 (1948); Coe v. Coe, 334 U.S. 378 (1948); Baldwin, 283 U.S. at 525–26. The policy precluding collateral attack by a defendant who appeared in the original action is that one who contested an issue, or appeared and had the opportunity to contest the issue, should be bound by the result. *See, e.g.,* Baldwin, 283 U.S. at 525–26.

Should a defendant who entered an appearance in a proceeding before a foreign court that had personal jurisdiction under its own law likewise be precluded from raising the absence of personal jurisdiction under U.S. standards in an enforcement proceeding brought in a U.S. court? In other words, does the distinction regarding the defendant's appearance make sense in the context of the enforcement of a foreign order? U.S. courts, of course, are not required to give full faith and credit to the judgments of foreign nations, and grant recognition instead when required by state statute or comity.

Therefore, the question regarding whether res judicata bars such a collateral attack is determined by the law of the forum state hearing the enforcement proceeding, and not by federal law. The Mississippi Supreme Court addressed this issue in Dep't of Hum. Serv. v. Shelnut, 772 So.2d 1041 (Miss. 2000), determining that finality concerns dictated that a child support obligor who had appeared and contested personal jurisdiction in a Canadian proceeding would not be permitted to collaterally attack the Canadian judgment in enforcement proceedings in Mississippi.

Whether other states will follow this lead remains to be seen. In general civil actions, there appears to be some authority permitting collateral attacks on foreign judgments in U.S. courts after a defendant appeared in the foreign tribunal solely to contest jurisdiction. See Uniform Foreign Money-Judgments Recognition Act §5 (2), 13 U.L.A. 272 (1986). Additional circumstances under which collateral attack of a foreign judgment will be allowed after an appearance by defendant in the foreign court, however, are not yet well defined. See Nippon Emo-Trans Co., Ltd., v. Emo-Trans, Inc., 744 F. Supp. 1215, 1229 (E.D. N.Y. 1990) (observing that *Baldwin* addressed federal constitutional issues, but state law controls recognition of foreign judgments; and that, despite defendant's appearance in the foreign proceeding, neither New York statutory nor common law prevented reexamination of a foreign court's resolution of a jurisdictional issue in appropriate, limited circumstances); Restatement (Third) of the Foreign Relations Law of the United States §482 cmt. c (1986) ("If the defendant appeared in the foreign court to challenge the jurisdiction of the court and failed to prevail, it is not clear whether such determination will be considered *res judicata* by a court in the United States asked to recognize the resulting judgement.").

(b) Necessity and Propriety of Applying U.S. Due Process Standards. In *Luxembourg,* enforcement of the child support order was sought under both UIFSA and under the doctrine of comity. Under UIFSA §607, lack of personal jurisdiction by the issuing court over the defendant in the first action is specifically listed as a ground for contesting the validity or enforcement of a registered support order. This section is, of course, one of general applicability to all support orders, domestic and foreign, and the Comments reveal no indication that any particular attention was given by the drafters to the enforcement of foreign orders. Nevertheless, the application of Section 607 to transnational enforcement proceedings is consistent with existing precedent. The determination of the court in *Luxembourg* to deny comity on public policy grounds to a foreign judgment that did not comply with U.S. constitutional standards for personal jurisdiction is also consistent with the decisions of other U.S. courts considering this issue.

When a U.S. court is asked to enforce a foreign judgment that satisfied the jurisdictional requirements of the issuing nation, does denial of enforcement for failure to satisfy U.S. constitutional standards for personal jurisdiction make sense as a matter of public policy? Is denial of recognition in this context constitutionally compelled?

In reflecting on these questions, consider that insistence upon compliance with U.S. standards for personal jurisdiction in the enforcement of foreign child support orders has been one of the obstacles to entering a multilateral child support enforcement treaty. Many nations recognize habitual residence of the child or of the obligee as the basis for personal jurisdiction in child support proceedings. Professor David Cavers argues that jurisdictional principles devised to allocate judicial authority within our federal system should not be the basis to spurn enforcement of orders under multilateral treaties. "[T]reaties allocating judicial authority among sovereign states," he asserts, "cannot be umpired for all the parties to them by a court of any one state simply on the basis of its views of fair play and wise policy among sister states." David F. Cavers, *International Enforcement of Family Support*, 81 Colum. L. Rev. 994 (1981).

Consider also whether fundamental fairness necessitates insistence upon the jurisdictional nexus that U.S. courts currently require. In Kulko v. Superior Court, 436 U.S. 48 (1978), the U.S. Supreme Court reaffirmed that in child support proceedings one of the traditional bases of jurisdiction over a defendant—service upon defendant in the forum state, domicile of defendant in the forum state, consent of defendant to jurisdiction, or minimum contacts of defendant with the forum state—must be satisfied. In *Kulko*, the Court determined that neither domicile of the obligee (the custodial parent) nor the domicile of the children in the forum state created sufficient contacts. The Court further concluded that defendant's consent to his child living in the forum state was insufficient to constitute a purposeful contact with the state that would subject him to jurisdiction.

Even as applied to domestic cases, many commentators in the United States have been critical of *Kulko's* application in child support actions of this traditional analytical framework developed in commercial suits, with its focus on purposeful contacts by the defendant with the forum. Several have urged that the child's residence in the forum state should be recognized as a sufficient basis for personal jurisdiction in child support actions. Rosemarie Ring, Comment, *Personal Jurisdiction and Child Support: Establishing the Parent-Child Relationship as Minimum Contacts*, 89 Calif. L. Rev. 1125 (2001); Carol S. Bruch, *Statutory Reform of Constitutional Doctrine: Fitting International Shoe to Family Law*, 28 Cal. Davis 1047 (1995); United States Commission on Interstate Child Support, *Supporting Our Children: A Blueprint for Reform* (1992). Their suggestion comports with notions of jurisdictional fairness adopted in many other regions of the world. Use of the child's residence as a basis for jurisdiction in child support proceedings would also be consistent with the approach taken in many multilateral treaties (see Section D), and greatly reduce the incidence of non-recognition of foreign judgments.

2. Applicability of UIFSA in Transnational Enforcement Proceedings. The question of when a foreign nation or political subdivision (such as a Canadian province) should be treated as a "state," entitling its support orders to UIFSA enforcement, has been the subject of much discussion. In *Haker*, the North Carolina Court of Appeals observes that the Comment to UIFSA § 101(19) interprets the requirement of "substantially similar procedures" to mean reciprocity, and finds the record submitted by petitioner insufficient to conclude that Switzerland is a state. The court, however, is less than clear as to what additional information about Swiss law would have satisfied the court that the Section 101 criteria had been satisfied.

The North Carolina Court of Appeals revisited the issue one month later, in Foreman v. Foreman, 550 S.E.2d 792 (N.C. App. 2001), *cert den.* 354 N.C. 68 (2001). In an opinion written by one of the concurring judges in *Haker*, the court affirmed a decision finding a British alimony order valid and enforceable, citing British statutory law that specifically afforded reciprocity to the maintenance orders of specific states in the United States, including North Carolina. Noting that *Haker* imposed a burden on the one seeking enforcement to submit into the record evidence that the law of the issuing nation governing enforcement of foreign orders is substantially similar to UIFSA, the *Foreman* court observed that this requirement was unnecessary when the foreign nation was given reciprocal status by law or international agreement.

The 2001 amendments to UIFSA § 101 (21) confirm this intent, defining state to include:

(B) a foreign country or political subdivision that:

    (i) has been declared to be a foreign reciprocating country or political sub-division under federal law;

    (ii) has established a reciprocal arrangement for child support with this State as provided in Section 308 [which authorizes designation of an agency or official with the power to make a statewide binding determination recognizing such an arrangement]; or

    (iii) has enacted a law or established procedures for the issuance and en-forcement of support orders which are substantially similar to procedures under this [Act].

The comments to this revised definitional section suggest that the third criteria is satis-fied when "the foreign jurisdiction also has laws and procedures that allow for a U.S. order to be recognized in that foreign jurisdiction independent of a formal reciprocity agreement." When this third criteria is employed, the North Carolina appellate court would place the burden on the petitioner to submit foreign law into the record in the enforcement action that would satisfy the "substantially similar" requirement. How spe-cific and "substantially similar" that law has to be is still open to question.

Gary Caswell, a nationally recognized expert in the area of international child sup-port, argues for a broad interpretation of "substantially similar." He suggests that it should be sufficient to show that a foreign nation's laws and procedures "generally afford foreigners access to its tribunals, even though there is no specific reciprocity arrange-ment for child support." Gary Caswell, *International Child Support—1999*, 32 Fam. L. Q. 525, 550 (1998). He further suggests that in comparing foreign laws, advocates should emphasize general principles the two systems share—such as the obligation of parents to support children, criteria such as ability to pay and the child's need, and due process pro-cedural protections. *Id.* at 550 & n.127. A stringent interpretation, he contends, defeats the goal of the Act to facilitate enforcement of child support. *Id.* at 538.

In *Luxembourg* the New Jersey trial court, finding that no federal or state reciprocity arrangement existed with Luxembourg, embarked upon an examination of Luxem-bourg's jurisdictional law to determine whether it was substantially similar to UIFSA standards for personal jurisdiction. In doing so, was the court collapsing together the analysis of two separate issues, the applicability of UIFSA and the existence of personal jurisdiction? Even if, as in *Haker*, the facts were such that the issuing court clearly had a basis for personal jurisdiction that would satisfy the jurisdictional standards of both Luxembourg and U.S. courts, the New Jersey court would still have been required to de-termine if Luxembourg's law regarding enforcement of foreign judgements was suffi-ciently "similar" in other respects to utilize UIFSA in the enforcement proceeding. Con-versely, even if Luxembourg was a foreign reciprocating country or had a PUPD with New Jersey, the judgment would not have been enforceable under either UIFSA or comity if the Luxembourg court's exercise of jurisdiction over Mr. Canderas failed to satisfy the standards of the Due Process Clause of the Fourteenth Amendment of the U.S. Constitution.

Regarding the point in time at which the foreign reciprocal law or reciprocity arrangement must be in effect, the Mississippi Supreme Court held in Dep't of Hum. Serv. v. Shelnut, 772 So.2d 1041, 1051(Miss. 2000), that the date of trial of the enforce-ment proceeding was the appropriate reference point. The court rejected the obligor's assertion that UIFSA was inapplicable because Canada had no reciprocal support act in effect when the child support order was issued.

3. *UIFSA Enforcement Procedures.* Enforcement of a child support order under UIFSA can be accomplished in three ways.

a. Registration. Upon filing the appropriate documents required by UIFSA § 602, a support order issued in a foreign nation that qualifies as a "state" under the Act becomes enforceable in the same manner as an order issued by a tribunal (court, administrative agency, or other quasi-judicial entity, UIFSA § 102) of the enforcing state. UIFSA § 603(b). Notice of registration must be sent to the nonregistering party, who then has 20 days to request a hearing to contest the validity or enforcement of the order. If no request is made within that period, the order is confirmed by operation of law. UIFSA §§ 605, 606. The grounds upon which registration and/or enforcement can be contested are limited:

- the issuing tribunal lacked personal jurisdiction over the contesting party;
- the order was obtained by fraud;
- the order was vacated, suspended, or modified by a later order;
- the order has been stayed by the issuing tribunal pending appeal;
- a defense exists under the law of the forum state to the particular enforcement remedy that is sought;
- full or partial payment has already been made;
- the statute of limitations precludes enforcement of some or all of the arrearages for which collection is sought;
- the order is not the controlling order [added by 2001 amendments].

Confirmation of the order, either by operation of law or after hearing, precludes the obligor from subsequently challenging the order regarding any matter that could have been asserted at the time of registration. UIFSA §§ 607, 608.

Failure to register a foreign support order has been found by one appellate court to deprive the trial court of subject matter jurisdiction to enforce under UIFSA. In Brannan v. Smith, 107 Wash. App. 1054, 2001 WL 950216, the appellate court reversed a trial judge who had attempted to enforce an unregistered 1987 Australian child support order, after determining that the registered 1991 Australian order that increased the support obligation was not entitled to enforcement because it had been entered without affording the obligor due process. The appellate court observed that its ruling did not preclude future enforcement if a valid order was subsequently registered.

b. Administrative Enforcement. UIFSA § 507 permits a state IV-D agency to use alternatively any administrative procedure available in the forum state to enforce a support order. However, if the obligor contests either the administrative enforcement or the validity of the order, the support enforcement agency must then register the order pursuant to the requirements of UIFSA §§ 601–608.

c. Direct Enforcement of Income Assignment Orders. When a child support order is issued in the United States, state tribunals are required by federal law to include an income assignment order unless the parties have a written agreement for an alternative payment arrangement or the court finds good cause not to include the assignment order. The assignment order is then sent to a "payor," a person or entity who owes the obligor periodic income, earnings or other periodic payments. Periodic income includes wages, salaries, and commissions, and also includes workers compensation payments, disability benefits, pension or other retirement payments, interest, and other types of periodic payments. The payor, most often the obligor's employer, is directed by the order to withhold from each payment a specified amount for child support and, when applicable, arrearages, and to send those funds to the centralized collection and disbursement unit of the state that issued the order. Employers may charge a fee for processing the income withholding order. 42 U.S.C. § 666 (b)(2000).

UIFSA §§ 501–506 permit income-withholding orders issued in another state to be enforced directly by sending the order to an obligor's employer, without requiring registration of the order or filing a proceeding in the employer's state. Income-withholding orders issued by the tribunals of a foreign nation that was regarded as a "state" under UIFSA should therefore also be entitled to direct enforcement by an obligor's U.S. employer. Foreign orders might encounter some resistance, however. To be entitled to direct enforcement, the order must appear "regular on its face," and contain certain basic information regarding the amount to be withheld and the name and address of the person or entity to which the payments are to be forwarded. UIFSA § 502(b)(c). Since the federal government has prepared model forms for income assignment orders, it is possible that an order that does not look like the expected form might not appear "regular on its face" to a U.S. employer. Moreover, if the amounts to be withheld are stated in a foreign currency, some employers may find it "irregular" and decline to attempt the conversion.

4. *Choice of Law.* UIFSA §§ 303 and 604 establish choice of law principles for interstate proceedings that would be applicable to proceedings brought under UIFSA for enforcement of foreign support orders as well. Under these principles, a U.S. tribunal establishing, modifying, or enforcing a child support order will apply its own law, i.e., the law of the forum state, with two exceptions. First, in an enforcement proceeding, the U.S. tribunal will apply the statute of limitations of the forum state or the issuing state or nation, whichever is longer. Second, when interpreting a child support order issued outside the forum state, issues regarding the nature, extent, amount and duration of payments and other obligations of support are determined by the law of the state or nation that issued the order. The 2001 amendments clarify that this latter exception includes the computation of arrearages and interest.

This last exception is of particular relevance to the enforcement of foreign orders. Some European countries permit support obligations to continue through postgraduate professional education. Gary Caswell, *Making Long-distance Parents Pay Up,* 23-Fall Fam. Advoc. 52, 53 (2000). In Canada also, an obligation for child support can continue while a child is attending a post-secondary institution. *E.g.,* McArthur v. McArthur, [1998] 235 A.R. 297, (Alta. Ct. Q.B.). See Chapter Nine, Section A. In some countries, including Mexico, because termination is governed by statute, it is not the custom to include termination dates in the orders. Therefore, introducing evidence of the law of the issuing nation regarding duration of child support may be required more frequently and entail more effort in international cases than is the case in interstate enforcement.

5. *Currency Conversion.* Because the law of the issuing nation governs the amount of payments and arrearages, the amounts owed must be calculated using the currency of the issuing country. UIFSA § 604; Caswell, *supra,* at 53. The 2001 amendments to UIFSA § 305 will set forth this obligation more explicitly:

> (f) If requested to enforce a support order, arrears, or judgment or modify a support order stated in a foreign currency, a responding tribunal of this State shall convert the amount stated in the foreign currency to the equivalent amount in dollars under the applicable official or market exchange rate as publicly reported.

As a general rule, foreign support amounts are converted using exchange rates in effect on the date of preparation of the notice of registration or on the date of the hearing. *Id.* When the value of the foreign currency is fluctuating as against the U.S. dollar, however, courts considering conversion issues in general civil judgments have selected the date for conversion rate that would make the injured party whole, relying upon the approach recommended by the Restatement (Third) of Foreign Relations Law of the United States, § 823, cmt. c (1987). *E.g.,* Aker Verdal A/S v. Lampson, 828 P.2d 610 (Wash. Ct. App. 1992); El Universal, Compania Periodistica Nacional, S.A. de C.V., v. Phoenician Imports, Inc., 802 S.W.2d 799 (Tex. App. 1991). Therefore, when converting arrearages, if the foreign currency has depreciated relative to the U.S. dollar since the date of breach, the rate of exchange applicable on the date of breach should be used. The obligor is therefore prevented from profiting by "a dilatorious pay history and the obligee is made whole in terms of U.S. dollars by receiving the breach date U.S. equivalence for each foreign support amount that was due and unpaid." Caswell, *supra,* at 53. On the other hand, if the foreign currency has appreciated since the date of breach, the exchange rate on the date of judgement or the date of payment is more appropriate. E.g., Aker, 828 P.2d at 613. For support payments coming due in the future, requiring payment in the currency in which the obligation is denominated, or conversion on the date of payment, would appear to be an equitable solution. *Cf.* Restatement (Third) of Foreign Relations Law of the United States § 823(1) and cmt. c (1987).

To establish the conversion rates for foreign currencies, entering a stipulation or requesting judicial notice of the exchange rates published in the Wall Street Journal or the New York Times on the selected date have been successfully employed by state support enforcement attorneys and in other civil proceedings in the past. Caswell, *supra,* at 53; Teca-Print A.G. v. Amacoil Machinery, Inc., 525 N.Y.S.2d 535 (N.Y. Sup. Ct. 1988).

6. *Comity.* The appellate courts in both *Luxembourg* and *Haker* recognized that in addition to bringing an enforcement proceeding under UIFSA, enforcement of a foreign support order can alternatively be sought under the common law doctrine of comity. Reciprocity is *not* a prerequisite to enforcement under comity. Office of Child Support v. Sholan, 782 A.2d 1199, 1203 (Vt. 2001). Therefore, comity provides a remedy even in those instances in which the court finds UIFSA inapplicable.

In *Sholan,* the Vermont Supreme Court permitted recognition and enforcement of a German child support order under the doctrine of comity, despite the fact that Germany at the time had not entered into a foreign reciprocating country agreement under 42 U.S.C. § 659a (2000), nor did it have a reciprocal arrangement with Vermont. In so holding, the court rejected the father's argument that recognition under the doctrine of comity was preempted by federal law, finding instead that application of comity was consistent with the goal of § 659a to promote the enforcement of foreign orders. Sholan, 782 A.2d at 1202–03.

Relying upon Restatement (Third) of the Foreign Relations Law of the United States § 482, the court in *Sholan* observed that in order to recognize a foreign judgment under the doctrine of comity, a court must find the following requirements satisfied:

- the judgment was rendered by an impartial tribunal utilizing procedures compatible with due process of law;
- the issuing court had subject matter jurisdiction;
- the issuing court had jurisdiction over the defendant on a basis that would satisfy the jurisdictional requirements for a court in the state in which the judgment is being enforced;
- the defendant was afforded adequate notice;
- the judgment was not obtained by fraud;

- the judgment did not conflict with another judgment entitled to recognition;
- the foreign proceeding did not violate an agreement of the parties to submit the matter to another forum; and
- the original action or judgment did not conflict with federal or state policy. *Id.* at 1203–04.

Litigating a proceeding to enforce a foreign judgement on the basis of comity will be greatly facilitated by enactment of the 2001 amendments to UIFSA. A newly added Section 210 permits a state court "recognizing a support order of a foreign country or political subdivision on the basis of comity" to "receive evidence from another State pursuant to Section 316, communicate with a tribunal of another State pursuant to Section 317, and obtain discovery through a tribunal of another State pursuant to Section 318." The amendment thus enables the foreign resident who initiates the action to take advantage of many of the special evidentiary and procedural provisions of UIFSA described in Section B.1. above, even when the foreign nation would not satisfy UIFSA's definition of a "state."

7. *Authentication and Translation of Foreign Law and Orders.* It is often necessary in proceedings to enforce foreign child support orders to introduce foreign law into evidence. In addition, registration of any order under UIFSA requires submission of at least one "certified" copy of the order. UIFSA § 602. Proper authentication of a foreign order would also be required in an action to enforce a foreign order on the basis of comity. Therefore, it is vital that an attorney seeking the enforcement of a foreign order be aware of the proper method for authenticating the orders and laws of the particular nation involved.

Over 75 countries, including the United States, are parties to the Hague Convention Abolishing the Requirement of Legalization of Foreign Public Documents, Oct. 5, 1961, T.I.A.S. No. 172, 527 U.N.T.S. 189, which permits public documents to be recognized by member countries on the basis of a certification (an apostille) executed by authorities designated by the nation in which the document originates. Countries that are not a party to the Convention typically authenticate documents by "chain authentication" or "triple authentication." Under such a process, a judge might sign an order, the court clerk then certifies the order was signed by the judge, and then the judge certifies that the clerk is the clerk. Gary Caswell, *International Child Support—1999*, 32 Fam. L.Q. 525, 552 & nn.140–41 (1998). The evidentiary rules of many states, as well as the federal rules, also permit the court to treat foreign official documents as presumptively authentic even when all of the legalization requirements have not been satisfied, if reasonable opportunity has been given to all parties to investigate their authenticity and accuracy. *Id. See, e.g.,* Okla. Stat. tit. 12, § 902(3)(2001); Fed. R. Evid. 902(3). Translations of foreign orders or law should also be certified as accurate by a qualified translator. Caswell, *supra,* at 552.

8. *Enforcement Mechanisms.* Once a foreign order has been registered and, if challenged, confirmed under UIFSA, or recognized and found to be enforceable under the doctrine of comity, it may then be enforced in the same manner as could a support order issued by the forum state. UIFSA § 603; Restatement (Third) of Foreign Relations Law of the United States § 481 cmt.c (1987). If no income assignment order issued by the foreign tribunal was directly enforced under UIFSA § 501, the forum court will usually issue an income assignment order, directing the obligor's employer to make periodic deductions from the obligor's paycheck, as described above in Note 3(c). A variety of other enforcement mechanisms are also available under federal and state law. For ex-

ample, bank accounts and other assets of the obligor may be attached. An obligor in arrears, depending upon the amount of the arrearages, could also be subject to: an intercept of any tax refunds, government benefits, judgements, or settlements due the obligor; issuance of a lien against the obligor's real or personal property or a workers compensation claim; revocation, suspension or refusal to issue a drivers, professional, recreational, or business license; denial of a passsport; or disqualification for food stamps. Unemployed obligors in arrears can be ordered to participate in job finding or job training programs. Willful noncompliance with a support order, once it has been registered, could also subject the obligor to contempt proceedings, and a subsequent fine or imprisonment.

4. Modification Restrictions

Read UIFSA §§ 205, 206, 609, 610, 611, 612, 613, and 614.

Grave v. Shubert
2000 WL 1221343 (Minn. App. Aug. 23, 2000)
(Unpublished Opinion)

Amundson, J.

Appellant father challenges the district court's denial of his motion to review the magistrate's order granting respondent mother's motions to reduce to judgment child support arrears and to sequester appellant's retirement funds. Specifically, appellant contends the district court...lacked jurisdiction to grant respondent's motions because Minnesota lost jurisdiction over the matter when an English court modified the original child-support order granting a reduction in child support and a partial remission of arrearages. Because Minnesota never lost its original jurisdiction over the matter, we affirm.

On June 18, 1993, the marriage of appellant L. Elliot Shubert and respondent Marilyn M. Grave was dissolved. The parties have two children, and the court granted the parties joint legal custody. Grave received physical custody of the children, and Shubert was granted reasonable and liberal visitation and was to pay child support of $775.97 per month. Shubert has consistently failed to pay child support since the dissolution. In 1994, Shubert moved to London, England.

In November 1996, the county sought to enforce its order for child support in England. On August 19, 1998, Shubert sought a reduction in child support and remission of arrearages in England. Grave did not respond and on May 26, 1999, the English court reduced Shubert's child-support obligation and partially remitted arrearages.

In 1999, the county, providing non-public assistance services to Grave, learned that Shubert has two retirement accounts in the United States. On August 25, 1999, the county moved to reduce to judgment appellant's child-support arrears and sequester Shubert's retirement funds. Shubert failed to respond to this motion and proposed order, and failed to request a hearing before the magistrate. The magistrate then granted the county's motion. On November 23, 1999, Shubert sought a review of the magistrate's order. Shubert also asked to have the English court's orders considered as new evidence. Both motions were denied. This appeal followed.

* * *

I. Jurisdiction

Minnesota issued the original child-support order, and thereby has continuing, exclusive jurisdiction over the order as long as this state remains the residence of the obligor, the individual obligee, or the child for whose benefit the support order is issued. [UIFSA § 205(a)(1)].... But Minnesota loses its continuing, exclusive jurisdiction "with regard to prospective enforcement of the order issued in this state" if the child-support order has been modified by a tribunal of another state with substantially similar laws. [UIFSA § 205(c)].... The definition of "state" includes a foreign jurisdiction that has enacted a law or established procedures for issuance and enforcement of support orders that are substantially similar to the procedures under this chapter.... Thus, a proceeding may be commenced in the appropriate English court if the United Kingdom has enacted a child support act substantially similar to Minnesota's version of the Uniform Interstate Family Support Act (UIFSA).

In evaluating whether England's laws governing child support are sufficiently similar to the UIFSA, it is necessary to examine their statutory provision regarding modification of maintenance orders registered in a English court:

> the registering court shall have the like power, on an application made by the payer or payee under a registered order, to vary the order as if it had been made by the registering court and as if that court had the jurisdiction to make it. Reciprocal Enforcement of Maintenance Orders (United States of America) Order 1995, Sch. 3 s 9(1)(a) (U.K.).

The parties do not dispute that the child-support order issued in Minnesota was registered in England. Accordingly, under the laws of the United Kingdom, the English court was permitted to modify the child-support order. Contrary to English law, however, the UIFSA provides that a child-support order issued in another state and registered in this state may be modified by this state only if it finds "that the child, the individual obligee, and the obligor do not reside in the issuing state." [UIFSA § 611(a)(1)(i)].... If the UIFSA principles operated in the English court [it] could modify a Minnesota child-support order only if it found that Graves and the parties' children no longer resided in Minnesota. Because Graves and the children continue to reside in Minnesota, a substantially similar provision in England would prohibit an English court from modifying the child-support order.

But that is not the case here; the two provisions are not substantially similar. Indeed, they are not similar at all. England's law allows for modification, while Minnesota clearly prohibits it. The UIFSA disfavors the displacement of one state's judgment of a party's obligation, without some indication the other state is in a better position to attend the child's interests. Given this approach, it appears that the laws are not "substantially similar" enough for Minnesota to have lost its continuing, exclusive jurisdiction per [UIFSA § 205 (c)].

II. Applicability of Minn. Stat. § 518C.612 [UIFSA § 612]

Shubert further argues that this issue is controlled by [UIFSA § 612]..., which provides:

> [A] tribunal of this state shall recognize a modification of its earlier child support order by a tribunal of another state which assumed jurisdiction according to this chapter or a law substantially similar to this chapter and, upon request, except as otherwise provided in this chapter, shall * * * * recognize the modifying order of the other state, upon registration, for the purpose of enforcement. *Id.*

Those reasons militate against application of this statute here. First, as discussed in the previous section, the statutory provisions of Minnesota and the United Kingdom pertaining to modification of child-support orders are not "substantially similar." Second, the district court found that Shubert failed to present any evidence that the English modification order was ever registered in Minnesota. Thus, Shubert fails to meet the statute's threshold requirement that the English order be registered in Minnesota before our courts are obligated to recognize it.

Shubert next argues that [UIFSA §614]...states that a foreign child-support order need not be registered to be both valid and enforceable. If "filing" is construed to be "registration," then the paucity of evidence regarding the proper Minnesota registration of the English order would not necessarily defeat the applicability of [UIFSA §612].... But such construction tortures the rules of statutory construction, because [UIFSA §612]...requires substantial similarity between the law of each jurisdiction, which does not exist in the present case. Accordingly, Minnesota is not obligated to recognize and enforce the English court's modification of the child-support order.

III. Did Minnesota Lose Jurisdiction when it Registered its Child Support Order in the United Kingdom?

Shubert also argues that because Minnesota lost jurisdiction when it registered its original child-support order in England, the English court now has exclusive jurisdiction in this matter. And that because the transmittal did not specifically preclude modification of the child-support order issued in Minnesota, the English court was free to modify it. But the child-support enforcement transmittal sent to England requested that the child-support order be registered and enforced, it did not request or give permission for its order to be modified. Additionally, Shubert provides no authority for the proposition that registration of a child-support order in another state strips the issuing state of its jurisdiction. Minnesota did not lose jurisdiction when its child-support order was registered for enforcement in England.

* * *

Affirmed.

Wentworth v. Wentworth
No. 26145-6-11, 2001 WL 1301535 (Wash. Ct. App. Oct. 26, 2001)
(Unpublished Opinion)

Houghton, J.

Charles G.V. Wentworth appeals the trial court's dismissal of his petition to modify child support, arguing that the trial court erred in basing its decision on forum non conveniens grounds. We affirm.

Charles and Mary Wentworth married in 1987. By 1989, the couple had two children, Emma and Kevin. In 1992, the Wentworths moved to England. Upon the death of his mother in 1993, Charles inherited over 2,000 acres of land in Suffolk and Yorkshire, England. He also inherited considerable trust fund monies.

In 1997, the English High Court of Justice granted the Wentworths a divorce. The English court ordered Charles to pay $10,000 per annum to Mary to support her daughter from a previous marriage and to pay $13,000 per annum each for Emma and Kevin. The High Court also ordered that "Emma and Kevin shall reside with {Mary} and have reasonable contact with {Charles}." ... Mary returned to the United States with the children.

Charles filed a petition on April 2, 1998, asking the Pierce County Superior Court to create a parenting plan. Mary moved to dismiss on jurisdictional grounds.... The dispute concerned the length of Charles's visitation and whether Emma and Kevin would travel to England unaccompanied. The trial court ordered Charles to schedule a telephone conference between Justice Holman of the English High Court of Justice and a superior court commissioner to determine whether England would retain or defer jurisdiction to alter Charles's visitation schedule with Emma and Kevin. Justice Holman deferred jurisdiction over the visitation conflict to Washington, and ... the [Washington court] required that Charles accompany the children on the flight to England and provide Mary with copies of round trip airline tickets. The children were permitted to return unaccompanied if the flight was non-stop from England to Seattle-Tacoma International Airport.

On February 19, 1999, Mary sought a judgment against Charles for unpaid English court-ordered child support. The trial court granted judgment in her favor on March 8, 1999. Page two of the judgment and order includes an interlineation, stating: "This court will exercise jurisdiction over issues of child support." ... Charles contends that Mary's lawyer wrote it and Mary and her lawyer initialed it. Mary contends that only counsel initialed it. There are two sets of initials next to the interlineation.

On February 9, 2000, Charles filed the petition for support modification that gave rise to this appeal. In his petition, he requested relief from the English child support order because it had been more than two years since the entry of the order and there had been a change in the parents' income. He generally sought to extinguish his support obligation for Mary's first daughter when she graduated from high school. He also sought to recalculate his child support payments for Emma and Kevin using the Washington child support schedule. Mary argued that Washington courts lacked subject matter jurisdiction or, alternatively, should decline jurisdiction in favor of the English courts on the basis of forum non conveniens. The trial court "decline[d] to exercise jurisdiction on the basis of forum non conveniens with respect to the Petition for Support Modification."

Charles contends that the trial court erred in dismissing the matter on forum non conveniens grounds. He asserts that Washington is the correct forum because both parents agreed to its jurisdiction, Mary and the children live here, and there was no credible evidence that England was a more convenient forum.[2]

---

2. As a preliminary matter, Mary argues that Washington lacks subject matter jurisdiction under [UIFSA § 611].... Washington courts may modify a registered child support order issued in another state in only three circumstances: (1) the child, the obligee, and the obligor do not reside in the issuing state, a nonresident petitioner seeks modification, and the respondent is subject to the personal jurisdiction of the tribunal of Washington; (2) the trial court has personal jurisdiction over the child or a party and all individual parties consent in writing in the issuing tribunal for a Washington court to modify the support order; or (3) the issuing state 'has not enacted a law or established procedures substantially similar to {those} under the Uniform Interstate Family Support Act{.}'... Although Mary's argument has merit, for purposes of our discussion, we assume subject matter jurisdiction, a necessary predicate to forum non conveniens analysis.... We further note that the record does not reveal whether Charles registered the English child support order in Washington, as [UIFSA § 609] ... requires.... But for purposes of our discussion, we assume that Charles properly registered the English order.

The doctrine of forum non conveniens contemplates the discretionary declination of jurisdiction where, in the court's view, the difficulties of litigation militate for the dismissal of the action subject to a stipulation that the defendant submit to jurisdiction in a more convenient forum.... We review the dismissal for abuse of discretion. Under that standard, the trial court abuses its discretion when its decision is manifestly unreasonable....

Under forum non conveniens analysis, the court considers and balances both private and public interest factors:

> the relative ease of access to sources of proof; availability of compulsory process for attendance of unwilling, and the cost of obtaining attendance of willing, witnesses; possibility of view of premises,... and all other practical problems that make a trial of a case easy, expeditious and inexpensive....

Furthermore, there may also be questions as to the enforcibility of a judgment if one is obtained. The court will weigh relative advantages and obstacles to fair trial. Myers v. Boeing Co. ,...94 P.2d 1272 (Wash. 1990) (quoting Gulf Oil Corp. v. Gilbert, 330 U.S. 501, 508 (1947). The court should also consider public interests, including administrative difficulties and the forum with the most familiarity with the governing substantive law....

We now turn to the facts before us. Although Mary and the children reside in Washington, as described by Justice Holman in his 22-page judgment, Charles's considerable assets are located on English soil and held in English banks. Some of the assets are in trust subject to English law and taxation. Finally, Charles now lives in England and is subject to its process and inquiry into his financial circumstances. Any inquiry into whether there had been a change in Charles's income requires an understanding of his English assets and analysis of English law. Thus, applying the forum non conveniens factors here, we hold that the trial court did not abuse its broad discretion in finding that England is the more convenient forum.[3]

* * *

Affirmed. Seinfeld, J., and Hunt, A.C.J., concur.

Notes and Questions

1. *UIFSA Modification Restrictions.* In contrast to previous uniform acts addressing interstate enforcement of child support, UIFSA was drafted to create a "one order" regime, in which only one child support order for a particular child against a particular obligor can be in effect in the United States at any one time. This goal is fostered by establishing continuing exclusive jurisdiction in the court that issues the initial child support order, and providing that this jurisdiction (and thus the ability to modify the order) can be lost only in very specific circumstances. UIFSA §§ 205, 611, 612, 613, 615 [2001 Amendments]. In the interstate context, when all fifty states are playing by the same rules, these restrictions, combined with rules for resolving conflicts among pre-UIFSA multiple orders (*see* UIFSA §§ 207, 602, 604, 605, 607 [2001 Amendments]), have effectively achieved the "one-order" goal. Because many countries recognize under

---

3. We are not persuaded by Charles' argument that both he and Mary consented to Washington jurisdiction. Even assuming that Mary consented, Washington is clearly an inconvenient forum given the facts of this case.

their own laws much greater flexibility to modify the orders of another country, however, UIFSA's restrictions create fertile ground for conflicting orders in the international arena, as the *Graves* case illustrates.

In *Graves*, an English father is requesting that a Minnesota court take into account the subsequent modification of a Minnesota child support order by an English court, when proceedings are brought in the Minnesota court to enforce the initial Minnesota order. Notice that UIFSA § 205, which establishes the criteria for continuing, exclusive jurisdiction, provides that such jurisdiction to modify can be lost if another tribunal has modified the initial order pursuant to a law substantially similar to UIFSA. As used in UIFSA § 205, "substantially similar" is interpreted by the court in *Graves* to require more than just reciprocity on the part of English courts. What aspects of English law were not "substantially similar" to UIFSA, thus justifying the view of the court that Minnesota had not lost continuing exclusive jurisdiction? Which requirements of UIFSA § 611 would not have been satisfied, if they had been imposed in the English modification proceeding?

As a mater of policy, does it make sense to apply in an international context rules initially conceived to resolve interstate disputes? Wouldn't England have had greater access to information regarding Mr. Shubert's ability to pay, a factor that influenced the court in *Wentworth*? Consider also that disparate grounds for modification have presented another obstacle to the ability of the United States to join existing multilateral child support conventions.

On the other hand, is ability to pay the only factor in setting the amount of child support? What other factors are usually relevant and where would evidence relevant to those factors be located? Consider also that in all likelihood, the English court applied its own substantive law in the English modification proceeding. Assuming each court will apply its own substantive law to the standards for modification, which law is it more appropriate to apply? Should that be a factor in establishing rules for determining which court has modification jurisdiction? We cannot ascertain from the *Graves* opinion the reason for the reduction and remission of arrearages by the English court. If the English judgment was affected by Ms. Graves' default, that highlights another concern. Should she be burdened with the necessity of hiring British counsel to defend the English modification proceeding, when she and the children have never left Minnesota? Would broader recognition for modified orders issued in foreign courts that do not operate under UIFSA restrictions return us to a system of multiple support orders in effect concurrently, as was the case domestically under UIFSA's predecessor, the Uniform Reciprocal Enforcement of Support Orders (URESA)?

In *Wentworth*, the Washington appellate court initially assumed the it had subject matter jurisdiction to modify a support order issued by an English court, because proper jurisdiction is a prerequisite to the forum non conveniens analysis in which the court wished to engage. In footnote 2, the court summarizes the three circumstances in which UIFSA permits a court to modify the support order issued in a tribunal outside the forum state. On which basis was the court assuming that it had subject matter jurisdiction to modify? Is there indication in the opinion that all of the requirements necessary to establish jurisdiction to modify on that basis under of UIFSA § 611 were satisfied? Note that the court in footnote 3 retracts its assumption to some extent.

Grave and *Wentworth* illustrate both sides of the foreign modification coin, from the perspective of U.S. courts. As in *Graves,* U.S. courts under UIFSA § 612 will refuse to recognize foreign modifications to their support orders, unless the modifying court exercised jurisdiction under UIFSA standards, which require that the state issuing the support order no longer have continuing exclusive jurisdiction at the time the modification proceeding is filed in the foreign court. U.S. courts will also decline to modify foreign support orders, as the *Wentworth* court suggests, unless modification is permitted by UIFSA §611 and §613.

2. *Forum non conveniens.* In *Wentworth*, the Washington appellate court chooses to deny the father's request to modify the English support order on the basis that Washington is not a convenient forum, despite the fact that the mother and children now live in Washington. Forum non conveniens is a doctrine created by common law, which permits a court to dismiss a case so that it can be brought in a more convenient forum. There are normally two prerequisites to consideration of a forum non conveniens dismissal by U.S. courts: first, there must exist an alternate forum in which the plaintiff can obtain adequate relief; and second, the forum court considering the motion must first find that it has proper subject matter jurisdiction, personal jurisdiction, and venue. Gulf Oil Corp. v. Gilbert, 330 U.S. 501, 504 (1947). When those are satisfied, the court then employs a balancing test, weighing the factors identified in *Gulf Oil*, as the *Wentworth* court did, to determine whether the forum chosen would be burdensome. Although courts generally acknowledge a strong presumption in favor of plaintiff's choice of forum, that presumption "applies with less force" when the plaintiff is foreign. Piper Aircraft v. Reyno, 454 U.S. 235 (1981). *Gulf Oil* and *Piper*, of course, establish the standards for use of the doctrine of forum non conveniens in federal courts. State courts are free to create their own forum non conveniens doctrine. As *Wentworth* indicates, however, many states have utilized federal precedent in fashioning their own forum non conveniens principles. These principles were developed, however, in the context of tort suits, and not in the context of family support proceedings. Conceding the paucity of information provided in the *Wentworth* opinion, do you agree with the court's assessment in this case that England is the more convenient forum?

There is some question as to whether UIFSA precludes a forum non conveniens dismissal by a court with jurisdiction to modify. The Uniform Child Custody Jurisdiction and Enforcement Act (UCCJEA) and its predecessor, the Uniform Child Custody Jurisdiction Act (UCCJA), both contain specific forum non conveniens sections setting forth factors relevant to declining jurisdiction in custody matters. A parallel forum non conveniens section is conspicuously absent from UIFSA. The drafters suggest in the Comment to UIFSA §611 that this omission was intentional:

> Modification of child support under subsection (a)(1) and (a)(2) is distinct from custody modification under the federal Parental Kidnapping Prevention Act, 42 U.S.C. §1738A, which provides that the court of continuing, exclusive jurisdiction may "decline jurisdiction." Similar provisions are found in the UCCJA §14. In those statutes the methodology for the declination of jurisdiction is not spelled out, but rather is left to the discretion of possibly competing courts for case-by-case determination. *The privilege of declining jurisdiction, thereby creating the potential for a vacuum, is not authorized under UIFSA.* Once an initial child support order is established, at all times thereafter there is an existing order in effect to be enforced. Even if the issuing tribunal no longer has continuing, exclusive jurisdiction, its order remains fully enforceable until a tribunal with modification jurisdiction issues a new order in conformance with this article. (emphasis added)

The *Wentworth* court was not the court with continuing exclusive jurisdiction, however, but rather a court being asked to modify the order of another country in which one of the individual contestants still resided. One could argue the drafters' concerns regarding a vacuum are therefore not applicable in this context. Moreover, the language of the UIFSA statutes do not specifically forbid a court to refuse to modify another court's order on forum non conveniens grounds. UIFSA § 611 says "may modify," and UIFSA § 104 provides that the remedies provided by UIFSA are cumulative and do not affect the availability of remedies under other law. The Comment to § 104 suggests that the existence of UIFSA procedures do not "preclude the application of the general law of the forum." Nevertheless, if both parties had in fact agreed to modification in a new forum, would it be appropriate for a court to decline on the basis of forum non conveniens? Was the court in *Wentworth* using forum non conveniens to avoid the necessity of resolving a prickly factual issue underlying subject matter jurisdiction?

3. *Choice of Law Issues and Nonmodifiable Provisions.* An unusual aspect of *Wentworth* is that the English father was the parent pursuing modification in the Washington court, and the mother residing in Washington was opposing the Washington court's jurisdiction. It is common in U.S. interstate proceedings after all parties have moved from the issuing state for a parent to seek modification in the state of residence of the other parent, because UIFSA §§ 611 and 613 require that a petitioner seeking modification of the order of another state must be a nonresident of the forum, unless the parties consent to the forum's jurisdiction or both individual parties are residents of the forum state. In *Wentworth,* however, even under UIFSA principles the father could have sought modification in the English court that issued the original order, because he still resided there. Obviously, the father, relying upon the choice of law principles set forth in UIFSA §§ 303, 604 (discussed above in Note 4), felt that he would achieve a more favorable outcome under Washington law. Look at the nature of the modifications he was seeking. Based on your knowledge of U.S. child support standards, what provisions of U.S. law might Mr. Wentworth have found more favorable? Was he correct in his assessment regarding what law would be applied?

Although a modifying court generally applies its own law regarding the duty of support and amount payable, UIFSA § 303, it cannot modify any aspect of the order that could not be modified under the law of the issuing state. UIFSA § 611(c). The 2001 amendments to this section clarify that this includes the duration of the obligation of support. The Comment to the 2001 amended section, as well as the 1996 Comment to Section 611, suggest that the duration of the support order is not modifiable unless the law of the state that initially issued the support order would permit modification of its duration. Because duration is typically nonmodifiable, the Comment observes that if support is initially ordered through age 21, another state may not modify to terminate support at age 18, even if that is the age of termination under the modifying state's substantive law. Therefore, if the duration of an initial support order is considered nonmodifiable under the law of the issuing nation, U.S. courts are not permitted to reduce the period of support even when modification is otherwise permitted by UIFSA. This is a provision of some importance in the international context, because, as discussed above in Note 4 and in Chapter Seven, Section A, many nations impose support obligations through post-secondary education.

4. *Special Modification Provision for Foreign Orders.* The drafters of UIFSA recognized that the restrictions created in UIFSA § 611 for interstate modification might in some instances prevent obligees residing in foreign nations from seeking modifications in ei-

ther U.S. tribunals or their own nation's courts, due to the combination of UIFSA restrictions and restrictions imposed by the law applicable in their own courts. The 1996 UIFSA therefore created an exception in §611 to permit modification in a U.S. tribunal of a support order issued by a nation that had not enacted laws or procedures similar to UIFSA, upon application or consent of the individual party that did not reside in the forum state. In such instances, the consent of the individual party residing in the forum state is not required.

The 2001 Amendments create a new Section 615, which incorporates and expands this exception:

> (a) If a foreign country or political subdivision that is a State will not or may not modify its order pursuant to its laws, a tribunal of this State may assume jurisdiction to modify the child-support order and bind all individuals subject to the personal jurisdiction of the tribunal whether or not the consent to modification of a child-support order otherwise required of the individual pursuant to Section 611 has been given or whether the individual seeking modification is a resident of this State or of the foreign country or political subdivision.
>
> (b) An order issued pursuant to this section is the controlling order.

The Comments to both the 1996 and 2001 versions of this exception suggest such a provision is needed, for example, when one of the parties has left the country that issued a support order and the foreign court can no longer modify because the prerequisites for a modification under its own law cannot be satisfied in the party's absence. The exception creates a U.S. forum in which the order can be modified, even if the respondent now residing in the U.S. forum state (1996 version) or subject to the personal jurisdiction of the U.S. tribunal (2001 amendments) fails to agree to the U.S. tribunal's jurisdiction.

C. Enforcing U.S. Support Orders Abroad

Child support orders are frequently obtained in U.S. courts against obligors who subsequently relocate outside of the United States. Support orders may also be entered in U.S. tribunals against obligors who reside outside the United States at the time the proceeding is brought, if the obligor is subject to personal jurisdiction in the forum state. In either situation, obligees located in the United States are often faced with the need to initiate enforcement measures against obligors located abroad.

In many instances, these child support orders can be enforced using remedies available through U.S. courts and governmental agencies. If an obligor is employed by the U.S. government or an American company, an income assignment order from a U.S. court can be used to require child support payments and any arrearages to be withheld from the obligor's paycheck and forwarded to the obligee, via the appropriate state centralized collection and disbursement unit. Foreign employers that are subsidiaries of U.S. companies have also shown willingness to voluntarily comply with U.S. income assignment orders that have been sent to them with a request for assistance, particularly if the obligor is a U.S. citizen. Gary Caswell, *Making Long-distance Parents Pay Up,* 23-Fall Fam. Advoc. 52, 55 (2000). Even if the obligor's foreign-based employer has no U.S. affiliation, state child support enforcement agencies have found it useful to contact the foreign employer, often by sending the request for assistance directly to the president of the company, and providing authenticated, translated copies of child support orders, warrants, and other court documents. Department of State, *Child Support Enforcement Abroad, at* http://travel.state.gov/child_support.html.

If the obligor has lived or worked in the United States, many of the enforcement methods available against domestic obligors, such as lien enforcement against U.S bank accounts, pensions, or other real or personal property; suspension or revocation of U.S. occupational, professional, recreational, or drivers licenses; intercepts on federal or state tax refunds or government benefits; and reporting of arrearages to credit agencies, may also motivate compliance by obligors located abroad. In particularly egregious cases, pursuing state or federal criminal felony charges may qualify non-support as an extraditable offense under some U.S. treaties with foreign nations. Caswell, *supra,* at 55–56.

Another enforcement mechanism available through the federal government is the Passport Denial Program. If a state child support enforcement agency certifies to the Department of Health and Human Services (DHHS) that an individual owes over $5000 in child support arrearages, the Department of State, upon receipt of that certification from the DHHS, *cannot* issue a passport to such an obligor until the state agency certifies that acceptable payment arrangements have been made, and DHHS removes the individual's name from the electronic list. If an individual's name is certified to the Department of State after an initial passport has been issued, the Department may revoke, restrict, or limit the passport already issued. 42 U.S.C. §652 (2000); 22 C.F.R. §51.70. Therefore, delinquent obligors applying for a passport or other consular services abroad will have their request denied or their passport revoked or limited if they do not clear the Passport Name Check System. A limited validity passport can be used only to return to the United States. The State Department reports that between 30 to 40 passports are denied per day and over 4 million in child support payments have been collected through that program in the first five years of its operation. Department of State, *Child Support Enforcement Abroad, at* http://travel.state.gov/child_support.html (visited March 29, 2002).

Sometimes an inability to locate an obligor abroad creates an additional obstacle to enforcement. State IV-D agencies can often provide assistance in this regard, because they have access not only to the Federal Parent Locator Service, which can search a multitude of federal and state governmental databases (e.g., Social Security Administration, Internal Revenue Service, Selective Service System, Department of Defense, Veteran's Administration, National Personnel Records Center, National Directory of New Hires, and state employment agency records), but also to some foreign reciprocating countries' location resources as well. State child support enforcement agencies can also request information regarding the location of U.S. citizens contained in passport records from the Department of State. State agencies are also permitted to request information from consular registration records regarding U.S. citizens registered with U.S. embassies or consulates abroad. *See* Department of State, *Child Support Enforcement Abroad, at* http://travel.state.gov/child_support.html.

In many instances, compliance with a U.S. child support order by an obligor located abroad can best be obtained by seeking enforcement in a foreign tribunal, with the assistance of foreign attorneys or the appropriate foreign support enforcement agency. If the obligor is located in a foreign reciprocating country or a nation with a reciprocal arrangement with the state in which the obligee or child resides, it may be helpful to seek the assistance of the State IV-D agency to forward the necessary paperwork to that nation's central authority or other appropriate governmental entity. Private counsel can also assist in facilitating foreign enforcement proceedings, and in fact, those who specialize in international practice are often particularly effective in providing assistance when the nation involved has no reciprocal arrangement with the United States. Gary Caswell, *International Child Support—1999*, 32 Fam. L.Q. 525, 545 (1998). Even nations with no formal reciprocity arrangement are often willing to enforce U.S. child support orders in their courts as a matter of comity, particularly if they are parties to multilateral enforcement agreements with other countries.

Each country has its own procedures and forms for initiating requests for services and enforcement proceedings. OCSE and the National Child Support Enforcement Association (NCSEA) have developed country-specific information and forms, some of which are bilingual, for use in nations that have reciprocal arrangements with the U.S. or some states.

When enforcement is sought in a country with which no federal or state reciprocal agreement is in force, letters rogatory are often utilized to seek judicial assistance from a foreign court. A "letter rogatory" is a request for assistance from the court of one country to the court of another country. Although perhaps best known as a mechanism to request service of process or assistance with obtaining evidence from a foreign tribunal, they are also used to request assistance with enforcement of a judgment. U. S. tribunals have inherent authority to issue letters rogatory. *E.g.*, United States v. Reagan, 453 F.2d 165, 172 (6th Cir. 1971), cert. den. 406 U.S. 946 (1972); Wooster Products, Inc. v. Magna-Tek Inc., 1990 WL 51973 (Ohio App. April 25, 1990). They may be transmitted directly from court to court or through the Department of State. 28 U.S.C. § 1781(a)(2), (b)(2) (2000). Drafting instructions and information on the procedures for routing them through diplomatic or other channels to specific countries can be obtained from the Office of Overseas Citizens Services of the Department of State. Letters rogatory may be particularly useful when assistance from a foreign support enforcement agency or private foreign counsel cannot be obtained. *See* Caswell, *supra*, at 546–47; Gary Caswell, *Making Long-distance Parents Pay Up*, 23-Fall Fam. Advoc. 52, 54 (2000).

Problems

10-1. Ana, who resides in Reykjavik, Iceland with her two-year-old daughter, has never received child support from the child's father, Eric, who moved to the United States shortly after the child's birth. Ana and Eric never married, and although he acknowledged paternity and is listed on the child's birth certificate, no child support order has ever been entered by a court or administrative tribunal in either Iceland or the United States. Ana believes Eric is living in Massachusetts, but is not certain. What options are available to Ana, who is in difficult financial straits and would like to receive child support?

10-2. Ted, a US citizen, and Audrey, a citizen of Ireland, married in Oklahoma and resided there for two years following the birth of their child. Ted was transferred to Ireland with an international company, and the family moved to Dublin for a year. When their son was three years old, the couple separated. Ted was transferred back to Oklahoma and Audrey and the child remained in Ireland, moving to Cork to live near Audrey's relatives. Ted periodically sent money, but no support order had been issued.

Seven months after Ted moved back to Oklahoma, Ted filed a petition for divorce in an Oklahoma state court and asked the court to establish a child support order. Two weeks later, Audrey filed a child support proceeding in Ireland. Within 20 days of receiving service of the Oklahoma summons and petition, Audrey timely filed an answer in the Oklahoma state court proceeding, along with a motion in which she sought dismissal of the child support claim, challenging the jurisdiction of the Oklahoma court to issue a child support order. The Republic of Ireland has been declared a foreign reciprocating country by the U.S. Department of State. How will the Oklahoma court rule on Audrey's motion?

10-3. Nash and Carol resided in Oklahoma with their children for two years. When they separated, Carol returned to London, where her parents live, and took the children. Nash raised no objection, and kept in touch with the children by phone. After four months, Carol filed a proceeding in the appropriate tribunal in London to establish a child support order. Two weeks later, Nash filed a divorce proceeding in state court in Oklahoma. In the divorce petition, Nash asked the Oklahoma court to include in the decree a child support order, as well as provisions for his visitation with the children and other relief. In her response to his petition, Carol challenged the jurisdiction of the court to determine child support. Assume Oklahoma has a reciprocal arrangement with the United Kingdom. How is the court likely to rule on Carol's motion?

10-4. Pierre and Claudette, French citizens, had one child together while living in France. Four years later they separated. Pierre visited the child and provided some support for over a year, but then moved to Massachusetts to accept a new job with an international computer firm. Claudette and the child moved a few months later to London, also for employment reasons. The cost of living in London is high, and Claudette found that she had difficulty affording rent and adequate day care. She brought a proceeding in the appropriate court in the United Kingdom to seek a child support award from Pierre. Pierre was served with notice, but did not respond or appear. A judgment was awarded to Claudette for past and future child support, and Pierre received notice of the judgement.

Six months after the support order was entered, Pierre had paid nothing. Claudette received assistance from a child support enforcement authority in Britain, which forwarded the British judgment and appropriate documentation to the Child Support Enforcement Office in Boston. That Massachusetts IV-D agency registered the judgment and brought enforcement proceedings in the appropriate state court. After receiving proper notice, Pierre requested a hearing to contest the validity and enforcement of the child support order. What authority might the mother's counsel be using to enforce the order, and what defenses is Pierre likely to assert? Who will be successful? Would it make a difference whether or not Massachusetts had a reciprocal arrangement with the United Kingdom?

10-5. Stella and Karl divorced in Poland. Karl was awarded primary custody of their two sons, and Stella was ordered to pay child support of 200 Polish zlotych per month for each child until each graduated from a university, or reached the age of 19, if he was no longer in school. Two years after the divorce, Stella moved to the United States to take a teaching position at an American university in Ohio. She and her sons had become estranged, and she ceased making payments after the move. One year after Stella's move, Karl contacted the appropriate government agency in Poland for assistance with collection of his back due child support. That agency contacted the Ohio IV-D agency for assistance. Poland has been declared a foreign reciprocating country by the US. Department of State. What methods are available to enforce the Polish order in the Ohio courts?

Assume that the duty to pay child support under Ohio law ceases on a child's eighteenth birthday, or upon graduation from high school. One of the sons is now age 20, and attending a university. Assume also that the Polish zloty has recently lost value in comparison to the U.S. dollar. Which law will the Ohio court apply in determining the amount of arrearages? How will the amount of the arrearages be calculated?

10-6. Jan and Katja married in Colorado and had one child. When the child was one year of age, they moved to the Czech Republic, Katja's home country. Three years later they divorced in the Czech Republic. Katja was awarded custody and Jan was awarded visitation and ordered to pay child support in a specified amount.

Six months later, Jan moved back to Colorado. Katja and their child remained in the Czech Republic. The following year Jan lost his job and was forced to take a lower paying job. He stopped paying child support. Katja, with the assistance of the appropriate governmental agency in the Czech Republic and the IV-D agency in Colorado, registered the order and brought an enforcement action in a Colorado court. Jan filed a motion to reduce the child support order in the Colorado proceeding, and Katja was properly served with Jan's motion.

The Czech Republic has been declared a foreign reciprocating country by the U.S. Department of State. Does the Colorado court have jurisdiction to modify the child support order?

10-7. Juanita and Pablo, the parents of three children, divorced in Costa Rica, and Pablo was ordered to pay child support in a specified amount. Pablo moved to Arizona six months later, and obtained a much higher paying job than he had in Costa Rica. Assume Costa Rican law would permit the enforcement of U.S. child support orders against Costa Rican residents, but that Costa Rican law also prohibits modification of any support awards, including those of its own tribunals, unless both parties appear before the Costa Rican tribunal in person for the modification proceeding.

Juanita, through a governmental enforcement agency in Costa Rica and the state IV-D agency in Arizona, filed a proceeding in Arizona to increase the child support. Juanita consented in writing to the jurisdiction of Arizona over the proceeding. Pablo was properly served, refused to consent to jurisdiction, and in fact, moved to dismiss the proceeding for lack of jurisdiction. How should the Arizona court rule?

10-8. Tomiko, a U.S. citizen, and her husband, Yoshihiro, separated in Washington, where they had lived all of their married lives, when their daughter was six years old. At the time of the separation, Yoshihiro was transferred from his position with a Washington regional office of Sony, Inc. back to Tokyo for an assignment at the corporation's headquarters. Tomiko filed a divorce action in a Washington state court and obtained proper service upon Yoshihiro. Following the final hearing, a child support order was included in the decree.

Yoshihiro has not paid child support for the past six months. Assume for purposes of this problem that Japan has not been declared a foreign reciprocating country and has no reciprocal arrangement with the State of Washington. Tomiko is an elementary school teacher with a moderate income. What are her options to obtain enforcement of her child support award?

D. Multilateral Child Support Conventions

Although the United States is currently not a party to a multilateral child support convention, there are several global and numerous regional conventions addressing the transnational creation and enforcement of support orders that have been widely ratified by other nations. Conflicts between the United States and parties to these major conventions regarding standards for personal jurisdiction, conflict of laws, jurisdictional bases for modification of child support orders, standards for recognition of default judgments, access to free legal assistance, and other procedural differences have all created obstacles to U.S. participation. Federalism concerns have also contributed to U.S. abstention, because until the mid-1970s the establishment and enforcement of child support obligations was viewed as a matter largely within the cognizance of state rather than federal government. Most of the major multilateral child support conventions currently in effect were negotiated during the 1950s, 1960s, and early 1970s, before the federal government became heavily involved in child support collection and developed expertise in this field. *See* David F. Cavers, *International Enforcement of Family Support,* 81 Colum. L. Rev. 994, 996–1000, 1005, 1013–23 (1981); Gary Caswell, *International Child Support—1999,* 32 Fam. L.Q. 525, 528–31 (1998). The following section presents a brief introduction to the major global and some of the regional conventions currently in force.

1. New York Convention on Recovery Abroad of Maintenance

Since 1957, when it first entered into force, almost sixty nations representing every continent have become parties to the Convention on the Recovery Abroad of Maintenance (New York Convention). Drafted at a conference convened by the Economic and Social Council of the United Nations in 1956, the operation of the Convention is similar to, and may have been modeled after, the Uniform Reciprocal Enforcement of Support Act (URESA), one of the predecessors in the United States to UIFSA. Cavers, *supra,* at 1003. The Convention permits a claimant who resides in one contracting nation to apply to a "Transmitting Agency," a designated judicial or administrative authority in the claimant's own country, for assistance in recovering child support or alimony from a respondent, an individual subject to the jurisdiction of another contracting nation.

The Convention offers a claimant the opportunity to obtain an order of support from a respondent located abroad, who may not be subject to the jurisdiction of a court located where the claimant resides, using a two-nation proceeding similar to the two-state proceeding available through UIFSA, and formerly through URESA. Nations that are parties to the Convention apprise the Secretary General of the United Nations regarding authorities they have designated as Transmitting Agencies and the private or public bodies that they have designated as their Receiving Agencies, as well as information regarding the evidence normally required under their law for proof of maintenance claims.(Articles 2, 3). To initiate the process, the claimant submits to the judicial or administrative authority operating as a Transmitting Agency an application for assistance, information regarding how to locate the respondent and the grounds upon which the claim is based, photographs of the parties, and, if required, a power of attorney. (Articles 3, 4). Following review by the Transmitting Agency, these documents are then forwarded to the appropriate Receiving Agency in a nation that has jurisdiction over the respondent, which must take appropriate steps to recover maintenance for the claimant.(Articles 4, 6). Such steps might include settlement of the claim, prosecution of an action, and execution of any order for maintenance that may result.

The New York Convention provides that in all proceedings arising under the Convention, the law of the receiving nation, including its private international law, applies. (Article 6). Therefore, if the respondent is a national of a third country, for example, the receiving nation might apply the law of the nation of the respondent's nationality, or the law of the nation of the claimant's habitual residence, if other conventions to which the receiving nation is a party would dictate such choices regarding applicable law. Cavers, *supra,* at 1004. Neither Transmitting Agencies nor Receiving Agencies are permitted to charge fees for services rendered under the Convention, and claimants must be accorded the same treatment with regard to payment of court costs that is accorded nationals and residents of the country in which maintenance proceedings are instituted. (Article 9).

If a claimant already has an order for support, the order can also be transmitted to the Receiving Agency, along with the other application papers, and can be registered, recognized, and executed in the receiving nation to the extent permitted by that nation's law. (Article 5). The focus of the New York Convention, however, is not to set standards for the recognition or enforcement of foreign support orders per se, but rather to create a transnational system for prosecuting support claims. Thus, the nation to which claimant's application is sent is free to issue a new order for support that may differ in terms from an order previously obtained in the claimant's home country, or to modify the earlier order, if the receiving nation's law so permits. Thus, the potential is created for multiple orders to be in existence. One of the reasons the URESA system in the United States was ultimately revised by UIFSA was to eliminate the multi-order system that previously existed under URESA, and RURESA, a revised version of URESA, within the United States.

2. The Hague Conventions

The two child support conventions most recently produced by the Hague Conference are the 1973 Convention on the Recognition and Enforcement of Decisions Related to Maintenance Obligations (the Hague Enforcement Convention) and the 1973 Convention on the Law Applicable to Maintenance Obligations (Applicable Law Convention). As of March 2003, twenty nations were parties to the Hague Enforcement Convention. All of the contracting nations were European countries except for Australia, which became a party in February 2002. Thirteen nations had ratified or acceded to the Applicable Law Convention by 2003, of which only Japan was a non-European nation.

Both of the 1973 conventions incorporate the provisions of earlier Hague child support conventions drafted in the mid-1950s, which were expanded in the 1973 versions to cover maintenance claims for adults (alimony) as well as child support. Although most of the states that were parties to the earlier conventions subsequently ratified or acceded to the 1973 conventions, there are still a handful of nations that chose not to join the 1973 conventions and are party only to the 1956 Convention on the Law Applicable to Obligations to Support Minor Children or the 1958 Convention Concerning the Recognition and Enforcement of Decisions Involving Obligations to Support Minor Children. Thus the 1950s conventions are still in effect between those nations and the other nations that were parties to them.

The 1973 Hague Enforcement Convention requires contracting nations to recognize and enforce maintenance decisions rendered by judicial or administrative authorities of other contracting nations, or maintenance settlements made before such authorities, if the decisions were rendered after proper notice based on any of the jurisdictional grounds recognized by the Convention. (Articles 1, 4, 6). Permissible bases of jurisdiction under the Convention include: (1) the habitual residence of either the maintenance creditor or the maintenance debtor, (2) the fact that both the maintenance creditor and the maintenance debtor were nationals of the country that issued the decision, (3) consent of the defendant to the jurisdiction of the issuing authority, or (4) the fact that the authority entering the maintenance decision was exercising jurisdiction over a divorce, annulment, or legal separation action on a basis that would satisfy the jurisdictional standards of the enforcing nation for such a proceeding. (Articles 7, 8).

The 1973 Applicable Law Convention, like its predecessor, provides that the applicable law to be applied in all maintenance proceedings in contracting nations must be the internal law of the nation that is the habitual residence of the maintenance creditor. If the maintenance creditor changes his or her habitual residence, the internal law of the new habitual residence applies from the moment the change occurs. (Article 4). However, if the creditor cannot obtain maintenance under the law of the creditor's habitual residence, the law of the common nationality of the debtor and creditor must be applied. (Article 5). Finally, the law of the forum must be applied if maintenance is unavailable under the law designated by Articles 4 or 5. The Act creates several exceptions, including a provision that maintenance obligations between divorced spouses is governed by the law applied to the divorce. (Article 8).

The law designated by the Convention determines such issues as whether, to what extent, and from whom a creditor may seek maintenance, the time limits for institution of proceedings, and the extent of a maintenance debtor's obligation to a public body that has provided benefits to a maintenance creditor. (Article 10).

Notes and Questions

1. *Comparison.* How do the provisions of the 1973 Hague Conventions differ from UIFSA regarding jurisdictional bases and applicable law? How do they differ from the New York Convention?

2. *A New Hague Convention on the Horizon?* At the Nineteenth Diplomatic Session of the Hague Conference in June 2001, a decision was made to include as a priority for the Twentieth Diplomatic Session the preparation of a worldwide convention on recovery of maintenance. The Hague Conference on Private International Law, *Maintenance Obligations,* http://www.hcch.net/e/workprog/maint.html. This decision was based on the Report and Conclusions of a Special Commission on Maintenance Obligations convened by the Hague in April 1999, which reviewed the operation of the Hague Conventions on maintenance and the New York Convention. Rather than revising existing conventions, the Commission recommended that a new and comprehensive instrument be designed to replace the existing Hague Conventions and the New York Convention.

Several reasons were identified for this more radical approach. One was the need for tighter integration than the current structure of multiple conventions provided. Proliferation of conventions has complicated transnational enforcement for national authorities. In addition, the New York Convention, viewed as innovative in its day, has been increasingly perceived as obsolete and, because of its relatively loose structure, vulnerable to inconsistent interpretation and practice. A new convention can take better account of recent developments at the national level that have improved the efficiency of support enforcement. The inadequacy of the current global conventions is demonstrated by the small number of cases processed through their international machinery in comparison with the need for transnational support enforcement that exists. *See* William Duncan, *The Hague Conference on Private International Law and Its Current Programme of Work Concerning the International Protection of Children and Other Aspects of Family Law,* in Sarcevic & Volken, 2 Yearbook of Private International Law 2000 41, 43 (2000). Commission members also noted that the Hague Conventions are not attracting many new ratifications. Permanent Bureau, *Report on and Conclusions of the Special Commission on Maintenance Obligations of April 1999* ¶ 44, available at http://www.hcch.net/e/workprog/maint.html.

The new international instrument, the Special Commission recommends, should be comprehensive, building upon the best features of the existing conventions, particularly in regard to recognition and enforcement. Advances in information technology and developments occurring at national and international levels are to be taken into account, and provisions relating to administrative cooperation must be an essential element. It is anticipated that this new global convention will be drafted in co-operation with the United Nations. *Id.* at ¶ 46.

3. Regional Conventions

a. *Inter-American Convention on Support Obligations*

In 1989 the Organization of American States (O.A.S.) adopted an Inter-American Convention on Support Obligations, which is intended to supplement the New York Convention. Carol S. Bruch, *The 1989 Inter-American Convention on Support Obligations,* 40 Am. J. Comp. L. 817, 819 (1992). Although the United States is not a signatory or party to the Inter-American Convention, Mexico and ten nations located in Central or South America had ratified or acceded to this Convention by March 2003, many of which are also party to the New York Convention. The Inter-American Convention applies to both child support and alimony proceedings, creating choice of law rules, jurisdictional bases, and provisions for the recognition and enforcement of qualifying orders.

The Inter-American Convention rejects the "cascade" approach of the 1973 Hague Applicable Law Convention, providing instead that regarding a support obligation, a judicial or administrative authority must apply the law it finds to be most favorable to the creditor from among the following four choices: the law of the creditor's domicile, the law of the creditor's habitual residence, the law of the debtor's domicile, or the law of the debtor's habitual residence. (Article 6). Article 21, however, provides that the Convention cannot be construed to restrict the rights of the creditor under forum law, which suggests that if domestic law is more favorable, it should control. The Convention appears to contemplate that the law of the selected nation will control all issues, although Article 21 creates some ambiguity about this point, as it could be interpreted to permit the substitution of domestic law on specific issues. Obviously, where the laws of different nations are more favorable to the creditor on different issues, determining which law is most favorable overall can sometimes be difficult. *Id.* at 823–24. Modification proceedings present a new opportunity to evaluate the most favorable law to the creditor in the context of different issues, such as duration of the support obligation, that might present themselves at the time of modification. *Id.* at 825.

The Inter-American Convention is the first multinational support convention to establish jurisdictional bases for support proceedings in contracting nations, rather than regulating jurisdiction indirectly, as the Hague and New York Conventions do, through their enforcement provisions. *Id.* at 827. A creditor's motion for support may be heard by judicial or administrative authorities in contracting parties in the nation of the creditor's domicile or habitual residence, the nation of the debtor's domicile or habitual residence, the nation in which the debtor "is connected by personal links such as possessing property, receiving income, or obtaining financial benefits," or any nation in which the debtor appears without challenging the jurisdiction. (Article 8). Although creditors may bring actions to increase support in any of the aforementioned nations, debtors may seek a termination or reduction of support obligation only before the authority that established the original support amount. (Article 8).

Contracting nations are required to recognize and enforce final orders entered consistently with the Convention's jurisdictional provisions, provided that the defendant in the original proceeding had notice and an opportunity to be heard and that the creditor complies with the Convention's formalities for certifying the order. (Articles 11, 12, 13). Execution can be ordered in an amount less than requested, if the needs of the creditor and the financial resources of the debtor so dictate, but the creditor retains the right to collect the remainder in the future. (Article 10). Less than full execution might be determined to be warranted, for example, in a country experiencing rampant inflation, such that enforcement of an order from another country at the current exchange rate would be financially disastrous for the debtor. *Id.* at 829.

In addition to provisions in the Convention that conflict with UIFSA's choice of law and jurisdictional provisions, another obstacle to U.S. ratification of the Convention is the requirement in Article 11 that notice in the original proceeding must have been given to the debtor in a "form substantially equivalent to that established by the law of the State" asked to enforce the order. Professor Bruch has observed that because service by private process server (rather than a marshal) and service by mail are not recognized in many nations that are party to the Convention, many orders issued by U.S. courts or administrative tribunals would be unenforceable in these nations under the Convention. *Id.* at 831.

b. European Union Instruments

For several decades, the European Union (E.U.) and its predecessor, the European Economic Community, have regulated jurisdiction over matters related to maintenance, which includes both child support and alimony, and recognition and enforcement of such decisions by member states. In 1968 the European Economic Community adopted the EC Convention on Jurisdiction and the Enforcement of Judgments in Civil and Commercial Matters, commonly referred to as "Brussels I." In December 2000, the Brussels I Convention was largely replaced by Council Regulation No. 44/2000, which is binding and directly applicable in all European Union member nations except Denmark. Denmark continues to be governed in its relations with other E.U. members by the Brussels I Convention.

Both instruments provide that in maintenance proceedings, a defendant domiciled in a member state may be sued in the courts of the nation in which defendant is domiciled, or the courts of the nation in which the maintenance creditor is domiciled or habitually resident. In addition, if a proceeding for divorce or annulment is brought between spouses in a different court, that court may also exercise jurisdiction over the maintenance matters if that nation's own jurisdictional law would so permit, unless that jurisdiction is based solely on the nationality of one of the parties. (Council Reg. No. 44/2001, Articles 2,3,5; Brussels I Convention, Articles 2,3,5). Jurisdiction may also be based on the entry of an appearance by the defendant, if defendant enters no objection to jurisdiction. (Council Reg. No. 44/2001, Article 24; Brussels I Convention, Article 18). The domicile of a party is to be determined by the forum nation's law, i.e., the law of the state in which proceedings are brought. (Council Reg. No. 44/2001, Article 59; Brussels I Convention, Article 52).

Member nations are required to recognize and enforce judgments of other member states, unless the judgment is manifestly contrary to public policy, entered by default without sufficient notice, or irreconcilable with an earlier judgment entitled to recognition. (Council Reg. No. 44/2001, Articles 32–34, 38–45; Brussels I Convention, Articles 26–27, 31–34).

In May 2002, the European Commission proposed a new Council Regulation Concerning Jurisdiction and the Recognition and Enforcement of Judgments in Matrimonial Matters and in Matters of Parental Responsibility, COM(2002) 222 final/2. If adopted, the new regulation would amend Regulation 44/2001 to also permit a court properly exercising jurisdiction over parental responsibility proceedings to hear matters related to maintenance. (Article 70).

Chapter 11

Adoption:
A Comparative Exploration

In this chapter we will take a brief look at the institution of adoption from both historical and comparative perspectives, and examine the impact that international law has had on domestic adoption practices around the globe. The regulation of transnational adoption, by contrast, under both international and U.S. domestic law, will be the focus of the following chapter, Chapter Twelve.

The institution of adoption has taken many forms throughout the ages, and served many purposes, not all of which were focused on the well-being of children. Section A of this chapter will provide a brief overview of the forms adoption has taken over time and the functions it has served; the historical development of modern adoption in Western nations; and its counterpart institution in Islamic societies, kafala.

Adoption law, like other areas within the field of domestic relations law, is shaped by conflicting conceptions of the proper definition of family and a child's place within it. Diverse adoption practices often reflect differing emphases on the importance of biological and social parenthood. Sections B and C of this chapter will explore this tension by focusing on two specific areas: (1) the termination of genetic parents' rights, through both voluntary and involuntary procedures, and (2) maintaining the link following adoption between a child and the child's biological family. Within each section, the prevailing constitutional and statutory regulation in American jurisdictions will be compared with approaches taken by other countries on selected issues, affording the opportunity to explore not only the resolution of the conflicting rights of the individual parties involved, but also the extent to which control over these issues by individual sovereigns has been affected by various international instruments, such as the United Nations Convention on the Rights of the Child and the European Convention on Human Rights.

A. A Glimpse at Adoption across
Time and Cultures

The institution of adoption has ancient roots. References to adoption are found in one of the earliest known written legal codes of law, the Babylonian Code of Hammurabi (2000 B.C.), as well as ancient Hindu, Egyptian, Greek, and Roman writings. Leo Albert Huard, *The Law of Adoption: Ancient and Modern*, 9 Vand. L. Rev. 743, 743–44 (1956). The primary purpose of these ancient forms was to ensure the continuity of family and the creation of an heir, rather than to serve the welfare of the person who was adopted. *Id.* at 745. Translations of the Code of Hammurabi, in fact, suggest that adoptees could have their tongues cut out if they openly stated that they were not born to their adoptive parents, and that they could be blinded if they attempted to search for their birth parents. Geraldine Van Bueren, *Children's Access to Adoption Records—State Discretion or an Enforceable International Right*, 58 Mod. L. Rev. 37, 39 (1995). One nineteenth century historian, Sir Henry Maine, suggests that the institution of adoption was critical to the survival of early patriarchal civilizations, allowing them to combine, or absorb each other, on terms other than the "absolute superiority on one side and the absolute subjection of the other." Stephen B. Presser, *The Historical Background of the American Law of Adoption*, 11 J. Fam. L. 443, 445 (1971) (quoting Henry Maine, Ancient Law 125 (1861)).

Acquiring male offspring to perpetuate the rites of ancestor worship was a strong motivation for adoption customs in some ancient cultures. In China, for example, a childless male was afforded the right by custom to claim the first-born male child of any of his younger brothers for this purpose. Presser, *supra*, at 445 n.11.

The development of adoption under ancient Roman law served both purposes: (1) avoiding "extinction of the family," and (2) perpetuating the "rites of family religious worship." *Id.* at 446. Although the Roman law of adoption took different forms over the centuries, adapting to changing social conditions, under one of the earlier forms a Roman could adopt only if he was at least sixty years of age and without an heir, and the adoptee was required to be an adult. Adoption severed relations with the former family, and the adoptee then inherited the name, the property, and the family rites of the adopter. *See id.* at 446; Huard, *supra*, at 744–45; Kerry Joseph O'Halloran, *Adoption in Two Jurisdictions of Ireland—A Case Study of Changes in the Balance Between Public and Private Law*, 3 Irish J. Fam. L. 34 (2001). The adoptee was also required to assume the domestic religion of his new family, and to "carry on the private worship of the household gods." Laura J. Schwartz, *Models for Parenthood in Adoption Law: The French Conception*, 28 Vand. J. Transnat'l L. 1069, 1092 (1995).

Unrecognized by canon law, adoption as a legal institution disappeared during the medieval period in many European nations. *See* Schwarz, *supra*, at 1092. Adoption was also never recognized by English common law. E. Wayne Carp, Family Matters: Secrecy and Disclosure in the History of Adoption 4 (1998). A variety of reasons have been proffered for its absence from British law, the most common being the extraordinary importance of blood lineage in the British social hierarchy and legal system. Moreover, the function served by the modern institution of adoption, the provision of homes for dependent children, was served to some extent by other social customs developed in the late middle ages for the training of all children, dependent or otherwise. Historians relate that by the sixteenth century, almost all young people were either placed in apprenticeships or "put out," a system that was practiced by middle class and poor alike. Apprenticed boys and girls were clothed, fed, and educated, and in return were required to work unpaid and forbidden to marry until the age of twenty-one. "Putting out" entailed sending a child (often between the ages of six and nine) to another family for service, so that he or she could learn the manners or the trade of that family. Putting out often involved living with a new family every few years. Presser, *supra*, at 448–55; Huard, *supra*, at 745–46.

In America, adoption was recognized by the customary law of many Native American tribes. Huard, *supra*, at 746. For example, in Oregon among the Walla Walla and Umatilla tribes, when an abandoned child was taken in and cared for by another, the child was regarded as the child of the caretaker, and both the child and the caretaker were treated under tribal custom as having all of the rights that would have been afforded a birth child and parent. *See* No-she-po v. Wa-win-ta, 65 P.15 (Or. 1900).

In the late eighteenth and early nineteenth centuries, adoptive relationships were occasionally created by private bills in the U.S. state legislatures. The first adoption statutes in the United States appeared in the mid-nineteenth century, in Mississippi (1846), and in Alabama, Texas, and Vermont (1850). *See* Lawrence Friedman, A History of American Law 211 (2d ed. 1985); Joan Heifetz Hollinger, *Introduction to Adoption Law and Practice*, 1 Adoption Law & Practice 1–19 (Joan Hollinger ed., 2000). These earliest statutes, however, merely created a legal procedure to authenticate a public record of private adoption agreements, in order to ease the legislative burden. Carp, *surpa*, at 11; Hollinger, *supra*, at 1–22.

Among those nations whose legal systems were predominantly influenced by English jurisprudence, the first modern adoption statute is usually credited to the State of Massachusetts, which enacted an adoption statue in 1851. The Massachusetts statute is widely recognized as the first to emphasize the child as the primary beneficiary of the proceeding, and to require judicial supervision over the process. The Massachusetts statute laid the foundation for a system intended to ensure the child's welfare by requiring: (1) written consent of the child's birth parents or legal guardian; (2) consent of the child if over 13 years of age; (3) the agreement of a married adopter's spouse to join in the petition; (4) a determination by a judge that the adopter is fit and "of sufficient ability to bring up a child"; (5) recognition that the child becomes the legal child of the adopters after the decree is issued for "all intents and purposes"; (6) termination of all legal rights on the part of the birth parent; and (7) a right of appeal for any petitioner or the child. Presser, *supra*, at 465. During the next quarter century, many states passed similar legislation. Historians note that although the purpose of this modern system is very different from its Roman predecessor, the notion from Roman law and subsequent civil law systems — that all of the rights of a birth child are conferred upon an adopted child — thus found its way into the American institution of adoption, and in fact early cases contain extensive references to Roman civil law. Huard, *supra*, at 748.

The practice of taking children from their birth families involuntarily developed later, growing out of the progressive movement in the late nineteenth and early twentieth centuries. Fueled by a combination of good intentions, the social pressures of increasing urbanization, and some anti-immigrant and class animus, "child-saving" societies, and later legislators and social workers, began gathering homeless children and progressed eventually to removing children from home situations considered harmful. Faced with overcrowded and poorly funded institutions and orphanages, reformers turned to adoption as an alternative. As a result, the number of children available for adoption swelled during the early twentieth century. *See* Papke, *Pondering Past Purposes: A Critical History of American Adoption Law*, 102 W. Va. L. Rev. 459, 464–68 (1999).

Other nations with Anglo-American legal systems were slower to enact statutory adoption schemes. Although one Canadian province enacted adoption legislation as early as 1873 and New Zealand did so by 1881, most Canadian provinces, as well as England and Wales (1926), Northern Ireland (1929), Australia (New South Wales, 1923), and Scotland (1930), all enacted their first modern adoption statutes after the First World War, when changing social conditions prompted a dramatic increase in the number of children born out of wedlock. *See* Nicholas Bala & Joanne Wildgoose, Canadian Children's Law: A Coursebook 371 (1985), *reprinted in* Berend Hovius, Family Law: Cases, Notes and Materials 1051 (5th ed. 2000). The thousands of orphans created by the First World War also prompted adoption legislation on the European continent.

In time, most Western nations created a legislative scheme for adoption intended to meet the needs of children requiring care.

Many nations with civil legal systems derived from Roman law recognize two forms of adoption, which scholars suggest may find their roots in forms of adoption existing in the late Roman Empire under the Code of Justinian. *See* Patricia Alzate Monroy, *Adoption Law in Colombia, in* The International Survey of Family Law 1996, 99, 102 (Andrew Bainham ed., 1998). Today many European nations, including France, Spain, Italy, Portugal, and Poland, as well as many Latin American nations recognize these forms, often referred to as "full" and "simple" adoption. Typically, in a simple adoption the adopted child's relationship with his birth family is not terminated, and the child retains the inheritance rights from the birth family to which an out-of-wedlock child would be entitled. A family relationship is created only between the adopter and the adopted child and the child's heirs. Full adoption, by contrast, severs the legal tie between the adoptee and the birth family, and a family relationship is established between the adopted person, the adopter, and all of the adopter's blood relatives. *Id.* at 102.

The characteristics and uses of full and simple adoption, in countries that recognize this distinction, will of course vary. A description of their meaning and application in French law is found in the following excerpt.

Laura J. Schwartz, *Models for Parenthood in Adoption Law: The French Conception*
28 Vand. J. Transnt'l L. 1069, 1094–98 (1995)

French law contains two forms of adoption. The first form is full adoption (*adoption plénière*), which is similar in structure to U.S. adoption. The second form is limited adoption (*adoption simple*). A child adopted "simply" (i.e., in the latter manner) usually adds the name of the adoptive parents to that of the natural parents and, for certain purposes, "remains in [the] family of origin." In an *adoption simple*, only the adoptive father and mother have parental authority and the power to make decisions involving the child's welfare. The relationship between the adoptee and the biological parents, however, is not completely severed. The adoptee may inherit from both families and reciprocal duties of material support continue to exist between the adoptee and the biological parents. Although an *adoption plénière* is irrevocable once pronounced, an *adoption simple* may be revoked under the following circumstances: (1) upon demand of the adopting parent before the adoptee reaches fifteen; (2) by the adoptee's biological family before the child reaches eighteen; and thereafter, (3) directly by the adoptee. During the adoptee's minority, an *adoption simple* may be transformed into an *adoption plénière* at the request of the adopting parent....

* * *

The vast majority of adoptions pronounced each year in France are *adoptions plénières*. Although EFA [a French organization of adoptive families] describes the choice between the two forms of adoption as "whether or not to make the adopted child...perfectly integrated, regardless of [the child's] ethnicity or origins, in the bosom of [the] adoptive family or country," such a characterization is both misleading and inaccurate. It presumes, not only that it is the adoptive parents, rather than a judge, who choose the form of adoption pronounced, but that, in all instances, *adoption simple* is inherently inferior to *adoption plénière*.

An *adoption simple* typically involves an older child or stepchild. The *Code Civil* permits an *adoption plénière* only until the age of fifteen and, following passage of a new law, forbids its pronouncement in stepparent adoptions where legally recognized ties exist between the child and the parent not married to the adopting individual. According to an EFA study, eighty-five percent of all *adoption simples* are either interfamilial or stepparent adoptions. Little is known about the former phenomenon, but, in the sample studied, eighty percent of the latter adoptions occurred when the child had reached majority. Presumably, in such cases, the adopting stepparent sought legal recognition (including inheritance rights) of emotional bonds developed during the adoptee's minority. Additionally, a small number of international adoptions result in the pronouncement of an *adoption simple*, usually against the adoptive parents' wishes.

In France, judges both determine the form of an adoption and make the formal pronouncement in open court. One court, describing the choice between *adoption plénière* and *adoption simple*, declared *adoption simple* to be the solution whenever granting an *adoption plénière* "would accentuate the discrepancy between biological reality and legal fiction and tend to jeopardize the psycho-emotional equilibrium of the child...." According to Jacqueline Rubellin-Devichi, a prominent French family law scholar, every adoption fits this description. Thus, she would expand the use of *adoption simple*. Rubellin-Devichi proposes—thus far unsuccessfully—a reformation of the *Code Civil*, requiring each adoption to begin as an *adoption simple* for a two- to three-year period, in order to foster the development of emotional ties between the child and the biological family.

Implicit in Rubellin-Devichi's proposal is the belief that adoptive affiliation differs so significantly from biological parenthood that it warrants different legal treatment. While this belief may be unsettling for many in the United States, it is, in fact, the same belief that underlies many "open adoptions" in the United States. Indeed, Rubellin-Devichi's proposed reform resembles an attempt to codify and foster "open adoption" in France.

Note

1. *Critique.* Consider the definition of *adoption simple* and the author's characterization of Rubellin-Devichi's proposal as an attempt to codify open adoption. Does that characterization underestimate the impact of the proposal? Do you think such a proposal would be usefully employed in the United States? Would the use of a mechanism such as *adoption simple* be a constructive option for step-parent adoptions? What would be the justification for employing this form in international adoptions, against the wishes of the adoptive parents?

In another part of the article, the author observes that "French adoption law and governmental family policy reflect a societal consensus on the central and intrinsic importance of biological relationships." *Id.* at 1069. Does the retention of *adoption simple* and its utilization in the manner described support this assessment?

Islamic nations have created an alternative institution, kafala, to provide for children in need of care. Kafala is a type of legal fostering, through which "a family may take a child to live with them on a permanent legal basis." Cynthia Price Cohen, Introductory Note to the United Nations Convention on the Rights of the Child, 28 I.L.M. 1448, 1451 (1989). Under Islamic law, kafala requires fulfilling the parental duties of feeding, educating, and caring for a child, "in the same way a father would do for his son."

Imad-ad-Dean Ahmad, *The Islamic View of Adoption, in* Adoption Factbook III 245 (Connaught Marshner ed., 1999). A child fostered through kafala may not use the name of the fostering family or inherit from them. Instead, the child retains inheritance rights from the birth family. Islamic law also requires that a child fostered through kafala be given information about his family of origin, as identity under Islamic law is defined by blood. *Id.* at 246; Cohen, *supra,* at 1451.

Some Muslim scholars contend that adoption itself is not prohibited by Islamic law, but merely classified as *mubah,* an act toward which religion is indifferent. Nevertheless, with the exception of Tunisia, the institution of adoption has not been incorporated into the legal system of most Islamic countries which apply the Shari'a personal status provisions. David Pearl, Textbook on Muslim Law 82 (1979); Jamal J. Nasir, The Islamic Law of Personal Status 166–67 (2d ed. 1990).

Differing views on adoption between Islamic and non-Islamic nations have been a factor that requires careful negotiation and drafting when creating multinational conventions regarding adoption practices. For example, because Islam does not recognize a "right to adoption," representatives from Islamic countries in the Working Group drafting the Convention on the Rights of the Child raised objections to the inclusion of some of the provisions related to adoption. Cohen, *supra,* at 1451. The language of the first sentence of Article 21, beginning "States that recognize and/or permit the system of adoption," reflects one compromise that was reached. Section C describes additional conflicts that emerged in the drafting process, reflecting these divergent views on the type of system that best serves the interests of a child in need of care.

B. Termination of Parental Rights

Although a myriad of issues are related to the topic of termination of parental rights, this section will address only two, both of which have received significant judicial, legislative, and media attention over the past two decades, within and outside of the United States: (1) the circumstances under which a birth mother can give and revoke a voluntary consent to adoption, and (2) the rights of putative fathers of children voluntarily placed by their birth mothers for adoption.

1. Giving and Revoking Voluntary Consent

In the United States, absent evidence of parental abandonment, mistreatment, or other sufficient grounds, a child cannot be placed for adoption without the consent of the child's birth mother. When the child is born in-wedlock, or, as will be explored in the next subsection, under some circumstances when the child is born out-of-wedlock, consent must similarly be obtained from the birth father as well. Severance of parental rights, absent consent or sufficient grounds for termination, would violate a parent's constitutional right, under substantive due process, to enjoy a relationship with his or her child.

The manner in which consent must be given, and the circumstances under which it can be revoked, however, are generally within the legislative powers of each state to determine, and thus vary significantly from state to state. In most states, a consent given by a birth mother prior to the birth of a child would not be valid, although Alabama permits a mother to give pre-birth consent, revocable within five days of the child's birth. Ala. Code § 26-10A-12 (2002). In some states, an irrevocable consent may be given by a birth mother immediately after birth. *E.g.,* Okla. Stat. tit. 10, § 7503-2.2 (2001). In many others, the waiting period for a birth mother to execute a valid consent is very short. *E.g.,* Ariz. Rev. Stat. Ann. § 8-107(B) (West Supp. 2002) (72 hours); Mass. Gen. Laws Ann. ch. 210, § 2 (West Supp. 2002) (4 days); Ohio Rev. Code Ann § 3107.08(A) (West 2002) (72 hours). Several states permit a father of a child born out of wedlock (frequently referred to as a putative father) to execute a consent prior to a child's birth. *E.g.,* Okla. Stat. tit. 10, § 7503-2.2 (2001); N.C. Gen. Stat. § 48-3-701 (2002). Valid consent may not be given for the adoption of an Indian child in any state, however, either before or within 10 days after the child's birth, as a matter of federal law. Indian Child Welfare Act, 25 U.S.C. § 1913(a) (1994).

Some states require that a consent be executed before a judge, *e.g,.* Ohio Rev. Code Ann. § 3107.081 (West 2002); Okla. Stat. tit. 10, § 7503-2.4 (2001), while others do not. *E.g.,* Ariz. Rev. Stat. Ann. § 8-107(B) (West Supp. 2002). Generally, the counseling afforded to a birth parent prior to giving consent is left to the discretion of the agency or other intermediary facilitating the adoption, rather than prescribed by statute. The majority of states permit adoptions to be facilitated independently, usually by private attorneys, as well as by licensed state agencies.

Traditionally in the United States, a valid consent to adoption could be revoked at any time for any reason, up until the time that the final decree of adoption was entered. In recent years, however, the majority of states have greatly reduced the time in which a consent may be revoked, or even made the consent irrevocable upon execution, absent proof of fraud or duress. Ira Ellman, Paul Kurtz & Elizabeth Scott, Cases and Materials on Family Law 1415 (2d ed. 2000). *See, e.g.,* Okla. Stat. tit. 10, § 7503-2.7 (2001) (consents signed before a judge after birth are irrevocable when signed); N.C. Gen. Stat. § 48-3-706 (2002) (revocable within 7 days). New York differentiates between consents executed before a judge, which are irrevocable immediately, and other consents, which are irrevocable thirty days after commencement of the adoption proceeding, unless a birth mother has given notice within the thirty days of her intent to revoke. Even when revocation is permitted, however, it does not always ensure that the child will be returned to the birth parent. In some states, including New York, revocation of parental consent merely triggers a "best interests" hearing, in which the court determines whether it is in the best interests of the child to proceed with the adoption or be returned to the parent. N.Y. Dom. Rel. Law § 115-b (McKinney Supp. 2002).

Some European nations take quite a different approach. In France, both birth parents have three months to revoke their consent to adoption. If a mother wishes to place a child for adoption at birth, the child is put in foster care for three months at state expense, affording the mother time to reconsider her decision. Schwartz, *supra,* at 1083. What policy interests are served by these different approaches?

Consider the following excerpt from a decision by the Supreme Court of Ireland, reflecting the concern of the Irish courts and legislature for affording a birth mother ample time to reach a decision.

E.F. & F.F. v. An Bord Uchtala
96/93 Transcript (Ir. Sup. Ct. 1996)

Keane, J.

The sad history of this matter began with the admission of the...Appellant (whom I shall call "the mother") to the National Maternity Hospital,...Dublin on a date in November, 1989, where, in the early hours of the following morning, she gave birth to a little girl. The latter, who is at the centre of this dispute, I shall refer to as "Mary."... The mother was not married but had a relationship of some years standing with Mary's father, DF (whom I shall refer to as "the father") and by whom she had another child, then aged just thirteen months.

On the mother's discharge from the hospital, Mary was placed in foster care. On January 11, 1990, the mother signed a form of consent to the placement of Mary for adoption. Four days later, Mary was placed with the Applicants/Respondents (whom I shall refer to as "the prospective adopters"). At some time subsequent to this, but certainly no later than September 18 1990, the mother withdrew her consent to Mary's adoption and has consistently refused since then to consent to Mary's adoption. On the 26 February, 1992 the prospective adopters issued the present proceedings seeking an order dispensing with the mother's consent to the making of an adoption order by the Respondents (whom I shall refer to as 'the Board'). After a hearing lasting four days in the High Court, Costello J., as he then was, made such an order. From that decision, the mother has now appealed to this court.

* * *

The Facts

[Ed. Note: At the time of the child's birth, the mother was living with her own mother and her thirteen-month-old son in a small house. The father slept there most nights and ate meals there, although he had his own house in the same town. The grandmother made it clear she was not happy about the prospect of a new baby coming home. Mother received no medical care during the pregnancy.

On the day of the baby's birth in early November 1989, the mother told a hospital social worker she wanted to have the baby adopted. She later testified at the hearing that while she knew she could not bring the baby home, she thought that the social worker would get somebody to mind her for a while. She said that while there was not really room for the baby in her mother's two bedroom house, she thought that perhaps she and the father could get public housing for the father, herself, and the two children.

The next day she was visited by Ms. Fahy, a social worker with St. Bridget's Adoption Society, whom she again told that she would like to have the baby adopted. Ms. Fahy testified that she explained to the mother at that time that adoption was a difficult decision, and the normal practice was to arrange foster care to give the mother time to think about what she would do. Although the mother initially desired immediate placement in an adoptive home, she then agreed to foster care. The mother later testified that at the time she thought adoption and fostering were the same, and that she understood the baby would be cared for by a nice family before she went to her adoptive parents. The mother subsequently signed a consent for foster placement, in the presence of Sister Benignus, the agency administrator, and the next day the baby was placed with a foster family. Ms. Fahy later testified that the mother told Ms. Fahy on the way to the foster home that the father had not taken any particular interest in the first baby, a statement the mother later denied, and that he was opposed to adoptive placement.

Ms. Fahy and Sister Benignus later testified that the normal period of foster care was six to eight weeks, and although the Health Boards made arrangements for longer periods of foster care, that option was not discussed with the mother.

The mother never requested contact with the baby, although she was advised she could have visits arranged through the agency.

Ms. Fahy visited the mother in late November, in which she asked if the father was willing to consent. In January, Ms. Fahy wrote the mother to ask if she had made a decision, and requested a letter from the father, in the form of a solicitor's letter, indicating he did not object. In mid-January, the mother met with Ms. Fahy and Sister Benignus at the agency office and signed a consent to place the child for adoption. Attached to the form was a memorandum explaining that an adoption order transfers all parental rights and duties to the adopters. It also stated that under the laws, an adoption order would not be made without the mother's consent. It further provided:

> Section 3 of the Adoption Act 1974 provides that if a child is given for adoption, and a person whose consent to the making of the adoption order is required fails, neglects or refuses to give consent, or withdraws a consent already given, the applicant for the adoption order may apply to the High Court and, if that court is satisfied that it is in the best interest of the child to do so, it may give custody of the child to the person who has applied for the adoption order and may authorise (the Board) to dispense with such consent, whereupon (the Board) may make the adoption order.
>
> A consent may be withdrawn at any time before the making of an adoption order.
>
> In order to ensure, therefore, that you will be informed of any proposal to have the child adopted, you should notify the Society of any change in address.

Ms. Fahy later testified that on the day the mother signed the consent to adoptive placement (Form 10), the mother had told Ms. Fahy that she wanted the child placed for adoption because the home was cramped, her son was "a handful," that she had to care for her elderly mother, and that the father would not be involved with the child's rearing. She also told Ms. Fahy that the father had initially objected, but that now he supported her decision. Ms. Fahy further testified that she went through the form with her to make sure she understood it. When asked during her testimony later about how she explained the paragraph about the meaning of the consent, Ms. Fahy replied:

> A. Right. That if a girl places her child for adoption and a couple who...sorry. If a girl places her child for adoption, her consent is required. Now, if she fails, neglects or refuses to give consent to [sic] takes back her consent that was already been given, [sic] the adopters may apply to the High Court for an adoption order, and if the court is satisfied that it is best for the child to remain with the adopters, that the High Court may authorise the Adoption Board to dispense with the natural mother's consent and to authorise the Adoption Board to make an adoption order.

Sister Benignus also later testified that on that same day, she had met with the mother, discussed other options for the baby's care, and satisfied herself that the mother wished to place the baby for adoption.

The mother later testified that she remembered being asked if she understood the form and had replied that she did, although she did not really understand it at the time. She testified later that she though she was just placing the baby for a while longer, because the form was titled Placement Form, although she admitted she had no idea how much longer that "while" would be. She took a copy of the form with her that day.

At the time the mother signed the form, she gave the agency a document signed by the father which stated, "I have no objections to (the child) being placed for adoption." The text was in the mother's handwriting. The mother later testified that the father signed it without knowing what it was, in blank, and that she wrote in the text afterwards.

The child was thereafter placed with the prospective adoptive family, a family with whom the agency had previously placed two boys.

In June, the social worker wrote to the mother asking for a meeting, and received no reply. In July, she wrote again, and later met with the mother at her home. Prior to this meeting, the mother had called Sister Benignus and suggested she might want the baby back. The mother's account was that she said she did want the baby back.

Ms. Fahy later testified that when she subsequently met with the mother in July 1990, the mother stated that she and the father were in the process of buying a house and thinking of asking for the baby back. Ms. Fahy testified that they discussed her original decision, and that at the end of the conversation the mother had said she would leave the baby where she was and sign the final papers. The mother's testimony about that meeting was that Ms. Fahy tried to persuade her to change her mind about seeking the baby's return, but that she would not.

Ms. Fahy, Sister Benignus, and the mother all testified, however, that at a subsequent meeting at the agency in mid-September 1990, the mother stated that she wanted the baby back and would not proceed with the adoption. In late September, she formally withdrew her consent in writing. The prospective adopters were subsequently informed, and on advice of their solicitor, refused to return the child.

In October, the government adoption board, An Bord Uchtala, having been informed of the situation by the agency, wrote to the mother advising her that if the adopters refused to give up custody, she could institute legal proceedings, and that it was in her interest to do so as quickly as possible. She was also advised that the adopters could apply to the High Court for an order dispensing with parental consent. Information concerning how to apply for legal aid was included.

Although Sister Benignus requested another meeting with the parents in October, the mother replied that the father was out of the country. No meeting occurred until March 1991, at which time the parents reaffirmed their desire to reclaim the child. Following that meeting, Sister Benignus wrote to them urging them to reconsider out of love for the child. In April the mother requested to see the child. Over the summer of 1991, the mother contacted a social worker in her home town about the situation. At another meeting with the parents and Ms. Fahy in February, 1992, it was clear that neither the parents nor the prospective adopters would change their minds about the situation. In February 1992, the prospective adopters sought an order to adopt without the mother's consent. In November 1992, a proceeding was filed by the mother seeking the child's return.

In addition to testimony regarding the above events, a child psychiatrist testified on behalf of the adoptive parents that the child was psychologically healthy and normal, that she only showed anxiety when separated from her prospective parents, that she was well settled in a happy home, and that he believed that separation from them would be like losing her parents, and would cause greatly heightened anxiety and have a gravely damaging effect on her. He further stated that "the absence of a blood link between the child and the prospective adopters was of little significance when compared to the depth of bonding which he considered had taken place after three years."

The trial judge found the testimony of the mother unreliable, and issued a finding that when she signed the consent on January 11, 1990, "she did so with full knowledge of the consequences, that she fully understood that the proposed adopters could apply to have her consent to have the adoption dispensed with and that if they succeeded she would thereby lose her baby...." He also found that he did not accept the mother's account of the circumstances under which the father signed the consent, and found that at the time he had no objection. He went on to find that even assuming that the mother and father would marry in the future, it was not in the child's best interests to be removed from the home in which she was living for the past three years. He thus granted the order dispensing with consent. Although the parents filed a notice of appeal promptly, the case was not heard by the Supreme Court for another three years, due to the inability of the parents to obtain a transcript because of the absence of legal aid. At the time of the Supreme Court hearing, the child was almost seven years old.]

* * *

On behalf of the mother, [her attorney]...submitted that the trial judge, in finding that the mother had made a fully informed and free decision, failed to have regard to a number of critical matters...:

(1) The absence of any pre-natal counselling of the mother and the failure of the adoption society to compensate for this failure by way of post-natal counselling;

(2) The signing of a consent to fostering the day after the birth of Mary;

(3) The failure of the [agency] to apprise the mother of the possibility of long-term fostering...;

(4) The almost total lack of communication by the [agency]...with the mother from the beginning of the fostering to the signing of the consent to placing for adoption;

(5) The decision of the [agency]...to proceed where they were aware that there was a continuing relationship between the father and the mother and the only evidence of the consent of the father was an unorthodox form...;

(6) the failure of the [agency] to explain to the mother in clear and unmistakable terms the consequences of her consent for placing Mary for adoption....

* * *

The principles of law applicable in this case are clear. As a result of the legal machinery provided by the Adoption Acts, 1952 to 1988, the consent of the natural mother of a child to its adoption is required at two stages of the process; first, when the child is being placed for adoption with prospective adopters and, secondly, when the Board are asked to make an adoption order. The second consent may not validly be given until six weeks after the birth and must be given not earlier than three months before the application for adoption. While the Board must satisfy itself before making the adoption order that, inter alia, the mother has consented and understands the nature and effect of the consent and of the adoption order, the combined effect of Section 15 of the 1952 Act, as amended by Section 8 of the 1974 Act, and Section 3 of the Adoption Act 1974 is to enable the Board to proceed with the adoption without the consent of the mother [pursuant to Section 3.]

* * *

Conclusions

...As to the first issue, i.e., the validity of the mother's consent to Mary's being placed for adoption, the conduct of the Adoption Society has been severely criticised on the hearing of the appeal and, it has to be said, with at least some justification. The mother agreed to Mary being placed in foster care almost within hours of her birth and at a stage when she must have undoubtedly been in a vulnerable condition. While, as she accepted herself, it was simply not a practical proposition to bring her baby home at that stage, the fact remained that she had a relationship with the father and had a child by him who was then thirteen months old. One would have expected the Society through its social workers within a relatively short period to visit both mother and father with a view to assessing the possibility of Mary being returned to them. Yet the only contact, apart from a Christmas card, established by the Society was the visit by Mrs. Fahy to the mother on November 23, the details of which she (Mrs. Fahy) did not recollect. The evidence of that meeting was that of the mother who said that the principal concern of Mrs. Fahy was with whether the father was prepared to consent to a placing for adoption. It is not unfair to say that, so far as the evidence goes, no serious consideration seems to have been given by the Adoption Society to the possibility of the child being restored to its parents at any time between the handing over to foster care and the signing of the Form 10 by the mother on January 11.

It must also be said that the letters written by Mrs. Fahy and Sister Benignus to the mother from July onwards (when she had evinced, at the very least, a tentative desire to have her baby back) reflect a somewhat disquieting approach on the part of the Adoption Society. Far from taking steps to see whether that obviously desirable reunion could be effected, at the cost of some natural disappointment and frustration to the prospective adopters, they seem to have seen their function as persuading the mother to continue with the adoption. It is regrettable that it is necessary to cite again the remarks of Walsh, J. in G v. An Bord Uchtala, at p 82:

> Doctors, nurses, social workers, those working in hospitals, adoption societies and others concerned in these cases must always keep uppermost in their minds that the unmarried mother and her baby each have all the fundamental rights of other human beings and also those rights which spring from the relationship of the mother to her child and of the child to her mother and that all these rights must be respected. Furthermore, it must never be overlooked that the Oireachtas instituted legal adoption in the interests of the child and not in the interests of those wishing to adopt a child legally, albeit for the most laudable reasons, and thereby to make a child, or additional children, members of their family.

Ultimately, however, the crucial issue on this appeal is as to whether, having regard to the legal principles already referred to, the clear and unambiguous finding by the trial judge that the consent of the mother was a free and fully informed surrender of her rights should be set aside by this court. The trial judge made it clear that, to the extent that the evidence of Sister Benignus and Mrs. Fahy was in conflict with that of the mother and father, he preferred to rely on the evidence of the former. That is patently a finding as to credibility with which this court cannot interfere.

It is, however, urged upon us that, even accepting all that Mrs. Fahy said in her evidence as to what transpired at the meeting with the mother on January 11, it remains the fact that she never (a) told the mother in plain and unequivocal language that if a successful Section 3 application was brought by the prospective adopters, she would never see her child again; and (b) told the mother in express language that the effect of a consent to placement was that her legal rights to custody of, or access to, her child were suspended for so long as the child remained lawfully in the custody of the prospective adopters and, in the event of a Section 3 order being made, would be extinguished forever, assuming the adoption order was duly made by the Board.

As to the first submission, it is undoubtedly the case that, while Mrs. Fahy said that she took the mother through every line of the Form 10 memorandum and did not content herself with simply reading the passage relating to Section 3 but endeavoured, as best she could, to explain its effect to her, she did not suggest that she said, in so many words, that if a successful Section 3 of the Adoption Act 1974 application were brought she (the mother) might never see her child again. It is also to be said that the wording of the passage relating to Section 3 in the Form 10 in use at the time might well have been confusing for someone unaccustomed to dealing with legal phraseology.... It would also be clearly preferable for a person explaining the effect of the placement to the mother to use blunt and uncompromising language: she should be told that, while she may withdraw her consent, the prospective adopters may always apply under Section 3 and that if an order is made under that Section followed by an adoption order, she will lose the custody of her child forever. However, while language of that precise nature was not used, on her own admission, by Mrs. Fahy in the present case, the trial judge, who had the opportunity of seeing and hearing the witnesses, was clearly satisfied that the consequences of a Section 3 order were fully explained to the mother and, most importantly, understood by her. That is a finding of fact with which this court cannot interfere.

* * *

It is accepted that, if the trial judge was correct in his view, as I am satisfied he was, that the consent to the placement was validly given, he had then to consider whether dispensing with the consent of the mother to adoption would be in the best interests of the child. I have already referred to the evidence of Dr. Byrne in this context and also to the evidence as to the circumstances of the adoptive parents. I am satisfied that there was clear and indeed cogent evidence on which the trial judge was entitled to conclude, as he did, that it would be in the best interests of Mary and the Board should be authorised to dispense with the mother's consent and that she should remain in the custody of the prospective adopters until such time as an adoption order was made.... [T]he order of the High Court must be affirmed.]

* * *

Notes and Questions

1. *Systemic Comparison.* Compare Ireland's consent and revocation procedures with the approach taken by many U.S. states and France, to the extent those systems are described above. What are the major advantages and drawbacks of each system? To the extent you can compare with the limited information provided, which system, in your opinion, most successfully serves the interests of the child? Does your view of that de-

pend on the extent to which you see the child's needs best served by biological or psychological relationships? Is that dichotomy too simplistic to evaluate the complexities of the relationships affected by the law of consent and revocation?

If this adoptive placement had occurred under the law of the various states described above, how might the subsequent conflict have been resolved? Are there aspects of each system from which you would choose to draw, if you were devising a new legislative scheme?

2. Rights of Putative Fathers

Traditionally, many nations, including the United States, permitted birth mothers to unilaterally place out-of-wedlock children for adoption, affording the birth father little or no say in the matter. In the early 1980s, within one year of each other, the U.S. Supreme Court and the European Court of Human Rights issued landmark decisions that would set the parameters for recognition of the rights of putative fathers in regard to the adoptive placement of their children.

Lehr v. Robertson, 463 U.S. 248 (1983), was actually the fourth in a line of U.S. Supreme Court cases to address the parental rights of fathers of children born out-of-wedlock. A decade earlier, in Stanley v. Illinois, 405 U.S. 645 (1972), the Court had examined the claim of a father who was denied custody of his two youngest children, who had been automatically made wards of the state following the death of their mother, his partner of eighteen years. Despite the fact that Mr. Stanley lived with these children all of their lives and fully participated in their rearing, under Illinois law, as an out-of-wedlock father, he had been presumed unfit. Finding that his custodial relationship with the children was denied without a hearing, the Court held that depriving him of the opportunity to present evidence regarding his fitness as a parent, a right afforded other parents, violated his rights under both procedural due process and equal protection.

Like *Lehr*, the next two decisions involved step-parent adoptions. In Quilloin v. Walcott, 434 U.S. 246 (1978), a father challenged the adoption of his eleven-year-old daughter, which the Georgia court granted despite his objection. Although Mr. Quilloin had received notice of the proceeding and had the opportunity to argue at the hearing that the adoption was not in the child's best interests, he asserted that his substantive due process rights were infringed when his parental rights were terminated without a finding that he was unfit. He also asserted a violation of equal protection, contending that Georgia law regarding the grounds for adoption afforded greater protection to mothers of out-of-wedlock children and married fathers. Because this father had supported and visited his child only sporadically and had never tried to bring a legitimation proceeding until after the adoption proceeding was filed, the Court rejected his claims, ruling that he was not similarly situated to either a mother or a married father. The next year, however, a successful constitutional challenge to a step-parent adoption was brought by an out-of-wedlock father who had lived with his partner and two children before their separation, supported his children thereafter, and had even had custody of the children following the separation for a period of time. In Caban v. Mohammed, 441 U.S. 380 (1979), the Court determined that Mr. Caban was denied equal protection by a New York statute that permitted adoption of his children without his consent or unfitness, but protected their mother from similar treatment. The stage was set for *Lehr*.

Lehr v. Robertson
463 U.S. 248 (1983)

[Ed. Note: Jonathon Lehr and Loraine Robertson lived together for two years before the birth of Jessica on November 9, 1976. The mother openly acknowledged Mr. Lehr was Jessica's father, and subsequently reported him as the father to the New York Social Services Department. Although Lehr visited the mother and child every day while they were in the hospital, after she was discharged, the mother terminated the relationship. Eight months later she married Mr. Robertson. During the first two years of Jessica's life, Mr. Lehr asserts that he had only sporadic success in locating the mother and child, and from August 1977 until August 1978 he was unable to locate them at all, until he found them with the help of a detective agency. He contends that at this time he offered to provide financial assistance and set up a trust fund for Jessica, but the mother refused, and would not permit him to visit. He hired an attorney, who in December 1978 contacted the mother on his behalf, threatening legal action. On December 21, 1978, perhaps in response to this letter, the mother and step-father brought an adoption proceeding in Ulster County, New York.

In January 1979, Mr. Lehr brought a paternity proceeding, seeking an order of support and reasonable visitation in Westchester County. Ms. Robertson was served in February, at which time her attorney informed the Ulster County judge of the paternity proceeding. The Ulster County judge then entered an order staying the Westchester County paternity action pending ruling on a motion to change its venue to Ulster County. Mr. Lehr's receipt of notice of that motion on March 3, 1979 was his first notification of the adoption proceeding. On March 7, 1979, Mr. Lehr's attorney phoned the Ulster County judge regarding his plans to seek a stay of the adoption proceeding, and learned that the Ulster County judge had entered the adoption order that morning. On the basis of the adoption order, the paternity action was dismissed. Mr. Lehr subsequently moved to vacate the adoption order, asserting it was obtained by fraud and in violation of his right to advance notice of the adoption proceeding under the Due Process and Equal Protection Clauses of the Federal Constitution.

New York law by statute afforded certain classes of out-of-wedlock fathers a right to notice of adoption proceedings. These included fathers who (1) registered with the state's putative father registry; (2) had been adjudicated the father; (3) had been identified on the child's birth certificate; (4) lived with the mother and child and held themselves out as the father; (5) had been identified as the father by the mother in a sworn statement; or (6) were married to the mother before the child was six months old.]

The Due Process Claim

The Fourteenth Amendment provides that no State shall deprive any person of life, liberty, or property without due process of law. When that Clause is invoked in a novel context, it is our practice to begin the inquiry with a determination of the precise nature of the private interest that is threatened by the State.... Only after that interest has been identified, can we properly evaluate the adequacy of the State's process....

The intangible fibers that connect parent and child have infinite variety. They are woven throughout the fabric of our society, providing it with strength, beauty, and flexibility. It is self-evident that they are sufficiently vital to merit constitutional protection in appropriate cases. In deciding whether this is such a case, however, we must consider the broad framework that has traditionally been used to resolve the legal problems arising from the parent-child relationship.

…The institution of marriage has played a critical role both in defining the legal entitlements of family members and in developing the decentralized structure of our democratic society. In recognition of that role, and as part of their general overarching concern for serving the best interests of children, state laws almost universally express an appropriate preference for the formal family.

In some cases, however, this Court has held that the Federal Constitution supersedes state law and provides even greater protection for certain formal family relationships....

There are also a few cases in which this Court has considered the extent to which the Constitution affords protection to the relationship between natural parents and children born out of wedlock.... This Court has examined the extent to which a natural father's biological relationship with his illegitimate child receives protection under the Due Process Clause in precisely three cases.... [The Court proceeded to review its holdings in *Stanley, Quilloin,* and *Caban.* Ed.]

The difference between the developed parent-child relationship that was implicated in *Stanley* and *Caban,* and the potential relationship involved in *Quilloin* and this case, is both clear and significant. When an unwed father demonstrates a full commitment to the responsibilities of parenthood by "com[ing] forward to participate in the rearing of his child," his interest in personal contact with his child acquires substantial protection under the due process clause.... At that point it may be said that he "act[s] as a father toward his children."... But the mere existence of a biological link does not merit equivalent constitutional protection. The actions of judges neither create nor sever genetic bonds. "[T]he importance of the familial relationship, to the individuals involved and to the society, stems from the emotional attachments that derive from the intimacy of daily association, and from the role it plays in 'promot[ing] a way of life' through the instruction of children as well as from the fact of blood relationship."...

The significance of the biological connection is that it offers the natural father an opportunity that no other male possesses to develop a relationship with his offspring. If he grasps that opportunity and accepts some measure of responsibility for the child's future, he may enjoy the blessings of the parent-child relationship and make uniquely valuable contributions to the child's development. If he fails to do so, the Federal Constitution will not automatically compel a state to listen to his opinion of where the child's best interests lie.

In this case, we are not assessing the constitutional adequacy of New York's procedures for terminating a developed relationship. Appellant has never had any significant custodial, personal, or financial relationship with Jessica, and he did not seek to establish a legal tie until after she was two years old. We are concerned only with whether New York has adequately protected his opportunity to form such a relationship.

The most effective protection of the putative father's opportunity to develop a relationship with his child is provided by the laws that authorize formal marriage and govern its consequences. But the availability of that protection is, of course, dependent on the will of both parents of the child. Thus, New York has adopted a special statutory scheme to protect the unmarried father's interest in assuming a responsible role in the future of his child.

After this Court's decision in *Stanley,* the New York Legislature appointed a special commission to recommend legislation that would accommodate both the interests of biological fathers in their children and the children's interest in prompt and certain adoption procedures. The commission recommended, and the legislature enacted, a statutory adoption scheme that automatically provides notice to seven categories of putative fathers who are likely to have assumed some responsibility for the care of their natural children. If this scheme were likely to omit many responsible fathers, and if qualification for notice were beyond the control of an interested putative father, it might be thought procedurally inadequate. Yet, as all of the New York courts that reviewed this matter observed, the right to receive notice was completely within appellant's control. By mailing a postcard to the putative father registry, he could have guaranteed that he would receive notice of any proceedings to adopt Jessica. The possibility that he may have failed to do so because of his ignorance of the law cannot be a sufficient reason for criticizing the law itself. The New York legislature concluded that a more open-ended notice requirement would merely complicate the adoption process, threaten the privacy interests of unwed mothers, create the risk of unnecessary controversy, and impair the desired finality of adoption decrees. Regardless of whether we would have done likewise if we were legislators instead of judges, we surely cannot characterize the state's conclusion as arbitrary.

Appellant argues, however, that even if the putative father's opportunity to establish a relationship with an illegitimate child is adequately protected by the New York statutory scheme in the normal case, he was nevertheless entitled to special notice because the court and the mother knew that he had filed an affiliation proceeding in another court. This argument amounts to nothing more than an indirect attack on the notice provisions of the New York statute. The legitimate state interests in facilitating the adoption of young children and having the adoption proceeding completed expeditiously that underlie the entire statutory scheme also justify a trial judge's determination to require all interested parties to adhere precisely to the procedural requirements of the statute. The Constitution does not require either a trial judge or a litigant to give special notice to nonparties who are presumptively capable of asserting and protecting their own rights. Since the New York statutes adequately protected appellant's inchoate interest in establishing a relationship with Jessica, we find no merit in the claim that his constitutional rights were offended because the family court strictly complied with the notice provisions of the statute.

The Equal Protection Claim.

The concept of equal justice under law requires the State to govern impartially. The sovereign may not draw distinctions between individuals based solely on differences that are irrelevant to a legitimate governmental objective.... Specifically, it may not subject men and women to disparate treatment when there is no substantial relation between the disparity and an important state purpose.

The legislation at issue in this case...is intended to establish procedures for adoptions. Those procedures are designed to promote the best interests of the child, protect the rights of interested third parties, and ensure promptness and finality. To serve those ends, the legislation guarantees to certain people the right to veto an adoption and the right to prior notice of any adoption proceeding. The mother of an illegitimate child is always within that favored class, but only certain putative fathers are included. Appellant contends that the gender-based distinction is invidious.

As we noted above, the existence or nonexistence of a substantial relationship between parent and child is a relevant criterion in evaluating both the rights of the parent and the best interests of the child.... Because, like the father in *Quilloin*, appellant has never established a substantial relationship with his daughter, the New York statutes at issue in this case did not operate to deny appellant equal protection.

We have held that these statutes may not constitutionally be applied in that class of cases where the mother and father are in fact similarly situated with regard to their relationship with the child. In *Caban*..., the Court held that it violated the Equal Protection Clause to grant the mother a veto over the adoption of a four-year-old girl and a six-year-old boy, but not to grant a veto to their father, who had admitted paternity and had participated in the rearing of the children. The Court made it clear, however, that if the father had not "come forward to participate in the rearing of his child, nothing in the Equal Protection Clause [would] preclude...the State from withholding from him the privilege of vetoing the adoption of that child."...

Jessica's parents are not like the parents involved in *Caban*. Whereas appellee had a continuous custodial responsibility for Jessica, appellant never established any custodial, personal, or financial relationship with her. If one parent has an established custodial relationship with the child and the other parent has either abandoned or never established a relationship, the Equal Protection Clause does not prevent a state from according the two parents different legal rights.

The judgment of the New York Court of Appeals is Affirmed.

The next year, a similar case came before the European Court of Human Rights. Mr. Keegan, the father of an out-of-wedlock child placed for adoption in infancy, challenged the decision of a court in the Republic of Ireland to permit the adoption of his child, without his knowledge or consent.

Keegan v. Ireland
290 Eur. Ct. H. R. (ser. A) (1994)

[Ed. Note: Mr. Keegan lived with his girlfriend, Miss V., from February 1987 to February 1988. Around Christmas 1987 they decided to have a child. On February 14, 1988, they became engaged to be married. One week later V. confirmed that she was pregnant. Shortly afterward, the relationship broke down and they separated. Their child was born on September 29, 1988 and Mr. Keegan visited V. and his daughter at the private nursing home when she was one day old. Two weeks later he attempted to visit them at the home of V.'s parents, but was not permitted to see either of them.

During the pregnancy, V. had made arrangements to have the child adopted. On November 17, 1988, she placed the child with an adoption agency, notifying Mr. Keegan of her action a week later. The relevant provisions of Irish law at that time permitted a child born out-of-wedlock to be placed for adoption without the consent of the father, unless he had been appointed a guardian. Mr. Keegan therefore filed legal proceedings to be appointed the child's guardian, in order to challenge the proposed adoption. He was subsequently appointed guardian by the Circuit Court and awarded legal custody. This decision was upheld by the High Court, but on appeal, the Irish Supreme Court ruled that the father's objection should not be considered if the prospective adopters could achieve a substantially better quality of welfare for the child. The case was remanded to the High Court, who heard testimony by a consulting psychiatrist that if the placement with the prospective adopters was disturbed after a period of over one year, the child would be likely to suffer trauma and have a difficult time forming trusting relationships. The High Court then declined to appoint Mr. Keegan guardian and the adoption order was subsequently made. Mr. Keegan then brought a proceeding with the

European Commission of Human Rights (*see* Chapter One, Section B.2.d., for a discussion of the former role of the Commission), which unanimously held that there had been a violation of Articles 8 and 6.1.]

* * *

II. Alleged violation of Article 8

41. The applicant alleged a violation of his right to respect for family life contrary to Article 8 of the Convention which provides:

> 1. Everyone has the right to respect for his private and family life, his home, and his correspondence.

> 2. There shall be no interference by a public authority with the exercise of this right except such as is in accordance with the law and is necessary in a democratic society in the interests of national security, public safety or the economic well-being of the country, for the prevention of disorder or crime, for the protection of health or morals, or for the protection of the rights and freedoms of others.

A. Applicability of Article 8

* * *

44. The Court recalls that the notion of the "family" in this provision is not confined solely to marriage-based relationships and may encompass other de facto "family ties" where the parties are living together outside of marriage.... A child born out of such a relationship is ipso iure part of that "family" unit from the moment of his birth and by the very fact of it. There thus exists between the child and his parents a bond amounting to family life even if at the time of his or her birth the parents are no longer co-habiting or if their relationship has then ended....

45. In the present case, the relationship between the applicant and the child's mother lasted for two years during one of which they co-habited. Moreover, the conception of their child was the result of a deliberate decision and they had also planned to get married.... Their relationship at this time had thus the hallmark of family life for the purposes of Article 8. The fact that it subsequently broke down does not alter this conclusion any more than it would for a couple who were lawfully married and in a similar situation. It follows that from the moment of the child's birth there existed between the applicant and his daughter a bond amounting to family life.

B. Compliance with Article 8

* * *

46. The applicant maintained that the State failed to respect his family life by facilitating the secret placement of his daughter for adoption without his knowledge or consent and by failing to create a legal nexus between himself and his daughter from the moment of birth.

Moreover, the test applied by the Supreme Court to determine the question of custody placed him at a considerable disadvantage vis-a-vis the adoptive parents by requiring him to show that any advantages that they had to offer the child were not important to her welfare. In his submission, to be consistent with Article 8 the law ought to have conferred on him a defeasible right to guardianship and, in any competition for custody with strangers, there ought to have existed a rebuttable legal presumption that the child's welfare was best served by being in his care and custody. He stressed, however, that he was not seeking to overturn the adoption order that had been made in respect of his child.

47. For the Government, Contracting States enjoy a wide margin of appreciation in the area of adoption. The right to respect for family life cannot be interpreted so broadly as

to embrace a right to impose the wishes of the natural father over the interests of the child in disregard of the findings of fact made by the courts.

The applicant, as the Supreme Court has held, had a right to apply to be made a guardian, which right he had exercised. Furthermore, the Supreme Court took into account the blood link between him and his daughter as one of the factors to be weighed in the balance in assessing the child's welfare. In addition, the applicant had every opportunity to present his case and to have his interests considered by the courts. However, in this process the rights and interests of the mother, who had wanted her child to be adopted, had also to be taken into account.

In particular, the Government emphasized that to grant a natural father a defeasible right to guardianship could give rise to complications, anguish and hardship in other cases and concerned a matter of social policy on which the European Court should be reluctant to intervene.

* * *

50. According to the principles set out by the Court in the caselaw, where the existence of a family tie with a child has been established, the State must act in a manner calculated to enable that tie to be developed and legal safeguards must be created that render possible as from the moment of birth the child's integration in his family.... In this context reference may be made to the principle laid down in Article 7 of the United Nations Convention on the Rights of the Child of 20 November 1989 that a child has, as far as possible, the right to be cared for by his or her parents. It is moreover, appropriate to recall that the mutual enjoyment by parent and child of each other's company constitutes a fundamental element of family life even when the relationship between the parents has broken down....

51. In the present case the obligations inherent in Article 8 are closely intertwined, bearing in mind the State's involvement in the adoption process. The fact that Irish law permitted the secret placement of the child for adoption without the applicant's knowledge or consent, leading to the bonding of the child with the proposed adopters and to the subsequent making of an adoption order, amounted to an interference with his right to respect for family life. Such interference is permissible only if the conditions set out in paragraph 2 of Article 8 are satisfied.

* * *

[Ed. Note: The Court concluded that the placement of the child was in accordance with Irish law and in pursuit of legitimate aims.]

55. The Court notes that the applicant was afforded an opportunity under Irish law to claim the guardianship and custody of his daughter and that his interests were fairly weighed in the balance by the High Court in its evaluation of her welfare. However, the essential problem in the present case is not with this assessment but rather with the fact that Irish law permitted the applicant's child to have been placed for adoption shortly after her birth without his knowledge or consent. As has been observed in a similar context, where a child is placed with alternative carers he or she may in the course of time establish with them new bonds which it might not be in his or her interests to disturb or interrupt by reversing a previous decision as to care.... Such a state of affairs not only jeopardised the proper development of the applicant's ties with the child but also set in motion a process which was likely to prove to be irreversible, thereby putting the applicant at a significant disadvantage in his contest with the prospective adopters for the custody of the child.

The Government has advanced no reasons relevant to the welfare of the applicant's daughter to justify such a departure from the principles that govern respect for family ties.

That being so, the Court cannot consider that the interference which it has found with the applicant's right to respect for family life, encompassing the full scope of the State's obligations, was necessary in a democratic society. There has thus been a violation of Article 8.

[Ed. Note: The Court also found a violation of Article 6, which provides a right to a fair hearing by an independent and impartial tribunal, because the father's only right to block the adoption came after he had completed a guardianship proceeding, by which time the scales concerning the child's welfare had tilted in favor of the provider. As a result of the trauma and distress that the proceedings had caused the applicant, the Court awarded him 10,000 Irish pounds in damages, plus reimbursement for legal costs.]

Notes and Questions

1. *Defining the Parameters.* If Johathon Lehr, under similar facts, had brought a claim against a nation that was a party to the European Convention on Human Rights, would he have been successful under the analysis applied in *Keegan?* Was the European Court saying that Article 8 requires that notice and the ability to veto be given to all fathers, regardless of the circumstances? If not, what guidance did the court provide in determining which fathers are entitled to notice and the right to veto an adoptive placement?

How would Mr. Keegan have fared under the test established by the U.S. Supreme Court in *Lehr* and *Quilloin* to determine when a father has a right to notice and the ability to veto an adoptive placement, assuming that he is a fit candidate for custody himself? In what way are the factors important in the *Lehr* analysis different than those used by the European Court in *Keegan?*

To what extent do you think the difference in the resolution of the two cases is due to the different analytical frameworks adopted by the courts under the U.S. constitutional doctrines of procedural due process and equal protection, and Articles 6 and 8 of the European Convention on Human Rights?

To what extent do you think they are a function of the different roles each court fulfills, one interpreting a domestic constitution in a federal government and the other an international convention ratified by numerous sovereign nations?

To what extent do you think the different remedies available to the two courts affected the different outcomes? As you contemplate this, consider the impact of a U.S. Supreme Court decision on the state legislatures and courts, as well as the impact of a decision of the European Court of Human Rights upon the legislative and judicial bodies of member nations.

Are there other factors, in your opinion, that contributed to the differences in outcome, to the extent that you believe actual differences exist?

2. *Irish Law*

a. *Constitutional.* Mr. Keegan's ability to successfully assert a claim under the Irish Constitution had been eliminated by a previous case, State (Nicolaou) v. An Bord Uchtala, [1966] I.R. 567, in which an out-of-wedlock father had challenged the constitutionality of an adoption order, alleging that it allowed the mother to surrender a right the Irish Constitution deems inalienable, and denied the child's right to the support and security of a parent. The Irish Supreme Court rejected this claim, holding that a father of a child born out-of-wedlock is not a member of the family, and thus is not entitled to special protection under Article 41 of the Irish Constitution; nor is he a parent within

Article 42 of the Constitution. Finally, the Court found that such a father has no personal rights in relation to the child under Article 40.3 of the Constitution.

This absence of constitutional protection ultimately doomed Mr. Keegan's efforts in the Irish courts, prior to asserting his claim under the European Convention on Human Rights. Recall that initially the High Court had found that Mr. Keegan was a fit parent to be a guardian. Questions were directed to the Irish Supreme Court, however, on the issue of what test should be used to determine if he should be appointed guardian. The High Court had initially determined that Mr. Keegan had a right to be guardian if he was fit and no circumstances regarding the child's welfare suggested that he not be appointed. The Supreme Court, however, rejected that test, in part influenced by an out-of-wedlock father's lack of constitutional rights. On remand, the High Court decided that the welfare of the child was the paramount consideration, and the child should remain with the adopters. *See* Paul O'Connor, *Constitution and the Family, in* The International Survey of Family Law 1994 271, 292–93 (Andrew Bainham ed., 1996).

b. Impact of Keegan on Irish Courts. In W.O'R v. E.H. and An Bord Uchtala, Unreported, Supreme Court, July 23, 1996, the Irish Supreme Court had the opportunity to revisit the right of unmarried fathers to block adoption orders. In this case, the father had lived with the mother for eleven years, during which time two children were born. After the birth of the second child, the parents subsequently separated and the mother married. Shortly afterwards, her husband applied to adopt the two children and the father applied for a guardianship order so that he could oppose the adoption. Reviewing the lower court's denial of his request, the Supreme Court reaffirmed that the father had no constitutional rights and that the issue regarding the guardianship was the welfare of the children. In the context of determining their welfare, the Supreme Court noted that a court may consider the relationship the father has with the children, and observed that a father who had raised the children in a stable relationship might have extensive interests, but they would still be subordinate to the children's interests.

In response to a question from the lower court about whether de facto family ties as recognized in *Keegan* were afforded recognition under the Irish Constitution, and what rights, if any, arose from those ties, the majority of the Supreme Court replied:

> The decision of the European Court is not part of the domestic law of Ireland. The family referred to in Articles 41 and 42 of the Constitution is the family based on marriage. The concept of a "de facto" family is unknown to the Irish Constitution.

However, the Court went on to note that it could recognize the existence of a de facto family, even if that status is accorded no constitutional protection. The Court acknowledged that the father in such a family might have extensive rights and interests, subject to the paramount concern which is the welfare of the children. Thus, *Keegan* has not affected the Irish Supreme Court's view as to the constitutional rights of putative fathers in Ireland. For further discussion of *W. O'R.*, see Helen O'Driscoll, *Rights of Unmarried Fathers*, 2 Irish J. Fam. L. 18 (1999).

c. Legislative Response. This is not to suggest that *Keegan* has been ignored in Ireland. In direct response to the decision, the Adoption Act of 1998 was passed, providing that: (1) an agency cannot place a child under four weeks of age for adoption; (2) a father can give notice to the Adoption Board of his wish to be notified of a proposal to place a particular child, or of an application for an order to adopt; (3) an agency must check this registry before placing a child; (4) an agency must consult any known father before placement and determine if he objects; and (5) if he objects, the agency must defer placement for three weeks to provide the father an opportunity to file for guardianship, and if he makes application within that time, defer the placement until the guardianship is concluded. In addition, the Act establishes the father's right to be heard at any hearing on an application for an adoption order. Of course, these procedural guarantees do not ensure that a father will be granted a guardianship, when he applies. That decision is still, according to *W.O'R.*, determined by the welfare of the child standard. Do you think that this legislative reform now satisfies the requirements of Article 8, as elucidated by the Court in *Keegan*?

3. *Subsequent Decisions. Keegan* was not the last word from the European Court of Human Rights on the rights of putative fathers. In Söderbäck v. Sweden, 1998-VII Eur. Ct. H.R. 3086, the Court held that the adoption of applicant's seven-year-old daughter by her step-father did not violate the rights of her out-of-wedlock father under Article 8, as he had never lived with the child, and had only seen her sporadically. The Court found the Swedish court's decision to grant the adoption to be within the margin of appreciation, observing that the child had been part of a family unit with the adopter for over six years and had had no contact with the father for years, in part due to the mother's objections, but also due in part to the father's own problems and lack of initiative. The father had been notified and had participated in the proceedings at all levels.

The Court has also held, in the context of a child protective proceeding. that unmarried fathers and married fathers do not have to be treated identically in order to satisfy Article 14, which forbids discrimination. Observing that the "relationship of natural fathers with their children will inevitably vary, from ignorance and indifference at one end of the spectrum to a close stable relationship indistinguishable from the conventional matrimonial-based family unit at the other," the Court found that the requirement under Scots law that an out-of-wedlock father seek an order for parental rights in order to have status as a party in a child protective hearing was reasonably justified, and therefore not discriminatory. McMichael v. United Kindom, 307 Eur. Ct. H.R. 27 (ser. A) (1995). How do these two decisions comport with the standards established by the U.S. Supreme Court in *Lehr*?

4. *Draft Principles.* In 2001, a Working Party of the Council of Europe Committee of Experts on Family Law issued their *Draft Report on Principles Concerning the Establishment and Legal Consequences of Parentage, available at* http://www.legal.coe.int/family/cjfa/GT2Rap7RepFiliationE.pdf. Principle 15 provides that an adoption should require the consent of both the father and the mother, but that the law may dispense with that consent if a parent is not the holder of parental responsibilities, or on exceptional grounds determined by law. The subsequent explanatory paragraph states that references to the "father" in common law systems referred to the man who is the holder of parental responsibilities. The drafters also observed that although the 1967 European Convention on the Adoption of Children required consent of only fathers of in-wedlock children, *Keegan* at the very least created the right of out-of-wedlock fathers to be consulted, and they queried the extent to which *Keegan* also creates the right to object.

C. Maintaining Links with the Family of Origin

In recent decades one of the most controversial topics in the field of adoption has been the extent to which identifying, and to a lesser extent, non-identifying information, should be exchanged between adopted individuals and their birth families. Particularly heated has been the debate among lawmakers and lobbyists concerning the release of birth records to adult adoptees. The development of disclosure norms through statutory and administrative regulation has been challenged and shaped not only by political and policy considerations, but in some nations by domestic constitutional mandates and, in recent years, the influence of international human rights conventions as well. To understand the context of this debate, an overview of the historical and current regulation of disclosure in the United States and other nations that permit full adoption might be helpful.

Although adoptions under nineteenth century U.S. statutory regimes were open to the parties, the press, and the public, a growing emphasis on confidentiality developed in the United States during the 1920s and 1930s that set the stage for the subsequent envelopment of adoption in a blanket of anonymity. During this period, U.S. states gradually passed legislation sealing adoption records and requiring the issuance of new birth certificates for adopted children, substituting the names of the adoptive parents for those of the birth parents. *See, e.g.*, Joan Heifetz Hollinger, *Introduction to Adoption Law and Practice*, *in* 1 Adoption Law and Practice 1-37, *Aftermath of Adoption: Legal and Social Consequences*, *in* 2 Adoption Law and Practice 13-5 (Joan Heifetz Hollinger ed., 2000). Inspired by what scholars have referred to as the "twin stigmata of infertility and illegitimacy," these reforms were prompted by the desire to shield birth parents, adoptive parents, and their children from embarrassment or potential blackmail. *E.g.*, Katrina Wegar, Adoption, Identity, & Kinship: The Debate Over Sealed Birth Records 36–37 (1997). It has also been observed that they served the interests of the developing profession of social workers, who saw implementation of confidentiality legislation as an opportunity to solidify their "occupational niche." E. Wayne Carp, Family Matters: Secrecy and Disclosure in the History of Adoption 42 (1998). Although under this initial wave of U.S. reform, adopted adults retained the right to obtain their original birth certificates, *id.* at 42, during the late 1950s and early 1960s U.S. states gradually revised their statutes to close birth certificates to everyone, including the adopted individuals themselves. Thereafter, identifying information could be obtained through adoption records and birth certificates only with a court order upon a showing of good cause. By 1960, only twenty U.S. states still permitted adult adoptees access to their birth records upon demand, and throughout the next thirty years all of the remaining U.S. states, with the exception of Alaska and Kansas, eventually closed their birth records to adoptees. Elizabeth Samuels, *The Idea of Adoption: An Inquiry into the History of Adult Adoptee Access to Birth Records*, 53 Rutgers L. Rev. 367, 373–84 (2001).

These statutory amendments imposing anonymity reflected the prevailing practices of adoption professionals, who, beginning in the 1930s and 1940s, routinely prevented birth parents from learning the identity of adopters, ostensibly to foreclose any possibility of harassment and ensure the stability of the adoptive placement for the child. *E.g.*, Carp, *supra*, at 102–07; Samuels, *supra*, at 385–86. The Child Welfare League of America (CWLA), described as the "international standard-setting body in the field of social welfare," promoted complete anonymity and the sealing of records in its published standards from the late 1930s onwards. Carp, *supra*, at 107. By the 1950s, the complete severance of birth and adoptive families was supported not only by professional social workers, but also by lawyers (who often facilitated independent adoptions) and psychologists. Wegar, *supra*, at 50; Rickie Solinger, Wake Up Little Susie: Single Pregnancy and Race Before Roe v. Wade 15–16 (1992).

This movement to permanently separate adoptees and their adoptive families from birth families was motivated not only by professed pragmatic considerations, but in part reflected a paradigm embraced during the mid-twentieth century that adoption constituted a rebirth, through which all ties with the birth family would be severed and an illusion created that the adoptee was born into the adoptive family. *See* Arthur Sorosky et.al., The Adoption Triangle 38 (1978). Children were matched with families on the basis of similar physical characteristics; birth certificates were altered to erase all trace of adoption; and adoption intermediaries by mid-century displayed increasing reluctance to provide even non-identifying information to adoptive families about a child's medical and social background, hoping to facilitate a "fresh start." *See* E. Wayne Carp, *Adoption Disclosure of Family Information: A Historical Perspective*, 74 Child Welfare 225–33 (1995). This approach was also consistent with social science literature during the mid-twentieth century that emphasized the importance of "nurture" over "nature." Samuels, *supra*, at 404.

An examination of many other nations in the English-speaking world reveals a similar history. Because most of the nations that were formerly part of the British Commonwealth did not enact adoption legislation until after the First World War, the same social conditions and prevailing professional philosophies that prompted the closure of records in the United States during the mid-twentieth century similarly influenced the development of legal norms that precluded access to adoption records and birth certificates in those nations as well. The exception to this pattern was Scotland. Nevertheless, social scientists conclude that Scotland's enactment of an open records provision in 1930 was more likely prompted by inheritance laws, which at the time permitted adopted individuals to inherit from their birth parents but not their adoptive parents, rather than by an early recognition of the psychological importance of identity. *See* John Triseliotis, In Search of Origins: The Experience of Adopted People 1 (1973).

Regional conventions addressing domestic adoption practices indicate that secrecy has been the norm in many other parts of the world as well. The European Convention on the Adoption of Children, April 24, 1967, 634 U.N.T.S. 255, which has been widely ratified in Europe (eighteen states were parties as of March 2003), provides that the identity of the adoptive family shall not be disclosed to the birth family, and that the records released to the adoptee and the adoptive family shall not reveal the identity of the birth parents. (Article 20). Similarly, the Inter-American Convention on Conflict of Laws Concerning the Adoption of Minors, May 24, 1984, O.A.S. Treaty Series No. 62, 24 I.L.M. 460, (six parties as of March 2003), also reflects the traditional approach of anonymity that has prevailed for full adoptions in most Latin American nations. In Article 7 it provides that: "Where called for, the secrecy of adoption shall be guaranteed." Many of the nations that were part of the former Soviet Union also have a history of restricting disclosure of adoption records.

Recent decades, however, have witnessed a growing worldwide awareness of the importance to many adopted individuals of securing access to information about their genetic origins. Beginning in the 1970s, hundreds of advocacy groups located across the globe have placed increasing pressure upon politicians to open birth records to adult adoptees. Their movement was fueled by changing social conditions in many Western nations that undermined the stigma of illegitimacy; and by the large number of adopted persons who for the first time were coming of age without access to their information. Eventually, they also found support within the social work profession. Influenced by the work of social scientists in the 1970s who emphasized the importance of acknowledging the differences between adoptive and biological parenthood, adoption professionals gradually replaced the "adoption as rebirth" paradigm with an appreciation of the importance to many adoptees of their connection to both their birth and adoptive families. The most recent edition of the CWLA Standards of Excellence for Adoption Services (rev. ed. 2000) encourages agencies to "promote policies that provide adopted adults with direct access to identifying information," *id.* at §6.22, and many agencies now assist adult adoptees with searches.

Though disclosure of information by mutual consent is now widely accepted, continuing controversy exists over the best method for ascertaining the wishes of a birth parent regarding disclosure, and whether disclosure should be made despite a birth parent's objection. Even though numerous studies indicate that the vast majority of birth parents desire contact, or at least do not object to being found, a small minority still oppose contact or the release of their identity, as evidenced by the significant number who file vetoes in jurisdictions that permit them. For example, over 2000 disclosure vetoes were filed by birth parents in British Columbia during the first three and a half years of operation of its registry, and over 1500 contact vetoes were filed in New South Wales, Australia during the first year of operation of its registry. *See* D. Marianne Blair, *The Impact of Family Paradigms, Domestic Constitutions, and International Conventions on Disclosure of an Adopted Person's Identities and Heritage: A Comparative Examination,* 22 Mich. J. Int'l L. 587, 605 (2001).

In the United States, most states still do not permit adult adoptees access to identifying information upon demand. Instead, within the past two decades, government-sponsored passive registries or active search programs have been created in almost every state to facilitate the exchange of information and reunions, if both parties consent. At least six states—Alaska, Kansas, Tennessee, Oregon, Alabama, and South Dakota—do permit adoptees unrestricted access to either birth certificates or court records. To protect the interests of birth parents who desire privacy, Tennessee operates a registry, modeled after the one in New South Wales, Australia, which permits birth parents and other birth relatives to file a veto to prevent an adoptee who has obtained a birth certificate from contacting the registering party, that person's spouse, and any of the registering party's relatives. Tenn. Code Ann. §36-1-128 (1996). Alabama and Oregon created instead contact preference registries, permitting birth parents to indicate their desire for contact, contact only through an intermediary, or no contact. Or. Rev. Stat. §432.240 (1999); Ala. Code §22-9A-12 (2000). In order to file a "no contact" preference, a birth parent must also file an updated medical history form. Unlike Tennessee's system, however, there is no civil or criminal penalty for violation of the preference. At least six other states—Maryland, Indiana, Delaware, Oklahoma, Montana, and Washington—recently amended their statutes to permit adult adoptees access to identifying information unless a birth parent has filed a disclosure veto, although most of the latter statutes apply prospectively only.

Thus, in the majority of U.S. states, unless adoptees locate their birth relatives through the state registry or search programs or through private searches, their only recourse to obtain identifying information is to file an action seeking court-ordered release for good cause shown. This standard has been very difficult to satisfy, in the eyes of most courts, unless the birth relative is contacted and consents to the disclosure. *E.g., In re* Dixon, 323 N.W.2d 549 (Mich. Ct. App. 1982) (severe depression and suicide attempts not sufficiently related to lack of information to merit disclosure); *In re* Application of George, 625 S.W.2d 151 (Mo. Ct. App. 1981) (when adopted adult needed a bone marrow donor, birth parent could be contacted only through intermediary); Golan v. Louise Wise Servs., 507 N.E.2d 275 (N.Y. 1987) (identifying information denied to adopted adult with heart condition who needed information for treatment and certification as commercial pilot).

In many parts of the world the movement to open adoption records has been more successful. England and Wales opened their birth records to adult adoptees as early as 1976; Northern Ireland followed suit in 1987. In addition, the majority of Western European nations, many of the Australian states and territories, Israel, Columbia, and Argentina are now reported to permit adoptees unequivocal access to identifying information. A handful of Canadian provinces have opened records to adult adoptees as well, and several others have opened their records prospectively only, or subject to a disclosure veto by birth parents. For a summary of the status of Canadian legislation, *see* Blair, *supra,* at 626–29. Many of these nations have also created search programs or registries to assist adoptees and birth families to find each other. On the other hand, there are sill several nations, including New Zealand, many South American countries, many Canadian provinces, and the Republic of Ireland, that join the majority of U.S. states in their refusal to provide adopted individuals unrestricted access to information identifying their birth parents.

1. Constitutional Rights

Both adult adoptees and birth parents have asserted that their constitutional rights are implicated in the governmental decision to disclose or withhold identifying information. Consider the manner in which the Supreme Court of Ireland addressed these issues in the following case.

I.O'T. v. B.
[1998] 2 I.R. 321

[Ed. Note: This decision is a consolidation of two actions brought by women who had been placed at birth for de facto adoption (before statutory adoption became available in Ireland in 1952). The names of the parents who raised the women were listed on their birth certificates, rather than the names of their birth mothers. As adults, each contacted the Defendant, The Rotunda Girls Aid Society, which had arranged the placements, and the agency put each in contact with Father Doyle, the custodian of the records. Father Doyle attempted to reach both birth mothers on their behalf. A letter sent to the address he had for one birth mother came back undelivered. The other birth mother telephoned him in response to his letter. She stated that "she was unable to cope with the situation" and requested that he not contact her again.

Each woman then sought an order directing the agency to reveal to her the identity of her birth mother. The Defendants, the agency and Father Doyle, opposed their petitions on the ground that the information was confidential. Following a hearing and preliminary ruling, the Circuit Court certified several questions to the Irish Supreme Court, some of which were procedural in nature, and are omitted herein, as well as those raised in the following excerpt, which address the constitutional rights of the parties involved. Two justices concurred with Chief Justice Hamilton, whose opinion is excerpted below. Justice Barron issued a separate opinion, expressing some reservations. Justice Keane issued a dissenting opinion.]

Hamilton, C.J.

* * *

It is now necessary to consider question 7 which is:

> [Whether]...the right of a natural child to know the identity of his or her natural parent is...an unenumerated right guaranteed by the Constitution.

If the right contended for exists, it can only exist by virtue of the provisions of Article 40.3.1 of the Constitution. This Article provides that:

> The State guarantees in its laws to respect, and, as far as practicable, by its laws to defend and vindicate the personal rights of the citizen.

* * *

...[R]ights arising from the relationship between a mother and her child born out of wedlock arise from and are governed by Article 40.3 of the Constitution and are not dependent on any other provision of the Constitution....

It is quite clear...that the action of the natural mother[s] of the applicant and... the plaintiff, though for the best of motives viz. ensuring proper care for their children, in placing them in the care of the respective foster parents, amounted to a decision to relinquish their rights and duties in regard to the said children. Such rights were relinquished by the natural parents when, through the offices of the Society they gave their children to the Society for the purpose of being placed with suitable foster parents who would assume the responsibility for rearing and educating them. As appears from the evidence before the learned Circuit Court Judge this was done by the mothers of both parties on the understanding that their identities would be kept confidential and that their identities would not be disclosed without their express consent.

In the course of my judgment in Kennedy v. Ireland [1987] IR 587, I stated...:

> Though not specifically guaranteed by the Constitution, the right of privacy is one of the fundamental personal rights of the citizen which flow from the Christian and democratic nature of the State. It is not an unqualified right. Its exercise may be restricted by the constitutional rights of others, by the requirements of the common good and is subject to the requirement of public order and morality.

The right to know the identity of one's natural mother is a basic right flowing from the natural and special relationship which exists between a mother and her child.... The existence of such right is not dependent on the obligation to protect the child's right to bodily integrity or such rights as the child might enjoy in relation to the property of his or her natural mother but stems directly from the aforesaid relationship.

It is not, however, an absolute or unqualified right: its exercise may be restricted by the constitutional rights of others, and by the requirement of the common good. Its exercise is restricted in the case of children who have been lawfully adopted in accordance with the provisions of the Adoption Act, 1952 as the effect of an adoption order is that all parental rights and duties of the natural parents are ended, while the child becomes a member of the family of the adoptive parents as if he or she had been their natural child.

The applicant and the plaintiff are not in the same position as children who have been adopted in accordance with the provisions of the Adoption Act, 1952. They remain the children of their natural mother and are entitled to the benefit of such rights as arise from such relationship.

While they enjoy the constitutional right to know the identity of their respective natural mothers, the exercise of such right may be restricted by the constitutional right to privacy and confidentiality of the natural mothers in respect of their dealings with the Society. Whether they are so restricted depends on the circumstances of the case and whether they, or either of them wish to exercise this right to privacy.

The answer to question 7 is "Yes," but such right is neither absolute nor unqualified.

While there is a conflict of constitutional rights, the obligation on the courts is to attempt to harmonise such rights having regard to the provisions of the Constitution and in the event of failure to so harmonise, to determine which right is the superior having regard to all the circumstances of the case. So far as the applicant and the plaintiff are concerned, the court must decide whether their constitutional rights outweigh the constitutional and legal rights of their natural mothers.

* * *

Question 10 of the case stated asks:

> Whether I was correct in holding that the natural mothers should be given an opportunity of asserting a claim of privilege and any other claim to privacy which the Constitution or law would leave open to them, without having their identities disclosed to the applicant or plaintiff

This question permits of only one answer, "Yes."

* * *

As it is not permissible at this stage to disclose to the applicant and the plaintiff the identity of their respective natural mothers, the learned Circuit Court Judge will have to evolve and adopt a procedure whereby he can hear the natural mothers without disclosing their identities to the natural children.... [T]he procedure is a matter for the learned Circuit Court Judge.

In the course of the preliminary judgment of the learned Circuit Court Judge, he... proposed that as the natural mother of the plaintiff has indicated that she does not want to be contacted by the Society again, a person such as a social worker or other appropriate person should be the person to make contact with the natural mother in the first place. He stated that:

> I would not be at all happy, nor do I think it would be a safe course for the court to adopt, to compel a natural mother of her age to endure what, may be for her a significantly traumatic and anxiety provoking participation in these proceedings without a full report from an appropriate professional skilled person in this area.

I agree that this approach should be adopted by the learned Circuit Court Judge as it is consistent with his sensitive approach to a difficult problem and his regard for the rights of the natural mother. This necessarily involves the disclosure to the court of the names and addresses of the natural mothers.

The learned Circuit Court Judge also posed the question (9):

> Whether I was correct in holding that the natural mothers...do not have an absolute constitutional or legal right to have the anonymity guaranteed them at the time they placed the applicant and the plaintiff respectively for adoption, preserved.

The said children were not placed for adoption and this question relates to their placement by the Society.

I would answer this question "Yes" as I am satisfied that neither the right to privacy nor to privilege in respect of confidential communications is absolute.

The learned Circuit Court Judge has posed the following question (11):

If both the plaintiff and the applicant have a constitutional or legal right to the information sought, and their natural mothers have a constitutional or legal right that the information should not be disclosed, what are the correct criteria to be applied in determining which should prevail in the circumstances of the case?

In the absence of evidence with regard to all the circumstances of the natural mother and her considered attitude with regard to the disclosure of her identity, it is neither possible nor desirable to lay down all the criteria to be applied in the balancing of the constitutional right of the child to know the identity of its natural mother and the constitutional right to privacy of the natural mother. In the particular circumstances of this case however, and having regard to the findings of fact already made by the learned Circuit Court Judge it is possible to indicate to him some of the matters which he is entitled to consider in determining which right should prevail.

He is entitled to consider:

(i) the circumstances giving rise to the natural mother relinquishing custody of her child;

(ii) the present circumstances of the natural mother and the effect thereon (if any) of the disclosure of her identity to her child;

(iii) the attitude of the natural mother to the disclosure of her identity to her natural child, and the reasons therefor;

(iv) the respective ages of the natural mother and her child;

(v) the reasons for the natural child's wish to know the identity of her natural mother and to meet her;

(vi) the present circumstances of the natural child; and

(vii) the views of the foster parents, if alive.

This list is not, nor is it intended to be, exhaustive. The learned Circuit Court Judge will have to consider all the circumstances which may be adduced in evidence.

The final question posed in the case stated was:

Should the Society be required to disclose the identity of their mothers to the applicant and the plaintiff, or any other person, without the consent of the respective mothers?

This question cannot be answered until there has been a determination by the learned Circuit Court Judge of the respective rights of the Society, the natural mothers and the natural children. However, pending such determination, the Society is obliged to disclose to the court the names and addresses of the natural mothers.

* * *

Keane, J. (dissenting)

* * *

I find it difficult to imagine an aspect of human experience which falls more clearly into the constitutional area of privacy, as thus defined, than the circumstances of the natural mothers in the present case. It is unnecessary to dwell on the social climate which prevailed when young women in the position of the natural mothers took such tragic and seemingly irreversible decisions. Some may have clung to the hope that at an unimaginably distant time they might be reunited with their children. All must have thought that, if they chose, they could carry their secret with them to the grave.

* * *

... [T]he claim on behalf of the applicants in the present case not merely necessitates a finding by this Court that a constitutional right of the nature asserted exists, however uncertain its jurisprudential origins: it must also of its nature be superior.... [to the right of privacy of the natural mothers.] I am satisfied that that claim is not well founded.

Clearly, most people in the position of the applicants, perhaps the overwhelming majority, would have a deep-seated wish to know the identity of their mother. But what is at issue is whether they have a discrete, unenumerated personal right to such knowledge which is one of the personal rights acknowledged by the Constitution and which imposes a corresponding duty on the mothers to reveal their identity to them. I am satisfied that they have not....

In the United States adopted individuals have also asserted a constitutional right, under a variety of theories, to disclosure of identifying information. The following decision is typical of the response these claims have received.

The Alma Society, Inc. v. Mellon
601 F.2d 1225 (2d Cir. 1979)

Oakes, C.J.

This appeal presents the question whether adopted persons upon reaching adulthood ("adult adoptees") are constitutionally entitled, irrespective of a showing of cause, to obtain their sealed adoption records, including the names of their natural parents. Appellants are adult adoptees and an association of such persons; and they urge that the New York statutes that require the sealing of adoption records are facially invalid on Fourteenth Amendment Due Process and Equal Protection grounds and on the further basis that those statutes impose upon them badges or incidents of slavery in violation of the Thirteenth Amendment....

Appellants argue that adult adoptees should be given access to the records of their adoptions with no showing of cause whatsoever. Their supporting affidavits, which we must take as true for present purposes, indicate that lack of access to such records causes some of them serious psychological trauma and pain and suffering, may cause in them or their children medical problems or misdiagnoses for lack of history, may create in some persons a consciousness of danger of unwitting incest, and in others a "crisis" of religious identity or what they feel is an impairment of religious freedom because they are unable to be reared in the religion of their natural parents. Appellants point out that only in the last fifty years has New York had sealed adoption records, that Scotland and Israel have had open records for some time, and that England and Wales have recently changed from closed to open records with access to adults who have obtained a certain age.

* * *

Substantive Due Process

What appellants assert is a right to "personhood." They rely on a series of Supreme Court cases involving familial relationships, rights of family privacy, and freedom to marry and reproduce. As they put it, "an adoptee is someone upon whom the State has, by sealing his records, imposed lifelong familial amnesia...injuring the adoptee in regard to his personal identity when he was too young to consent to, or even know, what was happening."...

We could readily take a "pigeon-hole" approach and in doing so, because appellants' novel claims do not fit into any as yet recognized category of "privacy," exclude them. For example, there is not involved a general "individual interest in avoiding disclosure of personal matters," Whalen v. Roe, 429 U.S. 589, 599,...(1977). Although it could be argued that appellants do have an "interest in independence in making certain kinds of important decisions,"...that categorization still would leave the question whether in a situation involving both natural parents and adoptive parents the adult adoptee should have "independence" in determining whether he or she shall obtain knowledge of the natural parents....

We think that it advances analysis, however, to examine more closely the character of the choices and information that we are asked to treat as special and the factual framework of the decision that we are asked to render.... We note, of course, that we are dealing with the "family" in general and with two families in particular[:] first, the natural parent(s) who has (have) surrendered custody of the adoptee child to the State and in turn an agency or other family, and second, the adopting family which has, presumably nurtured the child to the age of adulthood.... The information sought is information as to the identity of the real parent(s) that was concealed from one and all upon adoption as a matter of law and that may indeed have been a consideration in the willingness of the real parent(s) to give up the child for adoption. [T]wo recent Supreme Court cases have a bearing upon our deliberations.

The first of these is Quilloin v. Walcott, 434 U.S. 246 (1978). There the appellant, the natural father of an illegitimate child, sought to prevent the husband of the child's mother from adopting the child although the natural father had never attempted to legitimate the child who had always been in the mother's custody.... The Court expressed "little doubt" that the State's attempt "to force the break up of a natural family, over the objections of parents and children, without some showing of unfitness" would violate the Due Process Clause.... But the Court emphasized that "the result of the adoption in this case is to give full recognition to a family unit already in existence, a result desired by all concerned, except appellant."

...[T]he relevance of the [*Quilloin*] case is the Court's "full recognition (of) a family unit already in existence."...And even though appellants are adults we must assume that they are still part of their adoptive families, families still in existence as to each of them which might be adversely affected by the release of information as to the names of natural parents or the unsealing of the adoption records. At least it would seem that there is an interest on the part of the adopting parents that is of recognized importance, one that however, they surely can waive if they see fit to do so.

In Zablocki v. Redhail, 434 U.S. 374...(1978), the second recent case, a majority of the Court held that the right to marry, a "fundamental" interest under the Equal Protection Clause, was abridged by a statute requiring court permission to marry where the applicant has minor issue not in his custody and whom he is under obligation to support.... Thus the Court held in Zablocki that the decision to marry was "among the personal decisions protected by the right of privacy."...The Zablocki Court went on to say:

The woman whom appellee desired to marry had a fundamental right to seek an abortion of their expected child... or to bring the child into life to suffer the myriad social, if not economic, disabilities that the status of illegitimacy brings.... Surely, a decision to marry and raise the child in a traditional family setting must receive equivalent protection....

Again although *Zablocki* is not directly pertinent to this case, it does recognize that we must look to the nature of the relationships and that choices made by those other than the adopted child are involved.... [T]he State may take these choices into consideration and protect the natural mother's choice of privacy which not all have forsaken even if appellants are correct, as we are told, that many mothers would be willing in this day and age to have their adult adopted children contact them. So, too, a state may take into account the relationship of the adopting parents, even if, as appellants assert, many of them would not object to or would even encourage the adopted child's seeking out the identity of or relationship with a natural parent. The New York statutes in providing for release of the information on a "showing of good cause" do no more than to take these other relationships into account. As such they do not unconstitutionally infringe upon or arbitrarily remove appellants' rights of identity, privacy, or personhood. Upon an appropriate showing of psychological trauma, medical need, or of a religious identity crisis though it might be doubted upon a showing of "fear of unconscious incest" the New York courts would appear required under their own statute to grant permission to release all or part of the sealed adoption records.

Equal Protection

Appellants begin their equal protection analysis with the argument that adult adoptees are a suspect classification (and the correlative argument that the State has no compelling interests to support the validity of the sealed records laws).... [A]ppellants suggest that they are at least entitled to the same level of constitutional scrutiny as illegitimates who have been termed a "sensitive" or quasi-suspect category for which the appropriate level of scrutiny is "intermediate," not "strict".... But appellants cite us to no case holding that adoptees are a "sensitive" or quasi-suspect classification. Instead they argue that because the overwhelming majority of adoptees adopted by nonrelatives are illegitimate and because, they say, the State actually treats adoptees worse than non-adopted illegitimates, who at least know who their natural mothers are or were and often their natural fathers as well, strict scrutiny is the applicable standard of analysis under the Equal Protection Clause.... Second, appellants argue for application of "strict scrutiny" on the basis of suspect classification status under the Thirteenth Amendment on the theory that "(a)ny group upon which a State imposes...a badge or incident of slavery is ipso facto also a suspect category under the Equal Protection Clause."

We are not persuaded that strict or even intermediate scrutiny is the appropriate standard of review in this case. Appellants' second strict scrutiny argument requires little discussion. The Supreme Court has been loathe to expand the list of traits subject to this most rigorous level of review, and we are confident that the Court would not include a trait simply because it is a "badge or incident of slavery."...

Appellants' first argument for strict scrutiny, although more plausible, is also flawed. Simply because most adult adoptees are allegedly illegitimates, it does not follow that adoptees are subject to the same level of constitutional scrutiny as illegitimates, much less a greater level.... Here...the distinguishing trait between adult adoptees and non-adopted illegitimates, the allegedly similarly situated classes, is not illegitimacy indeed.

Both of these classes are largely comprised of illegitimates.... The trait, rather, is adopted status.

Appellants present no arguments in favor of treating classifications by adopted status as even quasi-suspect, entitled to an intermediate level of judicial scrutiny. Discrimination against illegitimates is generally so treated because of the illogic and injustice of stigmatizing a child in order to express disapproval of the parents' liaisons.... This rationale is less apposite to discrimination against adopted persons. If adopted persons experience social stigma, it is not as intense or pervasive as illegitimates suffer. Moreover, the present statute notwithstanding, the adopted are not generally subject to extensive legal disabilities and thus have less of a claim to judicial protection than illegitimates.

Even assuming that the classification here were subject to intermediate scrutiny, it would not violate equal protection; for we conclude that it is substantially related to an important state interest.... [T]he purpose of...Section 4138 of the Public Health Laws...was to erase the stigma of illegitimacy from the adopted child's life by sealing his original birth certificate and issuing a new one under his new surname. And the major purpose of adoption legislation is to encourage natural parents to use the process when they are unwilling or unable to care for their offspring. New York has established a careful legislative scheme...to encourage and facilitate the social policy of placing children in permanent loving homes when a natural family breaks up.... Forty-two other states, according to the State of New York, require that birth and adoption records be kept confidential, indicating the importance of the matter of confidentiality.... These significant legislative goals clearly justify the State's decision to keep the natural parents' names secret from adopted persons but not from non-adopted persons.

To be sure, once an adopted child reaches adulthood, some of the considerations that apply at the time of adoption and throughout the child's tender years no longer apply or apply with less force. Illegitimacy might stigmatize an adult less than a child, and the goal of encouraging adoption of unwanted and uncared for children might not be significantly affected if [a]dult adoptees could discover their natural parents' identities. But the state does have an interest that does not wane as the adopted child grows to adulthood, namely, the interest in protecting the privacy of the natural parents. "(T)he liberty interest in family privacy has its source, and its contours are ordinarily to be sought, not in state law, but in intrinsic human rights...." Smith v. Organization of Foster Families for Equality & Reform, 431 U.S. 816...(1977).... Whether or not the State's interest is "compelling,"...it is an important interest, and one which justifies keeping the records confidential regardless of the adopted child's age.

We also believe that the statutory classification is "substantially" related to this interest. To be sure, the law is somewhat overinclusive; for some natural parents undoubtedly would not object to revealing their identities to their children, and some adult adoptees have an extraordinary need for their records that might outweigh their natural parents' need for privacy. But a law does not violate equal protection simply because it results in overinclusion or underinclusion, i.e., some "misfit." The question, rather, is whether the differences between those burdened and those not burdened by a law are substantial enough to justify treating the two classes differently. Here, the legislature has not unreasonably concluded that a larger proportion of the natural parents of adopted children than of non-adopted children would want to keep their identities private. That is enough to make the statutory classification constitutional.

Moreover, we note that the provision for release of adoption records "on good cause shown" substantially mitigates the possible overbreadth of the statute. The New

York courts have granted access for aid in psychiatric or psychological treatment,... and for information about genetic conditions.... Thus this case presents an entirely different situation from what it would have if the State permitted no access on any ground. The permitted showing of good cause promotes individualized treatment, a form of structural justice.... We find, in short, no basis, even under the intermediate scrutiny standard, for holding that the New York statutes violate the Equal Protection Clause.

Thirteenth Amendment

Appellants make the novel argument...that the Thirteenth Amendment's prohibition of slavery and involuntary servitude gives them an absolute right to release of their adoption records.... Appellants liken their situation...to that of the antebellum South where a slave child was "sold off" while too young to remember his parents and grew up separated from them by inability to communicate as well as by distance. The analogy according to appellants is that however literate they may be, they cannot write to their natural parents, cannot visit them, and thereby wear a "badge or incident" of slavery.

This Thirteenth Amendment argument simply does not conform to the Supreme Court's interpretations of the Thirteenth Amendment. The Court has never held that the Amendment itself, unaided by legislation as it is here, reaches the "badges and incidents" of slavery as well as the actual conditions of slavery and involuntary servitude.... Moreover, the Court has indicated that for purposes of judicial enforcement under the express prohibition of the Amendment itself...the Court will define "slavery" narrowly....

* * *

As an additional matter, we point out the doubtful applicability of the second incident of slavery, upon which appellants rely, to the sealed records laws. Although it is doubtless true that an "incident" of slavery (in the original sense) was the abolition of the parental relation, i.e., the offspring of a slave was deprived of the care and attention of parents,...the New York sealed records laws do not deprive appellants of their parental relation. It is the New York adoption laws themselves that recognize the divestment by natural parents of their guardianship...; and it is the adoption laws that create a new parent-child relationship between appellants and their adoptive parents. Appellants do not challenge the constitutionality of the adoption laws; thus their challenge to the sealed records laws, even if cognizable under the Thirteenth Amendment in the absence of congressional legislation, is misdirected.... Judgment affirmed.

Alma is representative of a number of suits brought in the late 1970s and early 1980s in both federal and state courts in the United States challenging the constitutionality of statutory provisions that denied adult adoptees unrestricted access to identifying information regarding their birth parents. When these challenges were uniformly rejected by the courts, advocacy groups concentrated their efforts on achieving legislative reform. As mentioned above, they have met with some success in recent years in Tennessee, Oregon, and Alabama. The new statutes in Tennessee and Oregon then prompted litigation by birth parents. Compare the Irish Supreme Court's treatment of the interests of birth mothers with the Sixth Circuit's assessment of their constitutional challenge.

Promise Doe v. Sundquist
106 F.3d 702 (6th Cir. 1997)

Engel, C.J.

From 1951 to 1996, sealed adoption records were available in Tennessee only upon court order that disclosure was "in the best interest of the child or of the public." Under a recently enacted statute that was to go into effect July 1, 1996, [adoption records may now be released to an adopted person who is 21 years of age or older or that person's legal representative, and information may be released to the parents, sibling, ancestors or descendants of the adopted person only with the adopted person's express written consent.]. Tenn. Code Ann. § 36-1-127(c)(1). The new law also provides for a "contact veto," under which a parent, sibling, spouse, lineal ancestor, or lineal descendant of an adopted person may register to prevent contact by the adopted person.... The contact veto also can prohibit the adopted person from contacting any spouse, sibling, lineal descendant, or lineal ancestor of the person registering the veto.... A violator of the contact veto provision is subject to civil and criminal liability.... Before disclosure of the identity of an adopted person's relatives is made, the state "shall conduct a diligent search" for the relatives to give them a chance to register for the veto.... In any event, the relatives of an adopted person can veto only contact, not disclosure of their identities.

* * *

The plaintiffs claim that the new law violates their right of privacy under the United States and Tennessee Constitutions. They argue that the "zone of privacy" established in Griswold v. Connecticut, 381 U.S. 479...(1965), now encompasses familial privacy, reproductive privacy, and privacy against disclosure of confidential information and that the new statute violates each of these three. We will consider these theories in turn, but first we note our skepticism that information concerning a birth might be protected from disclosure by the Constitution. A birth is simultaneously an intimate occasion and a public event—the government has long kept records of when, where, and by whom babies are born. Such records have myriad purposes, such as furthering the interest of children in knowing the circumstances of their birth. The Tennessee legislature has resolved a conflict between that interest and the competing interest of some parents in concealing the circumstances of a birth. We are powerless to disturb this resolution unless the Constitution elevates the right to avoid disclosure of adoption records above the right to know the identity of one's parents.

...[T]he Due Process Clause guarantees the right to "marry, establish a home and bring up children."... Nothing in the Tennessee statute infringes on that right. Under the new scheme, people in Tennessee are still free not only to marry and to raise children, but also to adopt children and to give children up for adoption. We find that if there is a federal constitutional right of familial privacy, it does not extend as far as the plaintiffs would like.

Second, the plaintiffs claim that their right to reproductive privacy, as established in Roe v. Wade, 410 U.S. 113...(1973), and its progeny, is violated by the Tennessee statute. The freedom to make decisions about adoption, they argue, is sufficiently analogous to the freedom to decide whether to carry a baby to term to justify an extension of *Roe*. Even should it ultimately be held some day that the right to give up a baby for adoption or to adopt a child is protected by the Constitution, such a right would not be relevant to this case. Because the challenged law does not limit adoptions, cases striking down laws restricting abortions are not analogous. And even assuming that a law placing an undue burden on adoptions might conceivably be held to infringe on privacy rights in the *Roe* realm, much as laws placing "undue burden[s]" on abortions are unconstitutional under Planned Parenthood v. Casey, 505 U.S. 833...(1992), §36-1-127 does not unduly burden the adoption process. Whether it burdens the process at all is the subject of great dispute in two briefs submitted to this court by *amici curiae*. Any burden that does exist is incidental and not "undue."...

Third, the plaintiffs claim that the law violates their right to avoid disclosure of confidential information. They rely on a dictum in Whalen v. Roe, 429 U.S. 589...(1977), that describes one type of privacy right as "the individual interest in avoiding disclosure of personal matters."... This right has not been fleshed out by the Supreme Court. The plaintiffs' argument that it should be extended to cover this case runs counter to our [prior] decisions in [which] we read the *Whalen* dicta narrowly,...and held that "the Constitution does not encompass a general right to nondisclosure of private information." We concluded that no constitutional right was violated by the post-adjudication dissemination of juvenile court records.... [We have also] held that the disclosure of an inmate's HIV status was not unconstitutional, [and] reaffirmed the nonexistence of the right claimed by the plaintiffs here.... The plaintiffs distinguish these cases by arguing that the information released in each did not implicate fundamental rights. As discussed above, even if a court were someday to recognize adoption-related rights as fundamental, such recognition would not be relevant to this case because the challenged part of the new Tennessee law does not directly regulate when, how, or by whom a child may be adopted.

* * *

The element of public interest also weighs against enjoining enforcement of the Tennessee statute. The statute appears to be a serious attempt to weigh and balance two frequently conflicting interests: the interest of a child adopted at an early age to know who that child's birth parents were, an interest entitled to a good deal of respect and sympathy, and the interest of birth parents in the protection of the integrity of a sound adoption system. It is an issue of peculiar relevance to the primary police functions of the state as reserved to Tennessee under the Tenth Amendment.... Another aspect of public interest favoring the defendants' position is the interest of comity between states and federal governments, including the interest of the state in having the first opportunity to construe its own constitution and laws.

We remand to the district court to dismiss the plaintiffs' complaint with prejudice with respect to the federal constitutional issues but without prejudice to any right to seek relief from the Tennessee courts on the non-federal issues....

* * *

Notes and Questions

1. *Additional Constitutional Challenges by Birth Parents.* The birth mothers in *Promise Doe* accepted the Sixth Circuit's invitation, and brought a subsequent suit in Tennessee state court challenging the statute under the Tennessee State Constitution. The Tennessee Supreme Court similarly found no violation of a right to privacy under the Tennessee Constitution, observing that the impact of the law on future placement decisions was too speculative to qualify as an infringement of procreational liberty, and that the familial right to raise a child could not be violated by a statute that did not open records until the adoptee reached adulthood. The court also refused to recognize a state consti-

tutional right to nondisclosure of personal information. Doe v. Sundquist, 2 S.W.3d 919 (Tenn. 1999). A due process challenge to the constitutionality of the Oregon law opening records to adoptees was similarly rejected. Jane Does v. State, 993 P.2d 822 (Or. Ct. App. 1999), *rev. den.* 6 P.3d 1098 (Or. 2000). In addition, both the Oregon and Tennessee state courts rejected arguments that the new laws impaired contractual or vested rights in violation of the federal and state constitutions, as both courts determined that absolute confidentiality had never been guaranteed to birth parents under the laws of either state.

2. *Disclosure in Ireland.* Because the Republic of Ireland enacted its first adoption statute in 1952, at the peak of concern over anonymity in other Western nations, it is not surprising that similar social conditions in Ireland motivated enactment of a closed records law that prohibits the release of information from court records, except by court order. Adoption Act 1952, Section 22(5). The court and the national adoption board, An Bord Uchtala, are permitted to release records if they find it in the best interests of the child to do so. Adoption Act 1976, Section 8; C.R. v. An Bord Uchtala, [1993] 3 I.R. 535 (Ir. H. Ct.). Until the late 1990s, An Bord Uchtala rarely released records, but since that time, the Board has released information more frequently, on a case by case basis, after contacting the birth parent and providing counseling to the adopted individual. *E.g.,* Padraig O'Morain, *Adopted People May Get Access to Birth Certificates,* Ir. Times, May 21, 2001, at 1.

Adopted adults as of yet have no statutory right to access to information, however, and whatever they receive is at the discretion of the Board or individual agencies who arranged placement. In 2000, the Law Reform Committee of the Law Society of Ireland issued a position paper on adoption, in which they recommended enactment of an open records law with a disclosure veto system. They stated that although they favored providing an absolute right to identifying information to adult adoptees, with a contact veto system, they read *I.O'T.* as precluding that alternative. *Adoption Law: The Case for Reform,* available at http://www.lawsociety.ie/Adoption(report).htm. The Government ministers did not, apparently, feel similarly so constrained, as in 2001 the Government announced that the Cabinet had approved a bill that would permit all adult adopted individuals access to their birth certificates and personal information from their files. Press Release, Dep't of Health and Children, An Roinn Slainte Agus Leanai, Republic of Ireland, *Hanafin Announces New Draft Legislation on Adoption Information,* (May 24, 2001), *at* http://www.doh.ie/pressroom/pr20010524.html. However, over a year later, as this book goes to press, that bill has not yet become law.

3. *De facto adoption.* Chief Justice Hamilton in his opinion in *I.O'T.* emphasized that the applicants therein had been placed before statutory adoption was enacted in Ireland, and therefore their legal relationship with their birth mothers had never been terminated. Technically, they might still possess property rights derived from this legal relationship, such as inheritance rights upon their birth mothers' death. He distinguishes their situation from that of individuals statutorily adopted, whose bonds with their birth parents have been legally severed. While the decision thus does not technically establish a constitutional right to information on the part of an individual legally adopted, the rationale of *I.O'T.* would seem to support such an extension. What language from his opinion would you use to argue on behalf of legally adopted adults in subsequent litigation in Ireland?

One Irish academic has taken a critical view of Justice Hamilton's legalistic approach. *See* Owen McIntyre, *Adoption Law: The Case for Reform,* 1 Irish J. Fam. L. 6 (2001). Justice Barron, in a separate opinion not reprinted above, commented on the similarity in the positions of de facto and legal adoptees, and observed explicitly that it is the emotional impact of disclosure on the parties involved, rather than property rights, that is truly at stake in this case. Certainly, from an emotional perspective, the positions of de facto adoptees and legal adoptees, both placed in infancy, would appear indistinguishable.

4. *Comparison of Constitutional Treatment.* The Irish Supreme Court in *I.O'T.* recognized a child's constitutional right to identifying information and a parent's constitutional right to privacy, proffering a balancing test to harmonize those rights when they conflict. U.S. courts, by contrast, have uniformly rejected the constitutional claims of both adoptees and birth parents regarding disclosure of identifying information. Assuming that Irish courts subsequently find *I.O'T.* applicable to requests by legally adopted adults for identifying information, how would *I.O'T.* affect the court's resolution of such a claim? How would it differ from the manner in which a U.S. court would handle an action by an adult adoptee seeking an order for disclosure of identifying information, assuming it was filed in a state that had no open records law?

What, if any, are the advantages and disadvantages of "constitutionalizing" the conflicting rights of adopted adults and birth parents when a birth parent opposes release of identifying information?

Compare *Alma* and *Doe* in regard to the courts' discussions of the state's interests supporting the legislative decisions challenged in each. Beyond a reticence on the part of both courts to resolve this conflict constitutionally, what factors do you think account for the differences?

Then compare the treatment of the privacy interest of birth mothers in *I.O'T.* and *Doe*, which are virtually contemporaneous decisions. What factors might account for the different weight accorded by each court to those interests?

5. *Adoptive Parents' Interests.* Both *Alma* and *I.O'T.* explicitly mention the opinion of the adoptive parents of the adult seeking information as a factor to be taken into account. *I.O'T.* includes "the views of the foster parents," who are the de facto adoptive parents, as one consideration to be balanced, and in *Alma* the court discusses the adoptive family's interest as a factor weighing against finding a substantive due process right to identifying information. *Doe*, written almost two decades after *Alma*, virtually ignores any interest of adoptive parents, despite the fact that two of the plaintiffs were in fact adoptive parents challenging the Tennessee law. Should adoptive parents have any recognizable legal interest in this issue?

2. Influence of International Law

Another possible source of support for both adopted individuals seeking identifying information and birth parents seeking privacy can be found in international conventions addressing domestic as well as transnational adoption. As previously mentioned, some regional conventions drafted prior to the late 1980s support the notion that identifying information should remain confidential. On the other hand, advocates for adopted adults frequently assert that the right to information regarding one's identity is a human right, relying principally upon Articles 7, 8, and 21 of the Convention on the Rights of the Child (CRC), Nov. 20, 1989, 1577 U.N.T.S. 3. The Convention on the Rights of the Child has been ratified by virtually every nation in the world, with the notable exceptions of the United States and Somalia. *See* Cynthia Price Cohen & Susan Kilbourne, *Jurisprudence of the Committee on the Rights of the Child: A Guide for Re-*

search and Analysis, 19 Mich. J. Int'l L. 633, 635 (1998). Other aspects of the Convention are discussed throughout this book, and in detail in Chapter Fourteen, Section B.

It is interesting to look at the language, legislative history, and subsequent implementation of the Convention, both to assess the Convention's mandates regarding disclosure of identifying information, and also as an illustration more generally of the extent to which international law is influencing the development of national domestic norms in the field of family law.

Article 7 has been suggested as one possible source of a right to identifying information. It provides:

1. The child shall be registered immediately after birth and shall have the right from birth to a name, the right to acquire a nationality and, as far as possible, the right to know and be cared for by his or her parents.

2. States Parties shall ensure the implementation of these rights in accordance with their national law and their obligations under the relevant international instruments in this field, in particular where the child would be stateless.

Although the legislative history of this Article indicates that most of the discussion concerned other matters, at one point a conflict arose regarding adoption disclosure between the representatives of Islamic states and the representatives of the United States, the German Democratic Republic, and the U.S.S.R. The former group had proposed that an earlier draft provide that a "child shall have the right from his birth to know and belong to his parents...," language they felt was more consistent with Islamic law and kafala, which continues to recognize a child's relationship with his birth family. The latter group objected to the language on the grounds that it conflicted with their current adoption laws that required secrecy. A U.S. representative suggested the current language, qualifying the "right to know one's parents" with both the words "as far as possible" and the obligation in paragraph 2 that the right be implemented in accordance with national law. Rada Barnen, *Legislative History of the Convention on the Rights of the Child (1987–1989), Art. 7*, at 16–17.

Another article bearing on the issue is Article 8, which provides:

1. States Parties undertake to respect the right of the child to preserve his or her identity, including nationality, name and family relations as recognized by law, without unlawful interference.

2. Where a child is illegally deprived of some or all of the elements of his or her identity, States Parties shall provide appropriate assistance and protection, with a view to re-establishing speedily his or her identity.

This Article was originally proposed by an Argentinian representative, Dr. Jaime Sergio, to provide in part: "The child has the inalienable right to retain his true and genuine personal, legal and family identity." The proposal was inspired not by adoption per se, however, but by the abduction in Argentina of hundreds of children by force from their families by those in power during the junta, between 1975 and 1983. Poland made a similar proposal, inspired by the historical separation of children from their parents during World War II. Thus, the focus of the Article appears to be on the duty of nations to create mechanisms to rectify situations in which children are wrongfully or illegally separated from their parents. The insertion of the language defining the right as freedom from "unlawful interference" was an attempt to differentiate it from Article 21, which addressed lawful adoption methods. *Art. 8*, Barnen, *supra*, at 4–8; Jaime Sergio Cedra, *The Draft Convention on the Rights of the Child: New Rights*, 12 Hum. R. Q. 115, 116–17 (1990).

The final relevant article is Article 21 on adoption, wherein states parties pledge that, if they have a system of adoption, the best interests of the child shall be the paramount consideration. They also agree to five explicit principles. Reference to disclosure of identifying information is notable for its absence. The legislative history indicates that in 1982 representatives of the United States proposed language that would have required that measures be taken to safeguard the confidentiality of adoption records and permit access only by judicial order. However, this proposal was not accepted by the Working Group, several of whom felt that it "had no bearing on the rights of the child." Ultimately the United States withdrew the proposal with the understanding that the relevant provisions adopted in the convention were neutral on the subject. An amendment suggested by Latin American NGOs providing that "the adopted minor shall have the right to know which is his natural family," was circulated, but also never incorporated into the final draft. *Art. 21,* Barnen, *supra,* at 14–22. Thus, while the topic of disclosure of identifying information was raised at least twice during the drafting of Article 21, neither a provision mandating disclosure nor a provision mandating confidentiality were ultimately included.

The subsequent practice of the parties to an international agreement also plays a role in its interpretation. Restatement (Third) of the Foreign Relations Law of the United States § 325 (1987). Because the Committee on the Rights of the Child is charged with monitoring implementation of the CRC, a look at how the Committee has interpreted the treaty and how nations have interpreted their duty when ratifying and later submitting periodic reports is useful.

Examination of the reports of states parties regarding their implementation, however, reveals no clear pattern. Although some nations that permit adult adoptees access to their records mention that practice, and some nations that restrict access mention this as well, other nations that practice adoption do not mention their disclosure policies in their reports at all. A review of several of the reports that did raise the issue indicates that some nations believe that balancing the right to know one's identity with conflicting privacy interests is the appropriate approach, while other nations view the Convention as requiring unrestricted access. Germany, for example, implied in its report that its law permitting anyone over the age of fifteen to inspect state records was required by Article 8, and Poland felt compelled when it ratified the Convention to make a reservation to preserve their law of "secret" adoption. Canada, on the other hand, which does not permit adopted individuals unrestricted access to information in most of its provinces, did not include this issue in the reservations that it made to the Convention. During meetings to review the reports, the Committee itself has not raised the issue frequently with member nations who do not permit adoptees access to their information, and when it has come up the discussion reflected the complexity of the differing interests involved rather than ultimatums. Therefore, while some nations clearly seem to regard the Convention as supporting a right on the part of adoptees to information about their birth families, the variety of state reporting practices on this issue and the lack of insistence by the Committee suggests that subsequent practice does not yet definitively establish an unequivocal right to disclosure, although the records are certainly subject to alternative interpretations. *See* Blair, *supra,* at 650–55.

The Hague Convention on Protection of Children and Co-operation in Respect of Intercountry Adoption (Hague Intercountry Adoption Convention), May 29, 1993, 32 I.L.M. 1134, establishes norms and procedures to govern international adoptions between its states parties. Although the Convention mandates retention of identifying information, it does not require unrestricted disclosure. Article 16 of the Convention requires the Central Authority of the country of origin of the child to prepare a report including information about the child's identity, background, family, and medical history. This must be transmitted to the receiving country, but the country of origin is permitted to "tak[e] care not to reveal the identity of the mother and father, if, in the State of origin, these identities may not be disclosed." Article 30 requires contracting nations to ensure that the child or the child's representative "has access to such information, under appropriate guidance, in so far as it is permitted by the law of that State." Additional information about the Hague Intercountry Adoption Convention is presented in Chapter Twelve, Section B.2.

Recent decisions of the European Court of Human Rights suggest that the European Convention for the Protection of Human Rights and Fundamental Freedoms (European Convention on Human Rights), Nov. 4, 1950, 213 U.N.T.S. 221, may have some bearing on the disclosure issue as well. In the following case, the Court considered a claim for release of confidential information against the child welfare authorities of the City of Liverpool.

Gaskin v. United Kingdom
160 Eur. Ct. H.R. 2 (ser. A) (1989)

[Ed. Note: Mr. Gaskin spent a substantial portion of his childhood in foster care, following the death of his mother, during which he contends he was mistreated. As an adult, he applied to the Liverpool City Council to see his case records. Eventually, the City Council determined that information given by third parties would only be released if the provider of the information could be located and gave consent. On the basis of this policy, substantial portions of the records were withheld. Mr. Gaskin applied to the European Commission on Human Rights, which was in operation at that time (see Chapter One, Section B.2.d. for information regarding the Commission), asserting that the refusal of access to his records was in breach of his right to respect for his private and family life under Article 8 and his right to receive information under Article 10. The Commission ruled that there had been a violation of Article 8, observing that:

> [R]espect for private life requires that everyone should be able to establish details of their identity as individual human beings and that in principle they should not be obstructed by the authorities from obtaining such very basic information without specific justification.

The case was subsequently selected for hearing by the European Court of Human Rights, which issued an opinion containing the following finding.]

* * *

49. In the Court's opinion, persons in the situation of the applicant have a vital interest, protected by the Convention, in receiving the information necessary to know and to understand their childhood and early development. On the other hand, it must be borne in mind that confidentiality of public records is of importance for receiving objective and reliable information, and that such confidentiality can also be necessary for the protection of third persons. Under the latter aspect, a system like the British one, which makes access to records dependent on the consent of the contributor, can in principle be considered to be compatible with the obligations under Article 8..., taking into account the State's margin of appreciation. The Court considers, however, that under such a system the interests of the individual seeking access to records relating to his private and family life must be secured when a contributor to the records ei-

ther is not available or improperly refuses consent. Such a system is only in conformity with the principle of proportionality if it provides that an independent authority finally decides whether access has to be granted in cases where a contributor fails to answer or withholds consent. No such procedure was available to the applicant in the present case.

Accordingly, the procedures followed failed to secure respect for Mr. Gaskin's private and family life as required by Article 8...of the Convention....

50. ...Article 10...reads:

> Everyone has the right to freedom of expression. This right shall include freedom to hold opinions and to receive and impart information and ideas without interference by public authority....

* * *

52. The Court holds...that "the right to freedom to receive information basically prohibits a Government from restricting a person from receiving information that others wish or may be willing to impart to him."... [I]n the circumstances of the present case, Article 10 does not embody an obligation on the State concerned to impart the information in question to the individual.

* * *

58. The Court acknowledges that Mr. Gaskin may have suffered some emotional distress and anxiety by reason of the absence of any independent procedure such as that mentioned in paragraph 49 above. Making a determination on an equitable basis, the Court awards to Mr. Gaskin under this head the amount of £5000.

* * *

[Ed. Note: The Court held 11–6 that there had been a violation of Article 8 and unanimously that there had been no violation of Article 10.]

Notes

1. *Right to Privacy.* In a more recent decision, Z. v. Finland, 1997-I Eur. Ct. H.R. 323, the European Court of Human Rights recognized that the right to privacy under Article 8 includes, in some circumstances, the right to protection of personal data. The applicant claimed that a court order requiring her testimony in court regarding her medical condition (HIV positive), and the subsequent decision of the trial judge to make the trial record accessible to the public within ten years, was in violation of this right. Though the Court found that requiring applicant's testimony in court was justified by a legitimate governmental aim, the decision to reveal applicant's identity to the press, with details of her medical condition, served no legitimate governmental aim and constituted a violation of Article 8.

2. *Birth Parents' Right to Information.* Although the above materials have focused on the rights of adopted individuals to identifying information, frequently birth parents, and in particular, birth mothers, fervently wish to receive information about a child placed for adoption. In the United States, passive registries afford birth parents the opportunity to locate adult children, if both parties register, and many, though not all, of the confidential intermediary services will initiate searches at the request of birth parents and other birth relatives. Relatively few states afford birth parents a statutory right to information. Maryland law provides a birth parent whose child was adopted after January 1, 2000 a right to obtain the new as well as the old birth certificate and

the report of the adoption decree or judgement after the child's twenty-first birthday, subject to a disclosure veto by the adoptee. Md. Code Ann., Fam. Law § 5-3A-05 (2000). Tennessee will permit birth parents to access adoption records with the written consent of the adoptee, whom state officials will attempt to locate when a request is made. Tenn. Code Ann. § 36-1-127 (2000). Courts have also been unsympathetic to birth parents seeking identifying information through good cause hearings. *E.g., In re* Adoption of Baby S., 705 A.2d 822 (N.J. Super. Ct. Ch. Div. 1997); *In re* Christine, 397 A.2d 511 (R.I. 1979).

Birth parents have encountered similar obstacles in other nations. In England and Wales, at present, only passive registries and the discretionary efforts of adoption agencies afford birth mothers the opportunity to find children they have placed. A new Adoption and Children Bill, however, which was expected to receive royal assent in November 2002, will give birth parents the statutory right to use an intermediary service through which an adult adopted child can be located. David Cohen, *The Search for Kerrie*, Evening Standard, October 17, 2002. In Canada, most provincial governments also permit birth parents to use active intermediary programs, and the provinces that permit adoptees to obtain identifying information from state records, subject to a disclosure veto, also permit birth parents the same privilege. In addition, British Columbia by statute affords birth parents an unrestricted right to obtain adoption records that convey any change of name. British Columbia Adoption Act, R.S.B.C. ch 5, §§ 63–65 (1996).

The proposed bill under consideration in the Republic of Ireland is particularly progressive in the rights it would afford birth parents. If enacted, it would provide a birth parent with a statutory right to a copy of the adoption certificate, after the child's eighteenth birthday, subject only to a contact veto; and for prospective adoptions, birth parents would be entitled to information concerning their child's progress and well-being even while the child is a minor. *See* Press Release, Dep't of Health and Children, *supra*.

3. Nonidentifying Information. By the 1980s, it became apparent in the United States that the policy of withholding negative medical and social information from adoptive parents prior to and after placement had wrought tragic consequences for many families. Adopted children received delayed or inappropriate medical or psychiatric care, often resulting in permanent damage or institutionalization. Inappropriate placements with families unable to cope with a child's special needs sometimes led to disruption of the placement or the family, and sexual or physical attacks upon other siblings that parents had received no warning to expect. In response, almost every state in the United States has now enacted statutes compelling the disclosure of at least some health-related information to prospective adoptive parents. Most of these provide detailed guidance regarding the type of information that must be collected and disclosed, both prior to placement and subsequently. Disclosure of this information to adopted individuals when they reach adulthood is similarly mandated. Most of these legislative schemes also create a process for post-adoption supplementation of medical information and transmission to adoptive and birth families.

England, Wales, and Scotland mandate the appointment of medical advisors to consult with agencies, and require that a written report about a child's medical and social history be provided to prospective adopters before placement. Ireland's proposed new bill would also create a statutory right for adoptive parents to receive a child's medical and social history, a matter that previously has been left to Board policy and agency discretion.

Problem 11-1

A. As a staff attorney for a human rights organization in an Eastern European nation, you are representing Marta Kovacek in a proceeding before the highest appellate court in your nation. Ms. Kovacek was adopted thirty years ago as an infant, and has been seeking identifying information concerning her birth parents from the charitable organization that facilitated the adoption. The agency has records containing the information, and has contacted the birth mother, who refuses to give her permission for its release. Ms. Kovacek suffers from severe allergies, and her physician has informed her that a family medical history of close genetic relatives would be extremely helpful in diagnosing and treating her effectively. In addition, as she has just had a child of her own, she wishes to have medical and social history that would be helpful for her child. She also wants very much to know the identity of her birth parents, which for her is very important to her own emotional well-being.

Your nation has had a statute in effect for the past fifty years which provides that adoption records are to be sealed, and that information can be released only upon court order. The lower court, however, upon learning that the birth mother was opposed to releasing information, refused to grant Ms. Kovacek's application for an order.

Your nation has a relatively new constitution, which became effective just a decade ago. The section regarding individual rights incorporates many provisions of the U.S. Bill of Rights, including the guarantees of due process and equal protection. Your nation is also a state party to the Convention on the Rights of the Child, the European Convention on Human Rights, the International Covenant on Civil and Political Rights (*see* Article 17), and the U.N. Declaration on Social and Legal Principles relating to the Protection and Welfare of Children, with Special Reference to Foster Placement and Adoption Nationally and Internationally (*see* Articles 8 and 9).

What arguments will you make to the Supreme Court on your client's behalf?

B. You are the attorney for the charitable organization that placed Ms. Kovacek. Your organization has performed child welfare services in your country for the past forty years. Your policy is to release information to adoptees, when requested, only after contacting and receiving permission from a birth parent. In this case, a staff member of your client has contacted the birth mother, Mrs. Novak, a forty-seven year-old teacher in a parochial school, who lives in a small community approximately fifty miles away from the applicant, Ms. Kovacek. Ms. Novak has never told her other three children, who are now adults, about their eldest half-sibling. The community in which Ms. Novak lives and works is traditional and very religious, and she is concerned that she will lose her job if news of the placement becomes public. Although your agency will comply with whatever order the court issues, the officers have asked you to oppose the application, because they wish to support Ms. Novak, who placed her child with the understanding that the placement would be confidential, and because they fear that a court opinion opening records will deter other mothers from placing children in the future.

What arguments will you make to the Court on the agency's behalf?

C. You are the justice of the Supreme Court who has been assigned to write the opinion in the above case. How will you rule, and why?

Chapter 12

International Adoption

One of the deepest ties possible between human beings, the bond between parent and child, torn apart on one continent, is rewoven on another.

Karin Evans, The Lost
Daughters of China 6–7 (2000)

In the United States, the number of children who immigrate to this country as the result of international adoption has steadily grown from approximately 6,500 in 1991 to over 20,000 during 2002. *See* U.S. Dep't of State, Immigrant Visas Issued to Orphans Coming to the U.S., *at* http://www.travel.state.gov. Though Americans are reported to adopt more children from abroad than the citizens of all other nations combined, international adoption is becoming an increasingly common practice in many other Western countries as well. While these children bring great joy to their adoptive families and enrich their new communities, their departure is nevertheless mourned by their birth families and a loss to their countries of origin. Most importantly, the consequences for the children, though often positive in many ways, are not uniformly so. While complete prohibition of transnational adoption has few adherents in the international community, there is considerable debate regarding whether international and domestic law should foster or restrict its utilization. Section A of this chapter explores some of the arguments raised in this debate, and the divergent approaches reflected in the international conventions that address this institution.

There appears to be widespread agreement in the international community, however, that to the extent that transnational adoptions take place, they should be regulated by both international and domestic law. Section B of this chapter explores relevant international instruments, focusing primarily on the Hague Convention on Protection of Children and Co-operation in Respect of Intercountry Adoption (Hague Intercountry Adoption Convention), the most widely ratified multilateral convention governing transnational adoption. Federal legislation that will implement that Convention in the United States, following its ratification, is also examined.

Advising American clients undertaking an international adoption also requires knowledge of federal immigration law and state adoption law, as well as an understanding of the law of the child's country of origin or access to knowledgeable legal advisors within that nation. Section C will address the current process for adoption of a child born abroad by parents residing in the United States. The role of attorneys and adoption agencies in this process, immigration restrictions and documentation, eligibility for citizenship, the process for adoption and readoption in the United States, and recognition of foreign adoptions are among the topics discussed in this section.

A. Transnational Adoption:
Benevolent Option or Last Resort?

Before examining the legal regulation of transnational adoption, both internationally and domestically, it is useful to consider whether the institution should be promoted and facilitated by such regulation, or permitted only in the complete absence of humane alternatives. Different perspectives on this issue are reflected in academic discourse on the topic, some of which is authored by scholars who have been personally involved in the practice as either adoptive parents or adoptees. International instruments addressing transnational adoption also reflect varying degrees of acceptance.

Elizabeth Bartholet, *International Adoption: Propriety, Prospects and Pragmatics*
13 J. Amer. Acad. Matr. Lawyers 181, 182–183, 196–207, 210 (1996)

...Controversy surrounds the topic of international adoption. To some, it presents in extreme form problematic issues they see at the heart of all adoption. It can be viewed as the ultimate form of exploitation, the taking by the rich and powerful of the children born to the poor and powerless. It does tend to involve the adoption by the privileged classes in the industrialized nations, of the children of the least privileged groups in the poorest nations, the adoption by whites of black-and brown-skinned children from various Third World nations, and the separation of children not only from their birth parents, but from their racial, cultural, and national communities as well.

To others, however, international adoption is a particularly positive form of adoption. Prospective parents reach out to children in need, rather than fighting over the limited number of healthy infants available for adoption in this country. The fact that these families are built across lines of racial and cultural difference can be seen as a good thing, both for the parents and children involved and for the larger community. These are families whose members must learn to appreciate one another's differences, in terms of racial and cultural heritage, while at the same time experiencing their common humanity.... [T]he evidence indicates that they succeed in doing so.

* * *

The problems that should be seen as central to the international adoption debate are the misery and deprivation that characterize the lives of huge numbers of the children of the world. Millions of children die regularly of malnutrition and of diseases that should not kill. Millions more live in miserably inadequate institutions or on the streets. Their situations vary: some institutions are worse than others; some "street children" maintain a connection with a family while others are entirely on their own. But there can be no doubt that overwhelming numbers of children in the poor countries of the world are living and dying in conditions which involve extreme degrees of deprivation, neglect, exploitation, and abuse. These are the real problems of the children of the world. International adoption should be seen as an opportunity to solve some of these problems for some children. It should be structured to maximize this positive potential by facilitating the placement of children in need of nurturing homes with people in a position to provide those homes.

International adoption can, of course, play only a very limited role in addressing these problems. Solutions lie in reallocating social and economic resources both among countries and within countries, so that more children can be cared for by their birth families. But, given the fact that social reordering on a grand scale is not on the immediate horizon, international adoption clearly can serve the interests of at least those children in need of homes for whom adoptive parents can be found.

...Some have suggested that international adoption programs might conflict with programs designed to improve the lives of the millions of children now in need, or with efforts to accomplish the kind of social reordering that might help the children of the future. For example, some argue that instead of promoting and pursuing adoption, governments and individuals in the well-off, industrialized countries should devote increased resources to more cost-effective programs designed to promote the well-being of children in their native lands. These efforts could include improving foster care arrangements, sponsoring orphanages, and supporting various UNICEF projects.

Such efforts, however, are not inconsistent with supporting foreign adoption. Indeed, the opposite is true. Foreign adoption programs are likely to increase awareness in the United States and other receiving countries of the problems of children in the sending countries. Those who adopt have reason to identify, through their children, with the situations of other children not lucky enough to have found homes. Foreign adoption is thus likely to help create a climate more sympathetic to wide-ranging forms of support for children abroad.

Another argument voiced against international adoption is that it might relieve pressure within some sending countries to deal with social problems that need attention. But this argument also collapses upon analysis. Sending children abroad for adoption tends to highlight rather than to hide the fact that there are problems at home....

* * *

Care should be taken, of course, to prevent international adoption from creating new problems. Adoption must not be used to break up viable birth families, and those who want to adopt must not be allowed to use their financial advantage to induce impoverished birth parents to surrender their children. There is a need for the laws that prohibit baby buying, and for rules governing the process by which a child is removed from one parent to be given to another. The rules should ensure that the birth parents have voluntarily surrendered or abandoned their child, or have had their parental rights terminated for good reason.

But it is patently absurd to talk as if the real dangers for children were the dangers that they might be taken from their birth parents for purposes of abuse and exploitation. Nonetheless, public discourse about international adoption focuses overwhelmingly on its alleged risks. Concern is regularly expressed in this country and abroad about the dangers that children will be kidnapped or bought from their birth parents for sale to rich North Americans; the media in this country give headline coverage to stories of "kidnapping rings" and "baby trafficking." There are, of course, some documented instances of kidnappings and of improper payments to birth parents. But there is no evidence that these practices are widespread, and it is quite unlikely that they are. Current law makes it extremely risky for adoption intermediaries and would-be adopters to engage in baby buying or kidnapping. Even if some might be willing to engage in such activities if these were the only way or the easiest way to accomplish an adoption, the fact is that they are not. The world is, sadly, all too full of birth parents desperate to find homes for the children they cannot care for, and of children who have already been surrendered or abandoned. When one looks beneath the surface of most media and other stories of child trafficking, it becomes clear that the term "trafficking" is used very loosely. The stories sometimes involve claims that what is characterized as a "bribe" has been paid to an official, without disclosing the fact that small payments are traditional in the conduct of all official business in the country at issue. Often the trafficking headlines involve stories that reveal no more than that the adoptive parents paid a good deal of money to agencies or other adoption intermediaries, without indicating whether anything beyond legitimate fees for services were involved. Rarely is there any evidence that birth parents have been paid, or that children have been taken from birth parents capable of and interested in raising them.

...My point is not to justify everything that has been done in the name of international adoption, but that we need to look at even such abuses as occur in perspective. Recent events involving Romanian adoption are illustrative. The foreign adoptions that followed the fall of the Communist regime in Romania in 1989 became the source of the major adoption "scandal story" of the early 1990s. The story became a focal point for media discussions of international adoption and was used effectively by opponents of such adoption in the context of the Hague Convention negotiations and more generally. Would-be adopters from the United States and other countries were described as wandering through Romanian villages offering payments to induce baffled villagers to give up their children for adoption. There undoubtedly were some number of cases involving illicit payments to Romanian birth parents for their children, and I would agree that such transactions deserve condemnation. But the real story of the children in Romania, and the role of international adoption in their lives, is one in which baby buying deserves a limited amount of space. The real story has to do with a country in which tens of thousands of children lived in orphanages and state hospitals, where thousands acquired AIDS. It has to do with institutional conditions so horrible as to stun even the jaded reporters who first revealed them to the world. It also has to do with the fact that once news of the situation in Romania got out, thousands of people came forward who were eager to adopt some of the children they read about and saw on television. Thousands of children were adopted, both from these institutions and from birth parents who were unable to care for them.

It is true that international adoption was mishandled in Romania and that some abuses occurred. But the real scandal was that, when would-be adopters came forward, there was no system in place to handle adoptions in a way which would have facilitated placement while preventing abuses. The real tragedy has to do with the conditions in which Romanian children were and are living and dying, not with the fact that a limited number of birth parents received illegal payments....

...Critics of international adoption often voice concern that children will not receive appropriate care in their new families and countries. Arguments are made that it is unfair to separate children from their racial, ethnic, cultural, and national groups of origin. Loss of the group link and sense of group heritage is said to be a deprivation in itself. And growing up in a foreign land is said to pose risks of discrimination.

Those who voice these concerns again ignore the realities of children's current situations. International adoption represents an extraordinarily positive option for the homeless children of the world, compared to all other realistic options. Most of these children will not be adopted otherwise. They will continue to live in inadequate institutions or on the streets. Foster care is available only to a limited degree and sometimes results in little more than indentured servitude. The homeless children who survive to grow up often will face virulent forms of discrimination in their own country, based on their racial or ethnic status, or simply on the fact that they are illegitimate or orphaned.

The empirical studies that have focused on international adoption provide no basis for concern as to the welfare of the vast majority of international adoptees and their families. The studies show these children and their families functioning well, and comparing well on various measures of emotional adjustment with other adoptive families, as well as with biologic families. This is rather strikingly positive evidence since most international adoptees have had problematic preadoptive histories that could be expected to cause difficulties in adjustment. The studies show that adoption has for the most part been extraordinarily successful in enabling even those children who have suffered extremely severe forms of deprivation and abuse in their early lives, to recover and flourish. Thus one major study involved children caught up in the Vietnamese War who arrived in Norway for adoption at ages ranging from two to five. "Many could not walk. They were passive, apathetic, retarded and malnourished." At ages seventeen through twenty-two, these children were found to be in remarkably good shape: they were basically well-adjusted and strongly attached to their families. Some of the studies illuminate special challenges that many of these families face—challenges that have to do with adjusting to a new language and culture, or with overcoming the effects of traumatic preadoptive experiences and of early health problems. Other studies hint at the complex issues involved in being part of a biracial, bicultural, binational family. These families do have to deal with issues of discrimination. And the children do have to deal with complex identity issues in working through what it means to be an "Asian American" or a "Peruvian American" or a "Mexican American." But the problems of discrimination are not different in nature than the problems many of these children would face in their own lands. The challenges involved in developing an appropriate sense of group identity are not different in nature from those that all immigrants face. The studies provide no evidence that the challenge of establishing a satisfactory ethnic and cultural identity causes psychological harm to the international adoptee....

So the studies reveal no real negatives inherent in international adoption as compared to domestic adoption. From a real-world perspective, that is of course not the most relevant comparison. The key comparison would be between children adopted internationally and children denied the possibility of adoption—children destined for the most part to grow up in institutions or on the streets. But there is no need for comparative studies of this kind. They would simply bolster what common sense and professional opinion tell us already. A permanent adoptive family is vastly preferable from the child's perspective to even the best foster or institutional care. Most of the children without permanent families in the poor countries of the world are not living in "the best" temporary care situations, but rather in situations ranging from seriously inadequate to desperate.

There has been no focus in the studies on determining what special positives might inhere in international adoption for the children, their adoptive families, or the larger society. But some studies hint at the rich quality of the experience involved in being part of an international adoptive family, and the special perspective its members may develop on issues of community. One major nationwide study found that one-half of the international adoptees involved felt that as a result of their status, "they may be bridge-builders between the nations."...

* * *

...[R]estricting international adoption does not promote the interests of children or of their countries of origin. It does not put poor countries in a better economic or a better power position with respect to foreign governments. It is simply a symbolic gesture "for" the nation and "against" the foreigners that is easy and cheap to make. The children themselves have little political influence. Their voices are not heard.

The nations of the world should move beyond political hostilities and symbolic acts to focus on the real needs of children. If they did, they would accept international adoption as a good solution for at least some group of the world's homeless children and could begin to restructure their laws and policies so as to facilitate rather than impede such adoption. One side benefit would be that many more of the infertile who want to parent would be given the opportunity to do so through adoption. These people now feel under significant pressure to pursue biological parenthood through high-tech infertility treatment or complicated surrogacy arrangements—pressure that makes little sense in a world suffering in myriad ways from overpopulation. Another side benefit would be enrichment of our understanding of the meaning of family and of community.

Twila Perry, *Transracial and International Adoption: Mothers, Hierarchy, Race, and Feminist Legal Theory*
10 Yale J. L. & Feminism 101, 107–08, 132–137, 143–144, 147, 163–164 (1998)

I am not opposed to transracial or international adoption. Many women experience a powerful desire to become mothers. Not all women can conceive children biologically, and not all women choose to. It is also probably true that some women who place their children for adoption do not, in any sense, see their choice as dictated by anything other than their own free will. It must be remembered that adoption is an institution with ancient roots, and I suspect that even in a more humane and egalitarian society than the one that we now have, there would still be women who would choose to surrender their children. Finally, for some children, transracial or international adoption may be the option that is in their best interests at the particular time.

Still, there is a need for feminist theory to look more closely at the issues raised by adoption. As long as factors such as race, class, and patriarchy powerfully affect so many women's lives and choices, they must be a part of any meaningful analysis of this important and long-standing societal practice.

* * *

Some people in third world countries analogize international adoption to colonial exploitation. Rita Simon and Howard and Altstein, who have written extensively on transracial and international adoption, have observed that:

> [W]hat the West has generally regarded as charitable, humane—even noble— behavior, developing countries have come to define as imperialistic, self-serving and a return to a form of colonialism in which whites exploit and steal natural resources. In the 1970s and 1980s, children were the natural resources being exploited and out of which developing nations were being cheated.

* * *

There are important links to be drawn between the transracial adoption of Black children in the United States and the adoption of children of color from Asia and

Latin America. The factors of racism and economic discrimination that result in large numbers of Black children being separated from their biological parents in this country have counterparts in the international context, where a history of colonialism, neocolonialism, cultural imperialism, and economic exploitation often results in mothers being unable to keep the children to whom they have given birth. Thus, both domestically and internationally, transracial and international adoption often result in a pattern in which there is the transfer of children from the least advantaged women to the most advantaged women. Despite the differences between the specific circumstances of Black women in America and some other third world women, there is a connection in terms of a struggle by both to function as mothers under political and economic conditions which severely challenge their ability to adequately parent their own children. Moreover, many transracial adoptions, international adoptions, and adoptions in which racial and ethnic differences are not a factor, also share another connection—a link to the institution of patriarchy. Because poverty, racism and patriarchy are often factors when children become available for adoption, consideration of each of them is essential to the development of a feminist approach to adoption.

... [P]overty is often a factor in international adoption. Many women who surrender their children live in dire circumstances where disease, lack of education, and poor housing are part of everyday existence. Although the United States certainly cannot be held solely responsible for these conditions, there are relationships that exist between the United States and some of the countries from which internationally adopted children often come that should be troubling to feminists thinking about international adoption. These relationships have aspects that are economic, political/military, and cultural.

* * *

In recent years, some poor women, particularly in countries in Latin America, have found employment in factories which produce goods for companies in the United States. Unfortunately, the wages for which many of these women work are pitifully low, sometimes as low as forty cents per hour. What are the implications for international adoption of this trend of economic globalization? Clearly the wages these women earn are inadequate. Even if they are the highest wages the women have ever earned, they are not sufficient to lift the women out of poverty, and poverty is clearly a factor in so many children in Latin American [sic] being available for adoption by Americans....

...A number of countries from which children of color come have a history of colonialism—military and economic domination by western nations at some point in their histories. Obviously, colonial relationships exist to serve the needs of the colonizing countries; the result is generally exploitation of the people and resources of the country that is dominated. However, colonialism is not simply military and economic—it also has a cultural component. This cultural component often finds expression in the belief that the country that is being militarily and economically subjugated is comprised of an inferior people, and in the eyes of the conqueror, this inferiority justifies the conquest and continued domination.... While the era of actual colonialism may be over in much of the world, the racist and ethnocentric rationales for it linger.

The United States has never formally held colonies in Latin America. Nevertheless, our government has had strong military ties to numerous governments in that area of the world. It has often financed military endeavors favorable to United States' interests, and it has developed economic interests and relationships that favor American businesses. The United States has also been a dominant military force in a number of the Asian countries, such as Korea and Vietnam where many internationally adopted children have been born. The kind of economic and military relationships that the United States has had with some third-world countries can engender the same kind of cultural imperialism that results from more formal colonial relationships.

As troubling as it may be for many to admit, a conception of poor, third-world countries as subordinate nations fits very comfortably with the practice of international adoption. This kind of view translates easily into the idea that Western adoptive parents are simply saving unfortunate third-world children by bringing them out of primitive, impoverished and disease-ridden countries into the more affluent life that the West can offer. It permits a discourse that allows Westerners to take the high ground and portray their international adoptions as simple acts of humanitarianism and altruism.

Admittedly, there is a humanitarian aspect to many international adoptions. Obviously, there are children adopted from poor countries who would face a very bleak life or even death in their homelands. However, a feminist analysis of international adoption should go farther than a simple altruism narrative. Indeed, an appropriate question might not be what Westerners are giving to the children of impoverished countries, but what they are taking from those countries or from the poor women who live in them. "Taking" might appear to be a harsh word in the context of a situation in which women have voluntarily surrendered their children. However, the "voluntariness" of these surrenders must be examined in light of the economic, social, and political circumstances under which the mothers often live.

...Patriarchy and racism can also be important factors in the availability of children for international adoption, although these phenomena take different forms in different countries. In some countries, patriarchy may be the dominant factor. In Asian countries such as Korea, adoption historically has only been considered as a means to perpetuate family lines in families without a male heir. Because adoption has been unpopular as a general practice, it has been difficult to place children for adoption within the country.

In China, the availability of many baby girls for adoption is also largely a function of patriarchy. The Chinese tradition of favoring male children, combined with the policy limiting families to one child, results in many families choosing to keep a male child and putting female infants in orphanages, or sometimes even putting them to death. Adoption by foreigners has sometimes been a fortunate alternative to these fates. In Vietnam, children fathered by foreigners, often by American soldiers, have not been easily accepted by the society. Where the children have obviously been fathered by Blacks, racial prejudice can compound the factors of foreign blood and birth outside of marriage, placing on these children a triple burden....

* * *

The question of focus on the individual child versus a commitment to the group from which a child comes is also present in the context of international adoption. This was illustrated in the recent controversy over the conditions of babies in Chinese orphanages. Recently, Chinese dissidents and some Western journalists charged that some children in orphanages were being systematically neglected, abused, and even deliberately starved to death in order to control the population of the institutions. The Chinese government denied the allegations.

Although some Americans seeking or advocating the adoption of Chinese children by Americans vigorously sought to expose these conditions, others were reluctant to have the situation publicized for fear that it would anger the Chinese government and cause them to put an end to the adoptions. However, suppressing the controversy would not have been in the interests of the majority of children in these orphanages—children whose futures were in China and who were not going to be adopted by Americans. Obviously, there are questions as to whether the charges are true, and whether, or to what degree, it is appropriate for the United States to become involved in the matter.

In thinking about international adoption, I do not contend that American women alone have the power to change the complex circumstances that result in so many children needing homes. These circumstances stem from a complex mix of history, economics, patriarchy, and racism that has roots going back many centuries, and they admit of no easy solution. I do believe, however, that a feminist analysis must consist of more than the simple willingness to adopt the children of women who cannot care for them. Instead, there must be some acknowledgment that a Western woman's happiness in transacting an adoption may have been built upon a third-world woman's misery, and this must lead to some commitment to change the conditions that have created that state of affairs.

What might be the benefits of thinking about transracial and international adoption in this kind of a wider context? First of all, it might lead to action to improve the lives of children of color, both in this country and in some of the foreign countries from which many internationally adopted children come. Secondly, the demonstration of concern about the groups and societies from which adopted children come might diminish some of the reservations that women of color in this country and third world countries sometimes express about the white, western feminist movement not appearing interested in the problems faced by poor women of color. Any resulting improvement in solidarity between women, both worldwide and in this country, could increase the power of women to address a wide range of issues.

* * *

I am concerned that in the analysis of transracial and international adoption the focus in feminist theory on individual relationships of nurture and caretaking encourages an analysis of the transracial and international adoption that is essentially apolitical. The emphasis on the need of individual children for adoptive homes in which they will be nurtured on a one-on-one basis comes at the expense of thinking harder about the political and economic circumstances that shape the lives of so many more children in this society and in the world. The pattern of the transfer of children from poor women to women who are economically better off or from women who suffer racial subordination to women who possess racial privilege raises questions that must go beyond the need for nurturing in individual relationships. For feminists, adoption, like marriage, must be analyzed as a political institution in which issues of rights, inequality and the potential for exploitation must be central.

* * *

Adoption is an important institution. It provides an opportunity for people to experience the joys and challenges of parenthood. More importantly, it provides the opportunity for children to have homes who otherwise might not have them. A feminist analysis should support adoption as an institution, but at the same time should be willing to question the justice of a world which often results in the transfer of children of the least advantaged women to the most advantaged. There must be some commitment to eradicating the racism, economic exploitation and patriarchy that is often a factor that affects a woman's ability or choice to raise her own children.

* * *

Ryiah Lilith, *Buying a Wife But Saving a Child: A Deconstruction of Popular Rhetoric and Legal Analysis of Mail-Order Brides and Intercountry Adoptions*
9 Buff. Women's L.J.225, 229, 260–262 (2000–2001)

...[T]he modern phenomena of mail-order brides and intercountry adoptions are indistinguishable, at least in regards to U.S.—Asian transactions. Mail-order brides and intercountry adoptions are both by-products of Western/U.S. colonial and imperial activities in Asia and enduring Orientalism within U.S. culture....

* * *

...Imperialism creates a situation where the development of the subjugated nation is determined by the imperialist power.... Chinese social and cultural development will be shaped by the population's gender imbalance. According to a 1995 Chinese national sample population census, the ratio of male children under 5 to female children under 5 was 118 to 100.... Scholars are already investigating the sociological impact of the looming "bride shortage" in China....

It could be argued that adopting...Chinese girls does not create this gender imbalance—that this imbalance is instead caused by exogenous factors such as the cultural preference for male children and the one-child policy. However, while intercountry adoptions may not be the sole cause of the Chinese gender imbalance, they are a contributing factor: Logically, without intercountry adoptions, fewer female children would leave China. In addition, the possibility of intercountry adoptions may exacerbate the gender imbalance by encouraging families who want a son to place their daughter up for adoption; according to the International Social Service organization, the existence of intercountry adoption facilities in Korea in the 1960s and 1970s actually functioned as an incentive for the surrender of Korean children.

* * *

While relying on religious or humanitarian sentiment may give some American adoptive parents a sense of justification or entitlement to acquire Chinese orphans, such rationales mask the realty of imperialism and commodification.... The double standard of condemning mail-order brides as prostitutes, while uncritically supporting intercountry adoptions must be reconsidered, for when the historical notions and modern construction that enable mail-order brides and intercountry adoptions to be considered discrete practices are removed, what remains in both cases is the essential fact that white Americans, who cannot satisfy their desires for wives and children in the U.S., are paying billions of dollars to enable Asian women and children to immigrate to the U.S. in order to join these Americans' families.

David S. Rosettenstein, *Trans-racial Adoption in the United States and the Impact of Considerations Relating to Minority Population Groups on International Adoptions in the United States*
9 Int'l J.L. & Fam. 131, 146 (1995)

* * *

... [T]he Convention on the Prevention and Punishment of the Crime of Genocide [9 Dec. 1948, 78 U.N.T.S. 277] classifies as genocide the forcible transfer of children from one group to another group with the intent to destroy a national, ethnic or racial group. Although adopted in 1948, the Convention was only ratified and implemented in the United States in 1988. In the ordinary course it is unlikely, but not unknown historically, that a receiving state would be the initiator of the displacement process from the source state. However, the Convention does seem to leave open the possibility of an argument that a receiving state which creates a permanent placement for a child displaced by a known racial or ethnic purge in the source country is amenable to being characterized as an accessory to genocide. Such an argument raises the question of how, at the macro-level of global politics it is possible to regulate reprehensible behaviour, without ensnaring innocent children in the process. After all, a country seeking to avoid being classified as an accessory to genocide might well deny entry to the displaced children. Lest this analysis is seen as far-fetched, it is worth remembering that this is precisely the dilemma that has confronted the United States in the context of domestic debates on trans-racial adoption—down to the characterization of the process by the NABSW [National Association of Black Social Workers] as "genocide". The one substantial distinction between the domestic issue and the international question raised by the Convention is the reason why the children are in need of help. In the former the source of the problem is family disfunction, in the latter it is group oppression. Arguably, because of this, the proponents of domestic trans-racial adoption programmes ought to be accountable since the children's difficulties might be rectified by the channelling of additional resources to minority communities for family reinforcement or to promote intra-racial adoption. But, in the international arena, an unwillingness to accept the children and in the process denying them an opportunity for a permanent home, leaves them with the prospect of being victimized twice....

Susan R. Harris, *Race, Search, and My Baby-Self: Reflections of a Transracial Adoptee*
9 Yale J.L. & Feminism 5–10 (1997)

CAN YOU IMAGINE?
Have you ever spent time imagining
what it would have been like
to have been raised amongst individuals who were
racially different from you?

What it would have been like
to have gone FOR YEARS never having
spoken to a person who was of the same race as you;

What it would have been like
throughout the course of a typical day
never having encountered a person
who looked like you.

What it would have been like
to have Even your own Parents be
of a different race from you?
Can you imagine?

Let's think about this even though it might be hard to conceptualize. I am not talking about spending time abroad to experience different cultures or foods, knowing all the time that regardless of how you are treated, you will be able to return home and blend in with your family, friends, and peers. Nor am I talking about hanging out with friends of a different race, class, or culture and feeling different and sometimes uncomfortable for obvious and/or sometimes not-obvious reasons, yet knowing all the while that you can leave, and find a person

who will
understand you,
mirror you,
and once again, remind you,

that you are okay being the way you are. I am not talking about the choices you have made to become a more cultivated person. I am not talking about choices. And I am definitely not talking about a bad hair day. I am talking about growing up in a town where there might be one, two, three or four persons-if you're lucky-who look like you, but are not necessarily your age or even people with whom you are likely to come into contact. This is the situation for many transracial/transcultural adoptees who come from closed adoptions and who are raised in predominantly white communities. The added dimension for African American transracial adoptees is that they have facial features and/or skin coloring which have been historically exploited and oppressed.

* * *

What happens to the black male when he enters the adolescent years? This of course varies from male to male. How will he be viewed by various white people as he begins to look like a black man? Think of the confusion the adoptee might have if he is surrounded by white people who view him as a token, tell him that he isn't really black, and proceed to talk negatively about those other blacks. Or what must it be like to hear your white peers chat about getting a "black" one in the sack? How does the black male feel if he is viewed as a token one day, and then the next is falsely accused (like so many black males) of being a liar and/or a thief? Will he encounter fearful, racist white men who become angry and retaliate when he gets a position that they feel their white sons should have had? Will any of the white adults become concerned that the black male might date or rape their "superior or angelic" white daughters? Can you imagine the pain, rage, and confusion a black transracial adoptee has if and when he figures out that the environment he was raised in did not and does not value him or what he represents-black men.

What happens to the black female when dating begins? How does the black female feel about herself if all of her friends who are white begin to date and she is left dateless? How does she approach this subject with her white peers and white parents? Will anyone be sensitive to her? Or will people use the colorblind approach? Who knows? It really is the luck of the draw. Can you imagine having some of your friends say to you-"Maybe the boys don't ask you out because you're not friendly enough?" Could this be the case throughout all twelve years of schooling? I should say not! The black female, however, could easily believe her friends and think there is something wrong with her. Will the black female lose some friends if she says she doesn't get dates because she is not liked because she is black? Who knows? This can play out in numerous ways. What happens if the black female gets angry with her friends and family for not understanding her situation? Will they think she's crazy because Billy, the boy she likes, would never be prejudiced? Will they think she is just race obsessed, that she always blames these things on race? Will some of her friends feel justified to think of her as or call her a black bitch? Can you imagine going through twelve years of schooling supposedly like all of your white girlfriends, but never having a white boyfriend, or if you are gay, a white girlfriend? Or can you imagine being sexually exploited by so many boys, while all that you wanted was what your friends had-a boyfriend? Can you imagine none of your friends, parents, or even your white therapist (if you have one) ever bringing up the topic of race while things like this are happening to you? On an intellectual level, it would make sense because race does not play a significant part in their lives. But I strongly believe it does for many transracial adoptees whether they or their parents know it.

How does a white adoptive father and his adult black daughter make sense of a situation when they are together and someone believes her to be a prostitute? How does the daughter feel about her sense of worth if this is just one of many times that she has been told and made to feel worthless just because she wears a coat of color and has features that are African?

Can you imagine going through life being the target of discrimination when you have never seen or met a black person who is biologically related to you? How does one make sense of this? How can a person be called a nigger or a black bitch when she has been surrounded and only loved by white people? Race must be a social construct. So is this a colorblind society? Imagine at some point in your life being exposed to your same race and not being accepted because you are acting too "white." Is this an act? Why would anyone think that a child of any color raised by white parents in a white community would be anything other than a white person who has been spray painted one of the various shades of color? How do you think it feels when you begin to see that you have been too "socialized white" to feel "black," and too dark-skinned to ever be accepted as white?

Susan Soon-Keum Cox, *Ritual*

9 Yale J. L. & Feminism 17–21 (1997)

"You are the eldest child, you go first."

It's true, I was born first. I am the eldest. But I am new to this. I do not know how to lead in this ritual of respect and honor to our mother.

"You go first." The words are spoken again and my two brothers step back and motion me toward our mother's grave. I step in front of the mound of earth that comes nearly to my shoulders and is covered with stiff grass. Even the burial place of my mother is foreign to what I know from my life in a different place.

"You bow four times."

I am grateful for the direction, but feel awkward too. "Like this?" I bow stiffly. They nod "yes." I bow three more times, more aware of them than the spirit of our mother who receives this ritual.

It is my turn to step back, and my brother, the second-born, moves forward to bow low and reverently several times. He moves with grace and sureness. He has done this many times before. I watch him and realize that I did not bow properly.

* * *

This ritual, so clearly familiar to my brothers, is foreign to me. More Baptist than Buddhist, I have never honored the dead like this before. But it feels comforting. I look out over the rice fields that surround my mother's final rest and I am grateful to be here. I am certain this moment would bring happiness to our mother, wherever she is. I raise my glass to my brothers and say, "To our mother, Chung Kwan Ja. I am sure this would make her happy-the three of us here together."

The interpreter repeats my words in Korean. Hearing them, my brothers shake their heads vigorously. "No, no! Not Chung Kwan Ja. Chung Kwan Ja. You are not saying it correctly." As if they were speaking to a child they put their faces close to mine and say it slowly. I repeat it back to them. "No, no, still wrong." We go back and forth until I get it right, or they give up on me.

At first I am hurt. They did not hear what I said. All they heard was the wrong accent as I attempted to say my mother's name in a tender salute. And then it passes...I did say it wrong. It is because I did not have her to show me. I did not hear her name everyday as they did. But I am here now. With them, with her. And that is what matters in the big picture.

I reach out for my brothers' hands and we sit together quietly before our mother's grave.

* * *

I left Korea for my new life on October 9, 1956. I remember little about that trip. I do remember looking out a small round window, sitting next to a woman I could not understand, and feeling very, very scared.

I was the 167th child to be adopted from Korea. More than 60,000 Korean children in the last forty years have made the same journey. That trip across the ocean is much more than a journey of several thousand miles. For those of us who have been adopted, it is the birth into our family.

I grew up in a small rural community in Oregon. I was my parents' first child. A year later they adopted a son from Korea. We were followed by three biological siblings, so I am the oldest of five. Although we didn't look the same, I always knew I was very much my parents' daughter.

...In my community, I grew up knowing little about Korea, or my heritage. I rarely had an opportunity to see other Korean people. I did not eat Korean food, see beautiful Korean fan dancing, hear Korean music, or hold celedon pottery in my hands.

What my parents did give me was the essence of how they felt about Korea. It was unwavering and unconditional. I always knew they thought Korea was a most important place. They treasured its people, its history, everything about it; for the simple reasons that Korea was where I was from and I was their daughter.

As an interracial adoptee, I believe in the absolute appropriateness of interracial adoption for children who would otherwise be denied their birthright to have a family. My adoption experience was positive. I consider myself to have had a typical, normal childhood. I did not consider being Korean, or being adopted, as the most important aspects of my life. From my own personal life experience, however, I also believe that race is an issue. To deny that reality is naive, at best, and dishonest and condescending, at worst.

I am profoundly aware of how different my life might have been. I acknowledge and accept that my early life circumstances were difficult. The reality that I could not stay with the mother who gave birth to me was a sadness that I shared with my parents. They spoke of my life in Korea, and of my birth-mother, with nothing but respect and dignity.

* * *

I was 26 years old when I returned to Korea for the first time. It was exciting, but also frightening. The last time I had been in Korea I had carried a Korean passport. Twenty-two years later, I was returning with my husband to visit this place I could barely remember. Would it be familiar? Would I come to remember how to speak the first language I had known, but had since forgotten? I expected it might feel like an echo of an earlier time.

It did not feel familiar, but it did feel welcoming. I was filled with enormous pride by the wonderful spirit and graciousness of Korean people. I loved knowing that this was also my heritage.

* * *

Two years ago I completed the full cycle of adoption. Thirty-seven years after I left Korea at age four, I met my Korean brothers. We share biology through our birth mother, but no shared history, since we did not grow up together. I did not see my birth mother again. But I did find her. She died in 1978. I learned that her last words were to my younger Korean brother: "You have an older sister. She went to America." I cannot express what that means to me. To know I was my mother's last thought as she was dying. "Ritual" is a picture of all our lives rejoined all these years later. My family has been extended.

Notes and Questions

1. *Macro-level Concerns and Individual Needs.* While the social and economic forces that influence parental relinquishment or termination require consideration in the context of adoption in general, the placement of children in families of a different nationality, and often a different ethnicity or race, adds another layer of complexity. The reasons children are available for international adoptive placement are varied, but certainly poverty, patriarchy, racism, the vestiges of Western imperialism, cultural imperialism, and economic exploitation have played a role. The above excerpts from articles by Professors Bartholet, Perry, and Rosettenstein and Ms. Lilith all highlight the difficult tensions inherent in acknowledging and addressing global socio-political concerns and the very immediate needs of individual children.

Professor Bartholet emphasizes that the desperate situation of millions of children necessitates domestic and international laws that encourage international adoption, reforms she outlines in a portion of the article not reprinted herein. Moreover, she contends, international adoption actually focuses attention on these larger issues, and marshals resources to address them. It is certainly true that many reputable international adoption agencies not only facilitate adoptions, but also raise funds for orphanages and medical services for children who remain in the countries from which they place children.

Even if one accepts Professor Bartholet's contention that the immediate needs of children cannot be held in abeyance until the underlying complex geopolitical problems are resolved, those problems still must be addressed. One can also question the efficacy of transnational adoption to meet the needs of individual children if the institution is in fact diverting attention from the social and economic problems faced by the children and families remaining in impoverished countries, or worse, contributing to the number of children in need of homes. In what ways do Professor Perry and Ms. Lilith highlight those concerns? What measures, on both an individual level and a governmental level, might ameliorate them?

In the specific context of racial genocide, Professor Rosettenstein raises the intriguing question of whether receiving children for adoption who have been displaced by intentional ethnic or racial purging within their own countries renders the receiving country an accessory to genocide under international law? Could the same argument be made about receiving children who are in need of families as a result of gender discrimination, either officially sanctioned or cultural? [For an in-depth examination of the population control polies of China and the extent to which they might be addressed under international conventions, see Chapter Thirteen A.1.b. and A.2.] His own conclusion is that impeding such adoptions would simply punish the innocent victims of such practices. Do you agree?

2. *Commodification.* Ms. Lilith equates international adoption of Chinese infants with the practice of facilitating mail-order brides. Do you think this is a valid comparison?

One, though not the only, basis for her analogy is the fee paid for adoption. Adopting a child from China generally costs between $10,000 and $20,000. Karin Evans, The Lost Daughters of China 22 (2000). This is very comparable to adopting a child domestically through a private agency in the United States. Both domestic and international adoptions entail agency and legal fees, as well as fees for home studies and document preparation. The fact that international adoption involves two countries, and their immigration, emigration, and adoption laws, dictates that the document and travel costs are generally higher in international adoption. In addition to these expenses, international adoption often entails some fee to a foreign facilitator, agency, or government. In the case of China, the Chinese government requires a payment of $3,000, characterized as an orphanage donation. In the United States, fees to a private agency would include the costs of pre- and post-natal medical expenses and foster care prior to placement. Considering that the Chinese government has typically cared for a child in a governmental institution or in a foster placement for several months or several years prior to placement, would such fees be comparable in nature? The funds generated by these fees often enable Chinese orphanages to improve their facilities and provide additional medical care for the remaining children. If that is so, wouldn't concern for the issues raised by Professor Perry support an argument that such payments are not only justifiable, but perhaps morally compelled? On the other hand, could the potential for funding from such fees influence a decision of an administrator of an orphanage to place a child internationally rather than domestically?

3. *Child Trafficking.* Professor Bartholet notes the very real concern that international adoption creates opportunities for child trafficking and kidnapping. While this is a concern domestically as well, the extreme disparity of income levels in sending and receiving nations, coupled with insufficient regulation in some countries of origin, magnify the potential for these abuses in international adoption. Professor Bartholet is undoubtedly correct that the vast majority of international adoptions do not involve illegal payments to birth parents or kidnapping, and there are many very reputable agencies facilitating international adoptions. Nevertheless, serious abuses do occur with some frequency.

In December 2001, the INS suspended adoptions by U.S. parents of Cambodian children, following an investigation by INS and State Department officials that revealed a widespread practice of facilitators and orphanages offering mothers payments (usually $20–$100, in a country with a per capita annual income of $240) to relinquish their infants. Their investigation also confirmed cases of kidnapping for adoptive placement. U.S. Dep't of State, The Adoption Process in Cambodia—An Update, *at* http://www.travel.state.gov/cambodiaremarks.html.

Following an investigation in 1999, a Special Rapporteur reported to the U.N. Human Rights Commission that trafficking of babies and young children for international adoption existed in Guatemala "on a large scale," and frequently involved payments to birth parents. On occasion, threats to relinquish, trickery, and kidnapping were also employed by adoption facilitators. The practice of "false mothers" presenting babies for adoption was so prevalent that by the late 1990s, Canada, the United States, and the United Kingdom all required DNA testing for all babies adopted from Guatemala. Report of the Special Rapporteur on the Sale of Children, Child Prostitution and Child Pornography, presented to the UN Human Rights Commission on January 27, 2000, *available at* http://www.casa-alianza.org/EN/human-rights/sexual-exploit/ONU/sale.shtml. By 2001, several countries and Canadian provinces, including Netherlands, Iceland, Spain, British Columbia and Ontario, had all suspended adoptions from Guatemala. Robin Hilborn, Adoption News Briefs, *at* http://www.familyhelper.net/news.html.

Guatemala and Cambodia are not isolated areas of concern. Illegal adoption practices and charges of child selling led the Canadian province of Ontario to suspend processing of adoption applications for children from Vietnam in August, 2001. *Id.* Quebec's International Adoption Secretariat similarly halted adoptions from India in March 2001, after several Indian orphanages, including the one used by the agency approved by the Quebec government, were closed due to suspicions of child trafficking. *Id.* In 1998, a child-smuggling operation was uncovered in Taiwan, in which it was discovered that as many as 100 Chinese children had been illegally adopted in Taiwan, following illegal payments to birth parents and, in some instances, abduction. Curtis Kleem, *Airplane Trips and Organ Banks: Random Events and the Hague Convention on Intercountry Adoption*, 28 Ga. J. Int'l & Comp. L. 319, 329 (2000). Professor Bartholet refers to the international concern raised by adoption practices in Romania in the early 1990s. Nor is the United States immune from this problem, as the case of the "internet twins" so tragically illustrated. *See* Problem 12-3 below.

4. *Psychological Well-being of Children Adopted Transnationally.* The justification for permitting international adoption must be to serve the needs of children who would otherwise be denied the opportunity for a permanent family, and in many instances, adequate food, medical care, and education. The experience of transcultural, and often transracial adoption, however, creates challenges for these children as they mature in the nations in which they are placed, as reflected in the above excerpts from articles by Susan Harris, herself a transracial adoptee, and Susan Cox, an adoptee from Korea who at the time of the publication worked for Holt International Children's Services. In portions not included in the above excerpts, both authors affirmed that they were not opposed to transracial adoption, but stressed the need for sensitivity to and adequate support systems for the challenges interracial adoptees face. For an additional perspective from an interracial adoptee, see Asher D. Isaacs, *Interracial Adoption: Permanent Placement and Racial Identity—An Adoptee's Perspective*, 14 Nat'l Black L.J. 126 (1995) ((advocates preference for same-race placement).

In summarizing over fifteen different studies of children who have been adopted internationally, Anne Westhues and Joyce Cohen observed that "[t]he majority of research on intercountry adoption finds that children have adapted well with respect to a sense of belonging within the family," and that the children have also displayed "levels of self-esteem which are at least as positive as in the general population, and with some groups appear to be more positive." Anne Westhaus & Joyce S. Cohen, *Ethnic and Racial Identity of Internationally Adopted Adolescents and Young Adults: Some Issues in Relation to Children's Rights*, 1 Adoption Q. 33, 35 (1998). Several of these studies concluded, however, that individuals adopted across racial and cultural lines have a weaker sense of ethnic and racial identity than children raised within their own ethnic and racial groups. *Id.* at 36–37. The authors' own study of 155 adolescents adopted internationally found that although very few had developed a bicultural identity, a large majority were comfortable with their ethnic and racial background. *Id.* at 50–51.

The first United Nations instrument to specifically address the topic of international adoption was the Declaration on Social and Legal Principles relating to the Protection and Welfare of Children, with Special Reference to Foster Placement and Adoption Nationally and Internationally, G.A. Res. 41/85, U.N. GAOR, 41st Sess., U.N. Doc. A/Res/41/85 (1986). The principles espoused in that Declaration were incorporated two years later into the broader Convention on the Rights of the Child (CRC), Nov. 20, 1989, 1577 U.N.T.S. 3, a human rights treaty which has subsequently been ratified by almost every nation in the world, the United States being the notable exception. The broad panoply of rights contracting nations agree to afford children are discussed in various chapters of this book, and the Convention is covered extensively in Chapter Fourteen, Section B. Article 21 of the CRC imposes general obligations upon states parties in regard to their participation as sending or receiving countries, and calls for additional bilateral or multilateral agreements to promote these objectives.

The invitation to further regulate international adoption was accepted by the Hague Conference on Private International Law, which convened a Special Commission consisting of delegates from over 65 nations, including Hague member countries and thirty countries of origin, i.e., nations that had participated in international adoption as sending countries. In addition, five inter-governmental organizations and twelve non-governmental organizations (NGOs) participated in the negotiations. The result of their work, the Hague Intercountry Adoption Convention, May 29, 1993, S. Treaty Doc. No. 105-51, 32 I.L.M. 1134, entered into force in 1985. The Convention is discussed in detail in Section B of this chapter.

Problem 12-1

Read Article 21 of the Convention on the Rights of the Child; the Preamble and Articles 3, 4, 17, 18, 20, and 24 of The Declaration on Social and Legal Principles relating to the Protection and Welfare of Children, with special reference to Foster Placement and Adoption Nationally and Internationally; and the Preamble and Article 4 of the Hague Intercountry Adoption Convention.

All three documents accept the existence of international adoption and undertake to impose some regulation on the practice. Is there nevertheless a difference between the United Nations instruments and the Hague Intercountry Adoption Convention regarding the extent to which international adoption is viewed as an appropriate alternative? If you believe there is, what factors might have contributed to the difference in the drafters' eagerness to embrace this institution?

Problem 12-2

Assume that you were a delegate to the Special Commission convened by the Hague Conference on Private International Law, charged with drafting the Convention on Intercountry Adoption. The nation you were representing, up to this point, has not been very actively engaged in international adoption as either a sending or receiving country. Would you be in favor of drafting a Convention that regulates and encourages international adoption, severely restricts the practice (and if so, in what ways), or bans transnational adoption altogether?

What might your perspective be if you were a delegate from a nation that was formerly colonized by European powers, with limited economic resources, a large number of children in orphanages, and a recent incidence of black market international adoptions of children from your country? Alternatively, what might your perspective be if you were a delegate from a highly industrialized nation with a healthy economy, low birth rate, long waiting lists of prospective adoptive parents, and significant political pressure from organized pro-adoption groups?

B. Regulation of International Adoption by International Conventions

1. U.N. and Regional Conventions

The U.N. Convention on the Rights of the Child (CRC) was the first global convention to impose regulation on international adoption. One of the most important contributions of the CRC was its treatment of children as individuals with rights under international law, rather than simply as persons in need of care and protection. *See* Cynthia Price Cohen, *The Developing Jurisprudence of the Rights of the Child*, 6 St. Thomas L. Rev. 1, 7–10, 19 (1993). Consistent with this approach, Article 21, which addresses adoption, begins with the pronouncement that the best interests of the child must be the "paramount consideration" in any system of adoption. Beyond the provisions on which you focused when considering Problem 12-1 in Section A of this Chapter, Article 21 contains relatively few directives that address international adoption specifically. It directs that international adoptions be conducted with the safeguards and standards equivalent to those applicable to domestic adoptions. It provides that measures must be taken to ensure that those involved in international adoption do not derive improper financial gain. It also mandates that international placements be carried out by "competent authorities or organs."

Various regional conventions also address international adoption. The Organization of American States has been particularly productive on this issue. The Inter-American Convention on Conflict of Laws Concerning the Adoption of Minors, May 24, 1984, O.A.S. Treaty Series No. 62, 24 I.L.M. 460, establishes choice of law rules for adoptions between contracting nations. As of March 2003, only six nations were parties. The Inter-American Convention on International Traffic in Minors, Mar. 18, 1994, O.A.S. Treaty Series No. 79, 33 I.L.M. 721, provides for the creation in contracting nations of criminal penalties and civil remedies for international trafficking in minors, which includes the abduction, removal or retention of a minor by kidnapping, fraudulent or coerced consent, the giving or receipt of a benefit to obtain consent of parents or other caretakers, or any other unlawful means. Civil remedies include a proceeding for return of the child, annulment of adoptions, revocation of custody orders, and actions for costs and civil damages. Nine Central and South American countries were parties to this convention, as of March 2003, and Mexico, Bolivia, and Venezuela had signed but not yet ratified the treaty. The United States is currently not a party to either of these O.A.S. conventions.

Other regions have addressed the topic of international adoption as well. The African Charter on the Rights and Welfare of the Child, OAU Doc. CAB/LEG/24.9/49 (1990), modeled after the Convention on the Rights of the Child, in Article 24 refers to the option of international adoption as a last resort. In addition to incorporating almost verbatim the directives of Article 21 of the CRC, the African Charter also requires the establishment of machinery to monitor the well-being of an adopted child. The European Convention on the Adoption of Children, April 24, 1967, 634 U.N.T.S. 255, though focused primarily on general principles applying to all types of adoptions, also requires adopters of a child of a different nationality to facilitate the child's acquisition of their own nationality, and provides that loss of nationality resulting from an adoption must be conditioned upon the acquisition by the child of a new nationality. (Article 11). The European Convention also requires contracting nations to cooperate with each other in the transmission of information about the child and prospective adoptive parents necessary to facilitate appropriate pre-adoption investigation. (Article 14).

2. The Hague Intercountry Adoption Convention

The most widely adopted international convention devoted specifically to the regulation of international adoption today is the Hague Intercountry Adoption Convention, which entered into force on May 1, 1995. As of March 2003, over fifty nations were parties to this convention, and eleven additional nations had signed but not yet ratified. One of the latter group was the United States, which signed the convention on March 31, 1994. The U.S. Senate has given its advice and consent to ratification of this treaty, and the implementing legislation—The Intercountry Adoption Act of 2000, 42 U.S.C. 14901 et seq.—was passed and signed by President Clinton on October 6, 2000. Ratification by the United States is anticipated to occur in 2004. U.S. Dep't of State, *Hague Convention on International Adoption, at* http://www.travel.state.gov/hagueinfo2002.html.

a. Scope

Even after the United States ratifies, the Hague Convention may not apply in the short term to many of the international adoptions in which the United States is a receiving or a sending country. By its own terms (Article 2), as well as the provisions of the implementing legislation (42 U.S.C. § 14902(10)), the Convention only applies if both the sending country and the receiving country are contracting states. Of the top ten countries from which children immigrated to the United States for adoption in 2002, only Guatemala, Colombia, and Bulgaria were parties to the Convention as of March 2003. *See* U.S. Dep't of State, Immigrant Visas Issued to Orphans Coming to the U.S., *at* http://www.travel.state.gov. However, both Russia and China, which for the past several years have been the countries of origin of over 50% of the children immigrating to the United States, signed the Convention in the fall of 2000, and India signed in January 2003, so in the long term the Convention's scope could be quite significant. Moreover, the U.S. government appears to be influenced by Convention principles in its regulation of international adoption even when the Convention is not yet in effect, as evidenced recently by its reliance upon Hague Convention standards in its explanation of the decision in 2002 to suspend adoptions from Cambodia. *See* U.S. Dep't of State, The Adoption Process in Cambodia—An Update, *at* http://www.travel.state.gov/cambodiaremarks.html.

Several other provisions also affect the scope of the Hague Intercountry Adoption Convention. The Convention applies only to those adoptions for which the agreement of the prospective adoptive parents and the agreement of the necessary government officials have been obtained prior to the child's eighteenth birthday.(Article 3). Prospective adoptive parents must be habitually resident in a contracting nation (see Chapter Eight, Section A for a discussion of the meaning of habitual residence as developed under the Hague Abduction Convention), and the child must be habitually resident in another contracting state. Thus, residence in a state party, rather than citizenship, is the requisite connection to invoke the Convention's application. (Articles 2, 14).

b. Objectives

The drafters of the Hague Intercountry Adoption Convention sought to establish a framework for international adoptions consistent with the principles and objectives articulated by the Convention on the Rights of the Child. The Hague Convention reflects the CRC's respect for children as rights-bearing individuals, recognizing in its Preamble the necessity of safeguarding the "full and harmonious development" of the child's personality. *See* Alexandra Maravel, *The U.N. Convention on the Rights of the Child and the Hague Conference on Private International Law: The Dynamics of Children's Rights Through Legal Strata*, 6 Transnat'l L. & Contemp. Probs. 309, 316 (1996). The Convention articulates four primary objectives:

(1) to ensure that international adoptions take place in the best interests of the child, respecting throughout the process the child's fundamental rights under international law;

(2) to establish cooperation among the contracting parties to ensure safeguards formulated in pursuit of the first goal are followed;

(3) to prevent the abduction, sale, or trafficking of children; and

(4) to secure recognition of Convention adoptions by the contracting states. (Article 1).

c. Central Authorities

Following the model of the Hague Abduction Convention, the Hague Intercountry Adoption Convention requires each contracting nation to designate a governmental entity as its Central Authority, to be responsible for promoting intergovernmental cooperation and communication, exchanging information, eliminating obstacles to the Convention's application, and deterring child trafficking and other practices that would violate Convention standards. (Articles 6,7,8). The U.S. Department of State has been designated as the Central Authority for the United States. Within that Department, Convention duties will be performed by the Office of Consular Affairs, Office of Children's Issues. 42 U.S.C.A. § 14911 (2000). Some Central

Authority functions, however, such as reviewing applications of prospective adoptive parents (Article 14), have been delegated to the Attorney General, and will be performed, as they have been prior to implementation of the Convention, by the Immigration and Naturalization Service (INS). 42 U.S.C.A. § 14913 (2000).

The Office of Children's Issues will serve as the liason with other Central Authorities and coordinate Convention activities. This Office will be the point of contact within the United States and from abroad for matters related to the status of particular adoptions covered by the Convention, as well as systemic Convention-related matters. Information Paper Prepared by the Delegation of the United States, *The 1993 Hague Intercountry Adoption Convention: Status of and Concepts Underlying U.S. Federal Implementing Legislation, available at* http://travel.state.gov/status_concepts.html. The Office will also provide information regarding federal and state laws implementing the Convention and the agencies and approved persons that have been accredited to provide adoption services within the United States for Convention adoptions. It will gather information from other Central Authorities regarding their adoption requirements and Convention service providers, and make that information available to federal agencies, state courts, and those providing services regarding Convention adoptions. The Office of Children's Services will not operate as an adoption service provider for individual adoptions, but it will facilitate interaction between individual citizens and government officials of Convention countries in those instances in which an accredited agency or approved person is unwilling or unable to provide facilitation.

In addition, the Office of Children's Issues will operate a computer-based tracking system, in coordination with the INS, that will maintain a continuous step-by-step record of all incoming and outgoing international adoptions involving the United States, regardless of whether or not the adoption is covered by the Hague Convention. *Id.*; 42 U.S.C.A. § 14912 (2000). Following ratification of the Convention, the Office will prepare annual reports on all international adoptions involving the United States, which should provide valuable information in the future regarding such matters as the number of children who immigrate to and emigrate from the United States for adoption, the average time required to complete an adoption from each country, the range of fees charged, and the number and resolution of adoptions that disrupted after placement. 42 U.S.C.A. § 14914 (2000).

d. Accredited Bodies and Approved Persons or Bodies

Although many of the systemic duties of a Central Authority described above are nondelegable, most of the Convention responsibilities related to individual adoptions can be delegated to accredited bodies or approved persons or bodies. (Articles 9,11,15–22). Such duties would include the collection, preservation, and exchange of information about the child and the prospective adoptive parents, facilitation of the adoption, provision of adoption and post-adoption counseling, and responding to requests for information about particular adoptions they are facilitating. Within the United States, the Department of State is contracting with state agencies and other nonprofit entities to oversee the accreditation of adoption agencies to qualify as accredited bodies under the Convention, as well as the approval of persons or bodies who can perform certain Convention functions. These accrediting entities would also be responsible for ongoing monitoring of compliance by accredited agencies and approved persons or bodies with the Convention, enforcement proceedings against noncomplying agencies, persons, or bodies, and the collection of data and preparation of reports. 42 U.S.C.A. § 14922 (2000).

Broad standards for accreditation are found in Article 11 of the Convention, which provides that accredited bodies must be non-profit; directed and staffed by qualified individuals obligated to follow ethical standards and trained or experienced in intercountry adoption; and subject to supervision by a governmental entity regarding their operation, composition, and financial situation. More detailed requirements for accreditation within the United States are found in 42 U.S.C. § 14923 (2000), which contains specific requirements for such responsibilities as provision of medical records to prospective adoptive parents, completion and transmission of home studies of prospective adoptive parents, and provision of pre-adoption training to prospective adopters. Additional requirements address fee policies, staffing, record maintenance capacity, and mandatory liability insurance coverage. Further standards and procedures for accreditation will be included in regulations issued by the Department of State.

During negotiation of the Hague Intercountry Adoption Convention, there was much debate about whether the Convention should permit independent adoptions, i.e., those in which services are provided by individuals or bodies that are neither governmental entities nor accredited bodies. Several receiving countries, including the United States, have had a tradition of permitting private adoptions, in which the adoption is facilitated by an individual, often a lawyer, rather than an adoption agency licensed by a state. While the U.S. delegation included members personally opposed to this practice, there was concern that if the Convention prohibited such adoptions completely, it would never garner sufficient political support within the United States to achieve ratification. Delegates from the United States therefore pushed for provisions that would permit such independent adoptions under the Convention, but subject to Convention regulation. *See* Peter Pfund, *The Hague Intercountry Adoption Convention and Federal International Child Support Enforcement,* 30 U.C. Davis L. Rev. 647, 651–52 (1997). Some countries participating in the drafting strongly opposed such practices.

The resulting compromise was Article 22 of the Convention, which permits countries of origin to specify that their children may be placed internationally only if Convention functions are performed by a public authority or accredited body that satisfied the standards of Article 11. In the absence of such a designation, Article 22 permits most of the duties that could be performed by accredited bodies to also be handled by approved bodies or persons, such as lawyers or social workers, as long as they meet the standards of Article 22 and are subject to supervision by governmental authorities. Both the standards for such bodies or persons under Article 22, and U.S. standards for approving them under 42 U.S.§ 14923, are virtually identical to those for accredited bodies (i.e., accredited agencies), except that these approved entities are not required to be non-profit and are not required in the United States under § 14923 to be licensed by a State to provide adoption services.

Article 22 requires that in private adoptions facilitated by persons or entities that are not accredited bodies under the Convention, prospective adoptive parents must still make application to a Central Authority, another public authority, or an accredited body; and a governmental entity or accredited body must bear ultimate responsibility for the reports regarding the prospective adoptive parents (i.e., home studies) and the child, even if non-accredited bodies or individuals participate in their preparation. *See* G.Parra-Aranguren, Explanatory Report on the Convention on Protection of Children and Co-operation in Respect of Intercountry Adoption, ¶¶ 378–79, *available at* http://www.hcch.net/e/conventions/expl33e.html. In the United States these functions are performed by the INS for all adoptions involving the immigration of a child into the United States, whether or not the adoption is facilitated by an accredited agency.

e. Convention Requirements for Intercountry Adoptions

The Hague Intercountry Adoption Convention does not establish a uniform adoption law for all contracting nations. It does, however, establish certain minimum standards for adoption practices that must be followed by both countries of origin and receiving countries for adoptions covered by the Convention.

In the country of origin, the Convention requires that a competent governmental authority must establish that a child is adoptable and determine, after consideration of domestic placement options, that intercountry adoption is the alternative that best serves the interests of the child. A governmental authority must ensure that proper consent has been obtained from all persons, institutions, or authorities from whom consent is required. The governmental authority must also ensure that those consents are (1) voluntary; (2) in writing and in the required legal form; (3) given after counseling and with full information regarding the effect of the consent; (4) not induced by payment or compensation; and (5) have not been revoked; and, (6) if the consent of the birth mother is required, that it was not given before the birth of the child. In addition, if the child to be adopted is of sufficient age and maturity, a governmental entity must ensure (1) that the child must be counseled regarding the effect of the adoption and any consent the child is required to give; (2) that consideration has been given to the child's opinion and preferences; and (3) that the child's consent, when it is required by the applicable law, has been given voluntarily, in the required legal form, expressed or evidenced in writing, and not induced by payment or compensation. (Article 4). The governmental entity ensuring that these requirements have been met may be either administrative or judicial, or even the Central Authority itself. G. Parra-Aranguren, Explanatory Report ¶ 111, *supra*.

Issues such as when a child is "adoptable," which consents must be obtained, and the form requirements, are to be determined by the law that would be applicable in the country of origin, applying its own conflict of laws principles. G. Parra-Aranguren, Explanatory Report, *supra*, ¶¶ 119, 129. Thus, those issues not determined by the Convention's mandates will normally be resolved by domestic law, unless the circumstances are such that the sending nation's conflicts of law principles would apply another nation's law to resolve the issue.

Additional responsibilities of the country of origin may be performed by a governmental authority, an accredited body, or a person or body approved under Article 22. These include (1) preparation of a report concerning the child's identity, adoptability, background, social environment, family history, individual and family medical history, and special needs; (2) giving consideration to the child's upbringing and ethnic, religious, and cultural environment in determining an appropriate placement option; (3) ensuring the appropriate consents have been obtained; and (4) determining whether placement with particular prospective adoptive parents is in the child's best interests, based on the reports related to the child and the prospective adopters. Following a placement decision, a report on the child, proof the necessary consents have been obtained, and reasons for the placement determination must be forwarded to the Central Authority of the receiving state, and any necessary steps must be undertaken to ensure that the child will be permitted to emigrate. (Article 16)

In the receiving country, either a governmental authority, an accredited body, or an approved body or person must prepare a report for transmittal to the country of origin. In the United States, this report is often referred to as a home study. The Convention requires that it contain information about the adopters' identity, eligibility and suitability to adopt, background, family and medical history, reasons for adoption, social environment, ability to adopt internationally, and the characteristics of a child for whom they would be qualified to parent. (Article 15).

Following preparation of the home study, a competent governmental authority in the receiving country must determine that the prospective adoptive parents are eligible and suited to adopt, and that they have been counseled. After a child has been matched with prospective adoptive parents, competent governmental authorities in the receiving country must determine that the child who will be placed with them is authorized under that country's immigration laws to enter and reside permanently in that country. (Article 5). This last requirement is particularly important. As you will see in the next subsection, U.S. practices in non-Convention adoptions have in the past resulted in the discovery by U.S. parents, after an adoption in a foreign country, that their child is not eligible to enter the United States. Peter Pfund, *Implementation of the Hague Intercountry Adoption Convention in the United States: Issues and Pitfalls*, in E. Pluribus Unum 321, 331–32 (A. Borras et al. eds., 1996).

Before a child is transferred to prospective adoptive parents, governmental authorities, an accredited body, or an approved person or body in the country of origin must ensure (1) that the prospective adoptive parents have agreed to adopt the particular child with whom they have been matched; (2) that the proper authorities in the receiving nation have approved the placement decision, when the law of either nation requires such approval; (3) that such authorities of both states have agreed the adoption may proceed; (4) that the prospective adopters are eligible and suited to adopt; and (5) that the receiving country has determined that the child will be permitted to enter and reside permanently in that country. A governmental authority, accredited body, or approved person or body in the country of origin must also take whatever steps are necessary to ensure the child will be permitted to leave its home country. (Articles 17, 18). The Convention provides that the child should travel to the receiving nation in secure and appropriate circumstances, and if possible, in the company of the adoptive or prospective adoptive parents. (Article 19).

Once the child has reached the receiving country, those authorities, accredited agencies, or approved bodies or persons facilitating the adoption in each country must keep each other informed about the progress of the placement, if a probationary period is required, and about the adoption process and measures taken to complete it. (Article 20). Some countries of origin may require the adoption of a child to take place in their own country (Article 28), while others are willing to send a child to the receiving country after custody has been awarded to prospective adopters or an agency or intermediary, so that the adoption may take place in the receiving country. In the latter situation, if the governmental authority, accredited agency, or approved person or body facilitating the adoption in the receiving nation determines after placement, but prior to the adoption, that the placement is not in the child's best interests, it must remove the child from the prospective adopters with whom the child had been placed, arrange temporary care, and arrange a new placement, in consultation with the appropriate governmental authority, accredited body, or approved person or body in the country of origin who also facilitated the adoption. No adoption may take place by the new family until the appropriate authority, agency, or body in the country of origin has been notified. If the child is sufficiently mature, the child also must be consulted and, when appropriate, the child's consent to the new placement obtained as well. In those rare situations in which it becomes apparent that a new adoptive placement is not appropriate, the Convention dictates that arrangements must be made for the child's long term care, and only as a last resort and if the child's interests so require should the child be returned to the country of origin. (Article 21).

Following a Convention adoption, competent governmental authorities in both the sending and receiving states must ensure that they preserve any information they possess concerning a child's origin, including both medical history and identifying information regarding the child's parentage. They must also ensure that such information is available to the child or the child's representative to the extent permitted by their own law. (Article 30). Aside from the disclosure permitted to the child or his representative, other personal data gathered and transmitted pursuant to the Convention may not be used for any purpose beyond that permitted by applicable law of the sending and receiving nations. (Article 31).

Two provisions of the Convention, in particular, are intended to subvert child trafficking. The first is Article 29, which prohibits contact between prospective adoptive parents and the birth parents or other caretakers of the child until after (1) governmental authorities in the country of origin have established the child is adoptable, determined that intercountry adoption is the preferable option for the child, and obtained the necessary consents from everyone, other than the child, from whom applicable law requires a consent, and (2) the receiving country has determined the prospective adoptive parents eligible and suitable to adopt. The only exceptions to this mandate are family adoptions and contacts that are permitted by governmental authorities of the country of origin. (Article 29). The second restriction is that only reasonable professional fees, costs, and expenses may be charged or paid in connection with a Convention adoption. Directors, administrators, and other employees of bodies involved in an adoption are not permitted to receive unreasonably high remuneration for their services. The receipt of improper financial or other gain by anyone in connection with an intercountry adoption is strictly prohibited. (Article 32).

If a governmental authority discovers that any provision of the Convention has been violated, or that there is a serious risk that a provision will not be respected, it is required to inform the Central Authority, which is directed to take appropriate measures. (Article 33). Countries of origin as well as receiving countries that obtain information regarding serious irregularities can exercise their power under Article 17(c) prior to placement to prevent an adoption from proceeding. E.g., Roisin Pillay, *Implemelntation of the Hague Convention on Intercountry Adoption: The Law Reform Commission Report,* 1 Irish J. Fam. L. 19, 20 (1999). However, specific enforcement remedies are for the most part left to the applicable law of the nations involved, rather than included in the Convention. It is interesting to compare this approach with that of the Inter-American Convention on International Traffic in Minors, adopted just one year after the Hague Convention, which requires contracting nations to create severe penal remedies, extradite offenders to other contracting nations, return minors wrongfully removed or retained, annul adoptions and revoke custody orders resulting from trafficking, and recognize a civil action for damages and costs.

Within the United States, one of the primary systemic enforcement mechanisms is the suspension or cancellation of accreditation or approval, or temporary or permanent debarment of agencies or persons that had previously been accredited or approved to provide service in Hague Convention adoptions. Failure to comply with the requirements of the Intercountry Adoption Act in general, and specifically the failure to complete and transmit home studies in compliance with the Act's standards, are cited as grounds for such disciplinary action. 42 U.S.C.A. § 14924 (2000). In addition, the Intercountry Adoption Act creates both civil and criminal remedies for (1) providing services, without accreditation or approval, in connection with a Convention adoption, other than those services specifically permitted by 42 U.S.C. § 14921; or (2) making fraudulent statements or misrepresentations, or offering or accepting compensation, in order to influence the decision of an accrediting entity, the relinquishment of parental rights or parental consent, or any decision or act of a body performing a Central Authority function. Civil penalties may also be imposed for engaging an agent, within the United States or abroad, who takes any of the above actions. The Attorney General is authorized to bring actions for civil enforcement in any federal court. 42 U.S.C.A. § 14944 (2000).

f. Recognition of Convention Adoptions and U.S. Certification Procedures

An adoption certified as having been made in accordance with the Hague Intercountry Adoption Convention must be recognized by operation of law in all contracting nations. Certification of a Convention adoption is performed by a competent governmental authority in the nation in which the adoption takes place. Recognition can be refused only if the adoption is manifestly contrary to the recognizing nation's public policy, after taking into account the best interests of the child. (Articles 23, 24). The United States has specified that it will recognize adoptions between two other Convention countries even if the adoption became final before the date that the Convention enters into force for the United States. 42 U.S.C.A. § 14951 (2000).

If a child is adopted in a Convention country prior to immigrating to the United States, the U.S. Secretary of State, will issue to the adoptive citizen parent who is domiciled in the United States its own certificate that the adoption has been granted pursuant to the Convention, after the Office of Children's Issues has received notification from the Central Authority of the country of origin and has verified that the requirements of the Convention and the Intercountry Adoption Act have been satisfied. Any foreign adoption so certified by the Secretary of State is entitled to recognition as a valid final adoption for purposes of all federal, state, and local law within the United States. 42 U.S.C.A. § 14931 (2000).

When legal custody of a child is granted abroad to a prospective adoptive parent who is a U.S. citizen, so that the child may emigrate and be adopted in a United States court, the U.S. Secretary of State will issue a certificate that custody has been granted for purposes of an adoption pursuant to the Convention, after the Office of Children's Issues similarly receives notification from the sending nation's Central Authority and verifies that the requirements of the Convention and the Act have been met. The U.S. state court is prohibited from granting a final decree of adoption for the child until this certificate has been issued by the Secretary of State. 42 U.S.C.A. § 14931 (2000).

Documents originating in another Convention country related to a Convention adoption are admissible in any U.S. court without authentication, unless there is evidence to support an allegation that the document is false, altered, or otherwise unreliable. 42 U.S.C.A. § 14942 (2000).

Though most of the international adoptions in which the United States participates involve children immigrating to the United States, a small number of children born in the United States also emigrate to other countries for adoption. Precise statistics on the number of children adopted from the United States will not be available until the case-tracking registry of the Office of Children's Issues is fully implemented. Canadian immigration records indicate that between 65 and 100 children immigrated to Canada each year between 1999 and 2001 for relative or non-relative adoptions. Robin Hilborn, Adoption News Briefs, *at* http://www.familyhelper.net/news.html. State Department officials estimate that approximately 100–200 children are taken abroad annually for adoption in foreign courts, and no estimate is available regarding the number adopted in U.S. state courts prior to emigration. Peter Pfund, *supra*, at 324. Prior to implementation of the Hague Intercountry Adoption Convention, no federal laws regulated the adoption of U.S. children by foreign adoptive parents, and domestic state laws regulating adoption were applied only if the relinquishment or adoption occurred in the United States. *Id.*

The Intercountry Adoption Act now requires that when a child residing in the United States is to be placed for adoption in a Convention country, the accredited agency or approved person facilitating the adoption must:

(1) ensure that a background study on the child is prepared;

(2) certify that it has been unable to place the child in the United States in a timely manner, after making reasonable efforts to actively recruit U.S. adoptive parents;

(3) ensure that a determination is made that placement with the particular prospective adoptive parents identified is in the best interests of the child;

(4) furnish to a state court with appropriate jurisdiction (a) documentation regarding items (1)–(3); (b) a home study of the prospective adoptive parents; and (c) a declaration from the governmental authorities in the receiving country that the child will be permitted to enter and reside therein, and that any governmental consents necessary under the law of the receiving country for the adoption to be finalized have been obtained. 42 U.S.C.A. § 14932 (2000).

If the laws of the state in which the child resides and the law of the receiving country both permit parents or prospective adoptive parents to act on their own behalf, they are permitted by federal law to perform tasks (1), (3) and (4), but they must still obtain documentation that an accredited agency or approved person has searched for and been unable to find an adoptive home for the child within the United States. A state court cannot enter a final decree of adoption or grant custody for purposes of adoption of a child residing in the United States who will emigrate to a Convention country unless the court has received all of the documentation described above, as well as evidence that all of the requirements of the Hague Convention's Articles 4 and 15–21 have been satisfied, and has itself determined that the adoptive placement is in the best interests of the child. *Id.*

The agency or other approved person facilitating the adoption, or a parent or prospective adoptive parent must submit copies of the state court order of final adoption, or grant of custody for purposes of adoption, along with copies of the documentation furnished to the state court and any other information requested to the Office of Children's Issues of the Department of State. Upon verification, the Secretary of State will then issue an official certification that the child has been adopted, or that custody for purposes of adoption has been granted, in accordance with the Convention and the Intercountry Adoption Act. *Id.*

If a child residing in the United States is emigrating for purposes of adoption to a country that is not a party to the Hague Intercountry Adoption Convention, an accredited agency, approved person, governmental authority, or any other person providing adoption services is still obligated to provide information required by regulation to the Office of Children's Issues, so that the adoption may still be recorded in the case registry. *Id.*

Problems

Read the Hague Intercountry Adoption Convention and the Intercountry Adoption Act, 42 U.S.C. § 14901 et seq., and consider the following problems.

12-3. In 2001, the adoption of the "Internet twins" made international headlines. Infant girls born in Missouri were originally placed by their mother, Tranda Wecker, through a California adoption facilitator, Tina Johnson, with a California couple, the Allens, who are reported to have paid the facilitator a fee of $6,000. After the babies had lived with the Allens for approximately two months, the birth mother asked to see them, and then refused to return them to the Allens (a choice she was permitted to make under California law, which at that time afforded birth mothers an absolute right to revoke consent in an independent adoption within ninety days, Cal. Fam. Code § 8814.5 (West Supp. 2000)). Ms. Wecker subsequently transferred the babies to the Kilshaws, a couple from Wales who had paid Ms. Johnson $12,000 for their placement, allegedly with no foreknowledge about the previous placement with the Allens. Upon learning the babies were being placed with the Kilshaws, a confrontation between the Allens and Kilshaws occurred in a California hotel lobby when the transfer took place.

The Kilshaws and Ms. Johnson then reportedly drove to Arkansas with the babies, stopping in Missouri to collect documents. The Kilshaws filed an adoption proceeding, in which Ms. Johnson used the address of an aunt to allege in the Arkansas pleadings that she had been a resident of Arkansas for thirty days. Arkansas law at the time did not require that the adoptive parents live in the state, so a decree of adoption was granted, and the Kilshaws returned with the girls to Britain.

Ultimately, the story leaked to the British press. Both the Allens and the Kilshaws were on national television in the United States and Britain, asserting rights to the twins. As a result of the publicity, the British government temporarily placed the twins in foster care in Wales. The Arkansas court subsequently voided the adoption because neither the adoptive parents nor the birth mother were Arkansas residents, and the children were returned by the British government to state officials in Missouri, where they were again placed in foster care. By the time of their second birthday, the twins were still in foster care, the Missouri court having denied the requests of both of their birth parents to custody. *See* Sarah Lyall, *Battle by 2 Couples to Adopt U.S. Twins Moves to Britain*, N.Y. Times, Jan. 18, 2001, at A3; *British Couple That Lost Battle for 'Internet Twins' Now Loses House*, Associated Press Newswires, October 22, 2001; A.P., *Parents Denied Custody of Twins*, Philadelphia Inquirer, May 26, 2002, at A24.

At the time the adoption of the twins by the Kilshaws took place, both the United Kingdom and the United States were signatories to the Hague Intercountry Adoption Convention, but neither nation had yet ratified or implemented the Convention. How might the Convention and the Intercountry Adoption Act have impacted the Kilshaws' attempt to adopt the twins, if instead the Convention had been ratified by both nations at the time and had been already implemented in the United States? What specific provisions of each are relevant to your analysis?

Do you feel the provisions of the Convention and the Intercountry Adoption Act are sufficient to guard against intercountry adoption abuses? If not, what would be the benefits and burdens of additional regulations that you might propose?

12-4. Peter and Gwen adopted Teresa, a three-year-old from Ecuador, through Bridges Adoption Agency in Pittsburgh, Pennsylvania. Assume that both Ecuador and the United States had ratified and implemented the Hague Adoption Convention at the time of the adoption. Prior to placement, Peter and Gwen received from Bridges a medical history form describing Teresa as a happy, developmentally normal child with normal behavior and no remarkable illnesses. A brief medical history of the birth mother was provided, and the biological father was reported to be healthy. No identifying information regarding the birth parents was provided. Peter and Gwen proceeded with the placement, flew to Ecuador, and finalized the adoption in accordance with the Convention and Ecuadoran law.

After they returned to the United States, Peter and Gwen realized that Teresa's development was significantly behind, and she exhibited severe behavior disorders. Three years later, after multiple psychological evaluations and a battery of diagnostic testing, Teresa was diagnosed with bipolar disorder and severe attention deficit hyperactivity disorder. Two more years of intensive psychiatric treatment, both in-patient and out-patient, followed.

When Teresa was eight years old, the parents contacted the agency, at the request of one of Teresa's psychiatrists, to find out if there was any more medical history available. In response to this request, the agency released to them notes that the agency had received along with the initial report on Teresa from the orphanage at the time the placement was made, taken in Spanish by Teresa's caretakers at the orphanage. The notes indicated that Teresa had exhibited severe behavioral problems and developmental delay during her time at the orphanage as well. They also indicated that Teresa's biological father had been reported by paternal relatives to the orphanage staff to have severe mental problems. The adoption agency had staff at the time of the placement who spoke and read Spanish fluently, but had never before released these notes to Peter and Gwen.

Peter and Gwen immediately filed a lawsuit against Bridges Adoption Agency in Pennsylvania state court seeking compensatory and punitive damages for intentional and negligent misrepresentation and nondisclosure. Will any terms of the Convention or the Intercountry Adoption Act be of assistance to them in these claims? Could the nondisclosure have any other repercussions for the agency?

When Teresa is eighteen, if she wants to learn the identity of her birth parents, will the Convention or the Intercountry Adoption Act offer her any assistance?

C. Adopting a Child from Abroad — The Process

Though some children do emigrate from the United States to adoptive homes abroad, the vast majority of children affected by international adoption in the United States have immigrated to the United States to reside with their adoptive families. This section will examine the U.S. process for transnationally adopting a child, focusing on the many sources of legal regulation, including foreign law, state law, and federal law, which will continue, along with the Hague Intercountry Adoption Convention, to impact that process.

1. Role of Adoption Agencies and Lawyers

In the United States, agencies that facilitate international adoption are private rather than public entities. They are typically non-profit and licensed by the state in which they operate. However, in some states, for-profit individuals or entities are also permitted to facilitate both domestic and international adoptions, without meeting the state licensing requirements for adoption agencies.

After implementation of the Hague Convention, individuals or agencies will be precluded from providing services in connection with the adoption of children from countries that have ratified the Convention, unless they satisfy the standards for designation by the federal government as an accredited agency (non-profit, state-licensed) or approved person (for-profit individual or entity that need not be a state-licensed adoption agency). 42 U.S.C.A. § 14921 (2000). Exceptions to this requirement permit (1) the preparation of a background study of a child or a home study of prospective adopters by professional social workers, if the study or report is later approved by an accredited agency, (2) the provision of child welfare services, and (3) the provision of legal services, without federal accreditation or approval of the social workers or lawyers providing such services. Prospective adoptive parents are also permitted to act on their own behalf, to the extent such activities are not prohibited by state law. *Id.* Agencies or individuals providing services in non-Convention adoptions continue to be subject only to whatever regulation is imposed by the states in which they operate, and the foreign nations from which they facilitate adoptions.

When prospective adoptive parents work with a knowledgeable agency, agency staff can often guide them through the entire adoption process. Typically the agency advises clients regarding the adoption requirements of the foreign nations with which the agency works, assists clients with obtaining a home study that satisfies the requirements of both state and federal law, and provides pre-adoption training and counseling. The agency also normally assists prospective adopters with the paperwork required for U. S. immigration procedures, as well as the application to the appropriate governmental authorities, agencies, or orphanages in the foreign country for assignment. Harlan S. Tenenbaum, *Guiding Clients Through the Complexities of International Adoption,* 13 Am. J. Fam. L. 235 (1999).

International adoption agencies typically maintain relationships with a governmental entity, orphanage, or individual in a foreign country, with whom the agency has a child-placing agreement or contract. Through this agreement, individuals or entities in the country of origin identify a child, obtain the necessary consents or certify the abandonment, make the match, complete the paperwork on the child to forward to the United States for the prospective adopters to examine, arrange for the child to obtain passport and permission to emigrate, and provide the necessary documents for the child to obtain a visa. Most countries of origin require that at least one of the prospective adoptive parents travel to that country to take custody of the child and complete the adoption, and in these circumstances the agency typically assists with arrangements for travel and the services of interpreters or guides who facilitate the process in the foreign nation. Some countries of origin will transfer custody of the child to the agency itself, and permit the agency to provide for the child to be escorted to the United States. Upon arrival the agency then transfers custody to the prospective adoptive parents and adoption proceedings are filed in a U.S. court. Most agencies will also arrange for post-placement home studies, when required by state law, and provide post-adoption counseling. If the initial placement disrupts before the adoption is finalized, the agency then bears responsibility for finding another placement for the child in the United States. *See* Tenenbaum, *supra,* at 235–36; Kathleen M. Sullivan, *Intercountry Adoption, A Step-by-Step Guide for the Practitioner,* 95-09 Immigr. Briefings 1(1995). Many agencies also facilitate support groups and cultural activities for adoptees and their families.

If an adoption is being facilitated by an experienced international adoption agency, lawyers often play only a small role, assisting with an adoption, or in some cases, readoption, in a U.S. court. In many cases, when readoption is unnecessary, *see* Section C.4.*b. infra,* private lawyers may have no role at all, as a good agency is often able to provide the assistance necessary.

Clients thinking about international adoption sometimes approach an attorney for general advice, without having identified a particular child. In addition to providing general information about how the process works and some of the pitfalls, often the best advice an attorney can give is to steer the client to a reputable, experienced international adoption agency, and provide advice on how to choose an agency. Sometimes prospective adoptive parents will work with two agencies, one in their home state that prepares the home study, and an agency located in another state that facilitates the placement. *See* Elizabeth Bartholet, *International Adoption: Overview,* in 2 Adoption Law and Practice, 10-1, 10-24 (Joan Hollinger ed., 1997).

In order to choose an agency, clients should first give thought to the country from which they hope to adopt a child. Most agencies facilitate adoptions with only a limited number of countries, and some countries of origin will only work with a limited number of agencies. Most agencies will facilitate adoptions with prospective adoptive parents who reside anywhere in the United States, but some countries of origin by contract permit particular agencies to place children only in certain states.

Many issues affect the decision to pursue adoption in a particular sending country. Each country of origin has its own eligibility requirements for prospective adoptive parents, regarding such factors as age, marital status, health, fertility, and current parental status. The characteristics of children available for adoption in different countries also vary a great deal. Some countries place children as young as four to six months, while other countries only have older children available for adoption. Some nations permit only children with special needs to be placed internationally. Some have more children of one gender available for placement. The circumstances affecting the reasons children are available and the care they have received in the countries of origin also vary, as do the health risks and the type of background information available. The expense associated with international adoption varies as well. Adoptions from countries that permit agencies to escort children to the United States generally involve less expense than those that require travel. Some countries require several trips, and lengthy stays, to process an adoption. Waiting periods also fluctuate dramatically. Moreover, the availability of children from particular countries changes quickly, and over the past decade many countries of origin have periodically shut down their international adoption programs. In addition, the INS has on occasion halted adoptions from a particular country, as it did with Cambodia in January 2002.

All of these factors may influence prospective adopters' choices about the countries to which they wish to apply, and as a result, the agencies with which they choose to work. While no agency can circumvent all hazards, the selection of a reputable agency experienced in working with a country or countries from which one hopes to adopt is generally wise. In addition, selecting an agency that works with more than one country often permits that agency to facilitate an adoption with a different country, if the first country to which a prospective adopter applies shuts down before a placement is made.

Some prospective adoptive parents wish to pursue an independent adoption, i.e., one in which the prospective adopters, their attorney, or another intermediary who is not a licensed agency deal directly with a foreign child-placing source. While some countries of origin, particularly in Asia, refuse to place children through independent facilitators, other nations, particularly in Latin America, have historically permitted such practices. Often this route is attempted when the prospective adoptive parents wish to adopt a family member, a friend's child, or a child whom they have identified through their own overseas work or other international connections they have made.

When a client is pursuing an independent international adoption, the attorney's role is far more complicated, as the attorney often must provide the advice and assistance that normally is provided by an agency. The client will need guidance about immigration requirements, any applicable state law requirements, and the requirements of the country of origin, in addition to any Hague Convention requirements, if the adoption will be covered by the Convention. Assistance with obtaining a home study that satisfies all applicable state, federal, and foreign legal requirements; collection and transmittal of documents; and communication with the individual or entity facilitating the adoption in the country of origin will often be necessary, in addition to representation in a state court adoption proceeding, when one is required.

Attorneys who assist clients with international adoptions on a regular basis often seek advice regarding local law and other assistance from foreign counsel or other individuals in the country of origin who are authorized to facilitate international adoptions. Sullivan, *supra,* at 6. One practitioner also recommends that attorneys who regularly handle international adoptions should develop a questionnaire similar to those used by agencies, to obtain detailed information from clients regarding their background, marital history, citizenship, financial affairs, various areas that will be covered on the home study, and the type of child they seek to adopt. This will enable attorneys to advise clients of potential obstacles early in the process, and also enable the attorney to assist them in selecting a country, if they have not already done so. *Id.* at 4.

Note

1. *Law of the Countries of Origin.* A detailed examination of the foreign law governing the eligibility requirements and adoption procedures of the nations from which children are adopted and brought to the United States is beyond the scope of this chapter. Adoption laws in many of the countries of origin are frequently amended, and internationally adopted children come to the United States from many nations. Between 1989 and 2002, in every year except 1999 children immigrated to the United States in substantial numbers (50 or more) from 20 or more countries. U.S. Dep't of State, *Immigrant Visas Issued to Orphans Coming to the U.S., at* http://www.travel.state.gov/orphan_numbers.html.

For information concerning the requirements of specific countries, an excellent starting place is the website of the Department of State, which contains general information about many of the countries from which American citizens adopt children, as well as announcements regarding temporary or permanent cessation of international placements instigated by the countries of origin, or in some instances, the INS. *See* U.S. Dep't of State, http://www.travel.state.gov/adopt.html. International adoption agencies are also a useful source of information. In addition, many law review articles have been written about specific countries of origin, and recent reform efforts in some of them. *See, e.g.,* Curtis Kleem, *Airplane Trips and Organ Banks: Random Events and the Hague Convention on Intercountry Adoption,* 28 Ga. J. Int'l & Comp. L. 319 (2000) [China]; Crystal J. Gates, *China's Newly Enacted Intercountry Adoption Law: Friend or Foe,* 7 Ind. J. Global Legal Stud. 369 (1999); Shannon Thompson, *The 1998 Russian Federation Family Code Provisions on Intercountry Adoption Break the Hague Convention Ratification Gridlock: What Next? An Analysis of Post-Ratification Ramifications on Securing a Uniform Process of International Adoption,* 9 Trans. L. & Contemp. Prob. 703 (1999); Suzanne Hoelgaard, *Cultural Determinants of Adoption Policy: A Colombian Case Study,* 12 Int'l J.L. Pol. & Fam. 202 (1998).

2. U.S. Immigration Requirements

Often the most difficult legal issues for U.S. adopters involve satisfying the requirements of U.S. immigration law. In devising the statutes and regulations governing the immigration of adopted children, Congress and the INS sought to ensure that: (1) prospective adoptive parents are suitable to adopt; (2) the law of the state of the adoptive parents' residence and the law of the country of origin have been satisfied; (3) children are authorized to enter the United States on preferential visas; and, in Convention adoptions, (4) the requirements of the Hague Intercountry Adoption Convention have been met. *See* Bartholet, 2 Adoption Law and Practice, *supra,* at 10–26. The overarching aim of all of these goals is to deter fraudulent adoption practices and their devastating consequences for children and their families. U.S.Dep't of State, *International Adoption Safeguards, at* http://www.travel.state.gov/safeguards. html.

Children coming to the United States to join adoptive families are classified for immigration purposes as immigrants (those seeking permanent residence) rather than non-immigrants (those seeking admission for a limited period of time). Two types of visas are available for immigrants—those subject to numerical limitation and those that are not. 8 U.S.C. § 1151 (2000). Family preference visas subject to numerical limitation are allocated by country, and acquiring such a visa often entails a significant wait. Therefore, it is critical that children immigrating for adoption qualify to obtain a visa that is not subject to numerical limitation. Such visas are generally issued to two groups—special immigrants, a category usually inapplicable to adoptees, 8 U.S.C. § 1151(b)(1)(A), and immediate relatives, 8 U.S.C. § 1151 (b)(2)(A). *See* David Weissbrodt, Immigration Law and Procedure 109–112, 117–118 (4th ed.1998).

A child adopted abroad or entering the United States for adoption by a U.S. citizen may qualify for immediate relative immigration status if: (1) the child satisfies the statutory definition of orphan, 8 U.S.C. § 1101(b)(1)(F); (2) the child has been adopted and in the legal and residential custody of the adoptive parent for at least two years, 8 U.S.C. § 1101(b)(1)(E); or (3) the adoption is covered by the Hague Convention and satisfies the requirements of 8 U.S.C. § 1101(b)(1)(G), which will go into effect when the Hague Intercountry Adoption Convention enters into force for the United States. In the past, the vast majority of prospective adoptive parents sought immediate relative classification for their children through use of the orphan petition. This may continue to be the preferred basis for several years, until the Hague Convention is ratified by many of the nations from which children emigrate to the United States for adoption.

a. Qualifying for Immediate Relative Status as an Orphan

i. Eligibility

In order to obtain an immediate relative visa for a child who has been adopted abroad or is coming to the United States for adoption, the adoptive parent or parents filing an orphan petition must satisfy several criteria:

(1) If the adopters are a married couple, at least one spouse must be a U.S. citizen; and if the other spouse is an alien residing in the United States, he or she must be in lawful immigration status.

(2) If the adopter is single, he or she must be a U.S. citizen, at least 24 years of age when the I-600A advanced processing petition is filed, and at least 25 years of age when the I-600 orphan petition is filed.

In addition, prospective adopters must have submitted a home study satisfying federal criteria that convinces the INS that they are suitable to adopt and the child will receive proper care. 8 U.S.C. § 1101(b)(1)(F) (2000); 8 C.F.R. § 204.3(b) (2002).

The more difficult hurdle is obtaining classification of the child as an "orphan." Although in the common vernacular we normally refer to a child as an orphan only if the child's parents are deceased, immigration law defines a child as an orphan if:

(1) both of the child's parents have died, disappeared, abandoned or deserted the child; or if the child has been separated from them due to the involuntary termination of their parental rights by the country of origin; or if the child has lost them permanently due to civil unrest, a natural disaster, or some other calamitous event beyond the parents' control; or

(2) the sole surviving parent is not capable of providing the child with proper care and has irrevocably released the child for adoption and emigration.

If a child is born out of wedlock, the birth father is not considered a parent for purposes of the above definition if the father has disappeared, abandoned, or deserted the child, or irrevocably released the child in writing for adoption and emigration, unless the father has legitimated the child at a time when the child was in his legal custody. 8 U.S.C. § 1101(b)(1)(F) and (2) (2000); 8 C.F.R. § 204.3(b) (2002).

The terms used in the above criteria are defined narrowly in 8 C.F.R. § 204.3(b). Abandonment must include both the intent to and actual surrender of all parental rights, control and custody. Relinquishment of a child to prospective adoptive parents, or for a specific adoption, is not regarded as abandonment. Relinquishment to a third party for care in anticipation of an adoption also will not be considered abandonment, unless the third party is a government agency, court, adoption agency, or orphanage legally authorized by the country of origin to receive such a relinquishment. Desertion requires that the child has become a ward of a governmental authority because the parents have willfully forsaken the child and refused to fulfill their parental responsibilities. Disappearance means that following a reasonable effort to locate both parents, their whereabouts are unknown, their absence from the child's life is inexplicable, and there is no reasonable hope of their reappearance. The following case illustrates the difficulties many prospective adoptive parents have encountered with these restrictive criteria.

Rogan v. Reno

75 F. Supp.2d 63 (E.D.N.Y. 1999)

MEMORANDUM OF DECISION AND ORDER

Spatt, J.

This immigration matter involves the Defendant Immigration and Naturalization Service's ("INS") denial of the Plaintiff's [sic] visa petition to classify their niece, Sarah Elizabeth Ragob, as an immediate relative. Presently before the Court is the Defendants' motion to dismiss the complaint.

BACKGROUND

On February 23, 1998, the Plaintiffs filed a petition with the INS seeking to classify their adopted daughter, Sarah Elizabeth Ragob ("Sarah"), as an immediate relative, thus allowing her to emigrate from her home country of the Philippine Islands. On May 28, 1998, the INS determined that Sarah was not eligible for designation as an immediate relative pursuant to 8 U.S.C. § 1101(b)(1)(f), because she was not considered "orphaned" by her natural parents as that term is defined in the immigration statute.

On June 12, 1998, the Plaintiffs filed an appeal with the Board of Immigration Appeals ("BIA"), and on November 14, 1998, the BIA dismissed the appeal, holding that Sarah was not an orphan. The Plaintiffs then commenced this declaratory judgment action, seeking a declaration that Sarah is an orphan as defined by 8 U.S.C. § 1101(b)(1)(f), and is therefore eligible for classification as an immediate relative.

The Defendants now move to dismiss the Plaintiffs' complaint on two grounds. First, the Defendants allege that a 1996 Congressional statute, 8 U.S.C. § 1252(g) deprives this Court of subject matter jurisdiction to hear the case. Second, the government contends that decision of the INS on Sarah's status was not arbitrary or capricious.

The complaint alleges that Sarah was born on October 29, 1997 in the Philippine Islands to a woman named Zanaida Creado Rogob, with the birth certificate listing the father as "unknown." Plaintiff Ederlina Rogan, the sister of Zanaida, was present at the birth and Sarah lived with her, away from Zanaida for six months following the birth. Thereafter, the Plaintiffs petitioned a Philippine court to adopt Sarah, and such petition was granted, with the consent of Zanaida and without objection by the natural father, on February 16, 1998. Sarah currently lives with her grandmother in Leyte City, a 24 hour drive from Zanaida.

The post-investigation findings of the INS Officer in Charge in the Philippines, which were part of the record before the BIA and attached as an exhibit to the complaint, shed additional light on Sarah's situation. The INS found that Sarah's natural father was a man named Arnel Sorilla, and that he and Zanaida, although not legally married, live together as husband and wife. Arnel is employed by a security and investigation agency, and supports three other children with Zanaida in a lifestyle considered "well-off" by local standards. Zanaida admitted to the investigating officer that the decision to list the father as "unknown" on the birth certificate was made by Plaintiff Ederlina, at the suggestion of her lawyer to ease the immigration process.

DISCUSSION

The Defendants argue that this Court lacks subject matter jurisdiction to decide this case by virtue of 8 U.S.C. § 1252. That section, entitled "Judicial Review of Orders of Removal," contains sections restricting judicial review of actions by the Attorney General. In this regard, the Defendants point to § 1252(g), which states:

> Except as provided in this section and notwithstanding any other provision of law, no court shall have jurisdiction to hear any cause or claim by or on behalf of any alien arising from the decision or action by the Attorney General to commence proceedings, adjudicate cases, or execute removal orders against any alien under this chapter....

Several courts have held that the revocation of subject matter jurisdiction in 8 U.S.C. § 1252(g) applies only to removal proceedings, in which the INS attempts to deport or exclude an inadmissible alien.... This Court finds the logic in these cases to be sound. The title and content of § 1252 repeatedly refer to removal proceedings, and the section makes no mention of 8 U.S.C. § 1154, the procedure which the Plaintiffs invoked to obtain immediate relative status for Sarah. Therefore, the Court finds that § 1252(g) does not apply in cases such as this one, where the relief requested is simply re-classification of a petitioner's visa status, not removal or exclusion of an immigrant.

The Court now turns to the Defendants' second argument: that the decision by the INS that Sarah was not an "orphan" was not an abuse of discretion as a matter of law. An INS determination denying "immediate relative" status is within the broad discretion of the INS and "courts will not reverse its decision unless there has been an abuse of discretion."... The court will not find an abuse of discretion unless the BIA's decision was "made without a rational explanation, inexplicably departed from established policies, or rested on an impermissible basis, such as an invidious discrimination against a particular race or group." Douglas v. INS, 28 F.3d 241, 243 (2d Cir.1994). The Plaintiffs' complaint does not dispute the facts as found by the INS investigator in the Philippines regarding Sarah's family situation. Therefore, if the BIA's decision is an "abuse of discretion," it must be because the BIA's decision is a departure from established policies or a mis-application of the INS regulations.

The INS determined that Sarah was not eligible for a re-classification on the grounds that she was not an "orphan" as defined by the law. A child becomes an "orphan" under 8 U.S.C. § 1101(b)(1)(f) because of the death or disappearance of, abandonment or desertion by, or separation or loss from, both parents or for whom the sole or surviving parent is incapable of providing the proper care and has in writing irrevocably released the child for emigration and adoption.

The Plaintiffs argue that Sarah falls within this definition under both the "abandoned" and "sole or surviving parent" categories.

A. Whether Sarah was "abandoned" by both parents

"Abandonment," as used in 8 U.S.C. § 1101(b)(1)(f), occurs where

> The parents have wilfully forsaken all parental rights, obligations, and claims to the child...without intending to transfer, or without transferring, these rights to any specific person(s).... A relinquishment or release by the parents to the prospective adoptive parents or for a specific adoption does not constitute abandonment. Similarly, the relinquishment or release of the child by the parents to a third party for custodial care in anticipation of, or

preparation for, adoption does not constitute abandonment.... 8 C.F.R. § 204.3(b).

Under the facts alleged in the complaint, the decision by the INS that Sarah was not "abandoned," as that word is defined in the statute, was not an abuse of discretion. Under the definition of "abandonment," Zanaida's relinquishment of parental rights in Sarah had to occur independently of and prior to Ederlina's petition to adopt her. The language of 8 C.F.R. § 204.3(b) is clear: "release by the parents to the prospective adoptive parents... does not constitute abandonment."... The Plaintiffs do not contend that Zanaida "abandoned" Sarah before Ederlina petitioned for adoption; rather, the Plaintiffs allege that Zanaida "consented" to the adoption, a consent that would have been unnecessary if she had truly "abandoned" Sarah before that time. Moreover, review of the order of the Philippine court indicates that Ederlina filed her petition to adopt Sarah, with the consent of Zanaida, a mere 15 days after Sarah was born, further casting doubt on the proposition that Zanaida could have abandoned Sarah prior to that time.

On this basis, the Court finds that the BIA properly exercised its discretion to find, under the facts presented, that Sarah was not "abandoned" by her natural parents.

B. Whether Sarah was a child of a "sole parent" who was "incapable of providing proper care."

Nevertheless, the Plaintiffs could also demonstrate that Sarah was an "orphan" under the statute by showing that "the sole or surviving parent is incapable of providing the proper care and has in writing irrevocably released the child for emigration and adoption." 8 U.S.C. § 1101(b)(1)(f)....

Under 8 U.S.C. § 1101(b)(2), a child's natural father is not considered a "parent" if the father has "disappeared or abandoned or deserted the child...." The INS regulations interpreting this statutory section deviate from the above language somewhat, defining a child as having a "sole parent" where "her father has severed all parental ties, rights, duties, and obligations to the child...." 8 C.F.R. § 204.3(b).

The record before the INS indicated that Sarah's biological father shared the same house with her mother and Sarah's siblings, and was providing ample financial support to all of them. In addition, Sarah's mother informed the INS investigator that Sarah's father was listed as "unknown" only to ease Sarah's adoption and emigration. Under these facts as alleged in the complaint, the Court finds that Sarah's father has not "disappeared," "abandoned," or "deserted" Sarah. The INS regulations do not define what constitutes "severing all parental ties," but since the statute uses the term "abandoned," the definition of "abandonment" in 8 C.F.R. § 204.3(b) is helpful in interpreting it. The INS definition of abandonment specifically excludes relinquishment of parental rights made pursuant to consensual adoptions. 8 C.F.R. § 204.3(b). It is logical to interpret the statutory use of the expression "disappeared, abandoned, or deserted" consistently with the definition of "abandoned" used in the INS regulations. Both definitions are means to the same end, namely, determining whether the child is an "orphan."

Here, the Plaintiffs argue that Sarah's natural father's parental rights were severed when Sarah was adopted without objection by him. However, since the statute requires that Sarah's natural father "abandon" her before she can be considered to have a "sole parent," and because Sarah's parents turned her over to the Plaintiffs in anticipation of them adopting her, the Plaintiffs cannot show that Sarah's father's relinquishment of his parental rights amounted to "abandonment" under 8 U.S.C. § 1101(b)(2).

Thus, Sarah's father has not "severed all parental rights" to her in the manner contemplated by the statute. Therefore, the Plaintiffs cannot rely upon the "sole parent" test to prove that Sarah is an "orphan" under 8 U.S.C. § 1101(b)(1)(f)....

Even if Sarah's father's acts were sufficient to constitute relinquishment of his parental rights in her, Sarah still fails to fit the definition of "orphan" under the "sole parent" test in 8 U.S.C. § 1101(b)(1)(f) since there is no evidence in the record before the BIA that Sarah's mother is "incapable of providing proper care" for Sarah. A sole parent is "incapable of providing proper care" where the parent "is unable to provide for the child's basic needs, consistent with the local standards." 8 C.F.R. § 204.3(b). The record before the BIA reflects that Sarah's mother, although unemployed, enjoys an "above-average" standard of living because of Sarah's father's employment. Nothing in the definition suggests that the child's "sole parent" provide for the child's needs using only money earned by the parent. Rather, the regulation merely seeks to inquire whether the child's basic needs are being met without inquiring who is providing for them.

... Under this definition, because the record before the BIA shows that Zanaida is capable of providing proper care, ... Sarah cannot be considered an "orphan" under 8 U.S.C. § 1101(b)(1)(f), even if Sarah's mother otherwise meets the definition of "sole parent."

CONCLUSION

In sum, the Court finds that the decision made by the BIA is a reasonable application of the immigration statute, INS regulations, and past precedent to the facts before it. Further, the Plaintiffs' complaint fails to allege any facts that, if taken as true, would demonstrate that the BIA's decision was an abuse of discretion. The INS decision that Sarah was not an "orphan" has a rational basis and was not an abuse of discretion as a matter of law. Accordingly, the Government's motion to dismiss the complaint is GRANTED and the complaint is dismissed....

Notes and Questions

1. *Out-of-wedlock Children.* U.S. immigration law makes it somewhat easier for out-of-wedlock children than in-wedlock children to immigrate for adoption, by permitting the classification of out-of-wedlock children as orphans if the sole parent is incapable of providing proper care. A child whose parents are married cannot be classified as an orphan even though the child's parents are incapable of supporting the child and both are willing to consent to the child's adoption. 8 U.S.C. § 1101 (b) (2000) and 8 C.F.R § 204.3 (2002). *See, e.g.,* Sullivan, *supra,* at n.148.

In *Rogan* the birth mother was not considered a "sole parent" because the birth father was considered a parent under the statutory definition in 8 U.S.C. § 1102 (b)(2). Read that subsection, and the definition of "sole parent" in 8 C.F.R § 204.3(b). Why was this birth father considered a parent? Would the plaintiffs have been more successful if they had obtained the birth father's written consent to the adoption, rather than listing him as "unknown"?

A child with only one surviving parent is granted the same status as an out-of-wedlock child, in that the child can be classified as an orphan if the surviving parent consents to the adoption and is incapable of providing proper care. The definition of "surviving parent" in 8 C.F.R § 204.3(b) suggests that this classification will not be possible, however, if the child's parent is remarried and the child now has a step-parent. Sullivan, *supra,* at 15.

2. Too Restrictive? It appears that this adoption was legal in the Philippines. Assuming that proper notice had been given to the birth father, would it also have been a legal adoption in the state in which you attend law school?

The definition of orphan in U.S. immigration law has been criticized for omitting children that are legally available for adoption under the laws of their home countries, and precluding adoptions that would be legal if performed within the United States as well. What do you think is the rationale for adopting such restrictive criteria for the immigration of adopted children? Discontent with the orphan definition fueled the push for the new Hague Convention basis for immediate relative classification, described *infra* in Section C.2.(c).

3. Alternatives. What other options are open to parents in the Rogans' situation? One possibility would be for at least one of the adoptive parents to live with Sarah in the Philippines for two years, and then file for an adopted child petition, as described *infra* in Section C.2.b. According to their attorney, that was not a feasible alternative for the Rogans. Mr. Rogan was a New York City police officer and his wife was a nurse. (Telephone interview by Marianne Blair with Jerold Wolin, October 29, 2001). Two other possible remedies exist, but both are difficult to obtain.

a. Advance Parole. Occasionally the INS will permit an alien to enter the United States on "parole." Under this status, the alien is not officially "admitted," but is allowed to remain pending further investigation. The practice is utilized for humanitarian or public interest reasons, which include preventing the separation of families. Weissbrodt, *supra,* at 260–61. If an orphan petition is denied, adoptive parents may seek advance parole to permit a child to enter the United States pending completion of the requirement of two years of residence and legal custody, prior to petitioning for immediate relative status as an adopted child. Advance parole has also been used to permit a child needing urgent medical care to enter the United States pending approval of an orphan petition. In order to obtain advance parole, however, the circumstances must be unusual and compelling. Sometimes the influence of a U.S. Senator, a member of the House of Representatives, or a helpful case worker in the INS office for the adoptive parents' state of residence can facilitate conferral of parole. Sullivan, *supra,* at fn. 325 and accompanying text, *citing* Memorandum HQ 204.22-C from James A. Puleo, Executive Associate INS Commissioner (Nov. 25, 1994), *reported on and reproduced in* 71 Interpreter Releases 1644, 1650 (Dec. 12, 1994).

b. Private Congressional Immigration Bill. In very compelling circumstances and after all administrative remedies have been exhausted, it is possible to obtain admission for an adopted child through a private immigration bill. A private bill in effect exempts a particular alien from the general immigration laws. If the senator or congressperson who has been involved in the case agrees to initiate the process, a thorough presentation, similar to a brief, must be prepared for the House Subcommittee on Immigration and Claims and the Senate Subcommittee on Immigration, which in essence act like an equity court to grant special relief in individual cases. Former House Committee Chairman Mazzoli said of this procedure that "it must...reserve affirmative action to those [cases] of extraordinary merit and posing heavy hardship." Weissbrodt, *supra,* at 94. *See* Sulllivan, *supra,* at n.327 and accompanying text. Parents choosing this route are advised to stay in close contact with congressional staff members sponsoring the bill and work through several congressional sessions. *Id.*

Regarding the *Rogan* case, the petitioners' attorney explained that petitioners chose not to appeal the decision of the federal district court, but to contact their congressperson or senator instead for assistance. Fortunately, they knew their daughter was being well cared for by Ms. Rogan's mother while they pursued political assistance, presumably through one of the two channels described above. As of October 2001, their attorney did not know if they were ultimately successful. (Telephone interview with Jerold Wolin, October 29, 2001).

4. *Age Limitation.* In order for a child to be eligible for an immediate relative visa as an orphan, the orphan petition (I-600) must be filed before the child's sixteenth birthday. However, if a married couple or single person are adopting siblings and the orphan petition for at least one child is filed before that child's sixteenth birthday, the orphan petitions for siblings may be filed at any time prior to the siblings' eighteenth birthdays. 8 U.S.C. § 1101 (b)(1)(F) (2000).

ii. *Process of Obtaining an Orphan Visa*

For most Americans pursuing an international adoption, the next step after choosing an agency is to arrange for a home study. A petition for an orphan visa cannot be approved unless a public or private agency licensed by a state has favorably recommended the prospective adoptive parent or parents in a valid home study. 8 U.S.C. § 1154 (d) (2000). The INS therefore requires that a home study satisfying the criteria established in 8 C.F.R. § 204.3 be submitted as part of the process for applying for an orphan visa. In addition, the foreign country from which the child is to be adopted will in all likelihood require a home study, and may have additional criteria for the home study that must be satisfied. Certainly, if the adoption is covered by the Hague Intercountry Adoption Convention, the home study must satisfy the Convention's criteria in Article 15, as well as all requirements specified by the Central Authority of the country of origin. 42 U.S.C.A. § 14923 (b) (2000). If the child is going to be adopted or readopted in a U.S. state court, the home study submitted to the state court must satisfy the requirements of that state's law as well. The preparer may be subject to professional standards for performing a home study. Finally, the agency with which the prospective adopter is working may have its own internal requirements for a home study. Thus, the standards that a particular home study must satisfy will vary from case to case, depending upon how many of the above sources of criteria are applicable in any given situation. At a minimum, however, the requirements of 8 C.F.R. § 204.3 must be met before any orphan visa will be issued.

The research, interviews, and preparation for the home study must be performed by a person or entity licensed or authorized to conduct home studies under the law of the state in which the child will reside. 8 C.F.R. § 204.3 (b),(e) (2002). If the child is adopted in the country of origin by adoptive parents who reside abroad, the home study preparer may be licensed or authorized under the law of any U.S. state or the foreign country in which the adoption takes place, and the study must be reviewed and favorably recommended by a public or private adoption agency licensed or authorized by any U.S. state. 8 C.F.R. § 204.3 (b),(e) (2002).

The requirements specifying the manner in which the home study is to be prepared and the necessary contents are very specific. Each prospective adopter and any adult member of the adopters' household must be interviewed in person, and a home visit conducted. The home study must contain an assessment of each adopter's physical, mental, and emotional capabilities to parent, the adopters' financial circumstances, and the adopters' current living accommodations, as well as the living accommodations where the child will reside. Available child abuse registries must be checked regarding each adopter and any adult member of the adopters' household, to the extent permitted by state law. The home study preparer must inquire about any history on the part of the adopters or adult household members regarding arrests or convictions for any crime, as well as any history of substance abuse, sexual or child abuse, or domestic violence, even if it resulted in no arrests or convictions. The report must include all of this information, as well as any evidence of rehabilitation. Previous rejection for adoption or unfavorable home studies regarding any prospective adopter or adult household member must be attached. The home study must also summarize any counseling that has been given to prepare the adopters for international adoption and plans for post-placement counseling. Finally, if the findings are favorable, the home study must contain a specific approval of the prospective adoptive parent or parents, a discussion of the reasons for the approval, and any restrictions that apply. If the home study is for an adoption of a special needs child, the adopters' ability to properly care for a special needs child must be addressed and approval for special needs adoption included. If the state of the prospective adopters' residence requires review of the home study by state officials, this state review must occur before the home study is submitted to the INS. 8 C.F.R. § 204.3(e) (2002).

Most prospective adoptive parents seeking an orphan visa will begin the application process with the INS by first filing an Application for Advanced Processing of an Orphan Petition (Form I-600A), before a specific child is ever identified. If the prospective adoptive parents reside in the United States, the I-600A is filed at the INS office with jurisdiction over the state of the petitioners' residence. 8 C.F.R. § 204.3(g) (2002). The purpose of advanced processing is to obtain approval of the prospective adopters. Because this part of the process often takes many months, filing the I-600A early avoids delay later when a specific child has been identified and the adopters are eager to bring the child home to the United States as quickly as possible.

Along with the I-600A form, advanced processing requires extensive documentation. This includes evidence of the petitioner's U.S. citizenship, and if the spouse of a married citizen petitioner is an alien residing in the United States, evidence of the alien spouse's lawful immigration status. Married petitioners must submit a copy of their marriage certificate, and all petitioners and spouses must submit evidence of legal termination of all prior marriages. A favorable home study must be submitted within one year after the I-600A is filed. Often petitioners will file the I-600A while the home study is still being completed, and then submit it when it is done. A home study may be no more than six months old when it is submitted. If the petitioners have an older home study at the time they wish to apply for advanced processing, they must have the home study updated before it can be submitted. If the child must be adopted or readopted in a state court, the INS will also require proof that any preadoption requirements of the state where the child will reside have been satisfied, to the extent they can be met before the child has arrived. After the application is submitted, the INS will fingerprint each prospective adoptive parent and any other adult household member, to check against F.B.I. criminal records. 8 C.F.R. § 204.3 (c),(e)(9) (2002).

Decisions regarding whether to grant advanced processing applications are typically made by the INS district directors. Directors are responsible for making an independent determination regarding whether or not prospective adopters are capable of providing proper care, and are not bound by a favorable recommendation in the home study. 8 C.F.R. § 204.3(h) (2002). Advanced processing approval has been denied on the basis of irregular employment histories, criminal convictions, substance abuse, financial insolvency and a history of welfare receipt, and delinquency of other children of the petitioners. Sullivan, *supra,* at n.123 and accompanying text.

When petitioners for advanced processing are denied, they are advised by letter of the reasons and of their right to file an appeal with the Administrative Appeals Unit. This is obviously one point in the process in which prospective adopters might utilize the services of a lawyer, even if they are pursuing an agency adoption. The applicants or their attorney may file a letter of appeal stating their grounds for appeal and requesting a hearing. The appeal will be denied unless they can show the grounds for the decision were erroneous or no longer exist. Blanche Gelber, *International Adoption: Legal Requirements and Practical Considerations,* 2 Adoption Law & Practice 11-18 to 11-19 (Joan Hollinger ed., 1995).

In most cases, of course, the Application for Advanced Processing is successful. In these cases, after processing, a Notice of Favorable Determination Concerning Advanced Processing of Orphan Petition (I-171H) is sent to the petitioners. The application and supporting documents are then forwarded to the INS office with jurisdiction over the country of origin from which the prospective adopters hope to adopt, or if the Service has no office in that country, to the Department of State visa-issuing post for that nation [referred to collectively hereinafter as "the overseas site"]. In addition, if the prospective adopters plan to travel abroad to locate and/or adopt a child and file their orphan petition [I-600] at the overseas site, telegraphic notification of the approval of the application for advanced processing will be sent to the overseas site. 8 C.F.R. § 204.3 (b), (h)(3), (j) (2002). If circumstances change and the adopters find that they are traveling to another country to adopt, procedures exist to transfer the notification of the approval to the new overseas site. 8 C.F.R. § 204.3 (j) (2002).

While the advanced processing application is pending, the prospective adopters have in most cases been working with their agency or independent facilitator to locate a child to adopt. This entails compiling and forwarding the documentation required by the country of origin, a process that varies by country. Such documentation might include a letter or declaration of intent to adopt; a letter to the foreign authorities; certified copies of birth certificates, marriage certificates, and divorce decrees; power(s) of attorney; medical reports regarding examinations, history, and testing of prospective adopters for such diseases as tuberculosis, HIV virus, and venereal disease; local and state police clearances; tax returns; employers' letters; photographs of the prospective adopters and their homes; and a copy of the home study. Each document usually must be authenticated. Authentication requirements vary by country, but typically involve some or all of these steps—notarization, verification by the secretary of state or other state officials, verification by the U.S. Department of State Authentication Office, and then review by the embassy of the country of origin in the United States, before return of the documents to the agency or facilitator for forwarding to proper officials or liason in the country of origin. The prospective adopters then wait for a referral, which usually includes the child's picture, age, and medical information. Tennenbaum, *supra*, at 237. In Convention adoptions, the referral should include the information required by Article 16. Often the advanced processing petition is approved by the INS many months before the referral actually arrives. *Id.*

Some individuals pursuing independent adoption choose to travel to a country of origin, once they have received INS approval of their advanced processing application, and try to locate a child on their own to adopt. Such individuals are well advised to consult the Office of Citizens Consular Services at the U.S. consulate upon arrival in the foreign country, whose staff may help orient prospective parents to the nation's adoption laws. Orphanages operated by the government or reputable charitable or religious organizations are recommended as the best places to locate a child that will be adoptable under INS criteria, because they often keep formal records regarding how the child entered the orphanage and the parents' future intentions, if any, to reclaim the child.

The child welfare agency of the foreign government may be helpful in locating a reputable orphanage. Sullivan, *supra*, at nn.162–63 and accompanying text. Many countries, however, have not permitted such independent placements, and arranging this type of placement may become increasingly difficult in the future if more countries prefer to work through accredited bodies or approved entities under the Hague Convention for the "matching" process as well as the home study process.

Once a child has been identified, the second part of the immigration process requires the prospective adopters to submit a Petition to Classify Orphan as an Immediate Relative (Form I-600). This stage of the process is to determine if the child is eligible for entry as an orphan.

The site at which the I-600 may be filed depends upon whether at least one of the prospective adoptive parents travels abroad to locate or adopt the child. If neither is traveling to the country of origin, the I-600 must be filed in the INS office with jurisdiction over the adopters' state of residence. If at least one of the prospective adoptive parents is traveling abroad, the I-600 will normally be filed at the overseas site, which is typically a U.S. consulate in the country of origin. The petitioner must be physically present in the country of origin in order to file at the overseas site. If the adopters are a married couple and only one spouse is a U.S. citizen, it must be the U.S. citizen who travels to the country of origin so that the overseas site will have jurisdiction over the petition. 8 C.F.R. § 204.3 (g) (2002). Although adopters who travel have the option to file their I-600 with the INS office with jurisdiction over their state of residence, *id.*, they would rarely choose that option, as it would normally cause significant delay. Sullivan, *supra*, at n.208 and accompanying text. The overseas site, by contrast, usually processes the I-600 in a very short time, typically in a day or two.

Coordinating the filing of the I-600 with the advanced processing application process can present some bureaucratic complexities. If the prospective adoptive parents have already received approval of their advanced processing application, their I-600 orphan petition must be filed within eighteen months of the date the advanced processing application is approved. If the I-600 is not filed within that eighteen-month period, the advanced processing application is deemed abandoned, and the prospective adopters must reapply. 8 C.F.R. § 204.3 (d), (h)(7) (2002). An orphan petition filed outside of the eighteen-month period will be denied. *Id.* at (d), (h)(13). This eighteen-month window can sometimes be problematic, as it is not always possible to obtain a referral of a child from certain countries of origin in time to file the I-600 within that period.

On the other hand, sometimes a child is identified and the adopters are ready to petition for the orphan visa while the advanced processing application is still pending. In that event, the I-600 may be filed before the advanced processing application is approved, but normally it must be filed in the INS office in which the advanced processing application is pending. 8 C.F.R. § 204.3 (g)(3) (2002). There have been instances in which prospective adoptive parents have requested the INS office in which the advanced processing application is pending to expedite consideration of the application and telegraph or fax their approval to the consulate where the adopters wish to submit their I-600. Prospective adoptive parents who have sought such expedited review have often contacted their congressional representatives to obtain additional support for such requests. Sullivan, *supra*, at n.212 and accompanying text.

Sometimes prospective adoptive parents identify a particular child they wish to adopt before they have even filed an application for advanced processing. In such cases, they can file their orphan petition concurrently with the advanced processing application all on Form I-600, obviating the need to file a separate I-600A form. The supporting documentation normally required with the I-600A is submitted with the I-600 and its supporting documentation. 8 C.F.R. § 204.3(d) (2002).

Petitioners for an orphan visa must submit a variety of documents to accompany the I-600 form. These include the child's birth certificate or other proof of identity and age, and evidence supporting the child's classification as an orphan, such as death certificates of the birth parents, certification of the child's abandonment, or the consent of a sole or surviving parent to adoption and emigration, along with evidence the parent was unable to provide for the child's care. If the child has been adopted abroad, petitioners must submit a certified copy of the adoption decree, as well as evidence that the child was seen personally by the adopting parent or both spouses, if the adopters are married, prior to or during the adoption proceeding. If the child is to be adopted by the prospective adoptive parents in the United States, petitioners must submit evidence that they or an agency or entity working on their behalf have been awarded custody of the child in accordance with the law of the country of origin, and that the preadoption requirements, if any, of the state in which the child will reside have been satisfied. 8 C.F.R. § 204.3 (d)(1) (2002).

Preadoption requirements for foreign-born children immigrating for adoption vary from state to state. Illinios, for example, requires a medical report from authorized medical personnel in the country of origin; a valid home study; documentation of the child's legal adoptability; verification that the adoptive family is a licensed foster family; verification of compliance with the Interstate Compact on the Placement of Children, where applicable; and the posting of a $5000 bond as protection that the child will not become a public charge, or in lieu of the bond, a binding contract from a placement agency that assumes full responsibility for the child if the placement disrupts. 750 Ill. Comp. Stat. Ann. 50/4.1 (West 1999). Some states have no preadoption requirements, and in others they apply only to independent adoptions. For instance, before a child who has not been placed by an agency is admitted to the United States for adoption in New York, state law requires that prospective adopters file a petition, home study, and other documents with the New York court and appear for examination before a judge, who, if satisfied, will issue a pre-adoption certificate that the adoption appears to be in the best interests of the child. N.Y. Dom. Rel. § 115-a (McKinney 1999).

Even if an adoption took place in the country of origin, the INS will require that the child be readopted in the United States if the unmarried adopter or both spouses of a married couple did not personally see the child prior to the adoption. The INS will also require readoption if the adoption abroad was not full and final. 8 C.F.R. § 204.3 (d)(1)(iv) (2002). Some countries, particularly in Latin America, utilize what is sometimes referred to as a "simple" adoption, which does not fully terminate the rights of the birth parents. Sullivan, *supra*, at n.169 and accompanying text. In cases in which a readoption will be required, the I-600 must similarly be accompanied by evidence that the adopters or the agency or entity working on their behalf have been awarded custody, and that state preadoption requirements have been fulfilled, as described above. In addition, petitioners must prove that the state in which the child will reside permits readoption or provides for judicial recognition of the adoption abroad. Furthermore, if the adoption abroad was not full and final under the law of the nation in which it took place, petitioners must submit an irrevocable release of the child for emigration and adoption from the person or entity that had the immediately previous legal custody or control of the child. 8 C.F.R. § 204.3 (d)(1) (2002).

As part of the process of obtaining an orphan visa, an I-604 investigation is completed following submission of the I-600 and supporting documentation. If the I-600 has been filed overseas, the investigation is performed by a consular officer or, if it is submitted at an INS office overseas, an INS Service officer. 8 C.F.R. § 204.3 (k) (2002). Normally, this investigation is a routine paper check of the child's orphan status. However, it could include telephonic inquiries, interviews with the birth parents, blood tests of a birth parent, and/or a full field investigation. *Id.*, Sullivan, *supra*, at n.223 and accompanying text. If the I-600 is submitted to a U.S. consulate, upon completion of the investigation, the consular officer is authorized to approve the orphan petition. When discrepancies appear between the factual information in the 1-600A or I-600 and the facts uncovered by the investigation, however, the consular officer may consult with the appropriate overseas INS office. If the investigation reveals grounds for a revocation or denial of the petition, the adoptive parents are notified and the investigation report, supporting documents, and petition are forwarded to the appropriate overseas INS office for decision. *Id.* Potential problems could include that the adoption is not valid under the law of the nation in which it occurred; or that there is evidence of material fraud or misrepresentation in the I-600 or I-600A, or that the petitioners have experienced a material change in circumstances. Sullivan, *supra*, at n.223 and accompanying text. Evidence of child-buying, i.e., the payment of money or other consideration to a child's parent or someone else as inducement to release the child, is another ground for denial of an orphan petition. 8 C.F.R. § 204.3 (i) (2002).

If the I-600 was submitted to a stateside INS office with jurisdiction over the petitioners' state of residence, normally the I-604 investigation is completed after the case has been forwarded to the appropriate visa-issuing post in the country of origin. However, if a district director has concerns about the petition that can only be resolved through an I-604 investigation, the director can request an investigation prior to adjudication. 8 C.F.R. § 204.3 (k) (2002).

The denial of an orphan petition may be appealed to the Administrative Appeals Unit, and subsequently to federal court. 8 C.F.R. § 103.1 (2002), *amended by* 67 Fed. Reg. 4797 (Jan. 31, 2002); Gelber, *supra*, at 11–20. A revocation of a previous approval of an I-600A application or an I-600 petition can be appealed as well. Sullivan, *supra*, at n.225 and accompanying text. Revocation of a previous approval can occur if the director acquires information that would have caused a denial if it had been known at the time of the initial decision to approve. 8 C.F.R. § 204.3(h)(14) (2002).

Consular officers are responsible for the issuance of visas. Therefore, if the I-600 was submitted to and approved by the consular officer, that officer can then issue the child's visa. If the I-600 is approved by an INS officer, whether overseas or stateside, the INS then communicates their authorization through appropriate channels to the consular officer, so that the visa may be issued. Gelber, *supra*, at 11–21.

Prior to obtaining a visa, a child immigrating as an orphan must be examined by a physician authorized by the U.S. consulate to perform immigrant visa examinations. Sullivan, *supra*, at n.195 and accompanying text. The resulting report is attached to the child's visa. If a mental or physical defect is discovered, the petitioners are informed by the consular or INS officer involved. Before approving a visa, the officer will seek assurance from the adopters that they are aware of the child's mental or physical challenges and will undertake full responsibility for the child's care. Gelber, *supra*, at 11–22.

When the child arrives at a port of entry in the United States, the child is required to surrender his or her visa. The child will then receive from the INS an alien identification card, known as a green card, which proves the child is a legal resident of the United States. *Id.*

b. Qualifying for Immediate Relative Status as an Adopted Child

Though used as a basis less frequently than orphan status, an adoptive parent who is a U.S. citizen can also obtain an immediate relative visa for a child who has:

(1) been legally adopted before the child's sixteenth birthday, or adopted before the child's eighteenth birthday if the child is a sibling of another child adopted under the age of sixteen by the same adoptive parent or parents;

(2) been in the legal custody of an adoptive parent for at least two years; and

(3) resided with an adoptive parent for at least two years. 8 U.S.C. § 1101 (b)(1)(E) (2000).

In some ways obtaining an "adopted child" visa is an easier process, because the child need not satisfy the orphan criteria, and submission of a home study is not part of the INS process, although some type of home study would normally have been required by the country in which the adoption took place. On the other hand, obtaining an "adopted child" visa usually involves residing outside of the United States with the child for at least two years. In some cases, however, U.S. citizen parents have been able to use this route to obtain immigrant visas for children residing in the United States while undocumented or in non-immigrant status. Sullivan, *supra*, at n.274 and accompanying text. Such children are ineligible for orphan visas. 8 C.F.R. § 204.3(k)(3) (2002).

"Adopted child" petitions are also filed by adoptive parents who are lawful permanent residents of the United States. Because these petitioners are not U.S. citizens, their children are not entitled to immediate relative visas, which are not subject to numerical limitation. Instead, these parents are asserting that their child satisfies the criteria for an "adopted child" in order to qualify the child for a family-sponsored preference visa. This is normally the only avenue available for legal permanent residents to obtain an immigrant visa for an adopted child, since nonpreference visas were eliminated by Congress in 1990. 8 U.S.C. § 1151(a) (2000); Sullivan, *supra*, at n.274 and accompanying text; Weissbrodt, *supra*, at 115. If the adopted child is "accompanying" or "following to join" a parent who is immigrating with a family-sponsored, employment-related, or diversity immigrant visa, the child is admitted in the same preference category as the parent and is considered a derivative beneficiary for whom no separate petition must be filed. 8 C.F.R. § 204.2(d)(4) (2002). Derivative status was created to avoid separation of nuclear families who are attempting to immigrate. Weissbrodt, *supra*, at 117. A child of an alien admitted as an immediate relative, however, must have a separate petition approved on his or her behalf. 8 C.F.R. § 204.2(d)(4) (2002). A child adopted after the parent obtains lawful permanent residence is also not entitled to derivative status, and the parent must apply for a second preference family-sponsored visa for the child. Weissbrodt, *supra*, at 117.

In order for an adoption to be recognized for immigration purposes, it must be valid and recognized by the applicable law of the country or state in which it occurred. Even if the adoption would be legal in the United States, it cannot be used to create adopted child status if it was not legal in the place in which it occurred. Conversely, adoptions that would not be legal in the United States can still be recognized if valid in the country in which they took place.

Kaho v. Ilchert
765 F.2d 877 (9th Cir. 1985)

Wiggins, C.J.

[Ed. Note: Petitioner, Kuli Haapai Kaho, a lawful permanent resident of the United States, sought a family-sponsored preference visa for his two adopted daughters, whom he asserted had been adopted by him under the customary laws of Tonga. The girls had been entrusted to petitioner's care by their birth father upon the instructions of their birth mother, petitioner's cousin, who died when the girls were three and seven years of age.

A customary adoption is an adoption created by operation of custom, sometimes referred to as a "common law adoption." 765 F.2d at 879 n.2. Kaho's visa petition was denied by the INS District Director, David Ilchert, whose decision was affirmed by the Board of Immigration Appeals (BIA) based on the BIA's conclusion that customary adoption was not legally recognized in Tonga. The district court, observing that 8 U.S.C, § 1101(b)(1)(E) "requires that an adoption be legally recognized under the law of the country where the adoption took place," 765 F.2d at 880, reversed the BIA decision and remanded the matter to the INS to determine if the adoption by Kaho had been a bona fide customary adoption. Ilchert appealed the district court's remand order to the 9th Circuit.

In the first part of the opinion, the appellate court determined that the district court's judgment was a final appealable order, that the district court was entitled to review the issue of the validity of customary adoptions under Tongan law de novo, and that the appellate court could review the district court's ruling de novo. Turning to the merits, the appellate court first reviewed evidence that had been presented to the BIA in earlier cases regarding the validity of customary adoption under Tongan law.]

* * *

In Matter of Fakalata, 18 I. & N. Dec. 213 (BIA 1982), the BIA held that customary Tongan adoptions do not create a legal status or relationship under Tongan law and therefore are not legally valid.... In reaching this conclusion in *Fakalata*, the BIA relied heavily upon two letters of the Tongan Crown Solicitor, a section of the Tongan Constitution prohibiting the inheritance of land by customary adoptees, and an article entitled "Tongan Adoption" by Keith L. Morton, included in Transactions in Kinship—Adoption and Fosterage in Oceania (I. Brady ed. 1976)....

* * *

The second letter of the Crown Solicitor, dated July 18, 1980, reads in its entirety:

TO WHOM IT MAY CONCERN:

On January 16, I wrote a letter to Mr. Kersi B. Shroff of the Library of Congress of the United States responding to a letter he wrote me requesting my opinion concerning the legal effect of Tongan customary adoptions. In that letter I stated: "Such 'adoption' does not give the child any legal rights in the estate of the foster parent and is not recognised (sic) as legally valid under Tongan law."

In Tonga, there is no reported "law" concerning parental rights and duties and children's rights and duties when customarily adopted. Tongan customary adoptions are an important aspect of our traditional culture and continue to be practiced today very commonly. There is no need for anyone to go to the courts to enforce parental rights or duties or children's rights or duties because everyone understands that customarily adopted children are treated in all respects as if they were legally adopted except that they cannot inherit. Even illegitimate children adopted according to our statutory law cannot inherit, but they also are considered legally adopted.

Customary adoptions used to (sic) prior to our Constitution allow the adopted children to succeed to estates and titles, but the Constitution forbade the inheritance or succession by adopted children. But the Constitution did not outlaw customary adoptions. They have continued until this day. Many families in Tonga have one or more members who are adopted. The adopted children cannot succeed to the estates of their parents, but in all other ways, they are considered the real children of their adopting parents. Such adoptions have the effect in Tonga of creating a parent and child relationship.

The section of the Morton monograph primarily relied upon by the BIA...reads: "The Tongan government sanctions only a few of these adoptions. Few applications for legal adoptions are made to the courts because the circumstances of Tongan adoption are often incongruent with the European model of adoption applied in the courts."... The BIA also emphasized Morton's suggestion "that an adoption may be obtained through application to the courts which is recognized by Tongan law as according rights of succession to the adopted child."...In light of Morton's comments the BIA stated, "if a means of acquiring legal sanction for an adoption is available, we believe that our immigration laws would require a person seeking immigration benefits on the basis of an adoption in Tonga to obtain endorsement of law in that matter."...

* * *

In ruling on the issue whether customary adoptions are legally recognized under the laws of Tonga, the district court considered the material which the BIA had before it in *Fakalata* and additional evidence such as an extensive affidavit of Dr. George Marcus [hereinafter Marcus affidavit], an anthropologist and Chairman of the Department of Anthropology at Rice University in Houston, Texas....

In rejecting the BIA's determination regarding the validity of customary adoptions, [the] district court stated:

> The ironic effect of the INS's approach to Tongan customary adoptions may be that only those customary adoptees whose adoptive status was disputed in Tonga may acquire preference visas, because they are the only customary adoptees who would have sought and obtained Tongan judicial sanction. Customary adoptees whose good faith adoptive status no one disputed would never have required recourse to courts; lacking a judicial decree recognizing their adoptive status, they would be per se precluded from obtaining preference visas. The effect is contrary to congressional (sic) intent.

* * *

Our review of the Crown Solicitor's second letter convinces us that he has retracted his original conclusion that customary adoptions have no legal effect in Tongan law. In his second and most recent letter, the Crown Solicitor stated that customary adoptions have the effect of creating a parent/child relationship recognized under Tongan law. The

Crown Solicitor explained that there was no need to resort to courts to enforce the rights and responsibilities of such a relationship "because everyone understands that customarily adopted children are treated in all respects as if they were legally adopted except that they cannot inherit." This statement by the Crown Solicitor demonstrates that the BIA misconstrued Morton's comment regarding judicial approval of adoptions in Tonga.

* * *

... Dr. Marcus provides a reasonable explanation why there exists a statutory provision for the adoption of illegitimate children but no such provision for the adoption of legitimate children. Dr. Marcus explains that the statutory provision for adoption of illegitimate children was enacted in anticipation of challenges to the adoption by the parents of the illegitimate child. Adoption of illegitimate children under Tongan custom does not require the father's consent. The mother is frequently pressured into consenting to the adoption. Because such adoptions are "more a matter of expediency and necessity than a matter of consensual transaction as between two sets of parents as in the usual 'pusiaki' adoption" [an adoption by blood relatives], the parents are likely to attempt to reclaim their child. The statutory provision thus affords the adopting parents some measure of security. Such a safeguard is not necessary for customary adoption of legitimate children because of their consensual nature.

Dr. Marcus adds that Tongan courts will enforce the rights and duties stemming from "pusiaki" adoptions. Specifically, Dr.Marcus explains: "Where relevant to the case, a magistrate will measure the strength and validity of adoption by attempting to determine the circumstances of the adoption transaction and the history of role-playing between parent and child. If the adopter and adoptee have conformed to the behavioral rights and duties of parent-child relationship, and moreover, if the adopted child has performed the duties of siblings in its adopted family, then the validity of the adopted tie is not only recognized but takes precedence over any competing claims or versions of the relationship, whatever the specific issue in dispute." Dr. Marcus further explains that pusiaki adoptions may be given effect by the Tongan Land Courts.

The BIA has expressly held that it is not necessary for an adoption to be recognized by a juridical act before it can be recognized as valid for immigration purposes.... We find the BIA's position [on this issue]...consistent with the Act's purpose to reunite families.

In *Fakalata*, the BIA also found significant to its determination the Tongan constitutional prohibition against adopted children succeeding to the estates and titles of their adopted parents.... Closer study of this constitutional prohibition reveals that it does not support the conclusion that customary adoptions are not legally recognized in Tonga.

The second letter of the Crown Solicitor states that the constitutional prohibition applies to judicially adopted children as well as to customarily adopted children. Dr. Marcus further explains that the constitutional provision concerns the law of succession to title and estates and is not a complete bar to inheritance by adopted children. Dr. Marcus adds that the prohibition refers only to adoption between strangers not to pusiaki adoptions.

If the BIA concludes that it cannot recognize customary adoption of children because of this inheritance prohibition, it would be forced to conclude that adoptions of illegitimate children, which are expressly provided for by statute under Tongan law, also cannot be recognized. A conclusion that the statutory adoption of illegitimate children is not valid under Tongan law would be contrary to the BIA's interpretation of section 1101(b)(1)(E).

In *Fakalata*, the BIA also refused to recognize customary adoptions as legally valid because the relationship between the adopted child is not "exclusive."... In Tonga, an adopted child may maintain ties with his or her natural parents and may elect to emphasize those ties. In light of the "fluidity" of Tongan customary adoptions, the BIA concluded "a system which gives an adopted child the option to maintain a legal relationship with his natural parents is inconsistent with *our concept of adoption* and with [section 1101(b)(1)(E)]."... (emphasis added).

The flaw in the BIA's analysis is clear. For an adoption to be valid under section 1101(b)(1)(E), an adoption need not conform to the BIA's or Anglo-American notions of adoption; the adoption need only be recognized under the law of the country where the adoption occurred.... In addition, the BIA confuses the legal issue—whether Tongan customary adoptions are legally recognized—with the factual issue—whether a bona fide customary adoption ever took place in a given case.

* * *

... The record before us demonstrates that customary adoptions are valid under Tongan law.

The district court properly concluded that the INS abused its discretion in denying Kaho's visa petitions. A remand to the BIA for it to determine whether there existed a bona fide customary adoption of Valeti and Tupuo by Kaho was proper. AFFIRMED.

Notes and Questions

1. *Proof of Foreign Law.* As *Kaho* illustrates, it is not always easy to establish what the law of a foreign country is. The burden is on the petitioner for an "adopted child" visa to establish that the adoption was legally valid. Fed. R. Civ. P. 44.1, which addresses the type of evidence a court may consider in making a determination of foreign law, provides:

> A party who intends to raise an issue concerning the law of a foreign country shall give notice in his pleadings or other reasonable written notice. The court, in determining foreign law, may consider any relevant material or source, including testimony, whether or not submitted by a party or admissible under the Federal Rules of Evidence. The court's determination shall be treated as a ruling on a question of law.

What sources did the court consider in *Kaho*? Were all equally reliable? Note that the first letter of the Crown Solicitor was a response to a request for an opinion from the U.S. Library of Congress. The BIA and the courts commonly seek legal opinions from the Library of Congress regarding foreign law. Sulllivan, *supra*, at n.298 and accompanying text; Sarah Ignatius & Elisabeth Stickney, *Immigration Law & the Family* § 13:11 (2002), *available at* Westlaw, IMLF § 13.11. In addition to statutes, codes, regulations, and legal opinions of foreign courts or authoritative governmental entities, the opinions of legal officers in the country of the adoption and authoritative books are also useful sources of evidence.

2. *Appropriate Benchmark for Customary Adoption's Validity under Foreign Law.* The INS has affirmed in several cases that a customary adoption will be recognized for immigration purposes if valid where it took place. *E.g.,* Matter of Ng, 14 I. & N. Dec.

135 (B.I.A. 1972) (Hong Kong); Matter of Kwok, 14 I. & N. Dec. 127 (B.I.A. 1972) (China). While both the BIA and the courts agree that a judicial act is not necessary for a valid adoption, they disagree in *Kaho* about what other characteristics are important to determining an adoption's validity under foreign law. One commentator has suggested that the INS asserts that customary adoptions must confer upon adoptees the same rights that biological children possess, whereas the court in *Kaho* will find the adoption valid if it confers upon adoptees the rights accorded children adopted through the Tongan statutory method of adoption. Ignatius, *supra*, at § 13:4. Do you agree with this analysis? Which do you think is the better approach? Are their other characteristics upon which the BIA and the court express differing views? What do you think is the underlying concern of the INS in taking a more conservative approach?

The courts have not been uniform in their review of BIA decisions regarding Tongan customary adoptions. In Mila v. District Director of the Denver, Col. Dist. of the INS, 678 F.2d 123 (10th Cir. 1982), the Tenth Circuit affirmed a BIA refusal to recognize a Tongan adoption, in a case in which only the first letter of the Tongan Crown Solicitor was before the court.

3. *Applicability of Foreign Law to the Individual Adopter.* In some countries the validity of an adoption is affected by the religion of the parties involved. In Matter of Khatoon, 19 I. & N. Dec. 153 (B.I.A. 1984), the BIA denied a petition for a preferential visa for petitioner's adoptive mother because both the petitioner and the beneficiary were Moslems, and the Hindu Adoption Code in India, under which petitioner alleged he was adopted, applied only to Hindus. Basing its decision upon an advisory memorandum from the Library of Congress, the BIA found that in India "the personal law of each religion applies only to its respective followers," and that the Indian Muslim Personal Law does not legally recognize adoptions as valid. The opinion did not discuss the Muslim practice of kafala, which is discussed in Chapter Eleven. Should relationships created by kafala be recognized by U.S. immigration law as the basis for immediate relative or preferential immigrant status?

The fact that an adoption occurred in an Islamic country does not necessarily mean the adoption will not be valid under foreign law. In some Islamic countries, such as Egypt and Syria, Christians are permitted to adopt in accordance with the personal law of their religion, and a few other Islamic countries, such as Tunisia and Indonesia, do include some provision in their laws for adoption. J.H.A. van Loon, *Report on Intercountry Adoption*, 1990 Hague Conf. on Private Int'l L. 28.

4. *Proxy Adoptions.* The INS will recognize a foreign adoption of a child residing abroad by proxy, entered by adoptive parents who have already immigrated to the United States, if it is considered valid under the law of the country in which the adoption takes place. Matter of Cho, 16 I. & N. Dec. 188 (B.I.A. 1977) (recognizing Korean adoption by proxy). An adoption performed in the United States of a child still residing abroad will also be valid for immigration purposes, as long as the other criteria of 8 U.S.C. § 1101(b)(1)(E) have been satisfied. Matter of Cabucana, 16 I. & N. Dec. 217 (B.I.A. 1977), following Pascual v. O'Shea, No. 76-0081 (D. Hawaii, Sept. 30, 1976).

Unlike an orphan petition, which must be filed before a child's sixteenth birthday (or eighteenth birthday if he or she falls within the sibling exception), a petition on behalf of an adopted child need not be filed within these deadlines. As long as the adoption has been finalized by the child's sixteenth birthday (or eighteenth birthday for siblings satisfying the exception), a child may be admitted as an immediate relative as long as the Form I-130, Petition for Alien Relative, is filed and approved while the child is still under the age of twenty-one and unmarried. Dep't of Justice Immigration & Naturalization Service, *Other Procedures Concerning Adoptive Relationships,* in The Immigration of Adopted and Prospective Adopted Children, *available at* INS Adopt, Ch. VIII, 2000 WL 33596853 (INS). A U.S. citizen who is the adoptive parent of a person over the age of twenty-one who satisfies the criteria of an adopted child may file an I-130 to obtain a family-sponsored first preference visa for an unmarried adoptee and a third preference visa for a married adoptee. Lawful permanent residents may file an I-130 to obtain family sponsored second preference visas for their children or unmarried sons or daughters of any age who satisfy the criteria for adopted children. 8 U.S.C. § 1153 (2000).

The second requirement for "adopted child" status is that the child must have been in the legal custody of an adoptive parent for at least two years prior to filing the petition for an "adopted child" visa. "Legal custody" is defined as "the assumption of responsibility for a minor by an adult under the laws of the state and under the order or approval of a court of law or other appropriate government entity." 8 C.F.R. § 204.2(d)(2)(vii)(A) (2002). Despite the insistence in the regulations that a legal process through the courts or other governmental body occur, commentators and *Kaho* suggest that customary adoption can confer custody when it substitutes for a legal process of adoption. Ignatius, *supra,* at 13:8. Periods of legal custody that occurred prior to the adoption can count toward the two-year requirement, if custody was granted to the adoptive parent by a court or governmental entity prior to the adoption. Informal custodial or guardianship arrangements prior to the adoption, however, such as an affidavit conferring custody, will not be sufficient. If no award of custody is granted prior to the adoption, the adoption marks the commencement of legal custody. 8 C.F.R. § 204.2(d)(2)(vii)(A) (2002).

Finally, in order to qualify for an "adopted child" visa, the child must have resided with the adopted parent for at least two years prior to filing the petition. Just as with the period of legal custody, all or a portion of the period of residence may occur before or after the adoption. The petitioner must submit documentation that he or she resided with the child in a familial relationship during this period and exercised parental control. To establish this parental control, the adoptive parent may submit evidence that he or she owned or maintained the residence in which he or she lived with the child and that he or she financially supported the child and provided day-to-day supervision, although other types of evidence might be relevant as well. Most difficult are those situations in which the adoptive parent and child resided in the same home as the birth parent, which sometimes occurs in relative adoptions. In those cases, the burden is on the adoptive parent to prove that he or she exercised primary parental control during the period of residence. 8 C.F.R. § 204.2(d)(2)(vii)(B), (C) (2002).

When the child is adopted by a married couple, only one of the spouses needs to have legal custody and reside with the child for the respective two-year periods in order to satisfy the requirements of 8 U.S.C. § 1101 (b)(1)(E). The spouse who fulfills the custody and residency requirements need not be the petitioner, as long as both the spouse and the petitioner have adopted the child. Matter of Patel, 17 I. & N. Dec. 414 (B.I.A. 1980); INS, *Other Procedures Concerning Adoptive Relationships, supra,* at Ch. VIII.

The two-year periods of legal custody and residency need not be coterminous. Matter of Cho, 16 I. & N. Dec. 188 (B.I.A. 1977). Moreover, neither the two-year period of custody nor the two-year period of residence need be uninterrupted. The statutory requirements will be fulfilled as long as there has been two years in the aggregate of legal custody and residence. 8 C.F.R. §204.2(d)(2)(vii)(C) (2002). However, these two requirements are the means of ensuring that a bona fide parent-child relationship exists. Sullivan, *supra*, at n.279 and accompanying text. The Board of Immigration Appeals has shown its willingness to scrutinize these requirements in order to prevent fraudulent adoptions "entered into solely to confer immediate relative or preference status." Matter of Reputan, 19 I. & N. Dec. 119, 122 (B.I.A. 1984). Thus, the visa petition filed by an aunt who alleged she had resided with her adopted niece and nephew in the Philippines for seven periods of various durations totaling twenty-seven months in the aggregate over a sixteen-year time span was denied by the Board. Noting that "residence" is defined by 8 U.S.C. §1101(a)(33) as a person's "principal, actual dwelling place in fact, without regard to intent," the Board found periodic visits to a child's home insufficient to satisfy the two-year residency requirement. *Id.* at 120–21.

A lawful permanent resident who leaves the United States to reside abroad with an adopted child for two years must be careful not to trigger a presumption of abandonment of residency, which at the least would forgo his or her ability to petition for the beneficiary. *See* Sullivan, *supra*, at n.296 and accompanying text; Ignatius, *supra*, at §7:64. Immigration experts recommend that lawful permanent residents who plan to remain outside the United States for more than a year should obtain a reentry permit before they leave. *Id.* at n.7. For further information regarding abandonment of lawful permanent residency status, see Ignatious, *supra*, at Chapter 15.

An I-130 petition is normally filed in the INS office with jurisdiction over petitioners' state of residence, unless submitted simultaneously with a petition for adjustment of status for a beneficiary already residing in the United States, in which case the INS office with jurisdiction over the adoptee's place of residence would be appropriate. If the petitioner is residing abroad, then it is normally filed in the INS overseas office of the country of residence (except Canada), or if none, the U.S. consulate there. Ignatius, *supra*, at 7:64. Supporting documentation must include evidence of the petitioner's citizenship or permanent resident status, a copy of the adoption decree, evidence of the two years of legal custody and residence, certified copies of the parents' marriage certificate, and proof of termination of any prior marriages of the parents. 8 C.F.R. §204.2(d)(2)(vii) (2000); Ignatius, *supra*, at 7:69.

c. *Hague Convention Adoptions*

The Intercountry Adoption Act of 2000 amended 8 U.S.C. §1101 (b)(1) to create a third category of children immigrating for adoption purposes who could qualify for immediate relative status. The eligibility requirements for this group of children are set forth in a new subsection (G), which will go into effect upon entry into force of the Hague Intercountry Adoption Act for the United States. Subsection (G) permits a child to be classified as an immediate relative if:

> (1) the child is under the age of sixteen at the time the petition for an immediate relative visa is filed;

(2) the child has been adopted in, or is emigrating for adoption in the United States from a country that is a party to the Hague Intercountry Adoption Convention;

(3) the child is being adopted by a U.S. citizen and spouse, or by an unmarried U.S. citizen at least twenty-five years of age;

(4) the INS has determined that the child will receive proper care from the adoptive parent or parents;

(5) consent to termination of their legal relationship with the child, and to the child's emigration and adoption, has been freely given by the child's birth parents, or by the sole or surviving parent if the other parent has died, disappeared, or abandoned or deserted the child, or by any other individuals or institutions that have legal custody of the child;

(6) in cases in which the child has two living parents, the parents are incapable of providing proper care for the child;

(7) the INS determines that the purpose of the adoption is to form a bona fide parent-child relationship, and that such a relationship between the child and his birth parents has been terminated;

(8) in cases in which the child is not adopted in the country of origin, the child's emigration for adoption by the prospective adoptive parent or parents has been approved by the proper governmental authorities in the country of origin, and any pre-adoption requirements of the adopters' proposed state of residence have been satisfied.

In addition, new amendments to 11 U.S.C. § 1154 (d), which will also go into effect when the Hague Intercountry Adoption Convention enters into force for the United States, add two additional requirements:

(9) prior to approval of the petition for immediate relative status based upon a Convention Adoption, the Secretary of State under 42 U.S.C. § 14931 must certify that the Central Authority of the country of origin has notified the appropriate U.S. governmental authorities that an adoption occurred or custody was awarded for purposes of adoption in accordance with the Convention, and

(10) a valid home study must be performed that includes a favorable recommendation by a public or private adoption agency authorized by the state of the child's proposed residence, or, if the child is adopted abroad, by an agency licensed in the United States.

Despite this lengthy laundry list of requirements, the new "Convention" basis was added in an effort to facilitate the issuance of visas for some children who could be validly adopted under the laws of their own country, but were ineligible for visas under the stringent "orphan" requirements. Congress determined that when the additional safeguards of the Convention were in place, some of the abusive practices that the "orphan" restrictions were intended to deter were less likely to occur.

As this book goes to publication, the regulations implementing this new basis for immediate relative status for adopted children have not yet been issued. It would seem likely that the home study requirements, and perhaps many of the other requirements, will be very similar to those set forth in 8 C.F.R. § 204.3 for orphan petitions, but this remains to be seen.

Problem 12-5

The Hague Intercountry Adoption Convention entered into force for the Philippines in November 1996. Examine the amendments to 8 U.S.C. § 1101 (b)(1)(G) and (2) that go into effect when that Convention enters into force for the United States. If the adoption described in the *Rogan* case set forth above had occurred under the Convention, would the outcome have been different?

3. Citizenship

Prior to 2001, a child who was adopted internationally by a U.S. citizen did not become a U.S. citizen automatically. Instead, the child remained a lawful permanent resident, until the parent on the child's behalf, or the child as an adult, applied for naturalization.

After February 27, 2001, the effective date of the Child Citizenship Act of 2000, adopted children born abroad can become U.S. citizens automatically as of the date that all of the Act's requirements are met. These requirements are:

(1) at least one parent of the child is a U.S. citizen, by birth or naturalization;

(2) the child is under 18 years of age;

(3) the child is residing in the United States, in the legal and physical custody of the citizen parent, pursuant to a lawful admission for permanent residence by satisfying the requirements of 8 U.S.C. § 1101 (b)(1)(E), (F), or (G); and

(4) the adoption is final. 8 U.S.C. § 1431 (2000).

It does not matter in which order the requirements are met. Thus, children adopted abroad will become citizens as soon as they are residing with their U.S. citizen parent in the United States, and children who are entering the United States from abroad for adoption in U.S. courts will become citizens when their adoption is final. All of the requirements must be satisfied before the child's eighteenth birthday, however, in order for automatic citizenship to come into effect. U.S. Dep't of State, *Fact Sheet on Child Citizenship Act of 2000, available at* http:www.travel.state.gov/childcitfaq.html.

Adopted children who had not yet been naturalized on February 28, 2001, but who met all of the requirements of the Act on that date, became automatic citizens as long as they had not yet reached eighteen years of age. Those over the age of eighteen on February 28, 2001 are still required to apply for naturalization. *Id.*

Children who become automatic citizens under the Act will not have a certificate of citizenship, just as children born in the United States have no certificate of citizenship. However, if an adoptee wishes to obtain a U.S. passport, one can be obtained upon submission of a certified copy of the final adoption decree, the child's foreign passport with the INS I-551 stamp on it or the child's resident alien card (green card), and the parent's valid identification. *Id.*

Another section of the Citizenship Act of 2000 permits a parent to apply for citizenship for an adopted child who is born and resides abroad. This process is not automatic. Upon application and completion of the naturalization process, a certificate of citizenship will be awarded to such a child if the following requirements are satisfied:

(1) at least one parent is a United States citizen, by birth or naturalization;

(2) the U.S. citizen parent has been physically present in the United States for a total of at least five years, at least two of which were after the age of fourteen, or a parent of the U.S. citizen parent satisfies that requirement;

(3) the child is under the age of eighteen;

(4) the child resides abroad in the legal and physical custody of the U.S. citizen parent, is temporarily present in the United States after lawful admission as a nonimmigrant, and is maintaining lawful status; and

(5) the child satisfies the definition of an adopted child in 8 U.S.C. §1101 (b)(1)(E), (F), or (G). 8 U.S.C. §1433 (2000).

4. Adoption, Readoption, and Recognition of Foreign Orders in U.S. Courts

a. Initial Adoption in U.S. Court

When a child emigrates to the United States for adoption in U.S. state courts, the adoption requirements of the particular forum state must be satisfied. One issue an attorney handling such an adoption may need to address is whether a consent or relinquishment given by a parent in a foreign nation will be recognized as sufficient by the state court in which the adoption takes place. Some states will recognize a consent or relinquishment signed by a resident of a foreign country as long as the consent or relinquishment is valid under the law of the country in which such person resides, Okla. Stat. tit. 10, §§7503-2.3(K), 7503-2.4(J) (2001), or under the law of the country in which the consent or relinquishment is signed. Kan. Stat. Ann. §59-2117 (1995); Mich. Comp. L. Ann. §710.29 (West 2002).

If a consent or relinquishment has not been obtained from each birth parent, or if one or both were not given in a manner or form that would be recognized under the law of the forum state, then in some states a proceeding to terminate the parental rights of one or both birth parents must be commenced. Many states will recognize the order of a foreign court or other authorized governmental entity terminating the parental rights of the birth parents, and some will waive the requirement of notice and consent of a birth parent if the petitioners submit to the court a document issued by a foreign governmental entity stating that the birth parent has given consent to the adoption, or relinquished the child, or the parent's parental rights have been terminated, or the child has been abandoned. See Okla. Stat. tit. 10, §7502-1.4(d)(1) (2001). In a similar vein, the Kansas Supreme Court held that a proceeding to terminate parental rights was not necessary, and the petition for adoption without the consent of the parents should be granted, when the court had been presented with a Chinese decree of adoption and the certification of a Chinese orphanage director that the child had been abandoned, and the INS had issued a visa and permitted the child to enter the country. In the Matter of Adoption of W.J., 942 P.2d 37 (Kan. 1997).

b. Readoption in a U.S. Court

The INS will require a child who enters on an "orphan visa" to be readopted in the United States if the unmarried adopter or both spouses of a married couple did not personally see the child prior to an adoption in the country of origin, or if the adoption abroad was not full and final. 8 C.F.R. §204.3 (d) (2002). Even when the INS does not require it, however, there are other reasons that adoptive parents wish to pursue readoption. Sometimes foreign political instability motivates a desire for a state adoption decree that will provide additional emotional and legal security. Readoption has also been pursued to ensure recognition of the child's adoptive status under the law of states that do not recognize foreign decrees of adoption. Harlan S. Tennenbaum, *Guiding Clients Through the Complexities of International Adoption,* 13 Am J. Fam. L. 235, 243 (1999).

Another principal reason for seeking readoption is to obtain issuance of a birth certificate from the child's state of residence. Children adopted from some countries, such as China, typically have only certificates of abandonment. Even when a foreign birth certificate is available, however, obtaining a certificate of foreign birth issued by a U.S. state government provides a far more convenient method of identification throughout an adoptee's lifetime, because certified copies are more easily obtainable and need no translation. *Id.* Although some states issue a new birth certificate upon proof of a foreign adoption, *e.g.,* Cal. Fam. Code §8919 (West Supp. 2002), other states require readoption in their state courts in order to obtain a new birth certificate. *E.g.,* Okla. Stat. tit. 10, §7505-6.6 (2001). Readoption also provides an opportunity to change the child's name, and subsequently obtain a birth certificate or other legal identification under the new name. While name changes are often included in the foreign adoption process, this does not always occur, and children then immigrate with papers reflecting only the name they were given in their orphanage. *See* Philip Cordery, *Readoption in the UK—A Guide for Families who have Adopted Children in China,* May 2000 Int'l Fam. L. 74, 75.

Many states by statute recognize the right to readopt a child who has been adopted in a foreign country by a resident of the state. *E.g.,* Okla. Stat. tit. 10, §7502-1.4 (2001); Tenn. Code Ann. §36-1-106 (Supp. 2000). By statute or common law, often requirements that would normally be applicable in an adoption brought for the first time in the state court, such as a notice to birth parents or a proceeding to terminate parental rights, an interlocutory waiting period, or a home study, will be waived for a readoption subsequent to an adoption in a foreign country. *E.g.,* Okla. Stat. tit. 10, §7502-1.4 (2001) (termination of parental rights, six-month waiting period, if child has resided with petitioners for six months); Tenn. Code Ann. §36-1-106 (termination of parental rights, home study, court report, and waiting period); In the Matter of Adoption of W.J., 942 P.2d 37 (Kan. 1997) (termination proceeding); Adoption of Luis A.L.W., 620 N.Y.S.2d 219 (N.Y. Surr. Ct. 1994) (six-month waiting period).

c. *Recognition of Foreign Adoption Decrees by U.S. Courts*

Foreign orders of adoption are not entitled to full faith and credit under the U.S. Constitution. In the past, some state courts refused to recognize the adoptive status of a child adopted abroad, an issue which often arose in the context of inheritance rights. Today, the majority of state courts are now required by state statute to recognize a decree or order of adoption issued by a foreign court or other governmental authority with appropriate jurisdiction, and to ensure that the foreign decree will afford the same rights and obligations as if the adoption had taken place in the forum state. *E.g.,* Ind. Code Ann. §31-19-28-1 (Michie 1998). Some state courts have similarly recognized foreign adoption decrees under the common law doctrine of comity.

Once the Hague Intercountry Adoption Convention enters into force for the United States, foreign adoptions that take place in Convention countries will be certified by the Secretary of State pursuant to 42 U.S.C. §14931, and therefore entitled under federal law to recognition as valid final adoptions for all purposes under federal, state, and local law within the United States. 42 U.S.C.A. §14931(b) (2000). See Section B.2.f. of this Chapter, *supra*. The incidence of state court readoptions following foreign Convention adoptions will in all likelihood be far lower, as prospective adoptive parents are assured under the Convention and the Intercountry Adoption Act that all U.S. courts and all countries that are parties to the Convention will recognize the validity of their adoptions, and they will have a certification from a U.S. governmental authority that may serve many of the same purposes as would be met by a state certificate of foreign birth.

Problems

12-6. Claire Tucker, a twenty-four year old school teacher from Vermont who is a U.S. citizen, wishes to adopt a toddler from China through a local adoption agency that facilitates international adoptions. The agency has urged her to file her I-600A application and accompanying documentation as soon as possible. She has not finished the home study process yet, and is concerned about whether she can or should file the I-600A immediately. She understands from the agency orientation meetings that the birth parents of a child adopted from China are often married, and that consents from these birth parents will almost certainly be unavailable because the children are usually left in public places or government buildings and taken to the orphanage with no identification. She is wondering if she will have any difficulty obtaining approval of her I-600 petition, assuming she receives approval through advanced processing. Are her concerns valid?

12-7. Ellis Adams, a U.S. citizen aged thirty, and his wife, Sarah Cho, a twenty-three year old who is a lawful permanent resident from Taiwan, have contacted an agency to adopt a child from China. The two of them have been interviewed and approved for adoption in a home study completed a year ago for a domestic adoption, through a different agency, that never took place because the birth mother involved changed her mind. As part of that home study a social worker from the agency, who was licensed to perform home studies in their state, visited their home; assessed their financial situation and their physical, mental, and emotional capabilities as adoptive parents; determined that there was no entry regarding either of them in the child abuse registries; inquired from both about any history of abuse or violence or criminal history; and specifically approved them for adoption.

They have submitted this home study and the other necessary documentation with their I-600A application, and have been fingerprinted. They have also submitted their application for a referral to China, and hope to receive a referral soon.

When the referral comes, they plan that only one of them will travel to China to adopt their daughter and bring her back to the United States. The reason both do not plan to travel is that Ellis' mother recently moved in with them, following serious injuries in a car accident, and she requires significant care.

Are Ellis and Sarah likely to receive approval of their I-600A? If not, why not, and what is their recourse? If they are approved, will the INS permit only one of them to travel and adopt their child in China, and if so, does it matter which one?

12-8. Peter Gonsalves and his wife, Maria, both U.S. citizens over the age of thirty, contact their attorney for assistance with adopting a three-year-old boy from Mexico who has been identified to them through their church. The child is currently living with his elderly grandmother in Mexico, who has terminal cancer. The child is the youngest of seven children. His mother lives in a distant city, supporting six other children on her meager wages working in a factory. This child has asthma, so he has lived with his grandmother for the past year and a half to avoid the smog in the city in which his mother and siblings reside. The mother is willing to sign adoption papers. The child's birth parents never formally married. Peter and Maria have been told that the boy's birth father moved three months ago to seek work in another Mexican state, and his mother does not know his current whereabouts.

Knowing that Peter and Maria were hoping to adopt, the priest at their church told them about the boy, whom he had met on a recent trip to Mexico on an exchange project. The church in Mexico is trying to help the grandmother. Because Peter and Maria heard you assist clients with international adoption, they contacted you. What advice can you give them about whether it is possible to adopt this boy, and the steps they need to take. What additional information, if any, do you need?

12-9. Justin Trent and his wife, Meera, have been stationed in India for fifteen years on assignment with a U.S. corporation. Justin is a U.S. citizen and Meera, an Indian citizen, is a lawful permanent resident of the United States. The couple have been married for thirty years. Three years ago, their neighbors and best friends were killed in a car accident. The neighbors' sons, ages 13 and 15, came to live with Justin and Meera, and Meera was named legal guardian by an Indian court at that time. One year ago, when the boys were 15 and 17 years of age, Justin and Meera adopted the boys in India in a proceeding that was valid under Indian law. The religious heritage of Meera and the boys is Hindu and Justin's is Christian.

Justin and Meera are now being transferred back to their employer's headquarters in Texas, and they wish to petition to obtain visas for the boys, who at this time are almost 17 and almost 19 years of age. Is there any basis upon which they could successfully petition for immediate relative visas for the boys?

12-10. Amanda and Ian Patrick, both U.S. citizens, were stationed in Guatemala for four years with the U.S. foreign service. Their housekeeper, Anita, and her four-year-old daughter lived with them. Anita gave birth to a second daughter during this time, and when the infant was four months old, Anita asked Amanda and Ian if they would like to adopt this child. Anita's relationship with this child's birth father had deteriorated, and she wanted to return to her studies at a local university. The birth father had visited periodically, and would not consent to the adoption in writing.

When the baby was six months old, Amanda and Ian adopted her in an adoption that is valid under the law of Guatemala. Notice was given to the birth father, and he did not appear at the hearing to object. When the baby was eight months old, Anita and her older daughter moved out, and Anita returned to school.

When the baby was twenty-eight months old, Amanda and Ian were transferred back to the United States. They left the child with a close friend for a month while they moved back and got the household settled. Amanda then returned to Guatemala, and when the child was thirty months old, Amanda petitioned on her behalf for immediate relative status. Will she be successful?

Chapter 13

Reproductive Freedom, Assisted Conception, and Abortion

Reproductive rights and reproductive freedom are an integral part of the broader human rights discussion. The choice of whether, when, and how often to have children sometimes is tainted by economic coercion, threat of criminal prosecution, and/or invasive and involuntary medical procedures. Restrictive governmental policies that shape reproductive behavior fall into two broad categories: 1) physical coercion or threat of physical coercion and 2) financial incentives or disincentives. The first part of this chapter compares policies in Romania and China with policies in the West. The object is to gain a greater appreciation of the overlap in the countries' policies, despite the undeniable differences, and to explore reasons for the similarities and differences. The second part of this chapter examines assisted reproduction, an entirely different topic. However, this topic also has implications for the relationship between the individual and government. The government can facilitate the use of these technologies by a broad segment of society, often through the provision of financial assistance or through deregulation, or it can prohibit the use of a technology or technologies by all. Those who violate the prohibition may be criminally confined or denied their child's custody. Finally, this chapter analyzes the issue of access to abortion. It specifically examines ways in which governments regulate women's access to abortion and their ability to do so considering domestic, regional, and international law. Although this chapter's three topics differ greatly in many respects, you should try to attend to the underlying forces that may, in fact, tie these topics together within a country and between countries.

A. Legislating Reproductive Decision-Making

1. Direct Regulation of Reproductive Decision-Making

In some countries, the government is actively involved in reproductive decision-making. This was the case in Romania as recently as 1990, and continues to be so in China today. In these two countries, the national government has a policy regarding reproductive decision-making, and justifies its intrusion into personal autonomy with concerns about the collective good. Romania and China provide examples of policies that directly regulate the individual's right to make reproductive decisions freely, although the policies are diametrically opposed in their goals.

a. Romania

From 1966 to 1989, under the leadership of President Nicolae Ceausescu, the Romanian people were subject to one of the most repressive population policies in recent history. President Ceausescu believed that a large population was vital to a successful and healthy socialist state, and he issued Decree 770 when birth rates began to decline. Decree 770 banned most abortions, allowing exceptions only if the abortion occurred during the first trimester of the pregnancy and only if one of the following criteria were met:

> the pregnancy endangers the woman's life such that no other resolution is possible;
>
> one of the parents suffers from a serious hereditary illness, or from one that will predetermine a serious congenital malformation;
>
> the pregnant woman shows grave physical, psychological, or sensory disabilities;
>
> the woman is over 45 years of age;
>
> the woman has given birth to four children and has them in her care;
>
> the pregnancy is the result of rape or incest.

Gail Kligman, The Politics of Duplicity: Controlling Reproduction in Ceausescu's Romania 54, 55 (1998) (citing article 2). If the woman's life was threatened, she could abort until the end of the second trimester. Id. The law punished those who performed illegal abortions, intermediaries, and the women themselves. Id. at 57. Sanctions included imprisonment. Id.

The government justified the ban in the preamble of the decree: "The interruption of a pregnancy represents an act with grave consequences for the health of women, and is detrimental to fertility and the natural growth of the population." Id. at 52–53.

The effect of Decree 770 was to increase Romania's population immediately. Contraceptives were almost completely unavailable in Romania at this time. Id. at 45. The fertility rate rose from 1.9 children per woman in 1966 to 3.7 children per woman in 1967. Id. at 58. Put another way, there were 273,687 live births in 1966 and 527,764 live births in 1967. Sherri Poradzisz, The Society and Its Environment, in Romania: A Country Study 61, 72 (Ronald D. Bachman ed., 1991).

However, by 1973 the total fertility rate had dropped to 2.4 children per woman, due in large part to the resourcefulness of the Romanian people in finding ways around the restrictions on abortion. Id. Illegal abortions became commonplace, as did medical complications from the abortions. Abortion-related maternal deaths rose from approximately 83 deaths in 1966 to 469 deaths in 1977. Jerome S. Legge, Jr., Abortion Policy: An Evaluation of the Consequences for Maternal and Infant Health 59–65 (1985). One source reports, "Denials of reproductive choice in Romania led to over 10,000 deaths from illegally performed abortions and approximately 5.2 million cases of permanent sterility resulting from faulty abortion procedures." Paula Abrams, Population Politics: Reproductive Rights and U.S. Asylum Policy, 14 Geo. Immigr. L.J. 881, 887 (2000).

In the ensuing years, as birth rates continued to decline from the high point in 1967, Ceausescu instituted more legal reform to ensure the success of his demographic policies. In 1974, the labor code was revised to allow pregnant women and nursing mothers to have lighter work duties and more time off to care for their children. Poradzisz, *supra*, at 73. In 1984, the legal age of marriage for women was lowered to fifteen. *Id.* at 109. A variety of other pro-natalist policies were also initiated. People who were childless after age 25, regardless of their marital status, were subject to a tax of between ten and twenty percent of their income. *Id.* at 72. A decree restricting divorce was strictly enforced, resulting in a drop from 26,000 divorces in 1966 to only 28 in 1967. *Id.* Women giving birth to their third and subsequent children were granted monetary awards, and the income tax rate for families with three or more children was reduced by thirty percent. *Id.* at 72. At the height of Ceausescu's efforts to increase population,

> Monthly gynecological exams for all women of childbearing age were instituted, even for pubescent girls, to identify pregnancies in the earliest stages and to monitor pregnant women to ensure that their pregnancies came to term. Miscarriages were to be investigated and illegal abortions prosecuted.... Doctors and nurses involved in gynecology came under increasing pressure, especially after 1985, when "demographic command units" were set up to ensure that all women were gynecologically examined at their place of work. These units not only monitored pregnancies and ensured deliveries but also investigated childless women and couples, asked detailed questions about their sex lives and the general health of their reproductive systems, and recommended treatment for infertility.

Id.

Yet the efforts were largely ineffective:

> Although government expenditures on maternal incentives rose by 470 percent between 1967 and 1983, the birthrate actually decreased during that time by 40 percent. After 1983, despite the extreme measures taken by the regime to combat the decline, there was only a slight increase, from 14.3 to 15.5 per 1,000 in 1984 and 16 per 1,000 in 1985. After more than two decades of draconian anti-abortion regulation and expenditures for maternal incentives that by 1985 equalled half the amount budgeted for defense, Romanian birth rates were only a fraction higher than those rates in countries permitting abortion on demand.

Id. at 74.

Ceausescu was forcefully removed from office and executed in 1989. Immediately following his overthrow, Decree 770 was abrogated. "The rush to procure legal abortions in early 1990 was astounding. In the first three weeks after abortion was legalized, five thousand legal abortions were performed in the city of Bucharest alone. By the end of 1990, Romanian physicians performed more than one million abortions on about 600,000 women." Nicki Negrau, *Listening to Women's Voices: Living in Post-Communist Romania*, 12 Conn. J. Int'l L. 117, 123 (1996). Today "[a]bortion is the primary means of controlling births, and Romania has the highest rate in the world, with three abortions to every live birth." Reed Boland, *Symposium on Population Law: The Environment, Population, and Women's Human Rights*, 27 Envtl. L. 1137, 1141 (1997).

The Ceausescu era has had lingering effects. In 1995, the Committee on the Rights of the Child asked Romania to "[d]escribe steps taken to reduce the high number of abortions." *Summary of the 122nd Meeting: Romania, Comm. on the Rights of the Child*, 5th Sess., 122nd Mtg., ¶1, U.N. Doc. CRC/C/SR.122 (1995). The Romanian representative stated that Romania was expanding its efforts at encouraging family planning, and that international organizations were assisting it. Yet the representative explained, "[i]n Romania, reasons for voluntary termination of pregnancy included socio-economic factors, the absence of effective contraception and the general rejection of the statutory restrictions imposed during the traumatic years of pro-birth demographic policies." *Id.*

¶3. Myths and misperceptions about birth control attributed to propaganda during the Ceaucescu era is also one of the numerous obstacles to increased contraceptive use. Negrau, *supra*, at 124.

What lessons can one draw from the Romanian experience? Gail Kligman, author of *The Politics of Duplicity*, has concluded:

> The fundamental lesson of Romania's political demographic policies, the centerpiece of which was the re-criminalization of abortion [abortion was also illegal from 1948–57] is that legal and safe abortions must be protected by law. The comparative, historical records of maternal mortality in countries where abortion is banned make clear that women will seek illegal abortions when effective options to prevent and terminate unwanted pregnancies are not available to them. In short, women risk their lives in order to gain control over their fertility.

See Kligman, *supra*, at 245–46. Do you agree with Kligman that this is the fundamental lesson? What other lessons can one draw from this story? Does your answer to the foregoing questions assume that it was wrong for the government to try to increase Romania's population? If so, why was it wrong? What exactly bothers you, if anything at all, about the Ceausescu regime's policies?

b. The People's Republic of China
i. The Policy

The People's Republic of China (PRC) currently has one of the most restrictive anti-natalist population policies in the world. In 1979, faced with a rapidly growing population and a limited share of the world's natural resources, the government of the PRC instituted the "One-Child Policy." The One-Child Policy, called Wan Xishaoyou, emphasizes later marriages, fewer children, and high quality children. Marilyn Dalsimer & Laurie Nisonoff, *The Implications of the New Agricultural and One-Child Family Policies for Rural Chinese Women*, 13 Feminist Stud. 583, 586 n.14 (1987). Recently, the One-Child Policy was codified in the Population and Family Planning Law of the People's Republic of China. The new codification consolidates and memorializes what before was a conglomeration of directives, resolutions, and regulations from various levels of government. To understand the policy and its evolution over time, it is important to start with those pre-codification pieces.

The family planning policy has roots in the PRC Constitution, the 1980 Marriage Law, and the 1992 Law Safeguarding Women's Rights and Interests.

Constitution of the People's Republic of China
Ch. I–II, (1993), *available at*
http://www.qis.net/chinalaw/lawtran1.htm

[Article 25] The State promotes family planning so that population growth may fit the plans for economic and social development....

[Article 33] Every citizen is entitled to the rights and at the same time must perform the duties prescribed by the Constitution and the law....

[Article 49] Marriage, the family and mother and child are protected by the state. Both husband and wife have the duty to practice family planning....

[Article 51] Citizens of the People's Republic of China, in exercising their freedoms and rights, may not infringe upon the interests of the state, of society or of the collective, or upon the lawful freedoms and rights of other citizens....

[Article 54] It is the duty of citizens of the People's Republic of China to safeguard the security, honor and interests of the motherland; they must not commit acts detrimental to the security, honor and interest of the motherland.

Marriage Law of the People's Republic of China

No. 72 (1981), *available at*
http://www.unescap.org/pop/database/law_china/ch_record003.htm

[Article 1] This Law is the fundamental code governing marriage and family relations.

[Article 2] A marriage system based on the free choices of partners, on monogamy and on equality between man and woman shall be applied. The lawful rights and interests of women, children and old people shall be protected. Family planning shall be practiced....

[Article 5] No marriage may be contracted before the man has reached 22 years of age and the woman 20 years of age. Late marriage and late childbirth shall be encouraged....

[Article 9] Husband and wife shall have equal status in the family....

[Article 12] Both husband and wife shall have the duty to practice family planning....

[Article 15] Infanticide by drowning and any other acts causing serious harm to infants shall be prohibited.

Law Safeguarding Women's Rights and Interests of the People's Republic of China

Ch. VII (1992), *available at*
http://www.qis.net/chinalaw/prclaw49.htm

[Article 47] Women have the right to bear children in accordance with relevant provisions of the state. They also have the freedom of choosing not to bear children. Husband and wife of child-bearing age should practice family planning in accordance with relevant provisions of the state. The departments concerned should provide them with safe and effective contraceptive medicine, instruments and techniques as well as protect the health and safety of the women having birth control surgery.

Xiaorong Li, *License to Coerce: Violence Against Women, State Responsibility, and Legal Failures in China's Family-Planning Program*

8 Yale J.L. & Feminism 145, 152–153 (1996)

The "one birth" policy as spelled out in central government resolutions, directives and provincial regulations can be summarized as follows (specifics vary slightly between provinces and autonomous minority regions):

(1) Couples should apply for birth permits before they try to conceive a child.

(2) At least one spouse is required to use "long term" and "effective" contraception after having the permitted number of children. Women are to use an IUD after having the permitted number of children.

(3) Those who proceed with unauthorized pregnancies, especially after they have already had the permissible number of births, must have their pregnancies terminated. After out-of-plan births, one spouse must be sterilized.

These measures are guided by quantitative birth quotas (the number of permitted births per year for a particular community), that are normally assigned by the central authorities to each province, autonomous region, and major municipality. Such quotas are further subdivided among provinces, townships, villages, and working units. For example, in 1992, the State Council instituted a "Ten Year Plan" and "The Eighth Five-Year Plan," specifying the population quotas that each provincial government was expected to meet. According to the "Eighth Five-Year Plan," for example, population growth in Beijing between 1991 and 1995 was not to exceed 730,000, a growth-rate cap of 13.1% per year; the population of Tibet was to grow by no more than 230,000, a cap of 19.91% per year; and in Sichuan, population growth was not to exceed 7,160,000, with growth limited to 12.91% per year.

Though it has been known as the "one child policy," the national average targeted number of births per couple has actually been slightly higher. Rural couples in many provinces are allowed to have a second child if, for example, their first child was a daughter. A third child is, however, strictly forbidden under any circumstances.

The penalties and consequences of noncompliance fall under several categories:

(1) Penalties openly imposed by the policy: stiff fines; disqualification for benefits such as subsidized child day care, health care, housing and education; administrative demotion and dismissal from employment.

(2) Penalties and psychological intimidation sanctioned by the policy: policy-created pressures from co-workers or fellow villagers; intimidation and humiliation, including mandatory study sessions, visits by authorities, and public posting and monitoring of menstrual periods.

(3) Violence used by government agents: physical brutality and property destruction, including detention, beatings and the demolition of residence by local officials, militia acting in a governmental capacity, and the police.

Enforcement varies from region to region, partly according to the limited discretion of local officials and the social norms within each rural unit and workplace. In some areas, people who do not comply with the policy may be subjected to severe penalties, including physical assault and property destruction. In other areas, even the penalties imposed by national and regional policies may not be enforced.

In the early stages of implementation, local officials enjoyed significant discretion in enforcing the policy, with some fluctuations in the degree of pressure from the center for compliance. When politically decentralized policy implementation failed to produce the desired results, the Communist Party Central Committee and the State Council decided to mobilize the huge government bureaucracy to enforce compliance. The 1991 "Decision on Stepping Up Family Planning Work and Strictly Controlling Population Growth" entrusted senior party officials at each level with responsibility for supervising birth control in regions under their administration. According to the..."family-planning target management responsibility contract" (jihua shengyu mubiao guanli zerenzhi) announced in this Decision, the performance of party leaders and government officials is assessed on the basis of their "achievement" of the allocated birth quotas for their areas. Failure to keep the number of births within the quota could mean demotion, stiff fines, or the loss of bonuses.

Effective September 1, 2002, China's One-Child Policy was codified in the Law on Population and Family Planning passed by the Standing Committee of the National People's Congress. The act is quite detailed with its forty-seven articles. Most former aspects of the policy are reflected in the new law, and despite the statutory consolidation, local areas still have considerable discretion with regard to the policy's enforcement. The new law contains explicit references to rewards for couples who practice family planning, *see, e.g.,* art. 23 (recognition and rewards for couples who practice family planning); art. 26 (incentives for sterilization); art. 27 (incentives from employers); art. 28 (loan and work incentives for households in poverty) as well as penalties for couples who do not. *See* art. 41 (imposing social compensation fee); art. 42 (imposing administrative penalties including disciplinary measures for state employees). Implicit in the act is a recognition that various social programs and policies are important for the success of the One-Child Policy. *See, e.g.,* art. 3 (calling for expansion of women's education and employment opportunities); art. 24 (calling for the establishment and improvement of social security arrangements for old-age insurance, medical insurance, and childbearing insurance). Perhaps the most striking difference between the former policy and the codified law is that there are now explicit prohibitions against infringing citizens' legitimate rights and interests. *See* art. 4. The law also states that the policy is to be implemented through "publicity and education, advances in science and technology, comprehensive services and the establishment and improvement of the incentive and social security systems." *See* art. 3. Consider also the following provisions:

Population and Family Planning Law
of the People's Republic of China

(Dec. 29, 2001) (Unofficial Translation), at
http://www.unescap.org/pop/database/law_china/ch_record052.htm

Article 36. Anyone who violates this law by one of the following acts shall be ordered to rectify the violation and warned by the family planning or public health agency, and all gains derived from such illegal acts shall be confiscated by the family planning or public health administrative departments.

If the illegal gains exceed RMB 10,000, a fine of no less than two times and no more than six times the amount shall be imposed. If no illegal gains is involved or the amount is less than RMB 10,000, a fine of no less than RMB 10,000 and no more than RMB 30,000 shall be imposed. In serious cases, licenses shall be revoked by the issuing agency. Acts constituting a crime shall be referred for criminal prosecution.

(1) Illegal performance of a surgical procedure related to family planning at another's behest.

(2) Use of ultrasonography or other techniques to identify fetal gender for non-medical purposes or sex-selective pregnancy termination for non-medical purposes, at another's behest.

(3) Faking a birth control procedure related to family planning, falsifying a medical report, or counterfeiting certificates related to family planning....

Article 38. Family Planning service providers who commit malpractice or who delay emergency response, diagnosis or treatment with dire results shall be held liable under the applicable laws and regulations.

Article 39. Staff of state organs who commit one of the following acts in the course of family planning activities shall, if the act constitutes a crime, be referred for criminal prosecution; or, if the act does not constitute a crime, be subject to both administrative penalties and confiscation of any illegal gains.

(1) Infringing on a citizen's personal rights, property rights or other legitimate rights and interests.

(2) Abuse of power, dereliction of duty or graft.

(3) Seeking or accepting a bribe.

(4) Withholding, reducing, redirecting or embezzling family planning program funds or social compensation fees.

(5) Distorting, under-reporting, fabricating, modifying or refusing to report statistical data on population or family planning....

Article 44. Citizens, entities treated as legal persons or other organizations deeming that an administrative organ has infringed on their legitimate rights and interests while implementing family planning policy may appeal for review or sue for redress.

---

ii. Justifications and Criticisms of the Policy

China's vigorous attempts to control population growth has been met with both praise and condemnation. Understanding the justifications for the policy is critical to assessing the policy itself.

Information Office of The State Council of the People's Republic of China, *Human Rights in China*

ch. VIII (1991), *available at* http://www.china.org.cn/e-white/7/7-VIII.htm
(hereinafter State Council White Paper on Human Rights)

The Chinese government implements a family planning policy in the light of the Constitution, with the aim of promoting economic and social development, raising people's living standards, enhancing the quality of its population and safeguarding the people's rights to enjoy a better life.

China is a developing country with the biggest population in the world. Many people, little arable land, comparatively inadequate per-capita share of natural resources plus a relatively backward economy and culture—these features spell out China's basic national conditions.

The population which is expanding too quickly poses a sharp contradiction to economic and social development, [affects] the utilization of resources and environmental protection, places a serious constraint on China's economic and social development, and drags improvement of livelihood and the quality of the people. By the end of 1990, the mainland population had reached 1.14 [billion]. With such an immense population base, China, despite the implementation of birth control, still sees a yearly net increase of 17 [million] people, a number equal to the population of a medium-sized country. [Ed. Note: China's population as of July 2001 is estimated at 1.27 billion. *See* Central Intelligence Agency, The World Factbook 2001, *available at* http://www.cia.gov/cia/publications/factbook/index.html.]

As for the per-capita area of cultivated land, it had dropped to 1.3 mu, representing only 25% of the world average. Similarly, the per-capita share of freshwater resources is just one quarter of the world average. China's grain production ranks first in the world, but divided among the population, the amount of grain per person accounts for just 22% of that in the United States.

More than a quarter of the annual addition to the national income is consumed by the new population born during the same year. As a result, funds for accumulation have to be cut, and the speed of economic growth slowed down. The rapid swelling of the population has brought about many pressures on the country's employment, education, housing, medical care, and communications and transportation.

Faced with the gravity of this situation, the government, in order to guarantee people's minimum living conditions and to enable citizens not only to have enough to eat and wear but also to grow better off, cannot do as some people imagine—wait for a high level of economic development to initiate a natural decline in birthrate. If we did so, the population would grow without restriction, and the economy would deteriorate steadily.

Hence, China has to strive for economic growth by trying in every possible way to increase the productive forces, while at the same time practice the policy of family planning to strictly control population growth so that it may suit economic and social development. This is the only correct choice that any government responsible to the people and their descendants can make under China's given set of special circumstances.

It is universally acknowledged that China has achieved tremendous successes in family planning. The birthrate dropped by a big margin from 33.42 per thousand in 1970 to 21.06 per thousand in 1990, and the natural population growth dropped from 25.83 per thousand to 14.39 per thousand. [Ed. Note: The birth rate is now 15.95 per thousand and the death rate is 6.74 per thousand. *See* Central Intelligence Agency, *supra.*] In 1970 the childbearing rate of Chinese women was 5.81, and the figure decreased to 2.31 in 1990. At present, the above three indicators are lower than the average level of other developing countries. To a certain extent, this success has mitigated the contradiction between China's ballooning population and its economic and social development. It has played an important role in advancing socialist modernization and raising the living standard and the quality of the population. Also it has been an important contribution to the stability of the world's population....

China adheres to the principle of combining government guidance with the wishes of the masses when carrying out its family planning policy. Since it involves all families, it would be impossible to put the policy into effect in a county with more that 1.1 billion without the masses' understanding, support and conscientious participation. Family planning is also a reform of social custom and cannot possibly be carried out just by administrative orders. In the countryside, which is inhabited by 80% of the population, millenia-old traditional ideas remain influential, the economy is backward in some areas, and the social welfare and guarantee systems are still inadequate. People have real difficulties in their production and livelihood. Given these factors, the government has always given priority to tireless publicity and educational work among the masses to enhance the public awareness that birth control, as a fundamental policy, has a direct bearing on the nation's prosperity and people's happy family life.

Government officials are required to take the lead in carrying out the policy and set a good example. In recent years, the Chinese Family Planning Association has set up more than 600,000 grassroots branches with 32 [million] members to aid the masses in self-education, self-management, and self-service, combining ideological education with helping the masses solve practical problems. At the same time, the government has adopted some necessary economic and administrative measures as supplementary means. These measures are all adopted in keeping with the law, and with the ultimate aim of persuasion....

China's population policy has two objectives: control of population growth and improvement in quality of the population. Work in this field not only encourages couples of child bearing age to have fewer children but also provides them with mother care, baby care, and advice on optimum methods of childbearing and child-rearing. These services include pre-marriage check-ups, heredity consultation, pre-natal diagnosis and care during pregnancy to help couples have sound, healthy babies....

China's family planning policy fully conforms to Item 9 of the United Nations' Declaration of Mexico City on Population and Growth in 1984, which demands that "countries which consider that their population growth rate hinders their national development plans should adopt appropriate population plans and programmes." It also accords with the UN World Population Plan of Action which stresses that every country has the sovereign right to formulate and implement its own population policy.

Some people who censure China's family planning policy as "violating human rights" and being "inhuman" do not understand or consider China's real situation. But some others have deliberately distorted the facts in an attempt to put pressure on China and interfere in China's internal affairs. China has only two alternatives in handling its population problem: to implement family planning policy or to allow blind growth in births. The former choice enables children to be born and grow up healthily and live a better life, while the latter one leads to unrestrained expansion of population so that the majority of the people will be short on food and clothing, while some will even tend to die young. Which of the two pays more attention to human rights and is more humane? The answer is obvious.

To get a sense of why many have criticized the policy, consider one of the stories told by a man seeking asylum in the United States:

De You Chen and Lan-Zheng Sun were married in China. They had two girls. After their birth of the second girl, birth control authorities fined the couple 2,000 RMB (the PRC's currency) for having a second child within four years of the first. The authorities also required the implantation of an intra-uterine device in Sun. Because Chen and Sun wanted a boy, they had the device illegally removed. In 1990, Sun became pregnant again. Upon learning of her pregnancy, the authorities threatened to destroy the couple's home if she did not abort the child. Chen and Sun responded by fleeing to a nearby village. The authorities then destroyed the couple's home, extorted information from Chen's father, and fined him 2,000 RMB. After Sun gave birth, the couple returned to their original village. The authorities scheduled Sun for a sterilization surgery, imposed a 10,000 RMB fine, and barred all three children from attending school. Because Sun was too ill for surgery, the authorities ordered that Chen be sterilized instead. In

August, 1991, Chen fled his village to hide at his workplace. In November 1992, his sister warned him that the authorities would find him, jail him, and sterilize him. Chen then fled China aboard a boat headed for the United States. *See generally* Chen v. INS, 95 F.3d 801 (9th Cir. 1996).

iii. Redressing Policy Excesses

The facts in *Chen v. INS* suggest that local governmental officials have used violence to achieve the policy's objectives. Will the new Population and Family Planning Law halt these practices? It is important to recognize that the central government has historically denounced violence and threats of violence. Yet, in a 1996 report on China, Amnesty International reported that "despite assurances from the State Family Planning Commission that 'coercion is not permitted,' Amnesty International has been unable to find any instance of sanctions imposed on officials who perpetrated such violations." Amnesty International, China: No One Is Safe, ch. 3 (1996), *available at* http://www. amnesty.org/ailib/intcam/china/china96/report/cc3.htm. Some have suggested that China's size makes it simply impossible for the central government to control local excesses. Responding to such an argument, Justice La Forest, in *Chan v. Canada (Minister of Employment & Immigration)*, [1995] 128 D.L.R. 4th 213, 238 (Can.), stated: "The evidence does not lead to the conclusion that the central government of China is unable to protect its citizens from the excesses of the local authorities." Justice La Forest noted, "[W]hile local officials are rarely punished for abuses committed during the sterilization process, economic sanctions are levied against such officials when birth rates are too high." *Id.* at 239.

Recently, there have been sporadic reports of private lawsuits seeking redress for abuses. For example, a court in Yiyang awarded a woman an amount equivalent to $14,000 in damages and medical expenses after local officials forced her to have an abortion because her husband was ten days under the minimum age to have a child. The abortion had complications leading to sterility, and the mother became clinically depressed. *See A Forced Abortion Took Away Her Chance of Becoming a Mother*, The Straits Times, May 8, 2001, *available at* http://straitstimes.asia1.com.sg/mnt/html/women/issues26.html. The case is being appealed. *Id.*

The ability of the courts to effectively remedy governmental abuses has to be evaluated against the background of the Chinese judicial system more generally.

Donald C. Clarke, *What's Law Got to do With It? Legal Institutions and Economic Reform in China*
10 UCLA Pac. Basin L.J. 1, 21–22, 58–67 (1991)

[C]ourt personnel are essentially controlled by the government at the corresponding level.[83] Unlike federal judges in the United States, Chinese judges have no security of tenure and below the [Supreme People's Court] are not appointed by the central government. Hence, [Basic-Level People's Court] judges are beholden to the county-level

---

83. Officially, the court president is appointed by the People's Congress of the same level as the court; the vice-president and other judges are appointed by the Standing Committee of the same People's Congress. People's Congresses are rarely if ever anything more than rubber stamps for the local Party organization, particularly in matters of legal administration, which are handled by the same Party committee that handles public security matters.

government, and [Higher-Level People's Court] judges are beholden to the provincial-level government.

Officials in China's court system are generally poorly educated. China now has some seven "political-legal institutes" and thirty-three law departments which annually produce about 4,000 LL.B. graduates. Because very little legal education took place between the mid-1960s and the late 1970s, qualified persons who can serve as judges are scarce. Recent graduates, in their early twenties, are simply too young. A large number of judges, especially at the basic court level, are demobilized army officers, and some courts even draft their clerks into service as "substitute judges" (daili shenpanyuan) when manpower is short. No career judicial bureaucracy with clear, or even vague, standards of competency has been created, and no objective qualifications for judges have been established. Among Hunan's 8,308 judges, for example, only 756 (9.1%) have studied beyond high school. Of these, only 300 (3.6% of the total) specialized in law. Nationwide, one writer asserts that only 10% of all judges and procurators have been educated at or above the college level. Some efforts are being made to train judges on the job. In February 1988, the Supreme People's Court and the State Education Commission established a Training Center for Senior Judges....

Any incentive structure premised on protection of rights and enforcement of law by Chinese courts as currently constituted is problematic. The ability of Chinese courts to enforce legal standards is severely limited for several reasons....

1. Lack of Education

Many of China's judges and other legal officials have little or no professional training in law. Judicial ignorance of the law is particularly devastating in a system such as China's because so few ways exist to remedy it. Chinese judicial procedure is basically inquisitorial, leaving a great deal of initiative to the judge instead of to the parties and their lawyers. Just finding the applicable law can be an impossible task. Laws and regulations are promulgated by a bewildering variety of governmental and quasi-governmental bodies, and no comprehensive and up-to-date indexes are available. Indeed, it is illegal for individuals to compile collections of laws and regulations. No regular system of case reporting exists that would allow judges to see how other courts had handled similar problems. Quite often there will simply be no statutory rule directly on point, or there may exist contradictory rules. In these cases, guessing how an untrained and ill-educated judge will choose to decide the issue is impossible, and parties have no sense of what sorts of arguments should or should not count.

2. Corruption

Official corruption is a serious problem in China—indeed, it was one of the grievances that sent the people of Beijing and other cities into the streets in the spring of 1989—and it extends to the judiciary. The extent of corruption, however, cannot be quantified in a rigorous way....

3. Overriding of Judge's Decision Within the Court

Courts at all levels have as part of their structure an Adjudication Committee headed by the president of the court. It is the highest decision making body within the court as an institution. Official policy states that "judicial independence" means not that the particular judge or judges hearing the case should be independent from outside pressures (i.e., senior judges in the same court), but at most that the court as an institution should be free from outside pressures. The Adjudication Committee has the power, among other things, to override the decision of the judges who actually hear the case and conduct the trial and to order them to enter a different decision.[260] Reports in the legal press indicate that in many courts the Adjudication Committee routinely decides cases, with the result that "those who try the case do not decide it, and those who decide the case do not try it" (shenzhe bu pan, panzhe bu shen).

4. Vulnerability to Outside Pressures

Judges can be threatened with various unpleasant consequences if they do not decide as the threatener wishes. I shall look here at only one kind of vulnerability with a specific institutional basis, that is, the power of the local Party and government to dictate to courts how they shall decide cases. The local Party tends to judicial matters through its Political-Legal Committee (zheng-fa weiyuanhui). This Committee has traditionally been in charge of the police, the procuracy, the courts, other aspects of judicial administration, and civil affairs. The Committee often is headed by the leader of the local police or of the local Party and government.

A common practice in China is for local Party secretaries of Party committees to review and approve the disposition of cases by courts. This was the concrete manifestation of the principle of Party leadership. The official theory now is that Party leadership is to be exercised at the level of legislation or general policy making, not in the adjudication of specific cases. But breaking old habits has proved difficult....

Judges may find themselves out of a job if they do not do as they are told by the Political-Legal Committee or other local power holder. The formal power of appointment and dismissal of court personnel is lodged in the local People's Congresses. In practice, however, they act as rubber stamps for the local Party organizational department. The real power is in the hands of the local Party leadership. "This personnel power exercised by a small group of leaders hangs like the sword of Damocles over those who would do things according to law." Thus, "if the court insists on handling things according to law and disposes of certain cases in ways not satisfactory to these leaders, some of them will use their power to arbitrarily reassign the court's leadership."

Some Chinese analysts, noting the local government's power over personnel, have suggested putting the entire court system under vertical leadership. The Supreme People's Court is reported to be drafting regulations to reform the court personnel system, and basic-level court presidents may be placed directly under provincial leadership. This will not be enough to solve the problem, however. Even where there is no question of actually dismissing or transferring judges, local governments are often able to exert pressure on courts through their control over court finances and material supplies as well as other court personnel....

---

260. The relationship between the local Party authorities, the Adjudication Committee, and the individual judge(s) hearing a case can be expressed as follows. The Party committee has the right, and even the duty, to concern itself with the work of the court and to make suggestions. It has the actual power, but not the right, to order the court to make a particular decision. The Adjudication Committee has both the right and the actual power to order individual judges hearing a case to make a particular decision.

5. Obstacles to Enforcement

Enforcing court judgments against any determined defendant, to say nothing of a well-connected and politically powerful defendant, is frequently difficult. An impressionistic view is provided by a report to the Standing Committee of the Sixth National People's Congress. In Heilongjiang province, only 10% of court judgments are "conscientiously implemented"; 20% are implemented in a "relatively conscientious" way. In half the cases, a few results are achieved, but a "relatively large degree of difficulty" is encountered in implementation; and 20% of court judgments are implemented "fairly poorly." ...

Why is it so difficult to execute judgments? First, there are few penalties for refusing to obey a court order. Chinese courts have no contempt power, and refusing to obey a court order is not a crime. Article 157 of the Criminal Law makes criminal a refusal to carry out a judgment if the refusal is by means of threats or violence. This covers the person who interferes with the actions of others carrying out a judgment, but does not cover the person who is ordered to do something and simply does not do it....

Second, courts often lack sufficient bureaucratic clout to enforce their judgments against administrative units. Any clout they have comes from the bureaucratic rank of individual judges. Although courts and governments at any given level are supposed to be equal, court presidents generally have a lower bureaucratic rank than the chief executive of the government at the same level.... That a lower-level official from one bureaucracy should be able to give orders to a higher-level official from another is alien to the way China functions. A low-status judge does not have the prerogative to disobey, much less to command, a higher-status official. As one county Party secretary is reported to have said, "Tell me what matters more: official rank or the law? I can definitely tell you, rank matters more. Law is made by man; without man, how could there be law? Without man, how could law matter at all? That's why I say that rank matters more."

Third, the cooperation of local authorities is needed. Judicial independence is not much use if it results in nothing more than the issuance of a piece of paper. The enforcement of local court judgments may be supported by local authorities, if only because a judgment they opposed would likely not be issued in the first place....

Notes and Questions

1. *Exceptions.* To be clear, China's One-Child Policy has never been without its exceptions, and those exceptions have expanded over time. For example, many of the provinces, and some of the larger cities, have decided to offer second-born children the same rights as first-born children if these second children are born to parents who were only children. *See* Xinhua Eng, *Two-Child Law Does Not Mean Change of Birth Control Policy in China*, Newswire, June 25, 2000, *available at* 2000 WL 23071745; Damien McElroy, *Shanghai Sets Aside China's One-Baby Law*, The Sunday Telegraph, June 25, 2000, at 28. Another exception exists for ethnic minorities. People's Congresses in the ethnic minority autonomous areas have their own family planning policies, and these policies are more lenient than those for the Han people. "Under these policies, an ethnic minority family generally may have two or three children; in frontier areas and areas with adverse geographical conditions, families of ethnic minorities with very small populations may have more than three children each; and Tibetan farmers and herdsmen in the Tibet Autonomous Region may have as many children as they like. As a result, eth-

nic minority populations have been able to increase at a higher rate than the rest of the population." *See* Information Office of the State Council of the People's Republic of China, National Minorities Policy and Its Practice in China, Ch. IV (Sept. 1999). Despite these exceptions, the central government has reiterated its commitment to the One-Child Policy. McElroy, *supra*.

2. *Coercion.* Conflicting information exists about the extent coercion is used to further China's population policies. On the one hand, reports of forced abortions and forced sterilizations exist. *See, e.g.,* Central News Agency (Taiwan), *Poverty Drives People of Fujian Province to Seek Better Life Overseas,* World Reporter-Asia Intelligence Wire, June 21, 2000, *available at* 2000 WL 2362402; *Hearing on Forced Abortion and Sterilization in China: The View from the Inside,* Before the Subcommittee on International Operations and Human Rights, 105th Cong. 30 (1998) (statement of Gao Xiao Dvan, Planned-Birth Officer). On the other hand, some of these reports are false. *See, e.g.,* Wen Huang and Pin Ho, *The Roots of Dover's Immigrant Tragedy,* Christian Sci. Monitor, June 23, 2000, at 11. Moreover, some believe that the economic sanctions are losing their effectiveness as living standards rise. *See* Huang and Ho, *supra.* Assuming that at least some of the reports of forced abortion or sterilization are true, what is the problem with these procedures? Are these methods of population control more problematic than economic sanctions? If so, why?

3. *Non-judicial Solutions.* If the courts in China are beholden to local authorities, is there anything that China could do to diminish the abuses occurring in its population control policy?

4. *Socialism.* China was a feudal monarchy until 1911, when it became a Republic. In 1949, the People's Republic of China was founded after a revolution led by the Communist Party. China is now a socialist society. The National People's Congress claims that socialism has "considerably" improved the standard of living for the people. It sees "socialist modernization" as the "basic task of the nation in the years to come." Const. of the People's Republic of China, preamble (1993). During the Ceausescu regime, Romania was also a socialist country. Is there something about socialism that makes it more likely that the government will try to control the population's reproduction?

5. *Constitutionalism in China.* How does the Chinese Constitution differ from the United States Constitution? How does the concept of "rights" differ? What of the fact that the Constitution states, "The people's courts shall, in accordance with the law, exercise judicial power independently and are not subject to interference by administrative organs, public organizations or individuals." *Id.* art. 126, §VII.

6. *Implementation.* Much of the One-Child Policy is implemented at the local level. Article 107, section 1 of the Chinese Constitution specifies, "Local people's governments at and above the county level, within the limits of their authority as prescribed by law, conduct the administrative work concerning the...family planning in their respective administrative areas; issue decisions and orders; appoint, remove and train administrative functionaries, appraise their work and reward or punish them." Historically, the decentralized administration has been one of the policy's weaknesses. One reporter has stated, "Widespread localised corruption and sheer neglect of the rules has meant 80% of Chinese children have a sibling." John Schauble, *Shanghai Relaxes One-Child Policy,* The Age, June 16, 2000. The new Population and Family Law addresses localized corruption explicitly.

7. *Education.* What do you make of the fact that China had earlier educational campaigns that achieved "great success," but not sufficient success to eliminate the popula-

tion crisis in China? *See* Xizhe Peng, *Population Policy and Program in China: Challenge and Prospective*, 35 Tex. Int'l L.J. 51, 52–53 (2000) (noting that the 1971 Wan-Xi-Shao campaign emphasized later marriages, greater spacing between children, and fewer children which led the total fertility rate to decline "sharply from 5.8 in 1970 down to 2.8 in 1979").

8. *Comparing Policies.* By all accounts, China's efforts at controlling population have been somewhat successful, while similar tactics in Romania failed to produce the desired results. Both policies were restrictive. What factors distinguish the effectiveness of these policies? Are there greater human rights implications to Romania's policy than to China's policy? If so, why?

9. *Collateral Legal Consequences.* China's One-Child Policy so dominates life in China that the law even makes the policy relevant upon divorce. Article 46 of the Law Safeguarding Women's Rights and Interests of the People's Republic of China (1992) states: "In dealing with the question of rearing children at the time of divorce, favorable consideration should be given to the wife's reasonable demands and to the rights and interests of the children if she has lost child-bearing ability because of sterilization or other reasons."

10. *Collateral Social Consequences.* The One-Child Policy affects more than the rate of population growth. For example, Chinese authorities are concerned about the "quality" of the declining Chinese population and they are implementing eugenics policies. *See* Michael Palmer, *Caring for Young and Old: Developments in the Family Law of the People's Republic of China, 1996–1998, in* The International Survey of Family Law 95, 101–02 (2000). In addition, the older population is now much more numerous than the younger population, raising questions about how Chinese society will support the older population. As mentioned above, the new Population and Family Planning Law calls for enhanced social security programs such as old-age insurance. Also, it is a crime in China not to care for one's aged parents. *Id.* at 97.

11. *Collateral Social Consequences II.* Much has been made of the fact that China's One-Child Policy has encouraged female-infanticide, sex-selective abortion, and abandonment of girls. *See, e.g.,* Xiaorong Li, *License to Coerce: Violence Against Women, State Responsibility, and Legal Failures in China's Family-Planning Program*, 8 Yale J.L. & Feminism 145, 159 (1996) ("In the 1980s, in rural areas, forced compliance with the birth control policy has resulted in a rise in the rate of incidents of female infanticide and abandonment of girls, with five percent of female infants disappearing from the records in national surveys."); Ellen Keng, *Population Control Through the One-Child Policy in China; Its Effects on Women*, 18 Women's Rts. L. Rep. 205, 210 (1997) ("Further evidence from the State Statistical Bureau indicates that in 1987, the world average of boys was 106 per 100 girls at birth, yet China's ratio was 113 boys per 100 girls and has reached as high as 118.47 per 100 girls in some provinces."); *id.* at 206 ("Typically, unwanted daughters were given to orphanages."); Karin Evans, The Lost Daughters of China 108–116 (2000). In fact, the 2000 census revealed that the problem is getting worse: there were "117 boys born for every 100 girls in 2000, up from 114 in 1990." Antoaneta Bezlova, *China to Formalize One-Child Policy*, Asia Times, May 24, 2001, *at* http://www.atimes.com/china/CE24Ad02.html.

For various reasons, Chinese couples typically have a strong preference for a boy child. First, the marriage system is patrilocal. The daughter becomes a member of the husband's household upon marriage. In contrast, "sons remained within their household upon marriage and helped their parents financially." Keng, *supra*, at 207. Second, all ancestor worship is done by sons. Elisabeth Croll, Feminism and Socialism in China

23 (1978). These religious rites affect the welfare of the dead in the "spirit world." *Id.* Third, the Household Responsibility System, an agricultural reform that replaced the collective system, makes male children particularly valuable. Since most Chinese do not have any financial security in their old age, other than their children, boys represent a greater potential source of financial security than girls. *See* Gerrie Zhang, Comment, *U.S. Asylum Policy and Population Control in the People's Republic of China*, 18 Hous. J. Int'l L. 557, 564 (1996).

Sex-selective abortion, infanticide of female children, and child abandonment are all illegal in China. *See, e.g.,* Law on the Protection of Minors, No. 50, arts. 8, 52 (1991)(P.R.C.); Regulation Prohibiting Fetal Sex Identification and Selective Termination of Pregnancy for Non-Medical Reasons, art. 2 (1998)(P.R.C.). However, the statistics indicate that these laws have not ended these practices. The continuation of these practices has led to a shortage of prospective brides, which in turn has lead to trafficking in women, *i.e.,* the abduction of girls and women for sale as wives or prostitutes. *See* Keng, *supra,* at 210. Trafficking is prohibited by Chinese law, and local governments are directed to adopt measures to help rescue victims. Do these secondary effects mean that the One-Child Policy, on-balance, is unwise? Are there any positive social consequences of the policy, apart from controlling population growth? Some people have suggested that the One-Child Policy may contribute to gender equality in China.

Lawrence K. Hong, *Potential Effects of the One-Child Policy on Gender Equality in the People's Republic of China*
1 Gender & Soc'y 317, 319–20, 323 (1987)

[Ed. Note: The author explains how patrilineal traditions are very entrenched in China, especially in the rural areas where 80% of the population lives.]

If widely accepted, the policy could bring about the demise of the patrilineal system because single children do not have nephews and nieces, and their children will not have uncles, aunts, or close cousins. It only takes approximately 40 years...for the newest member in the family to find himself or herself without any collateral relatives within the fifth degree (the traditional boundaries for the lineage in China). The patrilineal network will be reduced to direct lineal kin—parents, grandparents, and surviving great grandparents. With the corporeal body of the patrilineal lineage stripped to its minimum, its power and sphere of influence on the individual, village, and work would be expected to dwindle.

[Ed. Note: The author explains how China is characterized by exogamous marriage that is patrilocal and virilocal. Exogamy is the custom of marrying outside of one's social unit, patrilocalism involves the home territory of the husband's family, and virilocalism involves the wife joining the husband's household. Uxorilocalism is where the husband joins the wife's household.]

Under the one-child policy, this rare and socially undesirable uxorilocal marital arrangement may successfully compete with virilocal marriage. For economic reasons, families with daughters are unlikely to let them go to the groom's village to live because they will be needed not only for the parents' old-age security but also to boost the life-long earning potential of the household [under the Responsibility Systems and the Household Sideline Production, economic schemes introduced in the late 70s that favor families with a large number of workers].

[Ed. Note: The author explains how women are underrepresented in nontraditional jobs outside the home.]

As long as women have to invest most of their adult lives in childbearing, they are less likely to be able to prepare themselves for and to commit themselves to novel careers for their gender; conversely, if childbearing is eliminated or is reduced to a relatively short period early in their adult lives, women my find it rewarding to prepare for and engage in many of the jobs traditionally held by men in China.

iv. International Human Rights

(a) Substantive Concerns — A Balance

Nations have worked together on international population issues for approximately fifty years. Initial cooperation focused on gathering and sharing population statistics, but by the early 1970s participants in international population conferences were concerned about the rapidly increasing world population and its implications for the environment, world hunger, infant and maternal mortality, and a host of other social ills. Nations came together to set policy goals and offer recommendations at the World Population Conference at Bucharest in 1974, the International Conference on Population at Mexico City in 1984, and again at the International Conference on Population and Development in Cairo in 1994.

Despite differences on particular issues, particularly the need for safe abortion, most countries agreed on most issues at the Cairo Conference, including that rapid unchecked population growth is harmful and that population stabilization is critical. As the Programme of Action from the Cairo Conference said:

> While it had taken 123 years for world population to increase from 1 billion to 2 billion, succeeding increments of 1 billion took 33 years, 14 years and 13 years. The transition from the fifth to the sixth billion, currently under way, is expected to take only 11 years and to be completed by 1998.

Report of the International Conference on Population and Development, U.N. Population Division, Dept. of Econ. & Soc. Affairs, with support from the U.N. Population Fund, 49th Sess., §6.1, U.N. Doc. A/CONF. 171/1 (1994). After the Conference reaffirmed the rights and freedoms in the Universal Declaration of Human Rights (principle 1), the right to an adequate standard of living (principle 2), the right to development (principle 3), and the right to gender equality (principle 4), among other things, the Conference adopted principle 5: "Population-related goals and policies are integral parts of cultural, economic and social development, the principal aim of which is to improve the quality of life of all people."

However, the Programme of Action also recognized limits to population policies. Participants recognized that family-planning programs should not involve any form of coercion, that governmentally-sponsored economic incentives and disincentives were only marginally effective, and that governmental goals "should be defined in terms of unmet needs for information and services" and not quotas or targets imposed on providers. *Id.* §7.12. The aim "should be to assist couples and individuals to achieve their reproductive goals and give them the full opportunity to exercise the right to have children by choice." *Id.* §7.16. Countries were to meet the family-planning needs of their populations as soon as possible, but no later than 2015. *Id.* §7.16. A number of countries entered reservations, specifically objecting to the word "individuals" in section 7.16.

In addition, the Cairo Programme of Action recognized "reproductive rights," as set out in international human rights documents. *Id.* §§7.2–7.3. The notion of "reproductive rights" includes *both* "the basic right of all couples and individuals to decide freely and responsibly the number, spacing and timing of their children, and to have the information and means to do so" *and* "the right to obtain the highest standard of sexual and reproductive health." *Id.* §7.3.

Although the Cairo Programme of Action emphasized human rights, it also emphasized individual responsibility and sovereign autonomy. For example, it stated: "The promotion of the responsible exercise of these rights for all people should be the fundamental basis for government and community-supported policies and programmes...." *Id.* §7.3. In addition, the preamble stated:

> The recommendations for action are made in a spirit of consensus and international cooperation, recognizing that the formulation and implementation of population-related policies is the responsibility of each country and should take into account the economic, social, and environmental diversity of conditions in each country, with full respect for the various religious and ethical values, cultural backgrounds and philosophical convictions of its people, as well as the shared but differentiated responsibilities of all the world's people for a common future.

Id. ¶1.11.

How does the Cairo Programme of Action affect the legality or morality of China's actions? The answer to this question requires that one answer two subsidiary questions. First, what is the legal status of the Programme of Action? Approximately 170 countries were represented at the Conference. The Programme of Action was endorsed by the General Assembly in resolution 49/128 in December 1994, General Assembly resolution 50/124 in December 1995, and Economic and Social Council resolution 1995/55 in July 1995. *See* G.A. Res. 49/128, U.N. GAOR, 49th Sess., Agenda Item 158, U.N. Doc. A/RES/49/128 (1995). Second, what is the meaning of the language in the Programme of Action? The following expert helps us answer this second question.

Reed Boland, *Symposium on Population Law: The Environment, Population, and Women's Human Rights*
27 Envtl. L. 1137, 1158–60 (1997)

The rights to decide freely and responsibly on the number and spacing of children, and to have the access to the education and means to exercise these rights are of particular interest. This phrase constitutes what one might call, at this point in the evolution of thinking on population issues, the classic formulation of reproductive rights in an international context.

The phrase's first recorded use was in the final document approved by the Teheran Conference on Human Rights in 1968. Since then, in various wordings, it has been a staple of population thinking, taken up by a number of individual governments in population policy statements and laws, and reiterated prominently in the documents adopted by the three international population conferences, held in Bucharest in 1974, in Mexico City in 1984, and, most recently in Cairo in 1994....

The primary issue is the interpretation of the contrasting words "freely" and "responsibly," linked together as delimiters of reproductive rights. This linkage has prompted a series of questions. Is there a true 'free' reproductive right if it must be exercised 'responsibly?' Who is to determine what constitutes responsible action; the individual, the couple, the family, the community, or the government? What are the limits of 'responsible' action? For example, does responsibility entail undergoing sterilization and abortion when not desired, bearing children that are unwanted, submitting to contraception (including contraception that may be harmful to health) or conversely, bearing more children than can be properly cared for? Does a government have a right to impose strict population control measures in the name of responsibility for the purpose of providing a better life for future generations? The answers to these questions have fueled recent debates over population, the environment and reproductive rights.

Most observers would probably agree that forcing a woman to undergo sterilization or abortion, or to bear a child, as the policies of Romania, China and India have done, constitutes a human rights violation. Agreement, however becomes more difficult when the issue is the forced use of contraception (which the Government of China does not deny), and much more difficult in the case of incentives or the application of psychological pressure. The task becomes one of balancing conflicting considerations, such as, how coercive are the measures adopted, how urgent is the need for action, and what will be the response of the population affected? Also, are there less coercive alternatives that could be applied, and if so, what is the probability that the measures adopted will actually achieve the result desired?

The extreme complexity of the task is well illustrated by the issues of incentives and the application of pressure. All governments, including our own, use incentives of various sorts to bring about policy change; one need only think of the manipulation of the United States Internal Revenue (Tax) Code as an example. In addition, incentives can vary enormously, from providing a desperately poor person with clothing or money to be sterilized, to paying family planning workers a sum for each acceptor they recruit, to denying health care and education to children born outside of birth plans, or to giving preference in new housing or additional family subsidies to families that accept limits on their size. Similarly, it is part of the human condition to receive pressure from family, colleagues, and the government over matters of public and private behavior. This sort of pressure is particularly common in the sphere of sexuality and marriage. There are also great gaps between public humiliation and ostracism and lengthy individual interrogations on the one hand, and strong educational campaigns or appeals to the common good, to friendship, or to family harmony on the other. The range in these areas is from the relatively benign to the deceptive, cruel and inhumane; exactly where the boundary of the permissible is crossed is highly problematic. However, I suggest that a warning flag be raised when incentives become punishment or disproportionate to the sacrifice being demanded and when pressure leaves an individual with no practical choice but to comply.

Reed Boland spoke mostly of government-initiated coercion. Coercion can also result from private parties' actions. What are the obligations of a state under international human rights instruments to curb cultural practices, for example, that inhibit the right to decide freely and responsibly on the number and spacing of children? For an expansive view, consider the following excerpt by Paula Abrams:

Paula Abrams, *Population Politics: Reproductive Rights and U.S. Asylum Policy*
14 Geo. Immigr. L.J. 881, 895–97 (2000)

Far less obvious violations of reproductive self-determination arise in many cultures where patriarchal laws and traditions vest control of women's reproductive functions in fathers and husbands. Control of women's reproduction in these societies may be reinforced by traditions which view the family, rather than the individual, as the primary unit of society. The pervasive discrimination against women which characterize these societies belies any concept of reproductive "choice." For example, in Saudi Arabia, discrimination against women denies them the right to travel without a male companion or to receive medical treatment in a hospital without the consent of a male relative. Polygamy and restrictions on work which lead to total financial dependence create a culture in which reproductive choice has no practical meaning.

Despite the significant violations of reproductive self-determination which may occur, legal recognition of this type of coercion has been problematic. The government's role is perceived as indirect, and therefore, less culpable. In addition, where patriarchal cultural traditions, rather than explicit laws, are the source of discrimination, denial of rights may be attributed to private parties rather than state action. These interpretations present persistent problems for the legal recognition of women's rights. Although women may be subject to traditional violations of civil and political rights where direct government action is easily recognized, most violations of women's rights result from pervasive discrimination which has both legal and cultural roots. Even though discrimination is clearly prohibited by international law, the consequences of discrimination, including violations of other rights, such as reproductive self-determination, are not as well recognized. Nonetheless, where the government actively perpetrates discrimination which results in the denial of rights, or refuses to provide legal protection for women's rights, coercive government action may be found.

As we reflect on the actual content of the "reproductive rights" in international human rights instruments, it is worth emphasizing that this sort of inquiry is relatively new, even for human rights advocates. *See* Reed Boland, *Civil and Political Rights and the Right to Nondiscrimination: Population Policies, Human Rights, and Legal Change,* 44 Am. U. L. Rev. 1257, 1258–59, 1263–64 (1995). Attention has historically focused, instead, on practical issues surrounding the best way to lower the birthrate and on whether abortion services are properly part of a family planning program. *Id.*

Do the conventional human rights instruments have much to say about countries' population policies? Consider the International Covenant on Civil and Political Rights, articles 7–8, 17–18, 23–24, and 26. Examine also the Universal Declaration on Human Rights, articles 3, 12, 16, 18, and 29. What arguments would you make that China's policy, for example, violated Mr. Chen's human rights?

The Convention on the Elimination of All Forms of Discrimination Against Women (CEDAW) specifically addresses reproductive rights. *See* CEDAW, arts. 1, 12, 16 (1)(e). Both China and Romania have signed and ratified CEDAW. Notably, Romania ratified CEDAW in 1982, at a time of some of its most restrictive and invasive reproduction policies. Notice that CEDAW does not guarantee the right to decide on the number and spacing of children, but only guarantees that men and women will have the same rights with regard to that decision. Is a prohibition on abortion a violation of CEDAW? Imagine a country took away completely the right of both men and women to control their reproductive destiny. Is taking away the right completely a violation of CEDAW? Put another way, when the government controls the decision about the number and spacing of children, are men's and women's rights affected equally?

Certain population policies may also give rise to violations of the U.N. Convention on the Rights of the Child. For example, the enforcement of the One-Child Policy can affect children themselves. "When couples have out-of-plan children, they invalidate the benefits for their first 'planned' child and have to pay back the benefits that they have enjoyed." Xiaorong Li, *License to Coerce: Violence Against Women, State Responsibility, and Legal Failures in China's Family-Planning Program*, 8 Yale J.L. & Feminism 145, 157 (1996). Assume that these benefits include admission to public school and access to public health care. Does this enforcement mechanism violate the U.N. Convention of the Rights of the Child?

Problem 13-1

The government of State X, a sovereign nation, implants Norplant in all women age 13-18 in order to reduce the number of pregnancies. Failure to have Norplant implanted is a misdemeanor and can subject the objector to six months in prison. State X is a small island, and it finds that the rapidly increasing population is threatening the quality of life for existing residents. In particular, it discovered that at least 33% of the country's births were to young women, aged 13-18, about half of whom were unmarried. In addition, State X also has a law that prohibits individuals with certain inheritable mental defects from reproducing. The legislative history indicates that legislators wanted to ensure the best quality population possible since the counrty was limiting the size of its population. Do State X's policies violate international law? Assume State X is a party to all United Nations' human rights instruments.

(b) China's Views of International Human Rights

The People's Republic of China has been criticized for human rights violations in connection with its restrictive population policies. The Chinese government has a different view of human rights than does the United States government. The government of China explains:

China has always maintained that human rights are essentially matters within the domestic jurisdiction of a country. Respect for each country's sovereignty and non-interference in internal affairs are universally recognized principles of international law, which are applicable to all fields of international relations, and of course, applicable to the field of human rights as well.... It is neither proper nor feasible for any country to judge other countries by the yardstick of its own mode or to impose its own mode on others. Therefore, the purpose of international protection of human rights and related activities should be to promote normal cooperation in the international field of human rights and international harmony, mutual understanding and mutual respect. Consideration should be given to the differing view of human rights held by countries with different political, economic and social systems, as well as different historical, religious and cultural backgrounds. International human rights activities should be carried on in the spirit of seeking common ground while preserving differences, mutual respect, and the promotion of understanding and cooperation. China has always held that to effect international protection of human rights, the international community should interfere with and stop acts that endanger world peace and security, such as gross human rights violations caused by colonialism, racism, foreign aggression and occupation, as well as apartheid, racial discrimination, genocide, slave trade and serious violation of human rights by international terrorist organizations.

Information Office of the State Council of the People's Republic of China, *Human Rights in China*, (1991), *at* http://www.chinaguide.org/e-white/7/7-vii/html. China cites in support of its position article 2(7) of the Charter of the United Nations, which states, "[n]othing in the present Charter shall authorize the United Nations to intervene in matters which are essentially within the domestic jurisdiction of any state...."

The 1991 *White Paper on Human Rights*, released by the Information Office of the State Council of the PRC, explained in detail the Chinese government's framework for evaluating human rights within China.

Information Office of the State Council of the People's Republic of China, *Human Rights in China*

ch. VII (1991), *at* http://www.chinaguide.org/e-white/7/7-vii/html

[T]he evolution of the situation in regard to human rights is circumscribed by the historical, social, economic and cultural conditions of various nations, and involves a process of historical development. Owing to tremendous differences in historical background, social system, cultural tradition and economic development, countries differ in their understanding and practice of human rights. From their different situations they have taken different attitudes towards the relevant UN conventions. Despite its international aspect, the issue of human rights falls by and large within the sovereignty of each country. Therefore, a country's human rights situation should not be judged in total disregard of its history and national conditions, nor can it be evaluated according to a preconceived model or the conditions of another country or region. Such is the practical attitude, the attitude of seeking truth from facts.

From their own historical conditions, the realities of their own country and their long practical experience, the Chinese people have derived their own viewpoints on the human rights issue and formulated relevant laws and policies. It is stipulated in the Constitution of the People's Republic of China that all power in the People's Republic of China belongs to the people. Chinese human rights have three salient characteristics.

First, extensiveness. It is not a minority of the people or part of a class or social stratum but the entire Chinese citizenry who constitutes the subject enjoying human rights. The human rights enjoyed by the Chinese citizenry encompass an extensive scope, including not only survival, personal and political rights, but also economic, cultural and social rights. The state pays full attention to safeguarding both individual and collective rights.

Second, equality. China has adopted the socialist system after abolishing the system of exploitation and eliminating the exploiting classes. The Chinese citizenry enjoys all civic rights equally irrespective of the money and property status as well as of nationality, race, sex, occupation, family background, religion, level of education and duration of residence.

Third, authenticity. The state provides guarantees in terms of systems, laws and material means for the realization of human rights. The various civic rights prescribed in the Constitution and other state laws are in accord with what people enjoy in real life. China's human rights legislation and policies are endorsed and supported by the people of all nationalities and social strata and by all the political parties, social organizations and all walks of life.

Reed Boland, *Symposium on Population Law: The Environment, Population, and Women's Human Rights*
27 Envtl. L. 1137, 1160–61 (1997)

Nor is cultural relativism to be taken lightly. It is a historical fact that the concept of universal human rights as understood by the human rights community is largely a product of the Western imagination, strongly influenced by 18th century Enlightenment philosophy and ideas of personal autonomy and freedom. The key issue has been how to keep the government from intruding on personal rights to which individuals are entitled. Although increased interest in social and economic rights has changed this formula somewhat, even these rights are most often approached from the perspective of governmental denial of personal entitlements.

To many developing societies these are unfamiliar if not alien ideas. Persons within these societies often think of themselves more as a part of the family or community than as individuals and value ideas of cooperation, compromise, and shared responsibility more than self-expression. Consensus and the well being of society are often more important than individual self-fulfillment and personal entitlement. Moreover, in many developing countries where day-to-day survival and the lack of basic health and educational services are uppermost concerns, the assertion of collective economic and social rights seems far more relevant than the expression of individual civil and political rights. Countries such as China that have implemented population policies with coercive features make just this point, arguing that the collective economic and social welfare of their population in the future justifies any denial of personal rights that may occur in the present.

Despite the complexity of these matters, several principles are worth keeping in mind, such as healthy skepticism about the claims of population policies...and compassion when possible human rights violations are involved. The arguments of governments about the need for restrictive measures are all too easy to accept at face value. If there was indisputable evidence that specific disasters would occur unless population growth rates were drastically and immediately curbed, strong measures might be warranted. There is again, however, little evidence of this translation of policy into result. Indeed, much evidence indicates the opposite. A number of highly coercive policies have not worked. They do not respond to the actual needs of the populations subjected to them. Rather, these policies create a backlash of resistance, dishonesty, and distrust. They reflect a fundamental pessimism as to the ability of people to make the right choices for themselves and their families when given security and the ability to choose.

Notes and Questions

1. *China's Participation in Human Rights Treaties.* Can China be held to international standards? What of the fact that China joined the United Nations in 1971 and has ratified the Convention on the Elimination of All Forms of Discrimination Against Women, the Convention on the Rights of the Child (and two optional protocols), and the International Covenant on Economic, Social and Cultural Rights? China has signed, but not ratified, the International Covenant on Political and Civil Rights. Assuming China can be held to international standards, how does it measure up?

2. *China's Position on Human Rights.* The Chinese government claims that the collective good mandates China's restrictive population policies. Can the need for economic

growth and security justify human rights abuses? Would the Chinese government dispute the formulation of the question?

3. *The 2001 Human Rights Report.* The PRC has issued several other White Papers since the one released in 1991. The most recent White Paper on Human Rights was released in 2001. It emphasizes, more than the earlier White Paper, China's willingness to improve its human rights situation. Information Office of the State Council of the People's Republic of China, *Human Rights in China*, part VII (2000), *available at* http:/www.chinadaily.com.ch/highlights/paper/2001right.html. Among other things, the report mentions the judicial role in enforcing human rights in China, given the "impartial judicature" that "strictly enforce[s] the law." *Id.* at part III. The White Paper does not address the population policy directly, other than to note improvement in the standard of living in China. *Id.* at part I. The report notes that China "spared no effort to develop the economy" because safeguarding people's rights to subsistence is on the top of its agenda. *Id.*

4. *Asian Human Rights.* In 1993, members of various Asian nations, including China, came together to discuss human rights. The participants issued a report called the "Bangkok Declaration." *See Report of the Regional Meeting for Asia of the World Conference on Human Rights*, G.A. 46, U.N. GAOR, 7th Sess., U.N. Doc. A/Conf. 157/ASRM/8A/CONF.157/PC/59 (1993). It emphasized that Asian countries "with their diverse and rich cultures and traditions" could contribute to world efforts on human rights, *see id.* at part I, but that "universal" human rights "must be considered in the context of a dynamic and evolving process of international norm setting, bearing in mind the significance of national and regional particularities and various historical, cultural and religious backgrounds." *Id.* at part I, no. 8. Asia is the only region in the world without a regional human rights treaty or enforcement agency, much to the chagrin of the United Nations. *See* Richard Klein, *Cultural Relativism, Economic Development and International Human Rights in the Asian Context*, 9 Touro Int'l L. Rev. 1, 29–30 (2001).

Some have criticized the underlying claim that there is a unique Asian approach to human rights. *See* Yash Ghai, *Human Rights & Governance: The Asia Debate, in* International Human Rights in Context: Law, Politics, Morals 236, 237 (Henry J. Steiner & Philip Alston eds., 1996) (arguing that the diversity of Asian culture and realities undermine any claim of a unique perspective). On the other hand, some have claimed to have documented the differences between Asian and western values. David Hitchcock conducted a study of academics, government officials, business leaders, journalists, religious leaders and cultural leaders. He explains his methodology and outcome:

> One hundred and one of the Asians from eight counties (including one from the Philippines) were given [a list of]... societal values or qualities, and asked to mark those they thought were "critically important to people in your country." (It should be noted that they were advised to estimate the views of others and *not* to focus simply of their *own* views, which, many implied, might have been different—perhaps less traditional.) Twenty-eight Americans from various U.S. foreign affairs agencies in Washington and East Asia were also asked... to complete the exercise. All respondents were to check no more than...6 of the 14 societal values....

> On the list of societal values, the top six Asian choices were, in descending priority: orderly society; harmony; accountability of public officials; openness to new ideas; freedom of expression; and respect for authority. The top American

choices were, in descending order: freedom of expression; personal freedom; rights of the individual; resolve conflicting political views through open debate; thinking for oneself; and official accountability.... The largest difference between Asians and Americans came in the percentages that checked as "critically important" orderly society (71 percent of the Asians versus 11 percent of the Americans); personal freedom (82 percent of the Americans versus 32 percent of the Asians); and individual rights (78 percent of the Americans versus 29 percent of the Asians). The percentages of Asians checking as "critically important" decision by majority and consensus were, however, approximately the same—37 percent versus 39 percent; and the numbers checking "resolve conflicting political views through open debate" versus "through private consultation" were the same—29 percent.

See David Hitchcock, Asian Values and the United States 21–22 (1994). What does this mean, if anything, for China's defense of its reproductive rights policy?

5. *Other Human Rights Implications.* Consider the following two provisions of the new Population and Family Planning Law of the People's Republic of China. What issues, if any, do these articles raise? Article 7 states: "Social organizations such as Trade Unions, Communist Youth Leagues, Women's Federations, and Family Planning Associations; enterprises; institutions; and individual citizens shall assist the people's government in carrying out population and family planning programs." Article 43 states: "Those who resist or hinder family planning administrative departments and staff in the performance of their legitimate duties shall be subject to criticism and ordered to amend their conduct by the family planning administrative departments involved. Conduct breaching public security regulations shall be subject to public security penalties. Acts constituting a crime shall be referred for criminal prosecution." Might China be legitimately criticized for these specific aspects of its policy? Are the rights implicated by these provisions closer to the Chinese notion of human rights and therefore less insulated from criticism?

v. The United States' Response to China's Policy

The United States' response to China's One-Child Policy is multifold. For example, the United States puts restrictions on the use of its contributions to the United Nations Population Fund (UNFPA) and U.S. Agency for International Development (U.S. AID) so that its funds are not used to support coercive family planning programs. For a description of the relevant laws, *see* Tara A. Gellman, Notes & Comments, *The Blurred Line Between Aiding Progress & Sanctioning Abuse: United States Appropriations, The UNFPA and Family Planning in the P.R.C.*, 17 N.Y.L. Sch. J. Hum. Rts. 1063 (2001). For a criticism of those programs, *see* Farida Akhter, Reproductive Rights: A Critique From the Realities Bangladeshi Women, Re/productions (issue #1), at http://www.hsph.harvard.edu/organizations/healthnet/SAsia/repro/farida.html (arguing that "reproductive rights" are a disguise of the Western capitalist "population controllers" who have impinged on women's freedom).

The United States also responds through its laws governing asylum requests. The Fourth Circuit in *Chen v. INS*, 195 F.3d 198 (4th Cir. 1999), explained how the law works:

The Immigration and Nationality Act provides the Attorney General with discretion to grant asylum to any alien who is a "refugee." 8 U.S.C.A. §1158(b)

(West 1999). The Act defines "refugee" as a person unable or unwilling to return to his home country "because of persecution or a well-founded fear of persecution on account of race, religion, nationality, membership in a particular social group, or political opinion...." 8 U.S.C.A. § 1101(a)(42)(A) (West 1999).

Prior to 1997, the Board of Immigration Appeals consistently held that persecution under China's "one child" family planning policy was not persecution "on account of political opinion," and that victims of these policies were therefore not entitled to asylum, *see In re Chang*, Interim Decision 3107, 1989 WL 247513 (B.I.A. 1989); that holding was affirmed on review by the courts. *See Chen v. INS*, 95 F.3d 801 (9th Cir. 1996).... Apparently in response to this interpretation, Congress amended the definition of "refugee" in the Illegal Immigration Reform and Immigrant Responsibility Act of 1996 (IIRIRA), effective April 1, 1997, to include those who had been persecuted under a coercive family planning program, or who legitimately feared such persecution:

> For purposes of determinations under this chapter, a person who has been forced to abort a pregnancy or to undergo involuntary sterilization, or who has been persecuted for failure or refusal to undergo such a procedure or for other resistance to a coercive population control program, shall be deemed to have been persecuted on account of political opinion, and a person who has a well founded fear that he or she will be forced to undergo such a procedure or subject to persecution for such failure, refusal, or resistance shall be deemed to have a well founded fear of persecution on account of political opinion.

Pub. L. No. 104-208, 601(a)(1), 110 Stat. 3009-689 (1996) (current version at 8 U.S.C.A. § 1101(a)(42)).

Although persecution under the One-Child Policy now counts as persecution on account of "political opinion" for purposes of obtaining asylum, petitioners must still establish a "well founded fear of persecution." A well-founded fear is both a subjective fear of persecution and an objectively reasonable fear of persecution. *See* INS v. Cardoza-Fonseca, 480 U.S. 421, 430–31 (1987). The objective component is often difficult to satisfy, as it requires specific, concrete facts that a reasonable person in like circumstances would fear persecution. *See, e.g.,* Huaman-Cornelio v. Board of Immigr. Appeals, 979 F.2d 995, 999 (4th Cir. 1992); M.A. v. INS, 899 F.2d 304, 311 (4th Cir. 1990). At times, petitioners who lack such specific evidence, either that they were individually targeted or that they belong to a broader class of individuals who have been subject to systematic persecution, have failed in their attempts to gain asylum. An example of how this requirement can thwart an application is found in *Chen v. Immigr. & Naturalization Serv.*, 195 F.3d 198 (4th Cir. 1999). There the applicant's fear of being subjected to an involuntary sterilization procedure, or of being persecuted for a refusal to undergo such a procedure, was not well-founded because the applicant failed to rebut the State Department report that couples returning to Shanghai from university study abroad had been excused from any penalties. The Fourth Circuit stated, "Although the Human Rights in China report offered by Chen details horrific practices that continue to take place, the report does not contradict the State Department's conclusion that the practice of forced sterilization is uncommon and increasingly limited to rural areas. The Human Rights in China report does not present a picture of systematic persecution under the 'one child' policy." *Id.* at

204. The court reached this conclusion despite the fact that the State Department's report on China "records conflicting insights from informants . . . and offers only tentative conclusions." *Id.* at 202.

The U.N. High Commissioner for Refugees issued a Handbook on Procedures and Criteria for Determining Refugee Status under the 1951 Convention and the 1967 Protocol relating to the Status of Refugees, HCR/IP/4/Eng/Rev.1 (reedited 1992). Under the heading "Establishing the facts" the following paragraphs appear:

> 196. It is a general legal principle that the burden of proof lies on the person submitting a claim. Often, however, an applicant may not be able to support his statements by documentary or other proof, and cases in which an applicant can provide evidence of all his statements will be the exception rather than the rule. In most cases a person fleeing from persecution will have arrived with the barest necessities and very frequently even without personal documents. Thus, while the burden of proof in principle rests on the applicant, the duty to ascertain and evaluate all the relevant facts is shared between the applicant and the examiner. Indeed, in some cases, it may be for the examiner to use all the means at his disposal to produce the necessary evidence in support of the application. Even such independent research may not, however, always be successful and there may also be statements that are not susceptible of proof. In such cases, if the applicant's account appears credible, he should, unless there are good reasons to the contrary, be given the benefit of the doubt.

> 197. The requirement of evidence should thus not be too strictly applied in view of the difficulty of proof inherent in the special situation in which an applicant for refugee status finds himself. Allowance for such possible lack of evidence does not, however, mean that unsupported statements must necessarily be accepted as true if they are inconsistent with the general account put forward by the applicant. . . .

> 204. The benefit of the doubt should, however, only be given when all available evidence has been obtained and checked and when the examiner is satisfied as to the applicant's general credibility. The applicant's statements must be coherent and plausible and must not run counter to generally known facts.

The Handbook on Procedures and Criteria for Determining Refugee Status sets forth the "benefit of the doubt" doctrine. Does the "benefit of the doubt" apply to the applicant's subjective fear, to the objective reasonableness of that fear, or both? Are the guidelines in this publication binding on U.S. courts? Why did the "benefit of the doubt" doctrine not aid Mr. Chen?

Other elements of an asylum claim were explored in detail in Chapter 6 on Violence Between Family Members and we refer you to that material for additional information.

Notes and Questions

1. *Nexus Requirement.* Prior to the adoption of Section 601 of IIRIRA, the Board of Immigration Appeals had routinely denied applicants' request for asylum, finding that applicants were not persecuted on account of their political opinions. What is the argument that the decision to have children is a "political opinion?"

2. *Statutory Categories.* The IIRIRA amendment to the definition of "refugee" is critical for asylum petitioners from China. The Board of Immigration Appeals had stated:

"[E]ven if involuntary sterilization was demonstrated to be a violation of internationally recognized human rights, that fact in itself would not establish that an individual subjected to such an act was a victim of persecution 'on account of race, religion, nationality, membership in a particular social group, or political opinion.'" *In re* Chang, 20 I. & N. Dec. 38, 46–47 (1989). What if the involuntary sterilization would have violated U.S. constitutional law had it occurred in the United States? Would that have allowed an applicant to fit within one of the persecution categories prior to enactment of IIRIRA?

3. *Breadth of Section 601.* Section 601 provides that a person "who has been persecuted for...resistance to a coercive population control program" has a separate basis for establishing asylum. What is a "coercive population control program"? Need it involve physical violence? Since forced abortion and sterilization are set forth as independent grounds for asylum under section 601, must it mean something else? Would the following policies qualify? (A) A regulation that said, "After the birth of an unauthorized child, the family shall have all utilities cut off, food coupons stopped, and business licenses revoked, until sterilization of at least one adult is performed." (B) Cultural practices that place almost all decisions about reproductive decision-making in the hands of men. (C) Decree 770 in Romania. On this topic, *see generally* Paula Abrams, *Population Politics: Reproductive Rights and U.S. Asylum Policy*, 14 Geo. Immigr. L.J. 881 (2000).

4. *Impact of Section 601.* Section 601 sets a ceiling of 1,000 people who may be granted refugee or asylee status under it. In fiscal year 1997, the INS granted asylum to 606 aliens pursuant to this provision. *See generally* INS, 1997 Statistical Yearbook of the Immigration and Naturalization Service 77 (1997), *available at* http://www.immigration.gov/graphics/shared/aboutus/statistics/97asyttl.pdf. There quickly became a backlog, however. For example, at the beginning of 2002, the INS granted asylum to 1,000 aliens pursuant to this provision, and acknowledged that there are more aliens with a "conditional asylee status" awaiting the next fiscal year in order to obtain their final grant of asylum. *See* INS, 2001 Statistical Yearbook of the Immigration and Naturalization Service 90 (2003), *available at* http://www.immigration.gov/graphics/shared/aboutus/statistics/Yearbook2001.pdf.

Problem 13-2

Reread Problem 13-1. Assume Hsien-Ye Wang is a sixteen-year-old girl from State X. She has been charged with a violation of the juvenile justice code for her failure to allow authorities to implant Norplant in her arm. She has been placed on probation, with the condition that she cannot be alone with any males who are not her family members until she submits to the procedure. Violation of the condition will result in her detention at a center for wayward girls. Hsien-Ye arrives at the U.S. border with no documentation of the prosecution or the conditions of her probation. She seeks asylum. Will she be entitled to it? Should she be?

2. Indirect Regulation of Reproductive Decision-Making

The discussion so far has focused on state policies that include the direct regulation of reproduction. Yet a government might stop short of outright regulation of reproductive decision-making and employ only incentives or disincentives for individuals to conform their reproductive behavior to governmental expectations. Does the human rights analysis differ when the law only indirectly regulates reproduction, for example, through economic incentives or disincentives? Think about this question as you read the next section.

a. The United States: Welfare Reform and Reproductive Freedom

In 1996, Congress enacted the Personal Responsibility and Work Opportunity Reconciliation Act (PRWORA), Pub. L. No. 104-193, 110 Stat. 2105 (1996). PRWORA abolished Aid to Families with Dependent Children (AFDC), and replaced it with Temporary Assistance for Needy Families (TANF), sec. 103(a)(1), 401-419, 110 Stat. at 2113–60 (codified at 42 U.S.C. §§ 601–619). TANF is a block-grant program that allows states to implement and fund programs that reduce welfare dependence. Some of the stated goals of the TANF block grant program are to encourage the formation and maintenance of two-parent families, promote independence through jobs, and to prevent out-of-wedlock pregnancy. See 42 U.S.C. §§ 601–604.

A "family cap" is one of the programs that states may implement without federal approval in their attempts to meet federal goals. Most generally, a family cap "bars welfare benefits for any child born to a mother on welfare." Kathleen A. Kost & Frank W. Munger, *Fooling All of the People Some of the Time: 1990s Welfare Reform and the Exploitation of American Values*, 4 Va. J. Soc. Pol'y & L. 3, 87 (1996). Non-TANF programs, such as food stamps and Medicaid, are unaffected by family cap policies. A family cap differs dramatically from the way in which welfare was awarded traditionally under AFDC. Under AFDC, cash assistance grants increased incrementally as the family size increased.

Prior to TANF, states had been allowed to request waivers from the federal government in order to conduct experimental welfare reforms that deviated from federal requirements. In 1992, New Jersey received a waiver and initiated a family cap policy. The New Jersey policy is described in *C.K. v. Shalala*, below. In 1997, New Jersey repealed the Family Development Plan at issue in *C.K. v. Shalala*. See Work First New Jersey Act, N.J. Stat. Ann. §§ 44:10-55 to -94 (West. Supp. 2002). New Jersey's current family cap program is codified at N.J.S.A. § 44:10-61. The new law is "nearly identical" to the cap under the Family Development Plan, and was passed as part of a comprehensive effort to reform the prior welfare system in response to the enactment of TANF by Congress. See Sojourner A ex rel. Y.A. v. New Jersey Dep't of Human Serv., 794 A.2d 822, 826 (N.J. Super. Ct. App. Div. 2002).

Under the New Jersey family cap, a woman who is receiving cash assistance benefits under TANF will not receive an additional incremental increase in benefits for a child born or conceived while she is receiving benefits. The current policy does not apply if the mother with dependent children "gives birth to a child fewer than 10 months after applying for and receiving cash assistance benefits," or if "the birth of a child... occurs as a result of rape or incest." N.J. Stat. Ann. § 44:10-61(e), (f). The New Jersey law also provides that the amount of earned income that is disregarded in calculating TANF benefits will increase with the birth of a child. See N.J.S.A. § 44:10-61(c).

One implication of the policy is that two families of the same size may receive different cash assistance amounts depending upon when their children were conceived. For example, a mother with two children who applies for cash assistance will receive a larger grant than a mother who has her second child while receiving cash assistance.

Before considering the international law implications of family caps, or comparing family caps in the United States to policies in China, we need to assess the permissibility of these caps under U.S. law. Do family cap provisions represent an unconstitutional governmental intrusion into the decision whether to bear or beget a child, or are family cap provisions merely a refusal by the government to subsidize the exercise of a fundamental right? Does it make a difference that Congress' stated purpose in enacting PRWORA, which allows the family cap provisions, was to reduce out-of-wedlock births?

C.K. v. Shalala
883 F. Supp. 991 (D.N.J. 1995)

Politan, J.

Plaintiffs, residents of New Jersey currently receiving welfare funding via the Aid to Families with Dependent Children ("AFDC") program, challenge the exercise by the Secretary of the United States Department of Health and Human Services ("HHS") of her discretionary authority pursuant to § 1115 of the Social Security Act, 42 U.S.C. § 1315(a), which permits the Secretary to waive state plan requirements of the Act to enable individual states to test reforms to their AFDC programs via demonstration projects. Specifically, plaintiffs challenge the Secretary's grant of waivers to the state of New Jersey in July 1992 to allow implementation of the state's Family Development Program ("FDP") which, inter alia, contains the so-called Family Cap provision, an amendment to existing state law that eliminates the standard increase provided by AFDC for any child born to an individual currently receiving AFDC.

[P]laintiffs assert that as a matter of law the Family Cap violates... (4) the Equal Protection and Due Process Clauses of the United States Constitution.

Defendants, the United States Department of Health and Human Services and its Secretary Donna Shalala, along with the New Jersey Department of Human Services ("DHS") and its Commissioner William Waldman,... argue that the Secretary's grant of waivers to the state of New Jersey to implement the FDP reflected a reasoned judgment that the reforms proposed by the state were likely to promote the salutary objective of the AFDC program, namely breaking the cycle of poverty for AFDC recipients, enhancing their individual responsibility, and strengthening their family structure.... For the reasons expressed herein, defendants' motion for summary judgment dismissing the Complaint is GRANTED and plaintiffs' motion for summary judgment is DENIED.

Background

AFDC is a joint federal and state program established under Title IV-A of the Social Security Act, 42 U.S.C. § 601 et seq., to "enabl[e] each State to furnish financial assistance and rehabilitation and other services, as far as practicable under the conditions in such State, to needy dependent children and the parents or relatives with whom they are living...." 42 U.S.C. § 601. Under that program, if the state submits an AFDC state plan that meets the requirements of 42 U.S.C. § 602, the federal government reimburses it for a portion of the benefits it provides to aid recipients....

"The AFDC provisions of the Social Security Act envision aid to strengthen the entire family unit, including the dependent child's parent, so as to encourage the care of the child within his [or her] own home." Doe v. Gillman, 479 F.2d 646, 648 (8th Cir. 1973), *cert. denied*, 417 U.S. 947, 94 S.Ct. 3073, 41 L.Ed.2d 668 (1974) (citing 42 U.S.C. § 601). Within the AFDC legislation itself Congress has declared that it authorized familial financial aid:

> [f]or the purpose of encouraging the care of dependent children in their own homes or in the homes of relatives by enabling each State to furnish financial assistance and rehabilitation and other services, as far as practicable under the conditions in such State, to needy dependent children and the parents or relatives with whom they are living to help maintain and strengthen family life and to help such parents or relatives to attain or retain capability for the maximum self-support and personal independence consistent with the maintenance of continuing parental care and protection.... 42 U.S.C. § 601....

New Jersey's AFDC program is administered by the state's DHS. Effective July 1, 1992, the New Jersey Legislature enacted the Family Development Plan ("FDP").... [A] FDP provision which defendants have dubbed the "Family Cap," an amendment to existing state law that eliminates the standard AFDC grant increase (e.g., $102 for a second child and $64 for a third child) for any child conceived by and born to an AFDC recipient. The intent behind this cap on family benefits is to enhance family structure while simultaneously fostering responsibility and self-sufficiency. Indeed, the New Jersey legislature declared in its policy statement regarding its alteration of the AFDC benefits schedule that: "[t]he welfare system in this State should be designed to promote family stability among AFDC recipients by eliminating the incentive to break up families created by AFDC regulations, which undermines the ability of AFDC-enrolled mothers to achieve economic self-sufficiency and thereby perpetuates their dependence, and that of their children, on welfare." N.J.S.A. 44:10-3.7(c).

This policy statement accompanied the enactment of the Family Cap provision, which is the only component of the FDP challenged in this case. Briefly stated, after an initial ten-month grace period to provide notice to affected recipients, the FDP denies additional benefits to families receiving AFDC upon the birth of an additional child conceived while the family is receiving AFDC. A family affected by this provision is entitled to retain a larger amount of earned income, purportedly permitting the family not only to offset the denial of additional benefits but to realize an overall increase in financial benefits through earnings. *See* N.J.S.A. 44:10-3.5 and -3.6. For example, a parent with one child can receive a grant up to $322 a month in New Jersey. Under the federal system, if the mother had an additional child her grant would increase to $424 a month. Under FDP, she will not receive this $102 increase. Similarly, a mother with two children would not receive the $64 increase in her grant that she would otherwise receive if she had a third child....

[O]n June 5, 1992, DHS submitted its formal application to HHS for a waiver.... While DHS conceded that depriving children of AFDC might seem "harsh," it nevertheless justified the Family Cap provision by stating that its purpose is to encourage parents to be responsible in their decision to have another child while receiving welfare. Indeed, DHS went so far as to describe the choice to have a child while one is still receiving the fruit of the taxpayers' labor [as] "irresponsible [and] not socially desirable." DHS stated that it would offer financial incentives to encourage AFDC parents with children born after the Family Cap to offset the benefit they would otherwise have received through priority for employment and training services in FDP-JOBS [the job training and education programs created by FDP] and through the increase in the earnings disregard....

On July 20, 1992 Secretary Sullivan approved the waiver to allow the entire FDP to be implemented as a five-year research experiment under § 1315(a)....

Discussion...

Plaintiffs contend that the Family Cap trammels impermissibly upon their rights to due process and equal protection of the laws. They argue that the cap is irrational because it penalizes children for the behavior of their parents. In addition, plaintiffs assert that the cap fails the heightened strict scrutiny review since what it deems the state's "overriding" purpose in enacting the cap—deterring childbirth by welfare recipients—is an illegitimate goal sought to be realized by broad and overly intrusive means.

The Supreme Court has held that a program which places a ceiling on welfare benefits will pass constitutional muster provided that it bears a rational relationship to a legitimate state interest. Plaintiffs argue that the Family Cap cannot meet this standard because in their view it "penalizes vulnerable and needy children for their parents' behavior over which they have no control: the circumstances of their conception and birth." In support of this position they cite to, inter alia, *Plyler v. Doe*, 457 U.S. 202 (1982), where the Court deemed unconstitutional a Texas statute which withheld from local school districts funding for the education of children not legally admitted into this nation. While the Court realized that undocumented status is a proper subject for legislative action, it found it "difficult to conceive of a rational justification for penalizing these children for their presence in the United States." *Plyler*, 457 U.S. at 220. It therefore overturned the law, holding that "[e]ven if the State found it expedient to control the conduct of adults by acting against their children, legislation directing the onus of a parent's misconduct against his children does not comport with fundamental conceptions of justice." *Id. See also* Jimenez v. Weinberger, 417 U.S. 628 (1974) (holding unconstitutional a provision of the Social Security Act which allowed an illegitimate child to obtain benefits if a disabled parent either contributed to the child's support or lived with the child prior to the disability); New Jersey Welfare Rights Organization v. Cahill, 411 U.S. 619 (1973) (per curiam) (finding statute limiting benefits to families in which parents are "ceremonially married" to deny equal protection to illegitimate children); Levy v. Louisiana, 391 U.S. 68 (1968) (finding that a state may not create a right of action in favor of children for the wrongful death of a parent and exclude illegitimate children from the benefit of the same right).

However, reliance on the aforementioned decisions is unavailing here because the Family Cap is not an example of a state's attempt to influence the behavior of men and women by imposing sanctions on the children born of their illegitimate relationships. The legislation here does not direct the onus of parental conduct against the child, nor does it completely deprive children of benefits which they might otherwise receive but for the conduct of their parents. Rather, New Jersey's cap merely imposes a ceiling on the benefits accorded an AFDC household while permitting any additional child to share in that "capped" family income. Accordingly, this case is simply not within the ambit of *Plyler* and its forefathers, which found "behavior-modification" statutes that penalized children to be irrational.

This Court's application of the rational basis test must be guided by the Supreme Court's pronouncement in *Jefferson v. Hackney*, 406 U.S. 535, 546-47, 92 S.Ct. 1724, 1731-32, 32 L.Ed.2d 285 (1972) which held that: "[s]o long as its judgments are rational, and not invidious, the legislature's efforts to tackle the problems of the poor and the needy are not subject to a constitutional straightjacket. The very complexity of the problems suggests that there will be more than one constitutionally permissible method of solving them." *See also* Dandridge v. Williams, [397 U.S. 471, 487 (1970)] ("the Constitution does not empower this Court to second-guess state officials charged with the difficult responsibility of allocating limited public welfare funds among the myriad of potential recipients") (citations omitted). As noted above, New Jersey's welfare cap must be rationally related to a legitimate governmental purpose. The state (and indeed, the societal) interest served by the Family Cap has been well chronicled in the record as well as in this Opinion: to give AFDC recipients the same structure of incentives as working people, to promote individual responsibility, and to strengthen and stabilize the family unit. See N.J.S.A. 44:10-3.7; 24 N.J. Reg. 2155 (June 15, 1992).

These interests are clearly legitimate. Placing welfare households on a par with working families is a reasonable and appropriate goal of welfare reform; indeed, as the Supreme Court found in *Dandridge*, a "solid foundation for [a] regulation can be found in the State's legitimate interest in encouraging employment and avoiding discrimination between welfare families and the families of the working poor." Dandridge, 397 U.S. at 486, 90 S.Ct. at 1162. The Family Cap, by maintaining the level of AFDC benefits despite the arrival of an additional child, puts the welfare household in the same situation as that of a working family, which does not automatically receive a wage increase every time it produces another child. This in turn reflects the reasoned legislative determination that a ceiling on benefits provides an incentive for parents to leave the welfare rolls for the work force, as any "advantage" of welfare in the form of the per child benefit increase is no longer available. This legislatively-inspired impetus to enter or return to employment further illustrates a rational decision by the state not only to encourage personal responsibility but also to assist AFDC beneficiaries in achieving self-sufficiency. In addition, it cannot be gainsaid that the Family Cap sends a message that recipients should consider the static level of their welfare benefits before having another child, a message that may reasonably have an ameliorative effect on the rate of out-of-wedlock births that only foster the familial instability and crushing cycle of poverty currently plaguing the welfare class.

Clearly there may be other means or methods that the legislature might have employed in seeking to implement changes in welfare benefits and welfare behavior. However, my inquiry does not address the outer limits of what might have been proposed, but rather is confined to reviewing what was in fact done. It is obvious that in this case, the state's interest in reforming welfare is legitimate. Indeed, as the Second Circuit noted in [*Aguayo v. Richardson, Sec'y of the U.S. Dep't of Health, Educ. and Welfare*], "[a] purpose to determine whether and how improvements can be made in the welfare system is as 'legitimate' or 'appropriate' as anything can be." Aguayo, 473 F.2d at 1109. It is equally plain from the foregoing discussion that New Jersey has sought to realize its reform goals in a reasonable and rational fashion. Consequently, I must dismiss plaintiffs' contention that the cap does not have a rational relationship to an appropriate state purpose.

Apparently recognizing the obstacles to their challenge to the rationality of the Family Cap, plaintiffs assert that the cap violates their fundamental right to make private procreative choices such that strict scrutiny review must be applied. They argue that the cap cannot meet this increased level of review because the state has no compelling interest in deterring child birth and because the cap is not narrowly tailored to meet this goal. Plaintiffs' claim, distilled to its essence, is that the Family Cap is a governmental attempt to alter recipients' reproductive behavior by denying them benefits should they make procreative decisions disfavored by the state.

It is well-settled that decisions about family composition, conception and child-birth fall into a constitutionally protected zone of privacy. An individual has the right "to be free from unwarranted governmental intrusion into matters so fundamentally affecting a person as the decision whether to bear or beget a child." Eisenstadt v. Baird, 405 U.S. 438, 453 (1972). Although the right to an abortion, for example, is not absolute and unfettered, the government may not actively interfere with the individual's exercise of that right by placing an undue burden on that individual's access to abortion services. Planned Parenthood v. Casey, 505 U.S. 833, 870 (1992). Thus, while a state may not hinder one's exercise of protected choices, it is not obligated to remove obstacles that it did not create, including a lack of financial resources. Rust v. Sullivan, 500 U.S. 173, 201 (1991); Harris v. McRae, 448 U.S. 297, 317 (1980). In addition, once the government decides to provide public benefits, it may not selectively deny those benefits in order to infringe a constitutional right, including the right to procreative choice free from government influence. See Perry v. Sindermann, 408 U.S. 593, 597 (1972).

This case, however, does not present a situation where New Jersey has unduly burdened the procreative choice of the plaintiff class, as the Family Cap in no way conditions receipt of benefits upon plaintiffs' reproductive choices. Although plaintiffs may claim that the state's failure to subsidize a recipient's choice to procreate intrudes upon that individual's reproductive freedom, this assertion misses the mark. An AFDC household is still entitled to and will still receive benefits whether or not a member of that household conceives and/or gives birth to an additional child. While benefits heretofore granted a recipient household to which another child is added will no longer be available, that family will not suffer any decrease in aid and in fact will continue receiving benefits at the same level as before. In other words, New Jersey's legislative action does nothing to bar an AFDC recipient from conceiving and/or bringing to term an additional child, but has merely removed the automatic benefit increase associated with an additional child under the federal program. Moreover, it should be noted that if New Jersey eliminated its AFDC program altogether, plaintiffs would be faced with the same choices concerning conception but with an even greater lack of financial resources.

Thus, while this Court recognizes that a woman has a right to be free from governmental intrusion vis-a-vis her procreative choices, "it simply does not follow that a woman's freedom of choice carries with it a constitutional entitlement to the financial resources to avail herself of the full range of protected choices." [Harris v. McRae, 448 U.S. 297, 316 (1980)]. See also Rust v. Sullivan, 500 U.S. 173, 201 (1991) ("the Government has no constitutional duty to subsidize an activity merely because it is constitutionally protected"). Accordingly, the Court finds that the Family Cap does not infringe plaintiffs' procreative rights. In addition, the Court finds that New Jersey's welfare reform efforts are rationally related to the legitimate state interests of altering the cycle of welfare dependency that it has determined AFDC engenders in its recipients as well as promoting individual responsibility and family stability.

C.K. v. New Jersey Dep't of Health & Human Servs.
92 F.3d 171 (3d Cir. 1996)

We have nothing to add to the district court's opinion on this point except to observe that it would be remarkable to hold that a state's failure to subsidize a reproductive choice burdens that choice. In short, there are no constitutional implications when the state does not pay a benefit to parents who have a child that it would not pay to parents who did not have a child. Rather than burdening the procreative choice of the plaintiff class, section 3.5 is neutral with respect to that choice....

The courts adjudicating the previous case concluded that the family cap was not an unconstitutional condition on the plaintiffs' reproductive freedom. The doctrine of unconstitutional conditions prohibits the government from imposing a penalty on a person's exercise of his or her constitutional rights, or from offering a benefit contingent upon the person restricting his or her constitutional rights. In the previous case, the district and appellate courts did not think that the government was restricting a woman's reproductive freedom; rather the government was merely refusing to fund her choice to have a child. Do you agree? What is the effect on the poor woman's ability to exercise her constitutional rights if the government fails to subsidize her choice? In addition, does the government's purpose matter? Can the government refuse to subsidize a choice because it wants to influence the birthrate? In the next case, the U.S. Supreme Court held that the District of Columbia could not restrict welfare benefits to immigrants in order to encourage work and to deter immigration into the District because the ability to travel interstate is a fundamental right. Can an analogy be made in the family cap area? What explains the different outcomes in *C.K. v. Shalala* and *Shapiro v. Thompson*? After *Shapiro v. Thompson*, there is an excerpt in which Professor Yvette Barksdale discusses the existing unconstitutional conditions doctrine and suggests that the Supreme Court should focus on the harm that these sorts of conditions impose. Is that a preferable solution?

Shapiro v. Thompson
394 U.S. 618 (1969)

Mr. Justice Brennan delivered the opinion of the Court.

These three appeals were restored to the calendar for reargument. Each is an appeal from a decision of a three-judge District Court holding unconstitutional a State or District of Columbia statutory provision which denies welfare assistance to residents of the State or District who have not resided within their jurisdictions for at least one year immediately preceding their applications for such assistance. We affirm the judgments of the District Courts in the three cases....

There is no dispute that the effect of the waiting-period requirement in each case is to create two classes of needy resident families indistinguishable from each other except that one is composed of residents who have resided a year or more, and the second of residents who have resided less than a year, in the jurisdiction. On the basis of this sole difference the first class is granted and the second class is denied welfare aid upon which may depend the ability of the families to obtain the very means to subsist—food, shelter, and other necessities of life....[6]

Primarily, appellants justify the waiting-period requirement as a protective device to preserve the fiscal integrity of state public assistance programs. It is asserted that people who require welfare assistance during their first year of residence in a State are likely to

---

6. This constitutional challenge cannot be answered by the argument that public assistance benefits are a 'privilege' and not a 'right.' *See* Sherbert v. Verner, 374 U.S. 398, 404, 83 S.Ct. 1790, 1794, 10 L.Ed.2d 965 (1963).

become continuing burdens on state welfare programs. Therefore, the argument runs, if such people can be deterred from entering the jurisdiction by denying them welfare benefits during the first year, state programs to assist long-time residents will not be impaired by a substantial influx of indigent newcomers....

We do not doubt that the one-year waiting period device is well suited to discourage the influx of poor families in need of assistance. An indigent who desires to migrate, resettle, find a new job, and start a new life will doubtless hesitate if he knows that he must risk making the move without the possibility of falling back on state welfare assistance during his first year of residence, when his need may be most acute. But the purpose of inhibiting migration by needy persons into the State is constitutionally impermissible.

This Court long ago recognized that the nature of our Federal Union and our constitutional concepts of personal liberty unite to require that all citizens be free to travel throughout the length and breadth of our land uninhibited by statutes, rules, or regulations which unreasonably burden or restrict this movement. That proposition was early stated by Chief Justice Taney in the Passenger Cases, 7 How. 283, 492, 12 L.Ed. 702 (1849): "For all the great purposes for which the Federal government was formed, we are one people, with one common country. We are all citizens of the United States; and, as members of the same community, must have the right to pass and repass through every part of it without interruption, as freely as in our own States."

We have no occasion to ascribe the source of this right to travel interstate to a particular constitutional provision.... "(The) right finds no explicit mention in the Constitution. The reason, it has been suggested, is that a right so elementary was conceived from the beginning to be a necessary concomitant of the stronger Union the Constitution created. In any event, freedom to travel throughout the United States has long been recognized as a basic right under the Constitution."

Thus, the purpose of deterring the in-migration of indigents cannot serve as justification for the classification created by the one-year waiting period, since that purpose is constitutionally impermissible. If a law has 'no other purpose... than to chill the assertion of constitutional rights by penalizing those who choose to exercise them, then it (is) patently unconstitutional.' United States v. Jackson, 390 U.S. 570, 581, 88 S.Ct. 1209, 1216, 20 L.Ed.2d 138 (1968)....

More fundamentally, a State may no more try to fence out those indigents who seek higher welfare benefits than it may try to fence out indigents generally. Implicit in any such distinction is the notion that indigents who enter a State with the hope of securing higher welfare benefits are somehow less deserving than indigents who do not take this consideration into account. But we do not perceive why a mother who is seeking to make a new life for herself and her children should be regarded as less deserving because she considers, among others factors, the level of a State's public assistance. Surely such a mother is no less deserving than a mother who moves into a particular State in order to take advantage of its better educational facilities....

We recognize that a State has a valid interest in preserving the fiscal integrity of its programs. It may legitimately attempt to limit its expenditures, whether for public assistance, public education, or any other program. But a State may not accomplish such a purpose by invidious distinctions between classes of its citizens. It could not, for example, reduce expenditures for education by barring indigent children from its schools. Similarly, in the cases before us, appellants must do more than show that denying welfare benefits to new residents saves money. The saving of welfare costs cannot justify an otherwise invidious classification....

At the outset, we reject appellants' argument that a mere showing of a rational relationship between the waiting period and these four admittedly permissible state objectives will suffice to justify the classification. The waiting-period provision denies welfare benefits to otherwise eligible applicants solely because they have recently moved into the jurisdiction. But in moving from State to State or to the District of Columbia appellees were exercising a constitutional right, and any classification which serves to penalize the exercise of that right, unless shown to be necessary to promote a compelling governmental interest, is unconstitutional. *Cf.* Skinner v. Oklahoma, 316 U.S. 535, 541, 62 S.Ct. 1110, 1113, 86 L.Ed. 1655 (1942); Korematsu v. United States, 323 U.S. 214, 216, 65 S.Ct. 193, 194, 89 L.Ed. 194 (1944); Bates v. Little Rock, 361 U.S. 516, 524, 80 S.Ct. 412, 417, 4 L.Ed.2d 480 (1960); Sherbert v. Verner, 374 U.S. 398, 406, 83 S.Ct. 1790, 1795, 10 L.Ed.2d 965 (1963)....

Pennsylvania suggests that the one-year waiting period is justified as a means of encouraging new residents to join the labor force promptly. But this logic would also require a similar waiting period for long-term residents of the State. A state purpose to encourage employment provides no rational basis for imposing a one-year waiting-period restriction on new residents only.

We conclude therefore that appellants in these cases do not use and have no need to use the one-year requirement for the governmental purposes suggested. Thus, even under traditional equal protection tests a classification of welfare applicants according to whether they have lived in the State for one year would seem irrational and unconstitutional. But, of course, the traditional criteria do not apply in these cases. Since the classification here touches on the fundamental right of interstate movement, its constitutionality must be judged by the stricter standard of whether it promotes a compelling state interest. Under this standard, the waiting-period requirement clearly violates the Equal Protection Clause....

Yvette Marie Barksdale, *And the Poor Have Children: A Harm Based Analysis of Family Caps and the Hollow Procreative Rights of Welfare Beneficiaries*
14 L. & Ineq. 1, 69–71 (1995)

Family cap plans raise the issue of whether government may constitutionally use rights-based benefit conditions as a tool to influence value choices otherwise constitutionally protected from government intrusion.

Traditional Supreme Court doctrine answers this question by asking whether the government benefit [or] condition is a burden or penalty (in other words, a government decision that takes away something to which the individual has a right), or a mere government refusal to subsidize (that is, a government decision to not pay for constitutionally protected activity). If the latter, the denial of funding is constitutional regardless of its link to constitutionally protected activity or its harmful impact on the recipient of the funding.

This bifurcated approach protects the "haves" while unleashing the power of the government to attack constitutional rights of those who are recipients of government aid. This is particularly true with subsistence welfare benefits where, by definition, the recipients are poor and dependent upon government funding for basic necessities such as food, clothing and shelter. This view thus gives government significant power to use poverty itself as leverage to affect otherwise constitutionally protected value choices.

Scholars have consistently criticized the Court's approach. However, they have focused on whether the government action has prevented, affected, coerced, or pressured the exercise of the constitutional right. In truth, the effect of the condition on exercise of the constitutional right is only a smoke screen. The underlying problem with both government fines or penalties and government funding conditions is the harm or suffering that government imposes because of the exercise of the constitutional right. In the former case, the harm is the fine or penalty on the exercise of the right; in the latter case, the harm is the loss of funding because of the exercise of the right. It is the rights-based harm that is the basis for invalidating government fines or penalties. Thus, fines or penalties are unconstitutional even if there is no effect on the individual's choice—that is, if the individual nevertheless elects to exercise the rights and incur the penalty. This rights-based harm should also be the basis for invalidating rights-based government funding conditions.

Accordingly,... the better analysis should assess the constitutionality of funding conditions on the basis of whether they impose right-based government harm. Under this view, government harm that is expressly or intentionally linked to the exercise of a constitutional right would be constitutionally problematic whether the harm is the deprivation of a right or the denial of a benefit. Thus, a government decision to specifically exclude rights-protected activity from funding should be impermissible if a direct fine or penalty on the exercise of that right would be.

An exception might be where some rights-based line drawing is necessary. However, child limitation plans do not fit within the limited exception. The plans involve AFDC payments that generally provide for the subsistence needs of poor families. There is no need for the government to draw a distinction in payment levels on the basis of the welfare mother's exercise of a constitutional right to procreate. The government can base payment levels on a myriad of other factors. Accordingly, such benefit plans should be recognized for what they are: rights-based, government-imposed harm and suffering. Accordingly, they should be subject to the same strict scrutiny as any other attack on the right would be.

This view does not mean that the government is stripped of power to attempt to encourage citizens to make wise procreative choices. However, the government, in its reformist zeal, should not be able to use unconstitutional means to achieve legitimate goals in disregard of the constitutional protection of the fundamental right to procreate. Instead, the government should seek constitutional, non-oppressive means to achieve legitimate ends—means that respectfully seek to persuade citizens to make wise choices rather than bludgeon them into compliance.

As applied to child limitation plans, the government should be held to violate the procreative rights of welfare recipients if it uses harm and suffering, the weapons of oppression, to substitute the government's own procreative value choice for that of the recipient. Otherwise, what price rescue?

Notes and Questions

1. *Family Caps Popularity.* New Jersey's family cap is fairly typical of the family caps in the twenty-three states that currently have them. Sixteen states deny the traditional

incremental increase in cash benefits to children born while the family is on assistance: Arizona, Arkansas, California, Delaware, Georgia, Illinois, Indiana, Massachusetts, Mississippi, Nebraska, New Jersey, North Carolina, North Dakota, South Dakota, Virginia, and Wyoming. Two states, Idaho and Wisconsin, provide a flat grant to all families receiving assistance, regardless of size. Two states, Connecticut and Florida, reduce the traditional increase for "capped" children. Three states, Indiana, Oklahoma, and South Carolina, provide for a "capped" child's benefit to be paid in the form of a voucher. Maryland provides for a "capped" child's benefit to be paid into a restricted account or to a third party payee. *See* Center for Law and Social Policy, *State Policy Documentation Project; Family Cap Overview* (Mar. 1999), *available at* http://www.spdp.org/reprexpl.htm.

2. *State Constitutional Challenges.* New Jersey's current family cap, N.J.S.A. §44:10-61, was upheld against an equal protection challenge initiated under the New Jersey state constitution. *See* Sojourner A *ex rel.* Y.A. v. New Jersey Dep't of Human Servs., 794 A.2d 822 (N.J. Super. Ct. App. Div. 2002). Other states' caps have been similarly upheld. *See., e.g.,* N.B. v. Sybinski, 724 N.E.2d 1103, 1108-09 (Ind. Ct. App. 2000) (upholding Indiana's program, which restricted benefits to a child born ten months after a family starts receiving TANF benefits but not if the child lives with a qualified caretaker other than a parent, against an equal protection and substantive due process claim that the statute "forces parents to break up the family unit to ensure that the child's most basic physical needs are met" and therefore violates the "fundamental right of family association").

3. *U.S. Policy on Family Planning at Home.* Apart from permitting the family cap provisions related to PRWORA, the federal government has enacted legislation designed to affect the reproductive decision-making of welfare recipients. For example, some states receive federal grants to fund abstinence education for purposes of reducing out-of-wedlock births. *See* 42 U.S.C. §710. PRWORA also provides states a "Bonus to Reward Decrease in Illegitimacy Ratio." 42 U.S.C. §603(A)(2). This bonus rewards the top five states that reduce out-of-wedlock births without abortion increasing. The formulation of the "illegitimacy ratio" includes all out-of-wedlock births in a state, not just those children born to unmarried welfare recipients. *Id.* These programs were enacted based upon Congressional findings that, among other things, marriage is the foundation of a successful society and that out-of-wedlock childbirth has negative consequences for the child, the mother, the family, and society. *See* 42 U.S.C. §601. Do these laws intrude on individuals' procreative rights? Is the intrusion permissible?

4. *Effectiveness.* Assume, for purposes of argument, that it is legitimate state interest to reduce the number of births to families receiving government assistance and to move families off of welfare. Is it permissible for states to continue their family cap programs if the programs are ineffective? What would be the measure of effectiveness? The evidence on the programs' effectiveness appears to be "mixed." Consider the following:

Sojourner A *ex rel.* Y.A. v. New Jersey Dep't of Human Servs.
794 A.2d 822, 827–28 (N.J. Super. Ct. App. Div. 2002)

Studies have been undertaken to investigate the effects of the welfare reform on an ongoing basis.... The results have been mixed. According to a study by Mathematics Policy Research, Inc., since the WFNJ Act [Work First New Jersey Act] took effect it has "expanded child care assistance and other services designed to ease welfare recipient's transition to the workforce. During the first two years,...in the context of a strong economy, New Jersey has experienced an unprecedented reduction in its welfare caseload,...declin[ing] by almost 40 percent from July 1997 (the time the State fully implemented WFNJ) through August 1999." The report also reveals that welfare receipt has fallen steadily while employment has increased steadily among WFNJ clients. Approximately a year and a half after entering the WFNJ program, more than one in three recipients were off welfare and working, and a third were no longer in poverty.

Another study by the Rutgers School of Social Work, which was primarily directed at FDP [the Family Development Plan] in general rather than at the family cap in particular, revealed that women do not move off welfare more quickly, stay off welfare longer, or earn more money when they leave welfare. Nor does FDP "significantly" improve employment prospects, employment stability, and earnings among program participants. Reduction of welfare benefits may lead to homelessness and malnutrition. Moreover, the study showed that the original FDP program did have a "statistically significant impact on birth, abortion and family planning decisions." It revealed that between October 1992 and the end of 1996, there were 1,429 more abortions and 14,057 fewer births among AFDC recipients than would have occurred in the absence of the FDP.

With regard to the family cap specifically, the researchers concluded that the program has "communicated a message of personal responsibility to welfare recipients," with many of the program's beneficiaries saying that the family cap "is a fair rule that promotes individual responsibility, stresses the financial responsibility of giving birth and keeps the recipient's focus on job and career training." A substantial number of recipients reported that the family cap "discourages out-of-wedlock births, provides more incentives to get off welfare and causes postponement or avoidance of pregnancy." However, the family cap and two-year Medicaid extension were not "effective in reducing recipiency and moving welfare recipients from welfare and into employment." Yet, while "the immediate impact of the imposition of the family cap was to increase abortions[,]...[there was] also...evidence of a growth over time in the use of family planning services and contraception...as well as a decline over time in birth rates...."

A Legal Services of New Jersey study on welfare reform drew no conclusions about the effects of the family cap specifically, but instead focused on the impact of the new welfare program in its entirety, finding that one-third of welfare recipients have their benefits reduced for not complying with program requirements. Of the respondents whose benefits were reduced, almost one-fifth reported a termination of benefits, and nearly eighty percent reported being unable to support themselves and their households financially after the reduction.

In Illinois, the family cap had no apparent effect on birthrates or abortion rates. *See* Shelley Stark and Jodie Levine-Epstein, Ctr. For Law and Soc. Policy, *Excluded Children: Family Cap in a New Era* (Feb. 1999). Are these types of studies important in judging the permissibility of the governmental intrusion into reproductive decision-making?

5. *Unconstitutional Conditions.* How does one reconcile *C.K. v. Shalala* with *Shapiro v. Thompson*? Do family caps impose unconstitutional conditions? Do you find Yvette Barksdale's analysis compelling? Is there a factual or legal difference between the government's refusal to pay for in vitro fertilization, its refusal to pay increased welfare benefits to a family who has another child, and its refusal to pay for an abortion?

6. *International Human Rights Treaties.* How consistent are family caps with CEDAW? In particular, look at article 11. Are they a violation of the letter or spirit of other international law instruments? Do family caps impinge on the right to decide freely and responsibly on the number and spacing of children? Do they discriminate since they only target the reproduction of the poor?

7. *Other Controls.* While this section has focused on family caps, there are other instances of state-controlled reproduction in the United States. Consider, for instance, *State v. Oakley,* 629 N.W.2d 200 (Wis. 2001). In that case, the Wisconsin Supreme Court upheld a requirement that the defendant, as a condition of probation, avoid having another child, unless he could show that he could support that child and his current children. The defendant, a father of nine children, had been convicted of intentionally refusing to pay child support—a felony in Wisconsin. The court disagreed with the defendant's argument that the probation condition violated his constitutional right to procreate, and was therefore subject to strict scrutiny. The court held that probation conditions are only subject to a much lower standard of review. *Id.* at 208 n.23. Since "a convicted felon does not stand in the same position as someone who has not been convicted of a crime," the "conditions of probation may impinge upon constitutional rights as long as they are not overly broad and are reasonably related to the person's rehabilitation." According to the court, the condition was constitutional when measured against this standard.

In *obiter dictum,* the court stated that the condition also survived strict scrutiny. It rejected the defendant's argument that the probation condition was not narrowly tailored since it eliminated, not restricted, his right to procreate. The court stated:

> It does not eliminate Oakley's ability to exercise his constitutional right to procreate. He can satisfy the condition of probation by making efforts to support his children as required by law. Judge Hazlewood placed no limit on the number of children Oakley could have. Instead, the requirement is that Oakley acknowledge the requirements of the law and support his present and any future children. If Oakley decides to continue his present course of conduct—intentionally refusing to pay child support—he will face eight years in prison regardless of how many children he has. Furthermore, this condition will expire at the end of his term of probation. He may then decide to have more children, but of course, if he continues to intentionally refuse to support his children, the State could charge him again under 948.22(2). Rather, because Oakley can satisfy this condition by not intentionally refusing to support his current nine children and any future children as required by the law, we find that the condition is narrowly tailored to serve the State's compelling interest of having parents support their children. It is also narrowly tailored to serve the State's compelling interest in rehabilitating Oakley through probation rather than prison. The alternative to probation with conditions—incarceration for eight years—would have further victimized his children. And it is undoubtedly much broader than this conditional impingement on his procreative freedom for it would deprive him of his fundamental right to be free from physical restraint. Simply stated, Judge Hazlewood preserved much of Oakley's liberty by imposing probation with conditions rather than the more punitive option of imprisonment.

Part of the majority's reasoning also rested on the fact that if Oakley were incarcerated, "he would be unable to exercise his constitutional right to procreate." *Id.* at 209 n.25. All of the cases cited by the court for this last proposition involved a prisoner's right to sexual intercourse. What of the fact that a person might become a father through artificial insemination? *But see Gerber v. Hickman*, 291 F.3d 617 (9th Cir. 2002) (rejecting constitutional challenge to rule prohibiting prisoner from using artificial insemination); Percy v. Dep't of Corrections, 651 A.2d 1044 (N.J. Super. Ct. 1995) (same). Moreover, what of the fact that Mr. Oakley had not yet been imprisoned? Does it follow that if the state can deprive him of certain constitutional rights when it restrains him that it can exercise control over those same rights when it elects not to restrain him?

The majority also emphasized the fact that the defendant had intentionally failed to pay child support, which indicates that he had the ability to do so. The Wisconsin Supreme Court documented in its opinion that the "refusal to pay child support by so-called 'deadbeat parents' has fostered a crisis with devastating implications for our children." Would it be constitutional to deny the right to reproduce to all individuals who wilfully refused to pay child support? Could this be extended to individuals who lack the means to support their children since the implications for the children are also potentially devastating? What of the fact that the defendant and circuit court knew that the defendant "could not reasonably be expected to fully support" the children? *Id.* at 486 (Bradley, J., dissenting).

Two justices authored stinging dissents in *State v. Oakley*. Justice Bradley pointed out that the majority's decision "allows, for the first time in our state's history, the birth of a child to carry criminal sanctions." *Id.* at 41. Justice Bradley thought the probation condition was not narrowly tailored and cited the United States Supreme Court decision in *Zablocki v. Redhail*, 434 U.S. 374 (1978). There the Supreme Court had held unconstitutional a Wisconsin statute that prohibited people from marrying until they established that their child support obligations had been met. The U.S. Supreme Court in *Zablocki* stated, "[T]he State already has numerous other means for exacting compliance with support obligations, means that are at least as effective as the instant statute's and yet do not impinge upon the right to marry." *Id.* at 389. Justice Bradley suggested that those means were still available today. In addition, Justice Bradley emphasized that "prohibiting a person from having children as a condition of probation [is] 'coercive of abortion.'" *Oakley*, 629 N.W.2d at 53. Do you agree? Is there any significance to the fact that all justices joining or concurring in the court's decision were men and all the dissenting justices were women?

8. *Public Opinion.* The following question was asked of 1,000 likely voters in the United States: "Today, some people believe that mothers on welfare continue to have children that they are financially unable to support. There is proposed federal legislation that would require all welfare recipients to use birth control as a condition of their public benefits. Do you strongly support, somewhat support, somewhat oppose, or strongly oppose requiring welfare recipients to use birth control?" The results were as follows: 46.5% would strongly support a requirement, 15.4% somewhat support it, 21.9% strongly oppose it, 11.4% somewhat oppose it and 4.9% said they were not sure. The poll has been criticized as biased and failing to meet professional polling standards, although the survey results received widespread coverage. *See generally* Cynthia L. Cooper, *Poll on Welfare, Birth Control Misleading*, Women's Enews, July 12, 2001, *available at* http://www.womensnews.org/article.cfm/dynaid/612/context/archive (poll by Zoogby Int'l, a political polling firm in D.C. & Utica).

9. *United States and China.* What similarities and differences are there, if any, between China's One-Child Policy and New Jersey's family caps? Although the constitution and judiciary in the United States are vastly different from the constitution and judiciary in China, do these differences matter given the decisions of the U.S. courts on the constitutionality of family caps?

10. *U.S. Policy on Family Planning Abroad.* As suggested above, the United States government cares about family planning activities in other countries. Apart from concern about coercive policies, the United States government has also at times been concerned about the use of its funds to facilitate abortions, whether coercive or not. These concerns were initially the executive branch's prerogative, since it was the President who had the power to impose conditions on foreign aid directed to population programs. The Foreign Assistance Act of 1961 says, "In order to increase opportunities and motivation for family planning and to reduce the rate of population growth, the President is authorized to furnish assistance, on such terms and conditions as he may determine, for voluntary population planning." *See* Foreign Assistance Act of 1961, 22 U.S.C. §2151b(b) (1994). However, an amendment later proposed by Jessie Helms passed; it prohibited the direct use of U.S. funds to perform abortions. *See* Foreign Assistance Act of 1973, ch. 1, sec. 2, §114, 87 Stat. 714, 716 (1973). In 1984, the "Mexico City Policy" was promulgated, which prohibited the United States from funding any nongovernmental organization that provided or promoted abortions abroad. *See* U.S. Policy Statement for the International Conference on Population, 2d Sess., (1984), *reprinted in* 10 Population and Dev. Rev. 57 (1985). President Clinton revoked this policy shortly after he assumed office. *See* Memorandum on the Mexico City Policy, 1 Pub. Papers 10 (1993). Just after taking office, President George W. Bush reinstated the ban on U.S. aid to nongovernmental organizations that actively promote or perform abortions overseas. Memorandum from George W. Bush to the Administer of the United States Agency for International Development (Jan. 22, 2001), *at* http://www.whitehouse.gov/news/releases/20010123-5.html.

Problem 13-3

State X is a state within the United States. Legislators in State X have decided that the rate of out-of-wedlock births in the state is too high. State X competes for federal money that rewards states if they reduce their rate of out-of-wedlock childbirth more than other states. State X passes a law whereby any person who has a child while on welfare will be denied welfare assistance for that child, and will have any preexisting welfare assistance reduced by 10%. Prior to the enactment of the law, welfare recipients in the state had out-of-wedlock children at the same rate as individuals who did not receive welfare. State X believes that the law will discourage out-of-wedlock childbearing, promote individual responsibility, and strengthen and stabilize the family unit. Mary receives public assistance. While on public assistance, she delivers her first baby and finds her own benefits were reduced by 10%. She wants to challenge the State X law. What are Mary's arguments and what is the chance they will be successful?

b. *Western Europe: Reproductive Decision-Making in Countries with Low Birth Rates*

In contrast to the policies which try to discourage child bearing, many countries in Western Europe have policies designed to make procreation more attractive to women, by subsidizing their decision to have and raise a child. For example, a single mother in Denmark receives cash assistance, free kindergarten for her child, and subsidized housing. *See* Katarina Tomasevski, *Reproduction, Rights and Reality: How Facts and Law Can Work for Women: European Approaches to Enhancing Reproductive Freedom*, 44 Am. U. L. Rev. 1037 (1995). In Austria, parents, regardless of marital status, are entitled to a family allowance for each child in their household, mothers are entitled to a maternity allowance of twelve weeks after giving birth, and either parent may elect to stay home to care for the child and receive a government-funded parental allowance. Single parents are entitled to a governmental allowance, whether or not they are employed. *See The Austrian ESWIN Social Welfare Summary Fact Sheet*, European Social Welfare Information Network (2000), *at* http://www.eswin.net/a/aswfs.html. Norway provides single-parent families with a universal family allowance and a birth grant for single mothers; the government also pays child support if the non-custodial parent defaults. Dan Keeton, *Progressive Social Policy in the Global Economy*, The Democrat, Nov. 1998. These sorts of policies were explored in Chapter Nine, which addressed the Financial Support of Children.

Notes and Questions

1. *Promotive or Facilitative?* Some policies may be designed to persuade individuals and couples to have children, other policies may simply provide a means of guaranteeing free choice in procreative decisions.

2. *United States.* The United States affords parents of certain employers twelve weeks of unpaid family leave after the birth of a child. Family and Medical Leave Act of 1993, 29 U.S.C. § 2601 et seq. The federal tax scheme also provides certain benefits for individuals with children. These U.S. policies and others were discussed in Chapter Nine. How would you describe United States law and policy regarding the procreative decision? Is it neutral? If not, should it be neutral? If not, should the policies be reflective of a pro-natal or anti-natal position? "The United States is the only industrialized country where the birth rate reaches a 'replacement level' of 2.1 children per woman." U.S. Dep't of State, Population Reference Bureau Projects 21st Century Trends, May 21, 2001, *at* http://us.info.state.gov/topical/global/immigration/01052201.html.

B. Assisted Reproduction

The government fosters population growth when it assists infertile individuals' efforts to have biological children. Today a variety of reproductive technologies exists to address infertility, including traditional surrogacy, gestational surrogacy, in vitro fertilization, artificial insemination, and egg donation. These technologies can raise profound moral and legal issues for a society. This part of the chapter tries to identify some of the questions that have arisen as well as the forces that are shaping answers to these often difficult moral and legal questions.

1. Artificial Insemination

Artificial insemination (AI) is one technology that generates less controversy than some of the other technologies: "Artificial insemination is generally permissible and acceptable worldwide. In part, this international consensus may be because the technique has now been in used by humans for close to 200 years, allowing social and legal systems the time to equilibrate." Elizabeth Ann Pitrolo, *The Birds, the Bees, and the Deep Freeze: Is There International Consensus in the Debate Over Assisted Reproductive Technologies?*, 19 Hous. J. Int'l L. 147, 198–99 (1996).

A few qualifications, however, are in order. AI is generally permissible if the woman uses the sperm of her husband (AIH). However, numerous countries prohibit artificial insemination by donor (AID), particularly those countries heavily influenced by or following Islamic law. For example, Libya makes it a criminal offense to partake in the process. *See* Robert Blank, *Regulation of Donor Insemination, in* Donor Insemination: International Social Science Perspectives 142 (Ken Daniels & Erica Haimes eds., 1999) (citing articles 304A and 304B of the Libyan criminal code). And despite the widespread permissibility of AID in the West, various legal issues still arise concerning the technology. These issues include whether the sperm donor or the mother's partner have parental rights and obligations, what level of secrecy surrounds the donor's identity, who has access to this technology (*i.e.*, single people or gay and lesbian couples), who can donate sperm, whether donors can be paid, and whether extensive regulation is appropriate. In addition, the permissibility of post-mortem insemination has arisen as a question in the context of AIH and AID. The material that follows is intended to give you a sense of some of these controversies.

Most of these controversies are being worked out country by country, often in a piecemeal fashion. One author concluded, "[Donor] insemination policy in most countries is the product of a patchwork and often haphazard combination of programme and professional guidelines, committee reports, court rulings and in some cases statutory regulations. Moreover, often the statutory requirements represent new interpretations of existing laws poorly fitted to [donor insemination]. This divergent and potentially conflicting combination of private and public actions results in ambiguous policy." *See* Blank, *supra*, at 147. To focus our AI inquiry, this section concentrates on European countries and tries to identify some trends; the endeavor is difficult precisely because of the ambiguous policies.

At present in Europe, there is some consensus on the topic of *parental responsibility* for a husband or a male partner of a woman who has used AID. Most European countries prohibit the husband who has consented to the use of AID from challenging paternity. *See* Jiří F. Haderka, *Affiliation and Bioethics, in* Legal Problems Relating to Parentage: Proceedings 27th Colloquy on European Law, part VII.3.1.2.1 (1997). "[W]here that concept is not accepted, the law or practice at least favours his financial responsibility to the child and the mother." *Id.* at 58. A few countries, such as France, Spain, and Sweden, impose parental responsibilities on the mother's unmarried partner if there is consent to the procedure, but in France and Sweden, for example, parental responsibilities can be imposed in this situation only if a medical facility is also involved. *Id.* at VII.3.2. The situation with respect to the donor's responsibilities is less clear: "Only a few countries (Austria, Spain, France and Hungary) make a provision in their domestic legislation for the relationships between a child born as a result of AID or in vitro fertilization (IVF) and the donor of gametes or of the embryo; these countries preclude, in whole or in part, the establishment of a link of affiliation. Up to now the majority of domestic legislation is silent on this point." *Id.* at VII.4.

The legal uncertainty in many countries, and the lack of consensus between countries, has motivated regional organizations to address the topic. For example, the Council of Europe has a Committee of Experts on Family Law, and the Committee has set forth principles dealing with legal parentage. The Draft report does not discuss whether AID should be legal or illegal, or what restrictions should apply to its use; rather, it merely assumes the existence of donor insemination. It states that its principles "apply in cases of medically assisted procreation." *See Draft Report on Principles Concerning the Establishment and Legal Consequences of Parentage, Draft No. 1,* Council of Europe: Committee of

Experts on Family Law, principle 9, 10 (2001), *available at* http://www.legal.coe.int/family/Default.asp?fd=general&fn=IntroReportParentageE.htm. These principles are not binding on countries, but are recommended guidelines for countries engaging in legal reform.

Under the guidelines, a child born to a married mother shall be presumed to be the child of the mother's husband, and a child born to an unmarried cohabiting mother shall be presumed to be the child of the mother's male partner. *Id.* at principles 3(1), 5. States are free to reject application of the presumption if the child is born after the factual or legal separation of the parties. *Id.* at principles 3(2), 5. If the presumption does not apply in a particular case, then the law must provide for the establishment of paternal affiliation by voluntary recognition, which may be conditional on the consent of the child or the mother or a competent authority, and by judicial decision. *Id.* at principles 7, 8, 10. In a judicial proceeding, "[t]he mother's husband or companion who gave his consent to the treatment cannot oppose the establishment of his paternity, unless the court finds that the child was not born as a result of the treatment he consented to." *Id.* at principle 10(2).

The Draft report is more equivocal about the obligations of the gamete donor. The Draft report does not incorporate the recommendation made in 1987 by the Comité Ad Hoc Pour La Bioéthique (the Ad Hoc Committee of Experts of Bioethics or CAHBI) in its report, *Human Artificial Procreation*, that a person donating sperm to an authorized establishment be protected against a maintenance order and be prohibited from establishing legal parentage. *See* Haderka, *supra*, at V. However, the commentary to the Draft explains that the "best interest of the child" is the paramount consideration in the interpretation and application of the principles, but that "other interests, such as the interest of the family as well as the public interest may also be taken into account in addition to the best interests of the child. Therefore the law may opt not to allow the parentage to be established on the basis of biological affiliation, for instance in cases of medically assisted procreation with an anonymous donor of sperm." *Draft Report, supra,* ¶ 10.

Human rights treaties are one of the influences on the development of the law in this area. Whatever guidelines are ultimately adopted by the Council of Europe and whatever law is eventually adopted by individual member states will need to comply with the European Convention on Human Rights. The same is true for any regulations or directives eventually passed by the European Union. As mentioned in Chapter One, the European Convention on Human Rights is not part of the Council of Europe in the formal sense. However, the membership to both is essentially identical, and membership to the Council of Europe has been made subject to a country's becoming party to the European Convention on Human Rights. *See generally* Heinrich Klebes, *Membership in International Organizations and National Constitutional Law: A Case Study of the Law and Practice of the Council of Europe*, 99 St. Louis-Warsaw Transatlantic L. J. 69, 74 (1999). The European Court of Justice, which adjudicates claims involving European Union law, refers to the European Convention on Human Rights in its decisions, although it is not technically bound by the Convention. *See generally* Jean M. Sera, *The Case for Accession by the European Union to the European Convention for the Protection of Human Rights*, 14 B.U. Int'l L. J. 151 (1996). Consequently, the jurisprudence of the European Convention will have an influence on the legal developments at the national and regional levels in Europe.

There have been two noteworthy cases arising under the European Convention that involve artificial insemination. In *J.R.M. v. The Netherlands*, 74 Eur. Comm'n H.R. Dec. & Rep. 120 (1993), a lesbian couple used a known sperm donor. During the pregnancy and after the child's birth, the sperm donor visited the couple "regularly" for approximately eight months, and babysat one day a week. When the biological father requested that the child spend one weekend per month with him, the couple broke off all contact with the donor. The courts in the Netherlands denied the donor visitation rights. The donor complained to the European Commission, alleging a violation under article 8 of the Convention, *e.g.*, a lack of respect for his family life. The European Commission of Human Rights concluded that the application was inadmissible. It stated, "[T]he situation in which a person donates sperm only to enable a woman to become pregnant through artificial insemination does not of itself give the donor a right to respect for family life with the child." It also rejected the argument that the donation plus the subsequent contacts were sufficient to establish "family life." The Commission noted that "these contacts were limited in time and intensity. Furthermore, the applicant has apparently not considered making any contribution, financially or otherwise, to the child's upbringing."

In *X, Y and Z v. United Kingdom*, 4 Eur. H.R. Rep. 143 (1997), the right to respect for "family life" under article 8 was again raised, this time in a case involving X, a female-to-male transsexual, Y, his permanent and stable partner, and Z, a child born to Y by artificial insemination by donor. The couple had jointly applied for and were granted treatment for the artificial insemination that produced Z. When X tried to register as the father of Z, the register general refused, saying that only a biological man could register as a father. English law defines a person's sex by reference to biological criteria at birth and does not recognize changes from sex reassignment surgery. The inability of X to register as Z's father led to various problems, including X's inability to be vested with certain parental rights. The European Court found that article 8 was not violated. The Court found that article 8 applied to this family, and emphasized that article 8 may encompass "de facto" relationships. However, the court refused to find a violation of article 8 because of the "wide margin of appreciation" that existed in this area. *Id.* ¶ 44. The Court found England struck a "fair balance...between the competing interests of the individual and of the community as a whole." *Id.* ¶ 41. The Court noted that changing the law might have "undesirable or unforeseen ramifications" for children like Z or for other areas of family law. *Id.* ¶ 47. It also noted that the disadvantages suffered in the instant case were not great, *e.g.*, Z could inherit from X through a will. The fact that X was not listed as the father on Z's birth certificate was not significant because many nonbiological de facto fathers are not listed on the child's birth certificate, and birth certificates are not used much in the United Kingdom. *See id.* ¶ 49. It also concluded that its ruling did not stop X from acting as Z's father in the social sense. *Id.* ¶ 50.

It is not clear from the Court's opinion in *X, Y and Z* whether the wide margin of appreciation existed because the facts involved transsexuality, AID, or both. On the one hand, the Court's conclusion only emphasized the lack of a shared approach among States Parties on the issue of transsexuality. *Id.* ¶ 53. On the other hand, the Court discussed in the body of the opinion that Z was conceived by AID and was not biologically related to X. *Id.* ¶ 43. It emphasized that the legal relationship between a child conceived by AID and the de facto father is the subject of debate in Europe, and there was no "generally shared approach" among the States Parties.

How does the legal landscape in Europe compare with the legal landscape in the United States on issues of parental rights and obligations for the parties involved in AID? Is there enough legal certainty regarding the rights and obligations of individuals involved with this technology? It should be noted that courts in some States Parties are interpreting article 8 more favorably for sperm donors who seek parental rights. *See X v. Y*, 2002 S.L.T. 161 (Scot. Sess. 2002) (recognizing parental rights of sperm donor under article 8).

The issue of *post-mortem insemination* first gained international attention with the *Parpalaix* case in France in 1984. There, a court ordered a sperm bank to turn over a deceased man's sperm to his widow. The sperm had been deposited before Mr. Parpalaix underwent treatment for cancer, but the center argued that Mr. Parpalaix did not specify in writing what he wanted done with the sperm in the event of his death. The family testified that Mr. Parpalaix's intent was to have his wife use the sperm in the event of his death, and the widow prevailed. No legislation existed in France on this issue at the time of the court's ruling. *See generally* E.J. Dionne, Jr., *Widow Wins Paris Case for Husband's Sperm*, N.Y. Times, Aug. 2, 1984, at A8.

Approximately ten years later, the same issue again gained international attention with the *Diane Blood* case in England. Mr. and Mrs. Blood were married in 1991. Towards the end of 1994 they decided to start a family. Before they were successful, Mr. Blood contracted meningitis and went into a coma. Mrs. Blood asked the doctor to take a sperm sample from her husband by electro-ejaculation. A second sample was taken the next day shortly before her husband was declared clinically dead. The Human Fertilisation and Embryology Act of 1990 (Eng.) provided that the use of sperm from a donor who had subsequently died could occur only if certain requirements were met, including the donor's written consent. The trial court denied Mrs. Blood's request to use the sperm because she lacked the donor's written consent, and she appealed.

> The Court of Appeal has allowed Mrs. Blood's appeal because, although the authority's decision was correct that treatment in the United Kingdom could not take place without Mr. Blood's written consent, the authority was not properly advised as to the importance of Community law as to treatment in Belgium. Mrs. Blood has the right to be treated in Belgium with her husband's sperm unless there are good public policy reasons for not allowing this to happen. The authority also appears not to have had sufficient regard to the fact that in the future it will not be possible for this problem to arise because under English law Mr. Blood's sperm should not have been preserved as he had not given his written consent. If the sperm had not been preserved, it could not have been exported. If the authority decides to reconsider the question of export of the sperm they will have to decide whether to allow the export or to refuse on grounds which are acceptable to Community law.

R. v. Human Fertilisation & Embryology Authority (HFEA), *ex parte* Blood, 2 C.M.L.R. 591, 609 (Eng. C.A. 1997). After the *Blood* decision, the HFEA issued a new Code of Practice. It requires that before a facility stores individuals' gametes, the facility must tell the individuals of "the options available to them in the event of their death or mental incapacity and the consent required to ensure their wishes are fulfilled." Human Fertilisation and Embryology Authority, Code of Practice ¶ 6.4(g) (5th ed. 2001). In addition, the Code states, "Anyone consenting to the storage of their gametes, or of embryos produced from them, *must*:...b) state what is to be done with the gametes or embryos if they die, or become incapable of varying or revoking their consent." *Id.* ¶ 7.11(b). The word "must" received new emphasis in the Code of Practice after *Blood*; it was underlined, unlike in the Human Fertilisation and Embryology Act 1990.

Not surprisingly, the ability to use the sperm of a deceased individual varies by country. The answer to a host of collateral legal issues also vary by country. For example, are children born of post-mortem AI legitimate? Is such a child the decedent's child for purposes of governmental benefits and property succession? In the United States, courts are addressing these questions, and frequently the answer turns on the donor's consent. *See*

Woodward v. Comm'r of Soc. Sec., 760 N.E.2d 257 (Mass. 2002) (holding that a child can be a legal heir if the decedent specifically consented to posthumous use of the sperm; "such children [are] 'entitled to the same rights and protections of the law' as children conceived before death"). Similarly, the 2000 Uniform Parentage Act, section 707 states: "Parental Status of Deceased Spouse. If a spouse dies before placement of eggs, sperm, or embryos, the deceased spouse is not a parent of the resulting child unless the deceased spouse consented in a record that if assisted reproduction were to occur after the death, the deceased spouse would be a parent of the child." Unif. Parentage Act (2000) § 707, 9B U.L.A. 358 (2000).

Is the emphasis on consent consistent with international human rights standards? After all, children conceived by AID are arguably entitled to be free from discrimination. See, e.g., U.N. Convention on the Rights of the Child, Nov. 20, 1989, art. 2. Would denying the biological father's paternity for lack of consent to the postmortem insemination violate the rights of the child who was conceived with that sperm? What about a country's need to have an orderly, timely, and accurate disposition of heirs' and creditors' claims? Should the importance of "consent" differ if the issue is use of sperm versus succession to property?

International law arguably has something to say about the *secrecy* that often surrounds the AID process. Most notably, article 7 of the U.N. Convention on the Rights of the Child, in relevant part states, "The child...shall have...as far as possible, the right to know and be cared for by his or her parents." Sweden is well known as a country that gives a child conceived by AID the ability to learn the identity of the AI donor when the child turns eighteen. See Act on Insemination, No. 1140 (1984) (Swed.). Sweden, however does not give the donor a right to know the child's identity. See, e.g., Linda Nielsen, *The Role of Ethics Committees in Framing Legislation on Assisted Reproduction and Embryo Research, in* Assisted Conception: Research, Ethics and Law 127, 135 (Jennifer Gunning ed., 2000). "Except for Austria, which has adopted the Swedish law as a model for its own, few other countries appear inclined to take steps in the direction of Sweden." See Blank, *supra,* at 146. What are the arguments for or against secrecy both as a matter of plicy and as a potential violation of the Rights of the Child Convention?

There is no European consensus on the issue of *access* to sperm. "Many countries [in Europe] do not allow the use of AID or IVF in the case of an unmarried couple." See Haderka, *supra,* at part 58. Some countries allow unmarried couples to use AID, but often require that the couple be heterosexual and/or meet an external marker of relationship stability. Consider, for example, the French Code of Public Health. For all procreation assistance by medical means, "[t]he man and the woman forming the couple must be alive, of an age to procreate, married or able to provide evidence of communal life of at least two years and consenting prior to the insemination or transfer of the embryo." See Pascal Kamina, *Legal Approaches: France, in* Assisted Conception, *supra,* at 108 (citing Code de la Santé Publique, art. L. 152-2). It is a crime for a medical provider to perform an insemination in violation of this section. *Id.* Similarly, in Norway, if the parties are not married, then they must be male and female and living together in a "stable partnership," evidenced by three to five years of cohabitation. An explanatory memorandum explains the restriction: "The involvement of medical science in the creation of human life and the allocation of technical, medical and economic resources from society is seen as an opportunity to take into account the interest of the child. While the creation of one-parent families cannot be averted, the deliberate use of assisted conception services in such circumstances is seen to offend against the rights of the individual child who will result." See Nielsen, *supra,* at 133.

In England, centers control access to treatment and "must" take account of the welfare of any child who may be born or who may be affected as a result of the treatment. Human Fertilisation and Embryology Act, Code of Practice ¶¶ 3.8–3.18 (5th ed. 2001). The HFEA does not exclude any category of women from being eligible for treatment. Rather the Code lists a variety of factors that centers should consider. Sexual orientation, marital status, and relationship stability are not explicitly among them. Instead the Code suggests the center should consider "the need of that child for a father" and whether the home is "a stable and supportive environment." *Id.* ¶¶ 3.8, 3.10. Other relevant factors include the parties' "commitment to having and bringing up a child or children," *id.* ¶ 3.13(a), and "their health and consequent future ability to look after or provide for a child's needs." *Id.* ¶ 3.13(d). Some factors even focus on third parties. For example, in considering the welfare of any child who may be born or affected by treatment, the center must consider "the effect of a new baby or babies upon any existing child of the family," *id.* ¶ 3.13(h), and where donated gametes are used, "the possible attitudes of other members of the family towards the child, and towards their status in the family." *Id.* ¶ 3.14(b).

These issues of "access" present a tension between "the rights of the individual child who will result from treatment" and the rights of the woman not to be discriminated against in her access to treatment. Both of these "rights" arguably find support in international law. How should the tension be resolved? In *McBain v. State of Victoria*, (2000) 99 F.C.R. 116 (Austl.), a challenge was brought to the Victorian Infertility Treatment Act, which required that women undergoing IVF be married or living with a man in a de facto relationship. The challenge was based on the Commonwealth's Sex Discrimination Act that prohibited discrimination on the basis of marital status. In *McBain*, the Federal Court of Australia confronted the argument of the Catholic Church as amici curiae that Parliament intended to legislate in accordance with its international human rights obligations, and Parliament could not have intended therefore to extend access to reproductive technologies to single women. The court disagreed with the Church, and invalidated the discriminatory provision. The Church's argument and the court's response are set forth here:

> The Catholic Church pointed out that various international instruments recognize the right of a child to be born into a family, to be raised by its mother and father, and to know its parents. For example, Principle 6 of the Declaration of the Rights of the Child states that a child "shall, wherever possible, grow up in the care and under the responsibility of his parents." Principle 7 states that the responsibility for a child's education lies in the first place with its parents. Article 10 of the International Covenant on Economic, Social and Cultural Rights states that "the widest possible protection and assistance should be accorded to the family, which is the natural and fundamental group unit of society." Similarly art. 23 of the International Covenant on Civil and Political Rights states that the family is the natural and fundamental group unit in society and is entitled to protection by society and the State, and endorses the right of men and women to marry and found a family.

> The Catholic Church submitted that the word "services" in s. 22 [of the Sex Discrimination Act 1984 which prohibits discrimination in the provision of "goods or services"] can be read consistently with the rights of a child as identified in these treaties, and need not be read so as to breach the fundamental rights they recognize. The difficulty with this argument is that the Commonwealth Act has the purpose of giving effect to a particular treaty—the Convention on the Elimination of All Forms of Discrimination Against Women. The Catholic Church's argument would give primacy to implications from other

treaties over the words of the very treaty to which the Commonwealth Act gives effect. Further, when the treaties relied on are read as a whole, they tell against the existence of an untrammelled right of the kind for which the Catholic Church contends. Thus art. 10 of the International Covenant on Economic, Social and Cultural Rights must be read in the light of art. 1, which preserves the entitlement of every person to his or her own right of self determination, including the right freely to determine their social and cultural development, and art. 2(2), which includes a guarantee that the rights enunciated in the Covenant will be exercised without discrimination of any kind as to race, colour, sex or other status. Articles 1 and 2(2) of the International Covenant on Civil and Political Rights are to the same effect. The preamble to the Declaration of the Rights of the Child contains a recital in the same terms as Article 1 of each Covenant. As appears from paragraph 11, Principle 6 is qualified by the words "wherever possible."

The words of the relevant part of the definition of "services" are clear and unqualified. They are eminently apt to pick up a service rendered by a medical practitioner, and there is no occasion to introduce into them a qualification derived from an assumption made in treaties dealing with other topics, namely that a child will be born into a family as a result of natural processes involving a married couple. The fact that those treaties proceed on that assumption does not mean they are to be taken to assert or imply a prohibition against the birth of a child as a result of some other, medically assisted, mechanism.

McBain v. State of Victoria, (2000) 99 F.C.R. 116 (Austl.). Did the court "get it right"? Is international law particularly helpful in resolving this issue? Is the denial of access to reproductive technology the sort of issue with which human rights treaties are, or should be, concerned? *See generally* Rachael Hamed, *Human Rights and Assisted Reproduction...A Question of Balance?*, Tirohia (Nov. 1997) (quarterly newsletter of the New Zealand Human Rights Commission), *available at* http://www.hrc.co.nz/org/pubs/tirohias/1997/tirohianov97/index.htm (citing Ministerial Committee on Assisted Reproductive Technologies report stating that the Human Rights Act is the basis for addressing discrimination in the field of assisted reproduction and that the Human Rights Act prohibits refusing to treat a person due to discriminatory purpose, including marital status, sex, or sexual orientation); Danny Sandor, *Children Born From Sperm Donations: Financial Support and Other Responsibilities in the Context of Discrimination*, 4 Austl. J. of Hum. Rts. 175, (1997), *available at* http://www.aust/ii.edu.au/otherahric/ajhr/V4N1/ajhr4lll.html#fnB1 (citing Australian cases).

There is also the issue of *who may donate sperm*. "[I]n France...the sperm donor must be married and of proven fertility," that is, the donor must already have a child. *See* Blank, *supra*, at 143. Additionally, in France, the donor's partner must consent. *See* Kamina, *supra*, at 108 (citing Code de la Santé Publique, art. L. 673-2, (July 29, 1994)). In England, there are restrictions on taking sperm from men under 18 and over 45. *See* Human Fertilisation & Embryology Authority, Code of Practice ¶¶ 3.4-3.6 (5th ed. 2001). Most states in the United States have no such requirements, although statutes may set forth medical criteria for sperm donors. *See, e.g.,* N.H. Rev. Stat. Ann. § 168-B:10 (2002); Mich. Comp. L. Ann. § 333.16273 (2001). The American Society for Reproductive Medicine has adopted guidelines, which relate primarily to the donor's health, although age parameters (between 18 and 40) and proven fertility are two factors listed as relevant to the selection of a donor. *See* American Society for Reproductive Medicine, Guidelines for Gamete and Embryo Donation (1997), *available at* http://www.asrm.

org/media/practice/gamete.html. Compliance with the guidelines is voluntary. In fact, a study in the late 1980s indicated that 26% of physicians surveyed would not reject a donor less than 18 years old and 40% would not reject a donor over 40 years old. *See* United States Congress, Office of Technology Assessment, Infertility: Medical and Social Choices tbl. 2-34 (1988). What are the justifications for such age requirements, and should more states in the United States adopt some or all of them? Is there gender discrimination if a state requires that a married woman have her husband's written consent before she has access to AID, but a married man can donate sperm without his wife's consent?

Finally, there is the question of whether the law should allow donors *to be paid*. "Although payment for sperm providers is routine in the United States and allowable in the United Kingdom and Japan, most countries that have addressed the issue reject payment." Blank, *supra*, at 145. Similarly, "The United States is the only western country in which there are no national restrictions on the marketing of human ova, although the selling of human organs is prohibited by statute." Mary Lyndon Shanley, Making Babies, Making Families 97 (2001). Professor Shanley elaborates:

> In France, sperm donors were initially paid, but when it became possible to freeze sperm (and so the donors could come to a fertility center at their convenience) they ceased being paid. The majority of the centers "maintained a policy that the semen donation be simply that, a gift for which no payment is received as is the case for organ donation." In 1979 doctors reported that "donations have kept pace with semen demands," although a constant recruitment effort was necessary as demand continually increased.... More recently, England prohibited remuneration of more than 15 pounds sterling (about 24 dollars) for egg donors.

Shanley, *supra*, at 96–97. In Europe, a Convention on Biomedicine states, "The human body and its parts shall not, as such, give rise to financial gain." *See* Council of Europe, Convention for the Protection of Human Rights and Dignity of the Human Being with regard to the Application of Biology and Medicine: Convention on Human Rights and Biomedicine, Apr. 4, 1997, art. 21, Europ. T.S. No. 16. Nearly identical language appears in article 3 of the European Parliament's Charter of Fundamental Rights of the European Union, 2000 O.J. (C 364) 1, 9. What are the advantages or disadvantages of payment to donors? Should the same rules apply to semen donation and egg donation?

Underlying many of the questions set forth above is a meta-question: To what extent should reproductive technology be *regulated* by the government? The states and the federal government in the United States hardly regulate the use of reproductive technologies at all.

> In the United States, the assisted reproductive technology industry, with an annual revenue of $4 billion, is growing to serve an estimated one in six American couples who are infertile. Annually, in the United States alone, approximately 60,000 births result from donor insemination; 15,000 from IVF, and at least 1,000 from surrogacy arrangements. By contrast, only about 30,000 healthy infants are available for adoption. What is so striking about this comparison is that every state has an elaborate regulatory mechanism in place for adoption while only three states, Florida, Virginia, and New Hampshire, have enacted legislation to comprehensively address assisted reproductive technologies. Yet, they are not even the states where the most high tech reproduction is conducted.

Lori B. Andrews, *Reproductive Technology Comes of Age*, 21 Whittier L. Rev. 375, 377 (1999). Federal law only requires that each facility administering assisted reproductive technology report annually to the Centers for Disease Control on pregnancy success rates achieved by its program, the identity of the embryo laboratory used by such program, and whether the laboratory is certified under the law or has applied for such certification. *See* 42 U.S.C. § 263A-1 (1994).

Other countries do not necessarily have such a laissez-faire approach. For example, England has extensively regulated reproductive technology use. The Human Fertilization and Embryology Act 1990 established the Human Fertilization and Embryology Authority (HFEA). The HFEA regulates, through licensing and a Code of Practice, all research and treatment that involves human embryos, eggs, or sperm. The HFEA is guided by "the respect which is due to human life at all stages of its development," the "right" of infertile people to the proper "consideration" of their request for treatment, a concern for "the welfare of children," and a recognition of the benefits from medical and scientific knowledge. *See* HFEA, Code of Practice ¶ 7 (5th ed. 2001). The Code of Practice is regularly reviewed and amended, and is currently in its fifth edition. *See id.* at ¶ 8. Provisions in its Code of Practice are extensive, and include items related to confidentiality, *id.* at ¶¶ 5.1–.5, information to be given to participants, *id.* at ¶¶ 6.1–.12, consent, *id.* at ¶¶ 7.1–.42, counseling, *id.* at ¶¶ 8.1–.34, use and storage of gametes and embryos, *id.* at ¶¶ 9.1–10.15, research, *id.* at ¶¶ 11.1–.9, and record-keeping, *id.* at ¶¶ 12.1–.16. As mentioned above, it also requires centers to take account of the welfare of any child who may be born or who may be affected as a result of treatment. *Id.* at ¶¶ 3.8–.18.

What are the justifications for formal regulation? As one author accurately points out, "[T]he lack of statutory regulation does not necessarily mean that there is no regulation. In most countries where assisted conception services are available there is some form of professional self-regulation." Jennifer Gunning, *Overview: Legislative Approaches, in* Assisted Conception 101, 104 (Jennifer Gunning ed., 2000). In addition, litigation between parties over their rights and obligations also acts as a form of informal regulation. Is professional self-regulation and ad hoc case law sufficient? What interest does the state have in the regulation of this technology? For an excellent essay discussing formal regulation, *see* Naomi Pfeffer, *Regulating Reproduction, in* Bodies of Technology: Women's Involvement with Reproductive Medicine 254 (Ann Rudinow Saetnan et al. eds., 2000).

2. In Vitro Fertilization

The 1978 birth of Louise Brown in England marked the first successful in vitro fertilization (IVF). Since then, the technology has been used around the world. Individuals in developed countries have the highest rate of use, *see* Alicia Ely Yamin & Deborah P. Maine, *Maternal Mortality as a Human Rights Issue: Measuring Compliance with International Treaty Obligations*, 21 Hum. Rts. Q. 563, 563–64 (1999), but the use of this technology is not confined to developed countries. *See, e.g.,* Ctr. for Reproductive Law & Policy, Women of the World: Laws and Policies Affecting the Reproductive Lives, Anglophone Africa, 2001 Progress Report 77 (2001), *available at* http://www.crlp.org/pub_bo_wowafrica.html#progreport ("[I]n July 2000, the federal government [of Nigeria] announced plans to establish a fertility center that would offer in-vitro fertilization treatments for women having difficulty conceiving."); Sola Ogundipe, *Infertility is No Longer a Lifelong Disorder,* The Vanguard, Jan. 15, 2002, *available at* http://fr.all.africa.com/stories/200201150256.html ("Today, a couple can obtain successful IVF treatment in Nigeria at reasonable cost without the need to go abroad."). "Even in China, where population control is a top state priority and population reduction policies are stringently enforced, the first IVF birth was announced in 1988. One major hospital in China boasted that by 1993, fifty-one babies had been born at its facilities using the technique." Elizabeth Ann Pitrolo, *The Birds, The Bees, and the Deep Freeze: Is There International Consensus in the Debate Over Assisted Reproductive Technologies?*, 19 Hous. J. Int'l L. 147, 149–50 (1996). *See also* Jyotsna Agnihotri Gupta, *Riddled with Secrecy and Unethical Practices: Assisted Reproduction in India, in* Bodies of Technology: Women's Involvement with Reproductive Medicine (Ann Rudinow Saetnan et al. eds., 2000) (discussing the use of IVF in India despite India's focus on population control).

One of the most interesting legal issues surrounding IVF is how a court should resolve a dispute over the destiny of frozen embryos if a couple breaks up. The resolution of this issue sometimes depends upon the decision-makers' views of reproductive autonomy, and specifically the importance of the right to parent versus the right not to parent. Consider, for example, how this issue has been dealt with in Israel, and compare the resolution there with how the issue has been resolved in the United States.

a. Israel

Janie Chen, *The Right to Her Embryos: An Analysis of Nahmani v. Nahmani and Its Impact on Israeli In Vitro Fertilization Law*

7 Cardozo J. Int'l & Comp. L. 325, 325–48 (1999)

Ruti and Danny Nahmani made legal history for the first time in 1988. They embarked on a battle in Israel's Supreme Court for the right to have Mrs. Nahmani's eggs fertilized in vitro with Mr. Nahmani's sperm and then implanted in a surrogate mother in the United States. In 1992, however—after the eggs had been fertilized, but before the Nahmanis could deliver the embryos to a surrogate—Mr. Nahmani left his wife and moved in with another woman, with whom he has since had two children. Mr. Nahmani subsequently made it known that he no longer wanted a child with his estranged wife, and denied Assuta Hospital, where the embryos were stored, permission to release the frozen embryos. The embryos represented Mrs. Nahmani's last chance to have a biological child of her own since she was unable to produce more eggs.

In 1993, Mrs. Nahmani filed suit to obtain custody of the embryos in Haifa District Court, which ruled in her favor. In the September 12 ruling, the District Court ordered that the embryos be turned over to Mrs. Nahmani, citing not only her right to them, but also criticizing her husband's "jealousy and callousness, accompanied by cynicism, egotism and no little [male] chauvinism." The Court held that Mr. Nahmani's opposition constituted breach of contract. It found this contract in Mr. Nahmani's initial agreement to have a child with his wife, and, according to the Court, he could not withdraw his agreement once the IVF had been performed. It was therefore ordered that the fertilized eggs be given to Mrs. Nahmani so that she could proceed with the surrogate.

Mr. Nahmani immediately appealed to the Supreme Court which, in a 4–1 decision, overturned the District Court's ruling in 1994. The majority anchored its ruling in basic human rights and equality between the sexes. It dealt first with a person's rudimentary right to freedom and privacy, together with "personal autonomy." The Court articulated that the right to parenthood imposed no duty on an unwilling spouse to be a parent or assist the other spouse to be one; there was an equal right not to be a parent. It held that parenthood imposed unique lifetime responsibilities. Based on this rationale, the majority maintained that it would not be proper for the Court to impose parentage on an unwilling party, as it would ultimately infringe upon his right to "personal autonomy."

The Court then deliberated over the maxim of equality in the present context. It articulated that, under certain circumstances, a woman is permitted to have an abortion. She does not require her husband's permission and could reject his opposition to the abortion. In that connection, the majority said, if motherhood could not be forced on a woman, analogously, fatherhood could not be forced on a man.... Thus the Court determined that it should not thrust parenthood on Mr. Nahmani, regardless of his initial agreement to be a father. The justices decided that if natural parenthood could not be forced upon a woman, neither could parenthood be imposed on a man by technological means.

Legal approaches taken in Canada, Australia, England and the United States guided the Court in its decision. It noted that the majority of these countries require mutual consent by both parties at every stage of the IVF process.

The Court then examined sections 8(b)(3) and 14(b) of the Public Health Regulations (IVF) of 1987. In Israel, the IVF issue is dealt with only in health regulations by the Ministry of Health, rather than in Knesset law. The Supreme Court held that the regulations are only intended as a directive for the health authorities and do not define personal rights and duties in the highly sensitive and complicated context of artificial fertilization.

Contract law was also contemplated by the Court in assessing the Nahmani dispute. Consideration was given to the framework of the "agreement" between the Nahmanis and Mr. Nahmani's right to renege on their agreement under their estranged circumstances. The Court then addressed whether the Nahmanis' agreement was legally "frustrated" by some outside influence beyond the parties' control. Mrs. Nahmani argued that the agreement fell under sections 25 and 26 of the Contracts (General Part) Law of 1973 and that this legislation could be used to find in her husband's consent an intent for culmination of the IVF process, which the Court rejected. Mrs. Nahmani also argued that her husband was estopped from reneging on the agreement. It could not be said, the Court maintained, that his consent encapsulated the possibility of their breaking up, or that Mrs. Nahmani had agreed to the process on the basis of Mr. Nahmani's promise to see it completed even if they became estranged....

Lastly, the Court examined the issue of whether the "point of no return" in a spouse's agreement to a surrogate pregnancy is at the time of in vitro fertilization or only after the embryos are implanted in the surrogate's womb. The majority concluded that, until and including the stage of implementation, a couple's joint and ongoing agreement "is called for from every possible legal standpoint." Based on the preceding analysis, the Court concluded that, despite Mrs. Nahmani's plight, granting her the relief she sought would ultimately be unlawful and an offense against Mr. Nahmani's basic rights as an individual. The Court said:

> We are conscious of and sensitive to Ruti Nahmani's part in this, her involvement in the IVF procedure which was greater—physically and emotionally—than Dani's, and her understandable expectations that the procedure would end with her achieving her long sought-after goal. But the procedure is only the beginning of a road which the couple would have to

travel together, making joint decisions. [Ruling against Dani Nahmani] would mean forcing someone who no longer wants to travel that road to do so for the rest of his life.

On March 30, 1995, the Supreme Court granted judgment for Mr. Nahmani....

Immediately after the 1994 Supreme Court case was decided, the Court granted Mrs. Nahmani a second hearing before an expanded panel of justices. Never before had a subsequent hearing been granted in the Supreme Court on a case originally heard by more than three judges. On September 12, 1996, a board of eleven justices overturned the 1993 adjudication in a 7–4 ruling. The seven justices unanimously agreed that the right to be a parent prevails over the right not to be a parent. [Ed. Note: Each of the eleven judges wrote a separate opinion. For a more nuanced description of some of the alliances on the court, see Dalia Dorner, *Human Reproduction: Reflections on the Nahmani Case*, 35 Tex. Int'l L.J. 1 (2000).]

With no legal criteria but the notion of justice to guide the Court in resolving the IVF issue at hand, the Majority fashioned a three-prong test to scrutinize (i) the conflicting interests of the parties; (ii) the parties' legitimate expectations; and (iii) the appropriate public policy to be applied.

In assessing the first prong, the Nahmani Court found that conflicting interests were based on the right to be a parent versus the right not to be a parent. Forced to rule between these two rights, the Court had to decide which prevailed over the other. The Majority therefore advanced three different courses of action it could take to resolve this conflict. The first action required a uniform rejection of parenthood under the existing circumstances; the second involved an assiduous partiality for parenthood; and the third option, which the Court eventually relied on, struck a balance between the parties' conflicting rights and the fundamental circumstances surrounding these rights.

The Nahmani Court contended that parenthood is a person's most basic goal. It postulated that as a general rule, the positive right of parentage prevailed over the negative right of refusal. The Court held that "in balancing [the Nahmanis'] conflicting interests, we must remember that despite the symmetrical language — 'to be a parent' and 'not to be a parent' — these interests are not equal.... The interest in parenthood is a basic and existential value, both for the individual and for society as a whole. In contrast, there is no intrinsic value to the absence of parenthood." The Majority then resorted to the Torah and the writings of religious sages which regard deprivation of parenthood as loss of a person's soul. "It was true an unwilling parent would have responsibilities but, onerous as they could be, they could not be compared with the loss of his soul," the Justices articulated. Antithetically, the Nahmani Court regarded the interests of not being a parent a right of unequal weight. It distinguished this right as a claim grounded on privacy and freedom to make intimate decisions, which is invalidated by the axiomatic right to be a parent.

The justices further explored the different categories of rights recognized, including basic versus fundamental, general versus specific, absolute versus relative, and narrow derivative rights. In this case, the Court characterized the rights of Mrs. Nahmani in the context of specific versus general. Mr. Nahmani sought to impose on what appeared to be a specific limitation of Mrs. Nahmani's right to be a parent by restricting her to the use of embryos fertilized from his semen. However, the majority contended, the limitation was in fact general since she had no practical alternative to create another child and adoption was also not a viable alternative since it was not available to her. On the contrary, since Mr. Nahmani could still retain his right to be or not to be a parent, the Justices concluded that the limitation being imposed on his right was specific, relating only to parentage in the particular framework of this case.

> Ordinarily, the party wishing to avoid procreation should prevail, assuming that the other party has a reasonable possibility of achieving parenthood by means other than use of the preembryos in question. If no other reasonable alternatives exist, then the argument in favor of using the preembryos to achieve pregnancy should be considered.... [T]he rule does not contemplate the creation of an automatic veto....

Hence, the Nahmani Court felt that the "scales of justice" leaned in Mrs. Nahmani's favor.

On the rights of the IVF parent as discerned in the context of abortion rights, the Court disagreed with the prior Nahmani ruling. The Justices asserted, "as a man may not demand the termination of...pregnancy even if based on fraud...so is he precluded from demanding the cessation of the fertilization and implantation process. Both cases involve intervention in a woman's body, desecrating her dignity and modesty, which the law will not recognize." [Ed. Note: Citing Planned Parenthood v. Danforth, 428 U.S. 52 (1976).]

> There is no legal, ethical or logical reason why an in vitro fertilization should give rise to additional rights on the part of the husband. From a propositional standpoint[,] it matters little whether the ovum/sperm union takes place in the private darkness of a fallopian tube or the public glare of a petri dish. Fertilization is fertilization and fertilization of the ovum is the inception of the reproductive process. Biological life exists from that moment forward...To deny a husband rights while an embryo develops in the womb and grant a right to destroy [it] while it is in a hospital freezer is to favor situs over substance.

The Court relied on additional U.S. sources to bolster its abortion analogy:

> There are several forms which a disagreement between progenitors could take. The woman may want the embryo to be brought to term, and the man may want the embryo terminated. In that case, it would seem appropriate for the woman to be allowed to gestate the embryo. The Supreme Court's abortion and contraception decisions have indicated that the right of procreation is the right of an individual which does not require the agreement of the individual's partner. In particular, the woman has been held to have a right to abort without the husband's consent and the right not to abort over the wish of the husband that she abort.

The Court continued:

> But what if the positions were reversed and the woman wished to terminate the embryo and her male partner wished to have it brought to term? When an embryo conceived naturally is developing within a woman during the first two trimesters, it is clear that the woman's decision whether or not to terminate it takes precedence over the desires of the man who provided the sperm.... [I]t is at least arguable that the man's wishes should be honored when the embryo's continued existence need not be balanced against the physical and psychological needs of the woman carrying it. The man clearly would not have the right to force the female progenitor to gestate the embryo, but there seems to be no reason not to give him custody of the embryo for gestation in a surrogate mother.

Furthermore, the Court did not deem the rights of a man and a woman equal in this situation because a woman had complete rights over her own body and she alone could decide whether to continue or terminate the pregnancy.

Propagating the inquiry on opposing rights, the Court opined that while imposing a duty of parenthood on an unwilling individual was a substantive breach of his freedom, it concluded there was no such duty being forced on Mr. Nahmani in this case. The majority reached this conclusion by making a "substantive and basic distinction" between forcing Mr. Nahmani to surrender his sperm to the IVF process in pursuit of parenthood (substantive) and denying him the right to impose a barrier on Mrs. Nahmani's desire to have a child (basic). In the majority's view, the only right Mr. Nahmani lost was his opportunity to restrain Mrs. Nahmani from using the contested embryos after he already consented to the IVF process. By leaving his marriage, he abandoned his right to prevent the inception of his child and the Court added that "at this stage [of the IVF process], nothing more was required of him."

The Court recognized that Mr. Nahmani could not be fully indemnified if he were required to support a child he did not want and since his family situation had changed, his emotional opposition to the continuation of the IVF process was understandable. In response, it proposed that Mrs. Nahmani be granted the embryos subject to the condition that she agree not to claim money from Mr. Nahmani to aid any child or children born from their embryos. After weighing the relevant factors, the Nahmani Court determined that Mrs. Nahmani's right to be a parent prevailed in the struggle between the opposing interests. "A woman's right to be a parent is stronger than a man's right not to be a father," proclaimed the Court.

The Nahmani Court next deliberated over the expectations of the parties. Since the Court posited that this matter was not covered by ordinary contracts law, it elected to find a "just" solution by analyzing the circumstances surrounding the Nahmani dispute. The Majority focused primarily on Mrs. Nahmani's reliance on Mr. Nahmani.

> The doctrine of reliance should be applied to resolve a dispute between the gamete providers. The consistent application of a reliance based theory of contract law to enforce promises to reproduce through IVF will enable IVF participants to assert control over their reproductive choices by enabling them to anticipate their rights and duties, and to know with reasonable certainty that their expectations will be enforced by the courts.

The Justices held that Mrs. Nahmani detrimentally relied on her husband's initial consent to the IVF process when she underwent a pre-fertilization procedure which the Court felt "caused [her] continuous severe physical suffering and even threatened her life." The Court also pointed out that the embryos most likely signified Mrs. Nahmani's final chance to become a biological mother since they represented her last remaining ova, which she fertilized with her husband's sperm in reliance of his consent to father her child.

> One fact is of vital importance in making this judgment; the spouse who opposes implantation wanted a child at one time and submitted to the IVF process with that end in mind. The two spouses once agreed on this issue and initiated the IVF procedure in reliance on that mutual wish. Given this background, the greater injustice would be to deny implantation to the spouse who detrimentally relied on the other's words and conduct.

Tapping into their "own principles and feelings," the Court expressed animosity toward Mr. Nahmani for leaving his wife to be with another woman only two months after signing the contract with the surrogate institute in the United States. The Court had no doubt that Mr. Nahmani's change of mind reflected a capriciousness that "destroy[ed] [Mrs. Nahmani's] last spark of hope." It asserted that to allow Mr. Nahmani to whimsically withdraw his consent at any time was to give a power of veto over the continuing IVF process which, to the Court, was "clearly unacceptable" in conjunction with equality before the law.

> One approach would be to require mutual spousal consent as a prerequisite to implantation of all preembryos created through IVF. This approach would require obtaining consent twice from each spouse—once when the IVF procedure is initiated and again before each implantation.... This rule would... have disadvantages, however. Most significantly, it would grant tremendous power to one spouse over the other. It would mean that even though both spouses initially consented to having a child through IVF, neither could proceed with certainty that the other would not truncate the process. Such an outcome would surely frustrate the spouse seeking implantation, who will have invested large financial expense, time, energy, and in the wife's case[,] physical pain. The required second consent for implantation could become a tool for manipulation and abuse between spouses, especially under circumstances of a pending divorce. Any spouse ultimately denied the chance to have a child through IVF would probably suffer considerable emotional stress.

To remedy Mrs. Nahmani's unjust detriment, the Court turned to the doctrine of estoppel.

> Protection against this sort of injustice is recognized by the well established doctrine of estoppel.... The knowing action of the objecting spouse is the undertaking of IVF for the purpose of producing a child. The prejudice to the other spouse consists of the time, money, and psychological commitment necessarily expended in pursuing the full procedure. The injury would include not only the time and money spent, but also the last opportunity to have a child.

Finally, addressing the last prong of their analysis, the Court held that public policy demanded the parties' consent be secured in as short a time as possible in order to maintain legal stability and certainty. The Majority noted that not only were the IVF couple involved, but also the medical institutions and the surrogate mother. It maintained that the prospect of a one-sided veto was likely to lead to various difficulties affecting the whole procedure. Following this logic, the Court examined when the "point of no return" was after both parties agreed to the IVF procedure. Contrary to the belief that [the] "point" is reached when the embryo is implanted in the womb, the Court asserted that once the ovum has been fertilized by the sperm, a party cannot back out of that agreement. The Court felt strongly that the possibility of a new "being" created during the point of fertilization warranted continuation of the IVF process in the face of a one-sided objection. Moreover, the Court wanted to encourage couples unable to procreate children naturally to utilize the IVF process by eliminating any obstacles that they may encounter.

Ergo, by majority decision, the 1994 Nahmani judgment was set aside and the Haifa District court's decision for Mrs. Nahmani was restored....

Later in the article the author analyzed how Judaism affected the Israeli Supreme Court's decision. That portion of the article, pages 352–57, is set forth next.

With the 1996 Nahmani decision, the Israeli Supreme Court ushered in a vision of reproductive rights so paramount as to override the intrinsic right of personal autonomy. Only before a Jewish court embodying judges "with a uniquely Jewish reverence for life" could Mrs. Nahmani have succeeded in her pursuit to have a child, using the frozen embryos fertilized by her estranged husband against his will. To understand the majority's "unique" perspective, one must canvass the rich social, cultural, and religious history of a society that has a "deeply rooted, unequivocal, imprinted commitment to children." ...

Judaism overwhelmingly values children, considering them the prospect for the future and the foundation for the perpetuation of the Torah. This enthusiastic spirit stems from the incessant perils (both from internal and external forces) the Jewish community faced throughout its extended career, and its consistent emphasis on the duty to procreate in order to survive developed as a result. "If self-preservation is the first law of nature, the injunction 'Be fruitful and multiply' is properly the first Commandment, but not merely because it occurs in the opening chapter of Genesis but because it is the cornerstone of Jewish life, upon which all else depends." This commandment (mitzvah) of procreation has undergone many changes, shifting with the four main stages of Jewish history which shall briefly be addressed.

All through the biblical period, when Jewish life was sound, laid open only to the common risks that are part of the human state of being, the sensibility toward reproduction was insouciant; children were regarded as blessings. During the Return after the Babylonian Exile until the end of the Tannaitic period, the third century C.E., the Jewish population was concentrated in Palestine where there were no significant threats to Jewish survival. This period marked the emergence of the Jewish belief and practice in the Halakhah [Ed. Note: traditional Jewish law and ethics] as the rudimentary composition of Jewish life. The blessing of procreation was subsequently metamorphosed into a mitzvah, an obligation binding upon the Jew. There was yet no demand for extensively abundant families since Jewish life still remained normal.

As time progressed to the Middle Ages, during the protracted period of the Galut, Jewish life no longer centered around Palestine. The Jews were scattered throughout Europe, North Africa, and western Asia, where they were looked upon as aliens, living at the expense of their host country. They became perpetual "victims of persecution, expropriation, expulsion, and massacre at the hands of their neighbors." As a consequence, Jewish preservation was always uncertain — for the mass numbers of east European Jewry, this plight continued into the twentieth century. Fearing extinction of the Jewish population, Medieval Jewish leaders, determining that more children were needed to replenish the diminishing populace, introduced the rule that the commandment "be fruitful and multiply" had to take priority "over other considerations of health, convenience, or personal desire." This attitude eventually became the norm in traditional Judaism. The remaining era, which lasted only 150 years, witnessed the French Revolution and the birth of Nazism. During this modern age, the mitzvah of procreation went into total eclipse on account of highly urbanized and mobile Jews — mostly situated in central and western Europe and North America — who curtailed their birthrate at a more excessive rate than did the rest of the population in that area. However, a majority of the world Jewry, living in Eastern Europe, still retained the Jewish lifestyle of the middle ages and were faithfully employed in replenishing the diminishing denomination of Jews in Germany, Austria, Holland, Belgium, France, Great Britain, and Italy, in addition to the United States. The advent of the Holocaust wiped out this fountain of replenishment and decreased the world Jewish population from sixteen million to eleven million.

In the aftermath of century-old discrimination, persecution, and mass extermination, "one of the hallmarks of modern Jews is their preoccupation—or obsession—with Jewish survival and the preservation of Jewish identity."

A number of contemporary Jewish thinkers have urged an increase in the Jewish birthrate on grounds which are essentially extra-theological. The calamitous losses of the Holocaust, coupled with defection as a result of assimilation and intermarriage, have decimated the Jewish population. If demographic trends are not reversed, it is argued, the prospects for Jewish survival are precarious. Thus, higher birthrates within the Jewish community must be encouraged if Jews are to remain a viable ethnic group capable of continuing the uniquely Jewish contribution to human civilization.

It should follow from the Jewish community's aggressive promotion of conception that infertility is declared an "illness." This posture has, consequently, led to a "less conservative and noninterventionalist stance on IVF and surrogacy" in Israel. The IVF procedure is reckoned to be "a meritorious deed" which helps couples fulfill its procreative mitzvah. "Where the natural alternative is not available, these resourceful ways of bringing about the desideratum become acceptable. Enabling a woman to fulfill the maternal yearning, or a couple to fulfill the mitzvah, is itself a mitzvah." IVF has met with great disapproval by some Catholic theologians on the assertion that it is immoral and violative of natural laws. However, this argument is foreign to Judaism since it does not postulate a doctrine of natural law but rather, examines IVF "solely in light of possible infraction of biblical proscriptions. In the absence of a specific prohibition, man is free to utilize scientific knowledge in order to overcome impediments of nature."

---

b. United States

J.B. v. M.B.
783 A.2d 707 (N.J. 2001)

Poritz, C.J.

In this case, a divorced couple disagree about the disposition of seven preembryos that remain in storage after the couple, during their marriage, undertook in vitro fertilization procedures. We must first decide whether the husband and wife have entered into an enforceable contract that is now determinative on the disposition issue. If not, we must consider how such conflicts should be resolved by our courts....

J.B. and M.B. were married in February 1992.... J.B. learned that she had a condition that prevented her from becoming pregnant....

The in vitro fertilization procedure was carried out in May 1995 and resulted in eleven preembryos. Four were transferred to J.B. and seven were cryopreserved. J.B. became pregnant, either as a result of the procedure or through natural means, and gave birth to the couple's daughter on March 19, 1996. In September 1996, however, the couple separated, and J.B. informed M.B. that she wished to have the remaining preembryos discarded. M.B. did not agree.

J.B. filed a complaint for divorce on November 25, 1996, in which she sought an order from the court "with regard to the eight frozen embryos." In a counterclaim filed on November 24, 1997, M.B. demanded judgment compelling his wife "to allow the (8) eight frozen embryos currently in storage to be implanted or donated to other infertile couples." J.B. filed a motion for summary judgment on the preembryo issue in April 1998 alleging, in a certification filed with the motion, that she had intended to use the preembryos solely within her marriage to M.B....:

J.B. also certified that "[t]here were never any discussions between the Defendant and I regarding the disposition of the frozen embryos should our marriage be dissolved."

M.B., in a cross-motion filed in July 1998, described his understanding very differently. He certified that he and J.B. had agreed prior to undergoing the in vitro fertilization procedure that any unused preembryos would not be destroyed, but would be used by his wife or donated to infertile couples. His certification stated:

> Before we began the I.V.F. treatments, we had many long and serious discussions regarding the process and the moral and ethical repercussions. For me, as a Catholic, the I.V.F. procedure itself posed a dilemma. We discussed this issue extensively and had agreed that no matter what happened the eggs would be either utilized by us or by other infertile couples. In fact, the option to donate [the preembryos] to infertile couples was the Plaintiff's idea. She came up with this idea because she knew of other individuals in her work place who were having trouble conceiving.

M.B.'s mother, father, and sister also certified that on several occasions during family gatherings J.B. had stated her intention to either use or donate the preembryos.

The couple's final judgment of divorce, entered in September 1998, resolved all issues except disposition of the preembryos. Shortly thereafter, the trial court granted J.B.'s motion for summary judgment on that issue. The court found that the reason for the parties' decision to attempt in vitro fertilization — to create a family as a married couple — no longer existed. J.B. and M.B. had become parents and were now divorced. Moreover, M.B. was not infertile and could achieve parenthood in the future through natural means. The court did not accept M.B.'s argument that the parties undertook the in vitro fertilization procedure to "create life," and found no need for further fact finding on the existence of an agreement between them, noting that there was no written contract memorializing the parties' intentions. Because the husband was "fully able to father a child," and because he sought control of the preembryos "merely to donate them to another couple," the court concluded that the wife had "the greater interest and should prevail." The Appellate Division affirmed.... We granted certification,...and now modify and affirm the judgment of the Appellate Division....

M.B. contends that he and J.B. entered into an agreement to use or donate the preembryos, and J.B. disputes the existence of any such agreement. As an initial matter, then, we must decide whether this case involves a contract for the disposition of the cryopreserved preembryos resulting from in vitro fertilization. We begin, therefore, with the consent form provided to J.B. and M.B. by the Cooper Center. Cf. Garfinkel v. Morristown Obstetrics & Gynecology, 168 N.J. 124, 135, 773 A.2d 665 (2001) (noting intent expressed in writing controls interpretation of contract); State Troopers Fraternal Assoc. v. State, 149 N.J. 38, 47, 692 A.2d 519 (1997) (noting fundamental canons of contract construction require examination of plain language of contract).... Clearly, the thrust of the document signed by J.B. and M.B. is that the Cooper Center obtains control over the preembryos unless the parties choose otherwise in a writing, or unless a court specifically directs otherwise in an order of divorce....

M.B. asserts, however, that he and J.B. jointly intended another disposition....

Assuming that it would be possible to enter into a valid agreement at that time irrevocably deciding the disposition of preembryos in circumstances such as we have here, a formal, unambiguous memorialization of the parties' intentions would be required to confirm their joint determination. The parties do not contest the lack of such a writing. We hold, therefore, that J.B. and M.B. never entered into a separate binding contract providing for the disposition of the cryopreserved preembryos now in the possession of the Cooper Center....

In essence, J.B. and M.B. have agreed only that on their divorce the decision in respect of control, and therefore disposition, of their cryopreserved preembryos will be directed by the court. In this area, however, there are few guideposts for decision-making.... [A]t the point when a husband and wife decide to begin the in vitro fertilization process, they are unlikely to anticipate divorce or to be concerned about the disposition of preembryos on divorce. As they are both contributors of the genetic material comprising the preembryos, the decision should be theirs to make. *See generally* Davis v. Davis, 842 S.W.2d 588, 597 (Tenn. 1992) (stating that donors should retain decision-making authority with respect to their preembryos)....

But what if, as here, the parties disagree. Without guidance from the Legislature, we must consider a means by which courts can engage in a principled review of the issues presented in such cases in order to achieve a just result. Because the claims before us derive, in part, from concepts found in the Federal Constitution and the Constitution of this State, we begin with those concepts.

Both parties and the ACLU *Amici* invoke the right to privacy in support of their respective positions. More specifically, they claim procreational autonomy as a fundamental attribute of the privacy rights guaranteed by both the Federal and New Jersey Constitutions. Their arguments are based on various opinions of the United States Supreme Court that discuss the right to be free from governmental interference with procreational decisions. *See* Eisenstadt v. Baird, 405 U.S. 438, 453 (1972); Griswold v. Connecticut, 381 U.S. 479, 485-86 (1965); Skinner v. Oklahoma, 316 U.S. 535, 541 (1942)....

Those decisions provide a framework within which disputes over the disposition of preembryos can be resolved. In *Davis, supra,* for example, a divorced couple could not agree on the disposition of their unused, cryopreserved preembryos. 842 S.W.2d at 589. The Tennessee Supreme Court balanced the right to procreate of the party seeking to donate the preembryos (the wife), against the right not to procreate of the party seeking destruction of the preembryos (the husband)....

We agree with the Tennessee Supreme Court that "[o]rdinarily, the party wishing to avoid procreation should prevail." *Ibid.* Here, the Appellate Division succinctly described the "apparent" conflict between J.B. and M.B.:

> In the present case, the wife's right not to become a parent seemingly conflicts with the husband's right to procreate. The conflict, however, is more apparent than real. Recognition and enforcement of the wife's right would not seriously impair the husband's right to procreate. Though his right to procreate using the wife's egg would be terminated, he retains the capacity to father children....

In other words, M.B.'s right to procreate is not lost if he is denied an opportunity to use or donate the preembryos. M.B. is already a father and is able to become a father to additional children, whether through natural procreation or further in vitro fertilization. In contrast, J.B.'s right not to procreate may be lost through attempted use or through donation of the preembryos. Implantation, if successful, would result in the birth of her biological child and could have life-long emotional and psychological repercussions.[7] *See* Patricia A. Martin & Martin L. Lagod, *The Human Preembryo, the Progenitors, and the State: Toward a Dynamic Theory of Status, Rights, and Research Policy*, 5 High Tech. L.J. 257, 290 (1990) (stating that "[g]enetic ties may form a powerful bond...even if the progenitor is freed from the legal obligations of parenthood"). Her fundamental right not to procreate is irrevocably extinguished if a surrogate mother bears J.B.'s child. We will not force J.B. to become a biological parent against her will....

The court below "conclude[d] that a contract to procreate is contrary to New Jersey public policy and is unenforceable."...As the Appellate Division opinion in this case points out, the laws of New Jersey also evince a policy against enforcing private contracts to enter into or terminate familial relationships. 331 N.J. Super. at 234–35, 751 A.2d 613. New Jersey has, by statute, abolished the cause of action for breach of contract to marry. N.J.S.A. 2A:23-1. Private placement adoptions are disfavored, Sees v. Baber, 74 N.J. 201, 217, 377 A.2d 628 (1977), and may be approved over the objection of a parent only if that parent has failed or is unable to perform "the regular and expected parental functions of care and support of the child." N.J.S.A. 9:3-46; *see* N.J.S.A. 9:3-48 (stating statutory requirements for private placement adoption).

That public policy also led this Court to conclude in *Baby M*, [109 N.J. 396, 433-34 (N.J. 1988)], that a surrogacy contract was unenforceable. We held that public policy prohibited a binding agreement to require a surrogate, there the biological mother, to surrender her parental rights. *Id.* at 411. The contract in *Baby M* provided for a $10,000 payment to the surrogate for her to be artificially inseminated, carry the child to term, and then, after the child's birth, relinquish parental rights to the father and his wife. *Id.* at 411–12. The surrogate mother initially surrendered the child to the father, but subsequently reconsidered her decision and fled with Baby M. *Id.* at 414–15. In an action by the father to enforce the surrogacy contract, we held that the contract conflicted with "(1) laws prohibiting the use of money in connection with adoptions; (2) laws requiring proof of parental unfitness or abandonment before termination of parental rights is ordered or an adoption is granted; and (3) laws that make surrender of custody and consent to adoption revocable in private placement adoptions." *Id.* at 423. Our decision was consistent with the policy expressed earlier in *Sees, supra*, that consent to terminate parental rights was revocable in all but statutorily approved circumstances. 74 N.J. at 212.[8]

---

7. The legal consequences for J.B. also are unclear. *See* N.J.A.C. 8:2-1.4(a) (stating "the woman giving birth shall be recorded as a parent"). We note without comment that a recent case before the Chancery Division in Bergen County concluded that seventy-two hours must pass before a non-biological surrogate mother may surrender her parental rights and the biological mother's name may be placed on the birth certificate. A.H.W. v. G.H.B., 339 N.J.Super. 495, 505, 772 A.2d 948 (2000). In Arizona, an appellate court determined that a statute allowing a biological father but not a biological mother to prove paternity violated the Equal Protection Clause. Soos v. Superior Court, 182 Ariz. 470, 897 P.2d 1356, 1361 (1994). In California, the legal mother is the person who "intended to bring about the birth of a child that she intended to raise as her own." Johnson v. Calvert, 5 Cal.4th 84, 19 Cal.Rptr.2d 494, 851 P.2d 776, 782 (1993), *cert. denied*, 510 U.S. 874, 114 S.Ct. 206, 126 L.Ed.2d 163, and *cert. dismissed*, Baby Boy J. v. Johnson, 510 U.S. 938, 114 S.Ct. 374, 126 L.Ed.2d 324 (1993).

8. Currently, a minority of states have passed legislation addressing in vitro fertilization. *See, e.g.*, Cal. Penal Code § 367g (West 1999) (permitting use of preembryos only pursuant to written consent form); Fla. Stat. ch. 742.17 (1997) (establishing joint decision-making authority regarding disposition of preembryos); La. Rev. Stat. Ann. §§ 121-33 (West 1991) (establishing fertilized human ovum as biological human being that cannot be intentionally destroyed); Okla. Stat. Ann.

Enforcement of a contract that would allow the implantation of preembryos at some future date in a case where one party has reconsidered his or her earlier acquiescence raises similar issues. If implantation is successful, that party will have been forced to become a biological parent against his or her will. We note disagreement on the issue both among legal commentators and in the limited case law on the subject. *Kass, supra,* held that "[a]greements between progenitors, or gamete donors, regarding disposition of their prezygotes should generally be presumed valid and binding, and enforced in a dispute between them...." 673 N.Y.S.2d 350, 696 N.E.2d at 180. The New York court emphasized that such agreements would "avoid costly litigation," "minimize misunderstandings and maximize procreative liberty by reserving to the progenitors the authority to make what is in the first instance a quintessentially personal private decision."...

We recognize that persuasive reasons exist for enforcing preembryo disposition agreements. Both the *Kass* and *Davis* decisions pointed out the benefits of enforcing agreements between the parties. *See Kass, supra,* 673 N.Y.S.2d 350, 696 N.E.2d at 179 (noting "need for clear, consistent principles to guide parties in protecting their interests and resolving their disputes"); *Davis, supra,* 842 S.W.2d at 597 (discussing benefit of guidance to parties undertaking in vitro fertilization procedures). We also recognize that in vitro fertilization is in widespread use, and that there is a need for agreements between the participants and the clinics that perform the procedure. We believe that the better rule, and the one we adopt, is to enforce agreements entered into at the time in vitro fertilization is begun, subject to the right of either party to change his or her mind about disposition up to the point of use or destruction of any stored preembryos.

The public policy concerns that underlie limitations on contracts involving family relationships are protected by permitting either party to object at a later date to provisions specifying a disposition of preembryos that that party no longer accepts. Moreover, despite the conditional nature of the disposition provisions, in the large majority of cases the agreements will control, permitting fertility clinics and other like facilities to rely on their terms. Only when a party affirmatively notifies a clinic in writing of a change in intention should the disposition issue be reopened. Principles of fairness dictate that agreements provided by a clinic should be written in plain language, and that a qualified clinic representative should review the terms with the parties prior to execution. Agreements should not be signed in blank,... or in a manner suggesting that the parties have not given due consideration to the disposition question. Those and other reasonable safeguards should serve to limit later disputes.

Finally, if there is disagreement as to disposition because one party has reconsidered his or her earlier decision, the interests of both parties must be evaluated.... Because ordinarily the party choosing not to become a biological parent will prevail, we do not anticipate increased litigation as a result of our decision. In this case, after having considered that M.B. is a father and is capable of fathering additional children, we have affirmed J.B.'s right to prevent implantation of the preembryos. We express no opinion in respect of a case in which a party who has become infertile seeks use of stored preembryos against the wishes of his or her partner, noting only that the possibility of adoption also may be a consideration, among others, in the court's assessment....

---

tit. 10, §556 (West 2001) (requiring written consent for embryo transfer); Tex. Family Code Ann. §151.103 (West 1996) (establishing parental rights over child resulting from preembryo).

Under the judgment of the Appellate Division, the seven remaining preembryos are to be destroyed....

Verniero, J., concurring.

I join in the disposition of this case and in all but one aspect of the Court's opinion. I do not agree with the Court's suggestion, in *dicta,* that the right to procreate may depend on adoption as a consideration.

I also write to express my view that the same principles that compel the outcome in this case would permit an infertile party to assert his or her right to use a preembryo against the objections of the other party, if such use were the only means of procreation. In that instance, the balance arguably would weigh in favor of the infertile party absent countervailing factors of greater weight. I do not decide that profound question today, and the Court should not decide it or suggest a result, because it is absent from this case.

[Ed. Note: Justice Zazzali's concurring opinion is omitted.]

Notes and Questions

1. *Comparisons.* Compare and contrast the approaches in *Nahmani* and *J.B. v. M.B.* How would the American case come out under the reasoning in *Nahmani* and how would the Israeli case come out under the reasoning in *J.B. v. M.B.*? What are the significant factors in each case that lead the courts to formulate the rules they do? What similarities and differences emerge from these cases?

2. *Degree of Infringement.* Both the Israeli and New Jersey supreme courts emphasize the degree of infringement that each party's position would impose on the other party. Underlying the analysis is an assumption about what right is being infringed. Can you articulate each litigant's position in a way so that the right infringed is more or less than the courts imagine?

3. *Woman's Contribution?* The retrieval of an egg for the purpose of in vitro fertilization is more invasive than the collection of semen. Does this give the woman greater rights than the man in either *Nahmani* or *J.B. v. M.B.*? Should it? In Hungary, a statute recognizes the differences in the contribution made, and gives widows and divorced women the right to continue with the assisted procreation. *See, e.g.,* Judit Sándor, *The Hungarian Legislative Approach to Assisted Procreation: An Attempt at Transparency?, in* Assisted Conception: Research, Ethics and Law 142–43 (Jennifer Gunning ed., 2000). The couple can *opt out* of this legal framework at the outset of treatment with a joint writing. *Id.*

4. *Status of the Embryo.* In *Nahmani* and *J.B. v. M.B.*, how is the embryo viewed? Consider for a moment some of the laws regulating IVF in France. In France, a couple can only donate an embryo to another couple with the consent of a judge. "The intent of Parliament was to create a procedure close to adoption." *See* Pascal Kamina, *Legal Approaches: France, in* Assisted Conception, Research, Ethics and Law 107, 111 (Jennifer Gunning ed., 2000). The law also provides that the embryo is to be stored for five years, but it does not specify what is to happen to it after that time. *Id.* at 110. The Conseil d'Etat has proposed that embryos be destroyed after the five year period if the couple does not want them or if the couple does not specify that they should be donated to another couple or to research. *Id.* at 115. The view embodied within France's system "is emerging as a worldwide majority consensus." Elizabeth Ann Pitrolo, *The*

Birds, the Bees and the Deep Freeze: Is There International Consensus in the Debate Over Assisted Reproductive Technologies?, 19 Hous. J. Int'l L. 147, 201 (1996). What is that view? If a couple can elect to destroy the embryo without court intervention, why require the couple to obtain court consent before they can donate the embryo to another couple?

5. *European Union Law: Frozen Embryos, Time Limits, and Informed Consent.* Use of reproductive technology is subject to European Union law to the extent that access to the technology falls within either the free movement of persons, goods, capital or services. *See, e.g.,* R v. Human Fertilisation and Embryology Authority, *ex parte* Blood, 2 All E.R. 687 (Eng. C.A. 1997). The Charter of Fundamental Rights of the European Union also has provisions that address the use of reproductive technology. In particular, article 3, on the Right to the Integrity of the Person, states that "Everyone has the right to respect for his or her physical and mental integrity." Charter of Fundamental Rights of the European Union, 2000 O.J. (C 364) 1, 9. It continues, "In the fields of medicine and biology, the following must be respected in particular: The free and informed consent of the person concerned, according to the procedures laid down by law...." *Id.* Would such a provision have had an impact on the outcome of either *Nahmani* or *J.B. v. M.B.*, assuming this provision existed in Israel and New Jersey?

The Council of Europe has also taken positions on IVF. For example, in 1989, the European Parliament issued its Resolution on Artificial Insemination 'In Vivo' and 'In Vitro.' This resolution stated, in part, that embryos should be frozen only when "the woman's state of health temporarily prevents her from having the embryo implanted." If implantation is out of the question because of refusal, illness or death of the woman, the embryos should be taken out of storage and allowed to die. Resolution on Artificial Insemination "In Vivo" and "In Vitro," 1989 O.J. (C 96) 171, 172. It also stated that cryopreservation should occur for a maximum of three years. *Id.* In 2000, the European Parliament, in a resolution on human cloning, "renews its call for human artificial insemination techniques that do not produce an excess number of embryos in order to avoid generating superfluous embryos." Resolution on Human Cloning, 2000 O.J. (C 135) 263, 264. Does a time-limit for storage minimize the problems that sometimes arise in these cases? How?

6. *Infertility in Jewish Tradition.* Apart from the importance of reproduction in the Jewish tradition, there is also a recognition of the problem of infertility. "[M]any of the most prominent people in the Bible had trouble procreating. Sarah could not conceive. Rebekah had trouble but ultimately bore twins. Rachel was so jealous of the ability of her sister, Leah, to bear children that she asked Jacob to have sex with her handmaid so that, through the handmaid, some children could at least indirectly be attributed to Rachel. Ultimately, Rachel herself bore Joseph and Benjamin, dying during the second delivery. Later, Hannah had trouble but ultimately delivered the prophet, Samuel. These problems of infertility, then, are nothing new to the tradition." Elliot Dorff, *A Jewish Approach to Assisted Reproductive Technologies*, 21 Whittier L. Rev. 391, 392 (1999).

---

c. Catholicism

The debate about IVF and its regulation often includes, at least in part, religious views. In countries that apply religious law, the connection is explicit. In Israel, the influence of Judaism is clear. IVF is permitted and, in fact, welcomed as a method to help Jewish couples fulfill a *Mitzvah*. In addition, Jewish law influenced the outcome of the Nahmani dispute. Jewish law has a recognized status in Israel. The Foundations of Law Act § 1 (1980) states, "Where a court finds that a legal issue requiring decision cannot be resolved by reference to legislation or judicial precedent, or by means of analogy, it shall reach its decision in the light of the principles of freedom, justice, equity, and peace of the Jewish heritage (*moreshet Yisra'el*)." *See* 4 Justice Menachem Elon, Jewish Law: History, Sources, Principles 1828 (Bernard Auerbach & Melvin J. Kykes trans., 1st Eng. ed., The Jewish Publication Society 1994) (1988). Even in countries with a strong tradition of the separation of church and state, religious views cannot be excluded from the dialogue, nor should they be. These views contribute to the debate. For example, the Ethics Committee of the American Fertility Society published a document responding to the Roman Catholic *The Instruction on Respect for Human Life in its Origin and on the Dignity of Procreation* (1987). *See* Ethics Committee of the American Fertility Society, *Ethical Considerations of the New Reproductive Technologies,* 53 Fertil. Steril. 6 (Supp. 2 1990). It is helpful, therefore, to understand those views in order to assess religion's influence in this area. In particular, we examine Catholicism, which voices the strongest opposition to IVF.

Symposium on Religious Law: Roman Catholic, Islamic, and Jewish Treatment of Familial Issues, Including Education, Abortion, In Vitro Fertilization, Prenuptial Agreements, Contraception, and Marital Fraud
19 Loy. L.A. Int'l & Comp. L. Rev. 9, 46–51 (1993)

In Vitro Fertilization — Fact Pattern

In their six years of marriage, Diane and George have been unsuccessful in starting a family. After a series of medical examinations, the couple discover that Diane has blocked fallopian tubes. Although ovulation takes place, the eggs are unable to move to the uterus. The condition cannot be corrected by surgery.

Diane and George find that their sole means of having a child of their own is to submit to in vitro fertilization. This is accomplished by George masturbating and ejaculating into a specimen jar. Diane's ova will be surgically removed from her ovaries. Later, the doctors will introduce the ova to the sperm in order to produce several embryos. Five live embryos are produced, which is more than necessary, in order to avoid the repetition of the procedures required to obtain ova and sperm specimens. It usually takes several attempts at implantation to impregnate the woman successfully. After successful implantation occurs, the remaining embryos are usually destroyed. Before submitting to this process, Diane and George come to you and seek your legal advice. What do you advise?

You never hear from Diane and George again, until you find out that they are currently battling each other in court. You learn that the couple is now divorced and Diane has claimed custody of the embryos. She wishes to have them implanted in her womb and hopes to give birth to children out of wedlock. If successful, Diane expects child support for these children from George. George, therefore, has brought this suit to either win custody of the embryos in order to have them destroyed or, failing that, to enjoin her from implantation. Should either option fail, he wants the court to find that he is not obligated in any way to provide support for the children that may result from Diane's unilateral action of implantation. What do you advise?

A. Roman Catholic Response (by Russell E. Smith, S.T.D.)

1. The Ethical Questions...

This Essay develops six ethical issues: (1) the ethical propriety of in vitro fertilization ("IVF") itself; (2) the concomitant issue of masturbation to obtain the husband's semen; (3) the retrieval of multiple in vitro conceptions of embryos; (4) the associated issue of freezing/storing excess embryos; (5) the destruction of unwanted embryos; and (6) the issues of custody, possession, parental obligation, survival, and destruction of frozen embryos in the event of divorce....

2. The Church's Teaching

The Catholic Church's long-standing teaching on the moral issues involved in this case has been rearticulated most recently in two magisterial documents: *The Declaration on Procured Abortion* and *The Instruction on Respect for Human Life in its Origin and on the Dignity of Procreation*, both from the Congregation for the Doctrine of the Faith. The content of the former is summarized in its own words: "The tradition of the Church has always held that human life must be protected and cherished from the beginning, just as at the various stages of its development.... [P]rocured abortion, even during the first days, [is] objectively a grave sin." This echoes the teaching of the Church's supreme magisterium, the Second Vatican Ecumenical Council, that "abortion and infanticide are abominable crimes (*nefanda crimina*)."

The Instruction provides a more expansive treatment of the issues involved in this case. The two phrases of its long title are the two principles by which certain questions of contemporary medical technology should be evaluated.

The Instruction highlights two foundational values: (1) human life itself; and (2) the means of transmitting human life....

Concerning the second value regarding the transmission of human life, the Church teaches that the covenant of heterosexual marriage is the only appropriate forum for sexual expression. It also holds that the loving union of the spouses and the "begetting of offspring" are the two essential purposes of marriage, expressed most dramatically in the conjugal act.

Two general moral implications follow from this. First, the foundational value of human life derives from the fact that there is no way to make a credible distinction between a human being and a human person; critics have severely criticized any attempt to do so. Second, the foundational value of the transmission of human life also carries a moral implication, namely, that one cannot deliberately separate the two meanings of the conjugal act without embracing (at least implicitly) in a utilitarian manner a philosophical dualism that renders the physical nature subordinate to the spiritual nature. This is the rational basis for the Catholic doctrine forbidding contraception.

The moral implications that apply in the area of suppressing fertility apply also in the area of achieving fertility. Paradoxically, the same mentality that champions contraception and abortion also supports fertility technology, as the same technological ideology presents both sets of possibilities. This ideology depersonalizes some patient populations, such as fetuses and the permanently unconscious, and then proceeds to depersonalize integral features of a patient's humanity. It is a depersonalization that claims dominion not just over pathology, but also over the "new medical commodities" of life and death. This ideology implies that we have a right to someone's death by abortion or physician-assisted suicide, as well as a right to someone else's life. The ideology is presupposed, explicitly or implicitly, by the technological imperative that states that we should do all that we are technologically capable of doing.... Science without moral reflection...is catastrophic.

These two perennial values and their moral implications, versus the dualism implied by technological culture, form the matrix in which the painful situation of infertility is examined. The basic conclusion of *The Instruction* is best summarized as follows: Whereas assisted insemination can be morally licit because it is essentially a therapeutic intervention, an act of technology cannot replace the conjugal act.

The Instruction then states the following regarding the arena of fertility intervention:

First, concerning fetal life and its dignity: (1) Fetal human life is inviolable. The pursuit of offspring cannot include an intention to terminate their life, such as if there is a defect or disease. Procured abortion terminates innocent, personal human life. Concretely, diagnosis of disease should not be tantamount to a death sentence. There should be no discarding of embryos once conceived.

(2) The dignity of fetal human life precludes freezing the embryo as well as non-therapeutic experimentation.

(3) The Church teaches that the unborn child has a right to be procreated, born and raised in a family composed of his/her parents. It is in the family that the child can discover his/her own identity and achieve his/her own proper human development.

(4) Fertility intervention, which replaces the conjugal act rather than therapeutically assisting it, offends the dignity of the offspring by treating a human person as a "product" of technology, rather than as an "offspring" of one's parent's conjugal act.

There is a world of difference between "reproducing" and "procreating." Making human persons a product of technological industry presumes that human life is a commodity about which "clients" may be selective. It emerges from a worldview in which life itself can be manufactured, marketed, and distributed with concern for the buyer, not the object. The Church teaches that, while the personal dignity and inherent worth of an individual are not cheapened or compromised by the way they are conceived, nevertheless, a petri dish is not a worthy site of creation.

Four issues exist concerning the worthy transmission of life (the second perennial value). First, procreation should take place only within marriage. This precludes all practices of heterologous fertilization, including all techniques that "obtain a human conception artificially by the use of gametes coming from at least one donor other than the spouses who are joined in marriage." These procedures include artificial insemination by a donor ("AID"), heterologous in vitro fertilization, and surrogate motherhood.

Second, the unitive and procreative aspects of the conjugal act are inseparable. Just as one cannot suppress the procreative aspect of the conjugal act by contraception, one also cannot suppress the unitive meaning of the marital goods in pursuit of the procreative by artificial fertility interventions. Consequently, all forms of homologous artificial fertilization are precluded. For example, artificial insemination by the husband ("AIH") and homologous in vitro fertilization are prohibited. Additionally, masturbation severs the two integral meanings of the conjugal act by depriving it of its unitive dimension.

Third, *The Instruction* analyzes the question of suffering caused by infertility in marriage. The Church teaches that "the suffering of spouses who cannot have children or who are afraid of bringing a handicapped child into the world is a suffering that everyone must understand and properly evaluate." The desire for a child is integral to the vocation to parenthood, which is inherent in conjugal love. Suffering is particularly acute, therefore, for those couples whose infertility appears to be incurable. Yet, in spite of what we have said so far, it is still true that the end does not justify the means....

On this score, *The Instruction* states:

[M]arriage does not confer upon the spouses the right to have a child.... A true and proper right to a child would be contrary to the child's dignity and nature. The child is not an object to which one has a right, nor can [s/he] be considered as an object of ownership; rather, a child is a gift (the supreme gift) and the most gratuitous gift of marriage, and is a living testimony of the mutual giving of...parents.

In other words, no one has a right to another person....

Notes and Questions

1. *Diane and George.* Analyze the problem of Diane and George in terms of Catholic law and Israeli law. How would the hypothetical be answered under each? The *Nahmani* case may help you arrive at a conclusion about the permissibility of the procedure and who would receive the embryos. *Nahmani* should at least suggest a series of questions that you would want to ask Diane and George.

2. *Catholicism.* The Church rarely permits the use of assisted reproductive technology. However, the Church does accept the use of Gamete Intrafallopian Transfer (GIFT). This technique places the mother's own egg and the father's sperm simultaneously into the mother's fallopian tubes through laparoscopy, thereby permitting insemination to occur in vivo. However, this technique is only approved "if sperm is collected in a perforated sheath during intercourse so that neither contraception nor masturbation occurs." Pitrolo, *supra*, at 198.

3. *Comparing Catholicism and Judaism.* What factors can explain the differences between the approaches of Judaism and Catholicism to IVF?

Sex as Reproduction. Although reproduction is highly valued in the Jewish tradition, one author explains that "sexual relations are not only for reproductive purposes. The Torah thus assumes that women have a right to sex in marriage just as men do, and that the purpose of sex within marriage is in part for the mutual pleasure and bonding of the couple, quite apart from reproduction. [W]ithin the Jewish tradition, sexuality is seen both for reproduction and for the couple's mutual bonding and pleasure. Accordingly, when it comes to issues of infertility, the Jewish tradition, on the one hand, wants to tell couples that having children is not the sum and substance of human life or even of sexual experience. Human beings primarily gain value not from anything they do, but from who they are—creatures of God created in the Divine image. At the same time, given the Jewish tradition's strongly positive attitude toward procreation and children, it seeks to be as supportive as possible to those couples who are trying to reproduce." Elliot Dorff, *A Jewish Approach to Assisted Reproductive Technologies*, 21 Whittier L. Rev. 391, 392 (1999). How does this view differ from the Catholic tradition?

Medical Technology and Reproduction. "Unlike the Catholic tradition, which is very heavily rooted in ancient and medieval natural law theories, including Aquinas, the Jewish tradition never saw the difference between natural and artificial means to advance medical goals as being germane. Human beings have been given the ability by God to respond to a variety of different incapacities, medical and otherwise. Moreover, the Jewish tradition teaches that human beings have been given the divine mandate to use their abilities toward good purposes to fix the world. Therefore, Judaism teaches us that we are really fulfilling our role as partners with God when we intervene in a natural process to overcome the various frustrations and limitations of life. Consequently, from a Jewish perspective, the natural/artificial division simply does not matter, and Jews are perfectly willing to use artificial means to try to overcome infertility." Dorff, *supra*, at 393.

Permissibility of Abortion. The Catholic Church believes that human life begins at conception and that abortion is a grave sin. In contrast, Judaism does not consider the fetus to be a human being, but rather part of the woman's body. This is true throughout the pregnancy, until the child's head emerges from the woman's vagina. In fact, before the 40th day after conception (quickening), the fetus is only "like water." The moral status of the fetus develops as the fetus develops physiologically, and at quickening the decision to abort takes on more moral significance. As one may not generally harm their body, Judaism also generally forbids abortion. However, abortion is mandatory if a pregnancy endangers a woman's life or health, including mental health, since a woman receives all the protection of Jewish law as a human being. "When there is an elevated risk to the woman beyond that of normal pregnancy, but insufficient risk to constitute a clear threat to her life or health, abortion is permitted, but it is not required." *See* Elliot N. Dorff, *Testimony, in* Nat'l Bioethics Advisory Comm., II Ethical Issues in Hum. Stem Cell Research C-3, 4 (2000). *See generally* Laurie Zoloth, *Testimony, in* Nat'l Bioethics Advisory Comm., II Ethical Issues in Hum. Stem Cell Research J (2000).

Incest. In Judaism, sexual relationships between half-siblings are considered incestuous only if the half-siblings have a common mother or a common Jewish father. If they only have a common non-Jewish father, their relationship is not incestuous regardless of the mother's religion. Therefore, religious Jewish couples using AID are sometimes counseled to seek a non-Jewish sperm donor. *See generally* Richard V. Grazi & Joel B. Wolowelsky, *Donor Gametes for Assisted Reproduction in Contemporary Jewish Law & Ethics*, 2 Assisted Reproduction Reviews 3 (1992), *available at* http://www.daat.ac.il/daat/english/ethic/donor-1.htm. In contrast, in Catholicism, all half-sibling relationships are incestuous. *See* Catholic Encyclopedia, Consanguinity (In Canon Law), *available at* http://www.newadvent.org/cathen/04264a.htm (last visited Aug. 21, 2002). Consequently, using sperm from an anonymous donor is problematic, among other reasons, because the woman's child might grow up and unknowingly marry his or her half-sibling.

4. *Comparing Islamic Law.* In Islamic law, "Treatment of infertility is allowed and recommended, provided it is performed by honest and experienced specialists. Islam allows in vivo insemination of a wife's egg with the semen of the husband. Artificial insemination using donor or mixed sperm is forbidden because it destroys the lineage in a family. Sperm banks are also against the purpose of lawful family formations in Islam and so they are forbidden. Muheenat I. Foresyth & Fatimah Biade Abdulkareem, Reproductive Health Within the Context of Islam 128, 140 (Lai Olurode ed., 2000) (quoting Sheik Jadel Hag, the Mufti of Egypt). Neither the Qur'an nor Sunna provide a clear directive on abortion, and juristic rulings on abortion differ between the legal schools. *See* Najma Moosa, *A Descriptive Analysis of South African and Is-*

lamic Abortion Legislation and Local Muslim Community Responses, 21 Med. & L. 257, 268 (2002). However, "the most widely accepted juristic ruling on abortion is that it is generally prohibited. Ensoulment, according to inferences from these sources, occurs only after 120 days after which the fetus is considered as being 'alive.' There are exceptions to the rule in that abortion is allowed up to 120 days after conception for valid reasons and even thereafter when the continuation of the pregnancy endangers the mother's life." *Id.* at 271. "Any excess number of pre-embryos can be preserved. The frozen pre-embryos are the property of the couple alone and may be transferred to the wife during the validity of the marriage contract." Gamal I. Serour, Reproductive Choice: A Muslim Perspective, in The Future of Human Reproduction: Ethics, Choice and Regulation 191, 197 (John Harris & Soren Holm eds., 1998). Egg donation is not permitted. *See generally* Ibrahim B. Hewitt, What Does Islam Say? 52–54 (1997).

5. *International Law.* Does international law require that states tolerate the use of reproductive technology like IVF? Is there an affirmative obligation to make such technology available to individuals who seek to use it? For example, the International Covenant on Economic, Social and Cultural Rights (ICESCR) contains article 12(1), in which States Parties recognize the "right of everyone to the enjoyment of the highest attainable standard of physical and mental health," and article 15(1)(b), which gives everyone the right "to enjoy the benefits of scientific progress and its applications." Similarly, the Universal Declaration of Human Rights, article 25(1), recognizes a right to an adequate standard of living, including medical care, and article 27(1), recognizes everyone's right to "share in scientific advancement and its benefits." The Committee on the Elimination of Discrimination against Women "asks about the State Party's approach to, and regulation of, new technologies with regard to human reproduction." *Report of the Committee on Progress Achieved in the Implementation of the Convention,* CEDAW, 14th Sess., ¶ 434, U.N. Doc. CEDAW/C/1995/7. Why would it do that?

3. Surrogacy

For a brief overview of the situation in the United States regarding surrogacy, legal and factual, consider the following:

Lori B. Andrews, *Reproductive Technology Comes of Age*
21 Whittier L. Rev. 375, 379–81 (1999)

In recent years, at least twenty-three states have adopted surrogacy laws. But these laws are not as facilitative of the arrangement as the earlier statutes were of donor insemination. Most of the surrogacy statutes refuse to honor paid surrogate mother contracts. The statutes differ, however, in how they tip the balance in the event of a dispute over custody. The Michigan and Washington laws embody a classic family law approach, making a determination in individual cases based on the child's best interest. New Hampshire and Virginia (as well as Florida for traditional surrogacy) have a presumption that the contracting couple are the legal parents, but give the surrogate a certain time period during which to change her mind. In contrast, in Arizona, North Dakota, and Utah, the surrogate and her husband are the child's legal parents.

The District of Columbia and Arizona ban surrogacy contracts. Eight more states—Florida, Michigan, Nevada, New Hampshire, New York, Virginia, Washington, and West Virginia—ostensibly ban payments to surrogates, but these laws contain wide exceptions that allow surrogates' expenses to be paid. Ten jurisdictions address the role of the intermediary—prohibiting compensation for bringing together couples and surrogates or otherwise facilitating these arrangements.

Virginia and New Hampshire provide an extensive regulatory structure for unpaid surrogacy contracts, which includes medical and psychological screening and a requirement that the contract be submitted to a judge for approval in advance of the pregnancy. In addition, under these laws there must be a home study of the intended parents, as well as of the surrogate and her husband, to determine all four parties' suitability for parenthood.

———————

The variety of approaches in the United States is mirrored internationally. "Acceptance of the practice of surrogate mothers varies throughout the world, and the frequency with which it occurs differs substantially. The practice seems to be more readily accepted in North America than in western and central Europe." *See* Jiří F. Haderka, *Affiliation and Bioethics, in* Legal Problems Relating to Parentage: Proceedings 27th Colloquy on European Law, part VIII.2 (1997). Not only does the law differ between countries, but it also can differ within a country. *See, e.g.,* Loane Skene, *An Overview of Assisted Reproductive Technology Regulation in Australia and New Zealand,* 35 Tex. Int'l L.J. 31, 31–32 (2000); Angie Godwin McEwen, Note, *So You're Having Another Woman's Baby: Economics and Exploitation in Gestational Surrogacy,* 32 Vand. J. Transnat'l L. 271, 285–86 (1999); Lisa L. Behm, *Legal, Moral and International Perspectives on Surrogate Motherhood: The Call for a Uniform Regulatory Scheme in the United States,* 2 DePaul J. Health Care L. 557, 593–94 (1999).

We will focus on two countries whose responses to surrogacy have been deliberate, yet different: England and Israel. In England, a comprehensive policy for surrogacy has existed since approximately 1985 when the Surrogacy Arrangements Act, 1985, c. 49 (Eng.) was adopted; in Israel, a policy has existed since approximately 1996. As you read the following materials, you will notice that neither country outlaws surrogacy contracts. Try to assess whether there are any other similarities in these countries' approaches. Also, try to evaluate whether some of the differences converge when each country's entire framework for surrogacy is considered.

a. *United Kingdom*

Briody v. St. Helen's & Knowsley Area Health Authority

E.W.C.A. Civ. 1010 (Eng. C.A. 2001)

[Ed. Note: This malpractice action was brought by a childless woman against her doctor for the doctor's negligence in delivering her child. The doctor's actions caused her child's death and the removal of the plaintiff's uterus. The action, brought many years later, included a claim for the costs of surrogacy. The plaintiff prevailed at trial on the issue of liability. Although she was awarded a substantial sum to compensate for her infertility, she was not awarded the costs of surrogacy treatment. The treatment would have involved the use of her own eggs, and if that failed, then donor eggs. The trial judge rejected this element of damages stating that the commercial surrogacy agreement with a California surrogate, governed by California law, would not be possible in England: "On any view of our law the Claimant seeks an award of damages to acquire a child by methods which do not comply with that law; that seems to me to be wrong.... It is one thing for a court retrospectively to sanction breaches of statute in the paramount interests of an existing child, it is quite another to award damages to enable such an unenforceable and unlawful contract to be entered into."

On appeal, the plaintiff said that she now intended to enter a surrogacy arrangement in compliance with English law. The Court of Appeals, however, affirmed the trial court, resting its decision on the law of damages and civil procedure. Because of the manner in which the appellate court decided the case, it did not need to address whether the plaintiff's proposal to enter into a surrogacy agreement in compliance with English law violated public policy. However, Lady Justice Hale did note that since the new proposed surrogacy agreement would comply with English law, the proposed course of action itself was not contrary to public policy. In this context, the judge explained the law of surrogacy in England.]

Hale, L.J.

10. English law on surrogacy is quite clear:

a) Surrogacy arrangements are not unlawful, nor is the payment of money to a surrogate mother in return for her agreeing to carry and hand over the child.

b) The activities of commercial surrogacy agencies are unlawful. It is an offence for any person to take part in negotiating surrogacy arrangements on a commercial basis, i.e. for payment to himself or another (apart from the surrogate mother); for a body of persons negotiating surrogacy arrangements to receive payment from either the proposed surrogate mother or the commissioning parents; or for a person to take part in the management or control of a body of persons which negotiates or facilitates surrogacy arrangements: Surrogacy Arrangements Act 1985, s. 2.

c) It is also a crime to advertise either for surrogate mothers or a willingness to enter into or make surrogacy arrangements: Surrogacy Arrangements Act 1985, s. 3.

d) The surrogate mother is always the child's legal mother, irrespective of whose eggs were used: Human Fertilisation and Embryology Act 1990, s. 27(1).

e) If the commissioning father supplied the sperm, he will be the child's legal father, unless section 28 of the Human Fertilisation and Embryology Act 1990 applies so as to make someone else the father. It should be possible, by treating him and the surrogate together, to avoid the exclusion from fatherhood of ordinary sperm donors: *see* 1990 Act, s. 28(6)(a) and Sched 3, para. 5.

f) If the child is born by IVF (in vitro fertilization), GIFT (gamete intra-fallopian transfer) or artificial (but not natural) insemination to a married surrogate mother, her husband will be the legal father unless it is shown that he did not consent to the treatment: Human Fertilisation and Embryology Act 1990, s. 28(2). If the treatment was given "...in the course of treatment services provided for her and a man together" by a licensed clinic, her partner will be the father: 1990 Act, s. 28(3). But this can easily be avoided by her partner taking no part in the treatment.

g) No surrogacy arrangement is enforceable by or against any of the persons making it: Surrogacy Arrangements Act 1985, s. 1A (*see also* Children Act 1989, s. 2(9), reflecting the common law).

h) The future of any child born, if disputed, will always be governed by the paramount consideration of the welfare of the child: Children Act 1989, s. 1(1). It is unlikely, although not impossible, that a court would decide that the child should go to the commissioning parents rather than stay with a mother who had changed her mind: see A v C [1985] FLR 445; Re P (Minors)(Wardship: Surrogacy) [1987] 2 FLR 421. If the mother does not want the child and the commissioning parents are able to offer a suitable home, the court is likely to allow them to do so: *see* Re C (A Minor)(Wardship: Surrogacy) [1985] FLR 846.

i) If the child is handed over in accordance with the arrangement, the court may be prepared retrospectively to authorize, under s. 57(3) of the Adoption Act 1976, any payment made to the surrogate mother and grant an adoption order which would otherwise be prohibited by s. 24(2) of the 1976 Act: *see* Re Adoption Application (Payment for Adoption) [1987] Fam 81.

j) There is now a special procedure, similar to adoption, whereby the commissioning parents may become the child's legal parents: they must be married to one another, the child must be born as result of IVF, GIFT or artificial (again not natural) insemination using the gametes of one or both of them, the child must be living with them, the surrogate mother (and any father of the child who is not the commissioning father) must agree, and no payment must have been made unless authorized by the court: Human Fertilisation and Embryology Act 1990, s. 30; *see* Re Q (Parental Order) [1996] 1 FLR 369.

k) If a surrogacy arrangement involves treatment in a clinic licensed by the Human Fertilisation and Embryology Authority (which will be the case in this country unless natural or private artificial insemination is used), this must not be provided "unless account has been taken of the welfare of any child who may be born as a result of the treatment (including the need of that child for a father), and of any other child who may be affected by the birth": Human Fertilisation and Embryology Act 1990, s. 13(5).

l) Clinics must observe the Code of Practice promulgated by the Human Fertilisation and Embryology Authority (*see* 4th ed., 1998). This provides that "The application of assisted conception techniques to initiate a surrogate pregnancy should only be considered where it is physically impossible or highly undesirable for medical reasons for the commissioning mother to carry the child" (para. 3.20).

It also gives guidance on the factors to be considered when taking account of the child's welfare (para. 3.17); and points out that in a surrogacy arrangement either the surrogate (and her husband or partner if any) or the commissioning parents may become the child's parents and so both should be assessed, along with any risk of disruption should there be a dispute, and the effect on any other children in either the surrogate's or the commissioning parents' family (para. 3.19.b).

11. These provisions do not indicate that surrogacy as such is contrary to public policy. They tend to indicate that the issue is a difficult one, upon which opinions are divided, so that it would be wise to tread with caution. This is borne out in the official publications which have considered the matter. If there is a trend, it is towards acceptance and regulation as a last resort rather than towards prohibition.

Lady Justice Hale reported that England has come quite far since the Warnock Report was issued in 1984, a report of the Committee of Inquiry into Human Fertilisation and Embryology established by the Parliament. "The 'moral and social objections to surrogacy' weighed heavily with the majority of the Warnock Committee." *Id.* ¶ 12 (citing *Report of the Committee of Inquiry into Human Fertilisation and Embryology*, 1984, Cmnd. 9314, ch. 8). The Warnock Committee, for example, had "recommended criminal liability 'for professionals and others who knowingly assist in the establishment of a surrogate pregnancy.'" *Id.* This last provision was never adopted; rather the Surrogacy Arrangements Act of 1985 took a "minimalist course." *Id.* Then, by enacting the Human Fertilisation and Embryology Act of 1990, Parliament made the atmosphere even more permissive. Special provision was made for commissioning parents to become legal parents. *See* Human Fertilisation and Embryology Act, 1990, c. 37, § 30.

In 1997, the Health Ministers asked Professor Brazier and others to review the law. They found "that incomplete implementation of the recommendations of either the majority or the minority of the Warnock Committee created a policy vacuum within which surrogacy has developed in a haphazard fashion." Report of the Review Team, *Surrogacy—Review for Health Ministers of Current Arrangements for Payments and Regulations*, Executive Summ. ¶ 3 (1998). "They recommended further regulation, through the registration of non-profit-making agencies, who would have to abide by a Code of Practice, the continued banning of commercial agencies, statutory limitations so that surrogate mothers could only be paid genuine expenses, and the tightening of the section 30 process, with no power retrospectively to authorize illegal payments. These recommendations have not, as yet, been implemented." Briody v. St. Helen's & Knowsley Area Health Auth., *supra*, ¶ 13 (Hale, L.J.). Her Ladyship concluded: "Thus, while there is general agreement that commercial agencies and advertising should be banned, that surrogacy for convenience or social rather than medical reasons is unacceptable, and that the agreement should be unenforceable, there is little discernible consensus on anything else." *Id.* ¶ 14. Although these points of agreement undergird the United Kingdom's legislation, consider how the last one plays out in a litigated dispute between parties to a surrogacy contract when the surrogate mother tries to maintain custody of the child. The following case arose in Scotland, which at the relevant time was also governed by the Human Fertilisation and Embryology Act, 1990.

C v. S

S.L.T. 1387 (Scot. Sess. 1996)

Hope, L. President.

The child who is the subject of these proceedings for adoption was born to the respondent GS as a result of a surrogacy arrangement which she entered into with the petitioners Mr. and Mrs. C. The child was born on 30 March 1995.... Later that day Mr. and Mrs. C took possession of the child and returned with him to their home in Dunfermline. He has remained in their care there ever since. In August 1995, Mr. and Mrs. C lodged a petition for his adoption, to which his mother GS has withheld her agreement.

On 28 February 1996, the sheriff, after a proof, held in terms of § 16(2)(b) of the Adoption (Scotland) Act 1978 that GS was withholding her agreement unreasonably, and that her agreement to the making of the adoption order should on this ground be dispensed with under § 16(1)(b)(ii) of that Act. But he also held that Mr. and Mrs. C had contravened § 51(1)(c) of the 1978 Act* and § 30(7) of the Human Fertilisation and

---

* Ed. Note: Section 51 of the Adoption (Scotland) Act 1978 states:
    (1) Subject to the provisions of this section, it shall not be lawful to make or give to any person any payment or reward for or in consideration of—(a) the adoption by that per-

Embryology Act 1990** because they had made to GS a payment amounting to £8,000. So he refused to make an adoption order in relation to the child. In order however to safeguard and promote the welfare of the child throughout his childhood, he found Mr. and Mrs. C entitled to the child's custody in terms of §53(1)(b) of the Children Act 1975,*** and he refused to allow GS access to the child. GS has now appealed against his interlocutor. She wishes to retain her parental rights to the child, and her position is that the sheriff should have dismissed the petition by Mr. and Mrs. C for the child's adoption. Mr. and Mrs. C have also appealed against the interlocutor. Their position is that the sheriff should have granted an adoption order.

[Ed. Note: There were various issues raised on appeal and cross-appeal. This excerpt focuses primarily on the last issue raised by the parents: "They submit that the sheriff ought to have held that any objection on grounds of public policy which resulted from the making of the payment was outweighed by the need to safeguard and promote the welfare of the child throughout his childhood, and that he should have granted an adoption order so as to vest in Mr. and Mrs. C the parental rights and duties relating to the child and thus bring to an end the child's relationship with GS." Before turning to that issue, it is important to note that the Court of Sessions did find that the birth mother's consent to the adoption was unreasonably withheld. The Lord President stated:

---

son of a child; (b) the grant by that person of any agreement or consent required in connection with the adoption of a child; (c) the transfer by that person of the care and possession of a child with a view to the adoption of the child; or (d) the making by that person of any arrangements for the adoption of a child.

(2) Any person who makes or gives, or agrees or offers to make or give, any payment or reward prohibited by this section, or who receives or agrees to receive or attempts to obtain any such payment or reward, shall be guilty of an offence and liable on summary conviction to imprisonment for a term not exceeding three months or to a fine not exceeding level 5 on the standard scale or to both; and the court may order any child in respect of whom the offence was committed to be removed to a place of safety until he can be restored to his parents or guardian or until other arrangements can be made for him.

(3) This section does not apply to any payment made to an adoption agency by a parent or guardian of a child or by a person who adopts or proposes to adopt a child, being a payment in respect of expenses reasonably incurred by the agency in connection with the adoption of the child, or to any payment or reward authorized by the court to which an application for an adoption order in respect of a child is made.

** Ed. Note: Section 30(7) of the Human Fertilisation and Embryology Act 1990 provides: The court must be satisfied that no money or other benefit (other than for expenses reasonably incurred) has been given or received by the husband or the wife for or in consideration of—(a) the making of the order, (b) any agreement required by subsection (5) above, (c) the handing over of the child to the husband and the wife, or (d) the making of any arrangements with a view to the making of the order, unless authorized by the court.

The "order" referred to in section 30(7)(a) is a "parental order," which is defined in section 30(1) as "an order providing for a child to be treated in law as the child of the parties to a marriage..." Parental orders are regulated by The Parental Orders (Human Fertilisation and Embryology) Regulations, 1994, No. 2767 (2), and The Family Proceedings (Amendment) (No. 2) Rules 1994, No. 2165 (L.13).

*** Ed. Note: The Children Act 1975, section 53, provides:

(1) Without prejudice to the provisions of section 19 (power to make an interim order giving custody), where on an application for an adoption order in respect of a child the court is of opinion...(b)...that the making of a custody order in favour of the applicant would be more appropriate than the making of an adoption order in his favour, the court shall direct that the application is to be treated as if it had been made for custody of the child.

In my opinion the sheriff was entitled to hold that the factors were not equally balanced in regard to the home environment and lifestyle which the parties could provide. While the ability of GS as a mother to her four children is not in doubt, it is a fact that their father does not live with her and that he does not support the family. She is in that sense alone, and she is also on state benefits. Mr. and Mrs. C on the other hand have a secure relationship. Mr. C is employed as a police constable, and his wife is a trained general and psychiatric nurse. There were reasons which the sheriff has described in his note for doubting GS's sense of personal responsibility, due to her past drug taking, her reaction to professional advice and her decision to involve a tabloid newspaper in her desire to recover possession of the child. The sheriff held that she had lied time and time again throughout the surrogacy arrangement, and that she continued to conduct herself in this manner in the witness box. In his opinion her whole approach towards recovering the child was self orientated and she had totally closed her mind as to the effects which this might have on the child. His impression of Mr. and Mrs. C on the other hand, in the light of reports and from hearing and observing them in the witness box, was that they were ideal parents for the child and had been so since taking possession of him shortly after his birth....

Great emphasis was laid by counsel for GS on the circumstances of the child's removal from the hospital, and on what she described as the pressure which had been placed on her while she was carrying the child to implement the surrogacy arrangements which she had entered into.... Counsel said that GS had not been in a position to decide to part with the child voluntarily, because she had been subjected to pressure by Mr. and Mrs. C during her pregnancy by the sending of flowers and other gifts and by other means, all of which were designed to persuade her to deliver the baby to them when born. Immediately after the birth she was too distressed to know what she was doing and any consent which she may have given at that stage should be disregarded.

But in my opinion,... nothing which Mr. and Mrs. C did while acting on that advice [of the surrogacy agency] could be described as devious or putting undue pressure on GS. In the form which she submitted to [Childlessness Overcome Through Surrogacy]* at the outset, GS stated that she had four children of her own and that she did not wish to have any more as she felt that she had a complete family. The sheriff was entitled to hold that the fact that the child has been with Mr. and Mrs. C since birth and is happily living with them as part of their family is the result of decisions which GS took at the very outset of the whole arrangement. There can be no argument about her ability to exercise her judgment freely and with a complete understanding of what she was doing at that stage.

The Court of Sessions also found, however, that the custody order was not proper. Since the sheriff found that he could not make an adoption order because of the payment to GS, even though making the adoption order would be more appropriate than making a custody order, he could not then make a custody order. The custody order was "an unsatisfactory solution" "to safeguard and promote the child's welfare," since GS would have retained various parental responsibilities.]

---

* Ed. Note: Childlessness Overcome Through Surrogacy, or COTS, is an unlicensed agency that facilitates contact between potential surrogates and individuals that want a child.

The Payment to GS

The sheriff's finding...of fact is that at the time of the handing over of the child to them, the intention of Mr. and Mrs. C was either to seek a parental order in terms of the Human Fertilisation and Embryology Act 1990 or to seek to adopt the child. This finding of fact provides the basis for finding...that the payment of £8,000 was an illegal payment in terms of §30(7)(c) of the 1990 Act and §24 and §51(1)(c) of the 1978 Act. The reason which he gives in his findings in fact and law for refusing to make an adoption order in terms of §24(2) of the 1978 Act is that Mr. and Mrs. C had contravened §51(1)(c) of the 1978 Act and §30(7) of the 1990 Act....*

I can find nothing in the 1978 Act to suggest that a person who is unable to obtain a parental order under the 1990 Act [as he has contravened §30(7)(c) of that Act, because money or other benefit, other than for expenses reasonably incurred, has been given... in consideration of the handing over of the child to the husband and the wife], is thereby disabled from obtaining an adoption order in relation to that child. Neither §24(2) nor §51(1) of the 1978 Act makes any reference to §30(7) of the 1990 Act, although that Act amended the 1978 Act in other respects.... In my opinion, it is only if the payment has contravened §51(1), because it was made in one or other of the respects mentioned in that subsection for the adoption of the child, that §24(2) applies and the court is thereby precluded from making an adoption order. The fact that the payment contravened §30(7) of the 1990 Act may give rise to an objection to the making of an adoption order on grounds of public policy. But there is no statutory bar, as the issue is one for the exercise of discretion by the court.

The sheriff says in his note that in his view the payment of £8,000 flew in the face of the surrogacy legislation as well as the adoption legislation, and in particular that it was a clear breach of §51(1)(c). But his finding of fact is equivocal, as [he] states that at the time of the handing over of the child, the intention of Mr. and Mrs. C was either to seek a parental order or to seek to adopt the child.... While both Acts prohibit the making of payments, it does not follow that a payment which was for a purpose which is struck at by one Act is struck at by them both. So it was necessary to examine the evidence with some care in order to identify precisely what Mr. and Mrs. C had in mind when they made the payment. It is unfortunate that the sheriff did not make a clear finding on this point, but as he has not done so it is open to us to review the evidence.

[Ed. Note: The Court then found, after fairly equivocal evidence, that "the evidence of Mr. and Mrs. C read as a whole points clearly to the conclusion that by the time when the payments were made it was a parental order which they had in mind as the means of obtaining parental rights when the child was born."]

For these reasons I do not think that the sheriff had a sound basis in the evidence for his view that the payment was struck at by both Acts. I do not think that it was proved on a balance of probabilities that when Mr. and Mrs. C made the payment of £8,000 they did so, in terms of §51(1)(c) of the 1978 Act, for or in consideration of the transfer by GS of the care and possession of the child with a view to the child's adoption. On

---

* Ed. Note: Section 24(2) provided that the court shall not make an adoption order in relation to a child unless it is satisfied that the applicants have not, as respects the child, contravened §51. After this case was decided, the subsection was amended by the Children (Scotland) Act (1995 c.36), Sch. 2 ¶16. Now the section specifically states, "The court may make an adoption order in relation to a child even where it is found that the applicants have, as respects the child, contravened section 51."

the other hand, I do consider that the sheriff was entitled to hold that the payments were made, in terms of § 30(7)(c) of the 1990 Act, for or in consideration of the handing over of the child to Mr. and Mrs. C. Accordingly I am of opinion that the sheriff misdirected himself when he held that the arrangement was struck at by § 51(1)(c) of the 1978 Act and, as there was a clear breach of that provision, that he was bound to give effect to the prohibition in § 24(2) against the making of an adoption order.

But the fact that the evidence showed that the arrangement was prohibited by § 30(7) of the 1990 Act, unless authorized by the court, raises further issues which need to be examined in view of the objection which has been raised on grounds of public policy. As the present application is for an adoption order and not for a parental order it is not, strictly speaking, necessary for the payment to be authorized under § 30(7) of the 1990 Act. But the provisions of that subsection reflect the objection to trafficking in children which is founded on grounds of public policy. That objection has not been written into the legislation about adoption, but I do not think that the court can ignore it where it forms part of the background. So the question whether or not the payment would be likely to have been authorized is relevant in these proceedings, because a payment which the court would have authorized could not be said to be objectionable on public policy grounds. It is also necessary in these proceedings to have regard to the need to safeguard and promote the welfare of the child throughout his childhood in terms of § 6 of the 1978 Act.* As § 6 of that Act states that first consideration shall be given to the child's welfare, I think that this factor must be taken into account when the court is assessing what weight to attach to an argument based on grounds of public policy.... The degree of blame to be attached to Mr. and Mrs. C for making the payment is relevant at the stage when the court has to decide whether or not to make an adoption order, even if it would not have been authorized under § 30(7).

It seems unlikely that, if matters had proceeded as had been planned by Mr. and Mrs. C, and GS had given her consent to the making of a parental order, any issue would have been raised about the payment of £ 8,000. It was recorded in the relevant form which contained the list of expenses as a payment for loss of earnings and inconvenience. It was the amount which GS had asked for.... The amount had not been volunteered by Mr. and Mrs. C. If the question of authorization had arisen under § 30(7) of the 1990 Act, it could no doubt have been said that Mr. and Mrs. C should have questioned GS about this figure more closely. But they said in their evidence that they took her figure at face value.... The advice which they received from COTS had been that they should expect a figure for loss of earnings of about this amount. There is no indication in the evidence that the sum of £8,000 was intended by Mr. and Mrs. C to be a bribe or a reward for handing over the child to them. In my opinion the failure to challenge the amount proposed by GS could in all the circumstances be regarded as excusable. I do not think that it is obvious that authorization under § 30(7) of the 1990 Act would have been refused if Mr. and Mrs. C had been able to apply for a parental order. But in any event, I do not regard the transaction which they entered into as so offensive as to be open to serious objection on grounds of public policy.

---

* Ed. Note: The Adoption (Scotland) Act 1978 § 6 provides:
In reaching any decision relating to the adoption of a child, a court or adoption agency shall have regard to all the circumstances, first consideration being given to the need to safeguard and promote the welfare of the child throughout his childhood; and shall so far as practicable ascertain the wishes and feelings of the child regarding the decision and give due consideration to them, having regard to his age and understanding....

In Re Adoption Application AA 212/86 (Adoption Payment), Latey J had to consider whether a payment made by a childless couple to a surrogate mother whose child was handed over to them after birth for adoption was struck at by §50(1) of the Adoption Act 1958 and if so whether it should be authorized retrospectively under §50(3) of that Act, the provisions of which were then the equivalents in England of those to be found in §51 of the 1978 Act. He held that, on the facts of that case, there had been no payment or reward within the meaning of §50(1) of the 1958 Act, since the adoption had been contemplated after the payment of the money and the birth of the child. He also held that, even if the payment did fall within the prohibited ambit of the section, the court would exercise its discretion under §50(3) and give retrospective authorization for the payment. With regard to the question of authorization retrospectively, he made this comment on the argument that the payments could not be authorized . . . :

> If that is the correct view the results . . . would be draconian indeed. It would mean, for example, that any payment, however modest and however innocently made, would bar an adoption and do so however much the welfare of the child cried aloud for adoption with all the security and legal rights and status it carried with it: and that, be it said, within the framework of legislation whose first concern is promoting the welfare of the children concerned.
>
> I do not believe that Parliament ever intended to produce such a result (nor, anticipating, has it done so in my judgment). The result it intended to produce is wise and humane. It produced a balance by setting its face against trafficking in children, on the one hand, but recognizing that there may be transactions which are venial and should not prohibit adoption, on the other hand.

In my opinion the approach which Latey J took in that case is closely in point in the present case also. . . .

As the sheriff has held that it would certainly be in the child's best interests for him to be adopted by Mr. and Mrs. C, the appropriate course here is for an adoption order to be made.

[Ed. Note: The opinions of Lord Weir and Lord Allanbridge, both concurring in the opinion by Lord President Hope, are omitted.]

Notes and Questions

1. *Scottish Law.* The Adoption Act, 1978, c. 28, §51 (Scot.) prohibits certain payments in connection with an adoption. England takes the same approach. *See* Adoption Act, 1976, c. 36, §57 (Eng.). Was it likely that the payment here was in violation of the statute? How does the court determine Mr. and Mrs. C's intent? How effective is the court's method for determining whether the statute has been violated?

2. *Parental Order.* Section 30 of the Human Fertilisation and Embryology Act 1990 mentions a "parental order." The parental order is granted by a court for a child who is born as a result of a surrogacy arrangement and who is the genetic child of at least one of the applicants for the parental order. Section 30 provides that a child subject to a parental order is to be treated in law as a child of the parties to the marriage. The Parental Orders (Human Fertilisation and Embryology) Regulations, 1994, No. 2767 (Eng.) employ certain provisions familiar in the adoption context, including that the child's welfare is foremost and must guide the court in its decision whether to grant a parental order. The regulations also establish a Parental Order Register, and indicate how entries are to be made.

3. *Expenses Reasonably Incurred.* Both section 51 of the Adoption (Scotland) Act 1978 and section 30 of the Human Fertilisation and Embryology Act 1990 permit payments if authorized by the court. However, section 30 exempts from prior court approval payments "for expenses reasonably incurred." The contract stated the £8,000 was for "loss of earnings and inconvenience." Mr. and Mrs. C. would have had difficulty establishing that the money was solely for GS's lost earnings since GS was unemployed and on public assistance. 1996 S.L.T. at 1391.

4. *Practical Difficulties.* What should a court do in this type of situation? Would it have been a satisfying solution to refuse to enter an order of adoption? What would you advise a client in the United Kingdom who wanted to enter into a surrogacy agreement with a particular woman, but the woman was insisting upon a payment larger than her actual expenses?

5. *Law Reform in England.* The Health Ministers' recommendations were issued on September 1997 and are forming the basis of a current law reform project. *See* Law Commission, Law Under Review No. 52, No. 52/12 (Winter 2000/2001). Recall that the Health Ministers seek statutory limits so that surrogates are paid only genuine expenses; they also want courts to be stripped of the power to authorize illegal payments retroactively. The reform efforts would not, however, necessarily preclude the granting of an adoption order in circumstances like in *C v. S.* Why not?

6. *Identification of Mother in Europe.* In the late 1970s and early 1980s, Germany introduced the notion of "parallel plurality of mothers," meaning that a child could have both a legally recognized genetic and gestational mother. Now, however, there is uniform agreement in Europe "behind the idea of one mother," and the "one mother" is the person who has given birth. *See* Jiŕi Haderka, *Affiliation and Bioethics, in* Legal Problems Relating to Parentage: Proceedings 27th Colloquy on European Law, part VII (1997). Nonetheless, countries in Europe have adopted "mechanisms which may be described as the renunciation of maternity, or the transfer of maternity to another woman." *Id.* (citing England, the Ukraine, and Russia as having these models). This model is endorsed in the *Draft Report on Principles Concerning the Establishment and Legal Consequences of Parentage* (2000), written by the Committee of Experts on Family Law in the Council of Europe. *See* http://www.legal.coe.int/family/cjfa/GT2Rap7RepFiliationE.pdf. Apparently no European country has accepted the notion that the woman who gives birth is only presumptively the mother, until maternity is rebutted by evidence of biology in another woman. In fact, while the Draft Report permits maternal affiliation to be contested, the *only* ground is that "the woman considered to be the mother was not the one who gave birth to the child." *See Draft Report, supra,* at principle 12(2).

------

b. Israel

David A. Frenkel, *Legal Regulation of Surrogate Motherhood in Israel*
20 Med. & L. 605, 605–09 (2001)

In 1996, the Knesset (the Israeli Parliament) enacted the Agreements to Carry Embryos (Approval of Agreements and Status of the New Born Child) Law, 5756-1996.

The Law deals with gestational surrogacy....

The Law demands, as one of the preconditions to the surrogacy arrangement, a preconception agreement, signed by the "intended parents" and the proposed gestational carrier. Such an agreement needs the approval of an "Approval Committee." The Approval Committee consists of seven members, all appointed by the Minister of Justice, and includes: two physicians holding a specialist qualification in obstetrics and gynecology, a physician holding a specialist qualification in internal medicine, a clinical psychologist, a social worker..., a lawyer...and a clergyman of the religion of the parties concerned.... At least three of each gender should be included in the committee.

The parties to the agreement should be of age and whose domicile is Israel. The gestational carrier should be unmarried. Nonetheless the Approval Committee is authorized to approve an arrangement with a married woman, if the Committee is convinced that the "intended parents" have not been able, after a reasonable effort, to come to an agreement with any unmarried woman who would be ready to become a gestational carrier.

However, the Law forbids any surrogacy arrangement between the "intended parents" and a family member. The definition in the Law of a "family member" for this matter includes "mother, daughter, granddaughter, sister, aunt and cousin" and specifically excludes any such relationship created by adoption. On the other hand, the Law allows and even encourages commercial surrogacy with unrelated women.

The Approval Committee is authorized to approve payments to be made by the "intended parents" to the gestational carrier mother. Such payments may even be made on a monthly basis or in any other way, in order "to cover expenses, including legal expenses and insurance costs, and to compensate for loss of time, loss of income or temporary loss of ability to work, suffering, and any other kind of reasonable compensation."...

The Law permits a person to act as an intermediary and to be paid for acting as such. In a case where a broker has negotiated the arrangement, the parties to the arrangement have to provide the Approval Committee with a copy of their agreement with the broker including his personal details. The broker's fees are left to the decision of the parties to the arrangement and do not need the approval of the Committee....

The Approval Committee receives, in addition to the "preconception agreement," four additional documents:

i) A medical opinion with respect to the incapability of the "intended mother" to physically gestate a pregnancy to term or that gestation will cause a substantive risk to her health;

ii) a medical opinion as to the suitability of all parties concerned to that procedure;

iii) a psychological evaluation regarding the suitability of all parties concerned with the procedure;

iv) a certification of a psychologist or a social worker that the "intended parents" have received suitable professional advice, including on alternative possibilities of parenthood.

The law stipulates that the Committee may approve the agreement, even by a majority, if the Committee is convinced:

i) That all parties consented and entered into the agreement out of free will, after having understood its meaning and results.

ii) That there is no danger to the health of the gestational carrier or to the best interests of the child to be born.

iii) That no stipulations that may harm or deprive the rights of the child to be born or any of the parties are included in the agreement.

The "intended parents" and the gestational carrier are obliged to inform a welfare officer, at the end of five months of pregnancy, of the place and the expected date of birth. They are obliged also to notify the welfare officer of the birth not later than 24 hours after the baby was born. Upon birth, the child is automatically put in the custody of the "intended parents," and the welfare officer is appointed as the child's legal guardian. The gestational carrier mother is obliged to surrender the child to the "intended parents" as soon as possible after birth. The "intended parents" should apply to the Family Court for a "Parenthood Order." The Law stipulates that this should take place no later than seven days after the birth. If the "intended parents" fail to do so, the welfare officer should apply to the Family Court for the "Parenthood Order." The Order is granted automatically unless the court is convinced, after being provided with a written opinion submitted by a welfare officer, that such a "Parenthood Order" is against the best interests of the child. Once a "Parenthood Order" is issued, the "intended parents" become the parents and sole guardians of the child, and the child is considered theirs for all purposes. However, such an Order does not affect any prohibitions and permits found in marriage and divorce laws.

In case a gestational carrier mother withdraws from the agreement and wishes to keep the child, the court may accept her petition only if the court is convinced that circumstances have changed in such a way that justifies the canceling of the agreement and it will not harm the best interests of the child. The court may then issue an order declaring her to be the mother and guardian of the child. The court may give any further orders regarding the status of the child and the relationship with the "intended parents" or with any of the parties. In such a case, the court may order the gestational carrier mother to return expenses to the "intended parents." However, once a "Parenthood Order" is given to the "intended parents," the court is not allowed to approve any withdrawal from the preconception agreement.

"Parenthood Orders" are registered in a special register kept in the Ministry of Justice. The child upon reaching the age of 18 is entitled to inspect the Register and get all details as to the identity of the gestational carrier, and in case she was declared his mother, the identity of the "intended parents." The Register is open also to the registrars of marriages, to the attorney general and to the chief welfare officer.

The Law states also that nothing in this Law derogates from the need to get an informed consent from the gestational carrier for any medical treatment given to her, or to prevent the gestational carrier mother from receiving any medical treatment or to agree to any medical procedure, including termination of pregnancy in accordance with the proper law. All other arrangements of gestational surrogacy are criminal offenses and the Law provides for penalties that include one-year imprisonment and a fine of 20,000 NIS....

Payments for adoption, as well as selling children, are prohibited in Israel.

Notes and Questions

1. *Additional Provisions.* Among other things, the Israeli statute also provides that the gestational mother cannot use her own ova. In addition, the gestational mother and the

intended mother must be of the same religion. In Judaism, a child is considered Jewish if his mother is Jewish. Therefore, certainty about the "mother's" religion is very important.

2. *Surrogacy in Israel.* On February 19, 1998, a pair of twins became the first children born to a surrogate mother under the 1996 Israeli law. Reportedly, the surrogate was a single mother who agreed to the arrangement "mostly out of economic pressures," and she regretted the arrangement at times during the pregnancy. *See* Judy Siegel, *First Local Surrogate Birth*, Jerusalem Post, Feb. 20, 1998, at 1. The surrogate was not allowed to see the babies at the time of delivery, and she later, "with tears in her eyes," asked about their health. *Id.* As of mid-2001, "Ninety arrangements have been approved by the special supervisory committee in the Health Ministry out of 108 applications; 30 babies have been borne by surrogate mothers for 22 commissioning couples." *See* Judy Siegel-Itzkovich, *Bearing the Greatest Gift of All*, Jerusalem Post, May 27, 2001, at 17. A researcher who has looked at these cases of surrogacy reported that the payments to surrogate mothers average between $20,000 and $30,000, and that the commissioning parents "are not typically well-to-do," but rather take out loans so that the procedure can be had. *See id.* (reporting on research completed by Elly Teman). The researcher also stated that in most cases the surrogates maintain "family-like" relationships with the commissioning parents, *e.g.*, the surrogate visits the family on holidays. *Id.*

3. *Commodification.* An often heard justification for restricting surrogacy is the fear of commodifying either reproductive services or children. Is this concern reflected in the Israeli or English legislation on surrogacy? How does the case law interpreting the United Kingdom's act address the issue?

4. *Access to Surrogacy and International Law.* Who has access to surrogacy, both implicitly and explicitly, under the English and Israeli statutory schemes? At the end of 2002, the Israeli High Court of Justice rejected a discrimination claim brought by a single woman who wanted to use the surrogacy process. See Dan Izenberg, *High Court Rejects Single Woman's Petition to Use Surrogate Mother*, Jerusalem Post, Dec. 24, 2002, at 4. Do governments have an obligation under international human rights instruments to make surrogacy available to all who need it?

5. *Other Concerns and Comparisons.* Apart from issues of commodification and access to the procedure, what other features of the law in Israel or the United Kingdom do you like and why? What factors might explain the differences between the approaches? What factors might explain the divergence of approaches in the United States?

---

c. International Law

So far the examination of surrogacy has not explicitly addressed transnational surrogacy, although the facts of *Briody v. St. Helen's & Knowsley Area Hospital Authority* suggest such arrangements exist. The following problems raise issues of private international law, particularly conflict of laws and choice of law. These topics were previously discussed within the context of specific subjects, *e.g.*, child support, custody, marriage and divorce. The legal framework operating in the context of surrogacy is more general because no private international law treaty yet governs this area. The relevant principles are taught in conflict of laws classes. If you have not taken that class, these problems may be difficult to do. However, if you are interested in conflict of laws issues as well as choice of law issues in the surrogacy context, we highly recommend Susan Frelich Appleton, *Surrogacy Arrangements and the Conflict of Laws*, 1990 Wis. L. Rev. 399 (1990).

Problem 13-4

Rachel and David tried to have children for ten years with no success. After five years of unassisted attempts, they used a variety of reproductive technologies and became very discouraged with each failed attempt. At the conclusion of year ten, David still desperately wanted a biological child and suggested to Rachel that they try surrogacy. Rachel reluctantly agreed. Rachel's sister, Mara, lives in Country Y, a country that permits all forms of surrogacy. Mara agreed to be their surrogate on the condition that she receive $25,000. Rachel and David agreed. Rachel and David flew from their home in Country X to Country Y, met Mara, and signed the contract. The contract states that in consideration of a $25,000 payment, Mara will act as a surrogate for Rachel and David, and that all parties intend for Rachel and David to adopt the child. The contract says the law of Country Y will govern all disputes arising under the contract. Rachel and David pay Mara a large advance on the $25,000 and then Mara is inseminated in Country Y with David's sperm. Rachel and David return home, and a healthy baby is born nine months later in Country Y. At the time of birth, Mara refused to turn over the child to her sister and brother-in-law. Mara and Paul, Mara's boyfriend, want to raise the child as their own. Rachel and David return to enforce their agreement and to secure an adoption decree. Should Country Y enforce the agreement and enter the adoption? Assuming that the court in Country Y enforces the contract and enters an adoption decree, will it be honored in Country X? Assume that Country X outlaws all forms of surrogacy. Alternatively, assume that the law in Country X mirrors the law in England? What result? What if the law in Country X mirrors the law in Israel? What result?

Problem 13-5

The facts for this problem are the same as for Problem 13-4. However, now assume that Mara changes her mind during her pregnancy, and will refuse to relinquish the child at its birth. What will be the result if Mara moves to Country X during month seven of her pregnancy and gives birth there? *See* Appleton, *supra*, at 464.

Iris Liebowitz-Dori, *Womb for Rent:*
The Future of International Trade in Surrogacy
6 Minn. J. Global Trade 329, 330–31 (1997)

In 1995, young Polish women were brought to the Netherlands to serve as surrogates for infertile couples. They were recruited through advertisements in Polish newspapers which promised "good fees" and "discretion" in return for their service as surrogate mothers. To participate, they were instructed to contact an "agent" on the docks of Szczecin who would then take them to the Netherlands to live with their prospective customers. This recruitment process occurred despite the fact that surrogate motherhood for commercial gain has been banned in the Netherlands for two years and carries a prison sentence of up to one year.

Illegal international trade in surrogacy is not unique to the Netherlands, and the demand for surrogates will only increase in the future. Surrogacy targets the same market as its counterpart, adoption, where demand greatly exceeds supply....

As with adoption...unregulated international trade in surrogacy can lead to the widespread abuse of women and children. The economic disparity of consumers of surrogacy and the women who offer their reproductive services for sale is so extreme that the potential for abuse is very high. Without safeguards, the international trade in surrogacy will only increase this abuse. While the exploitation of both surrogates and their babies already exists, no international regulation protects them. Ideally, there should be a treaty covering surrogacy to address this problem.

Problem 13-6

Assume the position of a governmental representative from the United States, England, Netherlands, Poland, or Israel at a meeting sponsored by the Hague Conference of Private International Law. Should there be such a convention? If so, what should be its provisions? Would a public international law treaty be preferable? Why or why not?

Notes and Questions

1. *Diversity.* Contrast surrogacy regulation in Israel with the position in Brazil. Brazil's guidelines on medical ethics only permit surrogacy if the social mother and the surrogate are relatives, and if the surrogate is not paid. Even then, the law does not make a surrogacy contract enforceable. Claudia Marques, *Assisted Reproductive Technology (Act) in South America and the Effect on Adoption*, 35 Tex. Int'l L.J. 65, 86 (2000); Dalia Dorner, *Human Reproduction: Reflections on the Nahmani Case*, 35 Tex. Int'l L.J. 1, 9–10 n.38 (2000). Given these sorts of differences in approach, would it ever be possible to draft an international treaty on surrogacy that was accepted by all states? *See* Problem 13-6, *supra*.

2. *Regional Systems.* In 1989, the European Parliament passed a resolution on reproductive technology, including surrogacy. It generally disapproved of surrogacy and advocated the criminal punishment of paid surrogates. Resolution on Artificial Insemination, 'In Vivo,' and 'In Vitro' Fertilization, 1989 O.J. (C 96) 171, 171–73.

3. *Maternal Mortality.* Do we spend too much time considering the legal issues associated with surrogacy and the other technologies that facilitate pregnancy? Should we instead focus our efforts on access to medical technology for those women who are already pregnant? A joint report by WHO, UNFPA, UNICEF, and the World Bank states: "Worldwide, nearly 600,000 women between the ages of 15 and 49 die every year as a result of complications arising from pregnancy and childbirth.... For every woman who dies, many more suffer from serious conditions that can affect them for the rest of their lives." World Health Organization, Reduction of Maternal Mortality 1 (1999). The same report states that the overwhelming majority of deaths and complications occur in developing countries. "In developed countries, the maternal mortality ratio averages around 27 maternal deaths per 100,000 live births; in developing countries the ratio is nearly 20 times higher, at 480 per 100,000, and may be as high as 1000 per 100,000 in some regions." *Id.* at 11. Stated another way, "In some developing countries one woman in 12 may die from a pregnancy-related problem compared with one in 4000 in industrialized settings." *Id.* The report explains: "Globally, around 80% of all maternal deaths are the direct result of complications arising during pregnancy, delivery, or the puerperium." *Id.* at 11. "Most of these deaths could be avoided if preventive measures were taken and adequate care were available." *Id.* at 1. Infertility can undoubtedly cause individuals and couples considerable anguish. Nonetheless, the absence of reproductive

technology can never in itself cause someone's death. Why not just let the market regulate the practice or ban it altogether and turn our attention to the problem of maternal mortality?

4. Cloning

Charles P. Kindregan, *The Challenge of Bioethics: Family Law Meets the Biological Revolution*
13 The Advocate 3 (1982)

Developments in biology, and their medical and social applications, will test the ability of man to control his own destiny. It will also test man's ability to govern himself while maintaining his individual liberty. The greatest development in family law over the past decade has been the promotion of free choice and individual liberty in family and reproductive matters, under the doctrine of privacy. But the promotion of individual liberty and freedom, especially in regard to human reproduction, will face a great challenge in the existence of governmental power to manipulate reproductive choices. The potential of genetic engineering, the need for governmental involvement in setting policy of population growth, and other pressures will combine in the future to present us with both an unlimited opportunity and excessive danger.

The governments of this world will inevitably take steps to become involved in the application of genetic engineering to social engineering. The problem of population growth presents an initial opportunity for government involvement. So does the movement which would limit medical application of biological research by governmental regulation. The deemphasis on the concept of nuclear family, combined with the demand for legal regulation of alternative social groups by which human beings channel their sexual and reproductive desires, point in the direction of more government—not less. Even in conservative societies such as China and India, where the nuclear family is accepted by most as the norm, there has been compulsive government action designed to inhibit and limit individual choice.

Greater government involvement in human reproduction is not necessarily wrong, but it presents certain dangers. The courts in this country have continued to assert the primacy of individual choice in the area of family and human reproduction. But the biological revolution cuts in the opposite direction by making available to government the means of influencing and even controlling the genetic quality of human life. The idea of mass sterilization, compulsory abortion and licensed child-bearing may seem remote to those of us who live in a climate of human freedom-but they are possible in a world tortured by overpopulation, starvation, and totalitarianism. Yet even these possibilities pale as against the power to control and direct human genetic selectivity. The idea of eugenically pure reproduction was first proposed by the Englishman Francis Galton a century ago, and was first utilized by the American states which adopted compulsory eugenic sterilization laws. It was then first attempted on a mass scale by the Nazi party in Germany. The death camps for those who were viewed as eugenically impure, the camps for selective breeding of a pure master race, etc. will hopefully never be seen on this earth again. But those who would exploit the biological advances for reasons of racial theory, economic superiority, social theory, or national advantage will have other and more sophisticated tools at their fingertips.

As lawyers we should begin to consider this in earnest:

> [N]o government could (or would) leave to the pure scientists the work of establishing the goals of planned genetic evolution and the means of achieving it. For a state to leave in the hands of private parties the power of radically altering the genetic quality of the population would require an act of political restraint of a character unknown in human history.

Notes and Questions

1. *Comparative Approach.* For more information on various countries' approaches to cloning, *see* Nicole Atwill, *Human Cloning: French Legislation and European Initiatives,* 28 Int'l J. Legal Info. 500, 545–51 (2000); Gerhold K. Becker, *Cloning Humans? The Chinese Debate and Why It Matters,* 7 Eubios J. Asian and Int'l Bioethics 175–78 (1997), *available at* http://www.biol.tsukuba.ac.jp/~macer/EJ76/ej76j.html; Craig M. Borowski, *Human Cloning Research in Japan: A Study in Science, Culture, Morality, and Patent Law,* 9 Ind. Int'l & Comp. L. Rev. 505, 530–34 (1999); Melissa K. Cantrell, *International Response to Dolly: Will Scientific Freedom Get Sheared?,* 13 J.L. & Health 69, 87–91, 99–100 (1998–99); Jason T. Corsover, *The Next Logical Step? An International Perspective on the Issues of Human Cloning and Genetic Technology,* 4 ILSA J. Int'l & Comp. L. 697 (1998); Erin P. George, *The Stem Cell Debate: The Legal, Political And Ethical Issues Surrounding Federal Funding of Scientific Research on Human Embryos,* 12 Alb. L.J. Sci. & Tech. 747, 768–773 (2002) (discussing various countries' views on cloning of embryos); Adam Greene, *The World After Dolly: International Regulation of Human Cloning,* 33 Geo. Wash. Int'l L.J. 341 (2001); Susan Greenlee, *Dolly's Legacy to Human Cloning: International Legal Responses and Potential Human Rights Violations,* 18 Wis. Int'l L.J. 537 (2000); Alexandra Hawkins, *Protecting Human Dignity and Individuality: The Need for Uniformity in International Cloning Legislation,* 14 Transnat'l Law 243, 268–80 (2001); Khristan A. Heagle, *Should There Be Another Ewe? A Critical Analysis of the European Union Cloning Legislation,* 17 Dick. J. Int'l L. 135 (1998); May Mon Post, *Human Cloning: New Hope, New Implications, New Challenges,* 15 Temp. Int'l & Comp. L.J. 171, 177–82 (2001); Glenn McGee, The Human Cloning Debate, Part Five: God and the Clone (Glenn McGee ed., 1998) (looking at various religious perspectives on human cloning).

2. *International Law.* Will existing human rights instruments be sufficient to check governmental excesses?

3. *Domestic Family Law.* At the end of 2002, a company called Clonaid, which was founded by a religious sect called the Raelians, announced that a baby girl named "Eve" had been born to an American mother as a result of cloning. Almost immediately after the announcement, a Florida attorney asked a Florida juvenile court to appoint a legal guardian for the baby, and, if necessary, to place the child in the state's protective custody. The attorney alleged that the baby was "being exploited and may have suffered birth defects." *No DNA Testing Yet of Clone Baby Girl,* Seattle Times, Jan. 4, 2003. The lawsuit allegedly frightened the parents into silence and secrecy, and at the time this book went to press there was never any verification of the birth. The Florida court dismissed the case for lack of jurisdiction when the chief executive officer of Clonaid assured the court that the child was not, and had never been, in the state of Florida.

C. Abortion

The topic of abortion can be approached from a number of different angles. Sometimes the topic arises within a discussion of a country's overt population policy. Consequently, we have already seen the official prohibition of compulsory abortion in the context of our discussion about China. We have also seen, in the context of our discussion about Romania, concern under international law about the high levels of abortion in that country. Yet the topic of abortion can also be studied independently of population policy. Access to the procedure, access to information about the procedure, and the availability of safe abortion are yet other concerns. These issues were briefly touched upon in the opening section on Romania, and we now return to them in greater detail.

Municipal law, international law, and regional agreements all have something to contribute to an analysis of these issues. At each of these levels lawmakers and judges struggle with the competing interests involved, especially the woman's interest in self-determination and the fetus's interest in being born. The tensions are not always resolved similarly at each level. The question, therefore, arises again about the proper role of international institutions in resolving these issues. The proper role of the courts, as opposed to the legislative bodies, also emerges as an important consideration.

1. Municipal Approaches

a. Legislative Measures

We start by examining the following statutes regulating abortion in Ethiopia, Italy, and Denmark. As you read the laws, try to classify the types of abortion restrictions that you see. In particular, pay attention to the circumstances, if any, when a state may permit abortion. It may help you compare statutory provisions if you analyze the following problem under each law.

Problem 13-7

Helga is unmarried and 24 years old. She is thirteen weeks pregnant and wants to abort the pregnancy. She has one child already, a six-year-old girl, and has been struggling financially to make ends meet. Helga is convinced that another child would require her to give up her new job and return to her parents' house. The thought of returning to her parents' house scares Helga because she was sexually molested by her father as a child. She also fears for her daughter's safety if they have to live there. Helga has been suffering severe depression ever since she found out about the pregnancy. Advise Helga on her ability to get an abortion under the law of each of the three countries set forth below, and what steps she must take to secure one if it is legally available.

Ethiopia. Penal Code, Proclamation No. 158 of 1957, § 2
available at
http://cyber.law.harvard.edu/population/abortion/ethiopia.abo.html
Art. 529. Abortion procured by the pregnant woman

(1) A pregnant woman who procures her own abortion is punishable with simple imprisonment from three months to five years.

(2) Any other person who procures for her the means of, or aids her in the abortion shall be punished in accordance with the general provisions as an accomplice or co-offender. In the latter case, the punishment is simple imprisonment from one to five years.

Art. 530. Abortion procured by another

(1) Whosoever performs an abortion on another, or assists in the commission of the offence, is punishable with rigorous imprisonment not exceeding five years.

(2) Rigorous imprisonment shall be from three to ten years, where the woman was incapable of giving her consent, or where such consent was extorted by threats, coercion or deceit, or where she was incapable of realizing the significance of her actions, or where the intervention was effected against her will.

Art. 531. Aggravated cases

(1) Where the offender has acted for gain, or where he has habitually made a profession of abortion within the meaning of Art. 90, the punishment prescribed in the preceding article shall apply and a fine shall be imposed in addition.

(2) Where the offender has improperly practised his or her profession, especially that of doctor, pharmacist, midwife or nurse, the Court shall, in addition, order prohibition of practice, either for a limited period, or, where the offence is repeatedly committed, for life (Art. 122).

Art. 533. Extenuating circumstances

Apart from the general extenuating circumstances justifying ordinary mitigation of the punishment (Art. 79), the Court may mitigate it without restriction (Art. 185) where the pregnancy has been terminated on account of an exceptionally grave state of physical or mental distress, especially following rape or incest, or because of extreme poverty.

Art. 534. Termination of pregnancy on medical grounds

(1) Termination of pregnancy is not punishable where it is done to save the pregnant woman from grave and permanent danger to life or health which it is impossible to avert in any other way, provided that it is performed in conformity with the following legal requirements.

(2) Except where impossible, the danger shall be diagnosed, and certified in writing, by a registered medical practitioner, after examination of the applicant's state of health.

(3) The termination of the pregnancy shall be conditional upon:

(a) the findings and concurrent opinion, after a prior period of observation where necessary, of a second doctor qualified as a specialist in the alleged defect of health from which the pregnant woman is suffering, and empowered by the competent authority, either generally or in each specific case, to issue the necessary authorisation; and

(b) the duly substantiated consent of the pregnant woman, or where she is incapable under the provisions of civil law or on account of her physical condition of giving it, that of her next of kin or legal representative.

(4) The doctor terminating the pregnancy cannot evade these conditions by invoking his professional duty (Art. 65); where he terminates the pregnancy without observing the legal safeguards, he becomes liable to the provisions relating to abortion.

Art. 535. Required formalities and penalties for non-observance

(1) The doctor who confirms the state of health justifying the termination of the pregnancy and authorizes the intervention, shall keep a duplicate of the findings and decision and transmit them to the competent official department within the period of time fixed by law. The doctor terminating the pregnancy shall notify that department forthwith. No doctor may in such a case invoke professional secrecy (Art. 407).

(2) In the event of omission to comply with these obligatory formalities, the relevant penalties apply (Art. 790). In the event of repeated omissions, the offending doctor may be temporarily deprived of the right to exercise his profession (Art. 122).

Art. 536. Emergencies

(1) In the case of grave and imminent danger which can be averted only by an immediate intervention, the provisions relating to state of necessity apply (Art. 71).

(2) The prior consent of the pregnant woman or, in default thereof, that of her next of kin or legal representative where it is possible to secure it, and subsequent notification to the competent official department, are none the less required in all cases of termination of pregnancy, under pain of the penalties prescribed in the preceding article. . . .

Italy. Law No. 194 of 22 May 1978 on the social protection of motherhood and the voluntary termination of pregnancy (Gazz. Uff.)

available at
http://cyber.law.harvard.edu/population/abortion/Italy.abo.htm.

1. The State guarantees the right to responsible and planned parenthood, recognizes the social value of motherhood, and shall protect human life from its inception. The voluntary termination of pregnancy as covered by this Law shall not be a means of birth control. The State, the regions, and local authorities, acting within their respective powers and areas of competence, shall promote and develop medicosocial services and shall take other measures necessary to prevent abortion from being used for purposes of birth control.

2. The family counselling centres [consultori familiari] established by Law No. 405 of 29 July 1975 shall assist any pregnant woman, subject to the provisions of that Law:

a) by informing her of her rights under State and regional legislation and of the social, health, and welfare services actually available from agencies in her areas;

b) by informing her of appropriate ways to take advantage of the provisions of labour legislation designed to protect the pregnant woman;

c) by taking special action, or suggesting such action to the competent local authority or social welfare agencies in the area, wherever pregnancy or motherhood create problems which cannot be satisfactorily dealt with by normal action under item (a);

d) by helping to overcome the factors which might lead the woman to have her pregnancy terminated.

For the purposes of this Law, the counselling centres may make use of voluntary assistance, on the basis of pertinent regulations or agreements, from appropriate basic social welfare organizations and voluntary associations, which may also assist mothers in difficulties after the child is born.

The necessary means for achieving freely chosen objectives with regard to responsible parenthood may also be supplied to minors by health agencies and counselling centres, against a medical prescription.

3. [Financial provisions.]

4. In order to undergo termination of pregnancy during the first 90 days, women whose situation is such that continuation of the pregnancy, childbirth, or mother-hood would seriously endanger their physical or mental health, in view of their state of health, their economic, social, or family circumstances, the circumstances in which conception occurred, or the probability that the child would be born with ab-normalities or malformations, shall apply to a public counselling centre established under item (a) of Section 2 of Law No. 405 of 29 Jul 1975 or to a fully authorized medicosocial agency [struttura socio-sanitaria] in the region, or to a physician of her choice.

5. In all cases, in addition to guaranteeing the necessary medical examinations, coun-selling centres and medicosocial agencies shall be required, especially when the request for termination of pregnancy is motivated by the impact of economic, social, or family circumstances upon the pregnant women's health, to examine possible solutions to the problems in consultation with the woman and, where the woman consents, with the fa-ther of the conceptus, with due respect for the dignity and personal feelings of the woman and the person named as the father of the conceptus, to help her to overcome the factors which would lead her to have her pregnancy terminated, to enable her to take advantage of her rights as a working woman and a mother, and to encourage any suitable measures designed to support the woman, by providing her with all necessary assistance both during her pregnancy and after the delivery.

Where the woman applies to a physician of her choice, he shall: carry out the necessary medical examinations, with due respect for the woman's dignity and freedom; assess, in consultation with the woman and, where the woman consents, with the father of the con-ceptus, with due respect for the dignity and personal feelings of the woman and of the person named as the father of the conceptus, if so desired taking account of the result of the examinations referred to above, the circumstances leading her to request that her pregnancy be terminated; and inform her of her rights and of the social welfare facilities available to her, as well as regarding the counselling centres and the medicosocial agencies.

Where the physician at the counselling centre or the medicosocial agency, or the physi-cian of the woman's choice, finds that in view of the circumstances termination is ur-gently required, he shall immediately issue the woman a certificate attesting to the ur-gency of the case. Once she has been issued this certificate, the woman may report to one of the establishments authorized to perform pregnancy terminations.

If termination is not found to be urgently required, the physician at the counselling cen-tre or the medicosocial agency, or the physician of the woman's choice, shall at the end of the consultation, if the woman requests that her pregnancy be terminated on account of circumstances referred to in Section 4, issue her a copy of a document signed by himself and the woman attesting that the woman is pregnant and that the request has been made, and shall request her to reflect for seven days. After seven days have elapsed, the woman may take the document issued to her under the terms of this paragraph and report to one of the authorized establishments in order for her pregnancy to be terminated.

6. Voluntary termination of pregnancy may be performed after the first 90 days:

a) where the pregnancy or childbirth entails a serious threat to the woman's life;

b) where the pathological processes constituting a serious threat to the woman's physical or mental health, such as those associated with serious abnormalities or malformations of the fetus, have been diagnosed.

7. The pathological processes referred to in the preceding Section shall be diagnosed and certified by a physician on the staff of the department of obstetrics and gynecology of the hospital establishment in which the termination is to be performed. The physician may call upon the assistance of specialists. The physician shall be required to forward the documentation on the case as well as his certificate to the medical director of the hospital in order for the termination to be performed immediately.

Where the termination of pregnancy is necessary in view of an imminent threat to the woman's life, it may be performed without observing the procedures referred to in the preceding paragraph and in a place other than those referred to in Section 8. In such cases, the physician shall be required to notify the provincial medical officer.

Where it is possible that the fetus may be viable [sussiste la possibilità di vita autonoma del feto], pregnancy may be terminated only in the case referred to in item (a) of Section 6, and the physician performing the termination shall take any appropriate action to save the life of the fetus.

8. [Designating who can perform abortions and where they can be performed.]

9. [Describing exemption from performing procedure for health personnel with a conscientious objection.]

10. [Administrative provisions.]

11. [Provisions regarding paperwork required by facility where abortion occurs.]

12. Requests for pregnancy termination under the procedures prescribed by this Law shall be made in person by the woman.

Where the woman is under 18 years of age, the consent of the person exercising parental authority over the woman or her guardian shall be required for the termination of pregnancy. However, during the first 90 days, if there are serious grounds rendering it impossible or inadvisable to consult the persons exercising parental authority or the guardian, or if those persons are consulted but refuse their consent or express conflicting opinions, the counselling centre or medicosocial agency, or the physician of the woman's choice, shall carry out the duties and procedures set out in Section 5 and submit to the magistrate responsible for matters of guardianship [giudice tutelare] in the locality in which it (he) operates, not later than seven days following the request, a report giving its (his) views on the matter. Within five days, after interviewing the woman and taking account of her wishes, the grounds which she puts forward, and the report submitted to him, the magistrate may issue a decision, which shall not be subject to appeal, authorizing the woman to have her pregnancy terminated.

Where the physician finds that termination is urgently required in view of a serious threat to the health of a woman under 18 years of age, he shall make out a certificate indicating the conditions justifying the termination of pregnancy, without requesting the consent of the persons exercising parental authority or the guardian and without applying to the magistrate. The certificate shall entitle the woman to obtain, on an emergency basis, the termination and, where necessary, hospitalization.

In the case of a pregnancy termination after the first 90 days, the procedures referred to in Section 7 shall likewise be applicable to women under 18 years of age, without regard to the consent of the persons exercising parental authority or the guardian.

13. [Women under a civil disability.]

14. The physician performing the pregnancy termination shall be required to supply the woman with information and instructions on birth control and to acquaint her with the abortion procedures....

15. [Continuing education for health personnel.]

16. [Reporting on law to parliament by minister of health.]

17. Any person who criminally causes a woman to terminate her pregnancy shall be liable to from three months' to two years' imprisonment....

18. [Criminal provisions for coerced abortion]

19. Any person who induces a voluntary termination of pregnancy while failing to observe the conditions laid down in Sections 5 or 8 shall be liable to up to three years' imprisonment.

The woman shall be liable to a fine of up to 100,000 lire.

Where voluntary termination of pregnancy occurs without the medical examination provided for under items (a) and (b) of Section 6 or in any event without observing the conditions laid down in Section 7, the person bringing about such termination shall be liable to from one to four years' imprisonment.

The woman shall be liable to up to six months' imprisonment.

Where voluntary termination of pregnancy is performed upon a woman who is under 18 years of age or who is under civil disability, in cases other than those laid down in Section 12 and 13 or while failing to observe the conditions laid down in those Sections, the person bringing about such termination shall be liable to the corresponding penalties laid down in the preceding paragraphs, increased by up to one-half. The woman shall not be liable to any penalty.

Where the woman dies as a result of the acts referred to in the preceding paragraphs, the penalty shall be from three to seven years' imprisonment; where very grave personal injury is the result, the penalty shall be from two to five years' imprisonment; where grave personal injury is the result, the latter penalty shall be reduced.

The penalties laid down under the preceding paragraph shall be increased if the woman dies or is injured as a result of the acts referred to in the fifth paragraph....

21. [Criminal provisions for professional disclosure of confidential information.]

Denmark. Law No. 350 of 13 June 1973 on the interruption of pregnancy

(Lovitidende for Kongeriget Danmark, Part A,
6 July 1973, No. 32, pp. 993–95), *available at*
http://cyber.law.harvard.edu/population/abortion/denmark.abo.htm

Chapter 1. Requirements to be satisfied

1. A woman domiciled in Denmark shall be entitled to undergo an abortion provided that the procedure can be performed during the first 12 weeks of pregnancy and that, after application of the provisions of Section 8, the woman persists in her desire to have her pregnancy terminated.

2. A woman may undergo an abortion without special authorization, even after the 12th week of pregnancy has elapsed, if the procedure is necessary to avert a risk to her

life or of serious deterioration of her physician or mental health, and this risk is based solely or principally on circumstances of a medical character.

3. (1) After the 12th week of pregnancy has elapsed, a woman domiciled in Denmark may be granted authorization for an abortion in the following cases:

1. pregnancy, childbirth, or care of the child entail a risk of deterioration of the woman's health on account of an existing or potential physical or mental illness or infirmity or as a consequence of other aspects of the conditions under which she is living;

2. the woman has become pregnant under the circumstances referred to in Section 210 or Sections 216–224 of the Civil Criminal Code;

3. there is a danger that, on account of a hereditary condition or of an injury or disease during embryonic or fetal life, the child will be affected by a serious physical or mental disorder;

4. the woman is incapable of giving proper care to a child, on account of a physical or mental disorder or feeble-mindedness;

5. on account of her youth or immaturity, the woman is for the time being incapable of giving proper care to a child;

6. it can be assumed that pregnancy, childbirth, or care of a child constitute a serious burden to the woman, which cannot otherwise be averted, and it therefore appears essential for the pregnancy to be terminated, taking into account the interests of the woman, the management of her household, or the care of her other children. In reaching the decision, consideration shall be paid to the woman's age, the effort involved in her occupation, and her personal circumstances in other respects, as well as the circumstances of the family from the point of view of housing, income and health.

(2) Authorization for abortion may be granted only if the grounds on which the application is based are sufficiently important to justify subjecting the woman to the increased risk to her health which the procedure entails.

Chapter 2. The committee and appeal board

4. (1) The Minister of Justice shall establish one or more committees within each maternity aid institution [modrehjÆlpsinstitution], with the task of deciding on the matters referred to in Section 3.... Each committee shall be composed of the institution's director or one of his colleagues with equivalent training, and two physicians....

(2) [Composition of Board of Appeal.]

(3) Authorization may be granted only where the committee or board of appeal is unanimously in favour....

Chapter 3. Procedures to be followed

5. [For a woman under mental disability]

6. (1) If the woman is under 18 years of age or is incapable of managing her own affairs, the person exercising parental authority or, as the case may be, the guardian, must give his consent to the application.

(2) Where this is justified by the circumstances, the committee may refrain from requiring the consent referred to in subsection 1....

(3) Where this is justified by the circumstances, the committee may authorize an abortion even if the consent referred to in sub-section 1 has been refused....

8. (1) The application for an abortion shall be presented to a physician or a maternity aid institution.

(2) If the application is presented to a physician, the latter shall draw the woman's attention to the fact that, by consulting a maternity aid institution, she may obtain information on the available possibilities for assistance in the event that the pregnancy is continued to term and for assistance after the birth of the child. If the application is presented to a maternity aid institution, the woman shall on request receive the information referred to in the first sentence of this sub-section.

(3) The woman must be informed by the physician of the nature of the procedure and its direct consequences as well as the risks which it may involve. The same information shall be given to the person required to submit the application under sub-section 2 of Section 5 or to grant consent under sub-section 1 of Section 6.

9. If it appears that the conditions prescribed in Sections 1 or 2 are satisfied, the physician or the maternity aid institution shall refer the woman to a hospital, account being taken of the provisions of Section 10. Where these conditions are not satisfied, the physician shall immediately forward the application, accompanied by his opinion, to the competent maternity aid institution.

10. (1) The abortion may only be performed by a physician in a State or communal hospital or in a clinic [ambulatorium] attached to the hospital.

(2) If the chief physician of the hospital or hospital department concerned refuses to perform the procedure, even if the conditions prescribed in Sections 1 or 2 are satisfied or authorization for the abortion has been granted, the woman shall be referred to another hospital or hospital department in which the procedure can be performed.

(3) Nurses or student nurses for whom the rendering of assistance at an abortion would be contrary to their ethical or religious convictions shall be exempted from such duties on request.

11. [Payment of costs of the abortion procedure]....

Chapter 5. Penal provisions

14. (1) A physician who performs an abortion without the conditions prescribed in Sections 1 or 2 being satisfied and without an authorization having been granted under Section 3 shall be liable, without prejudice to any more severe penalty imposed under the Civil Criminal code, to up to two years' deprivation of liberty [hÆfte] or imprisonment [fÆngsel] or, if there are mitigating circumstances, to a fine.

(2) A physician who performs an abortion without the conditions prescribed in Sections 5 and 6 and sub-section 3 of Section 8 being satisfied shall be liable to a fine, without prejudice to any more severe penalty imposed under the Civil Criminal Code.

(3) A physician who performs an abortion in violation of sub-section 1 of Section 10 shall be liable to a fine.

(4) Any person who, not being a physician, performs an abortion shall be liable to up to four years' imprisonment, without prejudice to any more severe penalty imposed under the Civil Criminal code.

(5) The provisions of sub-sections 1 and 4 shall be applicable, mutatis mutandis, to any person who provides assistance in the activity in question....

Notes and Questions

1. *Categorization of Approaches.* National laws are, not surprisingly, diverse when it comes to abortion. Yet, how are the laws similar? What are the major differences? How does the law in the United States compare? Professor Mary Ann Glendon studied the abortion law of twenty countries in the West and concluded "When American abortion law is viewed in comparative perspective, it presents several unique features. Not only do we have less regulation of abortion in the interest of the fetus than any other Western nation, but we provide less public support for maternity and child raising. And, to a greater extent than in any other country, our courts have shut down the legislative process of bargaining, education, and persuasion on the abortion issue." Mary Ann Glendon, Abortion and Divorce in Western Law 2 (1987). Are the materials you just read consistent with Professor Glendon's conclusion, at least in part?

2. *Judicial versus Legislative Approach.* In many countries, the judiciary has determined whether a statutory restriction on abortion is permissible under the country's constitution or under international instruments, or it has interpreted an ambiguous statutory provision. *See, e.g.,* Cons. Const. 1975 J.C.P. II, No. 18030 (Fr.) (upholding France's abortion law as consistent with art. 2 of the Declaration of the Rights of Man and of the Citizen); Orzeczenie Trybunalu Konstytucyjnego z Dnia 28 May 1997 r. (Sygn.akt K. 26/96) (Pol.) (decision of the Polish Constitutional Tribunal striking down legislation enacted to liberalize abortion citing, *inter alia,* Poland's Constitution, which protects human life even at the pre-natal stage, and the preamble to the Convention on the Rights of the Child); R. v. Morgentaler, [1988] 1 S.C.R. 30 (Can.) (ruling that a criminal penalty for providers or recipients of nontherapeutic abortion violated a woman's right to personal security under sections 1 and 7 of the Canadian Charter of Rights and Freedoms); Christian Lawyers Ass'n of South Africa v. Minister of Health, 1998 SA 1113 (T) (upholding legislation permitting abortion during first twelve weeks of pregnancy and stating that the constitutional provision guaranteeing the right to life did not apply to the fetus). The material included above from Ethiopia, Italy, and Denmark only reflects legislative measures; it does not include court decisions (if any) that might interpret the laws. As suggested in note 1, the extent to which courts constitutionalize the question affects the ability of the legislature to formulate laws regarding abortion.

Should legislatures have wide latitude to regulate abortion? Without a doubt, abortion is one of those issues for which public opinion can be pronounced and divided. At times, different countries with similar histories arrive at very different responses to this issue. For example, Finland has much more restrictive abortion laws than Sweden, which funds abortion on demand until the eighteenth week. Finland only permits an abortion through the twelfth week of pregnancy, unless the woman is under sixteen and special circumstances exist, or the embryo is seriously disabled. Even in these circumstances, an abortion must occur sooner than the end of twenty weeks and twenty-four weeks, respectively. See Law No. 239 of 24 March 1970 on the interruption of pregnancy, as amended by Law No. 564 of 19 July 1978 and Law No. 572 of 12 July 1985 (Finland), *available at* http://cyber.law.harvard.edu/population/abortion/Finland.abo. htm. Finland's more restrictive laws reflect its "more conservative culture," despite its "common legal heritage and close ties with Sweden." David Bradley, *Convergence In Family Law: Mirrors, Transplants and Political Economy,* 6 Maastricht J. Eur. & Comp. L. 127 (1999).

3. *Permissiveness of Abortion Laws in Europe.* Abortion is generally permitted in Europe. Professor Glendon has noted that the change from strict laws regulating abortion to the more liberal laws occurred in less than two decades, starting in the mid-1960s, in almost all of the countries that she examined. Glendon, *supra*, at 11, 13. Today, even Belgium, one of two countries mentioned by Professor Glendon in 1987 as having strict laws, has liberalized its laws. In 1990, Belgium amended its 1867 Penal Code, which only permitted abortion on general grounds of necessity. Necessity required three physicians to state that the mother's life was at stake. Dep't of Econ. & Soc. Affairs, Pop. Div., Abortion Policies: A Global Review 75 (2001), *at* www.un.org/esa/population/publications/abortion/doc/belgiu1.doc. Now a woman can obtain an abortion in the first trimester if she is "in a state of distress as a result of her situation," and no doctor need certify her distress. After the first trimester, two doctors must agree that abortion is required to preserve the woman's health or because the fetus is seriously impaired. All women must receive counselling before the procedure, and wait six days after the counselling. *See generally* Gov't of Ireland, Dep't of the Taoiseach, Green Paper on Abortion, App. 3, at 1 (1999) (The Law Relating to Abortion in Selected Other Jurisdictions), *at* http://193.178./.117/upload/publications/251.pdf (discussing the law in Belgium). Now, the only country in Europe that still has extremely strict laws with regard to abortion is Ireland. Abortion is illegal and is only permitted to save the life of the woman. It is not permitted even if it is necessary to preserve her physical or mental health, or if the pregnancy was caused by rape or incest, or if the fetus is disabled. Dep't of Econ. & Soc. Affairs, Pop. Div., Abortion Policies: A Global Review 75 (2001), *available at* www.un.org/esa/population/publications/abortion/doc/ireland.doc.

4. *Permissiveness of Abortion Laws in Africa.* "With the notable exception of South Africa, the countries in Anglophone Africa place severe limitations on a woman's ability to obtain an abortion." *See* Center for Reproductive Law & Policy, Women of the World: Law and Policies Affecting their Reproductive Lives: Anglophone Africa 163 (1997). For example, Kenya, Nigeria and Tanzania only allow abortion if the mother's life is endangered. Ethiopia, as indicated above, is slightly more permissive, as is Ghana and Zimbabwe, although not as permissive as South Africa. South Africa enacted the Choice on Termination of Pregnancy Act, 1996, which allows abortion on demand during the first twelve weeks of pregnancy and also allows midwives to perform them. *Id.* at 160. "All seven countries [in Francophone Africa] have retained the section of the 1920 French Law that considers induced abortion a criminal act and authorizes it only under very limited conditions." Center for Reproductive Law & Policy, Women of the World: Law and Policies Affecting Their Reproductive Lives: Francophone Africa 186 (2000).

5. *Permissiveness of Abortion Laws in Latin America.* Latin America and the Caribbean have relatively strict abortion laws. Only Cuba has elective abortion during the first 12 weeks of pregnancy. Almost all of the countries (*i.e.*, Argentina, Barbados, Belize, Brazil, Cuba, El Salvador, Jamaica, Mexico, and Peru) have an "indications approach," whereby abortion is legal only if certain indicated circumstances exist. All of these countries recognize risk to the mother's life as a sufficient indication, but not all countries recognize as sufficient a risk to the mother's physical or mental health, rape or incest, or risk of fetal deformity. Only Barbados, Belize and Cuba consider socioeconomic hardship a factor. The Dominican Republic and Honduras have the strictest laws, with the only exception being risk to the mother's life. *See* John M. Paxman et al., *The Clandestine Epidemic: The Practice of Unsafe Abortion in Latin America*, 24 Stud. Fam. Plan. 205, 217, tbl. 9 (1993).

6. *Worldwide Picture.* "Currently, 62% of the world's people live in countries where induced abortion is permitted either for a wide range of reasons or without restriction

as to reason. In contrast, 26% of all people reside in nations where abortion is generally prohibited." Center for Reproductive Law & Policy, The World's Abortion Laws (Feb. 1999), *available at* http://www.crlp.org/pub_fac_aborlicpd.html (listing countries). The authors classify Ethiopia's law as representative of laws that are neither the most restrictive nor generally permissive. The authors also suggest that countries with similar laws house 9.9% of the worlds population.

7. *Effects of Restrictive Abortion Laws.* The woman who lives in a country with repressive abortion laws has three options if she is determined to terminate her pregnancy. If she has the money, time, and relevant information, she can travel to a more permissive jurisdiction to obtain an abortion. If she lacks any of these, she can resort to a "back-alley" or self-inflicted abortion. A woman might also attempt to come within the exceptions provided by the law. What problems, if any, would the third option pose for a woman whose case for an abortion is arguable under the law?

8. *Counseling.* Will more women seek counseling regarding alternatives to abortion if abortions are legal or illegal in a country? Put another way, will a woman contemplating an illegal abortion seek out counseling?

9. *Illegal Abortion.* Just to be absolutely clear, laws restricting abortion do not necessarily work to stop those abortions prohibited by the law. For example, "Although the data are problematic, Latin America and the Caribbean appear to have one of the highest incidences of induced abortion in the developing world." Paxman, *supra*, at 207. Because of the restrictive laws, "abortion is more commonly induced by substandard methods ranging from the use of herbal abortifacients to the insertion of catheters or metal sounds into the uterus. Some of these methods are merely ineffective, some are relatively safe in the hands of skilled personnel, and some are lethal." *Id.* at 208. "In Latin America complications resulting from unsafe, illegally induced abortion are considered the principal cause of death in women aged 15 to 39 years." *Id.* at 209. Yet, one cannot conclude that the laws do not work at all. Not measured here is the number of women who decided to forego an abortion and the number of women who avoided pregnancy altogether because of the law.

---

b. Judicial Measures

As suggested above, judicial decisions may confine the way in which a country legislates the practice of abortion. Let's examine the case law of one country, Germany, to see how the judiciary affected the statutory provisions on abortion that existed.

At issue in the following case was the Fifth Statute to Reform the Penal Law of the 18th of June, 1974. Among other things, the law exempted from punishment the performance of an abortion by a doctor during the first twelve weeks of a pregnancy. Until twenty-two weeks, the abortion could occur if there existed an eugenic indication, *e.g.*, if the fetus was deformed to the degree that it would be unreasonable for the woman to carry it to term. Throughout the pregnancy, a woman could get an abortion if necessary to save her life or to avoid a serious impairment to her health. Among other things, the law subjected doctors to punishment for performing an abortion without ensuring that the woman had received social and medical counseling. The women themselves only faced punishment if they performed their own abortion. *See generally* Robert E. Jonas & John D. Gorby, *West German Abortion Decision: A Contrast to Roe v. Wade*, 9 J. Marshall J. Prac. & Proc. 605, 610–613 (1978) (providing translation of court decision that includes relevant law); Florian Miedel, *Is West Germany's 1975 Abortion Decision a Solution to the American Abortion Debate? A Critique of Mary Ann Glendon and Donald Kommers*, 20 N.Y.U. Rev. L. & Soc. Change 471, 475 (1993–94). At the time the Constitutional Court issued the following decision, numerous other countries had substantially similar laws, including Austria, France, Denmark, Sweden, Great Britain and the Netherlands. *See* Jonas & Gorby, *supra*, at 683 (providing dissenting opinion of Rupp von Brünneck and Dr. Simon, JJ.).

BVerfG [Constitutional Court], BVerfGE 39 (1975), 1 (1–68) (F.R.G.)
translated in Robert E. Jonas & John D. Gorby,
West German Abortion Decision: A Contrast to Roe v. Wade
9 J. Marshall J. Prac. & Proc. 605, 637–684 (1976)

1. Article 2, Paragraph 2, Sentence 1, of the Basic Law...protects the life developing itself in the womb of the mother as an intrinsic legal value.*

a) The express incorporation into the Basic Law of the self-evident right to life—in contrast to the Weimar Constitution—may be explained principally as a reaction to the "destruction of life unworthy of life," to the "final solution" and "liquidations," which were carried out by the National Socialistic Regime as measures of state. Article 2, Paragraph 2, Sentence 1, of the Basic Law, just as it contains the abolition of the death penalty in Article 102, includes "a declaration of the fundamental worth of human life and of a concept of the state which stands in emphatic contrast to the philosophies of a political regime to which the individual life meant little and which therefore practiced limitless abuse with its presumed right over life and death of the citizen" (Decisions of the Federal Constitutional Court, 18, 112, 117).

b) In contrasting Article 2, Paragraph 2, Sentence 1, of the Basic Law, one should begin with its language: "Everyone has a right to life...." Life, in the sense of historical existence of a human individual, exists according to definite biological-physiological knowledge, in any case, from the 14th day after conception.... The process of development which has begun at that point is a continuing process which exhibits no sharp demarcation and does not allow a precise division of the various steps of development of the human life. The process does not end even with birth; the phenomena of consciousness which are specific to the human personality, for example, appear for the first time a rather long time after birth. Therefore, the protection of Article 2, Paragraph 2, Sentence 1, of the Basic Law cannot be limited either to the "completed" human being after birth or to the child about to be born which is independently capable of living. The right to life is guaranteed to everyone who "lives"; no distinction can be made here between various stages of the life developing itself before birth, or between unborn and born life. "Everyone" in the sense of Article 1, Paragraph 2, Sentence 1, of the Basic Law is "everyone living"; expressed in another way: every life possessing human individuality; "everyone" also includes the yet unborn human being.

c) [T]he sense and purpose of this provision of the Basic Law require that the protection of life should also be extended to the life developing itself. The security of human

---

* Article 2 (Rights of liberty).
    (1) Everyone has the right to the free development of his personality insofar as he does not violate the rights of others or offend against the constitutional order or the moral code.
    (2) Everyone has the right to life and to inviolability of his person. The freedom of the individual is inviolable. These rights may only be encroached upon pursuant to a law.

existence against encroachments by the state would be incomplete if it did not also embrace the prior step of "completed life," unborn life.

This extensive interpretation corresponds to the principle established in the opinions of the Federal Constitutional Court, "according to which, in doubtful cases, that interpretation is to be selected which develops to the highest degree the judicial effectiveness of the fundamental legal norm.". . .

d) In support of this result the legislative history of Article 2, Paragraph 2, Sentence 1, of the Basic Law may be adduced here. . . .

In the written report of the Main Committee (page 7). . . Parliamentary Representative Dr. von Mangoldt (CDU) explained with regard to Article 2 of the Basic Law: "With the guaranteeing of the right to life, germinating life should also be protected. The motions introduced by the German Party in the Main Committee to attach a particular sentence about the protection of germinating life did not attain a majority only because, according to the view prevailing in the Committee, the value to be protected was already secured through the present version.". . .

At the third reading on May 8, 1949, both Parliamentary Representatives Dr. Seebohm as well as Dr. Weber state that, according to their conception, Article 2, Paragraph 2, of the Basic Law would also include germinating life within the protection of this fundamental right (proceedings of the Parliamentary Council Stenographic Reports, p. 218, 223). The comments of both speakers stood without opposition.

The history of the origin of Article 2, Paragraph 2, Sentence 1, of the Basic Law suggests that the formulation "everyone has the right to life" should also include "germinating" life. In any case, even less can be concluded from the materials on behalf of the contrary point of view. On the other hand, no evidence is found in the legislative history for answering the question whether unborn life must be protected by the penal law. . . .

2. The duty of the state to protect every human life may therefore be directly deduced from Article 2, Paragraph 2, Sentence 1, of the Basic Law. In addition to that, the duty also results from the explicit provision of Article 1, Paragraph 1, Sentence 2, of the Basic Law since developing life participates in the protection which Article 1, Paragraph 1, of the Basic Law guarantees to human dignity.* Where human life exists, human dignity is present to it; it is not decisive that the bearer of this dignity himself be conscious of it, and know personally how to preserve it. The potential faculties present in the human being from the beginning suffice to establish human dignity.

3. On the other hand, the question disputed in the present proceeding as well as in judicial opinions and in scientific literature whether the one about to be born himself is a bearer of the fundamental right or, on account of a lesser capacity to possess legal and fundamental rights is "only" protected in his right to life by the objective norms of the constitution need not be decided here. According to the constant judicial utterances of the Federal Constitutional Court, the fundamental legal norms contain not only subjective rights of defense of the individual against the state but embody, at the same time, an objective ordering of values, which is valid as a constitutionally fundamental decision for all areas of the law and which provides direction and impe-

---

* Article 1(1) states: "The dignity of man is inviolable. To respect and protect it is the duty of all state authority."

tus for legislation, administration, and judicial opinions.... Whether and, if so, to what extent the state is obligated by the constitution to legal protection of developing life can therefore be concluded from the objective-legal content of the fundamental legal norms.

II.

1. The duty of the state to protect is comprehensive. It forbids not only — self-evidently — direct state attacks on the life developing itself but also requires the state to take a position protecting and promoting this life, that is to say, it must, above all, preserve it even against illegal attacks by others. It is for the individual areas of the legal order, each according to its special function, to effectuate this requirement. The degree of seriousness with which the state must take its obligation to protect increases as the rank of the legal value in question increases in importance within the order of values of the Basic Law. Human life represents, within the order of the Basic Law, an ultimate value, the particulars of which need not be established; it is the living foundation of human dignity and the prerequisite for all other fundamental rights.

2. The obligation of the state to take the life developing itself under protection exists, as a matter of principle, even against the mother. Without doubt, the natural connection of unborn life with that of the mother establishes an especially unique relationship, for which there is no parallel in other circumstances of life. Pregnancy belongs to the sphere of intimacy of the woman, the protection of which is constitutionally guaranteed through Article 2, Paragraph 1, in connection with Article 1, Paragraph 1, of the Basic Law. Were the embryo to be considered only as a part of the maternal organism the interruption of pregnancy would remain in the area of the private structuring of one's life, where the legislature is forbidden to encroach (Decisions of the Federal Constitutional Court, 6, 32 41; 6, 389 433; 27, 344 350; 32, 373 379). Since, however, the one about to be born is an independent human being who stands under the protection of the constitution, there is a social interruption of the pregnancy which makes it amenable to and in need of regulation by the state. The right of the woman to the free development of her personality, which has as its content the freedom of behavior in a comprehensive sense and accordingly embraces the personal responsibility of the woman to decide against parenthood and the responsibilities flowing from it, can also, it is true, likewise demand recognition and protection. This right, however, is not guaranteed without limits — the rights of others, the constitutional order, and the moral law limit it. *A priori*, this right can never include the authorization to intrude upon the protected sphere of right of another without justifying reason or much less to destroy that sphere along with the life itself; this is even less so, if, according to the nature of the case, a special responsibility exists precisely for this life.

A compromise which guarantees the protection of the life of the one about to be born and permits the pregnant woman the freedom of abortion is not possible since the interruption of pregnancy always means the destruction of the unborn life. In the required balancing, "both constitutional values are to be viewed in their relationship to human dignity, the center of the value system of the constitution" (Decisions of the Federal Constitutional Court, 35, 202 225). A decision oriented to Article 1, Paragraph 1, of the Basic Law must come down in favor of the precedence of the protection of life for the child *en ventre sa mere* over the right of the pregnant woman to self-determination. Regarding many opportunities for development of personality, she can be adversely affected through pregnancy, birth and the education of her children. On the other hand, the unborn life is destroyed through the interruption of pregnancy. According to the principle of the balance which preserves most of competing constitutionally protected positions in view of the fundamental idea of Article 19, Paragraph 2, of the Basic Law;* precedence must be given to the protection of the life of the child about to be born. This precedence exists as a matter of principle for the entire duration of pregnancy and may not be placed in question for any particular time. The opinion expressed in the Federal Parliament during the third deliberation on the Statute to Reform the Penal Law, the effect of which is to propose the precedence for a particular time "of the right to self-determination of the woman which flows from human dignity vis-a-vis all others, including the child's right to life"...is not reconcilable with the value ordering of the Basic Law.

3. From this point, the fundamental attitude of the legal order which is required by the constitution with regard to the interruption of pregnancy becomes clear: the legal order may not make the woman's right to self-determination the sole guideline of its rulemaking. The state must proceed, as a matter of principle, from a duty to carry the pregnancy to term and therefore to view, as a matter of principle, its interruption as an injustice. The condemnation of abortion must be clearly expressed in the legal order. The false impression must be avoided that the interruption of pregnancy is the same social process as, for example, approaching a physician for healing an illness or indeed a legally irrelevant alternative for the prevention of conception. The state may not abdicate its responsibility even through the recognition of a "legally free area," by which the state abstains from the value judgment and abandons this judgment to the decision of the individual to be made on the basis of his own sense of responsibility.

III.

How the state fulfills its obligation for an effective protection of developing life is, in the first instance, to be decided by the legislature. It determines which measures of protection are required and which serve the purpose of guaranteeing an effective protection of life....

[T]he primary concern is to strengthen readiness of the expectant mother to accept the pregnancy as her own responsibility and to bring the child *en ventre sa mere* to full life. Regardless of how the state fulfills its obligation to protect, it should not be forgotten that developing life itself is entrusted by nature in the first place to the protection of the mother. To reawaken and, if required, to strengthen the maternal duty to protect, where it is lost, should be the principal goal of the endeavors of the state for the protection of life....

The legislature is not obligated, as a matter of principle, to employ the same penal measures for the protection of the unborn life as it considers required and expedient for born life. As a look at legal history shows, this was never the case in the application of penal sanctions and is also true for the situation in the law up to the Fifth Statute to Reform the Penal Law....

Punishment...can never be an end in itself. Its employment is in principle subject to the decision of the legislature. The legislature is not prohibited, in consideration of the

---

* Article 19(2) states: "In no case may a basic right be infringed upon in its essential content."

points of view set out above, from expressing the legal condemnation of abortion required by the Basic Law in ways other than the threat of punishment. The decisive factor is whether the totality of the measures serving the protection of the unborn life, whether they be in civil law or in public law, especially of a social-legal or of a penal nature, guarantees an actual protection corresponding to the importance of the legal value to be secured. In the extreme case, namely, if the protection required by the constitution can be achieved in no other way, the lawgiver can be obligated to employ the means of the penal law for the protection of developing life. The penal norm represents, to a certain extent, the "ultimate reason" in the armory of the legislature. According to the principle of proportionality, a principle of the just state, which prevails for the whole of the public law, including constitutional law, the legislature may make use of this means only cautiously and with restraint. However, this final means must also be employed, if an effective protection of life cannot be achieved in other ways. The worth and the importance of the legal value to be protected demand this. It is not a question of an "absolute" duty to punish but rather one of a "relative" duty to use the penal sanction, which grows out of the insight into the inadequacy of all other means....

The obligation of the state to protect the developing life exists—as shown—against the mother as well. Here, however, the employment of the penal law may give rise to special problems which result from the unique situation of the pregnant woman.... In individual cases, difficult, even life-threatening situations of conflict may arise. The right to life of the unborn can lead to a burdening of the woman which essentially goes beyond that normally associated with pregnancy.... In such a situation of conflict which, in general, does not allow an unequivocal moral judgment and in which the decision for an interruption of pregnancy can attain the rank of a decision of conscience worthy of consideration, the legislature is obligated to exercise special restraint. If, in these cases, it views the conduct of the pregnant woman as not deserving punishment and forgoes the use of penal sanctions, the result, at any rate, is to be constitutionally accepted as a balancing incumbent upon the legislature....

A continuation of the pregnancy appears to be non-exactable especially when it is proven that the interruption is required "to avert" from the pregnant woman "a danger for her life or the danger of a grave impairment of her condition of health" (§218b, No. 1, of the Penal Code in the version of the Fifth Statute to Reform the Penal Law). In this case her own "right to life and bodily inviolability" (Article 2, Paragraph 2, Sentence 1, of the Basic Law) is at stake, the sacrifice of which cannot be expected of her for the unborn life. Beyond that, the legislature has a free hand to leave the interruption of pregnancy free of punishment in the case of other extraordinary burdens for the pregnant woman, which, from the point of view of non-exactability, are as weighty as those referred to in §218b, No. 1. In this category can be counted, especially, the cases of the eugenic (cf. Section 218b, No. 2, of the Penal Code), ethical (criminological), and of the social or emergency indication for abortion which were contained in the draft proposed by the Federal Government in the sixth election period of the Federal Parliament and were discussed both in the public debate as well as in the course of the legislative proceedings.... The decisive viewpoint is that in all of these cases another interest equally worthy of protection, from the standpoint of the constitution, asserts its validity with such urgency that the state's legal order cannot require that the pregnant woman must, under all circumstances, concede precedence to the right of the unborn....

Even in these cases the state may not be content merely to examine, and if the occasion arises, to certify that the statutory prerequisites for an abortion free of punishment are present. Rather, the state will also be expected to offer counseling and assistance with the goal of reminding pregnant women of the fundamental duty to respect the right to life of the unborn, to encourage her to continue the pregnancy and—especially in cases of social need—to support her through practical measures of assistance.

In all other cases the interruption of pregnancy remains a wrong deserving punishment since, in these cases, the destruction of a value of the law of the highest rank is subjected to the unrestricted pleasure of another and is not motivated by an emergency. If the legislature wants to dispense (even in this case) with penal law punishment, this would be compatible with the requirement to protect of Article 2, Paragraph 2, Sentence 1, of the Basic Law, only on the condition that another equally effective legal sanction stands at its command which would clearly bring out the unjust character of the act (the condemnation by the legal order) and likewise prevent the interruptions of pregnancy as effectively as a penal provision....

If the challenged regulation of terms of the Fifth Statute to Reform the Penal Law is examined according to these standards, the result is that the statute does not do justice, to the extent required, to the obligation to protect developing life effectively which is derived from Article 2, Paragraph 2, Sentence 1, in conjunction with Article 1, Paragraph 1, of the Basic Law....

The legal condemnation of the interruption of pregnancy required by the constitution must clearly appear in the legal order existing under the constitution. Therefore, as shown, only those cases can be excepted in which the continuation of the pregnancy is not exactable from the woman in consideration of the value decision made in Article 2, Paragraph 2, Sentence 1, of the Basic Law. This absolute condemnation is not expressed in the provisions of the Fifth Statute to Reform the Penal Law with regard to the interruption of pregnancy during the first twelve weeks....

The objection against this is that women not subject to influence understand best from experience how to avoid punishment so that the penal sanction is often ineffective.... [T]he general preventive function of the penal law ought not be forgotten. If one views as the task of the penal law the protection of especially important legal values and elementary values of the community, a great importance accrues to its function. Just as important as the observable reaction in an individual case is the long range effect of a penal norm which in its principal normative content ("abortion is punishable") has existed for a very long time. No doubt, the mere existence of such a penal sanction has influence on the conceptions of value and the manner of behavior of the populace.... The consciousness of legal consequences which follows from its transgression creates a threshold which many recoil from crossing. An opposite effect will result if, through a general repeal of punishability, even doubtlessly punishable behavior is declared to be legally free from objection. This must confuse the concepts of "right" and "wrong" dominant in the populace. The purely theoretical announcement that the interruption of pregnancy is "tolerated," but not "approved," must remain without effect as long as no legal sanction is recognizable which clearly segregates the justified cases of abortion from the reprehensible. If the threat of punishment disappears in its entirety, the impression will arise of necessity in the consciousness of the citizens of the state that in all cases the interruption of pregnancy is legally allowed and, therefore, even from a socio-ethical point of view, is no longer to be condemned. The "dangerous inference of moral permissibility from a legal absence of sanction"...is too near not to be drawn by a large number of those subject to the law....

The counseling and instruction of the pregnant woman provided in §218c, Par. 1, of the Penal Code cannot, considered by itself, be viewed as suitable to effectuate a continuation of the pregnancy.... The counseling centers provided for in §105, Par. 1, No. 2, of the Fifth Statute to Reform the Penal Law should themselves have the means to afford financial, social, and family assistance. Furthermore, they should provide to the pregnant woman and her relatives emotional care through suitable co-workers, and work intensively for the continuation of the pregnancy....

[T]he counseling centers will give instruction about "the public and private assistance available for pregnant women, mothers, and children," "especially regarding assistance which facilitates the continuation of the pregnancy and alleviates the situation of mother and child." This could be interpreted to mean that the counseling centers should only inform, without exerting influence directed to the motivational process. If a protective effect in favor of developing life is to accrue to the counseling, it will depend, in any case, decisively upon such an exertion of influence....

Even if one might consider it thinkable that counseling of this kind could exercise a definite effect in the sense of an aversion from the decision for abortion, its structure, in particular, exhibits in any case deficiencies which do not allow the expectation of an effective protection of developing life.... Physicians are neither qualified for such counseling activity by their professional training nor do they generally have the time required for individual counseling. It is especially questionable that the instruction about social assistance can be undertaken by the same physician who will perform the interruption of pregnancy.... [I]t must be assumed that the majority of physicians decline to perform interruptions of pregnancy which are not indicated, [consequently] only those physicians will make themselves available who either see in the interruption of pregnancy a money-making business or who are inclined to comply with every wish of a woman for interruption of pregnancy because they see in it merely a manifestation of the right to self-determination or a means to the emancipation of women. In both cases, an influence by the physician on the pregnant woman for the continuation of the pregnancy is highly improbable....

IV.

The regulation encountered in the Fifth Statute to Reform the Penal Law at times is defended with the argument that in other democratic countries of the Western World in recent times the penal provisions regulating the interruption of pregnancy have been "liberalized" or "modernized" in a similar or an even more extensive fashion; this would be, as the argument goes, an indication that the new regulation corresponds, in any case, to the general development of theories in this area and is not inconsistent with fundamental socio-ethical and legal principles.

These considerations cannot influence the decision to be made here. Disregarding the fact that all of these foreign laws in their respective countries are sharply controverted, the legal standards which are applicable there for the acts of the legislature are essentially different from those of the Federal Republic of Germany.

Underlying the Basic Law are principles for the structuring of the state that may be understood only in light of the historical experience and the spiritual-moral confrontation with the previous system of National Socialism. In opposition to the omnipotence of the totalitarian state which claimed for itself limitless dominion over all areas of social life and which, in the prosecution of its goals of state, consideration for the life of the individual fundamentally meant nothing, the Basic Law of the Federal Republic of Germany has erected an order bound together by values which places the individual human being and his dignity at the focal point of all of its ordinances. At its basis lies the concept, as the Federal Constitutional Court previously pronounced...that human beings posses an inherent worth as individuals in order of creation which uncompromisingly demands unconditional respect for the life of every individual human being, even for the apparently socially "worthless," and which therefore excludes the destruction of such life without legally justifiable grounds. This fundamental constitutional decision determines the structure and the interpretation of the entire legal order. Even the legislature is bound by it; considerations of socio-political expediency, even necessities of state, cannot overcome this constitutional limitation (Decisions of the Federal Constitutional Court, 1, 14 36). Even a general change of the viewpoints dominant in the populace on this subject—if such a change could be established at all—would change nothing.... Therefore, no adverse judgment is being passed about other legal orders "which have not had these experiences with a system of injustice and which, on the basis of an historical development which has taken a different course and other political conditions and fundamental views of the philosophy of state, have not made such a decision for themselves" (Decisions of the Federal Constitutional Court, 18, 112 117)....

Dissenting Opinion of Justice Rupp von Brünneck and Justice Dr. Simon....

The life of each individual human being is self-evidently a central value of the legal order. It is uncontested that the constitutional duty to protect this life also includes its preliminary stages before birth. The debates in Parliament and before the Federal Constitutional Court dealt not with the *whether* but rather the *how* of this protection. This decision is a matter of legislative responsibility. Under no circumstances can the duty of the state to prescribe punishment for abortion in every stage of pregnancy be derived from the constitution. The legislature should be able to determine the regulations for counseling and the term solution as well as for the indications solution....

The authority of the Federal Constitutional Court to annul the decisions of the legislature demands sparing use, if an imbalance between the constitutional organs is to be avoided. The requirement of judicial self-restraint, which is designated as the "elixer of life" of the jurisprudence of the Federal Constitutional Court, is especially valid when involved is not a defense from overreaching by state power but rather the making, via constitutional judicial control, of provisions for the positive structuring of the social order for the legislature which is directly legitimatized by the people. The Federal Constitutional Court must not succumb to the temptation to take over for itself the function of a controlling organ and shall not in the long run endanger the authority to judicially review constitutionality.

The test proposed in this proceeding departs from the basis of classical judicial control. The fundamental legal norms standing in the central part of our constitution guarantee as rights of defense to the citizen in relation to the state a sphere of unrestricted structuring of one's life based on personal responsibility. The classical function of the Federal Constitutional Court lies in defending against injuries to this sphere of freedom from excessive infringement by the state power. On the scale of possible infringements by the state, penal provisions are foremost: they demand of a citizen a definite behavior and subdue him in the case of a violation with grievous restrictions of freedom or with financial burdens. Judicial control of the constitutionality of such provisions therefore means a determination whether the encroachment resulting either from the enactment or application of penal provisions into protected spheres of freedom is allowable; whether, therefore, the state, generally or to the extent provided, may punish.

In the present constitutional dispute, the inverse question is presented for the first time for examination, namely whether the state *must* punish, whether the abolition of punishment for the interruption of pregnancy in the first three months of pregnancy is compatible with fundamental rights. It is obvious, however, that the disregard of punishment is the opposite of state encroachment. Since the partial withdrawal of the penal provision did not occur to benefit interruptions of pregnancies but rather, because the previous penal sanction, according to the unrefuted assumption of the legislature which has been confirmed by experience, has thoroughly proved itself ineffective, an "attack" on the unborn life by the state is not even indirectly construable....

Our strongest reservation is directed to the fact that for the first time in opinions of the Constitutional Court an objective value decision should function as a *duty* of the legislature to enact *penal norms*, therefore to postulate the strongest conceivable encroachment into the sphere of freedom of the citizen. This inverts the function of the fundamental rights into its contrary. If the objective value decision contained in a fundamental legal norm to protect a certain legal value should suffice to derive therefrom the duty to punish, the fundamental rights could underhandedly, on the pretext of securing freedom, become the basis for an abundance of regimentation which restrict freedom. What is valid for the protection of life can also be claimed for other legal values of high rank— for example, inviolability of the body, freedom, marriage, and family....

The opposite interpretation of fundamental rights necessarily leads to an extension of judicial control of constitutionality which is subject to equal if not more doubt: it is no longer necessary merely to determine alone whether a penal provision encroaches too far into the sphere of rights of the citizens, but also the inverse, whether the state punishes *too little*. Therefore, the Federal Constitutional Court will, contrary to the majority opinion, not be able to restrict itself to the question whether the enactment of any particular penal norm regardless of its contents is required, but in addition must clarify which penal sanction suffices for the protection of the respective legal value. In the last consequence the Court may find it necessary to determine whether the application of a penal norm in the individual case satisfies the concept of protection.

A constitutional determination of penal norms—as the majority requires—is ultimately to be rejected, precisely because the guiding ideas concerning penal law, according to the experiences of the last decades and the expected developments in the field of social sciences, are subject to quick and powerful change. This shows not only a picture of fundamental changes in perhaps the judgments concerning moral offenses—*e.g.,* homosexuality, wife-pandering, exhibitionism—but also covers in a special way the penal provisions against abortion. The freedom from punishment for ethically (criminologically) indicated abortion, which today corresponds to the predominant legal view, was still sharply debated in the sixties. The drafts of a penal code submitted by the federal government in 1960 and 1962 expressly rejected this indication; for the social and eugenic indications they were content with the reference that the rejection was "self-explanatory." ...

Our most important objection is directed to the majority's failure to explain how the requirement of condemnation as an independent duty is constitutionally derived. According to our view the constitution nowhere requires that ethically objectionable behavior or conduct deserving of punishment must *per se* be condemned with the help of the statutory law without regard to the desired effect. In a pluralistic, ideologically neutral and liberal democratic community, it is a task for the forces of society to codify the postulates of opinion. The state must practice abstention in this matter; its task is the protection of the legal values guaranteed and recognized by the constitution. For the constitutional decision it matters only whether the penal provision is imperatively required to secure an effective protection of developing life, having taken into consideration the interests of the woman which are deserving of protection....

Notes and Questions

1. *Holding.* What was the holding of the Federal Constitutional Court?

2. *The Dissent.* Dissenting opinions are fairly rare in Germany. The Federal Constitutional Court only first published dissents in 1971. *See* Michael G. Mattern, Notes and Comments, *German Abortion Law: The Unwanted Child of Reunification*, 13 Loy. L.A. Int'l & Comp. L. Rev. 643, 678 (1991). The dissent was signed by the only woman then on the court. Florian Miedel, *Is West Germany's 1975 Abortion Decision a Solution to the American Abortion Debate?: A Critique of Mary Ann Glendon and Donald Kommers*, 20 N.Y.U. Rev. L. & Soc. Change 471, 478 (1993–94).

3. *Right to Life of the Unborn.* Is the fetus a person in German law? Does it have the same constitutional rights as a child who has been born? Does the dissent agree with the majority on this point? Why does the Court permit the state to punish the killing of a fetus differently than the killing of a young child?

4. *Status of the Fetus in Germany More Generally.* The initial report of the Federal Republic of Germany, submitted in accordance with article 44 of the Convention on the Rights of the Child, discussed the general legal status of the unborn child in Germany, apart from the constitutional protection afforded it.

> The unborn child enjoys protection in the Federal Republic of Germany pursuant to a number of different legal provisions. To be sure, a person does not, as a matter of principle, have legal capacity until his or her birth (sect. 1 of the Civil Code). Pursuant to section 1923, subsection 2, of the Civil Code, however, a child who has not yet been born must be considered to be a potential heir if he or she is born alive and had already been conceived at the time of the death of the person to whose estate he or she is to succeed; within the framework of section 823, subsection 1, of the Civil Code he or she is protected prior to birth against injury inflicted by tortious acts. Pursuant to section 844, subsection 2, of the Civil Code he or she has the right to claim damages in the event that the person obligated to provide his or her maintenance is killed and can furthermore be the beneficiary of contracts for the benefit of third parties or with protective effect for the benefit of third parties. A curator may be appointed for the child even prior to birth to exercise his or her future rights (sect. 1912 of the Civil Code).

Consideration of Reports Submitted by States Parties Under Article 44 of the Convention, Addendum Germany, U.N. CRC, ¶ 10, U.N. Doc. CRC/C/11/Add.5 (1994).

5. *Positive Rights.* Often times constitutions are silent about whether a fetus is entitled to the right to life, and courts have to resolve the issue. When a fetus is given constitutional protection or human rights protection, this may impose a duty on the state not to harm the fetus or, alternatively, to protect its life. The German Constitutional Court stated, "The duty of the state to protect is comprehensive. It forbids not only... direct attacks on the life developing itself but also requires the state to...preserve it even against illegal attacks by others." How does this compare with the government's obligation under the U.S. Constitution? Recall *DeShaney v. Winnebago Cnty.,* 489 U.S. 189 (1989), in which the U.S. Supreme Court suggested that the U.S. Constitution imposes very few obligations on the government to stop harm inflicted by private individuals on others, unless the victim is in the physical custody of the government. If the fetus were a "person" under the U.S. Constitution, what would be the impact of that classification? Would you ever see a case like *BverfGE 39* (1975) in the United States?

6. *The Objective Order of Values.* The opinion talks about the "objective order of values." This concept was judicially developed and has been explained by one commentator as follows: "The constitution must be interpreted in the light of public values derived from a reading of the Basic Law as a whole and particularly from its list of guaranteed rights, a list crowned by the inviolate principle of human dignity. Under this theory, the Basic Law includes both individual rights and public values. An individual right is a subjective right that can be asserted against the state and thus capable of judicial vindication. But the right also embodies an objective value (*i.e.*, a public value) and, as such is said to have an independent force or effect under the Constitution, thereby imposing an affirmative duty on the State to ensure that the public value is realized in practice." Donald P. Kommers, *The Constitutional Law of Abortion in Germany: Should Americans Pay Attention?* 10 J. Contemp. Health L. & Pol'y 1, 8–9 (1993). How does this concept differ from the idea that a constitution has a "horizontal application." For a discussion of the horizontal application of rights, see note 8 before the *Grootboom* case in Chapter 14.A.2.

7. *The Mother's Interest.* Is the mother's interest recognized in the German Constitution? From where in the German Constitution does her interest get protection? One author suggests that the mother's interest is recognized in article 2(1) of the Basic Law. "Article 2(1) of the Basic Law, which embodies the principle of personal self-determination...confers upon everyone the 'right to the free development of his or her personality in so far as he or she does not violate the rights of others or offend against the constitutional order or the moral code.'" Kommers, *supra*, at 7. Alternatively, perhaps article 1(1), which speaks of the inviolability of a person's dignity, or article 2(2), which speaks of the inviolability of a person's body, are implicated. As you read further in this section, consider whether subsequent developments in Germany adequately acknowledge these principles.

8. *Nazism.* The majority's reasoning heavily relies on the fact that the German Constitution was drafted against the background of the National Socialist regime. However, do the Nazi's eugenics policies really have any relevance to a woman's own decision to abort her child? Also, the Nazi experience suggests that governments should not employ criminal punishment for abortion, right?

9. *Separation of Powers.* The dissenting opinion was very concerned about the separation of powers in Germany. That concern was well grounded in the facts at hand. The case was brought before the Court by a minority of members from the Bundestag (parliament) whose abortion legislation was defeated by the legislature after lengthy debate. What competing consideration was the majority concerned about?

10. *Social Welfare State.* How important is it to the Court's decision that Germany is a social welfare state? One author has suggested that the abortion decision was "fully anchored in the social legislation existing in West Germany at the time." Miedel, *supra*, at 504.

11. *Purpose or Effect of the Legislation.* Part of the disagreement between the majority and the dissent centers on whether the court should be concerned with the purpose or the effect of a law. According to the dissent, the purpose of the Fifth Statute to Reform the Penal Law was benign. The dissent emphasized that the legislature had removed the penal sanction for abortions performed during the first three months of pregnancy (incarceration for up to three years) because it was "ineffective." In fact, there were between 75,000 and 300,000 illegal abortions prior to adoption of § 218 of the Penal Code in the Fifth Statute to Reform the Penal Law. *See* Jonas & Gorby, *supra*, at 683 (provid-

ing dissenting opinion of Rupp von Brünneck and Dr. Simon, JJ.). However, only a few hundred cases were prosecuted under the earlier statute. *Id.* at 611. The majority of the Constitutional Court, however, focused on the effect of removing ted penal provision. It thought the government presented insufficient evidence that the enactment of the Fifth Statute to Reform the Penal Law would diminish the number of abortions, particularly because the reform allowed the interruption of the pregnancy, with the woman's consent, up to twelve weeks after conception. Most abortions (nine out of ten) occurred in the first twelve weeks. *See generally* Jonas & Gorby, *supra,* at 611, 651, 658. The Court believed that the rate of abortions would increase, if anything. *Id.* at 657. Undoubtedly the majority would not permit a provision whose express purpose was to increase the number of abortions. When, if ever, might the dissent be concerned with the effect the new law would have on the number of abortions?

12. *East Germany.* Prior to unification, East Germany had a liberal abortion law. The law allowed abortion on demand until the twelfth week. The law's rationale was as follows:

> The equality of the woman in education and career, marriage and the family, requires that the woman be able to decide for herself about pregnancy and its continuation. The realization of this right is inseparably connected with the increasing responsibility of the socialist state and all its citizens for the constant improvement of health care for the woman, for the furtherance of the family and love of children.

Mattern, *supra,* at 672 (citing Gesetz uber die Unterbrechung der Schwangerschaft, 1972 Gesetzblatt der DDR [GB] I 89 (E. Ger.)). The post-unification legal milieu in the former East Germany is described immediately below.

Abortion II and Abortion III in Germany. The Constitutional Court has issued several other important decisions on the topic of abortion. The first of these (Abortion II, BVerfGE, 88 (1993), 203 (F.R.G.)) came as a challenge to the Pregnancy and Family Assistance Act [PFAA], an act passed as part of the German Parliament's effort to unify Germany after the fall of East Germany. *See* Richard E. Levy & Alexander Somek, *Paradoxical Parallels in the American and German Abortion Decisions,* 9 Tul. J. Int'l & Comp. L. 109, 131 (2001). The PFAA "permitted women to have an abortion within the first three months of pregnancy, subject to a requirement of counseling—which must be certified—and a three day waiting period after consulting with the physician carrying out the abortion. The counseling procedure outlined by the PFAA Act was relatively more demanding than the comparable provisions that were struck down in *Abortion I* [BVerfGE 39 (1975)]." *Id.* In short, the PFAA decriminalized first-trimester abortions that were preceded by certain formalities. The PFAA was challenged in court; the next two excerpts describe the 135-page decision of the Constitutional Court that resulted from that litigation.

Deborah Goldberg, *Developments in German Abortion Law: A U.S. Perspective*
5 UCLA Women's L. J. 531, 542–44 (1995)

On May 28, 1993, the Federal Constitutional Court, in a 6–2 decision, upheld the constitutionality of the provisions of the 1992 Act that decriminalized abortion and gave women the "ultimate responsibility" to decide whether or not to terminate a pregnancy. By decriminalizing abortions, the 1992 Act ensured that abortions performed by a doctor in the first twelve weeks of the pregnancy and after official counseling would no longer be punishable. The Court also held that an abortion in the first twelve weeks of the pregnancy, while not criminal, was legal only if a serious medical, eugenic or criminal indication existed. The Court did not explicitly recognize the social indication, but explained that an indication exists where circumstances create an "undue burden" for the woman to carry the fetus to term. The court also indicated that the legislature can further define circumstances constituting an "unreasonable burden" and thus left open the possibility of re-establishing the social indication. Because the Court held that an abortion performed by a doctor in the first twelve weeks of the pregnancy and after official counseling cannot be criminalized, this form of abortion is allowable.

Although the Court found that the legislative reforms did not provide the minimum constitutional standards to protect unborn life, it held that the state was not obligated to criminalize all illegal abortions. Instead, the state could create a comprehensive system of counseling with the goal of convincing the pregnant woman to carry the fetus to term. If, after counseling, the woman decided to proceed with a nonindicated (or merely counseled) abortion, within the first twelve weeks of the pregnancy, it would not be considered a criminal offense. Nevertheless, the Court held this nonindicated abortion could not be considered justified or legal since it is in direct conflict with the state's constitutional duty to protect unborn life. . . .

Through its holding, the Court attempted "to erect a normative bulwark to counteract the impression, conveyed by the frequent practice of abortion, that abortion is socially acceptable." The Court acknowledged that two sets of constitutional rights are involved in every abortion decision: the state's duty to protect the unborn, and the woman's constitutional right to the protection of her dignity, her bodily integrity, and the free development of her personality. However, the Court found that the state has a duty to uphold minimum constitutional standards to protect the unborn fetus, even if they are in conflict with the rights of the pregnant woman, since her rights, although legitimate, are clearly less compelling. The Court used the distinction between illegality and criminality in order to balance conflicting constitutional rights, thus finding a compromise. The Court held that in order to fulfill its duty to protect unborn life, the state must consider an abortion without the existence of an indication fundamentally "wrong," although "allowable," and encourage the woman to carry the fetus to term.

Gerald L. Neuman, *Casey in the Mirror: Abortion, Abuse and the Right to Protection in the United States and Germany*
43 Am. J. Comp. L. 273, 282–87 (1995)

[T]he majority concluded that the legislature had acted reasonably in changing over from the system based on third party determination of indications to a system based on counseling. A key element of its reasoning was the fact that in the early phase of pregnancy, outsiders could not perceive that a woman was pregnant. The fetus was undiscovered, helpless and dependent on the woman. A system that elicited the cooperation of the woman therefore had a greater chance of success in preventing abortion than a system that antagonized her and prompted evasion. The threat of criminal punishment and the subjection of the woman to third party evaluation of her need for an abortion had proved antagonizing. It would be more effective, as well as more respectful, to appeal to the woman's sense of responsibility through individual counseling, while leaving the ultimate decision to the woman herself. The counselor had to explain to the woman that only unreasonable demands could justify an abortion [*i.e.*, that the pregnancy would impose on her unreasonable demands], and had to explore frankly with her whether her situation corresponded to that standard. The counselor also had to offer her help in obtaining available forms of assistance and to encourage her to bear the child anyway. The majority expressed its crucial concern that, in cases of a "general situation of need," the frankness and open-mindedness of the discussion would be impaired if the pregnant woman were anticipating a third party evaluation, even a later evaluation relating only to allowance of a claim for payment. Finally, the majority noted that its approval of a system based on counseling depended on a prediction of future effects; the legislature had a continuing constitutional duty to monitor the operation of the new system and to improve it if necessary. (Indeed, the court struck down the repeal of the former requirement that abortions be reported to a central statistical office, because it found that gathering some of this information was essential to fulfillment of the legislature's monitoring duty.)

The court was not satisfied with the legislature's specification of the content and organization of the counseling process. The legislation should have specified that the counseling must be directed toward the protection of the fetus, by helping the woman resolve her conflicted feelings through a decision to bear the child. The woman could be expected to reveal her reasons, but must be permitted to preserve her anonymity. If it appeared useful to bring into the counseling process the father of the fetus, the parents of a pregnant minor, or other people close to the woman, the counselor was obliged to urge the woman to permit this; conversely, if the woman was accompanied by a person whose presence impaired the counseling process, the counselor was obliged to urge the woman to return unaccompanied. The counselor, not the woman, had to decide when the counseling was complete and could be so certified. Counseling could be performed by private organizations, but the state was then obliged to monitor their performance, to determine whether they counseled in the right spirit, and to assure their independence from undue influence by abortion providers.

Although the physician who performed an abortion was ineligible to serve as counselor, the state was obliged to ensure that the physician played a supplementary role in the protection of the fetus. The medical profession was dedicated to preserving human life, and physicians normally consulted with their patients before providing requested treatments. The physician was obliged to determine that the patient had undergone counseling and had observed the three-day waiting period, and was obliged to verify independently the age of the fetus. The physician had to inquire into the reasons for the abortion, and to make sure that the patient was not being pressured into abortion against her true wishes. The physician was obliged to inform the patient that abortion involved the destruction of human life. Unless medically indicated, the sex of the fetus could not be disclosed to the patient during the first trimester, to avoid the practice of gender choice. The physician had to be subject to criminal penalties for failure to comply with these duties. After all that, the physician was obliged to make an ethical decision whether, given the patient's answers, it would be professionally responsible to perform the abortion; unethical conduct was subject to professional sanction, but the state was not obliged to criminalize it.

This expanded role of the physician was not, however, equivalent to a third party determination that the abortion was justified by the unreasonable demands that continuation of the pregnancy would place upon the woman. A majority of the court viewed the absence of a third party determination as having fateful consequences for the legal treatment of these "unevaluated abortions." The woman's own decision that continuation of the pregnancy would impose unreasonable demands upon her could not be treated as legally conclusive. To do so would make her a judge in her own case, and would violate the rule of law. People sometimes tended to place undue value on their own interests, and the counseling system could not be guaranteed to exclude this possibility. Therefore the legislature could decriminalize unevaluated abortions, but it could not define them as justified or lawful. This conclusion applied principally to abortions founded on the "general situation of need" criterion, because the medical, criminological and embryopathic criteria were susceptible to an objective third party verification that would not endanger the counseling process. Treating every unevaluated abortion as justified and lawful would violate the state's duty to protect every fetus. It would also undermine the public's sense of justice, increasing the danger that more women would choose to abort for constitutionally insufficient reasons.

The majority added a key qualification to its conclusion that an unevaluated abortion could not be treated as lawful. The state was forbidden to treat the abortion as lawful except in those contexts where treating the abortion as unlawful would impair the effectiveness of the counseling system as a means of protecting the fetus. Decriminalization was already one example of this exception: because the threat of criminal punishment could induce women to prevaricate in counseling or to avoid the counselors altogether, withdrawal of the criminal sanction was proper. The opinion addressed a variety of legal rules implicating aspects of abortion, and evaluated where the success of the counseling system required that unevaluated abortions be treated as if they were lawful, and where it did not.

The majority invalidated the new § 218a(1) of the Criminal Code, because it declared that unevaluated abortions after counseling within the first twelve weeks of pregnancy were "not unlawful," rather than merely free of criminal sanction. The majority found that the success of the counseling system did not require that women be granted the solace of a favorable legal judgment on their decisions....

The most controversial portion of the decision concerned the financing of unevaluated abortions. Five justices concluded that the public medical insurance system could not cover the cost of an unevaluated abortion if the woman had sufficient funds to pay for it herself. The state would be participating in unlawful killing if it paid for abortions without ascertaining that they were justified; this would violate the rule of law at its core. Such coverage was not necessary to the success of the counseling system, and it would tend to give the erroneous impression that the abortion was lawful. The prohibited social insurance benefits included the cost of the abortion procedure, follow-up medical care in case of an abortion without complications, and sick pay for the period of absence from work. Nor could private insurance cover the cost of an abortion without a third party determination of its legality. If the woman did not personally have the means to pay for an abortion, however, state payment would be permissible, because it was necessary to the success of the counseling system: otherwise the woman might not obtain the services of a law-abiding physician, and then her health would be endangered and the physician's protective function would not be performed. The majority identified a provision of the welfare laws as supplying a current legal basis for financing abortions for needy women. In addition, the court held that employers could be required to provide sick pay to employees who were absent from work because of abortions—exclusion of such payments from the employer's sick pay obligation would not be possible without compromising the employee's privacy.

The majority also discussed the need for criminal sanctions to protect women from pressures leading them to have abortions. The state was obliged to impose criminal sanctions on family members who reprehensibly withheld support that could reasonably have been expected from them, or pressured the woman into having the abortion. The state also needed to consider whether criminal sanctions should apply to other persons, such as employers or landlords, who reprehensibly force a pregnant woman into a dilemma that could eventuate in abortion. The court's decision required the legislature to enact some form of criminal sanction on family members, but left the treatment of employers and landlords to the legislature's discretion.

Although the Federal Constitutional Court struck down the PFAA in its second major abortion decision, it gave sufficient guidance that a new law was passed. The law, the Pregnant Women's and Family Aid (Amendment) Act of 1995, "retains the principle that abortion should, as a general rule, be regarded as a criminal offence. The legislation re-enacts a provision from an earlier 1976 Act which permits abortion…if the termination of the pregnancy is necessary to save the life of a woman or to avert a danger of serious physical or mental damage to the pregnant woman, taking into account her current and future life conditions. There is no time limit in respect of these grounds.…The Code further provides that an abortion performed by a doctor with the consent of the pregnant woman within the first twelve weeks after conception will not be punished, provided the pregnant woman receives anti-abortion counselling from someone other than the doctor performing the procedure at least three days prior to the operation and provides a certificate to this effect to the doctor. This counselling must encourage the woman to continue her pregnancy. She must be told that the unborn has a right to life at all stages of pregnancy and that the law may only regard abortion as acceptable if the continuation of the pregnancy would be an extraordinary burden exceeding that which can reasonably be expected of her. The Pregnancy Conflict Act 1995 sets out in more detail the rules governing counselling of pregnant women seeking abortions." See Gov't of Ireland, Dep't of Taoiseach, Green Paper on Abortion (1999), *available at* www.irl-gov.ie/taoiseach/publication/greenpaper/appendix3.htm (describing German law). The new laws were passed against a backdrop of "relative ease" by which women could obtain abortions, since the "indications" (*i.e.*, the exception to the ban on abortions during the first twelve weeks of pregnancy) had been interpreted broadly. See Levy & Somek, *supra*, at 130–31. To be clear, there is no criminal penalty for an abortion within the first twelve weeks of pregnancy if the mother undergoes counseling; however, the abortion will be considered "illegal" unless it falls within one of the indications.

In its third major decision, *Abortion III*, BVerfG, 1 BvR 2306/96 (1998), the Federal Constitutional Court "invalidated provisions of a Bavarian law that prohibited medical doctors without training as gynecologists from performing abortions, even if these doctors had performed abortions in the past and therefore had the requisite experience. The Court concluded that this change unduly frustrated reliance interests that are protected by article 12 of the Basic Law, which protects the fundamental right to practice one's profession. Thus, transitional rules were constitutionally required to protect the right of these physicians to continue to perform abortions. This latter conclusion does not modify or further elaborate the constitutional regime of *Abortion II*, but the recognition of a reliance-based right of physicians to perform abortions is a sign of how far the Court has come in accommodating some right of autonomy concerning abortion matters." Levy & Somek, *supra*, at 154 n.189.

The new approach to abortion is important for many women in Germany. The reason why might surprise you. Prior to the *Abortion II* decision, one author reported that "A recent empirical study of abortion in West Germany showed that ninety percent of women seeking abortions were able to find a doctor to attest to a social indication. However, only fifty percent of all women polled were able to obtain an attestation of indication on their first visit to a doctor. Ten percent of the women questioned had to visit three or more doctors. Of the women who failed to find an attesting physician, about half obtained illegal or foreign abortions. The rest continued the pregnancy to term." Mattern, *supra*, at 686. However, even after the *Abortion II* decision, the ability of a German woman to obtain an abortion varies tremendously by state, with the women in the predominantly Catholic states finding it the most difficult. Miedel, *supra*, at 483.

Comparing the United States' Law on Abortion. What are the similarities and differences in the United States and German constitutional case law regarding abortion? There have been a series of constitutional cases in the United States on the topic. For our purposes, the two most important cases probably are *Roe v. Wade*, 410 U.S. 113 (1973) and *Planned Parenthood v. Casey*, 505 U.S. 833 (1992), although a fuller analysis would undoubtedly include *Rust v. Sullivan*, 500 U.S. 173, 193-94 (1991) (upholding against First Amendment challenge restrictions on doctors ability to discuss abortion with their patients when the doctors received federal funds).

In *Roe v. Wade*, 410 U.S. 113 (1973), the U.S. Supreme Court struck down a Texas criminal law that permitted abortion only for the purpose of saving the mother's life. The Court held that the law violated the mother's privacy rights, as embodied in the Due Process Clause of the Fourteenth Amendment. It recognized that the state has a legitimate interest in both the mother's health and the fetus's potential life, but held that each of these interests became "compelling" at different times during the woman's pregnancy. Consequently, it developed what became known as the "trimester" approach: 1) A woman has the right to an abortion up until approximately the end of the first trimester; 2) The state can regulate abortion practices up until the end of the second trimester to promote the mother's health; and 3) The state can regulate or proscribe abortion after viability to further its interest in the potential human life, except that it has to permit abortion if necessary for the life or health of the mother. In *Roe v. Wade*, the U.S. Supreme Court specifically addressed the argument that the fetus was a person entitled to constitutional protection. Here is an excerpt from the opinion responsive to that argument:

> The Constitution does not define "person" in so many words. Section 1 of the Fourteenth Amendment contains three references to "person." The first, in defining "citizens," speaks of "persons born or naturalized in the United States." The word also appears both in the Due Process Clause and in the Equal Protection Clause. "Person" is used in other places in the Constitution: in the listing of qualifications for Representatives and Senators, Art. I, §2, cl. 2, and §3, cl. 3; in the Apportionment Clause, Art. I, §2, cl. 3; in the Migration and Importation provision, Art. I, §9, cl. 1; in the Emolument Clause, Art. I, §9, cl. 8; in the Electors provisions, Art. II, §1, cl. 2, and the superseded cl. 3; in the provision outlining qualifications for the office of President, Art. II, §1, cl. 5; in the Extradition provisions, Art. IV, §2, cl. 2, and the superseded Fugitive Slave Clause 3; and in the Fifth, Twelfth, and Twenty-second Amendments, as well as in §§2 and 3 of the Fourteenth Amendment. But in nearly all these instances, the use of the word is such that it has application only postnatally. None indicates, with any assurance, that it has any possible prenatal application.

All this, together with our observation,...that throughout the major portion of the 19th century prevailing legal abortion practices were far freer than they are today, persuades us that the word "person," as used in the Fourteenth Amendment, does not include the unborn. This is in accord with the results reached in those few cases where the issue has been squarely presented. [Ed. Note: The Court cites lower court cases]. Indeed, our decision in United States v. Vuitch, 402 U.S. 62 (1971), inferentially is to the same effect, for we there would not have indulged in statutory interpretation favorable to abortion in specified circumstances if the necessary consequence was the termination of life entitled to Fourteenth Amendment protection.

410 U.S. at 157–59. Some commentators have noted, "If the viable fetus was not to be recognized as a 'person' for constitutional analysis, there is no constitutional explanation of why the state's interest in protecting his or her right to life should be given parity with the woman's fundamental constitutional right of privacy." Levy & Somek, *supra*, at 120.

In *Planned Parenthood v. Casey*, 505 U.S. 833 (1992), the U.S. Supreme Court upheld some of the contested provisions of the Pennsylvania Abortion Control Act of 1982. Among other things, it found the following provisions to be constitutional: requiring the woman's informed consent before an abortion was performed; requiring that she receive certain information at least 24 hours before the abortion; requiring minors to obtain the consent of one parent; imposing certain reporting requirements on doctors; and the definition of medical emergency. These requirements were upheld as furthering the state's legitimate interests in protecting the woman's health and the "life of the fetus that may become a child." *Id.* at 846. The Court found unconstitutional a provision which required married women to notify their husbands unless an exception applied.

Casey reaffirmed aspects of *Roe v. Wade*. For example, the right to choose an abortion remains protected by substantive due process. Yet a plurality advanced a new framework by which courts were to evaluate states' efforts to regulate abortion. Now women have a right to an abortion prior to viability without the state imposing an "undue burden" on them. An undue burden exists if the law has the "purpose or effect of placing a substantial obstacle in the path of a woman seeking an abortion." *Casey*, 505 U.S. at 877. A state could never justify prohibiting abortion altogether or placing substantial obstacles in women's paths prior to viability. In addition, the state must allow an abortion even post-viability in situations where the woman's life or health is threatened. How does the U.S. Supreme Court's "undue burden" test differ from the use of that term in the German *Abortion II* decision?

Compare the permissibility of abortion in Germany and the United States today. Are the outcomes similar? Does that surprise you? What does that tell you about constitutional adjudication? For an excellent article comparing the decisions, *see* Levy & Somek, *supra*. For more on Germany and its approach to abortion, *see* Caroline J. Forder, *Abortion: A Constitutional Problem in European Perspective*, 1 Maastricht J. Eur. & Comp. L. 56 (1994).

2. International Law

Some international instruments address the topic of *reproductive health* and contain provisions that may pertain to abortion. Often it is unclear, however, whether the instrument supports access to abortion. *See, e.g.*, International Covenant on Economic, Social and Cultural Rights (ICESCR), art. 12; Convention on the Rights of the Child, art. 24. Other instruments have general provisions from which one might deduce that there is a *right to reproductive autonomy*, including abortion, although no definitive interpretation of the instrument exists. For example, the Universal Declaration of Human Rights (UDHR) includes article 3, which recognizes everyone's right to life, liberty and security of person, and article 12, which recognizes everyone's right to privacy. *See also* International Covenant on Civil and Political Rights (ICCPR), art. 9(1) (recognizing everyone's right to liberty and security of the person); art. 17 (recognizing the right to privacy). Similarly, documents with the imprimatur of world opinion state that individuals have the right to decide "freely and responsibly on the number and spacing of children." *See Report of the International Conference on Population and Development*, U.N. Population Div., Dep't of Econ. & Soc. Affairs, principle 8, U.N. Doc. A/CONF.171/13 (1994), *at* www.un.org/popin/icpd/conference/offeng/poa.html (Cairo Programe of Action); *Proclamation of Tehran*, Final Act of the International Conference on Human Rights, Tehran, (Apr. 22–May 13), ¶ 16, U.N. Doc. A/CONF.32/41 (1968); *Report of the United Nations World Population Conference, Bucharest*, Sales No. E 75.XIII.2 (1974). Does that phrase necessarily encompass the right to terminate an unwanted pregnancy?

What about international law provisions that condemn forced pregnancy? Article 7(1)(g) of the Rome Statute of the International Criminal Court, U.N. Doc. A/CONF. 183/9 (1998), recognizes "forced pregnancy" as "a crime against humanity" if "committed as part of a widespread or systematic attack directed against any civilian population, with knowledge of the attack." However, "unlawful confinement" is required for a pregnancy to be forced. *See id.* art. 7(2)(f). The Fourth World Conference on Women also condemned "forced pregnancy." *Beijing Declaration and Platform for Action*, U.N. Fourth World Conference on Women, ¶¶ 114, 133, 136, U.N. Doc. A/CONF.177/20 (1995). However, forced pregnancy was linked to armed conflict, *id.* ¶ 144(d), and ethnic cleansing. *Id.* ¶ 13. Consequently, the context in which this phrase appears diminishes its effectiveness for abortion proponents.

Complicating matters are international instruments that talk about protection for the unborn. For example, the preamble to the Convention on the Rights of the Child (CRC) states that "the child, by reason of his physical and mental immaturity, needs special safeguards and care, including appropriate legal protection, before as well as after birth." This language was taken from the 1959 United Nations Declaration on the Rights of the Child. Similarly, a recommendation by the European Parliament states: "The rights of every…child to life from the moment of conception, to shelter, adequate food and congenial environment should be recognised, and national governments should accept as an obligation the task of providing for full realisation of such rights." Recommendation 874 (1979) on the European Charter on the Rights of the Child, Eur. Par. Ass., 31st Sess., Rec. No. 874, Part. VI.A (1979).

The CRC, with its treaty status, potentially offers the most promise for those opposed to abortion. Yet the substantive provisions of the CRC do not necessarily support an anti-abortion position. The articles of the Convention do not specifically refer to abortion. Rather the CRC merely refers to "children" or "childhood." The definition of "child" does not resolve the issue. A child is a "human being" under eighteen years old. *See* art. 1. *Accord* UDHR, art. 25(2) ("motherhood and childhood are entitled to special care and assistances"). Professor Sanford Fox has given the CRC, and particularly the preamble and the definition of child, a detailed examination. He has concluded that ratification of the Convention would not require the United States to alter its abortion law. *See* Sanford J. Fox, *The United Nations Convention on the Rights of the Child and the United States Abortion Law*, 2 Ann. Surv. Int'l & Comp. L. 15 (1995). Looking closely at the language of the preamble, can you make an argument that it does not call for the abolition of abortion? Professer Fox also informs the reader that the legislative history of the Convention does not support an anti-choice understanding of the preamble either. In particular, he states that there is a "long-standing global consensus...that it is inappropriate for international law, or even formal international aspiration, to take a position for or against fetal or abortion rights." *Id.* at 27. Assuming Professor Fox's conclusion is accurate, is an absence of international law in this area to be applauded or condemned?

Let's focus for a moment on the Convention for the Elimination of All Forms of Discrimination against Women (CEDAW). Does CEDAW guarantee women access to safe abortions? Can you make an argument that it does, or does not, guarantee women access to safe abortions? Examine article 12, in particular, and then consider the elaboration on article 12 provided by the Committee on the Elimination of Discrimination Against Women.

General Recommendation No. 24, Report of the Committee on the Elimination of Discrimination Against Women
U.N. GAOR, 54th Sess., Supp. 38, U.N. Doc. A/54/38/Rev.1 (1999)

11. Measures to eliminate discrimination against women are considered to be inappropriate if a health-care system lacks services to prevent, detect and treat illnesses specific to women. It is discriminatory for a State party to refuse to provide legally for the performance of certain reproductive health services for women. For instance, if health service providers refuse to perform such services based on conscientious objection, measures should be introduced to ensure that women are referred to alternative health providers....

13. The duty of States parties to ensure, on a basis of equality of men and women, access to health-care services, information and education implies an obligation to respect, protect and fulfil women's rights to health care. States parties have the responsibility to ensure that legislation and executive action and policy comply with these three obligations. They must also put in place a system that ensures effective judicial action. Failure to do so will constitute a violation of article 12.

14. The obligation to respect rights requires States parties to refrain from obstructing action taken by women in pursuit of their health goals. States parties should report on how public and private health-care providers meet their duties to respect women's rights to have access to health care. For example, States parties should not restrict women's access to health services or to the clinics that provide those services on the ground that women do not have the authorization of husbands, partners, parents or health authorities, because they are unmarried or because they are women. Other barriers to women's access to appropriate health care include laws that criminalize medical procedures only needed by women or punish women who undergo those procedures....

17. The duty to fulfil rights places an obligation on States parties to take appropriate legislative, judicial, administrative, budgetary, economic and other measures to the maximum extent of their available resources to ensure that women realize their rights to health care. Studies such as those that emphasize the high maternal mortality and morbidity rates worldwide and the large numbers of couples who would like to limit their family size but lack access to or do not use any form of contraception provide an important indication for States parties of possible breaches of their duties to ensure women's access to health care....

21. States parties should report on measures taken to eliminate barriers that women face in access to health-care services and what measures they have taken to ensure women timely and affordable access to such services. Barriers include requirements or

conditions that prejudice women's access, such as high fees for health-care services, the requirement for preliminary authorization by spouse, parent or hospital authorities, distance from health facilities and the absence of convenient and affordable public transport....

23. In their reports, States parties should state what measures they have taken to ensure timely access to the range of services that are related to family planning, in particular, and to sexual and reproductive health in general. Particular attention should be paid to the health education of adolescents, including information and counselling on all methods of family planning....

26. Reports should also include what measures States parties have taken to ensure women appropriate services in connection with pregnancy, confinement and the postnatal period. Information on the rates at which these measures have reduced maternal mortality and morbidity in their countries, in general, and in vulnerable groups, regions and communities, in particular, should also be included....

29. States parties should implement a comprehensive national strategy to promote women's health throughout their lifespan. This will include interventions aimed at both the prevention and treatment of diseases and conditions affecting women, as well as responding to violence against women, and will ensure universal access for all women to a full range of high-quality and affordable health care, including sexual and reproductive health services....

31. States parties should also, in particular:...

(c) Prioritize the prevention of unwanted pregnancy through family planning and sex education and reduce maternal mortality rates through safe motherhood services and prenatal assistance. When possible, legislation criminalizing abortion should be amended, in order to withdraw punitive measures imposed on women who undergo abortion....

Notes and Questions

1. *Meaning?* What exactly does CEDAW guarantee with respect to reproductive health? If the United States became a party to CEDAW, would it be in violation of the treaty? Is Ethiopia? Italy? Denmark? These countries' laws on abortion are set forth earlier in the chapter. The CEDAW Committee "monitors developments in States Parties with regard to abortion. Women's reproductive health, and changes in access to, and use of, family planning are areas monitored over time...." *See Report of the Committee on Progress Achieved in the Implementation of the Convention,* CEDAW, 14th Sess., ¶ 439, U.N. Doc. CEDAW/C/1995/7 (1995). The Committee "habitually" asks countries about abortion. *See id.* To be clear, "While the object of the Women's Convention includes women's interest in the equal enjoyment with men of good health, it also seeks the elimination of all forms of discrimination against women so that they may enjoy both health and liberty." *See* Rebecca J. Cook, *International Protection of Women's Reproductive Rights,* 24 N.Y.U. J. Int'l L. & Pol. 645, 655 (1992).

2. *General Recommendations Made by the Committee on the Elimination of Discrimination Against Women.* The Committee on the Elimination of Discrimination Against Women issues recommendations and comments that are intended to assist in the interpretation and implementation of CEDAW. General Recommendation No. 19 addresses violence against women. Paragraph 22 states that coerced abortion is harmful to the

health and well-being of women and infringes their right to decide on the number and spacing of their children. Paragraph 24(m) recommends that States prevent coercion with respect to fertility and reproduction and ensure that women do not have to undergo unsafe medical procedures, such as illegal abortion, because they have no access to adequate fertility control services. General Recommendation No. 19 is contained in the Statutory Supplement.

3. *Applicability to Minors.* General Recommendation No. 24 also states, "States parties are encouraged to address the issue of women's health throughout the woman's lifespan. For the purposes of the present general recommendation, therefore, 'women' includes girls and adolescents." Are the three countries' laws on abortion (set forth earlier in the chapter) consistent with CEDAW and the Report?

4. *Access to Information.* Whether or not a particular restriction on access to abortion violates international law, denial of information about abortion may violate international law. For example, article 19(2) of the ICCPR recognizes the right to freedom of expression and this encompasses the right to obtain and impart information and ideas of all kinds. *See also* CEDAW, art. 10.

5. *Culture.* What if abortion is permitted by a country, at least to some extent, but the predominant culture makes exercise of the option difficult. Think about Italy, for example, and the dominance of Catholicism there. In fact, "When Law No. 194 was approved, the Holy See immediately issued a warning that any person performing an abortion and any woman obtaining an abortion would be excommunicated. Owing to the political pressure exerted by the Catholic Church on members of the Christian Democratic Party and the fear of some physicians that their medical practice would consist largely of the performance of abortions, nearly 70 percent of the physicians in Italy and a majority of other health-care professionals have invoked the conscience clause. The situation is most dramatic in southern Italy, where in some regions the proportion of physicians resorting to the conscience clause exceeds 90 percent.... Because of the high proportion of gynecologists that are conscientious objectors and the lack of hospital facilities, in some areas of Italy the delay between the issuance of a certificate and the intervention is at least three weeks. In addition, not all areas have family planning centers, as provided by the law of 1975." Dep't of Econ. & Soc. Affairs, Pop. Div., Abortion Policies: A Global Review 75 (2001), *at* http://www.un.org/esa/population/publications/abortiondoc/italy.doc. Extra-legal forces may decrease the availability of abortion, but may not decrease the demand for abortion. For example, in Brazil, "[d]espite legal restrictions, and the fact that Brazil can be characterized as a mainly Catholic country where abortion is considered a sin, abortion is widely practiced." Axel I. Mundigo & Cynthia Indriso eds., Abortion in the Developing World 218 (1999). Do countries have an obligation to change these cultural forces? How far does a country's obligation extend? What if, for example, men in a particular culture oppose women's use of contraception. *See, e.g., id.* at 249 (discussing segment of Mexican society).

6. *Religion.* Just as the law changes its position on various social issues over time, so does religion. For example, the dissent in 39 BVerfGE 1975, 1 (1–68), emphasized that "canon law, based on the theory of ensoulment, considered until the end of the nineteenth century, abortions performed up to the 80th day after conception to be free from punishment...." Jonas & Gorby, *supra*, at 673 (dissenting opinion of Rupp von Brünneck and Dr. Simon, JJ.). The Church's present anti-abortion position "was started by Pope Pius IX in 1854 during his affirmation of the Immaculate Conception of Mary, which elevated the status of women—particularly the 'sacredness' of their child-bearing role in church dogma." Rishona Fleishman, Comment, *The Battle Against Reproduc-*

tive Rights: The Impact of the Catholic Church on Abortion Law in Both International and Domestic Arenas, 14 Emory Int'l L. Rev. 277, 308 (2000). The existing position of the Catholic Church on abortion is very influential. "The influence of the Catholic Church on reproductive rights is international.... The Catholic Church is the only religion with a permanent observer seat in the United Nations. As an observer, the Holy See sends representatives to the United Nations and to conferences sponsored by the United Nations." *Id.* at 283.

7. *Concerns Under the ICESCR and ICCPR, and the Influence of International Law.* As discussed above, countries are sometimes questioned about their abortion policies by those bodies that monitor compliance with international instruments. Monitoring is the main way countries' abortion policies and practices are evaluated for compliance with international law. The effectiveness of this process has been widely debated among human rights advocates. *See, e.g.,* Diana D.M. Babor, *Population Growth and Reproductive Rights in International Human Rights Law*, 14 Conn. J. Int'l L. 83, 102 (1999). Let's examine some of the substantive concerns members of monitoring bodies raised about Ireland's restrictive abortion law. Think about both the merit of these comments as well as the impact they might have had on the government of Ireland. As a preliminary matter, a brief description of Ireland's position on abortion is warranted.

As the result of several referenda in the early 1990s, the Irish Constitution was amended to allow travel outside of Ireland for purposes of obtaining an abortion and to permit information inside of Ireland about abortion services. These changes were implemented through legislation, which was upheld as constitutional by the Supreme Court of Ireland. An abortion may be obtained in Ireland, however, only if there is a real risk to the mother's life. *See* Attorney General v. X, [1992] I.R. 1, 16 (Ir. S.C.). A referendum was submitted to the Irish voters in 2002 seeking to overturn case law that had allowed the threat of suicide by a pregnant woman to count as a real risk to the mother's life, thereby providing grounds for abortion. *See id.* The referendum also proposed confining abortions to approved facilities. The referendum was defeated by 10,500 votes, with urban areas disfavoring the measure much more than rural areas. *See* BBC News, *Irish PM Concedes Abortion Defeat*, March 7, 2002 at http://news. bbc.co.uk/hi/english/world/europe/newsid_1859000/1859287.stm.

Recently, the Committee on Economic, Social and Cultural Rights has questioned Ireland about the mortality rates from illegal abortion, citing article 12 of the International Covenant on Economic, Social and Cultural Rights (the right to the highest attainable standard of physical and mental health). *See List of Issues: Ireland*, U.N. Comm. on Econ., Soc. & Cultural Rts., U.N. Doc. E/C.12/Q/IRE/2 (2001). However, the concluding observations of the Committee with regard to Ireland did not mention abortion at all. *See Concluding Observations of the Committee on Economic, Social and Cultural Rights: Ireland*, U.N. Doc. E/C.12/1/Add.77 (2002).

Similarly, members of the Human Rights Committee recently asked Ireland questions about abortion, in connection with Ireland's second report submitted pursuant to the International Covenant on Civil and Political Rights (ICCPR). The nature of the concerns vary substantially from member to member. Below are some of the comments made during questioning.

Mr. Klein stated that while he "welcomed the important developments with regard to abortion, it appeared that neither asylum-seekers nor under-age girls in the care of the authorities enjoyed the right to travel for an abortion, even if they were entitled to on the grounds that the life of the mother was at risk. He wondered whether that did not constitute discrimination." *See, e.g., Summary Record of the 1846th Meeting: Ireland,* UNHRC, 69th Sess., ¶66, U.N. Doc. CCPR/C/SR.1846 (2000) (considering second periodic report of Ireland).

Mr. Ando was "concerned by the prohibition of abortion, or rather the plight of women who were the victims of rape, an odious crime that was particularly tragic in Ireland. He wondered whether it was not inhuman to have to choose between giving birth to a child conceived as the result of rape and attempting suicide, which seemed to be the only condition on which a pregnancy could be terminated—in other words when the mother's life was in danger. That situation, which hardly differed from that of prisoners on death row, was tantamount to a violation of article 7 of the Covenant, which prohibited cruel, inhuman or degrading treatment or punishment." *Id.* §4.

Mr. Amor stated the following: "Lawmakers agreed that the question of abortion, and thus of the beginning of life, was a sensitive one, and the response to it varied from one country to another. It was nevertheless hard to accept that Irish women should have to go abroad to terminate a pregnancy—a situation which in fact excluded all those with insufficient resources—or threaten to kill themselves to be heard. Obviously, a whole process of sociological evolution had yet to start in Ireland, where the influence of the church was undeniable. The country's fervor should not, however, give rise to violations of the Covenant, and especially of women's rights, nor should the church's grip on the State become too strong. In that regard, he wished to know whether medically assisted contraception was authorized." *Id.* §7.

The Chairperson, Ms. Medina Quiroga, stated: "It seemed clear that Ireland needed to address issues relating to pregnancy and abortion in the light of article 3 of the Covenant. She drew the delegation's attention to the Committee's general comment 28 relating to that article." *Summary Record of the First Part (Public) of the 1848th Meeting: Ireland,* UNHRC, 69th Sess., ¶20, U.N. Doc. CCRP/SR.1848 (2000). General Comment 28 expands upon article 3 of the ICCPR: equality of rights between men and women. It states that when States Parties report on their compliance with article 6 (the right to life), they "should give information on any measures taken by the State to help women prevent unwanted pregnancies, and to ensure that they do not have to undertake life-threatening clandestine abortions." Equality of Rights Between Men and Women (art. 3): *CCPR General Comment 28,* UNHRC ¶10, U.N. Doc. CCPR/C/21/Rev.1/Add.10 (2000). In addition, when States Parties report on their compliance with articles 7 and 24, they should specify "whether the State Party gives access to safe abortion to women who have become pregnant as a result of rape." *Id.* ¶11.

In its concluding observations on the Irish report, the Committee stated: "The Committee is concerned that the circumstances in which women may lawfully obtain an abortion are restricted to when the life of the mother is in danger and do not include, for example, situations where the pregnancy is the result of rape. The State party should ensure that women are not compelled to continue with pregnancies where that is incompatible with obligations arising under the Covenant (art. 7) and General Comment No. 28." *Concluding Observations of the Human Rights Committee: Ireland,* U.N. GAOR, 55th Sess., Supp. No. 40 ¶¶444–45, U.N. Doc. A/55/40 (2000).

Ireland was also questioned about abortion in 1999 by the Committee on the Elimination of Discrimination Against Women. In its concluding observations, the Committee emphasized the hardship caused by Ireland's law and the need for the government "to facilitate a national dialogue on women's reproductive rights, including on the restrictive abortion laws." *See Concluding Observations of the Committee: Ireland, 01/07/99,* ¶¶25–26, U.N. Doc. CEDAW/C/1999/L.2/Add.4 (1999).

Assume you are a member of the Irish delegation to the United Nations. What legal reforms, if any, must be enacted to bring Ireland into conformity with the ICCPR, ICE-SCR, and CEDAW?

3. Regional Approaches

Regional instruments also may affect a country's view of whether women have a "right" to an abortion. The European Convention for the Protection of Human Rights and Fundamental Freedoms (ECHR) does not mention abortion. Yet article 2 (right to life) and article 8 (right to respect for private and family life) appear potentially relevant to the question. Also, article 10, which recognizes the right to freedom of expression, has been held to encompass the right to receive information about abortion. Similarly, the African Charter on Human and People's Rights does not mention abortion, but article 4 recognizes the right to life and integrity of person. Article 16 recognizes everyone's "right to enjoy the best attainable state of physical and mental health" and requires States to "take the necessary measures to protect the health of their people and to ensure that they receive medical attention when they are sick." *See also* art. 18(3) ("The State shall ensure the elimination of every discrimination against women and also ensure the protection of the rights of the woman and the child as stipulated in international declarations and conventions."). Similarly, the American Convention on Human Rights recognizes the right to privacy in article 11 and the right to personal liberty and security in article 7(1). However, in article 4(1), it states "every person has the right to have his life respected. This right shall be protected by law, and, in general, from the moment of conception. No one shall be arbitrarily deprived of his life." All of these conventions, of course, are subject to interpretation on the issue of abortion. Consider how the issue was resolved by the Inter-American Commission on Human Rights, when it interpreted the American Declaration of the Rights and Duties of Man, and incidentally the American Convention on Human Rights. Then consider the resolution of a similar issue by the European Commission of Human Rights. What similarities and differences exist between the regional organizations on the topic of abortion?

a. *Organization of American States*
The Baby Boy Case, Resolution 23/81
Case No. 2141, Inter-Am. C.H.R. 25-5 (1981)

1. On January 19, 1977, Christian B. White and Gary K. Potter, filed with the Inter-American Commission on Human Rights a petition against the United States of America and the Commonwealth of Massachusetts for the purposes established in the Statute and Regulations of the Commission. The petition is accompanied by a cover letter of the Catholics for Christian Political Action, signed by Gary Potter, President....

[Ed. Note: The petitioners were concerned about a judgment of acquittal entered by the Supreme Judicial Court of Massachusetts in the case of Dr. Edelin, described below, and the U.S. Supreme Court's decision in *Roe v. Wade*. The petitioners brought the petition on behalf of the "Baby Boy" Dr. Edelin aborted.]

On October 3, 1973, the defendant Dr. Renneth Edelin, Chief Resident in obstetrics and gynecology at Boston City Hospital, performed an abortion by hysterotomy on a seventeen year old, unmarried woman, she and her mother having requested an abortion and consented to the operation. For his conduct in connection with the operation, Dr. Edelin was indicted for manslaughter, and convicted after trial. He appeal[ed] from the judgment of conviction and from the trial judge's refusal of a new trial.

In Massachusetts, for many years, a criminal abortion statute...had had the effect in the Commonwealth of punishing as a crime the performance of any abortion except when carried out by a physician "in good faith and in an honest belief that it (was) necessary for the preservation of the life or health of a woman."

On January 22, 1973, the Supreme Court of the United States decided the cases of Roe v. Wade, 410 U.S. 113, and Doe v. Bolton, 410 U.S. 179. These decisions not only "rendered inoperative" the Massachusetts criminal abortion statute, as the State Court had occasion to say in Doe v. Doe, 365 Mass. 556, 560 (1974), but introduced a new regime affording Constitutional protections....

All six Justices of Supreme Judicial Court of Massachusetts who heard the appeal, holding that there was error in the proceedings at trial, vote to reverse the conviction. Five Justices also vote to direct the entry of a judgment of acquittal; the Chief Justice, dissenting in part in a separate opinion, would order a new trial. The five Justices are agreed that there was insufficient evidence to go to a jury on the overarching issue whether Dr. Edelin was guilty beyond a reasonable doubt of the "wanton" or "reckless" conduct resulting in a death required for a conviction herein, and that motions for a directed verdict of acquittal should have been granted accordingly....

The highest Court, in the conclusion of its opinion, states: "This opinion does not seek an answer to the question when abortions are morally justifiable and when not. That question is wholly beyond our province. Rather we have dealt with a question of guilt or innocence under a particular state of facts. We are conscious that the significance of our decision as precedent is still further reduced by the fact that the case arose in an interregnum between the Supreme Court's abortion decisions of 1973 and the adoption of legislation intended to conform to those decision—a kind of internal circumstance not likely to be repeated...."

15. The international obligation of the United States of America, as a member of the Organization of American States (OAS), under the jurisdiction of the Inter-American Commission on Human Rights (IACHR) is governed by the Charter of OAS (Bogotá 1948) as amended by the Protocol of Buenos Aires on February 27, 1967, ratified by United States on April 23, 1968.

16. As a consequence of articles 3(i), 16, 51(e), 112 and 150 of this Treaty, the provisions of other instruments and resolutions of the OAS on human rights, acquired binding force. Those instruments and resolutions approved with the vote of U.S. government, are the following:

- American Declaration of the Rights and Duties of Man (Bogotá, 1948)
- Statute and Regulations of the IACHR 1960, as amended by resolution XXII of the Second Special Inter-American Conference (Rio de Janeiro, 1965)
- Statute and Regulations of IACHR of 1979–1980.

17. Both Statutes provide that, for the purpose of such instruments, the IACHR is the organ of the OAS entrusted with the competence to promote the observance and respect of human rights. For the purpose of the Statutes, human rights are understood to

be the rights set forth in the American Declaration in relation to States not parties to the American Convention on Human Rights (San José, 1969) (Articles 1 and 2 of 1960 Statute and article 1 of 1979 Statute).

18. The first violation denounced in the petition concerns article I of the American Declaration of Rights and Duties of Man: "Every human being has the right to life...." The petitioners admitted that the Declaration does not respond "when life begins," "when a pregnancy product becomes a human being" or other such questions. However, they try to answer these fundamental questions with two different arguments:

a) The travaux préparatoires, the discussion of the draft Declaration during the IX International Conference of American States at Bogotá in 1948 and the final vote, demonstrate that the intention of the Conference was to protect the right to life "from the moment of conception."

b) The American Convention on Human Rights, promulgated to advance the Declaration's high purposes and to be read as a corollary document, gives a definition of the right to life in article 4.1: "This right shall be protected by law from the moment of conception."

A brief legislative history of the Declaration does not support the petitioner's argument, as may be concluded from the following information and documents:

a) Pursuant to Resolution XL of the Inter-American Conference on Problems of War and Peace (Mexico, 1945), the Inter-American Juridical Committee of Río de Janeiro, formulated a preliminary draft of an International Declaration of the Rights and Duties of Man to be considered by the Ninth International Conference of American States (Bogotá, 1948). This preliminary draft was used by the Conference as a basis of discussion in conjunction with the draft of a similar Declaration prepared by the United Nations in December, 1947.

b) Article 1—Right to Life—of the draft submitted by the Juridical Committee reads: "Every person has the right to life. This right extends to the right to life from the moment of conception; to the right to life of incurables, imbeciles and the insane. Capital punishment may only be applied in cases in which it has been prescribed by pre-existing law for crimes of exceptional gravity."...

c) A Working Group was organized to consider the observations and amendments introduced by the Delegates and to prepare an acceptable document. As a result of its work, the Group submitted to the Sixth Committee a new draft entitled American Declaration of the Fundamental Rights and Duties of Man, article I of which reads: "Every human being has the right to life, liberty, security and integrity of this person."

d) This completely new article I and some substantial changes introduced by the Working Group in other articles has been explained, in its Report of the Working Group to the Committee, as a compromise to resolve the problems raised by the Delegations of Argentina, Brazil, Cuba, United States of America, Mexico, Peru, Uruguay and Venezuela, mainly as consequence of the conflict existing between the laws of those States and the draft of the Juridical Committee....

e) In connection with the right to life, the definition given in the Juridical Committee's draft was incompatible with the laws governing the death penalty and abortion in the majority of the American States. In effect, the acceptance of this absolute concept—the right to life from the moment of conception—would imply the obligation to derogate the articles of the Penal Codes in force in 1948 in many countries because such articles excluded the penal sanction for the crime of abortion if performed in one or more

of the following cases: (A) when necessary to save the life of the mother; (B) to interrupt the pregnancy of the victim of a rape; (C) to protect the honor of an honest
woman; (D) to prevent the transmission to the fetus of a hereditary on contagious disease; (E) for economic reasons....

f) In 1948, the American States that permitted abortion in one of such cases and,
consequently, would be affected by the adoption of article I of the Juridical Committee,
were; Argentina...; Brasil...; Costa Rica...; Cuba...; Ecuador...; Mexico (Distrito y
Territorios Federales)...; Nicaragua...; Paraguay...; Peru...; Uruguay...;
Venezuela...; United States of America...; Puerto Rico....

g) On April 22, 1948, the new article I of the Declaration prepared by the Working
Group was approve by the Sixth Committee with a slight change in the wording of the
Spanish text (there was no official English text at that stage).... Finally, the definitive
text of the Declaration in Spanish, English, Portuguese and French was approved by
the 7th plenary Session of the Conference on April 30, 1948, and the Final Act was
signed May 2nd. The only difference in the final text is the elimination of the word
"integrity."...

h) Consequently, the defendant is correct in challenging the petitioners' assumption
that article 1 of the Declaration has incorporated the notion that the right of life exists
from the moment of conception. Indeed, the conference faced this question but chose
not to adopt language which would clearly have stated that principle.

20. The second argument of the petitioners, related to the possible use of the Convention as an element for the interpretation of the Declaration requires also a study of the
motives that prevailed at the San José Diplomatic Conference with the adoption of the
definition of the right to life.

21. The Fifth Meeting of Consultation of Ministers of Foreign Affairs of the OAS, held
at Santiago, Chile in 1959, entrusted the Inter-American Council of Jurists with the
preparation of a draft of the Convention on Human Rights....

22. The draft, concluded by the Commission in about two weeks, developed the American Declaration of Bogotá, but has been influenced also by other sources, including the
work in course at the United Nations. It consists of 88 articles, begin (sic) with a definition of the right to life (article 2), which reintroduced the concept that "This right shall
be protected by law from the moment of conception."...

23. The Second Special Conference of Inter-American States (Rio de Janeiro, 1965) considered the draft of the Council with two other drafts presented by the Governments of
Chile and Uruguay, respectively, and asked the Council of the OAS, in cooperation with
the IACHR, to prepare the draft of the Convention to be submitted to the diplomatic
conference to be called for this purpose.

24. The Council of the OAS, considering the Opinion enacted by the IACHR on the
draft convention prepared by the Council of Jurists, give a mandate to Convention to be
submitted as working document to the San José conference....

25. To accommodate the views that insisted on the concept "from the moment of conception," with the objection raised, since the Bogota Conference, based on the legislation of American States that permitted abortion, inter alia, to save the mother's life, and
in case of rape, the IACHR, redrafting article 2 (Right to Life), decided, by majority
vote, to introduce the words "in general." This compromise was the origin of the new
text of article 2: "1. Every person has the right to have his life respected. This right shall
be protected by law, in general, from the moment of conception."...

26. The rapporteur of the Opinion proposed, at this second opportunity for discussion of the definition of the right of life, to delete the entire final phrase "in general, from the moment of conception." He repeated the reasoning of his dissenting opinion in the Commission; based on the abortion laws in force in the majority of the American States, with an addition: "to avoid any possibility of conflict with article 6, paragraph 1, of the United Nations Covenant on Civil and Political Rights, which states this right in a general way only." ...

27. However, the majority of the Commission believed that, for reasons of principle, it was fundamental to state the provision on the protection of the right to life in the form recommended to the Council of the OAS in its Opinion (Part One). It was accordingly decided to keep the text of paragraph 1 without change....

28. In the Diplomatic Conference that approved the American Convention, the Delegations of Brazil and the Dominican Republic introduced separate amendments to delete the final phrase of paragraph 1 of article 3 (Right to Life) "in general, from the moment of conception." The United States delegation supported the Brazilian position....

29. Conversely, the Delegation of Ecuador supported the deletion of the words "and in general." Finally, by majority vote, the Conference adopted the text of the draft submitted by the IACHR and approved by the Council of the OAS, which became the present text of article 4, paragraph 1, of the American Convention....

30. In the light of this history, it is clear that the petitioners' interpretation of the definition given by the American Convention on the right of life is incorrect. The addition of the phrase "in general, from the moment of conception" does not mean that the drafters of the Convention intended to modify the concept of the right to life that prevailed in Bogota, when they approved the American Declaration. The legal implications of the clause "in general, from the moment of conception" are substantially different from the shorter clause "from the moment of conception" as appears repeatedly in the petitioners' briefs.

31. However, accepting gratia argumentandi, that the American Convention had established the absolute concept of the right to life from the moment of conception — it would be impossible to impose upon the United States Government or that of any other State Member of the OAS, by means of "interpretation," an international obligation based upon a treaty that such State has not duly accepted or ratified....

33. The other rights which the petitioners contend were violated — Articles II, VII and XI of the American Declaration — have no direct relation to the facts set forth in the petition, including the decision of the U.S. Supreme Court and the Supreme Judicial Court of Massachusetts which were challenged in this case.

The Inter-American Commission on Human Rights Resolves:

1. The decision of the U.S. Supreme Court and the Supreme Judicial Court of Massachusetts and other facts stated in the petition do not constitute a violation of articles I, II, VII and XI of the American Declaration of Rights and Duties of Man.

Monroy Cabra, Dr., dissenting:

I dissent from the majority opinion of the Inter-American Commission on Human Rights in Case 2141 for the following reasons:

1. Article 1 of the American Declaration of the Rights and Duties of Man reads: "Every human being has the right to life, liberty, and the security of his person." Since the text is not explicit, I think that the interpretation most in accord with the genuine protection of the right to life is that this protection begins at conception rather than at birth.

2. The historical argument, upon which the majority opinion of the Commission is based, is unclear. Indeed, a review of the report and the minutes of the Working Group of the Sixth Committee shows that no conclusion was reached to permit the unequivocal inference that the intention of the drafters of the Declaration was to protect the right to life from the time of birth — much less to allow abortion, since this topic was not approached....

5. Since Article 1 does not define when life begins, one can resort to medical science which has concluded that life has its beginning in the union of two series of chromosomes. Most scientists agree that the fetus is a human being and is genetically complete....

8. The intentional and illegal interruption of the physiological process of pregnancy, resulting in the destruction of the embryo or death of the fetus, is unquestionably an offense against life and, consequently, a violation of Article 1 of the American Declaration of the Rights and Duties of Man. The maternal womb in which the flame of life is lighted is sacred and may not be profane to extinguish what God has created in his image and in his likeness.

[The concurring opinion of Dr. Andres Aguilar is omitted.]

Notes and Questions

1. *Treaty Interpretation.* Of what significance is the fact that an international instrument may be incompatible with the laws of some of the signatories at the time of its formulation? Does that mean the instrument was not meant to change the law in those States Parties? Does it reflect a compromise between the signatories' diverse laws? What if the legislative history does not mention "compromise"?

2. *Treaty Interpretation II.* Can one safely conclude that the removal of the following sentence from the Declaration means that life from conception was not meant to be covered: "This right extends to the right to life from the moment of conception." Was any other language eliminated during the drafting, and what can one conclude from that? *See The Baby Boy Case, supra,* at ¶ 18.

3. *Treaty Interpretation III.* What of the fact that the U.N. Declaration of the Rights of the Child (1959) says, "Whereas: the child, by reason of his physical and mental immaturity, needs special safeguards and care, including appropriate legal protection, before as well as after birth." Assuming that this language were helpful to the petitioners, would it bind the OAS?

4. *Treaty Interpretation IV.* Examine the American Declaration and compare article 1 to the other rights enshrined therein. Is there any significance to the fact that article 1 uses the term "human beings" instead of "persons"? If the Commission had held that article 1 applied to the fetus, would its decision necessarily have come out differently?

5. *Binding Force of the Declaration.* You know that normally declarations by international bodies are not binding on states, and that the United States never signed the American Convention. How then is it legally bound by the Declaration of Bogotá, according to the IACHR? The Declaration is binding on the United States because on May 25 and June 8, 1960, the Council of the Organization of American States approved, without dissent, the Statute of the Inter-American Commission on Human Rights. Article 2 stated: "For the purpose of the present Statute, human rights are understood to be the rights set forth in the American Declaration of the Rights and Du-

ties of Man." The *Baby Boy* case was significant because it was the first time the Commission stated that the Declaration was legally binding on members not party to the American Convention. The U.S. government disputes that the American Declaration imposes legally binding obligations on the United States. The government's reasons are set forth in the Editor's Note to the American Declaration, which is contained in the Statutory Supplement.

6. *The Relationship between the American Convention and the American Declaration.* Should the Convention's language influence the interpretation of the Declaration? *See* American Convention, art. 19(1).

7. *Access to Abortion.* Does the American Declaration require that an OAS member state make abortion available to its citizens? What about article 11?

8. *Commentary.* For a thorough discussion of *The Baby Boy Case*, see Dinah Shelton, *Abortion and the Right to Life in the Inter-American System: The Case of "Baby Boy,"* 2 Hum. Rts. L.J. 309 (1981).

b. Council of Europe

Paton v. United Kingdom
3 Eur. H.R. Rep. 408 (1981) (Eur. Comm'n H.R.)

The Facts

1. The applicant is a citizen of the United Kingdom born in 1944. He is a steel worker by profession.

2. From his statements and the documents submitted by the applicant it appears that he was married to Joan Mary Paton on 10 October 1974. On 12 May 1978 he was told by his wife that she was eight weeks pregnant and intended to have an abortion. On 17 May 1978 the applicant applied to the High Court of Justice for an injunction to prevent the abortion from being carried out. The original defendants to the application were Dr. Peter Frederick Knight, the manager of the Merseyside Nursing Home at which two doctors had given certificates in accordance with section 1 of the Abortion Act 1967 (hereinafter called the '1967 Act'), and the applicant's wife.

3. Section 1(1) of the 1967 Act permits the termination of a pregnancy by a registered medical practitioner if two registered medical practitioners find: (a) that the continuance of the pregnancy would involve risk to the life of the pregnant woman, or of injury to the physical or mental health of the pregnant woman or any existing children of her family, greater than if the pregnancy were terminated; or (b) that there is a substantial risk that if the child were born it would suffer from such physical or mental abnormalities as to be seriously handicapped. The certificate in the present case was issued under paragraph (a) (injury to the physical or mental health of the pregnant woman).*...

6. As to the question whether, in English law, the unborn child has a right to life, which could be invoked by the father, reference was *inter alia* made, on the one hand,

---

* In an affidavit submitted to the High Court, the applicant's wife stated *inter alia:* "My marriage was increasingly unhappy...and...has broken down irretrievably. I left the plaintiff on legal advice as I feared for my safety and we live apart...and in future I will live as a single woman.... Because of the plaintiff's behaviour, life with him became increasingly impossible and my health suffered and I am receiving treatment from my doctor.... I could not cope and I verily believe that for months I have been close to a nervous breakdown."

to Roman law, where abortion without the father's consent was a crime, and, on the other, to the United States Supreme Court's decision in Planned Parenthood of Central Missouri v. Danforth where the Court, by a majority, held that the State of Missouri "may not constitutionally require the consent of the spouse...as a condition for an abortion...."

7. The President dismissed the application. He stated that an injunction could be granted only to restrain the infringement of a legal right; that in English law the foetus has no legal rights until it is born and has a separate existence from its mother, and that the father of a foetus, whether or not he is married to the mother, has no legal right to prevent the mother from having an abortion or to be consulted or informed about a proposed abortion, if the provisions of the 1967 Act have been complied with....

8. The abortion was carried out within hours of the dismissal of the application.

Complaints

The applicant contends that the law of England and Wales violates: (1) Articles 2 and/or 5 of the Convention in that it allows abortion at all, and/or that it denies the foetus any legal rights; (2) Articles 6 and/or 8 and/or 9 of the Convention in that, if the provisions of the 1967 Act are complied with, it denies the father of a foetus, whether or not he is married to the mother:

(a) a right to object to a proposed abortion of the foetus; and/or

(b) a right to apply to the Courts for an order to prevent or postpone the proposed abortion; and/or

(c) a right to be consulted about the proposed abortion; and/or

(d) a right to be informed about the proposed abortion; and/or

(e) a right to demand, in a case where registered medical practitioners have given certificates under section 1 of the 1967 Act, that the mother be examined by a different registered medical practitioner or practitioners appointed by the father or by and upon his application to a designated court, tribunal or other body; and/or

(f) a right to demand that the registered medical practitioners, who examine the mother to decide whether or not to give certificates under section 1 of the 1967 Act, should be independent of the institution or organization at or by which the abortion will be carried out should such certificates be given....

The Law

1. The applicant complains of the refusal, by the High Court of Justice, of his application for an injunction to prevent the termination of his wife's pregnancy. He submits that the Abortion Act 1967, under which this abortion was authorised and eventually carried out, violates Articles 2 and/or 5, 6, 8 and 9 of the Convention....

4. The Commission...here recalls that the abortion law of High Contracting Parties to the Convention has so far been the subject of several applications under Article 25.... One application, invoking Article 8, was declared admissible by the Commission, in so far as it had been brought by two women. [Bruggemann and Scheuten v. Germany (1978) 10 D. & R. 100 (App. No. 6959/75), 3 E.H.R.R. 244] The Commission, and subsequently the Committee of Ministers, concluded that there was no breach of Article 8. That conclusion was based on an interpretation of Article 8 which, *inter alia*, took into

account the High Contracting Parties' law on abortion as applied at the time when the Convention entered into force.

5. The question whether the unborn child is covered by Article 2 was expressly left open [in *Bruggemann,* para. 60] and has not yet been considered by the Commission in any other case. It has, however, been the subject of proceedings before the Constitutional Court of Austria, a High Contracting State in which the Convention has the rank of constitutional law. In those proceedings the Austrian Constitutional Court, noting the different view expressed on this question in legal writings, found that Article 2(1), first sentence, interpreted in the context of Article 2, paras. (1) and (2), does not cover the unborn life. [Decision of 11 October 1974, Erk. Slg. (*Collection of Decisions*) No. 7400, [1975] *Europaische Grundrechtezeitschrift* 74.]

6. Article 2(1), first sentence, provides: "Everyone's right to life shall be protected by law" (in the French text: 'Le droit de toute personne a la vie est protege par la loi'). The Commission, in its interpretation of this clause and, in particular, of the terms 'everyone' and 'life,' has examined the ordinary meaning of the provision in the context both of Article 2 and of the Convention as a whole, taking into account the object and purpose of the Convention.

7. The Commission first notes that the term 'everyone' ('toute personne') is not defined in the Convention. It appears in Article 1 and in Section I, apart from Article 2(1), in Articles 5, 6, 8 to 11 and 13. In nearly all these instances the use of the word is such that it can apply only postnatally. None indicates clearly that it has any possible prenatal application, although such application in a rare case—*e.g.* under Article 6(1)—cannot be entirely excluded.

8. As regards, more particularly, Article 2, it contains the following limitations of 'everyone's' right to life enunciated in the first sentence of paragraph (1):—a clause permitting the death penalty in paragraph (1), second sentence: 'No one shall be deprived of his life intentionally save in the execution of a sentence of a court following his conviction of a crime for which this penalty is provided by law'; and—the provision, in paragraph (2), that deprivation of life shall not be regarded as inflicted in contravention of Article 2 when it results from 'the use of force which is no more than absolutely necessary' in the following three cases: 'In defence of any person from unlawful violence'; 'in order to effect a lawful arrest or to prevent the escape of a person lawfully detained'; 'in action lawfully taken for the purpose of quelling a riot or insurrection.' All the above limitations, by their nature, concern persons already born and cannot be applied to the foetus.

9. Thus both the general usage of the term 'everyone' ('toute personne') of the Convention (para. 7 above) and the context in which this term is employed in Article 2 (para. 8 above) tend to support the view that it does not include the unborn.

10. The Commission has next examined, in the light of the above considerations, whether the term 'life' in Article 2(1), first sentence, is to be interpreted as covering only the life of persons already born or also the 'unborn life' of the foetus. The Commission notes that the term 'life', too, is not defined in the Convention.

11. It further observes that another, more recent international instrument for the protection of human rights, the American Convention on Human Rights of 1969, contains in Article 4(1), first and second sentences, the following provisions expressly extending the right to life to the unborn: "Every person has the right to have his life respected. This right shall be protected by law and, in general, from the moment of conception."

12. The Commission is aware of the wide divergence of thinking on the question of where life begins. While some believe that it starts already with conception others tend to focus upon the moment of nidation, upon the point that the foetus becomes 'viable,' or upon live birth.

13. The German Federal Constitutional Court, when interpreting the provision 'everyone has a right to life' in Article 2(2) of the Basic Law, stated as follows:

> Life in the sense of the historical existence of a human individual exists according to established biological and physiological knowledge at least from the 14th day after conception (Nidation, Individuation).... The process of development beginning from this point is a continuous one so that no sharp divisions or exact distinction between the various stages of development of human life can be made. It does not end at birth: for example, the particular type of consciousness peculiar to the human personality only appears a considerable time after the birth. The protection conferred by Article 2(2) first sentence of the Basic Law can therefore be limited neither to the 'complete' person after birth nor to the foetus capable of independent existence prior to birth. The right to life is guaranteed to every one who 'lives'; in this context no distinction can be made between the various stages of developing life before birth or between born and unborn children. 'Everyone' in the meaning of Article 2(2) of the Basic Law is 'every living human being', in other words: every human individual possessing life; 'everyone' therefore includes unborn human beings....

14. The Commission also notes that, in a case arising under the Constitution of the United States [Roe v. Wade, 410 U.S. 113 (1973)], the State of Texas argued before the Supreme Court that, in general, life begins at conception and is present throughout pregnancy. The Court, while not resolving the difficult question where life begins, found that, "with respect to the State's important and legitimate interest in potential life, the 'compelling' point is at viability."

15. The Commission finally recalls the decision of the Austrian Constitutional Court mentioned...above which, while also given in the framework of constitutional litigation, had to apply, like the Commission in the present case, Article 2 of the European Convention on Human Rights.

16. The Commission considers with the Austrian Constitutional Court that, in interpreting the scope of the term 'life' in Article 2(1), first sentence, of the Convention, particular regard must be had to the context of the Article as a whole. It also observes that the term 'life' may be subject to different interpretations in different legal instruments, depending on the context in which it is used in the instrument concerned.

17. The Commission has already noted, when discussing the meaning of the term 'everyone' in Article 2 (para. 8 above), that the limitations, in paragraphs (1) and (2) of the Article, of 'everyone's' right to 'life,' by their nature, concern persons already born and cannot be applied to the foetus. The Commission must therefore examine whether Article 2, in the absence of any express limitation concerning the foetus, is to be interpreted: — as not covering the foetus at all; — as recognising a 'right to life' of the foetus with certain implied limitations; or — as recognising an absolute 'right to life' of the foetus.

18. The Commission has first considered whether Article 2 is to be construed as recognising an absolute 'right to life' of the foetus and has excluded such an interpretation on the following grounds.

19. The 'life' of the foetus is intimately connected with, and cannot be regarded in isolation from, the life of the pregnant woman. If Article 2 were held to cover the foetus and its protection under this Article were, in the absence of any express limitation, seen as absolute, an abortion would have to be considered as prohibited even where the continuance of the pregnancy would involve a serious risk to the life of the pregnant woman. This would mean that the 'unborn life' of the foetus would be regarded as being of a higher value than the life of the pregnant woman. The 'right to life' of a person already born would thus be considered as subject not only to the express limitations mentioned in paragraph 8 above but also to a further, implied limitation.

20. The Commission finds that such an interpretation would be contrary to the object and purpose of the Convention. It notes that, already at the time of the signature of the Convention (4 November 1950), all High Contracting Parties, with one possible exception, permitted abortion when necessary to save the life of the mother and that, in the meanwhile, the national law on termination of pregnancy has shown a tendency towards further liberalization.

21. Having thus excluded, as being incompatible with the object and purpose of the Convention, one of the three different constructions of Article 2 mentioned in paragraph 17 above, the Commission has next considered which of the two remaining interpretations is to be regarded as the correct one — *i.e.* whether Article 2 does not cover the foetus at all or whether it recognizes a 'right to life' of the foetus with certain implied limitations.

22. The Commission here notes that the abortion complained of was carried out at the initial stage of the pregnancy — the applicant's wife was ten weeks pregnant — under section 1(1)(a) of the Abortion Act 1967 in order to avert the risk of injury to the physical or mental health of the pregnant woman. It follows that, as regards the second of the two remaining interpretations, the Commission is in the present case not concerned with the broad question whether Article 2 recognizes a 'right to life' of the foetus during the whole period of the pregnancy but only with the narrower issue whether such a right is to be assumed for the initial stage of the pregnancy. Moreover, as regards implied limitations of a 'right to life' of the foetus at the initial stage, only the limitation protecting the life and health of the pregnant woman, the so-called 'medical indication,' is relevant for the determination of the present case and the question of other possible limitations (ethic indication, eugenic indication, social indication, time limitation) does not arise.

23. The Commission considers that it is not in these circumstances called upon to decide whether Article 2 does not cover the foetus at all or whether it recognizes a 'right to life' of the foetus with implied limitations. It finds that the authorization, by the United Kingdom authorities, of the abortion complained of is compatible with Article 2(1), first sentence because, if one assumes that this provision applies at the initial stage of the pregnancy, the abortion is covered by an implied limitation, protecting the life and health of the woman at that stage, of the 'right to life' of the foetus.

24. The Commission concludes that the applicant's complaint under Article 2 is inadmissible as being manifestly ill-founded within the meaning of Article 27(2).

25. In its examination of the applicant's complaints concerning the Abortion Act 1967 and its application in this case, the Commission has next had regard to Article 8 of the Convention which, in paragraph (1), guarantees to everyone the right to respect for his family life. The Commission here notes, apart from his principal complaint concerning the permission of the abortion, the applicant's ancillary submission that the 1967 Act denies the father of the foetus a right to be consulted, and to make applications, about

the proposed abortion. The Commission also observes that the applicant, who under Article 2 claims to be the victim of a violation of the right to life of the foetus of which he was the potential father, under Article 8 invokes a right of his own.

26. As regards the principal complaint concerning the permission of the abortion, the Commission recalls that the pregnancy of the applicant's wife was terminated in accordance with her wish and in order to avert the risk of injury to her physical or mental health. The Commission therefore finds that this decision, in so far as it interfered in itself with the applicant's right to respect for his family life, was justified under paragraph (2) of Article 8 as being necessary for the protection of the rights of another person. It follows that this complaint is also manifestly ill-founded within the meaning of Article 27(2).

27. The Commission has next considered the applicant's ancillary complaint that the Abortion Act 1967 denies the father of the foetus a right to be consulted, and to make applications, about the proposed abortion. It observes that any interpretation of the husband's and potential father's right, under Article 8 of the Convention, to respect for his private and family life, as regards an abortion which his wife intends to have performed on her, must first of all take into account the right of the pregnant woman, being the person primarily concerned in the pregnancy and its continuation or termination, to respect for her private life. The pregnant woman's right to respect for her private life, as affected by the developing foetus, has been examined by the Commission in its Report in the *Bruggemann* and *Scheuten* case. In the present case the Commission, having regard to the right of the pregnant woman, does not find that the husband's and potential father's right to respect for his private and family life can be interpreted so widely as to embrace such procedural rights as claimed by the applicant, *i.e.* a right to be consulted, or a right to make applications, about an abortion which his wife intends to have performed on her. The Commission concludes that this complaint is incompatible *ratione materiae* with the provisions of the Convention within the meaning of Article 27 (2).

28. The Commission does not find that any of the other provisions invoked by the applicant (Articles 5, 6 and 9 of the Convention) are relevant for the examination of his complaints. For these reasons, The Commission declares this application inadmissible.

Notes and Questions

1. *Relevant Provisions.* When multiple and often conflicting provisions apply to a dispute, the litigant must consider not only which article best supports the argument advanced, but also which article best supports the particular result desired. The allowable limitations on each right vary by article. For example, examine articles 2, 8, 9, 10, 12 and 14 of the European Convention on Human Rights. Which articles give the States Parties the most leeway to regulate abortion? Put another way, which articles give the States Parties the broadest margin of appreciation?

2. *Article 2 and Legislative History.* "The travaux préparatoires yield little information as to the High Contracting Parties' intent regarding the definition of '[e]veryone's right to life.' [T]he primary discussion of Article 2 protections focused on eliminating genocide." *See* Katherine Freeman, Comment, *The Unborn Child and the European Convention on Human Rights: To Whom Does 'Everyone's Right to Life' Belong?* 8 Emory Int'l L. Rev. 615, 648 (1994). Of what significance is the fact that "[n]o member state entered a reservation regarding abortion when the European Convention was signed"? *Id.* at 658. At that time, all of the signatories had laws restricting access to abortion, but many signatories also permitted abortion under various circumstances.

3. *Article 8 and Abortion. Bruggemann and Scheuten v. Federal Republic of Germany*, 3 Eur. H.R. Rep. 244 (1981) (Eur. Comm'n H.R.), mentioned in the preceding case, involved two women who challenged the criminal law in Germany, which they claimed restricted access to abortion too much. They were challenging the law as it existed after the *Abortion I* decision in 1975, a decision produced at length above. *See* Chapter 13.C.1, *supra*. They objected to the fact that a doctor could be subject to criminal penalties if he or she performed an abortion during the first twelve weeks after conception and there was not the proper "indication." The pregnant woman herself was exempt from any punishment if the abortion was performed by a doctor within the first twenty-two weeks of pregnancy and if she had medical and social counseling. The applicants based their claim on Article 8, among others. The Commission explained:

> The right to respect for private life is of such a scope as to secure to the individual a sphere within which he can freely pursue the development and fulfillment of his personality. To this effect, he must also have the possibility of establishing relationships of various kinds, including sexual, with other persons. In principle, therefore, whenever the State sets up rules for the behaviour of the individual within this sphere, it interferes with the respect for private life and such interference must be justified in the light of Article 8(2).

> However, there are limits to the personal sphere. While a large proportion of the law existing in a given State has some immediate or remote effect on the individual's possibility of developing his personality by doing what he wants to do, not all of these can be considered to constitute an interference with private life in the sense of Article 8 of the Convention.... The Commission has held that the concept of private life in Article 8 was broader than the definition given by numerous Anglo-Saxon and French authors, namely, the 'right to live as far as one wishes, protected from publicity,' in that it also comprises, 'to a certain degree, the right to establish and to develop relationships with other human beings, especially in the emotional field for the development and fulfillment of one's own personality.' But it denied 'that the protection afforded by Article 8 of the Convention extends to relationships of the individual with his entire immediate surroundings.' It thus found that the right to keep a dog did not pertain to the sphere of private life of the owner because 'the keeping of dogs is by the very nature of that animal necessarily associated with certain interferences with the life of others and even with public life'.... The termination of an unwanted pregnancy is not comparable with the situation in any of the above cases. However, pregnancy cannot be said to pertain uniquely to the sphere of private life. Whenever a woman is pregnant, her private life becomes closely connected with the developing foetus....

> The Commission does not find it necessary to decide, in this context, whether the unborn child is to be considered as 'life' in the sense of Article 2 of the Convention, or whether it could be regarded as an entity which under Article 8(2) could justify an interference 'for the protection of others.' There can be no doubt that certain interests relating to pregnancy are legally protected, *e.g.* as shown by a survey of the legal order in 13 High Contracting Parties. This survey reveals that, without exception, certain rights are attributed to the conceived but unborn child, in particular the right to inherit. The Commission also notes that Article 6(5) of the United Nations Covenant on Civil and Political Rights prohibits the execution of death sentences on pregnant women....

The Commission therefore finds that not every regulation of the termination of unwanted pregnancies constitutes an interference with *the right to respect* for the private life of the mother. Article 8(1) cannot be interpreted as meaning that pregnancy and its termination are, as a principle, solely a matter of the private life of the mother. In this respect the Commission notes that there is not one member State of the Convention which does not, in one way or another, set up legal rules in this matter.

In view of this situation, the Commission does not find that the legal rules complained about by the applicants interfere with their right to respect for their private life.

Furthermore, the Commission has had regard to the fact that, when the European Convention of Human Rights entered into force, the law on abortion in all member States was at least as restrictive as the one now complained of by the applicants. In many European countries the problem of abortion is or has been the subject of heated debates on legal reform since. There is no evidence that it was the intention of the Parties to the Convention to bind themselves in favour of any particular solution under discussion — *e.g.* a solution of the kind set out in the Fifth Criminal Law Reform Act (*Fristenlosung*—time limitation) which was not yet under public discussion at the time the Convention was drafted and adopted.

Is the Commission saying that restrictions on abortion are not subject to analysis under article 8? Could a fetus have legal personality for purposes of article 8(2), but not article 2?

4. *European Court of Human Rights.* Since the Commission ruled inadmissible the petition in *Paton* and the petition in *Bruggemann*, the European Court of Human Rights did not have to decide whether permitting access to abortion violates article 2, or whether abortion restrictions are subject to challenge under article 8. The European Court, however, held in *Open Door Counselling & Dublin Well Woman Centre v. Ireland*, 15 Eur. H.R. Rep. 244 (1992), that an Irish law restricting the dissemination of information regarding abortion facilities outside of Ireland violated the freedom of expression found in article 10 of the Convention. In *Bowman v. United Kingdom*, 26 Eur. H.R. Rep. 1 (1998), the Court held that it was also a violation of article 10 to prosecute a pro-life activist for distributing leaflets to try to influence the electoral process.

5. *Article 5.* At first glance, article 5 might appear relevant to the abortion debate. However, article 5's language about "liberty" is not equivalent to the language in the Fourteenth Amendment to the U.S. Constitution. As suggested by the full text of article 5, including the six defined instances of when a state can deprive a person of her liberty, article 5 is concerned with situations in which the state is arresting or detaining someone pursuant to the criminal law.

6. *Comparing Approaches.* What comparisons are possible, and what conclusions can be drawn (however tentative), regarding regional influences on national abortion practices?

7. *National Courts Interpreting the Convention.* Several courts of member states have held that article 2, on the "right to life," does not prohibit abortion. *See, e.g.,* Judgment of Oct. 11, 1974, VfSlg 221 (Aus. VfGH); Juristenvereiniging Pro Vita v. De Staat der Nederlanden (Ministerie van Welzijn, Volksgezondheid en Cultuur) 8 Feb. 1990, NJ 2986 (Neth. Hof), *summarized in* 19 European L. Digest 179 (1991).

8. *The European Union.* To the extent that access to abortion falls within either the free movement of persons, goods, capital or services, members of the European Union

must conform their abortion laws to European Union law. The compatibility of Ireland's law with European Union law was an issue in *Attorney General v. X*, [1992] 2 C.M.L.R. 277 (Ir. S.C.), although the Irish Supreme Court managed to sidestep it. The facts involved X, a girl approximately 14 years old, who had been raped and wanted to travel to England to have an abortion. The Irish Attorney General sought to enjoin her from travelling for the abortion. The Irish Constitution provides: "The State acknowledges the right to life of the unborn and, with due regard to the equal right to life of the mother, guarantees in its laws to respect, and, as far as practicable by its laws to defend and vindicate that right." The Irish Supreme Court held that the trial court had erred in denying the girl her ability to obtain an abortion because the trial court misjudged the seriousness of the girl's suicide threat. "If it is established as a matter of probability that there is a real and substantial risk to the life as distinct from the health of the mother, which can only be avoided by the termination of her pregnancy, then such termination is permissible, having regard to the true interpretation of Article 40.3.3 of the Constitution." *Id.* ¶ 38. This judicial exception for suicidal women was new. Referring to the Preamble of the Irish Constitution, Chief Justice Finlay said that judges had to interpret the Constitution "in accordance with their ideas of prudence, justice and charity," which may gradually change over time. *Id.* ¶ 34–35. Finding that the Constitution permitted X to travel for an abortion, the conflict between EU law and the Irish Constitution was avoided, and the Court did not address whether the injunction violated the Treaty of Rome, articles 56 or 59, which effectively provided freedom for persons to travel between Member States to obtain a service. However, in *obiter dicta*, various justices of the Irish Supreme Court held that under article 40.3.3 of the Irish Constitution, a court could restrain travel undertaken for the purpose of receiving an abortion. (*See, e.g.,* Finlay, C.J. ¶ 32).

After the decision, X went to the U.K. to have the abortion. In fact, "officially 4,000 Irish women, and unofficially probably closer to 7,000 or 8,000 women, travel to Britain for abortions every year." *See* Ailbhe Smyth, *The 'X' Case: Women and Abortion in the Republic of Ireland*, 1 Fem. L. Stud. 163 (1993). As mentioned above (*See* Chapter 13.C.2), the Irish defeated a referendum that would have eliminated the risk of suicide as a justification for an abortion. For more on Ireland and the impact of European law, see David Cole, *"Going to England": Irish Abortion Law and the European Community*, 17 Hastings Int'l & Comp. L. Rev. 113 (1993).

9. *The European Court of Justice.* In *Society for the Protection of Unborn Children Ireland Ltd v. Grogan*, 1991 E.C.R. I-4685, the European Court of Justice (ECJ) held that there was no violation of European law when students where prohibited from providing information about abortion services in other Member States. The connection between a restriction on the distribution of information and the provision of abortions was "too tenuous" for the prohibition on the distribution of information to be "a restriction" within article 59 of the treaty. *Id.* ¶ 24. In addition, the information constituted "freedom of expression" and not an economic activity. *Id.* ¶ 26. As to the defendant's claim that the restriction violated the right to freedom of expression in article 10(1) of the European Convention on Human Rights, the ECJ reminded the parties that it has "no such jurisdiction with regard to national legislation lying outside the scope of Community law." *Id.* ¶ 28. *Grogan* was decided the year before the European Court of Human Rights decided *Open Door Counselling*, mentioned in note 4 above.

10. For an excellent review of international and national developments in the area of abortion, *see* Rebecca J. Cook, et al., *International Developments in Abortion Law from 1988 to 1998*, 89 Am. J. Pub. Health 579 (1999). The authors suggest that the worldwide

liberalization of abortion laws has been largely maintained, although there are still significant encroachments on access in the form of funding cutbacks, waiting periods, and third-party permission requirements.

11. *A Penultimate Consideration.* The chapter ends with a reminder that the issues contained herein are all interdependent. Some will be more important than others to a particular country or a particular individual depending upon a range of factors. Professor Gayatri Chakravorty Spivak, while perhaps overstating the point somewhat, explains, "In a situation where extreme poverty makes children mean social security, the right to abortion is immaterial. In a situation where coercive contraception lays waste a woman's reproductive and general health, a right to abortion is immaterial. In a situation where the absence of resources makes it impossible to think of male and female children becoming equally competitive in the future, the right to abortion may facilitate the removal of female fetuses, where internalized gendering is misrepresented as woman's choice." Gayatri Chakravorty Spivak, *International Public Hearing on Crimes Related to Population Policies,* Re/productions: Issue #1, *at* http://www.hsph.harvard. edu/Organizations/heathnet/SAsia/repro/gcspivak.html. Given the variety of issues and the differing contexts in which the issues emerge, is the best way to approach the topic of reproductive freedom from a local, regional, or international perspective?

12. *The Last Consideration.* The chapter also ends with a warning about keeping one's nose solely in the legal materials. In addressing the international law related to reproductive freedom and noticing the "widespread and serious abuse of women with respect to reproduction," one author asks rhetorically, "whether [international human rights] is the latest trap to contain women's powers, safely channelling them into endless legal/diplomatic dispute loops. By emphasizing the legal framework, are we diverting women from other paths that may be more challenging to current holders of power? Perhaps we should be exploring other options to assist women in terms of economic, military, and political power." Elizabeth Spahn, *Waiting for Credentials: Feminist Theories of Enforcement of International Human Rights*, 44 Am. U. L. Rev. 1053, 1066 (1995). What do you think?

Chapter 14

Balancing the Child's Rights, Family Members' Rights and Duties, and the Community's Responsibilities

A. Constitutional Rights for Children

The term "children's rights" is often used to describe three different topics of study: 1) how the constitutional rights of parents and children affect the dynamics between parents, children, and the state; 2) how abuse and neglect laws limit parental power and protect children; and, 3) how the criminal justice system treats the juvenile offender. This chapter focuses primarily on the first topic. The first part of the chapter uses comparative law, in particular the law of the United States and South Africa, to explore the notion of "children's rights." It then looks at the U.N. Convention on the Rights of the Child, the main international legal instrument that addresses children's rights. The chapter next takes one issue—the spanking of children—and looks at this issue through both comparative and international law lenses. Finally, the chapter explores whether the balance between parents, children, and the state differs when the parents themselves are divided on an issue that impacts their child.

1. A Description of Children's Rights in the United States

Barbara Bennett Woodhouse, *The Constitutionalization of Children's Rights: Incorporating Emerging Human Rights into Constitutional Doctrine*
2 U. Pa. J. Const. L. 1, 2–3, 8–9 (1999)

Children have few clearly articulated or firmly established constitutional rights in the United States of America. Children enjoy few independent rights outside the context of criminal or administrative proceedings, because children's rights (generally called "interests") are conceptualized as subsumed within the rights of parents. Children's interests are defined by parents, who exercise their constitutionally protected rights to physical custody and control of children's upbringing. Children have succeeded in asserting rights in various narrow areas, which are confined primarily to criminal procedure and equal protection law and based entirely in decisional doctrines rather than text. If children have few "first generation rights," they have absolutely no "second generation rights." They enjoy no federal constitutional rights to education or to programs of protection from abuse and exploitation, and no rights to the basic nutrition, income supports, shelter, and health care on which the right to life obviously depends. Children's federal welfare entitlements, addressed only by statute, have been increasingly "privatized" by Congress in keeping with contemporary market theories....

The process of incorporating the next generation of rights-bearers into the world's constitutions is taking place, in many stages and variations, all around the globe. In the United States, however, advocates seeking to secure a place for children in the constitutional scheme face substantial doctrinal and political barriers.

The doctrinal barriers are complex and rooted in our own Constitution's peculiar history and structure. Our written Constitution is silent on rights for juveniles, and many scholars and judges harbor great skepticism about the legitimacy of incorporating un-enumerated rights into the constitutional scheme. Parental rights established a constitutional foothold seventy-five years ago, during the heyday of substantive due process, in cases like *Meyer v. Nebraska* and *Pierce v. Society of Sisters*. But the same door may not be open to rights for children. Controversy over the Supreme Court's role in enunciating rights in the context of economics, labor, and, more recently, abortion has made judges wary of additional claims that substantive rights can be incorporated by judicial interpretation into the due process clause's guarantees against state deprivations of life, liberty and property. After extending heightened scrutiny beyond race to laws burdening other classes such as women and illegitimate children, it seems that the Justices have grown weary of discovering new "suspect classes," making it difficult to use the Constitution to challenge differential treatment of children as a class.

The political barriers are obvious. Children do not vote. In addition, many conservatives reject the concept of rights for children as a threat to family values. Conversely, critics on the left fear that rights for children will be used to invade family privacy and threaten women's autonomy. Finally, Americans harbor deeply ambivalent feelings towards children. While our rhetoric makes children our highest priority, we rate very low on the scale of industrialized nations when it comes to making these promises a reality. Racism and economics complicate all of our political responses, including our responses to children's rights. We tend to see children in shades of rich and poor, black and white, and "them" against "us." Our own children are our most precious personal possessions. Other people's children are armed and dangerous, alien and out of control. No wonder Americans have trouble knowing what to do with this newest claim of rights.

Notes and Questions

1. *Constitutional Litigation for Children in the United States.* For a compilation of the cases decided by the U.S. Supreme Court on children's rights, see Susan Gluck Mezey, *Constitutional Adjudication of Children's Rights Claims in the United States Supreme Court, 1953–92*, 27 Fam. L.Q. 307 (1993). She explains, "Children's constitutional litigation, defined as attempts to seek a declaration of rights for children under age eighteen, has largely revolved around three sets of claims: challenges to parental and/or state authority; challenges to legal classifications based on birth, class, or wealth status; and de-

mands for procedural fairness by the state." *Id.* at 308. She concludes, perhaps not surprisingly, "[t]his analysis of children's rights claims suggests that constitutional litigation on behalf of a 'disadvantaged' group can be fruitful as long as there is a receptive Court." *Id.* at 321. She notes that from 1953 to 1992, the cases indicate a "decreasing support for children's rights claims," a lot of "inconsistency in the way the Court handled children's rights issues," and the lack of a "coherent theory to guide the outcome of the cases." *Id.* at 321–22. The author explains:

> With the decisions favoring neither a belief in paternalism nor autonomy, perhaps the better explanation for the Court's rulings lies in traditional principles of constitutional law. The decisions appear to be motivated more by the jurisprudence of the constitutional claim than by adherence to a child welfare theory. Each Court's children's rights decisions followed the pattern of decisions made for adult litigants. Just as the Court granted more leeway to states in the areas of privacy, the death penalty, search and seizure, and social welfare legislation for adults, so it did with respect to children. Not even the spectre of a severely brain-damaged child caused the majority to depart from a restrictive view of the Due Process Clause. [Ed. Note: *See* DeShaney v. Winnebago County Dep't of Social Serv., 489 U.S. 189 (1989).] At first glance it might appear that by applying a more rigorous level of scrutiny to state illegitimacy laws, the Court departed from established constitutional principles for the sake of the child. But even in these cases, however, the Court followed its traditional equal protection analysis of using heightened scrutiny in classifications such as sex, alienage, or illegitimacy which are based on innate factors that bear little or no relation to ability.

Id.

2. A Description of Children's Rights in South Africa

South Africa stands in sharp contrast to the United States. South Africa is perhaps the most progressive country in terms of constitutional rights for children. Consider the South Africa Constitution, which entered into force in 1997. Its Bill of Rights appears at the front of the document, in the second of fourteen chapters. It contains numerous socio-economic rights that apply to all, including the right to have "access to health care services" and the right to have "access to adequate housing." The Bill of Rights also includes a separate section on children's rights.

Constitution of the Republic of South Africa, ch. 2 (1996)

Section 28

(1) Every child has the right

    (a) to a name and a nationality from birth;

    (b) to family care or parental care, or to appropriate alternative care when removed from the family environment;

    (c) to basic nutrition, shelter, basic health care services and social services;

(d) to be protected from maltreatment, neglect, abuse or degradation;

(e) to be protected from exploitative labour practices;

(f) not to be required or permitted to perform work or provide services that

   (i) are inappropriate for a person of that child's age; or

   (ii) place at risk the child's well-being, education, physical or mental health or spiritual, moral or social development;

(g) not to be detained except as a measure of last resort, in which case, in addition to the rights a child enjoys under sections 12 and 35, the child may be detained only for the shortest appropriate period of time, and has the right to be

   (i) kept separately from detained persons over the age of 18 years; and

   (ii) treated in a manner, and kept in conditions, that take account of the child's age;

(h) to have a legal practitioner assigned to the child by the state, and at state expense, in civil proceedings affecting the child, if substantial injustice would otherwise result; and

(i) not to be used directly in armed conflict, and to be protected in times of armed conflict.

(2) A child's best interests are of paramount importance in every matter concerning the child.

(3) In this section "child" means a person under the age of 18 years.

Section 36

(1) The rights in the Bill of Rights may be limited only in terms of law of general application to the extent that the limitation is reasonable and justifiable in an open and democratic society based on human dignity, equality and freedom, taking into account all relevant factors, including

(a) the nature of the right;

(b) the importance of the purpose of the limitation;

(c) the nature and extent of the limitation;

(d) the relation between the limitation and its purpose; and

(e) less restrictive means to achieve the purpose.

(2) Except as provided in subsection (1) or in any other provision of the Constitution, no law may limit any right entrenched in the Bill of Rights.

Section 39

(1) When interpreting the Bill of Rights, a court, tribunal or forum

(a) must promote the values that underlie an open and democratic society based on human dignity, equality and freedom;

(b) must consider international law; and

(c) may consider foreign law.

(2) When interpreting any legislation, and when developing the common law or customary law, every court, tribunal or forum must promote the spirit, purport and objects of the Bill of Rights.

(3) The Bill of Rights does not deny the existence of any other rights or freedoms that are recognised or conferred by common law, customary law or legislation, to the extent that they are consistent with the Bill.

Before analyzing what sort of difference a constitution like South Africa's can make for children, it is useful to consider how section 28 became part of the South Africa Constitution. Some of the factors that make children's rights a difficult proposition in the United States today, as identified by Barbara Bennett Woodhouse, presumably existed in South Africa too. For example, children in South Africa do not vote. How then did children's rights receive constitutional status?

Tshepo L. Mosikatsana, *Children's Rights and Family Autonomy in the South African Context: A Comment on Children's Rights under the Final Constitution*
3 Mich. J. Race & L. 341, 350–351 (1998)

Although children are a nonvoting constituency, it is hardly surprising that a child-centered approach is gaining momentum in South Africa. One reason is that the youth of South Africa played a special role in spearheading the struggle for liberation from apartheid. These contributions to the processes of political transformation received national recognition through South Africa's designation of June 16th as Youth Day, the ratification of the U.N. Convention on the Rights of the Child, and the inclusion of section 28 in the Constitution.

Julia Sloth-Nielsen, *Chicken Soup or Chainsaws: Some Implications of the Constitutionalisation of Children's Rights in South Africa*
1996 Acta Juridica 6, 10–12

One reason for unanimity about the need to protect children's rights extensively at the constitutional level lies in the apartheid history of South Africa, which had peculiarly harsh consequences for children. In their submission to the Theme Committee of the Constitutional Assembly, the Pan African Congress (PAC) preface their comments on a revised § 30 with the statement that '(o)ur country has had a bad history of ill-treating children, such as abuse, neglect, child labour especially on farms, the spectre of street kids and gaols full of children and so on.' [Ed. Note: Section 30 was the provision addressing children's rights in the Interim Constitution.] To this can be added such well-known institutions as the migrant labour system, which contributed to the disintegration of families, the creation of separate and inferior education regimes for race groups other than 'white,' and the unacceptably high infant and maternal mortality rates in the light of state spending on health. Logically, therefore, it is not surprising that there should be a very real concern for the plight of children evident in the general support for extensive provision for children's rights at the constitutional level.

Also despite the fact that support for children's rights does not deliver an individual voting constituency, from the perspective of the liberation movements, the contribution of the nation's children to the struggle[33] was an aspect that could not be overlooked.

However, these do not on their own adequately explain the phenomenon of unanimous support for children's rights on the political front. After all, the right to education was high on the agenda of the liberation movements after decades of 'Bantu Education.' Yet although the right to education was included in the interim Constitution, the right currently enshrined was to some extent pared down to avoid the state being forced to commit enormous resources to education, possibly at the expense of other reform programmes. But the socio-economic rights for children that were included in the constitution suggest the unavoidable expenditure of large sums of money too.

Therefore, additional reasons for the high constitutional profile of children's rights must be sought. It is submitted that another element of current political agreement lies in the 'sentimental' idea of protecting children, as observed by Du Plessis and Corder during the negotiation process which led to the adoption of the interim Constitution. The image of childhood engendered by the 'sentimental' notion of children's rights (in sharp contrast to the actual experiences of children during the struggle) is one of powerless, but grateful, recipients of the benefaction of constitutional rights. This 'sentimental' discourse continues to hold sway to a degree in children's rights debates. For instance, one public submission to the Theme Committee of the Constitutional Assembly on the final provision for children's rights uses such dramatic terminology as 'acutely vulnerable,' 'devastating consequences,' and 'tremendous disadvantage.' In another view, a political party prefaced its submission on children's rights with a statement that: "[t]he gift of children is, among other things, a *social grace* from god upon society. The pride of a nation is directly determined in proportion to the values it passes on to its generations."

The impact of the 'sentimental' lobby for the constitutionalisation of children's rights would go some way to explaining the support of the erstwhile National Party government at the negotiating table for an extended section on children's rights in the interim Constitution. It provides a reason for the initial triumph of socio-economic rights for children in an otherwise minimalist environment. And, for the while, it continues to influence the implementation of children's rights at a domestic level.

A further possible reason lies in a perception that a political commitment to children's rights is both a 'vote winning' and a 'non-vote alienating' cause to espouse. The last is easily explained: children's rights do not offend any known political constituency, such as trade unionists, property owners, pro-lifers, or death penalty supporters. The first category recognizes again that support for children's rights carries with it a powerful positive and moral force that is attractive to all sectors of society. (As Prof. Michael King has remarked, who would admit that they are against children?) Thus, along with the perception that support for children's rights does not lead to a sacrifice of the moral high ground, simultaneously, neither does supporting children's rights entail any potentially compromising action, duty or commitment.

---

33. A key factor in the student and scholar uprisings of 1976 and the 1980s.

Barbara Bennett Woodhouse, *The Constitutionalization of Children's Rights: Incorporating Emerging Human Rights into Constitutional Doctrine*
2 U. Pa. J. Const. L. 1, 3–5 (1999)

The South Africa and United States constitutions differ in many respects. The U.S. Constitution is over two hundred years old while South Africa's is barely three years old. In addition, the process of drafting was markedly different. The U.S. Constitutional Convention gathered several dozen propertied white men in Philadelphia to deliberate and draft their document in strictest secrecy. Not only social but also geographical distance burdened communications between the drafters and their constituencies. The U.S. Bill of Rights was an afterthought. By contrast, the drafting of the new South African Constitution involved the entire populace of South Africa and their Bill of Rights took a place of pride. If you log onto the South African Constitutional Assembly's web site, you will find megabytes of discussion papers, proposals by Non-Governmental Organizations ("NGOs"), letters from school children, and oral communications to the Constitutional Assembly hotline from citizens of every class and color....

Notes and Questions

1. *Interim and Final Constitutions.* South Africa's Interim Constitution, officially known as the Constitution of the Republic of South Africa 1993, was adopted to facilitate the transfer of power. The Interim Constitution embodied, among other things, the principles of universal franchise (for those 18 years old or older) and constitutional supremacy—major adjustments to the apartheid regime that preceded it. Chapter 5 of the Interim Constitution set up a process whereby the final Constitution would be drafted by democratically elected representatives, acting as a Constitutional Assembly. The final Constitution was adopted by the Constitutional Assembly in 1996. The Interim Constitution provided that the Constitutional Court of South Africa was to certify the final Constitution, and the Constitutional Court initially sent the text back to the Constitutional Assembly for reconsideration, claiming that the draft of the final Constitution failed to comply with all the Constitutional Principles set forth in Schedule 4 of the Interim Constitution. The text was then amended to comply with the Court's ruling, and the Court certified the text in 1996, allowing the Constitution to come into effect. The final Constitution was drafted after receiving widespread public comment. It has 243 sections, and is remarkable for its attention to detail. For discussions of the historical events related to the drafting of the final Constitution, see generally Jeremy Sarkin, *The Drafting of South Africa's Final Constitution from a Human-Rights Perspective*, 47 Am. J. Comp. L. 67 (1999); Albie Sachs, *The Creation of South Africa's Constitution*, 41 N.Y.L. Sch. L. Rev. 669 (1997); Lourens du Plessis & Hugh Corder, Understanding South Africa's Transitional Bill of Rights (1994); In re Certification of the Constitution of the Republic of South Africa, 1996 (10) BCLR 1253 (CC), 1996 (4) SA 744 (CC), ¶¶ 1–30.

2. *More Rights for Children?* The final Constitution expanded in some areas the rights given to children under the Interim Constitution. The Interim Constitution did not protect children from "maltreatment" or "degradation." Nor did it protect children

from work that placed the child's "moral or social development" at risk. The provision on detention was also made stronger, and the provisions in subsections (h) and (i) were totally new. On the other hand, some provisions were arguably weakened. Section 30 of the Interim Constitution gave each child the right to "parental care," whereas section 28 in the final Constitution expanded that to include "family care" or "appropriate alternative care when removed from the family environment." In addition, although section 30 in the Interim Constitution did not mention the child's right to "shelter," which the final Constitution does mention, the Interim Constitution did use the more general term "security."

3. *Comparative Law and International Law.* The formulation of the South Africa Constitution drew on comparative and international law sources, particularly the Universal Declaration of Human Rights, the International Covenant on Economic, Social and Cultural Rights, the International Covenant on Civil and Political Rights, and the European Convention for the Protection of Human Rights and Fundamental Freedoms, as well as more recent constitutions, such as those of Germany, Canada, and Namibia. These sources reflected "accumulated wisdom in international as well as domestic human rights jurisprudence." *See* Lourens du Plessis & Hugh Corder, Understanding South Africa's Transitional Bill of Rights 24, 47–48 (1994). In fact, one of the Constitutional Principles that guided the Constitutional Assembly in drafting the final Constitution was the following: "Everyone shall enjoy all universally accepted fundamental rights, freedoms and civil liberties, which shall be provided for and protected by entrenched and justiciable provisions in the Constitution, which shall be drafted after having given due consideration to *inter alia* the fundamental rights contained in Chapter 3 of this Constitution." *See* Constitutional Principle II. Judges interpreting the South Africa Constitution will also draw on international law and may draw on foreign law, *see* section 39, *supra.* Must South Africa have ratified an international human rights convention in order for its courts to consider it?

4. *Times of Emergency, Non-Derogable Rights, and Standards of Review.* Section 37 of the Bill of Rights makes provision for the suspension of the Bill of Rights when there is "a state of emergency" declared by Parliament. A state of emergency is defined as when "the life of the nation is threatened by war, invasion, general insurrection, disorder, natural disaster or other public emergency; and…the declaration is necessary to restore peace and order." *See* §37(1). Any derogation from the Bill of Rights during a state of emergency must meet certain conditions, including that it is "strictly required by the emergency" and consistent with international law. *See* §37(4). During the emergency, there are certain non-derogable rights. These include the following rights set forth in section 28: subsections (1)(d) and (e); subparagraphs (i) and (ii) of subsection (1)(g); and subsection 1(i) with respect to children of fifteen years and younger. Why are these rights "non-derogable" and not the others? What do the differing standards tell you about the nature of the rights in South Africa?

5. *Constitutionalizing Children's Rights.* You may recall from Chapter 2 that the South Africa Constitution does not include in its Bill of Rights the right to freely marry or the right to a family life. In certifying the final Constitution, the Constitutional Court of South Africa specifically mentioned the diversity of approaches throughout the world regarding the placement of these rights in foundational documents. It also mentioned the disadvantage of "constitutionalizing" these rights. Specifically, it mentioned that a court would need to define "family," and defining the term could adversely impact individuals in a multi-cultural and multi-faith society. The court thought the other constitutional rights, including the concepts of freedom and security, would adequately protect the rights to marry and to have a family life.

Is there an analogy here to children's rights? What are the disadvantages of constitutionalizing children's rights, or are the situations too different for the analysis to be applicable? What difference does it make if a constitutional text includes children's rights or the courts develop these rights pursuant to clauses of general application, like the Due Process Clause in the U.S. Constitution? Could the United States Supreme Court achieve through constitutional interpretation what the South Africa Constitution sets forth explicitly? Alternatively, would the South African constitutional provision make a difference if embodied in the U.S. Constitution? Finally, and quite differently, what are the advantages or disadvantages for children of a constitutional provision protecting the right to family life?

6. *Other Constitutional Rights Impacting Children.* Beyond the rights mentioned in section 28, the South Africa Constitution also embodies other rights that are of importance to children. These include, for example, the right of "access to adequate housing," *see* § 26, the right of "access to health care services," *see* § 27, the right to "sufficient food and water," *see* § 27, and the right to a "basic education," *see* § 29.

7. *The Best Interests of the Child.* What does section 28(2) mean? Would a court have to apply this principle if a child were a defendant in a criminal action? Isn't it in a child's best interest to be found innocent?

8. *Horizontal Effect.* The South Africa Bill of Rights clearly "binds the legislature, the executive, the judiciary and all organs of state." § 8(1). This is called "vertical application," and is familiar to students of U.S. constitutional law. The "state action" requirement in U.S. constitutional law makes the U.S. Constitution have vertical application. *See* G. Sidney Buchanan, A Conceptual History of the State Action Doctrine: The Search for Governmental Responsibility (pts. 1 & 2), 34 Hous. L. Rev. 333 (1997), 34 Hous. L. Rev. 665 (1997). The South Africa Constitution, however, may also have "horizontal application": it may bind private citizens. Consider the full text of section 8 of the South Africa Constitution:

(1) The Bill of Rights applies to all law, and binds the legislature, the executive, the judiciary and all organs of state.

(2) A provision of the Bill of Rights binds a natural or a juristic person if, and to the extent that, it is applicable, taking into account the nature of the right and the nature of any duty imposed by the right.

(3) When applying a provision of the Bill of Rights to a natural or juristic person in terms of subsection (2), a court—

(a) in order to give effect to a right in the Bill, must apply, or if necessary develop, the common law to the extent that legislation does not give effect to that right; and

(b) may develop rules of the common law to limit the right, provided that the limitation is in accordance with section 36(1).

(4) A juristic person is entitled to the rights in the Bill of Rights to the extent required by the nature of the rights and the nature of that juristic person.

When the Constitution was first submitted to the Constitutional Court, here is what the Constitutional Court said, in part, about section 8(2):

The second ground for the objection was that in rendering the chapter on fundamental rights binding on private persons, the [New Text] is inconsistent with [Constitutional Principle VI] which requires that there be a separation of powers between the legislature, the executive and the judiciary. The argument was that the effect of horizontality is to permit the courts to encroach upon the proper terrain of the legislature, in that it permits the courts to alter legislation and, in particular, the common law. However, that argument has two flaws. First, it fails to acknowledge that courts have always been the sole arm of government responsible for the development of the common law. There can be no separation of powers objection, therefore, to the courts retaining their power over the common law. Second, the objectors also fail to recognize that the courts have no power to "alter" legislation. The power of the judiciary in terms of the [New Text] remains the power to determine whether provisions of legislation are inconsistent with the [New Text] or not, not to alter them in ways which it may consider desirable. In any event, even where a bill of rights does not bind private persons, it will generally bind a legislature. In such circumstances all legislation is subject to review. The argument, then, that a "horizontal" application of the Bill of Rights will inevitably involve the courts in the business of the legislature to an extent that they would not be involved were the Bill of Rights to operate only "vertically," is misconceived.

In re Certification of the Constitution of the Republic of South Africa, 1996 (4) SA 744 (CC), 1996 (10) BCLR 1253, ¶54 (CC).

The Constitutional Court also addressed the following argument:

The objectors also argued that imposing obligations upon individuals in the Bill of Rights is in breach of [Constitutional Principle II] which contemplates that individuals would be beneficiaries only of universally accepted fundamental rights and freedoms. They argued that as bearers of obligations, individuals would necessarily suffer a diminution of their rights in a manner that is contrary to the contemplation of [Constitutional Principle II]. This argument, too, cannot be accepted. As long as a bill of rights binds a legislature, legislation which regulates the relationships between private individuals will be subject to constitutional scrutiny. In Germany and similar European countries where there is general codification of private law and constitutional review, the codes have to comply with constitutional standards. And even in the United States, the Bill of Rights affects private law. As stated in the previous paragraph, such scrutiny will often involve a court in balancing competing rights. It is also implicit in the indirect horizontal application of the rights required by [Interim Constitution Chapter 3], to which the [Constitutional Assembly] had to pay "due regard." [Constitutional Principle II] implicitly recognizes that even if only the state is bound, rights conferred upon individuals will justifiably be limited in order to recognize the rights of others in certain circumstances. The fact that horizontal application may also lead to justifiable limits on the rights of individuals does not mean that [Constitutional Principle II] has been breached.

Id. ¶56.

What would it mean if section 28 had horizontal application? One commentator stated that "At a minimum, however, the clause [in section 8(2)] will effectively ensure that the common law is developed in line with the Bill of Rights, which is vital for the development of a human-rights-based democracy." Jeremy Sarkin, *The Drafting of South Africa's Final Constitution from a Human-Rights Perspective*, 47 Am. J. Comp. L. 67, 80 (1999). Similarly, the words "all law" in section 8(1) might also be a "seepage clause," requiring the application of the Bill of Rights to the common or customary law often governing the relationship between private parties. Section 39(2) is also often referred to as a seepage clause because it too would allow the Bill of Rights to affect private obligations.

These provisions differ from the explicit requirement in the Interim Constitution, and now the final Constitution, and require that no person unfairly discriminate against any other. *See* Interim Constitution § 33(4); Final Constitution § 9(4). Lourens du Plessis & Hugh Corder, Understanding South Africa's Transitional Bill of Rights 113 (1994). This latter provision was adopted to ensure that a private form of apartheid did not develop.

9. *Standing to Enforce Rights.* Standing to allege a violation of the South Africa Constitution appears to be quite broad. Section 38 of the South Africa Constitution gives the following people or groups a "right to approach a competent court, alleging that a right in the Bill of Rights has been infringed or threatened": anyone acting in his or her own interest; anyone acting on behalf of another person who cannot act in his or her own name; anyone acting as a member of, or in the interest of, a group or class of persons; anyone acting in the public interest; and, an association acting in the interest of its members.

10. *Limitation Clauses.* Section 36 is called a limitation clause. Limitation clauses are quite common in international instruments. For example, look at article 29(2) of the Universal Declaration of Human Rights, article 4 of the International Covenant on Economic, Social and Cultural Rights, and article 11(2) of the European Convention on Human Rights. Does the limitation clause in the South Africa Constitution mirror these clauses? Does the Bill of Rights in the U.S. Constitution have a limitation clause?

11. *Commissions.* Section 181 of the South Africa Constitution establishes various commissions to help protect the values enshrined in the Constitution. For example, the Human Rights Commission has the power to investigate and report on human rights, to secure appropriate redress when human rights have been violated, to carry out research, and to educate. *See* § 184(2). In addition, "[E]ach year, the Human Rights Commission must require relevant organs of state to provide the Commission with information on the measures that they have taken towards the realization of the rights in the Bill of Rights concerning housing, health care, food, water, social security, education, and the environment." § 184(3). Other commissions include the Commission for the Promotion and Protection of the Rights of Cultural, Religious and Linguistic Communities and the Commission for Gender Equality. *See* §§ 185, 187.

12. *Customary Law.* The recognition of customary law in the South Africa Constitution was discussed in Chapter Two on marriage. Section 30 gives everyone the right "to participate in the cultural life of their choice," and section 211 requires courts to apply customary law when applicable. However, sections 30, 39(2) and 211 make customary law subject to the Bill of Rights. A tension between customary law and the Bill of Rights potentially exists in the context of children's rights, just as it did in the marriage context.

> The existing network of South African laws and practices pertaining to the rights of children is not, in theory or reality, child-centered. Indigenous law is rooted in the protection of the family, and its focus generally is on the community rather than on the individual....

A key question for the success of Section 28 is whether its child-centered regime is compatible with the communalism of African culture. Specifically, we do not yet know whether the fact that section 28 borrows heavily from the UN Convention on the Rights of the Child means that the Constitution contains an individualistic concept of rights, founded in Western liberalism, that is incompatible with an African communalistic way of living.

Tshepo L. Mosikatsana, *Children's Rights and Family Autonomy in the South African Context: A Comment on Children's Rights under the Final Constitution*, 3 Mich. J. Race & L. 341, 345–47 (1998). As identified by the South African Law Commission, "the idea of the child as an individual with enforceable rights against the state, the community and the family...is in potential conflict with the traditional African world view and value system, which focuses on the interests of the family group or household, and treats the child as a member of that household, the individual child's interests often being subsumed under those of the family or household as an integral societal structure." *Issue Paper 13: Review of the Child Care Act: First Issue Paper*, South African Law Commission Apr. 18, 1998, at §8.2, *available at* http://wwwserver.law.wits.ac.za/salc/issue/ip13.html#8.1. For example, will a child be able to refuse participation in a village ceremony if the child would rather attend school?

Similarly, what will happen when a court decides to use the best interest test in section 28(2) of the Constitution in order to determine custody, or another issue, and arrives at a different outcome than would result under customary law. *See, e.g.,* Hlophe v. Mahlalela, 1998 (1) SA 449 (T) (holding that best interest standard must guide custody determination and not Swazi law regarding delivery of lobolo to wife's family, assuming Swazi customary law could be ascertained); Sati v. Kitsile [1998] 1 A11 SA 530 (E). Do the provisions subordinating customaty law to the Bill of Rights potentially allow courts to trample upon customary law?

13. *Balance of Power.* Concerns about how the South Africa Constitution affects the separation of powers among the branches of government has been raised in various contexts. In note 8, *supra*, the concern was raised in connection with the Constitution's horizontal application. The concern also arises when attention turns to the social and economic rights found in the Constitution. One author said:

> Granting the courts the power to enforce socio-economic rights does not constitute an inappropriate interference in the political process. A court hearing a constitutional challenge concerning the right to basic nutrition or basic health care services will have to determine whether the level of the services delivered meets the basic needs. If it does not, the court will find a prima facie infringement of the right and inquire into whether the violation is justifiable in an open and democratic society. If the infringement cannot be justified, the court will order the state to comply with its obligations. The court, however, will not make decisions of implementation and resource allocation that should be left to local officials. As Erika de Wet notes: "It will not be able to tell the state how it should relieve the basic needs. It will only be able to indicate to the state that it is constitutionally bound to ensure the basic needs of children which must be met before the state begins to allocate funds for any other projects and expenditures."

Mosikatsana, *supra*, 353–54. Do you agree with the first line of the quotation? Perhaps you will be better able to form an opinion after you read the next case.

Government of the Republic of South Africa v. Grootboom

2001 (1) SA 46 (CC)

Yacoob, J.

Introduction

The people of South Africa are committed to the attainment of social justice and the improvement of the quality of life for everyone. The Preamble to our Constitution records this commitment. The Constitution declares the founding values of our society to be "[h]uman dignity, the achievement of equality and the advancement of human rights and freedoms."

The group of people with whom we are concerned in these proceedings lived in appalling conditions, decided to move out, and illegally occupied someone else's land. They were evicted and left homeless. The root cause of their problems is the intolerable conditions under which they were living while waiting in the queue for their turn to be allocated low-cost housing. They are the people whose constitutional rights have to be determined in this case.

Mrs. Irene Grootboom and the other respondents[2] were rendered homeless as a result of their eviction from their informal homes situated on private land earmarked for formal low-cost housing. They applied to the Cape of Good Hope High Court (the High Court) for an order requiring the government to provide them with adequate basic shelter or housing until they obtained permanent accommodation and were granted certain relief. The appellants were ordered to provide the respondents who were children and their parents with shelter. The judgment provisionally concluded that "tents, portable latrines and a regular supply of water (albeit transported) would constitute the bare minimum." The appellants who represent all spheres of government responsible for housing challenge the correctness of that order....

The cause of the acute housing shortage lies in apartheid. A central feature of that policy was a system of influx control that sought to limit African occupation of urban areas. Influx control was rigorously enforced in the Western Cape, where government policy favored the exclusion of African people in order to accord preference to the coloured community: a policy adopted in 1954 and referred to as the "coloured labour preference policy." In consequence, the provision of family housing for African people in the Cape Peninsula was frozen in 1962. This freeze was extended to other urban areas in the Western Cape in 1968. Despite the harsh application of influx control in the Western Cape, African people continued to move to the area in search of jobs. Colonial dispossession and a rigidly enforced racial distribution of land in the rural areas had dislocated the rural economy and rendered sustainable and independent African farming increasingly precarious. Given the absence of formal housing, large numbers of people moved into informal settlements throughout the Cape peninsula.... The legacy of influx control in the Western Cape is the acute housing shortage that exists there now. Although the precise extent is uncertain, the shortage stood at more than 100,000 units in the Cape Metro at the time of the inception of the interim Constitution in

---

2. The respondents are 510 children and 390 adults. Mrs. Irene Grootboom, the first respondent, brought the application before the High Court on behalf of all the respondents.

1994. Hundreds of thousands of people in need of housing occupied rudimentary informal settlements providing for minimal shelter, but little else.

Mrs. Grootboom and most of the other respondents previously lived in an informal squatter settlement called Wallacedene.... The conditions under which most of the residents of Wallacedene lived were lamentable. A quarter of the households of Wallacedene had no income at all, and more than two thirds earned less than R500 per month. About half the population were children; all lived in shacks. They had no water, sewage or refuse removal services and only 5% of the shacks had electricity. The area is partly waterlogged and lies dangerously close to a main thoroughfare. Mrs. Grootboom lived with her family and her sister's family in a shack about twenty meters square.

Many had applied for subsidized low-cost housing from the municipality and had been on the waiting list for as long as seven years. Despite numerous inquiries from the municipality, no definite answer was given. Clearly it was going to be a long wait. Faced with the prospect of remaining in intolerable conditions indefinitely, the respondents began to move out of Wallacedene at the end of September 1998. They put up their shacks and shelters on vacant land that was privately owned and had been earmarked for low-cost housing. They called the land "New Rust."

They did not have the consent of the owner and on 8 December 1998 he obtained an ejectment order against them in the magistrates' court. The order was served on the occupants but they remained in occupation beyond the date by which they had been ordered to vacate. Mrs. Grootboom says they had nowhere else to go: their former sites in Wallacedene had been filled by others. The eviction proceedings were renewed in March 1999.... Negotiations resulted in the grant of an order requiring the occupants to vacate New Rust and authorizing the sheriff to evict them and to dismantle and remove any of their structures remaining on the land on 19 May 1999. The magistrate also directed that the parties and the municipality mediate to identify alternative land for the permanent or temporary occupation of the New Rust residents.

The municipality had not been party to the proceedings but it had engaged attorneys to monitor them on its behalf. It is not clear whether the municipality was a party to the settlement and the agreement to mediate. Nor is it clear whether the eviction was in accordance with the provisions of the Prevention of Illegal Eviction from and Unlawful Occupation of Land Act, 19 of 1998.[9] The validity of the eviction order has never been challenged and must be accepted as correct. However, no mediation took place and on 18 May 1999, at the beginning of the cold, windy and rainy Cape winter, the respondents were forcibly evicted at the municipality's expense. This was done prematurely and inhumanely: reminiscent of apartheid-style evictions. The respondents' homes were bulldozed and burnt and their possessions destroyed. Many of the residents who were not there could not even salvage their personal belongings.

The respondents went and sheltered on the Wallacedene sports field under such temporary structures as they could muster. Within a week the winter rains started and the plastic sheeting they had erected afforded scant protection. The next day the respondents' attorney wrote to the municipality describing the intolerable conditions under

---

9. Section 4(6) provides:
    If an unlawful occupier has occupied the land in question for less than six months at the time when the proceedings are initiated, a court may grant an order for eviction if it is of the opinion that it is just and equitable to do so, after considering all the relevant circumstances, including the rights and needs of the elderly, children, disabled persons and households headed by women.

which his clients were living and demanded that the municipality meet its constitutional obligations and provide temporary accommodation to the respondents. The respondents were not satisfied with the response of the municipality[10] and launched an urgent application in the High Court on 31 May 1999. As indicated above, the High Court granted relief to the respondents and the appellants now appeal against that relief.

The case in the High Court

Mrs Grootboom and the other respondents applied for an order directing the appellants forthwith to provide:

(i) adequate basic temporary shelter or housing to the respondents and their children pending their obtaining permanent accommodation;

(ii) or basic nutrition, shelter, healthcare and social services to the respondents who are children.

The respondents based their claim on two constitutional provisions. First, on section 26 of the Constitution which provides that everyone has the right of access to adequate housing. Section 26(2) imposes an obligation upon the state to take reasonable legislative and other measures to ensure the progressive realization of this right within its available resources....* The second basis for their claim was section 28(1)(c) of the Constitution which provides that children have the right to shelter....

The High Court judgment consists of two separate parts. The first, under the heading "Housing" considered the claim in terms of section 26 of the Constitution. On this part of the claim the High Court concluded:

In short [appellants] are faced with a massive shortage in available housing and an extremely constrained budget. Furthermore in terms of the pressing demands and scarce resources [appellants] had implemented a housing program in an attempt to maximize available resources to redress the housing shortage. For this reason it could not be said that [appellants] had not taken reasonable legislative and other measures within its available resources to achieve the progressive realization of the right to have access to adequate housing.

The court rejected an argument that the right of access to adequate housing under section 26 included a minimum core entitlement to shelter in terms of which the state was obliged to provide some form of shelter pending implementation of the program to provide adequate housing. This submission was based on the provisions of certain international instruments that are discussed later.[13]

The second part of the judgment addressed the claim of the children for shelter in terms of section 28(1)(c). The court reasoned that the parents bore the primary obliga-

---

10. The municipality responded on 27 May 1999 stating that it had supplied food and shelter at the Wallacedene Community Hall to the respondents and that it was approaching Western Cape government for assistance to resolve the problem. The respondents, however, considered that the Community Hall provided inadequate shelter as it could only house 80 people.

* Ed. Note: Section 26 provides:

(1) Everyone has the right to have access to adequate housing.

(2) The state must take reasonable legislative and other measures, within its available resources, to achieve the progressive realization of this right.

(3) No one may be evicted from their home, or have their home demolished, without an order of court made after considering all the relevant circumstances. No legislation may permit arbitrary evictions.

13. The International Covenant on Economic, Social and Cultural Rights, and the general comments issued by the United Nations Committee on Social and Economic Rights.

tion to provide shelter for their children, but that section 28(1)(c) imposed an obligation on the state to provide that shelter if parents could not. It went on to say that the shelter to be provided according to this obligation was a significantly more rudimentary form of protection from the elements than is provided by a house and falls short of adequate housing. The court concluded that: "an order which enforces a child's right to shelter should take account of the need of the child to be accompanied by his or her parent. Such an approach would be in accordance with the spirit and purport of section 28 as a whole."

In the result the court ordered as follows:

(2) It is declared, in terms of section 28 of the Constitution that:

(a) the applicant children are entitled to be provided with shelter by the appropriate organ or department of state;

(b) the applicant parents are entitled to be accommodated with their children in the aforegoing shelter; and

(c) the appropriate organ or department of state is obliged to provide the applicant children, and their accompanying parents, with such shelter until such time as the parents are able to shelter their own children;

(3) The several respondents are directed to present under oath a report or reports to this Court as to the implementation of paragraph (2) above within a period of three months from the date of this order....

The relevant constitutional provisions and their justiciability...

These rights [section 26 and section 28(1)(c)] need to be considered in the context of the cluster of socio-economic rights enshrined in the Constitution. They entrench the right of access to land, to adequate housing and to health care, food, water and social security. They also protect the rights of the child and the right to education.

While the justiciability of socio-economic rights has been the subject of considerable jurisprudential and political debate, the issue of whether socio-economic rights are justiciable at all in South Africa has been put beyond question by the text of our Constitution as construed in the Certification judgment. During the certification proceedings before this Court, it was contended that they were not justiciable and should therefore not have been included in the text of the new Constitution. In response to this argument, this Court held:

[T]hese rights are, at least to some extent, justiciable. As we have stated in the previous paragraph, many of the civil and political rights entrenched in the [constitutional text before this Court for certification in that case] will give rise to similar budgetary implications without compromising their justiciability. The fact that socio-economic rights will almost inevitably give rise to such implications does not seem to us to be a bar to their justiciability. At the very minimum, socio-economic rights can be negatively protected from improper invasion.

Socio-economic rights are expressly included in the Bill of Rights; they cannot be said to exist on paper only. Section 7(2) of the Constitution requires the state "to respect, protect, promote and fulfil the rights in the Bill of Rights" and the courts are constitutionally bound to ensure that they are protected and fulfilled. The question is therefore not whether socio-economic rights are justiciable under our Constitution, but how to enforce them in a given case.[21] This is a very difficult issue which must be carefully explored on a case-by-case basis.... Although the judgment of the High Court in favor of the appellants was based on the right to shelter (section 28(1)(c) of the Constitution), it is appropriate to consider the provisions of section 26 first so as to facilitate a contextual evaluation of section 28(1)(c).

Obligations imposed upon the state by section 26

Approach to interpretation

Like all the other rights in Chapter 2 of the Constitution (which contains the Bill of Rights), section 26 must be construed in its context. The section has been carefully crafted. It contains three subsections. The first confers a general right of access to adequate housing. The second establishes and delimits the scope of the positive obligation imposed upon the state to promote access to adequate housing and has three key elements. The state is obliged: (a) to take reasonable legislative and other measures; (b) within its available resources; (c) to achieve the progressive realization of this right....

Interpreting a right in its context requires the consideration of two types of context. On the one hand, rights must be understood in their textual setting. This will require a consideration of Chapter 2 and the Constitution as a whole. On the other hand, rights must also be understood in their social and historical context.

Our Constitution entrenches both civil and political rights and social and economic rights. All the rights in our Bill of Rights are inter-related and mutually supporting. There can be no doubt that human dignity, freedom and equality, the foundational values of our society, are denied those who have no food, clothing or shelter. Affording socio-economic rights to all people therefore enables them to enjoy the other rights enshrined in Chapter 2. The realization of these rights is also key to the advancement of race and gender equality and the evolution of a society in which men and women are equally able to achieve their full potential.

The right of access to adequate housing cannot be seen in isolation. There is a close relationship between it and the other socio-economic rights. Socio-economic rights must all be read together in the setting of the Constitution as a whole. The state is obliged to take positive action to meet the needs of those living in extreme conditions of poverty, homelessness or intolerable housing. Their interconnectedness needs to be taken into account in interpreting the socio-economic rights, and, in particular, in determining whether the state has met its obligations in terms of them.

Rights also need to be interpreted and understood in their social and historical context. The right to be free from unfair discrimination, for example, must be understood against our legacy of deep social inequality. The context in which the Bill of Rights is to be interpreted was described by Chaskalson P in *Soobramoney*:

> We live in a society in which there are great disparities in wealth. Millions of people are living in deplorable conditions and in great poverty. There is a high level of unemployment, inadequate social security, and many do not have access to clean water or to adequate health services. These conditions already existed when the Constitution was adopted and a commitment to address them, and to transform our society into one in which there will be human dignity, freedom

---

21. Section 38 of the Constitution empowers the Court to grant appropriate relief for the infringement of any right entrenched in the Bill of Rights.

and equality, lies at the heart of our new constitutional order. For as long as these conditions continue to exist that aspiration will have a hollow ring.

The relevant international law and its impact

During argument, considerable weight was attached to the value of international law in interpreting section 26 of our Constitution. Section 39 of the Constitution obliges a court to consider international law as a tool of interpretation for the Bill of Rights. In *Makwanyane* Chaskalson P, in the context of section 35(1) of the interim Constitution,[27] said:

> [P]ublic international law would include non-binding as well as binding law. They may both be used under the section as tools of interpretation. International agreements and customary international law accordingly provide a framework within which [the Bill of Rights] can be evaluated and understood, and for that purpose, decisions of tribunals dealing with comparable instruments, such as the United Nations Committee on Human Rights, the Inter-American Commission on Human Rights, the Inter-American Court of Human Rights, the European Commission on Human Rights, and the European Court of Human Rights, and, in appropriate cases, reports of specialized agencies such as the International Labor Organization, may provide guidance as to the correct interpretation of particular provisions of [the Bill of Rights]. (Footnotes omitted)

The relevant international law can be a guide to interpretation but the weight to be attached to any particular principle or rule of international law will vary. However, where the relevant principle of international law binds South Africa, it may be directly applicable.

The amici submitted that the International Covenant on Economic, Social and Cultural Rights (the Covenant)[29] is of significance in understanding the positive obligations created by the socio-economic rights in the Constitution. Article 11.1 of the Covenant provides:

> The States Parties to the present Covenant recognize the right of everyone to an adequate standard of living for himself and his family, including adequate food, clothing and housing, and to the continuous improvement of living conditions. The States Parties will take appropriate steps to ensure the realization of this right, recognizing to this effect the essential importance of international co-operation based on free consent.

This Article must be read with Article 2.1 which provides:

> Each State Party to the present Covenant undertakes to take steps, individually and through international assistance and co-operation, especially economic and technical, to the maximum of its available resources, with a view to achieving progressively the full realization of the rights recognized in the present Covenant by all appropriate means, including particularly the adoption of legislative measures.

The differences between the relevant provisions of the Covenant and our Constitution are significant in determining the extent to which the provisions of the Covenant

---

27. Section 35(1) of the interim Constitution provides:
   In interpreting the provisions of this Chapter a court of law shall promote the values which underlie an open and democratic society based on freedom and equality and shall, where applicable, have regard to public international law applicable to the protection of the rights entrenched in this Chapter, and may have regard to comparable foreign case law.

29. The Covenant was signed by South Africa on 3 October 1994 but has as not yet been ratified.

may be a guide to an interpretation of section 26. These differences, in so far as they relate to housing, are:

(a) The Covenant provides for a *right to adequate housing* while section 26 provides for the *right of access* to adequate housing.

(b) The Covenant obliges states parties to take *appropriate* steps which must include legislation while the Constitution obliges the South African state to take *reasonable* legislative and other measures.

The obligations undertaken by states parties to the Covenant are monitored by the United Nations Committee on Economic, Social and Cultural Rights (the committee). The *amici* relied on the relevant general comments issued by the committee concerning the interpretation and application of the Covenant, and argued that these general comments constitute a significant guide to the interpretation of section 26. In particular they argued that in interpreting this section, we should adopt an approach similar to that taken by the committee in paragraph 10 of general comment 3 issued in 1990, in which the committee found that socio-economic rights contain a minimum core:

On the basis of the extensive experience gained by the Committee, as well as by the body that preceded it, over a period of more than a decade of examining States parties' reports, the Committee is of the view that a minimum core obligation to ensure the satisfaction of, at the very least, minimum essential levels of each of the rights is incumbent upon every State party. Thus, for example, a State party in which any significant number of individuals is deprived of essential foodstuffs, of essential primary health care, of basic shelter and housing, or of the most basic forms of education, is *prima facie*, failing to discharge its obligations under the Covenant. If the Covenant were to be read in such a way as not to establish such a minimum core obligation, it would be largely deprived of its raison d'etre. By the same token, it must be noted that any assessment as to whether a State has discharged its minimum core obligation must also take account of resource constraints applying within the country concerned. Article 2(1) obligates each State party to take the necessary steps "to the maximum of its available resources." In order for a State party to be able to attribute its failure to meet at least its minimum core obligations to a lack of available resources it must demonstrate that every effort has been made to use all resources that are at its disposition in an effort to satisfy, as a matter of priority, those minimum obligations.

It is clear from this extract that the committee considers that every state party is bound to fulfil a minimum core obligation by ensuring the satisfaction of a minimum essential level of the socio-economic rights, including the right to adequate housing.... However, it is to be noted that the general comment does not specify precisely what that minimum core is.

The concept of a minimum core obligation was developed by the committee to describe the minimum expected of a state in order to comply with its obligation under the Covenant.... Minimum core obligation is determined generally by having regard to the needs of the most vulnerable group that is entitled to the protection of the right in question. It is in this context that the concept of a minimum core obligation must be understood in international law....

The determination of a minimum core in the context of "the right to have access to adequate housing" presents difficult questions. This is so because the needs in the context of access to adequate housing are diverse: there are those who need land; others need both land and houses; yet others need financial assistance. There are difficult questions relating to the definition of a minimum core in the context of a right to have access to adequate housing, in particular whether the minimum core obligation should be defined generally or with regard to specific groups of people. As will appear from the discussion below, the real question in terms of our Constitution is whether the measures taken by the state to realize the right afforded by section 26 are reasonable. There may be cases where it may be possible and appropriate to have regard to the content of a minimum core obligation to determine whether the measures taken by the state are reasonable. However, even if it were appropriate to do so, it could not be done unless sufficient information is placed before a court to enable it to determine the minimum core in any given context. In this case, we do not have sufficient information to determine what would comprise the minimum core obligation in the context of our Constitution. It is not in any event necessary to decide whether it is appropriate for a court to determine in the first instance the minimum core content of a right.

Analysis of section 26

I consider the meaning and scope of section 26 in its context....

Subsections (1) and (2) are related and must be read together. Subsection (1) aims at delineating the scope of the right. It is a right of everyone including children. Although the subsection does not expressly say so, there is, at the very least, a negative obligation placed upon the state and all other entities and persons to desist from preventing or impairing the right of access to adequate housing. The negative right is further spelt out in subsection (3) which prohibits arbitrary evictions.

The right delineated in section 26(1) is a right of "access to adequate housing" as distinct from the right to adequate housing encapsulated in the Covenant. This difference is significant. It recognizes that housing entails more than bricks and mortar. It requires available land, appropriate services such as the provision of water and the removal of sewage and the financing of all of these, including the building of the house itself. For a person to have access to adequate housing all of these conditions need to be met: there must be land, there must be services, there must be a dwelling. Access to land for the purpose of housing is therefore included in the right of access to adequate housing in section 26. A right of access to adequate housing also suggests that it is not only the state who is responsible for the provision of houses, but that other agents within our society, including individuals themselves, must be enabled by legislative and other measures to provide housing. The state must create the conditions for access to adequate housing for people at all economic levels of our society. State policy dealing with housing must therefore take account of different economic levels in our society.

In this regard, there is a difference between the position of those who can afford to pay for housing, even if it is only basic though adequate housing, and those who cannot. For those who can afford to pay for adequate housing, the state's primary obligation lies in unlocking the system, providing access to housing stock and a legislative framework to facilitate self-built houses through planning laws and access to finance. Issues of development and social welfare are raised in respect of those who cannot afford to provide themselves with housing. State policy needs to address both these groups. The poor are particularly vulnerable and their needs require special attention. It is in this context that the relationship between sections 26 and 27 and the other socio-economic rights is most apparent.* If under section 27 the state has in place programmes

---

* Ed. Note: See footnote 49 *infra* for relevant text.

to provide adequate social assistance to those who are otherwise unable to support themselves and their dependents, that would be relevant to the state's obligations in respect of other socio-economic rights.

The state's obligation to provide access to adequate housing depends on context, and may differ from province to province, from city to city, from rural to urban areas and from person to person....

Subsection (2) speaks to the positive obligation imposed upon the state. It requires the state to devise a comprehensive and workable plan to meet its obligations in terms of the subsection. However subsection (2) also makes it clear that the obligation imposed upon the state is not an absolute or unqualified one....

Reasonable legislative and other measures

What constitutes reasonable legislative and other measures must be determined in the light of the fact that [Chapter 3 of] the Constitution creates different spheres of government: national government, provincial government and local government....

Thus, a co-ordinated state housing program must be a comprehensive one determined by all three spheres of government in consultation with each other as contemplated by Chapter 3 of the Constitution. It may also require framework legislation at the national level, a matter we need not consider further in this case as there is national framework legislation in place. Each sphere of government must accept responsibility for the implementation of particular parts of the program, but the national sphere of government must assume responsibility for ensuring that laws, policies, programs and strategies are adequate to meet the state's section 26 obligations. In particular, the national framework, if there is one, must be designed so that these obligations can be met. It should be emphasized that national government bears an important responsibility in relation to the allocation of national revenue to the provinces and local government on an equitable basis. Furthermore, national and provincial government must ensure that executive obligations imposed by the housing legislation are met.

The measures must establish a coherent public housing program directed towards the progressive realization of the right of access to adequate housing within the state's available means. The program must be capable of facilitating the realization of the right. The precise contours and content of the measures to be adopted are primarily a matter for the legislature and the executive. They must, however, ensure that the measures they adopt are reasonable.... It is necessary to recognize that a wide range of possible measures could be adopted by the state to meet its obligations....

The state is required to take reasonable legislative *and* other measures.... Mere legislation is not enough. The state is obliged to act to achieve the intended result, and the legislative measures will invariably have to be supported by appropriate, well-directed policies and programs implemented by the executive....

Reasonableness must also be understood in the context of the Bill of Rights as a whole.... A society must seek to ensure that the basic necessities of life are provided to all if it is to be a society based on human dignity, freedom and equality.... Those whose needs are the most urgent and whose ability to enjoy all rights therefore is most in peril, must not be ignored by the measures aimed at achieving realization of the right.

It may not be sufficient to meet the test of reasonableness to show that the measures are capable of achieving a statistical advance in the realization of the right. Furthermore, the Constitution requires that everyone must be treated with care and concern. If the measures, though statistically successful, fail to respond to the needs of those most desperate, they may not pass the test.

Progressive realization of the right

The extent and content of the obligation consist in what must be achieved, that is, "the progressive realization of this right."...The term "progressive realization" shows that it was contemplated that the right could not be realized immediately.... Housing must be made more accessible not only to a larger number of people but to a wider range of people as time progresses. The phrase is taken from international law and Article 2.1 of the Covenant in particular. The committee has helpfully analyzed this requirement in the context of housing as follows:

> Nevertheless, the fact that realization over time, or in other words progressively, is foreseen under the Covenant should not be misinterpreted as depriving the obligation of all meaningful content. It is on the one hand a necessary flexibility device, reflecting the realities of the real world and the difficulties involved for any country in ensuring full realization of economic, social and cultural rights. On the other hand, the phrase must be read in the light of the overall objective, indeed the raison d'être, of the Covenant which is to establish clear obligations for States parties in respect of the full realization of the rights in question. It thus imposes an obligation to move as expeditiously and effectively as possible towards that goal. Moreover, any deliberately retrogressive measures in that regard would require the most careful consideration and would need to be fully justified by reference to the totality of the rights provided for in the Covenant and in the context of the full use of the maximum available resources.

Although the committee's analysis is intended to explain the scope of states parties' obligations under the Covenant, it is also helpful in plumbing the meaning of "progressive realization" in the context of our Constitution. The meaning ascribed to the phrase is in harmony with the context in which the phrase is used in our Constitution and there is no reason not to accept that it bears the same meaning in the Constitution as in the document from which it was so clearly derived.

Within available resources

The third defining aspect of the obligation to take the requisite measures is that the obligation does not require the state to do more than its available resources permit. This means that both the content of the obligation in relation to the rate at which it is achieved as well as the reasonableness of the measures employed to achieve the result are governed by the availability of resources....

Description and evaluation of the state housing programme...

There is in place both national and provincial legislation concerned with housing.... There is a single housing policy and a subsidy system that targets low-income earners regardless of race. The White Paper on Housing aims to stabilize the housing environment, establish institutional arrangements, protect consumers, rationalize institutional capacity within a sustainable long-term framework, facilitate the speedy release and servicing of land and co-ordinate and integrate the public sector investment in housing. In addition, various schemes are in place involving public/private partnerships aimed at ensuring that housing provision is effectively financed.

The concept of housing development as defined is central to the [Housing Act, 107 of 1997]. Housing development, as defined, seeks to provide citizens and permanent residents with access to permanent residential structures [that have] convenient access to economic opportunities and to health, educational and social amenities.

The definition of housing development as well as the general principles that are set out do not contemplate the provision of housing that falls short of the definition of housing development in the Act. In other words there is no express provision to facilitate access to temporary relief for people who have no access to land, no roof over their heads, for people who are living in intolerable conditions and for people who are in crisis because of natural disasters such as floods and fires, or because their homes are under threat of demolition. These are people in desperate need. Their immediate need can be met by relief short of housing which fulfills the requisite standards of durability, habitability and stability encompassed by the definition of housing development in the Act.

What has been done in execution of this program is a major achievement. Large sums of money have been spent and a significant number of houses have been built.[47] ... It is a program that is aimed at achieving the progressive realization of the right of access to adequate housing.

A question that nevertheless must be answered is whether the measures adopted are reasonable within the meaning of section 26 of the Constitution. Allocation of responsibilities and functions has been coherently and comprehensively addressed. The program is not haphazard but represents a systematic response to a pressing social need....

[Ed. Note: The Court next analyzed the housing problem in the area in which the respondents lived.] Shacks in this area increased by 111 percent during the period 1993 to 1996 and by 21 percent from then until 1998.... The scope of the problem is perhaps most sharply illustrated by this: about 22,000 houses are built in the Western Cape each year while demand grows at a rate of 20,000 family units per year. The backlog is therefore likely to be reduced, resources permitting and, on the basis of the figures in this study, only by 2,000 houses a year.... As stated above, many of the families living in Wallacedene are living in intolerable conditions....

The Cape Metro has realized that this desperate situation requires government action that is different in nature from that encompassed by the housing development policy described earlier in this judgment. It drafted a program (the Cape Metro land program) in June 1999, some months after the respondents had been evicted....

Crucially, the program acknowledges that its beneficiaries are families who are to be evicted, those who are in a crisis situation in an existing area such as in a flood-line, families located on strategic land and families from backyard shacks or on the waiting list who are in crisis situations. Its primary objective is the rapid release of land for these families in crisis, with services to be upgraded progressively.... It is common cause that, except for the Cape Metro land programme, there is no provision in the nationwide housing programme as applied within the Cape Metro for people in desperate need....

The national government bears the overall responsibility for ensuring that the state complies with the obligations imposed upon it by section 26. The nationwide housing program falls short of obligations imposed upon national government to the extent that it fails to recognize that the state must provide for relief for those in desperate need.

---

47. Some 362,160 houses were built or under construction between March 1994 and September 1997, while an overall total of some 637,190 subsidies had been allocated for projects in various stages of planning or development by October 1997.

They are not to be ignored in the interests of an overall program focussed on medium and long-term objectives. It is essential that a reasonable part of the national housing budget be devoted to this, but the precise allocation is for national government to decide in the first instance.

This case is concerned with the Cape Metro and the municipality. The former has realized that this need has not been fulfilled and has put in place its land program in an effort to fulfil it. This program, on the face of it, meets the obligation which the state has towards people in the position of the respondents in the Cape Metro.... However, as with legislative measures, the existence of the program is a starting point only. What remains is the implementation of the program by taking all reasonable steps that are necessary to initiate and sustain it. And it must be implemented with due regard to the urgency of the situations it is intended to address.

Effective implementation requires at least adequate budgetary support by national government. This, in turn, requires recognition of the obligation to meet immediate needs in the nationwide housing program. Recognition of such needs in the nationwide housing program requires it to plan, budget and monitor the fulfillment of immediate needs and the management of crises. This must ensure that a significant number of desperate people in need are afforded relief, though not all of them need receive it immediately. Such planning too will require proper co-operation between the different spheres of government.

In conclusion it has been established in this case that as of the date of the launch of this application, the state was not meeting the obligation imposed upon it by section 26(2) of the Constitution in the area of the Cape Metro....

Section 28(1)(c) and the right to shelter

The judgment of the High Court amounts to this: (a) section 28(1)(c) obliges the state to provide rudimentary shelter to children and their parents on demand if parents are unable to shelter their children; (b) this obligation exists independently of and in addition to the obligation to take reasonable legislative and other measures in terms of section 26; and (c) the state is bound to provide this rudimentary shelter irrespective of the availability of resources....

This reasoning produces an anomalous result. People who have children have a direct and enforceable right to housing under section 28(1)(c), while others who have none or whose children are adult are not entitled to housing under that section, no matter how old, disabled or otherwise deserving they may be. The carefully constructed constitutional scheme for progressive realization of socio-economic rights would make little sense if it could be trumped in every case by the rights of children to get shelter from the state on demand. Moreover, there is an obvious danger. Children could become stepping stones to housing for their parents instead of being valued for who they are.

The respondents and the *amici* in supporting the judgment of the High Court draw a distinction between housing on the one hand and shelter on the other. They contend that shelter is an attenuated form of housing and that the state is obliged to provide shelter to all children on demand. The respondents and the *amici* emphasize that the right of children to shelter is unqualified and that the "reasonable measures" qualification embodied in sections 25(5) 26, 27 and 29 are markedly absent in relation to section 28(1)(c). The appellants disagree and criticize the respondents' definition of shelter on the basis that it conceives shelter in terms that limit it to a material object. They contend that shelter is more than just that, but define it as an institution constructed by the state in which children are housed away from their parents.

I cannot accept that the Constitution draws any real distinction between housing on the one hand and shelter on the other, and that shelter is a rudimentary form of housing. Housing and shelter are related concepts and one of the aims of housing is to provide physical shelter. But shelter is not a commodity separate from housing. There is no doubt that all shelter represents protection from the elements and possibly even from danger. There are a range of ways in which shelter may be constituted: shelter may be ineffective or rudimentary at the one extreme and very effective and even ideal at the other. The concept of shelter in section 28(1)(c) is not qualified by any requirement that it should be "basic" shelter. It follows that the Constitution does not limit the concept of shelter to basic shelter alone. The concept of shelter in section 28(1)(c) embraces shelter in all its manifestations. However, it does not follow that the Constitution obliges the state to provide shelter at the most effective or the most rudimentary level to children in the company of their parents.

The obligation created by section 28(1)(c) can properly be ascertained only in the context of the rights and, in particular, the obligations created by sections 25(5), 26 and 27 of the Constitution. Each of these sections expressly obliges the state to take reasonable legislative and other measures, within its available resources, to achieve the rights with which they are concerned.[49] Section 28(1)(c) creates the right of children to basic nutrition, shelter, basic health care services and social services. There is an evident overlap between the rights created by sections 26 and 27 and those conferred on children by section 28. Apart from this overlap, the section 26 and 27 rights are conferred on everyone including children while section 28, on its face, accords rights to children alone. This overlap is not consistent with the notion that section 28(1)(c) creates separate and independent rights for children and their parents.

The extent of the state obligation must also be interpreted in the light of the international obligations binding upon South Africa. The United Nations Convention on the Rights of the Child, ratified by South Africa in 1995, seeks to impose obligations upon state parties to ensure that the rights of children in their countries are properly protected. Section 28 is one of the mechanisms to meet these obligations. It requires the state to take steps to ensure that children's rights are observed. In the first instance, the state does so by ensuring that there are legal obligations to compel parents to fulfil their responsibilities in relation to their children. Hence, legislation and the common law impose obligations upon parents to care for their children. The state reinforces the observance of these obligations by the use of civil and criminal law as well as social welfare programs.

Section 28(1)(c) must be read in this context. Subsections 28(1)(b) and (c) provide:

Every child has the right—

(b) to family care or parental care, or to appropriate alternative care when removed from the family environment;

(c) to basic nutrition, shelter, basic health care services and social services.

They must be read together. They ensure that children are properly cared for by their parents or families, and that they receive appropriate alternative care in the absence of

---

49. Section 25(5) mandates the state to foster conditions which enable citizens to gain land on an equitable basis; section 26(2) is concerned with the right of access to adequate housing; section 27(2) with the right of access to health care services, sufficient food and water and social security including appropriate social assistance if people are unable to support themselves and their dependents.

parental or family care. The section encapsulates the conception of the scope of care that children should receive in our society. Subsection (1)(b) defines those responsible for giving care while subsection (1)(c) lists various aspects of the care entitlement.

It follows from subsection 1(b) that the Constitution contemplates that a child has the right to parental or family care in the first place, and the right to alternative appropriate care only where that is lacking. Through legislation and the common law, the obligation to provide shelter in subsection (1)(c) is imposed primarily on the parents or family and only alternatively on the state. The state thus incurs the obligation to provide shelter to those children, for example, who are removed from their families. It follows that section 28(1)(c) does not create any primary state obligation to provide shelter on demand to parents and their children if children are being cared for by their parents or families.

This does not mean, however, that the state incurs no obligation in relation to children who are being cared for by their parents or families. In the first place, the state must provide the legal and administrative infrastructure necessary to ensure that children are accorded the protection contemplated by section 28. This obligation would normally be fulfilled by passing laws and creating enforcement mechanisms for the maintenance of children, their protection from maltreatment, abuse, neglect or degradation, and the prevention of other forms of abuse of children mentioned in section 28. In addition, the state is required to fulfil its obligations to provide families with access to land in terms of section 25, access to adequate housing in terms of section 26 as well as access to health care, food, water and social security in terms of section 27. It follows from this judgment that sections 25 and 27 require the state to provide access on a programmatic and coordinated basis, subject to available resources. One of the ways in which the state would meet its section 27 obligations would be through a social welfare program providing maintenance grants and other material assistance to families in need in defined circumstances.

It was not contended that the children who are respondents in this case should be provided with shelter apart from their parents. Those of the respondents in this case who are children are being cared for by their parents; they are not in the care of the state, in any alternative care, or abandoned. In the circumstances of this case, therefore, there was no obligation upon the state to provide shelter to those of the respondents who were children and, through them, their parents in terms of section 28(1)(c). The High Court therefore erred in making the order it did on the basis of this section.

Evaluation of the conduct of the appellants towards the respondents

The final section of this judgment is concerned with whether the respondents are entitled to some relief in the form of temporary housing.... We must also remember that the respondents are not alone in their desperation; hundreds of thousands (possibly millions) of South Africans live in appalling conditions throughout our country.

Although the conditions in which the respondents lived in Wallacedene were admittedly intolerable and although it is difficult to level any criticism against them for leaving the Wallacedene shack settlement, it is a painful reality that their circumstances were no worse than those of thousands of other people, including young children, who remained at Wallacedene. It cannot be said, on the evidence before us, that the respondents moved out of the Wallacedene settlement and occupied the land earmarked for a low-cost housing development as a deliberate strategy to gain preference in the allocation of housing resources over thousands of other people who remained in intolerable conditions and who were also in urgent need of housing relief. It must be borne in mind however, that the effect of any order that constitutes a special dispensation for the respondents on account of their extraordinary circumstances is to accord that preference....

Section 26, read in the context of the Bill of Rights as a whole, must mean that the respondents have a right to reasonable action by the state in all circumstances and with particular regard to human dignity....

There is...no dispute that the municipality funded the eviction of the respondents. The magistrate who ordered the ejectment of the respondents directed a process of mediation in which the municipality was to be involved to identify some alternative land for the occupation for the New Rust residents. Although the reason for this is unclear from the papers, it is evident that no effective mediation took place. The state had an obligation to ensure, at the very least, that the eviction was humanely executed. However, the eviction was reminiscent of the past and inconsistent with the values of the Constitution.... [S]ection 26(1) of the Constitution burdens the state with at least a negative obligation in relation to housing. The manner in which the eviction was carried out resulted in a breach of this obligation.

In these circumstances, the municipality's response to the letter of the respondents' attorney left much to be desired. It will be recalled that the letter stated that discussions were being held with officials from the Provincial Administration in order to find an amicable solution to the problem. There is no evidence that the respondents were ever informed of the outcome of these discussions....

In all these circumstances, the state may well have been in breach of its constitutional obligations....

This judgment must not be understood as approving any practice of land invasion for the purpose of coercing a state structure into providing housing on a preferential basis to those who participate in any exercise of this kind. Land invasion is inimical to the systematic provision of adequate housing on a planned basis. It may well be that the decision of a state structure, faced with the difficulty of repeated land invasions, not to provide housing in response to those invasions, would be reasonable. Reasonableness must be determined on the facts of each case.

Summary and conclusion...

Neither section 26 nor section 28 entitles the respondents to claim shelter or housing immediately upon demand. The High Court order ought therefore not to have been made. However, section 26 does oblige the state to devise and implement a coherent, co-ordinated program designed to meet its section 26 obligations. The program that has been adopted and was in force in the Cape Metro at the time that this application was brought, fell short of the obligations imposed upon the state by section 26(2) in that it failed to provide for any form of relief to those desperately in need of access to housing.

In the light of the conclusions I have reached, it is necessary and appropriate to make a declaratory order. The order requires the state to act to meet the obligation imposed upon it by section 26(2) of the Constitution. This includes the obligation to devise, fund, implement and supervise measures to provide relief to those in desperate need.

The Human Rights Commission is an *amicus* in this case. Section 184(1)(c) of the Constitution places a duty on the Commission to "monitor and assess the observance of human rights in the Republic." Subsections (2)(a) and (b) give the Commission the power:

(a) to investigate and to report on the observance of human rights;

(b) to take steps to secure appropriate redress where human rights have been violated.

Counsel for the Commission indicated during argument that the Commission had the duty and was prepared to monitor and report on the compliance by the state of its section 26 obligations. In the circumstances, the Commission will monitor and, if necessary, report in terms of these powers on the efforts made by the state to comply with its section 26 obligations in accordance with this judgment.

[Ed. Note: The other ten judges concurred in Justice Yacoob's judgment.]

Notes and Questions

1. What is the holding in *Government of RSA v. Grootboom?* What does it mean for the other provisions of section 28? How would a court enforce the constitutional mandate that every child has the right to basic nutrition, if at all?

2. *Impact on Children.* What is the effect on children's lives of a constitutional document that enshrines children's rights? What effect did section 28 of the South Africa Constitution have in *Grootboom?* Sloth-Nielsen attributes some real gains to the existence of children's rights in the Constitution. As an example, she mentions the presidential pronouncement in 1994 that established free medical care for children under six and pregnant mothers, a nutritional assistance program for school children, "the countrywide cessation of juvenile whipping as a sentence, and...the legislative prohibition of pre-trial detention of juveniles in prisons or police cells." *See* Julia Sloth-Nielsen, *Chicken Soup or Chainsaws: Some Implications of the Constitutionalisation of Children's Rights in South Africa,* 1996 Acta Juridica 6, 12–14. Sloth-Nielsen notes that these results were the product of "the persona of the President, fragile political consensus, and a perception that support for children's rights is 'chicken soup,'" and she argues that these factors are "shallow foundations on which to pin long term hopes." Sloth-Nielsen suggests that the "constitutional guarantees [can] provide the vehicle for implementation of children's rights in practice in the future" so long as child advocacy groups and NGOs take up the cause for children's rights. *Id.* at 25. Will legal action be the most effective option for these groups? Does the South Africa Constitution guarantee social programs for children?

3. *Purposive Interpretation.* Consider what one author has said of the courts' interpretation of the new South Africa Constitution. "[C]ourts of the new Republic do not place great emphasis on the language and give limited weight to the intent of the framers. The Constitutional Court has already indicated that it will adopt a 'purposive' and 'generous' approach to constitutional interpretation." Jeremy Sarkin, *The Drafting of South Africa's Final Constitution from a Human-Rights Perspective,* 47 Am. J. Comp. L. 67, 77 (1999). Does *Grootboom* support the author's conclusion?

4. *Obligations. Grootboom* suggests that the government's obligation under section 28 is to "provide the legal and administrative structure necessary" for achieving the objectives of section 28. How far does the state's obligation extend? Must the state's action be effective? What of the fact that section 28, unlike section 26, does not have the following language: "reasonable legislative and other measures" and "progressive realization of this right."

Consider, for example, these questions in the context of child labor. The South Africa Constitution states that every child has the right "to be protected from exploitive labour practices." *See* §28(1)(e). Tshepo Mosikatsana commented on the practical difficulties with affording this protection. "Child labor is fairly common in poor countries, and South Africa is no exception.... In South Africa, largely among the underclasses where children are considered to be an economic resource, there are strong economic constraints against eliminating child labor, powerful vested interests in maintaining the current state of affairs, and widespread cultural and legal support for the use of children's work. South African indigenous law and common law both recognize a child's duty to provide support for indigent parents. Though fairly common, child labor remains hidden from public view. It tends to be intermittent and to take place in the informal sector (including domestic work and family business enterprises).... Legislative intervention provides a limited and ineffective response to a hidden and pervasive problem such as child labor." Tshepo L. Mosikatsana, *Children's Rights and Family Autonomy in the South African Context: A Comment on Children's Rights under the Final Constitution*, 3 Mich. J. Race & L. 341, 368 (1998). Would it be constitutionally sufficient merely to have laws that outlawed child labor and to have violators prosecuted?

5. *Education.* The topic of education is addressed in a separate section of the South Africa Constitution. Section 29 states, in part, "Everyone has the right (a) to a basic education, including adult basic education; and (b) to further education, which the state through reasonable measures, must make progressively available and accessible." *See* §29(1). What is a "basic" education in today's world? Is this right, like the right to housing, primarily the responsibility of parents? Is the state's main responsibility to ensure parents fulfill their duty?

6. *Parental Care and Parental Rights.* Notice that there is a right of parental care mentioned in section 28(1)(b) of the South Africa Constitution, and that this is a right of the child. Parents have no constitutional right to the care and companionship of their children. This was done purposefully so that removal of children from abusive and neglectful families would not be too difficult. *See* Lourens du Plessis & Hugh Corder, Understanding South Africa's Transitional Bill of Rights 186 (1994). If there are no parental rights or family rights expressly set forth in the Constitution, do parents have any right in South Africa to direct their children's upbringing? For example, do South African parents have the right to educate their children in religious schools as opposed to state schools? *Cf.* Pierce v. Society of Sisters, 269 U.S. 510, 534–35 (1925) (finding that act requiring all children between eight and sixteen to attend public school "unreasonably interferes with the liberty of parents and guardians to direct the upbringing and education of children under their control"). Parental rights in South Africa are considered further in part C.2., *infra*, when we explore the topic of corporal punishment in South Africa.

7. *Post-Grootboom Caselaw.* Recently, the Constitutional Court decided a case dealing with the child's right to adequate health care in the context of mother-to-child HIV. *See* Minister of Health v. Treatment Action Campaign, 2002 (5) SA 703 (CC) (S. Afr.). The High Court in Pretoria had ordered the South African government to make the drug Nevirapine available in the public health sector where the pregnant woman's attending doctor considered it medically indicated. *See* Treatment Action Campaign v. Minister of Health, 2002 (4) BCLR 356 (T) (S. Afr.). The drug was offered to the government by the manufacturer at no cost for five years, and had been shown to prevent mother-to-child transmission of HIV. However, before the lawsuit, the drug was only available in the private sector and in governmental test sites that handled "approximately 10% of all births in the public sector...." The High Court held that limiting the

drug in the public sector to test sites was unreasonable in light of the Bill of Rights, sections 27(1) and (2), which guarantee the right to access to health care services, and section 28(1), which guarantees the right of every child to basic health care. The government appealed, emphasizing that its test sites were designed to ensure the safety and efficacy of the drug as well as guarantee its administration in situations where it would be most effective.

The Constitutional Court rested its decision primarily on section 27, *see* ¶ 135, and declared that the government had violated the negative obligation imposed by section 27(1), *i.e.*, not to prevent or impair the right of access to health care. *See* ¶ 46. Specifically, the court held the policy was not reasonable. It reiterated *Grootboom*'s admonition that those with the most desperate needs cannot be ignored when the government attempts to implement measures to achieve realization of a right. *See* ¶ 68.

The Court concluded, "[s]ections 27(1) and (2) of the Constitution require the government to devise and implement within its available resources a comprehensive and co-ordinated programme to realize progressively the rights of pregnant women and their newborn children to have access to health services to combat mother-to-child transmission of HIV." *See* ¶ 135. "The programme...must include reasonable measures for counseling and testing pregnant women...and mak[e] appropriate treatment available to them...." *Id.*

The Constitutional Court, again citing *Grootboom*, reiterated that sections 28(1)(b) and (c) had to be read together. *See* ¶ 75. The child has the right to family care first, with the right to alternative care when that is insufficient. However, the court rejected the government's argument that section 28(1)(c) imposes an obligation on the parents, not the state, to provide basic health care. The court stated that the primary obligation is on the parents, but that the state also has an obligation when the family cannot provide for the children. Such was the situation here since the mothers are indigent, rely on the public health care system, and are unable to get private health care. "They and their children are in the main dependent on the state to make health care services available to them." *See* ¶ 79.

The following article facilitates our comprehension of the South Africa Constitution and our comparison of it to the United States Constitution.

Lee E. Teitelbaum, *Children's Rights and the Problem of Equal Respect*
27 Hofstra L. Rev. 799 (1999)

I. *Introduction*

Few areas present more difficult problems than does the definition of the rights of children and parents and the authority of the state regarding their conduct.... American courts, in particular the Supreme Court, have...recognized the complexity presented by the legal position of children and, consequently, have routinely disclaimed any effort to systematically "consider the impact of...constitutional [guarantees] upon the totality of the relationship of the minor and the state."...This Article seeks to identify some of the conditions that create the well-recognized problems encountered in analyses of those rights....

II. *Traditional Rights Theories and Children*

For liberal theorists, and often in law, rights are a reflection of a basic human right to equal respect in making decisions about one's life; a theory which, it has been argued, the Constitution is meant to express. This approach begins from the assumption that human beings have a special capacity to reason and engage in deliberative decision-making. They can evaluate arguments and form plans according to their rational acceptance or rejection of various possibilities. It is this capacity in each of us that is entitled to respect.

It is further assumed that each of us is entitled not only to respect but to the same respect due others. The principle of equal respect is variously articulated according to the context of the moral theory in which it is situated but it is also associated with the notion of autonomy. Both are found in Locke's propositions that "all men by nature are equal" and of the "equal right, that every man hath, to his natural freedom, without being subjected to the will or authority of any other man...."

Several characteristics of these approaches to rights bear emphasis. Rights based on capacity, or moral agency, or ability to engage in neutral dialogue, seem ultimately to be understood as categorical. The entitlement to respect is founded on the ability to think rationally, form plans, and make choices. If an individual possesses this capacity or agency, he or she is entitled to respect for choices about life, and not just to respect in some degree, but to equal respect that is to the same degree of respect accorded to all other rights holders. Absence of this capacity is likewise categorical, in most views. If a rights holder is entitled to the same respect as all others, then one either has the same rights as others or has none of those rights. You may have other rights, if the society decides to give them to you. Animals are protected from cruelty, infants from starvation; but neither animals nor infants have rights to self-determination.

A second characteristic of the traditional understanding of rights is its political function. "Rights" have sometimes been described as a militant concept. Standard rights theories based on a respect for the choices of others creates a "space" around the individual. To have a right to do something means at least that no one may intrude on your choice except in very limited circumstances. In fact, if I am a rights holder or a citizen, no one else has any general claim regarding my conduct, except when that conduct invades the space of the other, through coercion or injury. We are all freestanding, independent actors except to the extent we agree to have relationships with others.

It is not surprising that these formulations of rights theory find little place for talk about children.... Locke...observed that children were an exception to his general proposition that "all men by nature are equal." The human mind, at birth, is a "white [p]aper, void of all [c]haracters, without any [i]deas." That paper will be inscribed by experience over time but, because children lack reason in at least their early years, parents, he said, "have a sort of rule and jurisdiction over them," although temporary and (perhaps) proportionate to the child's level of reason....

III. *Children's Rights in Legal Doctrine...*

A. *Welfare Rights*

The most pervasively recognized rights of children are positive rights, rights to receive social goods, which find expression in the laws of every state and in international declarations of human rights. Grants of positive rights are recognized grudgingly and with some suspicion in connection with adults, but are readily accepted in relation to young people....

Recognition of these positive rights can be justified on various theoretical grounds. For social contractarians, they derive from a hypothetical social contract, as those things that every rational person would consider essential to have as a child. Even without the contractarian framework, a liberal may consider some such entitlements to be essential to achieving the capacity for rational choice on which membership in a liberal society is founded. Utilitarians can justify a broader range of such rights, as long as it appears that production of educated healthy children will maximize human happiness.

Adults have relatively few positive rights. Medicaid would illustrate the exceptional situation. But even where positive rights are available to adults, there is a very important difference between the posture of positive rights for adults and those rights for children. The adult holder of positive rights retains his autonomy with respect to those rights—he or she may take advantage of Medicaid, or may choose not to do so. By contrast, the United Nation Declaration does not end with creation of a governmental duty to provide education. It also presumes a duty on the child to accept the benefits of that right. Education is to be "compulsory" quite as much as it is to be free.

Claims of this sort, which I have called "integrative rights" elsewhere, are evidently based on principles concerning the needs rather than the preferences or choices of children, at the point at which the decision is made....

B. *Other Statutory Rights for Children*

State positive laws also typically recognize certain rights for older minors that are not based on welfare interests. These laws permit older children to engage in activities that are generally permitted for adults and generally prohibited for minors.... It is, moreover, important that most of these age-variant laws do not create rights in the usual adult sense. While a sixteen-year-old may marry in most states, he or she can only do so with parental permission.

C. *Supreme Court Doctrine and Children's Rights*

The strongest declarations of minors' rights, and the classes of rights that seem most indistinguishable from rights in traditional political and moral theory, are found in decisions of the United States Supreme Court. The Court has by this point recognized rights claims for children in many areas where autonomy-based rights have been recognized for adults. The core meaning of liberty—freedom from physical confinement—was held applicable to children in *In re Gault* and reaffirmed in *Breed v. Jones. Gault* extended the privilege against self-incrimination to minors, not solely from concern for untrustworthy confessions but because children are entitled to decide whether and how they will participate in proceedings affecting their liberty.

First Amendment rights to political expression have also been recognized for very young children. *Tinker v. Des Moines Independent Community School District*, for example, held that the suspension of students (in that case ages eight, eleven, thirteen, fifteen and sixteen), for wearing armbands to protest the Vietnam War infringed on their right "to freedom of expression of their views." The right of children to receive information as well as to express themselves was recognized in *Erznoznik v. City of Jacksonville....*

Children, of course, have been held to possess some interest in privacy, reflected in rights of access to contraception and abortion. The Court has struck down categorical legislative rules requiring the consent of a parent of an unmarried minor as a condition to obtaining an abortion and prohibiting the distribution of contraceptives to minors.

When claimed by adults, these rights are typically understood as reflecting values of autonomy and choice. They are "negative rights"—rights not to be controlled by others in our choice about the good life....

The above cases do seem to suggest that children are generally entitled to rights in the strong sense enjoyed by adults: to claims of self-determination and self-realization against all others, including the state. But how can the Supreme Court have held that children have autonomy-based rights in the midst of a legal setting that supposes that children are obliged to accept parental and governmental control regarding health, education, housing, and the like? Part of the answer to this dilemma is that, although rights to speech, procreation and the like are justified for adults in terms of their capacity for rational choice, the extension of these rights to minors has never been explained on grounds assuming the same capacity for choice....

Rather, the Court's analysis has begun textually with the observation that the Constitution talks of "persons." It has followed that minors have some claims arising from the due process clause, but not that the extent of state power to regulate is the same for minors and adults, as would be true on an assumption of equal capacity. On the contrary, the Court has long recognized greater governmental authority to regulate the activities of minors than would be allowable for adults. States may restrict religiously motivated activities of children when some danger exists, although adults probably could not be so controlled. They may require attendance at school by minors, and may limit minors' access to "objectionable" but not "obscene" material that could not constitutionally be kept from adults....

The thrust of the Supreme Court cases discussed above, however, is precisely to say that the rights of children are more limited in their extension than those of adults. Whatever their status as rights, children's rights are understood differently than are the rights of adults.

D. Rethinking Respect for Children...

A theory of rights that ignores parents is similarly incomplete without some attention to the general claims that parents may make with respect to the ways in which their children develop. Those rights may be said to belong to the parents themselves or to derive from rights held by their children. The choice of theory may make some difference in how we think about the rights of children, and on any theory, parents have considerable responsibility for influencing their choices and assessing their capacity for choice. Accordingly, the relationship between the claims of parents and those of children must be taken into account in talking about the rights of children and that may, as well, require rethinking of the premises of traditional rights theory....

These differences in how we think about children, moreover, carry normative significance in our society. At early stages, the relationship between parents and children is one of control, mediated by affection. This stage of intensely personal authority is so generally true that we can indeed regard that quality as universal, or nearly so. There is no conflict between spheres of personal autonomy, and limits on parental authority can only be justified to the extent that their conduct harms others; here, their children.

As the child grows older, however, the value of parental control weakens, as it confronts a conflicting value. Children must not only be kept safe and socialized to accept authority, but they must also develop a capacity for autonomous action within existing norms. A child who does not learn to make choices within our cultural framework is plainly unable to perform the adult role in society. Indeed, the emphasis on acceptance of authority that is valued during infancy gives way to a normative expectation that children will assert some degree of autonomy as they move through adolescence. Thus, a child who fails to assert that autonomy may be described as "tied to his mother's apron strings." That description is pejorative, and the criticism it conveys is directed to both the child and his or her parent....

If the justification for recognizing certain rights rests on what we know or believe about the course of moral development, it is appropriate for legal institutions to take account of the nature of development in determining the claims of children and those of parents, rather than ignoring that development in favor of dichotomous judgments about capacity for moral choice....

[I]t may be that the approach actually taken by the Court is justifiable despite its departure from the requirements of traditional rights theory. The Court's decisions do not assume that children are equal among themselves; some are capable themselves of making decisions to terminate their pregnancies and others are not. Nor are minors equal to adults; it is appropriate to take account of circumstances that are special to young people when doing so can be shown to be justified. But despite these inequalities within the class of minors and between minors and adults, it is nonetheless important to talk about rights if we are to show some appropriate level of respect for members of the community who have some, if not complete, capacity to reason and some, if not complete, capacity to engage in moral activity.

This takes us only part of the way, however. It is a useful first step to consider one of the ways in which developing an approach to rights that applies sensibly to children will require reconsideration of traditional rights theory itself. A revised theory will require a diminished emphasis on universality, greater specificity with respect to the relationship between rights and social institutions, and reconsideration of our understanding of parents' rights, among other things. But these are subjects for another day.

Notes and Questions

1. *Different Types of Rights.* The Constitutional Court in *Grootboom* talks about a child's right to housing as a "socio-economic" right. What sort of rights does the South Africa Constitution give specifically to children? What sort of rights are omitted? Does Professor Teitelbaum's reference to "integrative rights" help you categorize children's rights in South Africa? Notice how children are not "required or permitted" to perform work inappropriate for their age.

2. *Civil and Political Rights.* Section 28 of the South Africa Constitution embodies few civil and political rights for children. One such right that exists is the right of every child to a nationality from birth. "The apartheid State denied Black children a common citizenship with Whites and relegated them to second class citizenship through racist, non-child-centered legislation. The forced removal and homeland policies assigned Black children to a homeland on the basis of their ethnic and tribal origin. The political rationale for the homeland policy was to deny Blacks citizenship rights in the country of their birth." Tshepo L. Mosikatsana, *Children's Rights and Family in the South African Context: A Comment on Children's Rights under the Final Constitution*, 3. Mich. J. Race & L. 341, 373-74 (1998).

Apart from the political and civil rights mentioned in section 28, do children have other political and civil rights, such as those afforded adults? The Bill of Rights applies to "all the people" in the country. *See* § 7(1). Specific rights, such as the right to privacy (section 14), freedom of religion (section 15), freedom of expression (section 16), freedom of assembly (section 17), and freedom of association, apply to "everyone." Some political rights, however, are specifically allocated to "every adult citizen." *See, e.g.,* § 19(3)(a) (right to vote). Does the broad expression of some civil rights in the South Africa Constitution mean that these rights for children are co-extensive with the rights for adults? As Professor Teitelbaum suggests, many rights in the Bill of Rights to the U.S. Constitution are not limited to adults by the text, but the Supreme Court has held the rights of children are not co-extensive with the rights of adults. *See, e.g.,* Planned Parenthood v. Casey, 505 U.S. 833 (1992); Ginsberg v. N.Y., 390 U.S. 629 (1968). Consider what two South African experts have said about this issue:

> [Do] children have a composite right to individual self-determination under the Constitution, which would entitle them to choose their own lifestyle, religion and opinions, regardless of the authority their parents are entitled to exercise toward them[?]

> The interest of children in maintaining their own autonomy must be seen in the context of the relationship of dependence that of necessity exists between child and parent. The responsibilities of care and support a parent has toward a child, and the rights and powers a parent can exercise toward a child in order to meet those responsibilities, limit the extent to which a child can lay claim to his or her self-determination. [A]s section 28 provides no right to individual self-determination, any claim to personal autonomy and choice of lifestyle of belief of a child would have to be based on the ordinary rights of a child (for instance to privacy, freedom of religion or freedom of expression). If these rights are limited by the exercise of parental authority, this limitation can be justified by a parent's duty of care and support toward the child. However, as a child grows older, and the duty of care and support diminishes, it will become progressively more difficult to justify intrusions into the personal autonomy of a child.

Barry Bekink & Danie Brand, *Constitutional Protection of Children, in* Introduction to Child Law in South Africa 169, 181–82 (J. Davel ed., 2000). In fact, the South African Law Commission has called "parental power" arguably "the most significant common law rule pertaining to children." *Issue Paper 13: Review of the Child Care Act: First Issue Paper,* South African Law Commission, Apr. 18, 1998, at § 6.3.3, *available at* http://www.server. law.wits.ac.za/salc/issue/ip13.html#8.1 (describing parental power as including the power to assist the child in legal proceedings, the power of reasonable chastisement, and the power to control the child's day-to-day life including social interactions). As mentioned in note 6 after *Grootboom,* this topic will be revisited at the end of the chapter.

3. *Capacity.* Do any of the rights given to children in South Africa depend upon their capacity to exercise those rights responsibly? How so? Why was section 28 necessary to include in the Bill of Rights since the South Africa Constitution also has section 9(3), which says that the state many not unfairly discriminate directly or indirectly against anyone on the grounds of, among other things, age?

4. *Comparison.* How are children's rights in South Africa different or similar to children's rights in the United States?

Problem 14-1

Imagine that you are an attorney for a group of South African girls and their parents. Your clients have just attended an international conference on children and violence, and feel empowered by the declaration from that conference that called on national governments to deal with the problem of violence against children. They ask that you work with them to end the situation described in the following excerpt. What arguments would you make to governmental authorities based upon domestic and international law? South Africa has ratified the International Covenant on Civil and Political Rights, the Convention on the Elimination of All Forms of Discrimination against Women, and the Convention on the Rights of the Child. What difficulties will you encounter with your arguments? If you had to be selective because you could only make one argument under one international instrument, what would it be and why?

Erika George et al., Scared At School: Sexual Violence Against Girls in South African Schools

(Joe Saunders et al. eds., 2001),
available at http://www.hrw.org/reports/2001/safrica

Human Rights Watch found that sexual abuse and harassment of girls by both teachers and other students is widespread in South Africa. In each of the three provinces visited, we documented cases of rape, assault, and sexual harassment of girls committed by both teachers and male students. Girls who encountered sexual violence at school were raped in school toilets, in empty classrooms and hallways, and in hostels and dormitories. Girls were also fondled, subjected to aggressive sexual advances, and verbally degraded at school. We found that girls from all levels of society and among all ethnic groups are affected by sexual violence at school.

Schools have long been violent places for South African children. South Africa has only recently emerged from a history in which violence was routinely used by the state as a means of exerting power. Years of violent enforcement of apartheid era policies have fueled a culture of violence. This historical legacy presents a challenge for the government as violence remains high in many areas and schools are still ill-equipped to curb violence. Violence is often sexualized, with devastating consequences for women and girls who disproportionately bear the brunt of sexual violence, not only in society at large but in schools as well....

Human Rights Watch found that sexual violence has a profoundly destabilizing effect on the education of girl children. All the rape survivors Human Rights Watch interviewed reported that their school performance suffered. All of the girls told us it was harder to concentrate on their work after their assaults. Some girls reported losing interest in school altogether, many girls transferred to new schools, others simply left school entirely.

Social workers and therapists working with girls who were raped by teachers or classmates reported, among other problems, that the girls were failing their higher education matriculation exams and losing interest in other outside activities, such as sports. Parents told Human Rights Watch that their children had become depressed, disruptive, and anxious. Teachers expressed concern that girls they knew to have experienced sexual violence at school or at the hands of their teachers or classmates were not performing up to full potential....

Although some schools try hard to respond to the problem of violence, too often school officials have concealed sexual violence and delayed disciplinary action against perpetrators of such violence at great cost to victims. Rather than receiving redress from school officials, girls who do report abuse are often further victimized and stigmatized by teachers and students.

Rarely do school authorities take steps to ensure that girls have a sense of security and comfort at school or to counsel and discipline boys who commit acts of violence. Many girls leave school altogether because they feel unsafe and are unwilling to remain in an environment that has failed to protect them.

Many girls suffer the effects of sexual violence in silence, having learned submission as a survival skill. Their attackers continue to act with impunity, in part because no one takes responsibility for the problem. Human Rights Watch found a great deal of confusion over responsibility for resolving problems and repeatedly encountered breaks in the chain of communication between school officials, police, and prosecutors, with all actors shifting responsibility and sexually abused girls getting lost in the shuffle.

Some school officials told Human Rights Watch that they could not take independent disciplinary measures in their school unless the victim brought formal criminal charges. In other cases, where the victim had gone to the police, schools claimed they could not take action against the accused until the courts had convicted him of the crime. School officials told Human Rights Watch they could not do anything because many victims did not press their claims; but, at the same time, many schools refused to support girls who did come forward. We found great dissatisfaction among female students, parents of victims, and teachers who brought their problems to the attention of school administrators. There is a clear need for standardized national guidelines on how to respond to such cases....

Recently, the government has introduced initiatives designed to address crime and violence in the school environment. Corporal punishment has been declared illegal in South Africa and the National Department of Education has recently developed an instruction manual for teachers on alternative modes of discipline. The Secretariat for Safety and Security, a civilian body that advises the minister responsible for police, in cooperation with the Department of Education has developed a National Crime Prevention Strategy for schools. The legislature has amended the Employment of Educators Act to require dismissal of teachers found guilty of serious misconduct, including sexual assault of students.

South Africa has yet to implement a national policy on how to deal with the problem of sexual violence and harassment in schools....

Human Rights Watch acknowledges both that the South African government has made significant efforts to address issues surrounding violence against women and girls, especially within the criminal justice system, and that the challenges faced are enormous and to a great extent not of its own making.

For more on the problem, the national and provincial governments' responses, and South Africa's obligations under international and national law, see *id.*

B. Convention on the Rights of the Child

1. A Close Look at the Convention

The U.N. General Assembly unanimously adopted the Convention on the Rights of the Child (CRC) in November 1989. It entered into force in September 1990. The Convention was drafted by the Economic and Social Council's Commission on Human Rights. The Convention had its predecessors, including the 1924 Geneva Declaration, adopted by the General Assembly of the League of Nations, and the 1959 U.N. Declaration on the Rights of the Child, adopted unanimously by the U.N. General Assembly. Read the Geneva Declaration, the Declaration of the Rights of the Child, and the CRC, all set out in the Supplement. How would you characterize the types of rights that are guaranteed to children in each?

Other international instruments also deal with children. *See, e.g.,* ILO Convention (No. 138) concerning Minimum Age for Admission to Employment, June 26, 1973, 1015 U.N.T.S. 297; ILO Convention (No. 182) concerning the Worst Forms of Child Labour, June 17, 1999, S. Treaty Doc. No. 106-5, 38 I.L.M. 1207 (1999); the ICCPR (article 26); and ICESCR (article 10(3)). The CRC was meant to bring many of these disparate threads together. *See generally* Eugeen Verhellen, Convention on the Rights of the Child, Background, Motivation, Strategies, Main Themes (1994); Cynthia Price Cohen, *The Developing Jurisprudence of the Rights of the Child,* 6 St. Thomas L. Rev. 1 (1993).

The Geneva Declaration and the Declaration on the Rights of the Child obviously differ from the CRC because of the nature of each instrument. Evaluate the enforcement mechanism in the CRC. Look particularly at articles 42 to 45, and then read the following two excerpts:

Fact Sheet No. 10 (Rev. 1), The Rights of the Child, U.N. High Comm'r for Human Rights (1998)
available at http://www.unhchr.ch/html/menu6/2/fs10.htm

Committee on the Rights of the Child...

The Committee on the Rights of the Child currently holds three sessions a year, each of four weeks' duration. The last week is always reserved for preparation of the next session. The Committee is serviced by the United Nations Centre for Human Rights in Geneva.

Under article 44 of the Convention, States parties accept the duty to submit regular reports to the Committee on the steps they have taken to put the Convention into effect and on progress in the enjoyment of children's rights in their territories. First implementation reports are to be submitted within two years of ratification of or accession to the Convention and thereafter every five years. The first initial reports were due in September 1992. More than 70 State reports had reached the Committee by December 1995.

At its first session, in October 1991, the Committee adopted guidelines to help States parties writing and structuring their initial reports. Governments are recommended to prepare their reports according to these guidelines, which stress that the report should indicate "factors and difficulties" encountered by the State in the implementation of the Convention—in other words, that it should be problem-oriented and self-critical. States are also asked to specify "implementation priorities" and "specific goals for the future." Relevant legal texts and statistical data are to be submitted with the report.

In establishing its procedures, the Committee has emphasized the importance of a constructive dialogue with government representatives. In this context, it has also made clear that it seeks close cooperation with relevant United Nations bodies and specialized agencies, as well as with other competent bodies, including non-governmental organizations.

Working procedure

A working group of the Committee meets prior to each of its sessions for a preliminary examination of reports received from States parties, and to prepare the Committee's discussions with the representatives of reporting States. In addition to State reports, the working group considers information provided by other human rights treaty bodies. The Committee also receives information from mechanisms established by the Commission on Human Rights to investigate human rights problems in specific countries or on thematic issues, for example the Special Rapporteurs on torture, on extrajudicial, summary or arbitrary executions, and on violence against women. A key partner in this context is the Special Rapporteur on the sale of children, child prostitution and child pornography.

General discussions and studies....

United Nations bodies and specialized agencies may take part in the deliberations of the working group and provide information. On the basis of written information received from relevant non-governmental organizations, the Committee has also often invited such organizations to take part in the preparatory meetings on State reports.

The end result of the pre-sessional working group's discussion on a State report is a "list of issues." This list, which gives a preliminary indication of the issues which the Committee considers to be priorities for discussion, is sent to the Government concerned with an invitation to participate in a forthcoming plenary session of the Committee at which its report will be considered. The Government is invited to respond to the issues in writing, before the session.

This approach gives Governments the opportunity better to prepare themselves for the discussion with the Committee. Other points not included in the list of issues may emerge during the discussion, which is one reason why the Committee prefers to discuss with high level officials, such as ministers or deputy ministers, rather than with representatives who lack the authority to make decisions.

Discussions with States parties are concrete and detailed, and tend to deal with both results and processes. Although all Committee members usually take part in the deliberations, in most cases two members take the lead on each country as "rapporteurs."

At the very end of the process, the Committee adopts "concluding observations," which are a statement on its consideration of a State's report. Concluding observations are meant to be widely publicized in the State party and to serve as the basis for a national debate on how to improve the enforcement of the provisions of the Convention. They therefore constitute an essential document: Governments are expected to implement the recommendations contained therein.

Notes are taken at the meetings of the Committee. The United Nations publishes both press releases on the discussions and more detailed summary records of the proceedings. The Committee encourages the publication of the State party's report, the summary records and the concluding observations on each country as a consolidated document....

The whole process of discussion of States parties' reports is designed to promote public debate. The Committee's discussions are normally open to the public; only the preparatory discussions of the pre-sessional working group and the drafting of the Committee's concluding observations are conducted in private. Likewise, it is important that the national reporting procedure be open and transparent; the Committee encourages such an approach.

The reporting procedure is constructive and oriented towards international cooperation and exchange of information. The aim is to define problems and discuss what corrective measures should be taken. The Committee can also transmit requests for assistance to the specialized United Nations bodies and agencies, including UNHCR, ILO, UNICEF, WHO, the United Nations Educational, Scientific and Cultural Organization (UNESCO) and other competent bodies.

Urgent procedure

There is no procedure outlined in the Convention for individual complaints from children or their representatives. The Committee may, however, request "further information relevant to the implementation of the Convention" (art. 44, para. 4). Such additional information may be requested from Governments if, for instance, there are indications of serious problems. . . .

General measures of implementation

In drafting its reporting guidelines for States, the Committee on the Rights of the Child placed emphasis on concrete implementation measures which would make a reality of the principles and provisions of the Convention. More specifically, the Committee paid special attention to necessary reforms within the spirit of the Convention and procedures for constant scrutiny of progress.

Under article 4 of the Convention, States parties are required to undertake all appropriate legislative, administrative and other measures to implement the Convention. With regard to economic, social and cultural rights, they must "undertake such measures to the maximum extent of their available resources and, where needed, within the framework of international cooperation."

An early step in the implementation process is for a State party to review its legislation and ensure that laws are consistent with the Convention. For instance, laws are needed for the protection of children against exploitation, in both the formal and informal labour market, and to ensure free and compulsory primary education.

Mechanisms may be introduced at the national and local levels to coordinate policies and monitor the implementation of the Convention, including through an ombudsman's office. The political decision-making process is important. What procedures are there to ensure that children's affairs are taken seriously in all relevant governmental structures, as well as in both the parliament and local assemblies? Are there opportunities for children themselves and their representatives to make themselves heard?

The gathering of reliable and relevant information on the situation of children is another important step to be taken. With precise data, discussions regarding remedies will be better informed and focused. Improvement of the capacity of the national statistical office can therefore be an essential contribution to the implementation of the Convention.

Other means of genuine realization of the principles and rights enshrined in the Convention are education and training of personnel working with children, such as nursery school and other teachers, child psychologists, pediatricians and other health personnel, the police and other law enforcement personnel, social workers and others. A broader awareness and knowledge of the Convention among people at large can also serve as a basis for implementation. It is an obligation under the Convention (art. 42) for States parties to disseminate such information-to both children and adults-in understandable languages. States' reports on implementation must also be made "widely available to the public" (art. 44, para. 6)....

Cynthia Price Cohen, *The Developing Jurisprudence of the Rights of the Child*
6 St. Thomas L. Rev. 1, 35–38 (1993)

The Egyptian report consisted of sixty-nine pages and listed demographic indicators, explained Egypt's political structure and constitution, and cited relevant legislation, including the international human rights treaties to which Egypt is a State Party. The main body of the report followed the pattern of the Committee's Guidelines. The most extensive sections were those devoted to Education (thirteen pages) and to Health and Welfare (seven pages). Interestingly, the section on Civil Rights and Freedoms was comparatively brief (three pages).

The Committee prepared a list of fifty-three questions to be answered by the Egyptian representative that also followed the format of the Guidelines. In the first section, the Committee asked questions about such matters as how the Egyptian report was prepared, what was being done to make the Convention widely known, how economic factors affected children, and whether the Convention could be invoked in court.

Under the section on General Principles, the questions focused on discrimination against girls and intrafamilial relations in the context of discrimination. Questions with respect to the Civil Rights and Freedoms section were related to such matters as birth registration, freedom of religion and freedom of association. Elsewhere in the list of questions there were inquiries about intrafamilial relations and about the use of Kafalah, which is the Islamic substitute for adoption. Other questions for the Egyptian delegation touched on child labor, health, street children, refugees and education. In practice, the formal public review of the Egyptian report developed an air of informality. At intervals, as the representatives from Egypt answered questions from the list, the Committee would interrupt with requests for clarifications and further information. The Committee showed a great deal of interest in the matter of "family identity cards," because it was the "head of the household," i.e., the father, who held these identity cards. The Committee member from the former USSR wondered if family identity cards constituted a violation of the child's "right to identity" because only one identity card existed, belonging to the family, and not to the individual child; thus, the identity card implied that the child did not have an individual identity, but rather only that of the family.

This confusion was straightened out through further questioning that revealed the existence of a parallel system of identification cards for individuals. In practice, if a person cashes a check, he or she uses an individual identity card. On the other hand, if a family member goes for medical treatment, it is the family identity card that must be shown. Although it is not the exact equivalent to an individual identity card, a child does receive some sort of identification card through the schools.

The discussion of identity cards continued for quite some time, and led to questions concerning gender discrimination and the right to a name. The Committee inquired as to how the child's name and right to an identity was affected if the child was born out of wedlock. The representative from Egypt explained that in such a case, an attempt was always made to find the father of the child and to ascertain paternity. In cases where the father was unwilling to cooperate, the mother could bring a court case to force the father to accept responsibility. If circumstances made it impossible to find the child's father, the child could have the mother's name and in that situation, the mother could be the holder of the "family identity card."

As the discussion concluded, the representative from Egypt remarked that Egyptian law requires the child to have a "socially acceptable name." This aroused the curiosity of the Committee, and the member from Barbados asked for a clarification as to the meaning of "socially acceptable name." The Egyptian representative replied that infant mortality rates were extremely high among rural illiterates, and that superstition had led them to believe that a child would live if they used a non-human name like "little donkey" or "jackass." The law had been passed to prevent children from developing psychological problems associated with such peculiar names. The Committee member from the former USSR pursued the matter further by inquiring as to whether the child had to have a name of Muslim origin. The reply was that there is no such thing as a Muslim name, and names of Muslims are really Arabic names. The representative further explained that Egyptian names include both Arabic names and names of Turkish origin.

The Committee's review of the Egyptian report explored in great detail the basis for a child's nationality, and the impact of the Koran on such legal matters as the unequal inheritance rights between men and women. In discussing the importance of the Koran, the Committee member from Sweden asked whether the Koran's criminal penalties of flogging and cutting off of hands was still followed in Egypt. The representative from Egypt patiently explained that Egyptian law follows the French Code, with influences from the Italian law. He further stated that the described physical penalties for crime "had not been followed for millennia," and that they were no longer necessary because they had been instituted during a period when there was no State and before the establishment of prisons or theories of rehabilitation for prisoners.

The above example serves to illustrate the type of detailed questioning that transpired during one of the three half-day sessions which the Committee on the Rights of the Child devoted to examination of the Egyptian report. Questions of similar detail were asked in each of the other half-day meetings. With minor variations, these same procedures were followed in the examination of every State Party report.

At the conclusion of the examination of the Egyptian report, members of the Committee on the Rights of the Child commended Egypt for Egypt's active participation in the drafting of the Convention on the Rights of the Child, as well as for being among the first countries to ratify the Convention. The Egyptian representative was also complimented on Egypt's establishment of a National Commission on Childhood and Motherhood.

In concluding its examination of the Egyptian report, the Committee urged the Egyptian government to reduce discrimination against girls, to prevent children from participating in hazardous employment, and to give greater attention to problems of sexual abuse and drug use by young people. The Committee further recommended that children under the age of six and those who are disabled should be placed in foster homes, rather than in institutions. The Committee requested that future reports contain more details and statistics, in particular on standards of sanitation. Finally, the

Committee pressed the point that information about the Convention on the Rights of the Child should be more widely disseminated.

Notes and Questions

1. *Egypt's Second Report.* In 2001, the Committee on the Rights of the Child considered Egypt's second periodic report, submitted in 1998. *See* Concluding Observations of the Committee on the Rights of the Child: Egypt 21/02/2001, U.N. CRC, 26th Sess., U.N. Doc. CRC/C/15/ Add. 145 (2001). In its Concluding Observations, the Committee criticized Egypt for submitting a "legalistic" report that did not provide "a self-critical evaluation of the prevailing situation of the exercise of children's rights in the country." The Committee noted that many of the concerns that it had raised with respect to Egypt's initial report had not been sufficiently addressed. *Id.* at 7. The Committee did praise Egypt for a number of achievements, but what was most striking was the repeated recommendation that Egypt get technical assistance in various areas. For example, the Committee recommended technical assistance from UNICEF and WHO to combat domestic violence and to criminalize marital rape, *see* ¶39, from ILO and UNICEF to address child labor, *see* ¶48, and from the Office of the United Nations High Commissioner for Human Rights, the Centre for International Crime Prevention, the International Network on Juvenile Justice and UNICEF to better address the administration of juvenile justice.

2. *Technical Assistance.* As demonstrated by the Committee's response to Egypt's second periodic report, the offering of technical assistance is an important part of the Committee's function. The Committee can transmit to specialized agencies, like the U.N.'s Children's Fund, reports from States Parties that contain a request or indicate a need for technical advice. *See* CRC § 45(b). *See also Provisional Rules of Procedure: 14/11/91*, UNCRC, U.N. Doc. CRC/C/4 (1991).

3. *NGOs.* When the Commission on Human Rights of the Economic and Social Council decided to establish a working party to draft the convention, it permitted NGOs to participate. The participation of NGOs was unusual and meaningful. There were over 50 NGOs that participated, and they formed an Ad Hoc Group to coordinate their efforts. After the CRC was drafted, the group played an important role in the Convention's widespread acceptance. *See generally* Eugeen Verhellen, Convention on the Rights of the Child, Background, Motivation, Strategies, Main Themes 67–68 (1994); Cynthia Price Cohen, *The Role of Nongovernmental Organizations in the Drafting of the Convention on the Rights of the Child*, 12 Hum. Rts. Q. 137 (1990). Article 45 established an ongoing role for the NGOs. The language "other competent bodies" was specifically added to include NGOs. *See Considerations 1989 Working Group*, 125-27 U.N. Doc. E/CN.4/1989/48, *in* The United Nations Convention on the Rights of the Child: A Guide to the Travaux Préparatoires 588 (Sharon Detrick ed. 1992).

4. *Enforcement.* How does the CRC's enforcement mechanisms compare to other international human rights instruments, like the ICCPR and the ICESCR? One author has called the CRC's enforcement mechanism "positive sanctioning." States receive (and can request) advice, assistance, and co-operation in meeting their goals, and need not fear sanctions for an inability to implement all of the provisions immediately. *See* Verhellen, *supra*, at 82.

5. *Backlog and its Effect.* The efficacy of the monitoring mechanism has to be measured against the Committee's ability to review and assess states' reports:

The Committee began its examination of State Party reports at its January session in 1993 and approximately seven reports have been reviewed during each of the subsequent sessions. By the end of 1997 the Committee had only been able to examine about 80 of the anticipated 191 States Party reports, and although the Committee is already having difficulty staying current with the reporting process, this situation promises to become even more daunting as States Parties begin to submit their periodic reports. The systematic pace of the reviewing process may make it impossible for the Committee to fully synthesize its work and to create a general jurisprudence, such as that developed by the Human Rights Committee, which monitors the International Covenant on Civil and Political Rights. Over time, the Human Rights Committee has published a series of General Comments explaining how it interprets most of the Covenant's articles. These comments provide the basis for evaluating the State Party reports that are submitted to the Committee. Unfortunately, at the present time, defining the jurisprudence of the Committee on the Rights of the Child is largely a matter of guess work. It is extremely difficult for a scholar or researcher to state with any certainty exactly how the Committee interprets each article of the Convention.

Cynthia Price Cohen, *The Jurisprudence of the Committee on the Rights of the Child*, 5 Geo. J. Fighting Poverty 201, 204 (1998).

Several factors may help mitigate the backlog in the future. First, the Committee is increasing its membership from ten to eighteen in 2003. *See* Committee on the Rights of the Child, UNHCHR, *available at* http:www/unhchr.ch/html/menu2/6/CRC/. Second, others have taken up the task of synthesizing some of the Committee's work. In particular, this is being done under the auspices of UNICEF. *See* Rachel Hodgkin & Peter Newell, Implementation Handbook for the Convention on the Rights of the Child (1998). Nonetheless, the Committee does have a substantial backlog of reports to review. The backlog causes untimely review, which minimizes the effectiveness of monitoring because the information provided by States Parties can become stale. Also, addressing the backlog consumes Committee resources. Consequently, for example, the Committee has issued only two General Comments to date.

6. *Children's Ombudsman.* Fact Sheet No. 10, *supra*, mentions that national ombudsmen may help implement the CRC. "[O]mbudsman has become the word for a person or an office which deals with complaints from a defined, circumscribed group of people, speaks on behalf of that group, and tries to improve conditions for individuals within the group as well as for the group in toto." Malfrid Grude Flekkoy, *The Children's Ombudsman as an Implementor of Children's Rights*, 6 Transnat'l L. & Contemp. Probs. 353, 355 (1996). The Committee on the Rights of the Child has become very vocal in encouraging States Parties to adopt such an entity. *See* General Comment No. 2 (2002), *The Role of Independent National Human Rights Institutions in the Protection and Promotion of the Rights of the Child*, CRC, U.N. Doc. CRC/GC/2002/2 (2002). The Council of Europe has been similarly vocal. For example, the Parliamentary Assembly of the Council of Europe adopted a recommendation that invites member states to "envisage, if they have not yet done so, the appointment of a special ombudsman for children, who could inform them on their rights, counsel them, intervene and, possibly, take legal action on their behalf." Recommendation on the Rights of Children, Eur. Parl. Ass. 27th Sess., Doc. No. 1121 (1990). At the behest of the Assembly of the Council of Europe, the Committee of Ministers asked member states in 1998 to appoint ombudsmen. *See* Recommendation of the Comm. of Ministers, 641st Sess., Doc. No. R (98) 8 (1998); Rec-

ommendation on a European Strategy for Children, Eur. Parl. Ass., 4th Sess., Doc. No. 1286 (1996). As a result of these efforts, today there are over thirty independent human rights institutions for children in various countries. *See* Editorial, *Independent Institutions Protecting Children's Rights*, 8 Innocenti Digest 1 (June 2001). In the United States, some states, like Alaska, Iowa, and Nebraska, have ombudsman programs, although these seem to have a much narrower scope than those abroad. *See* Howard A. Davidson, *Applying an International Innovation to Help U.S. Children: The Child Welfare Ombudsman*, 28 Fam. L.Q. 117, 126–31 (1994). The "most striking difference between United States. and non-U.S. programs is whether they consider themselves to address the subject of 'children's participation in a democratic society.' Only one U.S. program responded that this was within its area of focus, whereas most ombudsman offices in other nations stated that they focused on this area." *Id.* at 131.

7. *Content of the U.N. Convention on the Rights of the Child.* One author has suggested "three P's" as a way to summarize the rights provided in the CRC: provision (rights providing access to certain goods and services); protection (rights providing protection from maltreatment, etc.); and participation (rights providing autonomy and involvement in certain decisions). *See* Verhellen, *supra*, at 74. Participation rights for children are a new category for international instruments addressing children. Articles 13–16 are said to lay the foundation for these rights, and the United States was the chief proponent of these provisions. *See* Cynthia Price Cohen, *Role of the United States in Drafting the Convention on the Rights of the Child: Creating a New World for Children*, 4 Loy. Poverty L.J. 9, 26 (1998). The United States was also the chief proponent of the language that obligates states to undertake measures in regard to economic, social and cultural rights "to the maximum extent of their available resources." *See* art. 4. *See also Report of the Working Group on a Draft Convention on the Rights of the Child*, UNCHR, ¶177, U.N. Doc. E/CN.4/1989/48 (1989).

8. *Key Provisions to Measure State's Compliance.* Although there is no hierarchy of rights in the Convention, the Committee on the Rights of the Child highlighted in its Provisional Rules of Procedure, Annex III ¶13, four guiding principles by which it measures State Party's compliance with all of the other provisions: Non-discrimination (article 2), Best Interests of the Child (article 3), The Right to Life, Survival and Development (article 6), The Respect for the Views of the Child (article 12). The General Guidelines adopted in 1996 further reduced the guiding principles to the first two. The Committee's thoughts on these two principles are reproduced here:

General Guidelines Regarding the Form and Contents of Periodic Reports to Be Submitted by States Parties Under Article 44, Paragraph 1(b), of the Convention

U.N. Comm. on the Rights of the Child, 13th Sess.,
343d mtg., U.N. Doc. CRC/C/58 (1996)

[a. Non-discrimination. (article 2).]

25) Reports should indicate whether the principle of non-discrimination is included as a binding principle in the constitution or in domestic legislation specifically for children and whether all the possible grounds for discrimination spelled out in article 2 of the Convention are reflected in such legal provisions. Reports should further indicate the measures adopted to ensure the rights set forth in the convention to each child under the jurisdiction of the State without discrimination of any kind, including non-nationals, refugees and asylum-seekers.

26) Information should be provided on steps taken to ensure that discrimination is prevented and combated, both in law and practice, including discrimination on the basis of race, colour, sex, language, religion, political or other opinion, national, ethnic or social origin, property, disability, birth or other status of the child, his/her parents or legal guardians.

27) Please indicate the specific measures adopted to reduce economic, social and geographical disparities, including between rural and urban areas, to prevent discrimination against the most disadvantaged groups of children, including children belonging to minorities or indigenous communities, disabled children, children born out of wedlock, children who are non-nationals, migrants, displaced, refugees or asylum-seekers, and children who are living and/or working on the streets.

28) Please provide information on the specific measures taken to eliminate discrimination against girls and when appropriate indicate measures adopted as a follow-up to the Fourth World Conference on Women.

29) Please indicate measures taken to collect disaggregated data for the various groups of children mentioned above.

30) What measures have been taken to prevent and eliminate attitudes to and prejudice against children contributing to social or ethnic tension, racism and xenophobia?

31) Information should also be provided on the measures pursuant to article 2, paragraph 2 taken to ensure that the child is protected against all forms of discrimination or punishment on the basis of the status, activities, expressed opinions or beliefs of the child's parents, legal guardians or family members.

32) Please indicate major problems encountered in implementing the provisions of article 2 and plans to solve these problems, as well as any evaluation of progress in preventing and combating all forms of discrimination, including those arising from negative traditional practices.

[b. Best Interests of the Child. (article 3). The best interests of the child is mentioned in arts. 3(1), 9(1), 9(3), 18(1), 20(1), 21(1) and 40(2)(iii).]

33) Reports should indicate whether the principle of the best interests of the child and the need for it to be a primary consideration in all actions concerning children is reflected in the Constitution and relevant national legislation and regulations.

34) Please provide information on the consideration given to this principle by courts of law, administrative authorities or legislative bodies, as well as by public or private social welfare agencies.

35) Please provide information on how the best interests of the child have been given primary consideration in family life, school life, social life and in areas such as: budgetary allocations, including at the central, regional and local levels, and where appropriate at the federal and provincial levels, and within governmental departments.

36) Information should be included on the measures taken in the light of article 3, paragraph 2, including of a legislative and administrative nature, to ensure children such protection and care as is necessary for their well-being.

37) Information should also be provided on the steps taken pursuant to article 3, paragraph 3, to establish appropriate standards for all public and private institutions, services and facilities responsible for the care and protection of children and to ensure that they conform with such standards, particularly in the areas of safety, health, number and suitability of their staff, as well as competent supervision.

38) In the light of the legislative and administrative measures taken to ensure the consideration of the best interests of the child, please indicate the main problems remaining in this respect.

39) Please indicate in what ways the principle of the best interests of the child is made part of the training of professionals dealing with children's rights.

---

9. *Best Interests of the Child.* As indicated above, one of the main principles of the CRC is found in article 3. After looking at article 3, think about the following:

a. *Scope?* Would the provision be implicated by the divorce of a child's parents? Would it be implicated when the legislature decides to allocate money to the military and not to schools? What if the government were deporting a mother and not her children?

b. *Horizontal or Vertical Effect?* Would the provision be implicated when parents decide to buy a new car instead of spend money on a better education for their child?

c. *The Guiding Principle?* Does article 3 require that a court always put the best interests of the child first? Need the child's best interests be the overriding factor in all instances? When might it be appropriate to deviate from the principle? What about the fact that the words "the primary consideration" were rejected by the Working Group that drafted the Convention? *See Report of the Working Group on a Draft Convention on the Rights of the Child*, UNCHR, at 121–25, U.N. Doc. E/CN.4/1989/48 (1989).

10. *Participation Rights.* Examine article 12(2) of the CRC. What is the scope of this legal obligation? Would appointment of a guardian ad litem suffice? Need a guardian ad litem be appointed? What are "proceedings affecting the child?" Would it include a divorce action between the child's parents? In the United States, "The appointment of a representative for the child is mandated in only nine states, and then only under certain conditions, like an allegation of abuse." Katherine Hunt Federle, *Looking Ahead: An Empowerment Perspective on the Rights of Children*, 68 Temp. L. Rev. 1585, 1600 n.76 (1995). Is article 12(2) applicable to county proceedings about which school in a district should be closed during a time of fiscal austerity? Is article 12(2) applicable to administrative proceedings addressing environmental regulations in the child's town? Must States Parties allow children to vote in political elections?

11. *Evolving Capacities.* Look at articles 5, 12(1), 14(2), 40(1), and 40(2)(b)(iii). What does "evolving capacities" mean? Does the CRC require an abandonment of age-based classifications for decisions such as marriage, alcohol use, or driving?

12. *Respect for the Child's Human Dignity.* Look at articles 23(1), 28(2), 39, and 40. What does "respect for the child's human dignity" mean?

13. *Who is a Child?* When do the rights under the Convention attach and when do they terminate? Does the Convention threaten a woman's right to choose an abortion? Or, alternatively, does the Convention require that minors have access to abortion? Whether a "fetus" is a child for purposes of the Convention is addressed in Chapter 13.C.2.

14. *Education.* Look at articles 28 and 29. Could the United States, assuming it became a party to the Convention, require that all private schools teach about the U.N. Convention on the Rights of the Child? What if some of the articles offended a particu-

lar religion and its schools refused to comply? The Committee on the Rights of the Child adopted its first General Comment at its 26th session in January 2001. That comment states that the child's right to education is both a matter of access and content. *See Convention Update*, Int'l Child. Rts. Monitor, May 2001, at 33.

15. *Nonmarital children.* The CRC has no provision on nonmarital children. There were various attempts to incorporate the rights of the illegitimate child, but these were rejected. *See* Cynthia Price Cohen, *The Developing Jurisprudence of the Rights of the Child*, 6 St. Thomas L. Rev. 1, 61 n.327 (1993). Does that mean states can discriminate between children on the basis of marital status? Consider what the Committee said to Uruguay with regard to its law on the naming of nonmarital children: "[T]he Committee is particularly concerned at the persisting discrimination against children born out of wedlock, including in regard to the enjoyment of their civil rights. It notes that the procedure for the determination of their names paves the way for their stigmatization and the impossibility of having access to their origins." Rachel Hodgkin & Peter Newell, Implementation Handbook for the Convention on the Rights of the Child 102 (1998). Note 13 after the *Marckx* case in Chapter 1.A has more information on this topic.

16. *Reservations.* Many States Parties have attached reservations and declarations to the CRC. Consider article 51 of the CRC, which addresses reservations. How does one determine whether a reservation is contrary to the object and purpose of the Convention? Are reservations that are very broad and vague contrary to the CRC's object and purpose? For example, Pakistan's reservation stated the "provisions of the Convention shall be interpreted in the light of the principles of Islamic laws and values." William A. Schabas, *Reservations to the Convention on the Rights of the Child*, 18 Hum. Rts. Q. 472, 478 (1996). Although Pakistan withdrew this reservation in 1997, some other Islamic countries entered similar reservations and have not yet withdrawn them. *See* Convention on the Rights of the Child, *at* http://www.un.org/Depts/Treaty/final/ts2/newfiles/part_boo/iv_boo/iv_ll.html. Can one even determine what legal obligations have been undertaken by Pakistan or countries with similar reservations? What if a country says, as Iran did, that it "reserves the right not to apply any provisions or articles of the Convention that are incompatible with Islamic laws and the internal legislation in effect." *Id.* Can one argue that Iran has not even ratified the treaty given its reservation? Article 27 of the Vienna Convention on the Law of Treaties states: "A party may not invoke the provisions of its internal law as justification for its failure to perform a treaty." What if another state does not object to a broad reservation? Does that mean the other state accepts that the relevant portions of the treaty between itself and the reserving state do not apply? The Committee on the Rights of the Child questions States Parties about their reservations when those States Parties come before it. For more information on reservations and their acceptable parameters, see Chapter 1.B.1.b.ii.

17. *Post-CRC Efforts.* Since 1989, other international instruments have addressed children's rights. For example, the African Charter on the Rights and Welfare of the Child was adopted by the Organization of African Unity. *See African Charter on the Rights and Welfare of the Child*, O.A.U. 26th Conf., OAU Doc. CAB/LEG/24.9/49 (1990). For a comparison between that Charter and the CRC, *see* Cohen, *The Developing Jurisprudence of the Rights of the Child, supra*, at 60–62. In 1996, the Council of Europe adopted a European Convention on the Exercise of Children's Rights. "The object of the present Convention is, in the best interests of children, to promote their rights, to grant them procedural rights and to facilitate the exercise of these rights by ensuring that children are, themselves or through other persons or bodies, informed and allowed to participate in proceedings affecting them before a judicial authority." *European Convention on the Exercise of Children's Rights*, art. 1(2), COE, ETS No. 160 (1996). The Convention entered into force in July 2000, and

Greece, Poland, and Slovenia have ratified it. Seventeen other countries have signed the Convention. *See* Council of Europe, Chart of Signatures and Ratifications, European Convention on the Exercise of Children's Rights, *at* http://www.conventions.coe.int/Treaty/EN/searchsig.asp?NT=160&CM=1&DF=.

Problem 14-2

Carla and Bill were married for five years when they conceived John using artificial insemination with sperm provided by a donor. The donor's semen was obtained from their doctor. Under the relevant statute, the donor's anonymity was assured, and all parental rights were vested in Carla and Bill exclusively. When John turned 16, he found out the method of his conception and he longed to find his biological father. His parents do not support his desire to search for his father; they fear that he will discover someone who does not want to know John. Does article 2 or article 7 of the CRC provide John with assistance? Why or why not? Assume all the individuals live in a country that is a party to the CRC.

Problem 14-3

Minnie and Fred are divorcing and fighting over who will have physical custody of the couple's three children, Beth, age two, Steven, age eight, and Vincent, age nine. There is no guardian ad litem appointed for the children. The judge calls Vincent into his chambers and asks him who he wants to live with after the divorce. Vincent says he wants to live with Fred. The judge then calls Steven in and asks him the same question. Steven cries and tells the judge he cannot choose. The judge repeats the question softly five times before Steven blurts out, "I guess I want to live with my dad." The judge considered all the other evidence in equipoise. He then awards all three children to Fred, for he does not want to separate them. Has there been a violation of the Convention? What if the other evidence was not in equipoise, but suggested that it was certainly in the youngest child's best interest to be awarded to her mother? Again, assume the CRC has been ratified by the country in which this divorce action is being litigated.

2. The Convention and the United States

There has been fairly vehement opposition to the U.N. Rights of the Child Convention in the United States. Although the United States signed the treaty in 1995, the United States has not ratified it. Consider the following resolution that was introduced in the United States Senate.

Senate Resolution 133
104th Cong. (1995)

Mr. Helms (for himself, Mr. Lott, Mr. Abraham, Mr. Ashcroft, Mr. Coats, Mr. Craig, Mr. DeWine, Mr. Faircloth, Mr. Frist, Mr. Gramm, Mr. Grams, Mr. Hatch, Mr. Kempthorne, Mr. McConnell, Mr. Murkowski, Mr. Nickles, Mr. Santorum, Mr. Smith, and Mr. Thurmond) submitted the following resolution; which was referred to the Committee on Foreign Relations.

Whereas the Senate affirms the commitment of the United States to work with other nations to enhance the protection of children, the advancement of education, the eradication of disease, and the protection of human rights; Whereas the Constitution and laws of the United States are the best guarantees against mistreatment of children in our country; Whereas the laws and traditions of the United States affirm the right of parents to raise their children and to transmit to them their values and religious beliefs; Whereas the United Nations Convention on the Rights of the Child, if ratified, would become the supreme law of the land, taking precedence over State and Federal laws regarding family life; Whereas that Convention establishes a "universal standard" which must be met by all parties to the Convention, thereby inhibiting the rights of the States and the Federal Government to enact child protection and support laws inconsistent with that standard; and Whereas the Convention's intrusion into national sovereignty was manifested by the Convention's 1995 committee report faulting the United Kingdom for permitting parents to make decisions for their children without consulting those children: Now, therefore, be it

Resolved, That it is the sense of the Senate that—

(1) the United Nations Convention on the Rights of the Child is incompatible with the God-given right and responsibility of parents to raise their children;

(2) the Convention has the potential to severely restrict States and the Federal Government in their efforts to protect children and to enhance family life;

(3) the United States Constitution is the ultimate guarantor of rights and privileges to every American, including children; and

(4) the President should not sign and transmit to the Senate that fundamentally flawed Convention.

Notes and Questions

1. *Federalism.* As mentioned above, the United States has not ratified the Convention. To what extent are the concerns raised by Senator Helms valid? If the United States became a party to the Convention, would it potentially violate federalism principles of the U.S. Constitution? After all, family law is traditionally an area left for the states to regulate. Would states be bound to abide by the treaty? What if Congress passed a law in furtherance of the treaty that obligated states to provide a minimum level of child protective services for children? Would such a mandate be constitutional? How would the CRC "severely restrict" efforts to "protect children" and "enhance family life"?

2. *Comparing the U.S. Constitution and the CRC.* To what extent does the substance of the Convention go beyond our Bill of Rights and the constitutional guarantees that the U.S. Supreme Court has afforded children? It is useful to imagine how some of the landmark Supreme Court cases might have come out if the CRC were ratified by the United States, and appropriate implementing legislation had been adopted. For example, think about *Reno v. Flores*, 113 S. Ct. 1439 (1993) (upholding INS regulations limiting release of alien minors detained at border crossing to parents or close relatives against, inter alia, a substantive due process challenge related to the "fundamental" right to be free from "physical restraint"), *DeShaney v. Winnebago County Dep't of Social Services*, 109 S. Ct. 998 (1989) (holding the state had no affirmative obligation under 14th Amendment due process clause to protect child against abusive father), *Michael H. v. Gerald D.*, 109 S. Ct. 2333 (1989) (upholding statute that precluded biological father from challenging paternity of mother's husband against, inter alia, child's due process claim to maintain her filial relationship), *Hodgson v. Minnesota*, 110 S. Ct. 2926 (1990)

(upholding parental notice requirement prior to minor's abortion, unless judge dispenses with notice, against minor's due process challenge), and *Troxel v. Granville*, 530 U.S. 57 (2000) (reversing application of Washington statute that permitted grandparents to receive visitation over fit mother's objection). *See generally* Roger J.R. Levesque, *International Children's Rights Grow Up: Implications for American Jurisprudence and Domestic Policy*, 24 Cal. W. Int'l L.J. 193 (1994).

3. *Substance: Parental Rights and the Treaty.* Does the Convention tell parents how to raise their children? Can children bring suit against their parents before the International Court of Justice or courts in the United States for violation of the Convention? Imagine a child who wants to listen to rap music to which the parents object. If the government allows parents to censor their children's music, will the state be in violation of the Convention? Review articles 3, 5, 13, 14, and 18.

4. *Form: Parental Rights and the Treaty.* Does the Convention trump "parental rights" that have been found to be part of the U.S. Constitution? Consider the Supremacy Clause in Article VI of the U.S. Constitution: "all Treaties made, or which shall be made, under the Authority of the United States, shall be the supreme Law of the Land; and the Judges in every State shall be bound thereby, any Thing in the Constitution or Laws of any State to the Contrary notwithstanding."

5. *Controversy.* What do you make of the following observation?

> [T]he United States was active in drafting the articles that are generating the most heated opposition. Articles 13, 14, 15, and 16 are the results of proposals submitted by the U.S. delegation. The United States was also active in the development of Articles 17 and 18, as well as other less contentious articles. In fact, the United States had actually proposed an even more comprehensive protection of the child's civil and political rights than was adopted. The original U.S. proposal required States Parties to:
>
>> ensure that the child shall enjoy civil and political rights and freedoms in public life to the fullest extent commensurate with his age including in particular, freedom from arbitrary governmental interference with privacy, family, home or correspondence; the right to petition for redress of grievances; and, subject only to such reasonable restrictions provided by law as are necessary for respect of the rights and legally protected interests of others or for the protection of national security, public safety and order, or public health and morals, freedom of association and expression; and the right of peaceful assembly.

This proposal was modified through several years of negotiation, and was finally adopted as Articles 13, 15, and 16.

Susan Kilbourne, *U.S. Failure to Ratify the U.N. Convention on the Rights of the Child: Playing Politics with Children's Rights*, 6 Transnat'l L. & Contemp. Probs. 437, 456–57 (1996).

6. *Website.* More information on the Convention, the Committee, and country reports can be accessed at http://www.unhchr.ch/.

7. *New Optional Protocols.* Recently, the U.N. General Assembly adopted two optional protocols to the CRC. One addresses the involvement of children in armed conflicts. It was adopted and opened for signature, ratification and accession by General Assembly Resolution A/RES/54/263 on May 25, 2000. It is aimed at ensuring that children in the armed forces do not take a direct part in hostilities (article 1), that persons younger than 18 are not compulsorily recruited into the armed forces (article 2), that

the minimum age for the voluntary recruitment of persons into the armed forces be raised from 15 years old, that such recruitment not be forced or coerced, that the minor's parents or legal guardians give the state informed consent (article 3), and that armed groups (distinct from the armed forces of a state) should not, under any circumstances, recruit or use those under 18 in hostilities (article 4). The treaty entered into force on February 12, 2002, and over forty-one countries have ratified it.

The other optional protocol relates to the sale of children, child prostitution and child pornography. This protocol was also adopted and opened for signature, ratification and accession by General Assembly Resolution, A/RES/54/263 on May 25, 2000. This protocol prohibits the sale of children, child prostitution, and child pornography (article 1), and, among other things, requires states to criminalize these and related practices (*e.g.*, forced labour) (article 3), and to make the criminal prosecution of offenders a "child-friendly" process (article 8). The protocol also has provisions related to adoption. *See, e.g.*, art. 3(5). This protocol entered into force on January 18, 2002, and over forty-one countries have ratified it.

———————

Given Senator Helms' concerns, should the United States ratify the U.N. Convention on the Rights of the Child? What are the reasons to do so? Various commentators have given reasons for U.S. ratification. Do you agree that these are persuasive reasons? Are there other, more persuasive, reasons for ratification?

Susan Kilbourne, *U.S. Failure to Ratify the U.N. Convention on the Rights of the Child: Playing Politics With Children's Rights*
6 Transnat'l L. & Contemp. Probs. 437, 459–60 (1996)

First, the Convention would provide guidance for evaluating inconsistent existing policies. U.S. policies regarding children's issues, such as health, education, welfare, and abuse, are currently administered by so many different agencies, departments, and political entities as to be almost incoherent. The Convention would provide a unifying framework for analyzing U.S. policy. Second, in fulfilling the Convention's reporting requirements, the United States would necessarily perform an assessment of its implementation of the Convention's provisions, which would focus attention on the condition of children in the United States. In other words, the government would be more accountable for its policies, and, perhaps, more likely to implement them. Third, ratification would give the United States the opportunity to be represented on the Committee on the Rights of the Child. It would further allow the United States to continue to participate in the ongoing international dialogue on children's issues and to maintain a credible presence in the international human rights arena.

———————

Roger J.R. Levesque, *Educating American Youth: Lessons from Children's Human Rights Law*
27 J.L. & Educ. 173, 194–201 (1998)

There are two approaches human rights experts use to envision and ensure compliance with international treaties: 1) A narrow approach which focuses on the actual black letter law of international treaties as it would be applied in the relevant nation state; and 2) A broad approach which focuses more on the spirit of the law—seeking different ways to circumvent narrow rulings and approaches. Both approaches offer important insights into the potential use of international principles....

Narrow approaches to international obligations

Ratified international treaties become the law of the land. Although this broad principle seemingly makes treaties considerably powerful, several factors could legitimately limit any treaty's eventual impact. Whether a particular treaty provision directly rules in domestic arenas actually depends on whether the provision is self-executing, limited by a reservation and constitutional. Application of such analyses to the Children's Convention illustrates international law's limited ability to directly impact American policy making. For example, most of the rights and entitlements covered by the treaty are not self-executing, indicating that further legislation was anticipated for implementation. The self-executing articles are already covered by treaties [to] which the United States is a party and which admittedly have had limited, if any, direct impact on domestic policy. Or, as several commentators suggest, any such self-executing provisions would be subjected to a reservation....

Other limitations impact the extent to which properly ratified treaties become the controlling law of the land. Two common considerations illustrate potential limitations. The first consideration relates to the treaty's relationship to federal and state law: If the treaty's provisions conflict with federal law, then the most recent provision prevails, if it conflicts with state law, then the treaty prevails. These straight-forward rules suggest several ways to limit a treaty's reach, such as adopting a federal-state reservation and simply passing new federal laws that could vitiate some of the treaty's rule. The second limiting factor relates to the manner courts actually use international law. For example, even if provisions are self-executing, their impact on United States courts remains uncertain. When treaties are used directly, as customary law, or as guiding principles, its use remains indeterminative. Courts rarely venture into the ambiguous realm of international law.

Also important to consider is the actual language of the treaty. Generally, actual obligations in the language of the treaty tend to be very circumscribed—as revealed in the considerably comprehensive Children's Convention. For example, the potentially expansive international right to provide all children education may be conceived mainly as a positive obligation. As with most positive rights, the standard formulation establishes that the right [is] recognized progressively. This limitation has the potential to create impressive obstacles, as recognized by several distinguished commentators who conclude that, as enumerated, the rights do not necessarily contribute to more legal actualization of rights. Thus, the actual language of "the right to education," coupled by the likely use of other limiting mechanisms, offers little hope to those who would argue that human rights law can directly impact youths' educational rights.

Broad approaches to international obligations

It would be easy to conclude that the domestic impact of ratifying treaties remains negligible, [but] international treaties like the Children's Convention still could influence United States law in two significant ways. First, international standards could have an effect on executive and administrative branches. Second, modern international law takes into account domestic avoidance devices and finds other methods of breathing legal life back into international human rights law....

Even though commentaries and legal analyses tend to ignore the potential effect international standards could have on executive and administrative policymakers, three reasons make the potential for nonjudicial use of international standards significant. First, the executive branch remains free to enter into international agreements which prevail over inconsistent state law by reason of the Supremacy Clause. Thus, both states and the federal government would be bound by executive agreements unless the federal legislature or executive branches decided to enact new rules. Second, statutes and regulations, especially those dealing with child welfare issues, necessarily leave considerable discretion to those entrusted with their implementation. Thus, thousands of national and local decision-makers who have discretion to enforce, interpret and implement laws could be encouraged to administer domestic laws consistently with human rights law. Third, international law, including the Children's Convention, mandates that parties take administrative and all other measures to ensure human rights. International law actually mandates a broad approach.

In addition to the use of international law by those who act domestically, it is important to address the international community's power. Although any ratifying party may carefully circumscribe its duties to enforce basic human rights standards, they cannot avoid the obligation to publicize, report on, and monitor the enforcement and failures of enforcement, of rights found in international treaties. Although this reliance on cooperative and educational approaches to enforcing international law may seem rather weak and unsophisticated, it remains a major weapon in the struggle to ensure human rights. If nations fail to respect standards, the international community typically encourages, pushes, prods, and ultimately embarrasses states into taking steps to guarantee the proper implementation of rights. Importantly, the international community's power derives from a broad base that includes nation states, formal quasi-governmental organizations with a global reach, non-governmental organizations (NGOs), international professional organizations, and citizens who form local social movements that ultimately have global repercussions. International human rights instruments necessarily open the United States to domestic and international scrutiny based on agreed international norms.

A treaty's impact on the nation states' obligations to foreign parties provides another important arena to consider. The attachment of reservations to a ratification only confines a treaty's domestic effect as a source of domestic law; they do not affect the obligations to other signatories. In this regard a basic requirement in the law of treaties, "good faith" in efforts to implement its core values and standards, becomes crucial. Thus other nation-states may use treaties like the Children's Convention as a lever to influence the United States' approach to children, both toward children in the United States and those abroad. To be sure, the black letter obligations set forth in the Convention may not impose direct obligations on the United States or subject it to foreign jurisdictions. But the rights enumerated in the Convention are, nonetheless, recognized rights. And, as human rights which have been negotiated among nation states, they are erga omnes: all states, all world citizens, have an interest in their recognition and enforcement. It would be unwise to discount the power of such rights.

The extent to which international standards could influence United States law and policy depends upon the extent to which governmental and nongovernmental organizations most susceptible to societal influences can be encouraged to support the principles. Domesticating international rights through the executive and legislative branches, federal, state, and local, offers fertile ground for implementation. Arguably, influencing those who have discretion in implementing children's policies remains the most realistic and promising route to domesticating international children's rights.

Sanford J. Fox, *Beyond The American Legal System for the Protection of Children's Rights*
31 Fam. L.Q. 237, 264–267 (1997)

How to best exploit the opportunities presented by international law is the central challenge facing children's lawyers....

A process that has been called "indirect incorporation" suggests using the international norms to influence the meaning courts adopt of statutes and constitutional provisions involved in children's rights litigation. The advocate's point here is that domestic courts should, whenever possible, interpret American law so as to be consistent with and not violative of international standards. As Professor Lillich wrote more than a decade ago, "To the lawyer anxious to obtain results it offers significant as well as virtually limitless possibilities for achieving greater protection of the rights of individuals."

Favorable results may also be possible in cases where the protection needs to be sought in state or local law or practice by applying indirect pressure to produce a remedy. To appreciate this possibility something needs to be said of the federalism aspects of children's international rights.

The federal government is responsible for respecting these rights to the same extent that it is responsible for ensuring U.S. compliance with other parts of international law. That under our federal system state and local law has the dominant share of providing for children's rights does not alter the international obligation of the federal government. State law that fails to meet the requirements of international law that is binding on the United States brings the country into violation of international law.

If, for example, the ICCPR violation implicates state or local governments, the federal government is nonetheless responsible under international law. That the United States has undertaken to have state and local law and practice comply with the ICCPR requirements is clear from the text of Article 50 of the ICCPR, which provides: "The provisions of the present Covenant shall extend to all parts of federal States without any limitations or exceptions." The United States has not reserved against Article 50, probably because such a reservation would be seen to fail the "object and purpose" test. However, in ratifying the ICCPR, the United States included a federalism "understanding" of almost impenetrable meaning:

> That the United States understands that this Covenant shall be implemented by the Federal Government to the extent that it exercises legislative and judicial jurisdiction over the matters covered therein, and otherwise by the state and local governments; to the extent that state and local governments exercise jurisdiction over such matters, the Federal Government shall take measures appropriate to the Federal system to the end that the competent authorities of the state or local governments may take appropriate measures for the fulfillment of the Covenant.

In its own terms, this Understanding relates only to implementation of the Covenant and does not limit or modify the Article 50 obligation. It serves, moreover, to clarify that the federal government sees itself as obliged to "take measures appropriate to the federal system" in order to bring state and local law in line with the Covenant's requirements.

That is the point to which children's lawyers need to apply the pressure. Depending on the nature of the violation involved, they can demand federal action in compliance with its international obligations from the Department of Health and Human Services to remedy a state's failure to provide protection from abuse, or from the Department of Labor for a state's failure to meet child labor standards, [or] from the Department of Housing and Urban Development for a state's failure to assure a minimum level of housing for children. Certainly, the State Department should be an addressee for all complaints since that department will be obliged to defend the U.S. human rights' record....

Martha Minow, *What Ever Happened to Children's Rights?*
80 Minn. L. Rev. 267, 297–98 (1995)

Human rights in the international sphere depend upon the development of a community that believes in them rather than an authority—court or legislature—that will enforce them.

The vulnerability of international human rights for children to the willingness and commitments of adults at first seems like a weakness, a failure to secure something with force. This vulnerability in another sense, however, becomes a strength because it reveals how dependent and interdependent children are upon adults. Organizing to influence and shape such a community may line up means and ends in precisely the way most important for children. Without adults who believe in the importance and entitlements of children, no phrase, judicial order, or legislative statement will alter their conditions.

In a basic sense, all rights—for adults as well as for children—require a commitment by others to recognize the claims of others and to behave accordingly. Freedoms of association and religion, rights to marry and to procreate, and rights to maintain relationships with family members all depend upon community commitments to include the rights-bearers in the group deserving respect and attention.

Rights rhetorics in the past have tended too often to imply only freedom from— freedom from state control, freedom from interference by others. Children may need some forms of such freedoms but they also need guidance, involvement, support, and even control to protect them from harms against which they cannot protect themselves. I suggest that nothing inherent in rights rhetorics prevents acknowledging these needs of children. At the same time, the rhetoric of rights is the coin of the realm in national, and increasingly in international, law and politics. Not only does invoking this language put children on the map of public concern, it also crucially "impl[ies] a respect which places one in the referential range of self and others, which elevates one's status from human body to social being."

Many may ask whether it is practical to press for human rights on behalf of children. A negative answer might arise given the considerable resources right-wing groups muster in opposing such rights as interference in their privacy. The history of the children's rights movements throughout this century casts further doubt on the practicality of a human rights effort for children. By the 1980s, children's rights, as a phrase in search of a program, encompassed many contrasting and even conflicting commitments to children without a notable improvement of circumstances for many, many children. Whether styled as children's liberation or child protection, or as social welfare redistribution programs, each effort found powerful opponents poised against it. Moreover, the conventional conception of rights as implying an autonomous person who needs freedom from interference seems ill-suited to meeting the needs of most children.

Yet the past does not determine our future, but instead offers a set of lessons about the relationship between ideals and contingent realities. Powerful concepts like rights are amenable to new interpretations and applications that may in turn make good on their earlier promise and deeper meanings. So I suggest we roll up our sleeves and work on every front—our own workplaces, schools, communities, and states, our Congress, our medical care, our world—to explore what it would mean to view children as human beings entitled to human rights, or else find a better way to summon attention and resources on their behalf.

Michael King, *Against Children's Rights*
1996 Acta Juridica 28, 38–39

[I]t is not perhaps surprising that the United Nations Convention on the Rights of the Child, and all the other constitutional instruments which seek to set down rights for children, tend to generate legal communications that go far beyond the scope of what is recognizable as law. Indeed, even to see them as law is something of a misreading. They are formulated as law, because and only because there is no other mode (or code) for modern society to make generally available its fears and hopes for children and their future and, at the same time, to hold out the possibility of allaying those fears and realizing those hopes. The romantic Christian idea that children who die in childhood can expect to play together for eternity in a heavenly paradise no longer has any credence. Similarly, the belief that people's lives are foreordained according to some grand scheme denies (or at least limits) any possibility of the forging of a causal connection between present child and future adult. In modern society this belief has been replaced by a scientific (and now common-sense) equivalence between childhood well-being and adult well-being, which tells us that the future destiny of our children lies in present decisions. Happy and fulfilled children, therefore, make for happy and fulfilled adults. This message concerning the relationship between the child and the adult, the present and the future, may well be common to all the sub-systems of modern society. Of these, however, only law has the capacity to reconstitute this relationship in the form of rights and obligations. Adults can *through law* be required to make sacrifices in order to make children and the future happy and secure. They may even *through law* be made to suffer penalties if they fail to meet their obligations.

The reason for this faith in the power of the law may stem more from a disillusionment and a lack of faith in other systems, such as politics, economics, science and religion, to protect children and their future well-being than from any widespread popularity of law or lawyers. Contemporary politics in both democratic and autocratic countries, both nationally and internationally, provides little evidence of its ability to treat children as a distinctive group, separate from adults and families, deserving preferential treatment....

Attributing to law in modern society a greater authority than any other of society's function systems to determine what is right and wrong is to misread legality as denoting simultaneously both what is morally acceptable and what is, according to current scientific knowledge, healthy for children. Yet in practice all that law can do is decide what is right and wrong in law, that is what is lawful and what is unlawful, what is legal and what is illegal. This may or [may] not correspond to what people believe to be moral and immoral.

Notes and Questions

1. *Value of a Dedicated Line.* To what extent would ratification impose new obligations on the United States assuming that the United States did not enter reservations and declarations negating the treaty's legal significance? After all, the United States is already a party to the International Covenant on Civil and Political Rights, the Convention Against Torture, and the International Convention on the Elimination of All Forms of Racial Discrimination. In addition, representatives from the United States continually state that the United States adheres to, and will continue to promote, the Universal Declaration of Human Rights. Perhaps one of the greatest benefits from ratification for children in the United States would be the arrival of a forum dedicated solely to considering their rights (*i.e.,* the Committee on the Rights of the Child), and that forum would examine conditions and practices they encounter. Most optimistically, the United States might even respond positively to the Committee's recommendation that all States Parties have an independent national human rights institution dedicated solely to the rights of the child. *See generally* Merle H. Weiner, *Beyond Other Treaties: The U.N. Convention on the Rights of the Child and the Value of a Dedicated Line, in* Ratification of the U.N. Convention on the Rights of the Child: Implications for U.S. Law and Policy (Amer. Bar Assoc., forthcoming 2003).

2. *Arguments For and Against Ratification.* What other arguments can you think of for ratification? Against ratification?

3. *Necessity of Ratification.* In a later portion of Sanford Fox's article, the author suggests that there are existing legal mechanisms by which advocates can advance children's rights. For example, he mentions that the jurisdiction of the U.N. Human Rights Commission is not limited "by the substantive law of human rights treaties." He also mentions that children's rights claims should be brought before the Inter-American Commission on Human Rights. Do these mechanisms render the CRC unnecessary?

4. *Customary International Law.* There are over 190 States Parties to the CRC. This makes the CRC the most ratified international convention. In fact, a year after the U.N. adopted the CRC, approximately 130 countries signed it, and approximately half of those countries ratified it. *See* Bruce C. Hafen & Jonathan O. Hafen, *Abandoning Children to their Autonomy: The United Nations Convention on the Rights of the Child,* 37 Harv. Int'l L.J. 449, 449 & n.2 (1996). Is the United States bound by the treaty as a matter of customary law despite the fact that the United States has not ratified it?

C. Corporal Punishment

As you now have a basic understanding of "children's rights," it is useful to focus on a particular topic and see what impact constitutional rights, regional agreements, and the U.N. Convention on the Rights of the Child have had for children. Corporal punishment seems like a particularly worthy topic to study because the practice is a direct exercise of state and/or parental power over children in a manner with which children themselves might object. Therefore, the topic raises questions about children's autonomy. In addition, since parents and the state may disagree with each other in a particular instance about the desirability of corporal punishment, the topic also raises questions about their power and obligations.

Corporal punishment of children is a controversial practice in the United States. As discussed below, for many parents the ability to administer corporal punishment to their children is tied up with their religious beliefs. For other proponents, the topic is "emotionally charged because opinions about these practices are formed in childhood. This learning occur[s] under emotional circumstances and is affected by parents' needs to justify their own parents' practices." American Academy of Pediatrics, *Guidance for Effective Discipline*, 101 Pediatrics 723 (1998). On the other hand, an increased sensitivity to children's welfare and the fear of child abuse has led some parents to become vehement opponents. *See* Janet Chiancone, *Corporal Punishment: What Lawyers Need to Know*, 16 ABA Child Law Practice 1 (1997). Even those parents who support the use of corporal punishment themselves sometimes draw the line when the government, embodied in public school authorities, administers the punishment.

In the United States, "forty-nine states permit parents to use 'reasonable' corporal punishment on their offspring, and approximately half of the states permit educators to do the same to students." Susan H. Bitensky, *Spare the Rod, Embrace Human Rights: International Law's Mandate Against All Corporal Punishment of Children*, 21 Whittier L. Rev. 147 (1999). In *Ingraham v. Wright*, 430 U.S. 651 (1977), the United States Supreme Court held that the Eighth Amendment's prohibition against cruel and unusual punishment did not apply when school officials paddled students as a means of maintaining school discipline. The Court suggested that "[t]he prisoner and the schoolchild stand in wholly different circumstances, separated by the harsh facts of criminal conviction and incarceration." In particular, the prisoner, unlike the child, is deprived of contact with family and friends, and encounters the reality of prison brutality. *Id.* at 669. Consequently, the "schoolchild has little need for the protection of the Eighth Amendment." *Id.* at 670. The Court also rejected the argument that the Due Process Clause of the Fourteenth Amendment required prior notice and an opportunity to be heard before the paddling. Not only was a de minimis level of physical pain an imposition "with which the Constitution is not concerned," *id.* at 674, but even the deliberate infliction of "appreciable physical pain" would not trigger the requested protection. Applying *Mathews v. Eldridge*, 424 U.S. 319, 682 (1976), the Court held, "In view of the low incidence of abuse, the openness of our schools, and the common-law safeguards that already exist, the risk of error that may result in violation of a school child's substantive rights can only be regarded as minimal. Imposing additional administrative safeguards as a constitutional requirement might reduce that risk marginally, but would also entail a significant intrusion into an area of primary educational responsibility." *Ingraham*, 430 U.S. at 682.

Some nations have been opposed to the corporal punishment of children for a long time. Sweden in 1979 passed a law which stated "Children are to be treated with respect for their person and individuality and may not be subjected to corporal punishment or any other humiliating treatment." *See Europe Turns Against Smacking*, BBC News, Jan. 18, 2000, *available at* http://www.nospank.net/europe.htm. Finland passed a similar law in 1983. Since then, Denmark, Norway, Austria, Cyprus, Latvia, and Croatia have also banned corporal punishment. In addition, Italy's Supreme Court of Cassazione rendered a decision in 1996 with the same result, *see* Bitensky, *supra*, at 159–60, as did the Israeli Supreme Court in 2000. *See* Dan Izenberg,

Supreme Court: Corporal Punishment of Children is Indefensible, Jerusalem Post, Jan. 26, 2000, p. 4.

One of the more interesting recent developments in this area is the effect regional human rights treaties are having on states with a rather entrenched commitment to corporal punishment. For example, English law, which recognizes a role for reasonable parental discipline, is being strongly influenced by the European Convention for the Protection of Human Rights and Fundamental Freedoms (ECHR).

1. The European Convention for the Protection of Human Rights and Fundamental Freedoms

As you read the following cases, remember that the European Commission's decisions are not judgments. Rather, when the Commission existed as an entity (for now it has been merged with the European Court of Human Rights), the Commission determined admissability of applications and attempted to help parties reach friendly settlements. If a settlement was not reached, the Commission issued an advisory opinion about how the Convention was violated. The opinion was transmitted to the Committee of Ministers. The Commission might also refer the case to the European Court of Human Rights. If the Commission did not refer the case to the Court within three months, then the Committee of Ministers was to render a judgment.

When the Court heard a case, it often included the Commission's opinion before it issued its judgment. Some of the Commission's opinions are included in this section because they help illuminate the issues being decided. Although both the Commission and the Court might reach the same conclusion in a case, sometimes the European Court's judgment is quite short compared to the Commission's opinion. At other times, the Commission's opinion is at odds with the Court's judgment, but the Commission's opinion is useful as evidence of alternative approaches that the Court could have taken.

Today only the European Court of Human Rights adjudicates disputes under the European Convention on Human Rights. In 1998, the European Commission of Human Rights and the European Court of Human Rights were consolidated. This reform was prompted by a tremendous increase in the number of applications brought before the Commission (from 404 in 1981 to over 12,000 in 1997). *See* Registrar, The European Court of Human Rights, at 6, *available at* http://www.echr.coe.int.Eng/Edocs/InfodocRevised2.htm. The filtering formally done by the Commission is now done by committees of three judges. *Id.* at 11. In addition, the Committee of Ministers' participation is now limited to the supervision and execution of judgments. *See* Protocol No. 11 to the European Convention for the Protection of Human Rights and Fundamental Freedoms, Restructuring the Control Machinery Established Thereby, 33 I.L.M. 943, arts. 46–47 (1994).

A. v. United Kingdom
27 Eur. H.R. Rep. 611 (1999)

I. *The circumstances of the case*

The applicant is a British citizen, born in 1984. In May 1990 he and his brother were placed on the local Child Protection Register because of "known physical abuse." The co-habitee of the boys' mother was given a police caution after he admitted hitting A. with a cane. Both boys were removed from the Child Protection Register in November 1991. The co-habitee subsequently married the applicant's mother and became his stepfather.

In February 1993, the head teacher at A.'s school reported to the local Social Services Department that A.'s brother had disclosed that A. was being hit with a stick by his stepfather. The stepfather was arrested on 5 February 1993 and released on bail the next day.

On 5 February 1993 the applicant was examined by a consultant pediatrician, who found the following marks on his body, inter alia: (1) a fresh red linear bruise on the back of the right thigh, consistent with a blow from the garden cane, probably within the preceding twenty-four hours; (2) a double linear bruise on the back of the left calf, consistent with two separate blows given some time before the first injury; (3) two lines on the back of the left thigh, probably caused by two blows inflicted one or two days previously; (4) three linear bruises on the right bottom, consistent with three blows, possibly given at different times and up to one week old; (5) a fading linear bruise, probably several days old.

The pediatrician considered that the bruising was consistent with the use of a garden cane, applied with considerable force, on more than one occasion.

The stepfather was charged with assault occasioning actual bodily harm and tried in February 1994. It was not disputed by the defence that the stepfather had caned the boy on a number of occasions, but it was argued that this had been necessary and reasonable since A. was a difficult boy who did not respond to parental or school discipline. In summing-up, the judge advised the jury on the law as follows:

> ...What is it the prosecution must prove? If a man deliberately and unjustifiably hits another and causes some bodily injury, bruising or swelling will do, he is guilty of actual bodily harm. What does unjustifiably mean in the context of this case? It is a perfectly good defence that the alleged assault was merely the correcting of a child by its parent, in this case the stepfather, provided that the correction be moderate in the manner, the instrument and the quantity of it. Or, put another way, reasonable. It is not for the defendant to prove it was lawful correction. It is for the prosecution to prove it was not....

The jury found by a majority verdict that the applicant's stepfather was not guilty of assault occasioning actual bodily harm.

II. *Relevant domestic law...*

The applicant's stepfather was charged with "assault occasioning actual bodily harm" contrary to section 47 of the Offenses Against the Person Act 1861, as amended....

In addition, it is an offence under section 1(1) of the Children and Young Persons Act 1933 to assault or ill-treat a child in a manner likely to cause him unnecessary suffering or injury to health. The maximum penalty on conviction is ten years imprisonment....

In criminal proceedings for the assault of a child, the burden of proof is on the prosecution to satisfy the jury, beyond a reasonable doubt, *inter alia* that the assault did not constitute lawful punishment.

Parents or other persons *in loco parentis* are protected by the law if they administer punishment which is moderate and reasonable in the circumstances. The concept of "reasonableness" permits the courts to apply standards prevailing in contemporary society with regard to the physical punishment of children....

Physical assault is actionable as a form of trespass to the person, giving the aggrieved party the right to recovery of damages. In civil proceedings for assault, whilst the elements of the tort are the same as those of the criminal offence, the burden of proof of establishing that punishment was reasonable is on the defendant, on the balance of probabilities.

Proceedings before the Commission

A. applied to the Commission on 15 July 1994. He complained that the State had failed to protect him from ill-treatment by his stepfather, in violation of Articles 3 and/or 8 of the Convention; that he had been denied a remedy for these complaints in violation of Article 13; and that the domestic law on assault discriminated against children, in violation of Article 14 in conjunction with Articles 3 and 8....

The Commission declared the application admissible on 9 September 1996. In its report of 18 September 1997, it expressed the opinion that there had been a violation of Article 3; that it was not necessary to consider the complaint under Article 8; that there had been no violation of Article 13 and that it was not necessary to consider the complaint under Article 14 in conjunction with Articles 3 and 8. The full text of the Commission's opinion and of the two separate opinions contained in the report follows.

[Commission's] Opinion...

Article 3 of the Convention provides as follows: "No one shall be subjected to torture or to inhuman or degrading treatment or punishment."...The applicant's complaint under Article 3 of the Convention accordingly gives rise to two principal issues: whether the applicant was subjected to degrading treatment or punishment within the meaning of Article 3 and, if so, whether State responsibility attaches to the United Kingdom in respect of such treatment or punishment, with the consequence that there has been a violation of that Article in the present case....

In its *Costello-Roberts* judgment, the Court recalled that it had already held that corporal punishment may constitute an assault on a person's dignity and physical integrity as protected under Article 3. However, the Court also recalled that, in order for punishment to be "degrading" and in breach of Article 3, the humiliation or debasement involved must attain a particular level of severity and must in any event be other than that usual element of humiliation inherent in any punishment:

> The assessment of this minimum level of severity depends on all the circumstances of the case. Factors such as the nature and context of the punishment, the manner and method of its execution, its duration, its physical and mental effects and, in some instances, the sex, age and state of health of the victim must all be taken into account.

In the *Costello-Roberts* case itself, both the Commission and the Court found that the punishment of the 7-year-old applicant, which consisted of three smacks on the buttocks, through shorts, with a soft-soled shoe apparently causing no visible injury, did not attain the minimum level of severity to amount to a violation of Article 3. By contrast, in two cases involving corporal punishment in the school context, the Commission found that the punishment had attained the Article 3 threshold of severity. In the case of *Warwick*, App. 9471/81, Comm. Rep. 18.7.86, D.R. 60, p. 5, the Commission found that the administering of one stroke of the cane to the hand of a 16-year-old girl by a man, in the presence of another man, and which left physical injury the effects of which were visible for over a week, was "degrading...punishment" within the meaning of Article 3. In the case of *Y v. United Kingdom*, (A/247-A): (1994) 17 E.H.R.R. 238, Comm. Rep. 8.10.91, paras 44, 45, the Commission found that the caning—four times, on the buttocks through trousers—of a 15-year-old schoolboy, which left marks for some time, amounted to "degrading treatment and punishment" within the meaning of Article 3.

The Commission notes that the punishment to which the applicant, a 9-year-old boy, was subjected in the present case was considerably more severe in degree and in its effects than that in the *Costello-Roberts* case. It appears from the uncontested evidence before the criminal court that the applicant was beaten with a garden cane on two or, more probably, three occasions in the course of one week and that at least some of the strokes were inflicted directly onto the bare skin. As in the cases of *Warwick* and *Y*, the strokes were severe enough to leave bruises which, in the present case, were visible several days later. According to the doctor who examined the applicant, for a cane to cause bruising, it must be used with considerable force, particularly if it is administered over clothing.... The Commission further notes the applicant's own evidence at the trial to the effect that the beatings were frequent and "hurt a lot," particularly when he was beaten on the legs. The severity of the punishment to which the applicant was subjected is further borne out by the fact that, in contrast to the case of *Costello-Roberts*, the prosecuting authorities deemed the applicant's injuries to be sufficiently serious to merit the initiation of criminal proceedings against the applicant's stepfather.

The Government places emphasis on the fact that the caning of the applicant was not administered in school or by public authorities but in the applicant's home by his stepfather and thus lacked the element of "institutionalized violence" which the Court in its above mentioned *Tyrer* judgment regarded as an aggravating factor. While it is true that the punishment was administered privately at home, rather than in the institutional setting of a school, this fact cannot in the view of the Commission be determinative. As the Commission observed in its Report in the case of *Y*, the injuries inflicted on the applicant (in this case, a young boy) are unacceptable "whoever were to inflict the punishment, be it parent or teacher."

The Commission accordingly considers that, having regard to the circumstances of the present case, the corporal punishment inflicted on the applicant caused him significant physical injury, pain and humiliation which attained such a level of seriousness that it constituted degrading treatment or punishment within the meaning of Article 3 of the Convention.

The question remains whether the State may be held responsible for such treatment or punishment, administered as it was not by an agent of the State or by a teacher but by the applicant's stepfather.

The Commission observes in the first place that no direct responsibility can attach to the United Kingdom under the Convention for the acts of the applicant's stepfather. In this respect the position differs from that involving the use of corporal punishment by a teacher in school, whether a State or independent school. In concluding in the *Costello-Roberts* case that the direct responsibility of the United Kingdom was engaged under Article 3 of the Convention for the acts of the headmaster of a private school, the Court placed emphasis on three factors: (1) the State had an obligation to secure to children their right to education under Article 2 of Protocol No. 1, and functions relating to the internal administration of a school, such as discipline, could not be said to be merely ancillary to the educational process; (2) the fundamental right of everyone to education was a right guaranteed equally to pupils in State and independent schools, no distinction being made between the two; (3) a State could not absolve itself from responsibility by delegating its obligations to private bodies or individuals. These factors led the Court to conclude that

> ... [i]n the present case, which relates to the particular domain of school disci-
> pline, the treatment complained of, although it was the act of a headmaster of
> an independent school, is none the less such as may engage the responsibility
> of the United Kingdom under the Convention if it proves to be incompatible
> with Article 3 or Article 8 or both.

No similar reasoning can, in the view of the Commission, apply in a case where the acts complained of are those of a parent or step-parent. Moreover, no direct responsibility for the treatment in question can attach to the State by reason of the jury's acquittal of the applicant's stepfather. In this regard a distinction is to be drawn between a case where the verdict or decision of a jury directly infringes a Convention right[16] and a case such as the present where a substantive right in the Convention is violated by a private individual who is acquitted in criminal proceedings by the verdict of a jury.

The Commission recalls, however, that it has previously held that, even in the absence of any direct responsibility for the acts of a private individual under Article 3 of the Convention, State responsibility may nevertheless be engaged through the obligation imposed by Article 1 of the Convention "to secure ... the rights and freedoms defined in Section 1 of this Convention." In its Report in the *Costello-Roberts* case, the Commission recalled that it had held in its decision on admissibility that "the United Kingdom was responsible under the Convention, Articles 1, 3 and 8 of which having imposed a positive obligation on High Contracting Parties to ensure a legal system which provides adequate protection for children's physical and emotional integrity." ...

While, as noted above, the Court in its *Costello-Roberts* judgment preferred to found its decision as to State responsibility on the direct responsibility of the United Kingdom for the disciplinary system operating within schools, the Court, too, observed that it had

> ... [c]onsistently held that the responsibility of a State is engaged if a violation
> of one of the rights and freedoms defined in the Convention is the result of
> non-observance by that State of its obligation under Article 1 to secure those
> rights and freedoms in its domestic law to everyone within its jurisdiction. ...

The Commission observes at the outset that, while the choice of means designed to secure compliance with Convention rights in the sphere of the relations between individuals themselves is in principle a matter that falls within the Contracting States' margin of appreciation, the effective protection of vulnerable individuals such as children against treatment or punishment falling within Article 3 of the Convention requires the deterrent effect of the criminal law. ...

On the other hand, the obligation on the State under Article 1 of the Convention cannot be interpreted as requiring the State to guarantee through its legal system that inhuman or degrading treatment is never inflicted by one individual on another or that, if it is, the perpetrator will be subjected to criminal sanctions. In order that a State may be held responsible it must in the view of the Commission be shown that the domestic

---

16. As, for example, by an excessive award of damages: Tolstoy Miloslavsky v. United Kingdom (A/323): (1995) 20 E.H.R.R. 442.

legal system, and in particular the criminal law applicable in the circumstances of the case, fails to provide practical and effective protection of the rights guaranteed by Article 3.

In determining whether such protection is provided, the Commission attaches importance to the international recognition of the need for the protection against all forms of physical ill-treatment of children, who by reason of their age and vulnerability are not capable of protecting themselves. The Commission has had particular regard to the UN Convention on the Rights of the Child, setting out as it does general standards as to the protection of children and children's rights. The Commission notes that by Article 19 of the UN Convention, States are enjoined to take all appropriate measures "to protect the child from all forms of physical or mental violence, injury or abuse."

In the present case, as noted by the Commission in the *Costello-Roberts* case, English law provides certain criminal and civil law safeguards against assault. However, the protection afforded in this area by the law to children within the home is significantly reduced by the defence open to parents and those in loco parentis that the acts in question were lawful, as involving the reasonable and moderate physical punishment of the child. Moreover, the Commission notes that in criminal proceedings the burden lies on the prosecution to negative the defence, by satisfying a jury beyond reasonable doubt that the punishment was not in all the circumstances reasonable or moderate and not on the defendant to substantiate the reasonable and moderate value of the punishment applied.

The Government argues that, even in the absence of any express reference to Convention standards in domestic law, the criteria applied by the domestic courts in determining whether punishment is reasonable and moderate are very similar to those applied by the Convention organs in determining whether punishment is inhuman or degrading. In this regard, reliance is placed by the Government on examples of eight reported cases over a period of some 30 years, in which convictions for assault resulted from the use of excessive corporal punishment of children, as demonstrating the effectiveness of domestic law in protecting the rights of the child.

As to the former argument, the Commission is not convinced that there is any true correlation between the Convention test of punishment which is inhuman or degrading and the domestic law test of punishment which is not reasonable and moderate. In this connection, the Commission notes that, in its concluding observations of 15 February 1995 on the initial report of the United Kingdom, the UN Committee on the Rights of the Child expressed concern about the national legal provisions dealing with reasonable chastisement within the family, observing that the "imprecise nature of the expression of reasonable chastisement as contained in these legal provisions may pave the way for it to be interpreted in a subjective and arbitrary manner." In the specific context of the present case, the Commission observes that, while directing the jury that under English law it was for the prosecution to prove that the beating of the applicant was not lawful correction, little guidance was provided as to the meaning of "reasonable and moderate chastisement"; in particular, no specific guidance was given as to the relevance of the age or state of health of the applicant, the appropriateness of the instrument used, the frequency of the punishment, or the physical or mental suffering of the applicant or as to the relevance, if any, of the defence claim that the punishment of the applicant was "necessary" and "justified."

The Commission further regards it as significant that, following the Court's *Costello-Roberts* judgment, the Government introduced legislation to improve the protection of children at private schools against excessive use of corporal punishment by providing in terms that punishment "cannot be justified if the punishment was inhuman or degrading" and by laying down the circumstances to which regard is to be had in determining whether punishment is inhuman or degrading.

As to the Government's reliance on reported cases where convictions have been obtained in cases involving the physical punishment of children, the Commission accepts that, notwithstanding the domestic law defence of lawful correction, prosecutions have successfully resulted in convictions. However, the Commission does not consider that these cases afford any reliable basis for concluding that domestic law adequately protects the rights guaranteed by Article 3 in this area. In particular, the Commission notes that no information has been or can be provided as to the number of similar cases which resulted in acquittals or the number of cases in which the prosecuting authorities decided not to bring proceedings because the defence of lawful correction was likely to result in an acquittal.

The Commission, accordingly, finds that the domestic law failed to provide the applicant with adequate and effective protection against corporal punishment which was in the circumstances of the case degrading within the meaning of Article 3 of the Convention and that the applicant was a victim of treatment or punishment contrary to Article 3 of the Convention for which the United Kingdom must be held responsible. The Commission would emphasize that this finding does not mean that Article 3 is to be interpreted as imposing an obligation on States to protect, through their criminal law, against any form of physical rebuke, however mild, by a parent of a child.

Conclusion

The Commission concludes unanimously that in the present case there has been a violation of Article 3 of the Convention....

Loucaides, Mr., concurring.

I agree with the majority that there has been a violation of Article 3 of the Convention in this case. In so concluding, however, I did not find it necessary to examine, like the majority, whether or not in the circumstances of the present case the corporal punishment inflicted on the applicant caused him physical injury, pain or any other effect so as to decide whether the punishment attained "such a level of seriousness" that it constituted "inhuman or degrading treatment or punishment" within the meaning of Article 3 of the Convention. I continue to hold the view which I have expressed in the *Costello-Roberts* case....

> In principle...any school corporal punishment amounts to a breach of Article 3.... Corporal punishment is nothing less than a deliberate assault on a person's dignity and physical integrity.... Beating any person as a method of punishment for whatever wrongdoing on his part...is nowadays an unacceptable form of punishment and it amounts in my view to inhuman and degrading treatment. The number, intensity or hardness of the strokes or the fact that they do or do not cause physical injuries are, in my view, immaterial factors in determining whether corporal punishment amounts to inhuman and degrading treatment. The nature of such punishment in itself is a sufficiently severe blow to and degradation of the personality of the individual as to amount to such treatment....

Alkema, Mr., concurring.

I voted with the majority that Article 3 has been violated in the present case.... Yet, I would have preferred to consider the application under Article 8 and to have found a violation of that provision....*

It covers the right to respect for both privacy (including a person's physical and mental integrity) and family life. Violent events within the family as occurred in the present case, which might result *e.g.* in dismissal from parental authority, are matters that come in the case law of the Court and Commission usually under Article 8.

Moreover, Article 8 is not as absolute as Article 3. It thus, more naturally, allows for a balancing exercise for which in particular the second paragraph of Article 8 contains explicit criteria. Even in cases as the instant one where Article 8 implies a positive obligation for the State the second paragraph "may be of a certain relevance."

One such criterion is the legality of the rule applied, notably the precision and foreseeability of the rule as well as the extent to which it corresponds to the requirements of the Convention.

Furthermore, "the rights of others" might be in certain circumstances, for instance where the protection of other children of the family are concerned, a factor in this balancing exercise.

Finally, Article 8 offers the basis for testing the proportionality of legislation seeking to protect children against abuse. Therewith is connected the "margin of appreciation," a certain discretion for the State which is indispensable where the State's responsibility— as in the present case—is an indirect one. This is particularly so, where the State policy to offer adequate protection is materialized through a set of legislative rules penal and civil, which have to be implemented through the administration and the courts.

Judgment [of the European Court of Human Rights]

I. *Alleged Violation of Article 3 of the Convention*

The applicant asked the Court to find a violation of Article 3 of the Convention.... The Court recalls that ill-treatment must attain a minimum level of severity if it is to fall within the scope of Article 3. The assessment of this minimum is relative: it depends on all the circumstances of the case, such as the nature and context of the treatment, its duration, its physical and mental effects and, in some instances, the sex, age and state of health of the victim. *See* Costello-Roberts v. United Kingdom....

The Court recalls that the applicant, who was then nine years old, was found by the consultant pediatrician who examined him to have been beaten with a garden cane which had been applied with considerable force on more than one occasion.

The Court considers that treatment of this kind reaches the level of severity prohibited by Article 3.

It remains to be determined whether the State should be held responsible, under Article 3, for the beating of the applicant by his stepfather.

---

* Ed. Note: Article 8 of the Convention, so far as relevant, provides as follows:
  1. Everyone has the right to respect for his private and family life....
  2. There shall be no interference by a public authority with the exercise of this right except such as is in accordance with the law and is necessary in a democratic society...for the prevention of disorder or crime, for the protection of health or morals, or for the protection of the rights and freedoms of others.

The Court considers that the obligation on the High Contracting Parties under Article 1 of the Convention to secure to everyone within their jurisdiction the rights and freedoms defined in the Convention, taken together with Article 3, requires States to take measures designed to ensure that individuals within their jurisdiction are not subjected to torture or inhuman or degrading treatment or punishment, including such ill-treatment administered by private individuals. Children and other vulnerable individuals, in particular, are entitled to state protection, in the form of effective deterrence against such breaches of personal integrity.

The Court recalls that under English law it is a defence to a charge of assault on a child that the treatment in question amounted to "reasonable chastisement." The burden of proof is on the prosecution to establish beyond reasonable doubt that the assault went beyond the limits of lawful punishment. In the present case, despite the fact that the applicant had been subjected to treatment of sufficient severity to fall within the scope of Article 3, the jury acquitted his stepfather, who had administered the treatment.

In the Court's view, the law did not provide adequate protection to the applicant against treatment or punishment contrary to Article 3. Indeed, the Government [has] accepted that this law currently fails to provide adequate protection to children and should be amended.

In the circumstances of the present case, the failure to provide adequate protection constitutes a violation of Article 3 of the Convention....

In these circumstances it is not necessary to examine whether the inadequacy of the legal protection provided to A. against the ill-treatment that he suffered also breached his right to respect for private life under Article 8.

Notes and Questions

1. *Holding.* What is the exact holding of this case? Does the European Convention on Human Rights prohibit corporal punishment? The Commission seems to suggest that part of the problem with English law was the insufficient guidance given by the trial court to the jury on the issue of "reasonable and moderate chastisement." If a trial judge gives the guidance suggested, can the defense of reasonable and moderate chastisement still be used?

2. *Degrading and Inhuman Treatment.* The majority of the Commission holds a different view of corporal punishment than Mr. Loucaides, the former requiring a factual assessment of its severity and the latter believing all corporal punishment is inhuman and degrading. Who does the Court agree with? Why exactly was the caning by the stepfather degrading punishment? The Court stated in the *Tyrer* case, 2 Eur. H.R. Rep. 1, ¶ 30 (1978), and repeated in *A. v. United Kingdom*, that the assessment of whether punishment is degrading and in breach of article 3 "depends on all the circumstances of the case and, in particular, on the nature and context of the punishment itself and the manner and method of its execution." In *Tyrer*, the Court found that the birching of a 15-year-old youth over his bare posterior by the police authorities constituted an assault on the child's dignity and physical integrity to such a degree as to constitute degrading treatment, notwithstanding that he did not suffer any severe or long-lasting physical effects. If one had to summarize those factors that suggest corporal punishment is degrading or not, what would those factors be? According to the Commission in *A. v. United Kingdom*, one of the factors seems to be age. Would A.'s punishment have been acceptable if A. were younger or older? How does the age of the child affect the analysis?

3. *Relationship and Degradation.* Neither the Commission nor Mr. Loucaides thought that the relationship between the parent and child might make the punishment less degrading or inhuman. Do you agree? Notice that the person administering A.'s punishment was his step-father. Section 1(7) of the Children and Young Persons Act 1933 allows anyone who has "the lawful control or charge of a child" the "punishment defence." One commentator has suggested that the stepfather did not have parental responsibility, and the lawfulness of his standing to invoke the defense was debateable. However, this argument was not made. *See* Chris Barton, *A. v. United Kingdom. The Thirty Thousand Pound Caning—An 'English Vice' in Europe,* 11 Child & Fam. L.Q. 63, 65 (1999).

4. *Test the Limits.* Imagine that a fourteen-year-old child and his parents sign a statement at the beginning of the school year agreeing that the child will abide by the school's rules, and permitting corporal punishment if the child breaks the rules. Imagine further that the child is repeatedly bullying another child in violation of the school's rules. What is the outcome under the reasoning of the Commission as well as the reasoning of Mr. Loucaides?

5. *Effect of Law I.* What impact will *A. v. United Kingdom* have on parental behavior in England? The government conducted a poll that showed eighty-eight percent of parents in the U.K. find it "sometimes necessary to smack a naughty child." *See Protecting Children, Supporting Parents: A Consultation Document on the Physical Punishment of Children,* Annex A (2000) (citing 1998 Office for National Statistics survey). What impact would a similar decision issued by the United States Supreme Court have in the United States, where popular sentiment is similar? *See* Murray A. Straus, *Discipline and Deviance: Physical Punishment of Children and Violence and Other Crime in Adulthood,* 38 Soc. Probs. 133, 140 (1991) (citing national Opinion Research Center survey from 1986 that found "84 percent agreed or strongly agreed that 'it is sometimes necessary to discipline a child with a good, hard spanking'"). *See also* Barbara A. Wachope & Murray A. Straus, *Physical Punishment and Physical Abuse of American Children: Incidence Rates by Age, Gender and Occupational Class, in* Physical Violence in American Families: Risk Factors and Adaptations to Violence in 8,145 Families 133 (Murray A. Straus & Richard J. Gelles eds., 1990) (ninety-seven percent of American three year olds are subject to corporal punishment by their parents); Murray A. Straus & Denise A. Donnelly, *Corporal Punishment of Adolescents by American Parents,* 24 Youth & Soc'y 419, 425 (1993) (half of all American adolescents experience corporal punishment).

6. *Effect of Law II and the HRA 98.* After *A. v. United Kingdom,* the government of the United Kingdom was obligated to change its law to take account of the Court's judgment. The government committed itself to outlawing the "harmful and degrading treatment of children," although it also adamantly refused to prohibit all corporal punishment. The government stated, "There is a common sense distinction to be made between the sort of mild physical rebuke which occurs in families and which most loving parents consider acceptable, and the beating of children. The law needs to be clarified to make sure that it properly reflects this common sense distinction." *See Protecting Children, Supporting Parents: A Consultation Document on the Physical Punishment of Children* § 1.5 (2000). After soliciting public comment, the government ultimately decided that it did not need to change the law in the United Kingdom at all. It explained that the Human Rights Act 1998, which had come into force in October 2000, obligated courts in the United Kingdom to follow the European Court's ruling. The Human Rights Act of 1998 was designed to make the rights protected by the European Convention on Human Rights (ECHR) accessible to litigants in the United

Kingdom without having to bring a case before the European Court of Human Rights. For more information on the Human Rights Act 1998, see the notes after *L v. Finland* in Chapter 1.B.2.d.

In discussing the impact of the Human Rights Act 1998, the U.K. government felt confident that domestic courts would be able to assess whether physical punishment was reasonable chastisement or not in a manner consistent with the European Court's judgment. In particular, a court would have to direct a jury to consider the following factors: "The nature and context of the treatment; its duration; its physical and mental effects; and in some instances, the sex, age and state of health of the victim." *Protecting Children, Supporting Parents, supra,* § 5.3. *See also Analysis of Responses to "Protecting Children, Supporting Parents" Consultation Document* ¶ 76 (2001), *available at* http://www.doh.gov.uk/scg/pcspresponse/childproconsrep.pdf. Simply, the test to assess whether punishment was reasonable and moderate chastisement would now be the same as the test applied by the European Court to determine whether punishment is inhuman or degrading. In fact, courts in the United Kingdom are now applying the standard set forth in *A. v. United Kingdom* in criminal cases when the defense of reasonable chastisement is raised. *See* R. v. H., [2002] 1 Cr. App. R. 7, ¶ 35 (Eng.) (approving a jury instruction that reflected those factors that were set out in *A. v. United Kingdom*).

7. *Medical Opinion on Spanking.* Many professional organizations in the United States have now officially disapproved of corporal punishment. In 1991, the American Academy of Pediatrics spoke out against corporal punishment of children in school and urged all states to prohibit corporal punishment in schools. Committee on School Health, *Corporal Punishment in Schools,* 88 Pediatrics 173 (1991). It said, "corporal punishment may affect adversely a student's self-image and his or her school achievement, and that it may contribute to disruptive and violent student behavior. Alternative methods of behavioral management have been shown to be more effective than corporal punishment." *Id.* More recently, the American Academy of Pediatrics recommended that parents forego spanking as a method of discipline. American Academy of Pediatrics, *Guidance for Effective Discipline,* 101 Pediatrics 723 (1998). The limited effectiveness of spanking as well as the deleterious effects were noted. "The more children are spanked, the more anger they report as adults, the more likely they are to spank their own children, the more likely they are to approve of hitting a spouse, and the more marital conflict they experience as adults. Spanking has been associated with higher rates of physical aggression, more substance abuse, and increased risk of crime and violence when used with older children and adolescents." *Id.* (footnotes omitted). Provocatively, the Academy concluded, "A broader view of discipline needs to include the entire social structure. For example, cultures with children with relatively few behavior problems have been characterized by clear role definitions, clear expectations for the child's active work role in the family, very stable family constellations, and involvement of other community members in child care and supervision." *Id.*

8. *Children's Views.* Is it important how children view spanking? The American Academy of Pediatrics reports that children have a mixed response to the activity. Some children view spanking "as justified and symbolic of parental concern for them," although the children also "generally experience anger at the adult." *Id.* at 727 n.5. However, children usually "come to accept spanking as a parent's right at an early age, making changes in adult acceptance of spanking more difficult." *Id.* What if the child and the parent disagree about the appropriateness of spanking and the child is corporally punished for this "defiance" as well as the child's views on other issues? *See* ECHR, arts. 9 & 10.

9. *Children's Right to Participation.* In England, an organization of youngsters demonstrated to "Stop the Smacking" after the government published *Protecting Children, Supporting Parents* (2000), its consultation document in response to *A. v. United Kingdom.* One fourteen-year-old said the consultation document "was in very complicated language that children could not understand and they did not even bother talking to children about it." *See Children in Anti-smacking Protest,* BBC News, April 15, 2000, *available at* http://news6.thdo.bbc.co.uk/hi/english/uk/newsid%5F713000/713992.stm. Was the government's document, which sought to consult about the appropriate level of parental rights (and which ultimately rejected the possibility that all smacking should be unlawful), an independent violation of either the CRC or ECHR? *See generally* Chris Barton, *Physical Punishment of Children — The Consultation Document,* 30 Fam. L. 257 (2000).

10. *Procedural Protection.* Can you fashion an argument that articles 5 and 6 of the ECHR require that certain procedural protections precede the infliction of corporal punishment?

11. *Article 3 and Affirmative Duties.* Why was the United Kingdom liable for a breach of article 3? *See* ECHR, art. 1. The concept of state responsibility was extended even further recently in *Z v. United Kingdom,* 34 Eur. H.R. Rep. 3 (2002). In that case, five siblings, all severely neglected and mistreated by their parents, claimed that the Bedfordshire County Council breached article 3, among others, when it failed to take effective measures to protect them from abuse and neglect by their parents. The Commission, in finding a violation of article 3, held that the Convention imposed a positive obligation on the authorities to protect children who were at risk of inhuman and degrading treatment and who were incapable of protecting themselves. The Court also recognized "the difficult and sensitive decisions facing social services and the important countervailing principle of respecting and preserving family life," but concluded that "the present case…leaves no doubt as to the failure of the system to protect these child applicants from serious, long-term neglect and abuse." [2001] 2 FLR 612, ¶74. *Z v. United Kingdom* was the "first case in which the Convention has been held to impose a positive obligation on the state to take operational measures in order to protect children from abuse and neglect in the family." *See* Joanna Miles, *Case Commentary: Z and Others v. United Kingdom; TP and KM v. United Kingdom, Human Rights and Child Protection,* 13 Child & Fam. L.Q. 431, 435 (2001). For an excellent overview of the ECHR and child protection issues, *see* Dr. Ursula Kilkelly, *Child Protection and the European Convention on Human Rights,* 2 I.J.F.L. 12 (2000).

12. *Direct and Indirect Liability.* In *Costello-Roberts,* mentioned in *A. v. United Kingdom,* the United Kingdom was held directly responsible for the acts of the headmaster of a private school. Explain why the United Kingdom cannot be directly responsible in *A. v. United Kingdom.* As far as the United Kingdom's indirect liability is concerned, why did the criminal acquittal of the father in *A. v. United Kingdom* not protect the United Kingdom from indirect liability? Wasn't the existence of a criminal prosecution evidence of a legal system that provides protection for children's physical and emotional integrity? What weight does the Commission give to the fact that some people were convicted under the law? Do we even know why the stepfather was acquitted? Would the United Kingdom's position have been stronger had it emphasized that civil remedies were available for excessive corporal punishment? In *Ingraham v. Wright,* 430 U.S. 651 (1977), the U.S. Supreme Court found the civil remedy very important in its assessment of the type of process due to children who were subject to corporal punishment at school. Perhaps this type of argument would have been fairly weak in the context of *A. v. United King-*

dom, however, since England has "little history of compensation," even when the punishment constitutes "child abuse." *See* Barton, *A. v. United Kingdom, supra,* at 65 n.26.

13. *Article 3 versus Article 8.* Would article 8 have been a preferable article under which to find a violation? Mr. Alkina's concurring opinion suggests so. As Mr. Alkina explains, a "margin of appreciation" exists for article 8 and not article 3. The margin of appreciation is a concept developed by the European Court that signals "the Convention leaves the Contracting Parties an area of discretion." J.G. Merrills, The Development of International Law by the European Court of Human Rights 136 (1988). The author explains that the width of the margin varies significantly from right to right, but that generally "[t]he margin of appreciation is...a broad one if the applicant's position is such that some restriction of his rights would normally be expected." *Id.* at 144. Also, the margin of appreciation tends to be broad if the case involves "a controversial political, economic or social issue." *Id.* at 145. While the doctrine is often used to analyze restrictions on rights, it has also been used to help define the scope of the rights themselves. *Id.* at 150.

14. *U.N. Convention on the Rights of the Child.* What role did the CRC play in this case? Look at the full text of article 19 of the CRC. Could you argue that article 19 did not, in fact, require the conclusion drawn by the European Commission of Human Rights about the CRC? Were there provisions in the CRC that might have supported the government's position? If that is your opinion, consider the following the statement by two scholars that have studied the responses of the Committee on the Rights of the Child to States Parties' reports: "The Committee on the Rights of the Child has indicated that the Convention on the Rights of the Child requires a review of legislation to ensure that no level of violence to children is condoned. In particular, the Committee has emphasized that corporal punishment in the family, or in schools and other institutions, or in the penal system is incompatible with the Convention." *See* Rachel Hodgkin & Peter Newell, Implementation Handbook for the Convention on the Rights of the Child 242 (1998); *see generally* Susan H. Bitensky, *Spare the Rod, Embrace Human Rights: International Law's Mandate Against All Corporal Punishment of Children,* 21 Whittier L. Rev. 147, 153 (1999). Does *A. v. United Kingdom* give you new insight into the importance of States Parties' reports under the CRC and the Committee's monitoring process? What of the fact that the United Kingdom has ratified the CRC, but has not really incorporated it into U.K. law?

15. *Other International Instruments.* Are there other international instruments that suggest that corporal punishment may violate international human rights law? *See, e.g.,* Universal Declaration of Human Rights, arts. 1, 3; International Covenant on Civil and Political Rights, arts. 7, 9(1). For a discussion of these provisions, *see generally* Cynthia Price Cohen, *Freedom from Corporal Punishment: One of the Human Rights of Children,* N.Y.L. Sch. J. Hum. Rts. 95 (1984). What about the U.N. Convention Against Torture and Other Cruel, Inhuman or Degrading Treatments or Punishments? The United States typically enters reservations, understandings and declarations when it becomes party to a treaty that has the effect of saying ratification will not change existing U.S. laws and practices. *See* Louis Henkin, *U.S. Ratification of Human Rights Conventions: The Ghost of Senator Bricker,* 89 Am. J. Int'l L. 341, 341 (1995). For example, the United States entered a reservation to the U.N. Convention Against Torture that stated, "the United States considers itself bound by the obligation under article 16 to prevent 'cruel, inhuman or degrading treatment or punishment,' only insofar as the term 'cruel, inhuman or degrading treatment or punishment' means the cruel, unusual and inhumane treatment or punishment prohibited by the Fifth, Eighth, and/or Fourteenth Amendments to the Constitution of the United States." What effect does this reservation have on the legality of corporal pun-

ishment in the United States under CAT? Recall *Ingrahm v. Wright*, 430 U.S. 651 (1977). If the United States entered a similar reservation to the CRC when, and if, it ratified the Convention, what would be the legality of corporal punishment in the United States?

16. *Regional Systems I.* The text of the European Convention on Human Rights, drafted in 1950, has few provisions specifically geared toward children. Article 5(1)(d) and article 6(1) are the only provisions that explicitly address children. Consequently, children have often had to develop their specific claims out of broad or general language, *e.g.,* "inhuman or degrading treatment or punishment." Fortunately for children claimants, the European Court, and historically the Commission, have turned to the CRC for guidance in applying the ECHR. In contrast, the African Charter on the Rights and Welfare of the Child, drafted in 1990, specifically addresses corporal punishment. *See* arts. 11(5) & 20(1)(c). This Charter is contained in the Statutory Supplement. Is the standard in the African Charter on the Rights and Welfare of the Child different from the standard articulated in the ECHR, as interpreted by the European Court in *A. v. United Kingdom?*

17. *Regional Systems II.* The United States is a member of the Organization of American States (OAS). Individuals as well as member states can petition the Inter-American Commission on Human Rights in Washington, D.C. for violations of the American Declaration of the Rights and Duties of Man. The American Declaration of the Rights and Duties of Man is reproduced in the Statutory Supplement. Which articles of the Declaration would best support the argument against corporal punishment of children in the United States by public school officials or their parents? One author has suggested that *Ingraham v. Wright*, 430 U.S. 651 (1977), would be appropriate to challenge as a violation of the American Declaration, and that children's lawyers may have an ethical obligation to consider relief under this system. *See* Sanford J. Fox, *Beyond the American Legal System for the Protection of Children's Rights*, 31 Fam. L.Q. 237, 253 (1997). Would a challenge be successful if the Senate attached a federalism reservation to its ratification of the Charter of the OAS, which according to the Inter-American Court on Human Rights, makes the American Declaration legally binding on OAS members? The reservation states that none of the Charter's provisions "shall be considered as enlarging the powers of the Federal Government of the United States or limiting the powers of the several states of the Federal Union with respect to any matters recognized under the Constitution as being within the reserved powers of the several states." *See* Charter of the Organization of American States, Apr. 30, 1948, 2 O.S.T. 2394, 119 U.N.T.S. 3. Would a challenge be successful if the United States has consistently stated that it does not believe the American Declaration imposes legally binding obligations on members of the OAS? *See, e.g.,* Case 11.139 (Andrews v. United States), Inter-Am. C.H.R., ¶59, OEA/Ser.L/V/11.98doc.6rev (1998)(The United States government "categorically rejects…that the American Declaration…has acquired legally binding force for all OAS countries."). The American Convention on Human Rights also has provisions that might be relevant to the topic, *see, e.g.,* arts. 5(1), 11(1), but the United States is not a party to the American Convention on Human Rights.

18. *Children's Rights in Europe Generally.* Apart from the European Convention on Human Rights and the U.N. Convention on the Rights of the Child, which has been separately ratified by the fifteen European Union member states, there are a variety of other initiatives on behalf of children in the European Union. For example, the Treaty of Amsterdam (1997), which amended and simplified the then-existing treaties establishing the European communities, recognized children's issues, albeit in a limited fashion. *See, e.g.,* art. K(1) (directing that safety for citizens shall be achieved, inter alia, by preventing and combating offenses against children); art. 13 (prohibiting discrimination on the basis,

inter alia, of age). In addition, the European Charter of the Rights of the Child, Eur. Par. Ass., 31st Sess., Rec. No. 874 (1979), addresses a variety of issues affecting children, including child abuse, prostitution and pornography, child labor, social and medical protection, sports, and the child's right to a "legal voice" in cases of conflicts between parents. However, the Charter lacks a monitoring or implementing mechanism and mostly has symbolic value. The Parliamentary Assembly of the Council of Europe has also adopted Recommendation 1121 (1990) on the rights of children. Apart from calling on member states to sign and ratify a variety of then-existing legal instruments giving rights and protection to children, the recommendation suggests the study and assessment of how children might better exercise the rights granted, including better informing children of these rights. The European Convention on the Exercise of Children's Rights, Jan. 25, 1996, E.T.S. No. 160, stresses the children's need for procedural rights in judicial proceedings that impact them.

So far our attention has focused primarily on article 3 of the European Convention on Human Rights. Whether corporal punishment is cruel and degrading to the child is not the only issue that might arise under the ECHR in connection with the practice. There might also be questions about the parents' ability to have their own rights vindicated in this context, particularly when the punishment is not a violation of article 3. Imagine, for instance, parents who oppose all corporal punishment, but whose child is subject to it at school. A parent might claim that this situation violates his or her own rights. Article 2 of Protocol No. 1 to the ECHR states that governments must respect the right of parents to ensure that their children's education is in conformity with their religious and philosophical convictions. Those convictions might include the belief that corporal punishment is wrong. In addition, article 8 guarantees everyone the right to "respect for his private and family life." Does article 8 prohibit punishment by schools if a parent objects, even if that punishment is not inhuman or degrading under article 3? What if the parents are opposed to the corporal punishment on religious grounds? Is article 9 then implicated? The issue can arise also on facts that there are exactly the opposite. So, for example, can a state outlaw corporal punishment in all schools? Are parents' rights violated when they want a school to punish their child corporally, but the state forbids it? The next two cases address the importance of parental rights under the ECHR in the context of corporal punishment. The first case, *Campbell & Cosans v. United Kingdom*, 4 Eur. H.R. Rep. 293 (1982) (Eur. Ct. H. R.), involves parents who oppose corporal punishment. They raise a claim under article 2 of Protocol No. 1. As *A. v. United Kingdom, supra*, indicated, the European Court did not find a violation of article 3 in *Campbell & Cosans v. United Kingdom*.

Campbell & Cosans v. United Kingdom
4 Eur. H.R. Rep. 293 (1982) (Eur. Ct. H. R.)

Both Mrs. Campbell and Mrs. Cosans live in Scotland. Each of them had one child of compulsory school age at the time when she applied to the Commission. The applicants' complaints concern the use of corporal punishment as a disciplinary measure in the State schools in Scotland attended by their children. For both financial and practical reasons, the applicants had no realistic and acceptable alternative to sending their children to State schools....

At the time of Mrs. Campbell's application to the Commission (30 March 1976), her son Gordon, who was born on 3 July 1969, was attending St. Matthew's Roman

Catholic Primary School in Bishopbriggs which is situated in the Strathclyde Region Education Authority area.... The Strathclyde Regional Council had refused Mrs. Campbell's requests for a guarantee that Gordon would not be subjected to [corporal punishment]. He was, in fact, never so punished whilst at that school, where he remained until July 1979....

Mrs. Cosans's son Jeffrey, who was born on 31 May 1961, used to attend Beath Senior High School in Cowdenbeath which is situated in the Fife Region Education Authority area. On 23 September 1976, he was told to report to the Assistant Headmaster on the following day to receive corporal punishment for having tried to take a prohibited short cut through a cemetery on his way home from school. On his father's advice, Jeffrey duly reported, but refused to accept the punishment. On that account, he was immediately suspended from school until such time as he was willing to accept the punishment.

On 1 October 1976, Jeffrey's parents were officially informed of his suspension. On 18 October, they had an inconclusive meeting with the Senior Assistant Director of Education of the Fife Regional Council during which they repeated their disapproval of corporal punishment. On 14 January 1977, the day after a further meeting, that official informed Mr. and Mrs. Cosans by letter that he had decided to lift the suspension in view of the fact that their son's long absence from school constituted punishment enough; however, he added the condition that they should accept, inter alia, that "Jeffrey will obey the rules, regulations or disciplinary requirements of the school." However, Mr. and Mrs. Cosans stipulated that if their son were to be readmitted to the school, he should not receive corporal punishment for any incident while he was a pupil. The official replied that this constituted a refusal to accept the aforesaid condition. Accordingly, Jeffrey's suspension was not lifted and his parents were warned that they might be prosecuted for failure to ensure his attendance at school.... Jeffrey never returned to school after 24 September 1976. He ceased to be of compulsory school age on 31 May 1977, his sixteenth birthday....

Judgment

[Ed. Note: As to the article 3 claim, the Court held that "a mere threat of conduct prohibited by article 3 may itself be in conflict with that provision," but that the applicants' situation did not violate article 3.]

The Alleged Violation of the Second Sentence of Article 2 of Protocol No. 1

Article 2 of Protocol No. 1 reads as follows:

> No person shall be denied the right to education. In the exercise of any functions which it assumes in relation to education and to teaching, the State shall respect the right of parents to ensure such education and teaching in conformity with their own religious and philosophical convictions....

The Government maintained in the first place that functions relating to the internal administration of a school, such as discipline, were ancillary and were not functions in relation to "education" and to "teaching," within the meaning of Article 2, these terms denoting the provision of facilities and the imparting of information, respectively. The Court would point out that the education of children is the whole process whereby, in any society, adults endeavor to transmit their beliefs, culture and other values to the young, whereas teaching or instruction refers in particular to the transmission of knowledge and to intellectual development.

It appears to the Court somewhat artificial to attempt to separate off matters relating to internal administration as if all such matters fell outside the scope of Article 2. The use of corporal punishment may, in a sense, be said to belong to the internal administration of a school, but at the same time it is, when used, an integral part of the process whereby a school seeks to achieve the object for which it was established, including the development and moulding of the character and mental powers of its pupils. Moreover, as the Court pointed out in *Kjeldsen, Busk Madsen and Pedersen v. Denmark* (1976), 1 E.H.R.R. 711, para. 50, the second sentence of Article 2 is binding upon the contracting States in the exercise of "each and every" function that they undertake in the sphere of education and teaching, so that the fact that a given function may be considered to be ancillary is of no moment in this context.

The Government further argued that in Scotland the "functions" assumed by central or local government in the educational field did not extend to matters of discipline. It may be true that the day-to-day maintenance of discipline in the schools in question is left to the individual teacher; when he administers corporal punishment he is exercising not a power delegated to him by the State but a power vested in him by the Common Law by virtue of his status as a teacher, and the law in this respect can be changed only by Act of Parliament.... Nevertheless, in regard to education in Scotland, the State has assumed responsibility for formulating general policy...and the schools attended by the applicants' children were State schools. Discipline is an integral, even indispensable, part of any educational system, with the result that the functions assumed by the State in Scotland must be taken to extend to questions of discipline in general, even if not to its everyday maintenance. Indeed, this is confirmed by the fact that central and local authorities participated in the preparation of the Code of Practice and that the Government themselves are committed to a policy aimed at abolishing corporal punishment.

Thirdly, in the submission of the Government, the obligation to respect philosophical convictions arises only in relation to the content of, and mode of conveying, information and knowledge and not in relation to all aspects of school administration. As the Government pointed out, the *Kjeldsen, Busk Madsen and Pedersen* judgment states:

> The second sentence of Article 2 implies...that the State, in fulfilling the functions assumed by it in regard to education and teaching, must take care that information or knowledge included in the curriculum is conveyed in an objective, critical and pluralistic manner. The State is forbidden to pursue an aim of indoctrination that might be considered as not respecting parents' religious and philosophical convictions. That is the limit that must not be exceeded.

However, that case concerned the content of instruction, whereas the second sentence of Article 2 has a broader scope, as is shown by the generality of its wording. This was confirmed by the Court in the same judgment when it held that the said sentence is binding upon the contracting States in the exercise, inter alia, of the function "consisting of the organisation and financing of public education." And in the present case the functions assumed by the respondent State in this area extend to the supervision of the Scottish educational system in general, which must include questions of discipline.

The Government also contested the conclusion of the majority of the Commission that the applicants' views on the use of corporal punishment amounted to "philosophical convictions," arguing, inter alia, that the expression did not extend to opinions on internal school administration, such as discipline, and that, if the majority were correct, there was no reason why objections to other methods of discipline, or simply to discipline in general, should not also amount to "philosophical convictions."

In its ordinary meaning the word "convictions," taken on its own, is not synonymous with the words "opinions" and "ideas" such as are utilised in Article 10 of the Convention, which guarantees freedom of expression; it is more akin to the term "beliefs" (in the French text: "convictions") appearing in Article 9—which guarantees freedom of thought, conscience and religion—and denotes views that attain a certain level of cogency, seriousness, cohesion and importance.

As regards the adjective "philosophical," it is not capable of exhaustive definition and little assistance as to its precise significance is to be gleaned from the travaux préparatoires. The Commission pointed out that the word "philosophy" bears numerous meanings: it is used to allude to a fully-fledged system of thought or, rather loosely, to views on more or less trivial matters. The Court agrees with the Commission that neither of these two extremes can be adopted for the purposes of interpreting Article 2: the former would too narrowly restrict the scope of a right that is guaranteed to all parents and the latter might result in the inclusion of matters of insufficient weight or substance.

Having regard to the Convention as a whole, including Article 17, the expression "philosophical convictions" in the present context denotes, in the Court's opinion, such convictions as are worthy of respect in a "democratic society" and are not incompatible with human dignity; in addition, they must not conflict with the fundamental right of the child to education, the whole of Article 2 being dominated by its first sentence.

The applicants' views relate to a weighty and substantial aspect of human life and behaviour, namely the integrity of the person, the propriety or otherwise of the infliction of corporal punishment and the exclusion of the distress which the risk of such punishment entails. They are views which satisfy each of the various criteria listed above; it is this that distinguishes them from opinions that might be held on other methods of discipline or on discipline in general.

The Government pleaded, in the alternative, that the obligation to respect the applicants' convictions had been satisfied by the adoption of a policy of gradually eliminating corporal chastisement. They added that any other solution would be incompatible with the necessity of striking a balance between the opinions of supporters and opponents of this method of discipline and with the terms of the reservation of Article 2 made by the United Kingdom at the time of signing the Protocol, which reads:

> ...in view of certain provisions of the Education Acts in force in the United Kingdom, the principle affirmed in the second sentence of Article 2 is accepted by the United Kingdom only so far as it is compatible with the provision of efficient instruction and training, and the avoidance of unreasonable public expenditure.

The Court is unable to accept these submissions. (a) Whilst the adoption of the policy referred to clearly foreshadows a move in the direction of the position taken by the applicants, it does not amount to "respect" for their convictions. As is confirmed by the fact that, in the course of the drafting of Article 2, the words "have regard to" were replaced by the word "respect." The latter word means more than "acknowledge" or "take into account;" in addition to a primarily negative undertaking, it implies some positive obligation on the part of the State. This being so, the duty to respect parental convictions in this sphere cannot be overridden by the alleged necessity of striking a balance between the conflicting views involved, nor is the Government's policy to move gradually towards the abolition of corporal punishment in itself sufficient to comply with this duty.

(b) As regards the United Kingdom reservation, the Court notes that the provision of domestic law cited in the present case by the Government is section 29(1) of the Education (Scotland) Act 1962.* Under Article 64 of the Convention, a reservation in respect of any provision is permitted only to the extent that any law in force in a State's territory at the time when the reservation is made is not in conformity with the provision. The Protocol was signed on behalf of the United Kingdom on 20 March 1952. However, section 29(1) was no more than a re-enactment of an identical provision in the Education (Scotland) Act 1946 and therefore goes no further than a law in force at the time when the reservation was made.

The Court accepts that certain solutions canvassed—such as the establishment of a dual system whereby in each sector there would be separate schools for the children of parents objecting to corporal punishment—would be incompatible, especially in the present economic situation, with the avoidance of unreasonable public expenditure. However, the Court does not regard it as established that other means of respecting the applicants' convictions, such as a system of exemption for individual pupils in a particular school, would necessarily be incompatible with "the provision of efficient instruction and training, and the avoidance of unreasonable public expenditure."

Mrs. Campbell and Mrs. Cosans have accordingly been victims of a violation of the second sentence of Article 2 of Protocol No. 1.

The Alleged Violation of the First Sentence of Article 2 of Protocol No. 1

Mrs. Cosans alleged that, by reason of his suspension from school, her son Jeffrey had been denied the right to education, contrary to the first sentence of Article 2.... The Government['s] principal submission was that the right of access to educational facilities which is guaranteed by the first sentence may be made subject to reasonable requirements and that, since Jeffrey's suspension was due to his and his parents' refusal to accept such a requirement, there had been no breach....

The suspension of Jeffrey Cosans—which remained in force for nearly a whole school year—was motivated by his and his parents' refusal to accept that he receive or be liable to corporal chastisement. His return to school could have been secured only if his parents had acted contrary to their convictions, convictions which the United Kingdom is obliged to respect under the second sentence of Article 2 (see paras. 35–36 above). A condition of access to an educational establishment that conflicts in this way with another right enshrined in Protocol No. 1 cannot be described as reasonable and in any event falls outside the State's power of regulation under Article 2.

There has accordingly also been, as regards Jeffrey Cosans, [a] breach of the first sentence of that Article....

Partly Dissenting Opinion of Judge Sir Vincent Evans:

I agree that no violation of Article 3 of the Convention is established. In my opinion, however, the majority of the Court have given too wide an interpretation to Article 2 of Protocol No. 1....

---

* Ed. Note: Section 29(1) states: "[I]n the exercise and performance of their powers and duties under this Act, the Secretary of State and education authorities shall have regard to the general principle that, so far as is compatible with the provision of suitable instruction and training and the avoidance of unreasonable public expenditure, pupils are to be educated in accordance with the wishes of their parents."

In the previous two cases in which the application of Article 2 has been in issue, the Court has found it indispensable to have recourse to the negotiating history of the Article as an aid to the interpretation of what is undeniably a very difficult text. In the *Kjeldsen, Busk Madsen and Pedersen* case, the Court observed that the travaux préparatoires are "without doubt of particular consequence in the case of a clause that gave rise to such lengthy and impassioned discussions." In both the cases cited, the Court after recourse to the travaux, adopted, in respects relevant to the present case, a restrictive view of the aim of the second sentence of Article 2. In the *Kjeldsen, Busk Madsen and Pedersen* case (in which parents sought unsuccessfully to have their children exempted from sex education in State schools on the ground that it was contrary to their beliefs as Christian parents) this was that the State is forbidden to pursue an aim of indoctrination that might be considered as not respecting parents' religious and philosophical convictions. "That," said the Court, "is the limit that must not be exceeded" and consequently it was held that legislation which "in no way amount[ed] to an attempt at indoctrination aimed at advocating a specific kind of sexual behaviour" did not offend the applicants' religious and philosophical convictions to the extent forbidden by the second sentence of Article 2. In the *Belgian Linguistic* case, [(1968),1 E.H.R.R. 252]

> it was held that this provision did not require of States that they should, in the sphere of education and teaching, respect parents' linguistic preferences, but only their religious and philosophical convictions and that to interpret the terms "religious" and "philosophical" as covering linguistic preferences would amount to a distortion of their ordinary and usual meaning and read into the Convention something that was not there.

In the course of the preparatory work on Article 2 in the Consultative Assembly of the Council of Europe, the expression "philosophical convictions" was criticised as being so vague that it should not be inserted in a legal instrument purporting to protect human rights. But this very criticism evoked from Mr. Teitgen, the Rapporteur of the Consultative Assembly's Committee on Legal and Administrative Questions to which a draft of the Protocol had been referred for advice, a very emphatic explanation in the light of which the text of Article 2 was finally settled and the Protocol adopted and opened for signature. Mr. Teitgen made it clear that the intention was to protect the rights of parents against the use of educational institutions by the State for the ideological indoctrination of children. This was precisely the interpretation put upon the text by the Court in the *Kjeldsen, Busk Madsen and Pedersen* case. In the light of this background, my understanding of the second sentence of Article 2 is that it is concerned with the content of information and knowledge imparted to the child through education and teaching and the manner of imparting such information and knowledge and that the views of parents on such matters as the use of corporal punishment are as much outside the intended scope of the provision as are their linguistic preferences. If there had been any intention that it should apply to disciplinary measures, and to the use of corporal punishment in particular, it is inconceivable that the implications of this would not have been raised in the course of the lengthy debates that preceded its adoption.

An interpretation of the second sentence of Article 2 extending its application beyond its intended scope could give rise to very considerable difficulties in practice.... If the sentence in question is interpreted in a sense wide enough to cover the views of parents opposed to corporal punishment, I do not see how it can reasonably be applied so as to exclude from its scope all manner of other strongly held views regarding the way in which schools are organised and administered. There may be very strongly held beliefs on such matters as the segregation of sexes, the streaming of pupils according to ability or the existence of independent schools, which could be claimed to have a religious or philosophical basis. The view in favour of the abolition of independent schools, for example, could be regarded as a philosophical conviction on the part of those who believe in the ideology of egalitarianism. It would surely create problems which were never intended by the authors of the Protocol if different and inevitably conflicting opinions of this order had to be accommodated within the State's educational system. There is an important difference between the kind of convictions which it is my understanding that Article 2 was aimed to protect and views of the kind just mentioned. Different religious and philosophical convictions relating to the content of instruction can be duly respected in the teaching process by presenting information in an objective way. But in regard to such matters as the segregation of the sexes, streaming and the abolition of independent schools, there would be insuperable practical difficulties in respecting equally the views of those who are opposed to and those who favour one system or the other....

However, even if the wider interpretation of the second sentence of Article 2 adopted by the Court in the present case were correct, it would be my opinion that there has been no violation of this provision in view of the reservation made by the United Kingdom on signature of the Protocol.

In respect of the United Kingdom, Article 2 must be interpreted and applied as modified by the reservation. This means that the obligation thereunder to respect the right of parents has been assumed by the United Kingdom only so far as this can be done compatibly with the provision of efficient instruction and training and the avoidance of unreasonable public expenditure.

In the light of the interpretation put by them on the second sentence of Article 2, the majority of the Court have held that the Government's policy to move gradually towards the abolition of corporal punishment is not in itself sufficient to comply with their duty to respect parental convictions. It is implicit in the Court's judgment that some more positive means of respecting the applicants' convictions is called for by the sentence in question. If so, it is my view that the State is entitled to invoke its reservation unless it is shown that some other practical solution is available which is compatible with both the provision of efficient instruction and training and the avoidance of unreasonable public expenditure. In the course of the proceedings, only three possible solutions have been canvassed which, apart from the reservation, would sufficiently comply with the State's obligation as interpreted by the Court. These are—

> 1. that separate schools should be provided within the State educational system for children of parents who object to corporal punishment;
>
> 2. that separate classes within the same school should be provided for such children;
>
> 3. that a system should be established in which children in the same class should be treated differently according to the views and wishes of their parents.

The Court accepts that the first solution would be incompatible with the avoidance of unreasonable public expenditure, especially in the present economic situation. The second solution too would surely involve unreasonable expense and hardly be compatible with the provision of efficient instruction and training.... There remains the third possible solution referred to above.... It seems to me essential that any system of discipline in a school should be seen to be fair and capable of being fairly administered, otherwise a sense of injustice will be generated with harmful consequences both for the up-bringing of the individual and for harmonious relations within the group. It will also place the teacher in an impractical position to administer discipline fairly if children in the same class have to be treated differently according to the views of their parents. It has been pointed out that, where corporal punishment is used, exceptions are in any event made in respect of girls and children suffering from a disability. I believe that children will readily understand the reasons for this, but I think they are likely to regard it as arbitrary and unjust if Johnny is exempted simply because his Mum or Dad says so....

In these circumstances the reservation made by the United Kingdom to the second sentence of Article 2 applies. I conclude therefore that there has been no breach of the second sentence of Article 2.

There remains the question whether there has been a breach of the first sentence of Article 2 in the case of Jeffrey Cosans on account of his suspension from school.... [T]he right of access may be made subject to reasonable requirements, including acceptance of the rules, regulations and disciplinary requirements of the school. Since in my view, contrary to that of the majority of the Court, the disciplinary requirements which Jeffrey Cosans and his parents refused to accept did not violate the second sentence of Article 2, I do not find that there has been a breach of the first sentence of that Article.

X, Y and Z v. Sweden
5 Eur. H.R. Rep. 147 (1983) (Eur. Comm'n H.R.)

The applicants, three couples and one divorcee, are all resident in Sweden and have children aged between 20 months and 12 years. They all belong to a Protestant free church congregation in Stockholm. As such the applicants believe in 'traditional' means of bringing up their children and in particular, as an aspect of their religious doctrine, they believe in the necessity of physical punishment of their children, which they justify by reference to Biblical texts (e.g. Proverbs 13:12, Hebrews 12:6) and doctrinal works such as Luther's Large Catechism and Summa Theologiae Moralis (Mekkelbach)....

On 1 January 1979, however, the Swedish Parliament adopted a new second paragraph to Chapter 6, section 3 of the Code of Parenthood (Foraldrabalken) as a result of which section 3 now reads: "A custodian shall exercise the necessary supervision over the child with due regard to the child's age and other circumstances. The child shall not be subjected to corporal punishment or any other form of humiliating treatment."

Although the Code of Parenthood is not part of the Penal Code and its obligations are incomplete, in that no sanction attaches to their breach, the applicants contend that their rights and freedoms under the Convention have been and continue to be prejudiced both by the express terms and effect of the addition to Chapter 6, section 3 of the Code of Parenthood and also by the effect which it has had on the interpretation of the criminal law and in particular of Chapter 3, section 5 of the Penal Code.... * The appli-

---

* Ed. Note: Under Chapter 3 of the Swedish Penal Code, sections 5 and 6 (Brottsbalken) the offenses of assault and aggravated assault are respectively defined.
  Section 5 provides:
  A person who inflicts bodily injury, illness or pain upon another person, or renders him unconscious or otherwise similarly helpless, shall be sentenced for assault to imprisonment for at most two years or in cases where the offence is a petty one, to pay a fine.
  Section 6 provides:

cants maintain that ordinary chastisement has now become included within the scope of 'assault' as a criminal offence in Sweden and that parents no longer have a greater immunity from criminal sanction in imposing such ordinary chastisement on their children than they have if the same acts were committed on a stranger. They also maintain that slight forms of chastisement, although not criminally punishable, are breaches of the Code of Parenthood which might lead the applicants to lose custody of their children.... The applicants also anticipate that they will be faced with a dilemma in the education of their children, who will be taught at school to regard their parents' values as antisocial and criminal.... None of the applicants has been prosecuted under the present state of Swedish criminal law nor have any of them lost the custody of their children....

The applicants complain that the present state of Swedish criminal law and the amendment of the Code of Parenthood interfere with their right to respect for private and family life as guaranteed by Article 8 which provides:

(1) Everyone has the right to respect for his private and family life, his home and his correspondence.

(2) There shall be no interference by a public authority with the exercise of this right except such as is in accordance with the law and is necessary in a democratic society in the interests of national security, public safety or the economic well-being of the country, for the prevention of disorder or crime, for the protection of health or morals, or for the protection of the rights and freedoms of others....

The Commission will examine first the applicants' complaints relating to the Code of Parenthood and in particular to the second paragraph to Chapter 6, section 3 of the Code. In the applicants' submission this provision makes even slight forms of corporal chastisement illegal. They maintain that the existence and operation of this law constitutes an interference with their right to respect for family life as guaranteed by Article 8(1) of the Convention.

The Commission recalls its analysis of the scope of the concept of interference in its Report on Application No. 7525/76, *Dudgeon v. United Kingdom*, where it found:

In accordance with the Court's case law in the *Klass* case...an applicant may only complain of the actual effects of the law on him. If in reality it does not affect him at all, he cannot complain. Or its effects may be slight and not such as to interfere with his right to private life. When he complains of the existence of penal legislation, the question whether he runs any risk of prosecution will be relevant in assessing the existence, extent and nature of any actual effects on him. On the other hand, the mere fact that a penal law has not been enforced by means of criminal proceedings, or is unlikely to be so enforced, does not of itself negate the possibility that it has effects amounting to interference with private life. A primary purpose of any such law is to prevent the conduct it proscribes, by persuasion or deterrence. It also stigmatizes the conduct as unlawful and undesirable. These aspects must also be taken into consideration.

If the offence mentioned in section 5 is considered grave, the sentence shall be for aggravated assault to imprisonment for at least one and at most 10 years.

The Commission must examine the scope and operation of the Code of Parenthood on the basis of the parties' submissions in the light of these criteria. It notes first that the applicants do not contend that light corporal rebukes are breaches of the Swedish criminal law of assault. Nor have they established any instance of such behavior being regarded as "molestation" [under Chapter 4, section 7, of the Swedish Penal Code].

The present case does not therefore concern the operation of the criminal law. No question arises of a "risk of prosecution" as a result of the operation of the Code of Parenthood as it did in *Dudgeon.* The Commission must therefore consider the effects of the Code on the applicants' ability to express and implement their own convictions in the upbringing of their children, in the light of the background and aims of the Code.

The Commission notes first that Sweden is the only member-State of the Council of Europe which has introduced legislation prohibiting all corporal punishment of children by their parents including light corporal rebukes.

The Commission's evaluation of the Code's effect must start from the premise that parental rights and choices in the upbringing and education of their children are paramount as against the state. This is inherent in the terms of the guarantee of respect for family life contained in Article 8(1), since the upbringing of children is a central aspect of family life. The same principle is clearly reasserted in Article 2, First Protocol, the text and interpretation of which by the organs of the Convention leaves the primacy of the parental role in no doubt.

The applicants concede that the scope of permissible parental punishment of their children was uncertain before the amendment to the Code in question and the Government sought by this provision to discourage acts of violence against children by the imposition of the Code's general prohibition of corporal punishment of all kinds....

The Government...has stressed that it has no accompanying sanction and that it has neither directly, nor indirectly, affected the scope or interpretation of Swedish criminal law. For this reason it has not been able to provide the Commission with any concrete example of the operation of the Code or its interpretation and application by Swedish courts or authorities....

The exact practical effects of the provision about which the applicants complain remain obscure. The applicants have not been directly subjected to any enforcement or other procedure arising from their disagreement with the Code which might constitute an interference with their rights. Nor have they provided any examples of its interpretation or application by the Swedish authorities in other cases. They have further contended that the provisions of the Code may be relied upon in deciding questions as to the custody of children, but again they have not illustrated this submission and the Commission must therefore find from the facts before it that this has not actually occurred. Furthermore the information provided by the Swedish Government tends to confirm that this incomplete law is without any direct practical effect beyond that of attempting to encourage a reappraisal of the treatment of children....

On the facts as presented by the applicants it does not appear to the Commission that their original fears as to the nature of the amendment were justified. The Commission does not regard the effects of the amendment which are the subject of this application as constituting an interference which amounts to a lack of respect for the applicants' family life.

It follows that this complaint is manifestly ill-founded within the meaning of Article 27(2) of the Convention.

The applicants also allege that the scope of the criminal law of assault and molesting fails to respect their right to respect for private and family life as guaranteed by Article 8.

The Commission recognizes that, whilst the upbringing of children remains essentially a parental duty, encapsulated within the concept of family life, it is inevitable that certain aspects of criminal law will affect the relationship between parents and children to a greater or lesser degree. Hence the assault of children by their parents is treated as criminal and although the applicants have drawn attention to the wider prohibition of all corporal punishment of children contained in the Code of Parenthood, they concede that it is not every corporal rebuke which would infringe the Penal Code.

However, the applicants have not shown that the provisions of Swedish law criminalising the assault of children are unusual or in anyway draconian. The fact that no distinction is made between the treatment of children by their parents and the same treatment applied to an adult stranger cannot, in the Commission's opinion, constitute 'an interference' with respect for the applicants' private lives since the consequences of an assault are equated in both cases.

Nor does the mere fact that legislation or the state of the law intervenes to regulate something which pertains to family life constitute a breach of Article 8(1) of the Convention unless the intervention in question fails to respect the applicants' right to family life. The Commission finds that the scope of the Swedish law of assault and molestation is a normal measure for the control of violence and that its extension to apply to the ordinary physical chastisement of children by their parents is intended to protect potentially weak and vulnerable members of society.

The Commission therefore concludes that the state of Swedish criminal law does not interfere with their right to respect for private and family life within the meaning of Article 8(1) of the Convention. It follows that this aspect of their complaint is manifestly ill-founded within the meaning of Article 27(2) of the Convention....

The applicants further complain that the legal position in question fails to respect their right to freedom of religion as guaranteed by Article 9 of the Convention....

The Commission considers that on the facts of the application before it the same reasoning applies, mutatis mutandis, to the applicants' complaints under this Article as to those under Article 8. It follows that there has been no interference with the applicants' rights as guaranteed by Article 9....

The applicants further complain that the amendment of the Code of Parenthood is to be incorporated into the school curriculum in order, in their view, to spread the view as widely as possible and even amongst their own children, that the applicants' attitude to corporal punishment is outdated, wrong and reprehensible. They maintain that such an approach fails to respect the guarantee contained in the second sentence of Article 2, First Protocol, which provides: "In the exercise of any functions which it assumes in relation to education and to teaching, the State shall respect the right of parents to ensure such education and teaching in conformity with their own religious and philosophical convictions."

[T]he Government maintains that if this Article is applicable, the second sentence must be given a reasonable interpretation and may not be read to protect extraordinary or unusual elements of religious or philosophical doctrine which may conflict with the State's duties to protect children from harm.

[T]he Commission was faced with a similar argument on behalf of the United Kingdom Government in... *Campbell and Cosans v. United Kingdom*, 3 E.H.R.R. 531, concerning the use of corporal punishment in schools in the United Kingdom, where... it concluded that, in the light of the unequivocal terms of Article 1 of the Convention and Articles 2 and 5, First Protocol, "it is precisely in their capacity as individual parents that the applicants are entitled to claim the right to respect for their philosophical convictions and this irrespective of whether their claim may conflict with the standards generally accepted by other parents in respect of discipline."

It is true that those applications concerned the respect for philosophical convictions, but the Commission recognizes that the same criteria must equally apply to religious convictions.

However, as the European Court of Human Rights confirmed in its judgment in the *Kjeldsen, Busk Madsen and Pedersen* case, 1 E.H.R.R. 711, ¶ 53, the second sentence of Article 2, First Protocol does not prevent States from imparting through teaching or education, information or knowledge of a directly or indirectly religious or philosophical kind. Nor does it permit parents to object to aspects of teaching on these grounds unless the information or knowledge in question is not conveyed in an objective, critical and pluralistic manner. Thus: "the State is forbidden to pursue an aim of indoctrination that might be considered as not respecting parents' religious and philosophical convictions. That is the limit that must not be exceeded."

In the present case the applicants have not complained that their children have in fact been subjected to what they regard as indoctrination on the question of the propriety of corporal punishment. They have merely adverted to references in official publications that account should be taken of the amendment to the Code of Parenthood in the educational sphere.

The respondent Government has expressly referred to the underlying purpose of the amendment as an attempt to strengthen the rights of children and encourage respect for them as individuals and has stressed that this humanitarian objective is to be pursued by way of a general policy of education in its broadest sense.

Furthermore the Commission recalls that, in accordance with its *jurisprudence constante* and that of the Court, Article 2, First Protocol must be read as a whole with the Convention and especially in the light of the guarantees contained in Articles 8, 9 and 10.

In the present case the Commission has found that no interference with either Article 8 or 9 arises and concludes that the applicants, who have not adverted to more than policy statements of a general character, which could in no sense be described as an attempt by the respondent Government to implement a policy of indoctrination in Swedish schools, have failed to show that their right to respect for their religious convictions protected by Article 2, First Protocol has been violated by any concrete provision or practice.

It follows that this aspect of their complaint is manifestly ill-founded within the meaning of Article 27(2) of the Convention.

For these reasons the Commission declares the application inadmissible.

————————

Notes and Questions

1. *Parental Right to Educate One's Child.* Why were the parents' rights under article 2 of Protocol No. 1 infringed in *Campbell & Cosans v. United Kingdom*, but not in *X, Y and Z v. Sweden*?

2. *Pluralism and Parental Rights.* The Court in *Campbell & Cosans* and the Commission in *X, Y and Z v. Sweden* cited *Kjeldsen, Busk Madsen and Pedersen* for the proposition that valuing pluralism in education is an important part of article 2 of Protocol No. 1. Apparently, it is essential for the preservation of a "democratic society" that information or knowledge included in the curriculum be conveyed in an objective, critical and pluralistic manner. *See, e.g.,* Valsamis v. Greece, 24 Eur. H.R. Rep. 294 (1997) (Eur. Ct. H.R.). Some parents do not want their children to learn in an "objective, critical and pluralistic manner." Could the United Kingdom mandate that such an approach be implemented, even in private schools?

3. *Parental Rights to Stop Corporal Punishment in School.* How does the right of parents under article 2 of Protocol No. 1 or article 8 differ from parental rights in the United States? Consider *Baker v. Owen*, 395 F. Supp. 294 (M.D.N.C. 1975). In *Baker*, the United States District Court for the Middle District of North Carolina considered the claim of a mother who argued that the corporal punishment of her child by his teacher over her objections violated her constitutional right to determine the disciplinary methods for her child. The court concluded that while Fourteenth Amendment liberty "embraces the right of parents generally to control means of discipline of their children...[,] the state has a countervailing interest in the maintenance of order in the schools...sufficient to sustain the right of teachers and school officials to administer reasonable corporal punishment for disciplinary purposes." *Id.* at 296. The court rejected Mrs. Baker's argument that her right was "fundamental," and that a compelling state interest must be shown. *Id.* at 299.

For a U.S. decision in which parental rights were seen expansively when coupled with a free exercise of religious claim, *see* Wisconsin v. Yoder, 406 U.S. 205 (1972). In *Yoder*, the Supreme Court reversed the convictions of Amish parents who refused to send their children to school past the eighth grade. The Court held that the compulsory education laws violated the parents' Fourteenth Amendment liberty interest in raising their children coupled with their First Amendment interest in the free exercise of their religion. *Yoder* made clear, however, that philosophical beliefs would not get the same level of protection. It also made clear that its holding was limited to the convincing factual showing regarding the sincerity of their beliefs, the relationship of these beliefs to their way of life, the needs of their community for its continuation, and the hazards of the state law that "probably few other religious groups or sects could make." *Id.* at 235–36.

4. *Opt-Out Mechanisms.* In *Campbell & Cosans*, the Court and Judge Sir Vincent Evans disagree about whether an "opt-out mechanism" would be feasible. An opt-mechanism would permit certain children to be exempted from corporal punishment upon their parents' request on a case-by-case basis. The judges respective answers influence their opinions about whether the U.K.'s reservation to the Protocol excuses its violation of article 2 of Protocol No. 1. Similar concerns about the feasibility of particular solutions might suggest a narrow interpretation of the right itself (*e.g.*, States Parties might have a wide margin of appreciation). Should matters related to the school curriculum and functions be left to Member States' discretion given administerability concerns? Can the Commission or Court really assess the relative benefits of an opt-out or other mechanism?

5. *Narrowness of Article 2 in Protocol No. 1 and Article 9.* In *Valsamis v. Greece,* 24 Eur. H.R. Rep. 294 (1997) (Eur. Ct. H.R.), a girl and her parents, all Jehovah's Witnesses, alleged violations of article 2 of Protocol No. 1, articles 3 and 9 of the Convention, and article 13 of the Convention taken together with the aforementioned articles. The girl, age 12, was punished by her school for failing to participate in a school parade during the National Day celebration on October 28, commemorating the outbreak of war between Greece and fascist Italy on October 28, 1940. The school parade followed an official Mass and was held on the same day as a military parade. The applicants claimed that pacifism was a fundamental tenet of their religion and that their religion prohibited any conduct or practice associated with war or violence, even indirectly. The parents had specifically requested that the girl be exempt from national-holiday celebrations and public processions because it was contrary to their religious views.

The Commission and Court rejected most of the applicant's arguments. In evaluating the alleged violation of article 2 of Protocol No. 1, the Court concluded that it could "discern nothing, either in the purpose of the parade or in the arrangements for it, which could offend the applicants' pacifist convictions to an extent prohibited" by the Convention. "Such commemorations of national events serve, in their way, both pacifist objectives and the public interest. The presence of military representatives at some of the parades which take place in Greece on the day in question does not in itself alter the nature of the parades. Furthermore, the obligation on the pupil does not deprive her parents of their right to enlighten and advise their child, to exercise with regard to their child natural parental functions as educators, or to guide their children on a path in line with the parents' own religious or philosophical convictions." Because the Court held that the obligation to participate in the school parade did not offend the parents' religious convictions, it concluded that neither did it amount to an interference with the girl's right to freedom of religion under article 9.

A dissenting opinion suggested that the Court had to accept the applicants' perception of the symbolism of the school parade and its religious and philosophical connotations "unless it is obviously unfounded and unreasonable," which it was not. Who should decide if participation in the parade offends a person's religious or philosophical convictions? Is the factual question on which *X, Y and Z* turns of the same type?

6. *Freedom of Conscience.* The Commission and Court have protected Jehovah Witnesses' right under article 9 to proselytize and worship without state approval, but have not protected pacifistic activities inconsistent with a nation's laws. *Compare* Kokkinakis v. Greece, 17 Eur. H.R. Rep. 397 (1994) and Manoussakis v. Greece, 23 Eur. H.R. Rep. 387 (1996) *with* A. v. Switzerland, DR 38/219, and Arrowsmith v. U.K., 3 Eur. H.R. Rep. 218 (1981). *See generally* Luke Clements et al., European Human Rights: Taking A Case Under the Convention 187–89 (1999). The Commission's opinion in *Valsamis v. Greece,* discussed *supra* in note 5, expounded on the meaning of article 9:

> Article 9 protects primarily the sphere of personal beliefs and religious creeds: that is, the area which is sometimes called the forum internum. In addition, it protects acts which are intimately linked to these attitudes, such as acts of worship or devotion which are aspects of the practice of a religion or belief in a generally recognized form. However, the term "practice" as employed in Article 9 does not cover any act which is motivated or influenced by a religion or belief. In other words, Article 9 does not necessarily guarantee the right to behave in the public sphere in a manner dictated by a religion or a conviction.

24 Eur. H.R. Rep. 294, 307 (1997). Assume for a moment that Sweden started prosecuting parents for the infliction of mild corporal punishment and the applicants in *X, Y, and Z* were subject to prosecution. The applicants again contended that the laws on corporal punishment had more teeth and they did infringe on the applicants' beliefs and religious practices. Would it be permissible anyway, given the interpretations of article 9(2), to prohibit the corporal punishment of the applicants' children?

7. *Respect for Private and Family Life.* An article 8 claim was made by the parents in *X, Y and Z v. Sweden* and addressed by the Commission. The article 8 claim was not addressed by the Court in *A. v. United Kingdom.* Could the parents in *A. v. United Kingdom* have made a successful argument under article 8?

8. *Asymmetrical Parental Rights.* Are the different outcomes in *Campbell & Cosans* and *X, Y and Z v. Sweden* explainable, in part, by the different positions each set of parents took about corporal punishment itself? Before you dismiss such a suggestion, consider the recent case of *Williamson v. Sec'y of State for the Educ. & Employment,* [2002] E.L.R. 214 (Q.B. (Admin. Ct.)). In that case, teachers and parents challenged section 548 of the Education Act 1996, as amended by section 131 of the Schools Standards and Framework Act 1998. The law completely abolished the use of corporal punishment in independent schools. The law accomplished this result by removing the defense of justification (reasonable chastisement) for the teacher. Without the defense, the intentional infliction of physical harm would be unlawful.

The litigants claimed that the imposition of reasonable physical discipline by teachers is part and parcel of their Christian belief and that Christian schools in the independent sector were established to further this view of Christian education. They challenged the law after the Human Rights Act 1998 came into force in the U.K. The litigants based their claim on articles 8, 9, and 12 of the Convention, and article 2 of the First Protocol.

The trial court rejected the article 8 claim noting that "there is no denial of the parents' rights reasonably to chastise the child in the home." *Id.* ¶ 35. It felt "this Article is engaged only in the most indirect way," and refused to address the argument in any more detail. The court also said that article 12 "has absolutely no relevance to the issues in this case whatsoever." *Id.* ¶ 36. Article 12 addresses the right to marry and found a family.

The court then turned to the article 9 claim. It found that the parents were not asserting a religious belief or conviction nor was their position the practical manifestation of a belief or a practice in conformity with a religious conviction. That part of the trial court's opinion is produced here.

Williamson v. Sec'y of State for the Educ. & Employment
[2002] E.L.R. 214 (Eng. Q.B. (Admin. Ct.))

The high watermark of the Claimants case was the decision of the ECHR in *Campbell and Cosans v the U.K.,* 4 E.H.R.R. 293. In that case two Scottish parents alleged that the imposition of corporal punishment by a school against their wishes constituted a breach both of Article 2 of the First Protocol and also Article 3, which forbids the infliction of cruel and inhuman treatment. The Article 3 allegation failed but the challenge relating to Article 2 of Protocol Number One was upheld by the court....

Mr. Keith, for the Secretary of State, submits that the beliefs relied upon here do not meet these criteria [for assessing whether a view is a "philosophical conviction," as set forth in *Campbell and Cosans*]. They do not respect the integrity of the person, nor do they exclude distress. On the contrary, they create it. The Claimants submit that they fall precisely into the defined category. They allege that they are concerned with something more important than the physical integrity, namely the moral integrity of the child; that modest chastisement does not offend the child's dignity; and that any distress is justified by the objective.

There is some attraction in this argument, but ultimately I reject it. It is seeking to equate the non-administration of corporal punishment with its administration and to say that both constitute a philosophical or religious conviction. In my judgment, as the European Court of Human rights appears to have thought, the two cannot simply be equated in that way since the law is not neutral about the imposition of physical force. The law has always shown a respect for the physical integrity of the individual: any intentional assault is unlawful unless there is a defence of justification. Accordingly, it requires a stronger case to justify the right to inflict physical injury than to justify a right not to have it inflicted.

In my view this reflects a more deep seated distinction between the two positions. The belief that no corporal punishment should be imposed can properly be described as a philosophical or (in some cases) religious conviction. It is a belief that in principle no one should be so punished. By contrast, I do not consider that a belief that corporal punishment should be imposed can properly be so described. This has got nothing to do with the genuineness of the belief or its intrinsic merits. Rather it has to do with its nature or character. Nobody suggests that the corporal punishment should automatically be applied to all children as a matter of principle. For some children it may never be necessary. It is envisaged that it will be needed only for rare cases of relatively serious indiscipline. The parents wish it to be administered in such circumstances because they consider it to be a more efficacious method of securing appropriate discipline. I do not think that it is appropriate to describe a belief that one measure is more effective than another as a philosophical or religious conviction even if the reason for holding that belief is that it is supported by a religious text. It is not one of the articles of faith. It may be accurate to say that someone has a religious conviction that everything in the Bible is true, but it would surely be odd to describe, say, a belief in angels as a religious conviction or as itself constituting an article of religious faith. It is a belief which is in accordance with the religious faith, but it does not embody or define the belief or conviction itself.

Even if the parents believe that effective discipline cannot be secured in any other way, that still does not, in my judgment, convert the belief in its value as more than a belief—albeit genuinely and strongly held—as to its efficacy. Corporal punishment is not being invoked for its own sake but in order to help secure the religious convictions that underpin the Christian convictions of these families. Accordingly I do not accept that the belief in the desirability of corporal punishment, even although it is derived from the Christian convictions held by these parents, can properly be defined as a religious conviction in its own right....

Even if the Claimants cannot say that the desire to impose corporal punishment is...itself a religious belief or conviction within the meaning of Article 9 or Article 2 of the First Protocol, can it be described as the manifestation in practice of such a belief or conviction? It may be argued that practices may be in conformity with a conviction, or be a manifestation of a belief, even though it may be wrong to describe it as constituting a religious belief itself.

The Claimants have relied on two cases in particular in support of the proposition that there is an interference with the practice of their religion. In *Kokkinakis v Greece,* 17 E.H.R.R. 397, the applicant was a Jehovah's witness who was arrested for proselytizing when he entered the home of an orthodox Christian and sought to discuss religion with him. Under Greek law, proselytism was a criminal offence. Broadly this covered certain conduct amounting to a direct or indirect attempt to intrude on the religious beliefs of a person of a different religious persuasion with the aim of undermining those beliefs. The applicant had in fact been arrested on over sixty occasions. He successfully contended that the State had interfered with his Article 9 rights. The Court accepted that improper proselytism would not be protected under the Article but that true evangelism was....

In my view the decision in *Valsamis v Greece,* 24 E.H.R.R. 294, is of more relevance.... The parents alleged that their rights under Article 2 of the First Protocol had been infringed and the child['s] Article 9 rights had been breached....

In *Valsamis,* the court concluded that there had been no breach of either provision. The court noted that the child had been permitted to be exempted from religious education lessons and the Orthodox Mass. Moreover, it concluded that there was nothing either in the purpose of the parade or in the arrangements for it, which would offend the applicants' pacifists convictions to the extent rendered unlawful by Article 2 of the First Protocol.

For similar reasons the court also held that there had been no infringement of Article 9 in respect of the child.... The child had not been required to do anything which offended her religious convictions.

In my judgment, the parent Claimants are in a similar position to the parents in that case. The State does not fail to respect the right for the parents to have their children taught in an environment which will inculcate their Christian values. It does not require the children to do anything that is offensive to their religious beliefs, nor does it deny the school the right to impose a disciplinary regime to achieve that objective. It simply refuses the right of teachers to impose a particular sanction which the parents consider is necessary to secure that discipline. In my view the refusal to permit the sanction of corporal punishment cannot fairly be described as an act of indoctrination that fails to respect the parents' religious and philosophical convictions. The children are in no sense being indoctrinated; their beliefs remain untarnished. Even in relation to the imposition of corporal punishment itself, the children are not being indoctrinated in the sense that they are being told that it is wrong for it to be used.

In my view this case shows that not every interference to which religious objection can be made will amount to an infringement of the Convention. Moreover, I would not describe the imposition of corporal punishment as a manifestation of the belief within Article 9, nor as being a practice which is in conformity with a religious conviction within Article 2 of the First Protocol. I do not consider that all actions which are motivated by, or are in accordance with, a particular belief or conviction can be said to constitute a manifestation of it. In my judgment this conclusion is supported by the decision of the European Court of Human Rights in *Arrowsmith v UK,* 3 E.H.R.R. 218. In that case a pacifist distributed leaflets which sought to persuade soldiers to desert from the Army and to refuse to serve in Northern Ireland. She was arrested and charged with a criminal offence. The leaflets themselves were not advancing pacifist views and in the circumstances the court held they did not constitute a manifestation of belief within the meaning of Article 9. The action was motivated by, and consistent with, the pacifist belief, but it was not a manifestation of it. Similarly here: sending ones child to an environment in which corporal punishment is permitted for disciplinary misdemeanors is an action which is motivated by the belief but it is not in my judgment a manifestation of the belief itself. It is not the outward manifestation in observance or practice of the fundamental tenets of the religion such as will occur during religious services or even when seeking to convert others to one's beliefs. It is an action which, put at its highest, is designed to reinforce a respect for the religious values involved rather than being a manifestation of those values.

Accordingly, I do not consider that the Claimants' human rights are engaged in this case....

In December 2002, the Court of Appeal issued a decision in this case. *See* Williamson v. Sec'y of State for Educ. & Employment, 1 All E.R. 385 (Eng. C.A. 2003). All three judges felt the appeal should be dismissed. The three judges differed in their reasoning, however. Lord Justice Buton essentially agreed with the reasoning of the trial court, set forth above. Lord Justice Rix, however, did not agree with the trial court and stated, in dictum, that the appellants had established that their beliefs were religious convictions for purposes of article 2 of the First Protocol and article 9, *see* ¶ 154, that the parents were manifesting their beliefs for purposes of article 9, *see* ¶ 9, and that the parents' beliefs were entitled to respect under article 2 of the First Protocol, *see* ¶ 176. However, he believed the appeal should be dismissed because the parents were not materially affected by section 548 (this is called the doctrine of "non-interference") *See id.* ¶ 98. The parents could administer the punishment themselves at the school, and the schools sometimes asked the parents to do just that. *See id.* ¶ 154. Consequently, Lord Justice Rix never engaged in the balancing of the applicants' rights and the government's interests that he thought was required explicitly under article 9(2), and implicitly under article 2 of the First Protocol. *See id.* ¶¶ 175–75. Lady Justice Arden's opinion aligned with Lord Justice Rix's, but differed in several respects. Instead of explicitly relying on the doctrine of "non-interference," she integrated aspects of that doctrine into her analysis of article 9 and article 2 of the First Protocol. She agreed that parents were manifesting their beliefs for the purposes of article 9, but felt that their beliefs were not being infringed because their beliefs did not require that they send their children to school or have the punishment carried out by the teachers. *See id.* ¶ 294. She also believed that article 2 of the First Protocol was not violated since the parents could still administer the punishment in the schools themselves. Teachers' rights were not implicated because they could have no better rights than the parents. Of particular interest is Lady Justice Arden's express rejection that the child's rights were implicated in this case, although she acknowledged that the U.N. Convention on the Rights of the Child was not relied upon by the parties and played no part in the case. *Id.* ¶ 243.

---

9. *Just Satisfaction.* Mrs. Campbell, Mrs. Cosans, and her son Jeffrey again came before the European Court in 1991. *See* Campbell and Cosans v. United Kingdom, 13 Eur. H.R. Rep. 441 (1991) (Eur. Ct. H.R.). The litigation involved article 50 of the Convention (now article 41), which ensures "just satisfaction" for violations of the Convention. In its 1982 judgment in *Campbell & Cosans*, the Court reserved jurisdiction on the

question of just satisfaction in order to afford the parties an opportunity to reach a settlement, which never occurred.

Mrs. Campbell sought an undertaking from the Government that her children would not be subjected to any form of corporal punishment at schools within the United Kingdom's jurisdiction. The Court rejected the request: "The Court's judgments leave to the Contracting State concerned the choice of the means to be utilised in its domestic legal system for performance of its obligation under Article 53. The Court is therefore not empowered to direct the United Kingdom to give the undertaking sought." Here Strathclyde Regional Council had decided that with effect from August 1982 corporal punishment would be abolished in the area for which it was responsible. In addition, the U.K. government was actively considering the implications of the Court's 1982 judgment for the whole of the United Kingdom.

Typically, the Court, pursuant to article 41, orders governments to compensate their victims. Compensation can include both pecuniary and non-pecuniary loss as well as legal costs and expenses.

Jeffrey Cosans sought £25,000. He alleged that "his suspension from school had prevented him from taking certain examinations and from continuing study and training at further education establishments or night school, with the result that he was denied the opportunity of acquiring a skill for the future." Since the suspension, he had been unemployed, except during a short period. He claimed that the suspension also caused him considerable embarrassment at the time, and impacted his employment opportunities and prospects. The Government vigorously contested the relief sought.

The Court awarded satisfaction of £3,000. The Court thought Jeffrey suffered some non-pecuniary loss apart from the initial mental anxiety. "[H]e must have felt himself to be at a disadvantage as compared with others in his age-group. Furthermore, his failure to complete his schooling perforce deprived him of some opportunity to develop his intellectual potential." It also thought he suffered some pecuniary damage, although its calculation was problematical: "[E]ven had the suspension not occurred, Jeffrey's schooling would probably have led to no more than a limited qualification," and Jeffrey bore much of the blame for his unemployment. In addition, Jeffrey was entitled to unemployment social security benefits.

The mothers received only a portion of their claimed legal costs and expenses because the Court made deductions for the amount received from legal aid. Mrs. Cosans' claim for "moral damage," i.e., for mental suffering caused by her son's suspension, was rejected. The Court thought just satisfaction was provided by its finding that her rights were breached.

Problem 14-4

John, age 14, attends a public school. His parents vehemently believe that all people should be peace loving. The parents have told the school that under no circumstances should John be corporally punished. John gets into a fight, and the school disciplines him corporally without informing his parents. The discipline occurs in front of the classroom, with a 12-inch wooden ruler. John received three "licks" on his bottom. No marks were left. Has there been a violation of anyone's rights under the ECHR? Is the parents' claim stronger if their beliefs about corporal punishment are rooted in their religion?

2. South Africa

We come full circle now and look at the issue of corporal punishment in South Africa. This exploration allows us to think a little bit more about the constitutional protection afforded children in South Africa, and what it means in fact.

As background to the next case, a brief explanation of the recent history of corporal punishment in South Africa is warranted. Prior to the 1995 decision of *S v. Williams*, 1995 (7) BCLR 861 (CC) (S. Afr.), children who had been criminally convicted could be sentenced to corporal punishment. The use of a rod was not banned, it was regulated. The Criminal Procedure Act imposed various procedural protections, including limiting the strokes to no more than seven at any one time, requiring that the strokes be over clothed buttocks, and permitting that a parent or guardian be present. A doctor also had to certify that the juvenile "is in a fit state of health to undergo the whipping." Notwithstanding these protections, the South African Constitutional Court held in 1995, under the interim Constitution, that it was unconstitutional to sentence convicted juveniles to receive a "moderate correction" using a number of strokes from a light cane. This ruling eliminated a "common penalty in juvenile criminal cases in South Africa, with some 35,000 children being sentenced to this form of punishment annually before the ban imposed by the Constitutional Court took effect." Julia Sloth-Nielsen, *The Juvenile Justice Law Reform Process in South Africa: Can a Children's Rights Approach Carry the Day?*, 18 Quinnipiac L. Rev. 469, 473 (1999).

The Court rested its decision on sections 10 and 11(2) of the interim Constitution, and declined to address the arguments based on section 30 (the predecessor to section 28 in the Final Constitution). Section 10 stated: "Every person shall have the right to respect for and protection of his or her dignity." Section 11 of the Constitution dealt with "freedom and security of the person" and subsection 2 provided that "[n]o person shall be subject to torture of any kind, whether physical, mental or emotional, nor shall any person be subject to cruel, inhuman or degrading treatment or punishment."

The Court explained that "the wording of this section [11(2)] conforms to a large extent with most international human rights instruments. Generally, the right is guaranteed in absolute, non-derogable and unqualified terms; justification in those instances is not possible...." The Court rejected the argument that "age in itself was a redeeming feature; that while an adult whose character and personality has already been formed was likely to be hardened by the infliction of judicial whipping, the position was the opposite in the case of a juvenile." The Court stated:

> One would have thought that it is precisely because a juvenile is of a more impressionable and sensitive nature that he should be protected from experiences which may cause him to be coarsened and hardened. If the State, as role model par excellence, treats the weakest and the most vulnerable among us in a manner which diminishes rather than enhances their self-esteem and human dignity, the danger increases that their regard for a culture of decency and respect for the rights of others will be diminished....

The Court wanted to "join the mainstream of a world community that is progressively moving away from punishments that place undue emphasis on retribution and vengeance rather than on correction, prevention and the recognition of human rights." Using a purposive approach, the Court said, "It is regrettable, but undeniable, that since the middle 1980's our society has been subjected to an unprecedented wave of violence." It continued, "The process of political negotiations which resulted in the

Constitution were a rejection of violence. In this context, it cannot be doubted that the institutionalized use of violence by the State on juvenile offenders as authorized by section 294 of the Act is a cruel, inhuman and degrading punishment. The government has a particular responsibility to sustain and promote the values of the Constitution."

After finding a violation of section 11(2), the Court then evaluated whether the violation "constitutes a permissible limitation of the right in question." Using a proportionality test, and by "weighing up the individual's right which the State wishes to limit against the objective which the State seeks to achieve by such limitation," the court concluded that neither state justification was sufficient. The State had argued that it "made good practical sense to have juvenile whipping as a sentencing option... particularly in view of a shortage of resources and the infrastructure required for the implementation of other sentencing options for juveniles," and that "juvenile whipping was a deterrent." The Court admitted that conserving resources and deterring crime were legitimate goals, but ultimately felt that the gains were not "sufficiently significant to enable the State to override a right entrenched in the Constitution."

The government told the Court that "parents often asked for this punishment to be imposed." This fact did not matter to the Court: "[T]his consideration falls far short of the justification required to entitle the State to override the prohibition against the infliction of cruel, inhuman or degrading punishment. Its implications for the dignity of the individual are also far too serious."

The Abolition of Corporal Punishment Bill 1997, Act No. 33, was subsequently enacted and abolishes corporal punishment as an acceptable punishment to be imposed by courts of law, including courts of traditional leaders. The year before this act was passed, the South African Schools Act 84 of 1996 banned the use of corporal punishment in any school.

Christian Education South Africa v. Minister of Education

2000 (4) SA 757 (CC)

Sachs, J.

The central question in this matter is: when Parliament enacted a law to prohibit corporal punishment in schools, did it violate the rights of parents of children in independent schools who, in line with their religious convictions, had consented to its use?

The issue was triggered by the passage of the South African Schools Act (the Schools Act) in 1996.... The appellant, a voluntary association, is an umbrella body of 196 independent Christian schools in South Africa with a total of approximately 14 500 pupils. Its parent body was originally established in the USA "to promote evangelical Christian education" and the appellant has been operating in South Africa since 1983....

The appellant cited the following verses in the Bible as requiring its community members to use "corporal correction." *Proverbs 22:6:* "Train up a child in the way it should go and when he is old he will not depart from it." *Proverbs 22:15:* "Foolishness is bound in the heart of a child, but the rod of correction shall drive it far from him."

Proverbs 19:18: "Chasten thy son while there is hope and let not thy soul spare for his crying." *Proverbs 23:13 and 14:* "Do not withhold discipline from a child, if you punish with a rod he will not die. Punish him with a rod and save his soul from death." In support of its contention that parents have a divinely imposed responsibility for the training and upbringing of their children, the appellant cites *Deuteronomy* 6:4 to 7.... It has further claimed that according to the Christian faith, parents continue to comply with their biblical responsibility by delegating their authority to punish their children to the teachers....

While not doubting the sincerity of the appellant's beliefs, Liebenberg J in the High Court found that the scriptures relied on provided "guidelines" to parents on the use of the rod, but did not sanction the delegation of that authority to teachers. He held that the authority to delegate to teachers was derived from the common law and the approach adopted by the appellant was merely "to clothe rules of the common law in religious attire." He held that in the circumstances it had not been established that administering corporal punishment at schools formed part of religious belief. The judge, however, decided that as it was a test case he should consider the other arguments raised by the appellants. He assumed for the purposes of those arguments that administering corporal punishment at schools concerned a serious religious belief. He concluded that section 10 of the Schools Act did not constitute a substantial burden on religious freedom. He also held that corporal punishment in schools infringed the children's right to dignity and security of the person and was accordingly not protected by section 31 of the Constitution. He therefore dismissed the application.

The appellant applied for and was granted leave to appeal to this Court on the grounds that the blanket prohibition in section 10 of the Schools Act infringes the following provisions of the Constitution: "14. Privacy: Everyone has the right to privacy...."; "15. Freedom of religion, belief and opinion: (1) Everyone has the right to freedom of conscience, religion, thought, belief and opinion...."; "29. Education:...(3) Everyone has the right to establish and maintain, at their own expense, independent educational institutions...."; "30. Language and culture: Everyone has the right to use the language and to participate in the cultural life of their choice, but no one exercising these rights may do so in a manner inconsistent with any provision of the Bill of Rights."; "31. Cultural, religious and linguistic communities: (1) Persons belonging to a cultural, religious or linguistic community may not be denied the right, with other members of that community—(a) to enjoy their culture, practice their religion and use their language; and (b) to form, join and maintain cultural, religious and linguistic associations and other organs of civil society. (2) The rights in subsection (1) may not be exercised in a manner inconsistent with any provision of the Bill of Rights."...

It is clear...that a multiplicity of intersecting constitutional values and interests are involved in the present matter—some overlapping, some competing. The parents have a general interest in living their lives in a community setting according to their religious beliefs, and a more specific interest in directing the education of their children. The child, who is at the centre of the enquiry, is probably a believer, and a member of a family and a participant in a religious community that seeks to enjoy such freedom. Yet the same child is also an individual person who may find himself "at the other end of the stick," and as such be entitled to the protections of sections 10, 12 and 28. Then, the broad community has an interest in reducing violence wherever possible and protecting children from harm. The overlap and tension between the different clusters of rights reflect themselves in contradictory assessments of how the central constitutional value of dignity is implicated. On the one hand, the dignity of the parents may be negatively affected when the state tells them how to bring up and discipline their children and limits the manner in which they may express their religious beliefs. The child who has grown up in the particular faith may regard the punishment, although hurtful, as designed to strengthen his character. On the other hand, the child is being subjected to what an outsider might regard as the indignity of suffering a painful and humiliating hitting deliberately inflicted on him in an institutional setting. Indeed, it would be unusual if the child did not have ambivalent emotions. It is in this complex factual and psychological setting that the matter must be decided.

Sections 15 and 31 of the Constitution

The appellant's basic argument was that its rights of religious freedom as guaranteed by sections 15 and 31 had been infringed, and that those rights should be viewed cumulatively....

I will start with section 15 which deals with freedom of religion, belief and opinion....

[F]reedom of religion includes both the right to have a belief and the right to express such belief in practice.... [F]reedom of religion may be impaired by measures that coerce persons into acting or refraining from acting in a manner contrary to their beliefs.

The interim Constitution, like the ICCPR, did not distinguish between personal and communal religious observances and practices. The final Constitution, however, makes specific provision in section 31 for the practice of religion in community with others....

There are a number of other provisions designed to protect the rights of members of communities.... Taken together, they affirm the right of people to be who they are without being forced to subordinate themselves to the cultural and religious norms of others, and highlight the importance of individuals and communities being able to enjoy what has been called the "right to be different."...

It should be observed, further, that special care has been taken in the text expressly to acknowledge the supremacy of the Constitution and the Bill of Rights.... These explicit qualifications may be seen as serving a double purpose. The first is to prevent protected associational rights of members of communities from being used to "privatize" constitutionally offensive group practices and thereby immunize them from external legislative regulation or judicial control.... The second relates to oppressive features of internal relationships primarily within the communities concerned, where section 8, which regulates the horizontal application of the Bill of Rights, might be specially relevant.

This is clearly an area where interpretation should be prudently undertaken so that appropriate constitutional analysis can be developed over time in the light of the multitude of different situations that will arise.... For the purposes of this judgment, I shall adopt the approach most favourable to the appellant and assume without deciding that appellant's religious rights under sections 15 and 31(1) are both in issue. I shall also assume, again without deciding, that corporal punishment as practiced by the appellant's members is not "inconsistent with any provision of the Bill of Rights" as contemplated by section 31(2). I assume therefore that section 10 of the Schools Act limits the parents' religious rights both under section 31 and section 15. I shall consider, on these assumptions, whether section 10 of the Schools Act constitutes a reasonable and justifiable limitation of the parents' practice rights under section 15 and section 31.[4]...

---

4. If the limitation of the religious rights protected by sections 15 and 31 proves to be reasonable and justifiable, it is clear that any limitations of the rights to privacy (section 14) and the right to establish independent schools (section 29(3)) would also be justifiable.

Justification of the limitation of the right to religious freedom and religious community practice

(a) The test to be applied....

The appellant argued that once it succeeded in establishing that the Schools Act substantially impacted upon its sincerely held religious beliefs, the state was required to show a compelling state interest in order to justify its failure to provide an appropriate exemption.... The proposed formulation imports into our law a rigid "strict scrutiny" test taken from American jurisprudence, a test which I add, has been highly controversial in the United States.... In the context of freedom of religion, however, the test has been rejected by a majority opinion of the Supreme Court.[5]...

Our Bill of Rights, through its limitations clause, expressly contemplates the use of a nuanced and context-sensitive form of balancing. [The Court then set forth section 36, which is found at the beginning of this chapter.] [L]imitations on constitutional rights can pass constitutional muster only if the Court concludes that, considering the nature and importance of the right and the extent to which it is limited, such limitation is justified in relation to the purpose, importance and effect of the provision which results in this limitation, taking into account the availability of less restrictive means to achieve this purpose....

The underlying problem in any open and democratic society based on human dignity, equality and freedom in which conscientious and religious freedom has to be regarded with appropriate seriousness, is how far such democracy can and must go in allowing members of religious communities to define for themselves which laws they will obey and which not. Such a society can cohere only if all its participants accept that certain basic norms and standards are binding. Accordingly, believers cannot claim an automatic right to be exempted by their beliefs from the laws of the land. At the same time, the state should, wherever reasonably possible, seek to avoid putting believers to extremely painful and intensely burdensome choices of either being true to their faith or else respectful of the law.

(b) The nature of the rights and the scope of their limitation

There can be no doubt that the right to freedom of religion, belief and opinion in the open and democratic society contemplated by the Constitution is important. The right to believe or not to believe, and to act or not to act according to his or her beliefs or

---

5. In *Employment Division, Department of Human Resources of Oregon et al. v. Smith et al.*, 494 U.S. 872 (1990), Scalia J for the majority stated the court's approach as follows:

"[I]f prohibiting the exercise of religion... is not the object of the tax [law] but merely the incidental effect of a generally applicable and otherwise valid provision, the First Amendment has not been offended."(at 878)

He explained that this was because:

"[I]f 'compelling interest' really means what it says (and watering it down here would subvert its rigor in the other fields where it is applied), many laws will not meet the test. Any society adopting such a system would be courting anarchy.... Precisely because 'we are a cosmopolitan nation made up of people of almost every conceivable religious preference'... and precisely because we value and protect that religious divergence, we cannot afford the luxury of deeming *presumptively invalid*, as applied to the religious objector, every regulation of conduct that does not protect an interest of the highest order. The rule respondents favor [sic] would open the prospect of constitutionally required religious exemptions from civic obligations of almost every conceivable kind...." (at 888) (emphasis in the original)....

non-beliefs, is one of the key ingredients of any person's dignity. Yet freedom of religion goes beyond protecting the inviolability of the individual conscience. For many believers, their relationship with God or creation is central to all their activities....

As far as the members of the appellant are concerned, what is at stake is not merely a question of convenience or comfort, but an intensely held sense about what constitutes the good and proper life and their place in creation.... The impact of section 10 of the Schools Act on their religious and parental practices is, in their view, far from trivial.

Yet, while they may no longer authorize teachers to apply corporal punishment in their name pursuant to their beliefs, parents are not being deprived by the Schools Act of their general right and capacity to bring up their children according to their Christian beliefs. The effect of the Schools Act is limited merely to preventing them from empowering the schools to administer corporal punishment.

(c) The purpose, importance and effect of the limitation, and the availability of less restrictive means

The respondent has established that the prohibition of corporal punishment is part and parcel of a national programme to transform the education system to bring it into line with the letter and spirit of the Constitution. The creation of uniform norms and standards for all schools, whether public or independent, is crucial for educational development. A coherent and principled system of discipline is integral to such development.

The state is further under a constitutional duty to take steps to help diminish the amount of public and private violence in society generally and to protect all people and especially children from maltreatment, abuse or degradation. More specifically, by ratifying the United Nations Convention on the Rights of the Child, it undertook to take all appropriate measures to protect the child from violence, injury or abuse.[9] The Declaration on the Elimination of All Forms of Intolerance and of Discrimination Based on Religion or Belief declares in article 5(5) that: "Practices of a religion or belief in which a child is brought up must not be injurious to his physical or mental health or to his full development...."

Courts throughout the world have shown special solicitude for protecting children from what they have regarded as the potentially injurious consequences of their parents' religious practices. It is now widely accepted that in every matter concerning the child, the child's best interests must be of paramount importance.... The principle is not excluded in cases where the religious rights of the parent are involved. As L'Heureux-Dube J pointed out in the Canadian case of *P v S* [108 D.L.R. (4th) 287 at 317]:

> "[I]n ruling on a child's best interests, a court is not putting religion on trial nor its exercise by a parent for himself or herself, but is merely examining the way in which the exercise of a given religion by a parent throughout his or her right to access affects the child's best interests.

> I am of the view, finally, that there would be no infringement of the freedom of religion provided for in s. 2(*a*) were the Charter to apply to such orders when they are made in the child's best interests. As the court has reiterated many times, freedom of religion, like any freedom, is not absolute. It is inherently limited by the rights and freedoms of others. Whereas parents are free to

---

9. Especially articles 4, 19 and 34....

choose and practice the religion of their choice, such activities can and must be restricted when they are against the child's best interests, without thereby infringing the parents' freedom of religion."

In [a] similar vein Rutledge J of the US Supreme Court stated in *Prince v Massachusetts*:

"And neither rights of religion nor rights of parenthood are beyond limitation. Acting to guard the general interest in youth's well being, the state as *parens patriae* may restrict the parent's control by requiring school attendance, regulating or prohibiting the child's labor [sic] and in many other ways. Its authority is not nullified merely because the parent grounds his claim to control the child's course of conduct on religion or conscience. Thus, he cannot claim freedom from compulsory vaccination for the child more than for himself on religious grounds. The right to practice religion freely does not include liberty to expose the community or the child to communicable disease or the latter to ill health or death ... [T]he state has a wide range of power for limiting parental freedom and authority in things affecting the child's welfare; and that this includes, to some extent, matters of conscience and religious conviction.... The state's authority over children's activities is broader than over like actions of adults. This is peculiarly true of public activities...."

[T]he state has an interest in protecting pupils from degradation and indignity. The respondent contended that the trend in Europe and neighboring African countries was firmly in the direction of abolition of corporal punishment, and that the core value of human dignity in our Bill of Rights did not countenance the use of physical force to achieve scholarly correction. Accordingly, respondent was under an obligation to prohibit such punishment, and to do so without exception and for the benefit of all children. The appellant replied that for believers, including the children involved, the indignity and degradation lay not in the punishment, but in the defiance of the scriptures represented by leaving the misdeeds unpunished; subjectively, for those who shared the religious outlook of the community, no indignity at all was involved. It argued further that internationally there was widespread judicial support for the view that physical punishment only became degrading when it passed a certain degree of severity. Appellant would be bound by limits set by the common law, and these limits would establish the standards to be applied. It did not contend that corporal punishment should be permitted in all schools, but asserted that its use should be allowed within reasonable limits in independent schools where parents, out of their religious convictions, had authorized it. The state interest, accordingly, did not extend to protecting the children in the appellant's schools.

The issue of whether corporal punishment in schools is in itself degrading was touched upon but not decided by this Court in *S v Williams and Others*.... [T]he trend in southern Africa has been strongly in favor of regarding corporal punishment in schools as in itself violatory of the dignity of the child. At the same time, ... the issue is subject to controversy, and in particular, that the express delegation of consent by the parents might have a bearing on the extent of the state interest. Section 12 of the Constitution now adds to the rights protected by the interim Constitution the following provisions: "(1) Everyone has the right to freedom and security of the person, which includes the right — .... (c) to be free from all forms of violence whether from public or private sources.... (2) Everyone has the right to bodily and psychological integrity, which includes the right — .... (b) to security in and control over their body...."

It should be noted that these rights to be violence-free are additional to and not substitutes for the right not to be punished in a cruel, inhuman or degrading way. Under section 7(2) the state is obliged to "respect, protect, promote and fulfil" these rights. It must accordingly take appropriate steps to reduce violence in public and private life. Coupled with its special duty towards children, this obligation represents a powerful requirement on the state to act.

The present matter does not oblige us to decide whether corporal correction by parents in the home, if moderately applied, would amount to a form of violence from a private source. Whether or not the common law has to be developed[15] so as further to regulate or even prohibit caning in the home, is not an issue before us.

We cannot, however, forget that, on the facts as supplied by the appellant, corporal punishment administered by a teacher in the institutional environment of a school is quite different from corporal punishment in the home environment.... Such conduct happens not in the intimate and spontaneous atmosphere of the home, but in the detached and institutional environment of the school. Equally, it is not possible to ignore either our painful past history when the claims of protesting youth were met with force rather than reason, or the extent of traumatic child abuse practiced in our society today.... [S]uch broad considerations taken from past and present are highly relevant to the degree of legitimate concern that the state may have in an area loaded with social pain. They also indicate the real difficulties the state may have when asked to make exemptions even for the most honorable of persons.

Proportionality analysis

The measure was part and parcel of a legislative scheme designed to establish uniform educational standards for the country. Educational systems of a racist and grossly unequal character and operating according to a multiplicity of norms in a variety of fragmented institutions, had to be integrated into one broad educational dispensation. Parliament wished to make a radical break with an authoritarian past. As part of its pedagogical mission, the Department sought to introduce new principles of learning in terms of which problems were solved through reason rather than force. In order to put the child at the centre of the school and to protect the learner from physical and emotional abuse, the legislature prescribed a blanket ban on corporal punishment. In its judgement, which was directly influenced by its constitutional obligations, general prohibition rather than supervised regulation of the practice was required. The ban was part of a comprehensive process of eliminating state-sanctioned use of physical force as a method of punishment. The outlawing of physical punishment in the school accordingly represented more than a pragmatic attempt to deal with disciplinary problems in a new way. It had a principled and symbolic function, manifestly intended to promote respect for the dignity and physical and emotional integrity of all children.... Even a few examples of authorized corporal punishment in an institution functioning in the public sphere would do more than simply inconvenience the state or put it to extra expense. The whole symbolic, moral and pedagogical purpose of the measure would be disturbed, and the state's compliance with its duty to protect people from violence would be undermined. There is a further factor of considerable practical importance. It relates to the difficulty of monitoring the administration of corporal punishment. It will inevitably be administered with different force at different institutions or by different teachers, and there is always the possibility that it will be excessive. Children are put in a very vulnerable situation because they (and their parents possibly) can only complain about excessive punishment at the risk of angering the school or the community.

---

15. Under section 8(3) of the Constitution.

I do not wish to be understood as underestimating in any way the very special meaning that corporal correction in school has for the self-definition and ethos of the religious community in question. Yet their schools of necessity function in the public domain so as to prepare their learners for life in the broader society. Just as it is not unduly burdensome to oblige them to accommodate themselves as schools to secular norms regarding health and safety, payment of rates and taxes, planning permissions and fair labor practices, and just as they are obliged to respect national examination standards, so is it not unreasonable to expect them to make suitable adaptations to non-discriminatory laws that impact on their codes of discipline. The parents are not being obliged to make an absolute and strenuous choice between obeying a law of the land or following their conscience. They can do both simultaneously. What they are prevented from doing is to authorize teachers, acting in their name and on school premises, to fulfill what they regard as their conscientious and biblically-ordained responsibilities for the guidance of their children. Similarly, save for this one aspect, the appellant's schools are not prevented from maintaining their specific Christian ethos.

Postscript: The Voice of the Child

There is one further observation to be made. We have not had the assistance of a *curator ad litem* to represent the interests of the children. It was accepted in the High Court that it was not necessary to appoint such a curator because the state would represent the interests of the child. This was unfortunate. The children concerned were from a highly conscientised community and many would have been in their late teens and capable of articulate expression. Although both the state and the parents were in a position to speak on their behalf, neither was able to speak in their name. A curator could have made sensitive enquiries so as to enable their voice or voices to be heard. Their actual experiences and opinions would not necessarily have been decisive, but they would have enriched the dialogue, and the factual and experiential foundations for the balancing exercise in this difficult matter would have been more secure.

Notes and Questions

1. *The Importance of Section 28.* Was section 28 of the South Africa Constitution relied upon by Justice Sachs? How significant was section 28 to the Court's resolution of the issue? The High Court believed that the South African Schools Act did no more than give effect to section 28(1)(d). Christian Educ. South Africa v. Minister of Educ., 1999 (9) BCLR 951 (SE).

2. *Parents' Use of Corporal Punishment.* Would a law that went further than Sweden's survive a constitutional challenge in South Africa? Imagine the new law prohibits all corporal punishment of children by parents and imposes a criminal penalty for any use of corporal punishment.

3. *Children's Voices.* Justice Sachs mentioned that no one was before the court representing the interests of the children. What difference might children's voices have made given the outcome? *See generally* Lourens du Plessis, *Freedom of or Freedom from Religion? An Overview of Issues Pertinent to the Constitutional Protection of Religious Rights & Freedoms in "The New South Africa,"* 2001 BYU L. Rev. 439, 455 (2001). For a discussion of children's free exercise claims in the United States, see Note, *Children as Believers: Minors' Free Exercise Rights and the Psychology of Religious Development,* 115 Harv. L. Rev. 2205 (2002).

4. *Religion and Corporal Punishment.* Religious affiliation is the strongest predictor of whether a parent will use corporal punishment. *See* Michael Frankline & Marian Hetherly, *How Fundamentalism Affects Society*, The Humanist, Sept.–Oct. 1997, at 25, 26 (citing studies). *See also* Christopher G. Ellison, *Conservative Protestantism and the Corporal Punishment of Children: Clarifying the Issues*, 35 J. Sci. Study of Religion 1 (1996) (reviewing studies and acknowledging that conservative Protestants are disproportionately likely to endorse and use corporal punishment); Henry Danso et al., *The Role of Parental Religious Fundamentalism and Right-Wing Authoritarianism in Child-Rearing Goals and Practices*, 36 J. Sci. Study of Religion 496, 502, 506 (1997) (citing studies establishing a "chain of influence" between "religious fundamentalism," a desire to socialize children to accept parent's religious faith, the greater valuation of obedience, and a greater reliance on corporal punishment to obtain obedience).

5. *Reform in the United States. S. v. Williams* reported on the status of whipping as a criminal punishment in the United States: "In 1790 Congress excluded whipping from the punishments that might be imposed by the Federal Courts for federal offenses. It, however, continued to be applied in some states as a method of enforcing discipline in prisons and against juveniles in institutions and reformatories. Only the State of Delaware still retains the 'whipping post.'" S. v. Williams, 1995 (7) BCLR 861 n.55 (CC) (S. Afr.). As mentioned above, many states in the United States have now prohibited the use of corporal punishment in public school. Do you see further restrictions on the use of corporal punishment being adopted in the United States? Will international law or comparative law make a difference at home?

The United States is a party to the ICCPR and CAT. Do either of these treaties help domestic opponents of corporal punishment? The United States has entered declarations and reservations to both treaties. Of particular relevance is that the United States entered a reservation to CAT that states, "[T]he United States considers itself bound by the obligation under article 16 to prevent 'cruel, inhuman or degrading treatment or punishment,' only insofar as the term 'cruel, inhuman or degrading treatment or punishment' means the cruel, unusual and inhumane treatment or punishment prohibited by the Fifth, Eighth, and/or Fourteenth Amendments to the Constitution of the United States." *See* U.S. Reservations, Declarations and Understandings, Convention Against Torture and Other Cruel, Inhuman or Degrading Treatment or Punishment, 136 Cong. Rec. S17486-92 (daily ed., Oct. 27, 1990). The United States entered the same reservation to ICCPR. *See* U.S. Reservations, Declarations and Understandings, International Covenant on Civil and Political Rights, 138 Cong. Rec. S4781-01 (daily ed., Ap. 2, 1992). The United States also submitted federalism understandings to both treaties: "That the United States understands that this Covenant shall be implemented by the Federal Government to the extent that it exercises legislative and judicial jurisdiction over the matters covered therein, and otherwise by the state and local governments...." Finally, the United States attached declarations to both treaties indicating that neither of the treaties were self-executing.

6. *Children's Rights in Opposition to the State and Parents.* So far, children's rights have been explored primarily in the context of the children's rights vis-à-vis their parents' rights or vis-à-vis the state's authority. Either the parental interest was aligned with the child's interest against the state (*e.g., Government of the Republic of South Africa v. Grootboom*) or the state and the child's interest were aligned against the parent (*e.g., A. v. United Kingdom*). What would happen if the child's interest were not aligned with either the state or the parents? This sort of conflict can arise when children assert their own right to the free exercise of religion or freedom of speech. *See, e.g.,* Floyd G. Delon, *Pupil Rights in the "New" South Africa: Comparisons and Contrasts with American Con-*

stitutional Law, 103 Ed. Law. Rep. 901 (1995). This type of conflict can also materialize when a child wants to make a medical decision opposed by the parent and the state. The question is whether the child has the autonomy to make his or her own decision.

In the United States, there are a series of Supreme Court cases that address these issues. Generally, the cases fall in one of two camps. Either the children are seen to have a strong interest, *see, e.g.,* Bellotti v. Baird (Bellotti II), 443 U.S. 622 (1979), or they are seen to have a weak interest, *see, e.g.,* Parham v. J.R., 442 U.S. 584 (1979). The child's interest varies depending upon the maturity of the child and the potential that the parents will act contrary to their child's best interest. Consequently, in *Bellotti II,* the Court afforded "mature minors" the right to make medical decisions about an abortion without parental consent. *Bellotti,* 433 U.S. at 651. In *Parham,* in contrast, the Court upheld a state statute that allowed parents to commit their child to a state mental hospital without an adversary hearing, emphasizing that "parents generally do act in the child's best interests." *See Parham,* 442 U.S. at 602-03. In the United States, the notion that parents generally can be trusted to make decisions in their children's best interest has grown up as a corollary of the parents' right "to make decisions concerning the care, custody, and control of their children." The interplay of these two concepts, to the exclusion of the child's interest, was recently seen in *Troxel v. Granville,* 530 U.S. 57 (2000) (plurality opinion), albeit in a different context. For more on the U.S. role in balancing children's interests, the state's interest, and their parents' interest, see Janet L. Dolgin, *The Constitution as Family Arbiter: A Moral in the Mess?,* 102 Colum. L. Rev. 337 (2002).

In England, the most famous decision addressing the balance between the relative rights of parent and child is the House of Lords' decision in *Gillick v. West Norfolk and Wisbech Area Health Authority. See* Gillick v. West Norfolk and Wisbech Area Health Authority, [1985] 3 All E.R. 402 (HL). That case involved a mother who had requested that her fifteen-year-old daughter, as well as her other daughters, be denied access to birth control pills. The House of Lords ruled that the child's parents could not deny the child access to the pills. That House of Lords held that mature minors may consent to health care services with the same independence as adults so long as the child has "a sufficient understanding and intelligence to be capable of making up his own mind on the matter requiring decision." *See Gillick,* 3 All E.R. 402 (Templeman, L.J., dissenting). The right of the child, however, seems to be more limited when the child is trying to refuse, as opposed to obtain, treatment. *See In re R,* [1991] 4 All E.R. 177; *see also In Re W (A Minor) (Medical Treatment: Court's Jurisdiction),* [1992] 4 All E.R. 627 (permitting adult to override decision of a sixteen-year-old girl stricken with anorexia to refuse treatment). For more on the topic of children's rights to guide their own health care decisions, *see* Dr. Yehiel S. Kaplan, *The Right of A Minor in Israel to Participate in the Decision-Making Process Concerning His or Her Medical Treatment,* 25 Fordham Int'l L.J. 1085 (2002).

Finally, in South Africa, sections 28(1)(d) and 28(2) of the Constitution might suggest a very parent-centered approach to the child's ability to make his or her own medical decisions. The issue is currently dictated by legislation that affords some minors autonomy rights. While the Child Care Act 74 of 1983, § 39(4), states that one must be over eighteen years old to consent to surgical procedures, minors over fourteen can consent to medical and non-surgical procedures. *See generally* Tshepo L. Mosikatsana, *Children's Rights and Family Autonomy in the South African Context: A Comment on Children's Rights Under the Final Constitution,* 3 Mich. J. Race & L. 341, 391–92 (1998). The Termination of Pregnancy Act 92 of 1996, section 2, also allows minors to consent to abortion, even against the wishes of their parents or guardians, regardless of age.

To the extent that the U.N. Convention on the Rights of the Child explicitly gives children autonomy and participation rights, these sorts of conflicts will receive more attention in years to come, especially in South Africa where international law plays an important role in interpreting the Constitution.

Problem 14-5

Reconsider problem 14-4. Has there been a violation of anyone's rights under the South Africa Constitution?

D. Children's Rights in the Divided Family

The final case in this chapter looks at the issue of children's rights in a different context. Here the issue of children's rights arises in the context of a parental dispute about the child. As you read this case, notice the attention given to and treatment of the child's rights.

Re J
1 Fam. 571 (Eng. C.A. 1999)

Thorpe, L.J.

On 23 April 1999 Wall J. gave a reserved judgment refusing a father's application for a specific issue order that his five year old son be circumcised.... The judge's factual summary could not be bettered. What follows is all extracted from his judgment....

The father is 27. He is Turkish by birth and upbringing, and retains his Turkish nationality, although he is permanently resident in the United Kingdom and also has a British passport. He is a Muslim, although, as he freely accepts, he does not actively observe many of the tenets of his faith.

The mother is 29. She is English and, apart from a short period around the time of her marriage to the father when she lived with him in Turkey, she has lived throughout her life in England. She is notionally a Christian and a member of the Church of England but, like the father, she is nonpractising.

The parents met whilst the mother was on holiday in Turkey in the Summer of 1992. Later that year she returned to Turkey, and she and the father were married in Turkey on 18 November 1992. It was a first marriage for both of them.

The father says that whilst the mother was pregnant with J she gave her agreement that any male child would be circumcised. I accept that evidence.

Following the parents return to England from Turkey in February 1993, the marriage, despite the birth of J in March 1994, did not endure, and they separated on 29 September 1996 when J was aged two and a half.

J is five and attending a local state primary school. He is being brought up in an essentially secular household. The only contact he has with Islam is through his father. The mother has no Muslim friends and no connections with any members of the Muslim community. The father, likewise, does not appear to have Muslim friends or mix in Muslim circles.

Against that factual background, the judge then posed the question: what is J's religion? He answered it thus, adopting a submission made by his Guardian ad litem, the Official Solicitor. I quote: "In English Law, therefore, J would seem to be being brought up as a nonpractising Christian in accordance with the convictions of his mother with whom he lives and as a nonpractising Muslim when he stays with his father. He therefore has a mixed heritage and an essentially secular lifestyle. He does not have a settled religious faith."

The judge turned to decide, first, a substantial issue as to whether the mother should be required to bring J up as a Muslim; an issue which is no longer alive in this court since both parties accept the judge's pragmatic resolution under which the father is free during periods of contact to deal with this aspect in his own way.

The judge's approach to the dispute over circumcision was characteristically thorough. He considered the lawfulness of ritual male circumcision, concluding that it was lawful for two parties jointly exercising parental responsibility to arrange the ritual circumcision of their male child.

The judge then recorded medical attitudes to ritual circumcision, having heard evidence from a consultant pediatrician and having read the GMC and BMA guidelines supplied by the Official Solicitor. He concluded that current mainstream medical opinion requires both parents' consent and, particularly, maternal consent when the father lacks parental responsibility. Additionally, he recorded in the consultant's report that circumcision was not medically indicated for J since he did not suffer from any of the three medical conditions that can make circumcision either necessary or advisable. He also accepted the consultant's advice that: "The procedure is not pain free and there are potential risks both physical and psychological, which may be small but which are nonetheless definite."

The judge's summary of the submissions of the parties is full and in many ways favourable to the father. I need quote only this sentence: "By comparison with what I have to say was the mother's pallid and unconvincing statement of her religious beliefs, the father's passionate plea for J to be given his proper identity as a Muslim and for him to be thereby enabled to identify fully with his father was impressive."

In an important section, the judge considered the likely effects on J of being circumcised. There, he made these significant findings:

> In Turkish society, a Muslim male child's peers will all be circumcised: in the circles in which J will grow up, he is likely to be in a small minority and he will not have the reassurance that all his contemporaries have been through—or will go through—the same experience.

> The incident I have described also makes it clear to me that the mother, as J's primary carer, would find it extremely difficult to present the question of circumcision to J in a positive light, and unlike ritual circumcision occurring in the context of a Muslim family, where the event would be one of celebration and fulfillment, J's circumcision would be likely to be surrounded by tension and stress, even though the mother was able to agree with the father's counsel

in cross examination that she would, of course, care for J after the operation and would have no difficulty changing dressings.

In my judgment the strained relationship between the parents, and the fact that as a circumcised child J would be unlike most of his peers, increases the risk that J will suffer adverse psychological effects from being circumcised.

Against that background, Mr Justice Wall stated his conclusions, marshalling them by reference to the statutory checklist in section 1(3) of the Children Act 1989.* However, he preceded that exercise with this concise passage:

The major benefit is that J will thereby be firmly identified with his father, and confirmed in the eyes of Islam as a Muslim. However his circumcision would not be part of a family celebration, and he would not, thereafter, be brought up in a Muslim family environment.

The disadvantages are that despite the father's passionate defence of the procedure, J may be traumatized by it; he will, moreover, be living in the household of his mother, who disagrees with the procedure, and will find great difficulty in presenting it to J in a positive light.

Finally, in refusing the application, the judge stressed that his conclusion was finely balanced and depended on the facts as he had found them. He summarized the factors which had influenced his conclusion in the following four numbered paragraphs:

(1) Although born a Muslim, it is clear to me that J is going to have an essentially secular upbringing in England. He is not going to mix in Muslim circles, and his main contact with Muslims and the Muslim ethos will be his contact with his father. J is therefore not going to grow up in an environment in which circumcision is a part of family life; or in which circumcision will be in conformity with the religion practiced by his primary carer; or in which his peers have all been circumcised and for him not to be so would render him either unusual or an outsider. To the contrary, circumcision in the circles in which J is likely to move will be the exception rather than the rule.

(2) Circumcision is an effectively irreversible surgical intervention which has no medical basis in J's case. It is likely to be painful and carries with it small but definable physical and psychological risks. For it to be ordered there would accordingly have to be clear benefits to J which would demonstrate that circumcision was in his interests notwithstanding the risks. The principal benefits put forward are J's identification as a Muslim and the strengthening of his bond with his father. The strength of each is substan-

---

* Children Act 1981, ch. 41 § 1(3) states that a court in making this sort of order "shall have regard in particular to—
    (a) the ascertainable wishes and feelings of the child concerned (considered in the light of his age and understanding);
    (b) his physical, emotional and educational needs;
    (c) the likely effect on him of any change in his circumstances;
    (d) his age, sex, background and any characteristics of his which the [guardian ad litem] considers relevant;
    (e) any harm which he has suffered or is at risk of suffering;
    (f) how capable each of his parents, and any other person in relation to whom the [guardian ad litem] considers the question to be relevant, is of meeting his needs;
    (g) the range of powers available to the court under this Act in the proceedings in question."

tially weakened, in my judgment, by the facts of J's lifestyle and his likely upbringing....

(3) J is in the middle of a hostile battle between his parents over contact. He is to that extent a vulnerable child. The operation and the period leading up to it are likely to be highly stressful for the mother, who would find it difficult to explain to J why it was being undertaken and would have grave difficulty presenting it to J in a positive light. Furthermore, J is of an age and understanding to feel pain and discomfort without at the same time being fully able to understand why the operation was being carried out.

(4) J's mother, who not only shares parental responsibility for him with his father but cares for him on a day to day basis and is currently the most important person in his life, is opposed to his circumcision, and there is a rational basis for her opposition. It is a strong thing to impose a medically unnecessary surgical intervention on a residential parent who is opposed to it. In my judgment, this should only be done if the evidence shows that J's welfare requires him to be circumcised. For the reasons I have given, I do not think that the evidence overall shows that it is in J's interests to be circumcised.

By way of postscript, the judge dealt with Article 9 of the European Convention on Human Rights and with Article 24.3 of the United Nation Convention on the Rights of the Child. The judge correctly held that the father's right to manifest his religion had to be balanced against the welfare of the child and the rights of the mother. That holding has not been challenged in the course of this appeal....

In presenting the father's appeal, Miss Kushner QC faced an uphill struggle with some fortitude. Her principal complaint was that the judge confused the child's religion with the child's religious upbringing. As the child of a Muslim father, J arrived in this world a Muslim. His family, during the first two years of his life, were practicing Muslims to a slight degree and the separation of his parents could not terminate his religion, particularly in the absence of any active step by his mother so to do.

That contention seems to me, at best, to be theoretically correct. For what it is worth, it weighs very light in the scale that the judge had to balance to determine whether the relief sought would advance J's welfare. Some faiths recognize their religion as a birthright derived from either the child's mother or the child's father. Some recognize religion by some ceremony of induction or initiation, but the newborn does not share the perception of his parents or of the religious community to which the parents belong. A child's perception of his or her religion generally depends on involvement in worship and teaching within the family. From this develops the emotional, intellectual, psychological and spiritual sense of belonging to a religious faith. So far, for all practical purposes, the courts have been right to focus upon religious upbringing and it is no surprise to me that there is no reported case focusing on a child's religion, as Miss Kushner defines it....

Miss Kushner finally accused the judge of setting a general standard that has denied her client success in this application and which would make future applications unlikely to succeed. She rests this submission on a single paragraph, where the judge said:

I repeat that my decision in this case turns on its particular facts. I do not think it can be said that the court would not, in any circumstances, order a child to be circumcised. The example which was put in argument was that of a Jewish mother and an agnostic father with a number of sons, all of whom, by agreement, had been circumcised as infants in accordance with Jewish laws; the parents then have another son who is born after they have separated;

the mother wishes him to be circumcised like his brothers; the father, for no good reason, refuses his agreement. In circumstances such as these, it seems to me that the court would be likely to grant the mother a specific issue order.

It is immediately obvious to me that the paragraph does not begin to justify the charge. It merely emphasizes that each case must turn on its particular facts. I would not wish to be taken as laying down any more general guidance than the judge. The only certainty is that social attitudes to male circumcision will remain extremely fluid. The only generalization I would feel confident to express is that, in those communities where it is the practice to carry out the circumcision of a male child within days of birth, there is much less likelihood of forensic dispute. Many of the issues in the present appeal could not have developed but for the practice of the father's community to defer circumcision to the age of about seven.

The only point of principle that this appeal decides is to endorse the judge's conclusion that section 2(7) of the Children Act does not enable a parent to arrange circumcision without the consent of the other. Section 2(7) provides:

> Where more than one person has parental responsibility for a child, each of them may act alone and without the other (or others) in meeting that responsibility; but nothing in this Part shall be taken to effect the operation of any enactment which requires the consent of more than one person in a matter affecting the child.

Mr Nicholls, for the Official Solicitor, submitted and the judge accepted that the operation of circumcision is of considerable consequence and irreversible. It must, therefore, join the exceptional categories where disagreement between holders of parental responsibility must be submitted to the court for determination.

For all those reasons I would dismiss this appeal.

[Ed. Note: The separate opinions of Schiemann, L.J. and the President, both agreeing with Lord Justice Thorpe's opinion, are omitted.]

Notes and Questions

1. *Holding.* What is the holding of the English Court of Appeal in *Re J*? What substantive standard did the trial court employ to reach its decision?

2. *Decision-Maker.* Who should be deciding whether J is to be circumcised? His mother? His father? The court? J himself? A broader group of relatives? Why?

3. *The Child's Religion?* Under Islamic law, a child's religion is the same as his father's, and the child cannot choose another religion. *See* Cynthia Price Cohen, *Role of the United States in Drafting the Convention on the Rights of the Child: Creating a New World for Children*, 4 Loy. Poverty L.J. 9, 30 n.83 (1998) (citing Egyptian delegate). How did Lord Justice Thorpe determine the child's religion in this context? Lord Justice Schiemann says that this issue "bristles with conceptual and philosophical difficulties." Is the complexity of the task a good reason to avoid it?

4. *The Child's Rights.* Lord Justice Thorpe's opinion suggests that the father had argued that his own right to manifest his religion would be violated by the court's refusal to order that his son be circumcised. Given the ECHR case law set forth earlier, did the father have a valid claim? In the end, the trial court resolves the father's claim by balancing the father's right against the child's welfare and the mother's rights. This approach

was not challenged on appeal. Should it have been? Did the child have a rights claim under the ECHR or CRC that should have been thrown into the balance?

5. *Circumcision.* Article 24(3) of the CRC directs States Parties to take "all effective and appropriate measures with a view to abolishing traditional practices prejudicial to the health of the children." Could the court have ruled in favor of the father given this provision?

6. *Child's Right to Be Heard.* The Council of Europe adopted the European Convention on the Exercise of Children's Rights, Jan. 25, 1996, Europ. T.S. 160. The Convention provides, in part, that "A child considered by internal law as having sufficient understanding, in the case of proceedings before a judicial authority affecting him or her, shall be granted, and shall be entitled to request, the following rights: (a) to receive all relevant information; (b) to be consulted and express his or her views; (c) to be informed of the possible consequences of compliance with these views and the possible consequences of any decision." *See* art. 3. The Convention defines "relevant information" as "information which is appropriate to the age and understanding of the child, and which will be given to enable the child to exercise his or her rights fully unless the provision of such information were contrary to the welfare of the child." *See* art. 2(d). This Convention has entered into force. Would this Convention have made a difference to the outcome if it were followed in *Re J*? What of the fact that J had a guardian ad litem who made a submission to the court?

7. *Children's Rights and Parental Disagreement.* Is this a stronger case for consideration of children's rights than in other contexts? In particular, consider a situation in which the parents and the child disagree with a policy of the government (*e.g., Campbell & Cosans v. United Kingdom, supra*) or the government and the child disagree with a policy of the parent (*e.g., A v. United Kingdom*). What about the situation in which the child disagrees with the parent and the government?

8. *Back to Whipping.* Reconsider *A. v. United Kingdom.* In that case, A.'s natural father, who had parental responsibility, "disapproved of the 'step-father' canings." Assuming that the step-father's canings were reasonable, should the non-custodial father's opinion matter? In a situation where the adults with parental responsibility disagree about the propriety of corporal punishment, could a court entertain an action about the disagreement under section 2(7) of the Children Act? If not, is the court's interpretation of section 2(7) suspect given that the United Kingdom has ratified the ECHR and the CRC?

9. *Disputes Between Parents.* More information about parental disputes regarding their children can be found in Chapter Seven.

Index